CPAG'S

CW00402333

Housing B~~enefit and~~

Council Tax Benefit

Legislation

Twenty third edition

2010/2011

Twenty third edition revised by
Richard Poynter, Carolyn George, Stewart Wright and Martin Williams
Commentary by
Lorna Findlay, *LL.B (Hons)*
Employment Judge
Stewart Wright, *MA, Dip. Law, Barrister*
Tribunal Judge
Richard Poynter, *BCL, MA(Oxon)*
District Tribunal Judge
Deputy Judge of the Upper Tribunal
Carolyn George, *MA*
Freelance writer on welfare rights
Martin Williams
Welfare rights worker, CPAG

Published by Child Poverty Action Group

CPAG promotes action for the prevention and relief of poverty among children and families with children. To achieve this, CPAG aims to raise awareness of the causes, extent, nature and impact of poverty, and strategies for its eradication and prevention; bring about positive policy changes for families with children in poverty; and enable those eligible for income maintenance to have access to their full entitlement. If you are not already supporting us, please consider making a donation, or ask for details of our membership schemes and publications.

Published by Child Poverty Action Group
94 White Lion Street, London N1 9PF
020 7837 7979
staff@cpag.org.uk
www.cpag.org.uk

Child Poverty Action Group is a charity registered in England and Wales (registration number 294841) and in Scotland (registration number SC039339), and is a company limited by guarantee, registered in England (registration number 1993854). VAT number: 690 808117

A CIP record for this book is available from the British Library

ISBN: 978 1 906076 41 2

Typeset by David Lewis XML Associates Limited
Printed in the UK by CPI William Clowes Beccles NR34 7TL

Contents

Acknowledgements vi
Foreword vii
Table of Cases viii
Table of Commissioners Decisions xv
Table of Upper Tribunal Decisions xx
Housing Benefit Regulations: Destinations Table xxii
Council Tax Benefit Regulations: Destinations Table xxvii
Table of comparative provisions xxxi
Table of abbreviations xxxiii

Part 1: Main primary legislation

Social Security Contributions and Benefits Act 1992 (c. 4) 3
Social Security Administration Act, 1992 (c. 5) 26
Social Security (Consequential Provisions) Act 1992 (c. 6) 106
Social Security Act 1998 (c. 14) 107
Human Rights Act 1998 (c. 42) 112
Child Support, Pensions and Social Security Act 2000 (c. 19)
Constitutional Reform Act 2005 160
Welfare Reform Act 2007 (c. 5) 162
Tribunals, Courts and Enforcement Act 2007 (c. 15) 168

Part 2: Main secondary legislation – Housing benefit

Housing Benefit Regulations 2006, S.I. 2006 No. 213 205
Rent Officers (Housing Benefit Functions) Order 1997, S.I. 1997 No. 1984 592
Rent Officers (Housing Benefit Functions) (Scotland) Order 1997, S.I. 1997 No. 1995 (S. 144) 614
Rent Officers (Housing Benefit Functions) (Local Housing Allowance) Amendment Order 2003, S.I. 2003 No. 2398 632
Rent Officers (Housing Benefit Functions) (Local Housing Allowance) Amendment Order 2005, S.I. 2005 No. 236 633
Rent Officers (Housing Benefit Functions) Amendment Order 2007, S.I. 2007 No. 2871 634

Part 3: Main secondary legislation – Council tax benefit

Council Tax Benefit Regulations 2006, S.I. 2006 No. 215 641

Part 4: Main secondary legislation

Housing Benefit (Persons who have attained the qualifying age for state pension credit) Regulations 2006, S.I. 2006 No. 214 767
Council Tax Benefit (Persons who have attained the qualifying age for state pension credit) Regulations 2006, S.I. 2006 No. 216 913

Part 5: Secondary legislation – Decision making and appeals

Housing Benefit and Council Tax Benefit (Decisions and Appeals) Regulations 2001, S.I. 2001 No. 1002 1005

Tribunal Procedure (First-tier Tribunal) (Social Entitlement Chamber) Rules 2008, S.I. 2008 No. 2685   **1047**

Qualifications for Appointment of Members to the First-tier Tribunal and Upper Tribunal Order 2008, S.I. 2008 No. 2692   **1076**

Tribunal Procedure (Upper Tribunal) Rules 2008, S.I. 2008 No. 2698   **1078**

Transfer of Tribunal Functions Order 2008, S.I. 2008 No. 2833   **1102**

Appeals from the Upper Tribunal to the Court of Appeal Order 2008, S.I. 2008 No. 2884   **1105**

First-tier Tribunal and Upper Tribunal (Composition of Tribunal) Order 2008, S.I. 2008 No. 2835   **1106**

The Contracting Out (Administrative Work of Tribunals) Order 2009, S.I. 2009 No. 121   **1108**

The First-tier Tribunal and Upper Tribunal (Chambers) Order 2010, S.I. 2010 No. 2655   **1109**

Part 6: **Other primary legislation**

Local Government Finance Act 1992 (c. 14)   **1113**

Housing Act 1996 (c. 52)   **1122**

Welfare Reform and Pensions Act 1999 (c. 30)   **1123**

Immigration and Asylum Act 1999 (c. 33)   **1129**

Children (Leaving Care) Act 2000 (c. 35)   **1132**

Social Security Fraud Act 2001 (c. 11)   **1134**

Tax Credits Act 2002 (c. 21)   **1147**

Civil Partnership Act 2004 (c. 33)   **1148**

Part 7: **Other secondary legislation: Common and transitional provisions**

Social Security (Persons from Abroad) Miscellaneous Amendments Regulations 1996, S.I. 1996 No. 30   **1153**

Housing Benefit (Permitted Totals) Order 1996, S.I. 1996 No. 677   **1156**

Council Tax Benefit (Permitted Totals) Order 1996, S.I. 1996 No. 678   **1161**

Housing Benefit (Information from Landlords and Agents) Regulations 1997, S.I. 1997 No. 2436   **1162**

Social Security (Penalty Notice) Regulations 1997, S.I. 1997 No. 2813   **1166**

New Deal (Miscellaneous Provisions) Order 1998, S.I. 1998 No. 217   **1167**

Social Security (Immigration and Asylum) Consequential Amendments Regulations 2000, S.I. 2000 No. 636   **1169**

New Deal (Miscellaneous Provisions) Order 2001, S.I. 2001 No. 970   **1174**

Discretionary Financial Assistance Regulations 2001, S.I. 2001 No. 1167   **1176**

New Deal (Lone Parents) (Miscellaneous Provisions) Order 2001, S.I. 2001 No. 2915   **1182**

Social Security (Notification of Change of Circumstances) Regulations 2001, S.I. 2001 No. 3252   **1183**

Social Security (Loss of Benefit) Regulations 2001, S.I. 2001 No. 4022   **1185**

Contracting Out (Functions of Local Authorities: Income-Related Benefits) Order 2002, S.I. 2002 No. 1888   **1190**

Social Security (Habitual Residence) Amendment Regulations 2004, S.I. 2004 No. 1232   **1192**

Civil Partnership (Pensions, Social Security and Child Support) Consequential, etc Provisions Order 2005, S.I. 2005 No. 2877   **1193**

Civil Partnership Act 2004 (Relationships Arising Through Civil Partnership) Order 2005, S.I. 2005 No. 3137   **1195**

Housing Benefit and Council Tax Benefit (Consequential Provisions) Regulations 2006, S.I. 2006 No. 217   **1196**

Social Security (Persons from Abroad) Amendment Regulations 2006, S.I. 2006 No. 1026   **1226**

Housing Benefit and Council Tax Benefit (War Pension Disregards) Regulations 2007, S.I. 2007 No. 1619 **1227**

Social Security (Claims and Information) Regulations 2007, S.I. 2007 No. 2911 **1229**

Housing Benefit (Local Housing Allowance and Information Sharing) Amendment Regulations 2007, S.I. 2007 No. 2868 **1231**

Housing Benefit (State Pension Credit) (Local Housing Allowance and Information Sharing) Amendment Regulations 2007, S.I. 2007 No. 2869 **1233**

Housing Benefit (Local Housing Allowance, Miscellaneous and Consequential) Amendment Regulations 2007, S.I. 2007 No. 2870 **1235**

Welfare Reform Act 2007 (Commencement No4, and Savings and Transitional Provisions) Order 2007, S.I. 2007 No. 2872 **1237**

Social Security (Local Authority Investigations and Prosecutions) Regulations 2008, S.I. 2008 No. 463 **1240**

Welfare Reform Act 2007 (Commencement No. 7, Transitional and Savings Provisions) Order 2008, S.I. 2008 No. 2101 **1241**

Social Security (Use of Information for Housing Benefit and Welfare Services Purposes) Regulations 2008, S.I. 2008 No. 2112 **1242**

Welfare Reform Act (Relevant Enactment) Order 2009, S.I. 2009 No. 2162 **1244**

The Flexible New Deal (Miscellaneous Provisions) Order 2009, S.I. 2009 No. 1562 **1245**

The Community Task Force (Miscellaneous Provisions) Order 2010, S.I. 2010 No. 349 **1246**

Jobseeker's Allowance (Work for Your Benefit Pilot Scheme) Regulations 2010, S.I. 2010 No. 1222 **1247**

Index **1249**

Acknowledgements

We would like to thank all those who assisted with this publication including staff in CPAG's Citizen's Rights Office, colleagues at the Tribunals Service and staff at the DWP who all provide information on a regular basis.

We would like to acknowledge the efforts of previous authors, Paul Stagg, Martin Ward and Lorna Findlay.

Also we would like to thank Nicola Johnston who edited and managed the production of this book, Katherine Dawson for the index and Kathleen Armstrong for proof reading. Thanks also to Richard Gillard at David Lewis XML.

Foreword

Welcome to the 23rd edition of *CPAG's Annotated Housing Benefit and Council Tax Benefit Legislation*.

Changes and new material in this 23rd edition include the following.

The process of increasing the pension age for women from 60 to 65, and hence the qualifying age for pension credit, began on 6 April 2010. There have been consequential amendments to the HB and CTB regulations.

Those claiming income support "on the grounds of disability", incapacity benefit and severe disablement allowance will be assessed for and, if they qualify, transferred to employment and support allowance (ESA) at some point between October 2010 and the end of March 2014. To ensure that a claimant continues to qualify for the same rate of HB and CTB as before the transfer, or in specified circumstances while s/he or her/his partner is appealing a conversion decision, rules for entitlement to a protected amount of HB and CTB – a transitional addition – have been introduced.

The commentary to the Social Security (Loss of Benefit) Regulations 2001 has been fully updated to take account of the addition of a "one-strike" rule to the existing "two strikes" rule, whereby HB and CTB can be paid at a reduced rate during a sanction period.

The rules on who is to be treated as a member of a claimant's household have been amended to provide that certain children or young people placed with a claimant (or her/his partner) under child protection legislation (eg, foster children) who are not to be treated as members of the claimant's household, and hence as part of her/his benefit family, are in addition not to be treated as occupying the claimant's dwelling. This reverses the decision in *Wirral MBC v AH and SSWP* (HB) [2010] UKUT 208 (AAC) and now prevents the children and young people being taken into account as occupiers for the purposes of the size criteria under the local housing allowance scheme rules.

Note that the Government intends to make a number of amendments to the HB scheme, between 2011 and 2014, which will affect the amount of HB to which individuals are entitled. These are referred to in the commentary where relevant.

This book, of necessity, has to focus in any individual place upon the particular statutory provision being commented upon. For a more general guide to the schemes, we recommend CPAG's *Welfare Benefits and Tax Credits Handbook* which is also available on CPAG's online services (see below).

We would like to thank all those who have taken the trouble to contact us with suggestions for improvements and notification of new developments since the last edition. We are always pleased to receive further such suggestions and information and can be contacted at the addresses below.

The legislation in this edition is up to date to 29 November 2010.

An online version of this book is available. CPAG's *Housing Benefit and Council Tax Benefit Law Online* contains the full text linked to relevant Upper Tribunal decisions, caselaw etc. The commentary is updated twice yearly (in line with the book) but the legislation and caselaw is updated throughout the year. For more information visit www.cpag.org.uk/onlineservices.

The Subsidy section of this book (Part 8) is not included in this print edition. It is, however, still included on the online version. It contains: the Income-related Benefits (Subsidy to Authorities) Order 1998 SI No 582; the Housing Benefit and Council Tax Benefit (Subsidy) Regulations 1994 SI No 781; the Discretionary Housing Payments (Grants) Order 2001 SI No 2340. If you require a PDF copy of the section, please email njohnston@cpag.org.uk.

RICHARD POYNTER, CAROLYN GEORGE, STEWART WRIGHT AND MARTIN WILLIAMS
c/o Publications Department
CPAG
94 White Lion Street
London
N1 9PF

Table of cases

Abdirahman and another v SSWP and another [2007] EWCA Civ 657 (reported as *R(IS) 8/07)*... **291, 289**
Abdulaziz v UK [1985] 7 EHRR 471 at 501, para 78, ECtHR... **132**
Airey v Ireland (1979) 2 EHRR 305... **126**
Andersson v Sweden [1986] 46 DR 251, ECmHR... **127**
Andronicou v Cyprus [1998] 25 EHRR 491, ECtHR... **126**
Attorney General's Reference No 2 of 2001 [2003] UKHL 68, [2004] 1 All ER 1041... **126**
Attorney General's Reference No 4 of 2002 [2004] UKHL 43... **113**
B v SSWP [2005] EWCA Civ 929, [2005] 1 WLR 3796 (reported as *R(IS) 9/06)*... **43, 487, 489, 490, 1034**
Barrass v Reeve [1981] 1 WLR 408, DC... **57, 60**
Barry v LB Southwark [2008] EWCA Civ 1440... **271, 272**
Begum v Tower Hamlets LBC [2003] 2 WLR 238, HL... **127**
Bellet v France (1995) unreported, case number A/333-B, ECtHR... **126**
Bland v Chief Supplementary Benefit Officer [1983] 1 WLR 262, CA (reported as *R(SB) 12/83)*... **177, 184**
Bradford MBC v Anderton [1991] RA 45, QBD... **654**
Braintree District Council v Thompson [2005] EWCA Civ 178, 7 March 2005, unreported... **185**
Bruton v London & Quadrant Housing Trust [1999] 3 WLR 150... **246**
Cameron v Cameron [1996] SLT 306 at 313F... **295**
Cameron v Henry [1992] SLT 586, IH... **654**
Campbell and others v South Northamptonshire District Council and SSWP [2004] EWCA Civ 409 *The Times*... **94, 129, 252**
Campbell v Secretary of State for Social Services [1983] 4 FLR 138, QBD... **20**
Carpenter v SSWP [2003] EWCA Civ 33 (reported as *R(IB) 6/03)*... **140, 146, 178**
Carson and Reynolds [2005] UKHL 37 *The Times*... **129, 130, 131**
Case C-75/73 Hoekstra (nee Unger)... **271**
Case C-53/81 Levin v Staatssecretaris van Justitie [1982] ECR 01035... **271, 271, 271**
Cases C-286/82 & C-26/83) Luisi & Carbone v Ministero del Tesoro [1984] ECR 00377... **287**
Case C-267/83 Assiatou Diatta v Land Berlin [1985] ECR 00567... **277, 293**
Case C-139/85 Kempf v Staatssecretaris van Justitie [1986] ECR 01741... **271**
Case C-39/86 Sylvie Lair v Universität Hannover [1988] ECR 03161... **271**
Case C-66/86 Lawrie-Blum v Land Baden-Wurtternberg [1986] ECR 02121... **271**
Case C-263/86 Belgian State v Humbel [1988] ECR 05365... **287**
Case C-196/87 Steymann v Staatssecretaris van Justitie [1988] ECR 06159... **271, 288**
Case C-125/89 Kits van Heijerungen v Staatssecretaris van Justitie [1990] ECR I-01753... **271**
Case C-292/89 Antonissen [1991] ECR I-00745... **269**
Case C-357/89 Raulin [1992] ECR I-01027... **272**
Case C-3/90 Bernini v Minister van Ouderings en Wetenschappen [1992] ECR I-01071... **271**
Case C-109/92 Wirth v Landeshauptstadt Hannover [1993] ECR I-06447... **287**
Case C-70/95 Sodemare SA v Regione Lombardia [1997] ECR I-03395... **288**
Case C-184/99 Grzelcyzk ECR I-06193... **284**
Case C-268/99 Jany and Others v Staatssecretaris van Justitie [2001] ECR I-08615... **272**
Case C-413/99 Baumbast & R v SSHD [2002] ECR I-07091... **288, 289, 292, 293**
Case C-200/02 Zhu and Chen [2004] ECR I-09925... **293**
Case C-456/02 Michel Trojani v Centre public d'aide sociale de Bruxelles [2004] ECR I-07573... **288, 289**
Case C-1/05 Jia v Migrationsverket [2007] ECR I-00001... **277**
Case C-219/05 Eind [2007] ECR I-10719... **270**
Case C-310/08 LB Harrow v Ibrahim [2010] ECR... **269, 288, 292, 293**
Case C-480/08 Teixeira v LB Lambeth [2010] ECR... **269, 288, 292, 293**

Case C-127/08 Metock [2008] ECR I-06241... **269**

Case C-14/09 Hava Genc v Land Berlin [2010] ECR... **272**

Case C-162/09 SSWP v Taous Lassal [2010] ECR... **285, 293**

Casewell v Secretary of State for Work and Pensions [2008] 11 March, WLR (D) 86, reported as *R(IS) 7/08*... **564**

Chief Adjudication Officer v Ahmed [1994] *The Times*... **296**

Chief Adjudication Officer v Bate [1996] 1 WLR 814... **157**

Chief Adjudication Officer v Carr [1994] 2 June, *The Times*... **244**

Chief Adjudication Officer v Combe [1998] SLT 15 at 17D-F, IH (reported as *R(IS) 8/98*)... **1014**

Chief Adjudication Officer v McKiernon [1993], 3 July, CA... **1022**

Clayton's case [1861] 1 Mer 572... **64**

Clear v Smith [1981] 1 WLR 399 at 406, DC... **60, 486, 494**

Clift v United Kingdom (Application No 7205/07), 13 July 2010... **130**

Codner v Wiltshire Valuation and Community Charge Tribunal [1994] 34 RVR 169, QBD... **654**

Cooke v Secretary of State for Social Security [2001] EWCA CIV 734 (reported as *R(DLA) 6/01*)... **170, 185**

Cottingham v Chief Adjudication Officer [1992] appendix to *R(P) 1/93*... **16**

Cox v London (South West) Valuation and Community Charge Tribunal [1994] 34 RVR 171, QBD... **654**

Crabtree v Fern Spinning Co Ltd [1901] 85 LT 549 at 552, DC... **58**

Crake and Butterworth v Supplementary Benefit Commission [1982] 1 All ER 498... **20**

Davies v Child Support Commissioner and Child Support Agency [2008] EWHC 334 (Admin), QBD... **1050**

Department of Work and Pensions v Richards [2005] EWCA Crim 491, 3 March... **46**

Deumeland v Germany [1986] 8 EHRR 448 at 468, para 74, ECtHR... **125**

DH and others v Czech Republic (Appln No: 57325/00), 13 November 2007 (ECtHR)... **131**

Dias v SSWP [2009] EWCA Civ 807... **274, 293**

Dombo Beheer BV v Netherlands (1993) 18 EHRR 213 at 226-8, ECtHR... **125**

Donaghue v Poplar Housing Association Ltd [2002] QB 58, CA... **117, 119**

Douglas v Phoenix Motors [1970] SLT 57 at 58, Sh Ct... **62**

DSS v Bavi [1996] COD 260 at 261, DC... **60**

DSS v Cooper [1994] 158 JPN 354, DC... **60**

Duggan v Chief Adjudication Officer [1988] *The Times*... **489**

E v Secretary of State for the Home Department [2004] EWCA Civ 49... **179**

Eba v Advocate General for Scotland [2010] CSIH 78... **170, 187**

Fairbank v Lambeth Magistrates' Court [2003] HLR 62... **60**

Fedje v Sweden [1994] 17 EHRR 14, para 32, ECtHR... **127**

Feldbrugge v Netherlands (1986) 8 EHRR 425... **125**

Foster v Chief Adjudication Officer [1992] QB 31 at 45... **16, 179, 660**

Francis v Secretary of State for Work and Pensions [2005] EWCA Civ 1303, 10 November (reported as *R(IS) 6/06*)... **130, 132**

Franklin v Chief Adjudication Officer [1995] *The Times*... **489, 490**

Frish Limited v Barclays Bank Limited [1955] 2 QB 541... **259**

Frost v Feltham [1981] 1 WLR 455... **12, 653**

Fryer-Kelsey v SSWP [2005] EWCA Civ 511 (reported as *R(IB) 6/05*))... **185**

Gargett, R (on the application of) v London Borough of Lambeth [2008] EWCA Civ 1450 (18 December 2008)... **1179**

Gaumont British Distributors Ltd v Henry [1939] 2 KB 711 at 719, 723, DC... **58**

General Legal Council ex parte Basil Whitter v Barrington Earl Frankson [2006] UKPC 42, 27 July... **1063**

Ghaidan v Godin-Mendoza [2004] UKHL 30, 3 All ER 411... **114, 129, 131**

Gillies v SSWP [2006] UKHL 2, *Times Law Report*... **124, 182**

Godwin v Rossendale BC [2002] *The Times*... **585**

Grant v Southwestern and County Properties Ltd [1975] Ch 185 at 197A-F, Ch D... **58**

Grice v Needs [1980] 1 WLR 45 at 47F-G... **55**

Guygusuz v Austria [1997] 23 EHRR 364, ECtHR... **130, 131**

Haringey LBC v Awaritefe [1999] 32 HLR 517... **64, 182**

Haringey LBC v Cotter [1996] 29 HLR 682, CA… **128**
Harrison v DSS [1997] COD 220 at 220-1, DC… **61**
Herbert v Byrne [1964] 1 WLR 519 at 527, 528, 529, CA… **239**
Hinchy v SSWP [2005] UKHL 16… **490**
Hobbs and others v UK (Application No. 63684/00), 14 November 2006… **132**
Hooper v SSWP [2007] EWCA Civ 495 (reported as *R(IB) 4/07*)… **148**
Howker v SSWP [2003] ICR 405… **94**
Insurance Officer v McCaffrey [1985] 1 WLR 1353 at 1355H-1356C, HL… **31**
James Miller & Partners Ltd v Whitworth Street Estates (Manchester) Ltd [1970] AC 572… **247**
Jones v City of Glasgow DC HBRB [1997] unreported, 4 July, CSOH… **264**
Kaczmarek v SSWP [2008] EWCA Civ 1310, (reported as *R(IS) 5/09*)… **289, 290**
Kerr v Department for Social Development [2004] UKHL 23 (reported as *R 1/04 (SF)*)… **140, 180, 277, 281, 482**
King v Kerrier District Council [2006] EWHC 500 (Admin), unreported, 27 February (DC)… **61**
Kingston-upon-Thames BC v Prince [1998] 31 HLR 794, CA… **248**
Kirij v SSWP … **286**
Kjeldsen Madsen v Denmark [1976] 1 EHRR 711, ECtHR… **130**
Kola and Another v Secretary of State for Work and Pensions [2007] 28 November, UKHL 54, reported as *R(IS) 1/08*… **1220**
Lambeth London BC v Kay [2006] 4 All ER 128… **246**
Lane v Esdaile [1891] AC 210, 212… **177**
Langley v Bradford MDC and SSWP [2004] EWCA Civ 1343, 15 October, CA, reported as *R(H) 6/05*… **128, 257**
Leeds City Council v Price [2006] UKHL 10, [2006] 4 All ER 128… **113**
Lekpo-Bozua v LB Hackney and Secretary of State for Communities and Local Government [2010] EWCA Civ 909… **291**
Locabail (UK) Ltd v Bayfield Properties Ltd [2000] QB 451 at 496F-497A, para 89, CA… **181**
M (A Minor) v Secretary of State for Social Security [2001] 1 WLR 1453… **1155**
Malcolm v Tweeddale District HBRB [1994] SLT 1212, CS(OH)… **1207, 1211, 1212, 1213**
Manorlike Ltd v Le Vitas Travel Agency and Consultancy Services Ltd [1986] 1 All ER 573 at 575e-h, 576b-d, CA… **1013**
Massachusetts Board of Retirement v Murgia [1976] 438 US 285… **131**
McCarthy v SSHD [2008] EWCA Civ 641… **270, 285**
McLeod v HBRB for Banff and Buchan District HBRB [1988] SLT 753, CS(OH)… **1207, 1212**
Michalak v Wandsworth LBC [2003] 1 WLR 617… **129**
Miller v Secretary of State for Social Security [2002] GWD 25-861, CSIH… **180**
Mongan v Department for Social Development [2005] NICA 16, 13 April (reported as *R3/05 (DLA)*)… **145, 148**
Monteil v Secretary of State for the Home Department [1983] Imm AR 149 at 152, IAT… **271**
Mooney v SSWP [2004] SLT 1141 (reported as *R(DLA) 5/04*)… **148**
Moore v Branton [1974] 118 SJ 40, DC… **60**
Mullaney v Watford BC [1997] RA 225, QBD… **654**
Müller v Austria (Commission) [1975] 3 D and R 25… **133, 492**
Mulvey v Secretary of State for Social Security [1997] SLT 753 at 756, HL… **100**
Munro v UK [1986] 48 DR 154, ECmHR… **126**
Nessa v Chief Adjudication Officer [1998] 2 All ER 728… **294, 295**
Nimmo v Alexander Cowan & Sons Ltd [1968] AC 107, HL… **140**
Osinunga v DPP [1997] 30 HLR 853 at 856, DC… **46**
Osman v UK [1998] 29 EHRR 245, ECtHR… **157**
Owen v Chief Adjudication Officer [1999] *The Independent*… **16**
Page v Chief Adjudication Officer [1991] *The Times* 4 July, CA… **490**
Parry v Derbyshire Dales District Council [2006] EWHC 988 (Admin), 5 May, unreported… **653**
Patmalniece v SSWP [2009] EWCA Civ 621… **291, 292**
Pedro v SSWP [2009] EWCA Civ 1358; [2010] AACR 18… **277**
Petrovic v Austria [1998] 4 BHRC 232, ECtHR… **128, 132**
Plymouth CCV v Gigg [1997] 30 HLR 284, CA… **494**
Poplar Housing Association Ltd v Donoghue [2002] QB 58, CA… **114, 116**

Porter v Magill [2002] 2 WLR 37 at 83D-84B, paras 102-103, HL... **181**

Pretty v UK [2002] 35 EHRR 1, ECHR... **125**

Procurator Fiscal v Dyer and Watson [2002] UKPC D1... **126**

Procureur du Roi v Royer Case C-48/75... **276**

R (Alconbury Developments Ltd) v Secretary of State for the Environment, Transport and the Regions [2003] 2 AC 295, HL... **113, 127**

R (Anufrijeva) v Secretary of State for the Home Department [2003] 3 WLR 353, HL... **120, 1220**

R (Anufrijeva) v Southwark LBC [2003] EWCA Civ 1406, CA... **120, 128**

R (Balding) v Secretary of State for Work and Pensions [2007] EWHC 759, 3 April 2007... **492**

R (Barber) v Secretary of State for Work and Pensions [2002] 2 FLR 1181... **131**

R (Beeson) v Dorset [2002] 6 CCLR 5, CA... **127**

R (Begum) v SSWP [2003] EWHC 3380 Admin, reported as *R(IS) 11/04*... **1131**

R (Ben-Abdelaziz) v Secretary of State for the Home Department [2001] 1 WLR 1485, CA... **124**

R (Bernard) v Enfield LBC [2002] 5 CCLR 589... **120**

R (Bono) v Harlow DC HBRB [2002] 1 WLR 2475 paras 34-35, Richards J... **116**

R (Carson) v Secretary of State for Work and Pensions [2003] 3 All ER 577... **129, 131**

R (Cart and others) v Upper Tribunal and others [2009] EWHC 3052... **170**

R (Cumpsty) v Rent Officer [2002] EWHC 2526 (Admin)... **125, 126**

R (Douglas) v North Tyneside MBC and another [2004] 1 All ER 709... **134**

R (Greenfield) v Secretary of State for the Home Department [2005] UKHL 14, [2005] 2 All ER 240, HL... **120**

R (Heather) v The Leonard Cheshire Foundation [2001] 4 CCLR 211, Stanley Burton J... **117**

R (Hooper) v Secretary of State for Work and Pensions [2003] 1 WLR 2623, CA... **81**

R (Iran) v Secretary of State for the Home Department [2005] EWCA Civ 982... **179**

R (Isle of Anglesey DC) v SSWP [2003] EWHC 2518 (Admin)... **93**

R (Murphy) v Westminster CC [2002] HLR 447... **256, 257**

R (Naghshbandi) v Camden LBC [2003] HLR 280... **240, 241**

R (Naghshbandi) v Camden LBC [2001] EWHC Admin 813; [2003] HLR 280, CA... **1181**

R (Nahar) v Social Security Commissioner [2002] 1 FLR 670... **153**

R (on the application of Heffernan)(FC) v The Rent Service [2008] UKHL 58, 30 July 2008... **603**

R (on the application of Tilianu) v Social Fund Inspector and SSWP [2010] EWHC 213 (Admin)... **276**

R (Painter) v Carmarthenshire CC HBRB [2002] HLR 447... **256, 257**

R (Reynolds) v Secretary of State for Work and Pensions [2002] EWHC Admin 426... **128**

R (Reynolds) v Secretary of State for Work and Pensions [2005], UKHL 37, *The Times*... **521**

R (RJM) v SSWP [2008] UKHL 63, 22 October 2008... **113, 128, 130, 132**

R (S) v a Social Security Commissioner and Another [2009] EWHC 2221 (Admin)... **1201**

R (S) v Chief Constable of South Yorkshire Police [2004] 1 WLR 2196... **129, 130**

R (Saeedi) v Secretary of State for the Home Department [2010] EWHC 705 (Admin)... **291**

R (Sier) v Cambridge CC HBRB [2001] EWHC Admin 160, QBD; [2001] EWCA Civ 1523, CA... **480, 481, 482, 488**

R (Sibley) v West Dorset DC [2001] EWHC Admin 365... **1181**

R (T) v Richmond-upon-Thames LBC HBRB [2000] 33 HLR 65, QBD... **247**

R (Tucker) v Secretary of State for Social Security [2001] EWHC Admin 260... **128**

R (Tucker) v Secretary of State for Social Security [2001] EWHC Admin 260... **258**

R (Waite) v London Borough of Hammersmith and Fulham [2003] HLR 24... **243**

R (Wall) v Appeals Service [2003] EWHC 465 Admin... **127**

R (Wiles) v Social Security Commissioner and another [2010] EWCA Civ 258, reported as [2010] AACR 30... **170**

R v A (No 2) [2001] 2 AC 91, HL... **114**

R v Allerdale DC HBRB ex p Doughty [2000] COD 462, QBD... **179, 513, 1210**

R v Armour [1997] 2 Cr App R(S) 240, CA... **46**

R v Barrow BC ex p Catnach [1997] unreported, 3 September, QBD... **266**

R v Beverley DC HBRB ex p Hare [1995] 27 HLR 637, QBD... **1207, 1208**

R v Brent LBC ex p Shah [1983] 2 AC 309 at 343H-344B, HL... **294, 295, 296**

R v Brent LBC HBRB ex p Connery [1989] 22 HLR 40 at 44, QBD... **43, 1208, 1209**

R v Cambridge CC ex p Thomas [1995] unreported, 10 February, QBD... **248**

R v Camden LBC HBRB ex p W [1999] 21 May, unreported, QBD… **1210, 1211**
R v Canterbury CC ex p Woodhouse [1994] unreported, 2 August, QBD… **1210, 1211, 1212**
R v Chainey [1914] 1 KB 137 at 142, DC… **58**
R v Coventry CC ex p Waite [1995] unreported, 7 July, QBD… **1207, 1209**
R v Coventry CC ex p Waite [1995] unreported, 7 October, QBD… **1208, 1211, 1213**
R v Department of Social Security ex p Okito [1998] COD 48 at 49, QBD… **1155**
R v Deputy Industrial Injuries Commissioner ex p Moore [1965] 1 QB 456… **180**
R v Derby CC ex p Third Wave Housing [2000] 33 HLR 61, QBD… **246, 247**
R v Doncaster BC ex p Boulton [1992] 25 HLR 195, QBD… **554**
R v East Devon DC HBRB ex p Gibson [1993] 25 HLR, CA… **1207, 1208, 1211, 1212, 1213**
R v East Devon DC HBRB ex p Preston [1998] 31 HLR 936, QBD… **1213**
R v Ghosh [1982] QB 1053 at 1064D-G, CA… **57**
R v Gloucestershire CC ex p Barry [1997] AC 584, HL… **1177**
R v Gloucestershire CC ex p Dadds [1996] 29 HLR 700, QBD… **264, 266**
R v Greenwich LBC ex p Dhadly [1999] 32 HLR 829… **252, 264**
R v Greenwich LBC ex p Moult [1998] unreported, 19 June, CA… **254**
R v Haringey LBC ex p Ayub [1992] 25 HLR 566, QBD… **492, 493, 500**
R v HMRC ex parte Wilkinson [2005] UKHL 30… **132**
R v Ipswich BC ex p Flowers [1994] unreported, 1 March, QBD… **1213**
R v Islington LBC HBRB ex p de Grey [1992] unreported, 11 February, QBD… **481**
R v Kensington and Chelsea RBC ex p Abou-Jaoude [1996] unreported, 10 May, QBD… **1207, 1213**
R v Kensington and Chelsea RBC ex p Carney [1997] COD 124 at 125, QBD… **1210, 1211**
R v Kensington and Chelsea RBC ex p Pirie [1997] unreported, 26 March, QBD… **1206, 1207, 1208, 1211**
R v Kensington and Chelsea RBC ex p Sheikh [1997] unreported, 14 January, QBD… **1210, 1212**
R v Kensington and Chelsea RBC HBRB ex p Robertson [1988] 28 RVR 84 at 85, QBD… **243**
R v Lambert [2002] 2 AC 545, para 80, HL… **114**
R v Lambeth LBC ex p Crookes [1998] 31 HLR 59, QBD… **1063**
R v Lambeth LBC HBRB ex p Harrington [1996] unreported 22 November, QBD… **1211**
R v Liverpool CC ex p Griffiths [1990] 22 HLR 312, QBD… **481**
R v Manchester CC ex p Baragrove Properties Ltd [1991] 23 HLR 337, QBD… **265, 265, 265, 266**
R v Manchester CC ex p Harcup [1993] 26 HLR 402 at 408, QBD… **1208**
R v Manchester City Council ex p Stennett [2002] UKHL 34… **569**
R v Middlesborough BC ex p Holmes [1995] unreported, 15 February, QBD… **1197**
R v Milton Keynes BC HBRB ex p Macklen [1996] unreported, 30 April, QBD… **264**
R v Oadby and Wigston DC ex p Dickman [1995] 28 HLR 807… **1210, 1211, 1213**
R v Oldham MBC ex p G [1993] 1 FLR 645 at 662, CA… **248**
R v Passmore [2007] EWCA Crim 2053, 18 June, CA… **58**
R v Penwith DC ex p Burt [1990] 22 HLR 292 at 296, QBD… **238, 242**
R v Penwith DC ex p Menear [1991] 24 HLR 115, QBD… **19, 282**
R v Poole Borough Council ex p Ross [1995] 28 HLR 351, QBD… **247, 253, 254, 264, 266**
R v Rugby BC HBRB ex p Harrison [1994] 28 HLR 36 at 48-9, QBD… **245, 246, 252, 254, 255**
R v Sandwell MBC ex p Wilkinson [1998] 31 HLR 22, QBD… **1208, 1213**
R v Secretary of State for Social Security ex p Association of Metropolitan Authoroties [1992] 25 HLR 131, QBD… **97**
R v Secretary of State for Social Security ex p B and JCWI [1997] 1 WLR 275… **1153, 1154**
R v Secretary of State for Social Security ex p Golding [1996] unreported, 1 July, CA… **65**
R v Secretary of State for Social Security ex p Grant [1997] unreported, 31 July, QBD… **1220**
R v Secretary of State for Social Security ex p Sarwar [1997] 3 CMLR 647, CA… **5**
R v Secretary of State for Social Security ex p Smithson (case C-243/90) [1992] ECR I-467, ECJ… **1198**
R v Secretary of State for Social Security ex p T [1996] unreported, 1 November, QBD… **1154**
R v Secretary of State for Social Security ex p Taylor and Chapman [1996] *The Times*… **492**
R v Secretary of State for Social Security ex p Vijeikis [1998] COD 49, QBD… **1154, 1155**
R v Secretary of State for Social Services ex p CPAG [1990] 2 QB 540, CA… **1064**

R v Secretary of State for the Environment ex p Hammersmith and Fulham LBC [1991] 1 AC 521 at 597E-H, HL... **91**

R v Secretary of State for the Home Department ex p Brind [1991] 1 AC 696 at 747G-748F, 760D-762B, HL... **114**

R v Secretary of State for the Home Department ex p Jeyeanthan [2000] 1 WLR 354... **182**

R v Secretary of State for the Home Department ex p Pinochet (No 2) [2000] 1 AC 129, HL... **181**

R v Secretary of State for the Home Department ex parte Limbuela and others [2005] UKHL 66, 3 November, HL... **125**

R v Secretary of State for the Home Department, ex p Anderson [2002] UKHL 46... **113**

R v Secretary of State for Work and Pensions ex parte Hooper and others [2005] UKHL 29... **130**

R v Sefton MBC ex p Cunningham [1991] 23 HLR 534 at 538, QBD... **1207, 1210**

R v Sefton MBC HBRB ex p Brennan [1996] 29 HLR 735 at 741, QBD... **1212, 1213**

R v Slough BC ex p Green [1996] unreported, 15 November, QBD... **1211, 1213**

R v Solihull MBC HBRB ex p Simpson [1995] 1 FLR 140 at 148E-F, CA... **262, 263, 264**

R v South Hams DC ex p Ash [1999] 32 HLR 405 at 409, QBD... **81**

R v South Ribble DC HBRB ex p Hamilton [2000] 33 HLR 102, CA... **19, 137, 282, 814**

R v South Tyneside MBC ex p Tooley [1996] COD 143 at 144, QBD... **264**

R v St Edmundsbury BC HBRB ex p Sandys [1997] 30 HLR 800; [1998] *The Times*... **109**

R v Stewart [1987] 2 All ER 363, CA... **46**

R v Stoke-on-Trent CC ex p Highgate Projects [1996] 29 HLR 271 at 278, CA... **513**

R v Stratford-upon-Avon DC HBRB ex p White [1997] 30 HLR 178, QBD... **263**

R v Stratford-upon-Avon DC HBRB ex p White [1998] 31 HLR 126... **245, 256, 264, 265, 266**

R v Sutton LBC ex p Partridge [1994] 28 HLR 315 at 319-320... **252, 255**

R v Sutton LBC HBRB ex p Keegan [1992] 27 HLR 92 at 99-100, QBD... **246, 264, 265**

R v Swale BC HBRB ex p Marchant [1999] 1 FLR 1087, QBD; [2000] 1 FLR 246, CA... **238, 242, 594**

R v Thanet DC ex p Warren Court Hotels Ltd [2000] 33 HLR 339, CA... **585**

R v Tilley [2009] EWCA Crim 1426... **58**

R v Tower Hamlets LBC HBRB ex p Kapur [2000] *The Times*... **574**

R v Waltham Forest LBC ex p Holder [1996] 29 HLR 71 at 78-9... **1211, 1212, 1213**

R v Warrington BC ex p Williams [1997] 29 HLR 872 at 876, QBD... **21, 247, 249**

R v Westminster CC ex p Castelli and Tristan-Garcia [1995] 8 Admin LR 73 at 92E-F, QBD... **287**

R v Westminster CC HBRB ex p Mehanne [1999] 2 All ER 319, CA... **255, 1209, 1210**

R v Westminster CC HBRB ex p Pallas [1997] unreported, 23 September, QBD... **1211, 1212**

R v Westminster CC HBRB ex p Sier [1999] 32 HLR 655 at 662-3, QBD... **245, 264**

R v Woking BC ex p Crawley [1996] unreported, 19 June, QBD... **245, 246**

R v Wyre BC ex p Lord [1997] unreported, 24 October, QBD... **496**

Re B (Minors) (Abduction) [1993] 1 FLR 993 at 995C-D, FD... **295**

Re C (minors) (Adoption: Residence Order) [1994] Fam 1, CA... **258**

Re Collins [1990] Fam 56, FD... **258**

Re Forest of Dean Coal Mining Co [1879] 10 Ch D 451 at 453... **259**

Re J (a minor) (Abduction: Custody Rights) [1990] 2 AC 562... **294, 296**

Re Prince Blucher [1931] 2 Ch D 70... **1063**

Re S [2002] 2 AC 291, HL... **114**

Re Wyvern Developments Ltd [1974] 1 WLR 1097 at 1103D, Ch D... **249**

Ready-Mixed Concrete (South East) Ltd v Minister of Pensions and National Insurance [1968] 2 QB 497, CA... **259**

Rickards v Rickards [1990] Fam 194... **177**

Rider v Chief Adjudication Officer [1996] *The Times*... **528**

Rinner-Kühn Rinner-Kühn... **271**

Robson v Secretary of State for Social Services [1982] 3 FLR 232, QBD... **20**

Ruiz Zambrano (Case C-34/09)... **270**

Ruiz-Mateos v Spain (1993) 16 EHRR 505... **125**

Saker v Secretary of State for Social Security [1988] 16 January *The Times*... **1014**

Salesi v Italy (1993) 26 EHRR 187 at 199, para 19, ECtHR... **125**

Secretary of State for Social Services v Solly [1974] 3 All ER 922... **489**

Sengupta v Holmes [2002] *The Times*... **127**

Shah v Secretary of State for Social Security [2002] EWCA Civ 285, CA (reported as *R(IS) 2/ 02*)... **1131, 1155, 1172**

Singh v Post Office [1973] ICR 437 at 440... **1029**

SSWP v Ahmed [2005] EWCA Civ 535 (reported as *R(IS) 8/05*)... **1131**

SSWP v Chiltern District Council [2003] EWCA Civ 508 (reported as *R(H) 2/03*)... **147, 497**

SSWP v Gillies [2003] 2004 SLT 14, reported at 2006 SC (HL) 71... **124, 181**

SSWP v Lassal [2009] EWCA Civ 157... **274, 285**

SSWP v M [2006] UKHL 11, 8 March 2006, reported as *R(CS) 4/06*... **128, 130**

SSWP v Miah (reported as *R(JSA) 9/03*)... **21**

SSWP v Morina and Borrowdale [2007] EWCA Civ 749 (reported as *R(IS) 6/07*)... **177, 184**

SSWP v Roach [2006] (reported as *R(CS) 4/07*))... **185**

SSWP v Selby District Council and another [2006] EWCA Civ 271... **242**

SSWP v Wilson [2006] EWCA Civ 882, 29 June 2006 (reported as *R(H) 7/06*)... **29**

Stec and others v United Kingdom (Application Nos: 65731/01 and 65900/01), 6 July 2005, ECtHR... **128, 132**

Stevenson v Rogers [1992] SLT 558, IH... **653, 654**

Street v Mountford [1995] AC 809, HL... **12**

Swaddling v Chief Adjudication Officer (Case C-90/97) [1999] 2 CMLR 679, ECJ... **295**

Szoma v Secretary of State for Work and Pensions [2005] UKHL 64, [2006] 1 All ER 1 (reported as *R(IS) 2/06*)... **1173**

Taylor's Central Garages (Exeter) Ltd v Roper [1951] 115 JP 445 at 449, 450, DC... **58, 60**

The Belgian Linguistics Case (No.2) [1967] 1 EHRR 252 at 283-4, para 9, ECtHR... **130**

The House of Lords [1999] 1 WLR 1937, [1999] 4 All ER 677... **294, 295**

The House of Lords [2001] 1 WLR 539... **1209**

Thlimmenos v Greece [2001] 31 EHRR 411... **131**

Thrasyvoulou v Secretary of State for the Environment [1990] 2 AC 273 at 289, HL... **152**

Tolfree v Florence [1971] 1 WLR 141 at 144, DC... **60**

Tsfayo v United Kingdom (application no: 60860/00) 2006, 14 November, unreported, ECtHR... **127, 140, 1034**

Uratemp Ventures Ltd v Collins [2001] 3 WLR 806... **21**

Van der Mussele v Belgium [1983] 6 EHRR 163, 179-180... **131**

W (China) & Another v Secretary of State for the Home Department [2006] EWCA Civ 1494... **284**

Walsh v Rother DC [1978] 1 All ER 510 at 514a-e, HC... **63**

Ward v Kingston upon Hull CC [1993] RA 71, QBD... **654**

Warwick DC v Freeman [1994] 27 HLR 616, CA... **63, 64, 482, 483, 494, 1166**

Watson and Belmann Case C-118/75... **276**

Westminister CC v Clarke [1992] 2 AC 288 at 299, HL... **21**

Westminister CC v Croyalgrange Ltd [1986] 1 WLR 674 at 684E, HL... **58**

White v Chief Adjudication Officer [1986] 2 All ER 905, CA (reported as an appendix to *R(S) 8/ 85*))... **177**

Williams v Bayley [1866] LR 1 HL 200, HL... **64**

Williams v Horsham District Council [2004] EWCA Civ 39, 21 January, CA... **653**

Wilson v First County Trust Ltd (No 2) [2003] WLR 586... **124**

Wood v SSWP [2003] EWCA Civ 53, CA (reported as *R(DLA) 1/03*)... **141, 146, 1014, 1021, 1022**

Wright v Howell [1947] 92 SJ 26, CA... **21**

X v Italy [1977] 11 DR 114... **133**

Yesiloz v LB Camden and SSWP [2009] EWCA Civ 145 (reported as *R(H)7/09*)... **1130**

Yildiz v Secretary of State for Social Security [2001] *The Independent*... **1154, 1155**

YL (by her litigation friend the Official Solicitor) v Birmingham City Council and others [2007] UKHL 27, 20 June, HL... **117**

Zalewska v Department for Social Development [2008] UKHL 67... **280**

Table of commissioners' decisions

C 10/1995 (IS)... **272**
CCS 7967/1995... **376**
CCS 1535/1997... **152**
CCS 565/1999... **180**
CCS 557/2005... **182**
CDLA 7980/1995... **353**
CDLA 1347/1999... **124**
CDLA 5413/1999... **125**
CDLA 3432/2001... **127**
CDLA 4895/2001... **1008**
CDLA 4977/2001... **463**
CDLA 1456/2002... **178, 179**
CDLA 2748/2002... **126, 181**
CDLA 2975/2002... **178, 179**
CDLA 4331/2002... **149**
CDLA 1685/2004... **1070**
CDLA 2014/2004... **1060**
CDLA 2999/2004... **1023**
CDLA 1589/2005... **457**
CF 6923/1999... **150**
CF 1863/2007... **277**
CFC 25/1989... **359**
CFC 1537/1995... **334**
CG 1479/1999... **1016**
CG 2122/2001... **1007**
CH 3776/2001... **585**
CH 3853/2001... **152, 261**
CH 4065/2001... **479, 484**
CH 4838/2001... **484**
CH 4943/2001... **455, 462, 463, 497**
CH 5135/2001... **452**
CH 5147/2001... **252**
CH 5217/2001... **462**
CH 5221/2001... **180**
CH 393/2002... **239**
CH 396/2002... **251, 261**
CH 474/2002... **452**
CH 627/2002... **178**
CH 716/2002... **252, 257, 260**
CH 843/2002... **251**
CH 844/2002... **303**
CH 999/2002... **455**
CH 1076/2002... **179, 254, 255**
CH 1085/2002... **181, 238**
CH 1129/2002... **145, 149**
CH 1171/2002... **146, 246, 247, 252**
CH 1172/2002... **484**
CH 1175/2002... **145, 149, 1177**
CH 1296/2002... **479**
CH 1325/2002... **255**
CH 1618/2002... **247**

CH 1992/2002... **1213**
CH 1993/2002... **1213**
CH 2191/2002... **452**
CH 2201/2002... **239, 240, 241, 479**
CH 2302/2002... **139, 182**
CH 2321/2002... **363, 367, 371, 380, 482, 558**
CH 2349/2002... **182, 497**
CH 2387/2002... **360**
CH 2443/2002... **490**
CH 2521/2002... **238, 239**
CH 2554/2002... **484, 485**
CH 2659/2002... **452**
CH 2888/2002... **484**
CH 3008/2002... **252, 253, 263**
CH 3009/2002... **145, 452, 1008, 1013, 1021**
CH 3376/2002... **245, 305**
CH 3629/2002... **484**
CH 3679/2002... **180, 1010**
CH 3679/2002... **481**
CH 4099/2002... **463**
CH 4465/2002... **484**
CH 4546/2002... **240**
CH 4922/2002... **246**
CH 4970/2002... **1209, 1213**
CH 4972/2002... **383**
CH 5125/2002... **94**
CH 5302/2002... **260**
CH 5553/2002... **421, 497**
CH 69/2003... **482**
CH 216/2003... **463**
CH 296/2003... **224**
CH 329/2003... **355**
CH 393/2003... **452**
CH 663/2003... **248, 253, 254**
CH 943/2003... **437, 481, 482**
CH 1176/2003... **485**
CH 1208/2003... **246, 327**
CH 1210/2003... **152**
CH 1278/2003... **223, 224**
CH 1953/2003... **392**
CH 2214/2003... **1215**
CH 2329/2003... **253, 255, 302**
CH 2516/2003... **264**
CH 2743/2003... **222**
CH 3110/2003... **303**
CH 3197/2003... **393**
CH 3616/2003... **223, 260**
CH 3743/2003... **253, 254**
CH 4354/2003... **478**

CH 4390/2003... **455**
CH 4574/2003... **128, 243**
CH 4733/2003... **258, 259, 260**
CH 4854/2003... **254**
CH 4918/2003... **483, 484**
CH 296/2004... **178, 253, 254**
CH 609/2004... **484**
CH 939/2004... **481**
CH 996/2004... **243, 451**
CH 1097/2004... **254**
CH 1237/2004... **243**
CH 1326/2004... **262**
CH 1586/2004... **251, 261**
CH 1762/2004... **421**
CH 1791/2004... **451**
CH 1854/2004... **242**
CH 2258/2004... **222**
CH 2517/2004... **556**
CH 2794/2004... **456, 458, 480, 481, 483**
CH 3439/2004... **479, 484**
CH 3656/2004... **256**
CH 3817/2004... **43, 177, 443, 451, 1010, 1043**
CH 3857/2004... **241**
CH 3893/2004... **242, 243**
CH 257/2005... **247**
CH 318/2005... **226**
CH 704/2005... **152**
CH 1419/2005... **265**
CH 1450/2005... **371**
CH 1561/2005... **339, 340, 437**
CH 1675/2005... **485**
CH 1786/2005... **238**
CH 2409/2005... **483**
CH 2484/2005... **289**
CH 2899/2005... **253, 254**
CH 2986/2005... **322, 469**
CH 3083/2005... **480**
CH 3220/2005... **260**
CH 3314/2005... **271, 274, 275**
CH 3497/2005... **1041**
CH 3761/2005... **480, 482**
CH 3900/2005... **1201**
CH 4108 2005... **471**
CH 48/2006... **430**
CH 180/2006... **471, 474**
CH 282/2006... **1029**
CH 361/2006... **329**
CH 532/2006... **157, 460**
CH 533/2006... **157**
CH 542/2006... **256**
CH 687/2006... **482**
CH 858/2006... **479**
CH 1363/2006... **241**
CH 1400/2006... **287**
CH 1556/2006... **518**
CH 1578/2006... **303**

CH 1822 2006... **387**
CH 1911/2006... **240**
CH 2121/2006... **248**
CH 2959/2006... **246**
CH 2995/2006... **1031, 1033, 1034, 1035**
CH 3076/2006... **719**
CH 3282/2006... **253**
CH 3528/2006... **302, 1211, 1212**
CH 3622/2006... **44, 443**
CH 3736/2006... **434, 1035**
CH 3744/2006... **487**
CH 4248/2006... **1172**
CH 4428/2006... **481**
CH 4429/2006... **416**
CH 39/2007... **262**
CH 1289/2007... **1201**
CH 1384/2007... **719**
CH 1672/2007... **342**
CH 2555/2007... **455**
CH 2805/2007... **1202**
CH 2943/2007... **484**
CH 3590/2007... **518**
CH 3631/2007... **1043, 1044**
CH 3729/2007... **379**
CH 4014/2007... **343**
CH 1096/2008... **253**
CH 1330/2008... **360**
CH 2198/2008... **452**
CH 2726/2008... **1201**
CH 3495/2008... **492**
CH 3670/2008... **379**
CIB 5227/1999... **180**
CIB 3985/2001... **126**
CIB 4427/2002... **150**
CIB 4667/2002... **180**
CIB 2949/2005... **150**
CIS 124/1990... **386**
CIS 159/1990... **489**
CIS 93/1991... **378**
CIS 195/1991... **254**
CIS 222/1991... **489**
CIS 754/1991... **248**
CIS 93/1992... **1018**
CIS 395/1992... **489**
CIS 522/1992... **497**
CIS 671/1992... **22**
CIS 30/1993... **386**
CIS 77/1993... **361**
CIS 87/1993... **20**
CIS 393/1993... **489**
CIS 590/1993... **343, 360**
CIS 166/1994... **5**
CIS 368/1994... **577**
CIS 372/1994... **489**
CIS 564/1994... **281**
CIS 683/1994... **494**
CIS 1460/1995... **514**

CIS 2326/1995... **294, 295, 296**
CIS 5136/1995... **296**
CIS 8111/1995... **294, 295, 296**
CIS 11304/1995... **22**
CIS 11481/1995... **294**
CIS 11293/1996... **1198**
CIS 12703/1996... **296**
CIS 13498/1996... **294, 295, 296**
CIS 13986/1996... **406**
CIS 14591/1996... **296**
CIS 14850/1996... **228**
CIS 15611/1996... **529**
CIS 15927/1996... **294**
CIS 16410/1996... **294**
CIS 16992/1996... **1154, 1155**
CIS 85/1997... **231**
CIS 1137/1997... **1220**
CIS 1304/1997... **295**
CIS 1586/1997... **386**
CIS 2575/1997... **392**
CIS 3283/1997... **392**
CIS 3287/1997... **17**
CIS 3955/1997... **1154**
CIS 6002/1997... **181**
CIS 3418/1998... **1170**
CIS 4341/1998... **1220**
CIS 114/1999... **376**
CIS 217/1999... **1016**
CIS 1077/1999... **1155**
CIS 1115/1999... **1154**
CIS 2428/1999... **149**
CIS 5825/1999... **496**
CIS 6088/1999... **1155**
CIS 6249/1999... **1013**
CIS 6258/1999... **1154**
CIS 2943/2000... **379**
CIS 3508/2001... **1131**
CIS 47/2002... **1131**
CIS 521/2002... **561**
CIS 1277/2002... **1027**
CIS 4901/2002... **1039**
CIS 1870/2003... **131**
CIS 1972/2003... **295**
CIS 2505/2003... **142**
CIS 2532/2003... **228**
CIS 3228/2003... **478**
CIS 4348/2003... **490**
CIS 4474/2003... **294, 295**
CIS 1675/2004... **1021**
CIS 1697/2004... **1130**
CIS 218/2005... **386**
CIS 2559/2005... **295**
CIS 3182/2005... **274**
CIS 3573/2005... **289**
CIS 3875/2005... **287**
CIS 3890/2005... **274**
CIS 34/2006... **282**

CIS 1068/2006... **564**
CIS 1757 2006... **387**
CIS 1934/2006... **276**
CIS 2317/2006... **335**
CIS 2431/2006... **277**
CIS 2448/2006... **569**
CIS 3232/2006... **281**
CIS 4010/2006... **274**
CIS 647/2007... **356, 357**
CIS 731/2007... **274**
CIS 1793/2007... **272**
CIS 1813/2007... **356, 372**
CIS 1833/2007... **286**
CIS 1915/2007... **573**
CIS 2100/2007... **277**
CIS 2911/2007... **274**
CIS 3655/2007... **1021, 1022**
CIS 3799/2007... **275**
CIS 3960/2007... **292**
CIS 4144/2007... **271**
CIS 4237/2007... **274**
CIS 4299/2007... **285, 286**
CIS 4304/2007... **274, 276, 283**
CIS 185/2008... **293**
CIS 612/2008... **286**
CIS 1042/2008... **273, 279**
CIS 2258/2008... **286**
CIS 2287/2008... **379, 391**
CIS 2357/2009... **293**
CJSA 3979/1999... **456, 457**
CJSA 2375/2000... **149**
CJSA 1332/2001... **457**
CJSA 5100/2001... **126, 179**
CJSA 549/2003... **372**
CJSA 825/2004... **407**
CJSA 1425/2004... **386, 387**
CJSA 1223/2006... **295**
CJSA 3832/2006... **233**
CJSA 3960/2006... **1039**
CJSA 1556/2007... **379**
CP 8001/1995... **20**
CP 5084/2001... **133**
CP 518/2003... **131, 132**
CPC 2920/2005... **289**
CPC 683/2007... **567**
CPC 2134/2007... **286**
CPC 3373/2007... **367, 368**
CPC 1433/2008... **277**
CPC 1446/2008... **228**
CPC 1935/2010... **293**
CS 249/1989... **353**
CS 130/1992... **489**
CS 12770/1996... **489**
CS 14430/1996... **149**
CS 2647/1997... **353**
CSB 150/1985... **20**
CSB 1006/1985... **489**

CSB 64/1986… **489**
CSB 598/1987… **386**
CSB 950/1987… **434, 782**
CSDLA 855/1997… **181**
CSDLA 1019/1999… **124, 181**
CSDLA 336/2000… **180**
CSDLA 2/2002… **149**
CSDLA 606/2003… **181**
CSG 336/2003… **1088**
CSH 499/2006… **242**
CSHB 718/2002… **248, 251, 263, 482**
CSHB 405/2005… **242**
CSHB 606/2005… **245**
CSIB 848/1997… **181**
CSIB 588/1998… **180**
CSIS 62/1991… **497**
CSIS 100/1993… **228**
CSIS 185/1995… **228**
CSIS 460/2002… **127**
CSIS 754/2002… **142**
CSIS 652/2003… **228**
CSPC 677/2007… **261**
CTC 626/2001… **360**
CTC 3646/2007… **352**
CU 47/1993… **180**
R(A) 1/72… **179**
R(CS) 5/96… **296**
R(CS) 5/02… **178**
R(CS) 3/04… **1007**
R(DLA) 2/01… **149**
R(DLA) 3/01… **142**
R(DLA) 4/02… **128**
R(DLA) 3/05… **1008**
R(FC) 2/90… **232**
R(FC) 1/91… **367**
R(FC) 3/98… **157**
R(G) 1/79… **20**
R(H) 1/02… **180, 462, 485**
R(H) 1/03… **179, 252, 253**
R(H) 2/03… **1046**
R(H) 3/03… **251, 478**
R(H) 1/04… **480, 482**
R(H) 2/04… **480, 482**
R(H) 3/04… **43, 44, 64, 141, 143, 144, 146, 147, 152, 462, 463, 1046**
R(H) 5/04… **455**
R(H) 6/04… **141, 261**
R(H) 7/04… **43, 44, 148**
R(H) 8/04… **129, 131, 252**
R(H) 9/04… **282**
R(H) 1/05… **496**
R(H) 2/05… **1211, 1212**
R(H) 3/05… **460**
R(H) 4/05… **660**
R(H) 5/05… **245, 341, 496, 554**
R(H) 6/05… **257**
R(H) 7/05… **223, 223, 251, 263**

R(H) 9/05… **238, 239, 240, 241**
R(H) 10/05… **253, 263**
R(H) 1/06… **386**
R(H) 2/06… **456**
R(H) 3/06… **1209**
R(H) 4/06… **242**
R(H) 5/06… **256**
R(H) 6/06… **43, 44, 147, 148, 487, 488, 1046**
R(H) 1/07… **1015, 1041, 1064**
R(H) 2/07… **1201**
R(H) 3/07… **222**
R(H) 4/07… **241**
R(H) 5/07… **367**
R(H) 6/07… **261**
R(H) 7/07… **1201**
R(H) 8/07… **223**
R(H) 9/07… **433, 450**
R(H) 10/07… **43**
R(H) 1/08… **471, 1013**
R(H) 2/08… **469, 1013**
R(H) 3/08… **12, 654**
R(H) 4/08… **1034, 1035, 1046**
R(H) 5/08… **367**
R(H) 6/08… **1201, 1202**
R(H) 7/08… **569**
R(H) 8/08… **339**
R(H) 9/08… **303**
R(H) 10/08… **481, 482, 483**
R(H) 1/09… **1034**
R(H) 2/09… **371**
R(H) 4/09… **1201, 1202**
R(H) 5/09… **5, 21**
R(H) 8/09… **518**
R(I) 56/54… **1022**
R(I) 7/62… **1044**
R(I) 2/83… **1044**
R(I) 2/88… **1022**
R(I) 2/94… **1022**
R(I) 5/02… **1007**
R(I) 1/03… **157**
R(I) 2/06… **179**
R(IB) 4/02… **1013**
R(IB) 3/03… **94**
R(IB) 2/04… **143, 145, 148, 463, 471, 478, 1013, 1014, 1021**
R(IB) 2/07… **94**
R(IS) 1/90… **379**
R(IS) 2/90… **383**
R(IS) 5/92… **497**
R(IS) 6/92… **360, 361**
R(IS) 12/92… **378**
R(IS) 1/93… **232**
R(IS) 3/93… **343**
R(IS) 14/93… **262, 387**
R(IS) 17/93… **244, 431**
R(IS) 21/93… **382**

R(IS) 17/94... **248**
R(IS) 5/95... **232**
R(IS) 8/95... **233**
R(IS) 16/95... **399**
R(IS) 21/95... **232**
R(IS) 22/95... **232**
R(IS) 1/96... **407**
R(IS) 6/96... **294, 295, 296**
R(IS) 8/96... **352**
R(IS) 12/96... **227**
R(IS) 3/97... **278**
R(IS) 11/98... **254**
R(IS) 12/98... **271, 274**
R(IS) 15/98... **405**
R(IS) 19/98... **399**
R(IS) 22/98... **341**
R(IS) 1/99... **22**
R(IS) 5/99... **399**
R(IS) 7/99... **406**
R(IS) 8/99... **16**
R(IS) 11/99... **179**
R(IS) 13/99... **232**
R(IS) 1/00... **405**
R(IS) 6/00... **272**
R(IS) 3/01... **857**
R(IS) 6/01... **1044**
R(IS) 10/01... **377**
R(IS) 2/02... **1172**
R(IS) 4/03... **392, 393**
R(IS) 5/03... **490**
R(IS) 6/03... **342**
R(IS) 1/04... **125, 126**
R(IS) 2/04... **126**
R(IS) 3/04... **1043**
R(IS) 6/04... **124, 125, 127**
R(IS) 6/04... **1044**
R(IS) 15/04... **125, 1013, 1016**
R(IS) 16/04... **857, 1039**
R(IS) 5/05... **567**
R(IS) 7/05... **490**
R(IS) 7/06... **295**
R(IS) 11/06... **131**
R(IS) 5/07... **393**
R(IS) 2/08... **145, 148**
R(IS) 3/08... **286**
R(IS) 5/08... **569**
R(IS) 9/08... **343**

R(IS) 6/09... **177**
R(JSA) 1/02... **393**
R(JSA) 2/02... **407**
R(JSA) 3/02... **407**
R(JSA) 4/03... **233**
R(JSA) 2/04... **452**
R(JSA) 1/07... **232, 233**
R(P) 1/06... **133**
R(P) 2/06... **129**
R(PC) 3/08... **343**
R(PC) 1/09... **1130**
R(S) 2/63(T)... **451**
R(S) 4/84... **352**
R(S) 4/86... **1014, 1022**
R(SB) 10/81... **239, 569**
R(SB) 17/81... **20**
R(SB) 13/82... **22**
R(SB) 21/82... **490**
R(SB) 2/83... **180**
R(SB) 4/83... **22**
R(SB) 20/83... **399**
R(SB) 30/83... **22**
R(SB) 41/83... **404**
R(SB) 54/83... **490**
R(SB) 13/84... **566**
R(SB) 25/84... **1044**
R(SB) 27/84... **566**
R(SB) 40/84... **490**
R(SB) 1/85... **379**
R(SB) 4/85... **152**
R(SB) 8/85... **22**
R(SB) 9/85... **490**
R(SB) 18/85... **489**
R(SB) 35/85... **20**
R(SB) 38/85... **386**
R(SB) 40/85... **386**
R(SB) 21/86... **343, 360**
R(SB) 12/87... **534**
R(SB) 15/87... **490**
R(SB) 22/87... **256**
R(SB) 25/87... **399**
R(SB) 2/88... **461**
R(SB) 2/89... **377, 388**
R(SB) 9/91... **386**
R(SB) 12/91... **386**
R(TC) 1/05... **1017**

Table of Upper Tribunal decisions

AA v Cheshire and Wirral Partnership NHS Foundation Trust [2009] UKUT 195 (AAC)... **1072, 1073**

AA v Leicester City Council [2009] UKUT 86 (AAC)... **1033, 1034**

AA v London Borough of Hounslow [2008] UKUT 13 (AAC)... **454, 1033**

AH v Mendip DC [2008] UKUT 18 (AAC), R(H) 3/09... **487**

AM v SSWP [2009] UKUT 224 (AAC)... **1073**

AP-H v SSWP [2010] UKUT 183 (AAC)... **149**

AR v Bradford MBC [2008] UKUT 30 (AAC), R(H) 6/09... **341, 366**

AW v Essex County Council (SEN) [2010] UKUT 74 (AAC)... **177**

Basildon DC v AM [2009] UKUT 113 (AAC)... **252**

BB v South London & Maudsley NHS Trust & MOJ [2009] UKUT 157 (AAC)... **183**

Bexley LB v LD (HB) [2010] UKUT 79 (AAC)... **313, 331, 592, 607**

Birmingham City Council v IB [2009] UKUT 116 (AAC)... **21, 238, 240**

BM v Cheshire West and Chester Council [2009] UKUT 162 (AAC)... **1214, 1215**

Bradford MDC v MR (HB) [2010] UKUT 315 (AAC)... **260**

Bristol CC v AW [2009] UKUT 109 (AAC)... **1202**

BS v SSWP [2009] UKUT 16 (AAC)... **273, 280**

CD v First-tier Tribunal (SEC) (CIC) [2010] UKUT 181 (AAC)... **1052**

CH 4085/2007 [2008] UKUT 14 (AAC)... **29, 30**

CH v Wakefield DC [2009] UKUT 20 (AAC)... **261**

Chorley BC v IT (HB) [2009] UKUT 107 (AAC); [2010] AACR 2... **1201, 1202**

CIB 8/2008 [2009] UKUT 47 (AAC)... **126, 127**

CM v SSWP [2009] UKUT 43 (AAC), R(IS) 7/09... **407**

CP v M Technology School (SEN) [2010] UKUT 314 (AAC)... **181**

CR v Wycombe DC [2009] UKUT 19 (AAC)... **222**

DL v LB Redbridge [2010] UKUT 293 (AAC)... **1072**

DL v Liverpool City Council [2009] UKUT 176 (AAC)... **44, 487, 488, 489**

DN v Leicester City Council (HB) [2010] UKUT 253 (AAC)... **144, 1022**

Dorset Healthcare NHS Foundation Trust v MH [2009] UKUT 4 (AAC)'13 **178**

EF v SSWP [2009] UKUT 92 (AAC); R(IB) 3/09... **187**

EM and KN v SSWP [2009] UKUT 44 (AAC)... **293**

EM v Waltham Forest LBC [2009] UKUT 245 (AAC)... **342, 482, 483**

EW v Neath Port Talbot County Borough Council [2009] UKUT 14 (AAC)... **496**

FL v First-tier Tribunal and CICA [2010] UKUT 158 (AAC)... **145**

IB v Barnsley Metropolitan Borough Council [2009] UKUT 279 (AAC)... **700**

JH v SSWP [2009] UKUT 1 (AAC)... **566**

Kingston upon Hull CC v DLM (HB) [2010] UKUT 234 (AAC)... **342, 483**

KS v SSWP (JSA) [2009] UKUT 122 (AAC); [2010] AACR 3... **379, 386**

KS v SSWP (PC) [2010] UKUT 156 (AAC)... **296**

LA v SSWP [2010] UKUT 109 (AAC)... **270**

LCC v SSWP [2009] UKUT 74 (AAC)... **30**

Leicester City Council v LG [2009] UKUT 155 (AAC)... **449, 450, 451, 845, 856**

LM v LB Lewisham [2009] UKUT 204 (AAC): [2010] AACR 12... **178, 1060**

LM v SSWP [2009] UKUT 185 (AAC)... **1073**

London Borough of Hackney v GA [2008] UKUT 26 (AAC); R(H) 5/09... **21, 238, 240, 566**

London Borough of Islington v SJ [2008] UKUT 31 (AAC)... **469, 477**

MA v SSWP [2009] UKUT 211 (AAC)... **1050, 1052**

MD v SSWP (Enforcement Reference) [2010] UKUT 202 (AAC)... **1054**

MH v Wirral MBC [2009] UKUT 60 (AAC)... **260**

Middlesbrough BC v DS [2009] UKUT 80 (AAC)... **483**

MP v SSWP (DLA) [2010] UKUT 103 (AAC)... **177, 1058, 1066, 1070**

MR v CMEC [2009] UKUT 284 (AAC), [2009] UKUT 285 (AAC), [2010] UKUT 38 (AAC)... **1054**

NC v Tonbridge & Malling Borough Council [2010] UKUT 12 (AAC)... **354**

OFSTED v GM and WM [2009] UKUT 89 (AAC)... **145**

PA v CMEC [2009] UKUT 283 (AAC)... **1054**

PM v SSWP [2009] UKUT 236 (AAC)... **281**

R (RB) v First-tier Tribunal (Review) [2010] UKUT 160 (AAC)... **1073**

RF v CMEC (CSM) [2010] UKUT 41 (AAC)... **1051**

RK v SSWP [2008] UKUT 34 (AAC)... **228**

RM v SSWP (IS) [2010] UKUT 238 (AAC)... **292**

RM v SSWP [2009] UKUT 256 (AAC)... **1066**

SA v LB Newham (HB) [2010] UKUT 191 (AAC)... **245, 250**

Salford CC v PF [2009] UKUT 150 (AAC)... **225, 1202**

SD v London Borough of Brent [2009] UKUT 7 (AAC)... **259**

SD v Newcastle City Council (HB) [2010] UKUT 306 (AAC)... **343**

SE v SSWP [2009] UKUT 163 (AAC)... **1073, 1074**

Secretary of State for Education v JN [2010] UKUT 248 (AAC)... **145**

SG v Tameside MBC (HB) [2010] UKUT 243 (AAC)... **284**

SK v South Hams DC (HB) [2010] UKUT 129 (AAC)... **238, 313, 331, 518**

SN v London Borough of Hounslow [2010] UKUT 57 (AAC)... **480**

SSWP v AA [2009] UKUT 249 (AAC)... **270**

SSWP v CA [2009] UKUT 169 (AAC)... **290**

SSWP v EM [2009] UKUT 146 (AAC)... **275**

SSWP v FE [2009] UKUT 287 (AAC)... **275**

SSWP v IA [2009] UKUT 35 (AAC)... **277**

SSWP v IG [2008] UKUT 5 (AAC)... **1130**

SSWP v IR [2009] UKUT 11 (AAC)... **276, 277**

SSWP v JP (JSA) [2010] UKUT 90 (AAC)... **342**

SSWP v JS (IS) [2010] UKUT 131 (AAC)... **274**

SSWP v JS (IS) [2010] UKUT 240 (AAC)... **273, 276**

SSWP v JS (IS) [2010] UKUT 347 (AAC)... **292**

SSWP v RK [2009] UKUT 209 (AAC)... **276**

SSWP v Sister IS & Sister KM [2009] UKUT 200 (AAC)... **262**

SSWP v ZA [2009] UKUT 294 (AAC)... **281**

SSWP v ZW [2009] UKUT 25 (AAC)... **275**

ST v SSWP [2009] UKUT 269 (AAC)... **227**

Stroud DC v JG [2009] UKUT 67 (AAC); R(H) 8/09... **238, 242, 328, 518, 594**

SW v SSWP (IB) [2010] UKUT 73 (AAC)... **182**

Synergy Child Services Ltd v Ofsted [2009] UKUT 125 (AAC)... **177**

TG v SSWP [2009] UKUT 58 (AAC)... **273**

Torbay BC v RF [2010] UKUT 7 (AAC)... **243**

UH v LB Islington [2010] UKUT 64 (AAC)... **452**

VH v Suffolk County Council [2010] UKUT 203 (AAC)... **1072**

Walsall BC v GP Ltd and others [2009] UKUT 247 AAC; [2010] AACR 16... **43**

Wirral MBC v AH and SSWP (HB) [2010] UKUT 208 (AAC)... **323, 336**

Wirral MBC v AL (HB) [2010] UKUT 254 (AAC)... **475, 477**

Housing Benefit Regulations: Destinations table

General

HB Regs 1987	HB Regs 2006		HB (SPC) Regs 2006	
Reg 1	1	p209	1	p771
Reg 2	2	p209	2	p771
Reg 2B	4	p229	4	p783
Reg 3	3	p226	3	p782
	New Reg 5	p230	New Reg 5	p783
Reg 4	6	p230	6	p784

Provisions affecting entitlement to housing benefit

HB Regs 1987	HB Regs 2006		HB (SPC) Regs 2006	
Reg 5	7	p233	7	p785
Reg 6	8	p244	8	p788
Reg 7	9	p249	9	p789
Reg 7A	10	p266	10	p790
Reg 7B	Sch 4 SI 2006 No 217	p1225	Sch 4 SI 2006 No 217	p1225

Payments in respect of a dwelling

HB Regs 1987	HB Regs 2006		HB (SPC) Regs 2006	
Reg 8	11	p298	11	p792
Reg 10	12	p300	12	p793
	New reg 12B	p304	New reg 12B	p794
	New reg 12C	p306	New reg 12C	p795
	New reg 12D	p307	New reg 12D	p795
	New regs 12F-12K	p586	New regs 12F-12K	p907
Reg 11	13	p312	13	p798
Old reg 12	Sch 3 paras 4 and 5 SI 2006 No 217	p1225	Sch 3 paras 4 and 5 SI 2006 No 217	p1197
	New reg 13ZA	p315	New reg 13ZA	p799
	New reg 13ZB	p316	New reg 13ZB	p800
	New reg 13C	p317	New reg 13C	p800
	New reg 13D	p319	New reg 13D	p801
	New reg 13E	p324	New reg 13E	p804
Reg 12A	14	p324	14	p804
Reg 12B	15	p329	15	p806
Reg 12C	17	p331	17	p808
Reg 12CA	16	p329	16	p807
Reg 12D	18	p331	18	p808
	New reg 18A	p332	New reg 18A	p808

Membership of a family

HB Regs 1987	HB Regs 2006		HB (SPC) Regs 2006	
Reg 13	19	p332	19	p809
Reg 14	20	p334	20	p809
Reg 15	21	p335	21	p809

Applicable amounts

HB Regs 1987	HB Regs 2006		HB&CTB (SPC) Regs 2003 substituted reg	HB (SPC) Regs 2006	
Reg 16	22	p337	Reg 16	22	p810
Reg 17	23	p338			
Reg 18	24 Now revoked	p339			

Income and capital

HB Regs 1987	HB Regs 2006		HB&CTB (SPC) Regs 2003 substituted reg	HB (SPC) Regs 2006	
Reg 19	25	p344	Reg 19	23	p811
Reg 20	26	p345		24	p812
Reg 21	27	p346	Reg 21	25	p812
Reg 21A	28	p347	Reg 22	26	p812
Reg 22	29	p353	Reg 23	27	p813
Reg 23	30	p355	Reg 24	28	p815
Reg 24	31	p355	Reg 25	29	p815
Reg 24A	32	p356	Reg 26	30	p817
Reg 25	33	p357	Reg 27	31	p818
Reg 28	35	p358	Reg 28	33	p822
Reg 29	36	p362	Reg 29	34	p824
Reg 30	37	p363	Reg 30	35	p824
Reg 31	38	p364	Reg 31	36	p825
Reg 32	39	p368	Reg 32	37	p826
Reg 33	40	p369	Reg 33	38	p827
Reg 34	41	p372	Reg 34	39	p827
Reg 35	42	p373	Reg 35	40	p829
Reg 37	43	p380	Reg 36	41	p830
Reg 38	44	p380	Reg 37	42	p832
Reg 39	45	p380	Reg 38	43	p832
Reg 40	46	p381	Reg 39	44	p833
Reg 41	47	p382	Reg 40	45	p833
Reg 42	48	p383	Reg 41	46	p833
Reg 43	49	p383	Reg 42	47	p833
Reg 43A	50	p388	Reg 43	48	p834
Reg 44	51	p391	Reg 44	49	p837
Reg 45	52	p393			

Students

HB Regs 1987	HB Regs 2006	
Reg 46	53	p395
Reg 47	54	p400
Reg 48	55	p401
Reg 48A	56	p401
Reg 50	57	p408
Reg 52	58	p409
Reg 53	59	p409
Reg 54	60	p412
Reg 55	61	p412
Reg 56	62	p413
Reg 57	63	p413
Reg 57A	64	p413
	New reg 64A	p416
Reg 57B	65	p416
Reg 58	66	p417
Reg 58A	67	p417
Reg 59	68	p417
Reg 60	69	p417

Amount of benefit

HB Regs 1987	HB Regs 2006		HB&CTB (SPC) Regs 2003 inserted reg	HB (SPC) Regs 2006	
Reg 61	70	p418		50	p837
Reg 62	71	p419		51	p837
				New reg 52	p837
Reg 62A	72	p419			
	New reg 72A	p421			
	New reg 72B	p421			
	New reg 72C	p423			
	New reg 72D	p424			
Reg 62ZB	73	p425		53	p838
	New reg 73A	p425		New reg 53A	p839
	New reg 73B	p426		New reg 53B	p839
	New reg 73C	p426		New reg 53C	p840
	New reg 73D	p427		New reg 53D	p840
			Reg 62B	54	p841
Reg 63	74	p427		55	p842
Reg 64	75	p432		56	p844

Calculation of weekly amounts and changes of circumstances

HB Regs 1987	HB Regs 2006		HB (SPC) Regs 2006	
Reg 65	76	p432	57	p844
Reg 65A	77	p434		
Reg 65B	78	p434	58	p845
Reg 66				
Reg 67				
Reg 68	79	p434	59	p845
Reg 68A				
Reg 68B			60	p847
Reg 69	80	p437	61	p850
Reg 70	81	p440	62	p851

Claims

HB Regs 1987	HB Regs 2006		HB (SPC) Regs 2006	
Reg 71	82	p442	63	p852
Reg 72	83	p443	64	p853
	New reg 83A	p452	New reg 64A	p416
Reg 72A	84	p452	65	p857
Reg 72B	85	p453	66	p857
Reg 72BA	No provision		64(1)	p853
Reg 73	86	p453	67	p857
Reg 74	87	p456	68	p858
Reg 75	88	p457	69	p859
	New reg 88A	p459	New reg 69A	p861

Decisions on questions

HB Regs 1987	HB Regs 2006		HB (SPC) Regs 2006	
Reg 76	89	p460	70	p861
Reg 77	90	p461	71	p861

Payments

HB Regs 1987	HB Regs 2006		HB (SPC) Regs 2006	
Reg 88	91	p464	72	p861
	New reg 91A	p465	New reg 72A	p862
Reg 90	92	p466	73	p862
Reg 91	93	p467	74	p863
Reg 92	94	p469	75	p863
Reg 93	95	p470	76	p864
Reg 94	96	p473	77	p864
Reg 96	97	p476	78	p865
Reg 97	98	p476	79	p866

Overpayments

HB Regs 1987	HB Regs 2006		HB (SPC) Regs 2006	
Reg 98	99	p477	80	p866
Reg 99	100	p478	81	p866
Reg 100	101	p486	82	p867
Reg 101	102	p490	83	p868
Reg 102	103	p494	84	p869
Reg 103	104	p496	85	p869
Reg 104	105	p498	86	p870
1997/2435 106	106	p499	87	p871
1997/2435 107	107	p500	88	p872

Information

Source	HB Regs 2006		HB (SPC) Regs 2006	
SI 2002 No 1132, reg 2	108	p501	89	p872
SI 2002 No 1132, reg 3	109	p501	90	p872
	New reg 109A	p501	New reg 90A	p873
SI 2002 No 1132, reg 4	110	p502	91	p873
SI 2002 No 1132, reg 5	111	p502	92	p873
SI 2002 No 1132, reg 6	112	p502	93	p873
SI 1997 No 2436, reg 1	113	p503	94	p874

Source	HB Regs 2006		HB (SPC) Regs 2006	
HB Regs 1987, Reg 106	114	p506	95	p877
	New reg 114A	p503	95A	p874
SI 1988 No 662, reg 5	115	p506	96	p877
SI 1988 No 662, reg 6	116	p507	97	p877
SI 1997 No 2436, reg 2	117	p507	98	p878
SI 1997 No 2436, reg 3	118	p508	99	p878
SI 1997 No 2436, reg 4	119	p508	100	p879
SI 1997 No 2436, reg 5	120	p511	101	p880
SI 1997 No 2436, reg 6	121	p511	102	p880
	121A	p511	102A	p881
	New reg 122	p512	New reg 103	p881

Schedules

HB Regs 1987	HB Regs 2006		HB&CTB (SPC) Regs 2003	HB (SPC) Regs 2006	
Sch A1	Sch 4 SI 2006 No 217	p1225		Sch 4 SI 2006 No 217	p1225
Sch 1	Sch 1	p512		Sch 1	p881
Sch 1A	Sch 2	p517		Sch 2	p884
Sch 2	Sch 3	p521			
			Sch 2A	Sch 3	p886
Sch 3	Sch 4	p542			
			Sch 3A	Sch 4	p890
Sch 4	Sch 5	p550			
			Sch 4A	Sch 5	p893
Sch 5	Sch 6	p565			
			Sch 5ZA	Sch 6	p898
Sch 5A	Sch7	p580			
Sch 5B	Sch 8	p580		Sch 7	p904
Sch 6	Sch 9	p580		Sch 8	p904
	New Sch 10	p586		New Sch 9	p907
	New Sch 11	p590		New Sch 10	p911

Council Tax Benefit Regulations: destinations table

CTB Regs 1992	CTB Regs 2006		CTB (SPC) Regs		
Reg 1	1	p644	1		p916
Reg 2	2	p644	2		p916
Reg 2B	4	p655	4		p925
Reg 3	3	p654	3		p924
	New reg 5	p655	New reg 5		p925
Reg 4	6	p656	6		p925
Reg 4A	7	p657	7		p926
	New reg 7A	p658	New reg 7A		p927
Reg 4C	8	p658	8		p928
Reg 4D	Sch 4 SI 2006 No 217	p1225	Sch 4 SI 2006 No 217		p1225

CTB Regs 1992	CTB Regs 2006		CTB (SPC) Regs		
Reg 5	9	p660	9		p929
Reg 6	10	p661	10		p930
Reg 7	11	p661	11		p930

Applicable amounts

CTB Regs 1992	CTB Regs 2006		HB&CTB (SPC) Regs 2003 substituted reg	CTB (SPC) Regs 2006	
Reg 8	12	p662	Reg 8	12	p931
Reg 9	13	p663			
Reg 10	14 Now revoked	p663			

Income and capital

CTB Regs 1992	CTB Regs 2006		HB&CTB (SPC) Regs 2003 substituted reg	CTB (SPC) Regs 2006	
Reg 11	15	p663		13	p932
Reg 12	16	p664		14	p932
Reg 13	17	p664	Reg 13	15	p932
Reg 13A	18	p665	Reg 14	16	p932
Reg 14	19	p669	Reg 15	17	p932
Reg 15	20	p669	Reg 16	18	p934
Reg 16	21	p669	Reg 17	19	p934
Reg 16A	22	p670	Reg 18	20	p936
Reg 17	23	p670	Reg 19	21	p936
Reg 18	24	p670	Reg 19A	22	p940
Reg 19	25	p671	Reg 20	23	p940
Reg 20	26	p671	Reg 21	24	p942

CTB Regs 1992	CTB Regs 2006		HB&CTB (SPC) Regs 2003 substituted reg	CTB (SPC) Regs 2006	
Reg 21	27	p673	Reg 23	25	p942
Reg 22	28	p673	Reg 23	26	p943
Reg 23	29	p675	Reg 24	27	p944
Reg 24	30	p675	Reg 25	28	p944
Reg 25	31	p677	Reg 26	29	p945
Reg 26	32	p678	Reg 27	30	p946
Reg 28	33	p680	Reg 28	31	p947
Reg 29	34	p680	Reg 29	32	p949
Reg 30	35	p681	Reg 30	33	p949
Reg 31	36	p681	Reg 31	34	p949
Reg 32	37	p681	Reg 32	35	p950
Reg 33	38	p681	Reg 33	36	p950
Reg 34	39	p681	Reg 34	37	p950
Reg 35	40	p683	Reg 35	38	p950
Reg 36	41	p686	Reg 36	39	p953
Reg 37	42	p686			

Students

CTB Regs 1992	CTB Regs 2006		
Reg 38	43		p687
Reg 39	44		p690
Reg 40	45		p690
Reg 42	46		p692
Reg 43	47		p693
Reg 44	48		p694
Reg 45	49		p694
Reg 46	50		p694
Reg 47	51		p695
	New reg 51A		p696
Reg 47A	52		p696
Reg 48	53		p696
Reg 48A	54		p697
Reg 49	55		p697
Reg 50	56		p697

Amount of benefit

CTB Regs 1992	CTB Regs 2006		HB&CTB (SPC) Regs 2003 inserted reg	CTB (SPC) Regs 2006	
Reg 51	57	p697		40	p953
				New reg 41	p954
Reg 52	58	p698		42	p954
Reg 53	59	p700		43	p956
Reg 53A	60	p700		No provision	
Reg 53ZB	61	p702		44	p956
			Reg 53B	45	p958
Reg 54	62	p704		46	p959
Reg 55	63	p705		47	p959

Changes of circumstances and increases for exceptional circumstances

CTB Regs 1992	CTB Regs 2006		CTB (SPC) Regs 2006	
Reg 56	64	p706	48	p960
Reg 56A	65	p706	No provision	
Reg 56B	66	p706	49	p960
Reg 59	67	p706	50	p960
Reg 59B	No provision		51	p961

Claims

CTB Regs 1992	CTB Regs 2006		CTB (SPC) Regs 2006	
Reg 61	68	p707	52	p963
Reg 62	69	p708	53	p964
	New reg 69A	p712	New reg 53A	p968
Reg 62A	70	p712	54	p968
Reg 62B	71	p712	55	p968
Reg 62BA	No provision		56	p969
Reg 63	72	p712	57	p969
Reg 64	73	p714	58	p970
Reg 65	74	p714	59	p970
	New reg 74A	p715	New reg 59A	p972

Decisions on questions

CTB Regs 1992	CTB Regs 2006		CTB (SPC) Regs 2006	
Reg 66	75	p716	60	p972
Reg 67	76	p716	61	p972

Awards or payments of benefit

CTB Regs 1992	CTB Regs 2006		CTB (SPC) Regs 2006	
Reg 77	77	p716	62	p973
Reg 78	78	p717	63	p974
Reg 79	79	p717	64	p974
Reg 81	80	p718	65	p974
Reg 82	81	p718	66	p974

Excess benefit

CTB Regs 1992	CTB Regs 2006		CTB (SPC) Regs 2006	
Reg 83	82	p718	67	p975
Reg 84	83	p719	68	p975
Reg 85	84	p720	69	p976
Reg 86	85	p720	70	p976
Reg 87	86	p720	71	p976
Reg 88	87	p721	72	p976
Reg 89	88	p721	73	p976
Reg 90	89	p721	74	p977
Reg 91	90	p722	75	p977

Information

Source	CTB Regs 2006			CTB (SPC) Regs 2006	
SI 2002 No 1132, reg 2	91		p723	76	p978
SI 2002 No 1132, reg 3	92		p723	77	p978
	New reg 92A		p723	New reg 77A	p978
SI 2002 No 1132, reg 4	93		p723	78	p978
SI 2002 No 1132, reg 5	94		p724	79	p979
SI 2002 No 1132, reg 6	95		p724	80	p979
Reg 95	96		p724	81	p979
Reg 96	97		p725	82	p980

Schedules

CTB Regs 1992	CTB Regs 2006		HB&CTB (SPC) Regs 2003	CTB (SPC) Regs 2006	
Sch A1	Sch 4 SI 2006 No 217	p1225		Sch 4 SI 2006 No 217	p1225
	Sch A1	p726		Sch A1	p981
Sch 1	Sch 1	p726			
			Sch 1A	Sch 1	p981
Sch 2	Sch 2	p736		Sch 6	p996
Sch 3	Sch 3	p737			
			Sch 3A	Sch 2	p985
Sch 4	Sch 4	p741			
			Sch 4A	Sch 3	p988
Sch 5	Sch 5	p751			
			Sch 5ZA	Sch 4	p991
Sch 5A	Sch 6	p759			
Sch 5B	Sch 7	p759		Sch 5	p996
Sch 6	Sch 8	p759		Sch 7	p997
	New Sch 9	p762		New Sch 8	p1000

Table of comparative provisions

HB Regs	CTB Regs	HB Regs	CTB Regs
1	1	54	44
2(1)	2(1)	55-58	
2(2)			45
	2(2) – (3)	59	46
2(3)	2(4)	60	47
2(4)		61	48
	2(5)-(6)	62	49
3	3	63	50
4	4	64	51
5	5	64A	51A
6	6	65	52
7	8	66	53
8-9		67	54
10	7	68	55
10A	7A	69	56
11-18A		70-71	
19	9		57
20	10	72-72D	60-60D
21	11	73-73D	61-61D
22	12	74	58
23	13	75	
25	15		59
26	16		62-63
27	17	76	64
28	18	77	65
29	19	78	66
30	20	79	67
31	21	80-81	
32	22	82	68
33	23	83	69
34	24	83A	96A
35	25	84	70
36	26	85	71
37	27	86	72
38	28	87	73
39	29	88	74
40	30	88A	74A
41	11	89	75
42	12	90	76
43	13	91-96	
44	34		77-79
45	35	97	80
46	36	98	81
47	37	99-102	
48	38		82-87
49	39	103	88
50	40	104	89
51	41	105	90
52	42	107	
53	43	108	91

HB Regs	CTB Regs	HB Regs	CTB Regs
109	92	Sch 5/6-17	Sch 4/7-18
109A	92A	Sch 5/18	Sch 4/64
110	93	Sch 5/19-22	Sch 4/19-22
111	94	Sch 5/23-35	Sch 4/24-36
112	95		Sch 4/37
113-114A		Sch 5/36-41	Sch 4/38-43
115	96	Sch 5/42	Sch 4/23
116	97	Sch 5/43-50	Sch 4/44-51
117-121		Sch 5/51	
121A	98	Sch 5/52-63	Sch 4/52-63
122		Sch 6/1-28	Sch 5/1-28
		Sch 6/29	Sch 5/30
Sch A1	Sch A1	Sch 6/30	Sch 5/29
Sch 1		Sch 6/43	Sch 5/31-43
Sch 2			Sch 5/44
Sch 3	Sch 1	Sch 6/44	Sch 5/45
	Sch 2		Sch 5/46
Sch 4/1-15	Sch 3/1-15	Sch 6/45-60	Sch 5/47-62
Sch 4/16	Sch 3/17	Sch 7	Sch 6
Sch 4/17	Sch 3/16	Sch 8	Sch 7
Sch 5/1-5	Sch 4/1-5	Sch 9	Sch 8
	Sch 4/6		

Table of abbreviations

Abbreviation	Meaning	Abbreviation	Meaning
AC	Appeal Cases Law Reports	First-tier	First-tier Tribunal (Social Security
All ER	All England Reports	Tribunal	and Child Support)
Art, Arts	Article, Articles	GM	*Housing Benefit and Council Tax*
BC	Borough Council		*Benefit Guidance Manual* (DWP
BHRC	Butterworth's Human Rights Cases		looseleaf publication, also
CA	Carer's allowance		available on the internet at the
CA	Court of Appeal		DWP website)
CCLR	Community Care Law Reports	HB	Housing benefit
Ch	Chancery Division Law Reports	HB Regs	Housing Benefit Regulations 2006
Ch D	Chancery Division	HB(SPC)	Housing Benefit (Persons who
CIS, CH etc	Unreported Commissioner's	Regs	have attained the qualifying age for
	decision (see introductory notes for		state pension credit) Regulations
	an explanation)		2006
Cm	Command Paper	HB Regs 1987	Housing Benefit (General)
CMLR	Common Market Law Reports		Regulations 1987
CPA	Civil Partnership Act 2004	HB&CTB	Housing Benefit and Council Tax
COD	Crown Office Digest	(CP) Regs	Benefit (Consequential Provisions)
CSIH	Inner House of the Court of		Regulations 2006
	Session	HB(LHA&	Housing Benefit (Local Housing
CSOH	Outer House of the Court of	IS)A Regs	Alloweance and Information
	Session		Sharing) Amendment Regulations
CSPSSA	Child Support, Pensions and Social		2007
	Security Act 2000	HB(LHA,M&	Housing Benefit (Local Housing
CTB	Council tax benefit	C)A Regs	Allowance, Miscellaneous and
CTB Regs	Council Tax Benefit Regulations		Consequential) Amendment
	2006		Regulations 2007
CTB(SPC)	Council Tax Benefit (Persons who	HBRB	Housing Benefit Review Board
Regs	have attained the qualifying age for	HHJ	His/Her Honour Judge
	state pension credit) Regulations	HL	House of Lords
	2006	HLR	Housing Law Reports
CTB Regs	Council Tax Benefit (General)	IAT	Immigration Appeal Tribunal
1992	Regulations 1992	Imm AR	Immigration Appeal Reports
CTC	Child tax credit	IS	Income support
D&A Regs	Housing Benefit and Council Tax	J, JJ	Mr/Mrs Justice, Justices
	Benefit (Decisions and Appeals)	JSA (IB)	Income-based jobseeker's
	Regulations 2001		allowance
D&A	Housing Benefit and Council Tax	LBC	London Borough Council
Transitional	Benefit (Decisions and Appeals)	LGFA	Local Government Finance Act
Regs	(Transitional and Savings)		1992
	Regulations 2001	LGR	Local Government Reports
DC	District Council	LHA	Local housing allowance
DHP	Discretionary housing payment	LJ, LJJ	Lord/Lady Justice, Lord/Lady
DSS	Department of Social Security		Justices
	(predecessor to the DWP)	MBC	Metropolitan Borough Council
DWP	Department of Work and Pensions	PC	State pension credit
ECJ	European Court of Justice	para, paras	Paragraph, Paragraphs
ECR	European Court Reports	Prot	Protocol (to European Convention
ECtHR	European Court of Human Rights		on Human Rights)
ECmHR	European Commission of Human	QB	Queen's Bench Law Reports
	Rights	QBD	Queen's Bench Division of the
EHRR	European Human Rights Reports		High Court
ESA	Employment and support	r, rr	rule, rules
	allowance	RBC	Royal Borough Council
EU	European Union	reg, regs	Regulation, Regulations
EWCA Civ	Court of Appeal Civil Division	the Revenue	HM Revenue and Customs
	transcript	*R(IS), R(H)*	Reported Commissioner's decision
EWHC	Administrative Court transcript	etc	(see the introductory notes for an
[number]			explanation)
(Admin),		RVR	Rating and Valuation Reporter
EWHC		s, ss	Section, Sections
Admin		Sch, Schs	Schedule, Schedules
Ex p	Ex parte	SI	Statutory Instrument
FLR	Family Law Reports	SLT	Scots Law Times

Abbreviation	Meaning	Abbreviation	Meaning
SPCA	State Pension Credit Act 2002	**TP(FTT)**	Tribunal Procedure (First-tier
SSA	Social Security Act (of relevant	**Rules**	Tribunal) (Social Entitlement
	year)		Chamber) Rules 2008
SSAA	Social Security Administration Act	**TP(UT)Rules**	Tribunal Procedure (Upper
	1992		Tribunal) Rules 2008
SSA(F)A	Social Security Administration	**Tribunals**	Tribunals Service Social Security
	(Fraud) Act 1997	**Service**	and Child Support Appeals
SSCBA	Social Security Contributions and	**Upper**	Upper Tribunal (Administrative
	Benefits Act 1992	**Tribunal**	Appeals)
SSFA	Social Security Fraud Act 2001	**vol**	Volume
SSWP	Secretary of State for Work and	**WLR**	Weekly Law Reports
	Pensions	**WRA**	Welfare Reform Act 2007
TCA	Tax Credits Act 2007	**WRA 2009**	Welfare Reform Act 2009
TCEA 2007	Tribunals, Courts and Enforcement	**WRPA**	Welfare Reform and Pensions Act
	Act 2007		1999
TFEU	Treaty on the Functioning of the	**WTC**	Working tax credit
	European Union		

Part 1

Main primary legislation

Social Security Contributions and Benefits Act 1992
(1992 c4)

ARRANGEMENT OF SECTIONS
PART VII
INCOME-RELATED BENEFITS
GENERAL

123.   Income-related benefits

HOUSING BENEFIT

130.   Housing benefit
130A.   Appropriate maximum housing benefit
130B.   Loss of housing benefit following eviction on certain grounds
130C.   Relevant orders for possession
130D.   Loss of housing benefit: supplementary
130E.   Couples
130F.   Information provision
130G.   Pilot schemes relating to loss of housing benefit
131.   Council tax benefit
132.   Couples
133.   Polygamous marriages

GENERAL

134.   Exclusions from benefit
135.   The applicable amount
136.   Income and capital
136A.   Effect of attaining qualifying age for state pension credit
137.   Interpretation of Part VII and supplementary provisions

PART XIII
GENERAL
INTERPRETATION

172.   Applications of Act in relation to territorial waters
173.   Age
174.   References to Acts

SUBORDINATE LEGISLATION

175.   Regulations, orders and schemes
176.   Parliamentary control

SHORT TITLE, COMMENCEMENT AND EXTENT

177.   Short title, commencement and extent

PART VII
Income-Related Benefits
General

Income-related benefits

123.–(1)   Prescribed schemes shall provide for the following benefits (in this Act referred to as ''income-related benefits'')–

(a)-(c) *[Omitted]*

(d)   housing benefit; and

[¹(e)   council tax benefit.]

(2)   *[Omitted]*

(3)   Every authority granting housing benefit–

    (a)   shall take such steps as appear to them appropriate for the purpose of securing that persons who may be entitled to housing benefit from the authority become aware that they may be entitled to it; and

    (b)   shall make copies of the housing benefit scheme, with any modifications adopted by them under the Administration Act, available for public inspection at their principal office at all reasonable hours without payment.

[²(4)   [⁴ Each billing authority and in Scotland each local authority]

    (a)   shall take such steps as appear to it appropriate for the purpose of securing that any person who may be entitled to council tax benefit in respect of council tax payable to the authority becomes aware that he may be entitled to it; and

    (b)   shall make copies of the council tax benefit scheme, with any modifications adopted by it under the Administration Act, available for public inspection at its principal office at all reasonable hours without payment.]

Definitions

"Administration Act" – s174.
"billing authority" – s137.

Amendments

1.   Substituted by LGFA Sch 9 para 1(1) (1.4.93).
2.   Substituted by LGFA Sch 9 para 1(2).
3.   Substituted by Local Government etc. (Scotland) Act 1994 Sch 13 para 174(4) (1.4.96).
4.   Substituted by WRA s40 and Sch 5 para 1(2) (3.7.07).

General Note

This section provides the core basis in primary legislation for the HB and CTB schemes.

    Subs (1) provides for the setting up of the HB and CTB schemes as two of the income-related benefits.

    Subs (3) and (4) oblige the relevant authorities to publicise the availability of assistance under the HB and CTB schemes. There are two separate obligations: to take steps to increase awareness of the availability of HB and CTB to those on low incomes; and to make copies of the schemes (this presumably being a reference to the relevant legislation) available for inspection free of charge. The duties are entirely general in nature and authorities adopt various methods of discharging them, from advertising to providing advice in courts where proceedings for possession of property are being heard.

    It seems likely that the duties would be regarded as "target duties" in public law terms and hence not enforceable by a member of the general public, but it might be possible for a claimant to pray in aid poor publicisation of HB or CTB entitlement in her/his locality as being a factor showing "good cause" for a late claim: see p451.

    For the power to make modifications to the HB and CTB schemes, see ss134(8) and 139(6) SSAA on pp79 and 82.

Housing benefit

Housing benefit

130.–(1)   A person is entitled to housing benefit if–

    (a)   he is liable to make payments in respect of a dwelling in Great Britain which he occupies as his home;

    (b)   there is an appropriate maximum housing benefit in his case; and

    (c)   either–

        (i)   he has no income or his income does not exceed the applicable amount; or

        (ii)   his income exceeds that amount, but only by so much that there is an amount remaining if the deduction for which subsection (3)(b) below provides is made.

    (2)   In subsection (1) above "payments in respect of a dwelling" means such payments as may be prescribed, but the power to prescribe payments does not include power to prescribe–

    [¹[⁴ (a) payments to a billing authority or to a local authority in Scotland in respect of council tax;]

    (b)   mortgage payments, or, in relation to Scotland, payments under heritable securities.]

(3)   Where a person is entitled to housing benefit, then–

(a)   if he has no income or his income does not exceed the applicable amount, the amount of the housing benefit shall be the amount which is the appropriate maximum housing benefit in his case; and

(b)   if his income exceeds the applicable amount, the amount of the housing benefit shall be what remains after the deduction from the appropriate maximum housing benefit of prescribed percentages of the excess of his income over the applicable amount.

(4)   [⁵]

(5)   [³ ...]

Amendments

1.   Substituted by LGFA Sch 9 para 3 (1.4.93).
2.   Substituted by Local Government etc. (Scotland) Act 1994 Sch 13 para 174(4) (1.4.96).
3.   Deleted by Housing Act 1996 s227 and Sch 19 Pt IV (1.4.97).
4.   Substituted by WRA s40 and Sch 5 para 1(3) (3.7.07).
5.   Ceased to have effect by WRA s30(1) and Sch 8 (7.4.08).

Definitions

"dwelling" – see s137.
"Great Britain" – s172(a).
"prescribe" – s137.

Modifications

Subsection (4) ceased to have effect by s30(1) Welfare Reform Act 2007 from 7 April 2008, save for the transitional and savings provisions in the Welfare Reform Act 2007 (Commencement No.4, and Savings and Transitional Provisions) Order 2007 No.2872 which could apply up to 6 April 2009 at the latest (see p1237).

General Note

Subs (1) and (2) set out the basic conditions of entitlement to HB. In case it were not obvious from the use of the word "and" after sub-paras (a) and (b), it was confirmed in *CIS 166/1994* that the conditions of entitlement in the comparable s124 in relation to IS are cumulative and must all be satisfied. The conditions, and the principal parts of the HB Regs specifying the detail, are as follows:

(1)   The claimant is liable to make payments in respect of a dwelling in Great Britain which s/he occupies as her/his home: sub-section (1)(a). "Dwelling" is defined in s137 (on p18). Note that the dwelling which the claimant occupies as a home may comprise more than one property: *R(H) 5/09*. See p21 for a discussion. The question of whether a claimant is liable is dealt with by regs 8, 9 and 10 of both the HB and the HB(SPC) Regs and reg 56 HB Regs, and the question of occupation by reg 7 of both the HB and the HB(SPC) Regs. "Great Britain" includes territorial waters by virtue of s172(a), a provision unlikely to be of relevance in this context, but excludes Northern Ireland which has its own benefit scheme. It is permissible to make regulations under s137(2)(i) to treat only a specified category of people as if they were not liable to make payments: *R v Secretary of State for Social Security ex p Sarwar* [1997] 3 CMLR 647, CA. Subs (2) prevents any regulations being made to allow council tax (dealt with by CTB) and mortgage payments or heritable securities (partially dealt with by housing costs payable as part of IS, income-based JSA, income-related ESA or PC) to be met by the HB scheme. The "payments" for which liability can attract HB are set out in reg 12(1) of both the HB and the HB(SPC) Regs.

(2)   There is an appropriate maximum HB in her/his case: sub-section (1)(b). Maximum HB is calculated under reg 70 HB Regs (see p418) and reg 50 HB(SPC) Regs (see p837).

(3)   The claimant's income is sufficiently low: sub-section (1)(c). Income is calculated under Part 6 of both the HB and the HB(SPC) Regs. For the "applicable amount" see Part 5 and Sch 3 of those regs. Sub-section (c)(ii) is awkwardly worded. The second time the word "amount" is used, it does not refer to the applicable amount but refers to what is left of the claimant's maximum HB once the appropriate proportion of her/his income has been deducted as provided for by sub-section (3)(b). Before a claimant is entitled to be paid any HB, her/his "amount" must be at least the figure fixed by reg 75 HB Regs (reg 56 HB(SPC) Regs) (currently 50 pence).

Subs (3) provides for the amount of HB payable. Where the claimant's income is less than or equal to the applicable amount, the maximum HB is payable. Where the income exceeds the applicable amount, sub-section (b) provides for a "taper" under which entitlement declines gradually rather than instantly to nil. This is designed to minimise the impact of any poverty trap. The current percentage prescribed by reg 71 HB Regs (reg 51 HB(SPC) Regs) is 65 per cent. Thus if the applicable amount is £100 a week, the claimant has income of £90 a week and maximum HB is £60 a week, the HB payable is the maximum HB minus 65 per cent of £10 (the difference between £100 and £90), namely £53.50 (£60 – £6.50) a week.

Subs (4) allowed for regulations defining maximum HB. See now s130A.

[¹ **Appropriate maximum housing benefit**

130A.–(1)   For the purposes of section 130 above, the appropriate maximum housing benefit (in this section referred to as "the AMHB") is determined in accordance with this section.

(2)   Regulations must prescribe the manner in which the AMHB is to be determined.

(3)   The regulations may provide for the AMHB to be ascertained in the prescribed manner by reference to rent officer determinations.

(4)   The regulations may require an authority administering housing benefit in any prescribed case–

(a)   to apply for a rent officer determination, and

(b)   to do so within such time as may be specified in the regulations.

(5)   The regulations may make provision as to the circumstances in which, for the purpose of determining the AMHB, the amount of the liability mentioned in section 130(1)(a) above must be taken to be the amount of a rent officer determination instead of the actual amount of that liability.

(6)   Regulations under subsection (5) may also make provision for the liability of a person who, by virtue of regulations under section 137(2)(j) below, is treated as having a liability mentioned in section 130(1)(a) above to be the amount of a rent officer determination.

(7)   A rent officer determination is a determination made by a rent officer in the exercise of functions under section 122 of the Housing Act 1996.]

Amendment

1.   Inserted by WRA s30(2) with effect from 1.10.07 (for making regulations) and 7.4.08.

[¹**Loss of housing benefit following eviction on certain grounds**

130B.–(1)   If the following conditions are satisfied, then housing benefit is payable in the case of a person ("the former occupier") subject to subsection (4)–

(a)   a court makes a relevant order for possession of a dwelling occupied by him as his home;

(b)   in consequence of the order he ceases to occupy the dwelling;

(c)   either of the conditions in subsections (2) and (3) is satisfied; and

(d)   the conditions for entitlement to housing benefit are or become satisfied with respect to him.

(2)   The condition in this subsection is that the former occupier fails, without good cause, to comply with a warning notice served on him by a relevant local authority in England and Wales after he has ceased to occupy the dwelling.

(3)   The condition in this subsection is that–

(a)   the former occupier was, after he ceased to occupy the dwelling, required by a relevant local authority in Scotland to take specified action with the aim mentioned in subsection (10),

(b)   the former occupier was warned by the relevant local authority that if he failed to comply with the requirement the amount of housing benefit payable to him would be affected,

(c)   the former occupier fails, without good cause, to comply with the requirement, and

(d)   the relevant local authority recommends that housing benefit be payable to the former occupier subject to subsection (4).

(4)   During the restriction period or such part of it as may be prescribed, one or both of the following applies–

(a)   the rate of the benefit is reduced in such a manner as may be prescribed;

(b)   the benefit is payable only if the circumstances are such as may be prescribed.

(5)   The restriction period begins with the earliest date on which the conditions set out in subsections (1) to (3) are satisfied.

(6)   That period stops running if the relevant local authority considers that the restriction set out in subsection (4) should no longer apply (whether because the former

occupier is taking action to improve his behaviour or for any other reason), but starts running again if–
- (a)   in England and Wales, the former occupier fails to comply with a further warning notice served on him;
- (b)   in Scotland, the condition in subsection (7) is satisfied.
- (7)   The condition is that–
- (a)   the former occupier fails to comply with a further requirement such as is mentioned in paragraph (a) of subsection (3), having been warned as mentioned in paragraph (b) of that subsection, and
- (b)   the relevant local authority recommends that the restriction period starts running again.
- (8)   The restriction period shall not include any period which falls more than five years after the date on which the order for possession was made.
- (9)   A former occupier may not be subject to more than one restriction period in respect of one order for possession.
- (10) A relevant local authority is–
- (a)   in England and Wales, a local authority within the meaning of section 1 of the Local Government Act 2000, or
- (b)   in Scotland, a council constituted under section 2 of the Local Government etc. (Scotland) Act 1994,

which provides or may provide services to a former occupier with the aim of ending, or preventing repetition of, the conduct which may lead or has led to the making of a relevant order for possession.
- (11) A warning notice is a notice in the prescribed form–
- (a)   requiring the former occupier to take specified action with the aim mentioned in subsection (10),
- (b)   specifying the time when, or within which, that action must be taken, and
- (c)   warning the former occupier that if he fails to take the action the amount of housing benefit payable to him would be affected.]

Amendment

1.   Inserted by WRA s31(1) (1.11.07). The provision has no effect after 31 December 2010 (see s31(3) and (4) WRA on p162).

General Note

HB sanctions for anti-social behaviour are not a new idea. The idea was first raised in a housing Green Paper, *Quality and choice; a decent home for all*, published in 2000, but the idea was dropped in the face of widespread opposition. A Private Members Bill on a similar issue in 2002 was unsuccessful. Regrettably, the proposals resurfaced and ss130B to 130G SSCBA now provide for the reduction, or non-payment, of a former occupier's HB following eviction for anti-social behaviour in certain circumstances.

The rules were piloted in eight local authority areas in England from 1 November 2007 to 31 October 2009. If the conditions in subs (1) were satisfied, then restricted HB was payable during a restriction period. It is understood that the intention was for a local authority to attempt to engage with the former occupier with the aim of ending, or preventing repetition of, the anti-social behaviour through the provision of rehabilitation. For further commentary on s130B, see the 22nd edition of this work, p7. For the detailed pilot rules, see the Housing benefit (Loss of Benefit) (Pilot Scheme) Regulations 2007 SI No.2202 and the Housing Benefit (Loss of Benefit) (Pilot Scheme) (Supplementary) Regulations 2007 SI No.2474 in the 22nd edition of this work at pp1183 and 1188 respectively.

By s31(3) Welfare Reform Act 2007, the provisions end on 31 December 2010. Further primary legislation will be needed for the provisions to operate after that date.

[1Relevant orders for possession

130C.–(1)   In section 130B a relevant order for possession is, in England and Wales–
- (a)   an order made under section 84 of the Housing Act 1985 (secure tenancies) on Ground 2 set out in Schedule 2 to that Act;
- (b)   an order made under section 7 of the Housing Act 1988 (assured tenancies) on Ground 14 set out in Schedule 2 to that Act;
- (c)   an order made under section 98 of the Rent Act 1977 (protected or statutory tenancies) in the circumstances specified in Case 2 in Schedule 15 to that Act.

(2)   In that section a relevant order for possession is, in Scotland–

(a)   an order made under section 16(2) of the Housing (Scotland) Act 2001 (secure tenancies) on one of the grounds set out in paragraphs 2 and 7 in Part 1 of Schedule 2 to that Act;

(b)   an order made in accordance with section 18 of the Housing (Scotland) Act 1988 (assured tenancies) on Ground 15 in Part 2 of Schedule 5 to that Act;

(c)   an order made in accordance with section 11 of the Rent (Scotland) Act 1984 (protected or statutory tenancies) in the circumstances specified in Case 2 in Part 1 of Schedule 2 to that Act.

(3)   For the purposes of subsections (1) and (2) it does not matter whether the order is made on the grounds or in the circumstances there mentioned alone or together with other grounds or circumstances.

(4)   Subsections (5) and (6) apply if the court–

(a)   stays (in Scotland, sists) or suspends the execution of a relevant order for possession, or postpones the date of possession under it, and

(b)   imposes a condition (or conditions) on that stay, sist, suspension or postponement.

(5)   If a condition relates to the behaviour of a person or persons occupying the dwelling, section 130B(4) applies only if the order takes effect as a result of a breach of that condition.

(6)   Section 130B(4) does not apply if the condition (or, if there is more than one, each of them) relates only to matters other than the behaviour of a person or persons occupying the dwelling.]

Amendment

1.   Inserted by WRA s31(1) (1.11.07). The provision has no effect after 31 December 2010 (see s31(3) and (4) WRA on p162).

General Note

See s130B above and p8 of the 22nd edition of this work.

[¹Loss of housing benefit: supplementary

130D.–(1)   Regulations may provide that, where housing benefit has been paid subject to the restriction set out in section 130B(4), in prescribed circumstances–

(a)   the former occupier must be paid some or all of the amount of the benefit which, by virtue of that subsection, has not been payable to him, and

(b)   such other adjustments must be made as are prescribed.

(2)   The Secretary of State may by order vary the definition of relevant order for possession by–

(a)   adding to or removing from it orders of a specified description;

(b)   specifying circumstances in which it includes orders of a specified description.

(3)   Regulations may prescribe–

(a)   matters which are, or are not, to be taken into account in determining whether a person has, or does not have, good cause for failing to take action specified in a warning notice or failing to comply with a requirement such as is mentioned in section 130B(3)(a);

(b)   circumstances in which a person is, or is not, to be regarded as having, or not having, such good cause.

(4)   Expressions used in this section and in section 130B have the meaning given in that section.]

Amendment

1.   Inserted by WRA s31(1) (1.11.07). The provision has no effect after 31 December 2010 (see s31(3) and (4) WRA on p162).

General Note

See s130B above and p9 of the 22nd edition of this work.

[¹Couples

130E.–(1)   This section applies where at any time the conditions for entitlement to housing benefit are satisfied with respect to a person who is a member of a couple.

(2)   Where paragraphs (a) and (b) of section 130B(1) are satisfied in relation to both members of the couple (whether or not in respect of the same dwelling), then for the purposes of subsection (2) or (3) of that section, the failure by one member of the couple to comply with a warning notice or with a requirement such as is mentioned in section 130B(3)(a) must be treated also as a failure by his partner to comply with it.

(3)   Where paragraph (a) of section 130B(1) is not satisfied in relation to one member of the couple, then subsection (4) of that section does not apply to his partner (even if paragraphs (a), (b) and (c) of section 130B(1) are satisfied in relation to the partner).

(4)   References to a person's partner are to the other member of the couple concerned.]

Amendment

1.   Inserted by WRA s31(1) (1.11.07). The provision has no effect after 31 December 2010 (see s31(3) and (4) WRA on p162).

General Note

See s130B above and p9 of the 22nd edition of this work.

[¹Information provision

130F.–(1)   The Secretary of State may by regulations require–

(a)   a court which makes a relevant order for possession, or

(b)   any other person or description of person who the Secretary of State thinks is or may be aware of the making of such an order,

to notify him of the making of the order and to provide him with such details of matters in connection with the order as may be prescribed.

(2)   The Secretary of State may provide–

(a)   information obtained under subsection (1), or

(b)   information which is relevant to the exercise by him of any function relating to housing benefit,

to a relevant local authority, or a person authorised to exercise any function of such an authority relating to services mentioned in section 130B(10), for use in the provision of such services.

(3)   The Secretary of State may by regulations require–

(a)   a relevant local authority, or

(b)   a person authorised to exercise any function of such an authority relating to services mentioned in section 130B(10),

to supply relevant information held by the authority or other person to, or to a person providing services to, the Secretary of State for use for any purpose relating to the administration of housing benefit.

(4)   The Secretary of State may by regulations require–

(a)   an authority administering housing benefit,

(b)   a person authorised to exercise any function of such an authority relating to such a benefit,

(c)   a relevant local authority, or

(d)   a person authorised to exercise any function of such an authority relating to services mentioned in section 130B(10),

to provide relevant information held by that authority or person to an authority or person mentioned in paragraph (a) or (b) for use for any purpose relating to the administration of housing benefit.

(5)   The Secretary of State may by regulations require–

(a)   an authotity administering housing benefit,

(b)   a person authorised to exercise any function of such an authority relating to such a benefit,

(c)   a relevant local authority, or

(d)   a person authorised to exercise any function of such an authority relating to services mentioned in section 130B(10),

to provide relevant information held by that authority or person to an authority or person mentioned in paragraph (c) or (d) for use in the provision of those services.

(6)   Relevant information is–

(a)   if the information is held by an authority administering housing benefit or a person authorised to exercise any function of such an authority, information which is relevant to the exercise of any function relating to housing benefit by the authority or person;

(b)   if the information is held by a relevant local authority or a person authorised to exercise any function of such an authority, information which is relevant to the exercise of any function relating to the provision of services mentioned in section 130B(10).

(7)   Information must be supplied under subsection (1), (3), (4) or (5) in such circumstances, in such manner and form, and in accordance with such requirements, as may be prescribed.

(8)   "Relevant order for possession" and "relevant local authority" have the same meaning as in section 130B.

(9)   Subsections (1) and (5) do not extend to Scotland.]

Amendment

    1.   Inserted by WRA s31(1) (1.11.07). The provision has no effect after 31 December 2010 (see s31(3) and (4) WRA on p162).

General Note

    See s130B above. The regulations made were:

        Subs (1): reg 10 Housing Benefit (Loss of Benefit) (Pilot Scheme) (Supplementary) Regulations 2007.

        Subs (2) to (5): regs 11, 12 and 13 Housing Benefit (Loss of Benefit) (Pilot Scheme) (Supplementary) Regulations 2007.

[¹ Pilot schemes relating to loss of housing benefit

130G.–(1)   Regulations to which this section applies may be made so as to have effect for a prescribed period.

(2)   Any regulations which, by virtue of subsection (1), have effect for a limited period are referred to in this section as a "pilot scheme".

(3)   A pilot scheme may provide that it applies only in relation to–

(a)   one or more prescribed areas;

(b)   one or more prescribed classes of person;

(c)   persons selected by reference to prescribed criteria.

(4)   A pilot scheme may make consequential or transitional provision.

(5)   A pilot scheme ("the previous scheme") may be replaced by a further pilot scheme making the same, or similar, provision (apart from the prescribed period) to that made by the previous scheme.

(6)   A pilot scheme may be amended or revoked by regulations under this section.

(7)   This section applies to–

(a)   regulations made under any of sections 130B to 130F above;

(b)   regulations made under any other enactment, so far as they relate to, or are made for purposes which relate to, loss or restriction of housing benefit in pursuance of section 130B above.

(8)   This section does not extend to Scotland.]

Amendment

    1.   Inserted by WRA s31(1) (1.11.07). The provision has no effect after 31 December 2010 (see s31(3) and (4) WRA on p162).

General Note

    See s130B above. The pilot scheme areas were listed in the Schedule to the Housing Benefit (Loss of Benefit) (Pilot Scheme) Regulations 2007.

['Council tax benefit

131.–(1)   A person is entitled to council tax benefit in respect of a particular day falling after 31st March 1993 if the following are fulfilled, namely, the condition set out in subsection (3) below and either–
- (a)   each of the two conditions set out in subsections (4) and (5) below; or
- (b)   the condition set out in subsection (6) below.

(2)   Council tax benefit–
- (a)   shall not be allowed to a person in respect of any day falling before the day on which his entitlement is to be regarded as commencing for that purpose by virtue of paragraph (l) of section 6(1) of the Administration Act; but
- (b)   may be allowed to him in respect of not more than 6 days immediately following the day on which his period of entitlement would otherwise come to an end, if his entitlement is to be regarded by virtue of that paragraph as not having ended for that purpose.

(3)   The main condition for the purposes of subsection (1) above is that the person concerned–
- (a)   is for the day liable to pay council tax in respect of a dwelling of which he is a resident; and
- (b)   is not a prescribed person or a person of a prescribed class.

(4)   The first condition for the purposes of subsection (1)(a) above is that there is an appropriate maximum council tax benefit in the case of the person concerned.

(5)   The second condition for the purposes of subsection (1)(a) above is that–
- (a)   the day falls within a week in respect of which the person concerned has no income;
- (b)   the day falls within a week in respect of which his income does not exceed the applicable amount; or
- (c)   neither paragraph (a) nor paragraph (b) above is fulfilled in his case but amount A exceeds amount B where–
  - (i)   amount A is the appropriate maximum council tax benefit in his case; and
  - (ii)   amount B is a prescribed percentage of the difference between his income in respect of the week in which the day falls and the applicable amount.

(6)   The condition for the purposes of subsection (1)(b) above is that–
- (a)   no other resident of the dwelling is liable to pay rent to the person concerned in respect of the dwelling; and
- (b)   there is an alternative maximum council tax benefit in the case of that person which is derived from the income or aggregate incomes of one or more residents to whom this subsection applies.

(7)   Subsection (6)above applies to any other resident of the dwelling who–
- (a)   is not a person who, in accordance with Schedule 1 to the Local Government Finance Act 1992, falls to be disregarded for the purposes of discount; and
- (b)   is not a prescribed person or a person of a prescribed class.

(8)   Subject to subsection (9) below, where a person is entitled to council tax benefit in respect of a day, the amount to which he is entitled shall be–
- (a)   if subsection (5)(a) or (b) above applies, the amount which is the appropriate maximum council tax benefit in his case;
- (b)   if subsection (5)(c) above applies, the amount found by deducting amount B from amount A, where "amount A" and "amount B" have the meanings given by that subsection; and
- (c)   if subsection (6) above applies, the amount which is the alternative maximum council tax benefit in his case.

(9)   Where a person is entitled to council tax benefit in respect of a day, and both subsection (5) and subsection (6) above apply, the amount to which he is entitled shall be whichever is the greater of–
- (a)   the amount given by paragraph (a) or, as the case may be, paragraph (b) of subsection (8) above; and
- (b)   the amount given by paragraph (c) of that subsection.

(10)   Regulations shall prescribe the manner in which–

(a)　the appropriate maximum council tax benefit;

(b)　the alternative maximum council tax benefit, are to be determined in any case.

(11)　In this section 'dwelling' and 'resident' have the same meanings as in Part I or II of the Local Government Finance Act 1992.]

Amendment

1.　Substituted by LGFA Sch 9 para 4.

General Note

This section, setting out the basic conditions of entitlement to CTB, is harder to understand than s131. Note that it is supplemented by ss132 and 133.

Subsections (1) and (3) to (7): Conditions of entitlement

There are two types of CTB: that known as "main" CTB and the "alternative maximum" CTB, sometimes referred to as "second adult rebate". Subs (1) provides that in order to be entitled to either type of CTB, a person must always fulfil the conditions in subs (3). Then, to qualify for main CTB, both conditions in subs (4) and (5) must be fulflilled and for alternative maximum CTB, the conditions in subs (6) must be fulfilled. See also the commentary to the definition of "resident" in reg 2(1) CTB Regs (on p653).

The general conditions

(1)　The claimant must be liable to pay council tax in respect of a dwelling of which s/he is a resident: subs (3)(a). Liability for council tax is defined by the LGFA and secondary legislation made thereunder. It is a subject outside the scope of this book: see CPAG's *Council Tax Handbook*. The principal sections that define liability, s6 (in relation to England and Wales) and s75 (in Scotland), are set out in the extracts from the LGFA (see pp1113 and 1116). Residence is also defined by reference to the LGFA: subs (11). Being "resident" in relation to any chargeable dwelling means where an individual has her/his sole or main residence, which is a question of fact and degree in every case: *Frost v Feltham* [1981] 1 WLR 455. Accordingly, where a family had to occupy two flats in one building because of the number of members of the family, and the father was liable for council tax in respect of both flats, the tribunal erred in holding the claimant not to be resident in both dwellings (and so not eligible for CTB for the second flat): *R(H) 3/08*. The tribunal had erred in law by conflating the meaning of "dwelling" with "residence". Commissioner Howell noted in *R(H) 3/08* (para 9) that if a person is a resident of a chargeable dwelling so as to be liable for council tax on it, then s/he must also meet the condition of being a resident of that dwelling to qualify for CTB. There was therefore a legal inconsistency in the local authority's case in, on the one hand, holding the claimant to be liable for council tax for the second flat because he was resident in it, but, on the other, hand denying him CTB on the basis that he was not resident in the second flat.

(2)　The claimant must not be a prescribed person or a member of a prescribed class: subs (3)(b). Three categories are currently prescribed. Persons from abroad are prescribed under reg 7 of both the CTB and CTB(SPC) Regs. Most full-time students are prescribed under reg 45 CTB Regs. Full-time students are *not* a prescribed person or class for claimants of at least the qualifying age for PC who are not (and whose partners are not) on IS, income-based JSA or income-related ESA. Finally, people who are absent from home are prescribed by reg 8 of both the CTB and the CTB(SPC) Regs unless the absence is temporary as defined in those regulations.

Main CTB

The additional conditions for main CTB are:

(1)　There is an appropriate maximum CTB: subs (4). See reg 57 CTB Regs (reg 40 CTB(SPC) Regs).

(2)　The claimant's income is sufficiently low: subs (5). Income is calculated under Part 4 and applicable amounts under Part 3 of both the CTB and the CTB(SPC) Regs. If the claimant's income is lower than or equal to the applicable amount, s/he qualifies under sub-para (a) or (b). If it is higher, s/he qualifies under sub-para (c) where the maximum CTB exceeds a figure obtained by the prescribed percentage of the difference between the income and the applicable amount. The daily prescribed percentage is currently two and six-sevenths per cent (which is 20 per cent weekly): see reg 59 CTB Regs (reg 43 CTB(SPC) Regs).

Alternative maximum CTB

The additional conditions for alternative maximum CTB are:

(1)　No other resident of the dwelling is liable to pay rent to the claimant: subs (6)(a). Note that the phrase "liable to pay rent" is used rather than the phrase "liable to make payments in respect of the dwelling" as used, for example, in s130(1)(a). It would seem to follow from the difference in the wording that the liability must be in respect of rent in the strict sense, that is payment made under a tenancy. Thus if the person liable is not a tenant but is a licensee or some other form of occupant, because s/he either does not have exclusive possession of any part of the property or because the nature of the occupancy is inconsistent with the nature of a tenancy, the claimant is not excluded from alternative maximum CTB. There is a great deal of caselaw on whether an occupant is a tenant or not. See *Street v Mountford* [1995] AC 809, HL and any standard textbook on landlord and tenant law for general guidance.

(2)   There is an alternative maximum CTB in the claimant's case: subs (6)(b). See reg 62 and Sch 2 CTB Regs and reg 46 and Sch 6 CTB(SPC) Regs. This is based on the income of "second adults" residing with the claimant, not the income of the claimant. The aim of alternative maximum CTB is to deal with cases of multiple occupancy where some residents have low incomes and others have higher incomes. Subs (7) sets out the other residents to be taken into account in calculating alternative maximum CTB. Those who fall within Sch 1 LGFA are excluded, as are prescribed persons under reg 63 CTB Regs (reg 47 CTB(SPC) Regs).

Subsection (2): Period of entitlement
For the dates on which entitlement begins, see Part 7 of the CTB Regs on p706 and Part 6 of the CTB(SPC) Regs on p960.

Subsections (8) and (9): Amount of CTB
By virtue of subs (8)(a) and (c), the amount of CTB payable is normally either the maximum CTB or alternative maximum CTB. By subs (8)(b), if a claimant qualifies by virtue of subs (5)(c) the amount payable is the figure obtained by deducting the percentage of the difference between her/his income and applicable amount from the maximum CTB.

Under subs (9), if a claimant qualifies for both main CTB and alternative maximum CTB, s/he will be awarded the higher amount of the two obtained under the subs (8) calculations.

Subsections (10) and (11): Regulations and definitions
Maximum and alternative maximum CTB are calculated under Part 6 CTB Regs on p697 and Part 5 CTB(SPC) Regs on p953.

Couples

132.–(1)   As regards any case where a person is a member of a [⁶ couple] throughout a particular day, regulations may make such provision as the Secretary of State sees fit as to–

(a)   the entitlement of the person to a [¹ council tax benefit] in respect of the day, and

(b)   the amount to which he is entitled.

(2)   Nothing in subsections (3) to (8) below shall prejudice the generality of subsection (1) above.

(3)   The regulations may provide that prescribed provisions shall apply instead of prescribed provisions of this Part of this Act, or that prescribed provisions of this Part of this Act shall not apply or shall apply subject to prescribed amendments or adaptations.

(4)   The regulations may provide that, for the purpose of calculating in the case of the person concerned the matters mentioned in subsection (5) below, prescribed amounts relating to the person and his partner are to be aggregated and the aggregate is to be apportioned.

(5)   The matters are income, capital, the applicable amount, and [² the appropriate maximum council tax benefit and the alternative maximum council tax benefit.]

(6)   The regulations may–

(a)   amend section 139(6) of the Administration Act so as to allow for disregarding the whole or part of any pension payable to the partner of the person concerned in determining the latter's income;

(b)   amend section 139(7) of that Act accordingly.

(7)   The regulations may contain different provision as to the following different cases–

(a)   cases where the [³ main] condition is fulfilled on the day concerned by the person concerned but not by his partner;

(b)   cases where the [⁴ main] condition is fulfilled on the day concerned by the person concerned and by his partner.

(8)   The regulations may include such supplementary, incidental or consequential provisions as appear to the Secretary of State to be necessary or expedient.

(9)   In this section–

(a)   references to a person's partner are to the other member of the couple concerned, and

[⁵ (b) references to the main condition are references to the condition mentioned in section 131(3) above.]

Amendments

1.	Substituted by LGFA Sch 9 para 5(1) as from 1.4.93.
2.	Substituted by LGFA Sch 9 para 5(2) as from 1.4.93.
3.	Substituted by LGFA Sch 9 para 5(3) as from 1.4.93.
4.	Substituted by LGFA Sch 9 para 5(3) as from 1.4.93.
5.	Substituted by LGFA Sch 9 para 5(4) as from 1.4.93.
6.	Substituted by CPA 2004 Sch 24 para 45 as from 5.12.05.

Definitions

"couple" – see s137.
"partner" – see subs (9).

General Note

This empowers the Secretary of State to make regulations in respect of the entitlement to CTB of a person who is a member of a couple and in respect of the amount to which s/he is entitled. Since 5 December 2005, it includes civil partners. This section does not apply to couples who were married under a law which permits polygamy where, at the time of the claim, there are more than two partners to the marriage (for such marriages, see s133).

Subs (1) gives a broad power to the Secretary of State to make provision for couples in whatever way is thought fit. The generality of this power is confirmed by subs (2). See regs 15 and 68 CTB Regs and regs 13 and 52 CTB(SPC) Regs for the main provisions.

Subs (3) permits the making of regulations which substitute different provisions for the provisions of this Part, or which provide that certain provisions of this Part shall not apply or shall apply subject to prescribed modifications.

Subs (4) and (5) together provide that, in relation to the entitlement of a person covered by this section, when calculating that person's income, capital, applicable amount and appropriate maximum CTB and the alternative maximum CTB, regulations may be made which provide that certain amounts relating to that person and her/his partner are to be aggregated and apportioned between the two.

Subs (6) permits the making of regulations which provide that, in calculating the entitlement of a person covered by this section, s139(6) and (7) SSAA are to be amended so that war widow's pension or war disablement pension payable to that person's partner is to be wholly or partly ignored in calculating that person's income.

Subs (7). "the main condition" is defined in subs (9) as being a reference to s131(3). Regulations may be made which make different rules for the situation where one partner satisfies the "main condition" on a particular day but the other does not, as opposed to the situation where both partners satisfy the "main condition" on a particular day.

Subs (8) makes it clear that the power in subs (1) includes the power to make provisions by regulations which are supplementary, incidental or consequential to the main object of the powers "as appears necessary or expedient".

Polygamous marriages

133.–(1)   This section applies to any case where–

(a)   throughout a particular day a person (the person in question) is a husband or wife by virtue of a marriage entered into under a law which permits polygamy; and

(b)   either party to the marriage has for the time being any spouse additional to the other party.

(2)   For the purposes of section 132 above neither party to the marriage shall be taken to be a member of a couple on the day.

(3)   Regulations under this section may make such provision as the Secretary of State sees fit as to–

(a)   the entitlement of the person in question to a [1 council tax benefit] in respect of the day, and

(b)   the amount to which he is entitled.

(4)   Without prejudice to the generality of subsection (3) above the regulations may include provision equivalent to that included under section 132 above subject to any modifications the Secretary of State sees fit.

Amendment

1.	Substitution made by LGFA Sch 9 para 6 (1.4.93).

General Note

This makes the same provision for persons married under a law which permits polygamy as s132 does for couples. It covers people married under such a law, where the marriage itself is polygamous at the relevant time.

Subs (1) and (2) deal with the applications of this section and rule out any overlap with s132 by stating that those covered by subs (1) are not members of a couple.

Subs (3) gives the Secretary of State the same powers in relation to the entitlement and extent of entitlement of people covered by this section to CTB as s132(1) does in relation to couples.

Subs (4) states that the powers in subs (3) include powers to make the same types of regulation as mentioned in s132 "subject to any modifications the Secretary of State sees fit".

General

Exclusions from benefit

134.–(1)   No person shall be entitled to an income-related benefit if his capital or a prescribed part of it exceeds the prescribed amount.

(2)   Except in prescribed circumstances the entitlement of one member of a family to any one income-related benefit excludes entitlement to that benefit for any other member for the same period.

(3)   [¹ . . .]

(4)   Where the amount of any income-related benefit would be less than a prescribed amount, it shall not be payable except in prescribed circumstances.

Amendment
1.	Deleted by LGFA Sch 9 para 7.

General Note
Subs (1) provides for a capital limit above which a claimant will not be entitled to HB or CTB. The prescribed figure is currently £16,000 for both HB and CTB: see reg 43 of both the HB and the HB(SPC) Regs and reg 33 of both the CTB and the CTB(SPC) Regs. Note that by reg 26 HB(SPC) Regs and reg 16 CTB(SPC) Regs, where a claimant or her/his partner is in receipt of the guarantee credit of PC, the whole of her/his capital (and income) is ignored. Note also that in claims for "second adult rebate", the whole of the claimant's capital is ignored: Sch 5 para 46(1) CTB Regs; reg 16 and Sch 4 para 26A CTB(SPC) Regs. This means that for those claimants, there is effectively no capital limit.

Subs (2) provides that generally if one member of a "family" receives an income-related benefit for a period, the other members may not receive the same benefit for that period (for the meaning of "family" see p22).

Subs (4) provides for the fixing of a minimum level below which HB or CTB is not payable. See reg 75 HB Regs (reg 56 HB(SPC) Regs) which provides a minimum level of fifty pence a week for HB. No minimum payment of CTB has been prescribed.

The applicable amount

135.–(1)   The applicable amount, in relation to any income-related benefit, shall be such amount or the aggregate of such amounts as may be prescribed in relation to that benefit.

(2)   The power to prescribe applicable amounts conferred by subsection (1) above includes power to prescribe nil as an applicable amount.

(3)-(4)   [¹ . . .]

(5)   [² . . .] the applicable amount for a severely disabled person shall include an amount in respect of his being a severely disabled person.

(6)   Regulations may specify circumstances in which persons are to be treated as being or as not being severely disabled.

Amendments
1.	Deleted by LGFA Sch 9 para 8 (1.4.93).
2.	Amended by TCA Sch 6 (8.4.03).

General Note
Subs (1) enables the making of regulations to quantify "applicable amounts". See Part 5 and Sch 3 of both the HB and the HB(SPC) Regs and Part 3 and Sch 1 of both the CTB and the CTB(SPC) Regs. This subsection is supplemented by paras (2), (5) and (6) which specify certain provisions that must be included in the regulations on applicable amounts.

Subs (2). Nil can be a valid applicable amount.

Subs (5). Specific provision is made for the addition of an extra amount for severely disabled claimants, by virtue of subs (6) and Sch 3 para 14 HB Regs, Sch 3 para 6 HB(SPC) Regs, Sch 1 para 14 CTB Regs and Sch 1 para 6 CTB(SPC) Regs, which define "severely disabled" for these purposes.

Income and capital

136.–(1)   Where a person claiming an income-related benefit is a member of a family, the income and capital of any member of that family shall, except in prescribed circumstances, be treated as the income and capital of that person.

(2)   Regulations may provide that capital not exceeding the amount prescribed under section 134(1) above but exceeding a prescribed lower amount shall be treated, to a prescribed extent, as if it were income of a prescribed amount.

(3)   Income and capital shall be calculated or estimated in such manner as may be prescribed.

(4)   A person's income in respect of a week shall be calculated in accordance with prescribed rules; and the rules may provide for the calculation to be made by reference to an average over a period (which need not include the week concerned).

(5)   Circumstances may be prescribed in which–

(a)   a person is treated as possessing capital or income which he does not possess;

(b)   capital or income which a person does possess is to be disregarded;

(c)   income is to be treated as capital;

(d)   capital is to be treated as income.

Definitions

"family" – s137.

"income-related benefits" – s123.

General Note

This section enables the making of regulations to quantify "income" and "capital" on the basis of which entitlement to HB and CTB are calculated.

Subs (1) deals with the aggregation of assets for members of a "family" – see reg 25 HB Regs (reg 23 HB(SPC) Regs) and reg 15 CTB Regs (reg 13 CTB(SPC) Regs).

Subs (2) enables the "tariff income rules" whereby capital between certain levels is deemed to produce income at a set level irrespective of the actual income received by the claimant. See reg 52 HB Regs, reg 29(2) HB(SPC) Regs, reg 42 CTB Regs and reg 19(2) CTB(SPC) Regs for the tariff income rules.

Subs (3) to (5) introduce wide powers as to the treatment of resources, as to which generally see Part 6 of both the HB and HB(CTB) Regs and Part 4 of both the CTB and CTB(SPC) Regs. For examples of the uses of the powers specified by subs (5), see reg 49, Part 6 and Schs 4 to 6, reg 46, and reg 41 HB Regs.

Analysis

The scope of the very wide powers conferred by s136 has been the subject of judicial comment. In *Foster v Chief Adjudication Officer* [1992] QB 31 at 45, Sir John Donaldson MR noted in passing that s136 permits the Secretary of State "to prescribe that black is white and that nothing is something and vice versa in the context of income and capital".

The wide scope of the provisions was confirmed in *Owen v Chief Adjudication Officer* [1999] *The Independent* 13 April, CA (appendix to *R(IS) 8/99*). This case concerned an anomaly in the Income Support (General) Regulations 1987. The claimant became terminally ill and was signed off work by his doctor, receiving statutory and contractual sick pay. He was dismissed by his employer and was paid four weeks' sick pay in arrears on the last day of his employment. Notwithstanding the fact that the sick pay was paid in arrears, the regulations required that the sick pay be taken into account as income for the first four weeks of the claim as it was not "earnings": see regs 29(1), 29(2), 31(1) and 35(2) IS Regs. It should be noted that the position under the HB and CTB Regs is different as statutory and contractual sick pay are treated as "earnings": see reg 35(1)(i) and (j) HB Regs; 35(1)(h) and (k) HB(SPC) Regs; 25(1)(i) and (j) CTB Regs; and reg 25(1)(h) and (k) CTB(SPC) Regs.

The argument in *Owen* was that the effect of the regulations was not authorised by s136 and that the closing words of reg 29(2) were therefore *ultra vires*. It is plain that subs (4) envisages such regulations being made. However, as the Secretary of State conceded and the Court of Appeal accepted, that provision could not authorise the offending words in reg 29(2) because s136(4) did not appear in s22 Social Security Act 1986 as originally enacted. It was inserted as s22(8A) with effect from 29 July 1988 by the Local Government Finance Act 1988. However, the IS Regs had come into force on 11 April 1988 and so the subsection could not retrospectively revive any regulations that had been *ultra vires* in the absence of s22(8A): *Cottingham v Chief Adjudication Officer* [1992] appendix to *R(P) 1/93*, CA. The same would apply to much of the HB Regs 1987, which came into force between 1 April 1988 and 4 April 1988. Thus any provision which appeared in the HB Regs 1987 as they stood on 28 July 1988 and which could only be justified by subs (4) would be *ultra vires*. Any provision that had been the subject of insertion or amendment since that date, however, could be validly made under subs (4).

It was, however, argued for the Chief Adjudication Officer that the scheme was justified by either subs (3) or (5)(a). As far as subs (5)(a) was concerned, it was submitted for the claimant that as he did possess the income in question (though most of it had been spent on the previous month's bills), subs (5)(a) could not be applicable. The Court rejected this submission:

"... it is a deeming provision prescribing circumstances in which a person is treated as possessing income he does not possess. He may not in fact possess income in a relevant period for a number of reasons: he may never have possessed the income at all; he may have in fact possessed the income at an earlier period, but he does not possess it at a later period. In the latter case a person may be treated as possessing income in a later period, even though it was paid in respect of an earlier period and even though he has already spent all the income that he did in fact possess at the earlier period... These enabling terms are framed widely enough to authorise a provision spreading or apportioning income possessed by a claimant over a stated period by treating it as possessed by the claimant in which he did not in fact possess it."

The difficulty with this approach is that it does not deal with the case where the income is still possessed in the later period. If the income is all spent (and the evidence was that Mr Owen had spent most, but not all of it) then, because s136(5)(a) refers to income being deemed to be possessed "which he does not possess", the Court's approach is justified. However, if the income is still possessed, it cannot be said that on any normal reading of the language, s136(5)(a) can apply because the income is possessed during the relevant period. If a regulation would be *intra vires* when applied to some claimants, but *ultra vires* when applied to others, it must be struck down. Against this, it might be argued that once income is possessed beyond the period in which it is received, it becomes part of the claimant's capital and so s/he does not possess it as income.

The Court of Appeal did not deal with the argument concerning s136(3), which centred around whether, if no income was received during a period but the claimant was deemed to have such income, such a scheme could be said to involve a "calculation or estimation" of income. In *CIS 3287/1997* (Appendix paras 12-13) Commissioner Goodman stated that the outcome had to bear some resemblance to the reality.

The Court also vigorously rejected a second submission for the claimant that the regulations were *ultra vires* as irrational. Although it was accepted that the scheme operated unfairly, it could not be said to be irrational so as to justify the striking-down of the regulations.

[¹Effect of attaining qualifying age for state pension credit

136A.–(1) Subsections (2) and (3) below apply in relation to housing benefit and council tax benefit in the case of any person who has attained the qualifying age for state pension credit.

(2) Regulations may make provision for section 134(1) or any provision of section 136 above not to have effect in relation to those benefits in the case of any such person.

(3) In relation to those benefits, regulations may make provision for the determination of the income and capital of any such person; and any such regulations may include provision applying (with such modifications as the Secretary of State thinks fit)–

(a) section 5 of the State Pension Credit Act 2002 (provision for treating income of spouse as income of claimant, etc), and

(b) section 15 of that Act (determination of income and capital for purposes of state pension credit).

(4) Regulations under subsection (3) above may also include provision–

(a) authorising or requiring the use of any calculation or estimate of a person's income or capital made by the Secretary of State for the purposes of the State Pension Credit Act 2002; or

(b) requiring that, if and so long as an assessed income period is in force under section 6 of that Act in respect of a person falling within subsection (1) above,–

(i) the assessed amount of any element of his retirement provision shall be treated as the amount of that element for the purposes of housing benefit or council tax benefit; and

(ii) his income shall be taken for those purposes not to include any element of retirement provision which it is taken not to include for the purposes of state pension credit by virtue of a determination under subsection (5) of section 7 of that Act.

(5) In subsection (4) above "assessed amount", "element" and "retirement provision" have the same meaning as in the State Pension Credit Act 2002.

(6) The Secretary of State may by regulations make provision for the preceding provisions of this section to apply with modifications in cases to which section 12 of the State Pension Credit Act 2002 (polygamous marriages) applies.

(7) The provision that may be made by regulations under subsection (6) above includes any provision that may be made by regulations under section 133 above.]

Amendment

　1.　　Inserted by SPCA Sch 2 para 3 (27.01.03 (for making regulations) and 6.10.03).

Definition

"qualifying age for state pension credit" – s137.

General Note

s136A SSCBA gives extensive regulation-making powers in relation to the calculation of income and capital for HB and CTB purposes for those who have attained the qualifying age for PC (see the commentary to the definition on p22). The provisions for such claimants are in the HB(SPC) Regs and the CTB(SPC) Regs.

Interpretation of Part VII and supplementary provisions

137.–(1)　In this Part of this Act, unless the context otherwise requires–

[¹ "billing authority" has the same meaning as in Part I of the Local Government Finance Act 1992;]

"child" means a person under the age of 16;

[⁷ "couple" means–

　(a)　a man and woman who are married to each other and are members of the same household

　(b)　a man and woman who are not married to each other but are living together as husband and wife otherwise than in prescribed circumstances

　(c)　two people of the same sexwho are civil partners of each other and are members of the same household; or

　(d)　two people of the same sex who are not civil partners of each other but are living together as if they were civil partners otherwise than in prescribed circumstances;]

"dwelling" means any residential accommodation, whether or not consisting of the whole or part of a building and whether or not comprising separate and self-contained premises;

"family" means–

　(a)　a [⁶ couple];

　(b)　a [⁶ couple] and a member of the same household for whom one of them is or both are responsible and who is a child or a person of a prescribed description;

　(c)　except in prescribed circumstances, a person who is not a member of a [⁶ couple] and a member of the same household for whom that person is responsible and who is a child or a person of a prescribed description;

"industrial injuries scheme" means a scheme made under Schedule 8 to this Act or section 159 of the 1975 Act or under the Old Cases Act;

[¹⁰ "local authority" in relation to Scotland means a council constituted under section 2 of the Local Government etc. (Scotland) Act 1994;]

[⁸ . . .]

[⁵ "pensionable age" has the meaning given by the rules in paragraph 1 of Schedule 4 to the Pensions Act 1995 (c. 26);]

"prescribed" means specified in or determined in accordance with regulations;

[⁵ "the qualifying age for state pension credit" is (in accordance with section 1(2)(b) and (6) of the State Pension Credit Act 2002)–

　(a)　in the case of a woman, pensionable age; or

　(b)　in the case of a man, the age which is pensionable age in the case of a woman born on the same day as the man;]

[⁵ "state pension credit" means state pension credit under the State Pension Credit Act 2002;]

[⁸ . . .]

"war pension scheme" means a scheme under which war pensions (as defined in section 25 of the Social Security Act 1989) are provided;

"week", in relation to [³ council tax benefit], means a period of 7 days beginning with a Monday.

　[⁹ (1A)　For the purposes of this Part, two people of the same sex are to be regarded as living together as if they were civil partners if, but only if, they would be regarded as living together as husband and wife were they instead two people of the opposite sex.]

(2)   Regulations may make provision for the purposes of this Part of this Act–
(a)   as to circumstances in which a person is to be treated as being or not being in Great Britain;
(b)   continuing a person's entitlement to benefit during periods of temporary absence from Great Britain;
(c)   as to what is or is not to be treated as remunerative work or as employment;
(d)   as to circumstances in which a person is or is not to be treated as
          (i)   engaged or normally engaged in remunerative work
          (ii)   [⁴ . . .]
(e)   as to what is or is not to be treated as relevant education;
(f)   as to circumstances in which a person is or is not to be treated as receiving relevant education;
(g)   specifying the descriptions of pension increases under war pension schemes or industrial injuries schemes that are analogous to the benefits mentioned in section 129(2)(b)(i) to (iii) above;
(h)   as to circumstances in which a person is or is not to be treated as occupying a dwelling as his home;
(i)   for treating any person who is liable to make payments in respect of a dwelling as if he were not so liable;
(j)   for treating any person who is not liable to make payments in respect of a dwelling as if he were so liable;
(k)   for treating as included in a dwelling any land used for the purposes of the dwelling;
(l)   as to circumstances in which persons are to be treated as being or not being members of the same household;
(m)   as to circumstances in which one person is to be treated as responsible or not responsible for another.

Amendments

1.   Substituted by LGFA Sch 9 para 9(a) (1.4.93).
2.   Definition of "levying authority" repealed by Local Government etc. (Scotland) Act 1994 Sch 13 para 174(5) and Sch 14 (1.4.96).
3.   Substituted by LGFA Sch 9 para 9(d) (1.4.93).
4.   Deleted by Jobseekers Act 1995 Sch 2 para 35(2).
5.   Inserted by SPCA Sch 2 para 4 (2.7.02 (for making regulations) and 6.10.03).
6.   Substituted by CPA Sch 24 para 46(2) (5.12.05).
7.   Inserted by CPA Sch 24 para 46(3) (5.12.05).
8.   Omitted by CPA Sch 24 para 46(4) (5.12.05).
9.   Inserted by CPA Sch 24 para 46(5) (5.12.05).
10.   Inserted by WRA reg 40 and Sch 5 para 1(4) (3.7.07).

General Note

Subs (1) and (1A) define certain terms for the purpose of this part of the Act. Subs (2) enables regulations to be made in order to implement the schemes set up under this Part of the Act.

Analysis

Subsection (1): Definitions

"billing authority". Section 1(2) of the 1992 Act interprets this to cover district councils, London borough councils, the Common Council or the Council of the Isles of Scilly.

"couple". This definition was introduced with effect from 5 December 2005 as a result of the changes brought in by the Civil Partnership Act 2004 (CPA 2004). There are four situations in which two people are treated as a "couple" for HB and CTB purposes. The first two definitions carry forward the old definitions of "married couple" and "unmarried couple". The third and fourth definitions, apply in respect of "same sex" couples.

On the question of when it is for the local authority to determine whether or not a claimant is a member of a couple (as opposed to the DWP), see the discussion of *R v Penwith DC ex p Menear* [1991] 24 HLR 115, QBD and *R v South Ribble DC HBRB ex p Hamilton* [2000] 33 HLR 102, CA in the General Note on p343.

Married couple: para (a). As to membership of the same household, see p22. Occasionally it may be necessary to consider the question of whether someone is actually married. If the marriage could be shown to be void, as distinct from voidable, under the relevant law of marriage in either England and Wales or in Scotland (which are markedly different), then it would be necessary to consider whether the two people in question were an unmarried couple: see below. The validity of foreign marriages can cause very difficult questions of law to arise. Note also the existence in Scotland of the doctrine of marriage by habit and repute. In cases where any of these issues arise, reference should be made to specialist textbooks on the subject. A useful short summary for advisers with references to caselaw can be found in the discussion of bereavement benefits (where these issues arise much more frequently) in CPAG's *Welfare Benefits and Tax Credits Handbook*.

Unmarried couple: para (b). The main issue which arises here concerns the meaning of the phrase "living together as husband and wife". The phrase has been used widely in various means-tested and non-means-tested benefits schemes and is subject to a large body of caselaw. Differences of interpretation led the predecessor of the DWP to issue guidance about indications as to whether the test is satisfied. The first six of the principles below are the factors listed in the guidance, which is reproduced in the HB and CTB guidance: see GM C1 Annex A. They are "admirable signposts" (*Crake and Butterworth v Supplementary Benefit Commission* [1982] 1 All ER 498) but *CIS 87/1993* emphasised the need to stand back once all the evidence has been considered and look at the overall quality of the relationship.

(1)   If the couple share a household, they will be more likely to be a "living together as husband and wife". For the meaning of "household", see p22. If they are not part of the same household, it is highly unlikely that they are "living together" in this sense. However, one of the most common pitfalls in these cases is to consider issues relating to the sharing of a household and stop the inquiry there. While the sharing of a household is consistent with a relationship akin to husband and wife, the caselaw is replete with examples where it has been held that the facts are equally consistent with other types of relationship such as simple friendship or brother and sister (*CP 8001/1995* para 10), patient and carer (*R(SB) 35/85* para 8), and landlord and lodger (*Campbell v Secretary of State for Social Services* [1983] 4 FLR 138, QBD, though rejected on the facts of that particular case).

(2)   The more stable the relationship, the more likely they are to be "living together as husband and wife". However, again caution needs to be applied because some of the other relationships mentioned in the previous paragraph may last for a long time: *CP 8001/1995* para 12. A degree of permanency in a landlord and lodger relationship may take it over the line into cohabitation: see *Campbell* for an example. Note, however, point (7) below.

(3)   The closer the financial arrangements, the more likely that a finding of "living together as husband and wife" will be justified. However, in any case where this issue arises there will be some degree of financial connection between the parties and so it will only be a compelling factor if the financial arrangements are particularly close and involve, for example, joint bank accounts.

(4)   The presence of a sexual relationship is of importance: *R(SB) 17/81* (para 7). Claimants who are not involved in a sexual relationship may need to make this clear to the authorities at the outset. In *CIS 87/1993* (para 12) it was said that if there had never been a sexual relationship, strong alternative grounds will be required to permit a conclusion that the man and woman are a couple. In *CSB 150/1985* it was said that two Mormons engaged to each other and living in the same house could not be an unmarried couple. That decision probably goes too far in apparently excluding evidence of other factors, but it is an illustration of the significance of this factor. Its importance may vary according to the ages of the people in question and cultural factors, but authorities should be careful not to make assumptions.

(5)   If the couple have children "of their union", in the antiquated phrase that was used in the old supplementary benefit guidance, that will be a strong indication that they are "living together as husband and wife".

(6)   The degree of public acknowledgement of the relationship is a factor which is often underplayed and is often illuminating as to the true nature of the relationship and as to the intention of the parties (see below). If one partner uses the name of the other, that will be highly persuasive: *R(G) 1/79* (para 9).

(7)   The relevance of the intention of the parties is controversial. In *Crake and Butterworth,* Woolf J (at 504d-f) placed considerable emphasis on what the intention of the parties was, and Webster J thought that if the intention of the parties was capable of ascertainment, it was significant: see *Robson v Secretary of State for Social Services.* Subsequently, it was suggested that the intention of the parties could only be ascertained from their actions: see *R(SB) 17/81* (para 8). No doubt it is true that it would be wrong for an authority simply to accept a claimant's account of what her/his intention was without examining such a statement against the background of the objective evidence. However, it is suggested that if the objective evidence, perhaps coupled with credible evidence given by a claimant, clearly indicates an intention to adopt a different relationship, the two people will not be "living together as husband and wife": *CIS 87/1993* (para 14).

(8)   The nature of a relationship can change over time. Thus it is wrong for an authority to assume, just because it concludes that on a particular date that two people are an unmarried couple, that the relationship has always had that quality: *CP 8001/1995* (para 11).

If the result of this complex inquiry is that the couple are "living together as husband and wife", only one of them may claim HB and CTB in respect of their dwelling and their needs and resources are aggregated.

Civil partners: para (c). Two people of the same sex are treated as a "couple" if they are members of the same household (see p22) and have entered into a contract of civil partnership under the CPA 2004.

Not civil partners: para (d). Two people of the same sex are treated as a "couple" if they have not entered into a civil partnership contract, but are living together as if they were civil partners. Under subsection (1A) this last test can only be satisfied if the same sex couple would have been regarded as "living together as husband and wife" were they of the opposite sex. Similar considerations to those in the definition of couple under para (b) are relevant to determining whether a same sex couple is living together as if they were civil partners.

As to when the new definitions of couple may start to apply to same sex couples claiming HB/CTB, see art 3 of SI 2005 No.2877 on p1193.

"dwelling". The House of Lords decision in *Uratemp Ventures Ltd v Collins* [2001] 3 WLR 806 sheds new light on the meaning of "dwelling". Previous authority had stated, in the context of statutory protection of residential tenants, that a room or rooms which a tenant was given a right to occupy could only be a "dwelling" if they provided for the three basic necessities of life: namely sleeping, cooking and eating. Of these, sleeping had been regarded as the most important factor: *Wright v Howell* [1947] 92 SJ 26, CA; *Westminister CC v Clarke* [1992] 2 AC 288 at 299, HL. In *Collins*, however, the House of Lords ruled that rooms were not excluded from the definition of "dwelling" simply by virtue of the fact that they did not contain cooking facilities. Lord Irvine stated (at 808D, para 3) that "dwelling . . . connotes a place where one lives, regarding and treating it as home". He said (at 808E, para 4) that it was not even necessary that the room or rooms should contain a bed if a person was sleeping there. Lord Bingham said (at 809G-H, para 12) that although premises would not normally be a "dwelling" unless the tenant sleeps there, there was no inflexible rule even as to this.

The House of Lords in *Collins* emphasised the importance of the statutory context in interpreting the word (at 808D, para 3, 809D-E, para 10, 810C, para 15, 822F-823A, para 57). The emphasis on the "residential" aspects in the definition given in s137 suggests that in the HB context it should be given a wide interpretation, because the essence of the HB scheme is to include all rent and allied payments for different types of accommodation. That this is the correct interpretation is further confirmed by the inclusive nature of the definition to include parts of a building and accommodation which is not self-contained. Some landlords of low-grade accommodation attempt to exclude it from the regime of statutory protection by, for example, providing that cooking facilities are not to be used. Even if these agreements are genuine, the absence of cooking facilities should not exclude the occupant from HB.

The dwelling which the claimant occupies as a home may comprise more than one property: *London Borough of Hackney v GA* [2008] UKUT 26 (AAC); *R(H) 5/09*. The definition of "dwelling" in the HB context (for which see s130) is inseparable from occupation as the claimant's home. Judge Jacobs decided that the words "a dwelling in Great Britain which he occupies as his home" give rise to a single question of fact: what is the extent of the dwelling occupied by the claimant? In so deciding, the judge considered the decision of the Court of Appeal in *SSWP v Miah* (reported as *R(JSA) 9/03*). He accepted that although *Miah* is not a binding authority on the interpretation of the HB legislation, it is an authority that it is permissible, in appropriate circumstances, to take a functional approach to the definition of "dwelling". He did not read it as a restrictive definition, as it has to cover all sorts of residential accommodation. He said:

"The housing benefit legislation largely avoids terms of art from property law. For example: regulation 9 refers to payments in respect of a dwelling rather than rent and to agreement rather than tenancy. This reflects the breadth of the arrangements that are covered by the legislation. It is concerned with the economic substance of an arrangement rather than with the precise legal form. In that context, it is appropriate to take account of the reality of the claimant's living arrangements and not place too much emphasis on the legal structure."

Birmingham City Council v IB [2009] UKUT 116 (AAC) is consistent with the decision in *R(H) 5/09*. The claimant was a disabled student entitled to HB. To ensure full time attendance at university he needed a live-in carer and hence two-bedroom accommodation. The university did not have such accommodation available and therefore provided the claimant with two adjacent rooms, each with en-suite facilities, so that the carer could be on call 24 hours a day. The issue was whether two rooms which were physically separated from one another but had access onto the same corridor and required use of a common kitchen could constitute part of the same dwelling for HB purposes. Deputy Judge Mark decided that the claimant was entitled to HB on the basis that the dwelling occupied by him as a home included the room rented by him for his carer. Applying the tests set out in *Miah*, functionally and purposively, the judge decided that the claimant needed two rooms for living – one for himself and one for his carer. He said:

"Commonsense dictates that it should not matter whether there is a connecting door between the two, which the claimant might in any event be incapable of crossing, or whether the two rooms are in a larger flat as in this case or in a two room flat, or even a duplex with the carer's room on the first floor and inaccessible to the claimant. Nor should it matter if the landlord's internal billing system meant that the two rooms were separately billed."

Besides the accommodation being residential in nature, it seems that the agreement under which the claimant occupies the home must reflect this fact. In *R v Warrington BC ex p Williams* [1997] 29 HLR 872 at 876, QBD, the claimant rented commercial premises and used them as a dwelling, in breach of the lease. He claimed that the landlord had orally agreed that he could stay overnight to act as a night watchman, and so was unable to assert the true character of the premises against the claimant. In view of that, it was contended that the premises had to be seen as having a joint residential and commercial use. This argument was rejected, as a waiver of a condition against use as a dwelling did not alter the commercial nature of the tenancy and so the premises were not a dwelling.

"family". This definition and its component parts determine the crucial question of who forms part of the assessment unit for HB and CTB purposes – eg, for the purposes of the "applicable amount". These are couples (para (a)), couples with children (para (b)) and lone parents (para (c)). Broadly speaking, a couple's resources are to be treated as the claimant's for the purposes of the assessment of those resources whereas those who do not form part of the family will only be taken into account as non-dependants, if at all.

For the critical issue of membership of a "household", see below. This is of equal importance to opposite sex and same sex couples.

Section 137(2)(l) permits the making of regulations to define the situations in which people are not to be treated as sharing a household for these purposes. See reg 21 of both the HB and the HB(SPC) Regs and the CTB equivalents. Reg 20 of both the HB and the HB(SPC) Regs sets out the circumstances in which adults are to be treated as responsible for children and young persons (for the issue of the identity of persons of prescribed description for these purposes, see reg 19 of both sets of regs).

Meaning of "household" in the definitions of "couple" and "family". This word is of significance in three respects in determining the question of membership of a family. First, in order for a child or young person to form part of a claimant's family, s/he must live in the same household. Note that reg 21 HB Regs deems continued residence in the household in certain circumstances, but does not itself define the circumstances in which a child forms part of the household. Secondly, the other member of a "married couple" or "civil partnership couple" only forms part of a claimant's family if s/he is living in the same household. Thirdly, the question of whether an unmarried man and woman are "living together as husband and wife" or whether a same sex couple are living together as if they are civil partners involves consideration of, but is not determined by, the question of whether they share a household.

There is a considerable body of caselaw considering whether two people are members of the same "household". As was observed in *R(SB) 4/83* (para 19), the word is an ordinary English word and the question is to be resolved by the use of common sense. More than one interpretation of the facts before the authority or the First-tier Tribunal may therefore be permissible. However, the following principles can be established from the caselaw.

(1)   A person cannot be a member of more than one household at once: *R(SB) 8/85* (para 12). However, it is possible for a person to follow a regular pattern of moving from one household to another: see *CIS 11304/ 1995* (para 10), where a claimant spent about six months in each year living with his wife and the other part of the year living with another partner.

(2)   The issue is not determined on a week-by-week basis but on the basis of the overall relationship between the parties: *R(SB) 30/83* (para 5) concerning a university student moving in and out of the accommodation, who was held to be resident with her partner during the periods of absence during term-time. Note the special rules in reg 7(6)(b) HB Regs that can apply in these circumstances.

(3)   If the two people are separately liable to pay for their accommodation, that is a good indication that they are not members of the same household: *R(SB) 13/82* (para 11).

(4)   If the two people have completely separate living arrangements, then they cannot be members of the same household: *R(SB) 4/83* (para 19).

(5)   However, even if two people share certain facilities, there must still be an element of domesticity about their arrangements. This is illustrated by *CIS 671/1992* (para 4) where the claimant and his wife had senile dementia and did not understand the fact that they were husband and wife. Accordingly, mere presence in the same room does not mean that the two people are sharing a household. There must be a reasonable level of independence and self-sufficiency: *R(IS) 1/99* (Appendix para 14). This will often be lacking where a person is living in communal accommodation and so it will be rare for the occupants to be sharing a single household: *CIS 671/1992*.

(6)   In considering whether the element of shared living is sufficiently strong to constitute a single household, a number of factors may be relevant. These may include: whether there are independent arrangements for the storage and cooking of food, whether there are independent financial arrangements (apart from the question of separate liabilities for the accommodation discussed above), whether the two people eat separately, and the general evidence of family life within the accommodation. Ultimately, however, it remains a question of fact and it will often not be easy to demonstrate an error of law in the approach taken by an authority or the First-tier Tribunal.

"The qualifying age for state pension credit". This age is relevant in determining whether the HB and CTB Regs or the HB(SPC) and CTB(SPC) Regs apply to a claimant. The age at which someone qualifies for state pension credit (PC) is linked to the pensionable age for a woman. The qualifying age for PC for a woman is the minimum age she can receive state retirement pension. The qualifying age for PC for a man is the minimum age a woman born on the same day as him can receive state retirement pension. So for both men and women, the qualifying age for PC is:

(1)   60, if s/he was born before 6 April 1950; *or*

(2)   an age from 60 and one month to 64 and 11 months depending on her/his date of birth, if s/he was born on or after 6 April 1950 but before 6 April 1955; *or*

(3)   65, if s/he was born on or after 6 April 1955.

Consequently, the rules in the HB(SPC) Regs and the CTB(SPC) Regs will apply to individual claimants at different ages. For claimants born on or after 6 April 1950 but before 6 April 1955, there is a helpful table, setting out the relevant birth dates and pension ages, in an appendix to CPAG's *Welfare Benefits and Tax Credits Handbook*. Once pensionable age is 65 for both men and women, the age for both will rise to 68 between 2024 and 2046. Note, however, that the present Government may bring forward the rise in pensionable age to 66, to 2016 for men and 2020 for women.

Subsection (2): Regulation-making powers

This sets out general regulation-making powers in relation to issues relating to entitlement to means-tested benefits. For regulation-making powers in relation to adjudication and administration, see ss5 and 6 SSAA. The principal regulations made under these powers are listed next to the letter of each paragraph below.

(a)   Reg 7(10) to (17) of both the HB and the HB(SPC) Regs and reg 8(1) to (6) of both the CTB and the CTB(SPC) Regs. No distinction is drawn between absences inside and outside the UK in the HB and CTB schemes.

(b)   See para (a).

(c)   Reg 6(1) to (4) HB, HB(CTB), CTB and CTB(SPC) Regs.

(d)   Reg 6(5) to (7) HB, HB(CTB), CTB and CTB(SPC) Regs.

(e)   Not relevant. This concept has nothing to do with the HB and CTB rules about students but is used in the comparable IS and income-based JSA exclusions for students and others in full-time study.

(f)   See para (e).

(g)   Not relevant.

(h)   See reg 7 of both the HB and HB(SPC) Regs and reg 8 of both the CTB and CTB(SPC) Regs.

(i)   See regs 7, 9, 10 and 56 HB Regs and regs 7, 9, and 10 HB(SPC) Regs.

(j)   See reg 8(1)(b) to (e) of both the HB and the HB(SPC) Regs.

(k)   See reg 2(4) of both the HB and the HB(SPC) Regs.

(l)   See reg 21 of both the HB and the HB(SPC) Regs and reg 11 of both the CTB and the CTB(SPC) Regs.

(m)   See reg 20 of both the HB and the HB(SPC) Regs and reg 10 of both the CTB and the CTB(SPC) Regs.

PART XIII

General

Interpretation

Applications of Act in relation to territorial waters

172.   In this Act–

(a)   any reference to Great Britain includes a reference to the territorial waters of the United Kingdom adjacent to Great Britain;

(b)   any reference to the United Kingdom includes a reference to the territorial waters of the United Kingdom.

Age

173.   For the purposes of this Act a person–

(a)   is over or under a particular age if he has or, as the case may be has not attained that age; and

(b)   is between two particular ages if he has attained the first but not the second;

and in Scotland (as in England and Wales) the time at which a person attains a particular age expressed in years is the commencement of the relevant anniversary of the date of his birth.

References to Acts

174.   In this Act–

''the 1975 Act'' means the Social Security Act 1975;

''the 1986 Act'' means the Social Security Act 1986;

''the Administration Act'' means the Social Security Administration Act 1992;

''the Consequential Provisions Act'' means the Social Security (Consequential Provisions) Act 1992;

''the Northern Ireland Contributions and Benefits Act'' means the Social Security Contributions and Benefits (Northern Ireland) Act 1992;

''the Old Cases Act'' means the Industrial Injuries and Diseases (Old Cases) Act 1975; and

''the Pensions Act'' means the Social Security Pensions Act 1975.

Subordinate legislation

Regulations, orders and schemes

175.–(1)   Subject to section 145(5) above, regulations and orders under this Act shall be made by the Secretary of State.

[(1A)   *[Omitted]*]

(2)   Powers under this Act to make regulations, orders or schemes shall be exercisable by statutory instrument.

(3)   Except in the case of an order under section 145(3) above and in so far as this Act otherwise provides, any power under this Act to make regulations or an order may be exercised–

(a)   either in relation to all cases to which the power extends, or in relation to those cases subject to specified exceptions, or in relation to any specified cases or classes of case;

(b)   so as to make, as respects the cases in relation to which it is exercised–

(i)   the full provision to which the power extends or any less provision (whether by way of exception or otherwise),

(ii)   the same provision for all cases in relation to which the power is exercised, or different provision for different cases or different classes of case or different provision as respects the same case or class of case for different purposes of this Act,

(iii)   any such provision either unconditionally or subject to any specified condition;

and where such a power is expressed to be exercisable for alternative purposes it may be exercised in relation to the same case or any or all of those purposes; and powers to make regulations or an order for the purposes of any one provision of this Act are without prejudice to powers to make regulations or an order for the purposes of any other provision.

(4)   Without prejudice to any specific provision in this Act, any power conferred by this Act to make regulations or an order (other than the power conferred in section 145(3) above) includes power to make thereby such incidental, supplementary, consequential or transitional provision as appears to the Secretary of State to be expedient for the purposes of the regulations or order.

(5)   Without prejudice to any specific provisions in this Act, a power conferred by any provision of this Act except–

(a)   sections 30, 47(6), 57(9)(a) and 145(3) above and paragraph 3(9) of Schedule 7 to this Act;

(b)   section 122(1) above in relation to the definition of "payments by way of occupational or personal pension"; and

(c)   Part XI,

to make regulations or an order includes power to provide for a person to exercise a discretion in dealing with any matter.

(6)   Any power conferred by this Act to make orders or regulations relating to housing benefit or [¹ council tax benefit] shall include power to make different provisions for different areas.

(7)   Any power of the Secretary of State under any provision of this Act, except the provisions mentioned in subsection (5)(a) and (b) above and Part IX, to make any regulations or order, where the power is not expressed to be exercisable with the consent of the Treasury, shall if the Treasury so direct be exercisable only in conjunction with them.

(8)   Any power under any of sections 116 to 120 above to modify provisions of this Act or the Administration Act extends also to modifying so much of any other provision of this Act or that Act as re-enacts provisions of the 1975 Act which replaced provisions of the National Insurance (Industrial Injuries) Acts 1965 to 1974.

(9)   A power to make regulations under any of sections 116 to 120 above shall be exercisable in relation to any enactment passed after this Act which is directed to be construed as one with this Act; but this subsection applies only so far as a contrary

intention is not expressed in the enactment so passed, and is without prejudice to the generality of any such direction.

(10) Any reference in this section or section 176 below to an order or regulations under this Act includes a reference to an order or regulations made under any provision of an enactment passed after this Act and directed to be construed as one with this Act; but this subsection applies only so far as a contrary intention is not expressed in the enactment so passed, and without prejudice to the generality of any such direction.

Amendment
1.   Substituted by LGFA para 10 Sch 9 (1.4.93).

Parliamentary control
176.–(1)-(2)   *[Omitted]*
(3)   A statutory instrument–
(a)   which contains (whether alone or with other provisions) any order, regulations or scheme made under this Act by the Secretary of State, other than an order under section 145(3) above; and
(b)   which is not subject to any requirement that a draft of the instrument shall be laid before and approved by a resolution of each House of Parliament,
shall be subject to annulment in pursuance of a resolution of either House of Parliament.

Short title, commencement and extent

Short title, commencement and extent
177.–(1)   This Act may be cited as the Social Security Contributions and Benefits Act 1992.
(2)   This Act is to be read, where appropriate, with the Administration Act and the Consequential Provisions Act.
(3)   The enactments consolidated by this Act are repealed, in consequence of the consolidation, by the Consequential Provisions Act.
(4)   Except as provided in Schedule 4 to the Consequential Provisions Act, this Act shall come into force on 1st July 1992.
(5)   The following provisions extend to Northern Ireland–
(a)   section 16 and Schedule 2;
(b)   section 116(2); and
(c)   this section.
(6)   Except as provided by this section, this Act does not extend to Northern Ireland.

Social Security Administration Act 1992
(1992 c5)

Arrangement of Sections
PART I
CLAIMS FOR AND PAYMENTS AND GENERAL ADMINISTRATION OF BENEFIT
Necessity of claim
1.   Entitlement to benefit dependent on claim
2.   Retrospective effect of provisions making entitlement to benefit dependent on claim

Work-focused interviews
2A.   Claim or full entitlement to certain benefits conditional on work-focused interview
2C.   Optional work-focused interviews

Claims and payments regulations
5.   Regulations about claims for and payments of benefit

Council tax benefits
6.   Regulations about council tax benefits administration
7.   Relationship between council tax benefit and other benefits
7A.   Sharing of functions as regards certain claims and information
7B.   Use of social security information

PART II
ADJUDICATION
Housing benefit and council tax benefit
63.   Adjudication

PART III
OVERPAYMENTS AND ADJUSTMENTS OF BENEFIT
Housing benefit
75.   Overpayments of housing benefit

Council tax benefit
76.   Excess benefit
77.   Shortfall in benefit

PART VI
Enforcement
109A.   Authorisations for investigators
109B.   Power to require information
109C.   Powers of entry
110A.   Authorisations by local authorities
110AA. Power of local authority to require electronic access to information
111.   Delay, obstruction etc. of inspector
111A.   Dishonest representations for the purpose of obtaining benefit etc.
112.   False representations for obtaining benefit etc
113.   Breach of regulations
115.   Offences by bodies corporate
115A.   Penalty as alternative to prosecution
115B.   Penalty as alternative to prosecution: colluding employers etc

Legal proceedings
116.   Legal proceedings

116A. Local authority powers to prosecute benefit fraud
121DA. Interpretation of Part VI

PART VII
PROVISION OF INFORMATION
Authorities administering housing benefit or council tax benefit
122C. Supply of information to authorities administering benefit
122D. Supply of information by authorities administering benefit
122E. Supply of information between authorities administering benefit

Rent officers and housing benefit
122F. Supply by rent officers of information relating to housing benefit
123.   Unauthorised disclosure of information relating to particular persons
126A. Information from landlords and agents

EXPEDITED CLAIMS FOR HOUSING AND COUNCIL TAX BENEFIT
128A. Disclosure of information by authorities

PART VIII
ARRANGEMENTS FOR HOUSING BENEFIT AND COUNCIL TAX BENEFITS AND RELATED
SUBSIDIES
Housing benefit
134.   Arrangements for housing benefit

Council tax benefit
138.   Nature of benefits
139.   Arrangements for council tax benefit

Reports
139A. Persons to report on administration
139B. Powers of investigation
139BA. Interaction with Audit Commission
139C. Reports

Directions by Secretary of State
139D. Directions
139DA. Directions: Variation and Revocation
139E. Information about attainment of standards
139F. Enforcement notices
139G. Enforcement determinations
139H. Enforcement determinations: supplementary

Subsidy
140A. Subsidy
140B. Calculation of amount of subsidy
140C. Payment of subsidy
140D. Rent rebate subsidy: accounting provisions

Supplementary provisions
140E. Financing of joint arrangements
140F. No requirement for annual orders
140G. Interpretation: Part VIII

PART XIII
ADVISORY BODIES AND CONSULTATION
The Social Security Advisory Committee and the Industrial Injuries Advisory Council
170.   Consultation with representative organisations

172.   Functions of Committee and Council in relation to regulations
173.   Cases in which consultation is not required
174.   Committee's report on regulations and Secretary of State's duties

Housing benefit and council tax benefit
176.   Consultation with representative organisations

PART XV
MISCELLANEOUS
182A.   Return of social security post
182B.   Requirement to supply information about redirection of post
187.   Certain benefit to be inalienable

PART XVI
GENERAL
Subordinate legislation
189.   Regulations and orders – general
190.   Parliamentary control of orders and regulations

Supplementary
191.   Interpretation – general
192.   Short title, commencement and extent

SCHEDULES
4.   Persons Employed in Social Security Administration or Adjudication
10.   Supplementary Benefit etc

PART I
Claims for and Payments and General Administration of Benefit
Necessity of claim

Entitlement to benefit dependent on claim

1.–(1)   Except in such cases as may be prescribed, and subject to the following provisions of this section and to section 3 below, no person shall be entitled to any benefit unless, in addition to any other conditions relating to that benefit being satisfied–

(a)   he makes a claim for it in the manner, and within the time, prescribed in relation to that benefit by regulations under this Part of this Act; or

(b)   he is treated by virtue of such regulations as making a claim for it.

[²(1A)   No person whose entitlement to any benefit depends on his making a claim shall be entitled to the benefit unless subsection (1B) below is satisfied in relation both to the person making the claim and to any other person in respect of whom he is claiming benefit.

(1B)   This subsection is satisfied in relation to a person if–

(a)   the claim is accompanied by–

(i)   a statement of the person's national insurance number and information or evidence establishing that that number has been allocated to the person; or

(ii)   information or evidence enabling the national insurance number that has been allocated to the person to be ascertained; or

(b)   the person makes an application for a national insurance number to be allocated to him which is accompanied by information or evidence enabling such a number to be so allocated.

(1C)   Regulations may make provision disapplying subsection (1A) above in the case of–

(a)   prescribed benefits;

(b)   prescribed descriptions of persons making claims; or

(c)   prescribed descriptions of persons in respect of whom benefit is claimed,
or in other prescribed circumstances.]
(2)   Where under subsection (1) above a person is required to make a claim or to be
treated as making a claim for a benefit in order to be entitled to it–
(a)   if the benefit is a widow's payment, she shall not be entitled to it in respect of a
death occurring more than 12 months before the date on which the claim is
made or treated as made, and
(b)   if the benefit is any other benefit except disablement benefit or reduced earnings
allowance, the person shall not be entitled to it in respect of any period more
than 12 months before that date,
except as provided by section 3 below.
(3)   *[Omitted]*
(4)   In this section and section 2 below "benefit" means–
(a)   benefit as defined in section 122 of the Contributions and Benefits Act; and
[¹(aa) a jobseeker's allowance;]
[³(ab) state pension credit;]
[⁴ (ac) an employment and support allowance;] and
(b)   any income-related benefit.
(5)   This section (which corresponds to section 165A of the 1975 Act, as it had
effect immediately before this Act came into force) applies to claims made on or after 1st
October 1990 or treated by virtue of regulations under that section or this section as
having been made on or after that date.
(6)   Schedule 1 to this Act shall have effect in relation to other claims.

Amendments

1.   Inserted by Jobseekers Act 1995 Sch 2 para 38 (22.4.96).
2.   Inserted by SSA(F) Act 1997, s19.
3.   Inserted by SCPA s11 and Sch 1 para 2 (2.7.02 for making regulations and 7.4.03).
4.   Inserted by WRA s28 and Sch 3 para 10(2) (18.3.08 for making regulations and 27.7.08).

Definitions

"benefit" – s1(4).
"claim" – s191.
"income-related benefit" – s191.
"prescribe" – s191.

General Note

Subs (1) sets out the general condition of entitlement to benefit that there must be a current claim. See Part 10 HB Regs, Part 9 HB(SPC) Regs, Part 8 CTB Regs and Part 7 CTB(SPC) Regs.

Subs (1A) to (1C) provide a general requirement in relation to entitlement for all benefits, including HB and CTB. By subs (1B), it is necessary that the claimant either supplies her/his national insurance number (NINO) or enough information to allow the number to be ascertained, or makes an application for a number.

The phrase "any other person in respect of whom he is claiming benefit" in subsection (1A) includes the claimant's partner with whom s/he lives: *Secretary of State for Work and Pensions v Wilson* [2006] EWCA Civ 882, 29 June 2006 (reported as *R(H) 7/06*). Reg 4 of each of the HB, HB(SPC), CTB and CTB(SPC) Regs sets out cases in which s1(1A) is disapplied. These include the case of a claimant's partner where the partner is a "person subject to immigration control" because s/he does not have leave to enter or remain in the UK, s/he is not "habitually resident" and s/he has not previously been allocated a NINO. See, for example, reg 4 HB Regs on p229.

CH 4085/2007 [2008] UKUT 14 (AAC) considered the meaning in s1(1B)(b) of "accompanied by information or evidence enabling such a number" to be allocated. The tribunal had taken the view that the terms of s1(1B)(b) were not satisfied because the failure of the claimant's husband to attend an interview in respect of his application for a NINO, and the subsequent refusal of a NINO, showed that he had not provided sufficient information or evidence to enable a NINO to be allocated. Judge Rowland allowed the claimant's appeal. The requirement is merely to have applied for a NINO with the requisite information or evidence; the refusal of the NINO does not show conclusively that the requirement was not satisfied. What the Secretary of State actually requires in order to allocate a NINO is sufficient evidence to show that the applicant does not already have one, information that a claim for a benefit requiring an application for a NINO has been, or is to be, made and information as to identity so that the Secretary of State can be satisfied that the claimant is genuine. A person can only be expected to send what s/he has been told to send and the source of that information is likely to be those administering the benefit being claimed (here the local authority). The information and evidence mentioned in the legislation is only that information and evidence that the person concerned could reasonably have been expected to send when the application was made. The phrase "information or evidence enabling [a national insurance] number to be so allocated" cannot extend to information and evidence provided at an interview. In the judge's view, if Parliament had intended to include the information that is provided at interview, it would have made entitlement conditional on a NINO being allocated. The judge also pointed out that evidence of a failure to attend an interview is insufficient to show that an application was not, or has ceased to be, genuine. Regard must at least be had to the cause of the failure but even a lack of good cause may not indicate a lack of intention to pursue an application.

LCC v SSWP [2009] UKUT 74 (AAC) considered the NINO requirement in the context of a claimant's partner who had applied for, but was refused, a NINO. Judge Mesher confirmed that the NINO requirement applies not only on an initial claim but also where a decision making an indefinite award is being revised or superseded (*CH 4085/2007* approved in this respect). The judge also said that *CH 4085/2007* was right to hold that subsection (1B)(b) might be satisfied, even though the NINO was itself refused. However, he disagreed with the finding in that decision that the requirement can be satisfied simply by the submission of a form requesting a NINO interview. Rather, the information or evidence enabling a NINO to be allocated was to be regarded as encompassing all the information and evidence provided by the applicant during the process, down to and including the signing of the CA5400 form at the conclusion of the interview. He accepted that the essence of the interview was to obtain evidence of identity (and that immigration status, including not having the right to work, was irrelevant). As here such evidence had been provided (eg, a passport, student ID and utility bills in the applicant's name), the requirement was satisfied.

Retrospective effect of provisions making entitlement to benefit dependent on claim

2.–(1)   This section applies where a claim for benefit is made or treated as made at any time on or after 2nd September 1985 (the date on which section 165A or the 1975 Act (general provision as to necessity of claim for entitlement to benefit), as originally enacted, came into force) in respect of a period the whole or any part of which falls on or after that date.

(2)   Where this section applies, any question arising as to–

(a)   whether the claimant is or was at any time (whether before, on or after 2nd September 1985) entitled to the benefit in question, or to any other benefit on which his entitlement to that benefit depends; or

(b)   in a case where the claimant's entitlement to the benefit depends on the entitlement of another person to a benefit, whether that other person is or was so entitled,

shall be determined as if the relevant claim enactment and any regulations made under or referred to in that enactment had also been in force, with any necessary modifications, at all times relevant for the purpose of determining the entitlement of the claimant, and, where applicable, of the other person, to the benefit or benefits in question (including the entitlement of any person to any benefit on which that entitlement depends, and so on).

(3)   In this section ''the relevant claim enactment'' means section 1 above as it has effect in relation to the claim referred to in subsection (1) above.

(4)   In any case where–

(a)   a claim for benefit was made or treated as made (whether before, on or after 2nd September 1985, and whether by the same claimant as the claim referred to in subsection (1) above or not), and benefit was awarded on that claim, in respect of a period falling wholly or partly before that date; but

(b)   that award would not have been made had the current requirements applied in relation to claims for benefit, whenever made, in respect of periods before that date; and

(c)   entitlement to the benefit claimed as mentioned in subsection (1) above depends on whether the claimant or some other person was previously entitled or treated as entitled to that or some other benefit,

then, in determining whether the conditions of entitlement to the benefit so claimed are satisfied, the person to whom benefit was awarded as mentioned in paragraphs (a) and (b) above shall be taken to have been entitled to the benefit so awarded, notwithstanding anything in subsection (2) above.

(5)   In subsection (4) above ''the current requirements'' means–

(a)   the relevant claim enactment, and any regulations made or treated as made under that enactment, or referred to in it, as in force at the time of the claim referred to in subsection (1) above, with any necessary modifications; and

(b) subsection (1) (with the omission of the words following "at any time") and subsections (2) and (3) above.

Definitions
"benefit" – s1(4).
"claim" – s191.
"current requirements" – s2(5).
"relevant claim enactment" – s2(1).

General Note
This section was introduced by the Social Security Act 1990 to confirm that the predecessor of s1 above had retrospective effect. It means that a claimant cannot claim HB from before September 1985 on the basis that before that date a claim was not a requirement of entitlement to benefit: *Insurance Officer v McCaffrey* [1985] 1 WLR 1353 at 1355H-1356C, HL.

Work-focused interviews

Claim or full entitlement to certain benefits conditional on work-focused interview

2A.–(1) Regulations may make provision for or in connection with–
(a) imposing, as a condition falling to be satisfied by a person who–
  (i) makes a claim for a benefit to which this section applies, and
  [⁴ (ii) has not attained pensionable age at the time of making the claim (but see subsection (1A)),]
  a requirement to take part in [⁴ one or more work-focused interviews];
(b) imposing, at a time when–
  (i) a person [⁴ has not attained pensionable age and is] entitled to such a benefit, and
  (ii) any prescribed circumstances exist,
  a requirement to take part in [⁴ one or more work-focused interviews] as a condition of that person continuing to be entitled to the full amount which is payable to him in respect of the benefit apart from the regulations.
[⁴ (1A) For the purposes of subsection (1) a man born before 6 April 1955 is treated as attaining pensionable age when a woman born on the same day as the man would attain pensionable age.]
(2) The benefits to which this section applies are–
(a) income support;
(b) housing benefit;
(c) council tax benefit;
(d) widow's and bereavement benefits falling within section 20(1)(e) and (ea) of the Contributions and Benefits Act (other than a bereavement payment);
(e) incapacity benefit;
(f) severe disablement allowance; and
(g) [¹ carer's allowance].
(3) Regulations under this section may, in particular, make provision–
(a) for securing, where a person would otherwise be required to take part in interviews relating to two or more benefits–
  (i) that he is only required to take part in one interview, and
  (ii) that any such interview is capable of counting for the purposes of all those benefits;
(b) for determining the persons by whom interviews are to be conducted;
(c) conferring power on such persons or the designated authority to determine when and where interviews are to take place (including power in prescribed circumstances to determine that they are to take place in the homes of those being interviewed);
(d) prescribing the circumstances in which persons attending interviews are to be regarded as having or not having taken part in them;

(e) for securing that the appropriate consequences mentioned in subsection (4)(a) or (b) below ensue if a person who has been notified that he is required to take part in an interview–
  (i) fails to take part in the interview, and
  (ii) does not show, within the prescribed period, that he had good cause for that failure;

(f) prescribing–
  (i) matters which are or are not to be taken into account in determining whether a person does or does not have good cause for any failure to comply with the regulations, or
  (ii) circumstances in which a person is or is not to be regarded as having or not having good cause for any such failure.

(4) For the purposes of subsection (3)(e) above the appropriate consequences of a failure falling within that provision are–

(a) where the requirement to take part in an interview applied by virtue of subsection (1)(a) above, that as regards any relevant benefit either–
  (i) the person in question is to be regarded as not having made a claim for the benefit, or
  (ii) if (in the case of an interview postponed in accordance with subsection (7)) that person has already been awarded the benefit, his entitlement to the benefit is to terminate immediately;

(b) where the requirement to take part in an interview applied by virtue of subsection (1)(b) above, that the amount payable to the person in question in respect of any relevant benefit is to be reduced by the specified amount until the specified time.

(5) Regulations under this section may, in relation to any such reduction, provide–

(a) for the amount of the reduction to be calculated in the first instance by reference to such amount as may be prescribed;

(b) for the amount as so calculated to be restricted, in prescribed circumstances, to the prescribed extent;

(c) where the person in question is entitled to two or more relevant benefits, for determining the extent, and the order, in which those benefits are to be reduced in order to give effect to the reduction required in his case.

(6) Regulations under this section may provide that any requirement to take part in an interview that would otherwise apply to a person by virtue of such regulations–

(a) is, in any prescribed circumstances, either not to apply or not to apply until such time as is specified;

(b) is not to apply if the designated authority determines that an interview–
  (i) would not be of assistance to that person, or
  (ii) would not be appropriate in the circumstances;

(c) is not to apply until such time as the designated authority determines, if that authority determines that an interview–
  (i) would not be of assistance to that person, or
  (ii) would not be appropriate in the circumstances, until that time; and the regulations may make provision for treating a person in relation to whom any such requirement does not apply, or does not apply until a particular time, as having complied with that requirement to such extent and for such purposes as are specified.

(7) Where–

(a) a person is required to take part in an interview by virtue of subsection (1)(a), and

(b) the interview is postponed by or under regulations made in pursuance of subsection (6)(a) or (c), the time to which it is so postponed may be a time falling after an award of the relevant benefit to that person.

[³ (7A) Information supplied in pursuance of regulations under this section shall be taken for all purposes to be information relating to social security.]

(8) In this section–

"the designated authority" means such of the following as may be specified, namely–

(a)   the Secretary of State,

(b)   a person providing services to the Secretary of State,

(c)   a local authority,

[² (ca) subject to subsection (9), a county council in England,]

(d)   [² subject to subsection (9),] a person providing services to, or authorised to exercise any function of, [² any authority mentioned in paragraph (c) or (ca)];

''interview'' (in subsections (3) to (7)) means a work-focused interview;

''relevant benefit'', in relation to any person required to take part in a work-focused interview, means any benefit in relation to which that requirement applied by virtue of subsection (1)(a) or (b) above;

''specified'' means prescribed by or determined in accordance with regulations;

''work-focused interview'', in relation to a person, means an interview conducted for such purposes connected with employment or training in the case of that person as may be specified; and the purposes which may be so specified include purposes connected with a person's existing or future employment or training prospects or needs, and (in particular) assisting or encouraging a person to enhance his employment prospects.

[² (9)   A county council in England or a person providing services to, or authorised to exercise any function of, such a council may be specified as the designated authority only in relation to interviews with persons to whom the council is required to make support services available under section 68(1) of the Education and Skills Act 2008 (support services: provision by local education authorities).]

Commencement

    11.11.99: see s89(4)(a) WRPA.

Amendments

    1.   Amended by Art 2(2) and the Sch para 3 of SI 2002 No 1457 as from 1.4.03.

    2.   Amended by s169 and Sch 1 para 45 Education and Skills Act 2008 as from 26.1.09.

    3.   Amended by s34(1) Welfare Reform Act 2009 as from 12.1.10.

    4.   Amended by s35(2) and (4) Welfare Reform Act 2009 as from 10.2.10.

General Note

    The principal innovation made by the WRPA in so far as the subject matter of this book is concerned was a greatly expanded role for local authorities as providers of benefit services. The Act sought to permit the implementation of the Single Work-Focused Gateway, or ONE as it was subsequently renamed.

    The aim of the scheme was to set up a number of offices to handle claims and inquiries relating to all benefits for which a person might be eligible. It is understood that there are no longer any ONE offices. The provisions are included in this book because some ONE offices were run by local authorities: see subs (8)(c). The offices also provided "work-focused interviews" (WFIs) designed to assist claimants in finding employment. As usual, the Act sets out the bare bones of the scheme with regulations providing the flesh.

Analysis

    Subs (1). No claimant of at least pensionable age can be required to attend a WFI. For these purposes, a man born before 6 April 1955 is treated as having attained pensionable age when a woman born on the same day as him would attain pensionable age: subs (1A). In respect of claimants under pensionable age, the regulations enable such a requirement both at the time of making a claim and at some time after benefit is awarded. In the latter case, conditions may be imposed by the regulations before a WFI may be required and if the claimant fails to comply, s/he will only lose part of her/his benefit. This is confirmed by the terms of subs (4)(b).

    Subs (2) confirms that HB and CTB are among the benefits which, if claimed, may trigger a requirement of a WFI, but there is not currently such a requirement.

    Subs (3) contains a number of regulation-making powers, which may be summarised as follows:

    (1)   Para (a) envisages that a claimant will receive only one WFI, even if claiming more than one benefit.

    (2)   Paras (b) and (c) deal with the administration of interviews. The words in brackets in sub-para (c) provide for regulations to permit interviews to take place in the claimant's home. However, on its face para (c) appears to authorise a requirement that the interview be granted in the home. If that is so, there may be an issue as to whether such a requirement might infringe Art 8 of the European Convention of Human Rights as being an unjustifiable invasion of the claimant's privacy.

    (3)   Para (d) permits people to be deemed to have or to have not taken part in an interview.

    (4)   Paras (e) and (f) are the big stick. They provide for sanctions to be imposed under subs (4) in a case where the conditions in para (e) are fulfilled.

Subs (4) and (5) provide for the consequences of falling foul of subs (3)(e) and (f). Para (4) operates in three different ways. A person who has claimed benefit is treated as not having made a claim: para (a)(i). A person whose interview has been postponed under subs (7) has her/his entitlement to benefit terminated: para (a)(ii). It appears, however, that such termination will not be retrospective so as to create an overpayment. Finally, under para (b) a person who has the requirement applied to her/him during a period of entitlement to benefit does not have benefit terminated altogether, but has a deduction made from her/his benefit under subs (5).

Subs (6) and (7) contain wide powers to exempt claimants from the requirement to attend an interview, either permanently or temporarily. Where there is a temporary exemption, subs (7) permits an award of benefit to be made in the interim.

Subs (8) and (9). Subs (8) contains definitions, subject to subs (9). Local authorities are one of those who may be authorised to conduct WFIs.

Optional work-focused interviews

2C.–(1)   Regulations may make provision for conferring on local authorities [² or, subject to subsection (3A), county councils in England] functions in connection with conducting work-focused interviews in cases where such interviews are requested or consented to by persons to whom this section applies.

(2)   This section applies to [¹

(a)   persons making claims for or entitled to any of the benefits listed in section 2A(2) above or any prescribed benefit; and

(b)   partners of persons entitled to any of the benefits listed in section 2AA(2) above or any prescribed benefit;]

and it so applies regardless of whether such persons have, in accordance with regulations under section 2A [¹ or 2AA] above, already taken part in interviews conducted under such regulations.

(3)   The functions which may be conferred on a local authority [² or on a county council in England] by regulations under this section include functions relating to–

(a)   the obtaining and receiving of information for the purposes of work-focused interviews conducted under the regulations;

(b)   the recording and forwarding of information supplied at, or for the purposes of, such interviews;

(c)   the taking of steps to identify potential employment or training opportunities for persons taking part in such interviews.

[² (3A)   Regulations under this section may confer functions on a county council in England only in relation to interviews with persons to whom the council is required to make support services available under section 68(1) of the Education and Skills Act 2008 (support services: provision by local education authorities).]

(4)   Regulations under this section may make different provision for different areas or different authorities.

(5)   In this section ''work-focused interview'', in relation to a person to whom this section applies, means an interview conducted for such purposes connected with employment or training in the case of such a person as may be prescribed; and the purposes which may be so prescribed include–

(a)   purposes connected with the existing or future employment or training prospects or needs of such a person, and

(b)   (in particular) assisting or encouraging such a person to enhance his employment prospects.

Commencement

11.11.99: see s89(4)(a) WRPA.

Amendments

1.   Amended by the Employment Act 2002 Sch 7 para 10 (5.7.03).
2.   Amended by s169 and Sch 1 para 47 Education and Skills Act 2008 as from 26.1.09.

General Note

This authorised the pilot schemes for ONE that were run by local authorities. The Social Security (Claims and Information) Regulations 1999 SI No.3108 were made under this provision. The important point to note is the absence of any compulsion to attend an interview: see subs (1).

Claims and payments regulations

Regulations about claims for and payments of benefit

5.–(1) Regulations may provide–

(a) for requiring a claim for a benefit to which this section applies to be made by such person, in such manner and within such time as may be prescribed;

(b) for treating such a claim made in such circumstances as may be prescribed as having been made at such date earlier or later than that at which it is made as may be prescribed;

(c) for permitting such a claim to be made, or treated as if made, for a period wholly or partly after the date on which it is made;

(d) for permitting an award on such a claim to be made for such a period subject to the condition that the claimant satisfies the requirements for entitlement when benefit becomes payable under the award;

(e) [⁴ for any such award to be revised under section 9 of the Social Security Act 1998, or superceded under section 10 of that Act, if any of those requirements are found not to have been satisfied;]

(f) for the disallowance on any ground of a person's claim for a benefit to which this section applies to be treated as a disallowance of any further claim by that person for that benefit until the grounds of the original disallowance have ceased to exist;

(g) for enabling one person to act for another in relation to a claim for a benefit to which this section applies and for enabling such a claim to be made and proceeded with in the name of a person who has died;

(h) for requiring any information or evidence needed for the determination of such a claim or of any question arising in connection with such a claim to be furnished by such person as may be prescribed in accordance with the regulations;

[⁶(hh) for requiring such person as may be prescribed in accordance with the regulations to furnish any information or evidence needed for a determination whether a decision on an award of benefit to which this section applies–

    (i) should be revised under section 9 of the Social Security Act 1998 [⁷ or, as the case may be, under paragraph 3 of Schedule 7 to the Child Support, Pensions and Social Security Act 2000]; or

    (ii) should be superseded under section 10 of that Act [⁷ or, as the case may be, under paragraph 4 of that Schedule];]

(i) for the person to whom, time when and manner in which a benefit to which this section applies is to be paid and for the information and evidence to be furnished in connection with the payment of such a benefit;

(j) for notice to be given of any change of circumstances affecting the continuance of entitlement to such a benefit or payment of such a benefit;

(k) for the day on which entitlement to such a benefit is to begin or end;

(l) for calculating the amounts of such a benefit according to a prescribed scale or otherwise adjusting them so as to avoid fractional amounts or facilitate computations;

(m) for extinguishing the right to payment of such a benefit if payment is not obtained within such period, not being less than 12 months, as may be prescribed from the date on which the right is treated under the regulations as having arisen;

[⁸. . .]

(p) for the circumstances and manner in which payments of such a benefit may be made to another person on behalf of the beneficiary for any purpose, which may be to discharge, in whole or in part, an obligation of the beneficiary or any other person;

(q) for the payment or distribution of such a benefit to or among persons claiming to be entitled on the death of any person and for dispensing with strict proof of their title;

(r) for the making of a payment on account of such a benefit

      (i)   where no claim has been made and it is impracticable for one to be made immediately;
      (ii)   where a claim has been made and it is impracticable for the claim or an appeal, reference, review or application relating to it to be immediately determined;
      (iii)   where an award has been made but it is impracticable to pay the whole immediately.

(2)   This section applies to the following benefits–
(a)   benefits as defined in section 122 of the Contributions and Benefits Act;
[¹(aa) a jobseeker's allowance;]
[¹² (ab) state pension credit;]
[¹³ (ac) an employment and support allowance;]
(b)   income support;
[⁹ . . .]
[⁹ . . .]
(e)   housing benefit;
(f)   any social fund payments such as are mentioned in section 138(1)(a) or (2) of the Contributions and Benefits Act;
(g)   child benefit; and
(h)   Christmas bonus.

[¹⁰ (2A)   The regulations may also require such persons as are prescribed to provide a rent officer with information or evidence of such description as is prescribed.

(2B)   For the purposes of subsection (2A), the Secretary of State may prescribe any description of information or evidence which he thinks is necessary or expedient to enable rent officers to carry out their functions under section 122 of the Housing Act 1996.

(2C)   Information or evidence required to be provided by virtue of subsection (2A) may relate to an individual claim or award or to any description of claims or awards.]

[¹¹ (3)]
[¹² (3A)   *[Omitted]*
[⁸ . . .]
(5)   *[Omitted]*
[² (6)   As it has effect in relation to housing benefit subsection (1)(p) above authorises provision requiring the making of payments of benefit to another person, on behalf of the beneficiary in such circumstances as may be prescribed.]

Definition
   "prescribed" – see s191.

Amendments
  1.   Inserted by Jobseekers Act 1996 Sch 2 para 39.
  2.   Inserted by the Housing Act 1996, s120(1) and deemed always to have had effect by s120(2).
  3.   Substituted by the Housing Act 1996 Sch 13 para 3(2).
  4.   Substituted by SSA 1998 Sch 7 para 79(1)(a)
  5.   Repealed by SSA 1998 Sch 7 para 79(1)(b) from 29.11.99. However, this repeal does not take effect in relation to HB and CTB: see Art 2(2)(a) and (b) of the Social Security Act 1998 (Commencement No 12 and Consequential and Transitional Provisions) Order 1999 SI No 3178.
  6.   Inserted by SSA 1998 s74 .
  7.   Amended by CSPSSA Sch 7 para 21(1) (2.7.01).
  8.   Repealed by SSA 1998 s86(2), Sch 8.
  9.   Repealed by TCA Sch 6 (6.4.03).
  10.   Inserted by WRA s35(2) (1.10.07 (for making regulations) and 7.4.08).
  11.   Ceased to have effect by WRA s35(3) (7.4.08).
  12.   Amended by SPCA s11 and Sch 1 para 3 (2.7.02 (for making regulations) and 7.4.03).
  13.   Amended by WRA s28 and Sch 3 para 10(4) (27.10.08).

General Note
   This enables the making of regulations in relation to the administration of claims and payments for HB and various other benefits.

For the authority's powers to treat claims not made on the required form as valid, see reg 83(1) HB Regs and reg 64(2) HB(SPC) Regs.

Analysis
Paragraph (1)
By subs (2)(e), this subsection applies to HB. It does not apply to CTB, which is dealt with by s6. The list below refers to the lettered subparagraphs and which regulations, broadly speaking, are made under the powers given by the subparagraph.
(a) See HB Regs regs 82 and 83 and HB(SPC) regs 63 and 64.
(b) See HB Regs reg 83(12) and HB(SPC) Regs reg 64(1).
(c) See HB Regs reg 83(10) and HB(SPC) Regs reg 64(11).
(d) See HB Regs reg 83(10) and HB(SPC) Regs reg 64(11).
(e) This power is not relevant to HB and CTB. See paras 3 and 4 of Sch 7 of the CSPSSA 2000 for the regulation-making powers for revisions and supersessions.
(f) This power does not appear to have been exercised.
(g) See HB Regs reg 82(2) to (6) and HB(SPC) Regs reg 63(2) to (6).
(h) See HB Regs reg 86 and HB(SPC) Regs reg 67 and see paragraph (3) below.
(hh) See HB Regs reg 86 and HB(SPC) Regs reg 67.
(i) See HB Regs regs 91, 94 and 97 and HB(SPC) Regs reg 72, 75, 77 and 78.
(j) See HB Regs regs 86 and 88 and HB(SPC) Regs 67 and 69.
(k) See HB Regs reg 76 and HB(SPC) Regs 57.
(l) See HB Regs reg 80(7) and HB(SPC) Regs reg 61(6).
(m) This power does not appear to have been exercised.
(p) See HB Regs regs 95 and 96 and HB(SPC) Regs reg 76 and 77. Note also subs (6).
(q) See HB Regs reg 97 and HB(SPC) Regs reg 78.
(r) See HB Regs reg 93 and HB(SPC) Regs reg 74.

Paragraphs (2A), (2B) and (2C)
These give power to make the provisions for a rent officer to require information: see the Rent Officers (Housing Benefit Functions) Order 1997 and the Rent Officers (Housing Benefit Functions) (Scotland) Order 1997 on pp592 and 614. The power was formerly in para (3).

Paragraph (6)
The amendment made by the Housing Act 1996 removes any doubts about whether reg 93(1) HB Regs 1987 (now reg 95(1) HB Regs and reg 76(1) HB(SPC) Regs) was validly made under subs (1)(p), which only refers to circumstances in which payments of HB *may* be made, not circumstances when they *shall* be made to a third party. The amendment has retrospective effect.

Council tax benefits

Regulations about council tax benefits administration
6.–(1) Regulations may provide as follows as regards any [¹ council tax benefits]–
(a) for requiring a claim for a benefit to be made by such person, in such manner and within such time as may be prescribed;
(b) for treating a claim made in such circumstances as may be prescribed as having been made at such date earlier or later than that at which it is made as may be prescribed;
(c) for permitting a claim to be made, or treated as if made, for a period wholly or partly after the date on which it is made;
(d) for permitting an award on a claim to be made for such a period subject to the condition that the claimant satisfies the requirements for entitlement when benefit becomes payable, or any right to a reduction [² . . .] becomes available, under the award;
(e) for a review of any award if those requirements are found not to have been satisfied;
(f) for the disallowance on any ground of a person's claim for a benefit to be treated as a disallowance of any further claim by that person for that benefit until the grounds of the original disallowance have ceased to exist;
(g) for enabling one person to act for another in relation to a claim for a benefit and for enabling such a claim to be made and proceeded with in the name of a person who has died;

(h)   for requiring any information or evidence needed for the determination of a claim or of any question arising in connection with a claim to be furnished by such person as may be prescribed in accordance with the regulations;

[6(hh) for requiring such person as may be prescribed in accordance with the regulations to furnish any information or evidence needed for a determination whether a decision on an award of a benefit–

    (i)   should be revised under paragraph 3 of Schedule 7 to the Child Support, Pensions and Social Security Act 2000; or

    (ii)   should be superseded under paragraph 4 of that Schedule;]

(i)   for the time when and manner in which any benefit (or part) which takes the form of a payment is to be paid, and for the information and evidence to be furnished in connection with the payment;

(j)   for the time when the right to make a reduction [2 . . .] may be exercised;

(k)   for notice to be given of any change of circumstances affecting the continuance of entitlement to a benefit;

(l)   for the day on which entitlement to a benefit is to begin or end;

(m)   for calculating the amount of a benefit according to a prescribed scale or otherwise adjusting it so as to avoid fractional amounts or facilitate computation; [7. . .];

(p)   in the case of any benefit (or part) which takes the form of a payment, for payment or distribution to or among persons claiming to be entitled on the death of any person, and for dispensing with strict proof of their title;

(q)   in the case of any benefit (or part) which takes the form of a payment, for the circumstances and manner in which payment may be made to one person on behalf of another for any purpose, which may be to discharge, in whole or in part, an obligation of the person entitled to the benefit or any other person;

(r)   for making a payment on account of a benefit, or conferring a right to make a reduction [3 . . .] on account, where no claim has been made and it is impracticable for one to be made immediately;

(s)   for making a payment on account of a benefit, or conferring a right to make a reduction [3 . . .] on account, where a claim has been made but it is impracticable for the claim or an appeal, reference, review or application relating to it to be determined immediately;

(t)   for making a payment on account of a benefit, or conferring a right to make a reduction [3 . . .] on account, where an award has been made but it is impracticable to institute the benefit immediately;

(u)   generally as to administration.

(2)   Regulations under this section may include [4 provision in relation to council tax benefit that prescribed provisions shall apply instead of prescribed provisions of Part I or II of the Local Government Finance Act 1992, or that prescribed provisions of either of those Parts shall not apply] or shall apply subject to prescribed amendments or adaptations.

[5 (3)   References in subsection (2) above to either of the Parts there mentioned include references to regulations made under the Part concerned.]

[7 . . .]

Amendments

1.   Substituted by LGFA Sch 9 para 12(1)(a) (1.4.93).
2.   Repealed by LGFA Sch 9 para 12(1)(b) and Sch 14 (1.4.93).
3.   Repealed by LGFA Sch 9 para 12(1)(c) and Sch 14 (1.4.93).
4.   Substituted by LGFA Sch 9 para 12(2) (1.4.93).
5.   Substituted by LGFA Sch 9 para 12(3) (1.4.93).
6.   Inserted by CSPSS Act 2000 Sch 7 para 21(2) (2.7.01).
7.   Repealed by SSA 1998 s86 (2), Sch 8 (2.7.01).

General Note

This section gives similar powers to make regulations in relation to CTB as are available under s5 in relation to the benefits listed in s5(2). For the authority's powers to treat claims not made on the required form as valid, see reg 69(1) CTB Regs and reg 53(1) CTB(SPC) Regs.

Analysis

Paragraph (1)

The following list gives the main regulations which are made under each lettered subparagraph.
(a)   See CTB Regs regs 68 and 69 and CTB(SPC) Regs reg 52 and 53.
(b)   See CTB Regs regs 69(14) and CTB(SPC) Regs reg 56.
(c)   See CTB Regs regs 69(12) and CTB(SPC) Regs reg 53(12).
(d)   See CTB Regs reg 69(10) and CTB(SPC) Regs reg 53(10).
(f)   This power does not appear to have been exercised.
(g)   See CTB Regs reg 68 and CTB(SPC) Regs reg 52.
(h)   See CTB Regs reg 72 and CTB(SPC) Regs reg 57.
(hh)   See CTB Regs reg 72 and CTB(SPC) Regs 57.
(i)   See CTB Regs Part 10 and CTB(SPC) Regs Part 9.
(j)   This power does not appear to have been exercised.
(k)   See CTB Regs reg 74 and CTB(SPC) Regs reg 59.
(l)   See CTB Regs Part 7 and CTB(SPC) Regs Part 6.
(m)   See CTB Regs Part 6 and CTB(SPC) Regs Part 5.
(p)   See CTB Regs reg 80 and CTB(SPC) Regs reg 65.
(r), (s) and (t) These powers do not appear to have been exercised.

Paragraphs (2) and (3)

These give powers to make regulations that alter the effect of Parts I and II of the Local Government Finance Act 1992 and regulations made thereunder.

Relationship between council tax benefit and other benefits

7.–(1) Regulations may provide for a claim for one relevant benefit to be treated, either in the alternative or in addition, as a claim for any other relevant benefit that may be prescribed.

(2)   Regulations may provide for treating a payment made or right conferred by virtue of regulations–

(a)   under section 5(1)(r) above; or

(b)   under section 6(1)(r) to (t) above,

as made or conferred on account of any relevant benefit that is subsequently awarded or paid.

(3)   For the purposes of subsections (1) and (2) above relevant benefits are–

(a)   any benefit to which section 5 above applies; and

(b)   any [¹ council tax benefit].

Definition

"prescribe" – see s191.

Amendment

1.   Substitution made by LGFA Sch 9 para 13 (1.4.93).

General Note

For an example of regulations made under subs (2), see reg 93 HB Regs (on p467). There is no equivalent in the CTB Regs. There is no power to treat a claim for HB or CTB as a claim for any other benefit, or *vice versa*. However, the Secretary of State retains a power under reg 4(1) Social Security (Claims and Payments) Regulations 1987 to treat any written claim sent to her/him as being sufficient in the circumstances. So if a claimant mistakenly claims HB instead of help with housing costs with IS, income-based JSA, income-related ESA or PC and the HB claim was made through the DWP, it might be possible to ask the Secretary of State to exercise discretion to treat that as a claim for help with housing costs.

Sharing of functions as regards certain claims and information

7A.–(1)   Regulations may, for the purpose of supplementing the persons or bodies to whom claims for relevant benefits may be made, make provision–

(a)   as regards housing benefit or council tax benefit, for claims for that benefit to be made to–
(i)   a Minister of the Crown, or
(ii)   a person providing services to a Minister of the Crown;

(b)   as regards any other relevant benefit, for claims for that benefit to be made to–
(i)   a local authority,

(ii)   a person providing services to a local authority, or

(iii)   a person authorised to exercise any function of a local authority relating to housing benefit or council tax benefit.

[² (c) as regards any relevant benefit, for claims for that benefit to be made to–

(i)   a county council in England,

(ii)   a person providing services to a county council in England, or

(iii)   a person authorised to exercise any function a county council in England has under this section.]

(2)   Regulations may make provision for or in connection with–

(a)   the forwarding by a relevant authority of–

(i)   claims received by virtue of any provision authorised by subsection (1) above, and

(ii)   information or evidence supplied in connection with making such claims (whether supplied by persons making the claims or by other persons);

(b)   the receiving and forwarding by a relevant authority of information or evidence relating to social security [¹ or work] matters supplied by, or the obtaining by a relevant authority of such information or evidence from–

(i)   persons making, or who have made, claims for a relevant benefit, or

(ii)   other persons in connection with such claims, including information or evidence not relating to the claims or benefit in question;

(c)   the recording by a relevant authority of information or evidence relating to social security [¹ or work] matters supplied to, or obtained by, the authority and the holding by the authority of such information or evidence (whether as supplied or obtained or as recorded);

(d)   the giving of information or advice with respect to social security [¹ or work] matters by a relevant authority to persons making, or who have made, claims for a relevant benefit.

[² (e) the verification by a relevant authority of information or evidence supplied to or obtained by the authority in connection with a claim for or an award of a relevant benefit.]

(3)   In paragraphs (b) [² , (d) and (e)] of subsection (2) above–

(a)   references to claims for a relevant benefit are to such claims whether made as mentioned in subsection [² (1)(a), (b) or (c)] above or not; and

(b)   references to persons who have made such claims include persons to whom awards of benefit have been made on the claims.

(4)   Regulations under this section may make different provision for different areas.

(5)   Regulations under any other enactment may make such different provision for different areas as appears to the Secretary of State expedient in connection with any exercise by regulations under this section of the power conferred by subsection (4) above.

(6)   In this section–

(a)   ''benefit'' includes child support or a war pension (any reference to a claim being read, in relation to child support, as a reference to an application under the Child Support Act 1991 for a maintenance assessment);

(b)   ''local authority'' means an authority administering housing benefit or council tax benefit;

[² (c) ''relevant authority'' means–

(i)   a Minister of the Crown,

(ii)   a local authority;

(iii)   a county council in England;

(iv)   a person providing services to a person mentioned in sub-paragraphs (i) to (iii);

(v)   a person authorised to exercise any function of a local authority relating to housing benefit or council tax benefit;

(vi)   a person authorised to exercise any function a county council in England has under this section;]

(d)   ''relevant benefit'' means housing benefit, council tax benefit or any other benefit prescribed for the purposes of this section;

[¹ (e) ''social security or work matters'' means matters relating to-
    (i)   social security, child support or war pensions, or
    (ii)   employment or training;]

Commencement
    11.11.99: see s89(4)(a) WRPA.

Amendments
    1.   Amended by the Employment Act 2002 Sch 7 para 12 (24.11.02).
    2.   Amended by WRA 2007 s41(2) (3.7.07).

General Note
    This is another provision that enabled the implementation of the ONE schemes (see p33) and its successors. It gave power to make regulations enabling such offices to receive claims for all benefits, to receive, forward and supply information to offices where claims were adjudicated. Note there are no longer any ONE offices.
    Since 3 July 2007, it has enabled claims for HB and CTB to be made to a county council: subs (1)(c). Note: this only applies in England and only if the local authority has arranged for claims to be received at the county council's offices: reg 83(4)(g) HB Regs, reg 64(5)(g) HB(SPC) Regs, reg 69(4)(g) CTB Regs and reg 53(4)(g) CTB(SPC) Regs.

Use of social security information
7B.–(1)   A relevant authority may use for a relevant purpose any social security information which it holds.

(2)   Regulations may make provision as to the procedure to be followed by a relevant authority for the purposes of any function it has relating to the administration of a specified benefit if the authority holds social security information which–
    (a)   is relevant for the purposes of anything which may or must be done by the authority in connection with a claim for or an award of the benefit, and
    (b)   was used by another relevant authority in connection with a claim for or an award of a different specified benefit or was verified by that other authority in accordance with regulations under section 7A(2)(e) above.

(3)   A relevant purpose is anything which is done in relation to a claim which is made or which could be made for a specified benefit if it is done for the purpose of–
    (a)   identifying persons who may be entitled to such a benefit;
    (b)   encouraging or assisting a person to make such a claim;
    (c)   advising a person in relation to such a claim.

(4)   Social security information means–
    (a)   information relating to social security, child support or war pensions;
    (b)   evidence obtained in connection with a claim for or an award of a specified benefit.

(5)   A specified benefit is a benefit which is specified in regulations for the purposes of this section.

(6)   Expressions used in this section and in section 7A have the same meaning in this section as in that section.

(7)   This section does not affect any power which exists apart from this section to use for one purpose social security information obtained in connection with another purpose.

Commencement
    1.10.07: see s41(1) WRA 2007.

PART II
Adjudication
Housing benefit and council tax benefit

Adjudication
[¹**63.** . . .]

Amendment
    1.   Repealed by SSA 1998 s86(2) and Sch 8 (18.10.99).

General Note
This was the enabling section for most of the regulations concerned with adjudication. See now s34 SSA 1998 on p107 and Sch 7 CSPSSA on p139.

PART III
Overpayments and Adjustments of Benefit
Housing benefit

Overpayments of housing benefit

75.–(1)   Except where regulations otherwise provide, any amount of housing benefit [¹ determined in accordance with regulations to have been] paid in excess of entitlement may be recovered [²] either by the Secretary of State or by the authority which paid the benefit.

(2)   Regulations may require such an authority to recover such an amount in such circumstances as may be prescribed.

[³ (3)   An amount recoverable under this section shall be recoverable–

(a)   except in such circumstances as may be prescribed, from the person to whom it was paid; and

(b)   where regulations so provide from such other person (as well as, or instead of, the person to whom it was paid) as may be prescribed.]

(4)   Any amount recoverable under this section may, without prejudice to any other method of recovery, be recovered by deduction from prescribed benefits.

[⁴ (5)   Where an amount paid to a person on behalf of another person is recoverable under this section, subsections (3) and (4) above authorise its recovery from the person to whom it was paid by deduction–

(a)   from prescribed benefits to which he is entitled;

(b)   from prescribed benefits paid to him to discharge (in whole or in part) an obligation owed to him by the person on whose behalf the recoverable amount was paid; or

(c)   from prescribed benefits paid to him to discharge (in whole or in part) an obligation owed to him by any other person.

(6)   Where an amount is recovered as mentioned in paragraph (b) of subsection (5) above, the obligation specified in that paragraph shall in prescribed circumstances be taken to be discharged by the amount of the deduction; and where an amount is recovered as mentioned in paragraph (c) of that subsection, the obligation specified in that paragraph shall in all cases be taken to be so discharged.

(7)   Where any amount recoverable under this section is to be recovered otherwise than by deduction from prescribed benefits–

(a)   if the person from whom it is recoverable resides in England and Wales and the county court so orders, it is recoverable by execution issued from the county court or otherwise as if it were payable under an order of that court; and

(b)   if he resides in Scotland, it may be enforced in the same manner as an extract registered decree arbitral bearing a warrant for execution issued by the sheriff court of any sheriffdom in Scotland.]

Amendments
1.   Amended by SSA(F) Act, 1997 Sch 1 para (31.7.97).
2.   Repealed by SSA(F) Act 1997 Sch 2.
3.   Substituted by CSPSSA 2000 s71 (1.10.01).
4.   Amended by SSA(F) Act 1997 s16.

Definition
"prescribe" – see s191.

General Note
This section provides for the scheme for recovery of overpaid HB to be provided for by Part 13 of the HB Regs and Part 12 of the HB(SPC) Regs.

As has been made clear by a tribunal of commissioners in *R(H) 3/04* and *R(H) 6/06* (the latter drawing on the Court of Appeal's decision in *B v Secretary of State for Work and Pensions* [2005] EWCA Civ 929, [2005] 1 WLR 3796 (reported as *R(IS) 9/06*)), recoupment of overpayments involves a two-stage process.

First, it is necessary for the local authority to decide that there has been an overpayment and that it is recoverable from someone. Secondly, there is the decision as to whether to enforce recovery and the method used to enforce recovery. Neither of the latter can be subject of challenge before the First-tier Tribunal: *R(H) 6/06* and *R(H) 7/04* respectively.

Note that HB paid under the pre-1988 scheme may be recovered by virtue of s75 and the regulations made thereunder: Sch 10 para 4(3). Note the effect of s68 Welfare Reform and Pensions Act 1999 on the recoverability of certain payments.

Guidance has been issued to local authorities on overpayments in the form of the *HB/CTB Overpayments Guide* (available at www.dwp.gov.uk/housingbenefit/manuals/).

Analysis
Subsection (1): The right to recover overpayments
This provides the basic power to prescribe the circumstances when an overpayment is recoverable in Part 13 of the HB Regs and Part 12 of the HB(SPC) Regs. There can be no recovery of HB by an authority unless a valid determination has been made that there is a recoverable overpayment. See the Analysis to reg 90 HB Regs on p462 regarding the validity of decisions. Note that subs (1) has not been amended by CSPSSA to refer to it being "decided" rather than "determined" that an overpayment is recoverable. This forms the basis of the decision of the tribunal of commissioners in *R(H) 3/04* that a right to appeal against an overpayment decision arises under Sch 7 para 6(6) CSPSSA rather than para 6(1). This, however, can cause its own difficulties: see the Analyses to Sch 7 paras 1 and 6 CSPSSA on pp140 and 145.
Subsection (2): Required to recover
Where an interim payment on account proves to be excessive and the claimant continues to be entitled to HB, the authority must reduce the continuing payments to recover the overpayment: reg 93(3) HB Regs (reg 76(3) HB(SPC) Regs). Apart from that situation, as yet there are no circumstances where an authority is *required* by the Regulations to recover an overpayment.
Discretion to recover
In all other cases, the authority has a discretion as to whether to exercise its right of recovery, though the subsidy rules provide a strong incentive. Such a decision can encompass whether to recover all or part of the overpayment and the period over which it is to be recovered.

It is now clear from the tribunal of commissioners decision in *R(H) 6/06* and the Court of Appeal's decision in *B v Secretary of State for Work and Pensions* [2005] EWCA Civ 929, [2005] 1 WLR 3796 (reported as *R(IS) 9/06*), that, whatever may have been said in *R(H) 3/04*, a local authority has a general discretion as to whether to recover an overpayment of benefit which has been found to be recoverable; but that decision is not appealable. However, it must be remembered that all other overpayment decisions (ie, has there in fact been an overpayment, is it recoverable, and from whom is it recoverable) are all appealable: see further below and Part 13 of the HB Regs.

Like all discretionary powers, the authority must consider the circumstances of each individual case. If an authority fails to exercise its discretion in recovering overpayments, its decision to recover an overpayment may be vulnerable to judicial review.

It is impossible to compile a list of the matters that an authority may need to consider, but they will commonly include: the moral culpability of the person from whom recovery is sought, the effect of recovery on her/his life, the effect of recovery on her/his family, the likelihood of the claimant losing her/his accommodation and the possible resulting financial burden on the authority, and the cost-effectiveness of recovery. It is probably also legitimate for the authority to have regard to the financial implications of non-recovery of the overpayment: see eg, *R v Brent LBC HBRB ex p Connery* [1989] 22 HLR 40 at 44, QBD. However, this, like any other factor, cannot be treated as determinative. Financial or hardship grounds will be the usual factors which are taken into account, and terminal illness, senility or low intelligence and severe medical conditions might lead to non-recovery.

The authority may have a policy on recovery, but it must be sufficiently flexible to enable each case to be examined on its merits. If it is not, it will be vulnerable to challenge on judicial review. Policies that recovery will always be made or always be made from specified categories of claimants are unlawful.
Subsection (3): From whom recoverable?
See reg 101 HB Regs for the circumstances as to when an overpayment may be recoverable from persons other than those to whom benefit was paid. Section 75(3) is wide enough to fix recoverability on a landlord's agent if the overpaid benefit was paid to that agent, notwithstanding that, as an agent, s/he may have accounted to her/his principal (ie, the landlord) for all or part of the sum: *R(H) 10/07*. This analysis was taken further in *Walsall BC v GP Ltd and others* [2009] UKUT 247 AAC; [2010] AACR 16, where it was held that the words "the person to whom" benefit was paid in s75(3)(a) did not require that only one person had had benefit paid to them and were was wide enough to allow an overpayment to be legally recoverable from a landlord and their agent, as well as the claimant. By way of contrast, as there is no such thing as a joint claim for couples for HB (*CH 3817/2004*), where a couple is involved, an overpayment will only be recoverable from the claimant if it has been specifically

decided that the overpayment is (also) recoverable from the claimants partner: reg 3(1)(d) D&A Regs and *CH 3622/2006*. Note also, in what the Upper Tribunal judge described as a provisional view, the perspective in *DL v Liverpool City Council* [2009] UKUT 176 (AAC) that, because section 75(3)(a) refers to an amount of HB being recoverable "from the person to whom it was paid", the section does not extend to make recoverable payments of HB made to a claimant's rent account after her/his death.

The approach to s75(3) was given extensive consideration in *R(H) 6/06*. The tribunal of commissioners said that s75(3)(b):

"requires that any regulation made under s75(3)(b) should specify whether a prescribed person is jointly liable with the person to whom the payment was made or is liable instead of that person. Under this construction the words in parentheses have a purpose. The construction is consistent with s75(3)(a) because, where the Secretary of State makes regulations providing that an overpayment is recoverable from a prescribed person instead of the person to whom it was made, he is, in effect, providing for additional, but defined, circumstances in which the person to whom the payment was made is not liable to repay an overpayment. The circumstances are defined by the terms in which the prescribed person is defined or by the circumstances in respect of which he is prescribed (see s189(4)). This construction is also consistent with para 6(6) of Schedule 7, which provides a right of appeal to a tribunal in terms that do not limit it to points of law, because all issues arising under regulations made under s75(3) as to from whom an overpayment is recoverable are justiciable. If the Secretary of State makes regulations having the effect that an overpayment is recoverable from a prescribed person as well as the person to whom it is made, the non-justiciable choice as to from which of them the overpayment should actually be recovered falls to be made by the local authority at the stage of enforcing the right of recovery and so is not within the scope of the right of appeal".

It therefore concluded:

"under the legislation in force from 1 October 2001 to 9 April 2006, an overpayment of housing benefit is always recoverable from any person within the scope of regulation 101(2) as well as, if different, the person to whom the overpayment was made, except where regulation 101(1) applies in which case it is recoverable only from any person within the scope of regulation 101(2). No non-justiciable issues fall within the scope of the right of appeal and so there is no longer any need to apply *R(H) 3/04* and construe that right as being limited to points of law."

So the only appealable point (apart from whether there has in fact been an overpayment and whether it is recoverable) under s73(3) and reg 101 HB Regs 1987 is whether the person does in fact fall within reg 101. Once that point has been finally decided, *R(H) 6/06* makes it clear that no appeal right attaches to the enforcement decision of the local authority as against whom the recoverable overpayment should actually be recovered from.

Subsections (4) to (7): Methods of recovery

These provide for various methods of recovery of HB. Decisions as to what method of recovery to use are not appealable: *R(H) 7/04*. For recovery by deduction from other benefits, see regs 102 and 105 HB Regs and regs 83 and 86 HB(SPC) Regs.

Subs (5), (6) and (7) were introduced by the 1997 Act. Subs (5) expands the scope for recovery by deduction from other benefits to include benefits paid on behalf of others to people from whom recovery is sought. The principal use of this new power will be directed at recovery from landlords by deduction of HB paid direct in respect of other tenants. Subs (6) makes provision for the consequences of such recovery. See the Analysis to HB Regs regs 95 and 102 on pp471 and 491.

Subs (7) allows authorities to use county court and sheriff court procedures for registration of the overpayment as a debt without having to bring an action against the person from whom recovery is sought. For convenience, further details are given in the Analysis to HB Regs reg 102 on p491.

Council tax benefit

Excess benefit

76.–(1) Regulations may make provision as to any case where a [¹ billing authority] or a [⁵ local authority in Scotland] has allowed a [¹ council tax benefit] to a person and the amount allowed exceeds the amount to which he is entitled in respect of the benefit.

(2) [² ...] The regulations may provide that–

(a) a sum equal to the excess shall be due from the person concerned to the authority (whatever the form the benefit takes);

(b) any liability under any provision included under paragraph (a) above shall be met by such method mentioned in subsection (3) below as is prescribed as regards the case concerned, or by such combination or two or all three of the methods as is prescribed as regards the case concerned.

(3) The methods are–

(a) payment by the person concerned;

(b) addition to any amount payable in respect of [³ council tax;]

(c)   deduction from prescribed benefits.

[⁴ (4)-(5) . . .]

(6)   In a case where the regulations provide that a sum or part of a sum is to be paid, and the sum or part is not paid on or before such day as may be prescribed, the regulations may provide that the sum or part shall be recoverable in a court of competent jurisdiction.

[⁴ (7)   . . .]

(8)   The regulations may provide that they are not to apply as regards any case falling within a prescribed category.

Definitions

"billing authority" – see s191.

"income-related benefit" – see s191.

"charge payer" – in subs (4), see Subs (7).

Amendments

1.   Substitutions by LGFA Sch 9 para 15(1) (1.4.93).
2.   Repealed by LGFA Sch 9 para 15(2) and Sch 14 (1.4.93).
3.   Substituted by LGFA Sch 9 para 15(3) (1.4.93).
4.   Repealed by LGFA Sch 9 para 15(4) and Sch 14 (1.4.93).
5.   Substituted by Local Government etc. (Scotland) Act 1994 Sch 13 para 175(3) (1.4.96).

General Note

This section deals with overpayments of CTB. An overpayment of CTB is termed an 'excess payment'. The rules on recoverability and recovery are very similar, but there are some differences. In particular, the Social Security Administration (Fraud) Act 1997 made no amendments to this section, so the powers of recovery are slightly more restricted.

Analysis

Subs (1) provides the basic power to make the Part 11 CTB Regs and Part 10 CTB(SPC) Regs, which set out the scheme for excess payments of CTB. Note, however, that in contrast with s75(1) above, this subsection does not of itself provide that an amount can be recovered.

Subs (2) and (3). Firstly, by para (a), liability is imposed on the 'person concerned'. This must be a reference to the person referred to in subs (1) and so can only be a reference to the person to whom the excess benefit was allowed. So regulations to permit recovery from third parties would not be permitted, since they cannot be justified by subs (1) above.

Once the liability is imposed para (b) sets out how the liability is to be met. It is suggested that *only* those methods prescribed by subs (3) may be used. The methods are:

(1)   Payment by the person concerned: see reg 86(2)(a) CTB Regs (reg 71(2)(a) CTB(SPC) Regs). This operates to create a debt owed to the authority, but note the way subs (6) affects the authority's right to sue for it (see below).

(2)   Addition to a council tax bill: see reg 86(2)(b) CTB Regs (reg 71(2)(b) CTB(SPC) Regs).

(3)   Deduction from prescribed benefits: see 86(3) CTB Regs (reg 71(3) CTB(SPC) Regs).

Subs (6). The regulations can only provide for court recovery after the person concerned has failed to pay within a prescribed time. Note that this provision only authorises the bringing of an action by the authority and does not authorise the registration of the debt as under s75(7), because the wording does not allow recovery "as if payable under an order of a county court": see the County Court Rules 1981 Ord 25 r12(1) in England and Wales, preserved by the Sch to the Civil Procedure Rules 1998, and the equivalent provision in the sheriff court in Scotland.

Subs (8) permits the exceptions to recoverability of excess payments. See 83(2)and (3) CTB Regs (reg 68(2) and (3) CTB(SPC) Regs).

Shortfall in benefit

77.–(1)   Regulations may make provision as to any case where a [¹ billing authority] or a [² local authority in Scotland] has allowed [¹ council tax benefit] to a person and the amount allowed is less than the amount to which he is entitled in respect of the benefit.

Definition

"billing authority" – see s191.

Amendments

1.   Substituted by LGFA Sch 9 para 16(2) and Sch 14 (1.4.93).
2.   Substituted by Local Government etc. (Scotland) Act 1994 Sch 13 para 175(3) (1.4.96).

General Note

See reg 79 CTB Regs on p717 or reg 64 CTB(SPC) Regs on p974.

PART VI

Enforcement

General Note on Part VI

Part VI of the Act deals with specific criminal sanctions for abuse of the benefits system. The offences created apply to HB and CTB as well as benefits paid by the Secretary of State, though offences are prosecuted by the local authority: see ss116 and 116A.

Part VI has been subject to amendment since 1992 by no less than 15 different statutes. The result is a bloated, incoherent set of provisions. The description given by the former Law Lord, Lord Brightman, of Part VI as being a "drafting quagmire" (*Hansard* (HL) vol 623 col 338) may be thought to be flattering.

This repeated amending has been a direct product of the priority given by successive governments to investigating and combating social security fraud. There have been two Acts of Parliament specifically directed towards this issue: the Social Security Administration (Fraud) Act 1997 and the Social Security Fraud Act 2001. The 1997 Act was rushed through Parliament shortly before dissolution for the 1997 General Election amongst competition between the two major political parties as to which was "toughest" on benefit fraud. As a result, the measure had cross-party support. Besides widening the scope of the offences in s112 and introducing a new range of offences under s111A with higher penalties, the Act introduced a system of penalties which authorities may offer where prosecution is not thought economical. Part VII of the Act was also substantially recast.

For its part, the 2001 Act significantly expanded the information-seeking powers of local authorities and introduced a new scheme of penalising claimants convicted of more than one offence of benefit fraud. It also reformulated the criminal offences.

Despite the enacting of more serious offences under the Act, the practice has been to continue to prosecute such offences as general offences of dishonesty. In England and Wales, the relevant statute is the Theft Act 1968. A number of offences under that Act may be committed: theft under s1, obtaining property by deception under s15(1), and false accounting under s17(1). As to the last, it has been held that a HB claim form is a document created for accounting purposes: *Osinunga v DPP* [1997] 30 HLR 853 at 856, DC. In Scotland, a claimant could be prosecuted for the common law offences of theft or fraud.

For sentencing guidelines for the more serious offences under ss111A and 112, see *R v Stewart* [1987] 2 All ER 363, CA and *R v Armour* [1997] 2 Cr App R(S) 240, CA. There has been a noticeable toughening in sentencing for social security fraud in recent years.

Note that in confiscation order proceedings under section 71(1B) Criminal Justice Act 1988 no offfset can be made for *other* benefits which the defendant may have been entitled to but for her/his dishonest conduct when assessing how much is due under the confiscation order: *Department of Work and Pensions v Richards* [2005] EWCA Crim 491, 3 March. However, statutory offsets will apply when calculating in the first place the amount of overpaid HB/CTB: see reg 104 HB Regs (reg 85 HB(SPC) Regs); 89 CTB Regs (reg 74 CTB(SPC) Regs).

[¹Authorisations for investigators

109A.–(1)   An individual who for the time being has the Secretary of State's authorisation for the purposes of this Part shall be entitled, for any one or more of the purposes mentioned in subsection (2) below, to exercise any of the powers which are conferred on an authorised officer by sections 109B and 109C below.

(2)   Those purposes are–

(a)   ascertaining in relation to any case whether a benefit is or was payable in that case in accordance with any provision of the relevant social security legislation;

(b)   investigating the circumstances in which any accident, injury or disease which has given rise, or may give rise, to a claim for–

(i)   industrial injuries benefit, or

(ii)   any benefit under any provision of the relevant social security legislation, occurred or may have occurred, or was or may have been received or contracted;

(c)   ascertaining whether provisions of the relevant social security legislation are being, have been or are likely to be contravened (whether by particular persons or more generally);

(d)   preventing, detecting and securing evidence of the commission (whether by particular persons or more generally) of benefit offences.

(3)   An individual has the Secretary of State's authorisation for the purposes of this Part if, and only if, the Secretary of State has granted him an authorisation for those purposes and he is–

(a) an official of a Government department;
(b) an individual employed by an authority administering housing benefit or council tax benefit;
(c) an individual employed by an authority or joint committee that carries out functions relating to housing benefit or council tax benefit on behalf of the authority administering that benefit; or
(d) an individual employed by a person authorised by or on behalf of any such authority or joint committee as is mentioned in paragraph (b) or (c) above to carry out functions relating to housing benefit or council tax benefit for that authority or committee.

(4)　An authorisation granted for the purposes of this Part to an individual of any of the descriptions mentioned in subsection (3) above–
(a) must be contained in a certificate provided to that individual as evidence of his entitlement to exercise powers conferred by this Part;
(b) may contain provision as to the period for which the authorisation is to have effect; and
(c) may restrict the powers exercisable by virtue of the authorisation so as to prohibit their exercise except for particular purposes, in particular circumstances or in relation to particular benefits or particular provisions of the relevant social security legislation.

(5)　An authorisation granted under this section may be withdrawn at any time by the Secretary of State.

(6)　Where the Secretary of State grants an authorisation for the purposes of this Part to an individual employed by a local authority, or to an individual employed by a person who carries out functions relating to housing benefit or council tax benefit on behalf of a local authority–
(a) the Secretary of State and the local authority shall enter into such arrangements (if any) as they consider appropriate with respect to the carrying out of functions conferred on that individual by or in connection with the authorisation granted to him; and
(b) the Secretary of State may make to the local authority such payments (if any) as he thinks fit in respect of the carrying out by that individual of any such functions.

(7)　The matters on which a person may be authorised to consider and report to the Secretary of State under section 139A below shall be taken to include the carrying out by any such individual as is mentioned in subsection (3)(b) to (d) above of any functions conferred on that individual by virtue of any grant by the Secretary of State of an authorisation for the purposes of this Part.

(8)　The powers conferred by sections 109B and 109C below shall be exercisable in relation to persons holding office under the Crown and persons in the service of the Crown, and in relation to premises owned or occupied by the Crown, as they are exercisable in relation to other persons and premises.

Commencement

1.11.00: see CSPSSA Sch 6 para 2 and 2001 SI No 1252.

General Note

The powers introduced by CSPSSA extended the powers of fraud inspectors. Section 109A deals with authorisation of officers acting on behalf of the Secretary of State. It permits officers employed by the local authority to act both on behalf of the Secretary of State or the local authority employing her/him. Note, however, the important restrictions in subs (3) and (4). Subs (3) restricts the identity of people who can be granted a certificate to act as an inspector, and subs (4) gives power to restrict the scope of a certificate.

By subs (7) and (8), the Secretary of State may authorise inspectors to look into local authorities' administration of the HB scheme for the purposes of Pt VIII.

Power to require information

109B.–(1)　An authorised officer who has reasonable grounds for suspecting that a person–

(a) is a person falling within subsection (2) [¹ or (2A)] below, and

(b) has or may have possession of or access to any information about any matter that is relevant for any one or more of the purposes mentioned in section 109A(2) above,

may, by written notice, require that person to provide all such information described in the notice as is information of which he has possession, or to which he has access, and which it is reasonable for the authorised officer to require for a purpose so mentioned.

(2) The persons who fall within this subsection are–

(a) any person who is or has been an employer or employee within the meaning of any provision made by or under the Contributions and Benefits Act;

(b) any person who is or has been a self-employed earner within the meaning of any such provision;

(c) any person who by virtue of any provision made by or under that Act falls, or has fallen, to be treated for the purposes of any such provision as a person within paragraph (a) or (b) above;

(d) any person who is carrying on, or has carried on, any business involving the supply of goods for sale to the ultimate consumers by individuals not carrying on retail businesses from retail premises;

(e) any person who is carrying on, or has carried on, any business involving the supply of goods or services by the use of work done or services performed by persons other than employees of his;

(f) any person who is carrying on, or has carried on, an agency or other business for the introduction or supply, to persons requiring them, of persons available to do work or to perform services;

(g) any local authority acting in their capacity as an authority responsible for the granting of any licence;

(h) any person who is or has been a trustee or manager of a personal or occupational pension scheme;

(i) any person who is or has been liable to make a compensation payment or a payment to the Secretary of State under section 6 of the Social Security (Recovery of Benefits) Act 1997 (payments in respect of recoverable benefits); and

(j) the servants and agents of any such person as is specified in any of paragraphs (a) to (i) above.

[² (2A) The persons who fall within this subsection are–

(a) any bank;

[⁵ (aa) the Director of National Savings;]

(b) any person carrying on a business the whole or a significant part of which consists in the provision of credit (whether secured or unsecured) to members of the public;

[⁶ (c) any insurer;]

(d) any credit reference agency (within the meaning given by section 145(8) of the Consumer Credit Act 1974 (c. 39));

(e) any body the principal activity of which is to facilitate the exchange of information for the purpose of preventing or detecting fraud;

(f) any person carrying on a business the whole or a significant part of which consists in the provision to members of the public of a service for transferring money from place to place;

(g) any water undertaker or sewerage undertaker, [¹⁰ Scottish Water or any local authority which is to collect charges by virtue of an order under section 37 of the Water Industry (Scotland) Act 2002 (asp 3);]

[⁶ (h) any person who;

(i) is the holder of a licence under section 7 of the Gas Act 1986 (c. 44) to convey gas through pipes, or

(ii) is the holder of a licence under section 7A(1) of that Act to supply gas through pipes;]

(i)   any person who (within the meaning of the Electricity Act 1989 (c. 29)) distributes or supplies electricity;]

(j)   any person who provides a telecommunications service;

(k)   any person conducting any educational establishment or institution;

(l)   any body the principal activity of which is to provide services in connection with admissions to educational establishments or institutions;

(m)   the Student Loans Company;

(n)   any servant or agent of any person mentioned in any of the preceding paragraphs.

(2B)   Subject to the following provisions of this section, the powers conferred by this section on an authorised officer to require information from any person by virtue of his falling within subsection (2A) above shall be exercisable for the purpose only of obtaining information relating to a particular person identified (by name or description) by the officer.

(2C)   An authorised officer shall not, in exercise of those powers, require any information from any person by virtue of his falling within subsection (2A) above unless it appears to that officer that there are reasonable grounds for believing that the identified person to whom it relates is–

(a)   a person who has committed, is committing or intends to commit a benefit offence; or

(b)   a person who (within the meaning of Part 7 of the Contributions and Benefits Act) is a member of the family of a person falling within paragraph (a) above.

(2D)   Nothing in subsection (2B) or (2C) above shall prevent an authorised officer who is an official of a Government department and whose authorisation states that his authorisation applies for the purposes of this subsection from exercising the powers conferred by this section for obtaining from–

(a)   a water undertaker or [[10] Scottish Water,]

(b)   any person who (within the meaning the Gas Act 1986) supplies gas conveyed through pipes,

(c)   any person who (within the meaning of the Electricity Act 1989) supplies electricity conveyed by distribution systems, or

(d)   any servant or agent of a person mentioned in any of the preceding paragraphs, any information which relates exclusively to whether and in what quantities water, gas or electricity are being or have been supplied to residential premises specified or described in the notice by which the information is required.

(2E)   The powers conferred by this section shall not be exercisable for obtaining from any person providing a telecommunications service any information other than information which (within the meaning of section 21 of the Regulation of Investigatory Powers Act 2000 (c. 23)) is communications data but not traffic data.

(2F)   Nothing in subsection (2B) or (2C) above shall prevent an authorised officer from exercising the powers conferred by this section for requiring information, from a person who provides a telecommunications service, about the identity and postal address of a person identified by the authorised officer solely by reference to a telephone number or electronic address used in connection with the provision of such a service.]

(3)   The obligation of a person to provide information in accordance with a notice under this section shall be discharged only by the provision of that information, at such reasonable time and in such form as may be specified in the notice, to the authorised officer who–

(a)   is identified by or in accordance with the terms of the notice; or

(b)   has been identified, since the giving of the notice, by a further written notice given by the authorised officer who imposed the original requirement or another authorised officer.

(4)   The power of an authorised officer under this section to require the provision of information shall include a power to require the production and delivery up and (if necessary) creation of, or of copies of or extracts from, any such documents containing the information as may be specified or described in the notice imposing the requirement.

[[3] (5)   No one shall be required under this section to provide–

(a) any information that tends to incriminate either himself or, in the case of a person who is [¹¹arried or is a civil partner, his spouse or civil partner]; or

(b) any information in respect of which a claim to legal professional privilege or, in Scotland, confidentiality as between client and professional legal adviser, would be successful in any proceedings;

and for the purposes of this subsection it is immaterial whether the information is in documentary form or not.]

[⁴ (6) Provision may be made by order–

(a) adding any person to the list of persons falling within subsection (2A) above;

(b) removing any person from the list of persons falling within that subsection;

(c) modifying that subsection for the purpose of taking account of any change to the name of any person for the time being falling within that subsection.

(7) In this section–

[⁷ "bank" means–

(a) a person who has permission under Part IV of the Financial Services and Markets Act 2000 to accept deposits;

(b) an EEA firm of the kind mentioned in paragraph 5(b) of Schedule 3 to that Act which has permission under paragraph 15 of that Schedule (as a result of qualifying for authorisation under paragraph 12 of that Schedule) to accept deposits or other repayable funds from the public; or

(c) a person who does not require permission under that Act to accept deposits, in the course of his business in the United Kingdom;]

"credit" includes a cash loan or any form of financial accommodation, including the cashing of a cheque;

[⁸ "insurer" means–

(a) a person who has permission under Part IV of the Financial Services and Markets Act 2000 to effect or carry out contracts of insurance; or

(b) an EEA firm of the kind mentioned in paragraph 5(d) of Schedule 3 to that Act, which has permission under paragraph 15 of that Schedule (as a result of qualifying for authorisation under paragraph 12 of that Schedule) to effect or carry out contracts of insurance;]

"residential premises", in relation to a supply of water, gas or electricity, means any premises which–

(a) at the time of the supply were premises occupied wholly or partly for residential purposes, or

(b) are premises to which that supply was provided as if they were so occupied; and

"telecommunications service" has the same meaning as in the Regulation of Investigatory Powers Act 2000 (c. 23).]

[⁹ (7A) The definitions of "bank" and "insurer" in subsection (7) must be read with–

(a) section 22 of the Financial Services and Markets Act 2000;

(b) any relevant order under that section; and

(c) Schedule 2 to that Act.]

Commencement

1.11.00: see CSPSSA Sch 6 para 2 and 2001 SI No 1252.

Amendments

1. Amended by SSFA s1(2) SSFA (30.4.02).
2. Inserted by SSFA s1(2) (30.4.02).
3. Substituted by SSFA s1(3) (30.4.02).
4. Inserted by SSFA s1(4) (26.2.02).
5. Inserted by Art 2(a) of SI 2002 No 817 as from 1.4.02.
6. Substituted by Art 2(b) to (d) of SI 2002 No 817 as from 1.4.02.
7. Substituted by Art 3(a)(i) of SI 2002 No 817 as from 1.4.02.
8. Inserted by Art 3(a)(ii) of SI 2002 No 817 as from 1.4.02.
9. Inserted by Art 3(b) of SI 2002 No 817 as from 1.4.02.

10. Amended by Art 2 and the Sch of SI 2004 No 1822 as from 14.7.04.
11. Amended by CPA s254 and Sch 24 para 64 (5.12.05).

General Note

The powers of an inspector to require information are expanded significantly by s109B. A written notice is required as a condition precedent to an obligation to provide information: subs (1). Subs (4) enables the information to be required in a form that suits the inspector. The only controls upon information requirements made under subs (2) are that they are limited to information to which a person has access, and that the requirement is reasonable. In the case of any dispute, the latter qualification is likely to prove vital. If, for example, an employee will be required to breach some confidence by disclosing information about a colleague, it will be unreasonable to require such steps since there are ample powers to require the employer to disgorge the same information. Similarly, if information can only be obtained following undue expense, it may be said to be unreasonable to require it to be furnished. The requirement of reasonableness qualifies the method of provision under subs (4) as well as the requirement to provide the information under subs (1). Thus, even if it would be reasonable to require a person to answer questions, it might be unreasonable to require a person to provide written answers, depending on the situation.

The breadth of the classes of people from whom information may be required under subs (2) is obvious. To take two examples, workers can be required to give information about colleagues, and charities may be required to reveal who is working for them.

Subs (2A) to (2F) vastly expand the range of bodies from which information may be sought. Subs (6) enables amendment of the bodies that may be required to supply information by statutory instrument, which requires an affirmative resolution under s190(1)(aza) SSAA.

There is some limitation in the powers under subs (2A). First, information may only be sought in relation to a specific person or a member of her/his family: subs (2B). Secondly, there must be "reasonable grounds" to suspect the commission of an offence by that person: subs (2C). Thirdly, the content of communications may not be disclosed to relevant officers but only the fact that communications are being made or the extent of the services provided: subs (2E). Subs (2D), which allows information regarding the services supplied to an address to be obtained from utility companies, cannot be utilised by local authority officers: see subs (5).

Note that a breach of a duty to provide information under s109B does not of itself constitute an offence under this section. There may, however, be an offence committed under s111. Note also that subs (5) preserves the privilege against self-incrimination, and has now been expanded to cover information which is confidential or covered by legal professional privilege. It is likely that the courts would have implied such a limitation in any event.

Powers of entry

109C.–(1)   An authorised officer shall be entitled, at any reasonable time and either alone or accompanied by such other persons as he thinks fit, to enter any premises which–

(a)   are liable to inspection under this section; and

(b)   are premises to which it is reasonable for him to require entry in order to exercise the powers conferred by this section.

(2)   An authorised officer who has entered any premises liable to inspection under this section may–

(a)   make such an examination of those premises, and

(b)   conduct any such inquiry there, as appears to him appropriate for any one or more of the purposes mentioned in section 109A(2) above.

(3)   An authorised officer who has entered any premises liable to inspection under this section may–

(a)   question any person whom he finds there;

(b)   require any person whom he finds there to do any one or more of the following–

(i)   to provide him with such information,

(ii)   to produce and deliver up and (if necessary) create such documents or such copies of, or extracts from, documents, as he may reasonably require for any one or more of the purposes mentioned in section 109A(2) above; and

(c)   take possession of and either remove or make his own copies of any such documents as appear to him to contain information that is relevant for any of those purposes.

(4)   The premises liable to inspection under this section are any premises (including premises consisting in the whole or a part of a dwelling house) which an authorised officer has reasonable grounds for suspecting are–

(a)   premises which are a person's place of employment;

(b)   premises from which a trade or business is being carried on or where documents relating to a trade or business are kept by the person carrying it on or by another person on his behalf;

(c)   premises from which a personal or occupational pension scheme is being administered or where documents relating to the administration of such a scheme are kept by the person administering the scheme or by another person on his behalf;

(d)   premises where a person who is the compensator in relation to any such accident, injury or disease as is referred to in section 109A(2)(b) above is to be found;

(e)   premises where a person on whose behalf any such compensator has made, may have made or may make a compensation payment is to be found.

(5)   An authorised officer applying for admission to any premises in accordance with this section shall, if required to do so, produce the certificate containing his authorisation for the purposes of this Part.

(6)   Subsection (5) of section 109B applies for the purposes of this section as it applies for the purposes of that section.]

Amendment

1.   Substituted by CSPSSA Sch 6 para 2 (2.4.01).

General Note

The powers of authorised officers to enter premises are also extended under s109C. Note, however, that there is no power to enter a person's home without consent, unless there are reasonable grounds for suspecting that the home also falls into one of the categories in subs (4). Subs (3) gives powers in relation to making inquiries on premises.

[¹Authorisations by local authorities

110A.–(1)   An individual who for the time being has the authorisation for the purposes of this Part of an authority administering housing benefit or council tax benefit (''a local authority authorisation'') shall be entitled, for [⁴ a relevant purpose], to exercise any of the powers which, subject to subsection (8) below, are conferred on an authorised officer by sections 109B and 109C above.

[⁴ (1A)   Each of the following is a relevant purpose–

(a)   a purpose mentioned in subsection (2) below;

(b)   a purpose mentioned in section 109A(2)(a), (c) or (d).

(1B)   If the Secretary of State prescribes conditions for the purposes of this section, an authority must not proceed under this section for a purpose mentioned in section 109A(2)(a), (c) or (d) unless any such condition is satisfied.

(1C)   An authorisation made for a purpose mentioned in section 109A(2)(a), (c) or (d)–

(a)   is subject to such restrictions as may be prescribed;

(b)   is not valid in such circumstances as may be prescribed.]

(2)   [⁴ The purposes in this subsection] are–

(a)   ascertaining in relation to any case whether housing benefit or council tax benefit is or was payable in that case;

(b)   ascertaining whether provisions of the relevant social security legislation that relate to housing benefit or council tax benefit are being, have been or are likely to be contravened (whether by particular persons or more generally);

(c)   preventing, detecting and securing evidence of the commission (whether by particular persons or more generally) of benefit offences relating to housing benefit or council tax benefit.

(3)   An individual has the authorisation for the purposes of this Part of an authority administering housing benefit or council tax benefit if, and only if, that authority have granted him an authorisation for those purposes and he is–

(a)   an individual employed by that authority;

(b)   an individual employed by another authority or joint committee that carries out functions relating to housing benefit or council tax benefit on behalf of that authority;

(c)   an individual employed by a person authorised by or on behalf of–
   (i)   the authority in question,
   (ii)   any such authority or joint committee as is mentioned in paragraph (b) above,
   to carry out functions relating to housing benefit or council tax benefit for that authority or committee;

(d)   an official of a Government department.

(4)   Subsection (4) of section 109A above shall apply in relation to a local authority authorisation as it applies in relation to an authorisation under that section.

(5)   A local authority authorisation may be withdrawn at any time by the authority that granted it or by the Secretary of State.

(6)   The certificate or other instrument containing the grant or withdrawal by any local authority of any local authority authorisation must be issued under the hand of either–

(a)   the officer designated under section 4 of the Local Government and Housing Act 1989 as the head of the authority's paid service; or

(b)   the officer who is the authority's chief finance officer (within the meaning of section 5 of that Act).

(7)   It shall be the duty of any authority with power to grant local authority authorisations to comply with any directions of the Secretary of State as to–

(a)   whether or not such authorisations are to be granted by that authority;

(b)   the period for which authorisations granted by that authority are to have effect;

(c)   the number of persons who may be granted authorisations by that authority at any one time; and

(d)   the restrictions to be contained by virtue of subsection (4) above in the authorisations granted by that authority for those purposes.

(8)   The powers conferred by sections 109B and 109C above shall have effect in the case of an individual who is an authorised officer by virtue of this section as if those sections had effect–

(a)   with the substitution for every reference to the purposes mentioned in section 109A(2) above of a reference to the purposes mentioned in subsection (2) above; [² . . .]

(b)   with the substitution for every reference to the relevant social security legislation of a reference to so much of it as relates to housing benefit or council tax benefit [³ ;and

(c)   with the omission of section 109B(2D)].

[⁴ but paragraphs (a) and (b) above do not apply in any case where the relevant purpose is as mentioned in subsection (1A)(b) above.]

(9)   Nothing in this section conferring any power on an authorised officer in relation to housing benefit or council tax benefit shall require that power to be exercised only in relation to cases in which the authority administering the benefit is the authority by whom that officer's authorisation was granted.]

Amendments

1.   Substituted by CSPSSA 2000 Sch 6 para 3 (2.4.01).
2.   Amended by SSFA s19 (30.4.02).
3.   Inserted by SSFA s1(5) (30.4.02).
4.   Amended by WRA s46 (19.2.08 (for making regulations) and 7.4.08).

General Note

Authorities are given the power to appoint inspectors under s110A. They have the same powers as those granted to the inspectors engaged by the Secretary of State. Note the certification requirements in subs (6). "Issued under the hand of" probably permits a junior officer directly under the supervision of the officers mentioned to sign the authorisation. Note also the power to issue directions in subs (7), a novel feature of the HB scheme. Local authority officers do not acquire any of the preserved powers under s109B(2D) by the back door.

[¹ **Power of local authority to require electronic access to information**

110AA.–(1)   Subject to subsection (2) below, where it appears to an authority administering housing benefit or council tax benefit–

(a)   that a person falling within section 109B(2A) keeps any electronic records,

(b)   that the records contain or are likely, from time to time, to contain information about any matter that is relevant for any one or more of the purposes mentioned in section 110A(2) above, and

(c)   that facilities exist under which electronic access to those records is being provided, or is capable of being provided, by that person to other persons,

that authority may require that person to enter into arrangements under which authorised officers are allowed such access to those records.

(2)   An authorised officer–

(a)   shall be entitled to obtain information in accordance with arrangements entered into under subsection (1) above only if his authorisation states that his authorisation applies for the purposes of that subsection; and

(b)   shall not seek to obtain any information in accordance with any such arrangements other than information which–

(i)   relates to a particular person; and

(ii)   could be the subject of any such requirement under section 109B above as may be imposed in exercise of the powers conferred by section 110A(8) above.

(3)   The matters that may be included in the arrangements that a person is required to enter into under subsection (1) above may include–

(a)   requirements as to the electronic access to records that is to be made available to authorised officers;

(b)   requirements as to the keeping of records of the use that is made of the arrangements;

(c)   requirements restricting the disclosure of information about the use that is made of the arrangements; and

(d)   such other incidental requirements as the authority in question considers appropriate in connection with allowing access to records to authorised officers.

(4)   An authorised officer who is allowed access in accordance with any arrangements entered into under subsection (1) above shall be entitled to make copies of, and to take extracts from, any records containing information which he is entitled to make the subject of a requirement such as is mentioned in subsection (2)(b) above.

(5)   An authority administering housing benefit or council tax benefit shall not–

(a)   require any person to enter into arrangements for allowing authorised officers to have electronic access to any records; or

(b)   otherwise than in pursuance of a requirement under this section, enter into any arrangements with a person specified in section 109B(2A) above for allowing anyone acting on behalf of the authority for purposes connected with any benefit to have electronic access to any private information contained in any records,

except with the consent of the Secretary of State and subject to any conditions imposed by the Secretary of State by the provisions of the consent.

(6)   A consent for the purposes of subsection (5) may be given in relation to a particular case, or in relation to any case that falls within a particular description of cases.

(7)   In this section "private information", in relation to an authority administering housing benefit or council tax benefit, means any information held by a person who is not entitled to disclose it to that authority except in compliance with a requirement imposed by the authority in exercise of their statutory powers.]

Amendment
  1.   Inserted by SSFA s2(2) (30.4.02).

Commencement
  1.4.02: SI 2002 No 1222.

General Note
Section 110AA enables a local authority to require access to electronic information. Subs (1) and (2) limit the scope of the powers to a similar extent to the powers in ss109B and 110A. By subs (3), there is power to impose requirements as to access, the keeping of records and the maintenance of confidentiality concerning the access arrangements. There is an important limitation in subs (5) to (7) which requires the Secretary of State to give consent for the use of the powers conferred by s110AA and also access agreed with those holding the information to "private information". The definition in subs (7) would cover "personal data" within the meaning of the Data Protection Act 1998 and information which was of a confidential nature so as to attract the protection of the law of breach of confidence.

A refusal to comply with a lawful request is an offence under s111(1)(ab).

Delay, obstruction etc of inspector

111.–(1)   If a person–
(a)   intentionally delays or obstructs an [² authorised officer] in the exercise of any power under this Act [¹ other than an Inland Revenue power];
[³ (ab) refuses or neglects to comply with any requirement under section 109BA or 110AA or with the requirements of any arrangements entered into in accordance with subsection (1) of that section, or]
(b)   refuses or neglects to answer any question or to furnish any information or to produce any document when required to do so under this Act [¹ otherwise than in the exercise of an Inland Revenue power],
he shall be guilty of an offence and liable on summary conviction to a fine not exceeding level 3 on the standard scale.

(2)   Where a person is convicted of an offence under [⁴ subsection (1)(ab) or (b)] above and the refusal or neglect is continued by him after his conviction, he shall be guilty of a further offence and liable on summary conviction to a fine not exceeding £40 for each day on which it is continued.

[¹ (3) and (4) *[Omitted]*]

Amendments
1.   Inserted by Transfer of Functions Act 1999 s5 and Sch 5 para 4 as from 1.4.99.
2.   Amended by SSFA s1(6) (30.4.02).
3.   Inserted by SSFA s2(3)(a) (30.4.02).
4.   Amended by SSFA s2(3)(b) (30.4.02).

General Note
Now that local authorities have power to appoint inspectors under s110A, this offence may be committed by anyone who obstructs an inspector or who fails to provide information when required to do so.

Analysis
Subs (1). The offence can only be committed when the inspector is acting within her/his powers. It is implicit in subs (1)(b) that the defendant either refused to answer a question or suppy information or failed to do so properly. A defendant who truthfully stated that s/he could not answer the question (whether because s/he did not know the answer or because there was some privilege in the information or documents) or did not have access to the information or documents does not commit the offence.

Subs (2). The fine is calculated on a daily rate between the date of conviction for the offence under subs (1) and the date of conviction under subs (2), not the date that the information is laid for the offence under subs (2): *Grice v Needs* [1980] 1 WLR 45 at 47F-G.

[¹Dishonest representations for the purpose of obtaining benefit etc

111A.–(1)   If a person dishonestly–
(a)   makes a false statement or representation; [⁴ or]
(b)   produces or furnishes, or causes or allows to be produced or furnished, any document or information which is false in a material particular;
[⁵ ...]
[⁵ ...]
with a view to obtaining any benefit or other payment or advantage under the [² relevant] social security legislation (whether for himself or for some other person), he shall be guilty of an offence.

[⁶ (1A)   A person shall be guilty of an offence if–

(a) there has been a change of circumstances affecting any entitlement of his to any benefit or other payment or advantage under any provision of the relevant social security legislation;

(b) the change is not a change that is excluded by regulations from the changes that are required to be notified;

(c) he knows that the change affects an entitlement of his to such a benefit or other payment or advantage; and

(d) he dishonestly fails to give a prompt notification of that change in the prescribed manner to the prescribed person.

(1B) A person shall be guilty of an offence if–

(a) there has been a change of circumstances affecting any entitlement of another person to any benefit or other payment or advantage under any provision of the relevant social security legislation;

(b) the change is not a change that is excluded by regulations from the changes that are required to be notified;

(c) he knows that the change affects an entitlement of that other person to such a benefit or other payment or advantage; and

(d) he dishonestly causes or allows that other person to fail to give a prompt notification of that change in the prescribed manner to the prescribed person.

(1C) This subsection applies where–

(a) there has been a change of circumstances affecting any entitlement of a person ('the claimant') to any benefit or other payment or advantage under any provision of the relevant social security legislation;

(b) the benefit, payment or advantage is one in respect of which there is another person ('the recipient') who for the time being has a right to receive payments to which the claimant has, or (but for the arrangements under which they are payable to the recipient) would have, an entitlement; and

(c) the change is not a change that is excluded by regulations from the changes that are required to be notified.

(1D) In a case where subsection (1C) above applies, the recipient is guilty of an offence if–

(a) he knows that the change affects an entitlement of the claimant to a benefit or other payment or advantage under a provision of the relevant social security legislation;

(b) the entitlement is one in respect of which he has a right to receive payments to which the claimant has, or (but for the arrangements under which they are payable to the recipient) would have, an entitlement; and

(c) he dishonestly fails to give a prompt notification of that change in the prescribed manner to the prescribed person.

(1E) In a case where that subsection applies, a person other than the recipient is guilty of an offence if–

(a) he knows that the change affects an entitlement of the claimant to a benefit or other payment or advantage under a provision of the relevant social security legislation;

(b) the entitlement is one in respect of which the recipient has a right to receive payments to which the claimant has, or (but for the arrangements under which they are payable to the recipient) would have, an entitlement; and

(c) he dishonestly causes or allows the recipient to fail to give a prompt notification of that change in the prescribed manner to the prescribed person.

(1F) In any case where subsection (1C) above applies but the right of the recipient is confined to a right, by reason of his being a person to whom the claimant is required to make payments in respect of a dwelling, to receive payments of housing benefit–

(a) a person shall not be guilty of an offence under subsection (1D) or (1E) above unless the change is one relating to one or both of the following–

  (i) the claimant's occupation of that dwelling;

  (ii) the claimant's liability to make payments in respect of that dwelling;

but

(b)   subsections (1D)(a) and (1E)(a) above shall each have effect as if after ''knows'' there were inserted ''or could reasonably be expected to know''.

(1G)   For the purposes of subsections (1A) to (1E) above a notification of a change is prompt if, and only if, it is given as soon as reasonably practicable after the change occurs.]

[[3]...]

(3)   A person guilty of an offence under this section shall be liable–

(a)   on summary conviction, to imprisonment for a term not exceeding six months, or to a fine not exceeding the statutory maximum, or to both; or

(b)   on conviction on indictment, to imprisonment for a term not exceeding seven years, or to a fine, or to both.

(4)   In the application of this section to Scotland, in [[7] subsections (1) to (1E)] for ''dishonestly'' substitute ''knowingly''.]

Amendments

1.   Inserted by s11 of the SSA(F) Act 1997 as from 1.7.97.
2.   Inserted by CSPSSA 2000 s67 (2.4.01).
3.   Repealed by CSPSSA 2000 s85 (2.4.01).
4.   Amended by SSFA s16(1)(a) (18.10.01 and 30.4.02).
5.   Repealed by SSFA ss16(1)(a) and 19 and Sch (18.10.01 and 30.4.02).
6.   Inserted by SSFA s16(1)(b) and (2) (29.9.01 and 18.10.01).
7.   Amended by SSFA s16(1)(c) (18.10.01).

General Note

This section, inserted by s13 Social Security Administration (Fraud) Act 1997 and extensively amended by the Social Security Fraud Act 2001, creates an offence relating to fraudulent acts to complement the offence in s112. At first glance, the two offences appear quite similar in their ambit, but it is clear that this offence is intended to be used in prosecuting more serious offenders. Three factors lead to this conclusion. First, dishonesty must be shown. Secondly, there is a requirement that the act or omission in question must have been done with a view to obtaining benefit (contrast the position under s112 – see below). Finally, the offence is triable either way and the maximum penalties are substantially heavier.

No offence may be committed under this section by virtue of any act or omission committed before the section came into force on 1 July 1997: s25(5) of the 1997 Act. There is no equivalent provision in the 2001 Act, but the common law and Art 7 of the European Convention on Human Rights means that the new offences cannot apply to conduct committed before 18 October 2001, when the new provisions were brought into force by SI 2001 No.3551.

Analysis

These offences can all be committed by a "person". That wording will apply to legal as well as natural persons, and so companies and other bodies with legal personality may be charged with the offence: Sch 1 Interpretation Act 1978. Note also s115 SSAA, which provides that officers or members of a body corporate can be charged individually with the offence if the body corporate committed it "with the consent or connivance of" that officer.

Subsection (1)

".... dishonestly ....". The meaning of "dishonesty" in English criminal law is well settled from its use in the Theft Act 1968. It must be shown that the defendant's actions would not have been seen as honest by ordinary people and that the defendant must have been aware of this: *R v Ghosh* [1982] QB 1053 at 1064D-G, CA. It is suggested that the requirement of dishonesty qualifies the whole of the subparagraph that follows. In other words, it is not just necessary for the prosecution to prove that the defendant was dishonest in relation to the act or omission alleged. It must also be shown that there was a dishonest intent to procure payment of benefit. This point is illustrated by the facts in *Barrass v Reeve* [1981] 1 WLR 408, DC. The claimant falsely claimed that he was incapable of work, but asserted that his objective in doing so was to deceive his employer. If he was believed, then that would require his acquittal on a charge under s111A, as he would have been dishonest in making a false statement, but not in relation to obtaining benefit. His dishonesty would not be "with a view" to obtaining benefit. Such a defendant can, however, be prosecuted under s112.

"(a) makes a false statement or representation". Proof of an actual statement is required, though the statement could presumably be oral or written.

"(b) produces or furnishes, or causes or allows to be produced or furnished ....". This is a very wide phrase. "Produces" means to personally hand something over. "Furnishes" has a slightly wider meaning and means that steps have been taken to ensure that the article in question has been handed over. It is questionable whether a defendant who has documents seized by an inspector "furnishes" them. A person "causes" documents or information to be given if s/he participates in the giving of the information. A person "allows" documents or information to be given if s/he passively stands by while the information is given. In the last case, care must be

57

taken to ensure that the requisite dishonest intent is really present in relation to the omission. Mere carelessness or oversight will not suffice.

"…. any document ….". This tends to be given a flexible meaning by the courts to include any means by which information is stored: *Grant v Southwestern and County Properties Ltd* [1975] Ch 185 at 197A-F, Ch D. It will therefore include things like computer discs.

"…. with a view to obtaining any benefit ….". The complete offence is committed even though no benefit was actually paid as a result of the dishonesty, and so a defendant in such a case need not merely be charged with an attempt. All that is required is that the purpose (or one of the purposes) of the dishonesty was to procure payment.

"…. or other payment ….". This phrase prevents any argument as to whether any payment made is a payment of benefit. For example, if a landlord conspired with an individual in the HB office to send out two cheques for each claim, it might be arguable that the extra cheque was not "benefit". However, the second cheque would certainly fall within the scope of "other payment".

Subsection (1A)

This deals with dishonest failures to disclose by a claimant. There are four requirements.

(1)   There has been a change of circumstances which has affected entitlement to benefit: para (a). Note that it is necessary that entitlement to benefit *was* affected and not merely that the change might have affected entitlement: *R v Passmore* [2007] EWCA Crim 2053, 18 June, CA. Where this is disputed, it may be necessary to adjourn criminal proceedings pending resolution of the issue through the appeals process.

(2)   The change is not exempted from a disclosure requirement: para (b). See reg 88(3) HB Regs (reg 69(3) HB(SPC) Regs) and reg 74(3) CTB Regs (reg 59(3) CTB(SPC) Regs) for the types of information which need not be disclosed.

(3)   The defendant knows that the change affects entitlement: para (c). This requirement is narrowly drawn. It is not enough that the defendant *ought* to have known that the change was relevant. That is clear from the modification made by subs (1F)(b). It must be proven by the prosecution that there was knowledge on the part of the defendant that there was a requirement to notify: *Gaumont British Distributors Ltd v Henry* [1939] 2 KB 711 at 719, 723, DC. It is suggested that there must have been knowledge at the time that the failure to notify occurred. This could lead to a number of difficult problems. First, it is suggested that where a defendant forgets about the obligation, having previously been aware of it, s/he does not have the requisite knowledge at that moment in time. If, of course, s/he subsequently remembers the duty and fails to notify, then s/he can be charged with the offence for that period of time. Secondly, it seems doubtful whether it can be said that a genuinely ignorant person who did not read the literature given to her/him and did not make any inquiries can be said to know what s/he is required to notify, unless it can be said that there was a deliberate attempt to refrain from seeking information: *Taylor's Central Garages (Exeter) Ltd v Roper* [1951] 115 JP 445 at 449, 450, DC; *Westminister CC v Croyalgrange Ltd* [1986] 1 WLR 674 at 684E, HL. Finally, if a person forms a false view that no disclosure is required, then provided that view is genuinely held, it cannot be said that he "knows" that such disclosure is necessary.

(4)   There is a dishonest failure to disclose. See above on the meaning of "dishonesty". See reg 4 Social Security (Notification of Change of Circumstances) Regulations 2002 on p1183 for the prescribed manner and person. The notification must be prompt, meaning as soon as reasonably practicable: subs (1G). In Scotland, the requirement "knowingly" is substituted: see subs (4).

Subsection (1B)

This deals with dishonestly allowing another person to omit disclosure. Again there are four requirements. The first three are identical to those in subs (1A)(a), (b) and (c) save that the change of circumstances and knowledge must relate to the effect on the other person's entitlement. "Causes or allows" requires that there must be some sort of implied permission given by the defendant to the person under the duty that s/he should not notify: *R v Chainey* [1914] 1 KB 137 at 142, DC. A person does not "allow" information to be given where s/he is unable to prevent it being given: *Crabtree v Fern Spinning Co Ltd* [1901] 85 LT 549 at 552, DC. So if a person knows that her/his partner is supplying false information or refraining from supplying information but s/he is threatened with violence, s/he does not "allow" that conduct. This issue was revisited by the Court of Appeal in *R v Tilley* [2009] EWCA Crim 1426, where the court said (paras 41-43) that "allowing" must mean something less than "causing" but for the prosecution to succeed it must be able to point to some action that the person could have taken that would have resulted in the other person making the relevant disclosure: simply doing nothing is not enough to establish the offence.

Subsections (1C) to (1F)

These create similar offences relating to those in receipt of benefit who are not claimants. They must be those having a right to receive payments in place of the claimant: see subs (1C)(b). These might be:

(1)   Landlords to whom rent allowance is paid directly: see regs 95 and 96 HB Regs (reg 76 and 77 HB(SPC) Regs).

(2)   Officials appointed to look after the affairs of those unable to act, and others so appointed: see regs 82(2), (3), (5) and 94(2) HB Regs (reg 63(2), (3), (5) and 75(2) HB(SPC) Regs) and reg 68(2), (3), (5) and 78(2) CTB Regs (reg 52(2), (3), (5) and 63(2) CTB(SPC) Regs).

(3)   Other people to whom the authority has agreed to pay benefit, notwithstanding that the claimant is capable of managing their affairs: see reg 94(3) HB Regs (reg 75(3) HB(SPC) Regs).

Subs (1D) creates an offence which may be committed by such an individual where the claimant's benefit entitlement is affected and the change is not excluded from notification. Knowledge of the effect of the change and dishonesty in failing to notify must normally be proved, but subs (1F) modifies their effect in relation to landlords in receipt of HB.

First, the relevant change must relate to the claimant's occupation of the dwelling or their liability to make payments. Given that this statute creates a criminal offence, it is suggested that these exceptions must be read narrowly. They cannot, therefore, relate to matters which affect the question of whether there is a legal liability at all or whether the liability falls within reg 9(1) of the HB and the HB(SPC) Regs. They can relate only to the question of whether the claimant is physically in occupation, or the amount of the liability for rent. Secondly, the requirement of knowledge is softened by requiring only proof that the landlord ought reasonably to have known, but given the requirement of dishonesty it seems unlikely that anything short of the landlord shutting his eyes to the obvious will suffice to constitute the criminal offence.

Subs (1E) creates a similar offence to that in subs (1B), and is similarly modified by subs (1F) in relation to landlords in receipt of HB.

Subsection (4)

On the meaning of "knowingly" in Scottish criminal law, see Gordon, *Criminal Law* (1978 2nd edn), para 8-22; *The Laws of Scotland* (1995) vol. 7, para 79.

False representations for obtaining benefit etc

112.–(1)   If a person for the purpose of obtaining any benefit or other payment under the [⁴ relevant] [³ social security legislation] whether for himself or some other person, or for any other purpose connected with that legislation–

(a)   makes a statement or representation which he knows to be false; or

(b)   produces or furnishes, or knowingly causes or knowingly allows to be produced or furnished, any document or information which he knows to be false in a material particular,

he shall be guilty of an offence.

[⁶(1A)   A person shall be guilty of an offence if–

(a)   there has been a change of circumstances affecting any entitlement of his to any benefit or other payment or advantage under any provision of the relevant social security legislation;

(b)   the change is not a change that is excluded by regulations from the changes that are required to be notified;

(c)   he knows that the change affects an entitlement of his to such a benefit or other payment or advantage; and

(d)   he fails to give a prompt notification of that change in the prescribed manner to the prescribed person.]–

(1B)   A person is guilty of an offence under this section if–

(a)   there has been a change of circumstances affecting any entitlement of another person to any benefit or other payment or advantage under any provision of the relevant social security legislation;

(b)   the change is not a change that is excluded by regulations from the changes that are required to be notified;

(c)   he knows that the change affects an entitlement of that other person to such a benefit or other payment or advantage; and

(d)   he causes or allows that other person to fail to give a prompt notification of that change in the prescribed manner to the prescribed person.

(1C)   In a case where subsection (1C) of section 111A above applies, the recipient is guilty of an offence if–

(a)   he knows that the change affects an entitlement of the claimant to a benefit or other payment or advantage under a provision of the relevant social security legislation;

(b)   the entitlement is one in respect of which he has a right to receive payments to which the claimant has, or (but for the arrangements under which they are payable to the recipient) would have, an entitlement; and

(c)   he fails to give a prompt notification of that change in the prescribed manner to the prescribed person.

(1D)   In a case where that subsection applies, a person other than the recipient is guilty of an offence if–

(a)   he knows that the change affects an entitlement of the claimant to a benefit or other payment or advantage under a provision of the relevant social security legislation;

(b)   the entitlement is one in respect of which the recipient has a right to receive payments to which the claimant has, or (but for the arrangements under which they are payable to the recipient) would have, an entitlement; and

(c)   he causes or allows the recipient to fail to give a prompt notification of that change in the prescribed manner to the prescribed person.

(1E)   Subsection (1F) of section 111A above applies in relation to subsections (1C) and (1D) above as it applies in relation to subsections (1D) and (1E) of that section.

(1F)   For the purposes of subsections (1A) to (1D) above a notification of a change is prompt if, and only if, it is given as soon as reasonably practicable after the change occurs.]

(2)   A person guilty of an offence under [⁴ this section] shall be liable on summary conviction to a fine not exceeding level 5 on the standard scale, or to imprisonment for a term not exceeding 3 months, or to both.

[⁵. . .]

Amendments

1.   Amended by SSA(F) Act 1997, s14(1A).
2.   Amended by SSA (F) Act 1997, s14(3).
3.   Substituted by SSA(F) Act 1997, Sch 1 para 4(2).
4.   Inserted by CSPSS Act, Sch 6 para 6 (2.4.01).
5.   Repealed by CSPSS Act 2000, s85 and Sch 9 (2.4.01).
6.   Substituted by SSFA s16(3) (29.9.01 and 18.10.01).

General Note

This sets out the less serious offences that may be committed in relation to obligations of disclosure of information to an authority. Section 14 Social Security Administration (Fraud) Act 1997 considerably widened the scope of the offences to cover omissions as well as positive misstatements and again the offences have been reformulated by the Social Security Fraud Act 2001. Note the temporal effect of the provisions in subs (1A) to (1F): see the commentary to s111A. Note also the time limits for prosecutions imposed by s116.

Analysis

Subsection (1)

"If a person ...". See Analysis to s111A on p57.

"... for the purpose of obtaining benefit ... or for any other purpose connected with that legislation ...". The latter phrase means that it need not be shown that the defendant intended to obtain benefit. It suffices if the statement was made for purposes relating to benefit: *Clear v Smith* [1981] 1 WLR 399 at 406, DC (statement that no work was being done when claimant asserted that work was unremunerated); *Barrass v Reeve* [1981] 1 WLR 408, DC (statement that claimant was incapable of work allegedly only used to deceive employer); *DSS v Bavi* [1996] COD 260 at 261, DC (statement that claimant not working allegedly result of misunderstanding).

"(a) makes a statement or representation ....". An actual statement, whether written or oral, must be proved by the prosecution, though the place and date of the statement need not be proven: *DSS v Cooper* [1994] 158 JPN 354, DC.

In deciding whether a question on a claim form has been answered incorrectly, it is not necessary to analyse the question in a legalistic manner by reference to the meaning of a particular word in the HB Regs, but rather by taking a common-sense view. So where a claimant stated that he did not own property, but in fact was the registered owner of a house, it did not matter whether or not the claimant was an "owner" for the purposes of reg 2(1) HB and the HB(SPC) Regs. The fact that he had an interest in the property that made him the owner as a matter of common sense was sufficient: *Fairbank v Lambeth Magistrates' Court* [2003] HLR 62.

"... which he knows to be false ...". The defendant must know of the falsity at the time the statement or representation is made: *Moore v Branton* [1974] 118 SJ 40, DC. It does not matter that a specific statement may have been true when made, if on a change of circumstances the claimant continues to sign forms stating that there has been no such change. The latter will be the requisite false statement: *Tolfree v Florence* [1971] 1 WLR 141 at 144, DC. Showing that a defendant was negligent or failed to make inquiries into facts does not establish knowledge of the falsity of those facts: *Taylor's Central Garages (Exeter) Ltd v Roper* [1951] 115 JP 445 at 449, 450, DC.

The prosecution must prove that the defendant knew that the statement was false, but as long as the defendant knows that the statement or representation is false, s/he need not know that the falsity was material to her/his entitlement to benefit, since there is no requirement of materiality in para (a), unlike para (b): *Harrison v DSS* [1997] COD 220 at 220-1, DC.

Para (b). See the requirement of knowledge discussed in the previous paragraph and see the Analysis of s111A(1)(b).

Subsections (1A) to (1F)

These subsections create similar criminal offences to those in s111A(1A) to (1G), except that there is no requirement of dishonesty. Each of the sub-paras (a) to (d) under subs (1A) must be established to the criminal standard of proof, and therefore it is for the prosecution to prove beyond a reasonable doubt that the defendant knew that the change *would* affect her/his benefit entitlement: simply showing that the change could affect entitlement will not be sufficient: *King v Kerrier District Council* [2006] EWHC 500 (Admin), unreported, 27 February (DC).

Subsection (2)

The offence is triable only summarily – ie, in the magistrates' court or sheriff court in Scotland.

[¹Breach of regulations

113.–(1) Regulations and schemes under any of the [² legislation to which this section applies] may provide that any person who contravenes, or fails to comply with, any provision contained in regulations made under [² that legislation]–
  (a) in the case of a provision relating to contributions, shall be liable to a penalty;
  (b) in any other case, shall be guilty of an offence under [² any enactment contained in the legislation in question].
[²(1A) The legislation to which this section applies is–
  (a) the relevant social security legislation; and
  (b) the enactments specified in section 121DA(1) so far as relating to contributions [³].]
  (2) *[Omitted]*
  (3) A person guilty of such an offence as is mentioned in subsection (1)(b) above shall be liable on summary conviction–
  (a) to a fine not exceeding level 3 on the standard scale;
  (b) in the case of an offence of continuing a contravention or failure after conviction, to a fine not exceeding £163.40 for each day on which it is so continued.
  (4) *[Omitted]*]

Amendments

  1.   Substituted by SSA 1998 s60 (4.3.99/6.4.99).
  2.   Amended by CSPSSA Sch 6 para 7 (1.11.00).
  3.   Omitted by the National Insurance Contributions and Statutory Payments Act 2004 s12 and Sch 2 (6.4.05).

General Note

The section allows regulations to provide that a failure to comply with requirements in such regulations amounts to a criminal offence under this section. Until 1997 there was no such provision in the HB or CTB schemes, but from 3 November 1997 the Social Security (Information from Landlords and Agents) Regulations 1997 made such a provision. This is now in regs 117-121 HB Regs (regs 98-102 HB(SPC) Regs). These regulations require landlords and their agents to furnish a wide range of information to an authority on request. A failure to comply with such a demand amounts to an offence under this section. See the commentary to those Regulations.

As to the penalties, see the commentary to s111 on p55.

Offences by bodies corporate

115.–(1) Where an offence under this Act [¹, or under the Jobseeker's Act 1995] which has been committed by a body corporate is proved to have been committed with the consent or connivance of, or to be attributable to any neglect on the part of, a director, manager, secretary or other similar officer of the body corporate, or any person who was purporting to act in any such capacity, he, as well as the body corporate, shall be guilty of that offence and be liable to be proceeded against accordingly.

  (2) Where the affairs of a body corporate are managed by its members, subsection (1) above applies in relation to the acts and defaults of a member in connection with his functions of management as if he were a director of the body corporate.

Amendment

1.   Amended by the Jobseekers Act 1995 Sch 2 para 116.

General Note

This section might apply in HB or CTB cases where a body corporate which is a landlord or an employer commits an offence under ss111A or 112 in relation to HB or CTB. It confirms that any officer or manager of such a body can be personally liable to prosecution if s/he has deliberately or negligently caused or contributed to the commission of the offence.

It does not appear to be necessary for a prosecution under this section that the body corporate is also prosecuted, provided that it is guilty of the offence.

A 'body corporate' is not defined in the Act. In England and Wales, it means a body which is incorporated under royal charter, Act of Parliament or the Companies Act 1985. In Scottish law, however, it may include a partnership: *Douglas v Phoenix Motors* [1970] SLT 57 at 58, Sh Ct, where both English and Scottish law are discussed.

[¹Penalty as alternative to prosecution

115A.–(1) This section applies where an overpayment is recoverable from a person by, or due from a person to, the Secretary of State or an authority under or by virtue of section 71, 71A, 75 or 76 above and it appears to the Secretary of State or authority that–

(a)   the making of the overpayment was attributable to an act or omission on the part of that person; and

(b)   there are grounds for instituting against him proceedings for an offence (under this Act or any other enactment) relating to the overpayment.

(2)   The Secretary of State or authority may give to the person a written notice–

(a)   stating that he may be invited to agree to pay a penalty and that, if he does so in the manner specified by the Secretary of State or authority, no such proceedings will be instituted against him; and

(b)   containing such information relating to the operation of this section as may be prescribed.

(3)   The amount of the penalty shall be 30 per cent. of the amount of the overpayment (rounded down to the nearest whole penny).

(4)   If the person agrees in the specified manner to pay the penalty–

(a)   the amount of the penalty shall be recoverable by the same methods as those by which the overpayment is recoverable; and

(b)   no proceedings will be instituted against him for an offence (under this Act or any other enactment) relating to the overpayment.

(5)   The person may withdraw his agreement to pay the penalty by notifying the Secretary of State or authority, in the manner specified by the Secretary of State or authority, at any time during the period of 28 days beginning with the day on which he agrees to pay it; and if he does so–

(a)   so much of the penalty as has already been recovered shall be repaid; and

(b)   subsection (4)(b) above shall not apply.

(6)   Where, after the person has agreed to pay the penalty, it is decided on a review or appeal or in accordance with regulations that the overpayment is not recoverable or due, so much of the penalty as has already been recovered shall be repaid.

(7)   Where, after the person has agreed to pay the penalty, the amount of the overpayment is revised on a review or appeal or in accordance with regulations–

(a)   so much of the penalty as has already been recovered shall be repaid; and

(b)   subsection (4)(b) above shall no longer apply by reason of the agreement;

but if a new agreement is made under this section in relation to the revised overpayment, the amount already recovered by way of penalty, to the extent that it does not exceed the amount of the new penalty, may be treated as recovered under the new agreement instead of being repaid.

[²(7A)   Subject to subsection (7B) below, the Secretary of State and an authority which administers housing benefit or council tax benefit may agree that, to the extent determined by the agreement, one may carry out on the other's behalf, or may join in the carrying out of, any of the other's functions under this section.

(7B)   Subsection (7A) above shall not authorise any delegation of–

(a)   the function of the person by whom any overpayment is recoverable, or to whom it is due, of determining whether or not a notice should be given under subsection (2) above in respect of that overpayment; or

(b)   the Secretary of State's power to make regulations for the purposes of paragraph (b) of that subsection.]

(8)   In this section ''overpayment'' means–

(a)   a payment which should not have been made;

(b)   a sum which the Secretary of State should have received;

(c)   an amount of benefit paid in excess of entitlement; or

(d)   an amount equal to an excess of benefit allowed;

and the reference in subsection (1)(a) above to the making of the overpayment is to the making of the payment, the failure to receive the sum, the payment of benefit in excess of entitlement or the allowing of an excess of benefit.]

Amendments

1.   Inserted by SSA(F) Act 1997, s15.

2.   Inserted by SSFA s14 (30.4.02).

General Note

One controversial innovation of the Social Security Administration (Fraud) Act 1997 was to enable an authority to offer a prospective defendant the option to pay a penalty rather than institute proceedings for the prosecution of that person. It may be argued that authorities might see this as a short-cut and a simple way of avoiding the expense of bringing criminal proceedings. In addition, there may be iniquity in the operation of the system if landlords are able to evade prosecution by accepting the penalty while impecunious claimants are unable to do so.

A penalty may not be offered in relation to an offence alleged to have been committed before 18 December 1997, when the section came into force: s25(7) of the 1997 Act.

The scheme, in outline, is as follows. The authority may only offer a penalty when there are grounds for prosecuting for an offence in relation to an overpayment: subs (1). A written notice offering the penalty must be given: subs (2). If the person in question agrees to pay, s/he receives immunity from prosecution and must pay an additional 30 per cent on top of the overpayment: subs (3) and (4).

The person may withdraw from the agreement within 28 days: subs (5). If there is subsequently a decision that there is no recoverable overpayment, the penalty is not payable: subs (6). If the amount of the overpayment is revised, the agreement is void, but a new agreement may be made: subs (7).

Analysis

Subsection (1)

"... where an overpayment is recoverable .... or due ...". An overpayment is not recoverable unless a valid determination has been issued by the local authority: *Warwick DC v Freeman* [1994] 27 HLR 616, CA. This is made clear beyond doubt, in relation to HB, by the amendment to Administration Act s75(1) made by Sch 1 para 3 of the 1997 Act.

It is difficult to see what "or due" adds to this. It cannot be said that it renders the penalty system operable before there has been a determination, because an overpayment cannot be "due" until it is recoverable, and until the amount has been calculated, it would not be possible to determine the level of the penalty. It might be thought that it is intended to cover situations where the overpayment arose before the Bill comes into force, but there is a specific provision against retrospectivity in relation to s115A in s25(7) of the 1997 Act. Finally, it was said in committee that "the definition of overpayment in [section 115A] does not go any wider than what is already covered by the 1992 Act": Oliver Heald MP, Standing Committee E, 21 January 1997, col. 319. There is no room for saying that it applies to overpayments that have yet to be determined to be recoverable.

It is suggested that the penalty system cannot come into operation until the local authority has made its initial determination under reg 89(1) HB Regs (reg 70(1) HB(SPC) Regs) or reg 75(1) CTB Regs (reg 60(1) CTB(SPC) Regs) as appropriate. However, there is no need to wait until the review procedure is exhausted: see subs (6).

"... it appears to the Secretary of State or authority that ...". The prosecuting authority must satisfy itself that the two conditions set out in subsection (1) are met. If they do not carry out this thought process, the section has no application and so any notice served would be invalid.

"... under or by virtue of section ... 75 or 76 ...". Overpayments of HB and CTB are recoverable under ss75 and 76 respectively.

"... the making of the overpayment was attributable to an act or omission ...". The word "attributable" requires some connection between the overpayment and the act or omission, but the latter need not be the sole cause of the former: *Walsh v Rother DC* [1978] 1 All ER 510 at 514a-e, HC.

"... there are grounds for instituting proceedings for an offence". This must mean that there is at least enough evidence before the prosecuting authority to suggest that there is a *prima facie* case for the defendant to answer.

Subsection (2)

"... may give ...". The power to offer a penalty is discretionary and there can be no question of the authority being under any duty to do so.

"... if he does so in the manner specified ...". This phrase is a little vague. The notice words "the manner specified" apply to the invitation to make an agreement, rather than the payment of the penalty under that agreement. In other words, the notice is only required to state how the agreement is to be made. It does not have to set out how the penalty has to be paid.

It appears that there is no power for the Secretary of State to prescribe the means by which an agreement is reached and so this will be a matter for authorities. Needless to say, it ought to be in writing and authorities should take care that the chosen procedure leaves all parties clear as to whether the invitation has been accepted or not.

Paras (a) and (b). The notice must contain the specified information. If it does not, the notice will be invalid if the recipient has been disadvantaged thereby: *Freeman* (above), *Haringey LBC v Awaritefe* [1999] 32 HLR 517 and *R(H) 3/04.* It is suggested that in these circumstances, any agreement to pay a penalty may be unenforceable by reason of the invalidity of the notice, since the issue of a notice is the trigger for the making of the agreement. For the information that must be included in a penalty notice, see reg 2 Social Security (Penalty Notice) Regulations 1997 on p1166.

Subsection (3)

The amount of the overpayment is the amount as specified by the authority in its original determination that the overpayment is recoverable. Subs (6) deals with situations where the overpayment is later found not to be recoverable and subs (7) deals with the situation where the amount changes on review.

Subsection (4)

"... agrees in the specified manner to pay the penalty ...". The "specified manner" relates to the making of the agreement, not the payment: see subs (2). The significance of this is that if there is an agreement as to how the penalty is paid, but the person paying the penalty fails to adhere to that agreement, her/his failure does not render the agreement void and so the authority will not then be able to institute proceedings for a criminal offence.

Para (a). For the methods by which the overpayment will be recoverable, see the Analysis to reg 102 HB Regs on p491.

Para (b). In return for paying the penalty, the person in question cannot be prosecuted under any of the offences set out above or under any other legislation, including in particular the Theft Act 1968. There could still be a prosecution under the common law, which may be relevant in Scotland, where there is no equivalent of the 1968 Act. Such a prosecution would probably be regarded as an abuse of process.

Subsection (5)

This gives a statutory 28-day 'cooling-off' period during which a person who has agreed to pay a penalty may withdraw from the agreement. Once that period has expired, it may still be possible to take civil proceedings to set the agreement aside if it was procured by undue influence on the part of the authority, namely the threat of prosecution: *Williams v Bayley* [1866] LR 1 HL 200, HL. It would have to be shown that the influence of the authority continued after the 28-day period (so that, for example, the paying person took no legal advice) and probably that there was some impropriety in the authority's actions. This latter requirement could be fulfilled by showing that the evidence would not have supported a criminal charge.

"... in the manner specified ...". By reg 2(1)(d) Social Security (Penalty Notice) Regulations 1997, a penalty notice served under subs (2) must contain a statement that the person in question may withdraw "in the manner specified by ... the authority". It is highly arguable that this requires the authority to specifically state in the notice how a person may withdraw from the agreement, rather than simply state "the manner specified" in the notice.

"... so much of the penalty as has already been recovered shall be repaid ...". In many cases, the overpayment plus the penalty will not be paid as a lump sum, but will be paid in instalments. If the payer withdraws from the agreement, do the instalments which s/he has already paid count towards the overpayment or to the penalty? Assuming the sums paid have not been specifically attributed to one or the other, the rule in *Clayton's case* [1861] 1 Mer 572 probably applies, so that payments are applied to the debt that first arose in time until it is extinguished.

The question then is which debt arose first in time. If there is no challenge to the recoverability of the overpayment, then that debt will have arisen before the penalty. However, it may be that review of the question of recoverability has been sought. It cannot be said that there is a debt in relation to the overpayment until it has been established that the overpayment is recoverable. In such a case, it may be that the penalty is the first debt in time and that the instalments will have been applied to reduce that debt. In that case, the instalments will have to be repaid.

Subsection (6)

If the overpayment is found not to be recoverable, then the penalty disappears. Any payments made will have been attributable to the penalty, because there has never been any debt in relation to the overpayment. Note that the subsection does not provide that the claimant's immunity from prosecution disappears: compare subs (7)(b).

Subsection (7)

A change in the amount of the overpayment on review or appeal removes the effect of the agreement. The reason for this is probably to allow an authority, where it is subsequently discovered that the amount of an overpayment is much higher, to take the decision to prosecute after all. Payments already made towards the penalty must be repaid, but if a new agreement is concluded, then those payments may be treated as being on account of the newly assessed penalty.

Subsection (8)

This subsection gives a wide definition to "overpayment" for the purposes of s115A. The following categories of payment are included in the definition.

(a)　It might be thought that it was arguable that if there was an award of benefit pursuant to which the payments of benefit were made, it could not be said that the payment "should not have been made" because there was a legal obligation on the authority to pay that benefit until such time as the award was revised. However, a similar phrase also occurs in Sch 9A para 11 of the Social Security (Claims and Payments) Regulations 1987 which deals with recovery of overpaid mortgage interest paid as, for example, IS housing costs. In *R v Secretary of State for Social Security ex p Golding* [1996] unreported, 1 July, CA, the Court of Appeal held that a payment "ought not to have been made" if it was an overpayment, even though the payment was made pursuant to an award of an adjudication officer.

(b)　This has no application to HB or CTB.

(c)　This refers to payments not made pursuant to an award of benefit, such as double payments.

(d)　This refers to excess payments of CTB.

[¹ Penalty as alternative to prosecution: colluding employers etc

115B.–(1) This section applies where it appears to the Secretary of State or an authority that administers housing benefit or council tax benefit–

(a)　that there are grounds for instituting proceedings against any person ('the responsible person') for an offence (whether or not under this Act) in respect of any conduct; and

(b)　that the conduct in respect of which there are grounds for instituting the proceedings is conduct falling within subsection (2) below.

(2)　Conduct in respect of which there appear to be grounds for instituting proceedings falls within this subsection if–

(a)　those proceedings would be for an offence under this Act in connection with an inquiry relating to the employment of relevant employees or of any one or more particular relevant employees; or

(b)　it is conduct which was such as to facilitate the commission of a benefit offence by a relevant employee (whether or not such an offence was in fact committed).

(3)　The Secretary of State or authority may give to the responsible person a written notice–

(a)　specifying or describing the conduct in question;

(b)　stating that he may be invited to agree to pay a penalty in respect of that conduct;

(c)　stating that, if he does so in the manner specified by the Secretary of State or authority, no criminal proceedings will be instituted against him in respect of that conduct; and

(d)　containing such information relating to the operation of this section as may be prescribed.

(4)　If the recipient of a notice under subsection (3) above agrees, in the specified manner, to pay the penalty–

(a)　the amount of the penalty shall be recoverable as a civil debt, and shall be capable of being set off against an amount of relevant benefit payable to the recipient of the notice; and

(b)　no criminal proceedings shall be instituted against him in respect of the conduct to which the notice relates;

and section 71(10) above (recovery by execution etc.) shall apply in relation to an amount recoverable by virtue of paragraph (a) above as it applies in relation to an amount recoverable under the provisions mentioned in section 71(8) above.

(5)　The amount of the penalty shall be–

(a)　in a case in which the conduct in question falls within paragraph (a) of subsection (2) above but not within paragraph (b) of that subsection, £1,000;

(b) in a case in which that conduct falls within paragraph (b) of that subsection and the number of relevant employees by reference to whom it falls within that subsection is five or more, £5,000; and

(c) in any other case, the amount obtained by multiplying £1,000 by the number of relevant employees by reference to whom that conduct falls within that subsection.

(6) The responsible person may withdraw his agreement to pay a penalty under this section by notifying the Secretary of State or authority, in the manner specified by the Secretary of State or authority, at any time during the period of 28 days beginning with the day on which he agrees to pay it.

(7) Where the responsible person withdraws his agreement in accordance with subsection (6) above–

(a) so much of the penalty as has already been recovered shall be repaid; and

(b) subsection (4)(b) above shall not apply.

(8) For the purposes of this section an individual is a relevant employee in relation to any conduct of the responsible person if–

(a) that conduct was at or in relation to a time when that individual was an employee of the responsible person;

(b) that conduct was at or in relation to a time when that individual was an employee of a body corporate of which the responsible person is or has been a director; or

(c) the responsible person, in engaging in that conduct, was acting or purporting to act on behalf of, in the interests of or otherwise by reason of his connection with, any person by whom that individual is or has been employed.

(9) In this section–

"conduct" includes acts, omissions and statements;

"director"–

(a) in relation to a company (within the meaning of the Companies Act 1985), includes a shadow director;

(b) in relation to any such company that is a subsidiary of another, includes any director or shadow director of the other company; and

(c) in relation to a body corporate whose affairs are managed by its members, means a member of that body corporate;

"employee" means any person who–

(a) is employed under a contract of service or apprenticeship, or in an office (including an elective office), or

(b) carries out any work under any contract under which he has undertaken to provide his work,

and "employment" shall be construed accordingly;

"relevant benefit" means benefit prescribed for the purposes of section 71(8) above;

"shadow director" means a shadow director as defined in [² section 251 of the Companies Act 2006];

"subsidiary" means a subsidiary as defined in section 736 of the Companies Act 1985.]

Amendments

1. Inserted by SSFA s15(1) (30.4.02).

2. Amended by Art 10 and Sch 4 para 68 of SI 2007 No 2194 as from 1.10.07.

Commencement

1.4.02: SI 2002 No 1222.

General Note

This makes special provision for penalties to be payable by employers who collude with employees to commit benefit fraud. Penalties are to be paid into the Consolidated Fund: see subs (2). As with s115A, penalties are payable only by way of agreement and give the person paying immunity from prosecution in relation to the conduct giving rise to the giving of the notice.

There is some doubt as to whether this provision may have effect in relation to conduct that took place prior to the commencement date of this section. There was no provision in the SSFA equivalent to s25(7) SSA(F)A which prevented penalties taking effect in relation to pre-commencement conduct. It is suggested that there is no reason in principle why a penalty could not be offered, provided it could be shown that there was evidence of an offence under the old law.

Analysis
Subsections (1) and (2): When a penalty may be offered
These subsections together impose two criteria which must be satisfied before a penalty may be offered. Any notice served under subs (3) in circumstances where they are not made out would be invalid.
(1)   There must be "grounds for instituting proceedings" against a person. As in s115A(1)(b) SSAA, "grounds" would require that there should be at least sufficient evidence for there to be a case to answer. "Person" includes both natural and legal persons, such as companies and other corporations: Sch 1 to the Interpretation Act 1978. It does not, however, include a partnership since a partnership has no legal personality. It would have to be shown that there were grounds for proceedings against an individual partner and the notice would have to relate to that partner alone.
(2)   The person is guilty of relevant conduct within subs (2). This may relate to "an inquiry relating to" the employment of a relevant employee under para (a) or conduct facilitating an offence by such an employee under para (b). Para (a) relates to offences under s111 SSAA for refusing to supply information when required to do so. Local authority officers are entitled to demand information from employers under ss110A(1) and 109B(2)(a) SSAA. "Relating to" will probably include any information linked with the employment, even if the connection with the employment is indirect. Similarly under para (b), "facilitating" is a loose word and will probably cover conduct which makes it possible or even merely easier to commit a benefit offence as well as conduct which actively encourages or requires the commission of such offences. The employee need not have actually committed an offence; note, however, that the employer's conduct must itself be criminal or the first criterion above will not be satisfied.
Subsections (3) and (4): Making an agreement
Subs (3) and (4) are similar to s115A(2) and (4), with a few differences. First, the notice offering a penalty must specify the conduct of which complaint is made in addition to explaining that a penalty is offered and that it offers immunity from prosecution. The power to make regulations under subs (3)(d) has not yet been exercised, though it is likely that the courts will expect the Social Security (Penalty Notice) Regulations 1997 to be complied with.
Under subs (4), the penalty may be recovered as a civil debt by enforcement in the County Court or Sheriff Court. The wording of s71(10) SSAA is virtually identical to that in s75(7) SSAA. It may also be set off against any amount owing to the employer by way of "relevant benefit". By subs (9) this refers to benefits prescribed for the purposes of s71(8) SSAA. The relevant benefits include virtually all social security benefits and are listed in reg 15(2) Social Security (Payments on Account, Overpayments and Recovery) Regulations 1988 SI No.664.
Subsection (5): The amount of the penalty
If the conduct falls within subs (2)(a) and relates to failure to respond to an inquiry, the penalty is £1,000. If it is facilitating the commission of offences by employees, it is £1,000 multiplied by the number of employees affected, up to a limit of £5,000.
Subsections (6) and (7): Withdrawing from an agreement
These are identical to s115A(5) and (6).
Subsections (8) and (9): Definitions
"Relevant employee" is given a very wide definition by subs (8). It relates not merely to employees in law by para (a), but also employees of companies of which the responsible person is a director under para (b) (thus confirming that directors may have a personal liability for a penalty) and employees of persons on behalf of whom the responsible person was acting under para (c). The latter situation would cover a situation where an agent of the employer facilitates criminal offences.
"Director" is also given a wide definition. It may include the directors of sister companies, shadow directors or members of other bodies corporate. See the commentary to reg 9(1)(e) HB Regs on p258.
"Employee", by virtue of subs (9), includes independent contractors who provide labour under a contract. It also includes those who are apprentices or who are acting in an office.

Legal proceedings

Legal proceedings
116.–(1)   Any person authorised by the Secretary of State in that behalf may conduct any proceedings [⁸ under any provision of this Act other than section 114 or under any provision of] [⁵ the Jobseekers Act 1995] before a magistrates' court although not a barrister or solicitor.
(2)   Notwithstanding anything in any Act–
(a)   proceedings for an offence under this Act [⁵ , or the Jobseekers Act 1995] other than an offence relating to housing benefit or [¹ council tax benefit] [⁵ , or for an offence under the Jobseekers Act 1995] may be begun at any time within the period of 3 months from the date on which evidence, sufficient in the opinion of

the Secretary of State to justify a prosecution for the offence, comes to his knowledge or within a period of 12 months from the commission of the offence, whichever period last expires; and

(b)   proceedings for an offence under this Act relating to housing benefit or [¹ council tax benefit] may be begun at any time within the period of 3 months from the date on which evidence, sufficient in the opinion of the appropriate authority to justify a prosecution for the offence, comes to the authority's knowledge or within a period of 12 months from the commission of the offence, whichever period last expires.

[⁴(2A)   Subsection (2) above shall not be taken to impose any restriction on the time when proceedings may begun for an offence under section 111A above.]

(3)   For the purposes of subsection (2) above–

(a)   a certificate purporting to be signed by or on behalf of the Secretary of State as to the date on which such evidence as is mentioned in paragraph (a) of the subsection came to his knowledge shall be conclusive evidence of that date; and

(b)   a certificate of the appropriate authority as to the date on which such evidence as is mentioned in paragraph (b) of that subsection came to the authority's knowledge shall be conclusive evidence of that date.

(4)   In subsections (2) and (3) above "the appropriate authority" means, in relation to an offence which relates to housing benefit and concerns any dwelling–

[⁶ (a) . . .]

(b)   if it relates to a rent rebate, the authority who are the appropriate housing authority by virtue of [⁷ section 134 below]; and

(c)   if it relates to rent allowance, the authority who are the appropriate local authority by virtue of [⁷ that section].

(5)   In subsections (2) and (3) above "the appropriate authority" means, in relation to an offence relating to [² council tax benefit], such authority as is prescribed in relation to the offence.

[⁸(5A)   [Omitted]]

(6)   [⁹ . . .]

(7)   In the application of this section to Scotland, the following provisions shall have effect in substitution for subsections (1) [⁸ to (5A)] above–

(a)   proceedings for an offence under this Act [⁵ , or the Jobseekers Act 1995] may, notwithstanding anything in [³ section 136 of the Criminal Procedure (Scotland) Act 1995], be commenced at any time within the period of 3 months from the date on which evidence, sufficient in the opinion of the Lord Advocate to justify proceedings, comes to his knowledge, or within the period of 12 months from the commission of the offence, whichever period last expires;

[¹⁰(aa) this subsection shall not be taken to impose any restriction on the time when proceedings may be commenced for an offence under section 111A above;]

(b)   for the purposes of this subsection–

(i)   a certificate purporting to be signed by or on behalf of the Lord Advocate as to the date on which such evidence as is mentioned above came to his knowledge shall be conclusive evidence of that date; and

(ii)   subsection (3) of section 331 of the said Act of 1975 (date of commencement of proceedings) shall have effect as it has effect for the purposes of that section.

Amendments

1.   Substituted by LGFA Sch 9 para 17(1) (1.4.93).
2.   Substituted by LGFA Sch 9 para 17(2) (1.4.93).
3.   Substituted by Criminal Procedure (Consequential Provisions) (Scotland) Act 1995 Sch 4 para 82 (1.4.96).
4.   Amended by SSA(F)A Sch 1 para 5.
5.   Amended by Jobseekers Act 1995 Sch 2 para 56.
6.   Deleted by Housing Act 1996 Sch 13 para 3(3).
7.   Substituted by Housing Act 1996 Sch 13 para 3(3).
8.   Amended by Social Security (Transfer of Functions etc) Act 1999 Sch 1 para 21.

9.　　Repealed bv SSA 1998 Sch 7 para 83.
10.　　Inserted by SSFA s17 (30.4.02).

General Note

This section deals with the prosecution of offences under the Act. It provides that officers of the authority may conduct proceedings in person if authorised by the Secretary of State and for time limits for certain prosecutions.

Analysis

Subsection (2)(b)

This places time limits upon certain prosecutions in England and Wales. It only applies to offences "under this Act", so it does not apply to prosecutions under the Theft Act 1968 or any other statute, and nor does it apply to charges under s111A: subs (2A). It therefore applies to s112. A prosecution must be brought within two time periods, whichever ends later:

(1)　　three months after the authority believes that it has sufficient evidence to justify a prosecution;

(2)　　12 months after the commission of the offence.

Under the first of the two periods, a certificate by the authority stating when it believed that it had sufficient evidence is to be treated as conclusive evidence of that date: subs (3)(b). A defendant may question that date by way of judicial review.

Subsection (7)

This makes equivalent provision to subs (2)(b) in relation to proceedings brought in Scotland.

[¹Local authority powers to prosecute benefit fraud

116A–(1)　　This section applies if an authority administering housing benefit or council tax benefit has power to bring proceedings for a benefit offence relating to that benefit.

(2)　　The authority may bring proceedings for a benefit offence relating to any other relevant social security benefit unless–

(a)　　the proceedings relate to any benefit or circumstances or any description of benefit or circumstances which the Secretary of State prescribes for the purposes of this paragraph, or

(b)　　the Secretary of State has directed that the authority must not bring the proceedings,

and a direction under paragraph (b) may relate to a particular authority or description of authority or to particular proceedings or any description of proceedings.

(3)　　If the Secretary of State prescribes conditions for the purposes of this section, an authority must not bring proceedings under this section unless any such condition is satisfied.

(4)　　The Secretary of State may continue proceedings which have been brought by an authority under this section as if the proceedings had been brought in his name or he may discontinue the proceedings if–

(a)　　he makes provision under subsection (2)(a), such that the authority would no longer be entitled to bring the proceedings under this section,

(b)　　he gives a direction under subsection (2)(b) in relation to the proceedings, or

(c)　　a condition prescribed under subsection (3) ceases to be satisfied in relation to the proceedings.

(5)　　In the exercise of its power under subsection (2), a local authority must have regard to the Code for Crown Prosecutors issued by the Director of Public Prosecutions under section 10 of the Prosecution of Offences Act 1985–

(a)　　in determining whether the proceedings should be instituted;

(b)　　in determining what charges should be preferred;

(c)　　in considering what representations to make to a magistrates' court about mode of trial;

(d)　　in determining whether to discontinue proceedings.

(6)　　An authority must not bring proceedings for a benefit offence which does not relate to housing benefit or council tax benefit otherwise than in accordance with this section.

(7)　　In subsection (2), "relevant social security benefit" has the same meaning as in section 121DA below.

(8)　　This section does not apply to Scotland.](1992 c5, s110A)

Amendment
1.   Inserted by WRA s47 (19.2.08 (for making regulations) and 7.4.08).

[¹Interpretation of Part VI

121DA.–(1) In this Part "the relevant social security legislation" means the provisions of any of the following, except so far as relating to contributions, [⁴ . . .] statutory sick pay or statutory maternity pay, that is to say–

(a)   the Contributions and Benefits Act;

(b)   this Act;

(c)   the Pensions Act, except Part III;

(d)   section 4 of the Social Security (Incapacity for Work) Act 1994;

(e)   the Jobseekers Act 1995;

(f)   the Social Security (Recovery of Benefits) Act 1997;

(g)   Parts I and IV of the Social Security Act 1998;

(h)   Part V of the Welfare Reform and Pensions Act 1999;

[⁵ (hh) the State Pension Credit Act 2002;]

[⁶ (hi)   Part 1 of the Welfare Reform Act 2007;]

(i)   the Social Security Pensions Act 1975;

(j)   the Social Security Act 1973;

(k)   any subordinate legislation made, or having effect as if made, under any enactment specified in paragraphs (a) to (j) above.]

[² (2)   In this Part "authorised officer" means a person acting in accordance with any authorisation for the purposes of this Part which is for the time being in force in relation to him.

(3)   For the purposes of this Part–

(a)   references to a document include references to anything in which information is recorded in electronic or any other form;

(b)   the requirement that a notice given by an authorised officer be in writing shall be taken to be satisfied in any case where the contents of the notice–

(i)   are transmitted to the recipient of the notice by electronic means; and

(ii)   are received by him in a form that is legible and capable of being recorded for future reference.

(4)   In this Part "premises" includes–

(a)   moveable structures and vehicles, vessels, aircraft and hovercraft;

(b)   installations that are offshore installations for the purposes of the Mineral Workings (Offshore Installations) Act 1971; and

(c)   places of all other descriptions whether or not occupied as land or otherwise;

and references in this Part to the occupier of any premises shall be construed, in relation to premises that are not occupied as land, as references to any person for the time being present at the place in question.

(5)   In this Part–

"benefit" includes any allowance, payment, credit or loan;

[² "benefit offence" means–

(a)   any criminal offence in connection with a claim for a relevant social security benefit;

(b)   any criminal offence in connection with the receipt or payment of any amount by way of such a benefit;

(c)   any criminal offence committed for the purpose of facilitating the commission (whether or not by the same person) of a benefit offence;

(d)   any attempt or conspiracy to commit a benefit offence;] and

"compensation payment" has the same meaning as in the Social Security (Recovery of Benefits) Act 1997.

(6)   In this Part–

(a)   any reference to a person authorised to carry out any function relating to housing benefit or council tax benefit shall include a reference to a person providing services relating to the benefit directly or indirectly to an authority administering it; and

(b)   any reference to the carrying out of a function relating to such a benefit shall include a reference to the provision of any services relating to it.]

[¹ (7)   In this section [³ "relevant social security benefit" means a benefit under any provision of the relevant social security legislation; and] "subordinate legislation" has the same meaning as in the Interpretation Act 1978.]

Amendments

1.   Inserted by CSPSS Act, Sch 6 para 8 (1.11.00 and 2.4.01).
2.   Amended by SSFA s1(7) (30.4.02).
3.   Amended by SSFA s1(8) (30.4.02).
4.   Amended by TCA Sch 6 (8.4.03).
5.   Amended by SPCA Sch 2 para 12 (October 2003).
6.   Amended by WRA s28 and Sch 3 para 10(12) (27.10.08).

PART VII
Provision of Information

General Note on Part VII

The Social Security Administration (Fraud) Act 1997 significantly expanded the powers of the DWP and local authorities to share information with each other and with other government departments in an attempt to combat benefit fraud. Concern was expressed during the passage of the Act about the implications of giving such wide powers to share information and the consequences for the subjects of the information if it is inaccurate. One concern is the sharing of information with people providing services to social security authorities, who may well have other commercial interests which could benefit from the use of such information. It was said by the government during the committee stage of the Act that there were no current plans for wholesale privatisation of the social security authorities, but the wording of the Act leaves this possibility open: Alistair Burt MP, Standing Committee E, 14 January 1997, col.174.

If information is wrongfully disclosed, the law offers several possible avenues to prevent such abuse. First, there seems little doubt that information held by public bodies of this nature will be classified by the law as confidential information. It was said at the committee stage of the Act that all commercial organisations involved in work for social security authorities are generally required to sign agreements that information will be kept confidential: Oliver Heald MP, Standing Committee E, 12 December 1996, col. 106. It would be possible to obtain an injunction to prevent the revealing of such information by a recipient.

Secondly, the Data Protection Act 1998, which replaced the Data Protection Act 1984, contains restrictions in relation to material held on computer or, under the 1998 Act, "recorded as part of a relevant filing system": see the definition of "data" in s1 of the 1998 Act. By s13, there is a right to compensation for damage resulting from "any contravention by a data controller of any of the requirements" of the 1998 Act. The Government resisted attempts at the committee stage of the Fraud Act to subject the information sharing provisions to the supervision of the Data Protection Registrar, asserting that the 1984 Act and the new EU Directive on Data Protection, which the 1998 Act is intended to implement, already provided sufficient safeguards. The DWP has published a Code of Practice on the use of the information sharing provisions.

Thirdly, there is a criminal sanction under s123 SSAA relating to unauthorised disclosure by officials. The Act extends the scope of this offence to local authority officials: see General note to s123. Unauthorised access is covered by the Computer Misuse Act 1990 s1(1)(b). It was said in Committee that DWP officers were authorised to use computer records only for work purposes and any personal use would therefore be an offence under the 1990 Act: Oliver Heald MP, Standing Committee E, 17 December 1996, col.144.

Despite the concerns of many, the scope of Part VII and other similar provisions has been slowly expanded to provide for increased data-matching between different bodies holding information on claimants.

Authorities administering housing benefit or council tax benefit

[¹Supply of information to authorities administering benefit

122C.–(1) This section applies to information relating to social security [² , child support or war pensions, or employment or training,] which is held–
(a)   by the Secretary of State or the Northern Ireland Department; or
(b)   by a person providing services to the Secretary of State or the Northern Ireland Department in connection with the provision of those services.
(2)   Information to which this section applies may be supplied to–
(a)   an authority administering housing benefit or council tax benefit; or
(b)   a person authorised to exercise any function of such an authority relating to such a benefit,

for use in the administration of such a benefit [⁴ or for the purposes of anything the authority is permitted to do in relation to any other benefit by virtue of section 110A or 116A above].

(3)   But where information to which this section applies has been supplied to the Secretary of State, the Northern Ireland Department or the person providing services under section 122 or 122B above, it may only be supplied under subsection (2) above–

(a)   for use in the prevention, detection, investigation or prosecution of [⁴ benefit offences (within the meaning of Part 6 above)]; or

(b)   for use in checking the accuracy of information relating to housing benefit or to council tax benefit and (where appropriate) amending or supplementing such information.

(4)   The Secretary of State or the Northern Ireland Department–

(a)   may impose conditions on the use of information supplied under subsection (2) above; and

(b)   may charge a reasonable fee in respect of the cost of supplying information under that subsection.

(5)   Where information is supplied to an authority or other person under subsection (2) above, the authority or other person shall have regard to it in the exercise of any function relating to housing benefit or council tax benefit.

(6)   Information supplied under subsection (2) above shall not be supplied by the recipient to any other person or body unless–

(a)   it is supplied–

(i)   by an authority to a person authorised to exercise any function of the authority relating to housing benefit or council tax benefit; or

(ii)   by a person authorised to exercise any function of an authority relating to such a benefit to the authority;

(b)   it is supplied for the purposes of any civil or criminal proceedings relating to the Contributions and Benefits Act, the Jobseekers Act 1995 [³ , Part 1 of the Welfare Reform Act 2007] or this Act or to any provision of Northern Ireland legislation corresponding to any of them; or

(c)   it is supplied under section 122D or 122E below.

(7)   This section does not limit the circumstances in which information may be supplied apart from this section (in particular by reason of section 122(4) or 122B(4) above).]

[² (8)   In this section and section 122D below "war pension" has the same meaning as in section 25 of the Social Security Act 1989.]

Amendments

1.   Inserted by SSA(F)A s3 (1.7.97).
2.   Amended by the Employment Act 2002 s50 and Sch 6 para 22 (9.9.02).
3.   Amended by WRA s28 and Sch 3 para 10(15) (27.10.08).
4.   Amended by WRA s48(1) (2.7.09).

General Note

This allows any information held by the Secretary of State or someone providing the DWP with services to be passed to an authority for use in the administration of HB and CTB or for the purposes of anything the authority is permitted to do in relation to other benefits under s110A or 116A. s110A deals with the appointment of inspectors and s116A gives authorities the powers to prosecute fraud. Information may also be passed to a person carrying out functions on behalf of an authority. See also Sch 8 para 34 WRPA (on p1128). This includes, for example, the now defunct London Organised Fraud Investigation Team: Oliver Heald MP, Standing Committee E, 12 December 1996, col. 107. By subs (4), restrictions can be imposed on its use and a charge may be levied.

A further restriction is imposed by subs (3) in relation to information which the DWP has itself only been supplied with under s122 or s122B. In such a case, the information may be disclosed for use in investigating fraud, or simply for comparison with information held by an authority. In relation to the latter, it appears at first sight that there must be some relevant information held by the local authority to be checked. However, it seems likely that "the accuracy of information" will be read as referring to the body of information held by an authority as a whole. So, where an authority has no information at all of the type which is supplied by the Secretary of State, it will be entitled to record that information under paragraph (b) as "supplementing" that body of information.

Subs (6) restricts the right of the authority to pass the information to other bodies. It must be supplied for the purposes of court proceedings under the social security legislation or pursuant to s122D or s122E.

[¹Supply of information by authorities administering benefit

122D.–(1) The Secretary of State or the Northern Ireland Department may require–
(a)   an authority administering housing benefit or council tax benefit; or
(b)   a person authorised to exercise any function of such an authority relating to such a benefit,
to supply [⁵ relevant benefit information] held by the authority or other person to, or to a person providing services to, the Secretary of State or the Northern Ireland Department for use for any purpose relating to social security [³ , child support or war pensions, [⁴ employment or training, private pensions policy or retirement planning].

(2)   The Secretary of State or the Northern Ireland Department may require–
(a)   an authority administering housing benefit or council tax benefit; or
(b)   a person authorised to exercise any function of such an authority relating to such a benefit,
to supply benefit policy information held by the authority or other person to, or to a person providing services to, the Secretary of State or the Northern Ireland Department.

[⁴ (2A)   Information supplied under subsection (2) [⁵ , in addition to any other purpose for which the information may be used,] may be used for any purpose relating to private pensions policy or retirement planning.]

(3)   Information shall be supplied under subsection (1) or (2) above in such manner and form, and in accordance with such requirements, as may be [² specified in directions given by the Secretary of State or, as the case may be, the Northern Ireland Department].

[⁵ (4)   In subsection (1) "relevant benefit information", in relation to an authority or other person, means any information which is relevant to the exercise of any function relating to a relevant social security benefit by the authority or other person.]

(5)   In subsection (2) above "benefit policy information" means any information which may be relevant to the Secretary of State or the Northern Ireland Department–
(a)   in preparing estimates of likely future expenditure on [⁵ any relevant social security benefit]; or
(b)   in developing policy relating to [⁵ any relevant social security benefit].]

[⁴ (6)   In this section–
"private pensions policy" means policy relating to occupational pension schemes or personal pension schemes (within the meaning given by section 1 of the Pension Schemes Act 1993);
"retirement planning" means promoting financial planning for retirement.]
[⁵ "relevant social security benefit" has the same meaning as in section 121DA above.]

Amendments
1.   Inserted by SSA(F)A s3 (1.7.97).
2.   Amended by SSFA s6 (30.4.02).
3.   Amended by the Employment Act 2002 s50 and Sch 6 para 22 (9.9.02).
4.   Amended by the Pensions Act 2004 s236 and Sch 10 para 3 (18.11.04).
5.   Amended by WRA s48(2) (2.7.09).

General Note
This section deals with information moving from local authority to DWP. See also Sch 8 para 34 WRPA (on p1128). The categories and uses of information are broader. "Relevant benefit information" is that relevant to any function relating to a relevant social security benefit (for the definition see s121DA) held by an authority, and it may be supplied for any purpose relating to social security. "Benefit policy information" is that helping the DWP forecast likely expenditure or to develop policy. There is little information relating to the benefits that could not be disclosed under these provisions.

[¹Supply of information between authorities administering benefit

122E.–(1) This section applies to [² relevant benefit information] which is held by–
(a)   an authority administering housing benefit or council tax benefit; or
(b)   a person authorised to exercise any function of such an authority relating to such a benefit.

(2)   Information to which this section applies may be supplied to another such authority or person–

   (a)   for use in the prevention, detection, investigation or prosecution of [² benefit offences (within the meaning of Part 6 above)]; or

   (b)   for use in checking the accuracy of information relating to housing benefit or to council tax benefit and (where appropriate) amending or supplementing such information.

(3)   The Secretary of State or the Northern Ireland Department may require information to which this section applies and which is of a prescribed description to be supplied in prescribed circumstances to another such authority or person for use in the administration of housing benefit or council tax benefit.

(4)   Information shall be supplied under subsection (3) above in such manner and form, and in accordance with such requirements, as may be prescribed.

(5)   Where information supplied under subsection (2) or (3) above has been used in amending or supplementing other information, it is lawful for it to be–

   (a)   supplied to any person or body to whom that other information could be supplied; or

   (b)   used for any purpose for which that other information could be used.

[² (6)   In this section "relevant benefit information", in relation to an authority or other person, means any information which is relevant to the exercise of any function relating to a relevant social security benefit (within the meaning of section 121DA above) by the authority or other person.]

(7)   This section does not limit the circumstances in which information may be supplied apart from this section.]

Amendments
   1.   Inserted by SSA(F)A s3 (1.7.97).
   2.   Amended by WRA s48(3) (2.7.09).

General Note
   Benefit administration information may be shared voluntarily by local authorities or at the direction of the Secretary of State. In the former case, subs (2) requires the information to be used for the detection of fraud or the checking of information. Information transferred by order under subs (3) can be used more generally for administration. See also Sch 8 para 34 WRPA (on p1128).
   The effect of subs (5) is that when information received is mixed with a body of information, it may be supplied to whoever is entitled to receive that body of information, even though the recipient would not be entitled to disclosure of the transferred information in the form in which it was received. This is to obviate the need for complex screening processes when mixed information is being passed on.

[¹ Rent officers and housing benefit

Supply by rent officers of information relating to housing benefit

122F.–(1)   The Secretary of State may require a rent officer to supply housing benefit information held by the rent officer to, or to a person providing services to, the Secretary of State for use for purposes relating to any of the following–

   (a)   social security;

   (b)   child support;

   (c)   war pensions;

   (d)   employment or training;

   (e)   private pensions policy or retirement planning.

(2)   Information must be supplied under subsection (1) in such manner and form, and in accordance with such requirements, as may be specified in directions given by the Secretary of State.

(3)   A person who receives information by virtue of subsection (1) must not disclose the information to any person unless the disclosure is made–

   (a)   for a purpose mentioned in that subsection (including disclosure to another rent officer in connection with any function he has under section 122 of the Housing Act 1996 relating to housing benefit),

(b)   in accordance with any other enactment, or

(c)   in accordance with the order of a court.

(4)   Housing benefit information is any information which relates to the exercise by the rent officer of any function he has under section 122 of the Housing Act 1996 relating to housing benefit.]

Amendment

1.   Inserted by WRA s36 (27.3.09).

Unauthorised disclosure of information relating to particular persons

123.–(1) A person who is or has been employed in social security administration or adjudication is guilty of an offence if he discloses without lawful authority any information which he acquired in the course of his employment and which relates to a particular person.

(2)   A person who is or has been employed in the audit of expenditure or the investigation of complaints is guilty of an offence if he discloses without lawful authority any information

(a)   which he acquired in the course of his employment;

(b)   which is, or is derived from, information acquired or held by or for the purposes of any of the government departments or other bodies or persons referred to in Part I of Schedule 4 to this Act or Part I of Schedule 3 to the Northern Ireland Administration Act; and

(c)   which relates to a particular person.

(3)   It is not an offence under this section–

(a)   to disclose information in the form of a summary or collection of information so framed as not to enable information relating to any particular person to be ascertained from it; or

(b)   to disclose information which has previously been disclosed to the public with lawful authority.

(4)   It is a defence for a person charged with an offence under this section to prove that at the time of the alleged offence

(a)   he believed that he was making the disclosure in question with lawful authority and had no reasonable cause to believe otherwise; or

(b)   he believed that the information in question had previously been disclosed to the public with lawful authority and had no reasonable cause to believe otherwise.

(5)   A person guilty of an offence under this section shall be liable

(a)   on conviction on indictment, to imprisonment for a term not exceeding two years or a fine or both; or

(b)   on summary conviction, to imprisonment for a term not exceeding six months or a fine not exceeding the statutory maximum or both.

(6)   For the purposes of this section the persons who are "employed in social security administration or adjudication" are

(a)   any person specified in Part I of Schedule 4 to this Act or in any corresponding enactment having effect in Northern Ireland;

(b)   any other person who carries out the administrative work of any of the government departments or other bodies or persons referred to in that Part of that Schedule or that corresponding enactment; and

(c)   any persons who provides, or is employed in the provision of, services to any of those departments, persons or bodies;

and "employment", in relation to any such person, shall be construed accordingly.

[¹(6A)   Subsection (6) above shall have effect as if any [⁸ health care professional] who, for the purposes of [⁴ section 19 of the Social Security Act 1998], is provided by any person in pursuance of a contract entered into with the Secretary of State were specified in Part I of Schedule 4 to this Act.]

(7)   For the purposes of subsections (2) and (6) above, any reference in Part I of Schedule 4 to the Act or any corresponding enactment having effect in Northern Ireland

to a government department shall be construed in accordance with Part II of that Schedule or any corresponding enactment having effect in Northern Ireland, and for this purpose "government department" shall be taken to include

(a)   the Commissioners of Inland Revenue; and

(b)   the Scottish Courts Administration.

(8)   For the purposes of this section, the persons who are "employed in the audit of expenditure or the investigation of complaints" are

(a)   the Comptroller and Auditor General;

(b)   the Comptroller and Auditor General for Northern Ireland;

(c)   the Parliamentary Commissioner for Administration;

(d)   the Northern Ireland Parliamentary Commissioner for Administration;

(e)   the Health Service Commissioner for England;

[⁶ (f)]

(g)   [⁵ the Scottish Public Services Ombudsman];

(h)   the Northern Ireland Commissioner for Complaints;

[² (ha) a member of the Local Commission for England;

[⁶ (hb)]

[⁵ (hc)]]

[⁶ (hd)]

[⁶ (he) the Public Services Ombudsman for Wales and any member of his staff;]

(i)   any member of the staff of the National Audit Office or the Northern Ireland Audit Office;

(j)   any other person who carries out the administrative work of either of those Offices, or who provides, or is employed in the provision of, services to either of them;

[²(ja) a member of the Audit Commission for Local Authorities and the National Health Service in England [⁷] and any auditor appointed by that Commission;

(jb)   a member of the Accounts Commission for Scotland and any auditor within the meaning of Part VII of the Local Government (Scotland) Act 1973;

(jc)   a Northern Ireland local government auditor; and]

(k)   any officer of any of the Commissioners [⁵ , Ombudsman] [² or Commissions referred to in paragraphs (c) to [⁶ (ha)], (ja) and (jb) above and any person assisting an auditor referred to in paragraph (ja), (jb) or (jc) above;]

and "employment", in relation to any such person, shall be construed accordingly.

(9)   For the purposes of this section a disclosure is to be regarded as made with lawful authority, if, and only if, it is made

(a)   in accordance with his official duty

(i)   by a civil servant; or

(ii)   by a person employed in the audit of expenditure or the investing-action of complaints, who does not fall within subsection (8)(j) above;

(b)   by any other person either

(i)   for the purposes of the function in the exercise of which he holds the information and without contravening any restriction duly imposes by the person responsible; or

(ii)   to, or in accordance with an authorisation duly given by, the person responsible;

(c)   in accordance with any enactment or order or a court;

(d)   for the purpose of instituting, or otherwise for the purposes of, any proceedings before a court or before any tribunal or other body or person referred to in Part I of Schedule 4 to this Act or Part I of Schedule 3 to the Northern Ireland Administration Act; or

(e)   with the consent of the appropriate person;

and in this subsection "the person responsible" means the Secretary of State, the Lord Chancellor or any person authorised by the Secretary of State or the Lord Chancellor for the purposes of this subsection and includes a reference to "the person responsible" within the meaning of any corresponding enactment having effect in Northern Ireland.

(10)   For the purposes of subsection (9)(e) above, "the appropriate person" means the person to whom the information in question relates, except that if the affairs of that person are being dealt with–

(a)   under a power or attorney;

(b)   by a receiver appointed under section 99 of the Mental Health Act 1983 or a controller appointed under Article 101 of the Mental Health (Northern Ireland) Order 1986;

(c)   by a Scottish mental health custodian, [³ that is to say a guardian or other person entitled to act on behalf of the person under the Adults with Incapacity (Scotland) Act 2000 (asp 4)]; and

(d)   by a mental health appointee, that is to say

    (i)   a person directed or authorised as mentioned in sub-paragraph (a) of rule 41(1) of the Court of Protection Rules 1984 or sub-paragraph (a) of rule 38(1) of Order 109 of the Rules of the Supreme Court (Northern Ireland) 1980; or

    (ii)   a receiver ad interim appointed under sub-paragraph (b) of the said rule 41(1) or a controller ad interim appointed under sub-paragraph (b) of the said rule 38(1),

the appropriate person is the attorney, receiver, controller, custodian or appointee, as the case may be, or, in a case falling within paragraph (a) above, the person to whom the information relates.

Amendments

1.   Inserted by Deregulation and Contracting Out Act 1994 (c.40) Sch 16 para 21 (3.1.95).
2.   Amended by SSA(F)A s4.
3.   Amended by art 3 of SI 2005 No 1790 as from 30.6.05.
4.   Amended by SSA 1998 Sch 7 para 88 (5.7.99).
5.   Amended by Art 12 of SI 2004 No. 1823 as from 14.7.04.
6.   Amended by the Public Services Ombudsman (Wales) Act 2005 s39, Sch 6 para 26 and Sch 7 (1.4.06).
7.   Amended by the Local Government and Public Involvement in Health Act 2007 s146 and Sch 9 para 2(h) (1.4.07).
8.   Substituted by WRA s63 and Sch 7 para 3(3) (3.7.07).

General Note

This section makes it a criminal offence for officials involved in the administration or audit of benefits, or the investigation of complaints, to make an unauthorised disclosure of information which relates to particular people. It is applicable to local authority officers in relation to acts committed on or after 1 July 1997, when the amendments to Sch 4 naming officers as persons to whom s123 applies came into force.

[¹Information from landlords and agents

126A.–(1) Regulations shall provide that where a claim for housing benefit in respect of a dwelling is made to an authority and the circumstances are such as are prescribed–

(a)   the authority; or

(b)   a person authorised to exercise any function of the authority relating to housing benefit,

may require any appropriate person to supply information of a prescribed description to the authority or other person.

(2)   Subject to subsection (4) below, for the purposes of subsection (1) above a person is an appropriate person in relation to a dwelling if he is–

(a)   a person to whom anyone is, or claims to be, liable to make relevant payments;

(b)   a person to whom, or at whose direction, a person within paragraph (a) above has agreed to make payments in consequence of being entitled to receive relevant payments; or

(c)   a person acting on behalf of a person within paragraph (a) or (b) above in connection with any aspect of the management of the dwelling.

(3)   In subsection (2) above "relevant payments", in relation to a dwelling, means payments in respect of the dwelling which are of a description in relation to which housing benefit may be paid.

(4)   Regulations may provide that any prescribed person, or any person of a prescribed description, is not an appropriate person for the purposes of subsection (1) above.

(5)   The descriptions of information which may be prescribed for the purposes of subsection (1) above include, in particular, any description of information relating to, or to any interest in or other connection with, dwellings and other property situated anywhere in the United Kingdom.

(6)   Information shall be supplied under subsection (1) above in such manner and form, and at such time and in accordance with such other requirements, as may be prescribed.

(7)   Information supplied to an authority or other person under subsection (1) above may be used by the authority or other person only in the exercise of any function relating to housing benefit or council tax benefit.

(8)   The provisions of sections 122D and 122E above apply in relation to any information supplied under subsection (1) above which is not [² relevant benefit information] (within the meaning of those provisions) as if it were.]

Amendments

1.   Inserted by SSA(F)A s11 (8.10.97).
2.   Amended by WRA s48(4) (2.7.09).

General Note

During the passage of the Social Security Administration (Fraud) Act 1997, one of the main concerns of the Labour members in Committee was the failure of the Bill to make specific provision for the problem of fraud by landlords. The creation of a landlord register was proposed with criminal sanctions for non-compliance, and a power to refuse to pay benefit where fraud was suspected.

The Government's response was s11 of the Act, which inserted s126A. The section gives power to the authority to require information in circumstances to be prescribed by regulations. By subsection (5), it is made clear that the principal use of the provision will be to obtain lists of the landlord's property portfolio to enable cross-checks to be made. See also Sch 8 para 34 WRPA (on p1128).

For the information that may be required from landlords, see regs 117-121 HB Regs (reg 98-102 HB(SPC) Regs).

Analysis

Subsection (2)

This sets out the categories of people from whom information may be required under s126A:

(a)   Refers to the landlord or any person to whom the claimant is liable to make relevant payments. "Relevant payments" is defined in subs (3) as any payment (usually rent) which may lead to HB being paid. See reg 8 of both the HB and the HB(SPC) Regs for where a tenant may be so liable.

(b)   This deals with situations where there is effectively a sub-letting arrangement. If A lets a flat to B, and B in turn takes in a lodger C after agreeing that A will receive a share of the rent in return for letting him take in C, A will be liable to provide information under s126A when C claims HB.

(c)   This is a reference to agents.

Subsection (7)

The information supplied under s126A may only be used for purposes relating to benefits. See s123 for the consequences of a breach of this provision.

Subsection (8)

This subsection allows information collected under s126A to be passed to the Secretary of State or to other authorities under the powers conferred by sections 122D and 122E.

Information for purposes of housing benefit
[¹127. . . .]

Amendment

1.   Repealed by the SSA(F) Act 1997.

Information for purposes of council tax benefit
[¹128. . . .]

Amendment

1.   Repealed by the SSA(F) Act 1997.

[¹ Expedited claims for housing and council tax benefit

Disclosure of information by authorities

128A.–(1) Regulations may make provision requiring the disclosure by one authority (''the disclosing authority'') to another authority (''the receiving authority''), in prescribed circumstances, of information of a prescribed description obtained by the disclosing authority in respect of persons who have been entitled to a jobseeker's allowance or to income support.

(2)   The regulations may in particular provide for–

(a)   information to be disclosed–
- (i)   at the request of the receiving authority;
- (ii)   at the request of any person who falls within a prescribed category; or
- (iii)   otherwise than in response to such a request;

(b)   the period within which information is to be disclosed; and

(c)   information to be disclosed only if it has been obtained by the disclosing authority in the exercise of any of their functions in relation to housing benefit or council tax benefit.]

Amendments

1.   Inserted by Jobseekers Act 1995, s28(2) (12.12.95 for regulation-making purposes, 1.4.96 for other purposes).

2.   Whole section to be repealed by SSA(F)A, s22 Sch 2 when brought into force.

General Note

This section was to be repealed by s22 Social Security Administration (Fraud) Act 1997, but the repealing provision has not yet been brought into force. It is not clear whether the reference to s128A in Sch 2 was a mistake. For regulations under this section, see reg 115 HB Regs (reg 96 HB(SPC) Regs) and reg 96 CTB Regs (reg 81 CTB(SPC) Regs).

PART VIII
Arrangements for Housing Benefit and Council Tax Benefits and Related Subsidies
Housing benefit

Arrangements for housing benefit

134.–[¹(1) Housing benefit provided by virtue of a scheme under section 123 of the Social Security Contributions and Benefits Act 1992 (in this Part referred to as ''the housing benefit scheme'') shall be funded and administered by the appropriate housing authority or local authority.

(1A)   Housing benefit in respect of payments which the occupier of a dwelling is liable to make to a housing authority shall take the form of a rent rebate or, in prescribed cases, a rent allowance funded and administered by that authority.
The cases that may be so prescribed do not include any where the payment is in respect of property within the authority's Housing Revenue Account.

(1B)   In any other case housing benefit shall take the form of a rent allowance funded and administered by the local authority for the area in which the dwelling is situated or by such other local authority as is specified by an order made by the Secretary of State.]

(2)   The rebates and allowances referred to in [² subsections (1A) and (1B)] above may take any of the following forms, that is to say–

(a)   a payment or payments by the authority to the person entitled to the benefit;

(b)   a reduction in the amount of any payments which that person is liable to make to the authority by way of rent; or

(c)   such a payment or payments and such a reduction;

and in any enactment or instrument (whenever passed or made) ''pay'', in relation to housing benefit, includes discharge in any of those forms.

[¹ (3)]
[¹ (4)]
[¹ (5)   Authorities may–

(a)   agree that one shall discharge functions relating to housing benefit on another's behalf; or

(b)   discharge any such functions jointly or arrange for their discharge by a joint committee.

(5A)   Nothing in this section shall be read as excluding the general provisions of the Local Government Act 1972 or the Local Government (Scotland) Act 1973 from applying in relation to the housing benefit functions of a local authority.]

[¹ (6)]

[¹ (7)]

(8)   An authority may modify any part of the housing benefit scheme administered by the authority

(a)   so as to provide for disregarding, in determining a person's income (whether he is the occupier of a dwelling or any other person whose income falls to be aggregated with that of the occupier of a dwelling), the whole or part of any [⁴ prescribed] war disablement pension or [⁴ prescribed] war widow's [⁴] pension payable to that person;

(b)   to such extent in other respects as may be prescribed, and any such modification may be adopted by resolution of an authority.

(9)   Modifications other than such modifications as are mentioned in subsection (8)(a) above shall be so framed as to secure that, in the estimate of the authority adopting them, the total of [¹ the housing benefit which will be paid by the authority in any year will not exceed the permitted total or any subsidiary limit specified by order of the Secretary of State.]

(10)   An authority who have adopted modifications may by resolution revoke or vary them.

(11)   If the housing benefit scheme includes power for an authority to exercise a discretion in awarding housing benefit, the authority shall not exercise that discretion so that the total of [¹ the housing benefit paid by them during the year exceeds the permitted total or any subsidiary limit specified by order of the Secretary of State.]

[¹ (12)   The Secretary of State–

(a)   shall by order specify the permitted total of housing benefit payable by any authority in any year; and

(b)   may by order specify one or more subsidiary limits on the amount of housing benefit payable by any authority in any year in respect of any matter or matters specified in the order.

The power to specify the permitted total or a subsidiary limit may be exercised by fixing an amount or by providing rules for its calculation.]

(13)   In this section ''modifications'' includes additions, omissions and amendments, and related expressions shall be construed accordingly.

[⁴ (14) In this section ''war widow's pension'' includes any corresponding pension payable to a widower or surviving civil partner.]

Definitions

"dwelling" – s191.

"housing authority" – s191.

"modifications" – s134(13).

"war widow's pension" – s134(14)

Amendments

1.   Amended by the Housing Act 1996 Sch 12 para 1 and partially repealed by Sch 19, Part VI (1.4.97).

2.   Amended by the LGA 2003 s127(1) and Sch 7 para 35 (deemed to come into force on 1.4.97).

3.   Inserted by Art 7 of SI 2005 No 2053 as from 5.12.05.

4.   Amended by WRA 2007 ss40 and 67 and Sch 5 para 3 and Sch 8 (3.7.07).

General Note

Subs (1A) and (1B) prescribe the two different forms that HB may take, depending on whether it is paid to a housing authority or to other types of landlord (eg, private or housing association). Note that under s191, "housing authority" means a local authority, a new town corporation or the Development Board for Rural Wales.

Subs (5) enables those administering the scheme to make arrangements whereby one will carry out the functions of the other (eg, where HB is payable in respect of two homes under reg 7(6)(d) of both the HB and the HB(SPC) Regs) the authority in the area the claimant has moved from may ask the authority in the new area to deal with HB in respect of both homes.

Subs (8)-(10) allow the authority to modify the basic HB scheme within limits. Subs (8) sets out the circumstances in which modifications may be made and how they may be adopted by the authority. Subs (10) permits the authority to revoke any modifications if its terms are complied with. Subs (9) sets a financial limit on the modifications which may be made.

Subs (11) puts a financial limit on the extent to which an authority may use its discretionary powers to award extra benefit. The financial limits in subs (9) and (11) are defined by subs (12).

Analysis

Subs (1) requires the HB scheme to be funded and administered by the appropriate "housing authority" or "local authority", both defined in s191.

Subs (1A) and (1B) specify the two types of HB: rent rebate which is generally paid to claimants who pay rent to the housing authority who administers the HB scheme, and rent allowance which is paid to those who pay rent to other landlords. This is not quite a rigid distinction, since certain prescribed occupiers who make payments to a housing authority may receive rent allowance instead: see reg 91A HB Regs and reg 72A HB (SPC) Regs. The proviso to subs (1A) limits the cases which by Secretary of State prescription may take the form of a rent allowance so as to exclude payments of HB in relation to properties within the authority's housing revenue account (HRA). Such properties are detailed in s74 Local Government and Housing Act 1989 (c.42) and include all mainstream council housing provided under Part II of the Housing Act 1985 and accommodation the authority has leased from the private sector of the same purpose where it has chosen to account for it within its HRA.

An important distinction in the treatment of claims in rent rebate and rent allowance cases is that the requirement to refer to the rent officer for determinations and then to apply rent restriction rules only applies to the latter, and not to the former: see regs 13, 13C and 14 of both the HB and the HB(SPC) Regs.

Subs (2) clarifies the forms of "payment" envisaged by the terms "rebate" and "allowance" and is also important in relation to overpayments of benefit. See note on the HB Regs reg 99 on p477.

Subs (8). In the assessment of income for HB (and CTB) £10 of certain war pensions must be disregarded. Subs 8 allows an authority to resolve to disregard more of (or all of) prescribed war pensions as income for the purposes of its HB scheme. The prescribed pensions are in the Schedule to the HB&CTB (War Pension Disregards) Regulations 2007 SI No.1619 (see p1227). Note that "war widow's pension" includes any corresponding pension payable to a widower or a surviving civil partner: subs (14).

The authority may change its mind by a further resolution: subs (10). For "occupier", see HB Regs reg 7 and for "income", see Section 1 of Part 6. No direct subsidy is paid in respect of extra benefit paid in accordance with this section.

Prior to the amendments made by SI 2007 No.1619 from 3 July 2007, reg 40(3) HB Regs (reg 33(13) HB(SPC) Regs) and reg 30(3) CTB Regs (reg 23(13) CTB(SPC) Regs), made under subs (8)(b), permitted a similar disregard in relation to a war widower's pension. A local authority would have to have found stringent justification for any disparity in treatment between widows and widowers if it was not to fall foul of Art 14 of the European Convention on Human Rights, and it would not be permitted a period of grace in order to carry out reforms: *R (Hooper) v Secretary of State for Work and Pensions* [2003] 1 WLR 2623, CA, affirmed on this point by the House of Lords in [2005] UKHL 29, *The Times,* 6 May.

A resolution will only usually have effect from the date it is expressed to take effect. Thus where a claimant had been overpaid due to a late payment of an increase in his war pension, a resolution of the council to ignore war pension as income did not have retrospective effect: *R v South Hams DC ex p Ash* [1999] 32 HLR 405 at 409, QBD.

Subs (11) forbids authorities to exceed the permitted total of expenditure by allowing discretionary increases in benefit.

Housing benefit finance
  [¹**135.** . . .]

Amendment
1.   Repealed by the Housing Act 1996 Sch 19, Part VI (1.4.97).

Rent allowance subsidy and determinations of rent officers
  [¹**136.** . . .]

Amendment
1.   Repealed by the Housing Act 1996 Sch 19, Part VI (1.4.97).

Council tax benefit

Nature of benefits

138.–[¹(1)   Regulations shall provide that where a person is entitled to council tax benefit in respect of council tax payable to a billing authority or [⁴ local authority in Scotland] the benefit shall take such of the following forms as is prescribed in the case of the person–

(a)   a payment or payments by the authority to the person;

(b)   a reduction in the amount the person is or becomes liable to pay to the authority in respect of the tax for the relevant or any subsequent financial year;

(c)   both such payment or payments and such reduction.]

[⁹ References in any enactment or instrument (whenever passed or made) to payment in relation to council tax benefit, include any of those ways of giving the benefit.]

[²(2)   ...]

[³(3)–(4)   ...]

(5)   For the purposes of [⁵ subsection (1)] above the relevant [⁵ financial year] is the [⁵ financial year] in which the relevant day falls; and the relevant day is the day in respect of which the person concerned is entitled to the benefit.

[⁶(6)–(8)   ...]

(9)   Regulations under subsection (1), [⁷ ...] above may include such supplementary, incidental or consequential provisions as appear to the Secretary of State to be necessary or expedient; and any such provisions may include provisions amending or adapting provisions of [⁸ Part I or II of the Local Government Finance Act 1992].

Definitions
   "billing authority" – s191.
   "prescribed" – *ibid.*

Amendments
   1.   Substituted by LGFA Sch 9 para 19(1) (1.4.93).
   2.   Deleted by LGFA Sch 9 para 19(1) (1.4.93).
   3.   Deleted by LGFA Sch 9 para 19(3) (1.4.93).
   4.   Substituted by Local Government etc. (Scotland) Act 1994 Sch 13 para 175(3)(1.4.96).
   5.   Substituted by LGFA Sch 9 para 19(3) (1.4.93).
   6.   Repealed by LGFA Sch 9 para 19(4) and Sch 14 (1.4.93).
   7.   Repealed by LGFA Sch 9 para 19(5) and Sch 14 (1.4.93).
   8.   Substituted by LGFA Sch 9 para 19(5) (1.4.93).
   9.   Amended by the Housing Act 1996 Sch 12 para 2 (1.4.97)

General Note
   This prescribes the forms which CTB is to take. Subs (1) provides that it may take the form of a reduction from a claimant's council tax bill (whether for the present or the future financial year), a payment or both.

Arrangements for council tax benefit

139.–(1) Any [¹ council tax benefit] provided for by virtue of a scheme under section 123 of the Contributions and Benefits Act (in this Act referred to as a [¹ council tax] scheme) is to be administered by the appropriate authority.

[² (2)   For the purposes of this section the appropriate authority is the billing or [⁶ local authority in Scotland] which levied the council tax as regards which a person is entitled to the benefit.]

(3)   [² ...]

(4)   [⁷ Nothing in this section shall be read as excluding the general provisions of the Local Government Act 1972 or the Local Government (Scotland) Act 1973 from applying in relation to the council tax benefit functions of a local authority.]

(6)   [³ A billing authority] or [⁶ local authority in Scotland] may modify any part of the [⁴ council tax benefit] scheme administered by the authority–

(a)   so as to provide for disregarding, in determining a person's income, the whole or part of any [¹⁰ prescribed] war disablement pension or [² prescribed] war widow's pension payable to that person or to his partner or to a person to whom he is polygamously married;

(b) to such extent in other respects as may be prescribed, and any such modifications may be adopted by resolution of an authority.

(7) Modifications other than such modifications as are mentioned in subsection (6)(a) above shall be so framed as to secure that, in the estimate of the authority adopting them, the total of [⁷ the amount of benefit which will be paid by them in any year will not exceed the permitted total or any subsidiary limit specified by order of the Secretary of State.]

(8) An authority which has adopted modifications may by resolution revoke or vary them.

(9) If the [⁵ council tax benefit scheme] includes power for an authority to exercise a discretion in allowing [⁵ council tax benefit] the authority shall not exercise that discretion so that the total of [⁷ the amount of benefit paid by them in any year exceeds the permitted total or any subsidiary limit specified by order of the Secretary of State.]

(10) [⁷ The Secretary of State–

(a) shall by order specify the permitted total of council tax benefit payable by any authority in any year; and

(b) may by order specify one or more subsidiary limits on the amount of council tax benefit payable by any authority in any year in respect of any matter or matters specified in the order.

The power to specify the permitted total or a subsidiary limit may be exercised by fixing an amount or by providing rules for its calculation.]

(11) In this section–

''modifications'' includes additions, omissions and amendments, and related expressions shall be construed accordingly;

''partner'', in relation to a person, means the other member of the couple concerned; [¹⁰]

[¹⁰ ''war widow's pension'' includes any corresponding pension payable to a widower or surviving civil partner.]

Amendments

1. Substituted by LGFA Sch 9 para 20(1) (1.4.93).
2. Substituted by LGFA Sch 9 para 20(2) (1.4.93).
3. Substituted by LGFA Sch 9 para 20(5) (1.4.93).
4. Substituted by LGFA Sch 9 para 20(6) (1.4.93).
5. Substituted by LGFA Sch 9 para 20(7) (1.4.93).
6. Substituted by Local Government etc. (Scotland) Act 1994 Sch 13 para 175(3) (1.4.96).
7. Amended from by the Housing Act 1996 Sch 12 para 3 (1.4.97).
8. Inserted by CPA Sch 24 para 65(a) (5.12.05).
9. Inserted by Sch 24 para 65(b) CPA 2004 as from 5.12.05.
10. Amended by WRA s40 and Sch 5 para 4 (3.7.07).

General Note

This is the CTB equivalent of s134.

[¹ Reports

Persons to report on administration

139A.–[²(1) The Secretary of State may authorise persons to consider and report to him on the administration by authorities of housing benefit and council tax benefit.

(2) The Secretary of State may ask persons authorised under subsection (1) to consider in particular–

(a) authorities' performance in the prevention and detection of fraud relating to housing benefit and council tax benefit;

(b) authorities' compliance with the requirements of Part I of the Local Government Act 1999 (best value).

(2A) A person may be authorised under subsection (1)–

(a)　　on such terms and for such period as the Secretary of State thinks fit;

(b)　　to act generally or in relation to a specified authority or authorities;

(c)　　to report on administration generally or on specified matters.]

(3)　　In sections 139B and 139C below–

"benefit" means housing benefit or council tax benefit; and

"authority" means an authority which is administering either of those benefits.]

Amendments

1.　　Inserted by the SSA(F)A 1997 s5.

2.　　Substituted by the Local Government Act 1999 s14(1) (1.4.00).

General Note

This section and those that follow it were introduced from 1 July 1997 by the Social Security Administration (Fraud) Act 1997 following concern at the apparent unwillingness of some authorities to tackle fraud. They give the Secretary of State extensive powers over recalcitrant authorities and, ultimately, to require an authority's HB and CTB functions to be privatised.

This section gives the Secretary of State the power to appoint inspectors to examine the prevention of fraud and generally the administration of HB and CTB. The Secretary of State may also require the Audit Commission in England and Wales and the Accounts Commissioner in Scotland to conduct studies of how authorities are administering HB and CTB: Local Government Finance Act 1982 s28AB and Local Government (Scotland) Act 1973 ss97(4E), 101A and 105A, both inserted from 1 July 1997 by ss6 and 7 of the 1997 Act.

The section was amended by the Local Government Act 1999 to permit reports to consider whether the local authority is complying with the 'best value' provisions in Part I of the 1999 Act.

[¹Powers of investigation

139B.–(1) A person authorised under section 139A(1) above–

(a)　　has a right of access at all reasonable times to any document relating to the administration of benefit;

(b)　　is entitled to require from any person holding or accountable for any such document such information and explanation as he thinks necessary; and

(c)　　is entitled, if he thinks it necessary, to require any such person to produce any such document or to attend before him in person to give such information or explanation.

(2)　　A person authorised under section 139A(1) above is entitled to require any officer or member of an authority or any person involved in the administration of benefit for an authority–

(a)　　to give him such information and explanation relating to the administration of benefit as he thinks necessary; and

(b)　　if he thinks it necessary, to require any such person to attend before him in person to give the information or explanation.

(3)　　A person who without reasonable excuse fails to comply with a requirement under subsection (1) or (2) above is guilty of an offence and liable on summary conviction to a fine not exceeding level 3 on the standard scale.

(4)　　A person authorised under section 139A(1) above may–

(a)　　require any document or information which is to be given to him under subsection (1) or (2) above to be given in any form reasonably specified by him; and

(b)　　take copies of any document produced to him.

(5)　　In this section "document" means anything in which information of any description is recorded.]

Amendment

1.　　Inserted by SSA(F)A s5.

General Note

Extremely wide powers are given to the inspectors to look at documents, to require explanation of them under subs (1) and more generally to require information relating to benefit administration from local authority officials under subs (2). Such documents and information must be supplied in such form as the inspector requires and copies may be taken: subs (4). The definition of "document" in subs (5) will cover items such as computer data as well as paperwork.

[¹ Interaction with Audit Commission

139BA.–(1)   A person authorised under section 139A(1) must from time to time, or at such times as the Secretary of State may specify by order, prepare–

(a)   a document setting out what inspections of English authorities he proposes to carry out (an ''inspection programme'');

(b)   a document setting out the way in which he proposes to carry out his functions of inspecting and reporting on such authorities (an ''inspection framework'').

(2)   The person authorised under section 139A(1) must–

(a)   consult the Audit Commission before preparing an inspection programme or an inspection framework; and

(b)   once an inspection programme or inspection framework is prepared, send a copy of it to–

(i)   the Secretary of State; and

(ii)   the Audit Commission.

(3)   The Secretary of State may by order specify the form that inspection programmes or inspection frameworks must take.

(4)   A person authorised under section 139A(1)–

(a)   must co-operate with the Audit Commission, and

(b)   may act jointly with the Audit Commission,

where it is appropriate to do so for the efficient and effective discharge of the person's functions in relation to English authorities.

(5)   In this section–

''the Audit Commission'' means the Audit Commission for Local Authorities and the National Health Service in England;

''English authorities'' means authorities administering housing benefit or council tax benefit in England;

''person'' does not include the Audit Commission.]

Amendment
1.   Inserted by of the Local Government and Public Involvement in Health Act 2007 s150 (1.4.08).

Reports

[¹**139C.**–(1)   A report about an authority by a person authorised under section 139A(1) above may include recommendations about improvements which could be made by that authority in its administration of benefit and, [² in particular–

(a)   in the prevention and detection of fraud relating to benefit, or

(b)   for the purposes of complying with the requirements of Part I of the Local Government Act 1999 (best value).]

(2)   When the Secretary of State receives a report about an authority from a person authorised under section 139A(1) above, he shall send a copy to the authority.]

Amendments
1.   Inserted by SSA(F)A s5.
2.   Substituted by the Local Government Act 1999 s4(2) (1.4.00).

General Note
By subs (2), the authority under investigation is entitled to receive a copy of any report made by the inspectors.

[¹ Directions by Secretary of State

[¹ Directions

139D.–(1)   This section applies where–

(a)   a copy of a report has been sent to an authority under section 139C(2) above;

(b)   a copy of a report has been sent to an authority under [² section 10(1) of the Audit Commission Act 1998] and to the Secretary of State under [² section 39 of that Act];

[³ (ba) a copy of a report has been sent to an authority under section 22(5) or (6) of the Public Audit (Wales) Act 2004 and to the Secretary of State under section 51(3) of that Act;]

[⁵ (bb) a copy of a report has been sent to a local authority under subsection (3) of section 13 of the Local Government Act 1999 and to the Secretary of State under subsection (4A) of that section;]

[⁴ (c) a copy of a report under section 102(1)(b) or (c) of the Local Government (Scotland) Act 1973 which to any extent relates to the administration of benefit has been sent to a local authority and the Secretary of State under section 102(2) of that Act;]

[⁴ (ca) a copy of a report which has been sent to a local authority under section 13A(3) of the Local Government Act 1999 and to the Secretary of State under section 13A(4A) of that Act;]

    (d)   a copy of a report has been sent to an authority under [² section 38(7) of the Audit Commission Act 1998] or section 105A(7) of the Local Government (Scotland) Act 1973.

    (2)   The Secretary of State may [⁴ require] the authority to consider the report and to submit proposals for–

    (a)   improving its performance in relation to the prevention and detection of fraud relating to benefit or otherwise in relation to the administration of benefit; and

    (b)   remedying any failings identified by the report.

[⁴ (2A)   A requirement under subsection (2) above may specify–

    (a)   any information or description of information to be provided;

    (b)   the form and manner in which the information is to be provided.

    (2B)   The authority must respond to a requirement under subsection (2) above before the end of such period (not less than one month after the day on which the requirement is made) as the Secretary of State specifies in the requirement.

    (2C)   The Secretary of State may extend the period specified under subsection (2B) above.]

[⁴ (3)   After considering–

    (a)   the report,

    (b)   any proposals made by the authority in response to it, and

    (c)   any other information he thinks is relevant,

the Secretary of State may give directions to the authority under subsection (3A) or (3B) or both.

    (3A)   Directions under this subsection are directions as to–

    (a)   standards which the authority is to attain in the prevention and detection of fraud relating to benefit or otherwise in the administration of benefit;

    (b)   the time within which the standards are to be attained.

    (3B)   Directions under this subsection are directions to take such action as the Secretary of State thinks necessary or expedient for the purpose of improving the authority's exercise of its functions–

    (a)   in relation to the prevention and detection of fraud relating to benefit;

    (b)   otherwise in relation to the administration of benefit.

    (3C)   A direction under subsection (3B) may specify the time within which anything is to be done.]

    (4)   When giving directions to an authority under [⁴ subsection (3A)] above, the Secretary of State may make recommendations to the authority setting out any course of action which he thinks it might take to attain the standards which it is directed to attain.

[⁴ (4A)   If the Secretary of State proposes to give a direction under this section he must give the authority to which the direction is to be addressed an opportunity to make representations about the proposed direction.

    (4B)   The Secretary of State may specify a period within which representations mentioned in subsection (4A) above must be made.

    (4C)   The Secretary of State may extend a period specified under subsection (4B) above.

(4D)   Subsections (4A) to (4C) do not apply if the Secretary of State thinks that it is necessary for a direction to be given as a matter of urgency.

(4E)   If the Secretary of State acts under subsection (4D) he must give in writing to the authority to which the direction is addressed his reasons for doing so.]

(5)   In this section ''benefit'' means housing benefit or council tax benefit.

Amendments

1.   Inserted by SSA(F)A s8.
2.   Amended by the Audit Commission Act 1998 Sch 3 para 23.
3.   Amended by the Public Audit (Wales) Act 2004 s66 and Sch 2 para 15 (1.4.05).
4.   Amended by WRA s39 (1.4.08).
5.   Inserted by the Local Government and Public Involvement in Health Act 2007 s147(2) (1.4.08).

General Note

Section 139D is the initial stage of the four-part enforcement process by which the Secretary of State can compel improvements in the detection of fraud and administration of HB and CTB generally, where the performance of a local authority is thought to be unsatisfactory. It will follow a report by an inspector under s139C(2) or by the appropriate local government auditor: subs (1). This section and the three following it were introduced at the last moment in Committee.

The starting point in the process is for the Secretary of State to invite the authority's response to the report and suggest how it thinks matters could be improved. If the minister is not happy with the response, s/he may issue directions under subs (3) requiring improvements.

Analysis

Before directions are given, it is an essential part of the process for the Secretary of State to seek the authority's views under subs (2). If this step is omitted, it would seem that directions under subs (3) would be *ultra vires* as these can only be given by the Secretary of State "after considering ... any proposals made by the authority".

The Secretary of State may require an authority to reach a certain standard within a certain period of time. In determining this standard, the Secretary of State must act reasonably but has the widest discretion and it would have to be shown that the standards set are wholly irrational before they can be subject to any challenge. However, the structure of subs (3) suggests that the Secretary of State may only have regard to the contents of the report and the authority's response in considering whether to make a direction, and if so what direction to make. If, for example, a direction was made following a petition, then it seems that such a direction could be challenged on grounds of procedural impropriety.

[¹ Directions: variation and revocation

139DA.–(1)   The Secretary of State may at any time in accordance with this section vary or revoke a direction under section 139D above.

(2)   A direction may be varied or revoked only if the Secretary of State thinks it is necessary to do so–

(a)   in consequence of representations made by the authority to which the direction is addressed,

(b)   to rectify an omission or error, or

(c)   in consequence of a material change in circumstances.

(3)   The Secretary of State must not vary a direction unless he first–

(a)   sends a copy of the proposed variation to the authority concerned,

(b)   gives the authority his reasons for making the variation, and

(c)   gives the authority an opportunity to make representations about the proposed variation.

(4)   The Secretary of State may specify a period of not less than one month within which representations mentioned in subsection (3)(c) above must be made.

(5)   The Secretary of State may extend a period specified under subsection (4) above.

Amendment

1.   Inserted by s39(9) WRA 2007 with effect from 1.04.08.

Information about attainment of standards

[¹**139E.**–(1)   Where directions have been given to an authority under [² section 139D(3A) or (3B)] above, the Secretary of State may require the authority to supply to him any information which he considers may assist him in deciding–

(a)   whether the authority has attained the standards which it has been directed to attain; or

[² (aa) whether the authority has taken the action which it has been directed to take;]

(b)   whether the authority is likely to attain those standards [² or take that action] within the time specified in the directions.

(2)   Information shall be supplied under subsection (1) above in such manner and form as the Secretary of State may require.]

Amendments
1.   Inserted by SSA(F)A s9.
2.   Amended by WRA s40 and Sch 5 para 5 (1.04.08).

General Note
This is the second part of the enforcement process. It enables the Secretary of State to monitor the progress of the authority by requiring information to be supplied to her/him.

Enforcement notices

[¹**139F.**–(1)   Where directions have been given to an authority under [² section 139D(3A) or (3B)] above and the Secretary of State–

(a)   is not satisfied that the authority has attained the standards which it has been directed to attain; or

[² (aa) is not satisfied that the authority has taken the action which it has been directed to take;]

(b)   is not satisfied that the authority is likely to attain those standards [² or take that action] within the time specified in the directions,

he may serve on the authority a written notice under this section.

(2)   The notice shall–

(a)   identify the directions and state why the Secretary of State is not satisfied as mentioned in paragraph (a) [² , (aa)] or (b) of subsection (1) above; and

(b)   require the authority to submit a written response to the Secretary of State within a time specified in the notice.

(3)   If any person (other than the authority) carrying out work relating to the administration of benefit may be affected by any determination which may be made under section 139G below, the authority shall–

(a)   consult that person before submitting its response; and

(b)   include in its response any relevant observations made by that person.

(4)   [² If the notice identifies directions under section 139D(3A),] The authority's response shall either–

(a)   state that the authority has attained the standards, or is likely to attain them within the time specified in the directions, and justify that statement; or

(b)   state that the authority has not attained the standards, or is not likely to attain them within that time, and (if the authority wishes) give reasons why a determination under section 139G below should not be made or should not include any particular provision.

[² (4A)   If the notice identifies directions under section 139D(3B), the authority's response shall either–

(a)   state that the authority has taken the action, or is likely to take it within the time specified in the directions, and justify that statement; or

(b)   state that the authority has not taken the action, or is not likely to take it within that time, and (if the authority wishes) give reasons why a determination under section 139G below should not be made or should not include any particular provision.]

(5)   The notice may relate to any one or more matters covered by the directions.

(6)   The serving of a notice under this section relating to any directions or matter does not prevent the serving of further notices under this section relating to the same directions or matter.

(7)   In this section ''benefit'' means housing benefit or council tax benefit.]

Amendments
1. Inserted by SSA(F)A s9.
2. Amended by WHA s40 and Sch 5 para 6 (1.04.08).

General Note
If it becomes clear to the Secretary of State that an authority has not taken action, or is unlikely to take action, it has been directed to take or has not attained, or is not going to attain, the standards set by a direction under s139D(3A) or (3B), an enforcement notice may be served on the authority. A notice may be served before the expiry of any time limit specified in the direction: subs (1)(b). The notice must state, under subs (2)(a), the reasons for the Secretary of State's dissatisfaction.

The local authority is required to respond to the notice and state whether it has, or is going to be able to comply with the direction: subs (4) and (4A). Before it does so, it must consult those involved in the administration of benefit and incorporate their views in its response.

Subs (5) and (6) loosen possible restrictions on the Secretary of State's power to issue enforcement notices. Under subs (5), a notice may relate to particular matters identified in the direction, rather than the whole direction. More than one notice may be served in relation to a direction, and subs (6) confirms that subsequent notices may deal with the same matters as previous notices.

Analysis
"... any person (other than the authority) carrying out work relating to the administration of benefit....".
On a wide reading, this might include the administrative staff employed by the local authority as well as people or business organisations outside the authority carrying out functions relating to the administration of HB and CTB.

Enforcement determinations

[[1]**139G.**–(1) Where, after the time specified in the notice under section 139F above has expired, the Secretary of State–
(a) is not satisfied that the authority has attained the standards [[2] or taken the action] in question; or
(b) is not satisfied that the authority is likely to attain those standards [[2] or take that action] within the time specified in the directions, he may make a determination under this section.
(2) The determination may be made whether or not the authority has responded to the notice under section 139F above.
(3) The determination shall be designed to secure the attainment of the standards [[2] or the taking of the action] in question and–
(a) shall include provision such as is specified in subsection (4) below; and
(b) may also include provision such as is specified in subsection (5) below.
(4) The provision referred to in paragraph (a) of subsection (3) above is provision that the authority must comply with specified requirements as to inviting, preparing, considering and accepting bids to carry out any work which–
(a) falls to be carried out in pursuance of the authority's functions relating to the administration of benefit; and
(b) is of a description specified in the determination.
(5) The provision referred to in paragraph (b) of that subsection is provision of any one or more of the following kinds relating to the work, or any specified category of the work, to which the determination relates–
(a) provision that it may not be carried out by the authority;
(b) provision that it may not be carried out by any person (other than the authority) who has been carrying it out; and
(c) provision that any contract made by the authority with any person for carrying it out shall include terms requiring a level of performance which will secure, or contribute to securing, the attainment of the standards [[2] or the taking of the action] in question.
(6) In this section ''benefit'' means housing benefit or council tax benefit.]

Amendments
1. Inserted by SSA(F)A s9.
2. Amended by WRA s40 and Sch 5 para 7 (1.04.08).

General Note

The final step in the procedure is an enforcement determination. By this draconian step, the Secretary of State is able to require an authority to put its administration of HB and CTB, or any part thereof, out to tender: subs (4).

The Secretary of State may also impose further conditions under subs (5). The authority may be forbidden to carry out the work itself, a person who has been carrying out the work (see s139F) may be excluded, and the authority may be required to specify attainment of the standards as conditions of the contract awarded. See also s139H(3).

Enforcement determinations: supplementary

[¹**139H.**–(1)   The provisions included in a determination under section 139G above shall take effect from a date specified in the determination; and different dates may be specified in relation to different provisions.

(2)   The making of a determination under section 139G above in relation to any directions does not prevent the making of further determinations under that section in relation to the same directions.

(3)   The provision included in a determination by virtue of section 139G(3) above may include–

(a)   requirements that the Secretary of State be satisfied as to any specified matter; and

(b)   requirements that the Secretary of State authorise or consent to any specified matter.

(4)   The provision so included may also include provision as to the time at which any contract for the carrying out of work to which the determination relates (and which is not previously discharged) is to be taken to be frustrated by the determination.

(5)   A determination under section 139G above shall have effect in spite of any enactment under or by virtue of which an authority is required or authorised to carry out any work to which the determination relates.

(6)   A determination under section 139G above may make provision having effect, in relation to the work to which it relates, instead of any requirement which (apart from the determination) would have effect in relation to that work under or by virtue of the Local Government Act 1988.]

Amendment

1.   Inserted by SSA(F)A s9 .

General Note

This section makes a number of additional provisions in relation to enforcement determinations. By subs (1), time limits may be set for the determination to come into effect. More than one determination may be made in relation to a direction: subs (2). Subs (5) and (6) make it clear that the determination overrides any statutory provision requiring the authority to carry out the work in question and the requirements of the Local Government Act 1988 in relation to compulsory competitive tendering.

Finally, subs (3) allows the Secretary of State to control virtually any aspect of the tendering process or the work carried out pursuant to an enforcement direction.

[¹ Subsidy

Subsidy

140A.–(1)   For each year the Secretary of State shall pay a subsidy to each authority administering housing benefit or council tax benefit.

(2)   He shall pay–

(a)   rent rebate subsidy to each housing authority;

(b)   rent allowance subsidy to each local authority; and

(c)   council tax benefit subsidy to each billing authority or levying authority.

(3)   In the following provisions of this Part ''subsidy'', without more, refers to subsidy of any of those descriptions.]

Amendment

1.   Inserted by the Housing Act 1996 Sch 12 para 4.

General Note
ss140A to 140G deal with the subsidy arrangements in respect of HB and CTB.

[¹Calculation of amount of subsidy

140B.–(1)   The amount of subsidy to be paid to an authority [⁴ determined in accordance with an] order made by the Secretary of State.

(2)   Subject as follows, the amount of subsidy shall be calculated by reference to the amount of relevant benefit paid by the authority during the year.
[³]

(3)   The order may provide that the amount of subsidy in respect of any matter shall be a fixed sum or shall be nil.

[² (4)   The Secretary of State may–
(a)   pay as part of subsidy an additional amount specified by, or calculated in a manner specified by, the order; or
(b)   deduct from the amount which would otherwise be payable by way of subsidy an amount specified by, or calculated in a manner specified by, the order.

(4A)   The additional amounts which may be paid by virtue of subsection (4)(a) above include amounts in respect of–
(a)   the costs of administering the relevant benefit; or
(b)   success in preventing or detecting fraud relating to the relevant benefit or action to be taken with a view to preventing or detecting such fraud.

(5)   The Secretary of State may–
(a)   where an application is made by an authority on his invitation, pay to the authority as part of the subsidy such additional amount as he considers appropriate in respect of–
(i)   success in preventing or detecting fraud relating to the relevant benefit; or
(ii)   action to be taken with a view to preventing or detecting such fraud; or
(b)   deduct from the subsidy which would otherwise be payable to an authority such amount as he considers it unreasonable to pay by way of subsidy.

(5A)   The amounts which may be deducted by virtue of subsection (4)(b) or (5)(b) above include amounts in respect of–
(a)   a failure to comply with directions under [⁵ section 139D(3A) or (3B)] above; and
(b)   other failures in preventing or detecting fraud relating to the relevant benefit.]
Any such additional amount shall be a fixed sum specified by, or shall be calculated in the manner specified by, an order made by the Secretary of State.

(6)   In this section ''relevant benefit'' means housing benefit or council tax benefit, as the case may be.
[³ (7)]

Amendments
1.   Inserted by the Housing Act 1996 Sch 12 para 4.
2.   Substituted by SSA(F)A s10.
3.   Omitted/repealed by the Local Government Act 2003, s127(1) and Sch 7 para 36 and s127(2) and Part 1 Sch 8 (18.11.03).
4.   Amended by SSA(F)A Sch 1 para 7 (1.7.97).
5.   Amended by WRA s40 and Sch 5 para 9 (1.04.08).

General Note
Subsection (3) permits any element of a subsidy calculation to be made on a fixed basis or to be nil.
     The subsidy scheme gives greater powers to the Secretary of State to determine the amount of subsidy paid to relevant authorities, and in particular to reward success and punish failure regarding the prevention of fraud by giving extra subsidy or reducing it.

Analysis
   Subs (5). The Secretary of State does not have to seek the approval of Parliament prior to making deductions from the amounts of subsidy under her/his powers. The analysis in *R v Secretary of State for the Environment ex p Hammersmith and Fulham LBC* [1991] 1 AC 521 at 597E-H, HL will not therefore apply and an order made by the Secretary of State can be subject to challenge on the grounds of unreasonableness. In particular, it is

suggested that there can be no deduction from the subsidy unless the Secretary of State has some form of reliable evidence to justify such an approach, whether it be on the ground that the normal amount would be "unreasonable" under subs (4)(b) or that there have been failures in preventing fraud under subs (5A)(b). It was said that the power was a "last resort": Alistair Burt MP, Standing Committee E, 14 January 1997, col 243.

Subs (5A). Note that the power to reduce subsidy is not limited to the two factors mentioned, they are merely "included" in the circumstances that can justify a reduction.

[¹Payment of subsidy

140C.–(1)   Subsidy shall be paid by the Secretary of State in such instalments, at such times, in such manner and subject to such conditions as to claims, records, certificates, audit or otherwise as may be provided by order of the Secretary of State.

[² (1A)   Conditions under subsection (1) above may (in particular) be imposed to obtain information for the purposes of the carrying-out by the Secretary of State of any of his functions relating to subsidy.]

(2)   The order may provide that if an authority has not, within such period as may be specified in the order, complied with the conditions so specified as to claims, records, certificate, audit or otherwise, the Secretary of State may estimate the amount of subsidy payable to the authority and employ for that purpose such criteria as he considers relevant.

(3)   Where subsidy has been paid to an authority and it appears to the Secretary of State–

(a)   that subsidy has been overpaid; or

(b)   that there has been a breach of any condition specified in an order under this section, he may recover from the authority the whole or such part of the payment as he may determine.

Without prejudice to other methods of recovery, a sum recoverable under this subsection may be recovered by withholding or reducing subsidy.

(4)   An order made by the Secretary of State under this section may be made before, during or after the end of the year or years to which it relates.]

Amendments

1.   Inserted by the Housing Act 1996 Sch 12 para 4 .

2.   Inserted by the Local Government Act 2003 s127(1) and Sch 7 para 37 (18.11.03).

General Note

This deals with the calculation of subsidy and recovery of payments of subsidy which have either been overpaid or where there has been a breach of any condition.

Analysis

Subs (1) and (2). The Secretary of State may require the maintenance and production of records by the authority in order to calculate its subsidy and carry out estimates in default.

Subs (3)(a) expands the powers for rectifying errors in the payment of subsidy. Hitherto, the statutory powers were restricted to adjusting the following year's subsidy to rectify the error: s137(6). Now the Secretary of State may require immediate repayment.

Subs (3)(b) appears to allow the Secretary of State a general discretion to recover part or the whole of a subsidy payment where an authority has failed to comply with requirements made under subs (1).

It is suggested, however, that this power cannot be exercised in a penal manner. Under subs (2), if it had been clear from the outset that the authority had failed to comply with the requirements, the Secretary of State would have had to estimate the amount of subsidy. Such method of estimation as was chosen would have to be rational and reasonable. It is not logical that the authority should be in a worse position if the failure only comes to light at a later stage. It is therefore suggested that subs (3)(b) does not allow the Secretary of State to recover so much of the subsidy that the authority has effectively received a lesser amount of subsidy than it would have received under an estimate carried out pursuant to subs (2).

This issue was to be considered in judicial review proceedings brought by Bridgnorth DC. That council had failed to implement a new version of reg 11 HB Regs 1987 properly, with the result that a large number of claims were determined without a proper reference from a rent officer. The Secretary of State decided to recover the full amount of subsidy paid in the relevant years, even though many of the claims must have been assessed correctly or even underpaid. This would have had dire consequences for the council. In its application for judicial review, the council argued that recovery of all the subsidy was disproportionate. The proceedings were settled with an agreed quashing of the decision to recover, the Secretary of State acknowledging flaws in the decision-making process and agreeing not to recover any of the subsidy.

Following a review of the Secretary of State's approach to this power, a new policy was set out in Circular S1/2002. The recovery of each overpayment of subsidy will depend on all the circumstances, and criteria are set out which will be taken into account. The implementation of the policy was challenged in *H (Isle of Anglesey DC) v SSWP* [2003] , EWHC 2518 (Admin). The applicant local authority had made similar mistakes to Bridgnorth DC in its administration, and the Secretary of State proposed to recover 20 per cent of the subsidy paid to the council in respect of the claims that had not been properly administered. Lindsay J rejected the suggestion that Sch 4 para 6 Income-Related Benefits (Subsidy to Authorities) Order 1998, which awards nil subsidy where a claim has not been referred to the Rent Officer, was *ultra vires* (para 40) and also held that the decision of the Secretary of State on the particular facts of the case could not be castigated as penal, disproportionate or irrational.

[¹Rent rebate subsidy: accounting provisions

140D.–(1)   Rent rebate subsidy is payable–
(a)   in the case of a local authority in England and Wales, for the credit of a revenue account of theirs other than their Housing Revenue Account or Housing Repairs Account;
(b)   in the case of a local authority in Scotland, for the credit of their rent rebate account;
[² (c)]
(d)   in the case of a new town corporation in Scotland or Scottish Homes, for the credit of the account to which rent rebates granted by them, or it, are debited.
[² (2)]]

Amendments
1.   Inserted by Housing Act 1996 Sch 12 para 4.
2.   Omitted/repealed by the Local Government Act 2003, s127(1) and Sch 7 para 38 and s127(2) and Part 1 Sch 8 (18.11.03).

[¹ Supplementary provisions

Financing of joint arrangements

140E.–(1)   Where two or more authorities make arrangements for the discharge of any of their functions relating to housing benefit or council tax benefit–
(a)   by one authority on behalf of itself and one or more other authorities; or
(b)   by a joint committee,
the Secretary of State may make such payments as he thinks fit to the authority or committee in respect of their expenses in carrying out those functions.
(2)   The provisions of sections 140B and 140C (subsidy: calculation and supplementary provisions) apply in relation to a payment under this section as in relation to a payment of subsidy.
(3)   The Secretary of State may (without prejudice to the generality of his powers in relation to the amount of subsidy) take into account the fact that an amount has been paid under this section in respect of expenses which would otherwise have been met in whole or in part by the participating authorities.}

Amendment
1.   Inserted by the Housing Act 1996 Sch 12 para 4.

[¹No requirement for annual orders

140F.–(1)   Any power under this Part to make provision by order for or in relation to a year does not require the making of a new order each year.
(2)   Any order made under the power may be revoked or varied at any time, whether before, during or after the year to which it relates.]

Amendment
1.   Inserted by the Housing Act 1996 Sch 12 para 4.

[¹Interpretation: Part VIII

140G.   In this Part, unless the context otherwise requires–
''Housing Repairs Account'' means an account kept under section 77 of the Local Government and Housing Act 1989;

"Housing Revenue Account" means the account kept under section 74 of the Local Government and Housing Act 1989, and–
  (a)   references to property within that account have the same meaning as in Part VI of that Act, [²]
[² (b)]
"rent rebate subsidy" and "rent allowance subsidy" shall be construed in accordance with section 134 above;
"year" means a financial year within the meaning of the Local Government Finance Act 1992.]

Amendments
  1.   Inserted by the Housing Act 1996 s4.
  2.   Omitted/repealed by the Local Government Act 2003, s127(1) and Sch 7 para 39 and s127(2) and Part 1 Sch 8 (18.11.03).

PART XIII
Advisory Bodies and Consultation
The Social Security Advisory Committee and the Industrial Injuries Advisory Council

General Note
The Social Security Advisory Committee (SSAC) is a body of experts, working on a voluntary basis, which advises the Secretary of State as to the implications of new legislation to be enacted. It serves a valuable function of bringing potential problems with proposals to the attention of officials of the DWP and in speaking with an authoritative voice in doing so. Historically, however, the SSAC has only rarely persuaded the DWP to drop controversial proposals or modify them significantly, although there are exceptions such as the backdating restrictions which were due to replace the "good cause" test in reg 72(15) HB Regs 1987 and which were withdrawn by the DWP mainly as a result of the SSAC's carefully reasoned opposition.

The process by which regulations are dealt with by the SSAC is that the Secretary of State first sends draft proposals to it. The Committee then decides whether or not the proposed regulations should be referred to it under s173(1)(b) and, if it concludes that they should be, consults the public if necessary and then produces a report under s174(1). When the regulations are laid, the Secretary of State is required to place a copy of the SSAC's report and the DWP's response before Parliament.

Certain categories of regulations are not required to be referred to the SSAC by virtue of s172(3). The categories are set out in Sch 7 SSAA, which is not reproduced in this book. The categories that are relevant to HB and CTB are uprating regulations (para 3), tribunal rules (para 9) in respect of which the Secretary of State is supposed to consult the Administrative Justice and Tribunals Council, and consolidating regulations (para 10). In addition, s173(1) does not require the Secretary of State to refer regulations where "urgency" makes it "inexpedient" (see the commentary to s176) or the SSAC decides that it is unnecessary.

The SSAC seeks the views of the public on major regulations referred to it and details of current consultations can be found at www.ssac.org.uk.

The significance of the SSAC for the purposes of advisers has increased as a result of the decision in *Howker v SSWP* [2003] ICR 405 (reported as *R(IB) 3/03*). In that decision, the Court of Appeal held that amendments to the regulations governing incapacity benefit were *ultra vires* because officials of the DWP had misled the SSAC as to the effect of the amending regulations, with the consequence that the SSAC did not ask for the amending regulations to be referred. It need not be shown that the misleading advice was given deliberately: para 37.

It is necessary to consider the significance of the advice: para 40, or to show that it was "seriously inaccurate": para 54. The correct approach to determining whether the SSAC was misled is to look at all the material placed before the SSAC by the Secretary of State as the basis for the amendment (including answers given by DWP officials to the SSAC) and consider whether the overall effect was misleading; and, if it was, whether there is a real possibility that (a) the information might have misled the SSAC as to the effect of the proposed regulation, and (b) had the SSAC been aware of the regulations true effect it would have wished to have the proposed regulation formally referred to it: *R(IB) 2/07*.

In *CH 5125/2002*, a challenge was made to the 1998 amendments to reg 7 HB Regs 1987 on the basis that the SSAC had been misled. Commissioner Jacobs rejected the challenge (paras 68-69), holding that the adverse effect of the amendments had been made clear.

The Court of Appeal in *Campbell and others v South Northamptonshire District Council and SSWP* [2004] EWCA Civ 409 *The Times* 6 May, CA (reported as *R(H) 8/04*) – the appeal from *CH 5125/2002* – rejected the appeal and endorsed Commissioner Jacob's view that, as a whole, the adverse affects of the amendment regulations had been made clear to the SSAC and so it could not be said to have been misled.

The Social Security Advisory Committee

170.–(1)   The Social Security Advisory Committee (in this Act referred to as "the Committee") constituted under section 9 of the Social Security Act 1980 shall continue in being by that name–

(a)   to give (whether in pursuance of a reference under this Act or otherwise) advice and assistance to the Secretary of State in connection with the discharge of his functions under the relevant enactments;

(b)   to give (whether in pursuance of a reference under this Act or otherwise) advice and assistance to the Northern Ireland Department in connection with the discharge of its functions under the relevant Northern Ireland enactments; and

(c)   to perform such other duties as may be assigned to the Committee under any enactment.

(2)   Schedule 5 to this Act shall have effect with respect to the constitution of the Committee and the other matters there mentioned.

(3)   The Secretary of State may from time to time refer to the Committee for consideration and advice such questions relating to the operation of any of the relevant enactments as he thinks fit (including questions as to the advisability of amending any of them).

(4)   The Secretary of State shall furnish the Committee with such information as the Committee may reasonably require for the proper discharge of its functions.

(5)   In this Act–

"the relevant enactments" means–

(a)   the provisions of the Contributions and Benefits Act and this Act, except as they apply to industrial injuries benefit and Old Cases payments; and

(aa)-(ab) *[Omitted]*

[⁴ (ac) the provisions of the Social Security (Recovery of Benefits) Act 1997; and]

(ad)-(ae) *[Omitted]*

[¹ (af)   section 42, [⁷] and sections 68 to 70 of the Child Support, Pensions and Social Security Act 2000, and Schedule 7 to that Act.]

[² (ag) [⁶ sections 6A to 11] of the Social Security Fraud Act 2001.]

[³ (ah) the provisions of the State Pension Credit Act 2002.]

(ai)-(aia) *[Omitted]*

[⁵ (aj) sections 32 and 33 of the Welfare Reform Act 2007;]

(b)   *[Omitted]*

Amendments

1.   Inserted by CSPSSA s73 (1.12.00).
2.   Inserted by SSFA s12(3) (1.4.02).
3.   Inserted by SPCA Sch 2 para 12 (6.10.03).
4.   Inserted by the Social Security (Recovery of Benefits Act 1997) Sch 3 para 8 (6.10.97).
5.   Inserted by WRA s33(7) (1.4.08 for making regulations and 6.10.08).
6.   Amended by WRA 2009 s24 and Sch 4 para 9 (12.1.10 for making regulations and 1.4.10).
7.   Amended by WRA 2009 s58 and Sch 7 (22.3.10).

Functions of Committee and Council in relation to regulations

172.–(1)   Subject–

(a)   to subsection (3) below; and

(b)   to section 173 below,

where the Secretary of State proposes to make regulations under any of the relevant enactments, he shall refer the proposals, in the form of draft regulations or otherwise, to the Committee.

(2)   *[Omitted]*

(3)   Subsection (1) above does not apply to the regulations specified in Part I of Schedule 7 to this Act.

(4)-(5)   *[Omitted]*

Cases in which consultation is not required

173.–(1) Nothing in any enactment shall require any proposals in respect of regulations to be referred to the Committee or the Council if–

  (a)   it appears to the Secretary of State that by reason of the urgency of the matter it is inexpedient so to refer them; or

  (b)   the relevant advisory body have agreed that they shall not be referred.

(2)   Where by virtue only of subsection (1)(a) above the Secretary of State makes regulations without proposals in respect of them having been referred, then, unless the relevant advisory body agrees that this subsection shall not apply, he shall refer the regulations to that body as soon as practicable after making them.

(3)   Where the Secretary of State has referred proposals to the Committee or the Council, he may make the proposed regulations before the Committee have made their report or, as the case may be the Council have given their advice, only if after the reference it appears to him that by reason of the urgency of the matter it is expedient to do so.

(4)   Where by virtue of this section regulations are made before a report of the Committee has been made, the Committee shall consider them and make a report to the Secretary of State containing such recommendations with regard to the regulations as the Committee thinks appropriate; and a copy of any report made to the Secretary of State on the regulations shall be laid by him before each House of Parliament together, if the report contains recommendations, with a statement–

  (a)   of the extent (if any) to which the Secretary of State proposes to give effect to the recommendations; and

  (b)   in so far as he does not propose to give effect to them, of his reasons why not.

(5)   Except to the extent that this subsection is excluded by an enactment passed after 25th July 1986, nothing in any enactment shall require the reference to the Committee or the Council of any regulations contained in either–

  (a)   a statutory instrument made before the end of the period of 6 months beginning with the coming into force of the enactment under which those regulations are made; or

  (b)   a statutory instrument–

    (i)   which states that it contains only regulations made by virtue of, or consequential upon, a specified enactment; and

    (ii)   which is made before the end of the period of 6 months beginning with the coming into force of that specified enactment.

(6)   In relation to regulations required or authorised to be made by the Secretary of State in conjunction with the Treasury, any reference in this section to the Secretary of State shall be construed as a reference to the Secretary of State and the Treasury.

(7)   In this section ''regulations'' means regulations under any enactment, whenever passed.

Committee's report on regulations and Secretary of State's duties

174.–(1) The Committee shall consider any proposals referred to it by the Secretary of State under section 172 above and shall make to the Secretary of State a report containing such recommendations with regard to the subject-matter of the proposals as the Committee thinks appropriate.

(2)   If after receiving a report of the Committee the Secretary of State lays before Parliament any regulations or draft regulations which comprise the whole or any part of the subject-matter of the proposals referred to the Committee, he shall lay with the regulations or draft regulations a copy of the Committee's report and a statement showing–

  (a)   the extent (if any) to which he has, in framing the regulations, given effect to the Committee's recommendations; and

  (b)   in so far as effect has not been given to them, his reasons why not.

(3)   In the case of any regulations laid before Parliament at a time when Parliament is not sitting, the requirements of subsection (2) above shall be satisfied as respects either House of Parliament if a copy of the report and statement there referred to are laid before

that House not later than the second day on which the House sits after the laying of the regulations.

(4) In relation to regulations required or authorised to be made by the Secretary of State in conjunction with the Treasury any reference in this section to the Secretary of State shall be construed as a reference to the Secretary of State and the Treasury.

Housing benefit and council tax benefit

Consultation with representative organisations

176.–(1) Subject to subsection (2) below, before making–

(a) regulations relating to housing benefit or [¹ council tax benefit] (other than regulations of which the effect is to increase any amount specified in regulations previously made);

[³(aa) regulations under section 69 of the Child Support, Pensions and Social Security Act 2000]

(b) an order under [² any provision of Part VIII above.]

the Secretary of State shall consult with organisations appearing to him to be representative of the authorities concerned.

(2) Nothing in subsection (1) above shall require the Secretary of State to undertake consultations if–

(a) it appears to him that by reason of the urgency of the matter it is inexpedient to do so; or

(b) the organisations have agreed that consultations should not be undertaken.

(3) Where the Secretary of State has undertaken such consultations, he may make any regulations or order to which the consultations relate without completing the consultations if it appears to him that by reason of the urgency of the matter it is expedient to do so.

Amendments

1.   Substitution made by the Local Government Finance Act 1992 para 23 Sch 9 (1.4.93).
2.   Amended by the Housing Act 1996 Sch 13 para 3(4) (1.4.97).
3.   Inserted by CSPSSA s69(6) (2.7.01).

Analysis

The Secretary of State invoked the predecessor to para (2)(a) as the reason for not consulting with the local authority associations when the Housing Benefit (General) Amendment Regulations 1992 SI No.201 were introduced. Those regulations followed the introduction by the London Borough of Hackney of a scheme whereby council tenants with rent arrears would be liable to a higher rent rise than those who were not. The amending regulations were aimed at ensuring that HB would not be paid with regard to the rent arrears supplement: see the Analysis of reg 11(3) HB Regs on p300.

In *R v Secretary of State for Social Security ex p Association of Metropolitan Authoroties* [1992] 25 HLR 131, QBD, Tucker J found that in relation to the making of the regulations the Secretary of State could not invoke the exemption (then s61(8)(a) Social Security Act 1986) by leaving a decision until the last moment and thus himself creating the emergency.

PART XV
Miscellaneous

[¹Return of social security post

182A.–(1) A social security authority may require–

(a) the Post Office; or

(b) any other person who conveys postal packets,

to return to the sender social security post sent by or on behalf of the authority which would otherwise be redirected.

(2) A social security authority shall make payments of such amount as the Secretary of State considers reasonable in respect of the return of social security post in compliance with a requirement imposed by the authority under subsection (1) above.

(3) In subsections (1) and (2) above ''social security authority'' means–

(a)   the Secretary of State;
(b)   the Northern Ireland Department; or
(c)   any local or other authority administering housing benefit or council tax benefit (including the Northern Ireland Housing Executive).
(4)   In subsections (1) and (2) above "social security post" means postal packets–
(a)   the contents of which relate to any benefit, contributions or national insurance number or to any other matter relating to social security; and
(b)   which are marked, in a manner approved by the Post Office or other person conveying them, with the name and address of the sender and with an indication that they are to be returned rather than redirected.
(5)   In this section–
(a)   "redirected", in relation to any postal packet, means delivered to an address other than that indicated by the sender on the packet; and
(b)   "postal packet" has the same meaning as in the Post Office Act 1953.
(6)   Any requirement imposed under subsection (1) above has effect subject to any order under–
(a)   section 371 of the Insolvency Act 1986 or Article 342 of the Insolvency (Northern Ireland) Order 1989 (redirection of bankrupt's letters to trustee in bankruptcy);
(b)   paragraph 10 of Schedule 1 to the Solicitors Act 1974 or paragraph 15 of Schedule 1 to the Solicitors (Northern Ireland) Order 1976 (redirection of letters following intervention by Law Society); or
(c)   paragraph 10 of Schedule 5 to the Administration of Justice Act 1985 (redirection of letters following intervention by Council for Licensed Conveyancers).]

Amendment
1.   Inserted by SSA(F)A s20 (27.3.99).

General Note
Prior to the insertion of s182A, with the aim of preventing fraud, many local authorities had adopted the practice of marking envelopes containing HB giros "Do Not Redirect", but the Post Office generally disregarded such instructions, taking the view that without specific authority not to do so, it was obliged to obey directions from an addressee to redirect mail.
    Subs (1) allows a "social security authority" to require return of mail which would be redirected. "Social security authority" includes a local authority: subs (3)(c). The requirement is imposed simply by indicating the requirement on the envelope: subs (4). The authority can be required by the Secretary of State to pay a fee for this service: subs (2).
    Subs (6) makes the scheme subject to certain other statutory schemes requiring mail to be redirected.

[¹Requirement to supply information about redirection of post
182B.–(1)   The Secretary of State or the Northern Ireland Department may require the Post Office or any other person who conveys postal packets to supply information relating to arrangements for the redirection of postal packets to, or to a person supplying services to, the Secretary of State or the Department–
(a)   for use in the prevention, detection, investigation or prosecution of offences relating to social security; or
(b)   for use in checking the accuracy of information relating to benefits, contributions or national insurance numbers or to any other matter relating to social security and (where appropriate) amending or supplementing such information.
(2)   A local or other authority administering housing benefit or council tax benefit (including the Northern Ireland Housing Executive) may require the Post Office or any other person who conveys postal packets to supply information relating to arrangements for the redirection of postal packets to the authority or a person authorised to exercise any function of the authority relating to housing benefit or council tax benefit–
(a)   for use in the prevention, detection, investigation or prosecution of offences relating to such a benefit; or
(b)   for use in checking the accuracy of information relating to such a benefit and (where appropriate) amending or supplementing such information.

(3)   Information shall be supplied under subsection (1) or (2) above in such manner and form, and in accordance with such requirements, as may be prescribed.

(4)   Payments of such amount as the Secretary of State considers reasonable shall be made by a person or authority imposing a requirement under subsection (1) or (2) above in respect of the supply of information in compliance with the requirement.

(5)   Information supplied under subsection (1) or (2) above shall not be supplied by the recipient to any other person or body unless–

(a)   it could be supplied to that person or body under either of those subsections; or

(b)   it is supplied for the purposes of any civil or criminal proceedings relating to the Contributions and Benefits Act, the Jobseekers Act 1995 or this Act or to any provision of Northern Ireland legislation corresponding to any of them.

(6)   But where information supplied under subsection (1) or (2) above has been used (in accordance with paragraph (b) of the subsection concerned) in amending or supplementing other information, it is lawful for it to be–

(a)   supplied to any person or body to whom that other information could be supplied; or

(b)   used for any purpose for which that other information could be used.

(7)   In subsections (1) and (2) above ''arrangements for the redirection of postal packets'' means arrangements made with the Post Office or other person conveying postal packets for the delivery of postal packets to addresses other than those indicated by senders on the packets.

(8)   In this section ''postal packet'' has the same meaning as in the Post Office Act 1953.]

Amendment

1.   Inserted by SSA(F)A s21 (27.3.99).

General Note

This section requires the Post Office to gather information about the redirection of mail and supply it to social security authorities at their request. It is similar in form to the provisions requiring and enabling the supply of information from one authority to another: see Part VII. A charge may be imposed for this service: subs (4).

    Subs (2) is in similar form to s122C(3), discussed in the General Note to s122C (on p71). Similarly, for discussion of the wording of subs (6), see the General Note to s122E as it relates to s122E(5) (on p73). Under subs (5) and (6), if the authority wishes to supply the information received to the Secretary of State or another authority, it must satisfy itself that the recipient would be entitled to receive the information under subs (1) or (2), or that it is being supplied for the purpose of civil or criminal proceedings under the social security legislation. Thus this provision could not, it appears, be used to justify the passing of information where a person is being prosecuted under the Theft Act 1968. See also Sch 8 para 34 WRPA (on p1128).

Certain benefit to be inalienable

187.–(1)   Subject to the provisions of this Act, every assignment of or charge on–

(a)   benefit as defined in section 122 of the Contributions and Benefits Act;

[¹ (ab) state pension credit;]

[² (ac) an employment and support allowance;]

(b)   ⁚ any income-related benefit; or

(c)   ⁚child benefit,

⁚⁚ and every agreement to assign or charge such benefit shall be void; and, on the bankruptcy of a beneficiary, such benefit shall not pass to any trustee or other person acting on behalf of his creditors.

(2)   In the application of subsection (1) above to Scotland–

(a)   the reference to assignment of benefit shall be read as a reference to assignation, ''assign'' being construed accordingly;

(b)   the reference to a beneficiary's bankruptcy shall be read as a reference to the sequestration of his estate or the appointment on his estate of a judicial factor under section 41 of the Solicitors (Scotland) Act 1980.

(3)   [. . .]

Amendments
1. Inserted by SPCA Sch 2 para 23 (commenced October 2003).
2. Inserted by WRA s28 and Sch 3 para 10(31) (27.10.08).

General Note
This provision prevents any assignment of a right to benefit by agreement or by operation of law. It does not prevent recovery of an overpayment by the Secretary of State (or a local authority) after the claimant has been made bankrupt: *Mulvey v Secretary of State for Social Security* [1997] SLT 753 at 756, HL. See further the Analysis to reg 102 HB Regs (p491).

PART XVI
General
Subordinate legislation

Regulations and orders – general

189.–(1) Subject to [⁷] any [⁵ . . .] express provision of this Act, regulations and orders under this Act shall be made by the Secretary of State.

[⁷ (2)]

(3) Powers under this Act to make regulations or orders are exercisable by statutory instrument.

(4) Except in the case of regulations under section [⁷] 175 above and in so far as this Act otherwise provides, any power conferred by this Act to make an Order in Council, regulations or an order may be exercised
(a) either in relation to all cases to which the power extends, or in relation to those cases subject to specified exceptions, or in relation to any specified cases or classes of case;
(b) so as to make, as respects the cases in relation to which it is exercised–
(i) the full provision to which the power extends or any less provision (whether by way of exception or otherwise);
(ii) the same provision for all cases in relation to which the power is exercised, or different provision for different cases or different classes of case or different provision as respects the same case or class of case for different purposes of this Act;
(iii) any such provision either unconditionally or subject to any specified condition;
and where such a power is expressed to be exercisable for alternative purposes it may be exercised in relation to the same case for any or all of those purposes; and powers to make an Order in Council, regulations or an order for the purposes of any one provision of this Act are without prejudice to powers to make regulations or an order for the purposes of any other provision.

(5) Without prejudice to any specific provision in this Act, a power conferred by this Act to make an Order in Council, regulations or an order [⁷] includes power to make thereby such incidental, supplementary, consequential or transitional provision as appears to Her Majesty, or the authority making the regulations or order, as the case may be, to be expedient for the purposes of the Order in Council, regulations or order.

(6) Without prejudice to any specific provisions in this Act, a power conferred by any provision of this Act, except sections 14, [⁷] 130 and 175, to make an Order in Council, regulations or an order includes power to provide for a person to exercise a discretion in dealing with any matter.

(7) Any power conferred by this Act to make orders or regulation relating to housing benefit or [¹ council tax benefit] shall include power to make different provision for different areas [² or different authorities].

[⁸ (7A) Without prejudice to the generality of any of the preceding provisions of this section, regulations under any of sections 2A to 2C and 7A above may provide for all or any of the provisions of the regulations to apply only in relation to any area or areas specified in the regulations.]

(8)   An order under section [³140B, 140C,] 150, [⁹ 150A,] 152, 165(4) or 169 above [⁶] above shall not be made [⁴ by the Secretary of State] without the consent of the Treasury.

(9)   Any power of the Secretary of State under any provision of this Act, except under sections 80, 154, 175 and 178, to make any regulations or order, where the power is not expressed to be exercisable with the consent of the Treasury, shall if the Treasury so direct be exercisable only in conjunction with them.

[⁷ (10)]

(11)   A power under any of sections 177 to 179 above to make provisions by regulations or Order in Council for modifications or adaptations of the Contributions and Benefits Actor this Act shall be exercisable in relation to any enactment passed after this Act which is directed to be construed as one with them, except in so far as any such enactment relates to a benefit in relation to which the power is not exercisable; but this subsection applies only so far as a contrary intention is not expressed in the enactment so passed, and is without prejudice to the generality of any such direction.

(12)   Any reference in this section or section 190 below to an Order in Council, or an order or regulations, under this Act includes a reference to an Order in Council, an order or regulations made under any provision of an enactment passed after this Act and directed to be construed as one with this Act; but this subsection applies only so far as a contrary intention is not expressed in the enactment so passed, and without prejudice to the generality of any such direction.

Amendments
1.   Substitution made by the Local Government Finance Act 1992 Sch 9 para 24 (1.4.93).
2.   Amended by SSA(F)A Sch 1 para 10.
3.   Amended by the Housing Act 1996 Sch 13 para 3(5) (1.4.97).
4.   Amended by TCA Sch 4 para 3 (6.4.03).
5.   Amended by TCA Sch 6 (8.4.03).
6.   Amended by the Social Security (Recovery of Benefits) Act 1997 Sch 3 para 11 (6.10.97).
7.   Amended by SSA 1998 Sch 7 para 109 (6.9.99).
8.   Inserted by WRPA Sch 12 para 83 (11.11.99).
9.   Amended by the Pensions Act 2007, Sch 1 para 29 (26.9.07).

Parliamentary control of orders and regulations

190.–(1)   Subject to the provisions of this section, a statutory instrument containing (whether alone or with other provisions)–

[⁸ (za) regulations under section 132A(4);]
(a)   an order under section 141, 143, [¹ 143A,] 145, 150, [⁹ 150A,] 152 or 162(7) above; or
[⁶(aa) the first regulations to be made under section 2A;]
[⁷ (ab) the first regulations to be made under section 2AA;]
[³(aza) any order containing provision adding any person to the list of persons falling within section 109B(2A) above;]
(b)   regulations under section [⁴] [⁵ 122B(1)(b) or] 154 above,

shall not be made unless a draft of the instrument has been laid before Parliament and been approved by a resolution of each House of Parliament.

(2)   Subsection (1) above does not apply to a statutory instrument by reason only that it contains regulations under section 154 above which are to be made for the purpose of consolidating regulations to be revoked in the instrument.

(3)   A statutory instrument–
(a)   which contains (whether alone or with other provisions) orders or regulations made under this Act by the Secretary of State; and
(b)   which is not subject to any requirement that a draft of the instrument be laid before and approved by a resolution of each House of Parliament,

shall be subject to annulment in pursuance of a resolution of either House of Parliament.

[² (4)   .....]

Amendments
1.   Inserted by SSA 1998 Sch 7 para 110 (8.10.98).

2.   Repealed by SSA 1998 Sch 7 para 110 (6.4.99).
3.   Inserted by SSFA s1(9) (26.2.02).
4.   Amended by the Social Security (Recovery of Benefits) Act 1997 Sch 3 para 11 (6.10.97).
5.   Amended by SSA(F)A Sch 1 para 11 (1.7.97).
6.   Inserted byWRPA Sch 12 para 83 (11.11.99).
7.   Inserted by the Employment Act 2002 Sch 7 para 15 (5.7.03).
8.   Amended by the National Insurance Contributions Act 2006 s7(3) (30.3.06).
9.   Amended by the Pensions Act 2007 Sch 1 para 30 (26.9.07).

Supplementary

Interpretation – general

191.   In this Act, unless the context otherwise requires–
"the 1975 Act" means the Social Security Act 1975;
"the 1986 Act" means the Social Security Act 1986;
"benefit" means benefit under the Contributions and Benefits Act [16 [20 , state pension credit and an employment and support allowance]];
[1 "billing authority" has the same meaning as in Part I of the Local Government Finance Act 1992;]
"the Consequential Provisions Act" means the Social Security (Consequential Provisions) Act 1992;
[5 "contribution-based jobseeker's allowance" has the same meaning as in the Jobseekers Act 1995;]
"the Contributions and Benefits Act" means the Social Security Contributions and Benefits Act 1992;
[20 "contributory employment and support allowance" means a contributory allowance under Part 1 of the Welfare Reform Act 2007 (employment and support allowance);]
[14 "council tax benefit scheme" shall be construed in accordance with section 139(1) above;]
"disablement benefit" is to be construed in accordance with section 94(2)(a) of the Contributions and Benefits Act;
"dwelling" means any residential accommodation, whether or not consisting of the whole or part of a building and whether or not comprising separate and self-contained premises;
[2 "financial year" has the same meaning as in the Local Government Finance Act 1992;]
"5 year general qualification" is to be construed in accordance with section 71 of the Courts and Legal Services Act 1990;
"housing authority" means a local authority [17 or a new town corporation] or the Development Board for Rural Wales;
"housing benefit scheme" is to be construed in accordance with section 134(1) above;
[6 "income-based jobseeker's allowance" has the same meaning as in the Jobseekers Act 1995;]
"income-related benefit" means–
    (a)   income support;
    [15 . . .]
    [15 . . .]
    (d)   housing benefit; and
    [3(e)   council tax benefit;]
[20 "income-related employment and support allowance" means an income-related allowance under Part 1 of the Welfare Reform Act 2007 (employment and support allowance);]
"industrial injuries benefit" means benefit under Part V of the Contributions and Benefits Act, other than under Schedule 8;
"invalidity benefit" has the meaning assigned to it by section 20(1)(c) of that Act;
"local authority" means–

(a)   in relation to England [⁸ . . .], the council of a district or London borough, the Common Council of the City of London or the Council of the Isles of Scilly; and

[⁸(aa) in relation to Wales, the council of a county or county borough;] and

(b)   in relation to Scotland, [⁹ a council constituted under section 2 of the Local Government etc. (Scotland) Act 1994];

"medical examination" includes bacteriological and radiographical tests and similar investigations, and "medically examined" has a corresponding meaning;

"medical practitioner" means–

(a)   a registered medical practitioner; or

(b)   a person outside the United Kingdom who is not a registered medical practitioner, but has qualifications corresponding (in the Secretary of State's opinion) to those of a registered medical practitioner;

"medical treatment" means medical, surgical or rehabilitative treatment (including any course of diet or other regimen), and references to a person receiving or submitting himself to medical treatment are to be construed accordingly;

"new town corporation" means–

[²¹ (a) in relation to England–

    (i)   a development corporation established under the New Towns Act 1981; or

    (ii)   the Homes and Communities Agency so far as exercising functions in relation to anything transferred (or to be transferred) to it as mentioned in section 52(1)(a) to (d) of the Housing and Regeneration Act 2008;

(ab)   in relation to Wales–

    (i)   a development corporation established under the New Towns Act 1981; and

    (ii)   the Welsh Ministers so far as exercising functions in relation to anything transferred (or to be transferred) to them as mentioned in section 36(1)(a)(i) to (iii) of that Act;] and

(b)   in relation to Scotland, a development corporation established under the New Towns (Scotland) Act 1968;

[¹⁸ "the Northern Ireland Department" means means the Department for Social Development but–

(a)   in section 122 and sections 122B to 122E also includes the Department of Finance and Personnel; and

(b)   in sections 121E, 121F, 122, 122ZA, 122C and 122D also includes the Department for Employment and Learning;]

"the Northern Ireland Administration Act" means the Social Security (Northern Ireland) Administration Act 1992;

"occupational pension scheme" has the same meaning as in section 66(1) of the Pensions Act;

"the Old Cases Act" means the Industrial Injuries and Diseases (Old Cases) Act 1975;

"Old Cases payments" means payments under Part I of Schedule 8 to the Contributions and Benefits Act;

[¹⁰ "pensionable age" has the meaning given by the rules in paragraph 1 of Schedule 4 to the Pensions Act 1995];

"the Pensions Act" means the[¹¹ Pension Schemes Act 1993];

"personal pension scheme" has the meaning assigned to it by [¹² section 1 of the Pensions Act] [¹² and "appropriate", in relation to such a scheme, shall be construed in accordance with section 7(4) of that Act];

"prescribe" means prescribe by regulations [¹⁹ and "prescribed" must be construed accordingly];

"rent rebate" and [¹³ . . .] "rent allowance" shall be construed in accordance with section 134 above;

[¹³ . . .] "tax year" means the 12 months beginning with 6th April in any year;

[¹⁶ "state pension credit" means state pension credit under the State Pension Credit Act 2002;]

"10 year general qualification" is to be construed in accordance with section 71 of the Courts and Legal Services Act 1990; and

"widow's benefit" has the meaning assigned to it by section 20(1)(e) of the Contributions and Benefits Act.

Amendments

1. Substituted by LGFA Sch 9 para 25(a) (1.4.93).
2. Inserted by LGFA Sch 9 para 25(b) (1.4.93).
3. Substituted by LGFA Sch 9 para 25(c) (1.4.93).
4. Substituted by LGFA Sch 9 para 25(d) (1.4.93).
5. Inserted by theJobseekers Act 1995 Sch 2 para 73(3) (22.4.96).
6. Inserted by the Jobseekers Act 1995 Sch 2 para 73(4) (22.4.96).
7. Definition of "levying authority" repealed by the Local Government etc. (Scotland) Act 1994 Sch 13 para 175(5)(a) and Sch 14 (1.4.96).
8. Amended by the Local Government (Wales) Act 1994 Sch 1 para 94.
9. Substituted bythe Local Government etc. (Scotland) Act 1994 Sch 13 para 175(5)(b) (1.4.96).
10. Substituted by the Pensions Act 1995 Sch 4 para 14 (19.7.95).
11. Substituted by the Pensions Schemes Act 1993 Sch 8 para 31(c) (7.2.94).
12. Amended by the Pensions Schemes Act 1993 Sch 8 para 31(d) (7.2.94).
13. Repealed by the Housing Act 1996 Sch 19 Part VI (1.4.97).
14. Inserted by the Housing Act 1996 Sch 13 para 6(a).
15. Amended by TCA Sch 6 (8.4.03).
16. Amended by SPCA Sch 2 para 24 (commenced October 2003).
17. Amended by the Housing (Scotland) Act 2001 Sch 10 para 17 (1.04.02).
18. Amended by the Employment Act 2002 Sch 7 para 16 (9.9.02).
19. Amended by WRA s40 and Sch 5 para 10 (3.7.07).
20. Amended by WRA s29 and Sch 3 para 10(32) (18.3.08 for making regulations and 27.7.08).
21. Amended by the Housing and Regeneration Act 2008 s56 and Sch 8 para 61 (1.12.08).

Short title, commencement and extent

192.–(1)   This Act may be cited as the Social Security Administration Act 1992.

(2)   This Act is to be read, where appropriate, with the Contributions and Benefits Act and the Consequential Provisions Act.

(3)   The enactments consolidated by this Act are repealed, in consequence of the consolidation, by the Consequential Provisions Act.

(4)   Except as provided in Schedule 4 to the Consequential Provisions Act, this Act shall come into force on 1st July 1992.

(5)   The following provisions extend to Northern Ireland–

[² . . .]

[¹ . . .]

[³ section 132A (and sections 189 and 190, but only for the purposes of regulations under section 132A);]

section 170 (with Schedule 5);

section 177 (with Schedule 8); and

this section.

Except as provided by this section, this Act does not extend to Northern Ireland.

Amendments

1. Amended by the Social Security (Recovery of Benefits) Act 1997 Sch 3 para 12 (6.10.97).
2. Amended by the SSA 1998 Sch 7 para 112 (29.11.99).
3. Inserted by the National Insurance Contributions Act 2006 s7(4) (3.3.06).

SCHEDULE 4

PERSONS EMPLOYED IN SOCIAL SECURITY ADMINISTRATION OR ADJUDICATION PART I

The Specified Persons

Government departments

A civil servant in

[² (a)   the Department for Work and Pensions;]

[² . . .]

(c)   the [⁴ Ministry of Justice].

Other public departments and offices

[Omitted]

[¹ Local authorities etc

A member, officer or employee of an authority administering housing benefit or council tax benefit.

A person authorised to exercise any function of such an authority relating to such a benefit or any employee of such a person.

A person authorised under section 139A(1) of this Act to consider and report to the Secretary of State on the administration of housing benefit or council tax benefit.]

[³ A member, officer or employee of a county council in England who exercises–

(a) any function conferred on the county council by regulations made under section 7A of this Act;

(b) any function in connection with a relevant purpose within the meaning of section 7B(3) of this Act.

A person authorised to exercise any such function of such a county council or an employee of such a person.]

Adjudicating bodies

The clerk to, or other officer or member of staff of, any of the following bodies–

[⁴ (a)]

[Omitted]

Amendments

1.   Inserted by SSA(F)A s4.
2.   Amended by Sch para 8(4) of SI 2002 No 1397 as from 27.6.02.
3.   Inserted by WRA s41(3) (3.7.07).
4.   Amended by Art 9 and Sch 3 para 104 of SI 2008 No 2833 as from 3.11.08.

General Note

See also Sch 8 para 34 WRPA (on p1128).

SCHEDULE 10
SUPPLEMENTARY BENEFIT ETC
Overpayments etc

4.–(1)-(2)   *[Omitted]*

(3)   The reference to housing benefit in section 75 above includes a reference to housing benefits under Part II of the Social Security and Housing Benefits Act 1982.

Social Security (Consequential Provisions) Act 1992
(1992 c6)

Meaning of "the consolidating Acts"
    1.   In this Act–
"the consolidating Acts" means the Social Security Contributions and Benefits Act 1992 ("the Contributions and Benefits Act"), the Social Security Administration Act 1992 ("the Administration Act") and, so far as it reproduces the effect of the repealed enactments, this Act; and
"the repealed enactments" means the enactments repealed by this Act.

Continuity of the law
    2.–(1)   The substitution of the consolidating Acts for the repealed enactments does not affect the continuity of the law.

    (2)   Anything done or having effect as if done under or for the purposes of a provision of the repealed enactments has effect, if it could have been done under or for the purposes of the corresponding provision of the consolidating Acts, as if done under or for the purposes of that provision.

    (3)   Any reference, whether express or implied, in the consolidating Acts or any other enactment, instrument or document to a provision of the consolidating Acts shall, so far as the context permits, be construed as including, in relation to the times, circumstances and purposes in relation to which the corresponding provision of the repealed enactments has effect, a reference to that corresponding provision.

    (4)   Any reference, whether express or implied, in any enactment, instrument or document to a provision of the repealed enactments shall be construed, so far as is required for continuing its effects, as including a reference to the corresponding provision of the consolidating Acts.

Social Security Act 1998
(1998 c14)

PART I
General
Appeals

Constitution of appeal tribunals
[²**7.**]

Amendments

1.   Amended by the Tribunals, Courts and Enforcement Act 2007 s50 and Sch 10 para 29(3) and (4) (21.7.08).
2.   Omitted by Art 9 and Sch 3 para 147 of SI 2008 No. 2833 (3.11.08).

General Note

Until 3 November 2008, this section provided for the constitution of appeal tribunals hearing benefit appeals under this act as well as HB and CTB appeals under Sch 7 para 6 CSPSSA. See now the Tribunals, Courts and Enforcement Act 2007 on p168.

For commentary on this former provision, see p109 of the 20th edition.

Social Security Decisions and Appeals
Housing benefit and council tax benefit

Determination of claims and reviews
34.–(1)   Regulations shall provide that, where a person claims–
(a)   housing benefit; or
(b)   council tax benefit,
the authority to whom the claim is made shall notify the person of its determination of the claim.

(2)   Any such notification shall be given in such form as may be prescribed.

(3)   Regulations may make provision requiring authorities to whom claims for housing benefit or council tax benefit are made by, or in respect of, persons who have been entitled to a jobseeker's allowance or to income support [² or state pension credit] to give priority, in prescribed circumstances, to those claims over other claims for any such benefit.

[¹ (4)]
[¹ (5)]

Amendments

1.   Repealed by CSPSSA Sch 9 Pt VII (2.7.01).
2.   Amended by SPCA Sch 2 para 41 (2.7.02 (for making regulations) and 6.10.03).

Commencement

18.10.99: Social Security Act 1998 (Commencement No 11, Savings and Consequential and Transitional Provisions) Order 1999 SI No.2860 Art 2(a).

General Note

This replaced s63 SSAA as the basic piece of primary legislation upon which the decision-making structure for HB and CTB is based. So far as the mechanism for changing decisions is concerned, it has now in its turn been replaced by Sch 7 CSPSSA.

Subs (1) to (3) are identical to the former subs (1), (2), (2A) and (3) SSAA s63. All regulations validly made under those provisions are treated by virtue of s17(2)(b) Interpretation Act 1978 as if they had been made under these provisions. The following list gives the principal regulations made under the powers granted by each numbered paragraph of this section.

(1)   See reg 90 HB Regs, reg 71 HB(SPC) Regs, reg 76 CTB Regs and reg 61 CTB(SPC) Regs.

(2)   See Sch 9 HB Regs, Sch 8 HB(SPC) Regs, Sch 8 CTB Regs and Sch 7 CTB(SPC) Regs.

(3)   See reg 89(3) HB Regs, reg 70(3) HB(SPC) Regs, reg 75(3) CTB Regs and reg 60(3) CTB(SPC) Regs. Also note the different system for claiming HB and CTB for recipients of IS, JSA, ESA and PC (see reg 83(4) HB Regs, reg 64(5) HB(SPC) Regs, reg 69(4) CTB Regs and reg 53(4) CTB(SPC) Regs).

Subs (4) and (5) formerly provided for regulations to make provision for reviews of determinations relating to HB and CTB (subs (4)) and matters arising out of the revision on review of such determinations (subs (5)). Both were repealed in July 2001, though preserved for certain purposes: to enable a Review Board to record its decision and send it out; to permit correction of accidental errors; to enable a Review Board to appear in judicial review proceedings; and to enable effect to be given to a Review Board's decision. The transitional provisions were in the Housing Benefit and Council Tax Benefit (Decisions and Appeals)(Transitional and Savings) Regulations 2001 SI No.1264. They governed what happened where the process for disputing an authority's determination commenced before 2 July 2001 but had not finished by that date.

See pp993-1000 of the 20th edition for the transitional rules and pp104-5 of the 18th edition for commentary on the repealed provisions.

PART III
Benefits

Validation of certain housing benefit determinations.

69.–(1) Subject to subsections (3) and (4) below, in so far as a housing benefit determination made before 18th August 1997 purported to determine that housing benefit was payable in respect of–

(a)   charges for medical care, nursing care or personal care; or

(b)   charges for general counselling or any other support services,

it shall be deemed to have been validly made if, on the assumption mentioned in subsection (2) below, it would have been so made.

(2)   The assumption is that, at all material times, such charges as are mentioned in subsection (1) above were eligible to be met by housing benefit where the claimant's right to occupy the dwelling was conditional on his payment of the charges.

(3)   Where the effect of a review carried out on or after 18th August 1997 was to revise the amount of housing benefit payable in respect of any validated charges–

(a)   the revision shall be deemed not to have been validly made in so far as it had the effect of increasing that amount; and

(b)   housing benefit shall cease to be payable in respect of those charges as from the beginning of the period for which the first payment of the revised amount of benefit was made.

(4)   Housing benefit shall not be payable in respect of any validated charges for any period falling after–

(a)   5th April 1998 where the rent is payable at intervals of a whole number of weeks; and

(b)   31st March 1998 in any other case.

(5)   In this section–

''the dwelling'', in relation to a housing benefit determination, means the dwelling in respect of which the determination was made;

''housing benefit determination'' means a determination under section 130 of the Contributions and Benefits Act or the corresponding provisions of the Social Security Act 1986, or a decision on a review of such a determination;

''medical care'' includes treatment or counselling related to mental disorder, mental handicap, physical disablement or past or present alcohol or drug dependence;

''personal care'' includes assistance at meal-times or with personal appearance or hygiene;

''validated charges'' means charges in respect of which housing benefit is payable only by virtue of subsection (1) above.

General Note

This provision was made to alleviate accounting and subsidy difficulties experienced by local authorities following the confusion over whether service charges for the types of services mentioned in subs (1) were properly payable under the then HB Regs 1987 Sch 1 para 1(f)(i). It is now clear, following *R v St Edmundsbury BC HBRB ex p Sandys* [1997] 30 HLR 800; [1998] *The Times* 9 September, CA that such services should not have been met under that provision. Since the payments were unlawful, in the absence of a provision such as this some authorities might have been faced with difficulties in justifying their expenditure on these items.

Subs (1) and (2) retrospectively justify HB awards in respect of such service charges. The effect of the retrospective validation is limited by subs (3) and (4). Subs (4) makes clear that the validation only lasted until the end of the 1997 to 1998 financial year.

For an analysis of these provisions, see pp117-118 of the 15th edition.

PART IV
Miscellaneous and Supplemental

Regulations and orders

79.–(1) [³ Subject to subsection (2A) below,] regulations under this Act shall be made by the Secretary of State.

[³ (2)]

[² (2A) Subsection (1) has effect subject to any provision providing for regulations to be made by the Treasury or the Commissioners of Inland Revenue.]

(3) Powers under this Act to make regulations or orders are exercisable by statutory instrument.

(4) Any power conferred by this Act to make regulations or orders may be exercised–

(a) either in relation to all cases to which the power extends, or in relation to those cases subject to specified exceptions, or in relation to any specified cases or classes of case;

(b) so as to make, as respects the cases in relation to which it is exercised–

(i) the full provision to which the power extends or any less provision (whether by way of exception or otherwise);

(ii) the same provision for all cases in relation to which the power is exercised, or different provision for different cases or different classes of case or different provision as respects the same case or class of case for different purposes of this Act;

(iii) any such provision either unconditionally or subject to any specified condition;

and where such a power is expressed to be exercisable for alternative purposes it may be exercised in relation to the same case for any or all of those purposes.

(5) Powers to make regulations for the purposes of any one provision of this Act are without prejudice to powers to make regulations for the purposes of any other provision.

(6) Without prejudice to any specific provision in this Act, a power conferred by this Act to make regulations includes power to make thereby such incidental, supplementary, consequential or transitional provision as appears to the authority making the regulations to be expedient for the purposes of those regulations.

(7) Without prejudice to any specific provisions in this Act, a power conferred by any provision of this Act to make regulations includes power to provide for a person to exercise a discretion in dealing with any matter.

(8) Any power conferred by this Act to make regulations relating to housing benefit or council tax benefit shall include power to make different provision for different areas or different authorities.

[³ (9)]

Amendments

1. Amended by TCA Sch 4 para 13(2) (6.4.03).
2. Inserted by TCA Sch 4 para 13(3) (6.4.03).
3. Amended by Art 9 and Sch 3 para 168 of SI 2008 No. 2833 (3.11.08).

Parliamentary control of regulations

80.–(1)   Subject to the provisions of this section, a statutory instrument containing (whether alone or with other provisions) regulations under–

(a)   section [³] 12(2) or 72 above; or

(b)   [³] paragraph 9 of Schedule 2 [³] to this Act,

shall not be made unless a draft of the instrument has been laid before Parliament and been approved by a resolution of each House of Parliament.

(2)   A statutory instrument–

(a)   which contains (whether alone or with other provisions) regulations made under this Act by the Secretary of State[¹ , the Treasury or the Commissioners of Inland Revenue]; and

(b)   which is not subject to any requirement that a draft of the instrument be laid before and approved by a resolution of each House of Parliament,

shall be subject to annulment in pursuance of a resolution of either House of Parliament.

[³ (3)]

[³ [² (4)]]

Amendments

1.   Amended by TCA Sch 4 para 14 (6.4.03).
2.   Amended by the Tribunals, Courts and Enforcement Act 2007 s50 and Sch 10 para 29(5) (21.7.08).
3.   Amended by Art 9 and Sch 3 para 169 of SI 2008 No. 2833 (3.11.08).

Interpretation: general

84.   In this Act–

''the Administration Act'' means the Social Security Administration Act 1992;

''the Child Support Act'' means the Child Support Act 1991;

''the Contributions and Benefits Act'' means the Social Security Contributions and Benefits Act 1992;

''the Jobseekers Act'' means the Jobseekers Act 1995;

''the Vaccine Damage Payments Act'' means the Vaccine Damage Payments Act 1979;

''prescribe'' means prescribe by regulations.

Short title, commencement and extent

87.–(1)   This Act may be cited as the Social Security Act 1998.

(2)   This Act, except–

(a)   sections 66, 69, 72 and 77 to 85, this section and Schedule 6 to this Act; and

(b)   subsection (1) of section 50 so far as relating to a sum which is chargeable to tax by virtue of section 313 of the Income and Corporation Taxes Act 1988, and subsections (2) to (4) of that section,

shall come into force on such day as may be appointed by order made by the Secretary of State; and different days may be appointed for different provisions and for different purposes.

(3)   An order under subsection (2) above may make such savings, or such transitional or consequential provision, as the Secretary of State considers necessary or expedient–

(a)   in preparation for or in connection with the coming into force of any provision of this Act; or

(b)   in connection with the operation of any enactment repealed or amended by a provision of this Act during any period when the repeal or amendment is not wholly in force.

SCHEDULE 5

REGULATIONS AS TO PROCEDURE: PROVISION WHICH MAY BE MADE

General Note

These provisions authorise various regulations governing procedure. See pp116 and 117 of the 20th edition for a list showing which regulations were made under which paragraphs.

1.   Provision prescribing the procedure to be followed in connection with–

(a)   the making of decisions or determinations by the Secretary of State [¹]; and

(b)   the withdrawal of claims, applications, appeals or references falling to be decided or determined by the Secretary of State [¹].

Amendment

1.   Amended by Art 9 and Sch 3 para 173(a) of SI 2008 No. 2833 (3.11.08).

[¹**2.**]

Amendment

1.   Omitted by Art 9 and Sch 3 para 173(b) of SI 2008 No. 2833 (3.11.08).

3.   Provision as to the form which is to be used for any document, the evidence which is to be required and the circumstances in which any official record or certificate is to be sufficient or conclusive evidence.

4.   Provision as to the time within which, or the manner in which–

(a)   any evidence is to be produced; or

(b)   any application, reference or appeal is to be made.

[¹**5.**]

Amendment

1.   Omitted by Art 9 and Sch 3 para 173(b) of SI 2008 No. 2833 (3.11.08).

[¹**6.**]

Amendment

1.   Omitted by Art 9 and Sch 3 para 173(b) of SI 2008 No. 2833 (3.11.08).

[¹**7.**]

Amendment

[¹   1.   Omitted by Art 9 and Sch 3 para 173(b) of SI 2008 No. 2833 (3.11.08).

8.]

Amendment

1.   Omitted by Art 9 and Sch 3 para 173(b) of SI 2008 No. 2833 (3.11.08).

9.   Provision for the non-disclosure to a person of the particulars of any medical advice or medical evidence given or submitted for the purposes of a determination.

Human Rights Act 1998
(1998 c42)

General Note to the Act

The Human Rights Act 1998 was the result of the expressed intention of the Labour Government elected in 1997 to give domestic force to the European Convention on Human Rights and Fundamental Freedoms. Despite suggestions at the time it was passed that the British constitution and its traditions were under threat and that it would lead to judges, rather than Parliament, making the law, its actual impact has been modest in the social welfare field. Many challenges have been brought and few have succeeded. This is as true of challenges in the social security field as elsewhere. This is due to the fact that the Convention rights provide little by way of social rights, being directed principally to ensuring personal freedoms.

No attempt is made below to deal with the implications of the Convention in criminal proceedings, for which reference should be made to specialist works on criminal law.

ARRANGEMENT OF SECTIONS

Introduction
1.   The Convention Rights
2.   Interpretation of Convention rights

Legislation
3.   Interpretation of legislation
4.   Declaration of incompatibility
5.   Right of Crown to intervene

Public authorities
6.   Acts of public authorities
7.   Proceedings
8.   Judicial remedies
9.   Judicial acts

Remedial action
10.   Power to take remedial action

Other rights and proceedings
11.   Safeguard for existing human rights
13.   Freedom of thought, conscience and religion

Derogations and reservations (Omitted)

Judges of the European Court of Human Rights (Omitted)

Supplemental
20.   Orders etc. under this Act
21.   Interpretation, etc
22.   Short title, commencement, application and extent

SCHEDULES
1.   The Articles
2.   Remedial Orders

Introduction

The Convention Rights

1.–(1) In this Act "the Convention rights" means the rights and fundamental freedoms set out in–

(a)   Articles 2 to 12 and 14 of the Convention,

(b)   Articles 1 to 3 of the First Protocol, and

(c)   Articles 1 and 2 of the Sixth Protocol,
as read with Articles 16 to 18 of the Convention.

(2)   Those Articles are to have effect for the purposes of this Act subject to any designated derogation or reservation (as to which see sections 14 and 15).

(3)   The Articles are set out in Schedule 1.

(4)   The Secretary of State may by order make such amendments to this Act as he considers appropriate to reflect the effect, in relation to the United Kingdom, of a protocol.

(5)   In subsection (4) ''protocol'' means a protocol to the Convention–

(a)   which the United Kingdom has ratified; or

(b)   which the United Kingdom has signed with a view to ratification.

(6)   No amendment may be made by an order under subsection (4) so as to come into force before the protocol concerned is in force in relation to the United Kingdom.

Interpretation of Convention rights

2.–(1)   A court or tribunal determining a question which has arisen in connection with a Convention right must take into account any–

(a)   judgment, decision, declaration or advisory opinion of the European Court of Human Rights,

(b)   opinion of the Commission given in a report adopted under Article 31 of the Convention,

(c)   decision of the Commission in connection with Article 26 or 27(2) of the Convention, or

(d)   decision of the Committee of Ministers taken under Article 46 of the Convention, whenever made or given, so far as, in the opinion of the court or tribunal, it is relevant to the proceedings in which that question has arisen.

(2)   Evidence of any judgment, decision, declaration or opinion of which account may have to be taken under this section is to be given in proceedings before any court or tribunal in such manner as may be provided by rules.

(3)   In this section ''rules'' means rules of court or, in the case of proceedings before a tribunal, rules made for the purposes of this section–

(a)   by the Lord Chancellor or the Secretary of State, in relation to any proceedings outside Scotland;

(b)   by the Secretary of State, in relation to proceedings in Scotland; or

(c)   by a Northern Ireland department, in relation to proceedings before a tribunal in Northern Ireland–

(i)   which deals with transferred matters; and

(ii)   for which no rules made under paragraph (a) are in force.

General Note

This section deals with the effect of decisions of the European Court of Human Rights and the European Commission on Human Rights. The key words in s2 are "must take into account". Decisions are not therefore binding. However, great respect is accorded to Strasbourg decisions by the domestic courts, and it has been held that there should be a "special reason" for a departure from the learning of the Court or Commission: *R (Alconbury Developments Ltd) v Secretary of State for the Environment, Transport and the Regions* [2003] 2 AC 295, HL. This will especially be the case if the Strasbourg decision is recent and authoritative: see *Attorney General's Reference No 4 of 2002* [2004] UKHL 43 (para 33); and *R v Secretary of State for the Home Department, ex p Anderson* [2002] UKHL 46 (paras 17-18).

However, in almost all cases where there is a conflict between Strasbourg caselaw and a decision of a superior court in the UK the inferior court or tribunal in the UK should follow the decision of the superior (UK) court: *Leeds City Council v Price* [2006] UKHL 10, [2006] 4 All ER 128 (paras 43-44). In *R(RJM) v SSWP* [2008] UKHL 63, 22 October 2008, the House of Lords confirmed that this is the correct approach where the Court of Appeal is faced with a conflict between a House of Lords decision and later Strasbourg caselaw. But the House of Lords went on to to say in *RJM* that the same constraints do not necessarily apply where the Court of Appeal is faced with a conflict between an earlier Court of Appeal decision and a later decision of the European Court of Human Rights "the Court of Appeal should be free (but not obliged) to depart from that decision" (*RJM* at para 66).

The most widely available, and most useful set of reports is the *European Human Rights Reports* (EHRR) published by Sweet and Maxwell. Butterworths' *Human Rights Cases* also publish some decisions which are not available in the EHRR. Reports of decisions are also available at http://hudoc.echr.coe.int/hudoc/.

Legislation

Interpretation of legislation

3.–(1)   So far as it is possible to do so, primary legislation and subordinate legislation must be read and given effect in a way which is compatible with the Convention rights.

(2)   This section–

(a)   applies to primary legislation and subordinate legislation whenever enacted;

(b)   does not affect the validity, continuing operation or enforcement of any incompatible primary legislation; and

(c)   does not affect the validity, continuing operation or enforcement of any incompatible subordinate legislation if (disregarding any possibility of revocation) primary legislation prevents removal of the incompatibility.

General Note

This is the first of the four sections that deal with the impact of the Convention on domestic law and administration. It is concerned with the technique for interpreting legislation that may be incompatible with a Convention right.

Analysis

Subs (1) states the general interpretative principle. It is a direction in strong terms: legislation must be read consistently with the Convention "so far as it is possible to do so". Before the 1998 Act came into force, resort could be had to the Convention as an aid to interpretation only to resolve an ambiguity in the meaning of a provision: see eg, *R v Secretary of State for the Home Department ex p Brind* [1991] 1 AC 696 at 747G-748F, 760D-762B, HL. It is clear that s3(1) requires a much more robust approach. The leading cases on the approach required by s3(1) are *R v A (No 2) [2001] 2 AC 91, HL, Re S* [2002] 2 AC 291, HL and *Ghaidan v Godin-Mendoza* [2004] UKHL 30, 3 All ER 411. In *R v A (No 2)*, a challenge was made to legislation excluding cross-examination of complainants in rape trials about previous sexual history, including any previous relationship with the accused. Lord Steyn set out the general approach required by s3(1):

".... the interpretative obligation under section 3 of the 1998 Act is a strong one. It applies even if there is no ambiguity in the language in the sense of the language being capable of two different meanings. ... Section 3 places a duty on the court to strive to find a possible interpretation compatible with Convention rights. Under ordinary methods of interpretation a court may depart from the language of the statute to avoid absurd consequences: section 3 goes much further. Undoubtedly, a court must always look for a contextual and purposive interpretation: section 3 is more radical in its effect. It is a general principle of the interpretation of legal instruments that the text is the primary source of interpretation ... Section 3 qualifies this general principle because it requires a court to find an interpretation compatible with Convention rights if it is possible to do so. In the progress of the Bill through Parliament the Lord Chancellor observed that 'in 99% of the cases that will arise, there will be no need for judicial declarations of incompatibility' and the Home Secretary said 'We expect that, in almost all cases, the courts will be able to interpret the legislation compatibility with the Convention'. ... In accordance with the will of Parliament as reflected in section 3 it will sometimes be necessary to adopt an interpretation which linguistically may appear strained. The techniques to be used will not only involve the reading down of express language in a statute but also the implication of provisions. A declaration of incompatibility [under s4] is a measure of last resort. It must be avoided unless it is plainly impossible to do so." (at para 44)

Lord Hutton emphasised (at para 162) that s3(1) had to be utilised unless it was "impossible" to achieve the objective set out therein.

There are, however, limits to the exercise required by s3(1). It is limited to interpreting legislation, and does not allow judges "to act as legislators" and to override express or implied prohibitions in the legislation against adopting the proposed interpretation: *Re S* paras 37-41. The decision in *Re S* requires the court to be sure that the proposed modification is workable before it operates s3. Moreover, it is a precondition of carrying out the exercise under s3(1) that the ordinary interpretation of the legislation should conflict with a Convention right: *R v A (No 2)* at para 37; *Poplar Housing Association Ltd v Donoghue* [2002] QB 58, CA. The modification of the ordinary meaning of the legislation should be the minimum possible to achieve compatibility with the Convention: *Donoghue*, para 75(b). It should be possible to formulate, in words, the way in which the legislation has to be read in order for a compatible interpretation to be adopted: *R v Lambert* [2002] 2 AC 545, para 80, HL.

Ghaidan emphasises that use of the interpretive tool provided by s3(1) is not dependent on finding an ambiguity in the legislation, and s3 may require the tribunal or court to depart from the unambiguous meaning the legislation would otherwise bear. s3 may therefore require the decision-making body to depart from the intention of Parliament which enacted the legislation. However, the duty under s3 does not extend to allowing the courts to legislate, in the sense of reading in words which Parliament did not intend or otherwise adopting a meaning which is inconsistent with the underlying thrust of the legislation in question.

Subs (2) preserves the sovereignty of Parliament. The 1998 Act is no different to any other statute. It does not enable other statutes to be disregarded, and does not affect the continuing validity of such statutes. The same applies to secondary legislation such as regulations but *only* if "primary legislation prevents the removal of the incompatibility". Thus secondary legislation which is made under the general powers in the SSCBA, SSAA and other primary legislation in this book will be struck down if it is incompatible with Convention rights, since those powers are permissive and not mandatory; they do not *require* the regulations to exist in the form that they exist. If it is alleged, therefore, that regulations are incompatible with the Convention and they cannot be read in a way which is consistent with Convention rights under s3(1), then they will have become *ultra vires* from the time that the 1998 Act came into force.

Declaration of incompatibility

4.–(1)   Subsection (2) applies in any proceedings in which a court determines whether a provision of primary legislation is compatible with a Convention right.

(2)   If the court is satisfied that the provision is incompatible with a Convention right, it may make a declaration of that incompatibility.

(3)   Subsection (4) applies in any proceedings in which a court determines whether a provision of subordinate legislation, made in the exercise of a power conferred by primary legislation, is compatible with a Convention right.

(4)   If the court is satisfied–

(a)   that the provision is incompatible with a Convention right, and

(b)   that (disregarding any possibility of revocation) the primary legislation concerned prevents removal of the incompatibility,

it may make a declaration of that incompatibility.

(5)   In this section "court" means–

(a)   the House of Lords;

(b)   the Judicial Committee of the Privy Council;

(c)   the Courts-Martial Appeal Court;

(d)   in Scotland, the High Court of Justiciary sitting otherwise than as a trial court or the Court of Session;

(e)   in England and Wales or Northern Ireland, the High Court or the Court of Appeal.

(6)   A declaration under this section ("a declaration of incompatibility")–

(a)   does not affect the validity, continuing operation or enforcement of the provision in respect of which it is given; and

(b)   is not binding on the parties to the proceedings in which it is made.

General Note

The second means by which the Convention rights can impact on the law is through a declaration of incompatibility. But the effect of such a declaration is limited. It does not affect the validity of the legislation and is not binding upon the parties: see subs (6). Its sole purpose is to allow the Secretary of State to make a remedial order under s10 and Sch 2.

A declaration of incompatibility may only be made by a "court" as defined in subs (5). Thus authorities, the First-tier Tribunal and the Upper Tribunal have no power to grant such declarations. The usual mode of seeking a declaration of incompatibility will be by way of a claim for judicial review. The same could be done on appeal from the Upper Tribunal.

Right of Crown to intervene

5.–(1)   Where a court is considering whether to make a declaration of incompatibility, the Crown is entitled to notice in accordance with rules of court.

(2)   In any case to which subsection (1) applies–

(a)   a Minister of the Crown (or a person nominated by him),

(b)   a member of the Scottish Executive,

(c)   a Northern Ireland Minister,

(d)   a Northern Ireland department,

is entitled, on giving notice in accordance with rules of court, to be joined as a party to the proceedings.

(3)   Notice under subsection (2) may be given at any time during the proceedings.

(4)   A person who has been made a party to criminal proceedings (other than in Scotland) as the result of a notice under subsection (2) may, with leave, appeal to the House of Lords against any declaration of incompatibility made in the proceedings.

(5)   In subsection (4)–

"criminal proceedings" includes all proceedings before the Courts-Martial Appeal Court; and

"leave" means leave granted by the court making the declaration of incompatibility or by the House of Lords.

General Note

For guidance as to the procedure to adopt under s5, see *Poplar Housing Association Ltd v Donoghue* [2002] QB 58, CA.

Public authorities

Acts of public authorities

6.–(1)   It is unlawful for a public authority to act in a way which is incompatible with a Convention right.

(2)   Subsection (1) does not apply to an act if–

(a)   as the result of one or more provisions of primary legislation, the authority could not have acted differently; or

(b)   in the case of one or more provisions of, or made under, primary legislation which cannot be read or given effect in a way which is compatible with the Convention rights, the authority was acting so as to give effect to or enforce those provisions.

(3)   In this section "public authority" includes–

(a)   a court or tribunal, and

(b)   any person certain of whose functions are functions of a public nature,

but does not include either House of Parliament or a person exercising functions in connection with proceedings in Parliament.

(4)   In subsection (3) "Parliament" does not include the House of Lords in its judicial capacity.

(5)   In relation to a particular act, a person is not a public authority by virtue only of subsection (3)(b) if the nature of the act is private.

(6)   "An act" includes a failure to act but does not include a failure to–

(a)   introduce in, or lay before, Parliament a proposal for legislation; or

(b)   make any primary legislation or remedial order.

General Note

This forbids public authorities, with important exceptions, from infringing Convention rights by the way in which they act on a day-to-day basis.

Analysis

Subsections (1), (2) and (6): The basic prohibition

Subs (1) sets out the basic prohibition, which is then qualified by subs (2) and (6). For enforcement of this obligation, see s7.

Subs (2) follows the same aim of preserving Parliament as the supreme legislative authority. Under para (a), any public body which "could not have" acted in a different way as a result of obedience to primary legislation will not act unlawfully under subs (1). However, the words "could not have" emphasise that where the public body is given a discretion as to how it acts, it may breach s6(1) by acting unlawfully. Para (b) is more problematic. It applies both to primary legislation and secondary legislation. However, it is suggested that it will only apply to secondary legislation if its existence in the incompatible form is made compulsory by primary legislation, since otherwise the secondary legislation will be rendered *ultra vires* as a result of its incompatibility with the Convention right: see *R(Bono) v Harlow DC HBRB* [2002] 1 WLR 2475 paras 34-35, Richards J.

Subs (6) makes it clear that "act" includes omissions. It then goes on to preserve Parliamentary sovereignty by excluding from the definition a failure by a minister or Parliament to legislate. A failure to make a remedial order may also not be impugned under s6, since this would have the effect of enforcing the court's declaration of incompatibility.

Subsections (3) to (5): "Public body"
The critical question is: what is a "public body" for the purposes of s6? The definition in subs (3) does not purport to be a complete guide. Clearly, a local authority or the Secretary of State for Work and Pensions is a "public body". However, in the context of HB and CTB, it may be important to know whether contractors performing functions on behalf of a local authority or social landlords assisting in verification work (see Circulars HB/CTB A21/2001 and A43/2001 for proposals about this) are "public bodies". For the purposes of possession proceedings, similarly, it will be necessary to know whether social landlords are constrained by the obligation in s6(1).

Subs (3)(a) and (4) confirm that courts, the First-tier Tribunal and the Upper Tribunal are public bodies and hence are bound by the prohibition in subs (1). Subs (4) confirms that the House of Lords, when acting in its judicial capacity, is obliged to comply with the Convention just as any other court must.

Subs (3)(b) and (5) introduce the concept of a "functional" public authority; a body existing under private law but which is exercising functions of a public nature. The words "certain of whose" make it clear that the body may exercise private functions alongside its public functions without taking it outside the scope of "public body". Such a body will only be a "public body" in relation to its public acts, however, as subs (5) makes clear.

This distinction has been illuminated by caselaw. In *Donaghue v Poplar Housing Association Ltd* [2002] QB 58, CA, a tenant sought to impugn the decision of her landlord, a housing association, to seek possession of her home. She was an assured shorthold tenant under a tenancy conferred on her pursuant to an obligation of the local authority and her tenancy had been terminated under s21 Housing Act 1988, which gives a landlord an absolute right to possession. She contended that this was a breach of her right to respect for her home under Art 8 of the Convention. The Court of Appeal held that the meaning of "public body" should be given "a generous interpretation" (para 58). It went on to say (para 59):

"The purpose of s6(3)(b) is to deal with hybrid bodies which have both public and private functions. It is not to make a body, which does not have responsibilities to the public, a public body merely because it performs acts on behalf of a public body which would constitute public functions were such acts to be performed by the public body itself. An act can remain of a private nature even though it is performed because another body is under a public duty to ensure that that act is performed."

The court concluded (para 66) that the close links between the local authority and the housing association in that case meant that the association was a public body for the purposes of granting and terminating the claimant's tenancy. However, it went on to hold (paras 67-72) that there was no breach of Art 8.

The close links between the housing association and the local authority did not exist in *R (Heather) v The Leonard Cheshire Foundation* [2001] 4 CCLR 211, Stanley Burton J. In that case the claimants challenged the closure of a care home on Art 8 grounds. The judge distinguished *Donaghue* on the ground that the special ties between the local authority and the landlord in Donaghue did not exist here. That decision was upheld by the Court of Appeal [2002] 2 All ER 936. That approach to the phrase "public authority" in the context of private care homes has been reaffirmed, albeit by a bare majority, by the House of Lords in *YL (by her litigation friend the Official Solicitor) v Birmingham City Council and others* [2007] UKHL 27, 20 June, HL.

It is suggested, however, that a private company carrying out HB functions on behalf of the local authority will be a "public body" in carrying out such functions. Furthermore, if a social landlord assists with verification work, it will be a "public body" for those purposes. However, a social landlord will not be a "public body" in acting as a landlord, without the special features present in *Donaghue v Poplar Housing Association Ltd* or something akin to them.

Proceedings

7.–(1)   A person who claims that a public authority has acted (or proposes to act) in a way which is made unlawful by section 6(1) may–

(a)   bring proceedings against the authority under this Act in the appropriate court or tribunal, or

(b)   rely on the Convention right or rights concerned in any legal proceedings,

but only if he is (or would be) a victim of the unlawful act.

(2)   In subsection (1)(a) "appropriate court or tribunal" means such court or tribunal as may be determined in accordance with rules; and proceedings against an authority include a counterclaim or similar proceeding.

(3)   If the proceedings are brought on an application for judicial review, the applicant is to be taken to have a sufficient interest in relation to the unlawful act only if he is, or would be, a victim of that act.

(4)   If the proceedings are made by way of a petition for judicial review in Scotland, the applicant shall be taken to have title and interest to sue in relation to the unlawful act only if he is, or would be, a victim of that act.

(5)   Proceedings under subsection (1)(a) must be brought before the end of–

(a) the period of one year beginning with the date on which the act complained of took place; or

(b) such longer period as the court or tribunal considers equitable having regard to all the circumstances,

but that is subject to any rule imposing a stricter time limit in relation to the procedure in question.

(6)   In subsection (1)(b) "legal proceedings" includes–

(a)   proceedings brought by or at the instigation of a public authority; and

(b)   an appeal against the decision of a court or tribunal.

(7)   For the purposes of this section, a person is a victim of an unlawful act only if he would be a victim for the purposes of Article 34 of the Convention if proceedings were brought in the European Court of Human Rights in respect of that act.

(8)   Nothing in this Act creates a criminal offence.

(9)   In this section "rules" means–

(a)   in relation to proceedings before a court or tribunal outside Scotland, rules made by the Lord Chancellor or the Secretary of State for the purposes of this section or rules of court,

(b)   in relation to proceedings before a court or tribunal in Scotland, rules made by the Secretary of State for those purposes,

(c)   in relation to proceedings before a tribunal in Northern Ireland–

    (i)   which deals with transferred matters; and

    (ii)   for which no rules made under paragraph (a) are in force,

rules made by a Northern Ireland department for those purposes,

and includes provision made by order under section 1 of the Courts and Legal Services Act 1990.

(10)   In making rules, regard must be had to section 9.

(11)   The Minister who has power to make rules in relation to a particular tribunal may, to the extent he considers it necessary to ensure that the tribunal can provide an appropriate remedy in relation to an act (or proposed act) of a public authority which is (or would be) unlawful as a result of section 6(1), by order add to–

(a)   the relief or remedies which the tribunal may grant; or

(b)   the grounds on which it may grant any of them.

(12)   An order made under subsection (11) may contain such incidental, supplemental, consequential or transitional provision as the Minister making it considers appropriate.

(13)   "The Minister" includes the Northern Ireland department concerned.

General Note

This deals with the procedure by which allegations of a breach of Convention rights can be raised for the consideration of the courts and tribunals.

Analysis

Subsections (1)(a), (2) to (5) and (7) to (13): Bringing proceedings for a breach of the Convention

Taken together, these subsections envisage the commencement of proceedings before a court or tribunal complaining of the breach of the Convention. By its terms, the right to commence proceedings under subs (1)(a) may apply even where the breach has not yet occurred, in which case an injunction (interdict in Scotland) may be sought to restrain the breach.

Subs (1)(a) and (2) restrict the right to bring proceedings to a court or tribunal that may be identified in accordance with rules as being the appropriate forum in which to proceed. By r7.11 of the Civil Procedure Rules 1998, in England and Wales proceedings may be issued in the High Court or the County Court, except where complaint is made about a judicial act in which case proceedings must be commenced in the High Court: see s9 below for complaints about judicial acts.

No rules have been made conferring a right to commence proceedings in the First-tier Tribunal or before the Upper Tribunal. However, Convention rights may be relied upon in an appeal under subs (1)(b).

Subs (1)(a), (3), (4) and (7) deal with the right to bring proceedings. A person must be a "victim" for the purposes of the Convention if s/he is to have the right to commence proceedings. That includes proceedings for judicial review, where the test of standing (England and Wales) or title and interest (Scotland) is different. Art 34 of the Convention, referred to in subs (7), does not define "victim". The following rules are a summary of the caselaw of the court and commissioner on the subject: see, for example, Starmer, *European Human Rights Law* (2000) paras 2.18-2.39.

(1)   The Convention applies to persons not in the country or acts taking place outside the country if they are done on behalf of the state.

(2)   A corporate body may be a victim. A governmental organisation, however, cannot bring proceedings.

(3)   Those potentially affected, as well as those who have already been affected, may bring proceedings as long as the risk of a breach of the Convention is not merely theoretical.

(4)   People indirectly affected, such as the family members of a claimant, or shareholders in a company that is a landlord, may be a "victim". Claims may also be brought by personal representatives on death or incapacity.

Subs (5) imposes a one-year limitation period in respect of the commencement of proceedings. That time limit is, however, subject to any stricter time limit provided for by relevant rules.

   Subs (9) to (13) deal with rule-making powers.

Subsections (1)(b) and (6): Relying on a breach of the Convention in proceedings
Breaches of Convention rights may be relied upon in any proceedings. These include appeals to the First-tier Tribunal or subsequent appeals to the Upper Tribunal or beyond. If proceedings are brought, for example for possession, it will be possible to allege that the court would act in breach of the Convention by granting possession as well as that the claimant is itself acting in breach of the Convention if it is a public body. For an example of this approach, see *Donaghue v Poplar Housing Association Ltd* [2002] QB 58, CA, where the tenant alleged that the court was in breach of Art 6 for proceeding in an unfair manner and the claimant landlord was in breach of Art 8 by seeking possession.

Judicial remedies

8.–(1)   In relation to any act (or proposed act) of a public authority which the court finds is (or would be) unlawful, it may grant such relief or remedy, or make such order, within its powers as it considers just and appropriate.

(2)   But damages may be awarded only by a court which has power to award damages, or to order the payment of compensation, in civil proceedings.

(3)   No award of damages is to be made unless, taking account of all the circumstances of the case, including–

(a)   any other relief or remedy granted, or order made, in relation to the act in question (by that or any other court), and

(b)   the consequences of any decision (of that or any other court) in respect of that act,

the court is satisfied that the award is necessary to afford just satisfaction to the person in whose favour it is made.

(4)   In determining–

(a)   whether to award damages, or

(b)   the amount of an award,

the court must take into account the principles applied by the European Court of Human Rights in relation to the award of compensation under Article 41 of the Convention.

(5)   A public authority against which damages are awarded is to be treated–

(a)   in Scotland, for the purposes of section 3 of the Law Reform (Miscellaneous Provisions) (Scotland) Act 1940 as if the award were made in an action of damages in which the authority has been found liable in respect of loss or damage to the person to whom the award is made;

(b)   for the purposes of the Civil Liability (Contribution) Act 1978 as liable in respect of damage suffered by the person to whom the award is made.

(6)   In this section–

''court'' includes a tribunal;

''damages'' means damages for an unlawful act of a public authority; and

''unlawful'' means unlawful under section 6(1).

General Note
This section deals with the remedies that a court or tribunal may grant when proceedings are brought under s7 against a public body.

Analysis
   Subs (1) and (2) allow a court (which includes, by virtue of subs (6), a tribunal) to grant remedies for acts which are unlawful under s6. However, the key phrase here is "within its powers". There is no additional power to grant remedies conferred by s8. It follows that tribunals and commissioners have no power to award damages or costs by virtue of the 1998 Act, as confirmed by subs (2).

Subs (3) to (5) deal with awards of damages. An award of damages is only to be made if it is necessary to give "just satisfaction" to the victim. This is a phrase which originates in Art 41, and indeed subs (4) requires a court to consider the caselaw under Art 41 in deciding whether to award damages and, if so, how much.

However, it is difficult to distil any clear principles from the Strasbourg caselaw. Domestic caselaw has now illuminated the situations in which damages will be awarded for breaches of Art 8 of the Convention. In *R (Anufrijeva) v Southwark LBC* [2003] EWCA Civ 1406, CA, the Court of Appeal gave guidance on this question. The court said (para 65) that a broad-brush approach should be adopted. Where there is pecuniary loss caused by the breach, that will ordinarily be calculated and awarded (para 59). However, non-pecuniary loss causes greater difficulty, as recognised by the Court at para 60:

"Infringements can involve a variety of treatment of an individual which is objectionable in itself. The treatment may give rise to distress, anxiety, and, in extreme cases, psychiatric trauma. The primary object of the proceedings will often be to bring the adverse treatment to an end. If this is achieved is this enough to constitute 'just satisfaction' or is it necessary to award damages to compensate for the adverse treatment that has occurred? More particularly, should damages be awarded for anxiety and distress that has been occasioned by the breach? It is in relation to these questions that Strasbourg fails to give a consistent or coherent answer."

In cases of maladministration such as those being considered by the Court, the "critical message is that the remedy has to be 'just and appropriate' and 'necessary' to afford 'just satisfaction'" (para 66). In deciding whether the breach of rights required an award of damages, the Court said that the scale and manner of the breach, and the conduct of the parties, would all be relevant (paras 66-68). As far as quantum was concerned, the amounts awarded should be modest but not minimal, and comparable awards by the Local Government Ombudsman are a useful comparator (paras 75, 78). It appears that the £10,000 awarded to the claimants in *R (Bernard) v Enfield LBC* [2002] 5 CCLR 589 for leaving a severely disabled woman and her family in appalling and degrading living conditions for a considerable period of time is the very maximum award that should be made for a breach of Art 8.

The court also gave guidance as to the procedure that should be followed in relation to damages claims, having expressed its concern at the cost of the litigation before it (paras 81). Damages claims for maladministration should ordinarily proceed by way of judicial review and the claimant should be prepared to justify not using the Ombudsman or Adjudicator instead. Claims for damages should be determined on the papers by the appropriate level of judge, if necessary separately to any claim for other relief (such as an order to compel a local authority to determine a claim).

However, in *R(Greenfield) v Secretary of State for the Home Department* [2005] UKHL 14, [2005] 2 All ER 240, HL, the House of Lords, albeit in the context of a claim for damages for breach of Art 6, rejected the claimant's argument, which was predicated at least in part on the approach said to have been adopted in *R (Bernard) v Enfield* and *Anufrijeva*, that courts in England and Wales, when exercising their power to award damages under s8, should apply domestic scales of damages. In Lord Bingham's opinion one of the broader reasons why this approach should not be followed was that the HRA is not a tort statute: its objects are different and broader. As such, even in a case where a finding of violation is not judged to afford the applicant just satisfaction (and in most Art 6 violation cases the finding of breach of Art 6 should, in Lord Bingham's view, of itself provide the just satisfaction or remedy), such a finding will be an important part of the claimant's remedy. Accordingly, in Art 6 cases at least awards of damages should be modestly low.

Overall, Lord Bingham's view in *Greenfield* was that courts in the UK, although not inflexibly bound by Strasbourg awards in what may be different cases, should not aim to be significantly more or less generous than the ECtHR might be expected to be, in a case where it was willing to make an award at all.

Judicial acts

9.–(1) Proceedings under section 7(1)(a) in respect of a judicial act may be brought only–

(a) by exercising a right of appeal;

(b) on an application (in Scotland a petition) for judicial review; or

(c) in such other forum as may be prescribed by rules.

(2) That does not affect any rule of law which prevents a court from being the subject of judicial review.

(3) In proceedings under this Act in respect of a judicial act done in good faith, damages may not be awarded otherwise than to compensate a person to the extent required by Article 5(5) of the Convention.

(4) An award of damages permitted by subsection (3) is to be made against the Crown; but no award may be made unless the appropriate person, if not a party to the proceedings, is joined.

(5)   In this section–
"appropriate person" means the Minister responsible for the court concerned, or a person or government department nominated by him;
"court" includes a tribunal;
"judge" includes a member of a tribunal, a justice of the peace and a clerk or other officer entitled to exercise the jurisdiction of a court;
"judicial act" means a judicial act of a court and includes an act done on the instructions, or on behalf, of a judge; and
"rules" has the same meaning as in section 7(9).

Remedial action

Power to take remedial action

10.–(1)   This section applies if–
(a)   a provision of legislation has been declared under section 4 to be incompatible with a Convention right and, if an appeal lies–
(i)   all persons who may appeal have stated in writing that they do not intend to do so;
(ii)   the time for bringing an appeal has expired and no appeal has been brought within that time; or
(iii)   an appeal brought within that time has been determined or abandoned; or
(b)   it appears to a Minister of the Crown or Her Majesty in Council that, having regard to a finding of the European Court of Human Rights made after the coming into force of this section in proceedings against the United Kingdom, a provision of legislation is incompatible with an obligation of the United Kingdom arising from the Convention.
(2)   If a Minister of the Crown considers that there are compelling reasons for proceeding under this section, he may by order make such amendments to the legislation as he considers necessary to remove the incompatibility.
(3)   If, in the case of subordinate legislation, a Minister of the Crown considers–
(a)   that it is necessary to amend the primary legislation under which the subordinate legislation in question was made, in order to enable the incompatibility to be removed, and
(b)   that there are compelling reasons for proceeding under this section,
he may by order make such amendments to the primary legislation as he considers necessary.
(4)   This section also applies where the provision in question is in subordinate legislation and has been quashed, or declared invalid, by reason of incompatibility with a Convention right and the Minister proposes to proceed under paragraph 2(b) of Schedule 2.
(5)   If the legislation is an Order in Council, the power conferred by subsection (2) or (3) is exercisable by Her Majesty in Council.
(6)   In this section "legislation" does not include a Measure of the Church Assembly or of the General Synod of the Church of England.
(7)   Schedule 2 makes further provision about remedial orders.

Other rights and proceedings

Safeguard for existing human rights

11.   A person's reliance on a Convention right does not restrict–
(a)   any other right or freedom conferred on him by or under any law having effect in any part of the United Kingdom; or
(b)   his right to make any claim or bring any proceedings which he could make or bring apart from sections 7 to 9.

Freedom of thought, conscience and religion

13.–(1)   If a court's determination of any question arising under this Act might affect the exercise by a religious organisation (itself or its members collectively) of the Convention right to freedom of thought, conscience and religion, it must have particular regard to the importance of that right.

(2)   In this section "court" includes a tribunal.

Supplemental

Orders etc under this Act

20.–(1)   Any power of a Minister of the Crown to make an order under this Act is exercisable by statutory instrument.

(2)   The power of the Lord Chancellor or the Secretary of State to make rules (other than rules of court) under section 2(3) or 7(9) is exercisable by statutory instrument.

(3)   Any statutory instrument made under section 14, 15 or 16(7) must be laid before Parliament.

(4)   No order may be made by the Lord Chancellor or the Secretary of State under section 1(4), 7(11) or 16(2) unless a draft of the order has been laid before, and approved by, each House of Parliament.

(5)   Any statutory instrument made under section 18(7) or Schedule 4, or to which subsection (2) applies, shall be subject to annulment in pursuance of a resolution of either House of Parliament.

(6)   The power of a Northern Ireland department to make–

(a)   rules under section 2(3)(c) or 7(9)(c), or

(b)   an order under section 7(11),

is exercisable by statutory rule for the purposes of the Statutory Rules (Northern Ireland) Order 1979.

(7)   Any rules made under section 2(3)(c) or 7(9)(c) shall be subject to negative resolution; and section 41(6) of the Interpretation Act Northern Ireland) 1954 (meaning of "subject to negative resolution") shall apply as if the power to make the rules were conferred by an Act of the Northern Ireland Assembly.

(8)   No order may be made by a Northern Ireland department under section 7(11) unless a draft of the order has been laid before, and approved by, the Northern Ireland Assembly.

Interpretation etc

21.–(1)   In this Act–

"amend" includes repeal and apply (with or without modifications);

"the appropriate Minister" means the Minister of the Crown having charge of the appropriate authorised government department (within the meaning of the Crown Proceedings Act 1947);

"the Commission" means the European Commission of Human Rights;

"the Convention" means the Convention for the Protection of Human Rights and Fundamental Freedoms, agreed by the Council of Europe at Rome on 4th November 1950 as it has effect for the time being in relation to the United Kingdom;

"declaration of incompatibility" means a declaration under section 4;

"Minister of the Crown" has the same meaning as in the Ministers of the Crown Act 1975;

"Northern Ireland Minister" includes the First Minister and the deputy First Minister in Northern Ireland;

"primary legislation" means any–

(a)   public general Act;

(b)   local and personal Act;

(c)   private Act;

(d)   Measure of the Church Assembly;

(e)   Measure of the General Synod of the Church of England;

(f)   Order in Council–
- (i)   made in exercise of Her Majesty's Royal Prerogative;
- (ii)   made under section 38(1)(a) of the Northern Ireland Constitution Act 1973 or the corresponding provision of the Northern Ireland Act 1998; or
- (iii)   amending an Act of a kind mentioned in paragraph (a), (b) or (c);

and includes an order or other instrument made under primary legislation (otherwise than by the National Assembly for Wales, a member of the Scottish Executive, a Northern Ireland Minister or a Northern Ireland department) to the extent to which it operates to bring one or more provisions of that legislation into force or amends any primary legislation;

"the First Protocol" means the protocol to the Convention agreed at Paris on 20th March 1952;

"the Sixth Protocol" means the protocol to the Convention agreed at Strasbourg on 28th April 1983;

"the Eleventh Protocol" means the protocol to the Convention (restructuring the control machinery established by the Convention) agreed at Strasbourg on 11th May 1994;

"remedial order" means an order under section 10;

"subordinate legislation" means any–
- (a)   Order in Council other than one–
  - (i)   made in exercise of Her Majesty's Royal Prerogative;
  - (ii)   made under section 38(1)(a) of the Northern Ireland Constitution Act 1973 or the corresponding provision of the Northern Ireland Act 1998; or
  - (iii)   amending an Act of a kind mentioned in the definition of primary legislation;
- (b)   Act of the Scottish Parliament;
- (c)   Act of the Parliament of Northern Ireland;
- (d)   Measure of the Assembly established under section 1 of the Northern Ireland Assembly Act 1973;
- (e)   Act of the Northern Ireland Assembly;
- (f)   order, rules, regulations, scheme, warrant, byelaw or other instrument made under primary legislation (except to the extent to which it operates to bring one or more provisions of that legislation into force or amends any primary legislation);
- (g)   order, rules, regulations, scheme, warrant, byelaw or other instrument made under legislation mentioned in paragraph (b), (c), (d) or (e) or made under an Order in Council applying only to Northern Ireland;
- (h)   order, rules, regulations, scheme, warrant, byelaw or other instrument made by a member of the Scottish Executive, a Northern Ireland Minister or a Northern Ireland department in exercise of prerogative or other executive functions of Her Majesty which are exercisable by such a person on behalf of Her Majesty;

"transferred matters" has the same meaning as in the Northern Ireland Act 1998; and

"tribunal" means any tribunal in which legal proceedings may be brought.

(2)   The references in paragraphs (b) and (c) of section 2(1) to Articles are to Articles of the Convention as they had effect immediately before the coming into force of the Eleventh Protocol.

(3)   The reference in paragraph (d) of section 2(1) to Article 46 includes a reference to Articles 32 and 54 of the Convention as they had effect immediately before the coming into force of the Eleventh Protocol.

(4)   The references in section 2(1) to a report or decision of the Commission or a decision of the Committee of Ministers include references to a report or decision made as provided by paragraphs 3, 4 and 6 of Article 5 of the Eleventh Protocol (transitional provisions).

(5)   Any liability under the Army Act 1955, the Air Force Act 1955 or the Naval Discipline Act 1957 to suffer death for an offence is replaced by a liability to imprisonment for life or any less punishment authorised by those Acts; and those Acts shall accordingly have effect with the necessary modifications.

Short title, commencement, application and extent

22.–(1)   This Act may be cited as the Human Rights Act 1998.

(2)   Sections 18, 20 and 21(5) and this section come into force on the passing of this Act.

(3)   The other provisions of this Act come into force on such day as the Secretary of State may by order appoint; and different days may be appointed for different purposes.

(4)   Paragraph (b) of subsection (1) of section 7 applies to proceedings brought by or at the instigation of a public authority whenever the act in question took place; but otherwise that subsection does not apply to an act taking place before the coming into force of that section.

(5)   This Act binds the Crown.

(6)   This Act extends to Northern Ireland.

(7)   Section 21(5), so far as it relates to any provision contained in the Army Act 1955, the Air Force Act 1955 or the Naval Discipline Act 1957, extends to any place to which that provision extends.

Analysis

Subs (3) provides that the bulk of the 1998 Act was to come into force on the making of orders. The Human Rights Act (Commencement) Order 1998 SI No 2882 brought s19 (which allows ministers presenting legislation to Parliament to make statements about the compatibility of Bills with the Convention) into force from 24 November 1998. The remainder of the Act was brought into force by the Human Rights Act (Commencement No.2) Order 2000 No.1851 from 2 October 2000.

Subs (4) applies a limited retrospectivity to the Act. It is clear that where a public authority brings proceedings, a breach of Convention rights may be relied upon whenever the breach occurred. Thus a claimant who is prosecuted, or a person sued for recovery of an overpayment of HB, may rely on breaches of the Convention occurring prior to 2 October 2000 in those proceedings. 'Proceedings' means legal proceedings and so s22(4) does not apply to supersession (or revision) decisions instigated by a Secretary of State decision-maker as s/he only exercises administrative, and not legal, functions: *CDLA 1347/1999* para 29.

Judicial review proceedings are only technically brought in the name of the Crown. The reality is that they are instituted by the claimant, and accordingly damages cannot be claimed by a person whose Convention rights were breached prior to 2 October 2000 in judicial review proceedings: *R (Ben-Abdelaziz) v Secretary of State for the Home Department* [2001] 1 WLR 1485, CA.

The strict limits on the retrospectivity of the 1998 Act have now been confirmed by the House of Lords in *Wilson v First County Trust Ltd (No 2)* [2003] WLR 586. In *Wilson (No 2)*, it was confirmed that the 1998 Act has no application to events occurring prior to 2 October 2000 and so cannot give rise to any cause of action arising before that date save in the strictly limited circumstances set out in subs (4). Neither can the interpretative obligation in s3 apply to the law governing such a case (paras 10-23). The House of Lords did not find it necessary to decide whether the Court of Appeal's approach, in which it had decided that s6(1) obliged it to act compatibly with the Convention on an appeal, was incorrect in all cases. It could not, however, be correct in *Wilson (No 2)* because the court had purported to disapply primary legislation, which was prohibited by s6(2)(a) (paras 24-25).

The latter argument is, of course, of importance where a claimant asserts on an appeal heard after 2 October 2000 that a decision at a lower level in the appellate hierarchy breaches Convention Rights. In *CSDLA 1019/1999* (paras 70-89), the tribunal of commissioners ruled that an alleged breach of Art 6 in the constitution of a tribunal sitting prior to 2 October 2000 could not be relied upon on appeal. The tribunal's conclusion that the inclusion of a doctor who also carried out medical assessments for the Benefits Agency breached the common law rule against bias was overturned by the Court of Session in *SSWP v Gillies* [2003] 2004 SLT 14, reported at 2006 SC (HL) 71 (the decision of the Court of Session was upheld by the House of Lords in *Gillies v SSWP* [2006] UKHL 2, *Times Law Report*, 30 January (reported as *R(DLA) 5/06*). However, if a tribunal sitting after 2 October 2000 breaches a claimant's Convention rights, it does not matter whether the decision under appeal was made before or after that date: *Wilson (No 2)* para 21 and *R(IS) 6/04*; though if the decision under appeal was made before 2 October 2000 it cannot be challenged on the ground that it breached the claimant's Convention rights.

SCHEDULE 1
THE ARTICLES

General Note on Schedule 1

Only the Articles which might conceivably be relevant to HB and CTB entitlement are set out below and discussion is limited to that which is reasonably necessary to consider the arguments that might arise.

Article 3
Prohibition of torture

No one shall be subjected to torture or to inhuman or degrading treatment or punishment.

Analysis

A refusal of HB will not of itself give rise to any breach of Art 3. It is now established that while a state may have a positive obligation under Art 3 to prevent an individual suffering from "degrading treatment", the individual's condition must be of the requisite severity: *Pretty v UK* [2002] 35 EHRR 1, ECHR, para 52, where the ECHR said:

"As regards the types of "treatment" which fall within the scope of Article 3 of the Convention, the Court's case law refers to "ill-treatment" that attains a minimum level of severity and involves actual bodily injury or intense physical or mental suffering. Where treatment humiliates or debases an individual showing lack of respect for, or diminishing, his or her human dignity or arouses feelings of fear, anguish or inferiority capable of breaking an individual's moral and physical resistance, it may be characterised as degrading and also fall within the prohibition of Article 3. The suffering which flows from naturally occurring illness, physical or mental, may be treatment, where it is, or risks being, exacerbated by treatment, whether flowing from conditions of detention, expulsion or other measures, for which the authorities can be held responsible."

A claimant who is refused HB will ordinarily be able to avail her/himself of other forms of welfare support, whether by moving to a property where a claim for HB is unobjectionable or by other means. However, the threat of destitution may give rise to a breach of Art 3: *R v Secretary of State for the Home Department ex parte Limbuela and others* [2005] UKHL 66, 3 November, HL. So, even homelessness or destitution may be sufficient.

Article 6
Right to a fair trial

1. In the determination of his civil rights and obligations or of any criminal charge against him, everyone is entitled to a fair and public hearing within a reasonable time by an independent and impartial tribunal established by law. Judgment shall be pronounced publicly but the press and public may be excluded from all or part of the trial in the interest of morals, public order or national security in a democratic society, where the interests of juveniles or the protection of the private life of the parties so require, or to the extent strictly necessary in the opinion of the court in special circumstances where publicity would prejudice the interests of justice.

2.-3. *[Omitted]*

Analysis

Paras 2 and 3 concern only criminal proceedings and accordingly are omitted here. A decision on recoverability of overpayments does not involve the determination of a "criminal charge": *R(IS) 1/04*. Art 6 is the cornerstone of the procedural protections envisaged by the Convention.

"... the determination of his civil rights and obligations ...". Art 6 only has application if the matter in dispute is a "civil right" or "civil obligation". It now seems to be clear that the determination of entitlements to welfare benefits is the determination of a "civil right". Early cases established this principle in relation to contributory benefits, in which a right of property was recognised (see Prot 1 Art 1 below): see eg, *Feldbrugge v Netherlands* (1986) 8 EHRR 425; *Deumeland v Germany* [1986] 8 EHRR 448 at 468, para 74, ECtHR. The objection taken by the states in those cases was that entitlement to benefits was a public law right and not "civil" in nature. The now generally accepted view is that where legislation confers an enforceable right to a benefit, Art 6 applies to proceedings in which entitlement to that benefit is considered. This is confirmed by *Salesi v Italy* (1993) 26 EHRR 187 at 199, para 19, ECtHR, which concerned a non-contributory pension. A similar perspective was adopted by the Tribunal of Commissioners in *R(IS) 15/04* in the context of a decision not to revise. The commissioners reasoned firstly that a claimant is entitled to apply for a revision on the grounds of official error and, if that ground is made out, is entitled to have the decision revised. Accordingly, there is a 'right' to the revision. Secondly, although the 'civil right' in question is the right to the social security benefit which was the subject of the decision on the claim, seeking a revision of that decision is part of the process whereby entitlement to the benefit is determined, and therefore falls within the scope of Art 6.

The issue of whether decisions relating to HB entitlement concern "civil rights and obligations" has been settled by the decision of Pitchford J in *R (Cumpsty) v Rent Officer* [2002] EWHC 2526 (Admin), paras 76-80. The judge decided that even though the rent officer's determination did not itself decide the claimant's HB entitlement, it was such a vital and integral part of that decision that it was itself a determination of civil rights and obligations. See to similar effect the reasoning in *R(IS) 6/04*.

"... a fair and public hearing ...". In many respects, the concept of a fair hearing mirrors the rules of natural justice in domestic law. The incorporation of Art 6, however, arguably broadens and emphasises these rules and, more importantly, gives them teeth where unfairness results from the application of a statutory rule.

The first aspect of a fair hearing is equality of arms. There must be equal opportunities on the two sides to a dispute to present their cases: *Dombo Beheer BV v Netherlands* (1993) 18 EHRR 213 at 226-8, ECtHR, paras 30-40. It is inherent in this that parties must ordinarily have sight of the evidence before the tribunal: *Ruiz-Mateos v Spain* (1993) 16 EHRR 505, para 63. In *CDLA 5413/1999* paras 49-51, it was suggested that the provisions for deemed notification of an oral hearing before a tribunal (and hence, presumably the similar provisions deeming receipt of a notification of a decision, a statement of reasons and so on) could offend against this principle if they caused injustice. In *CJSA 5100/2001* the appeal to an appeal tribunal turned on a contested issue of fact, namely whether an investigating officer from the DWP had seen the claimant working, but the investigating officer failed to attend at the hearing and so could not be cross-examined by the claimant. Applying the 'equality of arms' principle, the commissioner ruled that while there was nothing the claimant could do to get the officer to attend, the Secretary of State could have secured his attendance, and the appeal tribunal then compounded this problem, and thereby erred in law, in failing to adjourn the case to enable the Secretary of State to seek the attendance of the investigating officer: see para 13. See also *CIB 3985/2001* where similar reasoning was applied to the Secretary of State's failure to make available to the tribunal relevant evidence in the form of a medical report which only he, and not the claimant held. In *CDLA 2748/2002* (para 11), the commissioner held that if there were difficulties with interpretation that hampered the presentation of a claimant's case, Art 6 might be breached if the tribunal failed to take appropriate action to remedy the situation.

Secondly, the process of hearing a case must be reasonably accessible. If a party suffers the loss of her/his case through misleading rules of procedure, then there might be a violation of Art 6: *Bellet v France* (1995) unreported, case number A/333-B, ECtHR. This could apply if an appeal is inadvertently lodged out of time and not subsequently admitted.

The availability of legal aid is a controversial topic. In *Airey v Ireland* (1979) 2 EHRR 305, the Court found a violation in a family case where a woman was attempting to divorce a violent husband. The question posed was whether a claimant could effectively represent her/himself in the particular proceedings in question without legal representation. Since then, the court has qualified the effect of *Airey*. In *Munro v UK* [1986] 48 DR 154, ECmHR, which concerned defamation proceedings, the Commission contrasted the nature of those proceedings with the intimate nature of the family proceedings in *Airey* and the serious consequences for the family. Moreover, if there is some other means of assistance available, *Andronicou v Cyprus* [1998] 25 EHRR 491, ECtHR suggests that there will be no violation of Art 6. Since the consequences of the loss of HB entitlement are fairly intimate and serious, involving the potential loss of a home, it may be arguable that the absence of Community Legal Service funding for a sufficiently complex tribunal or commissioner hearing might infringe Art 6, particularly if an application for funding under the Access to Justice Act 1999 has been refused.

The concept of a fair hearing also involves the right to a reasoned decision and a public hearing, neither of which should present particular difficulties within the present adjudication system, save that commissioners should exercise caution in refusing an oral hearing if a claimant wants one.

One issue of particular concern within the HB system remains the rent officer system.

However, the question of whether the system of determinations by a rent officer was compliant with Art 6 was decided affirmatively in *Cumpsty*. There, the claimant had been given a re-determination, had been given reasons for the rent officer's conclusion as to the local reference rent level and had entered into extensive correspondence with the rent officer. Pitchford J held that the rent officer was "independent and impartial" (paras 81-82) and that there was sufficient involvement of the claimant in the process to give him a "fair hearing" (para 91). It remains open to question whether that would be so in a case where the rent officer refused to give reasons or gave insufficient reasons to enable a meaningful dialogue to take place, particularly in the light of *Tsfayo* (see below).

"... within a reasonable time ...". *Feldbrugge*, *Denneland* and *Salesi* (cited above) are all examples of complaints of breach of the right to a determination within a reasonable time. In each case, the delay was several years. In the context of HB, however, since a home can be lost in as little as three to four months if HB is not put into payment, and a claim is supposed to be decided within 14 days, it may be that the tolerable period of delay is considerably less. However, in *R(IS) 1/04* and *R(IS) 2/04* delays of seven months and two years respectively in having initial decisions heard on an appeal were held to have met the reasonable time criterion and so did not breach Article 6.

In *CIB 8/2008* [2009] UKUT 47 (AAC), the DWP had delayed five years in preparing the claimant's appeal and forwarding it to the Tribunal Service, the delay being caused solely by administrative failure to progress the appeal. Judge Lane held that there had been a breach of Art 6. Citing *Procurator Fiscal v Dyer and Watson* [2002] UKPC D1, she said that where there is unreasonable delay, a breach of Art 6 is not dependant on proof of prejudice or detriment arising from the delay; prejudice is presumed if the delay is unreasonable. *Dyer* also confirmed that the manner in which administrative authorities deal with a dispute can be material to the issue of whether there has been unreasonable delay in providing a hearing.

Although Judge Lane's conclusion on remedy (see below) is consistent with the caselaw on Art 6, it is suggested that her view about Art 6 being breached in a case of unreasonable delay even where that delay has not prejudiced the right to a fair hearing needs to be treated with some considerable caution. The reason for this is that the reasoning of *Dyer* on this point has been undercut, if not entirely removed, by the decision of the House of Lords in the later case (to which Judge Lane did not refer) of *Attorney Generals' Reference No2 of 2001* [2003] UKHL 68, [2004] 1 All ER 1041. In that case a nine member House of Lords held (by a majority of 7 to 2), in the context of the remedy for criminal trial which had been the subject of unreasonable pre-trial delay but where no prejudice woud have arisen to the defendant to proceed with the trial, that the hearing could only not proceed if a fair hearing was no longer possible. In other words, an unreasonable delay of itself is not enough and prejudice or lack of fairness has to be shown. The majority of the House of Lords held that the same considerations applied with equal (if not more) force to civil proceedings, and indicated that this analysis went not just to what remedy may be granted but whether Article 6 had been breached in the first place (see, for example, Lord Nicholls at paras [36-39], Lord Hobhouse at paras [116] to [120] and Lord Millett at paras [131] to [137]).

If the requirement of a hearing within "a reasonable time" is breached, it is not open to a tribunal to allow a claimant's appeal simply on that basis or even, in an overpayment case, to impose a permanent stay: *CSIS 460/ 2002* (paras 41-49). In *CIB 8/2008* [2009] UKUT 47 (AAC) (cited above), the claimant sought to have his appeal allowed or stayed indefinitely. Judge Lane decided this would be an inappropriate remedy. She said: "The jurisprudence of both the European Court of Human Rights and British courts indicates that, even where there has been very lengthy delay in cases involving serious criminal charges, it is disproportionate to stay or allow an appeal in all but the most exceptional cases, if at all. This appeal is manifestly not an example of an exceptional case . . . having regard to a balance between the appellant and the public interest in maintaining the integrity of welfare benefit funds."

"... by an independent and impartial tribunal ...". At the time that the 1998 Act came into force, it was thought to be self-evident that the old Review Board system contravened Art 6 because a tribunal composed of members of the local authority could not be "independent and impartial". That has at long last been confirmed by the European Court of Human Rights in *Tsfayo v United Kingdom* (application no: 60860/00) 2006, 14 November, unreported, ECtHR.

However, prior to *Tsfayo*, the courts in the UK had sought to limit this vital component of Art 6 as it is applied to decision-making by public authorities in social welfare matters. The reasoning of the UK courts rests on the decision of the House of Lords in *R (Alconbury Developments Ltd) v Secretary of State for the Environment, Transport and the Regions* [2003] 2 AC 295, HL, where it was held that although a planning inspector was not independent of the Secretary of State, Art 6 did not require a full appeal to an independent court on the facts as well as law and judicial review was a sufficient safeguard for those concerned with planning inquiries. A large part of the House of Lords' reasoning was that since planning matters raised matters of public interest as well as a dispute between individuals and the planning authority, it was right that the decisions on matters of fact should be taken by someone who was publicly accountable (such as the Secretary of State through her/his inspectors).

As a matter of principle, it is difficult to quarrel with such a conclusion. However, the same reasoning was then applied to situations where there is no general public interest in the outcome of the dispute between citizen and state beyond the question of expenditure of public funds. Thus in *Begum v Tower Hamlets LBC* [2003] 2 WLR 238, HL, it was held that no appeal on questions of fact was necessary in homelessness cases for compliance with Art 6, and in *R (Beeson) v Dorset* [2002] 6 CCLR 5, CA, a panel appointed by the local authority, controlled by judicial review, was held to be an adequate safeguard for a citizen aggrieved by a decision that he had deliberately disposed of capital in order to qualify for the provision of accommodation under s21 National Assistance Act 1948. The fears expressed by the courts of "over-judicialisation" of administrative procedures sit very uneasily with the existence of extensive rights of appeal on questions of fact in social security issues and the vital importance of the issues raised to the well-being of the individual. How much of *Alconbury* and *Begum* may read across to HB/CTB adjudication in a post-*Tsfayo* world but one where there is a right of appeal to an independent appeal tribunal against most decisions remains to be worked out.

In *R(IS) 6/04* (paras 36-49), the commissioner ruled that the exclusion of a right of appeal on questions relating to whether a valid claim had been made infringed Art 6. It is not a breach of Art 6 for a commissioner who has previously decided that leave to appeal against a tribunal's decision should be refused to decide whether or not to set aside the refusal of leave: see *CDLA 3432/2001* paras 2-3 and *Sengupta v Holmes* [2002] *The Times* 19 August, CA. The same will apply, therefore, to tribunal members sitting and determining whether to set aside their own decisions, unless perhaps there is some impropriety by the tribunal member alleged. Similarly, there can be no objection to a tribunal member hearing an appeal simply on the basis that the member has sat on a previous tribunal which dismissed an appeal by the same claimant: *R (Wall) v Appeals Service* [2003] EWHC 465 Admin, para 14. There must be some basis for satisfying the apparent bias test, as to which see the commentary to Sch 7 para 8 CSPSSA.

Application to appeals. While Art 6 does not require a state to provide a system of appeals from the court or tribunal which gives the initial independent determination required by Art 6, if such a system is provided then that system must also comply with the safeguards of the Article: *Fedje v Sweden* [1994] 17 EHRR 14, para 32, ECtHR.

Article 8
Right to respect for private and family life

1.   Everyone has the right to respect for his private and family life, his home and his correspondence.

2.   There shall be no interference by a public authority with the exercise of this right except such as is in accordance with the law and is necessary in a democratic society in the interests of national security, public safety or the economic well-being of the country, for the prevention of disorder or crime, for the protection of health or morals, or for the protection of the rights and freedoms of others.

Analysis

Art 8 is in far less absolute terms than Art 6. It confers a right only to "respect" for the matters set out therein. There is no absolute obligation on a state to provide welfare support of a particular kind: *Andersson v Sweden*

[1986] 46 DR 251, ECmHR; *Petrovic v Austria* [1998] 4 BHRC 232, ECtHR (para 26); *R (Tucker) v Secretary of State for Social Security* [2001] EWHC Admin 260 (para 22).

Art 8, however, might be of relevance to a case in which a local authority had failed to adjudicate a claim for HB and a claimant lost her/his home as a result. No claim for damages for breach of statutory duty would lie in such circumstances: *Haringey LBC v Cotter* [1996] 29 HLR 682, CA. However, it is arguable that by failing to comply with obligations created by the state for the protection of a claimant's home, the local authority breached Art 8 in such a situation and would be liable in damages. There is a distinction between a complaint that the HB Regs exclude a claimant from entitlement (as in *Tucker*) and a complaint that the claimant is entitled to benefit but the relevant authority failed to decide so quickly enough.

Guidance as to the circumstances in which maladministration of a statutory scheme could give rise to a breach of Art 8 was given in *R (Anufrijeva) v Southwark LBC* [2003] EWCA Civ 1406, CA. Although there is no positive duty to provide particular forms of welfare support, nevertheless if in failing to adjudicate an HB claim the local authority failed to show respect for the home, then Art 8 might be breached: compare *Anufrijeva* para 43, where it was said that if withholding welfare support resulted in a lack of respect for family life, Art 8 could be breached. It is suggested that by analogy, since HB is a scheme designed to protect a person's home and thereby show "respect" for it, a failure to administer the HB scheme properly may give rise to a claim under Art 8 in principle. In para 45, the court said:

"In so far as Article 8 imposes positive obligations, these are not absolute. Before inaction can amount to a lack of respect for private and family life, there must be some ground for criticising the failure to act. There must be an element of culpability. At the very least there must be knowledge that the claimant's private and family life were at risk . . . Where the domestic law of a State imposes positive obligations in relation to the provision of welfare support, breach of those positive obligations of domestic law may suffice to provide the element of culpability necessary to establish a breach of Article 8, provided that the impact on private or family life is sufficiently serious and was foreseeable."

If the word "home" is transposed for "private and family" it seems, for example, that there is no reason why a local authority which ignores repeated pleas by a claimant and her/his representatives to adjudicate a HB claim for no good reason and which is aware that possession proceedings are pending would not be in breach of Art 8. Problems caused by lack of resources may, however, be taken into account when deciding whether Art 8 is breached: para 47. In para 48, the court said:

"Newman J suggested . . . that it is likely that the acts of a public authority will have to have so far departed from the performance of its duty as to amount to a denial or contradiction of that duty before Article 8 will be infringed. We think that this puts the position somewhat too high, for in considering whether the threshold of Article 8 has been reached it is necessary to have regard both to the extent of the culpability of the failure to act and to the severity of the consequence. Clearly, where one is considering whether there has been a lack of respect for Article 8 rights, the more glaring the deficiency in the behaviour of the public authority, the easier it will be to establish the necessary want of respect. Isolated acts of even significant carelessness are unlikely to suffice."

It is also possible that Art 8 might be invoked in relation to a failure to adjudicate a claim to a discretionary housing payment (DHP). Refusal of a DHP alone could not constitute a breach of Art 8, unless perhaps the authority was refusing to administer the scheme properly.

But Art 8 cannot be invoked to challenge the level of HB or CTB that is payable under the statutory schemes. In *R (Reynolds) v Secretary of State for Work and Pensions* [2002] EWHC Admin 426, it was stated that: "the broadly worded principle in Article 8 is [not] apt to a challenge to the level of a social security payment", and the Court of Appeal, agreeing, said the IS scheme did not *per se* come within the ambit of Article 8 (for the purposes of mounting an argument under Art 14). None of this reasoning was doubted by the House of Lords on a further appeal in *Reynolds*.

However, *CH 4574/2003* and Sedley LJ in *Langley v Bradford MDC and Secretary of State for Work and Pensions* [2004] EWCA Civ 1343, 15 October, CA, reported as *R(H) 6/05* both hold that the HB scheme does enage Art 8 as it is about respect for the home.

Although the judgment of the House of Lords in *SSWP v M* [2006] UKHL 11, 8 March 2006, reported as *R(CS) 4/06* may have laid down a narrower approach to the ambit of Art 8, given the decision in *Stec and others v United Kingdom* (Application Nos: 65731/01 and 65900/01), 6 July 2005, ECtHR the House of Lords in *R(RJM) v SSWP* [2008] UKHL 63, 22 October 2008, in relation to Article 1 Protocol 1 (see commentary to that Article) it should no longer be a necessary step (in any Art 14 discrimination argument at least) to argue that HB or CTB (save for DHPs) come within the scope of Art 8.

It is not a breach of respect for private life under Art 8 for an authority to film a claimant in public as part of an investigation of her/his entitlement to benefit, as long as the film is only used for that purpose: *R(DLA) 4/02* (para 21).

Article 9
Freedom of Thought, Conscience and Religion

1.   Everyone has the right to freedom of thought, conscience and religion; this right includes freedom to change his religion or belief and freedom, either alone or in community with others and in public or private, to manifest his religion or belief, in worship, teaching, practice and observance.

2.   Freedom to manifest one's religion or beliefs shall be subject only to such limitations as are prescribed by law and are necessary in a democratic society in the interests of public safety, for the protection of public order, health or morals, or for the protection of the rights and freedoms of others.

Analysis

While Art 9 does require some positive action on the part of a state to protect religious beliefs, it does not require the state to subsidise the manifestation of those beliefs. Any challenge, for example, to reg 9(1)(j) of either the HB Regs or the HB(SPC) Regs, or to reg 9(2) on the ground that it aims to exclude living arrangements such as those adopted by the Jesus Fellowship Church from entitlement to HB are unlikely to succeed on Art 9 grounds alone. However, they might form a basis for an Art 14 challenge, particularly in the light of the exhortation in s13. In *R(H) 8/04* (para 30), the commissioner indicated that the exclusion of church members from HB on the ground that they had adopted a communal lifestyle for religious reasons engaged Art 14 in conjunction with Art 9. This conclusion is to be challenged by the Secretary of State on the claimants' appeal to the Court of Appeal.

However, the question of whether Art 9 was 'engaged' on the facts was not given any clear or compelling answer by the Court of Appeal in *Campbell and others v South Northamptonshire District Council and SSWP* [2004] EWCA Civ 409 *The Times* 6 May, CA (reported as *R(H) 8/04*). The only substantive judgment on this point was given by Jacobs LJ where he said that Art 14 was not engaged because there was no violation of Art 9 (or Arts 8 and 1 of Protocol 1). With respect this, however, is the wrong test: it is enough for Art 14 to come into play (or 'be engaged') if the facts of the case come within the ambit, or engage, one of the substantive articles of the Convention (see *The Belgian Linguistics* case), there is no need for that substantive article to itself have been breached. Moreover, in later parts of the judgment the judge considers (and rejects on the facts) arguments that reg 7(1)(a) HB Regs 1987 (now reg 9(1)(a) of both the HB and the HB(SPC) Regs) indirectly discriminated against members of the Jesus Fellowship in a disproportionate manner, all of which suggests that the Court of Appeal was proceeding on the footing that Art 14 could be in play. Perhaps the best explanation for this confusion lies in the Court's emphatic rejection of the claimants' argument that human rights considerations had any bearing on the factual assessment of whether the tenancy agreement was on a commercial basis (see the notes on p252 to reg 9(1) HB Regs), so that their comments on Arts 9, 8 and 14 are, strictly speaking, *obiter*.

Article 14
Prohibition of discrimination

The enjoyment of the rights and freedoms set forth in this Convention shall be secured without discrimination on any ground such as sex, race, colour, language, religion, political or other opinion, national or social origin, association with a national minority, property, birth or other status.

Analysis

Art 14 deals with discrimination in the enjoyment of Convention rights. The issues to be considered in ascertaining whether there is a breach of Art 14 in a particular case have been put in various ways. Perhaps the most straightforward formulation is the four questions posed by Brooke LJ in *Michalak v Wandsworth LBC* [2003] 1 WLR 617 (para 20):

"(i)   Do the facts fall within the ambit of one or more of the substantive Convention provisions . . .?

(ii)   If so, was there different treatment as respects that right between the complainant on the one hand and other persons put forward for comparison ("the chosen comparators") on the other?

(iii)   Were the chosen comparators in an analogous situation to the complainant's situation?

(iv)   If so, did the difference in treatment have an objective and reasonable justification: in other words, did it pursue a legitimate aim and did the differential treatment bear a reasonable relationship of proportionality to the aim sought to be achieved?"

In *R (Carson) v Secretary of State for Work and Pensions* [2003] 3 All ER 577, Laws LJ suggested that questions (iii) and (iv) should be conflated into a composite question: "are the circumstances of X and Y so similar as to call (in the mind of a rational and fair-minded person) for a positive justification for the less favourable treatment of Y in comparison with X?". However, a rigid adherence to these four tests has subsequently been deprecated by the House of Lords in cases such as *R(S) v Chief Constable of South Yorkshire Police* [2004] 1 WLR 2196 (para 24), *Ghaidan v Godin-Mendoza* [2004] UKHL 30, 3 All ER 411 (para 134) and *Carson and Reynolds* [2005] UKHL 37 *The Times* 27 May (para 3). A Tribunal of Commissioner adopted Lord Nicholls approach in this last case, in *R(P) 2/06*, where they quoted as correct his view that the better approach in benefits cases was:

"to keep formulation of the relevant issues in these cases as simple and non-technical as possible. Article 14 does not apply unless the alleged discrimination is in connection with a Convention right and on a ground stated in article 14. If this prerequisite is satisfied, the essential question for the court is whether the alleged discrimination, that is, the difference in treatment of which complaint is made, can withstand scrutiny. Sometimes the answer to this question will be plain. There may be such an obvious, relevant difference between the claimant and those with whom he seeks to compare himself that their situations cannot be regarded as analogous. Sometimes, where the position is not so clear, a different approach is called for. Then the court's scrutiny may best be directed at considering whether the differentiation has a legitimate aim and whether the means chosen to achieve the aim is appropriate and not disproportionate in its adverse impact".

Facts "within the ambit" of a Convention right. The major limitation on Art 14 is that it does not provide a free-standing right not to be discriminated against. On the other hand, it is not necessary to show that another Convention right has been breached, otherwise Art 14 would be devoid of meaning. It must be shown that the circumstances of the discrimination fall within the ambit of one of the other rights guaranteed by the Convention: *The Belgian Linguistics Case (No.2)* [1967] 1 EHRR 252 at 283-4, para 9, ECtHR; *Guygusuz v Austria* [1997] 23 EHRR 364, ECtHR.

In *Guygusuz*, the applicant complained that he had been denied entitlement to an emergency needs benefit on the basis of his nationality. Although the denial of benefit did not itself amount to a breach of Protocol 1 Art 1 (see below), his entitlement to benefit was a "pecuniary right" within the ambit of that article. It followed that while there was no entitlement to benefit under that article, as the state had chosen to provide that benefit it had to ensure it did so without discriminating against the claimant.

In *SSWP v M* [2006] UKHL 11, 8 March 2006, reported as *R(CS) 4/06*, the House of Lords rejected the view that even the most tenuous connection between the allegedly discriminatory rule or regulation under challenge and the rights protected by the other articles of the Convention will suffice to bring the rule or regulation within the ambit of the other article of the Convention. Lord Bingham stated (para 4):

"It is not difficult, when considering any provision of the Convention, including article 8 and article 1 of the First Protocol ("IFP"), to identify the core values which the provision is intended to protect. But the further a situation is removed from one infringing those core values, the weaker the connection becomes, until a point is reached when there is no meaningful connection at all. At the inner extremity a situation may properly be said to be within the ambit or scope of the right, nebulous though those expressions necessarily are. At the outer extremity, it may not. There is no sharp line of demarcation between the two. An exercise of judgment is called for . . . I cannot accept that even a tenuous link is enough. That would be a recipe for artificiality and legalistic ingenuity of an unacceptable kind".

Even this approach is not necessarily free from difficulty where the ambit of Art 8 is concerned, because of its core focus being on *respect* for the home, family and private life: see Lord Walker in *M* at paras 83–84.

Differential treatment. Brooke LJ's questions (ii) and (iii) overlap to a considerable extent.

The grounds of discrimination which can be impugned under Art 14 are limited to discrimination relating to some personal characteristic of the claimant: *Kjeldsen Madsen v Denmark* [1976] 1 EHRR 711, ECtHR (para 56); *R(S) v Chief Constable of South Yorkshire Police* [2004] 1 WLR 2196; *R v Secretary of State for Work and Pensions ex parte Hooper and others* [2005] UKHL 29 and *Carson and Reynolds*. However, this does not mean a personal attribute which is immutable or inherent to the claimant: see, eg, *Francis v Secretary of State for Work and Pensions* [2005] EWCA Civ 1303, 10 November (reported as *R(IS) 6/06*). It can be a characterstic which has been acquired (eg, nationality in some circumstances, language, religion or property), and may be "more concerned with what people do, or with what happens to them , than who they are: but they may still come within article 14": per Lord Walker at para [5] of *R(RJM) v SSWP* [2008] UKHL 63, 22 October 2008. Moreover, a generous meaning should be given to the phrase "or other status" and it should not be too closely limited by the grounds which are specifically prohibited in Art 14 (para [43] of *RJM*), and the absence of one of the specifically prohibited grounds (eg, being homeless so *not* having 'property') may be enough to amount to a personal characteristic (para [44] of *RJM*). The fact that the status arises as a matter of choice is of little significance, and whether or not it is a legal status or has not been recognised by the ECtHR are of little weight (para [47] of *RJM*).

However, the decision of the ECtHR in *Clift v United Kingdom* (Application No 7205/07), 13 July 2010, may mark a step away from the "personal characteristic" thesis by the Strasbourg court. Having examined the derivation of the "personal characteristic" thesis in its own caselaw, but noted other such cases where they had not applied it, the ECtHR said that Art 14 prohibited differences in treatment "based on an identifiable, objective or personal characteristic, or "status" by which person or groups person are distinguishable from one another" (para [55]), and went on:

"[t]he Court therefore considers it clear that while it has consistently referred to a need for a distinction based on a "personal" characteristic in order to engage Article 14...the protection conferred by that Article is not limited to different treatment based on characteristics which are personal in the sense that they are innate or inherent...The question whether there is a difference of treatment based on a personal or identifiable characteristic in any given case is a matter to be assessed taking into consideration all the circumstances of the case and bearing in mind that the aim of the Convention is to guarantee not rights that are theoretical or illusory but rights that are practical and effective...the general purpose of Article 14 is to ensure that where a State provides for rights falling within the ambit of the Convention which go beyond the minimum guarantees set out therein, those supplementary rights are applied fairly and consistently to all those within its jurisdiction unless a difference of treatment is objectively justified" (paras [59] and [60]).

Besides the need to bring the discrimination of which complaint is made within the scope of some other article, not all discrimination will result in a breach of Art 14. The state may escape censure if it is shown that the measure in question has a legitimate aim and the means adopted are proportionate to the aim: *The Belgian Linguistics Case (No.2)* (para 34).

Domestic discrimination law distinguishes between direct discrimination (discriminating against a woman because she is a woman) and indirect discrimination which, generally, involves the imposition of a requirement which fewer people of a particular group can comply with (discriminating against a woman by prohibiting pregnant people from participating in an activity). The Convention does not distinguish between direct and indirect discrimination and there has been some doubt as to whether Art 14 extends to the latter form of treatment. The Court In *Barber* doubted that it did but not all the relevant Strasbourg caselaw was cited and in *R(H) 8/04* (paras 39-52) the commissioner decided that the claimants, members of the Jesus Fellowship Church, could complain of the fact that it was impossible for them to follow their religion while complying with the requirement that their agreements should be made on a commercial basis. The view of the commissioner in *R(H) 8/04* has been followed by other commissioners in *CIS 1870/2003* and *CP 518/20033*. However, the Court of Appeal in *Esfandiari* (*R(IS) 11/06* – the appeal from *CIS 1870/2003*), stated that indirect discrimination claims under Art 14 should be treated with some care because the caselaw is limited. In its view, in so far as a uniform test can be distilled from the caselaw, the relevant test to be satisfied (in order to call for the discrimination to be justified) would seem to be whether the effects on the particular group are "disproportionately prejudicial". See also to similar effect para 175 of the Grand Chamber's decision in *DH and others v Czech Republic* (Appln No: 57325/00), 13 November 2007 (ECtHR).

Justification. In *Guygusuz*, the state did not attempt to justify the discrimination. Since the burden of proof in relation to justification rests firmly on the state, a breach of Art 14 was therefore established and the claimant recovered compensation for the loss of the benefit: at 380-1, paras 40-4. However, there are plenty of statements demonstrating the width of discretion accorded to governments in social welfare matters, for example the following statement of Laws LJ in *Carson* (para 73):

"In the field of what may be called macro-economic policy, certainly including the distribution of public funds upon retirement pensions, the decision-making power of the elected arms of government is all but at its greatest, and the constraining role of the courts, absent a florid violation by government of established legal principles, is correspondingly modest. I conceive this approach to be wholly in line with our responsibilities under the Human Rights Act 1998."

Upholding both *Carson and Reynolds* in the House of Lords, Lord Hoffmann stated what may now have to be viewed as the classic test for assessing justification in the social security field.

"14.   There is no doubt that Ms Carson is being treated differently from a pensioner who has the same contribution record but lives in the United Kingdom or a treaty country. But that is not enough to amount to discrimination. Discrimination means a failure to treat like cases alike. There is obviously no discrimination when the cases are relevantly different. Indeed, it may be a breach of article 14 not to recognise the difference: see *Thlimmenos v Greece* [2001] 31 EHRR 411. There is discrimination only if the cases are not sufficiently different to justify the difference in treatment. The Strasbourg court sometimes expresses this by saying that the two cases must be in an "analogous situation": see *Van der Mussele v Belgium* [1983] 6 EHRR 163, 179-180, para 46.

15.   Whether cases are sufficiently different is partly a matter of values and partly a question of rationality. Article 14 expresses the Enlightenment value that every human being is entitled to equal respect and to be treated as an end and not a means. Characteristics such as race, caste, noble birth, membership of a political party and (here a change in values since the Enlightenment) gender, are seldom, if ever, acceptable grounds for differences in treatment. In some constitutions, the prohibition on discrimination is confined to grounds of this kind and I rather suspect that article 14 was also intended to be so limited. But the Strasbourg court has given it a wide interpretation, approaching that of the 14th Amendment, and it is therefore necessary, as in the United States, to distinguish between those grounds of discrimination which prima facie appear to offend our notions of the respect due to the individual and those which merely require some rational justification: *Massachusetts Board of Retirement v Murgia* [1976] 438 US 285.

16.   There are two important consequences of making this distinction. First, discrimination in the first category cannot be justified merely on utilitarian grounds, eg that it is rational to prefer to employ men rather than women because more women than men give up employment to look after childen. That offends the notion that everyone is entitled to be treated as an individual and not a statistical unit. On the other hand, differences in treatment in the second category (eg on grounds of ability, education, wealth, occupation) usually depend upon considerations of the general public interest. Secondly, while the courts, as guardians of the right of the individual to equal respect, will carefully examine the reasons offered for any discrimination in the first category, decisions about the general public interest which underpin differences in treatment in the second category are very much a matter for the democratically elected branches of government.

17.   There may be borderline cases in which it is not easy to allocate the ground of discrimination to one category or the other and, as I have observed, there are shifts in the values of society on these matters. *Ghaidan v Godin-Mendoza* [2004] UKHL 30, 3 All ER 411 recognised that discrimination on grounds of sexual orientation was now firmly in the first category. Discrimination on grounds of old age may be a contemporary example of a borderline case. But there is usually no difficulty about deciding whether one is dealing with a case in which the right to respect for the individuality of a human being is at stake or merely a question of general social policy. In the present case, the answer seems to me to be clear."

In social security cases, therefore, if the discrimination in question does not fall within Lord Hoffmann's specially prohibited first category, it may be relatively easy to justify on general public interest grounds (but note that *Francis* was successful).

In *Petrovic v Austria* [1998] 4 BHRC 232, ECtHR, the Court held that the disparity of provision by signatory states meant that a wide margin of appreciation was enjoyed in the field of social security, and that accordingly sex discrimination in relation to access to maternity allowances could not be impugned. That conclusion may be said to be surprising, given the critical view that the court has taken of discrimination on such grounds. Where the discrimination is on the ground of race or sex, the burden on the state to justify discrimination is particularly heavy: see, eg, *Abdulaziz v UK* [1985] 7 EHRR 471 at 501, para 78, ECtHR. However, the decision of the House of Lords in *Carson and Reynolds* leaves open whether a different test or less weighty reasons apply where the sex or race discrimination arises in respect of general measures of economic or social strategy. The commissioner in *CP 518/2003* said that if the claim for (indirect) sex discrimination in the allocation of pension entitlement could be made out then weighty reasons would be needed to justify it. But in the final decision in *Stec* (12 April 2006) the Grand Chamber of the ECtHR set out what it described as the general approach to justification. That is, that although in general weighty reasons are required to justify discrimination based on sex (or race), a wide margin of appreciation will usually be allowed to national governments when it comes to general measures of economic or social strategy. In such cases, *Stec* seems to suggest that the legislature's policy choice should generally be respected, unless it is manifestly without reasonable foundation. A counter argument to this may be that *Stec* is not the appropriate test, or at least has to be modified, where what is in issue is not a general measure of economic or social strategy (such as pensionable age) but rather is a subsistence benefit rule, and so weighty reasons remain to be given for sex discrimination in relation to minimum safety net benefits.

Note, however, in terms of remedy, that just satisfaction may not require "levelling up" to award benefit to the discriminated party (if s/he has managed to show unjustified differential treatment) in all cases: *R v HMRC ex parte Wilkinson* [2005] UKHL 30 at paras [26] to [28] and [47] to [53], and *Hobbs and others v UK* (Application No. 63684/00), 14 November 2006.

Article 17
Prohibition of abuse of rights

Nothing in this Convention may be interpreted as implying for any State, group or person any right to engage in any activity or perform any act aimed at the destruction of any of the rights and freedoms set forth herein or at their limitation to a greater extent than is provided for in the Convention.

Article 18
Limitation on use of restrictions on rights

The restrictions permitted under this Convention to the said rights and freedoms shall not be applied for any purpose other than those for which they have been prescribed.

The First Protocol
Article 1
Protection of Property

Every natural or legal person is entitled to the peaceful enjoyment of his possessions. No one shall be deprived of his possessions except in the public interest and subject to the conditions provided for by law and by the general principles of international law.

The preceding provisions shall not, however, in any way impair the right of a State to enforce such laws as it deems necessary to control the use of property in accordance with the general interest or to secure the payment of taxes or other contributions or penalties.

Analysis

Art 1 of the First Protocol is breached if either (a) the State interferes with the peaceful enjoyment of the claimant's possessions; or (b) the claimant has been deprived of possessions by the State: or (c) the applicant's possessions have been subjected to control by the State.

By far the most important issue is whether benefits constitute 'possessions' under this article. All benefits which arise as a matter of right (such as HB and CTB) are now covered by Art 1 Prt 1: see *Stec and others v United Kingdom* (Application Nos: 65731/01 and 65900/01), 6 July 2005, ECtHR and *R(RJM) v SSWP* [2008] UKHL 63, 22 October 2008.

Given its importance, it is worthwhile setting out the reasoning of the Grand Chamber of the ECtHR in *Stec* in full.

"It is in the interests of the coherence of the Convention as a whole that the autonomous concept of 'possessions' in Article 1 of Protocol No. 1 should be interpreted in a way which is consistent with the concept of pecuniary rights under Article 6. It is moreover important to adopt an interpretation of Article 1 of Protocol No.1 which avoids inequalities of treatment based on distinctions which, at the present day, appear illogical or unsustainable.

The Court's approach to Article 1 of Protocol No.1 should reflect the reality of the way in which welfare provision is currently organised within the Member States of the Council of Europe. It is clear that within those

States, and within most individual States, there exists a wide range of social security benefits designed to confer entitlements which arise as of right. Benefits are funded in a large variety of ways: some are paid for by contributions to a specific fund; some depend on a claimant's contribution record; many are paid for out of general taxation on the basis of a statutorily defined status (see, with reference to the United Kingdom's system, Lord Hoffmann's comments in ex parte Carson). . . Given the variety of funding methods, and the interlocking nature of benefits under most welfare systems, it appears increasingly artificial to hold that only benefits financed by contributions to a specific fund fall within the scope of Article 1 of Protocol No.1. Moreover, to exclude benefits paid for out of general taxation would be to disregard the fact that many claimants under this latter type of system also contribute to its financing, through the payment of tax.

In the modern, democratic State, many individuals are, for all or part of their lives, completely dependent for survival on social security and welfare benefits. Many domestic legal systems recognise that such individuals require a degree of certainty and security, and provide for benefits to be paid – subject to the fulfilment of the conditions of eligibility – as of right. Where an individual has an assertable right under domestic law to a welfare benefit, the importance of that interest should also be reflected by holding Article 1 of Protocol No.1 to be applicable.

Finally . . . the Court considers that to hold that a right to a non-contributory benefit falls within the scope of Article 1 of Protocol No. 1 no more renders otiose the provisions of the Social Charter than to reach the same conclusion in respect of a contributory benefit. Whilst the Convention sets forth what are essentially civil and political rights, many of them have implications of a social or economic nature. The mere fact that an interpretation of the Convention may extend into the sphere of social and economic rights should not be a decisive factor against such an interpretation; there is no water-tight division separating that sphere from the field covered by the Convention (see Airey v. Ireland)."

The ECtHR then concluded:

"therefore, if any distinction can still be said to exist in the caselaw between contributory and non-contributory benefits for the purposes of the applicability of Article 1 of Protocol No. 1, there is no ground to justify the continued drawing of such a distinction.

If . . . a Contracting State has in force legislation providing for the payment as of right of a welfare benefit – whether conditional or not on the prior payment of contributions – that legislation must be regarded as generating a proprietary interest falling within the ambit of Article 1 of Protocol No. 1 for persons satisfying its requirements.

In cases, such as the present, concerning a complaint under Article 14 in conjunction with Article 1 of Protocol No. 1 that the applicant has been denied all or part of a particular benefit on a discriminatory ground covered by Article 14, the relevant test is whether, but for the condition of entitlement about which the applicant complains, he or she would have had a right, enforceable under domestic law, to receive the benefit in question. Although Protocol No. 1 does not include the right to receive a social security payment of any kind, if a State does decide to create a benefits scheme, it must do so in a manner which is compatible with Article 14."

However, Art 1 Prt 1 does not confer a general right to be paid a benefit constituting a 'possession' at a particular rate (or, put another way, no right not to be deprived of a larger amount), *unless* the reduction is of such a substantial amount that it affects 'the very substance of the right': *Müller v Austria* (Commission) [1975] 3 D and R 25. *CP 5084/2001* lists the factors to help determine whether there was deprivation in this sense. These are: (a) does the provision in question reduce a benefit previously in payment; (b) was that provision in force throughout the time when the claimant was paying relevant contributions (or, presumably post *Stec*, claiming the benefit in question or, perhaps, being liable to pay tax); (c) the closeness of the link between the benefit and payment of contributions (arguably, post *Stec*, this factor is no longer relevant, or at least should carry less weight); and (d) the amount of the reduction in benefit.

Moreover, a claimant cannot be said to have been deprived of a possession if they had no entitlement to the possession at all under the rules of entitlement: *X v Italy* [1977] 11 DR 114, applied by the Court of Appeal in *Carson and Reynolds* (and not argued on the further appeals to the House of Lords). Therefore, the rules limiting backdating of the retirement pension to three months before the date of claim do not mean that a person has been 'deprived' of his or her pension for the period more than three months before the date they claim it: *R(P) 1/06*. However, these decisions, and the approach to this particular point which they exemplify, have now to be read subject to *Stec* if an Art 14 challenge is in play (it was not in *R(P) 1/06*). Accordingly, if the backdating rules for a pension (or, indeed, any benefit) had been changed or introduced in a discriminatory manner (eg, allowing more backdating for men than women), then *Stec*, in principle, may enable an Art 1 Prt 1 and Art 14 argument to be made. *X v Italy, Carson and Reynolds* and *R(P) 1/06* remain good law, however, if all that is being raised is an argument under Art 1 Prt 1.

As with Art 8, even if it can be shown that there has been deprivation of a posession in the sense described above, that can nonetheless be justified by the State if it can show that the deprivation was in accordance with the 'public interest'. A 'fair balance' test is applied in answering this question, in which compensation is a key factor. Compensation need not be full.

Article 2
Right to Education

No person shall be denied the right to education. In the exercise of any functions which it assumes in relation to education and to teaching, the State shall respect the right of parents to ensure such education and teaching in conformity with their own religious and philosophical convictions.

Analysis

This does not require a state to establish or facilitate a certain degree of education at its expense. All it requires is the right to enjoy such education that the state provides: *The Belgian Linguistics Case (No 2)* at 280-1, para 3. Thus it is difficult for students to argue that the severe restrictions on their entitlements to HB and CTB infringe Prt 1 Art 2: see *R(Douglas) v North Tyneside MBC and another* [2004] 1 All ER 709.

SCHEDULE 2
REMEDIAL ORDERS
Orders

1.–(1) A remedial order may–

(a) contain such incidental, supplemental, consequential or transitional provision as the person making it considers appropriate;

(b) be made so as to have effect from a date earlier than that on which it is made;

(c) make provision for the delegation of specific functions;

(d) make different provision for different cases.

(2) The power conferred by sub-paragraph (1)(a) includes–

(a) power to amend primary legislation (including primary legislation other than that which contains the incompatible provision); and

(b) power to amend or revoke subordinate legislation (including subordinate legislation other than that which contains the incompatible provision).

(3) A remedial order may be made so as to have the same extent as the legislation which it affects.

(4) No person is to be guilty of an offence solely as a result of the retrospective effect of a remedial order.

Procedure

2. No remedial order may be made unless–

(a) a draft of the order has been approved by a resolution of each House of Parliament made after the end of the period of 60 days beginning with the day on which the draft was laid; or

(b) it is declared in the order that it appears to the person making it that, because of the urgency of the matter, it is necessary to make the order without a draft being so approved.

Orders laid in draft

3.–(1) No draft may be laid under paragraph 2(a) unless–

(a) the person proposing to make the order has laid before Parliament a document which contains a draft of the proposed order and the required information; and

(b) the period of 60 days, beginning with the day on which the document required by this sub-paragraph was laid, has ended.

(2) If representations have been made during that period, the draft laid under paragraph 2(a) must be accompanied by a statement containing–

(a) a summary of the representations; and

(b) if, as a result of the representations, the proposed order has been changed, details of the changes.

Urgent cases

4.–(1) If a remedial order (''the original order'') is made without being approved in draft, the person making it must lay it before Parliament, accompanied by the required information, after it is made.

(2) If representations have been made during the period of 60 days beginning with the day on which the original order was made, the person making it must (after the end of that period) lay before Parliament a statement containing–

(a) a summary of the representations; and

(b) if, as a result of the representations, he considers it appropriate to make changes to the original order, details of the changes.

(3) If sub-paragraph (2)(b) applies, the person making the statement must–

(a) make a further remedial order replacing the original order; and

(b) lay the replacement order before Parliament.

(4) If, at the end of the period of 120 days beginning with the day on which the original order was made, a resolution has not been passed by each House approving the original or replacement order, the order ceases to have effect (but without that affecting anything previously done under either order or the power to make a fresh remedial order).

Definitions

5.   In this Schedule–

''representations'' means representations about a remedial order (or proposed remedial order) made to the person making (or proposing to make) it and includes any relevant Parliamentary report or resolution; and

''required information'' means–

(a)   an explanation of the incompatibility which the order (or proposed order) seeks to remove, including particulars of the relevant declaration, finding or order; and

(b)   a statement of the reasons for proceeding under section 10 and for making an order in those terms.

Calculating periods

6.   In calculating any period for the purposes of this Schedule, no account is to be taken of any time during which–

(a)   Parliament is dissolved or prorogued; or

(b)   both Houses are adjourned for more than four days.

Child Support, Pensions and Social Security Act 2000
(2000 c19)

Arrangement of Sections
Part III
SOCIAL SECURITY
Housing benefit and council tax benefit etc.

68.   Housing benefit and council tax benefit: revisions and appeals
69.   Discretionary financial assistance with housing
70.   Grants towards cost of discretionary housing payments

Supplemental
84.   Expenses
85.   Repeals
86.   Commencement and transitional provisions
87.   Short title and extent

Schedules
7.   Housing benefit and council tax benefit: revisions and appeals

General Note

This Act made a number of important reforms to social security, child support and pensions law. For HB purposes, the most significant changes are the introduction by s69 of a system of discretionary financial assistance to replace exceptional hardship payments under the former HB Regs 1987 reg 61(3), and the introduction, by s68 and Sch 7, of a decision making and appeals system based on the Social Security Act 1998 (including the replacement of local authority Housing Benefit and Council Tax Benefit Review Boards by an independent appeal tribunal). The provisions governing appeals were further amended from 3 November 2008 by the establishment of the First-tier Tribunal and Upper Tribunal under the Tribunals Courts and Enforcement Act 2007.

PART III
Social Security
Housing benefit and council tax benefit etc

Housing benefit and council tax benefit: revisions and appeals

68.   Schedule 7 (which makes provision for the revision of decisions made in connection with claims for housing benefit or council tax benefit and for appeals against such decisions) shall have effect.

Discretionary financial assistance with housing

69.–(1)   The Secretary of State may by regulations make provision conferring a power on relevant authorities to make payments by way of financial assistance (''discretionary housing payments'') to persons who–

(a)   are entitled to housing benefit or council tax benefit, or to both; and

(b)   appear to such an authority to require some further financial assistance (in addition to the benefit or benefits to which they are entitled) in order to meet housing costs.

(2)   Regulations under this section may include any of the following–

(a)   provision prescribing the circumstances in which discretionary housing payments may be made under the regulations;

(b)   provision conferring (subject to any provision made by virtue of paragraph (c) or (d) of this subsection or an order under section 70) a discretion on a relevant authority–

(i)   as to whether or not to make discretionary housing payments in a particular case; and

(ii)   as to the amount of the payments and the period for or in respect of which they are made;

(c) provision imposing a limit on the amount of the discretionary housing payment that may be made in any particular case;

(d) provision restricting the period for or in respect of which discretionary housing payments may be made;

(e) provision about the form and manner in which claims for discretionary housing payments are to be made and about the procedure to be followed by relevant authorities in dealing with and disposing of such claims;

(f) provision imposing conditions on persons claiming or receiving discretionary housing payments requiring them to provide a relevant authority with such information as may be prescribed;

(g) provision entitling a relevant authority that are making or have made a discretionary housing payment, in such circumstances as may be prescribed, to cancel the making of further such payments or to recover a payment already made;

(h) provision requiring or authorising a relevant authority to review decisions made by the authority with respect to the making, cancellation or recovery of discretionary housing payments.

(3) Regulations under this section shall be made by statutory instrument, which shall be subject to annulment in pursuance of a resolution of either House of Parliament.

(4) Subsections (4) to (6) of section 189 of the Social Security Administration Act 1992 (supplemental and incidental powers etc.) shall apply in relation to any power to make regulations under this section as they apply in relation to the powers to make regulations that are conferred by that Act.

(5) Any power to make regulations under this section shall include power to make different provision for different areas or different relevant authorities.

(6) *[Omitted]*

(7) In this section–

"prescribed" means prescribed by or determined in accordance with regulations made by the Secretary of State; and

"relevant authority" means an authority administering housing benefit or council tax benefit.

General Note

This section gives power to set up the scheme for discretionary financial assistance with housing costs, which takes the form of discretionary housing payments (DHPs). DHPs replaced exceptional hardship payments which were formerly available under reg 61(3) HB Regs 1987.

Analysis

Subs (1) introduces the scheme and sets out the two basic conditions for qualifying for a DHP, which are that a person is entitled to HB or CTB and that they "appear to require" further assistance with housing costs. "Entitled" in this context will almost certainly be construed as "lawfully entitled" and will hence exclude those who have obtained a decision awarding them benefit by deception: compare *R v South Ribble DC HBRB ex p Hamilton* [2000] 33 HLR 102, CA.

Subs (2) confers the usual very broad discretions as to the making of regulations upon the Secretary of State. The relevant provisions made under each paragraph are as follows:

(a) Reg 3 DFA Regs.
(b) Regs 2(2) and 5 DFA Regs.
(c) Reg 4 DFA Regs.
(d) Reg 2(3) DFA Regs.
(e) Reg 6 DFA Regs.
(f) Reg 7 DFA Regs.
(g) Reg 8(2) DFA Regs.
(h) Reg 8(1) DFA Regs.

Grants towards cost of discretionary housing payments

70.–(1) The Secretary of State may, out of money provided by Parliament, make to a relevant authority such payments as he thinks fit in respect of–

(a) the cost to that authority of the making of discretionary housing payments; and

(b)   the expenses involved in the administration by that authority of any scheme for the making of discretionary housing payments.

(2)   The following provisions, namely–

(a)   subsections (1), (3), (4), (5)(b) [¹] and (8) of section 140B of the Social Security Administration Act 1992 (calculation of amount of subsidy payable to authorities administering housing benefit or council tax benefit), and

(b)   section 140C of that Act (payment of subsidy),

shall apply in relation to payments under this section as they apply in relation to subsidy under section 140A of that Act.

(3)   The Secretary of State may by order make provision–

(a)   imposing a limit on the total amount of expenditure in any year that may be incurred by a relevant authority in making discretionary housing payments;

(b)   imposing subsidiary limits on the expenditure that may be incurred in any year by a relevant authority in making discretionary housing payments in the circumstances specified in the order.

(4)   An order imposing a limit by virtue of subsection (3)(a) or (b) may fix that limit either by specifying the amount of the limit or by providing for the means by which it is to be determined.

(5)   An order under this section shall be made by statutory instrument, which shall be subject to annulment in pursuance of a resolution of either House of Parliament.

(6)   Subsections (4) to (6) of section 189 of the Social Security Administration Act 1992 (supplemental and incidental powers etc.) shall apply in relation to any power to make an order under this section as they apply in relation to the powers to make an order that are conferred by that Act.

(7)   Any power to make an order under this section shall include power to make different provision for different areas or different relevant authorities.

(8)   In this section–

"discretionary housing payment" means any payment made by virtue of regulations under section 69;

"relevant authority" means an authority administering housing benefit or council tax benefit;

"subsidy" has the same meaning as in sections 140A to 140G of the Social Security Administration Act 1992;

"year" means a financial year within the meaning of the Local Government Finance Act 1992.

Amendment

1.   Repealed by the Local Government Act 2003 s127(2) and Part 1 Sch 8 (18.11.03).

General Note

This authorises a system of subsidy by the Secretary of State for DHPs made by local authorities. Note subs (2) which applies most of the provisions in SSAA ss140B and 140C to DHP subsidy. For regulations under this section, see the Discretionary Housing Payments (Grants) Order 2001.

Supplemental

Expenses

84.   There shall be paid out of money provided by Parliament–

(a)   any expenditure incurred by the Secretary of State for or in connection with the carrying out of his functions under this Act; and

(b)   any increase attributable to this Act in the sums which are payable out of money so provided under any other Act.

Repeals

85.–(1)   The enactments mentioned in Schedule 9 (which include some spent provisions) are hereby repealed to the extent specified in the third column of that Schedule.

(2)   The repeals specified in that Schedule have effect subject to the commencement provisions and savings contained, or referred to, in the notes set out in that Schedule.

Commencement and transitional provisions

86.–(1)   This section applies to the following provisions of this Act–
(a)   Part I (other than section 24);
(b)   Part II (other than sections 38 and 39 and paragraphs 4 to 6, 8(1), (3) and (4) and 13 of Schedule 5);
(c)   Part III;
(d)   sections 82 and 83 and Schedule 8;
(e)   Parts I to VII and IX of Schedule 9.
(2)   The provisions of this Act to which this section applies shall come into force on such day as may be appointed by order made by statutory instrument; and different days may be appointed under this section for different purposes.
(3)   The power to make an order under subsection (2) shall be exercisable–
(a)   except in a case falling within paragraph (b), by the Secretary of State; and
(b)   in the case of an order bringing into force any of the provisions of sections 82 and 83, Schedule 8 or Part IX of Schedule 9, by the Lord Chancellor.
(4)   In the case of Part I (other than section 24) and of sections 62 to 66, the power under subsection (2) to appoint different days for different purposes includes power to appoint different days for different areas.
(5)   The Secretary of State may by regulations make such transitional provision as he considers necessary or expedient in connection with the bringing into force of any of the following provisions of this Act–
(a)   sections 43 to 46 and section (1) of Part III of Schedule 9;
(b)   sections 68 to 70 and Schedule 7 and Part VII of Schedule 9.
(6)   Regulations under subsection (5) shall be made by statutory instrument subject to annulment in pursuance of a resolution of either House of Parliament.
(7)   Section 174(2) to (4) of the Pensions Act 1995 (supplementary provision in relation to powers to make subordinate legislation under that Act) shall apply in relation to the power to make regulations under subsection (5) as it applies to any power to make regulations under that Act.
(8)   In this section "subordinate legislation" has the same meaning as in the Interpretation Act 1978.

Short title and extent

87.–(1)   This Act may be cited as the Child Support, Pensions and Social Security Act 2000.
(2)-(4)   *[Omitted]*

SCHEDULE 7
HOUSING BENEFIT AND COUNCIL TAX BENEFIT: REVISIONS AND APPEALS

General Note on Sch 7

Under reg 89 HB Regs, reg 70 HB(SPC) Regs, reg 75 CTB Regs and reg 60 CTB(SPC) Regs, any matter that needs to be determined in order to decide a claim for HB or CTB falls to be determined by the relevant authority – ie, by a local government officer. Sch 7 and the D&A Regs (which are made under Sch 7 para 10) are concerned with the circumstances in which the initial decisions of local authorites can be changed.

There are only three such mechanisms, revision under para 3, supersession under para 4, and appeal, initially to the First-tier Tribunal. Unless a decision can be revised, superseded or changed on appeal, then it is final (see para 11). Contrary to what some local authorities – and the suppliers of their computer software – still seem to believe, there is no power for an authority simply to "cancel" or "withdraw" an award of HB or CTB: see, for example, *CH 2302/2002*.

Except where otherwise stated below, Sch 7 came into force on 2 July 2001 (art 2(2) Child Support, Pensions and Social Security Act 2000 (Commencement No.8) Order 2001 No.1252) and replaced the previous system of HB and CTB adjudication, under which the determinations of local authorities were subject to review by (usually) a more senior officer under reg 79 HB Regs 1987 or reg 69 CTB Regs 1992, and then to a further review by a Review Board consisting of members (ie, councillors) of the authority concerned under regs 81-83 HB Regs 1987 and regs 70-72 CTB Regs 1992. That system did not comply with Art 6 of the European Convention on Human Rights (see *Tsfayo v United Kingdom* (application no: 60860/00) 2006, 14 November, unreported, ECtHR) and therefore could not remain in place after the Human Rights Act 1998 came into force.

Under Sch 7, those who are affected by a local authority decision on a claim for, or an award of, HB or CTB – and those from whom it is determined that an overpayment of HB or CTB is recoverable – have a right of appeal to the First-tier Tribunal and thereafter, on a point of law, to the Upper Tribunal and then (in England and Wales) the Court of Appeal or (in Scotland) the Inner House of the Court of Session. The effect is to align the appeal rights for HB and CTB with those for the social security benefits administered by the DWP and the Revenue. The scheme of Sch 7 thus follows that set out in Part I, Ch II SSA 1998 very closely and decisions of the former social security commissioners, the Upper Tribunal and the courts on the comparable provisions will be of highly persuasive force in interpreting Sch 7. Care should be taken to note the differences between the two sets of legislation, however.

A system of revisions and supersessions is found in paras 3 and 4 which is identical to ss8 and 9 SSA 1998. Paras 6 and 7 govern appeals to the First-tier Tribunal in a similar fashion to ss12 and 13, and paras 8 and 9 deal with further appeals to the Upper Tribunal and the courts in a similar fashion to ss14 and 15. There are also extensive powers to suspend benefit in paras 13 and 14 and an anti-test case rule in paras 16 to 18 which is not, however, being fully implemented.

The general approach to decision making in social security and, by implication, HB and CTB, was considered by the House of Lords in *Kerr v Department for Social Development* [2004] UKHL 23 (reported as *R 1/04 (SF)*). The House of Lords set out five propositions of general application to the field of benefits adjudication. First, the determination of claims should be an inquisitorial process rather than adversarial. Second, facts which may reasonably be supposed to be within the claimant's own knowledge are for the claimant to supply at each stage in the assessment of the claim. However, s/he must be given a reasonable opportunity to supply them. Third, the knowledge as to the information that is needed to deal with a claim lies with the DWP (and/or the HB/CTB authority) and not with the claimant: so it is for the former to ask the relevant questions and the claimant is not to be faulted if the relevant questions to show whether or not the claim is excluded are not asked. Fourth, the general rule is that it is for the party who alleges an affirmative to make good her/his allegation. Fifth, it is also a general rule that a party who desires to take advantage of an exception must bring her/himself within the provisions of the exception: exceptions (including grounds of disentitlement to benefit) are to be established by those who rely on them: *Nimmo v Alexander Cowan & Sons Ltd* [1968] AC 107, HL, so that in *Kerr* it was for the Department of Social Development in Northern Ireland to prove on the wording of the sub-regulation that was relevant in that case that the named close relatives of Mr Kerr were not in receipt of a relevant benefit, as proof of that condition acted as a ground of disentitlement to a social fund funeral payment.

Introductory

1.–(1)   In this Schedule ''relevant authority'' means an authority administering housing benefit or council tax benefit.

(2)   In this Schedule ''relevant decision'' means any of the following–

(a)   a decision of a relevant authority on a claim for housing benefit or council tax benefit;

(b)   any decision under paragraph 4 of this Schedule which supersedes a decision falling within paragraph (a), within this paragraph or within paragraph (b) of sub-paragraph (1) of that paragraph;

but references in this Schedule to a relevant decision do not include references to a decision under paragraph 3 to revise a relevant decision.

Analysis

"Relevant decision" is a decision of a local authority that either decides a claim for HB or CTB or that supersedes such a decision (or a decision of the First-tier Tribunal or Upper Tribunal) under para 4. The definition is important because it governs which decisions can be revised and superseded and which carry a right of appeal.

"Decision" in this context means what is sometimes described as an "outcome" decision – ie, that the claimant is not entitled to benefit or is so entitled at a specified weekly rate for a specified period. The decisions that an authority makes on the individual issues of fact and law that lead to a conclusion of entitlement or non-entitlement (eg, whether a claimant is liable to pay rent, the calculation of her/his applicable amount or the level of her/his income) are not outcome decisions but, rather, findings of fact or "determinations". Findings of fact and determinations cannot themselves be revised, superseded or (subject to what is said in the next paragraph) appealed: see *Carpenter v SSWP* [2003] EWCA Civ 33 (reported as *R(IB) 6/03*). However, if there are grounds on which to change a finding of fact or determination that may lead to a revision or supersession if the result is to change the outcome. Another way of putting the point is to say that what is revised, superseded or appealed against is the relevant decision itself and not the reason(s) for that decision.

For HB and CTB (but not for other social security benefits), there may be an exception to the principle that "determinations" cannot be appealed. As explained below, para 6(6) grants a right of appeal to "any person from whom it has been *determined* that [an amount of HB or CTB] is recoverable" (emphasis added). That formulation follows the wording of s75 SSAA, the primary legislation governing recover of HB overpayments (although s76 SSAA, the equivalent provision for CTB, does not use "determine" or any cognate term). This is an unfortunate quirk of the drafting. A decision that there has been an overpayment of HB or CTB and that it is recoverable from one or more persons is plainly one that provides an outcome: it is not merely a finding of fact. Moreover, the equivalent decision in relation to a DWP benefit would be a "decision" (see s8(1)(c) and (4) SSA 1998) even though s/1 SSAA uses the word "determine" in the same way as s75. It would have avoided confusion – and, in particular, would have avoided any argument about whether an overpayment "determination" can be revised or superseded by the local authority once it has been made – for the draftsman to have included overpayment "determinations" in the definition of "relevant decision" rather than to treat them as requiring a separate right of appeal. However, that course was not taken and it must therefore be remembered that, as it relates to HB and CTB overpayments, the nomenclature in this area is inconsistent.

Decisions to revise an earlier decision under para 3 are not included in the definition of "relevant decision" because the effect of a revising decision is to alter the terms of the original decision without replacing it. Any challenge (whether by way of an application for a further revision or an appeal) is therefore against the original decision as revised, rather than against the revising decision. This explains the words "whether as originally made or as revised under paragraph 3" in brackets in paras 4(1) and 6(1). By contrast, a superseding decision replaces the original decision, albeit (usually) with effect from a later date.

Because para 1(2)(a) is not limited to decisions taken by the authority under Sch 7, decisions taken by local government officers before 2 July 2001 under regs 76 or 79 HB Regs 1987 and regs 66 or 69 (which, at the time, were referred to as "determinations") are "relevant decisions" and can therefore be revised under para 3: *R(H) 6/04* (para 21). It follows that they can also be superseded under para 4. Decisions taken by review boards before 2 July 2001 under reg 83 HB Regs or reg 72 CTB Regs 1992 (which, at the time, were referred to as "decisions") were treated (by reg 4(4) D&A Transitional Regs – see pp993-1000 of the 20th edition) as having been made by an appeal tribunal under para 6. An authority was therefore able to supersede them (at least until 3 November 2008: see the Analysis of para 4), but they could not be revised under para 3.

Note that a determination that an overpayment is recoverable is not a "relevant decision" within the definition in sub-para (2): *R(H) 3/04* (para 34). See the commentary to para 6 below and to s75 SSAA 1992 (see p43).

Refusals to revise and supersede. To supersede a decision is to alter it: see the decision of the majority of the Court of Appeal in *Wood v SSWP* [2003] EWCA Civ 53, CA (reported as *R(DLA) 1/03*) paras 42-43 and 78. By the same reasoning, to revise a decision is also to alter it. It follows that where an authority reconsiders an existing decision and does not change the outcome then it is not revising or superseding it (or even, as used to be said before *Wood*, superseding it "at the same rate") but *refusing* to revise or supersede it. That is so even if the reasoning or findings of fact that led to the original decision are changed, as long as the outcome remains the same.

Is a refusal to revise or supersede a "relevant decision" that gives rise to further rights of challenge?

For a refusal to revise, the answer is no. As revision changes the terms of the original decision without replacing it, a refusal to revise leaves the orginal decsion unchanged. From 1 September 2009, where an application is made within one month of the original decision (or within that time limit as extended under reg 5 D&A Regs), the refusal has the effect of extending the time limit for an appeal against the original decision (see Sch 1 TP(FT) as amended by SI 2009/1975 on p1075). That was also the position before 3 November 2008 under the former reg 18(3) D&A Regs. For the position between those two dates, see pp148-149 of the 21st edition.

For a refusal to supersede, the question is more difficult but it is suggested that the answer must be yes. In *Wood*, the Court of Appeal was considering ss10(1) and 12(1) and (9) SSA 1998. In order to avoid infriging Art 6 of the European Convention on Human Rights, the majority adopted a strained construction of the phrase "decision superseding any such decision" in s12(9) as meaning "decision taken pursuant to the power to supersede". A refusal to supersede was therefore a "decision taken pursuant to the power to supersede". A refusal to supersede was therefore a "decision ... under section ... 10" for the purposes of the right of appeal in s12(1) even though no supersession had actually taken place (*Wood* paras 51 and 78). Paras 1, 4 and 6 of Sch 7 are not in the same terms as ss10 and 12 SSA 1998 and the analogy is therefore not exact. Nevertheless, it is suggested that the same approach should be applied to HB and CTB decisions. This would involve reading the words "any decision under paragraph 4 of this Schedule which supersedes a decision" in para 1(2)(b) as meaning "any decision *taken pursuant to the power* under paragraph 4 ...". Given the decision of the majority in *Wood* that to "supersede" an earlier decision the superseding decision must change it, any other approach would inevitably infringe the Convention rights of the person affected. The approach is therefore required by s3(1) Human Rights Act 1998.

Decisions on claims for benefit

2. Where at any time a claim for housing benefit or council tax benefit is decided by a relevant authority–

(a)   the claim shall not be regarded as subsisting after that time; and

(b)   accordingly, the claimant shall not (without making a further claim) be entitled to the benefit on the basis of circumstances not obtaining at that time.

Analysis

The effect of para 2 is that a decision refusing a claim for HB or CTB (sometimes called a "nil award") cannot be superseded on grounds of a change of circumstances that occurs after the *decision* was made. If someone is correctly refused benefit and her/his circumstances change, s/he must instead make a fresh claim for benefit. For the situation if someone's circumstances change after an appeal against a decision is made, see Sch 7 para 6(9).

Sub-para (a) confirms that the temporal effect of a claim ceases on the date that the authority makes its decision on the claim. The logical implication of the words "after that time" is that the claim does "subsist" prior to that time and so if a claimant is not entitled to benefit as at the date of claim but because of a change of circumstances becomes entitled on some later date before the authority makes its decision, the authority is obliged to award benefit from the later date. If this interpretation is correct, there may be some tension between sub-para (a) and reg 83(10) HB Regs (reg 64(11) HB(SPC) Regs) and the CB equivalents, which appear to restrict the power to make such an award to a period of 13 weeks after the date of claim. Delays of more than that period in adjudicating claims are, unfortunately, endemic in some authorities. However, it may be argued that the regulations do no more than give a power to make an advance award *after* the date of claim.

To minimise any injustice caused by sub-para (a), it is suggested that benefit may be awarded from any date between the date of claim and the date on which the decision is made, even if the latter date is more than 13 weeks after the former. If, however, the decision is made quickly but it is apparent that the claimant would have become entitled to benefit within the 13-week period specified in reg 83(10) HB Regs (64(11) HB(SPC) Regs), such an award should be made.

Sub-para (b), if interpreted literally, leads to some bizarre results. What does "circumstances not obtaining at that time" mean? It appears to require the authority to consider only the circumstances as at the date of its decision. If that was so, then a claimant entitled to benefit on the date of claim but who subsequently loses entitlement as a result of a change of circumstances could not be awarded benefit at all. Again, this would give the severe delays occurring in many authorities even more serious consequences than the delays themselves.

The wording of sub-para (b) is similar to that used in para 6(9)(b) and the decisions of commissioners on the scope of s12(8)(b) SSA 1998 (the equivalent to para 6(9)(b) in relation to DWP benefits) will therefore assist. It is suggested that the position postulated in the previous paragraph would give rise to absurdities similar to those discussed in *R(DLA) 3/01* (see the commentary to para 6(9)(b) on p148). It is therefore appropriate to construe sub-para (b) as not excluding consideration of the position as at the date of claim and between the date of claim and date of the authority's initial decision. On that interpretation, it excludes consideration only of circumstances arising after the initial decision.

Two elements of the wording of sub-para (b) support that interpretation. First, the word "accordingly" links sub-para (b) to the rest of the paragraph and so focuses attention on the period after the decision is made. Secondly, "without making a further claim" again calls attention to the true focus of the sub-paragraph. The intention is that if a claim is rejected but a claimant subsequently becomes entitled, the claimant's means of securing benefit is a further claim and not an application to supersede the initial refusal.

"Closed period" supersessions. Para 2 has sometimes been misunderstood as preventing an authority from carrying out a "closed period" supersession. The problem occurs where:

(1)   the claimant is awarded benefit;

(2)   there is a change of circumstances which removes that entitlement; *and*

(3)   before the superseding decision is taken, there is a further change which re-establishes entitlement.

A common example may help: A, who is on HB/CTB as a person on low wages, works overtime during the month before Christmas with the result that he no longer satisfies the means test. By the time he receives his pay slip at the end of January, he has resumed his normal working pattern and is entitled to benefit again. In the past, some authorities have taken the view that when they make the superseding decision in February, the correct decision is that A has not been entitled to HB/CTB from the beginning of December because once his entitlement ended in December he could not become entitled to benefit again without a fresh claim (which has not been made).

That is not correct. As authorities have been reminded by Circular HB/CTB A6/2009, the award may be superseded for the period of non-entitlement and the supersession only replaces the original decision to that extent: see *CIS 2505/2003* and the authorities cited in that decision, particularly *CSIS 754/2002*. The reason – which is not explained adequately either in the Circular or the caselaw – is simply that any other outcome is unjust and that nothing in the Act or the D&A Regs requires the authority to reach such an outcome. In particular, para 2 does not have that effect: it is not concerned with revising or superseding decisions but with the initial decision on a claim. It says that if the initial decision is *refused* then the claimant cannot become entitled to benefit on the basis of circumstances not obtaining at the date of refusal because the claim has ceased to exist. It has no practical consequences where the initial decision is to *award* benefit because in such cases, although the claim still ceases to exist, the claimant does not have to rely upon the claim as the basis of his or her continuing entitlement: s/he can rely upon the decision awarding benefit. If, by the time that decision is superseded, there has been more than one change in circumstance then each such change is a ground for supersession and the authority is entitled – in fact, it will normally be obliged – to take each of those changes into account when making the superseding decision.

Revision of decisions

3.–(1)   Any relevant decision may be revised or further revised by the relevant authority which made the decision–

(a)   either within the prescribed period or in prescribed cases or circumstances; and

(b)   either on an application made for the purpose by a person affected by the decision or on their own initiative;

and regulations may prescribe the procedure by which a decision of a relevant authority may be so revised.

(2)   In making a decision under sub-paragraph (1), the relevant authority need not consider any issue that is not raised by the application or, as the case may be, did not cause them to act on their own initiative.

(3)   Subject to sub-paragraphs (4) and (5) and paragraph 18, a revision under this paragraph shall take effect as from the date on which the original decision took (or was to take) effect.

(4)   Regulations may provide that, in prescribed cases or circumstances, a revision under this paragraph shall take effect as from such other date as may be prescribed.

(5)   Where a decision is revised under this paragraph, for the purposes of any rule as to the time allowed for bringing an appeal, the decision shall be regarded as made on the date on which it is so revised.

(6)   Except in prescribed circumstances, an appeal against a decision of the relevant authority shall lapse if the decision is revised under this paragraph before the appeal is determined.

Definition

"relevant decision" – see Sch 7 para 1 CSPSSA 2000.

Analysis

Para 3 provides the statutory basis for a revision. The basic distinction between a revision and supersession is that the former corrects the original decision without replacing it and usually does not change the date from which that decision takes effect. A supersession replaces the original decision but usually only from some date subsequent to the date on which the decision was made.

Note that it is only a "relevant decision" as defined in para 1(2) that can be revised, or further revised, by the relevant authority that made the decision. This means that an authority cannot revise the decision of the First-tier Tribunal or the Upper Tribunal (or of the former appeal tribunals or social security commissioners). Such a decision may only be altered by a supersession under para 4 or on appeal.

The detailed procedure in relation to revisions is to be found in the commentary to regs 4, 5 and 6 D&A Regs. Only the bare outline is given here.

Note that following the decision of the tribunal of commissioners in *R(H) 3/04*, it may not be possible to revise a determination that an overpayment is recoverable. See the commentary to para 6 below.

Sub-para (1) introduces the power to revise. It includes a power to revise a decision more than once: "may be . . . further revised". A claimant may apply for a revision or it may be carried out by the authority of its own motion. For the mode of making an application, see regs 4(8) and (9) D&A Regs. For the "prescribed period", see reg 4(1) D&A Regs and note reg 5 giving power to extend time for an application by a claimant. For the "prescribed cases or circumstances", see reg 4(2), (3), (5), (7) and (7A)-(7F) on p1010.

Sub-para (2) limits what the authority is required to consider in the course of a revision. The critical phrase here, however, is "need not" which confers a discretion: see *R(IB) 2/04*. Therefore, authorities should not shut their eyes where to do so would cause an injustice. However, claimants are best advised to raise all the points with which they disagree in their applications for revision and to provide relevant evidence and information to support the application. On an appeal against a revised decision (or against a refusal to revise) the First-tier Tribunal may exercise this discretion for itself. See commentary to Sch 7 para 6(9)(a) on p148.

Sub-paras (3) and (4) state the general rule that a revision takes effect from the same date as the original decision. Accordingly, where a claimant is seeking an increase in benefit, a revision is more advantageous than a supersession. For exceptions to the rule, see the anti-test case rule in para 18 on p156 and reg 6 D&A Regs on p1018.

Sub-para (5) is necessary because there is no right of appeal against a revising decision: any appeal is against the original decision as revised. Without the extension of time established by sub-para (5), the appeal would be out-of-time whenever the process leading to the revising decision took more than a month.

Sub-para (6). If a decision is revised while there is an appeal pending against it, then the appeal lapses (ie, with the effect that the First-tier Tribunal or Upper Tribunal no longer has jurisdiction to hear it) if the revised decision is *more advantageous* to the person affected than the orginal decision: see reg 17 D&A Regs on p1036. If the person affected remains dissatisfied with the revised decision (ie, because it remains less favourable than would have been the case had the appeal been completely successful), then s/he must make a fresh appeal against the decision as revised.

Decisions superseding earlier decisions

4.–(1)   Subject to [¹ sub-paragraphs (4) and (4A)], the following, namely–

(a)   any relevant decision (whether as originally made or as revised under paragraph 3), and

(b)   any decision under this Schedule [² of the First-tier Tribunal or any decision of the Upper Tribunal which relates to any such decision],

may be superseded by a decision made by the appropriate relevant authority, either on an application made for the purpose by a person affected by the decision or on their own initiative.

(2)   In this paragraph "the appropriate relevant authority" means the authority which made the decision being superseded, the decision appealed against to the [2 First-tier Tribunal] or, as the case may be, the decision to which the decision being appealed against to the [2 Upper Tribunal] relates.

(3)   In making a decision under sub-paragraph (1), the relevant authority need not consider any issue that is not raised by the application or, as the case may be, did not cause them to act on their own initiative.

(4)   Regulations may prescribe the cases and circumstances in which, and the procedure by which, a decision may be made under this paragraph.

[1 (4A)   Regulations may prescribe the cases and circumstances in which, and the procedure by which, a decision relating to housing benefit must be made by the appropriate relevant authority.]

(5)   Subject to sub-paragraph (6) and paragraph 18, a decision under this paragraph shall take effect as from the date on which it is made or, where applicable, the date on which the application was made.

(6)   Regulations may provide that, in prescribed cases or circumstances, a decision under this paragraph shall take effect as from such other date as may be prescribed.

Amendments

1.   Amended by s30(3) of the WRA 2007 with effect from 1.10.07 (for making regulations) and 7.4.08.
2.   Amended by Art 9 and Sch 3 para 190(2) of SI 2008 No. 2833 (3.11.08).

Definitions

"relevant decision" – see Sch 7 para 1 CSPSSA 2000.

Analysis

Sub-paras (1), (4) and (4A) permit a supersession of a decision of an authority, as originally made or as revised or superseded, or of the First-tier Tribunal or the Upper Tribunal. Again, this may occur on the initiative of either the claimant or the authority. See reg 7 D&A Regs on p1018 for the circumstances in which supersession is permitted, and note especially reg 7(6) which permits a notification of a change of circumstances to be treated as an application for a supersession. Note that, following the decision of the tribunal of commissioners in *R(H) 3/04*, it may not be possible to supersede a determination that an overpayment is recoverable. See the commentary to para 6 on p145. Note also that the inadequate drafting of Sch 3 para 190 Transfer of Tribunal Functions Order 2008 has, presumably inadvertently, removed the local authority's power to supersede a decision made by an appeal tribunal or a social security commissioner before 3 November 2008: see *DN v Leicester City Council (HB)* [2010] UKUT 253 (AAC) and the commentary to reg 7 D&A Regs on p1021.

Sub-para (3) is similar in terms to para 3(2) (see p143).

Sub-paras (5) and (6) state the general rule as to the effective date of a supersession decision. It will normally take effect from the date it was made or from the date on which the application for it was made. For the extensive exceptions to this general rule, see regs 8 and 9 D&A Regs on pp1024 and 1028.

Use of experts by relevant authorities

5.   Where it appears to a relevant authority that a matter in relation to which a relevant decision falls to be made by them involves a question of fact requiring special expertise, they may direct that, in dealing with that matter, they shall have the assistance of one or more persons appearing to them to have knowledge or experience which would be relevant in determining that question.

Analysis

It is unclear why this provision was thought necessary. Perhaps it was designed to prevent any allegation that a decision was invalid because the part of the decision that required expertise had been effectively delegated to the expert. It is unlikely that much use will be made of this power.

Appeal to [1 First-tier Tribunal]

6.–(1)   Subject to sub-paragraph (2), this paragraph applies to any relevant decision (whether as originally made or as revised under paragraph 3) of a relevant authority which–

(a)   is made on a claim for, or on an award of, housing benefit or council tax benefit; or
(b)   does not fall within paragraph (a) but is of a prescribed description.

(2)   This paragraph does not apply to–

(a)   any decision terminating or reducing the amount of a person's housing benefit or council tax benefit that is made in consequence of any decision made under regulations under section 2A of the Administration Act (work-focused interviews);
(b)   any decision of a relevant authority as to the application or operation of any modification of a housing benefit scheme or council tax benefit scheme under section 134(8)(a) or section 139(6)(a) of the Administration Act (disregard of war disablement and war widows' pensions);
(c)   so much of any decision of a relevant authority as adopts a decision of a rent officer under any order made by virtue of section 122 of the Housing Act 1996 (decisions of rent officers for the purposes of housing benefit);
(d)   any decision of a relevant authority as to the amount of benefit to which a person is entitled in a case in which the amount is determined by the rate of benefit provided for by law; or

(e)   any such other decision as may be prescribed.

(3)   In the case of a decision to which this paragraph applies, any person affected by the decision shall have a right to appeal to [¹ the First-tier Tribunal].

(4)   Nothing in sub-paragraph (3) shall confer a right of appeal in relation to–

(a)   a prescribed decision; or

(b)   a prescribed determination embodied in or necessary to a decision.

(5)   Regulations under sub-paragraph (4) shall not prescribe any decision or determination that relates to the conditions of entitlement to housing benefit or council tax benefit for which a claim has been validly made.

(6)   Where any amount of housing benefit or council tax benefit is determined to be recoverable under or by virtue of section 75 or 76 of the Administration Act (overpayments and excess benefits), any person from whom it has been determined that it is so recoverable shall have a right of appeal to [¹ the First-tier Tribunal].

(7)   A person with a right of appeal under this paragraph shall be given such notice of the decision in respect of which he has that right, and of that right, as may be prescribed.

(8)   Regulations may make provision as to the manner in which, and the time within which, appeals are to be brought.

(9)   In deciding an appeal under this paragraph, [¹ the First-tier Tribunal]–

(a)   need not consider any issue that is not raised by the appeal; and

(b)   shall not take into account any circumstances not obtaining at the time when the decision appealed against was made.

Amendment

1.   Amended by Art 9 and Sch 3 para 190(3) of SI 2008 No. 2833 (3.11.08).

Definitions

"relevant decision" – see para 1.

"relevant authority" – see para 1.

Analysis

The First-tier Tribunal

This paragraph sets out the scope of the right of appeal to the First-tier Tribunal. For the circumstances in which that tribunal was established and how it is constituted, see the commentary to the Tribunals, Courts and Enforcement Act 2007 on p168.

The approach to decision-making by the First-tier Tribunal

When it hears an appeal, the First-tier Tribunal (like the former appeal tribunals before it) is conducting a rehearing of the case: see *R(IB) 2/04* (paras 19-25), affirming *CH 1129/2002*, and the caselaw relating to other chambers of the First-tier Tribunal including *OFSTED v GM and WM* [2009] UKUT 89 (AAC) and *Secretary of State for Education v JN* [2010] UKUT 248 (AAC). Subject to the restrictions imposed by sub-para (9), it must decide whether it agrees the decision of the local authority was right, not (as the High Court used to do when considering judicial review challenges to the decisions of Review Boards) whether it thinks that the local authority was entitled to reach the decision that it did on the evidence before it: see *CH 1175/2002* (para 4). The First-tier Tribunal has power to remit issues to a local authority for consideration by it: *CH 3009/2002* (para 25).

A tribunal is entitled to, and must, ensure that it has jurisdiction to hear the case before it. That means that it must ensure that the challenge made by a claimant to the decision is one which the claimant is entitled to make: see the commentary to sub-para (1) below. It also means that it must satisfy itself that the decision challenged is one which has been validly made. A failure by the local authority to comply with the requirement to notify a decision to the claimant in a proper form or to follow the rules concerning supersession and revision may render the decision of no effect: see the commentary to reg 90 and Sch 9 HB Regs. Note, however, that the First-tier Tribunal should not decline jurisdiction simply because it considers the appeal is bound to fail: *FL v First-tier Tribunal and CICA* [2010] UKUT 158 (AAC).

Although a tribunal should consider every issue that is raised by the appeal, and that will include any issue that is "clearly apparent from the evidence" (per *Mongan v Department for Social Development* [2005] NICA 16, 13 April (reported as *R3/05 (DLA)*)), it does not follow that the tribunal must make a *decision* on *every* issue raised by the appeal if there is a more appropriate way of dealing with one or more issues: *R(IS) 2/08*. The tribunal of commissioners in that appeal went on to say:

"When an appeal against an outcome decision raises one issue on which the appeal is allowed but it is necessary to deal with a further issue before another outcome decision is substituted, a tribunal may set aside the original outcome decision without substituting another outcome decision, provided it deals with the original issue raised by the appeal and substitutes a decision on that issue."

It will then be for the Respondent authority to make a fresh decision on the new issue, against which new appeal rights will arise.

The tribunal of commissioners gave the following guidance:

–   in order to assist tribunals (now the First-tier Tribunal), the [Respondent's] submission to a tribunal should indicate whether it is considered that, if the appeal is allowed, there are any outstanding issues that need further consideration and whether the [Respondent] wishes the tribunal to deal with them;

- where a tribunal, having dealt with the issues originally raised in an appeal, is not able immediately to give an outcome decision, it must decide whether to adjourn or whether to remit the question of entitlement to the [Respondent] if [it] would be in a better position to decide the issue and to seek further information from the claimant;
- the tribunal's decision, as recorded on the decision notice issued at the conclusion of the hearing, should explicitly record what has and has not been decided and in particular, should make it absolutely clear whether the tribunal has made an outcome decision or has remitted the final decision on entitlement to the [Respondent authority].

For a more detailed discussion of the rules that must be followed by a tribunal, see the commentary to the SSCS D&A Regs and D&A Regs, in particular reg 53 SSCS D&A Regs.

Sub-para (1): Decisions that can be appealed

The first question that arises under para 6 is whether the decision of which complaint is made is one in respect of which the tribunal has jurisdiction. The tribunal has no jurisdiction beyond that conferred by legislation: *R(H) 3/04* (para 32). Sub-para (1) sets out the general rule, which is subject to sub-paras (2) and (3) discussed below.

"*. . . any relevant decision (whether as originally made or as revised . . .)*". See p140 for a discussion of a "relevant decision" and in particular for the question of whether a refusal to revise or to supersede is a relevant decision.

The tribunal must be careful, when determining an appeal against a decision which has been revised, to ensure that it is considering the decision as revised and not as it was originally made, otherwise it will err in law: *CH 1171/2002* (paras 3-8).

Sub-para (1) does not confer a right of appeal against a determination that an overpayment is recoverable: *R(H) 3/04* (para 33). The right of appeal arises under sub-para (6) instead: see below.

"*. . . made on a claim for, or on an award . . .*". An appeal may be brought against any decision (whether an original decision or a revised or superseded decision) "made on a claim for, or on an award of", HB or CTB. No regulations have been made under sub-para (1)(b) and so every appeal must fall within the quoted words. They are wide enough to extend to issues arising under other legislation that must be determined for the purposes of an HB claim. Therefore, for example, an appeal may be validly made against a decision that a claimant is excluded from benefit under s115 Immigration and Asylum Act 1999.

There is an unfortunate tension between the definition of "relevant decision" in para 1(2) and these words in para 6(1). Para 1(2) defines a relevant decision only in terms of a decision on a claim or a supersession decision. The words "on an award" in para 6(1) must therefore be taken to refer to a decision superseding or refusing to supersede an earlier decision in order to avoid inconsistency between the two provisions.

For the question as to whether there is a right of appeal against a refusal to supersede, see p141.

In *Carpenter v SSWP* [2003] EWCA Civ 33 (reported as *R(IB) 6/03*), the Court of Appeal had to consider whether a refusal by a tribunal to adjourn a hearing was of itself a "decision" which called for a statement of reasons under the former reg 53(4) SSCS D&A Regs. Laws LJ confirmed that a distinction had to be drawn between outcome decisions (which he described as "decisions upon the actual question whether an applicant is entitled to this or that benefit") on the one hand and "the many determinations which will fall to be made along the way to such a decision and which will inform it or indeed may determine it" and "procedural determinations": para 16. A refusal to adjourn fell within the latter category and was not appealable. Caution is required when applying the *Carpenter* decision to HB and CTB because of the anomaly whereby outcome decisions about the recovery of HB and CTB overpayments are not "relevant decisions" but are referred to using the verb "determine" (see p140). Even if such decisions are "determinations", they are not the type of determination to which Laws LJ was referring – ie, they are neither "findings of fact on particular issues" nor "procedural determinations".

The claimant's right to a fair hearing by an independent tribunal at common law and under Art 6 must always inform any decision as to the scope of appeal rights: *Wood v SSWP* [2003] EWCA Civ 53, CA (reported as *R(DLA) 1/03*). The tribunal's priority should at all times be to ensure that a person affected has a fair opportunity to challenge any aspect of a decision which affects her/him.

"*. . . of a prescribed description*". No regulations have yet been made under para 6(1)(b), so if a decision is to be appealable it must fall within either para 6(1)(a) or para 6(6).

Sub-paras (2), (4) and (5): Decisions which cannot be appealed

Sub-paras (2) and (4) then set out a number of circumstances in which no appeal lies to the First-tier Tribunal against a decision.

(1)   A decision terminating or reducing the amount of HB or CTB after a decision relating to a work-focused interview: head (a). However the decision relating to the interview attracted its own right of appeal: see reg 15 Social Security (Work-Focused Interviews) Regulations 2000 in the 2003/04 edition of this book. Note that work-focused interviews were only required in certain local authority areas operating within the ONE scheme, now largely replaced by Jobcentre Plus, which does not require work-focused interviews for HB and CTB.

(2)   A decision as to whether war disablement and war widows' (or widowers') pensions should be disregarded for HB and CTB purposes: head (b). Such decisions are taken by resolution of the whole local authority. See the Analysis to s134(8) SSAA 1992 on p81.

(3)   Any element of a decision relating to HB that follows inevitably from the conclusion reached by the rent officer: head (c). This prevents any indirect challenge to a rent officer's determinations. However, a danger can arise here if neither the appellant or the local authority in the appeal address the issue of whether the alternative version of reg 13 HB Regs (or of reg 13 HB(SPC) Regs) may apply (and hence that the rent officer's determination may not be determinative of the eligible rent). In such a situation, there is a danger that the appeal may be struck out by the tribunal under r8(2) TP(FT) Rules. It is therefore suggested that local authorities should set out in any response to an appeal raising issues under reg 13 that the alternative version of reg 13 does not apply and why that is the case. It is also suggested that, before striking out appeals for want of jurisdiction under para 6(2)(c), tribunal judges should ask for that information from local authorities if it has not already been provided.

(4)   Any element of a decision as to the rate of benefit: head (d). No one can therefore make an appeal on the ground that the benefit they are receiving is insufficient, or that a premium is insufficient to meet a need. This would include, it would seem, any argument relying on the Human Rights Act 1998. As any such appeal would be hopeless in any event, it seems that these are included so as to designate them as "out-of-jurisdiction" appeals and hence capable of being struck out under r8(2) TP(FT) Rules.

(5)   Any prescribed decision or determination: head (e). See the Schedule to the D&A Regs and the commentary thereto. Sub-para (5) forbids the exclusion of any decision relating to whether the conditions of entitlement have been fulfilled. The exclusion of "a prescribed determination embodied in or necessary to a decision" from any right of appeal in para 6(4)(b) is puzzling because there is no right of appeal against such a determination in the first place: para 6(3) only gives a right of appeal against "decisions" and although para 6(6) may give a right of appeal against an overpayment "determination", that type of "determination" is not "embodied in or necessary to a decision". However, the point is academic. No regulations have actually been made under para 6(6)(b).

Sub-paragraph (6): Appeals relating to recovery of overpayments

Sub-para (6) deals with the thorny subject of overpayment appeals. It was established by the decision of the tribunal of commissioners in *R(H) 3/04* (para 33) that the right to challenge decisions relating to recovery of overpayments arises under sub-para (6) and not under sub-para (1). The basis for that conclusion was that "determinations" that an overpayment is recoverable from a person does not fall within the definition of "relevant decision" in para 1. For the distinction between "decisions" and "determinations", see p140. That distinction would appear to lead to the conclusion that an overpayment "determination" cannot be altered once made by revision or supersession, other than on appeal. Two possible answers to this are as follows. First, it might be possible to argue that the former legislation was preserved. Secondly, since Sch 7 para 11 presumably does not apply (on the approach of the tribunal of commissioners) to overpayment determinations, reliance might be placed on the common law rule that a statutory power can be exercised repeatedly unless the legislation provides otherwise: s12 Interpretation Act 1978, though see Wade and Forsyth, *Administrative Law* (10th edition, 2009) pp193-196.

Most of the problems concerning the scope of the right of appeal under sub-para (6) have now been resolved by the tribunal of commissioners' decision in *R(H) 6/06*.

Challenging a decision that there has been an overpayment. Before a determination can be made that an overpayment is recoverable, it is normally a pre-condition that the decisions awarding benefit are altered: *R(H) 3/04* (para 34). Although the tribunal of commissioners referred only to the alteration being carried out by way of supersession, revision will be appropriate in the case of any award of benefit which is to be altered for the full period for which it was in effect.

There still seem to be some authorities who persist in asserting that a landlord has no right to challenge a decision that an overpayment has occurred but only that it is recoverable from her/him. That is plainly incorrect. The decision that an overpayment has occurred is made under ss75(1) or 76(1) SSAA and hence falls within the right of appeal conferred by sub-para (6). The tribunal of commissioners in *R(H) 3/04* (para 50) and *R(H) 6/06* have confirmed that a landlord may assert on an appeal that no overpayment has occurred, even if the claimant has not challenged the decision or decisions altering entitlement to benefit.

Challenging recovery of the overpayment. One of the most troublesome questions under the new adjudication regime has been the extent to which a decision to recover an overpayment (as distinct from a determination that it is recoverable) may be appealed.

Whatever the correctness of the Court of Appeal's decision in *SSWP v Chiltern District Council* [2003] EWCA Civ 508 (reported as *R(H) 2/03*) and the tribunal of commissioner's decision in *R(H) 3/04* in respect of the regime in place prior to October 2001 (and the correctness of the Court of Appeal's decision is strongly doubted in *R(H) 6/06*), the tribunal of commissioners' decision in *R(H) 6/06* holds that rights of appeal only attach to decisions going to the recoverability of an overpayment and do not attach to decisions concerning the recovery (or enforcement) of such recoverable overpayment decisions. See further the commentary to s75 SSAA 1992 on p42.

Challenging the method of recovery. The First-tier Tribunal has no jurisdiction over *how* an overpayment is recovered. Methods of recovery are determined under s75(5) to (7) SSAA in a way that is outside the decision-making process as to recovery. Judicial review remains the only viable method of challenge.

This has been confirmed in *R(H) 7/04*, where the commissioner ruled that landlords had no jurisdiction to challenge the decision to recover a recoverable overpayment by way of deduction from future payments of HB made to the landlords (per s75(4) SSAA 1992 and reg 102 HB Regs 1987 – now reg 102 HB Regs and reg 83 HB(SPC) Regs), where the decision that there had been an overpayment and that it was recoverable had been issued against the tenants. In the commissioner's view, a clear distinction needs to be made in such cases between the determination that there is a recoverable overpayment from a named person, and the means by which recovery is effected. The latter may have consequences on the amount of future HB received by the landlord but that does not constitute a decision that the overpayment is recoverable from the landlord.

Sub-paragraphs (3) and (7): Persons with a right of appeal

Sub-para (3) provides that any "person affected" will generally have the right of appeal. That phrase has the same meaning as in the D&A Regs: see para 23(2) on p159 and reg 3 D&A Regs on p1009.

Sub-para (7) requires a person affected to be given notice of appeal rights. See Sch 9 HB Regs, Sch 8 HB(SPC) Regs, Sch 8 CTB Regs and Sch 7 CTB(SPC) Regs and for the consequences of non-compliance with those provisions, see the Analysis to reg 90 HB Regs on p462. See also reg 10 D&A Regs on p1029.

Sub-paragraph (8): Making an appeal

See regs 19 and 20 D&A Regs (on pp1038 and 1040) and r23 and Sch 1 TP(FT) Rules (on pp1062 and 1075).

Sub-paragraph (9): Extent of a tribunal's jurisdiction

Head (a): Issues not raised "by the appeal". The First-tier Tribunal "need not" consider any issue not raised by the appeal. By implication, that rule has two consequences. First, it must consider all the issues which are "raised by the appeal". Second, it may consider issues which are not "raised by the appeal".

For these purposes, an issue is "raised by the appeal" if either:

–   it has been raised by one of the parties at or before the appeal tribunal's decision (*R(IB) 2/04* paras 32 and 193); *or*

–   if it is an issue which "obviously demands attention" (see *Mooney v SSWP* [2004] SLT 1141 (reported as *R(DLA) 5/04*)) or which is "clearly apparent from the evidence" (see *Mongan v Department for Social Development* [2005] NICA 16, 13 April (reported as *R3/05 (DLA)*) and *Hooper v SSWP* [2007] EWCA Civ 495 (reported as *R(IB) 4/07*)).

That is so even if the appellant is represented and the representative does not raise the issue. As the Court in *Mongan* stated (at para 18):

"In carrying out their inquisitorial function, the tribunal should have regard to whether the party has the benefit of legal representation. It need hardly be said that close attention should be paid to the possibility that relevant issues might be overlooked where the appellant does not have legal representation. Where an appellant is legally represented the tribunal is entitled to look to the legal representatives for elucidation of the issues that arise. But this does not relieve them of the obligation to enquire into potentially relevant matters. A poorly represented party should not be placed at any greater disadvantage than an unrepresented party."

Note, however, that although the tribunal may not refuse to deal with an issue that is "clearly apparent from the evidence", it is not always necessary for it to deal with such an issue by making a decision about it. In *R(IS) 2/08* (a decision concerning IS in which the decision maker was therefore the Secretary of State rather than a local authority) a tribunal of commissioners stated:

"47.   ...what a tribunal must not do is ignore an issue that is clearly apparent from the evidence. However, it does not follow that the tribunal must make a decision on every issue raised by the appeal if there is a more appropriate way of dealing with one or more issues.

48.   It is well established that a tribunal allowing an appeal because the decision under appeal was made without jurisdiction is entitled simply to set aside the decision without substituting another. So too may a tribunal when allowing an appeal on the ground that the original decision was not made against the correct parties and in such a case it is plainly open to the Sectretary of State to make another decision in place of the one that has been set aside (*R(H) 6/06*). In our judgment, the same approach can be applied where an issue first arises in the course of an appeal. When an appeal against an outcome decision raises one issue on which the appeal is allowed but it is necessary to deal with a further issue before another outcome decision is substituted, a tribunal may set aside the original outcome decision without substituting anotheroutcome decision, provided it deals with the original issue raised by the appeal and substitutes a decision on that issue. The Secretary of State must then consider the new issue and decide what outcome decision to give. In that outcome decision, he must give effect to the tribunal's decision on the original issue unless, at the time he makes the outcome decision, he is satisfied that there are grounds on which to supersede the tribunal's decision so as, for instance, to take account of any changes of circumstances that have occurred since he made the decision that was the subject of the appeal to the tribunal. Because his decision is an outcome decision, the claimant will have a right of appeal against it."

Although the First-tier Tribunal "need not" consider issues not raised by the appeal, it may do so. Para 6(9)(a) confers a discretion which must be exercised consciously and judicially, taking into account all relevant circumstances. If a statement of reasons is given, then reasons for the exercise of the discretion should be set out (whether the discretion is exercise to consider or not to consider the additional issue). In addition, the tribunal must be satisfied that there has been compliance with the requirements of Art 6 of the European Convention on Human Rights and of natural justice (*R(IB) 2/04* paras 88 to 97 and 194). Compliance with Art 6 requires that the parties should not be put at a disadvantage because they have been taken by surprise by a point which the tribunal takes of its own motion. (For example, in *CH 1129/2002*, the local authority refused benefit under reg 6 HB Regs 1987 (now reg 8 HB Regs) but the tribunal substituted a decision under reg 7 of those regs (now reg 9 HB Regs) without making it clear to the claimant's representative that it proposed to take that course. The commissioner held that to be a breach of natural justice (para 30).) This is particularly important if the effect of taking the new point may be to make a decision that is less favourable to the appellant than the decision appealed against. In such cases, fairness is likely to require an express warning and, at least where the appellant is unrepresented, an offer of an adjournment. For reasons to do with the structure of disability living allowance, the question whether to consider issues not raised by the appeal arises most often in appeals relating to that benefit. For a discussion of the issues raised by s12(8)(a) Social Security Act 1998 (equivalent to para 6(9)(a)) in that context, see *AP-H v SSWP* [2010] UKUT 183 (AAC) and the various decisions of the commissioners and the Upper Tribunal referred to in that case.

Head (b): Circumstances "not obtaining at the time when the decision . . . was made". The purpose of this provision is to oust the "down to the date of hearing" rule under which a decision maker or tribunal was required by the decision in *CS 14430/1996* (Appendix para 3) to consider the claimant's entitlement not merely at the date of claim, but also in relation to each date up until the date of the hearing of the appeal. For example, if a claimant was refused benefit on the basis that s/he was not habitually resident in the UK, then a tribunal might have found that habitual residence had not been established as at the date of claim or of the decision maker's decision but was obtained by some later date. This was a rule which, although sounding impractical, when properly applied enabled tribunals to do practical justice and avoided the need for claimants to make repeated claims. Its application to HB and CTB was never, however, fully settled: see the Analysis to reg 83 HB Regs 1987 on p388 of the 13th edition.

Where an application has been made for a revision of the decision, which has been refused and the claimant has appealed against that refusal, the relevant date for the purposes of para 6(9)(b) is the date of the original decision, not the date of the refusal to revise: *CSDLA 2/2002* (para 22). The same is true of an appeal against an original decision that has been revised, but with which the appellant remains dissatisfied.

The equivalent provision relating to DWP benefits, s12(8)(b) SSA 1998, has had its scope substantially restricted by a number of commissioners' decisions. First, "circumstances" are the facts relevant to the decision and not the *evidence* of those facts. It is therefore perfectly permissible for the tribunal to have regard to evidence which is only made available, or even evidence that only comes into existence, after the decision was made: *R(DLA) 2/01* (para 9); *R(DLA) 3/01* (paras 58-60); *CH 1175/2002* (para 6). Furthermore, circumstances arising between the date of claim and the date that the decision was made must be considered: *R(DLA) 3/01* (paras 58-60); *CIS 2428/1999* (para 20). In *CJSA 2375/2000* (para 31), this principle was extended further to include circumstances which relate to the period prior to the decision, even if those circumstances did not come to light until after the decision was made. That case related to an appeal against a disqualification from JSA. After the decision was made, a previous disqualification was overturned on appeal and so the second disqualification fell to be reduced to two weeks, even if upheld. The commissioner held that it was necessary to interpret the provision so as to avoid absurdity and this convoluted interpretation was the only way in which this could be achieved. In *CDLA 4331/2002* (para 9), Commissioner Rowland said that s12(8)(b) SSA 1998 should not be read so as to prevent changes of circumstance to be taken into account which the decision maker is entitled to anticipate because they are almost certain to occur. See reg 7(2)(a)(ii) D&A Regs (on p1021) which gives a local authority the power to supersede in such a situation.

The combined effect of this provision and that of Sch 7 para 2 above, along with the limits on backdating of benefit following a claim or a supersession (for these see reg 83(12) HB Regs; reg 64(1) HB(SPC) Regs; reg 69(14) CTB Regs; reg 56 CTB(SPC) Regs; and reg 8 D&A Regs) is that as a general rule, a claimant needs to consider making a fresh claim for benefit (or seeking a supersession) if circumstances change after the date of the decision being appealed. Once the appeal is determined, if the decision on the claim or supersession request (the new decision) would have been made differently by the decision maker had the result of the appeal been known, a revision of the new decision is possible. If the new decision has itself been appealed, see reg 4(1)(c) D&A Regs. If the new decision has not itself been appealed, see reg 4(7) D&A Regs on p1014.

Redetermination etc of appeals by tribunal

7.–(1) This paragraph applies where an application is made [¹ to the First-tier Tribunal for permission to appeal to the Upper Tribunal from any decision of the First-tier Tribunal under paragraph 6].

[¹ (2)]

(3) If each of the principal parties to the case expresses the view that the decision was erroneous in point of law, [¹ the First-tier Tribunal] shall set aside the decision and refer the case for determination by a differently constituted [¹ First-tier Tribunal].

(4) In this paragraph and paragraph 8 ''principal parties'' means–

(a) where he is the applicant for leave to appeal or the circumstances are otherwise such as may be prescribed, the Secretary of State;

(b) the relevant authority against whose decision the appeal to the appeal tribunal was brought; and

(c) the person affected by the decision against which the appeal to the appeal tribunal was brought or by the tribunal's decision on that appeal.

Amendment

1.   Amended by Art 9 and Sch 3 para 190(4) of SI 2008 No.2833 (3.11.08).

Analysis

Para 7 is equivalent, with the exception of sub-para (4), to s13 SSA 1998. As originally enacted, it contained two provisions. The first, in sub-para (2), permitted the person considering an application for leave to appeal against a decision of a former appeal tribunal to set that decision aside if it was "erroneous in point of law". The second, in sub-para (3), obliged that person to set aside the tribunal's decision if all the parties expressed the view that it was legally erroneous.

Sub-para (2) has now been replaced by the First-tier Tribunal's power of review in s9 TCEA (see p174).

Sub-para (3) is a provision that is capable of causing inconvenience. If *both* parties state that the decision contains an error of law, the member is *required* to set aside the decision. In such a case, the case *must* be remitted to a differently constituted tribunal. The reasonableness of the position taken by the parties is not, on the face of it, a factor; and the parties need not even agree that the same error of law has occurred.

Before 3 November 2008, the procedure by which appeal tribunals considered applications for leave to appeal meant that this provision was rarely used in practice. Although under reg 58 D&A Regs, an application for leave to appeal by the local authority had to be sent to every other party to the proceedings, there was no such requirement for applications made by the person affected by the decision. As such, the local authority was not usually in a position to comment on an application for leave by a claimant, preventing para 7(3) taking effect. Moreover, from 20 May 2002, reg 58(3) D&A Regs was revoked by SI 2002 No.1379 and a party who received a copy of an application for leave to appeal no longer had a right to make representations. However under regs 39(1) and 40(4) TP(FT) Rules, it may be that the First-tier Tribunal is faced with circumstances in which it must set aside the decision under sub-para (3) more frequently.

If one party makes an application for leave which is then refused, and the other party then makes an application, para 7(3) will not be applicable and the question as to whether leave should be granted must be determined in the normal way: *CF 6923/1999*. If, however, both parties to the appeal have expressed the view that the decision of the tribunal is erroneous before leave has been granted or refused to either party by the tribunal, then the mandatory terms of para 7(3) mean that the decision of the tribunal must be set aside and the commissioner can have no jurisdiction under para 8: *CIB 4427/2002* (paras 16-17). On the other hand, where one party is refused leave to appeal and renews the application for leave under para 8 of Sch 7, but at or about the same time the other party to the appeal applies for leave to appeal to the tribunal, whether para 7(3) or para 8 applies will depend upon the precise sequence of events: *CIB 2949/2005*. In that case the commissioner took the view that as the renewed application for leave to appeal had been registered with the Commissioners' Office, the commissioner became seised of the matter under para 8 of Sch 7 and para 7(3) therefore could no longer apply.

Appeal from [¹ First-tier Tribunal to Upper Tribunal]

8.– [¹ (1)]

(2)   An appeal[¹ to the Upper Tribunal under section 11 of the Tribunals, Courts and Enforcement Act 2007 from any decision of the First-tier Tribunal under paragraph 6 or 7 lies] at the instance of any of the following–

(a)   the Secretary of State;

(b)   the relevant authority against whose decision the appeal to the appeal tribunal was brought;

(c)   any person affected by the decision against which the appeal to the [¹ First-tier Tribunal] was brought or by the tribunal's decision on that appeal.

[¹ (3)]
[¹ (4)]
[¹ (5)]
[¹ (6)]
[¹ (7)]
[¹ (8)]

Amendment

1.   Amended by Art 9 and Sch 3 para 190(5) of SI 2008 No. 2833 (3.11.08).

Analysis

For the Upper Tribunal, see the commentary to ss3 (p170), 5 (p171) and 11 (p176) TCEA.

Sub-para (2) supplements with s11(2) TCEA. It is necessary because s11(2) confers a right of appeal to the Upper Tribunal on "[a]ny party to a case" without defining who is, or is not, a "party to a case": see the commentary on p176.

[¹ **Applications for permission to appeal against a decision of the Upper Tribunal**]
    9.–[¹ (1)]
    [¹ (2)]
    (3)   [¹ An application for permission to appeal from a decision of the Upper Tribunal in respect of a decision of the First-tier Tribunal under paragraph 6 or 7] may only be made by–
    (a)   a person who, before the proceedings before the [¹ Upper Tribunal] were begun, was entitled to appeal to the [¹ Upper Tribunal] from the decision to which the [¹ Upper Tribunal's] decision relates;
    (b)   any other person who was a party to the proceedings in which the decision to which the [¹ Upper Tribunal's] decision relates was given;
    (c)   any other person who is authorised by regulations to apply for [¹ permission];
    [¹]
    [¹ (4)]
    [¹ (5)]

Amendement
    1.   Amended by Art 9 and Sch 3 para 190(6) of SI 2008 No. 2833 (3.11.08).

Analysis
Under s13 TCEA 2008 a further appeal lies from the Upper Tribunal, with permission, to either the Court of Appeal or to the Court of Session as appropriate.
Sub-paragraph (3): Who has the right to appeal?
Under sub-para (3), the people with a right of appeal are set out. First, there is any person who had a right of appeal to the commissioner: see para 8(2). Secondly, there is any other person who was a party to the tribunal proceedings. In fact, for HB and CTB purposes these are exactly the same parties as those with a right to appeal to the commissioner, since "party" means "principal party" under para 7(4): see regs 1(2) and 23(3)(b) D&A Regs. No regulations have been made under sub-para (3)(c). Sub-para (2) overlaps with s13(2) TCEA 2008. It appears to have been retained because the reference in head (a) to a person who would have had an appeal to the Upper Tribunal, taken together with para 8(2), confers a right of appeal on the Secretary of State (who, in a HB/CTB case, may not have been a party to the appeal to the Upper Tribunal) which is not conferred by s13(2).

Procedure
    10.–(1)   Regulations may make for the purposes of this Schedule any such provision as is specified in Schedule 5 to the Social Security Act 1998, or as would be so specified if the references to the Secretary of State in paragraph 1 of that Schedule were references to a relevant authority.
    [¹ (2)]
    [¹ (3)]
    [¹ (4)]
    [¹ (5)]
    [¹ (6)]
    [¹ (7)]
    [¹ (8)]

Amendment
    1.   Omitted by Art 9 and Sch 3 para 190(7) of SI 2008 No. 2833 (3.11.08).

Analysis
From 3 November 2008, the power to make rules about tribunal procedure are contained in s22 and Sch 5 TCEA and this paragraph is largely *otiose*. Sub-para (1) appears to have been retained because it provides residual regulation-making powers for those parts of the D&A Regs that do not concern tribunals and are not authorised by other provisions of Sch 7 (eg, para 3(4) and (6) and para 4(4) and (6)).

Finality of decisions
    11.   Subject to the provisions of this Schedule [¹ and to any provision made by or under Chapter 2 of Part 1 of the Tribunals, Courts and Enforcement Act 2007] , any decision made in accordance with the preceding provisions of this Schedule shall be final.

Amendment
    1.   Inserted by Art 9 and Sch 3 para 190(8) of SI 2008 No. 2833 (3.11.08).

Analysis
Para 11 covers the same ground as s17 SSA 1998, but is markedly different in scope. It provides that a decision is final, except to the extent that it may be altered on revision, supersession or appeal. The main question arising is whether para 11 is restricted in scope to the actual decision in a case or whether it also extends to findings of fact and law embodied in such a decision. It is suggested that the first of these alternatives is correct. The

language of para 11 may be contrasted with that in para 6(4), which suggests a contrast between a decision and a "determination embodied in or necessary to a decision". Thus if claim A is rejected on the basis that the claimant has notional capital because s/he sold a capital asset at an undervalue so as to obtain HB, the decision is final as far as it affects claim A (subject to challenge). However, if the claimant makes claim B eight weeks later, the authority cannot simply rely on para 11 in rejecting claim B but must, at least in theory, reconsider the question of notional capital. Commissioner Jacobs confirmed this approach in *CH 1210/2003*. He said that a decision relates only to a claim. Although it may be taken into account when deciding a later claim, it is not conclusive on claims in respect of different periods. It would also seem that, following the approach of the tribunal of commissioners in *R(H) 3/04*, para 11 has no application to a "determination" that an overpayment is recoverable.

The commissioners have consistently held that appeal tribunals were not bound by previous decisions of other appeal tribunals. Two decisions of Commissioner Jacobs deal with the point. It was held in *CH 3853/2001* (paras 18-19) that a Review Board decision on a question of fact does not bind an appeal tribunal deciding the same question in relation to a different claim. The commissioner said:

> "Nor was the Tribunal bound by the Board's finding that the claimant was compelled to act as he did. That was so despite the fact that it was made in respect of the same claimant, the same premises, the same circumstances and the same arguments. The Board's finding was made on a different claim dealing with a different period."

The same must therefore be true of authorities determining subsequent claims, and of the First-tier Tribunal hearing an appeal where a previous tribunal has dismissed an appeal on the same facts: *CCS 1535/1997* (paras 24-27), where the commissioner suggested that the fact that tribunals exercised an inquisitorial jurisdiction meant that there could be no issue estoppel (under which a decision on a question between two parties is ordinarily binding on them in relation to future litigation) in tribunal proceedings.

This interpretation produces a desirable flexibility within the decision-making system. It is a common phenomenon for advisers to be consulted by claimants who have had an adverse decision on a question such as notional capital which cannot be challenged by the time that the adviser becomes involved. While any prospect of getting benefit on that claim may have been lost, it might cause serious injustice to such a claimant if s/he does not have the right to have the matter reconsidered on a fresh claim. The drawback of the interpretation is that it has the potential to cause administrative difficulties for authorities and the Tribunals Service where a claimant aggrieved by a decision adverse to her/him decides to make multiple claims at regular intervals. Authorities must adjudicate and decide each claim that is made in the correct time and manner and which satisfies the evidence requirements: reg 89 HB Regs; reg 70 HB(SPC) Regs; reg 75 CTB Regs; and reg 60 CTB(SPC) Regs. Authorities will probably simply rely on the reasoning of the first officer who determined the question under dispute and issue further decisions to identical effect. What authorities would have to be careful to avoid, in these circumstances, is ignoring any further information or evidence that may be presented on subsequent claims.

As far as repeated appeals are concerned, if there are several appeals outstanding at once, they can be listed for hearing and disposed of together: *R(SB) 4/85*. In cases where there is abuse of the appeals system, reg 8(3)(c) TP(FT) Rules permits the tribunal to strike out the appeal if it considers there is no reasonable prospect of the appellant's case, or part of it, succeeding.

It may be questionable whether the commissioners' decisions on this topic take sufficient account of the general law of issue estoppel in public law decision making. In *Thrasyvoulou v Secretary of State for the Environment* [1990] 2 AC 273 at 289, HL, Lord Bridge referred to the two maxims that there was a public interest in the finality of litigation and that no one should be vexed by litigation on the same question more than once. He said:

> "In principle, they must apply equally to adjudications in the field of public law. In relation to adjudications subject to a comprehensive self-contained statutory code, the presumption, in my opinion, must be that where the statute has created a specific jurisdiction for the determination of any issue which establishes the existence of a legal right, the principle of *res judicata* applies to give finality to that determination unless an intention to exclude that principle can properly be inferred as a matter of construction of the relevant statutory powers."

The question, therefore, would be whether the fact that para 11 only makes decisions on claims final and not determinations embodied in those decisions is sufficient to exclude this general principle. *CH 704/2005* decides that issue estoppel can apply in respect of an issue decided by the county court which is also an issue arising on a HB or CTB appeal. In that case the issue was whether the claimant had a beneficial interest in a property and thus had capital in excess of £16,000. The commissioner said that issue estoppel could only apply if the parties to the appeal tribunal hearing were the same parties as in the county court and acting in the same capacity, but that was the case here as no valid distinction could be made between the local authority exercising its housing functions and its benefit functions. Nothing, in the commissioner's view, in the limited statutory estoppel created by para 11 of Sch 7, or the lack of any estoppel arising from findings of fact or determinations embodied in an appeal tribunal decisions created by s17(2) SSA 1998, meant that decisions made by *courts* in the exercise of their jurisdictions cannot create an issue estoppel for a later statutory appeal concerning the same parties.

This decision also decides (para 14) that decisions of the statutory authorities (including tribunals) concerning HB and CTB (and all other benefits) cannot bind later decision makers within that statutory arena, save to the limited extent set out in Sch 7 para 11 (or s17(1) SSA 1998). What it seems to leave open is whether decisions of *other* statutory tribunals (such as an immigration appeal tribunal) can give rise to an issue estoppel: see, for example, *H (Nahar) v Social Security Commissioner* [2002] 1 FLR 670, paras 35-38 and the commentary to para 11 in the 18th edition.

Matters arising as respects decisions

12. Regulations may make provision as respects matters arising–
(a) pending any decision under this Schedule of a relevant authority [¹ or the First-tier Tribunal, or any decision of the Upper Tribunal which relates to any decision under this Schedule of the First-Tier Tribunal,] which relates to–
    (i) any claim for housing benefit or council tax benefit;
    (ii) any person's entitlement to such a benefit or its receipt; or
(b) out of the revision under paragraph 3, or on appeal, of any such decision.

Amendment
1. Amended by Art 9 and Sch 3 para 190(8) of SI 2008 No.2833 (3.11.08).

Suspension in prescribed circumstances
13.–(1) Regulations may provide for–
(a) suspending, in whole or in part, any payments of housing benefit or council tax benefit;
(b) suspending, in whole or in part, any reduction (by way of council tax benefit) in the amount that a person is or will become liable to pay in respect of council tax;
(c) the subsequent making, or restoring, in prescribed circumstances of any or all of the payments, or reductions, so suspended.
(2) Regulations made under sub-paragraph (1) may, in particular, make provision for any case where, in relation to a claim for housing benefit or council tax benefit–
(a) it appears to the relevant authority that an issue arises whether the conditions for entitlement to such a benefit are or were fulfilled;
(b) it appears to the relevant authority that an issue arises whether a decision as to an award of such a benefit should be revised (under paragraph 3) or superseded (under paragraph 4);
(c) an appeal is pending against a decision of [¹ the First-tier Tribunal, the Upper Tribunal] or a court; or
(d) it appears to the relevant authority, where an appeal is pending against the decision given by [¹ the Upper Tribunal] or a court in a different case, that if the appeal were to be determined in a particular way an issue would arise whether the award of housing benefit or council tax benefit in the case itself ought to be revised or superseded.
(3) For the purposes of sub-paragraph (2), an appeal against a decision is pending if–
(a) an appeal against the decision has been brought but not determined;
(b) an application for [¹ permission] to appeal against the decision has been made but not determined; or
(c) the time within which–
    (i) an application for [¹ permission] to appeal may be made, or
    (ii) an appeal against the decision may be brought,
  has not expired and the circumstances are such as may be prescribed.
(4) In sub-paragraph (2)(d) the reference to a different case–
(a) includes a reference to a case involving a different relevant authority; but
(b) does not include a reference to a case relating to a different benefit unless the different benefit is housing benefit or council tax benefit.

Amendment
1. Amended by Art 9 and Sch 3 para 190(10) of SI 2008 No. 2833 (3.11.08).

Analysis
See regs 11 and 12 D&A Regs on pp1030 and 1031. Note that the power in sub-para (3)(c) was only exercised with effect from 30 October 2008: reg 11(3) DA Regs inserted by SI 2008 No.2667. Until then, it appears that there was no power to suspend unless the authority had at least got to the stage of making an application for leave to appeal.

Note also the limited scope of the "different cases" which may trigger suspension under reg 11(2)(b)(ii) D&A Regs. Sub-para (4) provides that a case involving a different local authority may trigger a suspension, but cases involving other benefits may not give rise to suspension. Thus if the Upper Tribunal is due to give a ruling on the interpretation of a part of the IS legislation, it will not be open to the authority to impose a suspension on payment under HB claims which require consideration of an identical provision in the HB legislation.

Sub-para (4) does not, in terms, preclude suspension where a ruling is due in respect of legislation outside the area of social security. It would seem arguable that it would be legitimate for an authority to suspend payment where an authoritative ruling is due as to the meaning of a particular phrase replicated in the HB legislation. After all, the test is whether an issue would arise, not that the decision would make a difference for certain. Since "court" is not defined in the legislation, a pending appeal to the Court of Appeal from the High Court or some other statutory tribunal may well give a right to suspend payment.

Suspension for failure to furnish information etc

14.–(1)   The powers conferred by this paragraph are exercisable in relation to persons who fail to comply with information requirements.

(2)   Regulations may provide for–

(a)   suspending, in whole or in part, any payments of housing benefit or council tax benefit;

(b)   suspending, in whole or in part, any reduction (by way of council tax benefit) in the amount that a person is or will become liable to pay in respect of council tax;

(c)   the subsequent making, or restoring, in prescribed circumstances of any or all of the payments, or any right, so suspended.

(3)   In this paragraph and paragraph 15 "information requirement" means–

(a)   in the case of housing benefit, a requirement in pursuance of regulations made by virtue of section 5(1)(hh) of the Administration Act to furnish information or evidence needed for a determination whether a decision on an award of that benefit should be revised under paragraph 3 or superseded under paragraph 4 of this Schedule; and

(b)   in the case of council tax benefit, a requirement made in pursuance of regulations under section 6(1)(hh) of the Administration Act to furnish information or evidence needed for a determination whether a decision on an award of that benefit should be so revised or superseded.

Analysis

See reg 13 D&A Regs on p1032. Reg 86 HB Regs, reg 67 HB(SPC) Regs, reg 72 CTB Regs and reg 57 CTB(SPC) Regs are partly made under ss5(1)(hh) and 6(1)(hh) SSAA.

Termination in cases of a failure to furnish information

15.   Regulations may provide that, except in prescribed cases or circumstances–

(a)   a person whose benefit has been suspended in accordance with regulations under paragraph 13 and who subsequently fails to comply with an information requirement, or

(b)   a person whose benefit has been suspended in accordance with regulations under paragraph 14 for failing to comply with such a requirement,

shall cease to be entitled to the benefit from a date not earlier than the date on which payments were suspended.

Analysis

See reg 14 D&A Regs on p1034.

Decisions involving issues that arise on appeal in other cases

16.–(1)   This paragraph applies where–

(a)   a relevant decision, or a decision under paragraph 3 about the revision of an earlier decision, falls to be made in any particular case; and

(b)   an appeal is pending against the decision given in another case by [the Upper Tribunal] or a court.

(2)   A relevant authority need not make the decision while the appeal is pending if they consider it possible that the result of the appeal will be such that, if it were already determined, there would be no entitlement to benefit.

(3)   If a relevant authority consider it possible that the result of the appeal will be such that, if it were already determined, it would affect the decision in some other way–

(a)   they need not, except in such cases or circumstances as may be prescribed, make the decision while the appeal is pending;

(b)   they may, in such cases or circumstances as may be prescribed, make the decision on such basis as may be prescribed.

(4)   Where–

(a)   a relevant authority act in accordance with sub-paragraph (3)(b), and

(b)   following the making of the determination it is appropriate for their decision to be revised,

they shall then revise their decision (under paragraph 3) in accordance with that determination.

(5)   For the purposes of this paragraph, an appeal against a decision is pending if–

(a)   an appeal against the decision has been brought but not determined;

(b)   an application for leave to appeal against the decision has been made but not determined; or

(c)   the time within which–

(i) an application for leave to appeal may be made, or

(ii) an appeal against the decision may be brought,

has not expired and the circumstances are such as may be prescribed.

(6)   In paragraphs (a), (b) and (c) of sub-paragraph (5), any reference to an appeal against a decision, or to an application for leave to appeal against a decision, includes a reference to–

(a)   an application for judicial review of the decision under section 31 of the Supreme Court Act 1981 or for leave to apply for judicial review; or

(b)   an application to the supervisory jurisdiction of the Court of Session in respect of the decision.
(7)   In sub-paragraph (1)(b) the reference to another case–
(a)   includes a reference to a case involving a decision made, or falling to be made, by a different relevant authority; but
(b)   does not include a reference to a case relating to another benefit unless the other benefit is housing benefit or council tax benefit.

Amendment
1.   Amended by Art 9 and Sch 3 para 190(11) of SI 2008 No. 2833 (3.11.08).

Analysis
Para 16 is concerned with situations where an appeal in another case (known as a "test case") is pending and a decision falls to be made on a claim or through a revision (known as a "look-alike case"). It enables the local authority to postpone making the decision in the look-alike case until the decision is made in the test case. See para 18 where a decision has already been made on a test case.

Sub-para (2) temporarily absolves the authority from its duty to make the decision if it is *possible* that the result of the appeal would result in nil entitlement.

Sub-paras (3) and (4) deal with cases where there would be some other effect on the decision (such as a change in the rate of benefit). See reg 15 D&A Regs on p1036 for the cases in which a decision may nonetheless be made. If the decision turns out to be wrong following the decision on the pending appeal, sub-para (4) requires the decision to be revised.

Sub-paras (5) to (7) deal with the type of appeals with which the court is concerned. Sub-paras (5) and (7) are identical to paras 13(3) and (4): see the Analysis to those provisions. Sub-para (6) confirms that "appeal" includes pending applications for judicial review in these circumstances.

Appeals involving issues that arise on appeal in other cases
17.–(1)   This paragraph applies where–
(a)   an appeal ("appeal A") in relation to a relevant decision (whether as originally made or as revised under paragraph 3) is made to [¹ the First-tier Tribunal, or from the First-tier Tribunal to the Upper Tribunal]; and
(b)   an appeal ("appeal B") is pending against a decision given in a different case by [¹ the Upper Tribunal] or a court.
(2)   If the relevant authority whose decision gave rise to appeal A consider it possible that the result of appeal B will be such that, if it were already determined, it would affect the determination of appeal A, they may serve notice requiring the [¹ First-tier Tribunal or Upper Tribunal]–
(a)   not to determine appeal A but to refer it to them; or
(b)   to deal with the appeal in accordance with sub-paragraph (4).
(3)   Where appeal A is referred to the authority under sub-paragraph (2)(a), following the determination of appeal B and in accordance with that determination, they shall if appropriate–
(a)   in a case where appeal A has not been determined by the [¹ First-tier Tribunal], revise (under paragraph 3) their decision which gave rise to that appeal; or
(b)   in a case where appeal A has been determined by the [¹ First-tier Tribunal], make a decision (under paragraph 4) superseding the tribunal's decision.
(4)   Where appeal A is to be dealt with in accordance with this sub-paragraph, the [¹ First-tier Tribunal or Upper Tribunal] shall either–
(a)   stay appeal A until appeal B is determined; or
(b)   if the [¹ First-tier Tribunal or Upper Tribunal] considers it to be in the interests of the appellant to do so, determine appeal A as if–
(i)   appeal B had already been determined; and
(ii)   the issues arising on appeal B had been decided in the way that was most unfavourable to the appellant.
(5)   Where the [¹ First-tier Tribunal or Upper Tribunal] acts in accordance with sub-paragraph (4)(b), following the determination of appeal B the relevant authority whose decision gave rise to appeal A shall, if appropriate, make a decision (under paragraph 4) superseding the decision of the [¹ First-tier Tribunal or Upper Tribunal] in accordance with that determination.
(6)   For the purposes of this paragraph, an appeal against a decision is pending if–
(a)   an appeal against the decision has been brought but not determined;
(b)   an application for leave to appeal against the decision has been made but not determined; or
(c)   the time within which–
(i)   an application for leave to appeal may be made, or
(ii)   an appeal against the decision may be brought,
has not expired and the circumstances are such as may be prescribed.
(7)   In this paragraph–
(a)   the reference in sub-paragraph (1)(a) to an appeal to [¹ the Upper Tribunal] includes a reference to an application for leave to appeal to [¹ the Upper Tribunal];
(b)   the reference in sub-paragraph (1)(b) to a different case–

      (i)   includes a reference to a case involving a different relevant authority; but

      (ii)   does not include a reference to a case relating to a different benefit unless the different benefit is housing benefit or council tax benefit; and

(c)   any reference in paragraph (a), (b) or (c) of sub-paragraph (6) to an appeal, or to an application for leave to appeal, against a decision includes a reference to–

      (i)   an application for judicial review of the decision under section 31 of the Supreme Court Act 1981 or for leave to apply for judicial review; or

      (ii)   an application to the supervisory jurisdiction of the Court of Session in respect of the decision.

(8)   In sub-paragraph (4) "the appellant" means the person who appealed or, as the case may be, first appealed against the decision mentioned in sub-paragraph (1)(a).

(9)   Regulations may make provision supplementing the provision made by this paragraph.

Commencement

It is understood that the Government does not intend to bring para 17 into force.

Amendment

1.   Amended by Art 9 and Sch 3 para 190(12) of SI 2008 No. 2833 (3.11.08).

Restrictions on entitlement to benefit in certain cases of error

18.–(1)   Subject to sub-paragraph (2), this paragraph applies where–

(a)   the effect of the determination, whenever made, of an appeal [¹ to the Upper Tribunal] or the court ("the relevant determination") is that the relevant authority's decision out of which the appeal arose was erroneous in point of law; and

(b)   after the date of the relevant determination a decision falls to be made by that relevant authority or another relevant authority in accordance with that determination (or would, apart from this paragraph, fall to be so made)–

      (i)   in relation to a claim for housing benefit or council tax benefit;

      (ii)   as to whether to revise, under paragraph 3, a decision as to a person's entitlement to such a benefit; or

      (iii)   on an application made under paragraph 4 for a decision as to a person's entitlement to such a benefit to be superseded.

(2)   This paragraph does not apply where the decision mentioned in sub-paragraph (1)(b)–

(a)   is one which, but for paragraph 16(2) or (3)(a), would have been made before the date of the relevant determination; or

(b)   is one made in pursuance of paragraph 17(3) or (5).

(3)   In so far as the decision relates to a person's entitlement to benefit in respect of a period before the date of the relevant determination, it shall be made as if the relevant authority's decision had been found by [¹ the Upper Tribunal] or court not to have been erroneous in point of law.

(4)   Sub-paragraph (1)(a) shall be read as including a case where–

(a)   the effect of the relevant determination is that part or all of a purported regulation or order is invalid; and

(b)   the error of law made by the relevant authority was to act on the basis that the purported regulation or order (or the part held to be invalid) was valid.

(5)   It is immaterial for the purposes of sub-paragraph (1)–

(a)   where such a decision as is mentioned in paragraph (b)(i) falls to be made, whether the claim was made before or after the date of the relevant determination;

(b)   where such a decision as is mentioned in paragraph (b)(ii) or (iii) falls to be made on an application under paragraph 3 or (as the case may be) 4, whether the application was made before or after that date.

(6)   In this paragraph "the court" means–

(a)   the High Court;

(b)   the Court of Appeal;

(c)   the Court of Session;

(d)   the House of Lords; or

(e)   the Court of Justice of the European Community.

(7)   For the purposes of this paragraph, any reference to entitlement to benefit includes a reference to entitlement–

(a)   to any increase in the rate of a benefit; or

(b)   to a benefit, or increase of benefit, at a particular rate.

(8)   The date of the relevant determination shall, in prescribed cases, be determined for the purposes of this paragraph in accordance with any regulations made for that purpose.

(9)   Regulations made under sub-paragraph (8) may include provision–

(a)   for a determination of a higher court to be treated as if it had been made on the date of a determination by a lower court or by [¹ the Upper Tribunal]; or

(b)   for a determination of a lower court or of [¹ the Upper Tribunal] to be treated as if it had been made on the date of a determination by a higher court.

Commencement

2.7.01, with the exception of para 18(2)(b) which has not been brought into force and it is understood that, as with para 17 to which it refers, it will not be brought into force.

Amendment

1.   Amended by Art 9 and Sch 3 para 190(13) of SI 2008 No. 2833 (3.11.08).

Analysis

The aim of this para, known as the "anti-test case" rule, is to prevent large numbers of appellants taking advantage of a favourable ruling of the Upper Tribunal or of the court by deeming the law to have been as it had always previously been thought to be, except in relation to the successful appellant. It is an invidious and capricious concept and previous attempts by the then DSS to create a similar effect, principally in s69 SSAA (now repealed and replaced by s27 SSA 1998), caused a great deal of uncertainty and litigation.

It is suggested that para 18 may be vulnerable to challenge under Art 6 of the European Convention on Human Rights. In *Osman v UK* [1998] 29 EHRR 245, ECtHR, it was established that to create an exclusionary rule which prevented effective access to a court would infringe Art 6. As claimants caught by para 18 are effectively excluded from an effective remedy through the appeals system, it must be open to question whether para 18 complies with Art 6. Any challenge would, however, have to proceed by way of an application for a declaration of incompatibility since para 18 is primary legislation. The reasoning of the House of Lords in *Chief Adjudication Officer v Bate* [1996] 1 WLR 814 provides some support and justification for the existence of these rules.

See para 16 for the rules which allow a local authority to postpone making a decision pending a decision in a test case.

Sub-paragraphs (1), (2) and (4) to (6): Application of the rule

Sub-para (1) states the basic situation in which the rule takes effect. It deals with a decision ("decision B" – the "look-alike" case) that falls to be made after a decision of a court, as defined in sub-para (6), or the Upper Tribunal ("decision A" – the "test case"). This only applies where decision B is a decision on a claim, an application for a supersession under para 4 or as to whether to revise under para 3 (see sub-para (1)(b)). Where someone wants to challenge a decision on entitlement to HB or CTB as a result of a test case decision, the "anti-test case" rule can therefore be avoided by appealing against rather than seeking a revision or a supersession of the decision: see *CH 532/2006* and *CH 533/2006*.

First-tier Tribunal decisions are not, of course, binding and do not make the rule take effect. Decision A, termed "the relevant determination", must have been that the relevant authority's initial decision was erroneous in law. "Relevant authority" refers to the authority involved in the case before the court or commissioner, which may be different from the authority required to make decision B on which the rule bites.

The decision which was appealed to create decision A must have been "erroneous in point of law". In many cases, a point of principle is stated by a court or more often by a commissioner that was not considered by the authority at all. Thus it is entirely possible that an authority makes a decision which is overturned on the facts by the First-tier Tribunal. The authority then subsequently appeals to the Upper Tribunal, who in decision A upholds the First-tier Tribunal's decision on the facts and gives guidance as to the law. Unless it is clear that the commissioner finds some flaw in the *legal* approach of the council as opposed to its conclusions of fact, it would seem that the rule cannot bite in such a situation.

Another point of uncertainty concerns whether decision B is made "in accordance with that determination", that is in accordance with decision A. What happens if there is another binding decision, decision C, made prior to decision A but which the authority was bound to apply? In the past it has been common for commissioners to issue decisions the implications of which are not realised until a further decision which achieves a greater degree of publicity. In these circumstances, it is the earliest authoritative decision which must be looked at for the purposes of deciding the relevant date: *R(FC) 3/98* (para 7); *R(I) 1/03* (the latter is a decision of a tribunal of commissioners).

Sub-para (2) limits some of the most unfair effects of the rule by disapplying it in cases where a suspension was imposed under para 16 so as to avoid making a decision prior to decision A. However, there may be difficulties in ascertaining whether a decision "would have been made" prior to the date of decision A. It is suggested that it should be assumed that the authority is complying with the time limit imposed by reg 89(2) HB Regs and the HB(SPC), CTB and CTB(SPC) equivalents. There is no specific time limit for the carrying out of a revision or supersession but it is suggested that they ought to be carried out as soon as all relevant information is before the authority, which may be as soon as the application is made.

Sub-para (4) contains an extraordinary and profoundly undemocratic provision. Under this sub-paragraph, where the error of law that is identified in decision A is the application of a regulation which turns out to be *ultra vires*, the authority must assume the regulation to be valid for the purposes of applying this rule. Parliament appears to have effectively approved the making of any rules, even those clearly outside the scope of the enabling powers, as having what may be substantial effects on the entitlements of claimants. In this way, regulations may have effect prior to "the relevant determination" even if made in breach of consultation procedures designed to protect claimants or even, apparently, if made in bad faith or in breach of the European

Convention on Human Rights. It is the sort of legislation designed to recreate the discredited approach of the first half of the twentieth century, namely that it is the Secretary of State (and hence the local authorities acting under her/his guidance) who determines the validity of regulations rather than the courts. It is not an exaggeration to say that provisions such as sub-para (4) undermine the rule of law.

Sub-para (5) confirms that the rule bites whenever the claim or application for revision or supersession was made.

Sub-paragraphs (3) and (7): The effect of the rule

Sub-para (3) states the effect of the rule. In relation to the period prior to decision A being made (and therefore not from the date of that decision), entitlement to benefit must be determined in decision B as if the authority's decision under attack in the proceedings giving rise to decision A was correct. Thus if decision A means that there was entitlement to benefit when decision A was on an appeal from an initial refusal of benefit, no benefit will be payable prior to the date of decision A. Similarly, where more benefit is payable as a result of decision A, the rule takes effect so as to deprive the claimant in decision B of that additional benefit in relation to the period prior to decision A: sub-para (7).

Sub-paragraphs (8) and (9): Regulations

No regulations have yet been made under sub-paras (8) and (9) and it is accordingly suggested that the normal rules will apply for ascertaining when a judgment takes effect.

In England and Wales, a court judgment normally takes effect from the day on which it is made or such later date as the court may specify: r40.7 Civil Procedure Rules 1998. In Scotland a court decree is enforceable once the successful party has been issued with an extract decree. In the Sheriff Court this is normally 14 days after the date of the decree. In the Court of Session this is normally seven days after the date of the decree. In certain types of cases these periods can be shortened.

Correction of errors and setting aside of decisions

19.–(1) Regulations may make provision with respect to–

(a) the correction of accidental errors in any decision or record of a decision made [¹ by the relevant authority] under or by virtue of any relevant provision; [¹]

[¹ (b)]

(2) Nothing in sub-paragraph (1) shall be construed as derogating from any power to correct errors [¹] which is exercisable apart from regulations made by virtue of that sub-paragraph.

(3) In this paragraph "relevant provision" means–

(a) any of the provisions of this Schedule;

(b) any of the provisions of Part VII of the Social Security Contributions and Benefits Act 1992 so far as they relate to housing benefit or council tax benefit; or

(c) any of the provisions of Part VIII of the Administration Act or of any regulations under section 2A of that Act, so far as the provisions or regulations relate to, or to arrangements for, housing benefit or council tax benefit.

Amendment

1. Amended by Art 9 and Sch 3 para 190(14) of SI 2008 No. 2833 (3.11.08).

Analysis

This para permits local authorities to correct accidental errors in their decisions.

Until 3 November 2008, para 19 also governed the correction and setting aside of tribunal decisions: see now rr36 and 37 TP(FT) Rules on pp1069 and 1069.

Regulations

20.–(1) The power to make regulations under this Schedule shall be [¹ exercisable by the Secretary of State]

(2) Any power conferred by this Schedule to make regulations shall include power to make different provision for different areas or different relevant authorities.

(3) Subsections (3) to (7) of section 79 of the Social Security Act 1998 (supplemental provision in connection with powers to make subordinate legislation under that Act) shall apply to any power to make regulations under this Schedule as they apply to any power to make regulations under that Act.

(4) A statutory instrument containing (whether alone or with other provisions) regulations under paragraph 6(2)(e) or (4) shall not be made unless a draft of the instrument has been laid before Parliament and approved by a resolution of each House.

(5) A statutory instrument–

(a) which contains (whether alone or with other provisions) regulations made under this Schedule, and

(b) which is not subject to any requirement that a draft of the instrument be laid before and approved by a resolution of each House of Parliament,

shall be subject to annulment in pursuance of a resolution of either House of Parliament.

[¹ (6)]

Amendment

    1.   Amended by Art 9 and Sch 3 para 190(15) of SI 2008 No. 2833 (3.11.08).

Interpretation

    23.–(1)   In this Schedule–

"the Administration Act" means the Social Security Administration Act 1992;

"affected" shall be construed subject to any regulations under sub-paragraph (2);

[¹]

[¹]

[¹]

"prescribed" means prescribed by regulations under this Schedule;

"relevant authority" has the meaning given by paragraph 1(1);

"relevant decision" has the meaning given by paragraph 1(2).

    (2)   Regulations may make provision specifying the circumstances in which a person is or is not to be treated for the purposes of this Schedule as a person who is affected by any decision of a relevant authority.

    (3)   For the purposes of this Schedule any decision that is made or falls to be made–

    (a)   by a person authorised to carry out any function of a relevant authority relating to housing benefit or council tax benefit, or

    (b)   by a person providing services relating to housing benefit or council tax benefit directly or indirectly to a relevant authority,

shall be treated as a decision of the relevant authority on whose behalf the function is carried out or, as the case may be, to whom those services are provided.

Amendment

    1.   Amended by Art 9 and Sch 3 para 190(16) of SI 2008 No. 2833 (3.11.08).

Analysis

    Sub-para (3) permits delegation of decision making functions in relation to HB/CTB either to officers authorised by local authorities to carry out their functions, or to contractors. The wording "directly or indirectly" covers cases of employees of contractors or, indeed, of sub-contractors.

Constitutional Reform Act 2005
Part 2
Arrangements to Modify the Office of Lord Chancellor
Continued judicial independence

Guarantee of continued judicial independence

3.–(1)   The Lord Chancellor, other Ministers of the Crown and all with responsibility for matters relating to the judiciary or otherwise to the administration of justice must uphold the continued independence of the judiciary.

(2)   Subsection (1) does not impose any duty which it would be within the legislative competence of the Scottish Parliament to impose.

(3)   *[Omitted]*

(4)   The following particular duties are imposed for the purpose of upholding that independence.

(5)   The Lord Chancellor and other Ministers of the Crown must not seek to influence particular judicial decisions through any special access to the judiciary.

(6)   The Lord Chancellor must have regard to–

(a)   the need to defend that independence;

(b)   the need for the judiciary to have the support necessary to enable them to exercise their functions;

(c)   the need for the public interest in regard to matters relating to the judiciary or otherwise to the administration of justice to be properly represented in decisions affecting those matters.

(7)   In this section "the judiciary" includes the judiciary of any of the following–

(a)   the Supreme Court;

(b)   any other court established under the law of any part of the United Kingdom;

(c)   any international court.

[¹ (7A)   In this section " the judiciary" also includes every person who–

(a)   holds an office listed in Schedule 14 or holds an office listed in subsection (7B), and

(b)   but for this subsection would not be a member of the judiciary for the purposes of this section.

(7B)   The offices are those of–

(a)   Senior President of Tribunals;

(b)-(e) *[Omitted]*

(8)   In subsection (7) "international court" means the International Court of Justice or any other court or tribunal which exercises jurisdiction, or performs functions of a judicial nature, in pursuance of–

(a)   an agreement to which the United Kingdom or Her Majesty's Government in the United Kingdom is a party, or

(b)   a resolution of the Security Council or General Assembly of the United Nations.

Amendment

1.   Amended by s1 Tribunals, Courts and Enforcement Act 2007 (19.9.2007)

SCHEDULE 14
THE JUDICIAL APPOINTMENTS COMMISSION: RELEVANT OFFICES AND ENACTMENTS

Part 1
Appointments by her Majesty

[¹ *Judge of the Upper Tribunal by appointment under paragraph 1(1) of Schedule 3 to the Tribunals, Courts and Enforcement Act 2007*   *Paragraph 1(1) of Schedule 3 to the Tribunals, Courts and Enforcement Act 2007]*

Part 3

Appointments by The Lord Chancellor: Offices to which Paragraph 2(2)(d) of Schedule 12 Applies

[¹ *Chamber President of a chamber of the First-tier Tribunal, or of a chamber of the Upper Tribunal, by appointment under section 7(7) of the Tribunals, Courts and Enforcement Act 2007, but not where appointed in accordance with paragraph 2(2) to (5) of Schedule 4 to that Act*

Section 7(7) of the Tribunals, Courts and Enforcement Act 2007

Judge of the First-tier Tribunal by appointment under paragraph 1(1) of Schedule 2 to the Tribunals, Courts and Enforcement Act 2007

Paragraph 1(1) of Schedule 2 to the Tribunals, Courts and Enforcement Act 2007

Other member of the First-tier Tribunal by appointment under paragraph 2(1) of Schedule 2 to the Tribunals, Courts and Enforcement Act 2007

Paragraph 2(1) of Schedule 2 to the Tribunals, Courts and Enforcement Act 2007

Other member of the Upper Tribunal by appointment under paragraph 2(1) of Schedule 3 to the Tribunals, Courts and Enforcement Act 2007

Paragraph 2(1) of Schedule 3 to the Tribunals, Courts and Enforcement Act 2007

Deputy judge of the Upper Tribunal by appointment under paragraph 7(1) of Schedule 3 to the Tribunals, Courts and Enforcement Act 2007

Paragraph 7(1) of Schedule 3 to the Tribunals, Courts and Enforcement Act 2007

Deputy Chamber President of a chamber of the First-tier Tribunal, or of a chamber of the Upper Tribunal, but not where appointed in accordance with paragraph 5(5) to (8) of Schedule 4 to the Tribunals, Courts and Enforcement Act 2007

Paragraph 5(1) of Schedule 4 to the Tribunals, Courts and Enforcement Act 2007]

Amendment

1.   Amended by Sch 8 para 66 Tribunals, Courts and Enforcement Act 2007 (3.11. 2008).

Welfare Reform Act 2007
(2007 c5)

Loss of housing benefit following eviction for anti-social behaviour, etc.

31.–(1)-(2) *[Omitted]*

(3)   The preceding provisions of this section have no effect after 31st December 2010.

(4)   The Secretary of State may by order made by statutory instrument make such provision as he thinks necessary or expedient in consequence of the operation of subsection (3) for the purpose of securing that, with effect from 1st January 2011, housing benefit to which a person who is a former occupier (within the meaning of section 130B of the Contributions and Benefits Act) is entitled is not subject to any restriction as mentioned in subsection (4) of that section.

Commencement

14.6.07 for the purpose only of the exercise of the power to make regulations; 1.11.07 for all other purposes.

General Note

Section 31(1) of the this Act inserts ss130B-130G into the SSCBA 1992 and s31(2) amends s176 of that Act. By s31(3), these provisions have no effect after 31 December 2010.

Housing benefit and council tax benefit for persons taking up employment

32.–(1)   Subsection (2) applies if a person is entitled to housing benefit or council tax benefit (by virtue of the general conditions of entitlement) and–

   (a)   he is also entitled to a prescribed benefit or his partner is entitled to such a benefit,

   (b)   he or his partner ceases to be entitled to the prescribed benefit in prescribed circumstances, and

   (c)   the prescribed conditions are satisfied.

(2)   That person is entitled to housing benefit or council tax benefit in accordance with this section for a prescribed period.

(3)   Subsection (2) applies whether or not the person would be entitled to housing benefit or council tax benefit by virtue of the general conditions of entitlement for the whole or any part of the prescribed period.

(4)   A person who is entitled to housing benefit or council tax benefit by virtue of subsection (2) must be treated for all purposes–

   (a)   as having made a claim for that benefit, and

   (b)   as having complied with any requirement under or by virtue of any enactment in connection with the making of such a claim.

(5)   Housing benefit or council tax benefit to which a person is entitled by virtue of subsection (2) is to be funded and administered by the appropriate authority.

(6)   Subsection (5) applies whether or not, for the whole or any part of the prescribed period–

   (a)   for the purposes of establishing an entitlement to housing benefit, the person occupies as his home a dwelling in the area of the authority;

   (b)   for the purposes of establishing an entitlement to council tax benefit, the person is a resident of a dwelling in the area of the authority.

(7)   The amount of housing benefit or council tax benefit payable in respect of a person who is entitled to the benefit by virtue of subsection (2) is to be determined in accordance with regulations made for the purposes of this section.

(8)   If an amount of housing benefit or council tax benefit is, by virtue of subsection (2), payable in respect of a person by the appropriate authority for any period, no other amount of housing benefit or council tax benefit is (by virtue of the general conditions of entitlement) payable by that authority in respect of that person for the same period.

(9)   Regulations may make provision in connection with the effect of a person's entitlement to housing benefit or council tax benefit by virtue of subsection (2) on an

award of such benefit by virtue of the general conditions of entitlement in respect of that person or his partner.

(10)   Regulations may provide that where–

(a)   an amount of housing benefit or council tax benefit is, by virtue of subsection (2), payable in respect of a person by the appropriate authority for the whole or any part of a prescribed period, and

(b)   an amount of housing benefit or council tax benefit is (by virtue of the general conditions of entitlement) payable by a local authority which is not that appropriate authority in respect of that person for the whole or any part of that period,

the amount of the benefit payable by the local authority mentioned in paragraph (b) is to be reduced by an amount determined in such manner as is prescribed.

(11)   An amount determined for the purposes of subsection (10) may have the effect of reducing the amount mentioned in paragraph (b) of that subsection to nil.

(12)   Regulations may make provision as to circumstances in which–

(a)   subsection (8) does not apply;

(b)   entitlement to housing benefit or council tax benefit of a partner of the person mentioned in subsection (10) is to be treated as the entitlement of that person;

(c)   benefit is not to be reduced as mentioned in subsection (10).

(13)   For the purposes of subsection (1) a person must be treated as entitled to housing benefit or council tax benefit by virtue of the general conditions of entitlement if–

(a)   he is not so entitled to that benefit at the time he or his partner ceases to be entitled to the prescribed benefit as mentioned in subsection (1)(b), and

(b)   his entitlement to housing benefit or council tax benefit (as the case may be) ceased during the prescribed period before that time.

Commencement

6.10.08 (1.4.08. to make regulations).

General Note

Sections 32 to 34 WRA 2007 establish a scheme for "extended payments" of HB and CTB which can assist people who, having been on a specified benefit for a period, come off that benefit because they (or their partners) commence employment (or self-employment) or increase hours or earnings. The scheme provides financial assistance, in the form of continuing entitlement to HB and CTB, in the early weeks of that employment. Section 33 deals with administrative matters and s34 with interpretation.

There are two schemes for extended payments.

(1)   Extended payments of HB and CTB paid where the claimant or her/his partner was entitled to a "qualifying income-related benefit", defined as IS, income-based JSA (including joint-claim JSA) or income-related ESA: regs 2 and 72 to 72D HB Regs; regs 2 and 60 to 60D CTB Regs. Note that although there are no equivalent rules in the HB(SPC) Regs and CTB(SPC) Regs, claimants of at least the qualifying age for PC who were (or whose partners were) entitled to a qualifying income-related benefit and who satisfy the other rules of entitlement to extended payments would qualify for these under the HB Regs and CTB Regs: see reg 5(1)(b) of both the HB and CTB Regs. The amount of HB or CTB payable under the normal rules of entitlement can then be adjusted: reg 52 HB(SPC) Regs; reg 41 CTB(SPC) Regs.

(2)   Extended payments of HB and CTB paid where the claimant or her/his partner was entitled to a "qualifying contributory benefit", defined as incapacity benefit, contributory ESA or severe disablement allowance: regs 2 and 73 to 73D HB Regs; regs 2 and 53 to 53D HB(SPC) Regs; regs 2 and 61 to 61D CTB Regs; regs 2 and 44 to 44D CTB(SPC) Regs.

Note that prior to 6 October 2008, the scheme for extended payments of HB and CTB was broadly similar to the current scheme, but with an important difference: HB and CTB entitlement under the normal rules ended in the same circumstances in which a claimant qualified for extended payments. For entitlement to continue after the extended payment period a fresh claim was required. This is now no longer the case.

Analysis

Subss (1) to (3). Subs (1) sets out the general rules for entitlement to extended payments of HB and CTB. The prescribed benefits, circumstances and conditions are all to be found in regs 2, 72 and 73 HB Regs, regs 2 and 53 HB(SPC) Regs, regs 2, 60 and 61 CTB Regs and regs 2 and 44 CTB(SPC) Regs. The "general conditions of entitlement" are those in Part 7 of the SSCBA 1992: s34(2).

If the conditions for extended payments are met, HB and/or CTB entitlement continues for a prescribed period, even if it would otherwise cease (ie, if based on the claimant's new circumstances): subss (2) and (3).

The prescribed period is one of up to four weeks: regs 72A and 73A HB Regs; reg 53A HB(SPC) Regs; regs 60A and 61A CTB Regs; reg 44A CTB(SPC) Regs.

Subs (4) ensures that no claim for extended payments is required by deeming a person to have made such a claim and to have complied with any requirements for making a claim for HB and/or CTB.

Subss (5) and (6), extended payments are funded and administered by the "appropriate authority", defined in s34(3) and (4) as the authority that funded and administered, as the case may be, the claimant's HB or CTB immediately before entitlement to the qualifying income-related or contributory benefit ceased. This is particularly relevant to "movers", that is, certain claimants who move from the area of one authority to another: regs 72C and 73C HB Regs; reg 53C HB(SPC) Regs; regs 60C and 61C CTB Regs; reg 44C CTB(SPC) Regs.

Subss (7) and (8). The amount of extended payments is dealt with in regs 72B, 72C, 73B and 73C HB Regs, regs 53B and 53C HB (SPC) Regs, regs 60B, 60C, 61B and 61C CTB Regs and regs 44B and 44C CTB(SPC) Regs.

Subss (9) to (12) prevent duplication of payments – eg, where a claimant receiving extended payments has a partner who claims HB or CTB in respect of the same period. See regs 72B(7), 72C(4), 73B(7) and 73C(4) HB Regs, regs 52, 53B(7) and 53C(4) HB(SPC) Regs, regs 60B(3), 60C(4), 61B(3) and 61C(4) CTB Regs and regs 41, 44B(3) and 44C(4) CTB(SPC) Regs.

Section 32: supplemental

33.–(1)   The administration provisions apply in relation to housing benefit or council tax benefit to which a person is entitled by virtue of subsection (2) of section 32 subject to–

(a)   subsections (4), (5) and (6) of that section;

(b)   any prescribed modifications of those provisions which the Secretary of State thinks are necessary or expedient in connection with such housing benefit or council tax benefit.

(2)   Modifications under subsection (1)(b) may, in particular, provide that housing benefit or council tax benefit to which a person is entitled by virtue of section 32(2) must or may take the form of a payment by the appropriate authority to another local authority in prescribed circumstances.

(3)   In this section the administration provisions are–

(a)   the Administration Act;

(b)   subordinate legislation (within the meaning of the Interpretation Act 1978 (c. 30)) made in pursuance of that Act.

(4)   The power to make regulations under this section or section 32 is exercisable by the Secretary of State by statutory instrument.

(5)   A statutory instrument containing regulations under this section or section 32 is subject to annulment in pursuance of a resolution of either House of Parliament.

(6)   Section 175(3) to (7) of the Contributions and Benefits Act (supplemental provision as to regulations) applies in relation to regulations under this section and section 32 above as it applies in relation to regulations under that Act.

(7)   [Omitted]

(8)   For the purposes of any enactment other than a relevant enactment–

(a)   entitlement to housing benefit by virtue of section 32(2) above is to be treated as entitlement under section 130 of the Contributions and Benefits Act;

(b)   entitlement to council tax benefit by virtue of section 32(2) above is to be treated as entitlement under section 131 of that Act.

(9)   In subsection (8), the relevant enactments are–

(a)   the administration provisions, and

(b)   Part 7 of the Contributions and Benefits Act, except sections 123 and 134(2) and (4).

Commencement
6.10.08 (1.4.08. to make regulations).

General Note
This deals with administrative matters in respect of the scheme for extended payments of HB and CTB. See the commentary to s32.

Sections 32 and 33: interpretation

34.–(1)   This section has effect for the interpretation of sections 32 and 33.

(2)   The general conditions of entitlement are the conditions governing entitlement to housing benefit or council tax benefit provided for by Part 7 of the Contributions and Benefits Act.

(3)   The appropriate authority–

(a)   in relation to housing benefit is the local authority or housing authority which, immediately before the person concerned ceased to be entitled to the prescribed benefit, funded and administered the housing benefit to which he was entitled;

(b)   in relation to council tax benefit is the billing authority or, in Scotland, local authority which, immediately before the person concerned ceased to be entitled to the prescribed benefit, funded and administered the council tax benefit to which he was entitled.

(4)   The following expressions have the same meaning as in the Administration Act–

(a)   billing authority;

(b)   housing authority;

(c)   local authority.

(5)   Partner, in relation to a person, is a person who is a member of the same couple (within the meaning of Part 7 of the Contributions and Benefits Act) as that person.

(6)   Prescribed means prescribed by regulations.

Commencement

6.10.08 (1.4.08. to make regulations).

General Note

This provides relevant definitions for the scheme for extended payments of HB and CTB. See the commentary to s32 on p163.

Information relating to certain benefits

42.–(1)   Information falling within subsection (3) may be supplied by the person who holds it to a person falling within subsection (4) for purposes connected with the application of grant paid under a relevant enactment towards expenditure incurred by the recipient of the grant–

(a)   in providing, or contributing to the provision of, welfare services, or

(b)   in connection with such welfare services.

(2)   Information falling within subsection (3) which is held for a prescribed purpose by a person falling within any of paragraphs (c) to (h) of subsection (4) may be–

(a)   used by that person for another prescribed purpose;

(b)   provided to another such person for use in relation to the same or another prescribed purpose.

(3)   The information is any information which is held by a person falling within subsection (4) relating to–

(a)   income support;

(b)   income-based jobseeker's allowance;

(c)   income-related employment and support allowance;

(d)   state pension credit;

(e)   housing benefit;

(f)   welfare services.

(4)   The persons are–

(a)   the Secretary of State;

(b)   a person providing services to the Secretary of State;

(c)   an authority administering housing benefit;

(d)   a person authorised to exercise any function of such an authority relating to housing benefit;

(e)   a person providing to such an authority services relating to housing benefit;

(f)   a local authority to which any grant is or will be paid as mentioned in subsection (1);

    (g)   a person authorised to exercise any function of such an authority relating to the grant;

    (h)   a person providing to such an authority services relating to any such function.

    (5)   Information which is supplied under subsection (1) to an authority or other person falling within subsection (4)(f), (g) or (h) may be supplied by the authority or person to a person who provides qualifying welfare services for purposes connected with the provision of those services.

    (6)   A person provides qualifying welfare services if–

    (a)   he provides welfare services,

    (b)   a local authority contribute or will contribute to the expenditure incurred by him in providing those services, and

    (c)   that contribution is or will be derived (in whole or in part) from any grant which is or will be paid to the authority as mentioned in subsection (1).

    (7)   A relevant enactment is an enactment specified by order made by the Secretary of State; and the power to make an order under this subsection is exercisable by statutory instrument subject to annulment in pursuance of a resolution of either House of Parliament.

    (8)   In subsection (2) a prescribed purpose is a purpose relating to housing benefit or welfare services which is prescribed by regulations made by the Secretary of State by statutory instrument subject to annulment in pursuance of a resolution of either House of Parliament.

    (9)   The power to make an order or regulations under this section includes power–

    (a)   to make different provision for different purposes;

    (b)   to make such incidental, supplementary, consequential, transitional or saving provision as the Secretary of State thinks necessary or expedient.

    (10)   In this section–

"income-based jobseeker's allowance" has the same meaning as in the Jobseekers Act 1995 (c. 18);

"income-related employment and support allowance" means an income-related allowance under Part 1;

"local authority" means–

    (a)   in relation to England, a county council, a district council, a London borough council, the Common Council of the City of London or the Council of the Isles of Scilly;

    (b)   in relation to Wales, a county council or a county borough council;

"welfare services" includes services which provide support, assistance, advice or counselling to individuals with particular needs.

    (11)   *[Omitted]*

Commencement

5.8.08 for the purpose only of the exercise of the power to make orders or regulations; 1.9.08 for all other purposes.

General Note

The Local Government Act 2000, by s93, introduced a system of grants to organisations providing welfare services such as counselling and support. This system replaced the provision made by Sch 1B of the HB Regs 1987.

    Until 1 September 2008, ss94 and 95 of the 2000 Act contained provisions dealing with the disclosure of information. This is now dealt with in ss42 and 43 WRA 2007.

Unlawful disclosure of certain information

43.–(1)   A person to whom subsection (2) applies is guilty of an offence if he discloses without lawful authority any information–

    (a)   which comes to him by virtue of section 42(1), (2) or (5), and

    (b)   which relates to a particular person.

    (2)   This subsection applies to–

    (a)   a person mentioned in section 42(4)(f) to (h);

(b)   a person who provides qualifying welfare services (within the meaning of section 42(6));

(c)   a person who is or has been a director, member of the committee of management, manager, secretary or other similar officer of a person mentioned in paragraph (a) or (b);

(d)   a person who is or has been an employee of a person mentioned in paragraph (a) or (b).

(3)   A person guilty of an offence under this section shall be liable–

(a)   on conviction on indictment, to imprisonment for a term not exceeding 2 years or a fine or both, or

(b)   on summary conviction, to imprisonment for a term not exceeding 12 months or a fine not exceeding the statutory maximum or both.

(4)   It is not an offence under this section–

(a)   to disclose information in the form of a summary or collection of information so framed as not to enable information relating to any particular person to be ascertained from it;

(b)   to disclose information which has previously been disclosed to the public with lawful authority.

(5)   It is a defence for a person charged with an offence under this section to prove that at the time of the alleged offence–

(a)   he believed that he was making the disclosure in question with lawful authority and had no reasonable cause to believe otherwise, or

(b)   he believed that the information in question had previously been disclosed to the public with lawful authority and had no reasonable cause to believe otherwise.

(6)   A disclosure is made with lawful authority if it is so made for the purposes of section 123 of the Administration Act.

(7)   This section does not affect that section.

(8)   Until the commencement of section 282 of the Criminal Justice Act 2003 (c. 44) (increase in maximum term that may be imposed on summary conviction of offence triable either way) the reference in subsection (3)(b) to 12 months must be taken to be a reference to 6 months.

Commencement

5.8.08 (for making orders or regulations); 1.9.08 for all other purposes.

General Note

See the General Note to s42 on p166.

Loss of benefit for commission of benefit offences

49.–(1)   In section 7 of the Social Security Fraud Act 2001 (c. 11) (loss of benefit for commission of benefit offences) in subsection (1)(b) (period within which later offence must be committed), for "three years" substitute "five years".

(2)   The amendment made by subsection (1) shall be disregarded insofar as the application of section 7(1)(b) of that Act involves considering whether an offence committed before the day on which this section comes into force was committed within the relevant period.

Commencement

1.4.08.

Tribunals, Courts and Enforcement Act 2007
(2007 c15)

ARRANGEMENT OF SECTIONS
PART 1
TRIBUNALS AND INQUIRIES
CHAPTER 1: TRIBUNAL JUDICIARY: INDEPENDENCE AND SENIOR PRESIDENT

2.   Senior President of Tribunals

CHAPTER 2: FIRST-TIER TRIBUNAL AND UPPER TRIBUNAL
ESTABLISHMENT

3.   The First-tier Tribunal and the Upper Tribunal

MEMBERS AND COMPOSITION OF TRIBUNALS

4.   Judges and other members of the First-tier Tribunal
5.   Judges and other members of the Upper Tribunal
6.   Certain judges who are also judges of First-tier Tribunal and Upper Tribunal
7.   Chambers: jurisdiction and Presidents
8.   Senior President of Tribunals: power to delegate

REVIEW OF DECISIONS AND APPEALS

9.   Review of decision of First-tier Tribunal
10. Review of decision of Upper Tribunal
11. Right to appeal to Upper Tribunal
12. Proceedings on appeal to Upper Tribunal
13. Right to appeal to Court of Appeal etc.
14. Proceedings on appeal to Court of Appeal etc.

"JUDICIAL REVIEW"

15. Upper Tribunal's "judicial review" jurisdiction
16. Application for relief under section 15(1)
17. Quashing orders under section 15(1): supplementary provision
18. Limits of jurisdiction under section 15(1)

MISCELLANEOUS

22. Tribunal Procedure Rules
23. Practice directions
24. Mediation
25. Supplementary powers of Upper Tribunal
26. First-tier Tribunal and Upper Tribunal: sitting places
27. Enforcement
28. Assessors
29. Costs or expenses

CHAPTER 3: TRANSFER OF TRIBUNAL FUNCTIONS

30. Transfer of functions of certain tribunals
31. Transfers under section 30: supplementary powers
32. Power to provide for appeal to Upper Tribunal from tribunals in Wales
33. Power to provide for appeal to Upper Tribunal from tribunals in Scotland
34. Power to provide for appeal to Upper Tribunal from tribunals in Northern Ireland
35. Transfer of Ministerial responsibilities for certain tribunals
36. Transfer of powers to make procedural rules for certain tribunals
37. Power to amend lists of tribunals in Schedule 6
38. Orders under sections 30 to 36: supplementary

Chapter 4: Administrative matters in respect of certain tribunals
39.   The general duty
41.   Provision of accommodation
42.   Fees
43.   Report by Senior President of Tribunals

Chapter 5: Oversight of administrative justice system, tribunals and inquiries
44.   The Administrative Justice and Tribunals Council
45.   Abolition of the Council on Tribunals

Chapter 6: Supplementary
49.   Orders and regulations under Part 1: supplemental and procedural provisions
Schedule 5: Procedure in First-tier Tribunal and Upper Tribunal
Schedule 6: Tribunals for the purposes of sections 30 to 36
Schedule 10: Amendments relating to judicial appointments

PART 1
Tribunals and Inquiries
Chapter 2
First-tier Tribunal and Upper Tribunal
Establishment

Senior President of Tribunals
    2.–(1)   Her Majesty may, on the recommendation of the Lord Chancellor, appoint a person to the office of Senior President of Tribunals.
    (2)   Schedule 1 makes further provision about the Senior President of Tribunals and about recommendations for appointment under subsection (1).
    (3)   A holder of the office of Senior President of Tribunals must, in carrying out the functions of that office, have regard to–
    (a)   the need for tribunals to be accessible,
    (b)   the need for proceedings before tribunals–
        (i)   to be fair, and
        (ii)   to be handled quickly and efficiently,
    (c)   the need for members of tribunals to be experts in the subject-matter of, or the law to be applied in, cases in which they decide matters, and
    (d)   the need to develop innovative methods of resolving disputes that are of a type that may be brought before tribunals.
    (4)   In subsection (3) ''tribunals'' means–
    (a)   the First-tier Tribunal,
    (b)   the Upper Tribunal,
    (c)-(e) *[Omitted]*

Commencement
    19.9.07.

General Note
    The first Senior President of Tribunals is the Rt Hon Lord Justice Carnwath CVO.

The First-tier Tribunal and the Upper Tribunal
    3.–(1)   There is to be a tribunal, known as the First-tier Tribunal, for the purpose of exercising the functions conferred on it under or by virtue of this Act or any other Act.
    (2)   There is to be a tribunal, known as the Upper Tribunal, for the purpose of exercising the functions conferred on it under or by virtue of this Act or any other Act.
    (3)   Each of the First-tier Tribunal, and the Upper Tribunal, is to consist of its judges and other members.

(4) The Senior President of Tribunals is to preside over both of the First-tier Tribunal and the Upper Tribunal.

(5) The Upper Tribunal is to be a superior court of record.

Commencement

3.11.08.

General Note

The First-tier Tribunal and Upper Tribunal came into existence on 3 November 2008, as part of a programme of tribunal reform going far beyond social security appeals. On the same date:

(1) Appeal tribunals and the social security commissioners were abolished (except for certain purposes in Scotland that have nothing to do with HB or CTB) (see art 4 of, and Sch 1 to, SI 2008 No.2833 on p1102).

(2) The functions of appeal tribunals were transferred to the First-tier Tribunal and those of the commissioners to the Upper Tribunal (art 3 of, and Sch 1 to, SI 2008 No.2833 on p1102).

(3) Sch 7 of CSPSSA was amended so that new appeals against local authority decisions about HB or CTB lie to the First-tier Tribunal rather than to an appeal tribunal.

(4) Legally-qualified panel members of appeal tribunals became judges of the First-tier Tribunal and commissioners became judges of the Upper Tribunal.

(5) Medically-, disability-, and financially-qualified members of appeal tribunals became members of the First-tier Tribunal.

(6) New procedural rules came into force for both the First-tier Tribunal and the Upper Tribunal.

Administrative support for both the First-tier Tribunal and the Upper Tribunal is supplied by the Tribunals Service, an executive agency of the Ministry of Justice. However, the two tribunals are not themselves part of the Tribunals Service. Tribunals Service staff are civil servants responsible ultimately to the Lord Chancellor. The judges and members of the two tribunals are members of the judiciary with a guarantee of independence under s3 Constitutional Reform Act 2005.

Subs (5) provides that the Upper Tribunal is to be a "superior court of record". It is not clear what the practical consequences of this designation are or, indeed, whether it has any practical consequences. It has been suggested that the phrase may mean that the Upper Tribunal is not amenable to judicial review. However, that possibility has been rejected by both the Court of Appeal (in England and Wales) and the Inner House of the Court of Session (in Scotland) (see *R (Cart and others) v Upper Tribunal and others* [2009] EWHC 3052 at para 35 and [2010] EWCA Civ 859 at paras 16-17; *Eba v Advocate General for Scotland* [2010] CSIH 78 at para 48). It appears from these authorities that the expression is meaningless in Scotland and "a concept of uncertain import" in England and Wales.

The Court of Appeal in *Cart* and the Inner House of the Court of Session in *Eba* also considered whether the Upper Tribunal was immune from judicial review by virtue of its nature and powers – ie, not merely because of its deemed status as a "superior court of record". Their decisions suggest that Scots law and English and Welsh law differ on the question. *Eba* holds that, in Scotland, the Upper Tribunal is subject to judicial review on any of the established grounds. *Cart*, by contrast, holds that in England and Wales the Upper Tribunal is only subject to judicial review on the grounds of "outright excess of jurisdiction" (ie, adjudicating upon a matter over which it has no jurisdiction or making an order it has no power to make, as opposed to making an error of law in the course of deciding a matter over which it does have jurisdiction) or procedural irregularities amounting to the denial of a fair hearing. It is understood that the decision of the Court of Appeal in *Cart* is to be appealed to the Supreme Court. However, at the time of going to press, no further details are available. Neither is it known whether there will be a further appeal in *Eba*.

It should be emphasised that the decision in *Cart* does not apply to applications for judicial review of refusals of leave to appeal by the former social security commissioners. In *R(Wiles) v Social Security Commissioner and another* [2010] EWCA Civ 258, reported as [2010] AACR 30, the Court of Appeal upheld the "comparatively long line of authority" that the (non-appealable) decisions of commissioners are susceptible to judicial review for excess of jurisdiction in both the senses described above. However, Dyson LJ (with whom Sedley LJ agreed) stated that the discretion to grant judicial review of such decisions should be exercised in accordance with the principles established in *Cooke v Secretary of State for Social Security* [2001] EWCA CIV 734 (reported as *R(DLA) 6/01*) for granting permission to appeal to the Court of Appeal against a decision of a commissioner.

Members and composition of tribunals

Judges and other members of the First-tier Tribunal

4.–(1) A person is a judge of the First-tier Tribunal if the person–

(a) is a judge of the First-tier Tribunal by virtue of appointment under paragraph 1(1) of Schedule 2,

(b) is a transferred-in judge of the First-tier Tribunal (see section 31(2)),

(c) is a judge of the Upper Tribunal,

(d)-(e) *[Omitted]*
(2)   *[Omitted]*
(3)   A person is one of the other members of the First-tier Tribunal if the person–
(a)   is a member of the First-tier Tribunal by virtue of appointment under paragraph 2(1) of Schedule 2,
(b)   is a transferred-in other member of the First-tier Tribunal (see section 31(2)),
(c)   is one of the other members of the Upper Tribunal, or
(d)   is a member of a panel of members of employment tribunals that is not a panel of chairmen of employment tribunals.
(4)   Schedule 2–
contains provision for the appointment of persons to be judges or other members of the First-tier Tribunal, and
makes further provision in connection with judges and other members of the First-tier Tribunal.

Commencement
3.11.08.

General Note
People who were chairmen of appeal tribunals on 2 November 2008 automatically became "transferred-in" judges of the First-tier Tribunal the following day. Part-time, fee-paid, judges of the First-tier Tribunal (ie, those who were previously referred to as "Deputy District Chairmen") are known by the informal title of "Tribunal Judge". Salaried judges are known informally as either "District Tribunal Judge" or "Regional Tribunal Judge" depending on the level of their administrative responsibilities.

Judges and members of the Upper Tribunal are *ex officio* members of the First-tier Tribunal.

Judges and other members should, strictly, be addressed as "sir" or "madam" when sitting on the First-tier Tribunal (even if their judicial rank would otherwise entitle them to some other title: see s6). However – except, perhaps, from counsel or solicitors – they are unlikely to object to any other respectful form of address.

Judges and other members of the Upper Tribunal
5.–(1)   A person is a judge of the Upper Tribunal if the person–
(a)   is the Senior President of Tribunals,
(b)   is a judge of the Upper Tribunal by virtue of appointment under paragraph 1(1) of Schedule 3,
(c)   is a transferred-in judge of the Upper Tribunal (see section 31(2)),
(d)   *[Omitted]*
(e)   is the Chief Social Security Commissioner, or any other Social Security Commissioner, appointed under section 50(1) of the Social Security Administration (Northern Ireland) Act 1992 (c. 8),
(f)   is a Social Security Commissioner appointed under section 50(2) of that Act (deputy Commissioners),
(g)   is within section 6(1),
(h)   is a deputy judge of the Upper Tribunal (whether under paragraph 7 of Schedule 3 or under section 31(2)), or
(i)   is a Chamber President or a Deputy Chamber President, whether of a chamber of the Upper Tribunal or of a chamber of the First-tier Tribunal, and does not fall within any of paragraphs (a) to (h).
(2)   A person is one of the other members of the Upper Tribunal if the person–
(a)   is a member of the Upper Tribunal by virtue of appointment under paragraph 2(1) of Schedule 3,
(b)   is a transferred-in other member of the Upper Tribunal (see section 31(2)),
(c)-(d) *[Omitted]*
(3)   Schedule 3–
contains provision for the appointment of persons to be judges (including deputy judges), or other members, of the Upper Tribunal, and
makes further provision in connection with judges and other members of the Upper Tribunal.

Commencement

3.11.08.

General Note

People who were social security commissioners or deputy social security commissioners on 2 November 2008 automatically became "transferred-in" judges and deputy judges of the Upper Tribunal the following day.

Under s4(1)(c), judges (and other members) of the Upper Tribunal are *ex officio* members of the First-tier Tribunal. As ss4 and 5 contain no provision equivalent to s6(2), it would appear that this includes part-time judges.

It is no longer the practice to distinguish informally between a (full-time) "Upper Tribunal Judge" and a (part-time) "Deputy Upper Tribunal Judge". This is because of s5(1)(h) which provides that a "deputy judge of the Upper Tribunal" is a "judge of the Upper Tribunal".

Judges of the Upper Tribunal should be addressed as "sir" or "madam" when sitting (even if their judicial rank would otherwise entitle them to some other title – see s6).

Social security commissioners used to sit either alone or as one of a tribunal of commissioners. Upper Tribunal judges may sit with 'other members' who are not legally-qualified and subs-s(3) gives effect to Sch 3, which provides for the appointment of such members. In the Upper Tribunal the equivalent of a tribunal of commissioners is a "three-judge panel" of the Upper Tribunal.

Certain judges who are also judges of First-tier Tribunal and Upper Tribunal

6.–(1) A person is within this subsection (and so, by virtue of sections 4(1)(c) and 5(1)(g), is a judge of the First-tier Tribunal and of the Upper Tribunal) if the person–

(a) is an ordinary judge of the Court of Appeal in England and Wales (including the vice-president, if any, of either division of that Court),

(b) is a Lord Justice of Appeal in Northern Ireland,

(c) is a judge of the Court of Session,

(d) is a puisne judge of the High Court in England and Wales or Northern Ireland,

(e) is a circuit judge,

(f) is a sheriff in Scotland,

(g) is a county court judge in Northern Ireland,

(h) is a district judge in England and Wales or Northern Ireland, or

(i) is a District Judge (Magistrates' Courts).

(2) References in subsection (1)(c) to (i) to office-holders do not include deputies or temporary office-holders.

Commencement

3.11.08.

General Note

Almost every salaried judge in the UK is *ex officio* a judge of the First-tier Tribunal and the Upper Tribunal. However, they will only sit as such if ticketed to do so by a chamber's president. It seems unlikely that the senior members of the judiciary listed in heads (a) to (d) of para (1) will sit on social security appeals other than in exceptional circumstances.

The decision that district judges should automatically be judges of the Upper Tribunal is difficult to justify. District judges are of the same judicial rank (Group 7) as district tribunal judges and of lower rank than regional tribunal judges. District and regional tribunal judges, who are likely to have considerably more experience than district judges in the specialist law and procedures applied by the First-tier Tribunal, are judges of the First-tier Tribunal only, not the Upper Tribunal. Further, it is contrary to principle that a judge should hold a Group 6 office without having been appointed to it – or another equivalent or higher office – in an open competition by the Judicial Appointments Commission.

The judges listed in heads (a) to (d) of para (1) would normally be addressed as "my lord" or "my lady" in court and those in heads (e) to (g) as "your honour". However, when sitting as a judge of either the First-tier Tribunal or Upper Tribunal, they should be addressed as "sir" or "madam".

Chambers: jurisdiction and Presidents

7.–(1) The Lord Chancellor may, with the concurrence of the Senior President of Tribunals, by order make provision for the organisation of each of the First-tier Tribunal and the Upper Tribunal into a number of chambers.

(2) There is–

(a) for each chamber of the First-tier Tribunal, and

(b)   for each chamber of the Upper Tribunal,
to be a person, or two persons, to preside over that chamber.

(3)   A person may not at any particular time preside over more than one chamber of the First-tier Tribunal and may not at any particular time preside over more than one chamber of the Upper Tribunal (but may at the same time preside over one chamber of the First-tier Tribunal and over one chamber of the Upper Tribunal).

(4)   A person appointed under this section to preside over a chamber is to be known as a Chamber President.

(5)   Where two persons are appointed under this section to preside over the same chamber, any reference in an enactment to the Chamber President of the chamber is a reference to a person appointed under this section to preside over the chamber.

(6)   The Senior President of Tribunals may (consistently with subsections (2) and (3)) appoint a person who is the Chamber President of a chamber to preside instead, or to preside also, over another chamber.

(7)   The Lord Chancellor may (consistently with subsections (2) and (3)) appoint a person who is not a Chamber President to preside over a chamber.

(8)   Schedule 4 (eligibility for appointment under subsection (7), appointment of Deputy Chamber Presidents and Acting Chamber Presidents, assignment of judges and other members of the First-tier Tribunal and Upper Tribunal, and further provision about Chamber Presidents and chambers) has effect.

(9)   Each of the Lord Chancellor and the Senior President of Tribunals may, with the concurrence of the other, by order–
(a)   make provision for the allocation of the First-tier Tribunal's functions between its chambers;
(b)   make provision for the allocation of the Upper Tribunal's functions between its chambers;
(c)   amend or revoke any order made under this subsection.

Commencement

s7(1) and (9): 19.9.07; all other subsections: 3.11.08.

General Note

The power to organise the First-tier Tribunal and Upper Tribunal into chambers has been exercised by the First-tier Tribunal and Upper Tribunal (Chambers) Order 2008.

Since 15 February 2010, the First-tier Tribunal has been organised into the Social Entitlement Chamber, the War Pensions and Armed Forces Compensation Chamber, the Health Education and Social Care Chamber, the Immigration and Asylum Chamber, the Tax Chamber and the General Regulatory Chamber. Appeals against HB and CTB decisions (and other social security benefits and tax credits) are assigned to the Social Entitlement Chamber. From the same date, the Upper Tribunal has been organised into the Administrative Appeals Chamber, the Tax and Chancery Chamber, the Lands Chamber and the Immigration and Asylum Chamber. Appeals concerning HB and CTB (and other social security benefits and tax credits) are heard by the Administrative Appeals Chamber.

Under subs (2) each chamber of the First-tier Tribunal and Upper Tribunal must have at least one "Chamber President". The President of the Social Entitlement Chamber is the former President of Appeal Tribunals, His Honour Judge Robert Martin. The President of the Administrative Appeals Chamber is Mr Justice Walker.

Senior President of Tribunals: power to delegate

8.–(1)   The Senior President of Tribunals may delegate any function he has in his capacity as Senior President of Tribunals–
(a)   to any judge, or other member, of the Upper Tribunal or First-tier Tribunal;
(b)   to staff appointed under section 40(1).

(2)   Subsection (1) does not apply to functions of the Senior President of Tribunals under section 7(9).

(3)   A delegation under subsection (1) is not revoked by the delegator's becoming incapacitated.

(4)   Any delegation under subsection (1) that is in force immediately before a person ceases to be Senior President of Tribunals continues in force until varied or revoked by a subsequent holder of the office of Senior President of Tribunals.

(5)   The delegation under this section of a function shall not prevent the exercise of the function by the Senior President of Tribunals.

Commencement
    3.11.08.

General Note
    The Senior President of Tribunals may delegate the functions assigned to her/him by s2 as set out in this section.

Review of decisions and appeals

Review of decision of First-tier Tribunal

9.–(1)   The First-tier Tribunal may review a decision made by it on a matter in a case, other than a decision that is an excluded decision for the purposes of section 11(1) (but see subsection (9)).

(2)   The First-tier Tribunal's power under subsection (1) in relation to a decision is exercisable–
(a)   of its own initiative, or
(b)   on application by a person who for the purposes of section 11(2) has a right of appeal in respect of the decision.
(3)   Tribunal Procedure Rules may–
(a)   provide that the First-tier Tribunal may not under subsection (1) review (whether of its own initiative or on application under subsection (2)(b)) a decision of a description specified for the purposes of this paragraph in Tribunal Procedure Rules;
(b)   provide that the First-tier Tribunal's power under subsection (1) to review a decision of a description specified for the purposes of this paragraph in Tribunal Procedure Rules is exercisable only of the tribunal's own initiative;
(c)   provide that an application under subsection (2)(b) that is of a description specified for the purposes of this paragraph in Tribunal Procedure Rules may be made only on grounds specified for the purposes of this paragraph in Tribunal Procedure Rules;
(d)   provide, in relation to a decision of a description specified for the purposes of this paragraph in Tribunal Procedure Rules, that the First-tier Tribunal's power under subsection (1) to review the decision of its own initiative is exercisable only on grounds specified for the purposes of this paragraph in Tribunal Procedure Rules.
(4)   Where the First-tier Tribunal has under subsection (1) reviewed a decision, the First-tier Tribunal may in the light of the review do any of the following–
(a)   correct accidental errors in the decision or in a record of the decision;
(b)   amend reasons given for the decision;
(c)   set the decision aside.
(5)   Where under subsection (4)(c) the First-tier Tribunal sets a decision aside, the First-tier Tribunal must either–
(a)   re-decide the matter concerned, or
(b)   refer that matter to the Upper Tribunal.
(6)   Where a matter is referred to the Upper Tribunal under subsection (5)(b), the Upper Tribunal must re-decide the matter.
(7)   Where the Upper Tribunal is under subsection (6) re-deciding a matter, it may make any decision which the First-tier Tribunal could make if the First-tier Tribunal were re-deciding the matter.
(8)   Where a tribunal is acting under subsection (5)(a) or (6), it may make such findings of fact as it considers appropriate.
(9)   This section has effect as if a decision under subsection (4)(c) to set aside an earlier decision were not an excluded decision for the purposes of section 11(1), but the First-tier Tribunal's only power in the light of a review under subsection (1) of a decision under subsection (4)(c) is the power under subsection (4)(a).

(10)   A decision of the First-tier Tribunal may not be reviewed under subsection (1) more than once, and once the First-tier Tribunal has decided that an earlier decision should not be reviewed under subsection (1) it may not then decide to review that earlier decision under that subsection.

(11)   Where under this section a decision is set aside and the matter concerned is then re-decided, the decision set aside and the decision made in re-deciding the matter are for the purposes of subsection (10) to be taken to be different decisions.

Commencement
 s9(3): 19.9.07; all other subsections: 3.11.08.

General Note
 See the commentary to r40 TP(FT) Rules on p1072.

Review of decision of Upper Tribunal

10.–(1)   The Upper Tribunal may review a decision made by it on a matter in a case, other than a decision that is an excluded decision for the purposes of section 13(1) (but see subsection (7)).

(2)   The Upper Tribunal's power under subsection (1) in relation to a decision is exercisable–

(a)   of its own initiative, or

(b)   on application by a person who for the purposes of section 13(2) has a right of appeal in respect of the decision.

(3)   Tribunal Procedure Rules may–

(a)   provide that the Upper Tribunal may not under subsection (1) review (whether of its own initiative or on application under subsection (2)(b)) a decision of a description specified for the purposes of this paragraph in Tribunal Procedure Rules;

(b)   provide that the Upper Tribunal's power under subsection (1) to review a decision of a description specified for the purposes of this paragraph in Tribunal Procedure Rules is exercisable only of the tribunal's own initiative;

(c)   provide that an application under subsection (2)(b) that is of a description specified for the purposes of this paragraph in Tribunal Procedure Rules may be made only on grounds specified for the purposes of this paragraph in Tribunal Procedure Rules;

(d)   provide, in relation to a decision of a description specified for the purposes of this paragraph in Tribunal Procedure Rules, that the Upper Tribunal's power under subsection (1) to review the decision of its own initiative is exercisable only on grounds specified for the purposes of this paragraph in Tribunal Procedure Rules.

(4)   Where the Upper Tribunal has under subsection (1) reviewed a decision, the Upper Tribunal may in the light of the review do any of the following–

(a)   correct accidental errors in the decision or in a record of the decision;

(b)   amend reasons given for the decision;

(c)   set the decision aside.

(5)   Where under subsection (4)(c) the Upper Tribunal sets a decision aside, the Upper Tribunal must re-decide the matter concerned.

(6)   Where the Upper Tribunal is acting under subsection (5), it may make such findings of fact as it considers appropriate.

(7)   This section has effect as if a decision under subsection (4)(c) to set aside an earlier decision were not an excluded decision for the purposes of section 13(1), but the Upper Tribunal's only power in the light of a review under subsection (1) of a decision under subsection (4)(c) is the power under subsection (4)(a).

(8)   A decision of the Upper Tribunal may not be reviewed under subsection (1) more than once, and once the Upper Tribunal has decided that an earlier decision should not be reviewed under subsection (1) it may not then decide to review that earlier decision under that subsection.

(9)   Where under this section a decision is set aside and the matter concerned is then re-decided, the decision set aside and the decision made in re-deciding the matter are for the purposes of subsection (8) to be taken to be different decisions.

Commencement
s10(3): 19.9.07; all other subsections: 3.11.08.

General Note
See the commentary to r46 FT(UT) Rules on p1100.

Right to appeal to Upper Tribunal

11.–(1)   For the purposes of subsection (2), the reference to a right of appeal is to a right to appeal to the Upper Tribunal on any point of law arising from a decision made by the First-tier Tribunal other than an excluded decision.

(2)   Any party to a case has a right of appeal, subject to subsection (8).

(3)   That right may be exercised only with permission (or, in Northern Ireland, leave).

(4)   Permission (or leave) may be given by–

(a)   the First-tier Tribunal, or

(b)   the Upper Tribunal,

on an application by the party.

(5)   For the purposes of subsection (1), an ''excluded decision'' is–

(a)-(c) [Omitted]

(d)   a decision of the First-tier Tribunal under section 9–

    (i)   to review, or not to review, an earlier decision of the tribunal,

    (ii)   to take no action, or not to take any particular action, in the light of a review of an earlier decision of the tribunal,

    (iii)   to set aside an earlier decision of the tribunal, or

    (iv)   to refer, or not to refer, a matter to the Upper Tribunal,

(e)   a decision of the First-tier Tribunal that is set aside under section 9 (including a decision set aside after proceedings on an appeal under this section have been begun), or

(f)   any decision of the First-tier Tribunal that is of a description specified in an order made by the Lord Chancellor.

(6)   A description may be specified under subsection (5)(f) only if–

(a)   in the case of a decision of that description, there is a right to appeal to a court, the Upper Tribunal or any other tribunal from the decision and that right is, or includes, something other than a right (however expressed) to appeal on any point of law arising from the decision, or

(b)   decisions of that description are made in carrying out a function transferred under section 30 and prior to the transfer of the function under section 30(1) there was no right to appeal from decisions of that description.

(7)   Where–

(a)   an order under subsection (5)(f) specifies a description of decisions, and

(b)   decisions of that description are made in carrying out a function transferred under section 30,

the order must be framed so as to come into force no later than the time when the transfer under section 30 of the function takes effect (but power to revoke the order continues to be exercisable after that time, and power to amend the order continues to be exercisable after that time for the purpose of narrowing the description for the time being specified).

(8)   The Lord Chancellor may by order make provision for a person to be treated as being, or to be treated as not being, a party to a case for the purposes of subsection (2).

Commencement
s11(5)(f) and (6) to (8): 19.9.07; all other subsections: 3.11.08.

General Note
There is a right of appeal on a point of law to the Upper Tribunal against most decisions of the First-tier Tribunal. Permission to appeal (formerly called "leave to appeal") is required.

Analysis

Who may appeal?

Subs (2) confers a right of appeal on "any party to a case". The power conferred on the Lord Chancellor by subs (8) to provide that a person "to be treated as being . . . or not being a party to the case" for the purposes of subs (2) has not been exercised and the phrase "any party to a case" is not defined in the Act. However, for HB/CTB purposes, CSPSSA Sch 7 para 8(2) confers a right of appeal on the Secretary of State, the relevant authority and any "person affected" by the decision against which the appeal to the First-tier Tribunal was brought or by the First-tier Tribunal's decision on the appeal. "Person affected" is defined for the purposes of Sch 7 in reg 3 D&A Regs. However, that definition is not exhaustive (*CH 3817/2004*): see further the commentary to reg 3 on p1010.

Which decisions may be appealed against?

Under subs (1), the right of appeal is against "a decision made by the First-tier Tribunal other than an excluded decision", as defined in subs (5). The word "decision"' in that phrase will always encompass the tribunal's outcome decision – ie, to allow or refuse the appeal on the merits. But there is not always a right of appeal against procedural or interlocutory decisions – eg, decisions on whether to adjourn, extend time for a late appeal, strike out for lack of jurisdiction or direct (or refuse to direct) disclosure of documents.

Whether such a right of exists is a matter of statutory construction in each case (see Sir Anthony Clarke MR and Arden LJ in *SSWP v Morina and Borrowdale* [2007] EWCA Civ 749 (reported as *R(IS) 6/07*) at paras 50, and 42 and 47 respectively). Some decisions are inherently unappealable. In such cases, it is necessary to adopt a purposive construction of the word "decision" because to interpret that word in a way that confers a right of appeal would be to subvert the operation of other provisions that restrict or exclude that right. The leading case is the decision of the House of Lords in *Lane v Esdaile* [1891] AC 210, 212 which decided that there was no appeal to the House of Lords against a refusal by the Court of Appeal of leave to appeal to that court. By imposing the requirement of leave, the legislature intended that there should be a check on unnecessary or frivolous appeals. To allow a right of appeal against the refusal of leave itself would be to frustrate that intention because the higher court could not decide whether the lower court should have granted leave without hearing the case.

Lane v Esdaile has been applied in the field of social security law on a number of occasions. Before the establishment of the Upper Tribunal on 3 November 2008, it was decided that there is no right of appeal to a commissioner from the following decisions.

(1)   A decision refusing leave to appeal to the Court of Appeal against a decision of the commissioner refusing leave to appeal from an appeal tribunal: *Bland v Chief Supplementary Benefit Officer* [1983] 1 WLR 262, CA (reported as *R(SB) 12/83*).

(2)   A decision of the commissioner refusing to extend time so as to admit a late application for leave to appeal: *White v Chief Adjudication Officer* [1986] 2 All ER 905, CA (reported as an appendix to *R(S) 8/85*).

(3)   A decision refusing to extend time for appealing to an appeal tribunal under reg 36 SSCS D&A Regs, at least once the absolute 13-month time limit has expired (*Morina and Borrowdale*). It may be arguable that there is a right of appeal against a refusal to extend time within the 13-month limit: see the discussion of *Rickards v Rickards* [1990] Fam 194 at paras 35-37 and 45 of *Morina* and *Borrowdale*, but see also *White* above. However, the suggestion that there was a right of appeal against a decision refusing to extend time for appealing to an appeal tribunal where the application was made within the 13-month limit was rejected by a tribunal of commissioners in *R(IS) 6/09*.

(4)   A decision to strike out an appeal as "out of jurisdiction" under reg 46 SSCS D&A Regs: *Morina* and *Borrowdale*.

The Upper Tribunal has considered the scope of s11 in a number of cases involving decisions of the Health, Education and Social Care Chamber (HESC) of the First-tier Tribunal. In *Synergy Child Services Ltd v Ofsted* [2009] UKUT 125 (AAC), Upper Tribunal Judge Rowland accepted a concession that a decision refusing to reinstate an appeal that had been automatically struck out under the HESC equivalent of rules 8(1) and (5) TP(FTT) Rules "because it is a substantive decision that is not an 'excluded decision' within section 11(5)". A decision to strike out a case brought proceedings to an end and a refusal to reinstate an automatically struck out decision was to be viewed in the same light. He distinguished *Morina* on the grounds that:

"[i]t arose in the narrow context of social security legislation, there was no express power to exclude decisions from the scope of the relevant right of appeal and the strike-out cases considered by the Court of Appeal were cases that had been struck out on the grounds of lack of jurisdiction".

In *AW v Essex County Council* (SEN) [2010] UKUT 74 (AAC), Upper Tribunal Judge Jacobs allowed an appeal against a decision of the First-tier Tribunal to strike an appeal out for lack of jurisdiction. He accepted that the Upper Tribunal's jurisdiction "includes an appeal against decision to strike out a case, at least one that is not capable of being reinstated."

In *MP v SSWP* (DLA) [2010] UKUT 103 (AAC), Upper Tribunal Judge Turnbull accepted a concession from the Secretary of State for Work and Pensions that a refusal to set aside a decision of the Social Entitlement Chamber of the First-tier Tribunal under rule 37 of the TP(FTT) Rules was appealable.

In the examples listed above, the interlocutory decisions finally disposed of the appeal. If, for example, a necessary extension of time is refused or an appeal is struck out, the appeal cannot proceed further and the decision that the appellant wished to challenge remains in effect. But even when an interlocutory decision (or "determination" – it does not matter which word is used in the empowering legislation: see *R(CS) 5/02* (para 9)) does not finally dispose of the appeal and is not inherently unappealable (eg, a decision to adjourn (or refuse to adjourn), a decision granting an extension of time or refusing to strike out for lack of jurisdiction, or a decision to direct disclosure of documents), the statutory context may nevertheless exclude a right of appeal.

This is because, in such cases, the right of appeal against the tribunal's final, outcome, decision will usually be an adequate remedy. Parties who are refused adjournments or strike outs may nevertheless win the appeal: in fact the tribunal may have refused the application to adjourn, precisely because it considered it probable that the applicant would win without an adjournment. No purpose is served by interpreting the word "decision" to include an interlocutory or procedural decision in such cases: see (in a slightly different context) Laws LJ in *Carpenter v SSWP* [2003] EWCA Civ 33 (reported as *R(IB) 6/03*).

There may, however, be circumstances in which a right of appeal against the final decision is not an adequate remedy. In *Dorset Healthcare NHS Foundation Trust v MH* [2009] UKUT 4 (AAC), a three-judge panel of the Upper Tribunal (HHJ Hickinbottom CP, HHJ Sycamore CP and Judge Rowland) held that the Upper Tribunal had jurisdiction under s11 to consider an appeal against an interlocutory decision of the HESC Chamber of the First-tier Tribunal to direct disclosure of the medical records of a patient detained under s3 Mental Health Act 1983. The NHS Trust opposed that direction because those records contained material supplied by third parties to whom it owed an obligation of confidentiality. The panel distinguished *Carpenter* on the basis that by the time of the First-tier Tribunal's final decision irreparable damage may already have been done by the disclosure.

In *LM v London Borough of Lewisham* [2009] UKUT 204 (AAC): [2010] AACR 12, a three-judge panel of the Upper Tribunal allowed an appeal against a case management direction given by the First-tier Tribunal (HESC) to produce evidence on the ground that it did not make provision for evidence that was subject to legal professional privilege. On the jurisdiction point, the Upper Tribunal followed the earlier decision in *Dorset Healthcare* and assumed jurisdiction because the case management direction was not an "excluded decision" within s11(5), with no express consideration of whether it was a "decision" within s11(1) in the first place. Although the panel did not seek to do so, the decision can be supported on the basis that an eventual appeal against the First-tier Tribunal's substantive decision is not an adequate remedy for having been compelled to disclose privileged information in the course of the proceedings that led to that decision.

The statutory context in which such decisions are made has, of course, been changed by the coming into force of s11 and the repeal of Sch 7 para 8(1) CSPSSA. In particular, subs (5) expressly excludes certain decisions from the right of appeal. It is not clear whether this implies that decisions not specifically excluded carry a right of appeal. The specific exclusions in subs (5) all relate to types of 'decision' that did not exist before TCEA 2007 came into force (although the same is not true of the equivalent list in s13(8)) and may have been included to clarify the position in respect of such decisions without implying that "decision" in subs (1) includes the types of decision or determination that had previously been held to be unappealable.

Paras (a) to (c) of subs (5) are omitted from the text as relating to criminal injuries compensation, data protection and freedom of information. The other excluded decisions are:

– decisions taken by the First-tier Tribunal pursuant to the power of review conferred by s9 (paras (d) and (e)). Note that it is only the decision under s9 itself that is excluded. If the First-tier Tribunal does not review the earlier decision, or having reviewed it, does not set it aside then, subject to time limits and the requirement for permission, there is a right of appeal against the earlier decision. If the First-tier Tribunal sets the earlier decision aside, it is obliged to redecide the matter or refer it to the Upper Tribunal. In the former case, there will be a right of appeal against the new decision; in the latter, the matter will be decided by the Upper Tribunal in any event. A decision that is set aside under s9 is excluded even if appeal proceedings against it have already begun. In those circumstances, the appeal presumably lapses on the decision's being set aside;

– decisions specified in an order made by the Lord Chancellor (para (f)). The Lord Chancellor has made the Appeals (Excluded Decisions) Order 2008 SI No.2707 and the Appeals (Excluded Decisions) (Amendment) Order 2008 SI No.2780 which exclude decisions on appeals under ss103 and 103A Immigration and Asylum Act 1999, s63(6) Tax Credits Act 2002 and s24(2) Child Trust Funds Act 2004.

Procedural or interlocutory decisions that do not carry a right of appeal to the Upper Tribunal (or from the Upper Tribunal to the Court of Appeal) can only be challenged by judicial review. Note, however, that by virtue of a Practice Direction given under s18(6) most judicial reviews of First-tier Tribunal decisions fall to be decided by the Upper Tribunal rather than the High Court: see the General Note to ss15-21 on p186.

Grounds of appeal

Appeal lies to the Upper Tribunal "on any point of law arising from" the First-tier Tribunal decision. It cannot be over-emphasised that the First-tier Tribunal is the fact-finding forum and that unless an error of law can be identified in a tribunal's decision, the Upper Tribunal will not be able to intervene, except possibly in the limited circumstances set out in category (10) below. A tribunal does not err in law simply because another tribunal or the Upper Tribunal would have assessed the combined significance of the facts differently or come to a different conclusion: *CDLA 1456/2002; CH 627/2002; CH 296/2004*.

In *CDLA 2975/2002* (para 15), the commissioner emphasised the importance of clearly identifying points of law:

"Errors of law on the part of an experienced Tribunal . . . are not of course to be inferred, or imagined, simply because they reach a result on the questions of fact and degree they have to determine with which another Tribunal or professional person might possibly disagree; and appeals seeking to dispute the result on such grounds cannot of course succeed as all they are in effect doing is seeking to reargue the case again on the facts."

This illustrates the importance of claimants and authorities ensuring that they put all the points that they wish to put and call all the evidence they wish to call before the First-tier Tribunal, because unless an error of law is made by the First-tier Tribunal it will not be possible to remedy the situation at a later stage. See also the commentary to Sch 7 para 6(9)(a) CSPSSA on p148.

It is probably not possible to give an exhaustive summary of all the circumstances in which an error of law may arise. Nevertheless a number of different summaries exist, particularly in *R(A) 1/72*, *R(IS) 11/99* and the decision of the Court of Appeal in *R(Iran) v Secretary of State for the Home Department* [2005] EWCA Civ 982 (discussed by a tribunal of commissioners in *R(I) 2/06*). Those summaries are not inconsistent but may differ in emphasis and are inevitably influenced by the issues in the cases in which they are given. It is convenient to base this discussion on para 4 of *R(IS) 11/99*, which summaries the categories of error that can give rise to a right of appeal as follows.

(1)   A false proposition of law is evident from the tribunal's statement of reasons. This will include reliance on a provision in secondary legislation that is *ultra vires*: *Foster v Chief Adjudication Officer* [1993] AC 754, HL, though note CSPSSA Sch 7 para 18(4).

(2)   The tribunal has reached a decision that is supported by no evidence. Distinguishing between no evidence and little evidence is important in this context. A complaint in the latter category will only mean that there is an error of law if the conclusion reached is irrational: see below.

(3)   The tribunal has breached the relevancy principle, either by taking into account matters that should have been ignored, or ignoring matters that should have been taken into account. Where a tribunal is called upon to draw inferences from primary findings of fact, care must be taken to ensure that each of the factors relied upon in drawing the inference is relevant. A failure to do so will mean that the decision is erroneous in law, even if the tribunal has considered some of the relevant matters: *R v Allerdale DC HBRB ex p Doughty* [2000] COD 462, QBD. For that reason, the Upper Tribunal may feel more able to interfere with a tribunal's inferences rather than its findings of primary fact: see *CH 1076/2002* for an example.

(4)   The tribunal's decision is irrational, in that no tribunal properly instructed as to the law could have reached a conclusion of fact set out in the statement of reasons. There will be many types of case heard by tribunals in which different tribunals could quite legitimately come to different conclusions. There may be no "right" answer in law: see *R(H) 1/03* (paras 24-25); *CDLA 1456/2002* (paras 9-11); and the quotation from *CDLA 2975/2002* above. It is rare for an appeal to succeed on this ground. Very often, appeals made on this ground are, on proper analysis, in fact complaining of some other error of law such as misconstruction of the relevant statutory provision. See *CDLA 1456/2002* (paras 9-13) for another particularly trenchant expression of this fundamental principle by Commissioner Howell.

(5)   The tribunal has failed to exercise its inquisitorial jurisdiction (see p180).

(6)   There has been a breach of the rules of natural justice (see p180).

(7)   There has been a relevant breach of the procedural rules (see p182).

(8)   The tribunal has acted in breach of the claimant's rights under the European Convention on Human Rights. Since a tribunal is a "public body" under s6(3)(a) Human Rights Act 1998, by virtue of s6(1) it is obliged to act in a way which is compatible with a party's Convention rights. Domestic public law often protects the same rights as those protected by the Convention, in particular Art 6 thereof. However, the commissioners were noticeably more enthusiastic than the courts about framing complaints of unfairness in terms of breach of Convention rights rather than trying to shoehorn them into the established grounds for complaint under domestic law set out above. See Commissioner Jacobs' decision in *CJSA 5100/2001* (paras 5-9) for a vivid example. Attention should therefore be paid to caselaw under the Convention as a possible additional source of complaint, while not neglecting the more mundane approach under domestic law. See also the commentary to Art 6 on p125.

(9)   The tribunal has made a decision which it has no jurisdiction to make. This covers situations where a tribunal purports to hear appeals relating to matters over which it does not have jurisdiction under Sch 7 para 6 and the regulations made thereunder. It also covers a situation where there is no valid appeal because there is some fundamental defect in the Secretary of State's or local authority's decision making. This may arise where no proper revision or supersession has been carried out and the error cannot be corrected or where there has been a failure to give proper notification of a decision which has caused prejudice to a claimant: see the commentary to reg 90 and Sch 9 HB Regs (see pp461 and 580) for consideration of the question of when a decision is rendered invalid by virtue of a failure to revise or supersede or where there is a defective attempt at revision or supersession.

(10)   Despite what has been said above about the distinction between errors of law and fact, it is possible that errors of fact may amount to errors of law in certain circumstances. In *E v Secretary of State for the Home Department* [2004] EWCA Civ 49 (paras 63-69), the Court of Appeal held that where on appeal a fact-

finding tribunal could be shown to have made a clear and indisputable error of fact and injustice was caused to an appellant as a result, an appellate tribunal (in that case, the Immigration Appeal Tribunal) could intervene. "Injustice" would only be caused, however, in a case where the parties had a "common interest" in ensuring the correct result was reached. That test was satisfied in the context of E (claims for asylum) and it is highly arguable that it would also be satisfied in the context of social security appeals. The implications of this potentially ground-breaking decision for the social security appeals system will have to be fully worked out by the Upper Tribunal.

Scope of the right of appeal: failure to exercise inquisitorial jurisdiction. One of the fundamental distinctions between tribunals and courts is that the latter are generally concerned only with deciding disputes raised by the parties for their consideration. By contrast, tribunals are generally expected to be much more pro-active in identifying and resolving issues between the parties. They need not, therefore, come to a conclusion that is advocated by one of the parties to an appeal: *R v Deputy Industrial Injuries Commissioner ex p Moore* [1965] 1 QB 456 and *Kerr v Department for Social Development* [2004] UKHL 23 (reported as *R 1/04 (SF)*). The question of when a tribunal's decision can be subject to appeal on this ground depends on all the circumstances of the case: *R(SB) 2/83* (paras 10-11). In deciding whether there has been a failure to exercise the inquisitorial function, it is helpful to consider whether it is an issue that is alleged to have been overlooked or whether it is relevant evidence that has not been considered. As far as issues are concerned, the tribunal has discretion by virtue of para 6(9)(a) to decline to consider issues which are not raised by the parties or at least by the appeal (see the Analysis on p148). Authorities on the scope of a tribunal's duty to consider new issues for itself must be read in the light of para 6(9)(a), though it is suggested that an unreasonable exercise of the discretion conferred by para 6(9)(a) may still constitute an error of law. The scope of the duty depends on the extent to which it appears that the parties have presented the relevant material to it. Where a representative appears to be competent, the omission will have to be obvious before the tribunal will err in law in failing to consider the issue: see *CSDLA 336/ 2000* (para 15). See also *R(H) 1/02* (paras 8-9). Where a representative specifically declines an opportunity to have a point addressed, the tribunal will not err in law by failing to do so itself: *CSIB 588/1998* (para 13).

The duty to consider or call for further evidence, on the other hand, may well be slightly wider. This is the case particularly where a claimant is unrepresented and may not be aware of the nature of the evidence that will be relevant to the determination of a question before the tribunal. It seems clear that if there is something to alert a tribunal that relevant evidence may exist that is not before it, it will err in law if it does not give the party the chance to produce that evidence: *CU 47/1993* (paras 4-11).

A tribunal does not generally err in law by failing to take documents not placed before it into account: *CH 5221/2001* (para 3.1). However, if it needs to examine a document to decide what impression it would have given to the reader, it will err in law if it does not call for a copy of the document rather than assuming the form that it took: *CH 5221/2001* (para 5).

Scope of the right of appeal: breach of natural justice. The rules of natural justice, which are now bolstered by the right to a fair hearing under Art 6 of the European Convention on Human Rights, comprise two basic principles: the first is the right to be heard and the second the rule against bias.

The right to be heard

The most obvious breach of the right to be heard is a case where a "person affected" is not notified of the proceedings. In *CH 3679/2002*, a claimant appealed against a decision that an overpayment was recoverable from a landlord. Commissioner Fellner held that the tribunal had erred in law because the landlord had not been made a party to the appeal and notified of the hearing: para 3. Provision for 14 days' notice of an oral hearing is made in r29 TP(FT) Rules. In *CH 3679/2002*, the commissioner said that to ensure a fair hearing, this must apply to provision of the submissions and evidence as well as the notice of the time and date of the hearing. He said that was so "unless the appeal tribunal is prepared to take the time during the oral hearing itself to redress the unfairness by ensuring that all the evidence and submissions are presented orally by both parties." In the absence of one of the parties, this could mean that the tribunal will find it necessary to adjourn the hearing.

If a party does not appear at a hearing through no fault of her/his own, then the tribunal's decision may be vitiated by an error of law even if no other person can be shown to be at fault: *CIB 5227/1999* (paras 9 and 10). If the claimant fails to attend a hearing due to a deliberate decision, there is no breach of the right: *CCS 565/1999* (para 12). Similarly, if a claimant fails to attend through carelessness, there is no error of law.

In *CIB 4667/2002*, the appellant's representative freely admitted that he had failed to attend a hearing because of a mistake about the date. The commissioner said that whether to adjourn a hearing in such circumstances is for the good sense, judgement and discretion of the tribunal. As tribunals are accustomed to dealing with unrepresented appellants and people who are not familiar with the legal process, the fact that a representative does not turn up to a hearing does not, in principle, make it wrong to proceed in her/ his absence. In order to give rise to an appeal on a point of law, "what has to be shown is that the tribunal's exercise of judgement was so unreasonable as to be perverse and to have deprived the claimant of a substantive opportunity for a fair hearing of the relevant issues in his or her case."

Experienced representatives who do not seek oral hearings on behalf of their clients might not then be able to argue that a tribunal should have nevertheless held one. In *Miller v Secretary of State for Social Security* [2002] GWD 25-861, CSIH, the appellant complained that she had not been allowed an oral hearing of her appeal to provide further evidence. However, the Court held that as the appellant's experienced representative had not sought an oral hearing and had stated that s/he was relying on specified paragraphs in the application for leave to appeal, the commissioner could not be said to have erred in law for not allowing an oral hearing.

Note the right to apply to set aside a tribunal decision under r37(1) and (2)(c) TP(FT) Rules where a party to the proceedings or the party's representative was not present at a hearing (see p1069).

There is no obligation on a tribunal to adjourn a case to offer an unrepresented claimant a chance to obtain representation: *CSIB 848/1997* (para 9). However, if a claimant expresses the wish for an adjournment to be represented this ought ordinarily to be granted, particularly in a difficult case with serious consequences. Where a claimant suffers from difficulties such as illiteracy, this emphasises the need for a tribunal to decide whether it is appropriate to proceed in such circumstances: *CIS 6002/1997* (paras 9-11)

The right to be heard is not only relevant in cases where parties (or their representatives) do not attend the hearing. A fair procedure must be adopted in all cases and what fairness requires will differ according to the circumstances of the case. For example, local authorities all too frequently fail to explain their decision making processes with sufficient clarity in written submissions to a tribunal. If the process may have an impact on the outcome of the appeal, it is essential for a tribunal to explain it to an unrepresented claimant: *CH 1085/2002* (para 20).

Similarly, at a hearing, a party must be given a fair opportunity to present her/his case. The tribunal may exercise control over the presentation of the case to the extent of preventing disruption of its proceedings or the pursuit of irrelevant matters. It may also control undue length of presentation, though care must be taken to ensure that the case is not in reality more complex than it had first appeared. If insufficient time has been allocated for the hearing of the case and there is any danger that to restrict the amount of time available to a party to present its case would hamper its ability to place its full case before the tribunal, then the case should be adjourned and the clerk to the tribunal should be directed to list the case with a longer time estimate.

In order for a party to have a fair opportunity to present her/his, s/he must have sufficient notice of the opposing party's case and, in particular, what is in dispute and what is not. The tribunal must therefore be vigilant not to allow one party to "ambush" another. But ambushes do not always come from the other party. The tribunal itself, in the exercise of its inquisitorial jurisdiction and the judicial discretion conferred by para 6(9)(a) of Sch 7 CSPSSA 2000, may take points that have not been raised by the parties and, if it does so, must ensure the parties have adequate notice of those points: see *CP v M Technology School (SEN)* [2010] UKUT 314 (AAC).

Where the Tribunals Service appoints an interpreter to be used at a hearing, a claimant is entitled to expect the questions to her/him and her/his replies to be interpreted professionally. In *CDLA 2748/2002*, the commissioner did not accept that it was adequate to establish a fair hearing that the tribunal concluded it had "sufficient understanding". If the standard of interpretation appears inadequate, the tribunal should take appropriate action.

It is not part of the tribunal's judicial function to seek to bargain with an appellant or her/his representative as to which parts of the appeal the tribunal might accept if other parts are not pressed for at the hearing: *CSDLA 606/2003*. In this case the appeal tribunal's record of proceedings noted that an offer had been put to the appellant by the chair of the tribunal just to reinstate her higher rate mobility component of DLA if she did not seek to argue for the care component, and the case was adjourned for 10 minutes for her to think about this. On reconvening the hearing the appellant, who at that point said she wished to proceed with her appeal, was then told that if she went ahead and sought to argue for the care component then she could risk losing everything, and she was told to think again about the matter. After a further short adjournment of five minutes the appellant "accepted the offer". Unsurprisingly, the commissioner concluded that this was not a fair and proper hearing. In her view, a "travesty of justice" had occurred in which the tribunal had pressurised the appellant into giving up her right to a hearing on the care component and had awarded the mobility component without any proper application of the relevant legal tests.

The rule against bias

The second aspect of the rules of natural justice is the rule against bias. Bias may be actual or apparent. Cases where it can be shown that a tribunal member has a direct interest in the outcome will be rare but even remote connections may be held to vitiate the fairness of proceedings: *R v Secretary of State for the Home Department ex p Pinochet (No 2)* [2000] 1 AC 129, HL. Members who are, for example, councillors of the relevant local authority or who are instructed by a party in private practice should disclose their interest or prior involvement. The same would be true of a member that had expressed strong views in an academic context that impinged upon the merits of one party's position: *Locabail (UK) Ltd v Bayfield Properties Ltd* [2000] QB 451 at 496F-497A, para 89, CA. If other parties are happy to proceed in knowledge of the full facts, any breach of this rule would be taken to be waived.

In cases of apparent bias, the question is "whether the fair-minded and informed observer, having considered the facts, would conclude that there was a real possibility that the tribunal was biased": *Porter v Magill* [2002] 2 WLR 37 at 83D-84B, paras 102-103, HL. See the detailed discussion in *CSDLA 1019/1999* (paras 70-89) for further consideration of this test. Note also *CSDLA 855/1997* (para 8), where the fact that a member of a tribunal was the partner of an examining medical practitioner whose report was being called into question was a breach of natural justice. The decision in *CSDLA 1019/1999* was overturned by the Court of Session in *SSWP v Gillies* [2003] 2004 SLT 14, reported at 2006 SC (HL) 71, in which the Court emphasised that the fair-minded observer is someone who is "neither complacent nor unduly sensitive or suspicious". The House of Lords upheld the decision of the Court of Session in *Gillies v SSWP* [2006] UKHL 2, *Times Law Report*, 30 January (reported as *R(DLA) 5/06*).

Examples of successful challenges for apparent bias can be found in *CCS 557/2005* and *SW v SSWP (IB)* [2010] UKUT 73 (AAC).

Representatives will need to exercise caution and restraint in making allegations of apparent bias based on the way in which hearings are conducted by tribunals. The commissioners have been critical about unparticularised complaints of bias which amount to nothing more than a complaint about the tribunal doing that which is its primary function, namely to closely test a party's case by questioning before accepting it in cases where the facts are in dispute: *CH 2302/2002* (para 10); *CH 2349/2002* (paras 12-13). It is strongly recommended that any representative who feels that a tribunal member has gone beyond what is acceptable by expressing views during the hearing or by the mode or tone of her/his questioning should make careful notes of what was said either at the time or as soon as possible after the hearing. When applying for permission to appeal to the Upper Tribunal, the allegations should be fully and carefully set out in order to give the tribunal member an opportunity to respond and the notes should be annexed to the application for leave if possible. If a different tribunal member is asked to determine whether or not leave should be granted (as is now frequently the case), the tribunal member about whom complaint is made and, if relevant, the other members and the clerk to the tribunal should be asked for their comments. Following such a procedure will make it easier for the Upper Tribunal to ascertain whether there is any substance to the complaint.

Scope of the right of appeal: breach of procedure. The courts have emphasised in recent years the need to consider the extent, nature and effect of non-compliance rather than whether the procedural provision is set out in the form of a duty or discretion: *Haringey LBC v Awaritefe* [1999] 32 HLR 517; *R v Secretary of State for the Home Department ex p Jeyeanthan* [2000] 1 WLR 354. A breach of the terms of a procedural requirement will not, therefore, of itself render a decision erroneous in law. As a rule of thumb, if the claimant is or might be prejudiced by the non-compliance then that will vitiate the decision. Further discussion as to when a breach of the procedural provisions in the TP(FT) Rules is found in the commentary to those regulations. Note, however, that the First-tier Tribunal has power to waive any requirement of those Rules where it is just to do so: see r7(2)(a) on p1053.

A common ground on which tribunal decisions are set aside is failure to give adequate reasons, which is a breach of procedure under r34(2) TP(FT) Rules. However, if the shortcoming in the statement of reasons is immaterial because the case could only have been decided adversely to the claimant, the Upper Tribunal will either dismiss the appeal or will allow the appeal but substitute a decision to the same effect as that of the First-tier Tribunal.

Proceedings on appeal to Upper Tribunal

12.–(1) Subsection (2) applies if the Upper Tribunal, in deciding an appeal under section 11, finds that the making of the decision concerned involved the making of an error on a point of law.

(2) The Upper Tribunal–

(a) may (but need not) set aside the decision of the First-tier Tribunal, and

(b) if it does, must either–

  (i) remit the case to the First-tier Tribunal with directions for its reconsideration, or

  (ii) re-make the decision.

(3) In acting under subsection (2)(b)(i), the Upper Tribunal may also–

(a) direct that the members of the First-tier Tribunal who are chosen to reconsider the case are not to be the same as those who made the decision that has been set aside;

(b) give procedural directions in connection with the reconsideration of the case by the First-tier Tribunal.

(4) In acting under subsection (2)(b)(ii), the Upper Tribunal–

(a) may make any decision which the First-tier Tribunal could make if the First-tier Tribunal were re-making the decision, and

(b) may make such findings of fact as it considers appropriate.

Commencement

3.11.08.

General Note

This section sets out what the Upper Tribunal can do if it finds that the First-tier Tribunal's decision "involved the making of an error on a point of law". It is equivalent, and in similar terms, to the former Sch 7 paras 5 and 6 CSPSSA and s14(7) and (8) SSA 1998.

In those circumstances, the first decision for the Upper Tribunal is whether to set the First-tier Tribunal's decision aside: subs (2)(a). Although the Upper Tribunal has a discretion not to set the decision aside, justice to the party that is disadvantaged by the error will normally require that it do so, unless the error was not material – ie, it did not have any effect on the outcome of the appeal before the First-tier Tribunal. The discretion may also be a useful tool with which to do justice in other (rare) cases where it would be unjust to set aside the First-tier Tribunal's decision even though it was erroneous. For an example of circumstances in which (in a mental health case) a three-judge panel of the Upper Tribunal found a decision of the First-tier Tribunal to be wrong in law but declined to set it aside, see *BB v South London & Maudsley NHS Trust & MOJ* [2009] UKUT 157 (AAC).

Having decided to set the First-tier Tribunal's decision aside, the Upper Tribunal then has two possible courses of action: subs (2)(b).

The first is to remit the case to the First-tier Tribunal with directions for its reconsideration. In this case, it also has powers to direct that it is reconsidered by different members of the First-tier Tribunal from those who made the original decision and to give procedural directions: subs (3). The phrase "members of the First-tier Tribunal" in subs (3)(a) is presumably intended to include the judge who made the original decision, although elsewhere in the Act a sharp distinction is drawn between "judges" and "other members" of the First-tier Tribunal. In other words, the judge is a "member" of the First-tier Tribunal (using that word in its ordinary sense) even though s/he is not an "other member" as defined in s4(3).

Alternatively, the Upper Tribunal may "re-make" the decision, in which case it may make any decision that the First-tier Tribunal could have made and make new or additional findings of fact: subs (4).

Right to appeal to Court of Appeal etc.

13.–(1)   For the purposes of subsection (2), the reference to a right of appeal is to a right to appeal to the relevant appellate court on any point of law arising from a decision made by the Upper Tribunal other than an excluded decision.

(2)   Any party to a case has a right of appeal, subject to subsection (14).

(3)   That right may be exercised only with permission (or, in Northern Ireland, leave).

(4)   Permission (or leave) may be given by–

(a)   the Upper Tribunal, or

(b)   the relevant appellate court,

on an application by the party.

(5)   An application may be made under subsection (4) to the relevant appellate court only if permission (or leave) has been refused by the Upper Tribunal.

(6)   The Lord Chancellor may, as respects an application under subsection (4) that falls within subsection (7) and for which the relevant appellate court is the Court of Appeal in England and Wales or the Court of Appeal in Northern Ireland, by order make provision for permission (or leave) not to be granted on the application unless the Upper Tribunal or (as the case may be) the relevant appellate court considers–

(a)   that the proposed appeal would raise some important point of principle or practice, or

(b)   that there is some other compelling reason for the relevant appellate court to hear the appeal.

(7)   An application falls within this subsection if the application is for permission (or leave) to appeal from any decision of the Upper Tribunal on an appeal under section 11.

(8)   For the purposes of subsection (1), an ''excluded decision'' is–

(a)-(b) [Omitted]

(c)   any decision of the Upper Tribunal on an application under section 11(4)(b) (application for permission or leave to appeal),

(d)   a decision of the Upper Tribunal under section 10–

(i)   to review, or not to review, an earlier decision of the tribunal,

(ii)   to take no action, or not to take any particular action, in the light of a review of an earlier decision of the tribunal, or

(iii)   to set aside an earlier decision of the tribunal,

(e)   a decision of the Upper Tribunal that is set aside under section 10 (including a decision set aside after proceedings on an appeal under this section have been begun), or

(f)   any decision of the Upper Tribunal that is of a description specified in an order made by the Lord Chancellor.

(9)   A description may be specified under subsection (8)(f) only if–

(a)   in the case of a decision of that description, there is a right to appeal to a court from the decision and that right is, or includes, something other than a right (however expressed) to appeal on any point of law arising from the decision, or

(b)   decisions of that description are made in carrying out a function transferred under section 30 and prior to the transfer of the function under section 30(1) there was no right to appeal from decisions of that description.

(10)   Where–

(a)   an order under subsection (8)(f) specifies a description of decisions, and

(b)   decisions of that description are made in carrying out a function transferred under section 30,

the order must be framed so as to come into force no later than the time when the transfer under section 30 of the function takes effect (but power to revoke the order continues to be exercisable after that time, and power to amend the order continues to be exercisable after that time for the purpose of narrowing the description for the time being specified).

(11)   Before the Upper Tribunal decides an application made to it under subsection (4), the Upper Tribunal must specify the court that is to be the relevant appellate court as respects the proposed appeal.

(12)   The court to be specified under subsection (11) in relation to a proposed appeal is whichever of the following courts appears to the Upper Tribunal to be the most appropriate–

(a)   the Court of Appeal in England and Wales;

(b)   the Court of Session;

(c)   the Court of Appeal in Northern Ireland.

(13)   In this section except subsection (11), "the relevant appellate court", as respects an appeal, means the court specified as respects that appeal by the Upper Tribunal under subsection (11).

(14)   The Lord Chancellor may by order make provision for a person to be treated as being, or to be treated as not being, a party to a case for the purposes of subsection (2).

(15)   Rules of court may make provision as to the time within which an application under subsection (4) to the relevant appellate court must be made.

Commencement

s13(6), (8)(f), (9), (10), (14) and (15): 19.9.07; all other subsections: 3.11.08.

General Note

A further appeal lies from the Upper Tribunal, with permission, to the "relevant appellate court".

Analysis

Who may appeal?

The right of appeal is conferred on "any party to the case" subs (2). As with s11, that phrase is undefined. However, by subs (3) and (4), the right may only be exercised with permission to appeal and, under CSPSSA Sch 7 para 9(3), an application for permission to appeal may only be made by a person who was entitled to appeal to the Upper Tribunal (ie, under CSPSSA Sch 7 para 8(2)) or who was a party to the proceedings before the Upper Tribunal's (ie, who was added or substituted as a party under r9 TP(UT) Rules) or who is authorised by regulations to apply for permission. No such regulations have been made (SI 2005 No.2007 which was made under the previous version of para 9(3) was revoked by Sch 2 to SI 2008 No.2683 with effect from 3 November 2008).

The right of appeal conferred by subs (2) is subject to subs (14). However, no order has yet been made under that subsection.

Which decisions may be appealed against?

With two exceptions, subs (1) and (8) are in similar terms to s11(1) and (5): see the Analysis of s11 on p176. The exceptions are that:

–   under subs (8)(c), a decision of the Upper Tribunal granting or refusing permission to appeal under s11(4)(b) (ie, permission to appeal from the First-tier Tribunal to the Upper Tribunal) is an "excluded decision". Any such decision can only be challenged by judicial review (if at all, see the discussion of *Cart* and *Eba* on p170). This codifies the law as it was before 3 November 2008: see *Bland v Chief Supplementary Benefit Officer* [1983] 1 WLR 262, CA (reported as *R(SB) 12/83*) and *SSWP v Morina and Borrowdale* [2007] EWCA Civ 749 (reported as *R(IS) 6/07*) and the Analysis to s11; *and*

–   no order has been made by the Lord Chancellor under subs (8)(f).

Grounds of appeal

Under subs (1), an appeal lies on "any point of law arising from a decision" of the Upper Tribunal: see the Analysis to s11(1) on p176. In addition, it will be an error of law for the Upper Tribunal to exceed its own jurisdiction by interfering with the decisions of the First-tier Tribunal where the Upper Tribunal disagrees with the decision on the facts but there has been no error of law. See, by analogy, *SSWP v Roach* [2006] (reported as *R(CS) 4/07*) and *Braintree District Council v Thompson* [2005] EWCA Civ 178, 7 March 2005, unreported.

The requirement for permission

Permission to appeal must first be sought from the Upper Tribunal: see subs (4) and r44 TP(UT) Rules (on p1099). Leave may only be sought from the relevant appellate court if the Upper Tribunal refuses leave.

In HB/CTB cases (and other cases on appeal from the Social Entitlement Chamber of the First-tier Tribunal), the time limit for applying for permission is three months after the date on which the Upper Tribunal sent the party written notice of its decision or (which will necessarily be later) notice of amended reasons, or correction of, the decision following a review under s10 and r46 or that an application to set aside the decision (ie, under r43) has been unsuccessful. That time limit may be extended under r5(3)(a): see r44(6) on p1099.

In HB/CTB cases (and all cases in which the decision of the Upper Tribunal was made on an appeal under s11) where the "relevant appellate court" is the Court of Appeal in England and Wales or the Court of Appeal in Northern Ireland, permission to appeal may only be granted if the Upper Tribunal or, where the Upper Tribunal refuses permission, the relevant appellate court, considers that the proposed appeal would raise some important point of principle or practice or there is some other compelling reason for the relevant appellate court to hear the appeal: see the Appeals from the Upper Tribunal to the Court of Appeal Order 2008 SI No.2834 made by the Lord Chancellor under the power conferred by subs (6). That order codifies the position that existed in practice before 3 November 2008: see *Cooke v Secretary of State for Social Security* [2001] EWCA CIV 734 (reported as *R(DLA) 6/01*), *Fryer-Kelsey v SSWP* [2005] EWCA Civ 511 (reported as *R(IB) 6/05*) and the Analysis to Sch 7 para 9 CSPSSA on p167 of the 20th edition.

Which is the "relevant appellate court"?

Appeal under s13 lies to the "relevant appellate court" which may be the Court of Appeal in England and Wales, the Court of Session in Scotland or the Court of Appeal in Northern Ireland. Before the Upper Tribunal decides an application for permission to appeal, it must specify which of those courts is to be the "relevant appellate court" in that particular case: see subs (11) and (12). This will usually (but not necessarily) be the appellate court for the jurisdiction in which the claimant lives. Exceptions might be made where the claimant has moved or, possibly, where the parties were in the north of England and could more easily attend a hearing in Edinburgh rather than London.

What procedure must be followed on an appeal under s13?

For the requirements of an application to the Upper Tribunal for permission to appeal, see r44(7) TP(UT) Rules on p1099.

Procedure before the Court of Appeal or the Court of Session is beyond the scope of this book. Readers are referred to Part 52 of the Civil Procedure Rules 1998 SI No.3132 (in England and Wales) and Chapter 41 of the Act of Sederunt (Rules of the Court of Session 1994) 1994 SI No.1443 (in Scotland).

Proceedings on appeal to Court of Appeal etc.

14.–(1)   Subsection (2) applies if the relevant appellate court, in deciding an appeal under section 13, finds that the making of the decision concerned involved the making of an error on a point of law.

(2)   The relevant appellate court–

(a)   may (but need not) set aside the decision of the Upper Tribunal, and

(b)   if it does, must either–

   (i)   remit the case to the Upper Tribunal or, where the decision of the Upper Tribunal was on an appeal or reference from another tribunal or some other person, to the Upper Tribunal or that other tribunal or person, with directions for its reconsideration, or

   (ii)   re-make the decision.

(3)   In acting under subsection (2)(b)(i), the relevant appellate court may also–

(a)   direct that the persons who are chosen to reconsider the case are not to be the same as those who–

   (i)   where the case is remitted to the Upper Tribunal, made the decision of the Upper Tribunal that has been set aside, or

   (ii)   where the case is remitted to another tribunal or person, made the decision in respect of which the appeal or reference to the Upper Tribunal was made;

(b)   give procedural directions in connection with the reconsideration of the case by the Upper Tribunal or other tribunal or person.

(4)   In acting under subsection (2)(b)(ii), the relevant appellate court–

(a)   may make any decision which the Upper Tribunal could make if the Upper Tribunal were re-making the decision or (as the case may be) which the other tribunal or person could make if that other tribunal or person were re-making the decision, and

(b)   may make such findings of fact as it considers appropriate.

(5)   Where–

(a)   under subsection (2)(b)(i) the relevant appellate court remits a case to the Upper Tribunal, and

(b)   the decision set aside under subsection (2)(a) was made by the Upper Tribunal on an appeal or reference from another tribunal or some other person,

the Upper Tribunal may (instead of reconsidering the case itself) remit the case to that other tribunal or person, with the directions given by the relevant appellate court for its reconsideration.

(6)   In acting under subsection (5), the Upper Tribunal may also–

(a)   direct that the persons who are chosen to reconsider the case are not to be the same as those who made the decision in respect of which the appeal or reference to the Upper Tribunal was made;

(b)   give procedural directions in connection with the reconsideration of the case by the other tribunal or person.

(7)   In this section ''the relevant appellate court'', as respects an appeal under section 13, means the court specified as respects that appeal by the Upper Tribunal under section 13(11).

Commencement
3.11.08.

General Note
This section sets out the powers of the Court of Appeal when hearing an appeal against a decision of the Upper Tribunal under s13. Those powers are equivalent to those exercised by the Upper Tribunal under s12 when deciding an appeal against a decision of the First-tier Tribunal: see the Analysis to s12 on p182. The only exception is that the Court of Appeal or Court of Session may remit the case either to the Upper Tribunal or the First-tier Tribunal.

Under subs (5) and (6), where the Court of Appeal or Court of Session remits a case to the Upper Tribunal, the Upper Tribunal may in turn remit it to the First-tier Tribunal with the directions given by the Court and (if appropriate) further procedural directions.

"Judicial review"

General Note on ss15 to 21
One of the major changes introduced by the Act was the extension of the power of judicial review (which had previously only been exercisable by the High Court) to the Upper Tribunal. However, the power is limited. Under s15(2) the application must either satisfy s18 or have been transferred to the Upper Tribunal from the High Court under s31A of the Supreme Court Act 1981 (introduced by s19 TCEA, which is not reproduced in this book).

Section 18 sets out four conditions that must be satisfied if the Upper Tribunal is to have jurisdiction. If they are not satisfied then the application must be transferred to the High Court under s18(3). Conditions 1 and 2 (in s18(4) and (5)) are self-explanatory. By condition 3 (s18(6)) the Upper Tribunal only has jurisdiction where the application falls within a class specified in a Practice Direction given by the Lord Chief Justice of England and Wales or the Lord Chief Justice of Northern Ireland. The former has made the following Direction:

"It is ordered as follows:

1.   The following direction takes effect in relation to an application made to the High Court or Upper Tribunal on or after 3 November 2008 that seeks relief of a kind mentioned in section 15(1) of the Tribunals, Courts and Enforcement Act 2007 ("the 2007 Act")

2.   The Lord Chief Justice hereby directs that the following classes of case are specified for the purposes of section 18(6) of the 2007 Act–

a.   *[Omitted as relating to criminal injuries compensation]*

b.   Any decision of the First-tier Tribunal made under the Tribunal Procedure Rules or section 9 of the 2007 Act where there is no right of appeal to the Upper Tribunal and that decision is not an excluded decision under paragraph (b), (c) or (f) of section 11(5) of the 2007 Act.

3.   This Direction does not have effect where an application seeks (whether or not alone) a declaration of incompatibility under section 4 of the Human Rights Act 1998.

4.	This Direction is made by the Lord Chief Justice with the agreement of the Lord Chancellor. It is made in the exercise of powers conferred by section 18(6) of the 2007 Act and in accordance with Part 1 of Schedule 2 to the Constitutional Reform Act 2005."

Note that paragraphs (b), (c) and (f) of s11(5) have no application to HB/CTB or to social security appeals generally.

The terms of that Direction raise once again the vexed question of the extent of any right of appeal to the Upper Tribunal against interlocutory or procedural decisions made by the First-tier Tribunal: see the Analysis of s11 on p176. The effect of the Direction, however, is to resolve the difficulty. As pointed out by the three-judge panel of the Upper Tribunal in the *Dorset Healthcare* case (see p178), if there is no right of appeal against such a decision, the Upper Tribunal may treat the purported appeal as an application for permission to apply for judicial review.

Condition 4 is that the judge presiding at the hearing of the application is either a judge of the High Court, Court of Appeal or Court of Session, or a person agreed in accordance with s18(8)(b). The Chamber President of the Administrative Appeals Chamber is a High Court judge but it is anticipated that judicial reviews will normally be heard by ordinary judges of the Upper Tribunal. The purpose of extending the judicial review jurisdiction to the Upper Tribunal was to relieve the pressure on the resources of the Administrative Court. That purpose is defeated if every judicial review in the Upper Tribunal has to be heard by a High Court judge.

In cases where the Upper Tribunal has jurisdiction, it must apply the same principles as would be applied by the High Court in deciding an application for judicial review (s15(5) and any relief granted has the same effect as (and is enforceable as if it were) relief granted by the High Court on an application for judicial review (s15(4)).

For the procedure to be followed in applying to the Upper Tribunal for permission to apply for judicial review, see s16 (on p188) and Part 4 TP(UT) Rules (on p1093).

In Scotland, it is not possible for an application for judicial review to be made directly to the Upper Tribunal. Instead a petition must be presented to the Court of Session, which may then be transferred to the Upper Tribunal: see *EF v SSWP* [2009] UKUT 92 (AAC); R(IB) 3/09 and *Eba* (at para 9).

Upper Tribunal's "judicial review" jurisdiction

15.–(1)	The Upper Tribunal has power, in cases arising under the law of England and Wales or under the law of Northern Ireland, to grant the following kinds of relief–

(a)	a mandatory order;
(b)	a prohibiting order;
(c)	a quashing order;
(d)	a declaration;
(e)	an injunction.

(2)	The power under subsection (1) may be exercised by the Upper Tribunal if–

(a)	certain conditions are met (see section 18), or
(b)	the tribunal is authorised to proceed even though not all of those conditions are met (see section 19(3) and (4)).

(3)	Relief under subsection (1) granted by the Upper Tribunal–

(a)	has the same effect as the corresponding relief granted by the High Court on an application for judicial review, and
(b)	is enforceable as if it were relief granted by the High Court on an application for judicial review.

(4)	In deciding whether to grant relief under subsection (1)(a), (b) or (c), the Upper Tribunal must apply the principles that the High Court would apply in deciding whether to grant that relief on an application for judicial review.

(5)	In deciding whether to grant relief under subsection (1)(d) or (e), the Upper Tribunal must–

(a)	in cases arising under the law of England and Wales apply the principles that the High Court would apply in deciding whether to grant that relief under section 31(2) of the Supreme Court Act 1981 (c. 54) on an application for judicial review, and
(b)	in cases arising under the law of Northern Ireland apply the principles that the High Court would apply in deciding whether to grant that relief on an application for judicial review.

(6)	*[Omitted]*

Commencement
3.11.08.

Application for relief under section 15(1)

16.–(1)   This section applies in relation to an application to the Upper Tribunal for relief under section 15(1).

(2)   The application may be made only if permission (or, in a case arising under the law of Northern Ireland, leave) to make it has been obtained from the tribunal.

(3)   The tribunal may not grant permission (or leave) to make the application unless it considers that the applicant has a sufficient interest in the matter to which the application relates.

(4)   Subsection (5) applies where the tribunal considers–

(a)   that there has been undue delay in making the application, and

(b)   that granting the relief sought on the application would be likely to cause substantial hardship to, or substantially prejudice the rights of, any person or would be detrimental to good administration.

(5)   The tribunal may–

(a)   refuse to grant permission (or leave) for the making of the application;

(b)   refuse to grant any relief sought on the application.

(6)   The tribunal may award to the applicant damages, restitution or the recovery of a sum due if–

(a)   the application includes a claim for such an award arising from any matter to which the application relates, and

(b)   the tribunal is satisfied that such an award would have been made by the High Court if the claim had been made in an action begun in the High Court by the applicant at the time of making the application.

(7)   An award under subsection (6) may be enforced as if it were an award of the High Court.

(8)   Where–

(a)   the tribunal refuses to grant permission (or leave) to apply for relief under section 15(1),

(b)   the applicant appeals against that refusal, and

(c)   the Court of Appeal grants the permission (or leave),

the Court of Appeal may go on to decide the application for relief under section 15(1).

(9)   Subsections (4) and (5) do not prevent Tribunal Procedure Rules from limiting the time within which applications may be made.

Commencement
3.11.08.

Quashing orders under section 15(1): supplementary provision

17.–(1)   If the Upper Tribunal makes a quashing order under section 15(1)(c) in respect of a decision, it may in addition–

(a)   remit the matter concerned to the court, tribunal or authority that made the decision, with a direction to reconsider the matter and reach a decision in accordance with the findings of the Upper Tribunal, or

(b)   substitute its own decision for the decision in question.

(2)   The power conferred by subsection (1)(b) is exercisable only if–

(a)   the decision in question was made by a court or tribunal,

(b)   the decision is quashed on the ground that there has been an error of law, and

(c)   without the error, there would have been only one decision that the court or tribunal could have reached.

(3)   Unless the Upper Tribunal otherwise directs, a decision substituted by it under subsection (1)(b) has effect as if it were a decision of the relevant court or tribunal.

Commencement
3.11.08.

Limits of jurisdiction under section 15(1)

18.–(1)   This section applies where an application made to the Upper Tribunal seeks (whether or not alone)–

(a)   relief under section 15(1), or

(b)   permission (or, in a case arising under the law of Northern Ireland, leave) to apply for relief under section 15(1).

(2)   If Conditions 1 to 4 are met, the tribunal has the function of deciding the application.

(3)   If the tribunal does not have the function of deciding the application, it must by order transfer the application to the High Court.

(4)   Condition 1 is that the application does not seek anything other than–

(a)   relief under section 15(1);

(b)   permission (or, in a case arising under the law of Northern Ireland, leave) to apply for relief under section 15(1);

(c)   an award under section 16(6);

(d)   interest;

(e)   costs.

(5)   Condition 2 is that the application does not call into question anything done by the Crown Court.

(6)   Condition 3 is that the application falls within a class specified for the purposes of this subsection in a direction given in accordance with Part 1 of Schedule 2 to the Constitutional Reform Act 2005 (c. 4).

(7)   The power to give directions under subsection (6) includes–

(a)   power to vary or revoke directions made in exercise of the power, and

(b)   power to make different provision for different purposes.

(8)   Condition 4 is that the judge presiding at the hearing of the application is either–

(a)   a judge of the High Court or the Court of Appeal in England and Wales or Northern Ireland, or a judge of the Court of Session, or

(b)   such other persons as may be agreed from time to time between the Lord Chief Justice, the Lord President, or the Lord Chief Justice of Northern Ireland, as the case may be, and the Senior President of Tribunals.

(9)   Where the application is transferred to the High Court under subsection (3)–

(a)   the application is to be treated for all purposes as if it–

    (i)   had been made to the High Court, and

    (ii)   sought things corresponding to those sought from the tribunal, and

(b)   any steps taken, permission (or leave) given or orders made by the tribunal in relation to the application are to be treated as taken, given or made by the High Court.

(10)   Rules of court may make provision for the purpose of supplementing subsection (9).

(11)   The provision that may be made by Tribunal Procedure Rules about amendment of an application for relief under section 15(1) includes, in particular, provision about amendments that would cause the application to become transferrable under subsection (3).

(12)   *[Omitted]*

Commencement

s18(10) and (11): 19.9.07; all other subsections: 3.11.08.

Miscellaneous

Tribunal Procedure Rules

22.–(1)   There are to be rules, to be called ''Tribunal Procedure Rules'', governing–

(a)   the practice and procedure to be followed in the First-tier Tribunal, and

(b)   the practice and procedure to be followed in the Upper Tribunal.

(2)   Tribunal Procedure Rules are to be made by the Tribunal Procedure Committee.

(3)   In Schedule 5–

Part 1 makes further provision about the content of Tribunal Procedure Rules,

Part 2 makes provision about the membership of the Tribunal Procedure Committee,

Part 3 makes provision about the making of Tribunal Procedure Rules by the Committee, and

Part 4 confers power to amend legislation in connection with Tribunal Procedure Rules.

(4) Power to make Tribunal Procedure Rules is to be exercised with a view to securing–

(a) that, in proceedings before the First-tier Tribunal and Upper Tribunal, justice is done,

(b) that the tribunal system is accessible and fair,

(c) that proceedings before the First-tier Tribunal or Upper Tribunal are handled quickly and efficiently,

(d) that the rules are both simple and simply expressed, and

(e) that the rules where appropriate confer on members of the First-tier Tribunal, or Upper Tribunal, responsibility for ensuring that proceedings before the tribunal are handled quickly and efficiently.

(5) In subsection (4)(b) ''the tribunal system'' means the system for deciding matters within the jurisdiction of the First-tier Tribunal or the Upper Tribunal.

Commencement

19.9.07.

General Note

This section, together with Sch 5, establish the Tribunal Procedure Committee and empower it to make procedural rules for the First-tier Tribunal and the Upper Tribunal. Those powers have been exercised by the Committee to make the TP(FT) Rules and the TP(UT) Rules. See further the commentary to those Rules on pp1047 and 1078.

Practice directions

23.–(1) The Senior President of Tribunals may give directions–

(a) as to the practice and procedure of the First-tier Tribunal;

(b) as to the practice and procedure of the Upper Tribunal.

(2) A Chamber President may give directions as to the practice and procedure of the chamber over which he presides.

(3) A power under this section to give directions includes–

(a) power to vary or revoke directions made in exercise of the power, and

(b) power to make different provision for different purposes (including different provision for different areas).

(4) Directions under subsection (1) may not be given without the approval of the Lord Chancellor.

(5) Directions under subsection (2) may not be given without the approval of–

(a) the Senior President of Tribunals, and

(b) the Lord Chancellor.

(6) Subsections (4) and (5)(b) do not apply to directions to the extent that they consist of guidance about any of the following–

(a) the application or interpretation of the law;

(b) the making of decisions by members of the First-tier Tribunal or Upper Tribunal.

(7) Subsections (4) and (5)(b) do not apply to directions to the extent that they consist of criteria for determining which members of the First-tier Tribunal or Upper Tribunal may be chosen to decide particular categories of matter; but the directions may, to that extent, be given only after consulting the Lord Chancellor.

Commencement

3.11.08.

General Note

The Senior President of Tribunal has exercised the powers conferred by subs (1) to make two practice directions, *Child, Vulnerable Adult and Sensitive Witnesses* and *Use of the Welsh Language in Tribunals in Wales*. Both Directions apply to the First-tier Tribunal and the Upper Tribunal.

In addition there have been two 'Practice Statements': *Composition of Tribunals in Social Security and Child Support Cases in the Social Entitlement Chamber* and *Record of Proceedings in Social Security and Child*

Support Cases in the Social Entitlement Chamber. The former is made under powers conferred by art 2 First-tier Tribunal and Upper Tribunal (Composition of Tribunal) Order 2008 (see p1106). However, there is no specific power for the Senior President to make the latter and it is open to question whether he has a general power to issue Practice Statements, as opposed to Practice Directions (which normally require the Lord Chancellor's consent under subs (4)).

Mediation

24.–(1)   A person exercising power to make Tribunal Procedure Rules or give practice directions must, when making provision in relation to mediation, have regard to the following principles–

   (a)   mediation of matters in dispute between parties to proceedings is to take place only by agreement between those parties;

   (b)   where parties to proceedings fail to mediate, or where mediation between parties to proceedings fails to resolve disputed matters, the failure is not to affect the outcome of the proceedings.

   (2)   Practice directions may provide for members to act as mediators in relation to disputed matters in a case that is the subject of proceedings.

   (3)   The provision that may be made by virtue of subsection (2) includes provision for a member to act as a mediator in relation to disputed matters in a case even though the member has been chosen to decide matters in the case.

   (4)   Once a member has begun to act as a mediator in relation to a disputed matter in a case that is the subject of proceedings, the member may decide matters in the case only with the consent of the parties.

   (5)   Staff appointed under section 40(1) may, subject to their terms of appointment, act as mediators in relation to disputed matters in a case that is the subject of proceedings.

   (6)   In this section–

"member" means a judge or other member of the First-tier Tribunal or a judge or other member of the Upper Tribunal;

"practice direction" means a direction under section 23(1) or (2);

"proceedings" means proceedings before the First-tier Tribunal or proceedings before the Upper Tribunal.

Commencement
   3.11.08.

Supplementary powers of Upper Tribunal

25.–(1)   In relation to the matters mentioned in subsection (2), the Upper Tribunal–

   (a)   has, in England and Wales or in Northern Ireland, the same powers, rights, privileges and authority as the High Court, and

   (b)   has, in Scotland, the same powers, rights, privileges and authority as the Court of Session.

   (2)   The matters are–

   (a)   the attendance and examination of witnesses,

   (b)   the production and inspection of documents, and

   (c)   all other matters incidental to the Upper Tribunal's functions.

   (3)   Subsection (1) shall not be taken–

   (a)   to limit any power to make Tribunal Procedure Rules;

   (b)   to be limited by anything in Tribunal Procedure Rules other than an express limitation.

   (4)   A power, right, privilege or authority conferred in a territory by subsection (1) is available for purposes of proceedings in the Upper Tribunal that take place outside that territory (as well as for purposes of proceedings in the tribunal that take place within that territory).

Commencement
   3.11.08.

First-tier Tribunal and Upper Tribunal: sitting places

26.   Each of the First-tier Tribunal and the Upper Tribunal may decide a case–

(a)   in England and Wales,
(b)   in Scotland, or
(c)   in Northern Ireland,

even though the case arises under the law of a territory other than the one in which the case is decided.

Commencement

3.11.08.

Enforcement

27.–(1)   A sum payable in pursuance of a decision of the First-tier Tribunal or Upper Tribunal made in England and Wales–

(a)   shall be recoverable as if it were payable under an order of a county court in England and Wales;
(b)   shall be recoverable as if it were payable under an order of the High Court in England and Wales.

(2)   An order for the payment of a sum payable in pursuance of a decision of the First-tier Tribunal or Upper Tribunal made in Scotland (or a copy of such an order certified in accordance with Tribunal Procedure Rules) may be enforced as if it were an extract registered decree arbitral bearing a warrant for execution issued by the sheriff court of any sheriffdom in Scotland.

(3)   A sum payable in pursuance of a decision of the First-tier Tribunal or Upper Tribunal made in Northern Ireland–

(a)   shall be recoverable as if it were payable under an order of a county court in Northern Ireland;
(b)   shall be recoverable as if it were payable under an order of the High Court in Northern Ireland.

(4)   This section does not apply to a sum payable in pursuance of–

(a)   an award under section 16(6), or
(b)   an order by virtue of section 21(1).

(5)   The Lord Chancellor may by order make provision for subsection (1) or (3) to apply in relation to a sum of a description specified in the order with the omission of one (but not both) of paragraphs (a) and (b).

(6)   Tribunal Procedure Rules–

(a)   may make provision as to where, for purposes of this section, a decision is to be taken to be made;
(b)   may provide for all or any of subsections (1) to (3) to apply only, or not to apply except, in relation to sums of a description specified in Tribunal Procedure Rules.

Assessors

28.–(1)   If it appears to the First-tier Tribunal or the Upper Tribunal that a matter before it requires special expertise not otherwise available to it, it may direct that in dealing with that matter it shall have the assistance of a person or persons appearing to it to have relevant knowledge or experience.

(2)   The remuneration of a person who gives assistance to either tribunal as mentioned in subsection (1) shall be determined and paid by the Lord Chancellor.

(3)   The Lord Chancellor may–

(a)   establish panels of persons from which either tribunal may (but need not) select persons to give it assistance as mentioned in subsection (1);
(b)   under paragraph (a) establish different panels for different purposes;
(c)   after carrying out such consultation as he considers appropriate, appoint persons to a panel established under paragraph (a);
(d)   remove a person from such a panel.

Commencement

3.11.08.

Costs or expenses

29.–(1)   The costs of and incidental to–

(a)   all proceedings in the First-tier Tribunal, and

(b)   all proceedings in the Upper Tribunal,

shall be in the discretion of the Tribunal in which the proceedings take place.

(2)   The relevant Tribunal shall have full power to determine by whom and to what extent the costs are to be paid.

(3)   Subsections (1) and (2) have effect subject to Tribunal Procedure Rules.

(4)   In any proceedings mentioned in subsection (1), the relevant Tribunal may–

(a)   disallow, or

(b)   (as the case may be) order the legal or other representative concerned to meet,

the whole of any wasted costs or such part of them as may be determined in accordance with Tribunal Procedure Rules.

(5)   In subsection (4) "wasted costs" means any costs incurred by a party–

(a)   as a result of any improper, unreasonable or negligent act or omission on the part of any legal or other representative or any employee of such a representative, or

(b)   which, in the light of any such act or omission occurring after they were incurred, the relevant Tribunal considers it is unreasonable to expect that party to pay.

(6)   In this section "legal or other representative", in relation to a party to proceedings, means any person exercising a right of audience or right to conduct the proceedings on his behalf.

(7)   In the application of this section in relation to Scotland, any reference in this section to costs is to be read as a reference to expenses.

Commencement
3.11.08.

General Note
Rule 10 TP(FT) Rules (made under subs (3)) provides that the Social Entitlement Chamber of the First-tier Tribunal has no power to award costs. Rule 10 TP(UT) Rules (also made under subs (3)) provides that the Upper Tribunal may only make an order in respect of costs when hearing an appeal from another tribunal if that other tribunal had power to order costs. The effect is that the Upper Tribunal has no power to make an order for costs on an appeal from a decision of the Social Entitlement Chamber.

Chapter 3
Transfer of tribunal functions

General Note to Chapter 3
Section 30 (together with the supplementary powers in ss31 and 36) permits the Lord Chancellor to make Orders transferring the functions of other tribunals to the First-tier Tribunal or Upper Tribunal, abolishing those other tribunals and making ancillary, transitional and savings provisions. Note, in particular, that under s38, such an order may amend repeal or revoke both primary and secondary legislation.

The power has been exercised to make the Transfer of Tribunal Functions Order 2008 (see p1102).

Transfer of functions of certain tribunals

30.–(1)   The Lord Chancellor may by order provide for a function of a scheduled tribunal to be transferred–

(a)   to the First-tier Tribunal,

(b)   to the Upper Tribunal,

(c)   to the First-tier Tribunal and the Upper Tribunal with the question as to which of them is to exercise the function in a particular case being determined by a person under provisions of the order,

(d)   to the First-tier Tribunal to the extent specified in the order and to the Upper Tribunal to the extent so specified,

(e)   to the First-tier Tribunal and the Upper Tribunal with the question as to which of them is to exercise the function in a particular case being determined by, or under, Tribunal Procedure Rules,

(f)-(i) [Omitted]
(2)   In subsection (1) "scheduled tribunal" means a tribunal in a list in Schedule 6 that has effect for the purposes of this section.
(3)   The Lord Chancellor may, as respects a function transferred under subsection (1) or this subsection, by order provide for the function to be further transferred as mentioned in any of paragraphs (a) to (i) of subsection (1).
(4)   An order under subsection (1) or (3) may include provision for the purposes of or in consequence of, or for giving full effect to, a transfer under that subsection.
(5)   A function of a tribunal may not be transferred under subsection (1) or (3) if, or to the extent that, the provision conferring the function–
(a)   would be within the legislative competence of the Scottish Parliament if it were included in an Act of that Parliament, or
(b)   [Omitted]
(6)-(7)   *[Omitted]*
(8)   A function of a tribunal may be transferred under subsection (1) or (3) only with the consent of the Welsh Ministers if any relevant function is exercisable in relation to the tribunal by the Welsh Ministers (whether by the Welsh Ministers alone, or by the Welsh Ministers jointly or concurrently with any other person).
(9)   In subsection (8) "relevant function", in relation to a tribunal, means a function which relates–
(a)   to the operation of the tribunal (including, in particular, its membership, administration, staff, accommodation and funding, and payments to its members or staff), or
(b)   to the provision of expenses and allowances to persons attending the tribunal or attending elsewhere in connection with proceedings before the tribunal.

Commencement
19.9.07.

Transfers under section 30: supplementary powers
31.–(1)   The Lord Chancellor may by order make provision for abolishing the tribunal by whom a function transferred under section 30(1) is exercisable immediately before its transfer.
(2)   The Lord Chancellor may by order make provision, where functions of a tribunal are transferred under section 30(1), for a person–
(a)   who is the tribunal (but is not the Secretary of State), or
(b)   who is a member of the tribunal, or
(c)   *[Omitted]*
to (instead or in addition) be the holder of an office specified in subsection (3).
(3)   Those offices are–
(a)   transferred-in judge of the First-tier Tribunal,
(b)   transferred-in other member of the First-tier Tribunal,
(c)   transferred-in judge of the Upper Tribunal,
(d)   transferred-in other member of the Upper Tribunal, and
(e)   deputy judge of the Upper Tribunal.
(4)   Where functions of a tribunal are transferred under section 30(1), the Lord Chancellor must exercise the power under subsection (2) so as to secure that each person who immediately before the end of the tribunal's life–
(a)   is the tribunal,
(b)   is a member of the tribunal, or
(c)   is an authorised decision-maker for the tribunal,
becomes the holder of an office specified in subsection (3) with effect from the end of the tribunal's life (if the person is not then already the holder of such an office).
(5)   Subsection (4) does not apply in relation to a person–
(a)   by virtue of the person's being the Secretary of State, or
(b)   by virtue of the person's being a Commissioner for the general purposes of the income tax;

and a reference in subsection (4) to the end of a tribunal's life is to when the tribunal is abolished or (without being abolished) comes to have no functions.

(6)   *[Omitted]*

(7)   Where a function of a tribunal is transferred under section 30(1), the Lord Chancellor may by order provide for procedural rules in force immediately before the transfer to have effect, or to have effect with appropriate modifications, after the transfer (and, accordingly, to be capable of being varied or revoked) as if they were–

(a)   Tribunal Procedure Rules, or

(b)   [Omitted]

(8)   In subsection (7)–

''procedural rules'' means provision (whether called rules or not)–

(a)   regulating practice or procedure before the tribunal, and

(b)   applying for purposes connected with the exercise of the function;

''appropriate modifications'' means modifications (including additions and omissions) that appear to the Lord Chancellor to be necessary to secure, or expedient in connection with securing, that the procedural rules apply in relation to the exercise of the function after the transfer.

(9)   The Lord Chancellor may, in connection with provision made by order under section 30 or the preceding provisions of this section, make by order such incidental, supplemental, transitional or consequential provision, or provision for savings, as the Lord Chancellor thinks fit, including provision applying only in relation to cases selected by a member–

(a)   of the First-tier Tribunal,

(b)   of the Upper Tribunal,

(c)-(d) [Omitted]

(10)   Subsections (1), (2) and (7) are not to be taken as prejudicing the generality of subsection (9).

Commencement
> 19.9.07.

Power to provide for appeal to Upper Tribunal from tribunals in Wales
32.   *[Omitted]*

Commencement
> 19.9.07.

Power to provide for appeal to Upper Tribunal from tribunals in Scotland
33.   *[Omitted]*

Commencement
> 19.9.07.

Power to provide for appeal to Upper Tribunal from tribunals in Northern Ireland
34.   *[Omitted]*

Commencement
> 19.9.07.

Transfer of Ministerial responsibilities for certain tribunals
35.   *[Omitted]*

Commencement
> 19.9.07.

Transfer of powers to make procedural rules for certain tribunals
36.   *[Omitted]*

Commencement
19.9.07.

Power to amend lists of tribunals in Schedule 6

37.–(1)   The Lord Chancellor may by order amend Schedule 6–

(a)   for the purpose of adding a tribunal to a list in the Schedule;

(b)   for the purpose of removing a tribunal from a list in the Schedule;

(c)   for the purpose of removing a list from the Schedule;

(d)   for the purpose of adding to the Schedule a list of tribunals that has effect for the purposes of any one or more of sections 30, 32(3), 35 and 36.

(2)   The following rules apply to the exercise of power under subsection (1)–

(a)   a tribunal may not be added to a list, or be in an added list, if the tribunal is established otherwise than by or under an enactment;

(b)   a tribunal established by an enactment passed or made after the last day of the Session in which this Act is passed must not be added to a list, or be in an added list, that has effect for the purposes of section 30;

(c)   if any relevant function is exercisable in relation to a tribunal by the Welsh Ministers (whether by the Welsh Ministers alone, or by the Welsh Ministers jointly or concurrently with any other person), the tribunal may be added to a list, or be in an added list, only with the consent of the Welsh Ministers;

(d)   a tribunal may be in more than one list.

(3)   In subsection (2)(c) ''relevant function'', in relation to a tribunal, means a function which relates–

(a)   to the operation of the tribunal (including, in particular, its membership, administration, staff, accommodation and funding, and payments to its members or staff), or

(b)   to the provision of expenses and allowances to persons attending the tribunal or attending elsewhere in connection with proceedings before the tribunal.

(4)   In subsection (1) ''tribunal'' does not include an ordinary court of law.

(5)   In this section ''enactment'' means any enactment whenever passed or made, including an enactment comprised in subordinate legislation (within the meaning of the Interpretation Act 1978 (c. 30)).

Commencement
19.9.07.

Orders under sections 30 to 36: supplementary

38.–(1)   Provision in an order under any of sections 30 to 36 may take the form of amendments, repeals or revocations of enactments.

(2)   In this section ''enactment'' means any enactment whenever passed or made, including an enactment comprised in subordinate legislation (within the meaning of the Interpretation Act 1978).

(3)   Any power to extend enactments to a territory outside the United Kingdom shall have effect as if it included–

(a)   power to extend those enactments as they have effect with any amendments and repeals made in them by orders under any of sections 30 to 36, and

(b)   power to extend those enactments as if any amendments and repeals made in them under those sections had not been made.

Commencement
19.9.07.

Chapter 4
Administrative matters in respect of certain tribunals

The general duty

39.–(1)   The Lord Chancellor is under a duty to ensure that there is an efficient and effective system to support the carrying on of the business of–

(a)   the First-tier Tribunal,

(b)   the Upper Tribunal,

(c)-(e) [Omitted]

and that appropriate services are provided for those tribunals (referred to in this section and in sections 40 and 41 as ''the tribunals'').

(2)   Any reference in this section, or in section 40 or 41, to the Lord Chancellor's general duty in relation to the tribunals is to his duty under subsection (1).

(3)   The Lord Chancellor must annually prepare and lay before each House of Parliament a report as to the way in which he has discharged his general duty in relation to the tribunals.

Commencement

19.9.07.

Provision of accommodation

41.–(1)   The Lord Chancellor may provide, equip, maintain and manage such tribunal buildings, offices and other accommodation as appear to him appropriate for the purpose of discharging his general duty in relation to the tribunals.

(2)   The Lord Chancellor may enter into such arrangements for the provision, equipment, maintenance or management of tribunal buildings, offices or other accommodation as appear to him appropriate for the purpose of discharging his general duty in relation to the tribunals.

(3)   The powers under–

(a)   section 2 of the Commissioners of Works Act 1852 (c. 28) (acquisition by agreement), and

(b)   section 228(1) of the Town and Country Planning Act 1990 (c. 8) (compulsory acquisition),

to acquire land necessary for the public service are to be treated as including power to acquire land for the purpose of its provision under arrangements entered into under subsection (2).

(4)   In this section ''tribunal building'' means any place where any of the tribunals sits, including the precincts of any building in which it sits.

Fees

42.–(1)   The Lord Chancellor may by order prescribe fees payable in respect of–

(a)   anything dealt with by the First-tier Tribunal,

(b)   anything dealt with by the Upper Tribunal,

(c)   anything dealt with by the Asylum and Immigration Tribunal,

(d)   anything dealt with by an added tribunal, and

(e)   mediation conducted by staff appointed under section 40(1).

(2)   An order under subsection (1) may, in particular, contain provision as to–

(a)   scales or rates of fees;

(b)   exemptions from or reductions in fees;

(c)   remission of fees in whole or in part.

(3)   In subsection (1)(d) ''added tribunal'' means a tribunal specified in an order made by the Lord Chancellor.

(4)   A tribunal may be specified in an order under subsection (3) only if–

(a)   it is established by or under an enactment, whenever passed or made, and

(b)   is not an ordinary court of law.

(5)   Before making an order under this section, the Lord Chancellor must consult–

(a)   the Senior President of Tribunals, and

(b)   the Administrative Justice and Tribunals Council.

(6)   The making of an order under subsection (1) requires the consent of the Treasury except where the order contains provision only for the purpose of altering amounts payable by way of fees already prescribed under that subsection.

(7)   The Lord Chancellor must take such steps as are reasonably practicable to bring information about fees under subsection (1) to the attention of persons likely to have to pay them.

(8)   Fees payable under subsection (1) are recoverable summarily as a civil debt.

(9)   Subsection (8) does not apply to the recovery in Scotland of fees payable under this section.

(10)   Until the Administrative Justice and Tribunals Council first has ten members appointed under paragraph 1(2) of Schedule 7, the reference to that council in subsection (5) is to be read as a reference to the Council on Tribunals.

Commencement
19.9.07.

Report by Senior President of Tribunals

43.–(1)   Each year the Senior President of Tribunals must give the Lord Chancellor a report covering, in relation to relevant tribunal cases–

(a)   matters that the Senior President of Tribunals wishes to bring to the attention of the Lord Chancellor, and

(b)   matters that the Lord Chancellor has asked the Senior President of Tribunals to cover in the report.

(2)   The Lord Chancellor must publish each report given to him under subsection (1).

(3)   In this section "relevant tribunal cases" means–

(a)   cases coming before the First-tier Tribunal,

(b)   cases coming before the Upper Tribunal,

(c)-(d) *[Omitted]*

Commencement
3.11.08.

Chapter 5
Oversight of administrative justice system, tribunals and inquiries

The Administrative Justice and Tribunals Council
44.   *[Omitted]*

Abolition of the Council on Tribunals
45.   *[Omitted]*

Chapter 6
Supplementary

Orders and regulations under Part 1: supplemental and procedural provisions

49.–(1)   Power–

(a)   of the Lord Chancellor to make an order, or regulations, under this Part,

(b)   of the Senior President of Tribunals to make an order under section 7(9), or

(c)   of the Scottish Ministers, or the Welsh Ministers, to make an order under paragraph 25(2) of Schedule 7,

is exercisable by statutory instrument.

(2)   The Statutory Instruments Act 1946 (c. 36) shall apply in relation to the power to make orders conferred on the Senior President of Tribunals by section 7(9) as if the Senior President of Tribunals were a Minister of the Crown.

(3)   Any power mentioned in subsection (1) includes power to make different provision for different purposes.

(4)   Without prejudice to the generality of subsection (3), power to make an order under section 30 or 31 includes power to make different provision in relation to England, Scotland, Wales and Northern Ireland respectively.

(5)   No order mentioned in subsection (6) is to be made unless a draft of the statutory instrument containing it (whether alone or with other provision) has been laid before, and approved by a resolution of, each House of Parliament.

(6) Those orders are–

(a) an order under section 11(8), 13(6) or (14), 30, 31(1), 32, 33, 34, 35, 36, 37 or 42(3);

(b) an order under paragraph 15 of Schedule 4;

(c) an order under section 42(1)(a) to (d) that provides for fees to be payable in respect of things for which fees have never been payable;

(d) an order under section 31(2), (7) or (9), or paragraph 30(1) of Schedule 5, that contains provision taking the form of an amendment or repeal of an enactment comprised in an Act.

(7) A statutory instrument that–

(a) contains–

(i) an order mentioned in subsection (8), or

(ii) regulations under Part 3 of Schedule 9, and

(b) is not subject to any requirement that a draft of the instrument be laid before, and approved by a resolution of, each House of Parliament,

is subject to annulment in pursuance of a resolution of either House of Parliament.

(8) Those orders are–

(a) an order made by the Lord Chancellor under this Part;

(b) an order made by the Senior President of Tribunals under section 7(9).

(9) A statutory instrument that contains an order made by the Scottish Ministers under paragraph 25(2) of Schedule 7 is subject to annulment in pursuance of a resolution of the Scottish Parliament.

(10) A statutory instrument that contains an order made by the Welsh Ministers under paragraph 25(2) of Schedule 7 is subject to annulment in pursuance of a resolution of the National Assembly for Wales.

Commencement
19.9.07.

SCHEDULE 5

Commencement
19.9.07.

SECTION 22
PROCEDURE IN FIRST-TIER TRIBUNAL AND UPPER TRIBUNAL

Part 1
Tribunal Procedure Rules

Introductory

1.–(1) This Part of this Schedule makes further provision about the content of Tribunal Procedure Rules.

(2) The generality of section 22(1) is not to be taken to be prejudiced by–

(a) the following paragraphs of this Part of this Schedule, or

(b) any other provision (including future provision) authorising or requiring the making of provision by Tribunal Procedure Rules.

(3) In the following paragraphs of this Part of this Schedule ''Rules'' means Tribunal Procedure Rules.

Concurrent functions

2. Rules may make provision as to who is to decide, or as to how to decide, which of the First-tier Tribunal and Upper Tribunal is to exercise, in relation to any particular matter, a function that is exercisable by the two tribunals on the basis that the question as to which of them is to exercise the function is to be determined by, or under, Rules.

Delegation of functions to staff

3.–(1) Rules may provide for functions–

(a) of the First-tier Tribunal, or

(b) of the Upper Tribunal,

to be exercised by staff appointed under section 40(1).

(2) In making provision of the kind mentioned in sub-paragraph (1) in relation to a function, Rules may (in particular)–

(a)   provide for the function to be exercisable by a member of staff only if the member of staff is, or is of a description, specified in exercise of a discretion conferred by Rules;

(b)   provide for the function to be exercisable by a member of staff only if the member of staff is approved, or is of a description approved, for the purpose by a person specified in Rules.

Time limits

4.   Rules may make provision for time limits as respects initiating, or taking any step in, proceedings before the First-tier Tribunal or the Upper Tribunal.

Repeat applications

5.   Rules may make provision restricting the making of fresh applications where a previous application in relation to the same matter has been made.

Tribunal acting of its own initiative

6.   Rules may make provision about the circumstances in which the First-tier Tribunal, or the Upper Tribunal, may exercise its powers of its own initiative.

Hearings

7.   Rules may–

(a)   make provision for dealing with matters without a hearing;

(b)   make provision as respects allowing or requiring a hearing to be in private or as respects allowing or requiring a hearing to be in public.

Proceedings without notice

8.   Rules may make provision for proceedings to take place, in circumstances described in Rules, at the request of one party even though the other, or another, party has had no notice.

Representation

9.   Rules may make provision conferring additional rights of audience before the First-tier Tribunal or the Upper Tribunal.

Evidence, witnesses and attendance

10.–(1)   Rules may make provision aboutevidence (including evidence on oath and administration of oaths).

(2)   Rules may modify any rules of evidence provided for elsewhere, so far as they would apply to proceedings before the First-tier Tribunal or Upper Tribunal.

(3)   Rules may make provision, where the First-tier Tribunal has required a person–

(a)   to attend at any place for the purpose of giving evidence,

(b)   otherwise to make himself available to give evidence,

(c)   to swear an oath in connection with the giving of evidence,

(d)   to give evidence as a witness,

(e)   to produce a document, or

(f)   to facilitate the inspection of a document or any other thing (including any premises),

for the Upper Tribunal to deal with non-compliance with the requirement as though the requirement had been imposed by the Upper Tribunal.

(4)   Rules may make provision for the payment of expenses and allowances to persons giving evidence, producing documents, attending proceedings or required to attend proceedings.

Use of information

11.–(1)   Rules may make provision for the disclosure or non-disclosure of information received during the course of proceedings before the First-tier Tribunal or Upper Tribunal.

(2)   Rules may make provision for imposing reporting restrictions in circumstances described in Rules.

Costs and expenses

12.–(1)   Rules may make provision for regulating matters relating tocosts, or (in Scotland) expenses, of proceedings before the First-tier Tribunal or Upper Tribunal.

(2)   The provision mentioned in sub-paragraph (1) includes (in particular)–

(a)   provision prescribing scales of costs or expenses;

(b)   provision for enabling costs to undergo detailed assessment in England and Wales by a county court or the High Court;

(c)   provision for taxation in Scotland of accounts of expenses by an Auditor of Court;

(d)   provision for enabling costs to be taxed in Northern Ireland in a county court or the High Court;

(e)   provision for costs or expenses–
    (i)   not to be allowed in respect of items of a description specified in Rules;
    (ii)   not to be allowed in proceedings of a description so specified;
(f)   provision for other exceptions to either or both of subsections (1) and (2) of section 29.

Set-off and interest
13.–(1)   Rules may make provision for a party to proceedings to deduct, from amounts payable by him, amounts payable to him.
(2)   Rules may make provision for interest on sums awarded (including provision conferring a discretion or provision in accordance with which interest is to be calculated).

Arbitration
14.   Rules may provide for Part 1 of the Arbitration Act 1996 (c. 23) (which extends to England and Wales, and Northern Ireland, but not Scotland) not to apply, or not to apply except so far as is specified in Rules, where the First-tier Tribunal, or Upper Tribunal, acts as arbitrator.

Correction of errors and setting-aside of decisions on procedural grounds
15.–(1)   Rules may make provision for the correction of accidental errors in a decision or record of a decision.
(2)   Rules may make provision for thesetting aside of a decision in proceedings before the First-tier Tribunal or Upper Tribunal–
(a)   where a document relating to the proceedings was not sent to, or was not received at an appropriate time by, a party to the proceedings or a party's representative,
(b)   where a document relating to the proceedings was not sent to the First-tier Tribunal or Upper Tribunal at an appropriate time,
(c)   where a party to the proceedings, or a party's representative, was not present at a hearing related to the proceedings, or
(d)   where there has been any other procedural irregularity in the proceedings.
(3)   Sub-paragraphs (1) and (2) shall not be taken to prejudice, or to be prejudiced by, any power to correct errors or set aside decisions that is exercisable apart from rules made by virtue of those sub-paragraphs.

Ancillary powers
16.   Rules may confer on the First-tier Tribunal, or the Upper Tribunal, such ancillary powers as are necessary for the proper discharge of its functions.

Rules may refer to practice directions
17.   Rules may, instead of providing for any matter, refer to provision made or to be made about that matter by directions under section 23.

Presumptions
18.   Rules may make provision in the form of presumptions (including, in particular, presumptions as to service or notification).

Differential provision
19.   Rules may make different provision for different purposes or different areas.

SCHEDULE 6

Commencement
19.9.07.

SECTIONS 30 TO 37
TRIBUNALS FOR THE PURPOSES OF SECTIONS 30 TO 36

Part 1
Tribunals for the purposes of sections 30, 35 and 36

Tribunal	Enactment
Appeal tribunal	Chapter 1 of Part 1 of the Social Security Act 1998 (c. 14)
Social Security Commissioner	Schedule 4 to the Social Security Act 1998 (c. 14)

SCHEDULE 10
SECTION 50
AMENDMENTS RELATING TO JUDICIAL APPOINTMENTS

Part 1
Amendments

29. (1)   The Social Security Act 1998 (c. 14) is amended as follows.

(2)–(7)   *[Omitted]*

(8)   At any time before the coming into force of section 59(1) of the Constitutional Reform Act 2005 (c. 4) (renaming of Supreme Court), the reference to the Senior Courts in the section 7(2)(a) substituted by sub-paragraph (3) is to be read as a reference to the Supreme Court.

Commencement
21.7.08.

Part 2

Main secondary legislation
Housing benefit

The Housing Benefit Regulations 2006
(SI 2006 No.213)

ARRANGEMENT OF REGULATIONS
PART 1
General

1.   Citation and commencement
2.   Interpretation
3.   Definition of non-dependant
4.   Cases in which section 1(1A) of the Administration Act is disapplied
5.   Persons who have attained the qualifying age for state pension credit
6.   Remunerative work

PART 2
Provisions affecting entitlement to housing benefit

7.   Circumstances in which a person is or is not to be treated as occupying a dwelling as his home
8.   Circumstances in which a person is to be treated as liable to make payments in respect of a dwelling
9.   Circumstances in which a person is to be treated as not liable to make payments in respect of a dwelling
10. Persons from abroad
10A. Entitlement of a refugee to housing benefit

PART 3
Payments in respect of a dwelling

11.   Eligible housing costs
12.   Rent
12B. Eligible rent
12C. Eligible rent and maximum rent
12D. Eligible rent and maximum rent (LHA)
12L. Transitional protection – larger properties
13.   Maximum rent
13ZA. Protection on death and 13 week protection
13ZB. Change in reckonable rent
13C. When maximum rent (LHA) is to be determined
13D. Determination of a maximum rent (LHA)
13E. Publication of local housing allowances
14.   Requirement to refer to rent officers
15.   Applications to the rent officer for redeterminations
16.   Application for a redetermination by a rent officer
17.   Substitute determinations or substitute redeterminations
18.   Application of provisions to substitute determinations or substitute redeterminations
18A. Amended determinations

PART 4
Membership of a family

19. Persons of prescribed description
20. Circumstances in which a person is to be treated as responsible or not responsible for another
21. Circumstances in which a person is to be treated as being or not being a member of the household

PART 5
Applicable amounts
22. Applicable amounts
23. Polygamous marriages
24. Patients

PART 6
Income and capital
SECTION 1
General
25. Calculation of income and capital of members of claimant's family and of a polygamous marriage
26. Circumstances in which income of non-dependant is to be treated as claimant's

SECTION 2
Income
27. Calculation of income on a weekly basis
28. Treatment of child care charges
29. Average weekly earnings of employed earners
30. Average weekly earnings of self-employed earners
31. Average weekly income other than earnings
32. Calculation of average weekly income from tax credits
33. Calculation of weekly income
34. Disregard of changes in tax, contributions etc

SECTION 3
Employed earners
35. Earnings of employed earners
36. Calculation of net earnings of employed earners

SECTION 4
Self-employed earners
37. Earnings of self-employed earners
38. Calculation of net profit of self-employed earners
39. Deduction of tax and contributions of self-employed earners

SECTION 5
Other income
40. Calculation of income other than earnings
41. Capital treated as income
42. Notional income

SECTION 6
Capital
43. Capital limit
44. Calculation of capital
45. Disregard of capital of child and young person
46. Income treated as capital
47. Calculation of capital in the United Kingdom
48. Calculation of capital outside the United Kingdom
49. Notional capital
50. Diminishing notional capital rule
51. Capital jointly held
52. Calculation of tariff income from capital

PART 7
Students
SECTION 1
General

53.   Interpretation
54.   Treatment of students

SECTION 2
Entitlement and payments in respect of a dwelling

55.   Occupying a dwelling as a person's home
56.   Full-time students to be treated as not liable to make payments in respect of a dwelling
57.   Student's eligible housing costs
58.   Student partners

SECTION 3
Income

59.   Calculation of grant income
60.   Calculation of covenant income where a contribution is assessed
61.   Covenant income where no grant income or no contribution is assessed
62.   Relationship with amounts to be disregarded under Schedule 5
63.   Other amounts to be disregarded
64.   Treatment of student loans
64A.   Treatment of fee loans
65.   Treatment of payments from access funds
66.   Disregard of contribution and rent
67.   Further disregard of student's income
68.   Amounts treated as capital
69.   Disregard of changes occurring during summer vacation

PART 8
Amount of benefit

70.   Maximum housing benefit
71.   Housing benefit tapers
72.   Extended payments
72A.   Duration of extended payment period
72B.   Amount of extended payment
72C.   Extended payments – movers
72D.   Relationship between extended payment and entitlement to housing benefit under the general conditions of entitlement
73.   Extended payments (qualifying contributory benefits)
73A.   Duration of extended payment period (qualifying contributory benefits)
73B.   Amount of extended payment (qualifying contributory benefits)
73C.   Extended payments (qualifying contributory benefits) – movers
73D.   Relationship between extended payment (qualifying contributory benefits) and entitlement to housing benefit under the general conditions of entitlement
74.   Non-dependant deductions
75.   Minimum housing benefit

PART 9
Calculation of weekly amounts and changes of circumstances

76.   Date on which entitlement is to commence
77.   Date on which housing benefit is to end
78.   Date on which housing benefit is to end where entitlement to severe disablement allowance or incapacity benefit ceases
79.   Date on which change of circumstances is to take effect

80.   Calculation of weekly amounts
81.   Rent free periods

PART 10
Claims
82.   Who may claim
83.   Time and manner in which claims are to be made
83A.   Electronic claims for benefit
84.   Date of claim where claim sent or delivered to a gateway office
85.   Date of claim where claim sent or delivered to an office of a designated authority
86.   Evidence and information
87.   Amendment and withdrawal of claim
88.   Duty to notify changes of circumstances
88ZA. Alternative means of notifying changes of circumstances
88A.   Notice of changes of circumstances given electronically

PART 11
Decisions on questions
89.   Decisions by a relevant authority
90.   Notification of decisions

PART 12
Payments
91.   Time and manner of payment
91A.   Cases in which payment to a housing authority are to take the form of a rent allowance
92.   Frequency of payment of a rent allowance
93.   Payment on account of a rent allowance
94.   Payment to be made to a person entitled
95.   Circumstances in which payment is to be made to a landlord
96.   Circumstances in which payment may be made to a landlord
97.   Payment on death of the person entitled
98.   Offsetting

PART 13
Overpayments
99.   Meaning of overpayment
100.   Recoverable overpayments
101.   Person from whom recovery may be sought
102.   Method of recovery
103.   Diminution of capital
104.   Sums to be deducted in calculating recoverable overpayments
105.   Recovery of overpayments from prescribed benefits
106.   Prescribed benefits
107.   Restrictions on recovery of rent and consequent notifications

PART 14
Information
SECTION 1
Claims and information
108.   Interpretation
109A. Verifying information
109.   Collection of information
110.   Recording and holding information
111.   Forwarding of information
112.   Request for information

SECTION 2
Information from landlords and agents and between authorities etc.
113.   Interpretation
114A.   Information to be provided to rent officers
114.   Evidence and information required by rent officers
115.   Information to be supplied by an authority to another authority
116.   Supply of information: extended payments (qualifying contributory benefits)
117.   Requiring information from landlords and agents
118.   Circumstances for requiring information
119.   Relevant information
120.   Manner of supply of information
121.   Criminal offence
121A.   Supply of benefit administration information between authorities

PART 15
Former pathfinder authorities
122.   Modifications in respect of former pathfinder areas

SCHEDULES
A1.   Treatment of claims for housing benefit by refugees
1.   Ineligible service charges
2.   Excluded tenancies
3.   Applicable amounts
4.   Sums to be disregarded in the calculation of earnings
5.   Sums to be disregarded in the calculation of income other than earnings
6.   Capital to be disregarded
7.   Extended payments of housing benefit
8.   Extended Payments (severe disablement allowance and incapacity benefit) of housing benefit
9.   Matters to be included in decision notice
10.   Former pathfinder authorities
11.   Electronic communication

PART 1
General

General Note on Part I

This Part defines terms commonly used in the HB Regs. Some regulations also give their own specialist meaning to terms used in them, and this will be pointed out where necessary. In addition, some of the terms found in the regs are defined in s137 Social Security Contributions and Benefits Act 1992 (SSCBA – see p3) – an indication is also given where this applies.

Citation and commencement

1.–(1)   These Regulations may be cited as the Housing Benefit Regulations 2006.

(2)   These Regulations are to be read, where appropriate, with the Consequential Provisions Regulations and, in a case where regulation 5(2) applies, with the Housing Benefit (Persons who have attained the qualifying age for state pension credit) Regulations 2006.

(3)   Except as provided in Schedule 4 to the Consequential Provisions Regulations, these Regulations shall come into force on 6th March 2006.

(4)   The regulations consolidated by these Regulations are revoked, in consequence of the consolidation, by the Consequential Provisions Regulations.

Interpretation

2.–(1)   In these Regulations–

''the Act'' means the Social Security Contributions and Benefits Act 1992;

''the 1973 Act'' means the Employment and Training Act 1973;

[¹"the 2000 Act" means the Electronic Communications Act 2000;]

"Abbeyfield Home" means an establishment run by the Abbeyfield Society including all bodies corporate or incorporate which are affiliated to that Society;

"adoption leave" means a period of absence from work on ordinary or additional adoption leave by virtue of section 75A or 75B of the Employment Rights Act 1996;

"the Administration Act" means the Social Security Administration Act 1992;

"appropriate DWP office" means an office of the Department for Work and Pensions dealing with state pension credit or an office which is normally open to the public for the receipt of claims for income support [¹⁷ , a jobseeker's allowance or an employment and support allowance];

[⁹ "amended determination" means a determination made in accordance with article 7A of the Rent Officers Order;]

"assessment period" means such period as is prescribed in regulations 29 to 31 over which income falls to be calculated;

"attendance allowance" means–

   (a)   an attendance allowance under Part 3 of the Act;

   (b)   an increase of disablement pension under section 104 or 105 of the Act;

   (c)   a payment under regulations made in exercise of the power conferred by paragraph 7(2)(b) of Part 2 of Schedule 8 to the Act;

   (d)   an increase of an allowance which is payable in respect of constant attendance under paragraph 4 of Part 1 of Schedule 8 to the Act;

   (e)   a payment by virtue of article 14, 15, 16, 43 or 44 of the Personal Injuries (Civilians) Scheme 1983 or any analogous payment; or

   (f)   any payment based on need for attendance which is paid as part of a war disablement pension;

[²² "basic rate", where it relates to the rate of tax, has the same meaning as in the Income Tax Act 2007 (see section 989 of that Act);]

"the benefit Acts" means the Act [¹⁷ , the Jobseekers Act and the Welfare Reform Act];

"benefit week" means a period of 7 consecutive days commencing upon a Monday and ending on a Sunday;

[⁹ "broad rental market area" has the meaning specified in paragraph 4 of Schedule 3B to the Rent Officers Order;]

[⁹ "broad rental market area determination" means a determination made in accordance with article 4B(1A) of the Rent Officers Order;]

"care home" in England and Wales has the meaning assigned to it by section 3 of the Care Standards Act 2000 and in Scotland means a care home service within the meaning assigned to it by section 2(3) of the Regulation of Care (Scotland) Act 2001;

[⁹ "change of dwelling" means, for the purposes of regulations 13C and 14, a change of dwelling occupied by a claimant as his home during the award where the dwelling to which the claimant has moved is one in respect of which the authority may make a rent allowance;]

"child" means a person under the age of 16;

"child tax credit" means a child tax credit under section 8 of the Tax Credits Act;

"the Children Order" means the Children (Northern Ireland) Order 1995;

"claim" means a claim for housing benefit;

"claimant" means a person claiming housing benefit;

"close relative" means a parent, parent-in-law, son, son-in-law, daughter, daughter-in-law, step-parent, step-son, step-daughter, brother, sister, or if any of the preceding persons is one member of a couple, the other member of that couple;

[¹⁹]

"concessionary payment" means a payment made under arrangements made by the Secretary of State with the consent of the Treasury which is charged either to the National Insurance Fund or to a Departmental Expenditure Vote to which payments of benefit [²⁰ or tax credits under the benefit Acts or the Tax Credits Act] [¹²] are charged;

"the Consequential Provisions Regulations" means the Housing Benefit and Council Tax Benefit (Consequential Provisions) Regulations 2006;

[[18] "contributory employment and support allowance" means a contributory allowance under Part 1 of the Welfare Reform Act;]

"co-ownership scheme" means a scheme under which the dwelling is let by a housing association and the tenant, or his personal representative, will, under the terms of the tenancy agreement or of the agreement under which he became a member of the association, be entitled, on his ceasing to be a member and subject to any conditions stated in either agreement, to a sum calculated by reference directly or indirectly to the value of the dwelling;

[[33] "converted employment and support allowance" means an employment and support allowance which is not income-related and to which a person is entitled as a result of a conversion decision within the meaning of the Employment and Support Allowance (Existing Awards) Regulations;]

"couple" means–
  (a) a man and a woman who are married to each other and are members of the same household;
  (b) a man and a woman who are not married to each other but are living together as husband and wife;
  (c) two people of the same sex who are civil partners of each other and are members of the same household; or
  (d) two people of the same sex who are not civil partners of each other but are living together as if they were civil partners,
  and for the purposes of sub-paragraph (d), two people of the same sex are to be regarded as living together as if they were civil partners if, but only if, they would be regarded as living together as husband and wife were they instead two people of the opposite sex;

"Crown tenant" means a person who occupies a dwelling under a tenancy or licence where the interest of the landlord belongs to Her Majesty in right of the Crown or to a government department or is held in trust for Her Majesty for the purposes of a government department, except (in the case of an interest belonging to Her Majesty in right of the Crown) where the interest is under the management of the Crown Estate Commissioners;

"date of claim" means the date on which the claim is made, or treated as made, for the purposes of regulation 83 (time and manner in which claims are to be made);

"the Decisions and Appeals Regulations" means the Housing Benefit and Council Tax Benefit (Decisions and Appeals) Regulations 2001;

"designated authority" means any of the following–
  (a) the Secretary of State;
  (b) a person providing services to the Secretary of State;
  (c) a local authority;
  (d) a person providing services to, or authorised to exercise any functions of, any such authority;

"designated office" means the office designated by the relevant authority for the receipt of claims to housing benefit–
  (a) by notice upon or with a form approved by it for the purpose of claiming housing benefit; or
  (b) by reference upon or with such a form to some other document available from it and sent by electronic means or otherwise on application and without charge; or
  (c) by any combination of the provisions set out in sub-paragraphs (a) and (b) above;

"disability living allowance" means a disability living allowance under section 71 of the Act;

"earnings" has the meaning prescribed in regulation 35 or, as the case may be, 37;

"the Eileen Trust" means the charitable trust of that name established on 29th March 1993 out of funds provided by the Secretary of State for the benefit of persons eligible for payment in accordance with its provisions;

[¹ "electronic communication" has the same meaning as in section 15(1) of the 2000 Act;]

[⁸ "eligible rent" means, as the case may require, an eligible rent determined in accordance with–

(a)   regulations 12B (eligible rent), 12C (eligible rent and maximum rent) or 12D (eligible rent and maximum rent (LHA)); or

(b)   regulations 12 (rent) and 13 (restrictions on unreasonable payments) as set out in paragraph 5 of Schedule 3 to the Consequential Provisions Regulations in a case to which paragraph 4 of that Schedule applies;]

"employed earner" is to be construed in accordance with section 2(1)(a) of the Act and also includes a person who is in receipt of a payment which is payable under any enactment having effect in Northern Ireland and which corresponds to statutory sick pay or statutory maternity pay;

[¹⁸ "Employment and Support Allowance Regulations" means the Employment and Support Allowance Regulations 2008;]

[³³ "Employment and Support Allowance (Existing Awards) Regulations" means the Employment and Support Allowance (Transitional Provisions, Housing Benefit and Council Tax Benefit) (Existing Awards) (No, 2) Regulations 2010;]

"employment zone" means an area within Great Britain designated for the purposes of section 60 of the Welfare Reform and Pensions Act 1999 and an "employment zone programme" means a programme established for such an area or areas designed to assist claimants for a jobseeker's allowance to obtain sustainable employment;

"employment zone contractor" means a person who is undertaking the provision of facilities in respect of an employment zone programme on behalf of the Secretary of State for Work and Pensions;

[²⁶ "enactment" includes an enactment comprised in, or in an instrument made under, an Act of the Scottish Parliament;]

[¹⁴ "extended payment" means a payment of housing benefit payable pursuant to regulation 72;]

[¹⁵ "extended payment period" means the period for which an extended payment is payable in accordance with regulation 72A or 73A;]

[¹⁴ "extended payment (qualifying contributory benefits)" means a payment of housing benefit payable pursuant to regulation 73;]

"family" has the meaning assigned to it by section 137(1) of the Act;

"the former Regulations" means the Housing Benefit (General) Regulations 1987;

"the Fund" means moneys made available from time to time by the Secretary of State for the benefit of persons eligible for payment in accordance with the provisions of a scheme established by him on 24th April 1992 or, in Scotland, on 10th April 1992;

[¹³]

"a guaranteed income payment" means a payment made under article 14(1)(b) or article 21(1)(a) of the Armed Forces and Reserve Forces (Compensation Scheme) Order 2005;

"hostel" means a building–

(a)   in which there is provided for persons generally or for a class of persons, domestic accommodation, otherwise than in separate and self-contained premises, and either board or facilities for the preparation of food adequate to the needs of those persons, or both; and

(b)   which is–

(i)   managed or owned by a registered housing association; or

(ii)   operated other than on a commercial basis and in respect of which funds are provided wholly or in part by a government department or agency or a local authority; or

(iii)   managed by a voluntary organisation or charity and provides care, support or supervision with a view to assisting those persons to be rehabilitated or resettled within the community; and

(c)   which is not–
    (i)   a care home;
    (ii)   an independent hospital; or
    (iii)   an Abbeyfield Home;

[³⁶ "Housing Act functions" means functions under section 122 of the Housing Act 1996;]

[⁸ "housing association" has the meaning assigned to it by section 1(1) of the Housing Associations Act 1985;]

"Immigration and Asylum Act" means the Immigration and Asylum Act 1999;

"an income-based jobseeker's allowance" and "a joint-claim jobseeker's allowance" have the same meanings as they have in the Jobseekers Act by virtue of section 1(4) of that Act;

[¹⁸ "income-related employment and support allowance" means an income-related allowance under Part 1 of the Welfare Reform Act;]

"Income Support Regulations" means the Income Support (General) Regulations 1987;

[³⁴ "independent hospital" –
(a)   in England, means a hospital as defined by section 275 of the National Health Service Act 2006 that is not a health service hospital as defined by that section;
(b)   in Wales, has the meaning assigned to it by section 2 of the Care Standards Act 2000; and
(c)   in Scotland, means an independent healthcare service as defined in section 2(5)(a) and (b) of the Regulation of Care (Scotland) Act 2001;]

[¹⁹]

[⁵ "the Independent Living Fund (2006)" means the Trust of that name established by a deed dated 10th April 2006 and made between the Secretary of State for Work and Pensions of the one part and Margaret Rosemary Cooper, Michael Beresford Boyall and Marie Theresa Martin of the other part;]

[¹⁹]
[¹⁹]
[¹⁹]
[¹¹]

"invalid carriage or other vehicle" means a vehicle propelled by petrol engine or by electric power supplied for use on the road and to be controlled by the occupant;

"Jobseekers Act" means the Jobseekers Act 1995;

"Jobseeker's Allowance Regulations" means the Jobseeker's Allowance Regulations 1996;]

[¹⁸ "limited capability for work" has the meaning given in section 1(4) of the Welfare Reform Act;

[¹⁸ "limited capability for work-related activity" has the meaning given in section 2(5) of the Welfare Reform Act;]

[⁹ "linked person" means–
(a)   any member of the claimant's family;
(b)   if the claimant is a member of a polygamous marriage, any partners of his and any child or young person for whom he or a partner is responsible and who is a member of the same household; or
(c)   any relative of the claimant or his partner who occupies the same dwelling as the claimant, whether or not they reside with him, except for a relative who has a separate right of occupation of the dwelling which would enable them to continue to occupy it even if the claimant ceased his occupation of it;]

[⁹ "local housing allowance" means an allowance determined in accordance with paragraph 2 of Schedule 3B to the Rent Officers Order;]

"the London Bombings Relief Charitable Fund" means the company limited by guarantee (number 5505072) and registered charity of that name established on 11th July 2005 for the purpose of (amongst other things) relieving sickness, disability or financial need of victims (including families or dependants of victims) of the terrorist attacks carried out in London on 7th July 2005;

"lone parent" means a person who has no partner and who is responsible for and a member of the same household as a child or young person;

"long tenancy" means a tenancy granted for a term of years certain exceeding twenty one years, whether or not the tenancy is, or may become, terminable before the end of that term by notice given by or to the tenant or by re-entry, forfeiture (or, in Scotland, irritancy) or otherwise and includes a lease for a term fixed by law under a grant with a covenant or obligation for perpetual renewal unless it is a lease by sub-demise from one which is not a long tenancy;

[⁷]

"the Macfarlane (Special Payments) Trust" means the trust of that name, established on 29th January 1990 partly out of funds provided by the Secretary of State, for the benefit of certain persons suffering from haemophilia;

"the Macfarlane (Special Payments) (No. 2) Trust" means the trust of that name, established on 3rd May 1991 partly out of funds provided by the Secretary of State, for the benefit of certain persons suffering from haemophilia and other beneficiaries;

"the Macfarlane Trust" means the charitable trust, established partly out of funds provided by the Secretary of State to the Haemophilia Society, for the relief of poverty or distress among those suffering from haemophilia;

[¹⁸ "main phase employment and support allowance" means an employment and support allowance where the calculation of the amount payable in respect of the claimant includes a component under section 2(1)(b) or 4(2)(b) of the Welfare Reform Act [²³ except in Part 1 of Schedule 3];]

"maternity leave" means a period during which a woman is absent from work because she is pregnant or has given birth to a child, and at the end of which she has a right to return to work either under the terms of her contract of employment or under Part 8 of the Employment Rights Act 1996;

[⁸ "maximum rent" means the amount to which the eligible rent is restricted in a case where regulation 13 applies;]

[⁹ "maximum rent (LHA)" means the amount determined in accordance with regulation 13D;]

[²⁷ "MFET Limited" means the company limited by guarantee (number 7121661) of that name, established for the purpose in particular of making payments in accordance with arrangements made with the Secretary of State to persons who have acquired HIV as a result of treatment by the NHS with blood or blood products;]

[¹⁴ "mover" means a claimant who changes the dwelling occupied as the claimant's home from a dwelling in the area of the appropriate authority to a dwelling in the area of a second authority;]

"net earnings" means such earnings as are calculated in accordance with regulation 36 (calculation of net earnings of employed earners);

"net profit" means such profit as is calculated in accordance with regulation 38 (calculation of net profit of self-employed earners);

"the New Deal options" means the employment programmes specified in regulation 75(1)(a)(ii) of the Jobseeker's Allowance Regulations and the training scheme specified in regulation 75(1)(b)(ii) of those Regulations;

[¹⁵ "new dwelling" means, for the purposes of the definition of "second authority" and regulations 72C, 73C, 115 and 116, the dwelling to which a claimant has moved, or is about to move, which is or will be occupied as the claimant's new home;]

"non-dependant" has the meaning prescribed in regulation 3;

[⁸ "non-dependant deduction" means a deduction that is to be made under regulation 74 (non-dependant deductions);]

"occupational pension" means any pension or other periodical payment under an occupational pension scheme but does not include any discretionary payment out of a fund established for relieving hardship in particular cases;

"ordinary clothing or footwear" means clothing or footwear for normal daily use but does not include school uniforms or clothing or footwear used solely for sporting activities;

"owner" means–
  (a)   in relation to a dwelling in England and Wales, the person who, otherwise than as a mortgagee in possession, is for the time being entitled to dispose of the fee simple, whether or not with the consent of other joint owners;
  (b)   in relation to a dwelling in Scotland, the proprietor under udal tenure or the proprietor of the dominion utile or the tenant's or the lessee's interest in a long tenancy, a kindly tenancy, a lease registered or registerable under the Registration of Leases (Scotland) Act 1857 or the Land Registration (Scotland) Act 1979 or a tenant-at-will as defined in section 20(8) of that Act of 1979;
"partner" means–
  (a)   where a claimant is a member of a couple, the other member of that couple; or
  (b)   where a claimant is polygamously married to two or more members of his household, any such member;
"paternity leave" means a period of absence from work on leave by virtue of section 80A or 80B of the Employment Rights Act 1996;
"payment" includes part of a payment;
"pension fund holder" means with respect to a personal pension scheme or [³ an occupational pension scheme], the trustees, managers or scheme administrators, as the case may be, of the scheme [³] concerned;
"person affected" shall be construed in accordance with regulation 3 of the Decisions and Appeals Regulations;
"person on income support" means a person in receipt of income support;
[¹²]
[³ "personal pension scheme" means–
  (a)   a personal pension scheme as defined by section 1 of the Pension Schemes Act 1993;
  (b)   an annuity contract or trust scheme approved under section 620 or 621 of the Income and Corporation Taxes Act 1988 or a substituted contract within the meaning of section 622(3) of that Act which is treated as having become a registered pension scheme by virtue of paragraph 1(1)(f) of Schedule 36 to the Finance Act 2004;
  (c)   a personal pension scheme approved under Chapter 4 of Part 14 of the Income and Corporation Taxes Act 1988 which is treated as having become a registered pension scheme by virtue of paragraph 1(1)(g) of Schedule 36 to the Finance Act 2004;]
"policy of life insurance" means any instrument by which the payment of money is assured on death (except death by accident only) or the happening of any contingency dependent on human life, or any instrument evidencing a contract which is subject to payment of premiums for a term dependent on human life;
"polygamous marriage" means any marriage during the subsistence of which a party to it is married to more than one person and the ceremony of marriage took place under the law of a country which permits polygamy;
"the qualifying age for state pension credit" means (in accordance with section 1(2)(b) and (6) of the State Pension Credit Act 2002)–
  (a)   in the case of a woman, pensionable age; or
  (b)   in the case of a man, the age which is pensionable age in the case of a woman born on the same day as the man;
[²⁶ "public authority" includes any person certain of whose functions are functions of a public nature;]
[¹⁵ "qualifying contributory benefit" means–
  (a)   severe disablement allowance;
  (b)   incapacity benefit;]
    [¹⁷ (c) contributory employment and support allowance;]
[¹⁵ "qualifying income-related benefit" means–
  (a)   income support;
  (b)   income-based jobseeker's allowance;]

[¹⁸ (c) income-related employment and support allowance;]

"qualifying person" means a person in respect of whom payment has been made from the Fund, the Eileen Trust [²⁸, MFET Limited], the Skipton Fund or the London Bombings Relief Charitable Fund;

[⁹ "reckonable rent" means payments which a person is liable to make in respect of the dwelling which he occupies as his home, and which are eligible, or would, but for regulation 13, be eligible for housing benefit;]]]

[⁹ [¹⁰ [³¹ "registered housing association" means–

(a)   a private registered provider of social housing;

(b)   a housing association which is registered in a register maintained by the Welsh Ministers under Chapter 1 of Part 1 of the Housing Act 1996; or

(c)   a housing association which is registered by Scottish Ministers by virtue of section 57(3)(b) of the Housing (Scotland) Act 2001;]]]]

"relative" means a close relative, grandparent, grandchild, uncle, aunt, nephew or niece;

"relevant authority" means an authority administering housing benefit;

[⁹ "relevant information" means information or evidence forwarded to the relevant authority by an appropriate DWP office regarding a claim on which rent allowance may be awarded, which completes the transfer of all information or evidence held by the appropriate DWP office relating to that claim;]

"remunerative work" has the meaning prescribed in regulation 6 (remunerative work);

"rent" includes all those payments in respect of a dwelling specified in regulation 12(1);

[⁸ "Rent Officers Order" means the Rent Officers (Housing Benefit Functions) Order 1997 or, as the case may be, the Rent Officers (Housing Benefit Functions) (Scotland) Order 1997;]

[¹⁵ "second authority" means the authority to which a mover is liable to make payments for the new dwelling;]

[³]

[¹⁶]

"self-employed earner" is to be construed in accordance with section 2(1)(b) of the Act;

"self-employment route" means assistance in pursuing self-employed earner's employment whilst participating in–

(a)   an employment zone programme; or

(b)   a programme provided or other arrangements made pursuant to section 2 of the 1973 Act (functions of the Secretary of State) or section 2 of the Enterprise and New Towns (Scotland) Act 1990 (functions in relation to training for employment, etc.); *[or]*

[(c)   the Work for Your Benefit Pilot Scheme;]

[²⁶ "service user group" means a group of individuals that is consulted by or on behalf of–

(a)   a Health Board, Special Health Board or the Agency in consequence of a function under section 2B of the National Health Service (Scotland) Act 1978,

(b)   a landlord authority in consequence of a function under section 105 of the Housing Act 1985,

(c)   a public authority in consequence of a function under section 49A of the Disability Discrimination Act 1995,

(d)   a best value authority in consequence of a function under section 3 of the Local Government Act 1999,

(e)   a local authority landlord or registered social landlord in consequence of a function under section 53 of the Housing (Scotland) Act 2001,

(f)   a relevant English body or a relevant Welsh body in consequence of a function under section 242 of the National Health Service Act 2006,

(g)   a Local Health Board in consequence of a function under section 183 of the National Health Service (Wales) Act 2006,

(h)   the Commission or the Office of the Health Professions Adjudicator in consequence of a function under sections 4, 5, or 108 of the Health and Social Care Act 2008,

(i)   the regulator or a [³¹ private registered provider of social housing] in consequence of a function under sections 98, 193 or 196 of the Housing and Regeneration Act 2008, or

(j)   a public or local authority in Great Britain in consequence of a function conferred under any other enactment,

for the purposes of monitoring and advising on a policy of that body or authority which affects or may affect persons in the group, or of monitoring or advising on services provided by that body or authority which are used (or may potentially be used) by those persons;]

"shared ownership tenancy" means–

(a)   in relation to England and Wales, a [⁴ lease] granted on payment of a premium calculated by reference to a percentage of the value of the dwelling or the cost of providing it;

(b)   in relation to Scotland, an agreement by virtue of which the tenant of a dwelling of which he and the landlord are joint owners is the tenant in respect of the landlord's interest in the dwelling or by virtue of which the tenant has the right to purchase the dwelling or the whole or part of the landlord's interest therein;

"single claimant" means a claimant who neither has a partner nor is a lone parent;

[⁹ "single room rent" means the rent determined by a rent officer under paragraph 5 of Schedule 1 to the Rent Officers Order;]

"the Skipton Fund" means the ex-gratia payment scheme administered by the Skipton Fund Limited, incorporated on 25th March 2004, for the benefit of certain persons suffering from hepatitis C and other persons eligible for payment in accordance with the scheme's provisions;

[²⁷ "special account" means an account as defined for the purposes of Chapter 4A of Part 8 of the Jobseeker's Allowance Regulations or Chapter 5 of Part 10 of the Employment and Support Allowance Regulations;]

"sports award" means an award made by one of the Sports Councils named in section 23(2) of the National Lottery etc. Act 1993 out of sums allocated to it for distribution under that section;

[⁶ [²⁴]]

"student" has the meaning prescribed in regulation 53 (interpretation);

"subsistence allowance" means an allowance which an employment zone contractor has agreed to pay to a person who is participating in an employment zone programme;

"the Tax Credits Act" means the Tax Credits Act 2002;

"tax year" means a period beginning with 6th April in one year and ending with 5th April in the next;

"training allowance" means an allowance (whether by way of periodical grants or otherwise) payable–

(a)   out of public funds by a Government department or by or on behalf of the Secretary of State, [²⁵ Skills Development Scotland,] Scottish Enterprise or Highlands and Islands Enterprise, the [³⁵ Young People's Learning Agency for England, the Chief Executive of Skills Funding] or the [²⁰ Welsh Ministers];

(b)   to a person for his maintenance or in respect of a member of his family; and

(c)   for the period, or part of the period, during which he is following a course of training or instruction provided by, or in pursuance of arrangements made with, that department or approved by that department in relation to him or so provided or approved by or on behalf of the Secretary of State, [²⁵ Skills Development Scotland,] Scottish Enterprise or Highlands and Islands Enterprise or the [²⁰ Welsh Ministers],

but it does not include an allowance paid by any Government department to or in respect of a person by reason of the fact that he is following a course of full-time education, other than under arrangements made under section 2 of the 1973 Act or is training as a teacher;

"voluntary organisation" means a body, other than a public or local authority, the activities of which are carried on otherwise than for profit;

[²]
[²¹ "war disablement pension" means any retired pay or pension or allowance payable in respect of disablement under an instrument specified in section 639(2) of the Income Tax (Earnings and Pensions) Act 2003;

"war pension" means a war disablement pension, a war widow's pension or a war widower's pension;

"war widow's pension" means any pension or allowance payable to a woman as a widow under an instrument specified in section 639(2) of the Income Tax (Earnings and Pensions) Act 2003 in respect of the death or disablement of any person;

"war widower's pension" means any pension or allowance payable to a man as a widower or to a surviving civil partner under an instrument specified in section 639(2) of the Income Tax (Earnings and Pensions) Act 2003 in respect of the death or disablement of any person;]

"water charges" means–

(a)   as respects England and Wales, any water and sewerage charges under Chapter 1 of Part 5 of the Water Industry Act 1991,

(b)   as respects Scotland, any water and sewerage charges established by Scottish Water under a charges scheme made under section 29A of the Water Industry (Scotland) Act 2002

in so far as such charges are in respect of the dwelling which a person occupies as his home;

[¹⁸ "Welfare Reform Act" means the Welfare Reform Act 2007;]

[*"the Work for Your Benefit Pilot Scheme" means a scheme within section 17A(1) of the Jobseekers Act 1995 known by that name and provided pursuant to arrangements made by the Secretary of State that is designed to assist claimants to obtain employment, including self-employment, and which includes for any individual work experience and job search;*]

"working tax credit" means a working tax credit under section 10 of the Tax Credits Act;

"Working Tax Credit Regulations" means the Working Tax Credit (Entitlement and Maximum Rate) Regulations 2002;

[⁸ "young individual" means a single claimant who has not attained the age of 25 years, but does not include such a claimant–

(a)   whose landlord is a registered housing association;

(b)   who has not attained the age of 22 years and has ceased to be the subject of a care order made pursuant to section 31(1)(a) of the Children Act 1989 which had previously been made in respect to him either–

(i)   after he attained the age of 16 years; or

(ii)   before he attained the age of 16 years, but had continued after he attained that age;

(c)   who has not attained the age of 22 years and was formerly provided with accommodation under section 20 of the Children Act 1989;

(d)   who has not attained the age of 22 years and has ceased to be subject to a supervision requirement by a children's hearing under section 70 of the Children (Scotland) Act 1995 ("the 1995 Act") made in respect of him which had continued after he attained the age of 16 years, other than a case where–

(i)   the ground of referral was based on the sole condition as to the need for compulsory measures of care specified in section 52(1)(i) of the 1995 Act (commission of offences by child); or

(ii)   he was required by virtue of the supervision requirement to reside with a parent or guardian of his within the meaning of the 1995 Act, or with a friend or relative of his or of his parent or guardian;

(e)   who has not attained the age of 22 years and has ceased to be a child in relation to whom the parental rights and responsibilities were transferred to a local authority under a parental responsibilities order made in accordance with section

86 of the 1995 Act or treated as so vested in accordance with paragraph 3 of Schedule 3 to that Act, either–
(i)   after he attained the age of 16 years; or
(ii)   before he attained the age of 16 years, but had continued after he attained that age; or
(f)   who has not attained the age of 22 years and has ceased to be provided with accommodation by a local authority under section 25 of the 1995 Act where he has previously been provided with accommodation by the authority under that provision either–
(i)   after he attained the age of 16 years; or
(ii)   before he attained the age of 16 years, but had continued to be in such accommodation after he attained that age;]
"young person" has the meaning prescribed in regulation 19(1)(persons of prescribed description).

(2)   References in these Regulations to a person who is liable to make payments shall include references to a person who is treated as so liable under regulation 8 (circumstances in which a person is to be treated as liable to make payments in respect of a dwelling).

(3)   For the purposes of these Regulations, a person is on an income-based jobseeker's allowance on any day in respect of which an income-based jobseeker's allowance is payable to him and on any day–
(a)   in respect of which he satisfies the conditions for entitlement to an income-based jobseeker's allowance but where the allowance is not paid in accordance with [30 regulation 27A of the Jobseeker's Allowance Regulations or] section 19 or 20A *[or regulations made under section 17A]* of the Jobseekers Act (circumstances in which a jobseeker's allowance is not payable); or
(b)   which is a waiting day for the purposes of paragraph 4 of Schedule 1 to that Act and which falls immediately before a day in respect of which an income-based jobseeker's allowance is payable to him or would be payable to him but for [30 regulation 27A of the Jobseeker's Allowance Regulations or] section 19 or 20A *[or regulations made under section 17A]* of that Act; or
(c)   in respect of which he is a member of a joint-claim couple for the purposes of the Jobseekers Act and no joint-claim jobseeker's allowance is payable in respect of that couple as a consequence of either member of that couple being subject to sanctions for the purposes of section 20A of that Act; or
(d)   in respect of which an income-based jobseeker's allowance or a joint-claim jobseeker's allowance would be payable but for a restriction imposed pursuant to [29] [32 section 6B, 7, 8 or 9] of the Social Security Fraud Act 2001 (loss of benefit provisions).

[18 (3A)   For the purposes of these Regulations, a person is on an income-related employment and support allowance on any day in respect of which an income-related employment and support allowance is payable to him and on any day–
(a)   in respect of which he satisfies the conditions for entitlement to an income-related employment and support allowance but where the allowance is not paid in accordance with section 18 of the Welfare Reform Act (disqualification); or
(b)   which is a waiting day for the purposes of paragraph 2 of Schedule 2 to that Act and which falls immediately before a day in respect of which an income-related employment and support allowance is payable to him or would be payable to him but for section 18 of that Act.]

(4)   For the purposes of these Regulations, the following shall be treated as included in a dwelling–
(a)   subject to sub-paragraphs (b) to (d) any land (whether or not occupied by a structure) which is used for the purposes of occupying a dwelling as a home where either–
(i)   the occupier of the dwelling acquired simultaneously the right to use the land and the right to occupy the dwelling, and, in the case of a person

liable to pay rent for his dwelling, he could not have occupied that dwelling without also acquiring the right to use the land; or

(ii)   the occupier of the dwelling has made or is making all reasonable efforts to terminate his liability to make payments in respect of the land;

(b)   where the dwelling is a caravan or mobile home, such of the land on which it stands as is used for the purposes of the dwelling;

(c)   where the dwelling is a houseboat, the land used for the purposes of mooring it;

(d)   where in Scotland, the dwelling is situated on or pertains to a croft within the meaning of section 3(1) of the Crofters (Scotland) Act 1993, the croft land on which it is situated or to which it pertains.

Modifications

Definitions were substituted and inserted by reg 4(1) Housing Benefit (Local Housing Allowance and Information Sharing) Amendment Regulations 2007 SI No.2868, as amended by reg 4(3) of SI 2008 No.586, as from 7 April 2008, save that for a person to whom reg 1(5) of those regulations applied (see p1231), the amendments came into force on the day on or after 7 April 2008 when the first of the events specified in reg 1(6) applied to her/him, or on 6 April 2009 if none had before that date.

Definition of "eligible rent" modified and definition of "maximum rent (standard local rate)" inserted by Sch 10 para 2 (see p586). These apply only to former Pathfinder Authorities who administered the pilot local housing allowance scheme.

References to "step-parent", step-children and the various in-laws in the definition of "close relative" are modified by s246 Civil Partnership Act 2004 (see p1148) and Art 3 and Sch para 24 to SI 2005 No.3137 (see p1195).

Reg 2(1) and (3) is modified by regs 13 and 19 Jobseeker's Allowance (Work for Your Benefit Pilot Scheme) Regulations 2010 SI No.1222 (see p1247) as from 22 November 2010 but only for those ordinarily resident in a pilot area or whose address for payment of JSA is located within such an area. The modifications are shown in italics above. They cease to have effect on 21 November 2013.

Amendments

1.   Inserted by Art 2(2) of SI 2006 No 2968 as from 20.12.06.
2.   Omitted by Reg 4(a) of SI 2007 No 1619 as from 3.7.07.
3.   Amended by reg 4(2) of SI 2007 No 1749 as from 16.7.07.
4.   Amended by reg 2(2) of SI 2007 No 1356 as from 1.10.07.
5.   Amended by Art 8(2) of SI 2007 No 2538 as from 1.10.07.
6.   Inserted by reg 11(2) of SI 2007 No 2618 as from 1.10.07.
7.   Revoked by reg 2 and the Sch of SI 2007 No 2618 as from 1.10.07.
8.   Substituted by reg 4(1) of SI 2007 No 2868 as from 7.4.08 (or if reg 1(5) of that SI applies, on the day on or after 7.4.08 when the first of the events specified in reg 1(6) applies, or from 6.4.09 if none have before that date).
9.   Inserted by reg 4(1) of SI 2007 No 2868, as amended by reg 4(3) of SI 2008 No 586, as from 7.4.08 (or if reg 1(5) of that SI applies, on the day on or after 7.4.08 when the first of the events specified in reg 1(6) applies, or from 6.4.09 if none have before that date).
10.   Substituted by reg 4(3) of SI 2008 No 586 as from 7.4.08.
11.   Omitted by reg 6(2) of SI 2008 No 698 as from 14.4.08.
12.   Omitted by reg 3(2) of SI 2008 No 1042 as from 19.5.08.
13.   Omitted by reg 2(2) of SI 2008 No 2299 as from 1.10.08.
14.   Substituted by reg 4(2) of SI 2008 No 959 as from 6.10.08.
15.   Inserted by reg 4(2) of SI 2008 No 959 as from 6.10.08.
16.   Omitted by reg 4(2) of SI 2008 No 959 as from 6.10.08.
17.   Amended by reg 5(2) of SI 2008 No 1082, as amended by reg 27 of SI 2008 No 2428, as from 27.10.08.
18.   Inserted by reg 5(2) of SI 2008 No 1082, as amended by reg 27 of SI 2008 No 2428, as from 27.10.08.
19.   Omitted by reg 6(2) of SI 2008 No 2767 as from 17.11.08.
20.   Amended by reg 5(2) of SI 2008 No 3157 as from 5.1.09.
21.   Inserted by reg 5(2) of SI 2008 No 3157 as from 5.1.09.
22.   Inserted by reg 6(1)(a) of SI 2009 No 583 as from 6.4.09.
23.   Amended by reg 6(2)(b) of SI 2009 No 583 as from 1.4.09 (6.4.09 where rent payable weekly or at intervals of a week).
24.   Omitted by reg 6(2)(c) of SI 2009 No 583 as from 6.4.09.
25.   Amended by reg 6(3)(a) of SI 2009 No 683 as from 6.4.09.
26.   Inserted by reg 6(2) of SI 2009 No 2655 as from 2.11.09.
27.   Inserted by reg 8(2) of SI 2010 No 641 as from 1.4.10 (5.4.10 where rent payable weekly or in multiples of a week).

28. Amended by reg 8(3) of SI 2010 No 641 as from 1.4.10 (5.4.10 where rent payable weekly or in multiples of a week).

29. Amended by reg 8 of SI 2010 No 424 as from 2.4.10 (the first day of the benefit week on or after 22.3.10 so far as it relates to a person who is subject to a restriction under section 62 or 63 of the Child Support, Pensions and Social Security Act 2000).

30. Amended by reg 4(1)(a) and (2) of SI 2010 No 509 as from 6.4.10.

31. Amended by Art 4 and Sch 1 para 51 of SI 2010 No 671 as from 1.4.10.

32. Amended by reg 4 of SI 2010 No 1160 as from 1.4.10.

33. Inserted by reg 27 and Sch 5 para 1(2) of SI 2010 No 1907 as amended by reg 15 of SI 2010 No 2430 as from 1.10.10.

34. Substituted by Arts 2 and 20 of SI 2010 No 1881 as from 1.10.10.

35. Amended by Art 14(2) of SI 2010 No 1941 as from 1.9.10.

36. Substituted by reg 2(2) of SI 2010 No 2449 as from 1.11.10.

Definition

"dwelling" – see s137(1) SSCBA.

Analysis

Paragraph (1): General definitions

"benefit week". In general, entitlement to HB accrues on a weekly basis, and by virtue of this definition, each week of entitlement runs from Monday to Sunday.

"change of dwelling" is a change of dwelling occupied by a claimant, during an award of HB, to a dwelling in respect of which the authority may make a rent allowance – eg, to a housing association or private tenancy. The phrase is relevant for the local housing allowance scheme and the local reference rent scheme for rent restriction.

"close relative". The term "couple" is defined later in this regulation by reference to s137 SSCBA. See also the modifications cited above.

"concessionary payment". These include, for example, extra statutory payments made during a strike.

"*converted employment and support allowance*". If a claimant is entitled to converted ESA, or in specified circumstances is appealing a conversion decision, s/he may be entitled to a protected amount of HB (and CTB) – a transitional addition. See regs 22(f) and 23(g) and Sch 3 Parts 7 and 8.

"co-ownership scheme". The term "housing association" is defined later in the regulation; for land included with a "dwelling", see reg 2(4). The same wording was used in the 1985 HB Regs. A case based on those regs held that equity sharing schemes run by housing associations under the Housing Corporation's model rules, whereby on leaving the scheme after a minimum period of 12 months a participant would receive an equity share payment based on the increased value of the premises, were "co-ownership schemes": *R v Birmingham CC HBRB ex p Ellery* [1989] 21 HLR 398, QBD.

"couple". The definition is the same as in s137 SSCBA (see p19).

"crown tenant". See s137(1) SSCBA on p21 for "dwelling". There is a separate scheme of relief for Crown tenants, but Crown tenants entitled to IS, income-based JSA, income-related ESA or PC may be able to claim help with their 'rent' under the housing costs rules for those benefits: see Sch 3 para 17(1)(e) Income Support (General) Regulations 1987, Sch 2 para 16(1)(e) Jobseeker's Allowance Regulations 1996, Sch 6 para 18(1)(e) Employment and Support Allowance Regulations 2008 and Sch 2 para 13(1)(e) State Pension Credit Regulations 2002.

"earnings". See reg 35, which defines "earnings" for employees, and reg 37 for self-employed people.

"eligible rent". See the regulations cited.

"employed earner". SSCBA s2(1)(a) defines this as "a person who is gainfully employed in Great Britain either under a contract of service, or in an office (including elective office) with general earnings".

"the Fund" refers to money made available by the government from a trust set up by the relevant Secretary of State for persons infected (including infected partners and children) with HIV through NHS blood transfusions or tissue transfers.

"hostel". This definition serves two purposes. First, hostels receive special treatment under the rent restrictions legislation: see regs 13(5)(d)(ii) and 14(2)(a). Second, by reg 4, inhabitants of hostels are exempt from the "NINO requirement" imposed by s1(1A) SSAA.

The criteria that must be fulfilled if a building is to qualify as a "hostel" are:

(1) The accommodation must be for "persons generally or for a class of persons". In this context, in connection with the second criterion, this means that there must be a degree of multiple occupancy. However, there is no need for the persons to have any particular need (eg, treatment for addiction) although this will be a feature of many of the dwellings that qualify.

(2) It must provide "domestic accommodation, otherwise than in separate and self-contained premises". This appears to require that the facilities required for the basic functions of life must be shared to some degree. At minimum, it is suggested, to be "separate and self-contained" units would have to have facilities for eating, sleeping, cooking and washing.

(3)   There must either be board provided or facilities for the preparation of food adequate to the needs of the people accommodated, or both.

(4)   The condition in sub-para (b) as to ownership or management must be fulfilled in one of three ways. First, under head (i), a building qualifies if it is owned *or* managed (but not necessarily both) by a "registered housing association" (also defined in reg 2(1)).

Alternatively, under head (ii) a building will qualify if it is operated other than on a commercial basis. The caselaw set out in the Analysis to reg 9(1)(a) (see p252) may assist, although the running of the accommodation as a whole must be examined rather than just the agreement with the individual tenant in question. It must also be funded in whole or in part by one of the relevant public bodies listed. It would appear that anything more than minimal funding would suffice, so a modest local authority grant would allow the dwelling to qualify.

Finally, under head (iii), a building qualifies if it is managed by a "voluntary organisation" (defined later in this regulation) or a charity, by which is presumably meant a registered charity. It must also provide suitable "care, support or supervision" to allow inhabitants "to be "rehabilitated or resettled" into the community. These are general words that should be given a wide meaning. They carry no pejorative implication and so the newly disabled, for example, require rehabilitation or resettlement just as do those with addictions.

(5)   The building cannot be a "care home", "independent hospital" or an "Abbeyfield Home" (all defined elsewhere in this regulation).

"Housing Act functions". The definition says that this has the same meaning as in section 136(1) SSAA 1992. However, that section was repealed with effect from 1 April 1997 by Part VI of Sch 19 to the Housing Act 1996. Relying on s17(2)(a) Interpretation Act 1978, the correct reference should presumably be to s122 Housing Act 1996 (on p1122).

"housing association". By s1(1) Housing Associations Act 1985, this means a "society, body of trustees or a company (a) which is established for the purposes of, or amongst whose objects and powers are included, those of providing, constructing, improving or managing, or facilitating or encouraging the construction or improvement of, housing accommodation, and (b) which does not trade for profit or whose constitution or rules prohibit the issue of capital with interest or dividend exceeding such rate as may be prescribed by the treasury, whether with or without differentiation between share and loan capital". See also the definition of "registered housing association" below.

"linked person". The definition is relevant for determining whether rent restrictions can be delayed under reg 12D(3) or (5) or reg 13ZA.

"local housing allowance". Where reg 12D applies, HB can be calculated by reference to the appropriate local housing allowance, here defined as an allowance determined in accordance with para 2 Sch 3B Rent Officers Order. "Rent Officers Order" is defined later in this regulation.

"lone parent". "Partner" is defined later in this regulation. Part 4 of the Regs deals with membership of a family: "young person" is defined in reg 19; reg 20, deals with circumstances in which an adult is treated as "responsible" for a child or young person; reg 21 with those in which persons are to be treated as sharing a household. See also p21 for more on the meaning of household.

"long tenancy". HB is not payable in respect of payments made under a long tenancy, other than where this is a shared ownership tenancy: reg 12(2)(a). Note that reg 12(2)(a) does not exclude payments by someone entitled to dispose of the leasehold interest under a long lease – a formulation similar to that for excepting payment by an owner under reg 12(2)(c). If rent is payable by the claimant under, for example, an assured shorthold tenancy and not under the long leasehold interest, HB might be payable in respect of the rent: *CR v Wycombe DC* [2009] UKUT 19 (AAC). However, consideration will need to be given to whether the claimant is to be treated as not liable to pay rent under reg 9 (see p249) and to whether any of the rental income belongs to the claimant and is to be taken into account. A "term of years certain" means that the length of the lease may be ascertained and that it is intended to last for more than 21 years, subject to the potential terminating factors here set out. The term will be set out in the lease. "Re-entry" is a landlord's remedy for the breach of a condition in a lease which can no longer be exercised without a court order while someone is lawfully residing in the dwelling concerned: see Protection from Eviction Act 1977. "Forfeiture" is a similarly restricted remedy for non-payment of rent. A tenancy for life takes effect as a tenancy for 90 years in England and Wales by virtue of s149(6) Law of Property Act 1925, and so is a "long tenancy" for HB purposes: *CH 2743/2003* para 8 and *CH 2258/2004* para 16.

An oral agreement cannot create a long tenancy. Moreover, an agreement in writing (but not by deed) will not be enough to create a long tenancy, as ss52 and 53 Law of Property Act 1925 require leases in excess of three years to be made by deed. Accordingly, a written agreement purporting to create a long tenancy but which was not made by deed (ie, under seal), is not a "tenancy granted" for a term in excess of 21 years and is not, therefore, a long tenancy: *R(H) 3/07*.

The term "irritancy", used in the definition, is a Scots law remedy – the landlord's right to end the lease and repossess the property if certain terms of the lease are broken. "lease for a term fixed by law . . . perpetual renewal" refers to the provisions of s145 and Sch 15 Law of Property Act 1925 which convert perpetually renewable leases into leases lasting for a term of 2,000 years but such leases will not count as long tenancies if they are sub-leases and the person sub-letting does not have a long tenancy her/himself.

"main phase employment and support allowance". The components referred to in the definition are the support component and the work-related activity component.

"maximum rent" is the amount to which the eligible rent is restricted under regs 12C, 13 and 14 (referred to as the "local reference rent" rules).

"maximum rent (LHA)" is the amount to which eligible rent is restricted under regs 12D, 13C and 13D (referred to as the "local housing allowance" rules).

"mover", "new dwelling", "qualifying contributory benefit","qualifying income-related benefit" and *"second authority"* are relevant to the rules for extended payments of HB in regs 72 to 73D.

"the New Deal Options". The New Deal is a government's programme for tackling long-term unemployment and exclusion from the labour market and reducing welfare dependency. It consists of a number of different schemes to promote work among such groups.

The relevant parts of reg 75 JSA Regs 1996 refer to the following schemes.

(1)   The Self-Employed Employment Option.
(2)   The Voluntary Sector Option.
(3)   The Environment Task Force Option.
(4)   The Community Task Force.
(5)   The Full-Time Education and Training Option.

The significance of this definition relates to the treatment of payments made by the Secretary of State: see Sch 5 para 13.

"non-dependant" and *"non-dependant deduction"*. Reg 74 provides that the maximum amount of HB payable to a claimant shall be reduced by fixed amounts if s/he lives with certain "non-dependants".

"owner". Owners are excluded from HB by virtue of reg 12(2)(c). The definition of "owner" in reg 2(1) also applies to cognate expressions such as "own", "owned" and "ownership" elsewhere in the HB Regs: *CH 1278/2003* para 13; *CH 3616/2003* para 7. Reg 12(2)(c) renders any payments by an "owner" ineligible for HB. The mortgagee is the lending institution which lends the person money on mortgage to buy the home. The other persons who have the right to sell or otherwise dispose of the dwelling should be listed on the title deeds or on the office copies relating to the title in the property which are held at the Land Registry. The inclusion in this definition of persons who cannot sell without consent is designed to overturn the decision in *R v Sedgemoor DC HBRB ex p Weadon* [1986] 18 HLR 355, QBD. That decision had held that a co-owner was able to get HB for rent paid to the other owners in respect of her occupation of the dwelling.

In *R(H) 8/07*, the claimant was the registered proprietor of the freehold of a property. He occupied a flat in it, and paid rent to the person to whom he had granted a long lease of it. He claimed HB in respect of his liability for that rent. Commissioner Turnbull said that although, for most practical purposes, the long leaseholder, rather than the claimant, would be regarded as the "owner" of the flat, "owner" for HB purposes is defined by reference to the ability to dispose of the fee simple, and not by reference to the ability to dispose of any long leasehold interest in it which may have been granted. The claimant here had the right to dispose of the fee simple. Although the definition applies "unless the context otherwise requires", it was not possible to conclude that the context of what is now reg 12(2)(c) HB Regs requires that, where a long leasehold interest has been granted at a low rent, the person with the ability to dispose of that leasehold interest, rather than the person who is entitled to dispose of the freehold, is the owner.

In *R v Sheffield CC HBRB ex p Smith* [1994] 28 HLR 36 at 47-8, QBD, Blackburne J suggested that if a person has a joint beneficial interest giving her/him a right to a share in the proceeds of sale, it does not follow that s/he is a person "for the time being, entitled to dispose of the fee simple". If this is right, it appears from his rejection of the argument for the respondents (at 46-7) that it will probably be necessary to show that the individual claimant has a specific power to dispose of the legal title to the property.

In *Fairbank v Lambeth Magistrates' Court* [2003] HLR 62 the claimant asserted that he held a property as trustee for his father. The court ruled that it was not necessary for him to come within the definition of "owner" to be guilty of the offence with which he was charged but went on to hold that a claimant who merely needs to consult beneficiaries under a trust of land is an "owner" for the purposes of reg 2(1). That finding was technically *obiter* but is fully reasoned and was followed by Commissioner Fellner in *R(H) 7/05* paras 35-41 and Commissioner Mesher in *CH 1278/2003* para 16.

The claimant in *R(H) 7/05* appealed against the decision of the commissioner but his appeal was rejected by the Court of Appeal in *Burton v New Forest District Council* [2004] EWCA Civ 1510, 12 November, reported as *R(H) 7/05*. The commissioner had decided that the claimant came within the definition of "owner" – and was thus disqualified from receiving HB by virtue of reg 10(2)(c) HB regs 1987 (now reg 12(2)(c) HB Regs) – because the claimant was the registered proprietor of the property (on the Land Charges Register), and so by virtue of s20(1) Land Registration Act 1925 was "entitled to dispose of the fee simple" without the consent of other joint owners, regardless of whether so selling the property would give rise to a breach of trust.

In rejecting the further appeal, the Court of Appeal held that there is no true distinction between the words "entitled to dispose of the fee simple" in reg 2(1)(a) and being "able" to dispose of the fee simple under s20(1) LRA 1925. Given this, it was quite impossible to construe the term "owner" in reg 2(1) as meaning exclusively a beneficial owner. Because his name remained on the title at the Land Registry as sole owner with title absolute, he was, as a matter of law, entitled to dispose of the fee simple at any point up until the Land Registry was rectified. But until any such rectification, the claimant was the "owner" and not entitled to any HB. Moreover, in the Court of Appeal's view, nothing in the terms of reg 7 HB Regs 1987 (now reg 9 HB Regs) acted to alter this conclusion.

In *CH 1278/2003*, the commissioner commented that administrators of estates may also fall within the definition since they have a right to dispose of the fee simple: paras 18-19.

It appears that local authorities are having to deal with such unorthodox arrangements for the holding of property with increasing frequency. Rather than grapple with the complexities as to whether the claimant is an "owner", some are simply finding that the arrangements fall foul of the provisions in reg 9(1). However, it is important that authorities do not make an assumption of non-commerciality or contrivance simply on the basis of the unusual nature of the arrangement. Such arrangements for the holding of property are often the reflection of the values of religious or ethnic groups, and caution will be required to ensure that the relevant tests are met. See the Analysis to reg 9 on p252 for more details.

It is important to bear in mind that the definition of "owner" cannot apply to a person who is a leaseholder, as opposed to a freeholder, in England and Wales: *CH 296/2003* para 29. Long tenancy holders (defined above) are excluded from HB by virtue of reg 12(2)(a).

"Udal tenure" is a form of land holding only found in the Orkney and Shetland Islands. The "proprietor of the dominium utile" is the person with the right to use and occupy the land and who now or in the past, is or would have been liable to pay feu duty; again, this should be apparent from the title deeds. "Long tenancy" is defined above. "Registered" leases are registered at the Register of Sasines in Register House, Edinburgh. "Registrable" leases, in Scotland, are those: (1) executed in probative writing; and (2) lasting for a period of more than 20 years, or for a shorter period if there is an obligation to renew the lease so that it will actually endure for a period exceeding that number of years.

"partner". Couples are defined above and by s137(1) SSCBA (see p19).

"person on income support". *R v South Ribble DC HBRB ex p Hamilton* [2000] 33 HLR 102, CA confirmed that the definition of "person on income support" must be read as a person lawfully in receipt of IS.

Note that the definition of person "on an income-based jobseeker's allowance" is in reg 2(3) and of person "on an income-related employment and support allowance" is in reg 2(3A).

"polygamous marriage". This only covers marriages that are lawful where and when they occur. An authority faced with a problem as to the validity of a polygamous marriage should seek expert advice from a specialist lawyer.

"the qualifying age for state pension credit". This age is relevant in determining whether the HB Regs or the HB(SPC) Regs apply to a claimant: reg 5. The age at which someone qualifies for state pension credit (PC) is linked to pensionable age for a woman.

The process of equalising men's and women's pension ages began on 6 April 2010. From that date, women's pension age begins to rise, as does the qualifying age for pension credit (PC). The qualifying age for PC for a woman is the minimum age she can receive state retirement pension. The qualifying age for PC for a man is the minimum age a woman born on the same day as him can receive state retirement pension. So for both men and women, the qualifying age for PC is:

(1)   60, if s/he was born before 6 April 1950;

(2)   an age from 60 and one month to 64 and 11 months depending on her/his date of birth, if s/he was born on or after 6 April 1950 but before 6 April 1955; *or*

(3)   65, if s/he was born on or after 6 April 1955.

Consequently, the rules in the Housing Benefit (Persons who have attained the qualifying age for state pension credit) Regulations 2006 (SI No.214) and the Council Tax Benefit (Persons who have attained the qualifying age for state pension credit) Regulations 2006 (SI No.216) will apply to individual claimants at different ages. For claimants born on or after 6 April 1950 but before 6 April 1955, there is a helpful table, setting out the relevant birth dates and pension ages, in an Appendix to CPAG's *Welfare Benefits and Tax Credits Handbook*.

Once pensionable age is 65 for both men and women, the age for both will then rise to 68 between 2024 and 2046. Note that the Government has indicated that a rise to age 66 may begin earlier.

"qualifying person". "The Fund", "the Eileen Trust", "MFET Ltd", "the Skipton Fund" and the "London Bombings Relief Charitable Fund" are all defined elsewhere in this regulation. The significance of the term is in respect of certain income and capital disregards.

"registered housing association". The definition is relevant when determining whether a claimant's eligible rent for HB purposes is to be restricted under any of the three rent restriction schemes, for which see the general Note on Part 3 on p297 and regs 12C and 12D. The definition was substituted from 1 April 2010 as a consequence of changes to the registration process for providers of social housing in England. Such providers are covered by para (a). Sections 68-71 Housing and Regeneration Act 2008 define social housing as low cost rental accommodation (ie, accommodation that is available to rent at below the market rate) and low cost ownership accommodation (ie, accommodation occupied or made available to occupy in accordance with shared ownership or equity percentage arrangements or shared ownership trusts). Rental and ownership accommodation are only social housing if the accommodation is available to people whose needs are not adequately served by the

commercial housing market. A "registered provider of social housing" is a person or body registered by the the Office for Tenants and Social Landlords (the Regulator of Social Housing). Private registered providers can be either non-profit or profit-making.

In Wales and Scotland, there was no change to the registration process for housing associations. A registered housing association is one registered in a register maintained by the Welsh Ministers or the Scottish Ministers respectively.

"relative". "Close relative" is defined earlier in this regulation. Note that neither definition covers half-sisters and brothers.

"self-employed earner". SSCBA s2(1)(b) defines this as "a person who is gainfully employed in Great Britain otherwise than in employed earner's employment (whether or not he is also employed in such employment)". For "employed earner's employment", see above.

"service user group". The definition is relevant for certain disregards of expenses and notional expenses as income.

"shared ownership tenancy". For "dwelling", see SSCBA s137(1) (p21) and reg 2(4). For "owner", see above.

"special account". The definition is relevant for an income disregard under Sch 5 para 58.

"sports award". Since 1999, awards made by the Sports Councils have been ignored for benefit purposes.

"training allowance". Under the New Deal (Miscellaneous Provisions) Order 1998 and the New Deal (Miscellaneous Provisions) Order 2001, payments to a trainee under the training options of the New Deal are to be treated as paid under s2 Employment and Training Act 1973 and therefore fall within the definition of "training allowance" for HB purposes.

"voluntary organisation". In determining whether activities are "carried on otherwise than for profit" it is relevant to look not simply at the constitution of the body but at its actual activities: *Salford CC v PF* [2009] UKUT 150 (AAC).

"young individual". Reg 13(5) requires that where the claimant is a "young individual" as defined here and the rent officer has supplied the authority with a single room rent, the maximum rent will be based on that figure. Reg 13D(2)(a) specifies the category of dwelling normally applicable to a "young individual" which in turn sets the maximum rent (LHA) for such a claimant under the "local housing allowance" rules.

For "registered housing association", see above.

In England and Wales, a single claimant under 22 is not a "young individual" if s/he was the subject of a care order made under s31(l)(a) Children Act 1989 which was made after s/he turned 16 or made before age 16 but continued after that age. For this exemption to apply, the court must have made an order putting the child in the care of a designated authority. A single claimant is also not a "young individual" in England and Wales if s/he is under 22 years and was formerly provided with accommodation under s20 Children Act 1989. This requires social services departments to provide accommodation to children (anyone aged under 18 years) in need. It also permits social services to provide accommodation to any child within its area – eg, if it considers that doing so would safeguard or promote the child's welfare.

In Scotland a single claimant under 22 is not a "young individual" if parental rights were assumed by a local authority under s86 Children (Scotland) Act 1995 or s/he was provided with accommodation by a local authority under s25 of that Act, in both cases after s/he turned 16 or before age 16 but continuing after that age. A single claimant under 22 is also not a "young individual" if s/he was subject to a supervision requirement under s70 Children (Scotland) Act 1995 ("provided that the supervision requirement was not made as a result of the child having committed an offence"). For this exemption to apply the authority should be satisfied that the child was living away from her/his normal place of residence but not with friends or relatives.

Paragraph (2)

This confirms that persons liable to make payments include those deemed to be so liable under reg 8.

Paragraph (3)

Someone is considered to be on income-based JSA not only on any day in respect of which it is payable to her/him, but also in respect of the following.

(1)   Days on which the claimant is entitled to income-based (or joint-claim) JSA but is disqualified from payment under reg 27A Jobseeker's Allowance Regulations 1996 SI No.207 (JSA Regs) or ss19 or 20A Jobseekers Act 1995 (JSA 1995) – ie, because s/he failed to attend an interview as required or has been "sanctioned", for example, for failing to apply for a job or for losing a job through misconduct. See the commentary in the latest edition of *Social Security Legislation* Vol II for further details.

(2)   So-called "waiting days". Under Sch 1 para 4 JSA 1995, a claimant is generally not entitled to JSA for the first three days of any jobseeking period ("waiting days"). If the waiting days immediately precede a day for which income-based JSA is payable (or would be payable were it not for a sanction under reg 27A JSA Regs or ss19 or 20A JSA 1995, for which see above), the claimant is entitled to maximum HB and CTB for the waiting days.

(3)   Where income-based (or joint-claim) JSA would be payable but for the loss of JSA due the operation of the provisions for loss of benefit on repeat convictions for benefit fraud.

Paragraph (3A)

Someone is considered to be on income-related ESA not only on any day in respect of which it is payable to her/him, but also in respect of the following:

(1)   Days on which the claimant is entitled to income-related ESA but is disqualified from payment under s18 Welfare Reform Act 2007 (WRA 2007) – ie, because s/he has limited capability for work through misconduct or for failing without good cause to follow medical advice or where s/he has failed without good cause to observe "prescribed rules of behaviour".

(2)   So called "waiting days". Under Sch 2 para 2 WRA 2007 and reg 144 Employment and Support Allowance Regulations 2008 SI No.794, a claimant is generally not entitled to ESA for the first three days of any "period of limited capability for work".

Paragraph (4)

This does not define the term "dwelling" exclusively: the full definition is in s137 SSCBA (see p21). This paragraph merely lists certain areas of land which are to be treated as part of a dwelling. The main application will be to include the land in capital disregarded under Sch 6 para 1. The basic aim is to avoid the payment of HB in respect of commercially used land.

Sub-para (a) requires that land must be used "for the purposes of occupying the dwelling as a home" as opposed to occupation for business or other purposes. Additionally, if the occupier obtained the use of the land and the dwelling at the same time, it must not have been possible for her/him to obtain the use of the one without the other. Otherwise, if the use of the land and the dwelling were obtained at different times, or the dwelling could have been occupied without the land, s/he must have made or be making "all reasonable efforts" to get rid of the liability for the land before it can be treated as part of the dwelling for HB purposes.

Sub-paras (b) and (c) include land under a caravan or mobile home or where a houseboat is moored in the definition of "dwelling". Note *CH 318/2005* which, although not relying on this provision, decided that a narrowboat can constitute a "dwelling" for the purposes of the HB scheme.

Sub-para (d). The Crofters (Scotland) Act 1993 s3(1) sets out the conditions which must be complied with before land will count as a "croft". First, it must be situated in one of the former "crofting counties". These are "Argyll, Caithness, Inverness, Orkney, Ross and Cromarty, Sutherland and Zetland". Second, the land must amount to a "holding" in terms of s35 Agricultural Holdings Act 1908 – ie, it must be pastoral or agricultural land, a mixture of both, or a market garden; which is not let to the tenant in the capacity of the landlord's employee. Finally, these "holdings" must have been covered by the Landholders Acts prior to 1955 or be registered as crofts (on application to the Land Court) under s4 of the 1955 Act or constitue a croft by direction of the Secretary of State under s2(1) The Crofters (Scotland) Act 1961. "Registerable" holdings are those for which the annual rent does not exceed £50, or of which the area does not exceed 50 acres. The Landholders Acts applied to land of similar description.

Definition of non-dependant

3.–(1)   In these Regulations, ''non-dependant'' means any person, except someone to whom paragraph (2) applies, who normally resides with a claimant or with whom a claimant normally resides.

(2)   This paragraph applies to–

(a)   any member of the claimant's family;

(b)   if the claimant is polygamously married, any partner of his and any child or young person who is a member of his household and for whom he or one of his partners is responsible;

(c)   a child or young person who is living with the claimant but who is not a member of his household by virtue of regulation 21 (circumstances in which a person is to be treated as being or not being a member of the same household);

(d)   subject to paragraph (3), a person who jointly occupies the claimant's dwelling and is either a co-owner of that dwelling with the claimant or his partner (whether or not there are other co-owners) or is liable with the claimant or his partner to make payments in respect of his occupation of the dwelling;

(e)   subject to paragraph (3)–

(i)   any person who is liable to make payments on a commercial basis to the claimant or the claimant's partner in respect of the occupation of the dwelling;

(ii)   any person to whom or to whose partner the claimant or the claimant's partner is liable to make payments on a commercial basis in respect of the occupation of the dwelling; or

(iii) any other member of the household of the person to whom or to whose partner the claimant or the claimant's partner is liable to make payments on a commercial basis in respect of the occupation of the dwelling;

(f) a person who lives with the claimant in order to care for him or a partner of his and who is engaged by a charitable or voluntary organisation which makes a charge to the claimant or his partner for the services provided by that person.

(3) Sub-paragraphs (d) and (e) of paragraph (2) shall not apply to any person who is treated as if he were not liable to make payments in respect of a dwelling under paragraph (1) of regulation 9 (circumstances in which a person is to be treated as not liable to make payments in respect of a dwelling).

(4) For the purposes of this regulation [¹ , regulations 9 and 13(6)(c) and the definition of "linked person" in regulation 2] a person resides with another only if they share any accommodation except a bathroom, a lavatory or a communal area within the meaning prescribed in paragraph 8 of Schedule 1 but not if each person is separately liable to make payments in respect of his occupation of the dwelling to the landlord.

Modifications

Amendments were made to para (4) by reg 4(2) Housing Benefit (Local Housing Allowance and Information Sharing) Amendment Regulations 2007 SI No.2868 as from 7 April 2008, save that for a person to whom reg 1(5) of those regulations applied (see p1231), the amendments came into force on the day on or after 7 April 2008 when the first of the events specified in reg 1(6) applied to her/him, or on 6 April 2009 if none had before that date.

Amendment

1.   Amended by reg 4(2) of SI 2007 No 2868 as from 7.4.08 (or if reg 1(5) of that SI applies, on the day on or after 7.4.08 when the first of the events specified in reg 1(6) applies, or from 6.4.09 if none have before that date).

Definitions

"child" – see s137(1) SSCBA and reg 2(1).
"claimant" – see reg 2(1).
"communal area" – see para 8 of Sch 1.
"dwelling" – see s137(1) SSCBA and reg 2(4).
"linked person" – see reg 2(1).
"partner" – see reg 2(1).
"young person" – see regs 2(1) and 19.

General Note

This defines which of the people who "reside" with the claimant or with whom the claimant resides are to be treated as "non-dependants" and therefore in respect of whom a claimant's maximum HB may be reduced under reg 74. Note that all payments made to a claimant by a non-dependant are disregarded under Sch 5 para 21.

Para (1) provides the general rule, subject to the exceptions listed in para (2). In particular, para (2)(e), provides that those residing with the claimant or her/his partner (or with whom the claimant or the partner resides) on a commercial basis are not to be treated as non-dependants.

Para (4) defines the term "resides" for these purposes, and also for the purposes of reg 9 (circumstances in which a person is to be treated as not liable to make payments in respect of a dwelling), reg 13(6)(c) (a situation when, in the case of a "young individual", maximum rent is not restricted to the single room rent) and the definition of "linked person" in reg 2.

Analysis

Paragraphs (1) and (4): Persons normally residing with the claimant

The basic rule is that a "non-dependant" is anyone who normally resides with the claimant or with whom the claimant normally resides. If neither is the case, and none of the exceptions in para (2) apply, the person is *not* a non-dependant and maximum HB cannot be reduced under reg 74. The addition of the latter category excludes any possibility of arguing that the claimant resides with the supposed non-dependent rather than the other way round – an argument accepted by the Court of Appeal in *Bate v Chief Adjudication Officer* [1994] *The Times,* 12 December, but rejected by the House of Lords when overturning the decision of the Court of Appeal (*R(IS) 12/ 96*).

Whether someone "normally resides" with the claimant is a purely factual question. It involves no element of judgment on the quality of the residence: *ST v SSWP* [2009] UKUT 269 (AAC). Note, however, that where a person stays in other places besides the claimant's home, it is a matter of fact and degree as to whether s/he is *normally* resident with the claimant. A person must have lived there for long enough to regard it as her/his usual home: *CIS 14850/1996* para 7. Relevant factors for deciding whether a person is normally resident may include: the relationship between the parties, how much time s/he spends at the claimant's address, where her/his post is sent, where s/he keeps clothes and other belongings, whether the stay or absence is temporary, and whether there is another permanent base that s/he could regard as home. However, where a person has connections with more than one home, it is possible that s/he may not be normally residing in any of them: *CSIS 100/1993*.

Para (4) restricts the circumstances in which a person "resides with" another. There must be some shared accommodation other than a bathroom, lavatory or communal area (defined in Sch 1 para 8 as an area of common access including a hall or passageway and rooms of common use in sheltered accommodation). A person shares a kitchen with another even though s/he is never there at the same time as the other person and even though s/he pays for the use of the kitchen: *Thamesdown BC v Goonery* [1995] 1 CLY 2600, CA.

In *CPC 1446/2008*, the claimant lived in a "granny annexe" built on to the back of her son's house. She had her own lounge and bathroom but used the kitchen of her son's house to heat up food in a microwave. A kitchen clearly counts as "any accommodation except a bathroom, a lavatory or a communal area". The question was whether the claimant was sharing the kitchen with a non-dependant. Approving *CIS 2532/2003* and *CSIS 652/2003*, Deputy Commissioner Wikeley decided that if a claimant makes use of a kitchen, s/he shares it, even if s/he does not actually visit it. The contrary view taken in the earlier *CSIS 185/1995* was disapproved. The Deputy Commissioner said that this is in accord with the plain meaning of the expression "normally resides with". He thought that if the claimant's son were asked "Where does your mother live?" or "Where does your mother reside?" his answer most probably would be "She can't manage by herself any more; she lives [or resides] with me – we have had a granny annex built out the back of our house".

It is plain from the wording of para (4) that a person does not "reside with" another person unless there is relevant shared accommodation. However, the existence of such sharing is not determinative of the issue, and all that need be shown is that the two people "reside with" each other in normal use of that phrase.

RK v SSWP [2008] UKUT 34 (AAC) decided that people are only to be regarded as residing with each other if they are sharing accommodation in a way that is consistent with living in the same household. Judge Rowland said that "share" does not mean "use with another person", but means "have the use of with another person" in the sense of "have a shared right to use". Actual use of accommodation is evidence of a right to use it but is neither necessary nor conclusive. The members of a household have shared use of the accommodation the household has the right to occupy. Where members of a family (in the non-technical sense of that word) are living in the same household on a non-commercial basis, they can usually be regarded as sharing the whole of the dwelling. The way accommodation is actually used may also be relevant when considering whether people are residing together. In particular, the fact that one member of a family frequently cooks for another member may be powerful evidence that they live in the same household. The fact that adults and older children respect each other's privacy and do not in fact make use of each other's bedrooms is immaterial. However, it is not invariably the case that members of the same family living in the same building are living in the same household. They may deliberately constitute themselves into different households – eg, because they are estranged or wish to establish their independence. In those circumstances, a person resides only with the members of the family who are members of the same household and the fact that the household may share accommodation with other family members living in a different household does not mean that they also reside with those other family members. But where a claimant in receipt of attendance allowance (AA) lives in the same building as other members of her/his family, it is unlikely that they are living in separate households because the purpose of living in the same building will usually have been precisely so that the claimant can receive the attention or supervision that entitlement to AA implies is needed from those other members of the family, at least to some extent.

Paragraphs (2) and (3): The exceptions

The following categories of people are *not* non-dependants even if they fall within the definition set out above. For the meaning of "household", see p22.

(1) A member of the claimant's family: para (2)(a). "Family" means the claimant's partner (if s/he has one) and any dependent children and qualifying young people who live with her/him and for whom s/he or her/his partner is responsible: s137(1) SSCBA and regs 19-21. Reg 20 deals with the situations in which an adult is to be treated as responsible for a child or young person, and reg 21, with those in which s/he may be treated as sharing a household with such a person.

(2) Where a claimant is in a polygamous marriage, any partner and any dependent children (and qualifying young people) who live with her/him and for whom either s/he or a partner is responsible: para (2)(b). See regs 19-21 on p332.

(3) A child or young person living with the claimant, but excluded from counting as a member of the household under reg 21: para (2)(c).

(4) A joint occupier who is also either a co-owner with the claimant or her/his partner or is liable with the claimant or her/his partner to make payments in respect of her/his occupation of the dwelling: para (2)(d). A "joint occupier" is someone who has a joint legal right to occupy the property, rather than merely someone who occupies the property along with the claimant or her/his partner: *R v Chesterfield BC ex p Fullwood* [1993] 26 HLR 126 at 129, CA. Thus it covers joint tenants and people who have signed a single license agreement. It has been argued in previous editions that it may be possible to argue that "payments in respect of his occupation of the dwelling" does not mean the same as "payments in respect

of a dwelling" in reg 8(1) and could cover situations such as utility bills which are in joint names. In view of the fact that para (3) envisages that reg 9 may apply to the liability under this paragraph so as to render the person a non-dependent after all, this seems to be incorrect, and the payments must be payments of rent or similar.

(5)　Those residing with the claimant who are liable to make payments on a commercial basis to her/him or her/his partner: para (2)(e)(i). For liability to make payments, see reg 9 on p249. For whether such payments are "on a commercial basis", see the Analysis to reg 9(1)(a) on p252. Where the person is not a non-dependant, some (or all) of the payments made to the claimant can be disregarded. See in particular Sch 5 paras 22 and 42 on pp556 and 561.

(6)　The landlord or other person to whom the claimant or her/his partner are liable to make payments on a commercial basis: para (2)(e)(ii).

(7)　Any member of the household of a person excluded by (6): para (2)(e)(iii).

(8)　A person employed by a charity or voluntary organisation to care for the claimant or her/his partner, where a charge is made for her/his services: para (2)(f). This applies whether or not there is assistance with the charges from a public or local authority.

By para (3), anyone in categories (4) to (7) above may be a non-dependent if her/his liability to pay rent falls foul of any of the exclusions from HB in reg 9(1) – eg, where the liability was created to take advantage of the HB scheme or the claimant is a close relative.

Cases in which section 1(1A) of the Administration Act is disapplied

4.　Section 1(1A) of the Administration Act (requirement to state national insurance number) shall not apply–

(a)　to a claim for housing benefit where the person making the claim, or in respect of whom the claim is made, is liable to make payments in respect of a dwelling which is a hostel;

(b)　to any child or young person in respect of whom housing benefit is claimed.

[¹ (c)　to a person who–

(i)　is a person in respect of whom a claim for housing benefit is made;

(ii)　is subject to immigration control within the meaning of section 115(9)(a) of the Immigration and Asylum Act;

(iii)　is a person from abroad for the purposes of these Regulations as defined in regulation 10(2); and

(iv)　has not previously been allocated a national insurance number.]

Amendment

1.　Amended by reg 9 of SI 2009 No 471 as from 6.4.09.

Definitions

"child" – see reg 2(1).
"hostel" – see reg 2(1).
"young person" – see reg 2(1).

General Note

The National Insurance number (NINO) requirement imposed by s1(1A) SSAA (see p28) is removed by para (a) in respect of inhabitants of hostels. Hopefully the excessively complex definition of "hostel", discussed on p221, will not detract from the effect of this provision.

Para (b) clarifies that the NINO requirement does not apply to a child or young person included in the claim for HB.

Para (c) disapplies the NINO requirement for anyone in respect of whom a claim for HB is made (eg, a partner) where s/he has not previously been allocated a NINO and the following conditions are satisfied:

(1)　s/he is "subject to immigration control" because s/he requires leave to enter or remain in the UK but does not have it: s115(9)(a) Immigration and Asylum Act 1999; *and*

(2)　s/he is not "habitually resident" in the UK, the Channel Islands, the Isle of Man or the Republic of Ireland: reg 10(2). However, note that given that none of those who are subject to immigration control because they require leave to enter or remain and do not have it can count as "habitually resident" it appears that para (c)(iii) is *otiose.*

This ensures that in such a case, the claim for HB can still be allowed. However, it is important to note that where a claim for HB is made in respect of someone "subject to immigration control" there might be consequences for that person's immigration status. Immigration advice is essential in such a situation.

Persons who have attained the qualifying age for state pension credit

5.–(1)   These Regulations apply to a person who–

(a)   has not attained the qualifying age for state pension credit; or

(b)   has attained the qualifying age for state pension credit if he, or if he has a partner, his partner, is a person on income support [² , on an income-based jobseeker's allowance or on an income-related employment and support allowance].

[¹ (2)]

(3)   Except as provided in [¹ paragraph (1)], these Regulations shall not apply in relation to any person if he, or if he has a partner, his partner, has attained the qualifying age for state pension credit.

Amendments

1.   Amended by reg 4(3) of SI 2008 No 959 as from 6.10.08.
2.   Amended by reg 6 of SI 2008 No 1082 as from 27.10.08.

Definitions

"person on an income-based jobseeker's allowance" – see reg 2(3).
"person on an income-related employment and support allowance" – see reg 2(3A).
"person on income support" – see reg 2(1).
"qualifying age for state pension credit" – see reg 2(1).

General Note

The HB Regs apply where neither the claimant nor her/his partner has reached the qualifying age for pension credit (PC) or if either have reached that age, where one of them is in receipt of IS, or is a person on income-based JSA or income-related ESA (see reg 2(3) and (3A) for the extended defintions). Otherwise, where the claimant or her/his partner has reached the qualifying age for PC, the HB(SPC) Regs instead apply (see p767).

Note that because those born on or after 6 April 1950 may reach the qualifying age for PC on different dates, reg 5 may be relevant to claimants at different ages. See the note on the definition of "qualifying age for state pension credit" on p224.

Remunerative work

6.–(1)   Subject to the following provisions of this regulation, a person shall be treated for the purposes of these Regulations as engaged in remunerative work if he is engaged, or, where his hours of work fluctuate, he is engaged on average, for not less than 16 hours a week, in work for which payment is made or which is done in expectation of payment.

(2)   Subject to paragraph (3), in determining the number of hours for which a person is engaged in work where his hours of work fluctuate, regard shall be had to the average of hours worked over–

(a)   if there is a recognisable cycle of work, the period of one complete cycle (including, where the cycle involves periods in which the person does no work, those periods but disregarding any other absences);

(b)   in any other case, the period of 5 weeks immediately prior to the date of claim, or such other length of time as may, in the particular case, enable the person's weekly average hours of work to be determined more accurately.

(3)   Where, for the purposes of paragraph (2)(a), a person's recognisable cycle of work at a school, other educational establishment or other place of employment is one year and includes periods of school holidays or similar vacations during which he does not work, those periods and any other periods not forming part of such holidays or vacations during which he is not required to work shall be disregarded in establishing the average hours for which he is engaged in work.

(4)   Where no recognisable cycle has been established in respect of a person's work, regard shall be had to the number of hours or, where those hours will fluctuate, the average of the hours, which he is expected to work in a week.

(5)   A person shall be treated as engaged in remunerative work during any period for which he is absent from work referred to in paragraph (1) if the absence is either without good cause or by reason of a recognised, customary or other holiday.

(6)   A person on income support [¹ , an income-based jobseeker's allowance or an income-related employment and support allowance] for more than 3 days in any benefit week shall be treated as not being in remunerative work in that week.

(7)   A person shall not be treated as engaged in remunerative work on any day on which the person is on maternity leave, paternity leave or adoption leave, or is absent from work because he is ill.

(8)   A person shall not be treated as engaged in remunerative work on any day on which he is engaged in an activity in respect of which–

(a)   a sports award has been made, or is to be made, to him; and

(b)   no other payment is made or is expected to be made to him.

Amendment

1.   Amended by reg 7 of SI 2008 No 1082 as from 27.10.08.

Definitions

"benefit week" – see reg 2(1).

"claim" – see reg 2(1).

"maternity leave", "paternity leave" and "adoption leave" – see reg 2(1).

"payment" – see reg 2(1).

"person on an income-based jobseeker's allowance" – see reg 2(3).

"person on an income-related employment and support allowance" – see reg 2(3A).

"person on income support" – see reg 2(1).

"sports award" – see reg 2(1).

General Note

This defines the term "remunerative work" for the purposes of these regulations. The test is of much greater significance in the context of other means-tested benefits such as IS, income-based JSA, income-related ESA and tax credits, because it is a condition of entitlement to (or an exclusion from) those benefits. Its significance for HB arises in relation to the treatment of earned income (Sch 4 para 1), additional earnings disregards and childcare costs disregards (Sch 4 para 17 and regs 27(1)(c) and 28) and where a non-dependant is in remunerative work, to the appropriate non-dependant deduction (reg 74).

There were modifications to this provision between November 1999 and November 2001 for New Deal participants. See the 14th edition for details.

Analysis

Paragraphs (1) and (5) to (8): Definition of remunerative work

By para (1), a person is in "remunerative work" if s/he is engaged for at least 16 hours a week in paid work or work done in the expectation of payment. This is qualified as follows:

(1)   If someone is absent from work "without good cause" or on a "recognised, customary or other holiday", s/he is treated as being at work for the period of absence: para (5). "Good cause" is not defined for these purposes. It is suggested that whether or not the employer has authorised the absence is not conclusive, but if the absence is authorised the claimant is likely to have good cause.

(2)   A person on IS, income-based JSA or income-related ESA for more than three days in a benefit week (see the definitions in reg 2) is not in remunerative work for that week: para (6). Note that if this applies to a non-dependant, a lower (or no) non-dependant deduction is applicable: reg 74.

(3)   A person on maternity, paternity or adoption leave or sick leave is not treated as being in remunerative work for the days that s/he is absent from work: para (7). But see reg 28(2) to (4), (14) and (15) on p347 for situations when such a person *can* be treated as in remunerative work for the purpose of the childcare charge deduction from earnings.

(4)   A person is not treated as being in remunerative work in respect of any day where her/his sole remuneration is, or is expected to be, in the form of a "sports award" (defined in reg 2(1) on p217): para (8). The definition requires that the claimant "is engaged in an activity in respect of which" the sports award is payable. A broad reading should be taken of this wording. If, for example, a person is receiving treatment for injury or is engaged in promotional activities relating to her/his sport, then it should be found to be satisfied. It is also a requirement that no other payment is made to her/him (or is expected to be made) in respect of the sporting activities in respect of that day.

"Engaged". The person must be "engaged" in remunerative work. Thus if s/he is engaged in other activities awaiting an opportunity to work, it is arguable that s/he is in a different situation from being engaged in work. In *CIS 85/1997* para 7, the commissioner distinguished between a claimant who waited in her flat above her shop until a customer called and the claimant in the case before him, who was a self-employed taxi-driver who would wait in the cab company's office for customers. The former claimant was not engaged in work, the latter was. This is not a particularly easy distinction to draw, but if the claimant pursues activities at her/his own home while

awaiting a call from a client, it is hard to see how s/he can be said to be "engaged" in work. The commissioner's decision was upheld by the Court of Appeal in *Kazantzis v Chief Adjudication Officer* [1999] *The Times* 30 June (*R(IS) 13/99*). It was not possible to draw a dividing line between the waiting time and the time spent driving when determining entitlement to IS. The same will be true of the operation of reg 6.

"Work done in the expectation of payment". Even if the person is not receiving any payment for the work, it may be necessary to decide whether s/he is expecting payment for work, whether immediately or at some future time. There are a number of useful decisions on IS which must be seen as highly persuasive.

The work must be done in the *expectation*, not merely the hope, of payment. So there must be a realistic expectation of payment within the foreseeable future: *R(IS) 1/93* para 11. Usually, where the person in question is employed this will not present much difficulty, though two points should be noted. First, it is not necessary that the payment comes from the employer: *R(FC) 2/90* concerning receipt of religious covenants. Secondly, the payment must be received for the current work. It is not sufficient for someone to be doing voluntary work in the hope of being offered a paid job: *R(IS) 5/95* para 8.

The most difficult problems arise with self-employed people. Millett LJ gave useful guidance for such cases in *Chief Adjudication Officer v Ellis* [1995], 15 February, CA (appendix to *R(IS) 22/95*). The guidance can be summarised as follows.

(1)   The question whether the work is paid for, or done in the expectation of, payment must be judged on a week by week basis at the time the work is done.

(2)   The type of work is not important. The issue to be determined is whether the work was paid for or expected to be paid for.

(3)   If the person in question was actually paid for the work done, s/he is in remunerative work. Only when it is not paid for does the question of whether the business can be expected to be profitable come in for consideration. However, insignificant sums received may be ignored, such as the £200 received in a year by the would-be music agent in *Smith v Chief Adjudication Officer* [1994] unreported, 11 October, CA.

(4)   Remuneration may take many forms. Just because a person's expenses in running a business are greater than her/his income from it does not prevent the income from being remuneration: *Perrot v Supplementary Benefit Commissioner* [1980] 3 All ER 110 at 114j, 116a-e, 117b, CA. However, in the case of retail and similar businesses, remuneration comes from the profit made from the store and not from the sale of the goods therein. Receipt of an Enterprise Allowance or similar payment does not amount to "payment" for the work: *Smith (R(IS) 21/95)*.

(5)   Where the person in question is in a partnership, monies received by the partnership do not amount to remuneration until there is a distribution of profits. However, where the person is in business with her/his partner, the authority will be justified in viewing the partnership as a single economic unit.

(6)   If such a person draws on the funds of the business, this may be by way of wage, advance on profit or consumption of the capital of the business. Only if the nature of the drawings can be seen to represent the last of these can it be found that the person is not in remunerative work.

(7)   If the partners are not making drawings, they are in remunerative work if they expect to receive a share of the profits. This does not depend on the state of the annual accounts but on whether they have a realistic expectation that they will receive a share. But they must hope to be paid for the work they are currently doing, not that they will put themselves in a situation to be able to earn money from future work. Lord Bingham MR added (transcript at 16B) that the expectation of profit had to come from that financial year, when the accounts were finalised.

Paragraphs (2), (3) and (4): Determination of hours worked

"regard shall be had". Paras (2) and (4) appear to offer some discretion to authorities in the way they determine the hours of work where these fluctuate in that an authority need only pay "regard" to the hours (or average of hours) mentioned in those paras. The primary question is whether the person is working for at least 16 hours a week "on average": para (1). It is suggested that if the authority thinks that the provisions under paras (2) and (4) give an unfair or unrealistic result, it is open to it to adopt a different approach. Caution is therefore required in applying the extensive IS caselaw, for which reference should be made to the corresponding IS provisions in *Social Security Legislation Vol II*.

Paras (2) and (4). The first thing the authority must decide is whether the person has a recognisable cycle of work, despite the fact that the weekly hours fluctuate. If so, under para (2)(a), the average number of hours worked is obtained by dividing the total number of hours in the cycle by the number of weeks it lasts, ignoring weeks in which no work is done unless this is part of the cycle. For example, if someone works 30 hours one week, 20 the next and then has the next week off (on a regular basis), the total hours worked over the cycle would be divided by three. If the person has a four-week cycle but is off during the last week due to sickness, the hours worked in that particular cycle would be divided by three only, not four.

If the person works casually or intermittently (eg, as a seasonal worker who works in the summer but is unemployed the rest of the year), the "work cycle" is that part of the year in which s/he is working and does not include the period of unemployment. Commissioner Howell dealt with the similar provision for JSA in *R(JSA) 1/07* and two other appeals. The claimants worked from March to October in summer employment. During the out-of-season months they had no earnings or work at all. The decision maker said that as they had had their summer employment for more than one year in a row, they had a cycle of work of a year and as the average hours of work over this period was greater than 16 hours a week they were in "remunerative work". Commissioner Howell disagreed. He said that the recurrence of an inability to get work at all during the winter months could not turn the whole calendar year into one continuous period of the claimants being "engaged in work" so as to be able to call the whole year a "recognisable cycle of work". The real question is whether the person is "in" work at the material time. That means that there must be some sort of continuing relationship between the employee and the employer and, where a contract of employment has been terminated, a committment to resume the relationship: *CJSA 3832/2006*.

Paras (2)(b) and (4), at first sight, appear to contradict each other. The best way to resolve the difficulty is probably to follow the approach taken by the commissioner in *R(IS) 8/95* Appendix paras 10 to 12. A claimant who normally worked a full week was on a period of working one week on and one week off, although he might be called in on non-working days. The commissioner holds that para (4) addresses the situation where there is insufficient evidence of recent working hours to resolve the question of the average working hours. It is forward-looking, with reference to the number of hours (or average of hours) a person is *expected* to work. Para (2) applies where such evidence exists and shows a fluctuation. If a recognisable cycle of work has been "established", then para (2)(a) applies. If not, para (2)(b) requires consideration of the average hours worked in the period of five weeks immediately before the date of claim, unless a different period (shorter or longer) provides a more accurate average. It is therefore backward-looking. The commissioner states that the point at which the calculation moves from being made under para (4) to that under para (2)(b) depends on the circumstances.

Para (3) provides a particular method by which the average weekly number of hours worked is calculated where a person's recognisable cycle of work at a school, other educational establishment or any other place of employment, is one year and includes school holidays or similar vacations during which s/he does not work. In such cases, school holidays and any other periods during which s/he is not required to work must be disregarded in calculating the average weekly hours worked – ie, average weekly hours should generally be calculated by reference only to average weekly hours worked during term time.

It is not open to evade the effect of para (3) by treating the vacations as being excluded from the cycle of work on the basis that no work is being done at those times: *Chief Adjudication Officer v Stafford* [2000] 1 All ER 686 at 693g-694a, CA, upheld by a majority of three to two in *Banks v Chief Adjudication Officer* [2001] 1 WLR 1411, HL. That would mean that the "cycle" was effectively being ignored. Nevertheless, in the HB context it is suggested that the authority may adopt a different approach if it feels that the result of the calculation in para (3) is unfair. Although it is in mandatory terms, para (3) applies "for the purposes of paragraph (2)(a)" and so the authority is only required to have regard to the calculation and is not bound by it. Reference should be made to the very powerful dissenting speech of Lord Scott in the House of Lords in *Stafford* for the unfair results of reliance on the "cycle" and the differing (and fairer) result reached by a tribunal of commissioners in the context of JSA in *R(JSA) 4/03* in such cases. See also the commentary on *R(JSA) 1/07* above.

PART 2
Provisions affecting entitlement to housing benefit

General Note on Part 2

By virtue of s130 SSCBA 1992, a person is entitled to HB in respect of certain payments that s/he is liable to make in relation to the dwelling s/he occupies as her/his home. Reg 7 deals with the meaning of the phrase "occupies as his home". Regs 8 and 9 respectively deal with the situations in which a person is or is not to be treated as "liable" for payments on that home. Reg 10 provides that certain persons from abroad are to be treated as not being liable for payments. See also reg 56 for full-time students who are treated as not being liable for payments.

See the 20th edition for the text of reg 10A and Sch A1 in Sch 4 of SI 2006 No.217 for claims by asylum seekers recorded as refugees on or before 14 June 2007.

Circumstances in which a person is or is not to be treated as occupying a dwelling as his home

7.–(1) Subject to the following provisions of this regulation, a person shall be treated as occupying as his home the dwelling normally occupied as his home–

(a) by himself or, if he is a member of a family, by himself and his family; or

(b) if he is polygamously married, by himself, his partners and any child or young person for whom he or any partner of his is responsible and who is a member of that same household,

and shall not be treated as occupying any other dwelling as his home.

(2) In determining whether a dwelling is the dwelling normally occupied as a person's home for the purpose of paragraph (1) regard shall be had to any other dwelling occupied by that person or any other person referred to in paragraph (1) whether or not that dwelling is in Great Britain.

(3)　Where a single claimant or a lone parent is a student, other than one to whom regulation 56(1) applies (circumstances in which certain students are treated as not liable to make payments in respect of a dwelling), or is on a training course and is liable to make payments (including payments of mortgage interest or, in Scotland, payments under heritable securities or, in either case, analogous payments) in respect of either (but not both) the dwelling which he occupies for the purpose of attending his course of study or, his training course, or as the case may be, the dwelling which he occupies when not attending his course, he shall be treated as occupying as his home the dwelling in respect of which he is liable to make such payments.

(4)　Where a claimant has been required to move into temporary accommodation by reason of essential repairs being carried out to the dwelling normally occupied as his home, and is liable to make payments (including payments of mortgage interest or, in Scotland, payments under heritable securities or, in either case, analogous payments) in respect of either (but not both) the dwelling which he normally occupied as his home or the temporary accommodation, he shall be treated as occupying as his home the dwelling in respect of which he is liable to make payments.

(5)　Where a person is required to reside in a dwelling which is a bail hostel or probation hostel approved by the Secretary of State under [⁵ section 13 of the Offender Management Act 2007], he shall not be treated as occupying that dwelling as his home.

(6)　Where a person is liable to make payments in respect of two (but not more than two) dwellings, he shall be treated as occupying both dwellings as his home only–

(a)　for a period not exceeding 52 weeks in the case where he has left and remains absent from the former dwelling occupied as his home through fear of violence in that dwelling or by a former member of his family and–

　　(i)　it is reasonable that housing benefit should be paid in respect of both his former dwelling and his present dwelling occupied as the home; and

　　(ii)　he intends to return to occupy the former dwelling as his home; or

(b)　in the case of a couple or a member of a polygamous marriage, where he or one partner is a student, other than one to whom regulation 56(1) applies (circumstances in which certain students are treated as not liable to make payments in respect of a dwelling), or is on a training course and it is unavoidable that the partners should occupy two separate dwellings and reasonable that housing benefit should be paid in respect of both dwellings; or

(c)　in the case where, because of the number of persons referred to in paragraph (1), they have been housed by a housing authority in two separate dwellings; or

(d)　in the case where a person has moved into a new dwelling occupied as the home, except where paragraph (4) applies, for a period not exceeding 4 benefit weeks [¹ from the date on which he moved] if he could not reasonably have avoided liability in respect of two dwellings; or

(e)　in the case where a person–

　　(i)　is treated by virtue of paragraph (8) as occupying a dwelling as his home ("the new dwelling") and sub-paragraph (c)(i) of that paragraph applies; and

　　(ii)　he has occupied another dwelling as his home on any day within the period of 4 weeks immediately preceding the date he moved to the new dwelling,

for a period not exceeding 4 benefit weeks immediately preceding the date on which he moved.

(7)　Where–

(a)　a person has moved into a dwelling for which he is not liable to make payments ("the new dwelling"); and

(b)　immediately before that move, he was liable to make payments for the dwelling he previously occupied as his home ("the former dwelling"); and

(c)　that liability continues after he has moved into the new dwelling,

he shall be treated as occupying the former dwelling as his home for a period not exceeding 4 benefit weeks if he could not reasonably have avoided liability in respect of that former dwelling.

(8) [² Where]–
(a) [² a person] has moved into a dwelling and was liable to make payments in respect of that dwelling before moving in; and
[² (b) either–
    (i) that person had claimed housing benefit before moving in and either no decision has yet been made on that claim or it has been refused but a further claim has been made or treated as made within 4 weeks of the date on which the claimant moved into the new dwelling occupied as the home; or
    (ii) that person notified the move to the new dwelling as a change of circumstances under regulation 88 (duty to notify changes of circumstances) before the move, or the move to the new dwelling was otherwise notified before the move under that regulation; and]
(c) the delay in moving into the dwelling in respect of which there was liability to make payments before moving in was reasonable and–
    (i) that delay was necessary in order to adapt the dwelling to meet the disablement needs of that person or any member of his family; or
    (ii) the move was delayed pending the outcome of an application under [³ Part 8] of the Act for a social fund payment to meet a need arising out of the move or in connection with setting up the home in the dwelling and either a member of the claimant's family is aged 5 or under or the claimant's applicable amount includes a premium under paragraph [³] 12, 14 or 16 of Schedule 3 [⁴ or a component under paragraph 23 or 24 of that Schedule]; or
    (iii) the claimant became liable to make payments in respect of the dwelling while he was a patient or in residential accommodation,
[² the person shall be treated] as occupying the dwelling as his home for any period not exceeding 4 weeks immediately prior to the date on which he moved into the dwelling and in respect of which he was liable to make payments.

(9) Where a person is treated by virtue of paragraph (8) as occupying a dwelling as his home in respect of the period before moving in, his claim for housing benefit in respect of that dwelling shall be treated as having been made on either–
(a) in the case of a claim in respect of which a decision has not yet been made the date that claim was or was treated as made in accordance with regulation 83 (time and manner in which claims are to be made); or
(b) in the case of a claim for housing benefit in respect of that dwelling which has been refused and a further claim was or was treated as made in accordance with Part 10 (claims) within 4 weeks of the date on which he moved into the dwelling, the date on which the claim was refused or was treated as made; or
(c) the date from which he is treated by virtue of paragraph (8) as occupying the dwelling as his home,
whichever of those dates is the later.

(10) Where a person to whom neither paragraph (6)(a) nor (16)(c)(x) applies–
(a) formerly occupied a dwelling but has left and remains absent from it through fear of violence–
    (i) in the dwelling; or
    (ii) by a person who was formerly a member of the family of the person first mentioned; and
(b) has a liability to make payments in respect of that dwelling which is unavoidable, he shall be treated as occupying the dwelling as his home for a period not exceeding 4 benefit weeks.

(11) This paragraph shall apply to a person who enters residential accommodation–
(a) for the purpose of ascertaining whether the accommodation suits his needs; and
(b) with the intention of returning to the dwelling which is normally occupied by him as his home should, in the event, the residential accommodation prove not to suit his needs; and

(c)   while the part of the dwelling which is normally occupied by him as his home is not let, or as the case may be, sublet.

(12)   A person to whom paragraph (11) applies shall be treated as if he is occupying the dwelling he normally occupies as his home for a period not exceeding, subject to an overall limit of 52 weeks on the absence from that home, 13 weeks beginning from the first day he enters a residential accommodation.

(13)   Subject to paragraph (17) a person shall be treated as occupying a dwelling as his home while he is temporarily absent therefrom for a period not exceeding 13 weeks beginning from the first day of that absence from the home only if–

(a)   he intends to return to occupy the dwelling as his home; and
(b)   the part of the dwelling normally occupied by him has not been let or, as the case may be, sub-let; and
(c)   the period of absence is unlikely to exceed 13 weeks.

(14)   This paragraph applies to a person who is–

(a)   detained in custody pending sentence upon conviction or under a sentence imposed by a court, other than a person who is detained in hospital under the provisions of the Mental Health Act 1983, or, in Scotland, under the provisions of the Mental Health (Care and Treatment) (Scotland) Act 2003 or the Criminal Procedure (Scotland) Act 1995; and
(b)   on temporary release from such detention in accordance with Rules made under the provisions of the Prison Act 1952 or the Prisons (Scotland) Act 1989.

(15)   Where paragraph (14) applies to a person, then, for any day when he is on temporary release–

(a)   if such temporary release was immediately preceded by a period of temporary absence under paragraph (13) or (16), he shall be treated as if he continues to be absent from the dwelling, despite any occupation of the dwelling;
(b)   for the purposes of paragraph (16)(c)(i), he shall be treated as if he remains in detention; and
(c)   if he does not fall within sub-paragraph (a), he shall be treated as if he does not occupy his dwelling as his home despite any such occupation of the dwelling.

(16)   This paragraph shall apply to a person who is temporarily absent from the dwelling he normally occupies as his home (''absence''), if–

(a)   he intends to return to occupy the dwelling as his home; and
(b)   while the part of the dwelling which is normally occupied by him has not been let, or as the case may be, sublet; and
(c)   he is–
    (i)   detained in custody on remand pending trial or, as a condition of bail, required to reside–
        (aa)   in a dwelling, other than the dwelling he occupies as his home; or
        (bb)   in premises approved under [5 section 13 of the Offender Management Act 2007],
        or, detained pending sentence upon conviction; or
    (ii)   resident in a hospital or similar institution as a patient; or
    (iii) undergoing, or as the case may be, his partner or his dependant child is undergoing, in the United Kingdom or elsewhere, medical treatment, or medically approved convalescence, in accommodation other than residential accommodation; or
    (iv)   following, in the United Kingdom or elsewhere, a training course; or
    (v)   undertaking medically approved care of a person residing in the United Kingdom or elsewhere; or
    (vi)   undertaking the care of a child whose parent or guardian is temporarily absent from the dwelling normally occupied by that parent or guardian for the purpose of receiving medically approved care or medical treatment; or
    (vii) a person who is, in the United Kingdom or elsewhere, receiving medically approved care provided in accommodation other than residential accommodation; or
    (viii) a student to whom paragraph (3) or (6)(b) does not apply;

(ix)   a person who is receiving care provided in residential accommodation other than a person to whom paragraph (11) applies; or

(x)   a person who has left the dwelling he occupies as his home through fear of violence, in that dwelling, or by a person who was formerly a member of the family of the person first mentioned, and to whom paragraph (6)(a) does not apply; and

(d)   the period of his absence is unlikely to exceed 52 weeks or, in exceptional circumstances, is unlikely substantially to exceed that period.

(17)   A person to whom paragraph (16) applies shall be treated as occupying the dwelling he normally occupies at his home during any period of absence not exceeding 52 weeks beginning from the first day of that absence.

(18)   In this regulation–

"medically approved" means certified by a medical practitioner;

"patient" means a person who is undergoing medical or other treatment as an in-patient in any hospital or similar institution;

"residential accommodation" means accommodation which is provided in–

(a)   a care home;

(b)   an independent hospital;

(c)   an Abbeyfield Home; or

(d)   an establishment managed or provided by a body incorporated by Royal Charter or constituted by Act of Parliament other than a local social services authority;

"training course" means a course of training or instruction provided wholly or partly by or on behalf of or in pursuance of arrangements made with, or approved by or on behalf of, [6 Skills Development Scotland,] Scottish Enterprise, Highlands and Islands Enterprise, a government department or the Secretary of State.

Amendments

1. Amended by reg 5 of SI 2006 No 3274 as from 8.1.07.
2. Amended by reg 11(3) of SI 2007 No 2618 as from 1.10.07.
3. Amended by reg 3(3) of SI 2008 No 1042 as from 19.5.08.
4. Amended by reg 7A of SI 2008 No 1082, as inserted by reg 28 of SI 2008 No 2428, as from 27.10.08.
5. Amended by reg 6(3) of SI 2008 No 2767 as from 17.11.08.
6. Amended by reg 6(3)(b) of SI 2009 No 583 as from 6.4.09.

Definitions

"benefit week" – see reg 2(1).
"child" – see s137 SSCBA and reg 2(1).
"claim" – see reg 2(1).
"claimant" – see reg 2(1).
"course of study" – see reg 53.
"dwelling" – see s137 SSCBA and reg 2(4).
"family" – see s137 SSCBA.
"housing authority" – see s191 SSAA.
"lone parent" – see reg 2(1).
"partner" – see reg 2(1).
"polygamous marriage" see reg 2(1).
"single claimant" – see reg 2(1).
"student" – see regs 2(1) and 53.
"young person" – see reg 2(1).

General Note

To be entitled to HB, a claimant must be liable to make payments in respect of a dwelling which s/he occupies as her/his home: s130 SSCBA (see p4). Paras (1) and (2) set out the general rule that a claimant is only usually treated as occupying one home, namely that normally occupied by her/him. The remainder of the regulation provides for various exceptions to this rule.

(1)   Paras (3) and (4) provide situations where if a claimant has two homes but only pays for one of them, s/he will be treated as occupying the one that is paid for. Broadly, para (3) applies to students and people on training courses who occupy one home during their courses and one during vacations, and para (4) applies to claimants who have had to move into temporary accommodation due to essential repairs.

(2)   Residence in an approved bail or probation hostel is to be ignored in considering where a person's normal home is: para (5).

(3)   Para (6) sets out a number of cases in which a claimant can be treated as occupying two homes and therefore receive HB for both.

(4)   Paras (7) to (10) deal with situations where a claimant can be treated as occupying a property which s/he has moved from or is about to move (or has moved) into.

(5)   Paras (11) to (17) deal with when someone can be treated as occupying a dwelling during a temporary absence.

Two provisions deal with claimants who are "students" who are not excluded from eligibility to HB under reg 56(1), or who are on "training courses": paras (3) and (6)(b).

The application of reg 7 is not restricted to the question of whether or not the claimant is entitled to HB. As the headnote suggests, the regulation determines the issue of whether or not a person is occupying the home. Thus where a claimant's children spent most of their time with their mother and she received child benefit in respect of them, each child was resident in the property where her/his "family" lived and so could not be treated as occupying the father's home for the purposes of the rent officer's assessment: *R v Swale BC HBRB ex p Marchant* [1999] 1 FLR 1087, QBD; [2000] 1 FLR 246, CA.

Reg 7 is also relevant in determining whether someone is an occupier of a dwelling with the claimant for the purposes of determining the number of bedrooms allowed under the size criteria within the rent restriction schemes, and hence if there has been a change in the number of occupiers for the purposes of a reference to the rent officer under reg 14(1)(c): *Stroud DC v JG* [2009] UKUT 67 (AAC); *R(H) 8/09*; *SK v South Hams DC (HB)* [2010] UKUT 129 (AAC).

In *R(H) 8/09*, the claimant's son was a student who lived away from home during term time. Judge Williams concluded that he was to be treated as occupying the claimant's dwelling as his home under reg 7(16)(c)(viii) and (17) (student who is temporarily absent from home). As such, there was not a change in the number of occupiers in the claimant's home and a reference under reg 14 therefore could not be made. Note that where it is determined that someone occupies a dwelling with the claimant, it will also be necessary to determine whether a non-dependant deduction is to be made under reg 74.

Analysis
Paragraphs (1) and (2): The general rule
The home in question is that "normally occupied" by the people listed in paras (1)(a) or (b), as appropriate. There is no definition of "normally occupied". In *CH 1085/2002* para 13, the commissioner pointed out that "normally occupied" was a lower standard to "permanently occupied". He also suggested that the views of officers administering JSA or the social fund were relevant: para 14. It is suggested that this could only be the case if the issue has been specifically considered by such officers, and tribunals must not, of course, treat their views as binding. Note that from 1 November 2010, specified children and young people living with the claimant (eg, foster children) are not to be treated as occupying the claimant's dwelling: reg 21(3).

The dwelling which the claimant occupies as a home may comprise more than one property or more than one room in a property: *London Borough of Hackney v GA* [2008] UKUT 26 (AAC); *R(H) 5/09*; *Birmingham City Council v IB* [2009] UKUT 116 (AAC). See p21 for a discussion. Under para (2), the authority must take account of any other dwelling occupied by the claimant or by any of the other people listed in para (1) in order to decide which is the "normal" home. This includes dwellings outside Great Britain, but GM A3.356 warns authorities that this provision is not intended to exclude from entitlement someone who has set up home in this country but whose family is no longer part of her/his household and remains abroad. The GM says that the purpose of taking account of homes outside Great Britain is to avoid simultaneous payment of HB under both the Northern Irish and British schemes.

Some factors which are relevant to the question of which home is "normally occupied" if more than one property is involved are the following:

(1)   The amount of time that the claimant spends at the property, compared with other properties with which a comparison is being made under para (2): *R v Penwith DC ex p Burt* [1990] 22 HLR 292 at 296, QBD.

(2)   The reason for any absence from the property, though note the possible application of paras (10) to (16).

(3)   Where the claimant's personal belongings are kept. See on this *R(H) 9/05* below.

(4)   Where the claimant is registered to vote, registers with GPs and dentists, is liable for council tax and utilities bills, etc.

(5)   Whether the claimant has any local ties such as memberships of clubs and associations.

Previous versions of this book have suggested another relevant factor as being where the claimant regards the centre of her/his existence and where s/he intends it should be in the future. However, *CH 1786/2005* (rightly) points out that a "centre of interests" test is not a substitute for making an overall assessment of the circumstances and evidence in each case in deciding which home is "normally occupied" by the claimant (per *CH 2521/2002*); and warns against chopping up what is essentially a single factual issue into series of individual tests for particular factors.

In *R(H) 9/05*, the claimant took out a tenancy of a new flat from February 2004 but she could not move in immediately as the property needed to be adapted to met her needs as a disabled person. On 15 March 2004 the disabled adaptations had been completed and so she terminated her former tenancy and her family moved all her furniture and possessions into the new flat. However, the claimant herself was unable to move in on this date

– and did not in fact move in until 9 August 2004 – because she became ill and had to be admitted to hospital. On these facts, the deputy commissioner decided that the claimant had normally occupied the flat as her home within reg 5(1) HB Regs 1987 (now reg 7(1) HB Regs) from the date her furniture and possessions had been moved into it, notwithstanding that the claimant herself had not begun living in the flat until five months later. The use of the word "normally" did not speak to the length of time present in the property but was rather in place to help resolve cases where the claimant might be regarded as living in more than one property. Moreover, the claimant could be said to have "moved in" to the flat on 15 March, and so could be treated as occupying it for the four weeks beforehand: reg 7(8)(c)(i) HB Regs. Further the claimant's temporary absence from the propery (to August 2004) did not affect these conclusions because it is possible for the claimant to intend to return to occupy the flat as her home even though she had never physically lived there.

The decision in *R(H) 9/05*, although no doubt welcome on the facts, places a strained interpretation on the word "return" as used in sub-paras (13) to (17) of reg 7. *CH 2521/2002* rules that the comparable sub-paras in reg 5(1) HB Regs 1987 (now reg 7(1) HB Regs) could be used as an aid to construe the test. However, given that *R(H) 9/05* is a reported decision it must be preferred over any conflicting unreported decisions (such as, at least implicitly, *CH 2201/2002* and *CH 2521/2002*).

Evidence of a claimant having made a claim for HB and JSA in the area of another authority will be adequate evidence that a claimant is residing elsewhere, at least in the absence of contradictory evidence: *CH 2201/2002* para 10.

In *CH 2521/2002* para 10, Commissioner Fellner cautioned against over-heavy reliance on *Herbert v Byrne* [1964] 1 WLR 519 at 527, 528, 529, CA, noting that it was a case under a different statutory provision. She went on to question in paras 11-12 whether a person may have two dwellings and still qualify for benefit on their usual residence under reg 5(1) HB regs 1987 (now reg 7(1) HB Regs). It is suggested that it is plain from para (2) that this is possible.

Paragraph (3): Absence due to study or training

This provides for the situation in which an eligible student or person on a training course who is a single claimant or a lone parent, occupies two dwellings, one to enable her/him to attend the course, and one which s/he uses at other times, but is only *liable* for payments in respect of one of them. Note that para (3) can only apply to a single person if s/he is claiming HB: definition of "single claimant" in reg 2(1). Note also that the payments in question can be mortgage and similar payments as well as payments of the nature that could attract HB. So if a claimant pays rent for two homes, or rent for one and mortgage payments for the other, s/he does not come within the scope of this provision.

When the paragraph applies, the claimant is treated for HB purposes, as occupying the dwelling for which s/he has to pay. This is of benefit, for example, to a student who pays for term-time accommodation but stays at her/his parents' home, at no cost to her/himself, during the vacations (but see Part 7 of these Regulations). Note para (6)(b) for couples who are liable to make payments for two homes, where one member of the couple is an eligible student.

Paragraph (4): Absence due to essential repairs

This ensures that claimants required to leave their normal home due to essential repair work can qualify for HB provided that they make such payments as are referred to in respect of either the normal home or the temporary accommodation. If they make relevant payments on *both*, they are not covered by this paragraph, but see para (6). As with para (3), the payments in question can be mortgage and similar payments as well as payments of the nature that could attract HB. So if a claimant pays rent for both the normal and the temporary home, or rent for one and mortgage payments for the other, s/he does not come within the scope of this provision.

There is no guidance on the meaning of "essential", but when this term was used in relation to the old supplementary benefit scheme in respect of grants for redecoration, a commissioner interpreted the term as covering work which was "necessary" rather than a luxury, but not necessarily "indispensable if life was to be maintained": *R(SB) 10/81*.

Commissioner Williams approved the relevance of the test propounded in *R(SB) 10/81* in *CH 393/2002*. He also held that it was not necessary for all the repairs to be completed in order for the deeming provision in para (4) to cease to have effect, as long as the essential repairs had been completed and the property was habitable: paras 15-16. However, consideration of the claimant's illness would be relevant in determining whether the property was habitable.

Paragraph (5): Approved hostels

This provision effectively requires a local authority to ignore enforced residence in an approved bail or probation hostel when deciding where someone's "normal home" is. Residence in the hostel must be "required" which will normally mean that it will be a condition of the person's bail. In England and Wales, documentary evidence of this may be obtained from the relevant Magistrates' or Crown Court. See para (16)(c)(i)(bb) for the provision that allows HB to be paid in respect of the claimant's normal home during a temporary absence in approved premises.

Paragraph (6): HB on two homes

Para (6) allows the claimant to be treated as occupying two dwellings as her/his home, and hence to qualify for HB in respect of both of them, in the circumstances there set out. Note that para (6) is only relevant if the claimant is occupying two or more dwellings. If the claimant occupies a single "dwelling" it is not relevant even if the dwelling is comprised of more than one property: *London Borough of Hackney v GA* [2008] UKUT 26 (AAC); R(H) 5/09; *Birmingham City Council v IB* [2009] UKUT 116 (AAC). See p21 for a discussion.

Sub-para (a) enables people forced to leave home through fear of actual or threatened violence to receive benefit in respect of both the abandoned and the new home where this is considered reasonable. There must be an intention to return to occupy the former home. Once that intention no longer exists HB is not payable on the former home. Also see the commentary on para (10).

No violence need yet have occurred – the mere fear of violence is sufficient. GM A3.411 states that this fear of violence must be reasonably held and suggests that corroborative evidence may be obtained from the police or a supportive organisation to whom reports of violence may have been made. It is suggested that provided there is an honest fear of violence which has some basis, this would suffice. Furthermore, authorities should not fall into the trap of rejecting a claimant's assertions of fear of violence if no report is made to the police. Many victims of domestic violence find it very difficult to seek official help.

The fear of violence can come from either of two sources.

(1)   Fear of violence in the dwelling formerly occupied as a home. A "dwelling" can include some land – eg, that used for the purpose of occupying a dwelling or land on which a caravan or mobile home stands: s137 SSCBA and reg 2(4). So fear of violence in, for example, the garden of the former home should suffice. Fear of attacks in the street will not suffice. However, it is suggested that abuse in the street towards a claimant living in her/his home which gives rise to a fear of being attacked in the home should be enough to qualify. Note that a fear of violence in the former home need not come from a former member of the claimant's family; attacks on the home by neighbours or racial violence can come within this heading.

(2)   Fear of violence by a former member of the claimant's family. For the meaning of family, see p22. This does not have to be a fear of violence in the former home.

The period for which HB can be paid for two homes is restricted in such circumstances to 52 weeks.

Sub-para (b) deals with claims from people who are members of a couple or a polygamous relationship where one of the partners is a student who is not excluded from HB by reg 56(1) or on a training course. In this situation, HB can be paid in respect of both the term-time residence and the dwelling in which the other partner(s) live indefinitely, but the need for two homes must be "unavoidable" and payment of HB in respect of both homes must be reasonable in the circumstances of the particular claim.

The decision of the court of Appeal in *R (Naghshbandi) v Camden LBC* [2003] HLR 280 may produce a potential anomaly in the operation of sub-para (b). See the commentary to regs 12B(4) and 54 for a discussion of the decision. Since, following *Naghshbandi*, reg 56(1) only applies in relation to a student who is a claimant, it arguably cannot apply in any case where the claimant is the student's partner. Thus if the claimant becomes liable for the rent on the student partner's accommodation, provided that the other conditions in sub-para (b) are met it may be possible for the claimant to claim HB on both properties even though if the student made a claim her/himself in respect of the student accommodation, it would be rejected because s/he does not fall into any of the categories in reg 56(2).

Sub-para (c) caters for very large families. The dwellings need not be adjacent: GM A3.660. However, the housing must be provided by the local authority. But note the reference to *London Borough of Hackney v GA* [2008] UKUT 26 (AAC); R(H) 5/09 above where the dwelling a claimant occupies as a home may comprise more than one property.

Sub-para (d) makes provision for HB claimants who move home and who could not reasonably avoid liability for payments in respect of both the old and the new home – eg, where s/he had to move quickly to take advantage of better accommodation and so had to leave a former home without being able to give notice to her/his landlord. HB can be paid in respect of both dwellings for up to four weeks from the date on which the claimant moved. See para (7) where there is no liability in respect of the new home and paras (8) and (9) where there is a delay in moving. *CH 1911/2006* emphasises that the "person" to which reg 5(5)(d) HB Regs 1987 (now reg 7(6)(d)) refers must be the HB claimant. Accordingly, sub-para (d) cannot cover a situation where the partner of the claimant moves into the new dwelling to get it ready for the rest of the family to move in.

In previous editions it has been suggested that before a claimant can get HB on both the old and new homes, s/he must have actually moved – ie, HB can be paid to cover payments on the old home after a move but not on a new home before the claimant moves in. This approach was adopted in *CH 2201/2002*. The commissioner was considering a case where a claimant's move into a new housing association property from his council flat was delayed for just over three weeks from the start of the new tenancy due to his disability and a delay in obtaining a grant to cover removal expenses. The claimant sought HB on both properties for that period. The commissioner stated (para 6) that reg 5(5) HB Regs 1987 (now reg 7(6)) had no application. But note now the decision in *R(H) 9/05* and its view – albeit in a slightly different context – that a person can be said to have moved in once her/his furniture and personal possessions have been placed in the property.

In *CH 4546/2002*, the claimant's partner and carer took a tenancy of a property and sub-let a part of the property to the claimant, who then moved in with them. The commissioner held that on the facts, the dual liability could have been avoided (para 29) but more importantly for general purposes, decided that sub-para (d) could operate even where the new liability fell foul of reg 7(1) HB Regs 1987 (now reg 9(1)), as the deeming of non-liability under reg 7(1) had no impact on whether there is a liability in fact in respect of the new dwelling for the purposes of sub-para (d). It is not clear whether the commissioner considered *Naghshbandi* (see above). It is not mentioned in the decision and it is arguably inconsistent with the Court of Appeal's reasoning in that case.

Sub-para (e). Under this provision, where a person is treated as occupying a new home under para (8)(c)(i) (ie, because a move was delayed while adaptations were made to meet her/his disablement needs or those of any member of her/his family) and occupied another dwelling within the four weeks immediately preceding the move, HB can be paid for both dwellings for up to four weeks.

Paragraph (7): Moving to a new home in respect of which there is no liability for payments

Para (7) deals with situations where a claimant has moved from a home for which s/he was liable to make payments, to a new dwelling for which there is no such liability. The latter could include, for example, prison or hospital. It allows HB to be paid for the former home for up to four weeks where liability continues after the move, so long as the claimant could not reasonably have avoided the liability – eg, where s/he had to leave a former home without being able to give notice to her/his landlord. See para (6)(d) and (e) where there *is* liability for payments for both homes.

Paragraphs (8) and (9): Delays in moving into new home

Like para (6)(d), these paragraphs deals with the situation where a claimant has moved house, but this provision does not authorise the treatment of more than one dwelling as the claimant's home; only para (6) lists the situations in which this is possible: *CH 2201/2002* para 7. Since its effect is retrospective in that it permits payment of HB for a period before the claimant moves, unless para (6) applies, it can only apply to people who were not receiving HB in respect of their former home.

Where this provision does apply, it permits payment of HB in respect of rent due up to four weeks before the claimant actually moved into the new home (where s/he was liable to pay in respect of that period). This is done by deeming the claimant to occupy the accommodation during that period, even though s/he had not in fact moved in. In addition, the following conditions must be satisfied.

(1)   The provision may only take effect after the claimant moves in: para (8)(a). But note here the decision in *R(H) 9/05*, which holds, in effect, that this does not require personal presence by the claimant, but can be met by the claimant's furniture and possessions being "moved in".

(2)   The claimant must either have claimed HB or have notified the authority of the move to the new dwelling before the move: para (8)(b)(i) and (ii). In the former case, the claim must either have been refused or not yet have been determined. If the claim has been refused, the claimant must make a fresh claim within four weeks of moving to the new home. At first sight, para (9) appears to relax the second condition, by allowing a claim made within four weeks of the move to be treated as if made prior to it. But on a careful reading the paragraph does not have this effect, because it only applies if the conditions in para (8)(a) to (c) are satisfied. Para (9) therefore simply governs the date on which a claim which was made prior to moving is treated as being effective.

(3)   If (1) and (2) are satisfied, the delay between taking on liability for the home and moving in must have been "reasonable": para (8)(c).

(4)   One or more of the conditions in para (8)(c)(i)-(iii) must be fulfilled. *CH 3857/2004* confirms the, perhaps obvious, point that the adaptations under para (8)(c)(i) have to meet the needs of the claimant or family member which arise from or are particular to her/his disabilities (eg, handrails), rather than being works which would be necessary regardless of disability (eg, redecorating). This is emphasised in *R(H) 4/07*, where the commissioner follows an earlier decision of his (*CH 1363/2006*) in holding that the word "adapt" entails a change to the fabric or structure of the dwelling and so will not encompass furnishing (eg, carpeting) or decorating the dwelling. In respect of para (8)(c)(ii), the relevant paragraphs refer to people entitled to have a disability, severe disability or disabled child premium included in their applicable amounts and the components are the work-related activity component and the support component – see Sch 3 (on p521). Note that prior to the omission of pensioner premiums from the HB Regs on 19 May 2008, people entitled to have one of the those premiums included in their applicable amount also came within para (8)(c)(ii). This applied where a claimant or her/his partner was over the qualifying age for PC (then aged 60) and either of them were on IS or income-based JSA. Unless any of the remaining premiums mentioned are applicable, such a claimant cannot now meet the conditions of para (8)(c)(ii). See reg 7(8)(c)(ii) HB(SPC) Regs where the claimant or partner is at least the qualifying age for PC and neither is on IS, income-based JSA or income-related ESA.

For the definitions of "patient" and "residential accommodation" in para (8)(c)(iii), see para (18). See para (6)(e) where someone is treated as occupying a dwelling under para (8)(c)(ii) and is also liable to make payments in respect of her/his former home.

Para (9) governs the date on which payment of HB for a period prior to that on which the claimant actually occupied the dwelling may be authorised subject to the four-week maximum provided in para (8). That period commences on the later of the appropriate dates ascertained under (a) to (c). For "made or treated as made", see regs 76 and 83. Note also that reg 79(10) sets the effective date for a change of circumstances as the first day on which the person is treated as occupying the new dwelling as a home under reg 7(8).

Paragraph (10): Absence due to domestic violence

Where neither para (6)(a) nor (16)(c)(x) applies, if the claimant has left a former home through fear of relevant violence and has an unavoidable liability to make payments in respect of that former home, this provision requires the authority to treat the claimant as occupying the dwelling as a home (and therefore potentially entitled to HB) for up to four weeks. So where the claimant cannot be treated as occupying both the former and the new home (eg, because s/he is only liable for payments on the former home) or s/he is not temporarily absent from the former home (eg, because s/he does not intend to return to it), HB can be paid on the former home for the period specified. For the types of violence to which this provision applies, see the Analysis to para (6)(a). Unlike the circumstances covered by para (6)(a) this provision applies even where there is no liability to make payments in respect of the new dwelling and regardless of whether or not the claimant intends to return to the former home.

Paragraph (11) and (12): Absence for a trial period in residential accommodation

If a claimant enters residential accommodation, as defined in para (18), on a permanent basis s/he is no longer entitled to HB on the former home.

Where a claimant enters such accommodation with the intention of returning home s/he is entitled to benefit for up to 52 weeks: para 16(c)(ix). Some people, however, go into residential accommodation on a trial basis to see if it suits them. In these circumstances, paras (11) and (12) may allow them to continue to receive HB for up to 13 weeks. The Court of Appeal's decision in *SSWP v Selby District Council and another* [2006] EWCA Civ 271, reported as *R(H) 4/06*, 13 February (overturning *CH 1854/2004*) holds that the language used in in sub-para (7B)(b) HB Regs 1987 (now para (11)(b)) requires that the intention of returning to the dwelling which is normally occupied as the home must be present at the moment the person enters the residential accommodation; no more, no less. In other words, the intention to return home is to be gauged and fixed as at the date the person enters the residential accommodation.

On the other hand, the terms of sub-para (11)(c) are not confined to the present and have a temporal span which covers the whole of a person's time in residential accommodation. Accordingly, if at any time during the "trial" stay in residential accommodation the dwelling normally occupied is let, then the claimant will fall outside the parameters of para (11) and lose her/his entitlement to HB. But that will not arise if all that has happened is that the claimant has given in her/his notice to quit the dwelling.

What reg 5(7C) HB Regs 1987 provided for (now reg 7(12)), in the Court of Appeal's view, was to *treat* the claimant as if s/he was occupying the dwelling s/he normally occupied for 13 weeks, even though s/he had manifested the intention of not returning to it (or more accurately not returning to it after her/his right to exclusive possession has ended by operation of her/his notice to quit).

The Court of Appeal noted that its construction of reg 5(7B) and (7C) HB Regs 1987 was supported by the *different* language used in reg 5(8B) and (8C) HB Regs 1987 (now reg 7(16) and (17)), which, in the court's view, by inference, shows that the intention there has to be present throughout the whole of the period of temporary absence (therefore endorsing, though not expressly, the views in *CH 3893/2004*).

In *CSHB 405/2005*, the commissioner stated (para 30) that "desire" is not equivalent to "intention" in this statutory context, the former being a less certain or fixed state of mind than the latter. More controversially, perhaps, the commissioner said that in the context of reg 5 HB Regs 1987 (now reg 7) an intention to return to occupy the dwelling as the home must involve not only a subjective purpose to do so but also the objective fact that such a return is a realistic possibility. It is arguable that adding this gloss to the statutory words is both unnecessary and unhelpful. What has to be ascertained under reg 7 is the "intention" of the person, albeit to do a particular thing. As a matter of evidence the ability of the claimant to return and occupy the dwelling as her/his home may go to the cogency of her/his intention, and may reduce an intention to a desire to return, but this is all a matter of weight to be attached to the evidence when deciding whether the claimant has the relevant intention. If the commissioner is saying that, even if it is determined that a person has the relevant intention, the claim under reg 7 can still be defeated if it is decided that such a return is not a realistic possibility, it is suggested that the decision is wrong.

Paragraph (13) and (16) to (17): Temporary absence

Claimants who are absent from their homes for a temporary period can obtain HB for up to 13 weeks, and only in the particular circumstances specified in paras (16) is HB available for up to 52 weeks, in both cases from the first day of absence (paras (13) and (17)). Note that paras (13) and (16) to (17) may also be relevant in determining whether someone occupies a dwelling with the claimant. See the discussion of *Swale* and *Stroud DC v JG* [2009] UKUT 67 (AAC); R(H) 8/09 in the General Note on p237.

CSH 499/2006 considered the phrase "from the first day of that absence from home". The claimant had been treated as occupying his home during an absence while in prison on remand under reg 5(8B)(c)(i) HB Regs 1987 (now reg 7(16)(c)(i)). The issue was whether he could then be treated as occupying his home for 13 weeks from the date he was sentenced to a term of imprisonment under reg 5(8) HB Regs 1987 (now reg 7(13)). Commissioner May refused the claimant's appeal. He said that the calculation of temporary absence was dependent upon the application of reg 5(8) HB Regs 1987. For the purposes of that paragraph, "the first day of that absence from the home" was, as a matter of fact, the date the claimant had first been detained in prison.

In *R v Penwith DC ex p Burt* [1990] 22 HLR 292 at 296, QBD, it was held that the absence must be for a continuous unbroken period – ie, without any returns. In cases where a claimant is moving backwards and forwards between two properties, authorities must consider reg 7(1) in order to decide what is the "normal" home in respect of which HB should be paid. It follows that authorities cannot "aggregate" periods of absence so as to make up the 13 or 52-week period. Consequently if the claimant, with the exception of prisoners on temporary leave under paras (14) and (15), returns to and occupies the dwelling as a home, even for a short time, the allowable period of temporary absence starts again. The DWP suggests that a stay at home lasting, for example, only a few hours may not be acceptable but one that lasts for at least 24 hours may be acceptable: GM A3.460.

To be entitled to HB during a period of absence, paras (13) and (16) require the following:

(1)   The claimant must intend to return to live in the dwelling: paras (13)(a) and (16)(a). Often, a good indicator of an intention to return is personal belongings and furniture being left in the home: *R v Kensington and Chelsea RBC HBRB ex p Robertson* [1988] 28 RVR 84 at 85, QBD. Other factors might be where the claimant pays council tax, where s/he is registered to vote and other local connections. However, once a notice to quit has been given by a tenant in respect of the dwelling then s/he can no longer have a continuing intention to return to occupy the dwelling as her/his home: *CH 3893/2004* para 6. In such a situation the giving of the notice to quit cannot be treated simply as an expression of a future intention not to return to the dwelling upon the expiry of the tenancy, as the wording of (13)(a) and (16)(a) requires the continuance in the current benefit week of a positive intention to return to the dwelling: *CH 3893/2004* para 8. See also *CH 1237/2004* below which is to similar effect.

(2)   The part of the dwelling normally occupied by the claimant must not have been let or sublet: paras (13)(b) and (16)(b).

(3)   The period of absence must be unlikely to exceed 13 or 52 weeks as appropriate, or in the latter case, in exceptional circumstances, be unlikely to exceed substantially 52 weeks: paras (13)(c) and (16)(d). Once it becomes clear that a claimant is going to be away for more than the period allowed, HB entitlement ends. What is crucial is not whether the period does, in the event, exceed 13 or 52 weeks, but whether it is likely to do so on each successive day of the absence. This has been a source of confusion. There have been cases of claimants who took lengthy trips abroad, intending to return within 13 weeks (and usually booked on a return flight within that period) but who were unable to return within the period due to unforeseen circumstances. Such claimants remain entitled to HB until it is no longer likely that they will return within the 13-week period. This is confirmed by the deputy commissioner in *CH 1237/2004*. The main point of that decision is that the point from which the period of absence is to be calculated – for the purpose of determining whether the absence is likely to exceed 52 (or 13) weeks – is the date the claimant left the house (para 12), and not the date of claim. However, the decision goes on to say that continued entitlement has to be judged on a week by week basis, so that if at any date in the period of absence it becomes likely that the absence will exceed 52 (or 13) weeks, that is a change of circumstances allowing for a supersession of the entitlement decision from that date. The decision also emphasises that the test of likely period of absence is an objective one, to which the claimant's belief or opinion about the likely period of absence is relevant evidence but is not determinative.

For those claimants who may be absent for up to 52 weeks, the period of absence must be unlikely to exceed the 52-week period or, in exceptional circumstances, unlikely to substantially exceed that period: para (16)(d). GM A3.532 suggests that the term "unlikely to substantially exceed" relates to periods of absence of up to 15 months but it is for the individual authority to determine this, subject to appeal.

There is no requirement, however, that the intention to be temporarily absent from the dwelling needs to be notified in writing to the authority prior to departure: *CH 996/2004* para 17.

The categories of claimant who may be temporarily absent for up to 52 weeks and retain their HB entitlement are set out in para (16)(c). There must be some causal link between the reason for the absence from home and being within one of the categories: *Torbay BC v RF* [2010] UKUT 7 (AAC). They are:

(i)   Claimants on remand pending trial or detained pending sentence, as well as those required to live in approved premises (eg, a bail hostel) or at an address away from their normal home as a condition of bail. This latter category removes the prior restriction in reg 5(8B)(c)(i) HB Regs 1987 to persons in bail hostels only. That rule had been challenged – by a claimant who was required to live away from her home as a condition of her bail – in *CH 4574/2003*. The commissioner held, however, that the restriction of the rule to bail hostel cases only, did not discriminate in a way which infringed the claimant's Art 14 Convention rights, as the difference in treatment between the two categories of person was within the margin of judgement that is allowed to the legislature when enacting social legislation: paras 63-66 applying *H (Waite) v London Borough of Hammersmith and Fulham* [2003] HLR 24. See paras (14) and (15) for additional rules where a detained or sentenced prisoner is given temporary release.

(ii)   Those resident in a hospital or similar institution as a patient as defined in para (18). Note that, unlike in the definition of "patient" in reg 28(11)(e), the medical or other treatment need not be provided free.

(iii)   Those undergoing, or whose partner or dependant child is undergoing, medical treatment or medically approved convalescence in the UK or elsewhere, but not in residential accommodation. "Medically approved" and "residential accommodation" are defined in para (18).

(iv)   Those undertaking a training course, as defined in para (18), in the UK or elsewhere.

(v)   Those providing medically approved care, in the UK or elsewhere, as defined in para (18).

(vi)   Those providing care for a child, defined in reg 2(1) as a person under the age of 16, whose parent or guardian is temporarily away from home receiving medical treatment or medically approved care.

(vii)   Those receiving medically approved care in the UK or elsewhere but not in "residential accommodation".

(viii) Students to whom para (3) or (6)(b) do not apply.

(ix)   Claimants receiving temporary care in "residential accommodation" but not those residing there on a trial basis. For the latter, see paras (11) and (12).

(x)   Claimants in fear of violence who are not eligible for HB in the circumstances under para (6)(a) because, for example, they are staying with close relatives and are not liable to pay rent on two homes but intend to return to occupy their original homes. Where there is no intention to return home, see para (10).

Paragraphs (14) and (15): Temporary release from imprisonment

The purpose of this provision is to ensure that most people detained in custody who are temporarily released cannot claim HB for the home they are temporarily occupying. A similar provision in the HB Regs 1987 was inserted following the decision in *Chief Adjudication Officer v Carr* [1994] 2 June, *The Times*, CA which held that a prisoner on home release could claim IS.

Where para (14) applies:

(1)   If the person's temporary release was immediately preceded by a period of temporary absence under paras (13) or (16), 13 or 52 weeks as the case may be, s/he is treated as still absent. If not, s/he is treated as not occupying the dwelling as a home: sub-paras (a) and (c).

(2)   For the purposes of para (16)(c)(i) (temporary absence of up to 52 weeks), the person is treated as if still detained.

The provision only applies to a person "detained in custody" pending sentence or under a sentence. It does not therefore apply to someone required to reside in approved premises or some other address away from home pending sentence: *R(IS) 17/93*. In addition, it does not apply to somebody detained under the mental health legislation listed in para (14)(a). Note also that someone serving a very short sentence might still qualify under the temporary absence provision in para (13).

Circumstances in which a person is to be treated as liable to make payments in respect of a dwelling

8.–(1) Subject to regulation 9 (circumstances in which a person is to be treated as not liable to make payments in respect of a dwelling), the following persons shall be treated as if they were liable to make payments in respect of a dwelling–

(a)   the person who is liable to make those payments;

(b)   a person who is a partner of the person to whom sub-paragraph (a) applies;

(c)   a person who has to make the payments if he is to continue to live in the home because the person liable to make them is not doing so and either–

(i)   he was formerly a partner of the person who is so liable; or

(ii)   he is some other person whom it is reasonable to treat as liable to make the payments;

(d)   a person whose liability to make such payments is waived by his landlord as reasonable compensation in return for works actually carried out by the tenant in carrying out reasonable repairs or redecoration which the landlord would otherwise have carried out or be required to carry out but this sub-paragraph shall apply only for a maximum of 8 benefit weeks in respect of any one waiver of liability;

(e)   a person who is a partner of a student to whom regulation 56(1) (circumstances in which certain students are treated as not liable to make payments in respect of a dwelling) applies.

(2)   A person shall be treated as liable to make a payment in respect of a dwelling for the whole of the period in, or in respect of, which the payment is to be made notwithstanding that the liability is discharged in whole or in part either before or during that period and, where the amount which a person is liable to pay in respect of a period is varied either during or after that period, he shall, subject to regulations 79 to 81 (dates of relevant changes of circumstances, weekly amounts and housing benefit for rent free periods), be treated as liable to pay the amount as so varied during the whole of that period.

Definitions

"benefit week" – see reg 2(1).

"claimant" – see reg 2(1).

"dwelling" – see reg 2(4) and s137(1) SSCBA.

"partner" – see reg 2(1).

"payment" – see reg 2(1).

General Note
One of the basic conditions of HB entitlement is that the claimant must be liable to make payments in respect of a dwelling: s130(1)(a) SSCBA. Reg 8 deals with the circumstances in which a person is treated as "liable" to make payments on a dwelling. This regulation must be read subject to reg 9 – if reg 9 applies to exclude the people listed here, they cannot be treated as liable. Cases often raise issues under both regulations. As Judge Lane points out in *SA v LB Newham (HB)* [2010] UKUT 191 (AAC), if there is a question whether a genuine liability to make payments arises under reg 8, a decision should be made on that issue before analysis of whether the claimant is to be treated as not liable to make payments under reg 9 despite there being a genuine agreement. See p247 for a discussion of so-called "sham" agreements. See the General Note to reg 9 on p250 for how such cases should be dealt with.

Analysis
Paragraph (1)
Para (1) sets out the categories of people who are treated as liable to make payments in respect of a dwelling. This is subject to reg 9, which sets out the circumstances in which people are to be treated as *not* liable to make payments.
   The people that can be treated as being liable to make payments are as follows.
(1)   The person who is liable – ie, under an agreement: sub-para (a).
(2)   The partner of a person coming under (1): sub-para (b). This does not mean that *both* the claimant and her/his partner may claim HB in respect of the home, but offers them a choice of claimant: see reg 82.
(3)   A person who has to make the payments if s/he is to continue to live in the home because the person who is actually liable is not doing so: sub-para (c). Once these two factors are established, if the person now paying was formerly the partner of the person who is actually liable, the authority *must* treat the payer as liable. If the payer is not a former partner of the liable person, the authority need only treat her/him as liable if this seems "reasonable". Note that where consideration is being given to whether reg 8(1)(c)(ii) applies, the liable "person" can include a limited company and is not restricted to a natural person: *R(H) 5/05* para 33. It is not possible to deem a co-tenant to be liable for a co-tenant's share of the rent in addition to his own under this provision: *CH 3376/2002* para 37. In *CSHB 606/2005*, the commissioner accepted (para 15) that it was not reasonable to treat a child of 15 as liable to make payments in place of her mother who was the tenant, where the mother was ineligible for HB under the terms of (what is now) reg 9(1)(d). On the facts, the claim by the child was simply a device to circumvent reg 9(1)(d) and to hold otherwise would negate the effect of reg 9(1)(d).
(4)   A person given a rent-free period in return for carrying out repairs or decoration: sub-para (d). The work done must be reasonable and that which the landlord would have carried out or be required to carry out if the claimant had not. The duration of the rent-free period must be "reasonable compensation". However, even if all of these conditions are met, the claimant can only retain her/his HB for up to eight benefit weeks in any one rent-free period. There is nothing to stop a person claiming for a subsequent eight-week period, so works that will take longer can be split up into eight week portions. In *R v Westminster CC HBRB ex p Sier* [1999] 32 HLR 655 at 662-3, QBD (Latham J), it was pointed out that where the eight-week period pre-dated any payment for rent, the authority would have to satisfy itself that there was actually an obligation to pay rent (in the absence of the waiver) prior to the payments of rent starting. In that case there was no evidence to support the existence of any such pre-existing liability. The judge also ruled that the eight-week period had to run from the beginning of any rent-free period. Thus it is not possible to select a convenient eight-week period – eg, in order to preserve transitional protection.
(5)   Partners of students excluded from entitlement to HB by reg 56(1): sub-para (e).
The meaning of the basic terms needs to be clarified.
   "Liable" is not itself defined. The Oxford English Dictionary defines it as "legally bound, answerable for .... under obligation to do ....". The need for the obligation to be legal as opposed to moral was confirmed by Blackburne J in *R v Rugby BC HBRB ex p Harrison* [1994] 28 HLR 36 at 48-9, QBD. In that case, the claimants were members of a religious commune who signed a detailed agreement headed "Statement of Conditions of Residence". It was held that there was a question of law as to whether the agreement was intended to create legal relations between the claimants and the commune, and Blackburne J decided that there was such an intention (at 51). He also decided that it was not necessary to demonstrate that the landlord would probably take proceedings to recover unpaid payments, in order to demonstrate that the obligation was a legal one (at 51). The Court of Appeal approved this analysis in *R v Stratford-upon-Avon DC HBRB ex p White* [1998] 31 HLR 126 a case concerning the same commune (the Jesus Fellowship Church). The court stated that there was no reason why a relationship with a spiritual basis should not have legally enforceable aspects to it, and on a proper analysis of the commune's documents the obligation to make regular payments was a legal one.
   In *R v Woking BC ex p Crawley* [1996] unreported, 19 June, QBD, Sedley J confirmed that the distinction that has to be drawn is between arrangements for living which will usually be made between friends and family (and, one might add, religious communities such as those in *Harrison* and *White*) and legally enforceable arrangements. If payment were made in the former cases, it would be "no more than subsidising a family arrangement which would in any event have resulted in the claimant sharing someone else's accommodation" (transcript at 7H-8B).

The claimant had stayed with a friend who held an assured shorthold tenancy on condition that he paid half the rent. There was a clause in the tenancy prohibiting sub-letting.

There is a conflict in the approaches of Blackburne J and Sedley J as to whether the issue of whether an agreement gives rise to a legal liability is a question of law or of fact. *CH 1171/2002* para 11 held that it was a question of fact whether or not a legal liability is created by an agreement.

What is required for there to be a legal liability? The three basic elements of a binding contract must be shown.

(1) There must be a "consideration" (broadly, that both parties are giving up something in return for something). This will not be an issue in HB cases.

(2) There must be a settled agreement between the parties. Again, this will not usually present a problem. There is no need for the parties to reach a detailed written agreement (see under "Evidence of liabiliity" below). If A orally agrees to rent a room to B for £50 a week, that is all that is required to establish a settled agreement for HB purposes. If there is no specific agreement about what facilities B can use and about house rules, that does not prevent there being a binding agreement.

(3) There must be an intention to create legal relations. Did the parties intend their agreement to be legally enforceable? It is on this third element that cases such as *Harrison* and *Crawley* turned. In deciding whether there is such an intention, local authorities should be careful to separate their consideration of this question from the question as to whether any of the grounds in reg 9(1) applies.

Those who do not have an interest in land can nevertheless enter into a tenancy agreement with another party, with a consequent liability for rent. In *CH 2959/2006*, the claimant had said that his brother (MI), to whom he paid rent, was acting as agent for the landlord. His claim for HB was refused on the basis that he was not liable to pay rent to the registered owner of the property (A) and that MI had no right to grant occupation. The tribunal upheld the decision. It said that in the absence of clear evidence that MI was the agent of A, he had no legal ability to enter into any contract with the claimant for the renting out of the property and consequently there could be no legal liability to make payments in respect of it. Deputy Commissioner Whybrow QC had sympathy with the difficult task faced by the tribunal but said that it erred in law by misdirecting itself that there could be no valid agreement creating a liability to make payments where the grantor had no power to let the property. He said (at para 22) that *Bruton v London & Quadrant Housing Trust* [1999] 3 WLR 150 and *Lambeth London BC v Kay* [2006] 4 All ER 128 (both House of Lords decisions):

"establish that a party who does not have an interest in land such as to enable him to grant a leasehold estate or tenancy in favour of another party can nevertheless enter into a tenancy agreement with another party which is valid and effective between the parties to the agreement, albeit that the agreement will not be effective to create an interest or estate in land binding on third parties, including the registered owner of the relevant land. While *Bruton* and *Kaywere* concerned with cases where the landlord could not create an estate because he was only a licensee of the owner of the legal interest, in my judgement the principle in those cases apply equally to circumstances, as found by the tribunal in this case, where MI had no authority from the registered owner to let the premises. Thus, assuming that there was an otherwise valid agreement between MI and the claimants, such an agreement would be as binding and effective as between these parties, notwithstanding it could not confer on the claimants an interest or estate binding A. The tribunal in holding otherwise erred in law."

Identifying the source of the liability may be of difficulty in cases where claimants have been placed by local authorities in accommodation pursuant to their duties. In *CH 1208/2003*, the claimant argued that his HB was not subject to restriction because he had been placed in accommodation by a local authority and his obligation to pay rent was to the authority rather than the owner of the accommodation. The commissioner, reversing the decision of the tribunal, stated that the mere fact that the local authority owed a statutory duty to house the claimant did not mean that his liability for rent was to the local authority: para 17. It was necessary to analyse how the local authority had actually discharged its duty.

The mere fact that payments are made to a person does not mean that the payments are made pursuant to a legal liability to that person. It is possible that the claimant is making payments of rent to a third party for the convenience of the landlord and her/his creditor. Thus in *CH 4922/2002* paras 16-17, the mere fact that the claimant was making payments to the landlord's mortgagee did not mean that they had taken on a legal liability for those payments which was excluded from HB under s130(2)(b).

The fact that the liability must be legal can produce problems with young claimants and claimants with a degree of mental incapacity. These matters are discussed under separate headings below.

Evidence of liability for rent may take various forms – eg, letter from a landlord, receipts for payment, bank withdrawal slips. HB is paid not only in respect of payments under a lease but also in respect of payments referable to licence agreements and other types of arrangement: see reg 12(1). None of the agreements that attract entitlement to HB have to be in writing and so authorities should be prepared to take a broad view of the evidence required to establish liability for rent. Where the agreement is oral and the evidence is sparse, the authority should give due weight to the claimant's declaration on a claim form that s/he is liable to pay rent: *R v Sutton LBC HBRB ex p Keegan* [1992] 27 HLR 92 at 99-100, QBD. This cannot be carried too far, however; in *R v Derby CC ex p Third Wave Housing* [2000] 33 HLR 61, QBD, it was pointed out that although a party's stated understanding may be genuine, such a statement cannot be determinative of the legal status of an agreement.

There should be no need to produce a rent book, since a tenancy can exist without one: *R v Warrington BC ex p Williams* [1997] 29 HLR 872 at 876, QBD. In *R v Poole Borough Council ex p Ross* [1995] 28 HLR 351, QBD, the Review Board decided that the claimant was not "liable" to pay rent because "there was no tenancy agreement and no steps had been taken to recover rent". Sedley J held (at 357-8) that neither of these findings could form a basis for the conclusion reached. As to the absence of a written agreement, it was clear from reg 10 HB Regs 1987 (now reg 12) that any kind of legal obligation sufficed to show that the claimant was obliged to make a relevant payment. As to the fact that the claimant's landlady had not sought to take proceedings, the short delay before the Board hearing and the fact that the landlady was aware of the HB dispute and could expect to be paid backdated benefit negated this factor.

In *Third Wave Housing*, Gibbs J provided guidance as to the requirements of a valid Review Board decision in a case where liability was in dispute. The applicant landlord (no point having been taken about the landlord's right to bring proceedings) was a voluntary organisation that arranged for foreign nationals to come to the UK to do voluntary work. They stayed in a hostel and claimed HB to pay their rent. Gibbs J stated that in considering whether the Board's decision that there was no liability for rent could be upheld, three matters had to be considered:

(1)   Was there material on which the finding could be made, whether individually or cumulatively?
(2)   Had the Board failed to take into account any evidence that was relevant to the question of liability?
(3)   Had the Board given adequate reasons or were they invalid as being sufficiently inadequate "so as not properly to indicate the basis of its findings"?

In that case, the judge concluded that the Review Board did have material before it in the form of evidence from the claimant to the effect that she had understood that she would not be pursued for rent arrears, her documentation had promised free accommodation, and she had made arrangements with a sister company to meet any shortfall in HB.

A further illustration of the range of factors that may be relevant to a determination as to whether a true liability exists may be found in *R (T) v Richmond-upon-Thames LBC HBRB* [2000] 33 HLR 65, QBD. In that case, a claimant with Alzheimer's disease lived with his landlady, who acted as his carer. The Board gave three findings as reasons for its conclusion that there was no liability for rent: that the carer acted as appointee for benefit purposes, that there was a close friendship between them, and that it was unclear how much rent had been paid prior to the HB claim. The judge rejected submissions that these factors were irrelevant and that it was irrational to use them as a basis for its finding (paras 25 and 26).

In *CH 1618/2002* para 12, the commissioner suggested that it was not permissible to consider evidence as to how the parties actually implement an agreement in determining the question as to whether a legal liability was created. The decision of the House of Lords in *James Miller & Partners Ltd v Whitworth Street Estates (Manchester) Ltd* [1970] AC 572 was cited for that proposition, but *Chitty* para 12-124 points out that the decision only supports a proposition that subsequent conduct cannot be used as an aid to interpretation of the *terms* of the contract. Such conduct can be considered in determining whether in fact a legal liability was created at all. Such restrictions upon the evidence that may be considered seem to be inappropriate in the context of informal proceedings before a tribunal.

Note also the, arguably *obiter*, view in *CH 257/2005* which holds that a failure of the landlord to supply an address for service contrary to s48(1) Landlord and Tenant Act 1987 only postpones when the rent is in fact to be paid (until the address is in fact provided) but does not mean that the claimant is not liable for the rent. Regrettably, the decision gives no real guidance as to what a HB authority should in fact do where there is a continuing failure by the landlord to comply with s48(1) Landlord and Tenant Act 1987 at the time of its decision on the claim. It is not immediately obvious that payment of the HB in this situation could lawfully be suspended under either regs 11 or 13 of the D&A Regs.

'Sham' agreements. Particular difficulties may be created by cases in which a written agreement exists, but the local authority takes the view that it does not reflect the true intention of the parties. This was the issue in *CH 1171/2002*, where the commissioner referred to cases on general contract law as to the meaning of "sham": paras 10 and 11. *CH 1618/2002* was another such case. The commissioner stated that the first question was whether the document, on a proper interpretation and on the assumption that it was a genuine agreement, imposed a duty to pay rent: para 13. If that question was answered positively, then the issue of whether the obligation to pay rent was a sham needs to be considered:

"If as interpreted the document produced by the claimant does impose a duty to pay rent, the tribunal must consider whether the obligation to pay rent is a genuine part of the arrangement between the parties. If it is not, the term is a mere sham that was never intended to be implemented, but which was brought into existence to misrepresent the true arrangement between the parties and to conceal the truth from those dealing with them." (para 14)

The commissioner went on to give some useful guidelines as to the principles to be applied in answering this basic question.

(1)   It need not be shown that the whole document is a sham. "The sham may extend to the whole of the document or be confined to one or more of its terms": para 13. It is the term creating the liability for rent which is of importance, although the fact that other terms are intended to be genuine is probably at least some evidence that the whole document is genuine.

(2)   It is for the person alleging that a document is a sham to prove it. The local authority must therefore prove that the document is a sham: paras 15-16.

(3)   Whether a term is a sham is a question of fact: para 17.

(4)   The term is only a sham if neither party regards it as a genuine term: para 17.

(5)   If a term is genuine, the motivation behind the term is irrelevant to the question of whether there is a legal liability: para 17. So if an obligation to pay rent was only inserted to bring the claimant within the scope of the HB scheme, that does not mean that there is no liability for rent, although that may call into question whether the agreement falls foul of reg 9(1)(l).

(6)   The tribunal may take account of the way in which the contract has been implemented by the parties: para 18. However, a careful distinction must be drawn between a term which will never be implemented and one which might be implemented but has not in fact been enforced. Only the former terms are shams: para 19. Thus where a landlord does not enforce an obligation to pay rent while an appeal against a refusal of HB under reg 8 is outstanding, it does not necessarily follow that the obligation as to payment is a sham: paras 20-22.

CSHB 718/2002 considered the Scottish law on the subject of the creation of leases. Some of the points made in this decision are, however, of general application. The commissioner held (para 26) that where there is more than one agreement, each must be considered separately in deciding whether they are shams. He also said, correctly, that non-payment of rent was evidence that the agreement was a sham (para 28). However, any explanation for non-payment (eg, lack of resources) would need to be taken into account.

Liability of the young. There is no lower age limit for claiming HB so claims by those under the age of 18 are possible. The law in England and Wales and that in Scotland require separate explanation.

In England and Wales, the age of capacity is 18: s1 Family Law Reform Act 1969. It is not possible for a minor to hold any legal estate in land: s1(6) Law of Property Act 1925. So if a person under the age of 18 signs a tenancy agreement, the agreement is treated as an undertaking by the landlord to hold the property in trust for the tenant: Sch 1 para 1(1) Trusts of Land and Appointment of Trustees Act 1996. However, that would not mean that the minor was not liable to make payments of rent, since the minor would still be obliged to meet the consideration for the creation of the statutory trust: namely the payments set out in the agreement. This issue does not arise in the case of other types of contract for the occupation of property such as a contractual license, in which no estate in land passes. Note also that a minor may succeed to certain statutory tenancies: see, for example, *Kingston-upon-Thames BC v Prince* [1998] 31 HLR 794, CA.

A minor is bound by a contract for "necessities" and it is therefore likely that accommodation would be regarded as a necessity. However, in deciding whether a minor can make a contract for the provision of accommodation, bear in mind the following statement of Scott LJ in *R v Oldham MBC ex p G* [1993] 1 FLR 645 at 662, CA:

"If a minor is to enter into a contract with the limited efficacy that the law allows, the minor must at least be old enough to understand the nature of the transaction and, if the transaction involves obligations of a continuing nature, the nature of those obligations."

In Scotland, the position is governed by the Age of Legal Capacity (Scotland) Act 1991. Any contract entered into by a person under the age of 16 is void: s1(1)(a). A contract entered into by a person aged between 16 and 18 is merely voidable: s1(1)(b). In the latter case it is suggested that the analysis above applies. Even if the contract is void, *R(IS) 17/94* points out that the claimant might be liable under the law of reparation. Reference should be made to that decision for a detailed analysis.

Liability of the mentally incapacitated. This is now governed exclusively by the Mental Capacity Act 2005. It is not appropriate for this commentary to seek to summarsie the terms of that Act. Where issues of mental capacity arise, readers should refer to one of the standard works on this Act.

To date there has been no caselaw on the interaction between the Mental Capacity Act 2005 and reg 8.

Caselaw prior to the Mental Capacity Act 2005 held as follows. Firstly, where the claimant is contracting for accommodation, it is unlikely that a high degree of comprehension is required: see, for example, *CIS 754/1991* (an IS claimant with Down's syndrome had sufficient contractual capacity). In any event, in *CH 663/2003* paras 8-10, the commissioner held that a claimant incapable of making a contract could be entitled to HB, since the contract was only voidable and the claimant could not take the benefit of the contract for the provision of accommodation without accepting the burden of paying rent. Following on from *CH 663/2003*, *CH 2121/2006* emphasises that there is no minimum level of understanding of a party to a transaction that can act to render the contract void from the outset.

In Scotland, an agreement entered into by a person incapable of understanding the nature of her/his obligations is void and not merely voidable: *The Laws of Scotland* (1990) vol 15 para 661. The analysis in *R(IS) 17/94* would also apply in this situation however: see above.

"... to make payments in respect of a dwelling". It is not enough that some legal liability exists. The liability must have been undertaken in return for the occupation of a dwelling. In *R v Cambridge CC ex p Thomas* [1995] unreported, 10 February, QBD, a mother assisted one of her sons in raising funds to purchase a house. A declaration of trust was made in respect of the property, which included an obligation on the son to pay any rent received from lodgers to his mother. The property was registered solely in the son's name. The son lived there but the mother did not. Another son, the claimant, moved in and started to pay rent to the mother. It was held that since the mother had no legal title, she could not grant the claimant any right to reside in the property, and so the payments that he had agreed to make to her were not "payments in respect of a dwelling".

This conclusion seems rather dubious. It was not apparently in issue that the son was happy for his brother to move in, and it seems wrong to say that the claimant had no rights against the son. It is basic contract law that payments (or "consideration") made in return for goods or services need not be made to the person providing those goods and services. Payment to a third party is sufficient: see, for example, *re Wyvern Developments Ltd* [1974] 1 WLR 1097 at 1103D, Ch D. Therefore it is suggested that the claimant's payments in *Thomas* were indeed made in return for his occupation of the dwelling, the son having given the claimant a right to occupy in exchange for payments to the mother. The case would have been better dealt with as a "contrived tenancy" case under reg 7(1) HB Regs 1987 (now reg 9(1)).

The fact that payments must be made in respect of a "dwelling" confirms that if the payments are made under a business tenancy, they do not qualify. However, there may be difficulties where the tenancy is a mixed one or where there has been a change of use during the tenancy. With mixed tenancies, an apportionment must be made as to the rent payable for the business premises and for the residential premises and only the latter payments can be eligible rent under reg 12: see, for example, reg 12B(3).

A change of use during a tenancy could result in premises becoming eligible for HB. It would depend on the actual use to which the premises were now put and some evidence of conversion to living accommodation would be required. However, there must also be some change in the nature of the payments made. In *R v Warrington BC ex p Williams* [1997] 29 HLR 872 at 876, QBD, the claimant took garage premises under a commercial lease containing a covenant forbidding use of the premises as a dwelling. The claimant claimed that he had started to sleep on the premises as a night watchman, and therefore could claim HB in respect of the premises. The landlord's agents denied that the agreement was anything other than commercial. Hidden J held (at 875-6) that the agreement remained as a commercial one, even if the landlord was aware of the fact that the claimant was living on the premises. Accordingly, the claimant was not entitled to HB.

Paragraph (2)

This ensures that a claimant may receive HB in respect of all of the rent due for a particular period, even when payment is made wholly or partly in advance. Benefit is to be calculated on the basis of the period to which a payment *relates*, irrespective of when payment is actually *made*. Likewise, where rent is varied, HB is calculated on the basis of the period the variation affects, irrespective of when the variation is announced to, or paid by, the claimant. So, subject to regs 79-81, if rent is due on the first day of every month and the claimant's landlord informs her/him on the 15th that s/he is putting the rent up as of that month, for HB purposes the increase is treated as taking effect on the first day of the month.

Circumstances in which a person is to be treated as not liable to make payments in respect of a dwelling

9.–(1) A person who is liable to make payments in respect of a dwelling shall be treated as if he were not so liable where–

(a) the tenancy or other agreement pursuant to which he occupies the dwelling is not on a commercial basis;

(b) his liability under the agreement is to a person who also resides in the dwelling and who is a close relative of his or of his partner;

(c) his liability under the agreement is–

  (i) to his former partner and is in respect of a dwelling which he and his former partner occupied before they ceased to be partners; or

  (ii) to his partner's former partner and is in respect of a dwelling which his partner and his partner's former partner occupied before they ceased to be partners;

(d) he is responsible, or his partner is responsible, for a child of the person to whom he is liable under the agreement;

(e) subject to paragraph (3), his liability under the agreement is to a company or a trustee of a trust of which–

  (i) he or his partner;

  (ii) his or his partner's close relative who resides with him; or

  (iii) his or his partner's former partner;

  is, in the case of a company, a director or an employee, or, in the case of a trust, a trustee or a beneficiary;

(f) his liability under the agreement is to a trustee of a trust of which his or his partner's child is a beneficiary;

(g) subject to paragraph (3), before the liability was created, he was a non-dependant of someone who resided, and continues to reside, in the dwelling;

(h)   he previously owned, or his partner previously owned, the dwelling in respect of which the liability arises and less than five years have elapsed since he or, as the case may be, his partner, ceased to own the property, save that this sub-paragraph shall not apply where he satisfies the appropriate authority that he or his partner could not have continued to occupy that dwelling without relinquishing ownership;

[¹ (ha) he or his partner–
    (i)   was a tenant under a long tenancy in respect of the dwelling; and
    (ii)   less than five years have elapsed since that tenancy ceased,
except where he satisfies the appropriate authority that he or his partner could not have continued to occupy that dwelling without relinquishing the tenancy;]

(i)   his occupation, or his partner's occupation, of the dwelling is a condition of his or his partner's employment by the landlord;

(j)   he is a member of, and is wholly maintained (disregarding any liability he may have to make payments in respect of the dwelling he occupies as his home) by, a religious order;

(k)   he is in residential accommodation;

(l)   in a case to which the preceding sub-paragraphs do not apply, the appropriate authority is satisfied that the liability was created to take advantage of the housing benefit scheme established under Part 7 of the Act.

(2)   In determining whether a tenancy or other agreement pursuant to which a person occupies a dwelling is not on a commercial basis regard shall be had inter alia to whether the terms upon which the person occupies the dwelling include terms which are not enforceable at law.

(3)   Sub-paragraphs (e) and (g) of paragraph (1) shall not apply in a case where the person satisfies the appropriate authority that the liability was not intended to be a means of taking advantage of the housing benefit scheme.

(4)   In this regulation ''residential accommodation'' means accommodation which is provided in–

(a)   a care home; or

(b)   an independent hospital.

Modifications

Reg 9 applies as modified by Sch 3 para 9(3)(a) HB&CTB(CP) Regs (see p1223) to a claimant who on 3 October 2005 was someone to whom reg 7(2) HB Regs 1987 as then in force applied.

    Reg 9 applies as modified by Sch 3 para 9(5)(a) HB&CTB(CP) Regs (see p1223) to a claimant who on 3 October 2005 was someone to whom reg 7(5) HB Regs 1987 as then in force applied.

    Reg 9 applies as modified by Sch 3 para 9(7)(a) HB&CTB(CP) Regs (see p1223) to a claimant who on 3 October 2005 was someone to whom reg 7(7) HB Regs 1987 as then in force applied.

Amendment

1.   Inserted by reg 2(3) of SI 2007 No 1356 as from 1.10.07.

Definitions

"close relative" – reg 2(1).
"dwelling" – see reg 2(4) and s137(1) SSCBA.
"long tenancy" – see reg 2(1).
"partner" – reg 2(1).
"payment" – see reg 2(1).
"resides with" – see reg 3(4).

General Note

The question of whether there is a genuine liability to make payments is dealt with under reg 8. However, reg 9 (made under powers conferred by s137(2)(i) SSCBA 1992) treats certain classes of people who are (or may be) under a legal liability to make payments as not being liable, thereby disqualifying them from HB. In *SA v LB Newham (HB)* [2010] UKUT 191 (AAC), Judge Lane pointed out that the question of genuine liability needs to be considered first under reg 8 and the question of whether the claimant is to be treated as not having a liability to make payments then considered under reg 9. She said:

    "As a matter of practicality, a tribunal may bypass regulation 8 if it sees an obvious ground under regulation 9 upon which it can decide the appeal, but there are dangers in doing so. Bypassing regulation 8 may not amount to a material error of law if the tribunal gives a satisfactory explanation for disallowing the appeal under regulation 9, but if the tribunal turns out to be wrong under regulation 9, the Upper Tribunal may have no alternative but to set aside and remit the appeal."

The facts of particular cases may bring a case within the meaning of more than one of the sub-paras in reg 9(1). If the First-tier Tribunal forms the view that a sub-para other than that relied upon by the authority in reaching its decision may be applicable, it is under a duty to warn the parties of that possibility and give them a fair opportunity to deal with the point, otherwise there will be a breach of natural justice and its decision will be set aside on appeal: *CH 396/2002* para 7. It makes no difference that there is evidence to support the tribunal's alternative ground for its decision: *CH 843/2002* para 7. The same applies to cases where the tribunal overturns an authority's decision that there is no liability but then goes on to find that reg 9 applies without warning the claimant: *R(H) 3/03* para 8. In the latter case, at para 1.3, the commissioner suggested that separate hearings could be held on the reg 8 and reg 9 issues. It is suggested that this will rarely be an appropriate course, because the issues overlap sufficiently that it makes far more sense for the tribunal to determine all issues at once. In *CSHB 718/2002* para 21, the commissioner said that it would be "sensible" to deal with all issues in one hearing and this course was also approved in *R(H) 7/05* para 3. Note also the view of Commissioner Levenson in *CH 1586/2004* that where a local authority or an appeal tribunal has decided that none of the provisions in para (1)(a) to (1)(k) applies the authority or tribunal is under a duty to consider para (1)(l): para 14. In his view, this duty arose because of the structure of reg 7(1) HB Regs 1987 (now reg 9(1)) and because "the very fact that regulation 7(1) was raised at all put 7(1)(l) into issue". With respect, it is suggested that the commissioner is wrong on both of these points and the conclusion he then draws from them. There is nothing in the language of reg 9(1) which compels the decision maker to consider 9(1)(l) in every case where none of the sub-paras which proceed it apply. If it were otherwise, and the opening words in 9(1)(l) "in a case to which the preceding sub-paragraphs do not apply" were said to create the duty, then in order for the local authority or the appeal tribunal to be able to rely on reg 9(1)(l) it would first have to show that it had considered and rejected sub-paras (a) to (k). Moreover, it is suggested that on a reg 9(1) case the "issue" (eg, per Sch 7 para 6(9)(a) CSPSSA 2000) is not whether reg 9(1) in general is satisfied, but whether the claimant is not be be treated as liable to pay rent *because* s/he comes within one or more of the sub-paras in reg 9(1). The oddity of Commissioner Levenson's approach is arguably revealed by the use of an example. Suppose a local authority decides a case against a claimant on the basis that reg 9(1)(d) applies. No issue is taken by the authority on 9(1)(l). The claimant then appeals and produces evidence to the First-tier Tribunal, which it accepts, that the landlord is not the father of her child and, moreover, she has never had any prior relationship with her landlord. In fact, it turns out that the local authority misread the name of the father on the child's birth certificate. Here, the whole, indeed sole, basis for the local authority invoking reg 9(1) has fallen away; yet on Commissioner Levenson's analysis the tribunal would be under a duty to go on and consider reg 9(1)(l). It may have been on the facts in *CH 1586/2004* that the appeal tribunal wrongly failed to consider the issue of reg 7(1)(l) HB Regs 1987 (now reg 9(1)(l) HB Regs) under the discretion vested in it by Sch 7 para 6(9)(a) CSPSSA 2000, but it is a long way from that statement to say that the tribunal was under a legal duty to consider 7(1)(l).

In *CH 396/2002*, the commissioner also emphasised the need to use the correct terminology to avoid confusion of thought. He pointed out that speaking of any of the sub-paragraphs in terms of contrivance led to a danger of superimposing the test in sub-para (l) on the considerations appropriate to the other sub-paragraphs under consideration: para 11.

Reg 9(1) requires careful treatment by authorities to determine the question of whether an agreement falls foul of its provisions. Local authorities and the First-tier Tribunal may find the following systematic approach helpful.

(1) Consider which of the sub-paras may be applicable to the case under consideration. Examine carefully the various issues that arise under each and what must be proven and by whom.

(2) Ensure that the parties have had a fair opportunity to prepare cases on any new sub-paras identified by the First-tier Tribunal as being potentially relevant and which have not been dealt with in the submissions of the parties. Note the discretion in Sch 7 para 6(9)(b) CSPSSA to decline to consider fresh issues, and the fact that a failure to give such an opportunity to consider the evidence will render a tribunal decision erroneous in law: see below.

(3) Consider all the evidence and make full findings of fact on all evidence, particularly where the evidence is in conflict.

(4) Examine any of sub-paras (a) to (k) that may be applicable. Decide whether, on the findings of fact, the claimant's case falls within any of them. Give full reasons why this is found to be so, ensuring that all relevant factors have been explicitly considered.

(5) If the case is found to fall within either of sub-paras (e) or (g), consider the question of whether the claimant has proved that the liability was not intended to take advantage of the HB scheme: para (3).

(6) If none of the preceding sub-paras are found to be applicable, consider whether sub-para (l) applies (and see *CH 1586/2004* referred to below). Note the difference in language between sub-para (1)(l) and para (3) discussed below. Give full reasons for the conclusion on this issue. It may be prudent to consider sub-para (l) even if a case is found to fall within one of the other sub-paras.

In the discussion below, the words "landlord", "tenant", and "tenancy" are used as convenient shorthand for the person to whom payment is made, the person making payment for the home, and the agreement under which the home is occupied, even where the use of these words is not strictly correct as a matter of law.

Analysis
Paragraph (1): Introduction
The interpretation of the various sub-paras of para (1) must be informed by the fact that reg 9(1) has the potential to work "rough justice" and that "it is appropriate to give them [the sub-paras] the narrowest interpretation that is consistent with the policy of protecting the scheme": *CH 716/2002* para 11.

When considering sub-paras (a) to (l), it must be borne in mind that these offer 13 entirely separate grounds on which the authority may refuse HB on the basis that someone must be treated as if not liable for rent. As will appear from the Analysis below, certain issues will be of relevance to more than one of the grounds. However, it is important to consider the possible application of each of the sub-paras separately, to avoid confusion.

Issues under sub-paras (a) to (l) may also be linked with the issue as to whether there is a genuine liability, which falls for consideration under reg 8. The issues are different, and again it is important to consider the legal requirements separately so as to avoid confusion: *CH 1171/2002* para 12.

The need to draw a careful distinction between issues arising under reg 8 and reg 9 was vividly illustrated by *R v Greenwich LBC ex p Dhadly* [1999] 32 HLR 829. The claimant occupied a three-bedroom property owned by his son, who lived in America. The local authority initially refused HB on the basis that there was no true liability to pay rent (though referring to SSCBA s130 rather than reg 6 HB Regs 1987 – now reg 8) and also on the basis that if there was a liability to pay rent, it fell foul of the former reg 7(1)(b) HB Regs 1987, now reg 9(1)(l). On review, the refusal of HB was based solely on the absence of a liability. The Review Board stated that it was "not satisfied that Mr Dhadly was genuinely liable to pay rent".

Mr Dhadly applied in person for judicial review of the Board's decision. His application was refused at first instance by Collins J [1998] 31 HLR 446. The judge held that the Board was wrong to rely on reg 7 HB Regs 1987 but as it was possible to justify its decision on the basis that there was no genuine liability for rent (ie, by reliance on reg 6 HB Regs 1987 – now reg 8), permission to seek judicial review would be refused. However, that decision was overturned by the Court of Appeal, which granted permission and remitted the case to a High Court judge for hearing.

The substantive application was heard by Richards J [1999] 32 HLR 829. Counsel for the local authority argued that even if the Board's findings on reg 7 HB Regs 1987 could not be supported, judicial review should nevertheless be refused on the ground that the Board's findings clearly supported a conclusion that there was no liability to pay rent. Richards J rejected that submission in these terms:

"I am not persuaded that the matter can be dealt with as easily as that. The Board's decision fails to show that the Board has properly understood the legal issues and the precise legal test that it was applying at each stage of the analysis. If it was applying section 130, it has conspicuously failed to say so and has, on the contrary, purported to be applying regulation 7(1)(b). .... in circumstances where there is no mention of section 130, and the decision is expressed to be on a different basis, the court should be slow to hold that the Board did approach section 130 in the right way and that the decision can be upheld as a proper application of that provision."

Paragraphs (1)(a) and (2): Non-commercial agreements
It is to be noted that it is the agreement between the parties, and not just the payment made pursuant to that agreement, that must be assessed to ascertain whether it is made other than "on a commercial basis". The agreement, and the relationship between the parties, must be looked at as a whole: *R V Sutton LBC ex p Partridge* [1994] 28 HLR 315 at 319-320; *R v Rugby BC HBRB ex p Harrison* [1994] 28 HLR 36 at 48-9, QBD. See also *R(H) 1/03* para 16.4. In paras 21-22 of that decision, the commissioner described a finding as to commerciality as a "compound fact" which depended on the primary facts found by the tribunal. In *CH 5147/2001* para 9, the commissioner stated that "the regulation is in the most general terms, allowing decision makers to take a variety of circumstances into account." All the relevant circumstances must be taken into account, but the weight given to them is a matter for the tribunal and a challenge to the weight given to the factors will only succeed if no reasonable tribunal could have approached the case in the way that the tribunal did: *R(H) 8/04* paras 23, 29. On a further appeal, the Court of Appeal in *Campbell and others v South Northamptonshire District Council and SSWP* [2004] EWCA Civ 409 *The Times* 6 May, CA (reported as *R(H) 8/04*) ruled that the weighing of the relevant circumstances is not analogous to the exercise of a discretion (as to which factors to take into account or not); everything in the evaluation is purely factual. Accordingly, there can be no scope for ruling certain relevant facts out of consideration because to take them into account would be to infringe a claimant's rights under the European Convention on Human Rights (here, Art 9, concerning freedom of religion). See also the decision of Judge Wikeley in *Basildon DC v AM* [2009] UKUT 113 (AAC).

In *CH 3008/2002*, the commissioner pointed out that the first step under sub-para (a) is to identify the agreement which is alleged not to have a commercial basis. Unlike sub-para (l), it may be possible for an agreement to pass in and out of the scope of sub-para (a). In that case, the reversionary interest of the landlord under an assured tenancy agreement had been transferred to the claimant's sister during the contractual term. At the end of the contractual term, a statutory tenancy came into existence by the operation of the Housing Act

1988. The commissioner remarked that he could not "understand how a tenancy that is created by law cannot be on a commercial basis" (para 11). This, at best, misleading sentence has been held to be wrong in *R(H) 10/05*, which should now be preferred to *CH 3008/2002* on this point. As Commissioner Turnbull puts it in *R(H) 10/05*:

"the . . . words [in *CH 3008/2002*] would appear to mean that a statutory tenancy cannot, at the point when it arises, be non-commercial, and that it can only become so by virtue of factors subsequently occurring (eg the sorts of events which the commissioner went on to mention). That is in my view plainly not correct. The statutory periodic tenancy arising under the 1988 Act has essentially the same terms as those of the preceding fixed term tenancy (section 5(3)(e) of the 1988 Act). Further, it arises simply by reason of the termination of the previous contractual tenancy. If that contractual tenancy was not on a commercial basis, then it is likely that the statutory one will also not be so. For example, if, by reason of the relationship between the parties, the terms of the contractual tenancy are very unusual, those terms will be carried over into the statutory tenancy. It is true that either the landlord or the tenant can under section 6 of the 1988 Act serve a notice proposing different terms, in which case in the event of dispute a rent assessment committee is to fix such terms "as might reasonably be expected to be found in an assured tenancy". A failure to use those provisions might be an additional factor pointing to non-commerciality, but the mere fact that the tenancy had arisen by force of the statute would not mean that it would be necessary to point to such a failure, or to some other matter arising subsequent to the arising of the statutory tenancy, in order to demonstrate non-commerciality."

However, if the agreement under which a claimant occupies a dwelling is *genuinely* on commercial terms then it follows that the agreement is necessarily on a commercial basis: *CH 3282/2006* para 15.

It is for the authority to produce evidence to satisfy itself or the First-tier Tribunal that the agreement is not on a commercial basis. In dealing with a reg 9(1)(a) case, the tribunal should "ask themselves whether the evidence has satisfied them on the balance of probability that the principal basis on which the agreement was made was a non-commercial one. If the test is not met the liability is excluded.": *R v Poole Borough Council ex p Ross* [1995] 28 HLR 351, QBD at 358 (see below).

The word "commercial" is not susceptible of further elaboration and it is probably not possible to definitively state when an agreement is commercial and when it is not. An attempted formulation in *CH 2329/2003* para 7 that "the arrangement ... will be other than commercial only if it confers no benefit on the owner which is proportionate to the benefit conferred on the occupier" was rejected in *CH 3743/2003* paras 32-35. Commissioner Jacobs said in the latter case (para 34) that "rigid rules are inappropriate" when assessing whether or not an agreement was made on a commercial basis. However, in *CH 663/2003* the commissioner suggested that the term "on a commercial basis" connotes a financially justifiable relationship and also some generality as to who may take up the tenancy, which would shut out (as being "commercial") an arrangement set up exclusively for the benefit of a particular claimant. This test would also seem to fall foul of the broader approach advocated in *CH 3743/2003*, as it seeks to elevate one relevant factor to being a decisive factor. The approach in *CH 663/2003* conflicts directly with *CH 296/2004*, where Commissioner Jacobs again emphasised that no factor is decisive in deciding commerciality and, rightly it is suggested, pointed out that accepting less than the contractual rent rather than evicting the tenant may simply be bowing to reality and does not necessarily mean that the arrangment is non-commercial. *CH 296/2004* also makes the rather pithy point that "[Rachman] is not the only model of a commercial landlord". What this division in the caselaw seems to reflect is the truth of the statement made above that it is not possible to definitively state when an agreement is or is not "commercial". It is suggested that the approach advocated in *CH 3743/2003* and *CH 296/2004* should be preferred. This suggestion is given added force by *CH 2899/2005*, which holds that in so far as *CH 2329/2003* and *CH 663/2003* put forward what may be described as the *only* relevant factors for determining commerciality they are inconsistent with *R(H) 1/03* and should not be followed.

In *CH 1096/2008*, the claimant was a disabled person who was the beneficiary of a trust created for him by his mother and another of her sons. In *CH 663/2003* it had been held that the tenancy he had in accommodation rented to him by the trust was not on a commercial basis, in particular because the arrangement was essentially and strictly personal to him. Subsequently, the property was sold and another purchased, with the claimant's mother and the trust owners in the form of joint tenants in common. Accommodation was rented to the claimant, with his mother as landlord. Judge Mesher decided that the claimant's tenancy was not on a commercial basis. The existence of the family trust was an essential background. As tenants in common, the trust had a right to possession of the whole property and in practical terms the claimant was either living in the trustees' half of the property or in property in which the trustees were entitled to a half-share of the income. Secondly, the claimant's mother had testified to the tribunal that she would never evict the claimant. Thirdly, the claimant's mother had signed the agreement for the claimant as tenant and as landlord, and she had control (as trustee) of the account into which the claimant's DLA was paid, and so in effect she controlled how much rent was paid to her as landlord. Taken altogether, all these factors strongly indicated that there was something other than a commercial arrangement. However, the judge accepted that a motive other than profit and concern that the claimant had accommodation where he could receive the necessary care and attention did not make the arrangement non-commercial, nor did the mere fact that the claimant's landlord was his mother. Judge Mesher commented that the legislation "seems very ill-suited to providing humane outcomes in these cases."

The factors which may be relevant in assessing whether the agreement is on a commercial basis include the following.

The relationship between the parties. Even if the parties are not "close relatives" so as to bring them within the scope of sub-para (b), the authority may take into account the relationship between them: *R v Poole Borough Council ex p Ross* [1995] 28 HLR 351, QBD. However, as Sedley J in *Ross* makes clear, there is nothing inherently non-commercial about letting to a close friend or relative, though the closer the relationship, the more critically the agreement may be examined. This point was emphasised by Commissioner Howell in *CH 4854/ 2003* where, following *Ross*, he stressed (para 11) that what is important is the nature of the arrangement: "the fact that the parties are friendly or related to one another cannot by itself turn a commercial arrangement or agreement into a non-commercial one". It will also be relevant to have regard to factors such as the desire to have a reliable and trustworthy tenant and someone companionable, particularly in cases involving single elderly people such as *Ross*: see Sedley J at 359. Such factors may explain why friends have decided not to live on their own. In *CH 1076/2002*, the claimant's adult son was the half-brother of the landlord. The commissioner stated, at para 19.1, that such a fact was of very little significance in view of the time that had elapsed since the relationship between the claimant and the landlord's father. The mere fact that the parties knew each other and could trust each other "proves nothing".

The 1997 GM A3.66iv made the point that fostering children is a commercial arrangement and so former foster children who remain in the family home when they are no longer dependent should be treated as paying rent on a commercial basis.

The fact that a claimant is residing with her/his landlord should not, of itself, be a factor suggesting that the agreement is non-commercial. Anyone who has shared a property with a resident landlord will be aware how intensely commercial the relationship can sometimes be. It will be much more instructive to have regard to the personal ties, if any, between landlord and tenant. Not all cases where there is a close relationship between landlord and tenant will fall foul of sub-para (a). It depends on all the facts of the case.

In *CH 296/2004*, the commissioner considered what difference, if any, the fact that the claimant's father was his landlord made to whether the tenancy was on a commercial basis. He concluded that there is nothing necessarily incompatible in a commercial arrangement being made between a parent and adult child, though the close family element in the relationship may make such a finding less likely: see *R(IS) 11/98* para 8 and *CIS 195/ 1991*. Moreover, care and support being provided to a disabled adult son by a parent under the tenancy, although different in quality from that which a stranger would provide, is not necessarily incompatible with the arrangement being commercial. If it were otherwise – and the provision of care and counselling by the landlord to the tenant would render such a tenancy arrangement automatically non-commercial, then there would have been no need make such service charges ineligible under Sch 1 para 1(f) HB Regs. Thirdly, the commissioner noted that the motivation for such arrangements will be different. However, even if the sole motivation for the arrangement is to ensure that the adult son or daughter is properly housed and supported, this does not necessarily mitigate against it being a commercial arrangement. Indeed, arrangements for supported independent living are a recognised part of the commercial rented sector. Fourthly, the commissioner emphasised that when considering the issue of eviction a realistic view should be taken about whether a landlord who is not a family member would have taken steps towards eviction, particularly where (as on the facts of this case) the claimant is able to pay a significant part of her/his rent even without HB.

In *CH 1097/2004*, the deputy commissioner confirmed (para 15), following *CH 296/2004*, that there is nothing inherently non-commercial in a tenancy agreement between members of the same family or between a provider and recipient of personal care. Neither did the fact that the landlords would not have let a room to anyone other than the claimant (a friend of theirs) mean that the tenancy was not on a commercial basis, considering all the facts of the case (paras 18-20). The friends wanted a commercial return for the room and without that return they would ultimately want the room back. Although they only considered letting the room to the claimant to assist her in difficult times (and would not have let it to anyone else) the letting was on a commercial basis even though the motivation for it was largely non-commercial.

However, in *CH 663/2003*, the commissioner – following *R v Rugby BC HBRB ex p Harrison* [1994] 28 HLR 36 at 48-9, QBD, and what he characterised as the peculiar and personal rights of occupation in play in that case – agreed that the agreement was not on a commercial basis because, although the rent may have been a commercial rent in that it had been assessed as a 'fair rent', on the facts of the case the arrangement looked at as a whole was one which was strictly personal to, and set up for the benefit of the claimant and the claimant alone. It was not, therefore, an arrangement which would have been offered on the open market to anyone other than the claimant. "On a commercial basis" connotes a financially justifiable relationship and also some general class of person who may take the benefit of the arrangement, rather than one person for whom the arrangement is exclusively conceived. But see *CH 3743/2003* and *CH 2899/2005* above.

The living arrangements. If the living arrangements are of an unusual character, this may suggest that the agreement is not commercial. In *R v Greenwich LBC ex p Moult* [1998] unreported, 19 June, CA, the claimant's agreement gave him occupation of the sole bedroom, but the rest of the accommodation was stated to be shared with the landlady. On a renewed application for leave to move for judicial review, it was observed that the fact that the owner jointly occupied the common parts but kept no part of the property for her sole use was "not something which one would expect to find in a commercial letting". In such a case, however, the authority should give due weight to any explanation given by the claimant for an unusual arrangement.

The amount payable. In *Partridge* 319-320, Laws J rejected a submission that "commercial" simply meant that some payment which was more than minimal was made for the accommodation. The same point was made in *Harrison* at 55, where it was said that even if the rent was broadly a market rent, the rest of the agreement might still lead to the conclusion that it was non-commercial. Profit is not necessary, provided the recompense is reasonable. GM A3.262 correctly emphasises the need not to place too much importance on this factor:

"Charging a low rent does not on its own make an agreement non-commercial. Many charities, voluntary bodies, and some individuals, choose to let properties at below market rents or do not want to make a profit from letting, but their tenancies may still be commercial arrangements if that is what the parties to the agreement intended."

Evidence of the making and amount of payments under the agreement. If there is no such evidence, that will be a factor the authority may take into account in deciding that the agreement is not a commercial one: *Moult* (see above). Such evidence may, of course, call into question the existence of any legal liability at all as well as the commerciality of the agreement. See the commentary to reg 8.

A careful distinction needs, however, to be drawn between a case where there is no evidence that *any* payments have been made and cases where the landlord has been accepting less than the contractual rent. In *CH 1076/2002*, the contractual rent was £400 and had been subject to a restriction of about 25 percent by the rent officer. The landlord accepted the amount payable by way of HB. The only reason given by the tribunal for finding that the agreement in question was on a non-commercial basis was the fact that the landlord had declined to sue for the balance. The landlord adduced independent evidence from a letting agent who stated that it was not unusual for private landlords to accept the amount of HB payable and not enforce entitlement to the rest. The commissioner held that in the light of that evidence and his own experience to the same effect, the landlord's decision not to enforce the balance could not be castigated as a non-commercial decision: paras 18 and 19.3. It was not irrelevant to the commerciality issue, but neither was it conclusive as the tribunal had found. Furthermore, the fact that the parties had not formally varied the agreement so as to provide for the new lower agreed rent was of little significance, since "lay people do not always attach the same significance to legal form as lawyers do": para 19.2.

A very common issue arising in these cases concerns the significance of a landlord deciding not to take immediate possession proceedings but deciding to await the outcome of an appeal against a refusal of HB. Considerable caution needs to be exercised before heavy reliance is placed on this factor. HB claimants are generally impecunious, having little or no disposable income and few or no assets against which a judgment can be enforced. Local authorities argue that no commercial landlord would wait so long for rent; but the contrary argument in these circumstances is that if evicted, a tenant will have little incentive to pursue an appeal against a refusal of HB and there will be no chance, as against at least some chance, that a landlord will ever receive her/his money. A decision to await the outcome of a hearing by the First-tier Tribunal, even if that takes a few months, will rarely demonstrate non-commerciality. A decision to wait considerably longer, perhaps a year or more if the case gets to the Upper Tribunal, would have to be examined with more care. Legal advice received or the landlord's perceptions as to the prospects of success of the appeal would be of importance in such a case. Independent evidence from letting agents as to common practice in such a situation, similar to that adduced in *CH 1076/2002*, would also be of assistance.

If payments are made to a third party instead of the landlord, it does not necessarily follow that the agreement is uncommercial (or that the true liability is to the payee: see the commentary to reg 8). In *CH 2329/2003*, the claimant and his wife moved into their daughter's house while she was abroad and paid all the outgoings on it themselves. The commissioner upheld the tribunal's conclusion that the agreement was a commercial one, saying (para 7):

". . . .the arrangement between the owner of a property and the occupier will be other than commercial only if it confers no benefit on the owner which is proportionate to the benefit conferred on the occupier. In this case the owner clearly benefits from the arrangement because it enables her to retain the house while she is abroad and have it occupied by somebody whom she can trust to look after it and its contents."

The parties' views. How the parties view the agreement may be relevant, but their views as to the nature of the agreement cannot be conclusive: *Partridge* at 318 (see p252).

Bad faith. As with sub-para (l), if there is evidence of bad faith on the part of the parties, it may lead the First-tier Tribunal to view their evidence with suspicion. However, the conclusion that the agreement is non-commercial would not automatically follow. In *CH 1325/2002*, the parties had created a tenancy agreement which had been misleading backdated to 1998 to attempt to justify a claim for backdating. The commissioner held that despite that conduct, the tribunal had been entitled to decide that there was a binding commercial agreement from 2001, the year in which the agreement was created (paras 12-14).

Para (2): Non-enforceable terms. Para (2) explicitly requires the authority to consider whether the contract includes terms that are not enforceable at law. However, it must be emphasised that it is not determinative of the question of non-commerciality, but is merely a factor to be placed in the equation. On the other hand, the fact that the Secretary of State has identified this as a factor of relevance means that it should be given considerable weight in the scales: compare *R v Westminster CC HBRB ex p Mehanne* [1999] 2 All ER 319, CA.

The presence of this factor requires careful disentanglement of the consideration of reg 8 and reg 9(1)(a). Under reg 8, the question is whether there is a legal liability to make a payment. Provided that the landlord could sue for rent under the agreement, reg 8 is satisfied, whether or not there are extraneous, non-legal terms: see *R v Stratford-upon-Avon DC HBRB ex p White* [1998] 31 HLR 126. Under reg 9(2) the issue is whether *any* of the terms are incapable of enforcement in the courts, not merely those relating to the payment of the rent.

A number of points need to be made about the effect of para (2). First, only "terms upon which the person occupies the dwelling" are relevant. It might be, for example, that one agreement contained the terms of the claimant's tenancy and also provided for details of her/his employment. Provided that the agreement did not make the occupation of the accommodation conditional of the employment (as to which see sub-para (i) below) the terms of the employment cannot be considered under para (2).

The question of whether a term agreed between the parties is enforceable at law should be considered broadly. This is only one factor in determining commerciality and so authorities should not overly concern themselves with technical issues of whether a landlord or tenant could sue for breach of a particular term. It must also be borne in mind that contractual terms can be "enforceable" in a number of ways. Thus a term cannot be said to be unenforceable simply because a party would not suffer any financial loss as a result of a breach and so could not sue the other party for damages. It may well be that an injunction (interdict in Scotland) could be obtained to prevent the other party breaking the agreement.

Once non-enforceable terms have been identified, the issue arises as to how much weight they should be given. It is suggested that the more fundamental they are to the whole agreement between the parties, the stronger their presence suggests that the agreement is non-commercial. The clear thrust of para (2) is to deal with cases like *White* where the legal liability is merely incidental to the spiritual relationship between landlord and tenant.

Paragraph (1)(b): Payments to resident landlords who are close relatives

As the categories of unacceptable relationships between landlord and tenant have been more exhaustively defined than under an older version of the rule, it is suggested that it is even more questionable whether this provision is compatible with Art 8 of the European Convention on Human Rights.

"Who also resides in the dwelling". A subtle change in the wording of the provision may substantially change its effect. An older version of reg 7(1)(a)(i) HB Regs 1987 spoke of a claimant "who resides with" the landlord. That imported the definition in reg 3(4). Now, however, the reference is to a landlord "who also resides in the dwelling". This would appear to oust the definition in reg 3(4), though this may not have been intended.

The critical factor is what is meant by "the dwelling" for these purposes. Must the landlord share *all* the tenant's accommodation, or is it sufficient if common parts are shared? By SSCBA s137(1), "dwelling" is defined as follows:

"...any residential accommodation, whether or not consisting of the whole or part of a building and whether or not comprising separate and self-contained premises."

The effect of *R (Painter) v Carmarthenshire CC HBRB* [2002] HLR 447 and *R (Murphy) v Westminster CC* [2002] HLR 447 is that careful attention must be paid to the agreement between the parties and its legal effect and it is likely that most house-sharing arrangements will be construed as being an agreement to share a single dwelling, rather than an agreement to create two separate dwellings within the same building: see paras 11 and 12 of the judgment. The view stated in previous editions of this book – that if the claimant has a tenancy, rather than a licence, in the property, it is impossible to conclude that the landlord "resides in the dwelling" because that would be inconsistent with the exclusive possession that is the hallmark of a tenancy – was found in *CH 3656/2004* to constrain para (1)(b) too narrowly. Commissioner Fellner accepted that this view might apply where the claimant rented a bed-sit and shared only the common parts. It is not the case that the only circumstances which could come within para (1)(b) is where the claimant and landlord share a room; everything will depend on the facts. *CH 3656/2004* was followed in *R(H) 5/06*, where the claimant and her sister shared the living room, kitchen and common parts, and the commissioner said that the claimant and her sister were residing in the same dwelling: the test for the commissioner was whether the landlord and the claimant were sharing the majority of the accommodation in the residential unit. (The commissioner also rejected an argument that the terms of reg 7(1)(b) HB Regs 1987 (now reg 9(1)(b)) were discriminatory and breached Art 14 of the European Convention on Human Rights.) The same commissioner put the issue somewhat differently in *CH 542/2006* where he said (para 13) that where "a person is entitled to and does share essential living accommodation such as living rooms and a kitchen, it is not in my judgment right to regard the "dwelling" in respect of which he pays rent as being only the rooms of which he has exclusive occupation". On that basis the claimant in *CH 542/2006* was caught by para 1(b) because his son, who was his landlord, also resided in the dwelling. Following *CH 3656/2004*, it was not necessary that the landlord son was entitled to occupy all the accommodation comprised in that dwelling.

However, even where there is no tenancy, there may be sufficient physical separation between the parts occupied by the "landlord" and the parts occupied by the tenant to lead to the conclusion that sub-para (b) does not bite. An example of this might be a self-contained "granny flat" where there is insufficient evidence of a tenancy but where the elderly relative is left to live her/his own life.

"Close relative". This is defined in reg 2(1). GM A3.240 suggests, on the authority of *R(SB) 22/87*, that "brother" and "sister" includes half-brother and half-sister. That decision also establishes that a child, when adopted, no longer has any relation with her/his natural parents and other relatives. It is to be pointed out that

step-brothers and step-sisters (unlike step-parents and children) do not fall within the definition, and GM A3.243-245 give useful examples of how divorce and death can affect who a person's "close relatives" are. Broadly, divorce and death sever the links with the family by marriage, so that a parent-in-law, for example, is no longer to be treated as such.

Paragraph (1)(c): Liability to former partners

This excludes agreements between former partners of both the claimant and her/his partner, if any. The liability must be in respect of the dwelling formerly occupied by the claimant/partner and the former partner before they ceased to be partners.

It is regrettable that para (3) does not apply to these agreements. One of the most common forms of financial settlement on divorce consists of partner A, formerly the main breadwinner, taking on responsibility for the mortgage, and partner B living in the property until their children become independent (the so-called *Mesher* order). The agreement will often include some kind of contribution made by B towards the mortgage payments. Such arrangements are excluded from HB, and it is likely to cause substantial difficulties for those in the position of such claimants.

Note the definition of "partner" in reg 2(1). There is no explicit requirement that the two relationships be consecutive and not separated in time, or that the occupation of the accommodation is continuous, provided that the accommodation remains the same. However, the phrase used in sub-para (c)(i) is "his former partner", instead of "a former partner of his" or "one of his former partners". It is arguable that the phrase used suggests a focus upon *one* individual rather than one of a group of individuals. Put shortly, in this context "former" means "last". This narrow interpretation gains some support from GM A3.266, which identifies the type of case towards which sub-para (c)(i) is directed in the following terms:

> "If a couple, married or unmarried, separate and the claimant, or current partner if they have one, remains in the joint home and is charged 'rent' by the partner who left, then treat the claimant as not liable for housing costs."

If a relationship is in the distant past, the case for regarding such a liability as necessarily abusive is much reduced. That may justify a narrow interpretation of the sub-para under the principle identified in *CH 716/2002* para 11.

It appears that the liability must be to the former partner alone. If, for example, the former partner jointly owned the property with a third party, it would appear that sub-para (c) does not apply. It would, however, apply if the liability was to joint landlords who were *both* former cohabitees of the claimant and/or her/his partner, there being nothing to exclude the usual principle that the singular includes the plural: see s6(c) Interpretation Act 1978.

The argument that the "dwelling" occupied by the claimant must be the same as the "dwelling" occupied when the claimant and her/his landlord were a couple and that if the claimant occupies a bedroom plus the common parts in a property while being excluded from the landlord's bedroom, sub-para (c) does not bite, was rejected in *Painter* and *Murphy* by Lightman J. Mr Painter and Mr Murphy had lived as lodgers in properties owned by their landladies before forming relationships with them and sharing their bedrooms. When the relationships broke down, they reverted to their status as lodgers. In Mr Painter's case, a deed of separation between the parties declared that he had a right to live in the property on paying rent but that the parties would respect each others' privacy. Lightman J held, as a matter of construction, that the agreement gave Mr Painter a right to occupy the whole property and so he was occupying the same dwelling as he formerly occupied (para 11). The agreement to respect each other's privacy, while it effectively amounted to an agreement not to go into each other's bedrooms, did not define rights of occupation.

The judge went on to hold (para 12) that a similar agreement would be inferred in Mr Murphy's case in the absence of any evidence as to the precise terms that had been agreed between the parties. The judge then went on to decide that even if the "dwelling" presently occupied by the two claimants was only part of the "dwelling" formerly occupied by each of them, that would suffice to trigger the exclusion because "it is only necessary that it was in fact occupied by the claimant and his former partner during the period of their relationship" (para 13).

It was further argued that sub-para (c) discriminated against the claimants as being people who had formerly been in a relationship with their landlady, whereas a lodger who had never been involved in such a relationship would not be excluded from HB. The sub-para therefore infringed the claimants' rights under Art 14 of the European Convention on Human Rights, taken in conjunction with Art 8. Lightman J rejected that argument (paras 15-21 of his judgment, discussed in the commentary to Art 14 on p129).

A further human rights challenge to sub-para (c) was raised in *R(H) 6/05*. It was argued that since claimants with a liability for rent to their former same-sex partners were not caught by the sub-paragraph (because their former partners would not have been a "partner" as then defined in reg 2(1)), the regulation discriminated against heterosexual claimants. The challenge failed and a further appeal to the Court of Appeal was also unsuccessful: *Langley v Bradford MDC and SSWP* [2004] EWCA Civ 1343, 15 October, CA, reported as *R(H) 6/05* (see the commentary to Art 14 on p129). Note that same-sex partners *do now* come within the definition of "partner".

Paragraph (1)(d): Responsible for landlord's child

This excludes claimants whose liability is to the parent of a child for whom, s/he or her/his partner is responsible. A person is only "responsible" for a child if s/he falls to be treated as part of the responsible person's family for benefit purposes. See the commentary on Part 4 of the HB Regs and in particular reg 20 (see p334). It follows that it is not sufficient that the claimant or her/his partner spends a lot of time caring for the child.

One issue of interpretation under this sub-para is the meaning of "child of" the landlord. It must be broader than a child for whom the landlord is "responsible", because under reg 20 only one person can be "responsible" for a child. Logically, it would mean any child of which the landlord was the genetic parent. It will also apply to a child who is adopted, who will not be regarded as being the child of his genetic parents: s39(2) Adoption Act 1976 and *Re Collins* [1990] Fam 56, FD. The genetic parents will also cease to be regarded as parents of the child when a freeing order is made under the 1976 Act prior to adoption: *Re C (minors) (Adoption: Residence Order)* [1994] Fam 1, CA. Likewise, any child in respect of whom a parental order has been made pursuant to the Human Fertilisation and Embryology Act 1990 is regarded as being the child of those in favour of whom the parental order is made: see the Parental Orders (Human Fertilisation and Embryology) Regulations 1994 SI No.2767. However, a man who provides sperm for "licensed" treatment under the 1990 Act is not to be regarded as a father of the child: s28(6)(a). In such a case, if the woman receiving treatment has a partner, s/he is regarded as his child: s28(3).

Those are the statutory presumptions that can be stated with confidence. Other situations are not so clear. It is not clear whether step-children are properly to be regarded as a "child of" the step-parent. It is suggested that unless the step-parent has parental responsibility for the child, the definition does not apply. Any person in whose favour a residence order is made acquires parental responsibility for a child: s12(2) Children Act 1989. Guardians acquire parental responsibility for a child: s5(6) of the 1989 Act. In any of these cases, the child is probably to be regarded as a "child of" the guardian: s5(6) Children Act 1989.

The above concerns the legislation in England and Wales. Scottish family law is to be found in different statutes.

The validity of sub-para (d) was subjected to an attack in *R (Tucker) v Secretary of State for Social Security* [2001] EWHC Admin 260; [2002] HLR 500, CA. Maurice Kay J rejected arguments of invalidity in domestic law on the basis of conflict with the primary legislation governing child support (paras 5-9), that it offended against the principle of legality (paras 10-14), and that it was irrational (paras 15-20). He went on to hold that sub-para (d) did not infringe Art 8 of the European Convention on Human Rights on its own or in conjunction with Art 14 (paras 21-29, discussed on p129). The Court of Appeal rejected the claimant's appeal, essentially adopting the same approach as the judge.

Paragraph (1)(e): Liability to connected company or trustee

This seeks to exclude a number of devices that in the DWP's view have been adopted in the past to circumvent the definition of "owner" in reg 2(1) and an older version of reg 7(1)(a)(i) and (ii) HB Regs 1987. These schemes have typically used the separate legal personality of a company or a trust as a vehicle to hold the freehold or leasehold interest in the home. The sub-para excludes agreements with a landlord that is a trust or a company where there is some connection between the landlord and the claimant or someone close to her/him. For convenience, in the following discussion the landlord is referred to as a "connected" company or trust, A is the claimant and B is the claimant's partner.

Who must have the connection? There are three categories of people that can have a relationship with the connected company or trust that brings the claim within the scope of sub-para (e) (collectively referred to below as "a relevant person"):

(1)   A or B;

(2)   C, who is a "close relative" of A or B who "resides with" A. See reg 2(1) for the definition of "close relative", and reg 3(4) for the issue of whether C "resides with" A. Note that the use of that phrase excludes the argument discussed under sub-paras (b) and (c) above – there is no reference to the sharing of a dwelling in sub-para (e). So if A and B occupy a ground floor flat and C, B's elderly mother, occupies the basement flat, and they share only a kitchen, C may be a relevant person for the purposes of sub-para (e);

(3)   D, who is A or B's former partner. See the Analysis to sub-para (c) above, though note that there is no requirement here that the home be the same as the one that D formerly occupied.

Connection with a company. The legal and everyday uses of the word "company" are different. Many people use the word loosely to denote any arrangement under which people trade in company with other people. In this context, a "company" is a company registered under the Companies Act 2006.

The agreement falls within sub-para (e) if a connected person is a director or an employee of the company. A company is required by ss9(4)(c) and of the 2006 Act to register the names of the officers , including directors, of the company Details of a company's directors may be obtained by carrying out a company search. These are held at the relevant Companies House for England and Wales or for Scotland. Company searches are also carried out by many independent organisations providing business services. The registration requirements, however, are frequently flouted and a person may still be treated as being a director of a company even when s/he is not registered as such. A director "includes any person occupying the position of director, by whatever name called": s250 of the 2006 Act. This may not extend to include a "shadow director". A shadow director is "a person in accordance with whose directions or instructions the directors of a company are accustomed to act": s251. However, in *CH 4733/2003*, Commissioner Howell said that it was "for consideration whether the term "director" in reg 7(1)(e) HB Regs 1987 (now reg 9(1)(e)) may need extending to include the concept of "shadow director" which it does not ordinarily do": para 37. Apart from those provisions, the term is not defined and the closest that caselaw has come to a definition is probably the following definition in *Re Forest of Dean Coal Mining Co* [1879] 10 Ch D 451 at 453: "commercial men managing a trading concern for the benefit of themselves and all the other shareholders in it".

A person is not necessarily an "employee" of a company simply because s/he does work for it. It may be that s/he is correctly to be seen as an independent contractor. The principal indicia of a contract of employment are an undertaking to provide work *personally* in exchange for remuneration and a sufficient degree of control by the employer over the employee: *Ready-Mixed Concrete (South East) Ltd v Minister of Pensions and National Insurance* [1968] 2 QB 497, CA. Authorities may find examination of the treatment of the claimant by the tax authorities helpful, but must be careful to reach their own conclusions. In *CH 4733/2003*, the commissioner said that the term "employee" has to be understood in the absence of any more extended definition as a person with some form of contract of service or an office holder: para 37.

Connection with a trust. This is likely to be a much more troublesome concept for authorities to apply, and so a short summary of the nature of trusts will be attempted here. A trust may be defined as a relationship in which property is held by a person or persons (the trustees) for the benefit of a person or persons (known as beneficiaries). The law imposes strict obligations on trustees as to their dealings with the property that is the subject-matter of the trust and requires them to act absolutely in the interest of the beneficiaries. One person may be both a trustee and a beneficiary.

The trust is a flexible concept and trusts range from small trusts of family property right up to huge corporate trusts such as pension funds and charities. Under reg 9(1), it will be mainly the former category of trust with which authorities will be concerned. In England and Wales, where there is a trust of real property, there must be at least two trustees unless the trustee is a trust company.

Trusts may be express or implied. In the case of an express trust, there will be a document setting out the terms of the trust and usually spelling out who the trustees and beneficiaries are, though informal documents may suffice to create an express trust if sufficiently certain. In certain circumstances, the courts may substitute trustees or alter the terms of a trust, including who is to benefit thereunder. Placing property in a trust constitutes a "disposition" of property, and the express trust is therefore only valid if evidenced in writing: see s53(1) Law of Property Act 1925 and s2(1) Law of Property (Miscellaneous Provisions) Act 1989 in relation to trusts created before and after 1989. If there is no document complying with the statutory requirements, then an implied trust may exist. There is nothing in sub-para (e) to prevent it applying to implied trusts. Broadly speaking, implied trusts are of two types. A resulting trust is imposed by the law when Z purchases property, or contributes towards the purchase of property, and it is agreed or understood between the trustees and Z that Z will be entitled to the property or, in the latter case, a proportional interest in it. A constructive trust arises in the absence of an agreement wherever it is unconscionable for the trustees to ignore Z's interests in the property.

This is only the briefest sketch of the law in England and Wales and reference should be made to standard works on equity for a full treatment of the law of trusts. Scottish trusts law has many similarities but also many fundamental differences: see *The Laws of Scotland* (1992) vol 14 para 1 and the full discussion in that volume.

Under sub-para (e), the liability must be to "a trustee". The normal rule in s6(c) of the Interpretation Act 1978 will apply here, so liability to more than one trustee will fall within the scope of the provision. However, it is suggested that the liability must be to a trustee *as such*, otherwise the landlord is not properly described as a "trustee". Where the home is not trust property, the provision does not apply. This is best illustrated with an example. A, X and Y are the joint trustees of a charity assisting the blind. X makes his living by buying, selling and renting property and rents one of his properties to A. Although A's liability to X is to a trustee of a trust of which he is also a trustee, X is not acting as a trustee when he rents the property to A and the agreement does not fall foul of sub-para (e).

The claimant or her/his partner or former partner, or a close relative of the claimant or her/his partner who resides with her/him, must be a trustee or a beneficiary of the trust. In *SD v London Borough of Brent* [2009] UKUT 7 (AAC), Judge Bano rejected the claimant's contention that the term "beneficiary" does not extend to objects of a discretionary trust in whose favour no power of appointment has been exercised, but decided that for the purposes of reg 9(1)(e), a person is only a "beneficiary" of a trust if under the terms of the trust s/he can be permitted to occupy the dwelling which is the subject of the HB claim. He went on to consider and apply *Frish Limited v Barclays Bank Limited* [1955] 2 QB 541 and decided that reg 9(1)(e) is limited to cases where there is power under the trust (other than by the grant of a lease) to provide the claimant with the accommodation in respect of which the claim for HB has been made.

The exception. Para (3) applies to cases falling within sub-para (e).

Paragraph (1)(f): Liability to child's trustee

Sub-para (f) excludes liabilities to a trustee, where "his or his partner's child" is a beneficiary under the trust. For an explanation of the trust concept see the Analysis to sub-para (e) above. Again it is suggested that the provision only applies where the liability is to a trustee as such.

"His or his partner's child" is not to be equated with a child for whom either is responsible under Pt 4. It is wider than that. It would appear that it should be interpreted in the same way as the phrase "a child of the person" in sub-para (d): see the Analysis to that sub-paragraph.

Paragraph (1)(g): Liability of former non-dependent

This excludes any claimant (A) who, before the liability was created, was a non-dependant of someone (B) who lived and continues to live in the dwelling. For the definition of "non-dependant", see reg 3 and the commentary thereto. It appears that A could fall within this provision even if B has never claimed HB. B must, however, reside in "the dwelling": see the Analysis to sub-paras (b) and (c) for the suggested significance of this phrase.

The exception. Para (3) applies to sub-para (g).

Paragraph (1)(h): Former owners

Para (1)(h) applies in any case in which the claimant or her/his partner previously owned the dwelling. A person ceases to own property, in England and Wales in any event, when a sale is completed and not when a contract of sale is entered into. Again the phrase "the dwelling" is used: see the Analysis to sub-paras (b) and (c), although the distinction discussed there is less likely to be of significance in this context. This para applies regardless of whether there has been a continutiy of residence – ie, even if the claimant lived elsewhere before returning to the property in question: *CH 3616/2003;CH 3220/2005;MH v Wirral MBC* [2009] UKUT 60 (AAC). Continuity is only necessary to come within the exception to para (1)(h), for which see below.

Sub-para (h) may apply even if a property has been divided into two separate properties or extended since the claimant owned it: *CH 3616/2003* paras 14-16. So if a claimant continues to occupy only part of the dwelling that was sold then s/he still falls within the scope of this provision because the new dwelling was part of the old dwelling.

Unless the claimant or partner fell within the definition of "owner" in reg 2(1), s/he cannot fall within the provision. Note: there is no requirement that the ownership of the claimant or partner immediately preceded that of the landlord, though it might be possible to make a similar argument as was adopted by the commissioner in *CH 716/2002* para 11 to support a conclusion that an intervening owner or owners would make sub-para (h) inapplicable.

As originally enacted in the HB Regs 1987, sub-para (h) had no application where the claimant had lived elsewhere before returning to the property in question: *CH 716/2002* para 11; *CH 5302/2002* para 14. From 21 May 2001, the harsh effect of the provision was mitigated by applying it only to cases where less than five years have elapsed since the relevant person ceased to own the property. The provision did not have retrospective effect in relation to claims made prior to 21 May 2001, but the five years could start to run prior to that date. In *CH 3616/2003* para 12, the commissioner decided that there was no longer any reason to hold that the provision should be limited in its effect. This conclusion sits uneasily with the commissioner's view in the earlier decisions that the word "continued" supported a view that the occupation of the property had to be continuous in order for the provision to apply: *CH 716/2002* paras 8-9. Since the regulation had not been amended save as to impose the five-year limit of its operation, it does not seem logical or in accordance with the normal rule of interpretation (that phrases used in previous versions of legislation and retained for present versions should be given the same interpretation as was adopted under the previous version) to give a more restricted meaning to "continued" under the new form. However, in *CH 4733/2003* Commissioner Howell was of the view, albeit *obiter*, that the interpretation placed on the wording of the amended form of reg 7(1)(h) HB Regs 1987 (now reg 9(1)(h)) in *CH 3616/2003* was the correct interpretation of the wording both of the amended and the unamended form of regulation 7(1)(h). Commissioner Angus agreed with this interpretation in *CH 3220/2005*. He said that there is no ambiguity in the wording of either the old or the new version of sub-para (h) which would warrant reading into them a proviso or a precondition of continual occupation: para 10. In *MH v Wirral MBC* [2009] UKUT 60 (AAC), Judge Jacobs confirmed his interpretation in *CH 3616/2003* for the reasons given in that decision. The judge said that he gave a different interpretation to the previous version of the legislation in *CH 716/2002*, because it was open-ended in its operation. This is what led him to interpret the provision differently from the natural meaning of its language. That consideration no longer applies, as the provision is limited to five years.

The exception. There is an exception for anyone "who satisfies the appropriate authority that he or his partner could not have continued to occupy that dwelling without relinquishing ownership". Continuity of residence is needed to come within the exception (ie, the claimant must show that s/he was in occupation of the dwelling both before and after the sale); *CH 3616/2003; Bradford MDC v MR (HB)* [2010] UKUT 315 (AAC). The judge in *Bradford MDC v MR*, although he did not decide the issues, pointed out that para (1)(h) does not state that the occupation of the dwelling must be as a home (as is necessary for entitlement to HB under s130 SSCBA 1992) and that if all that is required is occupation of the dwelling by the claimant, and not occupation of it as a home, there would be a question whether gaining possession of a dwelling, while leaving it empty, could amount to occupying it for the purpose of the exception to para (1)(h).

GM A3.282 suggests that this exception is principally aimed at those who sell their home when a mortgage lender is "on the point of seeking possession". It is arguable that this is too strict an interpretation of the wording of the provision. A claimant who is in substantial mortgage arrears which are mounting (perhaps because IS housing costs do not meet the full mortgage) and who has no realistic prospect of stopping the increase in the arrears could be said to fall within the provision, even if the mortgage lender has not yet got around to taking proceedings. It would not be sound policy to require a claimant to run up a large amount of debt where s/he has a ready solution to the problem.

GM A3.282 also suggests that the rule applies in cases of shared-ownership, where a tenant cannot afford the payments on the percentage owned and the housing organisation agrees to take back a part of the ownership and enable the tenant to rent a larger share. However, as sub-para (h) treats the claimant as not liable only where s/he or her/his partner previously owned "the dwelling" and has ceased to own "the property", it is arguable that as the claimant (or partner) has not given up ownership of the whole dwelling sub-para (h) cannot apply at all in such cases

In *CH 3853/2001*, the claimant had inherited a house from his mother. He felt under a moral obligation to share the property with his sisters. He sold it and divided the proceeds of sale between them, and then agreed with the purchaser that he could continue to live in the property. The commissioner adopted a test (para 16) of whether the claimant was under a "practical compulsion" to sell the property. He held that the claimant was not, since it would have been possible for the claimant to take out a mortgage in order to meet the moral obligation. This will include consideration of both the reasonableness of the sale as well surrounding matters which could have acted to remove the need to relinquish ownership (eg, finding a new or alternative employment or sub-letting part of the property): *CH 1586/2004* para 12.

CH v Wakefield DC [2009] UKUT 20 (AAC) considered the relevance of whether the claimant has made enquiries as to alternatives, or has taken advice. Judge Ward thought that here, the tribunal may have applied the wrong test, concerning itself with the adequacy of enquiry of itself, rather than as a route to establishing what alternative options were open to the claimant. Although it is true that sub-para (h) is not applying a test based on a claimant's conduct of itself, showing what steps have been taken to explore alternatives, whether by direct action taken by a claimant or by the claimant obtaining suitable advice, may well be an integral part of establishing whether or not it was possible for the claimant and partner to remain in occupation without relinquishing ownership. Judge Ward pointed out that as it is for a claimant to make out her/his case on this aspect, a claimant who does not address what steps have been taken to explore alternatives does so at her/his peril. As indicated in *R(H) 6/07*, there may be exceptional cases where a claimant's circumstances mean that investigation of options may not be required, but it follows that in cases which are not exceptional, it is likely to be a material factor.

The motive of the claimant in disposing of the property is irrelevant in determining the applicability of sub-para (h): *CH 396/2002* para 7. It is also important to note that the "practical compulsion" in *CH 3853/2001* does not require some *legal* compulsion to dispose of the property: *CH 396/2002* para 15. However, although the claimant's perceptions may be relevant as evidence of what is actually possible – so that in an exceptional case a claimant may be under so much stress that it is the interests of her/his own mental health to dispose of ownership as quickly as possible without investigating other possibilities short of sale – it has to be borne in mind that the statutory test to be applied is "could not" and not "believes s/he could not": *R(H) 6/07*.

A further important limitation of sub-para (h) is demonstrated by *R(H) 6/04*, in which the former owner was the claimant's husband who had left the country at the time that the property was let by the new owner to the claimant. The commissioner held that in order for sub-para (h) to bite, the former owner had to be the claimant's *current* partner: para 31. There was evidence in the case that the husband might no longer be living in the same household as the claimant, which would mean that he was no longer her partner.

Paragraph (1)(ha): Former tenants of long tenancies

This is a similar provision to that in sub-para (h). It applies where the claimant or her/his partner was a tenant under a long tenancy of the dwelling, but only where less than five years have elapsed since the tenancy ceased. "Long tenancy" is defined in reg 2(1). There is an exception for anyone who satisfies the appropriate authority that s/he or her/his partner could not have continued to occupy that dwelling without relinquishing the tenancy. See above for commentary on the similar exception in sub-para (h).

Paragraph (1)(i): Tied accommodation

Where the claimant or her/his partner is employed by the landlord, and it is a condition of the employment that the home be occupied, any liability for rent cannot attract HB. There must be a relationship of employment: see the Analysis to sub-para (e) above. Furthermore the occupancy must be a *condition* of the employment. That means that it must be compulsory and not merely a "perk of the job" or provided by the employer to assist resettlement. Where the claimant or partner has a written contract of employment, it will normally be apparent from the terms and conditions therein whether occupying the property is truly a "condition". Otherwise the best indicator will come from considering the nature of the job: is there something about it which makes residence on a premises necessary? The classic example is a pub landlord.

Sub-para (i) only applies during the period of employment. Once the employment ends, a liability to the former employer for rent may attract HB.

Paragraph (1)(j): Members of religious orders

This excludes those who are members of, and wholly maintained by, a religious order. The words in brackets preclude any argument that the liability for rent prevents the claimant from being "wholly" maintained by the order. However, the maintenance must be whole and not partial.

"Religious order" is not defined. GM A3.256 suggests that a religious order "consists of a group of people who have given up all material belongings and have offered their services free for the benefit of the order". GM A3.257 draws a contrast with religious communities, which "may do paid work or keep their own possessions" and may therefore qualify for HB.

The principal question in *CSPC 677/2007* was whether the claimant was a member of a religious order who was "fully" maintained by the order for the purposes of pension credit (PC). Commissioner May decided that she was. The claimant was a member of a religious order of Carmelite Nuns in which each sister paid all her own income into the monastery's account. Although only certain people could withdraw the money from the bank, each sister retained the right to her share of the money and if anything was needed, she could request cash, or payment for what was needed out of the account. If any of the sisters could not contribute to the funds, her expenses were covered by others' contributions. Commissioner May said that once funds are held in common for their application for the accommodation and maintenance of the members, it was difficult to advance the proposition that the members who benefit from this are not fully maintained, albeit that they themselves have, in some instances, made a contribution towards the funds of the order. He decided that for the purposes of whether a sister is maintained fully, her income, and the contribution of that income to the order, must be ignored. The Government had (eg, through letters from the Minister at the time) given the impression that there was a distinction to be made between self-maintaining and other religious orders. However, the statutory language did not permit such a distinction. The commissioner considered whether, but did not accept that, the provisions were contrary to the European Convention on Human Rights, Art 1 Protocol 1 and Arts 8 and 14.

The meaning of "religious order" and the issue of being "fully" maintained by an order for PC purposes were considered by a three-judge panel in *SSWP v Sister IS & Sister KM* [2009] UKUT 200 (AAC). The claimants argued that they were not members of a religious order because their orders were without centralised authority. This was not accepted by the Upper Tribunal who said that the term was used in a broad sense. Both claimants were "fully" maintained by their orders even though they were themselves the source of funds for the order, via their work and state benefits. The focus is on who it is that maintains a claimant, not where the money comes from. Both claimants were bound by vows of poverty and had no personal benefit from income they generated or received. The income therefore did not maintain the claimants; they were wholly reliant on the religious order for maintenance. The Upper Tribunal also decided that the provision barring entitlement to PC was not unlawful discrimination under the Human Rights Act 1998 because the discriminatory effect of the provision could be removed without conferring any advantage on the claimants. As the claimants would still be caught by the provision if it referred to "members of orders" rather than "members of religious orders", they were not victims for the purpose of the Act.

Paragraphs (1)(k) and (4): People in residential care

"Residential accommodation" is defined in para (4). Note also the modifications made by para 9 Sch 3 HB&CTB(CP) Regs (see p1222).

In *CH 1326/2004* (which was dealing with the pre-October 2005 form of paras (1)(k) and (3) of reg 7 HB Regs 1987, but the reasoning may remain applicable), it was accepted that where a person is living in a home run by a person registered to run a care home but is not in fact receiving the care which is contemplated in the registration then para (1)(k) will not apply to that person, as it is the care provided to the person in such a home (and not just residence in such a home) which is key to whether they fall within the meaning of "residential accommodation".

Paragraph (1)(l): Contrived agreements

This excludes claimants whose liability was created to take advantage of the HB scheme. It only applies where none of the preceding sub-paragraphs apply. There is a reference to the HB scheme established under Part 7 of the SSCBA 1992. This would suggest that if the liability was created when one of the predecessor schemes was in force, the provision cannot apply: compare *R(IS) 14/93* para 15.

Authorities need to consider all the evidence and relevant factors in determining whether an agreement is contrived. Apart from the old rent restriction rules, the "contrived tenancy" rule under reg 9(1)(l) has probably given rise to more litigation than any other part of the scheme. The usual trap into which decision makers fall is to identify one factor which they find particularly persuasive and rely solely on that matter without considering the entire background to the agreement and its contents.

I. GENERAL PRINCIPLES. Before setting out the factors which will usually fall to be taken into account in para 9(1)(l) cases, it is useful to set out some points of general application. First, the meaning of "to take advantage" in this context means "to abuse" and not, as in some other parts of social security legislation such as SSCBA s73(1)(d), to benefit from or to avail oneself of the scheme. If that were the case, no one could qualify for HB.

Commissioner Jacobs dealt with the meaning of "to take advantage of the scheme" in *CH 39/2007*. He said that it means something akin to abuse of the scheme or taking improper advantage of it. It did not mean merely using the scheme, nor did it mean "make the most of the opportunities that it presents". If it did, there would be no market for tenants requiring financial support for their rent. He said at para 19: "Many landlords use the housing benefit scheme as a way of financing the purchase of property as an investment or of financing a business, but it is not the function of regulation 9(1)(l) to impede the proper operation of the private rented housing sector." The provision has to be interpreted in the context of other control mechanisms provided for in the legislation – eg, the various rules for restricting "eligible rent", now in regs 12C to 14 of both the HB and the HB(SPC) Regs and in Sch 3 paras 4 and 5 HB&CTB(CP) Regs.

In general, the mere fact of letting only to tenants who have a genuine need for support, and to whom the landlord will provide support, with a view to obtaining a higher rent eligible for HB, is not an abuse: *Salford CC v PF* [2009] UKUT 150 (AAC). However, there will be an abuse if the rent is unfairly or improperly high, having regard in particular to the cost of providing the accommodation.

In *R v Solihull MBC HBRB ex p Simpson* [1995] 1 FLR 140 at 148E-F, CA, Kennedy LJ in the Court of Appeal cited Sedley J at first instance (1993) 26 HLR 370 at 378 as describing the purpose of the former reg 7(1)(a), (b) and (c) HB Regs 1987 as being "to shut out certain arrangements which, in the Secretary of State's view, would amount to an abuse of the system" and added:

"I believe that to be a correct approach, provided that abuse is not equated with bad faith on the part of the applicant. Bad faith would, of course, be persuasive evidence of abuse, but the appropriate Authority might in some cases properly conclude that there was a breach of regulation 7[(1)(l)] without it. In other words, the use of the words "take advantage" shows that at least in the eye of the beholder there has to be conduct which appears to some extent improper."

In *R v Stratford-upon-Avon DC HBRB ex p White* [1997] 30 HLR 178, QBD, Dyson J criticised this test on a number of grounds. He asked who was to judge whether there was impropriety, by what criteria, and what the policy of reg 7 HB Regs 1987 (now reg 9 HB Regs) was. The decision was reversed on appeal (1998) 31 HLR 126, CA. Mr White was a member of a religious commune, the Jesus Fellowship Church, that required certain categories of members to live in a commune, maximise their income and pool it. The Review Board found that there was a legal liability between Mr White and the Trust set up by the commune for the purposes of reg 6 HB Regs 1987 (now reg 8) but found that the obligation to make payments was "inextricably bound up" with the obligation to pool income. The Court of Appeal, holding that Mr White did not fall foul of subpara (1)(l), endorsed the interpretation of the subparagraph in *Simpson*:

"In my judgement the precise language of subpara [(l)] indicates that there must have been some purposive conduct on the part of those seeking benefit, the liability must appear "to have been created to take advantage". This connotes that something has been contrived or devised for the purpose of taking advantage of or exploiting the scheme. There is no evidence to suggest that Mr White (and, I would add, the landlord) has behaved in such a manner or been motivated by dubious ingenuity to create the liability." (Otton LJ at 137)

"For my part I share the judge's unhappiness at attempts to graft onto the express language of regulation 7(1)[(l)] an additional requirement .... having said that, I have little difficulty in finding in the language of paragraph [(l)] the connotation of an abuse of the housing benefit scheme." (Peter Gibson LJ at 141)

The mere fact that the arrangements between landlord and tenant are unusual and involve the creation of a "device of some sort" does not necessarily lead to the conclusion that the agreement is contrived: *R(H) 7/05* paras 46-47, though obviously the use of such means will call for some sort of innocent explanation.

The second point that must be made is that what is being examined is the *creation* of the liability to make payments. It would follow that the importance of the factors must be judged as at that time and not in the light of events which only became known to the parties subsequently: *CSHB 718/2002* para 33. However, that decision also notes (para 34) that an intention to abuse the HB scheme in the future would suffice to bring sub-para (l) into play. In *CH 3008/2002,* the claimant took a tenancy from a landlord with whom she had no relationship. During the contractual term, the landlord transferred the property to the claimant's sister. The contractual term subsequently expired and a statutory tenancy came into force by virtue of the Housing Act 1988. The commissioner confirmed (para 14) that since the claimant was unrelated to her landlord at the time that the tenancy was created, sub-para (l) could not apply to the creation of the contractual agreement. However, as to whether the liability could be "created to take advantage" of the HB scheme thereafter, he said (para 14):

"But what about the statutory protected [this should probably be 'periodic'] tenancy? The claimant's liability for rent has arisen under that tenancy since 16th July 1995. That tenancy was created by operation of law. How can a tenancy that exists by operation of law have been created with the necessary purpose? One answer may be this. If the sisters allowed the tenancy to come into existence when it could have been prevented, then it may be possible to find that the liability arising under the tenancy was created to take advantage of the scheme."

It is suggested that this is contrary to the wording of sub-para (l). When a statutory periodic tenancy is created at the point that the contractual period elapses, it is created by the Housing Act 1988 and not by the parties. It is hard to see how the parties "create" anything when a statutory periodic tenancy is allowed to come into force; rather, they allow the legislation to extend the tenancy. Moreover, nothing which is said in *R(H) 10/05* about the correctness of parts of *CH 3008/2002* detracts from this argument.

Even if the commissioner is right, extreme caution is required before it will be legitimate to make a finding along the lines that he indicates. If the tenancy is not an assured shorthold tenancy giving an absolute right to terminate it under s21 of the 1988 Act, the landlord may be powerless to act. As to the tenant, it will be a rare case in which they can be blamed for choosing to stay in existing accommodation rather than face a move into new accommodation.

It should be borne in mind in similar cases that it may be necessary to examine the motivation of the original agreement. Thus, if the relative agreed with the original landlord that the property would be purchased shortly after the original tenancy, it might be possible to find that the original agreement fell foul of sub-para (l) if all the other circumstances justified such a finding.

Finally, there is no presumption against the claimant that s/he is guilty of abusing the scheme: see Sedley J in *Simpson* at 378. Once it is established that the claimant is under a liability to make the payments, the burden of proof is on the authority to show some grounds for believing that abuse exists. The words "the appropriate authority is satisfied" allow the authority to reach its own conclusion on the point but, as elsewhere in administrative law, it cannot make a decision for which there is insufficient evidence or which is not properly reasoned. In *White,*

Dyson J suggested that the concept of the onus of proof was unhelpful. However, it may well be useful in cases where evidence is sparse, since if there is not enough information before an authority or the First-tier Tribunal to give rise to an inference of impropriety, reg 9(1)(l) cannot be applied. If there is enough evidence to allow the inference to be drawn, however, it may then be legitimate to examine whether the claimant has any explanation for the circumstances which do not relate to the obtaining of HB: see Kennedy LJ in *Simpson* at 148F.

A failure by a Review Board to apply the burden of proof under subpara (1)(l) properly was Richards J's primary reason for the quashing of the Board's decision in *R v Greenwich LBC ex p Dhadly* [1999] 32 HLR 829. It is worthy of note that this step was taken even though the Board specifically reminded itself at the start of its statement of reasons that the burden of proof to show the applicability of subpara (1)(l) rested on the local authority. Richards J examined the whole of the decision and considered that it showed that the Board might well not have applied the principle it stated at the outset.

II. OBLIGATIONS OF THE FIRST-TIER TRIBUNAL. *R v South Tyneside MBC ex p Tooley* [1996] COD 143 at 144, QBD, Ognall J stated that a Review Board's decision letter relating to a decision that a claimant falls foul of reg 7(1)(l) HB regs 1987 (now reg 9(1)(l)) must include the following matters. It is suggested that the same approach is applicable to the First-tier Tribunal.

(1)   A summary of the claimant's case as to why s/he does not come within subpara (1)(l) (though note there is no presumption against the claimant).

(2)   An account of the evidence, if any, given by the claimant in support of her/his case.

(3)   The conclusion of the Review Board.

(4)   A reasoned statement as to why the Review Board concluded that the tenancy was a contrived one. The facts will often be open to a number of possible interpretations and if a review board concludes that a tenancy is "contrived" its decision must contain a statement of reasons which is sufficiently detailed for the claimant to be able to understand why an adverse interpretation has been preferred to an unfavourable one: see Sedley J in *Simpson* at 378 and *Sier* (Latham J). In *ex p Dhadly*, Richards J also emphasised failures by the Board to deal with aspects of the evidence called and submissions made by the claimant as a reason for quashing its decision. The message is clear: a decision must show that all relevant evidence and factors have been considered or it will be vulnerable to challenge.

It is not essential that the First-tier Tribunal should consider the intentions of landlord, tenant and any other relevant party separately in every case. What is necessary depends on the facts: *Jones v City of Glasgow DC HBRB* [1997] unreported, 4 July, CSOH.

III. THE RELEVANT FACTORS. Again it must be emphasised that the whole of the circumstances of the case must be considered and that none of the following can be determinative in any one case.

The means, circumstances and intention of the tenant. A tenant will often have a number of motives or purposes in entering into an agreement to pay rent. The relevant question for the purposes of reg 9(1)(l) is which of these purposes was the tenant's dominant purpose. In *Simpson*, Kennedy LJ observed, at 149A-C:

"Of course [attracting HB] was one of the aims. That is why the applicant properly made inquiries to try to establish if Housing Benefit would be payable before he made the agreement, but it is at least arguable that his dominant purpose when he entered into the tenancy agreement was not to obtain Housing Benefit but to provide accommodation for his family .... In my judgment, the Board had to reject that conclusion if it was to find that the applicant created his liability to make payments to take advantage of the Housing Benefit Scheme ...."

It follows that, subject to what is said below about the circumstances and intentions of the landlord, reg 9(1)(l) cannot apply where the claimant's dominant purpose is to provide a home for her/himself and her/his family. In cases where it is accepted that the claimant and her/his family are actually living in the accommodation, it will often be difficult for the authority to show that this was not the dominant purpose of the tenancy, even when the circumstances surrounding the creation of the tenancy seem to be unusual. Tenants who are reliant on income-related benefits do not have much bargaining power in the housing market and will often have to take whatever is available. This will often be the explanation for cases where relatives have purchased a house and rented it to the claimant. *Simpson* was one such case, where the applicant and his partner had a severely handicapped daughter and lived in unsatisfactory council accommodation. The council were unable to move the family, and the partner's father purchased the home so as to facilitate proximity to schools and the hospital. Other cases of this type are *R v Milton Keynes BC HBRB ex p Macklen* [1996] unreported, 30 April, QBD and *R v Gloucestershire CC ex p Dadds* [1996] 29 HLR 700, QBD.

In particular, it is not sufficient to establish abuse for the authority to show that one or both of the parties knew at the time the agreement was made that the claimant would be unable to pay the rent without recourse to HB. This may be taken into account: Sedley J in *Simpson* at 376; *R v Sutton LBC HBRB ex p Keegan* [1992] 27 HLR 92 at 99-100, QBD; *R v Poole Borough Council ex p Ross* [1995] 28 HLR 351, QBD; *CH 2516/2003* para 4. However, it will rarely be a factor of great weight. Many recipients of HB will be in this position and, as Sedley J stated in *Simpson* at 379:

"To use this fact to deny an applicant benefit is to undermine the whole purpose of the Scheme by making the claimant's need count against instead of for him."

This point was re-emphasised by Peter Gibson LJ in *White* (see above) at 142.

However, the converse to this, namely that the claimant did not anticipate having to claim HB when s/he took on the rent liability or has met the liability her/himself from time to time, may often be a very good indication that there was no attempt to take advantage of the HB scheme: Kennedy LJ in *Simpson* at 149E and Otton LJ in *White* at 137.

Whether or not the claimant has sought other accommodation on the open housing market before entering into the tenancy may be relevant in some circumstances but equally it may be entirely reasonable for someone who is offered a tenancy on beneficial terms by a friend or relative to take up that offer without bothering to search elsewhere. The absence of a prior search for accommodation elsewhere does not necessarily mean that the tenant's dominant purpose in entering into the agreement was other than to provide her/himself and any family with a roof over their heads.

In some cases, it may be appropriate to consider the conduct of someone other than the tenant: *CH 1419/2005* para 15. In that case the claimant was a young man who was severely mentally impaired and had severe learning difficulties. His mother worked in the HB section of the local authority and helped her son enter into a joint tenancy agreement with herself and her husband in respect of a flat the claimant had previously lived in with his grandmother. On these facts Commissioner Jacobs accepted that the mother's conduct could in principle be relevant to the question of whether the tenancy had been created to take advantage of the HB scheme. In his view, in a case where a tenant is unable to act wholly independently it is relevant to take account of the motives and purposes of those who help in setting up the tenancy.

The means, circumstances and intention of the landlord. In many cases the best pointers as to whether an agreement falls foul of reg 7(1)(l) will be found in analysing the landlord's motives. As Peter Gibson LJ said in *White* (see above):

"A liability cannot be created unilaterally, but the reality, as Sir Christopher Slade pointed out in the course of argument, is that the purpose of the landlord is likely to be more significant than that of the tenant who will usually be incurring the liability for the proper purpose of providing himself with accommodation."

The fact that the landlord will make a profit from the rent charged is not conclusive evidence of abuse, as profit is the usual purpose and effect of any commercial letting. However, it is clear from *White* and the decision in *R v Manchester CC ex p Baragrove Properties Ltd* [1991] 23 HLR 337, QBD, that the landlord's intentions and circumstances can give rise to a finding of abuse even in the absence of any complicity or impropriety on the part of the tenant.

In *Baragrove Properties*, the applicant was a property management company managing about 340 houses on behalf of 140 landlords. They applied for judicial review of a policy adopted by the council on October 22 1990 to the effect that where the rent payable exceeded the "market rent" fixed by the rent officer by 50 per cent plus £20, it would treat tenancies granted to persons covered by an older version of reg 11(3) HB Regs 1987 as having been "created to take advantage of the housing benefit scheme" pursuant to reg 7(1)(l) HB Regs 1987 (now reg 9(1)(l) HB Regs) and therefore no HB would be payable. Where such claimants renegotiated their rents after such a refusal, the council would continue to refuse benefit under reg 7(1)(l) HB Regs 1987 where the new rent exceeded the "market rent" by 50 per cent plus £20 "save in the most exceptional of circumstances".

It was not disputed by the applicants that they were deliberately "targeting" people in so-called "exempt groups" (ie, exempt from certain rent restrictions) in terms of offering tenancies by advertising for such tenants and that they were not willing to let the properties concerned to HB claimants outside these groups. Nor would they have been able to levy the sort of rents involved, between twice and five times the "market rent", from non-HB tenants. Further, it was again not disputed that the sole and specific purpose of letting these properties at these rents to "exempt groups" was in order to "charge very high rents which they could not otherwise command". The case must be viewed against these rather remarkable circumstances.

The applicants argued that restrictions on excessive rents were governed by regs 11 and 12 HB Regs 1987 (provisions now found in Sch 3 para 5 of the HB&CTB(CP) Regs – see p1198) and could not therefore be used as the foundation for a refusal under reg 7(1)(l) HB Regs 1987 (now reg 9(1)(l) HB Regs). The respondents argued that these tenancies at these rents simply would not have been created but for the so-called "exemption" provisions of reg 11(3) HB Regs 1987 and that they therefore came within reg 7(1)(l). It was part of the applicant's case that the rent officer set the market rent too low. This was rejected. Stuart-Smith LJ held (at 345-6) that "given that the applicants have been deliberately targeting the exempt groups .... for the purpose of charging very high rents" the creation of such tenancies could fall within reg 7(1)(l).

The tenancies in *Baragrove Properties* were found to be "contrived" even though the tenants did not benefit from the abuse and were unlikely to have been motivated to enter into the agreements by the prospect of extra profits which would accrue to their landlord. It seems to follow that an abusive intention on the part of the landlord can, in an appropriate case, bring the tenancy within reg 9(1)(l) even though the tenant's dominant purpose in entering the tenancy was to provide a home for her/himself and her/his family. In the more conventional case where the focus is on the tenant, it is important for the authority to investigate what the consequences will be for the landlord if HB is not payable. If the landlord will be forced, or will wish, to evict the claimant if rent is not paid and is unable to maintain the property without the receipt of rent, those factors will be suggestive of the agreement not being contrived: *R v Sutton LBC HBRB ex p Keegan* [1992] 27 HLR 92 at 99-100, QBD. However, if the evidence is that the landlord will take a commercial view and will not chase a tenant for rent where it would be uneconomical to do so, that will not justify a finding of contrivance: *R v Stratford-upon-Avon DC HBRB ex p White* [1998] 31 HLR 126.

Prior relationship of landlord and tenant. The fact that the landlord and tenant knew each other or were friends before the tenancy was created, while it may be relevant, is far from being conclusive evidence of abuse. It may be a reasonable and commercial decision for a landlord to let to someone s/he knows, as s/he will be more certain of having a good tenant. Likewise, a tenant may feel more secure with a landlord who is known to her/ him. If friends can reach a mutually acceptable agreement, then nothing in reg 9 compels them to go into the market, as long as the tenant's dominant purpose is to provide her/himself and her/his family with a home and the landlord's dominant purpose is to provide accommodation for a reasonable return: see *R v Poole Borough Council ex p Ross* [1995] 28 HLR 351, QBD. Similarly, it is of little relevance that the parties are related, unless they reside together in which case see sub-para (b). Contrary to what seems to be popular belief, there is no legal rule which prevents members of the same family entering into binding legal agreements with each other, as long as all the parties intend to create legal relations. Again the question is what the dominant purpose of the agreement was at the time it was entered into.

Whether or not the agreement is commercial. This is itself a ground for exclusion under sub-para (a), but an agreement which is commercial, but less commercial than is normal may be some indication of contrivance.

The rent charged. If the rent payable under the agreement is high in comparison with the market rates prevailing in the area or if the accommodation is larger than is needed by the claimant and any family, then that may be evidence (taken together with other relevant factors) that the liability was created to take advantage of the scheme: see *Dadds* at 705 and *R v Barrow BC ex p Catnach* [1997] unreported, 3 September, QBD. If these are the only factors which suggest abuse, the authority does not need to rely on reg 9 and can restrict the claimant's eligible rent under a rent restriction scheme (if relevant): regs 12C to 14. These schemes make it difficult to "take advantage" of the scheme by charging an excessive rent.

Where the rent officer has made a valuation which is not much lower than the contractual rent, it will be irrational for the authority to conclude that the agreement is contrived without other factors being present: *Dadds* at 705, where the contractual rent was £95 and the rent officer's assessment was £78.

Paragraph (3): The exception

This sets out an important escape route from sub-paras (e) and (g) (but not the others). The critical concept is again whether the liability "takes advantage" of the HB scheme: see sub-para (l). However, there are critical differences between sub-para (l) and this provision.

The first point is that the burden of proof is on the claimant. Para (3) states that s/he must satisfy the local authority that the liability was not intended to be a means of taking advantage of the HB scheme. However, where there is adequate evidence relating to the issue, this is unlikely to be of great significance: see the discussion under paragraph (l). Secondly, the question for consideration is whether "the liability was intended to be a means" of taking advantage of the HB scheme. It is suggested that this involves the authority in carrying out an inquiry into two matters.

(1)   Is the existence of the liability an abuse of the HB scheme? It is inherent in the language of para (3) that the agreement is actually contrived, as well as that there was the requisite intention.

(2)   Was there an intention to take advantage of the scheme? In considering this question, particularly close attention must be had to the knowledge of the claimant and the landlord of the HB scheme and its operation. The paradigm case of an intention to abuse the HB scheme is *Baragrove Properties*, discussed above. It does not appear that it is necessary for *both* landlord and tenant to have the requisite intention. It will be sufficient if one of them does. But it is entirely possible that an agreement could be contrived, without landlord or tenant necessarily having intended to produce that result. A bold assertion by the claimant or landlord that there was no intention to abuse the scheme need not be accepted if their actions give the lie to that assertion. Clearly, however, in such a case careful findings of fact and reasons will have to be given by authorities and the First-tier Tribunal.

Persons from abroad

10.–(1)   A person from abroad who is liable to make payments in respect of a dwelling shall be treated as if he were not so liable but this paragraph shall not have effect in respect of a person to whom and for a period to which regulation 10A (entitlement of a refugee to housing benefit) and Schedule A1 (treatment of claims for housing benefit by refugees) apply.

[¹ (2)   In paragraph (1), ''person from abroad'' means, subject to the following provisions of this regulation, a person who is not habitually resident in the United Kingdom, the Channel Islands, the Isle of Man or the Republic of Ireland.

(3)   No person shall be treated as habitually resident in the United Kingdom, the Channel Islands, the Isle of Man or the Republic of Ireland unless he has a right to reside in (as the case may be) the United Kingdom, the Channel Islands, the Isle of Man or the Republic of Ireland other than a right to reside which falls within paragraph (3A).

(3A)   A right to reside falls within this paragraph if it is one which exists by virtue of, or in accordance with, one or more of the following–

(a)   regulation 13 of the Immigration (European Economic Area) Regulations 2006;

(b)   regulation 14 of those Regulations, but only in a case where the right exists under that regulation because the person is–

    (i)   a jobseeker for the purpose of the definition of "qualified person" in regulation 6(1) of those Regulations, or

    (ii)   a family member (within the meaning of regulation 7 of those Regulations) of such a jobseeker;

(c)   Article 6 of Council Directive No. 2004/38/EC; or

(d)   Article 39 of the Treaty establishing the European Community (in a case where the person is seeking work in the United Kingdom, the Channel Islands, the Isle of Man or the Republic of Ireland).

(3B)   A person is not a person from abroad if he is–

(a)   a worker for the purposes of Council Directive No. 2004/38/EC;

(b)   a self-employed person for the purposes of that Directive;

(c)   a person who retains a status referred to in sub-paragraph (a) or (b) pursuant to Article 7(3) of that Directive;

(d)   a person who is a family member of a person referred to in sub-paragraph (a), (b) or (c) within the meaning of Article 2 of that Directive;

(e)   a person who has a right to reside permanently in the United Kingdom by virtue of Article 17 of that Directive;

[⁵ (f)   a person who is treated as a worker for the purpose of the definition of "qualified person" in regulation 6(1) of the Immigration (European Economic Area) Regulations 2006 pursuant to–

    (i)   regulation 5 of the Accession (Immigration and Worker Registration) Regulations 2004 (application of the 2006 Regulations in relation to a national of the Czech Republic, Estonia, Latvia, Lithuania, Hungary, Poland, Slovenia or the Slovak Republic who is an "accession State worker requiring registration"), or

    (ii)   regulation 6 of the Accession (Immigration and Worker Authorisation) Regulations 2006 (right of residence of a Bulgarian or Romanian who is an "accession State national subject to worker authorisation");]

(g)   refugee;

[⁴ (h)   a person who has exceptional leave to enter or remain in the United Kingdom granted outside the rules made under section 3(2) of the Immigration Act 1971;

(hh)   a person who has humanitarian protection granted under those rules;]

(i)   a person who is not a person subject to immigration control within the meaning of section 115(9) of the Immigration and Asylum Act and who is in the United Kingdom as a result of his deportation, expulsion or other removal by compulsion of law from another country to the United Kingdom;

(j)   a person in Great Britain who left the territory of Montserrat after 1st November 1995 because of the effect on that territory of a volcanic eruption; [⁷]

[⁷ (jj)   a person who–

    (i)   arrived in Great Britain on or after 28th February 2009 but before 18th March 2011;

    (ii)   immediately before arriving there had been resident in Zimbabwe; and

    (iii)   before leaving Zimbabwe, had accepted an offer, made by Her Majesty's Government, to assist that person to move to and settle in the United Kingdom; or]

(k)   in receipt of income support [⁶ , an income-based jobseeker's allowance or on an income-related employment and support allowance].]

(4)   Paragraph 1 of Part 1 of the Schedule to, and regulation 2 as it applies to that paragraph of, the Social Security (Immigration and Asylum) Consequential Amendments Regulations 2000 shall not apply to a person who has been temporarily without funds for any period, or the aggregate of any periods, exceeding 42 days during any one period of limited leave (including any such period as extended).

[²]

(6)   In this regulation–

[²]

''refugee'' means a person recorded by the Secretary of State as a refugee within the definition in Article 1 of the Convention relating to the Status of Refugees.

Modifications

Reg 10(3B)(a) to (e) applies in relation to a national of Norway, Iceland, Liechtenstein or Switzerland or a member of her/his family (within the meaning of Art 2 Council Directive 2004/38/EC) as if such a national were a national of a member state. See reg 10 of SI 2006 No.1026 (p1226).

The amendments made by SI 2006 No.1026 do not affect the continued operation of the transitional and savings provided for in reg 12 Social Security (Persons From Abroad) Miscellaneous Amendments Regulations 1996 (see p1153), reg 6 Social Security (Habitual Residence) Amendment Regulations 2004 (see p1192) or Sch 3 para 6 HB&CTB(CP) Regs (see p1215). See reg 11 of SI 2006 No.1026 (p1226).

From 25 July 2006 until 31 January 2007, a para (3B)(jj) was inserted by the Social Security (Lebanon) Amendment Regulations 2006 SI No.1981. See p241 of the 20th edition for the text of the insertion.

Amendments

1.   Substituted by reg 4(2)(a) of SI 2006 No 1026 as from 30.4.06.
2.   Omitted by reg 4(2)(b) and (c) of SI 2006 No 1026 as from 30.4.06.
3.   Amended by reg 5 of SI 2006 No 1981 from 25.7.06 until 31.1. 07 only.
4.   Amended by reg 5 of SI 2006 No 2528 as from 9.10.06.
5.   Substituted by reg 5 of SI 2006 No 3341 as from 1.1.07.
6.   Amended by reg 8 of SI 2008 No 1082 as from 27.10.08.
7.   Amended by reg 5 of SI 2009 No 362 as from 18.3.09.

General Note

The scheme of the regulation

This has the effect of excluding certain categories of "persons from abroad" from entitlement to HB by deeming them not to be liable to make payments in respect of their home.

Before dealing with this question, however, a prior question may need to be addressed, namely whether the claimant is excluded from benefit altogether under s115 Immigration and Asylum Act 1999 and the Social Security (Immigration and Asylum) Consequential Provisions Regulations 2000 (see pp1129 and 1169) as a "person subject to immigration control". A person falling within s115 of the 1999 Act is barred from HB/CTB unless s/he can take advantage of the provisions in reg 2 of the 2000 Regs.

It is only if the person is not excluded under s115 that it may become necessary to address whether s/he is caught by reg 10. To add to the difficulties, para (4) limits the effect of certain provisions in the 2000 Regs, and modified versions of reg 10 in Sch 3 para 6 HB&CTB(CP) Regs (see p1215) limit the effect of reg 10. Note that even if a person who is subject to immigration control can avoid the exclusion under s115 of the 1999 Act due to coming within the 2000 Regulations s/he will still need not to be a "person from abroad" under reg 10 – see *Yesiloz v LB Camden and Secretary of State for Work and Pensions* [2009] EWCA Civ 415.

The label of "person from abroad" should thus be confined to those falling foul of reg 10. The regulation is a classic example of obscure social security drafting, but once unpicked its meaning is relatively plain.

The starting point is para (1), which sets out that a "person from abroad" shall be treated as not liable to make payments in respect of a dwelling, and so is not entitled to HB. Who then is a "person from abroad"? The short answer is given in para (2), namely a person who is not habitually resident in the UK, the Channel Islands, the Isle of Man or the Republic of Ireland (referred to collectively as the Common Travel Area or CTA); unless that person falls within para (3B), in which case s/he is simply not a person from abroad. Para (3) then provides that a person cannot be treated as habitually resident unless s/he has a "right to reside" in the CTA, other than one of the rights to reside which falls within para (3A). This requires some elucidation. Firstly, the test in para (3) is a separate test from that in (3B), notwithstanding the fact that all of the heads under the latter (with the possible exception of (j) to (k) in some conceivable circumstances) concern categories of person who all have a right of residence in the UK in any event. Secondly, if the only right to reside a person has is one which falls within para (3A) then, in effect, it does not amount to a right to reside at all, and that person will be a "person from abroad" (because s/he is not habitually resident in the UK) and not entitled to HB. What para (3A) covers is non-UK EEA nationals, whose only right of residence is due to their being within their first three months of residence in the CTA (para (3A)(a) and (c)), or such non-UK EEA nationals (or their family members – (3A)(b)(ii)) who have never previously worked in the CTA and are here looking for work (para (3A)(b)(i) and (d)), but not getting income-based JSA (because if that was the case they would not be a "person from abroad" in any event under para (3B)(k)). Thirdly, for those not coming within (3B), having a right to reside in the CTA is a necessary but not a sufficent condition for being habitually resident in the CTA; to meet the latter s/he will also have to show that s/he is habitually resident in the UK as a matter of fact (see p293). This may most obviously apply to UK nationals returning to the UK from abroad. If, however, the person falls within para (3B), s/he cannot be a "person from abroad" and is exempted for the habitual residence test altogether. Para 3B covers:

(1)   Some of those who have a right of residence under EU law: para (3B)(a)-(f).

(2)   Those who have been recorded by the Secretary of State as refugees (defined in para (6)) under asylum law: para (3B)(g). Note that, perhaps confusingly and unnecessarily, such people are *also* said not to be "persons from abroad" at all under para (1) (see reg 10A and Sch A1 in Sch 4 HB&CTB(CP) Regs – on p1225 – and the special rules for retrospectively dealing with HB claims by refugees).

(3)   Those granted exceptional leave to enter or remain and those granted humanitarian protection under the Immigration Rules: para (3B)(h) and (hh).

(4)   Those who have been deported or removed *to* the UK from another country: para (3B)(i).

(5)   Those in receipt of IS, income-based JSA or on an income-related ESA: para (3B)(k).

(6)   Certain claimants from Zimbabwe, Montserrat and (until 31 January 2007 – see the Modifications on p268) the Lebanon: para (3B)(j) and (jj).

So, in summary, the claimant will not be a "person from abroad" (and so will be entitled to HB) if either:

(a)   s/he falls within para (3B) – eg, because s/he is in receipt of IS or is a person who has retained the status of a worker in EU law; *or*

(b)   s/he has a right to reside in the CTA (eg, as a British or Irish citizen, under the Immigration Act 1971, or under some provision of EU law that is not specifically provided for in (3B) such as those with a permanent right of residence under Article 16 Directive 2004/38/EC) *and* s/he is habitually resident in the CTA as a matter of fact.

Given that receipt of IS, income-related ESA or income-based JSA in effect allows a person to bypass the habitual residence/right to reside tests for HB (and CTB) purposes, in reality right to reside or habitual residence disputes for HB/CTB purposes are often bypassed on the basis of the outcome of a claim for one of those benefits. As a reflection of this, the commentary below is not as comprehensive as it is to the corresponding commentary to the IS rules in Volume II of Sweet and Maxwell's *Social Security Legislation*. It is suggested that reference should be made to the latter, as well as to the commentary here, in cases where the right to reside or habitual residence tests are genuinely determinative of the HB/CTB claim.

Analysis

As discussed in the General Note, anyone who comes within one of the heads of para (3B) cannot be a "person from abroad". All of the people whose circumstances bring them within one of the heads of para (3B) have a right of residence by virtue of those circumstances in any event. However, it is only those who do not come within para (3B) who are formally required to have a right to reside in order to count as habitually resident and therefore not be persons from abroad.

This analysis is therefore structured as follows.

(1)   Paragraph (3B): Groups who cannot be "persons from abroad"

(2)   Paragraph (3): Who has a right to reside in the CTA

(3)   Paragraph (2): "habitually resident in fact"

As this is a long note, for ease of reference, these broad headings have been further broken down with sub-headings.

[1] Paragraph (3B): Groups who cannot be persons from abroad

If a person is covered by one of the heads within para (3B), s/he is not a person from abroad. Accordingly, s/he does not need to have a right to reside or to be habitually resident in fact.

The first five heads, (a) to (e), all make reference to EC Directive 2004/38. This came into effect on 30 April 2006. It is a codifying measure which seeks to bring together the many previously disparate provisions of EU law concerning residence rights within the EU. It repeals and replaces many previous Directives (eg, Directive 68/360/EEC) and amends EC Regulation 1612/68. Although a codifying measure, it is important to realise that another purpose of the Directive is to strengthen residence rights and the ECJ approaches its interpretation in this light (see Case C-127/08 *Metock* [2008] ECR I-06241 at para 59). It is now the key starting point for determining the residence status of non-UK EU nationals in the UK; and thus their entitlement to HB and CTB.

The Directive does not, however, codify all rights of residence for EU nationals. For example, it plainly does not address the right to reside of EU workseekers, who can qualify for JSA by "signing-on" and seeking work; a right which arises directly under Art 39 of the EC Treaty (see Case C-292/89 *Antonissen* [1991] ECR I-00745). Similarly, it is now clear from the decisions in Case C-310/08 *LB Harrow v Ibrahim* [2010] ECR and Case C-480/08 *Teixeira v LB Lambeth* [2010] ECR that rights of residence for the children of former workers who are in education (and their primary carers) arise outside the Directive: the ECJ explicitly rejected the arguments of the UK and others that this was not the case (see *Teixeira* at paras 55 to 60).

In addition, it is important to note that the Directive provides a right to reside for many people who do not come within any of the heads (a) to (e) of para (3B): such people may have a right to reside sufficient to come within para (3) but will also need to be habitually resident in fact under para (2). Where a person does not come within para (3B), reference should therefore be made to the appropriate sections of the analysis below.

Finally, it is also important to be aware that the Immigration (European Economic Area) Regulations 2006 No.1003 (I(EEA) Regs 2006) have sought to implement the Directive within domestic law. However, the Directive can be relied upon directly by EU nationals in the UK. Furthermore, sub-paras (3B)(a) to (e) refer only to provisions of the Directive and not to the domestic regulations. In some cases the domestic regulations may provide for a right of residence which the Directive does not – ie, be more generous. Where a claimant has a right of residence under the domestic regulations which is not provided for specifically by the Directive, s/he will not be within para (3B)(a) to (e) but rather may have a right of residence sufficient to come within para (3).

A note on EEA nationals. The EEA is a larger grouping than the EU as it also includes Iceland, Norway and Liechtenstein. Reg 10(c) Social Security (Persons from Abroad) Amendment Regulations 2006 No.1026 provides that nationals of these states are to be treated as if they were EU nationals for the purposes of para (3B)(a) to (e) (see p1226). Note also that Swiss nationals are treated by the I(EEA) Regs 2006 as if they were EEA nationals.

A note on British Citizens and the Directive. The UK is an EU state. However, the Directive does not apply to British Citizens who have never moved to or lived in another EU state: see Art 3(1) on who can be a beneficiary of the Directive. Accordingly, British Citizens will not come within para (3B)(a) to (c) or (e) and the family members of a British Citizen cannot take advantage of (d) unless the Citizen has gone and exercised an EU right of residence in another member state and then returned.

The situation is, however, different for those who have dual citizenship of Britain and another EEA country. In *SSWP v AA* [2009] UKUT 249 (AAC), the judge considered the right of residence of the family member of a person who had dual British and Spanish nationality. The dual national had lived in Britain all his life and was working but had not exercised his right to move freely as a worker, etc, within the EEA. The judge concluded that the dual national did have a right of residence in the UK under both the Directive and the 2006 Regulations, despite the fact that there had been no movement within the EEA. This was held, in respect of the Directive following *obiter* comments in *McCarthy v SSHD* [2008] EWCA Civ 641 (at para 33) and in respect of the 2006 Regulations, on the basis of the plain wording of the Regulations themselves:

"There is no general provision disapplying the Regulations in the case of those holding British nationality. Instead, the Regulations apply to those who hold a nationality other than British and there is no indication that holding British nationality as well means that they do not apply."

The judge distinguishes the case from *McCarthy* as, in that case, the dual national could not point to any possible right acquired under Community law through her Irish nationality. Accordingly the claimant had a right of residence as the family member of the dual national.

The family members of British citizens have rights of residence in EU law if the British citizen has her/himself exercised EU rights of freedom of movement in another EU country and then returned to the UK: Case C-219/05 *Eind* [2007] ECR I-10719. Reg 9 I(EEA) Regs provides that the family members of a British citizen who have resided in another EEA state as workers or self-employed people will have the regulations applied to them as if that British citizen was a non-British EEA national. Thus, if the British citizen would count as a worker/self-employed person etc in the UK were s/he a non-British EEA national, her/his family members have a right of residence. However, in *Eind* it was held that there was no need for a Union citizen who had been a worker in another EU country to carry out an economic activity in order for his family members to have an EU law right of residence on the national's return, with them, to the home state.

In *LA v SSWP* [2010] UKUT 109 (AAC), the claimant was the Greek mother-in-law of a British citizen who had worked on a self-employed basis in Greece and then returned to the UK with his Greek wife and the claimant. Judge Lane remitted the case to the First-tier Tribunal to make findings about both the issue of dependency and whether the British citizen had been a worker in the UK at the date of the refusal of his mother-in-law's PC claim on the basis that she did not have a right of residence. The need to make such a finding as to whether the British citizen was a worker on his return to the UK is inconsistent with the judgment in *Eind*. The judge in *LA v SSWP* does not appear to have been referred to the decision in *Eind*, and it is suggested that her decision on this point should not be followed as it is contrary to clear authority from the ECJ.

Developments in the area of EU residence law for EU citizens who are resident in their home state and have never exercised a right of residence under EU law in another state may be imminent. Until now it has been fairly clear that an EU national in that situation does not have rights of residence in her/his own country arising under EU law. However, in *Ruiz Zambrano* (Case C-34/09) (ECJ judgment still awaited), the Advocate General has suggested that in fact Art 21 Treaty on the Functioning of the European Union ("TFEU" – the "Lisbon Treaty" is now the main EU treaty, and its coming into force from 1 December 2009 has resulted in the renumbering of the provisions, so Art 21 is the old Art 18 EC) creates two rights: one right to move and another, independent, right of residence. Thus, in AG Sharpston's view, UK nationals do have an EU law right of residence in the UK without having moved. The issue then is whether the non-British family members of "static" British citizens can derive rights through that right of residence. It is of note that the family members of such "static" British citizens have fewer rights than the family members of any EU national who has exercised rights of freedom of movement. The AG suggests that this "reverse discrimination" could be prevented by finding such family members did have an Art 21 TFEU right of residence in certain situations. However, certain safeguards are suggested.

(1)   Firstly, the family members of the static EU national, would have to be in a postion where they would have a right of residence under EU law but for the fact that the EU national was resident in her/his home state and would have to not have a right of residence under domestic law.

(2)   Secondly, the fact that no right of residence accrued to such family members would have to violate a fundamental right protected under EU law (see the discussion of the Charter of Fundamental Rights below).

(3)   Thirdly, the issue of an Art 21 right for such family members would only arise as a subsidiary remedy.

It remains to be seen what the ECJ will decide in Mr Zambrano's case. It is, however, likely to have implications for EU nationals who have been married to and supported by UK nationals, and then separated and been refused benefits under the right to reside requirement.

[1.1] Para (3B)(a): workers

Note: A8 nationals required to register and A2 nationals subject to worker authorisation do not come within this provision (see p278).

The Directive itself does not define who is a "worker" but uses that word to refer to people who are workers for the purposes of Art 45 TFEU (formerly Art 39 EC). Freedom of movement for workers and their families is one of the fundamental principles of EU law. As such, a liberal interpretation must be given to the phrase: Case C-53/81 *Levin v Staatssecretaris van Justitie* [1982] ECR 01035.

The term is to be construed in accordance with EU law rather than domestic law: Case C-75/73 *Hoekstra (née Unger)* [1964] ECR 00177; *Levin* paras 11-12. The ECJ has held that a worker is someone in an employment relationship and that this concept must be defined by objective criteria which distinguish it by reference to the rights and duties of the persons concerned. The essential features of an employment relationship are that for a certain period of time a person:

–   provides services;

–   in return for remuneration;

–   under the direction of another person (Case C-66/86 *Lawrie-Blum v Land Baden-Wurttemberg* [1986] ECR 02121).

Further questions then arise concerning how much remuneration must be received and how many services must be provided in order for a person to gain the privileged status of worker. In addition, there is the question of when someone ceases to be a worker. The issue of loss of status is better dealt with in section [1.3] on p273.

In terms of what makes someone a worker and how that status is acquired, then the work must be "genuine and effective" rather than "marginal or ancillary": *Levin* para 17. This will be a question of fact in each case. GM C4 Annex B (para 6) suggests five factors which need to be weighed in deciding whether the work is "genuine and effective". To the extent indicated below, the first four of these provide a useful guide, but it must be stressed that *all* the relevant factors must be taken into account (the fifth more properly relates to loss of status and is not considered here). None will be decisive of itself.

(1)   The period of employment. The shorter the period of employment, the less likely it is that the status of "worker" is acquired, but it will not require a long period of employment to acquire the status. In Case C-39/86 *Sylvie Lair v Universität Hannover* [1988] ECR 03161, the ECJ explicitly held that member states may not impose a fixed minimum period before worker status is obtained. In *Barry v LB Southwark* [2008] EWCA Civ 1440, the Court of Appeal held that Mr Barry's two weeks' work at the Wimbledon Tennis Championships were sufficient to have made him a worker.

(2)   The number of hours worked. A person may be a "worker" even if s/he only works part-time but there will be a point at which the length of time spent working is so short that the work can be described as "marginal". In Case C-171/88 *Rinner-Kuhn* [1989] ECR 02743, a claimant working 10 hours a week was a worker and in Case C-125/89 *Kits van Heijerungen v Staatssecretaris van Justitie* [1990] ECR I-01753, a man working four hours a week was not. In *R(IS) 12/98* (para 15), an au pair who had worked for 13 hours a week for a modest wage plus board and lodging was held to be a worker. See also the discussion of *Genc* below.

(3)   The level of earnings. If there is no remuneration, a person cannot be a worker. However, the fact that the level of earnings is not sufficient to maintain the worker without recourse to benefit is not relevant to whether the work is "genuine and effective": Case C-139/85 *Kempf v Staatssecretaris van Justitie* [1986] ECR 01/41. The same should arguably be true where the claimant is earning less than a subsidence wage. However, in *CH 3314/2005* Commissioner Rowland considered the question of whether the claimant was a workseeker. The issue was whether she got the work she was looking for that would have been sufficient to make her a worker. The commissioner separated out the question of whether the search for work is "genuine" from whether it is "effective", and in respect of the latter held that reference can be had to whether a person will continue to need to have recourse to social assistance even if s/he finds the work s/he is looking for in order to decide if the work is "effective". The commissioner was not, however, referred to Case C-3/90 *Bernini v Minister van Ouderings en Wetenschappen* [1992] ECR I-01071, and it is therefore suggested that his conclusion on this (arguably *obiter*) point may need to be treated with some caution. Commissioner Jacobs declined to follow Commissioner Rowland's approach in *CIS 4144/2007* (para 24). Remuneration may also be in kind: Case C-196/87 *Steymann v Staatssecretaris van Justitie* [1988] ECR 06159.

(4)   Whether the work is regular or erratic. Periods of work and unemployment will not prevent the acquisition of worker status: *Monteil v Secretary of State for the Home Department* [1983] Imm AR 149 at 152, IAT. However, some types of job where the worker is only given work at the whim of the employer may be too

ancillary. For example, in Case C-357/89 *Raulin* [1992] ECR I-01027, the claimant was a waitress who made herself available, and was to be paid only when her employer required her services. In *CIS 1793/ 2007*, the judge distinguishes between a situation where "work is undertaken for what is expected from the outset to be for a very short period and indefinite employment that has curtailed prematurely" (in such a case the claimant is obliged to keep looking for work and often should be regarded as not being a worker) and that of an agency worker where "short periods of temporary work are not separated by longer periods of no work" in which case the person could be a worker throughout. It is clear that undeclared work can still make a claimant a worker: *Barry v LB Southwark* [2008] EWCA Civ 1440 – here the appellant had not declared to the DWP his two weeks' work at the Wimbledon Tennis Championship.

The ECJ considered again the concept of "worker" in Case C-14/09 *Hava Genc v Land Berlin* [2010] ECR nyr. The Court refused to be drawn by a plea from the referring national court that it lay down a minimum threshold in terms of hours and pay below which work would be considered marginal and ancillary. However, the Court was prepared to declare that the very limited amount of work which Ms Genc had done was potentially capable of making her a worker. It is worth, therefore, looking at the facts of her case, which concerned the refusal to renew her residence permit in 2007:

"Since 18 June 2004, Ms Genc has been working as a cleaner ... According to the contract of employment, which was put down in writing on 9 November 2007, the working time per week is 5.5 hours at an hourly rate of EUR 7.87. That contract provides for entitlement to 28 days of paid leave and continued payment of wages in the event of sickness. The contract is, moreover, subject to the relevant collective agreement. For this employment, Ms Genc receives monthly wages of approximately EUR 175."

The Court referred again to its caselaw establishing that the fact that wages were so low that the worker was still dependent on benefits (para 20) was irrelevant and went on to say:

"26. Although the fact that a person works for only a very limited number of hours in the context of an employment relationship may be an indication that the activities performed are marginal and ancillary (Case C-357/89 *Raulin* [1992] ECR I-01027, paragraph 14), the fact remains that, independently of the limited amount of the remuneration for and the number of hours of the activity in question, the possibility cannot be ruled out that, following an overall assessment of the employment relationship in question, that activity may be considered by the national authorities to be real and genuine, thereby allowing its holder to be granted the status of 'worker' within the meaning of Article 39 EC.

27. The overall assessment of Ms Genc's employment relationship makes it necessary to take into account factors relating not only to the number of working hours and the level of remuneration but also to the right to 28 days of paid leave, to the continued payment of wages in the event of sickness, and to a contract of employment which is subject to the relevant collective agreement, in conjunction with the fact that her contractual relationship with the same undertaking has lasted for almost four years.

28. Those factors are capable of constituting an indication that the professional activity in question is real and genuine."

[1.2] Paragraph (3B)(b): self-employed

Note: A8 and A2 nationals have the same rights as any other EEA national as self-employed persons (see the note to (3B)(f) on p278).

The Directive does not provide a definition of who counts as self-employed, but plainly this is to be taken from the meaning attributed to that concept by the ECJ in consideration of rights under Art 49 TFEU (previously Art 43) on freedom of establishment, which includes the right to take up and pursue activities as a self-employed person in an EU state.

The ECJ has taken the approach of defining as self-employed all those who are providing services in return for remuneration *but not under the direction of another person* – in other words, the distinction between a worker and a self-employed person turns on whether or not the services are provided outside a relationship of subordination: where they are (ie, there is no subordination of the service provider to another) then that activity must be regarded as self-employment (*Jany*, para 33).

Furthermore, the ECJ in *Jany* is clear that the same considerations as to the activities being genuine and effective, as opposed to marginal and ancillary, apply to self-employment (see the discussion at [1.1] above in relation to workers).

Someone who is merely seeking opportunities to become self-employed will not count: see the Northern Ireland Commissioner's decision in *C 10/1995 (IS)*. However, what of those who have taken some positive steps towards becoming self-employed but are not yet trading? In *R(IS) 6/00*, Commissioner Mesher considered the case of a French national who returned to the UK while she was pregnant. She placed an advert in a newspaper advertising French tuition. It was argued that she had a right of residence under Directive 73/148 (now repealed but with similar rights existing in Directive 2004/38). The commissioner held that the conclusions and reasoning in *C 10/1995 (IS)* could not be accepted in their entirety. He stated (paras 29-31) that there had to be a right of residence before a self-employed person actually began to trade in order to give effect to the Community objective of freedom of movement. Thus a person taking preparatory steps to setting up a business would acquire a right of residence under Directive 73/148. He then considered whether a claimant with an intention to trade, but who had not yet taken any steps towards doing so, could qualify.

"The difficult question is whether the right extends not merely to those who are taking steps towards offering their services to the public (or whatever final step is appropriate to the nature of the business) in a Member State, but also to those who wish to do that, but have not yet taken any steps beyond arriving in the Member State concerned. In my judgment, it does not. It would be going further than justified by the purposes of the Directive to extend a right of residence, rather than the mere right of entry to the Member State under Article 3, to such persons. It also seems to me that the crucial factor is not so much whether the person's intentions are for the present or for the future or are conditional in some way, but whether the person is taking steps towards offering services to the public, or otherwise setting up as a self-employed person." (para 31)

In *TG v SSWP* [2009] UKUT 58 (AAC), at the date of decision under consideration (in July 2006) the claimant had been working for about two months as a self-employed interpreter. Most of his work had been marketing and preparation and he had only been doing three or four hours of work a week and had made no profit (his first payment came after the date of the decision and for work done after that date). He had not registered with the Revenue as a self-employed person. The judge held that the failure to register with the Revenue was not fatal to the claimant being counted as self-employed (although it "may in some circumstances be evidence from which it may be inferred that a person is not self-employed"). He held on these facts that the claimant was self-employed. It is therefore clear that someone who is taking steps to become self-employed, but has not yet had any income as a result of those steps, may count as self-employed. That is useful in considering when someone may acquire the status of a self-employed person.

How though does one determine whether someone has ceased to be self-employed?

In *CIS 1042/2008*, the commissioner held that a woman who takes a period of leave from her self-employment for reasons of maternity but intends to return, continues to count as self-employed (so the issue of whether she is a person who retains the status of a self-employed person and so comes within para (3B)(c) does not arise).

In *SSWP v JS (IS)* [2010] UKUT 240 (AAC), Judge Jacobs considered the situation of a Polish claimant who had been working on a self-employed basis providing language support in schools. At the date of decision on her claim for IS, she appeared not to have had any ongoing work (or very little such ongoing work). The judge held:

"5.   I do not accept that a claimant who is for the moment doing no work is necessarily no longer self-employed. There will commonly be periods in a person's self-employment when no work is done. Weekends and holiday periods are obvious examples. There may also be periods when there is no work to do. The concept of self-employment necessarily encompasses periods of both feast and famine. During the latter, the person may be engaged in a variety of tasks that are properly seen as part of continuing self-employment: administrative work, such as maintaining the accounts; in marketing to generate more work; or developing the business in new directions. Self-employment is not confined to periods of actual work. It includes natural periods of rest and the vicissitudes of business life. This does not mean that self-employment survives no matter how little work arrives. It does mean that the issue can only be decided in the context of the facts at any particular time. The amount of work is one factor. Whether the claimant is taking any other steps in the course of self-employment is also relevant. The claimant's motives and intentions must all be taken into account, although they will not necessarily be decisive."

Therefore, it seems that there are circumstances in which a claimant experiencing a period with no ongoing business can continue to count as self-employed, although, as the judge notes, "So much depends on the circumstances, and, therefore, on the evidence."

For the position of those who wish to receive rather than provide services, see below.

[1.3] Para (3B)(c): Those who retain worker/self-employed status

Note: A8 nationals required to register and A2 nationals subject to worker authorisation cannot retain status as workers (although they can as self-employed persons (see the notes to para (3B)(f) on p278).

Before considering whether a person retains the status of worker/self-employed person, it is first necessary to consider whether s/he is in fact still a worker or self-employed. Part of the answer to this seems to be that someone remains a worker while on a period of leave from work, even if that leave is unpaid: see *BS v SSWP* [2009] UKUI 16 (AAC). The other issue is whether the person has left the labour market, and the position seems to be that this does not happen automatically once a contract of employment ends (see [1.3.3] on p276).

Once a person is no longer a worker or self-employed, then Art 7(3) of Directive 2004/38 may allow her/him to retain that status in certain circumstances. Art 7(3) provides that a person who is no longer a worker/self-employed person continues to have that status if s/he is:

(a)   temporarily unable to work as a result of an illness or accident (see [1.3.1] below);

(b)   in duly recorded involuntary unemployment after having been employed for more than one year and has registered as a jobseeker with the relevant employment office;

(c)   in duly recorded involuntary unemployment after having worked for less than a year and has registered as a jobseeker with the relevant employment office. The Directive states that in such circumstances "the status of worker shall be retained for no less than six months";

(d)   embarked upon vocational training. Unless involuntarily unemployed, the retention of the status of worker requires that the training be related to the previous employment (see [1.3.2] below for discussion of Art 7(3)(b) to (d)).

Attempts to argue that the heads under Art 7(3) of the Directive are not exhaustive of the situations in which a person may retain her/his status as a worker after ceasing to be in an employment relationship have been made in two cases but have not succeeded.

(1)   *Dias v SSWP* [2009] EWCA Civ 807 – in this case the argument was put that a woman who had been a worker, and then became unemployed after a period of maternity leave and was unable for the time being to return to her former employment (which was being held for her should she be able to return) because of domestic violence and the need to care for a small child who for some of the time was not well, should retain the status of worker. The Court of Appeal ruled that this would be an "impermissible judicial extension of rules carefully formulated in Europe, first by the courts and latterly by Article 7(3) of Directive 2004/38" and that the situation of Ms Dias was not analogous to those heads set out under Art 7(3). Although the Court has referred a number of other questions to the ECJ, this issue is not covered by them. On the facts of her case, it now seems that Ms Dias must have a permanent right of residence following the ruling in *Lassal* (see below). It is therefore likely that the further progress of this case will not shed much more light on the specific issue discussed here.

(2)   *SSWP v JS (IS)* [2010] UKUT 131 (AAC) – Judge Ward rejected an argument that a woman who had been an agency worker and who was unable to work during the latter stages of pregnancy but not entitled to a period of maternity leave, and so not an employee, should be regarded as retaining her status as a worker. With respect, it is arguable that the facts in JS's case are more properly speaking analogous to the situations already catered for in Art 7(3): all of those heads represent situations where a person would be in work but for a situation that looks to be short term and is to some extent beyond the control of the worker, and in that respect the late stages of pregnancy or the need to care for a nursing infant seem similar. Furthermore, it is difficult to see how the failure to recognise the continuation of worker status in such circumstances aids freedom of movement. The claimant in this case has obtained permission to appeal to the Court of Appeal from the Upper Tribunal and the appeal has been filed.

[1.3.1] "temporarily unable to work as a result of an illness of accident"
The meaning of this provision was considered in *CIS 3890/2005*. In that case, the tribunal directed itself that an incapacity was only temporary if there was a certainty of recovery. In the view of the tribunal, this was not the case with the claimant's back problems. The commissioner allowed the claimant's appeal and held that while the tribunal was permitted to conclude that the back problems could be a permanent illness, the test was whether or not the inability to work produced by the illness was temporary. In *CIS 4304/2007*, the commissioner held that the test of whether a claimant was "unable to work" was not the same as the UK test for whether a person could receive benefits on the basis of incapacity for work, but was an autonomous EU concept:

> "in order to ensure uniformity in that legislation between Member States, it must be interpreted in the same way throughout the EU. It cannot, therefore, depend upon the particular domestic legislation governing incapacity benefits. The language of the legislation has to be interpreted and applied as it stands. The context provides some guidance. It ensures continuity of worker status for someone who would otherwise be employed or looking for work. That employment or search for employment provides the touchstone against which the claimant's disabilities must be judged. The question is: can she fairly be described as unable to do the work she was doing or the sort of work that she was seeking?"

It has been held that pregnancy per se is not an illness and therefore a pregnant woman who gives up work during pregnancy does not necessarily retain her status as a worker on the basis of being temporarily unable to work as a result of an illness: *CIS 4010/2006*. However, if there is pregnancy-related ill health which prevents work, status will be retained: *CIS 731/2007*. Note also that a woman on maternity leave remains a worker and so the question of retaining status does not arise: *CIS 4237/2007*. Arguments that the worker/self-employed person was temporarily unable to work as a result of an illness experienced by someone else for whom s/he had to care have failed: *CIS 3182/2005*, *CIS 2911/2007*. See also the discussion of *SSWP v JS (IS)* above at [1.3]. Note also that in that case the First-tier Tribunal had held that the claimant was to be treated as incapable of work in the latter stages of her pregnancy due to the operation of deeming provisions in reg 14 Social Security (Incapacity for Work) (General) Regulations 1995 (SI 1995 No.311). Counsel for JS conceded before the Upper Tribunal that such an interpretation would prevent Art 7(3)(a) from having a common meaning across the EU and thus could not be defended.

[1.3.2] Involuntary unemployment
It is necessary to consider:

1.   The meaning of "involuntary unemployment" in Art 7(3)(b)-(d) of the Directive and of "voluntary unemployment" in Art 7(3)(d) – see [1.3.2.1].

2.   The circumstances in which someone is to be regarded as having "registered as a jobseeker with the relevant employment office" – see [1.3.2.2].

3.   The issue of whether a self-employed person whose business folds can retain status under Article 7(3)(b)-(d) – see [1.3.2.3].

[1.3.2.1] "voluntary" and "involuntary unemployment". For Art 7(3)(b) and (c), in terms of retaining status as a worker/self-employed person while involuntarily unemployed, it is clear that "involuntarily" relates not to the circumstances of leaving work but to the ongoing relationship to the labour market: *CH 3314/2005* (para 11) and *R(IS) 12/98*.

In *SSWP v EM* [2009] UKUT 146 (AAC), the Upper Tribunal considered the distinction between being "voluntarily" and "involuntarily" unemployed for the purposes of Art 7(3)(d) of the Directive. That provision provides for worker status to be retained when the worker has entered vocational education. Importantly, if the unemployment is voluntary, then worker status can only be retained where the vocational education is related to the previous employment. It is only where the person is involuntarily unemployed that worker status can be retained regardless of any connection between the content of the vocational education and the content of previous employment. EM needed to show that she was involuntarily unemployed because she could not argue that her former employment in a chicken processing factory was related to her vocational education training to be a teaching assistant. It was argued for her that in this provision one must look at how the person became unemployed in order to determine whether she was involuntarily unemployed. However, the judge disagreed and held that someone is involuntarily unemployed for the purposes of this provision:

"Only where a person has to retrain in order to find work reasonably equivalent to his or her former employment. [.....] it does not look back at the circumstances in which the person has become unemployed, although that may be part of the background; it is concerned with the situation where a person cannot reasonably be expected to be in the labour market because there is no appropriate market."

It should also be noted with regard to Art 7(3)(d) that there is no requirement for the claimant to have registered her/his unemployment with the relevant employment office.

[1.3.2.2] "registered as a jobseeker with the relevant employment office". The requirement to have "registered as a jobseeker with the relevant employment office" can certainly be met by claiming JSA at a Jobcentre Plus and signing on thereafter.

What is less clear is what happens in situations where the claimant has not done this. Prior to 30 April 2006, the Secretary of State for Work and Pensions had conceded in *CH 3314/2005* that a requirement that a claimant be "duly recorded by the relevant employment office" was met by an IS claimant who declared that she was seeking work on her "Right to Reside Stencil" – ie, she was in the claim process. That concession has not been given since then and in *CIS 3799/2007* it was held the test could only be met where a claimant had claimed JSA. In *SSWP v ZW* [2009] UKUT 25 (AAC), the Upper Tribunal held that participation in a work-focused interview by an IS claimant did not constitute registration with a relevant employment office.

However, in *SSWP v FE* [2009] UKUT 287 (AAC), a three judge panel of the Upper Tribunal considered the situation of someone who had worked for six months and who had, on being made redundant, claimed IS as a lone parent, stating on the HRT2(R) form issued to her by the Jobcentre that she was looking for work. The Upper Tribunal concluded by a 2-1 majority as follows:

"29. We conclude that the Secretary of State has not shown that the UK has defined specific mechanisms as being the only ways in which an individual can, for the purposes of Article 7(3)(c) "register as a job-seeker with the relevant employment office". That being so, the tribunal was entitled to hold that the Secretary of State's factual concessions meant that the claimant succeeded in her appeal. In summary:

a. What the Directive contemplates is that a claimant has done what is needed in order to have his or her name recorded as looking for work by the relevant employment office

b. Whether or not this has been done is a question of fact

c. There is no rule of law that such registration can be effected only by way of registering for jobseeker's allowance or national insurance credits, less still only by successfully claiming one or other of those benefits

d.   Nor was there at the material time an administrative practice to that effect (even assuming – without deciding – that to be a lawful way of implementing the Directive)

e. Successfully claiming jobseeker's allowance or national insurance credits will no doubt provide sufficient evidence to satisfy Article 7(3)(c); but

f. Those who are able to show not merely that they were seeking work, but that they had done what is needed in order to have their name recorded as looking for work by the relevant employment office – will meet the registration requirement of Article 7(3)(c).

g.   It being conceded that the claimant had stated on the Habitual Residence Test documents that she was seeking work and that the extent of the work being sought was sufficient, it follows that she met the relevant test."

The Secretary of State has obtained permission to appeal against that decision (case to be called *SSWP v Elmi*). The window for hearing at the Court of Appeal is 16 November 2010 to 16 March 2011.

One might think that, in many cases, claimants who have, on the facts, done what is necessary to have their names recorded as looking for work by the relevant employment office should be getting either income-based JSA or IS, and therefore the issue of whether they are persons for abroad for HB/CTB purposes cannot arise (see the analysis of para (3B)(k) below at [1.9]). However, in practice it does not seem that the Secretary of State is applying the ruling of the majority of the Upper Tribunal (despite being bound to do so). Therefore, local authorities and tribunals dealing with HB/CTB appeals where the issue is right to reside may need to determine whether the claimant has sought to have themselves registered as a jobseeker with the relevant employment office.

It is of note that none of the decided cases have involved a claimant who was not entitled to claim JSA – eg, because s/he is a full time student, is a woman who has attained the qualifying age for PC, or because s/he is looking for less than 16 hours work a week. Many of the cases decided on this point have involved lone parents who have been incorrectly advised by the DWP to claim IS rather than JSA. If there is no other remedy, they may be able to seek compensation from the DWP (including for amounts of HB which they have not received due to that misadvice). It cannot be overemphasised that a claim for JSA will almost always be in the interests of a claimant who is involuntarily unemployed; not only can there be no argument that it allows her/him to retain worker status as set out here, but if income-based JSA is awarded, then s/he cannot be a person from abroad in any event as s/he comes within para (3B)(k) (see below). Many people who are not looking for work would do so if they were aware that this and a successful claim for JSA would ensure HB was payable.

[1.3.2.3] Self-employed and involuntary unemployment. The I(EEA) Regs 2006 do not provide for a self-employed person who stops working to be able to retain her/his status through looking for work and registering with the relevant employment office. In *SSWP v RK* [2009] UKUT 209 (AAC), the judge held that this was not a case where the drafter of those regulations had failed to properly implement the Directive and that Art 7(3)(b) to (d) did not apply to retaining status as a self-employed person. It is suggested this decision must be wrong. This is clear from the plain words of the Directive themselves: "a Union Citizen [...] shall retain the status of worker *or self-employed person* in the following *circumstances*" (emphasis added). It is also clear from the judge's speculation to the effect that it "would be surprising if the rights of self-employed persons had been aligned to those of workers without any indication of an intention to do so being included in the lengthy preamble to the Directive" that he was not referred to ECJ cases which hold precisely that the rights of workers and the self-employed are substantially the same in any event. Thus the preambles to the Directive do not need to make clear something which was already clear from the caselaw of the ECJ as it does not represent a change to the law: see in this regard, *Procureur du Roi v Royer* (Case C-48/75) (in particular paras 12-15) and *Watson and Belmann* Case C-118/75 (para 9). The judge also founded his reasoning on the fact that Art 7(3)(c) and (d) refer to the retention of status of a worker (but not a self-employed person). However, in the French text this difficulty does not arise as the word used, *travailleur,* covers workers both in an employed and a self-employed capacity. Furthermore, it is suggested that, given the fact the same person may often work as an employee or on a self-employed basis in substantially similar roles, retention of status in both categories should be broadly similar. It is also difficult to see how the denial of retention of status to the self-employed through this route aids the freedom of movement to provide services.

In *R (on the application of Tilianu) v Social Fund Inspector and SSWP* [2010] EWHC 213 (Admin), the High Court rejected the arguments in the preceding paragraph concerning the language used in the French (and other texts) and the reliance that could be placed upon this. The Court concurred with the decision of the Upper Tribunal in *SSWP v RK* [2009] UKUT 209 (AAC). Mr Tilianu was thus not able to retain his status as a self-employed person during a period of involuntary unemployment (which, as he was an A8 national required to register his employment, meant he was not entitled to any benefit as a jobseeker either).

Mr Tilianu's application for permission to appeal to the Court of Appeal (and subsequent appeal if successful) is to be heard on the 15 or 16 November 2010. However, until that case is decided, it appears that the position at First-tier Tribunal, and for local authority decision makers, must be that the only way in which a person who is no longer self-employed can retain "self-employed" status is during a period of temporary incapacity for work.

Note, however, that in many cases the prior question should be whether the person has in fact stopped being a self-employed person (in which case no question of retaining that status need arise). Because a person who is merely taking steps to establish self-employment may count as a self-employed person (see [1.2] above), it must be the case that someone who has in fact established her/himself in that capacity and worked on that basis for some time and who is then in a period where no work is coming in, but who is actively taking steps to obtain more work, will still be considered self-employed: that has now been confirmed in *SSWP v JS (IS)* [2010] UKUT 240 (AAC) discussed above. This argument does not appear to have arisen on the facts of *Tilianu* or *SSWP v RK* [2009] UKUT 209 (AAC).

[1.3.3] Gaps and switching between heads of Art 7(3)
In *CIS 4304/2007* and *SSWP v IR* [2009] UKUT 11 (AAC), it has been decided that a person may move from retaining status under one of the above heads to retaining status under another – ie, a person who had been a worker, then had a period of retaining status while claiming JSA and then became temporarily unable to work due to illness would count as a person who retained the status of worker.

What, though, of situations where there is a gap between the person ceasing to be a worker/self-employed person and coming within one of Art 7(3)(a)–(d)? In *CIS 1934/2006,* the commissioner commented that "it may well be that some gap between employment and a person starting to seek work again will not be fatal"; however on the facts of the case before him – where the gap was two years, which is longer than the time abroad allowed for a person who wishes not to lose her/his permanent right of residence (see below) – this had not occurred. Interestingly, the commissioner commented that gaps where the "person had taken time away from the labour market for a short holiday or while giving birth" could possibly count. A more concrete example arose in *SSWP v IR*. In that case there had been a gap of just over two months between the claimant finishing work and claiming JSA. The judge remitted the case to a fresh tribunal to determine whether this gap was fatal and held as follows:

"A gap between becoming involuntarily unemployed and claiming jobseeker's allowance is not necessarily fatal. Whether it is significant or not will depend on the length of the gap and the reasons for it. Put into the legal terms of the EC analysis, the question is whether the gap shows that the claimant has withdrawn from the labour market. A claimant may take a few days to think about the future or to rest after a stressful period leading to redundancy. That may be consistent with remaining in the labour market. In contrast, a claimant who decides to spend six months backpacking in the Australian oubback before looking for work has clearly left the labour market for the time being."

So the position for people having a gap between stopping work and signing on depends upon the specific facts of their case and whether those facts show they remained in the labour market. The position for people who have a short gap between stopping work and becoming temporarily incapable of work is less clear. In *SSWP v IA* [2009] UKUT 35 (AAC), the judge comments that:

"There is nothing in either the Directive or the Regulations that confers a right to reside on someone who becomes unable to work unless immediately before that the person was either a worker or retained worker status. Worker status can be gained and retained. There is no power for it to be revived after it has been lost other than by working."

This is somewhat odd as it seems to assume that worker status must have been lost. Take, as an example, the case of a person who stops work and takes a short rest after a stressful period leading up to a redundancy but intends to sign on after that (which the same judge accepted was permissible in *SSWP v IR*). Why should that claimant not retain status if, for example, she breaks a leg during that period of rest and is then unable to sign on? It is suggested that the same considerations as apply to people who can retain status through involuntary unemployment should apply to those who become temporarily incapable of work – particularly where the incapacity was unforeseen.

There are no cases yet highlighted on the Upper Tribunal website which deal with situations where the gap is not immediately after working but is instead between retaining status under one head of Art 7(3) and retaining it under another head. Again, it is suggested that there is no reason why this should be any different and that the crucial issue will be whether the facts show that the person has remained in the labour market.

[1.4] Paragraph (3B)(d): Family members of workers or the self-employed

Para (3B)(d) provides that the family member within the meaning of Art 2 of the Directive of a worker/self-employed person or person who retains that status cannot be a "person from abroad".

Art 2(2) defines a family member as:

(1)   a spouse or registered civil partner;

(2)   a descendant of the worker/self-employed person or her/his spouse or civil partner who is *either* under 21 *or* is dependant;

(3)   direct relatives in the ascendant line (parents, grandparents etc) of the worker/self-employed person (or their spouse or civil partner) who are dependent.

It is important to note that a person remains a spouse/civil partner even if separated from the worker/self-employed person. A spouse/civil partner will only cease to count as a family member on divorce/termination of the civil partnership): Case C-267/83 *Assiatou Diatta v Land Berlin* [1985] ECR 00567 and *CIS 2431/2006*. Similarly, a child aged under 21 is not required to live with the qualifying worker/self-employed person and there may be complete alienation: *CF 1863/2007*. In cases of separated spouses relying on the residence rights of their husband or wife, it can be difficult for the claimant to obtain information about whether that person is working/self-employed or retaining that status – eg, a woman who has fled her husband due to domestic violence cannot easily obtain his most recent wage-slip. It is suggested that in such cases the DWP or the Revenue be asked to provide what information they can by the local authority. Where the status of the spouse cannot be established, it may be the case that the local authority cannot show the claimant is a person from abroad. Given that being a person from abroad is an exception to the general principle that, if one is liable for rent, then it can be met by way of HB, it may be arguable that the correct decision in such cases would be to allow the claim – see *Kerr v Department for Social Development (Northern Ireland)* [2004] UKHL 23. That will certainly be the case if the local authority has not made any efforts to establish itself whether the separated spouse is working through contacting the DWP and asking it to check its systems of national insurance contributions and benefit payments from which an answer to that question may be derived.

In *CIS 2100/2007*, the commissioner considered a number of ECJ decisions on the meaning of dependence and concluded they stand for the following principles.

(1)   A person is only dependent who actually receives support from another.

(2)   There need be no right to that support and it is irrelevant that there are alternative sources of support available.

(3)   That support must be material, although not necessarily financial, and must provide for, or contribute towards, the basic necessities of life.

In *Pedro v SSWP* [2009] EWCA Civ 1358; [2010] AACR 18, the Court of Appeal considered an appeal from *CPC 1433/2008*, in which the deputy commissioner had held that Case C-1/05 *Jia v Migrationsverket* [2007] ECR I-00001 was authority that the relationship of dependence must have existed in the country of origin. The Court held that, following the introduction of the Directive, *Jia* did not have this effect. Further, it reasoned, following

Metock, that the Directive strengthened previous rights of residence. The Court also explains the purposive construction that must be given to the Directive:

"if a particular interpretation of the Directive would mean that a national of a Member State might realistically be discouraged from leaving that state and going to another Member State to work or if, when working or having worked, in another Member State, he might be encouraged to leave, that would not be consistent with the purpose of the Directive, or give effect to it."

The Court held that a Union citizen who wished to work in another member state may be deterred from doing so if he knows that his elderly, but not then dependent mother, will not be regarded as his dependent for the purposes of Art 2(2) if she joins him and later becomes dependent upon him: that would not be consistent with the purpose of the Directive. Accordingly, the Court held that a person would still be dependent on another (and hence her/his family member) even if the relationship of dependency existed for the first time in the UK. Note that for "extended family members" (see below at [2.4]) the requirement for the dependence to have existed in the country of origin will still exist.

It is hoped that the Court's approach to construing the Directive in a manner so that the interpretation arrived at is only acceptable if it would not discourage a potential worker from exercising rights of free movement will be applied in other cases where the issue of construing the Directive arises.

[1.5] Paragraph (3B)(e): Former workers/self-employed

Art 17 of Directive 2004/38/EC gives certain former workers/self-employed persons the right to remain permanently in the territory of the host state. The following people are covered.

(1)   A former worker/self-employed person who, at the time s/he stops working, has reached pensionable age (or has taken early retirement) and who has been employed in that state for the last 12 months and has resided there continuously for more than three years. Only work in the host state counts: *R(IS) 3/97* para 16.

(2)   A former worker/self-employed person who ceases to work as a result of permanent (as opposed to merely temporary) incapacity. In addition, s/he must have *either* resided continuously for two years in the host state *or* if the incapacity is the result of an accident at work or occupational disease entitling her/him to a benefit payable in full or in part by the UK state.

(3)   A former worker/self-employed person who has worked and resided for three years in the host state before working in another member state, while retaining her/his residence in the host state and returning there at least once a week.

Periods of involuntary unemployment, recorded by the relevant employment office and periods not worked for reasons not of the person's own making, or cessation of work due to illness or accident, must be regarded as periods of employment for the purposes of the rules as to the time for which a person must work to come within the above groups.

In addition, the conditions as to length of residence and employment in (1) and (2) above are waived where the former worker/self-employed person's spouse is a British citizen (or was but lost that nationality by marriage to the worker/self-employed person): Art 17(2).

Once acquired, a permanent right to reside under Art 17 can only be lost by absence from the UK in excess of two years. See below on Art 16 which gives a more general right of permanent residence (Art 17, properly considered, being a derogation from that general rule to allow the right of permanent residence to be gained more quickly by those to whom it applies).

The family members of the worker or self-employed person, residing with them in the host member state also acquire a permanent right of residence (Art 17(3)). Furthermore, if a worker or self-employed person dies having resided continuously for at least two years (or for any period if the death was the result of an accident at work or occupational disease), then the family members who were residing with the worker will also acquire a permanent right of residence.

[1.6] Paragraph (3B)(f): A8 and A2 workers

Before setting out who comes within para (3B)(f), it is necessary to consider the special position of A8 and A2 nationals in general.

On 1 May 2004, 10 new countries joined the EU. There were Malta, Cyprus, Czech Republic, Poland, Hungary, Estonia, Latvia, Lithuania, Slovakia and Slovenia. Citizens of all but the first two are referred to here as "A8 nationals". On 1 January 2007, Bulgaria and Romania joined; their citizens are referred to here as "A2 nationals".

The treaties under which these states joined allowed existing member states to limit access to their labour markets by nationals of the new states, subject to certain conditions being met, for a period of seven years from the date of accession. Thus the treaties allowed derogations from Art 39 EC (now Art 45 TFEU), which provides freedom of movement for workers and from (the now revoked) Arts 1–6 of EC Regulation 1612/68.

The UK did not derogate from the rights of free movement as workers for the citizens of Malta or Cyprus. However, it chose to impose restrictions on A8 and later on A2 nationals. For A8 nationals, these restrictions are found in the Accession (Immigration and Worker Registration) Regulations 2004 No.1219, and for A2 nationals in the Accession (Immigration and Worker Authorisation) Regulations 2006 No.3317. Both sets of regulations can be found in Volume II of Sweet and Maxwell's *Social Security Legislation*. They derogate from the rights of residence for A8 and A2 nationals *as workers and work seekers* provided for in Art 39 EC Treaty. They also modify the rights of residence set forth in the I(EEA) Regs 2006 for nationals of these states.

It is important to understand that these special rules do not effect any rights of residence which A8 or A2 nationals may have under other provisions of EU law (ie, as self-employed or retaining that status, self-sufficient people or students) – as shown by *CIS 1042/2008*.

The special rules provide that most A8 and A2 nationals are subject to the requirement (for A8 nationals) to register their work or (for A2 nationals) to be authorised to work. Where an A8 or A2 national is subject to this requirement, her/his rights under Art 39 (and the I(EEA) Regs 2006) are modified in the following ways.

(1)   There is no right to reside as a jobseeker (hence getting HB through the route of obtaining income-based JSA and coming within para (3B)(k) is ruled out).

(2)   The status of worker cannot be retained when out of work.

(3)   S/he does not count as a worker (and therefore does not have a right to reside through working) while in work unless complying with the conditions for registration or authorisation.

Para (3B)(f) in effect provides that those who are in work and are required to be and are compliant with the relevant registration or authorisation conditions (and therefore do count as "workers" within the meaning of reg 6(1) I(EEA) Regs 2006 as modified by the relevant set of Accession regulations) cannot be persons from abroad.

In order to determine whether a particular claimant comes within para (3B)(f) it is therefore necessary to examine which A8 and A2 nationals are required to be registered/authorised (see [1.6.1] below) and what counts as being in registered/authorised employment (see [1.6.2] on p280): it is only if a person is required to register/be authorised and is working in compliance with the relevant provisions that s/he will come within para (3B)(f). People not required to be registered/authorised may come within para (3B)(a) if they are in work in the same way as any other EEA national.

It can be seen that an A8 or A2 national will fall within one of the following groups for consideration.

(1)   S/he is not an A8/A2 national required to be registered or authorised – if this is the case, her/his right to reside should be considered in the same way as with any other EU national.

(2)   S/he is an A8/A2 national required to be registered or authorised – if this is the case, whether s/he is a person from abroad will depend on:

(a) if s/he is working and in registered or authorised work; then s/he will fall within para (3B)(f) and cannot be a person from abroad;

(b) if s/he is not working or is working but has not complied with the requirement to register/obtain authorisation, s/he cannot have a right of residence as a worker or as someone retaining her/his status as a worker (or as a jobseeker, although without JSA nothing turns on this given the exclusion in para (3A)) but s/he may have a right to reside on some other basis – eg, as a self-employed person or as someone with five years' legal residence (see below).

[1.6.1] Which A8/A2 nationals are required to be registered or authorised

An A8 national is not required to register if s/he falls within reg 2(2) to (6) of the 2004 Accession Regs if:

–   on 30 April 2004 s/he had leave to enter or remain in the UK under the Immigration Act 1971 which was not subject to any condition restricting her/his employment;

–   s/he was working legally (ie, in accordance with any conditions as to employment attached to her/his leave to enter or remain (if there were any): reg 2(7)(a)) on 30 April 2004 and who had been so working without interruption for the previous 12 months;

–   s/he has worked legally (ie, for periods prior to accession as above and for periods after accession in accordance with the conditions of the scheme) without interruption for a continuous period of 12 months – in essence this means that once an A8 national has worked in accordance with the scheme for 12 months, s/he is treated as any other EU national;

–   s/he is the spouse/civil partner/child under 18 of a person with leave to enter/remain in the UK that allows employment;

–   s/he has dual nationality with the UK or another (non-A8/A2) EEA state or Switzerland;

–   s/he is a family member of another EEA or Swiss national who has a right to reside under the I(EEA) Regs 2006 (other than an A8/A2 national subject to registration/authorisation if her/his only right to reside is for the first three months in the UK);

–   s/he is the member of a diplomatic mission, or the family member of such a person, or the person otherwise entitled to diplomatic immunity;

–   s/he is a posted worker – ie, is working in the UK providing services on behalf of an employer who is not established in the UK.

An A2 national is not subject to worker authorisation if s/he falls within reg 2(2)-(11) of the 2006 Accession Regs. This occurs where s/he:

–   has (or had on 31 December 2006) leave to enter/remain which has no restriction on employment;

–   was legally working in the UK for 12 months, up to and including 31 December 2006;

–   has legally worked for 12 months (beginning before or after 31 December 2006);

–   is a posted worker – ie, is working in the UK providing services on behalf of an employer who is not established in the UK;

- is the member of a diplomatic mission, or the family member of such a person, or a person otherwise entitled to diplomatic immunity;
- has dual nationality with the UK or another (non-A2) EEA state;
- is the spouse/civil partner of UK a national or of a person settled in the UK;
- is the spouse/civil partner/child under 18 of a person with leave to enter/remain in the UK that allows employment;
- has a permanent right of residence (see below);
- is a student with a registration certificate, which includes a statement that s/he shall not work more than 20 hours a week (unless it is part of vocational training or during vacations) and s/he complies with this. If the certificate confirms the student can work during the four months after the course ends, the exemption continues for this period;
- is a family member of an EEA national who has a right to reside unless the EEA national is an accession state national subject to worker authorisation (or the only reason s/he is not an accession state national subject to worker authorisation is because s/he is covered by the group below);
- is a family member of an accession state national subject to worker authorisation who has a right to reside as a worker, student, self-employed or self-sufficient person;
- is a highly skilled person with a registration certificate stating s/he has unconditional access to the UK's labour market (issued under reg 4 of the 2006 Accession Regs).

Both A8 and A2 nationals are legally working for an interrupted period of 12 months if they were working legally at the start and end of that period and the total of any days during the period when they were not so working is 30 or less. Work is legal for periods prior to accession if it was in accordance with any condition of their leave under the Immigration Act 1971. For periods after that, work is legal if it is in accordance with the requirement to be registered/authorised (see below), or if it is work done while the claimant is not an A8 or A2 national who is required to be registered or authorised (see above). The latter would apply, for example, in the case of a Polish national who was married to a Spanish worker. That Polish national would not be an A8 national requiring registration while married to the Spanish worker. If the couple then divorce, the Polish national would become an A8 national requiring registration unless s/he had done 12 months' work while married (which would have counted as legal work: see reg 2(7)(c) 2004 Accession Regs and reg 2(12)(b) 2006 Accession Regs). In *BS v SSWP* [2009] UKUT 16 (AAC), the judge held that a claimant was "legally working" for the purposes of the 2006 Accession Regulations when she was on unpaid sick leave (and in Bulgaria).

[1.6.2] What counts as registered/authorised work

A8 nationals who are required to register (ie, fall outside the circumstances set out in the above list) can only work for authorised employers. They will only count as workers for the purposes of reg 6(1) I(EEA) Regs or Art 39 EC (now Art 45 TFEU) when so doing (regs 4 and 5 of the 2004 Accession Regs). In other words, an A8 national who is required to register and is working but not for an authorised employer will, as stated above, not have a right of residence as a worker (and will not come within para (3B)(f)).

An employer is an authorised employer in relation to a worker in the circumstances set out in reg 7(2) of the 2004 Accession Regs if:

- the worker was legally working for that employer on 30 April 2004 and has not ceased working for it;
- the worker is within the first month of employment with that employer;
- the worker is outside the first month of employment but during that month applied for a registration certificate and has not received it;
- the worker has received a valid registration certificate in respect of that employer;
- where, during the period 1 May to 31 December 2004 only, the worker began working as a seasonal worker at an agricultural camp after 1 May 2004 but had been issued, prior to 1 May 2004, with leave to enter under the Immigration Act 1971 as a seasonal worker at such a camp, then the employer at such a camp is an authorised employer (this may seem archaic but could have some relevance to determining whether this person had a permanent right of residence several years later).

An A2 national subject to worker authorisation must be authorised to work, and where working but not in authorised work, is treated in the same way as an A8 national who is not working for an authorised employer: see regs 5 and 6 of the 2006 Accession Regs. An A2 national subject to worker authorisation is only authorised to work if s/he holds an accession worker authorisation document and is working in accordance with the rules set out in that document. These documents will either be passports which are stamped with visas showing limited leave to enter under the Immigration Act 1971 which give some (restricted) rights to work in a particular category or for a particular employer, seasonal agricultural worker cards or "accession worker cards" which are issued under reg 10 of the 2006 Accession Regs where the A2 national meets the conditions for work in a category of employment set out in Schedule 1 to those regulations (such as au pair, domestic worker, work permit employment etc).

In *Zalewska v Department for Social Development* [2008] UKHL 67, the House of Lords rejected an argument that an A8 national who had claimed IS after she had ceased working in registered employment for less than 12 months was protected by Art 7(2) of EC Regulation 1612/68. The court ruled, unanimously on this point, that the effect of the Annexes to the Accession Treaty was to modify the impact of the rights of migrant workers under Art 39 of the EC Treaty and Arts 1-6 of Regulation 1612/68 so as to enable national rules to be applied to regulate

A8 nationals' access to the state's employment markets. Of their very nature, these differential rules were intended to be, and were allowed to be, discriminatory. Once an A8 national had been admitted to the labour market in the UK (by taking up registered employment), s/he would be a "worker" and fall under the protection of Art 7(2) of Regulation 1612/68 (now a worker covered by para (3B)(a)). However, the central question in the appeal was whether Ms Zalewska remained as a "worker" and so was protected when she made her claim for IS. It was clear that the status of A8 nationals was intended to be different from that of other EU nationals and it was clearly not the intention of the Act of Accession to tie the hands of national authorities as to how they regulated their national labour markets. As the relevant Annexes to the Accession Treaty made plain, an A8 national properly admitted to the UK's labour market for 12 months would acquire full EU "worker" rights. But as the UK had been left to determine the conditions in which an A8 national has been properly admitted to the labour market for 12 months, whether Ms Zaleskwa had or had not had to be determined by considering UK law. That law showed that in order to be properly admitted to the labour market, Ms Zaleskwa would need to have been in registered employment for 12 months before her claim for IS, which she had not. By a bare majority of three to two, the House of Lords ruled that the registration scheme was a reasonable and proportionate concomitant of the permitted derogation. In so doing, the majority of the House of Lords followed and adopted Commssioner Rowland's reasoning in *CIS 3232/2006*. Further, if during the 12-month period, an A8 national worker ceases to qualify as a worker (by ceasing registered work), s/he falls within the derogation from Art 39 of the Treaty and Art 7(2) of Regulation 1612/68 and so ceases to be protected by either.

That, however, is not the end of arguments about the rules for A8 workers.

–   In *PM v SSWP* [2009] UKUT 236 (AAC), the claimant, an A8 national, had temporary admission as an asylum seeker prior to accession. He had obtained permission to work as an asylum seeker and worked from June 2003 to April 2005. He had not registered this work after accession. The issue in the case before the Upper Tribunal was whether the claimant was an A8 national required to register. Reg 2(7)(a)(i) of the 2004 Accession Regs provides that a person is legally working before accession if s/he had leave to enter (note temporary admission is not leave to enter) under the Immigration Act 1971 and was working in accordance with the conditions of that leave. The claimant sought to argue that this was not an exhaustive description of when a person was legally working. If the claimant was legally working at the date of accession, then he would not have been required to register that work at accession for it to be legal (see first bullet above and reg 7(2)(a)). The claimant's argument was to the effect that legally working (as it was a phrase which appeared in the Accession Treaty) must have a Community meaning. The judge dismissed this argument. The claimant has now obtained permission to appeal to the Court of Appeal (in *Miskovic v SSWP*) and the case was heard on 19 November 2010.

–   In *SSWP v ZA* [2009] UKUT 294 (AAC), the Upper Tribunal considered the Secretary of State's appeals against decisions in a number of cases where the A8 national claimants had not applied for their registration certificates within the first month of their employment commencing, but had subsequently received certificates – eg, following applications made after the first month of employment. The issue was whether possession of the certificate meant that the work was to be regarded as work for an authorised employer throughout (eg, that the issue of the certificate operated to retrospectively validate the work as for an authorised employer) or whether, properly speaking, the work, after the first month, was not for an authorised employer until the certificate was received. It is clear from the judgment that the Upper Tribunal regarded the issue as finely balanced but eventually determined that certificates, when finally issued, did not retrospectively authorise the work. Judge Ward notes that in general it would be for the DWP (or local authority in a HB case) to obtain evidence about when the certificate was applied for, so it could be determined whether the whole of a claimant's work was for an authorised employer (where the application was made within the first month of employment) or whether the work only had that character from the date of issue of the certificate (when the application was not made within the initial month). In cases where the local authority has failed to make the relevant enquiries, the matter may be determined in favour of the worker (see *Kerr* referred to above). One of the claimants in the case has applied for permission to appeal to the Court of Appeal (if permission is granted the case will be known as *Aleksandroviciute v SSWP*).

Finally, it should be noted that the restrictions for A8 workers cannot continue beyond 1 May 2011 (seven years after accession) because the Treaty of Accession does not allow restrictions beyond that period.

[1.7] Paragraph (3B)(g): Refugees

Prior to 15 October 1996, a "refugee" was defined as being a person who came within the meaning of that term under the Convention Relating to the Status of Refugees. In *CIS 564/1994* (paras 23-4) it was confirmed that a person who fulfilled the criteria under the Convention for being a refugee was a refugee even if the immigration authorities had yet to decide so. The suggestion to the contrary was described as "callous, unprincipled nonsense". Had that definition remained in place, it would therefore have been necessary for authorities and tribunals to decide for themselves whether a claimant was a refugee.

From that date, the definition in para (6) took effect, so that a person is only a "refugee" when the Secretary of State has recorded her/him as such. When this is done, the claimant is sent form GEN 22. There was special provision for the often lengthy period while refugees had their claims for asylum determined: see reg 10A and

Sch A1 in Sch 4 of the HB&CTB(CP) Regs on p1225. However, this provision no longer exists for those claimants not recorded as refugees by 14 June 2007.

[1.8] Paragraph (3B)(h) and (hh): Persons granted exceptional leave to remain or enter/humanitarian protection

Exceptional leave to remain was usually granted by the Secretary of State to those who could show compelling humanitarian reasons why they should not be deported. Humanitarian protection is now granted, within the rules, for similar reasons.

[1.9] Paragraph (3B)(k): Claimants in receipt of IS, income-based JSA or on income-related ESA

This is a most important category. This is not just because there is no need for an authority to enquire into the residence rights or ordinary habitual residence of a person in receipt of one of these benefits, but because the right to reside requirement, as it applies to entitlement to income-based JSA (reg 85A Jobseekers Allowance Regulations 1996), does not exclude from entitlement someone whose only right to reside is as an EEA jobseeker. In effect that means that any EEA national (other than an A8 national required to register or an A2 national subject to worker authorisation) whose only right to reside stems from the fact that s/he is looking for work and meets the means test requirement for income-based JSA can, by obtaining that benefit, get entitlement to HB. Note that a person "on income support or income-based jobseeker's allowance" includes those who are entitled but not being paid it due to a sanction, "waiting days" or because of the "loss of benefit" provisions, and a person "on an income-related ESA" includes those on "waiting days" as well as certain claimants disqualified from payment of ESA: reg 2(3) and (3A).

The view expressed in previous editions of this book that, if the claimant is receiving either of these benefits then the authority is not entitled to refuse benefit on the ground that s/he is a person from abroad (following *R v Penwith DC ex p Menear* [1991] 24 HLR 115, QBD), was expressly rejected by the deputy commissioner in *R(H) 9/04*. In the deputy commissioner's view, *Menear* is only authority for the proposition that an authority is bound by the DWP's decision on income and capital: para 24. However, he went on to stress (para 39) that, although the authority is not precluded from disagreeing with the DWP's decision on whether the claimant is a person from abroad, it is not obliged to decide the issue from scratch in every case and may follow the DWP's decision in the absence of anything to compel it taking a contrary view. Equally, if the DWP finds that a claimant is a person from abroad and refuses IS or income-based JSA, the authority is still under a duty to determine the HB claim. Moreover, if the information is not complete, the authority ought to ask the claimant to supply it and not blindly follow the decision maker's decision. Notwithstanding these qualifications, or the fact that the decision has been reported, it is respectfully suggested that *R(H) 9/04* is wrong in saying that an authority can come to to its own view about whether a claimant is a person from abroad, even if that person is in receipt of IS. To start with, the views expressed by the deputy commissioner on this point are plainly *obiter*, as no question arose in that case of whether the claimant was a person from abroad. More importantly, however, the terms of reg 10(2) and (3) when read together, it is suggested, show that if a person is in receipt of IS, and so falls within para (3), s/he cannot by the terms of para (2) fall within para (2), and so s/he cannot be a person from abroad. However inapt the analogy with *ex parte Menear* may have been in previous editions of this book (as it is only authority, as *R(H) 9/04* rightly holds, for the proposition that the means tests cannot be applied by a HB authority if the claimant is already in receipt of IS), it is suggested that the view in those previous editions, that a person in receipt of IS cannot be refused HB (or CTB) on the basis that s/he is a person from abroad, was and remains sound. The same deputy commissioner has now accepted these criticisms in *CIS 34/2006 and others* (para 47), and has recanted from what he said in *R(H) 9/04* (para 39). He went on to rule in *CIS 34/2006* that a person is not "in receipt" of IS for a period where it has later been established that s/he was not entitled to that benefit.

However, if the IS award was obtained by fraud, the local authority may be able to decide that there was no award from the outset, even where the DWP has not taken any action to revise or supersede the award (see *R v South Ribble DC HBRB ex p Hamilton* [2000] 33 HLR 102, CA); though the better advice in this situation would be for the local authority to refer its evidence of fraud to the DWP and get the DWP to carry out any revision or supersession of the IS (or income-based JSA) entitlement first, and suspend payment of HB/CTB in the meantime.

[1.10] Paragraph (3B)(j): Claimants from Montserrat

So long as the claimant left Montserrat after 1 November 1995, and it was due to the catastrophic volcanic activity on that island, s/he cannot be a "person from abroad". There is no requirement that s/he came straight to the UK from Montserrat.

[2] Paragraph (3): Who has a right to reside in the Common Travel Area

As detailed above, for those not coming within para (3B) then para (3) provides that they will not be habitually resident under para (2), unless they have a right to reside in the CTA.

Advisers should note the transitional protection which may allow some claimants to count as habitually resident without needing to have a right of residence (see pp1203 and 1215). A claimant who can take advantage of this protection does not need to have a right to reside (but will be subject to the requirement of habitual residence in fact, unless exempt under para (3B)).

British citizens, Irish citizens and citizens of the other states in the CTA clearly all have a right to reside in the CTA. So too do those who have valid leave to remain under the Immigration Act 1971 (although such persons may well be excluded on the separate basis that they are "persons subject to immigration control"). In reality, therefore, it is only non-British or Irish EEA nationals who may be found not to have a right to reside in the CTA: all other persons clearly have a right of residence or are excluded at an earlier stage because they are subject to immigration control.

As discussed above for EU nationals, the starting point for determining whether a right to reside exists is Directive 2004/38. As noted, the EEA is a larger grouping than the EU. It includes Norway, Iceland and Liechtenstein. EEA nationals enjoy the same rights of residence as EU nationals under the EEA Treaty (the "Oporto Agreement"). The I(EEA) Regs 2006 treat nationals from any EEA state (save Britain – see above) and Swiss nationals in the same manner.

The Directive, and the I(EEA) Regulations, set out three main types of residence right.

(1)   An initial right to reside for all EEA nationals (see [2.1] below).

(2)   An extended right to reside for EEA nationals and their family members who are workers, self-employed, self-sufficient or students (see [2.2] below).

(3)   A permanent right of residence for those who have resided legally for five years (or less if they come within Art 17 discussed above) (see [2.3] on p285).

It is helpful to consider each of these in turn before looking at:

–   the rights of extended family members (see [2.4] on p286);

–   certain other situations where a right of residence may be retained (see [2.5] on p285);

–   the difficult question of when someone may have a right to reside not provided for in the Directive or the I(EEA) Regs 2006 (see [2.6] on p287);

–   whether possession of an EU residence document issued by the Home Office can be relied upon to establish a right of residence (see [2.7] on p293).

[2.1] Initial right to reside

All EEA nationals have an initial right of residence for up to three months (Art 6 of the Directive and reg 13 I(EEA) Regs 2006). Art 24 of the Directive provides in general that those with a right of residence under the Directive are entitled to equal treatment. However, Art 24(2) allows member states to derogate from this requirement of equal treatment by stating that "the host Member State shall not be obliged to confer entitlement to social assistance during the first three months of residence". Thus, para (3A)(a) and (c) of this regulation provides that the initial right of residence is not a sufficient right to reside to satisfy para (3). The effect is that, where a claimant's *only* right to reside is because s/he is an EEA national within her/his first three months of residence in the UK, that right will not entitle her/him to HB.

[2.2] Extended right to reside

The Directive provides (Art 7(1)) that those who are workers, self-employed, self-sufficient, students or their family members shall have a right to reside for longer than the first three months. Similar provision is made by regs 6 and 14 I(EEA) Regs 2006. The I(EEA) Regs 2006 also give this right to jobseekers and their family members: however, para (3A)(b) and (d) again provide that this is not a sufficient right to reside to satisfy para (3). Note though that a jobseeker may be able to obtain income-based JSA, in which case s/he would not be a person from abroad under para (3B)(k). Thus, someone whose only right to reside is as a jobseeker, or the family member of a jobseeker, will not be entitled to HB unless s/he is in receipt of income-based JSA.

What then of the other groups with an extended right to reside? Workers, the self-employed and those who retain one of those statuses are specifically provided for under para (3B) and, with one qualification, do not need to be considered here (see above at [1.1] to [1.3]). The qualification is that reg 6(2)(b)(iii) I(EEA) Regs 2006 provides that a person who has been employed for less than a year before becoming involuntarily unemployed can retain the status of a worker indefinitely provided s/he has registered with the relevant unemployment office and has a genuine chance of being engaged. The Directive does not appear to provide for this as it says only that for such people the status of worker will be retained for "no less than" six months. According to the commissioner in *CIS 4304/2007*, the consequence of this is that such a person would not come within the equivalent of para (3B)(c) for the IS Regs but would need to be habitually resident under the para (2) equivalent. This is because s/he would be treated as retaining the status of worker (and the consequent right to reside) under domestic law but not under the Directive.

[2.2.1] Self-sufficient

Self-sufficient persons have an extended right of residence. The Directive and the I(EEA) Regs 2006 require that to be self-sufficient the person must have "sufficient resources for themselves and their family members not to become a burden on the social assistance system of the host Member State and have comprehensive sickness insurance cover in the host Member State" (Art 7(1)(a)).

Art 8(4) provides that member states may not lay down a fixed amount which they regard as "sufficient resources" and cannot in any event require a person to have more resources than the threshold below which nationals of the host state become eligible for social assistance. Reg 4(4) I(EEA) Regs 2006 is slightly different in that resources "are to be regarded as sufficient if they exceed the maximum level of resources which a UK national and his family members may possess if he is to become eligible for social assistance under the United Kingdom benefit system". Note that this says nothing about whether resources below this level *might* be regarded (as opposed to *must* be regarded) as sufficient. As HB does count as social assistance, any person who would qualify for some HB cannot automatically be regarded as having sufficient resources. However, there may be cases where a small amount of HB entitlement for a short period would not mean the person was a burden on the social assistance system and had sufficient resources.

The requirement for comprehensive sickness insurance was considered by the Court of Appeal in *W (China) & Another v Secretary of State for the Home Department* [2006] EWCA Civ 1494. In that case the Court held that the fact the appellant could rely on NHS treatment was not sufficient as the NHS is largely tax funded and not insurance based. Furthermore, as the purpose of the requirement that comprehensive health insurance was in place was precisely to prevent a burden on the host state, then the fact that free NHS services were obtainable in fact precisely created that burden. Note that this case did not consider whether the same would apply to a claimant who came within the personal scope of EC Regulation 1408/71 and had a right to access NHS treatment under the equal treatment provision of that Directive (as a sickness benefit in kind).

In *SG v Tameside MBC (HB)* [2010] UKUT 243 (AAC), the Upper Tribunal considered the case of a Swedish national who was in receipt of a Swedish invalidity pension of £121.68 a week. The claimant had lived in the UK since December 2007 and had initially stayed with her sister, before moving to stay with friends in February 2008. In May 2008, the claimant was given a tenancy of a housing association flat but HB was refused on the basis that she had no right to reside. Judge Ward summarised the issues arising for his decision, concerning whether the claimant came within Art 7(1)(a) of Directive 2004/38, as follows:

a.   do the provisions of Regulation (EEC) No.1408/71 applicable to the receipt by an EU citizen of National Health Service care mean that she has "comprehensive sickness insurance cover in the host member State"? and

b.   when and how does the test of "sufficient resources" fall to be applied?

With regard to the first question, the Upper Tribunal held, accepting a concession from the Secretary of State (who was joined as a party to the case), that as the claimant was in receipt of a Swedish invalidity benefit, the UK would be able, under Art 28a of EC Regulation 1408/71 and Art 95 of EC Regulations 574/72, to claim from the Swedish state. Accordingly, the purpose of the requirement that comprehensive sickness insurance, identified by the Court of Appeal in *W (China)*, was not frustrated by receipt of free NHS treatment as the UK would be reimbursed for that treatment.

Thus, provided that under these EC Regulations (or their replacements: EC Regulations 883/04 and 987/2009) the UK would be able to claim any NHS costs for treating someone from another member state, that will satisfy the requirement of comprehensive medical insurance. Note that this right to reclaim costs appears only to arise in limited circumstances – ie, where that other member state was the one whose legislation was applicable to the claimant (see Title II of EC Regulation 883/04 for when that is the case) and typically where that state is paying a benefit to the claimant.

With regard to the second issue, the Upper Tribunal noted Case C-184/99 *Grzelcyzk* ECR I-06193. The Upper Tribunal concluded (albeit tentatively) that, following that case, it is arguable that a claimant who can demonstrate that s/he was self-sufficient for a time but then ceased to be self-sufficient, might only lawfully be denied benefit if s/he has become an unreasonable burden on the social assistance system. That then left the judge to decide the sub-issues arising.

(1)   Whether the claimant had ever been self-sufficient? That involves asking how much resources she needed to count as self-sufficient.

(2)   Whether, if she had been, at the time of claim for HB she was likely to be an unreasonable burden on the social assistance system?

The judge notes that the requirement under Art 7(1)(a) of the Directive is to have sufficient resources not to become a burden *during her/his period of residence*. He then looked at how much resources a claimant would need to avoid being a burden on the social assistance scheme in that period. Judge Ward noted that the claimant had a higher income than the personal allowance for IS purposes. However, HB counts as social assistance and, to be self-sufficient, a person needs a roof over her/his head. Therefore, the judge rules that one can take into account whether the claimant has housing (or sufficient income to obtain housing) in determining sufficiency of resources (at para 50). That said, it is possible that where a claimant has accommodation provided by a third party for free, it will count as part of the claimant's resouces. However, the judge then ruled that in this case the arrangements the claimant had for the provision of accommodation from her sister, which had fallen through when her violent ex-husband discovered her location, and her later residence with friends in Manchester were not sufficiently secure to be able to say the claimant had sufficient accommodation. The judge also considered that if the level of resources required was thought to be the level above which the claimant would become eligible for some HB (arguably taking into account premiums that she would have included in her applicable amount to calculate this) then the claimant always had inadequate resources. Thus the judge found that the claimant did not have sufficient resources at any point.

However, the Upper Tribunal went on to consider whether the claimant would be, were he wrong on that, an unreasonable burden at the date of decision. He concluded that she would be. It is worth noting that the main factors the judge took into account in considering this were the fact that the claimant would in all likelihood be indefinitely in need of benefits and that these would be for a significant portion of her housing costs.

Thus, provided a claimant could, unlike SG, demonstrate that s/he had been self-sufficient at some point, then *SG v Tameside MBC (HB)* may allow them to claim HB and CTB when, for some reason, s/he ceases to be self-sufficient, *provided* s/he can show the reliance on such benefits is likely to be relatively short term and/or for a small overall proportion of her/his needs. Whether the analysis in *SG v Tameside MBC (HB)* is correct in the emphasis it places on the factors of length of period for which benefits are needed or the amount of recourse, and also whether it is correct to say a claimant must have resources sufficient to meet her/his housing costs, will undoubtedly arise in future cases.

[2.2.2] Students
Students also have an extended right of residence. Note, however, that they must have made a declaration to the Home Secretary to the effect that they have sufficient resources to avoid becoming a burden on the social assistance system (see above in [2.2.1] for what this means). They must also have comprehensive sickness insurance.

Note also that for a student's family members, it is only the spouse and dependent children who can derive a right of residence from the student (dependent direct relatives in the ascending line are treated as extended family members): see Art 7(4) and reg 7(2).

[2.2.3] Family members of anyone with extended right of residence
Art 7 provides that the family members of anyone with an extended right of residence also has a right of residence. The meaning of family members within the directive has been considered at [1.4] above. Reg 14(2) I(EEA) Regs 2006 makes similar provision. Note that the I(EEA) Regs 2006 provide that someone who is an "extended family member" (see [2.4] below) and has the required residence documentation counts as a family member and may therefore have a right to reside if the person of whom s/he is a family member has such a right.

[2.3] Permanent right to reside
Art 16 of the Directive provides that those who "have resided legally for a continuous period of five years in the host Member State shall have the right of permanent residence there". Once acquired, this right is not subject to the claimant meeting other conditions – eg, being a worker, self-employed person etc.

Once acquired, the right can only be lost by absence from the host state of more than two consecutive years.

Reg 15 I(EEA) Regs 2006 seeks to implement Art 16 in domestic law but fails to do so adequately. A person acquires a permanent right of residence when s/he has resided for five years "in accordance with these regulations". The Regulations treat residence before their coming into force (30 April 2006) as residence "in accordance with these regulations" if it was residence in accordance with the Immigration (European Economic Area) Regulations 2000 No.2326 (I(EEA) Regs 2000) (see Sch 4 para 6 I(EEA) Regs 2006). The 2000 Regulations were in force from 2 October 2000.

In *CIS 4299/2007*, the commissioner held that rights of residence from sources other than Directive 2004/38/EC (ie, as a jobseeker) could count towards the five-year period of residence required for Art 16, as could EU rights held prior to the coming into force of Directive 2004/38/EC.

In *SSWP v Lassal* [2009] EWCA Civ 157, the Secretary of State's appeal to the Court of Appeal against that decision, the Court referred to the ECJ the following question:

"Is Article 16(1) of Directive 2004/38 of the European Parliament and the Council of 29 April 2004 to be interpreted as entitling that EU citizen to a right of permanent residence by virtue of the fact that she had been legally resident, in accordance with earlier community law instruments conferring rights of residence on workers, for a continuous period of five years which ended prior to 30 April 2006 (the date by which member States had to transpose the Directive)?"

Ms Lassal had, after completing her five years' residence in accordance with earlier provisions, left the UK for a 10-month period before 30 April 2006 and the Court of Appeal also asked whether that could affect her permanent right of residence.

The ECJ gave its judgment on 7 March 2010 in Case C-162/09 *SSWP v Taous Lassal* [2010] ECR. The Court held in clear terms that:

"– continuous periods of five years' residence completed before the date of transposition of Directive 2004/38, namely 30 April 2006, in accordance with earlier European Union law instruments, must be taken into account for the purposes of the acquisition of the right of permanent residence pursuant to Article 16(1) thereof, and

– absences from the host Member State of less than two consecutive years, which occurred before 30 April 2006 but following a continuous period of five years' legal residence completed before that date do not affect the acquisition of the right of permanent residence pursuant to Article 16(1) thereof."

The ruling in *Lassal* should now be followed by all decision makers in HB/CTB cases. At the time of writing, the DWP has not yet issued new guidance to local authorities about the case. Bizarrely, guidance issued in February 2010 (Annex 1 to *HB Bulletin G2/2010*) ignored the strong views of the Court of Appeal, given when *Lassal* was referred to the ECJ, that the commissioner in *CIS 4299/2007* had been correct. Furthermore, that guidance at para 2, wrongly, stated that only the Home Secretary could "grant" a right of permanent residence. That is evidently not the case from consideration of Ms Lassal's case (and a host of other ECJ judgments): EU residence rights do not arise by virtue of an application but rather simply by the EU citizen meeting the conditions for having the right. Local authorities following the guidance in that *Bulletin* on the requirement for the Home Secretary to have granted a permanent residence right in order for it to exist will, therefore, be making legally incorrect decisons.

In *McCarthy v SSHD* [2008] EWCA Civ 641, the House of Lords has referred the following questions to the ECJ:

"(1)   Is a person of dual Irish and UK nationality who has resided in the UK for her entire life a 'beneficiary' within the meaning of article 3 of Directive 2004/38 . . . .?

(2)   Has such a person 'resided legally' within the host member State for the purpose of article 16 of the Directive in circumstances where she was unable to satisfy the requirement of article 7 of Directive 2004/38?"

In that case, the appellant is a person with dual Irish and British nationality who had lived in Britain all her life. She argued she had a permanent right to reside under the Directive enabling her Jamaican husband to obtain a right to reside as her family member. The Court of Appeal held: "The lawful residence contemplated in article 16 is residence which complies with community law requirements specified in the Directive". Claimants wishing to rely on an argument that they have been "lawfully resident" for five years other than through exercising an EU law right of residence are likely to have their cases stayed pending the outcome of this reference. Note that the Advocate General in *Teixeira* (paras 119 and 120) expressed a view that residence lawful under domestic law would count towards the five-year period.

In *R(IS) 3/08*, *CIS 1833/2007*, *CIS 4299/2007* and *CPC 2134/2007*, it has been held that periods of residence in the UK before the claimant was an EU national (ie, before the state of which s/he is a national acceded to the EU) cannot count towards the acquisition of a right of permanent residence – this is consistent with the finding in *McCarthy* that periods where there was only a domestic law right of residence do not assist a claimant to satisfy the five-year requirement. *CPC 2134/2007* is under appeal to the Court of Appeal (sub nom *Kirij v SSWP*). It is of note that the European Commission suggests that this is wrong in its report to the European Parliament and Council on the Application of the Directive (Brussels, COM(2008) 840/3). However, the view of the Commission, unlike that of the commissioners in the above decisions, does not bind a decision maker or tribunal considering a HB claim.

Art 16(1) and reg 15(1) I(EEA) Regs 2006 are at least the same in referring to those who have resided *continuously* for a five-year period. Art 16(3) and reg 3(2) both also provide that continuity of residence shall not be affected by absences, for any reason, of up to six months in total in any year, or one absence of up to 12 months for reason of pregnancy, childbirth, serious illness, study or vocational training or overseas posting. In *CIS 2258/2008,* the commissioner held that, although this means that such absences allow periods of residence to be linked up, they do not themselves count as periods spent legally residing. There is nothing in the Directive or the 2006 Regs which touches on what is to be made, for the purposes of continuity of residence to acquire a permanent right, of time spent in the UK where there is no right to reside. It is suggested that such gaps should be treated in the same way as absences abroad. Thus, if a person works for three years and then remains in the UK but ceases being economically active for five months before returning to work for a further two years, that gap should not be fatal to continuity of residence just as it would not be had s/he returned to her/his country of origin for that five-month period.

[2.4] The rights of extended family members

Art 3(2) of the Directive provides that member states shall, in accordance with national legislation, facilitate the entry and residence of those not coming within the narrow definition of family member set out in Art 2(2) (see [1.4] above) for the following:

–   any other family member who in the country from which they have come are dependants or members of the household of the Union citizen;
–   other such family members who strictly require personal care due to serious health grounds;
–   partners with whom the Union citizen has a durable relationship, duly attested.

The I(EEA) Regs 2009 provide that persons in such circumstances are "extended family members" (reg 8), and reg 7(3) provides that if they have obtained a residence certificate/card, they will count as family members. As family members they can derive a right of residence from the Union citizen of whom they are a family member who has such a right.

In *CIS 612/2008*, the commissioner comments, *obiter*, at para 53, that in the absence of the required residence documentation an extended family member cannot have a right of residence. This is because, although the ECJ has held that generally a residence document is not necessary to have the right of residence which it describes, the right of residence for an extended family member does not arise directly under Art 3(2) but is merely one which the UK is required to facilitate. Thus, unless the Home Secretary has granted such a right of residence (as shown by the issue of the residence document) it does not exist.

As it is only the claimant of HB who is required not to be a person from abroad, in many cases of unmarried/civil-partnered couples then the failure of the Directive to confer a right on such partners by virtue of their relationship will not be problematic, provided it is the partner who has the right of residence who has claimed benefit. It may be relevant if, for example, the claimant is the child of an extended family member (who has not obtained a residence document) of a worker, but is not the child of the worker. Similarly, it could be relevant in a case where the claimant's unmarried partner who was a worker has died.

[2.5] Retention of a right of residence: death, divorce and departure

Arts 12 and 13 of the Directive provide for the retention of the right of residence by a family member where the person who had a right of residence as a worker, self-employed person, self-sufficient person or student has died, divorced her/him or departed from the UK.

Art 12(1) provides that the death or departure of the EU citizen shall not affect the right of residence of her/his family members. The only qualification to this is that such persons cannot themselves acquire a right of permanent residence until they themselves are a worker, self-employed or self-sufficient person or a student.

For non-EU family members, Art 12(2) provides that the death of the EU citizen shall not affect the residence of the non-EU family member, but only provided they have resided in the host state for at least one year before the death. It appears that such non-EU family members must also be in a position whereby if they were EU citizens they themselves would count as workers, self-employed persons, self-sufficient or students (or be the family members of such people) at least until they acquire a permanent right of residence. Art 12(3) provides for the retention of the right of residence of a non-EU family member where the EU citizen on whose right of residence s/he relies departs from the UK, but only if s/he is the child of that EU citizen enrolled in education or the parent with actual custody of such a child.

Unfortunately, the retention of the right of residence in the event of death or departure provided for in Art 12 is another area where the I(EEA) Regs 2006 and the EU provisions diverge. Reg 14(3) provides that a "family member who has retained the right of residence" has a right to reside. Reg 10 then provides a definition of such a person. It seems that Reg 10(2) does provide an equivalent right for non-EU nationals to that of Art 12(3) in the event of the death of the EU citizen. Reg 10(3) I(EEA) Regs 2006 provides for the retention of the right of residence of the direct descendant or the spouse of either an EU or non-EU national where the EU national on who s/he relies has died or departed from the UK, but only where that person is attending an educational course when the EU national died or departed the UK or (under reg 10(4)) the person is the parent with custody of a child attending such a course in those circumstances. What is missing here, as compared to the Directive, is the right of an EU national whose family member with an EU law right of residence has died or departed from the UK to retain her/his status regardless of involvement in an educational course. In addition, no right to retain status is conferred on family members who are dependent and in the *ascendant* line. What is added here, again as compared to the Directive, is the right of a non-EU national family member to retain status where her/his EU family member with a right of residence has died, even if s/he has not resided in the UK for a year, provided s/he is in education or the parent with care of such a person (as stated above in the Directive, the rights of non-EU family members in the event of death of the EU family member only arise if there has been residence of a year).

Similar problems arise in relation to Art 13 which provides for the retention of residence in the event of divorce/termination of a registered partnership. Again, the Directive provides that the right to reside of EU national family members is not affected by such events. However, the UK rules contain absolutely no reference to this. At least Art 13(2) relating to non-EU family members who are divorced from, or have their registered partnership terminated with an EU national with a right to reside is faithfully transposed in reg 10(5) I(EEA) Regs 2006. Thus a non-EEA national who is the family member of a qualifying EEA national who divorces/terminates a partnership with her/him will retain her/his status if s/he would be a qualifying person if s/he were an EEA national (ie, a worker, self-employed person, self-sufficient or a student) if:

–   the marriage had lasted at least three years, at least one of which was spent in the UK; *or*

–   s/he is the former spouse/registered partner of the EEA national and has custody of their child; *or*

–   s/he is the former spouse/registered partner of the EEA national and has the right of access to a child of the EEA national where a court has ordered that such access takes place in the UK; *or*

–   the continued right of residence is warranted by particularly difficult circumstances such as the claimant or another family member having been a victim of domestic violence within the marriage or partnership.

Fortunately, if a claimant comes within Arts 12 or 13 of the Directive or reg 10 I(EEA) Regs 2006, s/he should still have a right to reside on the basis of whichever provision applies to her/him.

[2.6] EU Rights of residence other than those in the Directive

The subject of what rights of residence a person not coming within the Directive may have has proved a troubled one.

[2.6.1] Service recipients

EU nationals wishing to be recipients of services in other member states were previously covered by Art 1(1)(b) of Directive 73/148, but Directive 2004/38/EC is silent about recipients as is reg 10 HB Regs. This probably does not matter as recipients of services have a right to reside under EC Treaty Arts 49 and 50. "Services" are normally provided for remuneration: EC Treaty Art 60; *R v Westminster CC ex p Castelli and Tristan-Garcia* [1995] 8 Admin LR 73 at 92E-F, QBD (R Henderson QC) (EU national cannot seek to be recipient of NHS services to show right of residence). Examples of services which may be sought are tourism, business, education and medical treatment: Cases C-286/82 & C-26/83 *Luisi & Carbone v Ministero del Tesoro* [1984] ECR 00377. Note that the services received must be being provided for the purpose of making a profit: see *CH 1400/2006* in which the commissioner held, following cases C-263/86 *Belgian State v Humbel* [1988] ECR 05365 and C-109/92 *Wirth v Landeshauptstadt Hannover* [1993] ECR I-06447, that a claimant attending a postgraduate course at the University of London for which she had paid the foreign student fee rate was not a recipient of services.

The limitations of the derivative residence rights under Arts 49 and 50 for those seeking to claim benefits were revealed in *CIS 3875/2005*. The commissioner accepted that the provision of accommodation, social services and medical services are all capable of falling within the scope of Art 50. However, two important limiting factors then have to be considered. Firstly, the services must normally provided for remuneration. Secondly, Art 50 does not apply where a national of a member state goes to the territory of another member state and establishes her/his principal residence there in order to provide or receive services there for an *indefinite* period: Case C-196/87 *Steymann v Staatssecretaris van Justitie* [1988] ECR 06159 and Case C-70/95 *Sodemare SA v Regione Lombardia* [1997] ECR I-03395. The residence right only arises if the services are being sought for a temporary period. However, from a practical perspective, establishing that fact would itself undermine any claim (for the habitual residence test) that the claimant had a settled intention to remain in the UK. In addition, the right to reside for recipients of services can only arise if the claimant came to the UK in order to receive services here, and not simply whether the claimant travelled to the UK in circumstances where it was likely that s/he would receive services, even if that was not the purpose of the journey.

[2.6.2] Article 21 TFEU

All nationals of EU member states are citizens of the EU (Art 20 TFEU, formerly Art 17 EC Treaty). By Art 20(2)(a) and Art 21(1) (formerly Art 18), EU citizens have the right to move and reside freely within the EU. However, for both articles these rights are expressed to be subject to the "limitations and conditions defined by the Treaties and by the measures adopted to give them effect".

In addition, Art 18 TFEU (formerly Art 12 EC Treaty) provides that it is unlawful to discriminate on the basis of nationality within the scope of application of the Treaty.

The question of whether an EU national who does not meet the conditions set out in Directive 2004/38 for a right of residence should nonetheless, at least in some cases, be regarded as possessing such a right directly under Art 21 has proved a difficult one. Related to this question, is that of whether denial of benefits to someone who does not have a right of residence (even directly under Art 21) is consistent with the anti-discrimination provision in Art 18 TFEU.

Baumbast has had more attention of late for being the first in the line of cases which has culminated in *Teixeira* and *Ibrahim*. However, the ECJ in that case also considered the residence rights of Mr Baumbast. Mr Baumbast, a German national, had been a worker in the UK for several years but was, at the relevant time, employed by a German company to work in China. He thus had sufficient resources to avoid being a burden on the social assistance system of the UK. However, he did not meet the condition for a right of residence as a self-sufficient person in the then applicable Directive because his comprehensive medical insurance did not cover emergency treatment in the UK (in other words he did not satisfy the "limitations and conditions" in the measures adopted under the then Art 18 (now Art 21). Nonetheless, the ECJ held that:

"90.   In any event, the limitations and conditions which are referred to in Article 18 EC and laid down by Directive 90/364 are based on the idea that the exercise of the right of residence of citizens of the Union can be subordinated to the legitimate interests of the Member States. In that regard, according to the fourth recital in the preamble to Directive 90/364 beneficiaries of the right of residence must not become an 'unreasonable' burden on the public finances of the host Member State.

91.   However, those limitations and conditions must be applied in compliance with the limits imposed by Community law and in accordance with the general principles of that law, in particular the principle of proportionality. That means that national measures adopted on that subject must be necessary and appropriate to attain the objective pursued (see, to that effect, Joined Cases C-259/91, C-331/91 and C-332/91 *Allué and Others* [1993] ECR I-4309, para 15).

92.   In respect of the application of the principle of proportionality to the facts of the Baumbast case, it must be recalled, first, that it has not been denied that Mr Baumbast has sufficient resources within the meaning of Directive 90/364; second, that he worked and therefore lawfully resided in the host Member State for several years, initially as an employed person and subsequently as a self-employed person; third, that during that period his family also resided in the host Member State and remained there even after his activities as an employed and self-employed person in that State came to an end; fourth, that neither Mr Baumbast nor the members of his family have become burdens on the public finances of the host Member State and, fifth, that both Mr Baumbast and his family have comprehensive sickness insurance in another Member State of the Union.

93.   Under those circumstances, to refuse to allow Mr Baumbast to exercise the right of residence which is conferred on him by Article 18(1) EC by virtue of the application of the provisions of Directive 90/364 on the ground that his sickness insurance does not cover the emergency treatment given in the host Member State would amount to a disproportionate interference with the exercise of that right."

Mr Baumbast thus received his residence permit. The *Baumbast* judgment is therefore authority for the principle that a right of residence can arise directly under Art 21 where it is not proportionate to insist on satisfaction of the precise terms of Directive 2004/38. The UK courts, in the cases discussed below, have generally determined that the situations in which it would not be proportionate to deny a residence right to a person, due to a need to pursue the legitimate aim of protecting the public finances of the UK from an "unreasonable" burden, are extremely rare.

In Case C-456/02 *Michel Trojani v Centre public d'aide sociale de Bruxelles* [2004] ECR I-07573, the ECJ gives an example of where it is proportionate to insist on fulfilment of the conditions in the Directives. Mr Trojani was a French national living in a Salvation Army hostel in Belgium. He was not a worker. He claimed and was refused the minimex. The Court (at para 36) held clearly that, in those circumstances, it was not disproportionate to hold that he did not have a right of residence under then Art 18 (now Art 21). However, Mr Trojani had been given a residence permit by the local municipal authority. The Court went on to hold that an EU national who "has been lawfully resident in the host Member State for a certain time or possesses a residence permit" could rely on the anti-discrimination rule in Art 12 (now Art 18). As benefits were within the scope of the Treaty (see para 42), then it was unlawful discrimination to deny him the minimex.

The two main domestic cases which grapple with the principles in *Baumbast* and *Trojani* discussed above are *Abdirahman and another v SSWP and another* [2007] EWCA Civ 657 (reported as *R(IS) 8/07*) and *Kaczmarek v SSWP* [2008] EWCA Civ 1310, (reported as *R(IS) 5/09*). In *Abdirahman*, the Court of Appeal rejected appeals by two claimants whose appeals had been dismissed by a tribunal of commissioners in *CIS 3573/2005*, *CH 2484/2005* and *CPC 2920/2005*. The claimants were born in Somalia and were nationals of Sweden and Norway respectively and had entered the UK lawfully as EEA nationals. Neither claimant was at the relevant time a worker or economically self-sufficient. One claimed IS, HB and CTB, the other claimed PC. All claims were refused on the basis that the claimants did not have a right to reside in the UK.

The Court of Appeal held, firstly, that being lawfully present in the UK (as the claimants were) was not to be equated with a "right to reside", as UK law made a distinction between a right to reside and any lesser status (including, and here particularly, an EEA national who was in this country having entered lawfully and had committed no breach of immigration law, but who was not a "qualified person" under I(EEA) Regs 2000). The claimants in this case, although lawfully present, did not have a right to reside, under UK law, at the time relevant to the appeals, because they were not qualified persons. Having considered Art 18 (now Art 21) of the Treaty, Directive 90/364/EEC and ECJ caselaw thereunder (especially *Trojani* – the Court of Appeal noting with approval the view of the Advocate General in that case that "the basic principle of Community law is that persons who depend on social assistance will be taken care of in their own Member State"), the Court of Appeal concluded that Art 18 (now Art 21) does not create a right of residence for an EU citizen in another member state, in a case in which the limitations imposed under Directive 90/364 (note these are now the same limitations as those requiring self-sufficiency for those who are not workers or self-employed found in Directive 2004/38) are not satisfied, and where those limitations are proportionate to the legitimate objective in protecting the public finances of the host member state.

This then left the claimants' second argument, based on Art 12 of the EC Treaty (now Art 18 TFEU) and that article's prohibition on discrimination. The tribunal of commissioners below had found that the claimants' cases fell within Art 12 and thus called for the discrimination in not awarding them benefit on the grounds of nationality to be justified, but had found such justification. However, in the Court of Appeal's view, the appeals did not even get that far as the claims did not come "[w]ithin the scope of application of this Treaty", which are the opening words of Art 12. Surprisingly, they held (at para 43) that the benefits themselves were not within the scope of the Treaty (although this was said to be a "misreport" in *Kaczmarek* – see below). Nonetheless, they held that if they were wrong on this, then the discrimination was justified as a proportionate way to achieve the legitimate aim articulated by the SSWP to protect the UK finances from EU nationals coming to the UK in order to live off the benefit system.

In *Kaczmarek*, the Court of Appeal considered the case of a claimant who had lived in the UK since 2002, initially as a student and then as a worker for the period June 2003 to February 2005. She applied for IS in May 2005. It was argued for the claimant that she had been lawfully resident in the UK for a three-year period at the date of her claim, mostly as a worker, and had therefore demonstrated the sort of social integration that the ECJ had in mind in *Trojani* when it held that a person who had been "lawfully resident in the host Member State for a certain time" could rely upon the anti-discrimination measure in Art 12 (now Art 18). The Court of Appeal dismissed the appeal and held that the reference in *Trojani* to residence "for a certain time" did not "open the door to eligibility based on residence of unspecified but significant duration and of a type which evidences a degree of social integration in the host Member State" (para 16). The Court held that the reference to residence "for a certain time" was a reference to a specific qualifying period which gives rise to an express right of residence – "it would be wholly undesirable if Article 12 were to give rise to an open-textured temporal qualification of the kind suggested on behalf of the appellant. Eligibility is primarily and more appropriately a matter for normative regulation rather than discretion or subjective evaluation on a case by case basis". With respect to the Court, given that at the time that the ECJ decided in *Trojani* that there was no general rule about specific qualifying periods in EU law which gave rise to an express right of residence (Art 16 of Directive 2004/38 being a development which postdated that decision), it is difficult to see how this can be said to be what the ECJ actually had in mind.

The Court in *Kaczmarek* then revisited the issue of the proportionality of the denial of a right of residence to this claimant. The Court referred to those passages from *Baumbast* set out above. However, it agreed with the commissioner below who had held that the approach to the proportionality in such cases should be informed by the concept of whether there was a "lacuna" in the Directive. It is necessary to explain this in some detail.

–   At para 120 of the Advocate General's opinion in *Baumbast* it was observed that the rules on freedom of movement "had not kept up with the pace of developments". In particular, the Advocate General noted that when the legislation at issue in that case had been created (1968), no account was taken of a case where a person might live in one member state while working outside that state for a firm established in a different state.

–   In such a case there was an unintended lacuna (hole) in the rules which it would be proportionate to fill.

–   The Court of Appeal was of the view that the ECJ had been informed by that analysis.

– Residence rules were brought up to date by Directive 2004/38 (which was not in force at the time of the decision under consideration in *Kaczmarek*).

– That Directive now provides an "authoritative insight into the parameters of proportionality when applied to the economically inactive migrant".

– Where it appears, therefore, that the Directive has deliberately excluded a class of persons from the rights of residence it provides, it will not be proportionate to set those limitations aside on the grounds of proportionality. Or, in the words of the Court, "it would be inappropriate and presumptuous for us to characterize something as a lacuna when it was not identified by the Council when it most recently moved to enlarge eligibility".

An example of a case where there was a lacuna which ought to be filled is provided in *R(IS)4/09*: decided by the same commissioner whose lacuna-filling approach was subsequently endorsed by the Court of Appeal in *Kaczmarek*. There the claimant was a French national who had given up work to care for her husband, a national of Cameroon who had been working but had had to stop due to illness. The French national did not retain her status as a worker, and because her husband was a non-EEA national, he had no independent right of residence as a worker who was temporarily incapable of work on which she could rely as his family member. In these circumstances, the commissioner was satisfied that the claimant had a right of residence pursuant to Art 18 (now Art 21) notwithstanding the fact that she was not self-sufficient etc. For the commissioner, the questions to be asked in such cases are as follows:

"whether there is a lacuna in that directive, whether recognising a right of residence under Article 18(1) of the Treaty would be inconsistent with the directive and whether the principle of proportionality requires a right of residence to be recognised..."

He went on to set out the factors taken into account:

"54. In my judgment, having regard to all these considerations, the claimant's wife's right of free movement for the purpose of working, guaranteed to her by Article 39 of the Treaty, would be infringed if she and the claimant were not recognised as having the right to reside in the United Kingdom in the circumstances of this case. There was a lacuna in the directives in force at the time of the claimant's claim for income support and there is now a lacuna in Directive 2004/38/EC but I am satisfied that the claimant and his wife retained rights of residence by virtue of Article 18(1) of the Treaty. Where a worker exercising rights under Article 39 of the Treaty in the United Kingdom is obliged to cease work and cannot be available for alternative work due to a need to care for his or her spouse who is a not a citizen of the Union but who is temporarily seriously disabled, they both retain rights of residence in the United Kingdom in the circumstances that arise in this case. Among those circumstances are the facts that:

(a) the disabled person had been exercising his Community law right to work in the United Kingdom and had become temporarily incapable of work;

(b) the disability had first manifested itself some considerable time after the disabled person had arrived in the United Kingdom, after he had married and after he had started work;

(c) the disabled person had qualified for free National Health Service treatment by virtue of his period of residence in the United Kingdom, which was at least in part by virtue of his right of residence under Community law, and was continuing to undergo such treatment while being cared for by his wife;

(d) the recognition of the claimant's right of residence under Community law when he married had led to him losing the opportunity of establishing a right of residence in his own right as a refugee.

Whether any of those circumstances is determinative can be decided when the need arises. (If point (a) is not determinative, it may follow that a person retains a right of residence while temporarily unable to be available for work due to the need to care for a dependant child, although, I would suggest, only where the child's need for care is temporary and is wholly due to the seriousness of the disability rather than the child's age.)"

In *SSWP v CA* [2009] UKUT 169 (AAC), the judge holds that this type of "lacuna-filling" approach is the only correct approach to the question of proportionality in right to reside cases. However, the judge in *SSWP v AH (IS)* [2010] UKUT 265 (AAC) takes a different view. The judge in that case comments that, although the lacuna-filling approach is one way in which proportionality operates (although he would not have read the *Baumbast* judgment in that way), the other approach is that proportionality overrides conditions that normally apply:

"Freedom of movement for EU citizens is a fundamental right. Any exceptions or conditions must be narrowly interpreted and applied. They must not be given an effect out of proportion with the policy objective that they seek to fulfil."

However, on either approach to the facts of the case before him, the judge concluded that it would not be proportionate to deny an Art 18 (now Art 21) right of residence. The claimant in that case had come to the UK in 2000, aged 11, and was significantly disabled. His parents had received IS throughout their residence here (and so had been transitionally protected from the right to reside test). The appeal concerned entitlement to IS on a claim made in 2008. The judge held that in respect of proportionality then:

"The claimant has been in the United Kingdom for a long time and has integrated into life here. But neither he nor his family have ever had a right to reside. Even if Directive 2004/38 had been in force on their arrival, they would only have had an initial right for three months. They have received considerable public financial support. The family as a whole, and the claimant individually, will continue to need public support indefinitely.

Insisting on compliance with the conditions in Directive 2004/38 is not disproportionate in that context. The purpose of the conditions is to protect the public finances, and especially the social security system, of host States. This is a clear example of a case in which that objective should be respected."

Turning to the "lacuna-filling" approach, the judge held:

"Moreover, given how recently Directive 2004/38 was made, it is reasonable and appropriate to assume that the European legislators considered that in current conditions the scope of rights to reside beyond an initial three months should remain ultimately founded in economic or related activity."

That decision appears consistent with that of the Court of Appeal in *Lekpo-Bozua v LB Hackney and Secretary of State for Communities and Local Government* [2010] EWCA Civ 909. The case concerned whether Ms Lekpo-Bozua was owed what is known as the "full duty" as a homeless person in priority need by LB Hackney. Ms Lekpo-Bozua was British but the reason she argued she came within the "priority need" category was that she was looking after her niece, a French national aged 16 at the relevant time. The niece had lived with her for about nine years. The homelessness provisions provided that the full duty was not owed where the priority need situation would not have arisen if someone who did not have a right to reside was not included in the application. So the question was whether Ms Lekpo-Bozua's niece had a right of residence. The Court declared that she did not.

In both of the above cases, it is difficult to see how the decisions are proportionate in the sense that they go further than would seem necessary to comply with the legitimate policy objective which the insertion of a right to reside requirement as a condition for HB (or homelessness rights) was designed to achieve (eg, preventing people coming to the UK to live off the benefit system: see *Abdirahman*) – no one could argue that the EU nationals in these cases who had come to the UK as children had made such a decision. It is arguable that when the Directive was drafted, it was not foreseen that the UK would at that time have allowed nationals of other EU states to reside in the UK (and been happy to pay them benefits) for considerable periods of time despite those persons not having a right of residence under EU law. Furthermore, the Advocate General in *Teixeira* seemed to have been of the view (at paras 119 and 120) that a person who resided in the UK and was "entitled under national law" to do so could, after five years of such entitlement, acquire a permanent right of residence pursuant to Art 16 of Directive 2004/38. Finally, it appears from *Lassal* that the purpose of the permanent right of residence is to promote social cohesion and to strengthen the feeling of Union citizenship (para 32 and 36). It is difficult to see how that integrationist approach is consistent with the denial of a right of residence to those who have lived here (albeit not in exercise of an EU right of residence but without their residence being objected to by the UK state) for a considerable period of time as children.

The exact parameters of who may have a right of residence directly under Art 21 TFEU, or failing that, who may rely on Art 18 TFEU, therefore, remain to be worked out in further cases. At present it is suggested that the case of *R(IS) 4/09* provides one benchmark as to when an Art 21 TFEU right may arise. In other cases, it is apparent that, if there would need to be reliance on benefits for a considerable period of time were an Art 21 right recognised, that will present a significant barrier, at least before UK courts.

Finally, it is also worth noting that since the coming into force of the TFEU, the Charter of Fundamental Rights of the European Union now has the same legal value as the EU Treaties (see Art 6 TFEU). It is likely that the provisions of Title IV of the Charter, entitled "Solidarity", will increasingly be relied upon in cases where no clear right of residence exists and a claim for HB/CTB is made. In particular, a question to be asked is whether Article 34 of the Charter which states that the EU "recognises and respects the right to social and housing assistance so as to ensure a decent existence for all who lack sufficient resources" actually adds anything to existing law. It may be that the incorporation of the Charter shifts the tenor of judgments on these issues further towards the importance of recognising the solidarity that EU states have to display towards nationals of other EU states within their boundaries.

Note that although the UK has, with Poland, attempted to opt out of that rule under Protocol 30 to TFEU, this provision does not change the enforceability of the Charter before UK Courts: in *R (Saeedi) v Secretary of State for the Home Department* [2010] EWHC 705 (Admin), Cranston J had held that the Charter could not be "directly relied on as against the United Kingdom" by virtue of the Protocol (para 155). However, on appeal to the Court of Appeal, the Master of the Rolls recorded that the Home Secretary no longer supported that finding. She conceded that "the fundamental rights set out in the Charter can be relied on as against the United Kingdom and ... that [Cranston J] erred in holding otherwise". The Master of the Rolls referred to the concern expressed by the Equality and Human Rights Commission, which had intervened in the Court of Appeal proceedings specifically to address this aspect of Cranston J's judgment, that the Home Secretary's concession should be made known so that Cranston J's judgment was not followed by other courts which were unaware of the concession. A question was referred to the ECJ, so the final judgment of the Court of Appeal is still pending. However, the concession made can be relied upon now.

In *Patmalniece v SSWP* [2009] EWCA Civ 621, the Court of Appeal held that the justification accepted for any discrimination that did exist in *Abdirahman* was also sufficient to justify the discrimination that did arise for the purposes of Art 3 EC Regulation 1408/71. That article is the anti-discrimination provision within EC Regulation 1408/71 and can be relied upon by all those within the personal scope of the regulation as defined in Art 2. The Court of Appeal held (at para 24) that, although the right to reside test was indirectly discriminatory against non-UK EU nationals, that discrimination was not overt (ie, direct) because some EU nationals would pass the test.

The Court went on to hold that as PC (the benefit at issue in that case) was a special non-contributory benefit, then the justification advanced in *Abdirahman* sufficed here in as much as PC still had characteristics of social assistance. Where that leaves those benefits to which the right to reside test applies that are not special-contributory benefits or social assistance for the purposes of the Regulation (eg, child benefit) is not a subject for this volume as it is accepted that HB and CTB are not covered by EC Regulation 1408/71. *Patmalniece*has been appealed to the Supreme Court and is to be heard on 29 November 2010.

[2.6.3] Rights of carer's of the children in education of former workers

On 23 February 2010, in Case C-480/08 *Teixeira v LB Lambeth* [2010] ECR and Case C-310/08 *LB Harrow v Ibrahim* [2010] ECR, the ECJ confirmed its decision in Case C-413/99 *Baumbast & R v SSHD* [2002] ECR I-07091 and held that the children of EU workers or former workers and their primary carers have a right of residence by virtue of Article 12 of EEC Regulation 1612/68 and are thereby entitled to access social assistance in the UK. Article 12 provides that the children of a national of a member state who is, or has been, employed in the territory of another member state shall be admitted to that state's education system under the same conditions as the nationals of that State.

The principal issue in both cases was the same: namely, whether the appellants had a right of residence deriving directly from Article 12 of Regulation 1612/68, it being accepted by all parties that they could not derive such a right from EC Directive 2004/38.

The ECJ dismisses the UK's arguments (that such a right was dependent on self-sufficiency or that the Directive had limited the scope of *Baumbast*) in both judgments, holding that a national of a member state who was employed in the UK can claim a right of residence as the primary carer of a child in education solely on the basis of Article 12 of Regulation 1612/68, without being required to satisfy the conditions laid down in Directive 2004/38. Paragraphs 53 and 54 of *Teixeira* state that Article 12 must be applied independently of other rights of residence in EU law and para 58 notes that this interpretation is confirmed by the *travaux preparatoires* to Directive 2004/38, which show that the Directive was designed to be consistent with the judgment in *Baumbast*.

With regard to the requirement of self-sufficiency, the ECJ again refers to its judgment in *Baumbast* and notes that the right of residence accorded to the children and their mother in that case was not based on their self-sufficiency but on the purpose of Regulation 1612/68 to promote and facilitate freedom of movement for workers which necessitated the best possible conditions for the integration of the worker's family in the host state. The ECJ therefore holds that the right of residence deriving from Article 12 "is not conditional on that parent having sufficient resources not to become a burden on the social assistance system of that Member State during the period of residence and having comprehensive sickness cover there."

The Court also clarified in *Teixeira* that there was no requirement that the child first entered education when the EU citizen was a worker in order to have a right to reside under Art 12 of Regulation 1612/68. There was nothing in the wording of the Article that required that, and it was "enough that the child who is in education in the host Member State became installed there when one of his or her parents was exercising rights of residence there as a migrant worker" (para 74). In terms of the duration of the Art 12 right of residence, the Court notes that in terms of access to, and the completion of, education, the right extends to higher education. Consequently, the date a child completes her/his education may be after reaching the age of majority and also after ceasing to be dependent on a parent. In terms of the primary carer, the Court held (at para 86) that her right to reside may extend beyond the age of majority of the child "if the child continues to need the presence and the care of that parent in order to be able to pursue and complete his or her education."

Finally, it should be noted that there is no requirement that the primary carer is or was a worker, or continues to reside with the parent who was the worker (see *Ibrahim*). This means that a woman (of whatever nationality) who has separated from her partner who is an EEA national who has worked in the UK can establish a right to reside on the basis of being a lone parent of their child in education.

The judgments mean that claimants covered by the *Baumbast* principle are entitled to HB (providing they are also habitually resident in the ordinary sense), including new claimants, and those whose appeals are yet to be determined or have been stayed pending the ECJ judgments. In practical terms, the claimant will need to establish the following:

(1)   a parent has worked in the UK and attained the status of worker for the purposes of EU law; *and*

(2)   a child of that worker has resided in the UK at the same time as the worker; *and*

(3)   the child has entered and remains in the UK education system; *and*

(4)   the claimant is the child's primary carer.

Note that in *CIS 3960/2007*, it was held that enrolling in nursery education does not count as a child having entered education for the purposes of Art 12 of EC Reg 1612/68.

In *SSWP v JS (IS)* [2010] UKUT 347 (AAC), the Upper Tribunal held that the child in education of an A8 worker who has done some authorised work, but less than the 12 months (and is therefore still an A8 worker requiring registration or would be if s/he got a job), still has a right of residence under Art 12 of Regulation 1612/68, and therefore that the primary carer of that child also enjoys a right of residence.

Another issue, is whether the family member of the primary carer with a right of residence following the *Teixeira* and *Ibrahim* cases can have a right of residence. The judge in *RM v SSWP (IS)* [2010] UKUT 238 (AAC) suggests, *obiter*, at para 9 that they do. However, in the same paragraph the judge decides (without any reasoning) that an A8 worker who has done some work (the first month of which must be regarded as for an authorised employer) and is then the primary carer of children in education does not have a right of residence – ie, decides differently to the Upper Tribunal in the case of *JS* referred to above. The claimant, RM, has sought permission to appeal to the Court of Appeal on this and other grounds. The point about whether family members of the primary carer with a *Teixeira* right of residence themselves have a right to reside also arises in another case awaiting determination by the Upper Tribunal – file *CPC 1935/2010*).

A decision of the Upper Tribunal is awaited on the issue of whether the child in education (and therefore that child's primary carer) of someone who is or has been self-employed enjoys a similar right of residence to the child of someone who is or has been a worker (file reference – *CIS 2357/2009*).

[2.6.4] Rights of carer's of children who themselves have a right of residence
A further issue that may arise following *Teixeira* and *Ibrahim* (see above) concerns the situations of primary carers of children where the child has a right of residence as the family member of someone who has either an Art 7 extended right of residence or an Art 16 or Art 17 permanent right of residence but where **either** that child is not in education **and/or** the non-primary carer parent's right of residence is not as a worker or someone retaining that status.

In *Teixeira* and *Ibrahim,* the children had no right of residence as the family member of a worker, as their parents were not at the relevant time in work or retaining that status. However, as they were the children of people who had been workers and as they were in education, then they had a right of residence directly under Art 12 of EC Regulation 1612/68.

However, in many cases of separated unmarried partners, it may be that while the partner looking after the children has no right of residence in her/his own right, the other partner will have a right of residence as a worker or self-employed person. That is sufficient to give the child a right of residence as a family member (see the case of *Diatta*). However, it will not provide a right of residence to the ex-partner of that worker (as they are not married, they do not count as family members of each other under Art 2 of the Directive).

In such situations, the case of Case C-200/02 *Zhu and Chen* [2004] ECR I-09925 suggests that the primary carer of the child will still have a right of residence. While in the cases of *Baumbast*, *Teixeira* and *Ibrahim*, the ECJ had to locate the right of residence for the child in the fact that they were the children of those who had been workers and were in education, in *Chen*, the ECJ had found the child had a right of residence as a self-sufficient person. However, in all four cases the ECJ went on to find that the fact that the child had a right of residence meant that her/his primary carer too had to have such a right (to facilitate that of the child). It can, therefore, be argued that whenever a child has a right of residence (whether that arises because s/he is a child in education of a former worker or on some other basis, such as because s/he is the family member of a person who is in fact a worker albeit not living with that worker or s/he is the child of a self-employed person etc) then the primary carer of that child must have a right of residence.

[2.7] Residence documentation
In *CIS 185/2008,* the commissioner held that a valid residence permit, issued under the provisions in force before Directive 2004/38 must be accepted as proof that the bearer had a right of residence, despite the fact that the claimant was no longer pursuing the economic activity which had entitled her to the issue of the permit in the first place. The same commissioner, now a judge, in *EM and KN v SSWP* has held that the introduction of the Directive whose scheme for residence documentation for EU nationals is one which member states have a discretion to adopt, together with the fact that the I(EEA) Regs 2006 describe (reg 2) a residence certificate as being a document issued to someone "as proof of [...] right of residence [...] at the date of issue", and provide for residence permits issued under the old rules to become certificates issued under the new, means that from 30 April 2006, residence certificates can no longer be relied upon to serve this function. Note that in the latter case, it seems from the judge's reasoning that he would have held that a residence card issued to non-EEA nationals under the Directive does still serve as proof of a right of residence. In *Dias v SSWP* [2009] EWCA Civ 807, which is the Secretary of State's appeal from *CIS 185/2008*, the Court of Appeal has doubted that a residence permit did perform the function declared by the commissioner but has referred that as a question to the ECJ. Ms Dias' case also raised the same issue as that in *Lassal* – ie, whether a period of five years' residence in accordance with EU law prior to the coming into force of Directive 2004/38 provided a permanent right of residence under Art 16 of that instrument when it became law. It is unclear therefore whether the ECJ will determine the other issues in her case given that, following *Lassal,* she clearly has a permanent right of residence.

[3] Paragraph (2): "habitually resident in fact"
To repeat, for emphasis, the points made in the General Note above, habitual residence in fact will only arise as an issue for those people who have a right to reside and who do not fall within para (3B).

The phrase "habitual residence" has been frequently used in international conventions, many of which have been incorporated into English law by statute. As "habitual residence" does not have a special meaning for HB/CTB purposes (see below), caselaw on the meaning of the phrase in other contexts may be examined to determine the meaning in this context. In particular, there is a large amount of caselaw on the phrase as used in the Hague Convention on the Civil Aspects of Child Abduction 1980 Art 3 and the Child Abduction and Custody Act 1985. In addition, an identical test was introduced for IS claimants along with the amendments adding the HB/CTB test. There are now many decisions in relation to IS which must be regarded as highly persuasive authority.

[3.1] Basic principles

The basic principles established by this large body of caselaw are now enumerated below. For a helpful review of the law on habitual residence see *CIS 4474/2003*. The quotations constituting the first two principles are taken from the speech of Lord Brandon in In *Re J (a minor) (Abduction: Custody Rights)* [1990] 2 AC 562.

(1)   "... the expression "habitually resident", as used in Art 3 of the Convention, is nowhere defined. It follows, I think, that the expression is not to be treated as a term of art with special meaning, but is rather to be understood according to the ordinary and natural meaning of the two words which it contains." This statement was approved and followed in *R(IS) 6/96* (paras 17, 20) and *CIS 2326/1995* (para 17).

(2)   "... the question whether a person is or is not habitually resident in a specified country is a question of fact to be decided by reference to all the circumstances of any particular case". So it has been held that it is not possible to draw up a comprehensive list of factors to be considered: *R(IS) 6/96* (paras 17, 20); *CIS 13498/1996* (para 9). All the facts of the case must be considered.

(3)   It is possible for a claimant to be habitually resident in more than one state at once: *CIS 2326/1995* (para 27).

(4)   In deciding whether a claimant is habitually resident, authorities and tribunals must examine the whole period down to the date that the decision is made, because the time period between the claim and the decision being made may be sufficient to allow the "appreciable period of time" to have accrued: *CIS 2326/1995* (para 29); *CIS 11481/1995* (paras 10-12).

(5)   It is for the authority to justify a decision that the claimant is not habitually resident. It follows that if no evidence is available to support such a decision, the authority must accept the claimant as habitually resident: *R(IS) 6/96* (para 15).

(6)   A person cannot be habitually resident unless s/he is resident. If s/he is not resident, there is no need to consider the quality of the claimant's existence here. A future intention to reside here is insufficient: *CIS 15927/1996* (paras 6, 9). Residence may be in the CTA (see p268). The residence must be lawful: *R v Brent LBC ex p Shah* [1983] 2 AC 309 at 343H-344B, HL. Residence is not the same as physical presence. One may be resident without being present: see the discussion of loss of habitual residence below. It is possible for a claimant to be resident in more than one country: *CIS 16410/1996* (para 10). Likewise, one may be present without being resident. In *R(IS) 6/96* (para 19) the following was said:

"Residence to my mind involves a more settled state than mere physical presence in a country, so that a person who is a short stay visitor, or has come here for an operation or to receive medical treatment other than long-term care, is neither resident nor habitually resident. To count as resident, a person must be seen to be making a home here; even though it need not be his or her home, nor need it be intended to be a permanent one, provided that it is genuinely home for the time being."

In many cases, the claimant will not previously have spent any substantial period of time in the CTA. The sole question will then be whether the claimant has acquired habitual residence status. However, there will also be cases in which the claimant was present in the CTA for a substantial period or periods of time before going away to another country. In such cases, the claimant may have been habitually resident in the CTA before s/he left and before considering the present period of residence, it will be necessary to decide whether the status of habitual residence was ever lost: *R(IS) 6/96* (paras 31-2); *CIS 8111/1995* (para 11). If it was not lost, it will not be necessary for the claimant to show that s/he has acquired the status during the present period of residence. It is therefore necessary to consider both [3.2] how the status is acquired and [3.3] how it is lost.

[3.2] Acquisition of habitual residence

The starting point is the third point made by Lord Brandon in *Re J (a minor) (Abduction: Custody Rights)* [1990] 2 AC 562 at 578G-H:

"... there is a significant difference between a person ceasing to be habitually resident in country A, and his subsequently becoming resident in country B instead. A person may cease to be habitually resident in country A in a single day if he or she leaves it with a settled intention not to return to it but to take up long-term residence in country B instead. Such a person cannot, however, become habitually resident in country B in a single day. An appreciable period of time and a settled intention will be necessary to enable him or her to become so. During that appreciable period of time the person will have ceased to be habitually resident in country A but not yet have become resident in country B."

In essence, therefore, two basic requirements need to be fulfilled: [3.2.1] an appreciable period of time must elapse and the claimant must have [3.2.2] a settled intention to reside in the UK.

[3.2.1] "An appreciable period of time"

The need for an "appreciable period of time" to elapse before a person can become habitually resident has been a reasonably constant feature of the caselaw: see *R(IS) 6/96* (para 21) and *CIS 2326/1995* (paras 20-1), despite strenuous argument in the latter case that Lord Brandon's statement was *obiter* and of no assistance in the benefits context. This was confirmed by the majority in *Nessa v Chief Adjudication Officer* [1998] 2 All ER 728, which was an appeal from the latter decision, despite a powerful dissent from Thorpe LJ. *The House of Lords* [1999] 1 WLR 1937, [1999] 4 All ER 677 subsequently upheld the commissioner's decision unanimously. However, it is arguably noteworthy that Lord Slynn, in giving the only substantial judgment of the House of Lords in *Nessa* did not use the word "appreciable". Instead, he stated that it was "plain as a matter of ordinary language [that] a person is not habitually resident in any country unless he has taken up residence and lived there for a period". Although there would be some types of legislation which could not work if there could be a gap between leaving country A and establishing habitual residence in country B, the IS legislation (and hence the HB/CTB legislation) did not fall into that category. He then went on to give some general guidance:

"I do not consider that, when he spoke of residence for an appreciable period, Lord Brandon meant more than this. It is a question of fact to be determined on the date where the determination has to be made on the circumstances of each case whether and when that habitual residence had been established. Bringing possessions, doing everything necessary to establish residence before coming, having a right of abode, seeking to bring family, 'durable ties' with the country of residence or intended residence, and many other factors have to be taken into account.

The requisite period is not a fixed period. It may be longer where there are doubts. It may be short . . . There may indeed be special cases where the person concerned is not coming here from the first time, but is resuming an habitual residence previously had . . . On such facts, the adjudication officer may or of course may not be satisfied that the previous habitual residence has been resumed. This position is quite different from that of someone coming to the United Kingdom for the first time." (see *The House of Lords* [1999] 1 WLR 1937, [1999] 4 All ER 677 at 682f-683d)

The decision in *Nessa* therefore settles a number of points. First, unless the claimant falls within the scope of Regulation 1408/71 and can take advantage of the ruling in *Swaddling v Chief Adjudication Officer* (Case C-90/97) [1999] 2 CMLR 679, ECJ (see below), or in some cases is a returning resident (see below), the claimant must demonstrate that s/he has resided in the CTA for some period of time.

Secondly, it confirmed that the period of time may vary and depends on the facts of the individual case.

In *R(IS) 6/96* (para 28), the commissioner gave examples of periods of time which would normally be necessary for residence to have been for an appreciable period. This approach has been rejected in *CIS 2326/1995* (para 24) and *CIS 8111/1995* (para 17) as likely to lead to the suggested periods being treated as rules of thumb. In *Cameron v Cameron* [1996] SLT 306 at 313F, CS(IH) it was said that there was no minimum period of residence that could be described as "habitual". This approach was followed in *CIS 2326/1995* (para 24). In paras 25-7, the commissioner pointed out that Lord Brandon's statement that habitual residence could not be acquired in a single day had to be seen in the child abduction context, where a child was removed and where intention or preparation for her/him taking up residence in the country where s/he was taken by the abductor has to be ignored. If there is a "sharp-edged" change of residence, where the claimant unequivocally abandons the former state of residence and commits to the CTA, the period may be quite short. In *CIS 4474/2003*, the commissioner confirms that what constitutes the required period will depend on the circumstances of the particular case. However, he added that in the general run of cases the period will lie between one and three months and that cogent reasons would need to be given by a tribunal supporting a decision that required a significantly longer period. This approach was subsequently doubted by the tribunal of commissioners in *CIS 2559/2005* (para 17), a view echoed in *CIS 1972/2003* as reducing the relevant period of residence to a fixed tariff. In *R(IS) 7/06* (an appeal against which was dismissed by the Court of Appeal) the commissioner had supported the comments in *CIS 4474/2003* to the effect that cases outside the one- to three-month range were exceptional. The same commissioner who decided *CIS 4474/2003* has replied, in *CJSA 1223/2006*, by stating that his decision should not be regarded as setting a tariff, but that he remained of the view that for most cases an appreciable period is likely to be between one and three months. It is suggested that the fact that in most cases such a period will be appropriate that is not the same as setting a tariff but merely recognises what is decided in most cases. Thus a case outside this range is a strange one and will require a cogent explanation.

Note that in *CIS 1304/1997*, the commissioner held that a person who had previously been habitually resident in the UK and had stopped being habitually resident during a period of absence (see [3.3] below) could nonetheless be habitually resident immediately on return to the UK – ie, without the need for the new period of residence to have been for an appreciable period of time. This might be the case if the claimant is returning to take up a way of life previously settled. This was said to depend on factors such as (1) the circumstances of loss of habitual residence, (2) any links maintained while the claimant was away, and (3) the circumstances of the return to the UK.

The "length, continuity and nature" of the residence will be relevant to whether it has been for a sufficient period: *R(IS) 6/96* (para 21). However, in *CIS 2326/1995* (para 26), the commissioner suggested that the period need not be continuous and preparatory acts in other states or preparatory visits to the CTA may be relevant if they are evidence of the claimant's settled intention (see below). It seems to follow from this that a strongly settled intention will tend to reduce the necessary period: *Re B (Minors) (Abduction)* [1993] 1 FLR 993 at 995C-D, FD (Waite J).

The provisions of the United Nations Convention on the Rights of the Child have no direct application here as it does not form part of domestic UK law. However, it can be taken into account in deciding what on the facts of a particular case may amount to a sufficient period: *CIS 1972/2003* para 17.

[3.2.2] A "settled intention"

The claimant must also have a "settled intention" to reside in the CTA. The intention need not be to reside permanently in the CTA: *Shah* at 344C-D, *Cameron* at 313G-I, *CIS 13498/1996* (para 12). Evidence of settled intention usually comes from the claimant's actions before entering the CTA and between that time and claiming benefit. However, the actions between the claim and a tribunal hearing may be relied on to show that the intention was always there: *CIS 2326/1995* para 28. In addition, the claimant's behaviour during a previous period of residence in the CTA may assist: *CIS 8111/1995* para 15.

Factors which may be relevant in assessing "settled intention" include:

(1)   The claimant's employment or prospects of employment. Her/his education and qualifications may be highly significant: *CIS 5136/1995* para 4. A higher proportion of time spent working and a stable job are good evidence. The work done by the claimant's partner may also be relevant and an imminent offer of work will also be good evidence.

(2)   The claimant's reasons for coming to the CTA. A clear reason for presence is more likely to demonstrate a settled intention. 1997 GM C13 Annex 3 para 18 gave retirement, studying, medical treatment, visiting relatives or domestic political unrest as examples.

(3)   The claimant's intentions as to where her/his future lies, which can be shown by an intention to move family and property here.

(4)   Where the claimant's "centre of interest" lies: *CIS 2326/1995* (para 22). This means the strength of ties to this country. Is her/his immediate family in this country? What about extended family? Has s/he joined clubs or associations? Where does s/he hold real or personal property? Has s/he registered with a doctor? Is s/he seeking work? Has money been spent in this country with a view to establishing residence?

(5)   The viability of continued residence in the CTA. Note that this is a relevant factor and not a separate requirement. *R(IS) 6/96* (paras 28-9) suggested it was an additional requirement for the claimant to be able to demonstrate that s/he can maintain her/himself during the appreciable period without reliance on state benefits. The supposed requirement of viability has been heavily criticised. As was pointed out in *CIS 5136/1995* (para 4), it produces an "absurd circularity". A claimant cannot attain an appreciable period and hence be entitled to benefit unless s/he has had a viable existence, but many claimants cannot have a viable existence unless they receive benefit. This supposed requirement could result in the sick or retired never being habitually resident. It is now reasonably clear that the viability of residence without benefits is not a separate requirement, but is merely another factor giving evidence of settled intention: *CIS 2326/1995* (para 28); *CIS 12703/1996* (para 10); *CIS 2326/1995* (para 20 – where it was said to be of "considerable relevance"): see below.

(6)   In *CIS 2326/1995* (para 17) and *R(CS) 5/96* (para 9), it was stated that while habitual residence has a common meaning in all the statutory contexts in which it occurs, different factors may have different weight in different contexts. In the case of HB, it is suggested that the agreement pursuant to which HB is claimed will be of particular significance. Thus lodgers who can leave at will are less likely to have a settled intention to remain than tenants with statutory protection. The length of any lease or licence may also be relevant.

[3.3] Loss of habitual residence

In *Re J*, Lord Brandon stated that habitual residence may be lost in a day, but this will only happen where there is clear, unequivocal evidence of complete abandonment of the state by the claimant: see the comments in *CIS 2326/1995* referred to above. A "temporary absence" from the CTA will not prevent a claimant remaining habitually resident in the CTA: *R(IS) 6/96* (para 21); *Shah* at 342D-E. This is so whether the absence is short or long, provided that the absence can be described as "temporary". Holidays are usually regarded as "temporary": *CIS 5136/1995* para 5 (three weeks); 1997 GM C13 Annex 3 para 29(i) (three months). *CIS 12703/1996* (para 7) suggests that an absence was not "temporary" where the return date was uncertain and habitual residence was lost, though this suggestion may be in conflict with *Chief Adjudication Officer v Ahmed* [1994] *The Times* 6 April, CA. A five-year absence lost the claimant her habitual residence status in *CIS 13498/1996* (para 16). On the other side of the dividing line was *CIS 14591/1996* in which the claimant and his wife were resident in the UK for 15 months before leaving in October 1994 to be with their daughter-in-law pending her entry clearance. That process took 13 months. The family then returned and the claimant's IS claim was refused. It was held that as the absence abroad had always been intended to be temporary, the claimant had not lost his habitual residence status. Similarly, in *KS v SSWP (PC)* [2010] UKUT 156 (AAC), Judge Levenson held that a person who had left the UK on a two-year Voluntary Service Overseas assignment had not lost their habitual residence during the temporary absence.

Entitlement of a refugee to Housing Benefit
[¹ 10A]

Modification

Reg 10A was inserted by Sch 4 para 2(1) of the HB&CTB(CP) Regs. It only applied to claims for HB by some refugees. Sch A1 was also inserted by Sch 4 para 2(2) of the HB&CTB(CP) Regs.

Amendment

1.   Lapsed by s12(2)(e) of the Asylum and Immigration (Treatment of Claimants, etc.) Act 2004 (for those recorded as refugees after 14.6.07).

General Note
Reg 10A and Sch A1 as inserted by Sch 4 HB&CTB(CP) Regs dealt with a refugee's retrospective entitlement to HB.

Section 12 Asylum and Immigration (Treatment of Claimants, etc.) Act 2004 came into force on 14 June 2007 by the Asylum and Immigration (Treatment of Claimants, etc.) Act 2004 (Commencement No.7 and Transitional Provisions) Order 2007 SI No.1602. However, the commencement does not apply to those recorded as refugees on or before 14 June 2007. For these purposes, a person is "recorded as a refugee" on the day the Secretary of State notifies her/him that s/he has been recognised as a refugee and granted asylum in the UK.

See pp1126-1127 of the 20th edition for the full text of reg 10A and Sch A1 and commentary on these.

Note that reg 10A and paras 3 and 7 of Sch A1 of both the HB regs and the HB(SPC) Regs, as inserted by para 2, were substituted by reg 6 Housing Benefit (Local Housing Allowance, Miscellaneous and Consequential) Amendment Regulations 2007 SI No.2870 as from 7 April 2008, save that for a person to whom reg 1(3) of those regulations applied, the amendments came into force on the day on or after 7 April 2008 when the first of the events specified in reg 1(4) applied to her/him, or on 6 April 2009 if none had before that date. Sch 4 para 3(4) was amended by reg 7(5) Social Secuity (Miscellaneous Amendments)(No.2) Regulations 2008 SI No.1042 as from 19 May 2008.

PART 3
Payments in respect of a dwelling

General Note on Part 3
This Part of the Regulations deals with the type of payments in respect of which HB may be paid (and the amount of these). The power to make such regulations is granted by s130(2) SSCBA 1992. It is important to note the transitional protection and modifications that exist in relation to these regulations.

The starting point in deciding whether a particular payment will attract HB is reg 11(1), which confirms that HB is to be paid in respect of all those payments set out in reg 12(1). Categories of payments which HB will not meet are set out in regs 11(2) and (3) and 12(2). Note also s130(2) SSCBA which confirms that there is no power to make regulations extending HB coverage to council tax payments (which, of course, are met by CTB), or payments under mortgages or heritable securities in Scotland (which can be met as housing costs under the IS, income-based JSA, income-related ESA or PC schemes).

The amount of HB payable depends on, among other factors, the claimant's "maximum housing benefit" defined in reg 70 as the weekly "eligible rent" minus any deductions for non-dependants under reg 74.

Regs 12B to 12D set out what is "eligible rent" for HB purposes. Which of these regulations is to be used to determine eligible rent depends on whether HB is payable as a rent rebate or a rent allowance, and whether any of the rent restriction schemes are applicable.

There are three potential schemes that can restrict eligible rent where HB is paid as a rent allowance.
(1)   The "local housing allowance" (LHA) scheme, for which see regs 12D and 13C to 13E HB Regs. Under this scheme, eligible rent is determined by reference to the "maximum rent (LHA)".
(2)   The "local reference rent" scheme, for which see regs 12C, 13, 13ZA, 13ZB and 14 HB Regs. Under this scheme, eligible rent is determined by reference to the "maximum rent".
(3)   The "pre-January 1996" scheme, for which see Sch 3 paras 4 and 5 HB&CTB(CP) Regs (see p1198). Under this scheme, the form of the HB rules prior to 2 January 1996 applies and the authority can restrict eligible rent to the amount it considers appropriate.
The "LHA" rules, introduced from 7 April 2008, add a new layer of complexity to an already complicated situation. An added difficulty for local authorities, claimants and advisers was that until 6 April 2009, there were two versions of some of the HB Regs and the HB(SPC) Regs. See the commentary to reg 1 of the HB(LHA&IS)A Regs 2007 on p1232 and to reg 14 HB Regs on p324.

Note that in cases of hardship, where extra financial assistance is needed to meet housing costs, authorities can pay discretionary housing payments under the Discretionary Financial Assistance Regulations 2001 (see p1176).

Which rent restriction rules apply
Rent restriction rules do not apply at all on claims where HB is paid in the form of a "rent rebate" – ie, where the claimant is the tenant of the local authority that pays her/him HB. Note, however, that there is a general discretion to decrease eligible rent under reg 12B(6). Where HB is paid in the form of a "rent allowance" (ie, to private and social landlord tenants) and a claim for HB is made on or after 7 April 2008 (or where there is a change of dwelling during an award of HB on or after that date), whether rent restriction rules apply, and if so which ones is, can be summarised as follows.
(1)   Rent restriction rules do not apply at all if the claimant has an "excluded tenancy": regs 13C(5)(a) and (c) and 14(2)(b) and Sch 2 paras 3 to 12 HB Regs. These include, for example, regulated and protected tenanacies (ie, tenancies entered into before 15 January 1989 or, in Scotland, 2 January 1989) and many lettings by registered housing associations (see reg 2(1) for the definition). There is a general discretion to decrease eligible rent under reg 12B(6).

(2)   The "pre-January 1996" rules apply if the claimant lives in "exempt accommodation": reg 13C(5)(b) HB Regs and Sch 3 para 4(1)(b) HB&CTB(CP) Regs. Note that these rules also provide transitional protection for certain other claimants who have been entitled to HB since 1 January 1996 and who have not moved home, and certain claimants who inherit this protection: Sch 3 para 4(1)(a) and (2) to (7) HB&CTB(CP) Regs.

(3)   The "local reference rent" rules apply if the claimant lives in a hostel, houseboat, mobile home or caravan or her/his rent includes board and attendance. In some cases, the rules can also apply if the landlord is a registered housing association (see reg 2(1) for the definition) or the tenancy is a former local authority or new town letting which has been transferred to a new owner: regs 13(1), 13C(5)(a) to (e) and (6) and 14 and Sch 2 HB Regs.

(4)   In all other cases, the "LHA" rules apply: reg 13C HB Regs.

The "LHA" rules were piloted in 18 Pathfinder areas from late 2003. The "LHA" rules as now in force apply to those living in a former Pathfinder area to whom the pilot rules applied before 7 April 2008. The pilot rules were more generous in some respects. Some transitional protection is provided: regs 12E to 12K as inserted by Sch 10 para 6 HB Regs.

Other than where the pilot rules applied, the Government's intention is that if a claimant's eligible rent was being restricted under any of the rules that applied before 7 April 2008, it will continue to be restricted under the same rules, until there is a break in the claim or the claimant moves to a new home while entitled to HB. From that point, eligible rent will be restricted (if relevant) under whichever rules then apply. It is important for a claimant to assess any financial impact before a new claim, or a change of dwelling occurs.

It is understood that although the majority of claimants will be no better or worse off under the "LHA" scheme than under the "local reference rent" scheme, there will be some gainers. In these circumstances, a claimant may be able to surrender her/his HB claim and make a fresh claim which would then be assessed by reference to the "LHA" rules. DWP Guidance (HB/CTB G10/2008) reminds authorities that although there is no statutory mechanism expressly permitting a claim to be withdrawn once a decision has been made on it, a claimant should not be prevented from surrendering an award of benefit if s/he indicates that s/he no longer wishes to claim HB. However, the following should be borne in mind.

(1)   The claimant needs to be sure s/he *will* be better off if HB is assessed under the "LHA" scheme. The HB Regs apply in full whichever rent restriction scheme applies – eg, the usual income and capital rules apply and HB is calculated in the usual way.

(2)   As a new claim for HB would not appear to be possible while the claimant already has an award of HB, s/he would lose entitlement to HB for at least one week. This is because entitlement to HB would only end on the Monday following the change of circumstances (the surrender of the award) and entitlement on a claim after that would (generally) then not begin until the following Monday: reg 8(2) HB&CTB(DA) Regs and regs 76(1) and 79(1) HB Regs. If the claimant is entitled to a high rate of HB it could take time to recoup the loss.

(3)   The claimant may have some form of transitional protection which could be lost if s/he breaks her/his HB claim.

(4)   The "LHA" rules might not actually apply – eg, if the claimant lives in a houseboat or mobile home, or her/his landlord is a registered provider of social housing: see reg 13C(5) on p317.

Eligible housing costs

11.–[¹ (1)   Subject to the following provisions of this regulation, housing benefit shall be payable in respect of the payments specified in regulation 12(1) (rent) and a claimant's maximum housing benefit shall be calculated under Part 8 (amount of benefit) by reference to the amount of his eligible rent determined in accordance with–

(a)   regulation 12B (eligible rent);

(b)   regulations 12C (eligible rent and maximum rent), 13 (maximum rent), 13ZA (protection on death and 13 week protection) and 13ZB (change in reckonable rent);

(c)   regulations 12D (eligible rent and maximum rent (LHA)), 13C (when a maximum rent (LHA) is to be determined) and 13D (determination of a maximum rent (LHA)); or

(d)   regulations 12 (rent) and 13 (restrictions on unreasonable payments) as set out in paragraph 5 of Schedule 3 to the Consequential Provisions Regulations,

whichever is applicable in his case.]

(2)   Subject to paragraph (4), housing benefit shall not be payable in respect of payments made by a person on income support [³ , an income-based jobseeker's allowance or an income-related employment and support allowance] whose applicable amount for that benefit includes an amount in respect of those payments.

(3)   Where any payment for which a person is liable in respect of a dwelling and which is specified in regulation 12(1) (payments of rent for which housing benefit is payable), is increased on account of–

(a)   outstanding arrears of any payment or charge; or

(b)   any other unpaid payment or charge,

to which [² paragraphs (1) or (2) of that regulation or paragraph (2) of regulation 12B] or Schedule 1(ineligible service charges) refer and which is or was formerly owed by him in respect of that or another dwelling, a rent rebate or, as the case may be, a rent allowance shall not be payable in respect of that increase.

(4)   Where a person who has been awarded housing benefit in respect of a dwelling becomes entitled to income support [³ , an income-based jobseeker's allowance or an income-related employment and support allowance] and his applicable amount for the purpose of calculating his entitlement to that benefit includes an amount in respect of a payment made by him in respect of that dwelling, the payments made by him in respect of that dwelling shall continue to be eligible for housing benefit for a period of 4 benefit weeks beginning with the benefit week after the date on which he becomes entitled to income support [³ , an income-based jobseeker's allowance or an income-related employment and support allowance].

Modifications

Para (1) was substituted and para (3) amended by reg 4(3) Housing Benefit (Local Housing Allowance and Information Sharing) Amendment Regulations 2007 SI No.2868 as from 7 April 2008, save that for a person to whom reg 1(5) of those regulations applied (see p1231), the amendments came into force on the day on or after 7 April 2008 when the first of the events specified in reg 1(6) applied to her/him, or on 6 April 2009 if none had before that date.

Para (1) is modified by Sch 10 para 3 (see p586). This applies only to former Pathfinder Authorities who administered the pilot local housing allowance scheme.

Amendments

1.   Substituted by reg 4(3)(a) of SI 2007 No 2868 as from 7.4.08 (or if reg 1(5) of that SI applies, on the day on or after 7.4.08 when the first of the events specified in reg 1(6) applies, or from 6.4.09 if none have before that date).

2.   Amended by reg 4(3)(b) of SI 2007 No 2868 as from 7.4.08 (or if reg 1(5) of that SI applies, on the day on or after 7.4.08 when the first of the events specified in reg 1(6) applies, or from 6.4.09 if none have before that date).

3.   Amended by reg 9 of SI 2008 No 1082 as from 27.10.08.

Definitions

"applicable amount" – see s135 SSCBA.

"benefit week" – see reg 2(1).

"dwelling" – see reg 2(4) and s137(1) SSCBA.

"maximum housing benefit" – see reg 70.

"rent allowance" – see s134(1A) SSAA.

"rent rebate" – see s134(1B) SSAA.

"payment" – see reg 2(1).

"person on an income-based jobseeker's allowance" – see reg 2(3).

"person on an income-related employment and support allowance" – see reg 2(3A).

"person on income support" – see reg 2(1).

General Note

Even if a payment is covered by para (1), no HB may be paid in respect of it if paras (2) or (3) apply.

Analysis

Paragraph (1): The general rule

The general rule is that HB is payable in respect of all those categories of payment set out in reg 12(1). As will be seen from the commentary on that regulation, a wide variety of payments can be met by HB. "Eligible rent" for HB purposes is determined by the regulations listed in paras (a) to (d).

Reg 12B is the general rule.

Regs 12C, 13, 13ZA and 13ZB are the "local reference rent" scheme.

Regs 12D, 13C and 13D are the "LHA" scheme.

Regs 12 and 13 as set out in Sch 3 para 5 HB&CTB(CP) Regs are the "pre-January 1996" scheme.

Paragraphs (2) and (4): Exclusion for payments met by IS, income-based JSA or income-related ESA

Para (2) excludes payment of HB in respect of payments which are already covered by IS, income-based JSA or income-related ESA. Para (4) provides an exception to this rule for people already receiving HB for a dwelling who become entitled to IS, income-based JSA or income-related ESA with an applicable amount that includes amounts in respect of payments made for that dwelling – eg, where they buy a home that they formerly rented. In that situation, HB may continue to be paid for an overlap period of four benefit weeks.

Paragraph (3): Exclusion for increased rent to cover arrears

In the financial year 1991/92 a number of local housing authorities introduced rent setting arrangements for their dwellings that increased a tenant's weekly rent to include an amount in respect of her/his outstanding arrears from the existing or former tenancy. Para (3) provides that where a claimant's liability in respect of a dwelling is increased on account of outstanding arrears or unpaid sums which are owed or formerly owed by the claimant in respect of the current or former dwelling, then HB is not payable in respect of that increase. Nevertheless as a result of the rules relating to the housing authority's housing revenue account contained in Part VI of and the Schedule to the Local Government and Housing Act 1989, an authority has to increase the general level of rents for all tenants as the result of its need to provide for, or write off, bad debts and rent arrears. The general increase in rents due to such provision remains eligible for HB.

Rent

12.–(1) Subject to the following provisions of this regulation, the payments in respect of which housing benefit is payable in the form of a rent rebate or allowance are the following periodical payments which a person is liable to make in respect of the dwelling which he occupies as his home–

(a)   payments of, or by way of, rent;

(b)   payments in respect of a licence or permission to occupy the dwelling;

(c)   payments by way of mesne profits or, in Scotland, violent profits;

(d)   payments in respect of, or in consequence of, use and occupation of the dwelling;

(e)   payments of, or by way of, service charges payment of which is a condition on which the right to occupy the dwelling depends;

(f)   mooring charges payable for a houseboat;

(g)   where the home is a caravan or a mobile home, payments in respect of the site on which it stands;

(h)   any contribution payable by a person resident in an almshouse provided by a housing association which is either a charity of which particulars are entered in the register of charities established under section 3 of the Charities Act 1993 (register of charities) or an exempt charity within the meaning of that Act, which is a contribution towards the cost of maintaining that association's almshouses and essential services in them;

(i)   payments under a rental purchase agreement, that is to say an agreement for the purchase of a dwelling which is a building or part of one under which the whole or part of the purchase price is to be paid in more than one instalment and the completion of the purchase is deferred until the whole or a specified part of the purchase price has been paid; and

(j)   where, in Scotland, the dwelling is situated on or pertains to a croft within the meaning of section 3(1) of the Crofters (Scotland) Act 1993, the payment in respect of the croft land.

(2)   A rent rebate or, as the case may be, a rent allowance shall not be payable in respect of the following periodical payments–

(a)   payments under a long tenancy except a shared ownership tenancy [¹];

(b)   payments under a co-ownership scheme;

(c)   payments by an owner;

(d)   payments under a hire purchase, credit sale or conditional sale agreement except to the extent the conditional sale agreement is in respect of land; and

(e)   payments by a Crown tenant.

[¹ (f)   payments by a person in respect of a dwelling where his partner is an owner of that dwelling.]

[² (3)]

[²

(4)]

[² (5)]
[² (6)]
[² (7)]
(8)   In this regulation [³ , regulation 12B (eligible rent)] and Schedule 1 (ineligible service charges)–
"service charges" means periodical payments for services, whether or not under the same agreement as that under which the dwelling is occupied, or whether or not such a charge is specified as separate from or separately identified within other payments made by the occupier in respect of the dwelling; and
"services" means services performed or facilities (including the use of furniture) provided for, or rights made available to, the occupier of a dwelling.

Modifications

Paras (3) to (7) were omitted and para (8) amended by reg 4(4) Housing Benefit (Local Housing Allowance and Information Sharing) Amendment Regulations 2007 SI No.2868 as from 7 April 2008, save that for a person to whom reg 1(5) of those regulations applied (see p1231), the amendments came into force on the day on or after 7 April 2008 when the first of the events specified in reg 1(6) applied to her/him, or on 6 April 2009 if none had before that date.

A different version of reg 12 is substituted and used to determine eligible rent for some claimants entitled to HB on 1 January 1996. See Sch 3 paras 4 and 5(1) HB&CTB(CP) Regs (p1199).

Amendments

1.   Amended by reg 2(4) of SI 2007 No 1356 as from 1.10.07.
2.   Omitted by reg 4(4)(a) of SI 2007 No 2868 as from 7.4.08 (or if reg 1(5) of that SI applies, on the day on or after 7.4.08 when the first of the events specified in reg 1(6) applies, or from 6.4.09 if none have before that date).
3.   Amended by reg 4(4)(b) of SI 2007 No 2868 as from 7.4.08 (or if reg 1(5) of that SI applies, on the day on or after 7.4.08 when the first of the events specified in reg 1(6) applies, or from 6.4.09 if none have before that date).

Definitions

"co-ownership scheme" – see reg 2(1).
"dwelling" – see reg 2(4) and s137(1) SSCBA.
"housing association" – see reg 2(1).
"croft" – see "owner", reg 2.
"long tenancy" – see reg 2(1).
"owner" – see reg 2(1).
"payment" – see reg 2(1).
"rent rebate", "rent allowance" – see ss134(1A) and (1B).
"shared ownership tenancy" – see reg 2(1).

General Note

This deals with the payments that may be met by HB. For what is then "eligible rent" for HB purposes, see regs 12B, 12C and 12D.

Para (1) defines payments which qualify as rent, and therefore in respect of which HB, by way of rent rebate or rent allowance, may be paid. Para (2) sets out payments in respect of which HB is not payable. Para (8) defines the terms "services" and "service charges" for the purposes of this reg, reg 12B and Sch 1.

Note that the provisions in the former paras (3) to (7) are now to be found in other regulations as follows:
Para (3)(a): see reg 12C.
Para (3)(b): see reg 12B(2)(b).
Para (4): see reg 12B(3).
Para (5): see reg reg 12B(4).
Para (6): see reg 12B(5).
Para (7): see reg 12B(6).

Analysis

Paragraph (1): Payments that qualify for HB

In the same way that many people use "rent" as a portmanteau term for most types of payments that they make in return for occupying their home, the HB Regs use it as a convenient shorthand for various categories of payments. Some claimants may make payments falling into more than one of these categories, all of which will be eligible.

In order to attract HB, however, the payments must be "periodical". Thus in *CH 2329/2003*, the claimant and his wife were paying all the outgoings on their daughter's property while she was abroad. It was held that there was a commercial agreement: see the commentary to reg 9(1)(a) on p252. The payments made to the mortgagees on behalf of the daughter, therefore, could be met by HB, but the commissioner held that one-off payments for repairs fell outside the scope of the scheme (para 9). Discussing reg 10 HB Regs 1987 the commissioner said:

> "For the occupier's payments to or on behalf of the landlord to come within the scope of regulation 10 they must, therefore, be made at regular intervals and be of an ascertainable amount so that the weekly rental figure can be calculated in accordance with regulation 69 of the regulations."

Regs 10 and 69 HB regs 1987 are now regs 12 and 80 HB Regs.

For the issue of whether payments are those a person is "liable to make", see reg 8. For the question of whether a dwelling is occupied as the home, see reg 7.

Sub-para (a). "Rent" in this sub-para, of course, refers to rent properly so-called and not merely some payment that the claimant refers to as rent and which does not fall into one of the other categories. It refers, therefore, to payments made to a landlord under a tenancy. It includes all payments described as or deemed to be rent in the tenancy agreement. It can include charges for voids and long term maintenance: *CH 3528/2006*. Commissioner Jacobs said that the first question is whether a payment is a "service charge" (defined in reg 12(8)). If it is not, the charge *may* be taken into account as part of the rent under sub-para (a), if it relates to a matter that is properly considered in setting the rent.

Sub-para (b). The main indicators of a tenancy are that exclusive occupation is granted to the tenant or tenants for a certain period in return for periodic payments of rent. However, many claimants will not have tenancies because they have not been granted exclusive occupation of the premises. This is most obviously the case with lodgers, but may occur in cases where the landlord is not obviously resident. Although this can create headaches in other areas of law, such claimants occupy under a licence and so qualify for HB under sub-para (b). The use of the word "permission" is probably aimed at cases of tolerated trespassers, where no formal licence is granted but the landlord agrees to refrain from seeking possession for a period.

Reg 10 HB Regs 1987 (now reg 12) was the battleground between authorities and the Jesus Fellowship Church, following the leading cases on liability for rent and contrived tenancies (see the commentary to regs 8 and 9 on pp245 and 252). In *R v Milton Keynes CC HBRB ex p Saxby* [2000] unreported, 11 August, QBD; [2001] 33 HLR 82, CA, the courts were concerned with a claim by an Elder of the church. In broad terms, condition 4 required both "style 3" members (who are the rank and file members of the communities) and Elders (who are the heads of the communities and licensees of the trust property) to pay £55 to the common purse. Condition 6 required Elders to ensure that the payment due to the church's central trust fund from the common purse of £30 a resident, including themselves, was made.

The Review Board held that the Elder's liability for rent was that payable under condition 4 and not that under condition 6. Hidden J held that to be a wrong approach; the payments under condition 6 were sufficiently connected with the licence held by the Elders to enable it to be a payment "in respect of" that licence. The Court of Appeal upheld his decision. Hale LJ said:

"15.   The argument is therefore about whether "payments in respect of a dwelling which he occupies as his home" means "payments in respect of his own (or his own and his family's) occupation of a dwelling as his home". This would be to rewrite both section 123(1) of the Act and regulation 10(1). The non-dependant deduction provisions make it quite clear that the payments may relate to a dwelling in which other people also live. It would be strange indeed, and most unfair, if an Elder could only make a claim based upon his own contribution to the common purse, but then suffer fixed non-dependant deductions for all the adult residents (indeed that was what the local authority had earlier decided in this case).

16.   It is also quite clear that the clause 6 payments made by the Elders are the rent paid by them, as licensees, in respect of their licence to occupy the house. They have to make those payments irrespective of whether or not the residents make their clause 4 payments: it is not therefore the simple transmission of payments made by others."

It should, however, be noted that it would appear that the full amount of each condition 6 payment has to be made by the Elder. If that is so, the amount of HB payable may fall to be restricted under the rent restrictions provisions.

Sub-paras (c) and (d). "Mesne profits" in England and Wales are the damages for which a former tenant whose lease is forfeit may be liable to pay as compensation for depriving the landlord of the use or occupation of her/his land. They are usually assessed according to the ordinary letting value of the land. These categories of payment cannot include any interest which a claimant has been ordered to pay a landlord by a court: *R v Kensington and Chelsea RBC ex p Brandt* [1995] 28 HLR 528, QBD.

In Scotland, "violent profits" are damages which a possessor of land in bad faith is liable to pay to the true occupier. They are assessed according to the profit the latter could have made from letting the land during the period s/he was dispossessed, plus compensation for any damage caused.

Payments for "use and occupation" is another phrase borrowed from the law of real property. Such payments are assessed by a court in the same way as mesne profits except that they are paid by a trespasser for use of the land rather than a former tenant. Sub-para (d) is to be interpreted as referring to payments for use and occupation in that sense rather than according to the normal meaning of those words which might include payments that must be made as an incidence of the occupation. In *R v Bristol CC ex p Jacobs* (1999) 32 HLR

841 (Owen J), the claimant was liable to pay water rates as a consequence of her tenancy and argued that the rates fell within sub-para (d). The argument was rejected but leave to appeal was granted.

In *CH 844/2002*, for which see the notes to sub-para (f) below, the commissioner thought that a boat licence fee giving permission to use the boat on waterways fell within sub-para (d): para 13. That decision does not refer to the analysis in *ex p Jacobs* and it is suggested that it is erroneous.

Sub-para (e). "Service charges" are defined by para (8). The payments must be made in return for "services", also defined in para (8). Under this sub-para only those charges paid as a condition of occupying the premises are treated as rent. Thus if it is something the landlord provides at the tenant's request, it is not a service charge. The payments must be periodical, which means that they must relate to a specified period. The periods need not be even, however, and they need not correlate to the periods over which rent is paid.

See also reg 12B(2) which restricts the category of charges that can be included in a claimant's "eligible rent" under that regulation.

Sub-para (f). "Houseboat" is not defined in the HB legislation. In *R(H) 9/08*, Commissioner Levenson pointed out that the legislation could have defined the term but did not. He said (at para 19) that for HB purposes "houseboat" is an ordinary English word without a technical meaning and that it is a matter of fact in any particular case whether a boat is a "houseboat" in this sense. He found it difficult to imagine a case in which a reasonable tribunal would conclude that a boat which is fitted out as a dwelling suitable for permanent residence is not a houseboat. Definitions in other legislation or regulations for different purposes (eg, tax liability) are not relevant. These might reflect or inform common usage but cannot define "houseboat" for HB purposes. Neither can the classification for the purposes of licensing, or the operation of other schemes, such as the definition of a houseboat used in paragraph 38 of the British Waterways Boat Licence and Permit Conditions.

This provision was considered by Commissioner Williams in *CH 844/2002*, which concerned the question of whether the claimant could claim HB in respect of the cost of a mooring permit and a boat licence fee payable to British Waterways. The commissioner held (para 8) that a houseboat did not necessarily have no engine and could be capable of movement. The commissioner also held (para 13) that "mooring charges" could cover both a houseboat certificate granted by the British Waterways Board as well as a mooring fee.

Sub-para (g). Again, "caravan" and "mobile home" are not defined. This sub-para covers all payments, not just for the space occupied by the caravan or mobile home. It covers things like charges for electricity supply, toilet and shower facilities etc. Payments by mobile home owners are regulated by the Mobile Homes Act 1983. *CH 3110/2003* makes the valuable point that if the claimant's home does not count as a caravan or a mobile home (in this case it was a prefabricated chalet type structure resting on the land), s/he should nevertheless be entitled under reg 12(1)(a) to HB to meet the rent paid in respect of the land on which the home stands because it counts as "rent" for which s/he is "liable to make [periodical payments] in respect of the dwelling which he occupies as his home": per reg 12(1). The fact that the rent was called "ground rent" was irrelevant, since the tenancy of the land was not a "long tenancy" falling within reg 12(2)(a) (the rent under such a tenancy ordinarily being called "ground rent").

Sub-para (h). The "register of charities" is kept by the Charity Commission. "Exempt" charities are those listed in Sch 2 to the 1993 Act. This includes certain universities and colleges, the Church Commissioners, societies registered under the Industrial and Provident Societies Act 1893, and the Friendly Societies Act 1896. A registrar maintains a list of those bodies registered under each of those Acts.

Sub-para (i) is self-explanatory.

Sub-para (j) relates to agricultural land in Scotland.

Paragraph (2): Payments that do not qualify

This sets out categories of payments ineligible for HB. "Long tenancy", "co-ownership scheme" and "owner" are all defined in reg 2 and reference should be made to the commentary to that regulation, particularly in relation to ownership. Note that since 1 October 2007, the exception for shared ownership tenancies (also defined in reg 2) applies to all such tenancies – ie, private sector shared ownership leases as well as shared ownership tenancies granted by a housing association or a housing authority.

CH 1578/2006 dealt with issues of general principle about the liability of one co-owner to another and the treatment of any such liability for the purposes of HB. The legal position is governed by the Trusts of Land and Appointment of Trustees Act 1996. s13(6)(a) of that Act provides: "where entitlement of any beneficiary to occupy land under section 12 has been excluded or restricted, the conditions which may be imposed on any beneficiary in relation to his occupation of the land include conditions requiring him to make payments by way of compensation to the beneficiary whose entitlement has been excluded or restricted". The HB scheme is intended to cover payments made to secure occupation, not payments made to compensate another person for not exercising a right to occupy. Here, the payments which were made to the claimant's son were repayments of the mortgage loan and were not rent within the meaning of the HB Regs. The claimant's liability to make such payments arose as a result of acquiring a beneficial interest in the property, not in consequence of her use and occupation of the dwelling.

Crown tenants have their own scheme to assist with rent: see p221.

[¹ **Eligible rent**

12B.–(1)   The amount of a person's eligible rent shall be determined in accordance with the provisions of this regulation except where regulations 12C (eligible rent and maximum rent) or 12D (eligible rent and maximum rent (LHA)) apply, or paragraph 4 of Schedule 3 to the Consequential Provisions Regulations applies.

(2)   Subject to paragraphs (3), (4) and (6), the amount of a person's eligible rent shall be the aggregate of such payments specified in regulation 12(1) as that person is liable to pay less–

(a)   except where he is separately liable for charges for water, sewerage or allied environmental services, an amount determined in accordance with paragraph (5);

(b)   where payments include service charges which are wholly or partly ineligible, an amount in respect of the ineligible charges determined in accordance with Schedule 1; and

(c)   where he is liable to make payments in respect of any service charges to which regulation 12(1)(e) does not apply, but to which paragraph 3(2) of Part 1 of Schedule 1 (unreasonably low service charges) applies in the particular circumstances, an amount in respect of such charges determined in accordance with paragraph 3(2) of Part 1 of Schedule 1.

(3)   Where the payments specified in regulation 12(1) are payable in respect of accommodation which consists partly of residential accommodation and partly of other accommodation, only such proportion of those payments as is referable to the residential accommodation shall count as eligible rent for the purposes of these Regulations.

(4)   Where more than one person is liable to make payments in respect of a dwelling, the payments specified in regulation 12(1) shall be apportioned for the purpose of calculating the eligible rent for each such person having regard to all the circumstances, in particular, the number of such persons and the proportion of rent paid by each such person.

(5)   The amount of the deduction referred to in paragraph (2) shall be–

(a)   if the dwelling occupied by the claimant is a self-contained unit, except in a case to which sub-paragraph (c) applies, the amount of the charges;

(b)   in any other case, except one to which sub-paragraph (c) applies, the proportion of those charges in respect of the self-contained unit which is obtained by dividing the area of the dwelling occupied by the claimant by the area of the self-contained unit of which it forms part;

(c)   where the charges vary in accordance with the amount of water actually used, the amount which the appropriate authority considers to be fairly attributable to water, and sewerage services, having regard to the actual or estimated consumption of the claimant.

(6)   In any case where it appears to the relevant authority that in the particular circumstances of that case the eligible rent as determined in accordance with the preceding paragraphs of this regulation is greater than it is reasonable to meet by way of housing benefit, the eligible rent shall be such lesser sum as seems to that authority to be an appropriate rent in that particular case.]

Modifications

Reg 12B is modified by Sch 10 para 4 (see p586). This applies only to former Pathfinder Authorities who administered the pilot local housing allowance scheme.

Amendment

1.   Inserted by reg 5 of SI 2007 No 2868 as from 7.4.08 (or if reg 1(5) of that SI applies, on the day on or after 7.4.08 when the first of the events specified in reg 1(6) applies, or from 6.4.09 if none have before that date).

Definitions

"claimant" – see reg 2(1).
"dwelling" – see reg 2(4) and s137(1) SSCBA.
"payment" – see reg 2(1).
"service charges" – see reg 12(8).

General Note
Reg 12B, together with Sch 1, deals with the question of how much of the rent is to be "eligible rent" for calculating HB. It applies unless regs 12C or 12D HB Regs (respectively, the "local reference rent" and "local housing allowance" schemes) or Sch 3 para 4 HB&CTB(CP) Regs (the "pre-January 1996" scheme) apply. It can apply both where HB is paid as a rent rebate and where it is paid as a rent allowance – ie, in the latter case where the tenancy is excluded from the application of all of the rent restriction schemes.

Analysis
Paragraphs (2) to (5): Calculation of eligible rent
If reg 12B applies, these paragraphs set out the system of determining the claimant's "eligible rent". An apportionment under paras (3) and (4) may be relevant. Finally, there is a general discretion to restrict "eligible rent" under para (6).

The following stages need to be followed in making the calculation.
(1)   "Eligible rent" is the aggregate of the payments under reg 12(1) that a person is liable to pay, less the deductions set out in para (2)(a) to (c) – ie, it is the contractual rent, minus ineligible services.
(2)   The first deduction is for water, sewerage and allied environmental services, which is not made if (as is usually the case) a claimant is liable for such services separately from her/his tenancy: para (2)(a). If the deduction is to be made, the rules are set out in para (5). If the claimant lives in a self-contained unit, the whole of the charges are deducted under para (5)(a). If the dwelling is not self-contained, a share of the charges is deducted. This is calculated by dividing the total area of the unit in which the dwelling is contained (such as a block of flats) by the area of the dwelling: para (5)(b). It seems that common parts are included in the total area of the unit for the purposes of this calculation. If in either case, the amount of the charges varies, then the authority may deduct a sum that is fairly attributable to charges: para (5)(c).
(3)   The second deduction is in respect of ineligible service charges: para (2)(b). This is determined under Sch 1 para 1: see the commentary on p513. Note that "service charges" for these purposes are defined in reg 12(8).
(4)   Finally, a higher deduction must be made in respect of certain service charges: para (2)(c). They must be charges not falling within reg 12(1)(e) – ie, because occupation of the property is not conditional on payment. They must also be ineligible charges in respect of which the local authority has decided that the amounts levied are unreasonably low. See the commentary to Sch 1 para 3(2) on p515.

Paragraph (3): Apportionment where accommodation only partly residential
Where the accommodation occupied by the claimant is not solely residential accommodation, only that portion of the payments referable to the residential element can form part of the "eligible rent". This will typically arise in the case of accommodation that has both residential and commercial parts.

Paragraph (4): Apportionment of joint liabilities
This apportionment is only to be carried out if there is a joint liability – eg, where three tenants in a property have all signed the tenancy agreement. If each of the tenants has a separate tenancy agreement with the landlord, no apportionment is appropriate. The local authority has a discretion to decide the proportions to be attributed to each person, "having regard to" all the circumstances. It may not be appropriate to divide the amounts equally. This will be the case, for example, where one person occupies a much larger room than another. Particular regard must be paid to the number of such persons and to the amounts paid by each, but the weight given to the latter could be reduced, for example, where it was clear that the division of the amounts had been arranged deliberately to maximise benefit entitlement.

A problem that has arisen is whether a person who is deemed not to be liable for rent by virtue of regs 9, 10 or 56 must be excluded from the apportionment exercise under reg 12B(4) HB Regs. In *R (Naghshbandi) v Camden LBC* [2001] EWHC Admin 813; [2003] HLR 280, CA, Rafferty J decided that the apportionment must be between the people who are actually liable to pay the rent and any deemed non-liability should be ignored for these purposes. Rafferty J's decision was upheld by the Court of Appeal [2003] HLR 280.

In *CH 3376/2002*, the elderly claimant was a joint tenant of a property with his son, who had moved out some considerable time previously. He was no longer in contact with the son. He was in poor health. The local authority assessed his HB on the basis that he was liable for half the rent and he appealed.

Commissioner Jacobs first dealt with an argument for the claimant that he could be treated as liable for the son's share of the rent under reg 6(1)(c) HB Regs 1987 (now reg 8(1)(c)) as well as his own share under reg 6(1)(a) (now reg 8(1)(a)) and that no apportionment could therefore be made. He held that reg 10(5) HB Regs 1987 (a provision now in reg 12B(4)) required apportionment only of actual liabilities rather than liabilities which were deemed to exist under reg 6(1) HB Regs 1987: para 37.

He then went on to consider the discretion as to apportionment and concluded that the whole of the rent should be apportioned to the claimant: para 60. He gave useful general guidance on the exercise of the discretion:
(1)   The proportion of the rent that had been paid by each joint tenant might be an important factor, but was not an overriding or even the predominant factor in every case: para 45.

(2) The right to respect for the home under Art 8 European Convention on Human Rights was a relevant consideration: para 53. It was not determinative. Unless a failure to pay full HB would be a breach of Art 8.1, it is hard to see what the relevance of the Convention would be.

(3) The paragraph specifies the number of tenants and the total rent paid as relevant: para 54.

(4) The ability of the tenants to pay was relevant, but did not of itself justify placing a disproportionate responsibility on the claimant for HB: para 55.

(5) The views of the landlord as to who is expected to pay in practice are relevant, but the fact that a landlord has forborn to enforce the full rent pending the outcome of a dispute about HB should not be held against the claimant: para 56.

(6) Whether the claimant could be expected to move might be relevant. This would involve consideration of issues such as the claimant's age, state of health, connections with the local area and the availability of property in the locality: para 58.

The commissioner pointed out that it was possible for the local authority to make a different apportionment for a limited period only, to give the claimant a fair chance to move or to find another co-tenant: para 57. However, caution needs to be exercised over the latter course because most tenancies strictly control the right of the tenant to get another person into the property. He also stated that it was possible for an apportionment to be changed if a change of circumstances occurred: para 63.

Paragraph (6): Discretion to restrict eligible rent

Para (6) contains a general discretion to reduce the eligible rent still further. The power to reduce the eligible rent under para (6) is additional to the foregoing provisions of this regulation, but only where the "eligible rent" as determined under the provisions above is greater than it is reasonable to meet by way of HB. The generality of the power enables authorities to ensure that where reg 12B applies, HB should not be paid on any rent above a level which the authority considers to be appropriate in any particular case. In the case of council tenants, this provision could be used where the claimant is occupying a property larger than reasonably required, even though the rent is reasonable for that particular property.

Note: regs 12C and 12D(3)(a)(ii) and the definition of "cap rent" in reg 13D(12) are said to be subject to reg 12B(6). See the commentary to regs 12C and 13D on pp307 and 322 for a discussion.

Para (6) raises a number of questions of judgment that must be considered rationally. If the authority or the First-tier Tribunal reaches a decision that no sensible decision maker could reach then it may be held to be vulnerable to attack on appeal. There is no restriction in the paragraph as to which factors may be taken into account and so all facts relevant to the making of a restriction may be considered. No fixed rules or policies may be adopted. It is clear from the wording of the provision that each case must be considered individually. Decision makers should be prepared to give coherent reasons for imposing a restriction.

It was confirmed in *R (Laali) v Westminster CC HBRB* [2002] HLR 179, QBD that when deciding whether or not to make a reduction under reg 10(6B) HB Regs 1987 (now reg 12B(6)), the claimant's personal circumstances were relevant. The Review Board had therefore been in error to disregard the claimant's need to live in St John's Wood because his daughter lived nearby, because of the length of time he had lived in the area, because the accommodation was all on one floor and hence more suitable for him (he was disabled) and that he was unable to pay a deposit or rent in advance on another property. The authority's contention that those matters fell to be considered on an application for an exceptional hardship payment pursuant to a former version of reg 61 HB Regs 1987 (since substituted) was rejected, though permission to appeal was granted.

[¹ Eligible rent and maximum rent

12C.–(1) This regulation applies where a maximum rent has been, or is to be, determined in accordance with regulation 13 (maximum rent).

(2) Where this regulation applies, except where paragraph (3) applies, the amount of a person's eligible rent shall be the maximum rent, subject to paragraphs (3), (4) and (6) of regulation 12B.

(3) In a case where the maximum rent is derived from a single room rent determined by a rent officer under paragraph 5 of Schedule 1 to the Rent Officers Order the eligible rent shall be the maximum rent subject to paragraphs (3) and (6) of regulation 12B.]

Amendment

1. Inserted by reg 5 of SI 2007 No 2868 as from 7.4.08 (or if reg 1(5) of that SI applies, on the day on or after 7.4.08 when the first of the events specified in reg 1(6) applies, or from 6.4.09 if none have before that date).

Definitions

"maximum rent" – see reg 2(1).

"Rent Officers Order"– see reg 2(1).

"single room rent" – see reg 2(1).

General Note

"Eligible rent" for HB purposes is determined under reg 12C if "maximum rent" is determined under reg 13 (the "local reference rent" rules). "Maximum rent" is determined under reg 13 where reg 14 is relevant. See p313 for a summary of the "local reference rent" scheme. Note that the use of the maximum rent in calculating HB may be delayed under reg 13ZA.

Analysis

If reg 12C applies, the "eligible rent" is the "maximum rent" as calculated under reg 13. Where the claimant is a "young individual", broadly a single person under 25 (but see the full definition in reg 2(1) and the commentary on p225), this is the maximum rent derived from the "single room rent": see the commentary to reg 13(5). So in simple terms, eligible rent under the "local reference rent" scheme is the contractual rent, minus any amount above the level to which maximum rent is restricted. Note that except in the circumstances set out in reg 13(5) and (7), the authority does not make deductions under reg 12C for ineligible charges; these have generally been dealt with in the determinations made by the rent officer.

In all cases, where the accommodation occupied by the claimant is not solely residential accommodation, only that portion of the payments referable to the residential element can form part of the eligible rent: see reg 12(B)(3).

Where the claimant is jointly liable to make the payments set out in reg 12(1), an apportionment must be made: see see reg 12B(4). This of course does not apply where the maximum rent is derived from the single room rent.

Both paras (2) and (3) are said to be subject to reg 12B(6) which purports to give the authority a general discretion to reduce the eligible rent calculated under reg 12C. Note, however, the wording of reg 12B(6), which states it only applies where eligible rent has been determined in accordance with the preceding paragraphs of that regulation, so it may be arguable that it cannot apply here.

If reg 12C(2) and (3) *are* subject to reg 12B(6), caution is required where a rent officer's determinations have already restricted the claimant's eligible rent under reg 13: see the commentary on p314. After all, that process should mean that the claimant's rent has been reduced to a reasonable level already. However, in *R v Macclesfield BC HBRB ex p Temsamani* [1999] unreported, February 24, QBD, the High Court confirmed that, under the provisions as they applied before 7 April 2008, an authority could properly reduce the eligible rent even where the Rent Officer had not given a significantly high rent determination provided that it had sufficient evidential basis to do so.

[¹ **Eligible rent and maximum rent (LHA)**

12D.–(1)   This regulation applies where, by virtue of paragraphs (2) or (3) of regulation 13C (when a maximum rent (LHA) is to be determined), a maximum rent (LHA) has been, or is to be, determined in accordance with regulation 13D (determination of a maximum rent (LHA)).

(2)   Where this regulation applies, except where paragraphs (3)(a) (protection on death) or (5)(a) (13 week protection) apply,–

(a)   the amount of a person's eligible rent shall be the maximum rent (LHA); and

(b)   it shall apply until the earlier of–

    (i)   the determination of a maximum rent (LHA) by virtue of regulation 13C(2)(d) (change of category of dwelling, death or change of dwelling for an LHA case);

    (ii)   the determination of a maximum rent (LHA) by virtue of regulation 13C(3) (anniversary of LHA date); or

    (iii)   the determination of a maximum rent by virtue of regulation 13 or an eligible rent under regulation 12B.

(3)   Subject to paragraph (7), where the relevant authority is required to determine a maximum rent (LHA) by virtue of regulation 13C(2)(a), (b) (new claim on or after 7th April 2008) or (d)(i) or (ii) (change of category of dwelling or death relating to an LHA case) and the claimant occupies a dwelling which is the same as that occupied by him at the date of death of any linked person, the eligible rent shall be–

(a)   either–

    (i)   the eligible rent which applied on the day before the death occurred; or

    (ii)   in a case where there was no eligible rent, subject to regulation 12B(3) (mixed use accommodation), (4) (more than one person liable to make payments) and (6) (discretion in relation to eligible rent), the reckonable rent due on that day; or

(b)   the eligible rent determined in accordance with paragraph (2), where it is equal to or more than the eligible rent determined in accordance with sub-paragraph (a).

(4)   For the purpose of paragraph (3), a claimant shall be treated as occupying the dwelling if paragraph (13) of regulation 7 (circumstances in which a person is or is not to be treated as occupying a dwelling as his home) is satisfied and for that purpose paragraph (13) shall have effect as if sub-paragraph (b) of that paragraph were omitted.

(5)   Subject to paragraphs (6) and (7), where a relevant authority is required to determine a maximum rent (LHA) by virtue of regulation 13C(2)(a) or (b) (new claim on or after 7th April 2008) and the relevant authority is satisfied that the claimant or a linked person was able to meet the financial commitments for his dwelling when they were entered into, the eligible rent shall be–

(a)   an eligible rent determined in accordance with regulation 12B(2); or

(b)   the eligible rent determined in accordance with paragraph (2), where it is equal to or more than the eligible rent referred to in sub-paragraph (a).

(6)   Paragraph (5) shall not apply where a claimant or the claimant's partner, was previously entitled to benefit in respect of an award of housing benefit which fell wholly or partly less than 52 weeks before the commencement of the claimant's current award of housing benefit.

(7)   Where a person's eligible rent has been determined in accordance with–

(a)   paragraph (3)(a) (protection on death), it shall apply until the first of the following events occurs–

(i)   the period of 12 months from the date of death has expired;

(ii)   the relevant authority determines an eligible rent in accordance with paragraph (2) which is equal to or exceeds it or is based on a maximum rent (LHA) determined by virtue of regulation 13C(2)(d)(iii) (change of dwelling);

(iii) the determination of an eligible rent in accordance with paragraph (3)(a) (protection on death) in relation to a subsequent death; or

(iv)   the determination of a maximum rent by virtue of regulation 13 or an eligible rent under regulation 12B.

(b)   paragraph (5)(a) (13 week protection), it shall apply until the first of the following events occurs–

(i)   the first 13 weeks of the claimant's award of housing benefit have expired;

(ii)   the relevant authority determines an eligible rent in accordance with paragraph (2) which is equal to or exceeds it or is based on a maximum rent (LHA) determined by virtue of regulation 13C(2)(d)(iii) (change of dwelling);

(iii) the determination of an eligible rent in accordance with paragraph (3)(a) (protection on death); or

(iv)   the determination of a maximum rent by virtue of regulation 13 or an eligible rent under regulation 12B.

(8)   Where an eligible rent ceases to apply by virtue of paragraph (7)(a)(i) (expiry of protection on death) or (7)(b)(i) (expiry of 13 week protection), the eligible rent that shall apply instead shall be the one which would have applied but for paragraphs (3)(a) and (5)(a).]

Modifications

Reg 12D is modified by Sch 10 para 5 (see p586). This applies only to former Pathfinder Authorities who administered the pilot local housing allowance scheme.

Amendment

1.   Inserted by reg 5 of SI 2007 No 2868 as from 7.4.08 (or if reg 1(5) of that SI applies, on the day on or after 7.4.08 when the first of the events specified in reg 1(6) applies, or from 6.4.09 if none have before that date).

Definitions

"claimant" – see reg 2(1).

"dwelling" – see reg 2(4) and s137(1) SSCBA.

"the LHA date" – see reg 13C(6).
"linked person" – see reg 2(1).
"partner" – see reg 2(1).
"reckonable rent" – see reg 2(1).

General Note

"Eligible rent" for HB purposes is determined under reg 12D if "maximum rent (LHA)" is determined under reg 13D (the "LHA" rules). See p322 for a summary of the "LHA" scheme.

Reg 12D also sets out the the period over which the eligible rent applies (para (2)(b)). Note that local authorities can generally only reassess a claimant's eligible rent annually, even if the claimant's rent or the rate of the appropriate local housing allowance
  changes.

Reg 12D provides rules for delaying a restriction of eligible rent in specified circumstances (paras (3) to (8)).

Note the transitional protection that is provided to those living in former Pathfinder areas whose HB was calculated on the basis of the "maximum rent (standard local rate)": reg 122 and Sch 10.

Analysis

If reg 12C applies, the "eligible rent" is the "maximum rent (LHA)" as calculated under reg 13D: para (2)(a). So in simple terms, eligible rent under the "LHA" scheme is the contractual rent, minus any amount above the level to which maximum rent (LHA) is restricted. Note that the authority does not make deductions under reg 12D for ineligible charges; these are generally dealt with in the local housing allowances set by the rent officer upon which maximum rent (LHA) is based.

Unlike under the "local reference rent" scheme, eligible rent is not apportioned where the accommodation occupied by the claimant is not solely residential or where the claimant is jointly liable to make the payments set out in reg 12(1). However, an apportionment of the claimant's "cap rent" (an element in the calculation of maximum rent (LHA)) *is* made, which has the same effect: see see reg 13D(12).

Para (2). Under para (2), eligible rent is the maximum rent (LHA) unless the claimant has protection on death under para (3)(a) or 13-week protection under para (5)(a). This applies until the earliest of the three circumstances in para (2)(b), that is until:

(1)   A new maximum rent (LHA) has been determined following a specified change: para 2(b)(i). The specified changes are a change in the category of dwelling that applies to the claimant (ie, s/he is allowed more or fewer bedrooms), a member of the claimant's family (or a relative of the claimant or her/his partner living with the claimant) dieing or the claimant moving to a new home. For full details see reg 13C(2)(d).

(2)   A new maximum rent (LHA) has been determined following the anniversary of the LHA date: para (2)(b)(ii). The "LHA date" (defined in reg 13C(6)) is the date by reference to which the LHA used to determine the maximum rent (LHA) was identified.

(3)   A "maximum rent" has been determined under reg 13 (the "local reference rent" rules) or an eligible rent has been determined under reg 12B (the normal rules), that is, where the "LHA" rules no longer apply to the claimant (eg, because her/his landlord is now a registered provider of social housing or s/he has moved to a rented mobile home): para (2)(b)(iii).

Paras (3), (4), (7) and (8): Protection on death

Para (3) provides a degree of protection for the recently bereaved if a claimant is continuing to occupy a home which s/he occupied at the time a "linked person" died. Para (3) only applies where the authority is required to determine a new maximum rent (LHA) under any of reg 13C(2(a), (b) or (d)(i) or (ii) – eg, where because of the death of the "linked person" there is a change in the category of dwelling that applies to the claimant.

A "linked person" for these purposes is a member of the claimant's family (defined in s137(1) SSCBA), a partner in a polygamous marriage or a child or young person for whom s/he or a partner is responsible and who lives in the same household, or a relative of the claimant or her/his partner who occupies the same dwelling without a separate right to do so: reg 2(1). As to the last of these categories, "relative" is also defined in reg 2(1). The deceased person need not have been residing with the claimant, provided only that s/he occupied the same dwelling. Oddly, reg 3(4) specifies when a person "resides with" another for the purposes of the definition of "linked person", but the term used here is "occupies the same dwelling ... whether or not they reside with him". In this context, "occupies the same dwelling" arguably means someone living within the same building, provided that the living units of the claimant and the deceased are not completely self-contained. It might cover those who were sharing only a toilet, or some similar part of the accommodation. The relative should not have had a separate right of occupation. If the relative had her/his own tenancy from a landlord, the claimant cannot therefore take advantage of this provision. However, if the claimant and the relative were joint tenants, it could be argued that the relative's right of occupation was not "separate" because it was held jointly with the claimant.

By para (4), "occupation" of a home for the purposes of para (3) can include deemed occupation under reg 7(13), that is, where someone is treated as occupying a dwelling for up to 13 weeks while temporarily absent from it. The claimant need not, however, comply with sub-para (b) of that regulation, so it does not matter if the home was let or sublet.

Unless eligible rent determined on the basis of the new circumstances is the same or higher, eligible rent is either the eligible rent that applied on the day before the date of death, or in a case where there was no eligible rent in force, the "reckonable rent" on the date of death. "Reckonable rent" means the payments a person is liable to make in respect of the dwelling s/he occupies as her/his home and which are eligible (or but for reg 13 would be eligible) for HB. Note that where the eligible rent is the reckonable rent, this is subject to reg 12B(3), (4) and (6). See reg 12B for a discussion of these provisions. Note, however, the wording of reg 12B(6), which states it only applies where eligible rent has been determined in accordance with the preceding paragraphs of that regulation, so it may be arguable that it cannot apply here.

The protected eligible rent continues to apply until the first of the the events in para (7)(a) occurs, ie:

(1)   It is more than 12 months since the date of death. Where the protection ceases for this reason, the eligible rent that applies is that which would have applied but for the protection provided by para (3)(a): para (8).

(2)   The authority determines an eligible rent that is the same or higher than the protected eligible rent, or is based on a different maximum rent (LHA) because the claimant has moved.

(3)   The authority determines an eligible rent because another "linked person" has died.

(4)   A "maximum rent" has been determined under reg 13 (the "local reference rent" rules) or an eligible rent has been determined under reg 12B (the normal rules), that is, the "LHA" rules no longer apply.

Paras (5) to (7) and (8): 13 week protection

Para (5) can postpone the application of the eligible rent during the first 13 weeks of an HB award if the claimant or a "linked person" (see above) was able to meet the financial commitments for the dwelling (which includes things like bills as well as the rent) at the time they were taken on. Para (5) only applies on a new claim for HB on or after 7 April 2008. By para (6), the protection in para (5) does not apply where the claimant or her/his partner has been entitled to HB at some time within the 52 weeks prior to the commencement of the claimant's current HB award.

Unless eligible rent as determined under para (2) is the same or higher, eligible rent is to be determined under reg 12B(2) (the normal rules). See the commentary to reg 12B on p305.

The protected eligible rent continues to apply until the first of the the events in para (7)(b) occurs, ie:

(1)   It is more than 13 weeks since HB was awarded. Where the protection ceases for this reason, the eligible rent that applies is that which would have applied but for the protection provided by para (5)(a): para (8).

(2)   The authority determines an eligible rent that is the same or higher than the protected eligible rent, or is based on a different maximum rent (LHA) because the claimant has moved.

(3)   The authority determines an eligible rent because a "linked person" has died: see para (3)(a).

(4)   A "maximum rent" has been determined under reg 13 (the "local reference rent" rules) or an eligible rent has been determined under reg 12B (the normal rules), that is, the "LHA" rules no longer apply.

Basic transitional protection for pathfinder cases
12E.

Modification

Reg 12E is inserted by Sch 10 para 6 (see p586). It only applies to former Pathfinder Authorities who administered the pilot local housing allowance scheme.

Cases where the claimant enjoyed protection on death before 7th April 2008
12F.

Modification

Reg 12F is inserted by Sch 10 para 6 (see p586). It only applies to former Pathfinder Authorities who administered the pilot local housing allowance scheme.

Cases where the claimant enjoyed 13 week protection before 7th April 2008
12G.

Modification

Reg 12G is inserted by Sch 10 para 6 (see p586). It only applies to former Pathfinder Authorities who administered the pilot local housing allowance scheme.

Cases where a death occurs in the first year on or after 7th April 2008
12H.

Modification

Reg 12H is inserted by Sch 10 para 6 (see p586). It only applies to former Pathfinder Authorities who administered the pilot local housing allowance scheme.

Basic transitional protection in the second year and subsequent years after 7th April 2008
12I.

Modification

Reg 12I is inserted by Sch 10 para 6 (see p586). It only applies to former Pathfinder Authorities who administered the pilot local housing allowance scheme.

Transitional protection in the second year after 7th April 2008 where the claimant is already enjoying protection on death
12J.

Modification

Reg 12J is inserted by Sch 10 para 6 (see p586). It only applies to former Pathfinder Authorities who administered the pilot local housing allowance scheme.

Protection on death in the second and subsequent years after 7th April 2008
12K.

Modification

Reg 12K is inserted by Sch 10 para 6 (see p586). It only applies to former Pathfinder Authorities who administered the pilot local housing allowance scheme.

[¹ Transitional protection – larger properties
12L.–(1)   This regulation applies where–
(a)   reference was made to a maximum rent (LHA) in determining the amount of the eligible rent which applied immediately before 6th April 2009;
(b)   the category of dwelling for which that maximum rent (LHA) was determined corresponded to a category of six or more bedrooms; and
(c)   on or after 6th April 2009 the relevant authority is required to determine a maximum rent (LHA) by virtue of–
    (i)   regulation 13C(2)(d)(i) (change of category of dwelling), where it has not received notification of the death of a linked person; or
    (ii)   regulation 13C(3) (anniversary of the LHA date).
(2)   Where this regulation applies, the claimant's eligible rent is–
(a)   the maximum rent (LHA) where that is equal to or higher than the eligible rent that applied immediately before 6th April 2009; or
(b)   the amount of the eligible rent which applied immediately before 6th April 2009.
(3)   Where the eligible rent is the amount of the eligible rent which applied immediately before 6th April 2009, it will continue to apply until, on or after 6th April 2009, the first of the following events occurs–
(a)   the end of 26 weeks after the determination of the maximum rent (LHA) referred to in paragraph (1)(c);
(b)   the relevant authority is required to determine a maximum rent (LHA) by virtue of regulation 13C (when a maximum rent (LHA) is to be determined) because the claimant has become entitled to a smaller category of dwelling;
(c)   the relevant authority is required to determine an eligible rent following a change of dwelling; or
(d)   the relevant authority is required to determine an eligible rent in accordance with regulation 12D(3) (protection on death).
(4)   Where the eligible rent ceases to apply because of paragraph (3)(a), the eligible rent will be the maximum rent (LHA) which would have applied but for the transitional protection in paragraph (2)(b).
(5)   Where the eligible rent is the maximum rent (LHA), it shall be treated as if it had been determined in accordance with regulation 12D(2)(a) (eligible rent is maximum rent (LHA)) and shall apply according to the provisions of regulation 12D.]

Amendment

1.   Inserted by reg 2(2) of SI 2009 No 614 as from 6.4.09.

General Note

From 6 April 2009, the appropriate local housing allowance for a claimant is the one for the category of dwelling with the number of bedrooms s/he is allowed under the size criteria, to a maximum of five bedrooms: reg 13D(2)(c). Where a claimant's eligible rent was determined by reference to a maximum rent (LHA) for a category of dwelling of six or more bedrooms prior to 6 April 2009, reg 12L allowed for any reduction in HB to be delayed. This applies from the point where the authority was required to determine a maximum rent (LHA) because of a change circumstances which affected the category of dwelling applicable to the claimant (other than where the authority received notification of the death of a "linked person") or because it was the anniversary of the "LHA date" (defined in reg 13C(6)).

Unless the maximum rent (LHA) was the same or higher, eligible rent was the amount of eligible rent that applied immediately before 6 April 2009.

The protected eligible rent continued to apply for 26 weeks unless the events in para (3)(b) to (d) occurred sooner.

[¹ **Maximum rent**

13.–(1) The maximum rent shall be determined in accordance with paragraphs (2) to (8) where–

(a) a local authority has applied for a determination in accordance with regulation 14 (requirement to refer to rent officers), a redetermination in accordance with regulation 15 or 16, or a substitute determination or substitute redetermination in accordance with regulation 17 and a rent officer has made a determination, redetermination, substitute determination or substitute redetermination in exercise of the Housing Act functions; or

(b) an authority is not required to apply to the rent officer for a determination because–

(i) regulation 14(2)(a) applies; or

(ii) regulation 14(2)(b) applies because paragraph 2(2) of Schedule 2 applies.

(2) In a case where the rent officer has determined a claim-related rent, but is not required to notify the relevant authority of a local reference rent or a single room rent, the maximum rent shall be that claim-related rent.

(3) Subject to the limit specified in paragraph (4), in a case where the rent officer has determined both a local reference rent of which he is required to notify the relevant authority and a claim-related rent, the maximum rent shall be the local reference rent.

(4) In a case to which paragraph 8 of Schedule 3 to the Consequential Provisions Regulations applies, where the rent officer has determined and is required to notify the relevant authority of a local reference rent the maximum rent shall not exceed twice that local reference rent.

(5) Subject to paragraph (6), in the case of a young individual–

(a) except where sub-paragraph (b) applies, where the rent officer has determined a single room rent and is required to notify the relevant authority of it, the maximum rent shall not exceed that single room rent;

(b) where–

(i) the rent officer has determined a single room rent and a claim-related rent and is required to notify the authority of them;

(ii) the claim-related rent includes payment in respect of meals; and

(iii) the single room rent is greater than the claim-related rent less an amount in respect of meals determined in accordance with paragraph 2 of Part 1 of Schedule 1 (ineligible service charges),

the maximum rent shall not exceed the claim-related rent less that amount in respect of meals.

(6) Paragraph (5) shall not apply in the case of a claimant–

(a) to whom paragraph 4 of Schedule 3 to the Consequential Provisions Regulations (saving provision) applies;

(b) to whom paragraph 14 of Schedule 3 (severe disability premium) applies; or

(c) where a non-dependant resides with him.

(7) Where the maximum rent is derived from–

(a)   a claim-related rent and the notification under paragraph 9(1)(c) of Schedule 1 to the Rent Officers Order states that an ineligible amount in respect of meals has been included in that claim-related rent; or

(b)   a local reference rent and the notification under paragraph 9(1)(da) of Schedule 1 to the Rent Officers Order states that an ineligible amount in respect of meals has been included in that local reference rent,

in determining the maximum rent the relevant authority shall deduct an amount determined in accordance with paragraph 2 of Schedule 1 to these Regulations in respect of meals.

(8)   This regulation is subject to regulations 13ZA (protection on death and 13 week protection) and 13ZB (change in reckonable rent).

(9)

In this regulation–

"claim-related rent" means the rent notified by the rent officer under paragraph 9(1) of Schedule 1 to the Rent Officers Order;

"local reference rent" means the rent determined by a rent officer under paragraph 4 of Schedule 1 to the Rent Officers Order.]

Modifications

Reg 13 was substituted by reg 6 Housing Benefit (Local Housing Allowance and Information Sharing) Amendment Regulations 2007 SI No.2868 as from 7 April 2008, save that for a person to whom reg 1(5) of those regulations applied (see p1231), the amendments came into force on the day on or after 7 April 2008 when the first of the events specified in reg 1(6) applied to her/him, or on 6 April 2009 if none had before that date.

A different version of reg 13 is substituted for some claimants entitled to HB on 1 January 1996. See Sch 3 paras 4 and 5(2) HB&CTB(CP) Regs on p1199.

Reg 13 applies as modified by Sch 3 para 8 HB&CTB(CP) Regs (see p1205) for some claimants entitled to HB on or before 5 October 1997.

Amendment

1.   Substituted by reg 6 of SI 2007 No 2868 as from 7.4.08 (or if reg 1(5) of that SI applies, on the day on or after 7.4.08 when the first of the events specified in reg 1(6) applies, or from 6.4.09 if none have before that date).

Definitions

"non-dependant" – see reg 3.
"Rent Officers Order – see reg 2(1).
"single room rent" – see reg 2(1).
"young individual" – see reg 2(1).
"young person" – see reg 2(1).

General Note

Reg 13 deals with the calculation of the claimant's "maximum rent" for HB purposes under the "local reference rent" scheme. The significance of the maximum rent is that the claimant's "eligible rent" cannot exceed it: reg 12C.

The maximum rent is determined from the rent officer's determinations. The rent officer's determinations are extremely difficult to attack in judicial review proceedings and cannot, by virtue of Sch 7 para 6(2)(c) CSPSSA 2000, be appealed to the First-tier Tribunal. For further discussion of challenges to rent officer's decisions and of the possible human rights issues involved, see reg 16 for redeterminations by a rent officer and the Rent Officers (Housing Benefit Functions) Order 1997 on p592.) Note that although there is no right of appeal to the First-tier Tribunal against a decision of the rent officer, the claimant can appeal the local authority's decision on HB entitlement and, as such, can challenge the factual basis upon which the rent officer decision was made – eg, the number of occupiers given to the rent officer by the local authority: *Bexley LB v LD(HB)* [2010] UKUT 79 (AAC) and *SK v South Hams DC (HB)* [2010] UKUT 129 (AAC).

Summary of the maximum rent calculation

One of the difficult aspects of reg 13 is the terminology applied to the various figures used to calculate maximum rent. The terms are summarised here, with cross-reference to other commentary. Not all the various terms will be relevant in every case.

Maximum rent is calculated as follows:

(1)   The authority applies for a rent officer determination under reg 14 (unless not required to do so in the circumstances specified in para (1)(b) – broadly where there are existing determinations it can use): reg 13(1).

(2)   The following rent determinations are made by the rent officer:

(a)   A significantly high rent (SHR) determination is made if the claimant's rent is significantly higher than a reasonable rent: Sch 1 para 1 of the Rent Officer (Housing Benefit Functions) Order 1997 or its Scottish equivalent, which are referred to collectively as the RO Orders in this commentary.

(b)   A size-related rent determination is made (SizeRR) under Sch 1 para 2 of the RO Orders if it is decided that the property exceeds the size criteria set out in Sch 2 of the RO Orders.

(c)   An exceptionally high rent determination is made (EHR) if the rent officer decides under Sch 1 para 3 of the RO Orders that it needs to be given.

(d)   The local reference rent (LRR) is calculated under Sch 1 para 4 of the RO Orders. The LRR is broadly the mid-point of reasonable market rents for comparable assured tenancies in the same area (called the "broad rental market area (local reference rent)").

(e)   The single room rent (SRR) is calculated under Sch 1 para 5 of the RO Orders. It is used in the calculation of the maximum rent of a "young individual" (broadly, single people under 25 but see the full definition in reg 2(1) and the commentary on p225). It is assessed on the basis of the mid-point of reasonable rents for comparable assured tenancies in the same area (called the "broad rental market area (local reference rent)") comprising a single room occupied exclusively, with a shared, toilet, bathroom, kitchen and living room and which does not include payments for board and attendance.

(3)   The lowest of the determinations in (1)(a)-(c) above, or if none of them are determined, the rent payable under the tenancy, is the claim-related rent (CRR): Sch 1 para 6 of the RO Orders. The rent officer notifies the authority of the CRR (and if an ineligible amount in respect of meals has been included) and if lower, the LRR or SRR.

(4)   Unless Sch 3 paras 4 and 5 HB&CTB(CP) Regs apply, maximum rent is calculated by the authority using the determinations notified in (2) above: reg 13(2)-(7). Maximum rent is the lowest of the CRR, the LRR, or if relevant the SRR unless the claimant has transitional protection, for which, see Sch 3 para 8 HB&CTB(CP) Regs (on p1221) and the commentary to para (3).

(5)   The authority decides whether the use of the maximum rent in calculating HB entitlement can be delayed: reg 13ZA.

The eligible rent is then calculated by the authority in accordance with reg 12C above.

Analysis

Paragraph (1): The general rule

Reg 13 applies where an authority has applied for a rent officer determination under reg 14. It also applies where it is not required to do so because an application was made in respect of a claim within the previous 52 weeks or where the dwelling is a hostel and a determination has been made within the previous 12 months in respect of a similar dwelling in that hostel and there has been no change of circumstances in relation to the similar dwelling. In both of these situations, there will already be rent officer determinations the authority can use. See the commentary to reg 14 on p327 for when an authority must apply to the rent officer. The maximum rent is then to be determined as set out in the paras that follow.

Once maximum rent is set, HB is calculated using this figure until the next time the authority is required to apply to the rent officer for a determination. This is usually annually: reg 14(1)(f) and (g). Note, however that where a claimant's rent liability is reduced to an amount lower than the maximum rent, maximum rent can be reduced: reg 13ZB.

Paragraphs (2) to (8): Calculation of maximum rent

These paras set out the bases on which the maximum rent is calculated. Generally, the maximum rent is the lowest of the CRR, the LRR, or in the case of a "young individual", the SRR. Note that a restriction can be delayed in some circumstances: reg 13ZA. Some changes in rent can be taken into account: reg 13ZB.

Paras (2) to (4). The effect of paras (2) and (3) is that unless para (5) applies, maximum rent is the lower of the CRR and the LRR. There is transitional protection for some claimants. A "50 per cent taper" is preserved in relation to certain categories of claimants (broadly, those continuously entitled to, and in receipt of, HB for the same property since 5 October 1997): see para 8 Sch 3 HB&CTB(CP) Regs on p1221. For protected claimants, para (3) as modified provides that the maximum rent is the LRR plus half the difference between the CRR and the LRR. In this case, the maximum rent cannot be more than twice the LRR: para (4).

For example, if the rent officer's CRR for the dwelling is £100 and the rent officer's LRR figure is £40, the maximum rent is £70 if the claimant has the transitional protection but only £40 if s/he does not have it.

Paras (5) and (6). Para (5) applies where the claimant is a "young individual" as defined in reg 2(1) and the rent officer has notified a SRR. The maximum rent is restricted to the SRR, or the CRR minus any payments included for meals if this is lower. Note that someone does not count as a young individual if her/his landlord is a registered housing association or s/he is under 22 and was in the care of, or under the supervision of, a local authority under specified provisions after aged 16, or was provided with accommodation by a local authority under s20 Children Act 1989: see sub-paras (a) to (f) of the definition. The effect of this provision is softened by para (6), which provides that para (5) is not applicable where the "pre-January 1996" scheme rules apply or where the claimant qualifies for a severe disability premium or has a non-dependent residing with her/him, for which see reg 3.

Paragraph (7): Deductions

This sets out the rules for deducting amounts for meals from the maximum rent, where an ineligible amount in respect of these has been included in the CRR or LRR. In a decision concerning the old form of the rules, in *Shepherd v Dundee CC* [2002] SLT 1427, CS(IH), the claimant asserted that where eligible rent had already been restricted to a sum less than the contractual rent, it was not open to the local authority to make a further deduction in respect of the cost of board. Unsurprisingly, the court rejected that submission (paras 14-15).

[¹ Protection on death and 13 week protection

13ZA–(1)　　In a case where the claimant occupies a dwelling which is the same as that occupied by him at the date of death of a linked person, the maximum rent shall be either–

(a)　the maximum rent which applied before the death occurred; or

(b)　in a case where there was no maximum rent, the reckonable rent due before the death occurred,

(c)　for a period of 12 months from the date of such a death.

(2)　　For the purposes of paragraph (1), a claimant shall be treated as occupying the dwelling if paragraph (13) of regulation 7 (circumstances in which a person is or is not to be treated as occupying a dwelling as his home) is satisfied and for that purpose sub-paragraph (b) of that paragraph of that regulation shall be treated as if it were omitted.

(3)　　Subject to paragraph (4), where the relevant authority is satisfied that the claimant or a linked person was able to meet the financial commitments for his dwelling when they were entered into, there shall be no maximum rent during the first 13 weeks of the claimant's award of housing benefit.

(4)　　Paragraph (3) shall not apply where a claimant or the claimant's partner was previously entitled to benefit in respect of an award of housing benefit which fell wholly or partly less than 52 weeks before the commencement of the claimant's current award of housing benefit.]

Modifications

A different version of reg 13ZA is substituted for some claimants living in exempt accommodation or entitled to HB on 1 January 1996. It concerns restrictions on rent increases, not protection on death or 13 week protection. See Sch 3 paras 4 and 5(3) HB&CTB(CP) Regs on p1198.

Amendment

1.　　Inserted by reg 6 of SI 2007 No 2868 as from 7.4.08 (or if reg 1(5) of that SI applies, on the day on or after 7.4.08 when the first of the events specified in reg 1(6) applies, or from 6.4.09 if none have before that date).

Definitions

"child" – see reg 2(1).
"claimant" – see reg 2(1).
"dwelling" – see reg 2(4) and s137(1) SSCBA.
"linked person" – see reg 2(1).
"maximum rent" – see reg 13
"partner" – see reg 2(1).
"reckonable rent" – see reg 2(1).

Analysis

Delay in application of the maximum rent

Reg 13ZA provides for limited protection for two classes of claimants.

Paras (1) and (2): Protection on death. Para (1) provides a degree of protection for the recently bereaved. If a claimant is continuing to occupy a home which s/he occupied at the time a "linked person" died, the maximum rent that applied at the date of death continues to apply for 12 months from the date of death. In cases where there was no maximum rent in force, the maximum rent is the "reckonable rent". Again, this protection lasts for 12 months from the date of death. "Reckonable rent" means the payments a person is liable to make in respect of the dwelling s/he occupies as her/his home and which are eligible (or but for reg 13 would be eligible) for HB: reg 2(1).

A "linked person" for these purposes is a member of the claimant's family (defined in s137(1) SSCBA), a partner in a polygamous marriage or a child or young person for whom s/he or a partner is responsible and who lives in the same household, or a relative of the claimant or her/his partner who occupies the same dwelling without a separate right to do so: reg 2(1). As to the last of these categories, "relative" is also defined in reg 2(1).

The deceased person need not have been residing with the claimant, provided only that s/he occupied the same dwelling. Oddly, reg 3(4) specifies when a person "resides with" another for the purposes of the definition of "linked person", but the term used here is "occupies the same dwelling ... whether or not they reside with him". In this context, "occupies the same dwelling" arguably means someone living within the same building, provided that the living units of the claimant and the deceased are not completely self-contained. It might cover those who were sharing only a toilet, or some similar part of the accommodation. The relative should not have had a separate right of occupation. If the relative had her/his own tenancy from a landlord, the claimant cannot therefore take advantage of this provision. However, if the claimant and the relative were joint tenants, it could be argued that the relative's right of occupation was not "separate" because it was held jointly with the claimant. By para (2), "occupation" of a home for the purposes of para (1) can include deemed occupation under reg 7(13), that is, where someone is treated as occupying a dwelling for up to 13 weeks while temporarily absent from it. The claimant need not, however, comply with sub-para (b) of that regulation, so it does not matter if the home was let or sublet.

Paras (3) and (4): 13 week protection. Para (3) postpones the application of the maximum rent during the first 13 weeks of an HB award if the claimant or a "linked person" (see above) was able to meet the financial commitments for the dwelling (which will include things like bills as well as the rent) at the time they were taken on. By para (4), the protection in para (3) does not apply where the claimant or her/his partner has been entitled to HB at some time within the 52 weeks prior to the commencement of the claimant's current HB award.

[¹ Change in reckonable rent

13ZB.–(1)   In a case where–
(a)   the authority has determined a maximum rent under regulation 13 or 13ZA; and
(b)   during the period for which that maximum rent applies the reckonable rent in respect of the dwelling by reference to which that maximum rent was determined is reduced to a sum which is less than that maximum rent,
the maximum rent shall be reduced to an amount equal to the reduced reckonable rent.
(2)   This paragraph applies in a case where–
(a)   a rent officer has made a determination in exercise of the Housing Act functions pursuant to an application by an authority under regulation 14(1)(e) (pre-tenancy determination);
(b)   subsequent to that determination the reckonable rent for that dwelling is changed; and
(c)   a maximum rent is to be determined in relation to a claim for housing benefit by a claimant.
(3)   In a case to which paragraph (2) applies, where the reckonable rent is reduced to a figure below the figure that would have been the maximum rent if the reckonable rent had not changed, the maximum rent shall be the reckonable rent as so reduced.
(4)   In any other case to which paragraph (2) applies, the authority shall treat the reckonable rent to be that applicable to the determination by the rent officer referred to in paragraph (2)(a).]

Amendment
1.   Inserted by reg 6 of SI 2007 No 2868 as from 7.4.08 (or if reg 1(5) of that SI applies, on the day on or after 7.4.08 when the first of the events specified in reg 1(6) applies, or from 6.4.09 if none have before that date).

Definitions
"claimant" – see reg 2(1).
"dwelling" – see reg 2(4) and s137(1) SSCBA.
"maximum rent" – see reg 13.
"reckonable rent" – see reg 2(1).

Analysis
Reg 13ZB deals with the effect on the maximum rent of changes in the claimant's "reckonable rent" during an award of HB. "Reckonable rent" means the payments a person is liable to make in respect of the dwelling s/he occupies as her/his home and which are eligible (or but for reg 13 would be eligible) for HB: reg 2(1). Generally the maximum rent is only changed when the local authority is required to apply to the rent officer for a determination, usually annually, but under para (1), where the claimant's reckonable rent reduces during the award to a figure below the maximum rent figure determined by the authority under either reg 13 or reg 13ZA, the maximum rent is set to an amount equal to the new lower reckonable rent figure.

Para (2) deals with the situation where a maximum rent is to be determined after a claimant has obtained a pre-tenancy determination under reg 14(1)(e) and the reckonable rent is subsequently changed. If the reckonable rent is lower than the maximum rent would have been had the reckonable rent not changed, the maximum rent is the reckonable rent: para (3). In any other case (ie, where the reckonable rent is now higher than the maximum rent would have been), the authority must treat the reckonable rent to be that determined by the rent officer in the application for the pre-tenancy determination.

[¹ When a maximum rent (LHA) is to be determined

13C.–(1)   A relevant authority shall determine a maximum rent (LHA) in accordance with regulation 13D (determination of a maximum rent (LHA)) in any case where paragraphs (2) or (3) apply.

(2)   This paragraph applies where a relevant authority has received–

(a)   a claim on which a rent allowance may be awarded, where the date of claim falls on or after 7th April 2008;

(b)   relevant information regarding a claim on which a rent allowance may be awarded, where the date of claim falls on or after 7th April 2008;

(c)   in relation to an award of housing benefit where the eligible rent was determined without reference to regulation 13A or 13D, a notification of a change of dwelling (as defined in regulation 2) where the change occurs on or after 7th April 2008; or

(d)   in relation to an award of housing benefit where a maximum rent (LHA) was determined in accordance with regulation 13D–

   (i)   notification of a change of a kind which affects the category of dwelling applicable to the claim;

   (ii)   notification of the death of a linked person, where the notification does not fall within head (i); or

   (iii)   notification of a change of dwelling.

(3)   This paragraph applies on the anniversary of the LHA date.

(4)   Where the LHA date is 29th February, the anniversary of the LHA date shall be 28th February.

(5)   This regulation does not apply in a case where–

[³ (a)   the landlord is–

   (i)   a registered social landlord,

   (ii)   a non-profit registered provider of social housing, or

   (iii)   in relation to a dwelling which is social housing (within the meaning of sections 68 to 77 of the Housing and Regeneration Act 2008), a profit-making registered provider of social housing;]

(b)   paragraph 4(1)(b) of Schedule 3 to the Consequential Provisions Regulations (savings provision) applies;

(c)   the tenancy is an excluded tenancy of a type [² mentioned in any of paragraphs 4 to 11] of Schedule 2;

(d)   the claim or award relates to–

   (i)   periodical payments of kind falling within regulation 12(1) (rent) which a person is liable to make in relation to a houseboat, caravan or mobile home which he occupies as his home; or

   (ii)   rent payable in relation to a hostel; or

(e)   rent under the tenancy is attributable to board and attendance, and–

   (i)   the relevant authority has made an application to the rent officer in accordance with regulation 13D(10) (board and attendance determination), regulation 15 (applications to the rent officer for determinations) or regulation 17 (substitute determinations or substitute redeterminations); and

   (ii)   the rent officer has determined that a substantial part of the rent under the tenancy is fairly attributable to board and attendance and has notified the relevant authority of this in accordance with article 4C, 4D or 4E of the Rent Officers Order.

(6)   In this regulation–

"the LHA date" means the date by reference to which the local housing allowance used to determine the maximum rent (LHA) was identified;

"registered social landlord" has the same meaning as in Part 1 of the Housing Act 1996 or, in Scotland, sections 57 and 59 of the Housing (Scotland) Act 2001.]

Modifications

Reg 13C is modified by Sch 10 para 7 (see p586). This applies only to former Pathfinder Authorities who administered the pilot local housing allowance scheme.

Amendments

1.   Inserted by reg 7 of SI 2007 No 2868 as from 7.4.08 (or if reg 1(5) of that SI applies, on the day on or after 7.4.08 when the first of the events specified in reg 1(6) applies, or from 6.4.09 if none have before that date).

2.   Amended by reg 4(4)(a) of SI 2008 No 586 as from 7.4.08.

3.   Substituted by Art 4 and Sch 1 para 52 of SI 2010 No 671 as from 1.4.10.

Definitions

"change of dwelling" – see reg 2(1).
"hostel" – see reg 2(1).
"the LHA date" – see reg 13C(6).
"linked person" – see reg 2(1).
"relevant information" – see reg 2(1).
"rent allowance" – see s134(1B) SSAA 1992.

General Note

The starting point for deciding whether maximum rent (LHA) is to be calculated under reg 13D (the "LHA" rules), and hence eligible rent under reg 12D, is reg 13C. Reg 13C prescribes the circumstances in which this must be done, and those where the "LHA" rules do not apply.

Unless any of the circumstances in para (5) apply, broadly reg 13C will apply if, on or after 7 April 2008, a claim for HB is made or a claimant with an award of HB moves to a new home, and in both cases, HB would be paid as a rent allowance because the claimant lives in private rented accommodation. This can also include shared ownership tenancies with a private landlord: see the commentary to para (5)(c).

Claimants whose HB was assessed under the "local reference rent" rules before 7 April 2008, are effectively provided with transitional protection until there is a new claim (ie, following a break in claim) or the claimant moves. See p327 for a discussion of the issues.

Analysis

Paragraphs (2) to (4): When maximum rent (LHA) is to be determined under reg 13D

Paras (2) and (3) set out the circumstances in which a maximum rent (LHA) must be determined under reg 13D, unless excepted by para (5).

Para (2)(a) and (b): Claims. These sub-paras apply where a claim for HB is received or an authority has received "relevant information" regarding a claim on which a rent allowance may be awarded. In both cases, the date of claim must fall on or after 7 April 2008. Relevant information is defined in reg 2(1) as "information or evidence forwarded to the authority by an appropriate DWP office regarding a claim on which rent allowance may be awarded, which completes the transfer of all information or evidence held by the appropriate DWP office relating to that claim" – eg, where the claim for HB has been made with a claim to the DWP for IS, JSA, ESA or PC.

Para (2)(c): Change of dwelling to one where the "local housing allowance" rules apply. Sub-para (c) applies where the authority has received notification of a change of dwelling during an award of HB where eligible rent was determined otherwise than by reference to reg 13D or the local housing allowance pilot rules that applied in former Pathfinder areas. By the definition of "change of dwelling" in reg 2(1), the change must be to a dwelling in respect of which the authority may make a rent allowance. See sub-para (d)(iii) where there is a change of dwelling and eligible rent was already determined by reference to reg 13D.

Para (2)(d): Other changes. Sub-para (d) only applies where there is an award of HB made on the basis of a maximum rent (LHA) and one of the circumstances in sub-subparas (i) to (iii) occurs. These are self-explanatory.

Paras (3) and (4). Para (3) ensures that unless any of the circumstances in para (2) apply, maximum rent (LHA) is based on the local housing allowance (see the summary on p322) that is appropriate when the claim is assessed and HB is paid on this basis for at least 12 months. On the anniversary of "the LHA date" (defined in para (6)), the authority is required to determine a new maximum rent (LHA) under reg 13D. Para (4) is needed where the LHA date falls on 29 February, during a leap year.

Paragraph (5): The exceptions

Para (5) sets out a number of exceptions. Note that some of these are also excluded from other rent restriction schemes.

(1)   The landlord is a registered social landlord (since 1 April 2010, this applies in Wales and Scotland only) or a non-profit or a profit making registered provider of social housing (in England only): sub-para (a). Lettings by profit-making registered providers of social housing are only excepted if the claimant's dwelling is "social housing" within the meaning of ss68 to 77 Housing and Regeneration Act 2008, that is, low cost rental accommodation (ie, accommodation that is available to rent at below the market rate) and low cost ownership accommodation (ie, accommodation occupied or made available to occupy in accordance with shared ownership or equity percentage arrangements or shared ownership trusts) that is available to people whose needs are not adequately served by the commercial housing market.

A "registered provider of social housing" is is a person or body registered by the the Office for Tenants and Social Landlords (the Regulator of Social Housing). "Registered social landlord" is defined in para (6). Note that lettings by the landlords listed in sub-para (a) may also be excluded from the "local reference rent" scheme if they come within the definition of a registered housing association (in reg 2(1): reg 14(2)(b) and Sch 2 para 3(1)(a) and (1A).

(2)   The claimant occupies "exempt accommodation" as defined in Sch 3 para 4(10) HB&CTB(CP) Regs: sub-para (b) and Sch 3 para 4(1)(b) HB&CTB(CP) Regs. Broadly, this is supported accommodation. Note that such lettings are also excluded from the "local reference rent" scheme, but may be affected by the "pre-January 1996" rules found in Sch 3 paras 4 and 5 HB&CTB(CP) Regs.

Note that this exception does not cover the "exempt claimants" set out in Sch 3 para 4(1)(a) HB&CTB(CP) Regs. Such claimants lose their transitional protection under the "pre-January 1996" rules in any of the circumstances of reg 13C(2)(a) to (c). See the commentary to Sch 3 para 4 HB&CTB(CP) Regs on p1200.

(3)   The tenancy is an "excluded tenacy" under Sch 2 paras 4 to 11 HB Regs: sub-para (c). See the commentary to those provisions for details. Tenancies excluded under Sch 2 para 3 are not covered, but may come within the exception for registered social landlords and providers of social housing above. Tenancies excluded under Sch 2 para 12 (shared ownership tenancies) are not covered, but may come within other exceptions in reg 13C(5) – eg, where the landlord is a registered social landlord or provider of social housing. Note that tenancies excluded under Sch 2 paras 4 to 10 and 12 are also excluded from the "local reference rent" scheme, and that those excluded under Sch 2 para 11 generally are.

(4)   Periodical payments are made in relation to a houseboat, caravan or mobile home which is occupied as a home, or rent is payable in relation to a hostel: sub-para (d). For a discussion of the meaning of "periodical payments", see the commentary to reg 12(1).

(5)   Rent is attributable to board and attendance: sub-para (e). The authority must have made an application to the rent officer for a board and attendance determination under the provisions cited and the rent officer must have determined that a substantial part of the rent is "fairly attributable" to board and attendance. If so, the claimant's eligible rent may still be restricted under regs 12C and 13. See reg 14(1).

[¹ Determination of a maximum rent (LHA)

13D.–(1)   Subject to paragraph (3) to (11), the maximum rent (LHA) shall be the local housing allowance determined by the rent officer by virtue of article 4B(2A) or (4) of the Rent Officers Order which is applicable to–

(a)   the broad rental market area in which the dwelling to which the claim or award of housing benefit relates is situated at the relevant date; and

(b)   the category of dwelling which applies at the relevant date in accordance with paragraph (2).

(2)   The category of dwelling which applies is–

(a)   the category specified in paragraph 1(1)(a) of Schedule 3B to the Rent Officers Order (onebedroom shared accommodation) where–

(i)   the claimant is a young individual who has no non-dependant residing with him and to whom paragraph 14 of Schedule 3 (severe disability premium) does not apply; or

(ii)   paragraph (b) does not apply because neither sub-paragraph (b)(i) nor (ii) are satisfied in the claimant's case and neither the claimant nor his partner (where he has one) is a person to whom paragraph 14 of Schedule 3 (severe disability premium) applies, or to whom the circumstances in any of paragraphs (b) to (f) of the definition of young individual applies (certain care leavers);

(b)   except where paragraph (a)(i) applies, the category specified in paragraph 1(1)(b) of Schedule 3B to the Rent Officers Order (one bedroom self-contained

accommodation) where that applies in the claimant's case at the relevant date in accordance with the size criteria [² as set out in paragraph (3)] and–
(i)   the claimant (together with his partner where he has one) has the exclusive use of two or more rooms; or
(ii)   the claimant (together with his partner where he has one) has the exclusive use of one room, a bathroom and toilet and a kitchen or facilities for cooking,
and in this sub-paragraph "room" means a bedroom or room suitable for living in except for a room which the claimant shares with any person other than a member of his household, a non-dependant of his, or a person who pays rent to him or his partner;
(c)   in any other case, the category which corresponds with the number of bedrooms to which the claimant is entitled in accordance with paragraph (3) [³ to a maximum of five bedrooms].

(3)   The claimant shall be entitled to one bedroom for each of the following categories of occupier (and each occupier shall come within the first category only which applies to him)–
(a)   a couple (within the meaning of Part 7 of the Act);
(b)   a person who is not a child;
(c)   two children of the same sex;
(d)   two children who are less than 10 years old;
(e)   a child.
(4)   The relevant authority shall determine–
(a)   the cap rent (in accordance with the definition in paragraph (12)); and
(b)   whether the cap rent exceeds the applicable local housing allowance.
(5)   Where the applicable local housing allowance exceeds the cap rent, for the purpose of determining the appropriate maximum housing benefit, the amount of the claimant's liability shall be the amount of the applicable local housing allowance.
(6)   Where paragraph (5) applies, the maximum rent (LHA) shall be the lower of–
(a)   the applicable local housing allowance; or
(b)   the amount equal to the cap rent determined in accordance with paragraph (4)(a) plus £15.
[³ (7)]
(8)   Subject to paragraph (9), where–
(a)   the relevant authority receives a request from a person stating that–
(i)   he is contemplating occupying as his home a dwelling within the area of the relevant authority which contains a specified number of bedrooms, exceeding five, and
(ii)   that if he does so, he is likely to claim housing benefit; and
(b)   no local housing allowance determination is in effect for a broad rental market area falling within, in whole or in part, the area of the relevant authority for the category of dwelling containing the number of bedrooms specified in the request,
the relevant authority shall apply to the rent officer for local housing allowance determinations for each broad rental market area falling within its area, in whole or in part, for the category of dwelling containing the number of bedrooms specified in the request, and in this sub-paragraph "bedroom" means has the meaning specified in paragraph 1(2) of Schedule 3B to the Rent Officers Order.
(9)   The request must–
(a)   be made on a form approved by the relevant authority for the purpose of making a request under paragraph (8);
(b)   be properly completed; and
(c)   contain the following matters–
(i)   the signature of the prospective occupier;
(ii)   the signature of the person to whom the prospective occupier would incur liability to make such payments;
(iii)   a statement that the person in paragraph (ii) agrees to the application being made for that determination; and

      (iv)   an indication that the prospective occupier is contemplating occupying the dwelling as his home and that if he does so, he is likely to claim housing benefit.

(10)   The relevant authority shall apply to the rent officer for a board and attendance determination to be made in accordance with article 4C of the Rent Officers Order where–

    (a)   the relevant authority is required to determine a maximum rent (LHA) by virtue of regulation 13C; and

    (b)   part of the rent under the tenancy appears to the relevant authority to be likely to be attributable to board and attendance.

(11)   Where an application to a rent officer is required in accordance with paragraph (10) it shall be made within the same period following the day on which the relevant authority becomes obliged to determine a maximum rent (LHA) by virtue of regulation 13C as would be required if the application were to be made under regulation 14(1).

(12)   In this regulation–

"cap rent" means the aggregate of such payments specified in regulation 12(1) (rent) which the claimant is liable to pay, or is treated as liable to pay by virtue of regulation 8 (circumstances in which a person is treated as liable to make payments in respect of a dwelling), subject to regulation 12B(3) (mixed use accommodation), (4) (more than one person liable to make payments) and (6) (discretion in relation to eligible rent);

"occupiers" means the persons whom the relevant authority is satisfied occupy as their home the dwelling to which the claim or award relates except for any joint tenant who is not a member of the claimant's household;

"relevant date" means, as the case may require–

    (a)   the date of the claim to which the claim or relevant information referred to in regulation 13C(2)(a) or (b) relates;

    (b)   the date of the change of dwelling, change which affects the category of dwelling, or date of death, to which a notification referred to in regulation 13C(2)(c) or (d) relates; or

    (c)   the date on which the anniversary of the LHA date referred to in regulation 13C(3) falls.

"tenancy" includes

    (a)   in Scotland, any other right of occupancy; and

    (b)   in any other case, a licence to occupy premises,

and reference to a tenant, landlord or any other expression appropriate to a tenancy shall be construed accordingly.]

Modifications

Reg 13D is modified by Sch 10 para 8 (see p586). This applies only to former Pathfinder Authorities who administered the pilot local housing allowance scheme.

Amendments

1.   Inserted by reg 7 of SI 2007 No 2868 as from 7.4.08 (or if reg 1(5) of that SI applies, on the day on or after 7.4.08 when the first of the events specified in reg 1(6) applies, or from 6.4.09 if none have before that date).

2.   Amended by reg 4(4)(b) of SI 2008 No 586 as from 7.4.08.

3.   Amended by reg 2(3) of SI 2009 No 614 as from 6.4.09.

Definitions

"board and attendance determination" – see eg Art 2(1) of the relevant Rent Officer Order.

"broad rental market area" – see reg 2(1).

"child" – see reg 2(1).

"claimant" – see reg 2(1).

"the LHA date" – see reg 13C(6)

"local housing allowance" – see reg 2(1).

"non-dependant" – see reg 3

"partner" – see reg 2(1).

"rent allowance" – see s134(1B) SSAA 1992.

"young individual" – see reg 2(1).

General Note

Reg 13D deals with the calculation of the claimant's "maximum rent (LHA)" for HB purposes under the "LHA" scheme. The significance of the maximum rent (LHA) is that the claimant's "eligible rent" generally cannot exceed it: reg 12D. Reg 13D applies in the circumstances set out in reg 13C.

The DWP guidance to local authorities, the *Housing Benefit Local Housing Allowance Guidance Manual*, is available at www.dwp.gov.uk/docs/lha-guidance-manual.pdf

Summary of the scheme

It is important to remember that the "LHA" is not a new or different form of HB. Strictly speaking, it is a determination made by the rent officer upon which the calculation of HB for a relevant claimant is based. As Commissioner Williams points out in *CH 2986/2005*, the HB Regs apply in full, and the administrative provisions applying to decision making and appeals are the same as those applying to HB generally. Although the decision dealt with the pilot scheme rules in Pathfinder areas, the same would apply under the national scheme rules.

The scheme includes the following:

(1)   The "maximum rent (LHA)" is the local housing allowance that is appropriate for the claimant, or if lower, her/his "cap rent" plus £15: reg 13D(1), (5) and (6). Note: the Government has said it intends to remove the £15 excess from April 2011.

(2)   The "LHA" that is appropriate for a particular claimant depends on the category of dwelling that applies – ie, the number of bedrooms allowed under the size criteria (up to a maximum of five) and whether the claimant lives in shared accommodation: reg 13D(2) and (3). Note: the Government has indicated that the number of bedrooms allowed under the size criteria will be restricted to a maximum of four from April 2011. However, also from April 2011, HB claimants with a disability and a non-resident carer will be entitled to extra funding for an extra bedroom.

(3)   For those only allowed one bedroom under the size criteria who live in shared accommodation and for a "young individual" (defined in reg 2(1), broadly single claimants under 25), the local housing allowance is based on accommodation in which the tenant has exclusive use of one bedroom only and all or some of the other facilities are shared. This does not apply if the claimant (or her/his partner) qualifies for a severe disability premium or has a non-dependant living with her/him.

(4)   Local housing allowances for each size category of properties up to five bedrooms are set by the rent officer monthly and are based on the median of local market rents for assured tenancies in a "broad rental market area": reg 13D(1) HB Regs and Art 4B(2A) and (4) of the RO Orders. Note: the Government has indicated that from April 2011, LHA rates will be capped at £250 a week for a one-bedroom property, £290 a week for a two-bedroom property, £340 a week for a three-bedroom property and £400 a week for a four- or more bedroom property. It also says that from October 2011, LHA rates will be set at the 30th percentile of local rents and from 2013/2014, LHA rates will be uprated in line with the Consumer Price Index.

(5)   Local housing allowances are made public: reg 13E. These are available on the Valuation Office Agency website at https://lha-direct.voa.gov.uk/Secure/Default.aspx.

(6)   Maximum rent (LHA) is based on the local housing allowance that is appropriate when the claim is assessed, and this generally lasts for a year even if the allowance changes. The local authority reassesses claims annually, using the allowance that is then appropriate for the property. However, claims can be reassessed earlier if there are certain changes in circumstances and this means a different allowance is appropriate – eg, a change in the size of the household or a change in the category of dwelling that applies such as where a single claimant turns 25: regs 12D(2) and 13C(2) to (4) and (6).

(7)   If the appropriate local housing allowance for a claimant should be reduced, because of the death of a member of the claimant's family or a relative of the claimant or her/his partner who occupies the same dwelling, the decrease in "eligible rent" can be delayed for 12 months: reg 12D(3), (4), (7) and (8).

(8)   A restriction of a claimant's "eligible rent" can be delayed for 13 weeks if the claimant or a member of her/his family or a relative of the claimant or her/his partner who occupies the same dwelling could meet the costs of the dwelling when these were taken on: reg 12D(5) to (8).

(9)   If the amount of rent the claimant is liable to pay to her/his landlord is lower than her/his HB entitlement the claimant can keep the difference. The extra HB does not affect entitlement to other benefits.

(10)   In most cases, HB is paid to the claimant, not to the landlord (or agent). However, direct payments to landlords are still possible in some situations: regs 95 and 96. Note that in order to transfer payment of HB to a tenant from a landlord, a supersession decision is needed. The landlord has a right of appeal against the decision and the tenant is a party to any such appeal as a "person affected": *CH 2986/2005*.

Analysis

Paragraph (1): The general rule

Where reg 13C applies, maximum rent (LHA) is to be determined as set out in reg 13D. Maximum rent (LHA) is the local housing allowance determined by the rent officer that, at the "relevant date", is applicable to the "broad rental market area" in which the dwelling the claimant occupies is situated, and the category of dwelling that applies to the claimant. Note however the "cap" that can apply by virtue of paras (5) and (6) below. The "relevant date" is either the date of claim, the date of any of the changes specified in reg 13C(2)(c) or (d) (change of dwelling, etc) or the anniversary of the "LHA date" – ie, the date by reference to which a local housing allowance was last used to determine maximum rent (LHA): para (12).

A broad rental market area is defined as an area within which a person could reasonably be expected to live having regard to facilities and services for the purposes of health, education, recreation, personal banking and shopping and the travel distance by public and private transport. It must contain a variety of types of residential accommodation and types of lettings, and have sufficient private rented housing to ensure that the local housing allowance for the category of dwelling in the area is representative of the rents that a landlord might reasonably be expected to obtain in that area: Sch 3B para 4 of the RO Orders.

Once maximum rent (LHA) is set, HB is calculated on the basis of this until the next time the authority is required to redetermine maxuimum rent (LHA). This is usually annually: reg 12D(b)(ii) and reg 13C(3) and (4).

Paragraphs (2) and (3): The category of dwelling

Paras (2) and (3) set out the category of dwelling that applies in any particular case. There are three possibilities:

Para (2)(a): One-bedroom shared accommodation. This category applies if the claimant is a "young individual" (broadly single claimants under 25) who does not have any non-dependants residing with her/him (for which see reg 3), whether or not the claimant lives in shared accommodation. It also applies if the claimant (and her/his partner if any) is only allowed one bedroom under the size criteria and neither sub-paras (b)(i) or (ii) are satisfied – ie, s/he lives in shared accommodation. For the size criteria, see para (3).

This category does not apply if the claimant (or her/his partner) qualifies for a severe disability premium (for which see Sch 3 para 14). It also does not apply if the claimant (or her/his partner) is under 22 and was in the care of, or under the supervision of, a local authority under specified provisions after aged 16, or was provided with accommodation by a local authority under s20 Children Act 1989: see sub-paras (b) to (f) of the definition of "young individual" in reg 2(1). In both cases, the category in (2)(b) instead applies (one-bedroom self-contained accommodation), even if the claimant lives in shared accommodation.

Note that someone is not a "young individual" if her/his landlord is a registered housing association (defined in reg 2(1)), but such claimants are excepted from the "LHA" rules in any event: reg 13C(5)(a).

Para (2)(b): One-bedroom self-contained accommodation. Unless para (2)(a)(i) above applies, this category applies if the claimant is only allowed one bedroom under the size criteria – eg, s/he is a single claimant or a member of a couple without children and has no non-dependants residing with her/him. In addition, the claimant must not be living in shared accommodation – ie, s/he (and her/his partner) must have the exclusive use of at least two rooms or the exclusive use of one room, a bathroom and toilet and a kitchen or facilities for cooking. "Room" here means a bedroom or room suitable for living in, other than one the claimant shares with a member of her/his household, a non-dependant or someone who pays rent to the claimant or her/his partner.

Para (2)(c): Other cases. In any other case, the category that applies is that which corresponds with the number of bedrooms the claimant is entitled to under the size criteria in para (3), up to a maximum of five bedrooms. This category therefore applies, for example, if the claimant is a lone parent or a couple with children, or if the claimant has any non-dependants living with her/him.

Note: the five-bedroom limit has only existed since 6 April 2009. The amended rules apply to new claims from that date. Those with an award of HB based on a category of dwelling of more than five bedrooms had their claims reviewed at the anniversary of the claim. A reduction could be delayed for up to 26 weeks: reg 12L.

Para (3): The size criteria. Under the size criteria, the claimant is allowed one bedroom for each of the categories of occupier specified in sub-paras (a) to (e). "Bedroom" is not here defined. A person who is not a child is someone aged 16 or over: see the definition of "child" in reg 2(1). "Occupiers" is defined in para (12) as people who the authority is satisfied occupy the dwelling to which the claim or award relates as a home, other than a joint tenant who is not a member of the claimant's household. This therefore includes not only those who count as members of the claimant's family for benefit purposes (for which see s137(1) SSCBA), but also those who are not part of the family – eg, non-dependants or live-in carers. Prior to 1 November 2010, it could also include foster children: *Wirral MBC v AH and SSWP (HB)* [2010] UKUT 208 (AAC). This was because, although reg 21(3) prevented such children from counting as a member of claimant's household (and hence as a member of her/his family), it did not prevent the foster children from counting as occupying the claimant's dwelling. However, reg 21(3) was amended with effect from 1 November 2010 (see p335).

For a discussion of when a person might count as occupying a dwelling as a home, see reg 7 on p233.

Paragraphs (1) and (4) to (6): Calculation of maximum rent (LHA)

Under para (4), the authority is required to determine a "cap rent" and also whether this exceeds the local housing allowance that applies to the claimant. Maximum rent (LHA) is then the local housing allowance that applies, or if lower, the cap rent plus £15: paras (1) and (6). Note that the Government said it intends to remove the £15 excess from April 2011.

Cap rent is defined in para (12). It is the payments in reg 12(1) that the claimant is liable to pay (or treated as liable to pay – see reg 8). Where the accommodation occupied by the claimant is not solely residential accommodation, only that portion of the payments referable to the residential element can form part of the cap rent: reg 12(B)(3). Where the claimant is jointly liable to make the payments, an apportionment must be made: reg 12B(4).

The definition is also said to be subject to reg 12B(6) which purports to give the authority a general discretion to reduce the cap rent. Note, however, the wording of reg 12B(6), which states it only applies in cases where eligible rent, as determined in accordance with the preceding paragraphs of reg 12B, is greater than it is reasonable to meet by way of HB. Under the LHA scheme, eligible rent is set by reg 12D, so it may be arguable that there is no general discretion to decrease the cap rent, ie that the amount of the cap rent cannot be subject to reg 12B(6).

If the amount of the cap rent *is* subject to reg 12B(6), an authority will need to be cautious in using its discretion to decrease it. If the cap rent is relevant in the formula for calculating maximum rent (LHA) under reg 13D, this is because it is up to £15 lower than the appropriate LHA rate.

Para (5) is necessary to ensure that where a claimant's liability for rent is lower than the local housing allowance that applies, her/his HB can nevertheless be calculated on a higher figure, and the claimant's HB can include the amount by which HB exceeds her/his liability (if any).

Examples

(1)   The claimant is a joint tenant of a private flat with two friends. The rent for the flat is £150 a week. The local housing allowance that applies is that for one-bedroom shared accommodation, determined to be £75 by the rent officer. The cap rent is £50 (£150 divided by 3). Maximum rent (LHA) is therefore the cap rent plus £15 (£50 plus £15 = £65) as this figure is lower than the local housing allowance. This is also the "eligible rent": reg 12D(2)(a) and as the claimant does not have non-dependants residing with her/him, it is also the "maximum housing benefit" (reg 70). HB is then calculated using this figure: £65.

(2)   The claimant and her partner are joint tenants of a three-bedroom house. They live there with their daughter, aged 10. The rent for the house is £170 a week. The local housing allowance that applies is that for a two-bedroom dwelling, determined to be £135 by the rent officer. The cap rent is £170. Maximum rent (LHA) is therefore £135, the local housing allowance, because this is lower than the cap rent plus £15. This is also the "eligible rent": reg 12D(2)(a) and as the claimant does not have non-dependants residing with her, it is also the "maximum housing benefit" (reg 70). HB is then calculated using this figure: £135.

Paragraph (8): Where no local housing allowance has been set

Prospective occupiers. Under para (8), a prospective occupier of a dwelling with more than five bedrooms can ask the authority to apply to the rent officer for a local housing allowance determination, where no local housing allowance has been set for the relevant size of dwelling. This is meant to inform prospective tenants and landlords of the likely amount of rent that HB will meet for the property. The determination is not dependent on an actual HB claim being made at the time of application for the request for a local housing allowance, but a claim for HB must be likely. It is unclear when this provision will now be needed given that it can only be used where the home the applicant proposes to occupy is one of more than five bedrooms and the largest category of dwelling that can now apply is five-bedroom accommodation: see para (2)(c). The prospective occupier must submit her/his request to the authority on a properly completed form approved by the relevant authority which includes matters specified in para (9)(c), including the signatures of the prospective occupier and the landlord or letting agent.

Paragraphs (10) and (11): Board and attendance determinations

Paras (10) and (11) require the authority to apply to the rent officer for a board and attendance determination, that is, a determination on whether or not a substantial part of the rent under the tenancy is fairly attributable to board and attendance. If this is the case, the "local housing allowance" rules will not apply: reg 13C(5)(e). Instead, the "local reference rent" rules may apply (see regs 13 and 14). Note that where the rent officer decides that a substantial part of the rent under the tenancy is fairly attributable to board and attendance, s/he must treat the application for a determination as one made under reg 14(1): see, for example, Art 4C Rent Officers (Housing Benefit Functions) Order 1997 on p598.

[¹ Publication of local housing allowances

13E.–(1)   A relevant authority shall take such steps as appear to it to be appropriate for the purpose of securing that information in relation to broad rental market areas falling in whole or in part within its area, and local housing allowances applicable to such broad rental market areas, is brought to the attention of persons who may be entitled to housing benefit from the authority.

Amendment

1.   Inserted by reg 7 of SI 2007 No 2868 as from 7.4.08 (or if reg 1(5) of that SI applies, on the day on or after 7.4.08 when the first of the events specified in reg 1(6) applies, or from 6.4.09 if none have before that date).

[¹ Requirement to refer to rent officers

14.–(1)   Subject to the following provisions of this regulation, a relevant authority shall apply to a rent officer for a determination to be made in pursuance of the Housing Act functions where–

(a)   it has received a claim on which rent allowance may be awarded and any of the circumstances specified in regulation 13C(5)(a) to (e) (rent allowance cases for which a maximum rent (standard local rent) is not to be determined) apply;

(b)   it has received relevant information regarding a claim on which rent allowance may be awarded and any of the circumstances specified in regulation 13C(5)(a) to (e) apply;

(c)   it has received a notification of a change relating to a rent allowance and a maximum rent (LHA) does not fall to be determined under regulation 13C (determination of a maximum rent (LHA));

(d)   it has received a notification of a change of dwelling and any of the circumstances specified in regulation 13C(5)(a) to (e) apply;

(e)   it has received, except in the case where any liability to make payments in respect of a dwelling would be to a housing authority, a request from a person (''the prospective occupier''), on a properly completed form approved for the purpose by the relevant authority, which includes the specified matters and any of the circumstances specified in regulation 13C(5)(a) to (d) apply;

(f)   52 weeks have expired since it last made an application under sub-paragraph (a), (b), (c), (d) [² , (e) or (h)] in relation to the claim or award in question and–

    (i)   a maximum rent (LHA) determined under regulation 13D does not apply; and

    (ii)   a maximum rent (LHA) is not to be determined under regulation 13D; [²]

(g)   52 weeks have expired since an application was made under sub-paragraph (f) or a previous application was made under this sub-paragraph, whichever last occurred, and–

    (i)   a maximum rent (LHA) determined under regulation 13D does not apply; and

    (ii)   a maximum rent (LHA) is not to be determined under regulation 13D. [² or

(h)   has received notification that any of the circumstances in regulation 13C(5) apply.]

(2)   An application shall not be required under paragraph (1) where a claim, relevant information regarding a claim, notification or request relates to either–

(a)   a dwelling in a hostel if, during the period of 12 months ending on the day on which that claim, relevant information regarding a claim, notification or request is received by the relevant authority–

    (i)   a rent officer has already made a determination in the exercise of the Housing Act functions in respect of a dwelling in that hostel which is a similar dwelling to the dwelling to which the claim, relevant information regarding a claim, notification or request relates; and

    (ii)   there has been no change relating to a rent allowance that has affected the dwelling in respect of which that determination was made; or

(b)   an ''excluded tenancy'' within the meaning of Schedule 2 (excluded tenancies).

(3)   The provision of information to the rent officer in accordance with regulation 114A(5) shall be treated as an application to the rent officer under paragraph (1).

(4)   Where a relevant authority receives a request pursuant to paragraph (1)(e) (request from prospective occupier) and it is a case where, by reason of paragraph (2) (hostels or excluded tenancies), an application to a rent officer is not required, the authority shall–

(a)   return it to the prospective occupier, indicating why no such application is required; and

(b)   where it is not required by reason of either paragraph (2)(a) (hostels) of this regulation or paragraph 2 of Schedule 2 (cases where the rent officer has already made a determination), shall also send him a copy of that determination within 4 days of the receipt of that request by the authority.

(5)   Where an application to a rent officer is required by paragraph (1) it shall be made within 3 days, or as soon as practicable after that date, of–

(a)   the relevant authority receiving a claim on which rent allowance may be awarded;

(b)   the relevant authority receiving relevant information regarding a claim on which rent allowance may be awarded;

(c)   the relevant authority receiving a notification of a change relating to a rent allowance;

(d)   the relevant authority receiving a notification of a change of dwelling; or

(e)   the day on which the period mentioned in paragraph (1)(f) or (g) expired,

except that, in the case of a request to which paragraph (1)(e) (request from prospective occupier) applies, the application shall be made within 2 days of the receipt of that request by the authority.

(6)   In calculating any period of days mentioned in paragraphs (4) or (5), no regard shall be had to a day on which the offices of the relevant authority are closed for the purposes of receiving or determining claims.

(7)   For the purpose of this regulation a dwelling in a hostel shall be regarded as similar to another dwelling in that hostel if each dwelling provides sleeping accommodation for the same number of persons.

(8)   In this regulation–

"change relating to a rent allowance" means a change or increase to which paragraph 2(3)(a), (b), (c) or (d) of Schedule 2 applies;

"prospective occupier" shall include a person currently in receipt of housing benefit in respect of a dwelling which he occupies as his home and who is contemplating entering into a new agreement to occupy that dwelling, but only where his current agreement commenced 11 months or more before the request under paragraph (1)(e);

"specified matters" means–

(a)   the signature of the prospective occupier;

(b)   the signature of the person to whom the prospective occupier would incur liability to make such payments;

(c)   a statement that the person in paragraph (b) agrees to the application being made for that determination; and

(d)   an indication that the prospective occupier is contemplating occupying the dwelling as his home and that if he does so, he is likely to claim housing benefit;

"tenancy" includes–

(a)   in Scotland, any other right of occupancy; and

(b)   in any other case, a licence to occupy premises,

and reference to a tenant, landlord or any other expression appropriate to a tenancy shall be construed accordingly;

[²]]

Modifications

Reg 14 was substituted by reg 8 Housing Benefit (Local Housing Allowance and Information Sharing) Amendment Regulations 2007 SI No.2868 as from 7 April 2008, save that for a person to whom reg 1(5) of those regulations applied (see p1231), the amendments came into force on the day on or after 7 April 2008 when the first of the events specified in reg 1(6) applied to her/him, or on 6 April 2009 if none had before that date.

Amendments

1.   Substituted by reg 8 of SI 2007 No 2868 as from 7.4.08 (or if reg 1(5) of that SI applies, on the day on or after 7.4.08 when the first of the events specified in reg 1(6) applies, or from 6.4.09 if none have before that date).

2.   Amended by reg 4(5) of SI 2008 No 586 as from 4.7.08.

Definitions

"change of dwelling" – see reg 2(1).
"hostel" – see reg 2(1).
"maximum rent (LHA)" – see reg 2(1).
"relevant information" – see reg 2(1).
"rent allowance" – see s134(1B) SSAA 1992
"Housing Act functions" – see reg 2(1).

General Note

The starting point for deciding whether maximum rent is to be calculated under reg 13 (the "local reference rent" rules) is to consider whether the authority is required to apply to the rent officer for a determination under reg 14.

Reg 14, together with Sch 2, prescribes the circumstances in which the authority must ask the rent officer for a determination to be made and the time limits which must be observed. For the rent officer's functions under the Housing Act see the Rent Officers (Housing Benefit Functions) Order 1997 and the Rent Officers (Housing Benefit Functions) (Scotland) Order 1997. Reg 114A deals with the information which must be given to the rent officer. Although there is no right of appeal against rent officer determinations, authorities may ask for redeterminations on a claimant's behalf under reg 16. Other provisions for redeterminations and substitute determinations are found in regs 15, 17 and 18. Note also that where an application for a board and attendance determination is made under reg 13D(10) and the rent officer decides that a substantial part of the rent under the tenancy is fairly attributable to board and attendance, s/he must treat the application for a determination as one made under reg 14(1): see, for example, Art 4C Rent Officers (Housing Benefit Functions) Order 1997 on p598.

Unless the claimant has an "excluded tenancy" (for which see Sch 2) or the "pre-January 1996" rules apply (for which see Sch 3 paras 4 and 5 HB&CTB(CP) Regs), broadly, reg 14 will apply if, on or after 7 April 2008, a claim for HB is made or a claimant with an award of HB moves to a new home, HB would be paid as a rent allowance and one of the following applies: regs 13C(5)(a)-(e) and 14(1).

(1)   Rent is paid in relation to a hostel, a houseboat, a mobile home or a caravan: reg 13C(5)(d).

(2)   A substantial part of the rent is attributable to board and attendance: reg 13C(5)(e).

(3)   The landlord is a registered social landlord or a non-profit or profit-making registered provider of social housing (in the latter case, the claimant's dwelling must be "social housing", that is, low cost rental or ownership accommodation that is available to people whose needs are not adequately served by the commercial housing market): regs 13C(5)(a) and 14(2)(b). See the commentary to reg 13C(5)(a) on p319 for further information.

This only applies if the authority considers the accommodation to be unreasonably large or the rent unreasonably high. Otherwise, such a tenancy is an "excluded tenancy" under Sch 2 para 3.

(4)   The tenancy was a local authority or new town letting, that was transferred to a new owner.

This only applies if there has been a rent increase since the transfer and the authority considers the rent to be unreasonably high or, if the transfer took place before 7 October 2002, the authority considers the accommodation to be unreasonably large: regs 13C(5)(c) and 14(2)(b). Otherwise, the tenacy is an "excluded tenancy" under Sch 2 para 11.

Claimants entitled to HB before 7 April 2008

Reg 14 (in either its previous or substituted form) can also apply to other rent allowance cases not covered in the list above – ie, those who live in a private rented house or flat. If the claimant was entitled to HB immediately before 7 April 2008 under the "local reference rent" rules that then applied, these continue to apply until a new claim for HB is made (eg, after a break in entitlement) or the claimant moves to a new home: reg 13C(2)(a)-(c).

The "local reference rent" rules continue to apply, even following any of the changes of circumstance listed in Sch 2 para 2(3)(a) to (d) (and Sch 2 para 2(3)(a) to (d) HB Regs as substituted by reg 18 HB(LHA&IS)A Regs), and then when the local authority has to apply to the rent officer for determinations every 52 weeks thereafter: regs 13(1) and 14(1)(c), (f) and (g) HB Regs. However, if none of these changes have occurred (and the claimant has not made a new claim for HB or moved) and the only reason the local authority has to apply to the rent officer for determinations is because it is more than 52 weeks since it last did so, it appears that rent restriction rules may no longer apply and eligible rent should then be calculated under reg 12B. This is because the substituted version of reg 14 did not come into force for a particular claimant until the day on or after 7 April 2008 when the first of the events specified in reg 1(6) HB(LHA&IS)A Regs (see p1231) applied to her/him (or on 6 April 2009 if none had before that date). For this claimant, this would have been when the authority was required to apply to the rent officer under the former version of reg 14 for a determination (or on 6 April 2009): reg 1(6)(a), (7) and (8) HB(LHA&IS)A Regs. The authority's application to the rent officer would then have been made under the substituted version of reg 14 as it is now in force for the claimant. The substituted version of reg 14 can only apply where any of para (1)(a) to (h) apply. Although 52 weeks have passed since the local authority made an application for a rent officer determination, none of sub-paras (a) to (h) apply. Sub-para (1)(f) can only apply where the previous application was made under any of the other sub-paras in the substituted reg 14(1), and sub-para (g) can only apply where the previous application was made under sub-para (f) or (g). The "LHA" rules do not apply as a claim has not been made on or after 7 April 2008, nor has there been a change of dwelling: reg 13C(2). It is understood that this was not the Government's intention.

Analysis

Paragraph (1): When referrals are to be made

Pursuant to para (1), there are eight circumstances in which a local authority is obliged to apply to a rent officer for a determination. These are subject to para (2), which provides for circumstances in which no application is required.

In all of the circumstances, an application is only required where the "LHA" rules (for which see regs 13C and 13D) do not apply.

An application to the rent officer must only be made in cases where HB would be paid as a rent allowance and not as a rent rebate. This may cause difficulties in cases where claimants have been placed in accommodation by local housing authorities: for an example, see *CH 1208/2003* referred to in the commentary to reg 8. The situations when HB takes the form of rent allowance and rent rebate are in s134(1A) and (1B) SSAA 1992. Generally speaking, HB takes the form of a rent allowance in cases other than where rent is paid to the authority administering the HB scheme – eg, where a claimant is a private or housing association tenant.

Note that oddly, an application to the rent officer is required where Sch 3 para 4(1)(b) HB&CTB(CP) Regs applies, that is, where the claimant lives in "exempt accommodation": see paras (a), (b) and (d) to (h) below and reg 13C(5)(b). However, Sch 3 para 4(1)(b) HB&CTB(CP) Regs requires the authority to determine the eligible rent in such cases under the versions of reg 12 and 13 HB Regs set out in Sch 3 para 5 HB&CTB(CP) Regs.

Sub-paras (a) and (b): Claims. These sub-paras apply where a claim for HB is received or an authority has received "relevant information" regarding a claim on which a rent allowance may be awarded. Relevant information is defined in reg 2(1) as "information or evidence forwarded to the authority by an appropriate DWP office regarding a claim on which rent allowance may be awarded, which completes the transfer of all information or evidence held by the appropriate DWP office relating to that claim" – eg, where the claim for HB has been made with a claim to the DWP for IS, JSA, ESA or PC. In both cases, one of the circumstances in reg 13C(5)(a) to (e) must apply, in other words, the claimant must be exempt from the application of the "LHA" rules. See the commentary to reg 13C(5) for details of the circumstances.

Sub-para (c): Change relating to a rent allowance. This applies where the authority has received a notification of a change relating to a rent allowance. A "change relating to a rent allowance" is defined in para (8) by reference to various parts of Sch 2 and covers changes in the number of occupiers, changes in the condition of the dwelling, certain rent increases and changes in the composition of the household or a child becoming 10 or 16. See the commentary to those provisions for full details and note in particular the discussion of *Stroud DC v JG* [2009] UKUT 67 (AAC); R(H) 8/09. The words from "and a maximum rent (LHA)" to the end of the sub-para are needed to ensure that where a "maximum rent (LHA)" is to be determined under reg 13C, an application is not to be made under reg 14 which would lead to a "maximum rent" under reg 13 also being determined for the same claimant.

Sub-para (d): Change of dwelling. This sub-para applies where the authority has received a notification of a change of dwelling. "Change of dwelling" is defined in reg 2(1) as a change of dwelling during an award of HB, to a dwelling in respect of which the authority may make a rent allowance. As with sub-paras (a) and (b) above, one of the circumstances in reg 13C(5)(a) to (e) must apply.

Sub-para (e): Pre-tenancy determinations. This sub-para establishes a scheme of pre-tenancy determinations for prospective occupiers to whom one of the circumstances in reg 13C(5)(a) to (d) applies. The policy aim is to prevent a tenant taking on a tenancy and then finding that her/his eligible rent is restricted. The determinations inform prospective tenants, current tenants and landlords of the likely amount of rent that HB will meet.

Pre-tenancy determinations are available to "prospective occupiers". By para (8), this term does not just include those considering taking on a tenancy but also includes HB claimants who are already occupying accommodation and who are considering entering into a new agreement. In the latter case, however, any existing agreement must have started not less than eleven months prior to the request being made.

No claim for HB is required, but one must be likely: see sub-para (d) in the the definition of "specified matters" in para (8).

The prospective occupier must submit her/his request to the authority on a "properly completed form approved ... by the relevant authority" whch includes "specified matters", defined in para (8) as including the signature of the prospective occupier and the landlord or letting agent.

The pre-tenancy determinations are rent officer determinations for the purpose of reg 13 and are binding on the authority in the event of an HB claim in respect of that accommodation, either from the prospective tenant who made the original application or another tenant. However, in the latter case, the conditions under which the pre-tenancy determination was given by the rent officer must remain the same. For example, the size criteria should accord with the composition of the household.

Sub-paras (f) and (g): 52 weeks since previous application. These sub-paras apply where 52 weeks have elapsed since a previous application to the rent officer was made in relation to the claim or award in question under any of the other sub-paras in reg 14(1). This effectively provides for an annual re-assessment of maximum rent under reg 13. The qualification made by sub-subparas (i) and (ii) in both cases is needed to ensure that where a "maximum rent (LHA)" is to be (or has been) determined under reg 13D, an application is not to be made under reg 14 which would lead to a "maximum rent" also being determined for the same claimant.

Sub-para (h): Maximum rent (LHA) no longer applies. Sub-para (h) applies where HB has been determined by reference to the "LHA" rules under reg 13D, but these no longer apply – eg, where a claimant lives in private rented accommodation which has passed into the ownership of a registered housing association.

Paragraphs (2), (4) and (7): The exceptions
Para (2) sets out the two exceptions to the requirement to apply to a rent officer. Under para (a), no dwelling within a hostel need be referred if a determination has been made within the previous 12 months in respect of a similar dwelling in that hostel and there has been no change of circumstances in relation to the similar dwelling. "Similar dwelling" means one sleeping the same number of people: para (7). Under para (b), no "excluded tenancy" as set out in Sch 2 need be referred. Note that a number of the excluded tenancies are therefore excluded from the rent restriction schemes altogether. See the commentary to that Schedule on p517.

Under para (4), where a request for a pre-tenancy determination would relate to a case where application to the rent officer is not required by reason of para (2), the local authority must return the request indicating why a referral is not necessary and, where the reason is that a determination has already been made, enclose a copy of that determination.

Paragraphs (3), (5) and (6): Making the referral

Para (3) treats the provision of information to the rent officer under reg 114A(5) as an application for a determination under para (1). This applies in cases where a substantial part of rent is attributable to board and attendance.

Paras (5) and (6) set out the time limits with which the authority must comply. Applications for pre-tenancy determinations must be referred to the rent officer within two working days. In other cases, the referral to the rent officer must be made within three working days from the authority receiving the claim, relevant information or notification or "as soon as practicable after". Note that the two working day limit for pre-tenancy determinations is absolute and not subject to the "as soon as is practicable after" qualification.

By para (6), days on which the local authority's offices are closed do not count.

In *CH 361/2006*, the deputy commissioner pointed out that the intention is that the application to the rent officer should be one of the very first stages of the processing of a claim for HB and not something that need only be dealt with once it is established that all the other conditions of entitlement are satisfied. Although there may be cases and situations where it is not "practicable" for the authority to satisfy the time limit, what is not permissible is for an authority to take a conscious decision not to make a reference to a rent officer because it is believes that the claim will eventually fail on other grounds. Note that a failure to apply to the rent officer in respect of a claim may amount to an official error for the purposes of reg 100 (recoverable overpayments): para 34.

[¹ Application to the rent officer for redeterminations

15.–(1)   Subject to paragraph (2) and regulation 16 (application for redetermination by rent officer), where a relevant authority has obtained from a rent officer either or both of the following–

(a)   a determination on a reference made under regulation 13D(10) (board and attendance determination) or regulation 14 (requirement to refer to rent officers);

(b)   a redetermination on a reference made under regulation 16(2) (application for redetermination by rent officer),

the authority may apply to the rent officer for a redetermination of any determination or redetermination he has made which has effect at the date of the application.

(2)   No application shall be made for a further redetermination of a redetermination made in response to an application under paragraph (1).]

Modifications

Reg 15 was substituted by reg 9 Housing Benefit (Local Housing Allowance and Information Sharing) Amendment Regulations 2007 SI No.2868 as from 7 April 2008, save that for a person to whom reg 1(5) of those regulations applied (see p1231), the amendments came into force on the day on or after 7 April 2008 when the first of the events specified in reg 1(6) applied to her/him, or on 6 April 2009 if none had before that date.

Amendment

1.   Substituted by reg 9 of SI 2007 No 2868 as from 7.4.08 (or if reg 1(5) that SI applies, on the day on or after 7.4.08 when the first of the events specified in reg 1(6) applies, or from 6.4.09 if none have before that date).

General Note

Regs 15, 16, 17 and 18 allow for applications for redeterminations and substitute determinations. Under reg 15, an authority may apply for a redetermination of a determination, or for a second redetermination following one made at the person affected's request under reg 16(2). It may apply only once: see reg 15(2).

[¹ Application for a redetermination by a rent officer

16.–(1)   This paragraph applies where–

(a)   a person affected makes written representations which are signed by him, to a relevant authority concerning a decision which it makes in relation to him;

(b)   those representations relate, in whole or in part, to a rent officer's determination or redetermination in exercise of the Housing Act functions except for functions relating to broad rental market area determinations and local housing allowance determinations or amended determinations; and

(c)   those representations are made no later than one month after the day on which the person affected was notified of the decision by the relevant authority.

(2) Subject to paragraphs (3) and (4), where paragraph (1) applies, the relevant authority shall, within 7 days of receiving the representations, apply to the rent officer for a redetermination or, as the case may be, a further redetermination in exercise of the Housing Act functions and a copy of those representations shall accompany the local authority's application.

(3) Except where paragraph (4) applies, a relevant authority, in relation to any determination by a rent officer of an application under regulation 13D(10) (board and attendance determination) or 14(1) (requirement to refer to rent officers), shall not apply for a redetermination under paragraph (2) more than once in respect of an individual claimant's dwelling to which that determination relates.

(4) Paragraph (2) shall operate so as to require a relevant authority to make a second application where the following conditions are met in addition to those imposed by that paragraph–

(a) the written representations made under paragraph (1) relate to a redetermination by a rent officer made in response to an application by the relevant authority under regulation 15 (application to the rent officer for redetermination);

(b) by the time of that application, the rent officer has already provided a redetermination under this regulation of a determination made in response to an application under regulation 13D(10) or 14(1); and

(c) both the application under this regulation referred to in sub-paragraph (b) and the second application for which this paragraph provides relate to the same claimant.

(5) Where a decision has been revised in consequence of a redetermination, substitute determination or substitute redetermination by a rent officer in exercise of the Housing Act functions (except for those relating to broad rental market area determinations and local housing allowance determinations or amended determinations) and that redetermination, substitute determination or substitute redetermination has led to–

(a) a reduction in the maximum rent, the redetermination, substitute determination or substitute redetermination shall be a change of circumstances;

(b) an increase in the maximum rent, the redetermination, substitute determination or substitute redetermination shall have effect in place of the original determination.]

Modifications

Reg 16 was substituted by reg 9 Housing Benefit (Local Housing Allowance and Information Sharing) Amendment Regulations 2007 SI No.2868 as from 7 April 2008, save that for a person to whom reg 1(5) of those regulations applied (see p1231), the amendments came into force on the day on or after 7 April 2008 when the first of the events specified in reg 1(6) applied to her/him, or on 6 April 2009 if none had before that date.

Amendment

1. Substituted by reg 9 of SI 2007 No 2868 as from 7.4.08 (or if reg 1(5) of that SI applies, on the day on or after 7.4.08 when the first of the events specified in reg 1(6) applies, or from 6.4.09 if none have before that date).

General Note

Under para 6(2)(c) CSPSSA, "so much of any decision of a relevant authority as adopts a decision of a rent officer under any order made by virtue of section 122 of the Housing Act 1996" does not carry a right of appeal to the First-tier Tribunal. Reg 16 provides a limited opportunity for a "person affected" to challenge such a decision. "Person affected" is defined in reg 2(1) by reference to reg 3 D&A Regs and so can include, as well as a claimant, a landlord or her/his agent.

The procedure is for the "person affected" to make signed written representations to the authority about a decision, which relate to the rent officer's determination. These must be made no later than one month after the day on which s/he was notified of the authority's decision. The authority must then apply within seven days to the rent officer for a redetermination. Note that the time limit was six weeks for decisions notified by the relevant authority to the "person affected" before 1 October 2007.

Claimants and advisers should note that such representations may lead to a *decrease* in the maximum rent as well as to an increase. If that occurs, it is treated by para (5)(a) as a change of circumstances and will lead to the supersession of the earlier award. By contrast an increase in the maximum rent takes effect as a revision of the original award: para (5)(b). It therefore leads to a payment of back-dated benefit: see also regs 4(3), 7(2)(c) and 8(6) D&A Regs. Paras (3) and (4) make it clear that only one redetermination can be required for each original rent officer determination except where, in relation to the same claimant, there has been a first redetermination at the claimant's request, then a further redetermination at the authority's request, and the claimant then makes further representations about the second redetermination.

Note that although there is no right of appeal to the First-tier Tribunal against a decision of the rent officer, the claimant can appeal the local authority's decision on HB entitlement and, as such, can challenge the factual basis upon which the rent officer decision was made – eg, the number of occupiers given to the rent officer by the local authority: *Bexley LB v LD (HB)* [2010] UKUT 79 (AAC) and *SK v South Hams DC (HB)* [2010] UKUT 129 (AAC).

[¹ Substitute determinations or substitute redeterminations

17.–(1)   In a case where either–

(a)   the appropriate authority discovers that an application it has made to the rent officer contained an error in respect of any of the following–

(i)   the size of the dwelling;

(ii)   the number of occupiers;

(iii)   the composition of the household;

(iv)   the terms of the tenancy; or

(b)   the rent officer has, in accordance with article 7A(1) or (2) of the Rent Officers Order, notified an appropriate authority of an error he has made (other than in the application of his professional judgement),

the authority shall apply to the rent officer for a substitute determination, substitute redetermination, board and attendance redetermination, substitute board and attendance determination or substitute board and attendance redetermination, as the case may be.

(2)   In its application to the rent officer the relevant authority shall state the nature of the error and withdraw any previous application relating to the same case for a redetermination or substitute determination or substitute redetermination, which it has made but to which the rent officer has not yet responded.]

Modifications

Reg 17 was substituted by reg 9 of the Housing Benefit (Local Housing Allowance and Information Sharing) Amendment Regulations 2007 SI No.2868 as from 7 April 2008, save that for a person to whom reg 1(5) of those regulations applied (see p1231), the amendments came into force on the day on or after 7 April 2008 when the first of the events specified in reg 1(6) applied to her/him, or on 6 April 2009 if none had before that date.

Amendment

1.   Substituted by reg 9 of SI 2007 No 2868 as from 7.4.08 (or if reg 1(5) of that SI applies, on the day on or after 7.4.08 when the first of the events specified in reg 1(6) applies, or from 6.4.09 if none have before that date).

General Note

Reg 17 requires an authority to apply for a substitute determination where any of the errors listed in para (1) comes to light. It appears that the error may be one of law as well as fact, but it would seem that if the local authority reaches a conclusion from primary facts, for example as to the composition of a household, it cannot describe that conclusion as an "error" merely because another officer later takes a different view.

There is no mechanism for a claimant to apply for a substitute determination, but an authority could be invited to exercise its duty under reg 17 and could be vulnerable to judicial review if it refuses to do so.

The references to "the appropriate authority" in paras (1)(a) and (b) appear to have been overlooked by the draftsman of SI 2001 No.1605 which amended reg 12C HB Regs 1987 (now reg 17 HB Regs). s34 WRA 2007 now provides a definition, but only for the purposes of the interpretation of ss32 and 33 WRA 2007 (the scheme for extended payments of HB and CTB on a person taking up employment).

[¹ Application of provisions to substitute determinations or substitute redeterminations

18.   Regulations 15, 16 and 17 apply to a substitute determination or substitute redetermination as they apply to the determination or redetermination it replaces.]

Modifications

Reg 18 was substituted by reg 9 of the Housing Benefit (Local Housing Allowance and Information Sharing) Amendment Regulations 2007 SI No.2868 as from 7 April 2008, save that for a person to whom reg 1(5) of those regulations applied (see p1231), the amendments came into force on the day on or after 7 April 2008 when the first of the events specified in reg 1(6) applied to her/him, or on 6 April 2009 if none had before that date.

Amendment

1.   Substituted by reg 9 of SI 2007 No 2868 as from 7.4.08 (or if reg 1(5) of that SI applies, on the day on or after 7.4.08 when the first of the events specified in reg 1(6) applies, or from 6.4.09 if none have before that date).

General Note

Reg 18 confirms that substitute determinations may themselves be the subject of applications for redeterminations.

[¹ Amended determinations

18A.–(1)   This regulation applies where a decision has been revised in consequence of an amended broad rental market area determination or amended local housing allowance determination by a rent officer.

(2)   Where that amended determination has led to a reduction in the maximum rent (LHA) applicable to a claimant, the amended determination shall be a change of circumstances in relation to that claimant.

(3)   Where that amended determination has led to an increase in the maximum rent (LHA) applicable to a claimant, the amended determination shall have effect in place of the original determination.]

Amendment

1.   Inserted by reg 10 of SI 2007 No 2868 as from 7.4.08 (or if reg 1(5) of that SI applies, on the day on or after 7.4.08 when the first of the events specified in reg 1(6) applies, or from 6.4.09 if none have before that date).

Definitions

"amended determination" – see reg 2(1).
"claimant" – see reg 2(1).
"broad rental market area determination" – see reg 2(1).

General Note

The regulations do not provide a right of appeal or internal review against the broad rental market area determinations or the local housing allowance determinations made by the rent officer. However, where a rent officer is of the opinion that s/he has made an error (other than in the application of her/his professional judgement) in relation to either of these, s/he is required to notify the authority under Art 7A(4) of the Rent Officer Orders. S/he must also provide an amended determination, as soon as practicable.

Reg 18A then sets out when the amended determination applies. A decrease in the maximum rent (LHA) is treated by para (2) as a change of circumstances and will lead to the supersession of the earlier award. By contrast an increase in the maximum rent (LHA) takes effect as a revision of the original award: para (3). It therefore leads to a payment of backdated benefit: see also regs 4(3), 7(2)(c) and 8(6) D&A Regs.

PART 4
Membership of a family

General Note on Part 4

"Family" is defined in s137(1) SSCBA. Note that it has a specific meaning for HB purposes – ie, a "family" is a couple or lone parent and any child or "person of a prescribed condition" who is a member of the same household and for whom the claimant (or partner or both of them) is responsible. "Couple" and "child" are also defined in s137(1) SSCBA. Reg 19 sets out who is a person of a prescribed description for these purposes (a "qualifying young person"). Reg 20 provides circumstances in which the claimant and her/his partner are to be treated as responsible (or not responsible) for a child or young person. Reg 21 provides circumstances in which people (ie, the claimant, any partner and any child or young person) are to be treated as being (or not being) a member of the same household.

Being a member of the claimant's "family" is relevant for the following.

(1)   Working out the claimant's applicable amount: see Part 5.

(2)   Assessing the claimant's income and capital: see Part 6. Note: only the income and capital of a partner of the claimant is treated as the claimant's.

Note also that if someone is a member of the "family", s/he cannot be a non-dependant and hence no non-dependant deduction can be made for her/him: see regs 3(2)(a) and 74.

Persons of prescribed description

19.–(1)   Subject to paragraph (2), a person of a prescribed description for the purposes of section 137(1) of the Act as it applies to housing benefit (definition of family) is a person [¹ who falls within the definition of qualifying young person in section 142 of the Act (child and qualifying young person)], and in these Regulations such a person is referred to as a "young person".

(2)   Paragraph (1) shall not apply to a person who is–

(a)   on income support [³ , an income-based jobseeker's allowance or an income-related employment and support allowance]; [¹ or]

[² (b)]

(c)   a person to whom section 6 of the Children (Leaving Care) Act 2000 (exclusion from benefits) applies.

(3)   A person of a prescribed description for the purposes of section 137(1) of the Act as it applies to housing benefit (definition of the family) includes a child or young person in respect of whom section 145A of that Act applies for the purposes of entitlement to child benefit but only for the period prescribed under section 145A(1) of that Act.

Amendments

1.   Amended by reg 4(2)(a) and (b) of SI 2006 No 718 as from 10.4.06.
2.   Omitted by reg 4(2)(c) of SI 2006 No 718 as from 10.4.06.
3.   Amended by reg 10 of SI 2008 No 1082 as from 27.10.08.

Definitions

"person on income support" – see reg 2(1).
"person on an income-based jobseeker's allowance" – see reg 2(3).
"person on an income-related employment and support allowance" – see reg 2(3A).

General Note

s137(1) SSCBA refers to "child" and "person of a prescribed description" in the definition of "family" for HB purposes (see p18). The section and reg 2 define "child" and this reg deals with those covered by the latter term, and provides that they shall be referred to as a "young person" elsewhere in these regulations.

Analysis

Para (1). "Young person" is defined by reference to the definition of a "qualifying young person" for child benefit purposes. s142 SSCBA and the Child Benefit (General) Regulations 2006 SI No.223 (the CB Regs) prescribe who may be treated as a "qualifying young person" for these purposes.

First, the young person must be 16 or over and under 20 and on a course of "full-time non-advanced education" or in "approved training" (or having undertaken such a course or training, have been accepted or be enrolled to undertake a further such course or training). In most cases, s/he must have started the course or the training before reaching aged 19: regs 2(5) and 3 CB Regs.

The course of education must be at a school, college or similar institution (or elsewhere, for example, at home, if the Commissioners for Her Majesty's Revenue and Customs (HMRC) agree and the young person was receiving the education before reaching aged 16). "Full time" for these purposes means over 12 hours a week excluding meal breaks and unsupervised study: reg 1(3) CB Regs. "Non-advanced" means not above 'A' level or 'Higher' standard, but it is the nature of the course that matters, not where the student is studying, provided the Commissioners for the HMRC have approved the studies if s/he is not at a recognised educational establishment.

"Approved training" means arrangements made by the Government: in England known as "Entry to Employment" or "Programme Led Apprenticeships"; in Wales known as "Skillbuild", "Skillbuild+" or "Foundation Modern Apprenticeships" and in Scotland, known as "Get Ready for Work", "Skillseekers" or "Modern Apprenticeships": reg 1(3) CB Regs. The training cannot be provided under a contract of service: reg 3(2)(c) CB Regs.

If a young person leaves education or approved training before reaching age 20, s/he is still treated as a qualifying young person in any of the following circumstances.

(1)   If s/he is 16, up to and including 31 August following her/his 16th birthday or if her/his 16th birthday is on 31 August, up to and including the day after: reg 4 CB Regs.

(2)   If s/he is 16 or 17, is registered for work, education or training, is not in remunerative work (here defined as 24 hours or more a week), until the end of her/his "extension period" – ie, from the Monday after the course/training ends and ending 20 weeks later: reg 1(3) and 5 CB Regs.

(3)   If s/he is at least 16 but under 20, and has not yet passed the end of the week that includes her/his "terminal date", up to and including the week (Monday to Sunday) that includes her/his "terminal date" or, if s/he reaches 20 before that date, the week including the last Monday before her/his 20th birthday: reg 7 CB Regs. The "terminal date" is whichever of the following dates first follows the date s/he leaves the education or training: the last day in February, May, August or November: reg 7 CB Regs. A young person who is to return to take an external exam in connection with the education is treated as still being

in the education until the date of the last exam. In Scotland, a young person who has taken the Higher or Advanced Higher Certificate can be treated as still being in education until the date a comparable course in England would end if this is later.

Some interruptions in satisfying the conditions for being a "qualifying young person" can be ignored: reg 6 CB Regs.

Para (2). A young person is not part of the claimant's family if s/he is her/himself on IS, income-based JSA or income-related ESA. Neither is a person who is excluded from entitlement to benefits under s6 Children (Leaving Care) Act 2000 (see p1132).

Para (3). s145A SSCBA, inserted by s55 TCA 2002, provides for entitlement to child benefit to continue for a prescribed period after the death of a child or qualifying young person. The prescribed period is eight weeks for a child under 16. For a "qualifying young person" it is also eight weeks unless s/he would have attained the age of 20 during that period. In this case, if it is shorter, it is the period commencing the week in which the death occurred and finishing on the Monday in the week following the week in which the qualifying young person would have attained the age of 20: reg 20 CB Regs. The effect of reg 19(3) is that the deceased child continues to be treated as part of the claimant's family for HB purposes during that prescribed period.

Circumstances in which a person is to be treated as responsible or not responsible for another

20.–(1) Subject to the following provisions of this regulation a person shall be treated as responsible for a child or young person who is normally living with him and this includes a child or young person to whom paragraph (3) of regulation 19 applies.

(2) Where a child or young person spends equal amounts of time in different households, or where there is a question as to which household he is living in, the child or young person shall be treated for the purposes of paragraph (1) as normally living with–

(a) the person who is receiving child benefit in respect of him; or

(b) if there is no such person–

   (i) where only one claim for child benefit has been made in respect of him, the person who made that claim, or

   (ii) in any other case the person who has the primary responsibility for him.

(3) For the purposes of these Regulations a child or young person shall be the responsibility of only one person in any benefit week and any person other than the one treated as responsible for the child or young person under this regulation shall be treated as not so responsible.

Definitions
"benefit week" – see reg 2(1).
"child" – see s137(1) SSCBA and reg 2(1).
"household" – see note on s137 SSCBA.
"young person" – see reg 19.

General Note
For a child or young person to count as a member of a claimant's family for HB purposes, s/he must be a member of the claimant's household (see reg 21 on p335) and the claimant or her/his partner (or both of them) must be "responsible" for her/him: s137(1) SSCBA. A child or young person being a member of a claimant's family is important for a number of reasons, the main one being that the claimant's applicable amount will include allowances and premiums for her/him and hence the claimant's rate of HB is potentially higher.

Reg 20 sets out the situations in which a person is treated as responsible. By para (3) only one person can be treated as responsible for a particular child or young person in any benefit week. Para (1) sets out the general rule, that a person is responsible for a child or young person "normally living with" her/him. That includes a deceased child or young person falling within reg 19(3) above. Para (2) sets out the rules for deciding who the responsible person is, if there should be doubt or dispute.

Analysis
Para (1). The primary rule is that a person is responsible for a child or young person who is "normally living with" her/him. This means that the child or young person is spending more time with that person than with anyone else: *CFC 1537/1995.*

Para (2) contains deeming provisions to resolve doubtful cases. It only applies in two sets of circumstances.

(1) It applies where the amount of time spent in different households is equal. It need not be exactly equal in order to trigger the operation of para (2): *CFC 1537/1995.* Authorities should therefore consider the position in the round rather than carrying out an exact calculation.

(2)	It applies "where there is a question" as to which household a child or young person is living in. It is suggested that there must be a "question" of some difficulty, otherwise para (1) would be deprived of all effect.

Where para (2) applies, the test is determined in three stages. The child is treated as "normally living with:

(1)	The person who is in receipt of child benefit in respect of the child: sub-para (a). A person is not "receiving child benefit" where it is being paid to her/him, or, for example, paid into her/his bank account, by the person entitled to the child benefit: *CIS 2317/2006.*

(2)	If no one is receiving child benefit, the person who has claimed it in respect of the child: sub-para (b)(i).

(3)	In any other case (including where more than one person has claimed child benefit for the child), the person who has "primary responsibility" for the child: sub-para (b)(ii). This will require consideration of all the circumstances, financial and pastoral.

Circumstances in which a person is to be treated as being or not being a member of the household

21.–(1)	Subject to paragraphs (2) to (4), the claimant and any partner and, where the claimant or his partner is treated as responsible by virtue of regulation 20 (circumstances in which a person is to be treated as responsible or not responsible for another) for a child or young person, that child or young person and any child of that child or young person, shall be treated as members of the same household notwithstanding that any of them is temporarily living away from the other members of his family.

(2)	Paragraph (1) shall not apply to a person who is living away from the other members of his family where–

(a)	that person does not intend to resume living with the other members of his family; or

(b)	his absence from the other members of his family is likely to exceed 52 weeks, unless there are exceptional circumstances (for example where the person is in hospital or otherwise has no control over the length of his absence) and the absence is unlikely to be substantially more than 52 weeks.

(3)	A child or young person shall not be treated as a member of the claimant's household [¹ , nor as occupying the claimant's dwelling,] where he is–

(a)	placed with the claimant or his partner by a local authority under section 23(2)(a) of the Children Act 1989 or by a voluntary organisation under section 59(1)(a) of that Act, or in Scotland boarded out with the claimant or his partner under a relevant enactment; or

(b)	placed, or in Scotland boarded out, with the claimant or his partner prior to adoption; or

(c)	placed for adoption with the claimant or his partner in accordance with the Adoption and Children Act 2002 or the Adoption Agencies (Scotland) Regulations 1996.

(4)	Subject to paragraph (5), paragraph (1) shall not apply to a child or young person who is not living with the claimant and he–

(a)	is being looked after by, or in Scotland is in the care of, a local authority under a relevant enactment; or

(b)	has been placed, or in Scotland boarded out, with a person other than the claimant prior to adoption; or

(c)	has been placed for adoption in accordance with the Adoption and Children Act 2002 or the Adoption Agencies (Scotland) Regulations 1996.

(5)	An authority shall treat a child or young person to whom paragraph (4)(a) applies as being a member of the claimants' household in any benefit week where–

(a)	that child or young person lives with the claimant for part or all of that benefit week; and

(b)	the authority considers that it is reasonable to do so taking into account the nature and frequency of that child's or young person's visits.

(6)	In this regulation "relevant enactment" means the Army Act 1955, the Air Force Act 1955, the Naval Discipline Act 1957, the Matrimonial Proceedings Children Act 1958, the Social Work (Scotland) Act 1968, the Family Law Reform Act 1969, the Children and Young Persons Act 1969, the Matrimonial Causes Act 1973, the Children Act 1975, the Domestic Proceedings and Magistrates' Courts Act 1978, the Adoption

(Scotland) Act 1978, the Child Care Act 1980, the Family Law Act 1986, the Children Act 1989 and the Children (Scotland) Act 1995.

Amendment

1.　　Amended by reg 2(3) of SI 2010 No 2449 as from 1.11.10.

Definitions

"benefit week" – see reg 2(1).
"child" – see reg 2(1) and s137(1) SSCBA.
"claimant" – see reg 2(1).
"household" – see note to s137 SSCBA.
"partner" – see reg 2(1).
"relevant enactment" – see para (6).
"young person" – see reg 19.

General Note

Reg 21 deals with the situations in which a claimant's family for HB purposes (that is her/his partner and children or qualifying young people) are treated as being members of the same household and when they are not so treated, and when certain children and young people (specified in para (3)) are not to be treated as occupying the claimant's dwelling. Note that for a child or young person to count as a member of a claimant's family at all, s/he *must* be a member of the claimant's household and the claimant or her/his partner must be "responsible" for her/ him (see reg 20): s137(1) SSCBA. The first thing to notice is that this regulation does not define "household". See the Analysis to s137 SSCBA on p22. It does, however, set out the situations in which a person is to continue to be treated as a member of a household despite physical absence from it.

Analysis

Para (1). The general rule is that claimants, their partner(s), any child or young person for whom they are responsible, and any child of such a child or young person shall be treated as members of the same household even where one of them is temporarily living away from the other members of the family. The definition of "partner" in reg 2(1) means that this regulation applies equally to polygamous and non-polygamous relationships. Exceptions to the rule are found in paras (2) to (5).

Para (2) treats a person who is living away from the other members of the family (eg, a partner working abroad, or in another part of the country) as not being a member of the household, if s/he does not intend to resume living with the family or s/he is likely to be absent for more than 52 weeks (unless there are exceptional circumstances). Examples of exceptional circumstances are given in sub-para (b). If such a person is the claimant's partner, her/his income will no longer fall to be treated as the claimant's under reg 25 and any money actually received from her/him should be treated as maintenance under Section 5 of Part 6.

Para (3) provides that certain children or young people placed with a claimant (or her/his partner) under child protection legislation are not to be treated as members of the claimant's household, and and hence as part of her/ his benefit family. Para (3) was amended from 1 November 2010 and now also provides that these children and young people are not to be treated as occupying the claimant's dwelling. This reverses the decision in *Wirral MBC v AH and SSWP (HB)* [2010] UKUT 208 (AAC) and now prevents the children and young people being taken into account as occupiers for the purposes the size criteria under the local housing allowance scheme rules: see reg 13D(3).

Under sub-para (a), s23(1)(a) Children Act 1989 places a duty upon the local authority to provide accommodation for a child when s/he is in care. By s23(2)(a) of the Act, the authority is to provide that accommodation by placing the child with a family, a relative of hers/his, or any other suitable person. Where a voluntary organisation provides accommodation for a child under s59(1)(a) Children Act 1989 it must do so by placing the child with the same persons identified above. For the definition of "relevant enactment", see para (6).

Under sub-paras (b) and (c), a child placed with the claimant (boarded out in Scotland) as part of the adoption process is not to be treated as being a member of the claimant's family. The regulations referred to regulate adoption agencies and how they are to reach decisions.

Paras (4) and (5). Para (4) treats a child or young person who is being "looked after" (in care in Scotland) or is being prepared for adoption, as not being a member of the household (and hence part of the claimant's benefit family). However, if the child or young person is being "looked after" (or is in care) but lives with the claimant for part or all of any benefit week, then para (5) allows them to be treated as a member of the claimant's household, in that week. Para (5), however, only applies if the authority considers this reasonable taking into account the nature and frequency of the visits. The "nature" of the visits might refer to length of stay, and whether the child is treated as a member of the family during the stay, etc. Reading paras (4) and (5) together, the phrase "living with" seems to have the narrow meaning of physical presence, because if a child or young person is physically present in any particular week, if para (5) applies it may be used to override the effect of para (4).

PART 5
Applicable amounts

General Note on Part 5
This Part is made under s135 SSCBA and, together with Sch 3, prescribes the rules for ascertaining a claimant's applicable amount. The "applicable amount" is an essential component in the calculation of HB: see SSCBA s135 (p15) and Part 8 (p418).

   Sch 3 sets out the different elements that can make up an applicable amount. The "allowances" depend on whether a claimant is single, a lone parent, part of a couple or polygamously married, and whether s/he is responsible for a child or qualifying young person. In addition to these basic amounts, the claimant may qualify to have one or more of the premiums set out in Parts 3 and 4 of Sch 3 included in her/his applicable amount (see pp524 and 535) and one of the components set out in Parts 5 and 6 of Sch 3 (see pp536 and 538).

Applicable amounts
22. Subject to regulations 23, 24, 80 and 81 and Schedule A1 (polygamous marriages, patients, calculation of weekly amounts, rent free periods and treatment of claims for housing benefit by refugees), a claimant's weekly applicable amount shall be the aggregate of such of the following amounts as may apply in his case–
   (a)   an amount in respect of himself or, if he is a member of a couple, an amount in respect of both of them, determined in accordance with paragraph 1(1), (2) or (3), as the case may be, of Schedule 3;
   (b)   an amount determined in accordance with paragraph 2 of Schedule 3 in respect of any child or young person who is a member of his family;
   (c)   if he is a member of a family of which at least one member is a child or young person, an amount determined in accordance with Part 2 of Schedule 3 (family premium);
   (d)   the amount of any premiums which may be applicable to him, determined in accordance with Parts 3 and 4 of Schedule 3 (premiums).
   [1 (e)   the amount of either the–
      (i)   work-related activity component; or
      (ii)   support component,
      which may be applicable to him in accordance with Part 5 of Schedule 3 (the components).]
   [2 (f)   the amount of any transitional addition which may be applicable to him in accordance with Parts 7 and 8 of Schedule 3 (transitional addition).]

Amendments
   1.   Inserted by reg 11 of SI 2008 No 1082, as amended by reg 29 of SI 2008 No 2428, as from 27.10.08.
   2.   Inserted by Reg 27 and Sch 5 para 1(3) of SI 2010 No 1907 as amended by reg 15 of SI 2010 No 2430 as from 1.10.10.

Definitions
   "applicable amount" – see s135 SSCBA.
   "child" – reg 2(1).
   "claimant" – see reg 2(1).
   "couple" – see reg 2(1).
   "family" – see s137(1) SSCBA.
   "polygamous marriage" – see reg 2(1).
   "young person" – regs 2(1) and 19(1).

General Note
This regulation sets out the basic rules for ascertaining the applicable amounts for any claimant who is not polygamously married. The basic rules are subject to regs 23, 24, 80 and 81. A claimant's notional financial needs for the purpose of working out her/his HB entitlement are the total amounts applicable to her/him under paras (a)-(f). Note that reg 24 was revoked in April 2006 and that Sch A1 can only be relevant to those recorded as refugees on or before 14 June 2007. Reg 23 sets out the applicable amount for a claimant who is polygamously married.

Analysis
Para (a). The amount applicable under para (a) is the personal allowance which varies according to whether the claimant is a single person, a lone parent or a member of a couple. In all cases, the highest rate is applicable

where the claimant is entitled to ESA which includes a work-related activity component or a support component personally – ie, not simply on the basis of her/his partner's circumstances. The highest rate is also applicable for lone parents and couples if the claimant (or partner) is 18 or over, and for single people if the claimant is aged 25 or over.

Para (b). For membership of a "family", see p22 and Part 4 of these regulations. Sch 3 para 2 provides allowances for children and qualifying young people. Although there are two bands depending on the age of the child or young person, the amounts for both age-bands are currently the same.

Para (c). See note on para (b) and the analysis on the family premium in Sch 3 para 3 on p524.

Para (d). See the notes to Sch 3 for the details of the premiums. They are designed to meet the additional specific needs of some claimants. Note Sch 3 para 13(9) limits the award of the disability premium if the claimant has, or is treated as having, limited capabilty for work. In this case, s/he may instead be entitled to one of the components in para (e) below.

Para (e). See the notes to Sch 3 for details of the two components. They are designed to meet the additional needs of claimants who have, or are treated as having, limited capability for work. Sch 3 paras 21 and 21A prevent the award of more than one component. Para 22 limits the award of a component if the claimant is entitled to a disability premium.

Para (f). This amount is applicable where a claimant or her/his partner has been transferred from IS "on the grounds of disability", IB or SDA to ESA which is not income-related (the conversion), or in specified circumstances is appealing a conversion decision. The transitional addition (calculated under Sch 3 para 30) is meant to provide protection against a reduction in HB as a consequence of the conversion.

Polygamous marriages

23. Subject to regulations 24, 80 and 81 and Schedule A1 (patients, calculation of weekly amounts, rent free periods and treatment of claims for housing benefit by refugees), where a claimant is a member of a polygamous marriage, his weekly applicable amount shall be the aggregate of such of the following amounts as may apply in his case–

(a) the highest amount applicable to him and one of his partners determined in accordance with paragraph 1(3) of Schedule 3 as if he and that partner were a couple;

(b) an amount equal to the difference between the amounts specified in sub-paragraphs (3)(b) and (1)(b) of paragraph 1 of Schedule 3 in respect of each of his other partners;

(c) an amount determined in accordance with paragraph 2 of Schedule 3 (applicable amounts) in respect of any child or young person for whom he or a partner of his is responsible and who is a member of the same household;

(d) if he or another partner of the polygamous marriage is responsible for a child or young person who is a member of the same household, the amount specified in Part 2 of Schedule 3 (family premium);

(e) the amount of any premiums which may be applicable to him determined in accordance with Parts 3 and 4 of Schedule 3 (premiums).

[¹ (f) the amount of either the–

(i) work-related activity component; or

(ii) support component,

which may be applicable to him in accordance with Part 5 of Schedule 3 (the components).]

[² (g) the amount of any transitional addition which may be applicable to him in accordance with Parts 7 and 8 of Schedule 3 (transtional addition).]

Amendments

1. Inserted by reg 12 of SI 2008 No 1082, as amended by reg 30 of SI 2008 No 2428, as from 27.10.08.
2. Inserted by Reg 27 and Sch 5 para 1(4) of SI 2010 No 1907 as amended by reg 15 of SI 2010 No 2430 as from 1.10.10.

Definitions

"applicable amount" – see s135 SSCBA.

"child" – see reg 2(1).

"claimant" – see reg 2(1).

"partner" – see reg 2(1).

"polygamous marriage" – see reg 2(1).

"young person" – see reg 19.

General Note

These rules apply solely to claimants who are polygamously married: defined in reg 2(1). Because of the definition of "partner" in reg 2(1), an increased applicable amount can only be obtained under this regulation in respect of partners is a polygamous marriage who share the same household. The rules are subject to regs 24, 80 and 81. Note that reg 24 was revoked in April 2006 and that Sch A1 can only be relevant to those recorded as refugees on or before 14 June 2007.

Paras (c) to (g) of this regulation have the same effect as paras (b) to (f) of reg 22: see notes on that regulation. The applicable amount is the total due under paras (a) to (g).

Analysis

Paras (a) and (b). The basic personal allowance awarded in respect of polygamously married couples is calculated by taking the highest amount awarded under Sch 3 para 1(3) in respect of any of the couples (depending on age and whether the claimant is entitled to ESA which includes a work-related activity component or a support component). An additional personal allowance is then awarded for the other partner(s): the amount is the difference between the allowance for a single claimant aged not less than 25 and a couple aged not less than 18. So if a male claimant, A, aged 45 has two wives, B aged 37 and C aged 17, the couple allowance is calculated as between A and B and is for couples where at least one member is more than 18. A further amount is then awarded for C as stated above.

Paras (c) to (e) are identical to the premiums awarded under reg 22(b) to (d), save that in relation to family and child premiums the claimant is entitled if any of her/his partners is responsible for the children.

Patients
[¹24.]

Amendment

1.　　Omitted by reg 2(4) of SI 2005 No 2502 as amended by Sch 2 para 27 of SI 2006 No 217 as from 1.4.06 (3.4.06 where rent payable weekly or at intervals of a week).

General Note

Until omitted, reg 24 varied the applicable amounts due under regs 22 or 23 as appropriate, in relation to claimants who had been patients for more than 52 weeks. Whether someone is a patient is still of relevance in the treatment of childcare costs (under reg 28) and to entitlement to the disability and enchanced disability premiums (Sch 3 paras 13 and 15). The definition of "patient" for these purposes is in reg 28(11)(e) (see p352).

Long-term hospital patients may still be caught by the requirement in reg 7 that they must be occupying the home, but see reg 7(16)(c)(ii). The definition of "patient" for these purposes is in reg 7(18) (see p237). The definition there also applies in determining whether a non-dependant deduction is applicable under reg 74(7)(f).

PART 6
Income and capital

General Note on Part 6

The claimant's income and capital and that of her/his partner, together with her/his applicable amount (see Part 5) and her/his "eligible rent" (see Part 3) are the basic components of the HB calculation: see s130(1)(c) SSCBA (p4).

The income rules are very detailed and are largely in line with the rules for IS, income-based JSA and income-related ESA. Caselaw in relation to those benefits and that decided under the old supplementary benefit scheme will often be highly persuasive. There are a number of court judgments, and a volume of commissioners' and Upper Tribunal decisions. Only the most significant are examined in the commentary to Part 6. See the current volume of *Social Security Legislation Vol II* for a more comprehensive treatment.

There is provision for assessment of capital, and a capital limit on entitlement of £16,000.

Income and capital: the distinction

No attempt has been made at any sort of definition of the difference between income and capital. What is very clear is that a resource must be either one or the other; there is nothing inbetween. However, although a resource at any one time must be income or capital, it does not follow that such status is immutable as a sum of money can alter in status, particularly over time: *CH 1561/2005* paras 17 and 18. See also regs 41 and 46 on pp372 and 381 for the situations in which capital is to be treated as income and income is to be treated as capital, as well as the analysis to reg 32 on p356 for when payments of tax credits might not count as income.

In *R(H) 8/08*, the claimant's accountant had paid his rent, on a number of occasions, direct to his landlord, as a loan on a temporary basis while his HB application was being considered. The local authority took the rent payments into account as the claimant's income. Deputy Commissioner Mark reviewed the caselaw on the meaning of "income" and decided that, as stated by the Court of Appeal in *Morrell v SSWP* [2003] EWCA Civ 526 (reported as *R(IS) 6/03*), the word must be given its ordinary and natural meaning, subject only to specific provisions of the regulations giving it a different meaning. Loans can be income, but it is necessary to examine all the facts before coming to a conclusion. He said that while loans, in particular recurrent loans, may well be income if there is no immediate repayment obligation, all the facts and circumstances need to be examined to decide if this is the case. He made some useful points on the factors that need to be considered (at para 31).

(1)   If a claimant receives regular loans from family or friends to cover rent or other outgoings before applying for benefit, and is not expected to repay them until some time in the indefinite future, this suggests that the loans are "income".

(2)   If a claimant and another person (eg, her/his accountant) agree that s/he should lend the claimant money for her/his rent for a month or two, while a claim for HB is being processed, then this suggests the loans are not "income", particularly if the person would expect repayment as soon as the claim was processed and arrears of benefit paid.

(3)   If a person was lending money regularly in ignorance of an application for HB, or would have gone on lending it regardless of its outcome, then this may suggest the loans are "income".

(4)   The fact that loans are not made every month is a factor to be taken into account with all the other circumstances, both in considering whether all or some of the loans are income, and in considering what the claimant's income was at any particular time.

The deputy commissioner pointed out that it would not appear to be the intention of the legislation to penalise somebody in need who made a legitimate application for benefit, because, through no fault of her/his own, the application took time to process and s/he needed to borrow temporarily to cover her/his needs while the application was being considered.

In order to decide whether a particular resource is income or capital, careful note should be taken of the provisions for treatment of income as capital and *vice versa*: see regs 41 and 46 respectively. Further indications as to the nature of a resource may be found in Schs 5 and 6, which set out the categories of income and capital that are to be disregarded in the assessment process. If a resource is required to be partially disregarded as income or as capital, that is a good indication that the resource (or those of a similar nature) is intended by the regulations to be treated as such. For example, Sch 6 para 10(a) requires insurance payments relating to damage to the home to be ignored as capital for up to 26 weeks. It follows that such payments will be treated as capital, and it can be deduced from that that most insurance pay-outs will fall to be treated as capital rather than income.

However, *CH 1561/2005* warns against assuming that the provisions of the legislation can determine the classification of whether a sum of money is income or capital. Indeed the decision goes further than this and holds that the regulations do not provide any definition of income or capital (either expressly – which is true – or by implication) but instead are predicated on the classification already having been made. Even if this approach is correct, it is suggested that the provisions of the regulations may provide helpful guidance as to whether an initial classification of a sum of money into income or capital is correct (which the commissioner in *CH 1561/2005* himself would seem to have done when deciding in that case that arrears of working families' tax credit were to be treated as income).

Where the legislation does not specifically or implicitly define how a payment should be treated, resort must be had to the caselaw. A useful starting point is the decision of Bridge J in *R v Supplementary Benefit Commission ex p Singer* [1973] 1 WLR 713. He stated that the "essential feature of receipts by way of income is that they display an element of periodic recurrence. Income cannot include ad hoc receipts." This is a useful rule of thumb but it does not provide a complete answer, because periodic payments may constitute capital in certain circumstances. It is also necessary to consider the nature of the obligation under which the payments are made. In *Lillystone v Supplementary Benefits Commission* [1982] 3 FLR 52, CA, the claimant was receiving £70 a month for 10 years towards the purchase price of his house. Because the payments went towards the sale price of a capital asset, it was held that they constituted capital.

Two cases decided under a former version of the HB Regs 1987 may also be of assistance. In *R v Oxford CC ex p Jack* [1984] 17 HLR 419, QBD, the High Court considered the meaning of "income other than earnings" and quashed a decision of a review board to base its assessment of the claimant's income on withdrawals from his current account. This was because "the Board failed to enquire where the various sums paid into the account had come from". It might have been reasonable to base the claimant's income on his current account if no other evidence was available, but there was in this case. The judge referred to the definition of income in the Shorter Oxford English Dictionary. The current definition of income is:

"that which comes in as the periodical produce of one's work, business, lands or investment (commonly expressed in terms of money) annual or periodical receipts; revenue."

On the basis of the definition of "income", the judge made the following general remarks about the nature of income:

"income, in my view, is what would in the colloquial sense, be regarded as a person's income, including not merely periodical payments received as of legal right, but periodical payments received, not necessarily at regular intervals, as a result of parental or family feeling or as a result of an agreement not enforceable by law."

"[if] regular payments are made . . . it is much more likely that it will appear to be income than if it is an irregular amount which is paid at less regular intervals [although] the precise period for which payment is made is not critical".

Therefore, a lump sum paid at the start of a year with the expectation that it should gradually be drawn on for living expenses "would properly fall to be considered as income".

In *H v West Dorset DC ex p Poupard* [1988] 28 HVR 40, CA, Balcombe LJ considered the point and stated (at p43):

"if and insofar as what Glidewell J was saying was that it was a question of fact in any case, within the discretion of the review board, whether withdrawals from a bank account could be taken into account in estimating income, I respectfully agree [but] if he was intending to accept the concession 'prima facie that a withdrawal is not income', then in my judgment . . . his remarks were obiter and I do not accept them as laying down any general principle . . ."

In *Poupard,* the claimant's business was shown to have made a loss, but the claimant had made drawings both from the business receipts and from a bank overdraft facility in order to pay for living expenses, and those drawings were treated as income. Balcombe LJ's conclusions were as follows (at p43):

"(1)   Income is that which comes in to the applicant;

(2)   It may, depending on the facts of the case, be appropriate to take into account cash withdrawals from the gross receipts of an applicant's business, or withdrawals from an applicant's business, or withdrawals from an applicant's bank account or other moneys received by way of loan, notwithstanding that these may not be classified as income on accounting principles and notwithstanding that the loan may eventually be repaid out of capital.

(3)   Capital which is in no way utilised cannot be deemed to constitute or create income.

(4)   However, again depending on the facts of the particular case, the utilisation of capital, whether directly so as to pay for living expenses, or indirectly as security for a loan which is used to pay for living expenses, may thereby 'convert' the capital so used into 'income'."

Some care is required in using these cases, however, for two reasons. First, specific provision is now made to meet some of the points made: see, for example, reg 52(1) which *does* deem capital to create income. Secondly, the old HB scheme did not contain any capital limit. In *ex p Jack*, Glidewell J had referred extensively to Bridge J's views as to the nature of "income" in *Singer* (see above). In *Poupard*, Balcombe LJ found this case "of no help" because the supplementary benefit legislation had separate provision for the assessment of income and capital in the same way that the current HB Regs do. Consequently the comments in *Singer* are more relevant now than when they were considered in *Poupard*. Despite the fact that *Poupard* is a decision of the Court of Appeal, it is submitted that this case is of little assistance given the current HB scheme's distinction between capital and income.

Because income and capital are treated separately under these regulations, as they were in *Singer*, the relevance of *Poupard* to the current regulations must be debatable where, say, only sporadic withdrawals of differing amounts are made. The Court of Appeal held in *Poupard* that borrowings by way of a bank overdraft secured by capital and used for day-to-day living expenses constitute "income" for HB purposes. This decision is not necessarily inconsistent with *ex p Jack* as the Court did have regard to the source of the money and the fact that the loan was secured by capital. Certainly, the more general comments in *ex p Jack* regarding the nature of income payments have not been interfered with.

In *AR v Bradford MBC* [2008] UKUT 30 (AAC); R(H) 6/09, Judge Mesher went further. He said that the factors of the absence of any provision in the statute and regulations for taking capital into account and of any real definition of income that no doubt stood behind the impetus in *Poupard* to regard loans or the utilisation of a person's own capital for living expenses as income, are entirely absent from the current scheme. Nor is there room in that context for the adoption of a simplistic starting point like "income is that which comes in". The starting point must be the particular highly detailed statutory context. There is nothing in the statutory context here to point against the conclusion that drawings from a business are not to be taken into account as either income from self-employment or other income. *Poupard* never stood for any rigid rule that loans always have to count as income, but in Judge Mesher's judgment the decision should no longer be considered as of any relevance to the current HB and CTB schemes and should now be consigned to a historical footnote at most.

In *R(H) 5/05*, Commissioner Mesher held that "the resources provided by the use of the overdraft facility do not amount to income" (para 47); though it would appear that the contrary was not argued before him nor was *Poupard* cited to him. His reasoning, in paras 44 to 47, was as follows:

"It is just possible that it could have been argued that the claimant's use of the overdraft facility with his bank produced income in his hands. Nowhere in his comprehensive written and oral submissions did Mr Stagg make that specific argument, and it does not specifically appear anywhere else in the papers. In those circumstances I have not sought any further submissions and explain only briefly why I conclude that that argument would not work."

"The argument could have run as follows. On the statements before me, the first cheque paid by the bank without funds in the account to cover it was paid on 28 March 2001. By 18 April 2001 the overdraft stood at £2,799.55. The overdraft seems initially not to have been agreed, although it probably was by 18 April 2001. But it is established that the drawing of a cheque in excess of the amount standing to a customer's credit is a request for a loan and if the cheque is honoured the customer has borrowed money (see paragraph 11 of *R(IS) 22/98*). Money drawn down under an agreed limit is also borrowing, as is the honouring of cheques taking an overdraft over an agreed limit. The first two payments from Ms LB reduced the amount by which the claimant was overdrawn. The payments on 17 July 2001 and 7 November 2001 took him into credit, but the effect did not last for more than a few weeks in either case. The payment on 14 January 2002 did enable the claimant to stay in credit until 2 April 2002. It might have been argued that the approach endorsed by the Court of Appeal in *Morrell, R(IS) 6/03*, applied to the loans made to the claimant by his bank by way of overdraft. That would have been on the basis that a purpose must have been to allow the claimant to meet the recurrent expenses ordinarily met out of his current account. Chief among these was the monthly rent of £1,785.33, and there were other regular payments for items like home and contents insurance and water rates, as well as payments for cable services and credit card bills. It could have been argued that the provision of resources for such regularly recurring items resulted in the receipt of income."

"That on its face is a powerful argument. But it seems to me that it is undermined by the principles laid down in *Leeves v Chief Adjudication Officer*, R(IS) 5/99, as followed in *Morrell*). In that case, a student abandoned his course on 27 April 1995 having received the summer term's instalment of grant from his local education authority on 24 April 1995 (and spent it all on paying off mortgage arrears and debts). He had undertaken, in accordance with the legislation then in force on student grants, to repay such sum as might be determined by the authority if he ceased to attend the course before its normal termination date. On 24 May 1995 the authority wrote to the student terminating his grant with effect from 27 April 1995 and requiring repayment of a particular amount. Under the income support rules the payment of grant on 24 April 1995 would be attributed as income to the whole of the summer term. The Court of Appeal held that as from 24 May 1995 the grant monies were not income. The court agreed with counsel for the student that "income" should be given its natural and ordinary meaning and that moneys accruing or to be treated as accruing "under a certain obligation of immediate payment (ie, an equivalent debt) do not amount to income". From 27 April 1995 to 23 May 1995, although there was no reason to think that the discretion to call for repayment would not be exercised, it was not clear when the student would be required to repay or what the precise sum would be. So there was no "crystallised" obligation. But there was from 24 May 1995."

"Although I have no evidence in the present case of the precise terms on which the overdraft was granted to the claimant, I can take judicial notice of the fact that the standard terms are that bank overdrafts are repayable on demand, although the demand may be not be made while the amount stays within an agreed limit. Those terms bring the claimant's repayment obligation within the *Leeves* principles. The obligation is certain, as the amount overdrawn can be identified day by day, and is immediate, even though the bank chooses not to enforce the immediate obligation. Accordingly, the resources provided by the use of the overdraft facility do not amount to income. In my judgment, that result is also in accord with the ordinary and natural meaning of "income". One would not naturally speak of a person having an income from incurring expenditure and running up an overdraft".

In *CH 1672/2007*, there was a decree absolute of judicial separation in effect between the claimant and his wife. As part of the arrangements associated with the issue of the decree, he was ordered by the High Court to pay a monthly sum to his wife that was one half of his monthly occupational pension. The order was enforceable against him. However, the local authority decided that his income was his full pension income and that no account could be taken of the sums he paid to his wife. The claimant argued that his weekly income should be calculated after deducting the sum he had to pay to his wife. Commissioner Williams said that a review of the cases showed the difficulty that courts, tribunals and the Secretary of State have had in drawing a line between receipts by a claimant that are properly regarded as income as against those that are not income (and are termed by default of any alternative as capital). Within the category of payments that on receipt are regarded as income there was a further difficulty in deciding in what circumstances those receipts should be reduced fully or partly by reference to payments made by the recipient from those receipts, whether to the original payer or to some third party. The cases also all showed the importance of noting the immediate statutory context of the questions to be asked, and the terms to be applied, and in those contexts, the precise financial transactions taking place and the importance of distinguishing between informal arrangements and formal liabilities. The commissioner accepted that a literal interpretation of the rules would mean here, that the income transferred by the claimant to his wife would be regarded both as his income and as her income at the same time. In his view it militated against introducing an "ordinary" meaning of income that allowed the same income to be counted twice in the hands of different recipients as equally income of both of them. He therefore decided that the proper interpretation of the relevant statutory test of income, in its ordinary sense, but also in the context of the arrangements in this appeal, was that the claimant's income should be regarded as the amount he had left from his occupational pension after he had passed on the sums he was required to pay to his wife from that pension under the High Court pension-splitting order.

There have been a number of decisions on the treatment of payments made by local authority employers as arrears or compensation payments made in respect of equal pay, equal treatment, sex discrimination claims or similar, when the employee in question has also been in receipt of means-tested benefits during the period of the payment. *EM v Waltham Forest LBC* [2009] UKUT 245 (AAC) concerned treatment of bonus payments which were held to be capital payments. It is understood that permission to appeal to the Court of Appeal has been granted. *SSWP v JP (JSA)* [2010] UKUT 90 (AAC) concerned treatment of a payment made in offer of settlement under the Equal Pay Act 1970, which was held to be income (specifically "earnings"). It is understood that permission to appeal to the Court of Appeal is being sought. *Kingston upon Hull CC v DLM (HB)* [2010] UKUT

234 (AAC) (the most recent of the three decisions) concerned an equal pay "final settlement" compensation offer. Judge Howell held that the payment was "earnings". He said that the First-tier Tribunal was right to apply the principle of *R(SB) 21/86* which was followed in *CIS 590/1993* and in *SSWP v JP*.

When income converts to capital

Another important point is the effect of retention of income. The most common example of a capital asset is, perhaps, a bank account which contains the accumulated earnings of the account-holder, minus outgoings. Thus there comes a point at which income metamorphoses into capital. The general rule is that a payment is treated as income for a period equal to that to which it is attributable, whereon it becomes part of the claimant's capital: see *R(IS) 3/93*; *R(IS) 9/08*; *R(PC) 3/08*.

Decision-making on income and capital issues

The rules in this Part only apply, effectively, to claimants who are not in receipt of IS, income-based JSA or income-related ESA. Recipients of those benefits have already had their income and capital taken into account for the purposes of assessing entitlement to that benefit. By definition, IS, income-based JSA and income-related ESA claimants have capital worth less than £16,000 and income less than their applicable amounts, and whatever income or capital as such claimants *do* possess is disregarded under Schs 4, 5 and 6. They are therefore entitled to HB under s130(1)(c)(i) SSCBA, and there is no need for local authorities to assess income and capital under this Part to determine entitlement: see *R v Penwith DC ex p Menear* [1991] 24 HLR 115, QBD. In addition, as the deputy commissioner in *CH 4014/2007* pointed out, for these purposes, the local authority only needs to decide the question of whether a claimant is a member of a couple if s/he is *not* receiving IS, income-based JSA or income-related ESA. The question is not directly relevant to entitlement to HB and CTB in the same way as for those benefits; if the claimant is receiving one of them, s/he is automatically entitled to HB and CTB (if the qualifying conditions are met) and even if s/he has a partner, the partner's income and capital are disregarded. This means that the authority can, and usually must, consider itself bound by a DWP decision to award IS, income-based JSA or income-related ESA.

There are two exceptions to this cardinal rule. The first arises where an authority has evidence which has not already been considered by the DWP and which raises a reasonable doubt as to whether the DWP decision on the means test was correct. The authority may notify the DWP of its views under the information-sharing powers in Part VII SSAA and may suspend payment of HB pending consideration by the DWP as to whether the award of benefit should be revised or superseded: see reg 11 D&A Regs.

The second exception is a product of the decision of the Court of Appeal in *R v South Ribble DC HBRB ex p Hamilton* [2000] 33 HLR 102, CA. In that case, the Review Board upheld the council's determinations that HB should be refused to the claimant on the basis that he was fraudulently concealing income and capital from the then DSS and the local authority. There was, indeed, strong evidence before the Board to this effect, but the authority did not refer the matter to the DSS for investigation. The Court of Appeal approved the decision in *ex p Menear*, but said that the decision did not require a council to pay HB (or even to award it and then withhold benefit pending examination of the issue). If the authority can conclude that the claimant is fraudulently concealing resources from the DWP, it may lawfully refuse to award benefit.

On its facts, the decision is justifiable as a matter of public policy. However, caution is required in its application. In *Hamilton* there was apparently no evidence that the then DSS had ever considered whether it shared the local authority's view that the claimant was acting fraudulently. However, there may be cases where the DWP has examined a claim and has concluded that there is no basis for taking away the claimant's IS, JSA or ESA, or where a decision by a decision maker that a claimant has been acting fraudulently is reversed on appeal to the First-tier Tribunal. In that event, *Hamilton* should not be read as giving the local authority an entitlement to take a different view. The structure of the legislation, as emphasised in *Menear*, is that in such cases it is for the DWP (and subsequently the First-tier Tribunal) to make decisions on income and capital. It will only be if the DWP has not had an adequate opportunity to decide whether the claimant is concealing resources that the local authority will be justified in refusing benefit on the basis of the decision in *Hamilton*. This will apply both to cases where the DWP has been unaware of any basis for questioning the decision to award benefit and also to cases where the DWP (or tribunal) has decided that benefit should not be withdrawn but the authority has fresh evidence at its disposal.

What if the DWP fails to notify a claimant of a decision that her/his entitlement to, for example, IS has ended? In *SD v Newcastle City Council (HB)* [2010] UKUT 306 (AAC), Judge Mesher decided, applying *R v Secretary of State for the Home Department, ex parte Anufrijeva* [2003] UKHL 36 [2004] 1 AC 604, that such a decision could only have legal effect once notified and thus the claimant here was to continue to be considered as "on IS" until such time as she was notified. Judge Mesher appreciated the difficulty for local authorities when receiving information from the DWP that an award of IS or another passporting benefit has been terminated. He said (at para 15):

"A local authority cannot reasonably be expected to go behind such information at that stage and start making enquiries about whether the claimant has been notified of the income support decision. It seems to me that an authority would, unless there was some positive indication to the contrary, be entitled to take the information at face value and make the necessary housing benefit and CTB decisions in consequence. But once the issue of notification of the income support decision by the DWP is raised by or on behalf of the claimant or by some other evidence that comes before the local authority, things are different. Local authorities must then deal with the issue consistently with the approach of law set out above either in its own decisions or before tribunals on appeal."

Note, however, that once a claimant is notified by the DWP of a decision to end entitlement to a passporting benefit, the decision is effective. The local authority can then supersede the relevant HB and CTB decisions.

It should also be noted that if the DWP *refuses* IS, income-based JSA or income-related ESA on the basis of excess income or capital, there is nothing in the legislation that requires or entitles the authority to follow suit. It must carry out its own assessment of income and capital and is entitled to come to a different conclusion, though it is entitled to inquire of the DWP under Pt VII of the SSAA as to the basis for its refusal of benefit.

Structure of the Part

Section 1 contains general rules about when another person's income/capital may be treated as belonging to the claimant, and when the HB calculation may be based on a non-dependant's income and capital rather than the claimant's own. The provisions of Sections 2 to 5 apply to the claimant's income as defined by Section 1 (thus including that of her/his partner or partners falling within reg 25).

Section 2 contains general rules about the calculation of income on a weekly basis and what counts as "income" for these purposes. Regs 27 to 31 provide a definition of the different categories of income which are subject to the specific rules in Sections 3 to 5. Reg 33 applies generally to convert payments of assessable income into weekly amounts where they are paid for periods other than a week, as HB is calculated on a weekly basis. Reg 34 deals with the effect of changes in certain statutory deductions from income and is really a provision to help authorities administer the scheme more efficiently. The total amount of weekly income to be taken into account under this Part is the claimant's weekly income assessed under regs 29 to 32, plus any "tariff income" and capital treated as income.

Section 3 contains specific rules about the assessment of earnings from "employed earners" employment.

Section 4 contains specific rules about earnings from employment as a "self-employed" earner.

Section 5 sets out specific rules about the assessment of income which is not earnings.

Section 6 contains the rules about the assessment of capital.

SECTION 1
General

General Note on Section 1

This Section deals with two matters pursuant to s136 SSCBA 1992 (see p16) in relation to the calculation of a claimant's income and capital.

(1)   Reg 25, by authority of s136(1) SSCBA, prescribes the circumstances in which the income and capital of members of the claimant's family is or is not to be treated as the claimant's own. It also sets out the circumstances in which a claimant who is polygamously married is to be treated as possessing the income and capital of her/his partners.

(2)   Reg 26, in pursuance of s136(5)(a) and (b) SSCBA, enables the authority assessing HB to treat the claimant as possessing the income and capital of a non-dependant rather than her/his own resources, which are then disregarded. This is an anti-abuse provision.

Calculation of income and capital of members of claimant's family and of a polygamous marriage

25.–(1)   The income and capital of a claimant's partner which by virtue of section 136(1) of the Act is to be treated as income and capital of the claimant, shall be calculated or estimated in accordance with the following provisions of this Part in like manner as for the claimant; and any reference to the "claimant" shall, except where the context otherwise requires, be construed for the purposes of this Part as if it were a reference to his partner.

(2)   Where a claimant or the partner of a claimant is married polygamously to two or more members of his household–

(a)   the claimant shall be treated as possessing capital and income belonging to each such member; and

(b)   the income and capital of that member shall be calculated in accordance with the following provisions of this Part in like manner as for the claimant.

(3)   The income and capital of a child or young person shall not be treated as the income and capital of the claimant.

Definitions

"child" – see reg 2(1).

"claimant" – see reg 2(1).

"family" – see s137(1) SSCBA.

"household" – see "family".
"married polygamously" – see reg 2(1).
"partner" – see reg 2(1).
"young person" – see reg 19.

General Note

According to s136(1) SSCBA, a claimant is to be treated as possessing the income and capital of members of her/his "family" "except in prescribed circumstances". Under s136(5)(a) SSCBA, regulations may prescribe circumstances in which a claimant may be treated as possessing income which s/he does not in fact possess. This effectively only applies to the income and capital of any partner of the claimant as this regulation, together with the other provisions of this Part, prescribes that a child or young person's income and capital are *not* to be treated as the claimant's. Using the powers in s136(5)(a), reg 25 provides that claimants who are polygamously married are to be treated as possessing the income/capital of their partners who share their household.

Analysis

Para (1). The effect of para (1) is that whenever a reference to the claimant's capital or income is made it is to be treated as including the capital/income of her/his partner.

Para (2) provides that where the claimant is polygamously married s/he is to be treated as possessing the income and capital of all partners to the marriage with whom s/he shares a household (see p22).

Para (3) states that the income and capital of a child or young person is not treated as that of the claimant.

Circumstances in which income of non-dependant is to be treated as claimant's

26.–(1)   Where it appears to the relevant authority that a non-dependant and the claimant have entered into arrangements in order to take advantage of the housing benefit scheme and the non-dependant has more capital and income than the claimant, that authority shall, except where the claimant is on income support [¹ , an income-based jobseeker's allowance or an income-related employment and support allowance], treat the claimant as possessing capital and income belonging to that non-dependant and, in such a case, shall disregard any capital and income which the claimant does possess.

(2)   Where a claimant is treated as possessing capital and income belonging to a non-dependant under paragraph (1) the capital and income of that non-dependant shall be calculated in accordance with the following provisions of this Part in like manner as for the claimant and any reference to the ''claimant'' shall, except where the context otherwise requires, be construed for the purposes of this Part as if it were a reference to that non-dependant.

Amendment

1.   Amended by reg 13 of SI 2008 No 1082 as from 27.10.08.

Definitions

"claimant" – see reg 2(1).
"non-dependant" – see reg 3.

General Note

Made under s136(5)(a) and (b) SSCBA, this regulation gives an authority the power to assess entitlement to HB on the basis of a non-dependant's capital and income, rather than on the basis of the claimant's own, where the circumstances suggest to the authority that the claimant and non-dependant have made arrangements so as to take advantage of the HB scheme and the non-dependant has more income and capital than the claimant.

Analysis

Para (1). The language used in para (1), in particular the phrase "take advantage of the housing benefit scheme" are similar to that used in reg 9(1)(l) and so it is suggested that similar considerations arise and the caselaw will assist in resolving disputes on the application of this provision. Reference should be made to the Analysis on p262, but some modification will be necessary.

The first step is to identify some "arrangements" that the claimant and non-dependant have entered into. Some evidence of collusion will usually be required. Thus where A is a tenant whose uncle B lives with him and A becomes unemployed and claims HB to meet his rent liability, there is no basis for fixing him with B's resources. It is clear that the power cannot be used just because the non-dependant is wealthier than the claimant, and it is suggested that it should be used only where good reason exists.

If challenged, the onus is on the authority to show grounds for its belief that arrangements have been made so as to take advantage of the HB scheme. The words "appears to the relevant authority" do not absolve the authority from determining the question on proper principles and if it fails to do so, its decision will be vulnerable to challenge.

Note that this power may be used only where the non-dependant's income and capital *both* exceed that of the claimant and that it cannot be used where the claimant is on IS, income-based JSA or income-related ESA.

Para (2). If the authority does decide to use this power, it must base the HB calculation on the non-dependant's income and capital. Previous editions have suggested that this includes resources belonging to the non-dependant's family, but it is suggested that is incorrect. Para (2) requires the non-dependant's resources to be calculated under the "following provisions of this Part" and it would appear that phrase excludes consideration of reg 25 which deals with the treatment of the resources of family members and of reg 26 itself.

If the power is exercised, the claimant's income and capital is to be disregarded under para (1).

Every reference to claimant in the remainder of this part should be read as referring to the "non-dependant" unless the context of the regulation in question makes it clear that this is not intended. See particularly the note to Sch 4 para 3 on p545.

SECTION 2
Income

General Note on Section 2

This Section deals with the assessment of various types of income for HB purposes.

Calculation of income on a weekly basis

27.–(1) Subject to regulations 34 (disregard of changes in tax, contributions etc), and 80 and 81 (calculation of weekly amounts and rent free periods) for the purposes of section 130(1)(c) of the Act (conditions of entitlement to housing benefit) the income of a claimant shall be calculated on a weekly basis–

   (a)   by estimating the amount which is likely to be his average weekly income in accordance with this Section and Sections 3 to 5 of this Part and Sections 1 and 3 of Part 7;

   (b)   by adding to that amount the weekly income calculated under regulation 52 (calculation of tariff income from capital); and

   (c)   by then deducting any relevant child care charges to which regulation 28 (treatment of child care charges) applies from any earnings which form part of the average weekly income or, in a case where the conditions in paragraph (2) are met, from those earnings plus whichever credit specified in sub-paragraph (b) of that paragraph is appropriate, up to a maximum deduction in respect of the claimant's family of whichever of the sums specified in paragraph (3) applies in his case.

   (2)   The conditions of this paragraph are that–

   (a)   the claimant's earnings which form part of his average weekly income are less than the lower of either his relevant child care charges or whichever of the deductions specified in paragraph (3) otherwise applies in his case; and

   (b)   that claimant or, if he is a member of a couple either the claimant or his partner, is in receipt of either working tax credit or child tax credit.

   (3)   The maximum deduction to which paragraph (1)(c) above refers shall be–

   (a)   where the claimant's family includes only one child in respect of whom relevant child care charges are paid, [⁵ £175.00] per week;

   (b)   where the claimant's family includes more than one child in respect of whom relevant child care charges are paid, [⁵ £300] per week.

   (4)   For the purposes of paragraph (1) "income" includes capital treated as income under regulation 41 (capital treated as income) and income which a claimant is treated as possessing under regulation 42 (notional income).

Amendments

1.   Confirmed by Art 19(2) of SI 2006 No 645 and reg 8 of SI 2006 No 217 as from 1.4.06 (3.4.06 where rent payable weekly or at intervals of a week).
2.   Confirmed by Art 19(2) of SI 2007 No 688 as from 1.4.07 (2.4.07 where rent payable weekly or at intervals of a week).
3.   Confirmed by Art 19(3) of SI 2008 No 632 as from 1.4.08 (7.4.08 where rent payable weekly or in multiples of a week).

4.	Confirmed by Art 19(3) of SI 2009 No 497 as from 1.4.09 (6.4.09 where rent payable weekly or in multiples of a week).

5.	Confirmed by Art 19(2) of SI 2010 No 793 as from 1.4.10 (5.4.10 where rent payable weekly or in multiples of a week).

Definition
"claimant" – see reg 2(1).

General Note
Reg 27 sets out the basic formula for the calculation of income. It is the total income assessed under Sections 2 to 5 of this Part (and the special provisions for students in Part 7) plus any tariff income deemed to be generated by capital under reg 52, minus deductible child care charges up to the maximum figures stated in para (3). "Income" in this context includes notional income and capital deemed to be income as well as actual income: see para (4).

Analysis
Para (1)(b). Under reg 52, a claimant is treated as receiving income from her/his capital if the latter is worth more than £6,000 (£10,000 if living in residential accommodation) but less than £16,000 as assessed under Section 6 of this Part and Sch 6. Any actual income from capital is generally treated as capital under reg 46(4).

Paras (1)(c), (2) and (3) provide for relevant childcare charges (as defined by reg 28) to be deducted from earnings subject to weekly maxima of a set amount where those charges are incurred in respect of one child and a higher amount where they are incurred in respect of more than one child. Where the claimant's earnings are lower than the childcare charges or the amounts specified in para (3), any tax credit to which s/he is entitled will be added to the earnings for the purpose of calculating the deduction.

Para (4) confirms that notional income (reg 42) and capital treated as income (reg 41) should be included in the calculation of income on a weekly basis.

Treatment of child care charges

28.–(1)	This regulation applies where a claimant is incurring relevant child care charges and–

(a)	is a lone parent and is engaged in remunerative work;

(b)	is a member of a couple both of whom are engaged in remunerative work; or

(c)	is a member of a couple where one member is engaged in remunerative work and the other–

(i)	is incapacitated;

(ii)	is an in-patient in hospital; or

(iii)	is in prison (whether serving a custodial sentence or remanded in custody awaiting trial or sentence).

(2)	For the purposes of paragraph (1) and subject to paragraph (4), a person to whom paragraph (3) applies shall be treated as engaged in remunerative work for a period not exceeding 28 weeks during which he–

(a)	is paid statutory sick pay;

(b)	is paid short-term incapacity benefit at the lower rate under sections 30A to 30E of the Act;

[⁴ (ba) is paid an employment and support allowance;]

(c)	is paid income support on the grounds of incapacity for work under regulation 4ZA of, and paragraph 7 or 14 of Schedule 1B to, the Income Support Regulations; or

(d)	is credited with earnings on the grounds of incapacity for work [⁴ or limited capability for work] under regulation 8B of the Social Security (Credits) Regulations 1975.

(3)	This paragraph applies to a person who was engaged in remunerative work immediately before–

(a)	the first day of the period in respect of which he was first paid statutory sick pay, short-term incapacity benefit [⁴ , an employment and support allowance] or income support on the grounds of incapacity for work; or

(b)	the first day of the period in respect of which earnings are credited,

as the case may be.

(4)　In a case to which paragraph (2)(c) or (d) applies, the period of 28 weeks begins on the day on which the person is first paid income support or on the first day of the period in respect of which earnings are credited, as the case may be.

(5)　Relevant child care charges are those charges for care to which paragraphs (6) and (7) apply, and shall be calculated on a weekly basis in accordance with paragraph (10).

(6)　The charges are paid by the claimant for care which is provided–

(a)　in the case of any child of the claimant's family who is not disabled, in respect of the period beginning on that child's date of birth and ending on the day preceding the first Monday in September following that child's fifteenth birthday; or

(b)　in the case of any child of the claimant's family who is disabled, in respect of the period beginning on that person's date of birth and ending on the day preceding the first Monday in September following that person's sixteenth birthday.

(7)　The charges are paid for care which is provided by one or more of the care providers listed in paragraph (8) and are not paid–

(a)　in respect of the child's compulsory education;

(b)　by a claimant to a partner or by a partner to a claimant in respect of any child for whom either or any of them is responsible in accordance with regulation 20 (circumstances in which a person is treated as responsible or not responsible for another); or

(c)　in respect of care provided by a relative of a child wholly or mainly in the child's home.

(8)　The care to which paragraph (7) refers may be provided–

(a)　out of school hours, by a school on school premises or by a local authority–

(i)　for children who are not disabled in respect of the period beginning on their eighth birthday and ending on the day preceding the first Monday in September following their fifteenth birthday; or

(ii)　for children who are disabled in respect of the period beginning on their eighth birthday and ending on the day preceding the first Monday in September following their sixteenth birthday;

(b)　by a child care provider approved in accordance with the Tax Credit (New Category of Child Care Provider) Regulations 1999;

(c)　by persons registered under Part 10A of the Children Act 1989; or

(d)　in schools or establishments which are exempted from registration under Part 10A of the Children Act 1989 by virtue of paragraph 1 or 2 of Schedule 9A to that Act; or

(e)　by–

(i)　persons registered under section 7(1) of the Regulation of Care (Scotland) Act 2001; or

(ii)　local authorities registered under section 33(1) of that Act, where the care provided is child minding or daycare of children within the meaning of that Act; or

(f)　by a person prescribed in regulations made pursuant to section 12(4) of the Tax Credits Act. [⁶ or

(g)　by a person who is registered under Chapter 2 or 3 of Part 3 of the Childcare Act 2006; or .

(h)　by any of the schools mentioned in section 34(2) of the Childcare Act 2006 in circumstances where the requirement to register under Chapter 2 of Part 3 of that Act does not apply by virtue of section 34(2) of that Act; or .

(i)　by any of the schools mentioned in section 53(2) of the Childcare Act 2006 in circumstances where the requirement to register under Chapter 3 of Part 3 of that Act does not apply by virtue of section 53(2) of that Act; or .

(j)　by any of the establishments mentioned in section 18(5) of the Childcare Act 2006 in circumstances where the care is not included in the meaning of ''childcare'' for the purposes of Part 1 and Part 3 of that Act by virtue of that subsection; or .

(k) by a foster parent [⁷ or kinship carer]under the Fostering Services Regulations 2002, the Fostering Services (Wales) Regulations 2003 or the [⁷ Looked After Children (Scotland) Regulations 2009] in relation to a child other than one whom the foster parent is fostering [⁷ or kinship carer is looking after]; or .

(l) by a domiciliary care worker under the Domiciliary Care Agencies Regulations 2002 or the Domiciliary Care Agencies (Wales) Regulations 2004; or .

(m) by a person who is not a relative of the child wholly or mainly in the child's home.]

(9) In paragraphs (6) and (8)(a), ''the first Monday in September'' means the Monday which first occurs in the month of September in any year.

(10) Relevant child care charges shall be estimated over such period, not exceeding a year, as is appropriate in order that the average weekly charge may be estimated accurately having regard to information as to the amount of that charge provided by the child minder or person providing the care.

(11) For the purposes of paragraph (1)(c) the other member of a couple is incapacitated where–

[³ (a) the claimant's applicable amount includes a disability premium on account of the other member's incapacity [⁴ or the support component or the work-related activity component on account of the other member having limited capability for work];]

(b) the claimant's applicable amount would include a disability premium [³] on account of the other member's incapacity but for that other member being treated as capable of work by virtue of a determination made in accordance with regulations made under section 171E of the Act;

[⁴ (ba) the claimant's applicable amount would include the support component or the work-related activity component on account of the other member having limited capability for work but for that other member being treated as not having limited capability for work by virtue of a determination made in accordance with the Employment and Support Allowance Regulations;]

(c) the claimant (within the meaning of regulation 2) is, or is treated as, incapable of work and has been so incapable, or has been so treated as incapable, of work in accordance with the provisions of, and regulations made under, Part 12A of the Act (incapacity for work) for a continuous period of not less than 196 days; and for this purpose any two or more separate periods separated by a break of not more than 56 days shall be treated as one continuous period;

[⁴ (ca) the claimant (within the meaning of regulation 2(1)) has, or is treated as having, limited capability for work and has had, or been treated as having, limited capability for work in accordance with the Employment and Support Allowance Regulations for a continuous period of not less than 196 days and for this purpose any two or more separate periods separated by a break of not more than 84 days must be treated as one continuous period;]

(d) there is payable in respect of him one or more of the following pensions or allowances–

   (i) long-term incapacity benefit or short-term incapacity benefit at the higher rate under Schedule 4 to the Act;

   (ii) attendance allowance under section 64 of the Act;

   (iii) severe disablement allowance under section 68 of the Act;

   (iv) disability living allowance under section 71 of the Act;

   (v) increase of disablement pension under section 104 of the Act;

   (vi) a pension increase [⁵ paid as part of a war disablement pension or under] an industrial injuries scheme which is analogous to an allowance or increase of disablement pension under head (ii), (iv) or (v) above;

   [⁴ (vii) main phase employment and support allowance;]

(e) a pension or allowance to which head (ii), (iv), (v) or (vi) of sub-paragraph (d) above refers was payable on account of his incapacity but has ceased to be payable in consequence of his becoming a patient [¹ , which in this regulation shall mean a person (other than a person who is serving a sentence of imprisonment or detention in a youth custody institution) who is regarded as receiving free in-patient treatment within the meaning of [² regulation 2(4) and (5) of the Social Security (Hospital In-Patients) Regulations 2005].];

(f)   sub-paragraph (d) or (e) would apply to him if the legislative provisions referred to in those sub-paragraphs were provisions under any corresponding enactment having effect in Northern Ireland; or

(g)   he has an invalid carriage or other vehicle provided to him by the Secretary of State under section 5(2)(a) of and Schedule 2 to the National Health Service Act 1977 or by Scottish Ministers under section 46 of the National Health Service (Scotland) Act 1978 or provided by the [³ Department of Health, Social Services and Public Safety in Northern Ireland] under Article 30(1) of the Health and Personal Social Services (Northern Ireland) Order 1972.

(12)   For the purposes of paragraph (11), once paragraph (11)(c) applies to the claimant, if he then ceases, for a period of 56 days or less, to be incapable, or to be treated as incapable, of work, that paragraph shall, on his again becoming so incapable, or so treated as incapable, of work at the end of that period, immediately thereafter apply to him for so long as he remains incapable, or is treated as remaining incapable, of work.

[⁴ (12A)   For the purposes of paragraph (11), once paragraph (11)(ca) applies to the claimant, if he then ceases, for a period of 84 days or less, to have, or to be treated as having, limited capability for work, that paragraph is, on his again having, or being treated as having, limited capability for work at the end of that period, immediately thereafter to apply to him for so long as he has, or is treated as having, limited capability for work.]

(13)   For the purposes of paragraphs (6) and (8)(a), a person is disabled if he is a person–

(a)   in respect of whom disability living allowance is payable, or has ceased to be payable solely because he is a patient;

(b)   who is registered as blind in a register compiled under section 29 of the National Assistance Act 1948 (welfare services) or, in Scotland, has been certified as blind and in consequence he is registered as blind in a register maintained by or on behalf of a council constituted under section 2 of the Local Government (Scotland) Act 1994; or

(c)   who ceased to be registered as blind in such a register within the period beginning 28 weeks before the first Monday in September following that person's fifteenth birthday and ending on the day preceding the first Monday in September following that person's sixteenth birthday.

(14)   For the purposes of–

(a)   paragraph (1) a person on maternity leave, paternity leave or adoption leave shall be treated as if she is engaged in remunerative work for the period specified in sub-paragraph (b) ("the relevant period") provided that–

(i)   in the week before the period of maternity leave, paternity leave or adoption leave began she was in remunerative work;

(ii)   the claimant is incurring relevant child care charges within the meaning of paragraph (5); and

(iii)   she is entitled to statutory maternity pay under section 164 of the Act, statutory paternity pay by virtue of section 171ZA or 171ZB of the Act, statutory adoption pay by virtue of section 171ZL of the Act, maternity allowance under section 35 of the Act or qualifying support;

(b)   sub-paragraph (a) the relevant period shall begin on the day on which the person's maternity leave, paternity leave or adoption leave commences and shall end on–

(i)   the date that leave ends;

(ii)   if no child care element of working tax credit is in payment on the date that entitlement to maternity allowance, qualifying support, statutory maternity pay, statutory paternity pay or statutory adoption pay ends, the date that entitlement ends; or

(iii) if a child care element of working tax credit is in payment on the date that entitlement to maternity allowance, qualifying support, statutory maternity pay, statutory paternity pay or statutory adoption pay ends, the date that entitlement to that award of the child care element of working tax credit ends,

whichever shall occur first.

(15) In paragraph (14)–

(a) ''qualifying support'' means income support to which that person is entitled by virtue of paragraph 14B of Schedule 1B to the Income Support Regulations; and

(b) ''child care element'' of working tax credit means the element of working tax credit prescribed under section 12 of the Tax Credits Act (child care element).

Amendments

1. Amended by reg 2(5) of SI 2005 No 2502 as amended by Sch 2 para 27 of SI 2006 No 217 as from 1.4.06 (3.4.06 where rent payable weekly or at intervals of a week).
2. Amended by reg 5(2) of SI 2005 No 3360 as subsituted by Sch 2 para 30 of SI 2006 No 217 as from 10.4.06.
3. Amended by reg 3(4) of SI 2008 No 1042 as from 19.5.08.
4. Amended by reg 14 of SI 2008 No 1082 as from 27.10.08.
5. Amended by reg 5(3) of SI 2008 No 3157 as from 5.1.09.
6. Amended by reg 2 of SI 2009 No 1848 as from 5.8.09.
7. Amended by reg 7(2) of SI 2010 No 2429 as from 1.11.10.

Definitions

"claimant" – see reg 2(1).
"main phase employment and support allowance" – see reg 2(1).

General Note

This defines the circumstances in which childcare charges may be deducted (subject to the weekly maxima in reg 27(3)) from a claimant's earnings (and in some cases, WTC or CTC) under reg 27(1)(c).

Analysis

Para (1) lists the categories of people who are entitled to have child care charges deducted from their earnings (and in some cases from WTC or CTC). The relevant categories are lone parents who are in "remunerative work" (for which see reg 6 and paras (2) to (4), (14) and (15)), and couples with children where either both partners are in remunerative work or one partner is and the other is "incapacitated" as defined by paras (11), (12) and (12A), an in-patient in hospital as defined in para (11)(e) or in prison (on remand or serving a sentence).

Paras (2) to (4). A person who is absent from work because s/he is ill cannot be treated as in remunerative work under reg 6. However, for the purposes of the childcare charges disregard, paras (2) to (4) *can* treat someone as in remunerative work for the first 28 weeks of a period of sickness, so long as s/he was in such work immediately before getting one of the benefits specified in para (2)(a) to (c) or national insurance credits for incapacity or limited capability for work. Note that after the 28 week period, lone parents are no longer entitled to have a deduction made for childcare charges. However, couples are, if one of the couple is in remunerative work and the other is "incapacitated" as defined in paras (11), (12) and (12A).

Paras (5) to (9) define the type of child care charges ("relevant child care charges") which are eligible to be deducted. There are four basic rules.

(1) The charges must be paid by the claimant, or by the claimant's partner: see below.
(2) The child must be a member of the claimant's family: see s137 SSCBA (p22) and Part 4.
(3) The care must be provided by one of the care providers listed in para (8) – eg, by a registered child minder or through certain types of official scheme. There is no requirement for the claimant (or partner) to be working when the child care is being provided.
(4) The charges must relate to a period before the first Monday in September following the child's 15th birthday or, if the child is disabled within the definition in para (13), following her/his 16th birthday.

The charges cannot be made by the claimant to her/his partner (or vice versa) or made in respect of care provided by a relative of the child wholly or mainly in the child's home: para (7). Para (7) also says that payments made to the claimant by her/his partner are also ineligible but, given that the earlier part of the regulation suggests that payments can only be eligible in the first place if they are made "by the claimant" the effect of this part of the para is unclear. It seems to imply that payments made by a claimant's partner to, say, a registered child minder would be eligible and that the reference to "the claimant" rather than to "the claimant or the claimant's partner" is an oversight.

The charges cannot be payments for the child's "compulsory education". In *CTC 3646/2007*, a decision on the very similarly worded rule for working tax credit (WTC), the child attended a fee paying school that provided, at no additional cost, "classes" (called waiting classes) that pupils could attend before the start and at the end of the school day. The commissioner accepted that the "classes" were child care and were not compulsory education. However, the "classes" could only qualify as relevant child care charges if a separate charge was made for them. He said (at para 12):

" . . . [I]n circumstances where the charge covered compulsory education and was the same whether or not a particular child attended the waiting class, I do not consider that it is possible to say some proportion of the charge is not paid in respect of compulsory education, on the basis that the overall charge is set so as to cover the cost of the waiting class in addition to the cost of the education proper."

This was because, although the attendance amounted to childcare, the claimant was not incurring any cost in respect of that attendance that was not equally being incurred by the parents of a child who did not attend the "classes". Note, however, that the commissioner did accept that if the school had adopted a different charging policy under which there was a separate fee for the waiting class, this would not have been excluded from the definition.

Para (10) tells the authority to estimate the childcare charges over an appropriate period of no more than one year so as to reduce them accurately to a weekly amount for inclusion in the means test calculation.

Paras (11) to (13) define who is incapacitated and a patient for the purposes of para (1) and who is disabled for the purposes of paras (6) and (8). For a discussion on the definition of "patient", see below.

Paras (14) and (15). People who are absent from work on maternity, paternity or adoption leave cannot be treated as in remunerative work under reg 6. However, for the purposes of the childcare charge deduction, paras (14) and (15) *can* treat someone who is on such leave as in remunerative work. The person must have been in remunerative work immediately before the leave began, must be paying relevant childcare charges and must be entitled to statutory maternity, paternity or adoption pay or maternity allowance, or "qualifying support" (defined in para (15) as IS because of being on paternity leave). Para 14(b) provides that this special treatment ends when the leave ends (in which case it is no longer necessary) or, if earlier, when the claimant ceases to be entitled to statutory maternity, paternity or adoption pay or maternity allowance or "qualifying support" unless she was being paid a childcare element of WTC at that date. In the latter case, the special treatment continues until the end of entitlement to the childcare element of WTC.

Who is a patient?

Reg 2(4) and (5) Social Security (Hospital In-Patients) Regulations 2005 provide as follows:

"(4)   For the purposes of this regulation, a person shall be regarded as receiving or having received free in-patient treatment for any period for which he is or has been maintained free of charge while undergoing medical or other treatment as an in-patient–

(a)   in a hospital or similar institution under the National Health Service Act 1977, the National Health Service (Scotland) Act 1978 or the National Health Service and Community Care Act 1990, or

(b)   in a hospital or similar institution maintained or administered by the Defence Council,and such a person shall for the purposes of sub-paragraph (a) be regarded as being maintained free of charge in a hospital or similar institution unless his accommodation and services are provided under s65 National Health Service Act 1977, s57 National Health Service (Scotland) Act 1978 or para 14 Sch 2 National Health Service and Community Care Act 1990.

(5)   For the purposes of paragraph (4), a period during which a person is regarded as receiving or having received free in-patient treatment shall be deemed to begin on the day after the day on which he enters a hospital or similar institution referred to in that paragraph and to end on the day on which he leaves such a hospital or similar institution."

If a person is a prisoner or in youth custody s/he does not fall within the definition of "patient" for HB purposes. Other than that, however, a person is a "patient" if s/he falls within the scope of this definition. Four questions need to be posed.

Is the person an "in-patient"? A period of in-patient treatment begins on the day after the day of admission and ends on the day on which the person leaves. This affirms the commissioner's reasoning in *R(IS) 8/96*. There is an area of doubt in respect of the "day" on which a person enters hospital. The commissioner proceeded on the basis that a "day" for these purposes was the 24 hours between midnight and midnight. This interpretation does have the benefit of certainty, but is not necessarily inherent in the use of the word "day": *Halsbury's Laws of England* (1984 4th edn) vol 45 para 1113. The powerful arguments in favour of requiring a 24 hour stay in *R(S) 4/84* do not appear to be explicitly overridden by para (5).

Is the person receiving relevant treatment? The scope of the regulation is not confined to medical treatment. In *Botchett v Chief Adjudication Officer* [1996] 2 CCLR 121, CA the claimant had severe learning difficulties, although not a patient within the meaning of the Mental Health Act 1983, and required a high degree of care and supervision. She lived in a nursing home administered by a trust, which would take any amount of IS to which she was entitled over and above the standard nursing home rates. It was argued that the claimant was receiving care and not treatment in the home. However, the Court of Appeal ruled that the attention she received constituted "medical or other treatment".

Is the person in a "hospital or similar institution"? The definitions in s128 National Health Service Act 1977 must be applied: *White v Chief Adjudication Officer* [1993] *The Times* 2 August, CA. "Hospital" is "(a) any institution for the reception and treatment of persons suffering from illness; (b) any maternity home; and (c) any institution for the reception and treatment of persons during convalescence or persons requiring medical rehabilitation." "Illness" includes "mental disorder within the meaning of the Mental Health Act 1983 and any injury or disability requiring medical or dental treatment or nursing". It does not appear to cover those with disabilities if such disabilities do not of themselves require medical treatment – eg, blindness: *Jewish Blind Society Trustees v Henning* [1961] 1 WLR 24 at 30, 34, CA. In *Botchett*, it was held that the definition of "mental disorder" in the 1983 Act was wide enough to cover the claimant in that case. The home was therefore a "similar institution". In order to be an "institution", however, it would have to be a "building used by .... a society or organisation": see the *Shorter Oxford English Dictionary*. It might be possible to argue that very small, privately-run nursing homes are not therefore within the scope of the definition.

This suggestion is supported by *CDLA 7980/1995*, a decision on reg 8 Social Security (Disability Living Allowance) Regulations 1991, which is in similar terms to reg 2(4). In that case, the claimant had a learning disability and was epileptic. She lived in a privately rented house along with six people in a similar position. 24-hour care was provided by specialist carers from the local authority. Medication was provided by the claimant's GP. The tribunal decided that the house was not a "similar institution" and the commissioner upheld its ruling. He said (para 9):

"In my judgement, when those words are used in connection with the word 'hospital', they connote some sort of formal body or structure which controls all aspects of the treatment or care that is provided including the premises in which that treatment or care is carried out. They mean more than just a building in which care or treatment takes place. In this appeal, the treatment or care takes place in a private house which is let to the six occupants. They are the persons responsible for the payment of rent and other outgoings and for the purchase of their food. The appeal tribunal so found as they were bound to find on the evidence presented to them. .... On the appeal tribunal's findings there is simply no institution in the sense in which I consider the words must be construed. Further, no-one would suggest that the arrangements at No 167 could be described as 'a hospital' in any popular sense even though treatment and care is carried out there."

The authority of the decision is undermined slightly by the fact that *Botchett* was not apparently cited. However, it is suggested that it is correct. Note also that the treatment must be provided under one of the Acts mentioned in sub-para (a) or by the institutions mentioned in sub-para (b). If it is provided under the National Assistance Act 1948 or otherwise, the claimant will not be a "patient". Another authority supporting this interpretation of reg 2(4) is *CS 2647/1997* in which a resident at a hostel was held to fall outside its scope.

Is the person maintained free of charge? The effect of the closing words of para (4) is that a person is deemed to satisfy this condition unless s/he is a privately paying patient under the legislation mentioned there. Thus in *CS 249/1989* where the claimant's wife brought him meals every day because the hospital could not satisfy his dietary requirements, it was held that as he was not a private patient; he was deemed to be maintained free of charge even though it was costing his family money to feed him: para 11.

Average weekly earnings of employed earners

29.–(1) Where a claimant's income consists of earnings from employment as an employed earner his average weekly earnings shall be estimated by reference to his earnings from that employment–

(a) over a period immediately preceding the benefit week in which the claim is made or treated as made and being a period of–

    (i) 5 weeks, if he is paid weekly; or

    (ii) 2 months, if he is paid monthly; or

(b) whether or not sub-paragraph (a)(i) or (ii) applies, where a claimant's earnings fluctuate, over such other period preceding the benefit week in which the claim is made or treated as made as may, in any particular case, enable his average weekly earnings to be estimated more accurately.

(2) Where the claimant has been in his employment for less than the period specified in paragraph (1)(a)(i) or (ii)–

(a) if he has received any earnings for the period that he has been in that employment and those earnings are likely to represent his average weekly earnings from that employment his average weekly earnings shall be estimated by reference to those earnings;

(b) in any other case, the relevant authority shall require the claimant's employer to furnish an estimate of the claimant's likely weekly earnings over such period as the relevant authority may require and the claimant's average weekly earnings shall be estimated by reference to that estimate.

(3)   Where the amount of a claimant's earnings changes during an award the relevant authority shall estimate his average weekly earnings by reference to his likely earnings from the employment over such period as is appropriate in order that his average weekly earnings may be estimated accurately but the length of the period shall not in any case exceed 52 weeks.

(4)   For the purposes of this regulation the claimant's earnings shall be calculated in accordance with Section 3 of this Part.

Definitions

"benefit week" – see reg 2(1).
"claimant" – see reg 2(1).
"earnings" – see regs 2(1) and 35(1).
"employment as an employed earner" – see reg 2(1).
"income" – see General Note on this section.
"relevant authority" – reg 2(1).

General Note

This regulation deals with the earnings of an employed, as opposed to a self-employed, claimant. Para (4) refers to Section 3 for the assessment of earnings in this respect. Para (1) specifies the period over which a claimant's weekly earnings are to be averaged and reg 33 provides a mechanism for calculating weekly amounts of earnings where payment has been made for a period other than a week.

Para (2) modifies the rules in para (1) for people who have recently started work and para (3) deals with the situation where a claimant's earnings change during an award.

Remember that the earnings of a partner or partners of a claimant are included.

Earnings are usually verified from pay slips or a certificate of earnings. GM BW2.248 reminds authorities that because of the Government's overall policy of reducing the burden on business, they should avoid asking employers about a claimant's earnings unless no other source of information is available or there is doubt about the authenticity of the evidence provided by the claimant.

Analysis

Para (1). The wording of this regulation is unfortunate. The use of the word "consists" suggests that it only applies to claimants whose sole income is earnings from employment, although this cannot be the intention. For "benefit week in which the claim is made or treated as made", see reg 83 on p443.

If the claimant's weekly earnings fluctuate, the authority must use sub-para (b) to calculate her/his weekly average rather than sub-para (a). The wording suggests that where sub-para (b) applies, the periods mentioned in sub-para (a) cannot be used even if they do accurately reflect the claimant's weekly average. Note that the period chosen under sub-para (a) or sub-para (b) must precede the week in which the claim is made or treated as made, rather than be based on estimated future earnings.

See reg 33 if the claimant is paid in respect of a period other than a week, in order to work out the weekly amount due.

Para (2) deals with the situation where the claimant has not yet been in employment for the appropriate period under para (1)(a)(i) or (ii).

Sub-para (a) deals with claimants who have already been paid amounts which reflect their likely future earnings; for "earnings", see para (4). See also reg 33 where the amount paid relates to a period other than a week.

Sub-para (b) deals with claimants who have not yet been paid any earnings, or who have been paid but the amount received is not representative of what they will receive in the future. Note that it is the local authority that must require the employer to provide an estimate of the claimant's likely earnings, not the claimant. An award of HB can then be made on the basis of the estimate. The local authority may then instruct the claimant to notify it if s/he actually earns more than the estimate and adjust the original estimate accordingly under para (3): *NC v Tonbridge & Malling Borough Council* [2010] UKUT 12 (AAC).

For the treatment of advance earnings, see reg 46(5).

Para (3) deals with changes in a claimant's "earnings" during an award – ie, relevant changes of circumstance. Claimants are under a duty to report such changes: see reg 88. Reg 79 specifies the date on which the changes will take effect. This paragraph obliges the authority to amend the claimant's entitlement to HB when such a change becomes effective. The averaging process is not bound by para (1), which applies only to the determination of entitlement on a claim, but the authority must choose an appropriate period in order to estimate earnings accurately. The length of the period can in no case exceed 52 weeks. Reg 33 applies to help ascertain the weekly value of earnings for these purposes.

Para (4). See section 3 and Sch 4, for the assessment of earnings.

Average weekly earnings of self-employed earners

30.–(1)   Where a claimant's income consists of earnings from employment as a self-employed earner his average weekly earnings shall be estimated by reference to his earnings from that employment over such period as is appropriate in order that his average weekly earnings may be estimated accurately but the length of the period shall not in any case exceed a year.

(2)   For the purposes of this regulation the claimant's earnings shall be calculated in accordance with Section 4 of this Part.

Definitions
"claimant" – see reg 2(1).
"income" – see General Note on this Section.
"self-employed earner" – see reg 2(1).

General Note
This deals with the earnings from self-employment of claimants and their partners. Reg 33 applies to ascertain the weekly amounts of such earnings if payment is made for a period other than a week. Para (2) provides that earnings are to be assessed for these purposes under section 4 of this Part.

Analysis
Unlike the provisions in respect of *employed* earners, there is no mechanism for dealing with unforeseen changes in the claimant's income over the period of an award. Also there is no prescribed period over which income should be averaged. The authority must simply choose a period it thinks appropriate that will enable it to estimate the claimant's income from this source accurately. The averaging period must not exceed a year.

It was emphasised in *CH 329/2003* that it may not always be appropriate to use the last year's accounts.

Average weekly income other than earnings

31.–(1)   A claimant's income which does not consist of earnings shall, except where paragraph (2) applies, be estimated over such period as is appropriate in order that his average weekly income may be estimated accurately but the length of the period shall not in any case exceed 52 weeks; and nothing in this paragraph shall authorise an authority to disregard any such income other than that specified in Schedule 5.

(2)   The period over which any benefit under the benefit Acts is to be taken into account shall be the period in respect of which that benefit is payable.

(3)   For the purposes of this regulation income other than earnings shall be calculated in accordance with Section 5 of this Part.

Definitions
"benefit Acts" – see reg 2(1) and s123 SSCBA.
"claimant" – see reg 2(1).
"income" – see General Note on this Section.

General Note
This deals with income which is not "earnings" under regs 29 and 30. Para (3) provides that such income is to be taken into account as specified by section 5 of this Part. Under reg 27(1)(a), this "other income" is to be assessed on the basis of what a claimant is likely to receive on an average weekly basis. See reg 33 on p357 for the conversion of payments made in respect of periods other than a week into weekly amounts.

Analysis
As with regs 29 and 30, the authority must estimate such income over an appropriate period in order to estimate earnings accurately. Here the length of the period can in no case exceed 52 weeks. The authority can only disregard such amounts as are authorised by Sch 5.

The effect of para (2) is that benefits paid under the benefit Acts (as defined in reg 2(1)) should only be taken into account during the period in respect of which they are payable (eg, the two weeks before actual payment if made two-weekly in arrears); and if not paid for every week, they should only be taken into account in respect of the number of weeks for which they actually are paid.

Calculation of average weekly income from tax credits

32.–(1)   This regulation applies where a claimant receives a tax credit.

(2)   Where this regulation applies, the period over which a tax credit is to be taken into account shall be the period set out in paragraph (3).

(3)   Where the instalment in respect of which payment of a tax credit is made is–

(a)   a daily instalment, the period is 1 day, being the day in respect of which the instalment is paid;

(b)   a weekly instalment, the period is 7 days, ending on the day on which the instalment is due to be paid;

(c)   a two weekly instalment, the period is 14 days, commencing 6 days before the day on which the instalment is due to be paid;

(d)   a four weekly instalment, the period is 28 days, ending on the day on which the instalment is due to be paid.

(4)   For the purposes of this regulation "tax credit" means child tax credit or working tax credit.

Analysis

This provides the mechanism for taking tax credits income into account. "Tax credits" are child tax credit (CTC) and working tax credit (WTC): para (4). See reg 33 for the conversion of payments made in respect of periods other than a week into weekly amounts. Note that reg 34(e) allows a local authority to ignore legislative changes in the maximum rate of tax credits (ie, the annual uprating) for up to 30 weeks.

The regulation applies where the claimant "receives a tax credit". Para (2) then sets out how the instalments are to be calculated for HB purposes. The instalments should be set out in the claimant's tax credit award notice. There are some important implications:

(1)   Where an overpayment that occurred during the current year's award of tax credits is being recovered by the Revenue, it is the reduced amount of tax credits (the "instalment") that should be taken into account for HB purposes. Note that where an overpayment of tax credits from a previous year is being recovered from the current year's award, the amount of tax credits that is taken into account is similarly, the amount actually being paid: reg 40(6). But see below if tax credits are currently in payment, but are being overpaid.

(2)   Where the amount of an award of tax credits changes during the year, the local authority takes this into account when the instalment reflecting this is "due to be paid", not when the change occurs.

(3)   Where a payment is not a regular instalment, but a payment of arrears of tax credits (eg, at the beginning of an award or after a change in circumstances has been taken into account), it should be not be treated as income, but as capital and disregarded for up to 52 weeks: Sch 6 para 9(1)(e).

(4)   Tax credit "additional payments" or "top-up payments" (discretionary payments made by the Revenue where a reduced tax credits award causes hardship) are effected by increasing the tax credit award for the relevant year and hence the instalments due to be paid for the remainder of that year.

Are all payments of tax credits income?

In *CIS 1813/2007*, the claimant had been receiving WTC. She informed the Revenue immediately when she stopped working because she knew that she ceased to be eligible for WTC. Despite her best efforts to stop being paid, WTC continued to be paid for nearly two months. The Revenue then sought to recover the overpayment. When she had claimed IS on ceasing work, the WTC payments were taken into account as income in calculating her entitlement. The deputy commissioner decided, however, that the payments of WTC were not income, or if that was wrong, that they were "voluntary payments" to be disregarded. Although normally WTC does count as part of a claimant's income for IS purposes, it appeared to the deputy commissioner to be an abuse of language to treat payments as income, if they are payments the claimant has asked that s/he should not receive, having correctly explained why s/he should not be receiving them. As regards voluntary payments, he said (at para 12):

"The position would be different at a time before disclosure is made of facts which give [the Revenue] grounds to vary the award, and may be different if there is an element of uncertainty whether a variation can or should be made. But once there has been proper disclosure by the claimant which allows for only one decision, and even more so where the claimant has asked not to be paid, or for that decision to be made, it is entirely a matter for [the Revenue] whether the payments continue to be made or whether it varies the award and ceases the payments."

He distinguished the case from *CIS 647/2007* where it had been held that an overpayment of WTC did count as income for IS purposes. In that case, the claimant had *not* informed the Revenue of the change in her circumstances. Hence, the Revenue continued to be under an obligation to make the payments of WTC that had been awarded and had no basis on which to consider amending the WTC award. No question of the payment being a voluntary one, and no question of its stopping being her income, could therefore arise.

Although *CIS 1813/2007* was a decision concerning whether WTC payments were to be treated as income for the purposes of IS, in principle, it should apply to HB. Applying the case to HB, if a claimant is continuing to receive payments of tax credits to which s/he is not entitled and has reported relevant changes in her/his circumstances to the Revenue and/or asked that payments cease, an authority should not treat the payments as income and should not take them into account in calculating HB. This is despite the provision in reg 40(6) (see p369) under which, where an overpayment is being recovered from a tax credits award, it is the amount of tax credits in payment that is taken into account. However, where a claimant does not report a change in circumstances to the Revenue or ask for tax credits payments to stop, applying *CIS 647/2007*, the payments would be income. Likewise, where a claimant retains some entitlement to tax credits under an award, the amount of that entitlement would be income.

Calculation of weekly income

33.–(1) For the purposes of regulations 29 (average weekly earnings of employed earners), 31 (average weekly income other than earnings) and 32 (calculation of average weekly income from tax credits), where the period in respect of which a payment is made–

- (a) does not exceed a week, the weekly amount shall be the amount of that payment;
- (b) exceeds a week, the weekly amount shall be determined–
  - (i) in a case where that period is a month, by multiplying the amount of the payment by 12 and dividing the product by 52;
  - (ii) in any other case, by dividing the amount of the payment by the number equal to the number of days in the period to which it relates and multiplying the quotient by 7.

(2) For the purposes of regulation 30 (average weekly earnings of self-employed earners) the weekly amount of earnings of a claimant shall be determined by dividing his earnings over the assessment period by the number equal to the number of days in that period and multiplying the quotient by 7.

General Note

This provides the means for converting the sums to be taken into account under regs 29 to 32 into weekly amounts.

Analysis

Para (1)(a). Where a payment is made for a period of up to a week, the weekly amount is the amount of the payment.

Para (1)(b). Payments in respect of a month are to be converted by multiplying by 12 to give the annual figure then dividing by 52 to produce a weekly figure. Sub-para (b)(ii) converts payments in respect of periods not covered by para (a) or sub-para (b)(i) by dividing by the number of days in the period to which the payment relates and multiplying by seven. Note that days during weekends must also be counted as days for this purpose.

Para (2) deals with the earnings of a self-employed earner. These are based on the estimated average of earnings received over the assessment period (up to one year – see reg 30). The average weekly amount of earnings is obtained by dividing those earnings by the number of days in the assessment period and multiplying the result by seven.

Disregard of changes in tax, contributions etc

34. In calculating the claimant's income the appropriate authority may disregard any legislative change–

- (a) in the basic or other rates of income tax;
- (b) in the amount of any personal tax relief;
- (c) in the rates of social security contributions payable under the Act or in the lower earnings limit or upper earnings limit for Class 1 contributions under the Act, the lower or upper limits applicable to Class 4 contributions under the Act or the amount specified in section 11(4) of the Act (small earnings exception in relation to Class 2 contributions);
- (d) in the amount of tax payable as a result of an increase in the weekly rate of Category A, B, C or D retirement pension or any addition thereto or any graduated pension payable under the Act;
- (e) in the maximum rate of child tax credit or working tax credit,

for a period not exceeding 30 benefit weeks beginning with the benefit week immediately following the date from which the change is effective.

Definitions
"benefit weeks" – see reg 2(1).
"income" – see General Note on this Section.

General Note
This regulation is intended to assist the authority in administering the HB scheme by modifying the other provisions of this Part and reg 79 so that the effect of certain changes in the claimant's income are ignored for up to 30 benefit weeks after they take effect, giving an authority time to gather information and re-calculate an affected claimant's HB. The changes listed could reduce or increase a claimant's entitlement to HB. If an authority exercises its discretion under this paragraph it does not mean that the claimant has been over or under-paid, so when the authority does take the change into account there is no adjustment to be made to HB paid in the intervening period. This is because during that period entitlement has been correctly assessed according to the treatment of income rules.

See also reg 42(8), about changes in the rate of certain benefits.

Analysis
Note that the "changes" which may be ignored as set out in sub-paras (a) to (e) are only those arising from changes in the legislation, not extra-statutory concessions.

Para (b) covers changes in personal tax relief by which is meant the tax thresholds.

Para (d). Pensioners will only pay tax on these amounts if their total income is sufficient to use up their tax allowances. Therefore the change in the amount of tax payable may not change some pensioners' HB entitlement in any case. Note that most pensioner claimants have their HB assessed under the HB(SPC) Regs, so this provision will generally only have application where a claimant under the qualifying age for PC has a partner who is receiving one of the pensions listed.

SECTION 3
Employed earners

General Note on Section 3
See also regs 27 and 29 and the General Note to Section 2.

Reg 29(4) provides that for the purposes of that reg (ie, quantification of the employee's weekly earnings together with the earnings of any partner), this Section is to govern the amounts which are to be taken into account as earnings, and how they are to be assessed.

Reg 35 defines earnings for the purposes of this Chapter.

Reg 36 provides that for the purposes of reg 29 it is net earnings that are to be taken into account, minus the amounts which may be deducted under Sch 4, and sets out how "net" earnings are to be ascertained.

Earnings of employed earners

35.–(1) Subject to paragraph (2), "earnings" means in the case of employment as an employed earner, any remuneration or profit derived from that employment and includes–

(a) any bonus or commission;

(b) any payment in lieu of remuneration except any periodic sum paid to a claimant on account of the termination of his employment by reason of redundancy;

(c) any payment in lieu of notice or any lump sum payment intended as compensation for the loss of employment but only in so far as it represents loss of income;

(d) any holiday pay except any payable more than 4 weeks after termination or interruption of the employment;

(e) any payment by way of a retainer;

(f) any payment made by the claimant's employer in respect of expenses not wholly, exclusively and necessarily incurred in the performance of the duties of the employment, including any payment made by the claimant's employer in respect of–

    (i) travelling expenses incurred by the claimant between his home and place of employment;

    (ii) expenses incurred by the claimant under arrangements made for the care of a member of his family owing to the claimant's absence from home;

(g) any award of compensation made under section 112(4) or 117(3)(a) of the Employment Rights Act 1996 (remedies and compensation for unfair dismissal);

[¹ (gg) any payment or remuneration made under section 28, 34, 64, 68 or 70 of the Employment Rights Act 1996 (right to guarantee payments, remuneration on suspension on medical or maternity grounds, complaints to employment tribunals);]

(h)　any such sum as is referred to in section 112 of the Act (certain sums to be earnings for social security purposes);

(i)　any statutory sick pay, statutory maternity pay, statutory paternity pay or statutory adoption pay, or a corresponding payment under any enactment having effect in Northern Ireland;

(j)　any remuneration paid by or on behalf of an employer to the claimant who for the time being is on maternity leave, paternity leave or adoption leave or is absent from work because he is ill;

(k)　the amount of any payment by way of a non-cash voucher which has been taken into account in the computation of a person's earnings in accordance with Part 5 of Schedule 3 to the Social Security (Contributions) Regulations 2001.

(2)　Earnings shall not include–

(a)　subject to paragraph (3), any payment in kind;

(b)　any payment in respect of expenses wholly, exclusively and necessarily incurred in the performance of the duties of the employment;

(c)　any occupational pension.

[² (d) any payment in respect of expenses arising out of the claimant's participation in a service user group.]

(3)　Paragraph (2)(a) shall not apply in respect of any non-cash voucher referred to in paragraph (1)(k).

Amendments

1.　Inserted by reg 11(4) of SI 2007 No 2618 as from 1.10.07.
2.　Inserted by reg 6(3) of SI 2009 No 2655 as from 2.11.09.

Definitions

"employed earner" – see reg 2(1).
"occupational pension" – see reg 2(1).
"service user group" – see reg 2(1).

General Note

This regulation defines "earnings" for the purposes of this Part. It includes all those payments listed in para (1) but excludes those listed in para (2).

Analysis

Paragraph (1): General

"Remuneration or profit derived from ... employment". Sub-paras (a) to (k) of this paragraph do not exclusively define earnings; they are simply a list of items which are deemed to be earnings for these purposes. The true test of which other payments are "earnings" is the phrase "remuneration or profit derived from . . . employment".

The phrase is well known to tax lawyers as defining the payments which may become liable to tax as employment income. In *CFC 25/1989*, the commissioner held that the similarity of wording under Revenue and Social Security legislation "cannot be accidental" and that income tax cases were "a useful guide". "Remuneration or profit" would seem to exclude payments of expenses but see paras (1)(f) and (2)(b) for a detailed look at the treatment of expenses. The issue of whether a payment is "derived from" employment is constantly before the courts regarding the question of liability to tax. A number of tests have evolved to decide whether a payment is so derived.

Generally, the phrase has been widely interpreted in relation to tax so that it is unusual for a payment passing between employer and employee not to be treated as "derived from" employment. A payment made to an employee by a third party is less likely to be so regarded. See, for example, *Moore v Griffiths* [1972] 1 WLR 1024, Ch D, where a payment made to Bobby Moore after the 1966 World Cup by a company seeking publicity from the prize-giving was not "derived from" employment despite the "work" relationship.

Where the payment has been made by an employer, the case of *Hochstrasser v Mayes* [1959] Ch 22, CA, is often quoted. In that case, the test of derivation was held to be whether the payment was made in return for services "past, present or future". This case also established that, in relation to tax at least, the employment relationship need only be one reason for the payment before it will be treated as "derived from" employment. Other important factors in deciding whether a payment is "derived from" employment have been held to be:

(1)   Whether the employee has a contractual right to payment: *Moorhouse v Dooland* [1955] Ch 284, CA.

(2)   Whether the employer's purpose in making the payment was to provide an incentive to the employee to work harder: *Tyrer v Smart* [1979] 1 WLR 113, HL.

(3)   The fact that the payment relates to terms and conditions of employment: *Hamblett v Godfrey* [1987] 1 WLR 357, CA. In that case, payments of £1,000 made to GCHQ employees to give up trade union rights were held to be derived from employment on this basis.

(4)   Whether the payment was of a recurrent nature; if so, it is more likely to be treated as derived from employment: *Blakiston v Cooper* [1909] AC 104, HL.

In *CH 2387/2002*, Commissioner Fellner considered a case in which a company director had put forward accounts showing payment of directors' emoluments of £6,400. In fact, the claimant had only drawn just under £3,000 and the balance had been added to a loan account showing monies owed by the company to the claimant. This approach had been suggested by the company's accountants as a means of saving tax. The commissioner held (para 11) that it was not permissible to put forward one set of earnings figures for tax purposes and another set for benefits purposes. In *CTC 626/2001*, Commissioner Williams upheld a refusal of tax credit to a husband and wife who had adopted an artificial means of payment to themselves from their partnership to save tax, and then argued that for tax credits purposes the true position had to be taken into account. Commissioner Fellner applied that decision and held that the claimant's income for CTB purposes had to be calculated in accordance with the figure given in the accounts.

Payments made in respect of offices. "Employed earner" is defined in s2(1)(a) SSCBA: see reg 2(1) on p212. The definition provides as follows:

"a person who is gainfully employed in Great Britain either under a contract of service, or in an office (including elective office) with general earnings".

Thus it can be seen that the definition of "employed earner" does not solely relate to employment but also to office-holders, provided that they have "general earnings". "General earnings" are defined in s7(3) Income Tax (Earnings and Pensions) Act 2003. The reference to elective office means that councillors' allowances will be treated as "earnings" for the purposes of Part 6: see *R(IS) 6/92* para 5. There is important caselaw on the treatment of allowances: see the commentary to para (1)(f) below.

Paragraph (1): Categories of earnings

"Earnings" includes the payments listed in paragraphs (a) to (k) of para (1).

Sub-para (a) is self-explanatory.

Sub-para (b). Payments "in lieu of remuneration" include awards made by employment tribunals and courts to compensate for loss of earnings. It does not, however, apply to redundancy payments.

A compensatory award made by an employment tribunal falls under this sub-para, in so far as it consists of compensation for loss of earnings: *R(SB) 21/86* para 12. Similarly, where an applicant is awarded any compensation in a claim for discrimination which relates to lost earnings, it falls under sub-para (b): *CIS 590/1993* para 7. It was also decided in that case, however, that awards covering injury to feelings and the loss of a tax rebate did not fall within sub-para (b).

Sub-para (c) applies, for example, to basic awards for unfair dismissal, payments explicitly made in lieu of notice, or payments made by the Secretary of State under s167 Employment Rights Act 1996 to employees whose employer goes into liquidation before they can work their notice.

Sub-para (d). Note that holiday pay payable more than four weeks after employment terminates is treated as capital under reg 46(3).

Sub-para (e). "Retainer" is not defined, but GM BW2.70 says this is "a payment made for a period when no actual work is carried out, such as payment made to employees of the school meals service during school holidays". Payments made during a period of "garden leave" would probably also fall under this provision.

Sub-para (f). The wording "wholly exclusively and necessarily" is the same test as is applied to ascertain deductible expenditure from earnings in relation to income tax. For a discussion of the meaning of the phrase, see the note on para (2)(b) below, which provides that earnings which are so incurred are not to count as earnings for these purposes. That means that under this paragraph, all expenses not so incurred are to be seen as "earnings".

Heads (i) and (ii) deem that the items there specified are *not* to be treated as "wholly exclusively and necessarily" incurred for the purposes of the employment. So travelling expenses to work (but not those incurred while *at* work) are to be treated as earnings, and so are childminding and other care expenses necessitated when the carer goes to work. For the treatment of such expenses, see reg 28 above.

In *CH 1330/2008*, the claimant was a careworker whose contract of employment showed that her "place of work" was "at any location within [a specified London Borough]". The local authority decided that her place of employment for the purposes of reg 35 was the first place she went to work on any particular day. Expenses for that journey therefore counted as earnings under reg 35(1)(f). Commissioner Jacobs disagreed. He said that reg 35(1) only applies if the claimant *has* a place of employment. If there is no place of employment, which he accepted was the case here, the provision does not apply. Referring to the approach taken by Millett J in *Coates Brothers plc v General Accident Life Assurance Ltd* [1991] 1 WLR 712 at 717 he said that as a matter of interpretation, it is permissible to imply the words "if any" into reg 35(1)(f)(i) so that it reads: "travelling expenses incurred by the claimant between his home and place of employment *if any*". The commissioner accepted that everyone who works must work somewhere. However, that is not the sense of reg 35, which is referring to a fixed place at which work is done or a base from which work is undertaken. The distinction is between travelling done in order to get to work and travelling done while working. Put into the context of this case, the issue was whether, when the claimant left her home, she was travelling (i) in order to take up her duties or (ii) as part of her duties.

There is important caselaw on the treatment of councillor's allowances, concerning arguments that the allowances are supposed to cover expenses of councillors. The allowances are paid under s18 Local Government and Housing Act 1989 and, for example, the Local Authorities (Members' Allowances)(England) Regulations 2003. None of that legislation gives a clue as to how the allowances are to be treated. In *R(IS) 6/92* para 8, the commissioner concluded that the attendance allowance payable to councillors was "not a payment to meet expenses, but a payment to recompense a councillor for his attendance at authorised meetings". In *CIS 77/1993* para 8, however, the same commissioner pointed out that Department of the Environment Circular 2/91, which was issued following the introduction of the system of allowances in the 1991 Regulations, suggested that the purpose of the basic allowance was *both* to recompense a councillor for her/his efforts and for her/his expenses. He therefore concluded that if the councillor could show that s/he had incurred expenses which satisfied the stringent test set out in sub-para (f), the payment of the allowance could be regarded as falling within the provision.

It is therefore suggested that what is important is not the purpose for which any allowance is paid but rather whether the evidence shows that the councillor has incurred expenses "wholly exclusively and necessarily" as a consequence of her/his work as a councillor. Councillors claiming HB but not IS, JSA or income-related ESA are therefore advised to keep full records of their expenses. It should also be noted that they have the right to have income tax deducted from an attendance allowance at the basic rate and then to ask the Revenue to direct the council to deduct expenses from the tax.

Sub-para (g) covers compensation awards made under ss112(4) and 117(3)(a) Employment Rights Act 1996. The former provision refers to compensatory awards made by industrial tribunals where the complainant has established unfair dismissal but the tribunal does not recommend reinstatement or re-engagement. The latter provision refers to the higher rate awards made where reinstatement or re-engagement has been recommended but the employer has failed to comply.

Sub-para (gg) covers the payments or remuneration made under the sections of the Employment Rights Act 1996 listed. They are guarantee payments (ss28 and 34), remuneration to an employee who is suspended from work by her/his employer on medical grounds (ss64 and 70) or on maternity grounds (ss68 and 70).

Sub-para (h). The payments covered are:

(1)   Amounts representing arrears of pay paid in pursuance of an order for reinstatement or re-engagement under the Employment Rights Act 1996).

(2)   Amounts payable by way of pay in pursuance of an order for continuation of a contract of employment under the Employment Rights Act 1996 or the Trade Union and Labour Relations (Consolidation) Act 1992.

(3)   "Protective awards" made to employees where the employer has failed to comply with the consultation procedure for redundancies under the Trade Union and Labour Relations (Consolidation) Act 1992.

Sub-paras (i) and (j) confirm that sick pay and maternity, paternity and adoption pay, whether made under statute or as additional payments under contract, count as earnings.

Sub-para (k). The principle is that if a "non-cash voucher" counts as earnings when calculating liability to pay national insurance contributions under the regulations cited, it also counts as earnings for HB. Note that the contributions legislation is changed very frequently, so in any case of doubt reference should be made to the current version of the regulations set out in The Law of Social Security (the "Blue Volumes") published by the DWP (available at www.dwp.gov.uk) or current tax handbooks.

Paragraphs (2) and (3): Exclusions from the definition of earnings

Sub-paras (a) to (d) exclude certain types of payment from the definition of "earnings" in para (1). Such payments therefore count as "income other than earnings" to be assessed under Section 5, but note that under Sch 5 payments in kind, expenses "wholly exclusively and necessarily incurred" for the purposes set out and expenses for a claimant's participation in a service user group are to be disregarded completely: see paras (2), (3) and (2A) respectively.

Sub-para (a) excludes any payment in kind, with the exception of vouchers that fall to be taken into account under para (1)(k) above: see para (3).

Sub-para (b). The phrase "wholly exclusively and necessarily incurred in performing the duties of the employment" has been rigidly interpreted in relation to tax law. Before a payment may fall into this category it must display all three attributes referred to:

(1)   "Wholly" means that all of the payment in question must be dedicated to this purpose, not just part. However, if a lump sum is paid in respect of some expenses which qualify and others which do not, there would seem to be no reason why an apportionment cannot be made: see the authorities on councillors' allowances referred to under para (1)(f).

(2)   "Exclusively" means that the payment must be for no other purpose than the duties of the employment – eg, expenditure on an item which is to be used partly for domestic use would not qualify.

(3)   Finally, before expenditure may be excluded from the definition of earnings on this basis, it must be "necessary" for the performance of the duties of employment. In relation to tax, the case of *Brown v*

Bullock [1961] 1 WLR 1095, CA, decided that only expenditure necessitated by the duties themselves, and not simply the employer's policies, would qualify. For example, if the job is such that protective clothing is necessary, expenditure on that clothing which is reimbursed will not be "earnings", but if an employer insists that employees wear suits, when the job could be done adequately without the wearing of a suit, expenses in that respect will not be "necessarily" incurred for the purpose of performing the duties and so *will* count as earnings.

There is a vast amount of caselaw concerned with the phrase in relation to tax and reference should be made to textbooks on tax law in any case of doubt.

Note that expenses deemed not to be earnings by sub-para (b) are disregarded as "income other than earnings" by Sch 5 para 3.

Sub-para (c). See p214 for the definition of "occupational pension".

Sub-para (d). See p216 for the definition of "service user group".

Calculation of net earnings of employed earners

36.–(1) For the purposes of regulation 29 (average weekly earnings of employed earners), the earnings of a claimant derived or likely to be derived from employment as an employed earner to be taken into account shall, subject to paragraph (2), be his net earnings.

(2) There shall be disregarded from a claimant's net earnings, any sum, where applicable, specified in paragraphs 1 to 14 of Schedule 4.

(3) For the purposes of paragraph (1) net earnings shall, except where paragraph (6) applies, be calculated by taking into account the gross earnings of the claimant from that employment over the assessment period, less–

(a) any amount deducted from those earnings by way of–
   (i) income tax;
   (ii) primary Class 1 contributions under the Act;

(b) one-half of any sum paid by the claimant by way of a contribution towards an occupational pension scheme;

(c) one-half of the amount calculated in accordance with paragraph (5) in respect of any qualifying contribution payable by the claimant; and

(d) where those earnings include a payment which is payable under any enactment having effect in Northern Ireland and which corresponds to statutory sick pay, statutory maternity pay, statutory paternity pay or statutory adoption pay, any amount deducted from those earnings by way of any contributions which are payable under any enactment having effect in Northern Ireland and which correspond to primary Class 1 contributions under the Act.

(4) In this regulation ''qualifying contribution'' means any sum which is payable periodically as a contribution towards a personal pension scheme.

(5) The amount in respect of any qualifying contribution shall be calculated by multiplying the daily amount of the qualifying contribution by the number equal to the number of days in the assessment period; and for the purposes of this regulation the daily amount of the qualifying contribution shall be determined–

(a) where the qualifying contribution is payable monthly, by multiplying the amount of the qualifying contribution by 12 and dividing the product by 365;

(b) in any other case, by dividing the amount of the qualifying contribution by the number equal to the number of days in the period to which the qualifying contribution relates.

(6) Where the earnings of a claimant are estimated under sub-paragraph (b) of paragraph (2) of regulation 29 (average weekly earnings of employed earners), his net earnings shall be calculated by taking into account those earnings over the assessment period, less–

(a) an amount in respect of income tax equivalent to an amount calculated by applying to those earnings [2] the basic rate of tax applicable to the assessment period less only the personal relief to which the claimant is entitled under sections 257(1) of the Income and Corporation Taxes Act 1988 (personal allowances) as is appropriate to his circumstances but, if the assessment period is less than a year, the earnings to which the [1 [2 basic] rate] of tax is to be applied and the amount of the personal relief deductible under this sub-paragraph shall be calculated on a pro rata basis;

(b)   an amount equivalent to the amount of the primary Class 1 contributions that would be payable by him under the Act in respect of those earnings if such contributions were payable; and

(c)   one-half of any sum which would be payable by the claimant by way of a contribution towards an occupational or personal pension scheme, if the earnings so estimated were actual earnings.

Amendments
1.   Amended by reg 11(5) of SI 2007 No 2618 as from 1.10.07.
2.   Amended by reg 6(4) of SI 2009 No 583 as from 6.4.09.

Definitions
"claimant" – see reg 2(1).
"earnings" – see reg 35.
"employed earner" – see reg 2(1).
"occupational pension" – see reg 2(1).
"personal pension scheme" – see reg 2(1).

General Note
Paras (1) and (2) set out the general rule that "earnings" to be taken into account under reg 29 are "net" earnings minus the deductions authorised by Sch 4.

Paras (3) and (6) define "net" for these purposes. Para (3) relates to claimants whose earnings are to be averaged under reg 29(1). Their net earnings are to be ascertained by deducting income tax, national insurance (NI) contributions and half of occupational/personal pension contributions made by the employee from the gross figure. Para (6) deals with those whose earnings are estimated under reg 29(2).

Analysis
Para (2). In considering the scope of any disregard, decisions on similarly-worded disregards in other means-tested benefit schemes must be taken into account: *CH 2321/2002* para 8.

Paras (3) to (5) set out amounts which are to be deducted to generate a net earnings figure. See also reg 34 where the amounts of statutory deductions change during an award. The deductions are:
(1)   Amounts deducted by way of income tax and Class 1 NI contributions: para (3)(a).
(2)   Half of any contributions made by a claimant towards an occupational pension scheme: para (3)(b).
(3)   Half of any "qualifying contributions": para (3)(c). These are those made to a personal pension scheme: see para (4). Para (5) sets out the method of calculation.
(4)   Sums deducted from statutory sick and maternity pay in Northern Ireland which correspond to Class 1 contributions: para (3)(d).

Para (6)(a). The wording of para (6)(a) is odd, but the effect is that the appropriate personal allowance for tax purposes is deducted from gross earnings and the basic rate applied to what remains. Details of tax rates and NI contributions are available at www.hmrc.gov.uk/rates.

"on a pro-rata basis" requires, for example, that if the assessment period is six months, one half of the appropriate personal reliefs should be deducted. Notice that if the HB is being assessed outside the year of assessment in which the claim was made, the basic rate of tax due in that year is used, but the personal relief applying in the current tax year is to be applied.

SECTION 4
Self-employed earners

General Note on Section 4
This deals with the assessment of earnings from self-employment for the purposes of regs 27 and 30.

Reg 37 defines "earnings" so far as self-employed earners are concerned.

Reg 38 provides the rules under which such a person's "net profit" is to be calculated and reg 39 provides the details necessary in relation to reg 38 to enable deductions in respect of tax and NI contributions to be made.

The main disputes in relation to this Section are likely to be about the quantification of "profit". In particular it may be difficult for the claimant or those whose income is aggregated with the claimant's to provide adequate evidence of net profit.

Earnings of self-employed earners
37.–(1)   Subject to paragraph (2), "earnings", in the case of employment as a self-employed earner, means the gross income of the employment and shall include any

allowance paid under section 2 of the 1973 Act or section 2 of the Enterprise and New Towns (Scotland) Act 1990 to the claimant for the purpose of assisting him in carrying on his business unless at the date of claim the allowance has been terminated.

(2) "Earnings" shall not include any payment to which paragraph 26 or 27 of Schedule 5 refers (payments in respect of a person accommodated with the claimant under arrangements made by a local authority or voluntary organisation and payments made to the claimant by a health authority, local authority or voluntary organisation in respect of persons temporarily in the claimant's care) nor shall it include any sports award.

[¹ [² (3) This paragraph applies to–
(a) royalties or other sums paid as a consideration for the use of, or the right to use, any copyright, design, patent or trade mark; or
(b) any payment in respect of any–
  (i) book registered under the Public Lending Right Scheme 1982; or
  (ii) work made under any international public lending right scheme that is analogous to the Public Lending Right Scheme 1982,
where the claimant is the first owner of the copyright, design, patent or trade mark, or an original contributor to the book or work concerned.]

(4) Where the claimant's earnings consist of any items to which paragraph (3) applies, those earnings shall be taken into account over a period equal to such number of weeks as is equal to the number obtained (and any fraction shall be treated as a corresponding fraction of a week) by dividing the earnings by the amount of housing benefit which would be payable had the payment not been made plus an amount equal to the total of the sums which would fall to be disregarded from the payment under Schedule 4 (sums to be disregarded in the calculation of earnings) as appropriate in the claimant's case.]

Amendments
1. Inserted by reg 6(3) of SI 2008 No 698 as from, as it relates to a particular beneficiary, the first day of the benefit week on or after 7.4. 08.
2. Substituted by reg 6(5) of SI 2009 No 583 as from the first day of the first benefit week to commence for the claimant on or after 6.4.09.

Definitions
"claimant" – reg 2(1).
"self-employed earner" – see reg 2(1).

General Note
This regulation provides a general definition of the term "earnings" in relation to self-employed earners. Para (2) clarifies that local authority payments to foster parents should not be treated as self-employed earnings. Foster payments in fact are considered to be income other than earnings and are disregarded under Sch 5 para 26, as are certain payments made to those providing respite care (Sch 5 para 27). Paras (3) and (4) deal with the period over which royalties, copyright, design, patent, trade mark and Public Lending Right Scheme payments are to be taken into account.

The reference is to *gross* income and the other regulations in this Section provide for deductions from earnings to arrive at "net profit" for the purposes of reg 30.

Analysis
Para (1). s2 Employment and Training Act 1973 enables arrangements to be made that are considered appropriate for the purposes of assisting people to select, train for, obtain and retain employment.

Paras (3) and (4). Under para (4), any of the payments listed in para (3) are taken into account over a period of weeks obtained by dividing the amount of the payments by the amount of HB which would be payable had the claimant not received the payments, plus the amount that would have been disregarded from the earnings under Sch 4.

Calculation of net profit of self-employed earners
38.–(1) For the purposes of regulation 30 (average weekly earnings of self-employed earners) the earnings of a claimant to be taken into account shall be–
(a) in the case of a self-employed earner who is engaged in employment on his own account, the net profit derived from that employment;

(b) in the case of a self-employed earner whose employment is carried on in partnership or is that of a share fisherman within the meaning of the Social Security (Mariners' Benefits) Regulations 1975, his share of the net profit derived from that employment, less–

    (i) an amount in respect of income tax and of social security contributions payable under the Act calculated in accordance with regulation 39 (deduction of tax and contributions for self-employed earners); and

    (ii) one-half of the amount calculated in accordance with paragraph (11) in respect of any qualifying premium.

(2) There shall be disregarded from a claimant's net profit, any sum, where applicable, specified in paragraphs 1 to 14 of Schedule 4.

(3) For the purposes of paragraph (1)(a) the net profit of the employment shall, except where paragraph (9) applies, be calculated by taking into account the earnings of the employment over the assessment period less–

(a) subject to paragraphs (5) to (7), any expenses wholly and exclusively incurred in that period for the purposes of that employment;

(b) an amount in respect of–

    (i) income tax; and

    (ii) social security contributions payable under the Act,

    calculated in accordance with regulation 39 (deduction of tax and contributions for self-employed earners); and

(c) one-half of the amount calculated in accordance with paragraph (11) in respect of any qualifying premium.

(4) For the purposes of paragraph (1)(b) the net profit of the employment shall be calculated by taking into account the earnings of the employment over the assessment period less, subject to paragraphs (5) to (7), any expenses wholly and exclusively incurred in that period for the purposes of the employment.

(5) Subject to paragraph (6), no deduction shall be made under paragraph (3)(a) or (4), in respect of–

(a) any capital expenditure;

(b) the depreciation of any capital asset;

(c) any sum employed or intended to be employed in the setting up or expansion of the employment;

(d) any loss incurred before the beginning of the assessment period;

(e) the repayment of capital on any loan taken out for the purposes of the employment;

(f) any expenses incurred in providing business entertainment; and

(g) any debts, except bad debts proved to be such, but this sub-paragraph shall not apply to any expenses incurred in the recovery of a debt.

(6) A deduction shall be made under paragraph (3)(a) or (4) in respect of the repayment of capital on any loan used for–

(a) the replacement in the course of business of equipment or machinery; and

(b) the repair of an existing business asset except to the extent that any sum is payable under an insurance policy for its repair.

(7) The relevant authority shall refuse to make a deduction in respect of any expenses under paragraph (3)(a) or (4) where it is not satisfied given the nature and the amount of the expense that it has been reasonably incurred.

(8) For the avoidance of doubt–

(a) a deduction shall not be made under paragraph (3)(a) or (4) in respect of any sum unless it has been expended for the purposes of the business;

(b) a deduction shall be made thereunder in respect of–

    (i) the excess of any value added tax paid over value added tax received in the assessment period;

    (ii) any income expended in the repair of an existing business asset except to the extent that any sum is payable under an insurance policy for its repair;

    (iii) any payment of interest on a loan taken out for the purposes of the employment.

(9)   Where a claimant is engaged in employment as a child minder the net profit of the employment shall be one-third of the earnings of that employment, less–
  (a)   an amount in respect of–
    (i)   income tax; and
    (ii)   social security contributions payable under the Act,
    calculated in accordance with regulation 39 (deduction of tax and contributions for self-employed earners); and
  (b)   one-half of the amount calculated in accordance with paragraph (11) in respect of any qualifying premium.

(10)   For the avoidance of doubt where a claimant is engaged in employment as a self-employed earner and he is also engaged in one or more other employments as a self-employed or employed earner any loss incurred in any one of his employments shall not be offset against his earnings in any other of his employments.

(11)   The amount in respect of any qualifying premium shall be calculated by multiplying the daily amount of the qualifying premium by the number equal to the number of days in the assessment period; and for the purposes of this regulation the daily amount of the qualifying premium shall be determined–
  (a)   where the qualifying premium is payable monthly, by multiplying the amount of the qualifying premium by 12 and dividing the product by 365;
  (b)   in any other case, by dividing the amount of the qualifying premium by the number equal to the number of days in the period to which the qualifying premium relates.

(12)   In this regulation, ''qualifying premium'' means any premium which is payable periodically in respect of [1] a personal pension scheme and is so payable on or after the date of claim.

Amendment

1.   Omitted by reg 4(3) of SI 2007 No 1749 as from 16.7.07.

Definitions

"assessment period" – see reg 30.
"capital" – see General Note on Section 6.
"claimant" – see reg 2(1).
"date of claim" – reg 2(1).
"earnings" – see reg 37.
"employed earner" – see reg 2(1).
"partner" – reg 2(1).
"qualifying premium" – see para (11).
"relevant authority" – see reg 2(1).
"self-employed earner" – reg 2(1).

General Note

This deals with the assessment of "net profit" for the purposes of reg 30. It produces detailed rules as to what expenditure may be deducted from gross "earnings" (see reg 37 on p363) to arrive at the net figure. The wording follows the income tax law quite closely in relation to allowable deductions from chargeable income.

Analysis

Paragraphs (1) and (2): The basic calculation

Para (1) sets out the basic rule for what is to be taken into account as earnings for the self-employed under reg 30. See p359 for the meaning of "derived from". Earnings to be taken into account are "net profit" minus deductions authorised by Sch 4. Whether or not the business is in profit, any drawings cannot be regarded as earnings, nor can they be taken into account as other income. To do so would involve taking into account both the claimant's share of the profits (independent of whether any profits were withdrawn) and the actual drawings from that share of profits: *AR v Bradford MBC* [2008] UKUT 30 (AAC), R(H) 6/09. See also the commentary on *R v West Dorset DC ex p Poupard* [1988] 28 RVR 40, CA on p339.

There are two categories of self-employed.
(1)   Those who are in self-employment in their own account. Their net profit is calculated under para (3). See commentary to para 5(d) below.
(2)   Those who are in partnerships or are share fishermen. Their net profit is calculated under para (4).
Note that childminders are dealt with separately. Their net profit is calculated under para (9).

Para (2) requires the deduction of the disregarded amounts set out in paras 1 to 14 of Sch 4. Para 14 of Sch 4 ensures that where a self-employed claimant's earnings are paid in a currency other than sterling then any banking or commission charges made on converting those earnings into sterling are deducted from the value of the earnings to be taken into account. In considering the scope of any disregard, decisions on similarly-worded disregards in other means-tested benefit schemes must be taken into account: *CH 2321/2002* para 8.

Note that the deputy commissioner in *CPC 3373/2007*, dealing with the equivalent provision for PC purposes, pointed out that when the difference between receipts and expenditure is a positive figure the regulations refer to it as a "profit" and where it is a negative figure, they refer to it as a "loss". He said that it followed that when a loss is made the net "profit" of the employment for these purposes is nil and not a negative figure.

Paragraph (3): Those who are self-employed on their own account

Note that this does not apply to childminders, who are dealt with under para (9). The total of the amounts available under sub-paras (a) to (c) must be deducted to arrive at the net profit.

Sub-para (a) must be read together with paras (5) to (8) to ascertain exactly which expenses are deductible. The expenses set out in para (5) cannot be deducted, whereas those in para (6) must be deducted. There is a general requirement under para (7) that the expenses must be "reasonably incurred". Para (8) then sets out further deeming provisions. See the discussion of the terms "wholly" and "exclusively" in the commentary to reg 35(2)(b). Note that here there is no requirement that the expenses be necessary. Instead, the test of reasonableness is used.

In *R(H) 5/07*, the commissioner followed *R(FC) 1/91* in holding that the part of the interest on a car loan apportionable to business use could be allowed as an expense "wholly and exclusively incurred . . . for the purposes of [the] employment".

Only expenses incurred during the period over which the profit is averaged out under reg 30 may be considered.

Sub-para (b) requires deduction of income tax and NI contributions. See reg 39, which supplements this.

Sub-para (c) requires the deduction of half of a "qualifying premium" paid in respect of a personal pension scheme (defined in paras (11) and (12)).

Paragraph (4): Partners and share fishermen

Where someone is a partner or a share fisherman, this paragraph with para (1)(b)(i) and (ii), is used to calculate earnings. Under para (1)(b)(i) and (ii), from the claimant's share of the net profit, deductions are made corresponding to para (3)(b) and (c). Para (4) enables business expenses to be deducted on a similar basis to that provided by para (3)(a) in relation to all other self-employed people except child minders.

See also the note to para (10) below.

Paragraph (5): Items which are not expenses

This lists items which are deemed not to satisfy para (3)(a) or para (4), except to the extent that para (6) provides otherwise.

Sub-para (a) capital expenditure. Note that where para (6) applies, the expenditure to which it relates is deductible under para (3)(a) or para (4), despite this provision.

Sub-para (b) depreciation. There can be no deduction in this respect as tax relief and other allowances are already available.

Sub-para (d) losses incurred before the assessment period. Although losses incurred during the assessment period may be deducted as allowable expenses this can only ever take the net "profit" (per para (1)(a)) to a figure of nil; it cannot reduce the profit to a negative figure to be set off against any other income which the claimant may have: *R(H) 5/08* (paras 26-28).

Sub-para (e) excludes repayments of capital on loans taken out for the purposes of the employment. However, para (8)(b)(iii) states that interest on such a loan may be an allowable expense. See also para (6).

Sub-para (g) prevents debts owed to the business being taken into account when calculating net profit. "Bad debts", however, may be taken into account. Bad debts are irrecoverable in accounting terms – eg, because the debtor is insolvent. The requirement that bad debts be "proven to be such" indicates that the claimant must prove that a debt is a bad debt. Expenses incurred in recovering a business debt are deductible in assessing "net profit" if para (3)(a), or paras (4) and (7) are satisfied.

Paragraph (6): Items deemed to be expenses

This qualifies para (5) by providing that capital used to repay loans for the items listed shall be deducted under para (3)(a) or para (4) when calculating net profit.

Sub-para (a). Note that the replacement must be in the "course of business" and not for personal use.

However, in *R(H) 5/07* the commissioner held that capital repayments in respect of a replacement car are deductible as a car is perfectly capable of amounting to "business equipment or machinery", regardless of how good accounting practice may view it.

Sub-para (b). If a sum is "payable" (whether or not actually paid) under an insurance policy for the repair in question, para (5)(e) operates to prevent deduction of capital repayments in this respect, to the extent that the insurance payment would cover them. See also para (8)(b)(iii).

Paragraph (7): Reasonableness of expenses

In deciding whether a business expense has been "reasonably" incurred, the authority has to take account of the nature as well as the amount of the expense, given the character of the claimant's business. The question is whether expenditure of this kind is reasonable. If para (6) or para (8)(b) deems expenses to be deductible, they need to also satisfy the "reasonableness" test under para (7).

Paragraph (8): Deeming provisions

Para (8) contains a number of deeming provisions confirming the effect of paras (3) to (6). Any amounts referred to here which are deductible must still be subjected to the reasonableness test in para (7).

Sub-para (a) simply reinforces the use of the word "wholly" in para (3)(a), confirming that any expenditure of which any part is not for business purposes is not deductible.

Sub-para (b) confirms that net payments of VAT, repair expenditure (except sums paid under insurance policies) and interest payments on loan may be deducted when calculating net profit.

Paragraph (9): Childminders

Para (9) provides special rules for the assessment of the net profit of childminders. "Childminder" is not defined but as "child" is defined as any person under the age of 16, it is suggested that any person looking after a "child" at any period of the day by way of a business will fall within that provision. Paras (3) to (7) do not apply. Instead, childminders are deemed to have net profit of one-third of their earnings. Para (2) still applies and so the sums listed in Sch 4 paras 1 to 14 are deductible from a childminder's net profit for the purposes of reg 30.

As to deductions under sub-para (a), see reg 39. "Qualifying premiums" in sub-para (b) are defined in para (11). Half a qualifying premium may be deducted.

Paragraph (10): Offsetting

This paragraph provides that if a claimant has more than one employment, losses made in one during the averaging period cannot be offset against gains made in respect of another. It is, however, not possible to imply a general rule, that losses may be offset: *CPC 3373/2007*. Para (10) states expressly that it has been made "for the avoidance of doubt" and it is intended merely to clarify the law as it would exist even if the regulation had not been made.

Paragraphs (11) and (12): "Qualifying premiums"

Para (11) deals with calculation of qualifying premiums. Para (12) clarifies that the amount initially to be deducted should be based on the amounts payable on or after the date of claim.

Deduction of tax and contributions of self-employed earners

39.–(1)   The amount to be deducted in respect of income tax under regulation 38(1)(b)(i), (3)(b)(i) or (9)(a)(i) (calculation of net profit of self-employed earners) shall be calculated on the basis of the amount of chargeable income and as if that income were assessable to income tax at the [¹ starting rate] or, as the case may be, the [¹ starting rate] and the basic rate of tax applicable to the assessment period less only the personal relief to which the claimant is entitled under sections 257(1) of the Income and Corporation Taxes Act 1988 (personal allowances) as is appropriate to his circumstances; but, if the assessment period is less than a year, the earnings to which the [¹ starting rate] of tax is to be applied and the amount of the personal relief deductible under this paragraph shall be calculated on a pro rata basis.

(2)   The amount to be deducted in respect of social security contributions under regulation 38(1)(b)(i), (3)(b)(ii) or (9)(a)(ii) shall be the total of–

(a)   the amount of Class 2 contributions payable under section 11(1) or, as the case may be, 11(3) of the Act at the rate applicable to the assessment period except where the claimant's chargeable income is less than the amount specified in section 11(4) of the Act (small earnings exception) for the tax year applicable to the assessment period; but if the assessment period is less than a year, the amount specified for that tax year shall be reduced pro rata; and

(b)   the amount of Class 4 contributions (if any) which would be payable under section 15 of the Act (Class 4 contributions recoverable under the Income Tax Acts) at the percentage rate applicable to the assessment period on so much of the chargeable income as exceeds the lower limit but does not exceed the upper limit of profits and gains applicable for the tax year applicable to the assessment period; but if the assessment period is less than a year, those limits shall be reduced pro rata.

(3)   In this regulation "chargeable income" means–

(a)   except where sub-paragraph (b) applies, the earnings derived from the employment less any expenses deducted under paragraph (3)(a) or, as the case may be, (4) of regulation 38;

(b)   in the case of employment as a child minder, one third of the earnings of that employment.

Amendment

1.   Amended by reg 11(6) of SI 2007 No 2618 as from 1.10.07.

Definitions

"self-employed earner" – see reg 2(1).

General Note

This relates to the calculation of "net profit" under reg 38 and in particular to deductions for income tax and national insurance (NI) made under paras (1)(b), (3)(b) and (9)(a) of that regulation. Para (1) deals with the quantification of income tax to be deducted from "earnings" as defined in reg 37 under paras (1)(b)(i), (3)(b)(i) or (9)(a)(i) as appropriate.

Para (2) deals with the amount of NI contributions to be deducted from earnings; and para (3) defines the term "chargeable income" as used in this regulation.

Analysis

Para (2). A self-employed person may be liable to both class 2 and class 4 contributions depending on the level of her/his profits. The amount due is calculated on the basis of "chargeable income": see para (3) for the definition. Deductions for NI should be based on the rates applicable to the assessment period (see reg 2(1)).

Para (3) defines "chargeable income" as the amount remaining after the deductions in paras (3)(a) and (4) of reg 38, as appropriate, have been made from gross earnings. In the case of a child minder, it is one-third of her/his earnings. See the Analysis to reg 38(9) on p368.

SECTION 5
Other income

General Note on Section 5

This Section provides the rules under which income which is not "earnings" under Sections 3 or 4 is to be assessed. Note, however, that student income is dealt with in Part 7.

Calculation of income other than earnings

40.–(1)   For the purposes of regulation 31 (average weekly income other than earnings), the income of a claimant which does not consist of earnings to be taken into account shall, subject to paragraphs (2) to (7) be his gross income and any capital treated as income under regulation 41 (capital treated as income).

(2)   There shall be disregarded from the calculation of a claimant's gross income under paragraph (1), any sum, where applicable, specified in Schedule 5.

[² (3)]

[² (4)]

[² (4A)]

(5)   Where the payment of any benefit under the benefit Acts is subject to any deduction by way of recovery the amount to be taken into account under paragraph (1) shall be the gross amount payable.

[⁴ (5A) Where the claimant or, where the claimant is a member of a couple, his partner is receiving a contributory employment and support allowance and that benefit has been reduced under regulation 63 of the Employment and Support Allowance Regulations the amount of that benefit to be taken into account is the amount as if it had not been reduced.]

(6)   Where an award of any working tax credit or child tax credit under the Tax Credits Act is subject to a deduction by way of recovery of an overpayment of working tax credit or child tax credit which arose in a previous tax year the amount to be taken into account under paragraph (1) shall be the amount of working tax credit or child tax credit awarded less the amount of that deduction.

(7)   [³ Paragraphs (8) and (8A) apply] where–

(a)   a relevant payment has been made to a person in an academic year; and

(b)   that person abandons, or is dismissed from, his course of study before the payment to him of the final instalment of the relevant payment.

(8)   [³ Where a relevant payment is made quarterly, the] amount of a relevant payment to be taken into account for the assessment period for the purposes of paragraph (1) in respect of a person to whom paragraph (7) applies, shall be calculated by applying the formula–

$$\frac{A - (B \times C)}{D}$$

where–

A= the total amount of the relevant payment which that person would have received had he remained a student until the last day of the academic term in which he abandoned, or was dismissed from, his course, less any deduction under regulation 64(5);

B= the number of benefit weeks from the benefit week immediately following that which includes the first day of that academic year to the benefit week which includes the day on which the person abandoned, or was dismissed from, his course;

C= the weekly amount of the relevant payment, before the application of the £10 disregard, which would have been taken into account as income under regulation 64(2) had the person not abandoned or been dismissed from, his course and, in the case of a person who was not entitled to housing benefit immediately before he abandoned or was dismissed from his course, had that person, at that time, been entitled to housing benefit;

D= the number of benefit weeks in the assessment period.

[³ (8A)   Where a relevant payment is made by two or more instalments in a quarter, the amount of a relevant payment to be taken into account for the assessment period for the purposes of paragraph (1) in respect of a person to whom paragraph (7) applies, shall be calculated by applying the formula in paragraph (8) but as if–

A = the total amount of relevant payments which that person received, or would have received, from the first day of the academic year to the day the person abandoned the course, or was dismissed from it, less any deduction under regulation 64(5).]

(9)   [³ In this regulation]–

"academic year" and "student loan" shall have the same meanings as for the purposes of Part 7;

[³ "assessment period" means–

(a)   in a case where a relevant payment is made quarterly, the period beginning with the benefit week which includes the day on which the person abandoned, or was dismissed from, his course and ending with the benefit week which includes the last day of the last quarter for which an instalment of the relevant payment was payable to that person;

(b)   in a case where the relevant payment is made by two or more instalments in a quarter, the period beginning with the benefit week which includes the day on which the person abandoned, or was dismissed from, his course and ending with the benefit week which includes–

(i)   the day immediately before the day on which the next instalment of the relevant payment would have been due had the payments continued; or

(ii)   the last day of the last quarter for which an instalment of the relevant payment was payable to that person,

whichever of those dates is earlier;]

"relevant payment" means either a student loan or an amount intended for the maintenance of dependants referred to in regulation 59(7) or both.

[³ "quarter" in relation to an assessment period means a period in that year beginning on–

(a)   1st January and ending on 31st March;

(b   1st April and ending on 30th June;

(c)   1st July and ending on 31st August; or

(d)   1st September and ending on 31st December;]

(10)   For the avoidance of doubt there shall be included as income to be taken into account under paragraph (1)–

(a)   any payment to which regulation 35(2) (payments not earnings) applies; or

(b)   in the case of a claimant who is receiving support under section 95 or 98 of the Immigration and Asylum Act including support provided by virtue of regulations made under Schedule 9 to that Act, the amount of such support provided in respect of essential living needs of the claimant and his dependants (if any) as is specified in regulations made under paragraph 3 of Schedule 8 to the Immigration and Asylum Act.

Amendments

1.   Inserted by reg 2 of SI 2006 No 2813 as from 20.11.06.
2.   Omitted by reg 4(b) of SI 2007 No 1619 as from 3.7.07.
3.   Amended by reg 5(2) of SI 2008 No 1599 as from, for students whose period of study begins on or after 1.8.08 but before 1.9.08, on the day the period of study begins; in any other case 1.9.08.
4.   Inserted by reg 15 of SI 2008 No 1082 as from 27.10.08.

Definitions

"capital" – see General Note on Section 6.
"claimant" – see reg 2(1).
"earnings" – see regs 35 and 37.
"income" – see General Note on Section 2.

General Note

Unlike in sections 3 and 4 of this Part, the general rule is that gross, rather than net, income is to be taken into account together with any capital treated as income under reg 41. Amounts specified in Sch 5 are disregarded; this includes tax paid on the income.

Analysis

Para (1) confirms that, subject to paras (2) to (7), gross income is taken into account. Note, however, that tax paid on the income is to be disregarded under Sch 5 para 1. For general comments about the nature of income, see the General Note to this Part.

Para (2) permits the disregards in Sch 5. In considering the scope of any disregard, decisions on similarly-worded disregards in other means-tested benefit schemes must be taken into account: *CH 2321/2002* (para 8).

Paras (3) to (4A) permitted a local authority to modify the scheme so as to disregard war widow's and widower's pensions and certain payments made under the Armed Forces and Reserve Forces (Compensation Scheme) Order 2005. The Housing Benefit and Council Tax Benefit (War Pension Disregards) Regulations 2007 (see p1227) now prescribe the pensions that can be disregarded. See s134(8)(a) SSAA for a discussion of the authority's powers to modify the HB scheme.

Para (5) refers only to the situation where a "deduction by way of recovery" is made from gross benefit paid under the benefit Acts (defined in reg 2(1)) – eg, to recoup an overpayment – not to the situation where there is a *reduction* in benefit for some other reason such as a trade dispute or for a JSA sanction, or where IB is reduced where occupational pension is in payment: *R(H) 2/09*. Tax credits are not dealt with under this paragraph, but under para (6) instead.

Para (5A) means that where a claimant or her/his partner is receiving a reduced rate of contributory ESA under reg 63 ESA Regs 2008, the amount of ESA as if *not* reduced is to be taken into account. Reg 63 ESA Regs provides for a reduction in ESA where the ESA claimant is required to take part in a work-focused health-related assessment or a work-focused interview, but has failed to do so without good cause. ESA is reduced by 50 per cent of the amount of the work-related activity component for four weeks, and then by 100 per cent of that component thereafter.

Para (6) makes it plain that where an award of WTC or CTC for the current year is subject of a deduction in order to recover an overpayment of tax credits from the previous year (pursuant to s28(1) Tax Credits Act 2002), the amount of CTC or WTC to be taken into account in calculating the weekly level of income for HB purposes is the current year award of tax credits less the deduction for the overpayment: generally, the amount being paid. This is confirmed in *CH 1450/2005*, where the commissioner rejected an argument that as the claimant was putting the overpaid sums of tax credits aside pending recovery, she was holding the sums on trust for the Revenue, had no beneficial interest in the sums, and so they should have been ignored as income in the year in which they were actually paid. The sums were clearly received by the claimant and were her income, and any different result would mean that the overpaid sums stood to be disregarded both in the year in which they were received and the following year, which would amount to a double disregard.

However, note that where tax credits continue to be paid incorrectly after a claimant has asked that they cease, the continuing payments can be disregarded while the overpayment continues: see the commentary to reg 32 and in particular the discussion of *CIS 1813/2007* on p356. This means that, although there could in effect be a double deduction, even where incorrect payments of tax credits were disregarded as income in a past period, for a current period, an authority must make a deduction for the recovery of the overpayment if the conditions of para (6) are met, and only take into account the amount of tax credits being paid. It is therefore important for a claimant to ensure that s/he notifies the Revenue of relevant changes of circumstance timeously and to ask that payment of tax credits cease.

Paras (7) to (9) deal with students who leave their courses prematurely. Where the student has received a "relevant payment" (as defined in para (9)), that payment is apportioned according to the formula in para (8). The effect is that the former student is treated as having the same weekly income from the relevant payment as if s/he had completed the course but only for the period during which s/he was actually on the course. Para (8A) modifies the formula in para (8) where the student has received the relevant payment in two or more instalments in a quarter.

In *CJSA 549/2003* (para 6), the commissioner confirmed that the formula in para (8) has to be applied even in a case where the student had repaid a student loan that she had taken out in full. He was critical of the unfairness of this rule.

Para (10)(a) makes it clear that payments which are disregarded under reg 35(2) in the calculation of earnings are to be taken into account as "other income" under para (1). See, however, Sch 5 paras 3 and 23 for when these can be disregarded.

Capital treated as income

41.–(1) Any capital payable by instalments which are outstanding at the date on which the claim is made or treated as made, or, at the date of any subsequent revision or supersession, shall, if the aggregate of the instalments outstanding and the amount of the claimant's capital otherwise calculated in accordance with Section 6 exceeds £16,000, be treated as income.

(2) Any payment received under an annuity shall be treated as income.

(3) Any earnings to the extent that they are not a payment of income shall be treated as income.

(4) Any Career Development Loan paid pursuant to section 2 of the 1973 Act shall be treated as income.

(5) Where an agreement or court order provides that payments shall be made to the claimant in consequence of any personal injury to the claimant and that such payments are to be made, wholly or partly, by way of periodic payments, any such periodic payments received by the claimant (but not a payment which is treated as capital by virtue of this Part), shall be treated as income.

Definitions

"capital" – see General Note on Section 6.
"claimant" – see reg 2(1).
"earnings" – see regs 35 and 37.
"income" – see General Note on Section 2.

General Note

Reg 41 provides for the treatment as income of some payments which would normally be regarded as capital. They are disregarded as capital under para 22 of Sch 6.

Analysis

Para (1) aims to give a benevolent treatment of outstanding instalments of capital owed to a claimant. If the sum of the claimant's capital and the instalments outstanding is worth more than £16,000 (the capital limit) and hence would normally disqualify the claimant from benefit, the value of the right to receive the instalments is disregarded as a capital asset under Sch 6 para 18 and the outstanding instalments are treated as income. This question is decided both on the date of claim (see reg 83) and on any subsequent revision or supersession.

Para (2) deems payments under an annuity to be income.

Para (3) requires that earnings be treated as income in all cases.

Para (4) deems career development loans to be income rather than capital.

Para (5) deals with income from structured settlements in personal injury cases. It is frequently a term of settlement in cases involving very serious injuries that the defendant purchases an annuity which will yield a regular income for the claimant.

Notional income

42.–(1)   A claimant shall be treated as possessing income of which he has deprived himself for the purpose of securing entitlement to housing benefit or increasing the amount of that benefit.

(2)   Except in the case of–

(a)   a discretionary trust;

(b)   a trust derived from a payment made in consequence of a personal injury;

(c)   a personal pension scheme [¹ , occupational pension scheme] [² [⁵] or a payment made by the Board of the Pension Protection Fund] where the claimant [¹⁴ has not attained the qualifying age for state pension credit];

[⁴ (d) any sum to which paragraph 45(2)(a) of Schedule 6 (capital to be disregarded) applies which is administered in the way referred to in paragraph 45(1)(a);

(da)   any sum to which paragraph 46(a) of Schedule 6 refers;]

(e)   rehabilitation allowance made under section 2 of the 1973 Act;

(f)   child tax credit; or

(g)   working tax credit,

[¹² (h) any sum to which paragraph (12A) applies;]

any income which would become available to the claimant upon application being made, but which has not been acquired by him, shall be treated as possessed by the claimant but only from the date on which it could be expected to be acquired were an application made.

[⁸ (3)]

[⁸ [⁵ (3A)]]

[⁸ (4)]

[⁸ (5)]

(6)   Any payment of income, other than a payment of income specified in paragraph (7), made–

(a)   to a third party in respect of a single claimant or a member of the family (but not a member of the third party's family) shall, where that payment is a payment of an occupational pension [² , a pension or other periodical payment made under a personal pension scheme or a payment made by the Board of the Pension Protection Fund], be treated as possessed by that single claimant or, as the case may be, by that member;

(b)   to a third party in respect of a single claimant or in respect of a member of the family (but not a member of the third party's family) shall, where it is not a payment referred to in sub-paragraph (a), be treated as possessed by that single claimant or by that member to the extent that it is used for the food, household fuel or, subject to paragraph (13), rent or ordinary clothing or footwear, of that single claimant or, as the case may be, of any member of that family or is used for any council tax or water charges for which that claimant or member is liable;

(c)   to a single claimant or a member of the family in respect of a third party (but not in respect of another member of that family) shall be treated as possessed by that single claimant or, as the case may be, that member of the family to the extent that it is kept or used by him or used by or on behalf of any member of the family.

(7)   Paragraph (6) shall not apply in respect of a payment of income made–

(a)   under [¹³ or by] the Macfarlane Trust, the Macfarlane (Special Payments) Trust, the Macfarlane (Special Payments) (No. 2) Trust, the Fund, the Eileen Trust [¹³, MFET Limited] or the Independent Living [⁹ Fund (2006)];

(b)   pursuant to section 19(1)(a) of the Coal Industry Act 1994 (concessionary coal);

(c)   pursuant to section 2 of the 1973 Act in respect of a person's participation–

(i)   in an employment programme specified in regulation 75(1)(a)(ii) of the Jobseeker's Allowance Regulations;

(ii)   in a training scheme specified in regulation 75(1)(b)(ii) of those Regulations;

(iii)   in the Intensive Activity Period specified in regulation 75(1)(a)(iv) of those Regulations [⁷]; [¹¹]

> (iv) in a qualifying course within the meaning specified in regulation 17A(7) of those Regulations; [¹¹ or]
>
> [¹¹ (v) in the Flexible New Deal specified in regulation 75(1)(a)(v) of those Regulations;]

[(ca) *in respect of a person's participation in the Work for Your Benefit Pilot Scheme;*]

(d) under an occupational pension scheme [² , in respect of a pension or other periodical payment made under a personal pension scheme or a payment made by the Board of the Pension Protection Fund] where–

> (i) a bankruptcy order has been made in respect of the person in respect of whom the payment has been made or, in Scotland, the estate of that person is subject to sequestration or a judicial factor has been appointed on that person's estate under section 41 of the Solicitors (Scotland) Act 1980;
>
> (ii) the payment is made to the trustee in bankruptcy or any other person acting on behalf of the creditors; and
>
> (iii) the person referred to in (i) and any member of his family does not possess, or is not treated as possessing, any other income apart from that payment.

(8) Where a claimant is in receipt of any benefit (other than housing benefit) under the benefit Acts and the rate of that benefit is altered with effect from a date on or after 1st April in any year but not more than 14 days thereafter, the relevant authority shall treat the claimant as possessing such benefit at the altered rate–

(a) in a case in which the claimant's weekly amount of eligible rent falls to be calculated in accordance with regulation 80(2)(b) [³ or (c)] (calculation of weekly amounts), from 1st April in that year;

(b) in any other case, from the first Monday in April in that year,

to the date on which the altered rate is to take effect.

(9) Subject to paragraph (10), where–

(a) a claimant performs a service for another person; and

(b) that person makes no payment of earnings or pays less than that paid for a comparable employment in the area,

the relevant authority shall treat the claimant as possessing such earnings (if any) as is reasonable for that employment unless the claimant satisfies the authority that the means of that person are insufficient for him to pay or to pay more for the service.

(10) Paragraph (9) shall not apply–

(a) to a claimant who is engaged by a charitable or voluntary organisation or who is a volunteer if the relevant authority is satisfied in any of those cases that it is reasonable for him to provide those services free of charge; or

(b) in a case where the service is performed in connection with–

> (i) the claimant's participation in an employment or training programme in accordance with regulation 19(1)(q) of the Jobseeker's Allowance Regulations, other than where the service is performed in connection with the claimant's participation in the Intense Activity Period specified in regulation 75(1)(a)(iv) of those Regulations [⁷]; or
>
> (ii) the claimant's or the claimant's partner's participation in an employment or training programme as defined in regulation 19(3) of those Regulations for which a training allowance is not payable or, where such an allowance is payable, it is payable for the sole purpose of reimbursement of travelling or meal expenses to the person participating in that programme. [⁶ ; or

(c) to a claimant who is participating in a work placement approved by the Secretary of State (or a person providing services to the Secretary of State) before the placement starts.

(10A) In paragraph (10)(c) "work placement" means practical work experience which is not undertaken in expectation of payment.]

(11) Where a claimant is treated as possessing any income under any of paragraphs (1) to (8), the foregoing provisions of this Part shall apply for the purposes of calculating the amount of that income as if a payment had actually been made and as if it were actual income which he does possess.

(12)   Where a claimant is treated as possessing any earnings under paragraph (9) the foregoing provisions of this Part shall apply for the purposes of calculating the amount of those earnings as if a payment had actually been made and as if they were actual earnings which he does possess except that paragraph (3) of regulation 36 (calculation of net earnings of employed earners) shall not apply and his net earnings shall be calculated by taking into account those earnings which he is treated as possessing, less–

(a)   an amount in respect of income tax equivalent to an amount calculated by applying to those earnings the [¹⁰] the basic rate of tax applicable to the assessment period less only the personal relief to which the claimant is entitled under sections 257(1) of the Income and Corporation Taxes Act 1988 (personal allowances) as is appropriate to his circumstances; but, if the assessment period is less than a year, the earnings to which the [⁶ [¹⁰ basic] rate] of tax is to be applied and the amount of the personal relief deductible under this sub-paragraph shall be calculated on a pro rata basis;

(b)   an amount equivalent to the amount of the primary Class 1 contributions that would be payable by him under the Act in respect of those earnings if such contributions were payable; and

(c)   one-half of any sum payable by the claimant by way of a contribution towards an occupational or personal pension scheme.

[¹² (12A)   Paragraphs (1), (2), (6) and (9) shall not apply in respect of any amount of income other than earnings, or earnings of an employed earner, arising out of the claimant's participation in a service user group.]

(13)   In paragraph (6) ''rent'' means eligible rent less any deductions in respect of non-dependants which fall to be made under regulation 74 (non-dependant deductions).

Modifications

Reg 42(7) is modified by reg 14 Jobseeker's Allowance (Work for Your Benefit Pilot Scheme) Regulations 2010 SI No.1222 (see p1247) as from 22 November 2010 but only for those ordinarily resident in a pilot area or whose address for payment of JSA is located within such an area. The modifications are shown in italics above. They cease to have effect on 21 November 2013.

Amendments

1.   Amended by reg 5A(2) of SI 2005 No 2465 as inserted by Sch 2 para 28(5) of SI 2006 No 217 as from 6.4.06.
2.   Amended by reg 8(2)(a)-(c) of SI 2006 No 588 as from 6.4.06.
3.   Amended by reg 8(2)(d) of SI 2006 No 588 as from 1.4.06.
4.   Substituted by reg 6(2) of SI 2007 No 719 as from 2.4.07.
5.   Amended by reg 4(4) of SI 2007 No 1749 as from 16.7.07.
6.   Amended by reg 11(7) of SI 2007 No 2618 as from 1.10.07.
7.   Omitted by reg 6(4) of SI 2008 No 698 as from 14.4.08.
8.   Omitted by reg 3(5) of SI 2008 No 1042 as from 19.5.08.
9.   Amended by reg 6(4)(a) of SI 2008 No 2767 as from 17.11.08.
10.   Amended by reg 6(4) of SI 2009 No 583 as from 6.4.09.
11.   Amended by reg 3 of SI 2009 No 480 as from 5.10.09.
12.   Inserted by reg 6(4) of SI 2009 No 2655 as from 2.11.09.
13.   Amended by reg 8(3) and (5) of SI 2010 No 641 as from 1.4.10 (5.4.10 where rent payable weekly or in multiples of a week).
14.   Amended by reg 8(4) of SI 2010 No 641 as from 6.4.10.

Definitions

"benefit Acts" – see SSCBA.
"benefit week" – see reg 2(1).
"claimant" – see reg 2(1).
"earnings" – see regs 35 and 37.
"eligible rent" – see reg 2(1).
"family" – see s137(1) SSCBA.
"occupational pension/personal pension scheme" – see reg 2(1).
"relevant authority" – see reg 2(1).
"service user group" – see reg 2(1).
"the Fund", "the Macfarlane Trust", "the Independent Living Fund", "the Macfarlane (Special Payments) Trust", "MFET Ltd", "the Eileen Trust" – see reg 2(1).

General Note

This highly complex regulation deals with the situations in which a claimant may be treated as possessing income that s/he does not in fact possess. It covers a variety of situations.

Para (1) deals with income of which a claimant has deprived her/himself.

Para (2) deals with income which is available to a claimant on application.

Paras (6) and (7) deal with payments involving third parties. Para (6)(b) requires an equivalent amount of payments made to third parties on behalf of a claimant to cover basic living expenses to be taken into account as income. Para (6)(c) requires income paid to a claimant or a member of the family in respect of someone else who is not a member of the family to be taken into account if it is retained or used by the claimant or the member of the family.

Para (8) deals with the effect of changes in benefit rates.

Para (9) requires a claimant to be treated as possessing any earnings which would be reasonable if s/he is not paid or is paid too little; para (10) provides exceptions to para (9).

Para (12A) disapplies paras (1), (2), (6) and (9) for income other than earnings and earnings of employees arising out of participation in a "service user group".

Analysis

Paragraph (1): Income of which the claimant has deprived himself

The wording of this provision dates back to the old supplementary benefits scheme, though there is no discretion as there then was as to whether the consequences of the provision should apply. Caselaw decided by the commissioners and the Upper Tribunal will be highly relevant to deciding whether or not the terms of para (1) are met. That caselaw is summarised in the Analysis to reg 49(1) on p385.

The effect of the provision is that the claimant is deemed to possess income which s/he has got rid of in order to qualify for, or increase entitlement to, HB. That apparently simple question involves a fairly complex analysis and so careful reference needs to be made to the caselaw. Note that para (1) does not apply in respect of any amount of income other than earnings, or earnings from employment, arising out of participation in a service user group (see para (12A)).

A child support commissioner has decided, in relation to the equivalent child support provision, that a refusal to take up an offer of employment does not amount to deprivation of income: *CCS 7967/1995*. In relation to claimants who do carry out work for which they are not paid or are paid too little, see para (9).

Paragraph (2): Income available on application

This makes it clear that, unless excepted by sub-paras (a) to (h), income a claimant could obtain on application being made is treated as possessed by the claimant, even if it is has not actually been acquired by her/him. Note that para (2) does not apply in respect of any amount of income other than earnings, or earnings from employment, arising out of participation in a service user group (see para (12A)).

Certain payments from trusts falling within the sub-paras are excluded. In relation to potential payments from other types of trust, s31 Trustee Act 1925 must be borne in mind. In most cases trustees are under a duty to pay the income produced by property held in trust for a beneficiary who is aged 18 or more to that beneficiary, unless the terms of the trust itself exclude such payments. Accordingly, in such a case, a beneficiary *would* be entitled to the income on application and therefore it must be taken into account under this paragraph. *Actual* payments of this kind should be assessed under reg 40 instead. The section only gives trustees a *power* to pay income where the potential beneficiary is aged under 18 so there is no guarantee that a beneficiary *would* be entitled to income on application in such a case, and therefore the potential income will not be assessable under this paragraph.

Para (2) may apply to entitlement to social security benefits, but the authority would have to be certain not merely that application for the benefit would result in entitlement, but also as to the amount of any entitlement. Where benefits are concerned, entitlement decisions are for decision makers within the social security system. If there is any uncertainty, it is suggested that the wording of para (2) is not met because it is necessary for the authority to satisfy itself that income *would* be available on application.

Another point that needs to be borne in mind is that payments of benefits are often ignored in whole or in part as income for the purposes of assessing HB and CTB. If a benefit is disregarded under Sch 5, it cannot be taken into account as notional income under para (2).

With income from some sources, the problem will be in deciding what the claimant really could be paid if s/he applied. But if the authority decides that money would become available on application it must treat the claimant as possessing it, unless the source of the funds is set out in sub-paras (a) to (h).

Sub-para (a): Exclusion of discretionary trusts. This is because, by definition, a potential beneficiary has no right to payment. A discretionary trust is one in relation to which the trustees have a choice as to the beneficiary they should pay, or how much they pay. But if a claimant actually receives such a payment it is assessable under reg 40.

Sub-para (b): "Trust derived from a payment made in consequence of personal injury". This would cover a trust of funds from a vaccine damage payment, as well as an out-of-court settlement or actual damages under court order which are placed in a trust following a court order. The regulation does not apply to potential payments from such a source but reg 40 might apply to any actual payments of income: see *CIS 114/1999* para

21, upheld in *Beattie v Secretary of State for Social Security* [2001] 1 WLR 1404, CA, and both reported as *R(IS) 10/01*. Note, however, that some payments from trusts set up out of money paid because of personal injury to the claimant can be ignored under Sch 5 para 14 and that any payments from certain trusts (eg, the McFarlane Trust or the Eileen Trust) are ignored under Sch 5 para 35. In *R(SB) 2/89* para 15, it was held that "personal injury" included injury suffered as a result of a disease (as well as accidental injury).

Sub-para (c) requires income to which a claimant would be entitled from a personal pension scheme or occupational pension scheme or a payment by the Board of the Pension Protection Fund if it was applied for not to be taken into account, so long as s/he is under the qualifying age for PC. However, see reg 41(4) to (6) HB(SPC) Regs where the claimant is at least that age and neither s/he nor her /his partner is on IS, income-based JSA or income-related ESA.

Sub-paras (d) and (da) refer to funds derived from awards of damages for personal injury, administered either by a relevant court or by the Court of Protection on behalf of a claimant. See the Analysis to Sch 6 para 45 on p576.

Sub-para (e). Rehabilitation allowance is paid to those on full-time rehabilitation courses. They are designed to help those who have been incapable of work for long periods to return to work.

Sub-paras (f) and (g). A claimant cannot be treated as in possession of CTC or WTC if s/he does not claim them.

Sub-para (h) refers to payments of income other than earnings, and earnings of an employee arising out of participation in a "service user group" (defined in reg 2(1)).

Paragraphs (3) to (5): Income from retirement schemes

These provisions, which aimed to ensure that a person aged over 60 did not deprive her/himself of income available from a pension scheme, were deleted with effect from 19 May 2008. Claimants aged at least the qualifying age for PC are now dealt with under the HB(SPC) Regs unless the claimant or her/his partner is on IS, income-based JSA or income-related ESA (see reg 5), in which case, all income is ignored under Sch 5 para 4. See reg 41(4) to (6) HB(SPC) Regs.

Paragraphs (6), (7) and (13): Payments involving third parties

Para (6) deals with a number of different circumstances in which third parties are involved in relevant funds. The authority here is obliged to treat the claimant or family member as possessing income if one of the sub-paras applies. There is no discretion. However, if a payment to a third party is a voluntary payment (ie, one where the payer does not receive anything in return) this income or part of it may be disregarded under Sch 5 para 14. If the payment is made from one of the sources specified in para (7), it is ignored. Note also that para (6) does not apply in respect of any amount of income other than earnings, or earnings from employment, arising out of participation in a service user group (see para (12A)).

Para (6)(a) prevents a person depriving her/himself of income to which s/he is entitled from the pension schemes listed by assigning it to a third party. The amounts of any payments to third parties will be taken into account as the income of that person, but see para (7)(d).

Para (6)(b) deals with when income for the benefit of a single claimant or a member of the family is paid direct to a third party. The aim is to prevent third parties paying for basic items which are usually covered by means-tested benefits. But if the payment is for a purpose other than those listed (eg, for a leisure item or educational purposes), the payment should be disregarded. The relevant items are:

(1) Food.

(2) Household fuel. This will cover coal (though note the effect of para (7)(b) in relation to concessionary coal), gas and electricity but will not cover, for example, petrol for a car purchased by someone outside the claimant's family.

(3) Rent. This is defined in para (13) as being eligible rent less deductions made for non-dependants. For the determination of eligible rent see regs 12B, 12C and 12D as well as reg 12 as set out in Sch 3 para 5 HB&CTB(CP) Regs. The consequence of the wording of para (13) is that if the claimant's HB is reduced because certain payments of rent are not eligible or is restricted under the rent restrictions provisions in Part 3 or the HB&CTB(CP) Regs, the shortfall may be paid by a third party direct to the landlord without it being taken into account as the income of the claimant or other person liable for the rent.

(4) Ordinary clothing or footwear. This is defined in reg 2(1) as clothing or footwear "for normal daily use" but does not include school uniforms or clothing or footwear used solely for sporting activities. What "normal daily use" means will be a question of fact. Whether, for example, a suit would fall under this sub-para might depend on the person's circumstances. For example, if s/he is in low paid work and wears the suit every day, it is probably an item for "normal daily use". If a suit is purchased for a single event such as a wedding or a funeral, that is arguably not "normal daily use". The provision therefore has the perverse effect that the price of luxuries will often not be taken into account as income but the cost of basic items bought for someone will be.

Para (6)(c) is more restrictive in its terms than sub-para (b). It applies to payments made to a claimant or a member of her/his family in respect of a third party – eg, which actually belong to someone else, or are to be used for someone else's benefit. If the payee keeps the money or uses it for the benefit of her/himself or the member of the family, or any other member of her/his family so uses it, s/he will be treated as possessing it to the extent that it was so kept or used. This is the case no matter the purpose to which the money is put.

Para (7) states that any payments made from the Macfarlane Trust, Macfarlane (Special Payments) Trust, the Macfarlane (Special Payments) (No 2) Trust, the Fund, the Eileen Trust, MFET Limited or the Independent Living Fund (2006) are exempt from the treatment in para (6) as are payments in lieu of concessionary coal and certain payments under s2 Employment and Training Act 1973 and the New Deal and the Flexible New Deal.

Para (7)(d) constitutes an exception to the treatment of assigned pension entitlements under para (6)(a) above. If the person entitled to the payments has been made bankrupt or sequestrated and the payments are being made to her/his trustee in bankruptcy or other person administering her/his affairs, and no member of the family has any other income, the payments will not be taken into account.

Paragraph (8): Treatment of benefits

Para (8) provides that where a claimant receives a benefit other than HB and it is due to be altered between April 1 and 15 in any given year, the authority is obliged to treat the claimant as receiving the altered amount up to two benefit weeks before that week in which the different amount is paid to him. This rule is for the authority's administrative convenience to enable it to alter amounts so as to coincide with changes in rent, rather than cope with changes of circumstances later on.

Paragraphs (9), (10) and (10A): Notional earnings

Para (9), is sometimes known as the "notional earnings" rule. The effect is to treat the claimant as having an income from unpaid or low paid work which s/he does, with the limited exceptions in para (10). Note also that para (9) does not apply in respect of any amount of income other than earnings, or earnings from employment, arising out of participation in a service user group (see para (12A)).

The exceptions are work for charitable or voluntary bodies or other voluntary work (para (10)(a)), services performed in connection with certain employment or training schemes for which a training allowance is not payable or where the allowance is only for travel or meal expenses (para (1)(b)) and certain approved work placements (para (10)(c)). "Work placement" is defined in para (10A). See also Sch 5 para 2 on p551.

The provision is directed at employers who pay too little and aims to prevent low-paid work being subsidised by the public purse. It is not directed at claimants who declare less than they earn, yet the effect is to penalise the claimant.

In applying the paragraph, however, the authority has many value judgments to make.

(1)   If the claimant is working for a charitable or voluntary body or is a volunteer, the authority must decide if it is "reasonable" for her/him to work free of charge. A "volunteer" is a person who without any obligation performs a service for someone else without expecting payment: *R(IS) 12/92* para 6. It might be reasonable for such work to be done where the worker is trying to obtain work experience. Other relevant factors are the closeness of the relationship between the provider and beneficiary of the service, the expectations of family members if there is a family relationship, the housing arrangements of the parties and why, if s/he did, the service provider gave up employment: see *CIS 93/1991* para 4.

(2)   Does the person for whom the work is performed pay less than the amount paid for "comparable employment" in the area? If there is no "comparable employment" and something is paid, it is arguable that the paragraph cannot apply: see sub-para (b). A particular difficulty that has arisen concerns employees who are paid less than the national minimum wage. Some authorities have proceeded on the basis that since it is generally unlawful to pay less than the minimum wage, employees working for less than the minimum wage have to be treated as being in receipt of notional earnings. This seems particularly harsh and wholly out of touch with the reality of work in tight labour markets in areas of high unemployment, where workers may have little option but to accept low-paid work to keep themselves in the job market. Thus unless the authority has evidence of comparable jobs paying higher wages, authorities ought readily to find that it is not reasonable to treat the relevant person as receiving more money.

(3)   What is a "reasonable" amount to treat the claimant as possessing from the employment? In certain circumstances it may be "reasonable" to treat the claimant as possessing *no* income from this source.

Even if the authority considers the terms of sub-paras (a) and (b) to be satisfied, the claimant can still avoid the effect of the paragraph by satisfying the authority that the person for whom the work is done cannot afford to pay, or to pay more. It may be difficult to provide evidence of the other person's means.

Paragraphs (11) and (12): Quantification of notional income

Para (11) deals with the quantification of income which a claimant is treated as possessing under paras (1) to (8). Basically, the notional income is quantified as if it were real.

Para (12) quantifies notional earnings which a claimant is deemed to receive under para (9). The deductions made under sub-paras (a) to (c) are the same as those in reg 36(6). See the Analysis on p363.

Paragraph (12A): Payments to "service user groups"

Para (12A) disapplies paras (1), (2), (6) and (9) for the payments set out to a claimant who is a participant in a "service user group", defined in reg 2(1) (on p216).

SECTION 6
Capital

General Note on Section 6

This Section deals with the quantification of a claimant's "capital" for HB purposes. There is a bar on entitlement for anyone with capital exceeding £16,000 as assessed under this Section: see reg 43. If a claimant has capital worth between £6,000 (£10,000 if living in residential accommodation) and £16,000, s/he is treated as receiving "tariff income" from that capital: see reg 52. *Actual* income produced by capital which is taken into account is itself treated as capital and disregarded as income: see reg 46(4) and Sch 5 para 17. Income produced by some *disregarded* capital is taken into account under Section 5: Sch 5 para 17.

There is a total disregard of capital belonging to IS, income-based JSA and income-related ESA claimants as their capital has already been taken into account in the assessment of that benefit, though note the potential effect of the decision in *R v South Ribble DC HBRB ex p Hamilton* [2000] 33 HLR 102, CA: see the discussion on p343.

The term "capital" itself is not defined by the regulations. For the capital/income distinction, see p339.

It is important to remember that a capital resource which appears to belong to the claimant (eg, property in her/his name) may in fact legally belong to someone else because it is held subject to a trust or pursuant to some other form of equity. For example, a house in the claimant's name but purchased with someone else's money, not as a gift for the claimant, was held not to belong to the claimant, but to be held on "resulting trust" for the person advancing the money: *R(SB) 1/85* para 9. Likewise, if a claimant is paid money for a particular purpose in circumstances which make her/him a trustee for the carrying out of that purpose, and for some reason that purpose is not, or cannot, be carried out, s/he would normally not own the money but would hold it on trust for the person it originally belonged to. In *R(IS) 1/90*, the claimant tried to argue that he had transferred over £6,000 from a redundancy payment to his son, to pay for his education. It was held in a high interest account in the claimant's name as he feared his son might misuse the money. It was held that although the money was clearly earmarked for his son's education, he had done nothing to renounce ownership and control. A person should not be treated as voluntarily giving up an interest in property unless there is a very clear indication that this is his/her intention. There was no express or implied declaration of trust in this case. See the discussion in the commentary to reg 46 Income Support (General) Regulations 1987 in the current edition of vol II of *Social Security Legislation* for a more extensive analysis of the caselaw on beneficial ownership of capital.

In *Thomas v Chief Adjudication Officer* reported as an appendix to *R(SB) 17/87*, CA, it was held that money held by a solicitor for a client was an actual, not a notional resource, and that the solicitor should be looked at in the same way as a bank.

CIS 2287/2008 concerned, among other issues, the classification of an asset as capital. Agreeing with *CIS 2943/2000* and disagreeing with *CH 3729/2007*, Commissioner Jacobs decided that the decision in *Chief Adjudication Officer v Leeves* [1999] FLR 90, CA (reported as *R(IS) 5/99*), although a decision in respect of income, applied to capital, that is, that capital that should in law be immediately repaid is not capital, the focus being on the moment of receipt or notional attribution. However, he pointed out that as with income, it is relevant only to the classification of money or an asset as capital and only applies if the capital never became a resource in the claimant's hands from the moment of receipt or attribution. He said (at paras 27 and 28):

> "A claimant may receive capital in circumstances that render it immediately subject to a bare trust for the transferor. If so, the capital never comes into the beneficial ownership of the claimant. But if the circumstances do not create a trust, it is possible that the claimant is under a certain and immediate obligation to return the asset transferred. If so, *Leeves* applies. . . . However, it only applies at the moment of receipt or attribution and for the purpose of classification. It does not apply thereafter. In particular, it does not apply to reduce the amount on account of liability that has arisen after the payment (or attribution) but in respect of, or otherwise connected with, it."

Commissioner Jacobs said that a demand for repayment after something has become capital in the claimant's hands, is outside the scope of *Leeves*. In this appeal, the claimant had been overpaid benefit and the overpayment decisions had created liabilities. However, Commissioner Jacobs said that they did not affect the character of the assets held by the claimant. What the overpayment decisions did was to create new liabilities that reduced the net worth of the claimant's assets. That is outside the scope of *Leeves*, because they did not prevent the assets becoming capital.

In *KS v SSWP (JSA)* [2009] UKUT 122 (AAC); [2010] AACR 3, the claimant had been adjudged bankrupt and a trustee in bankruptcy had been appointed prior to his claim for JSA. He was refused JSA because he was said to have capital in excess of the limit. Under s284(1) to (3) Insolvency Act 1986, where a person is adjudged bankrupt, any disposition of property made by that person from the date of presentation of the petition to the vesting of her/his estate in a trustee, is void unless made with the consent of the court or subsequently ratified by the court. That includes payments in cash or otherwise by the bankrupt, so that where a payment is void by virtue of that section, the person paid holds the sum paid for the bankrupt as part of his estate. Prior to the making of a bankruptcy order, a claimant may deprive her/himself of her/his capital as explained by Judge Jacobs in *CH 3670/2008*. However, s/he cannot deprive her/himself of anything of value following the making of the order. Agreeing with the decision in *CJSA 1556/2007* (a case concerning a restraint order), Judge Mark said that in the context of bankruptcy proceedings, where the provisions of the Insolvency Act 1986 are designed to transfer property automatically to the trustee as soon as the necessary formalities have been gone through to appoint a trustee, the claimant has been stripped of his beneficial interest in the property once the bankruptcy order has been made, and the provisions invalidating subsequent transactions by him are designed to protect the interests of the trustee and the creditors. It was unnecessary for him to come to any firm conclusion on the question whether it remains capital with a nil value or ceases to be capital at all, as the effect on the claimant's entitlement to benefit will be the same in either case. That conclusion also was a reasonable one, as a bankrupt ought not to be at a disadvantage because there is a delay in appointing a trustee. The purpose of the provisions as to capital is to ensure that the state does not provide benefit to somebody with capital assets over a certain amount out of which s/he can legally provide for her/himself. It ought not to be able to say that the claimant cannot legally spend the money and at the same time that s/he is not entitled to benefit because s/he can spend it unlawfully. However, Judge Mark went on to say that a claimant may fall foul of the notional capital rule (for which see reg 49). If s/he presents a petition (or possibly, fails to resist a petition presented by a creditor) and is declared bankrupt as a result, s/he may be found to have deprived her/himself of capital for the purpose of the notional capital rule if s/he has taken this step, or held back from opposing the petition for the purpose of securing entitlement to benefit. He said that this may also be the case if the claimant fails to take reasonable steps either to ensure that the debts are paid off and the bankruptcy annulled, or if the claimant fails to co-operate with the trustee in bankruptcy to ensure that the bankruptcy proceeds smoothly, that all liabilities are discharged and that any surplus is paid to him.

Sch 6 provides a long list of disregards for a claimant's capital. Reg 41 provides that certain capital is treated as income.

Capital limit

43. For the purposes of section 134(1) of the Act as it applies to housing benefit (no entitlement to benefit if capital exceeds prescribed amount), the prescribed amount is £16,000.

General Note
The "prescribed amount" has been £16,000 since April 1990.

Calculation of capital

44.–(1) For the purposes of Part 7 of the Act (income-related benefits) as it applies to housing benefit, the capital of a claimant to be taken into account shall, subject to paragraph (2), be the whole of his capital calculated in accordance with this Part and any income treated as capital under regulation 46 (income treated as capital).

(2) There shall be disregarded from the calculation of a claimant's capital under paragraph (1), any capital, where applicable, specified in Schedule 6.

Definitions
"capital" – see General Note.
"claimant" – see reg 2(1).

General Note
This regulation provides the general authority for assessing capital according to the rules set out in the rest of this Part, not just this Section, so income treated as capital under reg 46 is specifically included. But para (2), together with Sch 6, provides for the disregard of certain items of capital. In considering the scope of any disregard, decisions on similarly-worded disregards in other means-tested benefit schemes must be taken into account: *CH 2321/2002* para 8. Note also the effect of reg 25 which treats the capital of the claimant's partner(s) as the claimant's.

Disregard of capital of child and young person

45. The capital of a child or young person who is a member of the claimant's family shall not be treated as capital of the claimant.

Definitions
"child" – see reg 2(1).
"family" – see s137(1) SSCBA.
"membership of a family" – see Part 4.
"young person" – see reg 19.

General Note

The effect of this regulation is that the capital of a child or young person for whom the claimant or her/his partner is "responsible" (for which, see reg 20), and who lives in the same household, is *not* to be treated as the claimant's.

Income treated as capital

46.–(1) Any bounty derived from employment to which paragraph 8 of Schedule 4 applies and paid at intervals of at least one year shall be treated as capital.

(2) Any amount by way of a refund of income tax deducted from profits or emoluments chargeable to income tax under Schedule D or E shall be treated as capital.

(3) Any holiday pay which is not earnings under regulation 35(1)(d) (earnings of employed earners) shall be treated as capital.

(4) Except any income derived from capital disregarded under paragraphs 1, 2, 4, 8, 14 [¹ , 25 to 28, 45 or 46] of Schedule 6, any income derived from capital shall be treated as capital but only from the date it is normally due to be credited to the claimant's account.

(5) In the case of employment as an employed earner, any advance of earnings or any loan made by the claimant's employer shall be treated as capital.

(6) Any charitable or voluntary payment which is not made or due to be made at regular intervals, other than a payment which is made under [³ or by] the Macfarlane Trust, the Macfarlane (Special Payments) Trust, the Macfarlane (Special Payments) (No. 2) Trust, the Fund, the Eileen Trust [³ , MFET Limited] or the Independent Living [² Fund (2006)], shall be treated as capital.

(7) There shall be treated as capital the gross receipts of any commercial activity carried on by a person in respect of which assistance is received under the self-employment route, but only in so far as those receipts were payable into a special account [³] during the period in which that person was receiving such assistance.

(8) Any arrears of subsistence allowance which are paid to a claimant as a lump sum shall be treated as capital.

(9) Any arrears of working tax credit or child tax credit shall be treated as capital.

Amendments

1. Amended by reg 15(2) of SI 2006 No 2378 from the first day of the first benefit week to commence on or after 2.10.06.
2. Amended by reg 6(4)(b) of SI 2008 No 2767 as from 17.11.08.
3. Amended by reg 8(3), (5) and (6) of SI 2010 No 641 as from 1.4.10 (5.4.10 where rent payable weekly or in multiples of a week).

Definitions

"claimant" – see reg 2(1).
"derived from" – see Analysis of reg 35.
"earnings" – see regs 35 and 36.
"employed earner" – reg 2(1).
"the fund" – see reg 2(1).
"self-employment route" – see reg 2(1).
"special account"– see reg 2(1).
"subsistence allowance" – see reg 2(1).

General Note

This regulation sets out certain types of income that are to be treated as capital and Sch 5 para 30 provides that these are to be *ignored* for the purposes of assessing a claimant's income, to avoid double counting.

Analysis

Para (1). The relevant employments are part-time firefighters, part-time coastguards and those involved in launching lifeboats, and reservists. Note that para (1) only applies where the bounty is paid at intervals of at least one year.

Para (2) deals with income tax refunded on earnings from employed earners or self-employment.

Para (3). Under regulation 35(1)(d), holiday pay payable more than four weeks after termination or interruption of employment is not treated as earnings. However, it is treated as capital under para (3).

Para (4). Most income from capital is treated as capital. Instead, capital is treated as producing "tariff income". See the General Note to reg 52 on p394. The word "normally" is used so that occasional deviations from this date may be ignored. See also Sch 5 para 17 on p555 and Sch 6 para 15 on p570.

Para (5) is self-explanatory.

Para (6). For "charitable or voluntary payment", see the Analysis of Sch 5 para 14 on p553. Regular charitable or voluntary payments are income and may be disregarded in whole or in part under that paragraph.

Para (6) treats *irregular* charitable or voluntary payments (other than those specified) as capital. They do not affect entitlement to benefit at all if the claimant's total capital after receipt is less than £6,000. If total capital after receipt is between £6,000 (or £10,000 if living in residential accommodation) and £16,000 the tariff income rule in reg 52 applies. Note that irregular payments from the Macfarlane Trusts etc are disregarded by Sch 6 para 24.

Para (7). "Self-employment route" is defined in reg 2(1). The definition of the special account referred to is in reg 102A Jobseeker's Allowance Regulations 1996 and reg 100 Employment and Support Allowance Regulations 2008. See also Sch 5 para 58 for payments to those following this route that can be disregarded as income.

Para (8). "Subsistence allowance" means that which an employment zone contractor has agreed to pay someone who is participating in an employment zone programme. "Employment zone" and "employment zone contractor" are defined in reg 2(1).

Para (9) is an important provision when the Revenue is experiencing delays in deciding claims for tax credits. It provides that "any arrears" of WTC and CTC are to be treated as capital. Note also that Sch 6 para 9(1)(e) provides for such arrears to be disregarded as capital for a period of 52 weeks from the date of receipt.

The Revenue pays tax credits by direct credit transfer either one week or four-weekly in arrears. It is clear that this provision is not intended to apply to such four-weekly payments (payments "in arrears") as distinct from payments made in respect of a period prior to the current period (payments "of arrears"). However, it may be open to argument that payments in arrears, at least in so far as they relate to the three weeks previous to the week in which the payments are made, are "arrears" and should be treated as capital rather than income.

Calculation of capital in the United Kingdom

[¹**47.** Capital which a claimant possesses in the United Kingdom shall be calculated at its current market or surrender value less–

(a) where there would be expenses attributable to the sale, 10 per cent; and

(b) the amount of any encumbrance secured on it.]

Amendment

1. Substituted by reg 11(8) of SI 2007 No 2618 as from 1.10.07.

Definitions

"capital" – see General Note on this Section.
"claimant" – see reg 2(1).

General Note

This deals with the quantification of capital which is taken into account for HB purposes and which is situated in the UK (a term which includes Northern Ireland). Until 1 October 2007, there was different rule for the valuation of National Savings Certificates. See p307 of the 19th edition for the former version of the rule.

Analysis

The authority has to decide what the current market or surrender value is. Authorities should avoid asking for evidence which would cause the claimant inordinate expenditure – eg, surveyor's reports.

GM BW1.513 suggests:

"[where capital consists of stocks and shares] valuation should relate to the value on the date the claim for benefit is made, or treated as made, and be based on relevant information, such as the Stock Market pages in a national newspaper. . ."

GM BW1.470 suggests that as regards valuation of property (eg, a second home or business premises), authorities should obtain a current market valuation unless one is already available.

Where there is a conflict of valuation evidence, the First-tier Tribunal is not obliged to give more weight to the lower valuation so as to grant rather than deny benefit. Valuation is "an art rather than a science" and, in an appropriate case, a tribunal is entitled to resolve the conflict by taking an average of the competing figures. The tribunal does not err by accepting valuation assumptions which were reasonable at the time the value of the capital has to be assessed, even if subsequent evidence has shown those assumptions to be incorrect: see *R v Doncaster MBC ex p Nortrop* [1998] unreported, 31 July, QBD.

From the current market/surrender value should be deducted the amounts referred to in sub-paras (a) and (b). In sub-para (b), the words "encumbrance secured on it" would include any debts secured on the capital – eg, a mortgage on a house. In *R(IS) 21/93* para 19(7)(a), the commissioner concluded that a mere unsecured loan could not be an "incumbrance". The word should therefore be read as it applies in the law of real property.

R(IS) 2/90 concerned the valuation of shares in a private company. The articles of association of the private company provided that the shares must be offered first to the other shareholders at a "fair" value, determined by the company's auditors. Commissioner Rice held that the DWP could not just come to its own, higher valuation and the value of the shares could not be more than that set by the auditor. The value could have been lower as IS presupposed a quick sale.

Calculation of capital outside the United Kingdom

48. Capital which a claimant possesses in a country outside the United Kingdom shall be calculated–

(a) in a case where there is no prohibition in that country against the transfer to the United Kingdom of an amount equal to its current market or surrender value in that country, at that value;

(b) in a case where there is such a prohibition, at the price which it would realise if sold in the United Kingdom to a willing buyer,

less, where there would be expenses attributable to sale, 10 per cent. and the amount of any encumbrances secured on it.

Definitions

"capital" – see General Note on this Section.
"claimant" – see reg 2(1).

General Note

This provides for the quantification of capital owned by the claimant outside the UK, with different rules depending on whether or not an amount equivalent to the value of that asset in the country in which it is situated may be transferred to the UK. There will undoubtedly be problems in quantifying the market value of such assets overseas and in converting the amount in question to sterling. GM BW1.400-407 gives some guidance.

If there is no prohibition on the transfer of the value of the asset to the UK from the country, para (a) applies and the claimant is treated as possessing an amount equal to the market or surrender value in that country, minus the deductions as available under reg 47 above. It is the "current market or surrender value *in that country*" which is relevant. Thus in *CH 4972/2002* (para 9) the commissioner stated that the market value of a property in France had to be assessed for a sale in France rather than the UK.

If there *is* a prohibition on the transfer of the value of the asset to the UK from the country in which it is situated, para (b) applies. The claimant is treated as possessing the amount, if any, which a "willing buyer" in the UK would pay to purchase the asset from the claimant, bearing in mind that such a buyer would not her/himself be able to liquidate the assets and transfer them here either. As with para (a), the deductions as available under reg 47 must be made. The amounts a claimant can be treated as possessing on this basis will usually be much smaller than the actual value of the asset if sold in the country in which it is situated.

Notional capital

49.–(1) A claimant shall be treated as possessing capital of which he has deprived himself for the purpose of securing entitlement to housing benefit or increasing the amount of that benefit except to the extent that that capital is reduced in accordance with regulation 50 (diminishing notional capital rule).

(2) Except in the case of–

(a) a discretionary trust; or

(b) a trust derived from a payment made in consequence of a personal injury; or

(c) any loan which would be obtained only if secured against capital disregarded under Schedule 6; or

(d) a personal pension scheme [¹ , occupational pension scheme] [² [⁴] or a payment made by the Board of the Pension Protection Fund]; or

[³ (e) any sum to which paragraph 45(2)(a) of Schedule 6 (capital to be disregarded) applies which is administered in the way referred to in paragraph 45(1)(a); or

(ea) any sum to which paragraph 46(a) of Schedule 6 refers; or]

(f) child tax credit; or

(g) working tax credit,

any capital which would become available to the claimant upon application being made, but which has not been acquired by him, shall be treated as possessed by him but only from the date on which it could be expected to be acquired were an application made.

(3) Any payment of capital, other than a payment of capital specified in paragraph (4), made–

- (a) to a third party in respect of a single claimant or a member of the family (but not a member of the third party's family) shall, where that payment is a payment of an occupational pension [² , a pension or other periodical payment made under a personal pension scheme or a payment made by the Board of the Pension Protection Fund], be treated as possessed by that single claimant or, as the case may be, by that member;
- (b) to a third party in respect of a single claimant or in respect of a member of the family (but not a member of the third party's family) shall, where it is not a payment referred to in sub-paragraph (a), be treated as possessed by that single claimant or by that member to the extent that it is used for the food, household fuel or, subject to paragraph (8), rent or ordinary clothing or footwear, of that single claimant or, as the case may be, of any member of that family or is used for any council tax or water charges for which that claimant or member is liable;
- (c) to a single claimant or a member of the family in respect of a third party (but not in respect of another member of the family) shall be treated as possessed by that single claimant or, as the case may be, that member of the family to the extent that it is kept or used by him or used by or on behalf of any member of the family.
- (4) Paragraph (3) shall not apply in respect of a payment of capital made–
- (a) under [⁸ or by] the Macfarlane Trust, the Macfarlane (Special Payments) Trust, the Macfarlane (Special Payments) (No. 2) Trust, the Fund, the Eileen Trust [⁸ , MFET Limited] , the Independent Living [⁶ Fund (2006)], the Skipton Fund or the London Bombings Relief Charitable Fund;
- (b) pursuant to section 2 of the 1973 Act in respect of a person's participation–
  - (i) in an employment programme specified in regulation 75(1)(a)(ii) of the Jobseeker's Allowance Regulations;
  - (ii) in a training scheme specified in regulation 75(1)(b)(ii) of those Regulations;
  - (iii) in the Intense Activity Period specified in regulation 75(1)(a)(iv) of those Regulations [⁵]; [⁷]
  - (iv) in a qualifying course within the meaning specified in regulation 17A(7) of those Regulations; [⁷ or]
  - [⁷ (v) in the Flexible New Deal specified in regulation 75(1)(a)(v) of those Regulations;]
- *[(ba) in respect of a person's participation in the Work for Your Benefit Pilot Scheme;]*
- (c) under an occupational pension scheme [² , in respect of a pension or other periodical payment made under a personal pension scheme or a payment made by the Board of the Pension Protection Fund] where–
  - (i) a bankruptcy order has been made in respect of the person in respect of whom the payment has been made or, in Scotland, the estate of that person is subject to sequestration or a judicial factor has been appointed on that person's estate under section 41 of the Solicitors (Scotland) Act 1980;
  - (ii) the payment is made to the trustee in bankruptcy or any other person acting on behalf of the creditors; and
  - (iii) the person referred to in (i) and any member of his family does not possess, or is not treated as possessing, any other income apart from that payment.
- (5) Where a claimant stands in relation to a company in a position analogous to that of a sole owner or partner in the business of that company, he may be treated as if he were such sole owner or partner and in such a case–
  - (a) the value of his holding in that company shall, notwithstanding regulation 44 (calculation of capital) be disregarded; and
  - (b) he shall, subject to paragraph (6), be treated as possessing an amount of capital equal to the value or, as the case may be, his share of the value of the capital of that company and the foregoing provisions of this Section shall apply for the purposes of calculating that amount as if it were actual capital which he does possess.

(6)   For so long as the claimant undertakes activities in the course of the business of the company, the amount which he is treated as possessing under paragraph (5) shall be disregarded.

(7)   Where a claimant is treated as possessing capital under any of paragraphs (1) to (3) the foregoing provisions of this Section shall apply for the purposes of calculating its amount as if it were actual capital which he does possess.

(8)   In paragraph (3) "rent" means eligible rent less any deductions in respect of non-dependants which fall to be made under regulation 74 (non-dependant deductions).

Modifications

Reg 49(4) is modified by reg 15 Jobseeker's Allowance (Work for Your Benefit Pilot Scheme) Regulations 2010 SI No.1222 (see p1247) as from 22 November 2010 but only for those ordinarily resident in a pilot area or whose address for payment of JSA is located within such an area. The modifications are shown in italics above. They cease to have effect on 21 November 2013.

Amendments

1.   Amended by reg 5A(3) of SI 2005 No 2465 as inserted by Sch 2 para 28(5) of SI 2006 No 217 as from 6.4.06.
2.   Amended by reg 8(3) of SI 2006 No 588 as from 6.4.06.
3.   Substituted by reg 6(3) of SI 2007 No 719 as from 2.4.07.
4.   Amended by reg 4(5) of SI 2007 No 1749 as from 16.7.07.
5.   Omitted by reg 6(4) of SI 2008 No 698 as from 14.4.08.
6.   Amended by reg 6(4)(c) of SI 2008 No 2767 as from 17.11.08.
7.   Amended by reg 3 of SI 2009 No 480 as from 5.10.09.
8.   Amended by reg 8(3) and (5) of SI 2010 No 641 as from 1.4.10 (5.4.10 where rent payable weekly or in multiples of a week).

Definitions

"capital" – see General Note on this section.
"claimant" – see reg 2(1).
"family" – see s137(1) SSCBA.
"Macfarlane (Special Payments) Trust, the Fund, the Eileen Trust, the Independent Living Fund (2006), etc" – see reg 2(1).
"membership of family" – see Part 4.
"ordinary clothing or footware" – see reg 2(1).

General Note

This regulation sets out the situations in which a claimant must or may be treated as possessing capital even when s/he does not actually possess it. This regulation corresponds to reg 42 in respect of income.

Paras (1) to (5) set out these situations, para (6) qualifies para (5), and para (7) provides how capital that a claimant is deemed to possess under this regulation is to be quantified. Para (8) defines the term "rent" as it is used in para (3).

Analysis

Paragraph (1): Capital of which a claimant has deprived her/himself

Para (1) is similar to reg 42(1) in its effect. The notes below on the wording of this paragraph will be equally applicable to reg 42(1).

Guidance. Much of the relevant DWP guidance is useful but care must be taken to give precedence to the wording of the regulation and the caselaw.

The key factors in reaching a decision that deprivation has occurred are (1) that the resource had actually belonged to the claimant and (2) that the dates and period over which disposal occurred indicate at least a partial motive for the deprivation.

GM BW1.714, lists certain circumstances where the DWP suggests deprivation may have occurred:

(1)   A lump sum payment made to someone else – eg, as a gift or to repay a debt.
(2)   Substantial expenditure incurred on a non-essential item – eg, on an expensive holiday.
(3)   Title deeds of property which is not, or will soon cease to be, the claimant's home transferred into someone else's name.
(4)   Money put into an irrevocable trust.
(5)   Money converted into a form (eg, personal possessions) which would fall to be disregarded.
(6)   Money reduced by extravagant living.

However, while the guidance provides a useful indication of the types of situation in which a claimant is likely to be subject to an inquiry as to the circumstances of the deprivation, the wording of the legislation and the relevant caselaw must always be followed. Note, therefore, some of the criticisms of the guidance set out below.

"A claimant shall be treated as possessing capital . . . ". The first point that needs to be made is that the capital of which the claimant is said to have deprived her/himself must be capital which would normally fall to be taken into account. Thus if the capital does not belong to the claimant in the first case (perhaps because it is subject to a trust: see the General Note on this Section) or if it falls to be disregarded under Sch 6, para (1) can have no application.

" . . . of which he has deprived himself . . . ". The word "deprived" is an ordinary English word and does not have any special meaning: *R(SB) 38/85* para 21. It is sufficient if a claimant ceases to possess the relevant asset, even if s/he receives something in exchange for the asset: *R(SB) 40/85* para 8.

It appears that a person can have "deprived himself" of an asset of which s/he was never in possession. So a deliberate failure to cash a cheque may amount to a "deprivation" (*CSB 598/1987*) as may a release of a debtor (*CIS 1586/1997*). A person may also have derpived her/himself of an asset if s/he presents a petition (or possibly fails to resist a petition by a creditor) and is declared bankrupt as a result: *KS v SSWP (JSA)* [2009] UKUT 122 (AAC); [2010] AACR 3.

" . . . for the purpose of securing entitlement to housing benefit or increasing the amount of that benefit . . . ". Three different issues arise from this part of the paragraph. First, there is the question of establishing the relevant "purpose". In deciding whether a person has deprived her/himself of capital to obtain HB, the authority must consider whether the obtaining of benefit was a "significant operative purpose" behind the decision to divest her/himself of the asset: *R(SB) 40/85* para 10. It is insufficient that the claimant knows that the obtaining of benefit is a natural consequence of the transaction: *R(SB) 9/91*. There must be a positive finding that the claimant actually knew of the capital limit in the light of all the facts, and it will not necessarily be sufficient for the authority to show that the information was available to the claimant in literature supplied by it: *CIS 124/1990* para 11; *CIS 30/1993*. These principles have been restated with force in *R(H) 1/06,* a case concerning a claimant with a severe and enduring mental illness. Commissioner Howell in considering reg 43 HB Regs 1987 (now reg 49 HB Regs) at para 13 stated:

"there is no doubt that the test of whether a claimant is shown to have deprived himself of capital "for the purpose of" securing entitlement to housing benefit so as to fall within the notional capital provisions of regulation 43 Housing Benefit (General) Regulations 1987 SI No 1971 is a subjective one, depending on the evidence about the particular claimant in question. It does not in my view adequately address or answer the point to say as the chairman did that because a person is not completely incapable of managing his affairs or of realising he was spending his money imprudently, it follows as a matter of course and without further analysis that all such spending is done for the purpose of securing entitlement to benefit. Such a jump is impermissible as it omits any real consideration of the actual purpose of the particular person involved".

This decision was endorsed and followed by Commissioner Bano in *CIS 218/2005* (para 7), where he said that "the issue requires a determination of the actual, or subjective, intention of the claimant".

Commissioner Howell returned to this point later in *R(H) 1/06*, where he said (para 22):

"Whether the securing of entitlement to benefit was, in this sense, among the purposes which led any particular claimant to act as he did is a question that must be determined by the tribunal of fact in the circumstances of each individual case, the test as already noted being one of subjective purpose: see in the housing benefit context *R (Beeson) v Dorset County Council* [2001] EWHC Admin 986, 30 November 2001, *per* Richards J at paragraphs 9, 37 (not challenged on this point in the Court of Appeal). In the great majority of cases this must be a matter of drawing such inferences as the tribunal of fact thinks fit from the surrounding circumstances, such as the claimant's state of knowledge of the rules, the nature and timing of the disposals he makes and the timing and manner of his claims for benefit; since direct evidence to show such a purpose is in the nature of things unlikely. Such a task is however a perfectly normal one for a tribunal of fact to have to undertake, and this is of course by no means the only instance in the law when the purpose for which a thing is done may not be express, and has to be ascertained "as a matter of substance and of fact": *re South African Supply and Cold Storage Company* [1904] 2 Ch 268, per Buckley J at p282. In using the word "significant" Mr Monroe may perhaps have had in mind what was said by Lord Morris of Borth-y-Gest in *Sweet v Parsley* [1970] AC 132, 155A:

"In my opinion, the words 'premises . . . used for the purposes of . . . ' denote a purpose which is other than quite incidental or casual or fortuitous: they denote a purpose which is or has become either a significant one or a recognised one though certainly not necessarily an only one."

The mere fact that an asset has been disposed of at a substantial undervalue is insufficient, of itself, for an authority to conclude that a claimant should be treated as having notional capital. The claimant's explanation for the disposition needs to be properly considered: *R v South Tyneside MBC ex p Tooley* [1996] COD 143 at 144, QBD.

The caselaw on the correct approach to be taken to "purpose" where the deprivation is constituted in paying off a commercial debt (in this case credit cards) was reviewed in *CJSA 1425/2004*. Commissioner Rowland stressed that the approach of the Court of Appeal in *Jones v SSWP* [2003] EWCA 964, unreported, does not undermine the point in *R(SB) 12/91* that, if the debtor has no practical choice but to pay her/his debt, the repayment of the debt cannot reasonably be regarded as having been for the purpose of obtaining benefit and that, normally, if a debt is immediately repayable, the debtor has no practical choice. Moreover, *Jones* is not authority for the proposition that if the debtor thought that the debt would not be called in for some time, payment of the debt would be for the purpose of obtaining benefit. Commissioner Rowland commented (at para 38) that he found it:

"difficult to envisage a case where it would be unreasonable for a claimant to pay a debt that had become due, merely because the creditor had decided not to enforce it for the time being, unless, perhaps, the decision not to enforce the debt was entirely unconnected to the claimant's lack of means and amounted, in effect, to a variation of the terms upon which the debt became repayable".

He went on (para 40) to conclude:

"The effect of all these decisions is therefore that, if a claimant realised that one consequence of depriving himself of capital was that he might become entitled to jobseeker's allowance or income support and he nonetheless deprived himself of that capital, there arises the question whether obtaining benefit was a significant operative purpose of the deprivation. Because there will almost always be some other purpose as well, that question is determined by deciding whether, given his knowledge, it was reasonable in all the circumstances for him to act as he did, bearing in mind not only his obligation to tax payers to support himself, but also his obligations to other people. Moreover, insofar as his obligation to support himself is concerned, it is necessary to have regard to the long term as well as the short term."

In approaching the facts of the case before him, Commissioner Rowland made a number of useful observations.

(1)   If a claimant has mixed motives, the question whether the purpose of obtaining benefits is a significant operative purpose is to be determined by deciding whether it was reasonable for the claimant to act in the way that he did: *CJSA 1425/2004* para 46.

(2)   The true significance of the timing of the deprivation is that the closer the deprivation was to the date of claim, the stronger the inference will be that the deprivation was made in the expectation that there would be a claim and with the knowledge that the deprivation would affect the claimant's entitlement to benefit: para 48.

(3)   Even if the appellant's forthcoming application for "review" of his benefit claim may have prompted him into paying his credit card debts when he did, that merely suggested that obtaining benefit was one purpose behind the payments; leaving the question whether it was a significant operative purpose still to be answered (and that was to be determined by considering whether making the payments was reasonable. In other words, although a claimant's desire to obtain benefit may explain the timing of the payments, it is not necessarily to be taken to have been a significant operative purpose behind the making of the payments: para 49.

(4)   The threat of having to make high interest payments is just as capable of making it reasonable to pay a debt as the threat of enforcement of a liability to repay: para 50.

The second point is that the intention must be to secure, or increase the amount of "housing benefit". The regulation does not operate where the claimant has deprived her/himself of capital in order to get other means-tested benefits. If, for example, it could be shown that a claimant had deprived her/himself of capital but that her/his purpose in doing so was to secure entitlement to IS, income-based JSA or income-related ESA rather than HB then s/he might be entitled to continue to receive HB even though the other benefit was stopped or reduced.

In practice, this would probably be difficult to establish but it might be possible to show in some cases that the claimant had no knowledge of the existence of HB (perhaps because s/he had never previously rented property). This principle also applies when one benefit is abolished and replaced by another: in *R(IS) 14/93* paras 16-17 it was held that a claimant who had deprived himself of substantial amounts of capital in 1987 in order to secure entitlement to supplementary benefit was nevertheless entitled to IS because, at the date of the deprivation, that benefit did not exist and therefore the deprivation could not have had the purpose of securing entitlement to it. It is not unknown for similar cases to emerge even now and it is suggested that the reference to "housing benefit" in reg 49(1) must be read as a reference to "housing benefit" under the HB Regs and not under the previous schemes: compare *R v Middlesborough BC ex p Graville* [1993] unreported, 26 March, QBD and *Andrew v City of Glasgow DC* [1996] SLT 814 at 817H-L.

Third, notional capital may exist where the claimant's intention was to increase entitlement as well as to create entitlement where none existed as long as the capital was held.

However, in some circumstances a claimant may be fixed with notional capital even though the deprivation was by her/his partner *before* they became a couple: *CH 1822 2006*, a decision refusing leave to appeal to a commissioner (decided with *CIS 1757 2006*). This is because the focus of reg 49 is at the time when entitlement is in issue but in respect of a past disposal of capital. In this situation the notional capital rule will only apply to a future partner when there has been conduct that is related to future entitlement to benefit either for the person alone or as a member of a family, and then only when there has been a deprivation of capital with the necessary intention. Note that the claimant failed in his application for a judicial review of the commissioner's decision: *R (Hook) v The Social Security Commissioner* [2007] EWHC 1705 (Admin), 3 July (reported as *R(IS) 7/07*).

Paragraph (2): Capital available on application

This is similar to reg 42(2): see the commentary on p376. The authority is obliged to treat the claimant as possessing any capital which would become available to her/him on application, unless it comes within the exceptions in sub-paras (a) to (g). If a claimant is a potential beneficiary under a discretionary trust or a trust derived from a payment made in consequence of personal injury (see reg 42), or could raise money on a loan, but only if the loan was secured by capital disregarded under Sch 6, s/he is not to be treated as possessing capital under this regulation. See also Sch 6 para 14 in respect of entitlement under a trust of funds paid in consequence of personal injury.

Actual payments made to the claimant under a discretionary or other type of trust will be dealt with under the rest of this Section and not this regulation.

If the trust or other source from which a claimant could obtain capital is not excluded from this regulation, it must still be established by the authority that s/he actually could get payment if s/he asked. This will cause problems. In relation to trusts, under s32 Trustee Act 1925, trustees have a restricted power to advance up to half a claimant's potential share of capital under a trust, whether or not the claimant's right to such capital is vested or subject to her/him satisfying a contingency. But the trustees cannot be *obliged* to exercise this power, so it is by no means certain that if a claimant is a potential beneficiary under a trust s/he *would* be paid on application. Further information will be necessary.

If the claimant is absolutely entitled to trust funds under the rule in *Saunders v Vautier* [1841] 4 Bear 115, s/he is treated as the legal owner of the funds so that it is arguable that the trust funds will be treated as *actual* capital and not be subject to this regulation. However, in *R(SB) 2/89*, which concerned a trust of personal injury compensation, the beneficiary of the trust was the sole beneficiary and therefore, under the law, absolutely entitled to the money in the trust fund, but this did not stop it being disregarded under the analogous provision. This makes sense, because otherwise sub-para (e) would be deprived of any effect.

Paragraphs (3), (4) and (8): Payments involving third parties

This is identical in effect to paras (6) and (7) of reg 42. See the Analysis on p377.

Paragraph (5) and (6): Business assets

The application of para (5) by an authority is discretionary. Sub-paras (a) and (b) and para (6) quantify how much capital a claimant is to be treated as possessing in this respect, if the authority decides to exercise its discretion.

If this paragraph applies while the claimant is actually working for the company, the capital value of her/his share of it is to be totally ignored in assessing the claimant's assets; if para (6) does *not* apply, under para (5)(a) and (b) s/he is treated as possessing the capital value of the company or her/his share of that value, rather than the actual value of her/his *holding* which is ignored.

The valuation is made according to the rules in the rest of this Section – ie, at market value, minus allowable deductions: see reg 47. If the claimant is the sole owner, see Sch 6 para 8, which allows its value to be ignored for a "reasonable" period after s/he stops work to allow the company to be sold.

Paragraph (7): Valuation

If a claimant is treated as possessing capital under paras (1) to (5), it is to be quantified according to the rules which pertain to *actual* capital assets under this Section.

Diminishing notional capital rule

50.–(1) Where a claimant is treated as possessing capital under regulation 49(1) (notional capital), the amount which he is treated as possessing–

(a) in the case of a week that is subsequent to–
  (i) the relevant week in respect of which the conditions set out in paragraph (2) are satisfied; or
  (ii) a week which follows that relevant week and which satisfies those conditions,
  shall be reduced by an amount determined under paragraph (3);

(b) in the case of a week in respect of which paragraph (1)(a) does not apply but where–
  (i) that week is a week subsequent to the relevant week; and
  (ii) that relevant week is a week in which the condition in paragraph (4) is satisfied,
  shall be reduced by the amount determined under paragraph (4).

(2) This paragraph applies to a benefit week where the claimant satisfies the conditions that–

(a) he is in receipt of housing benefit; and

(b) but for regulation 49(1), he would have received an additional amount of housing benefit in that week.

(3) In a case to which paragraph (2) applies, the amount of the reduction for the purposes of paragraph (1)(a) shall be equal to the aggregate of–

(a) the additional amount to which sub-paragraph (2)(b) refers;

(b) where the claimant has also claimed council tax benefit, the amount of any council tax benefit or any additional amount of council tax benefit to which he would have been entitled in respect of the benefit week to which paragraph (2) refers but for the application of regulation 39(1) of the Council Tax Benefit Regulations 2006 (notional capital);

(c)   where the claimant has also claimed income support, the amount of income support to which he would have been entitled in respect of the benefit week to which paragraph (2) refers but for the application of regulation 51(1) of the Income Support Regulations (notional capital); [²]

(d)   where the claimant has also claimed a jobseeker's allowance, the amount of an income-based jobseeker's allowance to which he would have been entitled in respect of the benefit week to which paragraph (2) refers but for the application of regulation 113 of the Jobseeker's Allowance Regulations (notional capital).

[² (e) where the claimant has also claimed an employment and support allowance, the amount of an income-related employment and support allowance to which he would have been entitled in respect of the benefit week to which paragraph (2) refers but for the application of regulation 115 of the Employment and Support Allowance Regulations (notional capital).]

(4)   Subject to paragraph (5), for the purposes of paragraph (1)(b) the condition is that the claimant would have been entitled to housing benefit in the relevant week but for regulation 49(1), and in such a case the amount of the reduction shall be equal to the aggregate of–

(a)   the amount of housing benefit to which the claimant would have been entitled in the relevant week but for regulation 49(1) and, for the purposes of this sub-paragraph, if the relevant week is a week to which [¹ regulation 80(3)(a)] refers (calculation of weekly amounts), that amount shall be determined by dividing the amount of housing benefit to which he would have been so entitled by the number of days in that week for which he was liable to make payments in respect of the dwelling he occupies as his home and multiplying the quotient so obtained by 7;

(b)   if the claimant would, but for regulation 39(1) of the Council Tax Benefit Regulations 2006, have been entitled to council tax benefit or to an additional amount of council tax benefit in respect of the benefit week which includes the last day of the relevant week, the amount which is equal to–

    (i)   in a case where no council tax benefit is payable, the amount to which he would have been entitled; or

    (ii)   in any other case, the amount equal to the additional amount of council tax benefit to which he would have been entitled;

and, for the purposes of this sub-paragraph, if the amount is in respect of a part-week, that amount shall be determined by dividing the amount of the council tax benefit to which he would have been so entitled by the number equal to the number of days in the part-week and multiplying the quotient so obtained by 7;

(c)   if the claimant would, but for regulation 51(1) of the Income Support Regulations, have been entitled to income support in respect of the benefit week, within the meaning of regulation 2(1) of those Regulations (interpretation), which includes the last day of the relevant week, the amount to which he would have been entitled and, for the purposes of this sub-paragraph, if the amount is in respect of a part-week, that amount shall be determined by dividing the amount of the income support to which he would have been so entitled by the number equal to the number of days in the part-week and multiplying the quotient so obtained by 7;

(d)   if the claimant would, but for regulation 113 of the Jobseeker's Allowance Regulations, have been entitled to an income-based jobseeker's allowance in respect of the benefit week, within the meaning of regulation 1(3) of those Regulations (interpretation), which includes the last day of the relevant week, the amount to which he would have been entitled and, for the purposes of this sub-paragraph, if the amount is in respect of a part-week, that amount shall be determined by dividing the amount of the income-based jobseeker's allowance to which he would have been so entitled by the number equal to the number of days in the part-week and multiplying the quotient so obtained by 7.

[² (e) if the claimant would, but for regulation 115 of the Employment and Support Allowance Regulations, have been entitled to an income-related employment and support allowance in respect of the benefit week, within the meaning of regulation 2(1) of those Regulations (interpretation), which includes the last day of the relevant week, the amount to which he would have been entitled and, for the purposes of this sub-paragraph, if the amount is in respect of a part-week, that amount must be determined by dividing the amount of the income-related employment and support allowance to which he would have been so entitled by the number equal to the number of days in that part-week and multiplying the quotient so obtained by 7.]

(5)   The amount determined under paragraph (4) shall be re-determined under that paragraph if the claimant makes a further claim for housing benefit and the conditions in paragraph (6) are satisfied, and in such a case–

(a)   sub-paragraphs (a) to (d) of paragraph (4) shall apply as if for the words "relevant week" there were substituted the words "relevant subsequent week"; and

(b)   subject to paragraph (7), the amount as re-determined shall have effect from the first week following the relevant subsequent week in question.

(6)   The conditions are that–

(a)   a further claim is made 26 or more weeks after–

  (i)   the date on which the claimant made a claim for housing benefit in respect of which he was first treated as possessing the capital in question under regulation 49(1);

  (ii)   in a case where there has been at least one redetermination in accordance with paragraph (5), the date on which he last made a claim for housing benefit which resulted in the weekly amount being re-determined; or

  (iii)   the date on which he last ceased to be entitled to housing benefit, whichever last occurred; and

(b)   the claimant would have been entitled to housing benefit but for regulation 49(1).

(7)   The amount as re-determined pursuant to paragraph (5) shall not have effect if it is less than the amount which applied in that case immediately before the redetermination and in such a case the higher amount shall continue to have effect.

(8)   For the purposes of this regulation–

(a)   "part-week" in paragraph (4)(b) means a period of less than a week for which council tax benefit is allowed;

(b)   "part-week" in paragraph (4)(c) [² , (d) and (e)] means–

  (i)   a period of less than a week which is the whole period for which income support [² an income-related employment and support allowance], or, as the case may be, an income-based jobseeker's allowance, is payable; and

  (ii)   any other period of less than a week for which it is payable;

(c)   "relevant week" means the benefit week in which the capital in question of which the claimant has deprived himself within the meaning of regulation 49(1)–

  (i)   was first taken into account for the purpose of determining his entitlement to housing benefit; or

  (ii)   was taken into account on a subsequent occasion for the purpose of determining or re-determining his entitlement to housing benefit on that subsequent occasion and that determination or redetermination resulted in his beginning to receive, or ceasing to receive, housing benefit;

  and where more than one benefit week is identified by reference to heads (i) and (ii) of this sub-paragraph the later or latest such benefit week;

(d)   "relevant subsequent week" means the benefit week which includes the day on which the further claim or, if more than one further claim has been made, the last such claim was made.

Modifications
Para (4)(a) was amended by reg 11 Housing Benefit (Local Housing Allowance and Information Sharing) Amendment Regulations 2007 SI No.2868 as from 7 April 2008, save that for a person to whom reg 1(5) of those regulations applied (see p1231), the amendments came into force on the day on or after 7 April 2008 when the first of the events specified in reg 1(6) applied to her/him, or on 6 April 2009 if none had before that date.

Amendments
1. Amended by reg 11 of SI 2007 No 2868 as from 7.4.08 (or if reg 1(5) of that SI applies, on the day on or after 7.4.08 when the first of the events specified in reg 1(6) applies, or from 6.4.09 if none have before that date).
2. Amended by reg 16 of SI 2008 No 1082 as from 27.10.08.

General Note
Although this regulation is lengthy, the principle is simple enough. Reg 49(1), if applied, could result in unfairness. Without a mechanism for reducing "notional capital", a claimant's HB entitlement could be affected permanently. In other words, had the claimant not disposed of capital, s/he would be able to use her/his capital resources and would eventually regain entitlement (or the increased rate of) HB. Reg 50 therefore provides the mechanism whereby the amount of notional capital which the claimant has as a result of the operation of reg 49(1) is reduced by the weekly amount of benefits lost as a result of the application of the rule.

Reg 50 does not apply to *actual* capital: *CIS 2287/2008*. However, Commissioner Jacobs said that although there is no formal "diminishing" rule for actual capital, a similar result can be attained using inferences in the fact finding process.

Analysis
Paragraphs (1) to (4): The basic calculation
Para (1) provides the source of the reductions to notional capital. The calculation starts at the "relevant week" which is defined in para (8)(c) and hence can apply retrospectively. The "relevant week" is ordinarily the first week in which the notional capital was taken into account for the purposes of determining entitlement to HB. If, however, there are one or more subsequent determinations and benefit is actually awarded under that determination, the "relevant week" is the week of the most recent determination.

First, under sub-para (a), in relation to any subsequent week where the conditions in para (2) are met, a reduction is made according to the calculation in para (3). In relation to any other week in which the condition in para (4) is met, a reduction is made under that paragraph.

Paras (2) and (3). Para (2) sets out two relevant conditions: that a person is in receipt of HB and that the effect of reg 49(1) has been to reduce her/his entitlement in that week. This would apply where the claimant's capital (notional and actual) is below the upper, but above the lower, capital limit and hence tariff income calculated under reg 52 reduces the amount to which s/he is entitled.

If para (2) applies, para (3) requires the amount of the notional capital in that week to be reduced by the additional amount of HB to which the claimant would have been entitled in the absence of reg 49(1) plus any CTB, IS, income-based JSA and income-related ESA to which s/he would have been entitled in the absence of operation of the equivalent provisions for those benefits. The claimant will need to show that a valid claim had been made, subject to the rules for deeming claims. See the current volume II of *Social Security Legislation* for the rules relating to claims for those benefits.

Para (4) imposes the condition for para (1)(b), which is that there would have been entitlement to HB but for the operation of reg 49(1). This would apply where there is no current entitlement to HB – ie, because the claimant's capital (notional and actual) is above the capital limit, or is below the upper, but above the lower, capital limit and hence tariff income calculated under reg 52 reduces the amount to which s/he is entitled to nil. The amount of notional capital is reduced in a similar way to para (3). Part-weeks are dealt with on a pro rata basis.

Paragraphs (5) to (7): Redeterminations
Under para (5), if the claimant then reclaims HB 26 or more weeks after the latest date set out in para (6), and is still not entitled due to the "notional capital" rule in reg 49(1), the rate of diminution is recalculated at that point. Any changes which would reduce the rate of diminution are ignored under para (7), although factors which would increase that rate (eg, annual uprating) are taken into account.

It follows that claimants excluded from benefit by this rule should reclaim at 26-week intervals to ensure that the "notional capital" reduces at the maximum rate. If the "diminishing capital" rule results in a claimant becoming entitled again at some later date any remaining "notional capital" reduces according to the rules in paras (1)(a), (2), (3) and (8)(b)(ii).

Capital jointly held
51. Except where a claimant possesses capital which is disregarded under regulation 49(5) (notional capital) where a claimant and one or more persons are beneficially entitled in possession to any capital asset they shall be treated as if each of them were entitled in

possession to the whole beneficial interest therein in an equal share and the foregoing provisions of this Section shall apply for the purposes of calculating the amount of capital which the claimant is treated as possessing as if it were actual capital which the claimant does possess.

General Note

The legal owner of an asset may be, but is not always, the same as the beneficial owner – eg, if one person buys a house in her/his name, but part of the purchase price is paid by someone else, and that person does not intend to make the nominal purchaser an outright gift, or only intends to lend the nominal purchaser the money, that other person has a "beneficial interest" in the house, despite the fact that the legal ownership is in the person whose name is on the title deeds. The term "in possession" means that ownership can be enjoyed at present and is not postponed to some other legal interest (eg, a life interest) or dependent on the satisfaction of some contingency. As the law on quantification of beneficial interests is complex, this paragraph simply deems each of those who have such an interest in a particular capital asset to have an equal share in it. See also Sch 5 para 17 in respect of income produced by such an asset.

Analysis

Reg 51 has what is probably the most chequered legislative history of any regulation in this book. Before 2 October 1995, the wording of reg 44 HB Regs 1987 (now reg 51) was exactly the same as it is now. Then, as part of a series of changes to the rules for all the income-related benefits, it was amended. Those amendments were designed to reverse the decision of the Court of Appeal in *Chief Adjudication Officer v Palfrey*, [1995] *The Times*, 8 February, reported as *R(IS) 5/98*, CA. Then, in May 1998 the equivalent amendment to the IS Regs was then held to be *ultra vires* in *CIS 3283/1997*. The then DSS did not appeal that decision and accepted the commissioner's reasoning by returning the regulation to its original wording.

The regulation deals with the common situation where property is owned by more than one person. Rather than become embroiled in difficult disputes as to the relative shares actually owned by each co-owner, the policy of the DWP has long been to calculate benefit entitlement as if the asset were owned in equal shares. However, whether or not reg 51 successfully carries that policy into effect is open to question. Two problems arise. The first is whether the wording of the regulation is apt to include all forms of co-ownership and the second is the basis on which the claimant's deemed equal share is to be valued.

Under English law, there are two forms of co-ownership, namely joint tenancy and tenancy in common. The word "tenancy" might seem to suggest leasehold ownership or entitlement under a tenancy agreement but in this context applies to freehold ownership as well. Under a joint tenancy, all co-owners own the whole property (and hence if one dies, her/his interest is simply subsumed in the interest(s) of the other(s) by a process known as "survivorship" rather than passing under the will of the deceased owner). By contrast each owner under a tenancy in common owns an undivided share in the property. There was disagreement between commissioners as to whether reg 44 HB Regs 1987 (now reg 51) applied to both forms of co-ownership or merely to joint tenancies. It was confirmed by the Court of Appeal in *SSWP v Hourigan* [2003] 1 WLR 608 (reported as *R(IS) 4/03*), paras 17-21, 30, 32 that reg 51 has no application to tenants in common.

In *CIS 2575/1997* the commissioner held that the regulation also applied to foreign property and covered all forms of co-ownership whether existing under English law or not. Whether or not the latter finding can stand with *Hourigan* remains to be seen. Logically, if a form of foreign co-holding is akin to tenancy in common, the regulation should be inapplicable. If that is correct, evidence from a local lawyer in the country where the property was held would be required to ascertain the nature of the co-ownership.

If the regulation does apply, there are two possible approaches to the valuation of the deemed share. These may be illustrated by the example of a house which is owned jointly by two people. The first approach values the house as a whole and then, after deductions for the costs of sale and any mortgages or other charges, divides that figure by two and values each co-owner's deemed share at an amount equal to the dividend. The second approach looks at the value which would be obtained on the open market if, rather than sell the house as a whole, the claimant's deemed equal share was sold but the deemed equal share of the co-owner was not. In other words the second approach values the claimant's share on the basis that any purchaser would have to continue to share the property with the co-owner. The difference between the approaches can be summed up as being between "half the value" and the "value of half".

The Court of Appeal in *Palfrey* favoured the "value of half" approach, the 1995 amendments purported to replace it with the "half the value" rule and, as a result of *CIS 3283/1997* and amendments in October 1998, the "value of half" rule has now regained supremacy.

The "value of half" approach has, for the claimant, the advantage of consistently returning a lower valuation. In the case of a jointly-owned house, common sense suggests that the value of half (or a third or any other part-share) will quite often be nil simply because there will be no evidence of an actual market in part shares of houses and because it would not be possible for the buyer of a part-share to take out a mortgage on it. The correctness of this view is reinforced by the decision in *CH 1953/2003* which concerned the former matrimonial home occupied by the claimant's wife. The tribunal had simply found that the claimant had to be treated as entitled to half the property which would take him over the capital limit. Following *Hourigan*, that approach was incorrect as the form of co-ownership had to be investigated (para 11). The tribunal was not entitled to assume that the claimant's wife would buy him out of the property on his request (para 14). In valuing the property, account had to be taken of the potential difficulties with sale in the light of the rights of the claimant's wife (para 15). The commissioner observed that "I would need evidence of the existence of a real market for the claimant's interest in his former home" (para 16).

Arrangements for authorities to obtain valuations of jointly owned property are described in GM BW1.491-493 but it is advisable for claimants involved in disputes to obtain their own valuation evidence. Although District Valuers can usually claim special expertise because details of every property purchase need to be produced to the Revenue as part of the conveyancing process, it is doubtful whether any such claim can be made in relation to sales of part shares. This is because there are unlikely to be many such sales. It is therefore always worth asking for the number of real-life examples on which the official valuation is based.

In *R(IS) 5/07*, Commissioner Williams sets out that the approach to be taken in assessing the capital value of a claimant's share in a former joint home. The question of the value of a former joint home is only to be considered if none of the relevant capital disregards apply on the facts of the case (for which see Sch 6). If none of the disregards apply, next one has to consider whether the claimant's interest in the former home is as a tenant in common or a joint tenant. A joint tenancy should not be assumed (because nowadays it is far more common, for tax planning reasons for example, for couples to be advised to buy as tenants in common). However, this factual issue can be resolved easily by payment of a small fee and searching the land registry (at www.landregisteronline.gov.uk). If the interest is as a joint tenant, it is the current market value of the claimant's half of the house that is relevant (ie, with the former partner still living in it and perhaps unwilling or unable to move out or buy out the claimant's half share), not half the value of the sale of proceeds of the whole house: *R(IS) 4/03*, *CH 3197/2003* and *R(JSA) 1/02* considered.

Calculation of tariff income from capital

52.–(1) Except where the circumstances prescribed in paragraph [¹] (4) apply to the claimant, where the claimant's capital calculated in accordance with this Part exceeds [¹ £6,000] it shall be treated as equivalent to a weekly tariff income of £1 for each complete £250 in excess of [¹ £6,000] but not exceeding £16,000.

[¹ (2)]

(3) Where the circumstances prescribed in paragraph (4) apply to a claimant and that claimant's capital calculated in accordance with this Part exceeds £10,000, it shall be treated as equivalent to a weekly tariff income of £1 for each complete £250 in excess of £10,000 but not exceeding £16,000.

(4) For the purposes of paragraph (3), the prescribed circumstances are that the claimant–
(a) occupies residential accommodation as his home; or
(b) is a person–
  (i) to whom on 3rd October 2005 paragraph (2) of regulation 7 of the former regulations as in force on that date applied; or
  (ii) to whom on 3rd October 2005, paragraph (5) or paragraph (7) of regulation 7 of those Regulations as in force on that date applied and continues to apply;

(5) For the purposes of paragraph (4), the claimant shall be treated as–
(a) occupying residential accommodation as his home; or
(b) a person to whom regulation 9(1A) as inserted by paragraph 9(3)(a) of Schedule 3 to the Consequential Provisions Regulations, applies; or
(c) a person to whom regulation 9(6) as inserted by paragraph 9(5)(a) of Schedule 3 to the Consequential Provisions Regulations, applies; or
(d) a person to whom regulation 9(6) as inserted by paragraph 9(7)(a) of Schedule 3 to the Consequential Provisions Regulations, applies,
in any period during which he is treated as occupying the accommodation as his home pursuant to regulation 7(12), (13) or (17).

(6) Notwithstanding paragraphs (1) [¹] and (3) where any part of the excess is not a complete £250 that part shall be treated as equivalent to a weekly tariff income of £1.

(7) For the purposes of paragraphs (1) [¹] and (3), capital includes any income treated as capital under regulation 46 (income treated as capital).

(8) For the purposes of this regulation and subject to paragraph (9), ''residential accommodation'' means accommodation which is provided by an establishment–

(a)   under sections 21 to 24 of the National Assistance Act 1948 (provision of accommodation) or under section 59 of the Social Work (Scotland) Act 1968 (provision of residential and other establishments) where board is not available to the claimant and the home in which the accommodation is provided is either owned or managed or owned and managed by a local authority;

(b)   which is managed or provided by a body incorporated by Royal Charter or constituted by Act of Parliament (other than a social services authority) and provides both board and personal care for the claimant; and in this sub-paragraph, "personal care" means care which includes assistance with bodily functions where such assistance is required;

(c)   which is an Abbeyfield Home,

and in this definition, "board" refers to the availability to the claimant in the home in which his accommodation is provided of cooked or prepared food, where the food is made available to him in consequence solely of his paying the charge for the accommodation or any other charge which he is required to pay as a condition of occupying the accommodation, or both those charges and is made available for his consumption without any further charge to him.

(9)   Paragraph (8) shall not apply to residential accommodation of the type referred to in sub-paragraphs (a) to (c) of paragraph (8) where such accommodation is residential accommodation for the purpose of regulation 9 unless the claimant is a person to whom paragraphs 10, 11 or 12 of Schedule 3 to the Social Security (Care Homes and Independent Hospitals) Regulations 2005 apply.

Modifications

Reg 52 applies as modified by Sch 3 para 9(3)(b) HB&CTB(CP) Regs (see p1223) to a claimant who on 3 October 2005 was someone to whom reg 7(2) of the HB Regs 1987 as then in force applied.

Reg 52 applies as modified by Sch 3 para 9(5)(b) HB&CTB(CP) Regs (see p1223) to a claimant who on 3 October 2005 was someone to whom reg 7(5) of the HB Regs 1987 as then in force applied.

Reg 52 applies as modified by Sch 3 para 9(7)(b) HB&CTB(CP) Regs (see p1224) to a claimant who on 3 October 2005 was someone to whom reg 7(7) of the HB Regs 1987 as then in force applied.

Amendment

1.   Amended by reg 5A(4) of SI 2005 No 2465 as inserted by Sch 2 para 28(5) of SI 2006 No 217 as from 1.4.06.

Definitions

"capital" – see General Note on this Part.

"claimant" – see reg 2(1).

General Note

This regulation applies to create "tariff income" which is deemed to be generated by capital held by a claimant which is nonetheless insufficient to take her/him over the capital limit. Actual income from assessable capital is usually treated as capital itself under reg 46. For income from disregarded capital, see Sch 5 para 17 and reg 46(4).

Analysis

Paras (1), (6) and (7) set out the normal rule. Where para (4) does not apply to a claimant, and the total capital falling to be assessed under this Section is between £6,000 and £16,000, the claimant is treated as having income of £1 a week from each £250 or part of £250 in excess of £6,000. For example, a claimant has £7,765 assessed under this Part. S/he is treated as receiving £1,750 divided by 250 = 7. £15 left over gives rise to another £1 and so s/he is deemed to have £8 a week income from that capital.

Paras (3) to (5), (8) and (9) set out a special rule for certain claimants in "residential accommodation" as defined in paras (8) and (9). By para (5), those who are deemed to be in occupation by relevant provisions in reg 7 also qualify. For these claimants the lower capital limit is increased from £6,000 to £10,000, and they are treated as having weekly tariff income of £1 for each £250, or part thereof, of capital in excess of £10,000.

PART 7
Students

General Note on Part 7

Since 1 September 1990, government policy has been to exclude most, but not all, full-time students from entitlement to HB by treating them (under reg 56) as not liable to make payments in respect of their dwelling.

These changes were part of a more general change in the structure of student finance, the aim of which was to provide for students' financial needs wholly through the system of grants and student loans. Educational establishments have been provided with further "access funds" to assist students suffering from financial hardship. Full-time students are not generally eligible for IS, income-related ESA or JSA (except for limited categories). For further information about other types of financial support available to students, see CPAG's *Student Support and Benefits Handbook: England, Wales and Northern Ireland* and *Benefits for Students in Scotland Handbook* (the latter can be accessed online for free at http://scottishhandbooks.cpag.org.uk).

There are no comparable rules for students in the HB(SPC) Regs so claimants covered by those regulatations are not excluded from entitlement to HB for being students. In addition, student loan and grant income is ignored; it does not come within the definition of "income" in reg 29 HB(SPC) Regs.

The excluded students

Reg 56(1) excludes anyone who is a "full-time student" from entitlement to HB subject to certain exceptions listed in reg 56(2). The definition of "full-time student" is found in reg 53.

It must be borne in mind that a claimant may fall within the definition of "full-time student" from the date on which her/his course starts until the day it ends or that s/he abandons it or is dismissed from it: reg 53(2) to (4). This means that the special rules for full-time students can apply even if the claimant is not studying at the material time – eg, during the summer vacation or absences from a course due to ill health or pregnancy. For the difficult questions arising for students who have taken time off in the middle of their courses, see the Analysis to reg 56.

The treatment of student claims

Even if a student is not excluded from entitlement to HB by reg 56, s/he must still satisfy the other rules in this Part before qualifying. The general rule is that claims by students will, subject to the special rules in this Part, be decided in the same way as claims by non-students. The special rules can be summarised as:

(1)   If a full-time student is absent from her/his home where s/he lives to study outside a period of study, then s/he is deemed not to occupy the dwelling, unless the absence is due to hospitalisation: reg 55.

(2)   Unless a full-time student is entitled to HB by virtue of the exceptions in reg 56(2), HB is not payable during a period of study in respect of payments made to the student's educational establishment, except in limited circumstances: reg 57.

(3)   There are detailed rules for the treatment of the sources of income for students – eg, grants, covenant income, student loans and access funds: regs 59 to 69. Note that education maintenance allowances (and similar payments) paid to young people on certain non-advanced courses are dealt with separately. They are disregarded as income under para 11 of Sch 5 and as capital under para 51 of Sch 6. Career development loans paid under s2 Employment and Training Act 1973 are taken into account as income (reg 41(4)) with provision for some or all of it to be disregarded (Sch 5 para 13).

Claimants with a student partner

The general exclusion of full-time students from HB does not prevent a claimant whose partner is a student from claiming HB. However, the provisions of reg 57 concerning claimants who pay rent to educational establishments apply to such claimants: reg 58.

SECTION 1
General

Interpretation

53.–(1)   In this Part–

"academic year" means the period of twelve months beginning on 1st January, 1st April, 1st July or 1st September according to whether the course in question begins in the winter, the spring, the summer or the autumn respectively but if students are required to begin attending the course during August or September and to continue attending through the autumn, the academic year of the course shall be considered to begin in the autumn rather than the summer;

"access funds" means–

(a)   grants made under section 68 of the Further and Higher Education Act 1992 for the purpose of providing funds on a discretionary basis to be paid to students;

(b)   grants made under sections 73(a) and (c) and 74(1) of the Education (Scotland) Act 1980; or

(c)   grants made under Article 30 of the Education and Libraries (Northern Ireland) Order 1993 or grants, loans or other payments made under Article 5 of the Further Education (Northern Ireland) Order 1997 in each case being grants, or grants, loans or other payments as the case may be, for the purpose of assisting students in financial difficulties;

(d) discretionary payments, known as "learner support funds", which are made available to students in further education by institutions out of funds provided by the [⁷ Young People's Learning Agency for England under sections 61 and 62 of the Apprenticeships, Skills, Children and Learning Act 2009 or the Chief Executive of Skills Funding under sections 100 and 101 of that Act]; or

(e) Financial Contingency Funds made available by the [⁴ Welsh Ministers];

"college of further education" means a college of further education within the meaning of Part I of the Further and Higher Education (Scotland) Act 1992;

[⁵ "contribution" means–

(a) any contribution in respect of the income of a student or any person which the Secretary of State, the Scottish Ministers or an education authority takes into account in ascertaining the amount of a student's grant or student loan; or

(b) any sums, which in determining the amount of a student's allowance or bursary in Scotland under the Education (Scotland) Act 1980, the Scottish Ministers or education authority takes into account being sums which the Scottish Ministers or education authority consider that it is reasonable for the following persons to contribute towards the holder's expenses–

(i) the holder of the allowance or bursary;

(ii) the holder's parents;

(iii) the holder's parent's spouse, civil partner or a person ordinarily living with the holder's parent as if he or she were the spouse or civil partner of that parent; or

(iv) the holder's spouse or civil partner;]

"course of study" means any course of study, whether or not it is a sandwich course and whether or not a grant is made for undertaking or attending it;

"covenant income" means the gross income payable to a full-time student under a Deed of Covenant by his parent;

"education authority" means a government department, [⁶ a local authority as defined in section 579 of the Education Act 1996 (interpretation)], a local education authority as defined in section 123 of the Local Government (Scotland) Act 1973, an education and library board established under Article 3 of the Education and Libraries (Northern Ireland) Order 1986, any body which is a research council for the purposes of the Science and Technology Act 1965 or any analogous government department, authority, board or body, of the Channel Islands, Isle of Man or any other country outside Great Britain;

"full-time course of study" means a full-time course of study which–

(a) is not funded in whole or in part by the [⁷ Young People's Learning Agency for England, the Chief Executive of Skills Funding] or by the [¹ [⁴ Welsh Ministers]] or a full-time course of study which is not funded in whole or in part by the Scottish Ministers at a college of further education or a full-time course of study which is a course of higher education and is funded in whole or in part by the Scottish Ministers;

(b) is funded in whole or in part by the [⁷ Young People's Learning Agency for England, the Chief Executive of Skills Funding] or by the [¹ [⁴ Welsh Ministers]] if it involves more than 16 guided learning hours per week for the student in question, according to the number of guided learning hours per week for that student set out–

[⁷ (i) in the case of a course funded by the Young People's Learning Agency for England or the Chief Executive of Skills Funding in the student's learning agreement signed on behalf of the establishment which is funded by either of those bodies for the delivery of that course; or]

(ii) in the case of a course funded by the [¹ [⁴ Welsh Ministers]], in a document signed on behalf of the establishment which is funded by that Council for the delivery of that course; or

(c) is not higher education and is funded in whole or in part by the Scottish Ministers at a college of further education and involves–

(i)   more than 16 hours per week of classroom-based or workshop-based programmed learning under the direct guidance of teaching staff according to the number of hours set out in a document signed on behalf of the college; or

(ii)   16 hours or less per week of classroom-based or workshop-based programmed learning under the direct guidance of teaching staff and it involves additional hours using structured learning packages supported by the teaching staff where the combined total of hours exceeds 21 hours per week, according to the number of hours set out in a document signed on behalf of the college;

"full-time student" means a person attending or undertaking a full-time course of study and includes a student on a sandwich course;

"grant" (except in the definition of "access funds") means any kind of educational grant or award and includes any scholarship, studentship, exhibition, allowance or bursary but does not include a payment from access funds or any payment to which paragraph 11 of Schedule 5 or [² paragraph 51] of Schedule 6 applies;

"grant income" means–

(a)   any income by way of a grant;

(b)   any contribution whether or not it is paid;

"higher education" means higher education within the meaning of Part 2 of the Further and Higher Education (Scotland) Act 1992;

"last day of the course" means–

(a)   in the case of a qualifying course, the date on which the last day of that course falls or the date on which the final examination relating to that course is completed, whichever is the later;

(b)   in any other case, the date on which the last day of the final academic term falls in respect of the course in which the student is enrolled;

"period of study" means–

(a)   in the case of a course of study for one year or less, the period beginning with the start of the course and ending with the last day of the course;

(b)   in the case of a course of study for more than one year, in the first or, as the case may be, any subsequent year of the course, other than the final year of the course, the period beginning with the start of the course or, as the case may be, that year's start and ending with either–

[⁵ (i)   the day before the start of the next year of the course in a case where the student's grant or loan is assessed at a rate appropriate to his studying throughout the year or, if he does not have a grant or loan, where a loan would have been assessed at such a rate had he had one; or]

(ii)   in any other case, the day before the start of the [⁵ normal] summer vacation appropriate to his course;

(c)   in the final year of a course of study of more than one year, the period beginning with that year's start and ending with the last day of the course;

"periods of experience" means periods of work experience which form part of a sandwich course;

"qualifying course" means a qualifying course as defined for the purposes of Parts 2 and 4 of the Jobseeker's Allowance Regulations;

[² "sandwich course" has the meaning prescribed in regulation 2(9) of the Education (Student Support) Regulations 2008, regulation 4(2) of the Education (Student Loans) (Scotland) Regulations 2007 or regulation 2(8) of the Education (Student Support) Regulations (Northern Ireland) 2007, as the case may be;]

"standard maintenance grant" means–

(a)   except where paragraph (b) or (c) applies, in the case of a student attending or undertaking a course of study at the University of London or an establishment within the area comprising the City of London and the Metropolitan Police District, the amount specified for the time being in paragraph 2(2)(a) of Schedule 2 to the Education (Mandatory Awards) Regulations 2003 ("the 2003 Regulations") for such a student;

(b)   except where paragraph (c) applies, in the case of a student residing at his parent's home, the amount specified in paragraph 3 thereof;

(c)   in the case of a student receiving an allowance or bursary under the Education (Scotland) Act 1980, the amount of money specified as "standard maintenance allowance" for the relevant year appropriate for the student set out in the Student Support in Scotland Guide issued by the Student Awards Agency for Scotland, or its nearest equivalent in the case of a bursary provided by a college of further education or a local education authority [³];

(d)   in any other case, the amount specified in paragraph 2(2) of Schedule 2 to the 2000 Regulations other than in sub-paragraph (a) or (b) thereof;

"student" means a person, other than a person in receipt of a training allowance, who is attending or undertaking–

(a)   a course of study at an educational establishment; or

(b)   a qualifying course;

"student loan" means a loan towards a student's maintenance pursuant to any regulations made under section 22 of the Teaching and Higher Education Act 1998, section 73 of the Education (Scotland) Act 1980 or Article 3 of the Education (Student Support) (Northern Ireland) Order 1998 and shall include, in Scotland, a young student's bursary paid under regulation 4(1)(c) of the [² Students' Allowances (Scotland) Regulations 2007].

(2)   For the purposes of the definition of "full-time student" in paragraph (1), a person shall be regarded as attending or, as the case may be, undertaking a full-time course of study or as being on a sandwich course–

(a)   subject to paragraph (3), in the case of a person attending or undertaking a part of a modular course which would be a full-time course of study for the purposes of this Part, for the period beginning on the day on which that part of the course starts and ending–

    (i)   on the last day on which he is registered with the educational establishment as attending or undertaking that part as a full-time course of study; or

    (ii)   on such earlier date (if any) as he finally abandons the course or is dismissed from it;

(b)   in any other case, throughout the period beginning on the date on which he starts attending or undertaking the course and ending on the last day of the course or on such earlier date (if any) as he finally abandons it or is dismissed from it.

(3)   For the purposes of sub-paragraph (a) of paragraph (2), the period referred to in that sub-paragraph shall include–

(a)   where a person has failed examinations or has failed to successfully complete a module relating to a period when he was attending or undertaking a part of the course as a full-time course of study, any period in respect of which he attends or undertakes the course for the purpose of retaking those examinations or that module;

(b)   any period of vacation within the period specified in that paragraph or immediately following that period except where the person has registered with the educational establishment to attend or undertake the final module in the course and the vacation immediately follows the last day on which he is required to attend or undertake the course.

(4)   In paragraph (2), "modular course" means a course of study which consists of two or more modules, the successful completion of a specified number of which is required before a person is considered by the educational establishment to have completed the course.

Amendments

1.   Amended by reg 2 of SI 2005 No 3238 as amended by Sch 2 para 31 of SI 2006 No 217 as from 1.4.06.
2.   Amended by reg 3(6) of SI 2008 No 1042 as from 19.5.08.
3.   Amended by reg 6(5) of SI 2008 No 2767 as from 17.11.08.
4.   Amended by reg 5(4) of SI 2008 No 3156 as from 5.1.09.
5.   Substituted by reg 6(6) of SI 2009 No 583 as from 6.4.09.
6.   Amended by Art 4 and Sch 3 para 64 of SI 2010 No 1172 as from 5.5.10.

7.   Amended by Art 14(3) of SI 2010 No 1941 as from 1.9.10.

Analysis

"academic year". This definition is relevant to the treatment of student loans. See reg 64(2) on p413.

"access funds". See reg 65 for the treatment of certain access funds.

"contribution". The definition includes any contribution in respect of the income of the student or any other person taken into account in the assessment of a student's grant or loan or in Scotland, allowance or bursary, including amounts which the student, her/his spouse, civil partner or parents (or in some cases in Scotland, parent's partners) could reasonably be expected to contribute. Note that this allows the reduction in the student's grant or loan on the basis of her/his own income to be treated as a "contribution". See regs 66 and 67 where the claimant or her/his partner is assessed as liable to make a contribution. See Sch 5 paras 19 and 20 for income disregards where the claimant is making a parental contribution in respect of a student.

"course of study". A course counts as a course of study whether or not it is a sandwich course and whether or not a grant is made for it. For the meaning of a "sandwich course", see below. It must be a course of study, and purely vocational work may not qualify: see, for example, *R(SB) 25/87* which decides that a pupil barrister is not studying; s/he is attending a barrister to assimilate vocational skills. However, where there is active tuition, the fact that the skills are vocational will not prevent the course being a course of study. Many such "courses" may be excluded by the requirement that no training allowance is being received (see the definition of "student" below). So in *R(IS) 19/98* para 11 it was held that a nurse on the Project 2000 scheme who was paid a bursary by the Department of Health during her training was on a course of study. For when a full-time student is treated as attending a full-time course of study, see para (2).

"covenant income". Notice that this covers only income covenanted by a parent, not grandparent, etc and that the beneficiary must be a full-time student. This definition refers to the gross amount of the payment.

"full-time course of study". See the Analysis to reg 56 on p404.

"full-time student". See the Analysis to reg 56 on p404.

"grant" means any kind of educational grant or award other than a payment from access funds or an education maintenance allowance which can be disregarded as income under Sch 5 para 11 or as capital under Sch 6 para 51 HB Regs. GM Annex A C2.11 advises local authorities not to include payments derived from funds made available by the Secretary of State to assist students in financial difficulties under s100 Education Act 1944, s65 Further and Higher Education Act 1992, s73 Education (Scotland) Act 1980 or s40 Further and Higher Education (Scotland) Act 1992.

There are conflicting decisions of the commissioners in relation to whether "award" can include loans made to students by educational authorities. In *R(SB) 20/83* para 10(3), it was held that it could, but in *R(IS) 16/95* para 10 it was pointed out that the word usually connoted an absolute gift when used in an educational context. It is suggested that this is plainly right in view of the examples of sources of income such as scholarships, which are almost invariably in the nature of gifts rather than loans. Likewise, it cannot apply to bank loans or overdrafts obtained by students. Note the special provisions for assessing income from student loans in reg 64.

"grant income". A contribution (see above) is deemed to have been received by the student whether paid or not.

Note that when a student abandons a course, s/he falls under an obligation to repay any grant made by the education authority. The amount of the grant which is repayable cannot be treated as income from that date: *R(IS) 5/99* para 12. Changes were made to the IS scheme to provide for such treatment, but no corresponding amendments were made to the HB and CTB regulations. The commissioner's decision was upheld on a different basis by the Court of Appeal in *Chief Adjudication Officer v Leeves* [1999] FLR 90, CA (reported as *R(IS) 5/99*). Potter LJ held that once the education authority demanded repayment of an ascertained sum, the amount of the grant could not be treated as income from that date.

"last day of the course". This clarifies the treatment of those cases where, for example, the student is able to leave the course a few weeks early after having taken final exams. For "qualifying courses" (see below), since these are not organised along the lines of terms, the last day of the course is the later of the date of the final exam or the last day of the course. In other cases "the last day of the course" always means the date on which the last day of the final academic term is scheduled to fall and not the earlier date on which the student actually left.

Note that GM C2.352-354 says that full-time postgraduate students cease to be treated as full-time students when their course is completed. The guidance goes on to say that whether such a student who is doing further research or writing a thesis after this should be regarded as a full-time student depends on the amount of work being undertaken, not on the fact that the course was full-time.

"period of study". In a "course of study" (see above) of more than one year, the date on which a "period of study" ends depends on whether grants or loans for that course are assessed on the basis of a full year's study, or whether no grant or loan is assessed for the summer vacation. In the latter case, which will be the norm, it ends at the beginning of that vacation and starts again when the vacation ends. This is the case whether or not the student in question receives a grant or loan. During the final year of a course, the "period of study" always ends on "the last day of the course" (see above). See further the Analysis to reg 56 on p404.

"periods of experience". "Periods of work experience", the definition of which is, for example, found in reg 2 Education (Student Support) Regulations 2008 SI No.529, means–

"(a)   periods of industrial, professional or commercial experience associated with full-time study at an institution but at a place outside the institution,

(b)   periods during which a student is employed and residing in a country whose language is one that he is studying for his course (provided that the period of residence in that country is a requirement of his course and the study of one or more modern languages accounts for not less than one half of the total time spent studying on the course)."

"qualifying course". These courses form part of the elaborate package aimed at assisting the long-term unemployed. The definition of such a course is to be found in reg 17A(7) Jobseeker's Allowance Regulations 1996 (JSA Regs). Certain claimants on such courses may continue to receive JSA throughout the period of study. Three conditions must be fulfilled.

(1)   It must be an "employment-related course". By reg 1(3) JSA Regs, this is defined as "a course the purpose of which is to assist persons to acquire or enhance skills required for employment, for seeking employment or for a particular occupation".

(2)   It must last for no more than 12 consecutive months.

(3)   It must be a course of an appropriate level. The definition of what is an appropriate level is different in England and Wales on one hand and Scotland on the other. In England and Wales, Sch 2 Further and Higher Education Act 1992 provides the definition. It covers vocational courses approved by the Secretary of State, GCSE and A-Level courses, preparation for further education, preparatory courses for the foregoing, English and Welsh classes, basic mathematics courses, and courses teaching independent living and communication skills. In Scotland, s6 Further and Higher Education (Scotland) Act 1992 lists courses that: prepare people for vocational qualifications, prepare for SEB or GCE exams, assist those with learning difficulties, assist access to higher education, assist with English for those for whom it is not their first language, and preparatory courses covering the above. Note that there are wide powers to add categories of course. Not all such courses are capable of fulfilling the first condition above. Note also that by reg 17A(8) JSA Regs, any courses of a higher standard may nonetheless be determined to be qualifying courses even if they do not fall within the scope of the definition above.

"sandwich course". Reg 2(9) Education (Student Support) Regulations 2008 SI No.529, for example, says that a course is a sandwich course if it is not a course for the initial training of teachers, it consists of alternate periods of full-time study in an institution and periods of work experience, and taking the course as a whole, the student attends the periods of full-time study for an average of not less than 18 weeks in each year. For the purposes of calculating the student's attendance, the course is treated as beginning with the first period of full-time study and ending with the last such period.

"student". A person in receipt of a training allowance does not come within the definition of student. For "training allowance", see reg 2(1). The definition of student includes those on "qualifying courses": see above. For "course of study", as defined in this regulation, see above.

Paras (2) to (4). By para (2), a full-time student is treated as attending the course throughout all vacations as well as during the term, or until s/he abandons or is dimissed from the course if earlier. The effect of this is partly offset by the use of the phrase "period of study" in various regulations: see above. See also the analysis of "course of study" above. Note that the rules differ for those on part of a modular course (defined in para (4)). Here, the student counts as a full-time student until the last day s/he is registered with the educational establishment as attending that part of the course full-time: para (2)(a). See para (3) where a student on a modular course fails exams or fails to complete a module.

Treatment of students

54.   The provisions of Parts 2, 3 and 4 (entitlement to housing benefit, payments in respect of a dwelling, membership of a family) shall have effect in relation to students subject to the following provisions of this Part.

General Note

See General Note to Part 7 on p394. These regulations also affect Part 6.

Analysis

In *R (Naghshbandi) v Camden LBC* [2001] EWHC Admin 813; [2003] HLR 280, CA, the court was considering the inter-relationship between Pts II and VII of the HB Regs 1987 (now Pts 2 and 7 HB Regs). The claimant had an adult son living in his household who was a student. There were a total of five members of the family who shared the rent liability and the issue was whether reg 48A(1) HB Regs 1987 (now reg 56(1) HB Regs) operated to deem the son not to be liable for rent and so to exclude him from the apportionment of the rent between those liable under reg 10(5) HB Regs 1987 (now reg 12B(4) HB Regs). The council and Rafferty J decided that the deemed non-liability did not apply to reg 10(5).

On appeal, the Secretary of State intervened to support the council's position. Counsel for the Secretary of State argued that the rule had to be read as if it said "shall have effect in relation to students who are claimants for housing benefit". The court accepted that argument and dismissed the claimant's appeal. But reading reg 54 in this way produces some potentially odd results. See the commentary to regs 7(6)(b) and 55 (on pp238 and 400).

SECTION 2
Entitlement and payments in respect of a dwelling

General Note on Section 2

See General Note on this Part. The rules in Parts 2, 3 and 4 apply to students, but they are modified as set out below.

This should be read together with regs 7(3) and 7(6)(b) (see p234), which also make provision for students.

Occupying a dwelling as a person's home

55.–(1) Subject to paragraph (2), a full-time student shall not be treated as occupying a dwelling as his home during any benefit week outside the period of study if he is absent from it for the whole of that week and if the main purpose of his occupation during the period of study would be to facilitate attendance on his course.

(2) The provisions of paragraph (1) shall not apply to any absence occasioned by the need to enter hospital for treatment.

Definitions

"benefit week" – see reg 2(1).
"dwelling" – see reg 2(4).
"full-time student" – see reg 53.
"period of study" – see reg 53.
"student" – see reg 53.

General Note

Even if a full-time student is able to claim HB, this regulation prevents her/him claiming in respect of accommodation occupied to enable her/him to attend the course, for any whole week s/he is absent from it outside her/his period of study (defined in reg 53).

This regulation does not apply where the student is in hospital for treatment: para (2).

It is suggested that where the student is not the claimant, reg 55 has no application because the application of this Part is limited to cases where the student is the claimant: *R (Naghshbandi) v Camden LBC* [2001] EWHC Admin 813; [2003] HLR 280, CA. Accordingly where a student's partner claims HB both in respect of the normal home and the student accommodation under reg 7(6)(b), HB will remain payable during the vacations.

Analysis

Para (1). For the meaning of "occupying a dwelling as his home", see reg 7 and particularly paras (3) and (6)(b) for special rules relating to students.

The student is only deemed not to be occupying the accommodation if the "main purpose" of her/his occupation during the "period of study" is to facilitate her/his attendance on the course – eg, if s/he would not normally be living there were it not for the course. So the provision cannot apply to a student who would stay in her/his term-time residence even if not attending a course, or who has other, equally important, reasons for staying at that place. Examples include where the claimant is fully independent of, does not have, or is estranged from her/his parents, or where s/he was already settled in the accommodation prior to study. GM C2.73 states that authorities may "readily accept" that the claimant's main purpose of residence is not study where the student's dependent children are living with her/him or where the student has no other accommodation which could be regarded as her/his home. Where the student is under 25, whether or not the student has parents is also relevant. Authorities should "look carefully" at other categories of case: GM C2.74.

Para (2). "Hospital" is not defined. It is suggested that it can cover a wider range of residential treatment than that offered by the NHS. It may cover private treatment and clinics where alternative medicine is practised, provided that there is a respectable medical basis for the treatment being given.

Full-time students to be treated as not liable to make payments in respect of a dwelling

56.–(1) A full-time student shall be treated as if he were not liable to make payments in respect of a dwelling.

(2) Paragraph (1) shall not apply to a full-time student–

(a) who is a person on income support [³ , an income-based jobseeker's allowance or an income-related employment and support allowance];

(b) who is a lone parent;

(c) whose applicable amount would, but for paragraph (1), include the [²] disability premium or severe disability premium;

(d)   whose applicable amount would include the disability premium but for his being treated as capable of work by virtue of a determination made in accordance with regulations made under section 171E of the Act;

(e)   who is, or is treated as, incapable of work and has been so incapable, or has been so treated as incapable, of work in accordance with the provisions of, and regulations made under, Part 12A of the Act (incapacity for work) for a continuous period of not less than 196 days; and for this purpose any two or more separate periods separated by a break of not more than 56 days shall be treated as one continuous period;

[³ (ea) who has, or is treated as having, limited capability for work and has had, or been treated as having, limited capability for work in accordance with the Employment and Support Allowance Regulations for a continuous period of not less than 196 days and for this purpose any two or more separate periods separated by a break of not more than 84 days must be treated as one continuous period;]

(f)   who has a partner who is also a full-time student, if he or that partner is treated as responsible for a child or young person;

(g)   who is a single claimant with whom a child is–

    (i)   placed by a local authority or voluntary organisation under section 23(2)(a) or section 59(1)(a) of the Children Act 1989 (provision of accommodation and maintenance); or

    (ii)   in Scotland, boarded out by a local authority or voluntary organisation within the meaning of the Social Work (Scotland) Act 1968;

[¹ (h) who is–

    (i)   aged under [⁴ 21] and whose course of study is not a course of higher education, or

    (ii)   a qualifying young person or child within the meaning of section 142 of the Act (child and qualifying young person);] or

(i)   in respect of whom–

    (i)   a supplementary requirement has been determined under paragraph 9 of Part 2 of Schedule 2 to the Education (Mandatory Awards) Regulations 2003; or

    [² (ii) an allowance or, as the case may be, bursary has been granted which includes a sum under paragraph (1)(d) of regulation 4 of the Students' Allowances (Scotland) Regulations 2007 or, as the case may be, under paragraph (1)(d) of regulation 4 of the Education Authority Bursaries (Scotland) Regulations 2007, in respect of expenses incurred; or]

    (iii)   a payment has been made under section 2 of the Education Act 1962 or under, or by virtue of regulations made under, the Teaching and Higher Education Act 1998; or

    (iv)   a grant has been made under [² regulation 37 of the Education (Student Support) Regulations 2008] or under [² regulation 39 of the Education (Student Support) Regulations (Northern Ireland) 2007]; or

    (v)   a supplementary requirement has been determined under paragraph 9 of Schedule 6 to the [² Students Awards Regulations (Northern Ireland) 2003] or a payment has been made under Article 50(3) of the Education and Libraries (Northern Ireland) Order 1986,

    on account of his disability by reason of deafness; or

(j)   who–

    (i)   immediately before 1st September 1990 was in receipt of income support by virtue of paragraph 7 of Schedule 1 to the Income Support (General) Regulations 1987 as then in force; or

    (ii)   on or after that date makes a claim for income support or housing benefit (or both) and at any time during the period of 18 months immediately preceding the date of that claim was in receipt of income support either by virtue of that paragraph or regulation 13(2)(b) of those Regulations, but this sub-paragraph shall cease to apply where the person has ceased to be in receipt of income support for a continuous period of 18 months or more.

[⁴ (2A)   For the purposes of paragraph (2)(h)(i) the student must have begun [⁵, or been enrolled or accepted onto] the course before attaining the age of 19.]

(3)   For the purposes of paragraph (2), once paragraph (2)(e) applies to a full-time student, if he then ceases, for a period of 56 days or less, to be incapable, or to be treated as incapable, of work, that paragraph shall, on his again becoming so incapable, or so treated as incapable, of work at the end of that period, immediately thereafter apply to him for so long as he remains incapable, or is treated as remaining incapable, of work.

(4)   In paragraph (2)(h) reference to a course of higher education is a reference to a course of any description mentioned in Schedule 6 to the Education Reform Act 1988 [²].

(5)   A full-time student to whom sub-paragraph (i) of paragraph (2) applies shall be treated as satisfying that sub-paragraph from the date on which he made a request for the supplementary requirement, allowance, bursary or payment, as the case may be.

(6)   Paragraph (1) shall not apply to a full-time student for the period specified in paragraph (7) if–

(a)   at any time during an academic year, with the consent of the relevant education establishment, he ceases to attend or undertake a course because he is–
  (i)   engaged in caring for another person; or
  (ii)   ill;
(b)   he has subsequently ceased to be engaged in caring for that person or, as the case may be, he has subsequently recovered from that illness; and
(c)   he is not eligible for a grant or a student loan in respect of the period specified in paragraph (7).

(7)   The period specified for the purposes of paragraph (6) is the period not exceeding one year beginning on the day on which he ceased to be engaged in caring for that other person or, as the case may be, the day on which he recovered from that illness and ending on the day before–

(a)   the day on which he resumes attending or undertaking the course; or
(b)   the day from which the relevant educational establishment has agreed that he may resume attending or undertaking the course,

whichever shall first occur.

Amendments
1. Inserted by reg 4(3) of SI 2006 No 718 as from 10.4.06.
2. Amended by reg 3(7) of SI 2008 No 1042 as from 19.5.08.
3. Amended by reg 17 of SI 2008 No 1082 as from 27.10.08.
4. Amended by reg 6(7) of SI 2009 No 583 as from 6.4.09.
5. Amended by reg 8(7) of SI 2010 No 641 as from 1.4.10 (5.4.10 where rent payable weekly or in multiples of a week).

Definitions
"disability premium" – see para 12 Sch 3.
"full-time student" – see reg 53.
"higher pensioner premium" – see para 11 Sch 3.
"lone parent" – see reg 2(1).
"partner" – see reg 2(1).
"pensioner premium" – see paras 9 and 10 Sch 3.
"person on income support" – see reg 2(1).
"person on an income-based jobseeker's allowance" – see reg 2(3).
"person on an income-related employment and support allowance" – see reg 2(3A).
"responsible for a child or young person" – see reg 20.
"severe disability premium" – see para 14 Sch 3.
"single claimant" – see reg 2(1).
"student" – see reg 53.

General Note
To qualify for HB, a claimant must be liable or treated as liable to make payments in respect of her/his dwelling (see s130(1)(a) SSCBA 1992 and reg 8 on pp10 and 244). Para (1) seeks to exclude most full-time students from entitlement to HB by treating them as not liable to make payments in respect of their dwelling. See the Analysis

below for the difficult question of what a full-time student is. Paras (2) to (7) define the exceptions to the general rule.

If someone comes within the definition of full-time student, s/he is then treated as attending or undertaking a full-time course of study for the duration of the course or until s/he abandons the course or is dismissed from it: reg 53(2). In limited circumstances, claims for HB can be made during breaks from study: paras (6) and (7).

Analysis
Para (1): The general exclusion

A "full-time student" is treated as not liable to make payments in respect of a dwelling by para (1). Note that even if the student falls within the exclusion, her/his partner can be treated as liable to make payments in respect of the dwelling (and can therefore qualify for HB) unless s/he is also an excluded student: see reg 8(1)(e) on p244.

Do all full-time students come within the definition? Under the definition in reg 53, a full-time student "means a person attending or undertaking a full-time course of study", including a sandwich course. As to the question of precisely what constitutes a "course of study", see the Analysis to reg 53 on p399. If the claimant is not on a "course of study", s/he cannot be affected by the general exclusion.

Note that unlike with IS and JSA, there are no special rules for those in "relevant education" (essentially full-time non-advanced education for those under 20 – eg, see s124(1)(d) SSCBA 1992 and reg 12 of the Income Support (General) Regulations 1987 SI No.1967). For this reason, a young person might be able to claim HB while in "relevant education" even if s/he cannot claim IS or JSA.

The phrase "full-time course of study" is defined in reg 53 as comprising three categories of course.

(1)   Sub-para (b) covers students whose courses at colleges of further education (CFEs) are funded in whole or in part by the Young People's Learning Agency for England or the Chief Executive of Skills Funding or the Welsh Ministers as appropriate. For such students, the categorisation of the course depends on the number of guided learning hours a week. A course of more than 16 guided learning hours a week is full-time; one of 16 or less is part-time.

The Skills Funding Agency defines guided learning hours as the times when a member of staff is present to give specific guidance towards the learning aim being studied on a programme, including lectures, tutorials and supervised study in – eg, open learning centres or learning workshops. It also includes time spent by staff assessing a learner's achievements – eg, in the assessment of competence for National Vocational Qualifications. The definition excludes hours where supervision or assistance is of a general nature and is not specific to the study of the learners, as well as time spent by staff in the day-to-day marking of assignments or homework where the learner is not present. CFEs provide a document, called a learning agreement in England, which makes it clear how many guided learning hours a course entails.

(2)   Sub-para (c) covers Scottish students on courses at a college of further education that are not higher education and are funded in whole or in part by the Scottish Ministers. For such students, the categorisation of a course depends on the number of hours of classroom-based or workshop-based "programmed learning" under the direct guidance of a teacher. A course of more than 16 hours a week is full-time. Also full-time is a course of more than 21 hours a week, 16 or less of which involve classroom-based or workshop-based "programmed learning" and the rest of which involve structured learning supported by a teacher. As in England and Wales, the CFE provides a document stating the number of hours of "learning" per week.

(3)   Sub-para (a) covers students on full-time courses of study at CFEs *not* funded in whole or in part by the Young People's Learning Agency for England or the Chief Executive of Skills Funding or the Welsh Ministers as appropriate. It also covers Scottish students on full-time courses of study:

(a)   at a college of further education that are not higher education and *not* funded in whole or in part by the Scottish ministers; *or*

(b)   which are courses of higher education funded in whole or in part by the Scottish Ministers.

This category was potentially troublesome in its meaning prior to amendments made in August 2001. For an argument that most Scottish higher education students did not then come within the definition of "full time student" at all, see pp311-312 of the 13th edition. That argument was not, as far as is known, tested in the courts. The definition now makes it clear that higher education courses will bring students within its scope provided that they are funded by the Scottish ministers.

In the first two categories, whether someone counts as a full- or part-time student depends on her/his personal pattern of attendance on the course. In the third category, this depends on the course as a whole.

The question as to how an authority is to judge whether a higher education course is full- or part-time arises frequently in courses coming under the third category (sub-para (a)). In the absence of any definition, local authorities seek the advice of the establishment where the student is studying. It is suggested that the view of the establishment as to whether the course is full-time or part-time is not conclusive, but it may require weighty evidence to rebut it. The assessment is based on the amount of time that is normally expected of a student on the course, not the time that the individual claimant devotes to her/his studies: *R(SB) 41/83* paras 11-12. A good indicator of whether a course is full-time, in relation to higher education courses, is whether or not the student is in receipt of a loan, since these are generally only available to full-time students. All the points in this paragraph were confirmed by the Court of Appeal in dismissing an application for leave to appeal in *Denton v Chief Adjudication Officer* [1999] ELR 86 at 87G-H.

Flexible (modular) courses. August 2000 reforms aimed to cope with the problems with modular courses posed by *Chief Adjudication Officer v Webber* [1998] 1 WLR 625 at 633E, CA (reported as *R(IS) 15/98*), and *R(IS) 1/00* paras 14-17. Paras (2) to (4) of reg 53 deal with full-time students on modular courses. "Modular course" is defined in reg 53(4) as a course of study of two or more modules, a specified number of which the student must complete successfully before the educational establishment considers her/him to have completed the course.

If the part of the modular course the student is attending "would be a full-time course of study" (see above), reg 53(2)(a) deems her/him to be a full-time student from the day on which that part of the course began until the last day s/he is registered with the educational establishment as attending or undertaking that part as a full-time course or until s/he abandons the course or is dismissed from it. Included are periods of attendance to retake examinations or the module: reg 53(3)(a). Also included are periods of vacation within the module as well as vacation that immediately follows it, unless this is the last day on which the student is required to attend or undertake the course: reg 53(3)(b).

The effect of the rules is that a claimant should not come within the definition of "full-time student" while studying part-time on a modular course or where s/he has changed from full-time to part-time or has taken time out from the course.

Paras (2) to (7): The exceptions

Para (2) exempts the following categories of student from the general exclusion from HB provided for by para (1).

(1)   Those on IS, income-based JSA or income-related ESA: sub-para (a). Once the claimant shows that s/he is on IS, income-based JSA or income-related ESA, the authority is not entitled to treat the claimant as a full-time student not liable to make payments in respect of a dwelling. It is not entitled to look into the position for itself: compare the income and capital case of *R v Penwith DC ex p Menear* [1991] 24 HLR 115, QBD. However, in *R v South Ribble DC HBRB ex p Hamilton* [2000] 33 HLR 102, CA, the Court of Appeal confirmed that the definition of "person on income support" must be read as a person lawfully in receipt of IS. If the authority suspects that the claimant should not be receiving IS, income-based JSA or income-related ESA, it ought to award HB, but could then suspend payment under reg 11 D&A Regs pending a query with the relevant DWP office. For a full discussion of *Menear* and *Hamilton*, see the General Note to Part 6 on p343.

(2)   Lone parents (defined in reg 2) and lone foster parents where the child has been formally boarded out with them by a local authority or voluntary agency: sub-paras (b) and (g).

(3)   Full-time students whose applicable amount would include the disability or severe disability premium: sub-para (c). Claimants who are not terminally ill do not normally qualify for disability premium on the basis of incapacity for work until they have been incapable of work for 364 days: see Sch 3 para 13(1)(b)(ii). So a student who has been incapacitated for between 196 days and 364 days cannot fall within this exception unless s/he qualifies for a severe disability premium, or for a disability premium for another reason – eg, receipt of a qualifying benefit such as DLA. Note that on the wording of sub-para (c), this exception would appear to apply to a full-time student whose applicable amount would include one of the premiums listed on the basis of her/his partner's circumstances, even if it would not include one of these based on the student's.

A claimant who has (or is treated as having) limited capability for work (eg, s/he is claiming ESA) cannot ever qualify for a disability premium (see Sch 3 para 13(9) on p528) so cannot fall within this exception unless s/he qualifies for the severe disability premium. However, the student may qualify under sub-paras (e) or (ea).

(4)   Full-time students who would be entitled to a disability premium but for being treated as capable of work under specified provisions: sub-para (d). This means that in situations where a DWP decision maker has made a determination under reg 18 Social Security (Incapacity for Work) Regulations 1995 (ie, where the claimant is disqualified from receiving benefit due to misconduct or failure to accept treatment), if the student is *actually* incapable of work, the determination is to be ignored.

(5)   Students who have been (or have been treated as) incapable of work, or who have (or have been treated as having) limited capability for work for a period of not less than 196 days: sub-paras (e) and (ea). In determining whether there has been incapacity or limited capability for 196 days, a number of periods may be added together if there are not more than 56 days (in the case of incapacity for work) or 84 days (in the case of limited capability for work) between them. Para (3) simply puts it beyond doubt that once the 196 day period has been attained, if the claimant becomes capable of work and then becomes incapable again within 56 days, s/he falls within sub-para (e) without having to build up a further period of 196 days first. It is suggested that on the wording of para (e), para (3) is not necessary.

The starting date for calculating the period will generally be the date shown on the first medical certificate furnished by the claimant. Such certificates can be granted retrospectively. The decision as to whether a claimant is incapable or is treated as incapable of work, or has or is treated as having limited capability for work, is one for the DWP. Note, however, that under reg 28 Social Security (Incapacity for Work) Regulations 1995, until the decision maker applies the "personal capability assessment" to the claimant, it can be deemed to be satisfied by virtue of the fact that medical certificates are being supplied. Likewise, until a decision is made as to whether a claimant has limited capability for work, s/he can be treated as having it under reg 30 ESA Regs pending the decision if s/he supplies medical certificates. Note also the transitional protection in Sch 3 paras 2 and 3 HB&CTB(CP) Regs (see p1197).

(6)   A full-time student claimant with a full-time student partner if either is "treated as responsible for a child or young person", as to which see reg 20: sub-para (f). Unlike with, for example IS, this exception applies throughout the year.

(7)   Claimants under the age of 21 who are not on a course of higher education who began, or were enrolled or accepted onto, the course before they were 19 (see para (2A)) and claimants who are qualifying young people or children within the meaning of s142 SSCBA 1992: sub-para (h).

"Higher education" is defined in para (4) by reference to Sch 6 Education Reform Act 1988. This includes the following types of course: teacher and youth worker training, first and postgraduate degree courses, HND and HNC courses as well as courses at a higher level in preparation for a professional qualification. See GM C2 Annex A C2.12-14 for a list of the types of courses regarded as providing higher education.

"Qualifying young person" is defined by regs 2 to 7 Child Benefit (General) Regulations 2006 SI No 223. It includes certain young people aged at least 16 but under 20 on full-time courses of non-advanced education or in approved training and some who have left courses or training. They must have begun their course or training (or be enrolled or accepted on it) before reaching the age of 19. 19 year olds must have reached that age on or after 10 April 2006. For further information, see CPAG's *Welfare Benefits and Tax Credits Handbook*.

(8)   Certain categories of students entitled to disabled students allowance (DSA) or a payment under the discretionary awards scheme on the same basis and the equivalents available in Scotland and Northern Ireland, because they are deaf: sub-para (i). This includes cases where the underlying conditions for the DSA are satisfied but no actual payment is made as a result of means-testing parental income, since what is required is that an additional requirement has been determined by the education authority, not that it has been paid. Note that this exception takes effect from the date of application for the payment.

(9)   Certain disabled students who fulfill either of two criteria in relation to receipt of IS: sub-para (j). This exception ensured that disabled students who were entitled to IS under the rules as they were prior to 1 September 1990 continued to qualify for HB. It is therefore unlikely that there are many (if any) students to whom this exception would still apply. For details see p374 of the 13th edition.

Paras (6) and (7): Breaks from study

A question which has caused acute controversy was whether students who take time out in the middle of their courses, for whatever reason, are deemed to retain the status of a full-time student for the period until they return to their courses. August 2000 reforms softened the harshest aspects of the treatment of such students, which had generated particularly sharp judicial criticism. See pp277-79 of the 12th edition for the caselaw in relation to the old provisions.

For the current rules, the starting point is to reproduce the definition of "full-time student" from reg 53. "Full-time student" means a person attending or undertaking a full-time course of study and includes a student on a sandwich course. For the purposes of the definition, someone continues to be treated as a undertaking a full-time course of study (or as being on a sandwich course) until the last day of the course or on such earlier date as s/he abandons or is dismissed from the course: reg 53(2) to (4).

Paras (6) and (7) of reg 56 provide welcome relief for full-time students who have to temporarily leave their courses with the consent of the educational establishment, due to illness or through having to care for another person. Such students cannot generally claim HB while caring or ill (however note the exceptions under paras (2)(c) to (ea)), but can when the illness or caring responsibilities come to an end. The relief is available for a period of up to one year, so long as the student is not eligible for a grant or loan in respect of the period. The period starts on the day the illness or caring ceased and ends on the earlier of the day the student resumes the course or the day from which the educational establishment has agreed s/he could do so: para (7). "Caring for another person" in sub-para (6)(a)(i) is not further defined. It is suggested that it is not necessary, for example, for the carer to fulfil the conditions of entitlement to carer's allowance or to be caring for a person in any specific circumstances. Nor does the sub-para set out the number of hours a person would have to be caring for another.

What, however, of other students such as those who fail their exams? If a student fails exams, or hits financial trouble and is forced to take a year out, it does not appear possible to revive the analysis of Commissioner Howell in *CIS 13986/1996* paras 10-14, which was disapproved by *O'Connor v Chief Adjudication Officer* [1999] ELR 209, CA (*R(IS) 7/99*). The reasoning of the majority in that case proceeded on the basis that a student taking time out would return to the same "course".

O'Connor does, however, leave open the position of students who have failed exams or otherwise broken off their studies and who know that they will be invited back (if at all) to follow what is undoubtedly a different course from the one they originally commenced (eg, because it is in a different subject or leads to a pass degree rather than an honours degree). It is suggested that such students must be treated as following a different course when they return and hence as not being full-time students when they are away from their studies.

In *R(IS) 1/96* the claimant was studying to be an architect. He had completed his university degree course, but then was to undertake a work placement prior to a further period of postgraduate study. Commissioner Howell said that as a matter of ordinary language "a course" is "a unified sequence of study, tuition and/or practical training, undertaken at or by arrangement with the education or training establishment, and intended to lead to one or more qualifications obtained on its completion," including modular courses leading to a single degree. He said that "a person who aspires to practice in a profession that requires more than one separately obtained qualification for which educational establishments do not provide a single sequence of tuition and/or experience, starts and completes one "course" and then moves on to another, rather than being engaged on one continuous "course" gaining intermediate qualifications and experience along the way": para 17. Thus if such a claimant has completed one course, s/he is not a full-time student in the period until s/he starts the next course. Note, however, the special rules for "sandwich courses".

R(JSA) 2/02 dealt with a claimant who had been attending a course at an educational establishment that provided training and education to enable her/him to take examinations that were set and marked by another, unconnected body. He failed the examinations and intended to re-sit them. Commissioner Williams said that it was possible to abandon, or be dismissed from, a course of training without abandoning or being dismissed from a course of examinations: para 11. This means that someone could cease to be a full-time student when a course is abandoned, even if s/he intends to re-sit the examinations at a later date.

If someone is taking time-out from study because of pregnancy, the rules do not provide relief. The JSA rules were challenged on the grounds that they directly discriminated against women. However, the Court of Appeal in *Secretary of State for Social Security v Walter* [2002] ICR 540 (reported as *R(JSA) 3/02*) rejected the arguments for the claimant. The Court did not, however, consider or decide on whether the rules were *indirectly* discriminatory (ie, whether they had a disproportionate impact on women) nor if such discrimination was proved, whether it could be objectively justified. It also did not consider whether the rules were incompatible with the Human Rights Act.

CJSA 825/2004 did consider the question of indirect discrimination in relation to a pregnant student who had taken leave of absence from her course but only EU law was raised. The commissioner held that the relevant pools for comparison were (1) male students who had taken leave of absence and (2) female students who had taken such leave, but that there was no statistical evidence to demonstrate that the latter class were disproportionately affected by the legislation.

Human Rights Act arguments were considered by the Upper Tribunal in *CM v SSWP* [2009] UKUT 43 (AAC); R(IS) 7/09. The claimant argued that the provision preventing a pregnant student claiming IS while taking a leave of absence from her course was indirectly discriminatory against women, alternatively pregnant women, because only women could become pregnant. Judge Lloyd Davies refused the claimant's appeal. He held as follows.

(1)   The right to claim a non-contributory social security benefit was within the scope or ambit of Art 1 of Protocol 1 to the European Convention on Human Rights so as to enable Art 14 to be engaged: *R(RJM) v SSWP* [2008] UKHL 63, 22 October 2008.

(2)   The denial of the claimant's claim was not within the ambit of Art 2 of Protocol 1 (right to education). The claimant had argued that the denial of IS to pregnant intercalating students meant that such students would be more likely to be forced to abandon their course (rather than take a leave of absence) so as to have means of subsistence. However, the claimant did not in fact abandon her course, but chose to intercalate. The judge therefore decided that there had been no denial of the right of education to the claimant (whose personal circumstances caused her to interrupt her course).

(3)   Statistics are not a necessary pre-condition for indirect discrimination to be adduced for the purposes of Art 14, taken with Art 1 of Protocol 1. Pregnancy is an "other status" for the purposes of Art 14. Rather than seeking to establish comparators, it is better to concentrate on the reasons for the difference in treatment and whether they amount to an objective and reasonable justification: *AL (Serbia) v Home Secretary* [2008] HL 42.

(4)   Having considered whether there was an objective and reasonable justification for the policy of disentitling pregnant intercalating students from IS (thereby distinguishing them from students who intercalate for other reasons), the judge held that there was. He said that, notwithstanding the lack of mention of pregnancy, "the policy behind the regulatory structure is that students who intercalate for essentially transient reasons (even through no fault of their own) should not receive benefit, but should rely on such support as might be available from the education authorities concerned. The later period of pregnancy cannot, given this policy, be distinguished from the periods (such as of illness or caring responsibilities) for which other students, who might also be regarded as hard cases, are denied benefit: once the policy of non-recognition of transient reasons for non-entitlement to benefit is accepted (and there was no general challenge to that policy before me), then I consider that there is objective and reasonable justification for the inclusion of intercalating students during the later term of their pregnancy within that policy."

Note that once the baby is born, the claimant may qualify for HB on the grounds of one of the exceptions in para (2) – eg, because s/he qualifies for IS or because s/he is a lone parent.

Student's eligible housing costs

57.–(1)   Subject to paragraphs (2) and (4), housing benefit shall not be payable during the period of study in respect of payments made by a student to an educational establishment which the student is attending.

(2)   Subject to paragraph (4), where the educational establishment itself pays rent for the dwelling occupied by the student as his home to a third party (other than to another educational establishment) the provisions of paragraph (1) shall only apply if rent is payable under the terms of a long tenancy or to an education authority which has provided the dwelling in exercise of its functions as an education authority.

(3)   Where it appears to the relevant authority that an educational establishment has arranged for accommodation to be provided by a person or body other than itself in order to take advantage of the housing benefit scheme, housing benefit shall not be payable during the period of study in respect of payments made to that person or body by a student.

(4)   Housing benefit shall be payable during the period of study in respect of payments made by a student to an educational establishment which the student is attending where the student–

(a)   is one who falls within a category specified in regulation 56(2); or

(b)   would fall within a category specified in regulation 56(2)(b) to (j) if he were a full-time student.

Definitions

"education authority" – see reg 53.
"dwelling" – see reg 2(4) and s137(1) SSCBA.
"long tenancy" – see reg 2(1).
"payments" – see reg 2(1).
"period of study" – see reg 53.
"rent" – see Part 3.
"student" – see reg 53.

General Note

The object of this regulation is to prevent students who pay rent to the educational establishment which they are attending, other than those to whom para (4) applies, from claiming HB, at least during their "period of study" (for which see reg 53(1)), whether they are full-time students or not. The rule also applies if a claimant's *partner* is a student but the claimant is not: see reg 58. In this case, the claimant is treated as if s/he is a student.

Para (2) provides an exception where the educational establishment is effectively acting as a letting agency for a third party, provided that third party is not another educational establishment, and that the establishment which is being paid does not have the property in question on a long tenancy from the third party.

Para (3) is an "anti-avoidance" device designed to stop bogus arrangements where the student pays a third party but the money ends up with the educational establishment.

Analysis

Para (1). The provision only has effect during the period of study, so students who rent from their institution during the summer vacation do not fall within its scope if the vacation is not part of their "period of study". Moreover, the institution from which the claimant rents must be the same one that the claimant is attending. However, such students may fall foul of para (3). An argument that para (1) is *ultra vires* was rejected by the High Court in *R (Bierman) v Secretary of State for Work and Pensions* [2004] EWHC 1024 (Admin), 23 April, unreported. Mr Justice Davis rejected the argument that ss130 and 137(2) SSCBA 1992 only empower the making of regulations which state that a person is not liable to pay rent and do not allow for regulations which speak of HB not being "payable". In the Court's view, the precise form of language used in reg 50(1) HB Regs 1987 (now reg 57(1) HB Regs) was not important; the intent was clearly to exclude entitlement for students who pay rent to the educational establishment which they are attending, and that intent is within the broad powers conferred by s130(2) SSCBA 1992. Moreover, the power to prescribe in s130(2) is not limited by the terms of s137(2) to regulations which speak about treating persons as not being 'liable' to make payments in respect of a dwelling.

Para (2). For the meaning of "dwelling occupied by the student as his home", see reg 7(3) and (6)(b), and reg 55. If the other establishment is not providing the accommodation in question "in the exercise of its functions", as where the institution has purchased property as an investment, the student should be able to claim HB if the rest of this paragraph is satisfied.

Para (3). It is suggested that the question of whether the institution has sought to "take advantage" of the HB scheme must be determined in the same way as a question as to whether a tenancy has been created for that purpose. See the Analysis to reg 9(1)(l) on p262. A student refused HB under this provision has the normal rights to challenge a decision. GM C2.94 states that the exclusion will not apply when rent is paid to a housing association. There is no statutory basis for this statement, but it is unlikely that an arrangement at arms' length will fall foul of this paragraph.

Para (4). The government recognised that living away from campus was preventing some students (in particular disabled students and lone parents) from having easy access to all the facilities that an educational establishment provides and to mix easily with other students. It also recognised that those who needed to live in accommodation provided by the educational establishment in order to attend a course, who could not afford such accommodation, might be prevented from taking up places on courses. Para (4) enables certain students to claim HB in respect of accommodation which they rent from their educational establishment. There are two categories:

(1) Full-time students who are exempt from the general exclusion from HB by reg 56(2): sub-para (a).
(2) Part-time students who would be exempt from the general exclusion from HB by reg 56(2) if they were full-time students, unless they would only be exempt because they are on IS, income-based JSA or income-related ESA: sub-para (b).

Note that students who are only exempt from the general exclusion from HB under reg 56(6) (ie, while waiting to return to a course following a period of incapacity or caring) do not come within either category. Presumably few of these students would be living in accommodation rented from the educational establishment during a "period of study" in any case, in which case reg 57 would not apply: see para(1).

Student partners

58.   Where a claimant is not, but his partner is, a student, the provisions of regulation 57 (student's eligible housing costs) shall apply as if the claimant were a student.

General Note

See commentary to reg 57 on p408.

SECTION 3
Income

General Note on Section 3

See General Note on this Part. This Section sets out the special rules for treatment of student income, namely grant, loan and fee loan income (regs 59, 64, 64A and 69) as well as covenant income (regs 60 and 61) and payments from access funds (reg 65). It supplements, and to some extent modifies, the provisions of Part 6 of these regulations. Regs 63, 66 and 67 provide for additional disregards from a student's income which is other than grants, loans or covenant income. Reg 68 sets out situations when certain student income is to be treated as capital.

Other types of income received by students are dealt with under the ordinary income and capital rules found in Part 6. Note that education maintenance allowances (and similar payments) paid to young people on certain non-advanced courses are excluded from the definition of "grant" and are dealt with separately. They are disregarded as income under Sch 5 para 11 and as capital under Sch 6 para 51. Career development loans paid under s2 Employment and Training Act 1973 are taken into account as income (reg 41(4)) with provision for some or all of such loans to be disregarded (Sch 5 para 13).

The effect of the apportionment rules on entitlement to HB

Grant income is in general spread over the weeks in a student's "period of study": see reg 53(1). A period of study can be a period of less than a calendar year – eg, it can exclude the summer vacation. Loan income is generally spread over the weeks in a student's "academic year": see reg 53(1). An academic year is a period of up to 12 months. Covenant income is spread over both the period of study and the academic year. For this reason, grant, loan and covenant income can be taken into account over different periods. This means that a student may be entitled to HB (or have increased entitlement to HB) outside her/his period of study. A fresh claim or a supersession request is required in these circumstances.

Calculation of grant income

59.–(1)   The amount of a student's grant income to be taken into account shall, subject to paragraphs (2) and (3), be the whole of his grant income.

(2)   There shall be excluded from a student's grant income any payment–

(a)   intended to meet tuition fees or examination fees;
(b)   in respect of the student's disability;
(c)   intended to meet additional expenditure connected with term time residential study away from the student's educational establishment;
(d)   on account of the student maintaining a home at a place other than that at which he resides during his course;

(e) on account of any other person but only if that person is residing outside of the United Kingdom and there is no applicable amount in respect of him;

(f) intended to meet the cost of books and equipment;

(g) intended to meet travel expenses incurred as a result of his attendance on the course;

(h) intended for the child care costs of a child dependant.

[⁴ (i) of higher education bursary for care leavers made under Part III of the Children Act 1989.]

(3) Where a student does not have a student loan and is not treated as possessing such a loan, there shall be excluded from the student's grant income–

(a) the sum of [⁵ £303] in respect of travel costs; and

(b) the sum of [⁵ £390] towards the costs of books and equipment,

whether or not any such costs are incurred.

[¹ (4) There shall also be excluded from a student's grant income the grant for dependants known as the parents' learning allowance paid pursuant to regulations made under Article 3 of the Education (Student Support) (Northern Ireland) Order 1998 or section 22 of the Teaching and Higher Education Act 1998.]

(5) Subject to paragraphs (6) and (7), a student's grant income shall be apportioned–

(a) subject to paragraph (8), in a case where it is attributable to the period of study, equally between the weeks in the period beginning with the benefit week, the first day of which coincides with, or immediately follows, the first day of the period of study and ending with the benefit week, the last day of which coincides with, or immediately precedes, the last day of the period of study;

(b) in any other case, equally between the weeks in the period beginning with the benefit week, the first day of which coincides with, or immediately follows, the first day of the period for which it is payable and ending with the benefit week, the last day of which coincides with, or immediately precedes, the last day of the period for which it is payable.

(6) Any grant in respect of dependants paid under section 63(6) of the Health Services and Public Health Act 1968 (grants in respect of the provision of instruction to officers of hospital authorities) and any amount intended for the maintenance of dependants under Part 3 of Schedule 2 to the Education (Mandatory Awards) Regulations 2003 shall be apportioned equally over the period of 52 weeks or, if there are 53 benefit weeks (including part-weeks) in the year, 53.

(7) In a case where a student is in receipt of a student loan or where he could have acquired a student loan by taking reasonable steps but had not done so, any amount intended for the maintenance of dependants to which neither paragraph (6) nor regulation 63(2) (other amounts to be disregarded) apply, shall be apportioned over the same period as the student's loan is apportioned or, as the case may be, would have been apportioned.

(8) In the case of a student on a sandwich course, any periods of experience within the period of study shall be excluded and the student's grant income shall be apportioned equally between the weeks in the period beginning with the benefit week, the first day of which immediately follows the last day of the period of experience and ending with the benefit week, the last day of which coincides with, or immediately precedes, the last day of the period of study.

Amendments

1. Substituted by reg 3(2) and (3) of SI 2006 No 1752 as from, for students whose period of study begins on or after 1.8.06 but before 1.9.06, on the day the period of study begins; in any other case 1.9.06.
2. Substituted by reg 4(2) of SI 2007 No 1632 as from, in the case of a person whose period of study begins on or after 1.8.07 but before 1.9.07, on the day the period of study begins; in any other case, 1.9.07.
3. Amended by reg 5(3) of SI 2008 No 1599 as from, for students whose period of study begins on or after 1.8.08 but before 1.9.08, on the day the period of study begins; in any other case 1.9.08.
4. Inserted by reg 6(8) of SI 2009 No 583 as from 6.4.09.
5. Amended by reg 2 of SI 2009 No 1575 as from, for students whose period of study begins on or after 1.8.09 but before 1.9.09, on the day the period of study begins; in any other case 1.9.09.

Definitions

"applicable amount" – see Part 5.

"benefit week" – see reg 2(1).

"child" – see reg 2(1).

"full-time student" – see reg 53.

"grant" and "grant income" – see reg 53.

"periods of experience" – see reg 53.

"period of study" – see reg 53.

"sandwich course" – see reg 53.

"student" – see reg 53.

"UK" – includes Northern Ireland.

General Note

Para (1) provides the general rule that a student's grant income is to be taken into account in full, whether or not s/he is in full-time education (see the definition of "student" in reg 53). Paras (2) to (4) list parts of the student's grant income which must be ignored.

Paras (5) to (7) set out the period over which grant income as calculated in paras (1) to (4) is to be taken into account, and how weekly amounts are to be calculated.

Reg 69 provides for treatment of changes in the amount of standard maintenance grant that occur in the recognised summer vacation. If that summer vacation does not form part of the student's period of study, the change is ignored from the date it occurs to the end of the vacation.

Note that if a student is eligible for a student loan in addition to a grant, the amounts disregarded for travel, books and equipment under para (3) are applied to the loan rather than the grant income under reg 64(5).

Analysis

Para (1). For the meaning of "grant income", see the Analysis to reg 53 on p399.

Paras (2) and (4). The total of any amounts listed under these paragraphs which apply to a claimant are to be disregarded. The categories are in general self-explanatory.

Under para (2)(b), payments in respect of the student's disability are to be disregarded. For example GM C2.322 tells local authorities to disregard Disabled Students Allowances as they are paid to provide help towards the costs of a non-medical helper, major items of equipment, travel costs and other items.

Under para (2)(e), payments "on account of any other person" outside the UK who is not residing with the claimant could include, for example, payments on account of a partner or child, but only if there is no HB applicable amount in respect of her/him.

Under para (2)(h), payments intended for the childcare costs of a child dependant may only be disregarded if they are for a child under the age of 16: see the definition of "child" in reg 2(1).

Note that the payments disregarded under para (2) are those "intended" for or paid "on account of" the types of expenditure mentioned or in respect of a student's disability, so there is no requirement that the student uses the payments for the items listed. See also regs 62, 63 and 67.

Para (3) permits the deductions from grant income listed, but only where a student does not have a loan and cannot be treated as having one – eg, under reg 64(3). These are flat-rate deductions in respect of books, equipment and travel, whether or not the costs are incurred. They are generally uprated annually, but are not to be uprated in 2010. If the student has a loan, see reg 64(5).

Apportionment of grant income

Para (5)(a). Except in the case of a sandwich course (see para (8)) where a grant is said to be in respect of the "period of study" (see reg 53) it is divided equally between the weeks which that period covers.

Para (5)(b). In any other case (ie, where a grant is not said to be in respect of the "period of study"), grant income is divided equally between the weeks in the period for which it is payable.

Para (6) deals with apportionment of grants for dependants paid under specific provisions. These are divided equally over 52 (or 53) benefit weeks.

Para (7) deals with grants for dependants not covered by para (6), paid to students in receipt of student loans or students who could receive a loan by taking reasonable steps. Note that reg 63(2) was omitted by SI 2009 No.583 from 6 April 2009.

The grant for dependants is apportioned over the same period as the loan (see reg 64). Note that where a claimant could have obtained a student loan but did not in fact do so, s/he is treated as being in receipt of one: reg 64(3)(b). If a student abandons or is dismissed from a course, the rules in reg 40(7), (8) and (9) specify how payments referred to in para (7) must be treated.

Para (8). If the student is on a "sandwich course" and the grant is said to be in respect of the "period of study", it should be divided equally over the weeks in that period during which the student is not on a "period of experience".

Calculation of covenant income where a contribution is assessed

60.–(1)   Where a student is in receipt of income by way of a grant during a period of study and a contribution has been assessed, the amount of his covenant income to be taken into account for that period and any summer vacation immediately following shall be the whole amount of the covenant income less, subject to paragraph (3), the amount of the contribution.

(2)   The weekly amount of the student's covenant income shall be determined–

(a)   by dividing the amount of income which falls to be taken into account under paragraph (1) by 52 or 53, whichever is reasonable in the circumstances; and

(b)   by disregarding from the resulting amount, £5.

(3)   For the purposes of paragraph (1), the contribution shall be treated as increased by the amount (if any) by which the amount excluded under regulation 59(2)(g) (calculation of grant income) falls short of the amount specified in paragraph 7(2) of Schedule 2 to the Education (Mandatory Awards) Regulations 2003 (travel expenditure).

Definitions
"contribution" – see reg 53.
"covenant income" – see reg 53.
"grant" – see reg 53.
"income" – see Part 6 also.
"period of study" – see reg 53.
"student" – see reg 53.

General Note
Prior to 1988, there was a provision for students to be paid under a deed of covenant whereby the payer could deduct the appropriate rate of tax from the gross amount of the payment and pay the student the net amount. The student could then claim a refund of the tax deducted, the refund being treated as capital under reg 68(1). Such tax relief has not been available since April 1988.

It is understood that it is now unlikely that there are any students still receiving covenant income. For general notes on, and an analysis of the rules for covenant income, see earlier editions of this work.

Covenant income where no grant income or no contribution is assessed

61.–(1)   Where a student is not in receipt of income by way of a grant the amount of his covenant income shall be calculated as follows–

(a)   any sums intended for any expenditure specified in regulation 59(2)(a) to (e) (calculation of grant income) necessary as a result of his attendance on the course shall be disregarded;

(b)   any covenant income, up to the amount of the standard maintenance grant, which is not so disregarded, shall be apportioned equally between the weeks of the period of study;

(c)   there shall be disregarded from the amount so apportioned the amount which would have been disregarded under regulation 59(2)(f) and (3) (calculation of grant income) had the student been in receipt of the standard maintenance grant; and

(d)   the balance, if any, shall be divided by 52 or 53 whichever is reasonable in the circumstances and treated as weekly income of which £5 shall be disregarded.

(2)   Where a student is in receipt of income by way of a grant and no contribution has been assessed, the amount of his covenanted income shall be calculated in accordance with sub-paragraphs (a) to (d) of paragraph (1), except that–

(a)   the value of the standard maintenance grant shall be abated by the amount of such grant income less an amount equal to the amount of any sums disregarded under regulation 59(2)(a) to (e); and

(b)   the amount to be disregarded under paragraph (1)(c) shall be abated by an amount equal to the amount of any sums disregarded under regulation 59(2)(f) and (g) and (3).

General Note
See General Note to reg 60.

Relationship with amounts to be disregarded under Schedule 5

62. No part of a student's covenant income or grant income shall be disregarded under [¹ paragraph 14] of Schedule 5 [²].

Amendments

1. Substituted by reg 3(4) of SI 2006 No 1752 as from, for students whose period of study begins on or after 1.8.06 but before 1.9.06, on the day the period of study begins; in any other case 1.9.06.
2. Amended by reg 15(3) of SI 2006 No 2378 from the 1st day of the 1st benefit week to commence on or after 2.10.06.

General Note

This provides that the disregard of, for example, charitable or voluntary payments under para 14 of Sch 5 cannot apply to a claimant's covenant or grant income at all.

Other amounts to be disregarded

63.–(1) For the purposes of ascertaining income other than grant income, covenant income and loans treated as income in accordance with regulation 64 (treatment of student loans), any amounts intended for any expenditure specified in regulation 59(2) (calculation of grant income), necessary as a result of his attendance on the course shall be disregarded but only if, and to the extent that, the necessary expenditure exceeds or is likely to exceed the amount of the sums disregarded under regulation 59(2) or (3), 60(3), 61 (1)(a) or (c) or 64(5) (calculation of grant income, covenant income and treatment of student loans) on like expenditure.

[² (2)]

Amendments

1. Amended by reg 3(8) of SI 2008 No 1042 as from 19.5.08.
2. Omitted by reg 6(9) of SI 2009 No 583 as from 6.4.09.

Definitions

"covenant income" – see reg 53.
"grant income" – see reg 53.

General Note

This deals with income other than grant income, covenant income and student loans treated as income under reg 64 – eg, gifts, etc. Any amounts intended for some or all of the items listed in reg 59(2) which are necessary for attendance on the student's course are disregarded, but only to the extent that the total necessary expenditure on these items exceeds (or is likely to exceed) the amounts actually disregarded (from grant, covenant and loan income) by the regulations listed: para (1).

It is unclear whether sums covered by this regulation, and which are not to be disregarded, are to be taken into account over a full year or just over the "period of study". It is submitted that how the money is intended to be used is relevant – eg, if a grandparent makes a gift for the student's maintenance during the period of study it should only be taken into account over that period.

Treatment of student loans

64.–(1) A student loan shall be treated as income.

(2) In calculating the weekly amount of the loan to be taken into account as income–

(a) in respect of a course that is of a single academic year's duration or less, a loan which is payable in respect of that period shall be apportioned equally between the weeks in the period beginning with–

(i) except in a case where head (ii) applies, the benefit week, the first day of which coincides with, or immediately follows, the first day of the single academic year;

(ii) where the student is required to start attending the course in August or where the course is less than an academic year's duration, the benefit week, the first day of which coincides with, or immediately follows, the first day of the course,

and ending with the benefit week, the last day of which coincides with, or immediately precedes, the last day of the course;

(b)   in respect of an academic year of a course which starts other than on 1st September, a loan which is payable in respect of that academic year shall be apportioned equally between the weeks in the period beginning with the benefit week the first day of which coincides with or immediately follows, the first day of that academic year and ending with the benefit week, the last day of which coincides with or immediately precedes, the last day of that academic year but excluding any benefit weeks falling entirely within the quarter during which, in the opinion of the Secretary of State, the longest of any vacation is taken and for the purposes of this sub-paragraph, ''quarter'' shall have the same meaning as for the purposes of the Education (Student Support) Regulations 2005;

(c)   in respect of the final academic year of a course (not being a course of a single year's duration), a loan which is payable in respect of that final academic year shall be apportioned equally between the weeks in the period beginning with–

(i)   except in a case where head (ii) applies, the benefit week, the first day of which coincides with, or immediately follows, the first day of that academic year;

(ii)   where the final academic year starts on 1st September, the benefit week, the first day of which coincides with, or immediately follows, the earlier of 1st September or the first day of the autumn term,

and ending with the benefit week, the last day of which coincides with, or immediately precedes, the last day of the course;

(d)   in any other case, the loan shall be apportioned equally between the weeks in the period beginning with the earlier of–

(i)   the first day of the first benefit week in September; or

(ii)   the benefit week, the first day of which coincides with, or immediately follows the first day of the autumn term,

and ending with the benefit week, the last day of which coincides with, or immediately precedes, the last day of June,

and, in all cases, from the weekly amount so apportioned there shall be disregarded £10.

(3)   A student shall be treated as possessing a student loan in respect of an academic year where–

(a)   a student loan has been made to him in respect of that year; or

(b)   he could acquire such a loan in respect of that year by taking reasonable steps to do so.

(4)   Where a student is treated as possessing a student loan under paragraph (3), the amount of the student loan to be taken into account as income shall be, subject to paragraph (5)–

(a)   in the case of a student to whom a student loan is made in respect of an academic year, a sum equal to–

(i)   the maximum student loan he is able to acquire in respect of that year by taking reasonable steps to do so; and

(ii)   any contribution whether or not it has been paid;

(b)   in the case of a student to whom a student loan is not made in respect of an academic year, the maximum student loan that would be made to the student if–

(i)   he took all reasonable steps to obtain the maximum student loan he is able to acquire in respect of that year; and

(ii)   no deduction in that loan was made by virtue of the application of a means test.

(5)   There shall be deducted from the amount of a student's loan income–

(a)   the sum of [4 £303] in respect of travel costs; and

(b)   the sum of [4 £390] towards the cost of books and equipment,

whether or not any such costs are incurred.

Amendments

1.   Substituted by reg 3(2) of SI 2006 No 1752 as from, for students whose period of study begins on or after 1.8.06 but before 1.9.06, on the day the period of study begins; in any other case 1.9.06.

2.   Substituted by reg 4(3) of SI 2007 No 1632 as from, in the case of a person whose period of study begins on or after 1.8.07 but before 1.9.07, on the day the period of study begins; in any other case, 1.9.07.

3. Amended by reg 5(4) of SI 2008 No 1599 as from, for students whose period of study begins on or after 1.8.08 but before 1.9.08, on the day the period of study begins; in any other case 1.9.08.
4. Amended by reg 2 of SI 2009 No 1575 as from, for students whose period of study begins on or after 1.8.09 but before 1.9.09, on the day the period of study begins; in any other case 1.9.09.

Definitions

"academic year" – see reg 53.
"benefit week" – see reg 2(1).
"contribution" – see reg 2(1).
"last day of course" – see reg 53.
"student loan" – see reg 53.
"year" – see reg 53.

General Note

Under para (1) a "student loan" is treated as income. It is disregarded as capital under para 22 of Sch 6.

Note: career development loans paid pursuant to s2 Employment and Training Act 1973 are dealt with under reg 41(4) and Sch 5 para 13.

Under para (2), the loan is apportioned on a weekly basis over the length of the course or the academic year. Note that the definition of "academic year" (reg 53(1)) specifies that where a course begins during August or September, the academic year of the course is considered to start on 1 September.

Under para (3), a student is treated as having a loan even where s/he has not applied for one, provided that s/he could obtain one. S/he is deemed to have the maximum loan available: para (4).

Under para (5), set deductions are made from loan income in respect of travel, books and equipment, whether or not the costs are incurred.

Note that if a student abandons or is dismissed from a course, the rules in reg 40(7) to (9) specify how a loan must be treated.

Loans paid to part-time students towards books and travel are dealt with under this regulation. So if they are paid at a lower rate than the combination of disregards available for books and equipment and travel costs they are disregarded in full.

Analysis

Para (2). How a student loan is to be apportioned, in general depends on whether the course lasts for one year or for a longer period. There are four possibilities.

(1) Courses that last for a single academic year or less: sub-para (a). The loan is divided equally between the weeks in the period beginning with the start of the academic year (or for courses starting in August or lasting less than a year, the first day of the course) and ending on the last day of the course.
(2) Courses that start other than on 1 September: sub-para (b). If the academic year of a course starts other than on 1 September, the loan is divided equally between the weeks in the period from the first to the last days of the academic year. Any benefit weeks falling entirely within the quarter during which, in the opinion of the DWP, the longest vacation is taken, must be disregarded. "Quarter" in relation to an academic year, means a period in that year from 1 January to 31 March, 1 April to 30 June, 1 July to 31 August, or 1 September to 31 December. If it is the final academic year of the course, see (3) below.
(3) The final academic year of a course: sub-para (c). Unless the course is for a single year (for which see (1) above), the loan payable in respect of the final academic year of a student's course is apportioned as follows. If the academic year starts on 1 September, the loan is to be divided equally between the weeks in the period beginning with the earliest of 1 September or the first day of the autumn term and ending with the benefit week the last day of which coincides with or immediately precedes the last day of the course. In other cases, the loan is divided equally between the weeks in the period from the first day of the academic year to the benefit week the last day of which coincides with or immediately precedes the last day of the course.
(4) Any other case: sub-para (d). Unless it is the final year of the course (for which see (3) above), sub-para (d) applies to courses of more than an academic year's duration where the academic year starts on 1 September. The loan is divided equally between the weeks in the period beginning with the earlier of the first benefit week in September or in the autumn term and ending on the benefit week the last day of which coincides with or immediately precedes the last day of June.

In all four cases, a £10 weekly disregard must be applied. Note, however, that this disregard can overlap with disregards from covenant income and access funds as well as disregards from certain types of war pension income. A combined maximum of £20 is allowed: Sch 5 para 34.

Paras (3) and (4). A student is treated as possessing a student loan where one has been made to her/him, as well as where s/he could acquire a loan by taking reasonable steps to do so: para (3). GM C2.120 points out that student loans are available to most eligible full-time British students in higher education, except for some students aged 50 to 55 and those over 55 when their course started. They are also available to postgraduate students studying for a Postgraduate Certificate of Education (PGCE).

The Housing Benefit Regulations 2006

The meaning of the phrase "he could acquire such a loan . . . by taking reasonable steps to do so" was considered in *CH 4429/2006*. The claimant's partner had not taken out a student loan because strongly held religious beliefs prohibited him from doing so. The claimant argued that it was therefore not reasonable for her partner to apply for a student loan. However, the commissioner said that the regulation refers to "reasonable steps", that is, it qualifies the steps which must be taken to acquire a loan. It is not concerned with other matters such as the motives and religious beliefs of the claimant. It is the mechanics of obtaining a loan that must be considered. The commissioner also decided that there was no breach of Art 14 of the European Convention on Human Rights.

The amount of loan then taken into account is the maximum amount of loan the student would be able to acquire if s/he took reasonable steps to do so, even if less than this amount (or no loan) is actually borrowed: para (4). In the case of a student who has taken out a loan, any contribution assessed is also taken into account, even if it has not been paid: para (4)(a)(ii). In the case of a student who has not taken out a loan, no account is taken of any deduction in that loan that could have been made as a result of the means-test.

Para (5). Under para (5), flat rate deductions must be made for travel costs, books and equipment, whether or not costs are incurred. These are generally uprated annually, but will not be uprated in 2010.

[¹ Treatment of fee loans

64A. A loan for fees, known as a fee loan or a fee contribution loan, made pursuant to regulations made under Article 3 of the Education (Student Support) (Northern Ireland) Order 1998, section 22 of the Teaching and Higher Education Act 1998 or section 73(f) of the Education (Scotland) Act 1980, shall be disregarded as income.]

Amendment

1.   Inserted by reg 3(5) of SI 2006 No 1752 as from, for students whose period of study begins on or after 1.8.06 but before 1.9.06, on the day the period of study begins; in any other case 1.9.06.

General Note

Eligible full-time higher education students can take out student loans to pay their fee contribution to the college or university. Reg 64A allows for these loans to be disregarded in full. Note that some students are eligible for means-tested fee grants. It is understood that these are paid directly to the college or university so would not count as the notional income or capital of the student (payments to a third party in respect of a claimant) under regs 42(6)(b) and 49(3)(a) HB Regs. See also reg 59(2)(a) on p409.

Treatment of payments from access funds

65.–(1)   This regulation applies to payments from access funds that are not payments to which regulation 68(2) or (3) (income treated as capital) applies.

(2)   A payment from access funds, other than a payment to which paragraph (3) applies, shall be disregarded as income.

(3)   Subject to paragraph (5) of this regulation and paragraph 34 of Schedule 5, any payments from access funds which are intended and used for food, household fuel or rent or ordinary clothing or footwear, of a single claimant or any other member of his family, and any payments from access funds which are used for any council tax or water charges for which that claimant or member is liable shall be disregarded as income to the extent of £20 per week.

(4)   For the purposes of paragraph (3), ''rent'' means eligible rent less any deductions in respect of non-dependants which fall to be made under regulation 74 (non-dependant deductions).

(5)   Where a payment from access funds is made–

(a)   on or after 1st September or the first day of the course, whichever first occurs, but before receipt of any student loan in respect of that year and that payment is intended for the purpose of bridging the period until receipt of the student loan; or

(b)   before the first day of the course to a person in anticipation of that person becoming a student,

that payment shall be disregarded as income.

General Note

Access funds are discretionary funds administered by colleges and universities who may call these funds by other names – eg, hardship funds, access bursaries, mature students' bursaries, childcare support, Access to Learning Fund, Financial Contigency Fund or Learner Support Fund.

Most payments from access funds which do not fall to be treated as capital under reg 68 (ie, which are not single lump sums) are disregarded: para (2). However, those intended for and used for specified basic necessities will be taken into account with a £20 disregard: para (3). Note, however, that this disregard can overlap with disregards from covenant income and student loan income as well as disregards from certain types of war pension income. A combined maximum of £20 is allowed: Sch 5 para 34. "Rent" is defined in para (4) and "ordinary clothing or footwear" in reg 2(1). Under para (5), an access fund payment used effectively as a bridging loan until a loan can be obtained is ignored, as is a payment made before the student commences study.

Disregard of contribution and rent

66. Where the claimant or his partner is a student and, for the purposes of assessing a contribution to the student's grant or student loan, the other partner's income has been taken into account, an amount equal to that contribution shall be disregarded for the purposes of assessing that other partner's income.

General Note

This provides for an income disregard where a student's partner has been assessed for a contribution to her/his grant or loan. That contribution is taken into account as income and so, to avoid double counting, an equal amount of the contributing partner's income is disregarded.

Further disregard of student's income

67. Where any part of a student's income has already been taken into account for the purposes of assessing his entitlement to a grant or student loan, the amount taken into account shall be disregarded in assessing that student's income.

General Note

This applies where a student has been assessed as liable to make a contribution towards his/her *own* grant or loan by the education authority. In this case, the amount of income taken into account is disregarded under this regulation.

Amounts treated as capital

68.–(1) Any amount by way of a refund of tax deducted from a student's covenant income shall be treated as capital.

(2) An amount paid from access funds as a single lump sum shall be treated as capital.

(3) An amount paid from access funds as a single lump sum which is intended and used for an item other than food, household fuel, rent, ordinary clothing or footwear of a single claimant or, as the case may be, of the claimant or any other member of his family, or which is used for any council tax or water charges for which that claimant or member is liable, shall be disregarded as capital but only for a period of 52 weeks from the date of the payment.

(4) In paragraph (3), "rent" means eligible rent less any deductions in respect of non-dependants which fall to be made under regulation 74 (non-dependant deductions).

General Note

See p412 on covenant income. Refunds of income tax deducted from a student's covenant income are treated as capital as are single payment access fund payments. An amount paid from access funds intended for and used for items other than specified basic necessities must be disregarded for 52 weeks from payment. "Rent" is defined in para (4) and "ordinary clothing and footware" in reg 2(1).

Disregard of changes occurring during summer vacation

69. In calculating a student's income the relevant authority shall disregard any change in the standard maintenance grant, occurring in the recognised summer vacation appropriate to the student's course, if that vacation does not form part of his period of study from the date on which the change occurred to the end of that vacation.

General Note

See the General Note to reg 59 on p411.

PART 8
Amount of benefit

General Note on Part 8

This Part provides the rules under which the amount of HB to which a person is entitled is calculated, as well as the two schemes for extended payments of HB.

Reg 70 sets out the rules for ascertaining the appropriate maximum HB to which a particular claimant may be entitled. Reg 71 prescribes the taper – the percentage of the claimant's excess income which is to be deducted from maximum HB.

Regs 72 to 73D make provisions for extended payments of HB, where HB was payable, in the circumstances prescribed – ie, where entitlement to IS, income-based JSA, ESA, IB or SDA ceases on account of the commencement of employment or self-employment or an increase in the hours or earnings from such.

Reg 74 is ancillary to reg 70 in that a person's maximum HB is arrived at by deducting certain amounts in respect of "non-dependants" from the "eligible rent" figure calculated under regs 12B, 12C or 12D or regs 12 and 13 as set out in Sch 3 para 5 HB&CTB(CP) Regs. Reg 74 sets out the appropriate amounts to be deducted in respect of different categories of non-dependant as well as the situations when no deduction can be made.

Reg 75 is made under s134(4) SSCBA and prescribes the minimum weekly amount of HB to which a claimant may be entitled and actually paid.

If sanctions apply, a lower amount of HB than as calculated in this Part might be payable in the following circumstances:

(1)   A reduction can be applied for four weeks where the claimant or a member of her/his family is convicted of one or more benefit offences or agrees to pay a penalty or accepts a formal caution instead of being prosecuted (the "one strike" rule) or for 13 weeks if convicted of two or more offences within five years (the "two strikes" rule). The reduction is 20 or 40 per cent of the appropriate personal allowance for a single person of the claimant's age: ss6A, 6B, 7 and 9 SSFA 2001 (see p1134) and the Social Security (Loss of Benefit) Regulations 2001 (see p1185).

(2)   From 1 November 2007 until 31 October 2009, in pilot areas in England only, a reduction could be applied following eviction on the grounds of anti-social behaviour, where the claimant failed to comply with a notice from a local authority to improve behaviour (10 per cent for the first four weeks, 20 per cent for the next four weeks, then 100 per cent until the local authority considered the sanction should no longer apply or a period of five years had expired (30 percent if the former occupier was a "person in hardship")): ss130B SSCBA 1992 (see p6) and the Housing Benefit (Loss of Benefit) (Pilot Scheme) Regulations 2007 SI No.2202 (see the 22nd edition of this work, p1183).

Note: the Government has indicated that from April 2013:

(1)   HB awards will be reduced by 90 percent of the initial award after 12 months for claimants receiving JSA.

(2)   "Housing entitlements" for working age people in the social sector will reflect family size.

[¹ Maximum housing benefit

70.   The amount of a person's appropriate maximum housing benefit in any week shall be 100 per cent. of his eligible rent calculated on a weekly basis in accordance with regulation 80 and 81 (calculation of weekly amounts and rent free periods) less any deductions in respect of non-dependants which fall to be made under regulation 74 (non-dependant deductions).]

Modifications

Reg 70 was substituted by reg 12 Housing Benefit (Local Housing Allowance and Information Sharing) Amendment Regulations 2007 SI No.2868 as from 7 April 2008, save that for a person to whom reg 1(5) of those regulations applied (see p1231), the amendments came into force on the day on or after 7 April 2008 when the first of the events specified in reg 1(6) applied to her/him, or on 6 April 2009 if none had before that date.

Amendment

1.   Substituted by reg 12 of SI 2007 No 2868 as from 7.4.08 (or if reg 1(5) of that SI applies, on the day on or after 7.4.08 when the first of the events specified in reg 1(6) applies, or from 6.4.09 if none have before that date).

Definitions

"eligible rent" – see reg 2(1).
"non-dependants" – see reg 3.

General Note

Where a claimant is entitled to HB under s130(1)(c)(i) SSCBA (where s/he has no income or her/his income does not exceed her/his applicable amount) the maximum HB is what s/he will actually receive. Where s/he is entitled under s130(1)(c)(ii) of SSCBA (ie, where her/his income exceeds her/his applicable amount) the HB due is to be calculated by deducting the percentage of the claimant's "excess income" prescribed by reg 71 from the maximum HB to which s/he is potentially entitled. "Excess income" is the amount by which a claimant's income assessed under Part 6 exceeds her/his "applicable amount" under Part 5.

Note that authorities have powers to top up HB with discretionary housing payments under the Discretionary Financial Assistance Regulations 2001 (see p1176).

Analysis

This regulation (together with reg 74) is determinative of the maximum HB which can be paid in any week (though note the situation where there is entitlement to "extended payments" of HB under reg 72 or 73).

A person's maximum HB is calculated by reference to her/his weekly eligible rent. "Eligible rent" is calculated under regs 12B, 12C or 12D HB Regs or regs 12 and 13 as set out in Sch 3 para 5 HB&CTB(CP) Regs. Note the three rent restriction schemes that can reduce eligible rent where HB is paid as a rent allowance.

Regs 80 and 81 set out how eligible rent is to be calculated on a weekly basis. Any of the non-dependant deductions listed in reg 74 which apply must be deducted from the eligible rent to produce the appropriate maximum HB in any case. Note that any actual payments made to the claimant by the non-dependant are disregarded under Sch 5 para 21.

Where the claimant has for any reason to pay interest on the eligible rent, that interest cannot form part of the HB: *R v Kensington and Chelsea RBC ex p Brandt* [1995] 28 HLR 528, QBD.

Housing benefit tapers

71. The prescribed percentages for the purpose of sub-section (3)(b) of section 130 of the Act (percentage of excess of income over applicable amount which is deducted from maximum housing benefit) shall be 65 per cent.

Analysis

Reg 71 provides the percentage of excess income to deduct from maximum HB when calculating HB entitlement where the claimant is covered by s130(1)(c)(ii) SSCBA. HB in such a case is calculated as follows.

(1)   Work out weekly "eligible rent" under the relevant provision (see Part 3 HB Regs and regs 80 and 81). Work out weekly maximum HB under reg 70 by deducting non-dependant deductions under reg 74 (if applicable) from "eligible rent".

(2)   Work out by how much the claimant's income exceeds her/his applicable amount (for which see Parts 5 and 6 and Sch 3).

(3)   To calculate HB due, deduct 65 per cent of the excess income so calculated from maximum HB.

Example

The claimant, aged 30, is the sole tenant of a private rented, one-bedroom self-contained flat where she lives alone. She has net earnings of £145.45 a week. The contractual rent is £120 a week. The appropriate local housing allowance is £95.

Eligible rent is £95: reg 12D.

Maximum HB is £95: reg 70 (the claimant has no non-dependants).

Applicable amount is £65.45: Sch 3 para 1.

Income to be taken into account is £140.45: £5 of her earnings are disregarded under Sch 4 para 10.

The difference between income and applicable amount is £75 (£140.45 − £65.45). 65 per cent of £75 is £48.75.

The claimant is entitled to HB of £46.25 (£95 − £48.75).

[²Extended payments

72.–(1)   A claimant who is entitled to housing benefit (by virtue of the general conditions of entitlement) shall be entitled to an extended payment where–

    (a)   the claimant or the claimant's partner was entitled to a qualifying income-related benefit;

    (b)   entitlement to a qualifying income-related benefit ceased because the claimant or the claimant's partner–

        (i)   commenced employment as an employed or self-employed earner;

        (ii)   increased their earnings from such employment; or

        (iii)   increased the number of hours worked in such employment,

    and that employment is or, as the case may be, increased earnings or increased number of hours are expected to last five weeks or more; and

    (c)   the claimant or the claimant's partner had been entitled to and in receipt of a qualifying income-related benefit, jobseeker's allowance or a combination of those benefits for a continuous period of at least 26 weeks before the day on which the entitlement to a qualifying income-related benefit ceased.

(2)   For the purpose of paragraph (1)(c), a claimant or a claimant's partner is to be treated as having been entitled to and in receipt of a qualifying income-related benefit or jobseeker's allowance during any period of less than five weeks in respect of which the claimant or the claimant's partner was not entitled to any of those benefits because the claimant or the claimant's partner was engaged in remunerative work as a consequence of their participation in an employment zone programme.

(3)   For the purpose of this regulation, where a claimant or a claimant's partner is entitled to and in receipt of joint-claim jobseeker's allowance they shall be treated as being entitled to and in receipt of jobseeker's allowance.

(4)   A claimant must be treated as entitled to housing benefit by virtue of the general conditions of entitlement where–

(a)   the claimant ceased to be entitled to housing benefit because the claimant vacated the dwelling occupied as the claimant's home;

(b)   the day on which the claimant vacated the dwelling was either in the week in which entitlement to a qualifying income-related benefit ceased, or in the preceding week; and

(c)   entitlement to the qualifying income-related benefit ceased in any of the circumstances listed in paragraph (1)(b).

(5)   This regulation shall not apply where, on the day before a claimant's entitlement to income support ceased, regulation 6(5) of the Income Support Regulations(11) (remunerative work: housing costs) applied to that claimant.]

Amendments

1.   Amended by reg 13 of SI 2007 No 2868 as from 7.4.08 (or if reg 1(5) of that SI applies, on the day on or after 7.4.08 when the first of the events specified in reg 1(6) applies, or from 6.4.09 if none have before that date).

2.   Substituted by reg 2(2) of SI 2008 No 959 as from 6.10.08.

Definitions

"employed earner" – see reg 2(1).

"general conditions of entitlement" – see s34(2) WRA 2007.

"qualifying income-related benefit" – see reg 2(1).

"self-employed earner" – see reg 2(1).

General Note

Sections 32 to 34 WRA 2007 and regs 72 to 72D provide a scheme for "extended payments" of HB to be made to certain people who have been on IS, income-based JSA or *income-related* ESA for at least 26 weeks, who come off that benefit because they or their partners commence employment or increase hours or earnings. Extended payments of HB can be made for up to four weeks: reg 72B. It is important to note that entitlement to HB does not end when the entitlement to the qualifying income-related benefit ends but continues until at least the end of the extended payment period: reg 72D(1). Entitlement can continue beyond the end of the extended payment period under the normal rules of entitlement to HB.

Reg 72 sets out the general rules of entitlement to extended payments. Reg 72A deals with the amount of the extended payments. Reg 72C provides special rules for "movers" (defined in reg 2(1) on p214). Reg 72D deals with the relationship between extended payments and HB entitlement under the normal rules of entitlement.

No separate claim for extended payments of HB is necessary: s32(4) WRA 2007.

Prior to 6 October 2008, the scheme for extended payments of HB was found in the former version of reg 72 and Sch 7. The scheme was broadly similar to the current scheme, but with an important difference; HB entitlement under the normal rules of entitlement ended in the same circumstances in which a claimant qualified for extended payments: reg 77, now omitted by the Housing Benefit and Council Tax Benefit (Extended Payments) Amendment Regulations 2008 SI No.959. For entitlement to continue after the extended payment period, a fresh claim was therefore required. Such claims were given priority under reg 89(3) (now also omitted by SI 2008 No.959). See the 20th edition for commentary on the former version of the rules.

See regs 73 to 73D for a similar scheme where entitlement to *contributory* ESA, incapacity benefit or severe disablement allowance ceases for employment reasons.

Analysis

Paras (1) to (3) Para (1) sets out the basic conditions of entitlement to extended payments. The conditions are that:

(1)   the claimant was entitled to HB under the general conditions of entitlement while either s/he or her/his partner was entitled to a "qualifying income-related benefit", defined in reg 2(1) as IS, income-based JSA

and income-related ESA: s32(1) and (3) WRA 2007 and para (1)(a). "Income-based JSA" includes "joint-claim JSA" (see reg 2(1)). The "general conditions of entitlement" are those in Part 7 of the SSCBA 1992: s34(2) WRA 2007. Note that certain claimants who move home are deemed to satisfy the general conditions of entitlement under para (4);

(2)   entitlement to the "qualifying income-related benefit" ceased because of the commencement of employment or self-employment, or an increase in earnings from, or hours in, the employment. This must be expected to last at least five weeks: para (1)(b); and

(3)   the claimant or her/his partner had been entitled to and receiving IS, JSA (either income-based, joint-claim or contribution-based) or income-related ESA or a combination of those benefits for a continuous period of 26 weeks. This includes periods of less than five weeks when the claimant or partner counted as in remunerative work because of being on an "employment zone programme": paras (1)(c), (2) and (3).

Para (4) The claimant is to be treated as entitled HB under the general conditions of entitlement where s/he ceased to be entitled because s/he moved home either in the week entitlement to a "qualifying income-related benefit" ceased, or the week before that, and s/he ceased to be entitled to the qualifying income-related benefit in any of the circumstances set out in para (1)(b). See also the additional rules for "movers" in reg 72C.

For the importance of meeting the precise timing in the former (similar) version of reg 72(1)(b), see *CH 1762/ 2004*, where the claimant failed to qualify for an extended payment because, although he had moved from his previous accommodation to take up employment, he did not do so either in the week in which he started his new job or in the previous week.

Para (5). This regulation does not apply to a person who, on the day before IS ceased, was being treated as not in remunerative work under reg 6(5) IS Regs. That regulation provides a similar scheme for extended payments of IS for home ownership costs (known as "mortgage interest run-on").

General issues

Prior to 6 October 2008, before entitlement to extended payments could be established various matters had to be certified by the DWP – eg, whether entitlement to a qualifying benefit had ceased. In addition, the claimant or her/his partner was required to notify the local authority or the DWP of specified matters within a strict time limit. This is no longer the case. However, the circumstances set out in para (1)(b) are changes that must be reported to both the DWP and the local authority under, respectively, reg 32 Social Security (Claims and Payments) Regulations 1987 and reg 88(1) HB Regs. A failure to report such a change would not affect entitlement to extended payments, but could result in an overpayment of HB from the end of the extended payment period.

Note: under the former scheme, there was no right of appeal against a failure by the Secretary of State to certify matters and hence a tribunal could not offset a supposed entitlement to extended payments against an overpayment of benefit: *CH 5553/2002* paras 15-18.

[¹ Duration of extended payment period

72A.–(1)   Where a claimant is entitled to an extended payment, the extended payment period starts on the first day of the benefit week immediately following the benefit week in which the claimant, or the claimant's partner, ceased to be entitled to a qualifying income-related benefit.

(2)   For the purpose of paragraph (1), a claimant or a claimant's partner ceases to be entitled to a qualifying income-related benefit on the day immediately following the last day of entitlement to that benefit.

(3)   The extended payment period ends–

(a)   at the end of a period of four weeks; or

(b)   on the date on which the claimant to whom the extended payment is payable has no liability for rent, if that occurs first.]

Amendment

1.   Inserted by reg 2(2) of SI 2008 No 959 as from 6.10.08.

Analysis

Under reg 72A, extended payments are made for four weeks, or until liability for rent ends if this is sooner: para (3). The period starts on the Monday following the benefit week in which entitlement to a qualifying income-related benefit ceased: paras (1) and (2). Note that even where the claimant moves, extended payments can in some cases continue to be paid until the end of the extended payment period: reg 72C.

[¹ Amount of extended payment

72B.–(1)   For any week during the extended payment period the amount of the extended payment payable to a claimant shall be the higher of–

(a) the amount of housing benefit to which the claimant was entitled under the general conditions of entitlement in the last benefit week before the claimant or the claimant's partner ceased to be entitled to a qualifying income-related benefit;

(b) the amount of housing benefit to which the claimant would be entitled under the general conditions of entitlement for any benefit week during the extended payment period, if regulation 72 (extended payments) did not apply to the claimant; or

(c) the amount of housing benefit to which the claimant's partner would be entitled under the general conditions of entitlement, if regulation 72 did not apply to the claimant.

(2) Paragraph (1) is subject to paragraphs (3) to (6) and does not apply in the case of a mover.

(3) Where the last benefit week referred to in paragraph (1)(a) fell, in whole or in part, within a rent free period, the last benefit week for the purposes of that paragraph is the last benefit week that did not fall within the rent free period.

(4) Where–

(a) a claimant is entitled to an extended payment by virtue of regulation 72(4) (early vacation of dwelling); and

(b) the last benefit week before the claimant ceased to be entitled to a qualifying income-related benefit was a week in which the claimant's eligible rent was calculated in accordance with regulation 80(3)(c) (calculation of rent for a partial week),

the last benefit week for the purpose of calculating the amount of the extended payment under paragraph (1)(a) shall be the benefit week before the partial week.

(5) Where–

(a) a claimant was treated as occupying two dwellings as the claimant's home under regulation 7(6) (liability to make payments in respect of two homes) at the time when the claimant's entitlement to a qualifying income-related benefit ceased; and

(b) the claimant's liability to pay rent for either of those dwellings ceases during the extended payment period,

the amount of the extended payment for any week shall be reduced by a sum equivalent to the housing benefit which was payable in respect of that dwelling.

(6) No extended payment is payable for any rent free period as defined in regulation 81(1)(13) (rent free periods).

(7) Where a claimant is in receipt of an extended payment under this regulation and the claimant's partner makes a claim for housing benefit, no amount of housing benefit shall be payable by the appropriate authority during the extended payment period.]

Amendment

1. Inserted by reg 2(2) of SI 2008 No 959 as from 6.10.08.

Definitions

"benefit week" – see reg 2(1).
"extended payment period" – see reg 2(1).
"the general conditions of entitlement" – see s34(2) WRA 2007.
"mover" – see reg 2(1).
"partner" – see reg 2(1).
"qualifying income-related benefit" – see reg 2(1).

Analysis

Paras (1) to (4). Other than for a "mover" (for which see reg 72C), para (1) sets out the amount of extended payments of HB that are payable during the extended payment period defined in reg 2(1) as the period for which an extended payment is payable in accordance with either reg 72A or 73A. For any week during the period, the amount payable is the higher of the following:

(1) the HB to which the claimant was entitled in the last (non-rent-free) benefit week before entitlement to a qualifying income-related benefit ceased: paras (1)(a) and (3). Note that where a claimant is entitled to an extended payment by virtue of reg 72(4) and the last benefit week is one in which HB was calculated

on a partial week, the amount of the extended payment is the HB in the week before the partial week: para (4). Note that a change in the claimant's circumstances during the extended payment period will not affect this: reg 72D(2) disapplies Part 9 HB Regs where extended payments are paid in accordance with reg 72B(1)(a); *or*

(2)   the weekly rate of HB to which the claimant would be entitled, as if the extended payment rules did not apply – ie, the amount of HB to which the claimant would be entitled on the basis of her/his new circumstances: para (1)(b); *or*

(3)   the weekly rate of HB to which the claimant's partner would be entitled, as if the extended payment rules did not apply – ie, the amount of HB to which the claimant's partner would be entitled if s/he claimed on the basis of her/his circumstances: para (1)(c).

At the end of the extended payment period, HB entitlement (if any) continues, but at the weekly rate of HB based on the new circumstances. Note that although the amount set by para (1)(a) cannot change, a change in the claimant's circumstances during the extended payment period can affect the weekly amount of the extended payments if, as a result of the change, the amount in either para (1)(b) or (c) is then higher or lower than that in (1)(a). The extended payment will then be whichever amount is now higher.

Example: The claimant is a local authority tenant with a non-dependant. She was entitled to HB of £75 in the week before her entitlement to IS ceased which takes into account a non-dependant deduction of £17. Her weekly entitlement based on her new circumstances in work is £69.21. Her extended payments are therefore £75 a week. In the second week of the extended payment period the non-dependant moves out. Her weekly entitlement based on her new circumstances is now £86.21 and as this is higher than the weekly rate of HB in the week before entitlement to IS ceased, this is now her weekly extended payment for the remainder of the period.

See also reg 72C where a claimant moves from the area of one authority to another during the extended payment period.

Para (5). A claimant may be treated as occupying two homes under reg 7(6) and can be entitled to HB (and therefore extended payments of HB) for both. Para (5) ensures that where liability to pay rent for either of the two dwelling ceases during the extended payment period, the extended payments are reduced by the amount of HB payable for that dwelling.

Para (6) prevents payment of extended payments during a rent-free period.

Para (7) prevents duplication of payments where the partner of the person being paid extended payments claims HB – ie, on the basis of the couple's new circumstances. See also reg 52 HB(SPC) Regs on p837 where the claimant claims HB under those rules while entitled to extended payments under reg 72 or reg 73.

[¹ Extended payments – movers

72C.–(1)   This regulation applies–

(a)   to a mover; and

(b)   from the Monday following the day of the move.

(2)   The amount of the extended payment payable from the Monday from which this regulation applies until the end of the extended payment period shall be the amount of housing benefit which was payable to the mover for the last benefit week before the mover, or the mover's partner, ceased to be entitled to a qualifying income-related benefit.

(3)   Where a mover's liability to make payments for the new dwelling is to the second authority, the extended payment may take the form of a payment from the appropriate authority to–

(a)   the second authority; or

(b)   the mover directly.

(4)   Where–

(a)   a mover, or the mover's partner, makes a claim for housing benefit to the second authority after the mover, or the mover's partner, ceased to be entitled to a qualifying income-related benefit; and

(b)   the mover, or the mover's partner, is in receipt of an extended payment from the appropriate authority,

the second authority shall reduce the weekly amount of housing benefit that the mover, or the mover's partner, is entitled to by a sum equal to the amount of the extended payment until the end of the extended payment period.

(5)   The reduction of housing benefit made by the second authority under paragraph (4) is subject to any entitlement the claimant may have pursuant to regulation 7(6) (liability to make payments in respect of two homes).

(6)   Where the last benefit week referred to in paragraph (2) fell, in whole or in part, within a rent free period, the last benefit week for the purposes of that paragraph is the last benefit week that did not fall within the rent free period.

(7)   No extended payment is payable for any rent free period as defined in regulation 81(1) (rent free periods).]

Amendment
1.   Inserted by reg 2(2) of SI 2008 No 959 as from 6.10.08.

Definitions
"appropriate authority" – see s34(3) WRA 2007.
"extended payment period" – see reg 2(1).
"mover" – see reg 2(1).
"partner" – see reg 2(1).
"qualifying income-related benefit" – see reg 2(1).
"second authority" – see reg 2(1).

Analysis
Reg 72C deals with the amount of extended payments paid to "movers". Movers, as defined by reg 2(1), are claimants who move home from the area of the "appropriate authority" (ie, the authority that was administering the HB claim immediately before entitlement to a qualifying income-related benefit ceased) to a home in the area of a "second authority". As a "second authority" (defined in reg 2(1)) is the authority "to which" (as opposed to *in* which) a mover is liable to make payments for the new dwelling (which in this context would appear to be a reference to payments of rent), reg 72C can only apply where the claimant pays rent to the second authority and therefore does not apply where the claimant pays rent to, for example, a private or housing association landlord. In such cases, there does not appear to be a provision as in paras (4) and (5) to reduce HB where a claim for HB is made to the second authority.

Paras (1), (2) and (6). The weekly amount of a mover's extended payments is the amount of HB which was payable in the last (non-rent free) benefit week before entitlement to a qualifying income-related benefit ceased: paras (2) and (6). This applies from the Monday following the move until the end of the extended payment period (see reg 72A): paras (1) and (2). Note that a change in the claimant's circumstances during the extended payment period will not affect the weekly amount of the extended payments: reg 72D(2) disapplies Part 9 HB Regs where extended payments are paid in accordance with reg 72C(2). However, a change might affect the amount by which the second authority can "top up" the extended payments under paras (4) and (5) below.

Para (3). Where the rent liability is to the second authority, the extended payments can be made either to the mover or to the second authority: para (3). But note that given the definition of "second authority" in reg 2(1), the mover will always be so liable.

Paras (4) and (5) require the second authority to reduce the amount of HB paid to the mover or her/his partner by the amount of the extended payments in the circumstances described in para (4)(a) and (b). This applies where the mover or her/his partner makes a claim for HB to the second authority while either of them is being paid extended payments by the appropriate authority after entitlement to a qualifying income-related benefit ceased. The effect of this is that if HB at the new home is higher than HB was at the former home, the extended payments are effectively "topped up" by any additional entitlement to HB based on the new circumstances. This is subject to any entitlement the claimant may have to HB for two homes under reg 7(6).

Para (7) prevents payment of extended payments during a rent-free period.

[¹Relationship between extended payment and entitlement to housing benefit under the general conditions of entitlement

72D.–(1)   Where a claimant's housing benefit award would have ended when the claimant ceased to be entitled to a qualifying income-related benefit in the circumstances listed in regulation 72(1)(b), that award will not cease until the end of the extended payment period.

(2)   Part 9 (calculation of weekly amounts and changes of circumstances) shall not apply to any extended payment payable in accordance with regulation 72B(1)(a) or 72C(2) (amount of extended payment – movers).]

Amendment
1.   Inserted by reg 2(2) of SI 2008 No 959 as from 6.10.08.

Analysis
Reg 72D confirms that entitlement to HB does not end until the end of the extended payment period, even if entitlement would have ended if based only on the claimant's new circumstances: para (1). It also confirms that

the general rules for calculating weekly amounts and for changes of circumstances do not apply to extended payments payable in accordance with reg 72B(1)(a) or 72C(2): para (2).

[²Extended payments (qualifying contributory benefits)

73.–(1)   A claimant who is entitled to housing benefit (by virtue of the general conditions of entitlement) shall be entitled to an extended payment (qualifying contributory benefits) where–

(a)   the claimant or the claimant's partner was entitled to a qualifying contributory benefit;

(b)   entitlement to a qualifying contributory benefit ceased because the claimant or the claimant's partner–
  (i)   commenced employment as an employed or self-employed earner;
  (ii)   increased their earnings from such employment; or
  (iii)   increased the number of hours worked in such employment,
  and that employment is or, as the case may be, increased earnings or increased number of hours are expected to last five weeks or more;

(c)   the claimant or the claimant's partner had been entitled to and in receipt of a qualifying contributory benefit or a combination of qualifying contributory benefits for a continuous period of at least 26 weeks before the day on which the entitlement to a qualifying contributory benefit ceased; and

(d)   the claimant or the claimant's partner was not entitled to and not in receipt of a qualifying income-related benefit in the last benefit week in which the claimant, or the claimant's partner, was entitled to a qualifying contributory benefit.

(2)   A claimant must be treated as entitled to housing benefit by virtue of the general conditions of entitlement where–

(a)   the claimant ceased to be entitled to housing benefit because the claimant vacated the dwelling occupied as the claimant's home;

(b)   the day on which the claimant vacated the dwelling was either in the week in which entitlement to a qualifying contributory benefit ceased, or in the preceding week; and

(c)   entitlement to the qualifying contributory benefit ceased in any of the circumstances listed in paragraph (1)(b).]

Amendments
1.   Amended by reg 13 of SI 2007 No 2868 as from 7.4.08 (or if reg 1(5) of that SI applies, on the day on or after 7.4.08 when the first of the events specified in reg 1(6) applies, or from 6.4.09 if none have before that date).
2.   Substituted by reg 3(2) of SI 2008 No 959 as from 6.10.08

General Note
Extended payments of HB are available to those who were not entitled to, or in receipt of, a "qualifying income-related benefit" (defined in reg 2 as IS, income-based JSA (including joint-claim JSA) and *income-related* ESA) whose entitlement to a "qualifying contributory benefit" (defined in reg 2 as IB, *contributory* ESA and SDA) ended because they started employment as an employed or self-employed earner, or increased earnings from, or hours of, the employment. See also regs 73A to 73D below.

The qualifying rules are broadly the same as the extended payment rules for those coming off a "qualifying income-related benefit" (see regs 72 to 72D above).

[¹ Duration of extended payment period (qualifying contributory benefits)

73A.–(1)   Where a claimant is entitled to an extended payment (qualifying contributory benefits), the extended payment period starts on the first day of the benefit week immediately following the benefit week in which the claimant, or the claimant's partner, ceased to be entitled to a qualifying contributory benefit.

(2)   For the purpose of paragraph (1), a claimant or a claimant's partner ceases to be entitled to a qualifying contributory benefit on the day immediately following the last day of entitlement to that benefit.

(3)   The extended payment period ends–

(a)   at the end of a period of four weeks; or

(b)   on the date on which the claimant to whom the extended payment (qualifying contributory benefits) is payable has no liability for rent, if that occurs first.]

Amendment

1.   Inserted by reg 3(2) of SI 2008 No 959 as from 6.10.08.

[¹ Amount of extended payment (qualifying contributory benefits)

73B.–(1)   For any week during the extended payment period the amount of the extended payment (qualifying contributory benefits) payable to a claimant shall be the higher of–

(a)   the amount of housing benefit to which the claimant was entitled under the general conditions of entitlement in the last benefit week before the claimant or the claimant's partner ceased to be entitled to a qualifying contributory benefit;

(b)   the amount of housing benefit to which the claimant would be entitled under the general conditions of entitlement for any benefit week during the extended payment period, if regulation 73 (extended payments (qualifying contributory benefits)) did not apply to the claimant; or

(c)   the amount of housing benefit to which the claimant's partner would be entitled under the general conditions of entitlement, if regulation 73 did not apply to the claimant.

(2)   Paragraph (1) is subject to the paragraphs (3) to (6) and does not apply in the case of a mover.

(3)   Where the last benefit week referred to in paragraph (1)(a) fell, in whole or in part, within a rent free period, the last benefit week for the purposes of that paragraph is the last benefit week that did not fall within the rent free period.

(4)   Where–

(a)   a claimant is entitled to an extended payment (qualifying contributory benefits) by virtue of regulation 73(2) (early vacation of dwelling); and

(b)   the last benefit week before the claimant ceased to be entitled to a qualifying contributory benefit was a week in which the claimant's eligible rent was calculated in accordance with regulation 80(3)(c)(15) (calculation of rent for a partial week),

the last benefit week for the purpose of calculating the amount of the extended payment (qualifying contributory benefits) under paragraph (1)(a) shall be the benefit week before the partial week.

(5)   Where–

(a)   a claimant was treated as occupying two dwellings as the claimant's home under regulation 7(6) (liability to make payments in respect of two homes) at the time when the claimant's entitlement to a qualifying contributory benefit ceased; and

(b)   the claimant's liability to pay rent for either of those dwellings ceases during the extended payment period,

the amount of the extended payment (qualifying contributory benefits) for any week shall be reduced by a sum equivalent to the housing benefit which was payable in respect of that dwelling.

(6)   No extended payment (qualifying contributory benefits) is payable for any rent free period as defined in regulation 81(1)(16) (rent free periods).

(7)   Where a claimant is in receipt of an extended payment (qualifying contributory benefits) under this regulation and the claimant's partner makes a claim for housing benefit, no amount of housing benefit shall be payable by the appropriate authority during the extended payment period.]

Amendment

1.   Inserted by reg 3(2) of SI 2008 No 959 as from 6.10.08.

[¹ Extended payments (qualifying contributory benefits) – movers

73C.–(1)   This regulation applies–

(a)   to a mover; and

(b)   from the Monday following the day of the move.

(2)   The amount of the extended payment (qualifying contributory benefits) payable from the Monday from which this regulation applies until the end of the extended payment period shall be the amount of housing benefit which was payable to the mover for the last benefit week before the mover, or the mover's partner, ceased to be entitled to a qualifying contributory benefit.

(3)   Where a mover's liability to make payments for the new dwelling is to the second authority, the extended payment (qualifying contributory benefits) may take the form of a payment from the appropriate authority to–

(a)   the second authority; or

(b)   the mover directly.

(4)   Where–

(a)   a mover, or the mover's partner, makes a claim for housing benefit to the second authority after the mover, or the mover's partner, ceased to be entitled to a qualifying contributory benefit; and

(b)   the mover, or the mover's partner, is in receipt of an extended payment (qualifying contributory benefits) from the appropriate authority,

the second authority shall reduce the weekly amount of housing benefit that the mover, or the mover's partner, is entitled to by a sum equal to the amount of the extended payment (qualifying contributory benefits) until the end of the extended payment period.

(5)   The reduction of housing benefit made by the second authority under paragraph (4) is subject to any entitlement the claimant may have pursuant to regulation 7(6) (liability to make payments in respect of two homes).

(6)   Where the last benefit week referred to in paragraph (2) fell, in whole or in part, within a rent free period, the last benefit week for the purposes of that paragraph is the last benefit week that did not fall within the rent free period.

(7)   No extended payment (qualifying contributory benefits) is payable for any rent free period as defined in regulation 81(1) (rent free periods).]

Amendment
1.   Inserted by reg 3(2) of SI 2008 No 959 as from 6.10.08.

[¹ **Relationship between extended payment (qualifying contributory benefits) and entitlement to housing benefit under the general conditions of entitlement**

73D.–(1)   Where a claimant's housing benefit award would have ended when the claimant ceased to be entitled to a qualifying contributory benefit in the circumstances listed in regulation 73(1)(b), that award will not cease until the end of the extended payment period.

(2)   Part 9 (calculation of weekly amounts and changes of circumstances) shall not apply to any extended payment (qualifying contributory benefits) payable in accordance with regulation 73B(1)(a) or 73C(2) (amount of extended payment – movers).]

Amendment
1.   Inserted by reg 3(2) of SI 2008 No 959 as from 6.10.08.

[¹ **Non-dependant deductions**

74.–(1)   Subject to the following provisions of this regulation, the deductions referred to in regulation 70 (maximum housing benefit) shall be–

(a)   in respect of a non-dependant aged 18 or over in remunerative work, [¹⁰ £47.75] per week;

(b)   in respect of a non-dependant aged 18 or over to whom sub-paragraph (a) does not apply, [¹⁰ £7.40] per week.

(2)   In the case of a non-dependant aged 18 or over to whom paragraph (1)(a) applies because he is in remunerative work, where it is shown to the appropriate authority that his normal weekly gross income is–

(a)   less than [¹⁰ £120.00], the deduction to be made under this regulation shall be that specified in paragraph 1(b);

(b)   not less than [¹⁰ £120.00] but less than [¹⁰ £178.00], the deduction to be made under this regulation shall be [¹⁰ £17.00];

(c)   not less than [¹⁰ £178.00] but less than [¹⁰ £231.00], the deduction to be made under this regulation shall be [¹⁰ £23.35];

(d)   not less than [¹⁰ £231.00] but less than [¹⁰ £306.00], the deduction to be made under this regulation shall be [¹⁰ £38.20];

(e)   not less than [¹⁰ £306.00] but less than [¹⁰ £382.00], the deduction to be made under this regulation shall be [¹⁰ £43.50].

(3)   Only one deduction shall be made under this regulation in respect of a couple or, as the case may be, members of a polygamous marriage and, where, but for this paragraph, the amount that would fall to be deducted in respect of one member of a couple or polygamous marriage is higher than the amount (if any) that would fall to be deducted in respect of the other, or any other, member, the higher amount shall be deducted.

(4)   In applying the provisions of paragraph (2) in the case of a couple or, as the case may be, a polygamous marriage, regard shall be had, for the purpose of paragraph (2) to the couple's or, as the case may be, all members of the polygamous marriage's joint weekly gross income.

(5)   Where a person is a non-dependant in respect of more than one joint occupier of a dwelling (except where the joint occupiers are a couple or members of a polygamous marriage), the deduction in respect of that non-dependant shall be apportioned between the joint occupiers (the amount so apportioned being rounded to the nearest penny) having regard to the number of joint occupiers and the proportion of the payments in respect of the dwelling payable by each of them.

(6)   No deduction shall be made in respect of any non-dependants occupying a claimant's dwelling if the claimant or his partner is–

(a)   blind or treated as blind by virtue of paragraph 13 of Schedule 3 (additional condition [⁹ for the disability premium]); or

(b)   receiving in respect of himself either–
   (i)   attendance allowance; or
   (ii)   the care component of the disability living allowance.

(7)   No deduction shall be made in respect of a non-dependant if–

(a)   although he resides with the claimant, it appears to the appropriate authority that his normal home is elsewhere; or

(b)   he is in receipt of a training allowance paid in connection with [⁶ youth training] established under section 2 of the 1973 Act or section 2 of the Enterprise and New Towns (Scotland) Act 1990; or

(c)   he is a full-time student during a period of study within the meaning of Part 7 (Students); or

(d)   he is a full time student and during a recognised summer vacation appropriate to his course he is not in remunerative work; or

(e)   he is a full-time student and the claimant or his partner has attained the age of 65; or

(f)   he is not residing with the claimant because he has been a patient for a period in excess of 52 weeks, or a prisoner, and for these purposes–
   (i)   "patient" has the meaning given in paragraph (18) of regulation 7 (circumstances in which a person is or is not to be treated as occupying a dwelling as his home);
   (ii)   where a person has been a patient for two or more distinct periods separated by one or more intervals each not exceeding 28 days, he shall be treated as having been a patient continuously for a period equal in duration to the total of those distinct periods; and
   (iii)   "prisoner" means a person who is detained in custody pending trial or sentence upon conviction or under a sentence imposed by a court other than a person who is detained in hospital under the provisions of the Mental Health Act 1983, or, in Scotland, under the provisions of the

Mental Health (Care and Treatment) (Scotland) Act 2003 or the Criminal Procedure (Scotland) Act 1995

(8)   No deduction shall be made in calculating the amount of a rent rebate or allowance in respect of a non-dependant aged less than 25 who is on income support [⁴ , an income-based jobseeker's allowance or an income-related employment and support allowance which does not include an amount under section 4(2)(b) of the Welfare Reform Act (the support component and the work-related activity component)].

(9)   In the case of a non-dependant to whom paragraph (2) applies because he is in remunerative work, there shall be disregarded from his weekly gross income–

(a)   any attendance allowance or disability living allowance received by him;

(b)   any payment made under [⁹ or by] the Macfarlane Trust, the Macfarlane (Special Payments) Trust, the Macfarlane (Special Payments) (No. 2) Trust, the Fund, the Eileen Trust [⁹ , MFET Limited] or the Independent Living [⁵ Fund (2006)] which had his income fallen to be calculated under regulation 40 (calculation of income other than earnings) would have been disregarded under paragraph 23 of Schedule 5 (income in kind); and

(c)   any payment which had his income fallen to be calculated under regulation 40 would have been disregarded under paragraph 35 of Schedule 5 (payments made under certain trusts and certain other payments).

(10)   No deduction shall be made in respect of a non-dependant who is on state pension credit.]

Modifications

Reg 74 was substituted by reg 14 Housing Benefit (Local Housing Allowance and Information Sharing) Amendment Regulations 2007 SI No.2868 as from 7 April 2008, save that for a person to whom reg 1(5) of those regulations applied (see p1231), the amendments came into force on the day on or after 7 April 2008 when the first of the events specified in reg 1(6) applied to her/him, or on 6 April 2009 if none had before that date.

Amendments

1.   Substituted by reg 14 of SI 2007 No 2868 as from 7.4.08 (or if reg 1(5) of that SI applies, on the day on or after 7.4.08 when the first of the events specified in reg 1(6) applies, or from 6.4.09 if none have before that date).
2.   Confirmed by Art 19(4) of SI 2008 No 632 as from 1.4.08 (7.4.08 where rent payable weekly or in multiples of a week).
3.   Amended by Art 19(4) of SI 2008 No 632 as from 1.4.08 (7.4.08 where rent payable weekly or in multiples of a week).
4.   Amended by reg 18 of SI 2008 No 1082 as from 27.10.08.
5.   Amended by reg 6(4)(d) of SI 2008 No 2767 as from 17.11.08.
6.   Amended by reg 6(6) of SI 2008 No 2767 as from 17.11.08.
7.   Confirmed by Art 19(4) of SI 2009 No 497 as from 1.4.09 (6.4.09 where rent payable weekly or in multiples of a week).
8.   Amended by Art 19(4) of SI 2009 No 497 as from 1.4.09 (6.4.09 where rent payable weekly or in multiples of a week).
9.   Amended by reg 8(3), (5) and (8) of SI 2010 No 641 as from 1.4.10 (5.4.10 where rent payable weekly or in multiples of a week).
10.   Confirmed by Art 19(3) of SI 2010 No 793 as from 1.4.10 (5.4.10 where rent payable weekly or in multiples of a week).

Definitions

"claimant" – see reg 2(1).
"couple" – see reg 2(1).
"disability living allowance" – see reg 2(1).
"dwelling" – see s137(1) of SSCBA and reg 2(4).
"the Macfarlane Trust", "the Macfarlane (Special Payments) Trust", "the Macfarlane (Special Payments)(No 2) Trust", "the Fund", "the Eileen Trust", "MFET Limited" and "the Independent Living Fund (2006)" – see reg 2(1).
"non-dependant" – see reg 3.
"partner"– see reg 2(1).
"period of study" – see reg 53.
"person on an income-based jobseeker's allowance" – see reg 2(3).
"person on income support" – see reg 2(1).
"person on an income-related employment and support allowance" — see reg 2(3A).

"polygamous marriage" – see reg 2(1).
"rent rebate/allowance" – see ss134(1A) and (1B) and 191 SSAA.
"remunerative work" – see reg 6.
"student" – see reg 53.

General Note

This regulation sets out the situations in which non-dependant deductions must be made from a claimant's "eligible rent" to arrive at maximum HB under reg 70, and the amounts of the relevant deductions. It is suggested that the appropriate procedure for determining whether a non-dependant deduction is to be made, and if so the amount of the deduction, is as follows.

(1)   The authority should first determine whether the claimant has any "non-dependants" normally residing with her/him. Reg 3 sets out who counts as a non-dependant and who does not. No deduction is applicable at *all* in respect of a person who does not come within the definition of "non-dependant".

(2)   If someone *is* a non-dependant, her/his age is relevant; it is only if s/he is aged 18 or over that a deduction can be applied: paras (1) and (2).

(3)   If someone is a non-dependant aged 18 or over, paras (6) to (8) and (10) set out the situations in which *no* deductions are to be made in respect of a non-dependant.

(4)   If someone is a non-dependant aged 18 or over and paras (6) to (8) or (10) do *not* apply, paras (1) and (2) set out the relevant amounts of the deductions for different categories of non-dependants. These depend on whether or not the non-dependant is in "remunerative work". If not in remunerative work, the lowest rate deduction is made, whatever the source of, and amount of, the non-dependant's income: para (1)(b). If the non-dependant is in remunerative work, the amount of the deduction depends on the gross income of the non-dependant, disregarding the amounts set out in para (9): paras (1)(a) and (2).

Paras (3) and (4) deal with non-dependants who are couples or partners to a polygamous marriage. Para (5) deals with the apportionment of non-dependant deductions where more than one person is liable for the rent on the dwelling in which the non-dependant is living.

Any actual payments made to the claimant by the non-dependant are disregarded under Sch 5 para 21.

The non-dependant deduction rates have not increased since 2001/2002. Note, however, that the Government has indicated that from April 2011, these will be uprated on the basis of prices.

Analysis

Paragraphs (1) to (4) and (9): Amounts of deductions

Para (1) sets out the general rule. The deductions provided by this paragraph shall only be made if the non-dependant is 18 or over, and if paras (6) to (8) and (10) do not apply. The lowest rate deduction is made where the non-dependant is not in remunerative work, whatever her/his income: para (1)(b). The highest rate deduction is made where the non-dependant is in remunerative work: (1)(a). This is qualified by para (2) where the non-dependant has income below set levels. Both sub-paras (a) and (b) are qualified by paras (3) to (5).

Higher rates of non-dependant deductions are specified in respect of people who are in "remunerative work" as defined in reg 6: see p230. It is suggested that it is for the authority to prove that a person is a non-dependant, and also that such a non-dependant is (or is to be treated as) in remunerative work.

A person is treated as not in remunerative work in various circumstances, under reg 6(5) to (8). These include where s/he has good cause for her/his absence from it, and where s/he is on, for example, sick leave or maternity, paternity or adoption leave. It would be wrong to assume that only "extended" absences should qualify as "good cause", although of course the absence will have to last at least one benefit week (Monday to Sunday) to be of significance. Likewise, a person on IS, income-based JSA or income-related ESA for more than three days in a benefit week is treated as not in remunerative work in that week. In such circumstances, paras (1)(a) and (2) do not apply.

Para (2) requires lower rate deductions than those provided by para (1)(a) to be made where the non-dependant is aged 18 or over and is in remunerative work with normal weekly gross income below the levels shown in sub-paras (a) to (e). It is suggested that the burden of proof is on the claimant to show that the non-dependant has a low income. This follows from the words "where it is shown to". However, authorities should bear in mind that non-dependants will often be reluctant to disclose personal financial details and should not just sit back and expect the claimant to obtain the information unassisted.

In *CH 48/2006* the local authority assumed, in the absence of any actual evidence as to what the non-dependant was earning, that the highest rate of non-dependent deduction was to be made from the claimant's maximum CTB. Both the local authority and the tribunal had proceeded on the basis that because no positive evidence from the non-dependant or the claimant had been produced, the very worst had to be assumed. The commissioner recognised that a local authority was entitled to require evidence from claimants under reg 63 CTB Regs 1992 (now reg 72 CTB Regs; the equivalent for HB is reg 86 HB Regs) and that, in the absence of such evidence, it may make adverse inferences. However, any such adverse inferences have to be based in some sense of reality. Authorities have the duty to assess what the likely level of a non-dependant's earnings are, on the evidence available and on the balance of probabilities, and estimate a non-dependant's income, with reasonable adverse assumptions being made where inferences have to be drawn because no evidence is available.

All the non-dependant's income under Part 6 and not just her/his wages must be taken into account.

It is income before the various deductions allowable for tax and other factors under Part 6 have been made, but para (9) provides that income from attendance allowance (AA) or disability living allowance (DLA) and certain other payments should be disregarded in calculating a non-dependant's gross weekly income.

Para (3) provides that there is to be only one non-dependant deduction made per couple or polygamous marriage. The deduction to be made is the highest amount that would apply to any of the individual partners under reg 74(1) or (2).

Para (4) must be read together with para (3). In deciding whether para (2) applies, the gross income of both/ all partners is to be taken into account.

Para (9) provides that in calculating the gross weekly income of a non-dependant in remunerative work income from AA or DLA is disregarded. Also disregarded are payments from any of the Macfarlane Trusts, the Fund, the Eileen Trust, MFET Limited or the Independent Living Fund (2006).

Paragraph (5): Apportionment

The authority must first decide on the appropriate non-dependant deduction, then apportion it, not simply according to the number of joint occupiers, but also according to the share of the rent each of them pays. Note that this para does not apply where joint occupiers are members of a couple or polygamous marriage as only one of them will be eligible for HB in any case. This para does not apply in respect of boarders who are not non-dependants: see reg 3(2)(e) on p226.

"Joint occupier" refers to a person with a joint legal right to occupy the property rather than a person who merely happens to live in the same building: see *R v Chesterfield BC ex p Fullwood* [1993] 26 HLR 126 at 129, CA cited in the Analysis to reg 3(2)(d) on p228.

Paragraphs (6) to (8) and (10): Exclusions

Para (6) sets out circumstances in which no non-dependant deduction is to be made for *any* of the claimant's non-dependants.

(1)   The claimant or her/his partner is blind, or is treated as blind: para (6)(a). See Sch 3 para 13 for the circumstances in which a person may be treated as blind. However, it is debatable whether the words "by virtue of" attach to "blind" as well as "treated as blind". If that is so, the claimant would have to show that s/he satisfies Sch 3 para 13(1)(a)(v). The better view is that registration need not be shown and so the sole question is whether on a common-sense view of the state of her/his eyesight, the relevant person can be said to be blind.

(2)   The claimant or her/his partner is receiving AA or DLA care component; any level will suffice: para (6)(b).

If para (6) does not apply, paras (7), (8) and (10) set out circumstances in which a deduction is not to be made in respect of a particular non-dependant.

(1)   The non-dependant's normal home is not with the claimant: para (7)(a). See p238 for a discussion of "normal home".

(2)   Where the non-dependant is in receipt of a training allowance in connection with youth training under the provisions listed, irrespective of her/his age: para (7)(b).

(3)   Where the non-dependant is a "full-time student" during a "period of study" or where the claimant or her/ his partner is 65 or over only, the non-dependant is a "full-time student", whether or not during a period of study: paras (7)(c) and (e). See reg 53 for the definition of those terms.

(4)   Where the non-dependant is a "full-time student", it is the summer vacation and s/he is not in remunerative work: para (7)(d).

(5)   Where the non-dependant has been a patient as defined in reg 7(18) for more than 52 weeks: para (7)(f). Note the linking rule in sub-para (f)(ii). This allows those who are continuously in and out of hospital to be treated as "patients" in due course. The effect of this is that separate periods spent as a patient which are not more than 28 days apart are added together when calculating the 52 weeks.

(6)   Where the non-dependant is a prisoner: para 7(f). A "prisoner" includes those who are remanded in custody pending trial or sentence as well as those actually serving sentences. It does not, however, include those detained under the mental health legislation listed, nor those resident in bail hostels: para (7)(f)(iii) and *R(IS) 17/93* para 6.

(7)   Where the non-dependant is aged under 25 and is on IS, income-based JSA or income-related ESA which does not include a support component or a work-related activity component: para (8). If the non-dependant is on income-related ESA, this para will only apply until a component is awarded by the DWP. For the situations when a person is deemed to be "on" IS, income-based JSA or income-related ESA, see reg 2(1), (3) and (3A) respectively. Note that someone is considered to be "on" income-based JSA not only on days when it is payable to her/him, but also on other days (eg, when sanctioned for losing a job through misconduct) and "on" income-related ESA (eg, when it is is not payable to a claimant who is disqualified in certain circumstances). See the note on reg 2(3) and (3A) on p225.

(8)   Where the non-dependant is on PC: para (10).

Minimum housing benefit

75. Where housing benefit is payable in the form of a rent rebate or allowance, it shall not be payable where the amount to which a person would otherwise be entitled is less than 50 pence per benefit week.

Definitions

"benefit week" – see reg 2(1).

"rent rebate"/"rent allowance" – see ss134(1A) and (1B) and 191 SSAA.

General Note

This prescribes the minimum weekly amount that may be paid to a claimant in respect of both forms of HB: rent rebate and rent allowance. If the claimant is entitled to less than 50p, that rebate or allowance shall not be paid.

PART 9
Calculation of weekly amounts and changes of circumstances

General Note on Part 9

Reg 76 provides the rules for deciding in which benefit week the claimant first becomes entitled to HB. Reg 79 sets out the dates on which changes of circumstance are to take effect for the purposes of calculating HB entitlement. Reg 80 deals with how eligible rent is to be worked out on a weekly basis. Reg 81 deals with the effect of "rent-free periods" on the calculation of weekly amounts of HB.

Date on which entitlement is to commence

76.–(1) Subject to [¹ paragraphs (2) and (3)], a person who makes a claim and is otherwise entitled to housing benefit shall be entitled to that benefit from the benefit week following the date on which his claim is or is treated as made.

(2) Where a claimant is otherwise entitled to housing benefit and becomes liable, for the first time, to make payments in respect of the dwelling which he occupies as his home in the benefit week in which his claim is or is treated as made, he shall be so entitled from that benefit week.

[¹ (3) A claimant shall become entitled to housing benefit from the benefit week in which the first day in respect of which his claim is made falls, where–

(a) he is otherwise entitled to housing benefit;

(b) paragraph (2) does not apply to him; and

[² (c) he becomes liable in that benefit week to make payments, which fall due on a daily basis, in respect of the accommodation listed in paragraph (4) which he occupies as his home.]]

[³ (4) The accommodation referred to in paragraph (3)(c) is–

(a) a hostel;

(b) board and lodging accommodation where the payments are to an authority under section 206(2) of the Housing Act 1996 or section 35(2)(b) of the Housing (Scotland) Act 1987;

(c) accommodation which the authority holds on a licence agreement where the payments are to an authority under section 206(2) of the Housing Act 1996 or section 35(2)(b) of the Housing (Scotland) Act 1987; or

(d) accommodation outside that authority's Housing Revenue Account which the authority holds on a lease granted for a term not exceeding 10 years.

(5) In this regulation–

"board and lodging accommodation" means–

(a) accommodation provided to a person or, if he is a member of a family, to him or any other member of his family, for a charge which is inclusive of the provision of that accommodation and at least some cooked or prepared meals which both are cooked or prepared (by a person other than a person to whom the accommodation is provided or by a member of his family) and are consumed in that accommodation or associated premises; or

(b) accommodation provided to a person in a hotel, guest house, lodging house or some similar establishment,

but it does not include accommodation in a care home, an Abbeyfield Home, an independent hospital or a hostel; and

''Housing Revenue Account'' has the same meaning as for the purposes of Part VIII of the Social Security Administration Act 1992.]

Amendments
1.   Amended by reg 8(4) of SI 2006 No 588 as from 1.4.06.
2.   Substituted by reg 2(2)(a) of SI 2007 No 294 as from 1.4.07.
3.   Inserted by reg 2(2)(b) of SI 2007 No 294 as from 1.4.07.

Definitions
"benefit week" – see reg 2(1).
"dwelling" – see s137(1) SSCBA and reg 2(4).

General Note
Reg 76 deals with when entitlement to HB commences and therefore from when it can be paid. Para (1) sets out the general rule and paras (2) and (3) provide exceptions where people who become liable for rent on their home claim (or are treated as claiming) HB during the same benefit week.

Analysis
Para (1). The general rule is that unless paras (2) or (3) apply, a claimant's entitlement to HB usually begins from the "benefit week" (running from Monday to Sunday) following the week in which the claim is made (or is treated as made) – ie, the Monday after the date of claim. Reg 83 determines the date on which a claim is, or is to be treated as, made. This can be a date earlier (or later) than the date the claim is actually received by the authority.

    Para (2). There are two conditions which must be satisfied before a claimant's entitlement to HB commences in the benefit week in which s/he claims rather than the one which follows.

(1)   S/he must become liable for rent on the dwelling she occupies as her/his home (see reg 7) for the *first time* during that benefit week (eg, s/he moves into a new home).

(2)   S/he must make her/his claim or be treated as doing so under reg 83 during that week.

The practical effect of this is that if para (2) applies, entitlement to HB starts from the same day the liability for rent began: see reg 80(2), (4)(a), (5) and (9).

    In *SSWP v Robinson* [2004], 11 February, CA (reported as *R(H) 4/04*), the Court of Appeal allowed the Secretary of State's appeal in a case where a claim had been made on 11 March, the same day on which the claimant became liable for rent, but had not moved into the property until 20 March. The commissioner had awarded benefit under para (2) from the benefit week in which 11 March fell. However, the Court of Appeal held that para (2) could not apply on the facts of Ms Robinson's case as, although in the week in which 11 March fell the claimant was liable for the rent on the new dwelling, she was not occupying it as her home, and reg 65(2) HB Regs 1987 (now reg 76(2) HB Regs) – by its use of the phrase "becomes liable for the first time" – only applies where the liability to make payments in respect of the property for the first time coincides with the benefit week in which the claimant meets the other conditions of entitlement to HB. In Ms Robinson's case that did not arise as her liability arose for the first time in the week before she met the other conditions of entitlement for HB (ie, occupying the dwelling as her home) and so the general rule in reg 65(1) HB Regs 1987 applied. However, see reg 7 which allows for some claimants who are moving (or have moved home) to be treated as occupying the new home although they are not actually doing so.

    In *R(H) 9/07*, the claimant had made a claim for HB in advance of satisfying the rules of entitlement. A few weeks later he moved into his new home. This was in the benefit week following the week his liability for rent began. Applying *Robinson*, the local authority awarded HB from the Monday following the date the claimant had moved into his new home. Commissioner Williams agreed this was the date on which this claimant's entitlement commenced. He gave detailed consideration to the interaction between an authorities discretion to treat a claim in advance of entitlement as made in the benefit week preceding the first week of entitlement under reg 76(11) HB Regs 1987 (now reg 83(10)), and the rules on commencement of entitlement to HB in reg 65(1) and (2) HB Regs 1987 (now reg 76(1) and (2)). The rules in reg 76(1) and (2) apply both to the actual date of claim and to the date treated as the date of claim. He therefore concluded that where a claim in advance is made, and reg 83(10) has been found to be relevant, it must be applied to both. The commissioner set out a helpful step-by-step approach authorities should take in reaching decisions in such cases. An authority should:

(1)   Identify the actual date of claim.

(2)   If the claim is made in the same week as that in which the claimant first becomes liable to make payments for her/his home, apply reg 76(2).

(3)   If on the facts reg 76(2) does not apply, apply reg 76(1).

(4)   Consider if reg 83(10) applies on the facts.

(5)   If reg 83(10) does not apply, the answer is that at step (3).

(6)   If reg 83(10) does apply, apply the date on which the claim is to be treated as made by reg 83(10) to reg 76(2).

(7)   If on the assumption in step (6), reg 76(2) is relevant to the claim, consider, as a matter of discretion, if reg 83(10) is to be applied.

(8)   If reg 76(2) is not relevant on the assumption in step (6), apply the assumption to reg 76(1). If the answer is different to that given at step (3) consider if that answer should, as a matter of discretion, be applied instead of the answer at step (3).

Note that para (3) was inserted into reg 76 in April 2006. Reg 76(1) is now subject to reg 76(2) *and* (3).

Para (3) provides assistance to those living in the types of accommodation listed in para (4), who become liable for daily payments in respect of that accommodation which they occupy as a home. Unless para (2) applies, entitlement to HB commences in the benefit week in which the first day in respect of which the claim is made falls, which could include where a claim is made for a past period: reg 83.

"Board and lodging accommodation" is defined as accommodation in which cooked or prepared meals are provided and consumed. This definition is identical to that found in reg 2(1) Income Support (General) Regulations 1987. Preparation, in the context of this definition, requires something more than merely leaving the ingredients out for the lodger: *CSB 950/1987*.

[¹Date on which housing benefit is to end
77.]

Amendment
1.   Omitted by reg 4(4)(a) of SI 2008 No 959 as from 6.10.08.

General Note
Until 6 October 2008, reg 77 provided a change of circumstances which terminated entitlement to HB, even where there would otherwise have been continued entitlement. This was that entitlement to IS or income-based (or joint-claim) JSA had ceased because of the commencement of employment (or self-employment) or because of increased earnings from, or hours worked in, such employment, the same circumstances that led to entitlement to extended payments of HB under the former version of reg 72. This meant that in such circumstances, a fresh claim for HB was necessary for entitlement to continue. For commentary, see pp367-386 of the 20th edition.

It is important to note that it was *only* in the circumstances described in reg 77 that entitlement to IS or income-based JSA ending had the effect of also ending entitlement to HB. If IS or income-based JSA entitlement ended (or ends) for other reasons, HB entitlement did *not* (and does not) end automatically, although there could be grounds for revision or supersession of the HB award – eg, where income has changed. This was confirmed in *CH 3736/2006*. The deputy commissioner reminded authorities that after the abolition of "benefit periods" in October 2003 (for claimants 60 or over) and in April 2004 (for other claimants), except in the circumstances contemplated by reg 77, the cessation of IS or income-based JSA is an ordinary change of circumstances that must be assessed like any other and it does not have the effect of automatically ending entitlement to HB. It cannot even be assumed that the cessation of IS or income-based JSA will reduce entitlement to HB. Until the authority knows why entitlement has ended, it cannot conclude that it ended in circumstances that provide grounds upon which to supersede the claimant's entitlement to HB. In cases where it is unclear why benefit has stopped, the correct approach is for the authority to suspend payment of benefit and make further enquiries to establish whether there are grounds for superseding the HB award.

[¹Date on which housing benefit is to end where entitlement to severe disablement allowance or incapacity benefit ceases
78.]

Amendment
1.   Omitted by reg 4(4)(b) of SI 2008 No 959 as from 6.10.08.

General Note
Until 6 October 2008, entitlement to HB ended, even where there would otherwise be continued entitlement, where entitlement to severe disablement allowance or incapacity benefit ceased because of employment or increased earnings. The rules were broadly the same as those in reg 77 – see in particular the General Note above.

Date on which change of circumstances is to take effect

79.–(1)   Except in cases where [⁵ regulation 34 (disregard of changes in tax, contributions, etc) applies, and subject to regulation 8(3) of the Decisions and Appeals Regulations and] the following provisions of this regulation, and to [⁷ regulation 80(5)], a change of circumstances which affects entitlement to, or the amount of, housing benefit ("change of circumstances") shall take effect from the first day of the benefit week following the date on which the change of circumstances actually occurs, and where that change is cessation of entitlement to any benefit under the benefit Acts, the date on which the change actually occurs shall be the day immediately following the last day of entitlement to that benefit.

[¹ (2) Subject to paragraph (8) [⁵ and regulation 8(3) of the Decisions and Appeals Regulations] where the change of circumstances is a change in the amount of rent payable in respect of a dwelling, that change shall take effect from the day on which it actually occurs.]

[² (2A) Subject to paragraphs (8) [⁶ to (10)], except in a case where regulation 8(3) of the Decisions and Appeals Regulations applies, where the change of circumstances is–

(a)   that a person moves into a new dwelling occupied as the home, or

(b)   any other event which–

    (i)   entitles a person to be treated as occupying two dwellings as his home under regulation 7(6), or

    (ii)   brings to an end a person's right to be treated as occupying two dwellings as his home under that regulation, in a case where he has, immediately prior to the event, been treated as occupying two dwellings as his home,

that change of circumstances shall take effect on the day on which it actually occurs.

(2B)   Subject to paragraph (8), where the change of circumstances is the expiry of a maximum period of time, referred to in regulation 7(6), for which a person can be treated as occupying two dwellings as his home, that change shall take effect on the day after the last day of that period]

(3)   Subject to paragraphs (8) [³], where the change of circumstances is an amendment to these Regulations that change, subject to [⁷ regulation 80(5)], shall take effect as follows–

(a)   where the amendment is made by an order under section 150 of the Administration Act (annual up-rating of benefits)–

    (i)   in a case in which the claimant's weekly amount of eligible rent falls to be calculated in accordance with regulation 80(2)(b) [³ or (c)] (calculation of weekly amounts), from 1st April;

    (ii)   in any other case, from the first Monday in April,

in the year in which that order comes into force;

(b)   in respect of any other amendment, from the date on which the amendment of these Regulations comes into force in the particular case.

[¹ (4) Subject to paragraph (8), if two or more changes of circumstances occurring in the same benefit week would, but for this paragraph, take effect in different benefit weeks in accordance with this regulation, they shall all take effect on the first day of the benefit week in which they occur, unless a change taking effect under paragraphs (2), (2A) or (2B) takes effect in that week, in which case the changes shall all take effect on the day on which that change takes effect.]

(5)   Where, during a benefit week commencing on the first Monday in April–

(a)   a change of circumstances takes effect in accordance with paragraph (3)(a)(ii);

(b)   one or more changes of circumstances occur to which paragraph (1) applies; and

(c)   no other change of circumstances occurs to which this regulation applies,

any change of circumstances to which paragraph (1) applies and which occurs in that benefit week shall take effect from the first day of that benefit week.

(6)   Where the change of circumstances is that income, or an increase in the amount of income, other than a benefit or an increase in the amount of a benefit under the Act, is paid in respect of a past period and there was no entitlement to income of that amount during that period, the change of circumstances shall take effect from the first day on which such income, had it been paid in that period at intervals appropriate to that income, would have fallen to be taken into account for the purposes of these Regulations.

(7)   Without prejudice to paragraph (6), where the change of circumstances is the payment of income, or arrears of income, in respect of a past period, the change of circumstances shall take effect from the first day on which such income, had it been timeously paid in that period at intervals appropriate to that income, would have fallen to be taken into account for the purposes of these Regulations.

[¹ (8) Subject to paragraph (9), where a change of circumstances occurs which has the effect of bringing entitlement to an end it shall take effect on the first day of the benefit week following the benefit week in which that change actually occurs except in a case where a person is liable to make payments, which fall due on a daily basis, [⁴] in which case that change shall take effect on the day on which it actually occurs.

(9) Where the change of circumstances is that a person moves to a new dwelling and immediately after the move he is treated as occupying his former dwelling as his home in accordance with regulation 7(7) or (10) then that change of circumstances shall take effect on the day after the last day for which he is treated as [⁸ occuping] the former dwelling in accordance with whichever of those regulations applies in his case.]

[⁶ (10) Where the change of circumstances is that the person moves to a new dwelling and immediately before the move that person is treated as occupying the new dwelling in accordance with regulation 7(8) then that change of circumstances shall take effect on the first day on which the person is treated as occupying the new dwelling as the home under that regulation.]

Modifications

Paras (1) and (3) were amended by reg 15 Housing Benefit (Local Housing Allowance and Information Sharing) Amendment Regulations 2007 SI No.2868 as from 7 April 2008, save that for a person to whom reg 1(5) of those regulations applied (see p1231), the amendments came into force on the day on or after 7 April 2008 when the first of the events specified in reg 1(6) applied to her/him, or on 6 April 2009 if none had before that date.

Reg 79 applies as if para (7) was omitted where a change of circumstances occurs as a result of the payment of arrears of any income which affects a determination or decision in respect of entitlement to, or the amount of, HB or CTB before 6 March 1995. See Sch 3 para 1 HB&CTB(CP) Regs on p1197.

Amendments

1.   Substituted by reg 2(10)(b), (e) and (f) of SI 2005 No 2502 as amended by Sch 2 para 27 of SI 2006 No 217 as from 1.4.06 (3.4.06 where rent payable weekly or at intervals of a week).
2.   Inserted by reg 2(10)(c) of SI 2005 No 2502 as amended by Sch 2 para 27 of SI 2006 No 217 as from 1.4.06 (3.4.06 where rent payable weekly or at intervals of a week).
3.   Amended by reg 2(10)(d) of SI 2005 No 2502 as amended by Sch 2 para 27 of SI 2006 No 217 as from 1.4.06 (3.4.06 where rent payable weekly or at intervals of a week).
4.   Amended by reg 2(3) of SI 2007 No 294 as from 1.4.07.
5.   Substituted by reg 4 of SI 2007 No 2470 as from 24.9.07.
6.   Amended by reg 11(9) of SI 2007 No 2618 as from 1.10.07.
7.   Substituted by reg 15 of SI 2007 No 2868 as from 7.4.08 (or if reg 1(5) of that SI applies, on the day on or after 7.4.08 when the first of the events specified in reg 1(6) applies, or from 6.4.09 if none have before that date).
8.   Substituted by reg 5 of SI 2008 No 2667 as from 30.10.08.

Definitions

"benefit Acts" – see reg 2(1).
"benefit week" – see reg 2(1).
"rent" – see Part 3.

General Note

Para (1) lays down the general rule as to the date on which changes take effect. Paras (2)–(5) and (8)–(10) set out some exceptional circumstances in which the change affects benefit from the benefit week in which the change actually occurs. But see also regs 34 and 42(8).

This regulation is to be read together with regs 80 and 81 (see pp437 and 440).

Analysis

Para (1) contains the general rule that changes in the claimant's circumstances, or those of anyone else whose circumstances affect the claimant's entitlement to HB or how much benefit s/he is due, are to take effect on the first day of the benefit week following the week in which the change takes place – ie, the Monday following the change. The changes referred to in this paragraph need not only be in the claimant's own circumstances. It is the effect of such a change on the claimant's entitlement to HB which is important, rather than who suffers the change.

The general rule does not apply where reg 34 applies. Reg 34 enables certain changes in a claimant's income to be ignored for up to 30 benefit weeks after the week in which they actually take effect.

Para (1) is subject to two provisions:

(1)   By reg 8(3) D&A Regs, where a change is one that is required to be notified and it is advantageous to the claimant, it must be notified within one month of the change (or a longer period in limited circumstances). If the change is notified outside this period, the date of notification is treated as if it is the date the change occurred.

(2)   Reg 80(5) sets the effective date for changes in applicable amounts, income or non-dependant deductions which occur in the same benefit week that a claimant has moved or her/his eligible rent has altered (in specified circumstances).

Paras (2) to (5) and (8) to (10) set out the exceptions to the general rule specified in para (1):

(1)   Changes in rent payable usually take effect from the day the change occurs: para (2). As with para (1) this is subject to reg 8(3) D&A Regs.

(2)   If the change is that the claimant has moved to a new home, or can be (or can no longer be) treated as occupying more than one home under reg 7(6), the change usually takes effect from the day the change occurs: para (2A). As with para (1) this is subject to reg 8(3) D&A Regs.

(3)   If the change is that the maximum period of time for which the claimant can be treated as occupying two homes under reg 7(6) has ended, the change usually takes effect on the day after the last day of the period: para (2B).

(4)   Changes consequent on benefit uprating usually take effect from the first Monday in April. However, where rent is payable monthly or daily, the change usually takes effect from 1 April: para (3)(a). Any other amendments to the regulations usually take effect on the date they come into force: para (3)(b).

(5)   Where more than one change of circumstances occurs in the same benefit week but would take effect in different weeks, they all take effect on the first day of the benefit week in which they occur: para (4). However, where a change referred to in either para (2), (2A) or (2B) takes effect that week, all the changes take effect on the day that change takes effect.

(6)   Where a change consequent on benefit uprating takes effect from the first Monday in April under para (3)(a) and there are changes falling under para (1) in the same week, all changes take effect on the same date if there are no others: para (5). The purpose of these complex rules is to minimise the need to issue multiple notices of determination each covering just a few days.

(7)   Where a change ends entitlement to HB, it usually takes effect from the first day of the benefit week following the benefit week in which the change occurred: para (8). However, where the claimant is liable for daily payments, the change takes effect on the day it occurs.

(8)   If the change is that the claimant has moved to a new home and immediately after this is treated as occupying a former home under regs 7(7) or (10) (ie, where liability for rent there continues and could not be avoided or where there was a fear of violence), the change takes effect on the day after the last day for which s/he is treated as occupying the former home: para (9).

(9)   If the change is that the claimant has moved to a new home and immediately before the move is treated as occupying the new home under reg 7(8) (ie, where a there was a delay in moving for specified reasons), the change takes effect on the day on which s/he is treated as occupying the new home.

Para (6) provides that arrears of non-benefit income should be taken into account over the period that they would have been taken into account if entitlement had existed and it had been paid on time. For example, if the claimant has a pay award finalised at the end of August which takes effect from May, the arrears should be treated as if received at the end of May.

Para (7) deals with difficulties posed by payment of benefit in arrears. Reg 31(2) provides that: "The period over which any benefit . . . is to be taken into account shall be the period in respect of which that benefit is payable." Where claimants have received awards of a benefit for past periods authorities may be able to retrospectively alter HB entitlement under the above rule and reg 4(2)(b) of the D&A Regs (and see also *CH 1561/2005*), thus creating potentially recoverable overpayments. But note the possible official error arguments-which may arise in these situations: see *CH 943/2003* and commentary to reg 100(2) on p479. Note also that arrears of some benefits as well as tax credits and discretionary housing payments count as capital not income and can be disregarded for a period after receipt (see Sch 6 para 9). Para (7) also applies to income other than benefits which was due earlier but paid late (ie, where entitlement existed all along): *EM v LB Waltham Forest* [2009] UKUT 245 (AAC) paras 63–69.

Reg 79 is modified by Sch 3 para 1 HB&CTB(CP) Regs on p1197 and the regulation applies as if para (7) was omitted where a change of circumstances occurs as a result of the payment of arrears of any income which affects a determination or decision about entitlement to, or the amount of, HB or CTB before 6 March 1995. This is a transitional provision, following amendments made by SI 1995 No.511 following the decision in *R v Middlesborough BC ex p Holmes* [1995] unreported, 15 February, QBD. It may be of continuing relevance in overpayment cases involving a failure to disclose receipt of income. See p407 of the 17th edition of this work.

[¹ Calculation of weekly amounts

80.–(1)   A person's entitlement to housing benefit in any benefit week shall be calculated in accordance with the following provisions of this regulation.

(2)   The weekly amount of a claimant's eligible rent shall be–

(a)   subject to paragraph (3), where rent is payable at intervals of one week or a multiple thereof, the amount of eligible rent payable weekly or, where it is payable at intervals of a multiple of a week, the amount determined by dividing the amount of eligible rent payable by the number equal to the number of weeks in respect of which it is payable; or

(b)   subject to paragraph (3), where the rent is payable at intervals of a calendar month or multiples thereof, the amount determined by dividing the amount payable by the number equal to the number of calendar months in respect of which it is payable, multiplying by 12 and dividing by 52;

(c)   subject to paragraph (3), where the rent is payable at intervals of a day or multiples thereof, the amount determined by dividing the amount payable by the number equal to the number of days in respect of which it is payable and multiplying by 7.

(3)   In a case–

(a)   to which regulation 76(2) or (3) (date on which entitlement is to commence) applies, his eligible rent for the benefit week in which he becomes liable to make payments in respect of a dwelling which he occupies as his home shall be calculated by multiplying his daily rent by the number equal to the number of days in that benefit week for which he is liable to make such payments;

(b)   where a change of circumstances takes effect in a benefit week under regulation 79(2A), (but is not a change described in sub-paragraph (c)(ii) of this regulation), (2B), (8) or (9) other than on the Monday of a benefit week then the claimant's eligible rent for that benefit week shall be calculated by multiplying his daily rent by the appropriate number of days in that benefit week;

(c)   where–

    (i)   the amount of eligible rent which the claimant is liable to pay in respect of a dwelling is altered and that change of circumstances takes effect under regulation 79(2); or

    (ii)   the claimant–

        (aa)   moves to a new dwelling occupied as the home,

        (bb)   he is not entitled to be treated, immediately after that move, as occupying two dwellings as his home or as occupying his former dwelling as his home, and

        (cc)   that change of circumstances takes effect under regulation 79(2A),

        other than on the Monday of a benefit week, then the claimant's eligible rent for that benefit week shall be calculated by multiplying his old and new daily rent by the number equal to the number of days in that week which relate respectively to the old and new amounts which he is liable to pay.

(4)   In the case of a claimant whose weekly eligible rent falls to be calculated in accordance with paragraph (3)(a) or (b) by reference to the daily rent in his case, his weekly applicable amount, weekly income, the weekly amount of any non-dependant deductions and the minimum amount payable in his case shall be calculated in the same manner as his weekly eligible rent by reference to the amounts determined in his case in accordance with Parts 5 to 8 (applicable amounts, income and capital, students and amount of benefit).

(5)   Where a change in the amount of a claimant's applicable amount, income or non-dependant deductions falls to be taken into account in the same benefit week as a change in his eligible rent to which paragraph (3)(c) applies, it shall be taken into account in that week on a daily basis in the same manner and as if it had occurred on the same day as that change in his eligible rent.

[² (6)]

(7)   Any amount determined under these Regulations may, if it is appropriate, be rounded to the nearest whole penny by disregarding any amount less than half a penny and treating any amount of half a penny or more as a whole penny.

(8)   In this regulation ''daily rent'' shall mean the amount determined by dividing by 7 the amount determined under whichever sub-paragraph of paragraph (2) is appropriate in each case.

(9)   Where a claimant is entitled to benefit in respect of two (but not more than two) dwellings in accordance with regulation 7(6) his eligible rent shall be calculated in respect of each dwelling in accordance with this regulation.]

Modifications

Reg 80 was substituted by reg 16 Housing Benefit (Local Housing Allowance and Information Sharing) Amendment Regulations 2007 SI No.2868 as from 7 April 2008, save that for a person to whom reg 1(5) of those regulations applied (see p1231), the amendments came into force on the day on or after 7 April 2008 when the first of the events specified in reg 1(6) applied to her/him, or on 6 April 2009 if none had before that date.

Amendments

1.   Substituted by reg 16 of SI 2007 No 2868 as from 7.4.08 (or if reg 1(5) of that SI applies, on the day on or after 7.4.08 when the first of the events specified in reg 1(6) applies, or from 6.4.09 if none have before that date).
2.   Omitted by reg 4(4)(c) of SI 2008 No 959 as from 6.10.08.

Definitions

"applicable amount" – see Part 5 and s135 SSCBA.
"benefit week" – see reg 2(1).
"claimant" – see reg 2(1).
"dwelling" – see reg 2(4) and s137(1) SSCBA.
"eligible rent" – see reg 2(1).
"non-dependant deductions" – see regs 3 and 74.

General Note

The calculation of HB is based on weekly amounts. This regulation deals with how a claimant's "eligible rent" (for which see regs 12B, 12C and 12D and regs 12 and 13 as set out in Sch 3 para 5 HB&CTB(CP) Regs) is to be calculated on a weekly basis for the purpose of the HB calculation. Note also reg 81 where a claimant has a "rent free period".

The other components in the calculation, namely applicable amounts (Part 5), income (Part 6) and amount of benefit (Part 8), are converted into weekly figures by the Parts which specifically deal with them, and are only affected by this regulation so far as paras (4) and (5) allow.

The interaction between reg 79 and reg 80(3) to (5) is that reg 79 operates to fix the benefit week in which changes of circumstances are to take effect, and paras (3) to (5) of reg 80 provide how such a change is to affect the weekly amount of benefit due for the benefit week in question.

Para (1) gives effect to the rest of this regulation.

Para (2) is the general rule. A distinction is drawn between claimants who pay rent on a weekly basis or for a period equivalent to a number of weeks (para (2)(a)) and those who pay rent at intervals of a month or a day or multiples of these (paras (2)(b) and (c)).

Para (3) deals with situations where eligible rent must be calculated for part-weeks (ie, where a claimant is not liable for rent for a full week) certain changes of circumstance affect rent due in a week or the amount of rent changes during a week.

Paras (4) and (5) are consequential on para (3) and refer to the quantification of the other components in the HB calculation where a change covered by para (3) has occurred.

Para (7) allows for the rounding of figures determined under the regulations.

Para (8) defines "daily rent" for the purpose of para (3).

Para (9) makes it clear that where a claimant is entitled to HB for two homes, the eligible rent for each dwelling is calculated separately under this regulation.

Analysis

Para (2) sets out the general rules for determining weekly amounts of eligible rent in circumstances where para (3) is not applicable.

Para (2)(a) provides that where rent is payable weekly, the weekly eligible rent is the weekly amount actually paid. Where rent is paid for a multiple of weeks, weekly eligible rent is the total payable for that period divided by the number of weeks in it – eg, where rent is paid fortnightly, the rent payable is divided by 2.

Para (2)(b) provides that the where rent is payable at intervals of (or in multiples of) a calendar month, weekly eligible rent is the total payable for the period divided by the number of months for that period, then multiplied by 12 and divided by 52.

Para (2)(c) provides that where rent is payable at intervals of (or in multiples of) a day, weekly eligible rent is the amount payable divided by the number of days in the period, then multiplied by 7.

Para (3) sets out the circumstances in which the normal rules in para (2) do not apply. The effect of para (3) combined with paras (4) and (5) is that for the week affected, eligible rent is calculated for a part-week on a daily basis. There are three situations:

(1)   Where a claimant's entitlement to HB commences in her/his week of claim (rather than the week after) – ie, s/he both claims (or is treated as claiming) HB and first becomes liable to pay rent on her/his dwelling in the same week or becomes liable for daily payments in specified types of accommodation which s/he occupies as a home (see reg 76(2) and (3)): sub-para (a). In such cases, eligible rent for the week in which s/he becomes liable (ie, the first week of claim) is calculated by multiplying "daily rent" by the number of days in the week for which the claimant is liable to make payments.

(2)   Where a change of circumstances takes effect other than on a Monday under reg 79(2A) (other than where para (c)(ii) of this reg applies, for which see below), (2B), (8) or (9) (all situations where the change takes effect during the week the change occurred rather than from the start of the next benefit week): sub-para (b). In such cases, eligible rent for the week in which the change takes effect is calculated by multiplying "daily rent" by the appropriate number of days in the benefit week.

(3)   Where a change in the rent payable takes effect on the day it occurs under reg 79(2) or a claimant moves, cannot be treated as occupying the former home for HB purposes and the change takes effect on the day it occurs under reg 79(2A) and in both cases, this is other than on the Monday of a benefit week: sub-para (c). In such cases, eligible rent for the week in which the change takes effect is calculated by multiplying the old and the new "daily rent" by the number of days in the week for which the claimant is liable to pay each of these.

"Daily rent" for all three purposes is defined in para (8).

Para (4). In the first two situations (where para (3)(a) or (b) applies), HB entitlement is calculated for the part-week only. The applicable amount, income, non-dependant deductions and the minimum amount of HB payable are adjusted in the same manner as her/his eligible rent so that they, too, only relate to the number of days for which the claimant is liable to rent.

Para (5). In the third situation (where para (3)(c) applies), and in the same benefit week as her/his eligible rent alters, a change in the applicable amount, income or non-dependant deductions takes effect, the weekly amount of any of these is calculated in the same way as the eligible rent, that is by apportioning the old and new amounts according to the number of days to which they relate.

Example: A claimant moves into a new home and claims HB in the same week (on a Friday). Her rent is £325 a calendar month. Applying reg 80(2)(b), her normal weekly eligible rent is £325 times 12 divided by 52 = £75. Applying reg 80(3)(a), her eligible rent for the first benefit week of entitlement is £75 divided by 7 times 3 days = £32.14. The other components determining the amount of HB are also apportioned for that week, applying reg 80(5).

Para (6), until 6 October 2008, together with the former versions of regs 72 and 73 and Schs 7 and 8, made provisions for adjusting ongoing HB entitlement where extended payments of benefit were paid.

[¹ Rent free periods

81.–(1) This regulation applies to a claimant for any period (referred to in this regulation as a rent free period) in, or in respect of, which he is not liable to pay rent except for any period to which regulation 8(1)(d) (waiver of rent by landlord in return for work done) applies.

(2)   In the case of the beginning or ending of a claimant's rent-free period, his eligible rent for the benefit week in which the rent free period begins and ends shall be calculated on a daily basis as if those benefit weeks were weeks to which regulation 80(3) applies.

(3)   For the purpose of determining the weekly applicable amount and income of a claimant to whom this regulation applies, the weekly amount of any non-dependant deductions and the minimum amount payable in his case–

(a)   in a case to which regulation 80(2)(a) applies, the amounts determined in his case in accordance with Parts 5 to 8 (applicable amounts, income and capital, students and amount of benefit) shall be multiplied by 52 or 53, whichever is appropriate, and divided by the number equal to the number of weeks in that 52 or 53 week period in respect of which he is liable to pay rent;

(b)   subject to paragraph (4), in a case to which regulation 80(2)(b) or (c) applies, the amounts determined in his case in accordance with Parts 5 to 8 shall be multiplied by 365 or 366, whichever is appropriate and divided by the number of days in that 365 or 366 day period in respect of which he is liable to pay rent.

(4)   In a case to which paragraph (3)(b) applies, where either regulation 80(4) or (5) also applies or it is the beginning or end of a rent-free period, the weekly amounts referred

to in paragraph (3) shall first be calculated in accordance with sub-paragraph (b) of that paragraph and then determined on a daily basis in the same manner as the claimant's eligible rent.]

Modifications

Reg 81 was substituted by reg 16 Housing Benefit (Local Housing Allowance and Information Sharing) Amendment Regulations 2007 SI No.2868 as from 7 April 2008, save that for a person to whom reg 1(5) of those regulations applied (see p1231), the amendments came into force on the day on or after 7 April 2008 when the first of the events specified in reg 1(6) applied to her/him, or on 6 April 2009 if none had before that date.

Amendment

1.	Substituted by reg 16 of SI 2007 No 2868 as from 7.4.08 (or if reg 1(5) of that SI applies, on the day on or after 7.4.08 when the first of the events specified in reg 1(6) applies, or from 6.4.09 if none have before that date).

Definitions

"applicable amount" – see reg 22 and s135 SSCBA.
"benefit week" – see reg 2(1).
"claimant" – see reg 2(1).
"eligible rent" – see reg 2(1).
"non-dependant deductions" – see regs 3 and 74.
"rent" – see Part 3.

General Note

Para (1) applies this regulation to a claimant in a "rent-free period". Those are periods in which (or in respect of which) a claimant who is normally liable to pay rent is not liable – eg, where a tenant pays rent over 48 weeks and has a rent-free period for the Christmas holidays. Reg 81 does not apply where the claimant is treated as liable for rent under reg 8(1)(d) – ie, where her/his rent has been waived temporarily to compensate for work done.

Para (2) deals with eligible rent for the weeks in which the rent free period begins and ends.

Paras (3) and (4) deal with adjustments to the applicable amount, income, non-dependant deductions and minimum amount of HB payable. Because the claimant will not be entitled to HB during a rent-free period because s/he is not then *liable* for rent as required by s130(1)(a) SSCBA and or treated as liable by reg 8, this regulation provides that these other components in the calculation of HB are adjusted to ensure that the claimant does not receive more HB than s/he otherwise would during a year on account of having rent-free weeks. It works by ensuring that *all* of her/his assessable income for that year including that paid in respect of rent-free weeks, is taken into account during the weeks in which s/he actually pays rent, and correspondingly that the non-dependant deductions and applicable amounts which would normally be taken into account over a whole year are taken into account during those same weeks.

Analysis

Para (2). In all cases, eligible rent in the benefit weeks in which the rent free period begins and ends is calculated on a daily basis as if reg 80(3) applies. See the note on that provision. Sch 1 para 7(2) also affects the calculation of weekly fixed rate ineligible service charges where there are rent free periods.

Para (3). A distinction is drawn between situations where rent is payable weekly (sub-para (a)) or monthly or daily (sub-para (b)) or in multiples of those periods. Where rent is payable weekly, weekly income, applicable amounts and non-dependant deductions are multiplied by 52 (or 53 as appropriate) to give annual amounts. These are then divided by the number of weeks in that 52 (or 53) week period in respect of which there is a liability to pay rent. Where rent is payable monthly or daily the figures are multiplied by 365 (or 366 as appropriate) and the result then divided by the number of days in that 365 (or 366) day period in respect of which there is a liability to pay rent. So for example, where rent is payable monthly other than in December (31 days), all the figures are multiplied by 365 and divided by 334 (365 – 31).

Para (4) qualifies the process under para (3)(b) where reg 80(4) or (5) apply or it is the beginning or end of the rent free period. Amounts produced under para (3)(b) are calculated first, then the daily rate is worked out in the same way as eligible rent under reg 80.

PART 10
Claims

General Note on Part 10

This Part regulates how, and by whom, claims for HB are to be made, the fixing of the date on which the claim is treated as having been made, the authority's rights to require supporting evidence and the duty of the claimant (and certain other people) to notify the authority of changes in circumstances.

Who may claim

82.–(1)   In the case of a couple or members of a polygamous marriage a claim shall be made by whichever one of them they agree should so claim or, in default of agreement, by such one of them as the relevant authority shall determine.

(2)   Where a person who is liable to make payments in respect of a dwelling is unable for the time being to act, and–

    (a)   a [¹ deputy] has been appointed by the Court of Protection with power to claim, or as the case may be, receive benefit on his behalf; or

    (b)   in Scotland, his estate is being administered by a judicial factor or any guardian acting or appointed under the Adults with Incapacity (Scotland) Act 2000 who has power to claim or, as the case may be, receive benefit on his behalf; or

    (c)   an attorney with a general power or a power to claim or as the case may be, receive benefit, has been appointed by that person under [¹ the Powers of Attorney Act 1971, the Enduring Powers of Attorney Act 1985 or the Mental Capacity Act 2005 or otherwise],

that [¹ deputy], judicial factor, guardian or attorney, as the case may be, may make a claim on behalf of that person.

(3)   Where a person who is liable to make payments in respect of a dwelling is unable for the time being to act and paragraph (2) does not apply to him, the relevant authority may, upon written application made to them by a person who, if a natural person, is over the age of 18, appoint that person to exercise on behalf of the person who is unable to act, any right to which that person might be entitled under the Act and to receive and deal on his behalf with any sums payable to him.

(4)   Where the relevant authority has made an appointment under paragraph (3) or treated a person as an appointee under paragraph (5)–

    (a)   it may at any time revoke the appointment;

    (b)   the person appointed may resign his office after having given 4 weeks notice in writing to the relevant authority of his intention to do so;

    (c)   any such appointment shall terminate when the relevant authority is notified that a receiver or other person to whom paragraph (2)(b) or (c) applies has been appointed.

(5)   Where a person who is liable to make payments in respect of a dwelling is for the time being unable to act and the Secretary of State has appointed a person to act on his behalf for the purposes of the Act the relevant authority may, if that person agrees, treat him as if he had been appointed by them under paragraph (3).

(6)   Anything required by these Regulations to be done by or to any person who is for the time being unable to act may be done by or to the [¹ deputy], judicial factor, guardian or attorney, if any, or by or to the person appointed or treated as appointed under this regulation and the receipt of any such person so appointed shall be a good discharge to the relevant authority for any sum paid.

    [² (7)]

Amendments

    1.   Substituted by reg 11(10) of SI 2007 No 2618 as from 1.10.07.

    2.   Omitted by reg 2(3) of SI 2008 No 2299 as from 1.10.08.

Definitions

    "claim" – see reg 2(1).

    "dwelling" – see reg 2(4) and s137(1) SSCBA.

    "liable to make payments" – see regs 8 and 9.

    "polygamous marriage" – see reg 2(1).

    "relevant authority" – see reg 2(1).

General Note

    The general rule (which is not expressly spelt out in the regulations) is that it is the person who "is liable to make payments in respect of a dwelling . . . which he occupies as his home" (see s130 SSCBA) who must make the claim for benefit required by s1 SSAA. Problems can arise, however, if that person is unable to manage her/his own affairs, or if more than one member of the household is potentially eligible to claim by virtue of reg 8(1). This regulation makes provision for such cases.

Analysis
Paragraph (1): The general rule
The effect of this paragraph is that only one partner in a couple or a polygamous marriage may claim HB in respect of the same dwelling. There is, therefore, no such thing as a joint claim for HB: *CH 3817/2004* (para 8); *CH 3622/2006*. If the parties to the relationship cannot agree who is to claim, the authority must decide.
Paragraphs (2) to (5): Claims on behalf of claimants
Paras (2) to (5) are made under powers given to the Secretary of State by s5(1)(g) and (2)(e) SSAA and cover the situation where the person who is liable to pay the rent is "unable for the time being to act". This will usually be because s/he is mentally or physically incapable of managing her/his affairs permanently, but it would also cover a temporary incapacity – eg, following an accident. The quoted phrase is apt to cover inability to act, however caused, and the regulation is not restricted either to medical incapacities or to mental illness or disability. It could, for example, apply to those with language difficulties.

Para (2) states that the representative of a person unable to act will be an attorney with powers to claim and receive benefit; or a deputy appointed by the Court of Protection in England and Wales with such powers; or a judicial factor or guardian in Scotland. The attorney, deputy, or judicial factor etc may claim and receive HB on the liable person's behalf. Note that if the conditions of para (2) are satisfied, the authority has no choice but to accept a claim from a person who comes within sub-paras (a) to (c).

Paras (3) to (5) permit the authority to appoint someone to act on the claimant's behalf if s/he is unable to act. An appointee must, if s/he is a natural person as opposed to a corporate body, be aged over 18 and must apply for the appointment in writing: para (3). The authority may revoke the appointment under para (4)(a) or the appointee may resign on four weeks' notice under para (4)(b). This is so even if there is no other person who is prepared to claim on behalf of the liable person. If a person falling within para (2) is appointed, any appointment made under para (3) ceases: para (4)(c). If an appointment has been made by the DWP, the appointee may also act in relation to HB: para (5). A person unable to act but otherwise eligible for HB will probably also be entitled to other benefits under SSCBA. This will usually be the most convenient course, but the authority is not under an absolute duty to accede to the request. Again, the only legal obligation is to exercise the discretion reasonably having regard to all the relevant circumstances of each individual case and directing itself properly as to the applicable law.

In most cases, the identity of the most suitable appointee will be readily apparent. If, however, there are competing candidates, or if the most obvious person is thought to be unsuitable (eg, because s/he is felt to be taking advantage of the liable person's vulnerability or has criminal convictions for benefit offences), the authority must exercise the discretion to appoint in accordance with the general principles of administrative law, having regard to all the relevant circumstances of each individual case. Although the paragraph is silent, it is doubted that an authority could lawfully stop a person who is unable to act from claiming HB by refusing everyone who applies to be appointed. If it is felt desirable to do so in order to protect the interests of the person who is unable to act, the authority could, in an appropriate case, appoint one of its own officers or an officer of the local social services authority to claim and receive HB (which would then usually be paid direct to the landlord). Any local government officer so appointed should always bear in mind her/his personal obligations under para (6) and possible liability to repay any benefit which may be overpaid.

Claims by agents. It may be that a liable person who is mentally competent is able to appoint an agent to claim benefit on her/his behalf whether or not s/he is "unable for the time being to act" and without formally granting the agent a power of attorney. It is a general principle of the common law that a person who may lawfully do an act her/himself may appoint another to do it for her/him as agent and in *R v Stoke-on-Trent CC ex p Highgate Projects* [1993] 26 HLR 551, QBD it was said in the context of an application for review that, as the claimants were legally competent, they could authorise their landlords to act for them as agent. In *Tkachuk v SSWP* [2007] EWCA Civ 515, reported as *R(IS) 3/07*, it was held that the common law of agency did apply in the context of claims for benefit.

As a matter of the law of agency there is no reason why the appointment of an agent should even be in writing but, in practical terms, an authority is unlikely to accept on a balance of probabilities that an agency has been created unless the agent can produce some written evidence of her/his authority.

Para (6) empowers anyone appointed under paras (2) or (3) (or treated as appointed under para (5)) to do anything the regulations require a claimant to do and allows the authority to act towards the appointee as if s/he were a claimant. A receipt for HB received by the appointee discharges the authority from any obligation under the regulations to pay that HB to the claimant.

Time and manner in which claims are to be made
83.–(1)   [¹ Subject to [⁴ paragraphs (4A) to (4AE)],] Every claim shall be in writing and made on a properly completed form approved for the purpose by the relevant authority or in such written form as the relevant authority may accept as sufficient in the circumstances of any particular case or class of cases having regard to the sufficiency of the written information and evidence.

(2) The forms approved for the purpose of claiming shall be provided free of charge by the relevant authority or such persons as they may authorise or appoint for the purpose.

(3) Each relevant authority shall notify the Secretary of State of the address to which claims delivered or sent to the appropriate DWP office are to be forwarded.

(4) A claim [¹ in writing]–

(a) may be sent or delivered to the appropriate DWP office where the claimant or his partner is also claiming income support, incapacity benefit, state pension credit [⁶ , a jobseeker's allowance or an employment and support allowance];

(b) where it has not been sent or delivered to the appropriate DWP office, shall be sent or delivered to the designated office;

(c) sent or delivered to the appropriate DWP office, other than one sent on the same form as a claim being made to income support, incapacity benefit [⁶ , a jobseeker's allowance or an employment and support allowance] and as approved by the Secretary of State for the purpose of the benefits being claimed, shall be forwarded to the relevant authority within two working days of the date of the receipt of the claim at the appropriate DWP office, or as soon as practicable thereafter;

[⁴ (d)]

[⁴ (e)]

(f) where the claimant has attained the qualifying age for state pension credit, may be sent or delivered to an authorised office.

[³ (g) may be sent or delivered to the offices of a county council in England if the council has arranged with the relevant authority for claims to be received at their offices ("county offices").]

[¹ (4A) Where the relevant authority has published a telephone number for the purpose of receiving claims for housing benefit, a claim may be made by telephone to that telephone number.

[⁴ (4AA) If the Secretary of State agrees, where–

(a) a person makes a claim for a benefit referred to in paragraph (4)(a); and

(b) the Secretary of State has made provision in the Social Security (Claims and Payments) Regulations 1987 for that benefit to be claimed by telephone,

that person may claim housing benefit by telephone to the telephone number specified by the Secretary of State.

(4AB) A claim for housing benefit may be made in accordance with paragraph (4AA) at any time before a decision has been made on the claim for the benefit referred to in paragraph (4)(a).

(4AC) If the Secretary of State agrees, where a person, in accordance with regulation 32 of the Social Security (Claims and Payments) Regulations 1987 (information to be given and changes to be notified)–

(a) furnishes the Secretary of State with such information or evidence as he may require; or

(b) notifies the Secretary of State of any change of circumstances,

that person may claim housing benefit in the same manner in which the information or evidence was furnished or the notification was given.

(4AD) If the Secretary of State agrees, where a person, in accordance with regulation 24 of the Jobseeker's Allowance Regulations (provision of information and evidence)(7)–

(a) furnishes the Secretary of State with such certificates, documents and other evidence as he may require; or

(b) notifies the Secretary of State of any change of circumstances,

that person may claim housing benefit in the same manner as the certificate, document and other evidence was furnished or the notification was given.

(4AE) A claim for housing benefit may be made in accordance with paragraphs (4AC) or (4AD) at any time before a decision has been made on the award of benefit to which the information, evidence, certificates, documents or notification relates.]

(4B) The relevant authority may determine, in any particular case, that a claim made by telephone [⁴ in accordance with paragraph (4A)] is not a valid claim unless the person making the claim approves a written statement of his circumstances, provided for the purpose by the relevant authority.

[⁴ (4BA) The relevant authority or the Secretary of State may determine that a claim made by telephone in accordance with paragraphs (4AA) to (4AE) is not a valid claim unless the person making the claim approves a written statement of his circumstances, provided for the purpose by the Secretary of State.]

[⁴ (4C) A claim made by telephone in accordance with paragraphs (4A) to (4AE) is defective unless the relevant authority or the Secretary of State is provided with all the information requested during that telephone call.]

(4D) Where a claim made by telephone in accordance with paragraph (4A) is defective, the relevant authority [⁴ must] provide the person making it with an opportunity to correct the defect.

[⁴ (4DA) Where a claim made by telephone in accordance with paragraphs (4AA) to (4AE) is defective–
- (a) the Secretary of State may provide the person making it with an opportunity to correct the defect;
- (b) the relevant authority must provide the person making it with an opportunity to correct the defect if the Secretary of State has not already done so, unless it considers that it has sufficient information to determine the claim.]

(4E) If the person corrects the defect within one month, or such longer period as the relevant authority considers reasonable, [⁴ of the date the relevant authority or the Secretary of State] last drew attention to it, the relevant authority shall treat the claim as if it had been duly made in the first instance.]

[⁴ (4F) If the person does not correct the defect within one month, or such longer period as the relevant authority considers reasonable, of the date the relevant authority or the Secretary of State last drew attention to it, the relevant authority may treat the claim as if it had been duly made in the first instance where it considers that it has sufficient information to determine the claim.]

(5) Subject to paragraph (10), [⁴] the date on which a claim is made shall be–
- (a) in a case where an award of income support [⁶ , an income-based jobseeker's allowance or an income-related employment and support allowance] has been made to the claimant or his partner and the claim for housing benefit is made within one month of the date on which the claim for that income support [⁶ , jobseeker's allowance or employment and support allowance] was received at the appropriate DWP office, the first day of entitlement to income support [⁶ , an income-based jobseeker's allowance or an income-related employment and support allowance] arising from that claim; [⁶]
- (b) in a case where the claimant or his partner is a person on income support [⁶ , an income-based jobseeker's allowance or an income-related employment and support allowance] and he becomes liable for the first time to make payments in respect of the dwelling which he occupies as his home, where the claim is received at the designated office or appropriate DWP office within one month of the claimant first becoming liable for such payments, the date he became liable for those payments;
- (c) in a case where the claimant is the former partner of a person who was, at the date of his death or their separation, entitled to housing benefit and the claimant makes a claim within one month of the date of the death or the separation, that date;
- [⁴ (d) except where sub-paragraph (a), (b) or (c) is satisfied, in a case where a properly completed claim is received in a designated office, an authorised office, county offices or an appropriate DWP office within one month, or such longer period as the relevant authority considers reasonable, of the date on which–
  - (i) a claim form was issued to the claimant following the claimant first notifying, by whatever means, a designated office, an authorised office or an appropriate DWP office of an intention to make a claim; or

(ii)   a claimant notifies, by whatever means, a designated office, an authorised office or an appropriate DWP office of an intention to make a claim by telephone in accordance with paragraphs (4A) to (4AE),

    the date of first notification; and]

(e)   in any other case, the date on which the claim is received at the designated office, authorised office [³ , county offices] or appropriate DWP office.

[⁶ (5A)   For the purposes only of sub-paragraph (5)(a) a person who has been awarded an income-based jobseeker's allowance or an income-related employment and support allowance is to be treated as entitled to that allowance for any days which immediately precede the first day in that award and on which he would have been entitled to that allowance but for regulations made under–

(a)   in the case of income-based jobseeker's allowance, paragraph 4 of Schedule 1 to the Jobseekers Act (waiting days); or

(b)   in the case of income-related employment and support allowance, paragraph 2 of Schedule 2 to the Welfare Reform Act (waiting days).]

(6)   Where a claim received at the designated office [⁷ or appropriate DWP office] has not been made in the manner prescribed in paragraph (1), that claim is for the purposes of these Regulations defective.

(7)   Where a claim [⁷ , which is received by a relevant authority,] is defective because–

(a)   it was made on the form approved for the purpose but that form is not accepted by the relevant authority as being properly completed; or

(b)   it was made in writing but not on the form approved for the purpose and the relevant authority does not accept the claim as being in a written form which is sufficient in the circumstances of the case having regard to the sufficiency of the written information and evidence,

the relevant authority may, in a case to which sub-paragraph (a) applies, request the claimant to complete the defective claim or, in the case to which sub-paragraph (b) applies, supply the claimant with the approved form or request further information or evidence.

[⁷ (7A)   Where a claim is received at an appropriate DWP office and it appears to the Secretary of State that the form has not been properly completed, the Secretary of State may request that the claimant provides the relevant authority with the information required to complete the form.]

[⁷ (8)   The relevant authority shall treat a defective claim as if it had been validly made in the first instance if, in any particular case, the conditions specified in sub-paragraph (a), (b) or (c) of paragraph (8A) are satisfied.

(8A)   The conditions are that–

(a)   where paragraph (7)(a) (incomplete form) applies, the authority receives at the designated office the properly completed claim or the information requested to complete it or the evidence within one month of the request, or such longer period as the relevant authority may consider reasonable; or

(b)   where paragraph (7)(b) (claim not on approved form or further information requested by relevant authority) applies–

(i)   the approved form sent to the claimant is received at the designated office properly completed within one month of it having been sent to him; or, as the case may be,

(ii)   the claimant supplies whatever information or evidence was requested under paragraph (7) within one month of the request,

or , in either case, within such longer period as the relevant authority may consider reasonable; or

(c)   where paragraph (7A) (further information requested by Secretary of State) applies, the relevant authority receives at the designated office the properly completed claim or the information requested to complete it within one month of the request by the Secretary of State or within such longer period as the relevant authority considers reasonable.]

(9)　A claim which is made on an approved form for the time being is, for the purposes of this regulation, properly completed if completed in accordance with the instructions on the form, including any instructions to provide information and evidence in connection with the claim.

[² (10)　Except in the case of a claim made by a person from abroad, where the claimant is not entitled to housing benefit in the benefit week immediately following the date of his claim but the relevant authority is of the opinion that unless there is a change of circumstances he will be entitled to housing benefit for a period beginning not later than the thirteenth benefit week following the date on which the claim is made, the relevant authority may treat the claim as made on a date in the benefit weekimmediately preceding the first benefit week of that period of entitlement and award benefit accordingly.]

(11)　In the case of a person who has attained, or whose partner has attained, [⁸ the age which is 17 weeks younger than the qualifying age for state pension credit], paragraph (10) shall apply as if for the reference to the thirteenth benefit week, there was substituted a reference to the seventeenth benefit week.

[⁹ (12)　Where a claimant ("C")–
(a)　makes a claim which includes (or which C subsequently requests should include) a period before the claim is made; and
(b)　from a day in that period, up to the date when C made the claim (or subsequently requested that the claim should include a past period), C had continuous good cause for failing to make a claim (or request that the claim should include that period),
the claim is to be treated as made on the date determined in accordance with paragraph (12A).

(12A)　That date is the latest of–
(a)　the first day from which C had continuous good cause;
(b)　the day 6 months before the date the claim was made;
(c)　the day 6 months before the date when C requested that the claim should include a past period.]

(13)　In this regulation "authorised office" means an office which is nominated by the Secretary of State and authorised by the relevant authority for receiving claims for decision by the relevant authority.

Amendments

1.	Inserted by reg 2(2) of SI 2006 No 2967 as from 20.12.06.
2.	Substituted by reg 3 of SI 2007 No 1331 as from 23.5.07.
3.	Amended by reg 7(2) of SI 2007 No 2911 as from 31.10.07.
4.	Amended by reg 2(4) of SI 2008 No 2299 as from 1.10.08.
5.	Substituted by reg 4 of SI 2008 No 2424 as from 6.10.08.
6.	Amended by reg 19 of SI 2008 No 1082 as from 27.10.08.
7.	Amended by reg 2(2) of SI 2008 No 2987 as from 22.12.08.
8.	Amended by reg 25 of SI 2009 No 1488 as from 6.4.10.
9.	Amended by reg 2(4) of SI 2010 No 2449 as from 1.11.10.

Definitions

"appropriate DWP office" – see reg 2(1).
"benefit week" – see reg 2(1).
"claimant" – see reg 2(1).
"claim" – see reg 2(1).
"partner" – see reg 2(1).
"person from abroad" – see reg 10.
"remunerative work" – see reg 6.

General Note

Paras (1) to (4AE) and (9) deal with how claims are to be made. Para (5) determines the date to be taken as the date of claim. Paras (4E), (4F), (8), (8A), (10) and (12) effectively qualify para (5) as they affect the date of claim.

447

Paras (4B) to (4D) deal with when a telephone claim is defective and paras (4D) to (4F) with how such claims can be rectified. Paras (6) to (8A) deal with rectification of written claims not made in the proper manner. Para (10) deals with claims made in advance of entitlement and para (12) and (12A) with backdating.

See also reg 86 for the evidence and information that can be required by an authority to support a claim and reg 87 for when a claim may be amended or withdrawn.

Analysis
Paragraphs (1) to (3): General requirements in relation to claims
Para (1) deals with the form a claim must take. Unless a telephone claim can be made, for which see paras (4A) and (4AA), claims must be in writing, and normally made on a form, approved by the local authority for this purpose, which has been "properly completed": see para (9). However, the authority has a discretion to accept a claim in some other written form, if it considers the written information and evidence to be "sufficient in the circumstances". Note also that a claim can be made by means of an electronic communication if the conditions in Sch 11 are satisfied: reg 83A.

In *Novitskaya v London Borough of Brent & Another* [2009] EWCA Civ 1260; [2010] AACR 6, the Court of Appeal, decided that a document may constitute a claim even where it does not use explicit wording or expressly name the benefit being claimed: the correct approach is that the meaning of a document (ie, whether it constitutes a claim) should be construed in the light of the relevant surrounding facts, including other documents. Distinguishing the decision in *R(S) 1/63* on the meaning of "claim", the Court said that excessive reliance should not be placed on the statement there that the intention to claim must appear on the face of the document. Distinguishing comments made in *CG 3844/2006*, the Court held that most situations would call for a "generous approach to the interpretation of such documents".

Local authorities may have their own approved forms. These may be (or be based on) the DWP model form: see www.direct.gov.uk/en/MoneyTaxAndBenefits/BenefitsTaxCreditsAndOtherSupport/On_a_low_income/index.htm.

A "rapid reclaim" form (HBRR1) can be accepted where a claimant is reclaiming IS, JSA or incapacity benefit (IB) at the same time as HB and this is within 26 weeks of a previous entitlement ending. This only applies if s/he is also re-claiming IS, JSA or IB, is entitled to IS, income-based JSA or IB and her/his circumstances have not changed since s/he was last claiming HB: GM A2.560-565. A rapid reclaim form can also be accepted where a claimant is reclaiming ESA at the same time as HB within 12 weeks of a previous entitlement ending. The form is issued by Jobcentre Plus offices to claimants who may be eligible.

Para (2) enables the authority to provide the approved forms referred to in para (1) itself, or to authorise or appoint someone else to provide them. Either way, the forms must be provided free of charge to claimants. Note para (7) where the claim is not made on an approved form.

Para (3) is linked with para (4) and deals with the situation in which an HB claim is sent by an IS, JSA, ESA, IB or PC claimant to a DWP office. The authority must tell the Secretary of State where it wishes the DWP to forward such claims.

Paragraph (4): Place of claim
Para (4) deals with the place to which a written HB claim may be sent or delivered. There are a number of possibilities according to the circumstances of the claimant.
(1) If the claimant (or her/his partner) is also claiming IS, JSA, ESA, IB or PC, the HB claim can be sent or delivered to either the "appropriate DWP office" or the authority's "designated office" (both defined in reg 2(1)): sub-paras (a) and (b). The standard practice where IS or income-based JSA are claimed on a written claim form, is to issue the claimant with a standard HB claim form. If claims for IS, income-based JSA, ESA or IB are made via a Jobcentre Plus contact centre, or a PC claim is made by telephone, the HB claim is usually completed at the same time (and is referred to as an "input document").
In these circumstances, authorities may then send a claimant its own form to fill in, but the date of claim remains that determined by para (5). See also Paras (4AA) to (4AE) for when a claim for HB made in connection with a claim for one of the benefits referred to in para (4)(a) can be made by telephone.
Sub-para (c) then provides that where a claim has been sent or delivered to the "appropriate DWP office", that office should send the claim to the authority within two working days of the date on which the HB claim is actually received. If this is not achieved, the claim must be sent on "as soon as practicable" after that. This requirement does not apply if the HB claim is made on the same form as that for IS, JSA, ESA or IB. The regulation does not set a time limit in such a situation.
Note that sub-paras (a) and (b) make reference to those claiming PC. The time and manner in which HB claims are to be made by those of at least the qualifying age for PC, not on IS, income-based JSA or income-related ESA are now dealt with by reg 64 HB(SPC) Regs. However, where someone is making an advance claim for PC prior to reaching the qualifying age, and an advance claim for HB under para (10), her/his claim would be dealt with under the HB Regs initially.
(2) Other HB claimants *must* send or deliver their claims to the authority's "designated office" (defined in reg 2(1): sub-para (b).
(3) Sub-paras (f) and (g) allow claims to be sent or delivered to an "authorised office" or the offices of a county council in the circumstances set out.

Paragraphs (4A) and (4B): Telephone claims to the local authority

Under para (4A), a claim for HB can be made by telephone where the local authority has published a telephone number for this purpose and the claim is made to that number. The local authority can decide in a particular case to provide a written statement of the claimant's circumstances for her/him to approve. The telephone claim might not be accepted as valid if the statement is not then approved: para (4B).

Note that even where a telephone claim is not permitted, a claimant can notify her/his intention to claim by telephone (or other means). If a written claim is then submitted within one month, the date of claim is the date of the notification of intention to claim: see para (5)(d).

Paragraphs (4AA) to (4AE) and (4BA): Telephone claims to the DWP

Under para (4AA), if the Secretary of State agrees, where a claim for IS, JSA, ESA, IB or PC is made by telephone under the provisions set out, a claim for HB can be also made by telephone to the number specified by the Secretary of State. This can be done at any time before a decision is made on the claim for the DWP benefit: para (4AB). See the commentary to para (4) above for a discussion on the position where there is a claim for PC.

A claim for HB can also be made, if the Secretary of State agrees, when a claimant is furnishing information or evidence as required or notifies a change of circumstances in accordance with either reg 32 Social Security (Claims and Payments) Regulations 1987 or reg 24 Jobseeker's Allowance Regulations 1996: paras (4AC) and (4AD). This can be done at any time before a decision is made on the award of the DWP benefit to which the evidence information or change of circumstances relates: para (4AE). Although there is no express reference here, it is understood the intention is for this provision to allow for a telephone claim for HB in this situation: explanatory memorandum to SI 2008 No.2299.

Where the HB claim is made by telephone, the DWP can decide in a particular case to provide a written statement of the claimant's circumstances for her/him to approve. The telephone claim might not be accepted as valid if the statement is not then approved: para (4BA).

Paragraphs (4C) to (4F): Validity of telephone claims

These mirror the rules in paras (6) to (9) which allow a claimant to remedy a defective written claim. A claim made by telephone is defective unless the claimant provides the local authority (or the DWP where the claim is made to the DWP) with all the information it requires during the telephone call: para (4C). Where a telephone claim is made in accordance with para (4A) and it is defective, the local authority must provide the claimant with an opportunity to correct the defect: para (4D). If the claim is made in accordance with paras (4AA) to (4AE) and it is defective, the DWP may provide the claimant the opportunity to correct the defect. However, if it does not, the local authority must do so, unless it considers it has sufficient information to determine the HB claim: para (4DA).

If the defect is corrected within one month of the last time it was drawn to the claimant's attention, or within a longer period considered "reasonable" by the authority, the claim *must* be treated as if it was properly made in the first instance: para (4E). If the defect is not corrected within the month (or longer period) although the local authority is not compelled to treat the claim as properly made in the first instance, it has the discretion to do so if it considers it has sufficient information to determine the claim: para (4F).

Paragraphs (5), (5A), (10) and (11): The date of claim

The date on which a claim is (or is treated as) made is important because, subject to para (12A), it is used to determine the date on which entitlement to HB commences under reg 76. Para (5) expressly provides what the date of claim shall be (be it in writing, by telephone or by electronic communication), other than where the claim is made in advance. Paras (10) and (11) provide the date a claim in advance is treated as made.

Para (5). It is important to note that the date of claim is not necessarily the date the claim is actually received by the authority – eg, the date the claimant submits a claim form or makes the telephone call which is the claim for HB. Para (5) is subject to para (10). It should also be read together with paras (4E), (4F), (8) and (8A). So, for example, if a claimant claims and is awarded IS from 1 October, makes a defective written claim for HB on 15 October, but then submits a properly completed claim form on 12 November, it can be argued that the date of claim for HB purposes is 1 October. This is because the HB claim is treated as if validly made on 15 October by para (8), and then as made on the first date of entitlement to IS under para 5(a). It is suggested that this is consistent with *Leicester City Council v LG* [2009] UKUT 155 (AAC). For a discussion of that decision, see p967.

Note also that a claim can be backdated under para (12).

Para (5)(d) and (e): The general rules. The date to be taken as the date on which a claim is made is usually the earliest of the following:

(1)   The date the claimant first notified a "designated office", an "authorised office" (see para (13)), or an "appropriate DWP office", by whatever means, of her/his intention to claim. This applies if a "properly completed claim" (only defined in para (9) if the claim is made on an approved form) is received in one of those offices (or a "county office", for which see para (4)(g)) within one month of the form being issued or the claimant notifying her/his intention to make a claim by telephone in accordance with paras (4A) to (4AE) (or a longer period if the authority considers this reasonable): sub-para (d).

"By whatever means" could include by telephone or in person, or where someone notifies the claimant's intention on her/his behalf.

However, claimants and advisers should note that in the event of a subsequent dispute, the absence of a written notification may cause evidential difficulties. Claimants should keep careful contemporaneous notes of any oral notification.

Note that where a claim form is issued for completion after a claimant notifies her/his intention to claim, the one month (or longer) time limit for returning the claim form runs from the date it was issued: sub-para (d)(i). If that time limit is met then the claim can be fixed as having been made on an earlier date than this even if there is a gap between the claimant contacting one of the offices saying s/he wants to claim HB and the claim form then being issued to her/him, thus insulating the claimant from any administrative delays on the part of the authority in issuing the claim form. Where the claimant notifies her/his intention to claim by telephone in accordance with paras (4A) to (4AE), the time limit for receipt of the "properly completed claim" runs from the date of notification: sub-para (d)(ii). It is presumed that a "properly completed claim" would be one that is not deemed defective, eg, by para (4C).

(2)   The date the claim is received at the "designated office", "authorised office", "county offices" or "appropriate DWP office": sub-para (e).

Para (5)(a) to (c): The exceptions. There are three exceptions to the general rule.

(1)   If a claimant (or her/his partner) has been awarded IS, income-based JSA or income-related ESA, and the HB claim is made within one month of the date on which the claim for IS, JSA or ESA was received at the "appropriate DWP", the date of claim for HB is the first day of entitlement to IS/income-based JSA/ income-related ESA – ie, the effective date of the award of IS/income-based JSA/income-related ESA: sub-para (a); *Leicester City Council v LG* [2009] UKUT 155 (AAC). For example, where the claim for IS is backdated, the date of claim for HB would be the date to which the IS claim was backdated.

On new claims for income-based JSA or income-related ESA, the claimant normally has to serve three waiting days before being entitled to that benefit. However, for the purposes of para (5)(a) claimants are to be treated as if they are entitled to income-based JSA or income-related ESA for any waiting days (which can be three or fewer if the claimant has interrupted the claim), if the waiting days immediately precede the first day in the award of income-based JSA or income-related ESA: para (5A). This means that they will be entitled to maximum HB (and CTB) from the outset. Liaison between the DWP and authorities in this respect could give rise to problems: both will have to be careful about recording the relevant dates.

(2)   If a claimant (or her/his partner) is on IS, income-based JSA or income-related ESA when s/he becomes liable for rent in a dwelling occupied as a home for the first time (eg, where s/he moves), her/his date of claim for HB is the date s/he first became liable, if the HB claim is received at a "designated office" or "appropriate DWP office" within one month of becoming liable: sub-para (b).

(3)   Sub-para (c) gives some relief from immediately having to claim when a couple relationship comes to an end either due to separation or the death of one of the couple. Where the claimant's former partner was entitled to HB at the time of her/his death or separation from the claimant, then if the claim is made within one month of the death or separation the date of claim for HB is the date of the death or separation.

Paragraphs (10) and (11): Advance claims

Other than where the claimant is a "person from abroad" (see reg 10), this paragraph gives an authority the discretion to treat an advance claim as made in the benefit week before the first week of entitlement to HB. This applies where a claimant is not entitled to HB in the benefit week after the actual date of claim, but the authority considers s/he will become entitled in the next 13 weeks unless there is a change in circumstances. Note that it is 17 weeks if the claimant or her/his partner is 17 weeks younger than the qualifying age for PC. See reg 76(1) and (2) for the effect of para (10) and, in particular, the note on *R(H) 9/07.* Excluding people from abroad from this advance claim rule reverses the effect of the Court of Appeal's decision in *SSWP v Bhakta* [2006] EWCA Civ 65, *(R(IS) 7/06).* See also reg 7(8) for claimants becoming entitled for the first time when they move to a new home.

Paragraphs (6) to (9): Validity of written claims

Paras (6) and (9). Under para (6), written claims which do not comply with para (1) are to be termed "defective" for the purposes of these regulations, but see paras (8) and (8A). Para (9) defines when a claim made on an approved form amounts to a "properly completed claim" – ie, when the claimant has followed the instructions as to its completion, including those as to provision of information and evidence. So s/he will not be penalised if the instructions are inadequate. See also reg 86 for situations when additional evidence and information must be provided when requested.

Para (7) goes on to say that if a claim received by the local authority is defective, for either of the reasons listed in sub-paras (a) (approved form but not properly completed) or (b) (not on approved form and not sufficient), the authority may give the claimant a chance to remedy things. It can return the form for completion, if sub-para (a) applies, or supply her/him with an approved form or request further information and evidence, if sub-para (b) applies. However, see also para (9).

Para (7A) allows the DWP, where the HB claim is received at an appropriate DWP office and appears not to have been completed properly, to request a claimant to provide information to the local authority needed to complete the form.

Paras (8) and (8A). A defective claim must be treated as if it had been validly made if any of the conditions in para (8A) are satisfied: para (8). So as regards the date to be taken as the date of claim, para (5) will apply, for example, to the date on which the claim was first sent or delivered, rather than the date on which a remedied form (or information or evidence), is returned or provided. The conditions are:

(1)   Where the authority gives the claimant a chance to remedy a defective claim under para (7)(a) or (b), the properly completed form, or the information or evidence requested, is returned within one month: para (8A)(a) and (b).

(2)   Where the DWP has requested the claimant to provide information to the local authority under para (7A), the properly completed form, or the information or evidence requested, is provided to the local authoritity within one month: para (8A)(c).

In all cases, the one-month period can be such longer period as the local authority considers "reasonable".

Paragraph (12) and (12A): Backdating

A claim made on or after 6 October 2008 can only be backdated for up to six months, rather than the 52 weeks that was possible before that date. Note that the DWP initially said, in the explanatory memorandum to SI 2008 No.2424, that the policy intention is to move to a three-month backdating period, in line with the period introduced from 6 October 2008 for people of pension age. It is introducing the reduction to a three-month backdating period for working age claimants on a staged basis, starting with the introduction of a six-month period, to provide more time to work with stakeholders on helping to mitigate any adverse impact. However, the Government has now decided not to move towards a three-month provision and so the six-month rule will stay for the time being.

Para (12) is amended, from 1 November 2010, and para (12A) is added. For para (12) to apply the claimant must have requested HB in respect of a past period (previously the rules required a "claim for backdating"); secondly, from a date in that past period up to the date on which the claimant requested HB for a past period, the claimant must have had continuous "good cause" for her/his failure to make a claim for HB. If these two conditions are met then the claim for the past period is treated as made on the latest of the days listed in para (12A): either the first day from which the claimant had continuous good cause, the day six months before HB was claimed or the day six months before HB in respect of a past period was requested.

Thus the regulations now deal with what is to be taken as the date of the "claim for backdating" under the old terminology. Prior to amendment that was important as it determined the date from which HB could be paid retrospectively. Was it the date the claim for backdating was actually made (ie, the date a claimant requests backdating, in writing or by telephone), or was the date to be determined by para (5) above? As the claim for backdating was a claim for HB, it was arguable that the date should have been determined by para (5). If this was right, it would have produced the same result as in *Leicester City Council v LG* [2009] UKUT 155 (AAC), such that the claimant could have the six months commence from, for example, the date of a claim for IS, income-based JSA or income-related ESA where a HB claim was then submitted within a month of that claim, or some other earlier date determined by para (5). For a discussion of the Upper Tribunal decision, see p967.

Now, however, it is clear that, where a claimant has made a claim for benefit and asks for HB in respect of a period of backdating before that claim was made, the earliest commencement of entitlement will be six months before that request was made (unless the date from which the continuous good cause is established is later). This provision sits somewhat uneasily alongside reg 87 which allows an amendment of an undecided claim to be treated as if it was made when the claim was made. It may be that this will mean that where a claim is amended to include a request for a backdated period before the claim is decided, the request for a past period will be treated as made on the same date the claim is made. That would seem to mitigate this rule to some extent.

Absent a person having been appointed under reg 82(3) to act on behalf of the claimant, the test of "good cause" applies to the claimant her/himself and not her/his landlord, even where the claimant is in supported housing and the landlord may, in fact, have been assisting the claimant with her/his claims for benefit: *CH 1791/ 2004* para 25. However, this decision emphasises that in the latter situation the actions or errors of the landlord will not be irrelevant, but have to be viewed from the perspective of whether the claimant acted reasonably in all the circumstances, in particular in allowing his or her landlord to act for her/him.

In the case of a couple (see reg 82(1)), it is for the member of the couple who makes the claim for backdating to show that s/he has "good cause" and it is irrelevant whether the other member of the couple can show good cause or not: *CH 3817/2004* para 8.

The Court of Appeal in *R v Aylesbury Vale DC ex p England* [1996] 29 HLR 303 held that ordinarily a claim for HB is to be treated as prospective only so an express request must be included if backdating is required. For the position where a request for backdating was made before 1 April 1996, see p236 of the 9th edition and p7 of the supplement to that edition.

CH 996/2004 states that the issue of backdating does not arise (and so need not be considered) if the other conditions of entitlement are not satisfied in any event. Although perhaps this will be an issue of little practical importance, it is respectfully suggested that *CH 996/2004* is wrong on this point and is putting the proverbial horse before the cart. Axiomatically, the other conditions of entitlement cannot arise unless and until a claim has been made (including for a backdated period), and so establishing if a claim has been made for a backdated period must be logically prior to deciding whether the other conditions of entitlement are met.

The phrase "good cause" has frequently been considered by social security commissioners and in *R(S) 2/ 63(T)* was defined by a tribunal of commissioners as:

". . . some fact which, having regard to all the circumstances (including the claimant's state of health and the information which he had received and that which he might have obtained) would probably have caused a reasonable person of his age and experience to act (or fail to act) as the claimant did."

CH 2198/2008 makes the point that the test is not how a reasonable person would have acted, but is rather whether *the claimant has good cause* for not claiming earlier. While whether, given a claimant's circumstances, it can be said s/he acted reasonably is a factor in whether s/he had good cause that is not necessarily determinative. In *UH v LB Islington* [2010] UKUT 64 (AAC), the Upper Tribunal agrees with that, but notes that the more reasonable a person's behaviour in not claiming earlier, given her/his age, experience and the information available to her/him, the more likely s/he will have good cause.

However, it is clear from *Chief Adjudication Officer v Upton* [1997] 2 CLY 4668, CA that, as long as the authority has regard to this legal test, the question of whether "good cause" exists is one of fact. The commissioner approved this view of *Upton* in *CH 2659/2002* para 24.

The burden of proof to establish "good cause" rests on the claimant: *CH 5135/2001* para 1.4. That case involved a claimant who relied on an illness from which he was suffering during the relevant period. The tribunal decided that an illness must be severe for a claimant to succeed in asserting "good cause", but the commissioner decided that was incorrect: para 6. The question was "whether the nature of the illness is sufficient to constitute or lead to good cause".

Where a claimant has a mental illness, the reasonableness of her/his actions must be judged by her/his mental age or capacity rather than chronological age, though medical evidence would be required: *CH 393/2003* para 5-6; *CH 474/2002* para 9. An illness is not rendered irrelevant just because a claimant does not have an appointee: *CH 393/2003* para 7.

In *CH 2191/2002*, the claimant failed to disclose to the DWP that her husband had started work. When the change of circumstances was discovered, her JSA was terminated retrospectively which led to a disallowance of HB during the same period. The commissioner held that the only conclusion that the tribunal could come to was that backdating should be refused, because she had failed to disclose the change of circumstances. This is to ask entirely the wrong question. The question is why the claimant did not make a claim earlier, not why she did not disclose a change of circumstances earlier. In any event, it is hard to see why she was not entitled to have her notional entitlement to HB offset under reg 104(1) HB Regs 1987 (now reg 104(1)).

A tribunal may, when hearing an appeal against refusal to backdate a claim to the date when a previous entitlement ended, treat that claim as an application for revision or appeal against the decision which brought the previous entitlement to HB to an end: *R(JSA) 2/04*; *CH 3009/2002*. In such a case, the tribunal needs to consider not just whether a claim can be backdated but also whether the decision to stop the benefit in the first place was correct.

For a discussion of the caselaw on the position for renewal claims prior to the abolition of benefit periods in April 2004, see pp460-61 of the 21st edition.

[¹Electronic claims for benefit

83A. A claim for housing benefit may be made by means of an electronic communication in accordance with Schedule 11.]

Amendment

1. Inserted by Art 2(3) of SI 2006 No 2968 as from 20.12.06.

Definitions

"electronic communication" – see reg 2(1).

General Note

If authorisation is given by means of a direction of the Chief Executive of the authority, a claim for HB can be made by electronic communication and such a claim is effectively dealt with as a written claim. The authorisation requirements and conditions for claims by electronic communication are found in Sch 11. By para 4 of Sch 11, any claim, certificate, notice, information or evidence which is delivered by means of an electronic communication must generally be treated as having been delivered in the manner or form required by any provision of the HB Regs, on the day the conditions imposed are satisfied.

The DWP reminds authorities in *HB/CTB General Information Bulletin G11/2007*, that claims made electronically where an authority has *not* obtained a Chief Executive's direction are not valid claims and that any benefit paid or credited as a result will not attract any subsidy.

[¹Date of claim where claim sent or delivered to a gateway office

84.]

Amendment

1. Omitted by reg 2(5) of SI 2008 No 2299 as from 1.10.08.

[¹**Date of claim where claim sent or delivered to an office of a designated authority 85.**]

Amendment
1. Omitted by reg 2(6) of SI 2008 No 2299 as from 1.10.08.

Evidence and information

86.–(1) Subject to [³ paragraphs (1A) and (2)] and to paragraph 5 of Schedule A1 (treatment of claims for housing benefit by refugees), a person who makes a claim, or a person to whom housing benefit has been awarded, shall furnish such certificates, documents, information and evidence in connection with the claim or the award, or any question arising out of the claim or the award, as may reasonably be required by the relevant authority in order to determine that person's entitlement to, or continuing entitlement to, housing benefit and shall do so within one month of [³ the relevant authority requiring him, or the Secretary of State requesting him, to do so] or such longer period as the relevant authority may consider reasonable.

[³ (1A) Where a person notifies a change of circumstances to the appropriate DWP office under regulation 88(6), the Secretary of State may request that the claimant provides to the relevant authority the information or evidence that the Secretary of State considers the relevant authority may require to determine the claimant's continuing entitlement to housing benefit.]

(2) Nothing in this regulation shall require a person to furnish any certificates, documents, information or evidence relating to a payment to which paragraph (4) applies.

(3) Where a request is made under paragraph (1), the relevant authority shall–

(a) inform the claimant or the person to whom housing benefit has been awarded of his duty under regulation 88 (duty to notify change of circumstances) to notify the designated office of any change of circumstances; and

(b) without prejudice to the extent of the duty owed under regulation 88, indicate to him either orally or by notice or by reference to some other document available to him on application and without charge, the kind of change or circumstances which is to be notified.

(4) This paragraph applies to any of the following payments–

(a) a payment which is–

   (i) disregarded under paragraph 23 of Schedule 5 (income in kind) or paragraph 34 of Schedule 6 (certain payments in kind); and

   (ii) made under [⁴ or by] the Macfarlane Trust, the Macfarlane (Special Payments) Trust, the Macfarlane (Special Payments) (No 2) Trust, the Fund, the Eileen Trust [⁴ , MFET Limited] , the Skipton Fund or the London Bombings Relief Charitable Fund;

(b) a payment which is disregarded under paragraph 35 of Schedule 5 or paragraph 24 of Schedule 6 (payments made under certain trusts and certain other payments), other than a payment made under the Independent Living [² Fund (2006)];

(c) a payment which is disregarded under regulation 74(9)(b) or (c) (income of non-dependant) other than a payment made under the Independent Living Funds.

(5) Where a claimant or a person to whom housing benefit has been awarded or any partner [⁵ has attained the qualifying age for state pension credit] and is a member of, or a person deriving entitlement to a pension under, a personal pension scheme, [¹] he shall where the relevant authority so requires furnish the following information–

(a) the name and address of the pension fund holder;

(b) such other information including any reference or policy number as is needed to enable the personal pension scheme [¹] to be identified.

(6) Where the pension fund holder receives from a relevant authority a request for details concerning a personal pension scheme [¹] relating to a person or any partner to whom paragraph (5) refers, the pension fund holder shall provide the relevant authority with any information to which paragraph (7) refers.

(7) The information to which this paragraph refers is–

(a) where the purchase of an annuity under a personal pension scheme has been deferred, the amount of any income which is being withdrawn from the personal pension scheme;

(b) in the case of–

    (i) a personal pension scheme where income withdrawal is available, the maximum amount of income which may be withdrawn from the scheme; or

    (ii) a personal pension scheme where income withdrawal is not available, [¹] the maximum amount of income which might be withdrawn from the fund if the fund were held under a personal pension scheme where income withdrawal was available,

calculated by or on behalf of the pension fund holder by means of tables prepared from time to time by the Government Actuary which are appropriate for this purpose.

Amendments

1. Amended by reg 4(6) of SI 2007 No 1749 as from 16.7.07.
2. Amended by reg 6(4)(e) of SI 2008 No 2767 as from 17.11.08.
3. Amended by reg 2(3) of SI 2008 No 2987 as from 22.12.08.
4. Amended by reg 8(3) and (5) of SI 2010 No 641 as from 1.4.10 (5.4.10 where rent payable weekly or in multiples of a week).
5. Amended by reg 8(9) of SI 2010 No 641 as from 6.4.10.

Definitions

"claim" – see reg 2(1).
"claimant" – see reg 2(1).
"designated office" – see reg 2(1).
"the Fund", "the Eileen Trust", "the Macfarlane Trust", "the Macfarlane (Special Payments) Trust", "the Macfarlane (Special Payments) (No 2) Trust", "MFET Limited", "the Independent Living Fund (2006)", "the Skipton Fund" and "the London Bombings Charitable Fund" – see reg 2(1).
"relevant authority" – see reg 2(1).

General Note

This obliges the claimant to provide evidence to support her/his claim if required to do so by the authority (either on the claim form or subsequently) or requested to do so by the DWP within one month of the request, or such longer period as the authority considers reasonable.

The authority must inform the claimant of her/his obligation (under reg 88) to report certain changes of circumstance. See also reg 83 for the information and evidence requirements for valid claims.

Analysis

Paragraphs (1), (1A), (2) and (4): Power to require information

The time at which information may be demanded is the whole period during which HB is being claimed. The claimant or person to whom HB is awarded must provide "certificates, documents, information and evidence" (not further defined) as may be reasonably required. This will depend upon the personal circumstances of each individual claimant and on whether the authority has reasonable cause to doubt any previous statements made, or information given, by her/him. However, the information must be required for the purpose of determining entitlement to HB and not for any other purpose. The requirement to supply information under reg 86 must actually have been communicated to the person in question; proof of posting to the last known address is not sufficient: *AA v London Borough of Hounslow* [2008] UKUT 13 (AAC).

Where there is a failure to comply with the requirements in reg 86(1), note the possibility of payment of HB being suspended under regs 11 or 13 D&A Regs (see pp1030 and 1032). Entitlement to HB might then be terminated under reg 14 of those regulations (see p1034).

Under para (1A), if a change of circumstances is notified to the DWP under reg 88(6), the DWP can request that a claimant provide information or evidence to the local authority if it is needed to determine the claimant's continuing entitlement to HB.

There is no duty to disclose details of certain specific payments which are wholly disregarded: para (2). These are listed in para (4), namely:

(1) Income or payments in kind disregarded under Sch 5 para 23 or Sch 6 para 34.

(2) Payments from any of the Macfarlane Trusts (which were established by the Secretary of State for Social Security for the benefit of haemophiliacs), the Fund, the Eileen Trust, MFET Limited, the Skipton Fund and the London Bombings Relief Charitable Fund.

(3)   Payments which are disregarded under Sch 5 para 34 or Sch 6 para 24 (except for payments from the Independent Living Funds). All such payments derive from payments made under the Macfarlane Trusts.

(4)   Payments to a non-dependant which are disregarded under reg 74(9)(b) or (c) (other than payments from the Independent Living Fund (2006)). Again these are payments under the Macfarlane Trusts, the Fund, MFET Limited or the Eileen Fund.

The power is to require information from "a person who makes a claim or a person to whom housing benefit has been awarded". This includes anyone claiming on behalf of a claimant as appointee under reg 82 or as a duly appointed agent. The fact that specific mention is made of such payments indicates that claimants are potentially under an obligation to disclose all other income and capital (even where it falls to be disregarded in its entirety), at least when requested to do so. It might be argued that the existence of the disregard means that the authority does not need to know the amount of such income or capital to determine the claim but the reality is otherwise: the authority needs to know the amount and nature of all such payments in order to be satisfied that the disregard applies in the first place. It is perfectly reasonable for a local authority to require information or evidence not only at the time the claim form is completed but also "from time to time in the form of a signed statement given in response to direct questions from a council officer at a home visit": *CH 4390/2003* para 11. Moreover, a local authority is entitled (and, indeed, required) to demand information under reg 86(1) notwithstanding the fact that entitlement had ceased in order to correctly calculate the amount of an overpayment: *CH 4943/2001* paras 65-70. The decision in *SSWP v Chiltern DC* [2003] HLR 1019, CA (reported as *R(H) 2/03*), which reversed Commissioner Jacobs' decision on two points, does not affect this conclusion. The Court of Appeal did not endorse the submission for the local authority before the commissioner to the effect that the only way in which it could obtain information in order to operate reg 104 HB Regs 1987 (now reg 104 HB Regs) was by inviting a fresh claim and that it could only operate reg 104 if backdating for "good cause" is granted. The Court of Appeal says "can use that fresh claim" and does not say "can only use that fresh claim" or that the local authority is precluded from obtaining information by other means. Moreover, such an approach would be inconsistent with the Court of Appeal's decision in *Adan* (*R(H) 5/04*): see the commentary to reg 104 on p497.

In *R v Liverpool CC ex p Johnson* (*No 2*) [1995] COD 200, QBD it was held that reg 73(1) HB Regs 1987 (now reg 86(1)) did not empower an authority to insist that a claimant attend for an interview or to decline to determine the claim if s/he did not do so. However, in the absence of such an interview, the authority may decide that it is not satisfied that the claimant has established her/his entitlement to HB, in which case the claim will be refused and the claimant left to her/his remedies of revision or appeal.

The authority may extend the one-month time limit within which the claimant must supply the evidence required or requested for as long as it considers reasonable. An authority's practice of never extending the time limit, however reasonable the request, would be liable to be overturned on judicial review as imposing a fetter on the authority's discretion. An individual refusal could also be challenged if it could be shown that the authority had failed to have regard to a relevant factor (eg, the claimant's state of health or the difficulty of obtaining the information).

Extensive guidance is given to local authorities by the DWP's Verification Framework as to the type of evidence they should require of claimants when a claim is made. However, the Verification Framework has no status in law other than that of general guidance. In particular, it cannot override the prohibition in para (2) to seek information of the types set out in para (4) and nor can it override the requirement in para (1) that information must be "*reasonably* required". *CH 999/2002* paras 13-15 upheld the reasonableness of a requirement to provide utility bills as proof of residence. However, the commissioner made it clear that the reasonableness of any requirement would depend on the circumstances of the individual case: para 14. In short, it is reg 86(1) with which the claimant must comply, not the Verification Framework.

The decision to seek certain information or seek it in certain ways (eg, a home visit) is not itself appealable. However, *CH 2555/2007* reminds the First-tier Tribunal that when an appeal has been made against a decision altering or stopping an award of benefit on the grounds of an alleged failure to provide information, the tribunal has to satisfy itself of the reasonableness of the request for information (or a home visit) in the individual case before it as part of its deciding whether the failure to provide the information provided sufficient grounds to alter or stop the benefit award. Accordingly, in cases where the need for a particular piece of information or a home visit is challenged on an appeal, the tribunal must decide for itself on the facts whether the information or home visit was reasonably required, rather than limiting itself to deciding (on judicial review type grounds) whether the request under reg 86(1) was one which a reasonable local authority could make.

Paragraph (3): The authority's obligations

This obliges the authority to inform the claimant of her/his duty to report changes of circumstances to the authority: sub-para (a), and also tell her/him what *kind* of change s/he should report: sub-para (b). The latter duty may be discharged by word of mouth but it is good practice to provide a written guide in every case and to get the claimant to sign to say that s/he has received and read it. A document is of more use to the claimant because s/he can refer to it in the future and if the duty is discharged by telling the claimant orally of the kinds of changes which should be reported, disputes may arise subsequently as to what was said and indeed whether such a conversation ever took place at all. Needless to say, the authority should be as explicit as possible so that the claimant is not misled in any way.

The duty under this para is stated to arise "where a request is made under paragraph (1)" but taken on its own this is apt to cause confusion. In practice, a request under para (1) is made in every case because information, documents and evidence, etc, are always requested by the questions in the authority's printed claim-form and there is no power other than reg 86(1) to require such information. It follows that the para (3) information should be given to the claimant at the time of the claim in every case and *again* if a supplementary request for further information or evidence is made.

The wording of para (3)(a) does not mean that a claimant is under a duty to provide information to an authority only where a prior request for information has been made by the authority: *CH 2794/2004* para 18. While the duty to provide evidence or information will only arise under reg 86(1) where that evidence or information has been requested, nothing in para (3) qualifies the claimant focused duty in reg 88(1).

Paragraphs (5) to (7): Pension funds

Para (5) entitles the authority to require a claimant or person to whom HB has been awarded (or any partner) who is at least the qualifying age for PC to supply information about pension fund holders and suppliers of pension schemes. Paras (6) and (7) require the provision of information by those administering the schemes. Such information may give rise to a finding of notional income under reg 42(3) if a claimant is failing to exercise her/his rights under the scheme.

Prior to 16 July 2007, reference was also made to "retirement annuity contracts". These were a method of saving for retirement. However, from April 2007 they were subsumed into "personal pension schemes" so it was no longer necessary to draw a distinction between retirement annuity contracts and personal pension schemes.

---

[2]Amendment and withdrawal of claim

[3]**87.**–(1)   person who has made a claim may amend it at any time before a decision has been made on it by a notice in writing delivered or sent to the designated office.

(2)   Where the claim was made by telephone in accordance with paragraphs (4A) to (4AE) of regulation 83, the amendment may also be made by telephone.

(3)   Any claim amended in accordance with paragraph (1) or (2) shall be treated as if it had been amended in the first instance.

(4)   A person who has made a claim may withdraw it at any time before a decision has been made on it by notice to the designated office.

(5)   Where the claim was made by telephone in accordance with paragraphs (4AA) to (4AE) of regulation 83, the withdrawal may also be made by telephone to the telephone number specified by the Secretary of State.

(6)   Any notice of withdrawal given in accordance with paragraph (4) or (5) shall have effect when it is received.]]

Amendments

1.   Inserted by reg 2(3) of SI 2006 No 2967 as from 20.12.06.
2.   Substituted by reg 6(4) of SI 2007 No 719 as from 2.4.07.
3.   Substituted by reg 2(7) of SI 2008 No 2299 as from 1.10.08.

Definitions

"claim" – see reg 2(1).
"designated office" – see reg 2(1).

Analysis

Paras (1) to (3). Before a decision has been made the claimant needs no permission to amend her/his claim provided s/he does so in writing. Where the claim was made by telephone in accordance with reg 83(4A) to (4AE), the amendment may also be done by telephone. The claim is then treated as if made as amended.

Para (4) to (6). A claim can be withdrawn by notice to the "designated office" at any time before a decision is made on it. There is no requirement as to the form of "notice" required to withdraw a claim; according to para (4) it need not even be in writing. Where the claim was made by telephone to the DWP in accordance with reg 83(4AA) to (4AE), it can be withdrawn by telephone to the number specified by the Secretary of State.

Once properly withdrawn the claim ceases to exist and no decision or award can be made on it, nor can the claim then be reinstated: *R(H) 2/06* para 9. It may be possible to show that the decision to withdraw was not freely made – thus depriving the withdrawal of legal effect – but this will only arise in an exceptional case where, for example, the claimant was acting under duress (*CJSA 3979/1999* para 26). However, even in a case of alleged duress, where a claimant is ordinarily able to understand the consequences of her/his actions, what will need to be shown is threatening or overbearing behaviour, or deception, leading to the claim being withdrawn: the fact that withdrawing the claim was not, with the benefit of hindsight, in the claimant's best interests will not be enough (*R(H) 2/06* para 11).

Although there is no statutory mechanism expressly permitting a claim to be withdrawn once a decision has been made on it, DWP Guidance (HB/CTB G10/2008) reminds authorities that a claimant should not be prevented from surrendering an award of benefit if s/he indicates that s/he no longer wishes to claim HB. See also: *CJSA 1332/2001, CDLA 1589/2005* and *CJSA 3979/1999* cited therein.

Duty to notify changes of circumstances

88.–(1) Subject to [³ [⁵ paragraphs (3) and (6)]], if at any time between the making of a claim and a decision being made on it, or during the award of housing benefit, there is a change of circumstances which the claimant, or any person by whom or on whose behalf sums payable by way of housing benefit are receivable, might reasonably be expected to know might affect the claimant's right to, the amount of or the receipt of housing benefit, that person shall be under a duty to notify that change of circumstances by giving notice [¹] to the designated office
[¹[² (a) in writing; or
(b) by telephone–
    (i) where the relevant authority has published a telephone number for that purpose or for the purposes of regulation 83 (time and manner in which claims are to be made) unless the authority determines that in any particular case or class of case notification may not be given by telephone; or
    (ii) in any case or class of case where the relevant authority determines that notice may be given by telephone; or
(c) by any other means which the relevant authority agrees to accept in any particular case.]]
[³ (2)]
(3) The duty imposed on a person by paragraph (1) does not extend to changes in–
(a) the amount of rent payable to a housing authority;
(b) the age of the claimant or that of any member of his family or of any non-dependants;
(c) these Regulations;
(d) in the case of a claimant on income support [² [⁴ , an income-based jobseeker's allowance or an income-related employment and support allowance]], any circumstances which affect the amount of income support [⁴ , an income-based jobseeker's allowance or an income-related employment and support allowance] but not the amount of housing benefit to which he is entitled, other than the cessation of that entitlement to income support [⁴ , an income-based jobseeker's allowance or an income-related employment and support allowance].
(4) Notwithstanding paragraph (3)(b) or (d) a claimant shall be required by paragraph (1) to notify the designated office of any change in the composition of his family arising from the fact that a person who was a member of his family is now no longer such a person because he ceases to be a child or young person.
[³ (5)]
[⁵ (6) Where–
(a) the claimant or the claimant's partner is in receipt of income support or jobseeker's allowance;
(b) the change of circumstance is that the claimant or the claimant's partner starts employment; and
(c) as a result of that change of circumstance, either entitlement to that benefit will end or, where the claimant or claimant's partner is in receipt of a contribution-based jobseeker's allowance, the amount of that benefit will be reduced,
the claimant may discharge the duty in paragraph (1) by notifying the change of circumstance by telephoning the appropriate DWP office if a telephone number has been provided for that purpose.]

Amendments
1. Amended by reg 2(4) of SI 2006 No 2967 as from 20.12.06.
2. Inserted by reg 3(9) of SI 2008 No 1042 as from 19.5.08.
3. Amended by reg 2(8) of SI 2008 No 2299 as from 1.10.08.
4. Amended by reg 20 of SI 2008 No 1082 as from 27.10.08.
5. Amended by reg 2(4) of SI 2008 No 2987 as from 22.12.08.
6. Amended by reg 2(5) of SI 2010 No 2449 as from 1.11.10.

Definitions
"appropriate DWP office – see reg 2(1).
"claimant" – reg 2(1).
"designated office" – see reg 2(1).
"designated authority" – see reg 2(1).
"family" – see s137(1) SSCBA and Part 4.
"housing authority" – see s191 SSAA.
"non-dependant" – see reg 3.
"rent" – see Part 3.

General Note
This regulation imposes a general duty on the claimant and anyone by whom, or on whose behalf, HB may be receivable to report to the authority any change of circumstances which might affect the claimant's right to, the amount of, or the payment of benefit.

The regulation links to the rules on overpayments: see Part 13. Local authorities should act promptly when notified of changes in circumstance as any subsequent overpayment may be irrecoverable as having been caused by official error.

Note also the possible offences where someone dishonestly fails to give a prompt notification of a change of circumstances: ss111A and 112 SSAA (on pp55 and 59). See also reg 4 Social Security (Notification of Change of Circumstances) Regulations 2001 (on p1183).

Analysis
Paragraph (1): The duty to report changes
The duty to report changes in circumstances is placed not merely on the claimant but on appointees and landlords who are in receipt of direct payment of HB: see regs 95 and 96. It is not contingent on a prior request being made by the local authority: *CH 2794/2004* para 18.

Notification must usually be given to the local authority (but see para (6) for an exception) and must be:
– in writing;
– by telephone where the relevant authority has published a telephone number for the purposes of telephone claims or notification of changes of circumstances or in other cases specified; *or*
– in a form other than in writing or by telephone.

Note that notice may also be given by means of an electronic communication in accordance with Sch 11 (if authorised) reg 88A and that there are alternative means for notice (reg 88ZA). Notice may be given to the DWP in specified circumstances under reg 88(6).

Telephoning the local authority with the information would, in many cases, be bad practice as it does not provide a permanent record. It is always best to ensure receipt of notifications by the authority by sending letters by recorded delivery post. Some authorities adopt a helpful practice of giving a receipt for documents handed over in person, and such documents should always be kept in a safe place.

The changes which must be reported are those which might effect the claimant's right to HB (eg, if s/he moves address or her/his capital increases above the capital limit), the amount of HB s/he is entitled to (eg, if her/his income increases, or s/he inherits capital which will increase her/his "tariff income" under reg 52); and his right to receive HB (eg, rent arrears which might justify payment to a landlord).

There are back up arrangements between local authorities and DWP local offices where the claimant is also in receipt of IS or income-based JSA. The DWP should notify the authority of any changes which are reported to them and, if the claimant ceases to be entitled to IS or income-based JSA. There is often delay in this happening so this should *not* be relied on. The primary duty is imposed on the claimant (and/or appointee or landlord as the case may be) to report all relevant changes to the correct office irrespective of whether the DWP also does so. A breakdown in the back-up procedure will not mean that a resulting overpayment is unrecoverable as being the result of an official error: see the Analysis to reg 100. Note that at the time of writing, the arrangement between authorities and the DWP where the claimant is also in receipt of income-related ESA were not yet known.

Paragraphs (3), (4) and (6): Exceptions to the general rule
Para (3) lists four types of change of circumstance which do not have to be reported to the local authority by someone under the general duty in para (1).
(1)   Changes in the rent charged by the authority to its own tenants: sub-para (a).
(2)   Changes in the ages of the claimant and her/his family or of any non-dependants: sub-para (b). This is subject to the qualification in para (4).
(3)   Changes in the regulations themselves: sub-para (c).
(4)   Changes which affect the amount of IS, income-based JSA or income-related ESA but not HB, other than the cessation of entitlement to one of those benefits: sub-para (d). This is subject to the qualification in para (4).

The changes in sub-paras (a), (b) and (c) are included because, although they do potentially affect entitlement, the authority will already be aware of them from other sources, as with those changes in sub-paras (a) and (c) or from the dates of birth supplied at the time of the claim.

The change set out in sub-para (d) would include, for example, a change in income or capital that reduces (but does not end) entitlement to IS, income-based JSA or income-related ESA. HB claimants who are also entitled to IS, income-based JSA or income-related ESA receive maximum HB whatever the amount of their IS, income-based JSA or income-related ESA (see s130(3)(a) of SSCBA, HB Regs Sch 4 para 12, Sch 5 para 4 and Sch 6 para 5 and the discussion on *R v Penwith DC ex p Menear* [1991] 24 HLR 115, QBD in the General Note to Part 6). Apart from the change set out in para (4) (to which this sub-paragraph is subject), changes in the amount of IS/income-based JSA/income-related ESA payable to the claimant have no effect on her/his entitlement to, nor the amount of, HB.

Para (4). Although the general rule in para (2)(b) is that changes in the age of members of the family do not need to be reported, this paragraph requires disclosure when someone ceases to be a "child" or a "young person" for HB purposes (for which see commentary to reg 19). This is because the effect of such a change could be that the person concerned ceases to be a member of the "family" and instead becomes a non-dependant: see reg 3 and s137(1) SSCBA.

The change from family member to non-dependant affects the level of HB payable even if the claimant continues to receive IS, income-based JSA or income-related ESA, because maximum HB is defined as eligible rent less non-dependant deductions: see reg 70. It must therefore be reported notwithstanding sub-para (3)(d).

Para (6). There is situation in which a claimant, instead of notifying the local authority, can report a change in circumstances by telephoning the DWP, if a telephone number has been provided for this purpose. This only applies where the change of circumstances is that the claimant or her/his partner has started employment, the claimant or her/his partner is in receipt of IS or JSA, and as a result of the change, entitlement to IS or JSA will end, or if the benefit is *contribution-based* JSA, the amount will be reduced.

[¹ Alternative means of notifying changes of circumstances

88ZA.–(1)   In such cases and subject to such conditions as the Secretary of State may specify, the duty in regulation 88(1) to notify a change of circumstances may be discharged by notifying the Secretary of State–

(a)   where the change of circumstances is a birth or death, through a relevant authority, or a county council in England, by personal attendance at an office specified by that authority or county council, provided the Secretary of State has agreed with that authority or county council for it to facilitate such notification; or

(b)   where the change of circumstances is a death, by telephone to a telephone number specified for that purpose by the Secretary of State.

(2)   Paragraph (1) only applies if the authority administering the claimant's housing benefit agrees with the Secretary of State that notifications may be made in accordance with that paragraph.

(3)   The Secretary of State must forward information received in accordance with paragraph (1) to the authority administering the claimant's housing benefit.]

Amendment

1.   Inserted by reg 5 of SI 2010 No 444 as from 5.4.10.

[¹Notice of changes of circumstances given electronically

88A.   A person may give notice of a change of circumstances required to be notified under regulation 88 by means of an electronic communication in accordance with Schedule 11.

Amendment

1.   Inserted by Art 2(4) of SI 2006 No 2968 as from 20.12.06.

General Note

If a local authority authorises it, notifications can be made by electronic communication. The authorisation requirements and conditions are found in Sch 11. By para 4 of Sch 11, any claim, certificate, notice, information or evidence which is delivered by means of an electronic communication must generally be treated as having been delivered in the manner or form required by any provision of the HB Regs, on the day the conditions imposed are satisfied.

PART 11
Decisions on questions

General Note on Part 11
This Part deals with decisions and their notification to those affected by them. Reg 89 provides that initial decisions are generally to be taken by the "relevant authority" and provides a flexible time limit for reaching decisions. Reg 90 prescribes how and when authorities are to notify any person affected by a decision (this is not just claimants) of their decisions and requires every notification to include a statement as to the matters set out in Sch 9.

Decisions by a relevant authority

89.–(1)   Unless provided otherwise by these Regulations, any matter required to be determined under these Regulations shall be determined in the first instance by the relevant authority.

(2)   The relevant authority shall make a decision on each claim within 14 days of the provisions of regulations 83 and 86 being satisfied or as soon as reasonably practicable thereafter.

[¹ (3)]

Amendment
1.   Omitted by reg 4(4)(d) of SI 2008 No 959 as from 6.10.08.

Definition
"relevant authority" – see reg 2(1).

General Note
This reinforces s34 SSA 1998 by providing that the relevant authority is to have primary responsibility for taking decisions under these regulations: para (1). Para (2) sets out a flexible time limit for taking decisions.

Analysis
Paragraph (1)
Decisions must be made by the "relevant authority", defined as the authority administering HB: reg 2(1). This rule is subject to other bodies being given decision-making powers by individual regulations: the rent officer's involvement in determining the claimant's maximum rent under reg 13 is an example. See also s134(5) SSAA.
Paragraph (2)
The relevant authority must make a decision on each claim. This includes where a claim is defective. The previous version of this paragraph in the HB Regs 1987 – which stated that an authority was under no duty to make a decision on a claim which had not been properly made or where the claimant had failed to provide evidence or information in connection with the claim – was ruled *ultra vires* and of no effect by a tribunal of commissioners in *R(H) 3/05*. The essence of the commissioners' decision was that there was no power given by primary legislation to local authorities to decide not to determine a claim. See *CH 532/2006* for the retrospective application of this decision.

   The effect of the decision and the subsequent amendments to reg 76 HB Regs 1987 (now consolidated in reg 88 HB Regs) is that a local authority must decide a defective claim at the point in time when the alleged defect will not or cannot reasonably be remedied, and when such a decision is made the claimant has a right of appeal to the First-tier Tribunal against the entitlement decision then arrived at. The decisions made by local authorities in these situations are simply decisions on claims, made on the evidence available, which in most cases will be negative decisions given the likely lack of evidence.

   If any support for this is needed it can be gained from what was said in Committee by the Parliamentary Under-Secretary of State (Maria Eagle) when reg 4(3) of (the then draft) SI 2004 No.3368 (which amended reg 76 HB Regs 1987) was being considered. She made it plain that the intent of the amendment was to implement in full *R(H) 3/05* and that the terms of reg 76(1) HB Regs 1987 required an authority to make a decision on every claim, defective or otherwise.

   The time limit for making a decision. Where the authority is under a duty to make a decision on the claim, the general rule is that it must be done within 14 days. However, the time limit is qualified by the phrase "or as soon as reasonably practicable thereafter".

   If the authority has made a decision on a claim but is delaying actual payment, see the Analysis to reg 91(3) on p465. Note also the obligation to make a payment on account in certain circumstances under reg 93 if the claim is not decided within 14 days. This does not require the claimant to make a further application for such payment: *R v Haringey LBC ex p Ayub* [1992] 25 HLR 566, QBD. See the Analysis to reg 93 on p468.

   Delays in making a decision can cause severe difficulties for private tenants. A threat to apply for judicial review may have a salutary effect on an authority failing to make a decision on a claim. In *R v Liverpool CC ex p*

Johnson (No 1) [1994] unreported, 23 June, QBD, it was said that it was "of the essence" that claims for HB should be determined speedily and an order of mandamus was granted to compel the authority to determine the claims. Of the corresponding provision for the adjudication of general benefits in SSAA s21(1), Commissioner Goodman stated that the word "imposes a fairly strict requirement ... and every effort should be made to secure compliance with the statutory provision ...": *R(SB) 2/88* (para 14).

Many authorities have sought to justify delays by staffing and financial constraints. In *R v Secretary of State for Social Services ex p CPAG* [1990] 2 QB 540, CA, a submission that the Secretary of State was under a duty to appoint enough adjudication officers (the term then used for decision makers) to enable every claim to be determined within 14 days was rejected. It was said, however, that s/he could not simply ignore the requirement and would be obliged to take it into account when determining how many officers to appoint. That discretion had to be exercised reasonably: at 555B-D. This suggests that a complete failure to have regard to the statutory duty under reg 89(2) will result in grounds for judicial review.

An alternative method of dealing with delays in assessment is to complain to a commissioner for Local Administration (local government ombudsman). If s/he considers the delay constitutes maladministration s/he may order compensation to be paid. As to when judicial review proceedings will be appropriate, note the suggestion in *R v Lambeth LBC ex p Crookes* [1995] 29 HLR 28 at 35, QBD that the ombudsman should normally be the first port of call in cases of delay. However, if the allegation is one of complete failure to make a decision rather than delay, the same analysis ought not to apply.

Paragraph (3)
Prior to 6 October 2008, a claimant's entitlement to HB ceased under reg 77 when her/his entitlement to IS or income-based JSA ceased on account of work or an increase in hours or earnings. Under para (3), a new claim for HB was given priority if the claimant was also treated as having claimed extended payments of HB under the version of reg 72(2) prior to 6 October 2008 and had given the authority or the DWP specified notice. The claim had to be made within 14 days of the IS or income-based JSA ceasing.

Reg 77 was omitted when the new form of the rules for extended payments were subsituted by SI 2008 No.959. Under the substituted rules (regs 72 to 72D), entitlement to HB continues at least until the end of the extended payment period, so no new claim (and therefore no priority) is needed.

Notification of decisions

90.–(1)   An authority shall notify in writing any person affected by a decision made by it under these Regulations–

(a)   in the case of a decision on a claim, forthwith or as soon as reasonably practicable thereafter;

(b)   in any other case, within 14 days of that decision or as soon as reasonably practicable thereafter,

and every notification shall include a statement as to the matters set out in Schedule 9.

(2)   A person affected to whom an authority sends or delivers a notification of decision may, by notice in writing signed by him [¹ within one month of the date of the notification of that decision (or, if the decision was notified before 1st November 2010, before 1st December 2010)], request the authority to provide a written statement setting out the reasons for its decision on any matter set out in the notice.

(3)   For the purposes of paragraph (2), where a person affected who requests a written statement is not a natural person, the notice in writing referred to in that paragraph shall be signed by a person over the age of 18 who is authorised to act on that person's behalf.

(4)   The written statement referred to in paragraph (2) shall be sent to the person requesting it within 14 days or as soon as is reasonably practical thereafter.

Amendment
1.   Amended by reg 2(6) of SI 2010 No 2449 as from 1.11.10.

Definition
"person affected" – see reg 2(1).

General Note
Once an authority has made a decision, reg 90 makes it mandatory for the authority to notify any person affected by the decision and sets out the rules which it must observe when notifying such a person (see also reg 93 in respect of payments on account of rent allowance).

Every notification must include a statement as to the matters set out in Sch 9. While Sch 9 obliges an authority to provide information in its notification in specified circumstances, paras (2) and (4) enable a person affected to ask for a statement of the *reasons* for a decision on any matter set out in the notice. Note also the additonal requirements for a notice of a decision against which there is a right of appeal in reg 10 D&A Regs (see p1029).

There are no specifications as to the form or content of the decision but authorities are encouraged to give full details rather than just quoting regulation numbers.

Analysis
Paragraph (1): General
"Person affected" is defined in reg 2(1) by reference to reg 3 D&A regs: see p1010 for a discussion of its meaning. See also the General Note to reg 95 on p471.

By reg 82(6) a notification to a deputy, judicial factor, guardian, attorney or appointee for a claimant who is unable to act is validly given even if (as will be usual) it is not also given to the claimant. A written notification can be validly given to a claimant who cannot read English, at least where such a claimant has assistance from friends, relatives or advisers available: *R v Newham LBC ex p Kaur* [1997] 29 HLR 776 at 784, QBD.

Sub-paras (a) and (b) give the time limits for making notifications in respect of claims and decisions on other matters.

Although the time limit for deciding on a claim is given by reg 89(2), once it is made the decision must be sent out "forthwith": sub-para (a). In any other case, the decision must be sent out within 14 days: sub-para (b). However, where this is not possible, both sub-paragraphs qualify the time periods. In this case, an authority must provide the notice "as soon as reasonably practicable thereafter". In respect of delays, see the Analysis to reg 89(2).

Paragraph (1): Validity of notifications
The duty in para (1) to provide a notification and the duty to ensure that the notification contains the matters prescribed by Sch 9 is mandatory. The question of whether a notification is valid has particular significance in the context of overpayments, but may also arise in other contexts. For example, a claimant may have missed the time limit for appealing and it may be necessary to decide upon the validity of a document purporting to be a decision, since if the decision has not been validly notified to the claimant, the authority can be compelled by judicial review proceedings to issue a proper notification which then attracts rights of appeal.

It must be borne in mind that a local authority is not precluded from issuing a valid decision by a tribunal's ruling that a previous purported decision is invalid and of no effect: *CH 5217/2001* para 12.

The form of the decision. The general approach of the High Court has been to look at the substance rather than the form of a communication to the claimant. Even if a communication to a claimant is not described as a "decision", the High Court has indicated that the communication will be examined to see whether it does in fact amount to a decision: *R v Islington LBC ex p Ewing* [1992] unreported, 5 February, QBD. In that case, letters from the authority refusing increases of benefit under what was reg 61(2) HB Regs 1987 (now revoked) were held arguably to be "decisions".

The Court of Appeal held that if a defect in a notice does not cause prejudice to a person affected, its validity should be upheld: *Haringey LBC v Awaritefe* [1999] 32 HLR 517. In that case the notice failed to refer to the defendant's right to seek a statement of reasons under reg 77(4) HB regs 1987 (now reg 90(2)), referred to the right to seek a review as a right of "appeal" and did not refer to a right to seek a further hearing before a Review Board. The Court held that as there was no evidence that these failures had prevented the defendant from challenging the decision that an overpayment was recoverable, she had not suffered any prejudice and so the non-compliance with the requirements of Sch 6 HB Regs 1987 (now Sch 9) did not invalidate the determination and the overpayment was recoverable.

However, *Awaritefe* and *R v Thanet DC ex p Warren Court Hotels Ltd* [2000] 33 HLR 339, CA may now need to be treated with a little caution as they were decided when the ultimate challenge to a decision was by way of judicial review, where the substantive factual basis of the overpayment decision could not be considered, whereas on an appeal, the First-tier Tribunal can consider the factual basis of the decision and, if necessary, adjourn the hearing of the appeal so as to give the appellant sufficient opportunity to address points which may not have been addressed in the initial decision notice. Accordingly, the better starting point for considering alleged deficiencies in the decision notice may be the commissioners' decisions referred to below, in particular *R(H) 3/04*.

Awaritefe was applied in *R(H) 1/02* para 10. Since there was no prejudice to the claimant in not having detailed calculations of an overpayment, if there had been a duty to state those details (which the commissioner held there was not) then the omission would not have rendered the overpayment irrecoverable: para 10.

Commissioner Jacobs applied *Awaritefe* in *CH 4943/2001* and held that although the constituent parts of the decision had emerged in dribs and drabs leading up to the appeal hearing, the landlord had sufficient information to be able to appeal and then argue its case before the tribunal (para 21). Accordingly the decision was not invalidated by the failure to provide all the required information at the outset. The same commissioner reached a consistent conclusion in *CH 5217/2001*, where the claimant complained that she had never been provided with a calculation of excess CTB alleged to have been paid to her. The commissioner held that the deprivation of a possible ground of appeal amounted to significant prejudice: paras 7, 9. Had the claimant been provided with a calculation before the tribunal, it would have been possible for her to address the point, with an adjournment if necessary, and the decision would not have been invalid. But it was too late to provide a calculation before the commissioner: para 13.

The terms of a decision may be proved by extraneous evidence even if the actual decision cannot be provided: *CH 4099/2002* paras 9-11; *CH 4943/2001* paras 10-11; *CH 216/2003* paras 12-16, though note para 20 where the commissioner is critical of the shortcomings of authorities' computer systems.

What impact deficiences in the decision notice may have on any subsequent appeal were considered by a tribunal of commissioners in *R(H) 3/04.* They concluded in respect of reg 77 HB Regs 1987 (now reg 90 HB Regs), at paras 74-76, as follows:

"74.   . . .the question of the effect of any procedural defect in the steps taken by the authority will only fall to be considered by an appeal tribunal on a properly constituted appeal, by a particular appellant against a recoverable overpayment determination for a particular amount made against him pursuant to section 75. Here the introduction of a full statutory right of appeal to a judicial tribunal having full jurisdiction to rehear and redetermine for itself the factual basis of the determination as to recoverability as well as its legality, coupled with the requirement to give a full statement of reasons for its decision if requested, means that many of the arguments which formerly occupied the courts on judicial review applications concerning procedural defects on the part of an authority will cease to have so much practical effect.

75.   Failures for example by a local authority to provide particulars of the facts, grounds, amount and period of the overpayment as required by regulation 77, or to notify the appellant of the existence of his rights of appeal, will for practical purposes in the normal case have ceased to cause any significant injustice to an appellant by the time a properly constituted appeal does get before the tribunal. This is because the appeal process affords him the opportunity to adduce evidence and have a full rehearing before a judicial body able to go into the factual basis of the claim that the money is legally recoverable from him, as well as any maintainable challenge to the lawfulness of the whole process. It may still be necessary, in an extreme case where the Council's attempt at operation of the procedure has been so far defective or non-existent that the tribunal is satisfied there has never been a valid basis for a determination against the appellant at all, for the whole process to be held abortive and the appeal summarily allowed on that ground; but such cases of total rejection where the authority will have to abandon its attempt at recovery or start again will now be rarer than in the days when the only judicial control was by way of review.

76.   Thus if the tribunal is satisfied on the facts before it that the case for a recoverable overpayment determination against the appellant is made out, incidental procedural defects in the local authority's determination that no longer have any continuing practical effect and have not caused any injustice still unremedied by the tribunal itself will not in our judgment prevent it confirming the authority's determination, or if necessary making its own findings and substituting its own decision as to the amount legally recoverable. Consequently we accept the arguments of the authorities and the Secretary of State summarised in paragraph 31 above, with the test of "significant prejudice" or "substantial compliance" explained in *Haringey LBC v Awaritefe* [1999] 32 HLR 517 applied as indicated above to take into account what happens in the tribunal appeal process itself. By the same token we reject the arguments for the landlords that any past failure of procedure must be fatal to recovery, or that past administrative cost and delay is a sufficient prejudice in this context to deprive a tribunal of the ability to confirm a determination or substitute its own, even where the original failures of notification, etc., have ceased to be of any practical effect".

Defective attempt at revision or supersession. The decision of the tribunal of commissioners in *R(IB) 2/04* has settled the law on defective attempts to make a decision to revise or supersede. It is suggested that these parts of the tribunal's decision will apply to the HB scheme. After detailed consideration of the statutory scheme under the SSA 1998, the tribunal concluded (para 55) that it was open to an appeal tribunal to substitute a revising decision for a superseding decision. It was also decided that defects in a revising or superseding decision would not generally render the decision invalid (para 72). It was said that:

". . . a decision should generally be regarded as having been made under Section 10, regardless of the form in which it may be expressed, if it has the effect of terminating an existing entitlement from the date of the decision (or from some later date than the effective date of the original decision). That is simply because there is no other general power which enables an existing entitlement to be terminated in that manner" (para 76).

The tribunal of commissioners' decision is not particularly helpful about the circumstances in which a revising or superseding decision would be invalid. It stated that:

"there may be some decisions made by the Secretary of State which have so little coherence or connection to legal powers that they do not amount to decisions under Section 10 at all. In the absence of specific facts, we do not consider it would be helpful here to seek to identify the characteristics which might lead to that conclusion in a particular case, but deal with the general principles below" (para 72).

Some assistance may be found in *CDLA 4977/2001* para 28, in which Commissioner Jacobs suggested cases where the officer took a decision without authority, where a similar decision had already been made by another officer, and where there had not been some step taken that was necessary to give the officer authority: para 28.

Paragraphs (2) to (4): Written statement of reasons

Para (2). The request for reasons must be in writing, within one month of the date of the notification of the decision. Prior to 1 November 2010, no time limit was specified. Note: if the decision was notified before that date, the request for reasons must be made before 1 December 2010.

The right to reasons extends to "any matter set out in the notice". Sch 9 deals with what should be included in the notice. Note that the requirement that the request is "signed by him" may mean that the person affected must sign it personally and it will be insufficient for it to be signed by a duly authorised agent such as a solicitor: *R v Lambeth LBC ex p Crookes* [1998] 31 HLR 59, QBD. But see the commentary to r23 of the TP(FTT) Rules on p1062 for a possible alternative argument.

Note that if a written statement is requested under reg 10 D&A Regs (where one has not already been provided): days between the date the authority receives the request and the date on which it is provided are ignored when calculating the time limit for seeking a revision (reg 4(4) D&A Regs); the time limit for appealing runs for 14 days after the later of the normal one-month time limit for appealing or after the written statement of reasons is provided (r23 and Sch 1 TP(FTT) Rules).

Para (3) requires that where a person affected is not a "natural person" (eg, a corporate body, such as a landlord that is a company), the notice seeking a written statement of reasons must be signed by an authorised person who is over aged 18.

Para (4). The authority does have a time limit for providing a written statement. This is 14 days or as soon as "reasonably practicable" after. See notes on reg 89(2) in respect of delays.

PART 12
Payments

General Note on Part 12

This Part governs when (reg 91(3)), how (regs 91(1) and 91A), how frequently (regs 91 and 92) and to whom (regs 94 to 96) HB shall be paid, and makes provision for payment on account of rent allowance if an authority is slow in calculating actual entitlement (reg 93).

Reg 97 deals with payment where the person entitled has died. Reg 98 provides for the offsetting of benefit already paid when the amount to which the claimant is entitled is revised.

Time and manner of payment

91.–(1)   Subject to paragraphs (2) and (3) and regulations 92 to 98 (frequency of payment of a rent allowance, and payment on account of a rent allowance, payment provisions, offsetting) the relevant authority shall pay housing benefit to which a person is entitled under these Regulations at such time and in such manner as is appropriate, having regard to–

(a)   the times at which and the frequency with which a person's liability to make payment of rent arises; and

(b)   the reasonable needs and convenience of the person entitled thereto.

(2)   Where a person's entitlement to housing benefit is less than £1 weekly the relevant authority may pay that benefit at 6 monthly intervals.

(3)   Subject to regulations 92 to 97 (frequency of payment of and payment on account of a rent allowance, payment provisions), every authority shall make the first payment of any housing benefit awarded by it within 14 days of the receipt of the claim at the designated office or, if that is not reasonably practical, as soon as possible thereafter.

Modifications

Reg 91(3) has effect as modified by Sch 3 para 7 of the HB&CTB(CP) Regs (see p1221) for some claimants entitled to and in receipt of HB in respect of their current home on 6 October 1996 and continuously since then.

Definitions

"payment" – see reg 2(1).

"rent" – see Part 3.

General Note

Although the language in which this regulation is expressed is mandatory, it merely sets out the boundaries within which the authority's discretion may be exercised.

Para (1) lists certain factors which the authority must consider in deciding how and when to pay HB; para (2) provides a discretion to pay at six monthly intervals where only a small amount of benefit is involved. Para (3) gives the time limit within which payment should be made after a successful claim.

Analysis

Para (1) is expressly subject to regs 92 to 98. The implication is that, if the authority's choice of time and method of payment is not "appropriate", it may be challenged. The factors in sub-paras (a) and (b) must be considered in deciding what is appropriate. Authorities who delay in paying rent rebates or allowances yet expect claimants to continue paying full rent in the meantime cannot be said to be taking account of a claimant's reasonable needs and convenience. In the case of private tenants, there will be no option but to pay in full despite outstanding HB entitlement. Such practices should be avoided.

Para (2) merely gives the authority a choice of paying at six monthly intervals when the claimant is entitled to less than £1 a week.

Para (3). The 14-day time limit for payment following a successful claim is qualified by the phrase "or if this is not reasonably practical . . . thereafter", and also by regs 92 to 97. For "reasonably practical" see reg 89(2) but note that payment must in any event be made "as soon as possible" after the 14-day limit expires, which may be an even more stringent test than that in reg 89(2). If it is impracticable for the authority to make a decision on a claim within 14 days, see reg 93 for when payments on account ("interim payments") must be made.

If a particular authority is persistently late in paying, legal action may be possible. See reg 89(2) in respect of dealing with delays. In an individual case, once entitlement to HB has been notified, that entitlement may be classed as a debt owed to the claimant, and if the authority delays unreasonably in paying thereafter, some success has been achieved in the past by suing in the county court for the HB owed.

It is clear from two decisions of the Court of Appeal that if an authority determines that a claimant is entitled to HB (or a landlord is entitled to direct payments) but then fails to make payment, the person entitled to receive the payment may bring an action in the County Court in England and Wales or the Sheriff Court in Scotland. First, the Court of Appeal has stated that where a public body has decided that sums should be payable to an individual pursuant to statute but then fails to do so, it may be sued in debt: *Trustees of the Dennis Rye Pension Fund v Sheffield CC* [1998] 1 WLR 840 at 849F-M, 850A, CA. This principle was applied in the HB context in *Jones v Waveney DC* [1999] 33 HLR 3, CA. The claimant, Mr Jones, was a landlord of a number of properties with tenants in receipt of HB from the defendant council. He was paid by regular cheques for the HB due to him from his tenants. The council took the view that one of his tenants was overpaid just over £1,000. No determination to that effect was issued and the sum was deducted from one of the regular cheques. Mr Jones brought proceedings in the County Court for the balance of the HB due to him. The County Court judge found in Mr Jones' favour and the council appealed. Pill LJ, dismissing the appeal, set out the position as follows:

"A claimant who seeks to obtain relief must normally follow the procedures set out in the Regulations, as this Court held in *Haringey LBC v Cotter* [1996] 29 HLR 682, CA. Where, however, as in this case, the Council have not themselves followed the procedures which they are obliged to follow under the regulations, and have thereby deprived the claimant of the protection and opportunities offered him by the regulations, he is entitled to bring a County Court action. In substance, by their defence the Council were seeking to "recover", under the regulations, what they had determined to be an overpayment under the regulations.

It is conceded that if a Council purported to make a payment by cheque of housing benefit they had determined to be due, but declined to sign the cheque, the sum determined to be due would be recoverable in the County Court. That would be a mere debt collecting exercise for which an ordinary action is appropriate."

The position can therefore be summarised as follows. Proceedings in the County Court or Sheriff Court may be brought by a claimant if benefit has been awarded to her/him but not paid. Proceedings may also be brought by a landlord where the benefit has been awarded and the council has also decided that direct payments should be made to her/him. Proceedings may be brought if a cheque has been issued but has been lost or, as Pill LJ suggested, not properly filled out with the result that it cannot be cashed by the intended recipient. However, proceedings may *never* be brought unless the council has actually awarded HB. If there is any dispute as to whether HB should have been awarded, the appeal process must be used to determine that issue.

[¹Cases in which payments to a housing authority are to take the form of a rent allowance

91A.–(1)   Where the occupier of a dwelling is liable to make payments in respect of that dwelling to a housing authority as a result of the making of an order specified in paragraph (2), housing benefit in respect of those payments shall take the form of a rent allowance.

(2)   The orders specified for the purposes of paragraph (1) are–

(a)   a management control order made in accordance with section 74 of the Antisocial Behaviour etc. (Scotland) Act 2004;

(b)   an interim management order made in accordance with section 102 of the Housing Act 2004;

(c)   a final management order made in accordance with section 113 of that Act;

(d)   an interim empty dwelling management order made in accordance with section 133 of that Act; and

(e)   a final empty dwelling management order made in accordance with section 136 of that Act.]

[² (3)   Where–

(a)   the occupier of a caravan, mobile home or houseboat is liable to make payments in respect of that caravan, mobile home or houseboat and housing benefit in relation to those payments takes the form of a rent allowance; and

(b)   the occupier is also liable to make payments to a housing authority in respect of the site on which that caravan or mobile home stands, or in respect of the mooring to which the houseboat is attached,

housing benefit in respect of payments to the housing authority shall take the form of a rent allowance.]

Amendments

1.   Inserted by reg 2 of SI 2006 No 644 as from 3.4.06.
2.   Inserted by reg 2(2) of SI 2008 No 2824 as from 6.4.09.

General Note

HB takes the form of a rent rebate where rent is paid to the authority paying the HB and otherwise takes the form of a rent allowance: s134(1A) and (1B) SSAA 1992. Various provisions within the HB Regs apply only where a rent allowance is payable.

    Paras (1) and (2). Where an occupier become liable to pay rent to an authority as a result of any of the orders specified in para (2) being made, rather than to her/his landlord, a rent rebate would ordinarily become payable. Reg 91A was inserted into the HB Regs to ensure that rent allowances continue to be paid so that claimants in this situation do not unfairly gain (eg, because their rent is not referred to the rent officer under reg 14) or lose (eg, if the LHA rules apply and they qualify for HB at a higher rate than their rent under regs 12D and 13D).

    Para (3) similarly deems HB paid in respect of payments made to the authority to be rent allowance in the situations set out.

Frequency of payment of a rent allowance

92.–(1)   Subject to the following provisions of this regulation any rent allowance other than a payment made in accordance with regulation 91(2) or (3) or 93 (time and manner of payment, payment on account of rent allowance) shall be paid at intervals of 2 or 4 weeks or one month or, with the consent of the person entitled, at intervals greater than one month.

(2)   Except in a case to which paragraph (3) applies, any payment of a rent allowance shall be made, in so far as it is practicable to do so, at the end of the period in respect of which it is made.

(3)   Except in a case to which regulation 96(2) applies and subject to paragraph (4), this paragraph applies where payment of a rent allowance is being made to a landlord (which for these purposes has the same meaning as in regulations 95 and 96 (payments to a landlord)), when that payment shall be made–

(a)   at intervals of 4 weeks; and

(b)   at the end of the period in respect of which it is made.

(4)   Where paragraph (3) applies–

(a)   in a case where the liability in respect of which the rent allowance is paid is monthly, the authority may make payment at intervals of 1 month;

(b)   in a case where the authority is paying a rent allowance to a landlord in respect of more than one claimant, then the first such payment in respect of any claimant may be made to that landlord at such lesser interval as that authority considers is in the best interest of the efficient administration of housing benefit.

(5)   Except in a case to which paragraph (3) applies, where a person's weekly entitlement to a rent allowance is more than £2 he may require payment at two weekly intervals and the relevant authority shall pay at two weekly intervals in such a case.

(6)   Except in a case to which paragraph (3) applies, the relevant authority may pay a rent allowance at weekly intervals where either–

(a)   it considers that unless the rent allowance is paid at weekly intervals an overpayment is likely to occur; or

(b)   the person entitled is liable to pay his rent weekly and it considers that it is in his interest that his allowance be paid weekly.

(7)   Subject to paragraphs (2), (3) and (5), the relevant authority may pay a rent allowance to a student once a term.

Modifications

Reg 92 has effect as modified by Sch 3 para 7 HB&CTB(CP) Regs (see p1221) for some claimants entitled to and in receipt of HB in respect of their current home on 6 October 1996 and continuously since then.

Definitions

"payment" – see reg 2(1).
"overpayment" – see reg 99.
"rent" – see Part 3.
"rent allowance" – see s134(1A) and (1B) SSAA.
"student" – see Part 7.

General Note

This applies solely to rent allowances (eg, HB paid to private and housing association tenants). It effectively limits the authority's choice in deciding how frequently to pay this form of HB. The regulation only applies where a claim is made or treated as made on or after 7 October 1996 and the claimant is not exempt from these payment rules. See Sch 3 para 7 HB&CTB(CP) Regs (p1221) for the saving provision.

Where the authority has a choice about how frequently to pay HB it must take into account the factors in reg 91(1).

Analysis

Paragraphs (1) and (2): Payments to claimants

Para (1). Under para (1), except where the claimant is entitled to less than £1 a week and the authority has used its powers in reg 91(2) or where an initial payment is made following a claim under reg 91(3), or where payment on account is made under reg 93, the authority may choose between the following periods of payment frequency: every two weeks, four weeks or monthly. Payment may only be made at longer intervals if the claimant agrees. If para (6) is satisfied, the authority can choose to pay weekly instead. This para is specifically qualified by paras (5) to (7). Where reg 91(2), 91(3), or 93 applies, this regulation is irrelevant. Where the "person entitled" is unable to consent see reg 82(3) and (6).

Para (2). The authority should make any payment of a rent allowance at the end of the period to which it relates ("in so far as it is practicable"), that is, in arrears.

Paragraphs (3) and (4): Payments to landlords

Para (3). Where HB takes the form of a rent allowance and payment is made to a landlord (excluding those cases where the authority is only making a first payment of benefit to the claimant by way of an instrument of payment payable to the landlord) payment must be made at intervals of four weeks under sub-para (a); and at the end of the period in respect of which it is made under sub-para (b).

Para (4) sets out two exceptions to the rule set out in para (3). First, where there is a calendar monthly rent liability, the authority has the discretion to make payment at calendar monthly intervals: sub-para (a). Second, where the authority is paying a rent allowance to a landlord in respect of more than one claimant, the first payment for any claimant may be made to that landlord at such shorter interval as the authority considers is in the best interest of the efficient administration of HB: sub-para (b). The latter might be appropriate where the authority has adopted a fixed cycle for a landlord with a number of properties – eg, agreeing to pay all monies due in respect of the tenants of that particular landlord on, say, every fourth Monday. The first direct payment in respect of any individual claimant could then be made in respect of a period of less than four weeks to bring it into cycle. Thereafter, payments should be made four-weekly in arrears on the pay-day agreed with the landlord.

Paragraphs (5) to (7): Special cases

Para (5). If this para applies, the authority must pay a rent allowance at two-weekly intervals if requested to do so. For "weekly entitlement", see regs 80 and 81 and Part 8.

Para (6). The authority has a discretion to pay a rent allowance weekly if either of the sub-paras apply. Under sub-para (a), see Part 13 for the rules about overpayments. This sub-para might apply where an authority is uncertain about a claimant's circumstances. Payment under sub-para (b) would be in a claimant's interest, for example, if rent is due weekly, to help her/him avoid getting into arrears.

Para (7) is expressly subject to paras (2), (3) and (5) above: eg, if this para is used, payment should be made on the date ascertained under para (2), and the claimant's right to request fortnightly payment under para (5) is protected. Even if para (5) does not apply, the authority is not obliged to use its powers under para (7) and may choose to pay a student at one of the intervals listed in para (1), or, impliedly, weekly under para (6).

Payment on account of a rent allowance

93.–(1)   Where it is impracticable for the relevant authority to make a decision on a claim for a rent allowance within 14 days of the claim for it having been made and that impracticability does not arise out of the failure of the claimant, without good cause, to furnish such information, certificates, documents or evidence as the authority reasonably requires and has requested or which has been requested by the Secretary of State, the authority shall make a payment on account of any entitlement to a rent allowance of such amount as it considers reasonable having regard to–

(a) such information which may at the time be available to it concerning the claimant's circumstances; and

(b) any relevant determination made by a rent officer in exercise of the Housing Act functions.

(2) The notice of award of any payment on account of a rent allowance made under paragraph (1) shall contain a notice to the effect that if on the subsequent decision of the claim the person is not entitled to a rent allowance, or is entitled to an amount of rent allowance less than the amount of the payment on account, the whole of the amount paid on account or the excess of that amount over the entitlement to an allowance, as the case may be, will be recoverable from the person to whom the payment on account was made.

(3) Where on the basis of the subsequent decision the amount of rent allowance payable differs from the amount paid on account under paragraph (1), future payments of rent allowance shall be increased or reduced to take account of any underpayment or, as the case may be, overpayment.

Definitions

"claimant" – see reg 2(1).
"overpayment" – see Part 13.
"payment" – see reg 2(1).
"rent allowance" – see ss134(1A) and (1B) SSAA.

General Note

This regulation only applies to claimants entitled to rent allowance – eg, HB paid to private and housing association tenants. Under it, the authority is obliged to make payments on account of HB to the claimant (interim payments) where it has been unable to make a formal decision on the claim under reg 89 and where the reason for the delay is not the claimant's failure to provide information or evidence, or, if it is, the claimant can show good cause for failing to do so.

The provision ensures that private tenants do not lose accommodation due to delays in benefit administration.

Subject only to the claimant not having failed to produce information or evidence without good cause when he has been required to do so, there is no exception of "reasonable practicability" in relation to this provision (see notes on regs 89 and 91). Payments are mandatory.

Under paras (2) and (3), if a claimant is paid more or less than s/he is entitled to under this provision, future payments of rent allowance are altered accordingly.

Analysis

Para (1). The authority's duty to make payment on account arises at the latest on the fourteenth day after the claim is made: that is, if no request for further information etc, has been made by that date or a request has been made, but the claimant has good cause for failing to supply the material requested, the authority must make a payment on account, although the amount of the payment is, to a certain extent, at the authority's discretion. In *R v Haringey LBC ex p Ayub* [1990] 25 HLR 566, QBD it was held that there is no need for a separate claim for a payment on account.

Reg 95(1)(b) can require an authority to pay HB to a landlord where the tenant is eight weeks or more in arrears of rent. Schiemann J went on to find that if the tenant is eight weeks or more in arrears of rent and the conditions in reg 91 HB regs 1987 (now reg 93) are satisfied, then the authority is under a duty to make payment on account to the *claimant's landlord*. But that duty only arises if the landlord or someone else informs the authority that there are eight weeks or more arrears – ie, it is not up to the authority to find this out for itself. He stated that if the tenant disputes that there are eight weeks arrears, the landlord can ask the council to make a determination on the issue. If it goes against the landlord the council's duty to pay the landlord direct would not arise unless and until the dispute was resolved in her/his favour.

The judge confirmed that there was no duty to pay rent allowance under reg 88 HB Regs 1987 (now reg 91), as opposed to making a payment on account, until a decision is made (but the claimant might be entitled to an order of mandamus requiring the council to make a decision if prejudiced by the amount or frequency of payments on account).

For the date on which a claim is treated as made, see reg 83. For the authority's powers to request information, see reg 86. Examples of "good cause" might be illness or difficulty in contacting someone who can supply the relevant information.

The amount of a payment depends on what the authority considers "reasonable" having regard to:

(1)   Such information which may at the time be available to it concerning the claimant's circumstances.

(2)   Any relevant determination made by a rent officer in exercise of the Housing Act functions – eg, the determination the authority must apply for under reg 14 (see that reg and the relevant Rent Officers (Housing Benefit Functions) Order).

Para (2) supplements reg 90 and Sch 9 by providing that the notice issued is to warn the claimant that if any excess payment to which he is not entitled is made under para (1), it can be recovered from the person to whom it was paid.

Para (3) supplements para (2) by providing that where a claimant is underpaid or overpaid under para (1), the overpayment shall be recovered or the under-payment made good by increasing or decreasing future payments of HB. There is no time limit specified in the regulation during which this must be done so that if a claimant is not actually entitled to HB when the para (1) payment is made, it may be recovered if s/he becomes entitled in the future.

If, on the "subsequent decision" referred to, it does transpire that the claimant is not entitled at all, however, the mere fact that he has been notified under para (2) that the payment made is a payment on account which may or may not be accurate does not of itself entitle the authority to recover the overpayment under reg 100: see *R v Liverpool CC ex p Griffiths* [1990] 22 HLR 312, QBD, and the note on reg 100.

Payment to be made to a person entitled

94.–(1)   Subject to regulations 95 to 97 (payment to landlords, payment on death) and the following provisions of this regulation, payment of any rent allowance to which a person is entitled shall be made to that person.

(2)   Where a person other than a person who is entitled to a rent allowance made the claim and that first person is a person referred to in regulation 82(2), (3) or (5) (persons appointed to act for a person unable to act), payment may be made to that person.

(3)   A person entitled to a rent allowance, although able to act on his own behalf, may request in writing that the appropriate authority make payments to a person, who if a natural person must be aged 18 or more, nominated by him, and the authority may make payments to that person.

Definitions

"payment" – see reg 2(1).
"rent allowance" – see s134(1A) and (1B) SSAA.

General Note

A rent allowance must be paid to a person entitled to it under para (1) or, if he is unable to act, may be paid to the person who claimed on her/his behalf under para (2). This is qualified by regs 95 and 96 (which set out when payments can or must be made to a landlord) and reg 97 (which deals with payment where the person entitled has died). A further exception is provided by para (3): an authority may agree to pay the rent allowance to someone else, aged 18 or over, nominated by the person entitled.

Analysis

Once a payment of HB has in fact been lawfully made to a claimant under this provision then a second payment may not be made to a landlord covering the same period, even though had the local authority been made aware of the true state of affairs at the time of the payment to the claimant (more than eight weeks' arrears of rent) it would have made the payment instead to the landlord under reg 95(1)(b): *R(H) 2/08* para 39, relying on reg 98. However, in most cases this problem should be avoided if local authorities properly notify both parties (ie, landlord and claimant) of the decision changing who is to be paid: see *CH 2986/2005*.

In *London Borough of Islington v SJ* [2008] UKUT 31 (AAC) an award of HB was made, with payment to be made to the claimant. The local authority later decided to backdate the award and pay the arrears of HB direct to the claimant's landlord. Nevertheless, the arrears of HB were paid to the claimant who did not use them to satisfy his liability for arrears of rent. When the landlord asked for payment of the arrears of HB, the local authority said that it could not pay these to the landlord because they had already been paid to the claimant and that it could not lawfully make payment of the same benefit twice. The First-tier Tribunal, allowing the landlord's appeal, decided that the arrears of HB were to be paid to the landlord on the basis that, although the principle stated in *R(H) 2/08* was accepted, namely that no second payment of HB can be made to a landlord once the claimant has been lawfully paid for the period in question, the local authority here did not lawfully pay arrears of HB to the claimant. Judge Turnbull upheld the tribunal's decision. The reasoning behind *R(H) 2/08* was that if HB has been paid in accordance with a decision (eg, to the claimant) and then that decision is revised so as to make the HB payable to another (eg, the landlord), the amount which has been paid to the claimant cannot be paid to the landlord, because that amount is required by reg 98 to be offset against the arrears which would otherwise be payable to the landlord under the revised decision. However, reg 98 can only apply where the first payment is made under and in accordance with a decision, that decision is then revised and payment is made in accordance with the revised decision. Here the decision was to pay HB to the landlord but this was incorrectly paid to the claimant. Further, the decision to pay to the landlord was never revised. The problem was simply that owing to an administrative error, payment had not been made in accordance with its terms. Note that the judge suggests (at para 16) that the payment made to the claimant was an "overpayment" within the definition in reg 99 and that it may be recoverable under reg 100. It is respectfully suggested that this is incorrect; "overpayment" means an amount paid to which there was no entitlement. The claimant here *was* entitled to the HB paid, it was simply paid to the wrong person.

Para (2). Payment to the appointee is discretionary so payment could still be made to the person entitled although this would be at the authority's risk as that person may not have mental capacity to give a valid receipt.

Para (3). For this to apply, the person entitled must be able to act for her/himself at the time the request is made. The reference to a "natural person" is to make a distinction between human beings and legal personalities such as companies. The authority has discretion whether or not to pay the nominee but the general principles of administrative law which govern the exercise of such discretions means that the authority must have a valid reason if it decides to depart from the claimant's wishes.

GM A6.181 refers to this procedure as nominating an "agent" and also misleadingly says that this power is to be used where the claimant is unable to collect money for her/himself – eg, when s/he is away from home or disabled. There is nothing in the regulation to restrict it in this way.

Circumstances in which payment is to be made to a landlord

95.–(1) Subject to paragraph (2) and paragraph 8(4) of Schedule A1 (treatment of claims for housing benefit by refugees), a payment of rent allowance shall be made to a landlord (and in this regulation the "landlord" includes a person to whom rent is payable by the person entitled to that allowance)–

(a) where under Regulations made under the Administration Act an amount of income support [² , a jobseeker's allowance or an employment and support allowance] payable to the claimant or his partner is being paid direct to the landlord; or

(b) where sub-paragraph (a) does not apply and the person is in arrears of an amount equivalent to 8 weeks or more of the amount he is liable to pay his landlord as rent, except where it is in the overriding interest of the claimant not to make direct payments to the landlord.

(2) Any payment of rent allowance made to a landlord pursuant to this regulation or to regulation 96 (circumstances in which payment may be made to a landlord) shall be to discharge, in whole or in part, the liability of the claimant to pay rent to that landlord in respect of the dwelling concerned, except in so far as–

(a) the claimant had no entitlement to the whole or part of that rent allowance so paid to his landlord; and

(b) the overpayment of rent allowance resulting was recovered in whole or in part from that landlord.

[¹ (2A) In a case where–

(a) a relevant authority has determined a maximum rent (LHA) in accordance with regulation 13D; and

(b) the rent allowance exceeds the amount which the claimant is liable to pay his landlord by way of rent,

any payment of rent allowance made to a landlord pursuant to this regulation or to regulation 96 may include all or part of any amount by which the rent allowance exceeds the amount which the claimant is liable to pay his landlord as rent but shall not include any amount by which the rent allowance exceeds the amount which the claimant is liable to pay his landlord as rent and arrears of rent.]

(3) Where the relevant authority is not satisfied that the landlord is a fit and proper person to be the recipient of a payment of rent allowance no such payment shall be made direct to him under paragraph (1).

Amendments

1. Amended by reg 17 of SI 2007 No 2868 as from 7.4.08 (or if reg 1(5) of that SI applies, on the day on or after 7.4.08 when the first of the events specified in reg 1(6) applies, or from 6.4.09 if none have before that date).

2. Amended by reg 21 of SI 2008 No 1082 as from 27.10.08.

Definitions
"claimant" – see reg 2(1).
"rent" – see Part 3.
"rent allowance" – see s134(1A) and (1B) SSAA.

General Note
Reg 95 is an exception to reg 94(1) which requires payment to be made to the "person entitled".

Under this regulation payment *must* be made to the landlord (as defined by the regulation itself) rather than the person entitled. By contrast, reg 96 provides instances in which payment *may* be made to the landlord.

Once an authority has made a decision, reg 90(1) requires it to notify any "person affected" by the decision. A landlord is a "person affected" where a decision is made under reg 95 whether or not to pay HB direct to her/ him: *CH 180/2006*.

Decisions made under reg 95 may be appealed to the First-tier Tribunal by either the claimant or the landlord, and it will be an error of law not to invite the claimant or landlord to the hearing of the other party's appeal as both are person's affected by such a decision: *CH 4108 2005*.

Like regs 92 to 94 this regulation only applies to payment of rent allowances.

Following a decision under reg 89(2), there is no duty to pay the landlord direct under reg 95 unless the DWP is paying part of the claimant's or her/his partner's IS, JSA or ESA direct to the landlord for rent arrears (para (1)(a)) or until the authority is told that eight or more weeks' arrears exist (para (1)(b)). Even then the duty does not arise until any dispute as to the amount of arrears has been resolved if necessary.

Major changes were made in the rules on the payment of HB, introduced with effect from 3 November 1997, in the context of a number of other regulations implementing the SSA(F)A 1997. These were described in guidance as measures to combat fraud. The regulations were, however, made under provisions of SSAA, principally ss5 and 6, which existed before the Fraud Act was passed.

The principal provisions are:

(1)   Authorities have discretion not to pay rent allowance to a landlord or agent who is not a "fit and proper person" to receive it: regs 95(3) and 96(3).

(2)   Landlords to whom direct payments are made are notified of their duty to report changes in the tenant's circumstances: Sch 9 Part 4.

Analysis
Paragraph (1): The duty to pay to the landlord
There are two circumstances in which the authority is obliged to make direct payments to the landlord (this includes a person to whom rent is payable), provided there has been no finding that the landlord is not a "fit and proper" person under para (3).

(1)   Where direct payments of IS, JSA or ESA are being made to the claimant's landlord by the DWP: sub-para (a). There is a power in Sch 9 Social Security (Claims and Payments) Regulations 1987 to make deductions from a claimant's IS, JSA or ESA to pay small amounts towards arrears of rent.

(2)   Where no IS, JSA or ESA is paid direct to the landlord, payment must be made to her/him where the person entitled to HB is in arrears equivalent to eight weeks' rent or more: sub-para (b). However, the authority can still decide *not* to do so where this would not be in the claimant's "overriding interest". Once the arrears have been reduced to less than eight weeks, compulsory payments to the landlord can no longer be made under this paragraph. However, the authority can make such payments under para (a) if relevant, or on a discretionary basis under reg 96. Note that what reg 95(1)(b) is concerned with is the tenant being eight weeks or more in arrears of liability for rent; it is not concerned with any set-off from that figure: *CH 4108 2005*. However, the view in that decision – that the decision of a local authority as to whether it is in the overriding interest of the claimant not to make direct payments to a landlord may only be interfered with on appeal on judicial review error of law grounds (ie, that it is not for the First-tier Tribunal to decide for itself whether payment direct is not in the overriding interest of the claimant) – has, rightly it is suggested, not been followed in *R(H) 1/08*. That later decision makes it plain that on an appeal it is for the First-tier Tribunal to exercise its normal decision making powers (per *R(IB) 2/04* para 25) on the evidence available and form its own judgment as to whether direct payment is not in the overriding interest of the claimant. *R(H) 1/08* also decides that it is permissible to suspend payment of HB (under reg 11(2)(a)(ii) of the D&A Regs) while enquiries are made as to which person the benefit should be paid to, as a change in payee requires the award to be revised or superseded.

Paragraph (2): Effect of recovery of an overpayment on rent liability
This purports to reverse the effect of *R v Haringey LBC ex p Ayub* [1992] 25 HLR 566, QBD by providing that where an overpayment is recovered from the landlord, rent arrears of the amount of the overpayment are created. It therefore purports to affect the substantive obligations and rights, under the general law of landlord and tenant, of the claimant and landlord *inter se*. It is strongly arguable that, in doing so, the paragraph is *ultra vires*. The regulation was made under s5(1)(p) SSAA which empowers the Secretary of State to make regulations which provide:

". . .for the circumstances and manner in which payments of such a benefit may be made to another person on behalf of the beneficiary for any purpose, which may be to discharge in whole or in part, an obligation of the beneficiary or any other person."

The enabling power therefore only provides for "the circumstances and manner" of payments to persons other than the claimant. Discharging an obligation is only a *purpose* for which payments can be made. Section 5(1)(p) does not give any power to prescribe *whether* an obligation is in fact discharged by the payment or, *a fortiori*, that an obligation which would under the general law be regarded as discharged should in the future revive upon the recovery of an overpayment from the landlord. See p491 for the changes brought in by the Social Security Administration (Fraud) Act 1997.

Paragraph (2A): Where a maximum rent (LHA) has been determined

This limits the amount that can be paid to a landlord where the "local housing allowance" rules apply and a maximum rent (LHA) has been determined in accordance with reg 13D. If HB exceeds the claimant's rent liability, the maximum that can be paid to her/his landlord is the amount which the claimant is liable to pay the landlord as rent and arrears of rent. The remainder must be paid to the claimant.

Paragraph (3): Landlord not a "fit and proper person"

Para (3) does not allow authorities to make direct payments to landlords under this regulation where they are not satisfied that the landlord is "a fit and proper person to be the recipient of a payment of rent allowance". This applies even if direct payments would otherwise be compulsory (eg, where the rent is more than eight weeks in arrears). A similar para is also in reg 96 where its effect is to allow authorities not to make direct payments to landlords who are not "fit and proper" even when the criteria for a discretionary direct payment would otherwise be met. Guidance as to the meaning of the words "fit and proper person" in the context of HB is given in GM A6.196-207 which identifies four basic principles.

(1)   The test only applies where the landlord's honesty in connection with HB is in doubt. It should not be applied in every case where a request for direct payments has been made.

(2)   The test must be applied on an individual basis. So, for example, an authority could not decide that all landlords of a particular class (eg, those who let houses in multiple occupation) are *ipso facto* not fit and proper persons.

(3)   Each case has to be decided on its own individual facts. The circumstances in which a landlord is not a fit and proper person cannot be listed exhaustively in advance and the examples in the Guidance are illustrative only.

(4)   Before a landlord can be said not to be a fit and proper person s/he must have engaged in undesirable activity in relation to HB. It is suggested that an authority cannot take non-HB-related behaviour into account (even, it would seem, where the behaviour is housing-related, for example, failure to comply with a Housing Act notice).

The Guidance's insistence that the undesirable activity should be HB-related is probably over-cautious. It is suggested that any serious dishonesty or criminality should suffice to make a landlord not "fit and proper" at least where such criminality or dishonesty is social security related. If a landlord has, for example, been convicted of a multiple-claim IS fraud, it is difficult to see an authority's decision that s/he is not a fit and proper person being overturned merely because benefits other than HB were involved.

On the other hand, some convictions may not suffice even when they are HB-related. The offences introduced by the Fraud Act have the effect, in some cases, of criminalising what would in other contexts amount to no more than a negligent omission. It is difficult to see how a single failure, by oversight, to report a change in a tenant's circumstances, which is now *prima facie* criminal under s112(1A) SSAA calls a landlord's honesty into sufficient question to make him or her not "fit and proper" (although the position would be different if there were habitual failures).

It is suggested that a failure or refusal to comply with a notice requiring information under s126A of the Administration Act would also be a factor which would legitimately be taken into account in reaching a decision. Such a failure or refusal is a criminal offence: see reg 121 and s113 SSAA.

It is unclear whether an agreement to pay an administrative penalty under s115A SSAA is a matter which can be taken into account in deciding whether or not a landlord is a fit and proper person. Such an agreement is not the same as accepting a caution for a criminal offence as it does not amount to an admission of guilt, and the local authority only needs grounds for commencing criminal proceedings before serving a penalty notice rather than proof beyond a reasonable doubt. In some cases, a landlord might agree to pay a penalty on the strictly commercial basis that to do so would be cheaper than to pay for legal representation against a criminal prosecution. On the other hand, the regulations clearly do not regard an agreement to pay a penalty as morally neutral. For example, reg 107 prevents a landlord who has agreed to pay an administrative penalty in respect of an overpayment from suing the tenant for any money which the authority has recovered under s75(5)(b) SSAA. It is therefore suggested that an agreement to pay a penalty is a factor which the authority can take into account but that it does not carry as much weight as a criminal conviction. One administrative penalty would probably not usually (depending on the precise circumstances) be sufficient on its own to prevent a landlord from being "fit and proper", but payment of a series of administrative penalties would almost certainly justify such a decision against a landlord.

Some behaviour which falls short of criminality may also justify a decision that a landlord is not a fit and proper person. The Guidance suggests that a habitual failure to repay an overpayment which the authority has decided is recoverable from him/her would be sufficient. However, before a decision is based on this ground, the authority should ensure that the notifications relating to the overpayments comply fully with the requirements of Sch 9 as otherwise the landlord would be within his/her rights not to have paid: see the decision of the Court of Appeal in *Warwick DC v Freeman* [1994] 27 HLR 616, CA.

It seems likely that there is an overlap between the "fit and proper test" and other anti-abuse provisions, in particular the contrived tenancy rules in HB Regs, reg 9(1)(l). The Court of Appeal has held in *R v Stratford-upon-Avon DC HBRB ex p White* [1998] 31 HLR 126 that the words "take advantage" in regulation 7 HB Regs 1987 (now reg 9 HB Regs) bear their "common meaning of avail oneself unfairly or improperly". In the circumstances, it would seem to be open to an authority to decide that a landlord who habitually created or was a party to contrived tenancies was not a fit and proper person. For example, although it would not today be possible to repeat the scheme devised by the landlords in *R v Manchester CC ex p Baragrove Properties Ltd* [1991] 23 HLR 337, QBD, a landlord who habitually targeted a particular class of claimant for no reason other than to exploit the favourable treatment afforded to that class by the HB scheme might be acting in a way which would justify a conclusion that s/he was not a fit and proper person.

The Guidance refers to circumstances in which a landlord has otherwise acted to obtain HB to which it is or was not entitled. One possible example of this would be the use of limited companies to avoid repayment of overpayments. Where one company had been closed down owing money to the authority and another set up with similar directors and/or shareholders, it might be possible for the authority to conclude that the second company was not a fit and proper person to receive direct payments even though it was the first company, which is a separate person from a legal point of view, which was responsible for the impropriety.

Whether or not a landlord is a fit and proper person to receive payments of rent allowance is a decision which can be made at the beginning of the claim and also during the period of an award if there are grounds for revision or supersession – eg, if there has been a change of circumstances or if the original decision was based on a mistake of fact or law.

Paradoxically, it does not follow automatically from a finding that a landlord is not a fit and proper person to receive payments of rent allowance, that rent allowance will not be paid to her/him. There is, of course, no question of payment to the landlord being mandatory in such circumstances but there is still a discretion to pay the landlord direct under reg 96. An authority might decide that the claimant's overriding interests require that direct payments be made to the landlord, but that the landlord is not "fit and proper" to receive them. In this unusual situation the authority would need to balance the risks and could decide to make direct payments. An authority could instead find alternative methods of payment. If direct payments are made, regular and frequent checks should be made on the claim.

Circumstances in which payment may be made to a landlord

96.–(1) Subject to paragraph 8(4) of Schedule A1 (treatment of claims for housing benefit by refugees), where regulation 95 (circumstances in which payment is to be made to a landlord) does not apply but subject to [¹ paragraphs (3) and (3A)] of this regulation, a payment of a rent allowance may nevertheless be made to a person's landlord where–

   (a)   the person has requested or consented to such payment;

   (b)   payment to the landlord is in the interest of the claimant and his family;

   (c)   the person has ceased to reside in the dwelling in respect of which the allowance was payable and there are outstanding payments of rent but any payment under this sub-paragraph shall be limited to an amount equal to the amount of rent outstanding.

(2)   Without prejudice to the power in paragraph (1), in any case where in the opinion of the authority–

   (a)   the claimant has not already discharged his liability to pay his landlord for the period in respect of which any payment is to be made; and

   (b)   it would be in the interests of the efficient administration of housing benefit,

a first payment of a rent allowance following the making of a decision on a claim or a supersession under paragraph 4 of Schedule 7 to the Child Support, Pensions and Social Security Act 2000 may be made, in whole or in part, [³] to that landlord.

(3)   In a case where the relevant authority is not satisfied that the landlord is a fit and proper person to be the recipient of a claimant's rent allowance, the authority may either–

   (a)   not make direct payments to the landlord in accordance with paragraph (1) [¹ , (3A) or (3B)]; or

(b)   make such payments to the landlord where the authority is satisfied that it is nonetheless in the best interests of the claimant and his family that the payments be made.

[² (3A)   In a case where a relevant authority has determined a maximum rent in accordance with regulation 13D–

(a)   sub-paragraphs (a) and (b) of paragraph (1) shall not apply; and

(b)   payment of a rent allowance to a person's landlord may be made where–

    (i)   the relevant authority considers that the claimant is likely to have difficulty in relation to the management of his financial affairs;

    (ii)   the relevant authority considers that it is improbable that the claimant will pay his rent; or

    (iii) a direct payment has previously been made by the relevant authority to the landlord in accordance with regulation 95 in respect of the current award of housing benefit.

(3B)   Where the relevant authority suspects that the grounds in paragraph (3A)(b)(i) or (ii) apply and is considering whether to make payments on one of those grounds, it may make a payment of a rent allowance to the person's landlord for a period not exceeding 8 weeks.]

(4)   In this regulation ''landlord'' has the same meaning as in regulation 95 and paragraph (2) of that regulation shall have effect for the purposes of this regulation.

Modifications

Paras (1) and (3) were amended and paras (3A) and (3B) inserted by reg 17 Housing Benefit (Local Housing Allowance and Information Sharing) Amendment Regulations 2007 SI No.2868 as from 7 April 2008, save that for a person to whom reg 1(5) of those regulations applied (see p1231), the amendments came into force on the day on or after 7 April 2008 when the first of the events specified in reg 1(6) applied to her/him, or on 6 April 2009 if none had before that date.

Amendments

1.   Amended by reg 17(2) of SI 2007 No 2868 as from 7.4.08 (or if reg 1(5) of that SI applies, on the day on or after 7.4.08 when the first of the events specified in reg 1(6) applies, or from 6.4.09 if none have before that date).

2.   Inserted by reg 17(2) of SI 2007 No 2868 as from 7.4.08 (or if reg 1(5) of that SI applies, on the day on or after 7.4.08 when the first of the events specified in reg 1(6) applies, or from 6.4.09 if none have before that date).

3.   Amended by reg 2(7) of SI 2010 No 2449 as from 1.11.10.

Definitions

"dwelling" – see reg 2(4) and s137(1) SSCBA.
"landlord" – see para (4) and reg 95.
"payment" – see reg 2(1).
"rent allowance" – see s134(1A) and (1B) SSAA.

General Note

Para (1) sets out three situations in which the authority has the discretion to pay rent allowance direct to the landlord, even though not obliged to do so under reg 95, or until it is obliged to do so under that regulation – eg, where eight weeks rent arrears have accrued.

Para (2) enables the authority to make the first payment of a rent allowance to the "landlord".

Para (3) sets out the options available to an authority which would otherwise be prepared to make discretionary direct payments but which is not satisfied that a landlord is a "fit and proper person to be the recipient of a claimant's rent allowance".

Paras (3A) and (3B) set out the situations in which the authority may not, and additional situations in which it may, pay rent allowance direct to the landlord, where the "local housing allowance" rules apply and a maximum rent (LHA) has been determined in accordance with reg 13D.

Para (4) defines "landlord" by reference to reg 95 and purports to apply the rule in reg 95(2) to cases where discretionary direct payments have been made and then recovered as overpayments.

See also the General Note to reg 95. Note that once an authority has made a decision, reg 90(1) requires it to notify any "person affected" by the decision. A landlord is a "person affected" where a decision is made under reg 96 whether or not to pay HB direct to her/him: *CH 180/2006*.

Analysis

Para (1) gives a discretion to the authority to make direct payments to the landlord (this includes a person to whom rent is payable) in three instances.

(1)   Where the claimant requests or consents to such payments: sub-para (a). Even if such a request is made, payment to the landlord is at the authority's discretion.

(2)   Where the authority considers it to be in the interest of the claimant and her/his family, if any: sub-para (b). Payment can be made under this sub-para without the consent of the claimant.

(3)   Sub-para (c) covers the situation where the claimant has moved, leaving arrears of rent. The authority can only pay HB due in respect of the *former* home to the landlord and then only to the extent necessary to clear outstanding rent. Payment can be made under this sub-para without the consent of the claimant.

Note that sub-paras (a) and (b) do *not* apply where a maximum rent (LHA) has been determined in accordance with reg 13D (see para (3A)) – ie, where the "local housing allowance" rules apply.

Para (2) enables the authority to make the first payment of a rent allowance following the determination of a claim or a supersession of an award, in whole or in part, to the landlord. This rule only applies however, if, in the authority's opinion, the following conditions are met.

(1)   The claimant has not already discharged her/his liability to pay the landlord for the period in respect of which any payment is to be made.

(2)   It would be in the interests of the "efficient administration" of HB.

The DWP described this power as tackling "an existing abuse when tenants abscond with the benefit without paying their rent", (*Social Security Departmental Report: The Government's Expenditure Plans, 1996-97 to 1998-99*, HMSO, March 1996, p40).

The authority's "opinion" should be based on information held at the time the claim (or supersession) is dealt with. The authority is not required to make special enquiries, for example, to establish from the landlord or specifically of the claimant whether the rental liability for the period in question has been discharged.

GM A6.163-166 advises authorities that they have a duty to safeguard the public purse by minimising the opportunities for fraud or abuse and that this duty would meet the criterion of the "efficient administration" of the benefit scheme. It suggests that an authority may wish to consider the amount of benefit payable and if there is evidence that the claimant has paid some or all of the rent for the period in question – the rent outstanding. If either the benefit due or the rent debt is small it may be inappropriate to invoke this power. Equally, it would be inappropriate to pay to the landlord more than the outstanding eligible rent. The Guidance suggests that the authority should consider paying the first payment to the landlord where, for example: the amount due is £100 or more, or the authority has reason to think that the claimant might default (perhaps because a previous landlord has reported non-payment), or there is a rent debt but the case is not appropriate for longer-term direct payment arrangements. The authority does not need to invoke this power where the claimant's circumstances warrant a permanent direct payment from the outset.

Para (3) applies the "fit and proper person" test to reg 96. See Analysis to reg 95(3).

Paras (3A) and (3B) are only relevant where the "local housing allowance" rules apply and a maximum rent (LHA) has been determined in accordance with reg 13D. In this case, the authority has the discretion to pay HB direct to a landlord under para (1)(c) (ie, where the claimant has moved leaving arrears of rent) but not (1)(a) or (b): para (3A)(a). In addition, it can do so in three further situations.

(1)   Where the authority considers that the claimant is likely to have difficulty managing her/his financial affairs: para (3A)(b)(i).

(2)   Where the authority considers that it is improbable that the claimant will pay her/his rent: para (3A)(b)(ii).

(3)   Where a direct payment has previously been made under reg 95 in respect of the current HB award: para (3A)(b)(iii).

If the authority suspects that paras (3A)(b)(i) or (ii) apply, it can pay rent allowance direct to the claimant's landlord while it considers whether to make payments on one of those grounds (for a maximum of eight weeks): para (3B).

In *Wirral MBC v AL (HB)* [2010] UKUT 254 (AAC) the questions arose whether a decision of the local authority not to exercise its discretion under reg 96(3A) was appealable by the landlord under Sch 7 para 6 CSPSSA 2000 and, if it was, what the scope of the appeal was – ie, whether the appeal was a complete re-exercise by the First-tier Tribunal of an administrative discretion given to the local authority, or something narrower. Judge Howell refrained from giving an actual decision on the questions, accepting that there was a right of appeal and that the nature of the appeal was a complete re-hearing. However, he said (at para 19):

"At some point the principles involved may need to be reconsidered, perhaps at a higher level, because it does seem odd and unusual if the discretionary and administrative matters housing benefit authorities are charged with considering for themselves under regulation 96, which must include non-justiciable questions, are to be reconsidered at large by a tribunal consisting of a lawyer without any of the responsibilities and constraints of such an authority, who is then supposed to substitute his or her own subjective view on the merits retrospectively: a far cry from the more normal judicial control of such matters by way of review to ensure administrative authorities invested with discretionary powers stay within them and act properly and legally."

Note that where a maximum rent (LHA) has been determined in accordance with reg 13D, if HB exceeds the claimant's rent liability, the maximum that can be paid to her/his landlord under either para (1) or (3A) is the amount which the claimant is liable to pay the landlord as rent and arrears of rent. The remainder must be paid to the claimant: reg 95(2A).

Para (4). If, as is argued above, reg 95(2) is *ultra vires*, it will be equally ineffective in the context of reg 96.

Payment on death of the person entitled

97.–(1)   Subject to paragraphs (3) and (5) where the person entitled to an allowance has died the relevant authority shall make payment either to his personal representative or, where there is none, his next of kin if aged 16 or over.

(2)   For the purposes of paragraph (1) "next of kin" means in England and Wales the persons who would take beneficially on an intestacy and in Scotland the persons entitled to the moveable estate on intestacy.

(3)   A payment under paragraph (1) or (5) shall not be made unless the landlord, the personal representative or the next of kin, as the case may be, makes written application for the payment of any sum of benefit to which the deceased was entitled, and such written application is sent to or delivered to the relevant authority at its designated office within 12 months of the deceased's death or such longer period as the authority may allow in any particular case.

(4)   The authority may dispense with strict proof of title of any person claiming under paragraph (3) and the receipt of such a person shall be a good discharge to the authority for any sum so paid.

(5)   Subject to paragraph (3), where the relevant authority determines, before the death of the person first mentioned in paragraph (1), that a rent allowance was payable to his landlord in accordance with regulation 95 or 96, that authority shall pay to that landlord so much of that allowance as does not exceed the amount of rent outstanding at the date of the person's death.

Definition

"designated office" – see reg 2(1).

General Note

This deals with the situation where a claimant has died before receiving HB to which s/he was entitled. Para (1) sets out to whom such benefit should be paid, para (3) how someone may apply for payment and paras (2) and (4) define those people and enables such a payee to give the authority a good receipt for payments made under this regulation. Para (5) deals with situations where HB was payable direct to a landlord before the claimant's death.

Analysis

Para (1) just talks about "an allowance" (presumably "rent allowance"). Subject to paras (3) and (5), payment to the personal representative (or next of kin) is mandatory.

Para (2) defines "next of kin". In England and Wales, the "persons who would take beneficially on an intestacy" are set out in the Administration of Estates Act 1925, the Intestates Act 1952, the Family Provision Act 1966 and the Family Law Reform Act 1969. In Scotland, the Succession (Scotland) Act 1964 provides the rules. A "personal representative" is someone appointed by a will (eg, an executor or executrix) to carry out the provisions of that will. Under para (4) the authority is not required to demand strict proof of whether the payee is a personal representative or next-of-kin.

Para (3). Before payment can be made to a landlord, personal representative or next-of-kin, s/he must apply in writing to the authority at its designated office, within 12 months of the deceased's death, or a longer period if the authority agrees.

Para (4). See also para (2) and the "General Note".

Para (5) makes clear that where the authority has decided to make HB payments direct to the landlord under regs 95 or 96, before the time of the claimant's death, any outstanding benefit, limited to the amount of rent outstanding at the time of the claimant's death, must be paid to the landlord if the landlord has made a written application for it: para (3).

Offsetting

98.–(1)   Where a person has been paid a sum of housing benefit under a decision which is subsequently revised or further revised, any sum paid in respect of a period covered by a subsequent decision shall be offset against arrears of entitlement under the subsequent decision except to the extent that the sum exceeds the arrears and shall be treated as properly paid on account of them.

(2)   Where an amount has been deducted under regulation 104(1) (sums to be deducted in calculating recoverable overpayments) an equivalent sum shall be offset against any arrears of entitlement under the subsequent decision except to the extent that the sum exceeds the arrears and shall be treated as properly paid on account of them.

(3)   No amount may be offset under paragraph (1) which has been determined to be an overpayment within the meaning of regulation 99 (meaning of overpayment).

General Note

This is an extremely tortuous piece of legislation designed, it seems, to cover the situation where a claimant has been underpaid for a period. See also the commentary on *London Borough of Islington v SJ* [2008] UKUT 31 (AAC) on p469.

Analysis

Paras (1) and (2). If someone has been paid a sum of HB under a decision which is later revised (or further revised), and it is decided to pay her/him more for a particular period, what s/he will get under para (1) is the difference between what s/he has already been paid and what s/he was actually entitled to. "Revised" includes a decision being revised by a tribunal altering it on appeal: *Wirral MBC v AL (HB)* [2010] UKUT 254 (AAC).

Where, in calculating the amount of a recoverable overpayment, a sum of HB has been deducted under reg 104(1) which should have been determined to be payable, the same sum is offset against the arrears of entitlement under the revised decision under para (2).

The phrase "except to the extent . . . arrears" means that this regulation cannot be used with the result that the claimant owes the authority money. HB can only be recovered from a claimant under reg 100. For example, if the claimant has been paid £100 for a period and on revision s/he should have got £95, s/he will not owe the authority anything. £95 of what s/he has been paid is offset against revised entitlement, but the extra £5 will be ignored unless reg 100 makes it recoverable.

Para (3). But under para (1), in computing what s/he has already been paid, anything which has been determined to be an overpayment (see reg 99) paid during the same period is to be left out of account. Under reg 102, however, such a recoverable overpayment may be deducted from arrears of HB paid so that in the end the claimant is no better off.

PART 13
Overpayments

General Note on 13

This part of the regulations deals with the calculation and recovery of overpayments of HB. Incentives to detect fraud, recover overpayments and avoid official errors are given by the percentages of subsidy which are payable in respect of different categories of overpayment.

Disputes about alleged overpayments (most often, whether an overpayment is recoverable) make up a large part, if not the majority, of HB and CTB appeals. A systematic approach is required by advisers, authorities and the First-tier Tribunal. The following stepped approach is suggested.

(1)   Has there been an overpayment? The definition is set out in reg 99.

(2)   What is the amount of the overpayment? This involves a complex process of calculation which is set out in the commentary to reg 103. Regs 103 and 104 set out deductions to be made from the gross amount of HB paid.

(3)   Is the overpayment recoverable? The test is different from that applicable to DWP benefits. The criteria for recoverability are set out in reg 100.

(4)   If there is a recoverable overpayment, from whom is it recoverable? The persons from whom it is recoverable are set out in reg 101.
[Note: disputes as to decisions given by a local authority on each of the above four questions may be appealed to a First-tier Tribunal. However, disputes arising under points (5) and (6) below cannot be appealed.]

(5)   Should the overpayment be recovered, and if so from whom? SSAA s75(2) and (3) give the local authority the power to recover.

(6)   How should the overpayment be recovered? SSAA s75(4)-(5) and regs 101(4), 102 and 105 provide for various means of recovery. A full guide is in the Analysis to reg 102.

Meaning of overpayment

99.   In this Part, "overpayment" means any amount which has been paid by way of housing benefit and to which there was no entitlement under these Regulations (whether on the initial decision [¹ or as subsequently revised or superseded or further revised or superseded]) and includes any amount paid on account under regulation 93 (payment on account of a rent allowance) which is in excess of the entitlement to housing benefit as subsequently decided.

Amendment

1.   Amended by reg 2 of SI 2005 No 2904 as amended by Sch 2 para 29 of SI 2006 No 217 as from 10.4.06.

General Note

This defines an "overpayment" for the purposes of Part 13. It must be borne in mind that just because an amount comes within the above definition it does not follow that it can be recovered. That question is dealt with by reg 100.

Analysis

"... any amount which has been paid by way of housing benefit . . . ". The provisions apply equally to rent allowance and rent rebate, though there are differences in the rules as to recoverability.

"... and to which there was no entitlement ... whether on the initial decision or as subsequently revised or superseded or further revised or superseded . . . ". It is fundamental to the social security benefits system, and HB and CTB are no exceptions to this, that a decision awarding benefit remains valid unless and until changed, and those changes can only be effected under the decision-making rules specifically provided for this purpose. Accordingly, an overpayment of HB can only arise if the decision awarding HB is first revised or superseded by the local authority. Hence, the compendious nature of the phrase above.

Following the decision of the tribunal of commissioners in *R(IB) 2/04*, where the commissioners concluded (para 55) that it was open to an appeal tribunal to substitute a revising decision for a superseding decision and also decided that defects in a revising or superseding decision would not generally render the decision invalid (para 72), and *CH 4354/2003*, a defective attempt by the local authority to revise or supersede the awarding decision can and should be corrected by a tribunal on any appeal against the resultant overpayment decision. Accordingly, the absence of a proper revision or supersession decision by the local authority is not to be equated with there being no revision or supersession decision at all, and so will not render void the overpayment decision. The only exceptions to this are where the revision or supersession decision of the local authority is so incoherent or lacking any legal basis that it does not amount to a decision at all: *R(IB) 2/04* para 72; or the evidence is not available to the tribunal to enable it to identify the details of the past awarding decision(s), without which the tribunal may not be able to identify any appropriate revision or supersession ground: *CIS 3228/2003*. But if there is no local authority revision or supersession decision at all, or no evidence of such a decision having been made (though this may not be too high a hurdle for the authority to pass – see para 76 of *R(IB) 2/04*), there is nothing for the tribunal to correct and there will be no overpayment.

In overpayment cases, it is also important to determine any question of whether the claimant was actually entitled to benefit according to the legislation as it stood at the time: *R(H) 3/03* para 8. Account must also be taken of any transitional protection conferred by subsequent amending legislation.

It must be borne in mind that when determining whether a claimant has been overpaid, it is the legislation in force at the date of the payment that determines her/his eligibility and not the version effective at the time that the authority comes to consider whether s/he has been overpaid. The only exception to this is where amending legislation is expressed to have retrospective effect.

"... any amount paid on account ... in excess of the entitlement ... as subsequently decided". The third broad category is excessive estimated payments. So if the local authority estimates the claimant's entitlement at £100 a week and it is subsequently found to be £80, the £20 a week excess constitutes an overpayment.

Recoverable overpayments

100.–(1)   Any overpayment, except one to which paragraph (2) applies, shall be recoverable.

(2)   Subject to paragraph (4) this paragraph applies to an overpayment [¹ which arose in consequence of] an official error where the claimant or a person acting on his behalf or any other person to whom the payment is made could not, at the time of receipt of the payment or of any notice relating to that payment, reasonably have been expected to realise that it was an overpayment.

(3)   In paragraph (2), ''overpayment which arose [¹ in consequence of an official error]'' means an overpayment caused by a mistake made whether in the form of an act or omission by–

(a)   the relevant authority;

(b)   an officer or person acting for that authority;

(c)   an officer of–

(i)   the Department for Work and Pensions; or
(ii)   Revenue and Customs,
acting as such; or
(d)   a person providing services to the Department for Work and Pensions or to the Commissioners for Her Majesty's Revenue and Customs,

where the claimant, a person acting on his behalf or any other person to whom the payment is made, did not cause or materially contribute to that mistake, act or omission.

(4)   Where in consequence of an official error, a person has been awarded rent rebate to which he was not entitled or which exceeded the benefit to which he was entitled, upon the award being revised [¹ or superseded] any overpayment of benefit, which remains credited to him by the relevant authority in respect of a period after the date on which the revision [¹ or supersession] took place, shall be recoverable.

Amendment
1.   Amended by reg 4 of SI 2005 No 2904 as amended by Sch 2 para 29 of SI 2006 No 217 as from 10.4.06.

Definitions
"claimant" – see reg 2(1).
"overpayment" – see reg 99.

General Note
The rules governing the recoverability of HB and CTB overpayments are arguably more stringent than the rules set out in s71 Administration Act for recovery of benefits paid by the DWP. Disputes about HB and CTB overpayments make up a significant number, if not the majority, of appeals to First-tier Tribunals against HB and CTB decisions.

For HB and CTB overpayments the starting point is that all overpayments are recoverable. The only exception to this general rule is if:
(1)   the overpayment was caused by an official error which no relevant person caused or contributed to; *and*
(2)   no relevant person could reasonably have been expected to realise that there was an overpayment either at the time it was made or when they were notified of the payment.

Analysis
Paragraph (1)
This states the general rule that, unless the criteria in para (2) apply, the overpayment is recoverable. Note that s68 Welfare Reform and Pensions Act 1999 renders certain overpayments irrecoverable even where the criteria specified in para (2) do not apply.

It is for the local authority to show that the overpayment is recoverable including, arguably, that it was not caused by official error: see *CH 4065/2001* para 1.3. However, it is for the claimant (or other relevant person) to prove that s/he could not reasonably have been expected to realise that s/he was being overpaid: *CH 3439/2004*.

Paragraphs (2) and (3)
These paragraphs together set out the criteria which have to be shown for the overpayment to be irrecoverable. Note that overpayments falling within para (4) will always be recoverable, regardless of whether the criteria are fulfilled. CTB Regs reg 83(4) and (5) specify further categories of overpayments of CTB to which the criteria do not apply.

Whether the criteria are met must be considered during the whole period of the overpayment not merely at the beginning. Thus an official error that occurs during the period of the overpayment may render part of an overpayment irrecoverable: *CH 1296/2002* para 4. The commissioner in *CH 858/2006* left open whether a recoverable overpayment may be split between differing causes of the overpayment which exist over the same period of time (in that case an overpayment which in part arose because of an increase in the claimant's earnings and in part because of a wrong award of tax credits), but the tenor of his reasoning suggests that it should be possible to do so.

First criterion: Official error which no relevant person caused or contributed to
The overpayment must be caused by an error or mistake made by the authority or a relevant person acting as such. Unless the person from whom recovery is sought can show such an error, the overpayment will always be recoverable regardless of the merits of the case: see, for example, *CH 2201/2002* para 9, where it was confirmed that an overpayment was recoverable where a claimant moved out without informing either the landlord or the local authority. (The only official error which might arise on these type of facts is if the local authority did not act timeously after it had been made aware that the claimant had moved out.) Equally, even if there is an error or mistake by a relevant official, it will not amount to an "official error" if the claimant or another relevant person caused or contributed to it, and so such an overpayment will also always be recoverable. But the caselaw has eschewed an overly refined approach to causation in this context. The result is that the key question to be asked

in a case where an overpayment has arisen after a mistake by an official is not whether the claimant (or other relevant person) caused or contributed to that mistake, but rather whether s/he caused or contributed to the overpayment. The starting point in this caselaw is the case of *Sier*.

In *R (Sier) v Cambridge CC HBRB* [2001] EWHC Admin 160, QBD; [2001] EWCA Civ 1523, CA (dealing with reg 99 HB Regs 1987 – now reg 100), the claimant lived in Cambridge and claimed HB for a long period while he was recovering from a long illness. On his recovery, he decided to seek accommodation in London and live there during the week to assist his search for work. He gave evidence to the Review Board that he had sought advice from two London authorities where he was proposing to live as to whether he would be entitled to claim HB on two homes and that he received (erroneous) advice that he would be able to do so. The Board accepted that evidence. As a result of the advice he received, he did not inform Cambridge City Council when he took a tenancy in London and it became his normal home. The council did not ask any questions directed to the location of the claimant's normal home on its claim form. The claimant also moved his IS claim to a London Employment Service office, but no form NHB 8 was sent to Cambridge City Council in accordance with the normal procedure. An overpayment resulted. On the facts, Mr Sier had not contributed to the "mistake" (the failure of the DSS (as it then was) to send the form NHB 8 to Cambridge City Council), and had that omission not occurred then Cambridge City Council would in all likelihood have stopped his HB. (Equally, on the facts it seemed that if there was an official error then the overpayment would not have been recoverable because of the erroneous advice which Mr Sier had been given upon which – per sub-para (3) – he could not reasonaby have been expected to realise that he was not entitled to get HB on his Cambridge and London homes and so could not have realised he was being overpaid.) But it was also true on the facts that Mr Sier had failed in his own duty to inform Cambdrige City Council that he had moved to London. On a literal reading of what is now reg 100(2) and (3), Mr Sier argued that the overpayment of HB on his Cambridge home was irrecoverable because he had not caused or contributed to the failure of the DSS to send the form NH8 to Cambridge City Council.

The High Court rejected this argument. It accepted that the failure to send the NHB 8 form was a relevant mistake, but it held that the mistake did not cause the overpayment. Accordingly, it was not an "official error" overpayment as defined in what is now reg 100(3) and was therefore recoverable from Mr Sier under what is now reg 100(1). The High Court accepted that an overpayment could have more than one cause but, as a matter of common sense, the cause of the overpayment was the claimant's failure to notify Cambridge City Council. The common sense approach was required by *Environmental Agency v Empress Cars (Abertillery) Ltd* [1999] 2 AC 22, HL. The Court of Appeal upheld the judge's approach.

> "In the present case, one has to have regard to the general legislative purpose, which seems to me to be clear. Parliament has laid down in the Regulations that a person is to be relieved of the obligation to repay an overpayment when that has been occasioned by an administrative mistake and not by any fault on the part of the recipient. That seems to me to be the basic thrust of the Regulation and one should approach the meaning of the word 'cause' and its application to the facts on that basis." (Latham LJ, para 25)

> "Such a result . . . seems to me so entirely surprising and unsatisfactory that it requires one to approach regulation 99(3) rather differently. In my judgment a single composite question falls to be asked under regulation 99(3). One must ask: 'was the overpayment the result of a wholly uninduced official error, or was it rather the result of the claimant's own failings, here his failure in breach of duty to report a change of circumstance?' The answer to that question on the facts of this case is, of course, self-evident . . . It would be remarkable indeed if the claimant was liable to make repayment in a case where he merely contributed to what might be a fundamental error on the part of the department, and yet wholly escapes such liability even when himself primarily responsible for the overpayment." (Simon Brown LJ, paras 30-31)

Sier has been followed and applied in a number of subsequent commissioner's decisions. In *R(H) 1/04*, the claimant had informed the local authority that he was in receipt of occupational pensions, but had failed to disclose that information on his claim forms for IS. IS was duly awarded and CTB was awarded as a result of the award of IS. The commissioner decided that even had there been an official error (as to which see the discussion below), the substantial cause of the overpayment was the claimant's failure to notify the DWP of the award of IS: para 26. No attempt was made by the claimant to argue that there was an error on the part of the DWP, and the commissioner held that the fact that he had not challenged the decision disallowing IS was some evidence that there was no such error: para 24.

A similar conclusion was reached in *R(H) 2/04* para 14. The true cause was the claimant's failure to disclose her new working families' tax credit (WFTC) award rather than the council's failure to await the level of the award before adjudicating her renewal claim for HB.

The paraphrasing of one paragraph in *CH 2794/2004* in previous editions of this book has been criticised (rightly) in *SN v London Borough of Hounslow* [2010] UKUT 57 (AAC) (at para 24) as oversimplifying, and thus potentially misleading, the approach on official error and causation following *Sier*. As the Upper Tribunal puts it in *SN v LB Hounslow*, "the test is the simple common sense one explained in *Sier* of what was the substantial (ie, not just a contributory) cause of the overpayment". What the previous commentary on *CH 2794/2004* was seeking to make clear was that even if a claimant did not cause or contribute to the official error that will not avail her/him if her/his act or omission was still the (substantial) cause of the overpayment occurring. Similar views to *SN v LB Hounslow* had previously been expressed in *CH 3083/2005* (para 38) and *CH 3761/2005*. In the latter case, at least for part of the period, the commissioner found that the substantial cause of the overpayment was the Jobcentre's mistakes in (i) telling the claimant that it would notify the local authority of his JSA stopping and he therefore did not need to do so, and (ii) its failure to then notify the local authority of that information. In *R(H) 10/08*, the deputy commissioner said that a tribunal must consider and determine whether the overpayment was caused by a wholly uninduced official error or was rather the result of the claimant's own failings – ie, her/his failure to inform the "designated office" of a change in circumstances under reg 88 (or reg 69 HB(SPC) Regs).

"... a mistake made, whether in the form of an act or omission ...". No fault is required for the act or omission to amount to a "mistake". All that is necessary is that, with the benefit of hindsight, something is done which should not have been done or something is not done which should have been. An example of this point, although it did not arise for decision in the case, is *R v Liverpool CC ex p Griffiths* [1990] 22 HLR 312, QBD, in which the authority's HB department was unable to implement changes to the HB scheme which had been brought in at very short notice. Estimated awards were made on review and reviewed again when the authority was able to work out claimants' exact entitlement. Some of the estimated awards were too high and the authority sought to recover the difference. Even though the authority could not have avoided making the error, it still amounted to a relevant mistake. It has been suggested that mere delay cannot amount to an "omission" so as to amount to an official error: *Griffiths.*

This broad statement needs clarification in one respect. If there is no duty on the authority or relevant official to take a step, and it is not reasonable to expect them to do it by way of investigating the claim, there is no "omission" if it is not done. Thus the authority is under no duty to demand a particular piece of information on its standard claim form and there is no official error if it does not do so: *R v Islington LBC HBRB ex p de Grey* [1992] unreported 11 February, QBD, where the form did not ask the claimant if he was a co-ownership tenant; *de Grey* was followed in *Sier*. In that case, the claim form failed to ask any questions designed to elicit information about where the claimant's normal home was. It was argued that as this was a basic issue under the HB scheme, it was a relevant mistake not to ask the relevant question. Richards J rejected the submission, holding that the very complexity of reg 5 HB Regs 1987 (now reg 7) and the rarity of claimants with two homes meant that it could not be said to be unreasonable not to ask any questions directed towards that point. That argument was not pursued before the Court of Appeal. However, note *CH 3679/2002*, where an overpayment occurred when a claimant continued to claim HB in respect of a liability to his ex-wife. The local authority's claim forms were not changed after January 1999 to seek information relevant to the then new form of reg 7 HB Regs 1987 (now reg 9). The commissioner held, accepting a concession by the local authority, that there was an "official error" in not changing the forms: paras 2, 7. The value of this holding was doubted in *CH 4428/2006* because it was based on a concession and was not decided by the commissioner, but in an inquisitorial jurisdiction it is a little difficult to see why this should wholly undermine the decision. Indeed, the commissioner in *CH 4428/2006* seemingly accepted (despite his stated rejection of *CH 3679/2002*) that "a failure to amend forms to accord with amending legislation may, in certain circumstances, amount to an official error but will not do so in every case" (para 33). However, for reasons which, with respect, are not particularly clear or convincing, he did not accept in the case before him that the failure to amend the claim forms promptly after the new form of reg 7(1)(d) HB Regs 1987 had come into effect amounted to an official error. The commissioner focused narrowly on whether it had been an error on the part of the local authority not to have changed its forms so as to seek information relevant to the reg 7(1)(d) issues (ie, whether the landlord is a parent of the claimant's child). However, with respect, it is surely arguable that the focus should have been on whether it had been an error not to have made any changes to its claims forms to capture all the information required after the wholesale changes to reg 7(1) HB Regs 1987, rather than just looking at whether the form should have been changed to elicit the reg 7(1)(d) information. It is suggested that, in the context of the complete reshaping of reg 7(1) HB Regs 1987 with effect from 25 January 1999, it is a false exercise to seek to ask whether the local authority erred in not changing its forms to obtain just one of the pieces of information requred for the new reg 7(1): not rewriting all claim forms may be quite justified for some period of time if the change required is quite a minor one or one which impacts on only a small minority of claimants; but not rewriting claim forms for a period of time may well not be justified where the changes are extensive.

However, where a tribunal on an appeal finds a decision on benefits or tax credits entitlement to have been wrongly made by the DWP or the Revenue, this, in effect, is binding authority that the benefits or tax credits decision was made in "error" or was a "mistake" for the purposes of reg 100(3), and it is not open to the HB authority to go behind the tribunal's decision to try and identify the exact basis on which it set aside the DWP's or Revenue's decision: *CH 943/2003*. The commissioner did, however, point out that the claimant might have contributed to the error if s/he failed to put evidence before the Revenue decision maker which led the tribunal to allow her/his appeal, or might be taken to be aware that s/he was being overpaid if the decision maker's decision was clearly wrong: para 39. It is suggested that only the most brazen of mistakes could possibly come into the latter category.

If an officer of the DWP undertakes to forward information to the local authority and fails to do so, s/he will be guilty of an official error even if the undertaking is given outside normal procedures: *CH 939/2004* para 11. Equally, a failure to operate the verification framework properly or at all is capable of amounting to a "mistake or omission": *CH 2794/2004* para 22; but this does not override the claimant's responsibility to answer the questions on claim forms accurately and completely.

When will there be an official error in a local authority failing to identify and query an apparent discrepancy in information before it? It is suggested that the problem will have to be clear and obvious before an official error will be made. In *R(H) 1/04* (see above), it was contended that the local authority should have queried the award of IS and it was an official error for them not to do so. Commissioner Turnbull rejected that contention (para 22), since the claimant might have been getting mortgage interest payments which would have entitled him to IS and "the information before the Council did not demonstrate that the income support award had been wrongly made".

This analysis will not, of course, be capable of application to a case involving an HB overpayment because the claimant ought not to be getting mortgage interest as part of an IS or JSA claim as well as HB. It is suggested that a failure to follow up a glaring discrepancy may involve an official error. See, however, the discussion on causation above.

To similar effect is the decision in *R(H) 2/04*, where a claimant was awarded HB on a renewal claim when her award of WFTC was about to expire. It was argued that the local authority should have realised that the new award of WFTC might be different and that benefit should not have been paid until the new award was made. Commissioner Howell rejected that submission, holding that it was the claimant's fault that the local authority had not been made aware of the new award: para 12. There had to be a "clear and obvious" error of fact as to the facts disclosed: para 13. A further illustration of the difficulty in demonstrating official error in cases of this nature is *CH 69/2003*, where the local authority was held to be under no duty to analyse the payments going into a bank account from statements before it (para 9). Nor can it be argued that there was an official error in not suspending payment on the basis of a suspicion: *CSHB 718/2002* para 42. *CH 687/2006* holds that nothing said by the House of Lords in *Kerr* [2004] 1 WLR 1374 cuts down on the "clear and obvious discrepancy" analysis in *R(H) 1/04* and *R(H) 2/04*.

Before 1 April 1997, this phrase was worded "a mistake made or something done or omitted to be done". It is arguable that this wording did not require a "mistake" at all and rendered it unnecessary for this criterion to be met, because there was always "something done" which caused the overpayment, namely the act of authorising the payment. There was nothing in the amending regulations (SI 1997 No.65) to suggest that the phrase applied to payments made before April 1997 and so this argument can still be used in relation to periods prior to that date.

Who must make the mistake? The overpayment must have been caused by a mistake made by the authority or a relevant official. The relevant official could be any of the following.

(1)	The relevant authority. "Relevant authority" is defined in reg 2 as an authority administering HB.

(2)	An officer or person acting for the "relevant authority". This includes employees of bodies carrying out HB functions which have been privatised or put out to tender under an enforcement determination issued by the Secretary of State (see s139G SSAA on p89). The officer need not be an officer working in the HB section: *CH 2321/2002* para 37. For example, if a claimant is visited by an officer from the social services department, who then promises to notify the HB department of a change in the claimant's circumstances and fails to do so, that will be a relevant mistake. In *R(H) 10/08*, the deputy commissioner agreed. He could see no justification for construing the term "relevant authority" in a way which confines it to one department within the authority. It would have been easy to limit the term expressly. He noted the contrast between the absence of a restrictive definition of the term "relevant authority" with the deliberately restrictive way in which the separate duty imposed on claimants to report change of circumstances was drafted. There, the claimant is required to report changes to the "designated office" as defined in reg 2, not to the authority generally. However, it would be insufficient to base a conclusion that a mistake had been made on the mere fact that information was given to a department, or an officer in a department, other than the HB department. A tribunal would need to be satisfied that either the claimant had a reasonably based expectation that the information would be passed on, for example, because s/he was told, or could reasonably infer, that this would happen, or because there were internal arrangements or practices within the authority for dealing with information potentially relevant to entitlement to HB and CTB and that those arrangements or practices had not been followed.

(3)	An officer of the DWP. The typical situation here will be where there has been a failure to follow the standard procedures for passing information between the departments and the authority in relation to claimants claiming IS or income-based JSA. In *Freeman* [1994] 27 HLR 616 at 621, Hale J said that it was "quite plain" that there was an official error, and the only possible mistake was the omission by the DSS to inform the authority of the cessation of the claimant's IS, and this was confirmed in *Sier* (in the High Court). Note *CH 943/2003*, which holds that an error here will include where the DWP (or Revenue – see para (4)) officer's decision is overturned by an appeal tribunal. But note also the comment of the commissioner in *CH 3761/2005* that the failure of an automatic computer notification system, without more, may not amount to an error on the part of an official of the DWP. As the Rent Service is an executive agency of the DWP, rent officers are also officers of the DWP and so a mistake made by a rent officer which leads to an overpayment may amount to an "official error".

(4)	An officer of Her Majesty's Revenue and Customs (the Revenue).

(5)	A person providing services to any of the above Departments. Again, this covers the possibility of privatisation of functions of the DWP and the Revenue.

"... acting as such ...". These words only qualify sub-paragraphs (c)(i) and (ii), and thus refer to DWP and Revenue officers acting as such. They would add nothing to sub-para (b) as it already has that qualification. *EM*

v Waltham Forest LBC [2009] UKUT 245 (AAC) was thus correct to point out (at para 82) that the commentary in previous editions of this book was wrong in referring to a "neighbour working for the council" when commenting on the phrase "acting as such". That commentary would have been perfectly apposite had it been referring to sub-para (b). However, in the context of sub-para (c) the phrase "acting as such" means that the DWP or Revenue official must be acting in her/his official capacity. Thus the claimant whose neighbour works for the DWP (or Revenue) and gives her/him wrong advice as to entitlement to HB cannot rely on his advice as the relevant mistake. This is for two reasons. Arguably these reasons depend on the same underpinning logic and so some of the criticisms of the previous commentary in *EM v Waltham Forest LBC* may, it is suggested, be misplaced. The first reason is because the neighbour was not acting in his official capacity as a DWP (or Revenue) officer when he gave the advice. Secondly, and perhaps alternatively, as *EM v Waltham Forest LBC* suggests (in para 82), because following *R(H) 10/08*, the claimant in the above example would not have a reasonable expectation that the neighbour's advice was advice that he could formally rely on. But, put this way, it is suggested this latter characterisation of the neighbour's advice collapses into the former; because it is only if the claimant can show that the neighbour was acting officially that he would have a reasonable expectation that the advice was correct and could be relied upon.

Does any mistake count? Despite the breadth of the wording in para (3), not every mistake made by a local authority will count. For example, errors in the calculation of employee pensions administered on behalf of the local authority in respect of its employees, or an error in a local authority's employee's wages, will not, without more, amount to an error by a relevant authority or a person acting for such an authority within the terms of reg 100(3): *Middlesbrough BC v DS* [2009] UKUT 80 (AAC) para 13, *EM v Waltham Forest LBC* paras 83-84 and *Kingston upon Hull CC v DLM (HB)* [2010] UKUT 234 (AAC) paras 38-41.

No contribution to the mistake. By para (3), the person from whom recovery is sought cannot rely on the mistake if a relevant person has contributed to it. Who is a relevant person? Para (3) provides that contribution to the mistake may be made by three categories of person.

(1)   The claimant.
(2)   A person acting on her/his behalf. People appointed under reg 82 to look after an incapacitated claimant's interests fall under this heading but it probably also includes those who are dealing with the authority on her/his behalf on an informal basis.
(3)   Any other person to whom the payment is made. This includes appointees who made the original claim paid under reg 94(2), landlords paid under regs 95 and 96, or personal representatives or next of kin of deceased claimants paid under reg 97. Where the person is the landlord and that landlord is a company or a housing association, the tests in reg 100(2) focus on, say, what the housing association as a whole could reasonably have been expected to realise and not what any particular employee of the association may reasonably have been expected top realise: *CH 4918/2003* (para 18).

The view expressed in previous editions of this book that, contrary to *Freeman*, the overpayment may only be recoverable from the person who caused or materially contibuted to the mistake was, it is suggested, wrong, and in any event arguably cannot sit with para 19 of *CH 4918/2003* (see below). This is for a number of reasons. Firstly, reg 100 is concerned with whether an overpayment is recoverable and not from whom it is recoverable (which falls to be determined under reg 101), and so it is arguably legally impermissible for the terms of reg 100 to constrain or calibrate the categories of person from whom an overpayment is recoverable, save where the wording of reg 100 clearly compels such a result. Secondly, the closing words of para (3) do not, without more, carry the import that it is only the person who causes or materially contributes to the mistake that the overpayment may be recoverable from. Suppose it is the claimant who has contributed to the mistake and the landlord has not. It is suggested that this, of itself, cannot render the overpayment irrecoverable from the landlord where the overpayment was paid to the landlord because, assuming the landlord cannot rely on the regulation 101(1) "defence", that would render the terms of reg 101(2) below *otiose*. Thirdly, the parallel wording in para (2) has been held not to be met if any one of the claimant, person acting on her/his behalf, or the person to whom the payment was made, could reasonably have been expected to realise that it was an overpayment, and, moreover, determination of that question is separate from the question of from whom the overpayment is recoverable (*CH 4918/2003* (paras 19 and 20 respectively).

"... did not cause or materially contribute ...". The relevant person need not be solely to blame. For the contribution to be "material", it must be shown that if the relevant person had acted differently s/he might have prevented the overpayment: *Saker v Secretary of State for Social Security* [1988] 16 January *The Times*, CA (reported as *R(I) 2/88)*. A claimant will not automatically have caused or materially contributed to the mistake if s/he notifies the authority of information other than in writing as required by reg 88(1): *CH 2409/2005* (para 22). In that case the claimant had not caused or materially contributed to the mistake, despite his breach of regulation 88(1), because he had given the authority the information by telephone, which it accepted, and had never been told by the authority that information had to be provided in writing. However, bear in mind the the view of the Court of Appeal in *Sier* (as explained in *CH 2794/2004* para 13), that the broad question to be asked is whether the claimant's act or omission caused or contributed to the overpayment being made; and so a more focused enquiry on whether the claimant contributed to the 'official error' is unlikely, in most cases, to lead to any different conclusion.

Second criterion: Knowledge of the overpayment

It must be shown that a relevant person could not reasonably have known that there was an overpayment. It is for the person seeking to rely on reg 100(2) to prove that s/he could not reasonably have been expected to realise that an overpayment was being made and not for the authority to prove that s/he could reasonably have been expected to realise that an overpayment was being made: *CH 4918/2003* (para 16) and *CH 3439/2004* (para 22 – applying ratio of *Kerr v Department for Social Development* [2004] UKHL 23 (reported as *R 1/04 (SF)*)). The "defence" under para (2) is not made out if any one of the claimant, person acting on her/his behalf, or the person to whom the payment was made, could reasonably have been expected to realise that it was an overpayment: *CH 4918/2003* (para 19).

"... could not ... reasonably have been expected to realise ...". It is not clear whether the test is objective or subjective. Is it whether the average person with average knowledge could reasonably be expected to know, or whether the particular person with her/his experience and education could have done? Because para (2) considers the knowledge of different specified categories of people, the latter test is probably correct. This has now been partially confirmed by Commissioner Jacobs in *CH 2554/2002*, in which he was critical of a statement by a tribunal that it did not impute "any more knowledge about the HB scheme than an ordinary reasonable person might have". He said (para 13):

> "The question of imputation of knowledge to the claimant did not arise. The issue for the Tribunal was what could reasonably be expected of *the claimant*. There may be exceptional cases in which it is reasonable to expect a claimant to find out more about the housing benefit scheme, probably from the local authority or (possibly) elsewhere. If those cases exist in reality rather than theory, they will involve claimants with a special knowledge of the scheme, such as former housing benefit officers. They will, in any event, be rare. This case is not one of them. In the overwhelming majority of cases, there is no scope for imputing any knowledge to the claimant. The issue will be what could reasonably be deduced from the information available to the claimant. What a claimant could reasonably have been expected to realise is a question of fact. It depends on the information available to the person and on an analysis of what that information could have revealed." (para 13). See also *CH 609/2004* at para 8.

This statement of principle is a useful rebuttal to the arguments put forward by some local authorities in overpayment cases as to what can be reasonably expected of claimants. Some authorities appear to believe that any HB claimant should know the legislation inside out and should know instinctively when s/he is being overpaid. Plainly, such an approach is preposterous. As the commissioner goes on to state, in most cases the claimant's only sources of knowledge are past experience with the scheme and the documents provided by the local authority: para 15.

On the facts of the case, which concerned a failure to report income, the commissioner did not regard as conclusive the warnings given in the HB award letter to report changes of income: paras 20-22. However, he decided that since it was clear from the award letter that tax credits reduced the HB entitlement, the claimant ought to have realised that her income from employment should also do so: para 23.

A number of decisions now illustrate how critical close attention to the facts of an individual case will be. In *CH 2888/2002* para 15, the commissioner held that where a claimant had disclosed an increase in income and his wife had repeatedly enquired as to when his HB was to be reduced, the only permissible conclusion was that he should have known that he was being overpaid. This conclusion requires caution, since it is possible for such a claimant eventually to form the view, reasonably, that the local authority does not regard the increased income as relevant to her/his HB entitlement.

In *CH 2943/2007*, the claimant had correctly stated her earnings in her HB and CTB claims and in later enquiries, but the local authority had calculated her benefit on incorrect (lower) earnings and these were shown on its decision notices. The commissioner pointed out that a claimant cannot reasonably be expected to seek advice about a local authority's decision notice because s/he does not understand all the figures unless s/he has some reason to believe that the figures are wrong. A claimant who has given clear and correct information is entitled to start from the basis that the local authority has such information when stating her/his weekly earnings.

Where a landlord was clearly informed that she should report the departure of a tenant from a property, her belief that she was entitled to receive HB during the claimant's notice period did not preclude a finding that she could reasonably be expected to know that she was being overpaid: *CH 1172/2002* para 8. Rather more obviously, in *CH 4465/2002* para 9 a landlord's argument that it could not reasonably be expected to know that it was being overpaid when it was aware of the claimant's departure from the premises and had indeed placed another tenant therein was rejected.

A less rigorous view was taken in *CH 3629/2002* where the claimant started low-paid work. She knew that her HB would decrease, but did not know when or by how much. The commissioner held that for a few weeks at least she could not reasonably have been expected to know that she was being overpaid.

If a claimant receives clear advice from a local authority that a certain income source is disregarded, then s/he cannot reasonably be expected to know that he is being overpaid: *CH 4838/2001* para 8. However, the effect of any contradictory advice in the documentation made available to a claimant should be taken into account in determining what is reasonable.

In *CH 4065/2001*, a claimant had been overpaid because the local authority had incorrectly calculated her income from IB. The authority alleged that she ought to have known that she was being overpaid and her response was that she had telephoned the local authority to query the award and had been told that it was correct. The authority's retort that there was no record of the call (as should have been the case on the office system) was held not to be a complete answer by Commissioner Jacobs. He said that "it is not my experience of life that administrative systems work perfectly in every case" (para 13). See also similar comments by the same commissioner in *CH 609/2004* para 24. It is implicit from the directions given to the tribunal in *CH 4065/2001,* that the commissioner took the view that if the claimant's evidence was accepted, the claimant could not reasonably have been expected to know that she was being overpaid. The directions (para 21) are a very useful summary of the correct approach to this very common type of case.

"*... at the time of receipt of the payment or of any notice relating to that payment ...*". It seems that the person whom it is alleged ought to have known should be the person receiving the payment or the notice. For example, a person should probably realise at the time of receipt of a duplicate payment that they s/he has overpaid: *R v Liverpool CC ex p Griffiths* [1990] 22 HLR 312, QBD (Nolan J).

The purpose of this part of reg 99(2) HB Regs 1987 (now reg 100(2)), and the basis for its interpretation, was explained clearly by Commissioner Jacobs in *CH 1176/2003* para 8:

"The context in which regulation 99(2) will operate is relevant. It only applies to cases in which the claimant was on low income at the time of the payment. And the payment involved will have been made to help the claimant pay rent on a dwelling. In those circumstances, it is likely that the money will be spent fairly quickly. That, I believe, accounts for the emphasis on the time of payment or notice relating to payment. If the claimant could not reasonably have been expected to realise that an overpayment had been made, it is likely that the money will have been spent and spent in reliance on the claimant being properly entitled to it. In other words, regulation 99(2) contains an element of protection for a claimant who has relied on being entitled to the payment. The provision is not worded in those terms or limited to cases where there has been reliance. But that rationale provides a context in which the terms of the legislation must be interpreted."

The phrase relating to notices causes difficulty. The amendment was apparently made to deal with rent rebate cases where the claimant never actually receives any rent: Circular HB/CCB 90/23, and see *CH 1675/2005*. The wording is not restricted to such cases: *CH 1176/2003* para 9. In the same case, the commissioner suggested that if notice of an erroneous payment is sent out but promptly corrected by a telephone call to the claimant, it might be possible to see the whole process as one transaction: para 32-33. This seems to be an unwarranted gloss on the legislation and adds an additional complication to a tribunal's task.

In *R(H) 1/02*, the commissioner was concerned with a case where a claimant had omitted to inform the local authority of an increase in her wages until she signed a review form some six weeks later. However, the authority recalculated her benefit on the basis of an incorrect figure being entered into its computer for the benefit calculations. That recalculation was carried out at a later stage, with a result that a lump sum was payable to the claimant. The claimant was sent notifications which set out the calculation with the incorrect figure used for the amount of her wages.

The commissioner held, at para 6(2)(a) of the decision, that where a claimant both receives a notice relating to a payment and receives it, knowledge or presumed knowledge on the date of either event will suffice to make the overpayment recoverable. He also held that "notice relating to that payment" requires that the notice in question be sufficiently closely related to the payment: para 6(2)(b).

This point was also addressed in *CH 1176/2003*, where the commissioner held (para 31) that, although the notice need not be the notice *of* payment, and so is wider than the actual decision notice, it must relate to the *payment* and not the overpayment, otherwise para (2) would provide no protection as, by definition, at the time of the overpayment notice the claimant must have been able to realise that it was an overpayment (see also *CH 1675/2005*). In *CH 1176/2003* a cheque for HB was mistakenly issued to the claimant's bank on 18 February and credited to her account on the following day. The claimant made a series of withdrawals from her bank account before being informed by the local authority on 26 February of the mistake. Commissioner Jacobs held that a payment made by cheque is only received when it is credited to the claimant's bank account and not when the cheque is received by the claimant or presented at the bank: paras 20-23. He also held, remitting the case to the tribunal for reconsideration, that the "time" of receipt should not be judged according to the split-second at which the cheque was credited: para 26. It was a question of fact for the tribunal but one possible approach was to examine the claimant's knowledge over the day of receipt: para 27.

"*... that it was an overpayment...*". It must be shown that the relevant person should have known that there was an overpayment, not that there might have been an overpayment. In *Griffiths* (above), the authority had sent out letters warning claimants that they might receive the wrong amount of benefit under the estimated award. It was argued that it was sufficient that Mrs Griffiths knew that she might be being overpaid. Nolan J held (at 317) that this was not enough. It was not reasonable to expect her to work out her entitlement herself to decide whether she was getting too much HB. This approach was confirmed in *CH 2554/2002* para 9. The corollary of this, as pointed out by Commissioner Jacobs in that case, is that the claimant need not be aware of the amount by which s/he is being overpaid. All that is necessary is that that the claimant "could reasonably have been expected to realise that the amount she was receiving definitely contained some element of overpayment".

Paragraph (4)

This provides that certain overpayments of rent rebate are always recoverable. There are four conditions for its operation.

(1)   There has been a revision of the award. It does not appear to apply if the award is correct but, for example, the claimant is credited twice on her/his account due to a clerical error.

(2)   It also appears that the claimant's rent account must be in credit for the paragraph to come into effect. So, if a claimant is wrongly awarded £100 rather than £50 rent rebate for four weeks, but incurs an annual service charge on the rent account of £500, the account will be £300 in the red and so the paragraph does not apply.

(3)   The credit is in respect of a period after the date of the revision. In respect of past periods, the exception does not apply and the three criteria can be considered.

(4)   Even if there is a credit after the date of the revision, that credit must be the overpayment and not subsequent payments of rent rebate or made by the claimant. If the latter is the case, then the surplus ought to be presumed to relate to the latest of the payments made into the rent account: *Clayton's case* [1861] 1 Mer 572. For example, a claimant wrongly awarded £100 rather than £80 for four weeks then has her/his rent rebate suspended for two weeks. After one week, the £80 credit has gone; after two, the claimant is £80 in the red. However, at the end of the two weeks, before a revision is carried out, the claimant pays £160 into the rent account. There is an £80 credit on the account when the review is carried out, but that represents the claimant's voluntary payment rather than the overpayment.

Person from whom recovery may be sought

101.–(1)   For the purposes of section 75(3)(a) of the Administration Act (prescribed circumstances in which an amount recoverable shall not be recovered from the person to whom it was paid), the prescribed circumstance is–

(a)   housing benefit has been paid in accordance with regulation 95 (circumstances in which payment is to be made to the landlord) or regulation 96 (circumstances in which payment may be made to a landlord);

(b)   the landlord has notified the relevant authority or the Secretary of State in writing that he suspects that there has been an overpayment;

[¹ (bb) the relevant authority is satisfied that the overpayment did not occur as a result of any change of dwelling occupied by the claimant as his home;]

(c)   it appears to the relevant authority that, on the assumption that there has been an overpayment–

    (i)   there are grounds for instituting proceedings against any person for an offence under section 111A or 112(1) of the Administration Act (dishonest or false representations for obtaining benefit); or

    (ii)   there has been a deliberate failure to report a relevant change of circumstances contrary to the requirement of regulation 88 (duty to notify a change of circumstances) and the overpayment occurred as a result of that deliberate failure; and

(d)   the relevant authority is satisfied that the landlord–

    (i)   has not colluded with the claimant so as to cause the overpayment;

    (ii)   has not acted, or neglected to act, in such a way so as to contribute to the period, or the amount, of the overpayment.

[² [⁴ (2)   For the purposes of section 75(3)(b) of the Administration Act (recovery from such other person, as well as or instead of the person to whom the overpayment was made), where recovery of an overpayment is sought by a relevant authority–

(a)   subject to paragraph (1) and where sub-paragraph (b) or (c) does not apply, the overpayment is recoverable from the claimant as well as the person to whom the payment was made, if different;

(b)   in a case where an overpayment arose in consequence of a misrepresentation of or a failure to disclose a material fact (in either case, whether fraudulently or otherwise) by or on behalf of the claimant, or by or on behalf of any person to whom the payment was made, the overpayment is only recoverable from any person who misrepresented or failed to disclose that material fact instead of, if different, the person to whom the payment was made; or

(c)   in a case where an overpayment arose in consequence of an official error where the claimant, or a person acting on the claimant's behalf, or any person to whom the payment was paid, or any person acting on their behalf, could reasonably have been expected, at the time of receipt of the payment or of any notice relating to that payment, to realise that it was an overpayment, the overpayment is only recoverable from any such person instead of, if different, the person to whom the payment was made.]

[³ (2A) Where an overpayment is made in a case where a relevant authority has determined a maximum rent (LHA) in accordance with regulation 13D (determination of a maximum rent (LHA)), and the housing benefit payable exceeds the amount which the claimant is liable to pay his landlord by way of rent, the relevant authority must not recover from the landlord more than the landlord has received.]

(3) For the purposes of [³ paragraphs (1) and (2A)], "landlord" shall have the same meaning as it has for the purposes of regulation 95.

[¹ (3A) For the purposes of [⁴ paragraph (2)(c)], "overpayment arose in consequence of an official error" shall have the same meaning as in regulation 100(3) above.]

[⁴ (4)]

Amendments

1. Inserted by reg 6(2) and (4) of SI 2005 No 2904 as amended by Sch 2 para 29 of SI 2006 No 217 as from 10.4.06.
2. Substituted by reg 6(3) of SI 2005 No 2904 as amended by Sch 2 para 29 of SI 2006 No 217 as from 10.4.06.
3. Amended by reg 2 of SI 2008 No 586 as from 7.4.08.
4. Amended by reg 4(2) of SI 2008 No 2824 as from 6.4.09.

Definitions

"claimant" – see reg 2(1).
"membership of household" – see Part 4 and note on s20(11).
"partner" – see reg 2(1).
"overpayment" – see reg 99.
"recoverable" – see reg 100.

General Note

SSAA s75(3) provides that a recoverable overpayment is recoverable from the person to whom it was paid unless regulations provide otherwise, and also gives a power to make regulations allowing recovery to be made from other persons in certain circumstances. This regulation exercises those powers. See commentary to s75 SSAA on p43 and the tribunal of commissioners' decision in *R(H) 6/06*. Note also the view in *DL v Liverpool City Council* [2009] UKUT 176 (AAC) that payments of HB made to a claimant's rent account after her/his death are not recoverable from the claimant under reg 101.

Despite the title of reg 101, it is clear that it is dealing with the recoverability stage rather than (the later) enforcement of recovery: *R(H) 6/06*.

Note also the commissioners' recommendation in para 60 of *R(H) 6/06* that in every case where reg 101 provides for joint liability, the local authority should make a single decision referring to all of those from whom the overpayment is recoverable, rather than separate decisions addressed to each of them. Moreover, where a local authority decides that an overpayment is not recoverable from the person to whom it was made, a proper decision to that effect should be made and included in the decision about the person from whom the overpayment is recoverable, and that decision issued to both parties. Unless and until this is done any alleged overpayment will not be recoverable from any person: *CH 3744/2006* (para 33).

R(H) 3/09 decided that it was not unfair for the immediately prior form of reg 101 to have retrospective effect, in the sense that if the reg 101 decision was made on or after 10 April 2006 then it would be the reg 101 in place at that time that would act to fix from whom the overpayment may be recoverable notwithstanding that the overpayment may be for a period arising wholly or partly before 10 April 2006 (when the result under the then version of reg 101 may have been different). Reg 101 (and para 2 in particular) has been amended again since the version of reg 101 that *R(H) 3/09* ruled on. However, as it would seem that the 6 April 2009 changes to reg 101(2) were intended merely to tidy up the wording of para (2), and as the scope of para (2) arguably remains the same, it is likely that *R(H) 3/09* remains good law.

One contentious issue which may still arise in respect of the post-9 April 2006 version of reg 101, however, is when a landlord may be said to have breached a legal duty to disclose so that s/he can be said to have failed to disclose (following *B v SSWP* [2005] EWCA Civ 929, [2005] 1 WLR 3796 (reported as *R(IS) 9/06*)). This is because regs 86(1) and 88(1) (and the equivalent regulations in the HB(SPC) Regs – regs 67(1) and 69(1)) would seem to only impose a legal duty on a landlord to disclose if there is a subsequent change in circumstances after the claim has been awarded, and then only if s/he knows about the change and "might reasonably be expected to know" that it "might affect" the claimant's HB.

Para (1) deals with the case where a person receiving HB will not be liable to repay benefit, namely a blameless landlord in certain limited cases.

All reg 101 is concerned with is fixing who, as a matter of law, is legally liable to repay the overpayment, and disputes as to whether a person falls within reg 101 are appealable. However, once those reg 101 issues have been finally decided there then arises one final decision to be made, namely who out of those people who are legally liable to repay the overpayment the local authority will actually seek to enforce recovery against as a matter of fact. That is a discretionary decision of the local authority and, as *R(H) 6/06* makes plain, it is *not* appealable.

Analysis

Paragraph (1): Cases where an overpayment is not recoverable from a landlord

As *R(H) 6/06* explains, para (1) provides a limited exception to the entitlement to recover from landlords. Para (1) sets out five conditions that must all be satisfied if the landlord is to escape liability.

If the five conditions in para (1) are satisfied, the overpayment is *irrecoverable* from the landlord even if the HB was paid to her/him. However, the five conditions must all be satisfied and, hence, if the landlord fails to meet just one of them it will lose the protection of para (1), and the question of whether the overpayment is recoverable from it will have to be determined under para (2).

Sub-para (a): Direct payments made to landlord. A landlord cannot take advantage of para (1) unless direct payments were made under reg 95 or 96.

Note, however, that the HB that has been paid direct arguably must be the same as the HB of which recovery is sought, given the scope of the enabling power in s75(3) (and see further the like reasoning in *DL v Liverpool City Council* above). So if the landlord received direct payments prior to the overpayment period but not during that period, the overpayment will not be recoverable (though not because the landlord has met the five conditions in reg 101(1) but because the overpayment does not fall within reg 101 in the first place).

Direct payments to a landlord's agent will satisfy this condition, since reg 101(3) imports the definition in reg 95: "a person to whom rent is payable". If a landlord appoints an agent to receive the rent, then for the purposes of reg 101, the agent will be treated as if s/he is the landlord.

Sub-para (b): Notification of overpayment. There must be a written notification. "Writing" should extend to communication by fax and also ought to extend to correspondence by email. It is also suggested that it will be sufficient if a landlord makes an oral statement to an officer which is recorded by that officer, as long as if it is then signed by the landlord.

A notice given by an agent or company director should be sufficient for the purposes of sub-para (b), certainly if it is explicitly made on behalf of the landlord.

Sub-para (bb): Not due to change of dwelling. If the authority, or on appeal the tribunal, is satisfied that the overpayment arose because of the claimant moving out of the dwelling for which s/he was getting HB, the landlord cannot rely on reg 101(1). The wording of sub-para (bb) would still seem to allow reg 101(1) to apply, however, to those parts of the overpayment that did not occur as a result of a change of dwelling.

Sub-para (c): Offence committed or deliberate failure to disclose. On appeal, the First-tier Tribunal must decide for itself whether it appears that the condition is satisfied.

The two limbs of sub-para (c) are alternatives. Under head (i), it is not necessary to prove that the relevant person is guilty of the offence, merely that there is a case for her/him to answer. See ss111A and 112(1) for the question of whether an offence is committed.

Under head (ii), there must have been a failure to report a change of circumstances by a claimant, a recipient of HB or an agent of a recipient. The breach must be deliberate. The *Shorter Oxford English Dictionary* defines "deliberate" as "carefully thought out, studied; intentional, done on purpose". A breach that is inadvertent or even negligent will not suffice. The breach must also have caused the overpayment. It need not be the sole cause. It will suffice if it is one of joint causes: *R (Sier) v Cambridge CC HBRB* [2001] EWHC Admin 160, QBD; [2001] EWCA Civ 1523, CA, Richards J, discussed on p480.

Sub-para (d): No fault of landlord. It appears that both limbs under sub-para (d) must be satisfied. Again the wording "the relevant authority is satisfied" does not confine the First-tier Tribunal to a review of the authority's decision; it must decide the question for itself afresh.

In head (i), "colluded" is not defined. The *Shorter Oxford English Dictionary* gives "conspire, plot, connive, act in secret concert . . . . stir up or bring about by collusion". Effectively, there must be an agreement to act in such a way that an overpayment occurs, but it may be that a specific intention to commit fraud is not required.

Under head (ii), it must be shown that the landlord "has not acted, or neglected to act" in a way that caused the claimant to be overpaid. One of two things must be shown: a positive action of the landlord (or, it would seem, the landlord's agent) or some degree of inaction. The latter must involve "neglect". So if the landlord did not know of the relevant facts or if a reasonable person in the landlord's position would not have informed the local authority of the position, then the overpayment does not become recoverable.

Paragraph (2): Targets for recovery

In most cases para (1) will not be satisfied. Therefore, for the vast majority of cases from whom the overpayment is recoverable will be governed by reg 101(2). The wording of para (2) was amended in April 2009. This rewriting of para (2) was not intended to alter its scope but to make clearer who para (2) was aimed at after criticism of the wording of prior versions of reg 101(2) by the Tribunal of Commissioners in *R(H) 6/06*.

Para (2) seeks to define the circumstances under s75(3)(b) SSAA in which an overpayment shall be recoverable from such other person as well as, or instead of, the person to whom it was paid. Thus the regulation making power in s75(3)(b) expressly contemplates that an overpayment may be recoverable from a person in addition to the person to whom the HB was paid or a person instead of the payee, and reg 101(2) then, in its now clearer terms, sets out how that is effected.

General rule: claimant and payee. The general rule is set out in para (2)(a). This provides that that an overpayment is recoverable from the claimant and the person, if different, to whom the overpayment was made.

However this general rule will not apply if reg 101(1) (above) applies, nor will it apply if either sub-paras (b) or (c) apply.

Note further, however, in respect of the claimant, what Judge Mesher called his "provisional view" in *DL v Liverpool City Council* that, although following *Secretary of State for Social Services v Solly* [1974] 3 All ER 922 an HB overpayment could in principle be recoverable from the claimant's estate after her/his death, this could only be where the overpayment was in respect of periods before the claimant's death, as only in that circumstance could the overpayment be said to be a liability of the claimant's estate.

First exception to general rule: person who fails to disclose or misrepresents. The first exception to the general rule is set out in sub-para (b) of para (2). The net effect of this exception is that where the overpayment has arisen in consequence of a misrepresentation of, or a failure to disclose, a material fact by a person then (a) the general rule above does not apply, and (b) the overpayment is (only) recoverable from the person who made the misrepresentation or failed to disclose. The misrepresentation may be made by or on behalf of the claimant or by or on behalf of the payee, but in either case the overpayment is only recoverable from the person who made the misrepresentation or failed to disclose. (See below, *inter alia,* for the meaning of "misrepresentation" and "failure to disclose".)

Thus, even where the HB was paid to a claimant (where, that is, normally s/he would be caught full square by the general rule described above), s/he may escape liability for the overpayment if the overpayment arose in consequence of someone other than her/him failing to disclose or misrepresenting a material fact. Likewise, where a landlord on the face of it falls within para (2)(a) with the claimant because HB was paid direct to them, they may escape liability if the overpayment arose because of a failure to disclose by the claimant – eg, failing to tell the authority that s/he had inherited £25,000.

Second exception – person who should realise official error overpayment being made. The second exception to the general rule is set out in sub-para (c). For it to apply at all, in contrast to the first exception, the overpayment must have arisen in consequence of an "official error" under reg 100(3). The net effect of the second exception is that where the overpayment has arisen in consequence of an official error then (a) the general rule above does not apply (nor can the first exception), and (b) the overpayment is (only) recoverable from those out of the claimant, the payee, or those acting on either's behalf, who under the reg 100(2) test could reasonably have been expected to realise that an overpayment was being made.

"... in consequence of ...". There must be a clear link between the misrepresentation or failure to disclose and the making of the overpayment. However, the misleading of the authority need not be the sole cause of the overpayment. It is sufficient if it is a significant contributing factor. So, where there has been a failure to disclose by a relevant person, it is not an answer that the authority could have discovered the true situation by contacting the DWP or some other person: *Duggan v Chief Adjudication Officer* [1988] *The Times* 18 December, CA; *CSB 64/1986* para 11.

On the other hand, where the authority knows of the true situation, the misleading may not be sufficiently significant. The "clear link" will not be established where it can be shown that the authority has actually been informed of the true situation by the DWP or some other third person: *CIS 159/1990* para 4; *CS 12770/1996* para 9. When the relevant person has previously informed the authority of the true facts but later inadvertently misleads the authority, provided it is reasonable for them to assume the previous information has been acted on, the later misrepresentation may not be an effective cause of the overpayment: *CS 130/1992* paras 15-16. Furthermore, where the information before the authority clearly makes it clear that there is a need for further inquiries, and those inquiries are not made, then the sole cause of the overpayment may be the authority's error: *CIS 222/1991* paras 4-5.

Where there has been criminal activity by a third person, such as the theft of a cheque, that activity may be found to be the true cause of a resulting overpayment: *CIS 395/1992* para 10.

"... a misrepresentation ...". A misrepresentation is an actual statement which is untrue or misleading: *CSB 1006/1985* para 5. It may be made in writing, orally or even by conduct if sufficiently unambiguous: *R(SB) 18/85* para 10.

Claim forms provided by authorities often require a person claiming on behalf of the claimant to sign a declaration at the end of the form. If the declaration is false then that may amount to a misrepresentation even if none of the details given on the form are untrue of themselves. However, the courts have tended to give a narrow reading to such declarations: see *Jones v Chief Adjudication Officer* [1994] 1 WLR 62 at 71H, 72F, CA; *Franklin v Chief Adjudication Officer* [1995] *The Times* 29 December, CA; *CIS 393/1993* para 7; *CIS 372/1994* para 6.

"... or failure to disclose ...". Following the case of *B* (see below for details) the authority must now establish only two matters; the additional test of whether disclosure was "reasonably to be expected" having been held to be unnecessary in *B.*

(1)   That the relevant person was under a duty to disclose. See reg 86 for the duty to provide information to the authority and reg 88 for the statutory duty to notify a change of circumstances. In *CH 2443/2002* para 14, the commissioner held that an employer could not be under a duty to disclose because reg 75 HB regs 1987 (now reg 88) had no application to an employer. More recently the Court of Appeal in *B v SSWP* [2005] EWCA Civ 929, [2005] 1 WLR 3796 (reported as *R(IS) 9/06*) – affirming the decision of the tribunal of commissioners in *CIS 4348/2003* – has held that a failure to disclose can only arise if the person was under a legal duty which s/he has breached *R(SB) 21/82*. However, there can be no duty to disclose information which is not known: *Franklin*; *R(SB) 54/83* para 13(2); *R(SB) 9/85* para 7.

(2)   That the relevant person did not disclose the relevant information. Disclosure means informing the authority in such a way that the information can be expected to come to the attention of a person with responsibility for handling the claim: *R(SB) 15/87* paras 25, 28 and *Hinchy v SSWP* [2005] UKHL 16 (*R(IS) 7/05*). Although HB Regs reg 88 and CTB Regs reg 74 require changes of circumstances to be notified "in writing to the designated office" oral disclosure has always been treated as sufficient in relation to DWP benefits, even before reg 32 Social Security (Claims and Payments) Regulations 1987 was amended to permit oral disclosure to be accepted: see *R(SB) 40/84* para 5; *R(SB) 15/87* para 13. Once disclosure has been made, there is no duty to disclose the same information again: *R(SB) 15/87* para 28.

"... a material fact ...". This is one that the relevant person ought reasonably to realise might affect benefit: HB Regs reg 75(1) and *Saker v Secretary of State for Social Security* [1988] 16 January *The Times*, CA (reported as *R(I) 2/88*).

"... in either case whether fraudulently or otherwise ...". No moral culpability need be shown on the part of the relevant person. The misleading of authority may have been entirely innocent: *Page v Chief Adjudication Officer* [1991] The Times 4 July, CA.

"... the person who misrepresented or failed to disclose that material fact ...". In all cases, this includes the individual responsible who misled the authority. It probably also includes corporate entities for whom the individual works: see Interpretation Act 1978 Sch 1.

Recovery from appointees. The mechanism in reg 82(3) for appointment of a person to act on behalf of another is similar to the procedure for appointment by the DWP under reg 33 Social Security (Claims and Payments) Regulations 1987. The question of whether appointees can be personally liable to repay an overpayment has caused controversy in relation to DWP benefits. This has now been settled by the decision of a tribunal of commissioners in *R(IS) 5/03*, in which it was held that such personal liability would ordinarily exist: para 57. Recovery will normally be available against both claimant and appointee: para 58. However, it was said that if the benefit was not paid over to the claimant, recovery could only be made from the appointee: para 59. It was also said that the appointee would have a right under general principles of agency law to be indemnified by her/his principal except in cases where s/he was guilty of negligence or a breach of duty: para 61. The principal is the local authority, because the local authority appoints the appointee to act. Accordingly, in cases where it is alleged that there is strict liability for a misrepresentation made by an appointee but the appointee acted with due diligence, the appointee will be able to counterclaim to proceedings brought by the local authority for an indemnity, and the claim for the amount of the overpayment and the counterclaim for the indemnity will cancel each other out.

Method of recovery

102.–(1)   Without prejudice to any other method of recovery, [² a relevant authority] may recover a recoverable overpayment from any person referred to in regulation 101 (persons from whom recovery may be sought) by deduction from any housing benefit to which that person is entitled (including arrears of entitlement after offsetting under regulation 98 (offsetting)) or, where it is unable to do so, may request the Secretary of State to recover any recoverable overpayment from the benefits prescribed in [³ regulation 105(1)] (recovery of overpayments from prescribed benefits).

[³ (1ZA)   Where an overpayment is recoverable from a claimant who has one or more partners, a relevant authority may recover the overpayment by deduction from any housing benefit payable to the claimant's partner, or where it is unable to do so, may request the Secretary of State to recover any recoverable overpayment from the benefits prescribed in regulation 105(1B) (recovery of overpayments from prescribed benefits), provided that the claimant and that partner were a couple both at the time of the overpayment and when the deduction is made.]

[² [⁴]]

(2)   Subject to paragraphs [² [⁴]] (4) and (5), where [¹ a relevant authority] makes deductions permitted by paragraph (1) [³ or (1ZA)] from the housing benefit it is paying to a claimant [³ or a claimant's partner] (other than deductions from arrears of entitlement), the deduction in respect of a benefit week shall be–

(a)   in a case to which paragraph (3) applies, not more than the amount there specified; and

(b)   in any other case, not more than three times five per cent. of the personal allowance for a single claimant aged not less than 25, that five per cent. being, where it is not a multiple of five pence, rounded to the next higher such multiple.

(3)   Where [¹ a relevant authority] makes deductions from housing benefit it is paying to a claimant [³ or a claimant's partner, where the claimant has] , in respect of the whole or part of the recoverable overpayment–

(a)   been found guilty of an offence whether under a statute or otherwise;

(b)   made an admission after caution of deception or fraud for the purpose of obtaining relevant benefit; or

(c)   agreed to pay a penalty under section 115A of the Administration Act (penalty as an alternative to prosecution) and the agreement has not been withdrawn,

the amount deducted under paragraph (2) shall be not more than four times five per cent. of the personal allowance for a single claimant aged not less than 25, but where that five per cent. is not a multiple of 10 pence, it shall be rounded to the nearest 10 pence or, if it is a multiple of 5 pence but not of 10 pence, the next higher multiple of 10 pence.

(4)   Where, in the calculation of housing benefit, the amount of earnings or other income falling to be taken into account is reduced by reason of paragraphs 3 to 10 of Schedule 4 (sums to be disregarded in the calculation of earnings) [⁴ , or paragraph 10A of that Schedule in a case where the amount of earnings to be disregarded under that paragraph is the amount referred to in regulation 45(2) of the Employment and Support Allowance Regulations or regulation 17(2) of the Social Security (Incapacity for Work) (General) Regulations 1995,] or paragraph 14 or 15 of Schedule 5 (sums to be disregarded in the calculation of income other than earnings), the deduction under paragraph (2) may be increased by not more than half the amount of the reduction.

(5)   No deduction made under this regulation [² [⁴]] shall be applied so as to reduce the housing benefit in respect of a benefit week to less than 50 pence.

(6)   In this regulation–

"admission after caution" means–

(i)   in England and Wales, an admission after a caution has been administered in accordance with a Code issued under the Police and Criminal Evidence Act 1984;

(ii)   in Scotland, admission after a caution has been administered, such admission being duly witnessed by two persons; and

"personal allowance for a single claimant aged not less than 25" means the amount specified in paragraph 1(1)(b) of column 2 of Schedule 3 (applicable amounts).

(7)   This regulation shall not apply in respect of an offence committed or an admission after caution or an agreement to pay a penalty made before 2nd October 2000.

Amendments

1.   Substituted by reg 7(2) of SI 2005 No 2904 as amended by Sch 2 para 29 of SI 2006 No 217 as from 10.4.06.

2.   Inserted by reg 7(3)-(5) of SI 2005 No 2904 as amended by Sch 2 para 29 of SI 2006 No 217 as from 10.4.06.

3.   Amended by reg 4(3) of SI 2008 No 2824 as from 6.4.09.

4.   Amended by reg 2(2) of SI 2009 No 2608 as from 1.4.10 (5.4.10 where rent payable weekly or in multiples of a week).

Definitions

"authority" – see reg 2(2) and s134(4) SSAA.

"overpayment" – see reg 99.

"recoverable" – see reg 100.

Analysis

In the detailed consideration of the various methods of recovery available that follows, the person from whom recovery is sought will be referred to as "D".

The fact that D has been declared bankrupt will not prevent recovery from benefits payable to her/him, since the specific statutory provisions dealing with recovery from benefit entitlement override the general law of bankruptcy in England and Wales: *R v Secretary of State for Social Security ex p Taylor and Chapman* [1996] *The Times* 5 February, QBD (Keene J), and the law of sequestration in Scotland: *Mulvey v Secretary of State for Social Security* [1997] SLT 753 at 756, HL. However, if an overpayment decision is made before a person is adjudged bankrupt, it will amount to a "contingent liability" under the Insolvency Act 1986 and a claimant should then be discharged from liability to repay that overpayment under s281 Insolvency Act 1986 if and when s/he is discharged from bankruptcy: *R(Balding) v SSWP* [2007] EWHC 759, 3 April 2007, (Admin). The Court of Appeal dismissed the Secretary of State's appeal against the decision in *SSWP v Balding* [2007] 13 December, EWCA Civ 1327. But if the overpayment decision is made after a person is adjudged bankrupt, even where the overpayment is for a period before s/he was adjudged bankrupt, the Insolvency Act 1986 has no application and the overpayment will remain a debt the person is liable to repay even after s/he has been discharged from bankruptcy: *CH 3495/2008*.

The authority may not add interest to the overpayment: *R v Kensington and Chelsea RBC ex p Brandt* [1995] 28 HLR 528, QBD (Dyson J).

Recovery from HB payable to D

Under reg 102, there may be recovery from any HB owing to D to which D is entitled. This can be arrears owed to D (even if the arrears are referable to dates outside the period of the overpayment) or future payments. The effect of reg 102 is duplicated by SSAA s75(5)(a) and reg 106(2).

Where D is a claimant in receipt of rent allowance, this should not cause any difficulties. When determining the appropriate rate of recovery, the authority will wish to balance the need for enforcement against the need to avoid making the tenant homeless and possibly liable to be housed by the authority. The authority may deduct from payments made to D's landlord. Since the landlord has never been paid, this will create rent arrears as between landlord and claimant.

Reg 102 only authorises deduction from HB where D is not a claimant, if it is HB paid to D in her/his role as claimant. In particular, where D is a landlord, reg 102 does not authorise recovery from HB paid to D in respect of tenants other than the overpaid claimant. The recovery is only from HB "to which that person [ie, the person from whom recovery is sought] is entitled". D is not entitled to HB; her/his tenants are.

In *R v Haringey LBC ex p Ayub* [1992] 25 HLR 566, QBD, the applicant was a landlord owning a large stock of housing in the authority's area. Many of his tenants received HB. When overpayments were made, the authority sought to withhold payment of HB payable in respect of other tenants. On judicial review, the authority admitted that this course of action was not sanctioned by reg 102. Instead, it was said that this was a convenient method of recovery. Furthermore, as the other tenants were debtors of the landlord, the authority could "garnish" their debts (that is, seize payments made to a debtor by his debtors). Schiemann J held that there was no right to garnish a debt until a court order was obtained, and then stated:

"When a council is making a payment to a landlord under regulations 93 or 94 *[now regs 95 and 96 HB Regs]* of rent allowance to which tenants B-Z are entitled it is in effect acting as the agent of those tenants and paying their rent for them. Upon such a payment being made the tenant's liability to the landlord is *pro tanto* extinguished and the latter cannot thereafter sue the former for more payment of that rent or repossess the property on the basis of non-payment of that rent. The authority is not allowed to use a tenant's rent allowance in order to extinguish any liability of the landlord to the authority. That is not a purpose for which Parliament has authorised the payment of rent allowance. The general right of set-off for which the authority contends would leave it totally unclear as to which unfortunate tenant's rent allowance is to be used for this purpose and indeed whether the choice of the unlucky tenant is to be in the hands of the landlord or in those of the authority."

However, s75(5)(b) and (c) SSAA (inserted by s16 Social Security (Administration) Fraud Act 1997) gives the authority the right to recover from "prescribed benefits" paid to D in respect of an obligation owed to him by another person. See reg 106(3) and note the effect of reg 107 on tenants' liabilities.

Paras (2) and (3) impose maximum weekly amounts that may be recovered from ongoing HB. This applies only to ongoing entitlement and not to arrears, as is clear from the words in parentheses in para (2). The maximum amount is subject to a needlessly complicated calculation. First, one takes the personal allowance for a single claimant aged over 25, then takes 5 per cent of that. That figure is then multiplied by three to give the maximum deduction.

A higher maximum applies wherever the claimant is convicted of an offence, admits the offence under caution or agrees to pay a penalty. However, that only applies where the offence, admission or agreement occurs after 2 October 2000: see para (7). An admission under caution must comply with Code C issued under the Police and Criminal Evidence Act 1984 in England and Wales. Some guidance is given on this in para 19 of Circular HB/CTB A42/2000, but careful reference should be made to the Code.

In either case, where the claimant has earnings which are being partially disregarded, a further amount of half of the disregard may be added to the amount being recovered.

It is to be noted, however, that these amounts remain the maxima and so authorities should give careful consideration to any hardship that may result in deciding whether to deduct the full amount: see para 20 of the Circular.

Recovery from HB payable to D's partner

Recovery from D's partner (S) is authorised by reg 101(2), provided the following conditions are met:

(1)   D is the claimant. The power cannot be used to recover, for example, from the partner of D who is an executor of the claimant's will and who has received benefit after the claimant's death.

(2)   D was receiving the HB. It does not apply where payment was made to the landlord under regs 93 or 94 or to any other payee.

(3)   D and S were living in the same household *both* at the time of the overpayment *and* at the time the deduction is made. It is suggested that the authority cannot make recovery of a proportion of the overpayment where S was only in the same household for some of the weeks of the period of the overpayment. The "overpayment" is the full amount found to be recoverable. S must have been living in the same household for the full period before the provision can be used.

Recovery from D's partner

There is some uncertainty as to whether, and if so in what circumstances, there may be recovery from D's partner other than by deduction from her/his HB entitlement. It is suggested that it is tolerably clear that there may be such recovery. Reg 101(4) is clearly only designed to make it clear that there may be deduction from benefit rather than prescribing this as the only method of recovery. The general rule is that specifically stated methods are without prejudice to other methods of recovery: reg 102(1).

On the other hand, it is suggested that reg 101(2)(b) restricts recovery to cases where the partner was the claimant's partner during the period of the overpayment. This appears to be clear from the present tense of the words "is" and "has" in the sub-paragraph. A counter-argument might be that reg 101(4) would then be superfluous, but it is suggested that it is the concomitant of reg 102(1) and merely makes it clear beyond doubt that there may be recovery by withholding HB due to a claimant. The restrictions on the amount so withheld under reg 102(2) will apply to a claimant's partner as well as a claimant.

Recovery from other benefits

The procedure for recovery from other benefits is specified by reg 105. It applies to benefits payable by the DWP and recovery is carried out by the Secretary of State on the authority's behalf.

There can be no recovery of overpaid HB from CTB or vice versa: 1997 GM A7.38. Neither can recovery be made of benefits payable to D's partner: 1997 GM A7.37iv.

Conditions for recovery from other benefits. The authority may only make a request to the Secretary of State to recover from other benefits payable to D when it is "unable" to recover by deduction from D's HB. It is suggested that this requires that there is no HB in payment which the authority can withhold, not merely that the authority consider that the amount is insufficient.

The Secretary of State may not recover the overpayment unless requested to by the authority, and must be satisfied of three conditions before making recovery. However, once the three conditions are present, the minister has no discretion to decline to recover.

(1)   That there is a recoverable overpayment of HB. The Secretary of State will invariably follow the authority's final determination, but ought to refuse recovery where D is still exercising statutory rights of review or is seeking judicial review. Where an application is made by the authority under reg 102 in this situation, D is well advised to inform the local office in writing of the fact that recoverability is in dispute.

(2)   The overpayment is due to the misleading of the authority. For the meaning of the wording in the phrase in para (3)(a), see the Analysis of reg 101. It appears that it is for the Secretary of State to decide whether this condition is met, even if the authority has already concluded that it has been misled.

(3)   D is receiving a "sufficient" amount of a relevant benefit to enable recovery. What is a "sufficient" amount depends on the facts of individual cases.

The relevant benefits. The following categories of benefit are prescribed by reg 105 as being candidates for recovery.

(1)   Any benefit except guardian's allowance: para (a). These are maternity allowance, widow's benefits, retirement pension, child's special allowance, carer's allowance, severe disablement allowance, industrial injuries benefits, disability living allowance and attendance allowance. It would also include arrears of defunct benefits such as mobility allowance and sickness, invalidity or unemployment benefit.

(2)   Income support: para (b).

(3)   Benefits payable to D from other EU member states under Regulation (EEC) No.1408/71, which provides for certain categories of benefit to be payable in other Member States when a claimant moves abroad. Benefits payable from overseas are administered by the DWP Overseas Benefit Directorate at Fylde: para (c).

(4)   JSA, whether income-based or contribution-based: para (d).

(5)   State pension credit: para (e)

Debit from D's rent account

Where D is in receipt of rent rebate, the authority may add the overpayment as a debit to the rent account. Caution is required, however. The debit must be carefully distinguished from any rent arrears that exist at the point of the debit and any that subsequently arise: 1997 GM A7.37.

The reason for this is that recovery of an overpayment of benefit from a landlord did not allow the landlord to recover the overpayment from the tenant as rent arrears. Once HB was paid to the landlord, the claimant's liability for rent is discharged to the extent of that HB payment: see the quotation from *Ayub* above. At most, the claimant owes the landlord a debt once there is recovery from the latter. But the debt is not rent arrears and the landlord cannot use the debt as the basis of a claim for possession for non-payment of rent.

This rule *may* have been abrogated in relation to rent allowance from April 1997 (see the Analysis to reg 95(2)), but the same principle applies to debits from the claimant's rent account. SSAA s134(2)(b) makes it clear that the effect of rent rebate is to reduce the claimant's liability to pay rent by the amount of the rebate. If the claimant fails to pay any balance, that will create rent arrears. However, once the rebate is credited to the rent account, the claimant's liability to pay the amount of the rebate is discharged, and it is not resurrected by a decision that the rebate should not have been paid. If an authority fails to distinguish between the overpayment and the rent arrears, it will be difficult to tell whether there is a valid claim for possession.

A further complication is the treatment of payments by the claimant after the overpayment is debited from the rent account. The general rule is that a debtor owing more than one debt to a creditor may elect to attribute a payment to any of the debts and in such proportions as s/he chooses. If, as will usually be the case, D does not indicate whether s/he is seeking to pay off the rent arrears or the overpayment, and the authority does not indicate to which debt it wishes to apply the payment, the debt is applied to the debt that first arose in time: *Clayton's case* [1861] 1 Mer 572. Two examples help clarify how this rule works.

(1)   In week 1, D is in rent arrears of £100. In week 2, a £500 overpayment is debited from the rent account, putting D £600 in the red. In week 3, D pays £200 into the rent account. Even though the account is in arrears to the sum of £400, the authority cannot seek possession on the basis of non-payment of rent, since the whole of that sum is attributable to the debited overpayment.

(2)   D's rent is £100 a week. In week 1, D's account is £200 in credit. In week 2, the day before the rent becomes due, a £500 overpayment is debited, making arrears of £300. D does not pay rent in either week 2 or week 3, but then pays £200 into the account in week 4. The account is £300 in the red. If D specifically states that s/he is paying off the rent arrears, then the £300 would represent part of the overpayment. If s/he does not, then the £200 s/he paid is treated as paying off the overpayment, since that preceded the rent arrears in time. Claimants in such situations are therefore advised to specifically state that they are paying off their rent arrears rather than the overpayment.

Court proceedings

Once a determination has been made that an overpayment is recoverable, a debt is created between the authority and D for which the authority may sue in the County Court. The claim must be brought within the relevant time limit, which is six years in England and Wales: s2 Limitation Act 1980. In Scotland, it is five years: s6, Sch 1 para 1 Prescription and Limitation (Scotland) Act 1973.

A number of recent cases have considered the extent to which D can raise a defence or counterclaim to such proceedings.

Defence alleging invalid determination. It is an essential pre-condition of recovery that a valid determination be issued by the authority complying with the requirements of Sch 9 para 15. If no such determination is issued, no debt is created and the authority may not sue for the amount: *Warwick DC v Freeman* [1994] 27 HLR 616, CA. In *Plymouth CC v Gigg* [1997] 30 HLR 284, CA, *Freeman* was distinguished and it is submitted that it remains good law on this point. The Court of Appeal so confirmed in *Haringey LBC v Awaritefe* [1999] 32 HLR 517.

Registration as a recoverable debt at court

SSAA s75(7) will permit the authority to avoid the need to bring proceedings by registering the overpayment at the relevant local court. Once registration is carried out, the authority may utilise the court's powers of enforcement such as the use of bailiffs and attachment of earnings orders.

In England and Wales, the relevant procedure is prescribed by Order 25 rule 12 of the County Court Rules 1981, now found in Sch 2 of the Civil Procedure Rules 1998. The authority must complete Form N322 certifying the amount due and attach a "copy of the award" which presumably means a copy of the final determination that the overpayment is recoverable and is to be recovered. This must be done within six years of the final determination: s7 Limitation Act 1980. The court order will be made by a court officer. If D wishes to challenge the validity of the determination, an application should be made to the District Judge to set aside the officer's order as one given in the absence of D.

There are equivalent procedures available in relation to the "extract registered decree arbitral" in the Sheriff Court in Scotland.

Compensation order

Where D is convicted of an offence in relation to the overpayment, the authority can ask the court to make a compensation order under s35 Powers of Criminal Courts Act 1973. This option is rarely used. Any authority with a compensation order in its favour must deduct the amount of the order from the amount it seeks to recover, otherwise there will be double recovery: *CIS 683/1994* para 5.

Diminution of capital

103.–(1)   Where in the case of a recoverable overpayment, in consequence of a misrepresentation or failure to disclose a material fact (in either case whether fraudulent or otherwise) as to a person's capital, or an error, other than one to which regulation 100(2) (effect of official error) refers, as to the amount of a person's capital, the overpayment was in respect of a period (''the overpayment period'') of more than 13 benefit weeks, the relevant authority shall, for the purpose only of calculating the amount of that overpayment–

(a)   at the end of the first 13 benefit weeks of the overpayment period, treat the amount of that capital as having been reduced by the amount of housing benefit overpaid during those 13 weeks;

(b)   at the end of each subsequent period of 13 benefit weeks, if any, of the overpayment period, treat the amount of that capital as having been further reduced by the amount of housing benefit overpaid during the immediately preceding 13 benefit weeks.

(2)   Capital shall not be treated as reduced over any period other than 13 benefit weeks or in any circumstances other than those for which paragraph (1) provides.

Definitions

"capital" – see Part 6, Section 6.
"overpayment" – see reg 99.

General Note

Regs 103 and 104 deal with three categories of deduction that may be made in calculating the amount of the recoverable overpayment. Calculation of amounts can be a complex process and a systematic approach is required. The following method should ensure that mistakes are minimised.

(1)   Determine the dates between which the claimant has been paid too much benefit.

(2)   Check that the criteria for recovery are met for the whole of that period. This will often not be the case. For example, A is overpaid for 10 weeks due to the authority failing to adjust her/his benefit after s/he told them about an award of incapacity benefit. On the facts of the case, it was not reasonable for A to realise that s/he was being overpaid until the fourth week. The first three weeks of benefit will not be recoverable and should be disregarded for the purposes of calculating the amount. The period that is left is the relevant period.

(3)   Calculate the full amount of benefit paid during the relevant period.

(4)   Determine whether the claimant should have been receiving any lesser amount during the relevant period. If so, this should be deducted from the amount of benefit obtained under step (3): reg 104(1).

(5)   In a rent rebate case, determine whether the claimant has paid too much rent for the period. If so, deduct the excess: reg 104(3).

(6)   Where the claimant has had too much capital, consider the application of the diminishing capital rule under reg 103.

The claimant is not entitled to have other amounts deducted, such as housing costs which ought to have been met under IS or income-based JSA where the claimant mistakenly claimed HB instead. However, the authority can be asked to consider exercising its discretion not to recover an appropriate portion of the overpayment in such circumstances.

Analysis

The injustice that reg 103 seeks to address concerns cases where overpayments arise through excess capital. Had HB been refused or reduced because of excess capital, the claimant would presumably have spent part of the capital on rent and eventually the level of capital would have reduced below the statutory limits. Without this provision, a claimant who would have fallen below one of the limits through such expenditure had the capital been properly taken into account would never qualify for the correct level of HB, since s/he did not in fact spend any of the capital.

Paragraph (1)

When the regulation applies. The rule comes into operation only where the relevant period is at least 13 weeks and then only in the following two cases.

(1)   Where the authority is misled as to an amount of the capital. For the meaning of "misrepresentation" and the other words and phrases in the first part of reg 103(1), see the Analysis to reg 101. It does not have to be the claimant who misled the authority about the amount of capital. Moreover, it does not have to be the claimant's capital.

(2)   Where there is an error as to the amount of the claimant's capital. It does not matter who makes the error. The reference to reg 100(2) means that if the error is an official error and the overpayment is irrecoverable because the other two criteria are met (see the Analysis to reg 100), the regulation has no application. If, however, there is more than one official error and the three criteria are met in relation to only one of them, then reg 103 will apply to such overpayment as has been made in consequence of the other error.

"... for the purpose only of calculating the amount of that overpayment ...". This makes it clear that reg 100 has no application in other cases. It cannot, for example, assist a claimant seeking to backdate a claim who had capital of just over one of the relevant limits. More importantly, it does not apply in respect of the claimant's future

entitlement to HB after the end of the overpayment period. Until the actual capital goes below the relevant limit, the claimant's actual capital will affect her/his entitlement.

The operation of the rule. At the end of each successive period of 13 weeks, the claimant's capital is treated as if reduced by the amount of the overpayment during that 13 weeks. However, in calculating the correct amount of HB which should have been payable (so as to calculate the amount actually overpaid), note the possible effect of the 65 per cent taper under s130(3)(b) SSCBA 1992 and reg 71 of these regulations if the tariff income from the capital gave the claimant an income figure in excess of her/his applicable amount.

It is not clear whether expenditure by the claimant during the same period should be taken into account, assuming that such expenditure is not caught by the diminishing capital rule. Para (2) probably does not mean that such expenditure should be ignored. It is suggested that it should be taken into account, since the regulation refers to "that capital" which is the capital that was not disclosed. As the claimant's capital, which was not disclosed, varied from time to time, logic would suggest that the reference to "that capital" must be read as being the capital (notional and actual) which the claimant actually had at the beginning of each 13-week period. If that is right, at the beginning of each 13-week period, any capital spent should be deducted and any capital acquired should be added. If this is not done, the diminishing capital rule would not work in such cases, because a claimant who reasonably purchased a car and reduced her/his capital from £7,000 to £3,500 would not get the benefit of the rule, whereas a claimant who received a legacy of £10,000 during the overpayment period could effectively insist that it was ignored. This interpretation is in accordance with the decision of the commissioner in *CIS 5825/ 1999* para 15.

Paragraph (2)

This makes it clear that no reduction can be applied where the overpayment period is less than 13 weeks or for any residue of less than that length of time. There is therefore no room to argue that the principle should be applied weekly.

Sums to be deducted in calculating recoverable overpayments

104.–(1) Subject to paragraph (2), in calculating the amount of a recoverable overpayment, the relevant authority shall deduct any amount of housing benefit which should have been determined to be payable in respect of the whole or part of the overpayment period–

(a) on the basis of the claim as presented to the authority;

(b) on the basis of the claim as it would have appeared had any misrepresentation or non-disclosure been remedied before the decision; or

(c) on the basis of the claim as it would have appeared if any change of circumstances [¹ , except a change of the dwelling which the claimant occupies as his home,] had been notified at the time that change occurred.

(2) In the case of rent rebate only, in calculating the amount of a recoverable overpayment the relevant authority may deduct so much of any payment by way of rent in respect of the overpayment period which exceeds the amount, if any, which the claimant was liable to pay for that period under the original erroneous decision.

Amendment

1.   Amended by reg 8 of SI 2005 No 2904 as amended by Sch 2 para 29 of SI 2006 No 217 as from 10.4.06.

Definitions

"payment" – see reg 2(1).
"rent" – see Part 3.
"rent rebate" – see ss134(1) and (2) and 191 SSAA.

General Note

This deals with two other deductions from the amount of an overpayment. See the General Note to reg 103. The rule was amended from 2 October 2000 to reverse the effect of the decision in *R v Wyre BC ex p Lord* [1997] unreported, 24 October, QBD (which itself was later overruled by the Court of Appeal in *R(H) 5/05*). The broad purpose of the new provisions is to ensure that an overpayment is "calculated with regard to the claimant's correct circumstances and any underlying entitlement deducted" (Circular HB/CTB A42/2000). In any case of doubt, regard should be had to that policy intent. However, *R(H) 1/05* holds (para 16) that it is for the claimant to prove the correct amount that s/he is entitled to for the overpayment period.

EW v Neath Port Talbot County Borough Council [2009] UKUT 14 (AAC) pointed out that although the First-tier Tribunal need not consider any issue not raised by an appeal, in a challenge to recoverability of an overpayment, it is always wise for the tribunal to satisfy itself as to the calculation of that overpayment, and in particular, that the local authority has taken steps to calculate any amounts which it might be appropriate to offset. However, claimants should beware: where the local authority seeks further information from the claimant to enable it to make an appropriate offset, and the information is not provided, the local authority and the tribunal are unable to apply the relevant offsetting provisions and it will be difficult for the claimant to argue that they have not complied with reg 104.

Analysis

Para (1) deals with the basic entitlement to an offset. The wording "which should have been determined to be payable" emphasises that the exercise is looking into the past with the benefit of hindsight to see what the true circumstances are and to award benefit on that basis. Para (1) bears some resemblance to reg 13(b) Social Security (Payments on Account, Overpayments and Recovery) Regulations 1988 and so the commissioners' decisions on that provision may provide some assistance. There are important differences, however. There is no equivalent of sub-para (c) in reg 13(b) of the 1988 Regulations. Moreover, an amount may only be deducted if it was payable "in respect of the whole or any part of the overpayment period", which words do not appear in reg 13(b). The ruling in *R(IS) 5/92* (para 6), that it was permissible to offset an amount which should have been payable in a period before the overpayment period, cannot therefore be applied here.

Bearing in mind those differences in the provisions and having regard to the policy intention, the three considerations set out in sub-paras (a) to (c) need to be examined as follows:

(1)   Any additional amount that should have been awarded "on the basis of the claim as presented to the authority" must be deducted. This may include additional amounts that have nothing to do with the overpayment. If, for example, a claimant can show that an additional premium should have been awarded on the basis of assertions in the initial claim, it is open to her/him to present further evidence to support those assertions: *CIS 522/1992* para 10. Furthermore, "the claim as presented" includes any information that would have been elicited on a reasonable enquiry by the local authority: *R(IS) 5/92* para 8. However, since there is no appeal against the Secretary of State's decision as to whether to issue a certificate under Sch 7 para 1, it will not be possible to offset an alleged entitlement to extended payments against an overpayment: *CH 5553/2002* paras 15-18.

(2)   Any additional amount that should have been awarded if any misrepresentation or non-disclosure had been remedied before determination. This obviously means, for example, that if a claimant has been claiming as a single person while living together as husband and wife with a partner, any entitlement on the basis of a claim as a couple should be awarded: *CSIS 62/1991* para 10. However, sub-para (b) potentially has a wider application. The word "any" is of importance. If there are other erroneous statements or omissions on the form besides the statement or statements that led to the overpayment, they can also be corrected. It might be arguable that if a claimant failed to state matters that might have led to a higher award of benefit, that could be said to be a non-disclosure which should allow the true facts to be brought into account.

(3)   Sub-para (c), as already noted, is not to be found in reg 13 of the 1988 Regulations and is at first sight worded a little strangely. When "change of circumstances" is being talked about, it is usually in the context of a change that occurs in the benefit period after the claim is made and so it seems odd to talk of how a claim would have appeared had a change been notified. The point, however, is that sub-para (c) applies both to the claim that was extant at the beginning of the overpayment period and to any renewal claims within the overpayment period.

The local authority is not entitled to absolve itself from applying reg 104 by the non-return of a fresh claim form sent to the claimant after HB had ceased. It was entitled to demand information under reg 86(1) notwithstanding the fact that the claim had ceased: *CH 4943/2001* paras 65-70. It is suggested that there is nothing in the Court of Appeal's reasoning in *SSWP v Chiltern DC* [2003] HLR 1019, CA (reported as *R(H) 2/03*) which allowed an appeal from some aspects of the commissioner's decision, which detracts from his reasoning on this point. See further the commentary to reg 87 on p456.

It appears from *CH 2349/2002* (para 11) that in considering non-disclosed income and the effect of it on the claimant's notional IID entitlement under reg 104, the claimant's income may be assessed on a week-by-week basis and need not be averaged out under reg 27(1)(a) HB Regs.

Para (2) will principally deal with errors in handling local authority rent accounts. If the overpayment has been wholly or partly caused by the claimant being asked to pay too much rent, as a result of which too much HB is credited to the rent account, then the extra rent is deductible from the amount. The authority will already have received the excess rent.

---

[1]Sums to be deducted in calculating recoverable overpayments where the claimant has changed dwelling

104A.–(1)   This regulation applies where an overpayment has occurred in the following circumstances–

(a)   a claimant has moved from the dwelling previously occupied as his home ("dwelling A") to another dwelling which he occupies as his home ("dwelling B");

(b)   the claimant has been awarded housing benefit in the form of a rent allowance in respect of dwelling A to which he is not entitled because he is no longer occupying or treated as occupying dwelling A as his home;

(c)   housing benefit is paid to the same person in respect of the claimant's occupation of dwelling B as it was paid to in respect of dwelling A; and

(d)   the same relevant authority is responsible for paying the housing benefit in respect of dwelling A and dwelling B.

(2)   Where this regulation applies, in calculating the amount of the overpayment which is recoverable the relevant authority may at its discretion deduct an amount equal to the claimant's weekly entitlement to housing benefit in respect of dwelling B for the number of benefit weeks equal to the number of weeks during which the claimant was overpaid housing benefit in respect of dwelling A.

(3)   Where a sum has been deducted under paragraph (2), an equivalent sum shall be treated as having been paid in respect of the claimant's entitlement to housing benefit in respect of dwelling B for the number of benefit weeks equal to the number of weeks during which the claimant was overpaid housing benefit in respect of dwelling A.]

Amendment

1.   Inserted by reg 2(3) of SI 2009 No 2608 as from 1.4.10 (5.4.10 where rent payable weekly or in multiples of a week).

Recovery of overpayments from prescribed benefits

105.–(1)   [³ Subject to paragraph (1B),] For the purposes of section 75(4) of the Administration Act (recovery of overpaid housing benefit by deduction from other benefits), the benefits prescribed by this regulation are–

(a)   any benefit except guardian's allowance;

(b)   income support under Part 7 of the Act;

(c)   any benefit payable under the legislation of any member State other than the United Kingdom concerning the branches of social security mentioned in Article 4(1) of Regulation (EEC) No 1408/71 on the application of social security schemes to employed persons, to self-employed persons and to members of their families moving within the Community, whether or not the benefit has been acquired by virtue of the provisions of that Regulation;

(d)   a jobseeker's allowance;

(e)   state pension credit.

[² (f)   an employment and support allowance.]

[¹ (1A)   For the purposes of paragraph (1)(c) the term "member State" shall be understood to include Switzerland in accordance with and subject to the provisions of Annex II of the Agreement between the European Community and its Member States and the Swiss Confederation on the free movement of persons, signed at Brussels on 21st June 1999.]

[³ (1B)   For the purposes of section 75(4) of the Administration Act, where recovery is sought from the claimant's partner under regulation 102(1ZA), the benefits prescribed by this regulation are–

(a)   income support under Part 7 of the Act;

(b)   income-based jobseeker's allowance;

(c)   state pension credit; and

(d)   income-related employment and support allowance.]

[³ (2)   The Secretary of State shall, if requested to do so by an authority under regulation 102 (method of recovery), recover a recoverable overpayment by deduction from any of the benefits prescribed in paragraph (1) or (in the case of the claimant's partner) any of the benefits prescribed in paragraph (1B) provided that the Secretary of State is satisfied that–

(a)   a recoverable overpayment has been made in consequence of a misrepresentation of or a failure to disclose a material fact (in either case whether fraudulently or otherwise), by a claimant or any other person to whom a payment of housing benefit has been made; and

(b)   the person from whom it is sought to recover the overpayment is receiving sufficient amounts of any of the benefits prescribed in paragraph (1) or (1B) (as the case may be) to enable deductions to be made for the recovery of the overpayment.]

(3)   In paragraph (1)(a), "benefit" has the meaning it has in section 122(1) of the Act.

Amendments

1.   Inserted by reg 9 of SI 2005 No 2904 as amended by Sch 2 para 29 of SI 2006 No 217 as from 10.4.06.

2.   Amended by reg 22 of SI 2008 No 1082 as from 27.10.08.

3.   Amended by reg 4(4) of SI 2008 No 2824 as from 6.4.09.

Definitions

"claimant" – see reg 2(1).

"member State" of the EEC – see para (1)(c) and (1A).

"recoverable overpayment" – see reg 100.

General Note

This specifies the categories of benefit from which the Secretary of State may make reductions to recover an overpayment of HB. See the Analysis to reg 102 for full details. See also reg 106.

Prescribed benefits

106.–(1)   The benefits prescribed for the purposes of section 75(5) and (7) of the Administration Act (recovery of overpayments) are those set out in the following paragraphs.

(2)   Prescribed benefits within section 75(5) of the Administration Act (benefits to which a landlord or agent is entitled) are–

(a)   housing benefit; and

(b)   those benefits prescribed from time to time in regulation 105(1) (recovery of overpayments from prescribed benefits), but only in cases where–

    (i)   an authority has, pursuant to regulation 102 (method of recovery), requested the Secretary of State to recover an overpayment of housing benefit from such benefits; and

    (ii)   the Secretary of State is satisfied as to the matters prescribed in paragraph (3)(a) and (b) of regulation 105.

(3)   Housing benefit is prescribed for the purposes of section 75(5)(b) or (c) of the Administration Act (benefits paid to a landlord or agent to discharge an obligation owed by another person).

(4)   Prescribed benefits within section 75(7) of the Administration Act (benefits recoverable from the county court or the sheriff court) are housing benefit and those benefits prescribed from time to time in regulation 105(1).

General Note

This specifies the benefits from which recovery may be made under SSAA s75(5). There is a certain amount of duplication of the powers which already exist under other regs in Part 13.

Analysis

Para (2). SSAA s75(5)(a) authorises recovery from benefits to which the landlord or agent is entitled personally. HB is prescribed, along with benefits falling within reg 105(1), provided the normal procedure prescribed by regs 102 and 105 is followed. This provision does not appear to add to the powers that authorities already had.

Para (3). SSAA s75(5)(b) authorises recovery from benefits which the landlord or agent is paid on behalf of claimant A, when claimant A was overpaid. SSAA s75(5)(c) authorises recovery from benefits paid on behalf of claimant A, when claimant B was overpaid. For the effect on rent obligations in the former case, see reg 107, and in the latter case see s75(6) whlch provldes that B's obligation is discharged. Note also Sch 9 para 15(2) that requires both landlord and claimant B to be informed of this fact.

Para (4). SSAA s75(7) provides that prescribed benefits may be recovered simply by registering the debt as recoverable under the respective procedures in the County Court and Sheriff Court. Para (4) provides that these powers apply to recovery of HB.

Restrictions on recovery of rent and consequent notifications

107.–(1)   Where, pursuant to section 75(5)(b) of the Administration Act, an amount has been recovered by deduction from housing benefit paid to a person (referred to as "the landlord" in this regulation) to discharge (in whole or in part) an obligation owed to him by the person on whose behalf the recoverable amount was paid (referred to as "the tenant" in this regulation) that obligation shall, in a case to which paragraph (2) applies, be taken to be discharged by the amount of the deduction.

(2)   This paragraph applies in a case where the amount recoverable from the landlord relates to an overpayment of housing benefit in relation to which the landlord has–

   (a)   agreed to pay a penalty pursuant to section 115A of the Administration Act (penalty as an alternative to prosecution); or

   (b)   been convicted of an offence arising under the Act or any other enactment.

(3)   In any case to which paragraph (2) applies or will apply when recovery is made the authority that has determined that there is an overpayment and that it is recoverable from the landlord shall notify both the landlord and the tenant that–

   (a)   the overpayment that it has recovered or that it has determined to recover ("that sum") is or will be one to which paragraph (2) applies; and

   (b)   the landlord has no right in relation to that sum against the tenant, and that his obligation to the landlord shall be taken to be discharged by the amount so recovered.

General Note

This provides for the effects of recovery from a landlord by deductions from future payments of HB in respect of a claimant, where the same claimant was the one overpaid. By s75(6), where recovery is made from a different claimant's HB, her/his obligation to pay rent is always discharged.

Analysis

The effect of recovery of an overpayment from a landlord on the extent of the overpaid tenant's rent arrears has always been a cause of controversy. See the Analysis to regs 95(2) and 105. Reg 95(2) is in conflict with the provisions in reg 107. Even if reg 95(2) is validly made (as to which see p471) it is suggested that reg 107, made as it is under a specific rather than a general enabling power, must take precedence in relation to overpayments made after 3 November 1997.

Para (1) confirms the effect of the regulation. If the case falls within para (2), then the tenant's obligation is to be treated as discharged by the amount of the deduction. Presumably, the time of deemed payment of rent is the time when the deduction is made. This may be significant in possession proceedings – eg, where the landlord is seeking a compulsory order under Ground 2 in Sch 2 Housing Act 1988.

Curiously, the regulation does not state what happens in cases that do not fall within para (2). If reg 95(2) is valid, then the tenant is in rent arrears. If it is not, then the analysis in *R v Haringey LBC ex p Ayub* [1992] 25 HLR 566, QBD suggests that the tenant's obligation will be discharged. If reg 95(2) is invalid, the question is whether s75(6) and reg 107 change the position by implication. Certainly it can be argued that by saying that the obligation is discharged in prescribed cases, s75(6) is saying that it is not discharged in other cases. However, s75(6) does not say that the obligation is discharged *only* in prescribed cases and so there would be a powerful contrary argument that Parliament cannot be deemed to have changed the existing law as between landlord and tenant without explicitly saying so.

Para (2). The requirement is that the landlord has been required to pay a penalty under SSAA s115A or convicted of an offence "in relation to" that overpayment. It is suggested that this would cover, for example, a conviction under SSAA s113 for failing to supply information under the Housing Benefit (Information from Landlords and Agents) Regulations 1997 that is connected with the making of the overpayment. It would appear that the landlord itself must be convicted of the offence. So if a company officer is convicted of an offence, that is insufficient to bring para (2) into effect because the company has a separate legal existence. On the other hand, as the singular must include the plural, conviction of one of joint landlords will bring para (2) into force, as will conviction of one of the partners in a partnership that holds property.

Para (3) provides that both landlord and tenant must be informed of the applicability of para (2) and that the landlord has no right to recover it from the tenant. It should logically have been an amendment to Sch 9.

PART 14
Information
SECTION 1
Claims and information

General Note on Section 1

The regulations in this Section, made principally under s7A SSAA, confirm the powers of local authorities in relation to the obtaining, retention and transmission of information in relation to claims for HB and CTB. This will prevent any allegation of a breach of the Data Protection Act 1998 where any dealing with information in the ways specified below takes place.

For powers to compel the provision of information, see Part 7 of the SSAA as amended by the SSFA (see p71). Reg 112 enables the Secretary of State or parties acting under her/his direction to demand information from a local authority.

Interpretation
108. In this Section–

[¹ "county council" means a county council in England, but only if the council has made an arrangement in accordance with regulation 83(4)(g) or 109(3);]

"local authority" means an authority administering housing benefit;

"relevant authority" means–

(a) the Secretary of State; or

(b) a person providing services to the Secretary of State; [¹ or

(c) a county council;]

"relevant information" means information or evidence relating to the administration of claims to or awards of housing benefit.

Amendment

1. Amended by reg 7(3) of SI 2007 No 2911 as from 31.10.07.

[¹Collection of information
109.–(1) The Secretary of State, or a person providing services to him, may receive or obtain relevant information from–

(a) persons making, or who have made, claims for housing benefit; or

(b) other persons in connection with such claims.

(2) In paragraph (1) references to persons who have made claims for housing benefit include persons to whom awards of benefit have been made on those claims.

(3) Where a county council has made an arrangement with a local authority, or a person authorised to exercise any function of a local authority relating to housing benefit or council tax benefit, to receive and obtain information or evidence relating to claims for housing benefit, the council may receive or obtain the information or evidence from–

(a) persons making claims for housing benefit; or

(b) other persons in connection with such claims.

(4) A county council may receive information or evidence relating to an award of housing benefit which is supplied by–

(a) the person to whom the award has been made; or

(b) other persons in connection with the award.]

Amendment

1. Substituted by reg 7(4) of SI 2007 No 2911 as from 31.10.07.

[¹Verifying information
109A. A relevant authority may verify relevant information supplied to, or obtained by, the authority in accordance with regulation 109.]

Amendment

1. Inserted by reg 7(5) of SI 2007 No 2911 as from 31.10.07.

[¹Recording and holding information

110. A relevant authority which obtains relevant information or to whom such information is supplied–

(a)   shall make a record of such information; and

(b)   may hold that information, whether as supplied or obtained or recorded, for the purpose of forwarding it to the person or authority for the time being administering housing benefit.]

Amendment

1.   Substituted by reg 7(6) of SI 2007 No 2911 as from 31.10.07.

Forwarding of information

111. A relevant authority which holds relevant information–

(a)   shall forward it to the person or authority for the time being administering claims to or awards of housing benefit to which the relevant information relates, being–

    (i)   a local authority;

    (ii)   a person providing services to a local authority; or

    (iii)   a person authorised to exercise any function of a local authority relating to housing benefit; and

[¹ (b)   may, if the relevant authority is the Secretary of State or a person providing services to the Secretary of State, continue to hold a record of such information, whether as supplied or obtained or recorded, for such period as he considers appropriate.]

Amendment

1.   Substituted by reg 7(7) of SI 2007 No 2911 as from 31.10.07.

Request for information

112. A relevant authority which holds information or evidence relating to social security matters shall forward such information or evidence as may be requested to the person or authority making that request, provided that–

(a)   the request is made by–

    (i)   a local authority;

    (ii)   a person providing services to a local authority; or

    (iii)   a person authorised to exercise any function of a local authority relating to housing benefit; and

(b)   the information or evidence requested includes relevant information;

(c)   the relevant authority is able to provide the information or evidence requested in the form in which it was originally supplied or obtained; and

(d)   provision of the information or evidence requested is considered necessary by the relevant authority to the proper performance by a local authority of its functions relating to housing benefit.

SECTION 2
Information from landlords and agents and between authorities etc.

General Note on Section 2

The Housing Benefit (Information from Landlords and Agents) Regulations 1997 SI No.2436 implemented s126A SSAA. These provisions are now in reg 113 (in part) and regs 117 to 121 HB Regs and reg 94 (in part) and regs 98 to 102 HB(SPC) Regs. These set out the circumstances in which local authorities may require information from landlords and agents, the information which must be supplied, the time limit for supplying it and the manner in which the information must be provided. Failure to comply with a notice requiring information under s126A is a criminal offence and would be a factor which a local authority could take into account when considering whether a landlord is a "fit and proper person" to receive payments of HB under regs 95 and 96 HB Regs (or regs 76 and 77 HB(SPC) Regs).

Interpretation
113. In this Section–
"the notice" means the notice prescribed in regulation 118(1)(b) (circumstances for requiring information);
"relevant information" means such information as is prescribed in regulation 119 (relevant information);
"the requirer" means a person within regulation 117 (requiring information from landlords and agents), who requires information pursuant to that regulation;
"the supplier" means an appropriate person who is required, pursuant to regulations 117 and 118, to supply relevant information and any person who is not so required is not, for the purpose of supplying information pursuant to section 126A of the Administration Act and these Regulations, an appropriate person.

[¹ Information to be provided to rent officers
114A.–(1) This paragraph applies to every claim for or award of housing benefit in the form of a rent allowance where the eligible rent has been, or is to be determined, in accordance with–
  (a) regulation 12(3)(a) (rent) or 12C (eligible rent and maximum rent), as the case may require;
  (b) [² regulation 12D] (eligible rent and the maximum rent (LHA)) or any of regulations 12E to 12K (transitional protection for pathfinder cases), as the case may require; or
  (c) regulations 12 (rent) and 13 (maximum rent) as set out in paragraph 5 of Schedule 3 to the Consequential Provisions Regulations.
  (2) No earlier than the first, and no later than the fifth, working day of every month a relevant authority shall provide the following information to the rent officer in relation to every claim for or award of housing benefit to which paragraph (1) applied in the preceding month–
  (a) the address, including any room or unit number, house or flat number or name, and the postcode of the dwelling to which the claim or award relates;
  (b) where the claim or award relates to mooring charges for a houseboat, or payments in respect of the site on which a caravan or mobile home stands, the mooring or plot number and the address of the mooring or site, including the postcode;
  (c) the date on which the tenancy began;
  (d) the amount of rent and the rental period, whether calendar monthly, four weekly, weekly or some other period;
  (e) where the claimant has the use of two or more bedrooms, the number of bedrooms and rooms suitable for living in that there are in the dwelling, and in this sub-paragraph "bedroom" does not include a bedroom which the claimant shares with any person other than a member of his household, a non-dependant of his, or a person who pays rent to him or his partner;
  (f) whether the tenant (together with his partner where he has one) has exclusive use of only one bedroom, and if so, whether they have exclusive use of a kitchen, bathroom, toilet and a room suitable for living in;
  (g) whether the tenant has exclusive use of only one bedroom, and if so, which, if any, of the following the tenancy provides for him to share–
    (i) a kitchen;
    (ii) a bathroom;
    (iii) a toilet; or
    (iv) a room suitable for living in;
  (h) the date on which entitlement to housing benefit began; and
  (i) where applicable, the date on which entitlement to housing benefit ended.
  (3) Where the relevant authority is required to apply to the rent officer for a board and attendance determination by virtue of regulation 13D(10) (determination of a maximum rent (LHA)), it shall provide the following information in the application to the Rent Officer–

(a) the address, including any room or unit number, house or flat number or name and the postcode of the dwelling to which the claim or award relates;

(b) the date on which the tenancy began;

(c) the length of the tenancy;

(d) the total amount of those payments referred to in regulation 12(1) (rent) which the claimant is liable to make in respect of the dwelling which he occupies as his home;

(e) whether those payments include any charges for water, sewerage or allied environmental services or charges in respect of meals or fuel which are ineligible for housing benefit; and

(f) where those payments include any charges that are ineligible for housing benefit by reason of paragraph 1(a)(iv) and (c) to (f) of Schedule 1 (ineligible service charges), that such charges are included, and the value of those charges as determined by that authority pursuant to regulation 12B(2) and that Schedule.

(4) Where the relevant authority has identified charges to which paragraph (3)(f) applies, it shall–

(a) deduct those charges from the total amount of those payments which, in accordance with paragraph (3)(d), it has stated that the claimant is liable to make in respect of the dwelling which he occupies as his home; and

(b) notify that total so reduced to the rent officer in its application.

(5) Where a relevant authority has received notification from the rent officer that a substantial part of the rent is attributable to board and attendance, it shall provide the information referred to in paragraphs (7) and (8), except for such information as it has already provided in accordance with paragraphs (3) and (4).

(6) Where the relevant authority is required to apply to the rent officer for a determination by virtue of regulation 14(1) (requirement to refer to rent officers), it shall provide the information referred to in paragraphs (7) to (9) in the application to the rent officer.

(7) In relation to the dwelling to which the claim or award relates, the relevant authority shall provide the following information–

(a) the address, including any room or unit number, house or flat number or name and the postcode of the dwelling;

(b) where the claim or award relates to mooring charges for a houseboat, or payments in respect of the site on which a caravan or mobile home stands, the mooring or plot number and the address of the mooring or site, including the postcode;

(c) whether the dwelling is–

(i)   a detached house;
(ii) a semi-detached house;
(iii) a terraced house;
(iv) a maisonette;
(v)   a detached bungalow;
(vi) a semi-detached bungalow;
(vii) a flat in a house;
(viii) a flat in a block;
(ix) a flat over a shop;
(x)   a bedsit or rooms or a studio flat;
(xi) a hostel;
(xii) a caravan, mobile home or houseboat;
(xiii) board and lodgings;
(xiv) a hotel;
(xv) a care home;
(xvi) an independent hospital; or
(xvii) some other description of dwelling, and if so what;

(d) whether the dwelling has central heating, a garden, a garage or a parking space;

(e) how many rooms suitable for living in there are–

(i)   in the dwelling;

    (ii)   in the dwelling which the claimant shares with any person other than a member of his household, a non-dependant of his, or a person who pays rent to him or his partner;

(f)   how many bedsitting rooms there are in the categories (e)(i) and (ii);

(g)   how many bedrooms there are in the categories (e)(i) and (ii);

(h)   how many bathrooms or toilets there are in the categories (e)(i) and (ii); and

(i)   such other information as the rent officer may reasonably require to make a determination.

(8)   In relation to the tenancy to which the claim or award relates, the relevant authority shall provide the following information–

(a)   the information referred to in paragraphs (3)(d) to (f) and (4);

(b)   if the tenancy is furnished, and if so, to what extent;

(c)   the rental period, whether calendar monthly, four weekly, weekly or some other period;

(d)   the length of the tenancy;

(e)   when the tenancy began and, if appropriate, when it ended;

(h)   the landlord's or letting agent's name;

(i)   the landlord's or letting agent's business address;

(j)   whether the landlord is a housing association [3 , private registered provider of social housing] or registered social landlord; and

(k)   such other information as the rent officer may reasonably require to make a determination.

(9)   In relation to the claimant and the other occupiers of the dwelling to which the claim or award relates, the relevant authority shall provide the following information–

(a)   such information regarding the relationship of the claimant to the occupiers and the occupiers to each other, as is necessary for the rent officer to make the determination;

(b)   the age and sex of each occupier under 18;

(c)   whether the claimant is or may be a young individual; and

(d)   any other information that is relevant to the rent officer in making the determination, including visits to the dwelling.

(10)   Where a rent officer serves a notice under article 5 (insufficient information) of the Rent Officers Order the relevant authority shall supply the further information required under this regulation, or confirm whether information already supplied is correct and, if it is not, supply the correct information.

(11)   Where the relevant authority refers a case to the rent officer in accordance with regulation 14 as in force before the coming into force of regulation 8 of the Housing Benefit (Local Housing Allowance and Information Sharing) Amendment Regulations 2007, it shall notify the rent officer that the referral is made in accordance with regulation 14 as in force before the coming into force of regulation 8 of those Regulations.

(12)   In this regulation–

"tenancy" includes–

(a)   in Scotland, any other right of occupancy; and

(b)   in any other case, a licence to occupy premises,

and reference to a tenant, landlord or any other expression appropriate to a tenancy shall be construed accordingly;

"working day" means any day other than a Saturday, a Sunday, Christmas Day, Good Friday or a day which is a bank holiday under the Banking and Financial Dealings Act 1971 in the jurisdiction in which the area of the relevant authority is situated.]

Amendments

1.   Inserted by reg 3(2) of SI 2007 No 2868, as amended by reg 4(2)(b) of SI 2008 No 586, as from 7.4.08.

2.   Amended by reg 4(2)(b) of SI 2008 No 586 as from 7.4.08.

3.   Amended by Art 4 and Sch 1 para 53 of SI 2010 No 671 as from 1.4.10.

General Note

The information required by para (3)(e) and (f) relates to applications for board and attendance determinations and whether the rent paid includes payments in respect of certain items that are ineligible to be met by HB. The authority must state the total amounts eligible to be met by HB under reg 12(1) and then set out information about ineligible charges relating to the following.

(1)   Water, sewerage and allied environmental services: sub-para (e).

(2)   Ineligible charges for meals and fuel: sub-para (e).

(3)   The cleaning of rooms and windows except the exterior of windows which cannot be cleaned by anyone in the household or communal areas: sub-para (f).

(4)   The provision of an emergency alarm system: sub-para (f).

(5)   Medical expenses: sub-para (f).

(6)   Nursing or personal care: sub-para (f).

(7)   General counselling or support services: sub-para (f).

Paras (6) to (9) set out the information which the local authority must give to the rent officer when it applies for a determination under reg 14(1) HB Regs. Note that under para (9), if the authority believes the claimant is or may be a "young individual" (see reg 2(1) for the definition), the authority must say so.

[¹ Evidence and information required by rent officers
114.]

Amendment

1.   Omitted by reg 3(3) of SI 2007 No 2868 as from 7.4.08.

[¹Information to be supplied by an authority to another authority

115.–(1)   This regulation applies for the purposes of section 128A of the Administration Act (duty of an authority to disclose information to another authority).

(2)   Information is to be disclosed by one authority to another where–

(a)   there is a mover who is or was in receipt of housing benefit from Authority "A";

(b)   either the mover's new dwelling is within the area of another Authority "B" or the mover is liable or treated as liable to make payments in respect of the new dwelling to housing authority B; and

(c)   the mover is entitled to an extended payment in accordance with regulation 72.

(3)   Authority A shall disclose to Authority B–

(a)   the amount of the extended payment calculated in accordance with regulation 72C(2) (amount of extended payment – movers);

(b)   the date that entitlement to the extended payment will commence or has commenced;

(c)   the date that entitlement to the extended payment ceased or will cease;

(d)   the date of the move from Authority A to Authority B;

(e)   where the extended payment will be paid by Authority A to Authority B in accordance with regulation 72C(3)(a) (payment of extended payment to the second authority)–

(i)   the amount that Authority A will pay to Authority B in accordance with that paragraph; and

(ii)   any other information required by Authority B to enable Authority A to make the payment in accordance with that paragraph; and

(f)   if any deduction was being made in respect of a recoverable overpayment.

(4)   Authority B shall disclose to Authority A–

(a)   if a mover's liability to make payments for the new dwelling is to Authority B; and

(b)   where the extended payment will be paid by Authority A to Authority B in accordance with regulation 72C(3)(a)–

(i)   any information required by Authority A to enable Authority A to make the payment in accordance with that paragraph; and

(ii)   the date on which Authority B receives any such payment.]

Amendment

1.   Substituted by reg 2(3) of SI 2008 No 959 as from 6.10.08.

General Note

This facilitates the passing of information between authorities where there is entitlement to extended payments of HB under regs 72 to 72D and the claimant moves from the area of the authority where s/he had previously been in receipt of HB to another. Reg 72C deals with these so-called "movers". See also s128A SSAA on p79, which is still in force. See reg 116 where there is entitlement to an extended payment under regs 73 to 73D.

[¹Supply of information – extended payments (qualifying contributory benefits)

116.–(1)   This regulation applies for the purposes of section 122E(3) of the Administration Act (duty of an authority to supply information to another authority).

(2)   Information is to be disclosed by one authority to another where–

(a)   there is a mover who is or was in receipt of housing benefit from Authority "A";

(b)   either the mover's new dwelling is within the area of another Authority "B" or the mover is liable or treated as liable to make payments in respect of the new dwelling to housing authority B; and

(c)   the mover is entitled to an extended payment (qualifying contributory benefits) in accordance with regulation 73.

(3)   Authority A shall disclose to Authority B–

(a)   the amount of the extended payment (qualifying contributory benefits) calculated in accordance with regulation 73C(2) (amount of extended payment – movers);

(b)   the date that entitlement to the extended payment will commence or has commenced;

(c)   the date that entitlement to the extended payment ceased or will cease;

(d)   the date of the move from Authority A to Authority B;

(e)   where the extended payment will be paid by Authority A to Authority B in accordance with regulation 73C(3)(a) (payment of the extended payment to the second authority)–

   (i)   the amount that Authority A will pay to Authority B in accordance with that paragraph; and

   (ii)   any other information required by Authority B to enable Authority A to make the payment in accordance with that paragraph; and

(f)   if any deduction was being made in respect of a recoverable overpayment.

(4)   Authority B shall disclose to Authority A–

(a)   if a mover's liability to make payments for the new dwelling is to Authority B; and

(b)   where the extended payment will be paid by Authority A to Authority B in accordance with regulation 73C(3)(a)–

   (i)   any information required by Authority A to enable Authority A to make the payment in accordance with that paragraph; and

   (ii)   the date on which Authority B receives any such payment.]

Amendment

1.   Substituted by reg 3(3) of SI 2008 No 959 as from 6.10.08.

General Note

This facilitates the passing of information between authorities where there is entitlement to extended payments of HB under regs 73 to 73D and the claimant moves from the area of the authority where s/he had previously been in receipt of HB to another. See reg 115 where there is entitlement to extended payments under reg 72.

Requiring information from landlords and agents

117.   Pursuant to section 126A of the Administration Act (information from landlords and agents), where a claim is made to an authority, on which a rent allowance may be awarded, then, in the circumstances prescribed in regulation 118 (circumstances for requiring information), that authority, or any person authorised to exercise any functions of the authority relating to housing benefit, may require an appropriate person to supply to that authority or person relevant information, in the manner prescribed in regulation 120 (manner of supply of information).

General Note

This confirms that the circumstances in which information may be sought are set out in reg 118 and the manner of the supply of information is set out in reg 120. Note that information may also be demanded by any body administering HB on behalf of an authority. Note also that it is not necessary that rent allowance has been awarded before the information may be required. The authority is probably entitled to delay determination of a claim pending the supply of the information by the landlord, but the delay must be reasonable in all the circumstances.

Circumstances for requiring information

118.–(1) A person is required to supply information in the following circumstances–

(a) he is an appropriate person in relation to any dwelling in respect of which–

(i) housing benefit is being paid to an appropriate person pursuant to regulation 95 or 96 (circumstances in which payment is to be or may be made to a landlord); or

(ii) a request has been made by an appropriate person or by the claimant for housing benefit to be so paid; and

(b) the requirer serves upon that appropriate person, whether by post or otherwise, a written notice stating that the requirer–

(i) suspects that there is or may be an impropriety in relation to a claim in respect of any dwelling wherever situate in relation to which he is an appropriate person; or

(ii) is already investigating an allegation of impropriety in relation to that person.

(2) In formation required to be supplied under paragraph (1) shall be supplied to the requirer at the address specified in the notice.

General Note

This sets out the circumstances in which information must be supplied by an "appropriate person".

Analysis

Para (1). A number of conditions must be fulfilled before the "appropriate person" comes under an obligation to supply the information requested.

(1) S/he must be an "appropriate person" in relation to a relevant dwelling. "Appropriate person" is defined in SSAA s126A(2) (see p77). It includes landlords and their agents.

(2) HB is being paid direct to the "appropriate person" under reg 95 or reg 96, or a request has been made for such payment by her/him or a claimant.

(3) A written notice is served in relation to the authority's grounds for making the request. This must be either that an impropriety in relation to a claim is suspected in respect of a dwelling where the "appropriate person" is involved, or that there is an investigation of impropriety in relation to the "appropriate person": sub-para (b). Under sub-para (b)(i), the impropriety need not relate to the same property, it need not be the same claimant and s/he need not be the "appropriate person" in respect of the same capacity. The authority is not obliged to inform the person of the reasons for its suspicion, nor is it restricted in seeking information that relates only to that suspicion. However, it is clear that the authority must have formed a suspicion, which provided it is held in good faith is probably immune from challenge. The only basis for a challenge would be judicial review.

Para (2). The notice must specify an address and the information must be supplied at that address.

Relevant information

119.–(1) The information the supplier is to supply to the requirer is that prescribed in paragraphs (2) and (3) (referred to in this Part as ''the relevant information'').

(2) For a supplier who falls within paragraph (4) or section 126A(2)(b) of the Administration Act (''the landlord''), the information is–

(a) where the landlord is a natural person–

(i) his appropriate details;

(ii) the relevant particulars of any residential property in which he has an interest; and

(iii) the appropriate details of any body corporate, in which he is a major shareholder or of which he is a director and which has an interest in residential property;

(b)   where the landlord is a trustee, except a trustee of a charity, in addition to any information that he is required to supply in accordance with sub-paragraph (a) or (c), as the case may be, the relevant particulars of any residential property held by the trust of which he is a trustee and the name and address of any beneficiary under the trust or the objects of that trust, as the case may be;

(c)   where the landlord is a body corporate or otherwise not a natural person, other than a charity–
- (i)   its appropriate details;
- (ii)   the relevant particulars of any residential property in which it has an interest;
- (iii)   the names and addresses of any directors of it;
- (iv)   the appropriate details of any person–
  - (aa)   who owns 20 per cent. or more of it; or
  - (bb)   of whom it owns 20 per cent. or more; and
- (v)   the names and addresses of its major shareholders;

(d)   where the landlord is a charity or is a recognised body, the appropriate details relating to the landlord and particulars of the landlord's registration as a charity.

(3)   For a supplier who falls within section 126A(2)(c) of the Administration Act or paragraph (5)(''the agent''), the information is–

(a)   the name and address of any person (''his principal'')–
- (i)   to whom the agent has agreed to make payments in consequence of being entitled to receive relevant payments: or
- (ii)   for whom the agent is acting on behalf of or in connection with any aspect of the management of a dwelling,

as the case may be;

(b)   the relevant particulars of any residential property in respect of which the agent–
- (i)   has agreed to make payments in consequence of being entitled to receive relevant payments; or
- (ii)   is acting on behalf of his principal in connection with any aspect of its management;

(c)   where the agent is a natural person–
- (i)   the relevant particulars of any residential property in which he has an interest;
- (ii)   the appropriate details of any body corporate or any person not a natural person, in which he is a major shareholder or of which he is a director and which has any interest in residential property; or

(d)   where the agent is a body corporate or other than a natural person–
- (i)   the relevant particulars of any residential property in which it has an interest;
- (ii)   the names and addresses of any directors of or major shareholders in the agent; and
- (iii)   the appropriate details of any person–
  - (aa)   who owns 20 per cent. or more of the agent; or
  - (bb)   of whom the agent owns 20 per cent. or more.

(4)   A supplier falls within this paragraph (landlord receiving rent), if he falls within section 126A(2)(a) of the Administration Act, but does not fall within paragraph (5).

(5)   A supplier falls within this paragraph (agent receiving the rent), if he falls within subsection (2)(a) of section 126A of the Administration Act and has agreed to make payments, in consequence of being entitled to receive relevant payments, to a person falling within subsection (2)(b) of that section.

(6)   For the purposes of this regulation–

''appropriate details'' means the name of the person and (in the case of a company) its registered office and, in any case, the full postal address, including post code, of the principal place of business of that person and the telephone and facsimile number (if any) of that place;

''charity'' means a charity which is registered under section 3 of the Charities Act 1993 and is not an exempt charity within the meaning of that Act;

"major shareholder" means, where a body corporate is a company limited by shares, any person holding one tenth or more of the issued shares in that company and, in any other case, all the owners of that body;

"recognised body" has the same meaning as in section 1(7) of the Law Reform (Miscellaneous Provisions) (Scotland) Act 1990;

"relevant particulars" means the full postal address, including post code, and number of current lettings of or within that residential property and, if that property includes two or more dwellings, that address and the number of such lettings for each such dwelling;

"residential property" includes any premises, situate within the United Kingdom–

(a)   used or which has, within the last six months, been used; or

(b)   which may be used or is adapted for use,

as residential accommodation,

and other expressions used in this regulation and also in the Companies Act 1985 shall have the same meaning in this regulation as they have in that Act.

General Note

This sets out the type of information that is to be supplied. It is worthy of note that all the information is to be supplied and there is no obligation on the authority to make a specific request for any of the information. However, it could presumably request only certain categories of information and if the rest was not supplied, a criminal prosecution might be regarded as an abuse of process. It would be useful for authorities to draw up questionnaires for different categories of suppliers of information to use.

A large amount of information may be supplied under this regulation about parties who will not be mixed up in the authority's investigation. It may be arguable that the low threshold in reg 118 for the requiring of the information is insufficient justification for the invasion of privacy that the supply of the information involves. There may well be grounds for challenge under the Human Rights Act 1998.

Analysis

Paragraph (2)

This sets out the information to be supplied by landlords. That expression is defined as covering both landlords directly receiving the rent and tenants that sublet. The former are under the obligation provided that they do not fulfil para (5) as being agents: see para (4). The latter fall within SSAA s126A(2)(b).

The information to be provided depends on the status of the landlord. Four cases are dealt with.

(1)   A "natural person" must supply her/his "appropriate details". S/he must also supply the "relevant particulars" of any residential property in which s/he has an interest. Those expressions are defined in para (6). The property must be residential, but it is suggested that information in relation to properties with both business and residential elements must be supplied. The word "interest" must relate to a property interest, but could be legal or equitable (ie, as a beneficiary under a trust). The "appropriate details" of any body corporate must be supplied provided that s/he is a "major shareholder" or a director, and the body corporate holds an interest in residential property. See para (6) for the meaning of "major shareholder".

(2)   Trustees must supply further information *in addition* to any other information supplied under one of the other heads. Details of residential property held by the trust, its beneficiaries and the objects of the trust must be supplied. The latter can be satisfied by supplying the requirer with a copy of the trust deed.

(3)   Bodies corporate (which will include partnerships in Scotland but not in England and Wales) must give their appropriate details, particulars of residential property, names and addresses of directors, the details of any person (which could be a natural or legal person) that owns 20 per cent or more of the body corporate or of which the body corporate owns 20 per cent or more, and the details of its major shareholders.

(4)   Charities must give their appropriate details and matters relating to their registration.

Paragraph (3)

This deals with the agent falling within s126A(2)(c) SSAA. Under sub-para (a), details of the principal must be given (ie, the person on whose behalf the agent is acting), along with particulars of any property in respect of which the agent is receiving HB or is acting on behalf of his principal: sub-para (b). This must be the same principal as the one whose name and address is disclosed under sub-para (a).

Where the agent is a natural person, details of any residential property in which he has an interest must be given. Again, "interest" can only refer to a legal or equitable interest in land and not merely a property that the agent is dealing with in the course of her/his business. S/he must also give details of interests in body corporate or "any person otherwise not a natural person" in which a major shareholding or directorship is held and which holds an interest in residential property. The latter expression would cover a partnership.

An agent that is a body corporate must give details of all residential property in which it is interested, the names and addresses of major shareholders and directors, and details of major ownership (see the Analysis to para (2) relating to bodies corporate).

Manner of supply of information

120.–(1)   Subject to paragraph (2), the relevant information shall be supplied–
(a)   in typewritten or printed form; or
(b)   with the written agreement of the requirer, in electronic or handwritten form,
within a period of 4 weeks commencing on the date on which the notice was sent or given.
(2)   Where–
(a)   within a period of 4 weeks commencing on the date on which the notice was sent or given, the supplier requests that the time for the supply of the relevant information be extended; and
(b)   the requirer provides written agreement to that request,
the time for the supply of the relevant information shall be extended to a period of 8 weeks commencing on the date on which the notice was sent or given.

General Note
The time limit for supplying the "relevant information" (for which see reg 119) is four weeks, which may be extended to eight weeks with the written agreement of the authority. It must normally be delivered in printed form but may, with the written agreement of the authority, be delivered in handwritten or electronic form.

Criminal offence

[¹**121.**   Any supplier who fails to supply relevant information to the requirer as, when and how required under regulations 117 to 120 shall be guilty of an offence under section 113 of the Administration Act.]

Amendment
1.   Substituted by reg 2(9) of SI 2008 No 2299 as from 1.10.08.

General Note
See the commentary to s113 SSAA on p61.

[¹ Supply of benefit administration information between authorities

121A.–(1)   For the purpose of section 122E(3) of the Administration Act (supply of information between authorities administering benefit) the circumstances in which information is to be supplied and the information to be supplied are set out in paragraph (2).
(2)   Where the functions of an authority (''Authority A'') relating to housing benefit are being exercised, wholly or in part, by another authority (''Authority B'')–
(a)   Authority A must supply to Authority B any benefit administration information it holds which is relevant to, and necessary for, Authority B to exercise those functions; and
(b)   Authority B must supply to Authority A any benefit administration information it holds which is relevant to, and necessary for, Authority A to exercise those functions.
(3)   The circumstances in which paragraph (2) applies include cases where the authorities have agreed to discharge functions jointly.
(4)   In paragraph (2) ''Authority A'' and ''Authority B'' include any person authorised to exercise functions relating to housing benefit on behalf of the authority in question.
(5)   This regulation shall not apply if the person or authority to whom the information is to be supplied agrees that the information need not be supplied.]

Amendment
1.   Inserted by reg 2(10) of SI 2008 No 2299 as from 1.10.08.

[¹ PART 15
Former pathfinder authorities

Modifications in respect of former pathfinder authorities

122.–(1)   In this regulation and in Schedule 10, ''former pathfinder authority'' means a relevant authority specified in Part 1 of that Schedule.

(2)   The provisions of Part 2 of Schedule 10 apply in relation to the area of a former pathfinder authority.]

Amendment

1.   Substituted by reg 20(1) of SI 2007 No 2868 as from 7.4.08.

General Note

The "local housing allowance" scheme for rent restriction, found in regs 12D, 13C and 13D, was piloted in 18 Pathfinder areas from late 2007 until 7 April 2008. The pilot rules were more generous in a number of respects than the current "local housing allowance" rules. Sch 10 provides transitional rules for determining eligible rent for those living in former Pathfinder areas where, prior to 7 April 2008, eligible rent was determined by reference to the maximum rent (standard local rate).

Prior to 7 April 2008, the HB Regs were modified by Sch 10 for those in Pathfinder areas as follows:

(1)   Regs 11, 12, 14-17, 95 and 96 HB Regs were amended.

(2)   Regs 11A, 12A, 13A and 13B, 18A HB Regs were inserted.

See pp510-518 of the 20th edition for the full text of the provisions and a summary of the Pathfinder scheme.

[¹ SCHEDULE A1]
TREATMENT OF CLAIMS FOR HOUSING BENEFIT BY REFUGEES

Modification

Sch A1 was inserted by Sch 4 para 2(2) HB&CTB(CP) Regs in respect of claims for HB by some refugees. Sch A1 was further modifed by Sch 4 para 4(2) for some HB claimants who were refugees who claimed asylum on or before 2 April 2000.

Amendment

1.   Lapsed by s12(2)(e) of the Asylum and Immigration (Treatment of Claimants, etc.) Act 2004 (for those recorded as refugees after 14.6.07).

General Note

Reg 10A and Sch A1 as inserted by Sch 4 HB&CTB(CP) Regs dealt with a refugee's retrospective entitlement to HB.

Section 12 Asylum and Immigration (Treatment of Claimants, etc.) Act 2004 came into force on 14 June 2007 by the Asylum and Immigration (Treatment of Claimants, etc.) Act 2004 (Commencement No.7 and Transitional Provisions) Order 2007 SI No.1602. However, the commencement does not apply to those recorded as refugees on or before 14 June 2007. For these purposes, a person is "recorded as a refugee" on the day the Secretary of State notifies her/him that s/he has been recognised as a refugee and granted asylum in the UK.

See the 20th edition pp1127-1129 for the full text of Sch A1 and pp1126-1127 for commentary on it.

Note that reg 10A and paras 3 and 7 of Sch A1 of both the HB regs and the HB(SPC) Regs, as inserted by para 2, were substituted by reg 6 Housing Benefit (Local Housing Allowance, Miscellaneous and Consequential) Amendment Regulations 2007 SI No.2870 as from 7 April 2008, save that for a person to whom reg 1(3) of those regulations applied, the amendments came into force on the day on or after 7 April 2008 when the first of the events specified in reg 1(4) applied to her/him, or on 6 April 2009 if none had before that date. Sch 4 para 3(4) HB&CTB(CP) Regs was amended by reg 7(5) Social Secuity (Miscellaneous Amendments)(No.2) Regulations 2008 SI No.1042 as from 19 May 2008.

SCHEDULE 1
REGULATION 11
Ineligible service charges

General Note

The general rule in reg 12(1)(e) is that services charges are "rent" for HB purposes and hence eligible to be met by HB under reg 11(1). This Schedule lists the exceptions to that rule. If a service charge is listed in the Schedule (and hence ineligible) a deduction must be made under reg 12B(2).

The scope of the concepts in the Schedule in the past caused variance in the approach to certain charges for assistance given by bodies to vulnerable tenants. Prompt action by the government allowed an interim scheme to be brought in by the Housing Benefit (General) Amendment (No.2) Regulations 1997, which was subsequently replaced by Supporting People: see the commentary to para 1(f).

PART 1
Service charges other than for fuel

Ineligible service charges
1.   The following service charges shall not be eligible to be met by housing benefit–
(a)   charges in respect of day-to-day living expenses including, in particular, all provision of–
   (i)   subject to paragraph 2 meals (including the preparation of meals or provision of unprepared food);
   (ii)   laundry (other than the provision of premises or equipment to enable a person to do his own laundry);
   [¹ (iii)   leisure items such as either sports facilities (except a children's play area), or television rental, licence and subscription fees (except radio relay charges and charges made in respect of the conveyance and installation and maintenance of equipment for the conveyance of a television broadcasting service);]
   (iv)   cleaning of rooms and windows except cleaning of–
     (aa)   communal areas; or
     (bb)   the exterior of any windows where neither the claimant nor any member of his household is able to clean them himself,
where a payment is not made in respect of such cleaning by a local authority (including, in relation to England, a county council) or the [² Welsh Ministers] to the claimant or his partner, or to another person on their behalf; and
   (v)   transport;
(b)   charges in respect of–
   (i)   the acquisition of furniture or household equipment; and
   (ii)   the use of such furniture or equipment where that furniture or household equipment will become the property of the claimant by virtue of an agreement with the landlord;
(c)   charges in respect of the provision of an emergency alarm system;
(d)   charges in respect of medical expenses (including the cost of treatment or counselling related to mental disorder, mental handicap, physical disablement or past or present alcohol or drug dependence);
(e)   charges in respect of the provision of nursing care or personal care (including assistance at meal-times or with personal appearance or hygiene);
(f)   charges in respect of general counselling or of any other support services, whoever provides those services;
(g)   charges in respect of any services not specified in sub-paragraphs (a) to (f) which are not connected with the provision of adequate accommodation.

Amendments
1.   Substituted by reg 6(5) of SI 2007 No 719 as from 2.4.07.
2.   Amended by reg 5(5) of SI 2008 No 3157 as from 5.1.09.

Analysis
This lists the ineligible services, including a catch-all para 1(g) which refers to charges in respect of services "which are not connected with the provision of adequate accommodation". Note the definition of "communal areas" in para 8. GM A4.730 provides a non-exhaustive list of the items which are *not* covered here and are therefore still "eligible": wardens and caretakers (in so far as they provide eligible services); removal of refuse; lifts; radio and TV relay (including ordinary UK channels and those where a satellite dish feeds the system); portering; communal telephone charges; entry-phones; cleaning of common areas; gardens; children's play areas.

It is for the claimant to satisfy the authority that a service charge is not ineligible: *R v Stoke-on-Trent CC ex p Highgate Projects* [1996] 29 HLR 271 at 278, CA.

Most of the categories of ineligible charge are self-explanatory, but the scope of sub-paras (e), (f) and (g) has caused considerable difficulty.

It is suggested that a service only falls under sub-para (e) if it involves a degree of physical proximity in the assistance that is given, and consists of doing something for the claimant rather than reminding or persuading the claimant to do it for her/himself. The distinction is perhaps easier to recognise than to state. A valid analogy might be the difference between "attention" and "supervision" in the context of awards of disability living allowance. Some assistance in drawing this distinction may also be obtained from the decision in *R v Allerdale DC HBRB ex p Doughty* [2000] COD 462, QBD. In that case, the applicant lived in a religious home. An application for registration of the home as a small residential home was rejected by the Registered Homes Tribunal. The Housing Benefit Review Board found that because the home was not registered under the Registered Homes Act 1984, it could not therefore be said to be providing "personal care" under the scope of the previous definition and so the home was not "supported accommodation".

The judge held this approach to be wrong. The effect of the rejection of registration was that the landlord could not provide "personal care" as defined in s20(1) of the 1984 Act: "care which includes assistance with bodily functions where such assistance is required".

"[Counsel for the applicant] accepts that the concept will also embrace other forms of care, such as psychiatric and certain physical care, but submits that it clearly does not extend to general counselling and support services such as fall within the scope of para 1(f)(iii). This is, in my view, plainly correct, and, as I have already indicated, in the schedule itself the concept of personal care is found in para (e) and the concept of 'general counselling' or 'any other support services' are found in para (f). In my view, the concept of 'personal care' in para (e) is the same as that found in the Registered Homes Act, but in any event, even if that were not so, it would be, in substance, a similar concept."

The scope of para 1(f) has been considered by the courts on a number of occasions and it was usually amended in consequence. Following the introduction of the Supporting People scheme, the complex former provisions have now been repealed and the question is now much simpler. For the old law, see pp397-398 of the 12th edition.

Under para 1(f), charges in respect of general counselling or any other support services are ineligible. It does not matter who provides the services.

CIS 1460/1995 provides valuable guidance on the scope of para 1(g). Although it excludes services which relate purely to meeting the personal needs of residents, this does not mean that in deciding whether a service is related to the provision of adequate accommodation the question of suitability for the personal needs of the residents is not relevant (as the cleaning of the outside of windows – per para 1(a)(iv) – is connected both with adequate accommodation and the personal needs of the claimant), and therefore the Schedule itself contemplates that some personal needs may be relevant to assessing what are eligible service charges. What constitutes "adequate accommodation" is a question of fact in each case. The terms of GM A4.730 set out above would suggest that the approach in *CIS 1460/1995* is accepted by the DWP as being correct.

Amount ineligible for meals

2.–(1)   Where a charge for meals is ineligible to be met by housing benefit under paragraph 1, the amount ineligible in respect of each week shall be the amount specified in the following provisions of this paragraph.

(2)   Subject to sub-paragraph (4), where the charge includes provision for at least three meals a day, the amount shall be–
    (a)   for a single claimant, [⁵ £23.25];
    (b)   if the claimant is a member of a family–
        (i)   for the claimant and for each member of his family aged 16 or over, [⁵ £23.35];
        (ii)   for each member of his family under age 16, [⁵ £11.80].

(3)   Except where sub-paragraph (5) applies and subject to sub-paragraph (4), where the charge includes provision for less than three meals a day, the amount shall be–
    (a)   for a single claimant, [⁵ £15.50];
    (b)   if the claimant is a member of a family–
        (i)   for the claimant and for each member of his family aged 16 or over, [⁵ £15.50];
        (ii)   for each member of his family under age 16, [⁵ £7.80].

(4)   For the purposes of sub-paragraphs (2)(b) and (3)(b), a person attains the age of 16 on the first Monday in September following his 16th birthday.

(5)   Where the charge for meals includes the provision of breakfast only, the amount for the claimant and, if he is a member of a family, for the claimant and for each member of his family, shall be [⁵ £2.85].

(6)   Where a charge for meals includes provision for meals for a person who is not a member of the claimant's family sub-paragraphs (2) to (5) shall apply as if that person were a member of the claimant's family.

(7)   For the avoidance of doubt where the charge does not include provision for meals for a claimant or, as the case may be, a member of his family, sub-paragraphs (2) to (5) shall not apply in respect of that person.

Amendments

    1.   Amended by Art 19(4) of SI 2006 No 645 and reg 8 of SI 2006 No 217 as from 1.4.06 (3.4.06 where rent payable weekly or at intervals of a week).
    2.   Amended by Art 19(4) of SI 2007 No 688 as from 1.4.07 (2.4.07 where rent payable weekly or at intervals of a week).
    3.   Amended by Art 19(5) of SI 2008 No 632 as from 1.4.08 (7.4.08 where rent payable weekly or in multiples of a week).
    4.   Amended by Art 19(5) of SI 2009 No 497 as from 1.4.09 (6.4.09 where rent payable weekly or at intervals of a week).
    5.   Amended by Art 19(4) of SI 2010 No 793 as from 1.4.10 (5.4.10 where rent payable weekly or in multiples of a week).

Analysis

Para 2 makes it clear that when a service charge is paid for meals, only the appropriate amounts shown in that paragraph are to be treated as ineligible, whatever the actual charge for meals. The leeway afforded by paras 3 and 4 in relation to other types of service charge does not apply here. The amount ineligible varies according to the number of meals per day included in the charge and the age of the members of the claimant's "family", defined in s137(1) SSCBA (see p22). However, where the charge does not include meals for the claimant or a member of her/his family, no deduction is made for that person: sub-para (7).

Where the charge for meals included in the claimant's charge includes meals not only for members of a claimant's family but for someone else (eg, a non-dependant), the appropriate deduction is to be made in respect of that person as though s/he was a member of the claimant's family: sub-para (6).

Amount of ineligible charges

3.–(1) Subject to paragraph 2 where an ineligible service charge is not separated from or separately identified within other payments made by the occupier in respect of the dwelling, the appropriate authority shall apportion such charge as is fairly attributable to the provision of that service, having regard to the cost of comparable services and such portion of those payments shall be ineligible to be met by housing benefit.

(2)   Subject to paragraph 2, where the relevant authority considers that the amount of any ineligible service charge which is separately identified within other payments made by the occupier in respect of the dwelling is unreasonably low having regard to the service provided, it shall substitute a sum for the charge in question which it considers represents the value of the services concerned and the amount so substituted shall be ineligible to be met by housing benefit.

(3)   In sub-paragraph (2) the expression "ineligible service charge" includes any service charge which does not qualify as a periodical payment under regulation 12(1)(e) (rent).

(4)   In any other case, the whole amount of the ineligible service charge shall be ineligible to be met by housing benefit.

Analysis

The general rule subject to para 2 above, as set out in para 3(4), is that the whole amount of an ineligible charge is ineligible for HB. However, this is subject to two qualifications. Firstly, in many cases, the amount of such a charge will not be identifiable and in such a case para 3(1) gives the authority power to make an amount "fairly attributable" to it ineligible for HB, having regard to the actual cost of comparable services.

Secondly, para 3(2) gives authorities the power to substitute their own valuation for ineligible service charges in a case where the amounts are considered to be unreasonably low for the services provided. See para 4 where *eligible* charges are thought to be excessive.

Excessive service costs

4.   Subject to paragraph 2, where the relevant authority considers that the amount of a service charge to which regulation 12(1)(e) (rent) applies is excessive in relation to the service provided for the claimant or his family, having regard to the cost of comparable services, it shall make a deduction from that charge of the excess and the amount so deducted shall be ineligible to be met by housing benefit.

Analysis

Where eligible charges are thought to be excessive, the excess is deducted and treated as ineligible.

PART 2
Payments in respect of fuel charges

5.   A service charge for fuel except a charge in respect of services for communal areas shall be ineligible to be met by housing benefit.

Analysis

Service charges relating to fuel are ineligible unless they relate to communal areas (as defined in para 8).

6.–(1)   Where a charge is ineligible to be met by housing benefit under paragraph 5–

(a)   in the calculation of entitlement to a rent rebate; or

(b)   in the calculation of entitlement to a rent allowance if the amount of the charge is specified or is otherwise readily identifiable (except where the amount of the charge is unrealistically low in relation to the fuel provided or the charge cannot readily be distinguished from a charge for a communal area),

the amount ineligible to be met by housing benefit shall be the full amount of the service charge.

(2)   In any other case, subject to sub-paragraphs (3) and (4) and paragraph 7, the amount ineligible to be met by housing benefit shall be the following amounts in respect of each week–

(a)   for heating (other than hot water) [⁵ £21.55];

(b)   for hot water [⁵ £2.50];

(c)   for lighting [⁵ £1.75];

(d)   for cooking [⁵ £2.50].

(3)   Where the accommodation occupied by the claimant or, if he is a member of a family, by the claimant and the members of his family, consists of one room only, the amount ineligible to be met by housing benefit in respect of each week where heating only is, or heating and either hot water or lighting (or both) are, provided, shall be one-half of the aggregate of the amounts specified in sub-paragraphs (2)(a), (b) and (c).

(4)   In a case to which sub-paragraph (2) or (3) applies, if a claimant provides evidence on which the actual or approximate amount of the service charge for fuel may be estimated, the amount ineligible to be met by housing benefit under this paragraph shall be that estimated amount.

Amendments

1.   Amended by Art 19(5) of SI 2006 No 645 and reg 8 of SI 2006 No 217 as from 1.4.06 (3.4.06 where rent payable weekly or at intervals of a week).

2.   Amended by Art 19(5) of SI 2007 No 688 as from 1.4.07 (2.4.07 where rent payable weekly or at intervals of a week).

3.   Confirmed by Art 19(6) of SI 2008 No 632 as from 1.4.08 (7.4.08 where rent payable weekly or in multiples of a week).

4.   Amended by Art 19(6) of SI 2009 No 497 as from 1.4.09 (6.4.09 where rent payable weekly or at intervals of a week).

5.   Confirmed by Art 19(5) of SI 2010 No 793 as from 1.4.10 (5.4.10 where rent payable weekly or in multiples of a week).

Analysis

Under para 6(1), the full amount of the service charge for fuel is ineligible in all cases where the claimant has a rent rebate, and in rent allowance cases where the charge is specified or can otherwise be readily identified. In the latter case, this does not apply if the charge is unrealistically low or if the charge cannot be distinguished from a portion relating to "communal areas" (defined in para 8).

If para 6(1) does not apply, regard must be had to sub-paras (2), (3) and (4) to work out the the the amount ineligible. Specified amounts are in sub-para (2). If, however, the claimant provides evidence to allow the actual amounts to be estimated, those amounts are to be taken instead: sub-para (4).

Under sub-para (3), where the claimant and her/his family (if applicable) occupy a single room, lower deductions apply. GM A4.912-913 suggests that this applies where the claimant occupies one room only, including cases where the room or other communal areas are shared and that the reference to "one room only" is not a reference to the number of rooms occupied solely by the claimant, that is that if a claimant has her/his own room and shared occupation of other rooms the higher amount is ineligible. However, the guidance also suggests that bathrooms, toilets and shared kitchens should not count as rooms occupied by the claimant and family.

The scope of sub-para (3) is uncertain in two respects. Firstly, this calculation only applies where "heating only is, or heating and either hot water or lighting (or both) are, provided", that is where there is a charge for heating, or heating and hot water, or heating and lighting, or heating, hot water and lighting.

Secondly, there are difficulties in determining how much is to be ineligible. Sub-para (3) provides that the ineligible amount is to be half the aggregate of the amounts set out in sub-para (2) for heating, hot water and lighting. What about, however, the case where a charge is only made for heating, or only for heating and one of the latter two categories of charge? On a literal reading of sub-para (3), it would appear that all the amounts are to be aggregated, yet this seems illogical in view of the fact that charges for hot water, lighting or both are not actually being made.

7.–(1)   Where rent is payable other than weekly, any amount ineligible to be met by housing benefit which is specified in this Schedule as a weekly amount shall–

(a)   where rent is payable in multiples of a week, be multiplied by the number equal to the number of weeks in respect of which it is payable; or

(b)   in any other case, be divided by 7 and multiplied by the number of days in the period to be used by the relevant authority for the purpose of calculating the claimant's weekly eligible rent under regulation 80 (calculation of weekly amounts).

(2)   In a case to which regulation 81 applies (rent free periods), any amount ineligible to be met by housing benefit which is specified in this Schedule as a weekly amount shall, where appropriate, be converted in accordance with sub-paragraph (1) and shall–

(a)   where rent is payable weekly, or in multiples of a week, be multiplied by 52 or 53, whichever is appropriate, and divided by the number equal to the number of weeks in that 52 or 53 week period in respect of which he is liable to pay rent; or

(b)   in any other case, be multiplied by 365 or 366, whichever is appropriate, and divided by the number of days in that 365 or 366 day period in respect of which he is liable to pay rent.

Analysis

Para 7 deals with the arithmetic of calculating ineligible charges where rent is paid other than weekly or where there are rent-free periods. Under para 7(1), the charges are converted to weekly amounts. Under para 7(2), where there are rent-free periods (see reg 81) the amount of ineligible charges is adjusted. Suppose, for example, the claimant has eligible rent of £50 a week and ineligible charges of £10 a week. She has a rent-free period of four weeks during a 52 week year. The £10 is multiplied by 52 and divided by 48, giving £10.84 as the ineligible amount during each week.

8. In this Schedule–
"communal areas" mean areas (other than rooms) of common access (including halls and passageways) and rooms of common use in sheltered accommodation;
"fuel" includes gas and electricity and a reference to a charge for fuel includes a charge for fuel which includes an amount in respect of the facility of providing it other than a specified amount for the provision of a heating system.

[¹ SCHEDULE 2
REGULATION 14
Excluded tenancies

Modifications

Schedule 2 was substituted by reg 18 Housing Benefit (Local Housing Allowance and Information Sharing) Amendment Regulations 2007 SI No.2868 as from 7 April 2008, save that for a person to whom reg 1(5) of those regulations applied (see p1231), the amendments came into force on the day on or after 7 April 2008 when the first of the events specified in reg 1(6) applied to her/him, or on 6 April 2009 if none had before that date.

Amendment

1. Substituted by reg 18 of SI 2007 No 2868 as from 7.4.08 (or if reg 1(5) of that SI applies, on the day on or after 7.4.08 when the first of the events specified in reg 1(6) applies, or from 6.4.09 if none have before that date).

General Note

This Schedule lists circumstances in which the general obligation in reg 14 (see p324) – requiring local authorities in claims for a rent allowance to seek determinations from the rent officer – does not apply. Although under para 1, these are referred to as "excluded tenancies", this is a misleading term because not all the agreements referred to in the Schedule relate to tenancies as distinct from licences and so on, and also because many of the exclusions relate not so much to the tenancy but to the person claiming. A tenancy may gain and lose its status as an "excluded tenancy" during its existence.

Note that in a number of cases, the "excluded tenancies" are not only excluded from the requirement to apply to the rent officer, but are excluded from the application of the "local reference rent" and the "local housing allowance" schemes altogether.

(1) A claimant is excluded from the application of the "local reference rent" scheme (see regs 12C and 13) where any of paras 4 to 9 or 12 apply. Where paras 3 or 11 apply, a claimant *may* be excluded from the application of that scheme.

(2) A claimant is excluded from the application of the "local housing allowance" scheme (see regs 12D, 13C and 13D) where any of paras 4 to 11 apply. Tenancies excluded under paras 3 and 12 are not covered, but may come within other exceptions in reg 13C(5).

These rules are quite complex and careful analysis will often be required to ascertain whether a decision to apply to the rent officer can be challenged. Even where that has been done, it may be to the claimant's advantage to allow an application to the rent officer in certain circumstances, particularly if rents have increased since a previous determination was made. The outcome of the application may well be a higher eligible rent and therefore entitlement to increased HB.

1. An excluded tenancy is any tenancy to which any of the following paragraphs applies.
2.–(1) Subject to the following sub-paragraphs, where a rent officer has made a determination, which relates to the tenancy in question or any other tenancy of the same dwelling this paragraph applies to–
(a) the tenancy in respect of which that determination was made; and
(b) any other tenancy of the same dwelling on terms which are substantially the same, other than the term relating to the amount of rent, as those terms were at the time of that determination or, if earlier, at the end of the tenancy.
(2) For the purposes of any claim, notification, request or application under regulation 14(1) ("the later application"), a tenancy shall not be an excluded tenancy by virtue of sub-paragraph (1) by reference to a rent officer's determination made in consequence of an earlier claim, notification, request or application ("the earlier application") where–
(a) the earlier and later applications were made in respect of the same claimant or different claimants; and
(b) the earlier application was made more than 52 weeks before the later application was made.

(3)   Sub-paragraph (1) shall not apply where subsequent to the making of the determination mentioned in that sub-paragraph–

(a)   the number of occupiers of the dwelling has changed and that dwelling is not in a hostel;

(b)   there has been a substantial change in the condition of the dwelling (including the making of improvements) or the terms of the tenancy other than a term relating to rent;

(c)   there has been a rent increase under a term of the tenancy and the term under which that increase was made was either included in the tenancy at the time when the application for that determination was made (or was a term substantially the same as such a term) and that determination was not made under paragraph 1(2), 2(2) or 3(3) of Schedule 1 to the Rent Officers Order;

(d)   in a case where the rent officer has made a determination under paragraph 2(2) of Schedule 1 to the Rent Officers Order (size and rent determinations), but since the date of the application for that determination–

    (i)   a child, who is a member of the household occupying the dwelling, has attained the age of 10 years; or

    (ii)   a young person, who is a member of the household occupying that dwelling, has attained the age of 16 years; or

    (iii)   there is a change in the composition of the household occupying the dwelling;

(e)   the claimant is a young individual, except in a case where the determination mentioned in sub-paragraph (1) was, or was made in conjunction with, a determination of a single room rent pursuant to paragraph 5 of Schedule 1 to the Rent Officers Order on or after 2nd July 2001.

Analysis

This is by far the most common type of "excluded tenancy" and is designed to avoid the need for constant applications to be made for properties where there are continual changes of tenant.

The general rule, as set out in sub-para (1), is that once a rent officer has made a determination in relation to accommodation, it remains valid during the term of the existing tenancy (which, it is suggested, will include any period during which the claimant becomes a statutory tenant by virtue of the operation of the Housing Act 1988 or similar legislation). It also remains valid in relation to subsequent tenancies, provided that they are on substantially the same terms as the tenancy in existence when the application was made, except in relation to the amount of rent payable. It is to be noted that it does not matter if the claimant changes.

However, the effect of this exclusion is limited. It applies only for 52 weeks: sub-para (2). Furthermore, sub-para (3) disapplies it in a case where any of the following changes of circumstance occur subsequent to the making of the determination:

(1)   Where the number of occupiers of the dwelling, whether or not they are members of the claimant's family, changes: sub-para (3)(a). This does not apply to hostel accommodation. There is no definition of "occupier" for these purposes. However, reg 7 determines the issue of whether a person is, or is not, to be treated as occupying a dwelling as a home: *Stroud DC v JG* [2009] UKUT 67 (AAC); *R(H) 8/09*; *SK v South Hams DC (HB)* [2010] UKUT 129 (AAC).

    In *R(H) 8/09*, the claimant's son was a student who lived away from home during term time. Judge Williams concluded that he was to be treated as occupying the claimant's dwelling as his home under reg 7(16)(c)(viii) and (17) (student who is temporarily absent from home). As such, there was not a change in the number of occupiers in the claimant's home and a reference under reg 14 could therefore not be made on this ground. Note:

(2)   Where there is a substantial change in the condition of the dwelling or the terms of the tenancy except in so far as they relate to rent: sub-para (3)(b).

(3)   Where there has been a rent increase under a term of the tenancy: sub-para (3)(c). This only applies where the term, or one like it, was in the tenancy when the previous application for a determination was made. It also only applies where the rent officer did not made a significantly high rent determination, an exceptionally high rent determination, or a size-related rent determination following the previous appplication. That should be clear from the terms of the rent officer's determination. It is important for the First-tier Tribunal to establish the correct legal basis for an increase in rent before going on to consider whether the authority is under a duty to apply to the rent officer under reg 14: *CH 1556/2006*.

    In *CH 3590/2007*, the claimant's rent was increased and he sought an increase in his HB. However, the authority decided it was unable to refer the increased rent to the rent officer until 52 weeks had expired since the previous referral and so his HB remained unchanged. The tribunal decided that, as the claimant had a monthly periodic assured shorthold tenancy that had arisen after a fixed term had ended, under a process set out in s13 Housing Act 1988 the rent could be increased once a year and that this was an implied term of the claimant's tenancy. Hence it decided that the 52 week rule could be displaced as sub-para (3)(c) applied. The deputy commissioner agreed that the "term" referred to in sub-para (3)(c) can be express or implied. However, he did not agree that s13 Housing Act 1988 operates by implying such a term. He said (para 11): "Rather it operates by establishing a free-standing statutory procedure under which a landlord may increase the rent payable under the tenancy even though it does not contain a term that would allow her to do so on a contractual basis. The tribunal was not correct to say that the rent could not be increased unless the process set out in section 13 was a term of the appellant's tenancy. The legal basis for the increased rent is section 13(4). Where it applies, that subsection imposes the increase in the rent as a matter of statute law and does not require contractual authority, whether express or implied, to do so." He concluded that the rent increase notified to the authority was not one to which sub-paras (3)(a)-(d) applied and was therefore not notification of a "change relating to a rent allowance" within reg 14(1)(c).

(4) Where the previous determination contained a size-related rent determination and there has been a specified change in circumstances: sub-para (3)(d). These are a change in the composition of the household occupying the dwelling, or a child becoming 10 or 16 which changes the rules about the number of bedrooms required: see Sch 2 para 1 Rent Officers (Housing Benefit Functions) Order 1997 on p609 and its Scottish equivalent on p628.

(5) Where the claimant is a "young individual" (defined in reg 2(1) as most claimants under the age of 25) and the previous determination did not include a single room rent: sub-para (3)(e). This would be the case if the previous tenant was not a young individual.

[¹**3.**–(1) Subject to [² sub-paragraphs (1A) and (2)], this paragraph applies where the landlord is–
(a) a registered housing association;
(b) a county council, with regard to gypsies' and travellers' caravan or mobile home sites and caravans or mobile homes provided on those sites; or
(c) a housing authority, with regard to caravan or mobile home sites or houseboat moorings, payments in respect of which are to take the form of a rent allowance in accordance with regulation 91A(3).

[² (1A) In relation to a profit-making registered provider of social housing, sub-paragraph (1)(a) only applies to its social housing (within the meaning of sections 68 to 77 of the Housing and Regeneration Act 2008).]

(2) Sub-paragraph (1) does not apply where the local authority considers that–
(a) the claimant occupies a dwelling larger than is reasonably required by the claimant and any others who occupy that dwelling (including any non-dependants of the claimant and any person paying rent to the claimant); or
(b) the rent payable for that dwelling is unreasonably high.

(3) Where the circumstances set out in head (a) or (b) of sub-paragraph (2) exist, the authority must state this in their application for a determination.

(4) In this Schedule ''gypsies and travellers'' means–
(a) persons with a cultural tradition of nomadism or of living in a caravan; and
(b) all other persons of a nomadic habit of life, whatever their race or origin, including–
(i) such persons who, on grounds only of their own or their family's or dependant's educational or health needs or old age, have ceased to travel temporarily or permanently; and
(ii) members of an organised group of travelling show people or circus people (whether or not travelling together as such).]

Amendments
1. Substituted by reg 2(3) of SI 2008 No 2824 as from 6.4.09.
2. Amended by Art 4 and Sch 1 paras 54 and 55 of SI 2010 No 671 as from 1.4.10.

Analysis
"Housing association" and "registered housing association" are defined in reg 2(1). Note that if the registered housing association is a profit-making registered provider of social housing, the exclusion only applies to the association's social housing; sub-para (1A).

The tenancies listed in sub-para (1) are excluded unless the authority considers the claimant's home to be unreasonably large or the rent to be unreasonably high: sub-para (2). The wording mirrors the wording in the version of reg 13(3)(a) and (b) HB Regs as in Sch 3 para 5(2) HB&CTB(CP) Regs, except that no specific comparison with suitable alternative accommodation is called for. However, it would be hard for a local authority to reach a conclusion that the home was unreasonably large or expensive without carrying out such a comparison. See p1205 for the extensive caselaw relating to these concepts.

---

4. This paragraph applies to a tenancy entered into before–
(a) in Scotland, 2nd January 1989; and
(b) in any other case, 15th January 1989.
5. This paragraph applies to a regulated tenancy within the meaning of–
(a) in Scotland, the Rent (Scotland) Act 1984; and
(b) in any other case, the Rent Act 1977.
6. This paragraph applies to a housing association tenancy which–
(a) in Scotland, is a tenancy to which Part 6 of the Rent (Scotland) Act 1984 applies; and
(b) in any other case, is a housing association tenancy to which Part 6 of the Rent Act 1977 applies.
7. This paragraph applies to a protected occupancy or statutory tenancy within the meaning of the Rent (Agriculture) Act 1976.

8. This paragraph applies to a tenancy at a low rent within the meaning of Part 1 of the Landlord and Tenant Act 1954 or Schedule 10 to the Local Government and Housing Act 1989.

9. This paragraph applies to a tenancy of any dwelling which is a bail hostel or probation hostel approved by the Secretary of State under [¹ section 13 of the Offender Management Act 2007].

Amendment

1.   Amended by reg 6(7) of SI 2008 No 2767 as from 17.11.08.

---

10. This paragraph applies to a tenancy of a housing action trust established under Part 3 of the Housing Act 1988.

11.–(1) Subject to sub-paragraphs (2) and (3) this paragraph applies to a tenancy–

(a)   in respect of a dwelling comprised in land which has been disposed of under section 32 of the Housing Act 1985 or section 12 of the Housing (Scotland) Act 1987;

(b)   in respect of a dwelling comprised in land which has been disposed of with the consent required by section 43 of the Housing Act 1985 or section 12 of the Housing (Scotland) Act 1987;

(c)   in respect of which the fee simple estate has been acquired, under the right conferred by Chapter 2 of Part 1 of the Housing Act 1996, otherwise than from a housing action trust within the meaning of Part 3 of the Housing Act 1988, or in respect of which the house has been acquired under the right conferred by Part 3 of the Housing (Scotland) Act 1988; or

(d)   in respect of a dwelling disposed of under the New Towns (Transfer of Housing Stock) Regulations 1990 to a person who is an approved person for the purposes of disposal under those Regulations or in respect of a dwelling disposed of pursuant to powers contained in the New Towns (Scotland) Act 1968 to a housing association.

(2)   This paragraph shall not apply to a tenancy to which sub-paragraph (1) refers if–

(a)   there has been an increase in rent since the disposal or acquisition, as the case may be, occurred; and

(b)   the local authority stated in the application for determination that–

(i)   the claimant occupies a dwelling larger than is reasonably required by him and any others who occupy that dwelling (including any non-dependant of his and any person paying rent to him); or

(ii)   the rent payable for that dwelling is unreasonably high.

(3)   Where the disposal or acquisition, as the case may be, took place on or after 7th October 2002, sub-paragraph (2)(b) shall apply to a tenancy to which sub-paragraph (1) refers as if head (i) were omitted.

12. This paragraph applies to a shared ownership tenancy.

Analysis

Paras 4 to 12 exclude a number of tenancies, most of which arose under old legislation. The common theme with tenancies under the old legislation is that the rent will usually be very low in any event. Reference should be made to the legislation mentioned in the paragraphs in any case of doubt.

Para 9 excludes a tenancy of a dwelling which is an approved bail hostel or probation hostel but note that those required to live in such accommodation are treated as not occupying the dwelling as a home and so cannot qualify for HB: reg 7(5).

Para 11 excludes former local authority or new town lettings which have been transferred to a new owner (eg, a housing association) under the powers cited. It also excludes properties the authority has a duty to sell to "approved landlords" under the "Tenants' Choice" provisions of the Housing Act 1988. The exclusion does not apply, however, if there has been an increase in rent since the transfer and the authority thinks that the rent unreasonably high or if the transfer took place before 7 October 2002, the accommodation is unreasonably large: para 11(3). See the commentary to para 3 and to the version of reg 13 mentioned there.

Para 12 excludes shared ownership tenancies (defined in reg 2(1)). Note, however, that the "local housing allowance" scheme may instead apply – eg, if the ownership is shared with a private landlord.

---

13. In this Schedule, "rent" shall be construed in accordance with paragraph (8) of regulation 14 (interpretation of "tenancy" and other expressions appropriate to a tenancy) and, subject to that paragraph, has the same meaning–

(a)   in Scotland, as in section 25 of the Housing (Scotland) Act 1988, except that the reference to the house in subsection (3) shall be construed as a reference to the dwelling;

(b)   in any other case, as in section 14 of the Housing Act 1988, except that the reference to the dwelling-house in subsection (4) shall be construed as a reference to the dwelling,

and–

(i)   other expressions have the same meanings as in regulation 14(8);

(ii)   in the case of a determination by a rent officer pursuant to a request for such a determination under regulation 14(1)(e), any reference to a "tenancy" shall be taken as a reference to a prospective tenancy and any reference to an "occupier" or any person "occupying" a dwelling shall, in the case of such a determination, be taken to be a reference to a potential occupier or potential occupation of that dwelling.]

SCHEDULE 3

REGULATION 22

Applicable amounts

Definitions

"claimant" – see reg 2(1).

"disability living allowance" – see reg 2(1).

"family" – see s137(1) SSCBA and Part 4.

"lone parent" – see reg 2(1).

"main phase employment and support allowance" – see reg 2(1).

"member of household" – see s137(1) SSCBA and reg 21.

"non-dependant" – see reg 3.

"partner" – see reg 2(1).

"person in receipt of benefit" – see para 19.

"polygamous marriage" – see reg 2(1).

"responsibility for a child" – see Part 4.

"single claimant" – see reg 2(1).

"training allowance" – see reg 2(1).

General Note on Schedule 3

This Schedule sets out the amounts of the various elements to be added together under regs 22 and 23 to arrive at a claimant's "applicable amount" on which the calculation of HB is based. The amounts are uprated each April. For the calculation of HB, see regs 70 to 75.

Part 1 sets out the personal allowances and allowances for children.

Part 2 sets out the conditions for the family premium.

Parts 3 and 4 set out the rules under which a claimant may qualify for one or more "premiums" and the amounts of the premiums.

Parts 5 and 6 set out the rules under which a claimant may qualify for a "component" and the amounts of the components.

Parts 7 and 8 set out the rules under which a claimant may qualify for a "transitional addition" when transferred to ESA from IS, IB or SDA, or appealing a decision not to transfer the claimant from one of those benefits to ESA, and the rules for calculating the transitional addition.

PART 1

Analysis

This Part sets out the amounts of the personal allowances and allowances for children and qualifying young people which form the primary part of the applicable amount. The highest rate personal allowance (for a single person, lone parent or couple, as the case may be) is applicable where the claimant is entitled to main phase ESA or converted ESA personally: para 1A. See the Analysis to para 1A below.

Otherwise, whether the highest rate personal allowance is applicable depends on: for single people, whether the claimant is aged at least 25; and for lone parents and members of couples, whether the claimant or her/his partner is at least 18.

The different personal allowances for single people under and over the age of 25 do not infringe Arts 8, 14 or Prot 1 Art 1 of the European Convention on Human Rights: *R (Reynolds) v Secretary of State for Work and Pensions* [2005], UKHL 37, *The Times*, 27 May.

Personal allowances

1.   The amounts specified in column (2) below in respect of each person or couple specified in column (1) shall be the amounts specified for the purposes of regulations 22(a) and 23(a) and (b)–

Column (1) Person or couple	Column (2) Amount
[4 (1) Single claimant who–	(1)
(a) is entitled to main phase employment and support allowance;	(a) [6 £65.45];
(b) is aged not less than 25;	(b) [6 £65.45];
(c) is aged less than 25	(c) [6 £51.85].
(2) Lone parent who–	(2)
(a) is entitled to main phase employment and support allowance;	(a) [6 £65.45];
(b) is aged not less than 18;	(b) [6 £65.45];
(c) is aged less than 18	(c) [6 £51.85].

(3) Couple where–

(a) the claimant is entitled to main phase employment and support allowance;

(b) at least one member is aged not less than 18;

(b) both members are aged less than 18.

(3)

(a) [⁶ £102.75];

(b) [⁶ £102.75];

(c) [⁶ £78.30.]

Amendments

1. Amended by Art 19(6) and Sch 6 para 1 of SI 2006 No 645 and reg 8 of SI 2006 No 217 as from 1.4.06 (3.4.06 where rent payable weekly or at intervals of a week).
2. Amended by Art 19(6) and Sch 6 para 1 of SI 2007 No 688 as from 1.4.07 (2.4.07 where rent payable weekly or at intervals of a week).
3. Amended by Art 19(7) and Sch 6 para 1 of SI 2008 No 632 as from 1.4.08 (7.4.08 where rent payable weekly or in multiples of a week).
4. Substituted by reg 23(a) of SI 2008 No 1082 as from 27.10.08.
5. Amended by Art 19(7) and Sch 5 para 1 of SI 2009 No 497 as from 1.4.09 (6.4.09 where rent payable weekly or in multiples of a week).
6. Amended by Art 19(6) and Sch 5 para 1 of SI 2010 No 793 as from 1.4.10 (5.4.10 where rent payable weekly or in multiples of a week).

[¹ [²**1A.** For the purposes of paragraph 1 a claimant is entitled to main phase employment and support allowance if–

(a) each of the conditions in paragraph 21 is satisfied in relation to the claimant personally; or

(b) the claimant personally is entitled to a converted employment and support allowance.]]

Amendments

1. Inserted by reg 6(10(a) of SI 2009 No 583 as from 1.4.09 (6.4.09 where rent payable weekly or at intervals of a week).
2. Substituted by reg 27 and Sch 5 para 1(5)(a) of SI 2010 No 1907 as amended by reg 15 of SI 2010 No 2430 as from 1.10.10.

Analysis

For the purposes of determining if the highest rate personal allowance is applicable, a claimant is treated as entitled to main phase ESA if:

(1) s/he personally satisifes para 21 – ie, s/he has claimed ESA and has, or is treated as having, limited capability for work. In addition, generally, the asessment phase (the first 13 weeks of entitlement to ESA) must have ended, although there are are exceptions – eg, where the claimant is terminally ill. The intention is that a claimant can satisfy para 21 where entitled to ESA and also where only entitled to national insurance credits. See para 21 for a discussion; *or*

(2) s/he is personally entitled to a converted ESA. Converted ESA (defined in reg 2(1)) is ESA which is not income-related to which the claimant is entitled on being transferred from IS "on the grounds of disability", IB or SDA. See Parts 7 and 8 for situations when there may be entitlement to a transitional addition.

2.–(1) The amount specified in column (2) below in respect of each person specified in column (1) shall, for the relevant period specified in column (1), be the amounts specified for the purposes of regulations 22(b) and 23(c)–

Column (1)
Child or young person
Persons in respect of the period–

Column (2)
Amount

(a) beginning on that person's date of birth and ending on the day preceding the first Monday in September following that person's sixteenth birthday;

(a) [⁶ £57.57];

(b) beginning on the first Monday in September following that person's sixteenth birthday and ending on the day preceding that person's [² twentieth] birthday.

(b) [⁶ £57.57].

(2) In column (1) of the table in paragraph (1), "the first Monday in September" means the Monday which first occurs in the month of September in any year.

Amendments

1. Amended by Art 19(6) and Sch 6 para 2 of SI 2006 No 645 and reg 8 of SI 2006 No 217 as from 1.4.06 (3.4.06 where rent payable weekly or at intervals of a week).
2. Amended by reg 4(4) of SI 2006 No 718 as from 10.4.06.
3. Amended by Art 19(6) and Sch 6 para 2 of SI 2007 No 688 as from 1.4.07 (2.4.07 where rent payable weekly or at intervals of a week).

4.   Amended by Art 19(7) and Sch 6 para 2 of SI 2008 No 632 as from 1.4.08 (7.4.08 where rent payable weekly or in multiples of a week).

5.   Amended by Art 19(7) and Sch 5 para 2 of SI 2009 No 497 as from 1.4.09 (6.4.09 where rent payable weekly or in multiples of a week).

6.   Amended by Art 19(6) and Sch 5 para 2 of SI 2010 No 793 as from 1.4.10 (5.4.10 where rent payable weekly or in multiples of a week).

PART 2
Family premium

3.–(1)   Subject to sub-paragraph (2), the amount for the purposes of regulations 22(c) and 23(d) in respect of a family of which at least one member is a child or young person shall be–

(a)   where the claimant is a lone parent to whom sub-paragraph (3) applies, [11 £22.20];

(b)   in any other case, [12 £17.40].

(2)   The amounts specified in sub-paragraph (1)(a) and (b) shall be increased by [11 £10.50] where at least one child is under the age of one year and for the purposes of this paragraph where the child's first birthday does not fall on a Monday he shall be treated as under the age of one year until the first Monday after his first birthday.

(3)   The amount in sub-paragraph (1)(a) shall be applicable to a lone parent–

(a)   who was entitled to housing benefit on 5th April 1998 and whose applicable amount on that date included the amount applicable under [7 sub-paragraph (1)(a)] as in force on that date; or

(b)   who was not entitled to housing benefit on 5th April 1998 because that date fell during a rent free period as defined in regulation 81(1) (rent free periods) and his applicable amount on that date would have included the amount applicable under [3 sub-paragraph (1)(a)] as in force on that date; or

(c)   on becoming entitled to housing benefit where that lone parent–

(i) had been treated as entitled to that benefit in accordance with sub-paragraph (5)(a) as at the day before the date of claim for that benefit; and

(ii) was entitled to council tax benefit as at the date of claim for housing benefit,

and in respect of whom, all of the conditions specified in sub-paragraph (4) have continued to apply.

(4)   The conditions specified for the purposes of sub-paragraph (3) are that, in respect of the period commencing on 6th April 1998–

(a)   the claimant has not ceased to be entitled, or has not ceased to be treated as entitled, to housing benefit;

(b)   the claimant has not ceased to be a lone parent;

(c)   where the claimant was entitled to income support or to an income-based jobseeker's allowance on 5th April 1998, he has [10 continuously, since that date, been entitled to income support, an income-based jobseeker's allowance or an income-related employment and support allowance or a combination of those benefits];

(d)   where the claimant was not entitled to income support or to an income-based jobseeker's allowance on 5th April 1998, he has not become entitled to [10 income support, an income-based jobseeker's allowance or an income-related employment and support allowance]; and

(e)   a premium under paragraph [7] 12 [10 or a component under paragraph 23 or 24] has not become applicable to the claimant.

(5)   For the purposes of sub-paragraphs (3)(c)(i) and (4)(a), a claimant shall be treated as entitled to housing benefit–

(a)   during any period where he was not, or had ceased to be, so entitled and throughout that period, he had been awarded council tax benefit and his applicable amount included the amount applicable under paragraph 3(1)(a) of Schedule 1 to the Council Tax Benefit Regulations 2006 (lone parent rate of family premium); or

(b)   during any rent free period as defined for the purposes of regulation 81(1).

Amendments

1.   Confirmed by Art 19(7) of SI 2006 No 645 and reg 8 of SI 2006 No 217 as from 1.4.06 (3.4.06 where rent payable weekly or at intervals of a week).

2.   Amended by Art 19(7) of SI 2006 No 645 and reg 8 of SI 2006 No 217 as from 1.4.06 (3.4.06 where rent payable weekly or at intervals of a week).

3.   Confirmed by Art 19(7) of SI 2007 No 688 as from 1.4.07 (2.4.07 where rent payable weekly or at intervals of a week).

4.   Amended by Art 19(7) of SI 2007 No 688 as from 1.4.07 (2.4.07 where rent payable weekly or at intervals of a week).

5.   Confirmed by Art 19(8) of SI 2008 No 632 as from 1.4.08 (7.4.08 where rent payable weekly or in multiples of a week).

6.   Amended by Art 19(8) of SI 2008 No 632 as from 1.4.08 (7.4.08 where rent payable weekly or in multiples of a week).

7.   Amended by reg 3(10)(a) and (b) of SI 2008 No 1042 as from 19.5.08.

8.   Confirmed by Art 19(8) of SI 2009 No 497 as from 1.4.09 (6.4.09 where rent payable weekly or in multiples of a week).

9.   Amended by Art 19(8) of SI 2009 No 497 as from 1.4.09 (6.4.09 where rent payable weekly or in multiples of a week).

10.   Amended by reg 6(10(b) of SI 2009 No 583 as from 1.4.09 (6.4.09 where rent payable weekly or at intervals of a week).

11.   Confirmed by Art 19(7)(a) and (c) of SI 2010 No 793 as from 1.4.10 (5.4.10 where rent payable weekly or in multiples of a week).

12.   Amended by Art 19(7)(b) of SI 2010 No 793 as from 1.4.10 (5.4.10 where rent payable weekly or in multiples of a week).

Analysis

A family premium is included in a claimant's applicable amount if at least one child or young person is a member of the family: see regs 22(c) and 23(d). It is additional to any other premiums and components that may be included. Only one family premium may be included, not one for each child. Note: an additional amount (sometimes referred to as a baby addition) is included where at least one member of the family is a child under the age of one: para (2).

The higher rate family premium for lone parents found in sub-para (1)(a) was abolished for most claimants in April 1998. Sub-paras (3) to (5) give transitional protection to certain groups of claimants. Claimants who do not fall within the scope of those provisions receive the lower rate under sub-para (1)(b).

Sub-paras (3) to (5). To be entitled to the transitional protection and so to the higher rate of family premium under sub-para (1)(a), the claimant must be in one of the categories in sub-para (3):

(1)   Claimants entitled to HB on 5 April 1998 and who had the higher rate of the family premium on that date: sub-para (3)(a).

(2)   Claimants who were not entitled on that date, but only because they were in a rent-free period (see reg 81), and would otherwise have had the higher rate of premium at that time: sub-para (3)(b).

(3)   Claimants who were not entitled on that date, but who were treated as if they were entitled on the day prior to their claim and who were entitled to CTB on the day of the claim: sub-para (3)(c). For these purposes, a person is treated as being entitled to HB for any period in which s/he was entitled to CTB and was getting the higher rate of family premium for that benefit: sub-para (5)(a).

Further, the claimant must have continuously from 6 April 1998 met all five of the conditions under sub-para (4):

(1)   The claimant has not ceased to be entitled or ceased to be *treated as* entitled to HB. For the purposes of deciding whether a person ceases to be treated as being entitled to HB, s/he can qualify under either limb of sub-para (5). So s/he will be treated as entitled if s/he is entitled to CTB including the higher rate of family premium for the whole of that period *and* during any rent-free period (see reg 81).

(2)   The claimant has not ceased to be a lone parent (see reg 2(1) for the definition).

(3)   The claimant was entitled to IS or income-based JSA on 5 April 1998 and has been continuously entitled to IS, income-based JSA or income-related ESA or a combination of those benefits since that date. Note that if the claimant switches from one benefit to another during that period (as may happen, for example, when someone comes out of a period of sickness and signs on) the condition is still fulfilled.

(4)   The claimant was not entitled to IS or income-based JSA on 5 April 1998 and has not become entitled to IS, income-based JSA or income-related ESA.

(5)   The claimant has not become entitled to a disability premium or a work-related activity component or a support component.

PART 3
Premiums

General Note to Part 3

This Part sets out the rules under which a claimant may qualify to have one or more "premiums" included in her/his applicable amount: see regs 22(d) and 23(e). The aim is to allow those claimants that have particular financial burdens or responsibilities arising out of their circumstances to qualify for higher rates of benefit. For a discussion of some issues to consider in respect of maximising entitlement to HB, see the commentary to para 13 on p530.

Paras 4 to 7, 18 and 19 set out some general rules governing entitlement to premiums, including the rules when a claimant qualifies for more than one premium: see paras 5 and 6. Paras 12 to 17 set out the specific rules relating to entitlement to individual premiums. The premiums that are available in addition to the family premium under Part 2 are:

(1)   Disability premium: paras 12 and 13.

(2)   Severe disability premium: para 14.

(3)   Enhanced disability premium: para 15.

(4)   Disabled child premium: para 16.

(5)   Carer premium: para 17.

Prior to 1 October 2007, a bereavement premium was available. Prior to 19 May 2008, pensioner premiums were available.

The rules of entitlement for some of the premiums are made more complicated by inconsistencies in the terminology used, specifically where a premium is affected by entitlement to, and/or receipt of, and/or payment of, another benefit – a "qualifying benefit". As a result, a number of issues arise, including:

(1)   A carer needs to consider how her/his claim for carer's allowance (CA) will affect the severe disability premium entitlement of the person s/he cares for, or of that person's partner (under para 14), particularly where the only financial advantage for the carer is the value of the carer premium (under para 17). For example, a single claimant will lose the severe disability premium if her/his carer is entitled to *and* receiving CA in respect of caring for her/him. However, a carer can qualify for the carer premium, and a severely disabled person can at the same time qualify for the severe disability premium, if the carer is entitled to, but *not* receiving, CA – eg, where CA overlaps with state retirement pension.

(2)   Severely disabled couples may qualify for two carer premiums, and at the same time the severe disability premium at the couple rate (under paras 14 and 17). This could be the case, for example, where both members of the couple are receiving attendance allowance or the highest or middle rate of disability living allowance and both members are entitled to (but not receiving) CA – eg, because it overlaps with state retirement pension.

Note that where there is an award of HB and a "qualifying benefit" is later awarded (or reinstated), regs 4(7B) and (7C), 7(2)(i) and 8(14) D&A Regs effectively allow for backdating of entitlement to premiums which depend on entitlement to (or receipt of) that qualifying benefit, for the period for which arrears of that benefit are paid. See the commentary to those provisions.

---

4.   Except as provided in paragraph 5, the premiums specified in Part 4 of this Schedule shall, for the purposes of regulations 22(d) and 23(e), be applicable to a claimant who satisfies the condition specified in paragraphs 8 to 17 in respect of that premium.

Analysis

Para 4 gives effect to the rates of the various premiums which are set out in Part 4 of the Schedule.

---

5.   Subject to paragraph 6, where a claimant satisfies the conditions in respect of more than one premium in this Part of this Schedule, only one premium shall be applicable to him and, if they are different amounts, the higher or highest amount shall apply.

Analysis

Para 5 states the general rule that where a claimant is entitled to more than one of the premiums in Part 3, only the highest is included in her/his applicable amount. This is subect to the exceptions in para 6. Therefore, since the omission of the bereavement premium and pensioner premiums from Part 3, the overall effect is as follows:

(1)   The severe disability premium, the enhanced disability premium, the disabled child premium and the carer premium may all be included in addition to each other, and in addition to the disability premium – the only "other premium which may apply" since the omission of the bereavement and pensioner premiums: para 6. They can also be paid in addition to the family premium, because it is included under Part 2 of the Schedule.

(2)   The transitional protection leading to the higher rate family premium for lone parents is lost if the disability premium is applicable: para 3(4)(e). In this case, the ordinary rate family premium is included.

Note also that a disability premium cannot be included if the claimant has, or is treated as having, "limited capability for work": para 13(9). However, the claimant may instead qualify for a work-related or support component under Part 5 of the Schedule. For a discussion of some issues to consider in respect of maximising entitlement to HB, see the commentary to para 13 on p530.

[¹**6.**   The following premiums, namely–

(a)   a severe disability premium to which paragraph 14 applies;

(b)   an enhanced disability premium to which paragraph 15 applies;

(c)   a disabled child premium to which paragraph 16 applies; and

(d)   a carer premium to which paragraph 17 applies,

may be applicable in addition to any other premium which may apply under this Schedule.]

Amendment

1.   Amended by reg 3(10)(c) of SI 2008 No 1042 as from 19.5.08.

7.–(1)   Subject to sub-paragraph (2), for the purposes of this Part of this Schedule, once a premium is applicable to a claimant under this Part, a person shall be treated as being in receipt of any benefit for–

(a)   in the case of a benefit to which the Social Security (Overlapping Benefits) Regulations 1979 applies, any period during which, apart from the provisions of those Regulations, he would be in receipt of that benefit; and

(b)   any period spent by a person in undertaking a course of training or instruction provided or approved by the Secretary of State under section 2 of the 1973 Act, or by [¹ Skills Development Scotland,] Scottish Enterprise or Highlands and Islands Enterprise under section 2 of the Enterprise and New Towns (Scotland) Act 1990 or for any period during which he is in receipt of a training allowance.

(2)   For the purposes of the carer premium under paragraph 17, a person shall be treated as being in receipt of carer's allowance by virtue of sub-paragraph (1)(a) only if and for so long as the person in respect of whose care the allowance has been claimed remains in receipt of attendance allowance, or the care component of disability living allowance at the highest or middle rate prescribed in accordance with section 72(3) of the Act.

Amendment

1.   Amended by reg 6(3)(c) of SI 2009 No 583 as from 6.4.09.

Analysis

Para 7 deals with the situation where entitlement to one of the premiums depends on the claimant being in receipt of some other benefit. The effect of para 7(1)(a) is that where a claimant is not receiving a benefit because the Social Security (Overlapping Benefits) Regulations 1979 apply, s/he will nevertheless be treated as being in receipt of that benefit for the purposes of Part 3. Under para 7(1)(b), if a claimant moves off benefit because s/he is participating in specified training, s/he is treated as being in receipt of benefit for the purposes of Part 3.

Para 7(2) was effectively made irrelevant by amendments to the carer premium rules (in April 2000 and October 2003). The issue for a carer premium under para 17 is whether the claimant or her/his partner is *entitled* to CA. The claimant or the partner are not required to be "in receipt" of that benefit. See the commentary to para 17. Note, however, that entitlement to CA will in any event end when the person being cared for is no longer in receipt of AA or the highest or middle rate of the care component of DLA.

[¹ Bereavement premium]

[¹ **8.**]

Amendment

1.   Revoked by reg 2 and the Sch of SI 2007 No 2618 as from 1.10.07.

Analysis

The bereavement premium was payable to widows and widowers who were, on 9 April 2001, aged between 55 and 60 and who were formerly entitled to bereavement allowance. From 9 April 2006, no claimants qualified for the bereavement premium. All such claimants were at least 60 and instead qualified for a pensioner premium (paid at a higher rate) under para 9. Para 8 was therefore revoked with effect from 1 October 2007. See the 18th edition for commentary.

[¹ Pensioner Premium for persons under 75

9.]

Amendment

1.   Omitted by reg 3(10)(d) of SI 2008 No 1042 as from 19.5.08.

Analysis

Until 19 May 2008, paras 9 and 10 provided two types of premiums for pensioners, both paid at the same rate.

Note that if the claimant or her/his partner is of at least the qualifying age for PC (defined in reg 2(1) and discussed on p224) and neither is on IS, income-based JSA or income-related ESA, her/his claim is assessed under the HB(SPC) Regs: reg 5. However, if s/he or her/his partner *is* on IS, income-based JSA or income-related ESA, pensioner premiums are not needed as the amount of entitlement is assessed without reference to an applicable amount.

[¹ Pensioner Premium for persons 75 and over

10.]

Amendment

1.   Omitted by reg 3(10)(d) of SI 2008 No 1042 as from 19.5.08.

[² Higher Pensioner Premium

11.]

Amendments
1.   Amended by reg 15(5) of SI 2006 No 2378 as from 9.10.06.
2.   Omitted by reg 3(10)(d) of SI 2008 No 1042 as from 19.5.08.

Analysis
Until 19 May 2008, para 11 provided for a higher pensioner premium. It was paid at the same rate as the pensioner premiums in paras 9 and 10 but effectively maintained the link with the claimant's (or her/his partner's) incapacity for work once retirement age was reached and a disability premium was no longer available under para 12. For the text of the provision and commentary on it, see pp457-458 of the 20th edition.

    Note that if the claimant or her/his partner is of at least the qualifying age for PC (defined in reg 2(1) and discussed on p224) and neither is on IS, income-based JSA or income-related ESA, her/his claim is assessed under the HB(SPC) Regs: reg 5. However, if s/he or her/his partner is on IS, income-based JSA or income-related ESA, the higher pensioner premium is not needed as the amount of entitlement is assessed without reference to an applicable amount. However, entitlement to the higher pensioner premium might still have been relevant, for example, because in claims for WTC, entitlement to it enabled the claimant to qualify for the disability element, itself a route into entitlement to WTC.

Disability Premium
    12.   The condition is that–
(a)   where the claimant is a single claimant or a lone parent, he [¹ has not attained the qualifying age for state pension credit] and the additional condition specified in paragraph 13 is satisfied; or
(b)   where the claimant has a partner, either–
    (i)   the claimant [¹ has not attained the qualifying age for state pension credit] and the additional condition specified in paragraph 13(1)(a) or (b) is satisfied by him; or
    (ii)   his partner [¹ has not attained the qualifying age for state pension credit] and the additional condition specified in paragraph 13(1)(a) is satisfied by his partner.

Amendment
1.   Amended by reg 26(2) of SI 2009 No 1488 as from 6.4.10.

Analysis
There are two conditions for entitlement to a disability premium. If the claimant is single or a lone parent, s/he must be under the qualifying age for PC (defined in reg 2(1) and discussed on p224) and satisfy the condition in para 13. If s/he has a partner, there are two ways to qualify. Either the claimant must be under the qualifying age for PC and satisfy a condition in para 13(1), or the partner must be under that age and satisfy the condition in para 13(1)(a). Satisfying para 13(1)(b) will not suffice in the case of a partner.

Additional Condition for the [³ Disability Premium]
    13.–(1)   Subject to sub-paragraph (2) and paragraph 7, the additional condition referred to in paragraphs 11 and 12 is that either–
(a)   the claimant or, as the case may be, his partner–
    (i)   is in receipt of one or more of the following benefits: attendance allowance, disability living allowance, the disability element or the severe disability element of working tax credit as specified in regulation 20(1)(b) and (f) of the Working Tax Credit Regulations, mobility supplement, long-term incapacity benefit under Part 2 of the Act or severe disablement allowance under Part 3 of the Act but, in the case of long-term incapacity benefit or severe disablement allowance only where it is paid in respect of him; or
    (ii)   was in receipt of long-term incapacity benefit under Part 2 of the Act when entitlement to that benefit ceased on account of the payment of a retirement pension under that Act and the claimant has since remained continuously entitled to housing benefit and, if the long-term incapacity benefit was payable to his partner, the partner is still a member of the family; or
    (iii)   [¹] was in receipt of attendance allowance or disability living allowance but payment of benefit has been suspended in accordance with regulations made under section 113(2) of the Act or otherwise abated as a consequence of the claimant or his partner becoming a patient within the meaning of [¹ regulation 28(11)(e) (treatment of child care charges)]; or
    (iv)   is provided by the Secretary of State with an invalid carriage or other vehicle under section 5(2) of the National Health Service Act 1977 (other services) or, in Scotland by the Scottish Ministers, under section 46 of the National Health Service (Scotland) Act 1978 (provision of services) or receives payments by way of grant from the Secretary of State under paragraph 2 of Schedule 2 to the Act of 1977 (additional provisions as to vehicles) or, in Scotland by the Scottish Ministers, under section 46 of the Act of 1978; or
    (v)   is blind and in consequence registered in a register compiled by a local authority under section 29 of the National Assistance Act 1948 (welfare services) or, in Scotland, has been certified as blind and in consequence he is registered in a register maintained by or on behalf of a council constituted under section 2 of the Local Government (Scotland) Act 1994; or

(b)   the claimant–
   (i)   is, or is treated as, incapable of work in accordance with the provisions of, and regulations made under, Part 12A of the Act (incapacity for work); and
   (ii)   has been incapable, or has been treated as incapable, of work for a continuous period of not less than–
      (aa)   in the case of a claimant who is terminally ill within the meaning of section 30B(4) of the Act, 196 days;
      (bb)   in any other case, 364 days.

(2)   For the purposes of sub-paragraph (1)(a)(v), a person who has ceased to be registered as blind on regaining his eyesight shall nevertheless be treated as blind and as satisfying the additional condition set out in that sub-paragraph for a period of 28 weeks following the date on which he ceased to be so registered.

(3)   For the purposes of sub-paragraph (1)(b), once [³] the disability premium is applicable to a claimant by virtue of his satisfying the additional condition specified in that provision, if he then ceases, for a period of 8 weeks or less, to be treated as incapable of work or to be incapable of work he shall, on again becoming so incapable of work, immediately thereafter be treated as satisfying the condition in sub-paragraph (1)(b).

[³ (4)]

(5)   For the purposes of sub-paragraph (1)(b), once the disability premium is applicable to a claimant by virtue of his satisfying the additional condition specified in that provision, he shall continue to be treated as satisfying that condition for any period spent by him in undertaking a course of training provided under section 2 of the 1973 Act or for any period during which he is in receipt of a training allowance.

(6)   For the purposes of sub-paragraph (1)(b), where any two or more periods of incapacity are separated by a break of not more than 56 days, those periods shall be treated as one continuous period.

(7)   For the purposes of this paragraph, a reference to a person who is or was in receipt of long-term incapacity benefit includes a person who is or was in receipt of short-term incapacity benefit at a rate equal to the long-term rate by virtue of section 30B(4)(a) of the Act (short-term incapacity benefit for a person who is terminally ill), or who would be or would have been in receipt of short-term incapacity benefit at such a rate but for the fact that the rate of short-term incapacity benefit already payable to him is or was equal to or greater than the long-term rate.

(8)   In the case of a claimant who is a welfare to work beneficiary [³ (a person to whom regulation 13A(1) of the Social Security (Incapacity for Work) (General) Regulations 1995 applies, and who again becomes incapable of work for the purposes of Part 12A of the Act)]–
(a)   the reference to a period of 8 weeks in sub-paragraph (3); and
(b)   the reference to a period of 56 days in sub-paragraph (6),
shall in each case be treated as a reference to a period of [² 104 weeks].

[⁴ (9)   The claimant is not entitled to the disability premium if the claimant has, or is treated as having, limited capability for work [⁵].]

Amendments

1.   Amended by reg 2(15)(b) of SI 2005 No 2502 as amended by Sch 2 para 27 of SI 2006 No 217 as from 1.4.06 (3.4.06 where rent payable weekly or at intervals of a week).
2.   Amended by reg 15(5) of SI 2006 No 2378 as from 9.10.06.
3.   Amended by reg 3(10)(e)-(h) of SI 2008 No 1042 as from 19.5.08.
4.   Inserted by reg 23(b) of SI 2008 No 1082 as from 27.10.08.
5.   Amended by reg 31(a) of SI 2008 No 2428 as from 27.10.08.

Analysis

This highly complex piece of legislation sets out the additional conditions for a disability premium specified in para 12. Prior to 19 May 2008, it also set out additional conditions for the higher pensioner premium specified in para 11.

To satisfy sub-para (1)(a), the claimant or her/his partner must fulfil any one of the five heads. To satisfy sub-para (1)(b), the claimant must fulfill all the criteria set out there. Note the deeming provisions in paras 7, 18 and 19 relating to receipt and payment of benefit.

Sub-para (1)(a)(i). The claimant or her/his partner must be receiving one of the benefits or elements of WTC listed. Note that the relevant person must be receiving incapacity benefit (IB) or severe disablement allowance for themselves and not on behalf of some other person. This prevents arguments such as those raised in *Rider v Chief Adjudication Officer* [1996] *Times* 30 January, CA. See also para 19.

In the case of IB, only long-term IB normally suffices but if a claimant is getting short-term IB as a terminally ill person or would qualify as such were s/he not already getting a higher rate than that applicable to the terminally ill, s/he is deemed to be getting long-term IB for this purpose: sub-para (7).

Sub-para (1)(a)(ii). The claimant or her/his partner must have been receiving long-term IB and subsequently retirement pension. If the IB was payable to the claimant's partner, the partner must still be a member of the family. Note the transitional protection in Sch 3 para 3 HB&CTB(CP) Regs (see p1198).

Only long-term IB normally suffices but if a claimant or her/his partner is getting short-term IB as a terminally ill person or would qualify as such were s/he not already getting a higher rate than that applicable to the terminally ill, s/he is deemed to be getting long-term IB for this purpose: sub-para (7).

Note that this sub-para will generally not be relevant, as if the claimant or her/his partner is of at least the qualifying age for PC (defined in reg 2(1)) and neither is on IS, income-based JSA or income-related ESA, her/his claim is assessed under the HB(SPC) Regs: reg 5. If the claimant or her/his partner is on one of those benefits, the amount of entitlement is assessed without reference to an applicable amount.

Sub-para (1)(a)(iii). This applies where the claimant or her/his partner are "patients". See reg 28(11)(e) on p352 for the meaning of patient. Either the claimant or her/his partner must have been in receipt of AA or DLA. Payment must then have been suspended under the Social Security (Attendance Allowance) Regulations 1991 or the Social Security (Disability Living Allowance) Regulations 1991 due to her/him being a "patient". Both sets of regulations do not speak in terms of suspension of benefit but rather as it being a "condition of receipt" of AA or DLA that the relevant person does not become a patient. Loss of benefit under the relevant provisions should be seen as a suspension of benefit for the purposes of this sub-paragraph.

Sub-para (1)(a)(iv). Under the 1977 Act, the Secretary of State may provide persons "suffering from a severe physical disability or defect" with such vehicles. Grants are also payable for "adapting, maintaining, repairing or insuring, paying road tax or providing a structure for a vehicle, or reimbursing duty paid in purchasing fuel for such a vehicle for a person suffering from a severe physical disability or defect".

The Secretary of State may also pay for driving lessons for a person with a severe physical disability or defect in order that s/he may drive the vehicle in question. The Scottish legislation is of the same effect as the English. Receipt of any assistance of this kind will mean that head (iv) is satisfied.

Sub-para (1)(a)(v) covers those who are blind and registered in a register as specified. Under sub-para (2), a person coming off the register is treated as fulfilling this condition for 28 weeks after her/his name is removed from the register.

Sub-para (1)(b) requires that the claimant is incapable of work for the purposes of the incapacity benefit legislation. Pursuant to Part 12A SSCBA, the question as to whether a claimant is, or is treated as, incapable for work is conclusively determined by the DWP decision maker. Therefore, if there is any dispute as to whether a claimant is incapable of work, it must be referred to the DWP even if the claimant is not claiming DWP benefits. A claimant who does not receive (and does not need to claim) DWP benefits (eg, IB or ESA) can apply for incapacity credits in order to obtain a determination that s/he is incapable of work which the local authority must then act upon. There would not appear to be anything in the HB regulations requiring such an application, which has implications for the question of entitlement to a disability premium under sub-para (1)(b) for a period starting on or after 27 October 2008. See below for a discussion. If the claimant does not want to claim either IB or ESA, and would not be better-off were s/he to qualify for one of the components in Part 5 (see p530 for a discussion), s/he should write to the DWP stating s/he wants the Secretary of State to assess her/his capacity for work under Part 12A SSCBA for the purposes of HB disability premium.

The claimant must be incapable or so treated for 365 days. The period is reduced to 196 days in the case of a claimant who is terminally ill. It seems that the question of whether someone is terminally ill must be resolved by the local authority and not by the DWP decision maker. By SSCBA s30B(4), "a person is terminally ill if he suffers from a progressive disease and his death in consequence of that disease can reasonably be expected within 6 months."

A prisoner may remain incapable of work. Serving as a prisoner prevents receipt of IB but does not deem her/him to be capable of work: *CIS 15611/1996.*

Once a claimant has qualified for a disability premium under sub-para (1)(b), there are deeming provisions that protect entitlement to the premium:

(1)   A period where the claimant is capable of work for eight weeks or less does not prevent the claimant satisfying this provision: sub-para (3). In the case of a "welfare to work beneficiary" (see below), this period is extended to 104 weeks: sub-para (8).

(2)   A claimant is treated as satisfying the conditions during a period spent undertaking training under the Employment and Training Act 1973 or in receipt of a training allowance (see reg 2(1) for a definition): sub-para (5).

(3)   A break in a period of incapacity of not more than 56 days is ignored: sub-para (6). In the case of a "welfare to work beneficiary" (see below), this period is extended to 104 weeks: sub-para (8).

Note the transitional protection in Sch 3 para 2 of the HB&CTB(CP) (see p1197).

From 27 October 2008 income support awarded "on the grounds of disability", IB and SDA were replaced with employment and support allowance (ESA). Under the Employment and Support Allowance (Transitional Provisions) Regulations 2008 SI No.795 and the Income Support (Prescribed Categories of Person) Regulations 2009 No.3152, people can still qualify for IS "on the grounds of disability", IB and SDA after 27 October 2008 in limited circumstances. However, if a claim is made for a period starting on or after 27 October 2008, the claim will generally be treated as a claim for ESA. There are a number of exceptions to the rule – eg, where the claim can be linked to a previous claim or where the claimant is a "welfare to work beneficiary".

For HB, if a claimant qualifies for the disability premium on the basis of incapacity for work before 27 October 2008, s/he will continue to do so at least until s/he is entitled to ESA or NI credits on the basis of *limited capability for work* (see sub-para (9) and the discussion on maximising entitlement). However, to enable the transitional provisions for IS, IB and SDA to continue, s67 and Sch 8 WRA 2007, which repeal ss171A to 171G SSCBA (ie, Part 12A SSCBA) have not yet been brought into force. This suggests that for HB, a claimant could still be, or could still be treated as, incapable of work, even where the issue arises for the first time on or after 27 October 2008 – ie, where s/he does not make a claim for ESA.

Note that those claiming IS "on the grounds of disability", IB and SDA will be assessed and, if they qualify, transferred to ESA at some point between 1 October 2010 and the end of March 2014. HB claimants who (or whose partners) are then entitled to "converted employment and support allowance" (defined in reg 2(1) as ESA which is not income-related and to which there is entitlement as a result of a "conversion decision", broadly ESA paid to those transferred from IS "on the grounds of disability", IB or SDA) will qualify for a component instead of a disability premium. As discussed below, in some cases, the HB entitlement of those who qualify for a disability premium is more generous than the HB entitlement of those who qualify for a component. To ensure a claimant is no worse off if s/he (or her/his partner) is entitled to converted ESA, or in specified circumstances is appealing a conversion decision, s/he may also be entitled to a protected amount of HB (and CTB) – a transitional addition: Sch 3 Parts 7 and 8.

Sub-para (8): welfare to work beneficiaries. A welfare to work beneficiary is someone falling within the scope of reg 13A(1) Social Security (Incapacity for Work) (General) Regulations 1995, which prescribes four conditions. First, the claimant must have been incapable of work for more than 196 days. Secondly, s/he must have stopped receiving the benefit s/he was receiving as a result of the incapacity (eg, IB or IS) on or after 5 October 1998. Thirdly, s/he must have commenced remunerative work or a training course for which training allowance is received within a month of benefit ceasing. Once a claimant then becomes incapable of work again, s/he is a welfare to work beneficiary for the purposes of this Schedule. For further information, see CPAG's *Welfare Benefits and Tax Credits Handbook.*

In cases of doubt, seek clarification from the DWP as to whether a claimant has acquired this status. However, it would appear that it is for the local authority and not the DWP to decide whether this condition is met for HB and CTB purposes (although the decision as to whether a claimant is incapable of work is made by the DWP: see above).

Sub-para (9). Under sub-para (9), a claimant is not entitled to a disability premium if s/he has, or is treated as having, limited capability for work (defined in reg 2(1) as having the meaning given in s1(4) of the WRA 2007). This is one of the basic conditions of entitlement to ESA, and to NI credits where the claimant is not fit for work. A claimant who has (or is treated as having) limited capability for work may instead be entitled to a work-related activity component or a support component: paras 21 to 26.

Note that sub-para (9) does *not* disentitle a claimant to the disability premium if it is only her/his *partner* who has, or is treated as having, limited capability for work. See below for a discussion of the potential effect of this.

Sub-para (9) applies even if a claimant would otherwise qualify for the disability premium on a ground not related to fitness for work – eg, under para 13(1)(a)(ii) on the basis of her/his (or her/his partner's) entitlement to DLA or under para 13(1)(a)(v) because s/he (or her/his partner) is registered blind.

For the position of those claiming IS "on grounds of disability", IB or SDA from 27 October 2008, see the discussion above. See also the commentary to sub-para (1)(b).

Maximising entitlement. On the face of it, the situation would appear to be straightforward: if a HB claimant is incapable of work for the purposes of incapacity benefit legislation, s/he qualifies for a disability premium under para 13(1)(b); if s/he has limited capability for work for the purposes of ESA legislation, s/he qualifies for a work-related activity component or a support component under paras 23 and 24. However, because (currently) the disability premium for a single claimant is higher in value than the work-related activity component, but lower in value than the support component, and because there is a higher rate of disability premium where the claimant is a member of a couple, but there is no couple rate of work-related activity component or support component, there are some important issues to bear in mind.

Unless a claimant is entitled to maximum HB because s/he or her/his partner is on IS, income-based JSA or income-related ESA, there are situations where consideration needs to be given to how the claimant can qualify for the highest rate of HB for her/him. If a single claimant is incapable of work, it may be beneficial not to claim ESA (or not to apply for NI credits on the basis of limited capability for work), to avoid a determination that may result in her/him failing to qualify for, or losing entitlement to, a disability premium – ie, if s/he would only qualify for the work-related activity component and not the support component. In the case of couples, it is only if the *claimant* has (or is treated as having) limited capability for work that there is no entitlement to the disability premium. It does not matter if the claimant's *partner* has (or is treated as having) limited capability for work. It may therefore be beneficial for a couple to consider which member should be the HB claimant if this would mean they would qualify for a disability premium (instead of a work-related component or a support component) – eg, if only one member of the couple (person A) has (or is treated as having) limited capability for work and receives DLA. In this case, if the other member of the couple (person B) claims HB, s/he qualifies for a disability premium at the rate for a couple under paras 13(1)(a)(i) and 20(5)(b). Note that where someone is on IS "on grounds of disability, IB or SDA, s/he will be assessed and, if s/he qualifies, transferred to ESA at some point between 1 October 2010 and the end of March 2014. When this happens, if s/he is an HB claimant, s/he will no longer qualify for a disability premium but will qualify for a component and possibly a transitional addition: Sch 3 Parts 5 to 8.

It is important to take the following into account.

(1)   The personal allowance of a single claimant under 25, a lone parent under 18 or a member of a couple both under 18 increases when the claimant is "entitled to main phase ESA": see paras 1 and 1A. Note,

however, that a claimant will normally only count as entitled to main phase ESA after what is known as the "assessment phase" (the first 13 weeks after a claim for ESA or NI credits).

(2)   Based on the 2010/2011 benefit rates, the amount of the disability premium for a single claimant is higher than the work-related activity component, but lower than the support component. However, the amount of the disability premium for a couple is higher than both components.

(3)   If a claimant qualifies for a support component, s/he also qualifies for an enhanced disability premium under para 15. Otherwise, to qualify for that premium for her/himself or her/his partner, the claimant or the partner must be aged less than the qualifying age for PC and qualify for the highest rate DLA care component.

(4)   A claimant cannot qualify for a disability premium if s/he has, or is treated as having, limited capability for work – ie, if s/he has qualified for ESA or NI credits on the basis of limited capability for work: para 13(9). This applies even if the claimant might qualify for a disability premium on grounds other than limited capability for work – eg, where s/he or her/his partner is receiving DLA. However, s/he also cannot qualify for either the work-related activity component or the support component until one of the conditions in para 21(c) is met, that is, when the "assessment phase" has ended, unless the claimant (or her his partner) is someone who can qualify for a component before it has ended. So potentially, there is a period during which HB will be calculated with neither the disability premium, nor one of the components.

(5)   Where both the claimant and her/his partner satisfy the conditions for a component, the component to be included is that to which the *claimant* is entitled, even if the partner qualifies for a higher rate component: para 22(2).

(6)   It may be important for the claimant to apply for NI credits. These help claimants satisfy the contribution conditions for certain contributory benefits. See CPAG's *Welfare Benefits and Tax Credits Handbook* for details.

Note: the claimant and her/his partner may need to consider swapping the claimant role to ensure entitlement to the highest possible rate of HB. It will be important to bear in mind not just issues in respect of maximising entitlement, but also whether any of the various forms of transitional protection will be lost.

Severe Disability Premium

14.–(1)   The condition is that the claimant is a severely disabled person.

(2)   For the purposes of sub-paragraph (1), a claimant shall be treated as being a severely disabled person if, and only if–

(a)   in the case of a single claimant, a lone parent or a claimant who is treated as having no partner in consequence of sub-paragraph (3)–

    (i)   he is in receipt of attendance allowance, or the care component of disability living allowance at the highest or middle rate prescribed in accordance with section 72(3) of the Act; and

    (ii)   subject to sub-paragraph (4), he has no non-dependants aged 18 or over normally residing with him or with whom he is normally residing; and

    (iii)   no person is entitled to, and in receipt of, a carer's allowance under section 70 of the Act in respect of caring for him;

(b)   in the case of a claimant who has a partner–

    (i)   the claimant is in receipt of attendance allowance, or the care component of disability living allowance at the highest or middle rate prescribed in accordance with section 72(3) of the Act; and

    (ii)   his partner is also in receipt of such an allowance or, if he is a member of a polygamous marriage, all the partners of that marriage are in receipt of such an allowance; and

    (iii)   subject to sub-paragraph (4), the claimant has no non-dependants aged 18 or over normally residing with him or with whom he is normally residing,

and either a person is [² entitled to and in receipt of a carer's allowance] in respect of caring for only one of a couple or, in the case of a polygamous marriage, for one or more but not all the partners of the marriage, or as the case may be, no person is entitled to and in receipt of such an allowance in respect of caring for either member of a couple or any partner of a polygamous marriage.

(3)   Where a claimant has a partner who does not satisfy the condition in sub-paragraph (2)(b)(ii), and that partner is blind or is treated as blind within the meaning of paragraph 13(1)(a)(v) and (2), that partner shall be treated for the purposes of sub-paragraph (2) as if he were not a partner of the claimant.

(4)   For the purposes of sub-paragraph (2)(a)(ii) and (2)(b)(iii) no account shall be taken of–

(a)   a person receiving attendance allowance, or the care component of disability living allowance at the highest or middle rate prescribed in accordance with section 72(3) of the Act; or

(b)   a person who is blind or is treated as blind within the meaning of paragraph 13(1)(a)(v) and (2).

(5)   For the purposes of sub-paragraph (2)(b) a person shall be treated–

(a)   as being in receipt of attendance allowance, or the care component of disability living allowance at the highest or middle rate prescribed in accordance with section 72(3) of the Act, if he would, but for his being a patient for a period exceeding 28 days, be so in receipt;

(b)   as being entitled to and in receipt of a carer's allowance if he would, but for the person for whom he was caring being a patient in hospital for a period exceeding 28 days, be so entitled and in receipt.

(6)   For the purposes of sub-paragraph (2)(a)(iii) and (2)(b), no account shall be taken of an award of carer's allowance to the extent that payment of such an award is backdated for a period before [¹ the date on which the award is first paid].

(7)   In sub-paragraph (2)(a)(iii) and (b), references to a person being in receipt of a carer's allowance shall include references to a person who would have been in receipt of that allowance but for the application of a restriction under section [³ 6B or] 7 of the Social Security Fraud Act 2001 (loss of benefit provisions).

Amendments

1.   Amended by reg 6(6) of SI 2007 No 719 as from 2.4.07.
2.   Amended by reg 6(10(c) of SI 2009 No 583 as from 6.4.09.
3.   Amended by reg 4 of SI 2010 No 1160 as from 1.4.10.

Analysis

To qualify for the severe disability premium, the claimant must be a "severely disabled person": sub-para (1). The claimant may be treated as such only in accordance with the terms of sub-para (2). See also the General Note to Part 3 of this Schedule (on p524).

Sub-para (2)(a) applies to single claimants and lone parents. It also applies to a claimant who is treated as having no partner under sub-para (3). There are three criteria, all of which must be fulfilled.

(1)   The claimant must be in receipt of attendance allowance (AA) or the care component of disability living allowance (DLA) at the highest or middle rate. Note the deeming provisions in paras 18 and 19 relating to receipt and payment of benefit. AA is defined in reg 2(1) and includes constant attendance allowance and exceptionally severe disablement allowance (or equivalent war pension).

(2)   There are no non-dependants living with her/him. For the meaning of "non-dependant" and "normally resides" see reg 3. Note that if such people are themselves receiving AA or highest or middle rate DLA care component or are blind or treated as blind for the purposes of para 13(1)(a)(v) and (2) then they are ignored: sub-para (4).

(3)   No one is entitled to and in receipt of carer's allowance (CA) in respect of caring for him/her. As with criterion (2), certain disabled people are ignored under sub-para (4). Backdated CA will not count: sub-para (6).

Sub-para (2)(b) applies to claimants with partners. There are four criteria which must be fulfilled. The claimant must satisfy the first two of the criteria listed under sub-para (2)(a) above: sub-paras (2)(b)(i) and (iii). In addition:

(1)   The partner, or all the parties to a polygamous marriage, must also be in receipt of AA or highest or middle rate DLA care component. Again, note the deeming provisions in paras 18 and 19 relating to receipt and payment of benefit.

(2)   Either someone is entitled to and in receipt of CA in respect of caring for only one member of the couple (or one but not all the members of a polygamous marriage) or no one is entitled to and in receipt of CA for either (or any) partner.

For the purposes of sub-para (2)(b) (ie, for a claimant with a partner), suspension of payment of AA or DLA due to the disabled person becoming a "patient" is ignored: sub-para (5). Likewise, any carer is treated as receiving CA if s/he would have been entitled to and receiving it, but for the fact that the disabled person has been a patient for longer than 28 days. This means that if someone is in receipt of CA for only one member of a couple (or polygamous marriage) or a claimant satisfies the conditions in sub-para (2)(b) only because of sub-para (5), a severe disability premium is included in the claimant's applicable amount at the single person's rate: para 20(6)(b)(i). Again, backdated CA is ignored: sub-para (6).

For the purposes of sub-paras (2)(a)(iii) and (b), a claimant's entitlement to the severe disability premium is only affected if a person is both entitled to *and* in receipt of CA, although, note that under sub-para (7), someone is treated as in receipt of CA if s/he would have been in receipt but for the "loss of benefit" provisions cited. So where the person is *not* receiving CA because s/he receives another "overlapping benefit" (sometimes known as an "underlying entitlement"), the claimant's entitlement to the severe disability premium is not affected. For the overlapping benefit rules, see the Social Security (Overlapping Benefits) Regulations 1979 SI No.597 (as amended). The benefits which overlap with CA are contribution-based JSA, contributory ESA, maternity allowance, incapacity benefit, retirement pension, widow's or bereavement benefits, severe disablement allowance and training allowances.

Sub-para (3). Under sub-para (3), where a claimant's partner is not in receipt of AA or highest or middle rate DLA care component, but is blind for the purposes of para 13(1)(a)(v) and (2), s/he is treated as not the claimant's partner for the purpose of sub-para (2). Note that, in practical terms, in order to qualify for a severe disability premium where one member of a couple is in receipt of a relevant benefit and the other is blind, the one who is in receipt of the benefit should be the HB claimant.

Enhanced disability premium

15.–[² (1)   Subject to sub-paragraph (2), the condition is that–

[³ (a)   the Secretary of State has decided that the claimant has, or is to be treated as having, limited capability for work-related activity; or]

(b)   the care component of disability living allowance is, or would, but for a suspension of benefit in accordance with regulations made under section 113(2) of the Act or but for an abatement as a consequence of hospitalisation be payable at the highest rate prescribed under section 72(3) of the Act in respect of–

     (i)   the claimant; or

     (ii)   a member of the claimant's family,

who [⁵ has not attained the qualifying age for state pension credit].]

(2)   An enhanced disability premium shall not be applicable in respect of–

(a)   a claimant who–

     (i)   is not a member of a couple or a polygamous marriage; and

     (ii)   is a patient within the meaning of [¹ regulation 28(11)(e)] and has been for a period of more than 52 weeks; or

(b)   a member of a couple or a polygamous marriage where each member is a patient within the meaning of [⁴ regulation 28(11)(e)] and has been for a period of more than 52 weeks.

Amendments

1.   Amended by reg 2(15)(c) of SI 2005 No 2502 as amended by Sch 2 para 27 of SI 2006 No 217 as from 1.4.06 (3.4.06 where rent payable weekly or at intervals of a week).
2.   Substituted by reg 23(c) of SI 2008 No 1082 as from 27.10.08.
3.   Substituted by reg 31(b) of SI 2008 No 2428 as from 27.10.08.
4.   Amended by reg 6(8) of SI 2008 No 2767 as from 17.11.08.
5.   Amended by reg 26(3) of SI 2009 No 1488 as from 6.4.10.

Analysis

The enhanced disability premium is included where either the Secretary of State has decided that the claimant has, or is to be treated as having, limited capability for work-related activity (defined in reg 2 as having the meaning given in s2(5) WRA 2007) or the highest rate of the care component of DLA is "payable" to the claimant or a member of her/his family who is under the qualifying age for PC (defined in reg 2(1)) (ie, a partner or child) or would be but for a stay in hospital. It is suggested that "payable" here must mean entitled to (or entitled to be paid) DLA, but does not necessarily mean that it is actually in payment. Note also the deeming provisions in paras 18 and 19 relating to receipt and payment of benefit.

    If the claimant is single, the enhanced disability premium is not applicable where s/he is a hospital in-patient, and has been for more than 52 weeks. See p352 for a discussion on the meaning of "patient". If the claimant is a member of a couple or of a polygamous marriage, the enhanced disability premium remains applicable unless both members of the couple or every member of the polygamous marriage are patients and have been so for more than 52 weeks. Note, however, that the claimant and partner may no longer count as a couple for HB purposes where one of them has been absent from the home for more than 52 weeks (see reg 21).

    For a discussion on maximising entitlement to HB, see p530.

Disabled child premium

16.   The condition is that a child or young person for whom the claimant or a partner of his is responsible and who is a member of the claimant's household–

(a)   is in receipt of disability living allowance or is no longer in receipt of such allowance because he is a patient, provided that the child or young person continues to be a member of the family; or

(b)   is blind or treated as blind within the meaning of paragraph 13; or

(c)   is a child or young person in respect of whom section 145A of the Act (entitlement to child benefit after death of child) applies for the purposes of entitlement to child benefit but only for the period prescribed under section 145A(1) of the Act and in respect of whom a disabled child premium was included in the claimant's applicable amount immediately before the death of that child.

Analysis

To get disabled child premium, the claimant or her/his partner must be responsible for a child or qualifying young person who is a part of the claimant's household (see Part 4). One of three critera must be satisfied.

(1)   The child or young person must be in receipt of DLA, or no longer be in receipt because s/he is a patient. In the latter case, s/he must still be a member of the family (see p22).

(2)   The child or young person is blind (or treated as blind) within the meaning in para 13.

(3)   The child or young person has died, the claimant was getting the disabled child premium immediately before the death and child benefit is paid for the child following the death. This only applies for a period of eight weeks.

Carer premium

17.–(1)   The condition is that the claimant or his partner is, or both of them are, entitled to a carer's allowance under section 70 of the Act.

(2)   Where a carer premium is awarded but–

(a)   the person in respect of whose care the carer's allowance has been awarded dies; or

(b)   in any other case the person in respect of whom a carer premium has been awarded ceases to be entitled to a carer's allowance,

the condition for the award of the premium shall be treated as satisfied for a period of eight weeks from the relevant date specified in sub-paragraph (3).

(3)   The relevant date for the purposes of sub-paragraph (2) shall be–

(a)   where sub-paragraph (2)(a) applies, the Sunday following the death of the person in respect of whose care a carer's allowance has been awarded or the date of death if the death occurred on a Sunday;

(b)   in any other case, the date on which the person who has been entitled to a carer's allowance ceases to be entitled to that allowance.

(4)   Where a person who has been entitled to a carer's allowance ceases to be entitled to that allowance and makes a claim for housing benefit, the condition for the award of the carer premium shall be treated as satisfied for a period of eight weeks from the date on which–

(a)   the person in respect of whose care the carer's allowance has been awarded dies;

(b)   in any other case, the person who has been entitled to a carer's allowance ceased to be entitled to that allowance.

Analysis

To qualify for the carer premium the claimant or her/his partner must be entitled to carer's allowance (CA). See also the General Note to Part 3 of this Schedule (on p524) and the Analysis of para 7(2) (on p526).

A carer premium is applicable even if the claimant or her/his partner is not actually receiving CA – ie, s/he already receives another "overlapping' benefit". This is sometimes referred to as "underlying entitlement" to CA. For the overlapping benefit rules, see the Social Security (Overlapping Benefits) Regulations 1979 SI No.597 (as amended). The benefits which overlap with CA are contribution-based JSA, contributory ESA, maternity allowance, incapacity benefit, retirement pension, widow's or bereavement benefits, severe disablement allowance and training allowances. It is important to note that for someone to be entitled to CA, a claim must be made: s1 SSAA. GM BW3.271 points out that claimants with an underlying entitlement to CA are notified by the DWP's CA Unit of that fact.

The premium is payable for each person who satisfies the condition, so both the claimant and her/his partner may qualify: para 20(8).

Where a carer is paid CA, the person being cared for might not be able to qualify for a severe disability premium. Careful benefit advice is therefore needed before a claim for CA is made.

Sub-paras (2), (3) and (4) allow entitlement to the premium to continue for eight weeks after caring or entitlement to CA ceases. This also applies where the person being cared for has died. The eight weeks runs from the same day if the death occurs on a Sunday and from the following Sunday if occurring on another day.

Persons in receipt of concessionary payments

18.   For the purpose of determining whether a premium is applicable to a person under paragraphs 13 to 17, any concessionary payment made to compensate that person for the non-payment of any benefit mentioned in those paragraphs shall be treated as if it were a payment of that benefit.

Analysis

Under para 18, a concessionary payment to compensate for non-payment of a benefit must be treated as a payment of that benefit. It has been suggested in previous editions that payment from non-governmental sources would suffice but that is not correct: see the definition of "concessionary payment" in reg 2(1) on p210.

Where a concessionary payment is "treated as if it were a payment of that benefit" under para 18, the benefit would be "payable" for the purpose of para 15 and a person would be "in receipt" of the benefit for the purposes of paras 13, 14 and 16. However, in para 17 the issue is whether someone is "entitled to" a benefit. It is suggested that where a payment is made in the circumstances set out in para 18, there has been a concession that there was an entitlement to the benefit concerned.

Person in receipt of benefit

19.   For the purposes of this Part of this Schedule, a person shall be regarded as being in receipt of any benefit if, and only if, it is paid in respect of him and shall be so regarded only for any period in respect of which that benefit is paid.

Analysis

This clarifies what it means to be "in receipt of" benefit, a concept that occurs in several places in Part 3 – eg, paras 13 to 16. It was added to reverse: *R(SB) 12/87*. Under para 19, a person is "in receipt" of benefit only if it is actually paid in respect of her/him. The words "in respect of" mean that it does not have to be paid *to* her/him: it might be paid to an appointee. However, the person "in receipt" is the one who is entitled to the benefit. So, for example, where a claimant is entitled to attendance allowance (AA) but it is being paid to another person on her/his behalf, it is the claimant who is "in receipt" of the AA, not the other person.

PART 4
Amounts of premiums specified in Part 3

Premium	Amount
20.–[⁴ (1)]	[⁴ (1)].
[⁶ (2)]	[⁶ (2)]
[⁶ (3)]	[⁶ (3)]
[⁶ (4)]	[⁶ (4)]
(5) Disability Premium–	(5)
(a) where the claimant satisfies the condition in paragraph 12(a);	(a) [⁸ £28.00];
(b) where the claimant satisfies the condition in paragraph 12(b).	(b) [⁸ £39.85].
(6) Severe Disability Premium–	(6)
(a) where the claimant satisfies the condition in paragraph 14(2)(a);	(a) [⁸ £53.65];
(b) where the claimant satisfies the condition in paragraph 14(2)(b)–	
(i) in a case where there is someone in receipt of carer's allowance or if he or any partner satisfies that condition only by virtue of paragraph 14(5);	(b) (i) [⁸ £53.65];
(ii) in a case where there is no one in receipt of such an allowance.	(b) (ii) [⁸ £107.30].
(7) Disabled Child Premium.	(7) [⁸ £52.08] in respect of each child or young person in respect of whom the condition specified in paragraph 16 of Part 3 of this Schedule is satisfied.
(8) Carer Premium.	(8) [⁸ £30.05] in respect of each person who satisfies the condition specified in paragraph 17.
(9) Enhanced Disability Premium [⁹].	(9) (a) [⁸ £21.00] in respect of each child or young person in respect of whom the conditions specified in paragraph 15 are satisfied;
	(b) [⁸ £13.65] in respect of each person who is neither–
	(i) a child or young person; nor
	(ii) a member of a couple or a polygamous marriage,
	in respect of whom the conditions specified in paragraph 15 are satisfied;
	(c) [⁸ £19.65] where the claimant is a member of a couple or a polygamous marriage and the conditions specified in paragraph 15 are satisfied in respect of a member of that couple or polygamous marriage.

Amendments

1. Amended by Art 19(8) and Sch 7 of SI 2006 No 645 and reg 8 of SI 2006 No 217 as from 1.4.06 (3.4.06 where rent payable weekly or at intervals of a week).
2. Confirmed by Art 19(8) and Sch 7 of SI 2007 No 688 as from 1.4.07 (2.4.07 where rent payable weekly or at intervals of a week).
3. Amended by Art 19(8) and Sch 7 of SI 2007 No 688 as from 1.4.07 (2.4.07 where rent payable weekly or at intervals of a week).
4. Revoked by reg 2 and the Sch of SI 2007 No 2618 as from 1.10.07.
5. Amended by Art 19(9) and Sch 7 of SI 2008 No 632 as from 1.4.08 (7.4.08 where rent payable weekly or in multiples of a week).
6. Omitted by reg 3(10)(i) of SI 2008 No 1042 as from 19.5.08.
7. Amended by Art 19(9) and Sch 6 of SI 2009 No 497 as from 1.4.09 (6.4.09 where rent payable weekly or in multiples of a week).

8. Amended by Art 19(8) and Sch 6 of SI 2010 No 793 as from 1.4.10 (5.4.10 where rent payable weekly or in multiples of a week).
9. Amended by reg 2(8)(b) of Si 2010 No 2449 as from 1.11.10.

Analysis
This simply quantifies the appropriate amounts for the premiums set out in Part 3.

[¹ PART 5

Amendment
1. Inserted by reg 23(d) of SI 2008 No 1082, as substituted by reg 31(c) of SI 2008 No 2428, as from 27.10.08.

General Note to Part 5
This Part sets out the rules under which a claimant may qualify to have one of two "components" included in her/his applicable amount: see regs 22(e) and 23(f). These components are only relevant where the claimant or her/his partner has, or is treated as having, limited capability for work under the ESA legislation. Paras 21, 21A and 22 set out some general rules governing entitlement to a component; there can only be entitlement to one of the components and not both. Paras 23 and 24 set out the specific rules relating to entitlement to the work-related activity component and the support component respectively.

Note that where there is an award of HB and a "qualifying benefit" (eg, ESA) is later awarded or reinstated regs 4(7B) and (7C), 7(2)(i) and 8(14) D&A Regs effectively allow for backdating of entitlement to components which depend on entitlement to (or receipt of) that qualifying benefit, for the period for which arrears of that benefit are paid – see the commentary to those provisions. Note also regs 7(2)(o) and 8(14D) D&A Regs where subsequent to the first day of entitlement to HB or CTB, the Secretary of State decides that the claimant or her/his partner has, or is to be treated as having, limited capability for work.

There may also be entitlement to a transitional addition if the claimant is on contributory ESA following being transferred from IS "on grounds of disability", IB or SDA: Sch 3 Parts 7 and 8.

The components
21. Subject to paragraph 22, the claimant is entitled to one, but not both, of the components in paragraphs 23 or 24 if–
(a) the claimant or the claimant's partner has made a claim for employment and support allowance;
(b) the Secretary of State has decided that the claimant or the claimant's partner has, or is to be treated as having, limited capability for work or limited capability for work-related activity; and
(c) either–
(i) the assessment phase as defined in section 24(2) of the Welfare Reform Act has ended; or
(ii) regulation 7 of the Employment and Support Allowance Regulations (circumstances where the condition that the assessment phase has ended before entitlement to the support component or the work related activity component arises does not apply) applies.
[¹**21A.** Subject to paragraph 22, the claimant is entitled to one, but not both, of the components in paragraphs 23 or 24 if the claimant or the claimant's partner is entitled to a converted employment and support allowance.]

Amendment
1. Inserted by reg 27 and Sch 5 para 1(5)(b) of SI 2010 No 1907 as amended by reg 15 of SI 2010 No 2430 as from 1.10.10.

22.–(1) The claimant has no entitlement under paragraph 23 or 24 if the claimant is entitled to the disability premium under paragraphs 12 and 13.
(2) Where the claimant and the claimant's partner each satisfies paragraph 23 or 24, the component to be included in the claimant's applicable amount is that which relates to the claimant.

Analysis to paras 21, 21A and 22
Under paras 21 and 21A, the claimant is entitled to one of the components in either para 23 or 24, but never both, if s/he or her/his partner satisfies the conditions.
Para 21. Under this para, the claimant or her/his parter must have made a claim for ESA and the Secretary of State must have decided that s/he or her/his partner has, or is to be treated as having, limited capability for work or limited capability for work-related activity (both defined in reg 2 by reference to the WRA 2007). Finally one of the following conditions must be met:

(1)   the "assessment phase" must have ended: sub-para (c)(i). The assessment phase is normally the first 13 weeks of entitlement to ESA, during which the claimant is paid ESA at a lower rate. During this phase, the DWP gathers further information relevant to the ESA claim (including assessing whether the claimant has "limited capability for work"). See CPAG's online service and the *Welfare Benefits and Tax Credits Handbook* for further details; *or*

(2)   the claimant must be someone to whom reg 7 of the Employment and Support Allowance Regulations (the ESA Regs) applies: sub-para (c)(ii). Reg 7 ESA Regs sets out situations when a claimant can qualify for a work-related activity component or support component before the end of the assessment phase – ie, if s/he is terminally ill, or where a period of limited capability for work is linked to an earlier one for which the assessment phase had ended.

Note that where neither of the two conditions above is yet met, there is no entitlement to a component, nor can there be entitlement to a disability premium – ie, where the claimant has claimed ESA (or applied for NI credits) and has, or is treated as having, limited capability for work: para 13(9). See p530 for a discussion.

The intention appears to be that a claimant can qualify for a component under para 21 if s/he (or her/his partner) does not qualify for ESA, but does qualify for NI credits for limited capability for work: explanatory memorandum to SI 2009 No.583. A claim for ESA must be made, but there is no requirement that the claimant (or partner) is entitled to that benefit. However, there is a question whether a claimant (or partner) getting NI credits only can satisfy the condition in sub-para (c)(i) if s/he or her/his partner is not entitled to ESA. The assessment phase cannot begin until the first day of entitlement to ESA: s24(2)(a) WRA. If it never begins, it cannot end.

Para 21A. Under this para, the claimant or her/his partner must be entitled to a "converted employment and support allowance". This is defined in reg 2(1) as ESA which is not income-related and to which there is entitlement as a result of a "conversion decision", broadly ESA paid to those transferred from IS "on the grounds of disability", IB or SDA. If a claimant is entitled to converted ESA, or in specified circumstances is appealing a conversion decision, s/he may also be entitled to protected amount of HB (and CTB) – a transitional addition: Sch 3 Parts 7 and 8.

Para 22. Both paras 21 and 21A are subject to para 22. Under para 22(1), there can be no entitlement to a component if the claimant is entitled to a disability premium (for which see paras 12 and 13 on p527 and the commentary). For example, where the claimant is receiving DLA and is capable of work and is therefore entitled to the disability premium, there would be no entitlement to a component, even if her/his partner has limited capability for work.

Where both the claimant and her/his partner satisfy the conditions for a component, the component to be included is that to which the claimant is entitled: para 22(2). This may mean that because the support component is of a higher value, the member of the couple who qualifies for that component should be the HB claimant. If a claimant and her/his partner are considering swapping the claiming role, it will be important to bear in mind not just issues in respect of maximising entitlement, but also whether any of the various forms of transitional protection would be lost.

See p528 for a discussion of other issues to consider in maximising entitlement to HB.

Note that the transitional protection leading to the higher rate family premium for lone parents is lost if a component under either para 23 or 24 is applicable: para 3(4)(e). In this case, the ordinary rate family premium is included.

The work-related activity component
23.   The claimant is entitled to the work-related activity component if the Secretary of State has decided that the claimant or the claimant's partner has, or is to be treated as having, limited capability for work.

The support component
24.   The claimant is entitled to the support component if the Secretary of State has decided that the claimant or the claimant's partner has, or is to be treated as having, limited capability for work-related activity.]

Analysis to paras 23 and 24
A claimant is entitled to a work-related activity component if the DWP has decided that either s/he or her/his partner has, or is to be treated as having, "limited capability for work" (defined in reg 2 by reference to s1(4) WRA 2007): para 23. This is one of the basic conditions of entitlement to ESA and to NI credits on new claims on or after 27 October 2008. However, entitlement to the component is initially precluded: see para 21(c). Limited capability for work is determined by the DWP by reference to reg 19 and Sch 2 of the Employment and Support Allowance Regulations 2008 SI No.794 (the ESA Regs). Claimants can be treated as having limited capability for work under regs 20 and 30 of the ESA Regs.

A higher rate of ESA is payable where the ESA claimant not only has limited capability for work, but has limited capability for work-related activity which makes it unreasonable to require the her/him to undertake such activity. This is determined by the DWP under reg 34 and Sch 3 of the ESA Regs. For HB purposes, this higher rate of ESA is offest by entitlement to the support component under para 24. A claimant is entitled to the support component if the DWP has decided that either s/he or her/his partner has limited capability for work-related activity.

Effectively all claimants who meet the conditions for the support component will also meet the conditions for the work-related activity component. However, a claimant is entitled to one, but not both, of the components: see para 21. The rules do not set out which component is applicable in this situation, but it is suggested that it is the support component.

Note that where the claimant's partner has limited capability for work but the claimant does not, the claimant may instead qualify for a disability premium under paras 12 and 13 – eg, if the claimant is receiving DLA or is incapable of work under the incapacity benefit legislation. See the commentary to para 13 on p530 for a discussion of some financial implications.

[¹ PART 6
Amount of components
25.   The amount of the work-related activity component is [³ £25.95].
26.   The amount of the support component is [³ £31.40].]

Amendments
1.   Inserted by reg 23(d) of SI 2008 No 1082, as substituted by reg 31(c) of SI 2008 No2428, as from 27.10.08.
2.   Amended by Art 19(10) of SI 2009 No 497 as from 1.4.09 (6.4.09 where rent payable weekly or in multiples of a week).
3.   Amended by Art 19(9) of SI 2010 No 793 as from 1.4.10 (5.4.10 where rent payable weekly or in multiples of a week).

Analysis
Paras 25 and 26 simply quantify the appropriate amounts for the components set out in Part 5.

[¹ PART 7

Amendment
1.   Inserted by reg 27 and Sch 5 para 1(5)(c) of SI 2010 No 1907 as amended by reg 15 of SI 2010 No 2430 as from 1.10.10.

General Note to part 7
Income support awarded "on the grounds of disability", incapacity benefit (IB) and severe disablement benefit (SDA) were replaced with employment and support allowance (ESA) on new claims from 27 October 2008. Under the Employment and Support Allowance (Transitional Provisions) Regulations 2008 SI No.795 and the Income Support (Prescribed Categories of Person) Regulations 2009 No.3152, people can still qualify for IS "on the grounds of disability", IB and SDA after that date in limited circumstances.

Those claiming IS "on the grounds of disability", IB and SDA will be assessed for and, if they qualify, transferred to ESA at some point between October 2010 and the end of March 2014. HB claimants who (or whose partners) are then entitled to "converted employment and support allowance" will qualify for a component instead of a disability premium. HB entitlement for those who qualify for a disability premium can in some cases be more generous than HB entitlement for those who qualify for a component. See p530 for a discussion of the issues. To ensure that a claimant continues to qualify for the same rate of HB as before the transfer to ESA, or in specified circumstances while s/he or her/his partner is appealing a conversion decision, s/he may be entitled to a protected amount of HB (and CTB) – a transitional addition under Part 7.

Para 27 sets out the rules of entitlement to a transitional addition and when the entitlement ends.
Para 28 provides a linking rule where there is a break in entitlement to HB.
Para 29 provides a linking rule where there is a break in entitlement to ESA.

Note that in all cases, entitlement to a transitional addition will end on 5 April 2020 if it has not already ended before that date.

The amount of the transitional addition is calculated under Part 8.

Transitional Addition
27.–(1)   The claimant is entitled to the transitional addition calculated in accordance with paragraph 30 where the claimant or the claimant's partner (''the relevant person'')–
(a)   is entitled to a converted employment and support allowance; or
(b)   is appealing a conversion decision as described in regulation 5(2)(b) of the Employment and Support Allowance (Existing Awards) Regulations and–

    (i)   is treated as having limited capability for work by virtue of regulation 30 of the Employment and Support Allowance Regulations as modified by the Employment and Support Allowance (Existing Awards) Regulations; and
    (ii)   is not in receipt of an income-related employment and support allowance,
unless the amount of the transitional addition calculated in accordance with paragraph 30 would be nil.
    (2)   The claimant's entitlement to a transitional addition by virtue of this paragraph ends on any of the following–
    (a)   the reduction of the transitional addition to nil in accordance with paragraph 31;
    (b)   the termination of the claimant's award of housing benefit;
    (c)   the relevant person ceasing to meet the requirements of sub-paragraph (1)(a) or (b), as the case may be;
    (d)   the claimant or the claimant's partner becoming entitled to an income-related employment and support allowance, an income-based jobseeker's allowance or income support;
    (e)   5th April 2020.

Analysis
Sub-para (1). An HB claimant can qualify for a transitional addition in two circumstances.
(1)   S/he or her/his partner is entitled to a "converted employment and support allowance": sub-para (1)(a). Converted ESA is defined in reg 2(1) as ESA to which there is entitlement as a result of a "conversion decision" (broadly ESA that is not income-related, paid to those transferred from IS "on the grounds of disability", incapacity benefit or severe disablement allowance).
(2)   S/he or her/his partner is appealing a conversion decision: sub-para (1)(b). In this case, the claimant or partner must be treated as having limited capability for work pending the appeal – ie, by providing medical evidence of limited capability for work. In addition, s/he must not be receiving income-related ESA. Note that where someone is appealing a conversion decision, if entitled, ESA is paid at the assessment phase rate – ie, without a work-related activity component or a support component.
There is no entitlement to a transitional addition if the claimant (or her/his partner) is entitled to converted *income-related* ESA, or is receiving income-related ESA while appealing a conversion decision. In such cases a transitional addition is not needed as someone entitled to income-related ESA has passported entitlement to maximum HB under reg 70 without reference to an applicable amount.
Sub-para (2). Entitlement to the transitional addition ends if any of the circumstances listed in sub-para (2)(a) to (d) occur, or on 5 April 2020 if none have occurred before that date. There are linking rules in paras 28 and 29 that may revive entitlement to a transitional addition where there is a break in entitlement to HB or to ESA.

28.–(1)   This paragraph applies where–
    (a)   the claimant's entitlement to a transitional addition ends, by virtue of the termination of the claimant's award of housing benefit, under–
    (i)   paragraph 27(2)(b);
    (ii)   sub-paragraph (3)(b) of this paragraph; or
    (iii)   paragraph 29(3)(b);
    (b)   within 104 weeks of that termination but before 5th April 2020 the claimant again becomes entitled to housing benefit;
    (c)   in the benefit week in which the claimant again becomes entitled to housing benefit the relevant person is entitled to an employment and support allowance which is not income-related;
    (d)   if the period between the events mentioned in paragraphs (a) and (b) is more than 12 weeks, the intervening period is one to which regulation 145(2) (linking period where claimant is a work or training beneficiary) of the Employment and Support Allowance Regulations applies in respect of the relevant person; and
    (e)   at the date on which the claimant again becomes entitled to housing benefit, neither the claimant nor the claimant's partner is entitled to an income-related employment and support allowance, an income-based jobseeker's allowance or income support.
    (2)   Where this paragraph applies, the claimant is entitled, with effect from the day on which the claimant again becomes entitled to housing benefit, to a transitional addition of the amount of the transitional addition that would have applied had the claimant's entitlement to a transitional addition not ended (but taking account of the effect which any intervening change of circumstances would have had by virtue of paragraph 31), unless the amount of the transitional addition would be nil.
    (3)   The claimant's entitlement to a transitional addition by virtue of this paragraph ends on any of the following–
    (a)   the reduction of the transitional addition to nil in accordance with paragraph 31;
    (b)   the termination of the claimant's award of housing benefit;
    (c)   the relevant person no longer being entitled to the employment and support allowance referred to in sub-paragraph (1)(c);
    (d)   the claimant or the claimant's partner becoming entitled to an income-related employment and support allowance, an income-based jobseeker's allowance or income support;
    (e)   5th April 2020.

Analysis

Sub-para (1). Para 28 provides a linking rule where a claimant's entitlement to a transitional addition ends under para 27(2)(b), para 28(3)(b) or para 29(3)(b) – ie, because her/his award of HB terminated. S/he will be entitled to a transitional addition again if the conditions in sub-para (1)(b) to (e) are satisfied. The effect of these is as follows:

(1) The original claimant must become entitled to HB again before 5 April 2020 and within twelve weeks of the termination of her/his award of HB (104 weeks if it is a linking period during which the "relevant person" is a "work or training beneficiary"): sub-para (1)(a), (b), and (d). The "relevant person" is the person who is entitled to converted ESA or is appealing a conversion decision – ie, the claimant or her/his partner as the case may be: para 27(1). Broadly, someone counts as a "work or training beneficiary" during a linking period of up to 104 weeks between two periods of limited capability for work, when s/he is in work or training: regs 145(2) and 148 ESA Regs.

(2) The "relevant person" must be entitled to ESA which is not income-related in the benefit week in which entitlement to HB begins again: sub-para (1)(c).

(3) Neither the claimant nor her/his partner can be entitled to IS, income-based JSA or income-related ESA on the date entitlement to HB begins again: sub-para (e).

Note that this linking rule can only apply if the person claiming HB when entitlement begins again is the person who was claiming HB before the award terminated: see the wording of sub-para (1)(b). For this reason, careful consideration needs to be given to the financial implications before the claimant and her/his partner swap the claimant role.

Sub-para (2). The amount of the transitional addition that applies is the amount that would have applied had entitlement to the addition not ended, taking into account any changes that would have decreased that transitional addition under para 31.

Sub-para (3). Entitlement to the transitional addition ends if any of the circumstances listed in sub-para (3)(a) to (d) occur, or on 5 April 2020 if none have occurred before that date. Note that where there is a break in entitlement to ESA or the HB award is terminated again, the linking rules both in this para and in para 29 may still apply.

29.–(1) This paragraph applies where–

(a) the claimant's entitlement to a transitional addition ends, by virtue of the relevant person ceasing to be entitled to an employment and support allowance, under–

(i) paragraph 27(2)(c);

(ii) paragraph 28(3)(c); or

(iii) sub-paragraph (3)(c) of this paragraph;

(b) before 5th April 2020 the relevant person again becomes entitled to an employment and support allowance which is not income-related;

(c) either–

(i) at the date on which the relevant person again becomes entitled to an employment support allowance which is not income-related regulation 145(1) of the Employment and Support Allowance Regulation applies to the relevant person; or

(ii) the period between the events mentioned in paragraphs (a) and (b) is one to which regulation 145(2) of the Employment and Support Allowance Regulations applies in respect of the relevant person; and

(d) at the date on which the relevant person again becomes entitled to an employment support allowance which is not income-related, neither the claimant nor the claimant's partner is entitled to an income-related employment and support allowance, an income-based jobseeker's allowance or income support.

(2) Where this paragraph applies, the claimant is entitled, with effect from the day that the relevant person's entitlement to employment and support allowance takes effect for housing benefit purposes, to a transitional addition of the amount of the transitional addition that would have applied had the claimant's entitlement to a transitional addition not ended (but taking account of the effect which any intervening change of circumstances would have had by virtue of paragraph 31), unless the amount of the transitional addition would be nil.

(3) The claimant's entitlement to a transitional addition by virtue of this paragraph ends on any of the following–

(a) the reduction of the transitional addition to nil in accordance with paragraph 31;

(b) the termination of the claimant's award of housing benefit;

(c) the relevant person no longer being entitled to the employment and support allowance referred to in sub-paragraph (1)(b);

(d) the claimant or the claimant's partner becoming entitled to an income-related employment and support allowance, an income-based jobseeker's allowance or income support;

(e) 5th April 2020.]

Analysis
Sub-para (1). Para 29 provides a linking rule where entitlement to HB continues, but entitlement to a transitional addition ends under paras 27(2)(c), 28(3)(c) or 29(3)(c) – ie, because the relevant person's entitlement to ESA ends, including where this is because s/he is no longer appealing a conversion decision. The "relevant person" is the person who is entitled to converted ESA or is appealing a conversion decision – ie, the claimant or her/his partner as the case may be: para 27(1). The HB claimant will be entitled to a transitional addition again if the conditions in sub-para (2)(b) to (e) are satisfied. The effect of these is as follows.
(1)   The "relevant person" must become entitled to ESA which is not income-related ESA again before 5 April 2020 and within 12 weeks of entitlement ceasing (104 weeks if the period is a linking period during which the "relevant person" is a "work or training beneficiary" for which see the analysis to para 28): sub-para (1)(a) to (c).
(2)   The claimant and her/his partner must not be entitled to IS, income-based JSA or income-related ESA on the date the "relevant person" becomes entitled to ESA again: sub-para (1)(d).
Note that where entitlement to HB ends (eg, as a consequence of entitlement to ESA ending), it appears that it is the linking rule in para 28 that is relevant, not the linking period in para 29.
Sub-para (2). The amount of the transitional addition that applies is the amount that would have applied had entitlement to the addition not ended, taking into account any changes that would have decreased that transitional addition under para 31.
Sub-para (3). Entitlement to the transitional addition ends if any of the circumstances listed in sub-para (3)(a) to (d) occur, or on 5 April 2020 if none have occurred before that date. Note that where there is a further break in entitlement to ESA or the HB award is terminated, the linking rules both in this para and in para 28 may still apply.

[¹ PART 8

Amendment
1.   Inserted by reg 27 and Sch 5 para 1(5)(c) of SI 2010 No 1907 as amended by reg 15 of SI 2010 No 2430 as from 1.10.10.

General Note to part 8
If an HB claimant is entitled to a transitional addition under Part 7, the amount of the addition is calculated under para 30. This is subject to para 31 which sets out how the amount of the transitional addition is to reduced where there are specified changes in circumstance. Once a claimant's transitional addition is reduced to nil, s/he cannot regain entitlement: paras 27(2)(a), 28(3)(a) and 29(3)(a).

Amount of transitional Addition
30.–(1)   Subject to paragraph 31, the amount of the transitional addition is the amount by which Amount A exceeds Amount B.
(2)   Where a conversion decision as described in regulation 5(2)(a) of the Employment and Support Allowance (Existing Awards) Regulations is made in respect of the relevant person–
(a)   Amount A is the basic amount that would have applied on the day that decision took effect had that decision not been made; and
(b)   Amount B is the basic amount that applied on that day as a result of that decision.
(3)   Where the relevant person is appealing a conversion decision as described in regulation 5(2)(b) of the Employment and Support Allowance (Existing Awards) Regulations and is treated as having limited capability for work by virtue of regulation 30 of the Employment and Support Allowance Regulations as modified by the Employment and Support Allowance (Existing Awards) Regulations–
(a)   Amount A is the basic amount that would have applied on the day the relevant person was first treated as having limited capability for work if the relevant person had not been so treated; and
(b)   Amount B is the basic amount that applied on that day as a result of the relevant person being so treated.
(4)   In this paragraph and paragraph 31, ''basic amount'' means the aggregate of such amounts as may apply in the claimant's case in accordance with regulation 22(a) to (e) or regulation 23(a) to (f).

Analysis
Simply put, the amount of the transitional addition is the difference between Amount A and Amount B: sub-para (1). This is subject to reduction under para 31.
Sub-para (2) defines Amount A and Amount B if the claimant or her/his partner was awarded converted ESA (see reg 2(1) for the definition). In this case, Amount A is the applicable amount under reg 22 or 23 that would have applied on the day the decision to award ESA took effect had that decision not been made – ie, the claimant's applicable amount immediately before entitlement to ESA began. Amount B is the applicable amount under reg 22 or 23 that applied on the day the decision to award ESA took effect.
Example. A single HB claimant aged 50 was entitled to long-term rate IB and was then awarded converted ESA which included a work-related activity component. Amount A is £65.45 (personal allowance) *plus* £28.00

(disability premium) = £93.45. Amount B is £65.45 (personal allowance) *plus* £25.95 (work-related activity component) = £91.40. The transitional addition is £2.05 (Amount A *minus* Amount B).

Sub-para (3) defines Amount A and amount B if the claimant or her/his partner is treated as having limited capability for work while appealing a decision not to award converted ESA. In this case, Amount A is the applicable amount under reg 22 or 23 that would have applied on the day the claimant or partner was first treated as having limited capability for work had s/he not been so treated – ie, the claimant's applicable amount immediately before appealing. Amount B is the applicable amount under reg 22 or 23 that applied on the day the claimant or partner was treated as having limited capability for work.

Example. A claimant who is a member of a couple is appealing a decision that he is not entitled to converted ESA. Prior to the decision, he was entitled to long-term rate IB and DLA. Amount A is £102.75 (personal allowance) *plus* £39.85 (disability premium) = £142.60. Amount B is £102.75 (personal allowance). The transitional addition is £39.85 (Amount A *minus* Amount B).

Para (4) defines "basic amount" for the purposes of both paras 30 and 31.

31.–(1)   Subject to sub-paragraph (2), where there is a change of circumstances which leads to an increase in the claimant's basic amount, the transitional addition that applies immediately before the change of circumstances shall be reduced by the amount by which Amount C exceeds Amount D.

(2)   If Amount C exceeds Amount D by more than the amount of the transitional addition that applies immediately before the change of circumstances, that transitional addition shall be reduced to nil.

(3)   Amount C is the basic amount that applies as a result of the increase.

(4)   Amount D is the basic amount that applied immediately before the increase.]

Analysis

The transitional addition as calculated under para 30 is subject to reduction if there is a change of circumstances which leads to an increase in the claimant's applicable amount under reg 22 or 23, until it the addition reduced to nil, when it is lost altogether. The reduction is the difference between the applicable amount as so increased (Amount C) and the applicable amount prior to the increase (Amount D). Note that "basic amount" is defined in para 30(4).

Example. A claimant who is a member of a couple was entitled to long-term rate IB and was then awarded converted ESA which included a work-related activity component. Her transitional addition is £13.90. Her partner is awarded carer's allowance and so her applicable amount should be increased by £30.05 to include a carer premium. Amount C is £102.75 (personal allowance) plus £25.95 (work-related activity component) plus £30.05 (carer premium) = £158.75. Amount D is £102.75 (personal allowance) plus £25.95 (work-related activity component) = £128.70. Amount C exceeds Amount D by more than £13.90 so the transitional addition is reduced to nil.

SCHEDULE 4
REGULATIONS 36(2) AND 38(2)
Sums to be disregarded in the calculation of earnings

Definitions

"applicable amount" – see Part 5.
"child" – see reg 2(1).
"claimant" – see reg 2(1).
"couple" – see s137(1) SSCBA.
"earnings" – see regs 35 and 37.
"employed earner" – see reg 2(1).
"family" – see s137(1) SSCBA.
"Great Britain" – excludes Northern Ireland.
"partner" – see reg 2(1).
"part-time employment" – see para 16.
"polygamous marriage" – see reg 2(1).
"remunerative work" – see reg 6.
"service user group" – see reg 2(1).
"support component" – see Sch 3 para 24.
"United Kingdom" – includes Northern Ireland.
"work-related activity component" – see Sch 3 para 23.
"young person" – see reg 19.

1.   In the case of a claimant who has been engaged in remunerative work as an employed earner or, had the employment been in Great Britain, would have been so engaged–

(a)   where–
     (i)   the employment has been terminated because of retirement; and
     (ii)   on retirement he is entitled to a retirement pension under the Act, or is not so entitled solely because of his failure to satisfy the contribution conditions,
any earnings [¹ paid or due to be paid] in respect of that employment, but only for a period commencing on the day immediately after the date on which the employment was terminated;

[¹ (b)   where before the first day of entitlement to housing benefit the employment has been terminated otherwise than because of retirement, any earnings paid or due to be paid in respect of that employment except–
     [² (i)   any payment of the nature described in–
          (aa)   regulation 35(1)(e), or
          (bb)   section 28, 64 or 68 of the Employment Rights Act 1996 (guarantee payments, suspension from work on medical or maternity grounds); and]
     (ii)   any award, sum or payment of the nature described in–
          (aa)   regulation 35(1)(g) or (h), or
          (bb)   section 34 or 70 of the Employment Rights Act 1996 (guarantee payments and suspension from work: complaints to employment tribunals),
including any payment made following the settlement of a complaint to an employment tribunal or of court proceedings;

(c)   where before the first day of entitlement to housing benefit–
     (i)   the employment has not been terminated, but
     (ii)   the claimant is not engaged in remunerative work,
any earnings paid or due to be paid in respect of that employment except any payment or remuneration of the nature described in [² paragraph 1(b)(i) or (ii)(bb) or regulation 35(1)(i)] or (j).]

Amendments

1.   Amended by reg 11(11)(a) of SI 2007 No 2618 as from 1.10.07.
2.   Amended by reg 6(5) of SI 2009 No 2655 as from 2.11.09.

Analysis

This paragraph applies only to claimants who have been in "remunerative work" as employed earners (see regs 2(1) and 6 for definitions), or who would have been had their employment been in Great Britain. Sub-paras (a) and (b) deal with situations where the employment terminates. Para (c) deals with situations where employment has *not* been terminated, but the person is no longer in "remunerative work" – eg, where s/he is no longer doing sufficient hours or is on sick leave. By reg 25, this para also applies to claimants' partners. It provides a complete disregard of earnings paid on retirement and a more restricted disregard for earnings received where employment has ceased or has been interrupted as at the first day of entitlement to HB. If a claimant receives wages or is due to receive wages on the termination or interruption of part-time work, see para 2. If s/he has been a self-employed earner, see para 2A.

    Sub-para (a) deals with the treatment of earnings on termination of employment because of retirement. In this case, if s/he is entitled to retirement pension when s/he retires (or would be but for failing to satisfy the contribution conditions), earnings (paid or due to be paid) from that employment are disregarded, but only for the period starting on the day after the day the employment ended. It is the date on which the employment terminated which is important, not the date on which the claimant last worked, which may be earlier. So where HB entitlement commences *after* the employment has terminated, all earnings from that employment should be disregarded. Note that by reg 5, this para is effectively redundant as the HB Regs do not apply to a claimant if s/he or her/his partner has reached the qualifying age for PC unless either is on IS, income-based JSA or income-related ESA. Claims by such claimants are instead dealt with under the HB(SPC) Regs. Note that if a claimant *is* on IS, income-based JSA or income-related ESA, earnings are disregarded under para 12 below.

    Sub-para (b) deals with the treatment of earnings on termination of employment before the first day of entitlement to HB, otherwise than on retirement. In this case, any earnings (paid or due to be paid) in respect of that employment should be disregarded, except those earnings shown in reg 35(1)(e), (g) and (h) (ie, retainers, compensation for unfair dismissal and payments deemed to be earnings by regulations made under s112 SSCBA) and guarantee payments and remuneration on suspension from work on medical or maternity grounds following a complaint to an employment tribunal under ss28, 34, 64, 68 or 70 Employment Rights Act 1996. So where the employment terminates *after* the first day of entitlement to HB, earnings from that employment should be taken into account, subject only to the appropriate earnings disregard below.

    Sub-para (c) deals with earnings that are disregarded on "remunerative work" ending but where the person's employment has not been terminated – eg, where working hours have decreased to less than 16, or the person is ill, or is on maternity leave. Where that person was not engaged in remunerative work at the first day of entitlement to HB, any earnings (paid or due to be paid) in respect of that employment are disregarded except those earnings shown in para 1(b)(i) and (ii)(bb) and reg 35(1)(i) and (j) (ie, retainers, any statutory sick pay, statutory maternity, paternity or adoption pay and any employer's sick pay or maternity, paternity or adoption pay). So where the remunerative work ceases *after* the first day of entitlement to HB, earnings from that employment should be taken into account, subject only to the appropriate earnings disregard below.

2. In the case of a claimant who, before the [¹ first day of entitlement to housing benefit]–

(a) has been engaged in part-time employment as an employed earner or, where the employment has been outside Great Britain, would have been so engaged had the employment been in Great Britain; and

(b) has ceased to be engaged in that employment, whether or not that employment has been terminated, any earnings [¹ paid or due to be paid] in respect of that employment except–

    (i) where that employment has been terminated, [¹ any payment of the nature described in [² paragraph 1(b)(i) or (ii)(bb))]];

    (ii) where that employment has not been terminated, [¹ any payment or remuneration of the nature described in [² paragraph 1(b)(i) or (ii)(bb) or regulation 35(1)(i)] or (j)].

Amendments

1. Amended by reg 11(11)(b) of SI 2007 No 2618 as from 1.10.07.
2. Amended by reg 6(5) of SI 2009 No 2655 as from 2.11.09.

Analysis

Para 2 deals with earnings disregarded on termination or interruption of part-time employment (less than 16 hours a week – see para 16). It clarifies that where a person has been in such employment (or would have been had her/his employment been in Great Britain) but this ceased before the first day of entitlement to HB, (irrespective of whether or not that employment has terminated), then any earnings (paid or due to be paid) from that employment should be disregarded, except for:

(1) Where the employment terminated, any payment of the nature of a retainer as well as any payments of the nature of those in para 1(b)(i) or (ii)(bb) (see above).

(2) Where, although that employment has not been terminated, that person has ceased to be engaged in that employment because, for example, s/he is ill, payments of the nature of those in para 1(b)(i) and (ii)(bb) (see above) and in reg 35(1)(i) and (j) of the HB Regs (ie, statutory sick pay, statutory maternity, paternity or adoption pay and any employer's sick pay or maternity, paternity or adoption pay).

So where the employment was terminated or interrupted *after* the first day of entitlement to HB, earnings from that employment should be taken into account, subject only to the appropriate earnings disregard below.

[¹2A. In the case of a claimant who has been engaged in remunerative work or part-time employment as a self-employed earner or, had the employment been in Great Britain would have been so engaged and who has ceased to be so employed, from the date of the cessation of his employment any earnings derived from that employment except earnings to which regulation 37(3) and (4) (earnings of self-employed earners) apply.]

Amendment

1. Inserted by reg 6(11) of SI 2009 No 583 as from 6.4.09.

Analysis

This deals with earnings disregarded when employment as a self-employed earner ends, whether this was remunerative work (for which see reg 6) or part-time employment (for which see para 16). In this case, all earnings derived from that employment are disregarded from the date it ended, other than royalties, sums paid for the use of, or the right to use, any copyright, design, patent or trade mark, or Public Lending Right Scheme payments.

3.–(1) In a case to which this paragraph applies and paragraph 4 does not apply, £20; but notwithstanding regulation 25 (calculation of income and capital of members of a claimant's family and of a polygamous marriage) if this paragraph applies to a claimant it shall not apply to his partner except where, and to the extent that, the earnings of the claimant which are to be disregarded under this paragraph are less than £20.

(2) This paragraph applies where the claimant's applicable amount includes an amount by way of the disability premium [², severe disability premium, work-related activity component or support component] under Schedule 3 (applicable amounts).

(3) This paragraph applies where–

[¹ (a) the claimant is a member of a couple and his applicable amount includes an amount by way of the disability premium under Schedule 3; and]

(b) he or his partner [³ has not attained the qualifying age for state pension credit] and at least one is engaged in employment.

[¹ (4)]

[¹ (5)]

Amendments

1. Amended by reg 3(11)(a) and (b) of SI 2008 No 1042 as from 19.5.08.
2. Amended by reg 24(a) of SI 2008 No 1082 as from 27.10.08.
3. Amended by reg 27 of SI 2009 No 1488 as from 6.4.10.

Analysis
This provides a flat-rate £20 disregard of the earnings of the claimant and/or his partner if any of the conditions in sub-paras (2) or (3) apply. It does not apply if the claimant qualifies for a lone parent disregard under para 4 or for an "exempt work" disregard under para 10A. Note that the claimant may also qualify for an additional earnings disregard under para 17.

There is a maximum £20 deduction, not a disregard of £20 of the earnings of each partner who has earnings. The disregard is first applied to the earnings of the claimant, then anything left over may be applied to the earnings, if any, of the partner(s). For example, if the claimant earns £10 a week and her/his partner earns £23, the claimant's earnings will be totally disregarded, but only £10 (balance of the disregard) of her/his partner's.

A £20 disregard applies if either of the conditions in sub-paras (2) or (3) applies. The condition in sub-para (2) is that the claimant's applicable amount includes the disability or severe disability premium or the work-related activity or support component (see paras 12, 13, 14, 23 and 24 of Sch 3). Even if a non-dependant's earnings are used (see reg 26) it is still the *claimant* who must satisfy these conditions as they relate to applicable amount, not resources. Note that para 3(3) was amended oddly when pensioner premiums were omitted on 19 May 2008. Where a claimant qualifies for a disability premium, s/he will qualify for a £20 earnings disregard under para 3(2) whether or not para 3(3) is satisfied.

---

4.   In a case where the claimant is a lone parent, £25.

Analysis
This provides a flat-rate disregard of £25 where the claimant is a lone parent (defined in reg 2(1)). It can only apply where the claimant is not on IS, income-based JSA or income-related ESA. If s/he is on one of those benefits, all of her/his earnings are disregarded under para 12.

5.–(1)   In a case to which neither paragraph 3 nor paragraph 4 applies to the claimant, and subject to sub-paragraph (2), where the claimant's applicable amount includes an amount by way of the carer premium under Schedule 3 (applicable amounts), £20 of the earnings of the person who is, or at any time in the preceding eight weeks was, in receipt of carer's allowance or treated in accordance with paragraph 17(2) of that Schedule as being in receipt of carer's allowance.

(2)   Where the carer premium is awarded in respect of the claimant and of any partner of his, their earnings shall for the purposes of this paragraph be aggregated, but the amount to be disregarded in accordance with sub-paragraph (1) shall not exceed £20 of the aggregated amount.

Analysis
Para 5 provides a £20 earnings disregard for claimants whose applicable amount includes the carer premium: see Sch 3 para 17. It does not apply if the claimant qualifies for a lone parent disregard under para 4 or for an "exempt work" disregard under para 10A. Para 5 applies to the earnings of the carer: sub-para (1). Where both the claimant and her/his partner qualifiy for the carer premium, £20 is disregarded from their combined earnings: sub-para (2). See para 6 where the claimant is a carer and her/his partner is engaged in employment. Note that the claimant may also qualify for an additional earnings disregard under para 17.

---

6.   Where the carer premium is awarded in respect of a claimant who is a member of a couple and whose earnings are less than £20, but is not awarded in respect of the other member of the couple, and that other member is engaged in an employment–
(a)   specified in paragraph 8(1), so much of the other member's earnings as would not when aggregated with the amount disregarded under paragraph 5 exceed £20;
(b)   other than one specified in paragraph 8(1), so much of the other member's earnings from such other employment up to £10 as would not when aggregated with the amount disregarded under paragraph 5 exceed £20.

Analysis
Where the claimant is the carer, has earnings less than £20 and is a member of a couple whose partner is engaged in any of the employments specified in para 8(1) (eg, part-time fire fighter or auxiliary coastguard), the remainder of the £20 disregard under para 5 can be applied to the partner's earnings: sub-para (a). If the partner is engaged in any other employment, up to £10 of her/his earnings can be disregarded: sub-para (b). The total can never exceed £20.

---

7.   In a case where paragraphs 3, 5, 6 and 8 do not apply to the claimant and he is one of a couple and a member of that couple is in employment, £10; but, notwithstanding regulation 25 (calculation of income and capital of members of claimant's family and of a polygamous marriage), if this paragraph applies to a claimant it shall not apply to his partner except where, and to the extent that, the earnings of the claimant which are to be disregarded under this paragraph are less than £10.

Analysis

This deals with the earnings of claimants who are members of a couple and who do not satisfy the provisions of paras 3, 5, 6 and 8. It does not apply if the claimant qualifies for a disregard under para 10A. Note that the claimant may also qualify for an additional earnings disregard under para 17.

It is not clear how this provision affects partners to polygamous marriages; presumably the claimant and one other partner would count as a "couple" for these purposes. A flat-rate disregard of £10 is available, irrespective of whether the earnings are from full-time or part-time work. Despite reg 25, the context requires that "partner" should not be substituted for "claimant" where the partner has earnings, as specific provision is made for the earnings of partners by the regulation. The effect is that there is only one disregard per couple, rather than a disregard of £10 of *each* of their earnings if each earn. See para 3 for an example of how this works. If reg 26 has been used, the rules apply to the earnings of the non-dependant and her/his partner as only the assessment of resources is involved. See para 8 if the claimant or her/his partner is engaged in any of the employments specified in para 8(1) (eg, part-time fire fighter or auxiliary coastguard). See para 9 if a claimant her/himself has earnings which would normally be covered by this paragraph as well as by para 8. See para 10A if the claimant or her/his partner is doing "exempt work" while receiving IB, ESA, SDA or NI credits for incapacity for work or limited capability for work.

8.–(1) In a case where paragraphs 3, 4, 5 and 6 do not apply to the claimant, £20 of earnings derived from one or more employments as–

(a) a part-time fire-fighter employed by a fire and rescue authority constituted by a scheme under section 2 of the Fire and Rescue Services Act 2004 or a scheme to which section 4 of that Act applies;

(b) a part-time fire-fighter employed by a fire and rescue authority (as defined in section 1 of the Fire (Scotland) Act 2005 or a joint fire and rescue board constituted by an amalgamation scheme made under section 2(1) of that Act;

(c) an auxiliary coastguard in respect of coast rescue activities;

(d) a person engaged part-time in the manning or launching of a life boat;

(e) a member of any territorial or reserve force prescribed in Part 1 of Schedule 6 to the Social Security (Contributions) Regulations 2001;

but, notwithstanding regulation 25 (calculation of income and capital of members of claimant's family and of a polygamous marriage), if this paragraph applies to a claimant it shall not apply to his partner except to the extent specified in sub-paragraph (2).

(2) If the claimant's partner is engaged in employment–

(a) specified in sub-paragraph (1), so much of his earnings as would not in aggregate with the amount of the claimant's earnings disregarded under this paragraph exceed £20;

(b) other than one specified in sub-paragraph (1), so much of his earnings from that employment up to £10 as would not in aggregate with the claimant's earnings disregarded under this paragraph exceed £20.

Analysis

This provides a £20 disregard in respect of the employments listed in para (1) if the claimant is not covered by paras 3, 4, 5 or 6 above. It does not apply if the claimant qualifies for a disregard under para 10A. Note that the claimant may also qualify for an additional earnings disregard under para 17. If the claimant has a partner and s/he or her/his partner has earnings from any other source of employment, see sub-para (2) of this paragraph if it is the partner who has such earnings, and para 9 if the claimant has earnings from other work. Because of para 9 it does not seem to be the intent that the claimant should be able to use the disregards in both paras 7 and 8, as paras 8 and 9 together provide a complete code where the claimant or her/his partner has earnings which would normally be covered by para 7 as well as by para 8(1) employment.

Sub-para (1) sets out the employments covered. Under sub-para (1)(e), the forces listed are: retired and emergency lists of officers of the Royal Navy; Royal Naval reserves; Royal Marines reserves; Army reserves; Territorial Army and Volunteer reserves; RAF reserves; Royal Auxiliary Air Force; Royal Irish Regiment. Note under that reg 46(1), payments of annual bounty in relation to these employments paid at intervals of at least one year are to be treated as capital.

Sub-para (2) deals with the situation where the claimant is in any of the employments specified in sub-para (1) and a partner of the claimant also has earnings from a listed employment (sub-para (2)(a)), or from other work (sub-para (2)(b)).

The partner's earnings will only be disregarded if the claimant's sub-para (1) earnings do not exhaust the disregard available under that sub-paragraph, and even then only up to the maximum amount specified.

Sub-para (2)(a). If the claimant's earnings from an employment listed in sub-para (1) are less than £20, the unused part of the disregard may be set against her/his partner's earnings from a listed employment.

Sub-para (2)(b). If the claimants earnings from listed employment do not exhaust the £20 disregard under sub-para (1), up to £10 of what remains of the disregard may be set against her/his partner's earnings from other work.

9. Where the claimant is engaged in [¹ one or more employments] specified in paragraph 8(1), but his earnings derived from such employments are less than £20 in any week and he is also engaged in any other employment so much of his earnings from that other employment, up to £5 if he is a single claimant, or up to £10 if he has a partner, as would not in aggregate with the amount of his earnings disregarded under [¹ paragraph 8] exceed £20.

Amendment

1.   Amended by reg 3(11)(c) of SI 2008 No 1042 as from 19.5.08.

Analysis

This appears to substitute for para 7 where the claimant has employment covered by para 8(1) and also does other work. Where such a claimant has not exhausted her/his £20 disregard under para 8(1) if s/he is single, s/he can offset up to £5 of what is left against earnings covered by this paragraph, or if s/he has a partner s/he can offset up to £10 against such earnings, subject to a total disregard of £20 of the claimant's earnings as assessed under this paragraph and para 8. The relationship between this paragraph and para 8(2) is not clear. It could be argued that this provision is in addition to, rather than in substitution for, para 8(2) on the basis that the claimant's earnings here cannot be intended also to refer to her/his partner's earnings as specific provision has been made for the partner's earnings under para 8(2) so that, if both have earnings, the claimant's earnings covered by this para and those of her/his partner under para 8(2), disregards under both para 8(2) and this para may be available. However, the "aggregate disregard" of the claimant's earnings covered by this paragraph and para 8 must not exceed £20, which implies that sums due to a partner and covered by para 8(2) are to be treated as the "claimant's" for these purposes, so no duplication occurs.

10.   In a case to which none of the paragraphs 3 to 9 applies, £5.

Analysis

This provides a £5 earnings disregard where none of paras 3 to 9 apply, that is, where a claimant is single, is not a lone parent and does not qualify for a £20 earnings disregard. See para 9 where the claimant also has earnings from any of the employments specified in para 8(1). This para does not apply if the claimant qualifes for a disregard under para 10A. Note that the claimant may also qualify for an additional earnings disregard under para 17.

[¹**10A.**–(1) Where–
(a)   the claimant (or if the claimant is a member of a couple, at least one member of that couple) is a person to whom sub-paragraph (5) applies;
(b)   the Secretary of State is satisfied that that person is undertaking exempt work as defined in sub-paragraph (6); and
(c)   paragraph 12 does not apply,
the amount specified in sub-paragraph (7) ("the specified amount").
(2)   Where this paragraph applies, paragraphs 3 to 10 do not apply; but in any case where the claimant is a lone parent, and the specified amount would be less than the amount specified in paragraph 4, then paragraph 4 applies instead of this paragraph.
(3)   Notwithstanding regulation 25 (calculation of income and capital of members of claimant's family and of a polygamous marriage), if sub-paragraph (1) applies to one member of a couple ("A") it shall not apply to the other member of that couple ("B") except to the extent provided in sub-paragraph (4).
(4)   Where A's earnings are less than the specified amount, there shall also be disregarded so much of B's earnings as would not when aggregated with A's earnings exceed the specified amount; but the amount of B's earnings which may be disregarded under this sub-paragraph is limited to a maximum of £20 unless the Secretary of State is satisfied that B is also undertaking exempt work.
(5)   This sub-paragraph applies to a person who is–
(a)   in receipt of a contributory employment and support allowance;
(b)   in receipt of incapacity benefit;
(c)   in receipt of severe disablement allowance; or
(d)   being credited with earnings on the grounds of incapacity for work or limited capability for work under regulation 8B of the Social Security (Credits) Regulations 1975.
(6)   "Exempt work" means work of the kind described in–
(a)   regulation 45(2), (3) or (4) of the Employment and Support Allowance Regulations; or (as the case may be)
(b)   regulation 17(2), (3) or (4) of the Social Security (Incapacity for Work) (General) Regulations 1995, and, in determining for the purposes of this paragraph whether a claimant or a member of a couple is undertaking any type of exempt work, it is immaterial whether that person or their partner is also undertaking other work.
(7)   The specified amount is the amount of money from time to time mentioned in any provision referred to in sub-paragraph (6) by virtue of which the work referred to in sub-paragraph (1) is exempt (or, where more

than one such provision is relevant and those provisions mention different amounts of money, the highest of those amounts).]

Amendment

1.   Inserted by reg 2(4)(a) of SI 2009 No 2608 as from 1.4.10 (5.4.10 where rent payable weekly or in multiples of a week).

Analysis

Para 10A provides a disregard where the claimant or her/his partner is undertaking "exempt work" (defined in sub-para (6)) while receiving contributory ESA, IB, SDA or NI credits for incapacity for work or limited capability for work, often referred to as "permitted work". This is to ensure that claimants (and partners) are not disadvantaged financially by attempting such work. Para 10A applies instead of paras 3 to 10, unless the claimant is a lone parent and the amount to be disregarded under para 4 would be higher than the disregard under this paragraph: sub-para (2). Note that the claimant may also qualify for an additional earnings disregard under para 17.

Para 10A does not apply if the claimant is on IS, income-based JSA or income-related ESA, in which case all of the claimant's (and partner's) earnings are disregarded under para 12.

"Exempt work" is any of the following:

(1)   Work as part of a treatment programme under medical supervision in a hospital or while regularly attending hospital as an outpatient for which earnings are no more than a set amount a week (currently £95).

(2)   Work for which earnings are no more than a set amount a week (currently £95) which is supervised by a public or local authority or by a voluntary organisation or community interest company engaged in the provision or procurement of work for people with disabilities – often referred to as "supported permitted work.

(3)   For up to 52 weeks (indefinitely in limited cases, for which see the regulations specified in para (6)), work done for less than 16 hours a week and for which earnings are no more than a set amount a week (currently £95) (often referred to as "permitted work higher limit").

(4)   Work for which earnings do not exceed £20 a week (often referred to as "permitted work lower limit").

Note: the higher limit is linked to the adult minimum wage and is generally increased every October.

The DWP must be satisfied that the person is undertaking exempt work as defined: para 10A(1)(b). It is understood that information on whether work falls into one of the categories and whether a time limit is appropriate is provided to local authorities clerically by Jobcentre Plus.

The disregard that applies is the amount of weekly earnings allowed for the type of exempt work being undertaken (currently £20 or £95 as the case may be), or where more than one type of exempt work is being undertaken, the highest of the amounts: sub-para (7). The disregard is not only applied to the earnings from the exempt work; it can be applied to any earnings from other work (see the wording of sub-para (1)). However, for a single claimant, the other work can only be other work s/he is permitted to do without affecting her/his entitlement to the benefits or NI credits specified – eg, work as a local councillor or disability member of the First-tier Tribunal. Where the claimant is a member of a couple and the earnings of the member doing exempt work are lower than the relevant disregard, the remainder can be used up on the earnings of the other member of the couple. This is limited to a maximum disregard of £20 unless the other member is also undertaking exempt work: sub-para (4).

---

11.   Any amount or the balance of any amount which would fall to be disregarded under paragraph 19 or 20 of Schedule 5 had the claimant's income which does not consist of earnings been sufficient to entitle him to the full disregarded thereunder.

Analysis

This applies where the claimant has insufficient income to use up the disregards under Sch 5 paras 19 and 20. Those paras deal with situations where the claimant is making a parental contirbution to a student's grant or loan or contributes to a student's maintenance. In such a case, the unused part of the disregards may be applied to the claimant's earnings. This provision is available in addition to any other disregard available under this Schedule.

---

12.   Where a claimant is on income support [, an income-based jobseeker's allowance or an income-related employment and support allowance], his earnings.

Amendment

1.   Amended by reg 24(b) of SI 2008 No 1082 as from 27.10.08.

Analysis

This paragraph is necessary as claimants on IS, income-based JSA or income-related ESA have already had their income taken into account for those purposes. "Person on income support" is defined by reg 2(1), "person on an income-based jobseeker's allowance" by reg 2(3) and "person on an income-related employment and support allowance" by reg 2(3A).

---

13.   Any earnings derived from employment which are payable in a country outside the United Kingdom for such period during which there is a prohibition against the transfer to the United Kingdom of those earnings.

14.   Where a payment of earnings is made in a currency other than Sterling, any banking charge or commission payable in converting that payment into Sterling.

15.   Any earnings of a child or young person.

16.   In this Schedule "part-time employment" means employment in which the person is engaged on average for less than 16 hours a week.

17.–(1)   In a case where the claimant is a person who satisfies at least one of the conditions set out in sub-paragraph (2), and his net earnings equal or exceed the total of the amounts set out in sub-paragraph (3), the amount of his earnings that falls to be disregarded under [⁷ paragraphs 3 to 10A] of this Schedule shall be increased by [⁸ £17.10].

(2)   The conditions of this sub-paragraph are that–

(a)   the claimant, or if he is a member of a couple, either the claimant or his partner, is a person to whom regulation 20(1)(c) of the Working Tax Credit Regulations applies; or

(b)   the claimant–

　(i)   is, or if he is a member of a couple, at least one member of that couple is aged at least 25 and is engaged in remunerative work for on average not less than 30 hours per week; or

　(ii)   is a member of a couple and–

　　(aa)   at least one member of that couple, is engaged in remunerative work for on average not less than 16 hours per week; and

　　(bb)   his applicable amount includes a family premium under paragraph 3 of Schedule 3; or

　(iii)   is a lone parent who is engaged in remunerative work for on average not less than 16 hours per week; or

　(iv)   is, or if he is a member of a couple, at least one member of that couple is engaged in remunerative work for on average not less than 16 hours per week; and–

　　[⁵ (aa)   the claimant's applicable amount includes a disability premium under paragraph 12, the work-related activity component under paragraph 23 or the support component under paragraph 24 of Schedule 3];]

　　(bb)   where he is a member of a couple, at least one member of that couple satisfies the qualifying conditions for the [⁴] [⁵ , a disability premium, the work-related activity component or the support component] referred to in sub-head (aa) above and is engaged in remunerative work for on average not less than 16 hours per week; or

(c)   the claimant is, or, if he has a partner, one of them is, a person to whom regulation 18(3) of the Working Tax Credit Regulations (eligibility for 50 plus element) applies, or would apply if an application for working tax credit were to be made in his case.

(3)   The following are the amounts referred to in sub-paragraph (1)–

(a)   the amount to be disregarded from the claimant's earnings under [⁹ paragraphs 3 to 10A] of this Schedule;

(b)   the amount of child care charges calculated as deductible under [⁴ regulation 27(1)(c)]; and

(c)   [⁸ £17.10].

(4)   The provisions of regulation 6 shall apply in determining whether or not a person works for on average not less than 30 hours per week, but as if the reference to 16 hours in paragraph (1) of that regulation were a reference to 30 hours.

Amendments

1.   Amended by Art 19(9) of SI 2006 No 645 and reg 8 of SI 2006 No 217 as from 1.4.06 (3.4.06 where rent payable weekly or at intervals of a week).

2.   Amended by Art 19(9) of SI 2007 No 688 as from 1.4.07 (2.4.07 where rent payable weekly or at intervals of a week).

3.   Amended by Art 19(10) of SI 2008 No 632 as from 1.4.08 (7.4.08 where rent payable weekly or in multiples of a week).

4.   Amended by reg 3(11)(d)-(f) of SI 2008 No 1042 as from 19.5.08.

5.   Amended by reg 24(c) of SI 2008 No 1082, as amended by reg 32 of SI 2008 No 2428, as from 27.10.08.

6.   Amended by Art 19(11) of SI 2009 No 497 as from 1.4.09 (6.4.09 where rent payable weekly or at intervals of a week).

7.   Amended by reg 2(4)(b) of SI 2009 No 2608 as from 1.4.10 (5.4.10 where rent payable weekly or in multiples of a week).

8.   Amended by Art 19(10) of SI 2010 No 793 as from 1.4.10 (5.4.10 where rent payable weekly or in multiples of a week).

9.   Amended by reg 2(9) of SI 2010 No 2449 as from 1.11.10.

Analysis

Para 17 provides an additional earnings disregard for some working claimants, broadly, those who qualify for a 30 hour element in the calculation of their working tax credit (WTC), or would do were they to claim. It lessens the impact of earnings on HB entitlement for those in low paid work. The categories of claimant who qualify are set out below.

If the claimant's (and partner's) net earnings are equal to or exceed the sum of the amounts set out in sub-para (3), the relevant disregard in paras 3 to 10A is to be increased by the amount of the additional disregard set out in sub-para (1). The amount is generally uprated annually, in April. The amounts in sub-para (3) are the amount to be disregarded under paras 3 to 10A, the claimant's deductible child care charges under reg 28(1)(c) and the amount of the additional disregard. See Sch 5 para 56 if net earnings are less than the sum. In this case, the equivalent of the additional earnings disregard is deducted from any WTC awarded.

Six categories of claimant qualify for an additional disregard.

(1)   Claimants to whom (or to whose partners) reg 20(1)(c) Working Tax Credit (Entitlement and Maximum Rate) Regulations 2002 applies: sub-para (2)(a). These are those who qualify for a 30-hour element with WTC, that is those who work 30 hours or more a week, or in the case of a couple with children, those who between them work 30 hours or more a week. The latter only applies if at least one of the couple is working 16 hours or more a week.

(2)   A claimant who is aged at least 25 and who works for at least 30 hours a week, or who has a partner who fulfils that description: sub-para (2)(b)(i).

(3)   A claimant who is a member of a couple, one of whom is working 16 hours or more a week, and who is entitled to a family premium – ie, s/he or her/his partner are responsible for at least one child or qualifying young person: sub-para (2)(b)(ii).

(4)   A claimant who is a lone parent working 16 hours or more per week: sub-para (2)(b)(iii).

(5)   A claimant who works, or whose partner (if any) works, 16 hours or more a week and whose applicable amount includes a disability premium, a work-related activity component or a support component. In the case of couples, the one of them that satisfies the conditions for a disability premium, a work-related activity component or a support component must be working at least 16 hours per week: sub-para (2)(b)(iv). It is important to note that a person who works in any week will be treated as not having limited capability for work under regs 40 and 44 ESA Regs, unless it is work s/he may do while claiming: reg 40(2) ESA Regs. To qualify for one of the components under Sch 3 paras 23 or 24, the claimant or her/his partner must have limited capability for work. So where there is entitlement to a component, this sub-para can only apply if the claimant (or partner) is doing work that is permitted by reg 40(2) ESA Regs.

(6)   A claimant who, or whose partner (if any), is a person to whom reg 18(3) Working Tax Credit Regulations applies, or would apply if an application for WTC were to be made. These are those who qualify (or would qualify) for a WTC 50 plus element: para (2)(c).

In deciding how many hours a week are worked, the averaging rules in reg 6 apply: sub-para (4).

SCHEDULE 5
REGULATION 40

Sums to be disregarded in the calculation of income other than earnings

Modifications

Para 51 was substituted by Sch 4 para 2(4) and paras 55A and 55B inserted by Sch 4 para 2(5) HB&CTB(CP) Regs in respect of claims for HB by some refugees.

A different version of para 55B was substituted for para 56 by Sch 4 para 4(2)(b) HB&CTB(CP) Regs for some HB claimants who were refugees who claimed asylum on or before 2 April 2000.

See also reg 10A and Sch A1 inserted by Sch 4 para 2 HB&CTB(CP) Regs.

Note that paras 55A and 55B lapsed by s12(2)(e) Asylum and Immigration (Treatment of Claimants, etc.) Act 2004 (for those recorded as refugees after 14 June 2007) and were deleted by reg 5(6)(k) of SI 2008 No.3157 as from 5 January 2009. For the full text of para 51 as substituted and paras 55A and 55B as inserted, see p1129 of the 20th edition.

Para A1 is inserted by reg 16 Jobseeker's Allowance (Work for Your Benefit Pilot Scheme) Regulations 2010 SI No.1222 (see p1247) as from 22 November 2010 but only for those ordinarily resident in a pilot area, or whose address for payment of JSA is located within such an area. The modification is shown in italics below. It ceases to have effect on 21 November 2013.

Definitions

"boarder" – see reg 2(1).
"capital" – see reg 2(1).
"child" – see reg 2(1).
"claimant" – see reg 2(1).

"dwelling" – see s137(1) SSCBA.
"earnings" – see regs 35 and 37.
"employment zone contractor" – see reg 2(1).
"employment zone programme" – see reg 2(1).
"family" – see reg 2(1).
"income"–see Part 6.
"Independent Living Fund (2006)" – see reg 2(1).
"Local Authority" – see s191 SSAA.
"Macfarlane Trust"–see reg 2(1).
"non-dependant" – reg 3.
"partner" – see reg 2(1).
"payment" – see reg 2(1).
"occupies as a home" – see reg 7.
"ordinary clothing or footwear – see reg 2(1).
"service user group" – see reg 2(1).
"student contribution" – see Part 7.
"subsistence allowance" – see reg 2(1).
"voluntary organisation" – see reg 2(1).
"the Work for Your Benefit Pilot Scheme" – see reg 2(1).
"young person" – see reg 19.

[A1.   Any payment made to the claimant in respect of any child care, travel or other expenses incurred, or to be incurred, by him in respect of his participation in the Work for Your Benefit Pilot Scheme.]
1.   Any amount paid by way of tax on income which is to be taken into account under regulation 40 (calculation of income other than earnings).

Analysis
This requires the deduction of any income tax *actually* paid on income other than earnings covered by reg 40.

---

2.   Any payment in respect of any expenses incurred or to be incurred by a claimant who is–
(a)   engaged by a charitable or voluntary organisation; or
(b)   a volunteer,
if he otherwise derives no remuneration or profit from the employment and is not to be treated as possessing any earnings under regulation 42(9) (notional income).

Analysis
Notice that the types of expenses to be disregarded are unrestricted, unlike under regs 35(2)(b) or 38, but that the requirement that no "remuneration or profit" be made excludes any element of *gain* from the disregard. See reg 42(9) for where someone can be treated as having "notional" earnings.

[¹**2A.**   Any payment in respect of expenses arising out of the claimant's participation in a service user group.]

Amendment
1.   Inserted by reg 6(6)(a) of SI 2009 No 2655 as from 2.11.09.

---

3.   In the case of employment as an employed earner, any payment in respect of expenses wholly, exclusively and necessarily incurred in the performance of the duties of the employment.

Analysis
The purpose is to avoid expenses which are deemed not to be "earnings" by reg 35(2)(b) being taken into account under any other regulation.

---

4.   Where a claimant is on income support [¹ , an income-based jobseeker's allowance or an income-related employment and support allowance] the whole of his income.

Amendment
1.   Amended by reg 25(a) of SI 2008 No 1082 as from 27.10.08.

Analysis
This para and para 5 are necessary as IS, income-based JSA and income-related ESA claimants have already had their income fully considered in relation to that benefit – see General Note on Part 6 on p339.

5. Where the claimant is a member of a joint-claim couple for the purposes of the Jobseekers Act and his partner is on an income-based jobseeker's allowance, the whole of the claimant's income.

6. Any disability living allowance.

Analysis
See para 7 for the treatment of concessionary payments of disability living allowance. See also Sch 6 para 9 where the concessionary payments are capital payments for arrears, or to compensate for arrears due.

7. Any concessionary payment made to compensate for the non-payment of–
(a) any payment specified in paragraph 6 or 9;
(b) income support;
(c) an income-based jobseeker's allowance.
[¹ (d) an income-related employment and support allowance.]

Amendment
1. Inserted by reg 25(a) of SI 2008 No 1082 as from 27.10.08.

Analysis
See also Sch 6 para 9 where the concessionary payments are capital payments for arrears, or to compensate for arrears due.

8. Any mobility supplement under [¹ article 20 of the Naval, Military and Air Forces Etc. (Disablement and Death) Service Pensions Order 2006] (including such a supplement by virtue of any other scheme or order) or under article 25A of the Personal Injuries (Civilians) Scheme 1983 or any payment intended to compensate for the non-payment of such a supplement.

Amendment
1. Amended by reg 5(6)(a) of SI 2008 No 3157 as from 5.1.09.

Analysis
Art 20 of the Order referred to relates to mobility supplement paid to members of the armed forces who are in receipt of retired pay or a pension due to a specified injury. Art 25A refers to similar payments made to civilians and former civil defence volunteers due to "war/war service injuries sustained during the period September 3, 1939 to March 19, 1946". Notice that the paragraph also covers sums paid as compensation for non-payment of the benefits referred to.

9. Any attendance allowance.

Analysis
See para 7 for the treatment of concessionary payments of attendance allowance. See also Sch 6 para 9 (on p568) where the concessionary payments are capital payments for arrears, or to compensate for arrears due.

10. Any payment to the claimant as holder of the Victoria Cross or of the George Cross or any analogous payment.

11.–(1) Any payment–
(a) by way of an education maintenance allowance made pursuant to–
   (i) regulations made under section 518 of the Education Act 1996 (payment of school expenses; grant of scholarships etc.);
   (ii) regulations made under section 49 or 73(f) of the Education (Scotland) Act 1980 (power to assist persons to take advantage of educational facilities);
   [¹ (iii) directions made under section 73ZA of the Education (Scotland) Act 1980 and paid under section 12(2)(c) of the Further and Higher Education (Scotland) Act 1992(45); or]
(b) corresponding to such an education maintenance allowance, made pursuant to–
   (i) section 14 or section 181 of the Education Act 2002 (power of Secretary of State and National Assembly for Wales to give financial assistance for purposes related to education or childcare, and allowances in respect of education or training); or
   (ii) regulations made under section 181 of that Act.
(2) Any payment, other than a payment to which sub-paragraph (1) applies, made pursuant to–
(a) regulations made under section 518 of the Education Act 1996;
(b) regulations made under section 49 of the Education (Scotland) Act 1980; or
[¹ (c) directions made under section 73ZA of the Education (Scotland) Act 1980 and paid under section 12(2)(c) of the Further and Higher Education (Scotland) Act 1992,]
in respect of a course of study attended by a child or a young person or a person who is in receipt of an education maintenance allowance made pursuant to any provision specified in sub-paragraph (1).

Amendment

1.　　Substituted by reg 5(6)(b) of SI 2008 No 3157 as from 5.1.09.

Analysis

This provides for a disregard of education maintenance allowance (in Wales payments corresponding to such an allowance) and payments made to people aged above compulsory school leaving age, whether or not that education is in, or equivalent to, secondary education. Also disregarded are payments paid to children below school leaving age to enable them to take part in activities at state schools, or, where appropriate, help pay fees for fee-paying schools, to avoid hardship to children or their parents. Note that the payments are also disregarded as capital under para 51 of Sch 6.

12.　　Any payment made to the claimant by way of a repayment under regulation 11(2) of the Education (Teacher Student Loans) (Repayment etc) Regulations 2002.

13.–(1)　Any payment made pursuant to section 2 of the 1973 Act or section 2 of the Enterprise and New Towns (Scotland) Act 1990 except–

(a)　　a payment made as a substitute for income support, a jobseeker's allowance, incapacity benefit [¹ , severe disablement allowance or an employment and support allowance];

(b)　　a payment of an allowance referred to in section 2(3) of the 1973 Act or section 2(5) of the Enterprise and New Towns (Scotland) Act 1990;

(c)　　a payment intended to meet the cost of living expenses which relate to any one or more of the items specified in sub-paragraph (2) whilst a claimant is participating in an education, training or other scheme to help him enhance his employment prospects unless the payment is a Career Development Loan paid pursuant to section 2 of the 1973 Act and the period of education or training or the scheme, which is supported by that loan, has been completed; or

(d)　　for the purpose only of assessing entitlement to housing benefit in respect of a dwelling other than the one which the claimant normally occupies as his home, a payment made to a person to whom regulation 7(5)(b) (circumstances in which a person is or is not to be treated as occupying a dwelling as his home) applies to the extent that the payment is made in respect of the cost of living away from home.

(2)　　The items specified in this sub-paragraph for the purposes of sub-paragraph (1)(c) are food, ordinary clothing or footwear, household fuel or rent of the claimant or, where the claimant is a member of a family, any other member of his family, or any council tax or water charges for which that claimant or member is liable.

(3)　　For the purposes of this paragraph, "rent" means eligible rent less any deductions in respect of non-dependants which fall to be made under regulation 74 (non-dependant deductions).

Amendment

1.　　Amended by reg 8(10)(a) of SI 2010 No 641 as from 1.4.10 (5.4.10 where rent payable weekly or in multiples of a week).

Analysis

This relates to any arrangements for training made under s2 of the Acts referred to. For an explanation of s2(1) Employment and Training Act 1973, see the note on reg 37 (on p364). Only the payments referred to in sub-paras (a) to (d) are to be taken into account.

14.–(1)　Subject to sub-paragraph (2), any of the following payments–

(a)　　a charitable payment;

(b)　　a voluntary payment;

(c)　　a payment (not falling within sub-paragraph (a) or (b) above) from a trust whose funds are derived from a payment made in consequence of any personal injury to the claimant;

(d)　　a payment under an annuity purchased–

　　(i)　　pursuant to any agreement or court order to make payments to the claimant; or

　　(ii)　　from funds derived from a payment made,

　　in consequence of any personal injury to the claimant; or

(e)　　a payment (not falling within sub-paragraphs (a) to (d)) received by virtue of any agreement or court order to make payments to the claimant in consequence of any personal injury to the claimant.

(2)　　Sub-paragraph (1) shall not apply to a payment which is made or due to be made by–

(a)　　a former partner of the claimant, or a former partner of any member of the claimant's family; or

(b)　　the parent of a child or young person where that child or young person is a member of the claimant's family.

Analysis

Note, firstly that para 35 provides a complete disregard of certain charitable payments, such as those made from the Macfarlane Trust, the Macfarlane (Special Payments) Trust, the Macfarlane (Special Payments) (No.2) Trust and the Independent Living Fund (2006). Note, secondly, that unlike previous versions of this paragraph, if the income payment falls within para (1) – this includes payments made in consequence of personal injury suffered by a claimant – and is not caught by para (2), all of the payment is ignored. There is no £20 limit under this para as there was under previous versions of this paragraph, nor does para 34 apply to limit the total amount of income that may be ignored.

Sub-para (c) covers payments from trusts whose funds are derived from payments made in consequence of personal injury to the claimant. The value of the trust itself is disregarded under para 14 of Sch 6, as is the value of the right to receive payments under it. See also para 14A Sch 6 for capital payments made from such a trust and paras 45 and 46 Sch 6 where damages paid to children or young people are administered by the Court.

The nature of charitable and voluntary payments was examined in detail in *R v Doncaster BC ex p Boulton* [1992] 25 HLR 195, QBD. Laws J held that:

"[t]he effect of specifying both charitable and voluntary payments is to enable payments which are not made for the payer's own benefit to be brought within the scope of the disregard without the need to engage with fine distinctions between charitable and non-charitable payments."

In addition it was found that the reference to charitable payments "must be to payments made under a charitable trust" – eg, those made by a registered charity. As with charitable payments, the Court decided that a payment is voluntary if it is made without anything being obtained by the payer in return.

The case itself dealt with the question of whether or not payments of cash in lieu of concessionary coal made to the widow of a miner by British Coal were voluntary payments which qualified for the disregard. This was found not to be the case on the basis that the agreement between British Coal and the Unions under which they are paid was entered into in the interests of good labour relations and for the efficient running of the coal industry. Laws J concluded that:

"This legitimate and proper purpose is, however, far away from the purpose and benevolence behind voluntary payments in the regulations . . . and that as a matter of the law the payments made to the applicant were not voluntary within the meaning of the relevant regulations."

Consequently authorities should take payments of cash in lieu of concessionary coal made by British Coal to ex-miners and their widows into account as "remuneration or profit derived from that employment" and should treat them as earnings. See also reg 42(6) and (7).

In *R(H) 5/05* Commissioner Mesher concluded that the phrase "voluntary payment" should have the same meaning here as it did in reg 40(6) HB Regs 1987 (now reg 46(6) HB Regs), even though the contexts are somewhat different, and that *Boulton* was correctly decided and applied as much to reg 40(6) HB Regs 1987 as it did to this para. However, on the facts of the case before him, where an "informal loan" had been made to the claimant, the commissioner concluded that there had been no intention to create legal relations and therefore no legally enforceable rights or obligations were created by the payments to the claimant. This was a crucial point which distinguished the case from *Boulton*, because here the person making the "loan" payments to the claimant got nothing in return, tangible or otherwise, whereas in *Boulton* the Coal Board did at least benefit from the payments of cash in lieu of concessionary coal in the sense of fostering good labour relations. The maintenance of a relationship of personal affection or of familial duty on the part of the payer, in Commissioner Mesher's view, did not constitute an intangible benefit for the payer sufficient to disqualify the payments as voluntary payments: para 42.

---

15. Subject to paragraph 34, £10 of any of the following, namely–

(a)   a war disablement pension (except insofar as such a pension falls to be disregarded under paragraph 8 or 9);

[¹ (b)   a war widow's pension or [³ war widower's pension] ;]

(c)   a pension payable to a person as a widow, widower or surviving civil partner under [²] any power of Her Majesty otherwise than under an enactment to make provision about pensions for or in respect of persons who have been disabled or have died in consequence of service as members of the armed forces of the Crown;

(d)   a guaranteed income payment [² and, if the amount of that payment has been abated to less than £10 by a [³ pension or payment falling within article 31(1)(a) or (b) of the Armed Forces and Reserve Forces (Compensation Scheme) Order 2005], so much of [³ that pension or payment] as would not, in aggregate with the amount of [³ any] guaranteed income payment disregarded, exceed £10];

(e)   a payment made to compensate for the non-payment of such a pension or payment as is mentioned in any of the preceding sub-paragraphs;

(f)   a pension paid by the government of a country outside Great Britain which is analogous to any of the pensions or payments mentioned in sub-paragraphs (a) to (d) above;

(g)   pension paid to victims of National Socialist persecution under any special provision made by the law of the Federal Republic of Germany, or any part of it, or of the Republic of Austria.

Amendments

1.   Substituted by reg 3(12)(a) of SI 2008 No 1042 as from 19.5.08.

2.   Amended by reg 5(6)(c of SI 2008 No 3157 as from 5.1.09.

3.   Amended by reg 6(6)(b) of SI 2009 No 2655 as from 2.11.09.

Analysis

A guaranteed income payment (defined in reg 2(1)) can be abated in part or in full by a payment under the Schemes set out in sub-para (d). The amendment made by SI 2008 No.3157 ensures that the claimant can benefit from the full £10 disregard in this situation. Great Britain does *not* include Northern Ireland. Para 15(f) extends the £10 statutory disregard to analogous payments made by the governments of other countries. This disregard can overlap with disregards from student covenant income and access funds as well as the disregard in para 16. A combined maximum of £20 is allowed: Sch 5 para 34.

Note: s134(8) SSAA allows an authority to resolve to disregard more than £10 of (or all of) prescribed war pensions.

---

16. Subject to paragraph 34, £15 of any–
(a) widowed mother's allowance paid pursuant to section 37 of the Act;
(b) widowed parent's allowance paid pursuant to section 39A of the Act.

Analysis

This disregard can overlap with disregards from student covenant income and access funds as well as the disregard in para 15. A combined maximum of £20 is allowed: Sch 5 para 34.

17.–(1) Any income derived from capital to which the claimant is or is treated under regulation 51 (capital jointly held) as beneficially entitled but, subject to sub-paragraph (2), not income derived from capital disregarded under paragraphs 1, 2, 4, 8, 14 or 25 to 28 of Schedule 6.
(2) Income derived from capital disregarded under paragraphs 2, 4 or 25 to 28 of Schedule 6 but only to the extent of–
(a) any mortgage repayments made in respect of the dwelling or premises in the period during which that income accrued; or
(b) any council tax or water charges which the claimant is liable to pay in respect of the dwelling or premises and which are paid in the period during which that income accrued.
(3) The definition of ''water charges'' in regulation 2(1) shall apply to sub-paragraph (2) of this paragraph with the omission of the words ''in so far as such charges are in respect of the dwelling which a person occupies as his home''.

Analysis

The effect of this para is that unless the *capital* to which the person is entitled is disregarded, under the provisions listed, the income produced by capital is to be disregarded. Income from capital disregarded under the provisions listed is to be taken into account, however, except so far as sub-para (2) provides otherwise. See also reg 51 (on p391). Note that reg 52 (on p393) provides a formula for calculating "tariff" (deemed) income from capital that is not disregarded.

Sub-para (2). Where income is produced from capital disregarded under paras 2, 4, or 25 to 28 of Sch 6, it can be disregarded to the extent that mortgage repayments (of capital as well as interest) were made in respect of the premises in question during the period to which the income relates. Deductions can also be made for any payments of council tax or water charges for which the claimant is liable during the period to which the income relates.

[¹**18.**]

Amendment

1. Omitted by reg 3(12)(b) of SI 2008 No 1042 as from 19.5.08.

---

19. Where the claimant makes a parental contribution in respect of a student attending a course at an establishment in the United Kingdom or undergoing education in the United Kingdom, which contribution has been assessed for the purposes of calculating–
(a) under, or pursuant to regulations made under powers conferred by, sections 1 or 2 of the Education Act 1962 or section 22 of the Teaching and Higher Education Act 1998, that student's award;
(b) under regulations made in exercise of the powers conferred by section 49 of the Education (Scotland) Act 1980, that student's bursary, scholarship, or other allowance under that section or under regulations made in exercise of the powers conferred by section 73 of that Act of 1980, any payment to that student under that section; or
(c) the student's student loan,
an amount equal to the weekly amount of that parental contribution, but only in respect of the period for which that contribution is assessed as being payable.

Analysis

Under this para, a parental contribution taken into account in computing a student's grant or loan under the provisions listed is disregarded in computing the payer's "other" income during the period for which the contribution is payable. If "other" income is insufficient to use up the disregard, the unused part can be disregarded from earnings: see Sch 4 para 11. See also para 20 below.

Sub-para (a). s1 of the 1962 Act deals with full time courses designated as first degree courses or comparable to these, at universities, colleges or other institutions in the UK.

Sub-para (b). Under s73 of the 1980 Act, the Secretary of State may award grants to assist the carrying out of educational research (Subs (1)(e)) or payments of allowances to persons attending "courses of education" (Subs (1)(f)).

Sub-para (c) refers to student loans. See reg 53 for the definition.

20.–(1)   Where the claimant is the parent of a student aged under 25 in advanced education who either–
(a)   is not in receipt of any award, grant or student loan in respect of that education; or
(b)   is in receipt of an award under section 2 of the Education Act 1962 or an award bestowed by virtue of the Teaching and Higher Education Act 1998, or regulations made thereunder, or a bursary, scholarship or other allowance under section 49(1) of the Education (Scotland) Act 1980, or a payment under section 73 of that Act of 1980,
and the claimant makes payments by way of a contribution towards the student's maintenance, other than a parental contribution falling within paragraph 19, an amount specified in sub-paragraph (2) in respect of each week during the student's term.
(2)   For the purposes of sub-paragraph (1), the amount shall be equal to–
(a)   the weekly amount of the payments; or
(b)   the amount by way of a personal allowance for a single claimant under 25 less the weekly amount of any award, bursary, scholarship, allowance or payment referred to in sub-paragraph (1)(b),
whichever is less.

Analysis

This provides a partial disregard in computing the payer's "other income" for payments made by a parent to a student in advanced education who is aged under 25 and is not receiving a grant or loan (or who gets one of the awards listed). If "other" income is insufficient to use up the disregard, the unused part can be disregarded from earnings: see Sch 4 para 11. See also para 19 above.

Note the, albeit very *obiter,* view in *CH 2517/2004* that the word "parent" in Sch 4 para 18 HB Regs 1987 (now Sch 5 para 20) should arguably not be restricted to a natural or adoptive parent.

Sub-para (2) quantifies how much of the parent's income may be disregarded in this respect.

---

21.   Any payment made to the claimant by a child or young person or a non-dependant.

Analysis

This provides a disregard of payments received by the claimant from a child, young person or non-dependant – but see reg 74 (on p427) for the deductions that can be made from "eligible rent" in respect of non-dependants. See also paras 22 and 42 if payments are being made by someone residing in the claimant's home who is other than a child, young person or non-dependant.

---

22.   Where the claimant occupies a dwelling as his home and the dwelling is also occupied by a person other than one to whom paragraph 21 or 42 refers and there is a contractual liability to make payments to the claimant in respect of the occupation of the dwelling by that person or a member of his family–
[³ (a)   where the aggregate of any payments made in respect of any one week in respect of the occupation of the dwelling by that person or a member of his family, or by that person and a member of his family, is less than £20, the whole of that amount; or
(b)   where the aggregate of any such payments is £20 or more per week, £20.]

Amendments

1.   Amended by Art 19(10)(a) of SI 2006 No 645 and reg 8 of SI 2006 No 217 as from 1.4.06 (3.4.06 where rent payable weekly or at intervals of a week).
2.   Amended by Art 19(10)(a) of SI 2007 No 688 as from 1.4.07 (2.4.07 where rent payable weekly or at intervals of a week).
3.   Substituted by reg 11(12) of SI 2007 No 2618 as from 1.4.08 (7.4.08 where rent payable weekly or at intervals of a week).

Analysis

This deals with payments from persons other than a child, young person or non-dependant (for which see para 21) or someone to whom the claimant is providing "board and lodging accommodation" (for which see para 42). There must be a contractual liability (ie, as a licensee or tenant) to pay the claimant in return for living in her/his home. Such income is *not* treated as "earnings" and the only disregards are those set out here.

23.–(1)   Any income in kind, except where regulation 40(10)(b) (provision of support under section 95 or 98 of the Immigration and Asylum Act in the calculation of income other than earnings) applies.

(2)   The reference in sub-paragraph (1) to ''income in kind'' does not include a payment to a third party made in respect of the claimant which is used by the third party to provide benefits in kind to the claimant.

Analysis

Income in kind is excluded from the calculation of HB, as long as it is not caught by sub-para (2) or income to be taken into account under reg 40(10(b).

---

24.   Any income which is payable in a country outside the United Kingdom for such period during which there is a prohibition against the transfer to the United Kingdom of that income.

25.–(1)   Any payment made to the claimant in respect of a person who is a member of his family–

(a)   pursuant to regulations under section 2(6)(b), 3 or 4 of the Adoption and Children Act 2002 or [¹ in accordance] with a scheme approved by the Scottish Ministers under [² section 51A] of the Adoption (Scotland) Act 1978 (schemes for payments of allowances to adopters);

[² (b)]

[³ (ba)   which is a payment made by a local authority in pursuance of section 15(1) of, and paragraph 15 of Schedule 1 to, the Children Act 1989 (local authority contribution to a child's maintenance where the child is living with a person as a result of a residence order) or in Scotland section 50 of the Children Act 1975 (payments towards maintenance of children);]

(c)   which is a payment made by an authority, as defined in Article 2 of the Children Order, in pursuance of Article 15 of, and paragraph 17 of Schedule 1 to, that Order (contribution by an authority to child's maintenance);

(d)   in accordance with regulations made pursuant to section 14F of the Children Act 1989 (special guardianship support services);

to the extent specified in sub-paragraph (3).

(2)   Any payment, other than a payment to which sub-paragraph (1)(a) applies, made pursuant to regulations under section 2(6)(b), 3 or 4 of the Adoption and Children Act 2002.

(3)   In the case of a child or young person, so much of the weekly amount of the payment as exceeds the amount included under Schedule 3 in the calculation of the claimant's applicable amount for that child or young person by way of the personal allowance and disabled child premium, if any.

Amendments

1.   Amended by reg 3(12)(c) of SI 2008 No 1042 as from 19.5.08.
2.   Amended by reg 5(6)(d) of SI 2008 No 3157 as from 5.1.09.
3.   Inserted by reg 6(6)(c) of SI 2009 No 2655 as from 2.11.09.

Analysis

The amount of the disregard allowed by para 25 is the amount by which the payments specified in para (1) and (2) *exceed* the personal allowance and disabled child premium (if any), applicable under Sch 3 to the child/young person in question (ie, such payments are to be taken into account *up to* that level): para (3). Note that where a payment is made in respect of a child or young person who does not count as a member of the claimant's "family" for HB purposes (eg, where the child or young person has not yet been placed with the claimant but is staying with her/him), the payment is fully disregarded in England: para (2). In Scotland and Wales, see reg 42(6)(c) under which any amount of the payment used by or spent on the child or young person is not to be treated as the claimant's income.

Until 5 January 2009, sub-para (1)(b) allowed for a disregard of contributions towards the cost of accommodation and maintenance of a child made by a local authority under s15(1) and para 15 Sch 1 Children Act 1989 where a child lived, or was to live, with someone as a result of a residence order. It also allowed a disregard (in Scotland) of certain payments made under s50 Children Act 1975 – eg, to "kinship carers". Sub-para (1)(b) was omitted in error and so the provision has now been re-inserted as sub-para (1)(ba).

[²**26.** Any payment made to the claimant with whom a person is accommodated by virtue of arrangements made–

(a)   by a local authority under–

(i)   section 23(2)(a) of the Children Act 1989 (provision of accommodation and maintenance for a child whom they are looking after),

(ii)   section 26 of the Children (Scotland) Act 1995 (manner of provision of accommodation to child looked after by local authority), or

(iii)   regulations 33 or 51 of the Looked After Children (Scotland) Regulations 2009 (fostering and kinship care allowances and fostering allowances); or

(b)   by a voluntary organisation under section 59(1)(a) of the Children Act 1989 (provision of accommodation by voluntary organisations).]

Amendments

1.   Amended by reg 15(6) of SI 2006 No 2378 as from 2.10.06.
2.   Substituted by reg 7(3) of SI 2010 No 2429 as from 1.11.10.

Analysis

This provides a total disregard for the payments referred to.

Sections 23 and 59 Children Act 1989 refer to the local authority powers to provide accommodation and maintenance for a child they are looking after and for the provision of accommodation by voluntary organisations. Section 26 of the Scottish Act gives authorities wide powers to make provision for children aged less than 18 where such arrangements would be: "likely to diminish the need to receive children into or keep them in care or the need to refer them to a children's hearing under Pt III of the Act."

The regulations provide the same in respect of children already in care.

27.　　Any payment made to the claimant or his partner for a person ("the person concerned"), who is not normally a member of the claimant's household but is temporarily in his care, by–

　(a)　　a health authority;

　(b)　　a local authority but excluding payments of housing benefit made in respect of the person concerned;

　(c)　　a voluntary organisation;

　(d)　　the person concerned pursuant to section 26(3A) of the National Assistance Act 1948; [1]

　(e)　　a primary care trust established under section 16A of the National Health Service Act [1 1977 or established by an order made under section 18(2)(c) of the National Health Service Act 2006]

　[¹ (f)　　a Local Health Board established under section 16BA of the National Health Service Act 1977 or established by an order made under section 11 of the National Health Service (Wales) Act 2006.]

Amendment

1.　　　　Amended by reg 5(6)(e) of SI 2008 No 3157 as from 5.1.09.

Analysis

For "membership of household", see p22, and Part 4 of these regulations.

This paragraph covers expenses plus any inducement element paid to enable a claimant to provide temporary respite care for someone (eg, an elderly or disabled person) so that, for example, a principal family carer can go for a holiday. There is a total disregard of such payments.

Sch 4 para 25 HB Regs 1987 (now Sch 5 para 27) was considered by Commissioner Williams in *CH 2321/ 2002*. He decided it was part of a set of disregards designed to enable landlords to receive income in return for caring for vulnerable people without their benefit being affected (para 21). The provisions were, between them, designed to apply to all such payments (para 23). Guidance was also given on the meaning of "temporarily in his care" (para 32).

28.　　Any payment made by a local authority in accordance with section 17, [¹ 23B, 23C or 24A] of the Children Act 1989 or, as the case may be, section 12 of the Social Work (Scotland) Act 1968 or section [² 22,] 29 or 30 of the Children (Scotland) Act 1995 (provision of services for children and their families and advice and assistance to certain children).

Amendments

1.　　　　Amended by reg 6(9)(a) of SI 2008 No 2767 as from 17.11.08.

2.　　　　Inserted by reg 7(4) of SI 2010 No 2429 as from 1.11.10.

Analysis

See Analysis of Sch 6 para 19 on p571.

　[¹**28A.**–(1)　　Subject to sub-paragraph (2), any payment (or part of a payment) made by a local authority in accordance with section 23C of the Children Act 1989(67) or section 29 of the Children (Scotland) Act 1995(68) (local authorities' duty to promote welfare of children and powers to grant financial assistance to persons in, or formerly in, their care) to a person ("A") which A passes on to the claimant.

　(2)　　　Sub-paragraph (1) applies only where A–

　(a)　　was formerly in the claimant's care, and

　(b)　　is aged 18 or over, and

　(c)　　continues to live with the claimant.]

Amendment

1.　　　　Inserted by reg 6(5)(a) of SI 2008 No 698 as from, as it relates to a particular beneficiary, the first day of the benefit week on or after 7.4.08.

Analysis

This provides a disregard of payments made by a local authority in accordance with the provisions listed. This only applies where the payment is made to someone formerly in the claimant's care as a child or young person, who is now aged 18 or over but continues to live with her/him, and who has passed the payment on to the claimant.

29.–(1)   Subject to sub-paragraph (2), any payment received under an insurancepolicy taken out to insure against the risk of being unable to maintain repayments–

   (a)   on a loan which is secured on the dwelling which the claimant occupies as his home; or

   (b)   under a regulated agreement as defined for the purposes of the Consumer Credit Act 1974 or under a hire-purchase agreement or a conditional sale agreement as defined for the purposes of Part 3 of the Hire-Purchase Act 1964.

   (2)   A payment referred to in sub-paragraph (1) shall only be disregarded to the extent that the payment received under that policy does not exceed the amounts, calculated on a weekly basis, which are used to–

   (a)   maintain the repayments referred to in sub-paragraph (1)(a) or, as the case may be, (b); and

   (b)   meet any amount due by way of premiums on–

       (i)   that policy; or

       (ii)   in a case to which sub-paragraph (1)(a) applies, an insurance policy taken out to insure against loss or damage to any building or part of a building which is occupied by the claimant as his home and which is required as a condition of the loan referred to in sub-paragraph (1)(a).

Analysis

Payments received under an insurance policy taken out to insure against the risk of being unable to maintain certain loan repayments are disregarded. The loan insured must be: (1) secured on the home or (2) an agreement of the types specified in sub-para (1)(b). The maximum disregarded is the total of the amounts in sub-para (2)(a) and (b).

30.   Any payment of income which by virtue of regulation 46 (income treated as capital) is to be treated as capital.

Analysis

This paragraph is necessary to aviod double counting.

31.   Any social fund payment made pursuant to Part 8 of the Act (the Social Fund).

32.   Any payment under Part 10 of the Act (Christmas bonus for pensioners).

33.   Where a payment of income is made in a currency other than sterling, any banking charge or commission payable in converting that payment into sterling.

34.   The total of a claimant's income or, if he is a member of a family, the family's income and the income of any person which he is treated as possessing under regulation 25(2) (calculation of income and capital of members of claimant's family and of a polygamous marriage) to be disregarded under regulation 60(2)(b) and regulation 61(1)(d) (calculation of covenant income where a contribution assessed), covenant income where no grant income or no contribution is assessed regulation 64(2) (treatment of student loans), regulation 65(3) (treatment of payments from access funds) and paragraphs 15 and 16 shall in no case exceed £20 per week.

Analysis

Under this paragraph, the combined maximum disregard for the types of income listed is £20.

35.–(1)   Any payment made under [³ or by] the Macfarlane Trust, the Macfarlane (Special Payments) Trust, the Macfarlane (Special Payments) (No. 2) Trust ("the Trusts"), the Fund, the Eileen Trust [³ , MFET Limited] or the Independent Living [¹ Fund (2006)].

   (2)   Any payment by or on behalf of a person who is suffering or who suffered from haemophilia or who is or was a qualifying person, which derives from a payment made under [³ or by] any of the Trusts to which sub-paragraph (1) refers and which is made to or for the benefit of–

   (a)   that person's partner or former partner from whom he is not, or where that person has died was not, estranged or divorced or with whom he has formed a civil partnership that has not been dissolved or, where that person has died, had not been dissolved at the time of that person's death;

   (b)   any child who is a member of that person's family or who was such a member and who is a member of the claimant's family; or

   (c)   any young person who is a member of that person's family or who was such a member and who is a member of the claimant's family.

   (3)   Any payment by or on behalf of the partner or former partner of a person who is suffering or who suffered from haemophilia or who is or was a qualifying person provided that the partner or former partner and that person are not, or if either of them has died were not, estranged or divorced or, where the partner or former partner and that person have formed a civil partnership, the civil partnership has not been dissolved or, if either of them has died, had not been dissolved at the time of the death, which derives from a payment made under [³ or by] any of the Trusts to which sub-paragraph (1) refers and which is made to or for the benefit of–

   (a)   the person who is suffering from haemophilia or who is a qualifying person;

   (b)   any child who is a member of that person's family or who was such a member and who is a member of the claimant's family; or

(c) any young person who is a member of that person's family or who was such a member and who is a member of the claimant's family.

(4) Any payment by a person who is suffering from haemophilia or who is a qualifying person, which derives from a payment under [³ or by] any of the Trusts to which sub-paragraph (1) refers, where–

(a) that person has no partner or former partner from whom he is not estranged or divorced or with whom he has formed a civil partnership that has not been dissolved, nor any child or young person who is or had been a member of that person's family; and

(b) the payment is made either–

(i) to that person's parent or step-parent; or

(ii) where that person at the date of the payment is a child, a young person or a student who has not completed his full-time education and has no parent or step-parent, to his guardian,

but only for a period from the date of the payment until the end of two years from that person's death.

(5) Any payment out of the estate of a person who suffered from haemophilia or who was a qualifying person, which derives from a payment under [³ or by] any of the Trusts to which sub-paragraph (1) refers, where–

(a) that person at the date of his death (the relevant date) had no partner or former partner from whom he was not estranged or divorced or with whom he had formed a civil partnership that had not been dissolved, nor any child or young person who was or had been a member of his family; and

(b) the payment is made either–

(i) to that person's parent or step-parent; or

(ii) where that person at the relevant date was a child, a young person or a student who had not completed his full-time education and had no parent or step-parent, to his guardian,

but only for a period of two years from the relevant date.

(6) In the case of a person to whom or for whose benefit a payment referred to in this paragraph is made, any income which derives from any payment of income or capital made under or deriving from any of the Trusts.

(7) For the purposes of sub-paragraphs (2) to (6), any reference to the Trusts shall be construed as including a reference to the Fund, the Eileen Trust [³ , MFET Limited] , the Skipton Fund or the London [² Bombings] Relief Charitable Fund.

Modifications

References to "step-parent" in sub-paras (4)(b)(i) and (ii) and (5)(b)(i) and (ii) are modified by s246 Civil Partnership Act 2004 and art 3 and para 25 Sch to SI 2005 No.3137.

Amendments

1. Amended by reg 6(4)(f) of SI 2008 No 2767 as from 17.11.08.
2. Amended by reg 5(6)(f) of SI 2008 No 3157 as from 5.1.09.
3. Amended by reg 8(3) and (5) of SI 2010 No 641 as from 1.4.10 (5.4.10 where rent payable weekly or in multiples of a week).

Analysis

Sub-para (1) provides an absolute disregard of payments from the Macfarlane Trust, the Macfarlane (Special Payments) Trust, the Macfarlane (Special Payments) (No.2) Trust, the Fund, the Eileen Trust, MFET Limited or the Independent Living Fund (2006).

Sub-paras (2)-(6) extend this disregard to certain situations where a payment made to someone who has (or had) haemophilia or who is (or was) a "qualifying person" (defined in reg 2(1)) from the Trusts referred to in sub-para (1) or included by sub-para (7), is passed on to someone else by the person who originally received it. The sub-paragraphs are relevant where the claimant or her/his partner is the person to whom the money has been passed.

---

36. Any payment made by the Secretary of State to compensate for the loss (in whole or in part) of entitlement to housing benefit.

[¹**37.**]

Amendment

1. Omitted by reg 6(5)(b) of SI 2008 No 698 as from 14.4.08.

[¹**38.**]

Amendment

1. Omitted by reg 5(6)(g) of SI 2008 No 3157 as from 5.1.09.

---

39. Any payment to a juror or witness in respect of attendance at a court other than compensation for loss of earnings or for the loss of a benefit payable under the benefit Acts.

Analysis
This would cover, for example, payments for travel, subsistence or accommodation.

[¹ **40.**]

Amendment
1.   Omitted by reg 6(9)(b) of SI 2008 No 2767 as from 17.11.08.

41.   Any payment in consequence of a reduction of council tax under section 13 or [¹] section 80 of the Local Government Finance Act 1992 (reduction of liability for council tax).

Amendment
1.   Omitted by reg 6(5)(c) of SI 2008 No 698 as from 14.4.08.

42.–(1)   Where the claimant occupies a dwelling as his home and he provides in that dwelling board and lodging accommodation, an amount, in respect of each person for whom such accommodation is provided for the whole or any part of a week, equal to–
(a)   where the aggregate of any payments made in respect of any one week in respect of such accommodation provided to such person does not exceed £20.00, 100 per cent. of such payments; or
(b)   where the aggregate of any such payments exceeds £20.00, £20.00 and 50 per cent. of the excess over £20.00.
(2)   In this paragraph "board and lodging accommodation" means accommodation provided to a person or, if he is a member of a family, to him or any other member of his family, for a charge which is inclusive of the provision of that accommodation and at least some cooked or prepared meals which both are cooked or prepared (by a person other than the person to whom the accommodation is provided or a member of his family) and are consumed in that accommodation or associated premises.

Analysis
This provides a disregard of a portion of the payments made to a claimant, by people to whom s/he provides "board and lodging accommodation" (as defined in sub-para (2)) in the dwelling s/he occupies as her/his home. The first £20 of each boarder's payment is ignored plus half of the amount in excess of £20. Where the claimant has a business partner, the paragraph does not say to apportion the disregard, even if the claimant's income includes just her/his share of the weekly charge to the boarders. The full disregard for each boarder as set out in this para should be made: *CIS 521/2002.*
There is no requirement that the board and lodgings be provided on a commercial basis, and no bar on this paragraph applying if, for example, the lodger is a close relative of the claimant. However, if the arrangement is not commercial, the lodger could come within the definition of a "non-dependant" in reg 3. If so, the payments made by her/him would instead be disregarded in full under para 21 above, but a non-dependant deduction would be made under reg 74 (see p427).

[¹**43.**]

Amendment
1.   Omitted by reg 5(6)(g) of SI 2008 No 3157 as from 5.1.09.

[²**44.**–(1)   Any payment or repayment made–
(a)   as respects England, under regulation 5, 6 or 12 of the National Health Service (Travel Expenses and Remission of Charges) Regulations 2003(48) (travelling expenses and health service supplies);
(b)   as respects Wales, under regulation 5, 6 or 11 of the National Health Service (Travelling Expenses and Remission of Charges) (Wales) Regulations 2007(49) (travelling expenses and health service supplies);
(c)   as respects Scotland, under regulation 3, 5 or 11 of the National Health Service (Travelling Expenses and Remission of Charges) (Scotland) (No. 2) Regulations 2003(50) (travelling expenses and health service supplies).
(2)   Any payment or repayment made by the Secretary of State for Health, the Scottish Ministers or the Welsh Ministers which is analogous to a payment or repayment mentioned in sub-paragraph (1).]

Amendments
1.   Amended by reg 3(12)(d)-(f) of SI 2008 No 1042 as from 19.5.08.
2.   Substituted by reg 5(6)(h) of SI 2008 No 3157 as from 5.1.09.

Analysis
Para 44 provides a disregard of payments made in respect of certain NHS charges (eg, dental treatment).

[²**45.** Any payment made to such persons entitled to receive benefits as may be determined by or under a scheme made pursuant to section 13 of the Social Security Act 1988 in lieu of vouchers or similar arrangements in connection with the provision of those benefits (including payments made in place of healthy start vouchers, milk tokens or the supply of vitamins).]

Amendments
1.   Amended by reg 3(12)(g) of SI 2008 No 1042 as from 19.5.08.
2.   Substituted by reg 5(6)(h) of SI 2008 No 3157 as from 5.1.09.

Analysis
Para 45 provides a disregard of payments made in lieu of vouchers for Healthy Start food and vitamins or for milk tokens. Healthy Start food is milk, fresh fruit and vegetables. Information is at www.healthystart.nhs.uk.

46. Any payment made by either the Secretary of State for [¹ Justice] or by Scottish Ministers under a scheme established to assist relatives and other persons to visit persons in custody.

Amendment
1.   Amended by Art 8 and the Sch para 23 of SI 2007 No 2128 as from 22.8.07.

[¹**47.**–(1)   Where a claimant's applicable amount includes an amount by way of family premium, £15 of any payment of maintenance, other than child maintenance, whether under a court order or not, which is made or due to be made by the claimant's former partner, or the claimant's partner's former partner.
    (2)   For the purpose of sub-paragraph (1) where more than one maintenance payment falls to be taken into account in any week, all such payments shall be aggregated and treated as if they were a single payment.
    (3)   A payment made by the Secretary of State in lieu of maintenance shall, for the purposes of sub-paragraph (1), be treated as a payment of maintenance made by a person specified in sub-paragraph (1).]

Amendment
1.   Substituted by reg 3(12)(h) of SI 2008 No 1042 as from 27.10.08.

Analysis
This provides a £15 disregard of maintenance payments other than child maintenance (for which see para 47A) where the claimant's applicable amount includes a family premium. In other words it only applies where the claimant is treated as responsible for a child or qualifying young person. To qualify for the disregard the maintenance payment must be made by the claimant's former partner or the claimant's partner's former partner.

[¹[²**47A.**–(1)   Any payment of child maintenance made or derived from a liable relative where the child or young person in respect of whom the payment is made is a member of the claimant's family, except where the person making the payment is the claimant or the claimant's partner.
    (2)   In paragraph (1)–
''child maintenance'' means any payment towards the maintenance of a child or young person, including any payment made voluntarily and payments made under–
    (a)   the Child Support Act 1991;
    (b)   the Child Support (Northern Ireland) Order 1991;
    (c)   a court order;
    (d)   a consent order;
    (e)   a maintenance agreement registered for execution in the Books of Council and Session or the sheriff court books;
''liable relative'' means a person listed in regulation 54 (interpretation) of the Income Support (General) Regulations 1987, other than a person falling within sub-paragraph (d) of that definition.]]

Amendments
1.   Inserted by reg 3(12)(h) of SI 2008 No 1042 as from 27.10.08.
2.   Substituted by reg 6(6)(d) of SI 2009 No 2655 as from 1.4.10 (5.4.10 where rent payable weekly or in multiples of a week).

Analysis
This provides a complete disregard of "child maintenance" payments, defined in sub-para (2) which are made by a "liable relative", except where the person making the payments is the claimant or her/his partner. Liable relatives as defined in reg 54 of the IS Regs include spouses, former spouses, civil partners and former civil partners of the claimant or of a member of her/his family. It also includes parents of a child or young person who is a member of the claimant's family and certain people who are contributing to the maintenance of a child or young person and who may reasonably be treated as the father of that child or young person.

[¹**48.**]

Amendment
1.   Omitted by reg 6(5)(b) of SI 2008 No 698 as from 14.4.08.

49.   Any payment (other than a training allowance) made, whether by the Secretary of State or any other person, under the Disabled Persons (Employment) Act 1944 to assist disabled persons to obtain or retain employment despite their disability.
50.   Any guardian's allowance.
[¹**51.**   Any council tax benefit.]

Amendment
1.   Substituted by reg 5(6)(i) of SI 2008 No 3157 as from 5.1.09.

[¹**52.**–(1)   If the claimant is in receipt of any benefit under Part 2, 3 or 5 of the Act, any increase in the rate of that benefit arising under Part 4 (increases for dependants) or section 106(a) (unemployability supplement) of the Act, where the dependant in respect of whom the increase is paid is not a member of the claimant's family.
(2)   If the claimant is in receipt of any pension or allowance under Part 2 or 3 of the Naval, Military and Air Forces Etc. (Disablement and Death) Service Pensions Order 2006, any increase in the rate of that pension or allowance under that Order, where the dependant in respect of whom the increase is paid is not a member of the claimant's family.]

Amendment
1.   Substituted by reg 5(6)(i) of SI 2008 No 3157 as from 5.1.09.

[¹**53.**   Any supplementary pension under article 23(2) of the Naval, Military and Air Forces Etc. (Disablement and Death) Service Pensions Order 2006 (pensions to surviving spouses and surviving civil partners) and any analogous payment made by the Secretary of State for Defence to any person who is not a person entitled under that Order.]

Amendment
1.   Substituted by reg 5(6)(i) of SI 2008 No 3157 as from 5.1.09.

54. In the case of a pension awarded at the supplementary rate under article 27(3) of the Personal Injuries (Civilians) Scheme 1983 (pensions to widows, widowers or surviving civil partners), the sum specified in paragraph 1(c) of Schedule 4 to that Scheme.
55.–(1)   Any payment which is–
(a)   made under any of the Dispensing Instruments to a widow, widower or surviving civil partner of a person–
(i)   whose death was attributable to service in a capacity analogous to service as a member of the armed forces of the Crown; and
(ii)   whose service in such capacity terminated before 31st March 1973; and
[¹ (b)   equal to the amount specified in article 23(2) of the Naval, Military and Air Forces Etc. (Disablement and Death) Service Pensions Order 2006.]
(2)   In this paragraph "the Dispensing Instruments" means the Order in Council of 19th December 1881, the Royal Warrant of 27th October 1884 and the Order by His Majesty of 14th January 1922 (exceptional grants of pay, non-effective pay and allowances).

Amendment
1.   Substituted by reg 5(6)(j) of SI 2008 No 3157 as from 5.1.09.

56.   Except in a case which falls under sub-paragraph (1) of paragraph 17 of Schedule 4, where the claimant is a person who satisfies any of the conditions of sub-paragraph (2) of that paragraph, any amount of working tax credit up to [⁵ £17.10].

Amendments
1.   Amended by Art 19(10)(b) of SI 2006 No 645 and reg 8 of SI 2006 No 217 as from 1.4.06 (3.4.06 where rent payable weekly or at intervals of a week).
2.   Amended by Art 19(10)(b) of SI 2007 No 688 as from 1.4.07 (2.4.07 where rent payable weekly or at intervals of a week).
3.   Amended by Art 19(11) of SI 2008 No 632 as from 1.4.08 (7.4.08 where rent payable weekly or in multiples of a week).

4. Amended by Art 19(12) of SI 2009 No 497 as from 1.4.09 (6.4.09 where rent payable weekly or at intervals of a week).

5. Amended by Art 19(11) of SI 2010 No 793 as from 1.4.10 (5.4.10 where rent payable weekly or in multiples of a week).

Analysis

This allows for a disregard of working tax credit up to the amount specified where earnings are too low to use the whole of the disregard allowed by Sch 4 para 17.

---

57. Any payment made [¹] under section 12B of the Social Work (Scotland) Act 1968 [² , or under sections 12A to 12D of the National Health Service Act 2006 (direct payments for health care)] or under regulations made under section 57 of the Health and Social Care Act 2001 (direct payments).

Amendments

1. Amended by reg 6(12) of SI 2009 No 583 as from 6.4.09.

2. Amended by reg 8(11) of SI 2010 No 641 as from 1.4.10 (5.4.10 where rent payable weekly or in multiples of a week).

Analysis

Rather than provide services to disabled people directly, local authorities can pay "direct payments" to them to buy their own services. Payments can also be made under the National Health Service Act directly to patients in lieu of their health care ("Direct Payments for Health Care"). Under this paragraph, direct payments are disregarded. They are also disregarded as capital under Sch 6 para 58.

Note that "direct payments" could count as "earnings" if the disabled person is a member of a couple and "employs" her/his partner as her/his carer. In *CIS 1068/2006*, the claimant was caring for his severely disabled wife, and claiming IS. Direct payments were made by the local authority to the claimant's wife. She used these to employ the claimant as her carer. The issue was whether the direct payments should be fully disregarded under Sch 9 para 58 Income Support (General) Regulations 1987 (the equivalent of this para) or taken into account as the claimant's earnings (making an appropriate earnings disregard). Allowing the Secretary of State's appeal, Commissioner Turnbull held that it was not open to the tribunal to hold on the evidence before it that the claimant was not in receipt of earnings from his wife in the form of the payment made to him. In determining the claimant's wife's income the "direct payments" to her had to be disregarded under Sch 9 para 58. However, the claimant's wife then used those payments to "employ" him as her carer. It did not matter whether she formally employed him or he was engaged as a self-employed earner to provide services for her: in either case the sums paid to the claimant were earnings and fell to be taken into account in calculating his IS. Nothing in s136(1) SSCBA 1992 altered this conclusion, or meant that the claimant had to be treated as receiving the payments as "direct payments" rather than earnings. The Court of Appeal upheld the decision in *Casewell v Secretary of State for Work and Pensions* [2008] 11 March, WLR (D) 86, reported as *R(IS) 7/08*.

58.–(1) Subject to sub-paragraph (2), in respect of a person who is receiving, or who has received, assistance under the self-employment route, any payment to that person–

(a) to meet expenses wholly and necessarily incurred whilst carrying on the commercial activity;

(b) which is used or intended to be used to maintain repayments on a loan taken out by that person for the purpose of establishing or carrying on the commercial activity,

in respect of which such assistance is or was received.

(2) Sub-paragraph (1) shall apply only in respect of payments which are paid to that person from the special account [¹].

Amendment

1. Amended by reg 8(10)(b) of SI 2010 No 641 as from 1.4.10 (5.4.10 where rent payable weekly or in multiples of a week).

Analysis

The payments set out in sub-para (1) to those following the "self-employment route" (defined in reg 2(1)) to meet expenses or to service loans are ignored, but only where paid into a special account referred to in sub-para (2) and also defined in reg 2(1). See also reg 46(7) for receipts paid to those following this route which are treated as capital.

59.–(1) Any payment of a sports award except to the extent that it has been made in respect of any one or more of the items specified in sub-paragraph (2).

(2) The items specified for the purposes of sub-paragraph (1) are food, ordinary clothing or footwear, household fuel or rent of the claimant or where the claimant is a member of a family, any other member of his family, or any council tax or water charges for which that claimant or member is liable.

(3)   For the purposes of sub-paragraph (2)–

"food" does not include vitamins, minerals or other special dietary supplements intended to enhance the performance of the person in the sport in respect of which the award was made;

"rent" means eligible rent less any deductions in respect of non-dependants which fall to be made under regulation 74 (non-dependant deductions).

Analysis

Sports awards (defined in reg 2(1)) are ignored as income except in so far as they provide for basic needs. On the wording of para (2), see the analysis to reg 42(6) on p377.

---

60.   Where the amount of subsistence allowance paid to a person in a benefit week exceeds the amount of income-based jobseeker's allowance that person would have received in that benefit week had it been payable to him, less 50p, that excess amount.

61.   In the case of a claimant participating in an employment zone programme, any discretionary payment made by an employment zone contractor to the claimant, being a fee, grant, loan or otherwise.

62.   Any discretionary housing payment paid pursuant to regulation 2(1) of the Discretionary Financial Assistance Regulations 2001.

63.–(1)   Any payment made by a local authority or by the [¹ Welsh Ministers], to or on behalf of the claimant or his partner relating to a service which is provided to develop or sustain the capacity of the claimant or his partner to live independently in his accommodation.

(2)   For the purposes of sub-paragraph (1) "local authority" includes, in England, a county council.

Amendment
1.   Amended by reg 5(6)(l) of SI 2008 No 3157 as from 5.1.09.

Analysis
Under this para, payments made by a local authority or the Welsh Ministers for support services to help the claimant or her/his partner live independantly (ie, under the Supporting People programme) are ignored as the claimant's income. This disregard does not apply to landlords receiving such payments for providing the services, although other paragraphs in this Schedule might apply.

[¹ [²**64.**]

Amendments
1.   Inserted by reg 4 of SI 2008 No 3140 as from 5.1.09.
2.   Revoked by reg 1(3) and (4) of SI 2008 No 3140 as from 6.4.09 (1.4.09 in relation to a claimant whose eligible rent falls to be calculated in accordance with reg 80(2)(b) or (c) HB Regs.

[¹**65.**   Any payment of child benefit.]

Amendment
1.   Inserted by reg 3 of SI 2009 No 2848 as from 2.11.09.

SCHEDULE 6
REGULATION 44
Capital to be disregarded

Modifications

Paras 48A and 48B were inserted by para 2(6) HB&CTB(CP) Regs in respect of claims for HB by some refugees.

A different version of para 48B was substituted for para 55B by Sch 4 para 4(2)(c) of the HB&CTB(CP) Regs for some HB claimants who are refugees who claimed asylum on or before 2 April 2000. See also reg 10A and Sch A1 inserted by Sch 4 para 2 HB&CTB(CP) Regs.

Note that paras 48A and 48B lapsed by s12(2)(e) of the Asylum and Immigration (Treatment of Claimants, etc.) Act 2004 (for those recorded as refugees after 14 June 2007) and were omitted by reg 5(7)(b) of SI 2008 No.3157 as from 5 January 2009. For the full text of paras 48A and 48B, see pp1129 and 1133 of the 20th edition.

Para A1 is inserted by reg 17 Jobseeker's Allowance (Work for Your Benefit Pilot Scheme) Regulations 2010 SI No.1222 (see p1247) as from 22 November 2010 but only for those ordinarily resident in a pilot area or whose address for payment of JSA is located within such an area. The modification is shown in italics below. It ceases to have effect on 21 November 2013.

Definitions
"claimant" – see reg 2(1).
"croft land" – see note on reg 2(4).

"dwelling" – see reg 2(4) and s137(1) SSCBA.
"family" – see s137(1) SSCBA.
"income related benefit" – see s123(1) SSCBA.
"Independent Living Fund (2006)" – see reg 2(1).
"Macfarlane Trust" – see reg 2(1).
"MFET Limited" – see reg 2(1).
"partner" – see reg 2(1).
"polygamous marriage" – see reg 2(1).
"relative" – see reg 2(1).
"self-employed earner" – see reg 2(1).
"the Work For Your Benefit Pilot Scheme" – see reg 2(1).
"young person" – see reg 19.

General Note on Schedule 6

This sets out the items of a claimant's and her/his partner's capital which must be ignored for the purposes of calculating HB. See reg 44(2) and, generally, Section 6 of Part 6. The disregards under the following paragraphs are cumulative unless specified otherwise. The effect is a mandatory disregard, but sometimes the *period* of the disregard is at the authority's discretion.

[A1.   Any payment made to the claimant in respect of any child care, travel or other expenses incurred, or to be incurred, by him in respect of his participation in the Work for Your Benefit Scheme but only for 52 weeks beginning with the date of receipt of the payment.]

1.   The dwelling together with any garage, garden and outbuildings, normally occupied by the claimant as his home including any premises not so occupied which it is impracticable or unreasonable to sell separately, in particular, in Scotland, any croft land on which the dwelling is situated; but, notwithstanding regulation 25 (calculation of income and capital of members of claimant's family and of a polygamous marriage), only one dwelling shall be disregarded under this paragraph.

Analysis

For the dwelling "normally occupied" by the claimant as her/his home, see reg 7. To be included as the home, provided they are part of the same "dwelling", are any premises it is "impractical or unreasonable" to sell separately.

This disregard is in addition to land already treated as a dwelling under reg 2(4). This wording was used in respect of the meaning of the word "home" in reg 2(1) of the Supplementary Benefit (Resources) Regs 1987. In *R(SB) 13/84* and *R(SB) 27/84*, it was said that whether it is "impractical or unreasonable" to sell is a subjective question – ie, to be looked at from the claimant's point of view and circumstances. A dwelling could include an extension built to accommodate a relative, but not where this is separately rated or self contained. Only one "dwelling" may be ignored under this paragraph. But note that the dwelling a claimant occupies as a home may comprise more than one property: *London Borough of Hackney v GA* [2008] UKUT 26 (AAC); *R(H) 5/09*.

Note: para 1 would cease to apply if the claimant no longer occupies a dwelling as a home (eg, s/he moves home) but other paras below might apply to the now former home so that its value can continue to be disregarded (see, for example, paras 4, 25, 26 and 28) or the proceeds of sale might be disregarded (see para 3).

2.   Any premises acquired for occupation by the claimant which he intends to occupy as his home within 26 weeks of the date of acquisition or such longer period as is reasonable in the circumstances to enable the claimant to obtain possession and commence occupation of the premises.

Analysis

Under this para, a claimant may have premises acquired for occupation as a home ignored for the purpose of calculating her/his entitlement to HB. The claimant must intend to occupy the premises as her/his home within 26 weeks of acquiring it (longer if reasonable). This is a week-by-week test and the disregard could cease to apply immediately if the claimant no longer intends to occupy the premises at all or within the 26-week (or longer) period: *JH v SSWP* [2009] UKUT 1 (AAC).

The words "as his home" show that only potential residential premises are covered. Once the claimant moves into the premises, para 2 would no longer apply, but para 1 would if they are "normally occupied" by the claimant.

3.   Any sum directly attributable to the proceeds of sale of any premises formerly occupied by the claimant as his home which is to be used for the purchase of other premises intended for such occupation within 26 weeks of the date of sale or such longer period as is reasonable in the circumstances to enable the claimant to complete the purchase.

Analysis
This covers the situation where the claimant has sold her/his former home, but has not yet purchased a new one. It applies where the proceeds of the sale are to be used to purchase premises which the claimant intends to occupy as a home, within 26 weeks of the date of sale. A longer period can be allowed if this is "reasonable", and is necessary to allow the claimant to complete the purchase. Once the new home is actually purchased, paras 1 or 2 could apply to the acquired premises, depending on whether the claimant moves in immediately or not. For the meaning of "occupied as home", see reg 7.

---

4.   Any premises occupied in whole or in part–
(a)   by a partner or relative of a single claimant or any member of the family as his home [¹ where that person has attained the qualifying age for state pension credit or is incapacitated];
(b)   by the former partner of the claimant as his home; but this provision shall not apply where the former partner is a person from whom the claimant is estranged or divorced or with whom he had formed a civil partnership that has been dissolved.

Amendment
1.   Amended by reg 28 of SI 2009 No 1488 as from 6.4.10.

Analysis
This allows the disregard of any dwelling owned by the claimant occupied by the people set out in sub-paras (a) or (b). This para is not restricted to the disregard of *one* dwelling only. It allows the whole premises to be ignored whether the partner/former partner/relative occupies all or part of them.

    Sub-para (a). The partner or relative in question must either be at least the qualifying age for PC (defined in reg 2(1)) or "incapacitated". "Incapacitated" is not defined here but would appear to have a broader meaning than those who would qualify for disability premium or for a component (see Sch 3).

    Sub-para (b) provides a disregard where the claimant's former partner occupies the premises as a home, so long as s/he and the claimant are not estranged or divorced nor their civil partnership dissolved. This would include situations where a couple continue to see themselves as a couple, but for HB purposes, are not treated as such – eg, because they are no longer members of the same household: regs 2(1) (definitions of "partner" and "couple") and 21.

    The meaning of "estranged" is not supplied by the regulation. In *R(IS) 5/05*, Commissioner Rowland said that it has a connotation of emotional disharmony. The question will be whether the parties have ceased to consider themselves to be a couple and not whether, despite that, they continue to maintain friendly relations. In *CPC 683/ 2007*, there was no emotional disharmony between the claimant and the former partner as adults, but there was emotional disharmony between them as partners. Commissioner Jacobs said that was a key distinction because the language used in the legislation is attempting to identify those cases in which the relationship between the parties is such that it is appropriate for their finances to be treated separately for the purposes of benefit entitlement.

    See para 25 below when the claimant *is* "estranged" or divorced from the former partner or where a civil partnership has been dissolved.

---

5.   Where a claimant is on income support [¹ , an income-based jobseeker's allowance or an income-related employment and support allowance], the whole of his capital.

Amendment
1.   Amended by reg 26(a) of SI 2008 No 1082 as from 27.10.08.

Analysis
This paragraph and para 6 are necessary to avoid double counting – see General Notes on Part 6 and Sch 4 para 12 and Sch 5 paras 4 and 5.

---

6.   Where the claimant is a member of a joint-claim couple for the purposes of the Jobseekers Act and his partner is on income-based jobseeker's allowance, the whole of the claimant's capital.
7.   Any future interest in property of any kind, other than land or premises in respect of which the claimant has granted a subsisting lease or tenancy, including sub-leases or sub-tenancies.

Analysis
A "future interest", or "reversionary interest", covers the situation where the claimant or her/his partner (see reg 25) will become entitled to possession of the asset at some future date, but someone else has that right at present – eg, where property has been left to another person for life, then to the claimant on that other person's death. The value of any such interest must be totally disregarded.

8.–(1)   The assets of any business owned in whole or in part by the claimant and for the purposes of which he is engaged as a self-employed earner, or if he has ceased to be so engaged, for such period as may be reasonable in the circumstances to allow for disposal of any such asset.

(2)   The assets of any business owned in whole or in part by the claimant where–

(a)   he is not engaged as a self-employed earner in that business by reason of some disease or bodily or mental disablement; but

(b)   he intends to become engaged or, as the case may be, re-engaged as a self-employed earner in that business as soon as he recovers or is able to become engaged or re-engaged in that business,

for a period of 26 weeks from the date on which the claim for housing benefit is made, or is treated as made, or, if it is unreasonable to expect him to become engaged or re-engaged in that business within that period, for such longer period as is reasonable in the circumstances to enable him to become so engaged or re-engaged.

(3)   In the case of a person who is receiving assistance under the self-employment route, the assets acquired by that person for the purpose of establishing or carrying on the commercial activity in respect of which such assistance is being received.

(4)   In the case of a person who has ceased carrying on the commercial activity in respect of which assistance was received as specified in sub-paragraph (3), the assets relating to that activity for such period as may be reasonable in the circumstances to allow for disposal of any such asset.

Analysis

This allows the disregard of business assets owned by the claimant while s/he is working for the business and also for a "reasonable" period after s/he ceases working for the business to allow time to sell or otherwise dispose of the assets: sub-para (1). What is a "reasonable" period will depend on the type of business as well as the current economic situation. See also reg 49(5). Sub-para (2) ensures the disregard is also applicable during any period a self-employed claimant is temporarily unable to work due to an illness or injury for a period of up to 26 weeks from the date the HB claim is, or is treated as, made. The initial 26 week period should be extended where it is considered unreasonable to expect the claimant to become (re-)engaged in that period.

9.–(1)   Subject to sub-paragraph (2), any arrears of, or any concessionary payment made to compensate for arrears due to the non-payment of–

(a)   any payment specified in paragraphs 6, 8 or 9 of Schedule 5;

[² (b)   an income-related benefit under Part 7 of the Act;]

(c)   an income-based jobseeker's allowance;

(d)   any discretionary housing payment paid pursuant to regulation 2(1) of the Discretionary Financial Assistance Regulations 2001;

(e)   working tax credit and child tax credit [¹],

[³ (f)   an income-related employment and support allowance,]

but only for a period of 52 weeks from the date of the receipt of arrears or of the concessionary payment.

(2)   In a case where the total of any arrears and, if appropriate, any concessionary payment referred to in sub-paragraph (1) relating to one of the specified payments, benefits or allowances amounts to £5,000 or more (referred to in this sub-paragraph and in sub-paragraph (3) as "the relevant sum") and is–

(a)   paid in order to rectify or to compensate for, an official error as defined in regulation 1(2) of the Decisions and Appeals Regulations; and

(b)   received by the claimant in full on or after 14th October 2001,

sub-paragraph (1) shall have effect in relation to such arrears or concessionary payment either for a period of 52 weeks from the date of receipt, or, if the relevant sum is received in its entirety during the award of housing benefit, for the remainder of that award if that is a longer period.

(3)   For the purposes of sub-paragraph (2), "the award of housing benefit" means–

(a)   the award in which the relevant sum is first received (or the first part thereof where it is paid in more than one instalment); and

(b)   where that award is followed by one or more further awards which, or each of which, begins immediately after the end of the previous award, such further award provided that for that further award the claimant–

(i)   is the person who received the relevant sum; or

(ii)   is the partner of the person who received the relevant sum, or was that person's partner at the date of his death.

Amendments

1.   Amended by reg 2(16) of SI 2005 No 2502 as amended by Sch 2 para 27 of SI 2006 No 217 as from 1.4.06 (3.4.06 where rent payable weekly or at intervals of a week).

2.   Substituted by reg 6(6)(a) of SI 2008 No 698 as from 14.4.08.

3.   Inserted by reg 26(b) of SI 2008 No 1082 as from 27.10.08.

Analysis

This allows payments of arrears of, or compensation in respect of, the benefits listed to be ignored for a period of up to 52 weeks after they are received. If anything is left of such a payment after the 52 weeks, the payment is taken into account as normal. WTC and CTC and discretionary housing payments also receive the same treatment.

In *CIS 2448/2006* the local authority had paid the claimant compensation because it had wrongly charged him for aftercare services pursuant to s117 Mental Health Act 1983: per *R v Manchester City Council ex p Stennett* [2002] UKHL 34. The claimant argued that the payment should be treated as arrears of compensation for non-payment of IS and so should be disregarded under Sch 10 para 7(1) IS Regs 1987 (the equivalent to para 9(1)) because, had the local authority not in fact charged him under the MHA for the costs of his residential accommodation, he would have received the full amount for IS and not just the sum for "personal expenses". The argument was rejected on the facts of the case. As the claimant had been paid full IS at all relevant times and then paid the residential fees element onto the care home, no arrears of IS were due. Even assuming that some of the IS was paid direct to the care home by the DWP, the argument was still ill-founded because whatever may have later been held in *Stennett*, at the time the IS would properly have been paid to the care home and so there could be no question of the claimant establishing that any sum of IS had been wrongfully withheld from him. Even if that was wrong, the payment here was not a payment of "arrears" of IS as that refers to a sum paid by the Secretary of State in satisfaction of an award of IS. The decision was approved by *R(IS) 5/08*.

See also Sch 5 para 7 where the concessionary payments are income payments.

---

10. Any sum–
(a) paid to the claimant in consequence of damage to, or loss of the home or any personal possession and intended for its repair or replacement; or
(b) acquired by the claimant (whether as a loan or otherwise) on the express condition that it is to be used for effecting essential repairs or improvement to the home,

which is to be used for the intended purpose, for a period of 26 weeks from the date on which it was so paid or acquired or such longer period as is reasonable in the circumstances to effect the repairs, replacement or improvement.

Analysis

This provides that certain sums for repairs to, or replacement of, personal possessions, or repairs or improvements to the home are to be ignored for a limited period. The initial 26-week period may be extended where this is considered reasonable where the claimant needs the extra time to get the repairs, etc done.

Sub-para (a) covers sums paid as a result of damage to, or the loss of, the claimant's home or personal possessions, intended for their repair or replacement. "Personal possession" is not defined but would cover, for example, a car. See the analysis to para 12 below.

Sub-para (b). This might even cover a payment from a relative – it is the terms of the payment which are important, not the source. "Essential" work was distinguished in *R(SB) 10/81* from that which is a luxury, but it need not be so vital as to be indispensable for life to be maintained (that case was about a single payment for "essential redecoration").

An "improvement" may be distinguished from a repair in that it connotes the adding of something new other than remedying a damaged, pre-existing feature.

---

11. Any sum–
(a) deposited with a housing association as defined in section 1(1) of the Housing Associations Act 1985 or section 338(1) of the Housing (Scotland) Act 1987 as a condition of occupying the home;
(b) which was so deposited and which is to be used for the purchase of another home, for the period of 26 weeks or such longer period as may be reasonable in the circumstances to enable the claimant to complete the purchase.

Analysis

Sub-para (a) provides a disregard for deposits held by a housing association, sub-para (b) for deposits which *were* so held until the claimant decided to purchase a home.

Sub-para (a). s1 Housing Act 1985 refers to s5 of that Act. The definition in s338(1) of the Scottish Act is precisely the same. The payment of the deposit must be a condition of occupying the home for the paragraph to apply.

Sub-para (b). Here the disregard is a limited one. The initial 26-week period may be extended where this is considered reasonable in view of the fact that the claimant needs the extra time to complete purchase.

---

12. Any personal possessions except those which have been acquired by the claimant with the intention of reducing his capital in order to secure entitlement to housing benefit or to increase the amount of that benefit.

Analysis

"Personal possessions" is not defined but could cover everything from clothing to paintings, furniture, cars or even a caravan based at a non-residential site. In *R(H) 7/08*, Commissioner Jacobs concluded that "personal possessions" means any physical assets other than land and assets used for business purposes. The only such items which cannot be ignored are those bought for the purposes of securing or increasing HB entitlement.

See the analysis of reg 49(1) on p385. See also para 10 where a sum has been paid to the claimant for damage to, or loss of, personal possessions.

13. The value of the right to receive any income under an annuity or the surrender value (if any) of such an annuity.

Analysis

This provides a total disregard of the surrender value of annuities or the right to receive income under them. For the treatment of income *actually* received under an annuity, see reg 41(2) and Sch 5 para 18.

14. Where the funds of a trust are derived from a payment made in consequence of any personal injury to the claimant [¹ or the claimant's partner], the value of the trust fund and the value of the right to receive any payment under that trust.

Amendment

1. Amended by reg 15(7)(a) of SI 2006 No 2378 from the first day of the first benefit week to commence on or after 2.10.06.

Analysis

"Payments made in consequence" of personal injury covers out of court settlements and insurance payments as well as damages under court order. The paragraph provides a disregard of the value of the trust fund, and the right to receive payments, for an indefinite period in all cases. See reg 42(2) in respect of income from such trusts. Payments of income are disregarded under Sch 5 para 14. See para 14A of this Schedule for capital payments and paras 45 and 46 where damages paid to children or young people are administered by the Court.

[¹**14A.**–(1) Any payment made to the claimant or the claimant's partner in consequence of any personal injury to the claimant or, as the case may be, the claimant's partner.

(2) But sub-paragraph (1)–

(a) applies only for the period of 52 weeks beginning with the day on which the claimant first receives any payment in consequence of that personal injury;

(b) does not apply to any subsequent payment made to him in consequence of that injury (whether it is made by the same person or another);

(c) ceases to apply to the payment or any part of the payment from the day on which the claimant no longer possesses it;

(d) does not apply to any payment from a trust where the funds of the trust are derived from a payment made in consequence of any personal injury to the claimant.

(3) For the purposes of sub-paragraph (2)(c), the circumstances in which a claimant no longer possesses a payment or a part of it include where the claimant has used a payment or part of it to purchase an asset.

(4) References in sub-paragraphs (2) and (3) to the claimant are to be construed as including references to his partner (where applicable).]

Amendment

1. Inserted by reg 15(7)(b) of SI 2006 No 2378 from the first day of the first benefit week to commence on or after 2.10.06.

Analysis

A payment made in consequence of a personal injury to the claimant or her/his partner is disregarded for 52 weeks from the day the claimant first receives any payment in consequence of that injury, though the amount of the disregard decreases as the payment is disposed of (eg, as the claimant spends it): sub-paras (1), (2)(a) and (c) and (3). This gives the claimant time to spend all or part of the payment, or to put it into a trust which can itself be disregarded under para 14. However, the paragraph does not apply to:

(1) Subsequent payments made in consequence of the same injury: sub-para (2)(b). However, it is suggested that the amount could be disregarded if put into a trust (see reg 49(2)(b) and para 14).

(2) Payments of capital made from a trust derived from payments made in consequence of a personal injury to the claimant or her/his partner: sub-para (2)(d). Note that payments of income from such a trust are disregarded under para 14 Sch 5.

Sub-para (4) confirms that in sub-paras (2) and (3) the references to "claimant" should also be read as "partner" where relevant.

15. The value of the right to receive any income under a life interest or from a life rent.

Analysis

The terms "life interest" or "life rent" (in Scots Law) cover the situation where a beneficiary under a trust gets the right to enjoy an asset during her/his lifetime, but that asset will pass on her/his death to someone else. Such a right can be bought and sold and is therefore given a capital value, but that value is to be ignored for the purpose of assessing HB. If, however, a claimant receives actual payments (eg, of income, under such a life interest or life rent) that income will be assessable under Section 5 of Part 6.

16. The value of the right to receive any income which is disregarded under [¹ paragraph 13 of Schedule 4] or paragraph 24 of Schedule 5.

Amendment
1.   Amended by reg 3(13)(a) of SI 2008 No 1042 as from 19.5.08.

Analysis
The right to receive income can be bought and sold and so has a capital value. However, where the right is to receive income disregarded under the paragraphs cited, that value is ignored for HB purposes. Para 13 Sch 4 and para 24 Sch 5 refer to earnings and income payable in a country outside the UK for a period during which there is a prohibition against the transfer of the earnings to the UK.

17. The surrender value of any policy of life insurance.
18. Where any payment of capital falls to be made by instalments, the value of the right to receive any outstanding instalments.

Analysis
Reg 41 deems capital payable by instalments which are outstanding as at the date of claim to be treated as income in certain circumstances. Under this paragraph, the value of the right to receive the outstanding instalments is ignored in the assessment of capital.

19. Any payment made by a local authority in accordance with section 17, [¹ 23B,] 23C or 24A of the Children Act 1989 or, as the case may be, section 12 of the Social Work (Scotland) Act 1968 or sections [² 22,] [¹ 29] or 30 of the Children (Scotland) Act 1995 (provision of services for children and their families and advice and assistance to certain children).

Amendments
1.   Amended by reg 6(10)(a) of SI 2008 No 2767 as from 17.11.08.
2.   Inserted by reg 7(4) of SI 2010 No 2429 as from 1.11.10.

Analysis
Section 17 Children Act enables the local authority to give children in need, their families and others cash payments "in exceptional circumstances". Section 12 of the Scottish legislation is to the same effect. Sections 23B, 23C and 24A enable the local authority to give individuals under 21 who at any time after reaching the age of 16 but while still a child had been looked after, accommodated or fostered by the local authority, cash payments "in exceptional circumstances". Sections 22, 29 and 30 of the Scottish legislation do also. For income payments, see Sch 5 para 28. For the circumstances in which payments made under s23C Children Act or s29 Children (Scotland) Act which are passed on to a former carer can be disreagrded, see para 19A below and Sch 5 para 28A.

[¹**19A.**–(1) Subject to sub-paragraph (2), any payment (or part of a payment) made by a local authority in accordance with section 23C of the Children Act 1989 or section 29 of the Children (Scotland) Act 1995 (local authorities' duty to promote welfare of children and powers to grant financial assistance to persons in, or formerly in, their care) to a person ("A") which A passes on to the claimant.
(2)   Sub-paragraph (1) applies only where A–
(a)   was formerly in the claimant's care, and
(b)   is aged 18 or over, and
(c)   continues to live with the claimant.]

Amendment
1.   Inserted by reg 6(6)(b) of SI 2008 No 698 as from, as it relates to a particular beneficiary, the first day of the benefit week on or after 7.4.08.

Analysis
This provides a disregard of payments made by a local authority in accordance with the provisions listed. This only applies where the payment is made to someone formerly in the claimant's care as a child or young person, who is now aged 18 or over but continues to live with her/him, and who has passed the payment on to the claimant.

20. Any social fund payment made pursuant to Part 8 of the Act.

21. Any refund of tax which falls to be deducted under section 369 of the Income and Corporation Taxes Act 1988 (deduction of tax from certain loan interest) on a payment of relevant loan interest for the purpose of acquiring an interest in the home or carrying out repairs or improvements to the home.

22. Any capital which by virtue of regulation 41 or 64 (capital treated as income and treatment of student loans) is to be treated as income.

Analysis

As capital under reg 41 and student loans under reg 64 are to be treated as part of the claimant's income, this paragraph is necessary to avoid double counting. See also para 18, above.

23. Where any payment of capital is made in a currency other than Sterling, any banking charge or commission payable in converting that payment into Sterling.

24.–(1) Any payment made under [² or by] the Macfarlane Trust, the Macfarlane (Special Payments) Trust, the Macfarlane (Special Payments) (No. 2) Trust (''the Trusts''), the Fund, the Eileen Trust [² , MFET Limited] , the Independent Living [¹ Fund (2006)], the Skipton Funds or the London Bombings Relief Charitable Fund.

(2) Any payment by or on behalf of a person who is suffering or who suffered from haemophilia or who is or was a qualifying person, which derives from a payment made under [² or by] any of the Trusts to which sub-paragraph (1) refers and which is made to or for the benefit of–

    (a)   that person's partner or former partner from whom he is not, or where that person has died was not, estranged or divorced or with whom he has formed a civil partnership that has not been dissolved or, where that person has died, had not been dissolved at the time of that person's death;

    (b)   any child who is a member of that person's family or who was such a member and who is a member of the claimant's family; or

    (c)   any young person who is a member of that person's family or who was such a member and who is a member of the claimant's family.

(3) Any payment by or on behalf of the partner or former partner of a person who is suffering or who suffered from haemophilia or who is or was a qualifying person provided that the partner or former partner and that person are not, or if either of them has died were not, estranged or divorced or, where the partner or former partner and that person have formed a civil partnership, the civil partnership has not been dissolved or, if either of them has died, had not been dissolved at the time of the death, which derives from a payment made under [² or by] any of the Trusts to which sub-paragraph (1) refers and which is made to or for the benefit of–

    (a)   the person who is suffering from haemophilia or who is a qualifying person;

    (b)   any child who is a member of that person's family or who was such a member and who is a member of the claimant's family; or

    (c)   any young person who is a member of that person's family or who was such a member and who is a member of the claimant's family.

(4) Any payment by a person who is suffering from haemophilia or who is a qualifying person, which derives from a payment under [² or by] any of the Trusts to which sub-paragraph (1) refers, where–

    (a)   that person has no partner or former partner from whom he is not estranged or divorced or with whom he has formed a civil partnership that has not been dissolved, nor any child or young person who is or had been a member of that person's family; and

    (b)   the payment is made either–

        (i)   to that person's parent or step-parent; or

        (ii)   where that person at the date of the payment is a child, a young person or a student who has not completed his full-time education and has no parent or step-parent, to his guardian,

but only for a period from the date of the payment until the end of two years from that person's death.

(5) Any payment out of the estate of a person who suffered from haemophilia or who was a qualifying person, which derives from a payment under [² or by] any of the Trusts to which sub-paragraph (1) refers, where–

    (a)   that person at the date of his death (the relevant date) had no partner or former partner from whom he was not estranged or divorced or with whom he had formed a civil partnership that had not been dissolved, nor any child or young person who was or had been a member of his family; and

    (b)   the payment is made either–

        (i)   to that person's parent or step-parent; or

        (ii)   where that person at the relevant date was a child, a young person or a student who had not completed his full-time education and had no parent or step-parent, to his guardian,

but only for a period of two years from the relevant date.

(6) In the case of a person to whom or for whose benefit a payment referred to in this paragraph is made, any capital resource which derives from any payment of income or capital made under or deriving from any of the Trusts.

(7) For the purposes of sub-paragraphs (2) to (6), any reference to the Trusts shall be construed as including a reference to the Fund, the Eileen Trust [² , MFET Limited] , the Skipton Fund or the London Bombings Relief Charitable Fund.

Modifications
References to "step-parent" in sub-paras (4)(b)(i) and (ii) and (5)(b)(i) and (ii) are modified by s246 Civil Partnership Act 2004 (see p I 148) and art 3 and para 26 of the Schedule to SI 2005 No.3137 (see p I 195).

Amendments
1.   Amended by reg 6(4)(g) of SI 2008 No 2767 as from 17.11.08.
2.   Amended by reg 8(3) and (5) of SI 2010 No 641 as from 1.4.10 (5.4.10 where rent payable weekly or in multiples of a week).

Analysis
See analysis of Sch 5 para 35.

25.–(1)   Where a claimant has ceased to occupy what was formerly the dwelling occupied as the home following his estrangement or divorce from, or dissolution of his civil partnership with, his former partner, that dwelling for a period of 26 weeks from the date on which he ceased to occupy that dwelling or, where the dwelling is occupied as the home by the former partner who is a lone parent, for so long as it is so occupied.

(2)   In this paragraph ''dwelling'' includes any garage, garden and outbuildings, which were formerly occupied by the claimant as his home and any premises not so occupied which it is impracticable or unreasonable to sell separately, in particular, in Scotland, any croft land on which the dwelling is situated.

Analysis
Sub-para (1) allows the disregard of a claimant's former home s/he left following estrangement or divorce from her/his partner or where her/his civil partnership with the partner has been dissolved. The home must be occupied by the former partner. For "occupied as the home": see the note to reg 7. See para 4 above for a discussion of the term "estranged" and where the claimant and the former partner are not estranged or divorced from the former partner or where a civil partnership has not been dissolved.
(1)   If the former partner is a lone parent, the dwelling can be disregarded indefinitely, so long as s/he continues to occupy it as a home. "Lone parent" is defined in reg 2(1).
(2)   In all other cases, the dwelling can be disregarded for 26 weeks from the date the claimant ceased to occupy it. There is no discretion to extend (although a claimant subject to this para may also be covered by other paras below – eg, paras 26 or 27). It may be difficult to ascertain on which date the claimant finally ceased to occupy the dwelling for these purposes.
This provision is likely to give rise to a number of practical difficulties where there are no children or the former partner leaves the home (eg, for it to be sold) not least because the short time during which the disregard is available will frequently be inadequate to enable a couple's financial affairs to be sorted out in the case of a divorce. At the end of the 26-week period, even if financial arrangements have been made following the breakdown of a relationship, matters may not be clear-cut as the divorce courts sometimes make what are known as "Mesher" orders which order that the former matrimonial home be held on trust for the former partners in their respective shares, but that it should not be sold until the occurrence of a particular event – eg, the death or remarriage of the partner who remains in residence. In such a case, the partner who has left will continue to have an interest in the home which, after the initial 26-week period, will not be disregarded unless the other partner is a lone parent and continues to live in the home, or one of the other paragraphs of Sch 6 applies. A practical solution lies in the method of valuation of such capital – see regs 47 and 51. The asset (here the claimant's share) is to be valued at its current market value less 10 per cent and the value of any incumbrance secured on it. If what a claimant possesses is an interest in a house which s/he is unable to sell because her/his partner is still living in it and/or because a court order forbids the sale, the market value of that asset is likely to be very low. Authorities should be careful to take a realistic and humane approach to this problem.
Sub-para (2) is the same definition of a "dwelling" as appears in para 1 above.

---

26.   Any premises where the claimant is taking reasonable steps to dispose of those premises, for a period of 26 weeks from the date on which he first took such steps, or such longer period as is reasonable in the circumstances to enable him to dispose of those premises.

Analysis
The question of what are "reasonable steps" to dispose of premises initially rests with the authority. Here the 26-week disregard runs from the date on which reasonable steps are first taken and may be extended where it appears "reasonable" to do so in the circumstances. In *CIS 1915/2007*, the claimant had fled domestic violence and an arranged marriage and began divorce proceedings. However, under family pressure these were temporarily suspended. The DWP decided that the value of her interest in the former matrimonial home could no longer be disregarded as she was no longer taking reasonable steps to dispose of it. Deputy Commissioner Mark allowed the claimant's appeal. He said that in considering the reasonableness of the period taken by the claimant to secure a divorce (and the resulting disposal of the premises), including any temporary suspension of such action, it was necessary to look at all the facts, including the pressures that were brought on her. The steps she

took to temporarily suspend her divorce proceedings until she had moved to a new address and changed her name to secure her safety did not mean that she was no longer taking reasonable steps to dispose of the premises through divorce proceedings.

Once the property has been disposed of, para 3 above may apply to the proceeds.

27.   Any premises which the claimant intends to occupy as his home, and in respect of which he is taking steps to obtain possession and has sought legal advice, or has commenced legal proceedings, with a view to obtaining possession, for a period of 26 weeks from the date on which he first sought such advice or first commenced such proceedings whichever is the earlier, or such longer period as is reasonable in the circumstances to enable him to obtain possession and commence occupation of those premises.

Analysis

The starting date for the period of disregard under this para is the date on which the claimant first sought legal advice if this is earlier (as it usually will be by several weeks if not months) than the date on which s/he commenced legal proceedings. There could be overlap between this para and para 25 above, in which case this para may operate to extend any period of disregard available under para 25: eg, if a claimant leaves the matrimonial home and 10 weeks later seeks advice on commencing divorce proceedings in which there is an application for the other partner, who is childless, to leave the premises and for the claimant to be permitted to re-enter, para 25 applies initially and then the full period in para 27 applies after advice is sought. In many cases, for reasons beyond the claimant's control, it is possible that possession proceedings will not be completed within six months of their commencement, and this should be reflected by the use of the discretion to extend the period of the disregard where necessary.

28.   Any premises which the claimant intends to occupy as his home to which essential repairs or alterations are required in order to render them fit for such occupation, for a period of 26 weeks from the date on which the claimant first takes steps to effect those repairs or alterations, or such longer period as is necessary to enable those repairs or alterations to be carried out.

Analysis

"Essential" repairs or alterations are not defined but they must be such as are necessary to make the premises fit for the claimant's occupation. It is possible that cases will arise where this paragraph overlaps with Sch 6 para 2, and the scheme should be operated with the claimant's interests in mind.

The scope of this paragraph was considered in *R v Tower Hamlets LBC HBRB ex p Kapur* [2000] *The Times* 28 June, QBD. The applicant owned a derelict house valued at £240,000 which was unfit for habitation. He wished to renovate the property and move back into it and made extensive efforts to obtain funding for the necessary works from lenders, relatives and public authorities in the form of various types of renovation grant. It took a great deal of time to assemble the funds. The Housing Benefit Review Board held that "the date on which the claimant first takes steps to effect those repairs" could not be earlier than the date on which works actually commenced. Scott Baker J quashed the Board's decision, holding that to be a wrong approach. The judge had regard to the *Adjudication Officer's Guide*, which stated, in relation to the similar Sch 10 para 28 Income Support (General) Regulations 1987, that the relevant "steps" could include getting a grant or loan to pay for repairs or alterations, employing an architect, getting planning permission or finding someone to do the work, and that the relevant "date" could be the first date on which inquiries about those matters were made. It was a question of fact for the authority as to when the first steps were taken, but the Board's approach was clearly too restrictive and its decision was therefore quashed.

[¹**29.**]

Amendment

1.   Omitted by reg 6(6)(c) of SI 2008 No 698 as from, as they relate to a particular beneficiary, the first day of the benefit week on or after 7.4.08.

30.   Any payment made by the Secretary of State to compensate for the loss (in whole or in part) of entitlement to housing benefit.

31.   The value of the right to receive an occupational or personal pension.

32.   The value of any funds held under a personal pension scheme [¹].

Amendment

1.   Amended by reg 4(7) of SI 2007 No 1749 as from 16.7.07.

33.   The value of the right to receive any rent except where the claimant has a reversionary interest in the property in respect of which rent is due.

34. Any payment in kind made by a charity or under [³ or by] the Macfarlane (Special Payments) Trust, the Macfarlane (Special Payments) (No. 2) Trust, [¹ the Fund [⁴ , MFET Limited] , [²] or the Independent Living Fund (2006)].

Amendments

1. Amended by Art 8(3) of SI 2007 No 2538 as from 1.10.07.
2. Amended by reg 6(9)(b) of SI 2008 No 2767 as from 17.11.08.
3. Amended by reg 8 (5) of SI 2010 No 641 as from 1.4.10 (5.4.10 where rent payable weekly or in multiples of a week).
4. Amended by reg 8(11) of SI 2010 No 641 as from 1.4.10 (5.4.10 where rent payable weekly or in multiples of a week).

Analysis

The implication of this para is that (except where the claimant is on IS, an income-based JSA or an income-related ESA – see Sch 4 para 12, Sch 5 paras 4 and 5 and Sch 6 paras 5 and 6) other, non-charitable capital payments in kind are to be taken into account. The regulations provide no mechanism for quantifying the value of other payments in kind.

---

35. Any payment made pursuant to section 2 of the 1973 Act or section 2 of the Enterprise and New Towns (Scotland) Act 1990, but only for the period of 52 weeks beginning on the date of receipt of the payment.
[¹ **36.**]

Amendment

1. Omitted by reg 6(9)(c) of SI 2008 No 2767 as from 17.11.08.

---

37. Any payment in consequence of a reduction of council tax under section 13 or, as the case may be, section 80 of the Local Government Finance Act 1992 (reduction of liability for council tax), but only for a period of 52 weeks from the date of the receipt of the payment.
38. Any grant made to the claimant in accordance with a scheme made under section 129 of the Housing Act 1988 or section 66 of the Housing (Scotland) Act 1988 (schemes for payments to assist local housing authority and local authority tenants to obtain other accommodation) which is to be used–
(a) to purchase premises intended for occupation as his home; or
(b) to carry out repairs or alterations which are required to render premises fit for occupation as his home,
for a period of 26 weeks from the date on which he received such a grant or such longer period as is reasonable in the circumstances to enable the purchase, repairs or alterations to be completed and the claimant to commence occupation of those premises as his home.
[¹ **39.** Any arrears of supplementary pension which is disregarded under paragraph 53 of Schedule 5 (sums to be disregarded in the calculation of income other than earnings) or of any amount which is disregarded under paragraph 54 or 55 of that Schedule, but only for a period of 52 weeks from the date of receipt of the arrears.]

Amendment

1. Substituted by reg 5(7)(a) of SI 2008 No 3157 as from 5.1.09.

[² **40.**–(1) Any payment or repayment made–
(a) as respects England, under regulation 5, 6 or 12 of the National Health Service (Travel Expenses and Remission of Charges) Regulations 2003 (travelling expenses and health service supplies);
(b) as respects Wales, under regulation 5, 6 or 11 of the National Health Service (Travelling Expenses and Remission of Charges) (Wales) Regulations 2007 (travelling expenses and health service supplies);
(c) as respects Scotland, under regulation 3, 5 or 11 of the National Health Service (Travelling Expenses and Remission of Charges) (Scotland) (No. 2) Regulations 2003 (travelling expenses and health service supplies),
but only for a period of 52 weeks from the date of receipt of the payment or repayment.
(2) Any payment or repayment made by the Secretary of State for Health, the Scottish Ministers or the Welsh Ministers which is analogous to a payment or repayment mentioned in sub-paragraph (1), but only for a period of 52 weeks from the date of receipt of the payment or repayment.]

Amendments

1. Amended by reg 3(13)(b)-(d) of SI 2008 No 1042 as from 19.5.08.
2. Substituted by reg 5(7)(a) of SI 2008 No 3157 as from 5.1.09.

Analysis

Paras 40, 41 and 42 provide a disregard on payments made in respect of certain NHS charges (eg, dental and optical treatment), hospital travel costs, payments in lieu of healthy start food vouchers (for which see Sch 5 para 45), milk tokens or the supply of vitamins, and for assisted prison visits. In all cases the disregard is only for 52 weeks.

[²**41.** Any payment made to such persons entitled to receive benefits as may be determined by or under a scheme made pursuant to section 13 of the Social Security Act 1988 in lieu of vouchers or similar arrangements in connection with the provision of those benefits (including payments made in place of healthy start vouchers, milk tokens or the supply of vitamins), but only for a period of 52 weeks from the date of receipt of the payment.]

Amendments

1. Amended by reg 3(13)(e) of SI 2008 No 1042 as from 19.5.08.
2. Substituted by reg 5(7)(a) of SI 2008 No 3157 as from 5.1.09.

[¹**41A.** Any payment made under Part 8A of the Act (entitlement to health in pregnancy grant).]

Amendment

1. Inserted by reg 6(13(a) of SI 2009 No 583 as from the first day of the first benefit week for the claimant on or after 6.4.09.

Analysis

Para 41 provides a complete and indefinite disregard of the health in pregnancy grant, a non-means-tested grant (currently £190) paid to pregnant women to help them prepare for the birth of the baby. Note: the Government intends to abolish health in pregnancy grants from January 2011.

42. Any payment made either by the Secretary of State for [¹ Justice] or Scottish Ministers under a scheme established to assist relatives and other persons to visit persons in custody, but only for a period of 52 weeks from the date of the receipt of the payment.

Amendment

1. Amended by Art 8 and the Sch para 23 of SI 2007 No 2128 as from 22.8.07.

43. Any payment (other than a training allowance) made, whether by the Secretary of State or any other person, under the Disabled Persons (Employment) Act 1944 [¹] to assist disabled persons to obtain or retain employment despite their disability.

Amendment

1. Amended by reg 3(13)(f) of SI 2008 No 1042 as from 19.5.08.

44. Any payment made by a local authority under section 3 of the Disabled Persons (Employment) Act 1958 to homeworkers assisted under the Blind Homeworkers' Scheme.

[¹ **45.** (1) Any sum of capital to which sub-paragraph (2) applies and–

(a) which is administered on behalf of a person by the High Court or the County Court under Rule 21.11(1) of the Civil Procedure Rules 1998 or by the Court of Protection;

(b) which can only be disposed of by order or direction of any such court; or

(c) where the person concerned is under the age of 18, which can only be disposed of by order or direction prior to that person attaining age 18.

(2) This sub-paragraph applies to a sum of capital which is derived from–

(a) an award of damages for a personal injury to that person; or

(b) compensation for the death of one or both parents where the person concerned is under the age of 18.]

Amendment

1. Substituted by reg 15(7)(c) of SI 2006 No 2378 from the 1st day of the 1st benefit week to commence on or after 2.10.06.

Analysis

An adult who receives compensation for personal injuries can prevent it from reducing her/his entitlement to HB by putting it in a trust (see para 14). However, where children and young people under 18 are awarded such compensation that is not possible as the money is not paid to them but retained in court until their 18th birthday. Paras 45 and 46 make it clear that compensation paid to children and young people for personal injury or the death of a parent is also disregarded while it is held by the court. At least as far as personal injury compensation is concerned they are probably unnecessary given the unreported decision of a commissioner in *CIS 368/1994*.

46. Any sum of capital administered on behalf of a person in accordance with an order made under section 13 of the Children (Scotland) Act 1995 or under Rule 36.14 of the Ordinary Cause Rules 1993 or under Rule 128 of those Rules, where such sum derives from–

(a) award of damages for a personal injury to that person; or

(b) compensation for the death of one or both parents where the person concerned is under the age of 18.

47. Any payment to the claimant as holder of the Victoria Cross or George Cross.

48. The amount of any child maintenance bonus payable by way of jobseeker's allowance or income support in accordance with section 10 of the Child Support Act 1995, or a corresponding payment under Article 4 of the Child Support (Northern Ireland) Order 1995, but only for a period of 52 weeks from the date of receipt.

49. In the case of a person who is receiving, or who has received, assistance under the self-employment route, any sum of capital which is acquired by that person for the purpose of establishing or carrying on the commercial activity in respect of which such assistance is or was received but only for a period of 52 weeks from the date on which that sum was acquired.

50.–(1) Any payment of a sports award for a period of 26 weeks from the date of receipt of that payment except to the extent that it has been made in respect of any one or more of the items specified in sub-paragraph (2).

(2) The items specified for the purposes of sub-paragraph (1) are food, ordinary clothing or footwear, household fuel or rent of the claimant or, where the claimant is a member of a family, any other member of his family, or any council tax or water charges for which that claimant or member is liable.

(3) For the purposes of sub-paragraph (2)–

"food" does not include vitamins, minerals or other special dietary supplements intended to enhance the performance of the person in the sport in respect of which the award was made;

"rent" means eligible rent less any deductions in respect of non-dependants which fall to be made under regulation 74 (non-dependant deductions).

Analysis

See Sch 5 para 59.

51.–(1) Any payment–

(a) by way of an education maintenance allowance made pursuant to–

    (i) regulations made under section 518 of the Education Act 1996 (payment of school expenses; grant of scholarships etc);

    (ii) regulations made under section 49 or 73(f) of the Education (Scotland) Act 1980 (power to assist persons to take advantage of educational facilities);

    [¹ (iii) directions made under section 73ZA of the Education (Scotland) Act 1980 and paid under section 12(2)(c) of the Further and Higher Education (Scotland) Act 1992; or]

(b) corresponding to such an education maintenance allowance, made pursuant to–

    (i) section 14 or section 181 of the Education Act 2002 (power of Secretary of State and National Assembly for Wales to give financial assistance for purposes related to education or childcare, and allowances in respect of education or training); or

    (ii) regulations made under section 181 of that Act.

(2) Any payment, other than a payment to which sub-paragraph (1) applies, made pursuant to–

(a) regulations made under section 518 of the Education Act 1996;

(b) regulations made under section 49 of the Education (Scotland) Act 1980; or

[¹ (c) directions made under section 73ZA of the Education (Scotland) Act 1980 and paid under section 12(2)(c) of the Further and Higher Education (Scotland) Act 1992,]

in respect of a course of study attended by a child or a young person or a person who is in receipt of an education maintenance allowance made pursuant to any provision specified in sub-paragraph (1).

Amendment

1. Amended by reg 5(7)(c) of SI 2008 No 3157 as from 5.1.09.

Analysis

See Sch 5 para 11.

---

52. In the case of a claimant participating in an employment zone programme, any discretionary payment made by an employment zone contractor to the claimant, being a fee, grant, loan or otherwise, but only for the period of 52 weeks from the date of receipt of the payment.

Analysis

Under paras 52 and 53, discretionary payments made to claimants who are participating in an employment zone programme, by an employment zone contractor (as defined in reg 2(1)) are disregarded for 52 weeks from the date of the payment, as is subsistence allowance (again, as defined in reg 2(1)).

53. Any arrears of subsistence allowance paid as a lump sum but only for the period of 52 weeks from the date of receipt of the payment.

54. Where an ex-gratia payment of £10,000 has been made by the Secretary of State on or after 1st February 2001 in consequence of the imprisonment or interment of–

(a) the claimant;

(b) the claimant's partner;

(c) the claimant's deceased spouse or deceased civil partner; or

(d) the claimant's partner's deceased spouse or deceased civil partner,

by the Japanese during the Second World War, £10,000.

Analysis

The ex gratia payment of £10,000 made to former Japanese prisoners of war is disregarded in full and indefinitely.

55.–(1) Subject to sub-paragraph (2), the amount of any trust payment made to a claimant or a member of a claimant's family who is–

(a) a diagnosed person;

(b) the diagnosed person's partner or the person who was the diagnosed person's partner at the [² date] of the diagnosed person's death;

(c) a parent of a diagnosed person, a person acting in place of the diagnosed person's parents or a person who was so acting at the date of the diagnosed person's death; or

(d) a member of the diagnosed person's family (other than his partner) or a person who was a member of the diagnosed person's family (other than his partner) at the date of the diagnosed person's death.

(2) Where a trust payment is made to–

(a) a person referred to in sub-paragraph (1)(a) or (b), that sub-paragraph shall apply for the period beginning on the date on which the trust payment is made and ending on the date on which that person dies;

(b) a person referred to in sub-paragraph (1)(c), that sub-paragraph shall apply for the period beginning on the date on which the trust payment is made and ending two years after that date;

(c) a person referred to in sub-paragraph (1)(d), that sub-paragraph shall apply for the period beginning on the date on which the trust payment is made and ending–

(i) two years after that date; or

(ii) on the day before the day on which that person–

(aa) ceases receiving full-time education; or

(bb) attains the age of [¹ 20],

whichever is the latest.

(3) Subject to sub-paragraph (4), the amount of any payment by a person to whom a trust payment has been made or of any payment out of the estate of a person to whom a trust payment has been made, which is made to a claimant or a member of a claimant's family who is–

(a) the diagnosed person's partner or the person who was the diagnosed person's partner at the date of the diagnosed person's death;

(b) a parent of a diagnosed person, a person acting in place of the diagnosed person's parents or a person who was so acting at the date of the diagnosed person's death; or

(c) a member of the diagnosed person's family (other than his partner) or a person who was a member of the diagnosed person's family (other than his partner) at the date of the diagnosed person's death,

but only to the extent that such payments do not exceed the total amount of any trust payments made to that person.

(4) Where a payment as referred to in sub-paragraph (3) is made to–

(a) a person referred to in sub-paragraph (3)(a), that sub-paragraph shall apply for the period beginning on the date on which that payment is made and ending on the date on which that person dies;

(b) a person referred to in sub-paragraph (3)(b), that sub-paragraph shall apply for the period beginning on the date on which that payment is made and ending two years after that date; or

(c) a person referred to in sub-paragraph (3)(c), that sub-paragraph shall apply for the period beginning on the date on which that payment is made and ending–

(i) two years after that date; or

(ii) on the day before the day on which that person–

(aa) ceases receiving full-time education; or

(bb) attains the age of [¹ 20],

whichever is the latest.

(5) In this paragraph, a reference to a person–

(a) being the diagnosed person's partner;

(b) being a member of a diagnosed person's family;

(c)   acting in place of the diagnosed person's parents,

at the date of the diagnosed person's death shall include a person who would have been such a person or a person who would have been so acting, but for the diagnosed person residing in a care home, an Abbeyfield Home or an independent hospital on that date.

(6)   In this paragraph–

"diagnosed person" means a person who has been diagnosed as suffering from, or who, after his death, has been diagnosed as having suffered from, variant Creutzfeld-Jakob disease;

"relevant trust" means a trust established out of funds provided by the Secretary of State in respect of persons who suffered, or who are suffering, from variant Creutzfeld-Jakob disease for the benefit of persons eligible for payments in accordance with its provisions;

"trust payment" means a payment under a relevant trust.

Amendments

1.   Amended by reg 4(5) of SI 2006 No 718 as from 10.4.06.

2.   Amended by reg 3(13)(g) of SI 2008 No 1042 as from 19.5.08.

Analysis

These provisions provide a complex disregard covering payments from trusts (referred to as "relevant trusts") set up by the Secretary of State to compensate those suffering from variant Creutzfeldt-Jakob disease. Part of the reason for the complexity is that some people may only be diagnosed as suffering from that disease after they have died and payments from such trusts may therefore need to be made to other family members.

Where a payment is made to someone who has the disease her/himself ("the diagnosed person") or to that person's partner or to a person who was the partner of a diagnosed person when the latter died, the disregard lasts for the life of the payee. In other cases, the disregard lasts for two years unless the payee is a child or young person for whom the diagnosed person is (or was at the date of her/his death) responsible: in the latter case, the period of the disregard ends on the day before the child or young person's 20th birthday, or the day before s/he leaves full-time education or two years from the date of payment, whichever is the latest. See para (5) for an extension of the definitions of "partner", member of the "family" and person acting in place of parents for these purposes.

Sub-para (3) establishes a similar disregard for payments made *by* a diagnosed person who has received money from a relevant trust to any of the people listed in heads (a) to (c). This includes payments made from the diagnosed person's estate after her/his death. The maximum amount which can be disregarded under sub-para (3) is the total sum received by the diagnosed person from any relevant trust.

---

56.   The amount of any payment, other than a war pension [¹], to compensate for the fact that the claimant, the claimant's partner, the claimant's deceased spouse or deceased civil partner or the claimant's partner's deceased spouse or deceased civil partner–

(a)   was a slave labourer or a forced labourer;

(b)   had suffered property loss or had suffered personal injury; or

(c)   was a parent of a child who had died,

during the Second World War.

Amendment

1.   Amended by reg 5(7)(d) of SI 2008 No 3157 as from 5.1.09.

Analysis

This paragraph provides a capital disregard of the amount of payments made to people who were slaves or forced labourers, suffered property loss or personal injury, or who were parents of a child who died during the Second World War. The disregard lasts for an unlimited time and even if there is a break in the claimant's benefit entitlement. It is additional to any other disregard, including the disregard for pensions for victims of persecution under Sch 5 para 15(g).

57.–(1)   Any payment made by a local authority, or by the [¹ Welsh Ministers], to or on behalf of the claimant or his partner relating to a service which is provided to develop or sustain the capacity of the claimant or his partner to live independently in his accommodation.

(2)   For the purposes of sub-paragraph (1) "local authority" includes in England a county council.

Amendment

1.   Amended by reg 5(7)(e) of SI 2008 No 3157 as from 5.1.09.

Analysis

See Sch 5 para 63.

58. Any payment made under [¹] regulations made under section 57 of the Health and Social Care Act 2001 or under section 12B of the Social Work (Scotland) Act 1968 [² , or under sections 12A to 12D of the National Health Service Act 2006 (direct payments for health care)].

Amendment
1. Amended by reg 6(13(b) of SI 2009 No 583 as from 6.4.09.
2. Amended by reg 8(11) of SI 2010 No 641 as from 1.4.10 (5.4.10 where rent payable weekly or in multiples of a week).

Analysis
See Sch 5 para 57.

59. Any payment made to the claimant pursuant to regulations under section 2(6)(b), 3 or 4 of the Adoption and Children Act 2002.
60. Any payment made to the claimant in accordance with regulations made pursuant to section 14F of the Children Act 1989 (special guardianship support services).

[² SCHEDULE 7]

Amendments
1. Amended by reg 19 of SI 2007 No 2868, as amended by reg 4(6) of SI 2008 No 586, as from 7.4.08 (or if reg 1(5) of that SI applies, on the day on or after 7.4.08 when the first of the events specified in reg 1(6) applies, or from 6.4.09 if none have before that date).
2. Omitted by reg 4(4)(e) of SI 2008 No 959 as from 6.10.08.

General Note
Prior to 6 October 2008, reg 72 and Sch 7 provided the rules for "extended payments" of HB. These are now found in ss32 to 32 WRA 2007 and regs 72 to 72D.

[² SCHEDULE 8]

Amendments
1. Amended by reg 19 of SI 2007 No 2868 as from 7.4.08 (or if reg 1(5) of that SI applies, on the day on or after 7.4.08 when the first of the events specified in reg 1(6) applies, or from 6.4.09 if none have before that date).
2. Omitted by reg 4(4)(f) of SI 2008 No 959 as from 6.10.08.

General Note
Prior to 6 October 2008, reg 73 and Sch 8 provided the rules for "extended payments" of HB where ther claimant ceased to be entitled to incapacity benefit or severe disablement allowance. These are now found in ss32 to 32 WRA 2007 and regs 73 to 73D.

SCHEDULE 9
REGULATION 90
Matters to be included in decision notice

Definitions
"applicable amount" – see Part 5.
"claimant" – see reg 2(1).
"earnings" – see regs 35 and 37.
"eligible rent" – see Part 3.
"income" – see General Note on Section 2 of Part 6.
"non-dependant" – see reg 3.
"rent allowance" "rent rebate" – see s134(1A) and (1B) SSAA.

General Note on Schedule 9
This lists matters to be included in written notices of decisions issued to "persons affected" by a relevant authority: see reg 90. Many authorities fail to provide all the information required by the various Parts of the Schedule. See the Analysis to reg 90 above for the effects of a failure to provide the necessary information. Note that reg 10(1) D&A Regs may require the inclusion of additional information where a decision carries a right of appeal.
There are seven parts specifying information to be included in a notice in different circumstances.

(1)   Part 1 lists general matters which *always* need to appear within the terms of a notice of decision.

(2)   Part 2 applies only to notifications of a successful claim made by an IS, income-based JSA or income-related ESA recipient or where "extended payments" of HB are payable. See Part 6 below where no HB award is made.

(3)   Part 3 applies only to notifications on a successful claim, this time when IS, income-based JSA and income-related ESA are *not* payable. See Part 6 where no HB award is made.

(4)   Part 4 applies where the authority has used its powers under regs 95 and 96 to pay HB direct to a landlord, whether or not on the decision of a claim.

(5)   Part 5 applies when the authority uses its powers to treat a non-dependant's income as if it was the claimant's under reg 26.

(6)   Part 6 only applies to notices informing a claimant that a claim for HB has been unsuccessful.

(7)   Part 7 applies to notifications informing a person affected that s/he has been overpaid where the overpayment is recoverable under reg 100.

PART 1
General

1.   The statement of matters to be included in any decision notice issued by a relevant authority to a person, and referred to in regulation 90 (notification of decisions) and in regulation 10 of the Decisions and Appeals Regulations are those matters set out in the following provisions of this Schedule.

Analysis
Para 1 makes it clear that the requirements of the Schedule are mandatory. They are not optional and they are not to be seen by authorities as a piece of unnecessary bureaucracy. Clear notices assist claimants in understanding how a decision has been reached and reduce confusion and dispute. On the question of validity of notifications, see the Analysis to reg 90(1).

     The requirements apply to decision notices issued under reg 90 and also under reg 10 D&A Regs. They apply both to initial decisions and decisions following revision or supersession, except as otherwise stated.

2.   Every decision notice shall include a statement as to the right of any person affected by that decision to request a written statement under regulation 90(2) (requests for statement of reasons) and the manner and time in which to do so.

Analysis
Para 2 requires every notice to state that persons affected have the right to request a statement of reasons under reg 90(2), and the time limit within, and manner in which, this must be done. This applies to initial decisions and decisions following a revision or supersession. For the meaning of "person affected", see reg 2(1).

3.   Every decision notice shall include a statement as to the right of any person affected by that decision to make an application for a revision in accordance with regulation 4(1)(a) of the Decisions and Appeals Regulations and, where appropriate, to appeal against that decision and the manner and time in which to do so.

Analysis
Para 3 requires every notice to set out the right to seek a revision under reg 4 of the D&A Regs. Note also reg 10 D&A Regs which specifies when a "person affected" must be notified of her/his right of appeal.

4.   Every decision notice following an application for a revision in accordance with regulation 4(1)(a) of the Decisions and Appeals Regulations shall include a statement as to whether the original decision in respect of which the person made his representations has been confirmed or revised and where the relevant authority has not revised the decision the reasons why not.

Analysis
If a claimant has requested a revision of an authority's decision under reg 4(1)(a) (an "any grounds" revision), this paragraph specifies the matters which must be included in the notice informing the person affected of the authority's decision on revision. Reasons need to be given only where the authority decides not to revise its original decision, but note the separate right to request reasons for a decision under reg 10 D&A Regs where there is a right of appeal against a decision.

5.   Every decision notice following an application for a revision in accordance with regulation 4(1)(a) of the Decisions and Appeals Regulations shall, if the original decision has been revised, include a statement as to the right of any person affected by that decision to apply for a revision in accordance with regulation 4(1)(a) of those Regulations and the manner and time in which to do so.

Analysis

Para 5 specifies that the notice sent out following an application for a revision must mention the right of any other person affected to apply for a further revision.

6.   An authority may include in the decision notice any other matters not prescribed by this Schedule which it sees fit, whether expressly or by reference to some other document available without charge to the person.

Analysis

The authority is not restricted to giving the information set out in the Schedule and there will be cases in which further information is appropriate.

7.   Parts 2, 3 and 6 of this Schedule shall apply only to the decision notice given on a claim.
8.   Where a decision notice is given following a revision of an earlier decision–
(a)   made of the authority's own motion which results in a revision of that earlier decision; or
(b)   made following an application for a revision in accordance with regulation 4(1)(a) of the Decisions and Appeals Regulations, whether or not resulting in a revision of that earlier decision,
that notice shall, subject to paragraph 6, contain a statement only as to all the matters revised.

Analysis

Para 8 refers to the notices covered by paras 4 and 5, whether or not the authority's decision is to revise. It also covers, by sub-para (a), notices which are issued following an authority's own decision to revise a decision. The interaction of this paragraph with paras 4 and 5 is not totally clear, but the net effect seems to be that, apart from the factors listed in these paragraphs, the authority should not put information about matters which were not involved in the revision in the notice. The exception is those matters that it sees fit to include under para 6, to which para 8 is expressly subject. Para 6 is sufficiently wide, however, to completely negate para 8.

PART 2
Awards where income support [², an income-based jobseeker's allowance, an income-related employment and support allowance] [¹, an extended payment or an extended payment (qualifying contributory benefits)] is payable

9.   Where a person on income support [², an income-based jobseeker's allowance or an income-related employment and support allowance] is awarded housing benefit [¹ or a claimant is entitled to an extended payment in accordance with regulation 72 or an extended payment (qualifying contributory benefits) in accordance with regulation 73], the decision notice shall include a statement as to–
(a)   his weekly eligible rent, if any; and
(b)   the amount and an explanation of any deduction made under paragraph 6(2) or (3) of Schedule 1 (fuel deductions), if any, and that the deduction may be varied if he provides to the authority evidence on which it may estimate the actual or approximate amount of that service charge; and
(c)   the amount of and the category of non-dependant deductions made under regulation 74, if any; and
(d)   the normal weekly amount of rent allowance, or rent rebate as the case may be, to which he is entitled; and
(e)   in the case of a rent allowance or a rent rebate paid as if it were a rent allowance, the day of payment, and the period in respect of which payment of that allowance is to be made; and
(f)   the first day of entitlement to an allowance or rebate; and
(g)   his duty to notify any change of circumstances which might affect his entitlement to, or the amount of, housing benefit and (without prejudice to the extent of the duty owed under regulation 88 (duty to notify changes of circumstances)) the kind of change of circumstances which is to be notified, either upon the notice or by reference to some other document available to him on application and without charge.

Amendments

1.   Amended by reg 4(5) of SI 2008 No 959 as from 6.10.08.
2.   Amended by reg 27(a) of SI 2008 No 1082 as from 27.10.08.

Analysis

IS, JSA and ESA claimants may claim HB via a local DWP or Jobcentre Plus office. Where one of those benefits is claimed, much of the authority's decision-making is simplified because it has no need to consider the question of the claimant's resources. However, the relevant authority is still responsible for taking all decisions on the HB claim (except those expressly reserved to someone else under these regulations or the primary legislation) and, by virtue of reg 90 and the D&A Regs, for issuing notices of those decisions.

The requirements of Part 2 only apply to initial decisions following a claim: see para 7. Moreover, they only apply to notices sent when the claimant is on IS, income-based JSA, income-related ESA and *successfully* claims

HB or where the claimant is entitled to extended payments of HB under either reg 72 or reg 73. If HB is refused, see Part 6. Paras 2, 3 and 6 of Part 1 of this Schedule also apply.

The following sub-paras specify the necessary information.

(a)   The weekly eligible rent: see Part 3 HB Regs.

(b)   The amount of any deductions made under Sch 1 para 6 in respect of fuel charges and the fact that the deductions may be varied if material is provided to allow the authority to estimate the service charge.

(c)   The amount and type of non-dependant deductions under reg 74. See reg 3 for who is a non-dependant.

(d)   The weekly amount of rent allowance or rent rebate: see Part 8 HB regs.

(e)   In the case of rent allowance, or a rent rebate that is paid to the claimant as if it were, the day of payment and period in respect of which payment is made: see Part 12 HB Regs.

(f)   The first day of entitlement: see reg 76.

(g)   Notification of the duty to notify changes of circumstances: see reg 88. The authority is obliged to give examples of the kinds of changes that must be notified. It would appear that it is also obliged to make it clear that the obligation under reg 88 is a general one and that the examples are just that. A failure to make such a statement could well constitute an "official error" for the purposes of overpayment recoverability: see reg 100. It may also affect the question of whether the claimant could reasonably be expected to know that s/he was being overpaid.

PART 3
Awards where no income support [¹ , an income-based jobseeker's allowance or an income-related employment and support allowance] is payable

10.   Where a person is not on income support [¹ , an income-based jobseeker's allowance or on an income-related employment and support allowance] but is awarded housing benefit, the decision notice shall include a statement as to–

(a)   the matters set out in paragraph 9; and

(b)   his applicable amount and how it is calculated; and

(c)   his weekly earnings; and

(d)   his weekly income other than earnings.

Amendment

1.   Amended by reg 27(b) of SI 2008 No 1082 as from 27.10.08.

Analysis

The requirements of Part 3 only apply to initial decisions following a claim: see para 7. In addition to the information set out in para 9, additional information must be given where the claimant is awarded HB but is not on IS, income-based JSA or income-related ESA (see reg 2 for the definitions), since the authority is required to carry out its own assessment of the claimant's resources. The following information is required, in addition to the matters in paras 2, 3, 6 and 9.

(1)   The applicable amount and "how it is calculated": sub-para (a). This means that the applicable amount itself must be stated, but a full breakdown should also be given of the personal allowances, premiums and components to which the claimant is entitled.

(2)   The claimant's weekly earnings: see regs 29, 30, 35 and 37.

(3)   The claimant's weekly income other than earnings: see regs 31 and 40.

It is curious that there is no requirement to state the amount of the capital that the claimant has. If there is capital between the lower limit and £16,000 and tariff income is calculated, without showing the source of the income, the claimant may well be left mystified.

PART 4
Awards where direct payments made to landlords

11.   Where a decision has been made under regulation 95 or 96 (circumstances in which payment is to be made, or may be made, direct to a landlord), the decision notice shall include a statement–

(a)   as to the amount of housing benefit which is to be paid direct to the landlord and the date from which it is to be paid; and

(b)   informing the landlord of the duty imposed upon him to notify the local authority of–

(i)   any change in circumstances which might affect the claimant's entitlement to housing benefit, or the amount of housing benefit payable in his case; and

(ii)   the kind of change of circumstances which is to be notified;

(c)   informing both landlords and claimants that where a payment of housing benefit is recoverable from a landlord and the recovery is made from housing benefit payable to the landlord to discharge (in whole or in part) an obligation owed to him by a claimant, then, in a case where that claimant is not the person on whose behalf the recoverable amount was paid, that obligation shall nonetheless be taken to be discharged by the amount so recovered,

and the notice shall be sent both to the claimant and to the landlord.

Analysis

The requirements as to content were substantially increased following the changes made by the Social Security Administration (Fraud) Act 1997 and the secondary legislation made thereunder.

"Landlord" in this paragraph has the same meaning as in reg 95: see para 12. The notice must be sent to both the landlord and the claimant and must contain the following information, in addition to the matters in paras 2, 3 and 6:

(1)   The amount of HB to be paid direct and the date from which it is to be paid: para 11(a).

(2)   A notification of the landlord's duty to notify changes of circumstances and the kind of changes that are to be notified: para 11(b). See the Analysis to para 9(g) above for commentary on this provision.

(3)   A warning to both landlord and tenant A that if payments in respect of tenant A's HB are withheld to recover an overpayment made to tenant B and recovered from the landlord, then tenant A's obligation is taken to be discharged: para 11(c). This is a consequence of SSAA s75(6). Note also the obligation in reg 107(3) when there is a decision that an overpayment is recoverable from the landlord.

Note that as a decision under regs 95 or 96 attracts a right of appeal (see para 1 Sch to the D&A Regs on p1044), notice of this right and the right to a written statement of reasons for the decision where not already provided) will also be required under reg 10 D&A Regs.

---

12.   In this Schedule, ''landlord'' has the same meaning as in regulation 95.

PART 5
Notice where income of non-dependant is treated as claimant's

13.   Where an authority makes a decision under regulation 26 (circumstances in which income and capital of a non-dependant is to be treated as claimant's) the decision notice shall contain a statement as to–

(a)   the fact that a decision has been made by reference to the income and capital of the claimant's non-dependant; and

(b)   the relevant authority's reasons for making that decision.

Analysis

Reg 26(1) permits an authority to treat a claimant as having her/his non-dependant's income and capital where it appears that they have entered into an arrangement to take advantage of the HB scheme. See the Analysis to reg 26 on p345.

Where such a decision is made, in addition to the matters in paras 2, 3 and 6, the decision notice must state the fact that reg 26(1) has been utilised and the reasons for making that decision, an unhelpfully vague phrase. It is suggested that authorities should give the following information:

(1)   The fact that it appears that the claimant and the non-dependant (who should be identified) have entered into an arrangement falling within reg 26 and a summary of the reasons why that view is taken. See the Analysis to reg 9(1)(l) on p262 for the meaning of "take advantage" in this context.

(2)   The assessment made by the authority of the income and capital of both the claimant and the non-dependant and details of the calculation made under the non-dependant's resources (which is probably required anyway by virtue of para 10).

It would appear that since a non-dependant is not a "person affected" within the meaning of reg 2(1), s/he is not entitled to receive notification of the decision or to challenge it.

PART 6
Notice where no award is made

14.   Where a person is not awarded housing benefit–

(a)   either on grounds of income or because the amount of any housing benefit is less than the minimum housing benefit prescribed by regulation 75, the decision notice shall include a statement as to–

(i)   the matters set out in paragraphs 9(a) to (c), and in a case where the amount of entitlement is less than the minimum amount of housing benefit prescribed, paragraph 9(d) also; and

(ii)   the matters set out in paragraphs 10(b) to (d) where the person is not on income support [, an income-based jobseeker's allowance or an income-related employment and support allowance]; and

(iii)   where the amount of entitlement is less than the minimum amount of housing benefit prescribed, that fact and that such entitlement is not payable;

(b)   for any reason other than one mentioned in sub-paragraph (a), the decision notice shall include a statement as to the reason why no award has been made.

Amendment

1.   Amended reg 27(c) of SI 2008 No 1082 as from 27.10.08.

Analysis

The requirements of Part 6 only apply to initial decisions following a claim: see para 7. Para 14 applies where HB is refused. Two categories of notices are set out. If the refusal is on income grounds, the information prescribed by paras 9(a) to (c) must be given, and where the claimant is not on IS, income-based JSA or income-related ESA (defined in reg 2), the information in paras 10(b) to (d). If HB is refused because the entitlement is less than the minimum HB payable under reg 75, the fact must be stated and the information in para 9(d).

If refusal is not for a reason specified in para (a), only the reason for the refusal need be given. It would be good practice for more information to be given under para 6, particularly where there has been a finding of no liability or of a contrived tenancy.

Paras 2, 3 and 6 apply to notices under para 14.

PART 7
Notice where recoverable overpayment

15.–(1)   Where the appropriate authority makes a decision that there is a recoverable overpayment within the meaning of regulation 100 (recoverable overpayments), the decision notice shall include a statement as to–

(a)   the fact that there is a recoverable overpayment; and

(b)   the reason why there is a recoverable overpayment; and

(c)   the amount of the recoverable overpayment; and

(d)   how the amount of the recoverable overpayment was calculated; and

(e)   the benefit weeks to which the recoverable overpayment relates; and

(f)   where recovery of the recoverable overpayment is to be made by deduction from a rent allowance or rebate, as the case may be, that fact and the amount of the deduction.

(2)   In a case where it is–

(a)   determined that there is a recoverable overpayment;

(b)   determined that that overpayment is recoverable from a landlord; and

(c)   decided that recovery of that overpayment is to be made by deduction from a rent allowance paid to that landlord to discharge (in whole or in part) an obligation owed to him by a claimant ("claimant A"), not being the claimant on whose behalf the recoverable amount was paid,

the decision notice sent to that landlord shall identify both–

(i)   the person on whose behalf the recoverable amount was paid to that landlord; and

(ii)   claimant A.

Analysis

Paras 2, 3 and 6 also apply to notices under para 15. The requirements of the notices were expanded following changes made by the Social Security Administration (Fraud) Act 1997 and the secondary legislation made thereunder. The following content is required:

(1)   The fact that there is a recoverable overpayment and the reason why there is one: sub-paras (1)(a) and (b). It is suggested that authorities should go systematically through each of the issues in reg 100 to determine the answer to this question. In *R v Thanet DC ex p Warren Court Hotels Ltd* [2000] 33 HLR 339, CA, the notifications of overpayment contained a statement that there had been a change in the claimant's circumstances, as a result of which an overpayment had occurred because the local authority was unaware of the change in circumstances. The council argued that for the purposes of Sch 6 para 14(1)(b) HB Regs 1987 (now Sch 9 para 15(1)(b) HB Regs), "the reason why there is a recoverable overpayment", it was sufficient to state, was that there had been a change in circumstances. Jackson J disagreed, holding that it was necessary to spell out what the change of circumstances was (see the Analyses to s75(2) SSAA on p43 and reg 90 on p462 for the effect of this defect and the other issues in the case).

"The phrase 'change of circumstances' in that letter could cover a multitude of events. To take one example, it could mean that Mr H was in paid employment from 12 October onwards. To take another example, it could mean that although Mr H was unemployed, there was a three-week break in his entitlement to housing benefit." (para 36).

The requirement to identify how an overpayment has occurred does not require detailed calculations of the revised amounts of benefit: *CH 3776/2001* para 10. All that is required is the old and new figures and the difference.

(2)   The amount of the overpayment and how it is calculated: sub-paras (1)(c) and (d). Enough detail should be given to enable the claimant to follow the calculation through. That should include a complete breakdown of how much benefit is recoverable in each week it was paid, and details of a diminishing capital calculation if necessary. See regs 103 and 104 on pp494 and 496.

(3)   The benefit weeks to which the overpayment relates: sub-para (1)(e).

(4)   Where recovery is to be made by deduction from ongoing payments of rent allowance or rent rebate, that fact and the amount of the deduction: sub-para (1)(f).

(5)   Where the overpayment is recoverable from the landlord and recovery is to be made from claimant A's benefit where claimant B was overpaid, the landlord must be told the identities of claimants A and B: sub-para (2). Under SSAA s75(6), claimant A's obligation is deemed to be discharged by the amount of the deduction.

In *Godwin v Rossendale BC* [2002] *The Times* 24 May, [2002] EWCA Civ 726, para 51, the court stated that a notice under Sch 6 para 14(2) HB Regs 1987 (now Sch 9 para 15(2) HB Regs) should be given before recovery is made. However, the court rejected the suggestion that a failure to do so rendered the recovery unlawful, since there was no prejudice to the landlord by the omission.

Note the additional information that has to be provided under reg 107(3) in certain cases.

[¹ SCHEDULE 10
REGULATION 122
Former pathfinder authorities

Amendment
1.   Substituted by reg 20(2) of SI 2007 No 2868 as from 7.4.08.

General Note
Until 7 April 2008, Sch 10 contained the modified rules for determining the maximum rent (standard local rate), and hence the maximum HB, for tenants in the deregulated private sector in Pathfinder areas – the pilot "local housing allowance" scheme. From that date, the "local housing allowance" scheme was introduced nationwide (see Part 3). As the national scheme is less generous in a number of respects than the pilot scheme, Sch 10 now contains modifications which provided transitional protection for claimants in former Pathfinder areas.

Para 6 inserts a number of regulations. A claimant may have transitional protection if, before 7 April 2008:

(1)   Her/his HB was calculated on the basis of the maximum rent (standard local rate): regs 12E and 12I.

(2)   A rent restriction was delayed because of the death of a member of the family or a relative: regs 12F and 12J.

(3)   A rent restriction was delayed for 13 weeks because the claimant or a member of the family or a relative could meet the costs of the dwelling: reg 12G.

Where a claimant has transitional protection and a member of the family or a relative of the claimant or her/his partner who lives in the same accommodation without a separate right to do so dies before 7 April 2009, a consequent rent restriction can be delayed: regs 12H and 12K.

PART 1
Former pathfinder authorities

Argyll and Bute
Blackpool
Brighton and Hove
Conwy
Coventry
East Riding of Yorkshire
Edinburgh
Guildford
Leeds
Lewisham
North East Lincolnshire
Norwich
Pembrokeshire
St Helens
Salford
South Norfolk
Teignbridge
Wandsworth

PART 2
Application of the Regulations

1.   These Regulations shall apply to former pathfinder authorities subject to the provisions of this Part of this Schedule.

Amendment of regulation 2
2.   In regulation 2(1) (interpretation)–

(a)   in the definition of ''eligible rent'', in sub-paragraph (a) for ''or 12D (eligible rent and maximum rent (LHA))'' substitute '', 12D (eligible rent and maximum rent (LHA)) or any of regulations 12E to 12K (transitional protection for pathfinder cases)'';

(b)   after the definition of ''maximum rent (LHA)'' insert–

''''maximum rent (standard local rent)'' means a maximum rent (standard local rate) determined in accordance with regulation 13A;''.

Amendment of regulation 11
3.   In regulation 11(1) (eligible housing costs)–

(a)   in paragraph (c) omit ''or''; and
(b)   after sub-paragraph (d) insert–

''; or
(e)   any of regulations 12E to 12K (transitional protection for pathfinder cases) and regulations 13C (when a maximum rent (LHA) is to be determined) and 13D (determination of a maximum rent (LHA)),''.

Amendment of regulation 12B

4.   In regulation 12B(1) (eligible rent) for ''or 12D (eligible rent and maximum rent (LHA))'' substitute '', 12D (eligible rent and maximum rent (LHA)) or any of regulations 12E to 12K (transitional protection for pathfinder cases)''.

Amendment of regulation 12D

5.   In regulation 12D (eligible rent and maximum rent (LHA)) before paragraph (1) insert–
''(A1)   This regulation shall not apply where any of regulations 12E to 12K (transitional protection for pathfinder cases) apply.''

Insertion of regulations 12E to 12K

6. After regulation 12D (eligible rent and maximum rent (LHA)) insert–
''Basic transitional protection for pathfinder cases
12E.–(1)   This regulation applies where–
(a)   reference was made to a maximum rent (standard local rate) in determining the amount of the eligible rent which applied immediately before 7th April 2008;
(b)   on 7th April 2008 the local authority determines a maximum rent (LHA) by virtue of regulation 13C(4A)(a); and
(c)   regulations 12F (cases where the claimant enjoyed protection on death before 7th April 2008) and 12G (cases where the claimant enjoyed 13 week protection before 7th April 2008) do not apply.
(2)   Where this regulation applies, the claimant's eligible rent is–
(a)   the maximum rent (LHA) where that is higher than the eligible rent which applied immediately before 7th April 2008; or
(b)   the amount of the eligible rent which applied immediately before 7th April 2008.
(3)   Where the eligible rent is the amount of the eligible rent which applied immediately before 7th April 2008, it will continue to apply until, on or after 7th April 2008, the first of the following events occurs–
(a)   the relevant authority is required to determine a maximum rent (LHA) by virtue of regulation 13C(2)(d)(i) (change of category of dwelling) because the claimant has become entitled to a larger category of dwelling and the maximum rent (LHA) is higher than that eligible rent;
(b)   the relevant authority is required to determine a maximum rent (LHA) by virtue of regulation 13C(2)(d)(i) (change of category of dwelling) because the claimant has become entitled to a smaller category of dwelling;
(c)   the relevant authority is required to determine an eligible rent following a change of dwelling;
(d)   the relevant authority is required to determine an eligible rent in accordance with regulation 12H (cases where a death occurs in the first year on or after 7th April 2008) following the death of a linked person;
(e)   the relevant authority determines a maximum rent (LHA) on 7th April 2009 by virtue of regulation 13C(4A)(b).
(4)   Where the eligible rent is the maximum rent (LHA), it shall be treated as if it had been determined in accordance with regulation 12D(2)(a) (eligible rent is maximum rent (LHA)) and shall apply according to the provisions of regulation 12D (eligible rent and maximum rent (LHA)).
Cases where the claimant enjoyed protection on death before 7th April 2008
12F.–(1)   This regulation applies where–
(a)   immediately before 7th April 2008 the claimant enjoyed protection on death in accordance with regulation 12A(4)(a)(ii) (pathfinder protection on death based on reckonable rent); and
(b)   on 7th April 2008 the local authority determines a maximum rent (LHA) by virtue of regulation 13C(4A)(a).
(2)   Where this regulation applies, the claimant's eligible rent is–
(a)   the maximum rent (LHA) where that is higher than the eligible rent which applied immediately before 7th April 2008; or
(b)   the amount of the eligible rent which applied immediately before 7th April 2008.
(3)   Where the eligible rent is the amount of the eligible rent which applied immediately before 7th April 2008, it will continue to apply until, on or after 7th April 2008, the first of the following events occurs–
(a)   the end of 12 months after the death to which the protection relates;
(b)   the relevant authority is required to determine a maximum rent (LHA) by virtue of regulation 13C(2)(d)(i) (change of category of dwelling) and it is higher than that eligible rent;

(c)   the relevant authority is required to determine an eligible rent following a change of dwelling;

(d)   the relevant authority is required to determine an eligible rent in accordance with regulation 12H (cases where a death occurs in the first year on or after 7th April 2008) following the death of a linked person;

(4)   Where the eligible rent ceases to apply because of paragraph (3)(a), the eligible rent will be the maximum rent (LHA) which would have applied but for the transitional protection.

(5)   Where the eligible rent is the maximum rent (LHA), it shall be treated as if it had been determined in accordance with regulation 12D(2)(a) (eligible rent is maximum rent (LHA)) and shall apply according to the provisions of regulation 12D (eligible rent and maximum rent (LHA)).

Cases where the claimant enjoyed 13 week protection before 7th April 2008

12G.–(1)   This regulation applies where–

(a)   immediately before 7th April 2008 the claimant enjoyed 13 week protection in accordance with regulation 12A(6)(a) (local housing allowance pathfinder 13 week protection); and

(b)   on 7th April 2008 the local authority determines a maximum rent (LHA) by virtue of regulation 13C(4A)(a).

(2)   Where this regulation applies, the claimant's eligible rent is–

(a)   the maximum rent (LHA) where that is higher than the eligible rent which applied immediately before 7th April 2008; or

(b)   the amount of the eligible rent which applied immediately before 7th April 2008.

(3)   Where the eligible rent is the amount of the eligible rent which applied immediately before 7th April 2008, it will continue to apply until, on or after 7th April 2008, the first of the following events occurs–

(a)   the end of the day when the protection expires, namely 13 weeks after the date of the claim;

(b)   the relevant authority is required to determine a maximum rent (LHA) by virtue of regulation 13C(2)(d)(i) (change of category of dwelling) and it is higher than that eligible rent;

(c)   the relevant authority is required to determine an eligible rent following a change of dwelling;

(d)   the relevant authority is required to determine an eligible rent in accordance with regulation 12H (cases where a death occurs in the first year on or after 7th April 2008) following the death of a linked person.

(4)   Where the eligible rent ceases to apply because of paragraph (3)(a), the eligible rent will be the maximum rent (LHA) which would have applied but for the transitional protection.

(5)   Where the eligible rent is the maximum rent (LHA), it shall be treated as if it had been determined in accordance with regulation 12D(2)(a) (eligible rent is maximum rent (LHA)) and shall apply according to the provisions of regulation 12D (eligible rent and maximum rent (LHA)).

Cases where a death occurs in the first year on or after 7th April 2008

12H.–(1)   This regulation applies where–

(a)   the eligible rent is that specified in regulation 12E(2)(b) (basic transitional protection for pathfinder cases), 12F(2)(b) (transitional protection where the claimant enjoyed protection on death before 7th April 2008), 12G(2)(b) (transitional protection where the claimant enjoyed 13 week protection before 7th April 2008) or paragraph (2)(b) of this regulation;

(b)   a linked person dies on or after 7th April 2008 and before 7th April 2009;

(c)   the claimant occupies the same dwelling as the linked person at the date of death; and

(d)   the relevant authority determines a maximum rent (LHA) by virtue of regulation 13C(2)(d)(i) or (ii) (change of category of dwelling or death of a linked person).

(2)   Where this regulation applies, the claimant's eligible rent is–

(a)   the maximum rent (LHA) where that is higher than the eligible rent which applied immediately before the date of the death; or

(b)   the amount of the eligible rent which applied immediately before the date of the death.

(3)   Where the eligible rent is the amount of the eligible rent which applied immediately before the date of death, it will continue to apply until, on or after the date of the death, the first of the following events occurs–

(a)   the end of 12 months from the date of the death;

(b)   the relevant authority is required to determine a maximum rent (LHA) by virtue of regulation 13C(2)(d)(i) (change of category of dwelling) and it is higher than that eligible rent;

(c)   the relevant authority is required to determine an eligible rent following a change of dwelling;

(d)   the relevant authority is required to determine an eligible rent in accordance with this regulation following the death of another linked person.

(4)   Where the eligible rent is the maximum rent (LHA), it shall be treated as if it had been determined in accordance with regulation 12D(2)(a) (eligible rent is maximum rent (LHA)) and shall apply according to the provisions of regulation 12D (eligible rent and maximum rent (LHA)).

(5)   For the purposes of paragraph (1)(c), a claimant shall be treated as occupying the dwelling if regulation 7(13) is satisfied and for that purpose paragraph (13) of regulation 7 shall have effect as if sub-paragraph (b) were omitted.

Basic transitional protection in the second year and subsequent years after 7th April 2008

12I.–(1) This regulation applies where–

(a)   immediately before 7th April 2009 the claimant was enjoying basic transitional protection under regulation 12E; and

(b)   the local authority determines a maximum rent (LHA) by virtue of 13C(4A)(b) on 7th April 2009.

(2)   Where this regulation applies, the claimant's eligible rent is–

(a)   the maximum rent (LHA) where it is higher than the eligible rent applying immediately before 7th April 2008; or

(b)   in any other case, the lower of–

    (i)   the amount of the eligible rent applying immediately before 7th April 2008; or

    (ii)   the amount of the cap rent by reference to which the maximum rent (LHA) was determined, plus £15.

(3)   Where the claimant's eligible rent is determined in accordance with paragraph (2)(b), it continues to apply until, on or after 7th April 2009, the first of the following events occurs–

(a)   the relevant authority is required to determine a maximum rent (LHA) by virtue of regulation 13C(2)(d)(i) (change of category of dwelling) because the claimant has become entitled to a larger category of dwelling or 13C(3) (anniversary of the LHA date) and the maximum rent (LHA) is higher than that eligible rent;

(b)   the relevant authority is required to determine a maximum rent (LHA) by virtue of regulation 13C(2)(d)(i) (change of category of dwelling) because the claimant has become entitled to a smaller category of dwelling;

(c)   the relevant authority is required to determine an eligible rent following a change of dwelling;

(d)   the relevant authority is required to determine an eligible rent in accordance with regulation 12K (protection on death in the second and subsequent years after 7th April 2008) following the death of a linked person.

(4)   Where the eligible rent is the maximum rent (LHA), it shall be treated as if it had been determined in accordance with regulation 12D(2)(a) (eligible rent is maximum rent (LHA)) and shall apply according to the provisions of regulation 12D (eligible rent and maximum rent (LHA)).

Transitional protection in the second year after 7th April 2008 where the claimant is already enjoying protection on death

12J.–(1) This regulation applies where–

(a)   immediately before 7th April 2009 the claimant was enjoying transitional protection on death under regulation 12H (cases where a death occurs in the first year on or after 7th April 2008); and

(b)   the local authority determines a maximum rent (LHA) by virtue of regulation 13C(4A)(b) on 7th April 2009 .

(2)   Where this regulation applies, the claimant's eligible rent is–

(a)   the maximum rent (LHA) where that is higher than the eligible rent which applied immediately before the date of the death to which the protection relates; or

(b)   the amount of the eligible rent which applied immediately before the date of the death.

(3)   Where the eligible rent which applies is the one that applied immediately before the date of the death, it continues to apply until, on or after the date of the death, the first of the following events occurs–

(a)   the end of 12 months after the date of the death to which the protection relates;

(b)   the relevant authority is required to determine a maximum rent (LHA) by virtue of regulation 13C(2)(d)(i) (change of category of dwelling) and it is higher than that eligible rent;

(c)   the relevant authority is required to determine an eligible rent following a change of dwelling;

(d)   the relevant authority is required to determine an eligible rent in accordance with regulation 12K (protection on death in the second and subsequent years after 7th April 2008) following the death of a linked person.

(4)   Where the eligible rent ceases to apply because of paragraph (3)(a) the eligible rent is the one that would have applied if the relevant authority not determined an eligible rent in accordance with regulation 12H(2)(b) (transitional protection where a death occurs in the first year on or after 7th April 2008).

(5)   Where the eligible rent is the maximum rent (LHA), it shall be treated as if it had been determined in accordance with regulation 12D(2)(a) (eligible rent is maximum rent (LHA)) and shall apply according to the provisions of regulation 12D (eligible rent and maximum rent (LHA)).

Protection on death in the second and subsequent years after 7th April 2008

12K.–(1)   This regulation applies where–

(a)   the claimant's eligible rent is that specified in regulation 12I(2)(b) (basic transitional protection in the second and subsequent years after 7th April 2008), 12J(2)(b) (transitional protection in the second year after 7th April 2008 where the claimant is already enjoying protection on death) or paragraph (2)(b) of this regulation;

(b)   a linked person dies on or after 7th April 2009;

(c)   the claimant occupies the same dwelling as the linked person at the date of death; and

(d)   the relevant authority determines a maximum rent (LHA) by virtue of regulation 13C(2)(d)(i) or (ii) (change of category of dwelling or death of a linked person).

(2)   Where this regulation applies, the claimant's eligible rent is–

(a)   the maximum rent (LHA) where that is higher than the eligible rent which applied immediately before the date of the death; or

(b)   the amount of eligible rent which applied immediately before the death.

(3)   Where the eligible rent which applies is the one that applied immediately before the date of the death, it will continue to apply until, on or after the date of the death, the first of the following events occurs–

(a)   the end of 12 months from the date of the death;

(b)   the relevant authority is required to determine a maximum rent (LHA) by virtue of regulation 13C(2)(d)(i) or (3) (change of category of dwelling or anniversary of the LHA date) and it is higher than that eligible rent;

(c)   the relevant authority is required to determine an eligible rent following a change of dwelling;

(d)   the relevant authority is required to determine an eligible rent in accordance with this regulation following the death of another linked person.

(4)   Where the eligible rent ceases to apply because of paragraph (3)(a) the eligible rent is the one that would have applied but had the relevant authority not determined an eligible rent in accordance with this regulation.

(5)   Where the eligible rent is the maximum rent (LHA), it shall be treated as if it had been determined in accordance with regulation 12D(2)(a) (eligible rent is maximum rent (LHA)) and shall apply according to the provisions of regulation 12D (eligible rent and maximum rent (LHA)).

(6)   For the purposes of paragraph (1)(c), a claimant shall be treated as occupying the dwelling if regulation 7(13) is satisfied and for that purpose paragraph (13) of regulation 7 shall have effect as if sub-paragraph (b) were omitted.''.

Amendment of regulation 13C

7.   In regulation 13C (when a maximum rent (LHA) is to be determined)–

(a)   in paragraph (1) for ''paragraphs (2) or (3)'' substitute ''paragraphs (2), (3) or (4A)'';

(b)   in paragraph (3) after ''LHA date'' insert ''except where paragraph (4A)(b) applies'';

(c)   after paragraph (4) insert–

''(4A)   This paragraph applies where it is–

(a)   7th April 2008 and reference was made to a maximum rent (standard local rate) in determining the amount of the eligible rent which applied immediately before 7th April 2008; or

(b)   7th April 2009 and the eligible rent which applies on that date was determined in accordance with regulation 12E(2)(b) (basic transitional protection for pathfinder cases) or 12H(2)(b) (transitional protection where a death occurs in the first year on or after 7th April 2008).''.

Amendment of regulation 13D

8.   In regulation 13D(12) (determination of a maximum rent (LHA)) in the definition of ''relevant date'' after sub-paragraph (c) insert–

''(d)   7th April 2008;

(e)   7th April 2009.'']

[¹SCHEDULE 11
ELECTRONIC COMMUNICATION

Amendment

1.   Inserted by Art 2(5) of SI 2006 No 2968 as from 20.12.06.

General Note to Schedule 11

Reg 83A allows claims for HB to be made by electronic communication. The authorisation requirements and conditions for such claims are found in Sch 11. See the General Note to reg 83A on p452.

PART 1
Introduction

Interpretation

1.   In this Schedule ''official computer system'' means a computer system maintained by or on behalf of the relevant authority or of the Secretary of State for sending, receiving, processing or storing of any claim, certificate, notice, information or evidence.

PART 2
Electronic Communication – General Provisions

Conditions for the use of electronic communication

2.–(1)   The relevant authority may use an electronic communication in connection with claims for, and awards of, benefit under these Regulations.

(2)   A person other than the relevant authority may use an electronic communication in connection with the matters referred to in sub-paragraph (1) if the conditions specified in sub-paragraphs (3) to (6) are satisfied.

(3)   The first condition is that the person is for the time being permitted to use an electronic communication by an authorisation given by means of a direction of the Chief Executive of the relevant authority.

(4)   The second condition is that the person uses an approved method of–

(a)   authenticating the identity of the sender of the communication;

(b)   electronic communication;

(c)   authenticating any claim or notice delivered by means of an electronic communication; and

(d)   subject to sub-paragraph (7), submitting to the relevant authority any claim, certificate, notice, information or evidence.

(5)   The third condition is that any claim, certificate, notice, information or evidence sent by means of an electronic communication is in a form approved for the purposes of this Schedule.

(6)   The fourth condition is that the person maintains such records in written or electronic form as may be specified in a direction given by the Chief Executive of the relevant authority.

(7)   Where the person uses any method other than the method approved of submitting any claim, certificate, notice, information or evidence, that claim, certificate, notice, information or evidence shall be treated as not having been submitted.

(8)   In this paragraph "approved" means approved by means of a direction given by the Chief Executive of the relevant authority for the purposes of this Schedule.

Use of intermediaries

3.   The relevant authority may use intermediaries in connection with–

(a)   the delivery of any claim, certificate, notice, information or evidence by means of an electronic communication; and

(b)   the authentication or security of anything transmitted by such means,

and may require other persons to use intermediaries in connection with those matters.

PART 3
Electronic Communication – Evidential Provisions

Effect of delivering information by means of electronic communication

4.–(1)   Any claim, certificate, notice, information or evidence which is delivered by means of an electronic communication shall be treated as having been delivered in the manner or form required by any provision of these Regulations, on the day the conditions imposed–

(a)   by this Schedule; and

(b)   by or under an enactment,

are satisfied.

(2)   The relevant authority may, by a direction, determine that any claim, certificate, notice, information or evidence is to be treated as delivered on a different day (whether earlier or later) from the day provided for in sub-paragraph (1).

(3)   Information shall not be taken to have been delivered to an official computer system by means of an electronic communication unless it is accepted by the system to which it is delivered.

Proof of identity of sender or recipient of information

5.   If it is necessary to prove, for the purpose of any legal proceedings, the identity of–

(a)   the sender of any claim, certificate, notice, information or evidence delivered by means of an electronic communication to an official computer system; or

(b)   the recipient of any such claim, certificate, notice, information or evidence delivered by means of an electronic communication from an official computer system,

the sender or recipient, as the case may be, shall be presumed to be the person whose name is recorded as such on that official computer system.

Proof of delivery of information

6.–(1)   If it is necessary to prove, for the purpose of any legal proceedings, that the use of an electronic communication has resulted in the delivery of any claim, certificate, notice, information or evidence this shall be presumed to have been the case where–

(a)   any such claim, certificate, notice, information or evidence has been delivered to the relevant authority, if the delivery of that claim, certificate, notice, information or evidence has been recorded on an official computer system; or

(b)   any such claim, certificate, notice, information or evidence has been delivered by the relevant authority, if the delivery of that certificate, notice, information or evidence has been recorded on an official computer system.

(2)   If it is necessary to prove, for the purpose of any legal proceedings, that the use of an electronic communication has resulted in the delivery of any such claim, certificate, notice, information or evidence, this shall be presumed not to be the case, if that claim, certificate, notice, information or evidence delivered to the relevant authority has not been recorded on an official computer system.

(3)   If it is necessary to prove, for the purpose of any legal proceedings, when any such claim, certificate, notice, information or evidence sent by means of an electronic communication has been received, the time and date of receipt shall be presumed to be that recorded on an official computer system.

Proof of content of information

7.   If it is necessary to prove, for the purpose of any legal proceedings, the content of any claim, certificate, notice, information or evidence sent by means of an electronic communication, the content shall be presumed to be that recorded on an official computer system.]

The Rent Officers (Housing Benefit Functions) Order 1997
(SI 1997 No.1984)

General Note

This order sets out the determinations to be made by rent officers when a tenancy is referred to them under regs 13D(10) and 14 of both the HB and the HB(SPC) Regs by an authority in England and Wales. It also sets out the determinations to be made by rent officers relating to the "local housing allowance" scheme for rent restriction used by authorities to determine eligible rent under regs 12D and 13D of both the HB and the HB(SPC) Regs. The equivalent Order for Scotland is SI 1997 No.1995 (see p614).

The determinations made by rent officers under this order are relevant in two ways. The first concerns the calculation of a claimant's "maximum housing benefit" (or the reduction of the "eligible rent") where HB is paid as a rent allowance (ie, to private sector and some social landlord lettings) and the second the amount of subsidy received by an authority. As to the first, for certain private sector and social landlord tenants whose tenancies commenced after 1 January 1996, the rent officers' figures are the basis on which a "maximum rent" is calculated under reg 13 of both the HB and the HB(SPC) Regs. For most private sector tenants who claim HB on or after 7 April 2008, or who move while awarded HB on or after that date, the rent officer figures are the basis on which a "maximum rent (LHA)" is calculated under reg 13D of both the HB and the HB(SPC) Regs. See the commentary to the regulations in Part 3 of the HB Regs for a summary of how "maximum rent" and "maximum rent (LHA)" are calculated (from p297).

For those tenants who live in "exempt accommodation" or who have the benefit of the transitional protection set out in Sch 3 paras 4 and 5 HB&CTB(CP) Regs (see p1197), a rent officer's determination is not determinative of maximum rent. It is a factor to which an authority may have regard when considering whether the dwelling occupied by the claimant is larger than reasonably required or that the rent is unreasonably high by comparison with the rent payable in respect of suitable alternative accommodation elsewhere: see paras (3)(a) and (b) of the version of reg 13 of both the HB and the HB(SPC) Regs in Sch 3 para 5 HB&CTB(CP) Regs and the Analysis thereto (from p1203).

There is no right of appeal to the First-tier Tribunal against a decision of the rent officer. However, the claimant can appeal the local authority's decision on HB entitlement and, as such, can challenge the factual basis upon which the rent officer decision was made – eg, the number of occupiers given to the rent officer by the local authority: *Borough of Bexley v LD (HB)* [2010] UKUT 79 (AAC).

The role of rent officers in rent allowance subsidy is governed by Art 16 of, and Sch 4, to the Income-Related Benefits (Subsidy) Order 1998 (SI 1998 No.562). There are financial incentives resting on local authorities to apply the rent restrictions scheme correctly.

Citation and commencement

1.–(1) This Order may be cited as the Rent Officers (Housing Benefit Functions) Order 1997.

(2)   This article and articles 8 and 10(1) shall come into force on 18th August 1997 and all the other articles shall come into force on 3rd September 1997.

Interpretation

2.–(1)   In this Order, unless the context otherwise requires–

"assured tenancy" has the same meaning as in Part I of the Housing Act 1988, except that it includes a tenancy which would be an assured tenancy but for paragraph 2 [³ , 8] or 10 of Schedule 1 to that Act and a licence which would be an assured tenancy (within the extended meaning given in this definition) were it a tenancy;

[² "board and attendance determination" means a determination made in accordance with article 4C;]

[⁹ "broad rental market area" has the meaning specified in paragraph 4 of Schedule 3B;]

[⁹ "broad rental market area determination" means a determination made in accordance with article 4B(1A);]

"child" means a person under the age of 16;

"determination" means a determination made in accordance with Part I or IV of Schedule 1 to this Order;

"dwelling" means any residential accommodation whether or not consisting of the whole or part of a building and whether or not comprising separate and self-contained premises;

[¹⁰ "hostel" has the same meaning as in regulation 2(1) of the Housing Benefit Regulations or, as the case may be, regulation 2(1) of the Housing Benefit (State Pension Credit) Regulations;]

[¹¹ "the Housing Benefit Regulations" mean the Housing Benefit Regulations 2006;

"the Housing Benefit (State Pension Credit) Regulations" means the Housing Benefit (Persons who have attained the qualifying age for state pension credit) Regulations 2006;]

"local authority" has the same meaning as in the Social Security Administration Act 1992 in relation to England and in relation to Wales;

[⁹ "local housing allowance determination" means a determination made in accordance with article 4B(2A);]

"occupier" means a person (whether or not identified by name) who is stated, in the application for the determination, to occupy the dwelling as his home;

[⁹]

"redetermination" means a redetermination made in accordance with article 4;

[⁹ "relevant date" means the date specified by a local authority in an application for a local housing allowance determination made in accordance with regulation 13D(7)(a) of the Housing Benefit Regulations or, as the case may be, regulation 13D(7)(a) of the Housing Benefit (State Pension Credit) Regulations;]

[¹ "relevant period" means–

(a) in relation to a determination, the period of five working days (or, where the determination does not relate to a prospective tenancy and the rent officer intends to inspect the dwelling before making the determination, 25 working days) beginning with-
    (i) where the rent officer requests further information under article 5, the date on which he receives the information; and
    (ii) in any other case, the date on which he receives the application for the determination; and

(b) in relation to a redetermination, the period of 20 working days beginning with-
    (i) where the rent officer requests further information under article 5, the date on which he receives the information; and
    (ii) in any other case, the date on which he receives the application for that redetermination;]

"relevant time" means the time the application for the determination [² or board and attendance determination] is made or, if earlier, the tenancy ends;

[¹⁰ "rent" means any of the periodical payments referred to in regulation 12(1) of the Housing Benefit Regulations or, as the case may be, regulation 12(1) of the Housing Benefit (State Pension Credit) Regulations;]

"size criteria" means the standards relating to bedrooms and rooms suitable for living in specified in Schedule 2 to this Order;

"tenancy" includes–

(a) a licence; and
(b) a prospective tenancy or licence; and
references to a tenant, a landlord or any other expression appropriate to a tenancy shall be construed accordingly; and

[⁸ "working day" means any day other than a Saturday, a Sunday, Christmas Day, Good Friday or a day which is a bank holiday in England and Wales under the Banking and Financial Dealings Act 1971.]

[¹²]

(2) In this Order any reference to a notice or application is to a notice or application in writing, except in a case where the recipient consents (whether generally or specifically) to the notice or application being transmitted by electronic means.

Modifications

Some definitions substituted and the definition of "pathfinder authority" omitted by Art 6(3) Rent Officers (Housing Benefit Functions) Amendment Order 2007 SI No.2871 as from 1 April 2008, save where Art 6(1)(a), (b) or (c) of that order applied (see p634).

Note that by Art 3 of SI 2007 No.2871, those provisions which on 19 March 2008 applied only in relation to the areas of former Pathfinder authorities, apply in the same way to the areas of every other local authority in England and Wales.

Amendments

1. Substituted by art 3 of SI 2000 No 1 as from 3.4.00.
2. Insertions made by Art 2 of SI 2003 No 2398 as from a date specified in Sch 1 to that SI in relation to each individual authority.
3. Inserted by Art 2(1) of SI 2004 No 2101 as from 31.8.04.
4. Substituted by Sch 1 para 11(2)(a), (c) and (d) of SI 2006 No 217 as from 6.3.06.
5. Inserted by Sch 1 para 11(2)(b) of SI 2006 No 217 as from 6.3.06.
6. Omitted by Sch 1 para 11(2)(e) of SI 2006 No 217 as from 6.3.06.
7. Amended by Art 4(1)(a)-(c) of SI 2007 No 2871 as from 20.3.08.
8. Inserted by Art 4(d) of SI 2007 No 2871 as from 20.3.08.
9. Substituted by Art 6(3) of SI 2007 No 2871 as from 7.4.08, save where Art 6(1)(a), (b) or (c) of that order applies.
10. Substituted by Art 10(1) of SI 2007 No 2871 as from 7.4.08.
11. Inserted by Art 10(1) of SI 2007 No 2871 as from 7.4.08.
12. Omitted by Art 10(1) of SI 2007 No 2871 as from 7.4.08.

Analysis

"Assured tenancy". By s1 Housing Act 1988 an "assured tenancy" is a tenancy of a dwelling house let to an individual or individuals as their "only or principal home". It has an extended definition in this section. Sch 1 para 2 of the 1988 Act excludes houses with an annual rent of more than a set amount from the Act, but tenancies of such properties fall within the definition for the purposes of this Order. Sch 1 para 10, broadly speaking, excludes properties where the landlord is resident. The very complex provisions of that paragraph and those accompanying it do not arise here either. Licenses also fall within the definition of "assured tenancy", so there will be no issue as to whether or not exclusive possession of the premises has been granted. Note that an assured shorthold tenancy is just a particular type of assured tenancy: see ss19A and 20 of the 1988 Act. Such tenancies therefore also fall within this definition.

"Occupier". The definition of "occupier" was discussed in *R v Swale BC HBRB ex p Marchant* [1999] 1 FLR 1087, QBD; [2000] 1 FLR 246, CA. The claimant was separated from his wife. Their children spent alternate weeks with the claimant and his wife. She received child benefit for them. The rent officer was instructed by the local authority to assess the claimant's rent on the basis that the children were not "occupiers" of his property. Kay J [1999] 1 FLR 1087 upheld that decision on the basis that as the wife was "responsible" for the children pursuant to reg 14 HB Regs 1987 (now reg 20 of both the HB and the HB(SPC) Regs), they were members of her family. Consequently reg 5(1) HB regs 1987 (now reg 7(1) of both the HB and the HB(SPC) Regs) proceeded on the basis that they were normally occupying the wife's home and that was the proper definition of "occupier" in Art 2.

The Court of Appeal heard and dismissed an appeal from that decision. Potter LJ stated that it was clear that resolution of the questions of with which parent a child normally lived and of whose household the child was a member should also be regarded as determinative of the question of which dwelling a child occupied for the purposes of the Rent Officers (Additional Functions) Order 1995 (which was in identical terms to the 1997 Order). To permit the children to be taken into account in examining the sizes of both households would lead to an "element of double provision" in the scheme.

It was also confirmed in the judgment of Potter LJ that the decision as to whether or not a person is an "occupier" is one for the local authority. This is made in the "application" to the rent officer pursuant to reg 14(1) of both the HB and the HB(SPC) Regs. See also the discussion on *Stroud DC v JG* [2009] UKUT 67 (AAC); R(H) 8/09 on p518.

"Relevant period". The rent officer must provide a determination within five working days and a redetermination within 20 working days of the relevant date. This period runs from the date of receipt of the request for the determination or, if the rent officer has to seek further information, the date on which that information is received. In the case of a determination, the "relevant period" is lengthened to 25 days where the determination sought is not a pre-tenancy determination under reg 14(1)(e) of both the HB and the HB(SPC) Regs and where the rent officer wishes to inspect the home first.

Determinations

3.–(1) Subject to [² articles 3A and 6], where a local authority, in accordance with regulations made under section 136(2) or (3) of the Social Security Administration Act 1992, [¹ or section 122(5) of the Housing Act 1996,] applies to a rent officer for determinations in respect of a tenancy of a dwelling, a rent officer shall–

(a) make the determinations in accordance with Part I of Schedule 1 (determinations);

(b) comply with Part II of Schedule 1 when making the determinations (assumptions etc.); and

(c) give notice in accordance with Part III of Schedule 1 (notifications) [¹ within the relevant period or as soon as is practicable after that period].

(2)   A rent officer for each registration area (within the meaning of section 62 of the Rent Act 1977), on the first working day of each month, shall–

(a)   make determinations in accordance with Part IV of Schedule 1 (indicative rent levels) in relation to the area of each local authority [⁴] within the registration area;

(b)   comply with paragraph 8(2) of Part II of Schedule 1 (assumptions etc.) when making the determinations; and

(c)   give to the local authority notice of the determinations relating to its area when they have been made.

Modifications

By Art 3 Rent Officers (Housing Benefit Functions) Amendment Order 2007 SI No.2871, those provisions which on 19 March 2008 applied only in relation to the areas of former Pathfinder authorities, apply in the same way to the areas of every other local authority in England and Wales.

Amendments

1.   Amended by art 4 of SI 2000 No 1 as from 3.4.00.
2.   Amended by reg 3 of SI 2001 No 1325 as from 2.7.01.
3.   Insertion made by Art 2 of SI 2003 No 2398 as from a date specified in Sch 1 to that SI in relation to each individual authority.
4.   Amended by Art 5(1) of SI 2007 No 2871 as from 7.4.08.

[¹ Transitional arrangements for determination of Single Room Rents with effect from 2nd July 2001

3A.   In a case where the rent officer has made and notified an authority of a determination of a single room rent pursuant to paragraph 5 of Schedule 1 in the period of 12 months before 2nd July 2001 that determination shall cease to have effect on [² . . .] 2nd July 2001 and a rent officer shall–

(a)   make a new determination of that single room rent in accordance with Part I of Schedule 1;

(b)   comply with Part II of Schedule 1; and

(c)   give notice in accordance with Part III of Schedule 1 within the relevant period or as soon as is practicable after that period;

without an application for a determination under [³ [⁴ regulation 14 of the Housing Benefit Regulations or, as the case may be, regulation 14 of the Housing Benefit (State Pension Credit) Regulations] having been made.]]

Amendments

1.   Inserted by reg 3 of SI 2001 No 1325 as from 2.7.01.
2.   Amended by reg 2(2) of SI 2001 No 2317 as from 2.7.01.
3.   Amended by reg 5 and Sch 2 para 11(3) of SI 2006 No 217 as from 6.3.06.
4.   Substituted by Art 10(2) of SI 2007 No 2871 as from 7.4.08.

General Note

The definition of the "single room rent" was amended on 2 July 2001 to be more generous to the claimants. Art 3A aimed to ensure that those who were affected by this change benefited from it immediately. For further information, see the commentary on p570 of the 18th edition.

[¹ Redeterminations

4.–(1)   Subject to article 6, where the local authority applies to a rent officer for a redetermination of any determination or redetermination in respect of a tenancy of a dwelling the rent officer shall, in accordance with Schedule 3–

(a)   make redeterminations of any effective determinations and any effective redeterminations in respect of that tenancy; and

(b)   give notice within the relevant period or as soon as is practicable after that period.

(2)   For the purposes of paragraph (1)–

(a)   ''effective determinations'' means any determinations made in accordance with Part I of Schedule 1 which have effect at the date of the application for a redetermination of a determination or redetermination; and

(b)   "effective redeterminations" means any redeterminations made in accordance with Schedule 3 which have effect at that date.

(3)   A rent officer whose advice is sought as provided for in Schedule 3 shall give that advice.

Amendment

1.   Substituted by Art 5 of SI 2000 No 1 as from 3.4.00.

General Note

Art 4 makes it clear that only "effective" determinations or redeterminations need to be redetermined – that is those that have effect at the time that the local authority applies for a redetermination.

[¹ Substitute determinations and substitute redeterminations

4A.–(1)   Where a local authority applies to a rent officer for a substitute determination, in accordance with [² [³ regulation 17 of the Housing Benefit Regulations or, as the case may be, regulation 17 of the Housing Benefit (State Pension Credit) Regulations]], the provisions of this Order shall apply to that substitute determination as they apply to a determination, but as if references to the relevant time were references to the date the application for the original determination was made or, if earlier, the date the tenancy ended.

(2)   Where a local authority applies to a rent officer for a substitute redetermination, in accordance with that regulation, the provisions of this Order shall apply to that substitute redetermination as they apply to a redetermination.]

Amendments

1.   Inserted by Art 5 of SI 2000 No 1 as from 3.4.00.
2.   Amended by reg 5 and Sch 2 para 11(4) of SI 2006 No 217 as from 6.3.06.
3.   Substituted by Art 10(3) of SI 2007 No 2871 as from 7.4.08.

General Note

Art 4A(1) allows for determinations to be substituted on an application under reg 17 of both the HB and the HB(SPC) Regs. Reg 17 permits substitute determinations where either the local authority or the rent officer has made an error.

[¹Broad rental market area determinations and local housing allowance determinations

4B.–[⁶ (1)]

[⁴ (1A)   On 20th March 2008 and so often thereafter as a rent officer considers appropriate, a rent officer shall, in relation to each local authority,–

(a)   determine one or more broad rental market areas which will (during the month which next begins after the determination is made) fall, in whole or in part, within the area of the local authority so that every part of the area of that local authority falls within a broad rental market area and no part of the area of that authority falls within more than one broad rental market area; and

(b)   give to that local authority a notice which–
    (i)   specifies the area contained within each broad rental market area as falls, in whole or in part, within the area of that authority, by reference to the postcodes for each such broad rental market area; and
    (ii)   identifies such of those postcodes as fall within the area of that authority.]

[⁶ (2)]

[⁴ (2A)   No more than 10 and not less than 8 working days before the end of each month a rent officer shall–

(a)   for each broad rental market area determine, in accordance with the provisions of Schedule 3B–
    (i)   a local housing allowance for each of the categories of dwelling set out in paragraph 1 of Schedule 3B; and
    (ii)   local housing allowances for such other categories of dwelling of more than five bedrooms as a rent officer believes are likely to be required for the purpose of calculating housing benefit; and

(b) give to each local authority notice of the local housing allowance determination made in accordance with paragraph (a) for each broad rental market area falling within, in whole or in part, the area of that authority.]

[⁶ (3)]

[⁴ (3A) Any broad rental market area determination made in accordance with paragraph (1A), or local housing allowance determination made in accordance with paragraph (2A) before 7th April 2008, shall take effect on 7th April 2008 and any subsequent determination shall take effect on the first [⁷ [⁸]] day of the month which begins after the day on which the determination is made.]

[⁶ (4) Where a local authority makes an application in accordance with regulation 13D(7)(a) of the Housing Benefit Regulations or, as the case may be, regulation 13D(7)(a) of the Housing Benefit (State Pension Credit) Regulations, a rent officer shall determine, in accordance with the provisions of Schedule 3B and as soon as is reasonably practicable, the local housing allowance for that category of dwelling at the relevant date, for each broad rental market area falling within, in whole or in part, the area of the local authority that made the application, at the relevant date.]

[⁶ (4A) Where a local authority makes an application in accordance with regulation 13D(8) of the Housing Benefit Regulations or, as the case may be, regulation 13D(8) of the Housing Benefit (State Pension Credit) Regulations, a rent officer shall determine in accordance with the provisions of Schedule 3B and as soon as is reasonably practicable, the local housing allowance for that category of dwelling for each broad rental market area falling within, in whole or in part, the areas of the local authority.]

(5) Where a rent officer has made a local housing allowance determination in accordance with paragraph (4)–

(a) he shall give notice of the determination to the [⁶ local authority] that made the application;

[⁶ (b) any local housing allowance determination made in accordance with paragraph (4) shall take effect for the month in which the relevant date falls, except that no such determination can have effect before 7th April 2008; and

(c) any local housing allowance determination made in accordance with paragraph (4A) shall take effect for the month in which notice is given in accordance with sub-paragraph (a), except that no such determination can have effect before 7th April 2008.]

[⁴ (6) Where a rent officer has made a local housing allowance determination in accordance with paragraph (2A) [⁵ , (4) or (4A)] he shall–

(a) make an approximate monthly allowance determination in relation to that local housing allowance determination; and

(b) give notice of the approximate monthly allowance determination to each authority to which he is required to give notice of the local housing allowance determination when he gives notice of that determination.]

Modifications

Paras (1), (2) and (3) omitted, para (4) substituted, para (4A) inserted and para (5) amended by Art 6(4) Rent Officers (Housing Benefit Functions) Amendment Order 2007 SI No.2871 as from 7 April 2008, save where Art 6(1)(a), (b) or (c) of that order applied (see p634).

Note that by Art 3 of SI 2007 No.2871, those provisions which on 19 March 2008 applied only in relation to the areas of former Pathfinder authorities, apply in the same way to the areas of every other local authority in England and Wales.

Amendments

1. Inserted by Art 2(5) of SI 2003 No 2398 as from a date specified in Sch 1 to that SI in relation to each individual authority.
2. Amended by reg 5 and Sch 2 para 11(5) of SI 2006 No 217 as from 6.3.06.
3. Amended by Art 4(2)(a) of SI 2007 No 2871 as from 20.3.08.
4. Inserted by Art 4(2)(b)-(e) of SI 2007 No 2871 as from 20.3.08.
5. Amended by Art 5(2) of SI 2007 No 2871 as from 7.4.08.
6. Amended by Art 6(4) of SI 2007 No 2871, as amended by Art 2(3) of SI 2008 No 587, as from 7.4.08, save where Art 6(1)(a), (b) or (c) of that order applies.
7. Amended by Art 2(2) of SI 2008 No 587 as from 7.4.08.

8.   Amended by Art 2(2) of SI 2008 No 3156 as from 5.1.09.

General Note

Art 4B sets out the determinations that a rent officer must make in connection with the "local housing allowance" (LHA) scheme for rent restriction (see regs 12C, 12D, 13C and 13D of both the HB and HB(SPC) Regs), and the time frame for these. The rent officer must determine:

(1)   One or more "broad rental market areas" in relation to each local authority. See p610 for a discussion of the definition. The first such determination was to be made on 20 March 2008, and thereafter the rent officer must determine these as often as s/he considers appropriate: para (1A).

(2)   A "local housing allowance" for the categories of dwelling set out in Sch 3B para 1: para (2A). The categories are: one-bedroom shared accommodation and one, two, three, four and five-bedroom dwellings. The LHAs must be determined monthly. The rent officer must also determine a LHA for other categories of more than five bedrooms if s/he believes these are likely to be required for calculating HB. It is unclear when this provision will now be needed given that the largest category of dwelling that can now apply is five-bedroom accommodation: see reg 13D(2)(c) of both the HB and the HB(SPC) Regs. Note: from April 2011 the Government intends to reduce the maximum number of bedrooms to four and to cap weekly LHA rates at £250 for a one-bedroom property, £290 for a two-bedroom property, £340 for a three-bedroom property and £400 for a four-bedroom property.

In both cases, the rent officer is required to notify the local authority as set out.

Paras (4), (4A) and (5) deal with determinations a rent officer must make when an authority has applied for a LHA determination under either reg 13D(7) or (8) of the HB regs (or HB(SPC) Regs). Note that reg 13D(7) was deleted from 5 April 2009.

See Art 7A for when a rent officer believes s/he has made an error (other than in the application of her/his professional judgement).

[¹Board and attendance determinations and notifications

[³**4C.**–(1)   Where a relevant authority makes an application to a rent officer in accordance with regulation 13D(10) of the Housing Benefit Regulations or, as the case may be, regulation 13D(10) of the Housing Benefit (State Pension Credit) Regulations, a rent officer shall determine whether or not a substantial part of the rent under the tenancy at the relevant time is fairly attributable to board and attendance.

(2)   Where a rent officer determines that a substantial part of the rent under the tenancy at the relevant time is fairly attributable to board and attendance, he shall–

(a)   notify the relevant authority accordingly; and

(b)   treat the application as if it had been made in accordance with regulation 14(1) of the Housing Benefit Regulations or, as the case may be regulation 14(1) of the Housing Benefit (State Pension Credit) Regulations.]

(3)   Where a rent officer determines that a substantial part of the rent under the tenancy at the relevant time is not fairly attributable to board and attendance, he shall notify the pathfinder authority accordingly.

[⁴ (4)   Where an application for a board and attendance determination is treated as if it had been made in accordance with regulation 14(1) of the Housing Benefit Regulations or, as the case may be, regulation 14(1) of the Housing Benefit (State Pension Credit) Regulations, then, for the purposes of paragraph (a)(ii) of the definition of "relevant period" in article 2(1), it shall be treated as having been received on the day on which the further information provided in accordance with regulation 114A(4) of the Housing Benefit Regulations or regulation 95A(4) of the Housing Benefit (State Pension Credit) Regulations is received.]]

Modifications

Paras (1) and (2) substituted by Art 6(5) Rent Officers (Housing Benefit Functions) Amendment Order 2007 SI No.2871 as from 7 April 2008, save where Art 6(1)(a), (b) or (c) of that order applied (see p634). Para (4) substituted by Art 7(2) Rent Officers (Housing Benefit Functions) Amendment Order 2007 SI No.2871 as from 7 April 2008, save where Art 7(1) of that order applied (see p634).

Note that by Art 3 SI 2007 No.2871, those provisions which on 19 March 2008 applied only in relation to the areas of former Pathfinder authorities, apply in the same way to the areas of every other local authority in England and Wales.

Amendments

1.   Inserted by Art 2(5) of SI 2003 No 2398 as from a date specified in Sch 1 to that SI in relation to each individual authority.

2. Amended by reg 5 and Sch 2 para 11(6) of SI 2006 No 217 as from 6.3.06.
3. Amended by Art 6(5) of SI 2007 No 2871 as from 7.4.08, save where Art 6(1)(a), (b) or (c) of that order applies.
4. Amended by Art 7(2) of SI 2007 No 2871 as from 7.4.08, save where Art 7(1) of that order applies.

General Note

Art 4C deals with the determinations that a rent officer must make when an authority has applied for a board and attendance determination under reg 13D(10) of either the HB Regs or HB(SPC) Regs. Note that if s/he decides that substantial part of the rent under the tenancy at the relevant time is fairly attributable to board and attendance, the application is treated as one under reg 14(1) of either the HB or the HB(SPC) Regs. This ensures that the determinations can then be used by the authority as appropriate in calculating eligible rent. See also Arts 4D and 4E for redeterminations and substitute determinations.

[¹Board and attendance redeterminations

4D.–(1)   Subject to article 6, where a [² local authority] applies to a rent officer for a redetermination of a board and attendance determination or board and attendance redetermination, the rent officer shall, in accordance with paragraph (2)–

(a)   make a redetermination of–

(i)   the board and attendance determination, provided it was made in accordance with article 4C and had effect at the date of the application for it to be redetermined; or

(ii)   the board and attendance redetermination provided it was made in accordance with head (i), and had effect at the date of the application for it to be redetermined; and

(b)   notify the [² local authority] of the redetermination.

(2)   When making a board and attendance redetermination under this article, the rent officer shall seek, and have regard to, the advice of one or two other rent officers in relation to the redetermination.

(3)   A rent officer whose advice is sought in accordance with paragraph (2) shall give that advice.

(4)   Article 4C shall apply in relation to a board and attendance redetermination but as if the references to the relevant time were references to the date on which the original application for a board and attendance determination was made, or if earlier, to the date on which the tenancy ended.]

Modifications

Para (1) amended by Art 6(6) Rent Officers (Housing Benefit Functions) Amendment Order 2007 SI No.2871 as from 7 April 2008, save where Art 6(1)(a), (b) or (c) of that order applied (see p634).

Note that by Art 3 SI 2007 No.2871, those provisions which on 19 March 2008 applied only in relation to the areas of former Pathfinder authorities, apply in the same way to the areas of every other local authority in England and Wales.

Amendments

1. Inserted by Art 2(5) of SI 2003 No 2398 as from a date specified in Sch 1 to that SI in relation to each individual authority.
2. Amended by Art 6(6) of SI 2007 No 2871 as from 7.4.08, save where Art 6(1)(a), (b) or (c) of that order applies.

[¹Substitute board and attendance determinations and substitute board and attendance redeterminations

4E.–(1)   Where a [³ local authority] applies to a rent officer for a substitute board and attendance determination in accordance with [²[⁴ regulation 17 of the Housing Benefit Regulations or, as the case may be, regulation 17 of the Housing Benefit (State Pension Credit) Regulations]], the provisions of this Order shall apply to that substitute board and attendance determination as they apply to a board and attendance determination but as if references to the relevant time were references to the date on which the original application for a board and attendance determination was made or, if earlier, the date on which the tenancy ended.

(2)   Where a [³ local authority] applies to a rent officer for a substitute board and attendance redetermination in accordance with [² [⁴ regulation 17 of the Housing Benefit

Regulations or, as the case may be, regulation 17 of the Housing Benefit (State Pension Credit) Regulations], the provisions of this Order shall apply to that substitute board and attendance redetermination as they apply to a board and attendance redetermination.]]

Modifications
Art 4E amended by Art 6(6) Rent Officers (Housing Benefit Functions) Amendment Order 2007 SI No.2871 as from 7 April 2008, save where Art 6(1)(a), (b) or (c) of that order applied (see p634).

Note that by Art 3 SI 2007 No.2871, those provisions which on 19 March 2008 applied only in relation to the areas of former Pathfinder authorities, apply in the same way to the areas of every other local authority in England and Wales.

Amendments
1.   Inserted by Art 2(5) of SI 2003 No 2398 as from a date specified in Sch 1 to that SI in relation to each individual authority.
2.   Amended by reg 5 and Sch 2 para 11(7) of SI 2006 No 217 as from 6.3.06.
3.   Amended by Art 6(6) of SI 2007 No 2871 as from 7.4.08, save where Art 6(1)(a), (b) or (c) of that order applies.
4.   Substituted by Art 10(4) of SI 2007 No 2871 as from 7.4.08.

Insufficient information

5.   If a rent officer needs further information in order to make a determination under article 3(1) [², a redetermination under article 4, a board and attendance determination under article 4C or a board and attendance redetermination under article 4D][³ where the information supplied under regulation 114A of the Housing Benefit Regulations or regulation 95A of the Housing Benefit (State Pension Credit) Regulations was incomplete or incorrect, he shall serve notice on the local authority requesting it to supply the further information required under regulation 114A or regulation 95A, as the case may be, or to confirm whether the information already supplied is correct and, if it is not, to supply the correct information] [¹ ...].

Modifications
Art 5 amended by Art 7(3) Rent Officers (Housing Benefit Functions) Amendment Order 2007 SI No.2871 as from 7 April 2008, save where Art 7(1) of that order applied (see p634).

Note that by Art 3 SI 2007 No.2871, those provisions which on 19 March 2008 applied only in relation to the areas of former Pathfinder authorities, apply in the same way to the areas of every other local authority in England and Wales.

Amendments
1.   Deleted by Art 6 of SI 2000 No 1 as from 3.4.00.
2.   Substituted by Art 2(6) SI 2003 No 2398 as from a date specified in Sch 1 to that SI in relation to each individual authority.
3.   Amended by Art 7(3) of SI 2007 No 2871 as from 7.4.08, save where Art 7(1) of that order applies.

Exceptions

6.–(1)   No determination [¹, redetermination, board and attendance determination or board and attendance redetermination] shall be made if the application for it is withdrawn.

(2)   No determination shall be made under paragraph 3, 4 or 5 of Part I of Schedule 1 if the tenancy is of residential accommodation, within the meaning of [² [³ regulation 9(4) of the Housing Benefit Regulations or, as the case may be, regulation 9(4) of the Housing Benefit (State Pension Credit) Regulations]] (registered homes etc.), or in a hostel.

(3)   No determination shall be made under paragraph 5 of Part I of Schedule 1 unless the local authority states in the application that the claimant is, or may be, a young individual (which has the same meaning as in [² [³ the Housing Benefit Regulations and the Housing Benefit (State Pension Credit) Regulations]]).

(4)   If the rent officer becomes aware that an application is not one which gives rise to a duty to make a determination [¹, redetermination, board and attendance determination or a board and attendance redetermination], the rent officer shall give the local authority notice to that effect.

Modifications

Note that by Art 3 Rent Officers (Housing Benefit Functions) Amendment Order 2007 SI No.2871, those provisions which on 19 March 2008 applied only in relation to the areas of former Pathfinder authorities, apply in the same way to the areas of every other local authority in England and Wales.

Amendments

1. Substituted by Art 2(7) of SI 2003 No 2398 as from a date specified in Sch 1 to that SI in relation to each individual authority.
2. Amended by reg 5 and Sch 2 para 11(8) of SI 2006 No 217 as from 6.3.06.
3. Substituted by Art 10(5) of SI 2007 No 2871 as from 7.4.08.

Special cases

7.–(1)   This Order shall apply as specified in Schedule 4 in relation to–

(a)   mooring charges payable for a houseboat;

(b)   payments in respect of the site on which a caravan or mobile home stands; or

(c)   payments under a rental purchase agreement.

(2)   Terms used in paragraph (1) have the same meaning in this article and in Schedule 4 as they have in [² [³ regulation 12(1) of the Housing Benefit Regulations or, as the case may be, regulation 12(1) of the Housing Benefit (State Pension Credit) Regulations]] (rents).[¹ ...]

Amendments

1. Omitted by Art 7 of SI 2000 No 1 as from 3.4.00.
2. Amended by reg 5 and Sch 2 para 11(9) of SI 2006 No 217 as from 6.3.06.
3. Substituted by Art 10(6) of SI 2007 No 2871 as from 7.4.08.

[¹**Errors**

7A.–[² (1)]   If a rent officer is of the opinion that he has made an error (other than in the application of his professional judgement) in relation to a determination or redetermination, he shall notify the local authority which made the application for that determination or redetermination of the error as soon as practicable after he becomes aware of it.]

[² (2)   If a rent officer is of the opinion that he has made an error (other than in the application of his professional judgement) in relation to a board and attendance determination or board and attendance redetermination, he shall notify the [⁵ local authority] which made the application for that board and attendance determination or board and attendance redetermination of the error as soon as practicable after he becomes aware of it.

[⁵ (3)]]

[⁴ (4)   If a rent officer is of the opinion that he has made an error (other than in the application of his professional judgement) in relation to a broad rental market area determination determined in accordance with article 4B(1A) or a local housing allowance determination determined in accordance with article 4B(2A), he shall notify any local authority to which notification of that determination was sent of the error, and the amended determination, as soon as practicable after he becomes aware of it.]

Modifications

Para (2) amended and para (3) omitted by Art 6(7) Rent Officers (Housing Benefit Functions) Amendment Order 2007 SI No.2871 as from 7 April 2008, save where Art 6(1)(a), (b) or (c) of that order applied (see p634).

Note that by Art 3 of SI 2007 No.2871, those provisions which on 19 March 2008 applied only in relation to the areas of former Pathfinder authorities, apply in the same way to the areas of every other local authority in England and Wales.

Amendments

1.   ˙ Inserted by Art 8 of SI 2000 No 1 as from 3.4.00.
2. Inserted by Art 2(8) of SI 2003 No 2398 as from a date specified in Sch 1 to that SI in relation to each individual authority.
3. Amended by Art 4(3)(a) of SI 2007 No 2871 as from 20.3.08.
4. Inserted by Art 4(3)(b) of SI 2007 No 2871 as from 20.3.08.

5.   Amended by Art 6(7) of SI 2007 No 2871 as from 7.4.08, save where Art 6(1)(a), (b) or (c) of that order applies.

General Note

Art 7A requires a rent officer to notify the local authority of an error in relation to determinations or redeterminations, which will then require the local authority to apply under reg 17 HB Regs or HB(SPC) Regs for a substitute determination under Art 4A. Likewise, Art 7A requires the rent officer to notify the local authority of error in relation to broad rental market area or local housing allowance determinations. In this case, the error, as well as the amended determination is notified.

The words in brackets, "other than in the application of his professional judgement", are important. A rent officer may not notify a local authority where s/he has second thoughts about a figure that s/he has assessed for a property. There must be some basic error of fact or law that vitiates the decision, or, for example, a slip of the pen.

Amendment to 1995 Order

8.   The Rent Officers (Additional Functions) Order 1995 shall be amended by the insertion at the end of article 6 (special cases) of the following–

"(3) In a case where the local authority states in the application that the rent includes charges for general counselling or any other support services which are eligible for housing benefit solely by virtue of paragraph 1(f)(iii) of Schedule 1 to the 1987 Regulations (landlord's support services: supported accommodation) or solely by virtue of that provision and paragraph 1(f)(ii) of that Schedule, the rent officer shall assume when making a determination on a redetermination that–

(a)   the services were not to be provided or made available; and

(b)   the rent payable under the tenancy at the relevant time is such amount as is specified in the application as the rent which would have been payable under the tenancy at that time if those items were not to be provided or made available.

(4)   In a case where the local authority states in the application that the rent includes charges for general counselling or any other support services and the charges–

(a)   are eligible for housing benefit by virtue of paragraph 1(f)(iii) of Schedule 1 to the 1987 Regulations (landlord's support services: supported accommodation) or that provision and paragraph 1(f)(ii) of that Schedule; and

(b)   are also eligible for housing benefit by virtue of paragraph 1(f)(i) of that Schedule (support services: other exceptions);

the rent officer shall include in the notice to the local authority, required under article 3(1)(c), a statement of the amount of the rent payable for the tenancy (which has the same meaning as in paragraph 3(1) of Schedule 1 to this Order) which relates to those charges.".

Revocations

9.   The Rent Officers (Additional Functions) Order 1995, the Rent Officers (Additional Functions) (Amendment) Order 1995, the Rent Officers (Additional Functions) (Amendment No. 2) Order 1995, the Rent Officers (Additional Functions) (Amendment) Order 1996 and the Rent Officers (Additional Functions) (Amendment) Order 1997 are hereby revoked.

Application

10.–(1)   The amendment made by article 8 does not have effect in a case where an application for a determination is made before the date that article comes into force.

(2)   The remaining articles of the Order (other than paragraph (1)) do not have effect in a case where an application is made for a determination before the date those articles come into force

SCHEDULE 1

Analysis

"Vicinity", "Neighbourhood" and "broad rental market area (local reference rent)"

Significantly high rent (SHR) and size related rent (SizeRR) figures are determined on the basis of rents in the "vicinity". Para 1(4) defines "vicinity" in fairly restrictive terms. "Immediately surrounding" must, on any view, connote a limited geographical area. It cannot, of course, be taken literally so as to preclude any comparators other than immediately neighbouring dwellings, but it cannot sensibly be extended to a zone extending further than, say, a few streets away. Only If there are no homes of a comparable size in that area may the "vicinity" be extended, but then only to an area where such homes exist: para 1(4)(b). It is not clear whether the "vicinity" is then expanded for the purpose of calculating the SHR as well as the SizeRR. It would appear from the wording of para 1(4)(b) that it is to be expanded for both purposes.

"Neighbourhood" is used for the purposes of an exceptionally high rent determination. Para 3(5)(a) defines "neighbourhood" in a town or city as the part of that town or city where the home is located that is a "distinct area of residential accommodation". This is an even more vague definition than that of "vicinity" and could cause much dispute, particularly in densely populated inner city areas where affluent areas and deprived areas are mixed freely and closely. And what is a "town or city"? Outside a town or city, the "neighbourhood" is expanded by para 3(5)(b) to as much as is required to incorporate comparator dwellings.

"Broad rental market area (local reference rent)" is used for the purposes of the determination of the local reference rent and the single room rent. The definition was inserted and amendments made to paras 4 and 5 from 5 January 2009, to reverse the effect of the House of Lords decision in *R(on the application of Heffernan)(FC) v The Rent Service* [2008] UKHL 58, 30 July 2008. Para 4(6) and (7) defines a "broad rental market area (local reference rent)" as an area within which a person could reasonably be expected to live having regard to facilities and services for the purposes of health, education, recreation, personal banking and shopping and the travel distance by public and private transport. It must contain a variety of types of residential accommodation and types of lettings, and have sufficient private rented housing to ensure that the local reference rents for tenancies in the area are representative of the rents that a landlord might reasonably be expected to obtain in that area.

Prior to 5 January 2009, "locality" was the zone of comparison for generating a local reference rent and the single room rent. This was defined as an area of more than one neighbourhood, including that where the relevant dwelling was situated, within which a claimant could be expected to live in the light of the available amenities, "neighbourhood" having the same meaning as in para 3(5). For a discussion of the definition and its context as well as the decision of the House of Lords in *Heffernan*, see pp612-613 of the 21st edition.

There is still considerable room for judgement here, both as to what the "vicinity", "neighbourhood" and "broad rental market area (local reference rent)" are and the area to which they should be expanded if applicable.

Significant amendments were made to Sch 1 from 6 November 2001. For commentary on the former provisions, see pp576-77 of the 18th edition.

Part I
Determinations

Significantly high rents

1.–(1)   The rent officer shall determine whether, in his opinion, the rent payable under the tenancy of the dwelling at the relevant time is significantly higher than the rent which the landlord might reasonably have been expected to obtain under the tenancy at that time.

(2)   If the rent officer determines under sub-paragraph (1) that the rent is significantly higher, the rent officer shall also determine the rent which the landlord might reasonably have been expected to obtain under the tenancy at the relevant time.

(3)   When making a determination under this paragraph, the rent officer shall have regard to the level of rent under similar tenancies of similar dwellings in the [¹ vicinity] (or as similar as regards tenancy, dwelling and [¹ vicinity] as is reasonably practicable) and shall assume that no one who would have been entitled to housing benefit had sought or is seeking the tenancy.

[²(4)   For the purposes of this paragraph and paragraph 2 ''vicinity'' means-

(a)   the area immediately surrounding the dwelling; or

(b)   where, for the purposes of sub-paragraph (2)(c) of paragraph 2, there is no dwelling in the area immediately surrounding the dwelling which satisfies the description in heads (i), (ii) and (iii) of that sub-paragraph, the area nearest to the dwelling where there is such a dwelling.]

Amendments

1.   Amended by art 2(2) of SI 2001 No 3561 as from 6.11.01.
2.   Inserted by art 2(2) of SI 2001 No 3561 as from 6.11.01.

Size and rent

2.–(1)   The rent officer shall determine whether the dwelling, at the relevant time, exceeds the size criteria for the occupiers.

(2)   If the rent officer determines that the dwelling exceeds the size criteria, the rent officer shall also determine the rent which a landlord might reasonably have been expected to obtain, at the relevant time, for a tenancy which is–

(a)   similar to the tenancy of the dwelling;

(b)   on the same terms other than the term relating to the amount of rent; and

(c)   of a dwelling which is in the same [¹ vicinity] as the dwelling, but which–

(i)   accords with the size criteria for the occupiers;

(ii)   is in a reasonable state of repair; and

(iii)   corresponds in other respects, in the rent officer's opinion, as closely as is reasonably practicable to the dwelling.

(3)   When making a determination under sub-paragraph (2), the rent officer shall have regard to the same matter and make the same assumption as specified in paragraph 1(3), except that in judging the similarity of other tenancies and dwellings the comparison shall be with the tenancy of the second dwelling referred to in sub-paragraph (2) and shall assume that no one who would have been entitled to housing benefit had sought or is seeking that tenancy.

Amendment

1.   Amended by art 2(3) of SI 2001 No 3561 as from 6.11.01.

Exceptionally high rents

3.–(1)   The rent officer shall determine whether, in his opinion, the rent payable for the tenancy of the dwelling at the relevant time is exceptionally high.

(2)   In sub-paragraph (1) "rent payable for the tenancy" means–

(a)   where a determination is made under sub-paragraph (2) of paragraph 2, the rent determined under that sub-paragraph;

(b)   where no determination is so made and a determination is made under sub-paragraph (2) of paragraph 1, the rent determined under that sub-paragraph; and

(c)   in any other case, the rent payable under the tenancy [¹ at the relevant time].

(3)   If the rent officer determines under sub-paragraph (1) that the rent is exceptionally high, the rent officer shall also determine the highest rent, which is not an exceptionally high rent and which a landlord might reasonably have been expected to obtain at the relevant time (on the assumption that no one who would have been entitled to housing benefit had sought or is seeking the tenancy) for an assured tenancy of a dwelling which–

(a)   is in the same [² neighbourhood] as the dwelling;

(b)   has the same number of bedrooms and rooms suitable for living in as the dwelling (or, where the dwelling exceeds the size criteria for the occupiers, accords with the size criteria); and

(c)   is in a reasonable state of repair.

(4)   For the purpose of determining whether a rent is an exceptionally high rent under this paragraph, the rent officer shall have regard to the levels of rent under assured tenancies of dwellings which–

(a)   are in the same [² neighbourhood] as the dwelling (or in as similar a locality as is reasonably practicable); and

(b)   have the same number of bedrooms and rooms suitable for living in as the dwelling (or, in a case where the dwelling exceeds the size criteria for the occupiers, accord with the size criteria).

[³ (5)   For the purposes of this paragraph and paragraph 4(6) "neighbourhood" means-

(a)   where the dwelling is in a town or city, the part of that town or city where the dwelling is located which is a distinct area of residential accommodation; or

(b)   where the dwelling is not in a town or city, the area surrounding the dwelling which is a distinct area of residential accommodation and where there are dwellings satisfying the description in sub-paragraph (4)(b).]

Amendments

1.   Inserted by arts 9 and 10 of SI 2000 No 1 as from 3.4.00.

2.   Amended by art 2(4) of SI 2001 No 3561 as from 6.11.01.

3.   Inserted by art 2(4) of SI 2001 No 3561 as from 6.11.01.

Local reference rents

4.–(1)   The rent officer shall make a determination of a local reference rent in accordance with the formula–

$$R = \frac{H+L}{2}$$

where–

R is the local reference rent;

H is the highest rent, in the rent officer's opinion–

(a)   which a landlord might reasonably have been expected to obtain, at the relevant time, for an assured tenancy of a dwelling which meets the criteria in sub-paragraph (2); and

(b)   which is not an exceptionally high rent; and

L is the lowest rent, in the rent officer's opinion,–

(a)   which a landlord might reasonably have been expected to obtain, at the relevant time, for an assured tenancy of a dwelling which meets the criteria in sub-paragraph (2); and

(b)   which is not an exceptionally low rent; and

(2)   The criteria are–

(a)   that the dwelling under the assured tenancy–
- (i)   is in the same [⁷ broad rental market area (local reference rent)] as the dwelling;
- (ii)   is in a reasonable state of repair, and
- (iii)   has the same number of bedrooms and rooms suitable for living in as the dwelling (or, in a case where the dwelling exceeds the size criteria for the occupiers, accords with the size criteria); and

(b)   if the tenant does not have the use under the tenancy of the dwelling[¹ at the relevant time] of more than one bedroom or room suitable for living in–
- (i)   that under the assured tenancy the tenant does not have the use of more than one bedroom or room suitable for living in;
- (ii)   if the rent under the tenancy [¹ at the relevant time] includes payments for board and attendance and the rent officer considers the amount fairly attributable to board and attendance is a substantial part of the rent, that a substantial part of the rent under the assured tenancy is fairly attributable to board and attendance;
- (iii)   if sub-paragraph (ii) does not apply and the tenant shares a [² kitchen, toilet, bathroom and room suitable for living in] with a person other than a member of his household, a non-dependant or a person who pays rent to the tenant, that the assured tenancy provides for the tenant to share a [² kitchen, toilet, bathroom and room suitable for living in]; and
- (iv)   if sub-paragraphs (ii) and (iii) do not apply, that the circumstances described in sub-paragraphs (ii) and (iii) do not apply in relation to the assured tenancy.

(3)   Where ascertaining H and L under sub-paragraph (1), the rent officer:

(a)   shall assume that no one who would have been entitled to housing benefit had sought or is seeking the tenancy; and

(b)   shall exclude the amount of any rent which, in the rent officer's opinion, is fairly attributable to the provision of services which are ineligible to be met by housing benefit

[⁴ . . .]

(4)   In sub-paragraph (2)(b)–

"bedroom or room suitable for living in" does not include a room which the tenant shares with any person other than–

(a)   a member of his household;

(b)   a non-dependant (as defined in this sub-paragraph); or

(c)   a person who pays rent to the tenant; and

[⁵ [⁶ "non-dependant" means a non-dependant of the tenant within the meaning of regulation 3 of the Housing Benefit Regulations or, as the case may be, regulation 3 of the Housing Benefit (State Pension Credit) Regulations;]]

(5)   In sub-paragraph (3), "services" means services performed or facilities (including the use of furniture) provided for, or rights made available to, the tenant, but not [¹ , in the case of a tenancy where a substantial part of the rent under the tenancy is fairly attributable to board and attendance, the provision of meals (including the preparation of meals or provision of unprepared food).]

[³ [⁷ (6)   For the purposes of this paragraph and paragraph 5 "broad rental market area (local reference rent)" means the area within which a tenant of the dwelling could reasonably be expected to live having regard to facilities and services for the purposes of health, education, recreation, personal banking and shopping, taking account of the distance of travel, by public and private transport, to and from those facilities and services.

(7)   A broad rental market area (local reference rent) must contain–

(a)   residential premises of a variety of types, including such premises held on a variety of tenures; and

(b)   sufficient privately rented residential premises, to ensure that, in the rent officer's opinion, the local reference rents for tenancies in the area are representative of the rents that a landlord might reasonably be expected to obtain in that area.]]

Amendments

1.   Inserted by arts 9 and 10 of SI 2000 No 1 as from 3.4.00.
2.   Amended by reg 2(3) of SI 2001 No 2317 as from 2.7.01.
3.   Amended by art 2(5) of SI 2001 No 3561 as from 6.11.01.
4.   Deleted by art 2 of SI 2003 No 478 as from 1.4.03 (7.4.03 where rent payable weekly or in multiples of a week).
5.   Substituted by reg 5 and Sch 2 para 11(10)(a) of SI 2006 No 217 as from 6.3.06.
6.   Substituted by Art 10(7)(a) of SI 2007 No 2871 as from 7.4.08.
7.   Amended by Art 2(3)(a) of SI 2008 No 3156 as from 5.1.09.

Single room rents

5.–(1)   The rent officer shall determine a single room rent in accordance with the following formula–

$$S = \frac{H+L}{2}$$

where–

S is the single room rent;

H is the highest rent, in the rent officer's opinion,–

(a)   which a landlord might reasonably have been expected to obtain, at the relevant time, for an assured tenancy of a dwelling which meets the criteria in sub-paragraph (2); and

(b)   which is not an exceptionally high rent.

L is the lowest rent, in the rent officer's opinion,–

(a)   which a landlord might reasonably have been expected to obtain, at the relevant time, for an assured tenancy of a dwelling which meets the criteria in sub-paragraph (2); and

(b)   which is not an exceptionally low rent.

(2)   The criteria are–

(a)   that the dwelling under the assured tenancy is in the same [⁴ broad rental market area (local reference rent)] as the dwelling and is in a reasonable state of repair;

(b)   that, under the assured tenancy, the tenant–

    (i)   has the exclusive use of one bedroom;

    (ii)   does not have the use of any other bedroom [¹...];

    [¹(iia) shares the use of a room suitable for living in;]

    (iii)   shares the use of a toilet [¹ and bathroom]; and

    (iv)   shares the use of a kitchen and does not have the exclusive use of facilities for cooking food; and

(c)   that the rent does not include any payment for board and attendance.

(3)   Sub-paragraphs [³ (3) and (5)] of paragraph 4 apply when ascertaining H and L under this sub-paragraph as if the reference in those sub-paragraphs to H and L were to H and L under [³ this paragraph].

Amendments

1.   Amended by reg 4 of SI 2001 No 1325 as from 2.7.01.
2.   Substituted by Art 2(9) of SI 2003 No 2398 as from a date specified in Sch 1 to that SI in relation to each individual authority.
3.   Amended by Arts 2(1) and 3 of SI 2005 No 236 as from 13.3.05.
4.   Amended by Art 2(3)(b) of SI 2008 No 3156 as from 5.1.09.

Analysis

The single room rent applies where the claimant is a "young individual" (see the definition in reg 2(1) HB Regs and the commentary to reg 13 HB Regs) which, in broad terms, means a single person under the age of 25. The policy is that HB should not pay for such people to live in self-contained accommodation but only in a single bedroom with shared facilities. Until 2 July 2001, sub-para (2) provided for the determination to be made on the basis of "bed-sitting" accommodation (ie, a single room with shared kitchen and toilet). The definition was extended from that date to include accommodation with a shared bathroom (surely an omission by oversight from the previous definition) and a shared living room.

Claim-related rent

[¹**6.**– [² (1)   In this paragraph, and in paragraph 9, "claim-related rent" means the claim-related rent determined by the rent officer in accordance with paragraph (2A).]

[² (2A)   The rent officer shall determine that the claim-related rent is–

(a)   where he makes a determination under sub-paragraph (2) of paragraph 1, sub-paragraph (2) of paragraph 2 and sub-paragraph (3) of paragraph 3, the lowest of the three rents determined under those sub-paragraphs;

(b)   where he makes a determination under only two of the sub-paragraphs referred to in paragraph (a), the lower of the two rents determined under those sub-paragraphs;

(c)   where he makes a determination under only one of the sub-paragraphs referred to in paragraph (a), the rent determined under that sub-paragraph;

(d)   where he does not make a determination under any of the sub-paragraphs referred to in sub-paragraph (a), the rent payable under the tenancy of the dwelling at the relevant time.]

[² (2)]

(3)   [²] the rent officer shall also determine the total amount of ineligible charges, as defined in paragraph 7, which he has not included in the claim-related rent because of the assumptions made in accordance with that paragraph.]

Modifications

Para (1) substituted, para (2A) inserted, para (2) omitted and para (3) is amended by Art 9(2) Rent Officers (Housing Benefit Functions) Amendment Order 2007 SI No.2871 as from 7 April 2008, save where Art 9(1)(a) or (b) of that order applied (see p635).

Amendments

1.   Substituted by arts 11 and 12 of SI 2000 No 1 as from 3.4.00.
2.   Amended by Art 9(2) of SI 2007 No 2871 as from 7.4.08, save where Art 9(1) of that order applies.

Analysis

The "claim-related rent" (CRR) is the lowest of the rent officer determinations, or if there are none, the rent payable under the tenancy. It is the lowest of the CHH, the local reference rent and, if relevant, the single room rent which determines maximum rent under reg 13.

There is a potential drawback in that claimants do not usually get an opportunity to examine the notifications given by the rent officer to the authority, still less the basis on which the rent officer has reached those calculations. This may make it questionable whether the procedure before the rent officer may infringe Art 6 of the European Convention on Human Rights, because the claimant has no effective means of challenging the determination. However, the claimant *can* appeal the local authority's decision on HB entitlement and, as such, can challenge the factual basis upon which the rent officer decision was made: *Borough of Bexley v LD (HB)* [2010] UKUT 79 (AAC).

Part II
Assumptions

Ineligible charges and support charges

[¹**7.**–[⁵ (1)   "ineligible charges" means service charges which are ineligible to be met by housing benefit by virtue of regulation 12B(2) (rent) of and Schedule 1 (ineligible service charges) to the Housing Benefit Regulations or, as the case may be, regulation 12B(2) of and Schedule 1 to the Housing Benefit (State Pension Credit) Regulations except in the case of a tenancy where the rent includes payments for board and attendance, and the rent officer considers that a substantial part of the rent under the tenancy is fairly attributable to board and attendance, charges specified in paragraph 1(a)(i) of Schedule 1 to the Housing Benefit Regulations or, as the case may be, in paragraph 1(a)(i) of Schedule 1 to the Housing Benefit (State Pension Credit) Regulations (charges for meals)]

(2)   When making a determination under paragraph 1, 2 or 3 of this Schedule, the rent officer shall assume that–

(a)   the items to which the ineligible charges relate;

[² . . .]

were not to be provided or made available.

[⁴ (3)   For the purposes of paragraphs 1, 2, 3, and 6 of Part 1 of this Schedule, the rent officer shall assume that the rent payable under the tenancy at the relevant time is–

(a)   where an amount is notified to the rent officer under regulation 114A(4)(b) of the Housing Benefit Regulations or, as the case may be, regulations 95A(4)(b) of the Housing Benefit (State Pension Credit) Regulations in respect of that tenancy, that notified amount less the total of any ineligible charges included in that amount; or

(b)   in any other case, the total amount stated under regulation 114A(3)(d) of the Housing Benefit Regulations or, as the case may be regulation 95A(3)(d) of the Housing Benefit (State Pension Credit) Regulations less the total of any ineligible charges included in that stated amount.]

(4)   The total of any ineligible charges, referred to in sub-paragraph (3), shall be the total of the amounts (excluding any amount which he considers is negligible) of any charges included in the notified amount or the stated amount, as the case may be, which, in the rent officer's opinion, are at the relevant time fairly attributable to any items to which ineligible charges relate.]

Modifications

Para 7(1) substituted by Art 8(2) Rent Officers (Housing Benefit Functions) Amendment Order 2007 SI No.2871 as from 7 April 2008, save where Art 8(1)(a) or (b) of that order applied (see p635).

Para 7(3) substituted by Art 7(4) of the Rent Officers (Housing Benefit Functions) Amendment Order 2007 SI No.2871 as from 7 April 2008, save where Art 7(1) of that order applied (see p634).

Amendments

1.   Substituted by arts 11 and 12 of SI 2000 No 1 as from 3.4.00.
2.   Deleted by art 2 of SI 2003 No 478 as from 1.4.03 (7.4.03 where rent payable weekly or in multiples of a week).
3.   Amended by reg 5 and Sch 2 para 11(10)(b) of SI 2006 No 217 as from 6.3.03.
4.   Substituted by Art 7(4) of SI 2007 No 2871 as from 7.4.08, save where Art 7(1) of that order applies.
5.   Substituted by Art 8(2) of SI 2007 No 2871 as from 7.4.08, save where Art 8(1) of that order applies.

Analysis

Para 7 specifies how ineligible charges are dealt with.

"Ineligible charges" are those which are ineligible under reg 12B(2) and Sch 1 of both the HB and the HB(SPC) Regs, with the exception of charges for meals in certain cases. These are where board and attendance are included in the rent and a "substantial" part of the rent is attributable to those elements. "Substantial" will be taken to mean "more than minimal". "Attendance", however, is not defined and it is not precisely clear what it refers to. In context, it is suggested that it must be intended to refer to the cooking and serving of meals, rather than the provision of some sort of physical attendance by way of nursing care or similar.

Para (2) requires the rent officer to leave out of account ineligible charges in determining what the various appropriate rents would be.

Para (3) sets out what the rent officer is to assume the rent payable by the claimant is. The normal rule, set out in sub-para (b), is that the rent is treated as being the amount stated by the local authority minus any ineligible charges. Sub-para (a) applies where the local authority states an amount under reg 114A(4)(b) HB Regs or reg 95A(4)(b) HB(SPC) Regs (or reg 14(9)(b) HB Regs or 14(8)(b) HB(SPC) Regs if Art 7(1) of SI 2007 No.2871 applies – see p634).

Para (4) specifies that "ineligible" charges for the purpose of para (3)(b) are those which the rent officer considers to be ineligible under the HB or HB(SPC) Regs.

Housing associations etc.

8.–(1)   In a case where the local authority states in the application that the landlord is a housing association or a charity, the rent officer shall assume that the landlord is not such a body.

(2)   The rent officer shall not take into account the rent under any tenancy where the landlord is a housing association or where the landlord is a charity and the dwelling is provided by the landlord in the pursuit of its charitable purposes.

(3)   In this paragraph–

"charity" has the same meaning as in the Charities Act 1993, except that it includes a Scottish charity (which has the same meaning as in section 1(7) of the Law Reform (Miscellaneous Provisions) (Scotland) Act 1990); and

"housing association" has the same meaning as in the Housing Associations Act 1985.

PART III
Notifications of Part I determinations

Notifications

9.–[¹ (1)   Subject to sub-paragraph (2), the rent officer shall give notice to the local authority of–
(a)   the claim-related rent determined under Part I;
(b)   where the dwelling is not in a hostel, the total amount of ineligible charges determined under paragraph 6(3) in relation to that claim-related rent;
[³ (c)   where that claim-related rent includes an amount which would be ineligible for housing benefit under paragraph 1(a)(i) of Schedule 1 to the Housing Benefit Regulations or, as the case may be, paragraph 1(a)(i) of Schedule 1 to the Housing Benefit (State Pension Credit) Regulations (charges for meals), the inclusion of an ineligible amount in respect of meals;]
(d)   any rent determined by the rent officer under paragraph 4 (local reference rents); and
[³ (da)   where any rent determined under paragraph 4 includes an amount which would be ineligible for housing benefit under the provisions referred to in sub-paragraph (c), the inclusion of an ineligible amount in respect of meals; and]
(e)   any rent determined by the rent officer under paragraph 5 (single room rents).]
(2)   If the rent officer determines a rent under–
(a)   paragraph 4 (local reference rents); or
(b)   paragraph 5 (single room rents);
which is equal to or more than the [¹ claim-related rent], the rent officer shall give notice to the local authority of this in place of giving notice of the determination made under paragraph 4 or, as the case may be, paragraph 5.

Modifications

Para (1) amended by Art 9(3) Rent Officers (Housing Benefit Functions) Amendment Order 2007 SI No.2871 as from 7 April 2008, save where Art 9(1)(a) or (b) of that order applied (see p635).

Amendments

1.   Amended by art 13 of SI 2000 No 1 as from 3.4.00.
2.   Amended by reg 5 and Sch 2 para 11(10)(c) of SI 2006 No 217 as from 6.3.06.
3.   Amended by Art 9(3) of SI 2007 No 2871 as from 7.4.08, save where Art 9(1) of that order applies.

Part IV
Indicative Rent Levels

11.–(1)   The rent officer shall determine the indicative rent level for each category described in sub-paragraph (3) in accordance with the following formula–

$$I = \frac{H+3L}{4}$$

where–
I is the indicative rent level;
H is the highest rent, in the rent officer's opinion,–

(a) which a landlord might reasonably be expected to obtain at the time the determination is being made for an assured tenancy of a dwelling meeting the criteria in sub-paragraph (2); and

(b) which is not an exceptionally high rent; and

L is the lowest rent, in the rent officer's opinion,–

(a) which a landlord might reasonably be expected to obtain at the time the determination is being made for an assured tenancy of a dwelling meeting the criteria in sub-paragraph (2); and

(b) which is not an exceptionally low rent.

(2) The criteria are that–

(a) the dwelling is in the area of the local authority;

(b) the dwelling is in a reasonable state of repair; and

(c) the dwelling and tenancy accord with the category to which the determination relates.

(3) The categories for the purposes of this paragraph are–

(a) a dwelling where the tenant does not have use of more than one room where a substantial part of the rent under the tenancy is fairly attributable to board and attendance;

(b) a dwelling where the tenant does not have use of more than one room, the tenancy provides for him to share a kitchen or toilet and paragraph (a) does not apply;

(c) a dwelling where the tenant does not have use of more than one room and where paragraphs (a) and (b) do not apply;

(d) a dwelling where the tenant does not have use of more than two rooms and where none of paragraphs (a) to (c) applies;

(e) a dwelling where the tenant does not have use of more than three rooms and where none of paragraphs (a) to (d) applies;

(f) a dwelling where the tenant does not have use of more than four rooms and where none of paragraphs (a) to (e) applies;

(g) a dwelling where the tenant does not have use of more than five rooms and where none of paragraphs (a) to (f) applies; and

(h) a dwelling where the tenant does not have use of more than six rooms and where none of paragraphs (a) to (g) applies.

(4) When ascertaining H and L under sub-paragraph (1), the rent officer:

(a) shall assume that no one who would have been entitled to housing benefit had sought or is seeking the tenancy; and

(b) shall exclude the amount of any rent which, in the rent officer's opinion, is fairly attributable to the provision of services which are ineligible to be met by housing benefit

[[1] . . .].]

(5) In this paragraph–

"room" means a bedroom or room suitable for living in and in paragraphs (a), (b) and (c) of sub-paragraph (3) does not include a room which the tenant shares with any person other than–

(a) a member of his household;

(b) a non-dependant of the tenant (within the meaning of [[2] [[3] regulation 3 of the Housing Benefit Regulations or, as the case may be, regulation 3 of the Housing Benefit (State Pension Credit) Regulations]]); or

(c) a person who pays rent to the tenant; and "services" has the meaning given by paragraph 4(5).

Amendments

1. Deleted by art 2 of SI 2003 No 478 as from 1.4.03 (7.4.03 where rent payable weekly or in multiples of a week).

2. Amended by reg 5 and Sch 2 para 11(10)(d) of SI 2006 No 217 as from 6.3.06.

3. Substituted by Art 10(7)(b) of SI 2007 No 2871 as from 7.4.08.

SCHEDULE 2
ARTICLE 2
Size Criteria

1. One bedroom or room suitable for living in shall be allowed for each of the following categories of occupier (and each occupier shall come within only the first category for which he is eligible)–

(a) [[1] a couple] (within the meaning of Part VII of the Social Security Contributions and Benefits Act 1992);

(b) a person who is not a child;

(c) two children of the same sex;

(d) two children who are less than ten years old;

(e) a child.

2. The number of rooms (excluding any allowed under paragraph 1) suitable for living in allowed are–

(a) if there are less than four occupiers, one;

(b) if there are more than three and less than seven occupiers, two; and

(c) in any other case, three.

Amendment

1. Substituted by art 29 of SI 2005 No 2877 as from 5.12.05.

SCHEDULE 3
REDETERMINATIONS

[¹1.   Schedules 1 and 2 shall apply in relation to a redetermination as they apply to a determination, but as if references in those Schedules to the relevant time were references to the date the application for the original determination was made or, if earlier, the date the tenancy ended.]

Amendment
1.   Substituted by SI 2000 No 1 from 3.4.00.

2.   The rent officer making the redetermination shall seek and have regard to the advice of one or two other rent officers in relation to the redetermination.

[² SCHEDULE 3A]

Modifications
Schedule 3A omitted by Art 6(8) Rent Officers (Housing Benefit Functions) Amendment Order 2007 SI No.2871 as from 7 April 2008, save where Art 6(1)(a), (b) or (c) of that order applied (see p634).

Amendments
1.   Schedule inserted by Art 2(10) of SI 2003 No 2398 as from a date specified in Sch 1 to that SI in relation to each individual authority.
2.   Omitted by Art 6(8) of SI 2007 No 2871 as from 7.4.08, save where Art 6(1)(a), (b) or (c) of that order applies.
3.   Substituted by Art 10(8) of SI 2007 No 2871 as from 7.4.08.

[¹ SCHEDULE 3B

Amendment
1.   Schedule inserted by Art 4(4) of SI 2007 No 2871 as from 20.3.08.

General Note
The rent officer determines local housing allowances (LHAs) in accordance with Sch 3B for each category of dwelling set out in Para 1: Art 4B. The authority then uses these to determine maximum rent (LHA) under reg 13D of both the HB and the HB(SPC) Regs. Note that a LHA for larger dwellings can also be set either because the rent officer believes it is likely to be required (Art 4B(2A)), or because the authority applies for one under reg 13D, but it is unclear when this would now be needed given that the largest category of dwelling that can now apply is five-bedroom accommodation: see reg 13D(2)(c) of both the HB and the HB(SPC) Regs. Note, also, that from April 2011 the Government intends to reduce the largest category of dwelling to four-bedroom accommodation.

Para 1 sets out the categories of dwelling.

Para 2 provides the process by which a LHA is determined, and the presumptions the rent officer is to use. Note that by this process, the LHA is the median rent of a list of rents for dwellings let under assured tenancies, payable at the date of the determination. The criteria for including an assured tenancy on the list are in sub-para (5). Note: from April 2011 the Government intends to cap weekly LHA rates at £250 for a one-bedroom property, £290 for a two-bedroom property, £340 for a three-bedroom property and £400 for a four-bedroom property and from October 2011 to amend the rules so that LHA rates are set at the 30th percentile (rather than the median). From 2013/2014, LHA rates will be uprated in line with the Consumer Price Index.

Para 3 deals with situations where the LHA for a category is lower than that for a category with a smaller number of bedrooms.

Para 4 defines "broad rental market area".

BROAD RENTAL MARKET AREA DETERMINATIONS AND LOCAL HOUSING ALLOWANCE DETERMINATIONS

Categories of dwelling
1.–(1)   The categories of dwelling for which a rent officer is required to determine a local housing allowance in accordance with article 4B(2A)(a)(i) are–
  (a)   a dwelling where the tenant has the exclusive use of only one bedroom and where the tenancy provides for him to share the use of one or more of–
      (i)   a kitchen;
      (ii)   a bathroom;
      (iii)   a toilet; or

  (iv) a room suitable for living in;
(b) a dwelling where the tenant (together with his partner where he has one) has the exclusive use of only one bedroom and exclusive use of a kitchen, a bathroom, a toilet and a room suitable for living in;
(c) a dwelling where the tenant has the use of only two bedrooms;
(d) a dwelling where the tenant has the use of only three bedrooms;
(e) a dwelling where the tenant has the use of only four bedrooms;
(f) a dwelling where the tenant has the use of only five bedrooms.
(2) In–
(a) sub-paragraph (1)(b) "partner" has the same meaning as in regulation 2 of the Housing Benefit Regulations or, as the case may be, regulation 2 of the Housing Benefit (State Pension Credit) Regulations;
(b) sub-paragraph (1)(c) to (f) "bedroom" means a bedroom, except for a bedroom which the tenant shares with any person other than–
  (i) a member of his household;
  (ii) a non-dependant of the tenant (within the meaning of regulation 3 of the Housing Benefit Regulations or, as the case may be, regulation 3 of the Housing Benefit (State Pension Credit) Regulations); or
  (iii) a person who pays rent to the tenant.

Local housing allowance for category of dwelling in paragraph 1

  2.–(1) Subject to paragraph 3 (anomalous local housing allowances), the rent officer must determine a local housing allowance for each category of dwelling in paragraph 1 in accordance with the following sub-paragraphs.
(2) The rent officer must compile a list of rents.
(3) A list of rents means a list in ascending order of the rents which, in the rent officer's opinion, are payable at the date of the determination for a dwelling let under an assured tenancy which meets the criteria specified in sub-paragraph (5).
(4) The list must include any rents which are of the same amount.
(5) The criteria for including an assured tenancy on the list of rents in relation to each category of dwelling specified in paragraph 1 are–
(a) that the dwelling let under the assured tenancy is in the broad rental market area for which the local housing allowance for that category of dwelling is being determined;
(b) that the dwelling is in a reasonable state of repair; and
(c) that the assured tenancy permits the tenant to use exclusively or share the use of, as the case may be, the same number and type of rooms as the category of dwelling in relation to which the list of rents is being compiled.
  [² (5A) Where the rent officer is not satisfied that the list of rents in respect of any category of dwelling would contain sufficient rents, payable at the date of the determination for dwellings in the broad rental market area, to enable a local housing allowance to be determined which is representative of the rents that a landlord might reasonably be expected to obtain in that area, the rent officer may add to the list rents for dwellings in the same category in other areas in which a comparable market exists.]
(6) Where rent is payable other than weekly the rent officer must use the figure which would be payable if the rent were to be payable weekly by–
(a) multiplying the rent by an appropriate figure to obtain the rent for a year;
(b) dividing the total in (a) by 365; and
(c) multiplying the total in (b) by 7.
(7) When compiling the list of rents for each category of dwelling, the rent officer must–
(a) assume that no one who would have been entitled to housing benefit had sought or is seeking the tenancy; and
(b) exclude the amount of any rent which, in the rent officer's opinion, is fairly attributable to the provision of services performed for, or facilities (including the use of furniture) provided for, or rights made available to, the tenant which are ineligible to be met by housing benefit.
  [¹ (8)]
(9) The local housing allowance for each category of dwelling specified in paragraph 1 is the amount of the median rent in the list of rents for that category of dwelling.
(10) The median rent is determined as follows–
(a) where there is an even number of rents on the list, the formula is–

$$\frac{\text{The amount of the rent at P + the amount of the rent at P1}}{2} = \text{the local housing allowance}$$

  where
P is the position on the list defined by dividing the number of rents on the list by 2 and P1 is the following position on the list.

(b)   where there is an odd number of rents on the list, the formula is–

$$\frac{\text{the number of rents on the list} + 1}{2} = L$$

where
L is the position on the list in which the rent used to identify the local housing allowance lies.

(11)   Where the median rent is not a whole number of pence, the rent must be rounded to the nearest whole penny by disregarding any amount less than half a penny and treating any amount of half a penny or more as a whole penny.

Amendments
1.   Omitted by Art 2(4)(a) of SI 2008 No 3156 as from 5.1.09.
2.   Inserted by Art 2(2) of SI 2009 No 2459 as from 12.10.09.

Anomalous local housing allowances
3.–(1)   Where–
(a)   the rent officer has determined the local housing allowance for each of the categories of dwelling in paragraph 1(1) in accordance with the preceding paragraphs of this Schedule; and
(b)   the local housing allowance for a category of dwelling in paragraph 1(1)(b) to (f) is lower than the local housing allowance for any of the categories of dwelling which precede it,
that local housing allowance shall be the same as the highest local housing allowance which precedes it.
(2)   Where–
(a)   the rent officer has determined a local housing allowance following an application made under article 4B(4); and
(b)   that local housing allowance is lower than the local housing allowance for the category of dwelling in paragraph 1(1)(f),
that local housing allowance shall be the same as the local housing allowance for the category of dwelling in paragraph 1(1)(f).

Broad rental market area
[¹4.   In this Schedule ''broad rental market area'' means an area within which a person could reasonably be expected to live having regard to facilities and services for the purposes of health, education, recreation, personal banking and shopping, taking account of the distance of travel, by public and private transport, to and from those facilities and services.]

Amendment
1.   Inserted by Art 2(4)(b) of SI 2008 No 3156 as from 5.1.09.

[¹5.   A broad rental market area must contain–
(a)   residential premises of a variety of types, including such premises held on a variety of tenures; and
(b)   sufficient privately rented residential premises to ensure that, in the rent officer's opinion, the local housing allowance for the categories of dwelling in the area for which the rent officer is required to determine a local housing allowance is representative of the rents that a landlord might reasonably be expected to obtain in that area.]

Amendment
1.   Inserted by Art 2(4)(b) of SI 2008 No 3156 as from 5.1.09.

SCHEDULE 4
SPECIAL CASES
Houseboats
1.   Where an application for a determination or a redetermination relates in whole or in part to mooring charges for a houseboat, this Order applies in relation to that application (or, as the case may be, to that part which relates to those charges) with the following modifications–
(a)   references to a tenancy, a tenancy of a dwelling or an assured tenancy are references to an agreement under which those charges are payable (and references to a landlord and a tenant shall be construed accordingly); and
(b)   no determination shall be made under paragraph 2 of Part I of Schedule 1 (size criteria) and references to the dwelling exceeding the size criteria shall not apply.

Mobile homes
2.   Where an application for a determination or redetermination relates in whole or in part to payments in respect of the site on which a caravan or a mobile home stands, this Order applies in relation to that application (or, as the case may be, that part which relates to those payments) with the following modifications–

(a)   references to a tenancy, a tenancy of a dwelling or an assured tenancy are references to an agreement under which those payments are payable (and references to a landlord and a tenant shall be construed accordingly), and

(b)   no determination shall be made under paragraph 2 of Part I of Schedule 1 (size criteria) and references to the dwelling exceeding the size criteria shall not apply.

Rental purchase agreements

3.   Where an application for a determination or a redetermination relates to a rental purchase agreement, the agreement is to be treated as if it were a tenancy.

The Rent Officers (Housing Benefit Functions) (Scotland) Order 1997
(SI 1997 No.1995 (S.144))

General Note

This Order is the Scottish equivalent of SI 1997 No.1984 and sets out the determinations to be made by rent officers when a tenancy is referred to them under regs 13D(10) and 14 of both the HB and the HB(SPC) Regs by an authority in Scotland. It also sets out the determinations to be made by rent officers relating to the "local housing allowance" scheme for rent restriction used by authorities to determine eligible rent under regs 12D and 13D of both the HB and the HB(SPC) Regs. See the commentary to SI 1997 No.1984.

Citation and commencement

1.–(1)   This Order may be cited as the Rent Officers (Housing Benefit Functions) (Scotland) Order 1997.

(2)   This Order shall come into force for the purposes of article 8 on 18th August 1997 and for all other purposes on 3rd September 1997.

Interpretation

2.–(1)   In this Order, unless the context otherwise requires–

"assured tenancy" has the same meaning as in Part II of the Housing (Scotland) Act 1988, except that it includes a tenancy which would be an assured tenancy but for paragraph [³ 7 or] 9 of Schedule 4 to that Act;

[² "board and attendance determination" means a determination made in accordance with article 4C;]

[⁹ "broad rental market area" has the meaning specified in paragraph 4 of Schedule 3B;]

[⁹ "broad rental market area determination" means a determination made in accordance with article 4B(1A);]

"child" means a person under the age of 16;

"determination" means a determination made in accordance with Part I or IV of Schedule 1 to this Order;

"dwelling" means any residential accommodation whether or not consisting of the whole or part of a building and whether or not comprising separate and self-contained premises;

[¹⁰ "hostel" has the same meaning as in regulation 2(1) of the Housing Benefit Regulations or, as the case may be, regulation 2(1) of the Housing Benefit (State Pension Credit) Regulations;]

[¹¹ "the Housing Benefit Regulations" mean the Housing Benefit Regulations 2006;

"the Housing Benefit (State Pension Credit) Regulations" means the Housing Benefit (Persons who have attained the qualifying age for state pension credit) Regulations 2006;]

"local authority" has the same meaning as in the Social Security Administration Act 1992 in relation to England and in relation to Wales;

[⁹ "local housing allowance determination" means a determination made in accordance with article 4B(2A);]

"occupier" means a person (whether or not identified by name) who is stated, in the application for the determination, to occupy the dwelling as his home;

[⁹]

"redetermination" means a redetermination made in accordance with article 4;

[⁹ "relevant date" means the date specified by a local authority in an application for a local housing allowance determination made in accordance with regulation 13D(7)(a) of the Housing Benefit Regulations or, as the case may be, regulation 13D(7)(a) of the Housing Benefit (State Pension Credit) Regulations;]

[¹ "relevant period" means–

(a)   in relation to a determination, the period of five working days (or, where the determination does not relate to a prospective tenancy and the rent officer intends to inspect the dwelling before making the determination, 25 working days) beginning with–

(i) where the rent officer requests further information under article 5, the date on which he receives the information; and

(ii) in any other case, the date on which he receives the application for the determination; and

(b) in relation to a redetermination, the period of 20 working days beginning with-

(i) where the rent officer requests further information under article 5, the date on which he receives the information; and

(ii) in any other case, the date on which he receives the application for that redetermination;]

"relevant time" means the time the application for the determination [² or board and attendance determination] is made or, if earlier, the tenancy ends;

[¹⁰ "rent" means any of the periodical payments referred to in regulation 12(1) of the Housing Benefit Regulations or, as the case may be, regulation 12(1) of the Housing Benefit (State Pension Credit) Regulations;]

"size criteria" means the standards relating to bedrooms and rooms suitable for living in specified in Schedule 2 to this Order;

"tenancy" includes any other right of occupancy and a prospective tenancy or right of occupancy and references to a tenant, a landlord or any other expression appropriate to a tenancy shall be construed accordingly; and

[⁸ "working day" means any day other than a Saturday, a Sunday or a day which is a bank holiday in Scotland under the Banking and Financial Dealings Act 1971.]

[¹²]

(2) In this Order any reference to a notice or application is to a notice or application in writing, except in a case where the recipient consents (whether generally or specifically) to the notice or application being transmitted by electronic means.

Modifications

Some definitions substituted and the definition of "pathfinder authority" omitted by Art 15(3) Rent Officers (Housing Benefit Functions) Amendment Order 2007 SI No.2871 as from 7 April 2008, save where Art 15(1)(a), (b) or (c) of that order applied (see p635).

Note that by Art 11 of SI 2007 No.2871, those provisions which on 19 March 2008 applied only in relation to the areas of former Pathfinder authorities, apply in the same way to the areas of every other local authority in Scotland.

Amendments

1. Inserted by Art 3 of SI 2000 No 3 as from 3.4.00.
2. Insertions made by Art 3 of SI 2003 No 2398 as from a date specified in Sch 1 to that SI in relation to each individual authority.
3. Inserted by Art 2(2) of SI 2004 No 2101 as from 31.8.04.
4. Substituted by reg 5 and Sch 2 para 12(2)(a), (c) and (d) of SI 2006 No 217 as from 6.3.06.
5. Inserted by reg 5 and Sch 2 para 12(2)(b) of SI 2006 No 217 as from 6.3.06.
6. Omitted by reg 5 and Sch 2 para 12(2)(e) of SI 2006 No 217 as from 6.3.06.
7. Amended by Art 13(1)(a)-(c) of SI 2007 No 2871 as from 20.3.08.
8. Inserted by Art 13(1)(d) of SI 2007 No 2871 as from 20.3.08.
9. Amended by Art 15(3) of SI 2007 No 2871 as from 7.4.08, save where Art 15(1)(a), (b) or (c) of that order applies.
10. Substituted by Art 19(1) of SI 2007 No 2871 as from 7.4.08.
11. Inserted by Art 19(1) of SI 2007 No 2871 as from 7.4.08.
12. Omitted by Art 19(1) of SI 2007 No 2871 as from 7.4.08.

Determinations

3.–(1) Subject to [² articles 3A and 6], where a local authority, in accordance with regulations made under section 136(2) or (3) of the Social Security Administration Act 1992 [¹ or section 122(5) of the Housing Act 1996], applies to a rent officer for determinations in respect of a tenancy of a dwelling, a rent officer shall–

(a) make the determinations in accordance with Part I of Schedule 1 (determinations);

(b) comply with Part II of Schedule 1 when making the determinations (assumptions etc.); and

(c) give notice in accordance with Part III of Schedule 1 (notifications) [¹ within the relevant period or as soon as is practicable after that period].

(2)   A rent officer for each registration area (within the meaning of section 43 of the Rent (Scotland) Act 1984) on the first working day of each month shall–

(a)   make determinations in accordance with Part IV of Schedule 1 (indicative rent levels) in the registration area [4 [5]];

(b)   comply with paragraph 8(2) of Part II of Schedule 1 (assumptions etc.) when making the determinations; and

(c)   give to the local authority notice of the determinations relating to its area when they have been made.

Modifications

Note that by Art 11 Rent Officers (Housing Benefit Functions) Amendment Order 2007 SI No.2871, those provisions which on 19 March 2008 applied only in relation to the areas of former Pathfinder authorities, apply in the same way to the areas of every other local authority in Scotland.

Amendments

1.   Amended by Art 4 of SI 2000 No 3 as from 3.4.00.
2.   Amended by Art 3(1) of SI 2001 No 1326 as from 2.7.01.
3.   Substitution made by Art 3 of SI 2003 No 2398 as from a date specified in Sch 1 to that SI in relation to each individual authority.
4.   Amended by art 5(2)(a) of SI 2005 No 236 as from 13.3.05.
5.   Omitted by Art 14(1) of SI 2007 No 2871 as from 7.4.08.

[1Transitional arrangements for determination of Single Room Rents with effect from 2nd July 2001

3A.   In a case where the rent officer has made and notified an authority of a determination of a single room rent pursuant to paragraph 5 of Schedule 1 in the period of 12 months before 2nd July 2001 that determination shall cease to have effect on [2 . . .] 2nd July 2001 and a rent officer shall–

(a)   make a new determination of that single room rent in accordance with Part I of Schedule 1;

(b)   comply with Part II of Schedule 1; and

(c)   give notice in accordance with Part III of Schedule 1 within the relevant period or as soon as is practicable after that period;

without an application for a determination under [3 [4 regulation 14 of the Housing Benefit Regulations or, as the case may be, regulation 14 of the Housing Benefit (State Pension Credit) Regulations]] having been made.]

Amendments

1.   Inserted by Art 3(2) of SI 2001 No 1326 as from 2.7.01.
2.   Amended by Art 2(2) of SI 2001 No 2318 as from 2.7.01.
3.   Amended by reg 5 and Sch 2 para 12(3) of SI 2006 No 217 as from 6.3.06.
4.   Substituted by Art 19(2) of SI 2007 No 2871 as from 7.4.08.

Redeterminations

[1**4**.–(1)   Subject to article 6, where the local authority applies to a rent officer for a redetermination of any determination or redetermination in respect of a tenancy of a dwelling the rent officer shall, in accordance with Schedule 3–

(a)   make redeterminations of any effective determinations and any effective redeterminations in respect of that tenancy; and

(b)   give notice within the relevant period or as soon as is practicable after that period.

(2)   For the purposes of paragraph (1)–

''effective determinations'' means any determinations made in accordance with Part I of Schedule 1 which have effect at the date of the application for a redetermination of a determination or redetermination; and

''effective redeterminations'' means any redeterminations made in accordance with Schedule 3 which have effect at that date.

(3)   A rent officer whose advice is sought as provided for in Schedule 3 shall give that advice.]

Amendment

1.   Substituted by Art 5 of SI 2000 No 3 as from 3.4.00.

Substitute determinations and substitute redeterminations

[¹**4A.**–(1)   Where a local authority applies to a rent officer for a substitute determination, in accordance with [² [³ regulation 17 of the Housing Benefit Regulations or, as the case may be, regulation 17 of the Housing Benefit (State Pension Credit) Regulations]], the provisions of this Order shall apply to that substitute determination as they apply to a determination, but as if references to the relevant time were references to the date the application for the original determination was made or, if earlier, the date the tenancy ended.

(2)   Where a local authority applies to a rent officer for a substitute redetermination, in accordance with that regulation, the provisions of this Order shall apply to that substitute redetermination as they apply to a redetermination.]

Amendments

1.   Inserted by Art 5 of SI 2000 No 3 as from 3.4.00.
2.   Amended by reg 5 and Sch 2 para 12(4) of SI 2006 No 217 as from 6.3.06.
3.   Substituted by Art 19(3) of SI 2007 No 2871 as from 7.4.08.

[¹Broad rental market area determinations and local housing allowance determinations

4B.   [⁶ (1)]

[⁴ (1A)   On 20th March 2008 and so often thereafter as a rent officer considers appropriate, a rent officer shall, in relation to each local authority,–

(a)   determine one or more broad rental market areas which will (during the month which next begins after the determination is made) fall, in whole or in part, within the area of the local authority so that every part of the area of that local authority falls within a broad rental market area and no part of the area of that authority falls within more than one broad rental market area; and

(b)   give to that local authority a notice which–

    (i)   specifies the area contained within each broad rental market area as falls, in whole or in part, within the area of that authority, by reference to the postcodes for each such broad rental market area; and

    (ii)   identifies such of those postcodes as fall within the area of that authority.]

[⁶   (2)]

[⁴ (2A)   No more than 10 and not less than 8 working days before the end of each month a rent officer shall–

(a)   for each broad rental market area determine, in accordance with the provisions of Schedule 3B–

    (i)   a local housing allowance for each of the categories of dwelling set out in paragraph 1 of Schedule 3B; and

    (ii)   local housing allowances for such other categories of dwelling of more than five bedrooms as a rent officer believes are likely to be required for the purpose of calculating housing benefit; and

(b)   give to each local authority notice of the local housing allowance determination made in accordance with paragraph (a) for each broad rental market area falling within, in whole or in part, the area of that authority.]

[⁶   (3)]

[⁴ (3A)   Any broad rental market area determination made in accordance with paragraph (1A), or local housing allowance determination made in accordance with paragraph (2A) before 7th April 2008, shall take effect on 7th April 2008 and any subsequent determination shall take effect on the first [⁷ [⁸]] day of the month which begins after the day on which the determination is made.]

[⁶ (4)   Where a local authority makes an application in accordance with regulation 13D(7)(a) of the Housing Benefit Regulations or, as the case may be, regulation 13D(7)(a) of the Housing Benefit (State Pension Credit) Regulations, a rent officer shall determine, in accordance with the provisions of Schedule 3B and as soon as is reasonably practicable, the local housing allowance for that category of dwelling at the relevant date, for each broad rental market area falling within, in whole or in part, the area of the local authority that made the application, at the relevant date.]

[⁶ (4A)   Where a local authority makes an application in accordance with regulation 13D(8) of the Housing Benefit Regulations or, as the case may be, regulation 13D(8) of the Housing Benefit (State Pension Credit) Regulations, a rent officer shall determine in accordance with the provisions of Schedule 3B and as soon as is reasonably practicable, the local housing allowance for that category of dwelling for each broad rental market area falling within, in whole or in part, the areas of the local authority.]

(5)   Where a rent officer has made a local housing allowance determination in accordance with paragraph (4)–

(a)   he shall give notice of the determination to the [⁶ local authority] that made the application;

[⁶ (b) any local housing allowance determination made in accordance with paragraph (4) shall take effect for the month in which the relevant date falls, except that no such determination can have effect before 7th April 2008; and

(c)   any local housing allowance determination made in accordance with paragraph (4A) shall take effect for the month in which notice is given in accordance with sub-paragraph (a), except that no such determination can have effect before 7th April 2008.]

[⁴ (6)   Where a rent officer has made a local housing allowance determination in accordance with paragraph (2A) [⁵ , (4) or (4A)] he shall–

(a)   make an approximate monthly allowance determination in relation to that local housing allowance determination; and

(b)   give notice of the approximate monthly allowance determination to each authority to which he is required to give notice of the local housing allowance determination when he gives notice of that determination.]

Modifications

Paras (1), (2) and (3) omitted, para (4) substituted, para (4A) inserted and para (5) amended by art 15(4) Rent Officers (Housing Benefit Functions) Amendment Order 2007 SI No.2871 as from 7 April 2008, save where art 15(1)(a), (b) or (c) of that order applied (see p635).

Note that by Art 11 of SI 2007 No.2871, those provisions which on 19 March 2008 applied only in relation to the areas of former Pathfinder authorities, apply in the same way to the areas of every other local authority in Scotland.

Amendments

1.   Inserted by Art 3(5) of SI 2003 No 2398 as from a date specified in Sch 1 to that SI in relation to each individual authority.

2.   Amended by reg 5 and Sch 2 para 12(5) of SI 2006 No 217 as from 6.3.06.

3.   Amended by Art 13(2)(a) of SI 2007 No 2871 as from 20.3.08.

4.   Inserted by Art 13(2)(b)-(e) of SI 2007 No 2871 as from 20.3.08.

5.   Amended by Art 14(2) of SI 2007 No 2871 as from 7.4.08.

6.   Amended by Art 15(4) of SI 2007 No 2871, as amended by Art 2(4) of SI 2008 No 587, as from 7.4.08, save where Art 15(1)(a), (b) or (c) of that order applies.

7.   Amended by Art 2(4) of SI 2008 No 587 as from 7.4.08.

8.   Amended by Art 3(2) of SI 2008 No 3156 as from 5.1.09.

[¹Board and attendance determinations and notifications

[³4C.–(1)   Where a relevant authority makes an application to a rent officer in accordance with regulation 13D(10) of the Housing Benefit Regulations or, as the case may be, regulation 13D(10) of the Housing Benefit (State Pension Credit) Regulations, a rent officer shall determine whether or not a substantial part of the rent under the tenancy at the relevant time is fairly attributable to board and attendance.

(2)   Where a rent officer determines that a substantial part of the rent under the tenancy at the relevant time is fairly attributable to board and attendance, he shall–

(a)   notify the relevant authority accordingly; and

(b)   treat the application as if it had been made in accordance with regulation 14(1) of the Housing Benefit Regulations or, as the case may be regulation 14(1) of the Housing Benefit (State Pension Credit) Regulations.]

(3)   Where a rent officer determines that a substantial part of the rent under the tenancy at the relevant time is not fairly attributable to board and attendance, he shall notify the pathfinder authority accordingly.

[⁴ (4)   Where an application for a board and attendance determination is treated as if it had been made in accordance with regulation 14(1) of the Housing Benefit Regulations or, as the case may be, regulation 14(1) of the Housing Benefit (State Pension Credit) Regulations, then, for the purposes of paragraph (a)(ii) of the definition of "relevant period" in article 2(1), it shall be treated as having been received on the day on which the further information provided in accordance with regulation 114A(4) of the Housing Benefit Regulations or regulation 95A(4) of the Housing Benefit (State Pension Credit) Regulations is received.]

Modifications

Paras (1) and (2) substituted by Art 15(5) Rent Officers (Housing Benefit Functions) Amendment Order 2007 SI No.2871 as from 7 April 2008, save where Art 15(1)(a), (b) or (c) of that order applied (see p635). Para (4) substituted by Art 16(2) of the Rent Officers (Housing Benefit Functions) Amendment Order 2007 SI No.2871 as from 7 April 2008, save where art 16(1) of that order applied (see p636).

Note that by Art 11 of SI 2007 No.2871, those provisions which on 19 March 2008 applied only in relation to the areas of former Pathfinder authorities, apply in the same way to the areas of every other local authority in Scotland.

Amendments

1.   Inserted by Art 3(5) of SI 2003 No 2398 as from a date specified in Sch 1 to that SI in relation to each individual authority.
2.   Amended by reg 5 and Sch 2 para 12(6) of SI 2006 No 217 as from 6.3.06.
3.   Substituted by Art 15(5) of SI 2007 No 2871 as from 7.4.08, save where Art 15(1)(a), (b) or (c) of that order applies.
4.   Substituted by Art 16(2) of SI 2007 No 2871 as from 7.4.08, save where Art 16(1) of that order applies.

[¹Board and attendance redeterminations

4D.–(1)   Subject to article 6, where a [² local authority] applies to a rent officer for a redetermination of a board and attendance determination or board and attendance redetermination, the rent officer shall, in accordance with paragraph (2)–

(a)   make a redetermination of–
    (i)   the board and attendance determination, provided it was made in accordance with article 4C and had effect at the date of the application for it to be redetermined; or
    (ii)   the board and attendance redetermination provided it was made in accordance with head (i), and had effect at the date of the application for it to be redetermined; and
(b)   notify the [² local authority] of the redetermination.

(2)   When making a board and attendance redetermination under this article, the rent officer shall seek, and have regard to, the advice of one or two other rent officers in relation to the redetermination.

(3)   A rent officer whose advice is sought in accordance with paragraph (2) shall give that advice.

(4)   Article 4C shall apply in relation to a board and attendance redetermination but as if the references to the relevant time were references to the date on which the original application for a board and attendance determination was made, or if earlier, to the date on which the tenancy ended.]

Modifications

Para (1) amended by Art 15(6) Rent Officers (Housing Benefit Functions) Amendment Order 2007 SI No.2871 as from 7 April 2008, save where Art 15(1)(a), (b) or (c) of that order applied (see p635).

Note that by Art 11 of SI 2007 No.2871, those provisions which on 19 March 2008 applied only in relation to the areas of former Pathfinder authorities, apply in the same way to the areas of every other local authority in Scotland.

Amendments
1.　　Inserted by Art 3(5) of SI 2003 No 2398 as from a date specified in Sch 1 to that SI in relation to each individual authority.
2.　　Amended by Art 15(6) of SI 2007 No 2871 as from 7.4.08, save where Art 15(1)(a), (b) or (c) of that order applies.

[¹Substitute board and attendance determinations and substitute board and attendance redeterminations

4E.–(1)　　Where a [³ local authority} applies to a rent officer for a substitute board and attendance determination in accordance with [² [³ regulation 17 of the Housing Benefit Regulations or, as the case may be, regulation 17 of the Housing Benefit (State Pension Credit) Regulations]], the provisions of this Order shall apply to that substitute board and attendance determination as they apply to a board and attendance determination but as if references to the relevant time were references to the date on which the original application for a board and attendance determination was made or, if earlier, the date on which the tenancy ended.

(2)　　Where a [³ local authority] applies to a rent officer for a substitute board and attendance redetermination in accordance with [² [³ regulation 17 of the Housing Benefit Regulations or, as the case may be, regulation 17 of the Housing Benefit (State Pension Credit) Regulations]], the provisions of this Order shall apply to that substitute board and attendance redetermination as they apply to a board and attendance redetermination.]

Modifications

Paras (1) and (2) amended by Art 15(6) Rent Officers (Housing Benefit Functions) Amendment Order 2007 SI No.2871 as from 7 April 2008, save where Art 15(1)(a), (b) or (c) of that order applied (see p635).

Note that by Art 11 of SI 2007 No.2871, those provisions which on 19 March 2008 applied only in relation to the areas of former Pathfinder authorities, apply in the same way to the areas of every other local authority in Scotland.

Amendments
1.　　Inserted by Art 3(5) of SI 2003 No 2398 as from a date specified in Sch 1 to that SI in relation to each individual authority.
2.　　Amended by reg 5 and Sch 2 para 12(7) of SI 2006 No 217 as from 6.3.06.
3.　　Amended by Art 15(6) of SI 2007 No 2871 as from 7.4.08, save where Art 15(1)(a), (b) or (c) of that order applies.
4.　　Substituted by Art 19(4) of SI 2007 No 2871 as from 7.4.08.

Insufficient information

5.　　If a rent officer needs further information in order to make a determination under article 3(1) or a [² redetermination under article 4, a board and attendance determination under article 4C or a board and attendance redetermination under article 4D], [³ where the information supplied under regulation 114A of the Housing Benefit Regulations or regulation 95A of the Housing Benefit (State Pension Credit) Regulations was incomplete or incorrect, he shall serve notice on the local authority requesting it to supply the further information required under regulation 114A or regulation 95A, as the case may be, or to confirm whether the information already supplied is correct and, if it is not, to supply the correct information.] [¹ ...]

Modifications

Art 5 amended by Art 16(3) Rent Officers (Housing Benefit Functions) Amendment Order 2007 SI No.2871 as from 7 April 2008, save where Art 16(1) of that order applied (see p636).

Note that by Art 11 of SI 2007 No.2871, those provisions which on 19 March 2008 applied only in relation to the areas of former Pathfinder authorities, apply in the same way to the areas of every other local authority in Scotland.

Amendments
1.　　Deleted by Art 6 of SI 2000 No 1 as from 3.4.00.
2.　　Substituted by Art 3(6) of SI 2003 No 2398 as from a date specified in Sch 1 to that SI in relation to each individual authority.
3.　　Amended by Art 16(1) of SI 2007 No 2871 as from 7.4.08, save where Art 16(1) of that order applies.

Exceptions

6.–(1)   No determination [¹, redetermination, board and attendance determination or board and attendance redetermination] shall be made if the application for it is withdrawn.

(2)   No determination shall be made under paragraph 3, 4 or 5 of Part I of Schedule 1 if the tenancy is of residential accommodation, within the meaning of [² [³ regulation 9(4) of the Housing Benefit Regulations or, as the case may be, regulation 9(4) of the Housing Benefit (State Pension Credit) Regulations]], or in a hostel.

(3)   No determination shall be made under paragraph 5 of Part I of Schedule 1 unless the local authority states in the application that the claimant is, or may be, a young individual (which has the same meaning as in [² [³ the Housing Benefit Regulations and the Housing Benefit (State Pension Credit) Regulations]]).

(4)   If the rent officer becomes aware that an application is not one which gives rise to a duty to make a determination [¹, redetermination, board and attendance determination or a board and attendance redetermination] , the rent officer shall give the local authority notice to that effect.

Modifications

Note that by Art 11 Rent Officers (Housing Benefit Functions) Amendment Order 2007 SI No.2871, those provisions which on 19 March 2008 applied only in relation to the areas of former Pathfinder authorities, apply in the same way to the areas of every other local authority in Scotland.

Amendments

1.   Substituted by Art 3(7) of SI 2003 No 2398 as from a date specified in Sch 1 to that SI in relation to each individual authority.
2.   Amended by reg 5 and Sch 2 para 12(8) of SI 2006 No 217 as from 6.3.06.
3.   Substituted by Art 19(5) of SI 2007 No 2871 as from 7.4.08.

Special cases

7.–(1)   This Order shall apply as specified in Schedule 4 in relation to–

(a)   mooring charges payable for a houseboat;

(b)   payments in respect of the site on which a caravan or a mobile home stands; or

(c)   payments under a rental purchase agreement.

(2)   Terms used in paragraph (1) have the same meaning in this article and in Schedule 4 as they have in [² [³ regulation 12(1) of the Housing Benefit Regulations or, as the case may be, regulation 12(1) of the Housing Benefit (State Pension Credit) Regulations]].

[¹ ...]

Amendments

1.   Deleted by Art 7 of SI 2000 No 3 as from 3.4.00.
2.   Amended by reg 5 and Sch 2 para 12(9) of SI 2006 No 217 as from 6.3.06.
3.   Substituted by Art 19(6) of SI 2007 No 2871 as from 7.4.08.

[¹Errors

7A.–[² (1)]   If a rent officer is of the opinion that he has made an error (other than in the application of his professional judgement) in relation to a determination or redetermination, he shall notify the local authority which made the application for that determination or redetermination of the error as soon as practicable after he becomes aware of it.]

[² (2)   If a rent officer is of the opinion that he has made an error (other than in the application of his professional judgement) in relation to a board and attendance determination or board and attendance redetermination, he shall notify the [⁵ local authority] which made the application for that board and attendance determination or board and attendance redetermination of the error as soon as practicable after he becomes aware of it.

[⁵ (3)]]

[⁴ (4)   If a rent officer is of the opinion that he has made an error (other than in the application of his professional judgement) in relation to a broad rental market area determination determined in accordance with article 4B(1A) or a local housing allowance determination determined in accordance with article 4B(2A), he shall notify any local authority to which notification of that determination was sent of the error, and the amended determination, as soon as practicable after he becomes aware of it.]

Modifications

Para (2) amended and para (3) omitted by Art 15(7) of the Rent Officers (Housing Benefit Functions) Amendment Order 2007 SI No.2871 as from 7 April 2008, save where Art 15(1)(a), (b) or (c) of that order applied (see p635).

Note that by Art 11 of SI 2007 No. 2871, those provisions which on 19 March 2008 applied only in relation to the areas of former Pathfinder authorities, apply in the same way to the areas of every other local authority in Scotland.

Amendments

1.   Inserted by Art 8 of SI 2000 No 3 as from 3.4.00.
2.   Inserted by Art 2(8) of SI 2003 No 2398 as from a date specified in Sch 1 to that SI in relation to each individual authority.
3.   Amended by Art 13(3)(a) of SI 2007 No 2871 as from 20.3.08.
4.   Inserted by Art 13(3)(b) of SI 2007 No 2871 as from 20.3.08.
5.   Amended by Art 15(7) of SI 2007 No 2871 as from 7.4.08, save where Art 15(1)(a), (b) or (c) of that order applies.

Amendment to 1995 Order

8.–(1) The Rent Officers (Additional Functions) (Scotland) Order 1995 shall be amended by the insertion at the end of article 6 (special cases) of the following:–

"(3) In a case where the local authority states in the application that the rent includes charges for general counselling or any other support services which are eligible for housing benefit solely by virtue of paragraph 1(f)(iii) of Schedule 1 to the 1987 Regulations (landlord's support services: supported accommodation) or solely by virtue of that provision and paragraph 1(f)(ii) of that Schedule, the rent officer shall assume when making a determination or a redetermination that–

(a)   the services were not to be provided or made available; and

(b)   the rent payable under the tenancy at the relevant time is such amount as is specified in the application as the rent which would have been payable under the tenancy at that time if those items were not to be provided or made available.

(4) In a case where the local authority states in the application that the rent includes charges for general counselling or any other support services and the charges–

(a)   are eligible for housing benefit by virtue of paragraph 1(f)(iii) of Schedule 1 to the 1987 Regulations, or that provision and paragraph 1(f)(ii) of that Schedule; and

(b)   are also eligible for housing benefit by virtue of paragraph 1(f)(i) of that Schedule (support services: other exceptions), the rent officer shall include in the notice to the local authority, required under article 3(1)(c), a statement of the amount of the rent payable for the tenancy (which has the same meaning as in paragraph 3(1) of Schedule 1 to this Order) which relates to those charges.".

(2) The amendment made by paragraph (1) above does not have effect in a case where an application for a determination is made before 18th August 1997.

Revocations and application

9.–(1) Subject to paragraph (2), article 8 of this Order and the Orders specified in Schedule 5 are hereby revoked.

(2) Nothing in articles 2 to 7 has effect in a case where an application for a determination is made before 3rd September 1997 and, in such a case, the Rent Officers (Additional Functions) (Scotland) Order 1995 shall continue to have effect.

SCHEDULE 1
PART I
Determinations

Significantly high rents

1.–(1)   The rent officer shall determine whether, in his opinion, the rent payable under the tenancy of the dwelling at the relevant time is significantly higher than the rent which the landlord might reasonably have been expected to obtain under the tenancy at that time.

(2)   If the rent officer determines under sub-paragraph (1) that the rent is significantly higher, the rent officer shall also determine the rent which the landlord might reasonably have been expected to obtain under the tenancy at the relevant time.

(3)   When making a determination under this paragraph, the rent officer shall have regard to the level of rent under similar tenancies of similar dwellings in the [¹ vicinity] (or as similar as regards tenancy, dwelling and [¹ vicinity] as is reasonably practicable) and shall assume that no one who would have been entitled to housing benefit had sought or is seeking the tenancy.

[²(4)   For the purposes of this paragraph and paragraph 2 ''vicinity'' means–

(a)   the area immediately surrounding the dwelling; or

(b)   where, for the purposes of sub-paragraph (2)(c) of paragraph 2, there is no dwelling in the area immediately surrounding the dwelling which satisfies the description in heads (i), (ii) and (iii) of that sub-paragraph, the area nearest to the dwelling where there is such a dwelling.]

Amendments

1.   Amended by art 3(2) of SI 2001 No 3561 as from 6.11.01.

2.   Inserted by art 3(2) of SI 2001 No 3561 as from 6.11.01.

Size and rent

2.–(1)   The rent officer shall determine whether the dwelling, at the relevant time, exceeds the size criteria for the occupiers.

(2)   If the rent officer determines that the dwelling exceeds the size criteria, the rent officer shall also determine the rent which a landlord might reasonably have been expected to obtain, at the relevant time, for a tenancy which is–

(a)   similar to the tenancy of the dwelling;

(b)   on the same terms other than the term relating to the amount of rent; and

(c)   of a dwelling which is in the same [¹ vicinity] as the dwelling, but which–

   (i)   accords with the size criteria for the occupiers;

   (ii)   is in a reasonable state of repair; and

   (iii) corresponds in other respects, in the rent officer's opinion, as closely as is reasonably practicable to the dwelling.

(3)   When making a determination under sub-paragraph (2), the rent officer shall have regard to the same matter and make the same assumption as specified in paragraph 1(3), except that in judging the similarity of other tenancies and dwellings the comparison shall be with the tenancy of the second dwelling referred to in sub-paragraph (2), and shall assume that no one who would have been entitled to housing benefit had sought or is seeking that tenancy.

Amendment

1.   Amended by art 3(3) of SI 2001 No 3561 as from 6.11.01.

Exceptionally high rents

3.–(1)   The rent officer shall determine whether, in his opinion, the rent payable for the tenancy of the dwelling at the relevant time is exceptionally high.

(2)   In sub-paragraph (1), ''rent payable for the tenancy'' means–

(a)   where a determination is made under sub-paragraph (2) of paragraph 2, the rent determined under that sub-paragraph;

(b)   where no determination is so made and a determination is made under sub-paragraph (2) of paragraph 1, the rent determined under that sub-paragraph; and

(c)   in any other case, the rent payable under the tenancy [¹ at the relevant time].

(3)   If the rent officer determines under sub-paragraph (1) that the rent is exceptionally high, the rent officer shall also determine the highest rent, which is not an exceptionally high rent and which a landlord might reasonably have been expected to obtain at the relevant time (on the assumption that no one who would have been entitled to housing benefit had sought or is seeking the tenancy) for an assured tenancy of a dwelling which–

(a)   is in the same [² neighbourhood] as the dwelling;

(b)   has the same number of bedrooms and rooms suitable for living in as the dwelling (or, where the dwelling exceeds the size criteria for the occupiers, accords with the size criteria); and

(c)   is in a reasonable state of repair.

(4)   For the purpose of determining whether a rent is an exceptionally high rent under this paragraph, the rent officer shall have regard to the levels of rent under assured tenancies of dwellings which–

(a)   are in the same [² neighbourhood] as the dwelling (or in as similar a locality as is reasonably practicable); and

(b)   have the same number of bedrooms and rooms suitable for living in as the dwelling (or, in a case where the dwelling exceeds the size criteria for the occupiers, accord with the size of criteria).

[³ (5)   For the purposes of this paragraph and paragraph 4(6) ''neighbourhood'' means-

(a)   where the dwelling is in a town or city, the part of that town or city where the dwelling is located which is a distinct area of residential accommodation; or

(b)   where the dwelling is not in a town or city, the area surrounding the dwelling which is a distinct area of residential accommodation and where there are dwellings satisfying the description in sub-paragraph (4)(b).]

Amendments

1.   Amended by Art 9 of SI 2000 No 3 as from 3.4.00.
2.   Amended by art 3(4) of SI 2001 No 3561 as from 6.11.01.
3.   Inserted by art 3(4) of SI 2001 No 3561 as from 6.11.01.

Local reference rents

4.–(1)   The rent officer shall make a determination of a local rent in accordance with the formula–

$$R = \frac{H+L}{2}$$

where–

R is the local reference rent;

H is the highest rent, in the rent officer's opinion–

(a)   which a landlord might reasonably have been expected to obtain, at the relevant time, for an assured tenancy of a dwelling which meets the criteria in sub-paragraph (2); and

(b)   which is not an exceptionally high rent; and

L is the lowest rent, in the rent officer's opinion–

(a)   which a landlord might reasonably have been expected to obtain, at the relevant time, for an assured tenancy of a dwelling which meets the criteria in sub-paragraph (2); and

(b)   which is not an exceptionally low rent.

(2)   The criteria are–

(a)   that the dwelling under the assured tenancy–

(i)   is in the same [⁸ broad rental market area (local reference rent)] as the dwelling;

(ii)   is in a reasonable state of repair; and

(iii)   has the same number of bedrooms and rooms suitable for living in as the dwelling (or, in a case where the dwelling exceeds the size criteria for the occupiers, accords with the size criteria); and

(b)   if the tenant does not have the use under the tenancy of the dwelling [¹ at the relevant time] of more than one bedroom or room suitable for living in–

(i)   that under the assured tenancy the tenant does not have the use of more than one bedroom or room suitable for living in;

(ii)   if the rent under the tenancy [¹ at the relevant time] includes payments for board and attendance and the rent officer considers that the amount fairly attributable to board and attendance is a substantial part of the rent, that a substantial part of the rent under the assured tenancy is fairly attributable to board and attendance;

(iii)   if sub-paragraph (ii) does not apply and the tenant shares a [⁴ kitchen, toilet, bathroom and room suitable for living in] with a person other than a member of his household, a non-dependant or a person who pays rent to the tenant, that the assured tenancy provides for the tenant to share a [⁴ kitchen, toilet, bathroom and room suitable for living in]; and

(iv)   if sub-paragraphs (ii) and (iii) do not apply, that the circumstances described in sub-paragraphs (ii) and (iii) do not apply in relation to the assured tenancy.

(3)   When ascertaining H and L under sub-paragraph (1), the rent officer–

(a)   shall assume that no one who would have been entitled to housing benefit had sought or is seeking the tenancy; and

(b)   shall exclude the amount of any rent which, in the rent officer's opinion, is fairly attributable to the provision of services which are ineligible to be met by housing benefit; [⁵. . .]

(4)   In sub-paragraph (2)(b)–

''bedroom or room suitable for living in'' does not include a room which the tenant shares with any person other than–

(a)   a member of his household;

(b)   a non-dependant (as defined in this sub-paragraph); or

(c)   a person who pays rent to the tenant; and

[⁶ [⁷ ''non-dependant'' means a non-dependant of the tenant within the meaning of regulation 3 of the Housing Benefit Regulations or, as the case may be, regulation 3 of the Housing Benefit (State Pension Credit) Regulations;]].

(5)   In sub-paragraph (3), ''services'' means services performed or facilities (including the use of furniture) provided for, or rights made available to, the tenant, but not [², in the case of a tenancy where a substantial part of the rent under the tenancy is fairly attributable to board and attendance, the provision of meals (including the preparation of meals or provision of unprepared food).]

[³[⁸ (6)   For the purposes of this paragraph and paragraph 5 ''broad rental market area (local reference rent)'' means the area within which a tenant of the dwelling could reasonably be expected to live having regard to facilities and services for the purposes of health, education, recreation, personal banking and shopping, taking account of the distance of travel, by public and private transport, to and from those facilities and services.

(7)   A broad rental market area (local reference rent) must contain–

(a)   residential premises of a variety of types, including such premises held on a variety of tenures; and

(b)   sufficient privately rented residential premises, to ensure that, in the rent officer's opinion, the local reference rents for tenancies in the area are representative of the rents that a landlord might reasonably be expected to obtain in that area.]]

Amendments

1.   Amended by Art 9 of SI 2000 No 3 as from 3.4.00.
2.   Substituted by Art 10 of SI 2000 No 3 as from 3.4.00.
3.   Inserted by art 3(5) of SI 2001 No 3561 as from 6.11.01.
4.   Amended by Art 2(3) of SI 2001 No2318 as from 2.7.01.
5.   Deleted by art 3 of SI 2003 No 478 as from 1.4.03 (7.4.03 where rent payable weekly or in multiples of a week).
6.   Amended by reg 5 and Sch 2 para 12(10)(a) of SI 2006 No 217 as from 6.3.06.
7.   Substituted by Art 19(7a) of SI 2007 No 2871 as from 7.4.08.
8.   Amended by Art 3(3)(a) of SI 2008 No 3156 as from 5.1.09.

Single room rents

5.–(1)   The rent officer shall determine a single room rent in accordance with the following formula–

$$S = \frac{H+L}{2}$$

where–

S is the single room rent;

H is the highest rent, in the rent officer's opinion–

(a)   which a landlord might reasonable have been expected to obtain, at the relevant time, for an assured tenancy of a dwelling which meets the criteria in sub-paragraph (2); and

(b)   which is not an exceptionally high rent; and

L is the lowest rent, in the rent officer's opinion–

(a)   which a landlord might reasonably have been expected to obtain, at the relevant time, for an assured tenancy of a dwelling which meets the criteria in sub-paragraph (2); and

(b)   which is not an exceptionally low rent.

(2)   The criteria are–

(a)   that the dwelling under the assured tenancy is in the same [⁴ broad rental market area (local reference rent)] as the dwelling and is in a reasonable state of repair;

(b)   that, under the assured tenancy, the tenant–

(i)   has the exclusive use of one bedroom;

(ii)   does not have the use of any other bedroom [¹ . . .] or room suitable for living in;

[² (iia)   shares the use of a room suitable for living in]

(iii)   shares the use of a toilet [¹ and bathroom]; and

(iv)   shares the use of a kitchen and does not have the exclusive use of facilities for cooking food; and

(c)   that the rent does not include any payment for board and attendance.

(3)   Sub-paragraphs [³ (3) and (5)] of paragraph 4 apply when ascertaining H and L under this sub-paragraph as if the reference in those sub-paragraphs to H and L were to H and L under [³ this paragraph].

Amendments

1.   Amended by reg 4 of SI 2001 No 1326 as from 2.7.01.
2.   Substituted by Art 2(9) of SI 2003 No 2398 as from a date specified in Sch 1 to that SI in relation to each individual authority.
3.   Amended by arts 5(1) and 6 of SI 2005 No 236 as from 13.3.05.
4.   Amended by Art 3(3)(b) of SI 2008 No 3156 as from 5.1.09.

Claim-related rent

[¹**6.**–[² (1) In this paragraph, and in paragraph 9, "claim-related rent" means the claim-related rent determined by the rent officer in accordance with paragraph (2A).]

[² (2A) The rent officer shall determine that the claim-related rent is–

(a) where he makes a determination under sub-paragraph (2) of paragraph 1, sub-paragraph (2) of paragraph 2 and sub-paragraph (3) of paragraph 3, the lowest of the three rents determined under those sub-paragraphs;

(b) where he makes a determination under only two of the sub-paragraphs referred to in paragraph (a), the lower of the two rents determined under those sub-paragraphs;

(c) where he makes a determination under only one of the sub-paragraphs referred to in paragraph (a), the rent determined under that sub-paragraph;

(d) where he does not make a determination under any of the sub-paragraphs referred to in sub-paragraph (a), the rent payable under the tenancy of the dwelling at the relevant time.]

[² (2)]

(3)   [²] the rent officer shall also determine the total amount of ineligible charges, as defined in paragraph 7, which he has not included in the claim-related rent because of the assumptions made in accordance with that paragraph.]

Modifications

Para 6(1) substituted, para 6(2A) inserted, para 6(2) omitted and para 6(3) amended by Art 18(2) Rent Officers (Housing Benefit Functions) Amendment Order 2007 SI No.2871 as from 7 April 2008, save where Art 18(1)(a) or (b) of that order applied (see p637).

Amendments

1.   Substituted by Art 11 of SI 2000 No 3 as from 3.4.00.
2.   Amended by Art 18(2) of SI 2007 No 2971 as from 7.4.08, save where Art 18(1)(a) or (b) of that order applies.

Part II
Assumptions

Ineligible charges and support charges

[¹**7.**[⁵ (1) "ineligible charges" means service charges which are ineligible to be met by housing benefit by virtue of regulation 12B(2) (rent) of and Schedule 1 (ineligible service charges) to the Housing Benefit Regulations or, as the case may be, regulation 12B(2) of and Schedule 1 to the Housing Benefit (State Pension Credit) Regulations except in the case of a tenancy where the rent includes payments for board and attendance, and the rent officer considers that a substantial part of the rent under the tenancy is fairly attributable to board and attendance, charges specified in paragraph 1(a)(i) of Schedule 1 to the Housing Benefit Regulations or, as the case may be, in paragraph 1(a)(i) of Schedule 1 to the Housing Benefit (State Pension Credit) Regulations (charges for meals).]

[². . .].

(2)   When making a determination under paragraph 1, 2 or 3 of this Schedule, the rent officer shall assume that–

(a)   the items to which the ineligible charges relate; [² . . .],

were not to be provided or made available.

[⁴ (3) For the purposes of paragraphs 1, 2, 3, and 6 of Part 1 of this Schedule, the rent officer shall assume that the rent payable under the tenancy at the relevant time is–

(a)   where an amount is notified to the rent officer under regulation 114A(4)(b) of the Housing Benefit Regulations or, as the case may be, regulations 95A(4)(b) of the Housing Benefit (State Pension Credit) Regulations in respect of that tenancy, that notified amount less the total of any ineligible charges included in that amount; or

(b)   in any other case, the total amount stated under regulation 114A(3)(d) of the Housing Benefit Regulations or, as the case may be regulation 95A(3)(d) of the Housing Benefit (State Pension Credit) Regulations less the total of any ineligible charges included in that stated amount.]

(4)   The total of any ineligible charges, referred to in sub-paragraph (3), shall be the total of the amounts (excluding any amount which he considers is negligible) of any charges included in the notified amount or the stated amount, as the case may be, which, in the rent officer's opinion, are at the relevant time fairly attributable to any items to which ineligible charges relate.]

Modifications

Para 7(3) substituted by Art 16(4) Rent Officers (Housing Benefit Functions) Amendment Order 2007 SI No.2871 as from 7 April 2008, save where Art 16(1) of that order applied (see p636). Para 7(1) substituted by Art 17(2) Rent Officers (Housing Benefit Functions) Amendment Order 2007 SI No.2871 as from 7 April 2008, save where Art 17(1) of that order applied (see p636).

Amendments

1. Amended by Art 9 of SI 2000 No 3 as from 3.4.00.
2. Deleted by art 3 of SI 2003 No 478 as from 1.4.03 (7.4.03 where rent payable weekly or in multiples of a week).
3. Amended by reg 5 and Sch 2 para 12(10)(b) of SI 2006 No 217 as from 6.3.06.
4. Substituted by Art 16(4) of SI 2007 No 2871 as from 7.4.08, save where Art 16(1) of that order applies.
5. Substituted by Art 17(2) of SI 2007 No 2871 as from 7.4.08, save where Art 17(1) of that order applies.

Housing associations etc.

8.–(1)   In a case where the local authority states in the application that the landlord is a housing association or a charity, the rent officer shall assume that the landlord is not such a body.

(2)   The rent officer shall not take into account the rent under any tenancy where the landlord is a housing association or where the landlord is a charity and the dwelling is provided by the landlord in the pursuit of its charitable purposes.

(3)   In this paragraph–

"charity" has the same meaning as in the Charities Act 1993, except that it includes a Scottish charity (which has the same meaning as in section 1(7) of the Law Reform (Miscellaneous Provisions) (Scotland) Act 1990); and

"housing association" has the same meaning as in the Housing Associations Act 1985.

Part III
Notifications of Part I Determinations

Notifications

9.–[¹(1)   Subject to sub-paragraph (2), the rent officer shall give notice to the local authority of–
(a)   the claim-related rent determined under Part I;
(b)   where the dwelling is not in a hostel, the total amount of ineligible charges determined under paragraph 6(3) in relation to that claim-related rent;
[³ (c)   where that claim-related rent includes an amount which would be ineligible for housing benefit under paragraph 1(a)(i) of Schedule 1 to the Housing Benefit Regulations or, as the case may be, paragraph 1(a)(i) of Schedule 1 to the Housing Benefit (State Pension Credit) Regulations (charges for meals), the inclusion of an ineligible amount in respect of meals;]
(d)   any rent determined by the rent officer under paragraph 4 (local reference rents); and
[³ (da)   where any rent determined under paragraph 4 includes an amount which would be ineligible for housing benefit under the provisions referred to in sub-paragraph (c), the inclusion of an ineligible amount in respect of meals;]
(e)   any rent determined by the rent officer under paragraph 5 (single room rents).]
(2)   If the rent officer determines a rent under–
(a)   paragraph 4 (local reference rents); or
(b)   paragraph 5 (single room rents),
which is equal to or more than the [¹ claim-related rent], the rent officer shall give notice to the local authority of this in place of giving notice of the determination made under paragraph 4 or, as the case may be, paragraph 5.

Modifications

Para 9(1)(c) substituted and para 9(1)(da) inserted by Art 18(3) of the Rent Officers (Housing Benefit Functions) Amendment Order 2007 SI No. 2871 as from 7 April 2008, save where Art 18(1)(a) or (b) of that order applied (see p637).

Amendments

1. Amended by Art 9 of SI 2000 No 3 as from 3.4.00.
2. Amended by reg 5 and Sch 2 para 12(10)(c) of SI 2006 No 217 as from 6.3.06.
3. Amended by Art 18(3) of SI 2007 No 2971 as from 7.4.08, save where Art 18(1)(a) or (b) of that order apply.

Part IV
Indicative Rent Levels

11.–(1)   The rent officer shall determine the indicative rent level for each category described in sub-paragraph (3) in accordance with the following formula–

$$I = \frac{H+3L}{4}$$

where–
I is the indicative rent level;
H is the highest rent, in the rent officer's opinion–

   (a)   which a landlord might reasonably be expected to obtain at the time the determination is being made for an assured tenancy of a dwelling meeting the criteria in sub-paragraph (2); and

   (b)   which is not an exceptionally high rent; and

L is the lowest rent, in the rent officer's opinion–

   (a)   which a landlord might reasonably be expected to obtain at the time the determination is being made for an assured tenancy of a dwelling meeting the criteria in sub-paragraph (2); and

   (b)   which is not an exceptionally low rent.

   (2)   The criteria are that–

   (a)   the dwelling is in the area of the local authority;

   (b)   the dwelling is in a reasonable state of repair; and

   (c)   the dwelling and tenancy accord with the category to which the determination relates.

   (3)   The categories for the purposes of this paragraph are–

   (a)   a dwelling where the tenant does not have use of more than one room where a substantial part of the rent under the tenancy is fairly attributable to board and attendance;

   (b)   a dwelling where the tenant does not have use of more than one room, the tenancy provides for him to share a kitchen or toilet and paragraph (a) does not apply;

   (c)   a dwelling where the tenant does not have use of more than one room and where paragraphs (a) and (b) do not apply;

   (d)   a dwelling where the tenant does not have use of more than two rooms and where none of paragraphs (a) to (c) applies;

   (e)   a dwelling where the tenant does not have use of more than three rooms and where none of paragraphs (a) to (d) applies;

   (f)   a dwelling where the tenant does not have use of more than four rooms and where none of paragraphs (a) to (e) applies;

   (g)   a dwelling where the tenant does not have use of more than five rooms and where none of paragraphs (a) to (f) applies; and

   (h)   a dwelling where the tenant does not have use of more than six rooms and where none of paragraphs (a) to (g) applies.

   (4)   When ascertaining H and L under sub-paragraph (1), the rent officer–

   (a)   shall assume that no one who would have been entitled to housing benefit had sought or is seeking the tenancy; and

   (b)   shall exclude the amount of any rent which, in the rent officer's opinion, is fairly attributable to the provision of services which are ineligible to be met by housing benefit; [¹ . . .]

   (5)   In this paragraph–

''room'' means a bedroom or room suitable for living in and in paragraphs (a), (b) and (c) of sub-paragraph (3) does not include a room which the tenant shares with any person other than–

   (a)   a member of his household;

   (b)   a non-dependant of the tenant (within the meaning of [² [³ regulation 3 of the Housing Benefit Regulations or, as the case may be, regulation 3 of the Housing Benefit (State Pension Credit) Regulations]]); or

   (c)   a person who pays rent to the tenant;

''services'' has the meaning given by paragraph 4(5).

Amendments

1.   Deleted by art 3 of SI 2003 No 478 as from 1.4.03 (7.4.03 where rent payable weekly or in multiples of a week).

2.   Amended by reg 5 and Sch 2 para 12(10)(d) of SI 2006 No 217 as from 6.3.06.

3.   Substituted by Art 19(7)(b) of SI 2007 No 2871 as from 7.4.08.

SCHEDULE 2
SIZE CRITERIA

1.   One bedroom or room suitable for living in shall be allowed for each of the following categories of occupier (and each occupier shall come within only the first category for which he is eligible)–

   (a)   [¹ a couple] (within the meaning of Part VII of the Social Security Contributions and Benefits Act 1992);

   (b)   a person who is not a child;

   (c)   two children of the same sex;

   (d)   two children who are less than ten years old;

   (e)   a child.

2.   The number of rooms (excluding any allowed under paragraph 1) suitable for living in allowed are–

   (a)   if there are less than four occupiers, one;

   (b)   if there are more than three and less than seven occupiers, two; and

   (c)   in any other case, three.

Amendment

1.   Substituted by art 30 of SI 2005 No 2877 as from 5.12.05.

SCHEDULE 3
REDETERMINATIONS
[¹**1.** Schedules 1 and 2 shall apply in relation to a redetermination as they apply to a determination, but as if references in those Schedules to the relevant time were references to the date the application for the original determination was made or, if earlier, the date the tenancy ended.]

Amendment

1.   Substituted by Art 12 of SI 2000 No 3 as from 3.4.00.

2.   The rent officer making the redetermination shall seek and have regard to the advice of one or two other rent officers in relation to the redetermination.

[² SCHEDULE 3A]

Modifications

Sch 3A omitted by Art 15(8) of the Rent Officers (Housing Benefit Functions) Amendment Order 2007 SI No.2871 as from 7 April 2008, save where Art 15(1)(a), (b) or (c) of that order applied (see p635).

Amendments

1.   Schedule inserted by Art 2(10) of SI 2003 No 2398 as from a date specified in Sch 1 to that SI in relation to each individual authority.
2.   Omitted by Art 15(8) of SI 2007 No 2871 as from 7.4.08, save where Art 15(1)(a), (b) or (c) of that order applies.
3.   Substituted by Art 19(8) of SI 2007 No 2871 as from 7.4.08.

[¹ SCHEDULE 3B

Amendment

1.   Schedule inserted by Art 13(4) of SI 2007 No 2871 as from 20.3.08.

Broad rental market area determinations and local housing allowance determinations

Categories of dwelling
1.–(1)   The categories of dwelling for which a rent officer is required to determine a local housing allowance in accordance with article 4B(2A)(a)(i) are–
- (a)   a dwelling where the tenant has the exclusive use of only one bedroom and where the tenancy provides for him to share the use of one or more of–
  - (i)   a kitchen;
  - (ii)   a bathroom;
  - (iii)   a toilet; or
  - (iv)   a room suitable for living in;
- (b)   a dwelling where the tenant (together with his partner where he has one) has the exclusive use of only one bedroom and exclusive use of a kitchen, a bathroom, a toilet and a room suitable for living in;
- (c)   a dwelling where the tenant has the use of only two bedrooms;
- (d)   a dwelling where the tenant has the use of only three bedrooms;
- (e)   a dwelling where the tenant has the use of only four bedrooms;
- (f)   a dwelling where the tenant has the use of only five bedrooms.
- (2)   In–
- (a)   sub-paragraph (1)(b) "partner" has the same meaning as in regulation 2 of the Housing Benefit Regulations or, as the case may be, regulation 2 of the Housing Benefit (State Pension Credit) Regulations;
- (b)   sub-paragraph (1)(c) to (f) "bedroom" means a bedroom, except for a bedroom which the tenant shares with any person other than–
  - (i)   a member of his household;
  - (ii)   a non-dependant of the tenant (within the meaning of regulation 3 of the Housing Benefit Regulations or, as the case may be, regulation 3 of the Housing Benefit (State Pension Credit) Regulations); or
  - (iii)   a person who pays rent to the tenant.

Local housing allowance for category of dwelling in paragraph 1
2.–(1)   Subject to paragraph 3 (anomalous local housing allowances), the rent officer must determine a local housing allowance for each category of dwelling in paragraph 1 in accordance with the following sub-paragraphs.

(2)   The rent officer must compile a list of rents.

(3)   A list of rents means a list in ascending order of the rents which, in the rent officer's opinion, are payable at the date of the determination for a dwelling let under an assured tenancy which meets the criteria specified in sub-paragraph (5).

(4)   The list must include any rents which are of the same amount.

(5)   The criteria for including an assured tenancy on the list of rents in relation to each category of dwelling specified in paragraph 1 are–

(a)   that the dwelling let under the assured tenancy is in the broad rental market area for which the local housing allowance for that category of dwelling is being determined;

(b)   that the dwelling is in a reasonable state of repair; and

(c)   that the assured tenancy permits the tenant to use exclusively or share the use of, as the case may be, the same number and type of rooms as the category of dwelling in relation to which the list of rents is being compiled.

[² (5A)   Where the rent officer is not satisfied that the list of rents in respect of any category of dwelling would contain sufficient rents, payable at the date of the determination for dwellings in the broad rental market area, to enable a local housing allowance to be determined which is representative of the rents that a landlord might reasonably be expected to obtain in that area, the rent officer may add to the list rents for dwellings in the same category in other areas in which a comparable market exists.]

(6)   Where rent is payable other than weekly the rent officer must use the figure which would be payable if the rent were to be payable weekly by–

(a)   multiplying the rent by an appropriate figure to obtain the rent for a year;

(b)   dividing the total in (a) by 365; and

(c)   multiplying the total in (b) by 7.

(7)   When compiling the list of rents for each category of dwelling, the rent officer must–

(a)   assume that no one who would have been entitled to housing benefit had sought or is seeking the tenancy; and

(b)   exclude the amount of any rent which, in the rent officer's opinion, is fairly attributable to the provision of services performed for, or facilities (including the use of furniture) provided for, or rights made available to, the tenant which are ineligible to be met by housing benefit.

[¹ (8)]

(9)   The local housing allowance for each category of dwelling specified in paragraph 1 is the amount of the median rent in the list of rents for that category of dwelling.

(10)   The median rent is determined as follows–

(a)   where there is an even number of rents on the list, the formula is–

(a)   where there is an even number of rents on the list, the formula is–

$$\frac{\text{The amount of the rent at P} + \text{the amount of the rent at P1}}{2} = \text{the local housing allowance}$$

where

P is the position on the list defined by dividing the number of rents on the list by 2 and P1 is the following position on the list.

(b)   where there is an odd number of rents on the list, the formula is–

$$\frac{\text{the number of rents on the list} + 1}{2} = \text{L}$$

where

L is the position on the list in which the rent used to identify the local housing allowance lies.

(11)   Where the median rent is not a whole number of pence, the rent must be rounded to the nearest whole penny by disregarding any amount less than half a penny and treating any amount of half a penny or more as a whole penny.

Amendments

1.   Omitted by Art 3(4)(a) of SI 2008 No 3156 as from 5.1.09.

2.   Inserted by Art 2(2) of SI 2009 No 2459 as from 12.10.09.

Anomalous local housing allowances

3.–(1)   Where–

(a)   the rent officer has determined the local housing allowance for each of the categories of dwelling in paragraph 1(1) in accordance with the preceding paragraphs of this Schedule; and

(b)   the local housing allowance for a category of dwelling in paragraph 1(1)(b) to (f) is lower than the local housing allowance for any of the categories of dwelling which precede it,

that local housing allowance shall be the same as the highest local housing allowance which precedes it.

(2)   Where–

(a)   the rent officer has determined a local housing allowance following an application made under article 4B(4); and

(b)   that local housing allowance is lower than the local housing allowance for the category of dwelling in paragraph 1(1)(f),

that local housing allowance shall be the same as the local housing allowance for the category of dwelling in paragraph 1(1)(f).

Broad rental market area
[¹**4.**   In this Schedule ''broad rental market area'' means an area within which a person could reasonably be expected to live having regard to facilities and services for the purposes of health, education, recreation, personal banking and shopping, taking account of the distance of travel, by public and private transport, to and from those facilities and services.]

Amendment
1.   Substituted by Art 3(4)(b) of SI 2008 No 3156 as from 5.1.09.

[¹**5.**   A broad rental market area must contain–
(a)   residential premises of a variety of types, including such premises held on a variety of tenures; and
(b)   sufficient privately rented residential premises to ensure that, in the rent officer's opinion, the local housing allowance for the categories of dwelling in the area for which the rent officer is required to determine a local housing allowance is representative of the rents that a landlord might reasonably be expected to obtain in that area.]]

Amendment
1.   Inserted by Art 3(4)(b) of SI 2008 No 3156 as from 5.1.09.

SCHEDULE 4
SPECIAL CASES
Houseboats
1.   Where an application for a determination or a redetermination relates in whole or in part to mooring charges for a houseboat, this Order applies in relation to that application (or, as the case may be, to that part which relates to those charges) with the following modifications–
(a)   references to a tenancy, a tenancy of a dwelling or an assured tenancy are references to an agreement under which those charges are payable (and references to a landlord and a tenant shall be construed accordingly); and
(b)   no determination shall be made under paragraph 2 of Part I of Schedule 1 (size criteria) and references to the dwelling exceeding the size criteria shall not apply.

Mobile homes
2.   Where an application for a determination or redetermination relates in whole or in part to payments in respect of the site on which a caravan or a mobile home stands, this Order applies in relation to that application (or, as the case may be, that part which relates to those payments) with the following modifications–
(a)   references to a tenancy, a tenancy of a dwelling or an assured tenancy are references to an agreement under which those payments are payable (and references to a landlord and a tenant shall be construed accordingly); and
(b)   no determination shall be made under paragraph 2 of Part I of Schedule 1 (size criteria) and references to the dwelling exceeding the size criteria shall not apply.

Rental purchase agreements
3.   Where an application for a determination or a redetermination relates to a rental purchase agreement, the agreement is to be treated as if it were a tenancy.

The Rent Officers (Housing Benefit Functions) (Local Housing Allowance) Amendment Order 2003
SI 2003 No.2398

General Note

This Order modified the Rent Officers (Housing Benefit Functions) Orders in respect of the implementation of the pilot housing allowance scheme in Pathfinder Authorities. Only the commencement dates are reproduced here.

Citation, commencement and interpretation

1.–(1) This Order may be cited as the Rent Officers (Housing Benefit Functions) (Local Housing Allowance) Amendment Order 2003 and shall come into force in relation to the area of a local authority specified in Schedule 1 to this Order on the date specified in that Schedule in relation to that local authority.

(2)   *[Omitted]*

SCHEDULE 1
DATE ON WHICH ORDER COMES INTO FORCE FOR LOCAL AUTHORITY AREAS

Local authority	Date
Blackpool	17th October 2003
Brighton and Hove	19th January 2004
Conwy	19th January 2004
Coventry	15th December 2003
Edinburgh	19th January 2004
Leeds	19th January 2004
Lewisham	17th November 2003
North East Lincolnshire	19th January 2004
Teignbridge	15th December 2003

The Rent Officers (Housing Benefit Functions) (Local Housing Allowance) Amendment Order 2005

(SI 2005 No.236)

Citation, commencement and interpretation

1.–(1)   This order may be cited as the Rent Officers (Housing Benefit Functions) (Local Housing Allowance) Amendment Order 2005.

(2)   This article and articles 2, 3, 5 and 6 shall come into force on 13th March 2005.

(3)   Articles 4 and 7 shall come into force in relation to the area of a local authority specified in the Schedule to this Order on the date specified in that Schedule in relation to that local authority.

(4)   In this Order–

(a)   ''local authority'' has the same meaning as in the Social Security Administration Act 1992; and

(b)   ''the 2003 Order'' means the Rent Officers (Housing Benefit Functions) (Local Housing Allowance) Amendment Order 2003.

The Rent Officers (Housing Benefit Functions) Order 1997: additional pathfinder authorities

4.   The Rent Officers (Housing Benefit Functions) Order 1997 shall apply in relation to the area of a local authority in England and Wales specified in the Schedule to this Order as it applies in relation to the area of a local authority in England and Wales specified in Schedule 1 to the 2003 Order.

The Rent Officers (Housing Benefit Functions) (Scotland) Order 1997: additional pathfinder authorities

7.   The Rent Officers (Housing Benefit Functions) (Scotland) Order 1997 shall apply in relation to the area of a local authority in Scotland specified in the Schedule to this Order as it applies in relation to the area of a local authority in Scotland specified in Schedule 1 to the 2003 Order.

SCHEDULE

ARTICLE 1(5)

DATE ON WHICH ARTICLES 4 AND 7 COME INTO FORCE FOR LOCAL AUTHORITY AREAS

Relevant authority	*Date*
Argyll and Bute	25th April 2005
East Riding of Yorkshire	21st March 2005
Guildford	6th June 2005
Norwich	16th May 2005
Pembrokeshire	23rd May 2005
St Helens	25th April 2005
Salford	20th June 2005
South Norfolk	9th May 2005
Wandsworth	14th March 2005.

The Rent Officers (Housing Benefit Functions) Amendment Order 2007

(SI 2007 No.2871)

Citation, commencement and interpretation

1.–(1) This Order may be cited as the Rent Officers (Housing Benefit Functions) Amendment Order 2007.

(2) This article and articles 2 (application of the Rent Officers Order), 3 (amendment of the Rent Officers Order), 11 (application of the Rent Officers (Scotland) Order) and 12 (amendment of the Rent Officers (Scotland) Order) shall come into force on 20th March 2008.

(3)-(4) *Omitted.*

(5) In this Order–

"local authority" has the same meaning as in the Social Security Administration Act 1992;

"the Rent Officers Order" means the Rent Officers (Housing Benefit Functions) Order 1997; and

"the Rent Officers (Scotland) Order" means Rent Officers (Housing Benefit Functions) (Scotland) Order 1997.

Application of the Rent Officers Order

2. Those provisions of the Rent Officers Order which on 19th March 2008 apply only in relation to the area of a local authority listed in the Schedule, shall apply in the same way to the area of every other local authority in England and Wales.

Amendments to the Rent Officers Order relating to the local housing allowance coming into force on 7th April 2008 save for certain purposes

6.–(1) This article shall not apply where–

(a) a board and attendance determination, board and attendance redetermination, substitute board and attendance determination or substitute board and attendance redetermination is to be made and the application for the board and attendance determination or original board and attendance determination was made by virtue of regulation 13A(6) of the Housing Benefit Regulations 2006 or, as the case may be, regulation 13A(6) of the Housing Benefit (Persons who have attained the qualifying age for state pension credit) Regulations 2006 as in force immediately before 7th April 2008;

(b) a local housing allowance determination is to be made and the application was made by virtue of regulation 13A(4) or (5) of the Housing Benefit Regulations 2006 or, as the case may be, regulation 13A(4) or (5) of the Housing Benefit (Persons who have attained the qualifying age for state pension credit) Regulations 2006 as in force immediately before 7th April 2008; or

(c) an error in relation to a broad rental market area determination, local housing allowance determination, board and attendance determination or a board and attendance redetermination is to be corrected and the original determination was made in accordance with the Rent Officers Order as in force immediately before 7th April 2008.

(2) For the purpose of sub-paragraph (1)(c) "original determination" means the broad rental market area determination, local housing allowance determination, board and attendance determination or board and attendance redetermination to which the correction of an error relates.

(3)-(8) *[Omitted]*

Amendments to the Rent Officers Order relating to information sharing coming into force on 7th April 2008 save for certain purposes

7.–(1) This article shall not apply where information is provided to the rent officer by virtue of regulation 14 or 114 of the Housing Benefit Regulations 2006 or, as the case may be, regulation 14 or 95 of the Housing Benefit (Persons who have attained the qualifying age for state pension credit) Regulations 2006 as in force immediately before 7th April 2008.

(2)-(4) *[Omitted]*

Amendments to the Rent Officers Order relating to ineligible service charges coming into force on 7th April 2008 save for certain purposes

8.–(1) This article shall not apply where the rent officer is required to make a determination under paragraphs 1, 2, 3, or 6 of Part 1 of Schedule 1 to the Rent Officers Order by virtue of–

(a) an application made under–
- (i) regulation 14 of the Housing Benefit Regulations 2006 as in force before the substitution of regulation 14 by virtue of regulation 8 of the Housing Benefit (Local Housing Allowance and Information Sharing) Amendment Regulations 2007; or
- (ii) regulation 14 of the Housing Benefit (Persons who have attained the qualifying age for state pension credit) Regulations 2006 as in force before the substitution of regulation 14 by virtue of regulation 8 of the Housing Benefit (State Pension Credit) (Local Housing Allowance and Information Sharing) Amendment Regulations 2007; or

(b) an application for a redetermination, substitute determination or substitute redetermination relating to a determination to which sub-paragraph (a) applies made under regulation 15, 16 or 17 of the Regulations referred to in sub-paragraph (a)(i) or (ii).

(2) *[Omitted]*

Amendments to the Rent Officers Order relating to claim-related rent coming into force on 7th April 2008 save for certain purposes

9.–(1) This article shall not apply where the rent officer has made a determination under paragraphs 1, 2, 3, 4 or 5 of Part 1 of Schedule 1 to the Rent Officers Order and that determination was made in relation to–

(a) an application under–
- (i) regulation 14 of the Housing Benefit Regulations 2006 as in force before the substitution of regulation 14 by virtue of regulation 8 of the Housing Benefit (Local Housing Allowance and Information Sharing) Amendment Regulations 2007; or
- (ii) regulation 14 of the Housing Benefit (Persons who have attained the qualifying age for state pension credit) Regulations 2006 as in force before the substitution of regulation 14 by virtue of regulation 8 of the Housing Benefit (State Pension Credit) (Local Housing Allowance and Information Sharing) Amendment Regulations 2007; or

(b) an application for a redetermination, substitute determination or substitute redetermination relating to a determination to which sub-paragraph (a) applies made under regulation 15, 16 or 17 of the Regulations referred to in sub-paragraph (a)(i) or (ii).

(2)-(3) *[Omitted]*

Application of the Rent Officers (Scotland) Order

11. Those provisions of the Rent Officers (Scotland) Order which on 19th March 2008 apply only in relation to the areas of the local authority of Argyll and Bute and the local authority of Edinburgh, shall apply in the same way to the area of every other local authority in Scotland.

Amendments to the Rent Officers (Scotland) Order relating to the local housing allowance coming into force on 7th April 2008 save for certain purposes

15.–(1) This article shall not apply where–

(a) a board and attendance determination, board and attendance redetermination, substitute board and attendance determination or substitute board and attendance redetermination is to be made and the application for the board and attendance determination or original board and attendance determination was made by virtue of regulation 13A(6) of the Housing Benefit Regulations 2006 or, as the case may be, regulation 13A(6) of the Housing Benefit (Persons who have attained the qualifying age for state pension credit) Regulations 2006 as in force immediately before 7th April 2008;

(b) a local housing allowance determination is to be made and the application was made by virtue of regulation 13A(4) or (5) of the Housing Benefit Regulations 2006 or, as the case may be, regulation 13A(4) or (5) of the Housing Benefit (Persons who have attained the qualifying age for state pension credit) Regulations 2006 as in force immediately before 7th April 2008; or

(c) an error in relation to a broad rental market area determination, local housing allowance determination, board and attendance determination or a board and attendance redetermination is to be corrected and the original determination was made in accordance with the Rent Officers (Scotland) Order as in force immediately before 7th April 2008.

(2) For the purpose of sub-paragraph (1)(c) "original determination" means the broad rental market area determination, local housing allowance determination, board and attendance determination or board and attendance redetermination to which the correction of an error relates.

(3)-(8) *[Omitted]*

Amendments to the Rent Officers (Scotland) Order relating to information sharing coming into force on 7th April 2008

16.–(1) where information is provided to the rent officer by virtue of regulation 14 or 114 of the Housing Benefit Regulations 2006 or, as the case may be, regulation 14 or 95 of the Housing Benefit (Persons who have attained the qualifying age for state pension credit) Regulations 2006 as in force immediately before 7th April 2008.

(2)-(4) *[Omitted]*

Amendments to the Rent Officers (Scotland) Order relating to ineligible service charges coming into force on 7th April 2008 save for certain purposes

17.–(1) This article shall not apply where the rent officer is required to make a determination under paragraphs 1, 2, 3, or 6 of Part 1 of Schedule 1 to the Rent Officers (Scotland) Order by virtue of–

(a) an application made under–
  (i) regulation 14 of the Housing Benefit Regulations 2006 as in force before the substitution of regulation 14 by virtue of regulation 8 of the Housing Benefit (Local Housing Allowance and Information Sharing) Amendment Regulations 2007; or
  (ii) regulation 14 of the Housing Benefit (Persons who have attained the qualifying age for state pension credit) Regulations 2006 as in force before the substitution of regulation 14 by virtue of regulation 8 of the Housing Benefit (State Pension Credit) (Local Housing Allowance and Information Sharing) Amendment Regulations 2007; or

(b) an application for a redetermination, substitute determination or substitute redetermination relating to a determination to which sub-paragraph (a) applies made under regulation 15, 16 or 17 of the Regulations referred to in sub-paragraph (a)(i) or (ii).

(2) *[Omitted]*

Amendments to the Rent Officers (Scotland) Order relating to claim-related rent coming into force on 7th April 2008 save for certain purposes

18.–(1)   This article shall not apply where the rent officer has made a determination under paragraphs 1, 2, 3, 4 or 5 of Part 1 of Schedule 1 to the Rent Officers (Scotland) Order and that determination was made in relation to–

(a)   an application under–
  (i)   regulation 14 of the Housing Benefit Regulations 2006 as in force before the substitution of regulation 14 by virtue of regulation 8 of the Housing Benefit (Local Housing Allowance and Information Sharing) Amendment Regulations 2007; or
  (ii)   regulation 14 of the as in force before the substitution of regulation 14 by virtue of regulation 8 of the Housing Benefit (State Pension Credit) (Local Housing Allowance and Information Sharing) Amendment Regulations 2007; or

(b)   an application for a redetermination, substitute determination or substitute redetermination relating to a determination to which sub-paragraph (a) applies made under regulation 15, 16 or 17 of the Regulations referred to in sub-paragraph (a)(i) or (ii).

(2)-(3)   *[Omitted]*

SCHEDULE
ARTICLE 2
LISTED AUTHORITIES

Blackpool
Brighton and Hove
Conwy
Coventry
East Riding of Yorkshire
Guildford
Leeds
Lewisham
North East Lincolnshire
Norwich
Pembrokeshire
St Helens
Salford
South Norfolk
Teignbridge
Wandsworth

Part 3

Main secondary legislation
Council tax benefit

The Council Tax Benefit Regulations 2006
(SI 2006 No.215)

Arrangement of Regulations

PART 1
General
1.   Citation and commencement
2.   Interpretation
3.   Definition of non-dependant
4.   Disapplication of section 1(1A) of the Administration Act
5.   Persons who have attained the qualifying age for state pension credit
6.   Remunerative work
7.   Persons from abroad
7A.   Entitlement of a refugee to council tax benefit
8.   Prescribed persons for the purposes of section 131(3)(b) of the Act

PART 2
Membership of a family
9.   Persons of prescribed description for the definition of family in section 137(1) of the Act
10.   Circumstances in which a person is to be treated as responsible or not responsible for another
11.   Circumstances in which a person is to be treated as being or not being a member of the household

PART 3
Applicable amounts
12.   Applicable amounts
13.   Polygamous marriages
14.   Patients

PART 4
Income and capital
SECTION 1
General
15.   Calculation of income and capital of members of claimant's family and of a polygamous marriage
16.   Circumstances in which capital and income of non-dependant is to be treated as claimant's

SECTION 2
Income
17.   Calculation of income on a weekly basis
18.   Treatment of child care charges
19.   Average weekly earnings of employed earners
20.   Average weekly earnings of self-employed earners
21.   Average weekly income other than earnings
22.   Calculation of average weekly income from tax credits
23.   Calculation of weekly income
24.   Disregard of changes in tax, contributions etc

SECTION 3
Employed earners
25.   Earnings of employed earners
26.   Calculation of net earnings of employed earners

SECTION 4
Self-employed earners
27.   Earnings of self-employed earners
28.   Calculation of net profit of self-employed earners
29.   Deduction of tax and contributions of self-employed earners

SECTION 5
Other income
30.   Calculation of income other than earnings
31.   Capital treated as income
32.   Notional income

SECTION 6
Capital
33.   Capital limit
34.   Calculation of capital
35.   Disregard of capital of child and young person
36.   Income treated as capital
37.   Calculation of capital in the United Kingdom
38.   Calculation of capital outside the United Kingdom
39.   Notional capital
40.   Diminishing notional capital rule
41.   Capital jointly held
42.   Calculation of tariff income from capital

PART 5
Students
SECTION 1
General
43.   Interpretation
44.   Treatment of students
45.   Students who are excluded from entitlement to council tax benefit

SECTION 2
Income
46.   Calculation of grant income
47.   Calculation of covenant income where a contribution is assessed
48.   Covenant income where no grant income or no contribution is assessed
49.   Relationship with amounts to be disregarded under Schedule 4
50.   Other amounts to be disregarded
51.   Treatment of student loans
51A.   Treatment of fee loans
52.   Treatment of payments from access funds
53.   Disregard of contribution
54.   Further disregard of student's income
55.   Income treated as capital
56.   Disregard of changes occurring during summer vacation

PART 6
Amount of benefit
57.   Maximum council tax benefit
58.   Non-dependant deductions
59.   Council tax benefit taper
60.   Extended payments
60A.   Duration of extended payment period
60B.   Amount of extended payment
60C.   Extended payments – movers

60D. Relationship between extended payment and entitlement to housing benefit under the general conditions of entitlement
61. Extended payments (qualifying contributory benefits)
61A. Duration of extended payment period (qualifying contributory benefits)
61B. Amount of extended payment (qualifying contributory benefits)
61C. Extended payments (qualifying contributory benefits) – movers
61D. Relationship between extended payment (qualifying contributory benefits) and entitlement to housing benefit under the general conditions of entitlement
62. Alternative maximum council tax benefit
63. Residents of a dwelling to whom section 131(6) of the Act does not apply

PART 7
Changes of circumstances and increases for exceptional circumstances
64. Date on which entitlement is to begin
65. Date on which council tax benefit is to end
66. Date on which council tax benefit is to end where entitlement to severe disablement allowance or incapacity benefit ceases
67. Date on which change of circumstances is to take effect

PART 8
Claims
68. Who may claim
69. Time and manner in which claims are to be made
69A. Electronic claims for benefit
70. Date of claim where claim sent or delivered to a gateway office
71. Date of claim where claim sent or delivered to an office of a designated authority
72. Evidence and information
73. Amendment and withdrawal of claim
74. Duty to notify changes of circumstances
74A. Notice of change of circunstances given electrinically

PART 9
Decisions on questions
75. Decisions by a relevant authority
76. Notification of decision

PART 10
Awards or payments of benefit
77. Time and manner of granting council tax benefit
78. Persons to whom benefit is to be paid
79. Shortfall in benefit
80. Payment on the death of the person entitled
81. Offsetting

PART 11
Excess benefit
82. Meaning of excess benefit
83. Recoverable excess benefit
84. Authority by which recovery may be made
85. Persons from whom recovery may be sought
86. Methods of recovery
87. Further provision as to recovery of excess benefit
88. Diminution of capital
89. Sums to be deducted in calculating recoverable excess benefit
90. Recovery of excess benefit from prescribed benefits

PART 12
Information
SECTION 1
Claims and information
91.   Interpretation
92.   Collection of information
92A.   Verifying information
93.   Recording and holding information
94.   Forwarding of information
95.   Request for information

SECTION 2
Information between authorities etc.
96.   Information to be supplied by an authority to another authority
97.   Supply of information – extended payments (qualifying contributory benefits)
98.   Supply of benefit administration information between authorities

SCHEDULES
A1.   Treatment of claims for council tax benefit by refugees
1.   Applicable amounts
2.   Amount of alternative maximum council tax benefit
3.   Sums to be disregarded in the calculation of earnings
4.   Sums to be disregarded in the calculation of income other than earnings
5.   Capital to be disregarded
6.   Extended payments of council tax benefit
7.   Extended payments (severe disablement allowance and incapacity benefit) of council tax benefit
8.   Matters to be included in decision notice
9.   Electronic communication

General Note

These regulations are largely similar to the Housing Benefit Regulations 2006 (SI 2006 No.213, referred to below as "the HB Regs"). Where a regulation is substantially the same as a corresponding regulation in the HB Regs, no commentary appears below and reference should be made to the table on pxxxii to ascertain the comparable HB regulation.

PART 1
General

Citation and commencement
    1.–(1)   These Regulations may be cited as the Council Tax Benefit Regulations 2006.
    (2)   These Regulations are to be read, where appropriate, with the Consequential Provisions Regulations.
    (3)   Except as provided in Schedule 4 to the Consequential Provisions Regulations, these Regulations shall come into force on 6th March 2006.
    (4)   The regulations consolidated by these Regulations are revoked, in consequence of the consolidation, by the Consequential Provisions Regulations.

Interpretation
    2.–(1)   In these Regulations–
"the Act" means the Social Security Contributions and Benefits Act 1992;
"the Administration Act" means the Social Security Administration Act 1992;
"the 1973 Act" means the Employment and Training Act 1973;
"the 1992 Act" means the Local Government Finance Act 1992;
[¹ "the 2000 Act" means the Electronic Communications Act 2000;]

"Abbeyfield Home" means an establishment run by the Abbeyfield Society including all bodies corporate or incorporate which are affiliated to that Society;

"adoption leave" means a period of absence from work on ordinary or additional adoption leave by virtue of section 75A or 75B of the Employment Rights Act 1996;

"alternative maximum council tax benefit" means the amount determined in accordance with regulation 62 and Schedule 2;

"appropriate DWP office" means an office of the Department for Work and Pensions dealing with state pension credit or claim office which is normally open to the public for the receipt of claims for income support [¹¹ , a jobseeker's allowance or an employment and support allowance];

"assessment period" means such period as is prescribed in regulations 19 to 21 over which income falls to be calculated;

"attendance allowance" means–

    (a)   an attendance allowance under Part 3 of the Act;

    (b)   an increase of disablement pension under section 104 or 105 of the Act;

    (c)   a payment under regulations made in exercise of the power conferred by paragraph 7(2)(b) of Part 2 of Schedule 8 to the Act;

    (d)   an increase of an allowance which is payable in respect of constant attendance under paragraph 4 of Part 1 of Schedule 8 to the Act;

    (e)   a payment by virtue of article 14, 15, 16, 43 or 44 of the Personal Injuries (Civilians) Scheme 1983 or any analogous payment; or

    (f)   any payment based on need for attendance which is paid as part of a war disablement pension;

[¹⁷ "basic rate", where it relates to the rate of tax, has the same meaning as in the Income Tax Act 2007 (see section 989 of that Act).]

"the benefit Acts" means the Act [¹² , the Jobseekers Act and the Welfare Reform Act];

"benefit week" means a period of 7 consecutive days commencing upon a Monday and ending on a Sunday;

"care home" in England and Wales has the meaning assigned to it by section 3 of the Care Standards Act 2000 and in Scotland means a care home service within the meaning assigned to it by section 2(3) of the Regulation of Care (Scotland) Act 2001;

"child" means a person under the age of 16;

"child tax credit" means a child tax credit under section 8 of the Tax Credits Act;

"the Children Order" means the Children (Northern Ireland) Order 1995;

"claim" means a claim for council tax benefit;

"claimant" means a person claiming council tax benefit;

"close relative" means a parent, parent-in-law, son, son-in-law, daughter, daughter-in-law, step-parent, step-son, step-daughter, brother, sister, or if any of the preceding persons is one member of a couple, the other member of that couple;

"community charge benefit" means community charge benefits under Part 7 of the Act as originally enacted;

[¹³ "contributory employment and support allowance" means a contributory allowance under Part 1 of the Welfare Reform Act;]

[²⁸ "converted employment and support allowance" means an employment and support allowance which is not income-related and to which a person is entitled as a result of a conversion decision within the meaning of the Employment and Support Allowance (Existing Awards) Regulations;]

"concessionary payment" means a payment made under arrangements made by the Secretary of State with the consent of the Treasury which is charged either to the National Insurance Fund or to a Departmental Expenditure Vote to which payments of benefit [¹⁵ or tax credits under the benefit Acts or the Tax Credits Act] are charged;

"the Consequential Provisions Regulations" means the Housing Benefit and Council Tax Benefit (Consequential Provisions) Regulations 2006;

"council tax benefit" means council tax benefit under Part 7 of the Act;

"couple" means–
  (a)   a man and a woman who are married to each other and are members of the same household;
  (b)   a man and a woman who are not married to each other but are living together as husband and wife;
  (c)   two people of the same sex who are civil partners of each other and are members of the same household; or
  (d)   two people of the same sex who are not civil partners of each other but are living together as if they were civil partners,
         and for the purposes of sub-paragraph (d), two people of the same sex are to be regarded as living together as if they were civil partners if, but only if, they would be regarded as living together as husband and wife were they instead two people of the opposite sex;
"date of claim" means the date on which the claim is made, or treated as made, for the purposes of regulation 69 (time and manner in which claims are to be made);
"the Decisions and Appeals Regulations" means the Housing Benefit and Council Tax Benefit (Decisions and Appeals) Regulations 2001;
"designated authority" means any of the following–
  (a)   the Secretary of State;
  (b)   a person providing services to the Secretary of State;
  (c)   a local authority;
  (d)   a person providing services to, or authorised to exercise any function of, any such authority;
"designated office" means the office designated by the relevant authority for the receipt of claims to council tax benefit–
  (a)   by notice upon or with a form approved by it for the purpose of claiming council tax benefit; or
  (b)   by reference upon or with such a form to some other document available from it and sent by electronic means or otherwise on application and without charge; or
  (c)   by any combination of the provisions set out in sub-paragraphs (a) and (b) above;
"disability living allowance" means a disability living allowance under section 71 of the Act;
"dwelling" has the same meaning in section 3 or 72 of the 1992 Act;
"earnings" has the meaning prescribed in regulation 25 or, as the case may be, 27;
"the Eileen Trust" means the charitable trust of that name established on 29th March 1993 out of funds provided by the Secretary of State for the benefit of persons eligible for payment in accordance with its provisions;
[¹ "electronic communication" has the same meaning as in section 15(1) of the 2000 Act;]
"employed earner" is to be construed in accordance with section 2(1)(a) of the Act and also includes a person who is in receipt of a payment which is payable under any enactment having effect in Northern Ireland and which corresponds to statutory sick pay or statutory maternity pay;
[¹³ "Employment and Support Allowance Regulations" means the Employment and Support Allowance Regulations 2008;]
[²⁸ "Employment and Support Allowance (Existing Awards) Regulations" means the Employment and Support Allowance (Transitional Provisions, Housing Benefit and Council Tax Benefit) (Existing Awards) (No. 2) Regulations 2010;]
"employment zone" means an area within Great Britain designated for the purposes of section 60 of the Welfare Reform and Pensions Act 1999 and an "employment zone programme" means a programme established for such an area or areas designed to assist claimants for a jobseeker's allowance to obtain sustainable employment;
"employment zone contractor" means a person who is undertaking the provision of facilities in respect of an employment zone programme on behalf of the Secretary of State for Work and Pensions;

[²¹ "enactment" includes an enactment comprised in, or in an instrument made under, an Act of the Scottish Parliament;]

[⁹ "extended payment" means a payment of council tax benefit payable pursuant to regulation 60;]

[¹⁰ "extended payment period" means the period for which an extended payment is payable in accordance with regulation 60A or 61A;]

[⁹ "extended payment (qualifying contributory benefits)" means a payment of council tax benefit payable pursuant to regulation 61;]

"family" has the meaning assigned to it by section 137(1) of the Act;

"the Fund" means moneys made available from time to time by the Secretary of State for the benefit of persons eligible for payment in accordance with the provisions of a scheme established by him on 24th April 1992 or, in Scotland, on 10th April 1992;

[¹¹]

"a guaranteed income payment" means a payment made under article 14(1)(b) or article 21(1)(a) of the Armed Forces and Reserve Forces (Compensation Scheme) Order 2005;

"housing benefit" means housing benefit under Part 7 of the Act;

"the Housing Benefit Regulations" means the Housing Benefit Regulations 2006;

"Immigration and Asylum Act" means the Immigration and Asylum Act 1999;

"an income-based jobseeker's allowance" and "a joint-claim jobseeker's allowance" have the same meaning as they have in the Jobseekers Act by virtue of section 1(4) of that Act;

[¹³ "income-related employment and support allowance" means an income-related allowance under Part 1 of the Welfare Reform Act;]

"Income Support Regulations" means the Income Support (General) Regulations 1987;

[²⁹ "independent hospital"–
    (a)   in England, means a hospital as defined by section 275 of the National Health Service Act 2006 that is not a health service hospital as defined by that section;
    (b)   in Wales, has the meaning assigned to it by section 2 of the Care Standards Act 2000; and
    (c)   in Scotland, means an independent healthcare service as defined in section 2(5)(a) and (b) of the Regulation of Care (Scotland) Act 2001;]

[¹⁴]

[⁴ "the Independent Living Fund (2006)" means the Trust of that name established by a deed dated 10th April 2006 and made between the Secretary of State for Work and Pensions of the one part and Margaret Rosemary Cooper, Michael Beresford Boyall and Marie Theresa Martin of the other part;]

[¹⁴]
[¹⁴]
[¹⁴]
[⁷]

"invalid carriage or other vehicle" means a vehicle propelled by a petrol engine or by electric power supplied for use on the road and to be controlled by the occupant;

"Jobseekers Act" means the Jobseekers Act 1995;

"Jobseeker's Allowance Regulations" means the Jobseeker's Allowance Regulations 1996;

[¹³ "limited capability for work" has the meaning given in section 1(4) of the Welfare Reform Act;]

[¹³ "limited capability for work-related activity" has the meaning given in section 2(5) of the Welfare Reform Act;]

"the London Bombings Relief Charitable Fund" means the company limited by guarantee (number 5505072), and registered charity of that name established on 11th July 2005 for the purpose of (amongst other things) relieving sickness, disability or financial need of victims (including families or dependants of victims) of the terrorist attacks carried out in London on 7th July 2005;

"lone parent" means a person who has no partner and who is responsible for and a member of the same household as a child or young person;

[6]

"the Macfarlane (Special Payments) Trust" means the trust of that name, established on 29th January 1990 partly out of funds provided by the Secretary of State, for the benefit of certain persons suffering from haemophilia;

"the Macfarlane (Special Payments) (No. 2) Trust" means the trust of that name, established on 3rd May 1991 partly out of funds provided by the Secretary of State, for the benefit of certain persons suffering from haemophilia and other beneficiaries;

"the Macfarlane Trust" means the charitable trust, established partly out of funds provided by the Secretary of State to the Haemophilia Society, for the relief of poverty or distress among those suffering from haemophilia;

[13 "main phase employment and support allowance" means an employment and support allowance where the calculation of the amount payable in respect of the claimant includes a component under section 2(1)(b) or 4(2)(b) of the Welfare Reform Act [18 except in Part 1 of Schedule 1]]

"maternity leave" means a period during which a woman is absent from work because she is pregnant or has given birth to a child, and at the end of which she has a right to return to work either under the terms of her contract of employment or under Part 8 of the Employment Rights Act 1996;

"member of a couple" means a member of a married or unmarried couple;

[22 "MFET Limited" means the company limited by guarantee (number 7121661) of that name, established for the purpose in particular of making payments in accordance with arrangements made with the Secretary of State to persons who have acquired HIV as a result of treatment by the NHS with blood or blood products;]

"mobility supplement" means a supplement to which paragraph 9 of Schedule 4 refers;

[10 "mover" means a claimant who changes the dwelling in which the claimant is resident and in respect of which the claimant liable to pay council tax from a dwelling in the area of the appropriate authority to a dwelling in the area of the second authority;]

"net earnings" means such earnings as are calculated in accordance with regulation 26;

"net profit" means such profit as is calculated in accordance with regulation 28;

"the New Deal options" means the employment programmes specified in regulation 75(1)(a)(ii) of the Jobseeker's Allowance Regulations and the training scheme specified in regulation 75(1)(b)(ii) of those Regulations;

[10 "new dwelling" means, for the purposes of the definition of "second authority" and regulations 60C, 61C, 96 and 97, the dwelling to which a claimant has moved, or is about to move, in which the claimant is or will be resident;]

"non-dependant" has the meaning prescribed in regulation 3;

"non-dependant deduction" means a deduction that is to be made under regulation 58;

"occupational pension" means any pension or other periodical payment under an occupational pension scheme but does not include any discretionary payment out of a fund established for relieving hardship in particular cases;

"ordinary clothing or footwear" means clothing or footwear for normal daily use, but does not include school uniforms, or clothing or footwear used solely for sporting activities;

"partner" means–
  (a) where a claimant is a member of a couple, the other member of that couple; or
  (b) where a claimant is polygamously married to two or more members of his household, any such member to whom he is married;

"paternity leave" means a period of absence from work on leave by virtue of section 80A or 80B of the Employment Rights Act 1996;

"payment" includes part of a payment;

"pension fund holder" means with respect to a personal pension scheme or [3 an occupational pension scheme], the trustees, managers or scheme administrators, as the case may be, of the scheme [3] concerned;

"person affected" shall be construed in accordance with regulation 3 of the Decisions
    and Appeals Regulations;
"person on income support" means a person in receipt of income support;
[⁸]
[³ "personal pension scheme" means–
    (a)   a personal pension scheme as defined by section 1 of the Pension Schemes Act
            1993;
    (b)   an annuity contract or trust scheme approved under section 620 or 621 of the
            Income and Corporation Taxes Act 1988 or a substituted contract within the
            meaning of section 622(3) of that Act which is treated as having become a
            registered pension scheme by virtue of paragraph 1(1)(f) of Schedule 36 to the
            Finance Act 2004;
    (c)   a personal pension scheme approved under Chapter 4 of Part 14 of the Income
            and Corporation Taxes Act 1988 which is treated as having become a registered
            pension scheme by virtue of paragraph 1(1)(g) of Schedule 36 to the Finance
            Act 2004;]
"policy of life insurance" means any instrument by which the payment of money is
    assured on death (except death by accident only) or the happening of any
    contingency dependent on human life, or any instrument evidencing a contract
    which is subject to payment of premiums for a term dependent on human life;
"polygamous marriage" means a marriage to which section 133(1) of the Act refers;
[²¹ "public authority" includes any person certain of whose functions are functions of a
    public nature;]
"qualifying age for state pension credit" means (in accordance with section 1(2)(b) and
    (6) of the State Pension Credit Act)–
    (a)   in the case of a woman, pensionable age; or
    (b)   in the case of a man, the age which is pensionable age in the case of a woman
            born on the same day as the man;
[¹⁰ "qualifying contributory benefit" means–
    (a)   severe disablement allowance;
    (b)   incapacity benefit;]
        [¹² (c) contributory employment and support allowance;]
[¹⁰ "qualifying income-related benefit" means–
    (a)   income support;
    (b)   income-based jobseeker's allowance;]
        [¹² (c) income-related employment and support allowance;]
"qualifying person" means a person in respect of whom payment has been made from
    the Fund, the Eileen Trust, [²³ MFET Limited], the Skipton Fund or the London
    Bombings Relief Charitable Fund;
"relative" means a close relative, grandparent, grandchild, uncle, aunt, nephew or niece;
"relevant authority" means an authority administering council tax benefit;
"remunerative work" has the meaning prescribed in regulation 6;
"rent" means "eligible rent" to which regulation 12 of the Housing Benefit Regulations
    refers less any deductions in respect of non-dependants which fall to be made
    under regulation 74 (non-dependant deductions) of those Regulations;
"resident" has the meaning it has in Part 1 or 2 of the 1992 Act;
[³]
"second adult" has the meaning given to it in Schedule 2;
[¹⁰ "second authority" means the authority to which a mover is liable to make payments
    for the new dwelling;]
"self-employed earner" is to be construed in accordance with section 2(1)(b) of the Act;
"self-employment route" means assistance in pursuing self-employed earner's employ-
    ment whilst participating in–
    (a)   an employment zone programme; or
    (b)   a programme provided or other arrangements made pursuant to section 2 of the
            1973 Act (functions of the Secretary of State) or section 2 of the Enterprise and

New Towns (Scotland) Act 1990 (functions in relation to training for employment, etc.); [*or*]

[(c) the Work for Your Benefit Pilot Scheme;]

[21 "service user group" means a group of individuals that is consulted by or on behalf of–

(a) a Health Board, Special Health Board or the Agency in consequence of a function under section 2B of the National Health Service (Scotland) Act 1978,

(b) a landlord authority in consequence of a function under section 105 of the Housing Act 1985,

(c) a public authority in consequence of a function under section 49A of the Disability Discrimination Act 1995,

(d) a best value authority in consequence of a function under section 3 of the Local Government Act 1999,

(e) a local authority landlord or registered social landlord in consequence of a function under section 53 of the Housing (Scotland) Act 2001,

(f) a relevant English body or a relevant Welsh body in consequence of a function under section 242 of the National Health Service Act 2006,

(g) a Local Health Board in consequence of a function under section 183 of the National Health Service (Wales) Act 2006,

(h) the Commission or the Office of the Health Professions Adjudicator in consequence of a function under sections 4, 5, or 108 of the Health and Social Care Act 2008,

(i) the regulator or a [26 private registered provider of social housing] in consequence of a function under sections 98, 193 or 196 of the Housing and Regeneration Act 2008, or

(j) a public or local authority in Great Britain in consequence of a function conferred under any other enactment,

for the purposes of monitoring and advising on a policy of that body or authority which affects or may affect persons in the group, or of monitoring or advising on services provided by that body or authority which are used (or may potentially be used) by those persons;]

"single claimant" means a claimant who neither has a partner nor is a lone parent;

"the Skipton Fund" means the ex-gratia payment scheme administered by the Skipton Fund Limited, incorporated on 25th March 2004, for the benefit of certain persons suffering from hepatitis C and other persons eligible for payment in accordance with the scheme's provisions;

[22 "special account" means an account as defined for the purposes of Chapter 4A of Part 8 of the Jobseeker's Allowance Regulations or Chapter 5 of Part 10 of the Employment and Support Allowance Regulations;]

"sports award" means an award made by one of the Sports Councils named in section 23(2) of the National Lottery etc Act 1993 out of sums allocated to it for distribution under that section;

[5 [19]]

"State Pension Credit Act" means the State Pension Credit Act 2002;

"student" has the meaning prescribed in regulation 43;

"subsistence allowance" means an allowance which an employment zone contractor has agreed to pay to a person who is participating in an employment zone programme;

[7]

"the Tax Credits Act" means the Tax Credits Act 2002;

"training allowance" means an allowance (whether by way of periodical grants or otherwise) payable–

(a) out of public funds by a Government department or by or on behalf of the Secretary of State, [20 Skills Development Scotland,] Scottish Enterprise or Highlands and Islands Enterprise, the [30 Young People's Learning Agency for England, the Chief Executive of Skills Funding] or the [15 Welsh Ministers];

(b) to a person for his maintenance or in respect of a member of his family; and

    (c)   for the period, or part of the period, during which he is following a course of training or instruction provided by, or in pursuance of arrangements made with, that department or approved by that department in relation to him or so provided or approved by or on behalf of the Secretary of State, [20 Skills Development Scotland,] Scottish Enterprise or Highlands and Islands Enterprise or the [15 Welsh Ministers],

but it does not include an allowance paid by any Government department to or in respect of a person by reason of the fact that he is following a course of full-time education, other than under arrangements made under section 2 of the 1973 Act or is training as a teacher;

"the Trusts" means the Macfarlane Trust, the Macfarlane (Special Payments) Trust and the Macfarlane (Special Payments) (No. 2) Trust;

"voluntary organisation" means a body, other than a public or local authority, the activities of which are carried on otherwise than for profit;

[2]

[20 "war disablement pension" means any retired pay or pension or allowance payable in respect of disablement under an instrument specified in section 639(2) of the Income Tax (Earnings and Pensions) Act 2003;

"war pension" means a war disablement pension, a war widow's pension or a war widower's pension;

"war widow's pension" means any pension or allowance payable to a woman as a widow under an instrument specified in section 639(2) of the Income Tax (Earnings and Pensions) Act 2003 in respect of the death or disablement of any person;

"war widower's pension" means any pension or allowance payable to a man as a widower or to a surviving civil partner under an instrument specified in section 639(2) of the Income Tax (Earnings and Pensions) Act 2003 in respect of the death or disablement of any person;]

"water charges" means–

    (a)   as respects England and Wales, any water and sewerage charges under Chapter 1 of Part 5 of the Water Industry Act 1991,

    (b)   as respects Scotland, any water and sewerage charges established by Scottish Water under a charges scheme made under section 29A of the Water Industry (Scotland) Act 2002,

            in so far as such charges are in respect of the dwelling which a person occupies as his home;

[13 "Welfare Reform Act" means the Welfare Reform Act 2007;]

[*"the Work for Your Benefit Pilot Scheme" means a scheme within section 17A(1) of the Jobseekers Act 1995 known by that name and provided pursuant to arrangements made by the Secretary of State that is designed to assist claimants to obtain employment, including self-employment, and which includes for any individual work experience and job search;*]

"working tax credit" means a working tax credit under section 10 of the Tax Credits Act;

"Working Tax Credit Regulations" means the Working Tax Credit (Entitlement and Maximum Rate) Regulations 2002; and

"young person" has the meaning prescribed in regulation 9(1).

    (2)   In these Regulations, references to a claimant occupying a dwelling or premises as his home shall be construed in accordance with regulation 7 of the Housing Benefit Regulations.

    (3)   In these Regulations, where an amount is to be rounded to the nearest penny, a fraction of a penny shall be disregarded if it is less than half a penny and shall otherwise be treated as a whole penny.

    (4)   For the purpose of these Regulations, a person is on an income-based jobseeker's allowance on any day in respect of which an income-based jobseeker's allowance is payable to him and on any day–

    (a)   in respect of which he satisfies the conditions for entitlement to an income-based jobseeker's allowance but where the allowance is not paid in accordance with

[²⁵ regulation 27A of the Jobseeker's Allowance Regulations or] section 19 or 20A *[or regulations made under section 17A]* of the Jobseekers Act (circumstances in which a jobseeker's allowance is not payable); or

(b)   which is a waiting day for the purposes of paragraph 4 of Schedule 1 to that Act and which falls immediately before a day in respect of which an income-based jobseeker's allowance is payable to him or would be payable to him but for [²⁵ regulation 27A of the Jobseeker's Allowance Regulations or] section 19 or 20A *[or regulations made under section 17A]* that Act;

(c)   in respect of which he is a member of a joint-claim couple for the purposes of the Jobseekers Act and no joint-claim jobseeker's allowance is payable in respect of that couple as a consequence of either member of that couple being subject to sanctions for the purposes of section 20A of that Act;

(d)   in respect of which an income-based jobseeker's allowance or a joint-claim jobseeker's allowance would be payable but for a restriction imposed pursuant to [²⁴] section [²⁷ 6B,] 7, 8 or 9 of the Social Security Fraud Act 2001 (loss of benefit provisions).

[¹³ (4A)   For the purposes of these Regulations, a person is on an income-related employment and support allowance on any day in respect of which an income-related employment and support allowance is payable to him and on any day–

(a)   in respect of which he satisfies the conditions for entitlement to an income-related employment and support allowance but where the allowance is not paid in accordance with section 18 of the Welfare Reform Act (disqualification); or

(b)   which is a waiting day for the purposes of paragraph 2 of Schedule 2 to that Act and which falls immediately before a day in respect of which an income-related employment and support allowance is payable to him or would be payable to him but for section 18 of that Act.].

(5)   For the purposes of these Regulations, two persons shall be taken to be estranged only if their estrangement constitutes a breakdown of the relationship between them.

(6)   In these Regulations, references to any person in receipt of state pension credit includes a person who would be in receipt of state pension credit but for regulation 13 of the State Pension Credit Regulations 2002 (small amounts of state pension credit).

Modifications

References to "step-parent", step-children and the various in-laws in the definition of "close relative" are modified by s246 Civil Partnership Act 2004 and Art 3 and para 44 of the Schedule to SI 2005 No.3137 (see pp1148 and 1195).

Reg 2(1) and reg 2(4) are modified by regs 13 and 19 Jobseeker's Allowance (Work for Your Benefit Pilot Scheme) Regulations 2010 SI No.1222 (see p1247) as from 22 November 2010 but only for those ordinarily resident in a pilot area or whose address for payment of JSA is located within such an area. The modifications are shown in italics above. They cease to have effect on 21 November 2013.

Amendments

1.   Inserted by Art 4(2) of SI 2006 No 2968 as from 20.12.06.
2.   Omitted by Reg 5(a) of SI 2007 No 1619 as from 3.7.07.
3.   Amended by reg 6(2) of SI 2007 No 1749 as from 16.7.07.
4.   Amended by Art 9(2) of SI 2007 No 2538 as from 16.7.07.
5.   Inserted by reg 13(2) of SI 2007 No 2618 as from 1.10.07.
6.   Revoked by reg 2 and the Sch of SI 2007 No 2618 as from 1.10.07.
7.   Omitted by reg 7(2) of SI 2008 No 698 as from 14.4.08.
8.   Amended by reg 5(2) of SI 2008 No 1042 as from 19.5.08.
9.   Substituted by reg 9(2) of SI 2008 No 959 as from 6.10.08.
10.   Amended by reg 9(2) of SI 2008 No 959 as from 6.10.08.
11.   Omitted by reg 4(2) of SI 2008 No 2299 as from 1.10.08.
12.   Amended by reg 43(2) of SI 2008 No 1082 as from 27.10.08.
13.   Inserted by reg 43(2) of SI 2008 No 1082, as amended by reg 36 of SI 2008 No 2428, as from 27.10.08.
14.   Amended by reg 8(2) of SI 2008 No 2767 as from 17.11.08.
15.   Amended by reg 7(2) of SI 2008 No 3157 as from 5.1.09.
16.   Inserted by reg 7(2) of SI 2008 No 3157 as from 5.1.09.
17.   Inserted by reg 8(2)(a) of SI 2009 No 583 as from 6.4.09.
18.   Amended by reg 8(2)(b) of SI 2009 No 583 as from 1.4.09.

19. Omitted by reg 8(2)(c) of SI 2009 No 583 as from 6.4.09.
20. Amended by reg 8(3)(a) of SI 2009 No 583 as from 6.4.09.
21. Inserted by reg 8(2) of SI 2009 No 2655 as from 2.11.09.
22. Inserted by reg 10(2) of SI 2010 No 641 as from 1.4.10 (5.4.10 where rent payable weekly or in multiples of a week).
23. Amended by reg 10(3) of SI 2010 No 641 as from 1.4.10 (5.4.10 where rent payable weekly or in multiples of a week).
24. Amended by reg 10 of SI 2010 No 424 as from 2.4.10.
25. Amended by reg 4(1)(c) and (2) of SI 2010 No 509 as from 6.4.10.
26. Amended by Art 4 and Sch 1 para 62 of SI 2010 No 671 as from 1.4.10.
27. Amended by reg 6 of SI 2010 No 1160 as from 1.4.10.
28. Inserted by reg 27 and Sch 5 para 2(2) of SI 2010 No 1907 as amended by reg 15 of SI 2010 No 2430 as from 1.10.10.
29. Substituted by Arts 2 and 22 of SI 2010 No 1881 as from 1.10.10.
30. Amended by Art 16(2) of SI 2010 No 1941 as from 1.9.10.

Analysis
Paragraph (1)
Many of the definitions in para (1) are shared with those for HB. Commentary is only given below on those that are unique to CTB. Reference should be made to the commentary to reg 2(1) HB Regs (see p221) for analysis of definitions that are common to HB and CTB.

"dwelling" – England and Wales definition. Section 3 Local Government Finance Act 1992 (the 1992 Act) provides that a dwelling for council tax and hence CTB purposes is any property which fulfils the following criteria.
(1) It would have been a hereditament (ie, a unit of accommodation) for the purposes of the General Rate Act 1967.
(2) It is not shown or required to be shown in local or a central non-domestic rating list.
(3) It is not exempt from local non-domestic rating.
A building is also a "dwelling" if it is a "composite hereditament" – ie, only part is used wholly for the purpose of living accommodation. Houses, flats, bungalows, cottages and maisonettes all normally count as dwellings. The pitch occupied by a caravan or a mooring occupied by a boat may also count as a dwelling, though holiday caravans and the like used for non-domestic purposes are subject to non-domestic rates.

"dwelling" – Scotland definition. In Scotland, by s72 of the 1992 Act a "dwelling" means any lands and heritages which fulfil the following criteria.
(1) It consists of one or more dwelling-houses with any garden, yard, garage, outhouse or pertinent other area belonging to and occupied with such dwelling-house or dwelling-houses.
(2) It would, but for the fact that it is a dwelling, be entered separately in the valuation roll. The valuation roll now only records the details of non-domestic and part residential subjects.
The Scottish dwelling includes the residential part of part residential subjects and that part of any premises which has been apportioned, as at 1 April 1989, as a dwelling house. It includes caravans but only if they are the sole or main residence. Certain types of property are explicitly included in or excluded from the Scottish definition of a dwelling by statutory instruments – eg, women's refuges by SI 1992 No.2955.

"resident". See ss6(5) (on p1113) and 99(1) of the 1992 Act.
"Resident" is defined in both the subsections as "an individual who has attained the age of 18 years and has his sole or main residence in the dwelling".

The critical part of the definition is the term "sole or main residence". This is not defined in the legislation, but there is a body of caselaw in relation to council tax and the community charge, which uses the same expression. In *Stevenson v Rogers* [1992] SLT 558, IH, it was said that the principal consideration in identifying a person's "main residence" was the length of time s/he spent in each place. This has to be read with the Court of Appeal decision in *Williams v Horsham District Council* [2004] EWCA Civ 39, 21 January, CA, which, drawing on *Frost v Feltham* [1981] 1 WLR 455 (and the latter's apparent acceptance that "main" means "principal" or "most important"), concludes that "sole or main residence" refers to premises in which a person actually resides rather than the dwelling itself. The Court of Appeal went on to state that it is probably impossible to produce a definition of "main residence" that will provide the appropriate test in all circumstances. However, the Court of Appeal said that usually a person's main residence will be the dwelling that a reasonable onlooker, with knowledge of the material facts, would regard as the person's home at the material time. Arguably, the factors identified in the cases below may now be seen as material facts which the hypothetical reasonable onlooker would be expected to have regard to under the *Williams* test.

Ownership of a dwelling is not equivalent to residence, and an owner of a dwelling is not, without more, resident in it: *Parry v Derbyshire Dales District Council* [2006] EWHC 988 (Admin), 5 May, unreported.

That case also decides (a) (see immediately following paragraph) that security of tenure may be relevant to the question whether the property is the person's main residence but is not relevant to whether s/he in fact resides there and (b) (see last but one paragraph on "resident" below) that Mr Parry ceased to reside in the property in question when he went abroad for a protracted period and let the property for two years.

The question of whether different accommodation was rented or owned was said in *Stevenson* to be irrelevant, though a comparison of security of tenure at two competing properties may be: *Ward v Kingston upon Hull CC* [1993] RA 71, QBD.

However, the authority is also entitled to take into account where the claimant's family live and where her/his children go to school: *Codner v Wiltshire Valuation and Community Charge Tribunal* [1994] 34 RVR 169, QBD; *Cox v London (South West) Valuation and Community Charge Tribunal* [1994] 34 RVR 171, QBD. A person who owns a property and continues a relationship with a person living in another may be found to be mainly resident in the latter: *Mullaney v Watford BC* [1997] RA 225, QBD.

There is conflicting authority on the position where a person maintains a home in this country and works for long periods outside the jurisdiction. In *Ward*, the fact that the charge payer worked for most of the year in Saudi Arabia did not prevent him being mainly resident here. Merchant seamen have also given rise to litigation: in *Bradford MBC v Anderton* [1991] RA 45, QBD it was said that the home had to be the main residence because a ship could not be a residence. In *Cameron v Henry* [1992] SLT 586, IH, the Court of Session reached the opposite conclusion and held that when the charge payer was at sea, he was not mainly resident on the mainland. Some of the "habitual residence" caselaw may also be helpful: see p269.

Because a "resident" is defined in the same terms for CTB as for council tax, it ought never to be an issue for CTB purposes. If someone is not a "resident", s/he is not liable for council tax and has no need to claim CTB. If someone is a "resident", and hence liable for council tax, s/he ought also to be treated as a "resident" for the purposes of CTB. This was confirmed in *R(H) 3/08*. The claimant and his family occupied two properties as a home. He was liable for council tax on both dwellings, but the authority only awarded CTB in respect of one of them. The issue was whether a person could be a "resident", in terms of s6(5) of the 1992 Act, in two properties being occupied and used together as one combined residence, when they were listed separately on the valuation list as two hereditaments and were taxed as two chargeable dwellings rather than a single one. The commissioner said that although the question of what is a person's "sole or main residence" is always a question of fact and degree for the tribunal of first instance to determine on the evidence, there is a material difference between the kind of case (such as *Mullaney*) where a person is dividing her/his time between two distinct homes and a decision has to be made on which is the "main" one, and cases such as this, where a person is occupying contiguous premises as a single combined home. Whereas it is true that a person can only have one "sole or main" *residence*, it did not follow that this always had to be identified with one single "chargeable dwelling".

Paragraph (2)

See reg 7 HB Regs (on p233) for the definition of when a claimant is occupying a dwelling and the Analysis to reg 8 of these regs (on p660) where the claimant is temporarilly absent from home.

Paragraphs (4) and (4A)

These are identical to reg 2(3) and (3A) HB Regs: see the Analysis on p225.

Paragraph (5)

This definition rather begs the question of when such a breakdown occurs.

Definition of non-dependant

3.–(1)   In these Regulations, ''non-dependant'' means any person, except someone to whom paragraph (2) applies, who normally resides with a claimant or with whom a claimant normally resides.

(2)   This paragraph applies to–

(a)   any member of the claimant's family;

(b)   if the claimant is polygamously married, any partner of his and any child or young person who is a member of his household and for whom he or one of his partners is responsible;

(c)   a child or young person who is living with the claimant but who is not a member of his household by virtue of regulation 11 (membership of the same household);

(d)   subject to paragraph (3), any person who, with the claimant, is jointly and severally liable to pay council tax in respect of a dwelling for any day under sections 6, 7 or 75 of the 1992 Act (persons liable to pay council tax);

(e)   subject to paragraph (3), any person who is liable to make payments on a commercial basis to the claimant or the claimant's partner in respect of the occupation of the dwelling;

(f)   a person who lives with the claimant in order to care for him or a partner of his and who is engaged by a charitable or voluntary organisation which makes a charge to the claimant or his partner for the services provided by that person.

(3)   Excepting persons to whom paragraph (2)(a) to (c) and (f) refer, a person to whom any of the following sub-paragraphs applies shall be a non-dependant–

(a)   a person who resides with the person to whom he is liable to make payments in respect of the dwelling and either–
    (i)   that person is a close relative of his or his partner; or
    (ii)   the tenancy or other agreement between them is other than on a commercial basis;

(b)   a person whose liability to make payments in respect of the dwelling appears to the relevant authority to have been created to take advantage of the council tax benefit scheme except someone who was, for any period within the eight weeks prior to the creation of the agreement giving rise to the liability to make such payments, otherwise liable to make payments of rent in respect of the same dwelling;

(c)   a person who becomes jointly and severally liable with the claimant for council tax in respect of a dwelling and who was, at any time during the period of eight weeks prior to his becoming so liable, a non-dependant of one or more of the other residents in that dwelling who are so liable for the tax, unless the relevant authority is satisfied that the change giving rise to the new liability was not made to take advantage of the council tax benefit scheme.

Analysis

This regulation is similar to reg 3 HB Regs, but there are a number of important differences.

(1)   Sub-para (2)(d) is different in that it exempts those who are jointly and severally liable to pay the council tax with the claimant instead of those who have a legal joint right of occupation: see Analysis to reg 3(2)(d) HB Regs on p228. In reality, these will usually be the same people.

(2)   There is no equivalent of reg 3(4) HB Regs. It seems the intention is that a person cannot "resides with" someone unless s/he is a "resident" within the meaning of that phrase in reg 2.

(3)   There is no equivalent of reg 3(2)(e)(ii) and (iii) HB Regs. It follows that resident landlords and their families may be treated as non-dependants.

(4)   The deeming provision in para (3) is similar, but again not identical. A person whose liability to pay rent to the claimant would fall foul of reg 9(1)(a) HB Regs if s/he claimed HB would count as a non-dependant for CTB purposes, just as s/he is for HB purposes: sub-para (a). However, sub-paras (b) and (c) refer to a liability created to take advantage of the CTB scheme rather than the HB scheme. It does not follow that an arrangement that falls foul of reg 9(1)(l) HB Regs will also have been created to take advantage of the CTB scheme. In most cases, the parties will probably not even have considered the council tax implications of the agreement. It is suggested that unless it can be shown that the dominant purpose of the parties was to secure CTB, as opposed to HB, the deeming provision in sub-para (b) cannot be satisfied: see the Analysis on p252.

Disapplication of section 1(1A) of the Administration Act

[¹**4.**   Section 1(1A) of the Administration Act (requirement to state a national insurance number) shall not apply–

(a)   in the case of a child or young person in respect of whom council tax benefit is claimed;

(b)   to a person who–
    (i)   is a person in respect of whom a claim for council tax benefit is made;
    (ii)   is subject to immigration control within the meaning of section 115(9)(a) of the Immigration and Asylum Act;
    (iii)   is a person from abroad for the purposes of these Regulations as defined in regulation 7(2); and
    (iv)   has not previously been allocated a national insurance number.]

Amendment

1.   Substituted by reg 11 of SI 2009 No 471 as from 6.4.09.

Persons who have attained the qualifying age for state pension credit

5.–(1)   These Regulations apply to a person who–

(a)   has not attained the qualifying age for state pension credit; or

(b)   has attained the qualifying age for state pension credit if he, or if he has a partner, his partner, is a person on income support [², on an income-based jobseeker's allowance or on an income-related employment and support allowance].

[¹ (2)]

(3) Except as provided in [¹ paragraph (1)(b)], these Regulations shall not apply in relation to any person if he, or if he has a partner, his partner, has attained the qualifying age for state pension credit.

Amendments

1.   Amended by reg 9(3) of SI 2008 No 959 as from 6.10.08.
2.   Amended by reg 44 of SI 2008 No 1082 as from 27.10.08.

General Note

The CTB Regs apply where neither the claimant nor her/his partner has reached the qualifying age for PC or if either have reached that age, where one of them is in receipt of IS, income-based JSA or income-related ESA. "Qualifying age for state pension credit" is defined in reg 2(1). This is the same definition as that in reg 2(1) HB Regs. See p224 for a discussion. Where the claimant or her/his partner has reached the qualifying age for PC and neither are in receipt of IS, income-based JSA or income-related ESA, the CTB(SPC) Regs instead apply (see p913).

Remunerative work

6.–(1) Subject to the following provisions of this regulation, a person shall be treated for the purposes of these Regulations as engaged in remunerative work if he is engaged, or, where his hours of work fluctuate, he is engaged on average, for not less than 16 hours a week, in work for which payment is made or which is done in expectation of payment.

(2) Subject to paragraph (3), in determining the number of hours for which a person is engaged in work where his hours of work fluctuate, regard shall be had to the average of hours worked over–

(a) if there is a recognisable cycle of work, the period of one complete cycle (including, where the cycle involves periods in which the person does no work, those periods but disregarding any other absences);

(b) in any other case, the period of 5 weeks immediately prior to the date of claim, or such other length of time as may, in the particular case, enable the person's weekly average hours of work to be determined more accurately.

(3) Where, for the purposes of paragraph (2)(a), a person's recognisable cycle of work at a school, other educational establishment or other place of employment is one year and includes periods of school holidays or similar vacations during which he does not work, those periods and any other periods not forming part of such holidays or vacations during which he is not required to work shall be disregarded in establishing the average hours for which he is engaged in work.

(4) Where no recognisable cycle has been established in respect of a person's work, regard shall be had to the number of hours or, where those hours will fluctuate, the average of the hours, which he is expected to work in a week.

(5) A person shall be treated as engaged in remunerative work during any period for which he is absent from work referred to in paragraph (1) if the absence is either without good cause or by reason of a recognised, customary or other holiday.

(6) A person on income support [¹ , an income-based jobseeker's allowance or an income-related employment and support allowance] for more than 3 days in any benefit week shall be treated as not being in remunerative work in that week.

(7) A person shall not be treated as engaged in remunerative work on any day on which the person is on maternity leave, paternity leave or adoption leave, or is absent from work because he is ill.

(8) A person shall not be treated as engaged in remunerative work on any day on which he is engaged in an activity in respect of which–

(a) a sports award has been made, or is to be made, to him; and

(b) no other payment is made or is expected to be made to him.

Amendment

1.   Amended by reg 45 of SI 2008 No 1082 as from 27.10.08.

Persons from abroad

7.–(1)   A person from abroad is a person of a prescribed class for the purposes of section 131(3)(b) of the Act but this paragraph shall not have effect in respect of a person to whom and for a period to which regulation 7A and Schedule A1 apply.

[¹ (2)   In paragraph (1), "person from abroad" means, subject to the following provisions of this regulation, a person who is not habitually resident in the United Kingdom, the Channel Islands, the Isle of Man or the Republic of Ireland.

(3)   No person shall be treated as habitually resident in the United Kingdom, the Channel Islands, the Isle of Man or the Republic of Ireland unless he has a right to reside in (as the case may be) the United Kingdom, the Channel Islands, the Isle of Man or the Republic of Ireland other than a right to reside which falls within paragraph (4).

(4)   A right to reside falls within this paragraph if it is one which exists by virtue of, or in accordance with, one or more of the following–

(a)   regulation 13 of the Immigration (European Economic Area) Regulations 2006;

(b)   regulation 14 of those Regulations, but only in a case where the right exists under that regulation because the person is–

   (i)   a jobseeker for the purpose of the definition of "qualified person" in regulation 6(1) of those Regulations, or

   (ii)   a family member (within the meaning of regulation 7 of those Regulations) of such a jobseeker;

(c)   Article 6 of Council Directive No. 2004/38/EC; or

(d)   Article 39 of the Treaty establishing the European Community (in a case where the person is seeking work in the United Kingdom, the Channel Islands, the Isle of Man or the Republic of Ireland).

(4A)   A person is not a person from abroad if he is–

(a)   a workerfor the purposes of Council Directive No. 2004/38/EC;

(b)   a self-employed personfor the purposes of that Directive;

(c)   a person who retains a status referred to in sub-paragraph (a) or (b) pursuant to Article 7(3) of that Directive;

(d)   a person who is a family member of a person referred to in sub-paragraph (a), (b) or (c) within the meaning of Article 2 of that Directive;

(e)   a person who has a right to reside permanently in the United Kingdom by virtue of Article 17 of that Directive;

[⁵ (f)   a person who is treated as a worker for the purpose of the definition of "qualified person" in regulation 6(1) of the Immigration (European Economic Area) Regulations 2006 pursuant to–

   (i)   regulation 5 of the Accession (Immigration and Worker Registration) Regulations 2004 (application of the 2006 Regulations in relation to a national of the Czech Republic, Estonia, Latvia, Lithuania, Hungary, Poland, Slovenia or the Slovak Republic who is an "accession State worker requiring registration"), or

   (ii)   regulation 6 of the Accession (Immigration and Worker Authorisation) Regulations 2006 (right of residence of a Bulgarian or Romanian who is an "accession State national subject to worker authorisation");]

(g)   a refugee;

[⁴ (h)   a person who has exceptional leave to enter or remain in the United Kingdom granted outside the rules made under section 3(2) of the Immigration Act 1971;

(hh)   a person who has humanitarian protection granted under those rules;]

(i)   a person who is not a person subject to immigration control within the meaning of section 115(9) of the Immigration and Asylum Act and who is in the United Kingdom as a result of his deportation, expulsion or other removal by compulsion of law from another country to the United Kingdom;

(j)   a person in Great Britain who left the territory of Montserrat after 1st November 1995 because of the effect on that territory of a volcanic eruption; [⁶]

[⁶ (jj)   a person who–

   (i)   arrived in Great Britain on or after 28th February 2009 but before 18th March 2011;

      (i)   immediately before arriving there had been resident in Zimbabwe; and

      (ii)   before leaving Zimbabwe, had accepted an offer, made by Her Majesty's Government, to assist that person to move to and settle in the United Kingdom; or]

  (k)   in receipt of income support [⁶ , an income-based jobseeker's allowance or on an income-related employment and support allowance].]

(5)   Paragraph 1 of Part 1 of the Schedule to, and regulation 2 as it applies to that paragraph of, the Social Security (Immigration and Asylum) Consequential Amendments Regulations 2000 shall not apply to a person who has been temporarily without funds for any period, or the aggregate of any periods, exceeding 42 days during any one period of limited leave (including any such period as extended).

(6)   In this regulation–

[²]

"refugee" in this regulation, regulation 7A (entitlement of a refugee to council tax benefit) and Schedule A1 (treatment of claims for council tax benefit by refugees), means a person recorded by the Secretary of State as a refugee within the definition in Article 1 of the Convention relating to the Status of Refugees.

Modifications

Reg 7(4A)(a) to (e) applies in relation to a national of Norway, Iceland, Liechtenstein or Switzerland or a member of her/his family (within the meaning of Art 2 Council Directive No.2004/38/EC) as if such a national were a national of a member state. See reg 10 of SI 2006 No.1026 on p1226.

    The amendments made by SI 2006 No.1026 do not affect the continued operation of the transitional and savings provided for in reg 12 Social Security (Persons From Abroad) Miscellaneous Amendments Regulations 1996 (see p1226), reg 6 Social Security (Habitual Residence) Amendment Regulations 2004 (see p1192) or Sch 3 para 6 HB&CTB(CP) Regs (see p1197). See reg 11 of SI 2006 No.1026 on p1226.

    From 25 July 2006 until 31 January 2007, a para (4A)(jj) was inserted by the Social Security (Lebanon) Amendment Regulations 2006 SI No.1981. See p576 of the 20th edition of this book for the insertion.

Amendments

1.   Substituted by reg 2(2)(a) of SI 2006 No 1026 as from 30.4.06.
2.   Omitted by reg 2(2)(b) of SI 2006 No 1026 as from 30.4.06.
3.   Amended by reg 7 of SI 2006 No 1981 from 25.7.06 until 31.1.07 only.
4.   Amended by reg 7 of SI 2006 No 2528 as from 9.10.06.
5.   Substituted by reg 7 of SI 2006 No 3341 as from 1.1.07.
6.   Amended by reg 46 of SI 2008 No 1082 as from 27.10.08.
7.   Amended by reg 7 of SI 2009 No 362 as from 18.3.09.

Entitlement of a refugee to council tax benefit
[¹ 7A]

Modification

Reg 7A was inserted by Sch 4 para 3(1) HB&CTB(CP) Regs. It only applied to claims for CTB by some refugees. See also Sch A1 inserted by Sch 4 para 3(2) HB&CTB(CP) Regs.

Amendment

1.   Lapsed by s12(2)(g) Asylum and Immigration (Treatment of Claimants, etc.) Act 2004 (for those recorded as refugees after 14.6.07).

Prescribed persons for the purposes of section 131(3)(b) of the Act

8.–(1)   Subject to paragraph (2), a person who is throughout any day referred to in section 131(3)(a) of the Act absent from the dwelling referred to in that section, shall be a prescribed person for the purposes of section 131(3)(b) of the Act in relation to that day.

(2)   A person shall not, in relation to any day which falls within a period of temporary absence from that dwelling, be a prescribed person under paragraph (1).

(3)	In paragraph (2), a "period of temporary absence" means–
(a)	a period of absence not exceeding 13 weeks, beginning with the first whole day on which a person resides in residential accommodation where and for so long as–
	(i)	the person resides in that accommodation;
	(ii)	the part of the dwelling in which he usually resided is not let or sub-let; and
	(iii)	that period of absence does not form part of a longer period of absence from the dwelling of more than 52 weeks,
	where he has entered the accommodation for the purpose of ascertaining whether it suits his needs and with the intention of returning to the dwelling if it proves not to suit his needs;
(b)	a period of absence not exceeding 13 weeks, beginning with the first whole day of absence from the dwelling, where and for so long as–
	(i)	the person intends to return to the dwelling;
	(ii)	the part of the dwelling in which he usually resided is not let or sub-let; and
	(iii)	that period is unlikely to exceed 13 weeks; and
(c)	a period of absence not exceeding 52 weeks, beginning with the first whole day of that absence, where and for so long as–
	(i)	the person intends to return to the dwelling;
	(ii)	the part of the dwelling in which he usually resided is not let or sub-let;
	(iii)	the person is a person to whom paragraph (4) applies; and
	(iv)	the period of absence is unlikely to exceed 52 weeks or, in exceptional circumstances, is unlikely substantially to exceed that period.
(4)	This paragraph applies to a person who is–
(a)	detained in custody on remand pending trial or required, as a condition of bail, to reside–
	(i)	in a dwelling, other than the dwelling referred to in paragraph (1), or
	(ii)	in premises approved under [¹ section 13 of the Offender Management Act 2007],
	or, detained in custody pending sentence upon conviction;
(b)	resident in a hospital or similar institution as a patient;
(c)	undergoing, or his partner or his dependent child is undergoing, in the United Kingdom or elsewhere, medical treatment, or medically approved convalescence, in accommodation other than residential accommodation;
(d)	following, in the United Kingdom or elsewhere, a training course;
(e)	undertaking medically approved care of a person residing in the United Kingdom or elsewhere;
(f)	undertaking the care of a child whose parent or guardian is temporarily absent from the dwelling normally occupied by that parent or guardian for the purpose of receiving medically approved care or medical treatment;
(g)	a person who is, in the United Kingdom or elsewhere, receiving medically approved care provided in accommodation other than residential accommodation;
(h)	a student;
(i)	a person who is receiving care provided in residential accommodation other than a person to whom paragraph (3)(a) applies; or
(j)	a person who has left the dwelling he resides in through fear of violence, in that dwelling, or by a person who was formerly a member of the family of the person first mentioned.
(5)	This paragraph applies to a person who is–
(a)	detained in custody pending sentence upon conviction or under a sentence imposed by a court (other than a person who is detained in hospital under the provisions of the Mental Health Act 1983, or, in Scotland, under the provisions of the Mental Health (Care and Treatment) (Scotland) Act 2003 or the Criminal Procedure (Scotland) Act 1995); and

    (b)   on temporary release from detention in accordance with Rules made under the provisions of the Prison Act 1952 or the Prisons (Scotland) Act 1989.

    (6)   Where paragraph (5) applies to a person, then, for any day when he is on temporary release–

    (a)   if such temporary release was immediately preceded by a period of temporary absence under paragraph (3)(b) or (c), he shall be treated, for the purposes of paragraph (1), as if he continues to be absent from the dwelling, despite any return to the dwelling;

    (b)   for the purposes of paragraph (4)(a), he shall be treated as if he remains in detention;

    (c)   if he does not fall within sub-paragraph (a), he shall be a prescribed person for the purposes of section 131(3)(b) of the Act.

    (7)   In this regulation–

"medically approved" means certified by a medical practitioner;

"patient" means a person who is undergoing medical or other treatment as an in-patient in any hospital or similar institution;

"residential accommodation" means accommodation which is provided–

    (a)   in a care home;

    (b)   in an independent hospital;

    (c)   in an Abbeyfield Home; or

    (d)   in an establishment managed or provided by a body incorporated by Royal Charter or constituted by Act of Parliament other than a local social services authority;

"training course" means a course of training or instruction provided wholly or partly by or on behalf of or in pursuance of arrangements made with, or approved by or on behalf of, [2 Skills Development Scotland,] Scottish Enterprise, Highlands and Islands Enterprise, a government department or the Secretary of State.

Amendments

1.   Amended by reg 8(3) of SI 2008 No 2767 as from 17.11.08.

2.   Amended by reg 8(3)(b) of SI 2009 No 583 as from 6.4.09.

Analysis

This provision was extensively modified in April 2005 in order to get round the difficulties created by the previous drafting of regs 4B and 4C CTB Regs 1992 (now reg 8 CTB Regs), and more particularly the decision of Commissioner Fellner in *R(H) 4/05* that reg 4C(3) Regs 1992 in its pre-April 2005 was *ultra vires* and of no effect. For a discussion of those difficulties and *R(H) 4/05*, see p630 of the 17th edition.

Reg 8 seeks to overcome *R(H) 4/05* by treating a person who is absent from the dwelling and not temporarily absent as being a prescribed person for the purposes of s131(3)(b) SSCBA 1992, and so not entitled to CTB under s131(10) of the same Act. Whether the prescription exercise is lawful may be open to some argument, but a similar (but stronger) type of argument was not successful in the case of *Foster v Chief Adjudication Officer* [1993] AC 754, HL.

Assuming it is lawful, then reg 8 is broadly similar in effect to reg 7(13), (16) and (17) HB Regs (ie, enabling entitlement to be retained if temporarily absent from the dwelling for up to 13 or 52 weeks in certain specified circumstances), to which reference should be made for the principles to be applied.

PART 2
Membership of a family

Persons of prescribed description for the definition of family in section 137(1) of the Act

    9.–(1)   Subject to paragraph (2), a person of a prescribed description for the purposes of section 137(1) of the Act (definition of family) as it applies to council tax benefit is a person [1 who falls within the definition of qualifying young person in section 142 of the Act (child and qualifying young person)], and in these Regulations such a person is referred to as a "young person".

    (2)   Paragraph (1) shall not apply to a person who is–

    (a)   on income support [4 , an income-based jobseeker's allowance or an income-related employment and support allowance]; [2 or]

[³ (b)]
(c)   a person to whom section 6 of the Children (Leaving Care) Act 2000 (exclusion from benefits) applies.

(3)   A person of a prescribed description for the purposes of section 137(1) of the Act as it applies to council tax benefit (definition of the family) includes a child or young person in respect of whom section 145A of the Act applies for the purposes of entitlement to child benefit but only for the period prescribed under section 145A(1) of the Act.

Amendments

1.	Amended by reg 5(2)(a) of SI 2006 No 718 as from 10.4.06.
2.	Inserted by reg 5(2)(b) of SI 2006 No 718 as from 10.4.06.
3.	Omitted by reg 5(2)(c) of SI 2006 No 718 as from 10.4.06.
4.	Amended by reg 47 of SI 2008 No 1082 as from 27.10.08.

Circumstances in which a person is to be treated as responsible or not responsible for another

10.–(1)   Subject to the following provisions of this regulation a person shall be treated as responsible for a child or young person who is normally living with him and this includes a child or young person to whom paragraph (3) of regulation 9 applies.

(2)   Where a child or young person spends equal amounts of time in different households, or where there is a question as to which household he is living in, the child or young person shall be treated for the purposes of paragraph (1) as normally living with–
(a)   the person who is receiving child benefit in respect of him; or
(b)   if there is no such person–
    (i)   where only one claim for child benefit has been made in respect of him, the person who made that claim; or
    (ii)   in any other case the person who has the primary responsibility for him.

(3)   For the purposes of these Regulations a child or young person shall be the responsibility of only one person in any benefit week and any person other than the one treated as responsible for the child or young person under this regulation shall be treated as not so responsible.

Circumstances in which a person is to be treated as being or not being a member of the household

11.–(1)   Subject to paragraphs (2) and (3), the claimant and any partner and, where the claimant or his partner is treated as responsible by virtue of regulation 10 (circumstances in which a person is to be treated as responsible or not responsible for another) for a child or young person, that child or young person and any child of that child or young person, shall be treated as members of the same household notwithstanding that any of them is temporarily absent from that household.

(2)   A child or young person shall not be treated as a member of the claimant's household where he is–
(a)   placed with the claimant or his partner by a local authority under section 23(2)(a) of the Children Act 1989 or by a voluntary organisation under section 59(1)(a) of that Act, or in Scotland boarded out with the claimant or his partner under a relevant enactment; or
(b)   placed, or in Scotland boarded out, with the claimant or his partner prior to adoption; or
(c)   placed for adoption with the claimant or his partner in accordance with the Adoption and Children Act 2002 or the Adoption Agencies (Scotland) Regulations 1996.

(3)   Subject to paragraph (4), paragraph (1) shall not apply to a child or young person who is not living with the claimant and he–
(a)   is being looked after by, or in Scotland is in the care of, a local authority under a relevant enactment; or
(b)   has been placed, or in Scotland boarded out, with a person other than the claimant prior to adoption; or

(c)   has been placed for adoption in accordance with the Adoption and Children Act 2002 or the Adoption Agencies (Scotland) Regulations 1996.

(4)   An authority shall treat a child or young person to whom paragraph (3)(a) applies as being a member of the claimant's household in any benefit week where–

(a)   that child or young person lives with the claimant for part or all of that benefit week; and

(b)   the authority considers that it is reasonable to do so taking into account the nature and frequency of that child's or young person's visits.

(5)   In this regulation "relevant enactment" means the Army Act 1955, the Air Force Act 1955, the Naval Discipline Act 1957, the Matrimonial Proceedings (Children) Act 1958, the Social Work (Scotland) Act 1968, the Family Law Reform Act 1969, the Children and Young Persons Act 1969, the Matrimonial Causes Act 1973, the Children Act 1975, the Domestic Proceedings and Magistrates' Courts Act 1978, the Adoption (Scotland) Act 1978, the Family Law Act 1986, the Children Act 1989 and the Children (Scotland) Act 1995.

General Note

This is similar to reg 21 HB Regs (see p335), except that reg 21(1) and (2) HB Regs is effectively combined in reg 11(1). The difference is that in relation to reg 21, when someone does not count as "temporarily living away" from the family is defined, whereas no definition of when someone does not count as "temporarily absent" from the household is given here. This means that authorities have more discretion in relation to CTB than they do in relation to HB in this respect.

As noted in reg 21, this regulation does not define household (see note on "family" on p22) but sets out the situations in which a member of a household will continue to be treated as such, despite physical absence from it.

Para (1) sets out the general rule that claimants, their partner(s), any child or young person for whom they are responsible, and any child of such a child or young person, shall continue to be treated as members of the same household even when one or more of them is "temporarily absent" from the household. "Child" is defined in reg 2(1) and "young person" in regs 2(1) and 9.

Para (2) excludes certain children and young people from the claimant's household even when they actually live there.

Para (3) excludes certain children and young people who are absent from the household and living in the circumstances set out in para (3)(a) to (c), but para (4) itself provides an exception to para (3)(a). That means that children or young people to whom both paras (3)(a) and (4) apply *are* to be treated as members of the claimant's household, that is certain children or young people who are being "looked after" but are living with the claimant for part or all of certain benefit weeks.

Para (5) defines "relevant enactment" for these purposes.

PART 3
Applicable amounts

Applicable amounts

12.   Subject to regulations 13 and 14 and Schedule A1 (polygamous marriages, patients and treatment of claims for council tax benefit by refugees), a claimant's weekly applicable amount shall be the aggregate of such of the following amounts as may apply in his case–

(a)   an amount in respect of himself or, if he is a member of a couple, an amount in respect of both of them, determined in accordance with paragraph 1(1), (2) or (3), as the case may be, of Schedule 1;

(b)   an amount determined in accordance with paragraph 2 of Schedule 1 in respect of any child or young person who is a member of his family;

(c)   if he is a member of a family of which at least one member is a child or young person, an amount determined in accordance with Part 2 of Schedule 1 (family premium);

(d)   the amount of any premiums which may be applicable to him, determined in accordance with Parts 3 and 4 of Schedule 1 (premiums).

[1 (e) the amount of either the–

(i)   work-related activity component; or

(ii)   [2] support component

[³ (f) the amount of any transitional addition which may be applicable to him in accordance with Parts 7 and 8 of Schedule 1 (transitional addition).] which may be applicable to him in accordance with Part 5 of Schedule 1 (the components).]

Amendments

1.   Amended by reg 48 of SI 2008 No 1082 as from 27.10.08.
2.   Amended by reg 37 of SI 2008 No 2428 as from 27.10.08.
3.   Inserted by reg 27 and Sch 5 para 2(3) of SI 2010 No 1907 as amended by reg 15 of SI 2010 No 2430 as from 1.10.10.

Polygamous marriages

13.   Subject to regulation 14 and Schedule A1 (patients and treatment of claims for council tax benefit by refugees), where a claimant is a member of a polygamous marriage, his weekly applicable amount shall be the aggregate of such of the following amounts as may apply in his case–

(a)   the amount applicable to him and one of his partners determined in accordance with paragraph 1(3) of Schedule 1 as if he and that partner were a couple;

(b)   an amount equal to the difference between the amounts specified in sub-paragraphs (3) and (1)(b) of paragraph 1 of Schedule 1 in respect of each of his other partners;

(c)   an amount determined in accordance with paragraph 2 of Schedule 1 (applicable amounts) in respect of any child or young person for whom he or a partner of his is responsible and who is a member of the same household;

(d)   if he or another partner of the polygamous marriage is responsible for a child or young person who is a member of the same household, the amount specified in Part 2 of Schedule 1 (family premium);

(e)   the amount of any premiums which may be applicable to him determined in accordance with Parts 3 and 4 of Schedule 1 (premiums).

[¹ (f)   the amount of either the–

(i)   work-related activity component; or

(ii)   [²] support component

which may be applicable to him in accordance with Part 5 of Schedule 1 (the components).]

[³ (g)   the amount of any transitional addition which may be applicable to him in accordance with Parts 7 and 8 of Schedule 1 (transitional addition).]

Amendments

1.   Amended by reg 49 of SI 2008 No 1082 as from 27.10.08.
2.   Amended by reg 38 of SI 2008 No 2428 as from 27.10.08.
3.   Inserted by reg 27 and Sch 5 para 2(4) of SI 2010 No 1907 as amended by reg 15 of SI 2010 No 2430 as from 1.10.10.

Patients

[¹**14.**]

Amendment

1.   Omitted by reg 3(4) of SI 2005 No 2502 as amended by Sch 2 para 27 of SI 2006 No 217 as from 1.4.06.

PART 4
Income and capital
SECTION 1
General

Calculation of income and capital of members of claimant's family and of a polygamous marriage

15.–(1)   The income and capital of a claimant's partner which by virtue of section 136(1) of the Act is to be treated as income and capital of the claimant, shall be calculated or estimated in accordance with the following provisions of this Part in like manner as for the claimant; and any reference to the ''claimant'' shall, except where the context otherwise requires, be construed for the purposes of this Part as if it were a reference to his partner.

(2)　Where a claimant or the partner of a claimant is married polygamously to two or more members of his household–

(a)　the claimant shall be treated as possessing capital and income belonging to each such member; and

(b)　the income and capital of that member shall be calculated in accordance with the following provisions of this Part in like manner as for the claimant.

(3)　The income and capital of a child or young person shall not be treated as the income and capital of the claimant.

Circumstances in which capital and income of non-dependant is to be treated as claimant's

16.–(1)　Where it appears to the relevant authority that a non-dependant and the claimant have entered into arrangements in order to take advantage of the council tax benefit scheme and the non-dependant has more capital and income than the claimant, that authority shall, except where the claimant is on income support [1 , an income-based jobseeker's allowance or an income-related employment and support allowance], treat the claimant as possessing capital and income belonging to that non-dependant and, in such a case, shall disregard any capital and income which the claimant does possess.

(2)　Where a claimant is treated as possessing capital and income belonging to a non-dependant under paragraph (1) the capital and income of that non-dependant shall be calculated in accordance with the following provisions of this Part in like manner as for the claimant and any reference to the ''claimant'' shall, except where the context otherwise requires, be construed for the purposes of this Part as if it were a reference to that non-dependant.

Amendment

1.　　Amended by reg 50 of SI 2008 No 1082 as from 27.10.08.

SECTION 2
Income

Calculation of income on a weekly basis

17.–(1)　Subject to regulation 24 (disregard of changes in tax, contributions etc.), for the purposes of section 131(5) of the Act (conditions of entitlement to council tax benefit) the income of a claimant shall be calculated on a weekly basis–

(a)　by estimating the amount which is likely to be his average weekly income in accordance with this Section and Sections 3 to 5 of this Part and Part 5;

(b)　by adding to that amount the weekly income calculated under regulation 42 (calculation of tariff income from capital); and

(c)　by then deducting any relevant child care charges to which regulation 18 (treatment of child care charges) applies from any earnings which form part of the average weekly income or, in a case where the conditions in paragraph (2) are met, from those earnings plus whichever credit specified in sub-paragraph (b) of that paragraph is appropriate, up to a maximum deduction in respect of the claimant's family of whichever of the sums specified in paragraph (3) applies in his case.

(2)　The conditions of this paragraph are that–

(a)　the claimant's earnings which form part of his average weekly income are less than the lower of either his relevant child care charges or whichever of the deductions specified in paragraph (3) otherwise applies in his case; and

(b)　that claimant or, if he is a member of a couple either the claimant or his partner, is in receipt of either working tax credit or child tax credit.

(3)   The maximum deduction to which paragraph (1)(c) above refers shall be–

(a)   where the claimant's family includes only one child in respect of whom relevant child care charges are paid, [⁵ £175.00] per week;

(b)   where the claimant's family includes more than one child in respect of whom relevant child care charges are paid, [⁵ £300] per week.

(4)   For the purposes of paragraph (1) ''income'' includes capital treated as income under regulation 31 (capital treated as income) and income which a claimant is treated as possessing under regulation 32 (notional income).

Amendments

1.   Confirmed by Art 21(2) of SI 2006 No 645 and reg 8 of SI 2006 No 217 as from 1.4.06.
2.   Confirmed by Art 21(2) of SI 2007 No 688 as from 1.4.07.
3.   Confirmed by Art 21(2) of SI 2008 No 632 as from 1.4.08.
4.   Confirmed by Art 21(2) of SI 2009 No 497 as from 1.4.09.
5.   Confirmed by Art 21(2) of SI 2010 No 793 as from 1.4.10.

Treatment of child care charges

18.–(1)   This regulation applies where a claimant is incurring relevant child care charges and–

(a)   is a lone parent and is engaged in remunerative work;

(b)   is a member of a couple both of whom are engaged in remunerative work; or

(c)   is a member of a couple where one member is engaged in remunerative work and the other–

  (i)   is incapacitated;

  (ii)   is an in-patient in hospital; or

  (iii)   is in prison (whether serving a custodial sentence or remanded in custody awaiting trial or sentence).

(2)   For the purposes of paragraph (1) and subject to paragraph (4), a person to whom paragraph (3) applies shall be treated as engaged in remunerative work for a period not exceeding 28 weeks during which he–

(a)   is paid statutory sick pay;

(b)   is paid short-term incapacity benefit at the lower rate under sections 30A to 30E of the Act;

[⁴ (ba)   is paid an employment and support allowance;]

(c)   is paid income support on the grounds of incapacity for work [⁴ or limited capability for work] under regulation 4ZA of, and paragraph 7 or 14 of Schedule 1B to, the Income Support Regulations; or

(d)   is credited with earnings on the grounds of incapacity for work under regulation 8B of the Social Security (Credits) Regulations 1975.

(3)   This paragraph applies to a person who was engaged in remunerative work immediately before–

(a)   the first day of the period in respect of which he was first paid statutory sick pay, short-term incapacity benefit [⁴ , an employment and support allowance] or income support on the grounds of incapacity for work; or

(b)   the first day of the period in respect of which earnings are credited,

as the case may be.

(4)   In a case to which paragraph (2)(c) or (d) applies, the period of 28 weeks begins on the day on which the person is first paid income support or on the first day of the period in respect of which earnings are credited, as the case may be.

(5)   Relevant child care charges are those charges for care to which paragraphs (6) and (7) apply, and shall be calculated on a weekly basis in accordance with paragraph (10).

(6)   The charges are paid by the claimant for care which is provided–

(a)   in the case of any child of the claimant's family who is not disabled, in respect of the period beginning on that child's date of birth and ending on the day preceding the first Monday in September following that child's fifteenth birthday; or

(b)   in the case of any child of the claimant's family who is disabled, in respect of the period beginning on that person's date of birth and ending on the day preceding the first Monday in September following that person's sixteenth birthday.

(7)   The charges are paid for care which is provided by one or more of the care providers listed in paragraph (8) and are not paid–

(a)   in respect of the child's compulsory education;

(b)   by a claimant to a partner or by a partner to a claimant in respect of any child for whom either or any of them is responsible in accordance with regulation 10 (circumstances in which a person is treated as responsible or not responsible for another); or

(c)   in respect of care provided by a relative of the child wholly or mainly in the child's home.

(8)   The care to which paragraph (7) refers may be provided–

(a)   out of school hours, by a school on school premises or by a local authority–

    (i)   for children who are not disabled in respect of the period beginning on their eighth birthday and ending on the day preceding the first Monday in September following their fifteenth birthday; or

    (ii)   for children who are disabled in respect of the period beginning on their eighth birthday and ending on the day preceding the first Monday in September following their sixteenth birthday; or

(b)   by a child care provider approved in accordance with by the Tax Credit (New Category of Child Care Provider) Regulations 1999;

(c)   by persons registered under Part 10A of the Children Act 1989; or

(d)   in schools or establishments which are exempted from registration under Part 10A of the Children Act 1989 by virtue of paragraph 1 or 2 of Schedule 9A to that Act; or

(e)   by–

    (i)   persons registered under section 7(1) of the Regulation of Care (Scotland) Act 2001, or

    (ii)   local authorities registered under section 33(1) of that Act, where the care provided is child minding or daycare within the meaning of that Act; or

(f)   by a person prescribed in regulations made pursuant to section 12(4) of the Tax Credits Act. [⁶ or

(g)   by a person who is registered under Chapter 2 or 3 of Part 3 of the Childcare Act 2006; or

(h)   by any of the schools mentioned in section 34(2) of the Childcare Act 2006 in circumstances where the requirement to register under Chapter 2 of Part 3 of that Act does not apply by virtue of section 34(2) of that Act; or

(i)   by any of the schools mentioned in section 53(2) of the Childcare Act 2006 in circumstances where the requirement to register under Chapter 3 of Part 3 of that Act does not apply by virtue of section 53(2) of that Act; or

(j)   by any of the establishments mentioned in section 18(5) of the Childcare Act 2006 in circumstances where the care is not included in the meaning of "childcare" for the purposes of Part 1 and Part 3 of that Act by virtue of that subsection; or

(k)   by a foster parent [⁷ or kinship carer] under the Fostering Services Regulations 2002, the Fostering Services (Wales) Regulations 2003 or the [⁷ Looked After Children (Scotland) Regulations 2009] in relation to a child other than one whom the foster parent is fostering [⁷ or kinship carer is looking after]; or .

(l)   by a domiciliary care worker under the Domiciliary Care Agencies Regulations 2002 or the Domiciliary Care Agencies (Wales) Regulations 2004; or

(m)   by a person who is not a relative of the child wholly or mainly in the child's home.]

(9)   In paragraphs (6) and (8)(a), "the first Monday in September" means the Monday which first occurs in the month of September in any year.

(10)   Relevant child care charges shall be estimated over such period, not exceeding a year, as is appropriate in order that the average weekly charge may be estimated accurately having regard to information as to the amount of that charge provided by the child minder or person providing the care.

(11)   For the purposes of paragraph (1)(c) the other member of a couple is incapacitated where–

[³ (a)   the claimant's applicable amount includes a disability premium on account of the other member's incapacity [⁴ or the support component or the work-related activity component on account of his having limited capability for work];]

(b)   the claimant's applicable amount would include a disability premium [³] on account of the other member's incapacity but for that other member being treated as capable of work by virtue of a determination made in accordance with regulations made under section 171E of the Act;

[⁴ (ba)   the claimant's applicable amount would include the support component or the work-related activity component on account of the other member having limited capability for work but for that other member being treated as not having limited capability for work by virtue of a determination made in accordance with the Employment and Support Allowance Regulations;]

(c)   the claimant (within the meaning of regulation 2) is, or is treated as, incapable of work and has been so incapable, or has been so treated as incapable, of work in accordance with the provisions of, and regulations made under, Part 12A of the Act (incapacity for work) for a continuous period of not less than 196 days; and for this purpose any two or more separate periods separated by a break of not more than 56 days shall be treated as one continuous period;

[⁴ (ca)   (within the meaning of regulation 2(1)) has, or is treated as having, limited capability for work and has had, or been treated as having, limited capability for work in accordance with the Employment and Support Allowance Regulations for a continuous period of not less than 196 days and for this purpose any two or more separate periods separated by a break of not more than 84 days must be treated as one continuous period;]

(d)   there is payable in respect of him one or more of the following pensions or allowances–

(i)   long-term incapacity benefit or short-term incapacity benefit at the higher rate under Schedule 4 to the Act;

(ii)   attendance allowance under section 64 of the Act;

(iii)   severe disablement allowance under section 68 of the Act;

(iv)   disability living allowance under section 71 of the Act;

(v)   increase of disablement pension under section 104 of the Act;

(vi)   a pension increase [⁵ paid as part of a war disablement pension or under] an industrial injuries scheme which is analogous to an allowance or increase of disablement pension under head (ii), (iv) or (v) above;

[⁴ (vii)   main phase employment and support allowance;]

(e)   a pension or allowance to which head (ii), (iv), (v) or (vi) of sub-paragraph (d) above refers was payable on account of his incapacity but has ceased to be payable in consequence of his becoming a patient, [¹ , which in this regulation shall mean a person (other than a person who is serving a sentence of imprisonment or detention in a youth custody institution) who is regarded as receiving free in-patient treatment within the meaning of [² regulation 2(4) and (5) of the Social Security (Hospital In-Patients) Regulations 2005].];

(f)   sub-paragraph (d) or (e) would apply to him if the legislative provisions referred to in those sub-paragraphs were provisions under any corresponding enactment having effect in Northern Ireland; or

(g)   he has an invalid carriage or other vehicle provided to him by the Secretary of State under section 5(2)(a) of and Schedule 2 to the National Health Service Act 1977 or under section 46 of the National Health Service (Scotland) Act 1978 or provided by the [³ Department of Health, Social Services and Public Safety in

Northern Ireland] under Article 30(1) of the Health and Personal Social Services (Northern Ireland) Order 1972.

(12) For the purposes of paragraph (11), once paragraph (11)(c) applies to the claimant, if he then ceases, for a period of 56 days or less, to be incapable, or to be treated as incapable, of work, that paragraph shall, on his again becoming so incapable, or so treated as incapable, of work at the end of that period, immediately thereafter apply to him for so long as he remains incapable, or is treated as remaining incapable, of work.

[⁴ (12A) For the purposes of paragraph (11), once paragraph (11)(ca) applies to the claimant, if he then ceases, for a period of 84 days or less, to have, or to be treated as having, limited capability for work, that paragraph is, on his again having, or being treated as having, limited capability for work at the end of that period, immediately thereafter apply to him for so long as he has, or is treated as having, limited capability for work.]

(13) For the purposes of paragraphs (6) and (8)(a), a person is disabled if he is a person–
(a)   in respect of whom disability living allowance is payable, or has ceased to be payable solely because he is a patient;
(b)   who is registered as blind in a register compiled under section 29 of the National Assistance Act 1948 (welfare services) or, in Scotland, has been certified as blind and in consequence he is registered as blind in a register maintained by or on behalf of a council constituted under section 2 of the Local Government (Scotland) Act 1994; or
(c)   who ceased to be registered as blind in such a register within the period beginning 28 weeks before the first Monday in September following that person's fifteenth birthday and ending on the day preceding that person's sixteenth birthday.

(14) For the purposes of paragraph (1) a woman on maternity leave, paternity leave or adoption leave shall be treated as if she is engaged in remunerative work for the period specified in paragraph (15) ("the relevant period") provided that–
(a)   in the week before the period of maternity leave, paternity leave or adoption leave began she was in remunerative work;
(b)   the claimant is incurring relevant child care charges within the meaning of paragraph (5); and
(c)   she is entitled to either statutory maternity pay under section 164 of the Act, statutory paternity pay by virtue of section 171ZA or 171ZB of the Act, statutory adoption pay by of section 171ZL of the Act, maternity allowance under section 35 of the Act or qualifying support.

(15) For the purposes of paragraph (14) the relevant period shall begin on the day on which the person's maternity, paternity leave or adoption leave commences and shall end on–
(a)   the date that leave ends;
(b)   if no child care element of working tax credit is in payment on the date that entitlement to maternity allowance, qualifying support, statutory maternity pay, statutory paternity pay or statutory adoption pay ends, the date that entitlement ends; or
(c)   if a child care element of working tax credit is in payment on the date that entitlement to maternity allowance or qualifying support, statutory maternity pay or statutory adoption pay ends, the date that entitlement to that award of the child care element of the working tax credit ends,
whichever shall occur first.

(16) In paragraphs (14) and (15)–
(a)   "qualifying support" means income support to which that person is entitled by virtue of paragraph 14B of Schedule 1B to the Income Support Regulations; and
(b)   "child care element" of working tax credit means the element of working tax credit prescribed under section 12 of the Tax Credits Act (child care element).

Amendments

1. Substituted by reg 3(5) of SI 2005 No 2502 as amended by Sch 2 para 27 of SI 2006 No 217 as from 1.4.06.
2. Amended by reg 5(2) of SI 2005 No 3360 as amended by Sch 2 para 30 of SI 2006 No 217 as from 10.4.06.
3. Amended by reg 5(3) of SI 2008 No 1042 as from 19.5.08.
4. Amended by reg 51 of SI 2008 No 1082 as from 27.10.08.
5. Amended by reg 7(3) of SI 2008 No 3157 as from 5.1.09.
6. Amended by reg 2 of SI 2008 No 1848 as from 5.8.09.
7. Amended by reg 9(2) of SI 2010 No 2429 as from 1.11.10.

Average weekly earnings of employed earners

19.–(1) Where a claimant's income consists of earnings from employment as an employed earner his average weekly earnings shall be estimated by reference to his earnings from that employment–
- (a) over a period immediately preceding the benefit week in which the claim is made or treated as made and being a period of–
  - (i) 5 weeks, if he is paid weekly; or
  - (ii) 2 months, if he is paid monthly; or
- (b) whether or not sub-paragraph (a)(i) or (ii) applies, where a claimant's earnings fluctuate, over such other period preceding the benefit week in which the claim is made or treated as made as may, in any particular case, enable his average weekly earnings to be estimated more accurately.

(2) Where the claimant has been in his employment for less than the period specified in paragraph (1)(a)(i) or (ii)–
- (a) if he has received any earnings for the period that he has been in that employment and those earnings are likely to represent his average weekly earnings from that employment his average weekly earnings shall be estimated by reference to those earnings;
- (b) in any other case, the relevant authority shall require the claimant's employer to furnish an estimate of the claimant's likely weekly earnings over such period as the relevant authority may require and the claimant's average weekly earnings shall be estimated by reference to that estimate.

(3) Where the amount of a claimant's earnings changes during an award the relevant authority shall estimate his average weekly earnings by reference to his likely earnings from the employment over such period as is appropriate in order that his average weekly earnings may be estimated accurately but the length of the period shall not in any case exceed 52 weeks.

(4) For the purposes of this regulation the claimant's earnings shall be calculated in accordance with Section 3 of this Part.

Average weekly earnings of self-employed earners

20.–(1) Where a claimant's income consists of earnings from employment as a self-employed earner his average weekly earnings shall be estimated by reference to his earnings from that employment over such period as is appropriate in order that his average weekly earnings may be estimated accurately but the length of the period shall not in any case exceed a year.

(2) For the purposes of this regulation the claimant's earnings shall be calculated in accordance with Section 4 of this Part.

Average weekly income other than earnings

21.–(1) A claimant's income which does not consist of earnings shall, except where paragraph (2) applies, be estimated over such period as is appropriate in order that his average weekly income may be estimated accurately but the length of the period shall not in any case exceed 52 weeks; and nothing in this paragraph shall authorise an authority to disregard any such income other than that specified in Schedule 4.

(2) The period over which any benefit under the benefit Acts is to be taken into account shall be the period in respect of which that benefit is payable.

(3)   For the purposes of this regulation income other than earnings shall be calculated in accordance with Section 5 of this Part.

Calculation of average weekly income from tax credits

22.–(1)   This regulation applies where a claimant receives a tax credit.

(2)   Where this regulation applies, the period over which a tax credit is to be taken into account shall be the period set out in paragraph (3).

(3)   Where the instalment in respect of which payment of a tax credit is made is–

(a)   a daily instalment, the period is 1 day, being the day in respect of which the instalment is paid;

(b)   a weekly instalment, the period is 7 days, ending on the day on which the instalment is due to be paid;

(c)   a two weekly instalment, the period is 14 days, commencing 6 days before the day on which the instalment is due to be paid;

(d)   a four weekly instalment, the period is 28 days, ending on the day on which the instalment is due to be paid.

(4)   For the purposes of this regulation "tax credit" means child tax credit or working tax credit.

Calculation of weekly income

23.–(1)   For the purposes of regulations 19 (average weekly earnings of employed earners), 21 (average weekly income other than earnings) and 22 (calculation of average weekly income from tax credits), where the period in respect of which a payment is made–

(a)   does not exceed a week, the weekly amount shall be the amount of that payment;

(b)   exceeds a week, the weekly amount shall be determined–

(i)   in a case where that period is a month, by multiplying the amount of the payment by 12 and dividing the product by 52;

(ii)   in any other case, by dividing the amount of the payment by the number equal to the number of days in the period to which it relates and multiplying the quotient by 7.

(2)   For the purposes of regulation 20 (average weekly earnings of self-employed earners) the weekly amount of earnings of a claimant shall be determined by dividing his earnings over the assessment period by the number equal to the number of days in that period and multiplying the quotient by 7.

Disregard of changes in tax, contributions etc

24.   In calculating the claimant's income the appropriate authority may disregard any legislative change–

(a)   in the basic or other rates of income tax;

(b)   in the amount of any personal tax relief;

(c)   in the rates of social security contributions payable under the Act or in the lower earnings limit or upper earnings limit for Class 1 contributions under the Act, the lower or upper limits applicable to Class 4 contributions under the Act or the amount specified in section 11(4) of the Act (small earnings exception in relation to Class 2 contributions);

(d)   in the amount of tax payable as a result of an increase in the weekly rate of Category A, B, C or D retirement pension or any addition thereto or any graduated pension payable under the Act;

(e)   in the maximum rate of child tax credit or working tax credit,

for a period not exceeding 30 benefit weeks beginning with the benefit week immediately following the date from which the change is effective.

SECTION 3
Employed earners

Earnings of employed earners

25.–(1) Subject to paragraph (2), "earnings" means in the case of employment as an employed earner, any remuneration or profit derived from that employment and includes–

(a) any bonus or commission;

(b) any payment in lieu of remuneration except any periodic sum paid to a claimant on account of the termination of his employment by reason of redundancy;

(c) any payment in lieu of notice or any lump sum payment intended as compensation for the loss of employment but only in so far as it represents loss of income;

(d) any holiday pay except any payable more than 4 weeks after termination or interruption of the employment;

(e) any payment by way of a retainer;

(f) any payment made by the claimant's employer in respect of expenses not wholly, exclusively and necessarily incurred in the performance of the duties of the employment, including any payment made by the claimant's employer in respect of–

(i) travelling expenses incurred by the claimant between his home and place of employment;

(ii) expenses incurred by the claimant under arrangements made for the care of a member of his family owing to the claimant's absence from home;

(g) any award of compensation made under section 112(4) or 117(3)(a) of the Employment Rights Act 1996 (remedies and compensation for unfair dismissal);

[¹ (gg) any payment or remuneration made under section 28, 34, 64, 68 or 70 of the Employment Rights Act 1996 (right to guarantee payments, remuneration on suspension on medical or maternity grounds, complaints to employment tribunals);]

(h) any such sum as is referred to in section 112 of the Act (certain sums to be earnings for social security purposes);

(i) any statutory sick pay, statutory maternity pay, statutory paternity pay or statutory adoption pay, or a corresponding payment under any enactment having effect in Northern Ireland;

(j) any remuneration paid by or on behalf of an employer to the claimant who for the time being is on maternity leave, paternity leave or adoption leave or is absent from work because he is ill;

(k) the amount of any payment by way of a non-cash voucher which has been taken into account in the computation of a person's earnings in accordance with Part 5 of Schedule 3 to the Social Security (Contributions) Regulations 2001.

(2) Earnings shall not include–

(a) subject to paragraph (3), any payment in kind;

(b) any payment in respect of expenses wholly, exclusively and necessarily incurred in the performance of the duties of the employment;

(c) any occupational pension.

[² (d) any payment in respect of expenses arising out of the claimant's participation in a service user group.]

(3) Paragraph (2)(a) shall not apply in respect of any non-cash voucher referred to in paragraph (1)(k).

Amendments

1. Amended by reg 13(3) of SI 2007 No 2618 as from 1.10.07.
2. Inserted by reg 8(3) of SI 2009 No 2655 as from 2.11.09.

Calculation of net earnings of employed earners

26.–(1) For the purposes of regulation 19 (average weekly earnings of employed earners), the earnings of a claimant derived or likely to be derived from employment as an employed earner to be taken into account shall, subject to paragraph (2), be his net earnings.

(2)   There shall be disregarded from a claimant's net earnings, any sum, where applicable, specified in paragraphs 1 to 14 of Schedule 3.

(3)   For the purposes of paragraph (1) net earnings shall, except where paragraph (6) applies, be calculated by taking into account the gross earnings of the claimant from that employment over the assessment period, less–

(a)   any amount deducted from those earnings by way of–

    (i)   income tax;

    (ii)   primary Class 1 contributions under the Act;

(b)   one-half of any sum paid by the claimant by way of a contribution towards an occupational pension scheme;

(c)   one-half of the amount calculated in accordance with paragraph (5) in respect of any qualifying contribution payable by the claimant; and

(d)   where those earnings include a payment which is payable under any enactment having effect in Northern Ireland and which corresponds to statutory sick pay, statutory maternity pay, statutory paternity pay or statutory adoption pay, any amount deducted from those earnings by way of any contributions which are payable under any enactment having effect in Northern Ireland and which correspond to primary Class 1 contributions under the Act.

(4)   In this regulation ''qualifying contribution'' means any sum which is payable periodically as a contribution towards a personal pension scheme.

(5)   The amount in respect of any qualifying contribution shall be calculated by multiplying the daily amount of the qualifying contribution by the number equal to the number of days in the assessment period; and for the purposes of this regulation the daily amount of the qualifying contribution shall be determined–

(a)   where the qualifying contribution is payable monthly, by multiplying the amount of the qualifying contribution by 12 and dividing the product by 365;

(b)   in any other case, by dividing the amount of the qualifying contribution by the number equal to the number of days in the period to which the qualifying contribution relates.

(6)   Where the earnings of a claimant are estimated under sub-paragraph (b) of paragraph (2) of regulation 19 (average weekly earnings of employed earners), his net earnings shall be calculated by taking into account those earnings over the assessment period, less–

(a)   an amount in respect of income tax equivalent to an amount calculated by applying to those earnings [2] the basic rate of tax applicable to the assessment period less only the personal relief to which the claimant is entitled under sections 257(1) of the Income and Corporation Taxes Act 1988 (personal allowances) as is appropriate to his circumstances but, if the assessment period is less than a year, the earnings to which the [1 [2 basic] rate] of tax is to be applied and the amount of the personal relief deductible under this sub-paragraph shall be calculated on a pro rata basis;

(b)   an amount equivalent to the amount of the primary Class 1 contributions that would be payable by him under the Act in respect of those earnings if such contributions were payable; and

(c)   one-half of any sum which would be payable by the claimant by way of a contribution towards an occupational or personal pension scheme, if the earnings so estimated were actual earnings.

Amendments

1.   Amended by reg 13(4) of SI 2007 No 2618 as from 1.10.07.

2.   Amended by reg 8(4) of SI 2009 No 583 as from 6.4.09.

SECTION 4
Self-employed earners

Earnings of self-employed earners

27.–(1)   Subject to paragraph (2), "earnings", in the case of employment as a self-employed earner, means the gross income of the employment and shall include any allowance paid under section 2 of the 1973 Act or section 2 of the Enterprise and New Towns (Scotland) Act 1990 to the claimant for the purpose of assisting him in carrying on his business unless at the date of claim the allowance has been terminated.

(2)   "Earnings" shall not include any payment to which paragraph 27 or 28 of Schedule 4 refers (payments in respect of a person accommodated with the claimant under arrangements made by a local authority or voluntary organisation and payments made to the claimant by a health authority, local authority or voluntary organisation in respect of persons temporarily in the claimant's care) nor shall it include any sports award.

[¹ [² (3)   This paragraph applies to–

(a)   royalties or other sums paid as a consideration for the use of, or the right to use, any copyright, design, patent or trade mark; or

(b)   any payment in respect of any–
  (i)   book registered under the Public Lending Right Scheme 1982; or
  (ii)   work made under any international public lending right scheme that is analogous to the Public Lending Right Scheme 1982,

where the claimant is the first owner of the copyright, design, patent or trade mark, or an original contributor to the book or work concerned.]

(4)   Where the claimant's earnings consist of any items to which paragraph (3) applies, those earnings shall be taken into account over a period equal to such number of weeks as is equal to the number obtained (and any fraction shall be treated as a corresponding fraction of a week) by dividing the earnings by the amount of council tax benefit which would be payable had the payment not been made plus an amount equal to the total of the sums which would fall to be disregarded from the payment under Schedule 3 (sums to be disregarded in the calculation of earnings) as appropriate in the claimant's case.]

Amendments

1.   Inserted by reg 7(3) of SI 2008 No 698 as from, as it relates to a particular beneficiary, the first day of the benefit week on or after 7.4.08.

2.   Substituted by reg 8(5) of SI 2009 No 583 as from, as it relates to a particular claimant, the first day of the first benefit week starting on or after 6.4.09.

Calculation of net profit of self-employed earners

28.–(1)   For the purposes of regulation 20 (average weekly earnings of self-employed earners) the earnings of a claimant to be taken into account shall be–

(a)   in the case of a self-employed earner who is engaged in employment on his own account, the net profit derived from that employment;

(b)   in the case of a self-employed earner whose employment is carried on in partnership or is that of a share fisherman within the meaning of the Social Security (Mariners' Benefits) Regulations 1975, his share of the net profit derived from that employment, less–
  (i)   an amount in respect of income tax and of social security contributions payable under the Act calculated in accordance with regulation 29 (deduction of tax and contributions for self-employed earners); and
  (ii)   one-half of the amount calculated in accordance with paragraph (11) in respect of any qualifying premium.

(2)   There shall be disregarded from a claimant's net profit, any sum, where applicable, specified in paragraphs 1 to 14 of Schedule 3.

(3)   For the purposes of paragraph (1)(a) the net profit of the employment shall, except where paragraph (9) applies, be calculated by taking into account the earnings of the employment over the assessment period less–

(a) subject to paragraphs (5) to (7), any expenses wholly and exclusively incurred in that period for the purposes of that employment;
(b) an amount in respect of–
　(i) income tax; and
　(ii) social security contributions payable under the Act,
　calculated in accordance with regulation 29 (deduction of tax and contributions for self-employed earners); and
(c) one-half of the amount calculated in accordance with paragraph (11) in respect of any qualifying premium.

(4) For the purposes of paragraph (1)(b) the net profit of the employment shall be calculated by taking into account the earnings of the employment over the assessment period less, subject to paragraphs (5) to (7), any expenses wholly and exclusively incurred in that period for the purposes of the employment.

(5) Subject to paragraph (6), no deduction shall be made under paragraph (3)(a) or (4), in respect of–
(a) any capital expenditure;
(b) the depreciation of any capital asset;
(c) any sum employed or intended to be employed in the setting up or expansion of the employment;
(d) any loss incurred before the beginning of the assessment period;
(e) the repayment of capital on any loan taken out for the purposes of the employment;
(f) any expenses incurred in providing business entertainment; and
(g) any debts, except bad debts proved to be such, but this sub-paragraph shall not apply to any expenses incurred in the recovery of a debt.

(6) A deduction shall be made under paragraph (3)(a) or (4) in respect of the repayment of capital on any loan used for–
(a) the replacement in the course of business of equipment or machinery; and
(b) the repair of an existing business asset except to the extent that any sum is payable under an insurance policy for its repair.

(7) The relevant authority shall refuse to make a deduction in respect of any expenses under paragraph (3)(a) or (4) where it is not satisfied given the nature and the amount of the expense that it has been reasonably incurred.

(8) For the avoidance of doubt–
(a) a deduction shall not be made under paragraph (3)(a) or (4) in respect of any sum unless it has been expended for the purposes of the business;
(b) a deduction shall be made thereunder in respect of–
　(i) the excess of any value added tax paid over value added tax received in the assessment period;
　(ii) any income expended in the repair of an existing business asset except to the extent that any sum is payable under an insurance policy for its repair;
　(iii) any payment of interest on a loan taken out for the purposes of the employment.

(9) Where a claimant is engaged in employment as a child minder the net profit of the employment shall be one-third of the earnings of that employment, less–
(a) an amount in respect of–
　(i) income tax; and
　(ii) social security contributions payable under the Act,
　calculated in accordance with regulation 29 (deduction of tax and contributions for self-employed earners); and
(b) one-half of the amount calculated in accordance with paragraph (11) in respect of any qualifying premium.

(10) For the avoidance of doubt where a claimant is engaged in employment as a self-employed earner and he is also engaged in one or more other employments as a self-employed or employed earner any loss incurred in any one of his employments shall not be offset against his earnings in any other of his employments.

(11)   The amount in respect of any qualifying premium shall be calculated by multiplying the daily amount of the qualifying premium by the number equal to the number of days in the assessment period; and for the purposes of this regulation the daily amount of the qualifying premium shall be determined–

(a)   where the qualifying premium is payable monthly, by multiplying the amount of the qualifying premium by 12 and dividing the product by 365;

(b)   in any other case, by dividing the amount of the qualifying premium by the number equal to the number of days in the period to which the qualifying premium relates.

(12)   In this regulation, "qualifying premium" means any premium which is payable periodically in respect of [¹] a personal pension scheme and is so payable on or after the date of claim.

Amendment

1.   Amended by reg 6(3) of SI 2007 No 1749 as from 16.7.07.

Deduction of tax and contributions of self-employed earners

29.–(1)   The amount to be deducted in respect of income tax under regulation 28(1)(b)(i), (3)(b)(i) or (9)(a)(i) (calculation of net profit of self-employed earners) shall be calculated on the basis of the amount of chargeable income and as if that income were assessable to income tax at [²] the basic rate of tax applicable to the assessment period less only the personal relief to which the claimant is entitled under sections 257(1) of the Income and Corporation Taxes Act 1988 (personal allowances) as is appropriate to his circumstances; but, if the assessment period is less than a year, the earnings to which the [¹ [² basic] rate]of tax is to be applied and the amount of the personal reliefs deductible under this paragraph shall be calculated on a pro rata basis.

(2)   The amount to be deducted in respect of social security contributions under regulation 28(1)(b)(i), (3)(b)(ii) or (9)(a)(ii) shall be the total of–

(a)   the amount of Class 2 contributions payable under section 11(1) or, as the case may be, 11(3) of the Act at the rate applicable to the assessment period except where the claimant's chargeable income is less than the amount specified in section 11(4) of the Act (small earnings exception) for the tax year applicable to the assessment period; but if the assessment period is less than a year, the amount specified for that tax year shall be reduced pro rata; and

(b)   the amount of Class 4 contributions (if any) which would be payable under section 15 of the Act (Class 4 contributions recoverable under the Income Tax Acts) at the percentage rate applicable to the assessment period on so much of the chargeable income as exceeds the lower limit but does not exceed the upper limit of profits and gains applicable for the tax year applicable to the assessment period; but if the assessment period is less than a year, those limits shall be reduced pro rata.

(3)   In this regulation "chargeable income" means–

(a)   except where sub-paragraph (b) applies, the earnings derived from the employment less any expenses deducted under paragraph (3)(a) or, as the case may be, (4) of regulation 28;

(b)   in the case of employment as a child minder, one-third of the earnings of that employment.

Amendments

1.   Amended by reg 13(5) of SI 2007 No 2618 as from 1.10.07.

2.   Amended by reg 8(4) of SI 2009 No 583 as from 6.4.09.

SECTION 5
Other income

Calculation of income other than earnings

30.–(1)   For the purposes of regulation 21 (average weekly income other than earnings), the income of a claimant which does not consist of earnings to be taken into account shall, subject to paragraphs (2) to (8), be his gross income and any capital treated as income under regulation 31 (capital treated as income).

(2)   There shall be disregarded from the calculation of a claimant's gross income under paragraph (1), any sum, where applicable, specified in Schedule 4.

[² (3)]

[² (4)]

[² (4A)]

(5)   Where the payment of any benefit under the benefit Acts is subject to any deduction by way of recovery the amount to be taken into account under paragraph (1) shall be the gross amount payable.

[⁴ (5A) Where the claimant or, where he is a member of a couple, his partner is receiving a contributory employment and support allowance and that benefit has been reduced under regulation 63 of the Employment and Support Allowance Regulations, the amount of that benefit to be taken into account is the amount as if it had not been reduced.]

(6)   Where an award of any working tax credit or child tax credit under the Tax Credits Act is subject to a deduction by way of recovery of an overpayment of working tax credit or child tax credit which arose in a previous tax year the amount to be taken into account under paragraph (1) shall be the amount of working tax credit or child tax credit awarded less the amount of that deduction.

(7)   In paragraph (6), "tax year" means a period beginning with 6th April in one year and ending with 5th April in the next.

(8)   [³ Paragraphs (9) and (9A) apply] where–

(a)   a relevant payment has been made to a person in an academic year; and

(b)   that person abandons, or is dismissed from, his course of study before the payment to him of the final instalment of the relevant payment.

(9)   [³ Where a relevant payment is made quarterly, the] amount of a relevant payment to be taken into account for the assessment period for the purposes of paragraph (1) in respect of a person to whom paragraph (8) applies, shall be calculated by applying the formula–

$$\frac{A - (B \times C)}{D}$$

where–

A = the total amount of the relevant payment which that person would have received had he remained a student until the last day of the academic term in which he abandoned, or was dismissed from, his course, less any deduction under regulation 51(5);

B = the number of benefit weeks from the benefit week immediately following that which includes the first day of that academic year to the benefit week which includes the day on which the person abandoned, or was dismissed from, his course;

C = the weekly amount of the relevant payment, before the application of the £10 disregard, which would have been taken into account as income under regulation 51(2) had the person not abandoned or been dismissed from, his course and, in the case of a person who was not entitled to council tax benefit immediately before he abandoned or was dismissed from his course, had that person, at that time, been entitled to housing benefit;

D = the number of benefit weeks in the assessment period.

[³ (9A)   Where a relevant payment is made by two or more instalments in a quarter, the amount of a relevant payment to be taken into account for the assessment period for the purposes of paragraph (1) in respect of a person to whom paragraph (8) applies, shall be calculated by applying the formula in paragraph (9) but as if–

A = the total amount of relevant payments which that person received, or would have received, from the first day of the academic year to the day the person abandoned the course, or was dismissed from it, less any deduction under regulation 51(5).]

(10)   [³ In this regulation]–

"academic year" and "student loan" shall have the same meanings as for the purposes of Part 5;

[³ "assessment period" means–
  (a) in a case where a relevant payment is made quarterly, the period beginning with the benefit week which includes the day on which the person abandoned, or was dismissed from, his course and ending with the benefit week which includes the last day of the last quarter for which an instalment of the relevant payment was payable to that person;
  (b) in a case where the relevant payment is made by two or more instalments in a quarter, the period beginning with the benefit week which includes the day on which the person abandoned, or was dismissed from, his course and ending with the benefit week which includes–
    (i)   the day immediately before the day on which the next instalment of the relevant payment would have been due had the payments continued; or
    (ii) the last day of the last quarter for which an instalment of the relevant payment was payable to that person,
  whichever of those dates is earlier;]
[³ "quarter" in relation to an assessment period means a period in that year beginning on–
  (a) 1st January and ending on 31st March;
  (b) 1st April and ending on 30th June;
  (c) 1st July and ending on 31st August; or
  (d) 1st September and ending on 31st December;].
"relevant payment" means either a student loan or an amount intended for the maintenance of dependants referred to in regulation 46(7) or both.
  (11) For the avoidance of doubt there shall be included as income to be taken into account under paragraph (1)–
  (a) any payment to which regulation 25(2) (payments not earnings) applies; or
  (b) in the case of a claimant who is receiving support under section 95 or 98 of the Immigration and Asylum Act including support provided by virtue of regulations made under Schedule 9 to that Act, the amount of such support provided in respect of essential living needs of the claimant and his dependants (if any) as is specified in regulations made under paragraph 3 of Schedule 8 to the Immigration and Asylum Act.

Amendments
  1.   Inserted by reg 4 of SI 2006 No 2813 as from 20.11.06.
  2.   Omitted by reg 5(b) of SI 2007 No 1619 as from 3.7.07.
  3.   Amended by reg 6(2) of SI 2008 No 1599 as from, for students whose period of study begins on or after 1.8.08 but before 1.9.08, on the day the period of study begins; in any other case 1.9.08.
  4.   Amended by reg 52 of SI 2008 No 1082 as from 27.10.08.

Capital treated as income
31.–(1) Any capital payable by instalments which are outstanding at the date on which the claim is made or treated as made, or, at the date of any subsequent revision or supersession, shall, if the aggregate of the instalments outstanding and the amount of the claimant's capital otherwise calculated in accordance with Section 6 exceeds £16,000, be treated as income.
  (2) Any payment received under an annuity shall be treated as income.
  (3) Any earnings to the extent that they are not a payment of income shall be treated as income.
  (4) Any Career Development Loan paid pursuant to section 2 of the 1973 Act shall be treated as income.
  (5) Where an agreement or court order provides that payments shall be made to the claimant in consequence of any personal injury to the claimant and that such payments are to be made, wholly or partly, by way of periodic payments, any such periodic payments received by the claimant (but not a payment which is treated as capital by virtue of this Part), shall be treated as income.

Notional income

32.–(1)   A claimant shall be treated as possessing income of which he has deprived himself for the purpose of securing entitlement to housing benefit or increasing the amount of that benefit.

(2)   Except in the case of–

(a)   a discretionary trust;

(b)   a trust derived from a payment made in consequence of a personal injury;

(c)   a personal pension scheme [¹ , occupational pension scheme] [² [⁴] or a payment made by the Board of the Pension Protection Fund] where the claimant [¹³ has not attained the qualifying age for state pension credit];

[³ (d) any sum to which paragraph 47(2)(a) of Schedule 5 (capital to be disregarded) applies which is administered in the way referred to in paragraph 47(1)(a);

(da)   any sum to which paragraph 48(a) of Schedule 5 refers;]

(e)   rehabilitation allowance made under section 2 of the 1973 Act;

(f)   child tax credit; or

(g)   working tax credit,

[¹¹ (h) any sum to which paragraph (13) applies;]

any income which would become available to the claimant upon application being made, but which has not been acquired by him, shall be treated as possessed by the claimant but only from the date on which it could be expected to be acquired were an application made.

[⁴ [⁷ (3)]

[⁴ [⁷ (3A)]]

[⁷ (4)]

[⁷ (5)]

(6)   Any payment of income, other than a payment of income specified in paragraph (7), made–

(a)   to a third party in respect of a single claimant or a member of the family (but not a member of the third party's family) shall, where that payment is a payment of an occupational pension [² , a pension or other periodical payment made under a personal pension scheme or a payment made by the Board of the Pension Protection Fund], be treated as possessed by that single claimant or, as the case may be, by that member;

(b)   to a third party in respect of a single claimant or in respect of a member of the family (but not a member of the third party's family) shall, where it is not a payment referred to in sub-paragraph (a), be treated as possessed by that single claimant or by that member to the extent that it is used for the food, ordinary clothing or footwear, household fuel or rent of that single claimant or, as the case may be, of any member of that family or is used for any council tax or water charges for which that claimant or member is liable;

(c)   to a single claimant or a member of the family in respect of a third party (but not in respect of another member of that family) shall be treated as possessed by that single claimant or, as the case may be, that member of the family to the extent that it is kept or used by him or used by or on behalf of any member of the family.

(7)   Paragraph (6) shall not apply in respect of a payment of income made–

(a)   under [¹² or by] the Macfarlane Trust, the Macfarlane (Special Payments) Trust, the Macfarlane (Special Payments) (No. 2) Trust, the Fund, the Eileen Trust [¹² , MFET Limited] or the Independent Living [⁸ Fund (2006)];

(b)   pursuant to section 19(1)(a) of the Coal Industry Act 1994 (concessionary coal);

(c)   pursuant to section 2 of the 1973 Act in respect of a person's participation–

(i)   in an employment programme specified in regulation 75(1)(a)(ii) of the Jobseeker's Allowance Regulations;

(ii)   in a training scheme specified in regulation 75(1)(b)(ii) of those Regulations;

(iii)   in the Intense Activity Period specified in regulation 75(1)(a)(iv) of those Regulations [⁶]; [¹⁰]

(iv)   in a qualifying course within the meaning specified in regulation 17A(7) of those Regulations; [¹⁰ or]

[¹⁰ (v) in the Flexible New Deal specified in regulation 75(1)(a)(v) of those Regulations;]

[(ca) in respect of a person's participation in the Work for Your Benefit Pilot Scheme;]

(d)   under an occupational pension scheme [² , in respect of a pension or other periodical payment made under a personal pension scheme or a payment made by the Board of the Pension Protection Fund] where–

    (i)   a bankruptcy order has been made in respect of the person in respect of whom the payment has been made or, in Scotland, the estate of that person is subject to sequestration or a judicial factor has been appointed on that person's estate under section 41 of the Solicitors (Scotland) Act 1980;

    (ii)   the payment is made to the trustee in bankruptcy or any other person acting on behalf of the creditors; and

    (iii) the person referred to in (i) and any member of his family does not possess, or is not treated as possessing, any other income apart from that payment.

(8)   Where a claimant is in receipt of any benefit (other than council tax benefit) under the benefit Acts and the rate of that benefit is altered with effect from a date on or after 1st April in any year but not more than 14 days thereafter, the relevant authority shall treat the claimant as possessing such benefit at the altered rate from either 1st April or the first Monday in April in that year, whichever date the relevant authority shall select to apply in its area, to the date on which the altered rate is to take effect.

(9)   Subject to paragraph (10), where–

(a)   a claimant performs a service for another person; and

(b)   that person makes no payment of earnings or pays less than that paid for a comparable employment in the area,

the relevant authority shall treat the claimant as possessing such earnings (if any) as is reasonable for that employment unless the claimant satisfies the authority that the means of that person are insufficient for him to pay or to pay more for the service.

(10)   Paragraph (9) shall not apply–

(a)   to a claimant who is engaged by a charitable or voluntary organisation or who is a volunteer if the relevant authority is satisfied in any of those cases that it is reasonable for him to provide those services free of charge; or

(b)   in a case where the service is performed in connection with–

    (i)   the claimant's participation in an employment or training programme in accordance with regulation 19(1)(q) of the Jobseeker's Allowance Regulations, other than where the service is performed in connection with the claimant's participation in the Intense Activity Period specified in regulation 75(1)(a)(iv) of those Regulations [⁶]; or

    (ii)   the claimant's or the claimant's partner's participation in an employment or training programme as defined in regulation 19(3) of those Regulations for which a training allowance is not payable or, where such an allowance is payable, it is payable for the sole purpose of reimbursement of travelling or meal expenses to the person participating in that programme. [⁵ or

(c)   to a claimant who is participating in a work placement approved by the Secretary of State (or a person providing services to the Secretary of State) before the placement starts.

(10A) In paragraph (10)(c) "work placement" means practical work experience which is not undertaken in expectation of payment.]

(11)   Where a claimant is treated as possessing any income under any of paragraphs (1) to (8), the foregoing provisions of this Part shall apply for the purposes of calculating the amount of that income as if a payment had actually been made and as if it were actual income which he does possess.

(12)   Where a claimant is treated as possessing any earnings under paragraph (9) the foregoing provisions of this Part shall apply for the purposes of calculating the amount of those earnings as if a payment had actually been made and as if they were actual

earnings which he does possess except that paragraph (3) of regulation 26 (calculation of net earnings of employed earners) shall not apply and his net earnings shall be calculated by taking into account those earnings which he is treated as possessing, less–

(a) an amount in respect of income tax equivalent to an amount calculated by applying to those earnings [⁹] the basic rate of tax applicable to the assessment period less only the personal relief to which the claimant is entitled under sections 257(1) of the Income and Corporation Taxes Act 1988 (personal allowances) as is appropriate to his circumstances; but, if the assessment period is less than a year, the earnings to which the [⁵ [⁹ basic] rate] of tax is to be applied and the amount of the personal relief deductible under this sub-paragraph shall be calculated on a pro rata basis;

(b) an amount equivalent to the amount of the primary Class 1 contributions that would be payable by him under the Act in respect of those earnings if such contributions were payable; and

(c) one-half of any sum payable by the claimant by way of a contribution towards an occupational or personal pension scheme.

[¹¹ (13) Paragraphs (1), (2), (6) and (9) shall not apply in respect of any amount of income other than earnings, or earnings of an employed earner, arising out of the claimant's participation in a service user group.]

Modifications

Reg 32(7) is modified by reg 14 Jobseeker's Allowance (Work for Your Benefit Pilot Scheme) Regulations 2010 SI No.1222 (see p1247) as from 22 November 2010 but only for those ordinarily resident in a pilot area or whose address for payment of JSA is located within such an area. The modifications are shown in italics above. They cease to have effect on 21 November 2013.

Amendments

1. Amended by reg 4A(2) of SI 2005 No 2465 as inserted by Sch 2 para 28(3) of SI 2006 No 217 as from 6.4.06.
2. Substituted by reg 9(2) of SI 2006 No 588 as from 6.4.06.
3. Substituted by reg 8(2) of SI 2007 No 719 as from 2.4.07.
4. Amended by reg 6(4) of SI 2007 No 1749 as from 16.7.07.
5. Amended by reg 13(6) of SI 2007 No 2618 as from 1.10.07.
6. Amended by reg 7(4)(a) of SI 2008 No 698 as from 14.4.08.
7. Omitted by reg 5(4) of SI 2008 No 1042 as from 19.5.08.
8. Amended by reg 8(4)(a) of SI 2008 No 2767 as from 17.11.08.
9. Amended by reg 8(4) of SI 2009 No 583 as from 6.4.09.
10. Amended by reg 3 of SI 2009 No 480 as from 5.10.09.
11. Inserted by reg 8(4) of SI 2009 No 2655 as from 2.11.09.
12. Amended by reg 10(3) and (5) of SI 2010 No 641 as from 1.4.10 (5.4.10 where rent payable weekly or in multiples of a week).
13. Amended by reg 10(6) of SI 2010 No 641 as from 6.4.10.

SECTION 6
Capital

Capital limit

33. For the purposes of section 134(1) of the Act as it applies to council tax benefit (no entitlement to benefit if capital exceeds prescribed amount), the prescribed amount is £16,000.

Calculation of capital

34.–(1) For the purposes of Part 7 of the Act as it applies to council tax benefit, the capital of a claimant to be taken into account shall, subject to paragraph (2), be the whole of his capital calculated in accordance with this Part and any income treated as capital under regulation 36 (income treated as capital).

(2) There shall be disregarded from the calculation of a claimant's capital under paragraph (1), any capital, where applicable, specified in Schedule 5.

Disregard of capital of child and young person
35. The capital of a child or young person who is a member of the claimant's family shall not be treated as capital of the claimant.

Income treated as capital
36.–(1) Any bounty derived from employment to which paragraph 8 of Schedule 3 applies and paid at intervals of at least one year shall be treated as capital.

(2) Any amount by way of a refund of income tax deducted from profits or emoluments chargeable to income tax under Schedule D or E shall be treated as capital.

(3) Any holiday pay which is not earnings under regulation 25(1)(d) (earnings of employed earners) shall be treated as capital.

(4) Except any income derived from capital disregarded under paragraphs 1, 2, 4, 8, 14 [¹ , 25 to 28, 47 or 48] of Schedule 5, any income derived from capital shall be treated as capital but only from the date it is normally due to be credited to the claimant's account.

(5) In the case of employment as an employed earner, any advance of earnings or any loan made by the claimant's employer shall be treated as capital.

(6) Any charitable or voluntary payment which is not made or due to be made at regular intervals, other than a payment which is made under [³ or by] the Trusts, the Fund, the Eileen Trust [³ , MFET Limited], the Independent Living [² Fund (2006)] or the London Bombings Charitable Relief Fund, shall be treated as capital.

(7) There shall be treated as capital the gross receipts of any commercial activity carried on by a person in respect of which assistance is received under the self-employment route, but only in so far as those receipts were payable into a special account [³] during the period in which that person was receiving such assistance.

(8) Any arrears of subsistence allowance which are paid to a claimant as a lump sum shall be treated as capital.

(9) Any arrears of working tax credit or child tax credit shall be treated as capital.

Amendments
1. Amended by reg 17(2) of SI 2006 No 2378 from the first day of the first benefit week to commence on or after 2.10.06.
2. Amended by reg 8(4)(b) of SI 2008 No 2767 as from 17.11.08.
3. Amended by reg 10(3), (5) and (6) of SI 2010 No 641 as from 1.4.10 (5.4.10 where rent payable weekly or in multiples of a week).

[¹Calculation of capital in the United Kingdom
37. Capital which a claimant possesses in the United Kingdom shall be calculated at its current market or surrender value less–

(a) where there would be expenses attributable to the sale, 10 per cent.; and

(b) the amount of any encumbrance secured on it.]

Amendment
1. Substituted by reg 13(7) of SI 2007 No 2618 as from 1.10.07.

Calculation of capital outside the United Kingdom
38. Capital which a claimant possesses in a country outside the United Kingdom shall be calculated–

(a) in a case where there is no prohibition in that country against the transfer to the United Kingdom of an amount equal to its current market or surrender value in that country, at that value;

(b) in a case where there is such a prohibition, at the price which it would realise if sold in the United Kingdom to a willing buyer,

less, where there would be expenses attributable to sale, 10 per cent. and the amount of any encumbrances secured on it.

Notional capital
39.–(1) A claimant shall be treated as possessing capital of which he has deprived himself for the purpose of securing entitlement to council tax benefit or increasing the

amount of that benefit except to the extent that that capital is reduced in accordance with regulation 40 (diminishing notional capital rule).

(2)   Except in the case of–

(a)   a discretionary trust; or

(b)   a trust derived from a payment made in consequence of a personal injury; or

(c)   any loan which would be obtained only if secured against capital disregarded under Schedule 5; or

(d)   a personal pension scheme [¹ , occupational pension scheme] [² [⁴] or a payment made by the Board of the Pension Protection Fund]; or

[³ (e)   any sum to which paragraph 47(2)(a) of Schedule 5 (capital to be disregarded) applies which is administered in the way referred to in paragraph 47(1)(a); or

(ea)   any sum to which paragraph 48(a) of Schedule 5 refers; or]

(f)   child tax credit; or

(g)   working tax credit,

any capital which would become available to the claimant upon application being made, but which has not been acquired by him, shall be treated as possessed by him but only from the date on which it could be expected to be acquired were an application made.

(3)   Any payment of capital, other than a payment of capital specified in paragraph (4), made–

(a)   to a third party in respect of a single claimant or a member of the family (but not a member of the third party's family) shall, where that payment is a payment of an occupational pension [² , a pension or other periodical payment made under a personal pension scheme or a payment made by the Board of the Pension Protection Fund], be treated as possessed by that single claimant or, as the case may be, by that member;

(b)   to a third party in respect of a single claimant or in respect of a member of the family (but not a member of the third party's family) shall, where it is not a payment referred to in sub-paragraph (a), be treated as possessed by that single claimant or by that member to the extent that it is used for the food, ordinary clothing or footwear, household fuel or rent of that single claimant or, as the case may be, of any member of that family or is used for any council tax or water charges for which that claimant or member is liable;

(c)   to a single claimant or a member of the family in respect of a third party (but not in respect of another member of the family) shall be treated as possessed by that single claimant or, as the case may be, that member of the family to the extent that it is kept or used by him or used by or on behalf of any member of the family.

(4)   Paragraph (3) shall not apply in respect of a payment of capital made–

(a)   under [⁸ or by] any of the Trusts, the Fund, the Eileen Trust [⁸ , MFET Limited], the Independent Living [⁶ Fund (2006)], the Skipton Fund, or the London Bombings Relief Charitable Fund;

(b)   pursuant to section 2 of the 1973 Act in respect of a person's participation–

(i)   in an employment programme specified in regulation 75(1)(a)(ii) of the Jobseeker's Allowance Regulations;

(ii)   in a training scheme specified in regulation 75(1)(b)(ii) of those Regulations;

(iii)   in the Intense Activity Period specified in regulation 75(1)(a)(iv) of those Regulations [⁵]; [⁷]

(iv)   in a qualifying course within the meaning specified in regulation 17A(7) of those Regulations; [⁷ or]

[⁷ (v) in the Flexible New Deal specified in regulation 75(1)(a)(v) of those Regulations;]

[(ba) in respect of a person's participation in the Work for Your Benefit Pilot Scheme;]

(c)   under an occupational pension scheme [² , in respect of a pension or other periodical payment made under a personal pension scheme or a payment made by the Board of the Pension Protection Fund] where–

(i)   a bankruptcy order has been made in respect of the person in respect of whom the payment has been made or, in Scotland, the estate of that person is subject to sequestration or a judicial factor has been appointed on that person's estate under section 41 of the Solicitors (Scotland) Act 1980;

(ii)   the payment is made to the trustee in bankruptcy or any other person acting on behalf of the creditors; and

(iii) the person referred to in (i) and any member of his family does not possess, or is not treated as possessing, any other income apart from that payment.

(5)   Where a claimant stands in relation to a company in a position analogous to that of a sole owner or partner in the business of that company, he may be treated as if he were such sole owner or partner and in such a case–

(a)   the value of his holding in that company shall, notwithstanding regulation 34 (calculation of capital) be disregarded; and

(b)   he shall, subject to paragraph (6), be treated as possessing an amount of capital equal to the value or, as the case may be, his share of the value of the capital of that company and the foregoing provisions of this Section shall apply for the purposes of calculating that amount as if it were actual capital which he does possess.

(6)   For so long as the claimant undertakes activities in the course of the business of the company, the amount which he is treated as possessing under paragraph (5) shall be disregarded.

(7)   Where a claimant is treated as possessing capital under any of paragraphs (1) to (3) the foregoing provisions of this Section shall apply for the purposes of calculating its amount as if it were actual capital which he does possess.

Modifications

Reg 34(4) is modified by reg 15 Jobseeker's Allowance (Work for Your Benefit Pilot Scheme) Regulations 2010 SI No.1222 (see p1247) as from 22 November 2010 but only for those ordinarily resident in a pilot area or whose address for payment of JSA is located within such an area. The modifications are shown in italics above. They cease to have effect on 21 November 2013.

Amendments

1.   Amended by reg 4A(3) of SI 2005 No 2465 as inserted by Sch 2 para 28(3) of SI 2006 No 217 as from 6.4.06.
2.   Amended by reg 9(3) of SI 2006 No 588 as from 6.4.06.
3.   Substituted by reg 8(3) of SI 2007 No 719 as from 2.4.07.
4.   Amended by reg 6(5) of SI 2007 No 1749 as from 16.7.07.
5.   Amended by reg 7(4)(b) of SI 2008 No 698 as from 14.4.08.
6.   Amended by reg 8(4)(c) of SI 2008 No 2767 as from 17.11.08.
7.   Amended by reg 3 of SI 2009 No 480 as from 5.10.09.
8.   Amended by reg 10(3) and (5) of SI 2010 No 641 as from 1.4.10 (5.4.10 where rent payable weekly or in multiples of a week).

Diminishing notional capital rule

40.–(1) Where a claimant is treated as possessing capital under regulation 39(1) (notional capital), the amount which he is treated as possessing–

(a)   in the case of a week that is subsequent to–

(i)   the relevant week in respect of which the conditions set out in paragraph (2) are satisfied; or

(ii)   a week which follows that relevant week and which satisfies those conditions,

shall be reduced by an amount determined under paragraph (3);

(b)   in the case of a week in respect of which paragraph (1)(a) does not apply but where–

(i)   that week is a week subsequent to the relevant week; and

(ii)   that relevant week is a week in which the condition in paragraph (4) is satisfied,

shall be reduced by the amount determined under paragraph (4).

(2)   This paragraph applies to a benefit week or part-week where the claimant satisfies the conditions that–

(a)   he is in receipt of council tax benefit; and

(b)   but for regulation 39(1), he would have received an additional amount of council tax benefit in that week.

(3)   In a case to which paragraph (2) applies, the amount of the reduction for the purposes of paragraph (1)(a) shall be equal to the aggregate of–

(a)   the additional amount to which sub-paragraph (2)(b) refers;

(b)   where the claimant has also claimed housing benefit, the amount of any housing benefit or any additional amount of that benefit to which he would have been entitled in respect of the whole or part of the benefit week to which paragraph (2) refers but for the application of regulation 49(1) of the Housing Benefit Regulations (notional capital);

(c)   where the claimant has also claimed income support, the amount of income support to which he would have been entitled in respect of the whole or part of the benefit week to which paragraph (2) refers but for the application of regulation 51(1) of the Income Support Regulations (notional capital); [¹]

(d)   where the claimant has also claimed a jobseeker's allowance, the amount of an income-based jobseeker's allowance to which he would have been entitled in respect of the whole or part of the benefit week to which paragraph (2) refers but for the application of regulation 113 of the Jobseeker's Allowance Regulations (notional capital).[¹ and

[¹ (e)   where the claimant has also claimed an employment and support allowance, the amount of an income-related employment and support allowance to which he would have been entitled in respect of the whole or part of benefit week to which paragraph (2) refers but for the application of regulation 115 of the Employment and Support Allowance Regulations (notional capital).]

(4)   Subject to paragraph (5), for the purposes of paragraph (1)(b) the condition is that the claimant would have been entitled to council tax benefit in the relevant week but for regulation 39(1), and in such a case the amount of the reduction shall be equal to the aggregate of–

(a)   the amount of council tax benefit to which the claimant would have been entitled in the relevant week but for regulation 39(1); and for the purposes of this sub-paragraph if the amount is in respect of a part-week, that amount shall be determined by dividing the amount of council tax benefit to which he would have been so entitled by the number equal to the number of days in the part-week and multiplying the quotient so obtained by 7;

(b)   if the claimant would, but for regulation 49(1) of the Housing Benefit Regulations, have been entitled to housing benefit or to an additional amount of housing benefit in respect of the benefit week which includes the last day of the relevant week, the amount which is equal to–

(i)   in a case where no housing benefit is payable, the amount to which he would have been entitled; or

(ii)   in any other case, the amount equal to the additional amount of housing benefit to which he would have been entitled,

and, for the purposes of this sub-paragraph, if the amount is in respect of a part-week, that amount shall be determined by dividing the amount of housing benefit to which he would have been so entitled by the number equal to the number of days in the part-week and multiplying the quotient so obtained by 7;

(c)   if the claimant would, but for regulation 51(1) of the Income Support Regulations, have been entitled to income support in respect of the benefit week, within the meaning of regulation 2(1) of those Regulations (interpretation), which includes the last day of the relevant week, the amount to which he would have been entitled and, for the purposes of this sub-paragraph, if the amount is in respect of a part-week, that amount shall be determined by dividing the amount of the income support to which he would have been so entitled by the number equal to the number of days in the part-week and multiplying the quotient so obtained by 7; [¹]

(d) if the claimant would, but for regulation 113 of the Jobseeker's Allowance Regulations, have been entitled to an income-based jobseeker's allowance in respect of the benefit week, within the meaning of regulation 1(3) of those Regulations (interpretation), which includes the last day of the relevant week, the amount to which he would have been entitled and, for the purposes of this sub-paragraph, if the amount is in respect of a part-week, that amount shall be determined by dividing the amount of the income-based jobseeker's allowance to which he would have been so entitled by the number equal to the number of days in the part-week and multiplying the quotient so obtained by 7. [¹ and

[¹ (e) if the claimant would, but for regulation 115 of the Employment and Support Allowance Regulations, have been entitled to an income-related employment and support allowance in respect of the benefit week, within the meaning of regulation 2(1) of those Regulations (interpretation), which includes the last day of the relevant week, the amount to which he would have been entitled and, for the purposes of this sub-paragraph, if the amount is in respect of a part-week, that amount must be determined by dividing the amount of the income-related employment and support allowance to which he would have been so entitled by the number equal to the number of days in that part-week and multiplying the quotient so obtained by 7.]

(5) The amount determined under paragraph (4) shall be re-determined under that paragraph if the claimant makes a further claim for council tax benefit and the conditions in paragraph (6) are satisfied, and in such a case–

(a) sub-paragraphs (a) to (d) of paragraph (4) shall apply as if for the words ''relevant week'' there were substituted the words ''relevant subsequent week''; and

(b) subject to paragraph (7), the amount as re-determined shall have effect from the first week following the relevant subsequent week in question.

(6) The conditions are that–

(a) a further claim is made 26 or more weeks after–

(i) the date on which the claimant made a claim for council tax benefit in respect of which he was first treated as possessing the capital in question under regulation 39(1);

(ii) in a case where there has been at least one re-determination in accordance with paragraph (5), the date on which he last made a claim for council tax benefit which resulted in the weekly amount being re-determined, or

(iii) the date on which he last ceased to be entitled to council tax benefit, whichever last occurred; and

(b) the claimant would have been entitled to council tax benefit but for regulation 39(1).

(7) The amount as re-determined pursuant to paragraph (5) shall not have effect if it is less than the amount which applied in that case immediately before the re-determination and in such a case the higher amount shall continue to have effect.

(8) For the purposes of this regulation–

(a) ''part-week''–

(i) in paragraph (4)(a) means a period of less than a week for which council tax benefit is allowed;

(ii) in paragraph (4)(b) means a period of less than a week for which housing benefit is payable;

(iii) in paragraph (4)(c) [¹ , (d) and (e)] means–

(aa) a period of less than a week which is the whole period for which income support [¹ , an income-related employment and support allowance] or, as the case may be, an income-based jobseeker's allowance is payable; and

(bb) any other period of less than a week for which it is payable;

(b) "relevant week" means the benefit week or part-week in which the capital in question of which the claimant has deprived himself within the meaning of regulation 39(1)–

    (i) was first taken into account for the purpose of determining his entitlement to council tax benefit; or

    (ii) was taken into account on a subsequent occasion for the purpose of determining or re-determining his entitlement to council tax benefit on that subsequent occasion and that determination or re-determination resulted in his beginning to receive, or ceasing to receive, council tax benefit;

and where more than one benefit week is identified by reference to heads (i) and (ii) of this sub-paragraph the later or latest such benefit week or, as the case may be, the later or latest such part-week;

(c) "relevant subsequent week" means the benefit week or part-week which includes the day on which the further claim or, if more than one further claim has been made, the last such claim was made.

Amendment

1.   Amended by reg 53 of SI 2008 No 1082 as from 27.10.08.

Capital jointly held

41.   Except where a claimant possesses capital which is disregarded under regulation 39(5) (notional capital) where a claimant and one or more persons are beneficially entitled in possession to any capital asset they shall be treated as if each of them were entitled in possession to the whole beneficial interest therein in an equal share and the foregoing provisions of this Section shall apply for the purposes of calculating the amount of capital which the claimant is treated as possessing as if it were actual capital which the claimant does possess.

Calculation of tariff income from capital

42.–[¹ (1)   Where the claimant's capital calculated in accordance with this Part exceeds £6,000, it shall be treated as equivalent to a weekly income of £1 for each complete £250 in excess of £6,000 but not exceeding £16,000.]

(2)   Notwithstanding paragraph (1) where any part of the excess is not a complete £250 that part shall be treated as equivalent to a weekly tariff income of £1.

(3)   For the purposes of paragraph (1), capital includes any income treated as capital under regulation 36 (income treated as capital).

Amendment

1.   Substituted by reg 4A(4) of SI 2005 No 2465 as inserted by Sch 2 para 28(3) of SI 2006 No 217 as from 6.4.06.

PART 5
Students
SECTION 1
General

General Note

Most full-time students are excluded from entitlement to CTB, as are students who are "persons from abroad" defined in reg 7: reg 45. Exceptions to the rule are found in reg 45(3). Full-time students are not precluded from claiming the alternative maximum CTB (second adult rebate): reg 45(1).

Even if a student is not excluded from entitlement to CTB, s/he must still satisfy the other rules set out in this Part before qualifying. The general rule is that claims by students are decided in the same way as claims by non-students, subject to the special income and capital rules found in regs 46–56.

The general exclusion of full-time students from CTB does not prevent a claimant whose partner is a student from claiming CTB.

There are no comparable rules for students in the CTB(SPC) Regs so claimants covered by those regulations are not excluded from entitlement to CTB for being students. In addition, student loan and grant income is ignored; it does not come within the definition of "income" in reg 19 CTB(SPC) Regs.

Interpretation

43.–(1)   In this Part–

"academic year" means the period of twelve months beginning on 1st January, 1st April, 1st July or 1st September according to whether the course in question begins in the winter, the spring, the summer or the autumn respectively but if students are required to begin attending the course during August or September and to continue attending through the autumn, the academic year of the course shall be considered to begin in the autumn rather than the summer;

"access funds" means–

(a)   grants made under section 68 of the Further and Higher Education Act 1992 for the purpose of providing funds on a discretionary basis to be paid to students;

(b)   grants made under sections 73(a) and (c) and 74(1) of the Education (Scotland) Act 1980;

(c)   grants made under Article 30 of the Education and Libraries (Northern Ireland) Order 1993 or grants, loans or other payments made under Article 5 of the Further Education (Northern Ireland) Order 1997 in each case being grants, or grants, loans or other payments as the case may be, for the purpose of assisting students in financial difficulties;

(d)   discretionary payments, known as "learner support funds", which are made available to students in further education by institutions out of funds provided by the [⁷ Young People's Learning Agency for England under sections 61 and 62 of the Apprenticeships, Skills, Children and Learning Act 2009 or the Chief Executive of Skills Funding under sections 100 and 101 of that Act]; or

(e)   Financial Contingency Funds made available by the [⁴ Welsh Ministers];

"college of further education" means a college of further education within the meaning of Part 1 of the Further and Higher Education (Scotland) Act 1992;

[⁵ "contribution" means–

(a)   any contribution in respect of the income of a student or any person which the Secretary of State, the Scottish Ministers or an education authority takes into account in ascertaining the amount of a student's grant or student loan; or

(b)   any sums, which in determining the amount of a student's allowance or bursary in Scotland under the Education (Scotland) Act 1980, the Scottish Ministers or education authority takes into account being sums which the Scottish Ministers or education authority consider that it is reasonable for the following persons to contribute towards the holder's expenses–

(i)   the holder of the allowance or bursary;

(ii)   the holder's parents;

(iii)   the holder's parent's spouse, civil partner or a person ordinarily living with the holder's parent as if he or she were the spouse or civil partner of that parent; or

(iv)   the holder's spouse or civil partner;]

"course of study" means any course of study, whether or not it is a sandwich course and whether or not a grant is made for attending or undertaking it;

"covenant income" means the gross income payable to a full-time student under a Deed of Covenant by his parent;

"education authority" means a government department, [⁶ a local authority as defined in section 579 of the Education Act 1996 (interpretation)], a local education authority as defined in section 123 of the Local Government (Scotland) Act 1973, an education and library board established under Article 3 of the Education and Libraries (Northern Ireland) Order 1986, any body which is a research council for the purposes of the Science and Technology Act 1965 or any analogous government department, authority, board or body, of the Channel Islands, Isle of Man or any other country outside Great Britain;

"full-time course of study" means a full-time course of study which–

(a)   is not funded in whole or in part by the [⁷ Young People's Learning Agency for England, the Chief Executive of Skills Funding] or by the [¹ [⁴ Welsh Ministers]] or a full-time course of study which is not funded in whole or in part by the

Scottish Ministers at a college of further education or a full-time course of study which is a course of higher education and is funded in whole or in part by the Scottish Ministers;

(b) is funded in whole or in part by the [⁷ Young People's Learning Agency for England, the Chief Executive of Skills Funding] or by the [¹ [⁴ Welsh Ministers]] if it involves more than 16 guided learning hours per week for the student in question, according to the number of guided learning hours per week for that student set out–

[⁷ (i) in the case of a course funded by the Young People's Learning Agency for England or the Chief Executive of Skills Funding, in the student's learning agreement signed on behalf of the establishment which is funded by either of those bodies for the delivery of that course; or]

(ii) in the case of a course funded by the [¹ [⁴ Welsh Ministers]], in a document signed on behalf of the establishment which is funded by that Council for the delivery of that course; or

(c) is not higher education and is funded in whole or in part by the Scottish Ministers at a college of further education and involves–

(i) more than 16 hours per week of classroom-based or workshop-based programmed learning under the direct guidance of teaching staff according to the number of hours set out in a document signed on behalf of the college; or

(ii) 16 hours or less per week of classroom-based or workshop-based programmed learning under the direct guidance of teaching staff and it involves additional hours using structured learning packages supported by the teaching staff where the combined total of hours exceeds 21 hours per week, according to the number of hours set out in a document signed on behalf of the college;

"full-time student" means a person attending or undertaking a full-time course of study and includes a student on a sandwich course;

"grant" (except in the definition of "access funds") means any kind of educational grant or award and includes any scholarship, studentship, exhibition, allowance or bursary but does not include a payment from access funds or any payment to which paragraph 12 of Schedule 4 or paragraph 53 of Schedule 5 applies;

"grant income" means–

(a) any income by way of a grant;

(b) any contribution whether or not it is paid;

"higher education" means higher education within the meaning of Part 2 of the Further and Higher Education (Scotland) Act 1992;

"last day of the course" means–

(a) in the case of a qualifying course, the date on which the last day of that course falls or the date on which the final examination relating to that course is completed, whichever is the later;

(b) in any other case, the date on which the last day of the final academic term falls in respect of the course in which the student is enrolled;

"period of study" means–

(a) in the case of a course of study for one year or less, the period beginning with the start of the course and ending with the last day of the course;

(b) in the case of a course of study for more than one year, in the first or, as the case may be, any subsequent year of the course, other than the final year of the course, the period beginning with the start of the course or, as the case may be, that year's start and ending with either–

[⁵ (i) the day before the start of the next year of the course in a case where the student's grant or loan is assessed at a rate appropriate to his studying throughout the year or, if he does not have a grant or loan, where a loan would have been assessed at such a rate had he had one; or]

(ii) in any other case, the day before the start of the [⁵ normal] summer vacation appropriate to his course;

(c)   in the final year of a course of study of more than one year, the period beginning with that year's start and ending with the last day of the course;

"periods of experience" means periods of work experience which form part of a sandwich course;

"qualifying course" means a qualifying course as defined for the purposes of Parts 2 and 4 of the Jobseeker's Allowance Regulations;

[² "sandwich course" has the meaning prescribed in regulation 2(9) of the Education (Student Support) Regulations 2008, regulation 4(2) of the Education (Student Loans) (Scotland) Regulations 2007(27) or regulation 2(8) of the Education (Student Support) Regulations (Northern Ireland) 2007(28), as the case may be;]

"standard maintenance grant" means–

(a)   except where paragraph (b) or (c) applies, in the case of a student attending or undertaking a course of study at the University of London or an establishment within the area comprising the City of London and the Metropolitan Police District, the amount specified for the time being in paragraph 2(2)(a) of Schedule 2 to the Education (Mandatory Awards) Regulations 2003 ("the 2003 Regulations") for such a student;

(b)   except where paragraph (c) applies, in the case of a student residing at his parent's home, the amount specified in paragraph 3 thereof;

(c)   in the case of a student receiving an allowance or bursary under the Education (Scotland) Act 1980, the amount of money specified as "standard maintenance allowance" for the relevant year appropriate for the student set out in the Student Support in Scotland Guide issued by the Student Awards Agency for Scotland, or its nearest equivalent in the case of a bursary provided by a college of further education or a local education authority [³];

(d)   in any other case, the amount specified in paragraph 2(2) of Schedule 2 to the 2003 Regulations other than in sub-paragraph (a) or (b) thereof;

"student" means a person, other than a person in receipt of a training allowance, who is attending or undertaking–

(a)   a course of study at an educational establishment; or

(b)   a qualifying course;

"student loan" means a loan towards a student's maintenance pursuant to any regulations made under section 22 of the Teaching and Higher Education Act 1998, section 73 of the Education (Scotland) Act 1980 or Article 3 of the Education (Student Support) (Northern Ireland) Order 1998 and shall include, in Scotland, a young student's bursary paid under regulation 4(1)(c) of the [² Students' Allowances (Scotland) Regulations 2007].

(2)   For the purposes of the definition of "full-time student" in paragraph (1), a person shall be regarded as attending or, as the case may be, undertaking a full-time course of study or as being on a sandwich course–

(a)   subject to paragraph (3), in the case of a person attending or undertaking a part of a modular course which would be a full-time course of study for the purposes of this Part, for the period beginning on the day on which that part of the course starts and ending–

(i)   on the last day on which he is registered with the educational establishment as attending or undertaking that part as a full-time course of study; or

(ii)   on such earlier date (if any) as he finally abandons the course or is dismissed from it;

(b)   in any other case, throughout the period beginning on the date on which he starts attending or undertaking the course and ending on the last day of the course or on such earlier date (if any) as he finally abandons it or is dismissed from it.

(3)   For the purposes of sub-paragraph (a) of paragraph (2), the period referred to in that sub-paragraph shall include–

(a)   where a person has failed examinations or has failed to successfully complete a module relating to a period when he was attending or undertaking a part of the course as a full-time course of study, any period in respect of which he attends or undertakes the course for the purpose of retaking those examinations or that module;

(b) any period of vacation within the period specified in that paragraph or immediately following that period except where the person has registered with the educational establishment to attend or undertake the final module in the course and the vacation immediately follows the last day on which he is required to attend or undertake the course.

(4) In paragraph (2), "modular course" means a course of study which consists of two or more modules, the successful completion of a specified number of which is required before a person is considered by the educational establishment to have completed the course.

Amendments

1.   Substituted by reg 3 of SI 2005 No 3238 as amended by Sch 2 para 31 of SI 2006 No 217 as from 1.4.06.
2.   Amended by reg 5(5) of SI 2008 No 1042 as from 19.5.08.
3.   Amended by reg 8(5) of SI 2008 No 2767 as from 17.11.08.
4.   Amended by reg 7(4) of SI 2008 No 3157 as from 5.1.09.
5.   Substituted by reg 8(6) of SI 2009 No 583 as from 6.4.09.
6.   Amended by Art 4 and Sch 3 para 65 of SI 2010 No 1172 as from 5.5.10.
7.   Amended by Art 16(3) of SI 2010 No.1941 as from 1.9.10.

General Note

See the commentary to reg 53 HB Regs on p395 for the definitions of "academic year", "access funds", "contribution", "course of study", "covenant income", "education authority", "full-time course of study", "full-time student", "grant", "grant income", "last day of the course", "period of study", "periods of experience", "qualifying course", "sandwich course" and "student". The definitions for HB purposes are the same as for CTB.

Treatment of students

44. These Regulations shall have effect in relation to students subject to the following provisions of this Part.

Students who are excluded from entitlement to council tax benefit

45.–(1) Except to the extent that a student may be entitled to an alternative maximum council tax benefit by virtue of section 131(3) and (6) of the Act, a student to whom paragraph (2) applies is a person of a prescribed class for the purposes of section 131(3)(b) of the Act (persons excluded from entitlement to council tax benefit).

(2) Subject to paragraph (3) and (7), this paragraph applies to a full-time student and students who are persons from abroad within the meaning of regulation 7 (persons from abroad).

(3) Paragraph (2) shall not apply to a student–

(a) who is a person on income support[² , an income-based jobseeker's allowance or an income-related employment and support allowance];

(b) who is a lone parent;

(c) whose applicable amount would, but for this regulation, include the disability premium or severe disability premium;

(d) whose applicable amount would include the disability premium but for his being treated as capable of work by virtue of a determination made in accordance with regulations made under section 171E of the Act;

(e) who is, or is treated as, incapable of work and has been so incapable, or has been so treated as incapable, of work in accordance with the provisions of, and regulations made under, Part 12A of the Act (incapacity for work) for a continuous period of not less than 196 days; and for this purpose any two or more separate periods separated by a break of not more than 56 days shall be treated as one continuous period;

[² (ea) who has, or is treated as having, limited capability for work and has had, or been treated as having, limited capability for work in accordance with the Employment and Support Allowance Regulations for a continuous period of not less than 196 days, and for this purpose any two or more separate periods separated by a break of not more than 84 days must be treated as one continuous period.]

(f)   who has a partner who is also a full-time student, if he or that partner is treated as responsible for a child or young person;

(g)   who is a single claimant with whom a child is placed by a local authority or voluntary organisation within the meaning of the Children Act 1989 or, in Scotland, boarded out within the meaning of the Social Work (Scotland) Act 1968;

[¹ (h) who is–
    (i)   aged under [³ 21] and whose course of study is not a course of higher education, or
    (ii)   a qualifying young person or child within the meaning of section 142 of the Act (child and qualifying young person);]

(i)   in respect of whom–
    (i)   a supplementary requirement has been determined under paragraph 9 of Part 2 of Schedule 2 to the Education (Mandatory Awards) Regulations 2003;
    (ii)   an allowance, or as the case may be, bursary has been granted which includes a sum under paragraph (1)(d) or regulation 4 of the Students' Allowances (Scotland) Regulations 1999 or, as the case may be, under paragraph (1)(d) of regulation 4 of the Education Authority (Bursaries) (Scotland) Regulations 1995, in respect of expenses incurred;
    (iii) a payment has been made under section 2 of the Education Act 1962 or under or by virtue of regulations made under the Teaching and Higher Education Act 1998;
    (iv)   a grant has been made under regulation 13 of the Education (Student Support) Regulations 2005 or under regulation 13 of the Education (Student Support) Regulations (Northern Ireland) 2000; or
    (v)   a supplementary requirement has been determined under paragraph 9 of Schedule 6 to the Students Awards Regulations (Northern Ireland) 1999 or a payment has been made under Article 50(3) of the Education and Libraries (Northern Ireland) Order 1986,
on account of his disability by reason of deafness.

[³ (3A)   For the purposes of paragraph (3)(h)(i) the student must have begun [⁴ , or been enrolled or accepted onto] the course before attaining the age of 19.]

(4)   For the purposes of paragraph (3), once paragraph (3)(e) applies to a full-time student, if he then ceases, for a period of 56 days or less, to be incapable, or to be treated as incapable, of work, that paragraph shall, on his again becoming so incapable, or so treated as incapable, of work at the end of that period, immediately thereafter apply to him for so long as he remains incapable or is treated as remaining incapable, of work.

(5)   In paragraph (3)(h) the reference to a course of higher education is a reference to a course of any description mentioned in Schedule 6 to the Education Reform Act 1988.

(6)   A full-time student to whom sub-paragraph (i) of paragraph (3) applies, shall be treated as satisfying that sub-paragraph from the date on which he made a request for the supplementary requirement, allowance, bursary or payment as the case may be.

(7)   Paragraph (2) shall not apply to a full-time student for the period specified in paragraph (8) if–

(a)   at any time during an academic year, with the consent of the relevant educational establishment, he ceases to attend or undertake a course because he is–
    (i)   engaged in caring for another person; or
    (ii)   ill;

(b)   he has subsequently ceased to be engaged in caring for that person or, as the case may be, he has subsequently recovered from that illness; and

(c)   he is not eligible for a grant or a student loan in respect of the period specified in paragraph (8).

(8)　The period specified for the purposes of paragraph (7) is the period, not exceeding one year, beginning on the day on which he ceased to be engaged in caring for that person or, as the case may be, the day on which he recovered from that illness and ending on the day before–

(a)　the day on which he resumes attending or undertaking the course; or

(b)　the day from which the relevant educational establishment has agreed that he may resume attending or undertaking the course,

whichever shall first occur.

Amendments

1.　Substituted by reg 5(3) of SI 2006 No 718 as from 10.4.06.
2.　Amended by reg 54 of SI 2008 No 1082 as from 27.10.08.
3.　Amended by reg 8(7) of SI 2009 No 583 as from 6.4.09.
4.　Amended by reg 10(7) of SI 2010 No 641 as from 1.4.10 (5.4.10 where rent payable weekly or in multiples of a week).

General Note

This regulation is similar to reg 56 HB Regs (see p401) in that it operates to exclude those students specified in para (2) from entitlement to CTB, though this is done simply by exclusion from benefit rather than treating them as not liable to make payments on their homes. Full-time students are *not* precluded from entitlement to an alternative maximum CTB – known as "second adult rebate": reg 45(1). This should be assessed in the normal way. The general exclusion of full-time students from CTB does not prevent a claimant whose partner is a student from claiming CTB.

Excluded from entitlement to CTB are full-time students (defined in reg 43) and students who are "persons from abroad" within the meaning of reg 7. The latter has no equivalent in reg 56 HB Regs, which merely bars full-time students. Para (2) confirms that even a part-time student is excluded from benefit if s/he is a "person from abroad". The end result is the same, since reg 7 excludes a student who is a "person from abroad" in any case.

The categories of students entitled to CTB are specified in para (3). These are the same as those entitled to HB in reg 56(2), save that there is no equivalent of reg 56(2)(j) here, which is spent in any case. See the commentary to reg 56 on p404.

In some cases, it does not matter that a student cannot claim CTB as some dwellings occupied by students are exempt from council tax (eg, dwellings where all of the residents are students and unoccupied dwellings owned by students): the Council Tax (Exempt Dwellings) Order 1993 as amended (for England and Wales); the Council Tax (Exempt Dwellings)(Scotland) Order 1997 (for Scotland). Where a dwelling is not exempt from council tax, students who share with non-students are not jointly and severally liable for council tax with the non-students: ss6(4) and 9(2) Local Government Finance Act 1992 as amended by s74 Local Government Act 2003 (for England and Wales); ss75 and 77 Local Government Finance Act 1992 as amended by s4 Education (Graduate Endowment and Student Support)(Scotland) Act 2001 (for Scotland). The definition of student is different for these purposes than for CTB: Sch 1 para 4(2) Local Government Finance Act 1992. Note: where a non-student claims CTB and s/he is sharing with a liable person who is a student excluded from CTB, the student is ignored in working out maximum CTB under reg 57. Alternatively, if the non-student is on IS, income-based JSA, income-related ESA or PC, the student will qualify for 100 per cent alternative maximum CTB: Sch 2 para 1.

SECTION 2
Income

Calculation of grant income

46.–(1)　The amount of a student's grant income to be taken into account shall, subject to paragraphs (2) and (3), be the whole of his grant income.

(2)　There shall be excluded from a student's grant income any payment–

(a)　intended to meet tuition fees or examination fees;

(b)　in respect of the student's disability;

(c)　intended to meet additional expenditure connected with term time residential study away from the student's educational establishment;

(d)　on account of the student maintaining a home at a place other than that at which he resides during his course;

(e)　on account of any other person but only if that person is residing outside of the United Kingdom and there is no applicable amount in respect of him;

(f)　intended to meet the cost of books and equipment;

(g)   intended to meet travel expenses incurred as a result of his attendance on the course;

(h)   intended for the child care costs of a child dependant.

[⁴ (i)   of higher education bursary for care leavers made under Part III of the Children Act 1989.]

(3)   Where a student does not have a student loan and is not treated as possessing such a loan, there shall be excluded from the student's grant income–

(a)   the sum of [⁵ £303] in respect of travel costs; and

(b)   the sum of [⁵ £390] towards the costs of books and equipment,

whether or not any such costs are incurred.

[¹ (4)   There shall also be excluded from a student's grant income the grant for dependants known as the parents' learning allowance paid pursuant to regulations made under Article 3 of the Education (Student Support) (Northern Ireland) Order 1998 or section 22 of the Teaching and Higher Education Act 1998.]

(5)   Subject to paragraphs (6) and (7), a student's grant income shall be apportioned–

(a)   subject to paragraph (8), in a case where it is attributable to the period of study, equally between the weeks in that period beginning with the benefit week, the first day of which coincides with, or immediately follows, the first day of the period of study and ending with the benefit week, the last day of which coincides with, or immediately precedes, the last day of the period of study;

(b)   in any other case, equally between the weeks in the period beginning with the benefit week, the first day of which coincides with, or immediately follows, the first day of the period for which it is payable and ending with the benefit week, the last day of which coincides with, or immediately precedes, the last day of the period for which it is payable.

(6)   Any grant in respect of dependants paid under section 63(6) of the Health Services and Public Health Act 1968 (grants in respect of the provision of instruction to officers of hospital authorities) and any amount intended for the maintenance of dependants under Part 3 of Schedule 2 to the Education (Mandatory Awards) Regulations 2003 shall be apportioned equally over the period of 52 weeks or, if there are 53 benefit weeks (including part-weeks) in the year, 53.

(7)   In a case where a student is in receipt of a student loan or where he could have acquired a student loan by taking reasonable steps but had not done so, any amount intended for the maintenance of dependants to which neither paragraph (6) nor regulation 50(2) (other amounts to be disregarded) apply, shall be apportioned over the same period as the student's loan is apportioned or, as the case may be, would have been apportioned.

(8)   In the case of a student on a sandwich course, any periods of experience within the period of study shall be excluded and the student's grant income shall be apportioned equally between the weeks in the period beginning with the benefit week, the first day of which immediately follows the last day of the period of experience and ending with the benefit week, the last day of which coincides with, or immediately precedes, the last day of the period of study.

Amendments

1.   Substituted by reg 2(2) and (3) of SI 2006 No 1752 as from, for students whose period of study begins on or after 1.8.06 but before 1.9.06, on the day the period of study begins; in any other case 1.9.06.

2.   Substituted by reg 5(2) of SI 2007 No 1632 as from, in the case of a person whose period of study begins on or after 1.8.07 but before 1.9.07, on the day the period of study begins; in any other case, 1.9.07.

3.   Amended by reg 6(3) of SI 2008 No 1599 as from, for students whose period of study begins on or after 1.8.08 but before 1.9.08, on the day the period of study begins; in any other case 1.9.08.

4.   Inserted by reg 8(8) of SI 2009 No 583 as from 6.4.09.

5.   Amended by reg 2 of SI 2009 No 1575 as from, for students whose period of study begins on or after 1.8.09 but before 1.9.09, on the day the period of study begins; in any other case 1.9.09.

Calculation of covenant income where a contribution is assessed

47.–(1)   Where a student is in receipt of income by way of a grant during a period of study and a contribution has been assessed, the amount of his covenant income to be taken into account for that period and any summer vacation immediately following shall be the whole amount of the covenant income less, subject to paragraph (3), the amount of the contribution.

(2)   The weekly amount of the student's covenant shall be determined–

(a)   by dividing the amount of income which falls to be taken into account under paragraph (1) by 52 or 53, whichever is reasonable in the circumstances; and

(b)   by disregarding from the resulting amount, £5.

(3)   For the purposes of paragraph (1), the contribution shall be treated as increased by the amount (if any) by which the amount excluded under regulation 46(2)(g) (calculation of grant income) falls short of the amount specified in paragraph 7(2) of Schedule 2 to the Education (Mandatory Awards) Regulations 2003 (travel expenditure).

Covenant income where no grant income or no contribution is assessed

48.–(1)   Where a student is not in receipt of income by way of a grant the amount of his covenant income shall be calculated as follows–

(a)   any sums intended for any expenditure specified in regulation 46(2)(a) to (e) (calculation of grant income) necessary as a result of his attendance on the course shall be disregarded;

(b)   any covenant income, up to the amount of the standard maintenance grant, which is not so disregarded, shall be apportioned equally between the weeks of the period of study;

(c)   there shall be disregarded from the amount so apportioned the amount which would have been disregarded under regulation 46(2)(f) and (3) (calculation of grant income) had the student been in receipt of the standard maintenance grant; and

(d)   the balance, if any, shall be divided by 52 or 53 whichever is reasonable in the circumstances and treated as weekly income of which £5 shall be disregarded.

(2)   Where a student is in receipt of income by way of a grant and no contribution has been assessed, the amount of his covenanted income shall be calculated in accordance with sub-paragraphs (a) to (d) of paragraph (1), except that–

(a)   the value of the standard maintenance grant shall be abated by the amount of such grant income less an amount equal to the amount of any sums disregarded under regulation 46(2)(a) to (e); and

(b)   the amount to be disregarded under paragraph (1)(c) shall be abated by an amount equal to the amount of any sums disregarded under regulation 46(2)(f) and (g) and (3).

Relationship with amounts to be disregarded under Schedule 4

49.   No part of a student's covenant income or grant income shall be disregarded under paragraph 15 of Schedule 4 [¹].

Amendment

1.   Amended by reg 17(3) of SI 2006 No 2378 from the first day of the first benefit week to commence on or after 2.10.06.

Other amounts to be disregarded

50.–(1)   For the purposes of ascertaining income other than grant income, covenant income and loans treated as income in accordance with regulation 51, any amounts intended for any expenditure specified in regulation 46(2) (calculation of grant income), necessary as a result of his attendance on the course shall be disregarded but only if, and to the extent that, the necessary expenditure exceeds or is likely to exceed the amount of the sums disregarded under regulation 46(2) or (3), 47(3), 48(1)(a) or (c) or 51(5) (calculation of grant income, covenant income and treatment of student loans) on like expenditure.

[² (2)]

Amendments

1.   Amended by reg 5(6) of SI 2008 No 1042 as from 19.5.08.

2.   Omitted by reg 8(9) of SI 2009 No 583 as from 6.4.09.

Treatment of student loans

51.–(1)   A student loan shall be treated as income.

(2)   In calculating the weekly amount of the loan to be taken into account as income–

(a)   in respect of a course that is of a single academic year's duration or less, a loan which is payable in respect of that period shall be apportioned equally between the weeks in the period beginning with–

(i)   except in a case where head (ii) applies, the benefit week, the first day of which coincides with, or immediately follows, the first day of the single academic year;

(ii)   where the student is required to start attending the course in August or where the course is less than an academic year's duration, the benefit week, the first day of which coincides with, or immediately follows, the first day of the course,

and ending with the benefit week, the last day of which coincides with, or immediately precedes, the last day of the course;

(b)   in respect of an academic year of a course which starts other than on 1st September, a loan which is payable in respect of that academic year shall be apportioned equally between the weeks in the period beginning with the benefit week, the first day of which coincides with or immediately follows, the first day of that academic year and ending with the benefit week, the last day of which coincides with or immediately precedes, the last day of that academic year but excluding any benefit weeks falling entirely within the quarter during which, in the opinion of the Secretary of State, the longest of any vacation is taken and for the purposes of this sub-paragraph, ''quarter'' shall have the same meaning as for the purposes of the Education (Student Support) Regulations 2005;

(c)   in respect of the final academic year of a course (not being a course of a single year's duration), a loan which is payable in respect of that final academic year shall be apportioned equally between the weeks in the period beginning with–

(i)   except in a case where head (ii) applies, the benefit week, the first day of which coincides with, or immediately follows, the first day of that academic year;

(ii)   where the final academic year starts on 1st September, the benefit week, the first day of which coincides with, or immediately follows, the earlier of 1st September or the first day of the autumn term,

and ending with the benefit week, the last day of which coincides with, or immediately precedes, the last day of the course;

(d)   in any other case, the loan shall be apportioned equally between the weeks in the period beginning with the earlier of–

(i)   the first day of the first benefit week in September; or

(ii)   the benefit week, the first day of which coincides with, or immediately follows the first day of the autumn term,

and ending with the benefit week, the last day of which coincides with, or immediately precedes, the last day of June,

and, in all cases, from the weekly amount so apportioned there shall be disregarded £10.

(3)   A student shall be treated as possessing a student loan in respect of an academic year where–

(a)   a student loan has been made to him in respect of that year; or

(b)   he could acquire such a loan in respect of that year by taking reasonable steps to do so.

(4)   Where a student is treated as possessing a student loan under paragraph (3), the amount of the student loan to be taken into account as income shall be, subject to paragraph (5)–

(a)   in the case of a student to whom a student loan is made in respect of an academic year, a sum equal to–

(i)   the maximum student loan he is able to acquire in respect of that year by taking reasonable steps to do so; and

(ii)   any contribution whether or not it has been paid to him;

(b)   in the case of a student to whom a student loan is not made in respect of an academic year, the maximum student loan that would be made to the student if–
   (i)   he took all reasonable steps to obtain the maximum student loan he is able to acquire in respect of that year; and
   (ii)   no deduction in that loan was made by virtue of the application of a means test.

(5)   There shall be deducted from the amount of income taken into account under paragraph (4)–
   (a)   the sum of [⁴ £303] in respect of travel costs; and
   (b)   the sum of [⁴ £390] towards the cost of books and equipment,
whether or not any such costs are incurred.

Amendments
1.   Substituted by reg 2(2) of SI 2006 No 1752 as from, for students whose period of study begins on or after 1.8.06 but before 1.9.06, on the day the period of study begins; in any other case 1.9.06.
2.   Substituted by reg 5(3) of SI 2007 No 1632 as from, in the case of a person whose period of study begins on or after 1.8.07 but before 1.9.07, on the day the period of study begins; in any other case, 1.9.07.
3.   Amended by reg 6(4) of SI 2008 No 1599 as from, for students whose period of study begins on or after 1.8.08 but before 1.9.08, on the day the period of study begins; in any other case 1.9.08.
4.   Amended by reg 2 of SI 2009 No 1575 as from, for students whose period of study begins on or after 1.8.09 but before 1.9.09, on the day the period of study begins; in any other case 1.9.09.

[¹ Treatment of fee loans

51A.   A loan for fees, known as a fee loan or a fee contribution loan, made pursuant to regulations made under Article 3 of the Education (Student Support) (Northern Ireland) Order 1998, section 22 of the Teaching and Higher Education Act 1998 or section 73(f) of the Education (Scotland) Act 1980, shall be disregarded as income.]

Amendment
1.   Inserted by reg 2(4) of SI 2006 No 1752 as from, for students whose period of study begins on or after 1.8.06 but before 1.9.06, on the day the period of study begins; in any other case 1.9.06.

Treatment of payments from access funds

52.–(1)   This regulation applies to payments from access funds that are not payments to which regulation 55 (2) or (3) (income treated as capital) applies.

(2)   A payment from access funds, other than a payment to which paragraph (3) applies, shall be disregarded as income.

(3)   Subject to paragraph (4) of this regulation and paragraph 35 of Schedule 4, any payments from access funds which are intended and used for an item of food, ordinary clothing or footwear, household fuel, or rent of a single claimant or, as the case may be, of the claimant or any other member of his family and any payments from access funds which are used for any council tax or water charges for which that claimant or member is liable, shall be disregarded as income to the extent of £20 per week.

(4)   Where a payment from access funds is made–
   (a)   on or after 1st September or the first day of the course, whichever first occurs, but before receipt of any student loan in respect of that year and that payment is intended for the purpose of bridging the period until receipt of the student loan; or
   (b)   before the first day of the course to a person in anticipation of that person becoming a student,
that payment shall be disregarded as income.

Disregard of contribution

53.   Where the claimant or his partner is a student and, for the purposes of assessing a contribution to the student's grant or student loan, the other partner's income has been taken into account, an amount equal to that contribution shall be disregarded for the purposes of assessing that other partner's income.

Further disregard of student's income
54. Where any part of a student's income has already been taken into account for the purposes of assessing his entitlement to a grant or student loan, the amount taken into account shall be disregarded in assessing that student's income.

Income treated as capital
55.–(1) Any amount by way of a refund of tax deducted from a student's covenant income shall be treated as capital.

(2) An amount paid from access funds as a single lump sum shall be treated as capital.

(3) An amount paid from access funds as a single lump sum which is intended and used for an item other than food, ordinary clothing or footwear, household fuel or rent, or which is used for an item other than any council tax or water charges for which that claimant or member is liable, shall be disregarded as capital but only for a period of 52 weeks from the date of the payment.

General Note

The CTB rule is the same as that for HB save that "ordinary clothing or footwear" and "rent" are defined in reg 2(1).

Disregard of changes occurring during summer vacation
56. In calculating a student's income the relevant authority shall disregard any change in the standard maintenance grant, occurring in the recognised summer vacation appropriate to the student's course, if that vacation does not form part of his period of study from the date on which the change occurred to the end of that vacation.

PART 6
Amount of benefit

Maximum council tax benefit
57.–(1) Subject to [¹ paragraphs (2) to (4)], the amount of a person's maximum council tax benefit in respect of a day for which he is liable to pay council tax, shall be 100 per cent. of the amount A/B where–
(a) A is the amount set by the appropriate authority as the council tax for the relevant financial year in respect of the dwelling in which he is a resident and for which he is liable, subject to any discount which may be appropriate to that dwelling under the 1992 Act; and
(b) B is the number of days in that financial year,
less any deductions in respect of non-dependants which fall to be made under regulation 58 (non-dependant deductions).

(2) In calculating a person's maximum council tax benefit any reduction in the amount that person is liable to pay in respect of council tax, which is made in consequence of any enactment in, or made under, the 1992 Act, shall be taken into account.

(3) Subject to paragraph (4), where a claimant is jointly and severally liable for council tax in respect of a dwelling in which he is resident with one or more other persons but excepting any person so residing with the claimant who is a student to whom regulation 45(2) (students who are excluded from entitlement to council tax benefit) applies, in determining the maximum council tax benefit in his case in accordance with paragraph (1), the amount A shall be divided by the number of persons who are jointly and severally liable for that tax.

(4) Where a claimant is jointly and severally liable for council tax in respect of a dwelling with only his partner, paragraph (3) shall not apply in his case.

[¹ (5)]

Amendment

1. Amended by reg 9(4) of SI 2008 No 959 as from 6.10.08.

Analysis
Reg 57 provides the basis for establishing a claimant's maximum CTB. The starting point is the net liability for council tax after deductions and discounts have been applied, less non-dependant deductions applicable under reg 58: paras (1) and (2).

Where the claimant is jointly and severally liable for council tax with one or more other persons (excluding any liable person residing with the claimant who is a student not entitled to CTB), such person not being her/his partner, her/his benefit is calculated only in respect of the appropriate proportion of the maximum: paras (3) and (4). This gives rise, potentially, to hardship in that, under the 1992 Act, a person who is jointly and severally liable can be pursued for the full amount of the tax due on the property while receiving benefit only on her/his "share".

Note: prior to 1 April 2004, the level of CTB allowable was restricted for those who were liable to pay council tax in respect of dwellings in valuation bands F, G and H. See reg 51 CTB Regs 1992 on p746 of the 16th edition for the former version of this reg and commentary on it.

Non-dependant deductions

58.–(1) Subject to the following provisions of this regulation, the non-dependant deductions in respect of a day referred to in regulation 57 (maximum council tax benefit) shall be–
   (a)   in respect of a non-dependant aged 18 or over in remunerative work, [¹⁴ £6.95] × 1/7;
   (b)   in respect of a non-dependant aged 18 or over to whom sub-paragraph (a) does not apply, [¹⁴ £2.30] × 1/7.

(2)   In the case of a non-dependant aged 18 or over to whom paragraph (1)(a) applies, where it is shown to the appropriate authority that his normal gross weekly income is–
   (a)   less than [¹⁴ £178.00], the deduction to be made under this regulation shall be that specified in paragraph (1)(b);
   (b)   not less than [¹⁴ £178.00] but less than [¹⁴ £306.00], the deduction to be made under this regulation shall be [¹⁴ £4.60];
   (c)   not less than [¹⁴ £306.00] but less than [¹⁴ £382.00], the deduction to be made under this regulation shall be [¹⁴ £5.80].

(3)   Only one deduction shall be made under this regulation in respect of a couple or, as the case may be, members of a polygamous marriage and, where, but for this paragraph, the amount that would fall to be deducted in respect of one member of a couple or polygamous marriage is higher than the amount (if any) that would fall to be deducted in respect of the other, or any other, member, the higher amount shall be deducted.

(4)   In applying the provisions of paragraph (2) in the case of a couple or, as the case may be, a polygamous marriage, regard shall be had, for the purpose of that paragraph, to the couple's or, as the case may be, all members of the polygamous marriage's joint weekly gross income.

(5)   Where in respect of a day–
   (a)   a person is a resident in a dwelling but is not himself liable for council tax in respect of that dwelling and that day;
   (b)   other residents in that dwelling (the liable persons) have joint and several liability for council tax in respect of that dwelling and that day otherwise than by virtue of section 9 or 77 or 77A of the 1992 Act (liability of spouses and civil partners); and
   (c)   the person to whom sub-paragraph (a) refers is a non-dependant of two or more of the liable persons,
the deduction in respect of that non-dependant shall be apportioned equally between those liable persons.

(6)   No deduction shall be made in respect of any non-dependants occupying a claimant's dwelling if the claimant or his partner is–
   (a)   blind or treated as blind by virtue of paragraph 13 of Schedule 1 (additional condition [¹³ for the disability premium]); or
   (b)   receiving in respect of himself either–
      (i)   attendance allowance; or
      (ii)   the care component of the disability living allowance.

(7)   No deduction shall be made in respect of a non-dependant if–

(a)   although he resides with the claimant, it appears to the relevant authority that his normal home is elsewhere; or

(b)   he is in receipt of a training allowance paid in connection with [¹⁰ youth training] established under section 2 of the 1973 Act or section 2 of the Enterprise and New Towns (Scotland) Act 1990; or

(c)   he is a full-time student within the meaning of Part 5 (Students); or

(d)   he is not residing with the claimant because he has been a patient for a period in excess of 52 weeks, and for these purposes–

    [¹ (i)   ''patient'' has the meaning given in paragraph (7) of regulation 8, and

    (ii)   where a person has been a patient for two or more distinct periods separated by one or more intervals each not exceeding 28 days, he shall be treated as having been a patient continuously for a period equal in duration to the total of those distinct periods.]

(8)   No deduction shall be made in respect of a non-dependant–

(a)   who is on income support, state pension credit [⁸ , an income-based jobseeker's allowance or an income-related employment and support allowance]; or

(b)   to whom Schedule 1 of the 1992 Act applies (persons disregarded for purposes of discount) but this sub-paragraph shall not apply to a non-dependant who is a student to whom paragraph 4 of that Schedule refers.

(9)   In the application of paragraph (2) there shall be disregarded from his weekly gross income–

(a)   any attendance allowance or disability living allowance received by him;

(b)   any payment made under [¹³ or by] the Trusts, the Fund, the Eileen Trust [¹³ , MFET Limited] or the Independent Living [⁹ Fund (2006)] which had his income fallen to be calculated under regulation 30 (calculation of income other than earnings) would have been disregarded under paragraph 24 of Schedule 4 (income in kind); and

(c)   any payment which had his income fallen to be calculated under regulation 30 would have been disregarded under paragraph 36 of Schedule 4 (payments made under certain trusts and certain other payments).

Amendments

1.   Substituted by reg 3(7) of SI 2005 No 2502 as amended by Sch 2 para 27 of SI 2006 No 217 as from 1.4.06.
2.   Confirmed by Art 21(3) of SI 2006 No 645 and reg 8 of SI 2006 No 217 as from 1.4.06.
3.   Amended by Art 21(3) of SI 2006 No 645 and reg 8 of SI 2006 No 217 as from 1.4.06.
4.   Confirmed by Art 21(3) of SI 2007 No 688 as from 1.4.07.
5.   Amended by Art 21(3) of SI 2007 No 688 as from 1.4.07.
6.   Confirmed by Art 21(3) of SI 2008 No 632 as from 1.4.08.
7.   Amended by Art 21(3) of SI 2008 No 632 as from 1.4.08.
8.   Amended by reg 55 of SI 2008 No 1082 as from 27.10.08.
9.   Amended by reg 8(4)(d) of SI 2008 No 2767 as from 17.11.08.
10.   Amended by reg 8(6) of SI 2008 No 2767 as from 17.11.08.
11.   Confirmed by Art 21(3) of SI 2009 No 497 as from 1.4.09.
12.   Amended by Art 21(3) of SI 2009 No 497 as from 1.4.09.
13.   Amended by reg 10(3), (5) and (8) of SI 2010 No 641 as from 1.4.10 (5.4.10 where rent payable weekly or in multiples of a week).
14.   Confirmed by Art 21(3) of SI 2010 No 793 as from 1.4.10.

Analysis

The rules on non-dependant deductions from CTB are broadly the same as those for HB (see reg 74 on p427). However, there are some differences in when no non-dependant deduction is to be made: paras (7) and (8).

(1)   No deduction is made for any non-dependant on IS, income-based JSA or income-related ESA, not just those under 25: para (8)(a). For CTB, unlike for HB, the income-related ESA can include a support component or a work-related activity component.

(2)   No deduction is made for non-dependants to whom Sch 1 Local Government Finance Act 1992 (LGFA 1992) applies: para (8)(b). These are people with what are known as "status discounts" – ie, those 18 or over for whom child benefit is payable and certain recent school and college-leavers, student nurses, foreign language assistants, apprentices, foreign spouses or dependants of students, people who are

"severely mentally impaired" (defined in Sch 1 LGFA 1992), people in detention, certain carers and members of visiting armed forces, international headquarters and defence organisations and their dependants.

(3)   No deduction is made for a non-dependant who is a full-time student, even if s/he works during the summer vacation: para (7)(b).

Council tax benefit taper

59.   The prescribed percentage for the purpose of sub-section (5)(c)(ii) of section 131 of the Act as it applies to council tax benefit, (percentage of excess of income over the applicable amount which is deducted from maximum council tax benefit), shall be 2 6/7 per cent.

General Note

Maximum CTB is calculated under reg 57 on a daily basis. The weekly equivalent of the taper is 2 and 6/7 times 7, which is 20 per cent. For a detailed analysis of the CTB calculation, see *IB v Barnsley Metropolitan Borough Council* [2009] UKUT 279 (AAC).

[¹Extended payments

60.–(1)   A claimant who is entitled to council tax benefit (by virtue of the general conditions of entitlement) shall be entitled to an extended payment where–
(a)   the claimant or the claimant's partner was entitled to a qualifying income-related benefit;
(b)   entitlement to a qualifying income-related benefit ceased because the claimant or the claimant's partner–
(i)   commenced employment as an employed or self-employed earner;
(ii)   increased their earnings from such employment; or
(iii)   increased the number of hours worked in such employment,
and that employment is or, as the case may be, increased earnings or increased number of hours are expected to last five weeks or more; and
(c)   the claimant or the claimant's partner had been entitled to and in receipt of a qualifying income-related benefit, jobseeker's allowance or a combination of those benefits for a continuous period of at least 26 weeks before the day on which the entitlement to a qualifying income-related benefit ceased.

(2)   For the purpose of paragraph (1)(c), a claimant or a claimant's partner is to be treated as having been entitled to and in receipt of a qualifying income-related benefit or jobseeker's allowance during any period of less than five weeks in respect of which the claimant or the claimant's partner was not entitled to any of those benefits because the claimant or the claimant's partner was engaged in remunerative work as a consequence of their participation in an employment zone programme.

(3)   For the purpose of this regulation, where a claimant or a claimant's partner is entitled to and in receipt of joint-claim jobseeker's allowance they shall be treated as being entitled to and in receipt of jobseeker's allowance.

(4)   A claimant must be treated as entitled to council tax benefit by virtue of the general conditions of entitlement where–
(a)   the claimant ceased to be entitled to council tax benefit because the claimant vacated the dwelling in which the claimant was resident;
(b)   the day on which the claimant vacated the dwelling was either in the week in which entitlement to a qualifying income-related benefit ceased, or in the preceding week; and
(c)   entitlement to the qualifying income-related benefit ceased in any of the circumstances listed in paragraph (1)(b).

(5)   This regulation shall not apply where, on the day before a claimant's entitlement to income support ceased, regulation 6(5) of the Income Support Regulations(27) (remunerative work: housing costs) applied to that claimant.]

Amendment

1.   Substituted by reg 7(2) of SI 2008 No 959 as from 6.10.08.

[¹ Duration of extended payment period

60A.–(1)   Where a claimant is entitled to an extended payment, the extended payment period starts on the first day of the benefit week immediately following the benefit week in which the claimant, or the claimant's partner, ceased to be entitled to a qualifying income-related benefit.

(2)   For the purpose of paragraph (1), a claimant or a claimant's partner ceases to be entitled to a qualifying income-related benefit on the day immediately following the last day of entitlement to that benefit.

(3)   The extended payment period ends–

(a)   at the end of a period of four weeks; or

(b)   on the date on which the claimant to whom the extended payment is payable has no liability for council tax, if that occurs first.]

Amendment

1.   Inserted by reg 7(2) of SI 2008 No 959 as from 6.10.08.

[¹ Amount of extended payment

60B.–(1)   For any week during the extended payment period the amount of the extended payment payable to a claimant shall be the higher of–

(a)   the amount of council tax benefit to which the claimant was entitled under the general conditions of entitlement in the last benefit week before the claimant or the claimant's partner ceased to be entitled to a qualifying income-related benefit;

(b)   the amount of council tax benefit to which the claimant would be entitled under the general conditions of entitlement for any benefit week during the extended payment period, if regulation 60 (extended payments) did not apply to the claimant; or

(c)   the amount of council tax benefit to which the claimant's partner would be entitled under the general conditions of entitlement, if regulation 60 did not apply to the claimant.

(2)   Paragraph (1) does not apply in the case of a mover.

(3)   Where a claimant is in receipt of an extended payment under this regulation and the claimant's partner makes a claim for council tax benefit, no amount of council tax benefit shall be payable by the appropriate authority during the extended payment period.]

Amendment

1.   Inserted by reg 7(2) of SI 2008 No 959 as from 6.10.08.

[¹ Extended payments – movers

60C.–(1)   This regulation applies–

(a)   to a mover; and

(b)   from the Monday following the day of the move.

(2)   The amount of the extended payment payable from the Monday from which this regulation applies until the end of the extended payment period shall be the amount of council tax benefit which was payable to the mover for the last benefit week before the mover, or the mover's partner, ceased to be entitled to a qualifying income-related benefit.

(3)   Where a mover's liability to pay council tax in respect of the new dwelling is to the second authority, the extended payment may take the form of a payment from the appropriate authority to–

(a)   the second authority; or

(b)   the mover directly.

(4)   Where–

(a)   a mover, or the mover's partner, makes a claim for council tax benefit to the second authority after the mover, or the mover's partner, ceased to be entitled to a qualifying income-related benefit; and

(b)   the mover, or the mover's partner, is in receipt of an extended payment from the appropriate authority, the second authority shall reduce the weekly amount of council tax benefit that the mover, or the mover's partner, is entitled to by a sum equal to the amount of the extended payment until the end of the extended payment period.]

Amendment

1.   Inserted by reg 7(2) of SI 2008 No 959 as from 6.10.08.

Analysis

The rules for extended payments of CTB are broadly the same as those for HB (see regs 72 to 72D HB Regs on p419). However, the rules for "movers" differ. Reg 60C deals with the amount of extended payments of CTB paid to "movers". Movers, as defined by reg 2(1), are claimants who change the dwelling in which they are resident from the area of the "appropriate authority" to a dwelling in the area of a "second authority". "Appropriate authority" is defined in s34(3) WRA as the authority that was administering the CTB claim immediately before entitlement to a qualifying income-related benefit ceased. "Second authority" is defined in reg 2(1) as the authority "to which" a mover is liable to make payments for the new dwelling (which in this context would appear to be a reference to payments of council tax). So the provision in para (4) for a reduction in CTB where a claim for CTB is made to the second authority applies whether the claimant is a tenant of the second authority or, for example, a private or housing association tenant.

[¹ Relationship between extended payment and entitlement to council tax benefit under the general conditions of entitlement

60D.–(1)   Where a claimant's council tax benefit award would have ended when the claimant ceased to be entitled to a qualifying income-related benefit in the circumstances listed in regulation 60(1)(b), that award will not cease until the end of the extended payment period.

(2)   Part 7 (changes of circumstances and increases for exceptional circumstances) shall not apply to any extended payment payable in accordance with regulation 60B(1)(a) or 60C(2) (amount of extended payment – movers).]

Amendment

1.   Inserted by reg 7(2) of SI 2008 No 959 as from 6.10.08.

[¹Extended Payments (qualifying contributory benefits)

61.–(1)   A claimant who is entitled to council tax benefit (by virtue of the general conditions of entitlement) shall be entitled to an extended payment (qualifying contributory benefits) where–

(a)   the claimant or the claimant's partner was entitled to a qualifying contributory benefit;

(b)   entitlement to a qualifying contributory benefit ceased because the claimant or the claimant's partner–

(i)   commenced employment as an employed or self-employed earner;

(ii)   increased their earnings from such employment; or

(iii)   increased the number of hours worked in such employment,

and that employment is or, as the case may be, increased earnings or increased number of hours are expected to last five weeks or more;

(c)   the claimant or the claimant's partner had been entitled to and in receipt of a qualifying contributory benefit or a combination of qualifying contributory benefits for a continuous period of at least 26 weeks before the day on which the entitlement to a qualifying contributory benefit ceased; and

(d)   the claimant or the claimant's partner was not entitled to and not in receipt of a qualifying income-related benefit in the last benefit week in which the claimant, or the claimant's partner, was entitled to a qualifying contributory benefit.

(2)   A claimant must be treated as entitled to council tax benefit by virtue of the general conditions of entitlement where–

(a)   the claimant ceased to be entitled to council tax benefit because the claimant vacated the dwelling in which the claimant was resident;

(b)   the day on which the claimant vacated the dwelling was either in the week in which entitlement to a qualifying contributory benefit ceased, or in the preceding week; and

(c)   entitlement to the qualifying contributory benefit ceased in any of the circumstances listed in paragraph (1)(b).]

Amendment

1.   Inserted by reg 8(2) of SI 2008 No 959 as from 6.10.08.

[¹ Duration of extended payment period (qualifying contributory benefits)

61A.–(1)   Where a claimant is entitled to an extended payment (qualifying contributory benefits), the extended payment period starts on the first day of the benefit week immediately following the benefit week in which the claimant, or the claimant's partner, ceased to be entitled to a qualifying contributory benefit.

(2)   For the purpose of paragraph (1), a claimant or a claimant's partner ceases to be entitled to a qualifying contributory benefit on the day immediately following the last day of entitlement to that benefit.

(3)   The extended payment period ends–

(a)   at the end of a period of four weeks; or

(b)   on the date on which the claimant to whom the extended payment (qualifying contributory benefits) is payable has no liability for council tax, if that occurs first.]

Amendment

1.   Inserted by reg 8(2) of SI 2008 No 959 as from 6.10.08.

[¹ Amount of extended payment (qualifying contributory benefits)

61B.–(1)   For any week during the extended payment period the amount of the extended payment (qualifying contributory benefits) payable to a claimant shall be the higher of–

(a)   the amount of council tax benefit to which the claimant was entitled under the general conditions of entitlement in the last benefit week before the claimant or the claimant's partner ceased to be entitled to a qualifying contributory benefit;

(b)   the amount of council tax benefit to which the claimant would be entitled under the general conditions of entitlement for any benefit week during the extended payment period, if regulation 61 (extended payments (qualifying contributory benefits)) did not apply to the claimant; or

(c)   the amount of council tax benefit to which the claimant's partner would be entitled under the general conditions of entitlement, if regulation 61 did not apply to the claimant.

(2)   Paragraph (1) does not apply in the case of a mover.

(3)   Where a claimant is in receipt of an extended payment (qualifying contributory benefits) under this regulation and the claimant's partner makes a claim for council tax benefit, no amount of council tax benefit shall be payable by the appropriate authority during the extended payment period.]

Amendment

1.   Inserted by reg 8(2) of SI 2008 No 959 as from 6.10.08.

[¹ Extended payments (qualifying contributory benefits) – movers

61C.–(1)   This regulation applies–

(a)   to a mover; and

(b)   from the Monday following the day of the move.

(2)   The amount of the extended payment (qualifying contributory benefit) payable from the Monday from which this regulation applies until the end of the extended payment period shall be the amount of council tax benefit which was payable to the mover for the last benefit week before the mover, or the mover's partner, ceased to be entitled to a qualifying contributory benefit.

(3)   Where a mover's liability to pay council tax in respect of the new dwelling is to the second authority, the extended payment (qualifying contributory benefits) may take the form of a payment from the appropriate authority to–

> (a)   the second authority; or
> (b)   the mover directly.
> (4)   Where–
> (a)   a mover, or the mover's partner, makes a claim for council tax benefit to the second authority after the mover, or the mover's partner, ceased to be entitled to a qualifying contributory benefit; and
> (b)   the mover, or the mover's partner, is in receipt of an extended payment (qualifying contributory benefits) from the appropriate authority,
> the second authority shall reduce the weekly amount of council tax benefit that the mover, or the mover's partner, is entitled to by a sum equal to the amount of the extended payment (qualifying contributory benefits) until the end of the extended payment period.]

Amendment

1.   Inserted by reg 8(2) of SI 2008 No 959 as from 6.10.08.

[¹ Relationship between extended payment (qualifying contributory benefits) and entitlement to council tax benefit under the general conditions of entitlement

61D.–(1)   Where a claimant's council tax benefit award would have ended when the claimant ceased to be entitled to a qualifying contributory benefit in the circumstances listed in regulation 61(1)(b), that award will not cease until the end of the extended payment period.

(2)   Part 7 (changes of circumstances and increases for exceptional circumstances) shall not apply to any extended payment (qualifying contributory benefits) payable in accordance with regulation 61B(1)(a) or 61C(2) (amount of extended payment – movers).]

Amendment

1.   Inserted by reg 8(2) of SI 2008 No 959 as from 6.10.08.

Alternative maximum council tax benefit

62.–(1)   Subject to paragraphs (2) and (3), the alternative maximum council tax benefit where the conditions set out in section 131(3) and (6) of the Act are fulfilled, shall be the amount determined in accordance with Schedule 2.

(2)   Subject to paragraph (3), where a claimant is jointly and severally liable for council tax in respect of a dwelling in which he is resident with one or more other persons, in determining the alternative maximum council tax benefit in his case, the amount determined in accordance with Schedule 2 shall be divided by the number of persons who are jointly and severally liable for that tax.

(3)   Where a claimant is jointly and severally liable for council tax in respect of a dwelling with only his partner, solely by virtue of section 9, 77 or 77A of the 1992 Act (liability of spouses and civil partners), paragraph (2) shall not apply in his case.

General Note

If the claimant does not qualify for CTB under s131(4) and (5) SSCBA (eg, because s/he has too much income or capital), in restricted circumstances s/he can claim benefit under s131(3) and (6) SSCBA based on the income of second adult(s) residing with her/him. Alternative maximum CTB is sometimes referred to as "second adult rebate". If the claimant would be entitled to CTB under s131(4) and (5) *and* using the "alternative maximum", s/he will get whichever is the higher amount: s131(9) SSCBA.

  Where a claimant satisfies the s131(3) and (6) conditions, the whole of her/his capital is disregarded under Sch 5 para 46. This means that even where a claimant has capital in excess of the limit provided by s134 SSCBA and reg 33, s/he is treated as having capital below that limit. The claimant's income makes no difference to entitlement to the alternative maximum CTB as the amount of this is calculated under Sch 2 CTB Regs by reference only to the income of the second adult(s).

  Reference should also be made to s131(3) and (6) SSCBA and reg 63 and Sch 2 (see pp11, 705 and 736).

Analysis

Para (1)

A claimant can qualify for alternative maximum CTB where a second adult is resident in the dwelling and none of the other residents are liable to pay the claimant rent: s131(6)(a) SSCBA. The other resident(s) whose income is used to calculate alternative maximum CTB must not be persons covered by Sch 1 to the 1992 Act (residents disregarded for the purposes of discounts): s131(7)(a) SSCBA. Reg 63 further restricts the categories of persons whose income can be used for these purposes (see below).

Perhaps the most common example of when there is potential entitlement to alternative maximum CTB is where the claimant is a single person and has a non-dependant young person or an elderly relative on a low income, living rent-free with her/him. If there is more than one other person residing with the claimant to whom s131(6) applies, their income may be aggregated (see Sch 2). The combined effect of s131 and this regulation is that non-dependant deductions do not apply where the "alternative maximum" applies.

Paras (2) and (3)

Where there is a joint liability for council tax, every liable person must make her/his own claim for a share of the alternative maximum CTB: para (2). This potentially raises the same difficulty as reg 57(3) (see Analysis on p698). However, where the joint liability is only with a partner, the claimant will receive the full alternative maximum CTB: para (3). On ss9, 77 or 77A, see below.

Residents of a dwelling to whom section 131(6) of the Act does not apply

63. Subsection (6) of section 131 of the Act (residents of a dwelling in respect of whom entitlement to an alternative maximum council tax benefit may arise) shall not apply in respect of any person referred to in the following paragraphs namely–

(a)   a person who is liable for council tax solely in consequence of the provisions of sections 9, 77 or 77A of the 1992 Act (spouse's or civil partner's joint and several liability for tax);

(b)   a person who is residing with a couple or with the members of a polygamous marriage where the claimant for council tax benefit is a member of that couple or of that marriage and–

(i)   in the case of a couple, neither member of that couple is a person who, in accordance with Schedule 1 to the 1992 Act, falls to be disregarded for the purposes of discount; or

(ii)   in the case of a polygamous marriage, two or more members of that marriage are not persons who, in accordance with Schedule 1 to the 1992 Act, fall to be disregarded for the purposes of discount;

(c)   a person who jointly with the claimant for benefit falls within the same paragraph of sections 6(2)(a) to (e) or 75(2)(a) to (e) of the 1992 Act (persons liable to pay council tax) as applies in the case of the claimant;

(d)   a person who is residing with two or more persons both or all of whom fall within the same paragraph of sections 6(2)(a) to (e) or 75(2)(a) to (e) of the 1992 Act and two or more of those persons are not persons who, in accordance with Schedule 1 to the 1992 Act, fall to be disregarded for the purposes of discount.

Analysis

Reg 63 should be read together with reg 62 and the Analysis on p704. Section 131(7) restricts the categories of people who count as "second adults" and hence whose income can be used as a basis for the alternative maximum CTB. Reg 63 provides further restrictions.

Sub-para (a). A spouse or civil partner who is jointly and severally liable for council tax under s9 (England and Wales) or s77 or 77A (Scotland) of the Local Government Finance Act 1992 cannot count as a "second adult". Sections 9, 77 and 77A do not apply to persons referred to in para 2 of Sch 1 to the 1992 Act.

Sub-para (b) excludes any person residing with a couple or partners in a polygamous marriage, where the claimant is a member of the couple or the marriage, save in the fairly unusual circumstances where the couple are both, or two or more members of the polygamous marriage, are disregarded under Sch 1 Local Government Finance Act 1992 (discounts). The effect of this is that the claimant cannot qualify for the alternative maximum CTB.

Sub-para (c) excludes people who are joint owners or joint tenants, or otherwise share the same status as the claimant under s6(2) (England and Wales) or s75(2) (Scotland) of the Act. Note that although such a person would not count as a second adult, s/he might her/himself qualify for ordinary CTB for her share of the council tax bill under s131(4) and (5).

Sub-para (d) excludes any person residing with two or more people who are not married or cohabiting but who share the same status under ss6 or 75 (ie, they are jointly liable for the council tax) and at least two of those liable are not disregarded under Sch 1 to the Local Government Finance Act 1992 (discounts). The effect of this is that the claimant cannot qualify for the alternative maximum CTB.

PART 7
Changes of circumstances and increases for exceptional circumstances

Date on which entitlement is to begin

64.–(1)   Subject to paragraph (2), any person to whom or in respect of whom a claim for council tax benefit is made and who is otherwise entitled to that benefit shall be so entitled from the benefit week following the date on which that claim is made or is treated as made.

(2)   Where a person is otherwise entitled to council tax benefit and becomes liable for the first time for a relevant authority's council tax in respect of a dwelling of which he is a resident in the benefit week in which his claim is made or is treated as made, he shall be so entitled from that benefit week.

[¹Date on which council tax benefit is to end
65.]

Amendment

1.   Omitted by reg 9(5)(a) of SI 2008 No 959 as from 6.10.08.

[¹Date on which council tax benefit is to end where entitlement to severe disablement allowance or incapacity benefit ceases
66.]

Amendment

1.   Omitted by reg 9(5)(b) of SI 2008 No 959 as from 6.10.08.

Date on which change of circumstances is to take effect

67.–(1)   Except in cases where regulation 24 (disregard of changes in tax, contributions, etc) [¹ applies, and subject to regulation 8(3) of the Decisions and Appeals Regulations, and] the following provisions of this regulation, a change of circumstances which affects entitlement to, or the amount of, council tax benefit (''change of circumstances''), shall take effect from the first day of the benefit week following the date on which the change actually occurs, and where that change is cessation of entitlement to any benefit under the benefit Acts, the date on which the change actually occurs shall be the day immediately following the last day of entitlement to that benefit.

(2)   Subject to paragraph (3), where the change of circumstances is a change in the amount of council tax payable, it shall take effect from the day on which it actually occurs.

(3)   Where the change of circumstances is a change in the amount a person is liable to pay in respect of council tax in consequence of regulations under section 13 or 80 of the 1992 Act (reduced amounts of council tax) or changes in the discount to which a dwelling may be subject under sections 11, 12 or 79 of that Act, it shall take effect from the day on which the change in amount has effect.

(4)   Where the change of circumstances is an amendment to these Regulations, it shall take effect from the date on which the amendment to these Regulations comes into force.

(5)   Where the change of circumstances is the claimant's acquisition of a partner, the change shall have effect on the day on which the acquisition takes place.

(6)   Where the change of circumstances is the death of a claimant's partner or their separation, it shall have effect on the day the death or separation occurs.

(7)   If two or more changes of circumstances occurring in the same benefit week would, but for this paragraph, take effect in different benefit weeks in accordance with paragraphs (1) to (6) they shall take effect from the day to which the appropriate paragraph from (2) to (6) above refers, or, where more than one day is concerned, from the earlier day.

(8)   Where the change of circumstances is that income, or an increase in the amount of income, other than a benefit or an increase in the amount of a benefit under the Act, is

paid in respect of a past period and there was no entitlement to income of that amount during that period, the change of circumstances shall take effect from the first day on which such income, had it been paid in that period at intervals appropriate to that income, would have fallen to be taken into account for the purposes of these Regulations.

(9)   Without prejudice to paragraph (8), where the change of circumstances is the payment of income, or arrears of income, in respect of a past period, the change of circumstances shall take effect from the first day on which such income, had it been timeously paid in that period at intervals appropriate to that income, would have fallen to be taken into account for the purposes of these Regulations.

Modifications

> Reg 67 applies as if para (9) was omitted where a change of circumstances occurs as a result of the payment of arrears of any income which affects a determination or decision in respect of entitlement to, or the amount of, HB or CTB before 6 March 1995. See Sch 3 para 1 HB&CTB(CP) Regs on p1197.

Amendment

> 1.   Substituted by reg 6 of SI 2007 No 2470 as from 24.9.07.

PART 8
Claims

Who may claim

68.–(1)   In the case of a couple or members of a polygamous marriage a claim shall be made by whichever one of them they agree should so claim or, in default of agreement, by such one of them as the relevant authority shall determine.

(2)   Where a person who is liable to pay council tax in respect of a dwelling is unable for the time being to act, and–

(a)   a [1 deputy] has been appointed by the Court of Protection with power to claim, or as the case may be, receive benefit on his behalf; or

(b)   in Scotland, his estate is being administered by a judicial factor or any guardian acting or appointed under the Adults with Incapacity (Scotland) Act 2000 who has power to claim or, as the case may be, receive benefit on his behalf; or

(c)   an attorney with a general power or a power to claim or as the case may be, receive benefit, has been appointed by that person under [1 the Powers of Attorney Act 1971, the Enduring Powers of Attorney Act 1985 or the Mental Capacity Act 2005] or otherwise,

that [1 deputy], judicial factor, guardian or attorney, as the case may be, may make a claim on behalf of that person.

(3)   Where a person who is liable to pay council tax in respect of a dwelling is unable for the time being to act and paragraph (2) does not apply to him, the relevant authority may, upon written application made to them by a person who, if a natural person, is over the age of 18, appoint that person to exercise on behalf of the person who is unable to act, any right to which that person might be entitled under the Act and to receive and deal on his behalf with any sums payable to him.

(4)   Where the relevant authority has made an appointment under paragraph (3) or treated a person as an appointee under paragraph (5)–

(a)   it may at any time revoke the appointment;

(b)   the person appointed may resign his office after having given 4 weeks notice in writing to the relevant authority of his intention to do so;

(c)   any such appointment shall terminate when the relevant authority is notified of the appointment of a person mentioned in paragraph (2).

(5)   Where a person who is liable to pay council tax in respect of a dwelling is for the time being unable to act and the Secretary of State has appointed a person to act on his behalf under regulation 33 of the Social Security (Claims and Payments) Regulations 1987 (persons unable to act), the relevant authority may if that person agrees, treat him as if he had been appointed by them under paragraph (3).

(6)   Anything required by these Regulations to be done by or to any person who is for the time being unable to act may be done by or to the persons mentioned in paragraph

(2) above or by or to the person appointed or treated as appointed under this regulation and the receipt of any such person so appointed shall be a good discharge to the relevant authority for any sum paid.

[² (7)]

Amendments

1. Amended by reg 13(8) of SI 2007 No 2618 as from 1.10.07.
2. Omitted by reg 4(3) of SI 2008 No 2299 as from 1.10.08.

Time and manner in which claims are to be made

69.–(1) [¹ Subject to [⁴ paragraphs (4A) to (4AE)],] every claim shall be in writing and made on a properly completed form approved for the purpose by the relevant authority or in such written form as the relevant authority may accept as sufficient in the circumstances of any particular case or class of cases having regard to the sufficiency of the written information and evidence.

(2)   The forms approved for the purpose of claiming shall be provided free of charge by the relevant authority or such persons as they may authorise or appoint for the purpose.

(3)   Each relevant authority shall notify the Secretary of State of the address to which claims delivered or sent to the appropriate DWP office are to be forwarded.

(4)   A claim [¹ in writing]–

(a)   may be sent or delivered to the appropriate DWP office where the claimant or his partner is also claiming income support, incapacity benefit, state pension credit [⁶ , a jobseeker's allowance or an employment and support allowance];

(b)   where it has not been sent or delivered to the appropriate DWP office, shall be sent or delivered to the designated office;

(c)   sent or delivered to the appropriate DWP office, other than one sent on the same form as a claim made to income support, incapacity benefit [⁶ , a jobseeker's allowance or an employment and support allowance] and as approved by the Secretary of State for the purpose of the benefits being claimed, shall be forwarded to the relevant authority within two working days of the date of the receipt of the claim at the appropriate DWP office, or as soon as practicable thereafter;

[⁴ (d)]

[⁴ (e)]

(f)   where the claimant has attained the qualifying age for state pension credit, may be sent or delivered to an authorised office.

[³ (g) may be sent or delivered to the offices of a county council in England if the council has arranged with the relevant authority for claims to be received at their offices ("county offices").]

[¹ (4A)   Where the relevant authority has published a telephone number for the purpose of receiving claims for council tax benefit, a claim may be made by telephone to that telephone number.

[⁴ (4AA)   If the Secretary of State agrees, where–

(a)   a person makes a claim for a benefit referred to in paragraph (4)(a); and

(b)   the Secretary of State has made provision in the Social Security (Claims and Payments) Regulations 1987 for that benefit to be claimed by telephone,

that person may claim council tax benefit by telephone to the telephone number specified by the Secretary of State.

(4AB)   A claim for council tax benefit may be made in accordance with paragraph (4AA) at any time before a decision has been made on the claim for the benefit referred to in paragraph (4)(a).

(4AC)   If the Secretary of State agrees, where a person, in accordance with regulation 32 of the Social Security (Claims and Payments) Regulations 1987 (information to be given and changes to be notified)–

(a)   furnishes the Secretary of State with such information or evidence as he may require; or

(b)   notifies the Secretary of State of any change of circumstances,
that person may claim council tax benefit in the same manner in which the information or evidence was furnished or the notification was given.

(4AD)   If the Secretary of State agrees, where a person, in accordance with regulation 24 of the Jobseeker's Allowance Regulations (provision of information and evidence)–

(a)   furnishes the Secretary of State with such certificates, documents and other evidence as he may require; or

(b)   notifies the Secretary of State of any change of circumstances,
that person may claim council tax benefit in the same manner as the certificate, document and other evidence was furnished or the notification was given.

(4AE)   A claim for council tax benefit may be made in accordance with paragraphs (4AC) or (4AD) at any time before a decision has been made on the award of benefit to which the information, evidence, certificates, documents or notification relates.]

(4B)   The relevant authority may determine, in any particular case, that a claim made by telephone [⁴ in accordance with paragraph (4A)] is not a valid claim unless the person making the claim approves a written statement of his circumstances, provided for the purpose by the relevant authority.

[⁴ (4BA)   The relevant authority or the Secretary of State may determine that a claim made by telephone in accordance with paragraphs (4AA) to (4AE) is not a valid claim unless the person making the claim approves a written statement of his circumstances provided for the purpose by the Secretary of State.]

[⁴ (4C)   A claim made by telephone in accordance with paragraphs (4A) to (4AE) is defective unless the relevant authority or the Secretary of State is provided with all the information requested during that telephone call.]

(4D)   Where a claim made by telephone in accordance with paragraph (4A) is defective, the relevant authority [⁴ must] provide the person making it with an opportunity to correct the defect.

[⁴ (4DA)   Where a claim made by telephone in accordance with paragraphs (4AA) to (4AE) is defective–

(a)   the Secretary of State may provide the person making it with an opportunity to correct the defect;

(b)   the relevant authority must provide the person making it with an opportunity to correct the defect if the Secretary of State has not already done so unless it considers that it has sufficient information to determine the claim.]

(4E)   If the person corrects the defect within one month, or such longer period as the relevant authority considers reasonable, [⁴ of the date the relevant authority or the Secretary of State] last drew attention to it, the relevant authority shall treat the claim as if it had been duly made in the first instance.]

[⁴ (4F)   If the person does not correct the defect within one month, or such longer period as the relevant authority considers reasonable, of the date the relevant authority or the Secretary of State last drew attention to it, the relevant authority may treat the claim as if it had been duly made in the first instance where it considers that it has sufficient information to determine the claim.]

(5)   Subject to paragraph (12), [⁴] the date on which a claim is made shall be–

(a)   in a case where an award of income support [⁶ , an income-based jobseeker's allowance or an income-related employment and support allowance] has been made to the claimant or his partner and the claim for council tax benefit is made within one month of the date on which the claim for that income support [⁶ , jobseeker's allowance or employment and support allowance] was received at the appropriate DWP office, the first day of entitlement to income support [⁶ , an income-based jobseeker's allowance or an income-related employment and support allowance] arising from that claim; [⁶];

(b)   in a case where a claimant or his partner is a person on income support [⁶ , an income-based jobseeker's allowance or an income-related employment and support allowance] and he becomes liable for the first time to pay council tax in respect of the dwelling which he occupies as his home, where the claim to the authority is received at the designated office or appropriate DWP office within one month of the date of the change, the date on which the change takes place;

(c)   in a case where the claimant is the former partner of a person who was, at the date of his death or their separation, entitled to council tax benefit and where the claimant makes a claim for council tax benefit within one month of the date of the death or the separation, that date;

[4 (d) except where sub-paragraph (a), (b) or (c) is satisfied, in a case where a properly completed claim is received in a designated office, an authorised office, county offices, or an appropriate DWP office within one month, or such longer period as the relevant authority considers reasonable, of the date on which–

    (i)   a claim form was issued to the claimant following the claimant first notifying, by whatever means, a designated office, an authorised office or an appropriate DWP office of an intention to make a claim; or

    (ii)   a claimant notifies, by whatever means, a designated office, an authorised office or an appropriate DWP office of an intention to make a claim by telephone in accordance with paragraphs (4A) to (4AE),

    the date of first notification;]

(e)   in any other case, the date on which the claim is received at the designated office, authorised office [3 , county offices] or appropriate DWP office.

[6 (5A)   For the purposes only of sub-paragraph (5)(a) a person who has been awarded an income-based jobseeker's allowance or an income-related employment and support allowance must be treated as entitled to that allowance for any days which immediately precede the first day in that award and on which he would, but for regulations made under–

(a)   in the case of income-based jobseeker's allowance, paragraph 4 of Schedule 1 to the Jobseekers Act (waiting days); or

(b)   in the case of income-related employment and support allowance, paragraph 2 of Schedule 2 to the Welfare Reform Act (waiting days),

have been entitled to that allowance.]

(6)   Where a claim received at the designated office [7 or appropriate DWP office] has not been made in the manner prescribed in paragraph (1), that claim is for the purposes of these Regulations defective.

(7)   Where a claim [7 , which is received by a relevant authority,] is defective because–

(a)   it was made on the form approved for the purpose but that form is not accepted by the relevant authority as being properly completed; or

(b)   it was made in writing but not on the form approved for the purpose and the relevant authority does not accept the claim as being in a written form which is sufficient in the circumstances of the case, having regard to the sufficiency of the written information and evidence,

the relevant authority may, in a case to which sub-paragraph (a) applies, request the claimant to complete the defective claim or, in a case to which sub-paragraph (b) applies, supply the claimant with the approved form or request further information or evidence.

[7 (7A) Where a claim is received at an appropriate DWP office and it appears to the Secretary of State that the form has not been properly completed, the Secretary of State may request that the claimant provides the relevant authority with the information required to complete the form.]

[7 (8) The relevant authority shall treat a defective claim as if it had been validly made in the first instance if, in any particular case, the conditions specified in sub-paragraph (a), (b) or (c) of paragraph (8A) are satisfied.

(8A) The conditions are that–

(a)   where paragraph (7)(a) (incomplete form) applies, the authority receives at the designated office the properly completed claim or the information requested to complete it or the evidence within one month of the request, or such longer period as the relevant authority may consider reasonable; or

(b)   where paragraph (7)(b) (claim not on approved form or further information requested by relevant authority) applies–

    (i)   the approved form sent to the claimant is received at the designated office properly completed within one month of it having been sent to him; or, as the case may be,

    (ii)   the claimant supplies whatever information or evidence was requested under paragraph (7) within one month of the request,

    or, in either case, within such longer period as the relevant authority may consider reasonable; or

(c)   where paragraph (7A) (further information requested by Secretary of State) applies, the relevant authority receives at the designated office the properly completed claim or the information requested to complete it within one month of the request by the Secretary of State or within such longer period as the relevant authority considers reasonable.]

(9)   A claim which is made on an approved form for the time being is, for the purposes of this regulation, properly completed if completed in accordance with the instructions on the form, including any instructions to provide information and evidence in connection with the claim.

[² (10)   Except in the case of a claim made by a person from abroad, where a person has not become liable for council tax to a relevant authority but it is anticipated that he will become so liable within the period of 8 weeks (the relevant period), he may claim council tax benefit at any time in that period in respect of that tax and, provided that liability arises within the relevant period, the authority shall treat the claim as having been made on the day on which the liability for the tax arises.]

(11)   Where, exceptionally, a relevant authority, has not set or imposed its council tax by the beginning of the financial year, if a claim for council tax benefit is properly made or treated as properly made and–

(a)   the date on which the claim is made or treated as made is in the period from the 1st April of the current year and ending one month after the date on which the authority sets or imposes the tax; and

(b)   if the tax had been determined, the claimant would have been entitled to council tax benefit either from–

    (i)   the benefit week in which the 1st April of the current year fell; or

    (ii)   a benefit week falling after the date specified in head (i) but before the claim was made,

    the relevant authority shall treat the claim as made in the benefit week immediately preceding the benefit week in which such entitlement would have commenced.

[² (12)   Except in the case of a claim made by a person from abroad, where the claimant is not entitled to council tax benefit in the benefit week immediately following the date of his claim but the relevant authority is of the opinion that unless there is a change of circumstances he will be entitled to council tax benefit for a period beginning not later than the thirteenth benefit week following the date on which the claim is made, the relevant authority may treat the claim as made on a date in the benefit week immediately preceding the first benefit week of that period of entitlement and award benefit accordingly.]

(13)   In the case of a person who has attained, or whose partner has attained, [⁸ the age which is 17 weeks younger than the qualifying age for state pension credit], paragraph (12) shall apply as if for the reference to the thirteenth benefit week, there was substituted a reference to the seventeenth benefit week.

[⁹ (14)   Where a claimant (''C'')–

(a)   makes a claim which includes (or which C subsequently requests should include) a period before the claim is made; and

(b)   from a day in that period, up to the date when C made the claim (or subsequently requested that the claim should include a past period), C had continuous good cause for failing to make a claim (or request that the claim should include that period),

the claim is to be treated as made on the date determined in accordance with paragraph (14A).

(14A) That date is the latest of–
(a) the first day from which C had continuous good cause;
(b) the day 6 months before the date the claim was made;
(c) the day 6 months before the date when C requested that the claim should include a past period.]
(15) In this regulation ''authorised office'' means an office which is nominated by the Secretary of State and authorised by the relevant authority for receiving claims for decision by the relevant authority.

Amendments
1. Inserted by reg 4(2) of SI 2006 No 2967 as from 20.12.06.
2. Substituted by reg 5 of SI 2007 No 1331 as from 23.5.07.
3. Amended by reg 9(2) of SI 2007 No 2911 as from 31.10.07
4. Amended by reg 4(3) of SI 2008 No 2299 as from 1.10.08, as corrected by correction slip July 2009.
5. Substituted by reg 6 of SI 2008 No 2424 as from 6.10.08.
6. Amended by reg 56 of SI 2008 No 1082 as from 27.10.08.
7. Amended by reg 4(2) of SI 2008 No 2987 as from 22.12.08.
8. Amended by reg 33 of SI 2009 No 1488 as from 6.4.10.
9. Amended by reg 4(2) of SI 2010 No 2449 as from 1.11.10.

[¹Electronic claims for benefit
69A. A claim for council tax benefit may be made by means of an electronic communication in accordance with Schedule 9.]

Amendment
1. Inserted by Art 4(3) of SI 2006 No 2968 as from 20.12.06.

[² Date of claim where claim sent or delivered to a gateway office
70.]

Amendments
1. Amended by reg 5(7) of SI 2008 No 1042 as from 19.5.08.
2. Omitted by reg 4(5) of SI 2008 No 2299 as from 1.10.08.

[² Date of claim where claim sent or delivered to an office of a designated authority
71.]

Amendments
1. Amended by reg 5(8) of SI 2008 No 1042 as from 19.5.08.
2. Omitted by reg 4(6) of SI 2008 No 2299 as from 1.10.08.

Evidence and information
72.–(1) Subject to [⁴ paragraphs (1A) and (2)] and to paragraph 4 of Schedule A1 (treatment of claims for council tax benefit by refugees), a person who makes a claim, or a person to whom council tax benefit has been awarded, shall furnish such certificates, documents, information and evidence in connection with the claim or the award, or any question arising out of the claim or the award, as may reasonably be required by the relevant authority in order to determine that person's entitlement to, or continuing entitlement to council tax benefit and shall do so within [² one month] of [⁴ the relevant authority requiring him, or the Secretary of State requesting him, to do so] or such longer period as the relevant authority may consider reasonable.
[⁴ (1A) Where a person notifies a change of circumstances to the appropriate DWP office under regulation 74(7), the Secretary of State may request that the claimant provides to the relevant authority the information or evidence that the Secretary of State considers the relevant authority may require to determine the claimant's continuing entitlement to housing benefit.]
(2) Nothing in this regulation shall require a person to furnish any certificates, documents, information or evidence relating to a payment to which paragraph (4) applies.
(3) Where a request is made under paragraph (1), the relevant authority shall–

(a)   inform the claimant or the person to whom council tax benefit has been awarded of his duty under regulation 74 (duty to notify change of circumstances) to notify the designated office of any change of circumstances; and

(b)   without prejudice to the extent of the duty owed under regulation 74, indicate to him either orally or by notice or by reference to some other document available to him on application and without charge, the kind of change of circumstances which are to be notified.

(4)   This paragraph applies to any of the following payments–

(a)   a payment which is–

    (i)   disregarded under paragraph 24 of Schedule 4 (income in kind) or paragraph 34 of Schedule 5 (certain payments in kind); and

    (ii)   made under [5 or by] the Trusts, the Fund, the Eileen Trust [5 , MFET Limited] , the Skipton Fund, or the London Bombings Relief Charitable Fund;

(b)   a payment which is disregarded under paragraph 36 of Schedule 4 or under paragraph 24 of Schedule 5 (payments made under certain trusts and certain other payments), other than a payment under the Independent Living [3 Fund (2006)];

(c)   a payment which is disregarded under regulation 58(9)(b) or (c) (non-dependant deductions) or paragraph 2(b) or (c) of Schedule 2 (second adult's gross income) other than a payment under the Independent Living [3 Fund (2006)].

(5)   Where a claimant or a person to whom council tax benefit has been awarded or any partner [6 has attained the qualifying age for state pension credit] and is a member of, or a person deriving entitlement to a pension under, a personal pension scheme, [1] he shall where the relevant authority so requires furnish the following information–

(a)   the name and address of the pension fund holder;

(b)   such other information including any reference or policy number as is needed to enable the personal pension scheme [1] to be identified.

(6)   Where the pension fund holder receives from a relevant authority a request for details concerning a personal pension scheme [1] relating to a person or any partner to whom paragraph (5) refers, the pension fund holder shall provide the relevant authority with any information to which paragraph (7) refers.

(7)   The information to which this paragraph refers is–

(a)   where the purchase of an annuity under a personal pension scheme has been deferred, the amount of any income which is being withdrawn from the personal pension scheme;

(b)   in the case of–

    (i)   a personal pension scheme where income withdrawal is available, the maximum amount of income which may be withdrawn from the scheme; or

    (ii)   a personal pension scheme where income withdrawal is not available, [1] the maximum amount of income which might be withdrawn from the fund if the fund were held under a personal pension scheme where income withdrawal was available,

calculated by or on behalf of the pension fund holder by means of tables prepared from time to time by the Government Actuary which are appropriate for this purpose.

Amendments

1.   Amended by reg 6(6) of SI 2007 No 1749 as from 16.7.07.
2.   Amended by reg 5(9) of SI 2008 No 1042 as from 19.5.08.
3.   Amended by reg 8(4)(e of SI 2008 No 2767 as from 17.11.08.
4.   Amended by reg 4(3) of SI 2008 No 2987 as from 22.12.08.
5.   Amended by reg 10(3) and (5) of SI 2010 No 641 as from 1.4.10 (5.4.10 where rent payable weekly or in multiples of a week).
6.   Amended by reg 10(9) of SI 2010 No 641 as from 6.4.10.

General Note

Like reg 86 HB Regs, reg 72 obliges the claimant to provide evidence to support her/his claim if requested to do so by the authority or the DWP. Note that prior to the amendment made from 19 May 2008, here the time limit for providing the evidence was four weeks rather than one month: para (1). It is understood that this was a drafting error at the time the regulations were consolidated. Note: the time limit in reg 63 CTB Regs 1992 (now reg 72) was amended by reg 3(15) of SI 2005 No.2894 as from 10 November 2005.

[²Amendment and withdrawal of claim

[³**73.**–(1)   A person who has made a claim may amend it at any time before a decision has been made on it by a notice in writing delivered or sent to the designated office.

(2)   Where the claim was made by telephone in accordance with paragraphs (4A) to (4AE) of regulation 69, the amendment may also be made by telephone.

(3)   Any claim amended in accordance with paragraph (1) or (2) shall be treated as if it had been amended in the first instance.

(4)   A person who has made a claim may withdraw it at any time before a decision has been made on it by notice to the designated office.

(5)   Where the claim was made by telephone in accordance with paragraphs (4AA) to (4AE) of regulation 69, the withdrawal may also be made by telephone to the telephone number specified by the Secretary of State.

(6)   Any notice of withdrawal given in accordance with paragraph (4) or (5) shall have effect when it is received.]]

Amendments

1.   Inserted by reg 4(3) of SI 2006 No 2967 as from 20.12.06.
2.   Substituted by reg 8(4) of SI 2007 No 719 as from 2.4.07.
3.   Substituted by reg 4(7) of SI 2008 No 2299 as from 1.10.08.

Duty to notify changes of circumstances

74.–(1)   Subject to [² paragraphs (3) [⁴ , (5) and (7)]], if at any time between the making of a claim and a decision being made on it, or during the award of council tax benefit there is a change of circumstances which the claimant, or any person by whom or on whose behalf sums payable by way of council tax benefit are receivable, might reasonably be expected to know might affect the claimant's right to, the amount of or the receipt of council tax benefit, that person shall be under a duty to notify that change of circumstances by giving notice [¹] to the designated office

[¹[⁵ (a)   in writing; or

(b)   by telephone–

(i)   where the relevant authority has published a telephone number for that purpose or for the purposes of regulation 69 (time and manner in which claims are to be made) unless the authority determines that in any particular case or class of case notification may not be given by telephone; or

(ii)   in any case or class of case where the relevant authority determines that notice may be given by telephone; or

(c)   by any other means which the relevant authority agrees to accept in any particular case.]]

[² (2)]

(3)   The duty imposed on a person by paragraph (1) does not extend to notifying changes–

(a)   in the amount of council tax payable to the relevant authority;

(b)   in the age of the claimant or that of any member of his family;

(c)   in these Regulations;

(d)   in the case of a claimant on income support [³ , an income-based jobseeker's allowance or an income-related employment and support allowance], in circumstances which affect the amount of income support [³ , an income-based jobseeker's allowance or an income-related employment and support allowance] but not the amount of council tax benefit to which he is entitled, other than the cessation of that entitlement to income support [³ , an income-based jobseeker's allowance or an income-related employment and support allowance].

(4) Notwithstanding paragraph (3)(b) or (d) a claimant shall be required by paragraph (1) to notify the designated office of any change in the composition of his family arising from the fact that a person who was a member of his family is now no longer such a person because he ceases to be a child or young person.

(5) Where the amount of a claimant's council tax benefit is the alternative maximum council tax benefit in his case, the claimant shall be under a duty to give written notice to the designated office of changes which occur in the number of adults in the dwelling or in their total gross incomes which might reasonably be expected to change his entitlement to that council tax benefit and where any such adult ceases to be in receipt of income support [3 , an income-based jobseeker's allowance or an income-related employment and support allowance] the date when this occurs.

[2 (6)]

[4 (7) Where–

(a) the claimant or the claimant's partner is in receipt of income support or jobseeker's allowance;

(b) the change of circumstance is that the claimant or the claimant's partner starts employment; and

(c) as a result of that change of circumstance either entitlement to that benefit will end or, where the claimant or claimant's partner is in receipt of a contribution-based jobseeker's allowance, the amount of that benefit will be reduced,

the claimant may discharge the duty in paragraph (1) by notifying the change of circumstance by telephoning the appropriate DWP office if a telephone number has been provided for that purpose.]

Amendments

1. Amended by reg 4(4) of SI 2006 No 2967 as from 20.12.06.
2. Amended by reg 4(8) of SI 2008 No 2299 as from 1.10.08.
3. Amended by reg 57 of SI 2008 No 1082 as from 27.10.08.
4. Amended by reg 4(4) of SI 2008 No 2987 as from 22.12.08.
5. Amended by reg 4(3) of SI 2010 N0 2449 as from 1.11.10.

General Note

For the alternatve maximum council tax referred to in para (5), see reg 62 on p704.

Reg 74 equates to reg 88 HB Regs, but there is no equivalent to reg 74(5) in those Regs.

[1 Alternative means of notifying changes of circumstances

74ZA.–(1) In such cases and subject to such conditions as the Secretary of State may specify, the duty in regulation 74(1) to notify a change of circumstances may be discharged by notifying the Secretary of State–

(a) where the change of circumstances is a birth or death, through a relevant authority, or a county council in England, by personal attendance at an office specified by that authority or county council, provided the Secretary of State has agreed with that authority or county council for it to facilitate such notification; or

(b) where the change of circumstances is a death, by telephone to a telephone number specified for that purpose by the Secretary of State.

(2) Paragraph (1) only applies if the authority administering the claimant's council tax benefit agrees with the Secretary of State that notifications may be made in accordance with that paragraph.

(3) The Secretary of State must forward information received in accordance with paragraph (1) to the authority administering the claimant's council tax benefit.]

Amendment

1. Inserted by reg 7 of SI 2010 No 444 as from 5.4.10.

[1Notice of changes of circumstances given electronically

74A. A person may give notice of a change of circumstances required to be notified under regulation 74 by means of an electronic communication in accordance with Schedule 9.]

Amendment

1.   Inserted by Art 4(4) of SI 2006 No 2968 as from 20.12.06.

PART 9
Decisions on questions

Decisions by a relevant authority

75.–(1)   Unless provided otherwise by these Regulations, any matter required to be determined under these Regulations shall be determined in the first instance by the relevant authority.

(2)   The relevant authority shall make a decision on each claim within 14 days of the provisions of regulations 69 and 72 (time and manner for making claims and evidence and information required) being satisfied or as soon as reasonably practicable thereafter.

[¹ (3)]

Amendment

1.   Omitted by reg 9(5)(c) of SI 2008 No 959 as from 6.10.08.

Notification of decision

76.–(1)   Except in cases to which paragraphs (a) and (b) of regulation 82 (excess benefit in consequence of a reduction of a relevant authority's council tax) refer, an Authority shall notify in writing any person affected by a decision made by it under these Regulations–

(a)   in the case of a decision on a claim, forthwith or as soon as reasonably practicable thereafter;

(b)   in any other case, within 14 days of that decision or as soon as reasonably practicable thereafter,

and every notification shall include a statement as to the matters set out in Schedule 8.

(2)   A person affected to whom an authority sends or delivers a notification of decision may [¹ , within one month of the date of the notification of that decision (or, if the decision was notified before 1st November 2010, before 1st December 2010),] request in writing the authority to provide a written statement setting out the reasons for its decision on any matter set out in the notice.

(3)   The written statement referred to in paragraph (2) shall be sent to the person requesting it within 14 days or as soon as is reasonably practical thereafter.

Amendment

1.   Amended by reg 4(4) of SI 2010 N0 2449 as from 1.11.10.

PART 10
Awards or payments of benefit

Time and manner of granting council tax benefit

77.–(1)   Subject to regulations 80 and 81 (payments on death and offsetting), where a person is entitled to council tax benefit in respect of his liability for a relevant authority's council tax as it has effect in respect of the relevant or any subsequent chargeable financial year, the relevant authority shall discharge his entitlement–

(a)   by reducing, so far as possible, the amount of his liability to which regulation 20(2) of the Council Tax (Administration and Enforcement) Regulations 1992 (the English and Welsh Regulations) or regulation 20(2) of the Council Tax (Administration and Enforcement) (Scotland) Regulations 1992 (the Scottish Regulations) refers; or

(b)   where–

(i)   such a reduction is not possible; or

(ii)   such a reduction would be insufficient to discharge the entitlement to council tax benefit; or

(iii) the person entitled to council tax benefit is jointly and severally liable for the tax and the relevant authority determines that such a reduction would be inappropriate,

by making payments to him of the benefit to which he is entitled, rounded where necessary to the nearest penny.

(2) The relevant authority shall notify the person entitled to council tax benefit of the amount of that benefit and how his entitlement is to be discharged in pursuance of paragraph (1).

(3) In a case to which paragraph (1)(b) refers–

(a) if the amount of the council tax for which he remains liable in respect of the relevant chargeable financial year, after any reduction to which paragraph (1)(a) refers has been made, is insufficient to enable his entitlement to council tax benefit in respect thereof to be discharged in that year, upon the final instalment of that tax becoming due any outstanding benefit–

(i) shall be paid to that person if he so requires; or

(ii) in any other case shall (as the relevant authority determines) either be repaid or credited against any subsequent liability of the person to make a payment in respect of the authority's council tax as it has effect for any subsequent year;

(b) if that person has ceased to be liable for the relevant authority's council tax and has discharged the liability for that tax, the outstanding balance (if any) of the council tax benefit in respect thereof shall be paid within 14 days or, if that is not reasonably practicable, as soon as practicable thereafter;

(c) in any other case, the council tax benefit shall be paid within 14 days of the receipt of the claim at the designated office or, if that is not reasonably practicable, as soon as practicable thereafter.

(4) For the purposes of this regulation "instalment" means any instalment of a relevant authority's council tax to which regulation 19 of either the English and Welsh Regulations or as the case may be the Scottish Regulations refers (council tax payments).

Persons to whom benefit is to be paid

78.–(1) Subject to regulation 80 (payment on death) and paragraph (2), any payment of council tax benefit under regulation 77(1)(b) shall be made to that person.

(2) Where a person other than a person who is entitled to council tax benefit made the claim and that first person is a person acting pursuant to an appointment under regulation 68(3) (persons appointed to act for a person unable to act) or is treated as having been so appointed by virtue of regulation 68(5), benefit may be paid to that person.

General Note

Para (1) provides that, unless a person entitled to CTB has died or someone has been appointed to act for her/him (for which see para (2)), if CTB is not paid under reg 77(1)(a) by reducing the claimant's council tax bill, CTB must be paid direct to that person.

Shortfall in benefit

79.–(1) Except in cases to which paragraph (2) refers, where, on the revision of a decision allowing council tax benefit to a person, it is determined that the amount allowed was less than the amount to which that person was entitled, the relevant authority shall either–

(a) make good any shortfall in benefit which is due to that person, by reducing so far as possible the next and any subsequent payments he is liable to make in respect of the council tax of the authority concerned as it has effect for the relevant chargeable financial year until that shortfall is made good; or

(b) where this is not possible or the person concerned so requests, pay any shortfall in benefit due to that person within 14 days of the revision of the decision being made or if that is not reasonably practicable, as soon as possible afterwards.

(2)   A shortfall in benefit need not be paid in any case to the extent that there is due from the person concerned to the relevant authority any recoverable excess benefit to which regulation 83(1) refers.

General Note

This regulation deals with the situation when an authority has underpaid a claimant. By para (1), unless para (2) applies and a recoverable overpayment under reg 83 is owed by the claimant, when it is decided that a claimant has been underpaid, the authority has a choice. If the claimant requests payment, the shortfall must be paid to her/him within 14 days or as soon as "reasonably practicable": see note on reg 89(2) HB Regs on p460. Otherwise, the amount outstanding should be deducted from the claimant's remaining liability for that chargeable financial year. If this is not possible (eg, because the remaining liability is less than the amount due to the claimant), payment should be made to the claimant within the timescale set out in para (1)(b).

Payment on the death of the person entitled

80.–(1)   Where the person entitled to any council tax benefit has died and it is not possible to award any council tax benefit which is due in the form of a reduction of the council tax for which he was liable, the relevant authority shall make payment either to his personal representative or, where there is none, his next of kin aged 16 or over.

(2)   For the purposes of paragraph (1), "next of kin" means in England and Wales the persons who would take beneficially on an intestacy and in Scotland the person entitled to the moveable estate on intestacy.

(3)   A payment under paragraph (1) may not be made unless the personal representative or the next of kin, as the case may be, makes written application for the payment of any sum of benefit to which the deceased was entitled, and such written application is sent to or delivered to the relevant authority at its designated office within 12 months of the deceased's death or such longer period as the authority may allow in any particular case.

(4)   The authority may dispense with strict proof of title of any person claiming under paragraph (3) and the receipt of such a person shall be a good discharge to the authority for any sum so paid.

Offsetting

81.–(1)   Where a person has been allowed or paid a sum of council tax benefit under a decision which is subsequently revised or further revised, any sum allowed or paid in respect of a period covered by the subsequent decision shall be offset against arrears of entitlement under the subsequent decision except to the extent that the sum exceeds the arrears and shall be treated as properly awarded or paid on account of them.

(2)   Where an amount has been deducted under regulation 89(1) an equivalent sum shall be offset against any arrears of entitlement under the subsequent determination.

(3)   No amount may be offset under paragraph (1) which has been determined to be excess benefit within the meaning of regulation 82 (meaning of excess benefit).

PART 11
Excess benefit

General Note on Part 11

Many of the provisions in this Part are equivalent to those in Part 13 of the HB Regs – see the General Note on p477. Overpayments of CTB are termed "excess benefit", but there is no particular significance about this. The rules on recovery are slightly different.

Meaning of excess benefit

82.   In this Part "excess benefit" means any amount which has been allowed by way of council tax benefit and to which there was no entitlement under these Regulations (whether on the initial decision [[1] or as subsequently revised or superseded or further revised or superseded]) and includes any excess which arises by reason of–

    (a)   a reduction in the amount a person is liable to pay in respect of council tax in consequence of–

(i)   regulations made under section 13 of the 1992 Act (reduction in the amount of a person's council tax); or

(ii)   any discount to which that tax is subject by virtue of section 11 or 79 of that Act;

(b)   a substitution under sections 31 or, in Scotland, section 94 of the 1992 Act (substituted amounts) of a lesser amount for an amount of council tax previously set by the relevant authority under section 30 or, in Scotland section 93 of that Act (amount set for council tax).

Amendment

1.   Amended by reg 3 of SI 2005 No 2904 as amended by Sch 2 para 29 of SI 2006 No 217 as from 10.4.06.

General Note

See reg 99 HB Regs on p477, although note that there is no equivalent to reg 93 HB Regs. For "overpayment" read "excess benefits".

Sub-paras (a) and (b) have no equivalent in the HB Regs. Sub-para (a) refers to cases where a claimant's liability for CTB is subsequently reduced due to a disability reduction, discount, transitional relief or charge-capping. Sub-para (b) deals with cases where an authority subsequently substitutes a lower council tax for the year. Any excess benefit falling within either of these sub-paras is always recoverable, whether or not there is an official error: reg 83(4).

It is common practice for local authorities to make awards of CTB until the end of the council tax year on the 31 March each year, and thus "credit" the claimant's council tax account with CTB up to the 31 March. However, in the context of excess CTB, Commissioner Rowland ruled in *CH 3076/2006* that such a credit may be treated as a credit of CTB only as each week of entitlement under the award passes. Accordingly where an award of CTB is superseded on, say, 1 November and entitlement to CTB removed from that date, then the amount credited to the council tax account for the period from 1 November to 31 March will not constitute excess CTB under reg 82. This is also the case, in the commissioner's view, where benefit is suspended and not then reinstated; so the credit is not a payment of excess CTB for the period of the suspension. Accordingly, there will only have been a payment of excess benefit in a "credit" case where entitlement to CTB has been removed retrospectively and payment of benefit was not suspended for that period.

However, in *CH 1384/2007* the deputy commissioner came to a contrary view in holding that a payment credited to the claimant's council tax account to the year end was a payment of CTB, and thus constituted excess CTB once it was established that the payment had been wrongly made.

Despite being decided within weeks of each other, neither decision refers to the other. Decision makers and tribunals can therefore choose which approach is correct. *CH 1384/2007* has the merit of pointing out that if an advance award is made at the outset for the whole of the year then there is nothing for the suspension powers in Part III of the D&A Regs (see p1030) to bite on. On the other hand, as *CH 1384/2007* points out, making awards of CTB to the end of the financial year would seem to be contemplated by s138(1)(b) SSAA and reg 83(5) below; and it is arguable that Commissioner Rowland in *CH 1384/2007* does not explain what excess benefit reg 83(5) applies to if his analysis is correct.

Recoverable excess benefit

83.–(1)   Any excess benefit, except benefit to which paragraph (2) applies, shall be recoverable.

(2)   Subject to paragraph (4) and (5) and excepting any excess benefit arising in consequence of a reduction in tax or substitution to which regulation 82 refers, this paragraph applies to excess benefit allowed in consequence of an official error, where the claimant or a person acting on his behalf or any other person to whom the excess benefit is allowed could not, at the time the benefit was allowed or upon the receipt of any notice relating to the allowance of that benefit, reasonably have been expected to realise that it was excess benefit.

(3)   In paragraph (2), "excess benefit allowed in consequence of an official error" means an overpayment caused by a mistake made whether in the form of an act or omission by–

(a)   the relevant authority;

(b)   an officer or person acting for that authority;

(c)   an officer of–

(i)   the Department for Work and Pensions; or

(ii)   the Commissioners for Her Majesty's Revenue and Customs,

acting as such; or

(d)   a person providing services to the Department or to the Commissioners referred to in (c),

where the claimant, a person acting on his behalf or any other person to whom the payment is made, did not cause or materially contribute to that mistake, act or omission.

(4)   Paragraph (2) shall not apply with respect to excess benefit to which regulation 82(a) and (b) refers.

(5)   Where in consequence of an official error a person has been awarded excess benefit, upon the award being revised [¹ or superseded] any excess benefit which remains credited to him by the relevant authority in respect of a period after the date of the revision [¹ or supersession], shall be recoverable.

Amendment

1.   Amended by reg 5 of SI 2005 No 2904 as amended by Sch 2 para 29 of SI 2006 No 217 as from 10.4.06.

General Note

It is suggested that the use of the phrase "in consequence of" in para (3) as opposed to "caused by" in reg 100(2) HB Regs is not significant.

Para (4) has no equivalent in reg 100 HB Regs and means that all of the excess payments referred to in sub-paras (a) and (b) of reg 82 are by definition recoverable. Para (5) is generally the equivalent of reg 100(4). For whether payments credited to a claimant's council tax account to the end of the council tax year can amount to excess benefit, see the discussion under reg 82.

Authority by which recovery may be made

84.   The relevant authority which allowed the recoverable excess benefit may recover it.

General Note

Reg 84 confirms the discretion to recover excess CTB by the authority that allowed it. See the Analysis to s75(2) SSAA on p42 for consideration of the discretion in the HB context.

Persons from whom recovery may be sought

[¹**85.**   Recoverable excess benefit shall be due from the claimant or the person to whom the excess benefit was allowed.]

Amendment

1.   Substituted by reg 6(2) of SI 2008 No 2824 as from 6.4.09.

General Note

Reg 85 is narrower than reg 101 HB Regs in that recovery cannot be made from a person who misrepresented or failed to disclose a material fact if s/he is not otherwise covered.

Methods of recovery

86.–(1)   Without prejudice to any other method of recovery a relevant authority may recover any recoverable excess benefit [¹] by any of the methods specified in paragraph (2) and (3) or any combination of those methods.

(2)   Excess benefit may be recovered [¹]–

(a)   by payment by or on behalf of the [¹ claimant or the person to whom the excess benefit was allowed]; or

(b)   by an addition being made by the relevant authority to any amount payable in respect of the council tax concerned.

[¹ (3)   Where recoverable excess benefit cannot be recovered by either of the methods specified in paragraph (2), the relevant authority may request the Secretary of State to recover the outstanding excess–

(a)   from the benefits prescribed in regulation 90(1); or

(b)   where the claimant has one or more partners, from the benefits prescribed in regulation 90(1A), provided that the claimant and that partner were a couple both at the time the excess benefit was allowed and when the deduction is made.

Amendment

1.   Amended by reg 6(3) of SI 2008 No 2824 as from 6.4.09.

General Note
Like reg 102 HB Regs, this regulation does not purport to be an exhaustive list of the methods of recovery. It simply sets out some permissible methods. Reg 87 sets out another. See the Analysis to reg 102 HB Regs on p491 for a complete guide to the methods of recovery, though see the General Note to reg 87 below.

Analysis
Para 2. Recovery of excess CTB may be effected by payment from the claimant or other person to whom the benefit was allowed or by an addition to the claimant's council tax bill. It is not possible to recover, as is the case with HB, by demand for payment from any other person whose misrepresentation or failure to disclose led to the overpayment.
Para 3 provides a further means of recovery, but only if para (2) cannot be used.

Further provision as to recovery of excess benefit

87. In addition to the methods for recovery of excess benefit which are specified in regulation 86, any sum or part of a sum which is due from the person concerned and which is not paid within 21 days of his being notified of the amount that is due, shall be recoverable in a court of competent jurisdiction by the authority to which the excess benefit is due.

General Note
This power is additional to any other methods of recovery adopted. Although HB overpayments can be recovered in a similar manner there is no such express power in the HB Regs.
Note that this regulation does not give the power to recover the excess benefit by registration as a recoverable debt at court, as to which see the Analysis on p491. This is because the wording of reg 87 does not conform with that specified in Sch 2 CCR Ord 25 in the procedure of the Sheriff Court in Scotland, to enable recovery under that rule.
Therefore all reg 87 does is confirm the right to sue for the debt in the appropriate court. Note that proceedings cannot be taken until 21 days after the notification of the amount due. This time period is a minimum and is less than the one-month period for seeking a revision or supersession of the decision. Authorities should consider the possibility of the claimant seeking such a revision or supersession when deciding whether to issue a demand notice for payment. In any event, it is arguable that a final decision is not made until any revision or supersession of, or appeal against, the decsion has been resolved, or the time limits for enabling such challenges to be made have expired (see *R(SB) 5/91*), and so the 21-day time limit can only begin to run from one month after the date of the decision that the excess benefit is recoverable.

Diminution of capital

88.–(1) Where in the case of recoverable excess benefit, in consequence of a misrepresentation or failure to disclose a material fact (in either case whether fraudulent or otherwise) as to a person's capital, or an error, other than one to which regulation 83(2) (effect of official error) refers, as to the amount of a person's capital, the excess benefit was in respect of a period (''the excess benefit period'') of more than 13 benefit weeks, the relevant authority shall, for the purpose only of calculating the amount of excess–

(a) at the end of the first 13 benefit weeks of the excess benefit period, treat the amount of the capital as having been reduced by the amount of excess council tax benefit allowed during those 13 weeks;

(b) at the end of each subsequent period of 13 benefit weeks, if any, of the excess benefit period, treat the amount of that capital as having been further reduced by the amount of excess council tax benefit allowed during the immediately preceding 13 benefit weeks.

(2) Capital shall not be treated as reduced over any period other than 13 benefit weeks or in any circumstances other than those, for which paragraph (1) provides.

Sums to be deducted in calculating recoverable excess benefit

89.–(1) In calculating the amount of recoverable excess benefit, the relevant authority shall deduct any amount of council tax benefit which should have been determined to be payable in respect of the whole or part of the overpayment period–

(a) on the basis of the claim as presented to the authority;

(b) on the basis of the claim as it would have appeared had any misrepresentation or non-disclosure been remedied before the decision; or

    (c)   on the basis of the claim as it would have appeared if any change of circumstances had been notified at the time that change occurred.

    (2)   In calculating the amount of recoverable excess benefit, the relevant authority may deduct so much of any payment of council tax in respect of the excess benefit period which exceeds the amount, if any, which the claimant was liable to pay for that period under the original erroneous decision.

Recovery of excess benefit from prescribed benefits

90.–(1)   [³ Subject to paragraph (1B),] For the purposes of section 76(3)(c) of the Administration Act (deduction of excess council tax benefit from prescribed benefits), the benefits prescribed by this regulation are–

    (a)   any benefit payable under the Act, except guardian's allowance or housing benefit;

    (b)   any benefit payable under the legislation of any member State, other than the United Kingdom, concerning the branches of social security mentioned in article 4(1) of Regulation (EEC) No. 1408/71 on the application of social security schemes to employed persons, to self-employed persons and to members of their families moving within the Community, whether or not the benefit has been acquired by virtue of the provisions of that Regulation;

    (c)   a jobseeker's allowance;

    (d)   state pension credit.

    [² (e) an employment and support allowance.]

    [¹ (1A)   For the purposes of paragraph (1)(b) the term ''Member State'' shall be understood to include Switzerland in accordance with and subject to the provisions of Annex II of the Agreement between the European Community and its Member States and the Swiss Confederation on the free movement of persons, signed at Brussels on 21st June 1999.]

    [³ (1B)   For the purposes of section 76(3)(c) of the Administration Act, where recovery is sought from the claimant's partner under regulation 86(3)(b), the benefits prescribed by this regulation are–

    (a)   income support under Part 7 of the Act;

    (b)   income-based jobseeker's allowance;

    (c)   state pension credit; and

    (d)   income-related employment and support allowance.]

    [³ (2)   The Secretary of State shall, if requested to do so by a relevant authority under regulation 86 (methods of recovery), recover excess benefit by deduction from any of the benefits prescribed in paragraph (1) or (in the case of the claimant's partner) any of the benefits prescribed in paragraph (1B) provided that the Secretary of State is satisfied that–

    (a)   recoverable excess benefit has been allowed in consequence of a misrepresentation of or a failure to disclose a material fact (in either case whether fraudulently or otherwise), by a claimant or any other person to whom council tax benefit has been allowed; and

    (b)   the person from whom it is sought to recover the excess benefit is receiving sufficient amounts of any of the benefits prescribed in paragraph (1) or (1B) (as the case may be) to enable deductions to be made for the recovery of the excess.]

Amendments

    1.   Inserted by reg 10 of SI 2005 No 2904 as amended by Sch 2 para 29 of SI 2006 No 217 as from 10.4.06.
    2.   Amended by reg 58 of SI 2008 No 1082 as from 27.10.08.
    3.   Amended by reg 6(4) of SI 2008 No 2824 as from 6.4.09.

PART 12
Information
SECTION 1
Claims and information

Interpretation

91. In this Section–

[¹ "county council" means a county council in England, but only if the council has made an arrangement in accordance with regulation 69(4)(g) or 92(3);]

"local authority" means an authority administering council tax benefit;

"relevant authority" means–

    (a)   the Secretary of State;

    (b)   a person providing services to the Secretary of State; [¹ or

    (c)   a county council;]

"relevant information" means information or evidence relating to the administration of claims to or awards of council tax benefit.

Amendment

1.   Amended by reg 9(3) of SI 2007 No 2911 as from 31.10.07.

[¹Collection of information

92.–(1)   The Secretary of State, or a person providing services to him, may receive or obtain relevant information from–

    (a)   persons making, or who have made, claims for council tax benefit; or

    (b)   other persons in connection with such claims.

    (2)   In paragraph (1) references to persons who have made claims for council tax benefit include persons to whom awards of benefit have been made on those claims.

    (3)   Where a county council has made an arrangement with a local authority, or a person authorised to exercise any function of a local authority relating to housing benefit or council tax benefit, to receive and obtain information and evidence relating to claims for council tax benefit, the council may receive or obtain the information or evidence from–

    (a)   persons making claims for council tax benefit; or

    (b)   other persons in connection with such claims.

    (4)   A county council may receive information relating to an award of council tax benefit which is supplied by–

    (a)   the person to whom an award has been made; or

    (b)   other persons in connection with the award.]

Amendment

1.   Substituted by reg 9(4) of SI 2007 No 2911 as from 31.10.07.

[¹Verifying information

92A.   A relevant authority may verify relevant information supplied to, or obtained by, the authority in accordance with regulation 92.]

Amendment

1.   Inserted by reg 9(5) of SI 2007 No 2911 as from 31.10.07.

[¹Recording and holding information

93.   A relevant authority which obtains relevant information or to whom such information is supplied–

    (a)   shall make a record of such information; and

    (b)   may hold that information, whether as supplied or obtained or recorded, for the purpose of forwarding it to the person or authority for the time being administering council tax benefit.]

Amendment

1.   Substituted by reg 9(6) of SI 2007 No 2911 as from 31.10.07.

Forwarding of information

94. A relevant authority which holds relevant information–

(a) shall forward it to the person or authority for the time being administering claims to or awards of council tax benefit to which the relevant information relates, being–

    (i) a local authority;

    (ii) a person providing services to a local authority; or

    (iii) a person authorised to exercise any function of a local authority relating to council tax benefit; and

[¹ (b) may, if the relevant authority is the Secretary of State or a person providing services to the Secretary of State, continue to hold a record of such information, whether as supplied or obtained or recorded, for such period as he considers appropriate.]

Amendment

1. Substituted by reg 9(7) of SI 2007 No 2911 as from 31.10.07.

Request for information

95. A relevant authority which holds information or evidence relating to social security matters shall forward such information or evidence as may be requested to the person or authority making that request, provided that–

(a) the request is made by–

    (i) a local authority;

    (ii) a person providing services to a local authority; or

    (iii) a person authorised to exercise any function of a local authority relating to council tax benefit; and

(b) the information or evidence requested includes relevant information;

(c) the relevant authority is able to provide the information or evidence requested in the form in which it was originally supplied or obtained; and

(d) provision of the information or evidence requested is considered necessary by the relevant authority to the proper performance by a local authority of its functions relating to council tax benefit.

SECTION 2
Information between authorities etc.

[¹Information to be supplied by an authority to another authority

96.–(1) This regulation applies for the purposes of section 128A of the Administration Act (duty of an authority to disclose information to another authority).

(2) Information is to be disclosed by one authority to another where–

(a) there is a mover who is or was allowed council tax benefit by appropriate Authority ''A'';

(b) the mover is liable to pay council tax in respect of the new dwelling to Authority ''B''; and

(c) the mover is entitled to an extended payment in accordance with regulation 60.

(3) Authority A shall disclose to Authority B–

(a) the amount of the extended payment calculated in accordance with regulation 60C(2) (amount of extended payment – movers);

(b) the date that entitlement to the extended payment will commence or has commenced;

(c) the date that entitlement to the extended payment ceased or will cease;

(d) the date of the move from Authority A to Authority B;

(e) where the extended payment will be paid by Authority A to Authority B in accordance with regulation 60C(3)(a) (payment of the extended payment to the second authority)–

    (i) the amount that Authority A will pay to Authority B in accordance with that paragraph; and

(ii)   any other information required by Authority B to enable Authority A to make the payment in accordance with that paragraph; and

(f)   if any deduction was being made in respect of a recoverable overpayment.

(4)   Authority B shall disclose to Authority A–

(a)   if a mover's liability to pay council tax for the new dwelling is to Authority B; and

(b)   where the extended payment will be paid by Authority A to Authority B in accordance with regulation 60C(3)(a)–

(i)   any information required by Authority A to enable Authority A to make the payment in accordance with that paragraph; and

(ii)   the date on which Authority B receives any such payment.]

Amendment

1.   Substituted by reg 7(3) of SI 2008 No 959 as from 6.10.08.

General Note

This regulation is made under s128A. Although s128A was to be repealed by the SSA(F)A (see General Note to the section on p79) the repeal has not yet been brought into force. It is the equivalent of reg 115 HB Regs (see the General Note on p507), except that the equivalent of reg 72 HB Regs is reg 60 CTB Regs and of reg 72C HB Regs is reg 60C CTB Regs.

['Supply of information – extended payments (qualifying contributory benefits)

97.–(1)   This regulation applies for the purposes of section 122E(3) of the Administration Act (duty of an authority to supply information to another authority).

(2)   Information is to be disclosed by one authority to another where–

(a)   there is a mover who is or was allowed council tax benefit by appropriate Authority ''A'';

(b)   the mover is liable to pay council tax in respect of the new dwelling to Authority ''B''; and

(c)   the mover is entitled to an extended payment (qualifying contributory benefits) in accordance with regulation 61.

(3)   Authority A shall disclose to Authority B–

(a)   the amount of the extended payment calculated in accordance with regulation 61C(2) (amount of extended payment – movers);

(b)   the date that entitlement to the extended payment will commence or has commenced;

(c)   the date that entitlement to the extended payment ceased or will cease;

(d)   the date of the move from Authority A to Authority B;

(e)   where the extended payment will be paid by Authority A to Authority B in accordance with regulation 61C(3)(a) (payment of the extended payment to the second authority)–

(i)   the amount that Authority A will pay to Authority B in accordance with that paragraph; and

(ii)   any other information required by Authority B to enable Authority A to make the payment required in accordance with that paragraph; and

(f)   if any deduction was being made in respect of a recoverable overpayment.

(4)   Authority B shall disclose to Authority A–

(a)   if a mover's liability to pay council tax for the new dwelling is to Authority B; and

(b)   where the extended payment will be paid by Authority A to Authority B in accordance with regulation 61C(3)(a)–

(i)   any information required by Authority A in order to enable Authority A to make the payment in accordance with that paragraph; and

(ii)   the date on which Authority B receives any such payment.]

Amendment

1.   Substituted by reg 8(3) of SI 2008 No 959 as from 6.10.08.

[¹ Supply of benefit administration information between authorities

98.–(1)   For the purpose of section 122E(3) of the Administration Act (supply of information between authorities administering benefit) the circumstances in which information is to be supplied and the information to be supplied are set out in paragraph (2).

(2)   Where the functions of an authority (''Authority A'') relating to council tax benefit are being exercised, wholly or in part, by another authority (''Authority B'')–

(a)   Authority A must supply to Authority B any benefit administration information it holds which is relevant to, and necessary for, Authority B to exercise those functions; and

(b)   Authority B must supply to Authority A any benefit administration information it holds which is relevant to, and necessary for, Authority A to exercise those functions.

(3)   The circumstances in which paragraph (2) applies include cases where the authorities have agreed to discharge functions jointly.

(4)   In paragraph (2), ''Authority A'' and ''Authority B'' include any person authorised to exercise functions relating to council tax benefit on behalf of the authority in question.

(5)   This regulation shall not apply if the person or authority to whom the information is to be supplied agrees that the information need not be supplied.]

Amendment

1.   Inserted by reg 4(9) of SI 2008 No 2299 as from 1.10.08, corrected by correction slip July 2009.

[¹ SCHEDULE A1]
Treatment of claims for council tax benefit by refugees

Modification

Sch A1 was inserted by Sch 4 para 3(2) HB&CTB(CP) Regs in respect of claims for CTB by some refugees. It was further modifed by Sch 4 para 4(4) for some CTB claimants who were refugees who claimed asylum on or before 2 April 2000. See also reg 7A inserted by Sch 4 para 3(1) HB&CTB(CP) Reg on p658.

Amendment

1.   Lapsed by s12(2)(g) Asylum and Immigration (Treatment of Claimants, etc.) Act 2004 (for those recorded as refugees after 14.6.07).

SCHEDULE 1
REGULATION 12
Applicable amounts

General Note

This Schedule is broadly equivalent to Sch 3 to the HB Regs. One difference of substance is the transitional protection for those who were entitled to the lone parent premium prior to the enactment of the Social Security (Lone Parents) Regulations 1998, in para 3(3). In the CTB Regulations, a person is deemed to be in receipt of CTB for a period during which s/he was getting HB or would have been but for the fact that s/he was then in a rent-free period for the purposes of reg 81 HB Regs.

PART 1
Personal Allowances

1.   The amounts specified in column (2) below in respect of each person or couple specified in column (1) shall be the amounts specified for the purposes of regulations 12(a) and 13(a) and (b)–

Column (1) Person or couple	Column (2) Amount
[⁴ (1) A single claimant who–	(1)
(a) is entitled to main phase employment and support allowance;	(a) [⁶ £65.45]
(b) is aged not less than 25;	(b) [⁶ £65.45];
(c) is aged not less than 18 but less than 25.	(c) [⁶ £51.85.]]
(2) Lone parent.	(2) [⁶ £65.45].
(3) Couple.	(3) [⁶ £102.75].

Amendments

1. Amended by Art 21(4) and Sch 10 of SI 2006 No 645 and reg 8 of SI 2006 No 217 as from 1.4.06.
2. Amended by Art 21(4) and Sch 10 of SI 2007 No 688 as from 1.4.07.
3. Amended by Art 21(4) and Sch 10 of SI 2008 No 632 as from 1.4.08.
4. Amended by reg 59(a) of SI 2008 No 1082 as from 27.10.08.
5. Amended by Art 21(4) and Sch 9 of SI 2009 No 497 as from 1.4.09.
6. Amended by Art 21(4) and Sch 9 of SI 2010 No 793 as from 1.4.10.

[¹ [²**1A.** For the purposes of paragraph 1 a claimant is entitled to main phase employment and support allowance if–
(a) paragraph 21 is satisfied in relation to the claimant; or
(b) the claimant is entitled to a converted employment and support allowance.]]

Amendments

1. Inserted by reg 8(10)(a) of SI 2009 No 583 as from 1.4.09.
2. Substituted by reg 27 and Sch 5 para 2(5)(a) of SI 2010 No 1907 as amended by reg 15 of SI 2010 No 2430 as from 1.10.10.

2.–(1) The amount specified in column (2) below in respect of each person specified in column (1) shall, for the relevant period specified in column (1), be the amounts specified for the purposes of regulations 12(b) and 13(c)–

Column (1)	*Column (2)*
Child or young person	*Amount*
Persons in respect of the period–	
(a) beginning on that person's date of birth and ending on the day preceding the first Monday in September following that person's sixteenth birthday;	(a) [⁶ £57.57];
(b) beginning on the first Monday in September following that person's sixteenth birthday and ending on the day preceding that person's [² twentieth] birthday.	(b) [⁶ £57.57].

(2) In column (1) of the table in paragraph (1), ''the first Monday in September'' means the Monday which first occurs in the month of September in any year.

Amendments

1. Amended by Art 21(4) and Sch 10 of SI 2006 No 645 and reg 8 of SI 2006 No 217 as from 1.4.06.
2. Amended by reg 5(4) of SI 2006 No 718 as from 10.4.06.
3. Amended by Art 21(4) and Sch 10 of SI 2007 No 688 as from 1.4.07.
4. Amended by Art 21(4) and Sch 10 of SI 2008 No 632 as from 1.4.08.
5. Amended by Art 21(4) and Sch 9 of SI 2009 No 497 as from 1.4.09.
6. Amended by Art 21(4) and Sch 9 of SI 2010 No 793 as from 1.4.10.

PART 2
Family Premium

3.–(1) Subject to sub-paragraph (2), the amount for the purposes of regulations 12(c) and 13(d) in respect of a family of which at least one member is a child or young person shall be–
(a) where the claimant is a lone parent to whom sub-paragraph (3) applies, [¹¹ £22.20];
(b) in any other case, [¹² £17.40].
(2) The amounts specified in sub-paragraph (1)(a) and (b) shall be increased by [¹¹ £10.50] where at least one child is under the age of one year and for the purposes of this paragraph where the child's first birthday does not fall on a Monday he shall be treated as under the age of one year until the first Monday after his first birthday.
(3) The amount in sub-paragraph (1)(a) shall be applicable to a lone parent–
(a) who was entitled to council tax benefit on 5th April 1998 and whose applicable amount on that date included the amount applicable under sub-paragraph (a) of this paragraph as in force on that date; or
(b) on becoming entitled to council tax benefit where that lone parent–
(i) had been treated as entitled to that benefit in accordance with sub-paragraph (4) as at the day before the date of claim for that benefit; and
(ii) was entitled to housing benefit as at the date of claim for council tax benefit or would have been entitled to housing benefit as at that date had that day not fallen during a rent free period as defined in regulation 81 of the Housing Benefit Regulations,
and in respect of whom, all of the conditions specified in sub-paragraph (4) have continued to apply.

(4)   The conditions specified for the purposes of sub-paragraph (3) are that, in respect of the period commencing on 6th April 1998–

- (a)   the claimant has not ceased to be entitled, or has not ceased to be treated as entitled, to council tax benefit;
- (b)   the claimant has not ceased to be a lone parent;
- (c)   where the claimant was entitled to income support or to an income-based jobseeker's allowance on 5th April 1998, he has [¹⁰ continuously, since that date, been entitled to income support, an income-based jobseeker's allowance or income-related employment and support allowance or a combination of those benefits];
- (d)   where the claimant was not entitled to income support or to an income-based jobseeker's allowance on 5th April 1998, he has not become entitled to [¹⁰ income support, an income-based jobseeker's allowance or an income-related employment and support allowance]; and
- (e)   a premium under paragraph [⁷] 12 [¹⁰ or a component under paragraph 23 or 24] has not become applicable to the claimant.

(5)   For the purposes of sub-paragraphs (3)(b)(i) and (4)(a), a claimant shall be treated as entitled to council tax benefit during any period where he was not, or had ceased to be, so entitled and–

- (a)   throughout that period, he had been awarded housing benefit and his applicable amount included the amount applicable under paragraph 3(1)(a) of Schedule 3 to the Housing Benefit Regulations (lone parent rate of family premium); or
- (b)   he would have been awarded housing benefit during that period had that period not been a rent free period as defined in regulation 81 of the Housing Benefit Regulations and his applicable amount throughout that period would have included the amount applicable under paragraph 3(1)(a) of Schedule 3 to those Regulations.

Amendments
1.   Confirmed by Art 21(5)(a) and (c) of SI 2006 No 645 and reg 8 of SI 2006 No 217 as from 1.4.06.
2.   Amended by Art 21(5)(b) and Sch 10 of SI 2006 No 645 and reg 8 of SI 2006 No 217 as from 1.4.06.
3.   Confirmed by Art 21(5)(a) and (c) of SI 2007 No 688 as from 1.4.07.
4.   Amended by Art 21(5)(b) of SI 2007 No 688 as from 1.4.07.
5.   Confirmed by Art 21(5)(a) and (c) of SI 2008 No 632 as from 1.4.08.
6.   Amended by Art 21(5)(b) of SI 2008 No 632 as from 1.4.08.
7.   Amended by reg 5(10)(a) of SI 2008 No 1042 as from 19.5.08.
8.   Confirmed by Art 21(5)(a) and (c) of SI 2009 No 497 as from 1.4.09.
9.   Amended by Art 21(5)(b) of SI 2009 No 497 as from 1.4.09.
10.   Amended by reg 8(10)(b) of SI 2009 No 583 as from 6.4.09.
11.   Confirmed by Art 21(5)(a) and (c) of SI 2010 No 793 as from 1.4.10.
12.   Amended by Art 21(5)(b) of SI 2010 No 793 as from 1.4.10.

PART 3
Premiums
4.   Except as provided in paragraph 5, the premiums specified in Part 4 of this Schedule shall, for the purposes of regulations 12(d) and 13(e), be applicable to a claimant who satisfies the condition specified in paragraphs 8 to 17 in respect of that premium.

5.   Subject to paragraph 6, where a claimant satisfies the conditions in respect of more than one premium in this Part of this Schedule, only one premium shall be applicable to him and, if they are different amounts, the higher or highest amount shall apply.

[¹**6.**   The following premiums, namely–
- (a)   a severe disability premium to which paragraph 14 applies;
- (b)   an enhanced disability premium to which paragraph 15 applies;
- (c)   a disabled child premium to which paragraph 16 applies; and
- (d)   a carer premium to which paragraph 17 applies,

may be applicable in addition to any other premium which may apply under this Schedule.]

Amendment
1.   Substituted by reg 5(10)(b) of SI 2008 No 1042 as from 19.5.08.

7.–(1)   Subject to sub-paragraph (2), for the purposes of this Part of this Schedule, once a premium is applicable to a claimant under this Part, a person shall be treated as being in receipt of any benefit for–

- (a)   in the case of a benefit to which the Social Security (Overlapping Benefits) Regulations 1979 applies, any period during which, apart from the provisions of those Regulations, he would be in receipt of that benefit; and
- (b)   any period spent by a person in undertaking a course of training or instruction provided or approved [¹ by the Secretary of State] under section 2 of the 1973 Act or [¹ by Skills Development Scotland, Scottish Enterprise or Highlands and Islands Enterprise under] section 2 of the Enterprise and New [¹ Towns] (Scotland) Act 1990 for any period during which he is in receipt of a training allowance.

(2)   For the purposes of the carer premium under paragraph 17, a person shall be treated as being in receipt of carer's allowance by virtue of sub-paragraph (1)(a) only if and for so long as the person in respect of whose care the allowance has been claimed remains in receipt of attendance allowance, or the care component of disability living allowance at the highest or middle rate prescribed in accordance with section 72(3) of the Act.

Amendment
1.   Amended by reg 8(10)(c) of SI 2009 No 583 as from 6.4.09.

[¹ Bereavement premium]
[¹**8.**]

Amendment
1.   Revoked by reg 2 and the Sch of SI 2007 No 2618 as from 1.10.07.

[¹ Pensioner Premium for persons under 75
9.]

Amendment
1.   Omitted by reg 5(10)(c) of SI 2008 No 1042 as from 19.5.08.

[¹ Pensioner Premium for persons 75 and over
10.]

Amendment
1.   Omitted by reg 5(10)(c) of SI 2008 No 1042 as from 19.5.08.

[² Higher Pensioner Premium
11.]

Amendments
1.   Amended by reg 17(4) of SI 2006 No 2378 as from 9.10.06.
2.   Omitted by reg 5(10)(c) of SI 2008 No 1042 as from 19.5.08.

Disability Premium
12.   The condition is that–
(a)   where the claimant is a single claimant or a lone parent, he [¹ has not attained the qualifying age for state pension credit] and the additional condition specified in paragraph 13 is satisfied; or
(b)   where the claimant has a partner, either–
    (i)   the claimant [¹ has not attained the qualifying age for state pension credit] and the additional condition specified in paragraph 13 (1)(a) or (b) is satisfied by him; or
    (ii)   his partner [¹ has not attained the qualifying age for state pension credit] and the additional condition specified in paragraph 13(1)(a) is satisfied by his partner.

Amendment
1.   Amended by reg 34(2) of SI 2009 No 1488 as from 6.4.10.

Additional Condition for the [⁴ Disability Premium]
13.–(1)   Subject to sub-paragraph (2) and paragraph 7, the additional condition referred to in paragraphs 11 and 12 is that either–
(a)   the claimant or, as the case may be, his partner–
    (i)   is in receipt of one or more of the following benefits: attendance allowance, disability living allowance, the disability element or the severe disability element of working tax credit as specified in regulation 20(1)(b) and (f) of the Working Tax Credit Regulations, mobility supplement, long-term incapacity benefit under Part 2 of the Act or severe disablement allowance under Part 3 of the Act but, in the case of long-term incapacity benefit or severe disablement allowance, only where it is paid in respect of him; or
    (ii)   was in receipt of long-term incapacity benefit under Part 2 of the Act when entitlement to that benefit ceased on account of the payment of a retirement pension under that Act and the claimant has since remained continuously entitled to [⁶] council tax benefit and, if the long-term incapacity benefit was payable to his partner, the partner is still a member of the family; or

(iii) [¹] was in receipt of attendance allowance or disability living allowance but payment of benefit has been suspended in accordance with regulations made under section 113(2) of the Act or otherwise abated as a consequence of the claimant or his partner becoming a patient within the meaning of [² regulation 18(11)(e) (treatment of child care charges)]; or

(iv) is provided by the Secretary of State with an invalid carriage or other vehicle under section 5(2) of the National Health Service Act 1977 (other services) or, in Scotland, under section 46 of the National Health Service (Scotland) Act 1978 (provision of services by Scottish Ministers) or receives payments by way of grant from the Secretary of State under paragraph 2 of Schedule 2 to the Act of 1977 (additional provisions as to vehicles) or, in Scotland, by Scottish Ministers under section 46 of the Act of 1978; or

(v) is blind and in consequence registered in a register compiled by a local authority under section 29 of the National Assistance Act 1948 (welfare services) or, in Scotland, has been certified as blind and in consequence he is registered in a register maintained by or on behalf of a council constituted under section 2 of the Local Government (Scotland) Act 1994; or

(b) the claimant–

(i) is, or is treated as, incapable of work in accordance with the provisions of, and regulations made under, Part 12A of the Act (incapacity for work); and

(ii) has been incapable, or has been treated as incapable, of work for a continuous period of not less than–

(aa) in the case of a claimant who is terminally ill within the meaning of section 30B(4) of the Act, 196 days;

(bb) in any other case, 364 days.

(2)   For the purposes of sub-paragraph (1)(a)(v), a person who has ceased to be registered as blind on regaining his eyesight shall nevertheless be treated as blind and as satisfying the additional condition set out in that sub-paragraph for a period of 28 weeks following the date on which he ceased to be so registered.

(3)   For the purposes of sub-paragraph (1)(b), once [⁴] the disability premium is applicable to a claimant by virtue of his satisfying the additional condition specified in that provision, if he then ceases, for a period of 8 weeks or less, to be treated as incapable of work or to be incapable of work he shall, on again becoming so incapable of work, immediately thereafter be treated as satisfying the condition in sub-paragraph (1)(b).

[⁴ (4)]

(5)   For the purposes of sub-paragraph (1)(b), once the disability premium is applicable to a claimant by virtue of his satisfying the additional condition specified in that provision, he shall continue to be treated as satisfying that condition for any period spent by him in undertaking a course of training provided under section 2 of the 1973 Act or section 2 of the Enterprise and New Towns (Scotland) Act 1990 or for any period during which he is in receipt of a training allowance.

(6)   For the purposes of sub-paragraph (1)(b), where any two or more periods of incapacity are separated by a break of not more than 56 days, those periods shall be treated as one continuous period.

(7)   For the purposes of this paragraph, a reference to a person who is or was in receipt of long-term incapacity benefit includes a person who is or was in receipt of short-term incapacity benefit at a rate equal to the long-term rate by virtue of section 30B(4)(a) of the Act (short-term incapacity benefit for a person who is terminally ill), or who would be or would have been in receipt of short-term incapacity benefit at such a rate but for the fact that the rate of short-term incapacity benefit already payable to him is or was equal to or greater than the long-term rate.

(8)   For the purposes of sub-paragraph (1)(b), once the disability premium is applicable to a claimant by virtue of his satisfying the additional condition specified in that provision, he shall continue to be treated as satisfying that condition for any period spent by him in undertaking a course of training provided under section 2 of the 1973 Act or section 2 of the Enterprise and New Towns (Scotland) Act 1990.

(9)   In the case of a claimant who is a welfare to work beneficiary [⁴ (a person to whom regulation 13A(1) of the Social Security (Incapacity for Work) (General) Regulations 1995 applies, and who again becomes incapable of work for the purposes of Part 12A of the Act)]–

(a) the reference to a period of 8 weeks in sub-paragraph (3); and

(b) the reference to a period of 56 days in sub-paragraph (6),

shall in each case be treated as a reference to a period of [³ 104 weeks].

[⁵ (10)   The claimant is not entitled to the disability premium if the claimant has, or is treated as having, limited capability for work.]

Amendments

1.   Omitted by reg 3(11)(a)(i) of SI 2005 No 2502 as amended by Sch 2 para 27 of SI 2006 No 217 as from 1.4.06.

2.   Amended by reg 3(11)(a)(ii) of SI 2005 No 2502 as amended by Sch 2 para 27 of SI 2006 No 217 as from 1.4.06.

3.   Amended by reg 17(4) of SI 2006 No 2378 as from 9.10.06.

4.   Amended by reg 5(10)(d)-(g) of SI 2008 No 1042 as from 19.5.08.

5.   Amended by reg 59(b) of SI 2008 No 1082, as amended by reg 39(a) of SI 2008 No 2428, as from 27.10.08.

6.   Amended by reg 8(8) of SI 2008 No 2767 as from 17.11.08.

Severe Disability Premium

14.–(1)   The condition is that the claimant is a severely disabled person.

(2)   For the purposes of sub-paragraph (1), a claimant shall be treated as being a severely disabled person if, and only if–

(a)   in the case of a single claimant, a lone parent or a claimant who is treated as having no partner in consequence of sub-paragraph (3)–

   (i)   he is in receipt of attendance allowance, or the care component of disability living allowance at the highest or middle rate prescribed in accordance with section 72(3) of the Act; and

   (ii)   subject to sub-paragraph (4), he has no non-dependants aged 18 or over normally residing with him or with whom he is normally residing; and

   (iii) no person is entitled to, and in receipt of, a carer's allowance under section 70 of the Act in respect of caring for him;

(b)   in the case of a claimant who has a partner–

   (i)   the claimant is in receipt of attendance allowance, or the care component of disability living allowance at the highest or middle rate prescribed in accordance with section 72(3) of the Act; and

   (ii)   his partner is also in receipt of such an allowance or, if he is a member of a polygamous marriage, all the partners of that marriage are in receipt of such an allowance; and

   (iii) subject to sub-paragraph (4), the claimant has no non-dependants aged 18 or over normally residing with him or with whom he is normally residing,

and either a person is [2 entitled to and in receipt of] a carer's allowance in respect of caring for only one of a couple or, in the case of a polygamous marriage, for one or more but not all the partners of the marriage, or as the case may be, no person is entitled to and in receipt of such an allowance in respect of caring for either member of a couple or any partner of a polygamous marriage.

(3)   Where a claimant has a partner who does not satisfy the condition in sub-paragraph (2)(b)(ii), and that partner is blind or is treated as blind within the meaning of paragraph 13(1)(a)(v) and (2), that partner shall be treated for the purposes of sub-paragraph (2)(b)(ii) as if he were not a partner of the claimant.

(4)   For the purposes of sub-paragraph (2)(a)(ii) and (2)(b)(iii) no account shall be taken of–

(a)   a person receiving attendance allowance, or disability living allowance by virtue of the care component at the highest or middle rate prescribed in accordance with section 72(3) of the Act; or

(b)   a person who is blind or is treated as blind within the meaning of paragraph 13(1)(a)(v) and (2).

(5)   For the purposes of sub-paragraph (2)(b) a person shall be treated–

(a)   as being in receipt of attendance allowance, or the care component of disability living allowance at the highest or middle rate prescribed in accordance with section 72(3) of the Act, if he would, but for his being a patient for a period exceeding 28 days, be so in receipt;

(b)   as being entitled to and in receipt of a carer's allowance if he would, but for the person for whom he was caring being a patient in hospital for a period exceeding 28 days, be so entitled and in receipt.

(6)   For the purposes of sub-paragraph (2)(a)(iii) and (2)(b), no account shall be taken of an award of carer's allowance to the extent that payment of such an award is back-dated for a period before [1 the date on which the award is first paid].

(7)   In sub-paragraph (2)(a)(iii) and (b), references to a person being in receipt of a carer's allowance shall include references to a person who would have been in receipt of that allowance but for the application of a restriction under section [3 6B or] 7 of the Social Security Fraud Act 2001 (loss of benefit provisions).

Amendments

1.   Amended by reg 8(5) of SI 2007 No 719 as from 2.4.07.
2.   Amended by reg 8(10)(d) of SI 2009 No 583 as from 6.4.09.
3.   Amended by reg 6 of SI 2010 No 1160 as from 1.4.10.

Enhanced disability premium

15.–[2 (1)   Subject to sub-paragraph (2), the condition is that–

(a)   the Secretary of State has decided that the claimant has, or is to be treated as having, limited capability for work-related activity; or

(b)   the care component of disability living allowance is, or would, but for a suspension of benefit in accordance with regulations made under section 113(2) of the Act or but for an abatement as a consequence of hospitalisation be payable at the highest rate prescribed under section 72(3) of the Act in respect of–

   (i)   the claimant; or

   (ii)   a member of the claimant's family,

who [3 has not attained the qualifying age for state pension credit].]

(2)   An enhanced disability premium shall not be applicable in respect of–

(a)   a claimant who–

   (i)   is not a member of a couple or a polygamous marriage; and

   (ii)   is a patient within the meaning of [1 regulation 18(11)(e)] (patients) and has been for a period of more than 52 weeks; or

(b)   a member of a couple or a polygamous marriage where each member is a patient within the meaning of [1 regulation 18(11)(e)] and has been for a period of more than 52 weeks.

Amendments
1. Amended by reg 3(11)(b) of SI 2005 No 2502 as amended by Sch 2 para 27 of SI 2006 No 217 as from 1.4.06.
2. Substituted by reg 59(c) of SI 2008 No 1082, as amended by reg 39(b) of SI 2008 No 2428, as from 27.10.08.
3. Amended by reg 34(3) of SI 2009 No 1488 as from 6.4.10.

Disabled Child Premium
    16.   The condition is that a child or young person for whom the claimant or a partner of his is responsible and who is a member of the claimant's household–
  (a)   is in receipt of disability living allowance or is no longer in receipt of such allowance because he is a patient, provided that the child or young person continues to be a member of the family; or
  (b)   is blind or treated as blind within the meaning of paragraph 13; or
  (c)   is a child or young person in respect of whom section 145A of the Act applies for the purposes of entitlement to child benefit but only for the period prescribed under section 145A(1) of the Act and in respect of whom a disabled child premium was included in the claimant's applicable amount immediately before the death of that child.

Carer Premium
    17.–(1)   The condition is that the claimant or his partner is, or both of them are, entitled to a carer's allowance under section 70 of the Act.
  (2)   Where a carer premium is awarded but–
  (a)   the person in respect of whose care the carer's allowance has been awarded dies; or
  (b)   in any other case the person in respect of whom a carer premium has been awarded ceases to be entitled to a carer's allowance,
the condition for the award of the premium shall be treated as satisfied for a period of eight weeks from the relevant date specified in sub-paragraph (3).
  (3)   The relevant date for the purposes of sub-paragraph (2) shall be–
  (a)   where sub-paragraph (2)(a) applies, the Sunday following the death of the person in respect of whose care a carer's allowance has been awarded or the date of death if the death occurred on a Sunday;
  (b)   in any other case, the date on which the person who has been entitled to a carer's allowance ceases to be entitled to that allowance.
  (4)   Where a person who has been entitled to a carer's allowance ceases to be entitled to that allowance and makes a claim for council tax benefit, the condition for the award of the carer premium shall be treated as satisfied for a period of eight weeks from the date on which–
  (a)   the person in respect of whose care the carer's allowance has been awarded dies;
  (b)   in any other case, the person who has been entitled to a carer's allowance ceased to be entitled to that allowance.

Persons in receipt of concessionary payments
    18.   For the purpose of determining whether a premium is applicable to a person under paragraphs 13 to 17, any concessionary payment made to compensate that person for the non-payment of any benefit mentioned in those paragraphs shall be treated as if it were a payment of that benefit.

Persons in receipt of benefit for another
    19.   For the purposes of this Part of this Schedule, a person shall be regarded as being in receipt of any benefit if, and only if, it is paid in respect of him and shall be so regarded only for any period in respect of which that benefit is paid.

PART 4
Amounts of premiums specified in Part 3

Premium	*Amount*
20.–[4 (1)]	[4 (1)].
[6 (2)]	[6 (2)]
[6 (3)]	[6 (3)]
[6 (4)]	[6 (4)]
(5) Disability Premium–	(5)
(a) where the claimant satisfies the condition in paragraph 12(a) [6];	(a) [8 £28.00];
(b) where the claimant satisfies the condition in paragraph 12(b).	(b) [8 £39.85].

(6) Severe Disability Premium–
    (a) where the claimant satisfies the condition in paragraph 14(2)(a),
    (b) where the claimant satisfies the condition in paragraph 14(2)(b)–
        (i) in a case where there is someone in receipt of carer's allowance or if he or any partner satisfies that condition only by virtue of paragraph 14(5);
        (ii) in a case where there is no one in receipt of such an allowance.

(7) Disabled Child Premium.

(8) Carer Premium.

(9) Enhanced Disability Premium [⁹].

(6)
    (a) [⁸ £53.65];

    (b)
        (i) [⁸ £53.65];

        (ii) [⁸ £107.30].

(7) [⁸ £52.08] in respect of each child or young person in respect of whom the condition specified in paragraph 16 of Part 3 of this Schedule is satisfied.

(8) [⁸ £30.05] in respect of each person who satisfies the condition specified in paragraph 17.

(9)
    (a) [⁸ £21.00] in respect of each child or young person in respect of whom the conditions specified in paragraph 15 are satisfied;
    (b) [⁸ £13.65] in respect of each person who is neither–
        (i) a child or young person; nor
        (ii) a member of a couple or a polygamous marriage,
    in respect of whom the conditions specified in paragraph 15 are satisfied;
    (c) [⁸ £19.65] where the claimant is a member of a couple or a polygamous marriage and the conditions specified in paragraph 15 are satisfied in respect of a member of that couple or polygamous marriage.

Amendments

1.   Amended by Art 21(6) and Sch 11 of SI 2006 No 645 and reg 8 of SI 2006 No 217 as from 1.4.06.
2.   Confirmed by Art 21(6) and Sch 11 of SI 2007 No 688 as from 1.4.07.
3.   Amended by Art 21(6) and Sch 11 of SI 2007 No 688 as from 1.4.07.
4.   Revoked by reg 2 and the Sch of SI 2007 No 2618 as from 1.10.07.
5.   Amended by Art 21(6) and Sch 11 of SI 2008 No 632 as from 1.4.08.
6.   Omitted by reg 5(10)(h) of SI 2008 No 1042 as from 19.5.08.
7.   Amended by Art 21(6) and Sch 10 of SI 2009 No 497 as from 1.4.09.
8.   Amended by Art 21(6) and Sch 10 of SI 2010 No 793 as from 1.4.10.
9.   Amended by reg 4(5)(b) of SI 2010 No 2449 as from 1.11.10.

[¹ PART 5
The components

Amendment

1.   Inserted by reg 59(d) of SI 2008 No 1082, as subsitututed by reg 39(c) of SI 2008 No 2428, as from 27.10.08.

21.   Subject to paragraph 22 the claimant is entitled to one, but not both, of the components in paragraph 23 or 24 if–
    (a)   the claimant or the claimant's partner has made a claim for employment and support allowance;
    (b)   the Secretary of State has decided that the claimant or the claimant's partner has, or is to be treated as having, limited capability for work or limited capability for work-related activity; and
    (c)   either–
        (i)   the assessment phase as defined in section 24(2) of the Welfare Reform Act has ended; or
        (ii)   regulation 7 of the Employment and Support Allowance Regulations (circumstances where the condition that the assessment phase has ended before entitlement to the support component or the work related activity component arises does not apply) applies.

[¹**21A.** Subject to paragraph 22, the claimant is entitled to one, but not both, of the components in paragraphs 23 and 24 if the claimant or his partner is entitled to a converted employment and support allowance.]

Amendment
1. Inserted by reg 27 and Sch 5 para 2(5)(b) of SI 2010 No 1907 as amended by reg 15 of SI 2010 No 2430 as from 1.10.10.

22.–(1) The claimant has no entitlement under paragraph 23 or 24 if the claimant is entitled to the disability premium under paragraphs 12 and 13.
(2) Where the claimant and the claimant's partner each satisfies paragraph 23 or 24, the component to be included in the claimant's applicable amount is that which relates to the claimant.

The work-related activity component
23. The claimant is entitled to the work-related activity component if the Secretary of State has decided that the claimant or the claimant's partner has, or is to be treated as having, limited capability for work.

The support component
24. The claimant is entitled to the support component if the Secretary of State has decided that the claimant or the claimant's partner has, or is to be treated as having, limited capability for work-related activity.]

[¹ PART 6

Amendments
1. Inserted by reg 59(d) of SI 2008 No 1082, as substituted by reg 39(c) of SI 2008 No 2428, as from 27.10.08.
2. Amended by Art 21(7) of SI 2009 No 497 as from 1.4.09.
3. Amended by Art 21(7) of SI 2010 No 793 as from 1.4.10.

Amount of components
25. The amount of the work-related activity component is [³ £25.95].
26. The amount of the support component is [³ £31.40].]

[¹ PART 7

Amendment
1. Inserted by reg 27 and Sch 5 para 2(5)(c) of SI 2010 No 1907 as amended by reg 15 of SI 2010 No 2430 as from 1.10.10.

Transitional Addition
27.–(1) The claimant is entitled to the transitional addition calculated in accordance with paragraph 30 where the claimant or the claimant's partner ("the relevant person")–
(a) is entitled to a converted employment and support allowance; or
(b) is appealing a conversion decision as described in regulation 5(2)(b) of the Employment and Support Allowance (Existing Awards) Regulations and–
    (i) is treated as having limited capability for work by virtue of regulation 30 of the Employment and Support Allowance Regulations as modified by the Employment and Support Allowance (Existing Awards) Regulations; and
    (ii) is not in receipt of an income-related employment and support allowance,
unless the amount of the transitional addition calculated in accordance with paragraph 30 would be nil.
(2) The claimant's entitlement to a transitional addition by virtue of this paragraph ends on any of the following–
(a) the reduction of the transitional addition to nil in accordance with paragraph 31;
(b) the termination of the claimant's award of council tax benefit;
(c) the relevant person ceasing to meet the requirements of sub-paragraph (1)(a) or (b), as the case may be;
(d) the claimant or the claimant's partner becoming entitled to an income-related employment and support allowance, an income-based jobseeker's allowance or income support;
(e) 5th April 2020.
28.–(1) This paragraph applies where–
(a) the claimant's entitlement to a transitional addition, ends by virtue of the termination of the claimant's award of council tax benefit, under–

        (i)   paragraph 27(2)(b);
        (ii)   sub-paragraph (3)(b) of this paragraph; or
        (iii)   paragraph 29(3)(b),

(b)   within 104 weeks of that termination but before 5th April 2020 the claimant again becomes entitled to council tax benefit;

(c)   in the benefit week in which the claimant again becomes entitled to council tax benefit the relevant person is entitled to an employment and support allowance which is not income-related;

(d)   if the period between the events mentioned in paragraphs (a) and (b) is more than 12 weeks, the intervening period is one to which regulation 145(2) (linking period where claimant is a work or training beneficiary) of the Employment and Support Allowance Regulations applies in respect of the relevant person; and

(e)   at the date on which the claimant again becomes entitled to council tax benefit, neither the claimant nor the claimant's partner is entitled to an income-related employment and support allowance, an income-based jobseeker's allowance or income support.

(2)   Where this paragraph applies, the claimant is entitled, with effect from the day on which the claimant again becomes entitled to council tax benefit, to a transitional addition of the amount of the transitional addition that would have applied had the claimant's entitlement to a transitional addition not ended (but taking account of the effect which any intervening change of circumstances would have had by virtue of paragraph 31), unless the amount of the transitional addition would be nil.

(3)   The claimant's entitlement to a transitional addition by virtue of this paragraph ends on any of the following–

(a)   the reduction of the transitional addition to nil in accordance with paragraph 31;

(b)   the termination of the claimant's award of council tax benefit;

(c)   the relevant person no longer being entitled to the employment and support allowance referred to in sub-paragraph (1)(c);

(d)   the claimant or the claimant's partner becoming entitled to an income-related employment and support allowance, an income-based jobseeker's allowance or income support;

(e)   5th April 2020.

29.–(1)   This paragraph applies where–

(a)   the claimant's entitlement to a transitional addition ends, by virtue of the relevant person ceasing to be entitled to an employment and support allowance, under–
        (i)   paragraph 27(2)(c);
        (ii)   paragraph 28(3)(c); or
        (iii)   sub-paragraph (3)(c) of this paragraph;

(b)   before 5th April 2020 the relevant person again becomes entitled to an employment and support allowance which is not income-related;

(c)   either–
        (i)   at the date on which the relevant person again becomes entitled to an employment support allowance which is not income-related regulation 145(1) of the Employment and Support Allowance Regulation applies to the relevant person; or
        (ii)   the period between the events mentioned in paragraphs (a) and (b) is one to which regulation 145(2) of the Employment and Support Allowance Regulations applies in respect of the relevant person; and

(d)   at the date on which the relevant person again becomes entitled to an employment support allowance which is not income-related, neither the claimant nor the claimant's partner is entitled to an income-related employment and support allowance, an income-based jobseeker's allowance or income support.

(2)   Where this paragraph applies, the claimant is entitled, with effect from the day that the relevant person's entitlement to employment and support allowance takes effect for council tax benefit purposes, to a transitional addition of the amount of the transitional addition that would have applied had the claimant's entitlement to a transitional addition not ended (but taking account of the effect which any intervening change of circumstances would have had by virtue of paragraph 31), unless the amount of the transitional addition would be nil.

(3)   The claimant's entitlement to a transitional addition by virtue of this paragraph ends on any of the following–

(a)   the reduction of the transitional addition to nil in accordance with paragraph 31;

(b)   the termination of the claimant's award of council tax benefit;

(c)   the relevant person no longer being entitled to the employment and support allowance referred to in sub-paragraph (1)(b);

(d)   the claimant or the claimant's partner becoming entitled to an income-related employment and support allowance, an income-based jobseeker's allowance or income support;

(e)   5th April 2020.]

[¹ PART 8

Amendment
1.   Inserted by reg 27 and Sch 5 para 2(5)(c) of SI 2010 No 1907 as amended by reg 15 of SI 2010 No 2430 as from 1.10.10.

Amount of transitional Addition

30.–(1)   Subject to paragraph 31, the amount of the transitional addition is the amount by which Amount A exceeds Amount B.

(2)   Where a conversion decision as described in regulation 5(2)(a) of the Employment and Support Allowance (Existing Awards) Regulations is made in respect of the relevant person–

(a)   Amount A is the basic amount that would have applied on the day that decision took effect had that decision not been made; and

(b)   Amount B is the basic amount that applied on that day as a result of that decision.

(3)   Where the relevant person is appealing a conversion decision as described in regulation 5(2)(b) of the Employment and Support Allowance (Existing Awards) Regulations and is treated as having limited capability for work by virtue of regulation 30 of the Employment and Support Allowance Regulations as modified by the Employment and Support Allowance (Existing Awards) Regulations–

(a)   Amount A is the basic amount that would have applied on the day the relevant person was first treated as having limited capability for work if the relevant person had not been so treated; and

(b)   Amount B is the basic amount that applied on that day as a result of the relevant person being so treated.

(4)   In this paragraph and paragraph 31, "basic amount" means the aggregate of such amounts as may apply in the claimant's case in accordance with regulation 12(a) to (e) or regulation 13(a) to (f).

31.–(1)   Subject to sub-paragraph (2), where there is a change of circumstances which leads to an increase in the claimant's basic amount, the transitional addition that applies immediately before the change of circumstances shall be reduced by the amount by which Amount C exceeds Amount D.

(2)   If Amount C exceeds Amount D by more than the amount of the transitional addition that applies immediately before the change of circumstances, that transitional addition shall be reduced to nil.

(3)   Amount C is the basic amount that applies as a result of the increase.

(4)   Amount D is the basic amount that applied immediately before the increase.]

SCHEDULE 2
REGULATION 62
Amount of alternative maximum council tax benefit

General Note
For Sch 1 Local Government Finance Act 1992, see p1119. See also the commentary to reg 62 on p704.

1.–(1)   Subject to paragraphs 2 and 3, the alternative maximum council tax benefit in respect of a day for the purpose of regulation 62 shall be determined in accordance with the following Table and in this Table [¹ –

(a)   "second adult" means any person or persons residing with the claimant to whom section 131(6) of the Act applies; and

(b)   "persons to whom regulation 45(2) applies" includes any person to whom that regulation would apply were they, and their partner if they had one, below the qualifying age for state pension credit.]

(2)   In this Schedule "council tax due in respect of that day" means the council tax payable under section 10 or 78 of the 1992 Act less [¹ –

(a)   any reductions made in consequence of any enactment in, or under, the 1992 Act; and

(b)   in a case to which sub-paragraph (c) in column (1) of the table below applies, the amount of any discount which may be appropriate to the dwelling under the 1992 Act.]

(1)	*(2)*
Second adult	*Alternative maximum council tax benefit*
(a) Where the second adult or all second adults are in receipt of income support [⁶ , an income-related employment and support allowance] or state pension credit or are persons on an income-based jobseeker's allowance;	(a) 25 per cent. of the council tax due in respect of that day;
(b) where the gross income of the second adult or, where there is more than one second adult, their aggregate gross income disregarding any income of persons on income support [⁶ , an income-related employment and support allowance], state pension credit or an income-based jobseeker's allowance–	(b)

(i) is less than [⁸ £175.00] per week;

(ii) is not less than [⁸ £175.00] per week but less than [⁸ £228.00] per week.

[² (c) Where the dwelling would be wholly occupied by one or more persons to whom regulation 45(2) applies but for the presence of one or more second adults who are in receipt of income support, state pension credit [⁶ , an income-related employment and support allowance] or are persons on an income-based jobseeker's allowance.]

(i) 15 per cent. of the council tax due in respect of that day;

(ii) 7.5 per cent. of the council tax due in respect of that day.

[² (c) 100 per cent. of the council tax due in respect of that day.]

Amendments

1. Amended by reg 9(4)(a) and (b) of SI 2006 No 588 as from 1.4.06.
2. Inserted by reg 9(4)(c) of SI 2006 No 588 as from 1.4.06.
3. Amended by Art 21(7) of SI 2006 No 645 and reg 8 of SI 2006 No 217 as from 1.4.06.
4. Amended by Art 21(7) of SI 2007 No 688 as from 1.4.07.
5. Amended by Art 21(7) of SI 2008 No 632 as from 1.4.08.
6. Amended by reg 60 of SI 2008 No 1082 as from 27.10.08.
7. Amended by Art 21(8) of SI 2009 No 497 as from 1.4.09.
8. Confirmed by Art 21(8) of SI 2010 No 793 as from 1.4.10.

General Note

The amount of the alternative maximum CTB is the relevant percentage (as set out in the table) of gross council tax liability minus the reductions and discounts listed in para 1(2). Note that this is not the same figure used for main CTB.

Para (a) of the table is self explanatory.

Under para (b) of the table, the combined gross income of all the second adults not on IS, income-based JSA, income-related ESA or PC (for the definitions see reg 2) is used. Paras 2 and 3 provide for some gross income to be disregarded.

Para (c) of the table applies to dwellings which would be occupied wholly by students excluded from entitlement to main CTB but for the presence of one or more second adults receiving IS, income-based JSA, income-related ESA or PC. Such a dwelling would not be exempt from council tax (as dwellings occupied wholly by students are), but the CTB claimant(s) will be entitled to 100 per cent alternative maximum CTB. For these purposes, someone counts as a student excluded from entitlement to main CTB if s/he would be so excluded were s/he (or her partner) under the qualifying age for PC: para 1(1)(b). See the General Note to reg 45 on p692 where the non-student is liable for council tax on a dwelling shared with students.

---

2. In determining a second adult's gross income for the purposes of this Schedule, there shall be disregarded from that income–

(a) any attendance allowance, or any disability living allowance under section 71 of the Act;

(b) any payment made under [² or by] the Trusts, the Fund, the Eileen Trust [² , MFET Limited] or the Independent Living [¹ Fund (2006)] which had his income fallen to be calculated under regulation 30 (calculation of income other than earnings) would have been disregarded under paragraph 24 of Schedule 4 (income in kind); and

(c) any payment which had his income fallen to be calculated under regulation 30 would have been disregarded under paragraph 36 of Schedule 4 (payments made under certain trusts and certain other payments).

Amendments

1. Amended by reg 8(4)(f) of SI 2008 No 2767 as from 17.11.08.
2. Amended by reg 10(3) and (5) of SI 2010 No 641 as from 1.4.10 (5.4.10 where rent payable weekly or in multiples of a week).

---

3. Where there are two or more second adults residing with the claimant for benefit and any such second adult falls to be disregarded for the purposes of discount in accordance with Schedule 1 of the 1992 Act, his income shall be disregarded in determining the amount of any alternative maximum council tax benefit, unless that second adult is a member of a couple and his partner does not fall to be disregarded for the purposes of discount.

SCHEDULE 3
REGULATION 26(2) AND 28(2)
Sums to be disregarded in the calculation of earnings

1. In the case of a claimant who has been engaged in remunerative work as an employed earner or, had the employment been in Great Britain, would have been so engaged–

(a)   where–
- (i)   the employment has been terminated because of retirement; and
- (ii)   on retirement he is entitled to a retirement pension under the Act, or is not so entitled solely because of his failure to satisfy the contribution conditions,

any earnings [¹ paid or due to be paid] in respect of that employment, but only for a period commencing on the day immediately after the date on which the employment was terminated;

[¹ (b)   where before the first day of entitlement to council tax benefit the employment has been terminated otherwise than because of retirement, any earnings paid or due to be paid in respect of that employment except–
- [² (i)   any payment of the nature described in–
  - (aa)   regulation 25(1)(e), or
  - (bb)   section 28, 64 or 68 of the Employment Rights Act 1996 (guarantee payments, suspension from work on medical or maternity grounds); and]
- (ii)   any award, sum or payment of the nature described in–
  - (aa)   regulation 25(1)(g) or (h), or
  - (bb)   section 34 or 70 of the Employment Rights Act 1996 (guarantee payments and suspension from work: complaints to employment tribunals),

including any payment made following the settlement of a complaint to an employment tribunal or of court proceedings;

(c)   where before the first day of entitlement to council tax benefit–
- (i)   the employment has not been terminated, but
- (ii)   the claimant is not engaged in remunerative work,

any earnings paid or due to be paid in respect of that employment except any payment or remuneration of the nature described in [² paragraph 1(b)(i) or (ii)(bb) or regulation 25(1)(i)] or (j).]

Amendments
1.   Amended by reg 13(9)(a) of SI 2618 No2 007 as from 1.10.07.
2.   Amended by reg 8(5) of SI 2009 No 2655 as from 2.11.09.

2.   In the case of a claimant who, before the [¹ first day of entitlement to council tax benefit]–
(a)   has been engaged in part-time employment as an employed earner or, where the employment has been outside Great Britain, would have been so engaged had the employment been in Great Britain; and
(b)   has ceased to be engaged in that employment, whether or not that employment has been terminated,
any earnings [¹ paid or due to be paid] in respect of that employment except–
- (i)   where that employment has been terminated, [¹ any payment of the nature described in [² paragraph 1(b)(i) or (ii)(bb)]];
- (ii)   where that employment has not been terminated, [¹ any payment or remuneration of the nature described in [² paragraph 1(b)(i) or (ii)(bb) or regulation 25(1)(i)] or (j)].

Amendments
1.   Amended by reg 13(9)(b) of SI 2618 No 2007 as from 1.10.07.
2.   Amended by reg 8(5) of SI 2009 No 2655 as from 2.11.09.

[¹2A.   In the case of a claimant who has been engaged in remunerative work or part-time employment as a self-employed earner or, had the employment been in Great Britain would have been so engaged and who has ceased to be so employed, from the date of the cessation of his employment any earnings derived from that employment except earnings to which regulation 27(3) and (4) (earnings of self-employed earners) apply.]

Amendment
1.   Inserted by reg 8(11) of SI 2009 No 583 as from 6.4.09.

3.–(1)   In a case to which this paragraph applies and paragraph 4 does not apply, £20; but notwithstanding regulation 15 (calculation of income and capital of members of a claimant's family and of a polygamous marriage) if this paragraph applies to a claimant it shall not apply to his partner except where, and to the extent that, the earnings of the claimant which are to be disregarded under this paragraph are less than £20.

(2)   This paragraph applies where the claimant's applicable amount includes an amount by way of the disability premium [², severe disability premium, work-related activity component or support component] under Schedule 1 (applicable amounts).

(3)   This paragraph applies where–
[¹ (a)   the claimant is a member of a couple and his applicable amount includes an amount by way of the disability premium under Schedule 1; and]
(b)   he or his partner [³ has not attained the qualifying age for state pension credit] and at least one is engaged in employment.
[¹ (4)-(5)]

Amendments

1. Amended by reg 5(11)(a) and (b) of SI 2008 No 1042 as from 19.5.08.
2. Amended by reg 61(a) of SI 2008 No 1082 as from 27.10.08.
3. Amended by reg 35 of SI 2009 No 1488 as from 6.4.10.

---

4.   In a case where the claimant is a lone parent, £25.

5.–(1)   In a case to which neither paragraph 3 nor paragraph 4 applies to the claimant and, subject to sub-paragraph (2), where the claimant's applicable amount includes an amount by way of the carer premium under Schedule 1 (applicable amounts), £20 of the earnings of the person who is, or at any time in the preceding eight weeks was, in receipt of carer's allowance or treated in accordance with paragraph 17(2) of that Schedule as being in receipt of carer's allowance.

(2)   Where the carer premium is awarded in respect of the claimant and of any partner of his, their earnings shall for the purposes of this paragraph be aggregated, but the amount to be disregarded in accordance with sub-paragraph (1) shall not exceed £20 of the aggregated amount.

6.   Where the carer premium is awarded in respect of a claimant who is a member of a couple and whose earnings are less than £20, but is not awarded in respect of the other member of the couple, and that other member is engaged in an employment–

(a)   specified in paragraph 8(1), so much of the other member's earnings as would not when aggregated with the amount disregarded under paragraph 5 exceed £20;

(b)   other than one specified in paragraph 8(1), so much of the other member's earnings from such other employment up to £10 as would not when aggregated with the amount disregarded under paragraph 5 exceed £20.

7.   In a case where paragraphs 3, 5, 6 and 8 do not apply to the claimant and he is one of a couple and a member of that couple is in employment, £10; but, notwithstanding regulation 15 (calculation of income and capital of members of claimant's family and of a polygamous marriage), if this paragraph applies to a claimant it shall not apply to his partner except where, and to the extent that, the earnings of the claimant which are to be disregarded under this paragraph are less than £10.

8.–(1)   In a case where paragraphs 3, 4, 5 and 6 do not apply to the claimant, £20 of earnings derived from one or more employments as–

(a)   as a part-time fire-fighter employed by a fire and rescue authority constituted by a scheme under section 2 of the Fire and Rescue Services Act 2004 or a scheme to which section 4 of that Act applies;

(b)   a part-time fire-fighter employed by a fire and rescue authority (as defined in section 1 of the Fire (Scotland) Act 2005) or a joint fire and rescue board constituted by an amalgamation scheme made under section 2(1) of that Act;

(c)   an auxiliary coastguard in respect of coast rescue activities;

(d)   a person engaged part-time in the manning or launching of a life boat;

(e)   a member of any territorial or reserve force prescribed in Part I of Schedule 6 to the Social Security (Contributions) Regulations 2001;

but, notwithstanding regulation 15 (calculation of income and capital of members of claimant's family and of a polygamous marriage), if this paragraph applies to a claimant it shall not apply to his partner except to the extent specified in sub-paragraph (2).

(2)   If the claimant's partner is engaged in employment–

(a)   specified in sub-paragraph (1), so much of his earnings as would not in aggregate with the amount of the claimant's earnings disregarded under this paragraph exceed £20;

(b)   other than one specified in sub-paragraph (1), so much of his earnings from that employment up to £10 as would not in aggregate with the claimant's earnings disregarded under this paragraph exceed £20.

9.   Where the claimant is engaged in [¹ one or more employments] specified in paragraph 8(1), but his earnings derived from such employments are less than £20 in any week and he is also engaged in any other employment so much of his earnings from that other employment, up to £5 if he is a single claimant, or up to £10 if he has a partner, as would not in aggregate with the amount of his earnings disregarded under paragraph 8 exceed £20.

Amendment

1. Amended by reg 5(11)(c) of SI 2008 No 1042 as from 19.5.08.

---

10.   In a case to which none of the paragraphs 3 to 9 applies, £5.

[¹**10A.**–(1)   Where–

(a)   the claimant (or if the claimant is a member of a couple, at least one member of that couple) is a person to whom sub-paragraph (5) applies;

(b)   the Secretary of State is satisfied that that person is undertaking exempt work as defined in sub-paragraph (6); and

(c)   paragraph 12 does not apply,

the amount specified in sub-paragraph (7) (''the specified amount'').

(2)   Where this paragraph applies, paragraphs 3 to 10 do not apply; but in any case where the claimant is a lone parent, and the specified amount would be less than the amount specified in paragraph 4, then paragraph 4 applies instead of this paragraph.

(3)   Notwithstanding regulation 15 (calculation of income and capital of members of claimant's family and of a polygamous marriage), if sub-paragraph (1) applies to one member of a couple (''A'') it shall not apply to the other member of that couple (''B'') except to the extent provided in sub-paragraph (4).

(4)   Where A's earnings are less than the specified amount, there shall also be disregarded so much of B's earnings as would not when aggregated with A's earnings exceed the specified amount; but the amount of B's earnings which may be disregarded under this sub-paragraph is limited to a maximum of £20 unless the Secretary of State is satisfied that B is also undertaking exempt work.

(5)   This sub-paragraph applies to a person who is–
(a)   in receipt of a contributory employment and support allowance;
(b)   in receipt of incapacity benefit;
(c)   in receipt of severe disablement allowance; or
(d)   being credited with earnings on the grounds of incapacity for work or limited capability for work under regulation 8B of the Social Security (Credits) Regulations 1975.

(6)   ''Exempt work'' means work of the kind described in–
(a)   regulation 45(2), (3) or (4) of the Employment and Support Allowance Regulations; or (as the case may be)
(b)   regulation 17(2), (3) or (4) of the Social Security (Incapacity for Work) (General) Regulations 1995, and, in determining for the purposes of this paragraph whether a claimant or a member of a couple is undertaking any type of exempt work, it is immaterial whether that person or their partner is also undertaking other work.

(7)   The specified amount is the amount of money from time to time mentioned in any provision referred to in sub-paragraph (6) by virtue of which the work referred to in sub-paragraph (1) is exempt (or, where more than one such provision is relevant and those provisions mention different amounts of money, the highest of those amounts).]

Amendment
1.   Inserted by reg 4(2)(a) of SI 2009 No 2608 as from 1.4.10.

---

11.   Any amount or the balance of any amount which would fall to be disregarded under paragraph 19 or 20 of Schedule 4 had the claimant's income which does not consist of earnings been sufficient to entitle him to the full disregard thereunder.

12.   Where a claimant is on income support [¹ , an income-based jobseeker's allowance or an income-related employment and support allowance], his earnings.

Amendment
1.   Amended by reg 61(b) of SI 2008 No 1082 as from 27.10.08.

---

13.   Any earnings derived from employment which are payable in a country outside the United Kingdom for such period during which there is a prohibition against the transfer to the United Kingdom of those earnings.

14.   Where a payment of earnings is made in a currency other than Sterling, any banking charge or commission payable in converting that payment into Sterling.

15.   Any earnings of a child or young person.

16.–(1)   In a case where the claimant is a person who satisfies at least one of the conditions set out in sub-paragraph (2), and his net earnings equal or exceed the total of the amounts set out in sub-paragraph (3), the amount of his earnings that falls to be disregarded under [⁷ paragraphs 3 to 10A] of this Schedule shall be increased by [⁸ £17.10].

(2)   The conditions of this sub-paragraph are that–
(a)   the claimant, or if he is a member of a couple, either the claimant or his partner, is a person to whom regulation 20(1)(c) of the Working Tax Credit Regulations applies; or
(b)   the claimant–
    (i)   is, or if he is a member of a couple, at least one member of that couple is aged at least 25 and is engaged in remunerative work for on average not less than 30 hours per week; or
    (ii)   is a member of a couple and–
        (aa)   at least one member of that couple, is engaged in remunerative work for on average not less than 16 hours per week; and
        (bb)   his applicable amount includes a family premium under paragraph 3 of Schedule 1; or
    (iii)   is a lone parent who is engaged in remunerative work for on average not less than 16 hours per week; or
    (iv)   is, or if he is a member of a couple, at least one member of that couple is engaged in remunerative work for on average not less than 16 hours per week; and–
        [⁵ (aa)   the claimant's applicable amount includes a disability premium under paragraph 12, the work-related activity component under paragraph 23 or the support component under paragraph 24 of Schedule 1 respectively;] and

> (bb)   where he is a member of a couple, at least one member of that couple satisfies the qualifying conditions for the [⁴] disability premium [⁵ or either of the components] referred to in sub-head (aa) above and is engaged in remunerative work for on average not less than 16 hours per week; or

(c)   the claimant is, or if he has a partner, one of them is, a person to whom regulation 18(3) of the Working Tax Credit Regulations (eligibility for 50 plus element) applies, or would apply if an application for working tax credit were to be made in his case.

(3)   The following are the amounts referred to in sub-paragraph (1)–

(a)   the amount calculated as disregardable from the claimant's earnings under [⁹ paragraphs 3 to 10A] of this Schedule;

(b)   the amount of child care charges calculated as deductible under regulation 17(1)(c); and

(c)   [⁸ £17.10].

(4)   The provisions of regulation 6 shall apply in determining whether or not a person works for on average not less than 30 hours per week, but as if the reference to 16 hours in paragraph (1) of that regulation were a reference to 30 hours.

Amendments

1.   Amended by Art 21(8) of SI 2006 No 645 and reg 8 of SI 2006 No 217 as from 1.4.06.
2.   Amended by Art 21(8) of SI 2007 No 688 as from 1.4.07.
3.   Amended by Art 21(8) of SI 2008 No 632 as from 1.4.08.
4.   Amended by reg 5(11)(c) of SI 2008 No 1042 as from 19.5.08.
5.   Amended by reg 61(c) of SI 2008 No 1082 as from 27.10.08.
6.   Amended by Art 21(9) of SI 2009 No 497 as from 1.4.09.
7.   Amended by reg 4(2)(b) of SI 2009 No 2608 as from 1.4.10.
8.   Amended by Art 21(9) of SI 2010 No 793 as from 1.4.10.
9.   Amended by reg 4(6) of SI 2010 No 2449 as from 1.11.10.

---

17.   In this Schedule "part-time employment" means employment in which the person is engaged on average for less than 16 hours a week.

SCHEDULE 4
REGULATION 30(2)
Sums to be disregarded in the calculation of income other than earnings

Modifications

Para 37 was substituted by Sch 4 para 3(4) and paras 56A and 56B inserted by para 3(5) HB&CTB(CP) Regs in respect of claims for CTB by some refugees.

A different version of para 56B was substituted for para 56B by Sch 4 para 4(4)(b) HB&CTB(CP) Regs for some CTB claimants who are refugees who claimed asylum on or before 2 April 2000. See also reg 7A and Sch A1 inserted by Sch 4 para 3 HB&CTB(CP) Regs.

Note that paras 56A and 56B lapsed by s12(2)(g) Asylum and Immigration (Treatment of Claimants, etc.) Act 2004 (for those recorded as refugees after 14 June 2007) and were omitted by reg 7(5)(n) of SI 2008 No.3157 as from 5 January 2009.

Para A1 is inserted by reg 16 Jobseeker's Allowance (Work for Your Benefit Pilot Scheme) Regulations 2010 SI No.1222 (see p1247) as from 22 November 2010 but only for those ordinarily resident in a pilot area or whose address for payment of JSA is located within such an area. The modification is shown in italics. It ceases to have effect on 21 November 2013.

[A1.   Any payment made to the claimant in respect of any child care, travel or other expenses incurred, or to be incurred, by him in respect of his participation in the Work for Your Benefit Pilot Scheme.]

1.   Any amount paid by way of tax on income which is to be taken into account under regulation 30 (calculation of income other than earnings).

2.   Any payment in respect of any expenses incurred or to be incurred by a claimant who is–

(a)   engaged by a charitable or voluntary organisation, or

(b)   volunteer,

if he otherwise derives no remuneration or profit from the employment and is not to be treated as possessing any earnings under regulation 32(8) (notional income).

[¹**2A.**   Any payment in respect of expenses arising out of the claimant's participation in a service user group.]

Amendment

1.   Inserted by reg 8(6)(a) of SI 2009 No 2655 as from 2.11.09.

---

3.   In the case of employment as an employed earner, any payment in respect of expenses wholly, exclusively and necessarily incurred in the performance of the duties of the employment.

4. Where a claimant is on income support [¹ , an income-based jobseeker's allowance or an income-related employment and support allowance] the whole of his income.

Amendment

1. Amended by reg 62(a) of SI 2008 No 1082 as from 27.10.08.

5. Where the claimant is a member of a joint-claim couple for the purposes of the Jobseekers Act and his partner is on an income-based jobseeker's allowance, the whole of the claimant's income.

6. Where the claimant, or the person who was the partner of the claimant on 31st March 2003, was entitled on that date to income support or an income-based jobseeker's allowance but ceased to be so entitled on or before 5th April 2003 by virtue only of regulation 13 of the Housing Benefit (General) Amendment (No. 3) Regulations 1999 as in force at that date, the whole of his income.

General Note

This disregard of the whole of the claimant's income is necessary to ensure that those whose entitlement to IS or income-based JSA ceased because help with housing costs within those benefits no longer included charges for support services continue to be passported to full CTB. It only applies if the claimant was entitled to IS or income-based JSA on 31 March 2003 (or someone who was her/his partner on that date was entitled to one of those benefits) and that entitlement ceased on or before 5 April 2003.

7. Any disability living allowance.

8. Any concessionary payment made to compensate for the non-payment of–

(a) any payment specified in paragraph 7 or 10;

(b) income support;

(c) an income-based jobseeker's allowance.

[¹ (d) an income-related employment and support allowance.]

Amendment

1. Inserted by reg 62(b) of SI 2008 No 1082 as from 27.10.08.

9. Any mobility supplement under [¹ article 20 of the Naval, Military and Air Forces Etc. (Disablement and Death) Service Pensions Order 2006] (including such a supplement by virtue of any other scheme or order) or under article 25A of the Personal Injuries (Civilians) Scheme 1983 or any payment intended to compensate for the non-payment of such a supplement.

Amendment

1. Amended by reg 7(5)(a) of SI 2008 No 3157 as from 5.1.09.

10. Any attendance allowance.

11. Any payment to the claimant as holder of the Victoria Cross or of the George Cross or any analogous payment.

12.–(1) Any payment–

(a) by way of an education maintenance allowance made pursuant to–

(i) regulations made under section 518 of the Education Act 1996 (payment of school expenses; grant of scholarships etc);

(ii) regulations made under section 49 or 73(f) of the Education (Scotland) Act 1980 (power to assist persons to take advantage of educational facilities);

[¹ (iii) directions made under section 73ZA of the Education (Scotland) Act 1980 and paid under section 12(2)(c) of the Further and Higher Education (Scotland) Act 1992; or]

(b) corresponding to such an education maintenance allowance, made pursuant to–

(i) section 14 or section 181 of the Education Act 2002 (power of Secretary of State and National Assembly for Wales to give financial assistance for purposes related to education or childcare, and allowances in respect of education or training); or

(ii) regulations made under section 181 of that Act.

(2) Any payment, other than a payment to which sub-paragraph (1) applies, made pursuant to–

(a) regulations made under section 518 of the Education Act 1996;

(b) regulations made under section 49 of the Education (Scotland) Act 1980; or

[¹ (c) directions made under section 73ZA of the Education (Scotland) Act 1980 and paid under section 12(2)(c) of the Further and Higher Education (Scotland) Act 1992,]

in respect of a course of study attended by a child or a young person or a person who is in receipt of an education maintenance allowance made pursuant to any provision specified in sub-paragraph (1).

Amendment

1. Substituted by reg 7(5)(b) of SI 2008 No 3157 as from 5.1.09.

13. Any payment made to the claimant by way of a repayment under regulation 11(2) of the Education (Teacher Student Loans) (Repayment etc) Regulations 2002.

14.–(1) Any payment made pursuant to section 2 of the 1973 Act or section 2 of the Enterprise and New Towns (Scotland) Act 1990 except a payment–

(a) made as a substitute for income support, a jobseeker's allowance, incapacity benefit or severe disablement allowance;

(b) of an allowance referred to in section 2(3) of the 1973 Act or section 2(5) of the Enterprise and New Towns (Scotland) Act 1990; or

(c) intended to meet the cost of living expenses which relate to any one or more of the items specified in sub-paragraph (2) whilst a claimant is participating in an education, training or other scheme to help him enhance his employment prospects unless the payment is a Career Development Loan paid pursuant to section 2 of the 1973 Act and the period of education or training or the scheme, which is supported by that loan, has been completed.

(2) The items specified in this sub-paragraph for the purposes of sub-paragraph (1)(c) are food, ordinary clothing or footwear, household fuel or rent of the claimant or, where the claimant is a member of a family, any other member of his family, or any council tax or water charges for which that claimant or member is liable.

15.–(1) Subject to sub-paragraph (2), any of the following payments–

(a) a charitable payment;

(b) a voluntary payment;

(c) a payment (not falling within sub-paragraph (a) or (b) above) from a trust whose funds are derived from a payment made in consequence of any personal injury to the claimant;

(d) a payment under an annuity purchased–

(i) pursuant to any agreement or court order to make payments to the claimant; or

(ii) from funds derived from a payment made,

in consequence of any personal injury to the claimant; or

(e) a payment (not falling within sub-paragraphs (a) to (d) received by virtue of any agreement or court order to make payments to the claimant in consequence of any personal injury to the claimant.

(2) Sub-paragraph (1) shall not apply to a payment which is made or due to be made by–

(a) a former partner of the claimant, or a former partner of any member of the claimant's family; or

(b) the parent of a child or young person where that child or young person is a member of the claimant's family.

16. Subject to paragraph 35, £10 of any of the following, namely–

(a) a war disablement pension (except insofar as such a pension falls to be disregarded under paragraph 9 or 10);

[¹ (b) a war widow's pension or [³ war widower's pension];]

(c) a pension payable to a person as a widow, widower or surviving civil partner under [²] any power of Her Majesty otherwise than under an enactment to make provision about pensions for or in respect of persons who have been disabled or have died in consequence of service as members of the armed forces of the Crown;

(d) a guaranteed income payment [² and, if the amount of that payment has been abated to less than £10 by a [³ pension or payment falling within article 31(1)(a) or (b) of the Armed Forces and Reserve Forces (Compensation Scheme) Order 2005], so much of [³ that pension or payment] as would not, in aggregate with the amount of [³ any] guaranteed income payment disregarded, exceed £10];

(e) a payment made to compensate for the non-payment of such a pension or payment as is mentioned in any of the preceding sub-paragraphs;

(f) a pension paid by the government of a country outside Great Britain which is analogous to any of the pensions or payments mentioned in sub-paragraphs (a) to (d) above;

(g) pension paid to victims of National Socialist persecution under any special provision made by the law of the Federal Republic of Germany, or any part of it, or of the Republic of Austria.

Amendments

1. Amended by reg 5(12)(a) of SI 2008 No 1042 as from 19.5.08.
2. Amended by reg 7(5)(c) of SI 2008 No 3157 as from 5.1.09.
3. Amended by reg 8(6)(b) of SI 2009 No 2655 as from 2.11.09.

---

17. Subject to paragraph 35, £15 of any–

(a) widowed mother's allowance paid pursuant to section 37 of the Act;

(b) widowed parent's allowance paid pursuant to section 39A of the Act.

18.–(1) Any income derived from capital to which the claimant is or is treated under regulation 41 (capital jointly held) as beneficially entitled but, subject to sub-paragraph (2), not income derived from capital disregarded under paragraphs 1, 2, 4, 8, 14 or 25 to 28 of Schedule 5.

(2) Income derived from capital disregarded under paragraphs 2, 4 or 25 to 28 of Schedule 5 but only to the extent of–

(a) any mortgage repayments made in respect of the dwelling or premises in the period during which that income accrued; or

(b) any council tax or water charges which the claimant is liable to pay in respect of the dwelling or premises and which are paid in the period during which that income accrued.

(3)   The definition of "water charges" in regulation 2(1) shall apply to sub-paragraph (2) of this paragraph with the omission of the words "in so far as such charges are in respect of the dwelling which a person occupies as his home".

19.   Where the claimant makes a parental contribution in respect of a student attending a course at an establishment in the United Kingdom or undergoing education in the United Kingdom, which contribution has been assessed for the purposes of calculating–

(a)   under, or pursuant to regulations made under powers conferred by, sections 1 or 2 of the Education Act 1962 or section 22 of the Teaching and Higher Education Act 1998, that student's award;

(b)   under regulations made in exercise of the powers conferred by section 49 of the Education (Scotland) Act 1980, that student's bursary, scholarship, or other allowance under that section or under regulations made in exercise of the powers conferred by section 73 of that Act of 1980, any payment to that student under that section; or

(c)   the student's student loan,

an amount equal to the weekly amount of that parental contribution, but only in respect of the period for which that contribution is assessed as being payable.

20.–(1)   Where the claimant is the parent of a student aged under 25 in advanced education who either–

(a)   is not in receipt of any award, grant or student loan in respect of that education; or

(b)   is in receipt of an award under section 2 of the Education Act 1962 (discretionary awards) or an award bestowed by virtue of the Teaching and Higher Education Act 1998, or regulations made thereunder, or a bursary, scholarship or other allowance under section 49(1) of the Education (Scotland) Act 1980, or a payment under section 73 of that Act of 1980,

and the claimant makes payments by way of a contribution towards the student's maintenance, other than a parental contribution falling within paragraph 19, an amount specified in sub-paragraph (2) in respect of each week during the student's term.

(2)   For the purposes of sub-paragraph (1), the amount shall be equal to–

(a)   the weekly amount of the payments; or

(b)   the amount by way of a personal allowance for a single claimant under 25 less the weekly amount of any award, bursary, scholarship, allowance or payment referred to in sub-paragraph (1)(b),

whichever is less.

21.   Any payment made to the claimant by a child or young person or a non-dependant.

22.   Where the claimant occupies a dwelling as his home and the dwelling is also occupied by a person other than one to whom paragraph 21 or 23 refers and there is a contractual liability to make payments to the claimant in respect of the occupation of the dwelling by that person or a member of his family–

[³ (a)   where the aggregate of any payments made in respect of any one week in respect of the occupation of the dwelling by that person or a member of his family, or by that person and a member of his family, is less than £20, the whole of that amount; or

(b)   where the aggregate of any such payments is £20 or more per week, £20.]

Amendments

1.   Amended by Art 21(9)(a) of SI 2006 No 645 and reg 8 of SI 2006 No 217 as from 1.4.06.
2.   Amended by Art 21(9)(a) of SI 2007 No 688 as from 1.4.07.
3.   Substituted by reg 13(10) of SI 2007 No 2618 as from 1.4.08.

23.–(1)   Where the claimant occupies a dwelling as his home and he provides in that dwelling board and lodging accommodation, an amount, in respect of each person for which such accommodation is provided for the whole or any part of a week, equal to–

(a)   where the aggregate of any payments made in respect of any one week in respect of such accommodation provided to such person does not exceed £20.00, 100 per cent. of such payments;

(b)   where the aggregate of any such payments exceeds £20.00, £20.00 and 50 per cent. of the excess over £20.00.

(2)   In this paragraph, "board and lodging accommodation" means accommodation provided to a person or, if he is a member of a family, to him or any other member of his family, for a charge which is inclusive of the provision of that accommodation and at least some cooked or prepared meals which both are cooked or prepared (by a person other than the person to whom the accommodation is provided or a member of his family) and are consumed in that accommodation or associated premises.

24.–(1)   Any income in kind, except where regulation 30(11)(b) (provision of support under section 95 or 98 of the Immigration and Asylum Act in the calculation of income other than earnings) applies.

(2)   The reference in sub-paragraph (1) to "income in kind" does not include a payment to a third party made in respect of the claimant which is used by the third party to provide benefits in kind to the claimant.

25.   Any income which is payable in a country outside the United Kingdom for such period during which there is a prohibition against the transfer to the United Kingdom of that income.

26.–(1)   Any payment made to the claimant in respect of a person who is a member of his family–

(a)   pursuant to regulations under section 2(6)(b), 3 or 4 of the Adoption and Children Act 2002 or in accordance or with a scheme approved by the Scottish Ministers under [¹ section 51A] of the Adoption (Scotland) Act 1978 (schemes for payments of allowances to adopters);

[¹ (b)]

[² (ba)   which is a payment made by a local authority in pursuance of section 15(1) of, and paragraph 15 of Schedule 1 to, the Children Act 1989 (local authority contribution to a child's maintenance where the child is living with a person as a result of a residence order) or in Scotland section 50 of the Children Act 1975 (payments towards maintenance of children);]

(c)   which is a payment made by an authority, as defined in Article 2 of the Children Order, in pursuance of Article 15 of, and paragraph 17 of Schedule 1 to, that Order (contribution by an authority to child's maintenance);

(d)   in accordance with regulations made pursuant to section 14F of the Children Act 1989 (special guardianship support services);

to the extent specified in sub-paragraph (3).

(2)   Any payment, other than a payment to which sub-paragraph (1)(a) applies, made to the claimant pursuant to regulations under section 2(6)(b), 3 or 4 of the Adoption and Children Act 2002.

(3)   In the case of a child or young person, so much of the weekly amount of the payment as exceeds the amount included under Schedule 1 in the calculation of the claimant's applicable amount for that child or young person by way of the personal allowance and disabled child premium, if any.

Amendments

1.   Amended by reg 7(5)(d) of SI 2008 No 3157 as from 5.1.09.
2.   Inserted by reg 8(6)(c) of SI 2009 No 2655 as from 2.11.09.

[²**27.** Any payment made to the claimant with whom a person is accommodated by virtue of arrangements made–

(a)   by a local authority under–
    (i)   section 23(2)(a) of the Children Act 1989 (provision of accommodation and maintenance for a child whom they are looking after),
    (ii)   section 26 of the Children (Scotland) Act 1995 (manner of provision of accommodation to child looked after by local authority), or
    (iii)   regulations 33 or 51 of the Looked After Children (Scotland) Regulations 2009 (fostering and kinship care allowances and fostering allowances); or
(b)   by a voluntary organisation under section 59(1)(a) of the Children Act 1989 (provision of accommodation by voluntary organisations).]

Amendments

1.   Amended by reg 17(5) of SI 2006 No 2378 as from 2.10.06.
2.   Substituted by reg 9(3) of SI 2010 No 2429 as from 1.11.10.

28.   Any payment made to the claimant or his partner for a person (''the person concerned''), who is not normally a member of the claimant's household but is temporarily in his care, by–

(a)   a health authority;
(b)   a local authority but excluding payments of housing benefit made in respect of the person concerned;
(c)   a voluntary organisation;
(d)   the person concerned pursuant to section 26(3A) of the National Assistance Act 1948; [¹]
(e)   a primary care trust established under section 16A of the National Health Service Act [¹ 1977 or established by an order made under section 18(2)(c) of the National Health Service Act 2006; or]
[¹ (f)   a Local Health Board established under section 16BA of the National Health Service Act 1977 or established by an order made under section 11 of the National Health Service (Wales) Act 2006.]

Amendment

1.   Amended by reg 7(5)(e) of SI 2008 No 3157 as from 5.1.09.

29.   Any payment made by a local authority in accordance with section 17, [¹ 23B,] 23C or 24A of the Children Act 1989 or, as the case may be, section 12 of the Social Work (Scotland) Act 1968 or section [² 22,] 29 or 30 of the Children (Scotland) Act 1995 (provision of services for children and their families and advice and assistance to certain children).

Amendments

1.   Amended by reg 8(9)(a) of SI 2008 No 2767 as from 17.11.08.
2.   Inserted by reg 9(4) of SI 2010 No 2429 as from 1.11.10.

[¹**29A.**–(1)   Subject to sub-paragraph (2), any payment (or part of a payment) made by a local authority in accordance with section 23C of the Children Act 1989(70) or section 29 of the Children (Scotland) Act 1995(71) (local authorities' duty to promote welfare of children and powers to grant financial assistance to persons in, or formerly in, their care) to a person (''A'') which A passes on to the claimant.

(2)   Sub-paragraph (1) applies only where A–
(a)   was formerly in the claimant's care, and

(b)   is aged 18 or over, and

(c)   continues to live with the claimant.]

Amendment

1.   Inserted by reg 7(5)(a) of SI 2008 No 698 as from, as it relates to a particular beneficiary, the first day of the benefit week on or after 7.4.08.

30.–(1)   Subject to sub-paragraph (2), any payment received under an insurance policy taken out to insure against the risk of being unable to maintain repayments–

(a)   on a loan which is secured on the dwelling which the claimant occupies as his home; or

(b)   under a regulated agreement as defined for the purposes of the Consumer Credit Act 1974 or under a hire-purchase agreement or a conditional sale agreement as defined for the purposes of Part 3 of the Hire-Purchase Act 1964.

(2)   A payment referred to in sub-paragraph (1) shall only be disregarded to the extent that the payment received under that policy does not exceed the amounts, calculated on a weekly basis, which are used to–

(a)   maintain the repayments referred to in sub-paragraph (1)(a) or, as the case may be, (b); and

(b)   meet any amount due by way of premiums on–

  (i)   that policy; or

  (ii)   in a case to which sub-paragraph (1)(a) applies, an insurance policy taken out to insure against loss or damage to any building or part of a building which is occupied by the claimant as his home and which is required as a condition of the loan referred to in sub-paragraph (1)(a).

31.   Any payment of income which by virtue of regulation 36 (income treated as capital) is to be treated as capital.

32.   Any social fund payment made pursuant to Part 8 of the Act (the Social Fund).

33.   Any payment under [¹ Part 10] of the Act (Christmas bonus for pensioners).

Amendment

1.   Amended by reg 7(5)(f) of SI 2008 No 3157 as from 5.1.09.

---

34.   Where a payment of income is made in a currency other than sterling, any banking charge or commission payable in converting that payment into sterling.

35.   The total of a claimant's income or, if he is a member of a family, the family's income and the income of any person which he is treated as possessing under regulation 15(2) (calculation of income and capital of members of claimant's family and of a polygamous marriage) to be disregarded under regulation 47(2)(b) and regulation 48(1)(d) (calculation of covenant income where a contribution assessed, covenant income where no grant income or no contribution is assessed), regulation 51(2) (treatment of student loans), regulation 52(3) (treatment of payments from access funds) and paragraphs 16 and 17 shall in no case exceed £20 per week.

36.–(1)   Any payment made under [² or by] any of the Trusts, the Fund, the Eileen Trust [² , MFET Limited] or the Independent Living [¹ Fund (2006)].

(2)   Any payment by or on behalf of a person who is suffering or who suffered from haemophilia or who is or was a qualifying person, which derives from a payment made under [² or by] any of the Trusts to which sub-paragraph (1) refers and which is made to or for the benefit of–

(a)   that person's partner or former partner from whom he is not, or where that person has died was not, estranged or divorced or with whom he has formed a civil partnership that has not been dissolved or, where that person has died, had not been dissolved at the time of that person's death;

(b)   any child who is a member of that person's family or who was such a member and who is a member of the claimant's family; or

(c)   any young person who is a member of that person's family or who was such a member and who is a member of the claimant's family.

(3)   Any payment by or on behalf of the partner or former partner of a person who is suffering or who suffered from haemophilia or who is or was a qualifying person provided that the partner or former partner and that person are not, or if either of them has died were not, estranged or divorced or, where the partner or former partner and that person have formed a civil partnership, the civil partnership has not been dissolved or, if either of them has died, had not been dissolved at the time of the death, which derives from a payment made under [² or by] any of the Trusts to which sub-paragraph (1) refers and which is made to or for the benefit of–

(a)   the person who is suffering from haemophilia or who is a qualifying person;

(b)   any child who is a member of that person's family or who was such a member and who is a member of the claimant's family; or

(c)   any young person who is a member of that person's family or who was such a member and who is a member of the claimant's family.

(4)   Any payment by a person who is suffering from haemophilia or who is a qualifying person, which derives from a payment under [² or by] any of the Trusts to which sub-paragraph (1) refers, where–

(a)   that person has no partner or former partner from whom he is not estranged or divorced or with whom he has formed a civil partnership that has not been dissolved, nor any child or young person who is or had been a member of that person's family; and

(b)   the payment is made either–
      (i)   to that person's parent or step-parent, or
      (ii)   where that person at the date of the payment is a child, a young person or a student who has not completed his full-time education and has no parent or step-parent, to his guardian,
but only for a period from the date of the payment until the end of two years from that person's death.

(5)   Any payment out of the estate of a person who suffered from haemophilia or who was a qualifying person, which derives from a payment under [² or by] any of the Trusts to which sub-paragraph (1) refers, where–
    (a)   that person at the date of his death (the relevant date) had no partner or former partner from whom he was not estranged or divorced or with whom he has formed a civil partnership that has not been dissolved, nor any child or young person who was or had been a member of his family; and
    (b)   the payment is made either–
      (i)   to that person's parent or step-parent, or
      (ii)   where that person at the relevant date was a child, a young person or a student who had not completed his full-time education and had no parent or step-parent, to his guardian,
but only for a period of two years from the relevant date.

(6)   In the case of a person to whom or for whose benefit a payment referred to in this paragraph is made, any income which derives from any payment of income or capital made under or deriving from any of the Trusts.

(7)   For the purposes of sub-paragraphs (2) to (6), any reference to the Trusts shall be construed as including a reference to the Fund, the Eileen Trust [², MFET Limited], the Skipton Fund and the London Bombings Relief Charitable Fund.

Modifications

References to "step-parent" in sub-paras (4)(b)(i) and (ii) and (5)(b)(i) and (ii) are modified by s246 Civil Partnership Act 2004 (see p1148) and art 3 and para 45 Schedule to SI 2005 No.3137 (see p1195).

Amendments

1.   Amended by reg 8(4)(g) of SI 2008 No 2767 as from 17.11.08.
2.   Amended by reg 10(3) and (5) of SI 2010 No 641 as from 1.4.10 (5.4.10 where rent payable weekly or in multiples of a week).

Analysis

Note that unlike for HB, there is a definition of "estranged". It is found in reg 2(5).

[¹**37.**   Any housing benefit.]

Amendment

1.   Substituted by reg 7(5)(g) of SI 2008 No 3157 as from 5.1.09.

---

38.   Any payment made by the Secretary of State to compensate for the loss (in whole or in part) of entitlement to housing benefit.

[¹**39.**]

Amendment

1.   Omitted by reg 7(5)(b) of SI 2008 No 698 as from 14.4.08.

[¹**40.**]

Amendment

1.   Omitted by reg 7(5)(h) of SI 2008 No 3157 as from 5.1.09.

---

41.   Any payment to a juror or witness in respect of attendance at a court other than compensation for loss of earnings or for the loss of a benefit payable under the benefit Acts.

[¹ **42.**]

Amendment

1.   Omitted by reg 8(9)(b) of SI 2008 No 2767 as from 17.11.08.

---

43.   Any payment in consequence of a reduction of council tax under section 13 [² or] [¹] section 80 of the 1992 Act (reduction of liability for council tax).

Amendments

1.   Amended by reg 7(5)(c) of SI 2008 No 698 as from 14.4.08.

2.   Amended by reg 8(12)(a) of SI 2009 No 583 as from 6.4.09.

[¹**44.**]

Amendment

1.   Omitted by reg 7(5)(h) of SI 2008 No 3157 as from 5.1.09.

[³**45.**–(1)   Any payment or repayment made–
(a)   as respects England, under regulation 5, 6 or 12 of the National Health Service (Travel Expenses and Remission of Charges) Regulations 2003 (travelling expenses and health service supplies);
(b)   as respects Wales, under regulation 5, 6 or 11 of the National Health Service (Travelling Expenses and Remission of Charges) (Wales) Regulations 2007 (travelling expenses and health service supplies);
(c)   as respects Scotland, under regulation 3, 5 or 11 of the National Health Service (Travelling Expenses and Remission of Charges) (Scotland) (No. 2) Regulations 2003 (travelling expenses and health service supplies).
(2)   Any payment or repayment made by the Secretary of State for Health, the Scottish Ministers or the Welsh Ministers which is analogous to a payment or repayment mentioned in sub-paragraph (1).]

Amendments

1.   Amended by reg 5(12)(b) of SI 2008 No 1042 as from 19.5.08.
2.   Inserted by reg 5(12)(b) of SI 2008 No 1042 as from 19.5.08.
3.   Substituted by reg 7(5)(i) of SI 2008 No 3157 as from 5.1.09.

[¹**46.**   Any payment made to such persons entitled to receive benefits as may be determined by or under a scheme made pursuant to section 13 of the Social Security Act 1988 in lieu of vouchers or similar arrangements in connection with the provision of those benefits (including payments made in place of healthy start vouchers, milk tokens or the supply of vitamins).]

Amendments

1.   Amended by reg 5(12)(c) of SI 2008 No 1042 as from 19.5.08.
2.   Substituted by reg 7(5)(i) of SI 2008 No 3157 as from 5.1.09.

---

47.   Any payment made by either the Secretary of State for [¹ Justice] or by the [¹ Scottish Ministers] under a scheme established to assist relatives and other persons to visit persons in custody.

Amendments

1.   Amended by Art 8 and the Sch para 24 of SI 2007 No 2128 as from 22.8.07.
2.   Amended by reg 7(5)(j) of SI 2008 No 3157 as from 5.1.09.

[¹**48.**–(1)   Where a claimant's applicable amount includes an amount by way of family premium, £15 of any payment of maintenance, other than child maintenance, whether under a court order or not, which is made or due to be made by the claimant's former partner, or the claimant's partner's former partner.
(2)   For the purpose of sub-paragraph (1) where more than one maintenance payment falls to be taken into account in any week, all such payments shall be aggregated and treated as if they were a single payment.
(3)   A payment made by the Secretary of State in lieu of maintenance shall, for the purpose of sub-paragraph (1), be treated as a payment of maintenance made by a person specified in sub-paragraph (1).]

Amendment

1.   Substituted by reg 5(12)(d) of SI 2008 No 1042 as from 27.10.08.

[¹[²[³**48A.**]–(1)   Any payment of child maintenance made or derived from a liable relative where the child or young person in respect of whom the payment is made is a member of the claimant's family, except where the person making the payment is the claimant or the claimant's partner.
(2)   In paragraph (1)–
"child maintenance" means any payment towards the maintenance of a child or young person, including any payment made voluntarily and payments made under–
(a)   the Child Support Act 1991;
(b)   the Child Support (Northern Ireland) Order 1991;
(c)   a court order;
(d)   a consent order;
(e)   a maintenance agreement registered for execution in the Books of Council and Session or the sheriff court books;
"liable relative" means a person listed in regulation 54 (interpretation) of the Income Support (General) Regulations 1987, other than a person falling within sub-paragraph (d) of that definition.]

Amendments
1.   Inserted by reg 5(12)(d) of SI 2008 No 1042 as from 27.10.08.
2.   Substituted by reg 8(6)(d) of SI 2009 No 2655 as from 1.4.10.
3.   Amended by reg 4(7)(a) of SI 2010 No 2449 as from 1.11.10.

General Note
This para was renumbered when it was substituted from 1 April 2010. It is presumed this was an error.

[¹**49.**]

Amendment
1.   Omitted by reg 7(5)(b) of SI 2008 No 698 as from 14.4. 08.

50.   Any payment (other than a training allowance) made, whether by the Secretary of State or any other person, under the Disabled Persons (Employment) Act 1944 to assist disabled persons to obtain or retain employment despite their disability.
51.   Any guardian's allowance.
[¹**52.**–(1)   If the claimant is in receipt of any benefit under Part 2, 3 or 5 of the Act, any increase in the rate of that benefit arising under Part 4 (increases for dependants) or section 106(a) (unemployability supplement) of the Act, where the dependant in respect of whom the increase is paid is not a member of the claimant's family.
(2)   If the claimant is in receipt of any pension or allowance under Part 2 or 3 of the Naval, Military and Air Forces Etc. (Disablement and Death) Service Pensions Order 2006, any increase in the rate of that pension or allowance under that Order, where the dependant in respect of whom the increase is paid is not a member of the claimant's family.]

Amendment
1.   Substituted by reg 7(5)(k) of SI 2008 No 3157 as from 5.1.09.

[¹**53.**   Any supplementary pension under article 23(2) of the Naval, Military and Air Forces Etc. (Disablement and Death) Service Pensions Order 2006 (pensions to surviving spouses and surviving civil partners) and any analogous payment made by the Secretary of State for Defence to any person who is not a person entitled under that Order.]

Amendment
1.   Substituted by reg 7(5)(k) of SI 2008 No 3157 as from 5.1.09.

54.   In the case of a pension awarded at the supplementary rate under article 27(3) of the Personal Injuries (Civilians) Scheme 1983 (pensions to widows, widowers or surviving civil partners), the sum specified in paragraph 1(c) of Schedule 4 to that Scheme.
55.–(1)   Any payment which is–
(a)   made under any of the Dispensing Instruments to a widow, widower or surviving civil partner of a person–
        (i)   whose death was attributable to service in a capacity analogous to service as a member of the armed forces of the Crown; and
        (ii)   whose service in such capacity terminated before 31st March 1973; and
[¹ (b)   equal to the amount specified in article 23(2) of the Naval, Military and Air Forces Etc. (Disablement and Death) Service Pensions Order 2006.]
(2)   In this paragraph ''the Dispensing Instruments'' means the Order in Council of 19th December 1881, the Royal Warrant of 27th October 1884 and the Order by His Majesty of 14th January 1922 (exceptional grants of pay, non-effective pay and allowances).

Amendment
1.   Amended by reg 7(5)(l) of SI 2008 No 3157 as from 5.1.09.

[¹**55A.**   Any council tax benefit to which the claimant is entitled.]

Amendment
1.   Inserted by reg 7(5)(m) of SI 2008 No 3157 as from 5.1.09.

56.   Except in a case which falls under sub-paragraph (1) of paragraph 16 of Schedule 3, where the claimant is a person who satisfies any of the conditions of sub-paragraph (2) of that paragraph, any amount of working tax credit up to [⁵ £17.10].

Amendments
1.   Amended by Art 21(9)(b) of SI 2006 No 645 and reg 8 of SI 2006 No 217 as from 1.4.06.
2.   Amended by Art 21(9)(b) of SI 2007 No 688 as from 1.4.07.
3.   Amended by Art 21(9) of SI 2008 No 632 as from 1.4.08.
4.   Amended by Art 21(10) of SI 2009 No 497 as from 1.4.09.
5.   Amended by Art 21(10) of SI 2010 No 793 as from 1.4.10.

57.   Any payment made [¹] under section 12B of the Social Work (Scotland) Act 1968 or under regulations made under section 57 of the Health and Social Care Act 2001 (direct payments).

Amendment
1.   Amended by reg 8(12)(b) of SI 2009 No 583 as from 6.4.09.

58.–(1)   Subject to sub-paragraph (2), in respect of a person who is receiving, or who has received, assistance under the self-employment route, any payment to that person–
(a)   to meet expenses wholly and necessarily incurred whilst carrying on the commercial activity;
(b)   which is used or intended to be used to maintain repayments on a loan taken out by that person for the purpose of establishing or carrying on the commercial activity,
in respect of which such assistance is or was received.
(2)   Sub-paragraph (1) shall apply only in respect of payments which are paid to that person from the special account as defined for the purposes of Chapter 4A of Part 8 of the Jobseeker's Allowance Regulations.
59.–(1)   Any payment of a sports award except to the extent that it has been made in respect of any one or more of the items specified in sub-paragraph (2).
(2)   The items specified for the purposes of sub-paragraph (1) are food, ordinary clothing or footwear, household fuel or rent of the claimant or where the claimant is a member of a family, any other member of his family, or any council tax or water charges for which that claimant or member is liable.
(3)   For the purposes of sub-paragraph (2) ''food'' does not include vitamins, minerals or other special dietary supplements intended to enhance the performance of the person in the sport in respect of which the award was made.
60.   Where the amount of subsistence allowance paid to a person in a benefit week exceeds the amount of income-based jobseeker's allowance that person would have received in that benefit week had it been payable to him, less 50p, that excess amount.
61.   In the case of a claimant participating in an employment zone programme, any discretionary payment made by an employment zone contractor to the claimant, being a fee, grant, loan or otherwise.
62.   Any discretionary housing payment paid pursuant to regulation 2(1) of the Discretionary Financial Assistance Regulations 2001.
63.–(1)   Any payment made by a local authority or by the [¹ Welsh Ministers], to or on behalf of the claimant or his partner relating to a service which is provided to develop or sustain the capacity of the claimant or his partner to live independently in his accommodation.
(2)   For the purposes of sub-paragraph (1) ''local authority'' includes, in England, a county council.

Amendment
1.   Amended by reg 7(5)(o) of SI 2008 No 3157 as from 5.1.09.

[¹**64.**]

Amendment
1.   Omitted by reg 5(12)(e) of SI 2008 No 1042 as from 19.5.08.

[¹ [² **65.**]]

Amendments
1.   Inserted by reg 5 of SI 2008 No 3140 as from 5.1.09.
2.   Revoked by reg 1(3) of SI 2008 No 3140 as from 6.4.09.

[¹**66.**   Any payment of child benefit.]

Amendment
1.   Inserted by reg 3 of SI 2009 No 2848 as from 2.11.09.

SCHEDULE 5
REGULATION 34(2)
Capital to be disregarded

Modifications

Paras 53A and 53B were inserted by Sch 4 para 3(6) HB&CTB(CP) Regs in respect of claims for CTB by some refugees.

A different version of para 53B was substituted for para 53B by Sch 4 para 4(4)(c) HB&CTB(CP) Regs for some CTB claimants who are refugees who claimed asylum on or before 2 April 2000. See also reg 7A and Sch A1 inserted by Sch 4 para 3 HB&CTB(CP) Regs.

Note that paras 53A and 53B lapsed by s12(2)(g) Asylum and Immigration (Treatment of Claimants, etc.) Act 2004 (for those recorded as refugees after 14 June 2007) and were omitted by reg 7(6)(e) of SI 2008 No.3157 as from 5 January 2009.

Para A1 is inserted by reg 17 Jobseeker's Allowance (Work for Your Benefit Pilot Scheme) Regulations 2010 SI No.1222 (see p1247) as from 22 November 2010 but only for those ordinarily resident in a pilot area or whose address for payment of JSA is located within such an area. The modification is shown in italics. It ceases to have effect on 21 November 2013.

[A1.   Any payment made to the claimant in respect of any child care, travel or other expenses incurred, or to be incurred, by him in respect of his participation in the Work for Your Benefit Scheme but only for 52 weeks beginning with the date of receipt of the payment.]

1.   The dwelling together with any garage, garden and outbuildings, normally occupied by the claimant as his home including any premises not so occupied which it is impracticable or unreasonable to sell separately, in particular [¹ , in Scotland,] any croft land on which the dwelling is situated; but, notwithstanding regulation 15 (calculation of income and capital of members of claimant's family and of a polygamous marriage), only one dwelling shall be disregarded under this paragraph.

Amendment

1.   Amended by reg 7(6)(a) of SI 2008 No 3157 as from 5.1.09.

2.   Any premises acquired for occupation by the claimant which he intends to occupy as his home within 26 weeks of the date of acquisition or such longer period as is reasonable in the circumstances to enable the claimant to obtain possession and commence occupation of the premises.

3.   Any sum directly attributable to the proceeds of sale of any premises formerly occupied by the claimant as his home which is to be used for the purchase of other premises intended for such occupation within 26 weeks of the date of sale or such longer period as is reasonable in the circumstances to enable the claimant to complete the purchase.

4.   Any premises occupied in whole or in part–

(a)   by a partner or relative of a single claimant or any member of the family as his home [¹ where that person has attained the qualifying age for state pension credit or is incapacitated];

(b)   by the former partner of the claimant as his home; but this provision shall not apply where the former partner is a person from whom the claimant is estranged or divorced or with whom he had formed a civil partnership that has been dissolved.

Amendment

1.   Amended by reg 36 of SI 2009 No 1488 as from 6.4.10.

Analysis

Note that unlike for HB, there is a definition of "estranged". It is found in reg 2(5) (see p652).

5.   Where a claimant is on income support [¹ , an income-based jobseeker's allowance or an income-related employment and support allowance], the whole of his capital.

Amendment

1.   Amended by reg 63(a) of SI 2008 No 1082 as from 27.10.08.

6.   Where the claimant is a member of a joint-claim couple for the purposes of the Jobseekers Act 1995 and his partner is on income-based jobseeker's allowance, the whole of the claimant's capital.

7.   Any future interest in property of any kind, other than land or premises in respect of which the claimant has granted a subsisting lease or tenancy, including sub-leases or sub-tenancies.

8.–(1)   The assets of any business owned in whole or in part by the claimant and for the purposes of which he is engaged as a self-employed earner, or if he has ceased to be so engaged, for such period as may be reasonable in the circumstances to allow for disposal of any such asset.

(2)   The assets of any business owned in whole or in part by the claimant where–

(a) he is not engaged as a self-employed earner in that business by reason of some disease or bodily or mental disablement; but

(b) he intends to become engaged or, as the case may be, re-engaged as a self-employed earner in that business as soon as he recovers or is able to become engaged or re-engaged in that business;

for a period of 26 weeks from the date on which the claim for council tax benefit is made, or is treated as made, or, if it is unreasonable to expect him to become engaged or re-engaged in that business within that period, for such longer period as is reasonable in the circumstances to enable him to become so engaged or re-engaged.

(3) In the case of a person who is receiving assistance under the self-employment route, the assets acquired by that person for the purpose of establishing or carrying on the commercial activity in respect of which such assistance is being received.

(4) In the case of a person who has ceased carrying on the commercial activity in respect of which assistance was received as specified in sub-paragraph (3), the assets relating to that activity for such period as may be reasonable in the circumstances to allow for disposal of any such asset.

9.–(1) Subject to sub-paragraph (2), any arrears of, or any concessionary payment made to compensate for arrears due to the non-payment of–

(a) any payment specified in paragraphs 7, 9 or 10 of Schedule 4;

[² (b) an income-related benefit under Part 7 of the Act;]

(c) an income-based jobseeker's allowance;

(d) any discretionary housing payment paid pursuant to regulation 2(1) of the Discretionary Financial Assistance Regulations 2001;

(e) working tax credit and child tax credit [¹],

[³ (f) an income-related employment and support allowance,]

but only for a period of 52 weeks from the date of the receipt of arrears or of the concessionary payment.

(2) In a case where the total of any arrears and, if appropriate, any concessionary payment referred to in sub-paragraph (1) relating to one of the specified payments, benefits or allowances amounts to £5,000 or more (referred to in this sub-paragraph and in sub-paragraph (3) as "the relevant sum") and is–

(a) paid in order to rectify or to compensate for, an official error as defined in regulation 1(2) of the Decisions and Appeals Regulations; and

(b) received by the claimant in full on or after 14th October 2001,

sub-paragraph (1) shall have effect in relation to such arrears or concessionary payment either for a period of 52 weeks from the date of receipt, or, if the relevant sum is received in its entirety during the award of council tax benefit, for the remainder of that award if that is a longer period.

(3) For the purposes of sub-paragraph (2), "the award of council tax benefit" means–

(a) the award in which the relevant sum is first received (or the first part thereof where it is paid in more than one instalment); and

(b) where that award is followed by one or more further awards which, or each of which, begins immediately after the end of the previous award, such further award provided that for that further award the claimant–

(i) is the person who received the relevant sum; or

(ii) is the partner of the person who received the relevant sum, or was that person's partner at the date of his death.

Amendments

1. Amended by reg 3(13) of SI 2005 No 2502 as amended by Sch 2 para 27 of SI 2006 No 217 as from 1.4.06.

2. Substituted by reg 7(6)(a) of SI 2008 No 698 as from 14.4.08.

3. Inserted by reg 63(b) of SI 2008 No 1082 as from 27.10.08.

---

10. Any sum–

(a) paid to the claimant in consequence of damage to, or loss of the home or any personal possession and intended for its repair or replacement; or

(b) acquired by the claimant (whether as a loan or otherwise) on the express condition that it is to be used for effecting essential repairs or improvement to the home,

which is to be used for the intended purpose, for a period of 26 weeks from the date on which it was so paid or acquired or such longer period as is reasonable in the circumstances to effect the repairs, replacement or improvement.

11. Any sum–

(a) deposited with a housing association as defined in section 1(1) of the Housing Associations Act 1985 or section 338(1) of the Housing (Scotland) Act 1987 as a condition of occupying the home;

(b) which was so deposited and which is to be used for the purchase of another home, for the period of 26 weeks or such longer period as may be reasonable in the circumstances to enable the claimant to complete the purchase.

12. Any personal possessions except those which have been acquired by the claimant with the intention of reducing his capital in order to secure entitlement to council tax benefit or to increase the amount of that benefit.

13. The value of the right to receive any income under an annuity or the surrender value (if any) of such an annuity.

14.   Where the funds of a trust are derived from a payment made in consequence of any personal injury to the claimant [¹ or claimant's partner], the value of the trust fund and the value of the right to receive any payment under that trust.

Amendment

1.   Amended by reg 17(6)(a) of SI 2006 No 2378 from the first day of the first benefit week to commence on or after 2.10.06.

[¹**14A.**–(1)   Any payment made to the claimant or the claimant's partner in consequence of any personal injury to the claimant or, as the case may be, the claimant's partner.

(2)   But sub-paragraph (1)–

(a)   applies only for the period of 52 weeks beginning with the day on which the claimant first receives any payment in consequence of that personal injury;

(b)   does not apply to any subsequent payment made to him in consequence of that injury (whether it is made by the same person or another);

(c)   ceases to apply to the payment or any part of the payment from the day on which the claimant no longer possesses it;

(d)   does not apply to any payment from a trust where the funds of the trust are derived from a payment made in consequence of any personal injury to the claimant.

(3)   For the purposes of sub-paragraph (2)(c), the circumstances in which a claimant no longer possesses a payment or a part of it include where the claimant has used a payment or part of it to purchase an asset.

(4)   References in sub-paragraphs (2) and (3) to the claimant are to be construed as including references to his partner (where applicable).]

Amendment

1.   Inserted by reg 17(6)(b) of SI 2006 No 2378 from the first day of the first benefit week to commence on or after 2.10.06.

---

15.   The value of the right to receive any income under a life interest or from a life rent.

16.   The value of the right to receive any income which is disregarded under paragraph 13 of Schedule 3 or paragraph 25 of Schedule 4.

17.   The surrender value of any policy of life insurance.

18.   Where any payment of capital falls to be made by instalments, the value of the right to receive any outstanding instalments.

19.   Any payment made by a local authority in accordance with section 17, [¹ 23B,] 23C or 24A of the Children Act 1989 or, as the case may be, section 12 of the Social Work (Scotland) Act 1968 or sections [² 22,] [¹ 29] or 30 of the Children (Scotland) Act 1995 (provision of services for children and their families and advice and assistance to certain children).

Amendments

1.   Amended by reg 8(10)(a) of SI 2008 No 2767 as from 17.11.08.

2.   Inserted by reg 9(4) of SI 2010 No 2429 as from 1.11.10.

[¹**19A.**–(1)   Subject to sub-paragraph (2), any payment (or part of a payment) made by a local authority in accordance with section 23C of the Children Act 1989 or section 29 of the Children (Scotland) Act 1995 (local authorities' duty to promote welfare of children and powers to grant financial assistance to persons in, or formerly in, their care) to a person (''A'') which A passes on to the claimant.

(2)   Sub-paragraph (1) applies only where A–

(a)   was formerly in the claimant's care, and

(b)   is aged 18 or over, and

(c)   continues to live with the claimant.]

Amendment

1.   Inserted by reg 7(6)(b) of SI 2008 No 698 as from, as it relates to a particular beneficiary, the first day of the benefit week on or after 7.4.08.

---

20.   Any social fund payment made pursuant to Part 8 of the Act.

21.   Any refund of tax which falls to be deducted under section 369 of the Income and Corporation Taxes Act 1988 (deduction of tax from certain loan interest) on a payment of relevant loan interest for the purpose of acquiring an interest in the home or carrying out repairs or improvements to the home.

22.   Any capital which by virtue of regulation 31 or 51 (capital treated as income, treatment of student loans) is to be treated as income.

23.   Where any payment of capital is made in a currency other than sterling, any banking charge or commission payable in converting that payment into sterling.

24.–(1)   Any payment made under [³ or by] the Trusts, the Fund, the Eileen Trust [³, MFET Limited], the Independent Living [¹ Fund (2006)], the Skipton Funds or the London Bombings Relief [² Charitable] Fund.

(2)   Any payment by or on behalf of a person who is suffering or who suffered from haemophilia or who is or was a qualifying person, which derives from a payment made under [³ or by] any of the Trusts to which sub-paragraph (1) refers and which is made to or for the benefit of–

(a)   that person's partner or former partner from whom he is not, or where that person has died was not, estranged or divorced or with whom he has formed a civil partnership that has not been dissolved or, where that person has died, had not been dissolved at the time of that person's death;

(b)   any child who is a member of that person's family or who was such a member and who is a member of the claimant's family; or

(c)   any young person who is a member of that person's family or who was such a member and who is a member of the claimant's family.

(3)   Any payment by or on behalf of the partner or former partner of a person who is suffering or who suffered from haemophilia or who is or was a qualifying person provided that the partner or former partner and that person are not, or if either of them has died were not, estranged or divorced or, where the partner or former partner and that person have formed a civil partnership, the civil partnership has not been dissolved or, if either of them has died, had not been dissolved at the time of the death, which derives from a payment made under [³ or by] any of the Trusts to which sub-paragraph (1) refers and which is made to or for the benefit of–

(a)   the person who is suffering from haemophilia or who is a qualifying person;

(b)   any child who is a member of that person's family or who was such a member and who is a member of the claimant's family; or

(c)   any young person who is a member of that person's family or who was such a member and who is a member of the claimant's family.

(4)   Any payment by a person who is suffering from haemophilia or who is a qualifying person, which derives from a payment under [³ or by] any of the Trusts to which sub-paragraph (1) refers, where–

(a)   that person has no partner or former partner from whom he is not estranged or divorced or with whom he has formed a civil partnership that has not been dissolved, nor any child or young person who is or had been a member of that person's family; and

(b)   the payment is made either–

(i)   to that person's parent or step-parent; or

(ii)   where that person at the date of the payment is a child, a young person or a student who has not completed his full-time education and has no parent or step-parent, to his guardian,

but only for a period from the date of the payment until the end of two years from that person's death.

(5)   Any payment out of the estate of a person who suffered from haemophilia or who was a qualifying person, which derives from a payment under [³ or by] any of the Trusts to which sub-paragraph (1) refers, where–

(a)   that person at the date of his death (the relevant date) had no partner or former partner from whom he was not estranged or divorced or with whom he had formed a civil partnership that had not been dissolved, nor any child or young person who was or had been a member of his family; and

(b)   the payment is made either–

(i)   to that person's parent or step-parent; or

(ii)   where that person at the relevant date was a child, a young person or a student who had not completed his full-time education and had no parent or step-parent, to his guardian,

but only for a period of two years from the relevant date.

(6)   In the case of a person to whom or for whose benefit a payment referred to in this paragraph is made, any capital resource which derives from any payment of income or capital made under or deriving from any of the Trusts.

(7)   For the purposes of sub-paragraphs (2) to (6), any reference to the Trusts shall be construed as including a reference to the Fund, the Eileen Trust [³ , MFET Limited], the Skipton Fund, and the London Bombings Relief Charitable Fund.

Modifications

References to "step-parent" in sub-paras (4)(b)(i) and (ii) and (5)(b)(i) and (ii) are modified by s246 Civil Partnership Act 2004 (see p1148) and art 3 and para 46 of the Sch to SI 2005 No.3137 (see p1195).

Amendments

1.   Amended by reg 8(4)(h) of SI 2008 No 2767 as from 17.11.08.

2.   Amended by reg 7(6)(b) of Si 2008 No 3157 as from 5.1.09.

3.   Amended by reg 10(3) and (5) of SI 2010 No 641 as from 1.4.10 (5.4.10 where rent payable weekly or in multiples of a week).

25.–(1)   Where a claimant has ceased to occupy what was formerly the dwelling occupied as the home following his estrangement or divorce from, or dissolution of his civil partnership with, his former partner, that dwelling for a period of 26 weeks from the date on which he ceased to occupy that dwelling or, where the dwelling is occupied as the home by the former partner who is a lone parent, for so long as it is so occupied.

(2)   In this paragraph "dwelling" includes any garage, garden and outbuildings, which were formerly occupied by the claimant as his home and any premises not so occupied which it is impracticable or unreasonable to sell separately, in particular, in Scotland, any croft land on which the dwelling is situated.

Analysis

Note that unlike for HB, there is a definition of "estranged". It is found in reg 2(5) (see p652).

---

26.   Any premises where the claimant is taking reasonable steps to dispose of those premises, for a period of 26 weeks from the date on which he first took such steps, or such longer period as is reasonable in the circumstances to enable him to dispose of those premises.

27.   Any premises which the claimant intends to occupy as his home, and in respect of which he is taking steps to obtain possession and has sought legal advice, or has commenced legal proceedings, with a view to obtaining possession, for a period of 26 weeks from the date on which he first sought such advice or first commenced such proceedings whichever is the earlier, or such longer period as is reasonable in the circumstances to enable him to obtain possession and commence occupation of those premises.

28.   Any premises which the claimant intends to occupy as his home to which essential repairs or alterations are required in order to render them fit for such occupation, for a period of 26 weeks from the date on which the claimant first takes steps to effect those repairs or alterations, or such longer period as is necessary to enable those repairs or alterations to be carried out.

29.   Any payment made by the Secretary of State to compensate for the loss (in whole or in part) of entitlement to housing benefit.

    [¹**30.**]

Amendment

1.   Omitted by reg 7(6)(c) of SI 2008 No 698 as from 14.4.08.

---

31.   The value of the right to receive an occupational or personal pension.

32.   The value of any funds held under a personal pension scheme [¹].

Amendment

1.   Amended by reg 6(7) of SI 2007 No 1749 as from 16.7.07.

---

33.   The value of the right to receive any rent except where the claimant has a reversionary interest in the property in respect of which rent is due.

34.   Any payment in kind made by a charity or under [³ or by] the Trusts, [¹ the Fund [³ , MFET Limited] [²] or the Independent Living Fund (2006)].

Amendments

1.   Amended by Art 9(3) of SI 2007 No 2538 as from 1.10.07.
2.   Amended by reg 8(10)(b) of SI 2008 No 2767 as from 17.11.08.
3.   Amended by reg 10(3), (5) and (12) of SI 2010 No 641 as from 1.4.10 (5.4.10 where rent payable weekly or in multiples of a week).

---

35.   Any payment made pursuant to section 2 of the 1973 Act or section 2 of the Enterprise and New Towns (Scotland) Act 1990, but only for the period of 52 weeks beginning on the date of receipt of the payment.

    [¹ **36.**]

Amendment

1.   Omitted by reg 8(10)(c) of SI 2008 No 2767 as from 17.11.08.

---

37.   Any payment in consequence of a reduction of council tax under section 13 or, as the case may be, section 80 of the Local Government Finance Act 1992 (reduction of liability for council tax), but only for a period of 52 weeks from the date of the receipt of the payment.

38.   Any grant made in accordance with a scheme made under section 129 of the Housing Act 1988 or section 66 of the Housing (Scotland) Act 1988 (schemes for payments to assist local housing authority and local authority tenants to obtain other accommodation) which is to be used–

(a)   to purchase premises intended for occupation as his home; or

(b)   to carry out repairs or alterations which are required to render premises fit for occupation as his home,

for a period of 26 weeks from the date on which he received such a grant or such longer period as is reasonable in the circumstances to enable the purchase, repairs or alterations to be completed and the claimant to commence occupation of those premises as his home.

[¹**39.**   Any arrears of supplementary pension which is disregarded under paragraph 53 of Schedule 4 (sums to be disregarded in the calculation of income other than earnings) or of any amount which is disregarded under paragraph 54 or 55 of that Schedule, but only for a period of 52 weeks from the date of receipt of the arrears.]

Amendment

1.   Substituted by reg 7(6)(c) of SI 2008 No 3157 as from 5.1.09.

[²**40.**–(1)   Any payment or repayment made–
(a)   as respects England, under regulation 5, 6 or 12 of the National Health Service (Travel Expenses and Remission of Charges) Regulations 2003 (travelling expenses and health service supplies);
(b)   as respects Wales, under regulation 5, 6 or 11 of the National Health Service (Travelling Expenses and Remission of Charges) (Wales) Regulations 2007 (travelling expenses and health service supplies);
(c)   as respects Scotland, under regulation 3, 5 or 11 of the National Health Service (Travelling Expenses and Remission of Charges) (Scotland) (No. 2) Regulations 2003 (travelling expenses and health service supplies),
but only for a period of 52 weeks from the date of receipt of the payment or repayment.
(2)   Any payment or repayment made by the Secretary of State for Health, the Scottish Ministers or the Welsh Ministers which is analogous to a payment or repayment mentioned in sub-paragraph (1), but only for a period of 52 weeks from the date of receipt of the payment or repayment.]

Amendments

1.   Amended by reg 5(13)(a)-(c) of SI 2008 No 1042 as from 19.5.08.
2.   Substituted by reg 7(6)(c) of SI 2008 No 3157 as from 5.1.09.

[²**41.**   Any payment made to such persons entitled to receive benefits as may be determined by or under a scheme made pursuant to section 13 of the Social Security Act 1988 in lieu of vouchers or similar arrangements in connection with the provision of those benefits (including payments made in place of healthy start vouchers, milk tokens or the supply of vitamins), but only for a period of 52 weeks from the date of receipt of the payment.]

Amendments

1.   Amended by reg 5(13)(d) of SI 2008 No 1042 as from 19.5.08.
2.   Substituted by reg 7(6)(c) of SI 2008 No 3157 as from 5.1.09.

[¹**41A.**   Any payment made under Part 8A of the Act (entitlement to health in pregnancy grant).]

Amendment

1.   Inserted by reg 8(13)(a) of SI 2009 No 583 as from, for any particular claimant, the first day of the first benefit week starting on or after 6.4.09.

42.   Any payment made either by the Secretary of State for [¹ the Justice] or by Scottish Ministers under a scheme established to assist relatives and other persons to visit persons in custody, but only for a period of 52 weeks from the date of the receipt of the payment.

Amendment

1.   Amended by Art 8 and the Sch para 24 of SI 2007 No 2128 as from 22.8.07.

43.   Any payment (other than a training allowance) made, whether by the Secretary of State or any other person, under the Disabled Persons (Employment) Act 1944 [¹] to assist disabled persons to obtain or retain employment despite their disability.

Amendment

1.   Amended by reg 5(13)(e) of SI 2008 No 1042 as from 19.5.08.

[¹**44.**]

Amendment

1.   Omitted by reg 7(6)(c) of SI 2008 No 698 as from 14.4.08.

45.   Any payment made by a local authority under section 3 of the Disabled Persons (Employment) Act 1958 to homeworkers assisted under the Blind Homeworkers' Scheme.
46.–(1)   Subject to sub-paragraph (2), where a claimant satisfies the conditions in section 131(3) and (6) of the Act (entitlement to alternative maximum council tax benefit), the whole of his capital.

(2)   Where in addition to satisfying the conditions in section 131(3) and (6) of the Act the claimant also satisfies the conditions in section 131(4) and (5) of the Act (entitlement to the maximum council tax benefit), sub-paragraph (1) shall not have effect.

[¹**47.**–(1)   Any sum of capital to which sub-paragraph (2) applies and–
(a)   which is administered on behalf of a person by the High Court or the County Court under Rule 21.11(1) of the Civil Procedure Rules 1998 or by the Court of Protection;
(b)   which can only be disposed of by order or direction of any such court; or
(c)   where the person concerned is under the age of 18, which can only be disposed of by order or direction prior to that person attaining age 18.
(2)   This sub-paragraph applies to a sum of capital which is derived from–
(a)   an award of damages for a personal injury to that person; or
(b)   compensation for the death of one or both parents where the person concerned is under the age of 18.]

Amendment

1.   Substituted by reg 17(6)(c) of SI 2006 No 2378 from the first day of the first benefit week to commence on or after 2.10.06.

48.   Any sum of capital administered on behalf of a person in accordance with an order made under section 13 of the Children (Scotland) Act 1995, or under Rule 36.14 of the Ordinary Cause Rules 1993 or under Rule 128 of those Rules, where such sum derives from–
(a)   award of damages for a personal injury to that person; or
(b)   compensation for the death of one or both parents where the person concerned is under the age of 18.

49.   Any payment to the claimant as holder of the Victoria Cross or George Cross.

50.   The amount of any child maintenance bonus payable by way of jobseeker's allowance or income support in accordance with section 10 of the Child Support Act 1995, or a corresponding payment under Article 4 of the Child Support (Northern Ireland) Order 1995, but only for a period of 52 weeks from the date of receipt.

51.   In the case of a person who is receiving, or who has received, assistance under the self-employment route, any sum of capital which is acquired by that person for the purpose of establishing or carrying on the commercial activity in respect of which such assistance is or was received but only for a period of 52 weeks from the date on which that sum was acquired.

52.–(1)   Any payment of a sports award for a period of 26 weeks from the date of receipt of that payment except to the extent that it has been made in respect of any one or more of the items specified in sub-paragraph (2).
(2)   The items specified for the purposes of sub-paragraph (1) are food, ordinary clothing or footwear, household fuel or rent of the claimant or, where the claimant is a member of a family, any other member of his family, or any council tax or water charges for which that claimant or member is liable.
(3)   For the purposes of sub-paragraph (2) ''food'' does not include vitamins, minerals or other special dietary supplements intended to enhance the performance of the person in the sport in respect of which the award was made.

53.–(1)   Any payment–
(a)   by way of an education maintenance allowance made pursuant to–
       (i)   regulations made under section 518 of the Education Act 1996;
       (ii)   regulations made under section 49 or 73(f) of the Education (Scotland) Act 1980;
       [¹ (iii) directions made under section 73ZA of the Education (Scotland) Act 1980 and paid under section 12(2)(c) of the Further and Higher Education (Scotland) Act 1992; or]
(b)   corresponding to such an education maintenance allowance, made pursuant to–
       (i)   section 14 or section 181 of the Education Act 2002 (power of Secretary of State and National Assembly for Wales to give financial assistance for purposes related to education or childcare, and allowances in respect of education or training); or
       (ii)   regulations made under section 181 of that Act.
(2)   Any payment, other than a payment to which sub-paragraph (1) applies, made pursuant to–
(a)   regulations made under section 518 of the Education Act 1996;
(b)   regulations made under section 49 of the Education (Scotland) Act 1980; or
[¹ (c) directions made under section 73ZA of the Education (Scotland) Act 1980 and paid under section 12(2)(c) of the Further and Higher Education (Scotland) Act 1992,]
in respect of a course of study attended by a child or a young person or a person who is in receipt of an education maintenance allowance made pursuant to any provision specified in sub-paragraph (1).

Amendment

1.   Amended by reg 7(6)(d) of SI 2008 No 3157 as from 5.1.09.

54.   In the case of a claimant participating in an employment zone programme, any discretionary payment made by an employment zone contractor to the claimant, being a fee, grant, loan or otherwise, but only for the period of 52 weeks from the date of receipt of the payment.

55.   Any arrears of subsistence allowance paid as a lump sum but only for the period of 52 weeks from the date of receipt of the payment.

56.   Where an ex-gratia payment of £10,000 has been made by the Secretary of State on or after 1st February 2001 in consequence of the imprisonment or interment of–

(a)   the claimant;

(b)   the claimant's partner;

(c)   the claimant's deceased spouse or deceased civil partner; or

(d)   the claimant's partner's deceased spouse or deceased civil partner,

by the Japanese during the Second World War, £10,000.

57.–(1)   Subject to sub-paragraph (2), the amount of any trust payment made to a claimant or a member of a claimant's family who is–

(a)   a diagnosed person;

(b)   the diagnosed person's partner or the person who was the diagnosed person's partner at the [² date] of the diagnosed person's death;

(c)   a parent of a diagnosed person, a person acting in place of the diagnosed person's parents or a person who was so acting at the date of the diagnosed person's death; or

(d)   a member of the diagnosed person's family (other than his partner) or a person who was a member of the diagnosed person's family (other than his partner) at the date of the diagnosed person's death.

(2)   Where a trust payment is made to–

(a)   a person referred to in sub-paragraph (1)(a) or (b), that sub-paragraph shall apply for the period beginning on the date on which the trust [³ payment] is made and ending on the date on which that person dies;

(b)   a person referred to in sub-paragraph (1)(c), that sub-paragraph shall apply for the period beginning on the date on which the trust payment is made and ending two years after that date;

(c)   a person referred to in sub-paragraph (1)(d), that sub-paragraph shall apply for the period beginning on the date on which the trust payment is made and ending–

    (i)   two years after that date; or

    (ii)   on the day before the day on which that person–

        (aa)   ceases receiving full-time education; or

        (bb)   attains the age of [¹ 20],

    whichever is the latest.

(3)   Subject to sub-paragraph (4), the amount of any payment by a person to whom a trust payment has been made or of any payment out of the estate of a person to whom a trust payment has been made, which is made to a claimant or a member of a claimant's family who is–

(a)   the diagnosed person's partner or the person who was the diagnosed person's partner at the date of the diagnosed person's death;

(b)   a parent of a diagnosed person, a person acting in place of the diagnosed person's parents or a person who was so acting at the date of the diagnosed person's death; or

(c)   a member of the diagnosed person's family (other than his partner) or a person who was a member of the diagnosed person's family (other than his partner) at the date of the diagnosed person's death,

but only to the extent that such payments do not exceed the total amount of any trust payments made to that person.

(4)   Where a payment as referred to in sub-paragraph (3) is made to–

(a)   a person referred to in sub-paragraph (3)(a), that sub-paragraph shall apply for the period beginning on the date on which that payment is made and ending on the date on which that person dies;

(b)   a person referred to in sub-paragraph (3)(b), that sub-paragraph shall apply for the period beginning on the date on which that payment is made and ending two years after that date; or

(c)   person referred to in sub-paragraph (3)(c), that sub-paragraph shall apply for the period beginning on the date on which that payment is made and ending–

    (i)   two years after that date; or

    (ii)   on the day before the day on which that person–

        (aa)   ceases receiving full-time education; or

        (bb)   attains the age of [¹ 20],

    whichever is the latest.

(5)   In this paragraph, a reference to a person–

(a)   being the diagnosed person's partner;

(b)   being a member of a diagnosed person's family;

(c)   acting in place of the diagnosed person's parents,

at the date of the diagnosed person's death shall include a person who would have been such a person or a person who would have been so acting, but for the diagnosed person residing in a care home, an Abbeyfield Home or an independent hospital on that date.

(6)   In this paragraph–

"diagnosed person" means a person who has been diagnosed as suffering from, or who, after his death, has been diagnosed as having suffered from, variant Creutzfeld-Jakob disease;

''relevant trust'' means a trust established out of funds provided by the Secretary of State in respect of persons who suffered, or who are suffering, from variant Creutzfeld-Jakob disease for the benefit of persons eligible for payments in accordance with its provisions;

''trust payment'' means a payment under a relevant trust.

Amendments

1. Amended by reg 5(5) of SI 2006 No 718 as from 10.4.06.
2. Amended by reg 5(13)(f) of SI 2008 No 1042 as from 19.5.08.
3. Amended by reg 7(6)(f) of SI 2008 No 3157 as from 5.1.09.

58. The amount of any payment, other than a war pension [¹], to compensate for the fact that the claimant, the claimant's partner, the claimant's deceased spouse or deceased civil partner or the claimant's partner's deceased spouse or deceased civil partner–

(a)   was a slave labourer or a forced labourer;

(b)   had suffered property loss or had suffered personal injury; or

(c)   was a parent of a child who had died,

during the Second World War.

Amendment

1. Amended by reg 7(6)(g) of SI 2008 No 3157 as from 5.1.09.

59.–(1) Any payment made by a local authority, or by the [¹ Welsh Ministers], to or on behalf of the claimant or his partner relating to a service which is provided to develop or sustain the capacity of the claimant or his partner to live independently in his accommodation.

(2)   For the purposes of sub-paragraph (1) ''local authority'' includes in England a county council.

Amendment

1. Amended by reg 7(6)(h) of SI 2008 No 3157 as from 5.1.09.

60. Any payment made under [¹] regulations made under section 57 of the Health and Social Care Act 2001 or under section 12B of the Social Work (Scotland) Act 1968.

Amendment

1. Amended by reg 8(13)(b) of SI 2009 No 583 as from 6.4.09.

61. Any payment made to the claimant pursuant to regulations under section 2(6)(b), 3 or 4 of the Adoption and Children Act 2002.

62. Any payment made to the claimant in accordance with regulations made pursuant to section 14F of the Children Act 1989 (special guardianship support services).

[¹ SCHEDULE 6]

Amendment

1. Omitted by reg 9(5)(d) of SI 2008 No 959 as from 6.10.08.

[¹ SCHEDULE 7]

Amendment

1. Omitted by reg 9(5)(e) of SI 2008 No 959 as from 6.10.08.

SCHEDULE 8
REGULATION 76(1)
Matters to be included in decision notice

PART 1
General

1. The statement of matters to be included in any decision notice issued by a relevant authority to a person, and referred to in regulation 76 (notification of decisions) and in regulation 10 of the Decisions and Appeals Regulations are those matters set out in the following provisions of this Schedule.

2. Every decision notice shall include a statement as to the right of any person affected by that decision to request a written statement under regulation 76(2) (requests for statement of reasons) and the manner and time in which to do so.

3. Every decision notice shall include a statement as to the right of any person affected by that decision to make an application for a revision in accordance with regulation 4(1)(a) of the Decisions and Appeals Regulations and, where appropriate, to appeal against that decision and the manner and time in which to do so.

4. Every decision notice following an application for a revision in accordance with regulation 4(1)(a) of the Decisions and Appeals Regulations shall include a statement as to whether the original decision in respect of which the person made his representations has been confirmed or revised and where the relevant authority has not revised the decision the reasons why not.

5. Every decision notice following an application for a revision in accordance with regulation 4(1)(a) of the Decisions and Appeals Regulations shall, if the original decision has been revised, include a statement as to the right of any person affected by that decision to apply for a revision in accordance with regulation 4(1)(a) of those Regulations and the manner and time in which to do so.

6. An authority may include in the decision notice any other matters not prescribed by this Schedule which it sees fit, whether expressly or by reference to some other document available without charge to the person.

7. Parts 2, 3 and 4 of this Schedule shall apply only to the decision notice given on a claim.

8. Where a decision notice is given following a revision of an earlier decision–

(a) made of the authority's own motion which results in a revision of that earlier decision; or

(b) made following an application for a revision in accordance with regulation 4(1)(a) of the Decisions and Appeals Regulations, whether or not resulting in a revision of that earlier decision,

that notice shall, subject to paragraph 6, contain a statement only as to all the matters revised.

PART 2
Awards where income support [² , an income-based jobseeker's allowance or an income-related employment and support allowance][¹ , an extended payment or an extended payment (qualifying contributory benefits)] is payable

9. Where a person on income support [² , an income-based jobseeker's allowance or an income-related employment and support allowance] is awarded council tax benefit [¹ or a claimant is entitled to an extended payment in accordance with regulation 60 or an extended payment (qualifying contributory benefits) in accordance with regulation 61], the decision notice shall include a statement as to–

(a) his normal weekly amount of council tax which may be rounded to the nearest penny;

(b) the normal weekly amount of the council tax benefit, which amount may be rounded to the nearest penny;

(c) the amount of and the category of non-dependant deductions made under regulation 58, if any;

(d) the first day of entitlement to the council tax benefit;

(e) his duty to notify any change of circumstances which might affect his entitlement to, or the amount of council tax benefit and, without prejudice to the extent of the duty owed under regulation 74 (duty to notify changes of circumstances) the kind of change of circumstances which is to be notified, either upon the notice or by reference to some other document available to him on application and without charge,

and in any case where the amount to which sub-paragraph (a) or (b) refers disregards fractions of a penny, the notice shall include a statement to that effect.

Amendments

1. Amended by reg 9(6) of SI 2008 No 959 as from 6.10.08.
2. Amended by reg 64(a) of SI 2008 No 1082 as from 27.10.08.

PART 3
Awards where no income support [¹ , an income-based jobseeker's allowance or an income-related employment and support allowance] is payable

10. Where a person is not on income support [² , an income-based jobseeker's allowance or an income-related employment and support allowance] but is awarded council tax benefit, the decision notice shall include a statement as to–

(a) the matters set out in paragraph 9;

(b) his applicable amount and how it is calculated;

(c) his weekly earnings; and

(d) his weekly income other than earnings.

Amendment

1. Amended by reg 64(b) of SI 2008 No 1082 as from 27.10.08.

PART 4
Notice where income of non-dependant is treated as claimant's income

11. Where an authority makes a decision under regulation 16 (circumstances in which income and capital of a non-dependant is to be treated as claimant's) the decision notice shall contain a statement as to–

(a)   the fact that a decision has been made by reference to the income and capital of the claimant's non-dependant; and

(b)   the relevant authority's reasons for making that decision.

PART 5
Notice where no award is made

12.   Where a person is not awarded council tax benefit under regulation 57 (maximum council tax benefit)–

(a)   on grounds of income, the decision notice shall include a statement as to–

    (i)   the matters set out in paragraphs 9(a); and

    (ii)   the matters set out in paragraphs 10(b) to (d) where the person is not on income support [¹ , an income-based jobseeker's allowance or on an income-related employment and support allowance];

(b)   on the grounds that the amount of the alternative maximum council tax benefit exceeds the appropriate maximum council tax benefit, the matters set our in paragraph 15;

(c)   for any reason other than one mentioned in sub-paragraphs (a) and (b), the decision notice shall include a statement as to the reason why no award has been made.

Amendment

1.   Amended by reg 64(c) of SI 2008 No 1082 as from 27.10.08.

PART 6
Awards where alternative maximum council tax benefit is payable in respect of a day

13.   Where a person is awarded council tax benefit determined in accordance with regulation 62 and Schedule 2 (alternative maximum council tax benefit) the decision notice shall include a statement as to–

(a)   the normal weekly amount of council tax, which amount may be rounded to the nearest penny;

(b)   the normal weekly amount of the alternative maximum council tax benefit, which amount may be rounded to the nearest penny;

(c)   the gross income or incomes and the rate of benefit which apply under Schedule 2;

(d)   the first day of entitlement to benefit;

(e)   the gross income of any second adult used to determine the rate of the alternative maximum council tax benefit or if any such adult is on income support [¹ , an income-related employment and support allowance], state pension credit or an income-based jobseeker's allowance;

(f)   the claimant's duty to notify any change of circumstances which might affect his entitlement to, or the amount of the alternative maximum council tax benefit and, without prejudice to the extent of the duty owed under regulation 74 (duty to notify changes of circumstances) the kind of change of circumstances which are to be notified, either upon the notice or by reference to some other document available to the claimant free of charge on application,

and in any case where the amount to which sub-paragraph (a) or (b) refers disregards fractions of a penny, the notice shall include a statement to that effect.

Amendment

1.   Amended by reg 64(d) of SI 2008 No 1082 as from 27.10.08.

Notice where no award of alternative maximum council tax benefit is made

14.   Where a person is not awarded council tax benefit in accordance with regulation 62 and Schedule 2 (alternative maximum council tax benefit)–

(a)   on the grounds that the gross income or as the case may be the aggregate gross incomes, of any second adult or adults in the claimant's dwelling is too high, the decision notice shall include a statement as to the matters set out in paragraphs 13(a), (c) and (e);

(b)   on the grounds that the appropriate maximum council tax benefit is higher than the alternative maximum council tax benefit, the decision notice shall include a statement as to the matters set out in paragraph 15 below;

(c)   for any reason not referred to in sub-paragraphs (a) and (b), the decision notice shall include a statement as to why no award has been made.

Notice where council tax benefit is awarded and section 131(9) of the Act applies

15.   Where the amount of a claimant's council tax benefit in respect of a day is the greater of the appropriate maximum council tax benefit and the alternative maximum council tax benefit in his case the notice shall in addition to the matters set out in paragraphs 9, 10 or 13, as the case may be, include a statement as to–

(a)   the amount of whichever is the lesser of the appropriate maximum council tax benefit or the alternative maximum council tax benefit in his case, which amount may be rounded to the nearest penny; and

(b)   that this amount has not been awarded in consequence of the award of council tax benefit at a higher rate, and in any case where the amount to which sub-paragraph (a) refers disregards fractions of a penny, the notice shall include a statement to that effect.

PART 7
Notice where there is recoverable excess benefit

16.–(1)   Except in cases to which paragraphs (a) and (b) of regulation 82 (excess benefit in consequence of a reduction in a relevant authority's council tax) refers, where the relevant authority makes a decision that there is recoverable excess benefit within the meaning of regulation 83 (recoverable excess benefits), the decision notice shall include a statement as to–

(a)   the fact that there is recoverable excess benefit;
(b)   the reason why there is recoverable excess benefit;
(c)   the amount of recoverable excess benefit;
(d)   how the amount of recoverable excess benefit was calculated;
(e)   the benefit weeks to which the recoverable excess benefit relates; and
(f)   the method or combination of methods by which the authority intends to recover the recoverable excess benefit, including–

(i)   payment by or on behalf of the person concerned of the amount due by the specified date;
(ii)   addition of the amount due to any amount in respect of the tax concerned for payment whether by instalments or otherwise by the specified date or dates; or
(iii)   if recovery cannot be effected in accordance with heads (i) or (ii), requesting the Secretary of State to recover the excess benefits by deduction from the benefit prescribed in regulation 90 (recovery of excess benefits from prescribed benefits).

[¹SCHEDULE 9
ELECTRONIC COMMUNICATION

Amendment
1.   Inserted by Art 4(5) of SI 2006 No 2968 as from 20.12.06.

PART 1
Introduction

Interpretation
1.   In this Schedule "official computer system" means a computer system maintained by or on behalf of the relevant authority or of the Secretary of State for sending, receiving, processing or storing of any claim, certificate, notice, information or evidence.

PART 2
Electronic Communication – General Provisions

Conditions for the use of electronic communication
2.–(1)   The relevant authority may use an electronic communication in connection with claims for, and awards of, benefit under these Regulations.
(2)   A person other than the relevant authority may use an electronic communication in connection with the matters referred to in sub-paragraph (1) if the conditions specified in sub-paragraphs (3) to (6) are satisfied.
(3)   The first condition is that the person is for the time being permitted to use an electronic communication by an authorisation given by means of a direction of the Chief Executive of the relevant authority.
(4)   The second condition is that the person uses an approved method of–
(a)   authenticating the identity of the sender of the communication;
(b)   electronic communication;
(c)   authenticating any claim or notice delivered by means of an electronic communication; and
(d)   subject to sub-paragraph (7), submitting to the relevant authority any claim, certificate, notice, information or evidence.
(5)   The third condition is that any claim, certificate, notice, information or evidence sent by means of an electronic communication is in a form approved for the purposes of this Schedule.
(6)   The fourth condition is that the person maintains such records in written or electronic form as may be specified in a direction given by the Chief Executive of the relevant authority.
(7)   Where the person uses any method other than the method approved of submitting any claim, certificate, notice, information or evidence, that claim, certificate, notice, information or evidence shall be treated as not having been submitted.
(8)   In this paragraph "approved" means approved by means of a direction given by the Chief Executive of the relevant authority for the purposes of this Schedule.

Use of intermediaries
   3.   The relevant authority may use intermediaries in connection with–
  (a)   the delivery of any claim, certificate, notice, information or evidence by means of an electronic communication; and
  (b)   the authentication or security of anything transmitted by such means,
and may require other persons to use intermediaries in connection with those matters.

PART 3
Electronic Communication – Evidential Provisions

Effect of delivering information by means of electronic communication
   4.–(1)   Any claim, certificate, notice, information or evidence which is delivered by means of an electronic communication shall be treated as having been delivered in the manner or form required by any provision of these Regulations, on the day the conditions imposed–
  (a)   by this Schedule; and
  (b)   by or under an enactment,
are satisfied.
   (2)   The relevant authority may, by a direction, determine that any claim, certificate, notice, information or evidence is to be treated as delivered on a different day (whether earlier or later) from the day provided for in sub-paragraph (1).
   (3)   Information shall not be taken to have been delivered to an official computer system by means of an electronic communication unless it is accepted by the system to which it is delivered.

Proof of identity of sender or recipient of information
   5.   If it is necessary to prove, for the purpose of any legal proceedings, the identity of–
  (a)   the sender of any claim, certificate, notice, information or evidence delivered by means of an electronic communication to an official computer system; or
  (b)   the recipient of any such claim, certificate, notice, information or evidence delivered by means of an electronic communication from an official computer system,
the sender or recipient, as the case may be, shall be presumed to be the person whose name is recorded as such on that official computer system.

Proof of delivery of information
   6.–(1)   If it is necessary to prove, for the purpose of any legal proceedings, that the use of an electronic communication has resulted in the delivery of any claim, certificate, notice, information or evidence this shall be presumed to have been the case where–
  (a)   any such claim, certificate, notice, information or evidence has been delivered to the relevant authority, if the delivery of that claim, certificate, notice, information or evidence has been recorded on an official computer system; or
  (b)   any such claim, certificate, notice, information or evidence has been delivered by the relevant authority, if the delivery of that certificate, notice, information or evidence has been recorded on an official computer system.
   (2)   If it is necessary to prove, for the purpose of any legal proceedings, that the use of an electronic communication has resulted in the delivery of any such claim, certificate, notice, information or evidence, this shall be presumed not to be the case, if that claim, certificate, notice, information or evidence delivered to the relevant authority has not been recorded on an official computer system.
   (3)   If it is necessary to prove, for the purpose of any legal proceedings, when any such claim, certificate, notice, information or evidence sent by means of an electronic communication has been received, the time and date of receipt shall be presumed to be that recorded on an official computer system.

Proof of content of information
   7.   If it is necessary to prove, for the purpose of any legal proceedings, the content of any claim, certificate, notice, information or evidence sent by means of an electronic communication, the content shall be presumed to be that recorded on an official computer system.]

Part 4

Main secondary legislation for people over state pension credit age

The Housing Benefit (Persons who have attained the qualifying age for state pension credit) Regulations 2006

2006 No.214

ARRANGEMENT OF REGULATIONS

PART 1
GENERAL

1. Citation and commencement
2. Interpretation
3. Definition of non-dependant
4. Cases in which section 1(1A) of the Administration Act is disapplied
5. Persons who have attained the qualifying age for state pension credit
6. Remunerative work

PART 2
PROVISIONS AFFECTING ENTITLEMENT TO HOUSING BENEFIT

7. Circumstances in which a person is or is not to be treated as occupying a dwelling as his home
8. Circumstances in which a person is to be treated as liable to make payments in respect of a dwelling
9. Circumstances in which a person is to be treated as not liable to make payments in respect of a dwelling
10. Persons from abroad
10A. Entitlement of a refugee to Housing Benefit

PART 3
PAYMENTS IN RESPECT OF A DWELLING

11. Eligible housing costs
12. Rent
12B. Eligible rent
12C. Eligible rent and maximum rent
12D. Eligible rent and maximum rent (LHA)
12L. Transitional prorection – larger properties
13. Maximum rent
12ZA. Protection on death and 13 week protection
13ZB. Change in reckonable rent
13C. When a maximum rent (LHA) is to be determined
13D. Determination of a maximum rent (LHA)
13E. Publication of local housing allowances
14. Requirement to refer to rent officers
15. Application to the rent officer for redeterminations
16. Application for redeterrmination by a rent officer
17. Substitute determinations or substitute redeterminations
18. Application of provisions to substitute determinations or substitute redeterminations
18A. Amended determinations

PART 4
MEMBERSHIP OF A FAMILY

19. Persons of prescribed description
20. Circumstances in which a person is to be treated as responsible or not responsible for another
21. Circumstances in which a person is to be treated as being or not being a member of the household

PART 5
APPLICABLE AMOUNTS
22.   Applicable amounts

PART 6
ASSESSMENT OF INCOME AND CAPITAL
SECTION 1
General
23.   Calculation of income and capital of members of claimant's family and of a polygamous marriage
24.   Circumstances in which income of non-dependant is to be treated as claimant's

SECTION 2
Income
25.   Calculation of income and capital
26.   Claimant in receipt of guarantee credit
27.   Calculation of claimant's income and capital in savings credit only cases
28.   Calculation of income and capital where state pension credit is not payable
29.   Meaning of ''income''
30.   Calculation of income on a weekly basis
31.   Treatment of child care charges
32.   Calculation of average weekly income from tax credits
33.   Calculation of weekly income
34.   Disregard of changes in tax, contributions etc

SECTION 3
Employed earners
35.   Earnings of employed earners
36.   Calculation of net earnings of employed earners

SECTION 4
Self-employed earners
37.   Calculation of earnings of self-employed earners
38.   Earnings of self-employed earners
39.   Calculation of net profit of self-employed earners
40.   Deduction of tax and contributions of self-employed earners

SECTION 5
Other income
41.   Notional income
42.   Income paid to third parties

SECTION 6
Capital
43.   Capital limit
44.   Calculation of capital
45.   Calculation of capital in the United Kingdom
46.   Calculation of capital outside the United Kingdom
47.   Notional capital
48.   Diminishing notional capital rule
49.   Capital jointly held

PART 7
Amount of benefit
50.   Maximum housing benefit
51.   Housing benefit tapers

52. Amount payable during extended payment period when an extended payment is payable pursuant to regulation 72 or 73 of the Housing Benefit Regulations
53. Extended payments (qualifying contributory benefits)
53A. Duration of extended payment period (qualifying contributory benefits)
53B. Amount of extended payment (qualifying contributory benefits)
53C. Extended payments (qualifying contributory benefits) – movers
53D. Relationship between extended payment (qualifying contributory benefits) and entitlement to housing benefit under the general conditions of entitlement
54. Continuing payments where state pension credit claimed
55. Non-dependant deductions
56. Minimum housing benefit

PART 8
Calculation of weekly amounts and changes of circumstances
57. Date on which entitlement is to commence
58. Date on which housing benefit is to end where entitlement to severe disablement allowance or incapacity benefit ceases
59. Date on which change of circumstances is to take effect
60. Change of circumstances where state pension credit payable
61. Calculation of weekly amounts
62. Rent free periods

PART 9
Claims
63. Who may claim
64. Time and manner in which claims are to be made
64A. Electronic claims for benefit
65. Date of claim where claim sent or delivered to a gateway office
66. Date of claim where claim sent or delivered to an office of a designated authority
67. Evidence and information
68. Amendment and withdrawal of claim
69. Duty to notify changes of circumstances
69A. Notice of changes of circumstances given electronically

PART 10
Decisions on questions
70. Decisions by a relevant authority
71. Notification of decision

PART 11
Payments
72. Time and manner of payment
72A. Cases in which payments to a housing authority are to take the form of a rent allowance
73. Frequency of payment of a rent allowance
74. Payment on account of a rent allowance
75. Payment to be made to a person entitled
76. Circumstances in which payment is to be made to a landlord
77. Circumstances in which payment may be made to a landlord
78. Payment on death of the person entitled
79. Offsetting

PART 12
Overpayments
80. Meaning of overpayment

81.   Recoverable overpayments
82.   Person from whom recovery may be sought
83.   Method of recovery
84.   Diminution of capital
85.   Sums to be deducted in calculating recoverable overpayments
86.   Recovery of overpayments from prescribed benefits
87.   Prescribed benefits
88.   Restrictions on recovery of rent and consequent notifications

PART 13
Information
SECTION 1
Claims and information
89.   Interpretation
90.   Collection of information
90A.   Verifying information
91.   Recording and holding information
92.   Forwarding of information
93.   Request for information

SECTION 2
Evidence and Information
94.   Interpretation
95A.   Information to be provided to rent officers
95.   Evidence and information required by rent officers
96.   Information to be supplied by an authority to another authority
97.   Supply of information – extended payments (qualifying contributory benefits)
98.   Requiring information from landlords and agents
99.   Circumstances for requiring information
100.   Relevant information
101.   Manner of supply of information
102.   Criminal offence
102A.   Supply of benefit administration information between authorities

PART 14
FormerPathfinder authorities
103.   Modifications in respect of former pathfinder authorities

SCHEDULES
A1.   Treatment of claims for housing benefit by refugees
1.   Ineligible service charges
2.   Excluded Tenancies
3.   Applicable amounts
4.   Sums disregarded from claimant's earnings
5.   Amounts to be disregarded in the calculation of income other than earnings
6.   Capital to be disregarded
7.   Extended payments (severe disablement allowance and incapacity benefit) of housing benefit
8.   Matters to be included in decision notice
9.   Former pathfinder authorities
10.   Electronic communication

PART 1
General

General Note to the HB(SPC) Regs
These regulations, rather than the HB Regs, apply where the claimant has attained the qualifying age for PC, as defined in reg 2. However, they do not apply in relation to any claimant who remains (or whose partner remains) in receipt of IS, income-based JSA or income-related ESA: reg 5 (see p783). It is vital to note that receipt of PC by an HB claimant is not a requirement for these regulations to apply to her/him.

Citation and commencement
1.–(1)   These Regulations may be cited as the Housing Benefit (Persons who have attained the qualifying age for state pension credit) Regulations 2006.

(2)   These Regulations are to be read, where appropriate, with the Consequential Provisions Regulations.

(3)   Except as provided in Schedule 4 to the Consequential Provisions Regulations, these Regulations shall come into force on 6th March 2006.

(4)   The regulations consolidated by these Regulations are revoked, in consequence of the consolidation, by the Consequential Provisions Regulations.

Interpretation
2.–(1)   In these Regulations–

"the Act" means the Social Security Contributions and Benefits Act 1992;

"the 1973 Act" means the Employment and Training Act 1973;

[² "the 2000 Act" means the Electronic Communications Act 2000;]

"Abbeyfield Home" means an establishment run by the Abbeyfield Society including all bodies corporate or incorporate which are affiliated to that Society;

"adoption leave" means a period of absence from work on ordinary or additional adoption leave by virtue of section 75A or 75B of the Employment Rights Act 1996;

"the Administration Act" means the Social Security Administration Act 1992;

[¹⁰ "amended determination" means a determination made in accordance with article 7A of the Rent Officers Order;]

"appropriate DWP office" means an office of the Department for Work and Pensions dealing with state pension credit or an office which is normally open to the public for the receipt of claims for income support [¹⁶ , a jobseeker's allowance or an employment and support allowance];

"assessment period" means the period determined–

(a)   in relation to the earnings of a self-employed earner, in accordance with regulation 37 (calculation of earnings of self-employed earners) for the purpose of calculating the weekly earnings of the claimant; or

(b)   in relation to any other income, in accordance with regulation 33 (calculation of weekly income) for the purpose of calculating the weekly income of the claimant;

"attendance allowance" means–

(a)   an attendance allowance under Part 3 of the Act;

(b)   an increase of disablement pension under section 104 or 105 of the Act;

(c)   a payment under regulations made in exercise of the power conferred by paragraph 7(2)(b) of Part 2 of Schedule 8 to the Act;

(d)   an increase of an allowance which is payable in respect of constant attendance under paragraph 4 of Part 1 of Schedule 8 to the Act;

(e)   a payment by virtue of article 14, 15, 16, 43 or 44 of the Personal Injuries (Civilians) Scheme 1983 or any analogous payment; or

(f)   any payment based on need for attendance which is paid as part of a war disablement pension;

[²¹ "basic rate", where it relates to the rate of tax, has the same meaning as in the Income Tax Act 2007 (see section 989 of that Act);]

"the benefit Acts" means the Act, the Jobseekers Act [¹⁶ , the Welfare Reform Act] and the State Pension Credit Act;

"benefit week" means a period of 7 consecutive days commencing upon a Monday and ending on a Sunday;

"board and lodging accommodation" means accommodation provided to a person or, if he is a member of a family, to him or any other member of his family, for a charge which is inclusive of the provision of that accommodation and at least some cooked or prepared meals which both are cooked or prepared (by a person other than the person to whom the accommodation is provided or a member of his family) and are consumed in that accommodation or associated premises;

[10 "broad rental market area" has the meaning specified in paragraph 4 of Schedule 3B to the Rent Officers Order;]

[10 "broad rental market area determination" means a determination made in accordance with article 4B(1A) of the Rent Officers Order;]

"care home" in England and Wales has the meaning assigned to it by section 3 of the Care Standards Act 2000 and in Scotland means a care home service within the meaning assigned to it by section 2(3) of the Regulation of Care (Scotland) Act 2001;

[10 "change of dwelling" means, for the purposes of regulations 13C and 14, a change of dwelling occupied by a claimant as his home during the award where the dwelling to which the claimant has moved is one in respect of which the authority may make a rent allowance;]

"child" means a person under the age of 16;

"child tax credit" means a child tax credit under section 8 of the Tax Credits Act;

"the Children Order" means the Children (Northern Ireland) Order 1995;

"claim" means a claim for housing benefit;

"claimant" means a person claiming housing benefit;

"close relative" means a parent, parent-in-law, son, son-in-law, daughter, daughter-in-law, step-parent, step-son, step-daughter, brother, sister, or if any of the preceding persons is one member of a couple, the other member of that couple;

[19 "concessionary payment" means a payment made under arrangements made by the Secretary of State with the consent of the Treasury which is charged to a Departmental Expenditure Vote to which payments of benefit or tax credits under the benefit Acts or the Tax Credits Act are charged;]

"the Consequential Provisions Regulations" means the Housing Benefit and Council Tax Benefit (Consequential Provisions) Regulations 2006;

[17 "contributory employment and support allowance" means a contributory allowance under Part 1 of the Welfare Reform Act;]

"co-ownership scheme" means a scheme under which the dwelling is let by a housing association and the tenant, or his personal representative, will, under the terms of the tenancy agreement or of the agreement under which he became a member of the association, be entitled, on his ceasing to be a member and subject to any conditions stated in either agreement, to a sum calculated by reference directly or indirectly to the value of the dwelling;

"couple" means–

    (a)   a man and a woman who are married to each other and are members of the same household;

    (b)   a man and a woman who are not married to each other but are living together as husband and wife;

    (c)   two people of the same sex who are civil partners of each other and are members of the same household; or

    (d)   two people of the same sex who are not civil partners of each other but are living together as if they were civil partners,

    and for the purposes of sub-paragraph (d), two people of the same sex are to be regarded as living together as if they were civil partners if, but only if, they would be regarded as living together as husband and wife were they instead two people of the opposite sex;

"course of study" means any course of study, whether or not it is a sandwich course and whether or not a grant is made for undertaking or attending it;

"Crown tenant" means a person who occupies a dwelling under a tenancy or licence where the interest of the landlord belongs to Her Majesty in right of the Crown or to a government department or is held in trust for Her Majesty for the purposes of a government department, except (in the case of an interest belonging to Her Majesty in right of the Crown) where the interest is under the management of the Crown Estate Commissioners;

"date of claim" means the date on which the claim is made, or treated as made, for the purposes of regulation 64 (time and manner in which claims are to be made);

"the Decisions and Appeals Regulations" means the Housing Benefit and Council Tax Benefit (Decisions and Appeals) Regulations 2001;

"the designated authority" means any of the following–
  (a) the Secretary of State;
  (b) a person providing services to the Secretary of State;
  (c) a local authority;
  (d) a person providing services to, or authorised to exercise any function of, any such local authority;

"designated office" means the office designated by the relevant authority for the receipt of claims to housing benefit–
  (a) by notice upon or with a form approved by it for the purpose of claiming housing benefit; or
  (b) by reference upon or with such a form to some other document available from it and sent by electronic means or otherwise on application and without charge; or
  (c) by any combination of the provisions set out in sub-paragraphs (a) and (b) above;

"disability living allowance" means a disability living allowance under section 71 of the Act;

"dwelling occupied as the home" means the dwelling, together with any garage, garden and outbuildings, normally occupied by the claimant as his home, including any premises not so occupied which it is impracticable or unreasonable to sell separately, in particular, in Scotland, any croft land on which the dwelling is situated;

"earnings" has the meaning prescribed in regulation 35 (earnings of employed earners) or, as the case may be, 38 (earnings of self-employed earners);

"the Eileen Trust" means the charitable trust of that name established on 29th March 1993 out of funds provided by the Secretary of State for the benefit of persons eligible for payment in accordance with its provisions;

[2 "electronic communication" has the same meaning as in section 15(1) of the 2000 Act;]

[9 "eligible rent" means as the case may require, an eligible rent determined in accordance with–
  (a) regulations 12B (eligible rent), 12C (eligible rent and maximum rent) or 12D (eligible rent and maximum rent (LHA)); or
  (b) regulations 12 (rent) and 13 (restrictions on unreasonable payments) as set out in paragraph 5 of Schedule 3 to the Consequential Provisions Regulations in a case to which paragraph 4 of that Schedule applies;]

"employed earner" is to be construed in accordance with section 2(1)(a) of the Act and also includes a person who is in receipt of a payment which is payable under any enactment having effect in Northern Ireland and which corresponds to statutory sick pay or statutory maternity pay;

[17 "Employment and Support Allowance Regulations" means the Employment and Support Allowance Regulations 2008;]

[24 "enactment" includes an enactment comprised in, or in an instrument made under, an Act of the Scottish Parliament;]

[13 "extended payment (qualifying contributory benefits)" means a payment of housing benefit payable pursuant to regulation 53 of these Regulations or regulation 73 of the Housing Benefit Regulations 2006;]

[¹⁴ "extended payment period" means the period for which an extended payment is payable in accordance with regulation 53A of these Regulations or regulation 72A or 73A of the Housing Benefit Regulations 2006;]

"family" has the meaning assigned to it by section 137(1) of the Act;

[¹²]

"the Fund" means moneys made available from time to time by the Secretary of State for the benefit of persons eligible for payment in accordance with the provisions of a scheme established by him on 24th April 1992 or, in Scotland, on 10th April 1992;

[¹⁵]

[¹ "the Graduated Retirement Benefit Regulations" means the Social Security (Graduated Retirement Benefit) Regulations 2005;]

"guarantee credit" is to be construed in accordance with sections 1 and 2 of the State Pension Credit Act;

"a guaranteed income payment" means a payment made under article 14(1)(b) or article 21(1)(a) of the Armed Forces and Reserve Forces (Compensation Scheme) Order 2005;

"hostel" means a building–

(a)   in which there is provided for persons generally or for a class of persons, domestic accommodation, otherwise than in separate and self-contained premises, and either board or facilities for the preparation of food adequate to the needs of those persons, or both; and

(b)   which is–

(i)   managed or owned by a registered housing association; or

(ii)   operated other than on a commercial basis and in respect of which funds are provided wholly or in part by a government department or agency or a local authority; or

(iii)   managed by a voluntary organisation or charity and provides care, support or supervision with a view to assisting those persons to be rehabilitated or resettled within the community; and

(c)   which is not–

(i)   a care home;

(ii)   an independent hospital; or

(iii)   an Abbeyfield Home;

[³³ "Housing Act functions" means functions under section 122 of the Housing Act 1996;]

[⁹ "housing association" has the meaning assigned to it by section 1(1) of the Housing Associations Act 1985;]

"an income-based jobseeker's allowance" and "a joint-claim jobseeker's allowance" have the same meaning as they have in the Jobseekers Act by virtue of section 1(4) of that Act;

[¹⁷ "income-related employment and support allowance" means an income-related allowance under Part 1 of the Welfare Reform Act;]

"Income Support Regulations" means the Income Support (General) Regulations 1987;

[³¹ "independent hospital" –

(a)   in England, means a hospital as defined by section 275 of the National Health Service Act 2006 that is not a health service hospital as defined by that section;

(b)   in Wales, has the meaning assigned to it by section 2 of the Care Standards Act 2000; and

(c)   in Scotland, means an independent healthcare service as defined in section 2(5)(a) and (b) of the Regulation of Care (Scotland) Act 2001;]

[¹⁸]

[⁶ "the Independent Living Fund (2006)" means the Trust of that name established by a deed dated 10th April 2006 and made between the Secretary of State for Work and Pensions of the one part and Margaret Rosemary Cooper, Michael Beresford Boyall and Marie Theresa Martin of the other part;]

[¹⁸]

[^{18}]
[^{18}]
''invalid carriage or other vehicle'' means a vehicle propelled by petrol engine or by electric power supplied for use on the road and to be controlled by the occupant;
''Jobseekers Act'' means the Jobseekers Act 1995;
''Jobseeker's Allowance Regulations'' means the Jobseeker's Allowance Regulations 1996;
[^{10} ''linked person'' means–
  (a)   any member of the claimant's family;
  (b)   if the claimant is a member of a polygamous marriage, any partners of his and any child or young person for whom he or a partner is responsible and who is a member of the same household; or
  (c)   any relative of the claimant or his partner who occupies the same dwelling as the claimant, whether or not they reside with him, except for a relative who has a separate right of occupation of the dwelling which would enable them to continue to occupy it even if the claimant ceased his occupation of it;]
[^{10} ''local housing allowance'' means an allowance determined in accordance with paragraph 2 of Schedule 3B to the Rent Officers Order;]
''the London Bombings Relief Charitable fund'' means the company limited by guarantee (number 5505072) and registered charity of that name established on 11th July 2005 for the purpose of (amongst other things) relieving sickness, disability or financial need of victims (including families or dependants of victims) of the terrorist attacks carried out in London on 7th July 2005;
''lone parent'' means a person who has no partner and who is responsible for and a member of the same household as a child or young person;
''long tenancy'' means a tenancy granted for a term of years certain exceeding twenty one years, whether or not the tenancy is, or may become, terminable before the end of that term by notice given by or to the tenant or by re-entry, forfeiture (or, in Scotland, irritancy) or otherwise and includes a lease for a term fixed by law under a grant with a covenant or obligation for perpetual renewal unless it is a lease by sub-demise from one which is not a long tenancy;
[^{8}]
''the Macfarlane (Special Payments) Trust'' means the trust of that name, established on 29th January 1990 partly out of funds provided by the Secretary of State, for the benefit of certain persons suffering from haemophilia;
''the Macfarlane (Special Payments) (No. 2) Trust'' means the trust of that name, established on 3rd May 1991 partly out of funds provided by the Secretary of State, for the benefit of certain persons suffering from haemophilia and other beneficiaries;
''the Macfarlane Trust'' means the charitable trust, established partly out of funds provided by the Secretary of State to the Haemophilia Society, for the relief of poverty or distress among those suffering from haemophilia;
[^{17} ''main phase employment and support allowance'' means an employment and support allowance where the calculation of the amount payable in respect of the claimant includes a component under section 2(1)(b) or 4(2)(b) of the Welfare Reform Act;]
''maternity leave'' means a period during which a woman is absent from work because she is pregnant or has given birth to a child, and at the end of which she has a right to return to work either under the terms of her contract of employment or under Part 8 of the Employment Rights Act 1996;
[^{9} ''maximum rent'' means the amount to which the eligible rent is restricted in a case where regulation 13 applies;]
[^{10} ''maximum rent (LHA)'' means the amount determined in accordance with regulation 13D;]
[^{25} ''MFET Limited'' means the company limited by guarantee (number 7121661) of that name, established for the purpose in particular of making payments in accordance

with arrangements made with the Secretary of State to persons who have acquired HIV as a result of treatment by the NHS with blood or blood products;]

[¹⁴ "mover" means a claimant who changes the dwelling occupied as the claimant's home from a dwelling in the area of the appropriate authority to a dwelling in the area of a second authority;]

"net earnings" means such earnings as are calculated in accordance with regulation 36 (calculation of net earnings of employed earners);

"net profit" means such profit as is calculated in accordance with regulation 39 (calculation of net profit of self-employed earners);

[¹⁴ "new dwelling" means, for the purposes of the definition of "second authority" and regulations 53C, 96 and 97, the dwelling to which a claimant has moved, or is about to move, which is or will be occupied as the claimant's new home;]

"non-dependant" has the meaning prescribed in regulation 3;

[⁹ "non-dependant deduction" means a deduction that is to be made under regulation 55 (non-dependant deductions);]

"occupational pension" means any pension or other periodical payment under an occupational pension scheme but does not include any discretionary payment out of a fund established for relieving hardship in particular cases;

"owner" means–
  (a)   in relation to a dwelling in England and Wales, the person who, otherwise than as a mortgagee in possession, is for the time being entitled to dispose of the fee simple, whether or not with the consent of other joint owners;
  (b)   in relation to a dwelling in Scotland, the proprietor under udal tenure or the proprietor of the dominion utile or the tenant's or the lessee's interest in a long tenancy, a kindly tenancy, a lease registered or registerable under the Registration of Leases (Scotland) Act 1857 or the Land Registration (Scotland) Act 1979 or a tenant-at-will as defined in section 20(8) of that Act of 1979;

"partner" means–
  (a)   where a claimant is a member of a couple, the other member of that couple; or
  (b)   where a claimant is polygamously married to two or more members of his household, any such member;

"paternity leave" means a period of absence from work on leave by virtue of section 80A or 80B of the Employment Rights Act 1996;

"payment" includes part of a payment;

"pension fund holder" means with respect to a personal pension scheme or [⁴ an occupational pension scheme], the trustees, managers or scheme administrators, as the case may be, of the scheme [⁴] concerned;

"person affected" shall be construed in accordance with regulation 3 of the Decisions and Appeals Regulations;

"person on income support" means a person in receipt of income support;

"person on state pension credit" means a person in receipt of state pension credit;

[⁴ "personal pension scheme" means–
  (a)   a personal pension scheme as defined by section 1 of the Pension Schemes Act 1993;
  (b)   an annuity contract or trust scheme approved under section 620 or 621 of the Income and Corporation Taxes Act 1988 or a substituted contract within the meaning of section 622(3) of that Act which is treated as having become a registered pension scheme by virtue of paragraph 1(1)(f) of Schedule 36 to the Finance Act 2004;
  (c)   a personal pension scheme approved under Chapter 4 of Part 14 of the Income and Corporation Taxes Act 1988 which is treated as having become a registered pension scheme by virtue of paragraph 1(1)(g) of Schedule 36 to the Finance Act 2004;]

"policy of life insurance" means any instrument by which the payment of money is assured on death (except death by accident only) or the happening of any contingency dependent on human life, or any instrument evidencing a contract which is subject to payment of premiums for a term dependent on human life;

"polygamous marriage" means any marriage during the subsistence of which a party to it is married to more than one person and the ceremony of marriage took place under the law of a country which permits polygamy;

[²⁴ "public authority" includes any person certain of whose functions are functions of a public nature;]

"qualifying age for state pension credit" means (in accordance with section 1(2)(b) and (6) of the State Pension Credit Act)–

  (a) in the case of a woman, pensionable age; or

  (b) in the case of a man, the age which is pensionable age in the case of a woman born on the same day as the man;

[¹⁴ "qualifying contributory benefit" means–

  (a) severe disablement allowance;

  (b) incapacity benefit;]

  [¹⁵ (c) contributory employment and support allowance;]

"qualifying course" means a qualifying course as defined for the purposes of Parts 2 and 4 of the Jobseeker's Allowance Regulations;

[¹⁴ "qualifying income-related benefit" means–

  (a) income support;

  (b) income-based jobseeker's allowance;]

  [¹⁵ (c) income-related employment and support allowance;]

"qualifying person" means a person in respect of whom payment has been made from the Fund, the Eileen Trust [²⁶ , MFET Limited], the Skipton Fund or the London Bombings Relief Charitable Fund;

[¹⁰ "reckonable rent" means payments which a person is liable to make in respect of the dwelling which he occupies as his home, and which are eligible, or would, but for regulation 13, be eligible for housing benefit;]

[¹⁰ [¹¹[²⁹ "registered housing association" means–

  (a) a private registered provider of social housing;

  (b) a housing association which is registered in a register maintained by the Welsh Ministers under Chapter 1 of Part 1 of the Housing Act 1996; or

  (c) a housing association which is registered by Scottish Ministers by virtue of section 57(3)(b) of the Housing (Scotland) Act 2001;]]]

"relative" means a close relative, grandparent, grandchild, uncle, aunt, nephew or niece;

"relevant authority" means an authority administering housing benefit;

[¹⁰ "relevant information" means information or evidence forwarded to the relevant authority by an appropriate DWP office regarding a claim on which rent allowance may be awarded, which completes the transfer of all information or evidence held by the appropriate DWP office relating to that claim;]

"remunerative work" has the meaning prescribed in regulation 6 (remunerative work);

"rent" includes all those payments in respect of a dwelling specified in regulation 12(1);

[⁹ "Rent Officers Order" means the Rent Officers (Housing Benefit Functions) Order 1997 or, as the case may be, the Rent Officers (Housing Benefit Functions) (Scotland) Order 1997;]

[⁴]

[¹² "sandwich course" has the meaning prescribed in regulation 2(9) of the Education (Student Support) Regulations 2008, regulation 4(2) of the Education (Student Loans) (Scotland) Regulations 2007 or regulation 2(8) of the Education (Student Support) Regulations (Northern Ireland) 2007, as the case may be;]

"savings credit" shall be construed in accordance with sections 1 and 3 of the State Pension Credit Act;

[¹⁴ "second authority" means the authority to which a mover is liable to make payments for the new dwelling;]

"self-employed earner" is to be construed in accordance with section 2(1)(b) of the Act;

[²⁴ "service user group" means a group of individuals that is consulted by or on behalf of–

  (a) a Health Board, Special Health Board or the Agency in consequence of a function under section 2B of the National Health Service (Scotland) Act 1978,

(b) a landlord authority in consequence of a function under section 105 of the Housing Act 1985,

(c) a public authority in consequence of a function under section 49A of the Disability Discrimination Act 1995,

(d) a best value authority in consequence of a function under section 3 of the Local Government Act 1999,

(e) a local authority landlord or registered social landlord in consequence of a function under section 53 of the Housing (Scotland) Act 2001,

(f) a relevant English body or a relevant Welsh body in consequence of a function under section 242 of the National Health Service Act 2006,

(g) a Local Health Board in consequence of a function under section 183 of the National Health Service (Wales) Act 2006,

(h) the Commission or the Office of the Health Professions Adjudicator in consequence of a function under sections 4, 5, or 108 of the Health and Social Care Act 2008,

(i) the regulator or a [29 private registered provider of social housing] in consequence of a function under sections 98, 193 or 196 of the Housing and Regeneration Act 2008, or

(j) a public or local authority in Great Britain in consequence of a function conferred under any other enactment,

for the purposes of monitoring and advising on a policy of that body or authority which affects or may affect persons in the group, or of monitoring or advising on services provided by that body or authority which are used (or may potentially be used) by those persons;]

"shared ownership tenancy" means–

(a) in relation to England and Wales, a [5 lease] granted on payment of a premium calculated by reference to a percentage of the value of the dwelling or the cost of providing it;

(b) in relation to Scotland, an agreement by virtue of which the tenant of a dwelling of which he and the landlord are joint owners is the tenant in respect of the landlord's interest in the dwelling or by virtue of which the tenant has the right to purchase the dwelling or the whole or part of the landlord's interest therein;

"single claimant" means a claimant who neither has a partner nor is a lone parent;

"the Skipton Fund" means the ex-gratia payment scheme administered by the Skipton Fund Limited, incorporated on 25th March 2004, for the benefit of certain persons suffering from hepatitis C and other persons eligible for payment in accordance with the scheme's provisions;

"sports award" means an award made by one of the Sports Councils named in section 23(2) of the National Lottery etc Act 1993 out of sums allocated to it for distribution under that section;

[7 [22]]

"State Pension Credit Act" means the State Pension Credit Act 2002;

"student" means a person, other than a person in receipt of a training allowance, who is attending or undertaking–

(a) a course of study at an educational establishment; or

(b) a qualifying course;

"the Tax Credits Act" means the Tax Credits Act 2002;

"tax year" means a period beginning with 6th April in one year and ending with 5th April in the next;

"training allowance" means an allowance (whether by way of periodical grants or otherwise) payable–

(a) out of public funds by a Government department or by or on behalf of the Secretary of State, [23 Skills Development Scotland,] Scottish Enterprise or Highlands and Islands Enterprise, the [32 Young People's Learning Agency for England, the Chief Executive of Skills Funding] or the [19 Welsh Ministers];

(b) to a person for his maintenance or in respect of a member of his family; and

(c)   for the period, or part of the period, during which he is following a course of training or instruction provided by, or in pursuance of arrangements made with, that department or approved by that department in relation to him or so provided or approved by or on behalf of the Secretary of State, [²³ Skills Development Scotland,] Scottish Enterprise or Highlands and Islands Enterprise or the [¹⁹ Welsh Ministers],

but it does not include an allowance paid by any Government department to or in respect of a person by reason of the fact that he is following a course of full-time education, other than under arrangements made under section 2 of the 1973 Act or is training as a teacher;

"voluntary organisation" means a body, other than a public or local authority, the activities of which are carried on otherwise than for profit;

[³]

[²⁰ "war disablement pension" means any retired pay or pension or allowance payable in respect of disablement under an instrument specified in section 639(2) of the Income Tax (Earnings and Pensions) Act 2003;

"war pension" means a war disablement pension, a war widow's pension or a war widower's pension;

"war widow's pension" means any pension or allowance payable to a woman as a widow under an instrument specified in section 639(2) of the Income Tax (Earnings and Pensions) Act 2003 in respect of the death or disablement of any person;

"war widower's pension" means any pension or allowance payable to a man as a widower or to a surviving civil partner under an instrument specified in section 639(2) of the Income Tax (Earnings and Pensions) Act 2003 in respect of the death or disablement of any person;]

"water charges" means–
    (a)   as respects England and Wales, any water and sewerage charges under Chapter 1 of Part 5 of the Water Industry Act 1991;
    (b)   as respects Scotland, any water and sewerage charges established by Scottish Water under a charges scheme made under section 29A of the Water Industry (Scotland) Act 2002,
    in so far as such charges are in respect of the dwelling which a person occupies as his home;

[¹⁷ "Welfare Reform Act" means the Welfare Reform Act 2007;]

"working tax credit" means a working tax credit under section 10 of the Tax Credits Act;

"Working Tax Credit Regulations" means the Working Tax Credit (Entitlement and Maximum Rate) Regulations 2002;

"young individual" means a single claimant who has not attained the age of 25 years, but does not include such a claimant–
    (a)   whose landlord is a registered housing association;
    (b)   who has not attained the age of 22 years and has ceased to be the subject of a care order made pursuant to section 31(1)(a) of the Children Act 1989 which had previously been made in respect to him either–
        (i)   after he attained the age of 16 years; or
        (ii)   before he attained the age of 16 years, but had continued after he attained that age;
    (c)   who has not attained the age of 22 years and was formerly provided with accommodation under section 20 of the Children Act 1989;
    (d)   who has not attained the age of 22 years and has ceased to be subject to a supervision requirement by a children's hearing under section 70 of the Children (Scotland) Act 1995 ("the 1995 Act") made in respect of him which had continued after he attained the age of 16 years, other than a case where–
        (i)   the ground of referral was based on the sole condition as to the need for compulsory measures of care specified in section 52(2)(g) of the 1995 Act (commission of offences by child); or

        (ii)   he was required by virtue of the supervision requirement to reside with a parent or guardian of his within the meaning of the 1995 Act, or with a friend or relative of his or of his parent or guardian;

(e)   who has not attained the age of 22 years and has ceased to be a child in relation to whom the parental rights and responsibilities were transferred to a local authority under a parental responsibilities order made in accordance with section 86 of the 1995 Act or treated as so vested in accordance with paragraph 3 of Schedule 3 to that Act, either–
    (i)   after he attained the age of 16 years; or
    (ii)   before he attained the age of 16 years, but had continued after he attained that age; or

(f)   who has not attained the age of 22 years and has ceased to be provided with accommodation by a local authority under section 25 of the 1995 Act where he has previously been provided with accommodation by the authority under that provision either–
    (i)   after he attained the age of 16 years; or
    (ii)   before he attained the age of 16 years, but had continued to be in such accommodation after he attained that age; and

"young person" has the meaning prescribed in regulation 19(1).

(2)   References in these Regulations to a person who is liable to make payments shall include references to a person who is treated as so liable under regulation 8 (circumstances in which a person is to be treated as liable to make payments in respect of a dwelling).

(3)   For the purposes of these Regulations, a person is on an income-based jobseeker's allowance on any day in respect of which an income-based jobseeker's allowance is payable to him and on any day–

(a)   in respect of which he satisfies the conditions for entitlement to an income-based jobseeker's allowance but where the allowance is not paid in accordance with [28 regulation 27A of the Jobseeker's Allowance Regulations or] section 19 or 20A *[or regulations made under section 17A]* of the Jobseekers Act (circumstances in which a jobseeker's allowance is not payable); or

(b)   which is a waiting day for the purposes of paragraph 4 of Schedule 1 to that Act and which falls immediately before a day in respect of which an income-based jobseeker's allowance is payable to him or would be payable to him but for [28 regulation 27A of the Jobseeker's Allowance Regulations or] section 19 or 20A *[or regulations made under section 17A]* of that Act; or

(c)   in respect of which he is a member of a joint-claim couple for the purposes of the Jobseekers Act and no joint-claim jobseeker's allowance is payable in respect of that couple as a consequence of either member of that couple being subject to sanctions for the purpose of section 20A of that Act; or

(d)   in respect of which an income-based jobseeker's allowance or a joint-claim jobseeker's allowance would be payable but for a restriction imposed pursuant to [27] section [30 6B,] 7, 8 or 9 of the Social Security Fraud Act 2001 (loss of benefit provisions).

[17 (3A)   For the purposes of these Regulations, a person is on an income-related employment and support allowance on any day in respect of which an income-related employment and support allowance is payable to him and on any day–

(a)   in respect of which he satisfies the conditions for entitlement to an income-related employment and support allowance but where the allowance is not paid in accordance with section 18 of the Welfare Reform Act (disqualification); or

(b)   which is a waiting day for the purposes of paragraph 2 of Schedule 2 to that Act and which falls immediately before a day in respect of which an income-related employment and support allowance is payable to him or would be payable to him but for section 18 of that Act.]

(4)   For the purposes of these Regulations, the following shall be treated as included in a dwelling–

(a)   subject to sub-paragraphs (b) to (d) any land (whether or not occupied by a structure) which is used for the purposes of occupying a dwelling as a home where either–

(i)   the occupier of the dwelling acquired simultaneously the right to use the land and the right to occupy the dwelling, and, in the case of a person liable to pay rent for his dwelling, he could not have occupied that dwelling without also acquiring the right to use the land; or

(ii)   the occupier of the dwelling has made or is making all reasonable efforts to terminate his liability to make payments in respect of the land;

(b)   where the dwelling is a caravan or mobile home, such of the land on which it stands as is used for the purposes of the dwelling;

(c)   where the dwelling is a houseboat, the land used for the purposes of mooring it;

(d)   where in Scotland, the dwelling is situated on or pertains to a croft within the meaning of section 3(1) of the Crofters (Scotland) Act 1993, the croft land on which it is situated or to which it pertains.

(5)   In these Regulations references to any person in receipt of a guarantee credit, a savings credit or state pension credit includes a reference to a person who would be in receipt thereof but for regulation 13 of the State Pension Credit Regulations 2002 (small amounts of state pension credit).

Modifications

Definitions substituted and inserted by reg 4(1) Housing Benefit (State Pension Credit) (Local Housing Allowance and Information Sharing) Amendment Regulations 2007 SI No.2869, as amended by reg 5(3) of SI 2008 No.586, as from 7 April 2008, save that for a person to whom reg 1(5) of those regulations applied (see p1233), the amendments came into force on the day on or after 7 April 2008 when the first of the events specified in reg 1(6) applies to her/him, or on 6 April 2009 if none had before that date.

Definition of "eligible rent" modified and definition of "maximum rent (standard local rate)" inserted by Sch 9 para 2 (see p907). These apply only to former Pathfinder Authorities who administered the pilot local housing allowance scheme.

References to "step-parent", step-children and the various in-laws in the definition of "close relative" are modified by s246 Civil Partnership Act 2004 (see p1148) and art 3 and Schedule para 24 to SI 2005 No.3137 (see p1195).

From 1 December 2008, in England and Wales, in the definition of "registered housing association", the reference to the Housing Corporation is to be treated as if it were a reference to the Regulator of Social Housing: Art 3 and Sch para 7 Transfer of Housing Corporation Functions (Modifications and Transitional Provisions) Order 2008 SI No.2839.

Reg 2(3) is modified by reg 19 Jobseeker's Allowance (Work for Your Benefit Pilot Scheme) Regulations 2010 SI No.1222 (see p1247) as from 22 November 2010 but only for those ordinarily resident in a pilot area or whose address for payment of JSA is located within such an area. The modifications are shown in italics above. They cease to have effect on 21 November 2013.

Amendments

1.   Inserted by reg 11(2) of SI 2005 No 2677 and reg 2 of SI 2006 No 217 as from 6.4.06.
2.   Inserted by Art 3(2) of SI 2006 No 2968 as from 20.12.06.
3.   Omitted by Reg 6(a) of SI 2007 No 1619 as from 3.7.07.
4   Amended by reg 5(2) of SI 2007 No 1749 as from 16.7.07.
5.   Amended by reg 3(2) of SI 2007 No 1356 as from 1.10.07.
6.   Amended by Art 9 of SI 2007 No 2538 as from 1.10.07.
7.   Inserted by reg 12(2) of SI 2007 No 2618 as from 1.10.07.
8.   Revoked by reg 2 and the Sch of SI 2007 No 2618 as from 1.10.07.
9.   Substituted by reg 4(1) of SI 2007 No 2869 as from 7.4.08 (or if reg 1(5) of that SI applies, on the day on or after 7.4.08 when the first of the events specified in reg 1(6) applies, or from 6.4.09 if none have before that date).
10.   Inserted by reg 4(1) of SI 2007 No 2869 as from 7.4.08 (or if reg 1(5) of that SI applies, on the day on or after 7.4.08 when the first of the events specified in reg 1(6) applies, or from 6.4.09 if none have before that date).
11.   Substituted by reg 5(3) of SI 2008 No 586 as from 7.4.08.
12.   Amended by reg 4(2) of SI 2008 No 1042 as from 19.5.08.
13.   Substituted by reg 6(2) of SI 2008 No 959 as from 6.10.08.
14.   Inserted by reg 6(2) of SI 2008 No 959 as from 6.10.08.
15.   Omitted by reg 3(2) of SI 2008 No 2299 as from 1.10.08.

16. Amended by reg 29(2) of SI 2008 No 1082 as from 27.10.08.
17. Inserted by reg 29(2) of SI 2008 No 1082, as amended by reg 33 of SI 2008 No 2428, as from 27.10.08.
18. Amended by reg 7(2) of SI 2008 No 2767 as from 17.11.08.
19. Amended by reg 6(2) of SI 2008 No 3157 as from 5.1.09.
20. Inserted by reg 6(2) of SI 2008 No 3157 as from 5.1.09.
21. Inserted by reg 7(2)(a) of SI 2009 No 583 as from 6.4.09.
22. Omitted by reg 7(2)(b) of SI 2009 No 583 as from 6.4.09.
23. Amended by reg 7(3)(a) of SI 2009 No 583 as from 6.4.09.
24. Inserted by reg 7(2) of SI 2009 No 2655 as from 2.11.09.
25. Inserted by reg 9(2) of SI 2010 No 641 as from 1.4.10 (5.4.10 where rent payable weekly or in multiples of a week).
26. Inserted by reg 9(3) of SI 2010 No 641 as from 1.4.10 (5.4.10 where rent payable weekly or in multiples of a week).
27. Amended by reg 8 of SI 2010 No 424 as from 2.4.10.
28. Amended by reg 4(1)(b) and (2) of SI 2010 No 509 as from 6.4.10.
29. Amended by Art 4 and Sch 1 para 57 of SI 2010 No 671 as from 1.4.10.
30. Amended by reg 5 of SI 2010 No 1160 as from 1.4.10.
31. Substituted by Arts 2 and 21 of SI 2010 No 1881 as from 1.10.10.
32. Amended by Art 15 of SI 2010 No 1941 as from 1.9.10.
33. Amended by reg 3(2) of SI 2010 No 2449 as from 1.11.10.

Analysis

"board and lodging accommodation" is defined as accommodation in which cooked or prepared meals are provided and consumed. This definition is identical to that found in reg 2(1) Income Support (General) Regulations 1987. Preparation, in the context of this definition, requires something more than merely leaving the ingredients out for the lodger: *CSB 950/1987*.

"qualifying age for state pension credit" is relevant in determining whether these regs or the HB Regs apply to a claimant: reg 5. The age at which someone qualifies for state pension credit (PC) is linked to pensionable age for a woman which will rise gradually to 65 by 2020 by virtue of s126 and Sch 4 Pensions Act 1995.

The process of equalising men's and women's pension ages began on 6 April 2010. From that date, women's pension age begins to rise, as does the qualifying age for PC. The qualifying age for PC for a woman is the minimum age she can receive state retirement pension. The qualifying age for PC for a man is the minimum age a woman born on the same day as him can receive state retirement pension. So for both men and women, the qualifying age for PC is:

(1) 60, if s/he was born before 6 April 1950;
(2) an age from 60 and one month to 64 and 11 months depending on her/his date of birth, if s/he was born on or after 6 April 1950 but before 6 April 1955; *or*
(3) 65, if s/he was born on or after 6 April 1955.

Consequently, the rules in the Housing Benefit (Persons who have attained the qualifying age for state pension credit) Regulations 2006 (SI No.214) and the Council Tax Benefit (Persons who have attained the qualifying age for state pension credit) Regulations 2006 (SI No.216) will apply to individual claimants at different ages. For claimants born on or after 6 April 1950 but before 6 April 1955, there is a helpful table, setting out the relevant birth dates and pension ages, in an Appendix to CPAG's *Welfare Benefits and Tax Credits Handbook*.

Definition of non-dependant

3.–(1) In these Regulations, ''non-dependant'' means any person, except someone to whom paragraph (2) applies, who normally resides with a claimant or with whom a claimant normally resides.

(2) This paragraph applies to–

(a) any member of the claimant's family;

(b) if the claimant is polygamously married, any partner of his and any child or young person who is a member of his household and for whom he or one of his partners is responsible;

(c) a child or young person who is living with the claimant but who is not a member of his household by virtue of regulation 21 (circumstances in which a person is to be treated as being or not being a member of the same household);

(d) subject to paragraph (3), a person who jointly occupies the claimant's dwelling and is either a co-owner of that dwelling with the claimant or his partner (whether or not there are other co-owners) or is liable with the claimant or his partner to make payments in respect of his occupation of the dwelling;

(e)   subject to paragraph (3)–
  (i)   any person who is liable to make payments on a commercial basis to the claimant or the claimant's partner in respect of the occupation of the dwelling;
  (ii)   any person to whom or to whose partner the claimant or the claimant's partner is liable to make payments on a commercial basis in respect of the occupation of the dwelling; or
  (iii)   any other member of the household of the person to whom or to whose partner the claimant or the claimant's partner is liable to make payments on a commercial basis in respect of the occupation of the dwelling;
(f)   a person who lives with the claimant in order to care for him or a partner of his and who is engaged by a charitable or voluntary organisation which makes a charge to the claimant or his partner for the services provided by that person.

(3)   Sub-paragraphs (d) and (e) of paragraph (2) shall not apply to any person who is treated as if he were not liable to make payments in respect of a dwelling under paragraph (1) of regulation 9 (circumstances in which a person is to be treated as not liable to make payments in respect of a dwelling).

(4)   For the purposes of this regulation and regulation 9 [¹ and the definition of "linked person" in regulation 2] a person resides with another only if they share any accommodation except a bathroom, a lavatory or a communal area within the meaning prescribed in paragraph 8 of Schedule 1 but not if each person is separately liable to make payments in respect of his occupation of the dwelling to the landlord.

Modifications

Amendments made to para (4) by reg 4(2) Housing Benefit (State Pension Credit) (Local Housing Allowance and Information Sharing) Amendment Regulations 2007 SI No.2869 as from 7 April 2008, save that for a person to whom reg 1(5) of those regulations applied (see p1233), the amendments came into force on the day on or after 7 April 2008 when the first of the events specified in reg 1(6) applied to her/him, or on 6 April 2009 if none had before that date.

Amendment

1.   Amended by reg 4(2) of SI 2007 No 2869 as from 7.4.08 (or if reg 1(5) of that SI applies, on the day on or after 7.4.08 when the first of the events specified in reg 1(6) applies, or from 6.4.09 if none have before that date).

Cases in which section 1(1A) of the Administration Act is disapplied

4.   Section 1(1A) of the Administration Act (requirement to state national insurance number) shall not apply–
(a)   to a claim for housing benefit where the person making the claim, or in respect of whom the claim is made, is liable to make payments in respect of a dwelling which is a hostel;
(b)   to any child or young person in respect of whom housing benefit is claimed.
[¹ (c)   to a person who–
  (i)   is a person in respect of whom a claim for housing benefit is made;
  (ii)   is subject to immigration control within the meaning of section 115(9)(a) of the Immigration and Asylum Act 1999;
  (iii)   is a person from abroad for the purposes of these Regulations as defined in regulation 10(2); and
  (iv)   has not previously been allocated a national insurance number.]

Amendment

1.   Amended by reg 10 of SI 2009 No 471 as from 6.4.09.

Persons who have attained the qualifying age for state pension credit

5.–(1)   Except as provided in paragraph (2), these Regulations apply to a person who has attained the qualifying age for state pension credit.

(2)   These Regulations shall not apply in relation to any person if he, or if he has a partner, his partner, is a person on income support [¹ , [² on] an income-based jobseeker's allowance or on an income-related employment and support allowance].

Amendments

   1.   Amended by reg 30 of SI 2008 No 1082 as from 27.10.08.

   2.   Amended by reg 34 of SI 2008 No 2428 as from 27.10.08.

Definitions

   "person on an income-based jobseeker's allowance" – see reg 2(3).

   "person on an income-related employment and support allowance" – see reg 2(3A).

   "person on income support" – see reg 2(3).

   "qualifying age for state pension credit" – see reg 2(1).

General Note

   The HB(SPC) Regs apply where a person has reached the qualifying age for PC (see p782). However, they do not apply if either the claimant or her/his partner is on IS, income-based JSA or income-related ESA. In this case, the HB Regs instead apply.

Remunerative work

6.–(1)   Subject to the following provisions of this regulation, a person shall be treated for the purposes of these Regulations as engaged in remunerative work if he is engaged, or, where his hours of work fluctuate, he is engaged on average, for not less than 16 hours a week, in work for which payment is made or which is done in expectation of payment.

(2)   Subject to paragraph (3), in determining the number of hours for which a person is engaged in work where his hours of work fluctuate, regard shall be had to the average of hours worked over–

   (a)   if there is a recognisable cycle of work, the period of one complete cycle (including, where the cycle involves periods in which the person does no work, those periods but disregarding any other absences);

   (b)   in any other case, the period of 5 weeks immediately prior to the date of claim, or such other length of time as may, in the particular case, enable the person's weekly average hours of work to be determined more accurately.

(3)   Where, for the purposes of paragraph (2)(a), a person's recognisable cycle of work at a school, other educational establishment or other place of employment is one year and includes periods of school holidays or similar vacations during which he does not work, those periods and any other periods not forming part of such holidays or vacations during which he is not required to work shall be disregarded in establishing the average hours for which he is engaged in work.

(4)   Where no recognisable cycle has been established in respect of a person's work, regard shall be had to the number of hours or, where those hours will fluctuate, the average of the hours, which he is expected to work in a week.

(5)   A person shall be treated as engaged in remunerative work during any period for which he is absent from work referred to in paragraph (1) if the absence is either without good cause or by reason of a recognised, customary or other holiday.

(6)   A person on income support [¹ , income-based jobseeker's allowance or an income-related employment and support allowance] for more than 3 days in any benefit week shall be treated as not being in remunerative work in that week.

(7)   A person shall not be treated as engaged in remunerative work on any day on which the person is on maternity leave, paternity leave or adoption leave, or is absent from work because he is ill.

(8)   A person shall not be treated as engaged in remunerative work on any day on which he is engaged in an activity in respect of which–

   (a)   a sports award has been made, or is to be made, to him; and

   (b)   no other payment is made or is expected to be made to him.

Amendment

   1.   Amended by reg 31 of SI 2008 No 1082 as from 27.10.08.

PART 2
Provisions affecting entitlement to housing benefit

Circumstances in which a person is or is not to be treated as occupying a dwelling as his home

7.–(1)   Subject to the following provisions of this regulation, a person shall be treated as occupying as his home the dwelling normally occupied as his home–

(a)   by himself or, if he is a member of a family, by himself and his family; or

(b)   if he is polygamously married, by himself, his partners and any child or young person for whom he or any partner of his is responsible and who is a member of that same household,

and shall not be treated as occupying any other dwelling as his home.

(2)   In determining whether a dwelling is the dwelling normally occupied as a person's home for the purpose of paragraph (1) regard shall be had to any other dwelling occupied by that person or any other person referred to in paragraph (1) whether or not that dwelling is in Great Britain.

(3)   Where a single claimant or a lone parent is a student, other than one to whom regulation 56(1) of the Housing Benefit Regulations 2006 applies (circumstances in which certain students are treated as not liable to make payments in respect of a dwelling), or is on a training course and is liable to make payments (including payments of mortgage interest or, in Scotland, payments under heritable securities or, in either case, analogous payments) in respect of either (but not both) the dwelling which he occupies for the purpose of attending his course of study or, his training course, or as the case may be, the dwelling which he occupies when not attending his course, he shall be treated as occupying as his home the dwelling in respect of which he is liable to make such payments.

(4)   Where a claimant has been required to move into temporary accommodation by reason of essential repairs being carried out to the dwelling normally occupied as his home, and is liable to make payments (including payments of mortgage interest or, in Scotland, payments under heritable securities or, in either case, analogous payments) in respect of either (but not both) the dwelling which he normally occupied as his home or the temporary accommodation, he shall be treated as occupying as his home the dwelling in respect of which he is liable to make payments.

(5)   Where a person is required to reside in a dwelling which is a bail hostel or probation hostel approved by the Secretary of State under [⁴section 13 of the Offender Management Act 2007], he shall not be treated as occupying that dwelling as his home.

(6)   Where a person is liable to make payments in respect of two(but not more than two) dwellings, he shall be treated as occupying both dwellings as his home only–

(a)   for a period not exceeding 52 weeks in the case where he has left and remains absent from the former dwelling occupied as his home through fear of violence in that dwelling or by a former member of his family and–

(i)   it is reasonable that housing benefit should be paid in respect of both his former dwelling and his present dwelling occupied as the home; and

(ii)   he intends to return to occupy the former dwelling as his home; or

(b)   in the case of a couple or a member of a polygamous marriage, where he or one partner is a student, other than one to whom regulation 56(1) of the Housing Benefit Regulations 2006 applies (circumstances in which certain students are treated as not liable to make payments in respect of a dwelling), or is on a training course and it is unavoidable that the partners should occupy two separate dwellings and reasonable that housing benefit should be paid in respect of both dwellings; or

(c)   in the case where, because of the number of persons referred to in paragraph (1), they have been housed by a housing authority in two separate dwellings; or

(d)   in the case where a person has moved into a newdwelling occupied as the home, except where paragraph (4) applies, for a period not exceeding four benefit weeks [¹ from the date on which he moved] if he could not reasonably have avoided liability in respect of two dwellings; or

    (e)   in the case where a person–
        (i)   is treated by virtue of paragraph (8) as occupying a dwelling as his home ("the new dwelling") and sub-paragraph (c)(i) of that paragraph applies; and
        (ii)   he has occupied another dwelling as his home on any day within the period of 4 weeks immediately preceding the date he moved to the new dwelling, for a period not exceeding 4 benefit weeks immediately preceding the date on which he moved.

    (7)   Where–
    (a)   a person has moved into a dwelling for which he is not liable to make payments ("the new dwelling"); and
    (b)   immediately before that move, he was liable to make payments for the dwelling he previously occupied as his home ("the former dwelling"); and
    (c)   that liability continues after he has moved into the new dwelling,

he shall be treated as occupying the former dwelling as his home for a period not exceeding four benefit weeks if he could not reasonably have avoided liability in respect of that former dwelling.

    (8)   [² Where]–
    (a)   [² a person] has moved into a dwelling and was liable to make payments in respect of that dwelling before moving in; and
    [² (b)   either–
        (i)   that person had claimed housing benefit before moving in and either no decision has yet been made on that claim or it has been refused but a further claim has been made or treated as made within 4 weeks of the date on which the claimant moved into the new dwelling occupied as the home; or
        (ii)   that person notified the move to the new dwelling as a change of circumstances under regulation 69 (duty to notify changes of circumstances) before the move, or the move to the new dwelling was otherwise notified before the move under that regulation; and]
    (c)   the delay in moving into the dwelling in respect of which there was liability to make payments before moving in was reasonable and–
        (i)   that delay was necessary in order to adapt the dwelling to meet the disablement needs of that person or any member of his family; or
        (ii)   the move was delayed pending the outcome of an application under [³ Part 8] of the Act for a social fund payment to meet a need arising out of the move or in connection with setting up the home in the dwelling and either a member of the claimant's family is aged 5 or under or the claimant is a person who has attained or whose partner has attained the qualifying age for state pension credit; or
        (iii)   the claimant became liable to make payments in respect of the dwelling while he was a patient or in residential accommodation,
        [² the person shall be treated] as occupying the dwelling as his home for any period not exceeding 4 weeks immediately prior to the date on which he moved into the dwelling and in respect of which he was liable to make payments.

    (9)   Where a person is treated by virtue of paragraph (8) as occupying a dwelling as his home in respect of the period before moving in, his claim for housing benefit in respect of that dwelling shall be treated as having been made on–
    (a)   in the case of a claim in respect of which a decision has not yet been made the date that claim was or was treated as made in accordance with regulation 64 (time and manner in which claims are to be made); or
    (b)   in the case of a claim for housing benefit in respect of that dwelling which has been refused and a further claim was or was treated as made in accordance with Part 9 (claims) within 4 weeks of the date on which he moved into the dwelling, the date on which the claim was refused or was treated as made; or
    (c)   the date from which he is treated by virtue of paragraph (8) as occupying the dwelling as his home,

whichever of those dates is the later.

(10)   Where a person to whom neither paragraph (6)(a) nor (16)(c)(x) applies–

(a)   formerly occupied a dwelling but has left and remains absent from it through fear of violence–

(i)   in the dwelling; or

(ii)   by a person who was formerly a member of the family of the person first mentioned; and

(b)   has a liability to make payments in respect of that dwelling which is unavoidable,

he shall be treated as occupying the dwelling as his home for a period not exceeding 4 benefit weeks.

(11)   This paragraph shall apply to a person who enters residential accommodation–

(a)   for the purpose of ascertaining whether the accommodation suits his needs; and

(b)   with the intention of returning to the dwelling which is normally occupied by him as his home should, in the event, the residential accommodation prove not to suit his needs; and

(c)   while the part of the dwelling which is normally occupied by him as his home is not let, or as the case may be, sublet.

(12)   A person to whom paragraph (11) applies shall be treated as if he is occupying the dwelling he normally occupies as his home for a period not exceeding, subject to an overall limit of 52 weeks on the absence from that home, 13 weeks beginning from the first day he enters a residential accommodation.

(13)   Subject to paragraph (17) a person shall be treated as occupying a dwelling as his home while he is temporarily absent therefrom for a period not exceeding 13 weeks beginning from the first day of that absence from the home only if–

(a)   he intends to return to occupy the dwelling as his home; and

(b)   the part of the dwelling normally occupied by him has not been let or, as the case may be, sub-let; and

(c)   the period of absence is unlikely to exceed 13 weeks.

(14)   This paragraph applies to a person who is–

(a)   detained in custody pending sentence upon conviction or under a sentence imposed by a court (other than a person who is detained in hospital under the provisions of the Mental Health Act 1983, or, in Scotland, under the provisions of the Mental Health (Care and Treatment) (Scotland) Act 2003 or the Criminal Procedure (Scotland) Act 1995); and

(b)   on temporary release from detention in accordance with Rules made under the provisions of the Prison Act 1952 or the Prisons (Scotland) Act 1989.

(15)   Where paragraph (14) applies to a person, then, for any day when he is on temporary release–

(a)   if such temporary release was immediately preceded by a period of temporary absence under paragraph (13) or (16), he shall be treated as if he continues to be absent from the dwelling, despite any occupation of the dwelling;

(b)   for the purposes of paragraph (16)(c)(i), he shall be treated as if he remains in detention; and

(c)   if he does not fall within sub-paragraph (a), he shall be treated as if he does not occupy his dwelling as his home despite any such occupation of the dwelling.

(16)   This paragraph shall apply to a person who is temporarily absent from the dwelling he normally occupies as his home ("absence"), if–

(a)   he intends to return to occupy the dwelling as his home; and

(b)   while the part of the dwelling which is normally occupied by him has not been let, or as the case may be, sublet; and

(c)   he is–

(i)   detained in custody on remand pending trial or, as a condition of bail, required to reside–

(aa)   in a dwelling, other than the dwelling he occupies as his home; or

(bb)   in premises approved under [⁴section 13 of the Offender Management Act 2007],

or, as the case may be, detained pending sentence upon conviction; or

      (ii)   resident in a hospital or similar institution as a patient; or

      (iii)   undergoing, or as the case may be, his partner or his dependant child is undergoing, in the United Kingdom or elsewhere, medical treatment, or medically approved convalescence, in accommodation other than residential accommodation; or

      (iv)   following, in the United Kingdom or elsewhere, a training course; or

      (v)   undertaking medically approved care of a person residing in the United Kingdom or elsewhere; or

      (vi)   undertaking the care of a child whose parent or guardian is temporarily absent from the dwelling normally occupied by that parent or guardian for the purpose of receiving medically approved care or medical treatment; or

      (vii) a person who is, in the United Kingdom or elsewhere, receiving medically approved care provided in accommodation other than residential accommodation; or

      (viii) a student to whom paragraph (3) or (6)(b) does not apply; or

      (ix)   a person who is receiving care provided in residential accommodation other than a person to whom paragraph (11) applies; or

      (x)   a person who has left the dwelling he occupies as his home through fear of violence, in that dwelling, or by a person who was formerly a member of the family of the person first mentioned, and to whom paragraph (6)(a) does not apply; and

   (d)   the period of his absence is unlikely to exceed 52 weeks or, in exceptional circumstances, is unlikely substantially to exceed that period.

(17)   A person to whom paragraph (16) applies shall be treated as occupying the dwelling he normally occupies at his home during any period of absence not exceeding 52 weeks beginning from the first day of that absence.

(18)   In this regulation–

"medically approved" means certified by a medical practitioner;

"patient" means a person who is undergoing medical or other treatment as an in-patient in any hospital or similar institution;

"residential accommodation" means accommodation which is provided in–

   (a)   a care home;

   (b)   an independent hospital;

   (c)   an Abbeyfield Home; or

   (d)   an establishment managed or provided by a body incorporated by Royal Charter or constituted by Act of Parliament other than a local social services authority;

"training course" means a course of training or instruction provided wholly or partly by or on behalf of or in pursuance of arrangements made with, or approved by or on behalf of, [5 Skills Development Scotland,] Scottish Enterprise, Highlands and Islands Enterprise, a government department or the Secretary of State.

Amendments

1.   Amended by reg 6 of SI 2006 No 3274 as from 8.1.07.
2.   Amended by reg 12(3) of SI 2007 No 2618 as from 1.10.07.
3.   Amended by reg 4(3) of SI 2008 No 1042 as from 19.5.08.
4.   Amended by reg 7(3) of SI 2008 No 2767 as from 17.11.08.
5.   Amended by reg 7(3)(b) of SI 2009 No 583 as from 6.4.09.

General Note

Reg 7 is nearly identical to reg 7 HB Regs (see p238). The only difference is in para (8)(c)(ii). Here, among the other conditions, rather than requiring that the claimant's applicable amount includes one of specific premiums or components, the claimant or her/his partner need only have reached the qualifying age for PC (defined in reg 2(1)).

Circumstances in which a person is to be treated as liable to make payments in respect of a dwelling

8.–(1)   Subject to regulation 9 (circumstances in which a person is to be treated as not liable to make payments in respect of a dwelling), the following persons shall be treated as if they were liable to make payments in respect of a dwelling–

(a) the person who is liable to make those payments;
(b) a person who is a partner of the person to whom sub-paragraph (a) applies;
(c) a person who has to make the payments if he is to continue to live in the home because the person liable to make them is not doing so and either–
   (i) he was formerly a partner of the person who is so liable; or
   (ii) he is some other person whom it is reasonable to treat as liable to make the payments;
(d) a person whose liability to make such payments is waived by his landlord as reasonable compensation in return for works actually carried out by the tenant in carrying out reasonable repairs or redecoration which the landlord would otherwise have carried out or be required to carry out but this sub-paragraph shall apply only for a maximum of 8 benefit weeks in respect of any one waiver of liability;
(e) a person who is a partner of a student to whom regulation 56(1) of the Housing Benefit Regulations 2006 (circumstances in which certain students are treated as not liable to make payments in respect of a dwelling) applies.

(2) A person shall be treated as liable to make a payment in respect of a dwelling for the whole of the period in, or in respect of, which the payment is to be made notwithstanding that the liability is discharged in whole or in part either before or during that period and, where the amount which a person is liable to pay in respect of a period is varied either during or after that period, he shall, subject to regulations 59 to 62 (dates of relevant changes of circumstances, weekly amounts and housing benefit for rent free periods), be treated as liable to pay the amount as so varied during the whole of that period.

Circumstances in which a person is to be treated as not liable to make payments in respect of a dwelling

9.–(1) A person who is liable to make payments in respect of a dwelling shall be treated as if he were not so liable where–
(a) the tenancy or other agreement pursuant to which he occupies the dwelling is not on a commercial basis;
(b) his liability under the agreement is to a person who also resides in the dwelling and who is a close relative of his or of his partner;
(c) his liability under the agreement is–
   (i) to his former partner and is in respect of a dwelling which he and his former partner occupied before they ceased to be partners; or
   (ii) to his partner's former partner and is in respect of a dwelling which his partner and his partner's former partner occupied before they ceased to be partners;
(d) he is responsible, or his partner is responsible, for a child of the person to whom he is liable under the agreement;
(e) subject to paragraph (3), his liability under the agreement is to a company or a trustee of a trust of which–
   (i) he or his partner;
   (ii) his or his partner's close relative who resides with him; or
   (iii) his or his partner's former partner,
is, in the case of a company, a director or an employee, or, in the case of a trust, a trustee or a beneficiary;
(f) is liability under the agreement is to a trustee of a trust of which his or his partner's child is a beneficiary;
(g) subject to paragraph (3), before the liability was created, he was a non-dependant of someone who resided, and continues to reside, in the dwelling;
(h) he previously owned, or his partner previously owned, the dwelling in respect of which the liability arises and less than five years have elapsed since he or, as the case may be, his partner, ceased to own the property, save that this sub-paragraph shall not apply where he satisfies the appropriate authority that he or

his partner could not have continued to occupy that dwelling without relinquishing ownership;

[¹ (ha) he or his partner–
- (i)   was a tenant under a long tenancy in respect of the dwelling; and
- (ii)   less than five years have elapsed since that tenancy ceased,

except where he satisfies the appropriate authority that he or his partner could not have continued to occupy that dwelling without relinquishing the tenancy;]

- (i)   his occupation, or his partner's occupation, of the dwelling is a condition of his or his partner's employment by the landlord;
- (j)   he is a member of, and is wholly maintained (disregarding any liability he may have to make payments in respect of the dwelling he occupies as his home) by, a religious order;
- (k)   he is in residential accommodation;
- (l)   in a case to which the preceding sub-paragraphs do not apply, the appropriate authority is satisfied that the liability was created to take advantage of the housing benefit scheme established under Part 7 of the Act.

(2)   In determining whether a tenancy or other agreement pursuant to which a person occupies a dwelling is not on a commercial basis regard shall be had inter alia to whether the terms upon which the person occupies the dwelling include terms which are not enforceable at law.

(3)   Sub-paragraphs (e) and (g) of paragraph (1) shall not apply in a case where the person satisfies the appropriate authority that the liability was not intended to be a means of taking advantage of the housing benefit scheme.

(4)   In this regulation "residential accommodation" means accommodation which is provided in–
- (a)   a care home; or
- (b)   an independent hospital.

Modifications

Reg 9 applies as modified by Sch 3 para 9(3)(a) HB&CTB(CP) Regs (see p1223) to a claimant who on 3 October 2005 was someone to whom reg 7(2) of the HB Regs 1987 as then in force applied.

Reg 9 applies as modified by Sch 3 para 9(5)(a) HB&CTB(CP) Regs (see p1223) to a claimant who on 3 October 2005 was someone to whom reg 7(5) of the HB Regs 1987 as then in force applied.

Reg 9 applies as modified by Sch 3 para 9(7)(a) HB&CTB(CP) Regs (see p1223) to a claimant who on 3 October 2005 was someone to whom reg 7(7) of the HB Regs 1987 as then in force applied.

Amendment

1.   Inserted by reg 3(3) of SI 2007 No 1356 as from 1.10.07.

Persons from abroad

10.–(1)   A person from abroad who is liable to make payments in respect of a dwelling shall be treated as if he were not so liable but this paragraph shall not have effect in respect of a person to whom and for a period to which regulation 10A (entitlement of a refugee to housing benefit) and Schedule A1 (treatment of claims for housing benefit by refugees) apply.

[¹ (2)   In paragraph (1), "person from abroad" means, subject to the following provisions of this regulation, a person who is not habitually resident in the United Kingdom, the Channel Islands, the Isle of Man or the Republic of Ireland.

(3)   No person shall be treated as habitually resident in the United Kingdom, the Channel Islands, the Isle of Man or the Republic of Ireland unless he has a right to reside in (as the case may be) the United Kingdom, the Channel Islands, the Isle of Man or the Republic of Ireland other than a right to reside which falls within paragraph (4).

(4)   A right to reside falls within this paragraph if it is one which exists by virtue of, or in accordance with, one or more of the following–
- (a)   regulation 13 of the Immigration (European Economic Area) Regulations 2006;
- (b)   regulation 14 of those Regulations, but only in a case where the right exists under that regulation because the person is–

      (i)   a jobseeker for the purpose of the definition of ''qualified person'' in regulation 6(1) of those Regulations, or

      (ii)   a family member (within the meaning of regulation 7 of those Regulations) of such a jobseeker;

(c)   Article 6 of Council Directive No. 2004/38/EC; or

(d)   Article 39 of the Treaty establishing the European Community (in a case where the person is seeking work in the United Kingdom, the Channel Islands, the Isle of Man or the Republic of Ireland).

(4A) A person is not a person from abroad if he is–

(a)   a worker for the purposes of Council Directive No. 2004/38/EC;

(b)   a self-employed person for the purposes of that Directive;

(c)   a person who retains a status referred to in sub-paragraph (a) or (b) pursuant to Article 7(3) of that Directive;

(d)   a person who is a family member of a person referred to in sub-paragraph (a), (b) or (c) within the meaning of Article 2 of that Directive;

(e)   a person who has a right to reside permanently in the United Kingdom by virtue of Article 17 of that Directive;

[⁵ (f)   a person who is treated as a worker for the purpose of the definition of ''qualified person'' in regulation 6(1) of the Immigration (European Economic Area) Regulations 2006 pursuant to–

      (i)   regulation 5 of the Accession (Immigration and Worker Registration) Regulations 2004 (application of the 2006 Regulations in relation to a national of the Czech Republic, Estonia, Latvia, Lithuania, Hungary, Poland, Slovenia or the Slovak Republic who is an ''accession State worker requiring registration''), or

      (ii)   regulation 6 of the Accession (Immigration and Worker Authorisation) Regulations 2006 (right of residence of a Bulgarian or Romanian who is an ''accession State national subject to worker authorisation'');]

(g)   a refugee;

[⁴ (h) a person who has exceptional leave to enter or remain in the United Kingdom granted outside the rules made under section 3(2) of the Immigration Act 1971;

(hh) a person who has humanitarian protection granted under those rules;]

(i)   a person who is not a person subject to immigration control within the meaning of section 115(9) of the Immigration and Asylum Act 1999 and who is in the United Kingdom as a result of his deportation, expulsion or other removal by compulsion of law from another country to the United Kingdom;

(j)   a person in Great Britain who left the territory of Montserrat after 1st November 1995 because of the effect on that territory of a volcanic eruption; [⁶]

[⁶ (jj) a person who–

      (i)   arrived in Great Britain on or after 28th February 2009 but before 18th March 2011;

      (ii)   immediately before arriving there had been resident in Zimbabwe; and

      (iii) before leaving Zimbabwe, had accepted an offer, made by Her Majesty's Government, to assist that person to move to and settle in the United Kingdom; or]

(k)   on state pension credit.]

(5)   Paragraph (1) of Part 1 of the Schedule to, and regulation 2 as it applies to that paragraph of, the Social Security (Immigration and Asylum) Consequential Amendments Regulations 2000 shall not apply to a person who has been temporarily without funds for any period, or the aggregate of any periods, exceeding 42 days during any one period of limited leave (including any such period as extended).

(6)   In this regulation–

[²]

''refugee'' in this regulation means a person recorded by the Secretary of State as a refugee within the definition in Article 1 of the Convention relating to the Status of Refugees.

Modifications

Reg 10(4A)(a) to (e) applies in relation to a national of Norway, Iceland, Liechtenstein or Switzerland or a member of her/his family (within the meaning of Art 2 of Council Directive No.2004/38/EC) as if such a national were a national of a member state. See reg 10 of SI 2006 No.1026 on p1226.

The amendments made by SI 2006 No.1026 do not affect the continued operation of the transitional and savings provided for in reg 12 Social Security (Persons From Abroad) Miscellaneous Amendments Regulations 1996 (see p1153), reg 6 Social Security (Habitual Residence) Amendment Regulations 2004 (see p1192) or Sch 3 para 6 HB&CTB(CP) Regs (see p1215). See reg 11 of SI 2006 No.1026 on p1226.

From 25 July 2006 until 31 January 2007, a para (4A)(jj) was inserted by the Social Security (Lebanon) Amendment Regulations 2006 SI No.1981. See p701 of the 20th edition for the text of the insertion.

Amendments

1.	Substituted by reg 5(2)(a) of SI 2006 No 1026 as from 30.4.06.
2.	Omitted by reg 5(2)(b) of SI 2006 No 1026 as from 30.4.06.
3.	Amended by reg 6 of SI 2006 No 1981 from 25.7.06 until 31.1.07 only.
4.	Amended by reg 6 of SI 2006 No 2528 as from 9.10.06.
5.	Substituted by reg 6 of SI 2006 No 3341 as from 1.1.07.
6.	Amended by reg 6 of SI 2009 No 362 as from 18.3.09.

Definition

"person on state pension credit" – see reg 2(1).

General Note

Claimants in receipt of PC are exempt from having the habitual residence test applied to them for HB purposes: para (4A)(k).

Entitlement of a refugee to Housing Benefit
[¹ 10A.]

Modification

Reg 10A was inserted by Sch 4 para 2(1) HB&CTB(CP) Regs. It only applied to claims for HB by some refugees.

Amendment

1.	Lapsed by s12(2)(e) of the Asylum and Immigration (Treatment of Claimants, etc.) Act 2004 (for those recorded as refugees after 14.6.07).

PART 3
Payments in respect of a dwelling

Eligible housing costs

[¹**11.**–(1) Subject to the following provisions of this regulation, housing benefit shall be payable in respect of the payments specified in regulation 12(1) (rent) and a claimant's maximum housing benefit shall be calculated under Part 7 (amount of benefit) by reference to the amount of his eligible rent determined in accordance with–

(a)	regulation 12B (eligible rent);

(b)	regulations 12C (eligible rent and maximum rent), 13 (maximum rent), 13ZA (protection on death and 13 week protection) and 13ZB (change in reckonable rent);

(c)	regulations 12D (eligible rent and maximum rent (LHA)), 13C (when a maximum rent (LHA) is to be determined) and 13D (determination of a maximum rent (LHA)); or

(d)	regulations 12 (rent) and 13 (restrictions on unreasonable payments) as set out in paragraph 5 of Schedule 3 to the Consequential Provisions Regulations,

whichever is applicable in his case.]

(2)	Where any payment for which a person is liable in respect of a dwelling and which is specified in regulation 12(1) (payments of rent for which housing benefit is payable), is increased on account of–

(a)	outstanding arrears of any payment or charge; or

(b)	any other unpaid payment or charge,

to which [¹ paragraphs (1) or (2) of that regulation or paragraph (2) of regulation 12B] or Schedule 1 (ineligible service charges) refer and which is or was formerly owed by him in respect of that or another dwelling, a rent rebate or, as the case may be, a rent allowance shall not be payable in respect of that increase.

Modifications

Para (1) substituted by reg 4(3)(a) Housing Benefit (State Pension Credit) (Local Housing Allowance and Information Sharing) Amendment Regulations 2007 SI No.2869 as from 7 April 2008, save that for a person to whom reg 1(5) of those regulations applied (see p1233), the amendments came into force on the day on or after 7 April 2008 when the first of the events specified in reg 1(6) applied to her/him, or on 6 April 2009 if none had before that date.

Reg 11 is modified by Sch 9 para 3 (see p907). This applies only to former Pathfinder Authorities who administered the pilot local housing allowance scheme.

Amendment

1.   Substituted by reg 4(3) of SI 2007 No 2869 as from 7.4.08 (or if reg 1(5) of that SI applies, on the day on or after 7.4.08 when the first of the events specified in reg 1(6) applies, or from 6.4.09 if none have before that date).

General Note

Reg 4(3)(b) Housing Benefit (State Pension Credit) (Local Housing Allowance and Information Sharing) Amendment Regulations 2007 SI No.2869 says in respect of reg 11 HB(SPC) Regs: in paragraph (3) for "paragraphs (1) to (3) of that regulation" substitute "paragraphs (1) or (2) of that regulation or paragraph (2) of regulation 12B". It is clear that this is meant to be an amendment to subparagraph (2).

Rent

12.–(1)   Subject to the following provisions of this regulation, the payments in respect of which housing benefit is payable in the form of a rent rebate or allowance are the following periodical payments which a person is liable to make in respect of the dwelling which he occupies as his home–

(a)   payments of, or by way of, rent;

(b)   payments in respect of a licence or permission to occupy the dwelling;

(c)   payments by way of mesne profits or, in Scotland, violent profits;

(d)   payments in respect of, or in consequence of, use and occupation of the dwelling;

(e)   payments of, or by way of, service charges payment of which is a condition on which the right to occupy the dwelling depends;

(f)   mooring charges payable for a houseboat;

(g)   where the home is a caravan or a mobile home, payments in respect of the site on which it stands;

(h)   any contribution payable by a person resident in an almshouse provided by a housing association which is either a charity of which particulars are entered in the register of charities established under section 3 of the Charities Act 1993 (register of charities) or an exempt charity within the meaning of that Act, which is a contribution towards the cost of maintaining that association's almshouses and essential services in them;

(i)   payments under a rental purchase agreement, that is to say an agreement for the purchase of a dwelling which is a building or part of one under which the whole or part of the purchase price is to be paid in more than one instalment and the completion of the purchase is deferred until the whole or a specified part of the purchase price has been paid; and

(j)   where, in Scotland, the dwelling is situated on or pertains to a croft within the meaning of section 3(1) of the Crofters (Scotland) Act 1993, the payment in respect of the croft land.

(2)   A rent rebate or, as the case may be, a rent allowance shall not be payable in respect of the following periodical payments–

(a)   payments under a long tenancy except a shared ownership tenancy [¹];

(b)   payments under a co-ownership scheme;

(c)   payments by an owner;

(d)   payments under a hire purchase, credit sale or conditional sale agreement except to the extent the conditional sale agreement is in respect of land; and

(e)   payments by a Crown tenant.

[¹ (f) payments by a person in respect of a dwelling where his partner is an owner of that dwelling.]

[² (3)]

[² (4)]

[² (5)]

[² (6)]

[² (7)]

(8)   In this regulation [³ , regulation 12B (eligible rent)] and Schedule 1 (ineligible service charges)–

"service charges" means periodical payments for services, whether or not under the same agreement as that under which the dwelling is occupied, or whether or not such a charge is specified as separate from or separately identified within other payments made by the occupier in respect of the dwelling; and

"services" means services performed or facilities (including the use of furniture) provided for, or rights made available to, the occupier of a dwelling.

Modifications

Paras (3) to (7) omitted and para (8) amended by reg 4(4) Housing Benefit (State Pension Credit) (Local Housing Allowance and Information Sharing) Amendment Regulations 2007 SI No.2869 as from 7 April 2008, save that for a person to whom reg 1(5) of those regulations applied (see p1233), the amendments came into force on the day on or after 7 April 2008 when the first of the events specified in reg 1(6) applied to her/him, or on 6 April 2009 if none had before that date.

A different version of reg 12 is substituted and used to determine eligible rent for some claimants entitled to HB on 1 January 1996. See Sch 3 paras 4 and 5 (1) HB&CTB(CP) Regs on p1199.

Amendments

1.   Inserted by reg 3(4) of SI 2007 No 1356 as from 1.10.07.

2.   Omitted by reg 4(4)(a) of SI 2007 No 2869 as from 7.4.08 (or if reg 1(5) of that SI applies, on the day on or after 7.4.08 when the first of the events specified in reg 1(6) applies, or from 6.4.09 if none have before that date).

3.   Amended by reg 4(4)(b) of SI 2007 No 2869 as from 7.4.08 (or if reg 1(5) of that SI applies, on the day on or after 7.4.08 when the first of the events specified in reg 1(6) applies, or from 6.4.09 if none have before that date).

[¹ **Eligible rent**

12B.–(1)   The amount of a person's eligible rent shall be determined in accordance with the provisions of this regulation except where regulations 12C (eligible rent and maximum rent) or 12D (eligible rent and maximum rent (LHA)) apply, or paragraph 4 of Schedule 3 to the Consequential Provisions Regulations applies.

(2)   Subject to paragraphs (3), (4) and (6), the amount of a person's eligible rent shall be the aggregate of such payments specified in regulation 12(1) as that person is liable to pay less–

(a)   except where he is separately liable for charges for water, sewerage or allied environmental services, an amount determined in accordance with paragraph (5);

(b)   where payments include service charges which are wholly or partly ineligible, an amount in respect of the ineligible charges determined in accordance with Schedule 1; and

(c)   where he is liable to make payments in respect of any service charges to which regulation 12(1)(e) does not apply, but to which paragraph 3(2) of Part 1 of Schedule 1 (unreasonably low service charges) applies in the particular circumstances, an amount in respect of such charges determined in accordance with paragraph 3(2) of Part 1 of Schedule 1.

(3)   Where the payments specified in regulation 12(1) are payable in respect of accommodation which consists partly of residential accommodation and partly of other accommodation, only such proportion of those payments as is referable to the residential accommodation shall count as eligible rent for the purposes of these Regulations.

(4)   Where more than one person is liable to make payments in respect of a dwelling, the payments specified in regulation 12(1) shall be apportioned for the purpose of

calculating the eligible rent for each such person having regard to all the circumstances, in particular, the number of such persons and the proportion of rent paid by each such person.

(5)   The amount of the deduction referred to in paragraph (2) shall be–

(a)   if the dwelling occupied by the claimant is a self-contained unit, except in a case to which sub-paragraph (c) applies, the amount of the charges;

(b)   in any other case, except one to which sub-paragraph (c) applies, the proportion of those charges in respect of the self-contained unit which is obtained by dividing the area of the dwelling occupied by the claimant by the area of the self-contained unit of which it forms part;

(c)   where the charges vary in accordance with the amount of water actually used, the amount which the appropriate authority considers to be fairly attributable to water, and sewerage services, having regard to the actual or estimated consumption of the claimant.

(6)   In any case where it appears to the relevant authority that in the particular circumstances of that case the eligible rent as determined in accordance with the preceding paragraphs of this regulation is greater than it is reasonable to meet by way of housing benefit, the eligible rent shall be such lesser sum as seems to that authority to be an appropriate rent in that particular case.]

Modifications

Reg 12B is modified by Sch 9 para 4 (see p907). This applies only to former Pathfinder Authorities who administered the pilot local housing allowance scheme.

Amendment

1.   Inserted by reg 5 of SI 2007 No 2869 as from 7.4.08 (or if reg 1(5) of that SI applies, on the day on or after 7.4.08 when the first of the events specified in reg 1(6) applies, or from 6.4.09 if none have before that date).

[¹ Eligible rent and maximum rent

12C.–(1)   This regulation applies where a maximum rent has been, or is to be, determined in accordance with regulation 13 (maximum rent).

(2)   Where this regulation applies the amount of a person's eligible rent shall be the maximum rent, subject to paragraphs (3), (4) and (6) of regulation 12B.]

Amendment

1.   Inserted by reg 5 of SI 2007 No 2869 as from 7.4.08 (or if reg 1(5) of that SI applies, on the day on or after 7.4.08 when the first of the events specified in reg 1(6) applies, or from 6.4.09 if none have before that date).

[¹ Eligible rent and maximum rent (LHA)

12D.–(1)   This regulation applies where, by virtue of paragraphs (2) or (3) of regulation 13C (when a maximum rent (LHA) is to be determined), a maximum rent (LHA) has been, or is to be, determined in accordance with regulation 13D (determination of a maximum rent (LHA)).

(2)   Where this regulation applies, except where paragraphs (3)(a) (protection on death) or (5)(a) (13 week protection) apply,–

(a)   the amount of a person's eligible rent shall be the maximum rent (LHA); and

(b)   it shall apply until the earlier of–

(i)   the determination of a maximum rent (LHA) by virtue of regulation 13C(2)(d) (change of category of dwelling, death or change of dwelling for an LHA case);

(ii)   the determination of a maximum rent (LHA) by virtue of regulation 13C(3) (anniversary of LHA date); or

(iii)   the determination of a maximum rent by virtue of regulation 13 or an eligible rent under regulation 12B.

(3)   Subject to paragraph (7), where the relevant authority is required to determine a maximum rent (LHA) by virtue of regulation 13C(2)(a), (b) (new claim on or after 7th

April 2008) or (d)(i) or (ii) (change of category of dwelling or death relating to an LHA case) and the claimant occupies a dwelling which is the same as that occupied by him at the date of death of any linked person, the eligible rent shall be–

(a)   either–

      (i)   the eligible rent which applied on the day before the death occurred; or

      (ii)   in a case where there was no eligible rent, subject to regulation 12B(3) (mixed use accommodation), (4) (more than one person liable to make payments) and (6) (discretion in relation to eligible rent), the reckonable rent due on that day; or

(b)   the eligible rent determined in accordance with paragraph (2), where it is equal to or more than the eligible rent determined in accordance with sub-paragraph (a).

(4)   For the purpose of paragraph (3), a claimant shall be treated as occupying the dwelling if paragraph (13) of regulation 7 (circumstances in which a person is or is not to be treated as occupying a dwelling as his home) is satisfied and for that purpose paragraph (13) shall have effect as if sub-paragraph (b) of that paragraph were omitted.

(5)   Subject to paragraphs (6) and (7), where a relevant authority is required to determine a maximum rent (LHA) by virtue of regulation 13C(2)(a) or (b) (new claim on or after 7th April 2008) and the relevant authority is satisfied that the claimant or a linked person was able to meet the financial commitments for his dwelling when they were entered into, the eligible rent shall be–

(a)   an eligible rent determined in accordance with regulation 12B(2); or

(b)   the eligible rent determined in accordance with paragraph (2), where it is equal to or more than the eligible rent referred to in sub-paragraph (a).

(6)   Paragraph (5) shall not apply where a claimant or the claimant's partner, was previously entitled to benefit in respect of an award of housing benefit which fell wholly or partly less than 52 weeks before the commencement of the claimant's current award of housing benefit.

(7)   Where a person's eligible rent has been determined in accordance with–

(a)   paragraph (3)(a) (protection on death), it shall apply until the first of the following events occurs–

      (i)   the period of 12 months from the date of death has expired;

      (ii)   the relevant authority determines an eligible rent in accordance with paragraph (2) which is equal to or exceeds it or is based on a maximum rent (LHA) determined by virtue of regulation 13C(2)(d)(iii) (change of dwelling);

      (iii)   the determination of an eligible rent in accordance with paragraph (3)(a) (protection on death) in relation to a subsequent death; or

      (iv)   the determination of a maximum rent by virtue of regulation 13 or an eligible rent under regulation 12B.

(b)   paragraph (5)(a) (13 week protection), it shall apply until the first of the following events occurs–

      (i)   the first 13 weeks of the claimant's award of housing benefit have expired;

      (ii)   the relevant authority determines an eligible rent in accordance with paragraph (2) which is equal to or exceeds it or is based on a maximum rent (LHA) determined by virtue of regulation 13C(2)(d)(iii) (change of dwelling);

      (iii)   the determination of an eligible rent in accordance with paragraph (3)(a) (protection on death); or

      (iv)   the determination of a maximum rent by virtue of regulation 13 or an eligible rent under regulation 12B.

(8)   Where an eligible rent ceases to apply by virtue of paragraph (7)(a)(i) (expiry of protection on death) or (7)(b)(i) (expiry of 13 week protection), the eligible rent that shall apply instead shall be the one which would have applied but for paragraphs (3)(a) and (5)(a).]

Modifications

Reg 12D is modified by Sch 9 para 5 (see p907). This applies only to former Pathfinder Authorities who administered the pilot local housing allowance scheme.

Amendment

1.   Inserted by reg 5 of SI 2007 No 2869 as from 7.4.08 (or if reg 1(5) of that SI applies, on the day on or after 7.4.08 when the first of the events specified in reg 1(6) applies, or from 6.4.09 if none have before that date).

Basic transitional protection for pathfinder cases
12E.

Modification

Reg 12E is inserted by Sch 9 para 6 (see p907). It only applies to former Pathfinder Authorities who administered the pilot local housing allowance scheme.

Cases where the claimant enjoyed protection on death before 7th April 2008
12F.

Modification

Reg 12F is inserted by Sch 9 para 6 (see p907). It only applies to former Pathfinder Authorities who administered the pilot local housing allowance scheme.

Cases where the claimant enjoyed 13 week protection before 7th April 2008
12G.

Modification

Reg 12G is inserted by Sch 9 para 6 (see p907). It only applies to former Pathfinder Authorities who administered the pilot local housing allowance scheme.

Cases where a death occurs in the first year on or after 7th April 2008
12H.

Modification

Reg 12H is inserted by Sch 9 para 6 (see p907). It only applies to former Pathfinder Authorities who administered the pilot local housing allowance scheme.

Basic transitional protection in the second year and subsequent years after 7th April 2008
12I.

Modification

Reg 12I is inserted by Sch 9 para 6 (see p907). It only applies to former Pathfinder Authorities who administered the pilot local housing allowance scheme.

Transitional protection in the second year after 7th April 2008 where the claimant is already enjoying protection on death
12J.

Modification

Reg 12J is inserted by Sch 9 para 6 (see p907). It only applies to former Pathfinder Authorities who administered the pilot local housing allowance scheme.

Protection on death in the second and subsequent years after 7th April 2008
12K.

Modification

Reg 12K is inserted by Sch 9 para 6 (see p907). It only applies to former Pathfinder Authorities who administered the pilot local housing allowance scheme.

[¹ Transitional protection – larger properties

12L.–(1)   This regulation applies where–

(a)   reference was made to a maximum rent (LHA) in determining the amount of the eligible rent which applied immediately before 6th April 2009;

(b)   the category of dwelling for which that maximum rent (LHA) was determined corresponded to a category of six or more bedrooms; and

(c)   on or after 6th April 2009 the relevant authority is required to determine a maximum rent (LHA) by virtue of–

    (i)   regulation 13C(2)(d)(i) (change of category of dwelling), where it has not received notification of the death of a linked person; or

    (ii)   regulation 13C(3) (anniversary of the LHA date).

(2)   Where this regulation applies, the claimant's eligible rent is–

(a)   the maximum rent (LHA) where that is equal to or higher than the eligible rent that applied immediately before 6th April 2009; or

(b)   the amount of the eligible rent which applied immediately before 6th April 2009.

(3)   Where the eligible rent is the amount of the eligible rent which applied immediately before 6th April 2009, it will continue to apply until, on or after 6th April 2009, the first of the following events occurs–

(a)   the end of 26 weeks after the determination of the maximum rent (LHA) referred to in paragraph (1)(c);

(b)   the relevant authority is required to determine a maximum rent (LHA) by virtue of regulation 13C (when a maximum rent (LHA) is to be determined) because the claimant has become entitled to a smaller category of dwelling;

(c)   the relevant authority is required to determine an eligible rent following a change of dwelling; or

(d)   the relevant authority is required to determine an eligible rent in accordance with regulation 12D(3) (protection on death).

(4)   Where the eligible rent ceases to apply because of paragraph (3)(a), the eligible rent will be the maximum rent (LHA) which would have applied but for the transitional protection in paragraph (2)(b).

(5)   Where the eligible rent is the maximum rent (LHA), it shall be treated as if it had been determined in accordance with regulation 12D(2)(a) (eligible rent is maximum rent (LHA)) and shall apply according to the provisions of regulation 12D.]

Amendment

1.   Inserted by reg 3(2) of SI 2009 No 614 as from 6.4.09.

Maximum rent

[¹ **13.**–1)   The maximum rent shall be determined in accordance with paragraphs (2) to (6) where–

(a)   a local authority has applied for a determination in accordance with regulation 14 (requirement to refer to rent officers), a redetermination in accordance with regulation 15 or 16, or a substitute determination or substitute redetermination in accordance with regulation 17 and a rent officer has made a determination, redetermination, substitute determination or substitute redetermination in exercise of the Housing Act functions; or

(b)   an authority is not required to apply to the rent officer for a determination because–

    (i)   regulation 14(2)(a) applies; or

    (ii)   regulation 14(2)(b) applies because paragraph 2(2) of Schedule 2 applies.

(2)   In a case where the rent officer has determined a claim-related rent, but is not required to notify the relevant authority of a local reference rent, the maximum rent shall be that claim-related rent.

(3)   Subject to the limit specified in paragraph (4), in a case where the rent officer has determined both a local reference rent of which he is required to notify the relevant authority and a claim-related rent, the maximum rent shall be the local reference rent.

(4)　In a case to which paragraph 8 of Schedule 3 to the Consequential Provisions Regulations applies, where the rent officer has determined and is required to notify the relevant authority of a local reference rent the maximum rent shall not exceed twice that local reference rent.

(5)　Where the maximum rent is derived from–

(a)　a claim-related rent and the notification under paragraph 9(1)(c) of Schedule 1 to the Rent Officers Order states that an ineligible amount in respect of meals has been included in that claim-related rent; or

(b)　a local reference rent and the notification under paragraph 9(1)(da) of Schedule 1 to the Rent Officers Order states that an ineligible amount in respect of meals has been included in that local reference rent,

in determining the maximum rent the relevant authority shall deduct an amount determined in accordance with paragraph 2 of Schedule 1 to these Regulations in respect of meals.

(6)　This regulation is subject to regulations 13ZA (protection on death and 13 week protection) and 13ZB (change in reckonable rent).

(7)　In this regulation–

"claim-related rent" means the rent notified by the rent officer under paragraph 9(1) of Schedule 1 to the Rent Officers Order;

"local reference rent" means the rent determined by a rent officer under paragraph 4 of Schedule 1 to the Rent Officers Order.]

Amendment

1.　Inserted by reg 6 of SI 2007 No 2869 as from 7.4.08 (or if reg 1(5) that SI applies, on the day on or after 7.4.08 when the first of the events specified in reg 1(6) applies, or from 6.4.09 if none have before that date).

Modifications

Reg 13 substituted by reg 6 Housing Benefit (State Pension Credit) (Local Housing Allowance and Information Sharing) Amendment Regulations 2007 SI No.2869 as from 7 April 2008, save that for a person to whom reg 1(5) of those regulations applied (see p1233), the amendments came into force on the day on or after 7 April 2008 when the first of the events specified in reg 1(6) applied to her/him, or on 6 April 2009 if none had before that date.

A different version of reg 13 is substituted for some claimants entitled to HB on 1 January 1996. See Sch 3 paras 4 and 5(2) HB&CTB(CP) Regs on p1199.

Reg 13 applies as modified by Sch 3 para 8 HB&CTB(CP) Regs (see p1205) for some claimants entitled to HB on or before 5 October 1997.

General Note

Reg 13 is nearly identical to reg 13 HB Regs (see p312). In these regs, there are naturally no rules in respect of a "young individual".

[¹ Protection on death and 13 week protection

13ZA.–(1)　In a case where the claimant occupies a dwelling which is the same as that occupied by him at the date of death of a linked person, the maximum rent shall be either–

(a)　the maximum rent which applied before the death occurred; or

(b)　in a case where there was no maximum rent, the reckonable rent due before the death occurred,

for a period of 12 months from the date of such a death.

(2)　For the purposes of paragraph (1), a claimant shall be treated as occupying the dwelling if paragraph (13) of regulation 7 (circumstances in which a person is or is not to be treated as occupying a dwelling as his home) is satisfied and for that purpose sub-paragraph (b) of that paragraph of that regulation shall be treated as if it were omitted.

(3)　Subject to paragraph (4), where the relevant authority is satisfied that the claimant or a linked person was able to meet the financial commitments for his dwelling when they were entered into, there shall be no maximum rent during the first 13 weeks of the claimant's award of housing benefit.

(4)　Paragraph (3) shall not apply where a claimant or the claimant's partner was previously entitled to benefit in respect of an award of housing benefit which fell wholly or partly less than 52 weeks before the commencement of the claimant's current award of housing benefit.]

Modifications

A different version of reg 13ZA is substituted for some claimants entitled to HB on 1 January 1996. See Sch 3 paras 4 and 5(3) HB&CTB(CP) Regs on p1198.

Amendment

1.   Inserted by reg 6 of SI 2007 No 2869 as from 7.4.08 (or if reg 1(5) that SI applies, on the day on or after 7.4.08 when the first of the events specified in reg 1(6) applies, or from 6.4.09 if none have before that date).

[¹ Change in reckonable rent

13ZB.–(1)   In a case where–

(a)   the authority has determined a maximum rent under regulation 13 or 13ZA; and

(b)   during the period for which that maximum rent applies the reckonable rent in respect of the dwelling by reference to which that maximum rent was determined is reduced to a sum which is less than that maximum rent,

the maximum rent shall be reduced to an amount equal to the reduced reckonable rent.

(2)   This paragraph applies in a case where–

(a)   a rent officer has made a determination in exercise of the Housing Act functions pursuant to an application by an authority under regulation 14(1)(e) (pre-tenancy determination);

(b)   subsequent to that determination the reckonable rent for that dwelling is changed; and

(c)   a maximum rent is to be determined in relation to a claim for housing benefit by a claimant.

(3)   In a case to which paragraph (2) applies, where the reckonable rent is reduced to a figure below the figure that would have been the maximum rent if the reckonable rent had not changed, the maximum rent shall be the reckonable rent as so reduced.

(4)   In any other case to which paragraph (2) applies, the authority shall treat the reckonable rent to be that applicable to the determination by the rent officer referred to in paragraph (2)(a).]

Amendment

1.   Inserted by reg 6 of SI 2007 No 2869 as from 7.4.08 (or if reg 1(5) that SI applies, on the day on or after 7.4.08 when the first of the events specified in reg 1(6) applies, or from 6.4.09 if none have before that date).

[¹ When a maximum rent (LHA) is to be determined

13C.–(1)   A relevant authority shall determine a maximum rent (LHA) in accordance with regulation 13D (determination of a maximum rent (LHA)) in any case where paragraphs (2) or (3) apply.

(2)   This paragraph applies where a relevant authority has received–

(a)   a claim on which a rent allowance may be awarded, where the date of claim falls on or after 7th April 2008;

(b)   relevant information regarding a claim on which a rent allowance may be awarded, where the date of claim falls on or after 7th April 2008;

(c)   in relation to an award of housing benefit where the eligible rent was determined without reference to regulation 13A or 13D, a notification of a change of dwelling (as defined in regulation 2) where the change occurs on or after 7th April 2008; or

(d)   in relation to an award of housing benefit where a maximum rent (LHA) was determined in accordance with regulation 13D–

(i)   notification of a change of a kind which affects the category of dwelling applicable to the claim;

(ii)   notification of the death of a linked person, where the notification does not fall within head (i); or

(iii)   notification of a change of dwelling.

(3)   This paragraph applies on the anniversary of the LHA date.

(4)   Where the LHA date is 29th February, the anniversary of the LHA date shall be 28th February.

(5)   This regulation does not apply in a case where–

[³ (a)   the landlord is–

   (i)   a registered social landlord,

   (ii)   a non-profit registered provider of social housing, or

   (iii)   in relation to a dwelling which is social housing (within the meaning of sections 68 to 77 of the Housing and Regeneration Act 2008), a profit-making registered provider of social housing;]

(b)   paragraph 4(1)(b) of Schedule 3 to the Consequential Provisions Regulations (savings provision) applies;

(c)   the tenancy is an excluded tenancy of a type [² mentioned in any of paragraphs 4 to 11] of Schedule 2;

(d)   the claim or award relates to–

   (i)   periodical payments of kind falling within regulation 12(1) (rent) which a person is liable to make in relation to a houseboat, caravan or mobile home which he occupies as his home; or

   (ii)   rent payable in relation to a hostel; or

(e)   rent under the tenancy is attributable to board and attendance, and–

   (i)   the relevant authority has made an application to the rent officer in accordance with regulation 13D(10) (board and attendance determination), regulation 15 (applications to the rent officer for determinations) or regulation 17 (substitute determinations or substitute redeterminations); and

   (ii)   the rent officer has determined that a substantial part of the rent under the tenancy is fairly attributable to board and attendance and has notified the relevant authority of this in accordance with article 4C, 4D or 4E of the Rent Officers Order.

(6)   In this regulation–

"the LHA date" means the date by reference to which the local housing allowance used to determine the maximum rent (LHA) was identified;

"registered social landlord" has the same meaning as in Part 1 of the Housing Act 1996 or, in Scotland, sections 57 and 59 of the Housing (Scotland) Act 2001.]

Modifications

Reg 13C is modified by Sch 9 para 7 (see p907). This applies only to former Pathfinder Authorities who administered the pilot local housing allowance scheme.

Amendments

1.   Inserted by reg 7 of SI 2007 No 2869 as from 7.4.08 (or if reg 1(5) that SI applies, on the day on or after 7.4.08 when the first of the events specified in reg 1(6) applies, or from 6.4.09 if none have before that date).

2.   Amended by reg 5(4)(a) of SI 2008 No 586 as from 7.4.08.

3.   Substituted by Art 4 and Sch 1 para 58 of SI 2010 No 671 as from 1.4.10.

[¹ Determination of a maximum rent (LHA)

13D.–(1)   Subject to paragraph (3) to (11), the maximum rent (LHA) shall be the local housing allowance determined by the rent officer by virtue of article 4B(2A) or (4) of the Rent Officers Order which is applicable to–

(a)   the broad rental market area in which the dwelling to which the claim or award of housing benefit relates is situated at the relevant date; and

(b)   the category of dwelling which applies at the relevant date in accordance with paragraph (2).

(2)   The category of dwelling which applies is–

(a)   the category specified in paragraph 1(1)(a) of Schedule 3B to the Rent Officers Order (one bedroom shared accommodation) where paragraph (b) does not apply because neither sub-paragraph (b)(i) nor (ii) are satisfied in the claimant's case and–

    (i)   neither the claimant nor his partner (where he has one) is a person to whom paragraph 6 of Schedule 3 (severe disability premium) applies; or

    [² (ii) the claimant's partner is not a care leaver;]

(b)   the category specified in paragraph 1(1)(b) of Schedule 3B to the Rent Officers Order (one bedroom self contained accommodation) where that applies in the claimant's case at the relevant date in accordance with the size criteria [² as set out in paragraph (3)] and–

    (i)   the claimant (together with his partner where he has one) has the exclusive use of two or more rooms; or

    (ii)   the claimant (together with his partner where he has one) has the exclusive use of one room, a bathroom and toilet and a kitchen or facilities for cooking,

and in this sub-paragraph "room" means a bedroom or room suitable for living in except for a room which the claimant shares with any person other than a member of his household, a non-dependant of his, or a person who pays rent to him or his partner; or

(c)   in any other case, the category which corresponds with the number of bedrooms to which the claimant is entitled in accordance with paragraph (3) [³ to a maximum of five bedrooms].

(3)   The claimant shall be entitled to one bedroom for each of the following categories of occupier (and each occupier shall come within the first category only which applies to him)–

(a)   a couple (within the meaning of Part 7 of the Act);

(b)   a person who is not a child;

(c)   two children of the same sex;

(d)   two children who are less than 10 years old;

(e)   a child.

(4)   The relevant authority shall determine–

(a)   the cap rent (in accordance with the definition in paragraph (12)); and

(b)   whether the cap rent exceeds the applicable local housing allowance.

(5)   Where the applicable local housing allowance exceeds the cap rent, for the purpose of determining the appropriate maximum housing benefit, the amount of the claimant's liability shall be the amount of the applicable local housing allowance.

(6)   Where paragraph (5) applies, the maximum rent (LHA) shall be the lower of–

(a)   the applicable local housing allowance; or

(b)   the amount equal to the cap rent determined in accordance with paragraph (4)(a) plus £15.

[³ (7)]

(8)   Subject to paragraph (9), where–

(a)   the relevant authority receives a request from a person stating that–

    (i)   he is contemplating occupying as his home a dwelling within the area of the relevant authority which contains a specified number of bedrooms, exceeding five, and

    (ii)   that if he does so, he is likely to claim housing benefit; and

(b)   no local housing allowance determination is in effect for a broad rental market area falling within, in whole or in part, the area of the relevant authority for the category of dwelling containing the number of bedrooms specified in the request,

the relevant authority shall apply to the rent officer for local housing allowance determinations for each broad rental market area falling within its area, in whole or in part, for the category of dwelling containing the number of bedrooms specified in the request, and in this sub-paragraph "bedroom" means has the meaning specified in paragraph 1(2) of Schedule 3B to the Rent Officers Order.

(9)   The request must–

(a)   be made on a form approved by the relevant authority for the purpose of making a request under paragraph (8);

(b)   be properly completed; and

(c)   contain the following matters–

    (i)   the signature of the prospective occupier;

    (ii)   the signature of the person to whom the prospective occupier would incur liability to make such payments;

    (iii)   a statement that the person in paragraph (ii) agrees to the application being made for that determination; and

    (iv)   an indication that the prospective occupier is contemplating occupying the dwelling as his home and that if he does so, he is likely to claim housing benefit.

(10)   The relevant authority shall apply to the rent officer for a board and attendance determination to be made in accordance with article 4C of the Rent Officers Order where–

(a)   the relevant authority is required to determine a maximum rent (LHA) by virtue of regulation 13C; and

(b)   part of the rent under the tenancy appears to the relevant authority to be likely to be attributable to board and attendance.

(11)   Where an application to a rent officer is required in accordance with paragraph (10) it shall be made within the same period following the day on which the relevant authority becomes obliged to determine a maximum rent (LHA) by virtue of regulation 13C as would be required if the application were to be made under regulation 14(1).

(12)   In this regulation–

"cap rent" means the aggregate of such payments specified in regulation 12(1) (rent) which the claimant is liable to pay, or is treated as liable to pay by virtue of regulation 8 (circumstances in which a person is treated as liable to make payments in respect of a dwelling) subject to regulation 12B(3) (mixed use accommodation), (4) (more than one person liable to make payments) and (6) (discretion in relation to eligible rent);

"care leaver" means a person who has not attained the age of 22 and–

(a)   has ceased to be the subject of a care order made pursuant to section 31(1)(a) of the Children Act 1989 which had previously been made in respect to him either–

    (i)   after he attained the age of 16 years; or

    (ii)   before he attained the age of 16 years, but had continued after he attained that age;

(b)   was formerly provided with accommodation under section 20 of the Children Act 1989;

(c)   has ceased to be subject to a supervision requirement by a children's hearing under section 70 of the Children (Scotland) Act 1995 ("the 1995 Act") made in respect of him which had continued after he attained the age of 16 years, other than a case where–

    (i)   the ground of referral was based on the sole condition as to the need for compulsory measures of care specified in section 52(1)(i) of the 1995 Act (commission of offences by child); or

    (ii)   he was required by virtue of the supervision requirement to reside with a parent or guardian of his within the meaning of the 1995 Act, or with a friend or relative of his or of his parent or guardian;

(d)   has ceased to be a child in relation to whom the parental rights and responsibilities were transferred to a local authority under a parental responsibilities order made in accordance with section 86 of the 1995 Act or treated as so vested in accordance with paragraph 3 of Schedule 3 to that Act, either–

    (i)   after he attained the age of 16 years; or

    (ii)   before he attained the age of 16 years, but had continued after he attained that age; or

(e)   has ceased to be provided with accommodation by a local authority under section 25 of the 1995 Act where he has previously been provided with accommodation by the authority under that provision either–

    (i)   after he attained the age of 16 years; or

(ii)   before he attained the age of 16 years, but had continued to be in such accommodation after he attained that age;

"occupiers" means the persons whom the relevant authority is satisfied occupy as their home the dwelling to which the claim or award relates except for any joint tenant who is not a member of the claimant's household;

"relevant date" means, as the case may require–

(a)   the date of the claim to which the claim or relevant information referred to in regulation 13C (2) (a) or (b) relates;

(b)   the date of the change of dwelling, change which affects the category of dwelling, or date of death, to which a notification referred to in regulation 13C(2)(c) or (d) relates; or

(c)   the date on which the anniversary of the LHA date referred to in regulation 13C(3) falls.

"tenancy" includes

(a)   in Scotland, any other right of occupancy; and

(b)   in any other case, a licence to occupy premises,

and reference to a tenant, landlord or any other expression appropriate to a tenancy shall be construed accordingly.]

Modifications

Reg 13D is modified by Sch 9 para 8 (see p907). This applies only to former Pathfinder Authorities who administered the pilot local housing allowance scheme.

Amendments

1.   Inserted by reg 7 of SI 2007 No 2869 as from 7.4.08 (or if reg 1(5) that SI applies, on the day on or after 7.4.08 when the first of the events specified in reg 1(6) applies, or from 6.4.09 if none have before that date).

2.   Amended by reg 5(4)(b) of SI 2008 No 586 as from 7.4.08.

3.   Amended by reg 3(3) of SI 2009 No 614 as from 6.4.09.

General Note

Reg 13D is nearly identical to reg 13D HB Regs (see p319). In these regs, there are naturally no rules in respect of a "young individual". However, here if the claimant (and any partner) live in shared accommodation, the LHA for one-bedroom shared accommodation only applies if neither the claimant nor her/his partner qualifies for a severe disability premium or the partner is not a "care leaver" (defined in para (12): para (2)(a)).

[¹Publication of local housing allowances

13E.–(1)   A relevant authority shall take such steps as appear to it to be appropriate for the purpose of securing that information in relation to broad rental market areas falling in whole or in part within its area, and local housing allowances applicable to such broad rental market areas, is brought to the attention of persons who may be entitled to housing benefit from the authority.]

Amendment

1.   Inserted by reg 7 of SI 2007 No 2869 as from 7.4.08 (or if reg 1(5) that SI applies, on the day on or after 7.4.08 when the first of the events specified in reg 1(6) applies, or from 6.4.09 if none have before that date).

[¹ Requirement to refer to rent officers

14.–(1)   Subject to the following provisions of this regulation, a relevant authority shall apply to a rent officer for a determination to be made in pursuance of the Housing Act functions where–

(a)   it has received a claim on which rent allowance may be awarded and any of the circumstances specified in regulation 13C(5)(a) to (e) (rent allowance cases for which a maximum rent (standard local rent) is not to be determined) apply;

(b)   it has received relevant information regarding a claim on which rent allowance may be awarded and any of the circumstances specified in regulation 13C(5)(a) to (e) apply;

(c)   it has received a notification of a change relating to a rent allowance and a maximum rent (LHA) does not fall to be determined under regulation 13C (determination of a maximum rent (LHA));

(d)   it has received a notification of a change of dwelling and any of the circumstances specified in regulation 13C(5)(a) to (e) apply;

(e)   it has received, except in the case where any liability to make payments in respect of a dwelling would be to a housing authority, a request from a person (''the prospective occupier''), on a properly completed form approved for the purpose by the relevant authority, which includes the specified matters and any of the circumstances specified in regulation 13C(5)(a) to (d) apply;

(f)   52 weeks have expired since it last made an application under sub-paragraph (a), (b), (c), (d) [² , (e) or (h)] in relation to the claim or award in question and–
    (i)   a maximum rent (LHA) determined under regulation 13D does not apply; and
    (ii)   a maximum rent (LHA) is not to be determined under regulation 13D; [²]

(g)   52 weeks have expired since an application was made under sub-paragraph (f) or a previous application was made under this sub-paragraph, whichever last occurred, and–
    (i)   a maximum rent (LHA) determined under regulation 13D does not apply; and
    (ii)   a maximum rent (LHA) is not to be determined under regulation 13D. [² or

(h)   has received notification that any of the circumstances in regulation 13C(5) apply.]

(2)   An application shall not be required under paragraph (1) where a claim, relevant information regarding a claim, notification or request relates to either–

(a)   a dwelling in a hostel if, during the period of 12 months ending on the day on which that claim, relevant information regarding a claim, notification or request is received by the relevant authority–
    (i)   a rent officer has already made a determination in the exercise of the Housing Act functions in respect of a dwelling in that hostel which is a similar dwelling to the dwelling to which the claim, relevant information regarding a claim, notification or request relates; and
    (ii)   there has been no change relating to a rent allowance that has affected the dwelling in respect of which that determination was made; or

(b)   an ''excluded tenancy'' within the meaning of Schedule 2 (excluded tenancies).

(3)   The provision of information to the rent officer in accordance with regulation 95A(5) shall be treated as an application to the rent officer under paragraph (1).

(4)   Where a relevant authority receives a request pursuant to paragraph (1)(e) (request from prospective occupier) and it is a case where, by reason of paragraph (2) (hostels or excluded tenancies), an application to a rent officer is not required, the authority shall–

(a)   return it to the prospective occupier, indicating why no such application is required; and

(b)   where it is not required by reason of either paragraph (2)(a) (hostels) of this regulation or paragraph 2 of Schedule 2 (cases where the rent officer has already made a determination), shall also send him a copy of that determination within 4 days of the receipt of that request by the authority.

(5)   Where an application to a rent officer is required by paragraph (1) it shall be madewithin 3 days, or as soon as practicable after that date, of–

(a)   the relevant authority receiving a claim on which rent allowance may be awarded;

(b)   the relevant authority receiving relevant information regarding a claim on which rent allowance may be awarded;

(c)   the relevant authority receiving a notification of a change relating to a rent allowance;

(d)   the relevant authority receiving a notification of a change of dwelling; or

(e)   the day on which the period mentioned in paragraph (1)(f) or (g) expired,

except that, in the case of a request to which paragraph (1)(e) (request from prospective occupier) applies, the application shall be made within 2 days of the receipt of that request by the authority.

(6)   In calculating any period of days mentioned in paragraphs (4) or (5), no regard shall be had to a day on which the offices of the relevant authority are closed for the purposes of receiving or determining claims.

(7)   For the purpose of this regulation a dwelling in a hostel shall be regarded as similar to another dwelling in that hostel if each dwelling provides sleeping accommodation for the same number of persons.

(8)   In this regulation–

"change relating to a rent allowance" means a change or increase to which paragraph 2(3)(a), (b), (c) or (d) of Schedule 2 applies;

"prospective occupier" shall include a person currently in receipt of housing benefit in respect of a dwelling which he occupies as his home and who is contemplating entering into a new agreement to occupy that dwelling, but only where his current agreement commenced 11 months or more before the request under paragraph (1)(e);

"specified matters" means–

(a)   the signature of the prospective occupier;

(b)   the signature of the person to whom the prospective occupier would incur liability to make such payments;

(c)   a statement that the person in paragraph (b) agrees to the application being made for that determination; and

(d)   an indication that the prospective occupier is contemplating occupying the dwelling as his home and that if he does so, he is likely to claim housing benefit;

"tenancy" includes–

(a)   in Scotland, any other right of occupancy; and

(b)   in any other case, a licence to occupy premises,

and reference to a tenant, landlord or any other expression appropriate to a tenancy shall be construed accordingly;

[²]]

Amendments

1.   Substituted by reg 8 of SI 2007 No 2869 as from 7.4.08 (or if reg 1(5) of that SI applies, on the day on or after 7.4.08 when the first of the events specified in reg 1(6) applies, or from 6.4.09 if none have before that date).

2.   Amended by reg 5(5) of SI 2008 No 586 as from 7.4.08.

Modifications

Reg 14 substituted by reg 8 Housing Benefit (State Pension Credit) (Local Housing Allowance and Information Sharing) Amendment Regulations 2007 SI No.2869, as amended by reg 5(5) of SI 2008 No.586, as from 7 April 2008, save that for a person to whom reg 1(5) of those regulations applied (see p1233), the amendments came into force on the day on or after 7 April 2008 when the first of the events specified in reg 1(6) applied to her/him, or on 6 April 2009 if none had before that date.

[¹ Application to the rent officer for redeterminations

15.–(1)   Subject to paragraph (2) and regulation 16 (application for redetermination by rent officer), where a relevant authority has obtained from a rent officer either or both of the following–

(a)   a determination on a reference made under regulation 13D(10) (board and attendance determination) or regulation 14 (requirement to refer to rent officers);

(b)   a redetermination on a reference made under regulation 16(2) (application for redetermination by rent officer),

the authority may apply to the rent officer for a redetermination of any determination or redetermination he has made which has effect at the date of the application.

(2)   No application shall be made for a further redetermination of a redetermination made in response to an application under paragraph (1).]

Modifications

Reg 15 substituted by reg 9 Housing Benefit (State Pension Credit) (Local Housing Allowance and Information Sharing) Amendment Regulations 2007 SI No.2869 as from 7 April 2008, save that for a person to whom reg 1(5) of those regulations applied (see p1233), the amendments came into force on the day on or after 7 April 2008 when the first of the events specified in reg 1(6) applied to her/him, or on 6 April 2009 if none had before that date.

Amendment

1. Substituted by reg 9 of SI 2007 No 2869 as from 7.4.08 (or if reg 1(5) of that SI applies, on the day on or after 7.4.08 when the first of the events specified in reg 1(6) applies, or from 6.4.09 if none have before that date).

[¹ Application for a redetermination by a rent officer

16.–(1)   This paragraph applies where–

(a)   a person affected makes written representations which are signed by him, to a relevant authority concerning a decision which it makes in relation to him;

(b)   those representations relate, in whole or in part, to a rent officer's determination or redetermination in exercise of the Housing Act functions except for functions relating to broad rental market area determinations and local housing allowance determinations or amended determinations; and

(c)   those representations are made no later than one month after the day on which the person affected was notified of the decision by the relevant authority.

(2)   Subject to paragraphs (3) and (4), where paragraph (1) applies, the relevant authority shall, within 7 days of receiving the representations, apply to the rent officer for a redetermination or, as the case may be, a further redetermination in exercise of the Housing Act functions and a copy of those representations shall accompany the local authority's application.

(3)   Except where paragraph (4) applies, a relevant authority, in relation to any determination by a rent officer of an application under regulation 13D(10) (board and attendance determination) or 14(1) (requirement to refer to rent officers), shall not apply for a redetermination under paragraph (2) more than once in respect of an individual claimant's dwelling to which that determination relates.

(4)   Paragraph (2) shall operate so as to require a relevant authority to make a second application where the following conditions are met in addition to those imposed by that paragraph–

(a)   the written representations made under paragraph (1) relate to a redetermination by a rent officer made in response to an application by the relevant authority under regulation 15 (application to the rent officer for redetermination);

(b)   by the time of that application, the rent officer has already provided a redetermination under this regulation of a determination made in response to an application under regulation 13D(10) or 14(1); and

(c)   both the application under this regulation referred to in sub-paragraph (b) and the second application for which this paragraph provides relate to the same claimant.

(5)   here a decision has been revised in consequence of a redetermination, substitute determination or substitute redetermination by a rent officer in exercise of the Housing Act functions (except for those relating to broad rental market area determinations and local housing allowance determinations or amended determinations) and that redetermination, substitute determination or substitute redetermination has led to–

(a)   a reduction in the maximum rent, the redetermination, substitute determination or substitute redetermination shall be a change of circumstances;

(b)   an increase in the maximum rent, the redetermination, substitute determination or substitute redetermination shall have effect in place of the original determination.]

Amendment

1. Substituted by reg 9 of SI 2007 No 2869 as from 7.4.08 (or if reg 1(5) of that SI applies, on the day on or after 7.4.08 when the first of the events specified in reg 1(6) applies, or from 6.4.09 if none have before that date).

Modifications
Reg 16 substituted by reg 9 Housing Benefit (State Pension Credit) (Local Housing Allowance and Information Sharing) Amendment Regulations 2007 SI No.2869 as from 7 April 2008, save that for a person to whom reg 1(5) of those regulations applied (see p1233), the amendments came into force on the day on or after 7 April 2008 when the first of the events specified in reg 1(6) applied to her/him, or on 6 April 2009 if none had before that date.

[¹ Substitute determinations or substitute redeterminations

17.–(1) In a case where either–

(a) the appropriate authority discovers that an application it has made to the rent officer contained an error in respect of any of the following–

    (i) the size of the dwelling;

    (ii) the number of occupiers;

    (iii) the composition of the household;

    (iv) the terms of the tenancy; or

(b) the rent officer has, in accordance with article 7A(1) or (2) of the Rent Officers Order, notified an appropriate authority of an error he has made (other than in the application of his professional judgement),

the authority shall apply to the rent officer for a substitute determination, substitute redetermination, board and attendance redetermination, substitute board and attendance determination or substitute board and attendance redetermination, as the case may be.

(2) In its application to the rent officer the relevant authority shall state the nature of the error and withdraw any previous application relating to the same case for a redetermination or substitute determination or substitute redetermination, which it has made but to which the rent officer has not yet responded.]

Modifications
Reg 17 substituted by reg 9 Housing Benefit (State Pension Credit) (Local Housing Allowance and Information Sharing) Amendment Regulations 2007 SI No.2869 as from 7 April 2008, save that for a person to whom reg 1(5) of those regulations applied (see p1233), the amendments came into force on the day on or after 7 April 2008 when the first of the events specified in reg 1(6) applied to her/him, or on 6 April 2009 if none had before that date.

Amendment
1. Substituted by reg 9 of SI 2007 No 2869 as from 7.4.08 (or if reg 1(5) of that SI applies, on the day on or after 7.4.08 when the first of the events specified in reg 1(6) applies, or from 6.4.09 if none have before that date).

[¹ Application of provisions to substitute determinations or substitute redeterminations

18. Regulations 15, 16 and 17 apply to a substitute determination or substitute redetermination as they apply to the determination or redetermination it replaces.]

Modifications
Reg 18 substituted by reg 9 Housing Benefit (State Pension Credit) (Local Housing Allowance and Information Sharing) Amendment Regulations 2007 SI No.2869 as from 7 April 2008, save that for a person to whom reg 1(5) of those regulations applied (see p1233), the amendments came into force on the day on or after 7 April 2008 when the first of the events specified in reg 1(6) applied to her/him, or on 6 April 2009 if none had before that date.

Amendment
1. Substituted by reg 9 of SI 2007 No 2869 as from 7.4.08 (or if reg 1(5) of that SI applies, on the day on or after 7.4.08 when the first of the events specified in reg 1(6) applies, or from 6.4.09 if none have before that date).

[¹ Amended determinations

18A.–(1) This regulation applies where a decision has been revised in consequence of an amended broad rental market area determination or amended local housing allowance determination by a rent officer.

(2) Where that amended determination has led to a reduction in the maximum rent (LHA) applicable to a claimant, the amended determination shall be a change of circumstances in relation to that claimant.

(3) Where that amended determination has led to an increase in the maximum rent (LHA) applicable to a claimant, the amended determination shall have effect in place of the original determination.]

Amendment

1.   Inserted by reg 10 of SI 2007 No 2869 as from 7.4.08 (or if reg 1(5) of that SI applies, on the day on or after 7.4.08 when the first of the events specified in reg 1(6) applies, or from 6.4.09 if none have before that date).

PART 4
Membership of a family

Persons of prescribed description

19.–(1)   Subject to paragraph (2), a person of a prescribed description for the purposes of section 137(1) of the Act as it applies to housing benefit (definition of family) is a person [¹ who falls within the definition of qualifying young person in section 142 of the Act (child and qualifying young person)], and in these Regulations such a person is referred to as a ''young person''.

(2)   Paragraph (1) shall not apply to a person who is–

(a)   on income support [⁴ , an income-based jobseeker's allowance or an income-related employment and support allowance]; [² or]

[³ (b)]

(c)   a person to whom section 6 of the Children (Leaving Care) Act 2000 (exclusion from benefits) applies.

(3)   A person of a prescribed description for the purposes of section 137(1) of the Act as it applies to housing benefit (definition of the family) includes a child or young person in respect of whom section 145A of that Act applies for the purposes of entitlement to child benefit but only for the period prescribed under section 145A(1) of that Act.

Amendments

1.   Substituted by reg 4(2)(a) of SI 2006 No 718 as from 10.4.06.
2.   Inserted by reg 4(2)(b) of SI 2006 No 718 as from 10.4.06.
3.   Omitted by reg 4(2)(c) of SI 2006 No 718 as from 10.4.06.
4.   Amended by reg 32 of SI 2008 No 1082 as from 27.10.08.

Circumstances in which a person is to be treated as responsible or not responsible for another

20.–(1)   Subject to the following provisions of this regulation a person shall be treated as responsible for a child or young person who is normally living with him and this includes a child or young person to whom paragraph (3) of regulation 19 applies.

(2)   Where a child or young person spends equal amounts of time in different households, or where there is a question as to which household he is living in, the child or young person shall be treated for the purposes of paragraph (1) as normally living with–

(a)   the person who is receiving child benefit in respect of him; or

(b)   if there is no such person–

    (i)   where only one claim for child benefit has been made in respect of him, the person who made that claim; or

    (ii)   in any other case the person who has the primary responsibility for him.

(3)   For the purposes of these Regulations a child or young person shall be the responsibility of only one person in any benefit week and any person other than the one treated as responsible for the child or young person under this regulation shall be treated as not so responsible.

Circumstances in which a person is to be treated as being or not being a member of the household

21.–(1)   Subject to paragraphs (2) to (4), the claimant and any partner and, where the claimant or his partner is treated as responsible by virtue of regulation 20 (circumstances

809

in which a person is to be treated as responsible or not responsible for another) for a child or young person, that child or young person and any child of that child or young person, shall be treated as members of the same household notwithstanding that any of them is temporarily living away from the other members of his family.

(2)   Paragraph (1) shall not apply to a person who is living away from the other members of his family where–

(a)   that person does not intend to resume living with the other members of his family; or

(b)   his absence from the other members of his family is likely to exceed 52 weeks, unless there are exceptional circumstances (for example where the person is in hospital or otherwise has no control over the length of his absence) and the absence is unlikely to be substantially more than 52 weeks.

(3)   A child or young person shall not be treated as a member of the claimant's household [¹ , nor as occupying the claimant's dwelling,]where he is–

(a)   placed with the claimant or his partner by a local authority under section 23(2)(a) of the Children Act 1989 or by a voluntary organisation under section 59(1)(a) of that Act, or in Scotland boarded out with the claimant or his partner under a relevant enactment; or

(b)   placed, or in Scotland boarded out, with the claimant or his partner prior to adoption; or

(c)   placed for adoption with the claimant or his partner in accordance with the Adoption and Children Act 2002 or the Adoption Agencies (Scotland) Regulations 1996.

(4)   Subject to paragraph (5), paragraph (1) shall not apply to a child or young person who is not living with the claimant and he–

(a)   is being looked after by, or in Scotland is in the care of, a local authority under a relevant enactment; or

(b)   has been placed, or in Scotland boarded out, with a person other than the claimant prior to adoption; or

(c)   has been placed for adoption in accordance with the Adoption and Children Act 2002 or the Adoption Agencies (Scotland) Regulations 1996.

(5)   An authority shall treat a child or young person to whom paragraph (4)(a) applies as being a member of the claimants' household in any benefit week where–

(a)   that child or young person lives with the claimant for part or all of that benefit week; and

(b)   the authority considers that it is reasonable to do so taking into account the nature and frequency of that child's or young person's visits.

(6)   In this regulation "relevant enactment" means the Army Act 1955, the Air Force Act 1955, the Naval Discipline Act 1957, the Matrimonial Proceedings Children Act 1958,the Social Work (Scotland) Act 1968, the Family Law Reform Act 1969, the Children and Young Persons Act 1969, the Matrimonial Causes Act 1973, the Children Act 1975, the Domestic Proceedings and Magistrates' Courts Act 1978, the Adoption (Scotland) Act 1978, the Child Care Act 1980, the Family Law Act 1986, the Children Act 1989 and the Children (Scotland) Act 1995.

Amendment

1.   Amended by reg 3(3) of SI 2010 No 2449 as from 1.11.10.

PART 5
Applicable amounts

Applicable amounts

22.–(1) Subject to regulations 61 and 62 and Schedule A1 (calculation of weekly amounts, rent free periods and treatment of claims for housing benefit by refugees), the applicable amount of a claimant shall be the aggregate of such of the following amounts as apply in his case–

(a)   an amount in respect of his personal allowance, determined in accordance with paragraph 1 of Schedule 3;

(b)   an amount in respect of any child or young person who is a member of his family, determined in accordance with paragraph 2 of that Schedule;

(c)   if he is a member of a family of which at least one member is a child or young person, an amount determined in accordance with paragraph 3(1) of Part 2 of that Schedule (family premium);

(d)   if he is a member of a family of which one member is a child under the age of one year, an additional amount determined in accordance with paragraph 3(2) of Part 2 of that Schedule;

(e)   the amount of any premiums which may be applicable to him, determined in accordance with Parts 3 and 4 of that Schedule (premiums).

[¹ (2)]

[¹ (3)]

[¹ (4)]

[² (5)   In [⁴ Schedule 3]–

"additional spouse" means a spouse of either party to the marriage who is additional to the other party to the marriage;

"patient" means a person (other than a person who is serving a sentence of imprisonment or detention in a youth custody institution) who is regarded as receiving free in-patient treatment within the meaning of [³ regulation 2(4) and (5) of the Social Security (Hospital In-Patients) Regulations 2005].]

[¹ (6)]

[¹ (7)]

Amendments

1.   Omitted by reg 2(3)(a) of SI 2005 No 2502 as amended by Sch 2 para 27 of SI 2006 No 217 as from 1.4.06 (3.4.06 where rent payable weekly or at intervals of a week).

2.   Substituted by reg 2(3)(b) of SI 2005 No 2502 as amended by Sch 2 para 27 of SI 2006 No 217 as from 1.4.06 (3.4.06 where rent payable weekly or at intervals of a week).

3.   Amended by reg 5(1) of SI 2005 No 3360 as amended by Sch 2 para 30 of SI 2006 No 217 as from 10.4.06.

4.   Amended by reg 4(5) of SI 2008 No 1042 as from 19.5.08.

Analysis

Para (1). The same technique for calculating applicable amounts is used as under regs 22 and 23 HB Regs. Note, however, that there is no entitlement to a component under the HB(SPC) Regs, nor is there entitlement to a "transitional amount" if the claimant or her/his partner is transferred from IS "on the grounds of disability", IB or SDA to ESA (see Parts 7 and 8 of Sch 3 HB Regs). The amounts and conditions of the premiums are as stated in Sch 3.

Paras (2) to (4), (6) and (7). Until omitted, these varied the applicable amounts due to claimants who had been patients for more than 52 weeks. See pp776-778 of the 18th edition for the text and commentary of the substituted version of reg 16 HB Regs 1987 (now reg 22 HB(SPC) Regs).

Para (5). The definition of "patient" here is still of relevance in the treatment of childcare costs (under reg 29). See p352 for a discussion of the meaning of "patient".

Long-term hospital patients may still be caught by the requirement that they be occupying the home in reg 7, but see reg 7(16)(c)(ii). The definition of patient for these purposes is in reg 7(18). The definition there also applies in determining whether a non-dependant deduction is applicable under reg 55(7)(f).

PART 6
Assessment of income and capital
SECTION 1
General

Calculation of income and capital of members of claimant's family and of a polygamous marriage

23.–(1)   The income and capital of a claimant's partner which by virtue of section 136(1) of the Act is to be treated as income and capital of the claimant, shall be calculated or estimated in accordance with the following provisions of this Part in like manner as for the claimant; and any reference to the ''claimant'' shall, except where the context otherwise requires, be construed for the purposes of this Part as if it were a reference to his partner.

(2) Where a claimant or the partner of a claimant is married polygamously to two or more members of his household–

(a) the claimant shall be treated as possessing capital and income belonging to each such member; and

(b) the income and capital of that member shall be calculated in accordance with the following provisions of this Part in like manner as for the claimant.

(3) The income and capital of a child or young person shall not be treated as the income and capital of the claimant.

Circumstances in which income of non-dependant is to be treated as claimant's

24.–(1) Where it appears to the relevant authority that a non-dependant and the claimant have entered into arrangements in order to take advantage of the housing benefit scheme and the non-dependant has more capital and income than the claimant, that authority shall, except where the claimant is on [¹ a guarantee credit], treat the claimant as possessing capital and income belonging to that non-dependant and, in such a case, shall disregard any capital and income which the claimant does possess.

(2) Where a claimant is treated as possessing capital and income belonging to a non-dependant under paragraph (1) the capital and income of that non-dependant shall be calculated in accordance with the following provisions of this Part in like manner as for the claimant and any reference to the ''claimant'' shall, except where the context otherwise requires, be construed for the purposes of this Part as if it were a reference to that non-dependant.

Amendment

1. Amended by reg 6(3) of SI 2008 No 3157 as from 5.1.09.

General Note

Note that prior to 5 January 2009, reg 24 applied except where the claimant was on IS or income-based JSA. Effectively this meant that there was no exception; the HB(SPC) Regs cannot apply where the claimant is on IS or income-based JSA: reg 5. It is understood that this was a drafting error when the regulations were being consolidated.

SECTION 2
Income

General Note to Section 2

Note that although the heading for Section 2 is "Income", the capital of some claimants is also dealt with in this section. Section 2 requires the treatment of resources in three ways:

(1) If a claimant (or her/his partner) is in receipt of the guarantee credit of PC all her/his income and capital are disregarded: reg 26. There is effectively no capital limit for such claimants. See p343 for the question of how far the decisions of the DWP are binding on the local authority.

(2) If a claimant (or her/his partner) is in receipt of the savings credit of PC but not the guarantee credit, the special rules in reg 27 apply. There is a £16,000 capital limit in such cases.

(3) If a claimant (or her/his partner) is not receiving either the guarantee credit or savings credit of PC, the rules in regs 29 to 49 apply: reg 28. There is a £16,000 capital limit in such cases.

Calculation of income and capital

25. The income and capital of–

(a) the claimant; and

(b) any partner of the claimant,

shall be calculated in accordance with the rules set out in this Part; and any reference in this Part to the claimant shall apply equally to any partner of the claimant.

Claimant in receipt of guarantee credit

26. In the case of a claimant who is in receipt, or whose partner is in receipt, of a guarantee credit, the whole of his capital and income shall be disregarded.

Calculation of claimant's income and capital in savings credit only cases

27.–(1)   In determining the income and capital of a claimant who has, or whose partner has, an award of state pension credit comprising only the savings credit, the relevant authority shall, subject to the following provisions of this regulation, use the calculation or estimate of the claimant's or, as the case may be, the claimant's partner's income and capital made by the Secretary of State for the purpose of determining that award.

(2)   The Secretary of State shall provide the relevant authority with details of the calculation or estimate–

(a)   if the claimant is on housing benefit or has claimed housing benefit, within the two working days following the day the calculation or estimate was determined, or as soon as reasonably practicable thereafter; or

(b)   if sub-paragraph (a) does not apply, within the two working days following the day he receives information from the relevant authority that the claimant or his partner has claimed housing benefit, or as soon as reasonably practicable thereafter.

(3)   The details provided by the Secretary of State shall include the amount taken into account in that determination in respect of the net income of the person claiming state pension credit.

(4)   The relevant authority shall modify the amount of the net income provided by the Secretary of State only in so far as necessary to take into account–

(a)   the amount of the savings credit payable;

(b)   in respect of any dependent children of the claimant, childcare charges taken into account under regulation 30(1)(c) (calculation of income on a weekly basis);

(c)   the higher amount disregarded under these Regulations in respect of–

   (i)   lone parent's earnings;

   (ii)   payments of maintenance, whether under a court order or not, which is made or due to be made by–

      (aa)   the claimant's former partner, or the claimant's partner's former partner; or

      (bb)   the parent of a child or young person where that child or young person is a member of the claimant's family except where that parent is the claimant or the claimant's partner;

(d)   any amount to be disregarded by virtue of [¹ paragraph 5A or 9(1)] of Schedule 4;

(e)   the income and capital of any partner of the claimant who is treated as a member of the claimant's household under regulation 21 (circumstances in which a person is to be treated as being or not being a member of the household) to the extent that it is not taken into account in determining the net income of the person claiming state pension credit;

(f)   regulation 24 (circumstances in which income of a non-dependent is to be treated as claimant's), if the relevant authority determines that this provision applies in the claimant's case;

(g)   any modification under section 134(8) of the Administration Act (modifications by resolution of an authority) which is applicable in the claimant's case.

(5)   Regulations 29 to 49 shall not apply to the amount of the net income to be taken into account by the local authority under paragraph (1), but shall apply (so far as relevant) for the purpose of determining any modifications which fall to be made to that amount under paragraph (4).

(6)   The relevant authority shall for the purpose of determining the claimant's entitlement of housing benefit use, except where paragraphs (7) and (8) apply, the calculation of the claimant's capital made by the Secretary of State, and shall in particular apply the provisions of regulation 43 if the claimant's capital is calculated as being in excess of £16,000.

(7)   If paragraph (8) applies, the relevant authority shall calculate the claimant's capital in accordance with regulations 43 to 49 below.

(8)   This paragraph applies if–
(a)   the Secretary of State notifies the relevant authority that the claimant's capital has been determined as being £16,000 or less;
(b)   subsequent to that determination the claimant's capital rises to more than £16,000; and
(c)   the increase occurs whilst there is in force an assessed income period within the meaning of sections 6 and 9 of the State Pension Credit Act.

Amendment

1.   Amended by reg 3(2) of SI 2009 No 2608 as from 1.4.10 (5.4.10 where rent payable weekly or in multiples of a week).

General Note

Reg 27 sets out the capital and income rules if the claimant or her/his partner has been awarded the savings credit of PC, but not the guarantee credit. In these cases, income and capital for HB purposes are the income and capital figure used by the DWP to work out PC, as modified by paras (4) to (8). The DWP figure is sometimes referred to as the "assessed income figure" or AIF.

Analysis

Paras (1) to (3). The general rule is that for the purpose of working out HB and CTB entitlement, authorities must use the calculation or estimate of income and capital made by the DWP in determining entitlement to the savings credit of PC. It is suggested that the mandatory wording of para (1) means that the reasoning of the Court of Appeal in *R v South Ribble DC HBRB ex p Hamilton* [2000] 33 HLR 102, CA cannot apply to such claimants. See p343 for a full discussion of the *Hamilton* decision, but it is suggested that the local authority is not entitled to disregard the DWP's assessment merely because it believes that there has been a failure by the claimant to disclose resources to the DWP. It must refer its evidence to the DWP with a view to revision or supersession of the award of savings credit, suspending HB entitlement if necessary.

See also reg 41(10) (where a claimant is in receipt of a benefit other than HB and the rate of that other benefit alters on or after 1 April in any year) and reg 60(6) (where there is a change in the DWP assessment of income and capital).

Para (2) imposes strict time limits for the provision of the information to the authority by the DWP on behalf of the Secretary of State.

Paras (4) and (5) deal with modifications an authority must make to the income figure provided by the DWP. By para (5), the rules in the remainder of Section 2 are used to determine the modifications (eg, reg 31 forms the basis for the calculation of childcare charges under para (4)(b)) but are not to be used to determine the amount of net income to be taken into account.

The following modifications must be made (if relevant):
(1)   The authority must add the savings credit that is payable: para (4)(a).
(2)   Childcare charges must be deducted from earnings under reg 30(1)(c): para (4)(b).
(3)   The more generous HB disregards for lone parents' earnings and maintenance must be applied: para (4)(c). For example, lone parents have only £20 of earnings disregarded for PC purposes but £25 is ignored for HB purposes (see Sch 4 para 1(a) on p890), so such claimants will have an additional £5 disregard applied to the assessment of income for HB purposes. For the maintenance disregards, see reg 29(1)(o) and Sch 5 para 20.
(4)   The additional earnings disregard under Sch 4 paras 5A and 9(1) for some claimants in work must be applied: para (4)(d).
(5)   The income and capital of the claimant's partner must be added, if it was not taken into account for PC purposes (eg, where the claimant is treated as a single claimant for PC purposes but under reg 21 is treated as having a partner): para (4)(e).
(6)   The income of a non-dependant must be added, but only if the authority decides the income of that non-dependant is to be treated as the claimant's under reg 24: para (4)(f). Note that in this case, the income and the capital of the claimant are disregarded under reg 24(1).
(7)   Any disregard of war pensions adopted by the authority must be applied: para (4)(g).

Paras (6) to (8) deal with the calculation of capital. The DWP's assessment must be used and the capital limit of £16,000 applies. The only time when the authority does its own capital assessment is where capital rises above £16,000 after entitlement to PC has been assessed and during an "assessed income period" – broadly, a set period during which the PC claimant is not required to report changes in retirement provision to the DWP, including the amount of her/his capital. Note that unless the increase in capital has the effect of disqualifying the claimant from HB, there can be no departure from the DWP's figure. For example, where there is an increase in capital but the amount is still less than the £16,000 limit, the authority is not permitted to add (or increase) deemed income from capital under reg 29(2); see para (5) above.

Calculation of income and capital where state pension credit is not payable
    28.   The income and capital of a person to whom neither regulation 26 nor regulation 27 applies shall be calculated or estimated by the relevant authority in accordance with regulations 29 to 49.

Meaning of "income"
    29.–(1)   For the purposes of these Regulations, "income" means income of any of the following descriptions–
(a)   earnings;
(b)   working tax credit;
(c)   retirement pension income within the meaning of the State Pension Credit Act;
(d)   income from annuity contracts (other than retirement pension income);
(e)   a war disablement pension or war widow's or widower's pension;
(f)   a foreign war disablement pension or war widow's or widower's pension;
(g)   a guaranteed income payment;
[4 (h)   a payment made under article 21(1)(c) of the Armed Forces and Reserve Forces (Compensation Scheme) Order 2005, in any case where article 23(2)(c) applies;]
(i)   income from capital, other than capital disregarded under Part 1 of Schedule 6;
(j)   social security benefits, other than retirement pension income or any of the following benefits–
    (i)   disability living allowance;
    (ii)   attendance allowance payable under section 64 of the Act;
    (iii)   an increase of disablement pension under section 104 or 105 of the Act;
    (iv)   a payment under regulations made in exercise of the power conferred by paragraph 7(2)(b) of Part 2 of Schedule 8 to the Act;
    (v)   an increase of an allowance payable in respect of constant attendance under paragraph 4 of Part 1 of Schedule 8 to the Act;
    (vi)   child benefit;
    (vii)   any guardian's allowance payable under section 77 of the Act;
    (viii)   any increase for a dependant, other than the claimant's partner, payable in accordance with Part 4 of the Act;
    (ix)   any social fund payment made under Part 8 of the Act;
    (x)   Christmas bonus payable under Part 10 of the Act;
    (xi)   housing benefit;
    (xii)   council tax benefit;
    (xiii)   bereavement payment;
    (xiv)   statutory sick pay;
    (xv)   statutory maternity pay;
    (xvi)   statutory paternity pay payable under Part 12ZA of the Act;
    (xvii)   statutory adoption pay payable under Part 12ZB of the Act;
    (xviii)   any benefit similar to those mentioned in the preceding provisions of this paragraph payable under legislation having effect in Northern Ireland;
(k)   all foreign social security benefits which are similar to the social security benefits prescribed above;
[4 (l)   a payment made–
    (i)   under article 30 of the Naval, Military and Air Forces Etc. (Disablement and Death) Service Pensions Order 2006, in any case where article 30(1)(b) applies; or
    (ii)   under article 12(8) of that Order, in any case where sub-paragraph (b) of that article applies;]
(m)   a pension paid to victims of National Socialist persecution under any special provision made by the law of the Federal Republic of Germany, or any part of it, or of the Republic of Austria;
(n)   payments under a scheme made under the Pneumoconiosis etc. (Worker's Compensation) Act 1979;
(o)   payments made towards the maintenance of the claimant by his spouse, civil partner, former spouse or former civil partner or towards the maintenance of the

claimant's partner by his spouse, civil partner, former spouse or former civil partner, including payments made–
    (i)   under a court order;
    (ii)   under an agreement for maintenance; or
    (iii) voluntarily;

(p)   payments due from any person in respect of board and lodging accommodation provided by the claimant;

[⁵ (q) royalties or other sums paid as a consideration for the use of, or the right to use, any copyright, design, patent or trade mark;]

[⁵ (r) any payment in respect of any–
    (i)   book registered under the Public Lending Right Scheme 1982; or
    (ii)   work made under any international public lending right scheme that is analogous to the Public Lending Right Scheme 1982;]

(s)   any payment, other than a payment ordered by a court or made in settlement of a claim, made by or on behalf of a former employer of a person on account of the early retirement of that person on grounds of ill-health or disability;

(t)   any sum payable by way of pension out of money provided under the Civil List Act 1837, the Civil List Act 1937, the Civil List Act 1952, the Civil List Act 1972 or the Civil List Act 1975;

(u)   any income in lieu of that specified in sub-paragraphs (a) to (r);

(v)   any payment of rent made to a claimant who–
    (i)   owns the freehold or leasehold interest in any property or is a tenant of any property;
    (ii)   occupies part of the property; and
    (iii) has an agreement with another person allowing that person to occupy that property on payment of rent; [¹]

(w)   any payment made at regular intervals under an equity release scheme.

[² (x) PPF periodic payments within the meaning of section 17(1) of the State Pension Credit Act.]

[⁶ (2) For the purposes of these Regulations and subject to regulation 44(2) (capital to be disregarded), a claimant's capital shall be treated as if it were aweekly income of–
(a)   £1 for each £500 in excess of £10,000; and
(b)   £1 for any excess which is not a complete £500.]

(3)   Where the payment of any social security benefit prescribed under paragraph (1) is subject to any deduction (other than an adjustment specified in paragraph (4)) the amount to be taken into account under paragraph (1) shall be the amount before the deduction is made.

(4)   The adjustments specified in this paragraph are those made in accordance with–
(a)   the Social Security (Overlapping Benefits) Regulations 1979;
(b)   the Social Security (Hospital In-Patients) Regulations 1975;
(c)   section 30DD or section 30E of the Act (reductions in incapacity benefit in respect of pensions and councillor's allowances).

[³ (d) section 3 of the Welfare Reform Act (deductions from contributory employment and support allowance in respect of pensions and councillor's allowances).]

(5)   Where an award of any working tax credit or child tax credit under the Tax Credits Act 2002 is subject to a deduction by way of recovery of an overpayment of working tax credit or child tax credit which arose in a previous tax year the amount to be taken into account under paragraph (1) shall be the amount of working tax credit or child tax credit awarded less the amount of that deduction.

[⁶ (6)]

[⁶ (7)]

(8)   In paragraph (1)(w), "equity release scheme" means a loan–
(a)   made between a person ("the lender") and the claimant;
(b)   by means of which a sum of money is advanced by the lender to the claimant by way of payments at regular intervals; and
(c)   which is secured on a dwelling in which the claimant owns an estate or interest and which he occupies as his home.

Amendments

1. Amended by reg 10(2)(a) of SI 2006 No 588 as from 6.4.06.
2. Inserted by reg 10(2)(b) of SI 2006 No 588 as from 6.4.06.
3. Amended by reg 33 of SI 2008 No 1082 as from 27.10.08.
4. Substituted by reg 6(4) of SI 2008 No 3157 as from 5.1.09.
5. Substituted by reg 7(4) of SI 2009 No 583 as from the first day of the first benefit week for a claimant on or after 6.4.09.
6. Amended by reg 5 of SI 2009 No 1676 as from 2.11.09.

Analysis

Paragraph (1): The definition of "income"

Unlike under the HB Regs, "income" is defined by reg 29(1). Therefore, any category of income that does not fall within any of the categories listed does not count as income and is not taken into account at all. Note that there are earnings disregards in Sch 4 (see p890) and amounts to be disregarded from income other than earnings in Sch 5 (see p893).

Most of the categories are self-explanatory but some require explanation.

"Retirement pension income" under sub-para (c) is defined in s16 SPCA. It includes Category A, B, C and D state retirement pension, occupational and personal pension schemes and other private arrangements.

Under sub-para (i), "income from capital" counts as income, unless it is from capital disregarded under Sch 6 Part 1. See also reg 33(11)(a) which confirms this. The combined effect of sub-para (1)(i) and Sch 5 paras 22 and 24 is that it is only actual income from the types of capital specified in Sch 6 Part 2 that is taken into account, and then only if the total value of the capital exceeds £10,000. Note that capital, other than capital disregarded under *either* Part of Sch 6, is deemed to produce a weekly income under para (2).

Under sub-para (j), social security benefits, other than retirement pension (which instead counts as income under sub-para (c)) and the benefits listed in sub-paras (j)(i) to (xviii), count as income.

Sub-para (s) seems to be directed at income from private health insurance schemes provided by an employer. Note that "equity release scheme" in sub-para (w) is defined in para (8).

Paragraph (2): Deemed income from capital

Para (2) deals with deemed income from capital, sometimes referred to as "tariff income". The tariff is lower than under the HB Regs: under the HB(SPC) Regs, a claimant is to be treated as having £1 weekly income for every £500 of capital over the lower capital limit (£10,000 since 2 November 2009). Because para (2) is subject to reg 44(2) and because of reg 33(11), it is only capital other than capital disregarded under Sch 6 that is treated as a producing a deemed weekly income as set out.

Prior to 2 November 2009, the lower limit was £6,000 (or £10,000 if the claimant resided in specified types of accommodation). Note: the rules for qualification for the £10,000 lower capital limit were different than under the HB Regs. See pp837-839 of the 21st edition for the text and commentary.

Paragraphs (3) to (5): Miscellaneous rules about income

Under paras (3) and (4), where there are adjustments in the amount of a social security benefit other than under the overlapping benefits provisions or the other circumstances listed in para (4), the unadjusted amount of income is taken into account.

Para (5) makes it plain that where an award of WTC or CTC for the current tax year is subject to a deduction in order to recover an overpayment of tax credit(s) from the previous year (pursuant to s28(1) Tax Credits Act 2002), the amount of WTC or CTC to be taken into account in calculating the weekly level of income for HB/CTB purposes is the current year award of tax credit(s) less the deduction for the overpayment.

Calculation of income on a weekly basis

30.–(1)   Subject to regulation 34 (disregard of changes in tax, contributions etc.) and 61 and 62 (calculation of weekly amounts and rent free periods), for the purposes of section 130(1)(c) of the Act (conditions for entitlement to housing benefit) the income of a claimant who has reached the qualifying age for state pension credit shall be calculated on a weekly basis–

(a)   by calculating or estimating the amount which is likely to be his average weekly income in accordance with this Part;

(b)   by adding to that amount the weekly income calculated under regulation 29(2);

(c)   by then deducting any relevant child care charges to which regulation 31 (treatment of child care charges) applies from any earnings which form part of the average weekly income or, in a case where the conditions in paragraph (2) are met, from those earnings plus whichever credit specified in sub-paragraph (b) of that paragraph is appropriate, up to a maximum deduction in respect of the claimant's family of whichever of the sums specified in paragraph (3) applies in his case.

(2)   The conditions of this paragraph are that–

(a)   the claimant's earnings which form part of his average weekly income are less than the lower of either his relevant child care charges or whichever of the deductions specified in paragraph (3) otherwise applies in his case; and

(b)   that claimant or, if he is a member of a couple either the claimant or his partner, is in receipt of working tax credit or child tax credit.

(3)   The maximum deduction to which paragraph (1)(c) above refers shall be–

(a)   where the claimant's family includes only one child in respect of whom relevant child care charges are paid, [⁵ £175.00] per week;

(b)   where the claimant's family includes more than one child in respect of whom relevant child care charges are paid, [⁵ £300] per week.

Amendments

1.   Confirmed by Art 20(3) of SI 2006 No 645 and reg 8 of SI 2006 No 217 as from 1.4.06 (3.4.06 where rent payable weekly or at intervals of a week).

2.   Confirmed by Art 20(2) of SI 2007 No 688 as from 1.4.07 (2.4.07 where rent payable weekly or at intervals of a week).

3.   Confirmed by Art 20(3) of SI 2008 No 632 as from 1.4.08 (7.4.08 where rent payable weekly or in multiples of a week).

4.   Confirmed by Art 20(3) of SI 2009 No 497 as from 1.4.09 (6.4.08 where rent payable weekly or in multiples of a week).

5.   Confirmed by Art 20(2) of SI 2010 No 793 as from 1.4.10 (5.4.10 where rent payable weekly or in multiples of a week).

General Note

This is, for practical purposes, identical to reg 27 HB Regs (see p346).

Treatment of child care charges

31.–(1)   This regulation applies where a claimant is incurring relevant child care charges and–

(a)   is a lone parent and is engaged in remunerative work;

(b)   is a member of a couple both of whom are engaged in remunerative work; or

(c)   is a member of a couple where one member is engaged in remunerative work and the other–

(i)   is incapacitated;

(ii)   is an in-patient in hospital; or

(iii)   is in prison (whether serving a custodial sentence or remanded in custody awaiting trial or sentence).

(2)   For the purposes of paragraph (1) and subject to paragraph (4), a person to whom paragraph (3) applies shall be treated as engaged in remunerative work for a period not exceeding 28 weeks during which he–

(a)   is paid statutory sick pay;

(b)   is paid short-term incapacity benefit at the lower rate under sections 30A to 30E of the Act;

[² (ba) is paid an employment and support allowance;]

(c)   is paid income support on the grounds of incapacity for work under regulation 4ZA of, and paragraph 7 or 14 of Schedule 1B to, the Income Support Regulations; or

(d)   is credited with earnings on the grounds of incapacity for work [² or limited capability for work] under regulation 8B of the Social Security (Credits) Regulations 1975.

(3)   This paragraph applies to a person who was engaged in remunerative work immediately before–

(a)   the first day of the period in respect of which he was first paid statutory sick pay, short-term incapacity benefit [² , an employment and support allowance] or income support on the grounds of incapacity for work; or

(b)   the first day of the period in respect of which earnings are credited, as the case may be.

(4)   In a case to which paragraph (2)(c) or (d) applies, the period of 28 weeks begins on the day on which the person is first paid income support or on the first day of the period in respect of which earnings are credited, as the case may be.

(5)   Relevant child care charges are those charges for care to which paragraphs (6) and (7) apply, and shall be estimated on a weekly basis in accordance with paragraph (10).

(6)   The charges are paid by the claimant for care which is provided–

(a)   in the case of any child of the claimant's family who is not disabled, in respect of the period beginning on that child's date of birth and ending on the day preceding the first Monday in September following that child's fifteenth birthday; or

(b)   in the case of any child of the claimant's family who is disabled, in respect of the period beginning on that person's date of birth and ending on the day preceding the first Monday in September following that person's sixteenth birthday.

(7)   The charges are paid for care which is provided by one or more of the care providers listed in paragraph (8) and are not paid–

(a)   in respect of the child's compulsory education;

(b)   by a claimant to a partner or by a partner to a claimant in respect of any child for whom either or any of them is responsible in accordance with regulation 20 (circumstances in which a person is treated as responsible or not responsible for another); or

(c)   in respect of care provided by a relative of a child wholly or mainly in the child's home.

(8)   The care to which paragraph (7) refers may be provided–

(a)   out of school hours, by a school on school premises or by a local authority–

   (i)   for children who are not disabled in respect of the period beginning on their eighth birthday and ending on the day preceding the first Monday in September following their fifteenth birthday; or

   (ii)   for children who are disabled in respect of the period beginning on their eighth birthday and ending on the day preceding the first Monday in September following their sixteenth birthday;

(b)   by a child care provider approved by an organisation accredited by the Secretary of State under the scheme established by the Tax Credit (New Category of Child Care Provider) Regulations 1999;

(c)   by persons registered under Part 10A of the Children Act 1989;

(d)   in schools or establishments which are exempted from registration under Part 10A of the Children Act 1989 by virtue of paragraph 1 or 2 of Schedule 9A to that Act;

(e)   by–

   (i)   persons registered under section 7(1) of the Regulation of Care (Scotland) Act 2001; or

   (ii)   local authorities registered under section 33(1) of that Act,

   where the care provided is childminding or day care of children within the meaning of that Act; or

(f)   by a person prescribed in regulations made pursuant to section 12(4) of the Tax Credits Act.[⁴ or

(g)   by a person who is registered under Chapter 2 or 3 of Part 3 of the Childcare Act 2006; or .

(h)   by any of the schools mentioned in section 34(2) of the Childcare Act 2006 in circumstances where the requirement to register under Chapter 2 of Part 3 of that Act does not apply by virtue of section 34(2) of that Act; or .

(i)   by any of the schools mentioned in section 53(2) of the Childcare Act 2006 in circumstances where the requirement to register under Chapter 3 of Part 3 of that Act does not apply by virtue of section 53(2) of that Act; or .

(j)   by any of the establishments mentioned in section 18(5) of the Childcare Act 2006 in circumstances where the care is not included in the meaning of "childcare" for the purposes of Part 1 and Part 3 of that Act by virtue of that subsection; or

(k) by a foster parent [5 or kinship carer] under the Fostering Services Regulations 2002, the Fostering Services (Wales) Regulations 2003 or the [5 Looked After Children (Scotland) Regulations 2009] in relation to a child other than one whom the foster parent is fostering [5 or kinship carer is looking after]; or

(l) by a domiciliary care worker under the Domiciliary Care Agencies Regulations 2002 or the Domiciliary Care Agencies (Wales) Regulations 2004; or

(m) by a person who is not a relative of the child wholly or mainly in the child's home.]

(9) In paragraphs (6) and (8)(a), "the first Monday in September" means the Monday which first occurs in the month of September in any year.

(10) Relevant child care charges shall be estimated over such period, not exceeding a year, as is appropriate in order that the average weekly charge may be estimated accurately having regard to information as to the amount of that charge provided by the child minder or person providing the care.

(11) For the purposes of paragraph (1)(c) the other member of a couple is to be treated as incapacitated where–

(a) he is aged not less than 80;

(b) he is aged less than 80 and–

(i) the additional conditions specified in paragraph 13 of Schedule 3 to the Housing Benefit Regulations 2006 are treated as applying in his case; and

(ii) he satisfies those conditions or would satisfy them but for his being treated as capable of work by virtue of a determination made in accordance with regulations made under section 171E of the Act;

[2 (ba) the claimant's applicable amount would include the support component or the work-related activity component on account of the other member having limited capability for work but for that other member being treated as not having limited capability for work by virtue of a determination made in accordance with the Employment and Support Allowance Regulations;]

(c) the claimant is, or is treated as, incapable of work and has been so incapable, or has been so treated as incapable, of work in accordance with the provisions of, and regulations made under, Part 12A of the Act (incapacity for work) for a continuous period of not less than 196 days; and for this purpose any two or more separate periods separated by a break of not more than 56 days shall be treated as one continuous period;

[2 (ca) the claimant (within the meaning of regulation 2(1)) has, or is treated as having, limited capability for work and has had, or been treated as having, limited capability for work in accordance with the Employment and Support Allowance Regulations for a continuous period of not less than 196 days and for this purpose any two or more separate periods separated by a break of not more than 84 days must be treated as one continuous period;]

(d) there is payable in respect of him one or more of the following–

(i) long-term incapacity benefit or short-term incapacity benefit at the higher rate specified in paragraph 2 of Part 1 of Schedule 4 to the Act;

(ii) attendance allowance under section 64 of the Act;

(iii) severe disablement allowance under section 68 of the Act;

(iv) disability living allowance under section 71 of the Act;

(v) increase of disablement pension under section 104 of the Act;

(vi) a pension increase [3 paid as part of a war disablement pension or under] an industrial injuries scheme which is analogous to an allowance or increase of disablement pension under head (ii), (iv) or (v) above;

[2 (vii) main phase employment and support allowance;]

(e) a pension or allowance to which head (ii), (iv), (v) or (vi) of sub-paragraph (d) above refers was payable on account of his incapacity but has ceased to be payable in consequence of his becoming a patient within the meaning of regulation 22(5) (applicable amounts);

(f)   [¹ sub-paragraph (d) or (e)] would apply to him if the legislative provisions referred to in those sub-paragraphs were provisions under any corresponding enactment having effect in Northern Ireland; or

(g)   he has an invalid carriage or other vehicle provided to him by the Secretary of State under section 5(2)(a) of and Schedule 2 to the National Health Service Act 1977 or by Scottish Ministers under section 46 of the National Health Service (Scotland) Act 1978 or provided by the Department of Health and Social Services for Northern Ireland under Article 30(1) of the Health and Personal Social Services (Northern Ireland) Order 1972.

(12)   For the purposes of paragraph (11), once paragraph (11)(c) applies to the claimant, if he then ceases, for a period of 56 days or less, to be incapable, or to be treated as incapable, of work, that paragraph shall, on his again becoming so incapable, or so treated as incapable, of work at the end of that period, immediately thereafter apply to him for so long as he remains incapable, or is treated as remaining incapable, of work.

[² (12A)   For the purposes of paragraph (11), once paragraph (11)(ca) applies to the claimant, if he then ceases, for a period of 84 days or less, to have, or to be treated as having, limited capability for work, that paragraph is, on his again having, or being treated as having, limited capability for work at the end of that period, immediately thereafter to apply to him for so long as he has, or is treated as having, limited capability for work.]

(13)   For the purposes of paragraphs (6) and (8)(a), a person is disabled if he is a person–

(a)   in respect of whom disability living allowance is payable, or has ceased to be payable solely because he is a patient;

(b)   who is registered as blind in a register compiled under section 29 of the National Assistance Act 1948 (welfare services) or, in Scotland, has been certified as blind and in consequence he is registered as blind in a register maintained by or on behalf of a council constituted under section 2 of the Local Government (Scotland) Act 1994; or

(c)   who ceased to be registered as blind in such a register within the period beginning 28 weeks before the first Monday in September following that person's fifteenth birthday and ending on the day preceding the first Monday in September following that person's sixteenth birthday.

(14)   For the purposes of paragraph (1) a person on maternity leave, paternity leave or adoption leave shall be treated as if he is engaged in remunerative work for the period specified in paragraph (15) ("the relevant period") provided that–

(a)   in the week before the period of maternity leave, paternity leave or adoption leave began he was in remunerative work;

(b)   the claimant is incurring relevant child care charges within the meaning of paragraph (5); and

(c)   he is entitled to statutory maternity pay under section 164 of the Act, statutory paternity pay by virtue of section 171ZA or 171ZB of the Act, statutory adoption pay by virtue of section 171ZL of the Act or maternity allowance under section 35 of the Act.

(15)   The relevant period shall begin on the day on which the person's maternity leave, paternity leave or adoption leave commences and shall end on–

(a)   the date that leave ends;

(b)   if no child care element of working tax credit is in payment on the date that entitlement to maternity allowance, statutory maternity pay, statutory paternity pay or statutory adoption pay ends, the date that entitlement ends; or

(c)   if a child care element of working tax credit is in payment on the date that entitlement to maternity allowance, statutory maternity pay, statutory paternity pay or statutory adoption pay ends, the date that entitlement to that award of the child care element of working tax credit ends,

whichever shall occur first.

(16) In paragraph (15), "child care element" of working tax credit means the element of working tax credit prescribed under section 12 of the Tax Credits Act (child care element).

Amendments

1. Amended by reg 4(5) of SI 2008 No 1042 as from 19.5.08.
2. Amended by reg 34 of SI 2008 No 1082 as from 27.10.08.
3. Amended by reg 6(5) of SI 2008 No 3157 as from 5.1.09.
4. Amended by reg 2 of SI 2008 No 1848 as from 5.8.09.
5. Inserted by reg 8(2) of SI 2010 No 2429 as from 1.11.10.

General Note

This is, for practical purposes, identical to reg 28 HB Regs (see p347).

Calculation of average weekly income from tax credits

32.–(1) This regulation applies where a claimant receives a tax credit.

(2) Where this regulation applies, the period over which a tax credit is to be taken into account shall be the period set out in paragraph (3).

(3) Where the instalment in respect of which payment of a tax credit is made is–

(a) a daily instalment, the period is 1 day, being the day in respect of which the instalment is paid;

(b) a weekly instalment, the period is 7 days, ending on the day on which the instalment is due to be paid;

(c) a two weekly instalment, the period is 14 days, commencing 6 days before the day on which the instalment is due to be paid;

(d) a four weekly instalment, the period is 28 days, ending on the day on which the instalment is due to be paid.

(4) For the purposes of this regulation "tax credit" means working tax credit.

General Note

This is, for practical purposes, identical to reg 32 HB Regs (see p356).

Calculation of weekly income

33.–(1) Except where paragraphs (2) and (4) apply, for the purposes of calculating the weekly income of the claimant, where the period in respect of which a payment is made–

(a) does not exceed a week, the whole of that payment shall be included in the claimant's weekly income;

(b) exceeds a week, the amount to be included in the claimant's weekly income shall be determined–

(i) in a case where that period is a month, by multiplying the amount of the payment by 12 and dividing the product by 52;

(ii) in a case where that period is three months, by multiplying the amount of the payment by 4 and dividing the product by 52;

(iii) in a case where that period is a year, by dividing the amount of the payment by 52;

(iv) in any other case, by multiplying the amount of the payment by 7 and dividing the product by the number of days in the period in respect of which it is made.

(2) Where–

(a) the claimant's regular pattern of work is such that he does not work the same hours every week; or

(b) the amount of the claimant's income fluctuates and has changed more than once, the weekly amount of that claimant's income shall be determined–

(i) if, in a case to which sub-paragraph (a) applies, there is a recognised cycle of work, by reference to his average weekly income over the period of the complete cycle (including, where the cycle involves periods in which the claimant does no work, those periods but disregarding any other absences); or

    (ii)   in any other case, on the basis of–

        (aa) the last two payments if those payments are one month or more apart;

        (bb) the last four payments if the last two payments are less than one month apart; or

        (cc) calculating or estimating such other payments as may, in the particular circumstances of the case, enable the claimant's average weekly income to be determined more accurately.

(3)   For the purposes of paragraph (2)(b) the last payments are the last payments before the date the claim was made or treated as made or, if there is a subsequent supersession under paragraph 4 of Schedule 7 to the Child Support, Pensions and Social Security Act 2000, the last payments before the date of the supersession.

(4)   If a claimant is entitled to receive a payment to which paragraph (5) applies, the amount of that payment shall be treated as if made in respect of a period of a year.

(5)   This paragraph applies to–

[³ (a) royalties or other sums paid as a consideration for the use of, or the right to use, any copyright, design, patent or trade mark;];

[³ (b) any payment in respect of any–

    (i)   book registered under the Public Lending Right Scheme 1982; or

    (ii) work made under any international public lending right scheme that is analogous to the Public Lending Right Scheme 1982; or]

(c)   any payment which is made on an occasional basis.

(6)   The period under which any benefit under the benefit Acts is to be taken into account shall be the period in respect of which that benefit is payable.

(7)   Where payments are made in a currency other than Sterling, the value of the payment shall be determined by taking the Sterling equivalent on the date the payment is made.

(8)   The sums specified in Schedule 4 shall be disregarded in calculating–

(a)   the claimant's earnings; and

[³ (b) any amount to which paragraph (5) applies where the claimant is the first owner of the copyright, design, patent or trademark, or an original contributor to the book or work referred to in paragraph (5)(b).]

[³ (8A)   For the purpose of paragraph (8)(b), and for that purpose only, the amounts specified in paragraph (5) shall be treated as though they were earnings.]

(9)   Income specified in Schedule 5 is to be disregarded in the calculation of a claimant's income.

[² (10)]

(11)   Schedule 6 shall have effect so that–

(a)   the capital specified in Part 1 shall be disregarded for the purpose of determining a claimant's income; and

(b)   the capital specified in Part 2 shall be disregarded for the purpose of determining a claimant's income under regulation 29(2) (weekly income from capital).

(12)   In the case of any income taken into account for the purpose of calculating a person's income, there shall be disregarded any amount payable by way of tax.

[² (13)]

[² (14)]

Amendments

1.   Inserted by reg 3 of SI 2006 No 2813 as from 20.11.06.

2.   Omitted by reg 6(b) of SI 2007 No 1619 as from 3.7.07.

3.   Amended by reg 7(5) of SI 2009 No 583 as from the first day of the first benefit week for a claimant on or after 6.4.09.

Analysis

Reg 33 contains a number of rules to facilitate the calculation of income on a weekly basis.

Para (1) contains the general rule and is similar in effect to reg 33 HB Regs (see p357). It is subject to the specific circumstances set out in paras (2) and (4) (and also para (6), though para (1) does not specifically state this).

Paras (2) and (3) deal with fluctuating income from work, whether employed or self-employed. Where the hours of work are different each week or income flucuates and has changed more than once, the first step is to look for a pattern of work under sub-para (b)(i). The wording is similar to that of reg 6(2)(a) HB Regs and caselaw under that and the equivalent IS and income-based JSA provisions are relevant to the question of whether a cycle exists and, if so, what it is.

In the absence of a cycle, either the last two or four payments may be taken according to their time period. There is also the option of using other means of estimating weekly income under (b)(ii)(cc). It appears that (b)(ii)(cc) is an alternative to (b)(ii)(aa) or (bb).

Paras (4) and (5) require royalty payments and Public Lending Right Scheme payments and analogous income, along with any payments made on an "occasional" basis, to be taken into account as referable to a year. It is inherent in the word "occasional" that the payments must be infrequent and irregular.

Para (6) requires payments of benefit to be taken into account over a period equivalent to that in respect of which it is payable. Note that reg 44(3) provides for certain arrears of PC to be treated as capital.

Para (7) requires foreign payments to be converted into Sterling for the purpose of assessment of income. The exchange rate at the date of payment is to be used.

Paras (8) to (9) and (11) bring in the schedules for disregards of income and capital. Note that Sch 6 Part 2 contains capital disregarded for the purposes of generating deemed income under reg 29(2).

Para (12) requires tax liabilities to be ignored when calculating income. "Tax" covers income tax and presumably also national insurance contributions, which are a form of taxation, as well as any other forms of tax that might apply to the particular type of income.

Paras (10), (13) and (14) contained a power to modify the HB scheme so as to disregard war widow's and widower's pensions and certain payments made under the Armed Forces and Reserve Forces (Compensation Scheme) Order 2005. s134(8) SSAA 1992 sets out the circumstances in which modifications can be made. The prescribed pensions are now found in the Schedule to the Housing Benefit and Council Tax Benefit (War Pension Disregards) Regulations 2007 (on p1227). See the commentary to s134(8) for a discussion of an authority's powers.

Disregard of changes in tax, contributions etc

34. In calculating the claimant's income the appropriate authority may disregard any legislative change–

(a)   in the basic or other rates of income tax;

(b)   in the amount of any personal tax relief;

(c)   in the rates of social security contributions payable under the Act or in the lower earnings limit or upper earnings limit for Class 1 contributions under that Act, the lower or upper limits applicable to Class 4 contributions under that Act or the amount specified in section 11(4) of the Act (small earnings exception in relation to Class 2 contributions);

(d)   in the amount of tax payable as a result of an increase in the weekly rate of Category A, B, C or D retirement pension or any addition thereto or any graduated pension payable under the Act; and

(e)   in the maximum rate of child tax credit or working tax credit,

for a period not exceeding 30 benefit weeks beginning with the benefit week immediately following the date from which the change is effective.

General Note

This is the equivalent of reg 34 HB Regs (see p357).

SECTION 3

Employed earners

Earnings of employed earners

35.–(1)   Subject to paragraph (2), "earnings" means in the case of employment as an employed earner, any remuneration or profit derived from that employment and includes–

(a)   any bonus or commission;

(b)   any payment in lieu of remuneration except any periodic sum paid to a claimant on account of the termination of his employment by reason of redundancy;

(c)   any payment in lieu of notice;

(d)   any holiday pay;

(e)   any payment by way of a retainer;

(f)   any payment made by the claimant's employer in respect of expenses not wholly, exclusively and necessarily incurred in the performance of the duties of the employment, including any payment made by the claimant's employer in respect of–

    (i)   travelling expenses incurred by the claimant between his home and place of employment;

    (ii)   expenses incurred by the claimant under arrangements made for the care of a member of his family owing to the claimant's absence from home;

(g)   the amount of any payment by way of a non-cash voucher which has been taken into account in the computation of a person's earnings in accordance with Part 5 of Schedule 3 to the Social Security (Contributions) Regulations 2001;

(h)   statutory sick pay and statutory maternity pay payable by the employer under the Act;

(i)   statutory paternity pay payable under Part 12ZA of the Act;

(j)   statutory adoption pay payable under Part 12ZB of the Act;

(k)   any sums payable under a contract of service–

    (i)   for incapacity for work due to sickness or injury; or

    (ii)   by reason of pregnancy or confinement.

(2)   Earnings shall not include–

(a)   subject to paragraph (3), any payment in kind;

(b)   any payment in respect of expenses wholly, exclusively and necessarily incurred in the performance of the duties of the employment;

(c)   any occupational pension;

(d)   any lump sum payment made under the Iron and Steel Re-adaptation Benefits Scheme;

(e)   any payment of compensation made pursuant to an award by an employment tribunal established under the Employment Tribunals Act 1996 in respect of unfair dismissal or unlawful discrimination.

[[1] (f)   any payment in respect of expenses arising out of the claimant's participation in a service user group.]

(3)   Paragraph (2)(a) shall not apply in respect of any non-cash voucher referred to in paragraph (1)(g).

Amendment

1.   Inserted by reg 7(3) of SI 2009 No 2655 as from 2.11.09.

Calculation of net earnings of employed earners

36.–(1)   For the purposes of regulation 30 (calculation of income on a weekly basis), the earnings of a claimant derived or likely to be derived from employment as an employed earner to be taken into account shall, subject to regulation 33(5) and Schedule 4, be his net earnings.

(2)   For the purposes of paragraph (1) net earnings shall, except in relation to any payment to which regulation 33(5) refers, be calculated by taking into account the gross earnings of the claimant from that employment over the assessment period, less–

(a)   any amount deducted from those earnings by way of–

    (i)   income tax;

    (ii)   primary Class 1 contributions under the Act;

(b)   one-half of any sum paid by the claimant by way of a contribution towards an occupational pension scheme;

(c)   one-half of the amount calculated in accordance with paragraph (4) in respect of any qualifying contribution payable by the claimant; and

(d)   where those earnings include a payment which is payable under any enactment having effect in Northern Ireland and which corresponds to statutory sick pay, statutory maternity pay, statutory paternity pay or statutory adoption pay, any amount deducted from those earnings by way of any contributions which are payable under any enactment having effect in Northern Ireland and which correspond to primary Class 1 contributions under the Act.

(3)   In this regulation "qualifying contribution" means any sum which is payable periodically as a contribution towards a personal pension scheme.

(4)   The amount in respect of any qualifying contribution shall be calculated by multiplying the daily amount of the qualifying contribution by the number equal to the number of days in the assessment period; and for the purposes of this regulation the daily amount of the qualifying contribution shall be determined–

(a)   where the qualifying contribution is payable monthly, by multiplying the amount of the qualifying contribution by 12 and dividing the product by 365;

(b)   in any other case, by dividing the amount of the qualifying contribution by the number equal to the number of days in the period to which the qualifying contribution relates.

(5)   Where the earnings of a claimant are determined under sub-paragraph (b) of paragraph (2) of regulation 33 (calculation of weekly income), his net earnings shall be calculated by taking into account those earnings over the assessment period, less–

(a)   an amount in respect of income tax equivalent to an amount calculated by applying to those earnings the [¹ [²] the basic rate of tax applicable to the assessment period less only the personal relief to which the claimant is entitled under section 257(1) of the Income and Corporation Taxes Act 1988 (personal allowances) as is appropriate to his circumstances but, if the assessment period is less than a year, the earnings to which the [¹ [² basic] rate] of tax is to be applied and the amount of the personal relief deductible under this sub-paragraph shall be calculated on a pro rata basis;

(b)   an amount equivalent to the amount of the primary Class 1 contributions that would be payable by him under the Act in respect of those earnings if such contributions were payable; and

(c)   one-half of any sum which would be payable by the claimant by way of a contribution towards an occupational or personal pension scheme, if the earnings so estimated were actual earnings.

Amendments
1.   Amended by reg 12(4) of SI 2007 No 2618 as from 1.10.07.
2.   Amended by reg 7(6) of SI 2009 No 583 as from 6.4.09.

General Note
This is equivalent to reg 36 HB Regs (see p362).

SECTION 4
Self-employed earners

Calculation of earnings of self-employed earners

37.–(1) Where a claimant's earnings consist of earnings from employment as a self-employed earner, the weekly amount of his earnings shall be determined by reference to his average weekly earnings from that employment–

(a)   over a period of one year; or

(b)   where the claimant has recently become engaged in that employment or there has been a change which is likely to affect the normal pattern of business, over such other period ("computation period") as may, in the particular case, enable the weekly amount of his earnings to be determined more accurately.

(2)   For the purposes of determining the weekly amount of earnings of a claimant to whom paragraph (1)(b) applies, his earnings over the computation period shall be divided by the number equal to the number of days in that period and multiplying the quotient by 7.

(3)   The period over which the weekly amount of a claimant's earnings is calculated in accordance with this regulation shall be his assessment period.

Analysis
This has no equivalent in the HB Regs. It simply states that self-employed earners have their weekly earnings calculated from average earnings over a year or where the business has recently started or there has been a change in the pattern of the business, such other period that enables the earnings to be determined more accurately.

Earnings of self-employed earners

38.–(1)   Subject to paragraph (2), ''earnings'', in the case of employment as a self-employed earner, means the gross receipts of the employment and shall include any allowance paid under section 2 of the 1973 Act or section 2 of the Enterprise and New Towns (Scotland) Act 1990 to the claimant for the purpose of assisting him in carrying on his business unless at the date of claim the allowance has been terminated.

(2)   ''Earnings'' in the case of employment as a self-employed earner does not include–

(a)   where a claimant occupies a dwelling as his home and he provides in that dwelling board and lodging accommodation for which payment is made, those payments;

(b)   any payment made by a local authority to a claimant–

    (i)   with whom a person is accommodated by virtue of arrangements made under section 23(2)(a) of the Children Act 1989(provision of accommodation and maintenance for a child whom they are looking after) or, as the case may be, section 26(1) of the Children (Scotland) Act 1995; or

    [² (ii) with whom a local authority foster a child under the Looked After Children (Scotland) Regulations 2009 or who is a kinship carer under those Regulations;]

(c)   any payment made by a voluntary organisation in accordance with section 59(1)(a) of the Children Act 1989 (provision of accommodation by voluntary organisations);

(d)   any payment made to the claimant or his partner for a person (''the person concerned'') who is not normally a member of the claimant's household but is temporarily in his care, by–

    (i)   a health authority;

    (ii)   a local authority, but excluding payments of housing benefit made in respect of the person concerned;

    (iii)   a voluntary organisation;

    (iv)   the person concerned pursuant to section 26(3A) of the National Assistance Act 1948; [¹]

    (v)   a primary care trust established under section 16A of the National Health Service Act [¹ 1977 or established by an order made under section 18(2)(c) of the National Health Service Act 2006; or]

    [¹ (vi) a Local Health Board established under section 16BA of the National Health Service Act 1977 or established by an order made under section 11 of the National Health Service (Wales) Act 2006;]

(e)   any sports award.

Amendments
1.   Amended by reg 6(6) of SI 2008 No 3157 as from 5.1.09.
2.   Substituted by reg 8(3) of SI 2010 No 2429 as from 1.11.10.

General Note
Para (1) is equivalent to reg 37(1) HB Regs. On para (2)(c) to (d), see Sch 5 paras 26 and 27 HB Regs on p557.

Calculation of net profit of self-employed earners

39.–(1)   For the purposes of regulation 30 (calculation of income on a weekly basis) the earnings of a claimant to be taken into account shall be–

   (a)   in the case of a self-employed earner who is engaged in employment on his own account, the net profit derived from that employment;

   (b)   in the case of a self-employed earner whose employment is carried on in partnership, his share of the net profit derived from that employment, less–

       (i)   an amount in respect of income tax and of social security contributions payable under the Act calculated in accordance with regulation 40 (deduction of tax and contributions for self-employed earners); and

       (ii)   one-half of the amount calculated in accordance with paragraph (10) in respect of any qualifying premium.

   (2)   For the purposes of paragraph (1)(a) the net profit of the employment shall, except where paragraph (8) applies, be calculated by taking into account the earnings of the employment over the assessment period less–

   (a)   subject to paragraphs (4) to (7), any expenses wholly and exclusively incurred in that period for the purposes of that employment;

   (b)   an amount in respect of–

       (i)   income tax; and

       (ii)   social security contributions payable under the Act,

       calculated in accordance with regulation 40 (deduction of tax and contributions for self-employed earners); and

   (c)   one-half of the amount calculated in accordance with paragraph (10) in respect of any qualifying premium.

   (3)   For the purposes of paragraph (1)(b) the net profit of the employment shall be calculated by taking into account the earnings of the employment over the assessment period less, subject to paragraphs (4) to (7), any expenses wholly and exclusively incurred in that period for the purposes of the employment.

   (4)   Subject to paragraph (5), no deduction shall be made under paragraph (2)(a) or (3), in respect of–

   (a)   any capital expenditure;

   (b)   the depreciation of any capital asset;

   (c)   any sum employed or intended to be employed in the setting up or expansion of the employment;

   (d)   any loss incurred before the beginning of the assessment period;

   (e)   the repayment of capital on any loan taken out for the purposes of the employment; and

   (f)   any expenses incurred in providing business entertainment.

   (5)   A deduction shall be made under paragraph (2)(a) or (3) in respect of the repayment of capital on any loan used for–

   (a)   the replacement in the course of business of equipment or machinery; and

   (b)   the repair of an existing business asset except to the extent that any sum is payable under an insurance policy for its repair.

   (6)   The relevant authority shall refuse to make a deduction in respect of any expenses under paragraph (2)(a) or (3) where it is not satisfied given the nature and the amount of the expense that it has been reasonably incurred.

   (7)   For the avoidance of doubt–

   (a)   a deduction shall not be made under paragraph (2)(a) or (3) in respect of any sum unless it has been expended for the purposes of the business;

   (b)   a deduction shall be made thereunder in respect of–

       (i)   the excess of any value added tax paid over value added tax received in the assessment period;

       (ii)   any income expended in the repair of an existing business asset except to the extent that any sum is payable under an insurance policy for its repair;

       (iii) any payment of interest on a loan taken out for the purposes of the employment.

   (8)   Where a claimant is engaged in employment as a child minder the net profit of the employment shall be one-third of the earnings of that employment, less–

   (a)   an amount in respect of–

       (i)   income tax; and

(ii)   social security contributions payable under the Act,

calculated in accordance with regulation 40 (deduction of tax and contributions for self-employed earners); and

(b)   one-half of the amount calculated in accordance with paragraph (10) in respect of any qualifying premium.

(9)   For the avoidance of doubt where a claimant is engaged in employment as a self-employed earner and he is also engaged in one or more other employments as a self-employed or employed earner any loss incurred in any one of his employments shall not be offset against his earnings in any other of his employments.

(10)   The amount in respect of any qualifying premium shall be calculated by multiplying the daily amount of the qualifying premium by the number equal to the number of days in the assessment period; and for the purposes of this regulation the daily amount of the qualifying premium shall be determined–

(a)   where the qualifying premium is payable monthly, by multiplying the amount of the qualifying premium by 12 and dividing the product by 365;

(b)   in any other case, by dividing the amount of the qualifying premium by the number equal to the number of days in the period to which the qualifying premium relates.

(11)   In this regulation, ''qualifying premium'' means any premium which is payable periodically in respect of [¹] a personal pension scheme and is so payable on or after the date of claim.

Amendment

1.   Omitted by reg 5(3) of SI 2007 No 1749 as from 16.7.07.

Deduction of tax and contributions of self-employed earners

40.–(1)   The amount to be deducted in respect of income tax under regulation 39(1)(b)(i), (2)(b)(i) or (8)(a)(i) (calculation of net profit of self-employed earners) shall be calculated on the basis of the amount of chargeable income and as if that income were assessable to income tax at the [¹ starting rate] or, as the case may be, the [¹ starting rate] and the basic rate of tax applicable to the assessment period less only the personal relief to which the claimant is entitled under sections 257(1) of the Income and Corporation Taxes Act 1988 (personal allowance) as is appropriate to his circumstances; but, if the assessment period is less than a year, the earnings to which the [¹ starting rate] of tax is to be applied and the amount of the personal reliefs deductible under this paragraph shall be calculated on a pro rata basis.

(2)   The amount to be deducted in respect of social security contributions under regulation 39(1)(b)(i), (2)(b)(ii) or (8)(a)(ii) shall be the total of–

(a)   the amount of Class 2 contributions payable under section 11(1) or, as the case may be, 11(3) of the Act at the rate applicable to the assessment period except where the claimant's chargeable income is less than the amount specified in section 11(4) of the Act (small earnings exception) for the tax year applicable to the assessment period; but if the assessment period is less than a year, the amount specified for that tax year shall be reduced pro rata; and

(b)   the amount of Class 4 contributions (if any) which would be payable under section 15 of the Act (Class 4 contributions recoverable under the Income Tax Acts) at the percentage rate applicable to the assessment period on so much of the chargeable income as exceeds the lower limit but does not exceed the upper limit of profits and gains applicable for the tax year applicable to the assessment period; but if the assessment period is less than a year, those limits shall be reduced pro rata.

(3)   In this regulation ''chargeable income'' means–

(a)   except where sub-paragraph (b) applies, the earnings derived from the employment less any expenses deducted under paragraph (2)(a) or, as the case may be, (3) of regulation 39;

(b)   in the case of employment as a child minder, one-third of the earnings of that employment.

Amendment
1.   Amended by reg 12(5) of SI 2007 No 2618 as from 1.10.07.

General Note
This is equivalent to reg 39 HB Regs (see p368).

SECTION 5
Other income

Notional income

41.–(1)   A claimant shall be treated as possessing–
(a)   subject to paragraph (2), the amount of any retirement pension income–
    (i)   for which no claim has been made; and
    (ii)   to which he might expect to be entitled if a claim for it were made;
(b)   income from an occupational pension scheme which the claimant elected to defer.

(2)   Paragraph (1)(a) shall not apply to the following where entitlement has been deferred–
(a)   Category A or Category B retirement pension payable under sections 43 to 55 of the Act;
(b)   a shared additional pension payable under section 55A of the Act; and
(c)   graduated retirement benefit payable under sections 36 or 37 of the National Insurance Act 1965.

(3)   For the purposes of paragraph (2), entitlement has been deferred–
(a)   in the case of a Category A or Category B pension, in the circumstances specified in section 55(3) of the Act;
(b)   in the case of a shared additional pension, in the circumstances specified in section 55C(3) of the Act;
(c)   in the case of graduated retirement benefit, in the circumstances specified in section 36(4) and (4A) of the National Insurance Act 1965.

[⁴ (4)   This paragraph applies where a person [⁶ who has attained the qualifying age for state pension credit] –
(a)   is entitled to money purchase benefits under an occupational pension scheme or a personal pension scheme;
(b)   fails to purchase an annuity with the funds available in that scheme; and
(c)   either–
    (i)   defers in whole or in part the payment of any income which would have been payable to him by his pension fund holder, or
    (ii)   fails to take any necessary action to secure that the whole of any income which would be payable to him by his pension fund holder upon his applying for it, is so paid, or
    (iii)   income withdrawal is not available to him under that scheme.

(4A)   Where paragraph (4) applies, the amount of any income foregone shall be treated as possessed by that person, but only from the date on which it could be expected to be acquired were an application for it to be made.]

(5)   The amount of any income foregone in a case [⁴ where paragraph (4)(c)(i) or (ii)] applies shall be the maximum amount of income which may be withdrawn from the fund and shall be determined by the relevant authority which shall take account of information provided by the pension fund holder in accordance with regulation 67(6) (evidence and information).

(6)   The amount of any income foregone in a case [⁴ where paragraph (4)(c)(iii)] applies shall be the income that the claimant could have received without purchasing an annuity had the funds held under the relevant scheme [⁴] been held under a personal pension scheme or occupational pension scheme where income withdrawal was available and shall be determined in the manner specified in paragraph (5).

(7)   In paragraph (4), "money purchase benefits" has the meaning it has in the Pension Schemes Act 1993.

(8)　[² Subject to paragraph (8A) [⁵ and (8C)],] A person shall be treated as possessing income of which he has deprived himself for the purpose of securing entitlement to housing benefit or increasing the amount of that benefit.

[² (8A)　Paragraph (8) shall not apply in respect of the amount of an increase of pension or benefit where a person, having made an election in favour of that increase of pension or benefit under Schedule 5 or 5A to the Contributions and Benefits Act or under Schedule 1 to the Graduated Retirement Benefit Regulations, changes that election in accordance with regulations made under Schedule 5 or 5A to that Act in favour of a lump sum.

(8B)　In paragraph (8A), "lump sum" means a lump sum under Schedule 5 or 5A to the Contributions and Benefits Act or under Schedule 1 to the Graduated Retirement Benefit Regulations.]

[⁵ (8C)　Paragraph (8) shall not apply in respect of any amount of income other than earnings, or earnings of an employed earner, arising out of the claimant's participation in a service user group.]

(9)　Where a claimant is in receipt of any benefit (other than housing benefit) under the benefit Acts and the rate of that benefit is altered with effect from a date on or after 1st April in any year but not more than 14 days thereafter, the relevant authority shall treat the claimant as possessing such benefit at the altered rate–
(a)　in a case in which the claimant's weekly amount of eligible rent falls to be calculated in accordance with regulation 61(2)(b) [¹ or (c)] (calculation of weekly amounts), from 1st April in that year;
(b)　in any other case, from the first Monday in April in that year,
to the date on which the altered rate is to take effect.

(10)　In the case of a claimant who has, or whose partner has, an award of state pension credit comprising only the savings credit, where a relevant authority treats the claimant as possessing any benefit (other than housing benefit) at the altered rate in accordance with paragraph (9), that authority shall–
(a)　determine the income and capital of that claimant in accordance with regulation 27(1) (calculation of claimant's income in savings credit only cases) where the calculation or estimate of that income and capital is altered with effect from a date on or after 1st April in any year but not more than 14 days thereafter; and
(b)　treat that claimant as possessing such income and capital at the altered rate by reference to the period referred to in paragraph (9)(a) or (b), as the case may be.

[³ (11)　For the purposes of paragraph (8), a person is not to be regarded as depriving himself of income where–
(a)　his rights to benefits under a registered pension scheme are extinguished and in consequence of this he receives a payment from the scheme, and
(b)　that payment is a trivial commutation lump sum within the meaning given by paragraph 7 of Schedule 29 to the Finance Act 2004.

(12)　In paragraph (11), "registered pension scheme" has the meaning given in section 150(2) of the Finance Act 2004.]

Amendments
1.　Amended by reg 2(7) of SI 2005 No 2502 as amended by Sch 2 para 27 of SI 2006 No 217 as from 1.4.06 (3.4.06 where rent payable weekly or at intervals of a week).
2.　Inserted by reg 11(3) of SI 2005 No 2677 and reg 2 of SI 2006 No 217 as from 6.4.06.
3.　Amended by reg 16(2) of SI 2006 No 2378 as from 2.10.06.
4.　Amended by reg 5(4) of SI 2007 No 1749 as from 16.7.07.
5.　Amended by reg 7(4) of SI 2009 No 2655 as from 2.11.09.
6.　Amended by reg 9(4) of SI 2010 No 641 as from 6.4.10.

Analysis
This, together with reg 42, is largely a simplified and re-ordered version of reg 42 HB Regs (see p373).

Paras (1) to (3) have no equivalent in reg 42 HB Regs. They deal with "retirement pension income" as defined in s16 SPCA (see reg 29(c)) or income from an occupational pension scheme. If a claimant or her/his partner fails to take up income from one of those sources, s/he will be treated as having income of that amount. Note the phrase "might expect to be entitled if a claim for it were made" in para (1)(a)(ii) which sets a lower burden of proof of availability. Para (1)(a) does not apply where entitlement to the types of pension listed in para (2) has been deferred in the circumstances set out in para (3).

Paras (4) to (6) aim to ensure that a claimant aged at least the qualifying age for PC (defined in reg 2(1)) does not deprive her/himself of income available from an occupational or personal pension scheme. The claimant or other relevant person is expected to purchase an annuity with the funds available in the pension scheme. If s/he does not do so, s/he will be treated as possessing the maximum amount that can be withdrawn from the scheme, as assessed under para (5) or (6) as appropriate. S/he is treated as possessing the income from the date it could be expected to be acquired were an application made for it: para (4A). The provision is only triggered if one of the conditions in heads (4)(c)(i) to (iii) are met.

Paras (8) to (8C). Para (8) is the equivalent of reg 42(1) HB Regs, but here it is subject to paras (8A), (8C) and (11). Under para (8A), where someone defers claiming a pension or benefit opting for an increase in it, then opts to take a lump sum instead, the deprivation rules do not apply to the increase. "Lump sum" is defined in para (8B). Para (11) concerns trivial lump sum payments made to a claimant in consequence of the ending of her/his right to receive benefits under a registered pension scheme: defined in para (12). The effect of para (11) is that the person cannot be treated as still receiving as income the benefits s/he used to receive under the registered pension scheme. The lump sum payment itself should be treated as capital. See Sch 6 para 26A for a disregard of lump sum payments made under Sch 5 or 5A SSCBA. Para (8C) concerns the payments set out made to claimants in respect of their participation in a service user group, defined in reg 2(1) (see p777).

Paras (9) and (10). Para (9) is designed to ease administration connected with the uprating of benefits. The increased amount of benefit is treated as possessed from 1 April each year unless rent is not payable weekly in which case it will apply from the first Monday in April. Where para (9) applies and a claimant or her/his partner has an award of the savings credit of PC only, para (10) tells an authority to redetermine such a claimant's income and capital and to treat the altered rate as the claimant's by reference to the relevant period in para (9).

Income paid to third parties

42.–(1) Any payment of income, other than a payment specified in paragraph (2), to a third party in respect of the claimant shall be treated as possessed by the claimant.

(2)   Paragraph (1) shall not apply in respect of a payment of income made under an occupational pension scheme [¹ , in respect of a pension or other periodical payment made under a personal pension scheme or a payment made by the Board of the Pension Protection Fund] where–

(a)   a bankruptcy order has been made in respect of the person in respect of whom the payment has been made or, in Scotland, the estate of that person is subject to sequestration or a judicial factor has been appointed on that person's estate under section 41 of the Solicitors (Scotland) Act 1980;

(b)   the payment is made to the trustee in bankruptcy or any other person acting on behalf of the creditors; and

(c)   the person referred to in sub-paragraph (a) and his partner does not possess, or is not treated as possessing, any other income apart from that payment.

Amendment
1.   Substituted by reg 10(3) of SI 2006 No 588 as from 6.4.06.

Analysis
This is significantly different in effect to the more complex reg 42(6) HB Regs (see p373). Under para (1), any payment of income (as defined in reg 29(1)) to a third party in respect of the claimant is treated as possessed by the claimant. Para (2) contains the only exception and is equivalent to reg 42(7)(d) HB Regs.

SECTION 6
Capital

Capital limit

43.   For the purposes of section 134(1) of the Act as it applies to housing benefit (no entitlement to benefit if capital exceeds a prescribed amount), the prescribed amount is £16,000.

General note
This is equivalent to reg 43 HB Regs (see p380). Note, however, that if a claimant or her/his partner is in receipt of the guarantee credit of PC, income and capital are ignored under reg 26; effectively, such claimants have no capital limit.

Calculation of capital

44.–(1) For the purposes of Part 7 of the Act as it applies to housing benefit, the capital of a claimant to be taken into account shall, subject to paragraph (2), be the whole of his capital calculated in accordance with this Part.

(2) There shall be disregarded from the calculation of the claimant's capital under paragraph (1) any capital, where applicable, specified in Schedule 6.

(3) A claimant's capital shall be treated as including any payment made to him by way of arrears of–

(a) child tax credit;

(b) working tax credit;

(c) state pension credit,

if the payment was made in respect of a period for the whole or part of which housing benefit was paid before those arrears were paid.

Analysis

Paras (1) and (2) are equivalent to reg 44 HB Regs (see p380). Para (3) requires arrears of CTC, WTC and PC to be treated as capital if HB was paid to the claimant in respect of the period to which the payment is attributable. This is to avoid the creation of overpayments.

Note that where a claimant or her/his partner is awarded the savings credit of PC but not the guarantee credit, the authority must use the assessment of income and capital the DWP used for PC purposes to calculate HB: reg 27(1) to (6). It is only where such a claimant's capital increases to more than £16,000 during an assessed income period that the authority is required to calculate capital for itself under regs 43 to 49: reg 27(7) and (8).

[¹Calculation of capital in the United Kingdom

45. Capital which a claimant possesses in the United Kingdom shall be calculated at its current market or surrender value less–

(a) where there would be expenses attributable to the sale, 10 per cent.; and

(b) the amount of any encumbrance secured on it.]

Amendment

1. Substituted by reg 12(6) of SI 2007 No 2618 as from 1.10.07.

General Note

This is equivalent to reg 47 HB Regs (see p382).

Calculation of capital outside the United Kingdom

46. Capital which a claimant possesses in a country outside the United Kingdom shall be calculated–

(a) in a case where there is no prohibition in that country against the transfer to the United Kingdom of an amount equal to its current market or surrender value in that country, at that value;

(b) in a case where there is such a prohibition, at the price which it would realise if sold in the United Kingdom to a willing buyer,

less, where there would be expenses attributable to sale, 10 per cent. and the amount of any encumbrance secured on it.

General Note

This is equivalent to the standard reg 48 HB Regs (see p383).

Notional capital

47.–(1) A claimant shall be treated as possessing capital of which he has deprived himself for the purpose of securing entitlement to housing benefit or increasing the amount of that benefit except to the extent that the capital which he is treated as possessing is reduced in accordance with regulation 48 (diminishing notional capital rule).

(2) A person who disposes of capital for the purpose of–

(a) reducing or paying a debt owed by the claimant; or

(b) purchasing goods or services if the expenditure was reasonable in the circumstances of the claimant's case,

shall be regarded as not depriving himself of it.

(3)   Where a claimant stands in relation to a company in a position analogous to that of a sole owner or partner in the business of that company, he shall be treated as if he were such sole owner or partner and in such a case–

(a)   the value of his holding in that company shall, notwithstanding regulation 44 (calculation of capital), be disregarded; and

(b)   he shall, subject to paragraph (4), be treated as possessing an amount of capital equal to the value or, as the case may be, his share of the value of the capital of that company and the foregoing provisions of this Part shall apply for the purposes of calculating that amount as if it were actual capital which he does possess.

(4)   For so long as a claimant undertakes activities in the course of the business of the company, the amount which he is treated as possessing under paragraph (3) shall be disregarded.

(5)   Where under this regulation a person is treated as possessing capital, the amount of that capital shall be calculated in accordance with the provisions of this Part as if it were actual capital which he does possess.

Analysis
> ***Para (1)*** is equivalent to reg 49(1) HB Regs (see p383) and paras (3) to (5) are equivalent to paras (5) to (7) of that regulation.
> ***Para (2)*** confirms the existing caselaw. There is no deprivation if the claimant is reducing or paying a debt or buying goods or services. The latter are subject to a test of reasonableness, the former is not.

Diminishing notional capital rule

48.–(1)   Where a claimant is treated as possessing capital under regulation 47(1) (notional capital), the amount which he is treated as possessing–

(a)   in the case of a week that is subsequent to–
   (i)   the relevant week in respect of which the conditions set out in paragraph (2) are satisfied; or
   (ii)   a week which follows that relevant week and which satisfies those conditions,
   shall be reduced by an amount determined under paragraph (3);

(b)   in the case of a week in respect of which paragraph (1)(a) does not apply but where–
   (i)   that week is a week subsequent to the relevant week; and
   (ii)   that relevant week is a week in which the condition in paragraph (4) is satisfied,
shall be reduced by the amount determined under paragraph (4).

(2)   This paragraph applies to a benefit week where the claimant satisfies the conditions that–

(a)   he is in receipt of housing benefit; and

(b)   but for regulation 47(1), he would have received an additional amount of housing benefit in that week.

(3)   In a case to which paragraph (2) applies, the amount of the reduction for the purposes of paragraph (1)(a) shall be equal to the aggregate of–

(a)   the additional amount to which paragraph (2)(b) refers;

(b)   where the claimant has also claimed state pension credit, the amount of any state pension credit or any additional amount of state pension credit to which he would have been entitled in respect of the benefit week to which paragraph (2) refers but for the application of regulation 21(1) of the State Pension Credit Regulations 2002 (notional capital);

(c)   where the claimant has also claimed council tax benefit, the amount of any council tax benefit or any additional amount of council tax benefit to which he would have been entitled in respect of the benefit week to which paragraph (2) refers but for the application of regulation 39(1) of the Council Tax Benefit Regulations 2006 or regulation 37(1) (notional capital)of the Council Tax Benefit (Persons who have obtained the qualifying age for state pensions credit) Regulations 2006;

(d)   where the claimant has also claimed a jobseeker's allowance, the amount of an income-based jobseeker's allowance to which he would have been entitled in respect of the benefit week to which paragraph (2) refers but for the application of regulation 113 of the Jobseeker's Allowance Regulations (notional capital).

[² (e) where the claimant has also claimed an employment and support allowance, the amount of an income-related employment and support allowance to which he would have been entitled in respect of the benefit week to which paragraph (2) refers but for the application of regulation 115 of the Employment and Support Allowance Regulations (notional capital).]

(4)   Subject to paragraph (5), for the purposes of paragraph (1)(b) the condition is that the claimant would have been entitled to housing benefit in the relevant week but for regulation 47(1), and in such a case the amount of the reduction shall be equal to the aggregate of–

(a)   the amount of housing benefit to which the claimant would have been entitled in the relevant week but for regulation 47(1) and, for the purposes of this sub-paragraph, if the relevant week is a week to which [¹ regulation 61(3)(a)] refers (calculation of weekly amounts), that amount shall be determined by dividing the amount of housing benefit to which he would have been so entitled by the number of days in that week for which he was liable to make payments in respect of the dwelling he occupies as his home and multiplying the quotient so obtained by 7;

(b)   if the claimant would, but for regulation 21 of the State Pension Credit Regulations 2002, have been entitled to state pension credit in respect of the benefit week, within the meaning of regulation 1(2) of those Regulations (interpretation), which includes the last day of the relevant week, the amount to which he would have been entitled and, for the purposes of this sub-paragraph, if the amount is in respect of a part-week, that amount shall be determined by dividing the amount of the state pension credit to which he would have been so entitled by the number equal to the number of days in the part-week and multiplying the quotient so obtained by 7;

(c)   if the claimant would, but for regulation 37(1) of the Council Tax Benefit (Persons who have attained the qualifying age for state pension credit) Regulations 2006, have been entitled to council tax benefit or to an additional amount of council tax benefit in respect of the benefit week which includes the last day of the relevant week, the amount which is equal to–

    (i)   in a case where no council tax benefit is payable, the amount to which he would have been entitled; or

    (ii)   in any other case, the amount equal to the additional amount of council tax benefit to which he would have been entitled;

and, for the purposes of this sub-paragraph, if the amount is in respect of a part-week, that amount shall be determined by dividing the amount of the council tax benefit to which he would have been so entitled by the number equal to the number of days in the part-week and multiplying the quotient so obtained by 7;

(d)   if the claimant would, but for regulation 113 of the Jobseeker's Allowance Regulations, have been entitled to an income-based jobseeker's allowance in respect of the benefit week, within the meaning of regulation 1(3) of those Regulations (interpretation), which includes the last day of the relevant week, the amount to which he would have been entitled and, for the purposes of this sub-paragraph, if the amount is in respect of a part-week, that amount shall be determined by dividing the amount of the income-based jobseeker's allowance to which he would have been so entitled by the number equal to the number of days in the part-week and multiplying the quotient so obtained by 7. [³ and]

[² (e) if the claimant would, but for regulation 115 of the Employment and Support Allowance Regulations, have been entitled to an income-related employment and support allowance in respect of the benefit week, within the meaning of regulation 2(1) of those Regulations (interpretation), which includes the last day of the relevant week, the amount to which he would have been entitled and, for the purposes of this sub-paragraph, if the amount is in respect of a part-week, that amount must be determined by dividing the amount of the income-related employment and support allowance to which he would have been so entitled by the number equal to the number of days in that part-week and multiplying the quotient so obtained by 7.]

(5) The amount determined under paragraph (4) shall be redetermined under that paragraph if the claimant makes a further claim for housing benefit and the conditions in paragraph (6) are satisfied, and in such a case–

(a) sub-paragraphs (a) to (d) of paragraph (4) shall apply as if for the words "relevant week" there were substituted the words "relevant subsequent week"; and

(b) subject to paragraph (7), the amount as redetermined shall have effect from the first week following the relevant subsequent week in question.

(6) The conditions are that–

(a) a further claim is made 26 or more weeks after–

    (i) the date on which the claimant made a claim for housing benefit in respect of which he was first treated as possessing the capital in question under regulation 47(1);

    (ii) in a case where there has been at least one redetermination in accordance with paragraph (5), the date on which he last made a claim for housing benefit which resulted in the weekly amount being redetermined; or

    (iii) the date on which he last ceased to be entitled to housing benefit, whichever last occurred; and

(b) the claimant would have been entitled to housing benefit but for regulation 47(1) of these Regulations or regulation 49(1) of the Housing Benefit Regulations 2006.

(7) The amount as re-determined pursuant to paragraph (5) shall not have effect if it is less than the amount which applied in that case immediately before the redetermination and in such a case the higher amount shall continue to have effect.

(8) For the purposes of this regulation–

(a) "part-week" in paragraph (4)(b) [² (d) and (e)] means–

    (i) a period of less than a week which is the whole period for which state pension credit [² , an income-related employment and support allowance] , or, as the case may be, an income-based jobseeker's allowance, is payable; and

    (ii) any other period of less than a week for which either of those benefits is payable;

(b) "part-week" in paragraph (4)(c) means a period of less than a week for which council tax benefit is allowed;

(c) "relevant week" means the benefit week in which the capital in question of which the claimant has deprived himself within the meaning of regulation 47(1)–

    (i) was first taken into account for the purpose of determining his entitlement to housing benefit; or

    (ii) was taken into account on a subsequent occasion for the purpose of determining or redetermining his entitlement to housing benefit on that subsequent occasion and that determination or redetermination resulted in his beginning to receive, or ceasing to receive, housing benefit, and where more than one benefit week is identified by reference to heads (i) and (ii) of this sub-paragraph, means the later or latest such benefit week;

(d) "relevant subsequent week" means the benefit week which includes the day on which the further claim or, if more than one further claim has been made, the last such claim was made.

Modifications

Para (4)(a) amended by reg 11 Housing Benefit (State Pension Credit) (Local Housing Allowance and Information Sharing) Amendment Regulations 2007 SI No.2869 as from 7 April 2008, save that for a person to whom reg 1(5) of those regulations applied (see p1233), the amendments came into force on the day on or after 7 April 2008 when the first of the events specified in reg 1(6) applied to her/him, or on 6 April 2009 if none had before that date.

Amendments
1.　Amended by reg 11 of SI 2007 No 2869 as from 7.4.08 (or if reg 1(5) of that SI applies, on the day on or after 7.4.08 when the first of the events specified in reg 1(6) applies, or from 6.4.09 if none have before that date).
2.　Amended by reg 35 of SI 2008 No 1082 as from 27.10.08.
3.　Amended by reg 35 of SI 2008 No 2428 as from 27.10.08.

Analysis
This is, for the most part, equivalent to reg 50 HB Regs (see p388). Paras (3) and (4) are different. Only notional entitlements to PC, CTB, income-based JSA and income-related ESA will be taken into account in calculating diminished notional capital.

Capital jointly held

49.　Where a claimant and one or more other persons are beneficially entitled in possession to any capital asset, other than a capital asset disregarded under regulation 47(3), they shall be treated as if each of them were entitled in possession to the whole beneficial interest therein in an equal share and the foregoing provisions of this Part shall apply for the purposes of calculating the amount of capital which the claimant is treated as possessing as if it were actual capital which the claimant does possess.

General Note
This is equivalent to reg 51 HB Regs (see p391).

PART 7
Amount of benefit

[¹ Maximum housing benefit

50.　The amount of a person's appropriate maximum housing benefit in any week shall be 100 per cent. of his eligible rent calculated on a weekly basis in accordance with regulation 61 and 62 (calculation of weekly amounts and rent free periods) less any deductions in respect of non-dependants which fall to be made under regulation 55 (non-dependant deductions).]

Modifications
Reg 50 substituted by reg 12 Housing Benefit (State Pension Credit) (Local Housing Allowance and Information Sharing) Amendment Regulations 2007 SI No.2869 as from 7 April 2008, save that for a person to whom reg 1(5) of those regulations applied (see p1233), the amendments came into force on the day on or after 7 April 2008 when the first of the events specified in reg 1(6) applied to her/him, or on 6 April 2009 if none had before that date.

Amendment
1.　Substituted by reg 12 of SI 2007 No 2869 as from 7.4.08 (or if reg 1(5) of that SI applies, on the day on or after 7.4.08 when the first of the events specified in reg 1(6) applies, or from 6.4.09 if none have before that date).

Housing benefit tapers

51.　The prescribed percentages for the purpose of sub-section (3)(b) of section 130 of the Act (percentage of excess of income over applicable amount which is deducted from maximum housing benefit) shall be 65 per cent.

[¹Amount payable during extended payment period when an extended payment is payable pursuant to regulation 72 or 73 of the Housing Benefit Regulations

52.–(1)　This regulation applies where–
  (a)　a claimant became entitled to an extended payment pursuant to regulation 72 of the Housing Benefit Regulations 2006 or an extended payment (qualifying contributory benefits) pursuant to regulation 73 of those Regulations; and
  (b)　during the extended payment period, these Regulations become applicable to the claimant or the claimant's partner in accordance with regulation 5 (persons who have attained the qualifying age for state pension credit).

(2)   Where this regulation applies, the amount of the extended payment or extended payment (qualifying contributory benefits) payable to a claimant for any week during the extended payment period shall be the higher of–

(a)   the amount of the extended payment payable in accordance with regulation 72B(1)(a) of the Housing Benefit Regulations 2006 or the extended payment (qualifying contributory benefits) payable in accordance with regulation 73B(1)(a) of those Regulations, as the case may be; or

(b)   the amount of housing benefit to which a claimant would be entitled under the general conditions of entitlement of these Regulations, if regulation 72 (extended payments) or 73 (extended payments (qualifying contributory benefits)) of the Housing Benefit Regulations 2006 did not apply to the claimant; or

(c)   the amount of housing benefit to which the claimant's partner would be entitled under the general conditions of entitlement of these Regulations, if regulation 72 or 73 of the Housing Benefit Regulations 2006 did not apply to the claimant.

(3)   Where this regulation applies, no amount of housing benefit shall be payable by the appropriate authority during the extended payment period to a claimant's partner under these Regulations for any week in the extended payment period.]

Amendment

1.   Substituted by reg 6(3) of SI 2008 No 959 as from 6.10.08.

Analysis

A claimant might claim (and be awarded) HB under these regs for the same period in which s/he is entitled to an extended payment under reg 72 or 73 HB Regs (see pp419 and 425). Reg 52 ensures that where an award of HB under these regulations is made, the amount of the extended payment is effectively offset against the amount of HB payable or the extended payment is topped up to the level of the new HB entitlement; only the higher of the extended payment or the amount of HB payable under these regulations to the claimant or her/his partner is payable as an extended payment: para (2). Para (3) prevents payment of HB to the extended payment claimant's partner during the extended payment period (defined in reg 2(1) on p774).

[²Extended payments (qualifying contributory benefits)

53.–(1)   Except in the case of a claimant who is in receipt of state pension credit, a claimant who is entitled to housing benefit (by virtue of the general conditions of entitlement) shall be entitled to an extended payment (qualifying contributory benefits) where–

(a)   the claimant or the claimant's partner was entitled to a qualifying contributory benefit;

(b)   entitlement to a qualifying contributory benefit ceased because the claimant or the claimant's partner–

(i)   commenced employment as an employed or self-employed earner;

(ii)   increased their earnings from such employment; or

(iii)   increased the number of hours worked in such employment,

and that employment is or, as the case may be, increased earnings or increased number of hours are expected to last five weeks or more;

(c)   the claimant or the claimant's partner had been entitled to and in receipt of a qualifying contributory benefit or a combination of qualifying contributory benefits for a continuous period of at least 26 weeks before the day on which the entitlement to a qualifying contributory benefit ceased;

(d)   the claimant or the claimant's partner was not entitled to and not in receipt of a qualifying income-related benefit in the last benefit week in which the claimant, or the claimant's partner, was entitled to a qualifying contributory benefit.

(2)   A claimant must be treated as entitled to housing benefit by virtue of the general conditions of entitlement where–

(a)   the claimant ceased to be entitled to housing benefit because the claimant vacated the dwelling occupied as the claimant's home;

(b)   the day on which the claimant vacated the dwelling was either in the week in which entitlement to a qualifying contributory benefit ceased, or in the preceding week; and

(c)   entitlement to the qualifying contributory benefit ceased in any of the circumstances listed in paragraph (1)(b).]

Amendments

1.   Amended by reg 13 of SI 2007 No 2869 as from 7.4.08 (or if reg 1(5) of that SI applies, on the day on or after 7.4.08 when the first of the events specified in reg 1(6) applies, or from 6.4.09 if none have before that date).

2.   Substituted by reg 5(2) of SI 2008 No 959 as from 6.10.08.

[¹ Duration of extended payment period (qualifying contributory benefits)

53A.–(1)   Where a claimant is entitled to an extended payment (qualifying contributory benefits), the extended payment period starts on the first day of the benefit week immediately following the benefit week in which the claimant, or the claimant's partner, ceased to be entitled to a qualifying contributory benefit.

(2)   For the purpose of paragraph (1), a claimant or a claimant's partner ceases to be entitled to a qualifying contributory benefit on the day immediately following the last day of entitlement to that benefit.

(3)   The extended payment period ends–

(a)   at the end of a period of four weeks; or

(b)   on the date on which the claimant to whom the extended payment (qualifying contributory benefits) is payable has no liability for rent, if that occurs first.]

Amendment

1.   Inserted by reg 5(2) of SI 2008 No 959 as from 6.10.08.

[¹ Amount of extended payment (qualifying contributory benefits)

53B.–(1)   For any week during the extended payment period the amount of the extended payment (qualifying contributory benefits) payable to a claimant shall be the higher of–

(a)   the amount of housing benefit to which the claimant was entitled under the general conditions of entitlement in the last benefit week before the claimant or the claimant's partner ceased to be entitled to a qualifying contributory benefit;

(b)   the amount of housing benefit to which the claimant would be entitled under the general conditions of entitlement for any benefit week during the extended payment period, if regulation 53 (extended payments (qualifying contributory benefits)) did not apply to the claimant; or

(c)   the amount of housing benefit to which the claimant's partner would be entitled under the general conditions of entitlement, if regulation 53 did not apply to the claimant.

(2)   Paragraph (1) is subject to the paragraphs (3) to (6) and does not apply in the case of a mover.

(3)   Where the last benefit week referred to in paragraph (1)(a) fell, in whole or in part, within a rent free period, the last benefit week for the purposes of that paragraph is the last benefit week that did not fall within the rent free period.

(4)   Where–

(a)   a claimant is entitled to an extended payment (qualifying contributory benefit) by virtue of regulation 53(2) (early vacation of dwelling); and

(b)   the last benefit week before the claimant ceased to be entitled to a qualifying contributory benefit was a week in which the claimant's eligible rent was calculated in accordance with regulation 61(3)(c)(21) (calculation of rent for a partial week),

the last benefit week for the purpose of calculating the amount of the extended payment (qualifying contributory benefits) under paragraph (1)(a) shall be the benefit week before the partial week.

(5)   Where–

(a)   a claimant was treated as occupying two dwellings as the claimant's home under regulation 7(6) (liability to make payments in respect of two homes) at the time when the claimant's entitlement to a qualifying contributory benefit ceased; and

(b)   the claimant's liability to pay rent for either of those dwellings ceases during the extended payment period,
the amount of the extended payment (qualifying contributory benefits) for any week shall be reduced by a sum equivalent to the housing benefit which was payable in respect of that dwelling.

(6)   No extended payment (qualifying contributory benefits) is payable for any rent free period as defined in regulation 62(1)(22) (rent free periods).

(7)   Where a claimant is in receipt of an extended payment (qualifying contributory benefits) under this regulation and the claimant's partner makes a claim for housing benefit, no amount of housing benefit shall be payable by the appropriate authority during the extended payment period.]

Amendment

1.   Inserted by reg 5(2) of SI 2008 No 959 as from 6.10.08.

[¹ Extended payments (qualifying contributory benefits) – movers

53C.–(1)   This regulation applies–

(a)   to a mover; and

(b)   from the Monday following the day of the move.

(2)   The amount of the extended payment (qualifying contributory benefits) payable from the Monday from which this regulation applies until the end of the extended payment period shall be the amount of housing benefit which was payable to the mover for the last benefit week before the mover, or the mover's partner, ceased to be entitled to a qualifying contributory benefit.

(3)   Where a mover's liability to make payments for the new dwelling is to the second authority, the extended payment (qualifying contributory benefits) may take the form of a payment from the appropriate authority to–

(a)   the second authority; or

(b)   the mover directly.

(4)   Where–

(a)   a mover, or the mover's partner, makes a claim for housing benefit to the second authority after the mover, or the mover's partner, ceased to be entitled to a qualifying contributory benefit; and

(b)   the mover, or the mover's partner, is in receipt of an extended payment(qualifying contributory benefits) from the appropriate authority,
the second authority shall reduce the weekly amount of housing benefit that the mover, or the mover's partner, is entitled to by a sum equal to the amount of the extended payment (qualifying contributory benefits) until the end of the extended payment period.

(5)   The reduction of housing benefit made by the second authority under paragraph (4) is subject to any entitlement the claimant may have pursuant to regulation 7(6) (liability to make payments in respect of two homes).

(6)   Where the last benefit week referred to in paragraph (2) fell, in whole or in part, within a rent free period, the last benefit week for the purposes of that paragraph is the last benefit week that did not fall within the rent free period.

(7)   No extended payment (qualifying contributory benefits) is payable for any rent free period as defined in regulation 62(1) (rent free periods).]

Amendment

1.   Inserted by reg 5(2) of SI 2008 No 959 as from 6.10.08.

[¹ Relationship between extended payment (qualifying contributory benefits) and entitlement to housing benefit under the general conditions of entitlement

53D.–(1)   Where a claimant's housing benefit award would have ended when the claimant ceased to be entitled to a qualifying contributory benefit in the circumstances listed in regulation 53(1)(b), that award will not cease until the end of the extended payment period.

(2)   Part 8 (calculation of weekly amounts and changes of circumstances) shall not apply to any extended payment (qualifying contributory benefits) payable in accordance with regulation 53B(1)(a) or 53C(2) (amount of extended payment – movers).]

Amendment
1.   Inserted by reg 5(2) of SI 2008 No 959 as from 6.10.08.

Continuing payments where state pension credit claimed

54.–(1)   This regulation applies where–

(a)   the claimant is entitled to housing benefit;

(b)   paragraph (2) is satisfied; and

(c)   either–

(i)   the claimant has attained the qualifying age for state pension credit or, if his entitlement to income-based jobseeker's allowance [¹ or income-related employment and support allowance] continued beyond that age, has attained the age of 65; or

(ii)   the claimant's partner has actually claimed state pension credit.

(2)   This regulation is only satisfied if the Secretary of State has certified to the relevant authority that the claimant's partner has actually claimed state pension credit or that–

(a)   the claimant's award of–

(i)   income support has terminated because the claimant has attained the qualifying age for state pension credit; or

(ii)   income-based jobseeker's allowance [¹ or income-related employment and support allowance] has terminated because the claimant has attained the qualifying age for state pension credit or the age of 65; and

(b)   the claimant has claimed or is treated as having claimed or is required to make a claim for state pension credit.

(3)   Subject to paragraph (4), in a case to which this regulation applies housing benefit shall continue to be paid for the period of 4 weeks beginning on the day following the day the claimant's entitlement to income support [¹ , income-related employment and support allowance] or, as the case may be, income-based jobseeker's allowance, ceased, if and for so long as the claimant otherwise satisfies the conditions for entitlement to housing benefit.

(4)   Where housing benefit is paid for the period of 4 weeks in accordance with paragraph (3) above, and the last day of that period falls on a day other than the last day of a benefit week, then housing benefit shall continue to be paid until the end of the benefit week in which the last day of that period falls.

(5)   Throughout the period of 4 weeks specified in paragraph (3) and any further period specified in paragraph (4)–

(a)   the whole of the income and capital of the claimant shall be disregarded;

(b)   subject to paragraph (6) the appropriate maximum housing benefit of the claimant shall be that which was applicable in his case immediately before that period commenced.

(6)   The appropriate maximum housing benefit shall be calculated in accordance with regulation 50 if, since the date it was last calculated–

(a)   the claimant's rent has increased; or

(b)   a change in the deduction under regulation 55 falls to be made.

Amendment
1.   Amended by reg 36 of SI 2008 No 1082 as from 27.10.08.

Analysis

Reg 54 provides a further scheme of extended payments to that in regs 53 to 53D, but are here called "continuing payments". Here, they are designed to ease the transition into retirement. To qualify for continuing payments, two conditions must be fulfilled:

(1)   Either the claimant has attained the qualifying age for PC (defined in reg 2(1) and discussed on p782) or has attained the age of 65 if entitlement to income-based JSA or income-related ESA continued beyond the qualifying age for PC, or the claimant's partner has claimed PC: para (1).

(2)   The Secretary of State certifies two matters: either that the claimant's partner has claimed PC; or that an award of IS has ceased because the claimant has attained the qualifying age for PC or an award of income-based JSA or income-related ESA has ceased because the claimant has attained the qualifying age for PC or the age of 65. In the latter case, the Secretary of State also certifies that the claimant has claimed (or has been treated as having claimed) PC or or is required to make such a claim: para (2).

Continuing payments last for four weeks from the day after the day IS, income-based JSA or income-related ESA ceases or if the four-week period ends before the end of a benefit week, until the end of the benefit week in which the end of the four-week period falls: paras (3) and (4). They are paid at the rate of the maximum HB applicable immediately preceding the start of the continuing payments: para (5). They may be adjusted, however, for rent increases or a change in applicable non-dependant deductions: para (6). Other changes of circumstances do not take effect until the first day of the benefit week after continuing payments end: reg 60(8).

Note that entitlement to HB can continue beyond the end of the continuing payment period under the normal rules of entitlement to HB. This may still be at the rate of maximum HB – eg, if the claimant or her/his partner is entitled to the guarantee credit of PC.

[¹ Non-dependant deductions

55.–(1)   Subject to the following provisions of this regulation, the deductions referred to in regulation 50 (maximum housing benefit) shall be–

(a)   in respect of a non-dependant aged 18 or over who is engaged in remunerative work, [⁹ £47.75];

(b)   in respect of a non-dependant aged 18 or over to whom sub-paragraph (a) does not apply, [⁹ £7.40] per week.

(2)   In the case of a non-dependant aged 18 or over to whom paragraph (1)(a) applies because he is in remunerative work, where it is shown to the appropriate authority that his normal weekly gross income is–

(a)   less than [⁹ £120.00], the deduction to be made under this regulation shall be that specified in paragraph 1(b);

(b)   not less than [⁹ £120.00] but less than [⁹ £178.00 , the deduction to be made under this regulation shall be [⁹ £17.00];

(c)   not less than [⁹ £178.00] but less than [⁹ £231.00], the deduction to be made under this regulation shall be [⁹ £23.35];

(d)   not less than [⁹ £231.00] but less than [⁹ £306.00], the deduction to be made under this regulation shall be [⁹ £38.20];

(e)   not less than [⁹ £306.00] but less than [⁹ £382.00], the deduction to be made under this regulation shall be [⁹ £43.50].

(3)   Only one deduction shall be made under this regulation in respect of a couple or, as the case may be, members of a polygamous marriage and, where, but for this paragraph, the amount that would fall to be deducted in respect of one member of a couple or polygamous marriage is higher than the amount (if any) that would fall to be deducted in respect of the other, or any other, member, the higher amount shall be deducted.

(4)   In applying the provisions of paragraph (2) in the case of a couple or, as the case may be, a polygamous marriage, regard shall be had, for the purpose of paragraph (2) to the couple's or, as the case may be, all members of the polygamous marriage's joint weekly gross income.

(5)   Where a person is a non-dependant in respect of more than one joint occupier of a dwelling (except where the joint occupiers are a couple or members of a polygamous marriage), the deduction in respect of that non-dependant shall be apportioned between the joint occupiers (the amount so apportioned being rounded to the nearest penny) having regard to the number of joint occupiers and the proportion of the payments in respect of the dwelling payable by each of them.

(6)   No deduction shall be made in respect of any non-dependants occupying a claimant's dwelling if the claimant or his partner is–

(a)   blind or treated as blind by virtue of paragraph 6(5) of Schedule 3 (severe disability premiums); or

(b)   receiving in respect of himself either–

(i)   attendance allowance; or

(ii)   the care component of the disability living allowance.

(7)   No deduction shall be made in respect of a non-dependant if–

(a)   although he resides with the claimant, it appears to the appropriate authority that his normal home is elsewhere; or

(b)   he is in receipt of a training allowance paid in connection with [⁵ youth training] established under section 2 of the 1973 Act or section 2 of the Enterprise and New Towns (Scotland) Act 1990; or

(c)   he is a full-time student during a period of study within the meaning of regulation 53(1) of the Housing Benefit Regulations 2006 (Students); or

(d)   he is a full time student and during a recognised summer vacation appropriate to his course he is not in remunerative work; or

(e)   he is a full-time student and the claimant or his partner has attained the age of 65; or

(f)   he is not residing with the claimant because he has been a patient for a period in excess of 52 weeks, or a prisoner, and for these purposes–

   (i)   "patient" has the meaning given in paragraph (18) of regulation 7 (circumstances in which a person is or is not to be treated as occupying a dwelling as his home);

   (ii)   where a person has been a patient for two or more distinct periods separated by one or more intervals each not exceeding 28 days, he shall be treated as having been a patient continuously for a period equal in duration to the total of those distinct periods; and

   (iii) "prisoner" means a person who is detained in custody pending trial or sentence upon conviction or under a sentence imposed by a court other than a person who is detained in hospital under the provisions of the Mental Health Act 1983, or, in Scotland, under the provisions of the Mental Health (Care and Treatment) (Scotland) Act 2003 or the Criminal Procedure (Scotland) Act 1995.

(8)   No deduction shall be made in calculating the amount of a rent rebate or allowance in respect of a non-dependant aged less than 25 who is on income support [⁴ , an income-based jobseeker's allowance or an income-related employment and support allowance which does not include an amount under section 4(2)(b) of the Welfare Reform Act (the support component and the work-related activity component)].

(9)   No deduction shall be made in respect of a non-dependant who is on state pension credit.

(10)   In the case of a non-dependant to whom paragraph (2) applies because he is in remunerative work, there shall be disregarded from his weekly gross income–

(a)   any attendance allowance or disability living allowance received by him;

(b)   any payment made under [⁸ or by] the Macfarlane Trust, the Macfarlane (Special Payments) Trust, the Macfarlane (Special Payments) (No. 2) Trust, the Fund, the Eileen Trust [⁸ , MFET Limited] or the Independent Living [⁵ Fund (2006)] which had his income fallen to be calculated under regulation 40 (calculation of income other than earnings) of the Housing Benefit Regulations 2006 would have been disregarded under paragraph 23 of Schedule 5 (income in kind) to those Regulations; and

(c)   any payment which had his income fallen to be calculated under regulation 40 of the Housing Benefit Regulations 2006 would have been disregarded under paragraph 35 of Schedule 5 to those Regulations (payments made under certain trusts and certain other payments).]

Modifications

Reg 55 substituted by reg 14 Housing Benefit (State Pension Credit) (Local Housing Allowance and Information Sharing) Amendment Regulations 2007 SI No.2869 as from 7 April 2008, save that for a person to whom reg 1(5) of those regulations applied (see p1233), the amendments came into force on the day on or after 7 April 2008 when the first of the events specified in reg 1(6) applied to her/him, or on 6 April 2009 If none had before that date.

Amendments

1. Substituted by reg 14 of SI 2007 No 2869 as from 7.4.08 (or if reg 1(5) of that SI applies, on the day on or after 7.4.08 when the first of the events specified in reg 1(6) applies, or from 6.4.09 if none have before that date).
2. Confirmed by Art 20(4) of SI 2008 No 632 as from 1.4.08 (7.4.08 where rent payable weekly or in multiples of a week).
3. Amended by Art 20(4) of SI 2008 No 632 as from 1.4.08 (7.4.08 where rent payable weekly or in multiples of a week).
4. Amended by reg 37 of SI 2008 No 1082 as from 27.10.08.
5. Amended by reg 7(4) of SI 2008 No 2767 as from 17.11.08.
6. Confirmed by Art 20(4) of SI 2009 No 497 as from 1.4.09 (6.4.08 where rent payable weekly or in multiples of a week).
7. Amended by Art 20(4) of SI 2009 No 497 as from 1.4.09 (6.4.08 where rent payable weekly or in multiples of a week).
8. Amended by reg 9(3) and (5) of SI 2010 No 641 as from 1.4.10 (5.4.10 where rent payable weekly or in multiples of a week).
9. Confirmed by Art 20(3) of SI 2010 No 793 as from 1.4.10 (5.4.10 where rent payable weekly or in multiples of a week).

Minimum housing benefit

56. Where housing benefit is payable in the form of a rent rebate or allowance, it shall not be payable where the amount to which a person would otherwise be entitled is less than 50 pence per benefit week.

PART 8
Calculation of weekly amounts and changes of circumstances

Date on which entitlement is to commence

57.–(1) Subject to paragraph (2), a person who makes a claim for, and is otherwise entitled to, housing benefit shall be entitled to that benefit from the benefit week following the first day in respect of which that claim is made.

[¹ (2) A claimant shall become entitled to housing benefit from the benefit week in which the first day in respect of which his claim is made falls, where he is otherwise entitled to housing benefit and–

(a) he becomes liable in that benefit week, for the first time, to make payments in respect of a dwelling which he occupies as his home; or,

[² (b) he becomes liable in that benefit week to make payments, which fall due on a daily basis, in respect of the accommodation listed in paragraph (3) which he occupies as his home.]]

(3) The accommodation referred to in paragraph (2)(b) is–

(a) a hostel;

(b) board and lodging accommodation where the payments are to an authority under section 206(2) of the Housing Act 1996 or section 35(2)(b) of the Housing (Scotland) Act 1987;

(c) accommodation which the authority holds on a licence agreement where the payments are to an authority under section 206(2) of the Housing Act 1996 or section 35(2)(b) of the Housing (Scotland) Act 1987; or

(d) accommodation outside that authority's Housing Revenue Account which the authority holds on a lease granted for a term not exceeding 10 years.

[³ (4) In this regulation–

"board and lodging accommodation" means–

(a) accommodation provided to a person or, if he is a member of a family, to him or any other member of his family, for a charge which is inclusive of the provision of that accommodation and at least some cooked or prepared meals which both are cooked or prepared (by a person other than a person to whom the accommodation is provided or by a member of his family) and are consumed in that accommodation or associated premises; or

(b) accommodation provided to a person in a hotel, guest house, lodging house or some similar establishment, but it does not include accommodation in a care home, an Abbeyfield Home, an independent hospital or a hostel; and

"Housing Revenue Account" has the same meaning as for the purposes of Part VIII of the Social Security Administration Act 1992.]

Amendments
1.   Substituted by reg 2(9) of SI 2005 No 2502 as amended by Sch 2 para 27 of SI 2006 No 217 as from 1.4.06 (3.4.06 where rent payable weekly or at intervals of a week).
2.   Substituted by reg 3(2)(a) SI 2007 No. 294 as from 1.4.07.
3.   Inserted by reg 3(2)(b) SI 2007 No. 294 as from 1.4.07.

Analysis
Para (1) sets the date on which entitlement to HB commences. Unlike under the HB Regs, this is the first day of the benefit week following the first day in respect of which the claim is made, provided the claimant is otherwise entitled to benefit. The earliest the date of entitlement can commence is determined by reg 64(1) – ie, currently three months before the date of claim determined under reg 64(6). See p967 for a discussion of *Leicester City Council v LG* [2009] UKUT 155 (AAC), a decision which dealt with the similar provisions under the CTB(SPC) Regs as they were prior to 1 November 2010.

Paras (2) to (4) have the same effect as reg 76(3) to (5) HB Regs (see p432).

[¹**Date on which housing benefit is to end where entitlement to severe disablement allowance or incapacity benefit ceases**
58.]

Amendment
1.   Omitted by reg 6(4)(a) of SI 2008 No 959 as from 6.10.08.

Date on which change of circumstances is to take effect

59.–(1) Except in cases where regulation 34 (disregard of changes in tax, contributions, etc) [⁶ applies, and subject to regulation 8(3) of the Decisions and Appeals Regulations and] the following provisions of this regulation and to [⁸ regulations 60 and 61(5)], a change of circumstances which affects entitlement to, or the amount of, housing benefit ("change of circumstances") shall take effect from the first day of the benefit week following the date on which the change of circumstances actually occurs, and where that change is cessation of entitlement to any benefit under the benefit Acts, the date on which the change actually occurs shall be the day immediately following the last day of entitlement to that benefit.

[¹ (2) Subject to paragraph (8) [⁶ and regulation 8(3) of the Decisions and Appeals Regulations] where the change of circumstances is a change in the amount of rent payable in respect of a dwelling, that change shall take effect from the day on which it actually occurs.]

[² (2A) Subject to paragraphs (8) [⁷ to (9A), except in a case where regulation 8(3) of the Decisions and Appeals Regulations applies, where the change of circumstances is–
(a)   that a person moves into a new dwelling occupied as the home, or
(b)   any other event which–
    (i)   entitles a person to be treated as occupying two dwellings as his home under regulation 7(6), or
    (ii)   brings to an end a person's right to be treated as occupying two dwellings as his home under that regulation, in a case where he has, immediately prior to the event, been treated as occupying two dwellings as his home,
that change of circumstances shall take effect on the day on which it actually occurs.

(2B)   Subject to paragraph (8), where the change of circumstances is the expiry of a maximum period of time, referred to in regulation 7(6), for which a person can be treated as occupying two dwellings as his home, that change shall take effect on the day after the last day of that period]

(3)   Subject to paragraphs (8) [³], where the change of circumstances is an amendment to these Regulations that change, subject to [⁸ regulation 61(5)], shall take effect as follows–

(a)   where the amendment is made by an order under section 150 of the Administration Act (annual up-rating of benefits)–

   (i)   in a case in which the claimant's weekly amount of eligible rent falls to be calculated in accordance with regulation 61(2)(b) [³ or (c)](calculation of weekly amounts), from 1st April;

   (ii)   in any other case, from the first Monday in April,

   in the year in which that order comes into force;

(b)   in respect of any other amendment, from the date on which the amendment of these Regulations comes into force in the particular case.

[¹ (4)   Subject to paragraph (8), if two or more changes of circumstances occurring in the same benefit week would, but for this paragraph, take effect in different benefit weeks in accordance with this regulation, they shall all take effect on the first day of the benefit week in which they occur, unless a change taking effect under paragraphs (2), (2A) or (2B) takes effect in that week, in which case the changes shall all take effect on the day on which that change takes effect.]

(5)   Where, during a benefit week commencing on the first Monday in April–

(a)   a change of circumstances takes effect in accordance with paragraph (3)(a)(ii);

(b)   one or more changes of circumstances occur to which paragraph (1) applies; and

(c)   no other change of circumstances occurs to which this regulation applies,

any change of circumstances to which paragraph (1) applies and which occurs in that benefit week shall take effect from the first day of that benefit week.

(6)   Where the change of circumstances is that income, or an increase in the amount of income, other than a benefit or an increase in the amount of a benefit under the Act, is paid in respect of a past period and there was no entitlement to income of that amount during that period, the change of circumstances shall take effect from the first day on which such income, had it been paid in that period at intervals appropriate to that income, would have fallen to be taken into account for the purposes of these Regulations.

(7)   Without prejudice to paragraph (6), where the change of circumstances is the payment of income, or arrears of income, in respect of a past period, the change of circumstances shall take effect from the first day on which such income, had it been timeously paid in that period at intervals appropriate to that income, would have fallen to be taken into account for the purposes of these Regulations.

[¹ (8)   Subject to paragraph (9), where a change of circumstances occurs which has the effect of bringing entitlement to an end it shall take effect on the first day of the benefit week following the benefit week in which that change actually occurs except in a case where a person is liable to make payments, which fall due on a daily basis, [⁵] in which case that change shall take effect on the day on which it actually occurs.

(9)   Where the change of circumstances is that a person moves to a new dwelling and immediately after the move he is treated as occupying his former dwelling as his home in accordance with regulation 7(7) or (10) then that change of circumstances shall take effect on the day after the last day for which he is treated as [⁹ occupying] the former dwelling in accordance with whichever of those regulations applies in his case.]

[⁷ (9A)   Where the change of circumstances is that the person moves to a new dwelling and immediately before the move that person is treated as occupying the new dwelling in accordance with regulation 7(8) then that change of circumstances shall take effect on the first day on which the person is treated as occupying the new dwelling as the home under that regulation.]

(10)   Paragraph (11) applies if–

(a)   the claimant or his partner has attained the age of 65; and

(b)   either–

   (i)   a non-dependant took up residence in the claimant's dwelling; or

   (ii)   there has been a change of circumstances in respect of a non-dependant so that the amount of the deduction which falls to be made under regulation 55 (non-dependant deductions) increased.

(11)   Where this paragraph applies, the change of circumstances [⁴ referred to in paragraph (10)(b)] shall take effect from the effective date.

(12) In paragraph (11) but subject to paragraph (13), "the effective date" means–
(a) where more than one change of a kind referred to in paragraph (10)(b) relating to the same non-dependant has occurred since–
  (i) the date on which the claimant's entitlement to housing benefit first began; or
  (ii) the date which was the last effective date in respect of such a change; whichever is the later, the date which falls 26 weeks after the date on which the first such change occurred;
(b) where sub-paragraph (a) does not apply, the date which falls 26 weeks after the date on which the change referred to in paragraph (10)(b) occurred.
(13) If in any particular case the date determined under paragraph (12) is not the first day of the benefit week, the effective date in that case shall be the first day of the next benefit week to commence after the date determined under that paragraph.

Modifications

Paras (1) and (3) amended by reg 15(1) Housing Benefit (State Pension Credit) (Local Housing Allowance and Information Sharing) Amendment Regulations 2007 SI No.2869, as amended by reg 5(6) of SI 2008 No.586, as from 7 April 2008, save that for a person to whom reg 1(5) of those regulations applied (see p1233), the amendments came into force on the day on or after 7 April 2008 when the first of the events specified in reg 1(6) applied to her/him, or on 6 April 2009 if none had before that date.

Reg 59 applies as if para (7) was omitted where a change of circumstances occurs as a result of the payment of arrears of any income which affects a determination or decision in respect of entitlement to, or the amount of, HB or CTB before 6 March 1995. See Sch 3 para 1 HB&CTB(CP) Regs on p1197.

Amendments

1. Substituted by reg 2(10)(b), (e) and, (f) of SI 2005 No 2502 as amended by Sch 2 para 27 of SI 2006 No 217 as from 1.4.06 (3.4.06 where rent payable weekly or at intervals of a week).
2. Inserted by reg 2(10)(c) of SI 2005 No 2502 as amended by Sch 2 para 27 of SI 2006 No 217 as from 1.4.06 (3.4.06 where rent payable weekly or at intervals of a week).
3. Amended by reg 2(10)(d) of SI 2005 No 2502 as amended by Sch 2 para 27 of SI 2006 No 217 as from 1.4.06 (3.4.06 where rent payable weekly or at intervals of a week).
4. Amended by reg 16(3) of SI 2006 No 2378 as from 2.10.06.
5. Amended by reg 3(3) SI 2007 No. 294 as from 1.4.07.
6. Substituted by reg 5 of SI 2007 No 2470 as from 24.9.07.
7. Amended by reg 12(7) of SI 2007 No 2618 as from 1.10.07.
8. Amended by reg 15 of SI 2007 No 2869, as amended by reg 5(6) of SI 2008 No 586,as from 7.4.08 (or if reg 1(5) of that SI applies, on the day on or after 7.4.08 when the first of the events specified in reg 1(6) applies, or from 6.4.09 if none have before that date).
9. Substituted by reg 6 of SI 2008 No 2667 as from 30.10.08.

General Note

Note the exceptions to the normal rules for determining the effective date of changes in circumstance in reg 59, set out in reg 60 immediately below.

Change of circumstances where state pension credit payable

60.–(1) Paragraphs (2) to (4) apply where–
(a) the claimant is also on state pension credit;
(b) the amount of state pension credit awarded to him is changed in consequence of a change in the claimant's circumstances or the correction of an official error; and
(c) the change in the amount of state pension credit payable to the claimant results in a change in the rate of housing benefit payable to the claimant.
(2) Where the change of circumstance is that an increase in the amount of state pension credit payable to the claimant results in–
(a) an increase in the rate at which housing benefit is payable to him, the change shall take effect from the first day of the benefit week in which state pension credit becomes payable at the increased rate; or
(b) a decrease in the rate at which housing benefit is payable to him, the change shall take effect from the first day of the benefit week next following the date on which–

(i) the local authority receives notification from the Secretary of State of the increase in the amount of state pension credit; or

(ii) state pension credit is increased,

whichever is the later.

(3) Where the change of circumstance is that the claimant's state pension credit is reduced and in consequence the rate of housing benefit payable to the claimant reduces–

(a) in a case where the claimant's state pension credit is reduced because the claimant failed to notify the Secretary of State timeously of the change of circumstances, the change shall take effect from the first day of the benefit week from which state pension credit was reduced; or

(b) in any other case the change shall take effect from the first day of the benefit week next following the date on which–

(i) the local authority receives notification from the Secretary of State of the reduction in the amount of state pension credit; or

(ii) state pension credit is reduced,

whichever is the later.

(4) Where the change of circumstance is that–

(a) state pension credit is reduced; and

(b) in consequence of the change the rate of housing benefit payable to the claimant is increased,

the change shall take effect from the first day of the benefit week in which state pension credit becomes payable at the reduced rate.

(5) Where a change of circumstances occurs in that an award of state pension credit has been made to the claimant or his partner and this would result in a decrease in the rate of housing benefit payable to the claimant, the change shall take effect from the first day of the benefit week next following the date on which–

(a) the local authority receives notification from the Secretary of State of the award; or

(b) entitlement to state pension credit begins,

whichever is the later.

(6) Where, in the case of a claimant who, or whose partner, is or has been awarded state pension credit comprising only the savings credit, there is–

(a) a change of circumstances of a kind described in any of paragraphs (2) to (5) which results from a relevant calculation or estimate; and

(b) a change of circumstances which is a relevant determination,

each of which results in a change in the rate of housing benefit payable to the claimant, the change of circumstances referred to in sub-paragraph (b) shall take effect from the day specified in paragraphs (2), (3), (4) or (5) as the case may be, in relation to the change referred to in sub-paragraph (a).

(7) Where a change of circumstance occurs in that a guarantee credit has been awarded to the claimant or his partner and this would result in an increase in the rate of housing benefit payable to the claimant, the change shall take effect from the first day of the benefit week next following the date in respect of which the guarantee credit is first payable.

(8) Where a change of circumstances would but for this paragraph take effect under the preceding provisions of this regulation within the 4 week period specified in regulation 54 (continuing payments where state pension credit claimed), that change shall take effect on the first day of the first benefit week to commence after the expiry of the 4 week period.

(9) Where the change of circumstances is an amendment of these Regulations, that change, subject to [² regulation 61(5)] (calculation of weekly amounts), shall take effect as follows–

(a) where the amendment is made by an order under section 150 of the Administration Act (annual uprating of benefits)–

(i) in a case in which the claimant's weekly amount of eligible rent falls to be calculated in accordance with regulation 61(2)(b) [¹ or (c)], from 1st April;

(ii)   in any other case, from the first Monday in April, in the year in which that order comes into force;

(b)   in respect of any other amendment, from the date on which the amendment of these Regulations comes into force in the particular case.

(10)   In this regulation–

"official error" has the meaning it has in the Decisions and Appeals Regulations by virtue of regulation 1(2) of those Regulations;

"relevant calculation or estimate" means the calculation or estimate made by the Secretary of State of the claimant's or, as the case may be, the claimant's partner's income and capital for the purposes of the award of state pension credit;

"relevant determination" means a change in the determination by the relevant authority of the claimant's income and capital using the relevant calculation or estimate, in accordance with regulation 27(1) (calculation of claimant's income and capital in savings credit only cases).

Modifications

Para (9) amended by reg 15 Housing Benefit (State Pension Credit) (Local Housing Allowance and Information Sharing) Amendment Regulations 2007 SI No.2869 as from 7 April 2008, save that for a person to whom reg 1(5) of those regulations applied (see p1233), the amendments came into force on the day on or after 7 April 2008 when the first of the events specified in reg 1(6) applied to her/him, or on 6 April 2009 if none had before that date.

Amendments

1.   Amended by reg 2(11) of SI 2005 No 2502 as amended by Sch 2 para 27 of SI 2006 No 217 as from 1.4.06 (3.4.06 where rent payable weekly or at intervals of a week).

2.   Amended by reg 15 of SI 2007 No 2869 as from 7.4.08 (or if reg 1(5) of that SI applies, on the day on or after 7.4.08 when the first of the events specified in reg 1(6) applies, or from 6.4.09 if none have before that date).

General Note

Reg 60 provides exceptions to the normal rules for determining the effective date of changes in circumstance in reg 59. The effect of reg 60 is that overpayments are not created where there has been a delay in the DWP passing information to authorities about a claimant's (or her/his partner's) PC. It applies when PC is awarded or a PC award is changed which in turn requires an HB award to be modified. Generally speaking, where HB increases as a result of the change in entitlement to PC, the change generally takes effect from the week the PC entitlement alters. However, where HB decreases, the change takes effect from the week the authority is notified of the change in entitlement to PC, or the date the PC changes if this is later. Exceptions are found in paras (8) and (9) where continuing payments are being made and where the change is an amendment to the HB(SPC) Regs.

Analysis

Paragraphs (1) to (5) and (7): The general rules

Where HB payable increases because the PC increases or decreases due to a change in circumstances or the correction of an official error, the change generally takes effect from the first day of the benefit week in which the rate of PC is altered: paras (2)(a) and (4). However, where HB increases because an award of guarantee credit of PC is made to the claimant or her/his partner, the change takes effect from the first day of the benefit week after the date the guarantee credit is payable: para (7).

Where HB payable decreases there are three possibilities. Where:

(1)   a claimant's PC increases due to a change in circumstances or the correction of an official error, the change takes effect from the first day in the benefit week following the later of the date the authority receives notification of the increase from the DWP or the date the PC increases: para (2)(b);

(2)   a claimant's PC decreases, the change takes effect from the first day in the benefit week following the later of the date the authority receives notification of the decreased PC from the DWP or the PC decreases, unless the reduction was due to a failure by the claimant to notify a change to the DWP "timeously". In this case it takes effect from the first day of the benefit week in which the PC decreased: para (3);

(3)   an award of PC is made to the claimant or her/his partner, the change takes effect from the first day of the benefit week following the later of the date the authority receives notification of the award of PC from the DWP or the date entitlement to PC begins: para (5).

Paragraph (6): Savings credit only cases

Where a claimant or her/his partner is getting the savings credit of PC only and the HB payable changes as a result of a change in the DWP assessment of income and capital and a change in the assessment of income and capital by the authority, the change in the authority's assessment takes effect under whichever of paras (2) to (5) applies in relation to the change in PC as a result of the DWP assessment. The definitions of "relevant calculation or estimate" and "relevant determination" are in para (10).

Paragraph (8): Where continuing payments are made

By virtue of para (8), a change taking place while continuing payments are being made under reg 54 above takes effect on the first day of the benefit week after continuing payments end.

Paragraph (9): Amendments to regulations

Where the change is an amendment to the HB(SPC) Regs, it takes effect from the date on which the amendment comes into force unless it is an amendment in respect of the annual uprating of benefits. In this case, if rent is payable monthly or daily, the change takes effect from 1 April or, in any other case, from the first Monday in April. Para (9) is subject to reg 61(5).

[¹ Calculation of weekly amounts

61.–(1)   A person's entitlement to housing benefit in any benefit week shall be calculated in accordance with the following provisions of this regulation.

(2)   The weekly amount of a claimant's eligible rent shall be–

(a)   subject to paragraph (3), where rent is payable at intervals of one week or a multiple thereof, the amount of eligible rent payable weekly or, where it is payable at intervals of a multiple of a week, the amount determined by dividing the amount of eligible rent payable by the number equal to the number of weeks in respect of which it is payable; or

(b)   subject to paragraph (3), where the rent is payable at intervals of a calendar month or multiples thereof, the amount determined by dividing the amount payable by the number equal to the number of calendar months in respect of which it is payable, multiplying by 12 and dividing by 52;

(c)   subject to paragraph (3), where the rent is payable at intervals of a day or multiples thereof, the amount determined by dividing the amount payable by the number equal to the number of days in respect of which it is payable and multiplying by 7.

(3)   In a case–

(a)   to which regulation 57(2) (date on which entitlement is to commence) applies, his eligible rent for the benefit week in which he becomes liable to make payments in respect of a dwelling which he occupies as his home shall be calculated by multiplying his daily rent by the number equal to the number of days in that benefit week for which he is liable to make such payments;

(b)   where a change of circumstances takes effect in a benefit week under regulation 59(2A), (but is not a change described in sub-paragraph (c)(ii) of this regulation), (2B), (8) or (9) other than on the Monday of a benefit week then the claimant's eligible rent for that benefit week shall be calculated by multiplying his daily rent by the appropriate number of days in that benefit week;

(c)   where–

(i)   the amount of eligible rent which the claimant is liable to pay in respect of a dwelling is altered and that change of circumstances takes effect under regulation 59(2); or

(ii)   the claimant–

(aa)   moves to a new dwelling occupied as the home,

(bb)   he is not entitled to be treated, immediately after that move, as occupying two dwellings as his home or as occupying his former dwelling as his home, and

(cc)   that change of circumstances takes effect under regulation 59(2A),

other than on the Monday of a benefit week, then the claimant's eligible rent for that benefit week shall be calculated by multiplying his old and new daily rent by the number equal to the number of days in that week which relate respectively to the old and new amounts which he is liable to pay.

(4)   In the case of a claimant whose weekly eligible rent falls to be calculated in accordance with paragraph (3)(a) or (b) by reference to the daily rent in his case, his weekly applicable amount, weekly income, the weekly amount of any non-dependant deductions and the minimum amount payable in his case shall be calculated in the same

manner as his weekly eligible rent by reference to the amounts determined in his case in accordance with Parts 5 to 7 (applicable amounts, income and capital, and amount of benefit).

(5)   Where a change in the amount of a claimant's applicable amount, income or non-dependant deductions falls to be taken into account in the same benefit week as a change in his eligible rent to which paragraph (3)(c) applies, it shall be taken into account in that week on a daily basis in the same manner and as if it had occurred on the same day as that change in his eligible rent.

(6)   Any amount determined under these Regulations may, if it is appropriate, be rounded to the nearest whole penny by disregarding any amount less than half a penny and treating any amount of half a penny or more as a whole penny.

[² (7)]

(8)   In this regulation "daily rent" shall mean the amount determined by dividing by 7 the amount determined under whichever sub-paragraph of paragraph (2) is appropriate in each case.

(9)   Where a claimant is entitled to benefit in respect of two (but not more than two) dwellings in accordance with regulation 7(6) his eligible rent shall be calculated in respect of each dwelling in accordance with this regulation.]

Amendments

1.   Substituted by reg 16 of SI 2007 No 2869 as from 7.4.08 (or if reg 1(5) of that SI applies, on the day on or after 7.4.08 when the first of the events specified in reg 1(6) applies, or from 6.4.09 if none have before that date).

2.   Omitted by reg 6(4)(b) of SI 2008 No 959 as from 6.10.08.

Modifications

Reg 61 substituted by reg 16 Housing Benefit (State Pension Credit) (Local Housing Allowance and Information Sharing) Amendment Regulations 2007 SI No.2869 as from 7 April 2008, save that for a person to whom reg 1(5) of those regulations applied (see p1233), the amendments came into force on the day on or after 7 April 2008 when the first of the events specified in reg 1(6) applied to her/him, or on 6 April 2009 if none had before that date.

[¹ Rent free periods

62.–(1)   This regulation applies to a claimant for any period (referred to in this regulation as a rent free period) in, or in respect of, which he is not liable to pay rent except for any period to which regulation 8(1)(d) (waiver of rent by landlord in return for work done) applies.

(2)   In the case of the beginning or ending of a claimant's rent-free period, his eligible rent for the benefit week in which the rent free period begins and ends shall be calculated on a daily basis as if those benefit weeks were weeks to which regulation 61(3) applies.

(3)   For the purpose of determining the weekly applicable amount and income of a claimant to whom this regulation applies, the weekly amount of any non-dependant deductions and the minimum amount payable in his case–

(a)   in a case to which regulation 61(2)(a) applies, the amounts determined in his case in accordance with Parts 5 to 7 (applicable amounts, income and capital, and amount of benefit) shall be multiplied by 52 or 53, whichever is appropriate, and divided by the number equal to the number of weeks in that 52 or 53 week period in respect of which he is liable to pay rent;

(b)   subject to paragraph (4), in a case to which regulation 61(2)(b) or (c) applies, the amounts determined in his case in accordance with Parts 5 to 7 shall be multiplied by 365 or 366, whichever is appropriate and divided by the number of days in that 365 or 366 day period in respect of which he is liable to pay rent.

(4)   In a case to which paragraph (3)(b) applies, where either regulation 61(4) or (5) also applies or it is the beginning or end of a rent-free period, the weekly amounts referred to in paragraph (3) shall first be calculated in accordance with sub-paragraph (b) of that paragraph and then determined on a daily basis in the same manner as the claimant's eligible rent.]

Amendment

1.　Substituted by reg 16 of SI 2007 No 2869 as from 7.4.08 (or if reg 1(5) of that SI applies, on the day on or after 7.4.08 when the first of the events specified in reg 1(6) applies, or from 6.4.09 if none have before that date).

Modifications

Reg 62 substituted by reg 16 Housing Benefit (State Pension Credit) (Local Housing Allowance and Information Sharing) Amendment Regulations 2007 SI No.2869 as from 7 April 2008, save that for a person to whom reg 1(5) of those regulations applied (see p1233), the amendments came into force on the day on or after 7 April 2008 when the first of the events specified in reg 1(6) applied to her/him, or on 6 April 2009 if none had before that date.

PART 9
Claims

Who may claim

63.–(1)　In the case of a couple or members of a polygamous marriage a claim shall be made by whichever one of them they agree should so claim or, in default of agreement, by such one of them as the relevant authority shall determine.

(2)　Where a person who is liable to make payments in respect of a dwelling is unable for the time being to act, and–

(a)　a [¹ deputy] has been appointed by the Court of Protection with power to claim, or as the case may be, receive benefit on his behalf; or

(b)　in Scotland, his estate is being administered by a judicial factor or any guardian acting or appointed under the Adults with Incapacity (Scotland) Act 2000 who has power to claim or, as the case may be, receive benefit on his behalf; or

(c)　an attorney with a general power or a power to claim or as the case may be, receive benefit, has been appointed by that person under [¹ the Powers of Attorney Act 1971, the Enduring Powers of Attorney Act 1985 or the Mental Capacity Act 2005 or otherwise],

that [¹ deputy], judicial factor, guardian or attorney, as the case may be, may make a claim on behalf of that person.

(3)　Where a person who is liable to make payments in respect of a dwelling is unable for the time being to act and paragraph (2) does not apply to him, the relevant authority may, upon written application made to them by a person who, if a natural person, is over the age of 18, appoint that person to exercise on behalf of the person who is unable to act, any right to which that person might be entitled under the Act and to receive and deal on his behalf with any sums payable to him.

(4)　Where the relevant authority has made an appointment under paragraph (3) or treated a person as an appointee under paragraph (5)–

(a)　it may at any time revoke the appointment;

(b)　the person appointed may resign his office after having given four week's notice in writing to the relevant authority of his intention to do so;

(c)　any such appointment shall terminate when the relevant authority is notified that a receiver or other person to whom paragraph (2)(b) or (c) applies has been appointed.

(5)　Where a person who is liable to make payments in respect of a dwelling is for the time being unable to act and the Secretary of State has appointed a person to act on his behalf for the purposes of the Act the relevant authority may if that person agrees treat him as if he had been appointed by them under paragraph (3).

(6)　Anything required by these Regulations to be done by or to any person who is for the time being unable to act may be done by or to the [¹ deputy], judicial factor, guardian or attorney, if any, or by or to the person appointed or treated as appointed under this regulation and the receipt of any such person so appointed shall be a good discharge to the relevant authority for any sum paid.

[² (7)]

Amendments

1. Amended by reg 12(8) of SI 2007 No 2618 as from 1.10.07.
2. Omitted by reg 3(3) of SI 2008 No 2299 as from 1.10.08.

Time and manner in which claims are to be made

64.–(1) [¹⁰ Subject to paragraph (1A),] The prescribed time for claiming housing benefit is as regards any day on which, apart from satisfying the condition of making a claim, the claimant is entitled to housing benefit, that day and the period of [⁵ three months] immediately following it.

[¹⁰ (1A)   In any case where paragraph (6)(a) applies, paragraph (1) does not entitle a claimant to claim housing benefit in respect of any day earlier than 3 months before the date on which the claim for state pension credit is made (or treated as made by virtue of any provision of the Social Security (Claims and Payments) Regulations 1987).]

(2)   [¹ Subject to [⁴ paragraphs (5A) to (5BD)],] Every claim shall be in writing and made on a properly completed form approved for the purpose by the relevant authority or in such written form as the relevant authority may accept as sufficient in the circumstances of any particular case or class of cases having regard to the sufficiency of the written information and evidence.

(3)   The forms approved for the purpose of claiming shall be provided free of charge by the relevant authority or such persons as they may authorise or appoint for the purpose.

(4)   Each relevant authority shall notify the Secretary of State of the address to which claims delivered or sent to the appropriate DWP office are to be forwarded.

(5)   A claim [¹ in writing]–

(a)   may be sent or delivered to the appropriate DWP office where the claimant or his partner is also claiming income support, incapacity benefit, state pension credit [⁶ , a jobseeker's allowance or an employment and support allowance];

(b)   where it has not been sent or delivered to the appropriate DWP office, shall be sent or delivered to the designated office;

(c)   sent or delivered to the appropriate DWP office, other than one sent on the same form as a claim made to income support, incapacity benefit [⁶ , a jobseeker's allowance or an employment and support allowance] and as approved by the Secretary of State for the purpose of the benefits being claimed, shall be forwarded to the relevant authority within two working days of the date of the receipt of the claim at the appropriate DWP office, or as soon as practicable thereafter;

[⁴ (d)]

[⁴ (e)]

(f)   where the claimant has attained the qualifying age for entitlement to state pension credit may be sent or delivered to an authorised office.

[³ (g) may be sent or delivered to the offices of a county council in England if the council has arranged with the relevant authority for claims to be received at their offices (''county offices'').]

[¹ (5A)   Where the relevant authority has published a telephone number for the purpose of receiving claims for housing benefit a claim may be made by telephone to that telephone number.

[⁴ (5B)   If the Secretary of State agrees, where–

(a)   a person makes a claim for a benefit referred to in paragraph (5)(a); and

(b)   the Secretary of State has made provision in the Social Security (Claims and Payments) Regulations 1987 for that benefit to be claimed by telephone,

that person may claim housing benefit by telephone to the telephone number specified by the Secretary of State.

(5BA)   A claim for housing benefit may be made in accordance with paragraph (5B) at any time before a decision has been made on the claim for the benefit referred to in paragraph (5)(a).

(5BB)   If the Secretary of State agrees, where a person, in accordance with regulation 32 of the Social Security (Claims and Payments) Regulations 1987 (information to be given and changes to be notified)–

    (a)   furnishes the Secretary of State with such information or evidence as he may require; or

    (b)   notifies the Secretary of State of any change of circumstances,

that person may claim housing benefit in the same manner in which the information or evidence was furnished or the notification was given.

    (5BC)   If the Secretary of State agrees, where a person, in accordance with regulation 24 of the Jobseeker's Allowance Regulations (provision of information and evidence)–

    (a)   furnishes the Secretary of State with such certificates, documents and other evidence as he may require; or

    (b)   notifies the Secretary of State of any change of circumstances,

that person may claim housing benefit in the same manner as the certificate, document and other evidence was furnished or the notification was given.

    (5BD)   A claim for housing benefit may be made in accordance with paragraphs (5BB) or (5BC) at any time before a decision has been made on the award of benefit to which the information, evidence, certificates, documents or notification relates.]

    (5C)   The relevant authority may determine, in any particular case, that a claim made by telephone [4 in accordance with paragraph (5A)] is not a valid claim unless the person making the claim approves a written statement of his circumstances, provided for the purpose by the relevant authority [4].

    [4 (5CA)   The relevant authority or the Secretary of State may determine that a claim made by telephone in accordance with paragraphs (5B) to (5BD) is not a valid claim unless the person making the claim approves a written statement of his circumstances, provided for the purpose by the Secretary of State.]

    [4 (5D)   A claim made by telephone in accordance with paragraphs (5A) to (5BD) is defective unless the relevant authority or the Secretary of State is provided with all the information requested during that telephone call.]

    (5E)   Where a claim made by telephone in accordance with paragraph (5A) [4] is defective, the relevant authority [4 must] provide the person making it with an opportunity to correct the defect.

    [4 (5EA)   Where a claim made by telephone in accordance with paragraphs (5B) to (5BD) is defective–

    (a)   the Secretary of State may provide the person making it with an opportunity to correct the defect;

    (b)   the relevant authority must provide the person making it with an opportunity to correct the defect if the Secretary of State has not already done so unless it considers that it has sufficient information to determine the claim.]

    (5F)   If the person corrects the defect within one month, or such longer period as the relevant authority considers reasonable, of the date the relevant authority [4 or the Secretary of State] last drew attention to it, the relevant authority shall treat the claim as if it had been duly made in the first instance.]

    [4 (5G)   If the person does not correct the defect within one month, or such longer period as the relevant authority considers reasonable, of the date the relevant authority or the Secretary of State last drew attention to it, the relevant authority may treat the claim as if it had been duly made in the first instance, where it considers that it has sufficient information to determine the claim.]

    (6)   Subject to paragraph (11) [4] the date on which a claim is made shall be–

    (a)   in a case where an award of state pension credit which comprises a guarantee credit has been made to the claimant or his partner and the claim for housing benefit is made within one month of the date on which the claim for state pension credit was received at the appropriate DWP office, the first day of entitlement to state pension credit arising from that claim;

    (b)   in a case where a claimant or his partner is a person in receipt of a guarantee credit and he becomes liable for the first time to make payments in respect of the dwelling which he occupies as his home, where the claim is received at the designated office or appropriate DWP office within one month of the claimant first becoming liable for such payments, the date he became liable for those payments;

(c)   in a case where the claimant is the former partner of a person who was, at the date of his death or their separation, entitled to housing benefit and the claimant makes a claim within one month of the date of the death or the separation, that date;

[⁴ (d)   except where sub-paragraph (a), (b) or (c) is satisfied, in a case where a properly completed claim is received in a designated office, an authorised office, county offices or an appropriate DWP office within one month, or such longer period as the relevant authority considers reasonable, of the date on which–

    (i)   a claim form was issued to the claimant following the claimant first notifying, by whatever means, a designated office, an authorised office or an appropriate DWP office of an intention to make a claim; or

    (ii)   a claimant notifies, by whatever means, a designated office, an authorised office or an appropriate DWP office of an intention to make a claim by telephone in accordance with paragraphs (5A) to (5BD),

the date of first notification;]

(e)   in any other case, the date on which the claim is received at the designated office, authorised office [³ , county offices] or appropriate DWP office.

(7)   Where a claim received at the designated office [⁸ or appropriate DWP office] has not been made in the manner prescribed in paragraph (2), that claim is for the purposes of these Regulations defective.

(8)   Where a claim [⁸ , which is received by a relevant authority,] is defective because–

(a)   it was made on the form approved for the purpose but that form is not accepted by the relevant authority as being properly completed; or

(b)   it was made in writing but not on the form approved for the purpose and the relevant authority does not accept the claim as being in a written form which is sufficient in the circumstances of the case having regard to the sufficiency of the written information and evidence,

the relevant authority may, in a case to which sub-paragraph (a) applies, request the claimant to complete the defective claim or, in the case to which sub-paragraph (b) applies, supply the claimant with the approved form or request further information or evidence.

[⁸ (8A)   Where a claim is received at an appropriate DWP office and it appears to the Secretary of State that the form has not been properly completed, the Secretary of State may request that the claimant provides the relevant authority with the information required to complete the form.]

[⁸ (9)   The relevant authority shall treat a defective claim as if it had been validly made in the first instance if, in any particular case, the conditions specified in sub-paragraph (a), (b) or (c) of paragraph (9A) are satisfied.

(9A)   The conditions are that–

(a)   where paragraph (8)(a) (incomplete form) applies, the authority receives at the designated office the properly completed claim or the information requested to complete it or the evidence within one month of the request, or such longer period as the relevant authority may consider reasonable; or

(b)   where paragraph (8)(b) (claim not on approved form or further information requested by relevant authority) applies–

    (i)   the approved form sent to the claimant is received at the designated office properly completed within one month of it having been sent to him; or, as the case may be,

    (ii)   the claimant supplies whatever information or evidence was requested under paragraph (8) within one month of the request,

or, in either case, within such longer period as the relevant authority may consider reasonable; or

(c)   where paragraph (8A) (further information requested by Secretary of State) applies, the relevant authority receives at the designated office the properly completed claim or the information requested to complete it within one month of the request by the Secretary of State or within such longer period as the relevant authority considers reasonable.]

(9) The relevant authority shall treat a defective claim as if it had been validly made in the first instance if–

(a) where paragraph (8)(a) applies, the authority receives at the designated office the properly completed claim or the information requested to complete it or the evidence within one month of the request, or such longer period as the relevant authority may consider reasonable; or

(b) where paragraph (8)(b) applies–

   (i) the approved form sent to the claimant is received at the designated office properly completed within one month of it having been sent to him; or, as the case may be,

   (ii) the claimant supplies whatever information or evidence was requested under paragraph (8) within one month of the request,

or within such longer period as the relevant authority may consider reasonable.

(10) A claim which is made on an approved form for the time being is, for the purposes of this regulation, properly completed if completed in accordance with the instructions on the form, including any instructions to provide information and evidence in connection with the claim.

[² (11) Except in the case of a claim made by a person from abroad, where the claimant is not entitled to housing benefit in the benefit week immediately following the date of his claim but the relevant authority is of the opinion that unless there is a change of circumstances he will be entitled to housing benefit for a period beginning not later than the seventeenth benefit week following the date on which the claim is made, the relevant authority may treat the claim as made on a date in the benefit week immediately preceding the first benefit week of that period of entitlement and award benefit accordingly.]

(12) Paragraph (11) applies in the case of a person who has attained, or whose partner has attained, [⁹ the age which is 17 weeks younger than the qualifying age for state pension credit].

[⁷ (13)]

(14) In this regulation "authorised office" means an office which is nominated by the Secretary of State and authorised by the relevant authority for receiving claims for decision by the relevant authority.

Amendments

1. Inserted by reg 3(2) of SI 2006 No 2967 as from 20.12.06.
2. Substituted by reg 4 of SI 2007 No 1331 as from 23.5.07.
3. Amended by reg 8(2) of SI 2007 No 2911 as from 31.10.07.
4. Amended by reg 3(4) of SI 2008 No 2299 as from 1.10.08.
5. Substituted by reg 5 of SI 2008 No 2424 as from 6.10.08.
6. Amended by reg 38 of SI 2008 No 1082 as from 27.10.08.
7. Omitted by reg 8 of SI 2008 No 2824 as from 27.11.08.
8. Amended by reg 3(2) of SI 2008 No 2987 as from 22.12.08.
9. Amended by reg 30 of SI 2009 No 1488 as from 6.4.10.
10. Amended by reg 3(4) of Si 2010 No 2449 as from 1.11.10.

Analysis

This is the equivalent of reg 83 HB Regs (see p443). There are some differences.

Paras (1), (1A) and (6)

Prior to 1 November 2010, the combined effect of these provisions and reg 57 could be generous as shown in *Leicester City Council v LG* [2009] UKUT 155 (AAC), an Upper Tribunal decision which dealt with the provisions under the CTB(SPC) Regs, which are effectively the same. See p967 for a discussion.

   Para (1) determines the earliest date of entitlement to HB; it is not a backdating provision as such. Accordingly, all the claimant has to show is that s/he was entitled to HB throughout the relevant three-month (or until 6 October 2008, 12-month) period; unlike under the HB Regs, there is no test of good cause, and so judgements as to why the claimant did not claim previously are irrelevant. If the claimant only qualified under the HB(SPC) Regs for part of the three-month period before the actual claim or was not entitled to HB for all of the three-month period, s/he should still benefit from this rule for that part of the period that s/he was entitled, as long as that period runs continuously up to the date of the actual claim, applying, by analogy, *R(IS) 3/01* and *R(IS) 16/04*.

Para (6) determines the date of claim for HB purposes, which is not necessarily the date the claim is actually received by the authority. The date on which entitlement to HB then commences is determined by reg 57. However, where para 6(a) applies (ie, where there is an award of PC guarantee credit and a claim for HB was made within one month of the claim for that credit), a claimant is not entitled to claim HB for any day earlier than three months before the claim for PC was made (or treated as made): para (1A). This would appear to mean that in such a case, the effective date for HB as determined by reg 57 (ie, the date on which entitlement to HB is to commence) cannot be earlier than the effective date of the PC award because the claimant cannot specify a date from which her/his claim is made that precedes that date.

Paras (11) and (12)

Paras (11) and (12) allow the authority to treat an advance claim for HB as made in the benefit week before the first week of entitlement where the claimant will become entitled to HB in the next 17 weeks if the claimant or her/his partner is 17 weeks (or fewer) younger than the qualifying age for PC (defined in reg 2(1)).

[¹Electronic claims for benefit

64A. A claim for housing benefit may be made by means of an electronic communication in accordance with Schedule 10.]

Amendment

1.   Inserted by Art 3(3) of SI 2006 No 2968 as from 20.12.06.

[¹ Date of claim where claim sent or delivered to a gateway office
65.]

Amendment

1.   Omitted by reg 3(5) of SI 2008 No 2299 as from 1.10.08.

[¹ Date of claim where claim sent or delivered to an office of a designated authority
66.]

Amendment

1.   Omitted by reg 3(6) of SI 2008 No 2299 as from 1.10.08.

Evidence and information

67.–(1)   Subject to [⁴ paragraphs (1A) and (2)] and to paragraph 5 of Schedule A1 (treatment of claims for housing benefit by refugees), a person who makes a claim, or a person to whom housing benefit has been awarded, shall furnish such certificates, documents, information and evidence in connection with the claim or the award, or any question arising out of the claim or the award, as may reasonably be required by the relevant authority in order to determine that person's entitlement to, or continuing entitlement to, housing benefit and shall do so within one month of [⁴ the relevant authority requiring him, or the Secretary of State requesting him, to do so] or such longer period as the relevant authority may consider reasonable.

[⁴ (1A)   Where a person notifies a change of circumstances to the appropriate DWP office under regulation 69(9), the Secretary of State may request that the claimant provides to the relevant authority the information or evidence that the Secretary of State considers the relevant authority may require to determine the claimant's continuing entitlement to housing benefit.]

(2)   Nothing in this regulation shall require a person to furnish any certificates, documents, information or evidence relating to a payment to which paragraph (4) applies.

(3)   Where a request is made under paragraph (1), the relevant authority shall–

(a)   inform the claimant or the person to whom housing benefit has been awarded of his duty under regulation 69 (duty to notify change of circumstances) to notify the designated office of any change of circumstances; and

(b)   without prejudice to the extent of the duty owed under regulation 69, indicate to him either orally or by notice or by reference to some other document available to him on application and without charge, the kind of change or circumstances which is to be notified.

(4)　This paragraph applies to any of the following payments–

(a)　a payment which is–

　　(i)　disregarded under paragraph 23 of Schedule 5 to the Housing Benefit Regulations 2006 (income in kind) or paragraph 34 of Schedule 6 to those Regulations (certain payments in kind); and

　　(ii)　made under [5 or by] the Macfarlane Trust, the Macfarlane (Special Payments) Trust, the Macfarlane (Special Payments) (No 2) Trust, the Fund, the Eileen Trust [5 , MFET Limited] , the Skipton Fund or the [2 London Bombings Relief Charitable Fund];

(b)　a payment which is disregarded under paragraph 35 of Schedule 5 to the Housing Benefit Regulations 2006 or paragraph 24 of Schedule 6 to those Regulations (payments made under certain trusts and certain other payments), other than a payment made under the Independent Living [3 Fund (2006)];

(c)　a payment which is disregarded under regulation 55(10)(b) or (c) (income of non-dependant) other than a payment made under the Independent Living [3 Fund (2006)].

(5)　Where a claimant or a person to whom housing benefit has been awarded or any partner is [5 has attained the qualifying age for state pension credit] and is a member of, or a person deriving entitlement to a pension under, a personal pension scheme, [1] he shall where the relevant authority so requires furnish the following information–

(a)　the name and address of the pension fund holder;

(b)　such other information including any reference or policy number as is needed to enable the personal pension scheme [1] to be identified.

(6)　Where the pension fund holder receives from a relevant authority a request for details concerning a personal pension scheme [1] relating to a person or any partner to whom paragraph (5) refers, the pension fund holder shall provide the relevant authority with any information to which paragraph (7) refers.

(7)　The information to which this paragraph refers is–

(a)　where the purchase of an annuity under a personal pension scheme has been deferred, the amount of any income which is being withdrawn from the personal pension scheme;

(b)　in the case of–

　　(i)　a personal pension scheme where income withdrawal is available, the maximum amount of income which may be withdrawn from the scheme; or

　　(ii)　a personal pension scheme where income withdrawal is not available, [1] the maximum amount of income which might be withdrawn from the fund if the fund were held under a personal pension scheme where income withdrawal was available,

calculated by or on behalf of the pension fund holder by means of tables prepared from time to time by the Government Actuary which are appropriate for this purpose.

Amendments

1.　Amended by reg 5(5) of SI 2007 No 1749 as from 16.7.07.

2.　Amended by reg 4(6) of SI 2008 No 1042 as from 19.5.08.

3.　Amended by reg 7(5(a) of SI 2008 No 2767 as from 17.11.08.

4.　Amended by reg 3(3) of SI 2008 No 2987 as from 22.12.08.

5.　Amended by reg 9(3), (5) and (6) of SI 2010 No 641 as from 1.4.10 (5.4.10 where rent payable weekly or in multiples of a week).

[2 **Amendment and withdrawal of claim**

[3 **68.**–(1)　A person who has made a claim may amend it at any time before a decision has been made on it by a notice in writing delivered or sent to the designated office.

(2)　Where the claim was made by telephone in accordance with paragraphs (5A) to (5BD) of regulation 64, the amendment may also be made by telephone.

(3)   Any claim amended in accordance with paragraph (1) or (2) shall be treated as if it had been amended in the first instance.

(4)   A person who has made a claim may withdraw it at any time before a decision has been made on it by notice to the designated office.

(5)   Where the claim was made by telephone in accordance with paragraphs (5B) to (5BD) of regulation 64, the withdrawal may also be made by telephone to the telephone number specified by the Secretary of State.

(6)   Any notice of withdrawal given in accordance with paragraph (4) or (5) shall have effect when it is received.]]

Amendments
1.   Inserted by reg 3(3) of SI 2006 No 2967 as from 20.12.06.
2.   Substituted by reg 7(2) of SI 2007 No 719 as from 2.4.07.
3.   Substituted by reg 3(7) of SI 2008 No 2299 as from 1.10.08.

Duty to notify changes of circumstances

69.–(1)   Subject to paragraphs [³ (3), (6) [⁴ , (7) and (9)]], if at any time between the making of a claim and a decision being made on it, or during the award of housing benefit, there is a change of circumstances which the claimant, or any person by whom or on whose behalf sums payable by way of housing benefit are receivable, might reasonably be expected to know might affect the claimant's right to, the amount of or the receipt of housing benefit, that person shall be under a duty to notify that change of circumstances by giving notice [²] to the designated office–

[²[⁵ (a)   in writing; or
(b)   by telephone–
    (i)   where the relevant authority has published a telephone number for that purpose or for the purposes of regulation 64 (time and manner in which claims are to be made) unless the authority determines that in any particular case or class of case notification may not be given by telephone; or
    (ii)   in any case or class of case where the relevant authority determines that notice may be given by telephone; or
(c)   by any other means which the relevant authority agrees to accept in any particular case.]

[³ (2)]

(3)   The duty imposed on a person by paragraph (1) does not extend to changes–
(a)   in the amount of rent payable to a housing authority;
(b)   in the age of the claimant or that of any member of his family or of any non-dependants;
(c)   in these Regulations.

(4)   Notwithstanding paragraph (3)(b) a claimant shall be required by paragraph (1) to notify the designated office of any change in the composition of his family arising from the fact that a person who was a member of his family is now no longer such a person because he ceases to be a child or young person.

[³ (5)]

(6)   A person on housing benefit who is also on state pension credit must report–
(a)   changes to his tenancy, but not changes in the amount of rent payable to a housing authority;
(b)   changes affecting the residence or income of any non-dependant normally residing with the claimant or with whom the claimant normally resides;
(c)   any absence from the dwelling which exceeds or is likely to exceed 13 weeks.

(7)   In addition to the changes required to be reported under paragraph (6) a person whose state pension credit comprises only a savings credit must also report
(a)   changes affecting a child living with him which may result in a change in the amount of housing benefit payable in his case, but not changes in the age of the child;

[¹ (b)]

(c)   any change in the amount of the claimant's capital to be taken into account which does or may take the amount of his capital to more than £16,000;
(d)   any change in the income or capital of–
    (i)   a non-dependant whose income and capital are treated as belonging to the claimant in accordance with regulation 24 (circumstances in which income of a non-dependant is to be treated as claimant's); or
    (ii)   a person to whom regulation 27(4)(e) refers,
and whether such a person or, as the case may be, non-dependant stops living or begins or resumes living with the claimant.

(8)   A person who is on housing benefit and on state pension credit need only report to the designated office the changes specified in paragraphs (6) and (7).

[⁴ (9)   Where–
(a)   the claimant or the claimant's partner is in receipt of jobseeker's allowance;
(b)   the change of circumstance is that the claimant or the claimant's partner starts employment; and
(c)   as a result of that change of circumstance either entitlement to that benefit will end or the amount of that benefit will be reduced,
the claimant may discharge the duty in paragraph (1) by notifying the change of circumstance by telephoning the appropriate DWP office if a telephone number has been provided for that purpose.]

Amendments

1.   Omitted by reg 2(14) of SI 2005 No 2502 as amended by Sch 2 para 27 of SI 2006 No 217 as from 1.4.06 (3.4.06 where rent payable weekly or at intervals of a week).
2.   Inserted by reg 3(3) of SI 2006 No 2967 as from 20.12.06.
3.   Amended by reg 3(8) of SI 2008 No 2299 as from 1.10.08.
4.   Amended by reg 3(4) of SI 2008 No 2987 as from 22.12.08.
5.   Amended by reg 3(5) of SI 2010 No 2449 as from 1.11.10.

Analysis

Paras (1) to (5) are identical to reg 88 HB Regs (see p457).

Paras (6) and (7) set out the types of change that PC recipients need to report to the local authority. All PC recipients must report changes relating to the residence or income of non-dependants, absences which exceed (or are likely to exceed) 13 weeks and "changes to his tenancy": para (6). This presumably includes changes to the demise, rent-free periods and so on, as well as increases or decreases in rent, other than the rent payable to a housing authority which is specifically excluded.

Para (7) lists further changes to be reported by PC recipients who are only getting savings credit. They must report changes in respect of dependant children (other than age), changes in the income and capital of the non-dependants and partners specified, and changes which may take capital over £16,000.

Para (9) differs slightly from reg 88(6) HB Regs. Under para (9) where the claimant or her/his partner is in receipt of JSA and starts employment and as a result entitlement to JSA ends or will be reduced, the claimant can report the change by telephoning the DWP, if a telephone number has been provided for that purpose.

[¹ Alternative means of notifying changes of circumstances

69ZA.–(1)   In such cases and subject to such conditions as the Secretary of State may specify, the duty in regulation 69(1) to notify a change of circumstances may be discharged by notifying the Secretary of State–
(a)   where the change of circumstances is a birth or death, through a relevant authority, or a county council in England, by personal attendance at an office specified by that authority or county council, provided the Secretary of State has agreed with that authority or county council for it to facilitate such notification; or
(b)   where the change of circumstances is a death, by telephone to a telephone number specified for that purpose by the Secretary of State.

(2)   Paragraph (1) only applies if the authority administering the claimant's housing benefit agrees with the Secretary of State that notifications may be made in accordance with that paragraph.

(3)   The Secretary of State must forward information received in accordance with paragraph (1) to the authority administering the claimant's housing benefit.]

Amendment
1.   Inserted by reg 6 of SI 2010 No 444 as from 5.4.10.

[¹Notice of changes of circumstances given electronically

69A.   A person may give notice of a change of circumstances required to be notified under regulation 69 by means of an electronic communication in accordance with Schedule 10.]

Amendment
1.   Inserted by Art 3(4) of SI 2006 No 2968 as from 20.12.06.

PART 10
Decisions on questions

Decisions by a relevant authority

70.–(1)   Unless provided otherwise by these Regulations, any matter required to be determined under these Regulations shall be determined in the first instance by the relevant authority.

(2)   The relevant authority shall make a decision on each claim within 14 days of the provisions of regulations 64 and 67 (time and manner in which claims are to be made and evidence and information) being satisfied or as soon as reasonably practicable thereafter.

[¹ (3)]

Amendment
1.   Omitted by reg 6(4)(c) of SI 2008 No 959 as from 6.10.08.

Notification of decision

71.–(1)   An authority shall notify in writing any person affected by a decision made by it under these Regulations–

(a)   in the case of a decision on a claim, forthwith or as soon as reasonably practicable thereafter;

(b)   in any other case, within 14 days of that decision or as soon as reasonably practicable thereafter,

and every notification shall include a statement as to the matters set out in Schedule 8.

(2)   A person affected to whom an authority sends or delivers a notification of decision may, by notice in writing signed by him, [¹ within one month of the date of the notification of that decision (or, if the decision was notified before 1st November 2010, before 1st December 2010)] request the authority to provide a written statement setting out the reasons for its decision on any matter set out in the notice.

(3)   For the purposes of paragraph (2), where a person affected who requests a written statement is not a natural person, the notice in writing referred to in that paragraph shall be signed by a person over the age of 18 who is authorised to act on that person's behalf.

(4)   The written statement referred to in paragraph (2) shall be sent to the person requesting it within 14 days or as soon as is reasonably practical thereafter.

Amendment
1.   Amended by reg 3(6) of SI 2010 No 2449 as from 1.11.10.

PART 11
Payments

Time and manner of payment

72.–(1)   Subject to paragraphs (2) and (3) and regulations 73 to 79 (frequency of payment of rent allowance, payment on account of a rent allowance, payment provisions, offsetting) the relevant authority shall pay housing benefit to which a person is entitled under these Regulations at such time and in such manner as is appropriate, having regard to–

(a)   the times at which and the frequency with which a person's liability to make payment of rent arises; and

(b)   the reasonable needs and convenience of the person entitled thereto.

(2)   Where a person's entitlement to housing benefit is less than £1 weekly the relevant authority may pay that benefit at 6 monthly intervals.

(3)   Subject to regulations 73 to 78 (frequency of payment of and payment on account of rent allowance, payment provisions), every authority shall make the first payment of any housing benefit awarded by it within 14 days of the receipt of the claim at the designated office or, if that is not reasonably practical, as soon as possible thereafter.

Modifications

Reg 72(3) has effect as modified by Sch 3 para 7 HB&CTB(CP) Regs (see p1221) for some claimants entitled to and in receipt of HB in respect of their current home on 6 October 1996 and continuously since that date.

[¹Cases in which payments to a housing authority are to take the form of a rent allowance

72A.–(1)   Where the occupier of a dwelling is liable to make payments in respect of that dwelling to a housing authority as a result of the making of an order specified in paragraph (2), housing benefit in respect of those payments shall take the form of a rent allowance.

(2)   The orders specified for the purposes of paragraph (1) are–

(a)   a management control order made in accordance with section 74 of the Antisocial Behaviour etc. (Scotland) Act 2004;

(b)   an interim management order made in accordance with section 102 of the Housing Act 2004;

(c)   a final management order made in accordance with section 113 of that Act;

(d)   an interim empty dwelling management order made in accordance with section 133 of that Act; and

(e)   a final empty dwelling management order made in accordance with section 136 of that Act.]

[² (3)   Where–

(a)   the occupier of a caravan, mobile home or houseboat is liable to make payments in respect of that caravan, mobile home or houseboat and housing benefit in relation to those payments takes the form of a rent allowance; and

(b)   the occupier is also liable to make payments to a housing authority in respect of the site on which that caravan or mobile home stands, or in respect of the mooring to which the houseboat is attached,

housing benefit in respect of payments to the housing authority shall take the form of a rent allowance.]

Amendments

1.   Inserted by reg 3 of SI 2006 No 644 as from 3.4.06.

2.   Inserted by reg 3(2) of SI 2008 No 2824 as from 6.4.09.

Frequency of payment of a rent allowance

73.–(1)   Subject to the following provisions of this regulation any rent allowance other than a payment made in accordance with regulation 72(2) or (3) or 74 (time and manner of payment, payment on account of rent allowance) shall be paid at intervals of 2 or 4 weeks or one month or, with the consent of the person entitled, at intervals greater than one month.

(2)   Except in a case to which paragraph (3) applies, any payment of a rent allowance shall be made, in so far as it is practicable to do so, at the end of the period in respect of which it is made.

(3)   Except in a case to which regulation 77(2) applies and subject to paragraph (4), this paragraph applies where payment of a rent allowance is being made to a landlord

(which for these purposes has the same meaning as in regulations 76 and 77 (payments to a landlord)), when that payment shall be made–

(a)   at intervals of 4 weeks; and

(b)   at the end of the period in respect of which it is made.

(4)   Where paragraph (3) applies–

(a)   in a case where the liability in respect of which the rent allowance is paid is monthly, the authority may make payment at intervals of 1 month;

(b)   in a case where the authority is paying a rent allowance to a landlord in respect of more than one claimant, then the first such payment in respect of any claimant may be made to that landlord at such lesser interval as that authority considers is in the best interest of the efficient administration of housing benefit.

(5)   Except in a case to which paragraph (3) applies, where a person's weekly entitlement to a rent allowance is more than £2 he may require payment at two weekly intervals and the relevant authority shall pay at two weekly intervals in such a case.

(6)   Except in a case to which paragraph (3) applies, the relevant authority may pay a rent allowance at weekly intervals where either–

(a)   it considers that unless the rent allowance is paid at weekly intervals an overpayment is likely to occur; or

(b)   the person entitled is liable to pay his rent weekly and it considers that it is in his interest that his allowance be paid weekly.

(7)   Subject to paragraphs (2), (3) and (5), the relevant authority may pay a rent allowance to a student once a term.

Modifications

Reg 73 has effect as modified by Sch 3 para 7 HB&CTB(CP) Regs (see p1221) for some claimants entitled to and in receipt of HB in respect of their current home on 6 October 1996 and continuously since that date.

Payment on account of a rent allowance

74.–(1)   Where it is impracticable for the relevant authority to make a decision on a claim for a rent allowance within 14 days of the claim for it having been made and that impracticability does not arise out of the failure of the claimant, without good cause, to furnish such information, certificates, documents or evidence as the authority reasonably requires and has requested or which has been requested by the Secretary of State, the authority shall make a payment on account of any entitlement to a rent allowance of such amount as it considers reasonable having regard to–

(a)   such information which may at the time be available to it concerning the claimant's circumstances; and

(b)   any relevant determination made by a rent officer in exercise of the Housing Act functions.

(2)   The notice of award of any payment on account of a rent allowance made under paragraph (1) shall contain a notice to the effect that if on subsequent decision of the claim the person is not entitled to a rent allowance, or is entitled to an amount of rent allowance less than the amount of the payment on account, the whole of the amount paid on account or the excess of that amount over the entitlement to an allowance, as the case may be, will be recoverable from the person to whom the payment on account was made.

(3)   Where on the basis of the subsequent decision the amount of rent allowance payable differs from the amount paid on account under paragraph (1), future payments of rent allowance shall be increased or reduced to take account of any underpayment or, as the case may be, overpayment.

Payment to be made to a person entitled

75.–(1)   Subject to regulations 76 to 78 (payment to landlords, payment on death) and the following provisions of this regulation, payment of any rent allowance to which a person is entitled shall be made to that person.

(2)   Where a person other than a person who is entitled to a rent allowance made the claim and that first person is a person referred to in regulation 63(2), (3) or (5) (persons appointed to act for a person unable to act), payment may be made to that person.

(3)   A person entitled to a rent allowance, although able to act on his own behalf, may request in writing that the appropriate authority make payments to a person, who if a natural person must be aged 18 or more, nominated by him, and the authority may make payments to that person.

Circumstances in which payment is to be made to a landlord

76.–(1)   Subject to paragraph (2) and paragraph 8(4) of Schedule A1 (treatment of claims for housing benefit by refugees), a payment of rent allowance shall be made to a landlord (and in this regulation the "landlord" includes a person to whom rent is payable by the person entitled to that allowance)–

(a)   where under Regulations made under the Administration Act an amount of state pension credit payable to the claimant or his partner is being paid direct to the landlord; or

(b)   where sub-paragraph (a) does not apply and the person is in arrears of an amount equivalent to 8 weeks or more of the amount he is liable to pay his landlord as rent, except where it is in the overriding interest of the claimant not to make direct payments to the landlord.

(2)   Any payment of rent allowance made to a landlord pursuant to this regulation or to regulation 77 (circumstances in which payment may be made to a landlord) shall be to discharge, in whole or in part, the liability of the claimant to pay rent to that landlord in respect of the dwelling concerned, except in so far as–

(a)   the claimant had no entitlement to the whole or part of that rent allowance so paid to his landlord; and

(b)   the overpayment of rent allowance resulting was recovered in whole or in part from that landlord.

[¹ (2A)   In a case where–

(a)   a relevant authority has determined a maximum rent (LHA) in accordance with regulation 13D; and

(b)   the rent allowance exceeds the amount which the claimant is liable to pay his landlord by way of rent,

any payment of rent allowance made to a landlord pursuant to this regulation or to regulation 77 may include all or part of any amount by which the rent allowance exceeds the amount which the claimant is liable to pay his landlord as rent but shall not include any amount by which the rent allowance exceeds the amount which the claimant is liable to pay his landlord as rent and arrears of rent.]

(3)   Where the relevant authority is not satisfied that the landlord is a fit and proper person to be the recipient of a payment of rent allowance no such payment shall be made direct to him under paragraph (1).

Amendment

1.   Inserted by reg 17 (1) of SI 2007 No 2869 as from 7.4.08 (or if reg 1(5) of that SI applies, on the day on or after 7.4.08 when the first of the events specified in reg 1(6) applies, or from 6.4.09 if none have before that date).

General Note

This is the equivalent of reg 95 HB Regs (see p470), though here the authority is obliged to make direct payments to the landlord where direct payments of PC are being made towards arrears of rent.

Circumstances in which payment may be made to a landlord

77.–(1)   Subject to paragraph 8(4) of Schedule A1 (treatment of claims for housing benefit by refugees), where regulation 76 (circumstances in which payment is to be made to a landlord) does not apply but subject to [¹ paragraphs (3) and (3A)], a payment of a rent allowance may nevertheless be made to a person's landlord where–

(a)   the person has requested or consented to such payment;

(b)   payment to the landlord is in the interest of the claimant and his family;

(c)   the person has ceased to reside in the dwelling in respect of which the allowance was payable and there are outstanding payments of rent but any payment under this sub-paragraph shall be limited to an amount equal to the amount of rent outstanding.

(2)   Without prejudice to the power in paragraph (1), in any case where in the opinion of the authority–

(a)   the claimant has not already discharged his liability to pay his landlord for the period in respect of which any payment is to be made; and

(b)   it would be in the interests of the efficient administration of housing benefit,

a first payment of a rent allowance following the making of a decision on a claim, or a supersession under paragraph 4 of Schedule 7 to the Child Support, Pensions and Social Security Act 2000 may be made, in whole or in part, [²] to that landlord.

(3)   In a case where the relevant authority is not satisfied that the landlord is a fit and proper person to be the recipient of a claimant's rent allowance, the authority may either–

(a)   not make direct payments to the landlord in accordance with paragraph (1) [² , (3A) or (3B)]; or

(b)   make such payments to the landlord where the authority is satisfied that it is nonetheless in the best interests of the claimant and his family that the payments be made.

[¹ (3A)   In a case where a relevant authority has determined a maximum rent in accordance with regulation 13D–

(a)   sub-paragraphs (a) and (b) of paragraph (1) shall not apply; and

(b)   payment of a rent allowance to a person's landlord may be made where–

(i)   the relevant authority considers that the claimant is likely to have difficulty in relation to the management of his financial affairs;

(ii)   the relevant authority considers that it is improbable that the claimant will pay his rent; or

(iii) a direct payment has previously been made by the relevant authority to the landlord in accordance with regulation 76 in respect of the current award of housing benefit.

(3B)   Where the relevant authority suspects that the grounds in paragraph (3A)(b)(i) or (ii) apply and is considering whether to make payments on one of those grounds, it may make a payment of a rent allowance to the person's landlord for a period not exceeding 8 weeks.]

(4)   In this regulation ''landlord'' has the same meaning as in regulation 76 and paragraph (2) of that regulation shall have effect for the purposes of this regulation.

Modifications

Paras (1) and (3) amended and paras (3A) and (3B) inserted by reg 17(2) Housing Benefit (State Pension Credit) (Local Housing Allowance and Information Sharing) Amendment Regulations 2007 SI No.2869 as from 7 April 2008, save that for a person to whom reg 1(5) of those regulations applied (see p1233), the amendments came into force on the day on or after 7 April 2008 when the first of the events specified in reg 1(6) applied to her/him, or on 6 April 2009 if none had before that date.

Amendments

1.   Amended by reg 17(2) of SI 2007 No 2869 as from 7.4.08 (or if reg 1(5) of that SI applies, on the day on or after 7.4.08 when the first of the events specified in reg 1(6) applies, or from 6.4.09 if none have before that date).

2.   Amended by reg 3(7) of Si 2010 No 2449 as from 1.11.10.

Payment on death of the person entitled

78.–(1)   Subject to paragraphs (3) and (5) where the person entitled to an allowance has died the relevant authority shall make payment either to his personal representative or, where there is none, his next of kin if aged 16 or over.

(2)   For the purposes of paragraph (1) ''next of kin'' means in England and Wales the persons who would take beneficially on an intestacy and in Scotland the persons entitled to the moveable estate on intestacy.

(3)   A payment under paragraph (1) or (5) shall not be made unless the landlord, the personal representative or the next of kin, as the case may be, makes written application for the payment of any sum of benefit to which the deceased was entitled, and such

written application is sent to or delivered to the relevant authority at its designated office within 12 months of the deceased's death or such longer period as the authority may allow in any particular case.

(4)   The authority may dispense with strict proof of title of any person claiming under paragraph (3) and the receipt of such a person shall be a good discharge to the authority for any sum so paid.

(5)   Subject to paragraph (3), where the relevant authority determines, before the death of the person first mentioned in paragraph (1), that a rent allowance was payable to his landlord in accordance with regulation 76 or 77, that authority shall pay to that landlord so much of that allowance as does not exceed the amount of rent outstanding at the date of the person's death.

Offsetting

79.–(1)   Where a person has been paid a sum of housing benefit under a decision which is subsequently revised or further revised, any sum paid in respect of a period covered by a subsequent decision shall be offset against arrears of entitlement under the subsequent decision except to the extent that the sum exceeds the arrears and shall be treated as properly paid on account of them.

(2)   Where an amount has been deducted under regulation 85(1) (sums to be deducted in calculating recoverable overpayments) an equivalent sum shall be offset against any arrears of entitlement under the subsequent decision except to the extent that the sum exceeds the arrears and shall be treated as properly paid on account of them.

(3)   No amount may be offset under paragraph (1) which has been determined to be an overpayment within the meaning of regulation 80 (meaning of overpayment).

PART 12
Overpayments

Meaning of overpayment

80.   In this Part, "overpayment" means any amount which has been paid by way of housing benefit and to which there was no entitlement under these Regulations (whether on the initial decision [¹ or as subsequently revised or superseded or further revised or superseded]) and includes any amount paid on account under regulation 74 (payment on account of a rent allowance) which is in excess of the entitlement to housing benefit as subsequently decided.

Amendment
1.   Amended by reg 2 of SI 2005 No 2904 as amended by Sch 2 para 29 of SI 2006 No 217 as from 10.4.06.

Recoverable overpayments

81.–(1)   Any overpayment, except one to which paragraph (2) applies, shall be recoverable.

(2)   Subject to paragraph (4) this paragraph applies to an overpayment caused by an official error where the claimant or a person acting on his behalf or any other person to whom the payment is made could not, at the time of receipt of the payment or of any notice relating to that payment, reasonably have been expected to realise that it was an overpayment.

(3)   In paragraph (2), "overpayment caused by official error" means an overpayment caused by a mistake made whether in the form of an act or omission by–
   (a)   the relevant authority;
   (b)   an officer or person acting for that authority;
   (c)   an officer of–
      (i)   the Department for Work and Pensions;
      (ii)   Revenue and Customs,
      acting as such; or
   (d)   a person providing services to the Department for Work and Pensions or to the Commissioners for Her Majesty's Revenue and Customs,

where the claimant, a person acting on his behalf or any other person to whom the payment is made, did not cause or materially contribute to that mistake, act or omission.

(4) Where in consequence of an official error, a person has been awarded a rent rebate to which he was not entitled or which exceeded the benefit to which he was entitled, upon the award being revised any overpayment of benefit, which remains credited to him by the relevant authority in respect of a period after the date on which the revision took place, shall be recoverable.

Amendment

1.   Amended by reg 2 of SI 2005 No 2904 as amended by Sch 2 para 29 of SI 2006 No 217 as from 10.4.06.

Person from whom recovery may be sought

82.–(1)   For the purposes of section 75(3)(a) of the Administration Act (prescribed circumstances in which an amount recoverable shall not be recovered from the person to whom it was paid), the prescribed circumstance is–

(a)   housing benefit has been paid in accordance with regulation 76 (circumstances in which payment is to be made to the landlord) or regulation 77 (circumstances in which payment may be made to a landlord);

(b)   the landlord has notified the relevant authority or the Secretary of State in writing that he suspects that there has been an overpayment;

[¹ (bb) the relevant authority is satisfied that the overpayment did not occur as a result of any change of dwelling occupied by the claimant as his home;]

(c)   it appears to the relevant authority that, on the assumption that there has been an overpayment–

(i)   there are grounds for instituting proceedings against any person for an offence under section 111A or 112(1) of the Administration (dishonest or false representations for obtaining benefit); or

(ii)   there has been a deliberate failure to report a relevant change of circumstances contrary to the requirement of regulation 69 (duty to notify a change of circumstances) and the overpayment occurred as a result of that deliberate failure; and

(d)   the relevant authority is satisfied that the landlord–

(i)   has not colluded with the claimant so as to cause the overpayment;

(ii)   has not acted, or neglected to act, in such a way so as contribute to the period, or the amount, of the overpayment.

[² [⁴ (2)   For the purposes of section 75(3)(b) of the Administration Act (recovery from such other person, as well as or instead of the person to whom the overpayment was made), where recovery of an overpayment is sought by a relevant authority–

(a)   subject to paragraph (1) and where sub-paragraph (b) or (c) does not apply, the overpayment is recoverable from the claimant as well as the person to whom the payment was made, if different;

(b)   in a case where an overpayment arose in consequence of a misrepresentation of or a failure to disclose a material fact (in either case, whether fraudulently or otherwise) by or on behalf of the claimant, or by or on behalf of any person to whom the payment was made, the overpayment is only recoverable from any person who misrepresented or failed to disclose that material fact instead of, if different, the person to whom the payment was made; or

(c)   in a case where an overpayment arose in consequence of an official error where the claimant, or a person acting on the claimant's behalf, or any person to whom the payment was paid, or any person acting on their behalf, could reasonably have been expected, at the time of receipt of the payment or of any notice relating to that payment, to realise that it was an overpayment, the overpayment is only recoverable from any such person instead of, if different, the person to whom the payment was made.]]

[³ (2A)   Where an overpayment is made in a case where a relevant authority has determined a maximum rent (LHA) in accordance with regulation 13D (determination of a maximum rent (LHA)), and the housing benefit payable exceeds the amount which the claimant is liable to pay his landlord by way of rent, the relevant authority must not recover from the landlord more than the landlord has received.]

(3)   For the purposes of [³ paragraphs (1) and (2A)], "landlord" shall have the same meaning as it has for the purposes of regulation 76.

[¹ (3A) For the purposes of [⁴ paragraph (2)(c)], "overpayment arose in consequence of an official error" shall have the same meaning as in regulation 81(3) above.]

[⁴ (4)]

Amendments

1.   Inserted by reg 6(2) and (4A) of SI 2005 No 2904 as amended by Sch 2 para 29 of SI 2006 No 217 as from 10.4.06.
2.   Substituted by reg 6(3) and (5) of SI 2005 No 2904 as amended by Sch 2 para 29 of SI 2006 No 217 as from 10.4.06.
3.   Amended by reg 3 of SI 2008 No 586 as from 7.4.08.
4.   Amended by reg 5(2) of SI 2008 No 2824 as from 6.4.09.

Method of recovery

83.–(1)   Without prejudice to any other method of recovery, [¹ a relevant authority] may recover a recoverable overpayment from any person referred to in regulation 82 (persons from whom recovery may be sought) by deduction from any housing benefit to which that person is entitled (including arrears of entitlement after offsetting under regulation 79 (offsetting)) or, where it is unable to do so, may request the Secretary of State to recover any recoverable overpayment from the benefits prescribed in [⁴ regulation 86(1)] (recovery of overpayments from prescribed benefits).

[⁴ (1ZA)   Where an overpayment is recoverable from a claimant who has one or more partners, a relevant authority may recover the overpayment by deduction from any housing benefit payable to the claimant's partner, or where it is unable to do so, may request the Secretary of State to recover any recoverable overpayment from the benefits prescribed in regulation 86(1B) (recovery of overpayments from prescribed benefits), provided that the claimant and that partner were a couple both at the time of the overpayment and when the deduction is made.]

[² [⁵]]

(2)   Subject to paragraphs [² [⁵]] (4) and (5), where [¹ a relevant authority] makes deductions permitted by paragraph (1) [⁴ or (1ZA)] from the housing benefit it is paying to a claimant [⁴ or a claimant's partner] (other than deductions from arrears of entitlement), the deduction in respect of a benefit week shall be–

(a)   in a case to which paragraph (3) applies, not more than the amount there specified; and

(b)   in any other case, not more than 3 times five per cent. of the personal allowance for a single claimant aged not less than 25, that five per cent. being, where it is not a multiple of five pence, rounded to the next higher such multiple.

(3)   Where [¹ a relevant authority] makes deductions from housing benefit it is paying to a claimant [⁴ or a claimant's partner, where the claimant has] , in respect of the whole or part of the recoverable overpayment–

(a)   been found guilty of an offence whether under a statute or otherwise;

(b)   made an admission after caution of deception or fraud for the purpose of obtaining relevant benefit; or

(c)   agreed to pay a penalty under section 115A of the Administration Act and the agreement has not been withdrawn,

the amount deducted under paragraph (2) shall be not more than four times five per cent. of the personal allowance for a single claimant aged not less than 25, but where that five per cent. is not a multiple of 10 pence, it shall be rounded to the nearest 10 pence or, if it is a multiple of 5 pence but not of 10 pence, the next higher multiple of 10 pence.

(4)   Where, in the calculation of housing benefit, the amount of earnings or other income falling to be taken into account is reduced by reason of [³ paragraphs 2 to 5 and 7] of Schedule 4 (sums to be disregarded in the calculation of earnings) [⁵ , or paragraph 5A of that Schedule in a case where the amount of earnings to be disregarded under that paragraph is the amount referred to in regulation 45(2) of the Employment and Support

Allowance Regulations or regulation 17(2) of the Social Security (Incapacity for Work) (General) Regulations 1995,] or paragraph 1 of Schedule 5 (sums to be disregarded in the calculation of income other than earnings), the deduction under paragraph (2) may be increased by not more than half the amount of the reduction.

(5)   No deduction made under this regulation [² [⁵]] shall be applied so as to reduce the housing benefit in respect of a benefit week to less than 50 pence.

(6)   In this regulation–

"admission after caution" means–

> (i)   in England and Wales, an admission after a caution has been administered in accordance with a Code issued under the Police and Criminal Evidence Act 1984;
>
> (ii)   in Scotland, admission after a caution has been administered, such admission being duly witnessed by two persons; and

"personal allowance for a single claimant aged not less than 25" means the amount specified in paragraph 1(1)(b) of column 2 of Schedule 3 to the Housing Benefit Regulations 2006 (applicable amounts).

(7)   This regulation shall not apply in respect of an offence committed or an admission after caution or an agreement to pay a penalty made before 2nd October 2000.

Amendments

1.   Substituted by reg 7(2) of SI 2005 No 2904 as amended by Sch 2 para 29 of SI 2006 No 217 as from 10.4.06.
2.   Inserted by reg 7(3), (4) and (5) of SI 2005 No 2904 as amended by Sch 2 para 29 of SI 2006 No 217 as from 10.4.06.
3.   Amended by reg 4(7) of SI 2008 No 1042 as from 19.5.08.
4.   Amended by reg 5(3) of SI 2008 No 2824 as from 6.4.09.
5.   Amended by reg 3(3) of SI 2009 No 2608 as from 1.4.10 (5.4.10 where rent payable weekly or in multiples of a week).

Diminution of capital

84.–(1)   Where, in the case of a recoverable overpayment, in consequence of a misrepresentation or failure to disclose a material fact (in either case whether fraudulent or otherwise) as to a person's capital, or an error, other than one to which regulation 81(2) (effect of official error) refers, as to the amount of a person's capital, the overpayment was in respect of a period ("the overpayment period") of more than 13 benefit weeks, the relevant authority shall, for the purposes only of calculating the amount of that overpayment–

> (a)   at the end of the first 13 benefit weeks of the overpayment period, treat the amount of that capital as having been reduced by the amount of housing benefit overpaid during those 13 weeks;
>
> (b)   at the end of each subsequent period of 13 benefit weeks, if any, of the overpayment period, treat the amount of that capital as having been further reduced by the amount of housing benefit overpaid during the immediately preceding 13 benefit weeks.

(2)   Capital shall not be treated as reduced over any period other than 13 benefit weeks or in any circumstances other than those for which paragraph (1) provides.

Sums to be deducted in calculating recoverable overpayments

85.–(1)   Subject to paragraph (2), in calculating the amount of a recoverable overpayment, the relevant authority shall deduct any amount of housing benefit which should have been determined to be payable in respect of the whole or part of the overpayment period–

> (a)   on the basis of the claim as presented to the authority;
>
> (b)   on the basis of the claim as it would have appeared had any misrepresentation or non-disclosure been remedied before the decision; or
>
> (c)   on the basis of the claim as it would have appeared if any change of circumstances [¹ , except a change of the dwelling which the claimant occupies as his home,] had been notified at the time that change occurred.

(2)   In the case of rent rebate only, in calculating the amount of a recoverable overpayment the relevant authority may deduct so much of any payment by way of rent in respect of the overpayment period which exceeds the amount, if any, which the claimant was liable to pay for that period under the original erroneous determination.

Amendment

1.   Inserted by reg 8 of SI 2005 No 2904 as amended by Sch 2 para 29 of SI 2006 No 217 as from 10.4.06.

[¹Sums to be deducted in calculating recoverable overpayments where the claimant has changed dwelling

85A.–(1)   This regulation applies where an overpayment has occurred in the following circumstances–

(a)   a claimant has moved from the dwelling previously occupied as his home (''dwelling A'') to another dwelling which he occupies as his home (''dwelling B'');

(b)   the claimant has been awarded housing benefit in the form of a rent allowance in respect of dwelling A to which he is not entitled because he is no longer occupying or treated as occupying dwelling A as his home;

(c)   housing benefit is paid to the same person in respect of the claimant's occupation of dwelling B as it was paid to in respect of dwelling A; and

(d)   the same relevant authority is responsible for paying the housing benefit in respect of dwelling A and dwelling B.

(2)   Where this regulation applies, in calculating the amount of the overpayment which is recoverable the relevant authority may at its discretion deduct an amount equal to the claimant's weekly entitlement to housing benefit in respect of dwelling B for the number of benefit weeks equal to the number of weeks during which the claimant was overpaid housing benefit in respect of dwelling A.

(3)   Where a sum has been deducted under paragraph (2), an equivalent sum shall be treated as having been paid in respect of the claimant's entitlement to housing benefit in respect of dwelling B for the number of benefit weeks equal to the number of weeks during which the claimant was overpaid housing benefit in respect of dwelling A.]

Amendment

1.   Inserted by reg 3(4) of SI 2009 No 2608 as from 1.4.10 (5.4.10 where rent payable weekly or in multiples of a week).

Recovery of overpayments from prescribed benefits

86.–(1)   [³ Subject to paragraph (1B),] For the purposes of section 75(4) of the Administration Act (recovery of overpaid housing benefit by deduction from other benefits), the benefits prescribed by this regulation are–

(a)   any benefit except guardian's allowance;

(b)   income support under Part 7 of the Act;

(c)   any benefit payable under the legislation of any member State other than the United Kingdom concerning the branches of social security mentioned in Article 4(1) of Regulation (EEC) No 1408/71 on the application of social security schemes to employed persons, to self-employed persons and to members of their families moving within the Community, whether or not the benefit has been acquired by virtue of the provisions of that Regulation;

(d)   a jobseeker's allowance;

(e)   state pension credit.

[² (f)   an employment and support allowance.]

[³ (1B)   For the purposes of section 75(4) of the Administration Act, where recovery is sought from the claimant's partner under regulation 83(1ZA), the benefits prescribed by this regulation are–

(a)   income support under Part 7 of the Act;

(b)   income-based jobseeker's allowance;

(c)   state pension credit; and

(d)   income-related employment and support allowance.]

[¹ (1A)   For the purposes of paragraph (1)(c) the term "member State" shall be understood to include Switzerland in accordance with and subject to the provisions of Annex II of the Agreement between the European Community and its Member States and the Swiss Confederation on the free movement of persons, signed at Brussels on 21st June 1999.]

[³ (2)   The Secretary of State shall, if requested to do so by an authority under regulation 83 (method of recovery), recover a recoverable overpayment by deduction from any of the benefits prescribed in paragraph (1) or (in the case of the claimant's partner) any of the benefits prescribed in paragraph (1B) provided that the Secretary of State is satisfied that–

(a)   a recoverable overpayment has been made in consequence of a misrepresentation of or a failure to disclose a material fact (in either case whether fraudulently or otherwise), by a claimant or any other person to whom a payment of housing benefit has been made; and

(b)   the person from whom it is sought to recover the overpayment is receiving sufficient amounts of any of the benefits prescribed in paragraph (1) or (1B) (as the case may be) to enable deductions to be made for the recovery of the overpayment.]

(2)   Where the Secretary of State is satisfied that–

(a)   a recoverable overpayment of housing benefit has been made, in consequence of a misrepresentation of or failure to disclose a material fact (in either case whether fraudulently or otherwise), by or on behalf of a claimant or any other person to whom a payment of housing benefit has been made; and

(b)   the person who misrepresented that fact or failed to disclose it is receiving a sufficient amount of one or more of the benefits prescribed in paragraph (1) to enable deductions to be made for the recovery of the overpayment,

he shall, if requested to do so by an authority under regulation 83 (method of recovery), recover the overpayment by deduction from any of those benefits.

(3)   In paragraph (1)(a), "benefit" has the meaning it has in section 122(1) of the Act.

Amendments

1.   Inserted by reg 9 of SI 2005 No 2904 as amended by Sch 2 para 29 of SI 2006 No 217 as from 10.4.06.
2.   Amended by reg 39 of SI 2008 No 1082 as from 27.10.08.
3.   Amended by reg 5(4) of SI 2008 No 2824 as from 6.4.09.

Prescribed benefits

87.–(1)   The benefits prescribed for the purposes of section 75(5) and (7) of the Administration Act (recovery of overpayments) are those set out in the following paragraphs.

(2)   Prescribed benefits within section 75(5)(a) of the Administration Act (benefits to which a landlord or agent is entitled) are–

(a)   housing benefit; and

(b)   those benefits prescribed from time to time in regulation 86(1) (recovery of overpayments from prescribed benefits), but only in cases where–

(i)   an authority has, pursuant to regulation 83 (method of recovery), requested the Secretary of State to recover an overpayment of housing benefit from such benefits; and

(ii)   the Secretary of State is satisfied as to the matters prescribed in paragraph (2)(a) and (b) of regulation 86.

(3)   Housing benefit is prescribed for the purposes of section 75(5)(b) or (c) of the Administration Act (benefits paid to a landlord or agent to discharge an obligation owed by another person).

(4)   Prescribed benefits within section 75(7) of the Administration Act (benefits recoverable from the county court or the sheriff court) are housing benefit and those benefits prescribed from time to time in regulation 86(1).

Restrictions on recovery of rent and consequent notifications

88.–(1)   Where, pursuant to section 75(5)(b) of the Administration Act, an amount has been recoveredby deduction from housing benefit paid to a person (referred to as "the landlord" in this regulation) to discharge (in whole or in part) an obligation owed to him by the person on whose behalf the recoverable amount was paid (referred to as "the tenant" in this regulation) that obligation shall, in a case to which paragraph (2) applies, be taken to be discharged by the amount of the deduction.

(2)   This paragraph applies in a case where the amount recoverable from the landlord relates to an overpayment of housing benefit in relation to which the landlord has–

(a)   agreed to pay a penalty pursuant to section 115A of the Administration Act (penalty as an alternative to prosecution); or

(b)   been convicted of an offence arising under the Act or any other enactment.

(3)   In any case to which paragraph (2) applies or will apply when recovery is made the authority that has determined that there is an overpayment and that it is recoverable from the landlord shall notify both the landlord and the tenant that–

(a)   the overpayment that it has recovered or that it has determined to recover ("the sum") is or will be one to which paragraph (2) applies; and

(b)   the landlord has no right in relation to that sum against the tenant, and that his obligation to the landlord shall be taken to be discharged by the amount so recovered.

PART 13
Information
SECTION 1
Claims and information

Interpretation

89.   In this Section–

[¹ "county council" means a county council in England, but only if the council has made an arrangement in accordance with regulation 64(5)(g) or 90(3);]

"local authority" means an authority administering housing benefit;

"relevant authority" means–

(a)   the Secretary of State;

(b)   a person providing services to the Secretary of State; [¹ or

(c)   a county council;]

"relevant information" means information or evidence relating to the administration of claims to or awards of housing benefit.

Amendment

1.   Amended by reg 8(3) of SI 2007 No 2911 as from 31.10.07.

[¹Collection of information

90.–(1)   The Secretary of State, or a person providing services to him, may receive or obtain relevant information from–

(a)   persons making, or who have made, claims for housing benefit; or

(b)   other persons in connection with such claims.

(2)   In paragraph (1) references to persons who have made claims for housing benefit include persons to whom awards of benefit have been made on those claims.

(3)   Where a county council has made an arrangement with a local authority, or a person authorised to exercise any function of a local authority relating to housing benefit or council tax benefit, to receive and obtain information and evidence relating to claims for housing benefit, the council may receive or obtain the information or evidence from–

(a)   persons making claims for housing benefit; or

(b)   other persons in connection with such claims.

(4)   A county council may receive information or evidence relating to an award of housing benefit which is supplied by–

(a)   the person to whom the award has been made; or

(b)   other persons in connection with the award.]

Amendment
1.   Substituted by reg 8(4) of SI 2007 No 2911 as from 31.10.07.

[¹Verifying information

90A.   A relevant authority may verify relevant information supplied to, or obtained by, the authority in accordance with regulation 90.]

Amendment
1.   Inserted by reg 8(5) of SI 2007 No 2911 as from 31.10.07.

[¹Recording and holding information

91.   A relevant authority which obtains relevant information or to whom such information is supplied–
(a)   shall make a record of such information; and
(b)   may hold that information, whether as supplied or obtained or recorded, for the purpose of forwarding it to the person or authority for the time being administering housing benefit.]

Amendment
1.   Substituted by reg 8(6) of SI 2007 No 2911 as from 31.10.07.

Forwarding of information

92.   A relevant authority which holds relevant information–
(a)   shall forward it to the person or authority for the time being administering claims to or awards of housing benefit to which the relevant information relates, being either–
    (i)   a local authority;
    (ii)   a person providing services to a local authority; or
    (iii)   a person authorised to exercise any function of a local authority relating to housing benefit; and
[¹ (b)   may, if the relevant authority is the Secretary of State or a person providing services to the Secretary of State, continue to hold a record of such information, whether as supplied or obtained or recorded, for such period as he considers appropriate.]

Amendment
1.   Substituted by reg 8(7) of SI 2007 No 2911 as from 31.10.07.

Request for information

93.   A relevant authority which holds information or evidence relating to social security matters shall forward such information or evidence as may be requested to the person or authority making that request, provided that–
(a)   the request is made by–
    (i)   a local authority;
    (ii)   a person providing services to a local authority; or
    (iii)   a person authorised to exercise any function of a local authority relating to housing benefit; and
(b)   the information or evidence requested includes relevant information;
(c)   the relevant authority is able to provide the information or evidence requested in the form in which it was originally supplied or obtained; and
(d)   provision of the information or evidence requested is considered necessary by the relevant authority to the proper performance by a local authority of its functions relating to housing benefit.

SECTION 2
Evidence and Information

Interpretation

94. In this Section–

"the notice" means the notice prescribed in regulation 99(1)(b) (circumstances for requiring information);

"relevant information" means such information as is prescribed in regulation 100 (relevant information);

"the requirer" means a person within regulation 98 (requiring information from landlords and agents), who requires information pursuant to that regulation;

"the supplier" means an appropriate person who is required, pursuant to regulations 98 and 99, to supply relevant information and any person who is not so required is not, for the purpose of supplying information pursuant to section 126A of the Administration Act and these Regulations, an appropriate person.

[¹ Information to be provided to rent officers

95A.–(1) This paragraph applies to every claim for or award of housing benefit in the form of a rent allowance where the eligible rent has been, or is to be determined, in accordance with–

(a) regulation 12(3)(a) (rent) or 12C (eligible rent and maximum rent), as the case may require;

(b) regulation 12A (eligible rent and the maximum rent (LHA)) or any of regulations 12E to 12K (transitional protection for pathfinder cases), as the case may require; or

(c) regulations 12 (rent) and 13 (maximum rent) as set out in paragraph 5 of Schedule 3 to the Consequential Provisions Regulations.

(2) No earlier than the first, and no later than the fifth, working day of every month a relevant authority shall provide the following information to the rent officer in relation to every claim for or award of housing benefit to which paragraph (1) applied in the preceding month–

(a) the address, including any room or unit number, house or flat number or name, and the postcode of the dwelling to which the claim or award relates;

(b) where the claim or award relates to mooring charges for a houseboat, or payments in respect of the site on which a caravan or mobile home stands, the mooring or plot number and the address of the mooring or site, including the postcode;

(c) the date on which the tenancy began;

(d) the amount of rent and the rental period, whether calendar monthly, four weekly, weekly or some other period;

(e) where the claimant has the use of two or more bedrooms, the number of bedrooms and rooms suitable for living in that there are in the dwelling, and in this sub-paragraph "bedroom" does not include a bedroom which the claimant shares with any person other than a member of his household, a non-dependant of his, or a person who pays rent to him or his partner;

(f) whether the tenant (together with his partner where he has one) has exclusive use of only one bedroom, and if so, whether they have exclusive use of a kitchen, bathroom, toilet and a room suitable for living in;

(g) whether the tenant has exclusive use of only one bedroom, and if so, which, if any, of the following the tenancy provides for him to share–

(i) a kitchen;

(ii) a bathroom;

(iii) a toilet; or

(iv) a room suitable for living in;

(h) the date on which entitlement to housing benefit began; and

(i) where applicable, the date on which entitlement to housing benefit ended.

(3)   Where the relevant authority is required to apply to the rent officer for a board and attendance determination by virtue of regulation 13D(10) (determination of a maximum rent (LHA)), it shall provide the following information in the application to the Rent Officer–

(a)   the address, including any room or unit number, house or flat number or name and the postcode of the dwelling to which the claim or award relates;

(b)   the date on which the tenancy began;

(c)   the length of the tenancy;

(d)   the total amount of those payments referred to in regulation 12(1) (rent) which the claimant is liable to make in respect of the dwelling which he occupies as his home;

(e)   whether those payments include any charges for water, sewerage or allied environmental services or charges in respect of meals or fuel which are ineligible for housing benefit; and

(f)   where those payments include any charges that are ineligible for housing benefit by reason of paragraph 1(a)(iv) and (c) to (f) of Schedule 1 (ineligible service charges), that such charges are included, and the value of those charges as determined by that authority pursuant to regulation 12B(2) and that Schedule.

(4)   where the relevant authority has identified charges to which paragraph (3)(f) applies, it shall–

(a)   deduct those charges from the total amount of those payments which, in accordance with paragraph (3)(d), it has stated that the claimant is liable to make in respect of the dwelling which he occupies as his home; and

(b)   notify that total so reduced to the rent officer in its application.

(5)   Where a relevant authority has received notification from the rent officer that a substantial part of the rent is attributable to board and attendance, it shall provide the information referred to in paragraphs (7) and (8), except for such information as it has already provided in accordance with paragraphs (3) and (4).

(6)   Where the relevant authority is required to apply to the rent officer for a determination by virtue of regulation 14(1) (requirement to refer to rent officers), it shall provide the information referred to in paragraphs (7) to (9) in the application to the rent officer.

(7)   In relation to the dwelling to which the claim or award relates, the relevant authority shall provide the following information–

(a)   the address, including any room or unit number, house or flat number or name and the postcode of the dwelling;

(b)   where the claim or award relates to mooring charges for a houseboat, or payments in respect of the site on which a caravan or mobile home stands, the mooring or plot number and the address of the mooring or site, including the postcode;

(c)   whether the dwelling is–
(i)   a detached house;
(ii)   a semi-detached house;
(iii)   a terraced house;
(iv)   a maisonette;
(v)   a detached bungalow;
(vi)   a semi-detached bungalow;
(vii)   a flat in a house;
(viii) a flat in a block;
(ix)   a flat over a shop;
(x)   a bedsit or rooms or a studio flat;
(xi)   a hostel;
(xii)   a caravan, mobile home or houseboat;
(xiii) board and lodgings;
(xiv)   a hotel;
(xv)   a care home;
(xvi)   an independent hospital; or

       (xvii) some other description of dwelling, and if so what;
- (d) whether the dwelling has central heating, a garden, a garage or a parking space;
- (e) how many rooms suitable for living in there are–
  - (i) in the dwelling;
  - (ii) in the dwelling which the claimant shares with any person other than a member of his household, a non-dependant of his, or a person who pays rent to him or his partner;
- (f) how many bedsitting rooms there are in the categories (e)(i) and (ii);
- (g) how many bedrooms there are in the categories (e)(i) and (ii);
- (h) how many bathrooms or toilets there are in the categories (e)(i) and (ii); and
- (i) such other information as the rent officer may reasonably require to make a determination.

(8) In relation to the tenancy to which the claim or award relates, the relevant authority shall provide the following information–
- (a) the information referred to in paragraphs (3)(d) to (f) and (4);
- (b) if the tenancy is furnished, and if so, to what extent;
- (c) the rental period, whether calendar monthly, four weekly, weekly or some other period;
- (d) the length of the tenancy;
- (e) when the tenancy began and, if appropriate, when it ended;
- (h) the landlord's or letting agent's name;
- (i) the landlord's or letting agent's business address;
- (j) whether the landlord is a housing association [² , private registered provider of social housing] or registered social landlord; and
- (k) such other information as the rent officer may reasonably require to make a determination.

(9) In relation to the claimant and the other occupiers of the dwelling to which the claim or award relates, the relevant authority shall provide the following information–
- (a) such information regarding the relationship of the claimant to the occupiers and the occupiers to each other, as is necessary for the rent officer to make the determination;
- (b) the age and sex of each occupier under 18; and
- (c) any other information that is relevant to the rent officer in making the determination, including visits to the dwelling.

(10) Where a rent officer serves a notice under article 5 (insufficient information) of the Rent Officers Order the relevant authority shall supply the further information required under this regulation, or confirm whether information already supplied is correct and, if it is not, supply the correct information.

(11) Where the relevant authority refers a case to the rent officer in accordance with regulation 14 as in force before the coming into force of regulation 8 of the Housing Benefit (State Pension Credit) (Local Housing Allowance and Information Sharing) Amendment Regulations 2007, it shall notify the rent officer that the referral is made in accordance with regulation 14 as in force before the coming into force of regulation 8 of those Regulations.

(12) In this regulation–

"tenancy" includes–
- (a) in Scotland, any other right of occupancy; and
- (b) in any other case, a licence to occupy premises,

and reference to a tenant, landlord or any other expression appropriate to a tenancy shall be construed accordingly;

"working day" means any day other than a Saturday, a Sunday, Christmas Day, Good Friday or a day which is a bank holiday under the Banking and Financial Dealings Act 1971 in the jurisdiction in which the area of the relevant authority is situated.]

Amendments

1.   Inserted by reg 3(2) of SI 2007 No 2869 as from 7.4.08.

2.   Amended by Art 4 and Sch 1 para 59 of SI 2010 No 671 as from 1.4.10.

General Note
Reg 5(2)(b) Housing benefit (Local Housing Allowance, Information Sharing and Miscellaneous) Amendment Regulations 2008 SI No.586 says to amend "regulation 114A" inserted by reg 3 Housing Benefit (State Pension Credit) (Local Housing Allowance and Information Sharing) Regulations 2007 SI No.2869. However, reg 3 inserted this regulation (reg 95A). Reg 5(2)(b) says: "in paragraph (1)(b) of the inserted regulation 114A for "regulation 12A" substitute "regulation 12D".

[¹ Evidence and information required by rent officers 95.]

Amendment
1.   Omitted by reg 3(3) of SI 2007 No 2869 as from 7.4.08.

[¹Information to be supplied by an authority to another authority

96.–(1)   This regulation applies for the purposes of section 128A of the Administration Act (duty of an authority to disclose information to another authority).
(2)   Information is to be disclosed by one authority to another where–
(a)   there is a mover who is or was in receipt of housing benefit from Authority "A";
(b)   either the mover's new dwelling is within the area of another Authority "B" or the mover is liable or treated as liable to make payments in respect of the new dwelling to housing authority B; and
(c)   the mover is entitled to an extended payment in accordance with regulation 72 of the Housing Benefit Regulations 2006.
(3)   Authority A shall disclose to Authority B–
(a)   the amount of the extended payment calculated in accordance with regulation 72C(2) of the Housing Benefit Regulations 2006 (amount of extended payment – movers);
(b)   the date that entitlement to the extended payment will commence or has commenced;
(c)   the date that entitlement to the extended payment ceased or will cease;
(d)   the date of the move from Authority A to Authority B;
(e)   where the extended payment will be paid by Authority A to Authority B in accordance with regulation 72C(3)(a) of the Housing Benefit Regulations 2006 (payment of extended payment to the second authority)–
    (i)   the amount that Authority A will pay to Authority B in accordance with that paragraph; and
    (ii)   any other information required by Authority B to enable Authority A to make the payment in accordance with that paragraph; and
(f)   if any deduction was being made in respect of a recoverable overpayment.
(4)   Authority B shall disclose to Authority A–
(a)   if a mover's liability to make payments for the new dwelling is to Authority B; and
(b)   where the extended payment will be paid by Authority A to Authority B in accordance with regulation 72C(3)(a) of the Housing Benefit Regulations 2006–
    (i)   any information required by Authority A to enable Authority A to make the payment in accordance with that paragraph; and
    (ii)   the date on which Authority B receives any such payment.]

Amendment
1.   Substituted by reg 5(3) of SI 2008 No 959 as from 6.10.08.

[¹Supply of information – extended payments (qualifying contributory benefits)

97.–(1)   This regulation applies for the purposes of section 122E(3) of the Administration Act (duty of an authority to supply information to another authority).
(2)   Information must be disclosed by one authority to another where–

(a) there is a mover who is or was in receipt of housing benefit from Authority "A";
(b) either the mover's new dwelling is within the area of another Authority "B" or the mover is liable or treated as liable to make payments in respect of the new dwelling to housing authority B; and
(c) the mover is entitled to an extended payment (qualifying contributory benefits) in accordance with regulation 53 of these Regulations or regulation 73 of the Housing Benefit Regulations 2006.
(3) Authority A shall disclose to Authority B–
(a) the amount of the extended payment (qualifying contributory benefits) calculated in accordance with regulation 53C(2) of these Regulations or regulation 73C(2) of the Housing Benefit Regulations 2006 (amount of extended payment – movers);
(b) the date that entitlement to the extended payment will commence or has commenced;
(c) the date that entitlement to the extended payment ceased or will cease;
(d) the date of the move from Authority A to Authority B;
(e) where the extended payment will be paid by Authority A to Authority B in accordance with regulation 53C(3)(a) of these Regulations or regulation 73C(3)(a) of the Housing Benefit Regulations 2006 (payment of the extended payment to the second authority)–
    (i) the amount that Authority A will pay to Authority B in accordance with that paragraph; and
    (ii) any other information required by Authority B to enable Authority A to make the payment in accordance with that paragraph; and
(f) if any deduction was being made in respect of a recoverable overpayment.
(4) Authority B shall disclose to Authority A–
(a) if a mover's liability to make payments for the new dwelling is to Authority B; and
(b) where the extended payment will be paid by Authority A to Authority B in accordance with regulation 53C(3)(a) of these Regulations or regulation 73C(3)(a) of the Housing Benefit Regulations 2006–
    (i) any information required by Authority A to enable Authority A to make the payment in accordance with that paragraph; and
    (ii) the date on which Authority B receives any such payment.]

Amendment
1.   Substituted by reg 5(3) of SI 2008 No 959 as from 6.10.08.

Requiring information from landlords and agents
98.   Pursuant to section 126A of the Administration Act, where a claim is made to an authority, on which a rent allowance may be awarded, then, in the circumstances prescribed in regulation 99 (circumstances for requiring information), that authority, or any person authorised to exercise any function of the authority relating to housing benefit, may require an appropriate person to supply to that authority or person relevant information, in the manner prescribed in regulation 101 (manner of supply of information).

Circumstances for requiring information
99.–(1)   A person is required to supply information in the following circumstances–
(a) he is an appropriate person in relation to any dwelling in respect of which–
    (i) housing benefit is being paid to an appropriate person pursuant to regulation 76 or 77 (circumstances in which payment is to be or may be made to a landlord); or
    (ii) a request has been made by an appropriate person or by the claimant for housing benefit to be so paid; and
(b) the requirer serves upon that appropriate person, whether by post or otherwise, a written notice stating that the requirer–

(i)   suspects that there is or may be an impropriety in relation to a claim in respect of any dwelling wherever situated in relation to which he is an appropriate person; or

(ii)   is already investigating an allegation of impropriety in relation to that person.

(2)   Information required to be supplied under paragraph (1) shall be supplied to the requirer at the address specified in the notice.

Relevant information

100.–(1)   The information the supplier is to supply to the requirer is that prescribed in paragraphs (2) and (3) (referred to in this Part as "the relevant information").

(2)   For a supplier who falls within paragraph (4) or section 126A(2)(b) of the Administration Act ("the landlord"), the information is–

(a)   where the landlord is a natural person–
- (i)   his appropriate details;
- (ii)   the relevant particulars of any residential property in which he has an interest; and
- (iii)   the appropriate details of any body corporate, in which he is a major shareholder or of which he is a director and which has an interest in residential property;

(b)   where the landlord is a trustee, except a trustee of a charity, in addition to any information that he is required to supply in accordance with sub-paragraph (a) or (c), as the case may be, the relevant particulars of any residential property held by the trust of which he is a trustee and the name and address of any beneficiary under the trust or the objects of that trust, as the case may be;

(c)   where the landlord is a body corporate or otherwise not a natural person, other than a charity–
- (i)   its appropriate details;
- (ii)   the relevant particulars of any residential property in which it has an interest;
- (iii)   the names and addresses of any directors of it;
- (iv)   the appropriate details of any person–
  - (aa)   who owns 20 per cent. or more of it; or
  - (bb)   of whom it owns 20 per cent. or more; and
- (v)   the names and addresses of its major shareholders;

(d)   where the landlord is a charity or is a recognised body the appropriate details relating to the landlord and particulars of the landlord's registration as a charity.

(3)   For a supplier who falls within section 126A(2)(c) of the Administration Act or paragraph (5) ("the agent"), the information is–

(a)   the name and address of any person ("his principal")–
- (i)   to whom the agent has agreed to make payments in consequence of being entitled to receive relevant payments; or
- (ii)   for whom the agent is acting on behalf of or in connection with any aspect of the management of a dwelling,

as the case may be;

(b)   the relevant particulars of any residential property in respect of which the agent–
- (i)   has agreed to make payments in consequence of being entitled to receive relevant payments; or
- (ii)   is acting on behalf of his principal in connection with any aspect of its management;

(c)   where the agent is a natural person–
- (i)   the relevant particulars of any residential property in which he has an interest;
- (ii)   the appropriate details of any body corporate or any person not a natural person, in which he is a major shareholder or of which he is a director and which has any interest in residential property; or

(d)   where the agent is a body corporate or other than a natural person–

      (i)   the relevant particulars of any residential property in which it has an interest;

     (ii)   the names and addresses of any directors of or major shareholders in the agent; and

    (iii) the appropriate details of any person–

          (aa) who owns 20 per cent. or more of the agent; or

          (bb) of whom the agent owns 20 per cent. or more.

    (4)   A supplier falls within this paragraph (landlord receiving rent), if he falls within section 126A(2)(a) of the Administration Act, but does not fall within paragraph (5).

    (5)   A supplier falls within this paragraph (agent receiving the rent), if he falls within subsection (2)(a) of section 126A of the Administration Act and has agreed to make payments, in consequence of being entitled to receive relevant payments, to a person falling within subsection (2)(b) of that section.

    (6)   For the purposes of this regulation–

"appropriate details" means the name of the person and (in the case of a company) its registered office and, in any case, the full postal address, including post code, of the principal place of business of that person and the telephone and facsimile number (if any) of that place;

"charity" means a charity which is registered under section 3 of the Charities Act 1993 and is not an exempt charity within the meaning of that Act;

"major shareholder" means, where a body corporate is a company limited by shares, any person holding one tenth or more of the issued shares in that company and, in any other case, all the owners of that body;

"recognised body" has the same meaning as in section 1(7) of the Law Reform (Miscellaneous Provisions) (Scotland) Act 1990;

"relevant particulars" means the full postal address, including post code, and number of current lettings of or within that residential property and, if that property includes two or more dwellings, that address and the number of such lettings for each such dwelling;

"residential property" includes any premises, situated within the United Kingdom–

      (i)   used or which has, within the last six months, been used; or

     (ii)   which may be used or is adapted for use,

as residential accommodation,

and other expressions used in this regulation and also in the Companies Act 1985 shall have the same meaning in this regulation as they have in that Act.

Manner of supply of information

    101.–(1)   Subject to paragraph (2), the relevant information shall be supplied–

    (a)   in typewritten or printed form; or

    (b)   with the written agreement of the inquirer, in electronic or handwritten form,

within a period of 4 weeks commencing on the date on which the notice was sent or given.

    (2)   Where–

    (a)   within a period of 4 weeks commencing on the date on which the notice was sent or given, the supplier requests that the time for the supply of the relevant information be extended; and

    (b)   the requirer provides written agreement to that request,

the time for the supply of the relevant information shall be extended to a period of 8 weeks commencing on the date on which the notice was sent or given.

Criminal offence

    [¹**102.**   Any supplier who fails to supply relevant information to the requirer as, when and how required under regulations 98 to 101 shall be guilty of an offence under section 113 of the Administration Act.]

Amendment

1.   Substituted by reg 3(9) of SI 2008 No 2299 as from 1.10.08.

[¹ Supply of benefit administration information between authorities

102A.–(1)   For the purpose of section 122E(3) of the Administration Act (supply of information between authorities administering benefit) the circumstances in which information is to be supplied and the information to be supplied are set out in paragraph (2).

(2)   Where the functions of an authority (''Authority A'') relating to housing benefit are being exercised, wholly or in part, by another authority (''Authority B'')–

  (a)   Authority A must supply to Authority B any benefit administration information it holds which is relevant to, and necessary for, Authority B to exercise those functions; and

  (b)   Authority B must supply to Authority A any benefit administration information it holds which is relevant to, and necessary for, Authority A to exercise those functions.

(3)   The circumstances in which paragraph (2) applies include cases where the authorities have agreed to discharge functions jointly.

(4)   In paragraph (2), ''Authority A'' and ''Authority B'' include any person authorised to exercise functions relating to housing benefit on behalf of the authority in question.

(5)   This regulation shall not apply if the person or authority to whom the information is to be supplied agrees that the information need not be supplied.]

Amendment
1.   Inserted by reg 3(10) of SI 2008 No 2299 as from 1.10.08.

[¹ PART 14
Former pathfinder authorities

Modifications in respect of former pathfinder authorities

103.–(1)   In this regulation and in Schedule 9, ''former pathfinder authority'' means a relevant authority specified in Part 1 of that Schedule.

(2)   The provisions of Part 2 of Schedule 9 apply in relation to the area of a former pathfinder authority.]

Amendment
1.   Substituted by reg 20 of SI 2007 No 2869 as from 7.4.08.

[¹ SCHEDULE A1]
TREATMENT OF CLAIMS FOR HOUSING BENEFIT BY REFUGEES

Modifications
  Sch A1 was inserted by Sch 4 para 2(2) as modified by Sch 4 para 2(3) HB&CTB(CP) Regs in respect of claims for HB by some refugees. Sch A1 was further modifed by Sch 4 para 4(2) and (3) for some HB claimants who were refugees who claimed asylum on or before 2 April 2000.

Amendment
1.   Lapsed by s12(2)(e) of the Asylum and Immigration (Treatment of Claimants, etc.) Act 2004 (for those recorded as refugees after 14.6.07).

SCHEDULE 1
REGULATION 11
Ineligible service charges

PART 1
Service charges other than for fuel

Ineligible service charges
  1.   The following service charges shall not be eligible to be met by housing benefit–
  (a)   charges in respect of day-to-day living expenses including, in particular, all provision of–
      (i)   subject to paragraph 2 meals (including the preparation of meals or provision of unprepared food);

(ii) laundry (other than the provision of premises or equipment to enable a person to do his own laundry);

[¹ (iii) leisure items such as either sports facilities (except a children's play area), or television rental, licence and subscription fees (except radio relay charges and charges made in respect of the conveyance and installation and maintenance of equipment for the conveyance of a television broadcasting service);]

(iv) cleaning of rooms and windows except cleaning of–

    (aa) communal areas; or

    (bb) the exterior of any windows where neither the claimant nor any member of his household is able to clean them himself,

where a payment is not made in respect of such cleaning by a local authority (including, in relation to England, a county council) or the [² Welsh Ministers] to the claimant or his partner, or to another person on their behalf; and

(v) transport;

(b) charges in respect of–

    (i) the acquisition of furniture or household equipment; and

    (ii) the use of such furniture or equipment where that furniture or household equipment will become the property of the claimant by virtue of an agreement with the landlord;

(c) charges in respect of the provision of an emergency alarm system;

(d) charges in respect of medical expenses (including the cost of treatment or counselling related to mental disorder, mental handicap, physical disablement or past or present alcohol or drug dependence);

(e) charges in respect of the provision of nursing care or personal care (including assistance at meal-times or with personal appearance or hygiene);

(f) charges in respect of general counselling or of any other support services, whoever provides those services;

(g) charges in respect of any services not specified in sub-paragraphs (a) to (f) which are not connected with the provision of adequate accommodation.

Amendments

1. Substituted by reg 7(3) of SI 2007 No 719 as from 2.4.07.
2. Amended by reg 6(7) of SI 2008 No 3157 as from 5.1.09.

Amount ineligible for meals

2.–(1) Where a charge for meals is ineligible to be met by housing benefit under paragraph 1, the amount ineligible in respect of each week shall be the amount specified in the following provisions of this paragraph.

(2) Subject to sub-paragraph (4), where the charge includes provision for at least three meals a day, the amount shall be–

(a) for a single claimant, [⁵ £23.35];

(b) if the claimant is a member of a family–

    (i) for the claimant and for each member of his family aged 16 or over, [⁵ £23.35];

    (ii) for each member of his family under age 16, [⁵ £11.80].

(3) Except where sub-paragraph (5) applies and subject to sub-paragraph (4), where the charge includes provision for less than three meals a day, the amount shall be–

(a) for a single claimant, [⁵ £15.50];

(b) if the claimant is a member of a family–

    (i) for the claimant and for each member of his family aged 16 or over, [⁵ £15.50];

    (ii) for each member of his family under age 16, [⁵ £7.80].

(4) For the purposes of sub-paragraphs (2)(b) and (3)(b), a person attains the age of 16 on the first Monday in September following his 16th birthday.

(5) Where the charge for meals includes the provision of breakfast only, the amount for the claimant and, if he is a member of a family, for the claimant and for each member of his family, shall be [⁵ £2.85].

(6) Where a charge for meals includes provision for meals for a person who is not a member of the claimant's family sub-paragraphs (2) to (5) shall apply as if that person were a member of the claimant's family.

(7) For the avoidance of doubt where the charge does not include provision for meals for a claimant or, as the case may be, a member of his family, sub-paragraphs (2) to (5) shall not apply in respect of that person.

Amendments

1. Amended by Art 19(4) of SI 2006 No 645 and reg 8 of SI 2006 No 217 as from 1.4.06 (3.4.06 where rent payable weekly or at intervals of a week).
2. Amended by Art 20(4) of SI 2007 No 688 as from 1.4.07 (2.4.07 where rent payable weekly or at intervals of a week).
3. Amended by Art 20(5) of SI 2008 No 632 as from 1.4.08 (7.4.08 where rent payable weekly or in multiples of a week).

4.   Amended by Art 20(5) of SI 2009 No 497 as from 1.4.09 (6.4.09 where rent payable weekly or at intervals of a week).

5.   Amended by Art 20(4) of SI 2010 No 793 as from 1.4.10 (5.4.10 where rent payable weekly or in multiples of a week).

Amount of ineligible charges

3.–(1)   Subject to paragraph 2 where an ineligible service charge is not separated from or separately identified within other payments made by the occupier in respect of the dwelling, the appropriate authority shall apportion such charge as is fairly attributable to the provision of that service, having regard to the cost of comparable services and such portion of those payments shall be ineligible to be met by housing benefit.

(2)   Subject to paragraph 2, where the relevant authority considers that the amount of any ineligible service charge which is separately identified within other payments made by the occupier in respect of the dwelling is unreasonably low having regard to the service provided, it shall substitute a sum for the charge in question which it considers represents the value of the services concerned and the amount so substituted shall be ineligible to be met by housing benefit.

(3)   In sub-paragraph (2) the expression "ineligible service charge" includes any service charge which does not qualify as a periodical payment under regulation 12(1)(e) (rent).

(4)   In any other case, the whole amount of the ineligible service charge shall be ineligible to be met by housing benefit.

Excessive service costs

4.   Subject to paragraph 2, where the relevant authority considers that the amount of a service charge to which regulation 12(1)(e) (rent) applies is excessive in relation to the service provided for the claimant or his family, having regard to the cost of comparable services, it shall make a deduction from that charge of the excess and the amount so deducted shall be ineligible to be met by housing benefit.

PART 2
Payments in respect of fuel charges

5.   A service charge for fuel except a charge in respect of services for communal areas shall be ineligible to be met by housing benefit.

6.–(1)   Where a charge is ineligible to be met by housing benefit under paragraph 5–

(a)   in the calculation of entitlement to a rent rebate; or

(b)   in the calculation of entitlement to a rent allowance if the amount of the charge is specified or is otherwise readily identifiable (except where the amount of the charge is unrealistically low in relation to the fuel provided or the charge cannot readily be distinguished from a charge for a communal area),

the amount ineligible to be met by housing benefit shall be the full amount of the service charge.

(2)   In any other case, subject to sub-paragraphs (3) and (4) and paragraph 7, the amount ineligible to be met by housing benefit shall be the following amounts in respect of each week–

(a)   for heating (other than hot water) [5 £21.55];

(b)   for hot water [5 £2.50];

(c)   for lighting [5 £1.75];

(d)   for cooking [5 £2.50].

(3)   Where the accommodation occupied by the claimant or, if he is a member of a family, by the claimant and the members of his family, consists of one room only, the amount ineligible to be met by housing benefit in respect of each week where heating only is, or heating and either hot water or lighting (or both) are, provided, shall be one-half of the aggregate of the amounts specified in sub-paragraphs (2)(a), (b) and (c).

(4)   In a case to which sub-paragraph (2) or (3) applies, if a claimant provides evidence on which the actual or approximate amount of the service charge for fuel may be estimated, the amount ineligible to be met by housing benefit under this paragraph shall be that estimated amount.

Amendments

1.   Amended by Art 19(5) of SI 2006 No 645 and reg 8 of SI 2006 No 217 as from 1.4.06 (3.4.06 where rent payable weekly or at intervals of a week).

2.   Amended by Art 20(5) of SI 2007 No 688 as from 1.4.07 (2.4.07 where rent payable weekly or at intervals of a week).

3.   Confirmed by Art 20(6) of SI 2008 No 632 as from 1.4.08 (7.4.08 where rent payable weekly or in multiples of a week).

4.   Amended by Art 20(6) of SI 2009 No 497 as from 1.4.09 (6.4.09 where rent payable weekly or at intervals of a week).

5.   Confirmed by Art 20(5) of SI 2010 No 793 as from 1.4.10 (5.4.10 where rent payable weekly or in multiples of a week).

7.–(1)   Where rent is payable other than weekly, any amount ineligible to be met by housing benefit which is specified in this Schedule as a weekly amount shall–

(a)   where rent is payable in multiples of a week, be multiplied by the number equal to the number of weeks in respect of which it is payable; or

(b)   in any other case, be divided by 7 and multiplied by the number of days in the period to be used by the relevant authority for the purpose of calculating the claimant's weekly eligible rent under regulation 61 (calculation of weekly amounts).

(2)   In a case to which regulation 62 applies (rent free periods), any amount ineligible to be met by housing benefit which is specified in this Schedule as a weekly amount shall, where appropriate, be converted in accordance with sub-paragraph (1) and shall–

(a)   where rent is payable weekly, or in multiples of a week, be multiplied by 52 or 53, whichever is appropriate, and divided by the number equal to the number of weeks in that 52 or 53 week period in respect of which he is liable to pay rent; or

(b)   in any other case, be multiplied by 365 or 366, whichever is appropriate, and divided by the number of days in that 365 or 366 day period in respect of which he is liable to pay rent.

8.   In this Schedule–

"communal areas" mean areas (other than rooms) of common access (including halls and passageways) and rooms of common use in sheltered accommodation;

"fuel" includes gas and electricity and a reference to a charge for fuel includes a charge for fuel which includes an amount in respect of the facility of providing it other than a specified amount for the provision of a heating system.

[¹ SCHEDULE 2
REGULATION 14
Excluded tenancies

Modifications

Sch 2 substituted by reg 18 Housing Benefit (State Pension Credit) (Local Housing Allowance and Information Sharing) Amendment Regulations 2007 SI No.2869 as from 7 April 2008, save that for a person to whom reg 1(5) of those regulations applied (see p1231), the amendments came into force on the day on or after 7 April 2008 when the first of the events specified in reg 1(6) applied to her/him, or on 6 April 2009 if none had before that date.

Amendment

1.   Substituted by reg 18 of SI 2007 No 2869 as from 7.4.08 (or if reg 1(5) of that SI applies, on the day on or after 7.4.08 when the first of the events specified in reg 1(6) applies, or from 6.4.09 if none have before that date).

---

1.   An excluded tenancy is any tenancy to which any of the following paragraphs applies.

2.–(1)   Subject to sub-paragraphs (2) to (3), where a rent officer has made a determination, which relates to the tenancy in question or any other tenancy of the same dwelling this paragraph applies to–

(a)   the tenancy in respect of which that determination was made; and

(b)   any other tenancy of the same dwelling on terms which are substantially the same, other than the term relating to the amount of rent, as those terms were at the time of that determination or, if earlier, at the end of the tenancy.

(2)   For the purposes of any claim, notification, request or application under regulation 14(1) ("the later application"), a tenancy shall not be an excluded tenancy by virtue of sub-paragraph (1) by reference to a rent officer's determination made in consequence of an earlier claim, notification, request or application ("the earlier application") where–

(a)   the earlier and later applications were made in respect of the same claimant or different claimants; and

(b)   the earlier application was made more than 52 weeks before the later application was made.

(3)   Sub-paragraph (1) shall not apply where subsequent to the making of the determination mentioned in that sub-paragraph–

(a)   the number of occupiers of the dwelling has changed and that dwelling is not in a hostel;

(b)   there has been a substantial change in the condition of the dwelling (including the making of improvements) or the terms of the tenancy other than a term relating to rent;

(c)   there has been a rent increase under a term of the tenancy and the term under which that increase was made was either included in the tenancy at the time when the application for that determination was made (or was a term substantially the same as such a term) and that determination was not made under paragraph 1(2), 2(2) or 3(3) of Schedule 1 to the Rent Officers Order;

(d)   in a case where the rent officer has made a determination under paragraph 2(2) of Schedule 1 to the Rent Officers Order (size and rent determinations), but since the date of the application for that determination–

(i)   a child, who is a member of the household occupying the dwelling, has attained the age of 10 years;

(ii)   a young person, who is a member of the household occupying that dwelling, has attained the age of 16 years; or

(iii)   there is a change in the composition of the household occupying the dwelling.

[¹**3.**–(1)   Subject to [² sub-paragraphs (1A) and (2)], this paragraph applies where the landlord is–

(a)   a registered housing association;

(b)   a county council, with regard to gypsies' and travellers' caravan or mobile home sites and caravans or mobile homes provided on those sites; or

(c)   a housing authority, with regard to caravan or mobile home sites or houseboat moorings, payments in respect of which are to take the form of a rent allowance in accordance with regulation 72A(3).

[² (1A)   In relation to a profit-making registered provider of social housing, sub-paragraph (1)(a) only applies to its social housing (within the meaning of sections 68 to 77 of the Housing and Regeneration Act 2008).]

(2)   Sub-paragraph (1) does not apply where the local authority considers that–

(a)   the claimant occupies a dwelling larger than is reasonably required by the claimant and any others who occupy that dwelling (including any non-dependants of the claimant and any person paying rent to the claimant); or

(b)   the rent payable for that dwelling is unreasonably high.

(3)   Where the circumstances set out in head (a) or (b) of sub-paragraph (2) exist, the authority must state this in their application for a determination.

(4)   In this Schedule "gypsies and travellers" means–

(a)   persons with a cultural tradition of nomadism or of living in a caravan; and

(b)   all other persons of a nomadic habit of life, whatever their race or origin, including–

(i)   such persons who, on grounds only of their own or their family's or dependant's educational or health needs or old age, have ceased to travel temporarily or permanently; and

(ii)   members of an organised group of travelling show people or circus people (whether or not travelling together as such).]

Amendment

1.   Substituted by reg 3(3) of SI 2008 No 2824 as from 6.4.09.

2.   Amended by Art 4 and Sch 1 paras 60 and 61 of SI 2010 No 671 as from 1.4.10.

---

4.   This paragraph applies to a tenancy entered into before–

(a)   in Scotland, 2nd January 1989; and

(b)   in any other case, 15th January 1989.

5.   This paragraph applies to a regulated tenancy within the meaning of–

(a)   in Scotland, the Rent (Scotland) Act 1984; and

(b)   in any other case, the Rent Act 1977.

6.   This paragraph applies to a housing association tenancy which–

(a)   in Scotland, is a tenancy to which Part 6 of the Rent (Scotland) Act 1984 applies; and

(b)   in any other case, is a housing association tenancy to which Part 6 of the Rent Act 1977 applies.

7.   This paragraph applies to a protected occupancy or statutory tenancy within the meaning of the Rent (Agriculture) Act 1976.

8.   This paragraph applies to a tenancy at a low rent within the meaning of Part 1 of the Landlord and Tenant Act 1954 or Schedule 10 to the Local Government and Housing Act 1989.

9.   This paragraph applies to a tenancy of any dwelling which is a bail hostel or probation hostel approved by the Secretary of State under [¹ section 13 of the Offender Management act 2007].

Amendment

1.   Amended by reg 7(6) of SI 2008 No 2767 as from 17.11.08.

---

10.   This paragraph applies to a tenancy of a housing action trust established under Part 3 of the Housing Act 1988.

11.–(1)   Subject to sub-paragraphs (2) and (3) this paragraph applies to a tenancy–

(a)   in respect of a dwelling comprised in land which has been disposed of under section 32 of the Housing Act 1985 or section 12 of the Housing (Scotland) Act 1987;

(b)   in respect of a dwelling comprised in land which has been disposed of with the consent required by section 43 of the Housing Act 1985 or section 12 of the Housing (Scotland) Act 1987;

(c)   in respect of which the fee simple estate has been acquired, under the right conferred by Chapter 2 of Part 1 of the Housing Act 1996, otherwise than from a housing action trust within the meaning of Part 3 of the Housing Act 1988, or in respect of which the house has been acquired under the right conferred by Part 3 of the Housing (Scotland) Act 1988; or

(d)   in respect of a dwelling disposed of under the New Towns (Transfer of Housing Stock) Regulations 1990 to a person who is an approved person for the purposes of disposal under those Regulations or in respect of a dwelling disposed of pursuant to powers contained in the New Towns (Scotland) Act 1968 to a housing association.

(2)   This paragraph shall not apply to a tenancy to which sub-paragraph (1) refers if–

(a)   there has been an increase in rent since the disposal or acquisition, as the case may be, occurred; and

(b)   the local authority stated in the application for determination that–
    (i)   the claimant occupies a dwelling larger than is reasonably required by him and any others who occupy that dwelling (including any non-dependant of his and any person paying rent to him); or
    (ii)   the rent payable for that dwelling is unreasonably high.

(3)   Where the disposal or acquisition, as the case may be, took place on or after 7th October 2002, sub-paragraph (2)(b) shall apply to a tenancy to which sub-paragraph (1) refers as if head (i) were omitted.

12.   This paragraph applies to a shared ownership tenancy.

13.   In this Schedule, "rent" shall be construed in accordance with paragraph (8) of regulation 14 (interpretation of "tenancy" and other expressions appropriate to a tenancy) and, subject to that paragraph, has the same meaning–

(a)   in Scotland, as in section 25 of the Housing (Scotland) Act 1988, except that the reference to the house in subsection (3) shall be construed as a reference to the dwelling;

(b)   in any other case, as in section 14 of the Housing Act 1988, except that the reference to the dwelling-house in subsection (4) shall be construed as a reference to the dwelling,

(c)   and–
    (i)   other expressions have the same meanings as in regulation 14(8);
    (ii)   in the case of a determination by a rent officer pursuant to a request for such a determination under regulation 14(1)(e), any reference to a "tenancy" shall be taken as a reference to a prospective tenancy and any reference to an "occupier" or any person "occupying" a dwelling shall, in the case of such a determination, be taken to be a reference to a potential occupier or potential occupation of that dwelling.]

SCHEDULE 3
REGULATION 22
Applicable amounts

General Note to Schedule 3

The amounts of the personal allowances and premiums are different than for those to whom the HB Regs apply.

The adult personal allowances are higher than under the HB Regs and those for single claimants aged 65 or over and couples where at least one is 65 or over are higher than those for claimants and couples aged under 65: para 1. Of the premiums, only family premium, severe disability premium (SDP), enhanced disability premium (EDP), disabled child premium and carer premium are available: paras 3 to 11. Note also that there is no equivalent to the components provided in Sch 3 Part 5 HB Regs and no equivalent to the transitional addition provided in Sch 3 Parts 7 and 8 HB Regs.

The rules for SDP are identical to those in the HB Regs: see p532. EDP is only available for specified children or young persons.

For commentary on paras 6 to 11, see the equivalent provisions in the HB Regs on pp531-534.

PART 1
Personal allowances

1.   The amount specified in column (2) below in respect of each person or couple specified in column (1) shall be the amount specified for the purposes of regulation 22–

Column (1)	*Column (2)*
Person, couple or polygamous marriage;	*Amount*
(1) Single claimant or lone parent–	(1) –
(a) aged under 65;	(a) [⁵ £132.60];
(b) aged 65 or over.	(b) [⁵ £153.15].
(2) Couple–	(2) –
(a) both members aged under 65;	(a) [⁵ £202.40];
(b) one member or both members aged 65 or over.	(b) [⁵ £229.50].
(3) If the claimant is a member of a polygamous marriage and none of the members of the marriage have attained the age of 65–	(3) –
(a) for the claimant and the other party to the marriage;	(a) [⁵ £202.40];
(b) for each additional spouse who is a member of the same household as the claimant.	(b) [⁵ £69.80].
(4) If the claimant is a member of a polygamous marriage and one or more members of the marriage are aged 65 or over–	(4) –
(a) for the claimant and the other party to the marriage;	(a) [⁵ £229.50];
(b) for each additional spouse who is a member of the same household as the claimant.	(b) [⁵ £76.35].

Amendments

1.   Amended by Art 20(4) and Sch 8 para 1 of SI 2006 No 645 and reg 8 of SI 2006 No 217 as from 1.4.06 (3.4.06 where rent payable weekly or at intervals of a week).

2.   Amended by Art 20(6) and Sch 8 of SI 2007 No 688 as from 1.4.07 (2.4.07 where rent payable weekly or at intervals of a week).

3.   Amended by Art 20(7) and Sch 8 of SI 2008 No 632 as from 1.4.08 (7.4.08 where rent payable weekly or in multiples of a week).

4.   Amended by Art 20(7) and Sch 7 of SI 2009 No 497 as from 1.4.09 (6.4.09 where rent payable weekly or in multiples of a week).

5.   Amended by Art 20(6) and Sch 7 of SI 2010 No 793 as from 1.4.10 (5.4.10 where rent payable weekly or in multiples of a week).

2.–(1)   The amounts specified in column (2) below in respect of each person specified in column (1) shall, for the relevant period specified in column (1), be the amounts specified for the purposes of regulation 22–

Column (1)	*Column (2)*
Child or young person	*Amount*
Person in respect of the period–	
(a) beginning on that person's date of birth and ending on the day preceding the first Monday in September following that person's sixteenth birthday;	[6 £57.57];;
(b) beginning on the first Monday in September following that persons 16th birthday and ending on the day preceding that person's [2 twentieth] birthday.	[6 £57.57].

(2)   In column (1) of the Table above, "the first Monday in September" means the Monday which first occurs in the month of September in any year.

Amendments
1.   Amended by Art 20(4) and Sch 8 para 2 of SI 2006 No 645 and reg 8 of SI 2006 No 217 as from 1.4.06 (3.4.06 where rent payable weekly or at intervals of a week).
2.   Amended by reg 4(4) of SI 2006 No 718 as from 10.4.06.
3.   Amended by Art 20(6) and Sch 8 of SI 2007 No 688 as from 1.4.07 (2.4.07 where rent payable weekly or at intervals of a week).
4.   Amended by Art 20(7) and Sch 8 of SI 2008 No 632 as from 1.4.08 (7.4.08 where rent payable weekly or in multiples of a week).
5.   Amended by Art 20(7) and Sch 7 of SI 2009 No 497 as from 1.4.09 (6.4.09 where rent payable weekly or in multiples of a week).
6.   Amended by Art 20(6) and Sch 7 of SI 2010 No 793 as from 1.4.10 (5.4.10 where rent payable weekly or in multiples of a week).

PART 2
Family premium
3.–(1)   The amount for the purposes of regulations 22(1)(c) and (d) in respect of a family of which at least one member is a child or young person shall be [9 £17.40].

(2)   The amount specified in sub-paragraph (1) shall be increased by [10 £10.50] where at least one child is under the age of one year and for the purposes of this sub-paragraph where that child's first birthday does not fall on a Monday he shall be treated as under the age of one year until the first Monday after his first birthday.

Amendments
1.   Amended by Art 20(5)(a) of SI 2006 No 645 and reg 8 of SI 2006 No 217 as from 1.4.06 (3.4.06 where rent payable weekly or at intervals of a week).
2.   Confirmed by Art 20(5)(b) of SI 2006 No 645 and reg 8 of SI 2006 No 217 as from 1.4.06 (3.4.06 where rent payable weekly or at intervals of a week).
3.   Amended by Art 20(7)(a) of SI 2007 No 688 as from 1.4.07 (2.4.07 where rent payable weekly or at intervals of a week).
4.   Confirmed by Art 20(7)(b) of SI 2007 No 688 as from 1.4.07 (2.4.07 where rent payable weekly or at intervals of a week).
5.   Amended by Art 20(8)(a) of SI 2008 No 632 as from 1.4.08 (7.4.08 where rent payable weekly or in multiples of a week).
6.   Confirmed by Art 20(8)(b) of SI 2008 No 632 as from 1.4.08 (7.4.08 where rent payable weekly or in multiples of a week).
7.   Amended by Art 20(8)(a) of SI 2009 No 497 as from 1.4.09 (6.4.09 where rent payable weekly or in multiples of a week).
8.   Confirmed by Art 20(8)(b) of SI 2009 No 497 as from 1.4.09 (6.4.09 where rent payable weekly or in multiples of a week).

9.   Amended by Art 20(7)(a) of SI 2010 No 793 as from 1.4.10 (5.4.10 where rent payable weekly or in multiples of a week).

10.   Confirmed by Art 20(7)(b) of SI 2010 No 793 as from 1.4.10 (5.4.10 where rent payable weekly or in multiples of a week).

PART 3
Premiums

4.   The premiums specified in Part 4 shall, for the purposes of regulation 22(1)(e), be applicable to a claimant who satisfies the condition specified in this Part in respect of that premium.

5.–(1)   Subject to sub-paragraph (2), for the purposes of this Part of this Schedule, once a premium is applicable to a claimant under this Part, a person shall be treated as being in receipt of any benefit for–

(a)   in the case of a benefit to which the Social Security (Overlapping Benefits) Regulations 1979 applies, any period during which, apart from the provisions of those Regulations, he would be in receipt of that benefit; and

(b)   any period spent by a person in undertaking a course of training or instruction provided or approved by the Secretary of State under section 2 of the 1973 Act, or by [¹ Skills Development Scotland,] Scottish Enterprise or Highlands and Islands Enterprise under section 2 of the Enterprise and New Towns (Scotland) Act 1990 or for any period during which he is in receipt of a training allowance.

(2)   For the purposes of the carer premium under paragraph 9, a person shall be treated as being in receipt of a carer's allowance under section 70 of the Act by virtue of sub-paragraph (1)(a) only if and for so long as the person in respect of whose care the allowance has been claimed remains in receipt of attendance allowance, or the care component of disability living allowance been at the highest or middle rate prescribed in accordance with section 72(3) of the Act.

Amendment
1.   Amended by reg 7(3)(c) of SI 2009 No 583 as from 6.4.09.

Severe disability premium

6.–(1)   The condition is that the claimant is a severely disabled person.

(2)   For the purposes of sub-paragraph (1), a claimant shall be treated as being a severely disabled person if, and only if–

(a)   in the case of a single claimant, lone parent or a claimant who is treated as having no partner in consequence of sub-paragraph (3)–

        (i)   he is in receipt of attendance allowance, or the care component of disability living allowance at the highest or middle rate prescribed in accordance with section 72(3) of the Act; and

        (ii)   subject to sub-paragraph (6), he has no non-dependants aged 18 or over normally residing with him or with whom he is normally residing; and

        (iii)   no person is entitled to, and in receipt of, a carer's allowance in respect of caring for him;

(b)   in the case of a claimant who has a partner–

        (i)   the claimant is in receipt of attendance allowance, or the care component of disability living allowance at the highest or middle rate prescribed in accordance with section 72(3) of the Act; and

        (ii)   his partner is also in receipt of such an allowance or, if the claimant is a member of a polygamous marriage, each other member of that marriage is in receipt of such an allowance; and

        (iii)   subject to sub-paragraph (6), the claimant has no non-dependants aged 18 or over normally residing with him or with whom he is normally residing,

and either a person is entitled to and in receipt of a carer's allowance in respect of caring for only one of the couple or, if he is a member of a polygamous marriage, for one or more but not all the members of the marriage, or as the case may be, no person is entitled to and in receipt of such an allowance in respect of caring for either member of a couple or any of the members of the marriage.

(3)   Where a claimant has a partner who does not satisfy the condition in sub-paragraph (2)(b)(ii), and that partner is blind or is treated as blind within the meaning of sub-paragraph (4), that partner shall be treated for the purposes of sub-paragraph (2) as if he were not a partner of the claimant.

(4)   For the purposes of sub-paragraph (3), a person is blind if he is registered in a register compiled by a local authority under section 29 of the National Assistance Act 1948 (welfare services) or, in Scotland, has been certified as blind and in consequence he is registered in a register maintained by or on behalf of a council constituted under section 2 of the Local Government (Scotland) Act 1994.

(5)   For the purposes of sub-paragraph (4), a person who has ceased to be registered as blind on regaining his eyesight shall nevertheless be treated as blind and as satisfying the additional condition set out in that sub-paragraph for a period of 28 weeks following the date on which he ceased to be so registered.

(6)   For the purposes of sub-paragraph (2)(a)(ii) and (2)(b)(iii) no account shall be taken of–

(a)   a person receiving attendance allowance, or the care component of disability living allowance at the highest or middle rate prescribed in accordance with section 72(3) of the Act; or

(b)   a person who is blind or is treated as blind within the meaning of sub-paragraphs (4) and (5).

(7)   For the purposes of sub-paragraph (2)(b) a person shall be treated–

(a)   as being in receipt of attendance allowance, or the care component of disability living allowance at the highest or middle rate prescribed in accordance with section 72(3) of the Act, if he would, but for his being a patient for a period exceeding 28 days, be so in receipt;

(b)   as being entitled to and in receipt of a carer's allowance if he would, but for the person for whom he was caring being a patient in hospital for a period exceeding 28 days, be so entitled and in receipt.

(8)   For the purposes of sub-paragraph (2)(a)(iii) and (2)(b)–

(a)   no account shall be taken of an award of a carer's allowance to the extent that payment of such an award is backdated for a period before [¹ the date on which the award is first paid]; and

(b)   references to a person being in receipt of a carer's allowance shall include references to a person who would have been in receipt of that allowance but for the application of a restriction under section [² 6B or] 7 of the Social Security Fraud Act 2001 (loss of benefit).

Amendments

1.   Amended by reg 7(4) of SI 2007 No 719 as from 2.4.07.
2.   Amended by reg 5 of SI 2010 No 1160 as from 1.4.10.

Enhanced disability premium

7.   The condition is that the care component of disability living allowance is, or would, but for a suspension of benefit in accordance with regulations under section 113(2) of the Act or but for an abatement as a consequence of hospitalisation, be payable at the highest rate prescribed under section 72(3) of the Act in respect of a child or young person who is a member of the claimant's family.

Disabled child premium

8.   The condition is that a child or young person for whom the claimant or a partner of his is responsible and who is a member of the claimant's household–

(a)   is in receipt of disability living allowance or is no longer in receipt of such allowance because he is a patient, provided that the child or young person continues to be a member of the family; or

(b)   is blind within the meaning of paragraph 6(4) or is treated as blind in accordance with paragraph 6(5);

(c)   is a child or a young person in respect of whom section 145A of the Act (entitlement to child benefit after death of child) applies for the purposes of entitlement to child benefit, but only for the period prescribed under that section, and in respect of whom a disabled child premium was included in the claimant's applicable amount immediately before the death of that child.

Carer premium

9.–(1)   The condition is that the claimant or his partner is, or both of them are, entitled to a carer's allowance.

(2)   Where a carer premium has been awarded but–

(a)   the person in respect of whose care the carer's allowance has been awarded dies; or

(b)   the person in respect of whom the premium was awarded ceases to be entitled, or ceases to be treated as entitled, to a carer's allowance,

this paragraph shall be treated as satisfied for a period of eight weeks from the relevant date specified in sub-paragraph (3).

(3)   The relevant date for the purposes of sub-paragraph (2) is–

(a)   the Sunday following the death of the person in respect of whose care the carer's allowance has been awarded (or beginning with the date of death if the date occurred on a Sunday);

(b)   where head (a) above does not apply, the date on which that person who was entitled to a carer's allowance ceases to be entitled to it.

(4)   For the purposes of this paragraph, a person shall be treated as being entitled to and in receipt of a carer's allowance for any period not covered by an award but in respect of which a payment is made in lieu of an award.

Persons in receipt of concessionary payments

10.   For the purpose of determining whether a premium is applicable to a person under paragraphs 6 to 9, any concessionary payment made to compensate that person for the non-payment of any benefit mentioned in those paragraphs shall be treated as if it were a payment of that benefit.

Person in receipt of benefit

11.   For the purposes of this Part of this Schedule, a person shall be regarded as being in receipt of any benefit if, and only if, it is paid in respect of him and shall be so regarded only for any period in respect of which that benefit is paid.

PART 4
Amounts of premiums specified in Part 3

Premium	*Amount*;
12.–(1) Severe Disability Premium	(1)
(a) where the claimant satisfies the condition in paragraph 6(2)(a);	(a) [5 £53.65];
(b) where the claimant satisfies the condition in paragraph 6(2)(b)–	
(i) in a case where there is someone in receipt of a carer's allowance or if he or any partner satisfies that condition only by virtue of paragraph 6(7);	(b) (i) [5 £53.65];
(ii) in a case where there is no-one in receipt of such an allowance	(b) (ii) [5 £107.30].
(2) Enhanced disability premium.	(2) [5 £21.00] in respect of each child or young person in respect of whom the conditions specified in paragraph 7 are satisfied.
(3) Disabled child premium.	(3) [5 £52.08] in respect of each child or young person in respect of whom the condition specified in paragraph 8 is satisfied.
(4) Carer premium.	(4) [5 £30.05] in respect of each person who satisfies the condition specified in paragraph 9.

Amendments

1.   Amended by Art 20(5) and Sch 9 of SI 2006 No 645 and reg 8 of SI 2006 No 217 as from 1.4.06 (3.4.06 where rent payable weekly or at intervals of a week).
2.   Amended by Art 20(8) and Sch 9 of SI 2007 No 688 as from 1.4.07 (2.4.07 where rent payable weekly or at intervals of a week).
3.   Amended by Art 20(9) and Sch 9 of SI 2008 No 632 as from 1.4.08 (7.4.08 where rent payable weekly or in multiples of a week).
4.   Amended by Art 20(9) and Sch 8 of SI 2009 No 497 as from 1.4.09 (6.4.08 where rent payable weekly or in multiples of a week).
5.   Amended by Art 20(8) and Sch 8 of SI 2010 No 793 as from 1.4.10 (5.4.10 where rent payable weekly or in multiples of a week).

SCHEDULE 4
REGULATION 36(1)
Sums disregarded from claimant's earnings

General Note to Schedule 4

The general rule, found in para 7, is that a single claimant qualifies for an earnings disregard of £5 and a claimant with a partner qualifies for an earnings disregard of £10. However, the earnings disregard for a lone parent is £25 and for certain categories of people is £20 . Note the potentially higher earnings disregard in para 5A where the claimant or her/his partner is undertaking "exempt work". See the Analysis of the equivalent Sch 4 para 10A HB Regs on p548.

The categories of people qualifying for a disregard of £20 are the following:

(1)   Claimants working for the rescue services and reserve armed forces: para 3. If the claimant is earning less than £20, any earnings of her/his partner will be disregarded up to that amount.

(2)   Carers who are in employment: para 4. Again, the earnings of both partners may be added together for the purposes of the disregard.

(3)   Certain sick or disabled claimants: para 5(1). Much of para 5(1) is similar to Sch 3 para 13(1) HB Regs, to which reference should be made.

(4)   Claimants who had a £20 disregard in an award of HB or CTB in the eight weeks before attaining the qualifying age for PC and where employment continues after the termination of that award: para 5(2). That disregard continues as long as HB entitlement continues: para 5(3).

There are then a number of other disregards. Para 6 requires the disregarding of any balance of parental contributions made to a student which are not disregarded under Sch 5 paras 18 and 19. Para 8 requires earnings derived from employment pre-dating the claim to be ignored, save for royalties and analogous payments. Para 9 is equivalent to Sch 4 para 17 HB Regs, and para 10 is equivalent to Sch 4 para 14 HB Regs.

1.   Where two or more of paragraphs 2 to 5 apply in any particular case the overall maximum sum which falls to be disregarded in that case under those paragraphs is restricted to–
  (a)   £25 in the case of a lone parent;

(b)   £20 in any other case.

2.   In a case where a claimant is a lone parent, £25 of earnings.

3.–(1)   In a case of earnings from any employment or employments to which sub-paragraph (2) applies, £20.

(2)   This paragraph applies to employment–

(a)   as a part-time fire-fighter employed by a fire and rescue authority constituted by a scheme under section 2 of the Fire and Rescue Services Act 2004 or a scheme to which section 4 of that Act applies;

(b)   as a part-time fire-fighter employed by a fire and rescue authority (as defined in section 1 of the Fire (Scotland) Act 2005) or a joint fire and rescue board constituted by an amalgamation scheme made under section 2(1) of that Act;

(c)   as an auxiliary coastguard in respect of coast rescue activities;

(d)   in the manning or launching of a lifeboat if the employment is part-time;

(e)   as a member of any territorial or reserve force prescribed in Part 1 of Schedule 6 to Social Security (Contributions) Regulations 2001.

(3)   If–

(a)   any of the earnings of the claimant or, if he has a partner, his partner, or both of them, are disregarded under sub-paragraph (1); and

(b)   either of them has, or they both have, other earnings,

so much of those other earnings as would not, in aggregate with the earnings disregarded under that sub-paragraph, exceed £20.

4.–(1)   If the claimant or, if he has a partner, his partner is a carer, or both are carers, £20 of any earnings received from his or their employment.

(2)   Where the carer premium is awarded in respect of the claimant and of any partner of his, their earnings shall for the purposes of this paragraph be aggregated, but the amount to be disregarded in accordance with sub-paragraph (1) shall not exceed £20 of the aggregated amount.

(3)   In this paragraph the claimant or his partner is a carer if paragraph 9 of Part 3 of Schedule 3 (amount applicable for carers) is satisfied in respect of him.

5.–(1)   £20 is disregarded if the claimant or, if he has a partner, his partner–

(a)   is in receipt of–

(i)   long-term incapacity benefit under Section 30A of the Act;

(ii)   severe disablement allowance under section 68 of the Act;

(iii)   attendance allowance;

(iv)   disability living allowance under sections 71 to 76 of the Act;

(v)   any mobility supplement under [² article 20 of the Naval, Military and Air Forces Etc. (Disablement and Death) Service Pensions Order 2006] (including such a supplement by virtue of any other scheme or order) or under article 25A of the Personal Injuries (Civilians) Scheme 1983; [¹]

(vi)   the disability element or the severe disability element of working tax credit under Schedule 2 to the Working Tax Credit Regulations; or

[¹ (vii) main phase employment and support allowance; or]

(b)   is or are registered as blind in a register compiled by a local authority under section 29 of the National Assistance Act 1948 (welfare services) or, in Scotland, has been certified as blind and in consequence is registered as blind in a register maintained by or on behalf of a council constituted under section 2 of the Local Government (Scotland) Act 1994; or

(c)   is, or is treated as, incapable of work in accordance with the provisions of, and regulations made under, Part 12A of the Act (incapacity for work), and has been incapable, or has been treated as incapable, of work for a continuous period of not less than–

(i)   in the case of a claimant who is terminally ill within the meaning of section 30B(4) of that Act, 196 days;

(ii)   in any other case, 364 days.[³ or]

[³ (d)   has, or is treated as having, limited capability for work within the meaning of section 1(4) of the Welfare Reform Act or limited capability for work-related activity within the meaning of section 2(5) of that Act and either–

(i)   the assessment phase as defined in section 24(2) of the Welfare Reform Act has ended; or

(ii)   regulation 7 of the Employment and Support Allowance Regulations (circumstances where the condition that the assessment phase has ended before entitlement to the support component or the work-related activity component arises does not apply) applies.]

(2)   Subject to sub-paragraph (3), £20 is disregarded if the claimant or, if he has a partner, his partner has, within a period of 8 weeks ending on the day in respect of which the claimant or his partner attains the qualifying age for state pension credit, had an award of housing benefit or council tax benefit and–

(a)   £20 was disregarded in respect of earnings taken into account in that award;

(b)   the person whose earnings qualified for the disregard continues in employment after the termination of that award.

(3)   The disregard of £20 specified in sub-paragraph (2) applies so long as there is no break, other than a break which does not exceed 8 weeks, in a person's entitlement to housing benefit or council tax benefit or in employment following the first day in respect of which that benefit is awarded.

(4)   £20 is the maximum amount which may be disregarded under this paragraph, notwithstanding that, where the claimant has a partner, both the claimant and his partner satisfy the requirements of this paragraph.

Amendments
1.   Amended by reg 40 of SI 2008 No 1082 as from 27.10.08.
2.   Amended by reg 6(8) of SI 2008 No 3157 as from 5.1.09.
3.   Amended by reg 7(7)(a) of SI 2009 No 583 as from 1.4.09 (6.4.09 where rent payable weekly or at intervals of a week).

[¹**5A.**   (1)   Where–
(a)   the claimant (or if the claimant is a member of a couple, at least one member of that couple) is a person to whom sub-paragraph (5) applies;
(b)   the Secretary of State is satisfied that that person is undertaking exempt work as defined in sub-paragraph (6); and
(c)   regulation 26 does not apply,
the amount specified in sub-paragraph (7) (''the specified amount'').
(2)   Where this paragraph applies, paragraphs 1 to 5 and 7 do not apply; but in any case where the claimant is a lone parent, and the specified amount would be less than the amount specified in paragraph 2, then paragraph 2 applies instead of this paragraph.
(3)   Notwithstanding regulation 23 (calculation of income and capital of members of claimant's family and of a polygamous marriage), if sub-paragraph (1) applies to one member of a couple (''A'') it shall not apply to the other member of that couple (''B'') except to the extent provided in sub-paragraph (4).
(4)   Where A's earnings are less than the specified amount, there shall also be disregarded so much of B's earnings as would not when aggregated with A's earnings exceed the specified amount; but the amount of B's earnings which may be disregarded under this sub-paragraph is limited to a maximum of £20 unless the Secretary of State is satisfied that B is also undertaking exempt work.
(5)   This sub-paragraph applies to a person who is–
(a)   in receipt of a contributory employment and support allowance;
(b)   in receipt of incapacity benefit;
(c)   in receipt of severe disablement allowance; or
(d)   being credited with earnings on the grounds of incapacity for work or limited capability for work under regulation 8B of the Social Security (Credits) Regulations 1975.
(6)   ''Exempt work'' means work of the kind described in–
(a)   regulation 45(2), (3) or (4) of the Employment and Support Allowance Regulations; or (as the case may be)
(b)   regulation 17(2), (3) or (4) of the Social Security (Incapacity for Work) (General) Regulations 1995,
and, in determining for the purposes of this paragraph whether a claimant or a member of a couple is undertaking any type of exempt work, it is immaterial whether that person or their partner is also undertaking other work.
(7)   The specified amount is the amount of money from time to time mentioned in any provision referred to in sub-paragraph (6) by virtue of which the work referred to in sub-paragraph (1) is exempt (or, where more than one such provision is relevant and those provisions mention different amounts of money, the highest of those amounts).]

Amendment
1.   Inserted by reg 3(5) of SI 2009 No 2608 as from 1.4.10 (5.4.10 where rent payable weekly or in multiples of a week).

6.   Any amount or the balance of any amount which would fall to be disregarded under paragraph 18 or 19 of Schedule 5 had the claimant's income which does not consist of earnings been sufficient to entitle him to the full disregarded thereunder.
7.   Except where the claimant or his partner qualifies for a £20 disregard under the preceding provisions of this Schedule–
(a)   £5 shall be disregarded if a claimant who has no partner has earnings;
(b)   £10 shall be disregarded if a claimant who has a partner has earnings.
8.   Any earnings, other than earnings referred to in regulation 33(8)(b) (copyright [¹ design], patent or trade mark), derived from employment which ended before the day in respect of which the claimant first satisfies the conditions for entitlement to housing benefit.

Amendment
1.   Amended by reg 7(7)(b) of SI 2009 No 583 as from the first day of the first benefit week for a claimant on or after 6.4.09.

9.–(1)   In a case where the claimant is a person who satisfies at least one of the conditions set out in sub-paragraph (2), and his net earnings equal or exceed the total of the amounts set out in sub-paragraph (3), the amount of his earnings that falls to be disregarded under this Schedule shall be increased by [⁵ £17.10].

(2)   The conditions of this sub-paragraph are that–

(a)   the claimant, or if he has a partner, either the claimant or his partner, is a person to whom regulation 20(1)(c) of the Working Tax Credit Regulations applies; or

(b)   the claimant–

     (i)   is, or any partner of his is, aged at least 25 and is engaged in remunerative work for on average not less than 30 hours per week; or

     (ii)   if he is a member of a couple–

          (aa)   at least one member of that couple is engaged in remunerative work for on average not less than 16 hours per week; and

          (bb)   his applicable amount includes a family premium under paragraph 3 of Schedule 3; or

     (iii)   is a lone parent who is engaged in remunerative work for on average not less than 16 hours per week; or

     (iv)   is, or if he has a partner, one of them is, engaged in remunerative work for on average not less than 16 hours per week, and paragraph 5(1) above is satisfied in respect of that person; or

(c)   the claimant is, or, if he has a partner, one of them is, a person to whom regulation 18(3) of the Working Tax Credit Regulations (eligibility for 50 plus element) applies, or would apply if an application for working tax credit were to be made in his case.

(3)   The following are the amounts referred to in sub-paragraph (1)–

(a)   any amount disregarded under this Schedule;

(b)   the amount of child care charges calculated as deductible under regulation 31(1)(c) (treatment of child care charges); and

(c)   [⁵ £17.10].

(4)   The provisions of regulation 6 (remunerative work) shall apply in determining whether or not a person works for on average not less than 30 hours per week, but as if the reference to 16 hours in paragraph (1) of that regulation was a reference to 30 hours.

Amendments

1.   Amended by Art 20(7) of SI 2006 No 645 and reg 8 of SI 2006 No 217 as from 1.4.06 (3.4.06 where rent payable weekly or at intervals of a week).

2.   Amended by Art 20(9) of SI 2007 No 688 as from 1.4.07 (2.4.07 where rent payable weekly or at intervals of a week).

3.   Amended by Art 20(10) of SI 2008 No 632 as from 1.4.08 (7.4.08 where rent payable weekly or in multiples of a week).

4.   Amended by Art 20(10) of SI 2009 No 497 as from 1.4.09 (6.4.09 where rent payable weekly or at intervals of a week).

5.   Amended by Art 20(9) of SI 2010 No 793 as from 1.4.10 (5.4.10 where rent payable weekly or in multiples of a week).

---

10.   Where a payment of earnings is made in a currency other than Sterling any banking charge or commission payable in converting that payment into Sterling.

SCHEDULE 5
REGULATION 33(9)
Amounts to be disregarded in the calculation of income other than earnings

1.   In addition to any sum which falls to be disregarded in accordance with paragraphs 2 to 6, £10 of any of the following, namely–

(a)   a war disablement pension (except insofar as such a pension falls to be disregarded under paragraph 2 or 3);

[¹ (b)   a war widow's pension or [³ war widower's pension];]

(c)   a pension payable to a person as a widow, widower or surviving civil partner under [²] any power of Her Majesty otherwise than under an enactment to make provision about pensions for or in respect of persons who have been disabled or have died in consequence of service as members of the armed forces of the Crown;

(d)   a guaranteed income payment [² and, if the amount of that payment has been abated to less than £10 by a [³ pension or payment falling within article 31(1)(a) or (b) of the Armed Forces and Reserve Forces (Compensation Scheme) Order 2005], so much of [³ that pension or payment] as would not, in aggregate with the amount of [³ any] guaranteed income payment disregarded, exceed £10];

(e)   a payment made to compensate for the non-payment of such a pension or payment as is mentioned in any of the preceding sub-paragraphs;

(f)   a pension paid by the government of a country outside Great Britain which is analogous to any of the pensions or payments mentioned in sub-paragraphs (a) to (d) above;

(g)   a pension paid to victims of National Socialist persecution under any special provision made by the law of the Federal Republic of Germany, or any part of it, or of the Republic of Austria.

Amendments
1.   Amended by reg 4(8)(a) of SI 2008 No 1042 as from 19.5.08.
2.   Amended by reg 6(9)(a) of SI 2008 No 3157 as from 5.1.09.
3.   Amended by reg 7(5) of SI 2009 No 2655 as from 2.11.09.

Analysis
See Sch 5 para 15 HB Regs (see p554), but note para 2 below.

---

2.   The whole of any amount included in a pension to which paragraph 1 relates in respect of–
(a)   the claimant's need for constant attendance;
(b)   the claimant's exceptionally severe disablement.

Analysis
These are supplements payable in respect of various war pensions for the exceptional needs of a recipient. The whole of such supplements are disregarded.

---

3.   Any mobility supplement under [¹ article 20 of the Naval, Military and Air Forces Etc. (Disablement and Death) Service Pensions Order 2006] (including such a supplement by virtue of any other scheme or order) or under article 25A of the Personal Injuries (Civilians) Scheme 1983 or any payment intended to compensate for the non-payment of such a supplement.

Amendment
1.   Amended by reg 6(9)(b) of SI 2008 No 3157 as from 5.1.09.

Analysis
This is equivalent to Sch 5 para 8 HB Regs (see p554).

[¹**4.**   Any supplementary pension under article 23(2) of the Naval, Military and Air Forces Etc. (Disablement and Death) Service Pensions Order 2006 (pensions to surviving spouses and surviving civil partners) and any analogous payment made by the Secretary of State for Defence to any person who is not a person entitled under that Order.]

Amendment
1.   Substituted by reg 6(9)(c) of SI 2008 No 3157 as from 5.1.09.

Analysis of paras 4, 5 and 6
Note that under Sch 6 paras 18 and 26B, arrears of supplementary pension disregarded under para 4, and any amount disregarded under paras 5 or 6, are disregarded as capital for one year from the date of receipt.

---

5.   In the case of a pension awarded at the supplementary rate under article 27(3) of the Personal Injuries (Civilians) Scheme 1983 (pensions to widows, widowers or surviving civil partners), the sum specified in paragraph 1(c) of Schedule 4 to that Scheme.
6.–(1)   Any payment which is–
(a)   made under any of the Dispensing Instruments to a widow, widower or surviving civil partner of a person–
    (i)   whose death was attributable to service in a capacity analogous to service as a member of the armed forces of the Crown; and
    (ii)   whose service in such capacity terminated before 31st March 1973; and
[¹ (b)   equal to the amount specified in article 23(2) of the Naval, Military and Air Forces Etc. (Disablement and Death) Service Pensions Order 2006.]
(2)   In this paragraph "the Dispensing Instruments" means the Order in Council of 19th December 1881, the Royal Warrant of 27th October 1884 and the Order by His Majesty of 14th January 1922 (exceptional grants of pay, non-effective pay and allowances).

Amendment
1.   Substituted by reg 6(9)(d) of SI 2008 No 3157 as from 5.1.09.

---

7.   £15 of any widowed parent's allowance to which the claimant is entitled under section 39A of the Act.
8.   £15 of any widowed mother's allowance to which the claimant is entitled under section 37 of the Act.
9.   Where the claimant occupies a dwelling as his home and he provides in that dwelling board and lodging accommodation, an amount, in respect of each person for whom such accommodation is provided for the whole or any part of a week, equal to–

(a)   where the aggregate of any payments made in respect of any one week in respect of such accommodation provided to such person does not exceed £20, 100 per cent. of such payments; or

(b)   where the aggregate of any such payments exceeds £20, £20 and 50 per cent. of the excess over £20.

10.   If the claimant–

(a)   owns the freehold or leasehold interest in any property or is a tenant of any property; and

(b)   occupies a part of that property; and

(c)   has an agreement with another person allowing that person to occupy another part of that property on payment of rent and–

    (i)   the amount paid by that person is less than £20 per week, the whole of that amount; or

    (ii)   the amount paid is £20 or more per week, £20.

Analysis

This has no equivalent in Sch 5 HB Regs (but see Sch 5 paras 22 and 42 HB Regs). Up to £20 of rent payable by a lodger may be disregarded whether or not board is also provided.

---

11.   Where a claimant receives income under an annuity purchased with a loan, which satisfies the following conditions–

(a)   that the loan was made as part of a scheme under which not less than 90 per cent. of the proceeds of the loan were applied to the purchase by the person to whom it was made of an annuity ending with his life or with the life of the survivor of two or more persons (in this paragraph referred to as "the annuitants") who include the person to whom the loan was made;

(b)   that at the time the loan was made the person to whom it was made or each of the annuitants had attained the age of 65;

(c)   that the loan was secured on a dwelling in Great Britain and the person to whom the loan was made or one of the annuitants owns an estate or interest in that dwelling;

(d)   that the person to whom the loan was made or one of the annuitants occupies the dwelling on which it was secured as his home at the time the interest is paid; and

(e)   that the interest payable on the loan is paid by the person to whom the loan was made or by one of the annuitants,

the amount, calculated on a weekly basis, equal to–

    (i)   where, or insofar as, section 369 of the Income and Corporation Taxes Act 1988 (mortgage interest payable under deduction of tax) applies to the payments of interest on the loan, the interest which is payable after deduction of a sum equal to income tax on such payments at the applicable percentage of income tax within the meaning of section 369(1A) of that Act;

    (ii)   in any other case, the interest which is payable on the loan without deduction of such a sum.

Analysis

The basic effect of this paragraph is to provide a disregard from the income produced by an annuity under a "Home Income Plan", of an amount equal to the interest payments (net of tax) on the loan used to purchase the annuity.

    Sub-paras (a) to (e) set out the conditions which must be satisfied before the disregard can apply and sub-paras (i) and (ii) deal with how much of the annuity can be ignored.

(1)   The person to whom the loan was made (payee) must have used 90 per cent of it at least to purchase the annuity which must last for the life of the payee or another person (annuitant): sub-para (a).

(2)   The interest on the loan must be payable by the payee or one of the annuitants: sub-para (e).

(3)   The payee or any annuitant(s) must have been aged 65 at the time the loan in question was made: sub-para (b).

(4)   The loan must have been secured on a dwelling in Great Britain which the payee or one of the annuitants owns (or owns an interest in): sub-para (c).

(5)   The payee or one of the annuitants must actually occupy the dwelling: sub-para (d).

Sub-paras (i) and (ii). s369 Income and Corporation Taxes Act 1988 allows tax relief on certain interest payments; where the section applies, the interest paid net of tax should be disregarded. Otherwise, all of the interest may be disregarded.

12.–(1)   Any payment, other than a payment to which sub-paragraph (2) applies, made to the claimant by Trustees in exercise of a discretion exercisable by them.

(2)   This sub-paragraph applies to payments made to the claimant by Trustees in exercise of a discretion exercisable by them for the purpose of–

(a)   obtaining food, ordinary clothing or footwear or household fuel;

(b)   the payment of rent, council tax or water charges for which that claimant or his partner is liable;

(c)   meeting housing costs of a kind specified in Schedule 2 to the State Pension Credit Regulations 2002.

(3)   In a case to which sub-paragraph (2) applies, £20 or–

(a)   if the payment is less than £20, the whole payment;

(b)   if, in the claimant's case, £10 is disregarded in accordance with paragraph 1(a) to (g), £10 or the whole payment if it is less than £10; or

(c)   if, in the claimant's case, £15 is disregarded under paragraph 7 or paragraph 8 and–

   (i)   he has no disregard under paragraph 1(a) to (g), £5 or the whole payment if it is less than £5;

   (ii)   he has a disregard under paragraph 1(a) to (g), nil.

(4)   For the purposes of this paragraph–

[¹ "ordinary clothing or footwear"] means clothing or footwear for normal daily use, but does not include school uniforms, or clothing and footwear used solely for sporting activities; and

"rent" means eligible rent for the purposes of these Regulations less any deductions in respect of non-dependants which fall to be made under regulation 55 (non-dependant deductions).

Amendment

1.   Amended by reg 4(8)(b) of SI 2008 No 1042 as from 19.5.08.

Analysis

This paragraph has no equivalent in Sch 5 HB Regs. All payments under a discretionary trust are ignored, except for those which are used for the essentials set out in para (2), which receive only a limited disregard calculated according to the amounts of other disregards.

---

13.   Any increase in [¹ pension or allowance under Part 2 or 3 of the Naval, Military and Air Forces Etc. (Disablement and Death) Service Pensions Order 2006] paid in respect of a dependent other than the pensioner's [¹] partner.

Amendment

1.   Amended by reg 6(9)(e) of SI 2008 No 3157 as from 5.1.09.

Analysis

This paragraph deals with increases in war pensions for dependants, which are to be ignored completely.

---

14.   Any payment ordered by a court to be made to the claimant or the claimant's partner in consequence of any accident, injury or disease suffered by the person or a child of the person to or in respect of whom the payments are made.

15.   Periodic payments made to the claimant or the claimant's partner under an agreement entered into in settlement of a claim made by the claimant or, as the case may be, the claimant's partner for an injury suffered by him.

Analysis to paras 14 and 15

The phrase "any accident, injury or disease" used in para 14 is probably wider than the phrase used in reg 42(2)(b) HB Regs "a personal injury". It might, for example, cover wrongful birth claims which can be said to arise from an "accident" such as a negligently carried out sterilisation.

   Para 15 does not appear to include payments from an annuity purchased by a defendant's insurer, since those are payments made under the annuity contract rather than under the settlement agreement.

---

16.   Any income which is payable outside the United Kingdom for such period during which there is a prohibition against the transfer to the United Kingdom of that income.

17.   Any banking charges or commission payable in converting to Sterling payments of income made in a currency other than Sterling.

18.   Where the claimant makes a parental contribution in respect of a student attending a course at an establishment in the United Kingdom or undergoing education in the United Kingdom, which contribution has been assessed for the purposes of calculating–

(a)   under, or pursuant to regulations made under powers conferred, by section 1 or 2 of the Education Act 1962, or section 22 of the Teaching and Higher Education Act 1998, that student's award;

(b)   under regulations made in exercise of the powers conferred by section 49 of the Education (Scotland) Act 1980, that student's bursary, scholarship, or other allowance under that section or under regulations made in exercise of the powers conferred by section 73 of that Act of 1980, any payment to that student under that section; or

(c)   the student's student loan,

an amount equal to the weekly amount of that parental contribution, but only in respect of the period for which that contribution is assessed as being payable.

Analysis

This is equivalent to Sch 5 para 19 HB Regs (see p555).

19.–(1)   Where the claimant is the parent of a student aged under 25 in advanced education who either–
(a)   is not in receipt of any award, grant or student loan in respect of that education; or
(b)   is in receipt of an award under section 2 of the Education Act 1962 (discretionary awards) or an award bestowed by virtue of the Teaching and Higher Education Act 1998, or regulations made thereunder, or a bursary, scholarship or other allowance under section 49(1) of the Education (Scotland) Act 1980, or a payment under section 73 of that Act of 1980,
and the claimant makes payments by way of a contribution towards the student's maintenance, other than a parental contribution falling within paragraph 18, an amount specified in sub-paragraph (2) in respect of each week during the student's term.
(2)   For the purposes of sub-paragraph (1), the amount shall be equal to–
(a)   the weekly amount of the payments; or
(b)   the amount by way of a personal allowance for a single claimant under 25 less the weekly amount of any award, bursary, scholarship, allowance or payment referred to in sub-paragraph (1)(b),
whichever is less.

Analysis
This is equivalent to Sch 5 para 20 HB Regs (see p556).

20.–(1)   Where a claimant's applicable amount includes an amount by way of a family premium, £15 of any payment of maintenance, whether under a court order or not, which is made or due to be made by the claimant's spouse, civil partner, former spouse or former civil partner or the claimant's partner's spouse, civil partner, former spouse, or former civil partner.
(2)   For the purposes of sub-paragraph (1), where more than one maintenance payment falls to be taken into account in any week, all such payments shall be aggregated and treated as if they were a single payment.

Analysis
This is equivalent to Sch 5 para 47 HB Regs, though there is no equivalent to para 47(3).
Note that other kinds of maintenance (eg, for a child) do not count as income and are ignored completely: reg 29(1)(o).

21.   Except in a case which falls under paragraph 9 of Schedule 4, where the claimant is a person who satisfies [⁴ any of] the conditions of sub-paragraph (2) of that paragraph, any amount of working tax credit up to [⁶ £17.10].
1.   Amended by Art 20(8) of SI 2006 No 645 and reg 8 of SI 2006 No 217 as from 1.4.06 (3.4.06 where rent payable weekly or at intervals of a week).
2.   Amended by Art 20(10) of SI 2007 No 688 as from 1.4.07 (2.4.07 where rent payable weekly or at intervals of a week).
3.   Amended by Art 20(11) of SI 2008 No 632 as from 1.4.08 (7.4.08 where rent payable weekly or in multiples of a week).
4.   Amended by reg 6(9)(f) of SI 2008 No 3157 as from 5.1.09.
5.   Amended by Art 20(11) of SI 2009 No 497 as from 1.4.09 (6.4.09 where rent payable weekly or at intervals of a week).
6.   Amended by Art 20(10) of SI 2010 No 793 as from 1.4.10 (5.4.10 where rent payable weekly or in multiples of a week).

Analysis
See the commentary to Sch 4 para 17 HB Regs on p550 and Sch 5 para 56 on p564).

22.   Except in the case of income from capital specified in Part 2 of Schedule 6, any actual income from capital.

Analysis
The combined effect of reg 29(1)(i) (which defines "income from capital" other than capital disregarded under Sch 6 Part 1 as income) and para 22 is that it is only actual income from any capital not specified in either Part 1 or Part 2 of Sch 6 that is disregarded. Instead, reg 29(2) provides a formula for calculating "deemed" income from the capital. Actual income from capital is only taken into account if the capital is specified in Sch 6 Part 2, but see para 24 below for a partial disregard.

[¹**23.**]

Amendment
1.   Omitted by reg 6(9)(g) of SI 2008 No 3157 as from 5.1.09.

[¹**24.** Where the total value of any capital specified in Part 2 (capital disregarded only for the purposes of determining deemed income) of Schedule 6 does not exceed £10,000, anyincome actually derived from such capital.]

Amendment

1.   Substituted by reg 6 of SI 2009 No 1676 as from 2.11.09.

Analysis

Under para 24, actual income from capital listed in Sch 6 Part 2 is disregarded, but only where the total value of it does not exceed £10,000. If the total value does exceed that amount, actual income from the capital is taken into account under reg 29(1)(i). See para 22 above for a disregard of actual income from capital not specified in Sch 6 Part 2.

SCHEDULE 6
REGULATION 44(2)
Capital to be disregarded

General Note to Sch 6

Sch 6 sets out the capital that is to be disregarded. It serves more than one purpose:
(1)   Capital listed in either Part 1 or Part 2 is not to be taken into account in working out if a claimant's capital exceeds the £16,000 capital limit: regs 43 and 44(2).
(2)   The capital specified in Part 1 is disregarded for the purposes of determining a claimant's income: reg 33(11)(a). In any event, actual income from the capital is not to be treated as "income": reg 29(1)(i).
(3)   Actual income from capital listed in Part 2 and from any other capital not disregarded under Part 1, is treated as income under reg 29(1)(i). Note however it is only taken into account if it is income from capital disregarded under Part 2 and then only if the total value exceeds £10,000: see Sch 5 para 24. Otherwise actual income from the capital is disregarded under Sch 5 para 22.
(4)   The capital specified in either Part 1 or Part 2 is disregarded for the purposes of determining "deemed" income: reg 33(11)(a) and (b). Other capital can be deemed to produce a weekly income under reg 29(2).

PART 1

General Note

Part 1 of Sch 6 lists capital that can be disregarded generally. If capital is in Part 1, actual income from it does not count as "income": reg 29(1)(i). In addition, the capital is not "deemed" to produce a weekly income under reg 29(2). This is confirmed by reg 33(11)(a).

Capital to be disregarded generally
1.   Any premises acquired for occupation by the claimant which he intends to occupy as his home within 26 weeks of the date of acquisition or such longer period as is reasonable in the circumstances to enable the claimant to obtain possession and commence occupation of the premises.
2.   Any premises which the claimant intends to occupy as his home, and in respect of which he is taking steps to obtain possession and has sought legal advice, or has commenced legal proceedings, with a view to obtaining possession, for a period of 26 weeks from the date on which he first sought such advice or first commenced such proceedings whichever is the earlier, or such longer period as is reasonable in the circumstances to enable him to obtain possession and commence occupation of those premises.
3.   Any premises which the claimant intends to occupy as his home to which essential repairs or alterations are required in order to render them fit for such occupation, for a period of 26 weeks from the date on which the claimant first takes steps to effect those repairs or alterations, or such longer period as is necessary to enable those repairs or alterations to be carried out.
4.   Any premises occupied in whole or in part–
(a)   by a person who is a relative of the claimant or of his partner as his home [¹ where that person has attained the qualifying age for state pension credit or is incapacitated];
(b)   by the former partner of the claimant as his home; but this provision shall not apply where the former partner is a person from whom the claimant is estranged or divorced or with whom he had formed a civil partnership that has been dissolved.

Amendment

1.   Amended by reg 31 of SI 2009 No 1488 as from 6.4.10.

5.   Any future interest in property of any kind, other than land or premises in respect of which the claimant has granted a subsisting lease or tenancy, including sub-leases or sub-tenancies.

6. Where a claimant has ceased to occupy what was formerly the dwelling occupied as the home following his estrangement or divorce from his former partner or the dissolution of a civil partnership with his former partner, that dwelling for a period of 26 weeks from the date on which he ceased to occupy that dwelling or, where the dwelling is occupied as the home by the former partner who is a lone parent, for so long as it is so occupied.

7. Any premises where the claimant is taking reasonable steps to dispose of the whole of his interest in those premises, for a period of 26 weeks from the date on which he first took such steps, or such longer period as is reasonable in the circumstances to enable him to dispose of those premises.

Analysis to paras 1 to 7
These are equivalent to HB Regs Sch 6 paras 2, 27, 28, 4, 7, 25 and 26 respectively (see p565).

---

8. All personal possessions.

Analysis
This is different to Sch 6 para 12 HB Regs because it contains no exception for possessions purchased in order to reduce capital and increase benefit. Unless the notional capital provision in reg 47 applies, the value of such possessions must be completely ignored.

---

9. The assets of any business owned in whole or in part by the claimant and for the purposes of which he is engaged as a self-employed earner or, if he has ceased to be engaged, for such period as may be reasonable in the circumstances to allow for disposal of those assets.

10. The assets of any business owned in whole or in part by the claimant if–

(a) he is not engaged as a self-employed earner in that business by reason of some disease or bodily or mental disablement; but

(b) he intends to become engaged (or, as the case may be, re-engaged) as a self-employed earner in that business as soon as he recovers or is able to become engaged, or re-engaged, in that business,

for a period of 26 weeks from the date on which the claim for housing benefit is made or, if it is unreasonable to expect him to become engaged or re-engaged in that business within that period, for such longer period as is reasonable in the circumstances to enable him to become so engaged or re-engaged.

Analysis to paras 9 and 10
These are equivalent to Sch 6 para 8 HB Regs (see p568).

---

11. The surrender value of any policy of life insurance.

12. The value of any funeral plan contract; and for this purpose, "funeral plan contract" means a contract under which–

(a) the claimant makes one or more payments to another person ("the provider");

(b) the provider undertakes to provide, or secure the provision of, a funeral in the United Kingdom for the claimant on his death; and

(c) the sole purpose of the plan is to provide or secure the provision of a funeral for the claimant on his death.

Analysis
This has no equivalent in Sch 6 HB Regs but is self-explanatory.

---

13. Where an ex-gratia payment has been made by the Secretary of State on or after 1st February 2001 in consequence of the imprisonment or internment of–

(a) the claimant;

(b) the claimant's partner;

(c) the claimant's deceased spouse or deceased civil partner; or

(d) the claimant's partner's deceased spouse or deceased civil partner,

by the Japanese during the Second World War, an amount equal to that payment.

14.–(1) Subject to sub-paragraph (2), the amount of any trust payment made to a claimant or a claimant's partner who is–

(a) a diagnosed person;

(b) a diagnosed person's partner or was a diagnosed person's partner at the time of the diagnosed person's death;

(c) a parent of a diagnosed person, a person acting in place of the diagnosed person's parents or a person who was so acting at the date of the diagnosed person's death.

(2) Where a trust payment is made to–

(a) a person referred to in sub-paragraph (1)(a) or (b), that sub-paragraph shall apply for the period beginning on the date on which the trust payment is made and ending on the date on which that person dies;

(b)   a person referred to in sub-paragraph (1)(c), that sub-paragraph shall apply for the period beginning on the date on which the trust payment is made and ending two years after that date.

(3)   Subject to sub-paragraph (4), the amount of any payment by a person to whom a trust payment has been made or of any payment out of the estate of a person to whom a trust payment has been made, which is made to a claimant or a claimant's partner who is–

(a)   the diagnosed person;

(b)   a diagnosed person's partner or was a diagnosed person's partner at the date of the diagnosed person's death; or

(c)   a parent of a diagnosed person, a person acting in place of the diagnosed person's parents or a person who was so acting at the date of the diagnosed person's death.

(4)   Where a payment such as referred to in sub-paragraph (3) is made to–

(a)   a person referred to in sub-paragraph (3)(a) or (b), that sub-paragraph shall apply for the period beginning on the date on which the payment is made and ending on the date on which that person dies;

(b)   a person referred to in sub-paragraph (3)(c), that sub-paragraph shall apply for the period beginning on the date on which the payment is made and ending two years after that date.

(5)   In this paragraph, a reference to a person–

(a)   being the diagnosed person's partner;

(b)   acting in place of the diagnosed person's parents,

at the date of the diagnosed person's death shall include a person who would have been such a person or a person who would have been so acting, but for the diagnosed person residing in a care home or an independent hospital.

(6)   In this paragraph–

"diagnosed person" means a person who has been diagnosed as suffering from, or who, after his death, has been diagnosed as having suffered from, variant Creutzfeldt-Jakob disease;

"relevant trust" means a trust established out of funds provided by the Secretary of State in respect of persons who suffered, or who are suffering, from variant Creutzfeldt-Jakob disease for the benefit of persons eligible for payments in accordance with its provisions;

"trust payment" means a payment under a relevant trust.

15.   The amount of any payment, other than a [¹ war pension], to compensate for the fact that the claimant, the claimant's partner, the claimant's deceased spouse or civil partner or the claimant's partner's deceased spouse or civil partner–

(a)   was a slave labourer or a forced labourer;

(b)   had suffered property loss or had suffered personal injury; or

(c)   was a parent of a child who had died,

during the Second World War.

Amendment

1.   Amended by reg 6(10)(a) of SI 2008 No 3157 as from 5.1.09.

16.–(1)   Any payment made under [² or by] –

(a)   the Macfarlane Trust, the Macfarlane (Special Payments) Trust, the Macfarlane (Special Payments) (No. 2) Trust, the Fund, the Eileen Trust [² , MFET Limited] , the Skipton Fund or the London Bombings Relief Charitable Fund (collectively referred to in this paragraph as "the Trusts"); or

(b)   the Independent Living [¹ Fund (2006)].

(2)   Any payment by or on behalf of a person who is suffering or who suffered from haemophilia or who is or was a qualifying person, which derives from a payment made under [² or by] any of the Trusts and which is made to or for the benefit of that person's partner or former partner from whom he is not, or where that person has died was not, estranged or divorced or with whom he has formed a civil partnership that has not been dissolved or, where that person has died, had not been dissolved at the time of that person's death.

(3)   Any payment by or on behalf of the partner or former partner of a person who is suffering or who suffered from haemophilia or who is or was a qualifying person provided that the partner or former partner and that person are not, or if either of them has died were not, estranged or divorced or, where the partner or former partner and that person have formed a civil partnership, the civil partnership has not been dissolved or, if either of them has died, had not been dissolved at the time of the death, which derives from a payment made under [² or by] any of the Trusts and which is made to or for the benefit of the person who is suffering from haemophilia or who is a qualifying person.

(4)   Any payment by a person who is suffering from haemophilia or who is a qualifying person, which derives from a payment under [² or by] any of the Trusts, where–

(a)   that person has no partner or former partner from whom he is not estranged or divorced or with whom he has formed a civil partnership that has not been dissolved nor any child who is or had been a member of that person's household; and

(b)   the payment is made either–

(i)   to that person's parent or step-parent; or

(ii)   where that person at the date of the payment is a child or a student who has not completed his full-time education and has no parent or step-parent, to any person standing in the place of his parent, but only for a period from the date of the payment until the end of two years from that person's death.

(5) Any payment out of the estate of a person who suffered from haemophilia or who was a qualifying person, which derives from a payment under [² or by] any of the Trusts, where–

   (a)   that person at the date of his death (''the relevant date'') had no partner or former partner from whom he was not estranged or divorced or with whom he had formed a civil partnership that had not been dissolved, nor any child who was or had been a member of his household; and

   (b)   the payment is made either–

      (i)   to that person's parent or step-parent; or

      (ii)   where that person at the relevant date was a child or a student who had not completed his full-time education and had no parent or step-parent, to any person standing in place of his parent,

but only for a period of two years from the relevant date.

(6) In the case of a person to whom or for whose benefit a payment referred to in this paragraph is made, any capital resource which derives from any payment of income or capital made under or deriving from any of the Trusts.

Modifications

References to "step-parent" in sub-paras (4)(b)(i) and (ii) and (5)(b)(i) and (ii) are modified by s246 Civil Partnership Act 2004 (see p1148) and Art 3 and Sch para 27 to SI 2005 No 3137 (see p1195).

Amendments

1.   Amended by reg 7(5)(b) of SI 2008 No 2767 as from 17.11.08.

2.   Amended by reg 9(3) and (5) of SI 2010 No 641 as from 1.4.10 (5.4.10 where rent payable weekly or in multiples of a week).

Analysis to paras 13 to 16

These are equivalent to HB Regs Sch 6 paras 54 (although there is no reference to the amount of the payment being £10,000), 55, 56 and 24 respectively (see p565).

17.–(1)   An amount equal to the amount of any payment made in consequence of any personal injury to the claimant or, if the claimant has a partner, to the partner.

(2)   Where the whole or part of the payment is administered–

[¹ (a)   by the High Court or the County Court under Rule 21.11(1) of the Civil Procedure Rules 1998, or the Court of Protection, or on behalf of a person where the payment can only be disposed of by order or direction of any such court;]

   (b)   in accordance with an order under Rule 36.14 of the Ordinary Cause Rules 1993 or under Rule 128 of those Rules; or

   (c)   in accordance with the terms of a trust established for the benefit of the claimant or his partner,

the whole of the amount so administered.

Amendment

1.   Substituted by reg 16(4) of SI 2006 No 2378 from the first day of the first benefit week to commence on or after 2.10.06.

Analysis

On sub-para (2), see Sch 6 paras 45 and 46 HB Regs on p576. For the words "in consequence of any personal injury" see reg 42(2) HB Regs on p373.

---

18.   Any amount specified in paragraphs 19, 20 [¹ , 21 or 26B] for a period of one year beginning with the date of receipt.

Amendment

1.   Amended by reg 6(10)(b) of SI 2008 No 3157 as from 5.1.09.

---

19.   Amounts paid under a policy of insurance in connection with the loss of or damage to the property occupied by the claimant as his home and to his personal possessions.

Analysis

By para 18, the amounts are disregarded for one year from the date of receipt.

---

20.   So much of any amounts paid to the claimant or deposited in the claimant's name for the sole purpose of–

   (a)   purchasing premises which the claimant intends to occupy as his home; or

(b)   effecting essential repairs or alterations to the premises occupied or intended to be occupied by the claimant as his home.

Analysis
By para 18, the amounts are disregarded for one year from the date of receipt.

21.–(1)   Subject to paragraph 22 any amount paid–
(a)   by way of arrears of benefit;
(b)   by way of compensation for the late payment of benefit;
(c)   in lieu of the payment of benefit;
(d)   to rectify, or compensate for, an official error, as defined for the purposes of paragraph 22, being an amount to which that paragraph does not apply;
(e)   by a local authority (including, in relation to England, a county council), or by the National Assembly for Wales, to or on behalf of the claimant or his partner relating to a service which is provided to develop or sustain the capacity of the claimant or his partner to live independently in his accommodation.
(2)   In sub-paragraph (1), "benefit" means–
(a)   attendance allowance under section 64 of the Act;
(b)   disability living allowance;
(c)   income support;
(d)   income-based jobseeker's allowance;
(e)   state pension credit;
(f)   housing benefit;
(g)   council tax benefit;
(h)   child tax credit;
(i)   an increase of a disablement pension under section 104 of the Act (increase where constant attendance is needed), and any further increase of such a pension under section 105 of the Act (increase for exceptionally severe disablement);
(j)   any amount included on account of the claimant's exceptionally severe disablement or need for constant attendance in a war disablement pension or a war widow's or widower's pension.
[¹ (k)   any discretionary housing payment paid pursuant to regulation 2(1) of the Discretionary Financial Assistance Regulations 2001; [²]
(l)   working tax credit.] [² or
[² (m)   income-related employment and support allowance.]

Amendments
1.   Inserted by reg 2(17) of SI 2005 No 2502 as amended by Sch 2 para 27 of SI 2006 No 217 as from 1.4.06 (3.4.06 where rent payable weekly or at intervals of a week).
2.   Amended by reg 41 of SI 2008 No 1082 as from 27.10.08.

Analysis
By para 18, the amounts are disregarded for one year from date of receipt. Para 21 covers arrears of benefit or compensatory payments and payments under the Supporting People scheme.
See also para 22 below where arrears of benefit are paid to compensate for "official error".

22.–(1)   Subject to sub-paragraph (3), any payment of £5,000 or more which has been made to rectify, or to compensate for, an official error relating to a relevant benefit and has been received by the claimant in full on or after the day on which he became entitled to benefit under these Regulations or the Housing Benefit Regulations 2006.
(2)   Subject to sub-paragraph (3), the total amount of any payments disregarded under–
(a)   paragraph 7(2) of Schedule 10 to the Income Support Regulations;
(b)   paragraph 12(2) of Schedule 8 to the Jobseeker's Allowance Regulations;
(c)   paragraph 9(2) of [¹ Schedule 6] to the Housing Benefit Regulations 2006;
(d)   paragraph 20A of Schedule 5 to the State Pension Credit Regulations 2002,
[² (e)   paragraph 11(2) of Schedule 9 to the Employment and Support Allowance Regulations,]
where the award in respect of which the payments last fell to be disregarded under those Regulations either terminated immediately before the relevant date or is still in existence at that date.
(3)   Any disregard which applies under sub-paragraph (1) or (2) shall have effect until the award comes to an end.
(4)   In this paragraph–
"the award", except in sub-paragraph (2), means–
(a)   the award of benefit under these Regulations during which the relevant sum or, where it is paid in more than one instalment, the first instalment of that sum is received; and
(b)   where that award is followed by one or more further awards which, or each of which, begins immediately after the previous award ends, such further awards until the end of the last such award, provided that, for such further awards, the claimant–

(i)   is the person who received the relevant sum;

(ii)   is the partner of that person; or

(iii)   was the partner of that person at the date of his death;

"official error" –

(a)   where the error relates to housing benefit or council tax benefit, has the meaning given by regulation 1(2) of the Decisions and Appeals Regulations;

(b)   where the error relates to any other relevant benefit, has the meaning given by regulation 1(3) of the Social Security and Child Support (Decisions and Appeals) Regulations 1999;

"the relevant date" means–

(a)   in the case of an existing award of benefit under these Regulations or the Housing Benefit Regulations 2006, 6th October 2003; and

(b)   in any other case, the date on which the claim for benefit under these Regulations or the Housing Benefit Regulations 2006 was made;

"relevant benefit" means any benefit specified in paragraph 21(2); and

"the relevant sum" means the payment referred to in sub-paragraph (1) or the total amount referred to in sub-paragraph (2).

Amendments

1.   Amended by reg 4(9) of SI 2008 No 1042 as from 19.5.08.

2.   Amended by reg 41(b) of SI 2008 No 1082 as from 27.10.08.

Analysis

Arrears of relevant benefits (for which see para 21(2)) are disregarded for longer than the year allowed under para 21 if the payment is £5,000 or more and was made to rectify or compensate for an "official error" (defined in sub-para (4)). The arrears must have been received in full on or after the day the claimant became entitled to HB or if paid before then, the current award of HB must follow immediately from a previous award of IS, income-based JSA, income-related ESA, PC or HB, or must still be being disregarded in an award of one of those benefits: paras (1) and (2) and the definition of "relevant date" in para (4). The arrears are disregarded until the award ends: sub-para (3).

---

23.   Where a capital asset is held in a currency other than Sterling, any banking charge or commission payable in converting that capital into Sterling.

24.   The value of the right to receive income from an occupational pension scheme or a personal pension scheme.

[¹**25.**]

Amendment

1.   Omitted by reg 5(6) of SI 2007 No 1749 as from 16.7.07.

---

26.   The dwelling occupied as the home; but only one dwelling shall be disregarded under this paragraph.

[¹**26A.**   Where a person elects to be entitled to a lump sum under Schedule 5 or 5A to the Contributions and Benefits Act or under Schedule 1 to the Graduated Retirement Benefit Regulations, or is treated as having made such an election, and a payment has been made pursuant to that election, an amount equal to–

(a)   except where sub-paragraph (b) applies, the amount of any payment or payments made on account of that lump sum;

(b)   the amount of that lump sum,

but only for so long as that person does not change that election in favour of an increase of pension or benefit.]

Amendment

1.   Inserted by reg 11(4) of SI 2005 No 2677 and reg 2 of SI 2006 No 217 as from 6.4.06.

[¹**26B.**   Any arrears of supplementary pension which is disregarded under paragraph 4 of Schedule 5 (amounts to be disregarded in the calculation of income other than earnings) or of any amount which is disregarded under paragraph 5 or 6 of that Schedule.]

Amendment

1.   Inserted by reg 6(10)(d) of SI 2008 No 3157 as from 5.1.09.

Analysis

By para 18, the arrears are disregarded for one year from the date of receipt.

[¹**26C.** Any payment made under Part 8A of the Act (entitlement to health in pregnancy grant).]

Amendment

1.   Inserted by reg 7(8) of SI 2009 No 583 as from 6.4.09.

PART 2

General Note

Part 2 lists capital that is disregarded "only for the purposes of determining deemed income" under reg 29(2). See also reg 33(11)(b). However, note that it is also disregarded for the purposes of the capital limit by reg 44(2). If capital is in this list, although it is not treated as producing a weekly deemed income, actual income from the capital can be taken into account, subject to para 24 of Sch 5.

Capital disregarded only for the purposes of determining deemed income

27.   The value of the right to receive any income under a life interest or from a life rent.

Analysis

This is the equivalent, save for the fact that the disregard only operates for the calculation of tariff income and the capital limit, of HB Regs Sch 6 para 15 (see p570).

28.   The value of the right to receive any rent except where the claimant has a reversionary interest in the property in respect of which rent is due.

29.   The value of the right to receive any income under an annuity or the surrender value (if any) of such an annuity.

Analysis

This is the equivalent, save for the fact that the disregard only operates for the calculation of tariff income and the capital limit, of HB Regs Sch 6 para 13 (see p570).

30.   Where property is held under a trust, other than–

(a)   a charitable trust within the meaning of the Charities Act 1993; or

(b)   a trust set up with any payment to which paragraph 16 of this Schedule applies,

and under the terms of the trust, payments fall to be made, or the trustees have a discretion to make payments, to or for the benefit of the claimant or the claimant's partner, or both, that property.

Analysis

Para 30 requires beneficial interests under a trust to be ignored.

[² SCHEDULE 7

Amendments

1.   Amended by reg 19 of SI 2007 No 2869 as from 7.4.08 (or if reg 1(5) of that SI applies, on the day on or after 7.4.08 when the first of the events specified in reg 1(6) applies, or from 6.4.09 if none have before that date).

2.   Omitted by reg 6(4)(d) of SI 2008 No 959 as from 6.10.08.

SCHEDULE 8
REGULATION 71
Matters to be included in decision notice

PART 1
General

1.   The statement of matters to be included in any decision notice issued by a relevant authority to a person, and referred to in regulation 71 (notification of decisions) and in regulation 10 of the Decisions and Appeals Regulations are those matters set out in the following provisions of this Schedule.

2.   Every decision notice shall include a statement as to the right of any person affected by that decision to request a written statement under regulation 71(2) (requests for statement of reasons) and the manner and time in which to do so.

3.   Every decision notice shall include a statement as to the right of any person affected by that decision to make an application for a revision in accordance with regulation 4(1)(a) of the Decisions and Appeals Regulations and, where appropriate, to appeal against that decision and the manner and time in which to do so.

4.   Every decision notice following an application for a revision in accordance with regulation 4(1)(a) of the Decisions and Appeals Regulations shall include a statement as to whether the original decision in

respect of which the person made his representations has been confirmed or revised and where the relevant authority has not revised the decision the reasons why not.

5. Every decision notice following an application for a revision in accordance with regulation 4(1)(a) of the Decisions and Appeals Regulations shall, if the original decision has been revised, include a statement as to the right of any person affected by that decision to apply for a revision in accordance with regulation 4(1)(a) of those Regulations and the manner and time in which to do so.

6. An authority may include in the decision notice any other matters not prescribed by this Schedule which it sees fit, whether expressly or by reference to some other document available without charge to the person.

7. Parts 2, 3 and 6 of this Schedule shall apply only to the decision notice given on a claim.

8. Where a decision notice is given following a revision of an earlier decision–

(a) made of the authority's own motion which results in a revision of that earlier decision; or

(b) made following an application for a revision in accordance with regulation 4(1)(a) of the Decisions and Appeals Regulations, whether or not resulting in a revision of that earlier decision,

that notice shall, subject to paragraph 6, contain a statement only as to all the matters revised.

PART 2
Awards where state pension credit [³ or an extended payment (qualifying contributory benefits] is payable

9.–(1) Where a person on state pension credit is awarded housing benefit, the decision notice shall include a statement as to–

(a) his weekly eligible rent, if any; and

(b) the amount and an explanation of any deduction made under paragraph 6(2) or (3) of Schedule 1 (fuel deductions), if any, and that the deduction may be varied if he provides to the authority evidence on which it may estimate the actual or approximate amount of that service charge; and

(c) the amount of and the category of non-dependant deductions made under regulation 55 (non-dependant deductions), if any; and

(d) the normal weekly amount of rent allowance, or rent rebate as the case may be, to which he is entitled; and

(e) in the case of a rent allowance and a [² rent rebate] paid as if it were a rent allowance, the day of payment, and the period in respect of which payment of that allowance is to be made; and

(f) the first day of entitlement to an allowance or rebate; and

(g) his duty to notify any change of circumstances which might affect his entitlement to, or the amount of, housing benefit and (without prejudice to the extent of the duty owed under regulation 69 (duty to notify changes of circumstances)) the kind of change of circumstances which is to be notified, either upon the notice or by reference to some other document available to him on application and without charge.

(2) In a case where a person on state pension credit has entitlement only to the savings credit, the following additional matters shall also be set out–

(a) the applicable amount and the basis of calculation;

(b) the amount of the savings credit [¹] taken into account;

(c) the amount of the person's income and capital as notified to the local authority by the Secretary of State and taken into account for the purposes of the housing benefit assessment;

(d) any modification of the claimant's income or capital made in accordance with regulation 27 (calculation of claimant's income in savings credit only cases); and

(e) the amount of the claimant's capital if paragraph (7) of regulation 27 applies in his case.

[³ (3) Where a claimant is entitled to an extended payment (qualifying contributory benefits) in accordance with regulation 53, the decision notice shall include a statement as to the matters set out in paragraph 9(1).]

Amendments

1. Amended by reg 2(18) of SI 2005 No 2502 as amended by Sch 2 para 27 of SI 2006 No 217 as from 1.4.06 (3.4.06 where rent payable weekly or at intervals of a week).

2. Amended by reg 4(10) of SI 2008 No 1042 as from 19.5.08.

3. Amended by reg 6(5) of SI 2008 No 959 as from 6.10.08.

PART 3
Awards where no state pension credit is payable

10. Where a person is not on state pension credit but is awarded housing benefit, the decision notice shall include a statement as to–

(a) the matters set out in paragraph 9; and

(b) his applicable amount and how it is calculated; and

(c) his weekly earnings; and

(d) his weekly income other than earnings.

PART 4
Awards where direct payments made to landlords
11. Where a decision has been made under regulation 76 or 77 (circumstances in which payment is to be made, or may be made, direct to a landlord), the decision notice shall include a statement–
(a) as to the amount of housing benefit which is to be paid direct to the landlord and the date from which it is to be paid; and
(b) informing the landlord of the duty imposed upon him to notify the local authority of–
  (i) any change in circumstances which might affect the claimant's entitlement to housing benefit, or the amount of housing benefit payable in his case; and
  (ii) the kind of change of circumstances which is to be notified,
and the notice shall be sent both to the claimant and to the landlord; and
(c) informing both landlords and claimants that where a payment of housing benefit is recoverable from a landlord and the recovery is made from housing benefit payable to the landlord to discharge (in whole or in part) an obligation owed to him by a claimant, then, in a case where that claimant is not the person on whose behalf the recoverable amount was paid, that obligation shall nonetheless be taken to be discharged by the amount so recovered.
12. In this Schedule, "landlord" has the same meaning as in regulation 76.

PART 5
Notice where income of non-dependant is treated as claimant's
13. Where an authority makes a decision under regulation 24 (circumstances in which income of non-dependant is to be treated as claimant's) the decision notice shall contain a statement as to–
(a) the fact that a decision has been made by reference to the income and capital of the claimant's non-dependant; and
(b) the relevant authority's reasons for making that decision.

PART 6
Notice where no award is made
14. Where a person is not awarded housing benefit–
(a) either on grounds of income or because the amount of any housing benefit is less than the minimum housing benefit prescribed by regulation 56, the decision notice shall include a statement as to–
  (i) the matters set out in paragraphs 9(1)(a) to (c), and in a case where the amount of entitlement is less than the minimum amount of housing benefit prescribed, paragraph 9(1)(d) also; and
  (ii) the matters set out in paragraphs 10(b) to (d) where the person is not on [¹ state pension credit]; and
  (iii) where the amount of entitlement is less than the minimum amount of housing benefit prescribed, that fact and that such entitlement is not payable;
(b) for any reason other than one mentioned in sub-paragraph (a), the decision notice shall include a statement as to the reason why no award has been made.

Amendment
1. Amended by reg 7(7) of SI 2008 No 2767 as from 6.4.09.

PART 7
Notice where recoverable overpayment
15.–(1) Where the appropriate authority makes a decision that there is a recoverable overpayment within the meaning of regulation 81 (recoverable overpayments), the decision notice shall include a statement as to–
(a) the fact that there is a recoverable overpayment; and
(b) the reason why there is a recoverable overpayment; and
(c) the amount of the recoverable overpayment; and
(d) how the amount of the recoverable overpayment was calculated; and
(e) the benefit weeks to which the recoverable overpayment relates; and
(f) where recovery of the recoverable overpayment is to be made by deduction from a rent allowance or rebate, as the case may be, that fact and the amount of the deduction.
(2) In a case where it is–
(a) determined that there is a recoverable overpayment;
(b) determined that that overpayment is recoverable from a landlord; and
(c) decided that recovery of that overpayment is to be made by deduction from a rent allowance paid to that landlord to discharge (in whole or in part) an obligation owed to him by a claimant ("claimant A"), not being the claimant on whose behalf the recoverable amount was paid,
the decision notice sent to that landlord shall identify both–
  (i) the person on whose behalf the recoverable amount was paid to that landlord; and
  (ii) claimant A.

[¹ SCHEDULE 9
REGULATION 103

Former pathfinder authorities

Amendment
1. Substituted by reg 20(2) of SI 2007 No 2869 as from 7.4.08.

PART 1
Former pathfinder authorities

Argyll and Bute
Blackpool
Brighton and Hove
Conwy
Coventry
East Riding of Yorkshire
Edinburgh
Guildford
Leeds
Lewisham
North East Lincolnshire
Norwich
Pembrokeshire
St Helens
Salford
South Norfolk
Teignbridge
Wandsworth

PART 2
Application of the Regulations
1.   These Regulations shall apply to former pathfinder authorities subject to the provisions of this Part of this Schedule.

Amendment of regulation 2
2.   In regulation 2(1) (interpretation)–
(a)   in the definition of ''eligible rent'', in sub-paragraph (a) for ''or 12D (eligible rent and maximum rent (LHA))'' substitute '', 12D (eligible rent and maximum rent (LHA)) or any of regulations 12E to 12K (transitional protection for pathfinder cases)'';
(b)   after the definition of ''maximum rent (LHA)'' insert–

'' ''maximum rent (standard local rent)'' means a maximum rent (standard local rate) determined in accordance with regulation 13A;''.

Amendment of regulation 11
3.   In regulation 11(1) (eligible housing costs)–
(a)   in paragraph (c) omit ''or''; and
(b)   after sub-paragraph (d) insert–

''or
(e)   any of regulations 12E to 12K (transitional protection for pathfinder cases), and regulations 13C (when a maximum rent (LHA) is to be determined) and 13D (determination of a maximum rent (LHA)),''.

Amendment of regulation 12B
4.   In regulation 12B(1) (eligible rent) for ''or 12D (eligible rent and maximum rent (LHA))'' substitute '', 12D (eligible rent and maximum rent (LHA)) or any of regulations 12E to 12K (transitional protection for pathfinder cases)''.

Amendment of regulation 12D
5.   In regulation 12D (eligible rent and maximum rent (LHA)) before paragraph (1) insert–

'' (A1) This regulation shall not apply where any of regulations 12E to 12K (transitional protection for pathfinder cases) apply.''

907

Insertion of regulations 12E to 12K

6.   After regulation 12D (eligible rent and maximum rent (LHA)) insert–

'' **Basic transitional protection for pathfinder cases**

12E.–(1)   This regulation applies where–

(a)   reference was made to a maximum rent (standard local rate) in determining the amount of the eligible rent which applied immediately before 7th April 2008;

(b)   on 7th April 2008 the local authority determines a maximum rent (LHA) by virtue of regulation 13C(4A)(a); and

(c)   regulations 12F (cases where the claimant enjoyed protection on death before 7th April 2008) and 12G (cases where the claimant enjoyed 13 week protection before 7th April 2008) do not apply.

(2)   Where this regulation applies, the claimant's eligible rent is–

(a)   the maximum rent (LHA) where that is higher than the eligible rent which applied immediately before 7th April 2008; or

(b)   the amount of the eligible rent which applied immediately before 7th April 2008.

(3)   Where the eligible rent is the amount of the eligible rent which applied immediately before 7th April 2008, it will continue to apply until, on or after 7th April 2008, the first of the following events occurs–

(a)   the relevant authority is required to determine a maximum rent (LHA) by virtue of regulation 13C(2)(d)(i) (change of category of dwelling) because the claimant has become entitled to a larger category of dwelling and the maximum rent (LHA) is higher than that eligible rent;

(b)   the relevant authority is required to determine a maximum rent (LHA) by virtue of regulation 13C(2)(d)(i) (change of category of dwelling) because the claimant has become entitled to a smaller category of dwelling;

(c)   the relevant authority is required to determine an eligible rent following a change of dwelling;

(d)   the relevant authority is required to determine an eligible rent in accordance with regulation 12H (cases where a death occurs in the first year on or after 7th April 2008) following the death of a linked person;

(e)   the relevant authority determines a maximum rent (LHA) on 7th April 2009 by virtue of regulation 13C(4A)(b).

(4)   Where the eligible rent is the maximum rent (LHA), it shall be treated as if it had been determined in accordance with regulation 12D(2)(a) (eligible rent is maximum rent (LHA)) and shall apply according to the provisions of regulation 12D (eligible rent and maximum rent (LHA)).

Cases where the claimant enjoyed protection on death before 7th April 2008

12F.–(1) This regulation applies where–

(a)   immediately before 7th April 2008 the claimant enjoyed protection on death in accordance with regulation 12A(4)(a)(ii) (pathfinder protection on death based on reckonable rent); and

(b)   on 7th April 2008 the local authority determines a maximum rent (LHA) by virtue of regulation 13C(4A)(a).

(2)   Where this regulation applies, the claimant's eligible rent is–

(a)   the maximum rent (LHA) where that is higher than the eligible rent which applied immediately before 7th April 2008; or

(b)   the amount of the eligible rent which applied immediately before 7th April 2008.

(3)   Where the eligible rent is the amount of the eligible rent which applied immediately before 7th April 2008, it will continue to apply until, on or after 7th April 2008, the first of the following events occurs–

(a)   the end of 12 months after the death to which the protection relates;

(b)   the relevant authority is required to determine a maximum rent (LHA) by virtue of regulation 13C(2)(d)(i) (change of category of dwelling) and it is higher than that eligible rent;

(c)   the relevant authority is required to determine an eligible rent following a change of dwelling;

(d)   the relevant authority is required to determine an eligible rent in accordance with regulation 12H (cases where a death occurs in the first year on or after 7th April 2008) following the death of a linked person;

(4)   Where the eligible rent ceases to apply because of paragraph (3)(a), the eligible rent will be the maximum rent (LHA) which would have applied but for the transitional protection.

(5)   Where the eligible rent is the maximum rent (LHA), it shall be treated as if it had been determined in accordance with regulation 12D(2)(a) (eligible rent is maximum rent (LHA)) and shall apply according to the provisions of regulation 12D (eligible rent and maximum rent (LHA)).

Cases where the claimant enjoyed 13 week protection before 7th April 2008

12G.–(1)   This regulation applies where–

(a)   immediately before 7th April 2008 the claimant enjoyed 13 week protection in accordance with regulation 12A(6)(a) (lo cal housing allowance pathfinder 13 week protection); and

(b)   on 7th April 2008 the local authority determines a maximum rent (LHA) by virtue of regulation 13C(4A)(a).

(2)   Where this regulation applies, the claimant's eligible rent is–

(a)   the maximum rent (LHA) where that is higher than the eligible rent which applied immediately before 7th April 2008; or

(b)   the amount of the eligible rent which applied immediately before 7th April 2008.

(3)   Where the eligible rent is the amount of the eligible rent which applied immediately before 7th April 2008, it will continue to apply until, on or after 7th April 2008, the first of the following events occurs–

(a)   the end of the day when the protection expires, namely 13 weeks after the date of the claim;

(b)   the relevant authority is required to determine a maximum rent (LHA) by virtue of regulation 13C(2)(d)(i) (change of category of dwelling) and it is higher than that eligible rent;

(c)   the relevant authority is required to determine an eligible rent following a change of dwelling;

(d)   the relevant authority is required to determine an eligible rent in accordance with regulation 12H (cases where a death occurs in the first year on or after 7th April 2008) following the death of a linked person.

(4)   Where the eligible rent ceases to apply because of paragraph (3)(a), the eligible rent will be the maximum rent (LHA) which would have applied but for the transitional protection.

(5)   Where the eligible rent is the maximum rent (LHA), it shall be treated as if it had been determined in accordance with regulation 12D(2)(a) (eligible rent is maximum rent (LHA)) and shall apply according to the provisions of regulation 12D (eligible rent and maximum rent (LHA)).

Cases where a death occurs in the first year on or after 7th April 2008

12H.–(1)   This regulation applies where–

(a)   the eligible rent is that specified in regulation 12E(2)(b) (basic transitional protection for pathfinder cases), 12F(2)(b) (transitional protection where the claimant enjoyed protection on death before 7th April 2008), 12G(2)(b) (transitional protection where the claimant enjoyed 13 week protection before 7th April 2008) or paragraph (2)(b) of this regulation;

(b)   a linked person dies on or after 7th April 2008 and before 7th April 2009;

(c)   the claimant occupies the same dwelling as the linked person at the date of death; and

(d)   the relevant authority determines a maximum rent (LHA) by virtue of regulation 13C(2)(d)(i) or (ii) (change of category of dwelling or death of a linked person).

(2)   Where this regulation applies, the claimant's eligible rent is–

(a)   the maximum rent (LHA) where that is higher than the eligible rent which applied immediately before the date of the death; or

(b)   the amount of the eligible rent which applied immediately before the date of the death.

(3)   Where the eligible rent is the amount of the eligible rent which applied immediately before the date of death, it will continue to apply until, on or after the date of the death, the first of the following events occurs–

(a)   the end of 12 months from the date of the death;

(b)   the relevant authority is required to determine a maximum rent (LHA) by virtue of regulation 13C(2)(d)(i) (change of category of dwelling) and it is higher than that eligible rent;

(c)   the relevant authority is required to determine an eligible rent following a change of dwelling;

(d)   the relevant authority is required to determine an eligible rent in accordance with this regulation following the death of another linked person.

(4)   Where the eligible rent is the maximum rent (LHA), it shall be treated as if it had been determined in accordance with regulation 12D(2)(a) (eligible rent is maximum rent (LHA)) and shall apply according to the provisions of regulation 12D (eligible rent and maximum rent (LHA)).

(5)   For the purposes of paragraph (1)(c), a claimant shall be treated as occupying the dwelling if regulation 7(13) is satisfied and for that purpose paragraph (13) of regulation 7 shall have effect as if sub-paragraph (b) were omitted.

Basic transitional protection in the second year and subsequent years after 7th April 2008

12I.–(1)   This regulation applies where–

(a)   immediately before 7th April 2009 the claimant was enjoying basic transitional protection under regulation 12E; and

(b)   the local authority determines a maximum rent (LHA) by virtue of 13C(4A)(b) on 7th April 2009.

(2)   Where this regulation applies, the claimant's eligible rent is–

(a)   the maximum rent (LHA) where it is higher than the eligible rent applying immediately before 7th April 2008; or

(b)   in any other case, the lower of–

(i)   the amount of the eligible rent applying immediately before 7th April 2008; or

(ii)   the amount of the cap rent by reference to which the maximum rent (LHA) was determined, plus £15.

(3)   Where the claimant's eligible rent is determined in accordance with paragraph (2)(b), it continues to apply until, on or after 7th April 2009, the first of the following events occurs–

(a)   the relevant authority is required to determine a maximum rent (LHA) by virtue of regulation 13C(2)(d)(i) (change of category of dwelling) because the claimant has become entitled to a larger category of dwelling or 13C(3) (anniversary of the LHA date) and the maximum rent (LHA) is higher than that eligible rent;

(b)   the relevant authority is required to determine a maximum rent (LHA) by virtue of regulation 13C(2)(d)(i) (change of category of dwelling) because the claimant has become entitled to a smaller category of dwelling;

(c)   the relevant authority is required to determine an eligible rent following a change of dwelling;

HB (Persons who have attained the qualifying age for state pension credit) Regulations 2006

(d)   the relevant authority is required to determine an eligible rent in accordance with regulation 12K (protection on death in the second and subsequent years after 7th April 2008) following the death of a linked person.

(4)   Where the eligible rent is the maximum rent (LHA), it shall be treated as if it had been determined in accordance with regulation 12D(2)(a) (eligible rent is maximum rent (LHA)) and shall apply according to the provisions of regulation 12D (eligible rent and maximum rent (LHA)).

Transitional protection in the second year after 7th April 2008 where the claimant is already enjoying protection on death

12J.–(1)   This regulation applies where–

(a)   immediately before 7th April 2009 the claimant was enjoying transitional protection on death under regulation 12H (cases where a death occurs in the first year on or after 7th April 2008); and

(b)   the local authority determines a maximum rent (LHA) by virtue of regulation 13C(4A)(b) on 7th April 2009 .

(2)   Where this regulation applies, the claimant's eligible rent is–

(a)   the maximum rent (LHA) where that is higher than the eligible rent which applied immediately before the date of the death to which the protection relates; or

(b)   the amount of the eligible rent which applied immediately before the date of the death.

(3)   Where the eligible rent which applies is the one that applied immediately before the date of the death, it continues to apply until, on or after the date of the death, the first of the following events occurs–

(a)   the end of 12 months after the date of the death to which the protection relates;

(b)   the relevant authority is required to determine a maximum rent (LHA) by virtue of regulation 13C(2)(d)(i) (change of category of dwelling) and it is higher than that eligible rent;

(c)   the relevant authority is required to determine an eligible rent following a change of dwelling;

(d)   the relevant authority is required to determine an eligible rent in accordance with regulation 12K (protection on death in the second and subsequent years after 7th April 2008) following the death of a linked person.

(4)   Where the eligible rent ceases to apply because of paragraph (3)(a) the eligible rent is the one that would have applied if the relevant authority not determined an eligible rent in accordance with regulation 12H(2)(b) (transitional protection where a death occurs in the first year on or after 7th April 2008).

(5)   Where the eligible rent is the maximum rent (LHA), it shall be treated as if it had been determined in accordance with regulation 12D(2)(a) (eligible rent is maximum rent (LHA)) and shall apply according to the provisions of regulation 12D (eligible rent and maximum rent (LHA)).

Protection on death in the second and subsequent years after 7th April 2008

12K.–(1)   This regulation applies where–

(a)   the claimant's eligible rent is that specified in regulation 12I(2)(b) (basic transitional protection in the second and subsequent years after 7th April 2008), 12J(2)(b) (transitional protection in the second year after 7th April 2008 where the claimant is already enjoying protection on death) or paragraph (2)(b) of this regulation; and

(b)   a linked person dies on or after 7th April 2009;

(c)   the claimant occupies the same dwelling as the linked person at the date of death; and

(d)   the relevant authority determines a maximum rent (LHA) by virtue of regulation 13C(2)(d)(i) or (ii) (change of category of dwelling or death of a linked person).

(2)   Where this regulation applies, the claimant's eligible rent is–

(a)   the maximum rent (LHA) where that is higher than the eligible rent which applied immediately before the date of the death; or

(b)   the amount of eligible rent which applied immediately before the death.

(3)   Where the eligible rent which applies is the one that applied immediately before the date of the death, it will continue to apply until, on or after the date of the death, the first of the following events occurs–

(a)   the end of 12 months from the date of the death;

(b)   the relevant authority is required to determine a maximum rent (LHA) by virtue of regulation 13C(2)(d)(i) or (3) (change of category of dwelling or anniversary of the LHA date) and it is higher than that eligible rent;

(c)   the relevant authority is required to determine an eligible rent following a change of dwelling;

(d)   the relevant authority is required to determine an eligible rent in accordance with this regulation following the death of another linked person.

(4)   Where the eligible rent ceases to apply because of paragraph (3)(a) the eligible rent is the one that would have applied but had the relevant authority not determined an eligible rent in accordance with this regulation.

(5)   Where the eligible rent is the maximum rent (LHA), it shall be treated as if it had been determined in accordance with regulation 12D(2)(a) (eligible rent is maximum rent (LHA)) and shall apply according to the provisions of regulation 12D (eligible rent and maximum rent (LHA)).

(6)   For the purposes of paragraph (1)(c), a claimant shall be treated as occupying the dwelling if regulation 7(13) is satisfied and for that purpose paragraph (13) of regulation 7 shall have effect as if sub-paragraph (b) were omitted.''.

Amendment of regulation 13C

7. In regulation 13C (when a maximum rent (LHA) is to be determined)–

(a) in paragraph (1) for ''paragraphs (2) or (3)'' substitute ''paragraphs (2), (3) or (4A)'';

(b) in paragraph (3) after ''LHA date'' insert ''except where paragraph (4A)(b) applies'';

(c) after paragraph (4) insert–

'' (4A) This paragraph applies where it is–

(a) 7th April 2008 and reference was made to a maximum rent (standard local rate) in determining the amount of the eligible rent which applied immediately before 7th April 2008; or

(b) 7th April 2009 and the eligible rent which applies on that date was determined in accordance with regulation 12E(2)(b) (basic transitional protection for pathfinder cases) or 12H(2)(b) (transitional protection where a death occurs in the first year on or after 7th April 2008).''.

Amendment of regulation 13D

8. In regulation 13D(12) (determination of a maximum rent (LHA)) in the definition of ''relevant date'' after sub-paragraph (c) insert–

'' (d) 7th April 2008;

(e) 7th April 2009.'']

[¹SCHEDULE 10
ELECTRONIC COMMUNICATION

Amendment

1. Inserted by Art 3(5) of SI 2006 No 2968 as from 20.12.06.

PART 1
Introduction

Interpretation

1. In this Schedule ''official computer system'' means a computer system maintained by or on behalf of the relevant authority or of the Secretary of State for sending, receiving, processing or storing of any claim, certificate, notice, information or evidence.

PART 2
Electronic Communication – General Provisions

Conditions for the use of electronic communication

2.–(1) The relevant authority may use an electronic communication in connection with claims for, and awards of, benefit under these Regulations.

(2) A person other than the relevant authority may use an electronic communication in connection with the matters referred to in sub-paragraph (1) if the conditions specified in sub-paragraphs (3) to (6) are satisfied.

(3) The first condition is that the person is for the time being permitted to use an electronic communication by an authorisation given by means of a direction of the Chief Executive of the relevant authority.

(4) The second condition is that the person uses an approved method of–

(a) authenticating the identity of the sender of the communication;

(b) electronic communication;

(c) authenticating any claim or notice delivered by means of an electronic communication; and

(d) subject to sub-paragraph (7), submitting to the relevant authority any claim, certificate, notice, information or evidence.

(5) The third condition is that any claim, certificate, notice, information or evidence sent by means of an electronic communication is in a form approved for the purposes of this Schedule.

(6) The fourth condition is that the person maintains such records in written or electronic form as may be specified in a direction given by the Chief Executive of the relevant authority.

(7) Where the person uses any method other than the method approved of submitting any claim, certificate, notice, information or evidence, that claim, certificate, notice, information or evidence shall be treated as not having been submitted.

(8) In this paragraph ''approved'' means approved by means of a direction given by the Chief Executive of the relevant authority for the purposes of this Schedule.

Use of intermediaries

3. The relevant authority may use intermediaries in connection with–

(a) the delivery of any claim, certificate, notice, information or evidence by means of an electronic communication; and

(b)   the authentication or security of anything transmitted by such means,
and may require other persons to use intermediaries in connection with those matters.

PART 3
Electronic Communication – Evidential Provisions

Effect of delivering information by means of electronic communication
4.–(1)   Any claim, certificate, notice, information or evidence which is delivered by means of an electronic communication shall be treated as having been delivered in the manner or form required by any provision of these Regulations, on the day the conditions imposed–
(a)   by this Schedule; and
(b)   by or under an enactment,
are satisfied.
(2)   The relevant authority may, by a direction, determine that any claim, certificate, notice, information or evidence is to be treated as delivered on a different day (whether earlier or later) from the day provided for in sub-paragraph (1).
(3)   Information shall not be taken to have been delivered to an official computer system by means of an electronic communication unless it is accepted by the system to which it is delivered.

Proof of identity of sender or recipient of information
5.   If it is necessary to prove, for the purpose of any legal proceedings, the identity of–
(a)   the sender of any claim, certificate, notice, information or evidence delivered by means of an electronic communication to an official computer system; or
(b)   the recipient of any such claim, certificate, notice, information or evidence delivered by means of an electronic communication from an official computer system,
the sender or recipient, as the case may be, shall be presumed to be the person whose name is recorded as such on that official computer system.

Proof of delivery of information
6.–(1)   If it is necessary to prove, for the purpose of any legal proceedings, that the use of an electronic communication has resulted in the delivery of any claim, certificate, notice, information or evidence this shall be presumed to have been the case where–
(a)   any such claim, certificate, notice, information or evidence has been delivered to the relevant authority, if the delivery of that claim, certificate, notice, information or evidence has been recorded on an official computer system; or
(b)   any such claim, certificate, notice, information or evidence has been delivered by the relevant authority, if the delivery of that certificate, notice, information or evidence has been recorded on an official computer system.
(2)   If it is necessary to prove, for the purpose of any legal proceedings, that the use of an electronic communication has resulted in the delivery of any such claim, certificate, notice, information or evidence, this shall be presumed not to be the case, if that claim, certificate, notice, information or evidence delivered to the relevant authority has not been recorded on an official computer system.
(3)   If it is necessary to prove, for the purpose of any legal proceedings, when any such claim, certificate, notice, information or evidence sent by means of an electronic communication has been received, the time and date of receipt shall be presumed to be that recorded on an official computer system.

Proof of content of information
7.   If it is necessary to prove, for the purpose of any legal proceedings, the content of any claim, certificate, notice, information or evidence sent by means of an electronic communication, the content shall be presumed to be that recorded on an official computer system.]

The Council Tax Benefit (Persons who have attained the qualifying age for state pension credit) Regulations 2006

2006 No.216

ARRANGEMENT OF REGULATIONS

PART 1
General

1. Citation and commencement
2. Interpretation
3. Definition of non-dependant
4. Section 1(1A) of the Administration Act disapplied
5. Application of Regulations
6. Remunerative work
7. Persons from abroad
7A. Entitlement of a refugee to council tax benefit
8. Prescribed persons for the purposes of section 131(3)(b) of the Act

PART 2
Membership of a family

9. Persons of prescribed description for the definition of family in section 137(1) of the Act
10. Circumstances in which a person is to be treated as responsible or not responsible for another
11. Circumstances in which a person is to be treated as being or not being a member of the household

PART 3
Applicable amounts

12. Applicable amounts

PART 4
Income and capital
SECTION 1
General

13. Calculation of income and capital of members of claimant's family and of a polygamous marriage
14. Circumstances in which income of non-dependant is to be treated as claimant's

SECTION 2
Income and capital

15. Calculation of income and capital
16. Claimant in receipt of guarantee credit
17. Calculation of claimant's income in savings credit only cases
18. Calculation of income and capital where state pension credit is not payable
19. Meaning of "income"
20. Calculation of income on a weekly basis
21. Treatment of child care charges
22. Calculation of average weekly income from tax credits
23. Calculation of weekly income
24. Disregard of changes in tax, contributions etc

SECTION 3
Employed earners

25. Earnings of employed earners
26. Calculation of net earnings of employed earners

SECTION 4
Self-employed earners
27.   Calculation of earnings of self-employed earners
28.   Earnings of self-employed earners
29.   Calculation of net profit of self-employed earners
30.   Deduction of tax and contributions for self-employed earners

SECTION 5
Other income
31.   Notional income
32.   Income paid to third parties

SECTION 6
Capital
33.   Capital limit
34.   Calculation of capital
35.   Calculation of capital in the United Kingdom
36.   Calculation of capital outside the United Kingdom
37.   Notional capital
38.   Diminishing notional capital rule
39.   Capital jointly held

PART 5
Amount of benefit
40.   Maximum council tax benefit
41.   Amount payable during extended payment period when an extended payment is payable pursuant to regulation 60 or 61 of the Council Tax Benefit Regulations
42.   Non-dependant deductions
43.   Council tax benefit taper
44.   Extended payments (qualifying contributory benefits)
44A.   Duration of extended payment period (qualifying contributory benefits)
44B.   Amount of extended payment (qualifying contributory benefits)
44C.   Extended payments (qualifying contributory benefits) – movers
44D.   Relationship between extended payment (qualifying contributory benefits) and entitlement to council tax benefit under the general conditions of entitlement
45.   Continuing payments where state pension credit claimed
46.   Alternative maximum council tax benefit
47.   Residents of a dwelling to whom section 131(6) of the Act does not apply

PART 6
Period of entitlement, changes of circumstances and increases for exceptional circumstances
48.   Date on which entitlement is to begin
49.   Date on which council tax benefit is to end where entitlement to severe disablement allowance or incapacity benefit ceases
50.   Date on which change of circumstances is to take effect
51.   Change of circumstances where state pension credit in payment

PART 7
Claims
52.   Who may claim
53.   Time and manner in which claims are to be made
53A.   Electronic claims for benefit
54.   Date of claim where claim sent or delivered to a gateway office

55.	Date of claim where claim sent or delivered to an office of a designated authority
56.	Time for claiming council tax benefit
57.	Evidence and information
58.	Amendment and withdrawal of claim
59.	Duty to notify changes of circumstances
59A.	Notice of change of circumstances given electronically

PART 8
Decisions on questions

60.	Decisions by a relevant authority
61.	Notification of decision

PART 9
Awards or payments of benefit

62.	Time and manner of granting council tax benefit
63.	Person to whom benefit is to be paid
64.	Shortfall in benefit
65.	Payment on the death of the person entitled
66.	Offsetting

PART 10
Excess benefit

67.	Meaning of excess benefit
68.	Recoverable excess benefit
69.	Authority by which recovery may be made
70.	Persons from whom recovery may be sought
71.	Methods of recovery
72.	Further provision as to recovery of excess benefit
73.	Diminution of capital
74.	Sums to be deducted in calculating recoverable excess benefit
75.	Recovery of excess benefit from prescribed benefits

PART 11
Information
SECTION 1
Claims and information

76.	Interpretation
77.	Collection of information
78.	Recording and holding information
79.	Forwarding of information
80.	Request for information

SECTION 2
Information between authorities etc.

81.	Information to be supplied by an authority to another authority
82.	Supply of information – extended payments (qualifying contributory benefits)
83.	Supply of benefit administration information between authorities

SCHEDULES

1.	Applicable amounts
2.	Sums disregarded from claimant's earnings
3.	Amounts to be disregarded in the calculation of income other than earnings
4.	Capital disregards
5.	Extended payments (severe disablement allowance and incapacity benefit) of council tax benefit

6.   Amount of alternative maximum council tax benefit
7.   Matters to be included in the decision notice
8.   Electronic communication

PART 1
General

Citation and commencement

1.–(1)   These Regulations may be cited as the Council Tax Benefit (Persons who have attained the qualifying age for state pension credit) Regulations 2006.

(2)   These Regulations are to be read, where appropriate, with the Consequential Provisions Regulations.

(3)   Except as provided in Schedule 4 to the Consequential Provisions Regulations, these Regulations shall come into force on 6th March 2006.

(4)   The regulations consolidated by these Regulations are revoked, in consequence of the consolidation, by the Consequential Provisions Regulations.

Interpretation

2.–(1)   In these Regulations–

"the Act" means the Social Security Contributions and Benefits Act 1992;

"the Administration Act" means the Social Security Administration Act 1992;

"the 1973 Act" means the Employment and Training Act 1973;

"the 1992 Act" means the Local Government Finance Act 1992;

[2 "the 2000 Act" means the Electronic Communications Act 2000;]

"Abbeyfield Home" means an establishment run by the Abbeyfield Society including all bodies corporate or incorporate which are affiliated to that Society;

"adoption leave" means a period of absence from work on ordinary or additional adoption leave by virtue of section 75A or 75B of the Employment Rights Act 1996;

"alternative maximum council tax benefit" means the amount determined in accordance with regulation 46 and Schedule 6;

"appropriate DWP office" means an office of the Department for Work and Pensions dealing with state pension credit or an office which is normally open to the public for the receipt of claims for income support [12 , a jobseeker's allowance or an employment and support allowance];

"assessment period" means the period determined–
   (a)   in relation to the earnings of a self-employed earner, in accordance with regulation 27 for the purpose of calculating the weekly earnings of the claimant; or
   (b)   in relation to any other income, in accordance with regulation 23 for the purpose of calculating the weekly income of the claimant;

"attendance allowance" means–
   (a)   an attendance allowance under Part 3 of the Act;
   (b)   an increase of disablement pension under section 104 or 105 of the Act;
   (c)   a payment under regulations made in exercise of the power conferred by paragraph 7(2)(b) of Part 2 of Schedule 8 to the Act;
   (d)   an increase of an allowance which is payable in respect of constant attendance under paragraph 4 of Part 1 of Schedule 8 to the Act;
   (e)   a payment by virtue of article 14, 15, 16, 43 or 44 of the Personal Injuries (Civilians) Scheme 1983 or any analogous payment; or
   (f)   any payment based on need for attendance which is paid as part of a war disablement pension;

[17 "basic rate", where it relates to the rate of tax, has the same meaning as in the Income Tax Act 2007 (see section 989 of that Act).]

"the benefit Acts" means the Act, the Jobseekers Act [12 , the Welfare Reform Act] and the State Pension Credit Act;

"benefit week" means a period of 7 consecutive days commencing upon a Monday and ending on a Sunday;

"board and lodging accommodation" means accommodation provided to a person or, if he is a member of a family, to him or any other member of his family, for a charge which is inclusive of the provision of that accommodation and at least some cooked or prepared meals which both are cooked or prepared (by a person other than the person to whom the accommodation is provided or a member of his family) and are consumed in that accommodation or associated premises;

"care home" in England and Wales has the meaning assigned to it by section 3 of the Care Standards Act 2000 and in Scotland means a care home service within the meaning assigned to it by section 2(3) of the Regulation of Care (Scotland) Act 2001;

"carer's allowance" means carer's allowance under section 70 of the Act;

"child" means a person under the age of 16;

"child tax credit" means a child tax credit under section 8 of the Tax Credits Act;

"the Children Order" means the Children (Northern Ireland) Order 1995;

"claim" means a claim for council tax benefit;

"claimant" means a person claiming council tax benefit;

"close relative" means a parent, parent-in-law, son, son-in-law, daughter, daughter-in-law, step-parent, step-son, step-daughter, brother, sister, or if any of the preceding persons is one member of a couple, the other member of that couple;

[15 "concessionary payment" means a payment made under arrangements made by the Secretary of State with the consent of the Treasury which is charged to a Departmental Expenditure Vote to which payments of benefit or tax credits under the benefit Acts or the Tax Credits Act are charged;]

"the Consequential Provisions Regulations" means the Housing Benefit and Council Tax Benefit (Consequential Provisions) Regulations 2006;

[13 "contributory employment and support allowance" means a contributory allowance under Part 1 of the Welfare Reform Act;]

"council tax benefit" means council tax benefit under Part 7 of the Act;

"couple" means–

    (a)   a man and a woman who are married to each other and are members of the same household;

    (b)   a man and a woman who are not married to each other but are living together as husband and wife;

    (c)   two people of the same sex who are civil partners of each other and are members of the same household; or

    (d)   two people of the same sex who are not civil partners of each other but are living together as if they were civil partners,

and for the purposes of sub-paragraph (d), two people of the same sex are to be regarded as living together as if they were civil partners if, but only if, they would be regarded as living together as husband and wife were they instead two people of the opposite sex;

"course of study" means any course of study, whether or not it is a sandwich course and whether or not a grant is made for undertaking or attending it;

"date of claim" means the date on which the claim is made, or treated as made, for the purposes of regulation 53 (time and manner in which claims are to be made);

"the Decisions and Appeals Regulations" means the Housing Benefit and Council Tax Benefit (Decisions and Appeals) Regulations 2001;

"designated authority" means any of the following–

    (a)   the Secretary of State;

    (b)   a person providing services to the Secretary of State;

    (c)   a local authority;

    (d)   a person providing services to, or authorised to exercise any functions of, any such authority;

"designated office" means the office designated by the relevant authority for the receipt of claims to council tax benefit–

    (a)   by notice upon or with a form approved by it for the purpose of claiming council tax benefit; or

    (b)   by reference upon or with such a form to some other document available from it and sent by electronic means or otherwise on application and without charge; or

    (c)   by any combination of the provisions set out in sub-paragraphs (a) and (b) above;

"disability living allowance" means a disability living allowance under section 71 of the Act;

"dwelling" has the same meaning in section 3 or 72 of the 1992 Act;

"earnings" has the meaning prescribed in regulation 25 or, as the case may be, 28;

"the Eileen Trust" means the charitable trust of that name established on 29th March 1993 out of funds provided by the Secretary of State for the benefit of persons eligible for payment in accordance with its provisions;

[2 "electronic communication" has the same meaning as in section 15(1) of the 2000 Act;]

"employed earner" is to be construed in accordance with section 2(1)(a) of the Act and also includes a person who is in receipt of a payment which is payable under any enactment having effect in Northern Ireland and which corresponds to statutory sick pay or statutory maternity pay;

[13 "Employment and Support Allowance Regulations" means the Employment and Support Allowance Regulations 2008;]

[20 "enactment" includes an enactment comprised in, or in an instrument made under, an Act of the Scottish Parliament;]

[10 "extended payment (qualifying contributory benefits)" means a payment of council tax benefit payable pursuant to regulation 44 of these Regulations or regulation 61 of the Council Tax Benefit Regulations 2006;]

[11 "extended payment period" means the period for which an extended payment is payable in accordance with regulation 44A of these Regulations or regulation 60A or 61A of the Council Tax Benefit Regulations 2006;]

"family" has the meaning assigned to it by section 137(1) of the Act;

"the Fund" means moneys made available from time to time by the Secretary of State for the benefit of persons eligible for payment in accordance with the provisions of a scheme established by him on 24th April 1992 or, in Scotland, on 10th April 1992;

[9]

[1 "the Graduated Retirement Benefit Regulations" means the Social Security (Graduated Retirement Benefit) Regulations 2005;]

"guarantee credit" is to be construed in accordance with sections 1 and 2 of the State Pension Credit Act;

"a guaranteed income payment" means a payment made under article 14(1)(b) or article 21(1)(a) of the Armed Forces and Reserve Forces (Compensation Scheme) Order 2005;

"housing benefit" means housing benefit under Part 7 of the Act;

"the Housing Benefit Regulations" means the Housing Benefit Regulations 2006;

"Immigration and Asylum Act" means the Immigration and Asylum Act 1999;

"an income-based jobseeker's allowance" and "a joint-claim jobseeker's allowance" have the same meaning as they have in the Jobseekers Act by virtue of section 1(4) of that Act;

[13 "income-related employment and support allowance" means an income-related allowance under Part 1 of the Welfare Reform Act;]

"Income Support Regulations" means the Income Support (General) Regulations 1987;

[27 "independent hospital"–

    (a)   in England, means a hospital as defined by section 275 of the National Health Service Act 2006 that is not a health service hospital as defined by that section;

    (b)   in Wales, has the meaning assigned to it by section 2 of the Care Standards Act 2000; and

(c)   in Scotland, means an independent healthcare service as defined in section 2(5)(a) and (b) of the Regulation of Care (Scotland) Act 2001;]

[^{14}]

[^{5} "the Independent Living Fund (2006)" means the Trust of that name established by a deed dated 10th April 2006 and made between the Secretary of State for Work and Pensions of the one part and Margaret Rosemary Cooper, Michael Beresford Boyall and Marie Theresa Martin of the other part;]

[^{14}]

[^{14}]

[^{14}]

"invalid carriage or other vehicle" means a vehicle propelled by petrol engine or by electric power supplied for use on the road and to be controlled by the occupant;

"Jobseekers Act" means the Jobseekers Act 1995;

"Jobseeker's Allowance Regulations" means the Jobseeker's Allowance Regulations 1996;

"The London [^{15} Bombings] Relief Charitable Fund" means the company limited by guarantee (number 5505072) and registered charity of that name established on 11th July 2005 for the purpose of (amongst other things) relieving sickness, disability or financial need of victims (including families or dependants of victims) of the terrorist attacks carried out in London on 7th July 2005;

"lone parent" means a person who has no partner and who is responsible for and a member of the same household as a child or young person;

[^{7}]

"the Macfarlane (Special Payments) Trust" means the trust of that name, established on 29th January 1990 partly out of funds provided by the Secretary of State, for the benefit of certain persons suffering from haemophilia;

"the Macfarlane (Special Payments) (No. 2) Trust" means the trust of that name, established on 3rd May 1991 partly out of funds provided by the Secretary of State, for the benefit of certain persons suffering from haemophilia and other beneficiaries;

"the Macfarlane Trust" means the charitable trust, established partly out of funds provided by the Secretary of State to the Haemophilia Society, for the relief of poverty or distress among those suffering from haemophilia;

[^{13} "main phase employment and support allowance" means an employment and support allowance where the calculation of the amount payable in respect of the claimant includes a component under section 2(1)(b) or 4(2)(b) of the Welfare Reform Act;]

"maternity leave" means a period during which a woman is absent from work because she is pregnant or has given birth to a child, and at the end of which she has a right to return to work either under the terms of her contract of employment or under Part 8 of the Employment Rights Act 1996;

"member of a couple" means a member of a married or unmarried couple;

[^{21} "MFET Limited" means the company limited by guarantee (number 7121661) of that name, established for the purpose in particular of making payments in accordance with arrangements made with the Secretary of State to persons who have acquired HIV as a result of treatment by the NHS with blood or blood products;]

"mobility supplement" means a supplement to which paragraph 5(1)(a)(v) of Schedule 2 refers;

[^{11} "mover" means a claimant who changes the dwelling in which the claimant is resident and in respect of which the claimant is liable to pay council tax from a dwelling in the area of the appropriate authority to a dwelling in the area of the second authority;]

"net earnings" means such earnings as are calculated in accordance with regulation 26;

"net profit" means such profit as is calculated in accordance with regulation 29;

[^{11} "new dwelling" means, for the purposes of the definition of "second authority" and regulations 44C, 81 and 82, the dwelling to which a claimant has moved, or is about to move, in which the claimant is or will be resident ;]

"non-dependant" has the meaning prescribed in regulation 3;

"non-dependant deduction" means a deduction that is to be made under regulation 42;

"occupational pension" means any pension or other periodical payment under an occupational pension scheme but does not include any discretionary payment out of a fund established for relieving hardship in particular cases;

"partner" means–

    (a)   where a claimant is a member of a couple, the other member of that couple; or

    (b)   where a claimant is polygamously married to two or more members of his household, any such member to whom he is married;

"paternity leave" means a period of absence from work on leave by virtue of section 80A or 80B of the Employment Rights Act 1996;

"payment" includes part of a payment;

"pension fund holder" means with respect to a personal pension scheme or [4 an occupational pension scheme], the trustees, managers or scheme administrators, as the case may be, of the scheme [4] concerned;

"person affected" shall be construed in accordance with regulation 3 of the Decisions and Appeals Regulations;

"person on income support" means a person in receipt of income support;

"person on state pension credit" means a person in receipt of state pension credit;

[4 "personal pension scheme" means–

    (a)   a personal pension scheme as defined by section 1 of the Pension Schemes Act 1993;

    (b)   an annuity contract or trust scheme approved under section 620 or 621 of the Income and Corporation Taxes Act 1988 or a substituted contract within the meaning of section 622(3) of that Act which is treated as having become a registered pension scheme by virtue of paragraph 1(1)(f) of Schedule 36 to the Finance Act 2004;

    (c)   a personal pension scheme approved under Chapter 4 of Part 14 of the Income and Corporation Taxes Act 1988 which is treated as having become a registered pension scheme by virtue of paragraph 1(1)(g) of Schedule 36 to the Finance Act 2004;]

"policy of life insurance" means any instrument by which the payment of money is assured on death (except death by accident only) or by the happening of any contingency dependent on human life, or any instrument evidencing a contract which is subject to payment of premiums for a term dependent on human life;

"polygamous marriage" means any marriage to which section 133(1) of the Act refers;

[20 "public authority" includes any person certain of whose functions are functions of a public nature;]

"qualifying age for state pension credit" means (in accordance with section 1(2)(b) and (6) of the State Pension Credit Act)–

    (a)   in the case of a woman, pensionable age; or

    (b)   in the case of a man, the age which is pensionable age in the case of a woman born on the same day as the man;

[11 "qualifying contributory benefit" means–

    (a)   severe disablement allowance;

    (b)   incapacity benefit;]

    [12 (c) contributory employment and support allowance;]

"qualifying course" means a qualifying course as defined for the purposes of Parts 2 and 4 of the Jobseeker's Allowance Regulations;

[11 "qualifying income-related benefit" means–

    (a)   income support;

    (b)   income-based jobseeker's allowance;]

    [13 (c)   income-related employment and support allowance;]

"qualifying person" means a person in respect of whom payment has been made from the Fund, the Eileen Trust [22 , MFET Limited]; the Skipton Fund or the London Bombings Relief Charitable Fund;

"relative" means a close relative, grandparent, grandchild, uncle, aunt, nephew or niece;

"relevant authority" means an authority administering council tax benefit;

"remunerative work" has the meaning prescribed in regulation 6;

"rent" means "eligible rent" to which regulation 12 of the Housing Benefit (Persons who have attained the qualifying age for state pension credit) Regulations 2006 refers, less any deductions in respect of non-dependants which fall to be made under regulation 55 (non-dependant deductions) of those Regulations;

"resident" has the meaning it has in Part 1 or 2 of the 1992 Act;

[4]

[8 "sandwich course" has the meaning prescribed in regulation 2(9) of the Education (Student Support) Regulations 2008, regulation 4(2) of the Education (Student Loans)(Scotland) Regulations 2007 or regulation 2(8) of the Education (Student Support) Regulations (Northern Ireland) 2007, as the case may be;]

"savings credit" shall be construed in accordance with sections 1 and 3 of the State Pension Credit Act;

"second adult" has the meaning given to it in Schedule 6;

[11 "second authority" means the authority to which a mover is liable to make payments for the new dwelling;]

"self-employed earner" is to be construed in accordance with section 2(1)(b) of the Act;

[20 "service user group" means a group of individuals that is consulted by or on behalf of–

(a)   a Health Board, Special Health Board or the Agency in consequence of a function under section 2B of the National Health Service (Scotland) Act 1978,

(b)   a landlord authority in consequence of a function under section 105 of the Housing Act 1985,

(c)   a public authority in consequence of a function under section 49A of the Disability Discrimination Act 1995,

(d)   a best value authority in consequence of a function under section 3 of the Local Government Act 1999,

(e)   a local authority landlord or registered social landlord in consequence of a function under section 53 of the Housing (Scotland) Act 2001,

(f)   a relevant English body or a relevant Welsh body in consequence of a function under section 242 of the National Health Service Act 2006,

(g)   a Local Health Board in consequence of a function under section 183 of the National Health Service (Wales) Act 2006,

(h)   the Commission or the Office of the Health Professions Adjudicator in consequence of a function under sections 4, 5, or 108 of the Health and Social Care Act 2008,

(i)   the regulator or a [25 private registered provider of social housing] in consequence of a function under sections 98, 193 or 196 of the Housing and Regeneration Act 2008, or

(j)   a local authority or any a public authority in Great Britain (not being a body or authority mentioned in paragraphs (a) to (i) above) in consequence of a function conferred under any enactment,

for the purposes of monitoring and advising on a policy of that body or authority which affects or may affect persons in the group, or of monitoring or advising on services provided by that body or authority which are used (or may potentially be used) by those persons;]

"single claimant" means a claimant who neither has a partner nor is a lone parent;

"the Skipton Fund" means the ex-gratia payment scheme administered by the Skipton Fund Limited, incorporated on 25th March 2004, for the benefit of certain persons suffering from hepatitis C and other persons eligible for payment in accordance with the scheme's provisions;

"sports award" means an award made by one of the Sports Councils named in section 23(2) of the National Lottery etc Act 1993 out of sums allocated to it for distribution under that section;

[6 [18]]

"State Pension Credit Act" means the State Pension Credit Act 2002;

"student" means a person, other than a person in receipt of a training allowance, who is attending or undertaking–

(a)   a course of study at an educational establishment; or

(b)   a qualifying course;

"tax year" means a period beginning with 6th April in one year and ending with 5th April in the next;

"the Tax Credits Act" means the Tax Credits Act 2002;

"training allowance" means an allowance (whether by way of periodical grants or otherwise) payable–

(a)   out of public funds by a Government department or by or on behalf of the Secretary of State, [¹⁹ Skills Development Scotland,] Scottish Enterprise or Highlands and Islands Enterprise, the [²⁸ Young People's Learning Agency for England, the Chief Executive of Skills Funding] or the [¹⁵ Welsh Ministers];

(b)   to a person for his maintenance or in respect of a member of his family; and

(c)   for the period, or part of the period, during which he is following a course of training or instruction provided by, or in pursuance of arrangements made with, that department or approved by that department in relation to him or so provided or approved by or on behalf of the Secretary of State, [¹⁹ Skills Development Scotland,] Scottish Enterprise or Highlands and Islands Enterprise or the [¹⁵ Welsh Ministers],

but it does not include an allowance paid by any Government department to or in respect of a person by reason of the fact that he is following a course of full-time education, other than under arrangements made under section 2 of the 1973 Act or is training as a teacher;

"the Trusts" means the Macfarlane Trust, the Macfarlane (Special Payments) Trust and the Macfarlane (Special Payments) (No. 2) Trust;

"voluntary organisation" means a body, other than a public or local authority, the activities of which are carried on otherwise than for profit;

[³]

[¹⁶ "war disablement pension" means any retired pay or pension or allowance payable in respect of disablement under an instrument specified in section 639(2) of the Income Tax (Earnings and Pensions) Act 2003;

"war pension" means a war disablement pension, a war widow's pension or a war widower's pension;

"war widow's pension" means any pension or allowance payable to a woman as a widow under an instrument specified in section 639(2) of the Income Tax (Earnings and Pensions) Act 2003 in respect of the death or disablement of any person;

"war widower's pension" means any pension or allowance payable to a man as a widower or to a surviving civil partner under an instrument specified in section 639(2) of the Income Tax (Earnings and Pensions) Act 2003 in respect of the death or disablement of any person;]

"water charges" means–

(a)   as respects England and Wales, any water and sewerage charges under Chapter 1 of Part 5 of the Water Industry Act 1991;

(b)   as respects Scotland, any water and sewerage charges established by Scottish Water under a charges scheme made under section 29A of the Water Industry (Scotland) Act 2002,

in so far as such charges are in respect of the dwelling which a person occupies as his home;

[¹³ "Welfare Reform Act" means the Welfare Reform Act 2007;]

"working tax credit" means a working tax credit under section 10 of the Tax Credits Act;

"Working Tax Credit Regulations" means the Working Tax Credit (Entitlement and Maximum Rate) Regulations 2002;

"young person" has the meaning prescribed in regulation 9(1).

(2)   In these Regulations, references to a claimant occupying a dwelling or premises as his home shall be construed in accordance with regulation 7 of the Housing Benefit Regulations.

(3)   In these Regulations, where an amount is to be rounded to the nearest penny, a fraction of a penny shall be disregarded if it is less than half a penny and shall otherwise be treated as a whole penny.

(4)   For the purpose of these Regulations, a person is on an income-based jobseeker's allowance on any day in respect of which an income-based jobseeker's allowance is payable to him and on any day–

   (a)   in respect of which he satisfies the conditions for entitlement to an income-based jobseeker's allowance but where the allowance is not paid in accordance with [²⁴ regulation 27A of the Jobseeker's Allowance Regulations or] section 19 or 20A *[or regulations made under section 17A]* of the Jobseekers Act (circumstances in which a jobseeker's allowance is not payable); or

   (b)   which is a waiting day for the purposes of paragraph 4 of Schedule 1 to that Act and which falls immediately before a day in respect of which an income-based jobseeker's allowance is payable to him or would be payable to him but for [²⁴ regulation 27A of the Jobseeker's Allowance Regulations or] section 19 or 20A *[or regulations made under section 17A]* of that Act;

   (c)   in respect of which he is a member of a joint-claim couple for the purposes of the Jobseekers Act and no joint-claim jobseeker's allowance is payable in respect of that couple as a consequence of either member of that couple being subject to sanctions for the purposes of section 20A of that Act;

   (d)   in respect of which an income-based jobseeker's allowance or a joint-claim jobseeker's allowance would be payable but for a restriction imposed pursuant to [²³] section [²⁶ 6B,] 7, 8 or 9 of the Social Security Fraud Act 2001 (loss of benefit provisions).

[¹³ (4A)   For the purposes of these Regulations, a person is on an income-related employment and support allowance on any day in respect of which an income-related employment and support allowance is payable to him and on any day–

   (a)   in respect of which he satisfies the conditions for entitlement to an income-related employment and support allowance but where the allowance is not paid in accordance with section 18 of the Welfare Reform Act (disqualification); or

   (b)   which is a waiting day for the purposes of paragraph 2 of Schedule 2 to that Act and which falls immediately before a day in respect of which an income-related employment and support allowance is payable to him or would be payable to him but for section 18 of that Act.]

(5)   For the purposes of these Regulations, two persons shall be taken to be estranged only if their estrangement constitutes a breakdown of the relationship between them.

(6)   In these Regulations references to any person in receipt of a guarantee credit, a savings credit or state pension credit includes a reference to a person who would be in receipt thereof but for regulation 13 of the State Pension Credit Regulations 2002 (small amounts of state pension credit).

Modifications

Reg 2(4) is modified by reg 19 Jobseeker's Allowance (Work for Your Benefit Pilot Scheme) Regulations 2010 SI No.1222 (see p1247) as from 22 November 2010 but only for those ordinarily resident in a pilot area or whose address for payment of JSA is located within such an area. The modifications are shown in italics above. They cease to have effect on 21 November 2013.

Amendments

   1.   Inserted by reg 12(2) of SI 2005 No 2677 and reg 2 of SI 2006 No 217 as from 6.4.06.
   2.   Inserted by Art 5(2) of SI 2006 No 2968 as from 20.12.06.
   3.   Omitted by Reg 7(a) of SI 2007 No 1619 as from 3.7.07.
   4.   Amended by reg 7(2) of SI 2007 No 1749 as from 16.7.07.
   5.   Amended by Art 10 of SI 2007 No 2538 as from 1.10.07.
   6.   Inserted by reg 14(2) of SI 2007 No 2618 as from 1.10.07.
   7.   Revoked by reg 2 and the Sch of SI 2007 No 2618 as from 1.10.07.

8.   Amended by reg 6(2) of SI 2008 No 1042 as from 19.5.08.
9.   Omitted by reg 5(2) of SI 2008 No 2299 as from 1.10.08.
10.   Substituted by reg 11(2) of Si 2008 No 959 as from 6.10.08.
11.   Inserted by reg 11(2) of Si 2008 No 959 as from 6.10.08.
12.   Amended by reg 66 of SI 2008 No 1082, as amended by reg 40(b) SI 2008 No 2428, as from 27.10.08.
13.   Inserted by reg 66 of SI 2008 No 1082, as amended by reg 40(a) SI 2008 No 2428, as from 27.10.08.
14.   Omitted by reg 9(2) of SI 2008 No 2767 as from 17.11.08.
15.   Amended by reg 8(2) of SI 2008 No 3157 as from 5.1.09.
16.   Inserted by reg 6(2) of SI 20008 No 3157 as from 5.1.09.
17.   Inserted by reg 9(2)(a) of SI 2009 No 583 as from 6.4.09.
18.   Omitted by reg 9(2)(b) of SI 2009 No 583 as from 6.4.09.
19.   Amended by reg 9(3)(a) of SI 2009 No 583 as from 6.4.09.
20.   Inserted by reg 9(2) of SI 2009 No 2655 as from 2.11.09.
21.   Inserted by reg 11(2) of SI 2010 No 641 as from 1.4.10 (5.4.10 where rent payable weekly or in multiples of a week).
22.   Amended by reg 11(3) of SI 2010 No 641 as from 1.4.10 (5.4.10 where rent payable weekly or in multiples of a week).
23.   Amended by reg 11 of SI 2010 No 424 as from 2.4.10.
24.   Amended by reg 4(1)(d) and (2) of SI 2010 No 509 as from 6.4.10.
25.   Amended by Art 4 and Sch 1 para 63 of SI 2010 No 671 as from 1.4.10.
26.   Amended by reg 7 of SI 2010 No 1160 as from 1.4.10.
27.   Substituted by Arts 2 and 23 of SI 2010 No 1881 as from 1.10.10.
28.   Amended by Art 17 of SI 2010 No 1941 as from 1.9.10.

Definition of non-dependant

3.–(1)   In these Regulations, ''non-dependant'' means any person, except someone to whom paragraph (2) applies, who normally resides with a claimant or with whom a claimant normally resides.

(2)   This paragraph applies to–

(a)   any member of the claimant's family;

(b)   if the claimant is polygamously married, any partner of his and any child or young person who is a member of his household and for whom he or one of his partners is responsible;

(c)   a child or young person who is living with the claimant but who is not a member of his household by virtue of regulation 11 (membership of the same household);

(d)   subject to paragraph (3), any person who, with the claimant, is jointly and severally liable to pay council tax in respect of a dwelling for any day under sections 6, 7 or 75 of the 1992 Act (persons liable to pay council tax);

(e)   subject to paragraph (3), any person who is liable to make payments on a commercial basis to the claimant or the claimant's partner in respect of the occupation of the dwelling;

(f)   a person who lives with the claimant in order to care for him or a partner of his and who is engaged by a charitable or voluntary organisation which makes a charge to the claimant or his partner for the services provided by that person.

(3)   Excepting persons to whom paragraph (2)(a) to (c) and (f) refer, a person to whom any of the following sub-paragraphs applies shall be a non-dependant–

(a)   a person who resides with the person to whom he is liable to make payments in respect of the dwelling and either–

   (i)   that person is a close relative of his or his partner; or

   (ii)   the tenancy or other agreement between them is other than on a commercial basis;

(b)   a person whose liability to make payments in respect of the dwelling appears to the relevant authority to have been created to take advantage of the council tax benefit scheme except someone who was, for any period within the eight weeks prior to the creation of the agreement giving rise to the liability to make such payments, otherwise liable to make payments of rent in respect of the same dwelling;

(c)   a person who becomes jointly and severally liable with the claimant for council tax in respect of a dwelling and who was, at any time during the period of eight weeks prior to his becoming so liable, a non-dependant of one or more of the other residents in that dwelling who are so liable for the tax, unless the relevant authority is satisfied that the change giving rise to the new liability was not made to take advantage of the council tax benefit scheme.

Section 1(1A) of the Administration Act disapplied
[¹**4.** Section 1(1A) of the Administration Act (requirement to state a national insurance number) shall not apply–
- (a) in the case of a child or young person in respect of whom council tax benefit is claimed;
- (b) to a person who–
  - (i) is a person in respect of whom a claim for council tax benefit is made;
  - (ii) is subject to immigration control within the meaning of section 115(9)(a) of the Immigration and Asylum Act;
  - (iii) is a person from abroad for the purposes of these Regulations as defined in regulation 7(2); and
  - (iv) has not previously been allocated a national insurance number.]

Amendment
1. Substituted by reg 12 of SI 2009 No 471 as from 6.4.09.

Application of Regulations
5.–(1) Except as provided in paragraph (2), these Regulations apply in relation to a person who has attained the qualifying age for state pension credit.

(2) These Regulations shall not apply in relation to any person if he or, if he has a partner, his partner, is a person on income support [¹ , an income-based jobseeker's allowance or on an income-related employment and support allowance].

Amendment
1. Amended by reg 67 of SI 2008 No 1082 as from 27.10.08.

Remunerative work
6.–(1) Subject to the following provisions of this regulation, a person shall be treated for the purposes of these Regulations as engaged in remunerative work if he is engaged, or, where his hours of work fluctuate, he is engaged on average, for not less than 16 hours a week, in work for which payment is made or which is done in expectation of payment.

(2) Subject to paragraph (3), in determining the number of hours for which a person is engaged in work where his hours of work fluctuate, regard shall be had to the average of hours worked over–
- (a) if there is a recognisable cycle of work, the period of one complete cycle (including, where the cycle involves periods in which the person does no work, those periods but disregarding any other absences);
- (b) in any other case, the period of 5 weeks immediately prior to the date of claim, or such other length of time as may, in the particular case, enable the person's weekly average hours of work to be determined more accurately.

(3) Where, for the purposes of paragraph (2)(a), a person's recognisable cycle of work at a school, other educational establishment or other place of employment is one year and includes periods of school holidays or similar vacations during which he does not work, those periods and any other periods not forming part of such holidays or vacations during which he is not required to work shall be disregarded in establishing the average hours for which he is engaged in work.

(4) Where no recognisable cycle has been established in respect of a person's work, regard shall be had to the number of hours or, where those hours will fluctuate, the average of the hours, which he is expected to work in a week.

(5) A person shall be treated as engaged in remunerative work during any period for which he is absent from work referred to in paragraph (1) if the absence is either without good cause or by reason of a recognised, customary or other holiday.

(6)   A person on income support [¹ , an income-based jobseeker's allowance or an income-related employment and support allowance] for more than 3 days in any benefit week shall be treated as not being engaged in remunerative work in that week.

(7)   A person shall not be treated as engaged in remunerative work on any day on which the person is on maternity leave, paternity leave or adoption leave, or is absent from work because he is ill.

(8)   A person shall not be treated as engaged in remunerative work on any day on which he is engaged in an activity in respect of which–

(a)   a sports award has been made, or is to be made, to him; and

(b)   no other payment is made or is expected to be made to him.

Amendment

1.   Amended by reg 68 of SI 2008 No 1082 as from 27.10.08.

Persons from abroad

7.–(1)   A person from abroad is a person of a prescribed class for the purposes of section 131(3)(b) of the Act but this paragraph shall not have effect in respect of a person to whom and for a period to which regulation 7A and Schedule A1 apply.

[¹ (2)   In paragraph (1), "person from abroad" means, subject to the following provisions of this regulation, a person who is not habitually resident in the United Kingdom, the Channel Islands, the Isle of Man or the Republic of Ireland.

(3)   No person shall be treated as habitually resident in the United Kingdom, the Channel Islands, the Isle of Man or the Republic of Ireland unless he has a right to reside in (as the case may be) the United Kingdom, the Channel Islands, the Isle of Man or the Republic of Ireland other than a right to reside which falls within paragraph (4).

(4)   A right to reside falls within this paragraph if it is one which exists by virtue of, or in accordance with, one or more of the following–

(a)   regulation 13 of the Immigration (European Economic Area) Regulations 2006;

(b)   regulation 14 of those Regulations, but only in a case where the right exists under that regulation because the person is–

(i)   a jobseeker for the purpose of the definition of "qualified person" in regulation 6(1) of those Regulations, or

(ii)   a family member (within the meaning of regulation 7 of those Regulations) of such a jobseeker;

(c)   Article 6 of Council Directive No. 2004/38/EC; or

(d)   Article 39 of the Treaty establishing the European Community (in a case where the person is seeking work in the United Kingdom, the Channel Islands, the Isle of Man or the Republic of Ireland).

(4A)   A person is not a person from abroad if he is–

(a)   a worker for the purposes of Council Directive No. 2004/38/EC;

(b)   a self-employed person for the purposes of that Directive;

(c)   a person who retains a status referred to in sub-paragraph (a) or (b) pursuant to Article 7(3) of that Directive;

(d)   a person who is a family member of a person referred to in sub-paragraph (a), (b) or (c) within the meaning of Article 2 of that Directive;

(e)   a person who has a right to reside permanently in the United Kingdom by virtue of Article 17 of that Directive;

[⁵ (f)   a person who is treated as a worker for the purpose of the definition of "qualified person" in regulation 6(1) of the Immigration (European Economic Area) Regulations 2006 pursuant to–

(i)   regulation 5 of the Accession (Immigration and Worker Registration) Regulations 2004 (application of the 2006 Regulations in relation to a national of the Czech Republic, Estonia, Latvia, Lithuania, Hungary, Poland, Slovenia or the Slovak Republic who is an "accession State worker requiring registration"), or

(ii) regulation 6 of the Accession (Immigration and Worker Authorisation) Regulations 2006 (right of residence of a Bulgarian or Romanian who is an "accession State national subject to worker authorisation");]

(g) a refugee;

[⁴ (h) a person who has exceptional leave to enter or remain in the United Kingdom granted outside the rules made under section 3(2) of the Immigration Act 1971;

(hh) a person who has humanitarian protection granted under those rules;]

(i) a person who is not a person subject to immigration control within the meaning of section 115(9) of the Immigration and Asylum Act and who is in the United Kingdom as a result of his deportation, expulsion or other removal by compulsion of law from another country to the United Kingdom;

(j) a person in Great Britain who left the territory of Montserrat after 1st November 1995 because of the effect on that territory of a volcanic eruption; [⁶]

[⁶ (jj) a person who–

(i) arrived in Great Britain on or after 28th February 2009 but before 18th March 2011;

(i) immediately before arriving there had been resident in Zimbabwe; and

(ii) before leaving Zimbabwe, had accepted an offer, made by Her Majesty's Government, to assist that person to move to and settle in the United Kingdom; or]

(k) on state pension credit.]

(5) Paragraph 1 of Part 1 of the Schedule to, and regulation 2 as it applies to that paragraph of, the Social Security (Immigration and Asylum) Consequential Amendments Regulations 2000 shall not apply to a person who has been temporarily without funds for any period, or the aggregate of any periods, exceeding 42 days during any one period of limited leave (including any such period as extended).

(6) In this regulation–

[²]

"refugee" in this regulation, regulation 7A (entitlement of a refugee to council tax benefit) and Schedule A1 (treatment of claims for council tax benefit by refugees), means a person recorded by the Secretary of State as a refugee within the definition in Article 1 of the Convention relating to the Status of Refugees.

Modifications

Reg 7(4A)(a) to (e) applies in relation to a national of Norway, Iceland, Liechtenstein or Switzerland or a member of her/his family (within the meaning of Article 2 of Council Directive No. 2004/38/EC) as if such a national were a national of a member State. See reg 10 of SI 2006 No.1026 on p1226.

The amendments made by SI 2006 No.1026 do not affect the continued operation of the transitional and savings provided for in reg 12 Social Security (Persons From Abroad) Miscellaneous Amendments Regulations 1996 (see p1153), reg 6 Social Security (Habitual Residence) Amendment Regulations 2004 (see p1192) or Sch 3 para 6 HB&CTB(CP) Regs (see p1215). See reg 11 of SI 2006 No.1026 on p1226.

From 25 July 2006 until 31 January 2007, a para (4A)(jj) was inserted by the Social Security (Lebanon) Amendment Regulations 2006 SI No.1981. See p824 of the 20th edition for the text of the insertion.

Amendments

1. Substituted by reg 3(2)(a) of SI 2006 No 1026 as from 30.4.06.
2. Omitted by reg 3(2)(b) of SI 2006 No 1026 as from 30.4.06.
3. Amended by reg 8 of SI 2006 No 1981 from 25.7.06 until 31.1.07 only.
4. Amended by reg 8 of SI 2006 No 2528 as from 9.10.06.
5. Substituted by reg 8 of SI 2006 No 3341 as from 1.1.07.
6. Amended by reg 8 of SI 2009 No 362 as from 18.3.09.

Entitlement of a refugee to council tax benefit
7A.

Modification

Reg 7A was inserted by Sch 4 para 3(1) HB&CTB(CP) Regs. It only applied to claims for CTB by some refugees. See also Sch A1 inserted by Sch 4 para 3(2) HB&CTB(CP) Regs on p981.

Amendment

1.   Lapsed by s12(2)(g) of the Asylum and Immigration (Treatment of Claimants, etc.) Act 2004 (for those recorded as refugees after 14.6.07).

Prescribed persons for the purposes of section 131(3)(b) of the Act

8.–(1)   Subject to paragraph (2), a person who is throughout any day referred to in section 131(3)(a) of the Act absent from the dwelling referred to in that section, shall be a prescribed person for the purposes of section 131(3)(b) of the Act in relation to that day.

(2)   A person shall not, in relation to any day which falls within a period of temporary absence from that dwelling, be a prescribed person under paragraph (1).

(3)   In paragraph (2), a "period of temporary absence" means–

(a)   a period of absence not exceeding 13 weeks, beginning with the first whole day on which a person resides inresidential accommodation where and for so long as–

    (i)   the person resides in that accommodation;

    (ii)   the part of the dwelling in which he usually resided is not let or sub-let; and

    (iii)   that period of absence does not form part of a longer period of absence from the dwelling of more than 52 weeks,

where he has entered the accommodation for the purpose of ascertaining whether it suits his needs and with the intention of returning to the dwelling if it proves not to suit his needs;

(b)   a period of absence not exceeding 13 weeks, beginning with the first whole day of absence from the dwelling, where and for so long as–

    (i)   the person intends to return to the dwelling;

    (ii)   the part of the dwelling in which he usually resided is not let or sub-let; and

    (iii)   that period is unlikely to exceed 13 weeks; and

(c)   a period of absence not exceeding 52 weeks, beginning with the first whole day of that absence, where and for so long as–

    (i)   the person intends to return to the dwelling;

    (ii)   the part of the dwelling in which he usually resided is not let or sub-let;

    (iii)   the person is a person to whom paragraph (4) applies; and

    (iv)   the period of absence is unlikely to exceed 52 weeks or, in exceptional circumstances, is unlikely substantially to exceed that period.

(4)   This paragraph applies to a person who–

(a)   is detained incustody on remand pending trial or required, as a condition of bail, to reside–

    (i)   in a dwelling, other than the dwelling referred to in paragraph (1); or

    (ii)   in premises approved under [1 section 13 of the Offender Management act 2007];

or, is detained in custody pending sentence upon conviction;

(b)   is resident in a hospital or similar institution as a patient;

(c)   is undergoing, or his partner or his dependent child is undergoing, in the United Kingdom or elsewhere, medical treatment, or medically approved convalescence, in accommodation other than residential accommodation;

(d)   is following, in the United Kingdom or elsewhere, a training course;

(e)   is undertaking medically approved care of a person residing in the United Kingdom or elsewhere;

(f)   is undertaking the care of a child whose parent or guardian is temporarily absent from the dwelling normally occupied by that parent or guardian for the purpose of receiving medically approved care or medical treatment;

(g)   is, in the United Kingdom or elsewhere, receiving medically approved care provided in accommodation other than residential accommodation;

(h)   is a student;

(i)   is receiving care provided in residential accommodation other than a person to whom paragraph (3)(a) applies; or

(j)   has left the dwelling he resides in through fear of violence, in that dwelling, or by a person who was formerly a member of the family of the person first mentioned.

(5)   This paragraph applies to a person who is–

(a)   detained in custody pending sentence upon conviction or under a sentence imposed by a court (other than a person who is detained in hospital under the provisions of the Mental Health Act 1983, or, in Scotland, under the provisions of the Mental Health (Care and Treatment) (Scotland) Act 2003 or the Criminal Procedure (Scotland) Act 1995); and

(b)   on temporary release from detention in accordance with Rules made under the provisions of the Prison Act 1952 or the Prisons (Scotland) Act 1989.

(6)   Where paragraph (5) applies to a person, then, for any day when he is on temporary release–

(a)   if such temporary release was immediately preceded by a period of temporary absence under paragraph (3)(b) or (c), he shall be treated, for the purposes of paragraph (1), as if he continues to be absent from the dwelling, despite any return to the dwelling;

(b)   for the purposes of paragraph (4)(a), he shall be treated as if he remains in detention;

(c)   if he does not fall within sub-paragraph (a), he shall be a prescribed person for the purposes of section 131(3)(b) of the Act.

(7)   In this regulation–

"medically approved" means certified by a medical practitioner;

"patient" means a person who is undergoing medical or other treatment as an in-patient in any hospital or similar institution;

"residential accommodation" means accommodation which is provided–

(a)   in a care home;

(b)   in an independent hospital;

(c)   in an Abbeyfield Home; or

(d)   in an establishment managed or provided by a body incorporated by Royal Charter or constituted by Act of Parliament other than a local social services authority;

"training course" means a course of training or instruction provided wholly or partly by or on behalf of or in pursuance of arrangements made with, or approved by or on behalf of, [² Skills Development Scotland,] Scottish Enterprise, Highlands and Islands Enterprise, a government department or the Secretary of State.

Amendments

1.   Amended by reg 9(3) of SI 2008 No 2767 as from 17.11.08.

2.   Amended by reg 9(3)(b) of SI 2009 No 583 as from 6.4.09.

PART 2
Membership of a family

Persons of prescribed description for the definition of family in section 137(1) of the Act

9.–(1)   Subject to paragraph (2), a person of a prescribed description for the purposes of section 137(1) of the Act (definition of family) as it applies to council tax benefit is a person [¹ who falls within the definition of qualifying young person in section 142 of the Act (child and qualifying young person)], and in these Regulations such a person is referred to as a "young person".

(2)   Paragraph (1) shall not apply to a person who is–

(a)   on income support [⁴ , an income-based jobseeker's allowance or an income-related employment and support allowance]; [² or]

[³ (b)]

(c)   a person to whom section 6 of the Children (Leaving Care) Act 2000 (exclusion from benefits) applies.

(3)   A person of a prescribed description for the purposes of section 137(1) of the Act as it applies to council tax benefit (definition of the family) includes a child or young person in respect of whom section 145A of the Act applies for the purposes of entitlement to child benefit but only for the period prescribed under section 145A(1) of the Act.

Amendments
1.   Amended by reg 5(2)(a) of SI 2006 No 718 as from 10.4.06.
2.   Inserted by reg 5(2)(b) of SI 2006 No 718 as from 10.4.06.
3.   Omitted by reg 5(2)(c) of SI 2006 No 718 as from 10.4.06.
4.   Amended by reg 69 of SI 2008 No 1082 as from 27.10.08.

Circumstances in which a person is to be treated as responsible or not responsible for another

10.–(1)   Subject to the following provisions of this regulation a person shall be treated as responsible for a child or young person who is normally living with him this includes a child or young person to whom paragraph (3) of regulation 9 applies.

(2)   Where a child or young person spends equal amounts of time in different households, or where there is a question as to which household he is living in, the child or young person shall be treated for the purposes of paragraph (1) as normally living with–

(a)   the person who is receiving child benefit in respect of him; or
(b)   if there is no such person–
    (i)   where only one claim for child benefit has been made in respect of him, the person who made that claim, or
    (ii)   in any other case the person who has the primary responsibility for him.

(3)   For the purposes of these Regulations a child or young person shall be the responsibility of only one person in any benefit week and any person other than the one treated as responsible for the child or young person under this regulation shall be treated as not so responsible.

Circumstances in which a person is to be treated as being or not being a member of the household

11.–(1)   Subject to paragraphs (2) and (3), the claimant and any partner and, where the claimant or his partner is treated as responsible by virtue of regulation 10 (circumstances in which a person is to be treated as responsible or not responsible for another) for a child or young person, that child or young person and any child of that child or young person, shall be treated as members of the same household notwithstanding that any of them is temporarily absent from that household.

(2)   A child or young person shall not be treated as a member of the claimant's household where he is–

(a)   placed with the claimant or his partner by a local authority under section 23(2)(a) of the Children Act 1989 or by a voluntary organisation under section 59(1)(a) of that Act, or in Scotland boarded out with the claimant or his partner under a relevant enactment; or
(b)   placed, or in Scotland boarded out, with the claimant or his partner prior to adoption; or
(c)   placed for adoption with the claimant or his partner in accordance with the Adoption and Children Act 2002 or the Adoption Agencies (Scotland) Regulations 1996.

(3)   Subject to paragraph (4), paragraph (1) shall not apply to a child or young person who is not living with the claimant and he–

(a)   is being looked after by, or in Scotland is in the care of, a local authority under a relevant enactment; or
(b)   has been placed, or in Scotland boarded out, with a person other than the claimant prior to adoption; or

(c)   has been placed for adoption pursuant to a decision under the [¹ Adoption and Children Act 2002] or the Adoption Agencies (Scotland) Regulations 1996

(4)   An authority shall treat a child or young person to whom paragraph (3)(a) applies as being a member of the claimants' household in any benefit week where–

(a)   that child or young person lives with the claimant for part or all of that benefit week; and

(b)   the authority considers that it is reasonable to do so taking into account the nature and frequency of that child's or young person's visits.

(5)   In this regulation "relevant enactment" means the Army Act 1955, the Air Force Act 1955, the Naval Discipline Act 1957, the Matrimonial Proceedings (Children) Act 1958, the Social Work (Scotland) Act 1968, the Family Law Reform Act 1969, the Children and Young Persons Act 1969, the Matrimonial Causes Act 1973, the Children Act 1975, the Domestic Proceedings and Magistrates' Courts Act 1978, the Adoption (Scotland) Act 1978, the Family Law Act 1986, the Children Act 1989 and the Children (Scotland) Act 1995.

Amendment

1.   Amended by reg 5(2) of SI 2010 No 2449 as from 1.11.10.

PART 3
Applicable amounts

Applicable amounts
12.–(1)   Subject to Schedule A1 (treatment of claims for council tax benefit by refugees), the applicable amount of a person shall be the aggregate of such of the following amounts as apply in his case–

(a)   an amount in respect of his personal allowance, determined in accordance with paragraph 1 of Schedule 1;

(b)   an amount in respect of any child or young person who is a member of his family, determined in accordance with paragraph 2 of that Schedule;

(c)   if he is a member of a family of which at least one member is a child or young person, an amount determined in accordance with paragraph 3(1) of Part 2 of that Schedule (family premium);

(d)   if he is a member of a family of which one member is a child under the age of one year, an additional amount determined in accordance with paragraph 3(2) of Part 2 of that Schedule;

(e)   the amount of any premiums which may be applicable to him, determined in accordance with Parts 3 and 4 of that Schedule (premiums).

[¹ (2)]
[¹ (3)]
[¹ (4)]
[² (5)   In Schedule 1–
"additional spouse" means a spouse by the party to the marriage who is additional to the party to the marriage;
"patient" means a person (other than a person who is serving a sentence of imprisonment or detention in a youth custody institution) who is regarded as receiving free in-patient treatment within the meaning of [³ regulation 2(4) and (5) of the Social Security (Hospital In-Patients) Regulations 2005].]
[¹ (6)]
[¹ (7)]

Amendments

1.   Omitted by reg 3(3)(a) and (c) of SI 2005 No 2502 as amended by Sch 2 para 27 of SI 2006 No 217 as from 1.4.06.

2.   Inserted by reg 3(3)(b) of SI 2005 No 2502 as amended by Sch 2 para 27 of SI 2006 No 217 as from 1.4.06.

3.   Amended by reg 5(1) of SI 2005 No 3360 as amended by Sch 2 para 30 of SI 2006 No 217 as from 10.4.06.

PART 4
Income and capital
SECTION 1
General

Calculation of income and capital of members of claimant's family and of a polygamous marriage

13.–(1)   The income and capital of a claimant's partner which by virtue of section 136(1) of the Act is to be treated as income and capital of the claimant, shall be calculated or estimated in accordance with the following provisions of this Part in like manner as for the claimant; and any reference to the "claimant" shall, except where the context otherwise requires, be construed for the purposes of this Part as if it were a reference to his partner.

(2)   Where a claimant or the partner of a claimant is married polygamously to two or more members of his household–

(a)   the claimant shall be treated as possessing capital and income belonging to each such member; and

(b)   the income and capital of that member shall be calculated in accordance with the following provisions of this Part in like manner as for the claimant.

(3)   The income and capital of a child or young person shall not be treated as the income and capital of the claimant.

Circumstances in which income of non-dependant is to be treated as claimant's

14.–(1)   Where it appears to the relevant authority that a non-dependant and the claimant have entered into arrangements in order to take advantage of the council tax benefit scheme and the non-dependant has more capital and income than the claimant, that authority [¹ , except where the claimant is on a guarantee credit,] shall treat the claimant as possessing capital and income belonging to that non-dependant and, in such a case, shall disregard any capital and income which the claimant does possess.

(2)   Where a claimant is treated as possessing capital and income belonging to a non-dependant under paragraph (1) the capital and income of that non-dependant shall be calculated in accordance with the following provisions of this Part in like manner as for the claimant and any reference to the "claimant" shall, except where the context otherwise requires, be construed for the purposes of this Part as if it were a reference to that non-dependant.

Amendment

1.   Amended by reg 8(3) of SI 2008 No 3157 as from 5.1.09.

SECTION 2
Income and capital

Calculation of income and capital

15.   The income and capital of–

(a)   the claimant; and

(b)   any partner of the claimant,

shall be calculated in accordance with the rules set out in this Section; and any reference in this Part to the claimant shall apply equally to any partner of the claimant.

Claimant in receipt of guarantee credit

16.   In the case of a claimant who is in receipt, or whose partner is in receipt, of a guarantee credit, the whole of his capital and income shall be disregarded.

Calculation of claimant's income in savings credit only cases

17.–(1)   In determining the income and capital of a claimant who has, or whose partner has, an award of state pension credit comprising only the savings credit, the relevant authority shall, subject to the following provisions of this regulation, use the calculation or estimate of the claimant's or as the case may be, the claimant's partner's income and capital made by the Secretary of State for the purpose of determining that award.

(2)   The Secretary of State shall provide the relevant authority with details of the calculation or estimate–

(a)   if the claimant is allowed council tax benefit or claimed council tax benefit, within the two working days following the day the calculation or estimate was determined, or as soon as reasonably practicable thereafter; or

(b)   if sub-paragraph (a) does not apply, within the two working days following the day he receives information from the relevant authority that the claimant or his partner has claimed council tax benefit, or as soon as reasonably practicable thereafter.

(3)   The details provided by the Secretary of State shall include the amount taken into account in that determination in respect of the net income of the person claiming state pension credit.

(4)   The relevant authority shall modify the amount of the net income provided by the Secretary of State only in so far as necessary to take into account–

(a)   the amount of any savings credit payable;

(b)   in respect of any dependent children of the claimant, child care charges taken into account under regulation 20(1)(c);

(c)   the higher amount disregarded under these Regulations in respect of–

    (i)   lone parent's earnings; or

    (ii)   payments of maintenance, whether under a court order or not, which is made or due to be made by–

        (aa)   the claimant's former partner, or the claimant's partner's former partner; or

        (bb)   the parent of a child or young person where that child or young person is a member of the claimant's family except where that parent is the claimant or the claimant's partner;

(d)   any amount to be disregarded by virtue of paragraph 9(1) of Schedule 2;

(e)   the income and capital of any partner of the claimant who is treated as a member of the claimant's household under regulation 11, to the extent that it is not taken into account in determining the net income of the person claiming state pension credit;

(f)   regulation 14 (circumstances in which income of a non-dependant is to be treated as claimant's), if the relevant authority determines that this provision applies in the claimant's case;

(g)   any modification under section 139(6) of the Administration Act (modifications by resolution of an authority) which is applicable in the claimant's case.

[¹ (h)   any amount to be disregarded by virtue of paragraph 5A of Schedule 2.]

(5)   Regulations 19 to 39 shall not apply to the amount of the net income to be taken into account by the local authority under paragraph (1), but shall apply (so far as relevant) for the purpose of determining any modifications which fall to be made to that amount under paragraph (4).

(6)   The relevant authority shall for the purpose of determining the claimant's entitlement to council tax benefit use, except where paragraphs (7) and (8) apply, the calculation of the claimant's capital made by the Secretary of State, and shall in particular apply the provisions of regulation 33 if the claimant's capital is calculated as being in excess of £16,000.

(7)   If paragraph (8) applies, the relevant authority shall calculate the claimant's capital in accordance with regulations 33 to 39 below.

(8)   This paragraph applies if–

(a)   the Secretary of State notifies the relevant authority that the claimant's capital has been determined as being £16,000 or less;

(b)   subsequent to that determination the claimant's capital rises to more than £16,000; and

(c)   the increase occurs whilst there is in force an assessed income period within the meaning of sections 6 and 9 of the State Pension Credit Act.

Amendment

1.   Amended by reg 5(2) of SI 2009 No 2608 as from 1.4.10.

Calculation of income and capital where state pension credit is not payable

18.   Where neither regulation 16 nor 17 applies in the claimant's case, his income and capital shall be calculated or estimated by the relevant authority in accordance with regulations 19 to 39 below.

Meaning of "income"

19.–(1)   For the purposes of these Regulations, "income" means income of any of the following descriptions–

(a)   earnings;

(b)   working tax credit;

(c)   retirement pension income within the meaning of the State Pension Credit Act;

(d)   income from annuity contracts (other than retirement pension income);

(e)   a war disablement pension or war widow's or widower" pension;

(f)   a foreign war disablement pension or war widow's or widower's pension;

(g)   a guaranteed income payment;

[⁴ (h) a payment made under article 21(1)(c) of the Armed Forces and Reserve Forces (Compensation Scheme) Order 2005, in any case where article 23(2)(c) applies;]

(i)   income from capital other than capital disregarded under Part 1 of Schedule 4;

(j)   social security benefits, other than retirement pension income or any of the following benefits–

    (i)   disability living allowance;

    (ii)   attendance allowance payable under section 64 of the Act;

    (iii)   an increase of disablement pension under section 104 or 105 of the Act;

    (iv)   a payment under regulations made in exercise of the power conferred by paragraph 7(2)(b) of Part 2 of Schedule 8 to the Act;

    (v)   an increase of an allowance payable in respect of constant attendance under paragraph 4 of Part 1 of Schedule 8 to the Act;

    (vi)   child benefit;

    (vii)   any guardian's allowance payable under section 77 of the Act;

    (viii) any increase for a dependant, other than the claimant's partner, payable in accordance with Part 4 of the Act;

    (ix)   any social fund payment made under Part 8 of the Act;

    (x)   Christmas bonus payable under Part 10 of the Act;

    (xi)   housing benefit;

    (xii)   council tax benefit;

    (xiii) bereavement payment;

    (xiv)   statutory sick pay;

    (xv)   statutory maternity pay;

    (xvi)   statutory paternity pay payable under Part 12ZA of the Act;

    (xvii) statutory adoption pay payable under Part 12ZB of the Act;

    (xviii) any benefit similar to those mentioned in the preceding provisions of this paragraph payable under legislation having effect in Northern Ireland;

(k)   all foreign social security benefits which are similar to the social security benefits prescribed above;

[⁴ (l)   a payment made–

    (i)   under article 30 of the Naval, Military and Air Forces Etc. (Disablement and Death) Service Pensions Order 2006, in any case where article 30(1)(b) applies; or

    (ii)   under article 12(8) of that Order, in any case where sub-paragraph (b) of that article applies;]

(m)   a pension paid to victims of National Socialist persecution under any special provision made by the law of the Federal Republic of Germany, or any part of it, or of the Republic of Austria;

(n)   payments under a scheme made under the Pneumoconiosis etc. (Worker's Compensation) Act 1979;

(o)   payments made towards the maintenance of the claimant by his spouse, civil partner, former spouse or former civil partner or towards the maintenance of the claimant's partner by his spouse, civil partner, former spouse or former civil partner, including payments made–

    (i)   under a court order;

    (ii)   under an agreement for maintenance; or

    (iii)   voluntarily;

(p)   payments due from any person in respect of board and lodging accommodation provided by the claimant;

[5 (q) royalties or other sums paid as a consideration for the use of, or the right to use, any copyright, design, patent or trade mark;]

[5 (r) any payment in respect of any–

    (i)   book registered under the Public Lending Right Scheme 1982; or

    (ii)   work made under any international public lending right scheme that is analogous to the Public Lending Right Scheme 1982;]

(s)   any payment, other than a payment ordered by a court or made in settlement of a claim, made by or on behalf of a former employer of a person on account of the early retirement of that person on grounds of ill-health or disability;

(t)   any sum payable by way of pension out of money provided under the Civil List Act 1837, the Civil List Act 1937, the Civil List Act 1952, the Civil List Act 1972 or the Civil List Act 1975;

(u)   any income in lieu of that specified in sub-paragraphs (a) to (r);

(v)   any payment of rent made to a claimant who–

    (i)   owns the freehold or leasehold interest in any property or is a tenant of any property;

    (ii)   occupies part of the property; and

    (iii)   has an agreement with another person allowing that person to occupy that property on payment of rent; [1]

(w)   any payment made at regular intervals under an equity release scheme.

[2 (x) PPF periodic payments within the meaning of section 17(1) of the State Pension Credit Act.]

[6 (2)   For the purposes of these Regulations and subject to regulation 34(2) (capital to be disregarded), a claimant's capital shall be treated as if it were a weekly income of–

(a)   £1 for each £500 in excess of £10,000; and

(b)   £1 for any excess which is not a complete £500.]

(3)   Where the payment of any social security benefit prescribed under paragraph (1) is subject to any deduction (other than an adjustment specified in paragraph (5)) the amount to be taken into account under paragraph (1) shall be the amount before the deduction is made.

(4)   Where an award of any working tax credit or child tax credit is subject to a deduction by way of recovery of an overpayment of working tax credit or child tax credit which arose in a previous tax year the amount to be taken into account under paragraph (1) shall be the amount of working tax credit or child tax credit awarded less the amount of that deduction.

(5)   The adjustments specified in this paragraph are those made in accordance with–

(a)   the Social Security (Overlapping Benefits) Regulations 1979;

(b)   the Social Security (Hospital In-Patients) Regulations 1975;

(c)   section 30DD or section 30E of the Act (reductions in incapacity benefit in respect of pensions and councillor's allowances).

[3 (d) section 3 of the Welfare Reform Act (deductions from contributory employment and support allowance in respect of pensions and councillor's allowances) and regulations made under it.]

[⁶ (6)]

[⁶ (7)]

(8)   In paragraph (1)(w), "equity release scheme" means a loan–

(a)   made between a person ("the lender") and the claimant;

(b)   by means of which a sum of money is advanced by the lender to the claimant by way of payments at regular intervals; and

(c)   which is secured on a dwelling in which the claimant owns an estate or interest and which he occupies as his home.

Amendments

1.   Omitted by reg 11(2)(a) of SI 2006 No 518 as from 6.4.04.
2.   Inserted by reg 11(2)(b) of SI 2006 No 518 as from 6.4.04.
3.   Amended by reg 70 of SI 2008 No 1082 as from 27.10.08.
4.   Amended by reg 8(4) of SI 2008 No 3157 as from 5.1.09.
5.   Substituted by reg 9(4) of SI 2009 No 583 as from, for a particular claimant, the first day of the first benefit week starting on or after 6.4.09.
6.   Amended by reg 8 of SI 2009 No 1676 as from 2.11.09.

Calculation of income on a weekly basis

20.–(1)   Subject to regulation 24 (disregard of changes in tax, contributions etc.), for the purposes of section 131(5) of the Act (conditions for entitlement to council tax benefit) the claimant's income shall be calculated on a weekly basis–

(a)   by calculating or estimating the amount which is likely to be his average weekly income in accordance with this Part;

(b)   by adding to that amount the weekly income calculated under regulation 19(2);

(c)   by then deducting any relevant child care charges to which regulation 21 (treatment of child care charges) applies from any earnings which form part of the average weekly income or, in a case where the conditions in paragraph (2) are met, from those earnings plus whichever credit specified in sub-paragraph (b) of that paragraph is appropriate, up to a maximum deduction in respect of the claimant's family of whichever of the sums specified in paragraph (3) applies in his case.

(2)   The conditions of this paragraph are that–

(a)   the claimant's earnings which form part of his average weekly income are less than the lower of either his relevant child care charges or whichever of the deductions specified in paragraph (3) otherwise applies in his case; and

(b)   that claimant or, if he is a member of a couple either the claimant or his partner, is in receipt of working tax credit or child tax credit.

(3)   The maximum deduction to which paragraph (1)(c) above refers shall be–

(a)   where the claimant's family includes only one child in respect of whom relevant child care charges are paid, [⁵ £175.00] per week;

(b)   where the claimant's family includes more than one child in respect of whom relevant child care charges are paid, [⁵ £300] per week.

Amendments

1.   Confirmed by Art 22(3) of SI 2006 No 645 and reg 8 of SI 2006 No 217 as from 1.4.06.
2.   Confirmed by Art 22(2) of SI 2007 No 688 as from 1.4.07.
3.   Amended by Art 22(2) of SI 2008 No 632 as from 1.4.08.
4.   Confirmed by Art 22(2) of SI 2009 No 497 as from 1.4.09.
5.   Confirmed by Art 22(2) of SI 2010 No 793 as from 1.4.10.

Treatment of child care charges

21.–(1)   This regulation applies where a claimant is incurring relevant child care charges and–

(a)   is a lone parent and is engaged in remunerative work;

(b)   is a member of a couple both of whom are engaged in remunerative work; or

(c)   is a member of a couple where one member is engaged in remunerative work and the other–

(i) is incapacitated;
(ii) is an in-patient in hospital; or
(iii) is in prison (whether serving a custodial sentence or remanded in custody awaiting trial or sentence).

(2) For the purposes of paragraph (1) and subject to paragraph (4), a person to whom paragraph (3) applies shall be treated as engaged in remunerative work for a period not exceeding 28 weeks during which he–

(a) is paid statutory sick pay;
(b) is paid short-term incapacity benefit at the lower rate under sections 30A to 30E of the Act;
[² (ba) is paid an employment and support allowance;]
(c) is paid income support on the grounds of incapacity for work under regulation 4ZA of, and paragraph 7 or 14 of Schedule 1B to, the Income Support (General) Regulations 1987; or
(d) is credited with earnings on the grounds of incapacity for work [² or limited capability for work] under regulation 8B of the Social Security (Credits) Regulations 1975.

(3) This paragraph applies to a person who was engaged in remunerative work immediately before–

(a) the first day of the period in respect of which he was first paid statutory sick pay, short-term incapacity benefit [² , an employment and support allowance] or income support on the grounds of incapacity for work; or
(b) the first day of the period in respect of which earnings are credited,
as the case may be.

(4) In a case to which paragraph (2)(c) or (d) applies, the period of 28 weeks begins on the day on which the person is first paid income support or on the first day of the period in respect of which earnings are credited, as the case may be.

(5) Relevant child care charges are those charges for care to which paragraphs (6) and (7) apply, and shall be estimated on a weekly basis in accordance with paragraph (10).

(6) The charges are paid by the claimant for care which is provided–

(a) in the case of any child of the claimant's family who is not disabled, in respect of the period beginning on that child's date of birth and ending on the day preceding the first Monday in September following that child's fifteenth birthday; or
(b) in the case of any child of the claimant's family who is disabled, in respect of the period beginning on that person's date of birth and ending on the day preceding the first Monday in September following that person's sixteenth birthday.

(7) The charges are paid for care which is provided by one or more of the care providers listed in paragraph (8) and are not paid–

(a) in respect of the child's compulsory education;
(b) by a claimant to a partner or by a partner to a claimant in respect of any child for whom either or any of them is responsible in accordance with regulation 10 (circumstances in which a person is treated as responsible or not responsible for another); or
(c) in respect of care provided by a relative of a child wholly or mainly in the child's home.

(8) The care to which paragraph (7) refers may be provided–

(a) out of school hours, by a school on school premises or by a local authority–
(i) for children who are not disabled in respect of the period beginning on their eighth birthday and ending on the day preceding the first Monday in September following their fifteenth birthday; or
(ii) for children who are disabled in respect of the period beginning on their eighth birthday and ending on the day preceding the first Monday in September following their sixteenth birthday;

(b)   by a child care provider approved in accordance with the Tax Credit (New Category of Child Care Provider) Regulations 1999;

(c)   by persons registered under Part 10A of the Children Act 1989;

(d)   in schools or establishments which are exempted from registration under Part 10A of the Children Act 1989 by virtue of paragraph 1 or 2 of Schedule 9A to that Act;

(e)   by–

      (i)   persons registered under section 7(1) of the Regulation of Care (Scotland) Act 2001; or

      (ii)   local authorities registered under section 33(1) of that Act,

      where the care provided is childminding or day care of children within the meaning of that Act; or

(f)   by a person prescribed in regulations made pursuant to section 12(4) of the Tax Credits Act. [⁴ or

(g)   by a person who is registered under Chapter 2 or 3 of Part 3 of the Childcare Act 2006; or

(h)   by any of the schools mentioned in section 34(2) of the Childcare Act 2006 in circumstances where the requirement to register under Chapter 2 of Part 3 of that Act does not apply by virtue of section 34(2) of that Act; or

(i)   by any of the schools mentioned in section 53(2) of the Childcare Act 2006 in circumstances where the requirement to register under Chapter 3 of Part 3 of that Act does not apply by virtue of section 53(2) of that Act; or

(j)   by any of the establishments mentioned in section 18(5) of the Childcare Act 2006 in circumstances where the care is not included in the meaning of "childcare" for the purposes of Part 1 and Part 3 of that Act by virtue of that subsection; or

(k)   by a foster parent [⁵ or kinship carer] under the Fostering Services Regulations 2002, the Fostering Services (Wales) Regulations 2003 or the [⁵ Looked After Children (Scotland) Regulations 2009] in relation to a child other than one whom the foster parent is fostering [⁵ or kinship carer is looking after]; or

(l)   by a domiciliary care worker under the Domiciliary Care Agencies Regulations 2002 or the Domiciliary Care Agencies (Wales) Regulations 2004; or

(m)   by a person who is not a relative of the child wholly or mainly in the child's home.]

(9)   In paragraphs (6) and (8)(a), "the first Monday in September" means the Monday which first occurs in the month of September in any year.

(10)   Relevant child care charges shall be estimated over such period, not exceeding a year, as is appropriate in order that the average weekly charge may be estimated accurately having regard to information as to the amount of that charge provided by the child minder or person providing the care.

(11)   For the purposes of paragraph (1)(c) the other member of a couple is to be treated as incapacitated where–

(a)   he is aged not less than 80;

(b)   he is aged less than 80; and–

      (i)   the additional conditions specified in paragraph 13 of Schedule 1 of the Council Tax Benefit Regulations are treated as applying in his case; and

      (ii)   he satisfies those conditions or would satisfy them but for his being treated as capable of work by virtue of a determination made in accordance with regulations made under section 171E of the Act;

[² (ba) the claimant's applicable amount would include the support component or the work-related activity component on account of the other member having limited capability for work but for that other member being treated as not having limited capability for work by virtue of a determination made in accordance with the Employment and Support Allowance Regulations;]

(c)   the claimant (within the meaning of regulation 2(1)) is, or is treated as, incapable of work and has been so incapable, or has been so treated as incapable, of work in accordance with the provisions of, and regulations made under, Part 12A of the Act (incapacity for work) for a continuous period of not less than 196 days; and for this purpose any two or more separate periods separated by a break of not more than 56 days shall be treated as one continuous period;

[² (ca) the claimant (within the meaning of regulation 2(1)) has, or is treated as having, limited capability for work and has had, or been treated as having, limited capability for work in accordance with the Employment and Support Allowance Regulations for a continuous period of not less than 196 days ; and for this purpose any two or more separate periods separated by a break of not more than 84 days must be treated as one continuous period;]

(d) there is payable in respect of him one or more of the following–
    (i) long-term incapacity benefit or short-term incapacity benefit at the higher rate specified in Schedule 4 to Act;
    (ii) attendance allowance under section 64 of the Act;
    (iii) severe disablement allowance under section 68 of the Act;
    (iv) disability living allowance under section 71 of the Act;
    (v) increase of disablement pension under section 104 of the Act;
    (vi) a pension increase [³ paid as part of a war disablement pension or under] an industrial injuries scheme which is analogous to an allowance or increase of disablement pension under head (ii), (iv) or (v) above;
    [² (vii) main phase employment and support allowance;]

(e) a pension or allowance to which head (ii), (iv), (v) or (vi) of sub-paragraph (d) above refers was payable on account of his incapacity but has ceased to be payable in consequence of his becoming a patient within the meaning of regulation 12(5) (applicable amounts);

(f) [¹ sub-paragraph (d) or (e)] would apply to him if the legislative provisions referred to in those sub-paragraphs were provisions under any corresponding enactment having effect in Northern Ireland; or

(g) he has an invalid carriage or other vehicle provided to him by the Secretary of State under section 5(2)(a) of and Schedule 2 to the National Health Service Act 1977 or by Scottish Ministers under section 46 of the National Health Service (Scotland) Act 1978 or provided by the Department of Health and Social Services for Northern Ireland under Article 30(1) of the Health and Personal Social Services (Northern Ireland) Order 1972.

(12) For the purposes of paragraph (11), once paragraph (11)(c) applies to the claimant, if he then ceases, for a period of 56 days or less, to be incapable, or to be treated as incapable, of work, that paragraph shall, on his again becoming so incapable, or so treated as incapable, of work at the end of that period, immediately thereafter apply to him for so long as he remains incapable, or is treated as remaining incapable, of work.

[² (12A) For the purposes of paragraph (11), once paragraph (11)(ca) applies to the claimant, if he then ceases, for a period of 84 days or less, to have, or to be treated as having, limited capability for work, that paragraph is, on his again having, or being treated as having, limited capability for work at the end of that period, immediately thereafter to apply to him for so long as he has, or is treated as having, limited capability for work.]

(13) For the purposes of paragraphs (6) and (8)(a), a person is disabled if he is a person–

(a) in respect of whom disability living allowance is payable, or has ceased to be payable solely because he is a patient;

(b) who is registered as blind in a register compiled under section 29 of the National Assistance Act 1948 (welfare services) or, in Scotland, has been certified as blind and in consequence he is registered as blind in a register maintained by or on behalf of a council constituted under section 2 of the Local Government (Scotland) Act 1999; or

(c) who ceased to be registered as blind in such a register within the period beginning 28 weeks before the first Monday in September following that person's fifteenth birthday and ending on the day preceding the first Monday in September following that person's sixteenth birthday.

(14) For the purposes of paragraph (1) a person on maternity leave, paternity leave or adoption leave shall be treated as if she is engaged in remunerative work for the period specified in paragraph (15) ("the relevant period") provided that–

(a) in the week before the period of maternity, paternity leave or adoption leave began she was in remunerative work;

(b) the claimant is incurring relevant child care charges within the meaning of paragraph (5); and

(c) she is entitled to statutory maternity pay under section 164 of the Act, statutory paternity pay by virtue of section 171ZA or 171ZB of the Act, statutory adoption pay by virtue of section 171ZL of the Act or maternity allowance under section 35 of the Act.

(15) The relevant period shall begin on the day on which the person's maternity leave, paternity leave or adoption leave commences and shall end on–

(a) the date that leave ends;

(b) if no child care element of working tax credit is in payment on the date that entitlement to maternity allowance, statutory maternity pay, statutory paternity pay or statutory adoption pay ends, the date that entitlement ends; or

(c) if a child care element of working tax credit is in payment on the date that entitlement to maternity allowance, statutory maternity pay, statutory paternity pay or statutory adoption pay ends, the date that entitlement to that award of the child care element of working tax credit ends,

whichever shall occur first.

(16) In paragraph (15), "child care element" of working tax credit means the element of working tax credit prescribed under section 12 of the Tax Credits Act (child care element).

Amendments

1.   Amended by reg 6(3) of SI 2008 No 1042 as from 19.5.08.
2.   Amended by reg 71 of SI 2008 No 1082 as from 27.10.08.
3.   Amended by reg 8(5) of SI 2008 No 3157 as from 5.1.09.
4.   Amended by reg 2 of SI 2008 No 1848 as from 5.8.09.
5.   Amended by reg 10(2) of SI 2010 No 2429 as from 1.11.10.

Calculation of average weekly income from tax credits

22.–(1) This regulation applies where a claimant receives a tax credit.

(2) Where this regulation applies, the period over which a tax credit is to be taken into account shall be the period set out in paragraph (3).

(3) Where the instalment in respect of which payment of a tax credit is made is–

(a) a daily instalment, the period is 1 day, being the day in respect of which the instalment is paid;

(b) a weekly instalment, the period is 7 days, ending on the day on which the instalment is due to be paid;

(c) a two weekly instalment, the period is 14 days, commencing 6 days before the day on which the instalment is due to be paid;

(d) a four weekly instalment, the period is 28 days, ending on the day on which the instalment is due to be paid.

(4) For the purposes of this regulation "tax credit" means working tax credit.

Calculation of weekly income

23.–(1) Except where paragraphs (2) and (4) apply, for the purposes of calculating the weekly income of the claimant, where the period in respect of which a payment is made–

(a) does not exceed a week, the whole of that payment shall be included in the claimant's weekly income;

(b) exceeds a week, the amount to be included in the claimant's weekly income shall be determined–

(i) in a case where that period is a month, by multiplying the amount of the payment by 12 and dividing the product by 52;

(ii)   in a case where that period is three months, by multiplying the amount of the payment by 4 and dividing the product by 52;

(iii)   in a case where that period is a year, by dividing the amount of the payment by 52;

(iv)   in any other case, by multiplying the amount of the payment by 7 and dividing the product by the number of days in the period in respect of which it is made.

(2)   Where–

(a)   the claimant's regular pattern of work is such that he does not work the same hours every week; or

(b)   the amount of the claimant's income fluctuates and has changed more than once, the weekly amount of that claimant's income shall be determined–

    (i)   if, in a case to which sub-paragraph (a) applies, there is a recognised cycle of work, by reference to his average weekly income over the period of the complete cycle (including, where the cycle involves periods in which the claimant does no work, those periods but disregarding any other absences); or

    (ii)   in any other case, on the basis of–

        (aa)   the last two payments if those payments are one month or more apart;

        (bb)   the last four payments if the last two payments are less than one month apart; or

        (cc)   calculating or estimating such other payments as may, in the particular circumstances of the case, enable the claimant's average weekly income to be determined more accurately.

(3)   For the purposes of paragraph (2)(b) the last payments are the last payments before the date the claim was made or treated as made or, if there is a subsequent supersession under paragraph 4 of Schedule 7 to the Child Support, Pensions and Social Security Act 2000, the last payments before the date of the supersession.

(4)   If a claimant is entitled to receive a payment to which paragraph (5) applies, the amount of that payment shall be treated as if made in respect of a period of a year.

(5)   This paragraph applies to–

[³ (a) royalties or other sums paid as a consideration for the use of, or the right to use, any copyright, design, patent or trade mark;]

[³ (b) any payment in respect of any–

    (i)   book registered under the Public Lending Right Scheme 1982; or

    (ii)   work made under any international public lending right scheme that is analogous to the Public Lending Right Scheme 1982;]

(c)   any payment which is made on an occasional basis.

(6)   The period under which any benefit under the benefit Acts is to be taken into account shall be the period in respect of which that benefit is payable.

(7)   Where payments are made in a currency other than Sterling, the value of the payment shall be determined by taking the Sterling equivalent on the date the payment is made.

(8)   The sums specified in Schedule 2 shall be disregarded in calculating–

(a)   the claimant's earnings; and

[³ (b) any amount to which paragraph (5) applies where the claimant is the first owner of the copyright, design, patent or trademark, or an original contributor to the book or work referred to in paragraph (5)(b).]

[³ (8A)   For the purposes of paragraph (8)(b), and for that purpose only, the amounts specified in paragraph (5) shall be treated as though they were earnings.]

(9)   Income specified in Schedule 3 is to be disregarded in the calculation of a claimant's income.

[² (10)]

(11)   Schedule 4 shall have effect so that–

(a)   the capital specified in Part 1 shall be disregarded for the purpose of determining a claimant's income; and

   (b)   the capital specified in Part 2 shall be disregarded for the purpose of determining a claimant's income under regulation 19(2).

   (12) In the case of any income taken into account for the purpose of calculating a person's income, there shall be disregarded any amount payable by way of tax.

[² (13)]

[² (14)]

Amendments

   1.   Inserted by reg 5 of SI 2006 No 2813 as from 20.11.06.

   2.   Omitted by Reg 7(b) of SI 2007 No 1619 as from 3.7.07.

   3.   Amended by reg 9(5) of SI 2009 No 583 as from, for a particular claimant, the first day of the first benefit week starting on or after 6.4.09.

Disregard of changes in tax, contributions etc

   24.   In calculating the claimant's income the appropriate authority may disregard any legislative change–

   (a)   in the basic or other rates of income tax;

   (b)   in the amount of any personal tax relief;

   (c)   in the rates of social security contributions payable under the Act or in the lower earnings limit or upper earnings limit for Class 1 contributions under that Act, the lower or upper limits applicable to Class 4 contributions under that Act or the amount specified in section 11(4) of that Act (small earnings exception in relation to Class 2 contributions);

   (d)   in the amount of tax payable as a result of an increase in the weekly rate of Category A, B, C or D retirement pension or any addition thereto or any graduated pension payable under the Act; and

   (e)   in the maximum rate of child tax credit or working tax credit,

for a period not exceeding 30 benefit weeks beginning with the benefit week immediately following the date from which the change is effective.

SECTION 3
Employed earners

Earnings of employed earners

   25.–(1)   Subject to paragraph (2), "earnings" means in the case of employment as an employed earner, any remuneration or profit derived from that employment and includes–

   (a)   any bonus or commission;

   (b)   any payment in lieu of remuneration except any periodic sum paid to a claimant on account of the termination of his employment by reason of redundancy;

   (c)   any payment in lieu of notice;

   (d)   any holiday pay;

   (e)   any payment by way of a retainer;

   (f)   any payment made by the claimant's employer in respect of expenses not wholly, exclusively and necessarily incurred in the performance of the duties of the employment, including any payment made by the claimant's employer in respect of–

       (i)   travelling expenses incurred by the claimant between his home and place of employment;

       (ii)   expenses incurred by the claimant under arrangements made for the care of a member of his family owing to the claimant's absence from home;

   (g)   the amount of any payment by way of a non-cash voucher which has been taken into account in the computation of a person's earnings in accordance with Part 5 of Schedule 3 to the Social Security (Contributions) Regulations 2001;

   (h)   statutory sick pay and statutory maternity pay payable by the employer under the Act;

   (i)   statutory paternity pay payable under Part 12ZA of the Act;

(j)   statutory adoption pay payable under Part 12ZB of the Act;

(k)   any sums payable under a contract of service–

    (i)   for incapacity for work due to sickness or injury; or

    (ii)   by reason of pregnancy or confinement.

(2)   Earnings shall not include–

(a)   subject to paragraph (3), any payment in kind;

(b)   any payment in respect of expenses wholly, exclusively and necessarily incurred in the performance of the duties of the employment;

(c)   any occupational pension;

(d)   any lump sum payment made under the Iron and Steel Re-adaptation Benefits Scheme;

(e)   any payment of compensation made pursuant to an award by an employment tribunal established under the Employment Tribunals Act 1996 in respect of unfair dismissal or unlawful discrimination.

[¹ (f)   any payment in respect of expenses arising out of the claimant's participation in a service user group.]

(3)   Paragraph (2)(a) shall not apply in respect of any non-cash voucher referred to in paragraph (1)(g).

Amendment

1.   Inserted by reg 9(3) of SI 2009 No 2655 as from 2.11.09.

Calculation of net earnings of employed earners

26.–(1)   For the purposes of regulation 20 (calculation of income on a weekly basis), the earnings of a claimant derived or likely to be derived from employment as an employed earner to be taken into account shall, subject to regulation 23(4) and Schedule 2, be his net earnings.

(2)   For the purposes of paragraph (1) net earnings shall, except where paragraph (5) applies, be calculated by taking into account the gross earnings of the claimant from that employment over the assessment period, less–

(a)   any amount deducted from those earnings by way of–

    (i)   income tax;

    (ii)   primary Class 1 contributions under the Act;

(b)   one-half of any sum paid by the claimant by way of a contribution towards an occupational pension scheme;

(c)   one-half of the amount calculated in accordance with paragraph (4) in respect of any qualifying contribution payable by the claimant; and

(d)   where those earnings include a payment which is payable under any enactment having effect in Northern Ireland and which corresponds to statutory sick pay, statutory maternity pay, statutory paternity pay or statutory adoption pay, any amount deducted from those earnings by way of any contributions which are payable under any enactment having effect in Northern Ireland and which correspond to primary Class 1 contributions under the Act.

(3)   In this regulation ''qualifying contribution'' means any sum which is payable periodically as a contribution towards a personal pension scheme.

(4)   The amount in respect of any qualifying contribution shall be calculated by multiplying the daily amount of the qualifying contribution by the number equal to the number of days in the assessment period; and for the purposes of this regulation the daily amount of the qualifying contribution shall be determined–

(a)   where the qualifying contribution is payable monthly, by multiplying the amount of the qualifying contribution by 12 and dividing the product by 365;

(b)   in any other case, by dividing the amount of the qualifying contribution by the number equal to the number of days in the period to which the qualifying contribution relates.

(5)   Where the earnings of a claimant are determined under sub-paragraph (b) of paragraph (2) of regulation 23 (calculation of weekly income), his net earnings shall be calculated by taking into account those earnings over the assessment period, less–

(a) an amount in respect of income tax equivalent to an amount calculated by applying to those earnings [²] the basic rate of tax applicable to the assessment period less only the personal relief to which the claimant is entitled under sections 257(1) of the Income and Corporation Taxes Act 1988 (personal allowances) as is appropriate to his circumstances but, if the assessment period is less than a year, the earnings to which the [¹ [² basic] rate] of tax is to be applied and the amount of the personal relief deductible under this sub-paragraph shall be calculated on a pro rata basis;

(b) an amount equivalent to the amount of the primary Class 1 contributions that would be payable by him under the Act in respect of those earnings if such contributions were payable; and

(c) one-half of any sum which would be payable by the claimant by way of a contribution towards an occupational or personal pension scheme, if the earnings so estimated were actual earnings.

Amendments

1. Amended by reg 13(3) of SI 2007 No 2618 as from 1.10.07.
2. Amended by reg 9(6) of SI 2009 No 583 as from 6.4.09.

SECTION 4
Self-employed earners

Calculation of earnings of self-employed earners

27.–(1)   Where a claimant's earnings consist of earnings from employment as a self-employed earner, the weekly amount of his earnings shall be determined by reference to his average weekly earnings from that employment–

(a) over a period of one year; or

(b) where the claimant has recently become engaged in that employment or there has been a change which is likely to affect the normal pattern of business, over such other period ("computation period") as may, in the particular case, enable the weekly amount of his earnings to be determined more accurately.

(2)   For the purposes determining the weekly amount of earnings of a claimant to whom paragraph (1)(b) applies, his earnings over the computation period shall be divided by the number equal to the number of days in that period and multiplying the quotient by 7.

(3)   The period over which the weekly amount of a claimant's earnings is calculated in accordance with this regulation shall be his assessment period.

Earnings of self-employed earners

28.–(1)   Subject to paragraph (2), "earnings", in the case of employment as a self-employed earner, means the gross receipts of the employment and shall include any allowance paid under section 2 of the 1973 Act or section 2 of the Enterprise and New Towns (Scotland) Act 1990 to the claimant for the purpose of assisting him in carrying on his business unless at the date of claim the allowance has been terminated.

(2)   "Earnings" in the case of employment as a self-employed earner does not include–

(a) where a claimant occupies a dwelling as his home and he provides in that dwelling board and lodging accommodation for which payment is made, those payments;

(b) any payment made by a local authority to a claimant–

   (i)   with whom a person is accommodated by virtue of arrangements made under section 23(2)(a) of the Children Act 1989 (provision of accommo-dation and maintenance for a child whom they are looking after) or, as the case may be, section 26(1) of the Children (Scotland) Act 1995; or

   [² (ii) with whom a local authority foster a child under the Looked After Children (Scotland) Regulations 2009 or who is a kinship carer under those Regulations;]

(c)   any payment made by a voluntary organisation in accordance with section 59(1)(a) of the Children Act 1989 (provision of accommodation by voluntary organisations);

(d)   any payment made to the claimant or his partner for a person ("the person concerned") who is not normally a member of the claimant's household but is temporarily in his care, by–
  (i)   a health authority;
  (ii)   a local authority but excluding payments of housing benefit made in respect of the person concerned;
  (iii)   a voluntary organisation;
  (iv)   the person concerned pursuant to section 26(3A) of the National Assistance Act 1948; [¹]
  (v)   a primary care trust established under section 16A of the National Health Service Act [¹ 1977 or established by an order made under section 18(2)(c) of the National Health Service Act 2006; or]
  [¹ (vi) a Local Health Board established under section 16BA of the National Health Service Act 1977 or established by an order made under section 11 of the National Health Service (Wales) Act 2006;]

(e)   any sports award.

Amendments
1.   Amended by reg 8(6) of SI 2008 No 3157 as from 5.1.09.
2.   Substituted by reg 10(3) of Si 2010 No 2429 as from 1.11.10.

Calculation of net profit of self-employed earners

29.–(1)   For the purposes of regulation 20 (calculation of income on a weekly basis) the earnings of a claimant to be taken into account shall be–

(a)   in the case of a self-employed earner who is engaged in employment on his own account, the net profit derived from that employment;

(b)   in the case of a self-employed earner whose employment is carried on in partnership, his share of the net profit derived from that employment, less–
  (i)   an amount in respect of income tax and of social security contributions payable under the Act calculated in accordance with regulation 30 (deduction of tax and contributions of self-employed earners); and
  (ii)   one-half of the amount calculated in accordance with paragraph (10) in respect of any qualifying premium.

(2)   For the purposes of paragraph (1)(a) the net profit of the employment shall, except where paragraph (8) applies, be calculated by taking into account the earnings of the employment over the assessment period less–

(a)   subject to paragraphs (4) to (7), any expenses wholly and exclusively incurred in that period for the purposes of that employment;

(b)   an amount in respect of–
  (i)   income tax; and
  (ii)   social security contributions payable under the Act,
  calculated in accordance with regulation 30 (deduction of tax and contributions of self-employed earners); and

(c)   one-half of the amount calculated in accordance with paragraph (10) in respect of any qualifying premium.

(3)   For the purposes of paragraph (1)(b), the net profit of the employment shall be calculated by taking into account the earnings of the employment over the assessment period less, subject to paragraphs (4) to (7), any expenses wholly and exclusively incurred in that period for the purposes of the employment.

(4)   Subject to paragraph (5), no deduction shall be made under paragraph (2)(a) or (3), in respect of–

(a)   any capital expenditure;
(b)   the depreciation of any capital asset;
(c)   any sum employed or intended to be employed in the setting up or expansion of the employment;

(d)   any loss incurred before the beginning of the assessment period;

(e)   the repayment of capital on any loan taken out for the purposes of the employment; and

(f)   any expenses incurred in providing business entertainment.

(5)   A deduction shall be made under paragraph (2)(a) or (3) in respect of the repayment of capital on any loan used for–

(a)   the replacement in the course of business of equipment or machinery; and

(b)   the repair of an existing business asset except to the extent that any sum is payable under an insurance policy for its repair.

(6)   The relevant authority shall refuse to make a deduction in respect of any expenses under paragraph (2)(a) or (3) where it is not satisfied given the nature and the amount of the expense that it has been reasonably incurred.

(7)   For the avoidance of doubt–

(a)   a deduction shall not be made under paragraph (2)(a) or (3) in respect of any sum unless it has been expended for the purposes of the business;

(b)   a deduction shall be made thereunder in respect of–

(i)   the excess of any value added tax paid over value added tax received in the assessment period;

(ii)   any income expended in the repair of an existing business asset except to the extent that any sum is payable under an insurance policy for its repair;

(iii)   any payment of interest on a loan taken out for the purposes of the employment.

(8)   Where a claimant is engaged in employment as a child minder the net profit of the employment shall be one-third of the earnings of that employment, less–

(a)   an amount in respect of–

(i)   income tax; and

(ii)   social security contributions payable under the Act,

calculated in accordance with regulation 30 (deduction of tax and contributions of self-employed earners); and

(b)   one-half of the amount calculated in accordance with paragraph (10) in respect of any qualifying premium.

(9)   For the avoidance of doubt where a claimant is engaged in employment as a self-employed earner and he is also engaged in one or more other employments as a self-employed or employed earner any loss incurred in any one of his employments shall not be offset against his earnings in any other of his employments.

(10)   The amount in respect of any qualifying premium shall be calculated by multiplying the daily amount of the qualifying premium by the number equal to the number of days in the assessment period; and for the purposes of this regulation the daily amount of the qualifying premium shall be determined–

(a)   where the qualifying premium is payable monthly, by multiplying the amount of the qualifying premium by 12 and dividing the product by 365;

(b)   in any other case, by dividing the amount of the qualifying premium by the number equal to the number of days in the period to which the qualifying premium relates.

(11)   In this regulation, "qualifying premium" means any premium which is payable periodically in respect of [1] a personal pension scheme and is so payable on or after the date of claim.

Amendment

1.   Amended by reg 7(3) of SI 2007 No 1749 as from 16.7.07.

Deduction of tax and contributions for self-employed earners

30.–(1)   The amount to be deducted in respect of income tax under regulation 29(1)(b)(i), (2)(b)(i) or (8)(a)(i) (calculation of net profit of self-employed earners) shall be calculated on the basis of the amount of chargeable income and as if that income were assessable to income tax at the [1 starting rate] or, as the case may be, the [1 starting rate] and the basic rate of tax applicable to the assessment period less only the personal relief to which the claimant is entitled under sections 257(1) of the Income and Corporation Taxes Act 1988 (personal allowances) as is appropriate to his circumstances; but, if the assessment period is less than a year, the earnings to which the [¹ starting rate] of tax is to be applied and the amount of the personal reliefs deductible under this paragraph shall be calculated on a pro rata basis.

(2)　The amount to be deducted in respect of social security contributions under regulation 29(1)(b)(i), (2)(b)(ii) or (8)(a)(ii) shall be the total of–
(a)　the amount of Class 2 contributions payable under section 11(1) or, as the case may be, 11(3) of the Act at the rate applicable to the assessment period except where the claimant's chargeable income is less than the amount specified in section 11(4) of that Act (small earnings exception) for the tax year applicable to the assessment period; but if the assessment period is less than a year, the amount specified for that tax year shall be reduced pro rata; and
(b)　the amount of Class 4 contributions (if any) which would be payable under section 15 of the Act (Class 4 contributions recoverable under the Income Tax Acts) at the percentage rate applicable to the assessment period on so much of the chargeable income as exceeds the lower limit but does not exceed the upper limit of profits and gains applicable for the tax year applicable to the assessment period; but if the assessment period is less than a year, those limits shall be reduced pro rata.

(3)　In this regulation "chargeable income" means–
(a)　except where sub-paragraph (b) applies, the earnings derived from the employment less any expenses deducted under paragraph (2)(a) or, as the case may be, (3) of regulation 29;
(b)　in the case of employment as a child minder, one third of the earnings of that employment.

Amendment
1.　　Amended by reg 13(4) of SI 2007 No 2618 as from 1.10.07.

SECTION 5
Other income

Notional income
31.–(1)　A claimant shall be treated as possessing–
(a)　subject to paragraph (2), the amount of any retirement pension income–
　(i)　for which no claim has been made; and
　(ii)　to which he might expect to be entitled if a claim for it were made;
(b)　income from an occupational pension scheme which the claimant elected to defer.

(2)　Paragraph (1)(a) shall not apply to the following where entitlement has been deferred–
(a)　a Category A or Category B retirement pension payable under sections 43 to 55 of the Act;
(b)　a shared additional pension payable under section 55A of the Act;
(c)　graduated retirement benefit payable under sections 36 and 37 of the National Insurance Act 1965.

(3)　For the purposes of paragraph (2), entitlement has been deferred–
(a)　in the case of a Category A or Category B pension, in the circumstances specified in section 55(3) of the Act;
(b)　in the case of a shared additional pension, in the circumstances specified in section 55C(3) of the Act; and
(c)　in the case of graduated retirement benefit, in the circumstances specified in section 36(4) and (4A) of the National Insurance Act 1965.

[³ (4)　This paragraph applies where a person [⁵ who has attained the qualifying age for state pension credit]–

   (a)   is entitled to money purchase benefits under an occupational pension scheme or a personal pension scheme;

   (b)   fails to purchase an annuity with the funds available in that scheme; and

   (c)   either–

       (i)   defers in whole or in part the payment of any income which would have been payable to him by his pension fund holder, or

       (ii)   fails to take any necessary action to secure that the whole of any income which would be payable to him by his pension fund holder upon his applying for it, is so paid, or

       (iii) income withdrawal is not available to him under that scheme.

(4A)   Where paragraph (4) applies, the amount of any income foregone shall be treated as possessed by that person, but only from the date on which it could be expected to be acquired were an application for it to be made.]

(5)   The amount of any income foregone in a case [³ where paragraph (4)(c)(i) or (ii)] applies shall be the maximum amount of income which may be withdrawn from the fund and shall be determined by the relevant authority which shall take account of information provided by the pension fund holder in accordance with regulation 57(6) (evidence and information).

(6)   The amount of any income foregone in a case [³ either paragraph (4)(c)(iii)] applies shall be the income that the claimant could have received without purchasing an annuity had the funds held under the relevant scheme [³] been held under a personal pension scheme or occupational pension scheme where income withdrawal was available and shall be determined in the manner specified in paragraph (5).

(7)   In paragraph (4), "money purchase benefits" has the meaning it has in the Pensions Scheme Act 1993.

(8)   [¹ Subject to paragraph (8A [⁴ and (8C)]),] A person shall be treated as possessing income of which he has deprived himself for the purpose of securing entitlement to council tax benefit or increasing the amount of that benefit.

[¹ (8A)   Paragraph (8) shall not apply in respect of the amount of an increase of pension or benefit where a person, having made an election in favour of that increase of pension or benefit under Schedule 5 or 5A to the Contributions and Benefits Act 1992 or under Schedule 1 to the Graduated Retirement Benefit Regulations, changes that election in accordance with regulations made under Schedule 5 or 5A to that Act in favour of a lump sum.

(8B)   In paragraph (8A), "lump sum" means a lump sum under Schedule 5 or 5A to the Contributions and Benefits Act 1992 or under Schedule 1 to the Graduated Retirement Benefit Regulations.]

[⁴ (8C)   Paragraph (8) shall not apply in respect of any amount of income other than earnings, or earnings of an employed earner, arising out of the claimant's participation in a service user group.]

(9)   Where a claimant is in receipt of any benefit (other than council tax benefit) under the benefit Acts and the rate of that benefit is altered with effect from a date on or after 1st April in any year but not more than 14 days thereafter, the relevant authority shall treat the claimant as possessing such benefit at the altered rate from either 1st April or the first Monday in April in that year, whichever date the relevant authority shall select to apply in its area, to the date on which the altered rate is to take effect.

(10)   In the case of a claimant who has, or whose partner has, an award of state pension credit comprising only the savings credit, where a relevant authority treats the claimant as possessing any benefit (other than council tax benefit) at the altered rate in accordance with paragraph (9), that authority shall–

   (a)   determine the income and capital of that claimant in accordance with regulation 17(1) (calculation of claimant's income in savings credit only cases) where the calculation or estimate of that income and capital is altered with effect from a date on or after 1st April in any year but not more than 14 days thereafter; and

   (b)   treat that claimant as possessing such income and capital at the altered rate by reference to the date selected by the relevant authority to apply in its area, for the purposes of establishing the period referred to in paragraph (9).

[² (11)   For the purposes of paragraph (8), a person is not to be regarded as depriving himself of income where–
- (a)   his rights to benefits under a registered pension scheme are extinguished and in consequence of this he receives a payment from the scheme, and
- (b)   that payment is a trivial commutation lump sum within the meaning given by paragraph 7 of Schedule 29 to the Finance Act 2004.

(12)   In paragraph (11), ''registered pension scheme'' has the meaning given in section 150(2) of the Finance Act 2004.]

Amendments

1.	Inserted by reg 12(3) of SI 2005 No 2677 and reg 2 of SI 2006 No 217 as from 6.4.06.
2.	Inserted by reg 18(2) of SI 2006 No 2378 as from 2.10.06.
3.	Amended by reg 7(4) of SI 2007 No 1749 as from 16.7.07.
4.	Amended by reg 9(4) of SI 2009 No 2655 as from 2.11.09.
5.	Amended by reg 11(4) of SI 2010 No 641 as from 6.4.10.

Income paid to third parties
32.–(1)   Any payment of income, other than a payment specified in paragraph (2), to a third party in respect of the claimant shall be treated as possessed by the claimant.

(2)   Paragraph (1) shall not apply in respect of a payment of income made under an occupational pension scheme [¹ , in respect of a pension or other periodical payment made under a personal pension scheme or a payment made by the Board of the Pension Protection Fund] where–
- (a)   a bankruptcy order has been made in respect of the person in respect of whom the payment has been made or, in Scotland, the estate of that person is subject to sequestration or a judicial factor has been appointed on that person's estate under section 41 of the Solicitors (Scotland) Act 1980;
- (b)   the payment is made to the trustee in bankruptcy or any other person acting on behalf of the creditors; and
- (c)   the person referred to in sub-paragraph (a) and his partner does not possess, or is not treated as possessing, any other income apart from that payment.

Amendment

1.	Amended by reg 11(3) of SI 2006 No 518 as from 6.4.04.

SECTION 6
Capital

Capital limit
33.   For the purposes of section 134(1) of the Act as it applies to council tax benefit (no entitlement to benefit if capital exceeds a prescribed amount), the prescribed amount is £16,000.

Calculation of capital
34.–(1)   For the purposes of Part 7 of the Act as it applies to council tax benefit, the capital of a claimant to be taken into account shall, subject to paragraph (2), be the whole of his capital calculated in accordance with this Part.

(2)   There shall be disregarded from the calculation of the claimant's capital under paragraph (1) any capital, where applicable, specified in Schedule 4.

(3)   A claimant's capital shall be treated as including any payment made to him by way of arrears of–
- (a)   child tax credit;
- (b)   working tax credit;
- (c)   state pension credit,

if the payment was made in respect of a period for the whole or part of which council tax benefit was allowed before those arrears were paid.

[¹Calculation of capital in the United Kingdom

35. Capital which a claimant possesses in the United Kingdom shall be calculated at its current market or surrender value less–

(a) where there would be expenses attributable to the sale, 10 per cent.; and

(b) the amount of any encumbrance secured on it.]

Amendment

1. Substituted by reg 13(5) of SI 2007 No 2618 as from 1.10.07.

Calculation of capital outside the United Kingdom

36. Capital which a claimant possesses in a country outside the United Kingdom shall be calculated–

(a) in a case where there is no prohibition in that country against the transfer to the United Kingdom of an amount equal to its current market or surrender value in that country, at that value;

(b) in a case where there is such a prohibition, at the price which it would realise if sold in the United Kingdom to a willing buyer,

less, where there would be expenses attributable to sale, 10 per cent. and the amount of any encumbrance secured on it.

Notional capital

37.–(1) A claimant shall be treated as possessing capital of which he has deprived himself for the purpose of securing entitlement to council tax benefit or increasing the amount of that benefit except to the extent that the capital which he is treated as possessing is reduced in accordance with regulation 38 (diminishing notional capital rule).

(2) A person who disposes of capital for the purpose of–

(a) reducing or paying a debt owed by the claimant; or

(b) purchasing goods or services if the expenditure was reasonable in the circumstances of the claimant's case,

shall be regarded as not depriving himself of it.

(3) Where a claimant stands in relation to a company in a position analogous to that of a sole owner or partner in the business of that company, he shall be treated as if he were such sole owner or partner and in such a case–

(a) the value of his holding in that company shall, notwithstanding regulation 34 (calculation of capital), be disregarded; and

(b) he shall, subject to paragraph (4), be treated as possessing an amount of capital equal to the value or, as the case may be, his share of the value of the capital of that company and the foregoing provisions of this Section shall apply for the purposes of calculating that amount as if it were actual capital which he does possess.

(4) For so long as a claimant undertakes activities in the course of the business of the company, the amount which he is treated as possessing under paragraph (3) shall be disregarded.

(5) Where under this regulation a person is treated as possessing capital, the amount of that capital shall be calculated in accordance with the provisions of this Part as if it were actual capital which he does possess.

Diminishing notional capital rule

38.–(1) Where a claimant is treated as possessing capital under regulation 37(1) (notional capital), the amount which he is treated as possessing–

(a) in the case of a week that is subsequent to–

(i) the relevant week in respect of which the conditions set out in paragraph (2) are satisfied; or

(ii) a week which follows that relevant week and which satisfies those conditions,

shall be reduced by an amount determined under paragraph (3);

(b)   in the case of a week in respect of which paragraph (1)(a) does not apply but where–
    (i)   that week is a week subsequent to the relevant week; and
    (ii)   that relevant week is a week in which the condition in paragraph (4) is satisfied,
    shall be reduced by the amount determined under paragraph (4).

(2)   This paragraph applies to a benefit week where the claimant satisfies the conditions that–
(a)   he is in receipt of council tax benefit; and
(b)   but for regulation 37(1), he would have received an additional amount of council tax benefit in that week.

(3)   In a case to which paragraph (2) applies, the amount of the reduction for the purposes of paragraph (1)(a) shall be equal to the aggregate of–
(a)   the additional amount to which paragraph (2)(b) refers;
(b)   where the claimant has also claimed state pension credit, the amount of any state pension credit or any additional amount of state pension credit to which he would have been entitled in respect of the benefit week to which paragraph (2) refers but for the application of regulation 21(1) of the State Pension Credit Regulations 2002 (notional capital);
(c)   where the claimant has also claimed housing benefit, the amount of any housing benefit or any additional amount of housing benefit to which he would have been entitled in respect of the whole or part of that benefit week to which paragraph (2) refers but for the application of regulation 47(1) of the Housing Benefit (Persons who have attained the qualifying age for state pension credit) Regulations 2006 (notional capital);
(d)   where the claimant has also claimed a jobseeker's allowance, the amount of an income-based jobseeker's allowance to which he would have been entitled in respect of the benefit week to which paragraph (2) refers but for the application of regulation 113 of the Jobseeker's Allowance Regulations (notional capital).
[¹ (e) where the claimant has also claimed an employment and support allowance, the amount of an income-related employment and support allowance to which he would have been entitled in respect of the benefit week to which paragraph (2) refers but for the application of regulation 115 of the Employment and Support Allowance Regulations (notional capital).]

(4)   Subject to paragraph (5), for the purposes of paragraph (1)(b), the condition is that the claimant would have been entitled to council tax benefit in the relevant week but for regulation 37(1), and in such a case the amount of the reduction shall be equal to the aggregate of–
(a)   the amount of council tax benefit to which the claimant would have been entitled in the relevant week but for regulation 37(1); and for the purposes of this sub-paragraph if the amount is in respect of a part-week that amount shall be determined by dividing the amount of council tax benefit to which he would have been so entitled by the number equal to the number of days in the part-week and multiplying the quotient so obtained by 7;
(b)   if the claimant would, but for regulation 21 of the State Pension Credit Regulations 2002, have been entitled to state pension credit in respect of the benefit week, within the meaning of regulation 1(2) of those Regulations (interpretation), which includes the last day of the relevant week, the amount to which he would have been entitled and, for the purposes of this sub-paragraph, if the amount is in respect of a part-week, that amount shall be determined by dividing the amount of the state pension credit to which he would have been so entitled by the number equal to the number of days in the part-week and multiplying the quotient so obtained by 7;
(c)   if the claimant would, but for regulation 47(1) of the Housing Benefit (Persons who have attained the qualifying age for state pension credit) Regulations 2006, have been entitled to housing benefit or to an additional amount of housing

benefit in respect of the benefit week which includes the last day of the relevant week, the amount which is equal to–

    (i)   in a case where no housing benefit is payable, the amount to which he would have been entitled; or

    (ii)   in any other case, the amount equal to the additional amount of housing benefit to which he would have been entitled,

and, for the purposes of this sub-paragraph, if the amount is in respect of a part-week, that amount shall be determined by dividing the amount of the housing benefit to which he would have been so entitled by the number equal to the number of days in the part-week and multiplying the quotient so obtained by 7;

(d)   if the claimant would, but for regulation 113 of the Jobseeker's Allowance Regulations, have been entitled to an income-based jobseeker's allowance in respect of the benefit week, within the meaning of regulation 1(3) of those Regulations (interpretation), which includes the last day of the relevant week, the amount to which he would have been entitled and, for the purposes of this sub-paragraph, if the amount is in respect of a part-week, that amount shall be determined by dividing the amount of the income-based jobseeker's allowance to which he would have been so entitled by the number equal to the number of days in the part-week and multiplying the quotient so obtained by 7.

[¹ (e)   if the claimant would, but for regulation 115 of the Employment and Support Allowance Regulations, have been entitled to an income-related employment and support allowance in respect of the benefit week, within the meaning of regulation 2(1) of those Regulations (interpretation), which includes the last day of the relevant week, the amount to which he would have been entitled and, for the purposes of this sub-paragraph, if the amount is in respect of a part-week, that amount must be determined by dividing the amount of the income-related employment and support allowance to which he would have been so entitled by the number equal to the number of days in that part-week and multiplying the quotient so obtained by 7.]

(5)   The amount determined under paragraph (4) shall be redetermined under that paragraph if the claimant makes a further claim for council tax benefit and the conditions in paragraph (6) are satisfied, and in such a case–

(a)   sub-paragraphs (a) to (d) of paragraph (4) shall apply as if for the words ''relevant week'' there were substituted the words ''relevant subsequent week''; and

(b)   subject to paragraph (7), the amount as redetermined shall have effect from the first week following the relevant subsequent week in question.

(6)   The conditions are that–

(a)   a further claim is made 26 or more weeks after–

    (i)   the date on which the claimant made a claim for council tax benefit in respect of which he was first treated as possessing the capital in question under regulation 37(1);

    (ii)   in a case where there has been at least one redetermination in accordance with paragraph (5), the date on which he last made a claim for council tax benefit which resulted in the weekly amount being redetermined; or

    (iii)   the date on which he last ceased to be entitled to council tax benefit, whichever last occurred; and

(b)   the claimant would have been entitled to council tax benefit but for regulation 37(1).

(7)   The amount as redetermined pursuant to paragraph (5) shall not have effect if it is less than the amount which applied in that case immediately before the redetermination and in such a case the higher amount shall continue to have effect.

(8)   For the purposes of this regulation–

(a)   ''part-week'' in paragraph (4)(a) means a period of less than a week for which council tax benefit is allowed;

(b)   ''part-week'' in paragraph (4)(b) [¹ , (d) and (e)] means–

(i)   a period of less than a week which is the whole period for which state pension credit [¹ , an income-related employment and support allowance], or, as the case may be, an income-based jobseeker's allowance, is payable; and

(ii)   any other period of less than a week for which either of those benefits is payable;

(c)   ''part-week'' in paragraph (4)(c) means a period of less than a week for which housing benefit is payable;

(d)   ''relevant week'' means the benefit week or part-week in which the capital in question of which the claimant has deprived himself within the meaning of regulation 37(1)–

(i)   was first taken into account for the purpose of determining his entitlement to council tax benefit; or

(ii)   was taken into account on a subsequent occasion for the purpose of determining or re-determining his entitlement to council tax benefit on that subsequent occasion and that determination or redetermination resulted in his beginning to receive, or ceasing to receive, council tax benefit,

and where more than one benefit week or part week is identified by reference to heads (i) and (ii) of this sub-paragraph the later or latest such benefit week or, as the case may be, the later or latest such part-week;

(e)   ''relevant subsequent week'' means the benefit week or part-week which includes the day on which the further claim or, if more than one further claim has been made, the last such claim was made.

Amendment

1.   Amended by reg 72 of SI 2008 No 1082 as from 27.10.08.

Capital jointly held

39. Where a claimant and one or more other persons are beneficially entitled in possession to any capital asset, other than a capital asset disregarded under regulation 37(4), they shall be treated as if each of them were entitled in possession to the whole beneficial interest therein in an equal share and the foregoing provisions of this Section shall apply for the purposes of calculating the amount of capital which the claimant is treated as possessing as if it were actual capital which the claimant does possess.

PART 5

Amount of benefit

Maximum council tax benefit

40.–(1) Subject to [¹ paragraphs (2) to (4)], the amount of a person's maximum council tax benefit in respect of a day for which he is liable to pay council tax, shall be 100 per cent. of the amount A/B where–

(a)   A is the amount set by the appropriate authority as the council tax for the relevant financial year in respect of the dwelling in which he is a resident and for which he is liable, subject to any discount which may be appropriate to that dwelling under the 1992 Act; and

(b)   B is the number of days in that financial year,

less any deductions in respect of non-dependants which fall to be made under regulation 42 (non-dependant deductions).

(2) In calculating a person's maximum council tax benefit any reduction in the amount that a person is liable to pay in respect of council tax, which is made in consequence of any enactment in, or made under, the 1992 Act, shall be taken into account.

(3) Subject to paragraph (4), where a claimant is jointly and severally liable for council tax in respect of a dwelling in which he is resident with one or more other persons but excepting any person so residing with the claimant who is a student to whom

regulation 45(2) of the Council Tax Benefit Regulations 2006 (students who are excluded from entitlement to council tax benefit) applies, in determining the maximum council tax benefit in his case in accordance with paragraph (1), the amount A shall be divided by the number of persons who are jointly and severally liable for that tax.

(4)   Where a claimant is jointly and severally liable for council tax in respect of a dwelling with only his partner, paragraph (3) shall not apply in his case.

[¹ (5)]

Amendment

1.   Amended by reg 11(3) of SI 2008 No 959 as from 6.10.08.

[¹**Amount payable during extended payment period when an extended payment is payable pursuant to regulation 60 or 61 of the Council Tax Benefit Regulations**

41.–(1)   This regulation applies where–

(a)   a claimant became entitled to an extended payment pursuant to regulation 60 of the Council Tax Benefit Regulations 2006 or an extended payment (qualifying contributory benefits) pursuant to regulation 61 of those Regulations; and

(b)   during the extended payment period, these Regulations become applicable to the claimant or the claimant's partner in accordance with regulation 5 (persons who have attained the qualifying age for state pension credit).

(2)   Where this regulation applies, the amount of the extended payment payable to a claimant for any week during the extended payment period shall be the higher of–

(a)   the amount of the extended payment payable in accordance with regulation 60B(1)(a) of the Council Tax Benefit Regulations 2006 or the extended payment (qualifying contributory benefits) payable in accordance with regulation 61B(1)(a) of those Regulations, as the case may be;

(b)   the amount of council tax benefit to which a claimant would be entitled under the general conditions of entitlement of these Regulations, if regulation 60 (extended payments) or regulation 61 (extended payments (qualifying contributory benefits)) of the Council Tax Benefit Regulations 2006 did not apply to the claimant; or

(c)   the amount of council tax which the claimant's partner would be entitled to under the general conditions of entitlement of these Regulations, if regulation 60 or regulation 61 of the Council Tax Benefit Regulations 2006 did not apply to the claimant.

(3)   Where this regulation applies, no amount of council tax benefit shall be payable by the appropriate authority during the extended payment period to a claimant's partner under these Regulations for any week in the extended payment period.]

Amendment

1.   Substituted by reg 11(4) of SI 2008 No 959 as from 6.10.08.

Non-dependant deductions

42.–(1)   Subject to the following provisions of this regulation, the non-dependant deductions in respect of a day referred to in regulation 40 (maximum council tax benefit) shall be–

(a)   in respect of a non-dependant aged 18 or over in remunerative work, [¹³ £6.95] × 1/7;

(b)   in respect of a non-dependant aged 18 or over to whom sub-paragraph (a) does not apply, [¹³ £2.30] × 1/7.

(2)   In the case of a non-dependant aged 18 or over to whom paragraph (1)(a) applies, where it is shown to the appropriate authority that his normal gross weekly income is–

(a)   less than [¹³ £178.00], the deduction to be made under this regulation shall be that specified in paragraph (1)(b);

(b)   not less than [¹³ £178.00] but less than [¹³ £306.00], the deduction to be made under this regulation shall be [¹³ £4.60];

(c)   not less than [¹³ £306.00] but less than [¹³ £382.00], the deduction to be made under this regulation shall be [¹³ £5.80].

(3)   Only one deduction shall be made under this regulation in respect of a couple or, as the case may be, members of a polygamous marriage and, where, but for this paragraph, the amount that would fall to be deducted in respect of one member of a couple or polygamous marriage is higher than the amount (if any) that would fall to be deducted in respect of the other, or any other, member, the higher amount shall be deducted.

(4)   In applying the provisions of paragraph (2) in the case of a couple or, as the case may be, a polygamous marriage, regard shall be had, for the purpose of that paragraph, to the couple's or, as the case may be, all members of the polygamous marriage's joint weekly gross income.

(5)   Where in respect of a day–

(a)   a person is a resident in a dwelling but is not himself liable for council tax in respect of that dwelling and that day;

(b)   other residents in that dwelling (the liable persons) have joint and several liability for council tax in respect of that dwelling and that day otherwise than by virtue of section 9, 77 or 77A of the 1992 Act (liability of spouses and civil partners); and

(c)   the person to whom sub-paragraph (a) refers is a non-dependant of two or more of the liable persons,

the deduction in respect of that non-dependant shall be apportioned equally between those liable persons.

(6)   No deduction shall be made in respect of any non-dependants occupying a claimant's dwelling if the claimant or his partner is–

(a)   blind or treated as blind by virtue of paragraph 13 of Schedule 1 (additional condition of the higher pensioner and disability premiums) to the Council Tax Benefit Regulations 2006; or

(b)   receiving in respect of himself either–

(i)   attendance allowance; or

(ii)   the care component of the disability living allowance.

(7)   No deduction shall be made in respect of a non-dependant if–

(a)   although he resides with the claimant, it appears to the relevant authority that his normal home is elsewhere; or

(b)   he is in receipt of a training allowance paid in connection with [⁹ youth training] established under section 2 of the 1973 Act or section 2 of the Enterprise and New Towns (Scotland) Act 1990; or

(c)   he is a full-time student within the meaning of Part 5 (Students) of the Council Tax Benefit Regulations 2006; or

(d)   he is not residing with the claimant because he has been a patient for a period in excess of 52 weeks, and for these purposes–

[¹ (i)   "patient" has the meaning given in paragraph (7) of regulation 8, and

(ii)   where a person has been a patient for two or more distinct periods separated by one or more intervals each not exceeding 28 days, he shall be treated as having been a patient continuously for a period equal in duration to the total of those distinct periods.]

(8)   No deduction shall be made in respect of a non-dependant–

(a)   who is on income support, on state pension credit [⁸ , an income-based jobseeker's allowance or an income-related emplyoment and support allowance]; or

(b)   to whom Schedule 1 of the 1992 Act applies (persons disregarded for purposes of discount) but this sub-paragraph shall not apply to a non-dependant who is a student to whom paragraph 4 of that Schedule refers.

(9)   In the application of paragraph (2) there shall be disregarded from his weekly gross income–

(a)   any attendance allowance or disability living allowance received by him;

(b)   any payment made under [¹² or by] the Trusts, the Fund, the Eileen Trust [¹² , MFET Limited] or the Independent Living [⁹ Fund (2006)] which had his income fallen to be calculated under regulation 30 of the Council Tax Benefit Regulations 2006 (calculation of income other than earnings) would have been disregarded under paragraph 24 of Schedule 4 to those Regulations (income in kind); and

(c)   any payment which had his income fallen to be calculated under regulation 30 of those Regulations would have been disregarded under paragraph 36 of Schedule 4 to those Regulations (payments made under certain trusts and certain other payments).

Amendments

1.   Substituted by reg 3(7) of SI 2005 No 2502 as amended by Sch 2 para 27 of SI 2006 No 217 as from 1.4.06.
2.   Confirmed by Art 21(3) of SI 2006 No 645 and reg 8 of SI 2006 No 217 as from 1.4.06.
3.   Amended by Art 21(3) of SI 2006 No 645 and reg 8 of SI 2006 No 217 as from 1.4.06
4.   Confirmed by Art 22(3) of SI 2007 No 688 as from 1.4.07.
5.   Amended by Art 22(3) of SI 2007 No 688 as from 1.4.07.
6.   Confirmed by Art 22(3) of SI 2008 No 632 as from 1.4.08.
7.   Amended by Art 22(3) of SI 2008 No 632 as from 1.4.08.
8.   Amended by reg 73 of SI 2008 No 1082 as from 27.10.08.
9.   Amended by reg 9(4) of SI 2008 No 2767 as from 17.11.08.
10.   Confirmed by Art 22(3) of SI 2009 No 497 as from 1.4.09.
11.   Amended by Art 22(3) of SI 2009 No 497 as from 1.4.09.
12.   Amended by reg 11(3) and (5) of SI 2010 No 641 as from 1.4.10 (5.4.10 where rent payable weekly or in multiples of a week).
13.   Confirmed by Art 22(3) of SI 2010 No 793 as from 1.4.10.

Council tax benefit taper

43.   The prescribed percentage for the purpose of sub-section (5)(c)(ii) of section 131 of the Act as it applies to council tax benefit, (percentage of excess of income over the applicable amount which is deducted from maximum council tax benefit)(a), shall be 2 6/7 per cent.

[¹Extended Payments (qualifying contributory benefits)

44.–(1)   Except in the case of a claimant who is in receipt of state pension credit, a claimant who is entitled to council tax benefit (by virtue of the general conditions of entitlement) shall be entitled to an extended payment (qualifying contributory benefits) where–

(a)   the claimant or the claimant's partner was entitled to a qualifying contributory benefit;

(b)   entitlement to a qualifying contributory benefit ceased because the claimant or the claimant's partner–
        (i)   commenced employment as an employed or self-employed earner;
        (ii)   increased their earnings from such employment; or
        (iii)   increased the number of hours worked in such employment,
        and that employment is or, as the case may be, increased earnings or increased number of hours are expected to last five weeks or more;

(c)   the claimant or the claimant's partner had been entitled to and in receipt of a qualifying contributory benefit or a combination of qualifying contributory benefits for a continuous period of at least 26 weeks before the day on which the entitlement to a qualifying contributory benefit ceased; and

(d)   the claimant or the claimant's partner was not entitled to and not in receipt of a qualifying income-related benefit in the last benefit week in which the claimant, or the claimant's partner, was entitled to a qualifying contributory benefit.

(2)   A claimant must be treated as entitled to council tax benefit by virtue of the general conditions of entitlement where–

(a)   the claimant ceased to be entitled to council tax benefit because the claimant vacated the dwelling in which the claimant was resident;

(b)   the day on which the claimant vacated the dwelling was either in the week in which entitlement to a qualifying contributory benefit ceased, or in the preceding week; and

(c)   entitlement to the qualifying contributory benefit ceased in any of the circumstances listed in paragraph (1)(b).]

Amendment

1.   Substituted by reg 10(2) of SI 2008 No 959 as from 6.10.08.

[¹ Duration of extended payment period (qualifying contributory benefits)

44A.–(1)   Where a claimant is entitled to an extended payment (qualifying contributory benefits), the extended payment period starts on the first day of the benefit week immediately following the benefit week in which the claimant, or the claimant's partner, ceased to be entitled to a qualifying contributory benefit.

(2)   For the purpose of paragraph (1), a claimant or a claimant's partner ceases to be entitled to a qualifying contributory benefit on the day immediately following the last day of entitlement to that benefit.

(3)   The extended payment period ends–

(a)   at the end of a period of four weeks; or

(b)   on the date on which the claimant to whom the extended payment (qualifying contributory benefits) is payable has no liability for council tax, if that occurs first.]

Amendment

1.   Inserted by reg 10(2) of SI 2008 No 959 as from 6.10.08.

[¹ Amount of extended payment (qualifying contributory benefits)

44B.–(1)   For any week during the extended payment period the amount of the extended payment (qualifying contributory benefits) payable to a claimant shall be the higher of–

(a)   the amount of council tax benefit to which the claimant was entitled under the general conditions of entitlement in the last benefit week before the claimant or the claimant's partner ceased to be entitled to a qualifying contributory benefit;

(b)   the amount of council tax benefit to which the claimant would be entitled under the general conditions of entitlement for any benefit week during the extended payment period, if regulation 44 (extended payments (qualifying contributory benefits)) did not apply to the claimant; or

(c)   the amount of council tax benefit to which the claimant's partner would be entitled under the general conditions of entitlement, if regulation 44 did not apply to the claimant.

(2)   Paragraph (1) does not apply in the case of a mover.

(3)   Where a claimant is in receipt of an extended payment (qualifying contributory benefits) under this regulation and the claimant's partner makes a claim for council tax benefit, no amount of council tax benefit shall be payable by the appropriate authority during the extended payment period.]

Amendment

1.   Inserted by reg 10(2) of SI 2008 No 959 as from 6.10.08.

[¹ Extended payments (qualifying contributory benefits) – movers

44C.–(1)   This regulation applies–

(a)   to a mover; and

(b)   from the Monday following the day of the move.

(2)   The amount of the extended payment (qualifying contributory benefit) payable from the Monday from which this regulation applies until the end of the extended payment period shall be the amount of council tax benefit which was payable to the mover for the last benefit week before the mover, or the mover's partner, ceased to be entitled to a qualifying contributory benefit.

(3)   Where a mover's liability to pay council tax in respect of the new dwelling is to the second authority, the extended payment (qualifying contributory benefits) may take the form of a payment from the appropriate authority to–

(a)   the second authority; or

(b)   the mover directly.

(4)   Where–

(a)   a mover, or the mover's partner, makes a claim for council tax benefit to the second authority after the mover, or the mover's partner, ceased to be entitled to a qualifying contributory benefit; and

(b)   the mover, or the mover's partner, is in receipt of an extended payment (qualifying contributory benefits) from the appropriate authority,

the second authority shall reduce the weekly amount of council tax benefit that the mover, or the mover's partner, is entitled to by a sum equal to the amount of the extended payment (qualifying contributory benefits) until the end of the extended payment period.]

Amendment

1.   Inserted by reg 10(2) of SI 2008 No 959 as from 6.10.08.

[1 Relationship between extended payment (qualifying contributory benefits) and entitlement to council tax benefit under the general conditions of entitlement

44D.–(1)   Where a claimant's council tax benefit award would have ended when the claimant ceased to be entitled to a qualifying contributory benefit in the circumstances listed in regulation 44(1)(b), that award will not cease until the end of the extended payment period.

(2)   Part 6 (period of entitlement, changes of circumstances and increases for exceptional circumstances) shall not apply to any extended payment (qualifying contributory benefits) payable in accordance with regulation 44B(1)(a) or regulation 44C(2) (amount of extended payment – movers).]

Amendment

1.   Inserted by reg 10(2) of SI 2008 No 959 as from 6.10.08.

Continuing payments where state pension credit claimed

45.–(1)   This regulation applies where–

(a)   the claimant is entitled to council tax benefit;

(b)   paragraph (2) is satisfied; and

(c)   either–

(i)   the claimant has attained the qualifying age for state pension credit or, if his entitlement to income-based jobseeker's allowance [1 or income-related employment and support allowance] continued beyond that age, has attained the age of 65; or

(ii)   the claimant's partner has actually claimed state pension credit.

(2)   This regulation is only satisfied if the Secretary of State has certified to the relevant authority that the claimant's partner has actually claimed state pension credit or that–

(a)   the claimant's award of–

(i)   income support has terminated because the claimant has attained the qualifying age for state pension credit; or

(ii)   income-based jobseeker's allowance [1 or income-related employment and support allowance] has terminated because the claimant has attained the qualifying age for state pension credit or the age of 65; and

(b)   the claimant has claimed or is treated as having claimed or is required to make a claim for state pension credit.

(3)   Subject to paragraph (4), in a case to which this regulation applies, council tax benefit shall continue to be paid for the period of 4 weeks beginning on the day following the day the claimant's entitlement to income support or, as the case may be, income-based jobseeker's allowance [1 , income-related employment and support allowance],

ceased, if and for so long as the claimant otherwise satisfies the conditions for entitlement to council tax benefit.

(4) Where council tax benefit is paid for the period of 4 weeks in accordance with paragraph (3) above, and the last day of that period falls on a day other than the last day of a benefit week, then council tax benefit shall continue to be paid until the end of the benefit week in which the last day of that period falls.

(5) Throughout the period of 4 weeks specified in paragraph (3) and any further period specified in paragraph (4)–

(a) the whole of the income and capital of the claimant shall be disregarded;

(b) the appropriate maximum council tax benefit of the claimant shall be that which was applicable in his case immediately before that period commenced.

(6) The appropriate maximum council tax benefit shall be calculated in accordance with regulation 40(1) if, since the date it was last calculated–

(a) the claimant's council tax liability has increased; or

(b) a change in the deduction under regulation 42 falls to be made.

Amendment

1. Amended by reg 74 of SI 2008 No 1082 as from 27.10.08.

Alternative maximum council tax benefit

46.–(1) Subject to paragraphs (2) and (3), the alternative maximum council tax benefit where the conditions set out in section 131(3) and (6) of the Act are fulfilled, shall be the amount determined in accordance with Schedule 6.

(2) Subject to paragraph (3), where a claimant is jointly and severally liable for council tax in respect of a dwelling in which he is resident with one or more other persons, in determining the alternative maximum council tax benefit in his case, the amount determined in accordance with Schedule 6 shall be divided by the number of persons who are jointly and severally liable for that tax.

(3) Where a claimant is jointly and severally liable for council tax in respect of a dwelling with only his partner, solely by virtue of section 9, 77 or 77A of the 1992 Act (liability of spouses and civil partners), paragraph (2) shall not apply in his case.

General Note

See the commentary to reg 62 and Sch 2 CTB Regs on pp704 and 736. However, note that prior to 19 May 2008, there was no equivalent in the CTB(SPC) Regs to Sch 5 para 46 CTB Regs. This meant that unless the claimant or her/his partner was in receipt of the guarantee credit of PC (in which case the whole of her/his capital is ignored under reg 16) the capital limit provided by s134 SSCBA and reg 33 applied. This is understood to have been an error, not the intention, as the Social Security (Miscellaneous Amendments)(No.2) Regulations 2008 SI No.1042 inserted para 26A into Sch 4 from 19 May 2008. Under that paragraph, the whole of the claimant's capital is disregarded where s/he satisfies the conditions in s131(3) and (6) (alternative maximum CTB), but not those in s131(4) and (5) SSCBA 1992 (main CTB).

Residents of a dwelling to whom section 131(6) of the Act does not apply

47. Subsection (6) of section 131 of the Act (residents of a dwelling in respect of whom entitlement to an alternative maximum council tax benefit may arise) shall not apply in respect of any person referred to in the following paragraphs namely–

(a) a person who is liable for council tax solely in consequence of the provisions of sections 9, 77 or 77A of the 1992 Act (spouse's or civil partner's joint and several liability for tax);

(b) a person who is residing with a couple or with the members of a polygamous marriage where the claimant for council tax benefit is a member of that couple or of that marriage and–

(i) in the case of a couple, neither member of that couple is a person who, in accordance with Schedule 1 to the 1992 Act, falls to be disregarded for the purposes of discount; or

(ii) in the case of a polygamous marriage, two or more members of that marriage are not persons who, in accordance with Schedule 1 to the 1992 Act, fall to be disregarded for the purposes of discount;

(c)   a person who jointly with the claimant for benefit falls within the same paragraph of sections 6(2)(a) to (e) or 75(2)(a) to (e) of the 1992 Act (persons liable to pay council tax) as applies in the case of the claimant;

(d)   a person who is residing with two or more persons both or all of whom fall within the same paragraph of sections 6(2)(a) to (e) or 75(2)(a) to (e) of the 1992 Act and two or more of those persons are not persons who, in accordance with Schedule 1 to the 1992 Act, fall to be disregarded for the purposes of discount.

PART 6
Period of entitlement, changes of circumstances and increases for exceptional circumstances

Date on which entitlement is to begin

48.–(1)   Subject to paragraph (2), any person by whom or in respect of whom a claim for council tax benefit is made and is otherwise entitled to that benefit shall be entitled from the benefit week following the first day in respect of which that claim is made.

(2)   A claimant who is otherwise entitled to council tax benefit and becomes liable, for the first time, for a relevant authority's council tax in respect the dwelling of which he is a resident in the benefit week in which the first day in respect of which his claim was made falls, shall be so entitled from that benefit week.

Analysis

Reg 48 determines the date on which entitlement to CTB commences. See the analysis to reg 53 on p967 for a discussion on the combined effect of this regulation and reg 53.

[¹Date on which council tax benefit is to end where entitlement to severe disablement allowance or incapacity benefit ceases
49.]

Amendment

1.   Omitted by reg 11(5)(a) of SI 2008 No 959 as from 6.10.08.

Date on which change of circumstances is to take effect

50.–(1)   Except in cases where regulation 24 (disregard of changes in tax, contributions, etc) [² applies, and subject to regulation 8(3) of the Decisions and Appeals Regulations, and] the following provisions of this regulation and regulation 51, a change of circumstances which affects entitlement to, or the amount of, council tax benefit ("change of circumstances"), shall take effect from the first day of the benefit week following the date on which the change actually occurs, and where that change is cessation of entitlement to any benefit under the benefit Acts, the date on which the change actually occurs shall be the day immediately following the last day of entitlement to that benefit.

(2)   Subject to paragraph (3), where the change of circumstances is a change in the amount of council tax payable, it shall take effect from the day on which it actually occurs.

(3)   Where the change of circumstances is a change in the amount a person is liable to pay in respect of council tax in consequence of regulations under section 13 or 80 of the 1992 Act (reduced amounts of council tax) or changes in the discount to which a dwelling may be subject under sections 11, 12 or 79 of that Act, it shall take effect from the day on which the change in amount has effect.

(4)   Where the change of circumstances is an amendment to these Regulations, it shall take effect from the date on which the amendment to these Regulations comes into force.

(5)   Where the change of circumstances is the claimant's acquisition of a partner, the change shall have effect on the day on which the acquisition takes place.

(6)   Where the change of circumstances is the death of a claimant's partner or their separation, it shall have effect on the day the death or separation occurs.

(7)   If two or more changes of circumstances occurring in the same benefit week would, but for this paragraph, take effect in different benefit weeks in accordance with paragraphs (1) to (6) they shall take effect from the day to which the appropriate paragraph from (2) to (6) above refers, or, where more than one day is concerned, from the earlier day.

(8)   Where the change of circumstances is that income, or an increase in the amount of income, other than a benefit or an increase in the amount of a benefit under the Act, is paid in respect of a past period and there was no entitlement to income of that amount during that period, the change of circumstances shall take effect from the first day on which such income, had it been paid in that period at intervals appropriate to that income, would have fallen to be taken into account for the purposes of these Regulations.

(9)   Without prejudice to paragraph (8), where the change of circumstances is the payment of income, or arrears of income, in respect of a past period, the change of circumstances shall take effect from the first day on which such income, had it been timeously paid in that period at intervals appropriate to that income, would have fallen to be taken into account for the purposes of these Regulations.

(10)   Paragraph (11) applies if–

(a)   the claimant or his partner has attained the age of 65; and

(b)   either–

  (i)   a non-dependant took up residence in the claimant's dwelling; or

  (ii)   there has been a change of circumstances in respect of a non-dependant so that the amount of the deduction which falls to be made under regulation 42 increased.

(11)   Where this paragraph applies, the change of circumstances [¹ referred to in paragraph (10)(b)] shall take effect from the effective date.

(12)   In paragraph (11) but subject to paragraph (13), "the effective date" means–

(a)   where more than one change of a kind referred to in paragraph (10)(b) relating to the same non-dependant has occurred since–

  (i)   the date on which the claimant's entitlement to council tax benefit first began; or

  (ii)   the date which was the last effective date in respect of such a change, whichever is the later, the date which falls 26 weeks after the date on which the first such change occurred;

(b)   where sub-paragraph (a) does not apply, the date which falls 26 weeks after the date on which the change referred to in paragraph (10)(b) occurred.

(13)   If in any particular case the date determined under paragraph (12) is not the first day of a benefit week, the effective date in that case shall be the first day of the next benefit week to commence after the date determined under that paragraph.

Modifications

Reg 50 applies as if para (9) was omitted where a change of circumstances occurs as a result of the payment of arrears of any income which affects a determination or decision in respect of entitlement to, or the amount of, HB or CTB before 6 March 1995. See Sch 3 para 1 HB&CTB(CP) Regs on p1197.

Amendments

1.   Amended by reg 18(3) of SI 2006 No 2378 as from 2.10.06.
2.   Substituted by reg 7 of SI 2007 No 2470 as from 24.9.07.

Change of circumstances where state pension credit in payment

51.–(1)   Paragraphs (2) to (4) apply where–

(a)   the claimant is also on state pension credit;

(b)   the amount of state pension credit awarded to him is changed in consequence of a change in the claimant's circumstances or the correction of an official error; and

(c)   the change in the amount of state pension credit payable to the claimant results in a change in the rate at which council tax benefit is allowed to him.

(2)   Where the change of circumstance is that an increase in the amount of state pension credit payable to the claimant results in–

(a)   an increase in the rate at which council tax benefit is allowed to him, the change shall take effect from the first day of the benefit week in which state pension credit becomes payable at the increased rate; or

(b)   a decrease in the rate at which council tax benefit is payable to him, the change shall take effect from the first day of the benefit week next following the date on which–

    (i)   the local authority receives notification from the Secretary of State of the increase in the amount of state pension credit; or

    (ii)   state pension credit is increased,

    whichever is the later.

(3)   Where the change of circumstance is that the claimant's state pension credit has been reduced and in consequence the rate of council tax benefit allowed to the claimant reduces–

(a)   in a case where the claimant's state pension credit is reduced because the claimant failed to notify the Secretary of State timeously of the change of circumstances, the change shall take effect from the first day of the benefit week from which state pension credit was reduced; or

(b)   in any other case the change shall take effect from the first day of the benefit week next following the date on which–

    (i)   the local authority receives notification from the Secretary of State of the reduction in the amount of state pension credit; or

    (ii)   state pension credit is reduced,

    whichever is the later.

(4)   Where the change of circumstance is that state pension credit is reduced and in consequence of the change, the rate of council tax benefit allowed to the claimant is increased, the change shall take effect from the first day of the benefit week in which state pension credit becomes payable at the reduced rate.

(5)   Where a change of circumstance occurs in that an award of state pension credit has been made to the claimant or his partner and this would result in a decrease in the rate of council tax benefit payable to the claimant, the change shall take effect from the first day of the benefit week next following the date on which–

(a)   the local authority receives notification from the Secretary of State of the award of state pension credit; or

(b)   entitlement to state pension credit begins,

    whichever is the later.

(6)   Where, in the case of a claimant who, or whose partner, is or has been awarded state pension credit comprising only the savings credit, there is–

(a)   a change of circumstances of a kind described in any of paragraphs (2) to (5) which results from a relevant calculation or estimate; and

(b)   a change of circumstances which is a relevant determination,

    each of which results in a change in the rate of council tax benefit payable to the claimant, the change of circumstances referred to in sub-paragraph (b) shall take effect from the day specified in paragraphs (2), (3), (4) or (5) as the case may be, in relation to the change referred to in sub-paragraph (a).

(7)   Where a change of circumstance occurs in that a guarantee credit has been awarded to the claimant or his partner and this would result in an increase in the rate of council tax benefit payable to the claimant, the change shall take effect from the first day of the benefit week next following the date in respect of which the guarantee credit is first payable.

(8)   Where a change of circumstances would, but for this paragraph, take effect under the preceding provisions of this regulation within the 4 week period specified in regulation 45 (continuing payments where state pension credit claimed), that change shall take effect on the first day of the first benefit week to commence after the expiry of the 4 week period.

(9)   Where the change of circumstances is an amendment of these Regulations that change shall take effect from the date on which the amendment to these Regulations, comes into force.

(10)   In paragraph (1) "official error" has the meaning it has in the Decisions and Appeals Regulations by virtue of regulation 1(2) of those Regulations

(11)   In this regulation–

"relevant calculation or estimate" means the calculation or estimate made by the Secretary of State of the claimant's or, as the case may be, the claimant's partner's income and capital for the purposes of the award of state pension credit;

"relevant determination" means a change in the determination by the relevant authority of the claimant's income and capital using the relevant calculation or estimate, in accordance with regulation 17(1).

PART 7
Claims

Who may claim
52.–(1)   In the case of a couple or members of a polygamous marriage a claim shall be made by whichever one of them they agree should so claim or, in default of agreement, by such one of them as the relevant authority shall determine.

(2)   Where a person who is liable to pay council tax in respect of a dwelling is unable for the time being to act, and–
- (a)   a [¹ deputy] has been appointed by the Court of Protection with power to claim, or as the case may be, receive benefit on his behalf; or
- (b)   in Scotland, his estate is being administered by a judicial factor or any guardian acting or appointed under the Adults with Incapacity (Scotland) Act 2000 who has power to claim or, as the case may be, receive benefit on his behalf; or
- (c)   an attorney with a general power or a power to claim or, as the case may be, receive benefit, has been appointed by that person under [¹ the Powers of Attorney Act 1971, the Enduring Powers of Attorney Act 1985 or the Mental Capacity Act 2005] or otherwise,

that [¹ deputy], judicial factor, guardian or attorney, as the case may be, may make a claim on behalf of that person.

(3)   Where a person who is liable to pay council tax in respect of a dwelling is unable for the time being to act and paragraph (2) does not apply to him, the relevant authority may, upon written application made to them by a person who, if a natural person, is over the age of 18, appoint that person to exercise on behalf of the person who is unable to act, any right to which that person might be entitled under the Act and to receive and deal on his behalf with any sums payable to him.

(4)   Where the relevant authority has made an appointment under paragraph (3) or treated a person as an appointee under paragraph (5)–
- (a)   it may at any time revoke the appointment;
- (b)   the person appointed may resign his office after having given 4 weeks notice in writing to the relevant authority of his intention to do so;
- (c)   any such appointment shall terminate when the relevant authority is notified of the appointment of a person mentioned in paragraph (2).

(5)   Where a person who is liable to pay council tax in respect of a dwelling is for the time being unable to act and the Secretary of State has appointed a person to act on his behalf under regulation 33 of the Social Security (Claims and Payments) Regulations 1987 (persons unable to act), the relevant authority may if that person agrees, treat him as if he had been appointed by them under paragraph (3).

(6)   Anything required by these Regulations to be done by or to any person who is for the time being unable to act may be done by or to the persons mentioned in paragraph (2) above or by or to the person appointed or treated as appointed under this regulation and the receipt of any such person so appointed shall be a good discharge to the relevant authority for any sum paid.

[² (7)]

Amendments
1.   Amended by reg 13(6) of SI 2007 No 2618 as from 1.10.07.
2.   Omitted by reg 5(3) of SI 2008 No 2299 as from 1.10.08.

Time and manner in which claims are to be made

53.–[¹ (1ZA)   [¹¹ Subject to paragraph (1ZB),] The prescribed time for claiming council tax benefit is as regards any day on which, apart from satisfying the condition of making a claim, the claimant is entitled to council tax benefit, that day and the period of [⁸ three months] immediately following it .]

[¹¹ (1ZB)   In any case where paragraph (5)(a) applies, paragraph (1ZA) does not entitle a claimant to claim council tax benefit in respect of any day earlier than 3 months before the date on which the claim for state pension credit is made (or treated as made by virtue of any provision of the Social Security (Claims and Payments) Regulations 1987).]

(1)   [¹ Subject to [⁵ paragraphs (4A) to (4BD)],] Every claim shall be in writing and made on a properly completed form approved for the purpose by the relevant authority or in such written form as the relevant authority may accept as sufficient in the circumstances of any particular case or class of cases having regard to the sufficiency of the written information and evidence.

(2)   The forms approved for the purpose of claiming shall be provided free of charge by the relevant authority or such persons as they may authorise or appoint for the purpose.

(3)   Each relevant authority shall notify the Secretary of State of the address to which claims delivered or sent to the appropriate DWP office are to be forwarded.

(4)   A claim [¹ in writing]–

(a)   may be sent or delivered to the appropriate DWP office where the claimant or his partner is also claiming income support, incapacity benefit, state pension credit [⁷ , a jobseeker's allowance or an employment and support allowance];

(b)   where it has not been sent or delivered to the appropriate DWP office, shall be sent or delivered to the designated office;

(c)   sent or delivered to the appropriate DWP office, other than one sent on the same form as a claim being made to income support, incapacity benefit [⁷ , a jobseeker's allowance or an employment and support allowance] and as approved by the Secretary of State for the purpose of the benefits being claimed, shall be forwarded to the relevant authority within two working days of the date of the receipt of the claim at the appropriate DWP office, or as soon as practicable thereafter;

[⁵ (d)]
[⁵ (e)]

(f)   where the claimant has attained the qualifying age for state pension credit, may be sent or delivered to an office which is an authorised office.

[³ (g) may be sent or delivered to the offices of a county council in England if the council has arranged with the relevant authority for claims to be received at their offices (''county offices'').]

[¹ (4A)   Where the relevant authority has published a telephone number for the purpose of receiving claims for council tax benefit, a claim may be made by telephone to that telephone number.

[⁵ (4B)   If the Secretary of State agrees, where a person is–

(a)   making a claim for a benefit referred to in paragraph (4)(a); and

(b)   the Secretary of State has made provision in the Social Security (Claims and Payments) Regulations 1987 for that benefit to be claimed by telephone,

that person may claim council tax benefit by telephone to the telephone number specified by the Secretary of State.

(4BA)   A claim for council tax benefit may be made in accordance with paragraph (4B) at any time before a decision has been made on the claim for the benefit referred to in paragraph (4)(a).

(4BB)   If the Secretary of State agrees, where a person, in accordance with regulation 32 of the Social Security (Claims and Payments) Regulations 1987 (information to be given and changes to be notified)–

(a)   furnishes the Secretary of State with such information or evidence as he may require; or

(b)   notifies the Secretary of State of any change of circumstances,

that person may claim council tax benefit in the same manner in which the information or evidence was furnished or the notification was given.

(4BC)   If the Secretary of State agrees, where a person, in accordance with regulation 24 of the Jobseeker's Allowance Regulations (provision of information and evidence)–

(a)   furnishes the Secretary of State with such certificates, documents and other evidence as he may require; or

(b)   notifies the Secretary of State of any change of circumstances,

that person may claim council tax benefit in the same manner as the certificate, document and other evidence was furnished or the notification was given.

(4BD)   A claim for council tax benefit may be made in accordance with paragraphs (4BB) or (4BC) at any time before a decision has been made on the award of benefit to which the information, evidence, certificates, documents or notification relates.]

(4C)   The relevant authority may determine, in any particular case, that a claim made by telephone [⁵ in accordance with paragraph (4A)] is not a valid claim unless the person making the claim approves a written statement of his circumstances, provided for the purpose by the relevant authority [⁵].

[⁵ (4CA)   The relevant authority or the Secretary of State may determine that a claim made by telephone in accordance with paragraphs (4B) to (4BD) is not a valid claim unless the person making the claim approves a written statement of his circumstances, provided for the purpose by the Secretary of State.]

(4D)   [⁵ A claim made by telephone in accordance with paragraphs (4A) to (4BD) is defective unless the relevant authority or the Secretary of State is provided with all the information requested during that telephone call.]

(4E)   Where a claim made by telephone in accordance with paragraph (4A) [⁵] is defective, the relevant authority [⁵ must] provide the person making it with an opportunity to correct the defect.

[⁵ (4EA)   Where a claim made by telephone in accordance with paragraphs (4B) to (4BD) is defective–

(a)   the Secretary of State may provide the person making it with an opportunity to correct the defect;

(b)   the relevant authority must provide the person making it with an opportunity to correct the defect if the Secretary of State has not already done so unless it considers that it has sufficient information to determine the claim.]

(4F)   If the person corrects the defect within one month, or such longer period as the relevant authority considers reasonable, [⁵ of the date the relevant authority or the Secretary of State] last drew attention to it, the relevant authority shall treat the claim as if it had been duly made in the first instance.]

[⁵ (4G)   If the person does not correct the defect within one month, or such longer period as the relevant authority considers reasonable, of the date the relevant authority or the Secretary of State last drew attention to it, the relevant authority may treat the claim as if it had been duly made in the first instance where it considers that it has sufficient information to determine the claim.]

(5)   Subject to paragraph (12), [⁵] the date on which a claim is made shall be–

(a)   in a case where an award of state pension credit which comprises a guarantee credit has been made to the claimant or his partner and the claim for council tax benefit is made within one month of the date on which the claim for that state pension credit which comprises a guarantee credit was received at the appropriate DWP office, the first day of entitlement to, state pension credit which comprises a guarantee credit arising from that claim;

(b)   in a case where a claimant or his partner is a person in receipt of a guarantee credit and he becomes liable for the first time to pay council tax in respect of the dwelling he occupies as his home, where the claim to the authority is received at the designated office or appropriate social security office within one month of the date of the change, the date on which the change takes place;

(c) in a case where the claimant is the former partner of a person who was, at the date of his death or their separation, entitled to council tax benefit and where the claimant makes a claim for council tax benefit within one month of the date of the death or the separation, that date;

[⁵ (d) except where sub-paragraph (a), (b) or (c) is satisfied, in a case where a properly completed claim is received in a designated office, an authorised office, county offices or an appropriate DWP office within one month, or such longer period as the relevant authority considers reasonable, of the date on which–

    (i) a claim form was issued to the claimant following the claimant first notifying, by whatever means, a designated office, an authorised office or an appropriate DWP office of an intention to make a claim; or

    (ii) a claimant notifies, by whatever means, a designated office, an authorised office or an appropriate DWP office of an intention to make a claim by telephone in accordance with paragraphs (4A) to (4BD),

the date of first notification; and]

(e) in any other case, the date on which the claim is received at the designated office [¹ or authorised office [³ , county offices] or appropriate DWP office].

(6) Where a claim received at the designated office [⁹ or appropriate DWP office] has not been made in the manner prescribed in paragraph (1), that claim is for the purposes of these Regulations defective.

(7) Where a claim [⁹ , which is received by a relevant authority,] is defective because–

(a) it was made on the form approved for the purpose but that form is not accepted by the relevant authority as being properly completed; or

(b) it was made in writing but not on the form approved for the purpose and the relevant authority does not accept the claim as being in a written form which is sufficient in the circumstances of the case having regard to the sufficiency of the written information and evidence,

the relevant authority may, in a case to which sub-paragraph (a) applies, request the claimant to complete the defective claim or, in the case to which sub-paragraph (b) applies, supply the claimant with the approved form or request further information and evidence.

[⁹ (7A) Where a claim is received at an appropriate DWP office and it appears to the Secretary of State that the form has not been properly completed, the Secretary of State may request that the claimant provides the relevant authority with the information required to complete the form.]

[(8) The relevant authority shall treat a defective claim as if it had been validly made in the first instance if, in any particular case, the conditions specified in sub-paragraph (a), (b) or (c) of paragraph (8A) are satisfied.

(8A) The conditions are that–

(a) where paragraph (7)(a) (incomplete form) applies, the authority receives at the designated office the properly completed claim or the information requested to complete it or the evidence within one month of the request, or such longer period as the relevant authority may consider reasonable; or

(b) where paragraph (7)(b) (claim not on approved form or further information requested by relevant authority) applies–

    (i) the approved form sent to the claimant is received at the designated office properly completed within one month of it having been sent to him; or, as the case may be,

    (ii) the claimant supplies whatever information or evidence was requested under paragraph (7) within one month of the request,

or, in either case, within such longer period as the relevant authority may consider reasonable; or

(c) where paragraph (7A) (further information requested by Secretary of State) applies, the relevant authority receives at the designated office the properly completed claim or the information requested to complete it within one month of the request by the Secretary of State or within such longer period as the relevant authority considers reasonable.]

(9) A claim which is made on an approved form for the time being is, for the purposes of this regulation, properly completed if completed in accordance with the instructions on the form, including any instructions to provide information and evidence in connection with the claim.

[² (10) Except in the case of a claim made by a person from abroad, where a person has not become liable for council tax to a relevant authority but it is anticipated that he will become so liable within the period of 8 weeks (the relevant period), he may claim council tax benefit at any time in that period in respect of that tax and, provided that liability arises within the relevant period, the authority shall treat the claim as having been made on the day on which the liability for the tax arises.]

(11) Where, exceptionally, a relevant authority, has not set or imposed its council tax by the beginning of the financial year, if a claim for council tax benefit is properly made or treated as properly made and–

(a) the date on which the claim is made or treated as made is in the period from the 1st April of the current year and ending one month after the date on which the authority sets or imposes the tax; and

(b) if the tax had been determined, the claimant would have been entitled to council tax benefit either from–

    (i) the benefit week in which the 1st April of the current year fell; or

    (ii) a benefit week falling after the date specified in head (i) but before the claim was made,

the relevant authority shall treat the claim as made in the benefit week immediately preceding the benefit week in which such entitlement would have commenced.

[² (12) Except in the case of a claim made by a person from abroad, where the claimant is not entitled to council tax benefit in the benefit week immediately following the date of his claim but the relevant authority is of the opinion that unless there is a change of circumstances he will be entitled to council tax benefit for a period beginning not later than the seventeenth benefit week following the date on which the claim is made, the relevant authority may treat the claim as made on a date in the benefit week immediately preceding the first benefit week of that period of entitlement and award benefit accordingly.]

[⁴ (12A) Paragraph (12) applies in the case of a person who has attained, or whose partner has attained, [¹⁰ the age which is 17 weeks younger than the qualifying age for state pension credit].]

[⁸ (13)]

(14) In this regulation "authorised office" means an office which is nominated by the Secretary of State and authorised by relevant authority for receiving claims for decision by the relevant authority.

Amendments

1. Inserted by reg 5(2) of SI 2006 No 2967 as from 20.12.06.
2. Substituted by reg 6 of SI 2007 No 1331 as from 23.5.07.
3. Amended by reg 10(2) of SI 2007 No 2911 as from 31.10.07.
4. Inserted by reg 6(4) of SI 2008 No 1042 as from 19.5.08.
5. Amended by reg 5(4) of SI 2008 No 2299 as from 1.10.08.
6. Substituted by reg 7(2) of SI 2008 No 2424 as from 6.10.08.
7. Amended by reg 75 of SI 2008 No 1082 as from 27.10.08.
8. Amended by reg 9 of SI 2008 No 2824 as from 27.11.08.
9. Amended by reg 5(2) of SI 2008 No 2987 as from 22.12.08.
10. Amended by reg 38 of SI 2009 No 1488 as from 6.4.10.
11. Amended by reg 5(3) of SI 2010 No 2449 as from 1.11.10.

Analysis

This is the equivalent of reg 60 CTB Regs. There are differences.

Paragraphs (1ZA), (1ZB) and (5)

Para (5) determines the date of claim for CTB purposes and para (1ZA) determines the earliest date of entitlement to CTB; it is not a backdating provision as such. See the commentary to reg 64(1) HB(SPC) Regs on p856. The date on which entitlement to CTB then commences is determined by reg 48.

Prior to 1 November 2010, the combined effect of these provisions could be generous, as shown in *Leicester City Council v LG* [2009] UKUT 155 (AAC). A request to the Pension Service to visit the claimant and assist with backdated claims for PC and CTB was made on 4 July 2007. The visit did not take place until 21 February 2008, when claim forms for both benefits were completed at the same time. The claimant was awarded PC with effect from 6 July 2006, based on her claim for PC being accepted as made in July 2007 (at the time a claim for PC could be backdated 12 months). The local authority determined the date of claim for CTB as 26 February 2007, the date 12 months before the date it received the CTB claim form, 12 months being the maximum period a CTB claim could then be "backdated" under regs 53(1ZA) and 56. Judge Jacobs disagreed. He decided that the date of claim for CTB was 6 July 2006 and that the claimant's entitlement to CTB was to be determined from a date 12 months before that date. His analysis of the issues was as follows:

(1)   Once a claim for CTB is made, the date of that claim is determined by reg 53. Para (5) expressly provides what the date of claim shall be. As the claimant here had been awarded PC and had claimed CTB within one month of her claim for that benefit, under para (5)(a) her date of claim was the effective date of the PC award – ie, 6 July 2006, the date to which her PC claim had been backdated.

(2)   The earliest date of entitlement to CTB is determined by regs 53(1ZA) and 56. Those regulations deal in form with the date of claim but in substance with the start of entitlement to CTB. The effect of those provisions is to give the claimant a period of time in which to make a claim from the time when the other conditions of entitlement to CTB were satisfied. At the time of the decision this was 12 months (ie, 12 months before the date of claim), but has since been shortened to three months.

(3)   The effective date (ie, the date on which entitlement to CTB is to commence) is determined by reg 48. If the claimant is otherwise entitled to CTB, it is the first day of the benefit week following the first day in respect of which the claim was made. "In respect of" caters for the possibility that the claim may have been made in respect of a period before the date of claim. The claimant may specify a date from which the claim is made. If so, that is the effective date, provided the other conditions of entitlement are satisfied. If the claimant does not specify a date, the local authority has two choices. It may ask the claimant to specify the date, or it may take the most favourable date, which is the maximum set by regs 53(1ZA) and 56.

Judge Jacobs accepted that this analysis produced an outcome that was very generous to claimants but said that is not a reason for rejecting it. He said: "No one can have missed the publicity about low take up of entitlement to council tax benefit and benefits for pensioners generally. The legislation clearly allows generous periods within which to claim, although they have now been significantly reduced, and my analysis is merely the logical consequence of the provisions."

Para (1ZB) was inserted from 1 November 2010 to reverse the effect of the decision in *Leicester City Council v LG*. Now, in a case where para 5(a) applies (ie, where there is an award of PC guarantee credit and a claim for CTB was made within one month of the claim for that credit), a claimant is not entitled to claim CTB for any day earlier than three months before the claim for PC was made (or treated as made). This would appear to mean that in such a case, the effective date for CTB as determined by reg 48 (ie, the date on which entitlement to CTB is to commence) cannot be earlier than the effective date of the PC award because the claimant cannot specify a date from which her/his claim is made that precedes that date.

Note that reg 56 was omitted from 1 November 2010.

[¹Electronic claims for benefit

53A.   A claim for council tax benefit may be made by means of an electronic communication in accordance with Schedule 8.]

Amendment

1.   Inserted by Art 5(3) of SI 2006 No 2968 as from 20.12.06.

[¹ Date of claim where claim sent or delivered to a gateway office

54.]

Amendment

1.   Omitted by reg 5(5) of SI 2008 No 2299 as from 1.10.08.

[¹ Date of claim where claim sent or delivered to an office of a designated authority

55.]

Amendment

1.   Omitted by reg 5(6) of SI 2008 No 2299 as from 1.10.08.

[¹Time for claiming council tax benefit
56.]

Amendments

1. Inserted by reg 7(3) of SI 2008 No 2424 as from 6.10.08.
2. Omitted by reg 5(4) of SI 2010 No 2449 as from 1.11.10.

General Note

Reg 56 was identical to reg 53(1ZA). It is not clear why this duplication was felt to be necessary. The regulation was omitted from 1 November 2010.

Evidence and information

57.–(1) Subject to [³ paragraphs (1A) and (2)] and to paragraph 4 of Schedule A1 (treatment of claims for council tax benefit by refugees), a person who makes a claim, or a person to whom council tax benefit has been awarded, shall furnish such certificates, documents, information and evidence in connection with the claim or the award, or any question arising out of the claim or the award, as may reasonably be required by the relevant authority in order to determine that person's entitlement to, or continuing entitlement to council tax benefit and shall do so within one month of [³ the relevant authority requiring him, or the Secretary of State requesting him, to do so] or such longer period as the relevant authority may consider reasonable.

[³ (1A) Where a person notifies a change of circumstances to the appropriate DWP office under regulation 59(10), the Secretary of State may request that the claimant provides to the relevant authority the information or evidence that the Secretary of State considers the relevant authority may require to determine the claimant's continuing entitlement to housing benefit.]

(2) Nothing in this regulation shall require a person to furnish any certificates, documents, information or evidence relating to a payment to which paragraph (4) applies.

(3) Where a request is made under paragraph (1), the relevant authority shall–

(a) inform the claimant or the person to whom council tax benefit has been awarded of his duty under regulation 59 (duty to notify change of circumstances) to notify the designated office of any change of circumstances; and

(b) without prejudice to the extent of the duty owed under regulation 59, indicate to him either orally or by notice or by reference to some other document available to him on application and without charge, the kind of change of circumstances which is to be notified.

(4) This paragraph applies to any of the following payments–

(a) a payment which is made under [⁴ or by] the Trusts, the Fund, the Eileen Trust [⁴, MFET Limited], the Skipton Fund or the London Bombings Relief Charitable Fund;

(b) a payment which is disregarded under paragraph 16 of Schedule 4 (payments made under certain trusts and certain other payments), other than a payment under the Independent Living [² Fund (2006)];

(c) a payment which is disregarded under regulation 42(9)(b) or (c) (non-dependant deductions) or paragraph 2(b) or (c) of Schedule 6 (second adult's gross income) other than a payment under the Independent Living [² Fund (2006)].

(5) Where a claimant or a person to whom council tax benefit has been awarded or any partner [⁴ has attained the qualifying age for state pension credit] and is a member of, or a person deriving entitlement to a pension under, a personal pension scheme, [¹] he shall where the relevant authority so requires furnish the following information–

(a) the name and address of the pension fund holder;

(b) such other information including any reference or policy number as is needed to enable the personal pension scheme [¹] to be identified.

(6) Where the pension fund holder receives from a relevant authority a request for details concerning a personal pension scheme [¹] relating to a person or any partner to whom paragraph (5) refers, the pension fund holder shall provide the relevant authority with any information to which paragraph (7) refers.

(7) The information to which this paragraph refers is–

(a)   where the purchase of an annuity under a personal pension scheme has been deferred, the amount of any income which is being withdrawn from the personal pension scheme;

(b)   in the case of–

    (i)   a personal pension scheme where income withdrawal is available, the maximum amount of income which may be withdrawn from the scheme; or

    (ii)   a personal pension scheme where income withdrawal is not available, [¹] the maximum amount of income which might be withdrawn from the fund if the fund were held under a personal pension scheme where income withdrawal was available,

calculated by or on behalf of the pension fund holder by means of tables prepared from time to time by the Government Actuary which are appropriate for this purpose.

Amendments

    1.   Amended by reg 7(5) of SI 2007 No 1749 as from 16.7.07.
    2.   Amended by reg 9(5)(a) of SI 2008 No 2767 as from 17.11.08.
    3.   Amended by reg 5(3) of SI 2008 No 2987 as from 22.12.08.
    4.   Amended by reg 11(3), (5) and (6) of SI 2010 No 641 as from 1.4.10 (5.4.10 where rent payable weekly or in multiples of a week).

[²Amendment and withdrawal of claim

[³**58.**–(1)   A person who has made a claim may amend it at any time before a decision has been made on it by a notice in writing delivered or sent to the designated office.

(2)   Where the claim was made by telephone in accordance with paragraphs (4A) to (4BD) of regulation 53, the amendment may also be made by telephone.

(3)   Any claim amended in accordance with paragraph (1) or (2) shall be treated as if it had been amended in the first instance.

(4)   A person who has made a claim may withdraw it at any time before a decision has been made on it by notice to the designated office.

(5)   Where the claim was made by telephone in accordance with paragraphs (4B) to (4BD) of regulation 53, the withdrawal may also be made by telephone to the telephone number specified by the Secretary of State.

(6)   Any notice of withdrawal given in accordance with paragraph (4) or (5) shall have effect when it is received.]

Amendments

    1.   Inserted by reg 5(3) of SI 2006 No 2967 as from 20.12.06.
    2.   Substituted by reg 9(2) of SI 2007 No 719 as from 2.4.07.
    3.   Substituted by reg 5(7) of SI 2008 No 2299 as from 1.10.08.

Duty to notify changes of circumstances

59.–(1)   Subject to paragraphs (3), (5) to (8) [⁶ and (10)] , if at any time between the making of a claim and a decision being made on it, or during the award of council tax benefit, there is a change of circumstances which the claimant or any person by whom or on whose behalf sums payable by way of council tax benefit are receivable might reasonably be expected to know might affect the claimant's right to, the amount of, or the receipt of council tax benefit, that person shall be under a duty to notify that change of circumstances by giving notice [²] to the designated office

[² [⁷ (a) in writing; or

(b)   by telephone–

    (i)   where the relevant authority has published a telephone number for that purpose or for the purposes of regulation 53 (time and manner in which claims are to be made) unless the authority determines that in any particular case or class of case notification may not be given by telephone; or

    (ii)   in any case or class of case where the relevant authority determines that notice may be given by telephone; or

(c) by any other means which the relevant authority agrees to accept in any particular case.]]

[³ (2)]

(3) The duty imposed on a person by paragraph (1) does not extend to notifying changes in–

(a) the amount of a council tax payable to the relevant authority;

(b) the age of the claimant or that of any member of his family;

(c) in these Regulations.

(4) Notwithstanding paragraph (3)(b) a claimant shall be required by paragraph (1) to notify the designated office of any change in the composition of his family arising from the fact that a person who was a member of his family is now no longer such a person because he ceases to be a child or young person.

(5) Where the amount of a claimant's council tax benefit is the alternative maximum council tax benefit in his case, the claimant shall be under a duty to give written notice to the designated office of changes which occur in the number of adults in the dwelling or in their total gross incomes which might reasonably be expected to change his entitlement to that council tax benefit and where any such adult ceases to be in receipt of [⁵ state pension credit,] income support [⁴ , an income-based jobseeker's allowance or an income-related employment and support allowance] the date when this occurs.

[³ (6)]

(7) A person entitled to council tax benefit who is also on state pension credit must report–

(a) changes affecting the residence or income of any non-dependant normally residing with the claimant or with whom the claimant normally resides;

(b) any absence from the dwelling which exceeds or is likely to exceed 13 weeks.

(8) In addition to the changes required to be reported under paragraph (7), a person whose state pension credit comprises only a savings credit must also report–

(a) changes affecting a child living with him which may result in a change in the amount of council tax benefit allowed in his case, but not changes in the age of the child;

[¹ (b)]

(c) any change in the amount of the claimant's capital to be taken into account which does or may take the amount of his capital to more than £16,000;

(d) any change in the income or capital of–

(i) a non-dependant whose income and capital are treated as belonging to the claimant in accordance with regulation 14 (circumstances in which income of a non-dependant is to be treated as claimant's); or

(ii) a person to whom regulation 17(4)(e) refers,

and whether such a person or, as the case may be, non-dependant stops living or begins or resumes living with the claimant.

(9) A person who is entitled to council tax benefit and on state pension credit need only report to the designated office the changes specified in paragraphs (7) and (8).

[⁶ (10) Where–

(a) the claimant or the claimant's partner is in receipt of jobseeker's allowance;

(b) the change of circumstance is that the claimant or the claimant's partner starts employment; and

(c) as a result of the change of circumstance either entitlement to that benefit will end or the amount of that benefit will be reduced,

the claimant may discharge the duty in paragraph (1) by notifying the change of circumstance by telephoning the appropriate DWP office if a telephone number has been provided for that purpose.]

Amendments

1. Omitted by reg 3(9) of SI 2005 No 2502 as amended by Sch 2 para 27 of SI 2006 No 217 as from 1.4.06.
2. Amended by reg 5(4) of SI 2006 No 2967 as from 20.12.06.
3. Omitted by reg 5(8) of SI 2008 No 2299 as from 1.10.08.
4. Amended by reg 76 of SI 2008 No 1082 as from 27.10.08.
5. Amended by reg 9(6) of SI 2008 No 2767 as from 17.11.08.

6.   Amended by reg 5(4) of SI 2008 No 2987 as from 22.12.08.
7.   Amended by reg 5(5) of SI 2010 No 2449 as from 1.11.10.

[¹ Alternative means of notifying changes of circumstances

59ZA.–(1)   In such cases and subject to such conditions as the Secretary of State may specify, the duty in regulation 59(1) to notify a change of circumstances may be discharged by notifying the Secretary of State–

(a)   where the change of circumstances is a birth or death, through a relevant authority, or a county council in England, by personal attendance at an office specified by that authority or county council, provided the Secretary of State has agreed with that authority or county council for it to facilitate such notification; or

(b)   where the change of circumstances is a death, by telephone to a telephone number specified for that purpose by the Secretary of State.

(2)   Paragraph (1) only applies if the authority administering the claimant's council tax benefit agrees with the Secretary of State that notifications may be made in accordance with that paragraph.

(3)   The Secretary of State must forward information received in accordance with paragraph (1) to the authority administering the claimant's council tax benefit.]

Amendment
1.   Inserted by reg 8 of SI 2010 No 444 as from 5.4.10.

[¹Notice of changes of circumstances given electronically

59A.   A person may give notice of a change of circumstances required to be notified under regulation 59 by means of an electronic communication in accordance with Schedule 8.]

Amendment
1.   Inserted by Art 5(4) of SI 2006 No 2968 as from 20.12.06.

PART 8
Decisions on questions

Decisions by a relevant authority

60.–(1)   Unless provided otherwise by these Regulations, any matter required to be determined under these Regulations shall be determined in the first instance by the relevant authority.

(2)   The relevant authority shall make a decision on each claim within 14 days of the provisions of regulations 53 and 57 (time and manner in which claims are to be made and evidence and information) being satisfied or as soon as reasonably practicable thereafter.

[¹ (3)]

Amendment
1.   Omitted by reg 11(5)(b) of SI 2008 No 959 as from 6.10.08.

Notification of decision

61.–(1)   Except in cases to which paragraphs (a) and (b) of regulation 67 (excess benefit in consequence of a reduction of a relevant authority's council tax) refer, an Authority shall notify in writing any person affected by a decision made by it under these Regulations–

(a)   in the case of a decision on a claim, forthwith or as soon as reasonably practicable thereafter;

(b)   in any other case, within 14 days of that decision or as soon as reasonably practicable thereafter,

and every notification shall include a statement as to the matters set out in Schedule 7.

(2)   A person affected to whom an authority sends or delivers a notification of decision may [¹ , within one month of the date of the notification of that decision (or, if the decision was notified before 1st November 2010, before 1st December 2010),] request in writing the authority to provide a written statement setting out the reasons for its decision on any matter set out in the notice.

(3)   The written statement referred to in paragraph (2) shall be sent to the person requesting it within 14 days or as soon as is reasonably practical thereafter.

Amendment

1.   Amended by reg 5(4) of SI 2010 No 2449 as from 1.11.10.

PART 9
Awards or payments of benefit

Time and manner of granting council tax benefit

62.–(1)   Subject to regulations 65 and 66 (payments on death and offsetting), where a person is entitled to council tax benefit in respect of his liability for a relevant authority's council tax as it has effect in respect of the relevant or any subsequent chargeable financial year, the relevant authority shall discharge his entitlement–

(a)   by reducing, so far as possible, the amount of his liability to which regulation 20(2) of the Council Tax (Administration and Enforcement) Regulations 1992 (the English and Welsh Regulations) or regulation 20(2) of the Council Tax (Administration and Enforcement) (Scotland) Regulations 1992 (the Scottish Regulations) refers; or

(b)   where–

(i)   such a reduction is not possible; or

(ii)   such a reduction would be insufficient to discharge the entitlement to council tax benefit; or

(iii)   the person entitled to council tax benefit is jointly and severally liable for the tax and the relevant authority determines that such a reduction would be inappropriate,

by making payments to him of the benefit to which he is entitled, rounded where necessary to the nearest penny.

(2)   The relevant authority shall notify the person entitled to council tax benefit of the amount of that benefit and how his entitlement is to be discharged in pursuance of paragraph (1).

(3)   In a case to which paragraph (1)(b) refers–

(a)   if the amount of the council tax for which he remains liable in respect of the relevant chargeable financial year, after any reduction to which paragraph (1)(a) refers has been made, is insufficient to enable his entitlement to council tax benefit in respect thereof to be discharged in that year, upon the final instalment of that tax becoming due any outstanding benefit–

(i)   shall be paid to that person if he so requires; or

(ii)   in any other case shall (as the relevant authority determines) either be repaid or credited against any subsequent liability of the person to make a payment in respect of the authority's council tax as it has effect for any subsequent year;

(b)   if that person has ceased to be liable for the relevant authority's council tax and has discharged the liability for that tax, the outstanding balance (if any) of the council tax benefit in respect thereof shall be paid within 14 days or, if that is not reasonably practicable, as soon as practicable thereafter;

(c)   in any other case, the council tax benefit shall be paid within 14 days of the receipt of the claim at the designated office or, if that is not reasonably practicable, as soon as practicable thereafter.

(4)   For the purposes of this regulation "instalment" means any instalment of a relevant authority's council tax to which regulation 19 of either the English and Welsh Regulations or as the case may be the Scottish Regulations refers (council tax payments).

Person to whom benefit is to be paid

63.–(1)   Subject to regulation 65 (payment on death) and paragraph (2), any payment of council tax benefit under regulation 62(1)(b) shall be made to that person.

(2)   Where a person other than a person who is entitled to council tax benefit made the claim and that first person is a person acting pursuant to an appointment under regulation 52(3) (persons appointed to act for a person unable to act) or is treated as having been so appointed by virtue of regulation 52(5), benefit may be paid to that person.

Shortfall in benefit

64.–(1)   Except in cases to which paragraph (2) refers, where, on the revision of a decision allowing council tax benefit to a person, it is determined that the amount allowed was less than the amount to which that person was entitled, the relevant authority shall either–

(a)   make good any shortfall in benefit which is due to that person, by reducing so far as possible the next and any subsequent payments he is liable to make in respect of the council tax of the authority concerned as it has effect for the relevant chargeable financial year until that shortfall is made good; or

(b)   where this is not possible or the person concerned so requests, pay any shortfall in benefit due to that person within 14 days of the revision of the decision being made or if that is not reasonable practicable, as soon as possible afterwards.

(2)   A shortfall in benefit need not be paid in any case to the extent that there is due from the person concerned to the relevant authority any recoverable excess benefit to which regulation 68(1) refers.

Payment on the death of the person entitled

65.–(1)   Where the person entitled to any council tax benefit has died and it is not possible to award any council tax benefit which is due in the form of a reduction of the council tax for which he was liable, the relevant authority shall make payment either to his personal representative or, where there is none, his next of kin aged 16 or over.

(2)   For the purposes of paragraph (1), "next of kin" means in England and Wales the persons who would take beneficially on an intestacy and in Scotland the person entitled to the moveable estate on intestacy.

(3)   A payment under paragraph (1) may not be made unless the personal representative or the next of kin, as the case may be, makes written application for the payment of any sum of benefit to which the deceased was entitled, and such written application is sent to or delivered to the relevant authority at its designated office within 12 months of the deceased's death or such longer period as the authority may allow in any particular case.

(4)   The authority may dispense with strict proof of title of any person claiming under paragraph (3) and the receipt of such a person shall be a good discharge to the authority for any sum so paid.

Offsetting

66.–(1)   Where a person has been allowed or paid a sum of council tax benefit under a decision which is subsequently revised or further revised, any sum allowed or paid in respect of a period covered by the subsequent decision shall be offset against arrears of entitlement under the subsequent decision except to the extent that the sum exceeds the arrears and shall be treated as properly awarded or paid on account of them.

(2)   Where an amount has been deducted under regulation 74(1) an equivalent sum shall be offset against any arrears of entitlement under the subsequent determination.

(3)   No amount may be offset under paragraph (1) which has been determined to be excess benefit within the meaning of regulation 67 (meaning of excess benefit).

PART 10
Excess benefit

Meaning of excess benefit

67. In this Part "excess benefit" means any amount which as been allowed by way of council tax benefit and to which there was no entitlement under these Regulations (whether on the initial decision [¹ or as subsequently revised or superseded or further revised or superseded]) and includes any excess which arises by reason of–

(a) a reduction in the amount a person is liable to pay in respect of council tax in consequence of–

    (i) regulations made under section 13 of the 1992 Act (reduction in the amount of a person's council tax); or

    (ii) any discount to which that tax is subject by virtue of section 11 or 79 of that Act;

(b) a substitution under sections 31 or 60 or, in Scotland, section 94 of the 1992 Act (substituted amounts) of a lesser amount for an amount of council tax previously set by the relevant authority under section 30 or, in Scotland section 93 of that Act (amount set for council tax).

Amendment

1. Amended by reg 3 of SI 2005 No 2904 as amended by Sch 2 para 29 of SI 2006 No 217 as from 10.4.06.

Recoverable excess benefit

68.–(1) Any excess benefit, except benefit to which paragraph (2) applies, shall be recoverable.

(2) Subject to paragraph (4) and (5) and excepting any excess benefit arising in consequence of a reduction in tax or substitution to which regulation 67 refers, this paragraph applies to excess benefit allowed in consequence of an official error, where the claimant or a person acting on his behalf or any other person to whom the excess benefit is allowed could not, at the time the benefit was allowed or upon the receipt of any notice relating to the allowance of that benefit, reasonably have been expected to realise that it was excess benefit.

(3) In paragraph (2), "excess benefit allowed in consequence of an official error" means an overpayment caused by a mistake made whether in the form of an act or omission by–

(a) the relevant authority;

(b) an officer or person acting for that authority;

(c) an officer of–

    (i) the Department for Work and Pensions; or

    (ii) the Commissioners for Her Majesty's Revenue and Customs,

    acting as such; or

(d) a person providing services to the Department or to the Commissioners referred to in (c),

    where the claimant, a person acting on his behalf or any other person to whom the payment is made, did not cause or materially contribute to that mistake, act or omission.

(4) Paragraph (2) shall not apply with respect to excess benefit to which regulation 67(a) and (b) refers.

(5) Where in consequence of an official error a person has been awarded excess benefit, upon the award being revised [¹ or superseded] any excess benefit which remains credited to him by the relevant authority in respect of a period after the date of the revision [¹ or supersession], shall be recoverable.

Amendment

1. Amended by reg 5 of SI 2005 No 2904 as amended by Sch 2 para 29 of SI 2006 No 217 as from 10.4.06.

Authority by which recovery may be made

69. The relevant authority which allowed the recoverable excess benefit may recover it.

Persons from whom recovery may be sought

[¹**70.** Recoverable excess benefit shall be due from the claimant or the person to whom the excess benefit was allowed.]

Amendment

1. Substituted by reg 7(2) of SI 2008 No 2824 as from 6.4.09.

Methods of recovery

71.–(1) Without prejudice to any other method of recovery a relevant authority may recover any recoverable excess benefit [¹] by any of the methods specified in paragraph (2) and (3) or any combination of those methods.

(2) Excess benefit may be recovered [¹]–

(a) by payment by or on behalf of the [¹ claimant or the person to whom the excess benefit was allowed]; or

(b) by an addition being made by the relevant authority to any amount payable in respect of the council tax concerned.

[¹ (3) Where recoverable excess benefit cannot be recovered by either of the methods specified in paragraph (2), the relevant authority may request the Secretary of State to recover the outstanding excess–

(a) from the benefits prescribed in regulation 75(1); or

(b) where the claimant has one or more partners, from the benefits prescribed in regulation 75(1A), provided that the claimant and that partner were a couple both at the time the excess benefit was allowed and when the deduction is made.]

Amendment

1. Amended by reg 7(3) of SI 2008 No 2824 as from 6.4.09.

Further provision as to recovery of excess benefit

72. In addition to the methods for recovery of excess benefit which are specified in regulation 71, any sum or part of a sum which is due from the person concerned and which is not paid within 21 days of his being notified of the amount that is due, shall be recoverable in a court of competent jurisdiction by the authority to which the excess benefit is due.

Diminution of capital

73.–(1) Where in the case of recoverable excess benefit, in consequence of a misrepresentation or failure to disclose a material fact (in either case whether fraudulent or otherwise) as to a person's capital, or an error, other than one to which regulation 68(2) (effect of official error) refers, as to the amount of a person's capital, the excess benefit was in respect of a period ("the excess benefit period") of more than 13 benefit weeks, the relevant authority shall, for the purpose only of calculating the amount of excess–

(a) at the end of the first 13 benefit weeks of the excess benefit period, treat the amount of the capital as having been reduced by the amount of excess council tax benefit allowed during those 13 weeks;

(b) at the end of each subsequent period of 13 benefit weeks, if any, of the excess benefit period, treat the amount of that capital as having been further reduced by the amount of excess council tax benefit allowed during the immediately preceding 13 benefit weeks.

(2) Capital shall not be treated as reduced over any period other than 13 benefit weeks or in any circumstances other than those, for which paragraph (1) provides.

Sums to be deducted in calculating recoverable excess benefit

74.–(1)   In calculating the amount of recoverable excess benefit, the relevant authority shall deduct any amount of council tax benefit which should have been determined to be payable in respect of the whole or part of the overpayment period–

(a)   on the basis of the claim as presented to the authority;

(b)   on the basis of the claim as it would have appeared had any misrepresentation or non-disclosure been remedied before the decision; or

(c)   on the basis of the claim as it would have appeared if any change of circumstances had been notified at the time that change occurred.

(2)   In calculating the amount of recoverable excess benefit, the relevant authority may deduct so much of any payment of council tax in respect of the excess benefit period which exceeds the amount, if any, which the claimant was liable to pay for that period under the original erroneous decision.

Recovery of excess benefit from prescribed benefits

75.–(1)   [³ Subject to paragraph (1B),] For the purposes of section 76(3)(c) of the Administration Act (deduction of excess council tax benefit from prescribed benefits), the benefits prescribed by this regulation are–

(a)   any benefit payable under the Act, except guardian's allowance or housing benefit;

(b)   any benefit payable under the legislation of any member State, other than the United Kingdom, concerning the branches of social security mentioned in article 4(1) of Regulation (EEC) No. 1408/71 on the application of social security schemes to employed persons, to self-employed persons and to members of their families moving within the Community, whether or not the benefit has been acquired by virtue of the provisions of that Regulation;

(c)   a jobseeker's allowance;

(d)   state pension credit.

[² (e) an employment and support allowance.]

[¹ (1A)   For the purposes of paragraph (1)(b) the term ''member State'' shall be understood to include Switzerland in accordance with and subject to the provisions of Annex II of the Agreement between the European Community and its Member States and the Swiss Confederation on the free movement of persons, signed at Brussels on 21st June 1999.]

[³ (1B)   For the purposes of section 76(3)(c) of the Administration Act, where recovery is sought from the claimant's partner under regulation 71(3)(b), the benefits prescribed by this regulation are–

(a)   income support under Part 7 of the Act;

(b)   income-based jobseeker's allowance;

(c)   state pension credit; and

(d)   income-related employment and support allowance.]

[³ (2)   The Secretary of State shall, if requested to do so by a relevant authority under regulation 71 (methods of recovery), recover excess benefit by deduction from any of the benefits prescribed in paragraph (1) or (in the case of the claimant's partner) any of the benefits prescribed in paragraph (1B) provided that the Secretary of State is satisfied that–

(a)   recoverable excess benefit has been allowed in consequence of a misrepresentation of or a failure to disclose a material fact (in either case whether fraudulently or otherwise), by a claimant or any other person to whom council tax benefit has been allowed; and

(b)   the person from whom it is sought to recover the excess benefit is receiving sufficient amounts of any of the benefits prescribed in paragraph (1) or (1B) (as the case may be) to enable deductions to be made for the recovery of the excess.]

Amendments

1.   Inserted by reg 10 of SI 2005 No 2904 as amended by Sch 2 para 29 of SI 2006 No 217 as from 10.4.06.

2.   Amended by reg 77 of SI 2008 No 1082 as from 27.10.08.

3.   Amended by reg 7(4) of SI 2008 No 2824 as from 6.4.09.

PART 11
Information
SECTION 1
Claims and information

Interpretation

76. In this Section–

[¹ "county council" means a county council in England, but only if the council has made an arrangement in accordance with regulation 53(4)(g) or 77(3);]

"local authority" means an authority administering council tax benefit;

"relevant authority" means–

    (a)   the Secretary of State;

    (b)   a person providing services to the Secretary of State; [¹ or

    (c)   a county council;]

"relevant information" means information or evidence relating to the administration of claims to or awards of council tax benefit.

Amendment
1.   Amended by reg 10(3) of SI 2007 No 2911 as from 31.10.07.

[¹Collection of information

77.–(1) The Secretary of State, or a person providing services to him, may receive or obtain relevant information from–

    (a)   persons making, or who have made, claims for council tax benefit; or

    (b)   other persons in connection with such claims.

    (2) In paragraph (1) references to persons who have made claims for council tax benefit include persons to whom awards of benefit have been made on those claims.

    (3)   Where a county council has made an arrangement with a local authority, or a person authorised to exercise any function of a local authority relating to housing benefit or council tax benefit, to receive and obtain information and evidence relating to a claim for council tax benefit, the council may receive or obtain the information or evidence from–

    (a)   persons making claims for council tax benefit; or

    (b)   other persons in connection with such claims.

    (4)   A county council may receive information relating to an award of council tax benefit which is supplied by–

    (a)   the person to whom the award has been made; or

    (b)   other persons in connection with the award.]

Amendment
1.   Substituted by reg 10(4) of SI 2007 No 2911 as from 31.10.07.

[¹Verifying information

77A.   A relevant authority may verify relevant information supplied to, or obtained by, the authority in accordance with regulation 77.]

Amendment
1.   Inserted by reg 10(5) of SI 2007 No 2911 as from 31.10.07.

[¹Recording and holding information

78.   A relevant authority which obtains relevant information or to whom such information is supplied–

    (a)   shall make a record of such information; and

    (b)   may hold that information, whether as supplied or obtained or recorded, for the purpose of forwarding it to the person or authority for the time being administering council tax benefit.]

Amendment
1.   Substituted by reg 10(6) of SI 2007 No 2911 as from 31.10.07.

Forwarding of information

79. A relevant authority which holds relevant information–

(a) shall forward it to the person or authority for the time being administering claims to or awards of council tax benefit to which the relevant information relates, being–

   (i) a local authority;

   (ii) a person providing services to a local authority; or

   (iii) a person authorised to exercise any function of a local authority relating to council tax benefit; and

[¹ (b) may, if the relevant authority is the Secretary of State or a person providing services to the Secretary of State, continue to hold a record of such information, whether as supplied or obtained or recorded, for such period as he considers appropriate.]

Amendment

1.   Substituted by reg 10(7) of SI 2007 No 2911 as from 31.10.07.

Request for information

80. A relevant authority which holds information or evidence relating to social security matters shall forward such information or evidence as may be requested to the person or authority making that request, provided that–

(a) the request is made by–

   (i) a local authority;

   (ii) a person providing services to a local authority; or

   (iii) a person authorised to exercise any function of a local authority relating to council tax benefit; and

(b) the information or evidence requested includes relevant information;

(c) the relevant authority is able to provide the information or evidence requested in the form in which it was originally supplied or obtained; and

(d) provision of the information or evidence requested is considered necessary by the relevant authority to the proper performance by a local authority of its functions relating to council tax benefit.

SECTION 2
Information between authorities etc.

[¹Information to be supplied by an authority to another authority

81.–(1) This regulation applies for the purposes of section 128A of the Administration Act (duty of an authority to disclose information to another authority).

(2) Information is to be disclosed by one authority to another where–

(a) there is a mover who is or was allowed council tax benefit by appropriate Authority "A";

(b) the mover is liable to pay council tax in respect of the new dwelling to Authority "B"; and

(c) the mover is entitled to an extended payment in accordance with regulation 60 of the Council Tax Benefit Regulations 2006.

(3) Authority A shall disclose to Authority B–

(a) the amount of the extended payment calculated in accordance with regulation 60C(2) of the Council Tax Benefit Regulations 2006 (amount of extended payment – movers);

(b) the date that entitlement to the extended payment will commence or has commenced;

(c) the date that entitlement to the extended payment ceased or will cease;

(d) the date of the move from Authority A to Authority B;

(e) where the extended payment will be paid by Authority A to Authority B in accordance with regulation 60C(3)(a) of the Council Tax Benefit Regulations 2006 (payment of the extended payment to second authority)–

        (i)   the amount that Authority A will pay to Authority B in accordance with that paragraph; and

        (ii)   any other information required by Authority B to enable Authority A to make the payment in accordance with that paragraph; and

(f)   if any deduction was being made in respect of a recoverable overpayment.

(4)   Authority B shall disclose to Authority A–

(a)   if a mover's liability to pay council tax for the new dwelling is to Authority B; and

(b)   where the extended payment will be paid by Authority A to Authority B in accordance with regulation 60C(3)(a) of the Council Tax Benefit Regulations 2006–

        (i)   any information required by Authority A to enable Authority A to make the payment in accordance with that paragraph; and

        (ii)   the date on which Authority B receives any such payment.]

Amendment

1.   Substituted by reg 10(3) of SI 2008 No 959 as from 6.10.08.

[¹Supply of information – extended payments (qualifying contributory benefits)

82.–(1) This regulation applies for the purposes of section 122E(3) of the Administration Act (duty of an authority to supply information to another authority).

(2)   Information is to be disclosed by one authority to another where–

(a)   there is a mover who is or was allowed council tax benefit by appropriate Authority "A";

(b)   the mover is liable to pay council tax in respect of the new dwelling to Authority "B"; and

(c)   the mover is entitled to an extended payment (qualifying contributory benefits) in accordance with regulation 44 of these Regulations or regulation 61 of the Council Tax Benefit Regulations 2006.

(3)   Authority A shall disclose to Authority B–

(a)   the amount of the extended payment calculated in accordance with regulation 44C(2) of these Regulations or regulation 61C(2) of the Council Tax Benefit Regulations 2006 (amount of extended payment – movers);

(b)   the date that entitlement to the extended payment will commence or has commenced;

(c)   the date that entitlement to the extended payment ceased or will cease;

(d)   the date of the move from Authority A to Authority B;

(e)   where the extended payment will be paid by Authority A to Authority B in accordance with regulation 44C(3)(a) of these Regulations or regulation 61C(3)(a) of the Council Tax Benefit Regulations 2006 (payment of the extended payment to the second authority)–

        (i)   the amount that Authority A will pay to Authority B in accordance with that paragraph; and

        (ii)   any other information required by Authority B to enable Authority A to make the payment in accordance with that paragraph; and

(f)   if any deduction was being made in respect of a recoverable overpayment.

(4)   Authority B shall disclose to Authority A–

(a)   if a mover's liability to pay council tax for the new dwelling is to Authority B; and

(b)   where the extended payment will be paid by Authority A to Authority B in accordance with regulation 44C(3)(a) of these Regulations or regulation 61C(3)(a) of the Council Tax Benefit Regulations 2006–

        (i)   any information required by Authority A to enable Authority A to make the payment in accordance with that paragraph; and

        (ii)   the date on which Authority B receives any such payment.]

Amendment

1.   Substituted by reg 10(3) of SI 2008 No 959 as from 6.10.08.

[¹ Supply of benefit administration information between authorities

83.–(1) For the purpose of section 122E(3) of the Administration Act (supply of information between authorities administering benefit) the circumstances in which information is to be supplied and the information to be supplied are set out in paragraph (2).

(2) Where the functions of an authority ("Authority A") relating to council tax benefit are being exercised, wholly or in part, by another authority ("Authority B")–

(a) Authority A must supply to Authority B any benefit administration information it holds which is relevant to, and necessary for, Authority B to exercise those functions; and

(b) Authority B must supply to Authority A any benefit administration information it holds which is relevant to, and necessary for, Authority A to exercise those functions.

(3) The circumstances in which paragraph (2) applies include cases where the authorities have agreed to discharge functions jointly.

(4) In paragraph (2), "Authority A" and "Authority B" include any person authorised to exercise functions relating to council tax benefit on behalf of the authority in question.

(5) This regulation shall not apply if the person or authority to whom the information is to be supplied agrees that the information need not be supplied.]

Amendment
1.   Inserted by reg 5(9) of SI 2008 No 2299 as from 1.10.08.

[¹ SCHEDULE A1]

Modification
Sch A1 was inserted by Sch 4 para 3(2) as modified by Sch 4 para 3(3) HB&CTB(CP) Regs in respect of claims for CTB by some refugees. Sch A1 was further modifed by Sch 4 para 4(4) and (5) for some CTB claimants who were refugees who claimed asylum on or before 2 April 2000. See also reg 7A inserted by Sch 4 para 3(1) HB&CTB(CP) Regs.

Amendment
1.   Lapsed by s12(2)(g) of the Asylum and Immigration (Treatment of Claimants, etc.) Act 2004 (for those recorded as refugees after 14.6.07).

SCHEDULE 1
REGULATION 12
Applicable amounts

PART 1
Personal allowances

1.   The amounts specified in column (2) below in respect of each person or couple specified in column (1) shall be the amount specified for the purposes of regulation 12–

Column (1) *Person, couple or polygamous marriage*	*Column (2)* *Amount*
(1) Single claimant or lone parent–	(1)
(a) aged under 65;	(a) [⁵ £132.60];
(b) aged 65 or over.	(b) [⁵ £153.15].
(2) Couple–	(2)
(a) both members aged under 65;	(a) [5 £202.40];
(b) one member or both members aged 65 or over.	(b) [⁵ £229.50].

(3) If the claimant is a member of a polygamous marriage and none of the members of the marriage have attained the age of 65–

    (a) for the claimant and the other party to the marriage;

    (b) for each additional spouse who is a member of the same household as the claimant.

(3)

    (a) [5 £202.40];

    (b) [5 £69.80].

(4) If the claimant is a member of a polygamous marriage and one or more members of the marriage are aged 65 or over–

    (a) for the claimant and the other party to the marriage;

    (b) for each additional spouse who is a member of the same household as the claimant.

(4)

    (a) [5 £229.50];

    (b) [5 £76.35].

Amendments

1.   Amended by Art 22(4) and Sch 12 of SI 2006 No 645 and reg 8 of SI 2006 No 217 as from 1.4.06.
2.   Amended by Art 22(4) and Sch 12 of SI 2007 No 688 as from 1.4.07.
3.   Amended by Art 22(4) and Sch 12 of SI 2008 No 632 as from 1.4.08.
4.   Amended by Art 22(4) and Sch 11 of SI 2009 No 497 as from 1.4.09.
5.   Amended by Art 22(4) and Sch 11 of SI 2010 No 793 as from 1.4.10.

2.–(1)   The amount specified in column (2) below in respect of each person specified in column (1) shall, for the relevant period specified in column (1), be the amounts specified for the purposes of regulation 12(1)(b)–

Column (1)

Child or young person

Persons in respect of the period–

    (a) beginning on that person's date of birth and ending on the day preceding the first Monday in September following that person's sixteenth birthday;

    (b) beginning on the first Monday in September following that person's sixteenth birthday and ending on the day preceding that person's [2 twentieth] birthday.

Column (2)

Amount

    (a) [6 £57.57];

    (b) [6 £57.57].

(2)   In column (1) of the table above, "the first Monday in September" means the Monday which first occurs in the month of September in any year.

Amendments

1.   Amended by Art 22(4) and Sch 12 of SI 2006 No 645 and reg 8 of SI 2006 No 217 as from 1.4.06.
2.   Amended by reg 5(4) of SI 2006 No 718 as from 10.4.06.
3.   Amended by Art 22(4) and Sch 12 of SI 2007 No 688 as from 1.4.07.
4.   Amended by Art 22(4) and Sch 12 of SI 2008 No 632 as from 1.4.08.
5.   Amended by Art 22(4) and Sch 11 of SI 2009 No 497 as from 1.4.09.
6.   Amended by Art 22(4) and Sch 11 of SI 2010 No 793 as from 1.4.10.

PART 2
Family premium

3.–(1)   The amount for the purposes of regulation 12(1)(c) and (d) in respect of a family of which at least one member is a child or young person shall be [9 £17.40].

(2)   The amounts specified in sub-paragraph (1) shall be increased by [10 £10.50] where at least one child is under the age of one year and for the purposes of this sub-paragraph where that child's first birthday does not fall on a Monday he shall be treated as under the age of one year until the first Monday after his first birthday.

Amendments

1.   Amended by Art 22(4)(a) and Sch 12 of SI 2006 No 645 and reg 8 of SI 2006 No 217 as from 1.4.06.
2.   Confirmed by Art 22(4)(b) and Sch 12 of SI 2006 No 645 and reg 8 of SI 2006 No 217 as from 1.4.06.
3.   Amended by Art 22(5)(a) of SI 2007 No 688 as from 1.4.07.
4.   Confirmed by Art 22(5)(b) of SI 2007 No 688 as from 1.4.07.
5.   Amended by Art 22(5)(a) of SI 2008 No 632 as from 1.4.08.
6.   Confirmed by Art 22(5)(b) of SI 2008 No 632 as from 1.4.08.
7.   Amended by Art 22(5) of SI 2009 No 497 as from 1.4.09.
8.   Confirmed by Art 22(5) of SI 2009 No 497 as from 1.4.09.
9.   Amended by Art 22(5) of SI 2010 No 793 as from 1.4.10.
10.   Confirmed by Art 22(5) of SI 2010 No 793 as from 1.4.10.

PART 3
Premiums
4. The premiums specified in Part 4 shall, for the purposes of regulation 12(1)(e), be applicable to a claimant who satisfies the condition specified in this Part in respect of that premium.

5.–(1) Subject to sub-paragraph (2), for the purposes of this Part of this Schedule, once a premium is applicable to a claimant under this Part, a person shall be treated as being in receipt of any benefit for–
- (a) in the case of a benefit to which the Social Security (Overlapping Benefits) Regulations 1979 applies, any period during which, apart from the provisions of those Regulations, he would be in receipt of that benefit; and
- (b) any period spent by a person in undertaking a course of training or instruction provided or approved by the Secretary of State under section 2 of the 1973 Act, or by [¹ Skills Development Scotland,] Scottish Enterprise or Highlands and Islands Enterprise under section 2 of the Enterprise and New Towns (Scotland) Act 1990 or for any period during which he is in receipt of a training allowance.

(2) For the purposes of the carer premium under paragraph 9, a person shall be treated as being in receipt of a carer's allowance by virtue of sub-paragraph (1)(a) only if and for so long as the person in respect of whose care the allowance has been claimed remains in receipt of attendance allowance, or the care component of disability living allowance at the highest or middle rate prescribed in accordance with section 72(3) of the Act.

Amendment
1. Amended by reg 9(3)(c) of SI 2009 No 583 as from 6.4.09.

Severe Disability Premium
6.–(1) The condition is that the claimant is a severely disabled person.

(2) For the purposes of sub-paragraph (1), a claimant shall be treated as being a severely disabled person if, and only if–
- (a) in the case of a single claimant, lone parent or a claimant who is treated as having no partner in consequence of sub-paragraph (3)–
  - (i) he is in receipt of attendance allowance, or the care component of disability living allowance at the highest or middle rate prescribed in accordance with section 72(3) of the Act; and
  - (ii) subject to sub-paragraph (6), he has no non-dependants aged 18 or over normally residing with him or with whom he is normally residing; and
  - (iii) no person is entitled to, and in receipt of, a carer's allowance in respect of caring for him;
- (b) in the case of a claimant who has a partner–
  - (i) the claimant is in receipt of attendance allowance, or the care component of disability living allowance at the highest or middle rate prescribed in accordance with section 72(3) of the Act; and
  - (ii) his partner is also in receipt of such an allowance or, if he is a member of a polygamous marriage, each other member of that marriage is in receipt of such an allowance; and
  - (iii) subject to sub-paragraph (6), the claimant has no non-dependants aged 18 or over normally residing with him or with whom he is normally residing,
  and either a person is [² entitled to and in receipt of] a carer's allowance in respect of caring for only one of the couple or, if he is a member of a polygamous marriage, for one or more but not all the members of the marriage, or as the case may be, no person is entitled to and in receipt of such an allowance in respect of caring for either member of a couple or any of the members of the marriage.

(3) Where a claimant has a partner who does not satisfy the condition in sub-paragraph (2)(b)(ii), and that partner is blind or is treated as blind within the meaning of sub-paragraph (4), that partner shall be treated for the purposes of sub-paragraph (2) as if he were not a partner of the claimant.

(4) For the purposes of sub-paragraph (3), a person is blind if he is registered in a register compiled by a local authority under section 29 of the National Assistance Act 1948 (welfare services) or, in Scotland, has been certified as blind and in consequence he is registered in a register maintained by or on behalf of a council constituted under section 2 of the Local Government (Scotland) Act 1994.

(5) For the purposes of sub-paragraph (4), a person who has ceased to be registered as blind on regaining his eyesight shall nevertheless be treated as blind and as satisfying the additional condition set out in that sub-paragraph for a period of 28 weeks following the date on which he ceased to be so registered.

(6) For the purposes of sub-paragraph (2)(a)(ii) and (2)(b)(iii) no account shall be taken of–
- (a) a person receiving attendance allowance, or the care component of disability living allowance at the highest or middle rate prescribed in accordance with section 72(3) of the Act; or
- (b) a person who is blind or is treated as blind within the meaning of sub-paragraphs (4) and (5).

(7) For the purposes of sub-paragraph (2)(b) a person shall be treated–
- (a) as being in receipt of attendance allowance, or the care component of disability living allowance at the highest or middle rate prescribed in accordance with section 72(3) of the Act, if he would, but for his being a patient for a period exceeding 28 days, be so in receipt;

(b)   as being entitled to and in receipt of a carer's allowance if he would, but for the person for whom he was caring being a patient in hospital for a period exceeding 28 days, be so entitled and in receipt.
(8)   For the purposes of sub-paragraph (2)(a)(iii) and (2)(b)–
(a)   no account shall be taken of an award of carer's allowance to the extent that payment of such an award is back-dated for a period before [¹ the date on which the award is first paid]; and
(b)   references to a person being in receipt of a carer's allowance shall include references to a person who would have been in receipt of that allowance but for the application of a restriction under section [³ 6B or] 7 of the Social Security Fraud Act 2001 (loss of benefit).

Amendments
1.   Amended by reg 9(3) of SI 2007 No 719 as from 2.4.07.
2.   Amended by reg 9(7) of SI 2009 No 583 as from 6.4.09.
3.   Amended by reg 7 of SI 2010 No 1160 as from 1.4.10.

Enhanced disability premium
7.   The condition is that the care component of disability living allowance is, or would, but for a suspension of benefit in accordance with regulations under section 113(2) of the Act or but for an abatement as a consequence of hospitalisation, be payable at the highest rate prescribed under section 72(3) of the Act in respect of a child or young person who is a member of the claimant's family.

Disabled Child Premium
8.   The condition is that a child or young person for whom the claimant or a partner of his is responsible and who is a member of the claimant's household–
(a)   is in receipt of disability living allowance or is no longer in receipt of such allowance because he is a patient, provided that the child or young person continues to be a member of the family; or
(b)   is blind within the meaning of paragraph 6(4) or treated as blind in accordance with paragraph 6(5); or
(c)   is a child or a young person in respect of whom section 145A of the Act applies for the purposes of entitlement to child benefit, but only for the period prescribed under that section, and in respect of whom a disabled child premium was included in the claimant's applicable amount immediately before the death of that child.

Carer Premium
9.–(1) The condition is that the claimant or his partner is, or both of them are, entitled to a carer's allowance.
(2)   Where a carer premium has been awarded but–
(a)   the person in respect of whose care the carer's allowance has been awarded dies; or
(b)   the person in respect of whom the premium was awarded ceases to be entitled, or ceases to be treated as entitled, to a carer's allowance,
this paragraph shall be treated as satisfied for a period of eight weeks from the relevant date specified in sub-paragraph (3).
(3)   The relevant date for the purposes of sub-paragraph (2) is–
(a)   the Sunday following the death of the person in respect of whose care the carer's allowance has been awarded (or beginning with the date of death if the date occurred on a Sunday);
(b)   where head (a) above does not apply, the date on which that person who was entitled to a carer's allowance ceases to be entitled to it.
(4)   For the purposes of this paragraph, a person shall be treated as being entitled to and in receipt of a carer's allowance for any period not covered by an award but in respect of which a payment is made in lieu of an award.

Persons in receipt of concessionary payments
10.   For the purpose of determining whether a premium is applicable to a person under paragraphs 6 to 9, any concessionary payment made to compensate that person for the non-payment of any benefit mentioned in those paragraphs shall be treated as if it were a payment of that benefit.

Person in receipt of benefit
11.   For the purposes of this Part of this Schedule, a person shall be regarded as being in receipt of any benefit if, and only if, it is paid in respect of him and shall be so regarded only for any period in respect of which that benefit is paid.

PART 4
Amounts of premiums specified in Part 3

Premium	*Amount*
12.–(1) Severe Disability Premium–	(1)
(a) where the claimant satisfies the condition in paragraph 6(2)(a);	(a) [⁵ £53.65];
(b) where the claimant satisfies the condition in paragraph 6(2)(b)–	(b)
(i) in a case where there is someone in receipt of carer's allowance or if he or any partner satisfies that condition only by virtue of paragraph 6(7);	(i) [⁵ £53.65];
(ii) in a case where there is no one in receipt of such an allowance.	(ii) [⁵ £107.30].
(2) Enhanced disability premium	(2) [⁵ £21.00] in respect of each child or young person in respect of whom the conditions specified in paragraph 7 are satisfied.
(3) Disabled Child Premium	(3) [⁵ £52.08] in respect of each child or young person in respect of whom the condition specified in paragraph 8 is satisfied.
(4) Carer Premium	(4) [⁵ £30.05] in respect of each person who satisfies the condition specified in paragraph 9.

Amendments

1.   Amended by Art 22(6) and Sch 13 of SI 2006 No 645 and reg 8 of SI 2006 No 217 as from 1.4.06.
2.   Amended by Art 22(6) and Sch 13 of SI 2007 No 688 as from 1.4.07.
3.   Amended by Art 22(6) and Sch 13 of SI 2008 No 632 as from 1.4.08.
4.   Amended by Art 22(6) and Sch 12 of SI 2009 No 497 as from 1.4.09.
5.   Amended by Art 22(6) and Sch 12 of SI 2010 No 793 as from 1.4.10.

SCHEDULE 2
REGULATION 23(8)
Sums disregarded from claimant's earnings

1.   Where two or more of paragraphs 2 to 5 apply in any particular case the overall maximum sum which falls to be disregarded in that case under those paragraphs is restricted to–

(a)   £25 in the case of a lone parent;

(b)   £20 in any other case.

2.   In a case where a claimant is a lone parent, £25 of earnings.

3.–(1)   In a case of earnings from any employment or employments to which sub-paragraph (2) applies, £20.

(2)   This paragraph applies to employment–

(a)   as a part-time fire-fighter employed by a fire and rescue authority constituted by a scheme under section 2 of the Fire and Rescue Services Act 2004 or a scheme to which section 4 of that Act applies;

(b)   a part-time fire-fighter employed by a fire and rescue authority (as defined in section 1 of the Fire (Scotland) Act 2005) or a joint fire and rescue board constituted by an amalgamation scheme made under section 2(1) of that Act;

(c)   as an auxiliary coastguard in respect of coast rescue activities;

(d)   in the manning or launching of a lifeboat if the employment is part-time;

(e)   as a member of any territorial or reserve force prescribed in Part I of Schedule 6 to Social Security (Contributions) Regulations 2001.

(3)   If–

(a)   any of the earnings of the claimant or, if he has a partner, his partner, or both of them, are disregarded under sub-paragraph (1); and

(b)   either of them has, or both of them have, other earnings,

so much of those other earnings as would not, in the aggregate with the earnings disregarded under that sub-paragraph, exceed £20.

4.–(1)   If the claimant or, if he has a partner, his partner is a carer, or both are carers, £20 of any earnings received from his or their employment.

(2)   Where the carer premium is awarded in respect of the claimant and of any partner of his, their earnings shall for the purposes of this paragraph be aggregated, but the amount to be disregarded in accordance with sub-paragraph (1) shall not exceed £20 of the aggregated amount.

(3)   In this paragraph the claimant or his partner is a carer if paragraph 9 of Part 3 of Schedule 1 (amount applicable for carers) is satisfied in respect of him.

5.–(1)   £20 is disregarded if the claimant or, if he has a partner, his partner–

    (a)   is in receipt of–
        (i)   long-term incapacity benefit under section 30A of the Act;
        (ii)   severe disablement allowance under section 68 of the Act;
        (iii)   attendance allowance;
        (iv)   disability living allowance under section 71 to 76 of the Act;
        (v)   any mobility supplement under [² article 20 of the Naval, Military and Air Forces Etc. (Disablement and Death) Service Pensions Order 2006] (including such a supplement by virtue of any other scheme or order) or under article 25A of the Personal Injuries (Civilians) Scheme 1983; [¹]
        (vi)   the disability element or the severe disability element of working tax credit under Schedule 2 to the Working Tax Credit Regulations; or
        [¹ (vii) main phase employment and support allowance; or]
    (b)   is or are registered as blind in a register compiled by a local authority under section 29 of the National Assistance Act 1948 (welfare services) or, in Scotland, has been certified as blind and in consequence is registered in a register maintained by or on behalf of a council constituted under section 2 of the Local Government (Scotland) Act 1994; or
    (c)   is, or is treated as, incapable of work in accordance with the provisions of, and regulations made under, Part 12A of the Act (incapacity for work), and has been incapable, or has been treated as incapable, of work for a continuous period of not less than–
        (i)   in the case of a claimant who is terminally ill within the meaning of section 30B(4) of the Act, 196 days;
        (ii)   in any other case, 364 days. [³ or]
    [³ (d)   has, or is treated as having, limited capacity for work within the meaning of section 1(4) of the Welfare Reform Act or limited capability for work-related activity within the meaning of section 2(5) of that Act and either–
        (i)   the assessment phase as defined in section 24(2) of the Welfare Reform Act has ended; or
        (ii)   regulation 7 of the Employment and Support Allowance Regulations (circumstances where the condition that the assessment phase has ended before entitlement to the support component or the work-related activity component arising does not apply) applies.]
    (2)   Subject to sub-paragraph (3), £20 is disregarded if the claimant or, if he has a partner, his partner has, within a period of 8 weeks ending on the day in respect of which the claimant or his partner attains the qualifying age for state pension credit, had an award of housing benefit or council tax benefit and–
    (a)   £20 was disregarded in respect of earnings taken into account in that award;
    (b)   the person whose earnings qualified for the disregard continues in employment after the termination of that award.
    (3)   The disregard of £20 specified in sub-paragraph (2) applies so long as there is no break, other than a break which does not exceed 8 weeks, in a person's entitlement to housing benefit or council tax benefit or in employment following the first day in respect of which that benefit is awarded.
    (4)   £20 is the maximum amount which may be disregarded under this paragraph, notwithstanding that, where the claimant has a partner, both the claimant and his partner satisfy the requirements of this paragraph.

Amendment
    1.   Amended by reg 78 of SI 2008 No 1082 as from 27.10.08.
    2.   Amended by reg 8(7) of SI 2008 No 3157 as from 5.1.09.
    3.   Inserted by reg 9(8) of SI 2009 No 583 as from 1.4.09.

[¹5A. (1)   Where–
    (a)   the claimant (or if the claimant is a member of a couple, at least one member of that couple) is a person to whom sub-paragraph (5) applies;
    (b)   the Secretary of State is satisfied that that person is undertaking exempt work as defined in sub-paragraph (6); and
    (c)   regulation 16 does not apply,
    the amount specified in sub-paragraph (7) ("the specified amount").
    (2)   Where this paragraph applies, paragraphs 1 to 5 and 7 do not apply; but in any case where the claimant is a lone parent, and the specified amount would be less than the amount specified in paragraph 2, then paragraph 2 applies instead of this paragraph.
    (3)   Notwithstanding regulation 13 (calculation of income and capital of members claimant's family and of a polygamous marriage), if sub-paragraph (1) applies to one member of a couple ("A") it shall not apply to the other member of that couple ("B") except to the extent provided in sub-paragraph (4).
    (4)   Where A's earnings are less than the specified amount, there shall also be disregarded so much of B's earnings as would not when aggregated with A's earnings exceed the specified amount; but the amount of B's earnings which may be disregarded under this sub-paragraph is limited to a maximum of £20 unless the Secretary of State is satisfied that B is also undertaking exempt work.
    (5)   This sub-paragraph applies to a person who is–
    (a)   in receipt of a contributory employment and support allowance;
    (b)   in receipt of incapacity benefit;
    (c)   in receipt of severe disablement allowance; or

(d)   being credited with earnings on the grounds of incapacity for work or limited capability for work under regulation 8B of the Social Security (Credits) Regulations 1975.

(6)   "Exempt work" means work of the kind described in–

(a)   regulation 45(2), (3) or (4) of the Employment and Support Allowance Regulations; or (as the case may be)

(b)   regulation 17(2), (3) or (4) of the Social Security (Incapacity for Work) (General) Regulations 1995,

and, in determining for the purposes of this paragraph whether a claimant or a member of a couple is undertaking any type of exempt work, it is immaterial whether that person or their partner is also undertaking other work.

(7)   The specified amount is the amount of money from time to time mentioned in any provision referred to in sub-paragraph (6) by virtue of which the work referred to in sub-paragraph (1) is exempt (or, where more than one such provision is relevant and those provisions mention different amounts of money, the highest of those amounts).]

Amendment

1.   Inserted by reg 5(3) of SI 2009 No 2608 as from 1.4.10.

---

6.   Any amount or the balance of any amount which would fall to be disregarded under paragraph 18 or 19 of Schedule 3 had the claimant's income which does not consist of earnings been sufficient to entitle him to the full disregarded thereunder.

7.   Except where the claimant or his partner qualifies for a £20 disregard under the preceding provisions of this Schedule–

(a)   £5 shall be disregarded if a claimant who has no partner has earnings;

(b)   £10 shall be disregarded if a claimant who has a partner has earnings.

8.   Any earnings, other than earnings referred to in regulation 23(8)(b), derived from employment which ended before the day in respect of which the claimant first satisfies the conditions for entitlement to council tax benefit.

9.–(1)   In a case where the claimant is a person who satisfies at least one of the conditions set out in sub-paragraph (2), and his net earnings equal or exceed the total of the amounts set out in sub-paragraph (3), the amount of his earnings that falls to be disregarded under this Schedule shall be increased by [⁵ £17.10].

(2)   The conditions of this sub-paragraph are that–

(a)   the claimant, or if he has a partner, either the claimant or his partner, is a person to whom regulation 20(1)(c) of the Working Tax Credit Regulations applies; or

(b)   the claimant–

    (i)   is, or any partner of his is, aged at least 25 and is engaged in remunerative work for on average not less than 30 hours per week; or

    (ii)   if he is a member of a couple–

        (aa)   at least one member of that couple is engaged in remunerative work for on average not less than 16 hours per week; and

        (bb)   his applicable amount includes a family premium under paragraph 3 of Schedule 1; or

    (iii)   is a lone parent who is engaged in remunerative work for on average not less than 16 hours per week; or

    (iv)   is, or if he has a partner, one of them is, engaged in remunerative work for on average not less than 16 hours per week and paragraph 5(1) above is satisfied in respect of that person; or

(c)   the claimant is, or, if he has a partner, one of them is, a person to whom regulation 18(3) of the Working Tax Credit Regulations (eligibility for 50 plus element) applies, or would apply if an application for working tax credit were to be made in his case.

(3)   The following are the amounts referred to in sub-paragraph (1)–

(a)   any amount disregarded under this Schedule;

(b)   the amount of child care charges calculated as deductible under regulation 20(1)(c); and

(c)   [⁵ £17.10].

(4)   The provisions of regulation 6 shall apply in determining whether or not a person works for on average not less than 30 hours per week, but as if the reference to 16 hours in paragraph (1) of that regulation was a reference to 30 hours.

Amendments

1.   Amended by Art 22(7) of SI 2006 No 645 and reg 8 of SI 2006 No 217 as from 1.4.06.

2.   Amended by Art 22(7) of SI 2007 No 688 as from 1.4.07.

3.   Amended by Art 22(7) of SI 2008 No 632 as from 1.4.08.

4.   Amended by Art 22(7) of SI 2009 No 497 as from 1.4.09.

5.   Amended by Art 22(7) of SI 2010 No 793 as from 1.4.10.

---

10.   Where a payment of earnings is made in a currency other than Sterling, any banking charge or commission payable in converting to that payment into Sterling.

SCHEDULE 3
REGULATION 23(9)
Amounts to be disregarded in the calculation of income other than earnings

1.   In addition to any sum which falls to be disregarded in accordance with paragraphs 2 to 6, £10 of any of the following, namely–

(a)   a war disablement pension (except insofar as such a pension falls to be disregarded under paragraph 2 or 3);

[¹ (b)   a war widow's pension or [³ war widower's pension];]

(c)   a pension payable to a person as a widow, widower or surviving civil partner under [²] any power of Her Majesty otherwise than under an enactment to make provision about pensions for or in respect of persons who have been disabled or have died in consequence of service as members of the armed forces of the Crown;

(d)   a guaranteed income payment [and, if the amount of that payment has been abated to less than £10 by a [³ pension or payment falling within article 31(1)(a) or (b) of the Armed Forces and Reserve Forces (Compensation Scheme) Order 2005], so much of [³ that pension or payment] as would not, in aggregate with the amount of [³ any] guaranteed income payment disregarded, exceed £10];

(e)   a payment made to compensate for the non-payment of such a pension or payment as is mentioned in any of the preceding sub-paragraphs;

(f)   a pension paid by the government of a country outside Great Britain which is analogous to any of the pensions or payments mentioned in sub-paragraphs (a) to (d) above;

(g)   a pension paid to victims of National Socialist persecution under any special provision made by the law of the Federal Republic of Germany, or any part of it, or of the Republic of Austria.

Amendments

1.   Substituted by reg 6(5)(a) of SI 2008 No 1042 as from 19.5.08.

2.   Amended by reg 8(8)(a) of SI 2008 No 3157 as from 5.1.09.

3.   Amended by reg 9(5) of SI 2009 No 2655 as from 2.11.09.

2.   The whole of any amount included in a pension to which paragraph 1 relates in respect of–

(a)   the claimant's need for constant attendance;

(b)   the claimant's exceptionally severe disablement.

3.   Any mobility supplement under [¹ article 20 of the Naval, Military and Air Forces Etc. (Disablement and Death) Service Pensions Order 2006] (including such a supplement by virtue of any other scheme or order) or under article 25A of the Personal Injuries (Civilians) Scheme 1983 or any payment intended to compensate for the non-payment of such a supplement.

Amendment

1.   Amended by reg 8(8)(b) of SI 2008 No 3157 as from 5.1.09.

[¹4.   Any supplementary pension under article 23(2) of the Naval, Military and Air Forces Etc. (Disablement and Death) Service Pensions Order 2006 (pensions to surviving spouses and surviving civil partners) and any analogous payment made by the Secretary of State for Defence to any person who is not a person entitled under that Order.]

Amendment

1.   Substituted by reg 8(8)(c) of SI 2008 No 3157 as from 5.1.09.

5.   In the case of a pension awarded at the supplementary rate under article 27(3) of the Personal Injuries (Civilians) Scheme 1983 (pensions to widows, widowers or surviving civil partners), the sum specified in paragraph 1(c) of Schedule 4 to that Scheme.

6.–(1)   Any payment which is–

(a)   made under any of the Dispensing Instruments to a widow, widower or surviving civil partner of a person–

     (i)   whose death was attributable to service in a capacity analogous to service as a member of the armed forces of the Crown; and

     (ii)   whose service in such capacity terminated before 31st March 1973; and

[¹ (b)   equal to the amount specified in article 23(2) of the Naval, Military and Air Forces Etc. (Disablement and Death) Service Pensions Order 2006.]

(2)   In this paragraph ''the Dispensing Instruments'' means the Order in Council of 19th December 1881, the Royal Warrant of 27th October 1884 and the Order by His Majesty of 14th January 1922 (exceptional grants of pay, non-effective pay and allowances).

Amendment

1.   Substituted by reg 8(8)(d) of SI 2008 No 3157 as from 5.1.09.

7. £15 of any widowed parent's allowance to which the claimant is entitled under section 39A of the Act.

8. £15 of any widowed mother's allowance to which the claimant is entitled under section 37 of the Act.

9. Where the claimant occupies a dwelling as his home and he provides in that dwelling board and lodging accommodation, an amount, in respect of each person for whom such accommodation is provided for the whole or any part of a week, equal to–

(a) where the aggregate of any payments made in respect of any one week in respect of such accommodation provided to such person does not exceed £20.00, 100 per cent. of such payments; or

(b) where the aggregate of any such payments exceeds £20.00, £20.00 and 50 per cent. of the excess over £20.00.

10. If the claimant–

(a) owns the freehold or leasehold interest in any property or is a tenant of any property; and

(b) occupies a part of that property; and

(c) has an agreement with another person allowing that person to occupy another part of that property on payment of rent and–

    (i) the amount paid by that person is less than £20 per week, the whole of that amount; or

    (ii) the amount paid is £20 or more per week, £20.

11. Where a claimant receives income under an annuity purchased with a loan, which satisfies the following conditions–

(a) that the loan was made as part of a scheme under which not less than 90 per cent. of the proceeds of the loan were applied to the purchase by the person to whom it was made of an annuity ending with his life or with the life of the survivor of two or more persons (in this paragraph referred to as "the annuitants") who include the person to whom the loan was made;

(b) that at the time the loan was made the person to whom it was made or each of the annuitants had attained the age of 65;

(c) that the loan was secured on a dwelling in Great Britain and the person to whom the loan was made or one of the annuitants owns an estate or interest in that dwelling;

(d) that the person to whom the loan was made or one of the annuitants occupies the dwelling on which it was secured as his home at the time the interest is paid; and

(e) that the interest payable on the loan is paid by the person to whom the loan was made or by one of the annuitants,

the amount, calculated on a weekly basis, equal to–

    (i) where, or insofar as, section 369 of the Income and Corporation Taxes Act 1988 (mortgage interest payable under deduction of tax) applies to the payments of interest on the loan, the interest which is payable after deduction of a sum equal to income tax on such payments at the applicable percentage of income tax within the meaning of section 369(1A) of that Act;

    (ii) in any other case, the interest which is payable on the loan without deduction of such a sum.

12.–(1) Any payment, other than a payment to which sub-paragraph (2) applies, made to the claimant by Trustees in exercise of a discretion exercisable by them.

(2) This sub-paragraph applies to payments made to the claimant by Trustees in exercise of a discretion exercisable by them for the purpose of–

(a) obtaining food, [¹ ordinary clothing or footwear] or household fuel;

(b) the payment of rent, council tax or water charges for which that claimant or his partner is liable;

(c) meeting housing costs of a kind specified in Schedule 2 to the State Pension Credit Regulations 2002.

(3) In a case to which sub-paragraph (2) applies, £20 or–

(a) if the payment is less than £20, the whole payment;

(b) if, in the claimant's case, £10 is disregarded in accordance with paragraph 1 (a) to (g), £10 or the whole payment if it is less than £10; or

(c) if, in the claimant's case, £15 is disregarded under paragraph 7 or paragraph 8 and–

    (i) he has no disregard under paragraph 1(a) to (g), £5 or the whole payment if it is less than £5;

    (ii) he has a disregard under paragraph 1(a) to (g), nil.

(4) For the purposes of this paragraph, "[¹ ordinary clothing or footwear]" means clothing or footwear for normal daily use, but does not include school uniforms, or clothing and footwear used solely for sporting activities.

Amendment

1. Amended by reg 6(5)(b) of SI 2008 No 1042 as from 19.5.08.

---

13. Any increase in [¹ pension or allowance under Part 2 or 3 of the Naval, Military and Air Forces Etc. (Disablement and Death) Service Pensions Order 2006] paid in respect of a dependent other than the pensioner's [¹] partner.

Amendment

1. Amended by reg 8(8)(e) of SI 2008 No 3157 as from 5.1.09.

---

14. Any payment ordered by a court to be made to the claimant or the claimant's partner in consequence of any accident, injury or disease suffered by the person or a child of the person to or in respect of whom the payments are made.

15. Periodic payments made to the claimant or the claimant's partner under an agreement entered into in settlement of a claim made by the claimant or, as the case may be, the claimant's partner for an injury suffered by him.

16. Any income which is payable outside the United Kingdom for such period during which there is a prohibition against the transfer to the United Kingdom of that income.

17. Any banking charges or commission payable in converting to Sterling payments of income made in a currency other than Sterling.

18. Where the claimant makes a parental contribution in respect of a student attending a course at an establishment in the United Kingdom or undergoing education in the United Kingdom, which contribution has been assessed for the purposes of calculating–

(a) under, or pursuant to regulations made under powers conferred by, sections 1 or 2 of the Education Act 1962 or section 22 of the Teaching and Higher Education Act 1998, that student's award;

(b) under regulations made in exercise of the powers conferred by section 49 of the Education (Scotland) Act 1980, that student's bursary, scholarship, or other allowance under that section or under regulations made in exercise of the powers conferred by section 73 of that Act of 1980, any payment to that student under that section; or

(c) the student's student loan,

an amount equal to the weekly amount of that parental contribution, but only in respect of the period for which that contribution is assessed as being payable.

19.–(1) Where the claimant is the parent of a student aged under 25 in advanced education who either–

(a) is not in receipt of any award, grant or student loan in respect of that education; or

(b) is in receipt of an award under section 2 of the Education Act 1962 (discretionary awards) or an award bestowed by virtue of the Teaching and Higher Education Act 1998, or regulations made thereunder, or a bursary, scholarship or other allowance under section 49(1) of the Education (Scotland) Act 1980, or a payment under section 73 of that Act of 1980,

and the claimant makes payments by way of a contribution towards the student's maintenance, other than a parental contribution falling within paragraph 18, an amount specified in sub-paragraph (2) in respect of each week during the student's term.

(2) For the purposes of sub-paragraph (1), the amount shall be equal to–

(a) the weekly amount of the payments; or

(b) the amount by way of a personal allowance for a single claimant under 25 less the weekly amount of any award, bursary, scholarship, allowance or payment referred to in sub-paragraph (1)(b),

whichever is less.

20.–(1) Where a claimant's applicable amount includes an amount by way of a family premium, £15 of any payment of maintenance, whether under a court order or not, which is made or due to be made by the claimant's spouse, civil partner, former spouse or former civil partner or the claimant's partner's spouse, civil partner, former spouse, or former civil partner.

(2) For the purposes of sub-paragraph (1), where more than one maintenance payment falls to be taken into account in any week, all such payments shall be aggregated and treated as if they were a single payment.

21. Except in a case which falls under paragraph 9 of Schedule 2, where the claimant is a person who satisfies [⁴ any of] the conditions of sub-paragraph (2) of that paragraph, any amount of working tax credit up to [⁶ £17.10].

Amendments

1. Amended by Art 22(8) of SI 2006 No 645 and reg 8 of SI 2006 No 217 as from 1.4.06.
2. Amended by Art 22(8) of SI 2007 No 688 as from 1.4.07.
3. Amended by Art 22(8) of SI 2008 No 632 as from 1.4.08.
4. Amended by reg 8(8)(f) of SI 2008 No 3157 as from 5.1.09.
5. Amended by Art 22(8) of SI 2009 No 497 as from 1.4.09.
6. Amended by Art 22(8) of SI 2010 No 793 as from 1.4.10.

[¹**22.**]

Amendment

1. Omitted by reg 8(8)(g) of SI 2008 No 3157 as from 5.1.09.

[¹**23.** Where the total value of any capital specified in Part 2 (capital disregarded only for the purposes of determining deemed income) of Schedule 4 does not exceed £10,000, any income actually derived from such capital.]

Amendment

1.   Substituted by reg 9 of SI 2009 No 1676 as from 2.11.09.

---

24.   Except in the case of income from capital specified in Part 2 of Schedule 4, any actual income from capital.

[¹**25.**   Where the claimant, or the person who was the partner of the claimant on 31st March 2003, was entitled on that date to income support or an income-based jobseeker's allowance but ceased to be so entitled on or before 5th April 2003 by virtue only of regulation 13 of the Housing Benefit (General) Amendment (No 3) Regulations 1999 as in force at that date, the whole of his income.]

Amendment

1.   Inserted by reg 6(5)(c) of SI 2008 No 1042 as from 19.5.08.

General Note

This is the equivalent of Sch 4 para 6 CTB Regs. It is understood to have been omitted in error when the regulations were consolidated in 2006.

SCHEDULE 4
REGULATION 34(2)
Capital disregards

PART 1
Capital to be disregarded

1.   Any premises acquired for occupation by the claimant which he intends to occupy as his home within 26 weeks of the date of acquisition or such longer period as is reasonable in the circumstances to enable the claimant to obtain possession and commence occupation of the premises.

2.   Any premises which the claimant intends to occupy as his home, and in respect of which he is taking steps to obtain possession and has sought legal advice, or has commenced legal proceedings, with a view to obtaining possession, for a period of 26 weeks from the date on which he first sought such advice or first commenced such proceedings whichever is the earlier, or such longer period as is reasonable in the circumstances to enable him to obtain possession and commence occupation of those premises.

3.   Any premises which the claimant intends to occupy as his home to which essential repairs or alterations are required in order to render them fit for such occupation, for a period of 26 weeks from the date on which the claimant first takes steps to effect those repairs or alterations, or such longer period as is necessary to enable those repairs or alterations to be carried out.

4.   Any premises occupied in whole or in part–

(a)   by a person who is a relative of the claimant or his partner as his home [¹ where that person has attained the qualifying age for state pension credit or is incapacitated];

(b)   by the former partner of the claimant as his home; but this provision shall not apply where the former partner is a person from whom the claimant is estranged or divorced or with whom he had formed a civil partnership that has been dissolved.

Amendment

1.   Amended by reg 39 of SI 2009 No 1488 as from 6.4.10.

---

5.   Any future interest in property of any kind, other than land or premises in respect of which the claimant has granted a subsisting lease or tenancy, including sub-leases or sub-tenancies.

6.   Where a claimant has ceased to occupy what was formerly the dwelling occupied as the home following his estrangement or divorce from his former partner or the dissolution of a civil partnership with his former partner, that dwelling for a period of 26 weeks from the date on which he ceased to occupy that dwelling or, where the dwelling is occupied as the home by the former partner who is a lone parent, for so long as it is so occupied.

7.   Any premises where the claimant is taking reasonable steps to dispose of the whole of his interest in those premises, for a period of 26 weeks from the date on which he first took such steps, or such longer period as is reasonable in the circumstances to enable him to dispose of those premises.

8.   All personal possessions.

9.   The assets of any business owned in whole or in part by the claimant and for the purposes of which he is engaged as a self-employed earner or, if he has ceased to be so engaged, for such period as may be reasonable in the circumstances to allow for disposal of those assets.

10.   The assets of any business owned in whole or in part by the claimant if–

(a)   he is not engaged as a self-employed earner in that business by reason of some disease or bodily or mental disablement; but

(b)   he intends to become engaged (or, as the case may be, re-engaged) as a self-employed earner in that business as soon as he recovers or is able to become engaged, or re-engaged, in that business, for a period of 26 weeks from the date on which the claim for council tax benefit is made or, if it is unreasonable to expect him to become engaged or re-engaged in that business within that period, for such longer period as is reasonable in the circumstances to enable him to become so engaged or re-engaged.

11. The surrender value of any policy of life insurance.

12. The value of any funeral plan contract; and for this purpose, "funeral plan contract" means a contract under which–

    (a) the claimant makes one or more payments to another person ("the provider");

    (b) the provider undertakes to provide, or secure the provision of, a funeral in the United Kingdom for the claimant on his death; and

    (c) the sole purpose of the plan is to provide or secure the provision of a funeral for the claimant on his death.

13. Where an ex-gratia payment has been made by the Secretary of State on or after 1st February 2001 in consequence of the imprisonment or internment of–

    (a) the claimant;

    (b) the claimant's partner;

    (c) the claimant's deceased spouse or deceased civil partner; or

    (d) the claimant's partner's deceased spouse or deceased civil partner,

by the Japanese during the Second World War, an amount equal to that payment.

14.–(1) Subject to sub-paragraph (2), the amount of any trust payment made to a claimant or a claimant's partner who is–

    (a) a diagnosed person;

    (b) a diagnosed person's partner or was a diagnosed person's partner at the time of the diagnosed person's death; or

    (c) a parent of a diagnosed person, a person acting in place of the diagnosed person's parents or a person who was so acting at the date of the diagnosed person's death.

    (2) Where a trust payment is made to–

    (a) a person referred to in sub-paragraph (1)(a) or (b), that sub-paragraph shall apply for the period beginning on the date on which the trust payment is made and ending on the date on which that person dies;

    (b) a person referred to in sub-paragraph (1)(c), that sub-paragraph shall apply for the period beginning on the date on which the trust payment is made and ending two years after that date.

    (3) Subject to sub-paragraph (4), the amount of any payment by a person to whom a trust payment has been made or of any payment out of the estate of a person to whom a trust payment has been made, which is made to a claimant or a claimant's partner who is–

    (a) the diagnosed person;

    (b) a diagnosed person's partner or was a diagnosed person's partner at the date of the diagnosed person's death; or

    (c) a parent of a diagnosed person, a person acting in place of the diagnosed person's parents or a person who was so acting at the date of the diagnosed person's death.

    (4) Where a payment such as referred to in sub-paragraph (3) is made to–

    (a) a person referred to in sub-paragraph (3)(a) or (b), that sub-paragraph shall apply for the period beginning on the date on which the payment is made and ending on the date on which that person dies;

    (b) a person referred to in sub-paragraph (3)(c), that sub-paragraph shall apply for the period beginning on the date on which the payment is made and ending two years after that date.

    (5) In this paragraph, a reference to a person–

    (a) being the diagnosed person's partner;

    (b) acting in place of the diagnosed person's parents,

at the date of the diagnosed person's death shall include a person who would have been such a person or a person who would have been so acting, but for the diagnosed person residing in a care home or an independent hospital.

    (6) In this paragraph–

"diagnosed person" means a person who has been diagnosed as suffering from, or who, after his death, has been diagnosed as having suffered from, variant Creutzfeldt-Jakob disease;

"relevant trust" means a trust established out of funds provided by the Secretary of State in respect of persons who suffered, or who are suffering, from variant Creutzfeldt-Jakob disease for the benefit of persons eligible for payments in accordance with its provisions;

"trust payment" means a payment under a relevant trust.

15. The amount of any payment, other than a [¹ war pension], to compensate for the fact that the claimant, the claimant's partner, the claimant's deceased spouse or civil partner or the claimant's partner's deceased spouse or civil partner–

    (a) was a slave labourer or a forced labourer;

    (b) had suffered property loss or had suffered personal injury; or

    (c) was a parent of a child who had died,

during the Second World War.

Amendment
1.   Amended by reg 8(9)(a) of SI 2008 No 3157 as from 5.1.09.

16.–(1)   Any payment made under [² or by]–
(a)   the Macfarlane Trust, the Macfarlane (Special Payments) Trust, the Macfarlane (Special Payments) (No. 2) Trust, the Fund, the Eileen Trust [², MFET Limited], the Skipton Fund, or the London Bombings Relief Charitable Fund (collectively referred to in this paragraph as ''the Trusts''); or
(b)   the Independent Living [¹ Fund (2006)].
(2)   Any payment by or on behalf of a person who is suffering or who suffered from haemophilia or who is or was a qualifying person, which derives from a payment made under [² or by] any of the Trusts and which is made to or for the benefit of that person's partner or former partner from whom he is not, or where that person has died was not, estranged or divorced or with whom he has formed a civil partnership that has not been dissolved or, where that person has died, had not been dissolved at the time of that person's death.
(3)   Any payment by or on behalf of the partner or former partner of a person who is suffering or who suffered from haemophilia or who is or was a qualifying person provided that the partner or former partner and that person are not, or if either of them has died were not, estranged or divorced or, where the partner or former partner and that person have formed a civil partnership, the civil partnership has not been dissolved or, if either of them has died, had not been dissolved at the time of the death, which derives from a payment made under [² or by] any of the Trusts and which is made to or for the benefit of the person who is suffering from haemophilia or who is a qualifying person.
(4)   Any payment by a person who is suffering from haemophilia or who is a qualifying person, which derives from a payment under [² or by] any of the Trusts, where–
(a)   that person has no partner or former partner from whom he is not estranged or divorced or with whom he has formed a civil partnership that has not been dissolved, nor any child who is or had been a member of that person's household; and
(b)   the payment is made either–
    (i)   to that person's parent or step-parent; or
    (ii) where that person at the date of the payment is a child or a student who has not completed his full-time education and has no parent or step-parent, to any person standing in the place of his parent,
but only for a period from the date of the payment until the end of two years from that person's death.
(5)   Any payment out of the estate of a person who suffered from haemophilia or who was a qualifying person, which derives from a payment under [² or by] any of the Trusts, where–
(a)   that person at the date of his death (''the relevant date'') had no partner or former partner from whom he was not estranged or divorced or with whom he had formed a civil partnership that had not been dissolved, nor any child who was or had been a member of his household; and
(b)   the payment is made either–
    (i)   to that person's parent or step-parent; or
    (ii) where that person at the relevant date was a child or a student who had not completed his full-time education and had no parent or step-parent, to any person standing in place of his parent,
but only for a period of two years from the relevant date.
(6)   In the case of a person to whom or for whose benefit a payment referred to in this paragraph is made, any capital resource which derives from any payment of income or capital made under or deriving from any of the Trusts.

Modifications
References to "step-parent" in sub-paras (4)(b)(i) and (ii) and (5)(b)(i) and (ii) are modified by s246 Civil Partnership Act 2004 and article 3 and para 27 of the Schedule to SI 2005 No 3137 (in Parts 6 and 7 respectively).

Amendments
1.   Amended by reg 9(5)(b) of SI 2008 No 2767 as from 17.11.08.
2.   Amended by reg 11(3) and (5) of SI 2010 No 641 as from 1.4.10 (5.4.10 where rent payable weekly or in multiples of a week).

17.–(1)   An amount equal to the amount of any payment made in consequence of any personal injury to the claimant or, if the claimant has a partner, to the partner.
(2)   Where the whole or part of the payment is administered–
[¹ (a)   by the High Court or the County Court under Rule 21.11(1) of the Civil Procedure Rules 1998, or the Court of Protection, or on behalf of a person where the payment can only be disposed of by order or direction of any such court;]
(b)   in accordance with an order made under Rule 36.14 of the Ordinary Cause Rules 1993 or under Rule 128 of those Rules; or
(c)   in accordance with the terms of a trust established for the benefit of the claimant or his partner,
the whole of the amount so administered.

Amendment

1.　　Substituted by reg 18(4) of SI 2006 No 2378 from the 1st day of the 1st benefit week to commence on or after 2.10.06.

18.　　Any amount specified in paragraph 19, 20 [¹ , 21 or 25A] for a period of one year beginning with the date of receipt.

Amendment

1.　　Amended by reg 8(9)(b) of SI 2008 No 3157 as from 5.1.09.

19.　　Amounts paid under a policy of insurance in connection with the loss of or damage to the property occupied by the claimant as his home and to his personal possessions.

20.　　So much of any amounts paid to the claimant or deposited in the claimant's name for the sole purpose of–

(a)　　purchasing premises which the claimant intends to occupy as his home; or

(b)　　effecting essential repairs or alterations to the premises occupied or intended to be occupied by the claimant as his home.

21.–(1)　　Subject to paragraph 22 any amount paid–

(a)　　by way of arrears of benefit;

(b)　　by way of compensation for the late payment of benefit;

(c)　　in lieu of the payment of benefit;

(d)　　to rectify, or compensate for, an official error, as defined for the purposes of paragraph 22, being an amount to which that paragraph does not apply;

(e)　　by a local authority out of funds provided under either section 93 of the Local Government Act 2000 under a scheme known as "Supporting People" or section 91 of the Housing (Scotland) Act 2001.

(2)　　In sub-paragraph (1), "benefit" means–

(a)　　attendance allowance under section 64 of the Act;

(b)　　disability living allowance;

(c)　　income support;

(d)　　income-based jobseeker's allowance;

(e)　　state pension credit;

(f)　　housing benefit;

(g)　　council tax benefit;

(h)　　child tax credit;

(i)　　an increase of a disablement pension under section 104 of the Act (increase where constant attendance is needed), and any further increase of such a pension under section 105 of the Act (increase for exceptionally severe disablement);

(j)　　any amount included on account of the claimant's exceptionally severe disablement or need for constant attendance in a war disablement pension or a war widow's or widower's pension.

[¹ (k)　　any discretionary housing payment paid pursuant to regulation 2(1) of the Discretionary Financial Assistance Regulations 2001; [²]

(l)　　working tax credit.] [² or

[² (m)　　income-related employment and support allowance,]

Amendments

1.　　Inserted by reg 3(14) of SI 2005 No 2502 as amended by Sch 2 para 27 of SI 2006 No 217 as from 1.4.06.

2.　　Amended by reg 79(a) of SI 2008 No 1082 as from 27.10.08.

22.–(1)　　Subject to sub-paragraph (3), any payment of £5,000 or more which has been made to rectify, or to compensate for, an official error relating to a relevant benefit and has been received by the claimant in full on or after the day on which he became entitled to benefit under these Regulations or under the Council Tax Benefit Regulations 2006.

(2)　　Subject to sub-paragraph (3), the total amount of any payments disregarded under–

(a)　　paragraph 7(2) of Schedule 10 to the Income Support (General) Regulations 1987;

(b)　　paragraph 12(2) of Schedule 8 to the Jobseeker's Allowance Regulations;

(c)　　paragraph 9(2) of Schedule 5 to the Council Tax Benefit Regulations 2006;

(d)　　paragraph 20A of Schedule 5 to the State Pension Credit Regulations 2002,

[² (e)　　paragraph 11(2) of Schedule 9 to the Employment and Support Allowance Regulations,]

where the award in respect of which the payments last fell to be disregarded under those Regulations either terminated immediately before the relevant date or is still in existence at that date.

(3)　　Any disregard which applies under sub-paragraph (1) or (2) shall have effect until the award comes to an end.

(4)　　In this paragraph–

"the award", except in sub-paragraph (2), means–

(a) the award of benefit under these Regulations during which the relevant sum or, where it is paid in more than one instalment, the first instalment of that sum is received; and

(b) where that award is followed by one or more further awards which, or each of which, begins immediately after the previous award ends, such further awards until the end of the last such award, provided that, for such further awards, the claimant–
    (i) is the person who received the relevant sum;
    (ii) is the partner of that person; or
    (iii) was the partner of that person at the date of his death;

''official error''–

(a) where the error relates to housing benefit or council tax benefit, has the meaning given by regulation 1(2) of the Decisions and Appeals Regulations; and

(b) where the error relates to any other relevant benefit, has the meaning given by regulation 1(3) of the Social Security and Child Support (Decisions and Appeals) Regulations 1999;

''the relevant date'' means–

(a) in the case of an existing award of benefit under these Regulations or the Council Tax Benefit Regulations 2006, 6th October 2003; and

(b) in any other case, the date on which the claim for benefit under these Regulations or the Council Tax Benefit Regulations 2006 was made;

''relevant benefit'' means any benefit specified in paragraph 21(2); and

''the relevant sum'' means the payment referred to in sub-paragraph (1) or the total amount referred to in sub-paragraph (2).

Amendment

1. Amended by reg 79(b) of SI 2008 No 1082 as from 27.10.08.

23. Where a capital asset is held in a currency other than Sterling, any banking charge or commission payable in converting that capital into Sterling.

24. The value of the right to receive income from an occupational pension scheme or a personal pension scheme.

[¹**25.**]

Amendment

1. Omitted by reg 7(6) of SI 2007 No 1749 as from 16.7.07.

[¹**25A.** Any arrears of supplementary pension which is disregarded under paragraph 4 of Schedule 3 (amounts to be disregarded in the calculation of income other than earnings) or of any amount which is disregarded under paragraph 5 or 6 of that Schedule.]

Amendment

1. Inserted by reg 8(9)(c) of SI 2008 No 3157 as from 5.1.09.

26. The dwelling occupied as the home; but only one dwelling shall be disregarded under this paragraph.

[¹**26A.**–(1) Subject to sub-paragraph (2), where a claimant satisfies the conditions in section 131(3) and (6) of the Act (entitlement to alternative maximum council tax benefit), the whole of his capital.

(2) Sub-paragraph (1) does not apply, where in addition to satisfying the conditions in section 131(3) and (6) of the Act the claimant also satisfies the conditions in section 131(4) and (5) of the Act (entitlement to the maximum council tax benefit).]

Amendment

1. Inserted by reg 6(6) of SI 2008 No 1042 as from 19.5.08.

General Note

Prior to 19 May 2008, there was no equivalent in the CTB(SPC) Regs to Sch 5 para 46 CTB Regs which allows for the disregard of the capital of those claiming alternative maximum CTB ("second adult rebate"). This meant that unless the claimant or her/his partner was in receipt of the guarantee credit of PC (in which case the whole of her/his capital is ignored under reg 16) the capital limit provided by s134 SSCBA and reg 33 applied. This is understood to have been an error, not the intention, as the Social Security (Miscellaneous Amendments)(No.2) Regulations 2008 SI No.1042 inserted para 26A into Sch 4 from 19 May 2008. Under para 26A, the whole of the claimant's capital is disregarded where s/he satisfies the conditions in s131(3) and (6) (alternative maximum CTB), but not those in s131(4) and (5) SSCBA 1992 (main CTB).

[¹**26B.** Any payment made under Part 8A of the Act (entitlement to health in pregnancy grant).]

Amendment

1. Inserted by reg 9(8) of SI 2009 No 583 as from, for any particular claimant, the first day of the first benefit week starting on or after 6.4.09.

[¹[²**26C.**] Where a person elects to be entitled to a lump sum under Schedule 5 or 5A to the Contributions and Benefits Act 1992 or under Schedule 1 to the Graduated Retirement Benefit Regulations, or is treated as having made such an election, and a payment has been made pursuant to that election, an amount equal to–

(a) except where sub-paragraph (b) applies, the amount of any payment or payments made on account of that lump sum;

(b) the amount of that lump sum,

but only for so long as that person does not change that election in favour of an increase of pension or benefit.

Amendments

1. Inserted by reg 12(4) of SI 2005 No 2677 and reg 2 of SI 2006 No 217 as from 6.4.06.
2. Amended by reg 5(4) of SI 2009 No 2608 as from 1.4.10.

PART 2
Capital disregarded only for the purposes of determining deemed income

27. The value of the right to receive any income under a life interest or from a life rent.

28. The value of the right to receive any rent except where the claimant has a reversionary interest in the property in respect of which rent is due.

29. The value of the right to receive any income under an annuity or the surrender value (if any) of such an annuity.

30. Where property is held under a trust, other than–

(a) a charitable trust within the meaning of the Charities Act 1993; or

(b) a trust set up with any payment to which paragraph 16 of this Schedule applies,

and under the terms of the trust, payments fall to be made, or the trustees have a discretion to make payments, to or for the benefit of the claimant or the claimant's partner, or both, that property.

[¹ SCHEDULE 5]

Amendment

1. Omitted by reg 11(5)(c) of SI 2008 No 959 as from 6.10.08.

SCHEDULE 6
REGULATION 46
Amount of alternative maximum council tax benefit

1.–(1) Subject to paragraphs 2 and 3, the alternative maximum council tax benefit in respect of a day for the purpose of regulation 46 shall be determined in accordance with the following Table and in this Table [¹–

(a) "second adult" means any person or persons residing with the claimant to whom section 131(6) of the Act applies; and

(b) "persons to whom regulation 45(2) of the Council Tax Benefit Regulations 2006 applies" includes any person to whom that regulation would apply were they, and their partner if they had one, below the qualifying age for state pension credit.]

(2) In this Schedule "council tax due in respect of that day" means the council tax payable under section 10 or 78 of the 1992 Act less [¹–

(a) any reductions made in consequence of any enactment in, or under, the 1992 Act; and

(b) in a case to which sub-paragraph (c) in column (1) of the table below applies, the amount of any discount which may be appropriate to the dwelling under the 1992 Act.]

Table

(1) Second adult	(2) Alternative maximum council tax benefit
(a) Where the second adult or all second adults are in receipt of income support [⁵ , income-related employment and support allowance] or state pension credit or are persons on an income based jobseeker's allowance;	(a) 25 per cent. of the council tax due in respect of that day;
(b) Where the gross income of the second adult or, where there is more than one second adult, their aggregate gross income disregarding any income of person on income support, [⁵ income-related employment and support allowance,] state pension credit or an income based jobseeker's allowance–	(b)

(i) is less than [⁷ £175.00] per week;

(ii) is not less than [⁷ £175.00 per week but less than [⁷ £228.00] per week.

[² (c) Where the dwelling would be wholly occupied by one or more persons to whom regulation 45(2) of the Council Tax Benefit Regulations 2006 applies but for the presence of one or more second adults who are in receipt of income support, state pension credit [⁵ , an income-related employment and support allowance] or are persons on an income-based job-seeker's allowance.]

(i) 15 per cent. of the council tax due in respect of that day;

(ii) 7.5 per cent. of the council tax due in respect of that day.

[² (c) 100 per cent. of the council tax due in respect of that day.]

Amendments
1. Amended by reg 11(4)(a) and (b) of SI 2006 No 588 as from 1.4.06.
2. Inserted by reg 11(4)(c) of SI 2006 No 588 as from 1.4.06.
3. Amended by Art 22(9) of SI 2007 No 688 as from 1.4.07.
4. Amended by Art 22(9) of SI 2008 No 632 as from 1.4.08.
5. Amended by reg 80 of SI 2008 No 1082 as from 27.10.08.
6. Amended by Art 22(9) of SI 2009 No 497 as from 1.4.09.
7. Confirmed by Art 22(9) of SI 2010 No 793 as from 1.4.10.

2. In determining a second adult's gross income for the purposes of this Schedule, there shall be disregarded from that income–
(a) any attendance allowance, or any disability allowance under section 71 of the Act;
(b) any payment made under [² or by] the Trusts, the Fund, the Eileen Trust [² , MFET Limited] or the Independent Living [¹ Fund (2006)] which had his income fallen to be calculated under regulation 30 of the Council Tax Benefit Regulations 2006 (calculation of income other than earnings) would have been disregarded under paragraph 24 of Schedule 4 to those Regulations (income in kind); and
(c) any payment which had his income fallen to be calculated under regulation 30 of the Council Tax Benefit Regulations 2006 would have been disregarded under paragraph 36 of Schedule 4 to those Regulations (payments made under certain trusts and certain other payments).

Amendments
1. Amended by reg 9(5)(c) of SI 2008 No 2767 as from 17.11.08.
2. Amended by reg 11(3) and (5) of SI 2010 No 641 as from 1.4.10 (5.4.10 where rent payable weekly or in multiples of a week).

3. Where there are two or more second adults residing with the claimant for benefit and any such second adult falls to be disregarded for the purposes of discount in accordance with Schedule 1 to the 1992 Act, his income shall be disregarded in determining the amount of any alternative maximum council tax benefit, unless that second adult is a member of a couple and his partner does not fall to be disregarded for the purposes of discount.

SCHEDULE 7
REGULATION 61(1)
Matters to be included in the decision notice

PART 1
General
1. The statement of matters to be included in any decision notice issued by a relevant authority to a person, and referred to in regulation 61 (notification of decision) and in regulation 10 of the Decisions and Appeals Regulations are those matters set out in the following provisions of this Schedule.
2. Every decision notice shall include a statement as to the right of any person affected by that decision to request a written statement under regulation 61(2) (requests for statement of reasons) and the manner and time in which to do so.
3. Every decision notice shall include a statement as to the right of any person affected by that decision to make an application for a revision in accordance with regulation 4(1)(a) of the Decisions and Appeals Regulations and, where appropriate, to appeal against that decision and the manner and time in which to do so.
4. Every decision notice following an application for a revision in accordance with regulation 4(1)(a) of the Decisions and Appeals Regulations shall include a statement as to whether the original decision in respect of which the person made his representations has been confirmed or revised and where the relevant authority has not revised the decision the reasons why not.

5.   Every decision notice following an application for a revision in accordance with regulation 4(1)(a) of the Decisions and Appeals Regulations shall, if the original decision has been revised, include a statement as to the right of any person affected by that decision to apply for a revision in accordance with regulation 4(1)(a) of those Regulations and the manner and time in which to do so.

6.   An authority may include in the decision notice any other matters not prescribed by this Schedule which it sees fit, whether expressly or by reference to some other document available without charge to the person.

7.   Parts 2, 3 and 4 of this Schedule shall apply only to the decision notice given on a claim.

8.   Where a decision notice is given following a revision of an earlier decision–

(a)   made of the authority's own motion which results in a revision of that earlier decision; or

(b)   made following an application for a revision in accordance with regulation 4(1)(a) of the Decisions and Appeals Regulations, whether or not resulting in a revision of that earlier decision,

that notice shall, subject to paragraph 6, contain a statement only as to all the matters revised.

PART 2
Awards where state pension credit [² or an extended payment (qualifying contributory benefits)] is payable

9.–(1)   Where a person on state pension credit is awarded council tax benefit, the decision notice shall include a statement as to–

(a)   the normal weekly amount of council tax which may be rounded to the nearest penny;

(b)   the normal weekly amount of the council tax benefit, which amount may be rounded to the nearest penny;

(c)   the amount of and the category of non-dependant deductions made under regulation 42, if any;

(d)   the first day of entitlement to the council tax benefit; and

(e)   his duty to notify any change of circumstances which might affect his entitlement to, or the amount of council tax benefit and, without prejudice to the extent of the duty owed under regulation 59 (duty to notify changes of circumstances), the kind of change of circumstances which is to be notified, either upon the notice or by reference to some other document available to him on application without charge,

and in any case where the amount to which sub-paragraph (a) or (b) refers disregards fractions of a penny, the notice shall include a statement to that effect.

(2)   In a case where a person on state pension credit has entitlement only to the savings credit, the following additional matters shall also be set out–

(a)   the applicable amount and the basis of calculation;

(b)   the amount of the savings credit [¹] taken into account;

(c)   the amount of the person's income and capital as notified to the local authority by the Secretary of State and taken into account for the purposes of the council tax benefit assessment;

(d)   any modification of the claimant's income or capital made in accordance with regulation 17 (calculation of claimant's income in savings credit only cases); and

(e)   the amount of the claimant's capital if paragraph (7) of regulation 17 applies in his case.

[² (3)   Where a claimant is entitled to an extended payment (qualifying contributory benefits) in accordance with regulation 44, the decision notice shall include a statement as to the matters set out in paragraph 9(1).]

Amendments
1.   Omitted by reg 3(15) of SI 2005 No 2502 as amended by Sch 2 para 27 of SI 2006 No 217 as from 1.4.06.
2.   Amended by reg 11(6) of SI 2008 No 959 as from 6.10.08.

PART 3
Awards of council tax benefit where state pension credit not in payment

10.   Where a person is not on state pension credit but is awarded council tax benefit, the decision notice shall include a statement as to–

(a)   the matters set out in paragraph 9;

(b)   his applicable amount and how it is calculated;

(c)   his weekly earnings; and

(d)   his weekly income other than earnings.

PART 4
Notice where income of non-dependant is treated as claimant's income

11.   Where an authority makes a decision under regulation 14 (circumstances in which income of non-dependant is to be treated as claimant's) the decision notice shall contain a statement as to–

(a)   the fact that a decision has been made by reference to the income and capital of the claimant's non-dependant; and

(b)   the relevant authority's reasons for making that decision.

PART 5
Notice where no award is made
12. Where a person is not awarded council tax benefit under regulation 40 (maximum council tax benefit)–
  (a) on grounds of income, the decision notice shall include a statement as to–
    (i) the matters set out in paragraph 9(1)(a); and
    (ii) the matters set out in paragraph 10(b) to (d) where the person is not on state pension credit;
  (b) on the grounds that the amount of the alternative maximum council tax benefit exceeds the appropriate maximum council tax benefit, the matters set out in paragraph 15;
  (c) for any reason other than one mentioned in sub-paragraph (a) or (b), the decision notice shall include a statement as to the reason why no award has been made.

PART 6
Awards where alternative maximum council tax benefit is payable in respect of a day
13. Where a person is awarded council tax benefit determined in accordance with regulation 46 and Schedule 6 (alternative maximum council tax benefit) the decision notice shall include a statement as to–
  (a) the normal weekly amount of council tax, which amount may be rounded to the nearest penny;
  (b) the normal weekly amount of the alternative maximum council tax benefit, which amount may be rounded to the nearest penny;
  (c) the gross income or incomes and the rate of benefit which apply under Schedule 6;
  (d) the first day of entitlement to benefit;
  (e) the gross income of any second adult used to determine the rate of the alternative maximum council tax benefit or if any such adult is on income support, state pension credit [¹ , an income-based jobseeker's allowance or an income-related employment and support allowance];
  (f) the claimant's duty to notify any change of circumstances which might affect his entitlement to, or the amount of the alternative maximum council tax benefit and, without prejudice to the extent of the duty owed under regulation 59 (duty to notify changes of circumstances) the kind of change of circumstances which are to be notified, either upon the notice or by reference to some other document available to the claimant free of charge on application,
and in any case where the amount to which sub-paragraph (a) or (b) refers disregards fractions of a penny, the notice shall include a statement to that effect.

Amendment
1.   Amended by reg 81 of SI 2008 No 1082 as from 27.10.08.

Notice where no award of alternative maximum council tax benefit is made
14. Where a person is not awarded council tax benefit in accordance with regulation 46 and Schedule 6 (alternative maximum council tax benefit)–
  (a) on the grounds that the gross income or as the case may be the aggregate gross incomes, of any second adult or adults in the claimant's dwelling is too high, the decision notice shall include a statement as to the matters set out in paragraphs 13(a), (c) and (e);
  (b) on the grounds that the appropriate maximum council tax benefit is higher than the alternative maximum council tax benefit, the decision notice shall include a statement as to the matters set out in paragraph 15 below;
  (c) for any reason not referred to in sub-paragraphs (a) and (b), the decision notice shall include a statement as to why no award has been made.

Notice where council tax benefit is awarded and section 131(9) of the Act applies
15. Where the amount of a claimant's council tax benefit in respect of a day is the greater of the appropriate maximum council tax benefit and the alternative maximum council tax benefit in his case the notice shall in addition to the matters set out in paragraphs 9, 10 or 13, as the case may be, include a statement as to–
  (a) the amount of whichever is the lesser of the appropriate maximum council tax benefit or the alternative maximum council tax benefit in his case, which amount may be rounded to the nearest penny; and
  (b) that this amount has not been awarded in consequence of the award of council tax benefit at a higher rate,
and in any case where the amount to which sub-paragraph (a) refers disregards fractions of a penny, the notice shall include a statement to that effect.

PART 7
Notice where there is recoverable excess benefit
16. Except in cases to which paragraphs (a) and (b) of regulation 67 (excess benefit in consequence of a reduction in a relevant authority's council tax) refers, where the relevant authority makes a decision that there is recoverable excess benefit within the meaning of regulation 68 (recoverable excess benefit), the decision notice shall include a statement as to–

(a)   the fact that there is recoverable excess benefit;
(b)   the reason why there is recoverable excess benefit;
(c)   the amount of recoverable excess benefit;
(d)   how the amount of recoverable excess benefit was calculated;
(e)   the benefit weeks to which the recoverable excess benefit relates; and
(f)   the method or combination of methods by which the authority intends to recover the recoverable excess benefit, including–
> (i)   payment by or on behalf of the person concerned of the amount due by the specified date;
> (ii)   addition of the amount due to any amount in respect of the tax concerned for payment whether by instalments or otherwise by the specified date or dates; or
> (iii)   if recovery cannot be effected in accordance with heads (i) or (ii), requesting the Secretary of State to recover the excess benefits by deduction from the benefit prescribed in regulation 75 (recovery of excess benefits from prescribed benefits).

[¹SCHEDULE 8
ELECTRONIC COMMUNICATION

Amendment
1.   Inserted by Art 5(5) of SI 2006 No 2968 as from 20.12.06.

PART 1
Introduction

Interpretation
1.   In this Schedule "official computer system" means a computer system maintained by or on behalf of the relevant authority or of the Secretary of State for sending, receiving, processing or storing of any claim, certificate, notice, information or evidence.

PART 2
Electronic Communication – General Provisions

Conditions for the use of electronic communication
2.–(1)   The relevant authority may use an electronic communication in connection with claims for, and awards of, benefit under these Regulations.
(2)   A person other than the relevant authority may use an electronic communication in connection with the matters referred to in sub-paragraph (1) if the conditions specified in sub-paragraphs (3) to (6) are satisfied.
(3)   The first condition is that the person is for the time being permitted to use an electronic communication by an authorisation given by means of a direction of the Chief Executive of the relevant authority.
(4)   The second condition is that the person uses an approved method of–
(a)   authenticating the identity of the sender of the communication;
(b)   electronic communication;
(c)   authenticating any claim or notice delivered by means of an electronic communication; and
(d)   subject to sub-paragraph (7), submitting to the relevant authority any claim, certificate, notice, information or evidence.
(5)   The third condition is that any claim, certificate, notice, information or evidence sent by means of an electronic communication is in a form approved for the purposes of this Schedule.
(6)   The fourth condition is that the person maintains such records in written or electronic form as may be specified in a direction given by the Chief Executive of the relevant authority.
(7)   Where the person uses any method other than the method approved of submitting any claim, certificate, notice, information or evidence, that claim, certificate, notice, information or evidence shall be treated as not having been submitted.
(8)   In this paragraph "approved" means approved by means of a direction given by the Chief Executive of the relevant authority for the purposes of this Schedule.

Use of intermediaries
3.   The relevant authority may use intermediaries in connection with–
(a)   the delivery of any claim, certificate, notice, information or evidence by means of an electronic communication; and
(b)   the authentication or security of anything transmitted by such means,
and may require other persons to use intermediaries in connection with those matters.

PART 3
Electronic Communication – Evidential Provisions

Effect of delivering information by means of electronic communication

4.–(1)   Any claim, certificate, notice, information or evidence which is delivered by means of an electronic communication shall be treated as having been delivered in the manner or form required by any provision of these Regulations, on the day the conditions imposed–

(a)   by this Schedule; and

(b)   by or under an enactment,

are satisfied.

(2)   The relevant authority may, by a direction, determine that any claim, certificate, notice, information or evidence is to be treated as delivered on a different day (whether earlier or later) from the day provided for in sub-paragraph (1).

(3)   Information shall not be taken to have been delivered to an official computer system by means of an electronic communication unless it is accepted by the system to which it is delivered.

Proof of identity of sender or recipient of information

5.   If it is necessary to prove, for the purpose of any legal proceedings, the identity of–

(a)   the sender of any claim, certificate, notice, information or evidence delivered by means of an electronic communication to an official computer system; or

(b)   the recipient of any such claim, certificate, notice, information or evidence delivered by means of an electronic communication from an official computer system,

the sender or recipient, as the case may be, shall be presumed to be the person whose name is recorded as such on that official computer system.

Proof of delivery of information

6.–(1)   If it is necessary to prove, for the purpose of any legal proceedings, that the use of an electronic communication has resulted in the delivery of any claim, certificate, notice, information or evidence this shall be presumed to have been the case where–

(a)   any such claim, certificate, notice, information or evidence has been delivered to the relevant authority, if the delivery of that claim, certificate, notice, information or evidence has been recorded on an official computer system; or

(b)   any such claim, certificate, notice, information or evidence has been delivered by the relevant authority, if the delivery of that certificate, notice, information or evidence has been recorded on an official computer system.

(2)   If it is necessary to prove, for the purpose of any legal proceedings, that the use of an electronic communication has resulted in the delivery of any such claim, certificate, notice, information or evidence, this shall be presumed not to be the case, if that claim, certificate, notice, information or evidence delivered to the relevant authority has not been recorded on an official computer system.

(3)   If it is necessary to prove, for the purpose of any legal proceedings, when any such claim, certificate, notice, information or evidence sent by means of an electronic communication has been received, the time and date of receipt shall be presumed to be that recorded on an official computer system.

Proof of content of information

7.   If it is necessary to prove, for the purpose of any legal proceedings, the content of any claim, certificate, notice, information or evidence sent by means of an electronic communication, the content shall be presumed to be that recorded on an official computer system.]

Part 5

Secondary legislation
Decision making and appeals

The Housing Benefit and Council Tax Benefit (Decisions and Appeals) Regulations 2001

(SI 2001 No.1002)

Arrangement of Regulations

PART I
General

1. Citation, commencement and interpretation
2. Service of notices or documents
3. Person treated as a person affected by a decision

PART II
Revisions and supersessions

4. Revision of decisions
5. Late application for a revision
6. Date from which a revision takes effect
7. Decisions superseding earlier decisions
8. Date from which a decision superseding an earlier decision takes effect
9. Effective date for late notification of change of circumstances
10. Notice of a decision against which an appeal lies

PART III
Suspension and termination of benefit and other matters

11. Cases where a relevant authority may suspend
12. Making or restoring of payments or reductions suspended
13. Suspension for failure to furnish information etc.
14. Termination in cases of a failure to furnish information
15. Decisions involving issues that arise on appeal in other cases

PART IV
Rights of appeal and procedure for bringing appeals

16. Decisions against which no appeal lies
17. Appeal against a decision which has been revised
18. Time within which an appeal is to be brought
19. Late appeals
20. Making of appeals and applications
21. Death of a party to an appeal

PART V
Appeal Tribunals

22. Composition of appeal tribunals
23. Procedure in connection with appeals

SCHEDULE
Decisions against which no appeal lies

PART I
General

Citation, commencement and interpretation

1.–(1) These Regulations may be cited as the Housing Benefit and Council Tax Benefit (Decisions and Appeals) Regulations 2001 and shall come into force on 2nd July 2001.

(2) In these Regulations, unless the context otherwise requires–

''the Act'' means the Child Support, Pensions and Social Security Act 2000;

[³ "the 1998 Act" means the Social Security Act 1998;]

"the Administration Act" means the Social Security Administration Act 1992;

"appeal" means an appeal to [⁸ the First-tier Tribunal];

"appropriate relevant authority" has the meaning it has in paragraph 4 of Schedule 7 to the Act;

"benefit week" means a period of seven consecutive days commencing on a Monday and ending on a Sunday;

"claimant" means a person claiming housing benefit or council tax benefit or both;

[⁸]

[⁶ "Council Tax Benefit Regulations" means the Council Tax Benefit Regulations 2006;]

[⁶ "Council Tax Benefit (State Pension Credit) Regulations" means the Council Tax Benefit (Persons who have attained the qualifying age for state pension credit) Regulations 2006;]

[⁴ "couple" means–

    (a)   a man and woman who are married to each other and are members of the same household;

    (b)   a man and woman who are not married to each other but are living together as husband and wife;

    (c)   two people of the same sex who are civil partners of each other and are members of the same household; or

    (d)   two people of the same sex who are not civil partners of each other but are living together as if they were civil partners,

and for the purposes of paragraph (d), two people of the same sex are to be regarded as living together as if they were civil partners if, but only if, they would be regarded as living together as husband and wife were they instead two people of the opposite sex;]

"Decisions and Appeals Regulations 1999" means the Social Security and Child Support (Decisions and Appeals) Regulations 1999;

[² . . .]

[³ "family" has the same meaning as in section 137 of the Social Security Contributions and Benefits Act 1992;]

[⁸]

[⁶ "Housing Benefit Regulations" means the Housing Benefit Regulations 2006;]

[⁶ "Housing Benefit (State Pension Credit) Regulations" means the Housing Benefit (Persons who have attained the qualifying age for state pension credit) Regulations 2006;]

[⁸]

"official error" means an error made by–

    (a)   a relevant authority or a person–

        (i)   authorised to carry out any function of a relevant authority relating to housing benefit or council tax benefit; or

        (ii)   providing services relating to housing benefit or council tax benefit directly or indirectly to a relevant authority;

    [¹ (b)   an officer of–

        (i)   the Department for Work and Pensions; or

        (ii)   the Commissioners of Inland Revenue,

    acting as such;]–

    [²(c) . . .]

but excludes any error caused wholly or partly by any person or body not specified in sub-paragraphs (a) to (c) of this definition and any error of law which is shown to have been an error only by virtue of a subsequent decision of [⁸ the Upper Tribunal] or the court;

[⁸]

"partner" means–

    (a)   where a claimant is a member of [⁵ a couple], the other member of that couple; or

(b)   where a claimant is polygamously married to two or more members of his household, any such member;

"person affected" shall be construed in accordance with regulation 3;

[⁸]

"principal parties" has the same meaning as in paragraph 7(4) of Schedule 7 to the Act;

"relevant authority" has the same meaning as in paragraph 1(1) of Schedule 7 to the Act;

"relevant decision" has the same meaning as in paragraph 1(2) of Schedule 7 to the Act;

[⁷ "the Welfare Reform Act" means the Welfare Reform Act 2007.]

[²...]

[²...]

(3)   In these Regulations, unless the context otherwise requires, a reference–

(a)   to a numbered regulation is to the regulation in these Regulations bearing that number;

(b)   in a regulation to a numbered paragraph is to the paragraph in that regulation bearing that number.

Amendments

1.   Amended by reg 23 of SI 2002 No 1379 as from 20.5.02.
2.   Deleted by Sch 2 para 8 (a) of SI 2002 No 1703 as from 30.9.02.
3.   Inserted by reg 5(2)(a) of SI 2003 No 2275 as from 6.10.03.
4.   Inserted by reg 9(2)(a) of SI 2005 No 2878 as from 5.12.05.
5.   Substituted by reg 9(b) of SI 2005 No 2878 as from 5.12.05.
6.   Amended by reg 5 and Sch 2 para 17(2) of SI 2006 No 217 as from 6.3.06.
7.   Inserted by reg 3 of SI 2008 No 1082, as substituted by reg 26 of SI 2008 No 2428, as from 27.10.08.
8.   Amended by Sch 1 para 149 of SI 2008 No 2683 as from 3.11.08.

Analysis

"Official error" is a ground for revision under reg 4(2)(a). It is an error wholly caused by one of the named categories of people. Those falling into sub-paras (a) and (b) are equivalent to the categories in sub-paras (a) to (c) of reg 100(3) HB Regs and reference should be made to the commentary to that provision on p479. Since 30 September 2002, "official error" no longer includes errors made by someone employed by an authority acting on behalf of the relevant HB and CTB authority for the area: sub-para (c) deleted.

The tailpiece excludes an error caused by a person not falling within the categories listed in the definition. That person may be wholly or only partly to blame for the error occurring.

Official errors include errors of law. However, an error of law is not an official error if it is "shown to have been" a mistake by a subsequent decision of the Upper Tribunal or a court. "Court" is not defined but will inevitably be interpreted to cover all superior courts in England, Scotland and Wales. If, however, as often occurs, there is a pre-existing commissioner's decision which gives a ruling on the point but the significance of which was not fully appreciated at the time, the failure to follow that decision will still be an official error. Before 3 November 2008, the reference to "the Upper Tribunal" was to "a Commissioner". The way in which the regulation has been amended appears to have the effect that where, on or after 3 November 2008, an authority or a tribunal is considering an error of law that is "shown to have been" a mistake by a decision of a commissioner before that date, the exclusion from the definition of official error no longer applies. In order to reflect what was almost certainly the policy intention, the words "a Commissioner" should have been replaced by the words "a Commissioner or the Upper Tribunal" rather than merely "the Upper Tribunal".

It is suggested that official error also includes situations where there is specific evidence which the authority or person had but which was not taken into account even though it was relevant, and where there is documentary or other written evidence of entitlement which the authority had but failed to give to the person making the decision at the time it was made.

Note that the difference in wording in sub-para (a) means that the restrictive reasoning in *R(I) 5/02* – error of law made by an adjudication officer on a decision made prior to the inception of the SSA 1998 does not fall within the definition and so that decision cannot ever be revised for "official error" – has no application to HB/CTB decisions. Note, in any case, that in *CG 2122/2001* Commissioner Mesher was reluctant to accept the tribunal's reasoning on this point in *R(I) 5/02* and in *R(CS) 3/04* Commissioner Turnbull decided that *R(I) 5/02* was wrongly decided on this point and he did not need to follow it.

Service of notices or documents

2.   Where, by, or in consequence of, any provision of these Regulations or Schedule 7 to the Act–

(a)   any notice or other document is required to be given or sent to [¹] the Secretary of State or the relevant authority, that notice or document shall be treated as having been so given or sent on the day that it is received by [¹] the Secretary of State or the relevant authority, as the case may be; and

(b)   any notice (including notification of a decision of a relevant authority) or other document is required to be given or sent to any person other than [¹] the Secretary of State or the relevant authority, as the case may be, that notice or document shall, if sent by post to that person's last known address, be treated as having been so given or sent on the day it was posted.

Amendment
1.   Amended by Sch 1 para 150 of SI 2008 No 2683 as from 3.11.08.

General Note
Reg 2 governs when notices and other documents are to be treated as having been served. It applies to all documents that are "required to be given or sent" by, or in consequence of, "any provision of these Regulations or Schedule 7" to CSPSSA.

There are two rules:

(1)   Under para (a), documents sent to the local authority are served when they are received.

(2)   Under para (b), a document sent to other parties (eg, by a local authority to a claimant) is deemed to be served on the day that it is posted.

Analysis
Para (a). The fact that a document given/sent to a local authority is only treated as having been given/sent when it is actually received is a constant source of dispute, and a trap for claimants who are often placed in the position of having to establish that it was more likely than not that a document was received by an authority when all the evidence relevant to that issue lies in the hands of the authority. The best advice for claimants is to either deliver all documents in person and obtain a receipt or send them by recorded delivery so that the Royal Mail can be approached for evidence of delivery if necessary. Unfortunately, that advice will often be impracticable either in terms of time (the claimant may well be in full-time low-waged work) or money (as recorded delivery greatly increases the cost of posting a letter and many letters may be necessary during the course of a claim). A compromise may be to advise claimants to send letters by ordinary post but obtain a free certificate of posting from the Post Office counter: proof of posting may help persuade a tribunal that it is more likely than not that the authority received the letter and subsequently misplaced it. But even if it does not, a claimant who can prove that s/he committed a document to the post is in a much stronger position to argue for any necessary extension of time if that document subsequently goes astray.

Local authorities are under a duty to ensure that those who are entitled to benefit receive it as well as to ensure that those with no entitlement do not. As entitlement may depend upon when they receive a particular document, it is important that all authorities should have rigorous and documented procedures for the opening of post. It is not unusual for the First-tier Tribunal to question presenting officers in detail about such procedures.

Documents sent by fax can raise particular difficulties. Provided a fax is sent prior to midnight and successfully transmitted, it will have been "received" on that day: *CDLA 4895/2001* (para 7). This issue was further considered in *R(DLA) 3/05*, in the context of a request for a statement of the appeal tribunal's reasons for its decision being faxed to a tribunal venue within the relevant time limit, but where that faxed request had not been picked up by the clerk to the tribunal – to whom such applications had to be made, see the former reg 53(4) SSCS D&A Regs – until after that time limit had expired, because the venue was not used on a daily basis. Commissioner Jacobs decided that, in such circumstances, an application is made when it is received by a fax machine, and that this is the case regardless of when the clerk actually collects the fax from the machine, which may be hours or days later (para 18). However, the fax machine used must relate in some way to the case to which the application relates, and at the very least it must be a fax machine within the relevant Tribunals Service Region (para 19). Nor is it sufficient to send an application to a fax machine at a casual venue, such as a town hall, as the fax machine there will belong to the owner or occupier of the premises and not the tribunal (para 20). In this case the application had been made to a dedicated appeals venue (albeit one that was not used for appeals each and every day), where the claimant's appeal had been heard and where the fax number for that venue had been made available to those with appeals at that venue. In these circumstances, and in the absence of any directions to the contrary, service on that fax machine was good service, and so the request for the statement of reasons had been made within time.

Para (b). The effect of this is that where on service of a document, a time limit begins to run, it runs from the date of posting, not date of receipt of the document. This presumes that if the document was sent to the correct address, it has been delivered. Extensions of time ought readily to be granted where a document is lost in the post or has been sent to an incorrect address. As Commissioner Williams pointed out in *CH 3009/2002*, there is no matching presumption that a document which it was intended to be posted was actually posted. He said that where, as in this case, an appellant challenges whether something has been posted for good reason, evidence of office practice is required to show that on the balance of probabilities, the document was posted: paras 12 and 13.

Before 3 November 2008, reg 2 also applied to documents sent to and by the clerk to an appeal tribunal. Sending and delivery of documents in proceedings before the First-tier Tribunal is now governed by r13 TP(FT) Rules 2008 (see p1058).

The divergent treatment of documents sent to local authorities and documents sent to other parties to the appeal would seem to raise issues about the "equality of arms" (see the commentary to Art 6 European Convention on Human Rights on p125). Reg 2 means that the risk of documents going astray in the post is always borne by the claimant or appellant, never by the local authority, and that, in the event of a dispute, the claimant or appellant either has to prove that s/he did not receive the document (which involves proving a negative) or that the authority did receive the document (which involves proving a fact when all the potential evidence for that fact is in the possession of the other party). The harsh effects of reg 2 will often, but not always, be mitigated by the possibility of obtaining an extension of time. Nevertheless, it is wrong in principle for procedural rules to overtly favour one party over another. That is particularly so when the advantaged party is the more powerful (in this case the state) and the disadvantaged the citizen.

Person treated as a person affected by a decision

3.–(1) For the purposes of Schedule 7 to the Act and subject to paragraph (2), a person is to be treated as a person affected by a relevant decision of a relevant authority where that person is–

(a) a claimant;

(b) in the case of a person who is liable to make payments in respect of a dwelling and is unable for the time being to act–

  (i) a [² deputy] appointed by the Court of Protection with power to claim, or as the case may be, receive benefit on his behalf,

  (ii) in Scotland, a tutor, curator, judicial factor or other guardian acting or appointed in terms of law administering that person's estate, or

  (iii) an attorney with a general power or a power to receive benefit appointed by the person liable to make those payments under [² the Powers of Attorney Act 1971, the Enduring Powers of Attorney Act 1985 or the Mental Capacity Act 2005 or otherwise];

[¹ (c) a person appointed by the relevant authority under regulation 82(3) of the Housing Benefit Regulations, regulation 63(3) of the Housing Benefit (State Pension Credit) Regulations, regulation 68(3) of the Council Tax Benefit Regulations or, as the case may be, regulation 52(3) of the Council Tax Benefit (State Pension Credit) Regulations (appointments for persons unable to act);

(d) a person from whom the relevant authority determines that–

  (i) an overpayment is recoverable in accordance with Part 13 of the Housing Benefit Regulations or Part 12 of the Housing Benefit (State Pension Credit) Regulations; or

  (ii) excess benefit is recoverable in accordance with Part 11 of the Council Tax Benefit Regulations or Part 10 of the Council Tax Benefit (State Pension Credit) Regulations; or

(e) a landlord or agent acting on behalf of that landlord and that decision is made under–

  (i) regulation 95 (circumstances in which payment is to be made to the landlord) of the Housing Benefit Regulations;

  (ii) regulation 96 (circumstances in which payment may be made to the landlord) of those Regulations;

  (iii) regulation 76 (circumstances in which payment is to be made to the landlord) of the Housing Benefit (State Pension Credit) Regulations;

  (iv) regulation 77 (circumstances in which payment may be made to the landlord) of those Regulations.]

(2) Paragraph (1) only applies in relation to a person referred to in paragraph (1) where the rights, duties or obligations of that person are affected by a relevant decision.

Amendments

1.   Substituted by reg 5 and Sch 2 para 17(3) of SI 2006 No 217 as from 6.3.06.

2.   Amended by reg 9 of SI 2007 No 2618 as from 1.10.07.

Analysis

Para (1) sets out the categories of "person affected". This definition is of vital importance, since it is a "person affected" who has the right to challenge decisions and appeal under Sch 7 CSPSSA and these regulations. The categories are:

(1)   The claimant: sub-para (a).

(2)   A deputy or attorney in England and Wales, or the Scottish equivalents, who is acting on behalf of the person who is liable to make payments: sub-para (b). The deemed non-liability in regs 9(1) and 10(1) of both the HB and the HB(SPC) Regs and reg 56(1) HB Regs will not preclude such a person acting on an appeal against such a decision.

(3)   An appointee appointed by the relevant authority: sub-para (c).

(4)   A person from whom it is decided that an overpayment is recoverable: sub-para (d). This could be a landlord. In *CH 3679/2002* (para 3) it was held that a landlord would be a "person affected" in relation to an appeal by a claimant against a decision that an overpayment was recoverable from a landlord. The failure to notify the landlord of the appeal rendered the decision erroneous in law.

(5)   A landlord or her/his agent, where the decision relates to direct payments (including a decision that the landlord is not a "fit and proper person" – see commentary to regs 95 and 96 HB Regs on pp471 and 475: sub-para (e)).

In *CH 3817/2004*, Commissioner Mesher holds that the list in para (1) is not exhaustive. Sch 7 para 23(2) CSPSSA allows regulations to specify who is to be treated as a person affected and who is not to be so treated and reg 3 only gives effect to the first part of that power. Para (1) does not say that those listed are the *only* persons affected and there is no list of persons who are *not* to be treated as persons affected. In those circumstances, the effect of para (1) is to put the status of the listed categories of person beyond argument. But it is still open to a person to argue that s/he is a person affected by a relevant decision for the purposes of para 6(3) Sch 7 CSPSSA in the ordinary meaning to be given to that term (para 14). In *CH 3817/2004* itself, a woman who was jointly and severally liable with her partner to pay rent and council tax was held to be a person affected by a decision to refuse a claim for backdating that the local authority had treated as having been made by her partner.

Para (2) provides that a person will only be a "person affected" if her/his rights, duties and obligations are affected by the decision in question. As far as the people listed in para (1) are concerned, this will always be the case. The rights of the claimant are affected by a decision to pay HB directly to a landlord or agent, or to recover an overpayment from such a person, because (in the former case) the entitlement to benefit is the claimant's and s/he is *prima facie* entitled to receive payment (see reg 94 HB Regs and reg 75 HB (SPC) Regs) and (in the latter) because recovery of an HB overpayment from the landlord or agent will create a debt from the claimant to the recoveree and (at least if reg 95(2)(b) HB Regs and reg 76(2)(b) of the HB (SPC) Regs are validly made: reg 95(2)(b)) will create arrears of rent that could lead to eviction (see p471). The rights of deputies (etc) and appointees (para (1)(b) and (c)) are affected because they are acting in the place of the claimant.

Para (2) will, however, be relevant in cases in which a person who is not on the list in para (1) seeks to argue that s/he is a person affected within the ordinary meaning of that phrase (see *CH 3817/2004* above). See also the commentary to reg 21 on p1043 in relation to who has a right of appeal where the claimant has died.

P ART II
Revisions and Supersessions

General Note on Part II

Pt II contains the very detailed provisions for revisions and supersessions, which are two of the three means by which a decision can be altered. The third is for the decision to be reversed or varied on appeal.

Reference should be made to Sch 7 paras 3 and 4 for the enabling provisions governing revisions and supersessions. Regs 4 to 6 contain the detailed provisions for the operation of revisions under Sch 7 para 4 CSPSSA. Reg 4 deals with grounds on which a revision can be made and the procedure for doing so. Reg 5 deals with applications for revision made outside the time limit in reg 4(1), and reg 6 deals with the effective date of a decision which has been revised. Regs 7 and 8 deal with the grounds and procedure (reg 7) and the effective date (reg 8) of a supersession. Reg 9 deals with late notifications of changes of circumstances (which are under reg 7(2)(a) grounds for a supersession) and reg 10 deals with notifications of decisions generally.

Revision of decisions

4.–(1)   Subject to the provisions in this regulation, a relevant decision ("the original decision") may be revised or further revised by the relevant authority which made the decision where–

(a)   [² subject to regulation 10A(3),] the person affected makes an application for a revision within–

(i)   one month of the date of notification of the original decision; or

(ii)   such extended time as the relevant authority may allow under regulation 5;

(b)   within one month of the date of notification of the original decision that authority has information which is sufficient to show that the original decision was made in ignorance of, or was based upon a mistake as to, some material fact; or

(c)   an appeal is made under paragraph 6 of Schedule 7 to the Act against the original decision within the time prescribed [¹⁰ by Tribunal Procedure Rules] but the appeal has not been determined.

(2)   An original decision may be revised or further revised by the relevant authority which made the decision, at any time by that authority, where that decision–

(a)   arose from an official error; or

(b)   was made in ignorance of, or was based upon a mistake as to, some material fact and as a result of that ignorance of or mistake as to that fact, the decision was more advantageous to the person affected than it would otherwise have been but for that ignorance or mistake.

(3)   Notwithstanding the provisions in paragraph (1), a relevant decision which adopts a rent officer's determination [⁶ , board and attendance determination, broad rental market area determination or local housing allowance determination] may be revised or further revised by the relevant authority which made the decision at any time in consequence of a rent officer's redetermination, substitute determination [⁶substitute redetermination, board and attendance redetermination, substitute board and attendance determination, substitute board and attendance redetermination, amended broad rental market area determination or amended local housing allowance determination] made under the Rent Officers (Housing Benefit Functions) Order 1997 or the Rent Officers (Housing Benefit Functions) (Scotland) Order 1997 which resulted in an increase in the amount which represents the rent for the purposes of calculating entitlement to benefit.

(4)   For the purposes of calculating the period in paragraph (1)(a)(i), where a written statement is requested under regulation 10, no account shall be taken of any period beginning with the day on which the relevant authority received the request for a statement and ending with the day on which that statement was provided to that person.

(5)   Where the relevant authority requires further evidence or information in order to consider all the issues raised by an application under paragraph (1)(a) ("the original application"), that authority shall notify the applicant that further evidence or information is required and, if it does so, the decision may be revised–

(a)   where the evidence or information so requested is provided within one month of the date of the notification or such longer period as the relevant authority may allow; or

(b)   where such evidence or information is not provided within the period referred to in sub-paragraph (a), on the basis of the original application.

(6)   A relevant decision that is prescribed under paragraph 6(2)(e) or (4)(a) of Schedule 7 to the Act may be revised at any time.

(7)   A relevant decision made in respect of a claim or an award may be revised where–

(a)   a decision in respect of that claim or that award is given by [¹⁰ the First-tier Tribunal, Upper Tribunal] or court on appeal against a decision ("decision A");

(b)   the relevant decision was made after decision A; and

(c)   the relevant decision would have been made differently had the relevant authority been aware of that appeal decision at the time it made the relevant decision.

[¹[¹¹ (7A)   Where–

(a)   a restriction is imposed on a person under section 6B, 7, 8 or 9 of the Social Security Fraud Act 2001 (loss of benefit provisions) as a result of the person–

(i)   being convicted of an offence by a court; or

(ii)   agreeing to pay a penalty as an alternative to prosecution under section 115A of the Administration Act or section 109A of the Social Security Administration (Northern Ireland) Act 1992, and

(b)   that conviction is quashed or set aside by that or any other court, or the person withdraws his agreement to pay a penalty,

a decision of the relevant authority made in accordance with regulation 7(2)(g) or (h) may be revised at any time.]]

[⁴ (7B)   Where–

(a)   the relevant authority makes an original decision awarding housing benefit or council tax benefit to a claimant; and

(b)   entitlement to a relevant benefit within the meaning of section 8(3) of the 1998 Act or to an increase in the rate of that relevant benefit is awarded to the claimant or a member of his family for a period which includes the date on which the original decision took effect,

the relevant authority may revise or further revise that original decision at any time.

(7C)   Where entitlement to housing benefit or council tax benefit has ceased ("decision A") because entitlement to a relevant benefit within the meaning of section 8(3) of the 1998 Act has ceased ("decision B"), decision A may be revised at any time if the entitlement to the relevant benefit to which decision B applies has been reinstated in consequence of a decision made under [⁵ section 9 or 10 of the 1998 Act or on an appeal under section 12 of that Act.]]

[⁸ (7D)   Where–

(a)   a person elects for an increase of–

  (i)   a Category A or Category B retirement pension in accordance with paragraph A1 or 3C of Schedule 5 to the Contributions and Benefits Act (pension increase or lump sum where entitlement to retirement pension is deferred);

  (ii)   a shared additional pension in accordance with paragraph 1 of Schedule 5A to that Act (pension increase or lump sum where entitlement to shared additional pension is deferred); or, as the case may be,

  (iii) graduated retirement benefit in accordance with paragraph 12 or 17 of Schedule 1 to the Social Security (Graduated Retirement Benefit) Regulations 2005 (further provisions replacing section 36(4) of the National Insurance Act 1965: increases of graduated retirement benefit and lump sums);

(b)   the relevant authority decides that the person or his partner is entitled to housing benefit or council tax benefit and takes into account the increase of pension or benefit in making or superseding that decision; and

(c)   the person's election for an increase is changed so that he is entitled to a lump sum,

the relevant authority may revise the housing benefit or council tax benefit decision.]

[⁹ (7E)   Where a court makes an order under section 71 of the Antisocial Behaviour etc. (Scotland) Act 2004 and that order is set aside by the sheriff principal following an appeal under section 72(1) of that Act, a decision made in accordance with regulation 7(2)(a) may be revised at any time.

(7F)   Where a local authority has served a notice in accordance with section 94 of the Antisocial Behaviour etc. (Scotland) Act 2004 and that notice is set aside by a court following an appeal under section 97(1) of that Act, a decision made in accordance with regulation 7(2)(a) may be revised at any time.]

(8)   An application for a revision shall be made in writing and delivered, by whatever means, to the relevant authority [³ . . .].

(9)   The relevant authority may treat an application for a supersession as an application for a revision.

(10)   Paragraph (1) shall not apply in respect of a change of circumstances which occurred since the decision [⁷ had effect] or where the relevant authority has evidence or information which indicates that a relevant change of circumstances will occur.

Amendments
1.   Inserted by reg 9(a) of SI 2002 No 490 as from 1.4.02.
2.   Amended by reg 24 of SI 2002 No 1379 as from 20.5.02.

3.   Deleted by Sch 2 para 8(b) of SI 2002 No 1703 as from 30.9.02.

4.   Inserted by reg 5(3) of SI 2003 No 2275 as from 6.10.03.

5.   Amended by reg 2 of SI 2003 No 2526 as from 5.10.03.

6.   Inserted by reg 16 of SI 2003 No 2399 as from a date specified in Sch 8 in relation to each particular authority.

7.   Amended by reg 3(2) of SI 2005 No 337 as from 18.3.05.

8.   Inserted by Reg 10(2) of SI 2005 No 2677 as from 6.4.06.

9.   Inserted by Reg 4 of SI 2006 No 644 as from 3.4.06.

10.   Amended by Sch 1 para 151 of SI 2008 No 2683 as from 3.11.08.

11.   Substituted by reg 9(2) of SI 2010 No 1160 as from 1.4.10.

Definition

"family" – see reg 1(2) and s137(1) SSCBA 1992.

General Note

A decision can be revised by a relevant authority following an application made by a "person affected" (defined in reg 3 – see p1009) on any ground: para (1)(a).

A decision can also be revised by a relevant authority in specific circumstances. Under paras (1)(b) and (c), a revision is only possible within a specific time frame. Under paras (2), (3), (6), (7) and (7A)-(7F) a revision is only possible if specific grounds apply – referred to here as "any time revisions".

Authorities may treat an application for a supersession as one for revision: para (9).

Authorities cannot, in general, supersede a decision where it can be revised: see reg 7(4) – the exception is where there are grounds for revision and further grounds for supersession that are not also grounds for a revision – eg, a subsequent change of circumstances. In receiving any application for revision or supersession, a local authority should therefore first consider whether a revision under para (1) is possible, including whether an extension of time for the application can be granted under reg 5. If this is not possible, a revision under any of the other grounds provided by reg 4 should be considered before consideration of any grounds for supersession under reg 7.

If the decision is one which carried a right of appeal, the authority must issue a new decision under reg 10. In the past, reg 18(3) provided that where an authority revises, or – following an application for revision – does not revise, a decision, the one-month time limit for appealing begins to run from the date on which notice is given of the revised decision or the decision not to revise. From 1 September 2009, that is again the position (see r23 of and Sch 1 TP(FT) Rules 2008 and Sch 7 para 3(5) CSPSSA 2000). For the position between 3 November 2008 and 1 September 2009, see p1036 of the 21st edition.

Commissioner Williams, applying the decision in *R(IB) 2/04*, said that appeal tribunals have the power to take any decision that the initial decision maker could have taken. This includes "considering in appropriate cases whether a claim should be considered as a request for a revision or supersession of a decision on a previous claim, subject to time limits and other statutory provisions": *CH 3009/2002* (para 21). The general limit is that this must be raised by the appeal or be a matter that the tribunal acting in its investigatory role decides it should consider. Further, he said that if the point is in issue before the tribunal or if it identifies the point as significant, it must consider any revision necessary to correct an official error in a decision before it, where there has been no decision on this point: *R(H) 1/08*, per *R(IS) 15/04* (para 78).

Analysis

In *CIS 6249/1999* (paras 21-25) – a case decided under the system of social security adjudication that was in place before SSA 1998 – the commissioner decided that if it would be so unfair to a claimant to "review" a decision that it would be an abuse of process to do so, the Secretary of State (and, on appeal, an appeal tribunal) could decline to do so. It is unclear whether this decision applies to the revision of decisions under SSA 1998 or Sch 7 CSPSSA. Certainly, it will be a rare case where it will be legitimate for an authority to refrain from revising an earlier decision on this ground. See also the commentary to paras (2), (3), (6), (7) and (7A)-(7F). The use of the word 'may' in paras (1) and (2) does not mean that a HB/CTB authority has a general discretion to refuse to revise a decision. Where the grounds of revision are made out, particularly where the ground is 'official error', the authority must revise: *R(IS) 15/04*.

Paragraphs (1)(a), (4) and (5): Applications for revision

Para (1)(a) sets out circumstances in which a person affected can apply for a revision on "any grounds". A person affected may apply for a revision within one month of the date of notification of the decision which is sought to be revised. If an accidental error in a decision has been corrected under reg 10A, any day falling before the day on which notice of the correction is given must be ignored in calculating the one-month period. For the date of notification, see reg 2. Where something must be done "within" a certain period of time, time runs from the day after notification: *R(IB) 4/02* (para 15). An act is done "within" a certain period of time if it is done at midnight on the last day of the period: *Manorlike Ltd v Le Vitas Travel Agency and Consultancy Services Ltd* [1986] 1 All ER 573 at 575e-h, 576b-d, CA.

Where a request is made for a written statement of reasons for a decision under reg 10(2), para (4) effectively stops the clock in respect of the one-month time limit for seeking a revision. The period from the date on which the request is received until the date on which the statement of reasons is provided to the person affected must be ignored in calculating whether an application was made within the one-month time limit. Reg 10 obliges authorities to "provide" a written statement to a claimant who has requested one. The use of the word "provide" (and the phrase "provided to" in para (4)) is to be contrasted with the words "given or sent to" in reg 2. It is suggested that the effect is that the deemed service rules in reg 2 do not apply and that the written statement of reasons will not have been "provided to" the claimant until s/he has actually received it: something is not "provided" to a person until it is actually in the possession of that person. If that is correct, the one-month period will not start running until the date of receipt. In practical terms, however, it will often be difficult for a claimant to prove the date of receipt. To avoid unnecessary disputes, it will – where possible – be preferable for a claimant to seek a revision on the basis that the written statement was "provided" on the date it was sent out by the authority.

Although a person affected may believe a written statement of reasons has not been included with a decision or that what has been provided is inadequate, the local authority could disagree. If there is any doubt about the situation, it is advisable to presume the clock has not stopped and to apply for a revision within the time limit as if it has not done so.

The time limit can be extended in the restricted circumstances set out in reg 5.

Where a decision carries a right of appeal, revision is only one of the two means of disputing the decision, the other being an appeal under Sch 7 para 6 CSPSSA. Revision is not a mandatory step that must be taken prior to an appeal. A "person affected" can exercise her/his right of appeal without having first sought a revision. Authorities can then revise a decision, if appropriate, pending determination of that appeal: see para (1)(c) below. However, an appeal should not be held up while this is done as appears to be the practice with some local authorities. The Local Government Ombudsman has made it clear in a report in Complaint No.01/C/13400 against Scarborough BC that authorities should aim to refer all appeals to the Tribunals Service within 28 days.

Para (5) gives an authority a power to require further evidence or information to be furnished within one month or a further period that may be allowed. If the evidence or information is not forthcoming, a decision as to whether to revise must be made on the existing material before the authority.

Paragraph (1)(b): Revision of decisions made on basis of incorrect facts

A local authority may revise a decision if, within one month of the date of notification of the original decision, it has information before it showing that the original decision was made on the wrong factual basis. There will be some overlap between this provision and revision for official error under para (2)(a). Outside of the one-month period, a revision under para (2)(b) or a supersession under reg 7(2)(b) may be appropriate instead.

In *Saker v Secretary of State for Social Security* [1988] 16 January *The Times*, CA (reported as *R(I) 2/88*) – decided under the old "review" regime in place prior to the SSA 1998 – it was held that a material fact is one which may affect the extent of entitlement. However, under the SSA 1998 and the CSPSSA 2000, as explained by the Court of Appeal in *Wood v SSWP* [2003] EWCA Civ 53, CA (reported as *R(DLA) 1/03*), for a revision or supersession to be made the award must change. In the tribunal of commissioners' decision *R(IB) 2/04*, the commissioners further explained *Wood* by stating that: (i) there can be no revision or supersession unless one of the grounds for revision or supersession is actually found to exist, and (ii) that ground forms the basis of the revision or supersession decision, in the sense that the original decision can only be altered in a way which follows from that ground. For appeal rights on revision or supersession decisions, see the commentary to Sch 7 para 1 CSPSSA on p149. A distinction must be drawn between facts and the inference to be drawn from those facts. Again, if the authority simply changes its mind about how it sees the evidence, the original determination is not open to revision on the ground of a mistake of fact: *R(S) 4/86* (para 6).

A distinction also needs to be drawn between mistakes of fact and law, though the distinction is not always easy to make. In addition, if a fact did not exist at the time a decision was made, that decision cannot be said to have been taken in ignorance of that fact: *Chief Adjudication Officer v Combe* [1998] SLT 15 at 17D-F, IH (reported as *R(IS) 8/98*). Supersession will be appropriate instead in such a situation.

Paragraph (1)(c): Revision while appeal pending

An authority may revise a decision which has been appealed within the time limit, where the appeal is still pending. The process of deciding whether to revise pending an appeal has, confusingly, been termed "reconsideration" by the DWP and local authorities, and is carried out as a matter of course whenever an appeal is made. An appeal will lapse if a revision is carried out and the new decision is more advantageous to the appellant: see Sch 7 para 3 CSPSSA on p142 and reg 17 on p1036.

At least in the past, some local authorities have abused the possibility of "reconsideration" created by para (1)(c) to delay, sometimes virtually indefinitely, the submission of the appeal to the tribunal. The technique involves asking a large number of supplementary questions, often in tendentious terms, so that the "reconsideration" can be carried out. If the questions are not answered, or information is not supplied, the appellant is told – quite unlawfully – that the claim has been treated as withdrawn or that the award has been terminated. If the questions are answered, further questions are asked seeking to exploit supposed inconsistencies with information previously given. In extreme cases, the claimant is then told that a decision has been taken not to change the original decision and that as this is a "revision" (which it is not: see the commentary to para 3 Sch 7 CSPSSA on p149) the appeal has therefore lapsed (which is also wrong because there has not in fact been a revision and, anyway, the new decision is not more advantageous to the claimant than the old: see the commentary to reg 17 on p1037). The hapless appellant then makes a fresh appeal and the whole sorry process starts all over again.

The primary duty on a local authority that receives an appeal is to prepare a submission and send it to the Tribunals Service without delay. The Local Government Ombudsman requires that this should normally be done within 28 days. Where there is delay (which would, in practice, have to be considerably longer than 28 days) or wilful refusal to submit an appeal the tribunal has a residual power to hear the appeal without such a submission: see *R(H) 1/07*.

If, in the course of preparing the submission, it becomes clear that the decision was wrong then the authority should, of course, revise it under para (1)(c). But if all that can be said is that there are unanswered questions that, if answered, might make a difference to the decision, then the best practice is for the authority to list those questions in the submission (so that the appellant will be aware of the type of further evidence that might be relevant) and, in an appropriate case, to apply for an interlocutory direction from the tribunal that the appellant should produce such evidence.

Paragraphs (2), (3), (6), (7) and (7A)-(7F): "Any time" revisions
There are several further grounds for revision which can be applied by the authority at any time. They apply in the following circumstances:
(1) Where the decision "arose from an official error": para (2)(a). For the definition of "official error", see reg 1(2) on p1005. The official error must have influenced the outcome of the decision in question.
(2) The decision was made on the wrong factual basis and was more advantageous to a person affected as a result: para (2)(b). For the meaning of "material fact" see the commentary to para (1)(b). Reg 17(2) does not specifically apply to para (2)(b) but will no doubt give a good guide as to the types of case where a decision is more "advantageous". It will include situations where on the correct factual basis, the claimant was not entitled to as much benefit as originally determined. This ground will therefore often be used in overpayment situations. In other circumstances, revision is possible under para (1)(b) or supersession is possible under reg 7(2)(b).
(3) Where a rent officer's redetermination or other subsequent decision has resulted in an *increase* in "the rent for the purposes of calculating entitlement to benefit": para (3). The latter phrase must refer to the maximum rent under reg 13 of both the HB and the HB(SPC) Regs. A reduction in the maximum rent is grounds for a supersession under reg 7(2)(c).
(4) Where the decision revised is one against which there is no right of appeal: para (6). See the Schedule on p1044 for decisions against which an appeal does not lie to a tribunal.
(5) Where an appeal is made against a decision to the First-tier Tribunal or Upper Tribunal or a court and after its decision (decision A), a fresh claim is decided or the decision is changed, for example, by a supersession (decision B): para (7). However, a revision is only possible on this ground if decision B would have been made differently had the relevant authority been aware of decision A at the time it made its decision. It does not appear that this ground can apply where the decision maker was aware of the decision but did not appreciate its significance. However, such an approach would constitute an "official error" and a revision could be made under para (2)(a) instead. Before 3 November 2008, this ground for revision applied where decision A was made by an appeal tribunal or a commissioner. The amendments made from that date appear to have the effect that there is no longer any power to revise in those circumstances. This is unfortunate. Even after 3 November 2008, there could still be circumstances in which it is desirable to revise a relevant decision made before that date in ignorance of a "decision A" that were both made before that date. Once again, the amendment should have substituted the words "an appeal tribunal or the First-tier Tribunal" for the words "an appeal tribunal" and the words "Commissioner or the Upper Tribunal" for the word "Commissioner".
(6) Where a conviction resulted in benefit being restricted under ss7, 8 or 9 Social Security Fraud Act 2001 (loss of benefit provisions) and that conviction has since been quashed or set aside: para (7A). Only decisions made in accordance with regs 7(2)(g) or (h) (grounds for supersession) can be revised on this ground.
(7) Where a local authority awards HB or CTB and, for a period which includes the date that award took effect, the claimant or a member of her/his family is awarded a "relevant benefit" or an increase in its rate: para (7B). "Relevant benefit" is defined in s8(3) SSA 1998 as any benefit under Parts II to V SSCBA 1992, JSA, PC, IS, a social fund grant for maternity or funeral expenses, child benefit and other benefits which may be prescribed. This is a welcome addition of what is known as a "qualifying benefit" rule. It allows HB and CTB awards to be increased and arrears to be paid back to the date the awards took effect where a relevant benefit is awarded or its rate is increased for a period including that date – eg, where an award of DLA (a relevant benefit) is made to a claimant and thus a disability premium should be included in her/his HB and CTB applicable amount. Where entitlement to a relevant benefit or an increase in its rate commences *after* the date the HB or CTB award took effect, the decision awarding HB or CTB can instead be superseded under reg 7(2)(i).
This ground for revision is only available where there is an existing award of HB and/or CTB. Where there is no entitlement to HB or CTB until an award of a relevant benefit (or increase in its rate) is made, a claimant will be wise to make a claim for HB and/or CTB while the claim for the relevant benefit is being

considered, asking the local authority to delay making a decision until the claim for the relevant benefit is determined – known as "stockpiling" a claim. If a decision maker fails to delay making a decision until the result of the claim for a relevant benefit is known, *CG 1479/1999* and *CIS 217/1999* suggest that this may be an error of law, giving rise to a ground for revision under para (2)(a). Alternatively, a claim for backdated HB and CTB will be required under reg 83(12) HB Regs, reg 64(1) HB(SPC) Regs, reg 69(14) CTB Regs or reg 56 CTB(SPC) Regs as the case may be. See also para (7C) for the situation where HB or CTB ceases when entitlement to a relevant benefit ceases.

(8)   Where entitlement to HB or CTB ceases because entitlement to a "relevant benefit" ceases, and the relevant benefit is re-instated in consequence of a revision or supersession decision or an appeal: para (7C). For the definition of "relevant benefit", see the commentary to para (7B) above. In some cases, a claimant is only entitled to HB or CTB because s/he or a member of her/his family is entitled to a relevant benefit – eg, where s/he would not be entitled to HB or CTB but for the fact that a carer premium should be included in her/his applicable amount because s/he is entitled to carer's allowance (a relevant benefit). In such a situation, if entitlement to the relevant benefit ceases, so does the entitlement to HB and CTB. However, where the relevant benefit is re-instated because of a revision, a supersession or an appeal, para (7C) allows the decision ceasing entitlement to HB and CTB to be revised. The effect of this is that HB and CTB can be reinstated and arrears paid back to the date from which entitlement ceased.

(9)   Where the claimant or her/his partner deferred claiming Category A or B retirement pension, shared additional pension or graduated retirement benefit and originally opted for an increase in the pension, but then opts for a lump sum instead: para (7D). This only applies where the authority has made a decision on her/his entitlement to HB or CTB and takes the increase in pension or benefit into account in making or superseding that decision.

(10)   Where a court makes an order under s71 Antisocial Behaviour etc. (Scotland) Act 2004 (or a local authority has served a notice in accordance with s94 of that Act) and that order is set aside by the sheriff principal (or that notice is set aside by a court) following an appeal: paras (7E) and (7F). Since 30 April 2006, in Scotland, where a local authority serves an anti-social behaviour notice on a landlord and s/he has failed to take reasonable management steps to deal with the behaviour, the local authority can ask a court to make a "no rent payable order" or a management control order (in the latter case rent then becomes payable to the local authority under reg 91A HB Regs or reg 72A HB(SPC) Regs). In addition, if a landlord fails to register with the local authority, it can serve a notice stating that no rent is payable on the property – known as a "no rent payable" notice. Where the order or notice is then set aside following an appeal, paras (7E) and (7D) enable a decision ending HB entitlement under reg 7(2)(a) below to be revised. In practice, this means that a claimant does not have to make a fresh claim for HB in these circumstnaces. A helpful explanation of the Antisocial Behaviour etc (Scotland) Act 2004 provisions and their impact on HB is available in Circular HB/CTB A10/2006.

Is an authority obliged to carry out an "any time" revision?

The above grounds all confer, on the face of it, a discretion on the local authority as to whether it goes ahead and revises. However, a HB/CTB authority does not have a general discretion to refuse to revise a decision. Where the grounds of revision are made out, particularly where the ground is 'official error', the authority must revise: *R(IS) 15/04* (para 39). Sometimes the person affected will not want the revision to be made, because it will inevitably be less advantageous. However, sometimes it may benefit the person affected, but s/he will not be able to apply for a revision under para (1) and will wish the authority to exercise its power to carry out the revision.

If the application cannot be treated as made within the time limit under para (1), an authority may simply reject the application as being out of time under that provision or refuse to extend the time for applying under reg 5. That rejection or refusal would not be a decision giving rise to a right of appeal. The only remedy is judicial review.

Paragraphs (8), (9) and (10): Procedural matters

Applications for revision are to be made in writing to the authority "by whatever means", for the significance of which, see the commentary to reg 20(1) on p1041.

Para (9) is a welcome power to treat an application for supersession as an application for revision. For the corresponding power, see reg 7(6) on p1018.

A decision can only be revised under para (1) on the basis of the circumstances at the time the decision had effect: para (10). Where a change of circumstances occurs after the decision took effect or the authority has evidence or information that indicates a change is due to take place, supersession under reg 7(2)(a) is appropriate instead. An application for revision on such grounds should be treated as an application for supersession under reg 7(6).

Late application for a revision

5.–(1)   The time limit for making an application for a revision specified in regulation 4 may be extended where the conditions specified in the following paragraphs of this regulation are satisfied.

(2)   An application for an extension of time (''the application'') shall be made in writing by the person affected by a relevant decision.

(3)   The application shall–
(a)   contain particulars of the grounds on which the extension of time is sought and shall contain sufficient details of the decision which it is sought to have revised to enable that decision to be identified;
(b)   [² subject to regulation 4(4)] be made within 13 months of the date of notification of the decision which it is sought to have revised; and
(c)   be delivered, by whatever means, to the relevant authority [¹ . . .].
(4)   The application shall not be granted unless the person affected satisfies the relevant authority that–
(a)   it is reasonable to grant the application;
(b)   the application for revision has merit; and
(c)   special circumstances are relevant to the application and as a result of those special circumstances it was not practicable for the application to be made within the time limit specified in regulation 4.
(5)   In determining whether it is reasonable to grant the application for an extension of time, no account shall be taken of the following–
(a)   that the person affected was unaware of or misunderstood the law applicable to his case (including ignorance or misunderstanding of the time limits imposed by these Regulations); or
(b)   that [³ the Upper Tribunal] or a court has taken a different view of the law from that previously understood and applied.
(6)   In determining whether it is reasonable to grant an application, the relevant authority shall have regard to the principle that the greater the amount of time that has elapsed between the expiration of the time specified in regulation 4 for applying for a revision and the making of the application for an extension of time, the more compelling should be the special circumstances on which the application is based.
(7)   An application under this regulation for an extension of time which has been refused may not be renewed.

Amendments
1.   Deleted by Sch 2 para 8(c) of SI 2002 No 1703 as from 30.9.02.
2.   Amended by reg 3(3) of SI 2005 No 337 as from 18.3.05.
3.   Amended by Sch 1 para 152 of SI 2008 No 2683 as from 3.11.08.

Analysis
Reg 5 deals with extensions of time for making an application for a revision under reg 4(1)(a).

It refers to the authority "determining" the question of whether an extension of time should be granted. The ruling is not a "decision" and no appeal to a tribunal lies against it. What is appealable is the original decision made under Sch 7 para 2 or 4 CSPSSA, either as revised under para 3, or – if no extension of time is granted – as originally made.

In *R(TC) 1/05*, Commissioner Turnbull said that an appeal tribunal does not have any jurisdiction to determine whether a decision maker ought to have exercised the power to extend time for applying for a revision and that a refusal or failure to extend the time was not a decision capable of being appealed. That reasoning was in the context of reg 4 SSCS D&A Regs, but would seem to apply four square to the same rule that reg 5 here embodies.

If, by the time an extension has been refused, fewer than 13 months have passed since the original decision, the person affected should consider applying to the tribunal for an extension of time in which to appeal against that decision. The rules for admitting late appeals in rr23(4) and (5) and 5(3)(a) TP(FT) Rules are less stringent than the rules for a late revision in para (4) and it may be to the advantage of the claimant to have the decision taken by an independent tribunal judge rather than an officer of the authority that made the original decision.

If, on the other hand, more than 13 months have passed since the original decision, the only remedy is judicial review.

Paras (2) and (3) set out the procedural requirements. An application must be made in writing with sufficient detail of the decision under attack to enable it to be identified and the grounds on which the late application is made. It must be made within 13 months of the date of notification of the decision (subject to reg 4(4) which extends the normal time limit where a written statement of reasons is requested). See p1013 on the meaning of "within". It must be delivered to the authority "by whatever means": see the commentary to reg 20(1) on p1041.

Paras (4) to (6) set out the criteria under which a late revision may be carried out. Under para (4), there are four principal conditions that must be met:
(1)   It must be reasonable to grant the application. Paras (5) and (6) are similar to reg 19(8) and (9): see the commentary on p1040.

(2)   There must be merit in the application for revision. It need not be certain to succeed, but it must be shown that a serious issue is raised for consideration.

(3)   There are "special circumstances" relevant to the application. "Special circumstances" are not defined, but are likely to be interpreted in a similar way to "special reasons" under the former reg 78(3) HB Regs 1987.

(4)   It was not practicable, as a result of the circumstances, to make the application within the time limit. Reg 19(6) contains similar wording, see p1039.

Para (7) appears to prevent a second bite at the cherry of an extension of time for applying for a revision. However, *CIS 93/1992*, held (at para 16) that reg 3(4) Social Security Adjudication Regulations 1986, which was in similar terms, "does not . . . prohibit a reconsideration by the chairman. It merely provides that a chairman is not *obliged* to consider a renewed application for extension of time". Although that was necessary to prevent repeated applications, if the chairman did consider a further application for extension of time after an earlier refusal of such extension, then s/he was entitled to do so and to change her/his mind if s/he wished. It is nevertheless important that all relevant matters are placed before the authority on the initial application.

Date from which a revision takes effect

6.   Where, on a revision under paragraph 3 of Schedule 7 to the Act, the relevant authority decides that the date from which a relevant decision ("the original decision") took effect was erroneous, the decision under that paragraph shall take effect on the date the original decision would have taken effect had the error not been made.

Analysis

The general rule is that a revised decision has effect from the same date as the original decision took effect, regardless of how long ago the original decision was made: Sch 7 para 3(3) CSPSSA. Where on a revision it is decided that the effective date of the original decision was wrong, the correct date will be taken.

Decisions superseding earlier decisions

7.–(1)   Subject to the provisions in this regulation, the prescribed cases and circumstances in which a decision may be made under paragraph 4 of Schedule 7 to the Act (decisions superseding earlier decisions) are as set out in paragraph (2).

(2)   The appropriate relevant authority may make a decision under paragraph 4 of Schedule 7 to the Act upon its own initiative or on an application made for the purpose on the basis that the decision to be superseded is a decision–

(a)   in respect of which–
   (i)   there has been a change of circumstances [³ since the decision had effect]; or
   (ii)   it is anticipated that a change of circumstances will occur;

(b)   which is erroneous in point of law or made in ignorance of, or was based upon a mistake as to, some material fact provided that the decision–
   (i)   cannot be revised on the basis of that error, ignorance or mistake; and
   (ii)   is not a decision prescribed in regulations under paragraph 6(2)(e) or (4)(a) of Schedule 7 to the Act;

(c)   which adopts a rent officer's determination [⁶ , board and attendance determination, broad rental market area determination or local housing allowance determination] and in consequence of a rent officer's redetermination, substitute determination, [⁶ substitute redetermination, board and attendance redetermination, substitute board and attendance determination, substitute board and attendance redetermination, amended broad rental market area determination or amended local housing allowance determination] made under the Rent Officers (Housing Benefit Functions) Order 1997 or the Rent Officers (Housing Benefit Functions) (Scotland) Order 1997 the amount which represents the rent for the purposes of calculating entitlement to benefit is reduced;

[³ (d) of [¹⁴ the First-tier Tribunal or of the Upper Tribunal]–
   (i)   that was made in ignorance of, or was based upon a mistake as to, some material fact; or
   (ii)   that was made in accordance with paragraph 17(4)(b) of Schedule 7 to the Act, in a case where paragraph 17(5) of that Schedule to the Act applies;]

(e)   which is prescribed in regulations made under paragraph 6(2)(e) or (4)(a) of Schedule 7 to the Act;

[² (f)]

[¹(g) which is affected by a decision of the Secretary of State that a sanctionable benefit payable to a claimant ceases to be payable or falls to be reduced under section [¹⁵ 6B,] 7 or 9 of the Social Security Fraud Act 2001 and for this purpose "sanctionable benefit" has the [¹⁵ meaning given in section 6A] of that Act; or

(h) which is affected by a decision of the Secretary of State that a joint-claim jobseeker's allowance ceases to be payable or falls to be reduced under section 8 of the Social Security Fraud Act 2001.]

[⁵ (i) [¹³ except where sub-paragraph (o) [¹⁶ , (p) or (q)] applies,] where–
    (i) the claimant has been awarded entitlement to housing benefit or council tax benefit; and
    (ii) subsequent to the first day of the period to which that entitlement relates, the claimant or a member of his family becomes entitled to an award of a relevant benefit within the meaning of section 8(3) of the 1998 Act or an increase in the rate of that relevant benefit.]

[⁹ (j) where–
    (i) the claimant or his partner makes, or is treated as having made, an election for a lump sum in accordance with–
        (aa) paragraph A1 or 3C of Schedule 5 to the Contributions and Benefits Act;
        (bb) paragraph 1 of Schedule 5A to that Act; or, as the case may be,
        (cc) paragraph 12 or 17 of Schedule 1 to the Social Security (Graduated Retirement Benefit) Regulations 2005; or
    (ii) such a lump sum is repaid in consequence of an application to change an election for a lump sum in accordance with regulation 5 of the Social Security (Deferral of Retirement Pensions, Shared Additional Pension and Graduated Retirement Benefit) (Miscellaneous Provisions) Regulations 2005 or, as the case may be, paragraph 20D of Schedule 1 to the Social Security (Graduated Retirement Benefit) Regulations 2005.]

[(k) – (n) See Modifications below]

[¹³ (o) where–
    (i) the claimant has been awarded entitlement to housing benefit or council tax benefit;
    (ii) the claimant or the claimant's partner has made a claim for employment and support allowance;
    (iii) subsequent to the first day of the period to which entitlement to housing benefit or council tax benefit relates, the Secretary of State has decided that the claimant or the claimant's partner has, or is to be treated as having, limited capability for work within the meaning of section 1(4) of the Welfare Reform Act or limited capability for work-related activity within the meaning of section 2(5) of that Act; and
    (iv) either–
        (aa) the assessment phase as defined in section 24(2) of the Welfare Reform Act has ended; or
        (bb) regulation 7 of the Employment and Support Allowance Regulations 2008(23) (circumstances where the condition that the assessment phase has ended before entitlement to the support component or the work related activity component arises does not apply) applies.]

[¹⁶ (p) where–
    (i) the claimant has been awarded entitlement to housing benefit or council tax benefit;
    (ii) the claimant or the claimant's partner has had an award of benefit converted to an employment and support allowance in accordance with regulation 5(2)(a) of the Employment and Support Allowance (Transitional Provisions, Housing Benefit and Council Tax Benefit) (Existing Awards) Regulations 2010; and

      (iii)   subsequent to the first day of the period to which that entitlement to housing benefit or council tax benefit relates, the Secretary of State makes a decision to supersede the award of employment and support allowance to award a different component;

(q)   where the claimant has been awarded entitlement to housing benefit or council tax benefit and subsequent to the first day of the period to which that entitlement relates–

      (i)   a conversion decision of the kind set out in regulation 5(2)(a) of the Employment and Support Allowance (Transitional Provisions, Housing Benefit and Council Tax Benefit) (Existing Awards) Regulations 2010 takes effect in respect of the claimant or the claimant's partner; or

      (ii)   [¹⁷ the claimant or the claimant's partner is appealing a conversion decision] as described in regulation 5(2)(b) of the Employment and Support Allowance (Transitional Provisions, Housing Benefit and Council Tax Benefit) (Existing Awards) Regulations 2010 and is treated as having limited capability for work by virtue of regulation 30 of the Employment and Support Allowance Regulations 2008 as modified by the Employment and Support Allowance (Transitional Provisions, Housing Benefit and Council Tax Benefit) (Existing Awards) Regulations 2010.]

[¹² [⁷ (2ZA)]]

[⁸ [¹¹ (2A)]]

[¹² [⁶ (2B)]]

[¹² [⁶ (2C)]]

(3)   The reference to a change of circumstances in paragraph (2)(a) shall include changes of circumstances specified in [¹⁰ [¹²], regulation 74(3) of the Council Tax Benefit Regulations or regulation 59(3) of the Council Tax Benefit (State Pension Credit) Regulations (changes of circumstances which do not need to be notified)].

(4)   A decision which may berevised under regulation 4 may not be superseded under this regulation except where–

(a)   circumstances arise in which the appropriate relevant authority may revise that decision under regulation 4; and

(b)   further circumstances arise in relation to that decision which are not specified in regulation 4 but are specified in paragraph (2) or (5).

(5)   Where the appropriate relevant authority requires further evidence or information from the applicant in order to consider all the issues raised by an application under paragraph (2) ("the original application"), the authority shall notify the applicant that further evidence or information is required and, if it does so, the decision may be superseded–

(a)   where the applicant provides further relevant evidence or information within one month of the date of notification or such longer period of time as the appropriate relevant authority may allow; or

(b)   where the applicant does not provide such evidence or information within the time allowed under sub-paragraph (a), on the basis of the original application.

(6)   The appropriate relevant authority may treat an application for a revision or a notification of a change of circumstances as an application for a supersession.

(7)   An application under this regulation shall be made in writing and delivered, by whatever means, to the relevant authority [² . . .].

Modifications

Paras (2ZA), (2B) and (2C) omitted and para (3) amended by reg 4(2) Housing Benefit (Local Housing Allowance, Miscellaneous and Consequential) Amendment Regulations 2007 SI No.2870 as from 7 April 2008, save that for a person to whom reg 1(3) of those regulations applied (see p1235), the amendments came into force on the day on or after 7 April 2008 when the first of the events specified in reg 1(4) applied to her/him, or on 6 April 2009 if none had before that date.

    Sub-paras 2(k) to (n) were inserted but only in respect of people to whom the Housing Benefit (Loss of Benefit)(Pilot Scheme)(Supplementary) Regulations 2007 SI No.2474 applied and only until 31 October 2009.

Amendments
1.   Inserted by reg 9(b) of SI 2002 No 490 as from 1.4.02.
2.   Deleted by Sch 2 para 8(d) of SI 2002 No 1703 as from 30.9.02.
3.   Amended by reg 4(1) of SI 2003 No 1050 as from 5.5.03.
4.   Amended by reg 24(1) of SI 2003 No 1338 as from 6.10.03.
5.   Amended by reg 5(4) of SI 2003 No 2275 as from 6.10.03.
6.   Inserted by reg 16 of SI 2003 No 2399 as from a date specified in Sch 8 in relation to each particular authority.
7.   Inserted by reg 34(1) of SI 2004 No 14 as from 5.4.04.
8.   Revoked by reg 33 of SI 2004 No 14 as from 5.4.04.
9.   Inserted by reg 10(3) of SI 2005 No 2677 as from 6.4.06.
10.   Amended by reg 5 and sch 2 para 17(3) of SI 2006 No 217 as from 6.3.06.
11.   Revoked by reg 8 of SI 2007 No 2470 as from 24.9.07.
12.   Omitted by reg 4(2) of SI 2007 No 2870 as from 7.4.08 (or if reg 1(3) of that SI applies, on the day on or after 7.4.08 when the first of the events specified in reg 1(4) applies, or from 6.4.09 if none have before that date).
13.   Amended by reg 3(3) of SI 2008 No 1082, as substituted by reg 26 of SI 2008 No 2428, as from 27.10.08.
14.   Amended by Sch 1 para 153 of SI 2008 No 2683 as from 3.11.08.
15.   Amended by reg 9(3) of SI 2010 No 1160 as from 1.4.10.
16.   Amended by reg 27 and Sch 5 para 3(2) of SI 2010 No 1907 as amended by reg 15 of SI 2010 No 2430 as from 1.10.10.
17.   Amended by reg 20 of SI 2010 No 2430 as from 1.11.10.

Definition
"family" – see reg 1(2) and s137(1) SSCBA 1992.

General Note
A decision can be superseded by a relevant authority on its own initiative or following an application made by a "person affected" by it (defined in reg 3). There must be grounds for supersession: paras (2), (2ZA) and (2B). See *Wood v SSWP* [2003] EWCA Civ 53, CA (reported as *R(DLA) 1/03*) for an authoritative analysis of the supersession scheme. *Wood* was further explained by the tribunal of commissioners in *R(IB) 2/04*. The commissioners ruled that: (i) there can be no supersession unless one of the grounds for supersession is actually found to exist; and (ii) that ground forms the basis of the supersession decision, in the sense that the original decision can only be altered in a way which follows from that ground: and see further *CIS 3655/2007*. See also the commentary to reg 90 HB Regs on p462 for consideration of the question of whether a decision is rendered invalid by virtue of a failure to revise or supersede or where there is a defective attempt at revision or supersession.

There is no time limit for applying for a supersession. However, where the ground for supersession is a change in circumstances (para (2)(a)) and the superseding decision is to the advantage of the claimant, the change must be reported within one month of it occurring (or any longer period allowed by the authority) for full arrears of benefit to be paid. See regs 8(3) and reg 9.

Authorities may treat an application for a revision as one for supersession: para (6).

By virtue of reg 7(4), there is no power to supersede a decision that could be revised except where there are grounds for revision and further grounds for supersession that are not also grounds for revision – eg, a subsequent change of circumstances. In those circumstances, local authorities that receive an application to supersede a decision should first consider whether a revision under reg 4(1) is possible, including whether an extension of time for the application can be granted under reg 5. If this is not possible, a revision under any of the other grounds provided by reg 4 should be considered before consideration of any grounds for supersession under reg 7.

Commissioner Williams, applying *R(IB) 2/04*, said that appeal tribunals have the power to take any decision that the initial decision maker could have taken. This includes "considering in appropriate cases whether a claim should be considered as a request for a revision or supersession of a decision on a previous claim, subject to time limits and other statutory provisions": *CH 3009/2002* (para 21). The general limit is that this must be raised by the appeal or be a matter that the tribunal acting in its investigatory role decides it should consider. Interestingly, however, the same commissioner took a different view on the facts in *CIS 1675/2004*, because the errors in the appeal were so extensive that the only safe course was to declare that none of the "decisions" were operative, and the matter (which was an overpayment "decision") was referred back to the Secretary of State for fresh consideration.

Analysis
Paragraph (2): Grounds for supersession
Para (2) sets out the various bases on which a supersession of a decision can be made.

(1)   Where there has been a change of circumstances since the decision had effect, or where such a change is expected in the future: sub-para (a). The words added with effect from 5 May 2003 confirm that a supersession of a decision can be made not only where there has been a change of circumstances since the decision was made, but also after it took effect – eg, after a tribunal's decision.
The wording omits the word "relevant" that was formerly present in reg 79(1)(a) HB Regs 1987, but nothing turns on this. A change of circumstances will be relevant if it is one that would affect the claimant's entitlement to HB, the extent of entitlement or to whom it should be paid. A change in the law is a relevant change of circumstances, but a court decision that changes the authority's view of the law is not: *Chief Adjudication Officer v McKiernon* [1993], 3 July, CA (reported as *R(I) 2/94*). Such issues are dealt with under sub-para (b) or by way of revision. Furthermore, the fact that an officer of the authority disagrees with the inferences to be drawn from the evidence is not a relevant change of circumstances, but if new evidence shows that there has been a change in the claimant's status, there can be a supersession: *R(S) 4/86* (para 5). A change of circumstances includes the types of changes which need not be disclosed: para (3).

(2)   Where the decision is based on incorrect facts or a mistake as to the law: sub-para (b). For the meaning of "material fact", see the commentary to reg 4(1)(b). This ground is subject to two qualifications. Head (i) prohibits its use if a revision is possible on the same grounds (see reg 4(1)(b) and (2)(b)) and head (ii) renders it non-available where no appeal lies against the decision (see the Schedule). In the latter case, sub-para (e) can apply instead.

(3)   Where a rent officer's redetermination or other further determination has resulted in a *reduction* in "the rent for the purposes of calculating entitlement to benefit": sub-para (c). The latter phrase must refer to the maximum rent under reg 13 of both the HB and the HB(SPC) Regs. An increase in the maximum rent is grounds for a revision: see reg 4(3).

(4)   Where a decision of the First-tier Tribunal or Upper Tribunal was based on incorrect facts or was made pending a "test case" under Sch 7 para 17(4)(b) CSPSSA where the "test case" has subsequently been decided: sub-para (d). However, the latter of these grounds for supersession is not currently relevant as Sch 7 para 17 is not yet in force. It is understood that the Government does not intend to bring it into force. Superseding a First-tier Tribunal or Upper Tribunal decision on the basis that it was made in ignorance of, or was based upon a mistake as to some material fact involves identifying on the evidence a fact which the First-tier Tribunal or Upper Tribunal was not aware of and that fact *would* justify a different outcome decision: *CIS 3655/2007* (at para 29, following *Wood v SSWP* [2003] EWCA Civ 53, CA (reported as *R(DLA) 1/03*) and, in effect, restoring *R(I) 56/54* to orthodoxy). The decision of the Court of Appeal in *R(I) 2/88*, in which it was held that a fact was "material" if it might make a difference to the decision being sought to be reviewed is, accordingly, no longer applicable.
Note that by replacing the words "of an appeal tribunal or of a Commissioner" with the words "of the First-tier Tribunal or of the Upper Tribunal", the 3 November 2008 amendments have removed the power to supersede decisions of the former appeal tribunals and social security commissioners: see *DN v Leicester City Council (HB)* [2010] UKUT 253 (AAC) at paras 28-34.
That is an astonishing drafting error. By Sch 7 para 11 CSPSSA such decisions are final. As they are not subject to revision, they can only be changed by a further appeal, by supersession or as a result of the annual up-rating of social security benefits under Part X SSAA 1992. In addition to being final, the abolition of benefit periods with effect from April 2004 means that they will also be indefinite. The effect of removing the power to supersede such decisions is therefore that – except by appeal or up-rating – an award of HB/CTB made by an appeal tribunal or a commissioner cannot ever be changed for any reason at all. That is so irrespective of whether the change is beneficial or adverse to the claimant. It is even so if the claimant no longer has any entitlement at all because – eg, s/he is no longer liable to pay rent or has died: those are both changes of circumstance and the mechanism for giving effect to them is by supersession.
It is not even possible for the authority to use the power of "termination" under Part III as it is now established that a decision to terminate under reg 14 operates by superseding the earlier decision: see the Analysis on p1034.
When SSA 1998 replaced social security appeal tribunals with appeal tribunals in 1999, this potential problem was dealt with by transitional provisions, which provided that after the change, any decision of a social security appeal tribunal, disability appeal tribunal or medical appeal tribunal was to be treated as a decision of an appeal tribunal – see, for example, Sch 16 para 12 Social Security Act 1998 (Commencement No.11, and Savings and Consequential and Transitional Provisions) Order 1999 No.2860. None of the Commencement Orders bringing TCEA 2007 into force makes any such provision. The Transfer of Tribunal Functions Order 2008 (see p1102), treats appeal tribunal decisions and commissioners decisions as, respectively, decisions of the First-tier Tribunal and Upper Tribunal for the purposes of a further appeal (see Sch 4 paras 4 and 5 on p1103) but makes no such provision (either in Sch 4 or anywhere else) for the purposes of supersession.
The problem cannot be overcome by reference to primary legislation. A similar error was made in the amendments to Sch 7 para 4(1)(b) CSPSSA 2000. As a result, not only are there no regulations permitting

the decisions of appeal tribunals and commissioners to be superseded: there is no longer even a power to make such regulations.

Neither is it guaranteed that the Upper Tribunal will be able to solve the problem by adopting a strained construction of the legislation. At least one similar error has occurred in the past (which makes it all the more extraordinary that it should have been permitted to recur). On that occasion, the commissioner confirmed that there was no power to change the earlier decision: see *CDLA 2999/2004.*

(5)   Where the decision is one against which there is no right of appeal: sub-para (e). See the Schedule on p1044 for details of the decisions against which an appeal does not lie to the First-tier Tribunal.

(6)   Where a decision is affected by a DWP decision stopping or restricting benefit under ss7 or 9 Social Security Fraud Act 2001 (loss of benefit provisions): sub-paras (g) and (h).

(7)   Where a local authority awards HB or CTB and, after the first day of the period of that award, the claimant or a member of her/his family becomes entitled to a "relevant benefit" or an increase in its rate: sub-para (i). "Relevant benefit" is defined in s8(3) SSA 1998 as any benefit under Parts II to V SSCBA 1992, JSA, PC, IS, a social fund grant for maternity or funeral expenses, child benefit and other benefits which may be prescribed. This is a welcome addition of what is known as a "qualifying benefit" rule. It allows HB and CTB awards to be increased and arrears to be paid back to the date of entitlement to a relevant benefit or an increase in its rate – eg, where an award of DLA is made to a claimant and thus a disability premium should be included in her/his HB and CTB applicable amount. Where the claimant or family member is awarded a relevant benefit or an increase in its rate for a period which includes the date the HB or CTB award took effect, the decision awarding HB or CTB can instead be revised under reg 4(7B). See the commentary to reg 4(7B) for the situation when there is no entitlement to HB and/or CTB until an award of a relevant benefit (or an increase in its rate) is made.

(8)   Where the claimant or her/his partner deferred claiming Category A or B retirement pension, shared additional pension or graduated retirement benefit and originally opted (or is treated as opting) for and is paid a lump sum or repays a lump sum because she opts instead for an increase in the pension: sub-para (j).

Paragraph (4): Relationship between revision and supersession

Para (4) provides that if a revision is possible as well as supersession, a revision must be carried out unless there are grounds for supersession which are not covered by the revision rules in reg 4. On receiving an application for revision or supersession, an authority should therefore first consider whether a revision under reg 4 is possible. It may be necessary to carry out a supersession at the same time as a revision, if some of the matters raised can be the subject matter of a revision but not all of them.

Paragraphs (5) to (7): Procedure

Paras (5) and (7) are in similar terms to reg 4(5) and (8): see the commentary on pp1013 and 1016. Para (6) entitles an authority to treat an application for revision or a notification of a change in circumstances as being an application for a supersession.

[¹ Decisions superseding earlier decisions in accordance with paragraph 4(4A) of Schedule 7 to the Act

7A.–(1)   The prescribed cases and circumstances in which a decision must be made under paragraph 4 of Schedule 7 to the Act (decisions superseding earlier decisions) are set out in paragraphs (2) to (4).

(2)   The appropriate relevant authority must make a decision superseding an earlier decision where it is required to determine a maximum rent (LHA) in accordance with [² regulation 13C(3)] of the Housing Benefit Regulations and [² regulation 13C(3)] of the Housing Benefit (State Pension Credit) Regulations (when a maximum rent (LHA) is to be determined).

(3)   The appropriate relevant authority must make a decision superseding an earlier decision in any case to which regulation 14(1)(f) or (g) or the Housing Benefit Regulations or regulation 14(1)(f) or (g) of the Housing Benefit (State Pension Credit) Regulations (requirement to refer to rent officers) applies.

(4)   The appropriate relevant authority must make a decision superseding an earlier decision where a change of circumstances specified in regulation 88(3) of the Housing Benefit Regulations or regulation 69(3) of the Housing Benefit (State Pension Credit) Regulations (changes of circumstances which do not need to be notified) occurs.]

Modifications

    Reg 7A inserted by reg 4(3) Housing Benefit (Local Housing Allowance, Miscellaneous and Consequential) Amendment Regulations 2007 SI No.2870, as amended by reg 6(2)(a) of SI 2008 No.586, as from 7 April 2008, save that for a person to whom reg 1(3) of those regulations applied (see p1235), the amendments came into force on the day on or after 7 April 2008 when the first of the events specified in reg 1(4) applied to her/him, or on 6 April 2009 if none had before that date.

Amendments

1.   Inserted by reg 4(3) of SI 2007 No 2870 as from 7.4.08 (or if reg 1(3) of that SI applies, on the day on or after 7.4.08 when the first of the events specified in reg 1(4) applies, or from 6.4.09 if none have before that date).

2.   Amended by reg 6(2()(a) of SI 2008 No 586 as from 7.4.08.

Date from which a decision superseding an earlier decision takes effect

8.–(1)   A decision made by virtue of paragraph 4 of Schedule 7 to the Act (''the superseding decision'') shall take effect on a date other than the date on which it is made or the date on which the application was made in the cases or circumstances prescribed in paragraphs (2) to (7).

(2)   Subject to paragraphs (3) and (6), where the superseding decision is made on the ground that there has been, or it is anticipated that there will be, a change of circumstances, the superseding decision shall take effect on the date on which the change of circumstances is to take effect [¹⁰ in accordance with–

(a)   regulation 79 of the Housing Benefit Regulations;

(b)   regulation 59 or 60 of the Housing Benefit (State Pension Credit) Regulations;

(c)   regulation 67 of the Council Tax Benefit Regulations; or

(d)   regulation 50 or 51 of the Council Tax Benefit (State Pension Credit) Regulations as the case may be.]

(3)   For the purposes of determining the date on which a superseding decision is to take effect in accordance with paragraph (2), in a case where–

(a)   the change of circumstances is a change of circumstances that is required by regulations to be notified, other than any change of circumstances to which regulation 68A [² or 68B] of the Housing Benefit Regulations or regulation 59A [² or 59B] of the Council Tax Benefit Regulations applies; and

(b)   that change of circumstances is notified more than one month after it occurs, or such longer period as may be allowed under regulation 9; and

(c)   the superseding decision is advantageous to the claimant,

the date of notification of the change of circumstances shall be treated as the date on which the change of circumstances occurred.

(4)   Where the superseding decision is advantageous to the claimant and is made on the ground that the superseded decision was made in ignorance of, or was based upon a mistake as to, some material fact, the superseding decision shall take effect from the first day of the benefit week in which–

(a)   except where sub-paragraph (b) applies, the appropriate relevant authority first has information which is sufficient to show that the superseded decision was made in ignorance of, or was based upon a mistake as to, some material fact;

(b)   where the superseding decision was made pursuant to an application, that application was received by the appropriate relevant authority.

(5)   For the purpose of paragraphs (3)(c) and (4), the reference to the decision which is advantageous to the claimant includes a decision specified in regulation 17(2).

(6)   A superseding decision made in consequence of a rent officer's redetermination, substitute determination, [⁶ substitute redetermination, board and attendance redetermination, substitute board and attendance determination, substitute board and attendance redetermination, amended broad rental market area determination or amended local housing allowance determination] under the Rent Officers (Housing Benefit Functions) Order 1997 or the Rent Officers (Housing Benefit Functions) (Scotland) Order 1997 shall take effect on the date on which a change of circumstances is to take effect in accordance with [¹⁸ regulation 79 of the Housing Benefit Regulations or, as the case may be, regulation 59 or 60 of the Housing Benefit (State Pension Credit) Regulations] as if that determination or redetermination were the relevant change of circumstances.

[⁷ (6A)   Except in a case where entitlement to housing benefit ceases, where a rent officer has made a determination in exercise of the Housing Act functions pursuant to an application by a relevant authority under [¹⁰ regulation 14(1)(f) or (g) of the Housing

Benefit Regulations or, as the case may be, regulation 14(1)(f) or (g) of the Housing Benefit (State Pension Credit) Regulations, any decision to which [¹² regulation 7A(3)] applies which adopts that determination shall take effect from–

    (a)   in a case where the amount of the rent officer's determination has increased or remains unchanged, and–

        (i)   rent is payable weekly or in multiples of weeks, the first day of the benefit week in which the day following the last day of the period mentioned in [¹⁰ regulation 14(1)(f) or (g) of the Housing Benefit Regulations or, as the case may be, regulation 14(1)(f) or (g) of the Housing Benefit (State Pension Credit) Regulations] occurs;

        (ii)   rent is payable other than in accordance with head (i), the first day following the last day of the period mentioned in [¹⁰ regulation 14(1)(f) or (g) of the Housing Benefit Regulations or, as the case may be, regulation 14(1)(f) or (g) of the Housing Benefit (State Pension Credit) Regulations];

    (b)   in a case where the amount of the rent officer's determination has decreased, the first day of the benefit week following the date on which that determination was received by a relevant authority;

    (6B)   For the purposes of paragraph (6A) "Housing Act functions" has the same meaning as in regulation 2(1) of the Housing Benefit Regulations [¹⁰ or, as the case may be, regulation 2(1) of the Housing Benefit (State Pension Credit) Regulations.].]

    (7)   Where a decision is made superseding a decision of [¹⁵ the First-tier Tribunal or of the Upper Tribunal] ("the appeal decision") which–

    (a)   was made in ignorance of, or was based upon a mistake as to, some material fact; and

    (b)   was more advantageous to the claimant than it would otherwise have been but for that ignorance or mistake,

that superseding decision shall take effect on the date on which the appeal decision took or was to take effect.

    (8)   A superseding decision made as a consequence of a determination which is a relevant determination for the purposes of paragraph 18 of Schedule 7 to the Act (restrictions on entitlement to benefit in certain cases of error) shall take effect from the date of the relevant determination.

    [¹(9)   A decision to which regulation 7(2)(g) or (h) applies shall take effect from the first day of the disqualification period prescribed for the purposes of section [¹⁶ 6B or] 7 of the Social Security Fraud Act 2001.]

    [³ (10)   Where the decision is superseded in accordance with regulation 7(2)(a)(i) and the relevant circumstances are that there has been a change in the legislation in relation to housing benefit or council tax benefit, the superseding decision shall take effect from the date on which that change in the legislation had effect.

    (11)   Where a superseding decision is made in a case to which regulation 7(2)(d)(ii) applies the superseding decision shall take effect from the date on which the [¹⁵ First-tier Tribunal or the Upper Tribunal's] decision would have taken effect had it been decided in accordance with the determination of the [¹⁵ Upper Tribunal] or the court in the appeal referred to in paragraph 17(1)(b) of Schedule 7 to the Act.]

    [⁸ [¹¹ (12)]]

    [⁸ [¹¹ (13)]]

    [⁵ (14)   Where the decision is superseded in accordance with regulation 7(2)(i) the superseding decision shall take effect from the date on which entitlement arises to the relevant benefit referred to in regulation 7(2)(i)(ii) or to an increase in the rate of that relevant benefit.]

    [⁹ (14A)   Where a decision is superseded in accordance with regulation 7(2)(j), the superseding decision shall take effect from the day on which a lump sum, or a payment on account of a lump sum, is paid or repaid if that day is the first day of the benefit week but, if it is not, from the next following such day.]

    [¹⁴ (14D)   Where the decision is superseded in accordance with regulation 7(2)(o) [¹⁷ or (p)], the decision shall take effect from–

(a)   the first day of entitlement to an amount in consequence of the decision of the Secretary of State referred to in regulation 7(2)(o)(iii) [¹⁷ or (p)(iii)]; or

(b)   the first day that there would have been such entitlement had the claimant or the claimant's partner been entitled to an employment and support allowance by virtue of section 1 of the Welfare Reform Act,

if that day is the first day of the benefit week but, if it is not, from the next following such day.]

[¹⁷ (14E)   Where a decision is superseded in accordance with regulation 7(2)(q) the decision shall take effect–

(a)   where the decision made in accordance with the Employment and Support Allowance (Transitional Provisions, Housing Benefit and Council Tax Benefit) (Existing Awards) Regulations 2010 takes effect on or after 1st April in any year but before 16th April of that year–

   (i)   from 1st April for a council tax benefit award;

   (ii)   from 1st April for a housing benefit award in which the claimant's weekly amount of eligible rent falls to be calculated in accordance with regulation 80(2)(b) or (c) of the Housing Benefit Regulations or, as the case may be, regulation 61(2)(b) or (c) of the Housing Benefit (State Pension Credit) Regulations;

   (iii)   from the first Monday in April for a housing benefit award to which sub-paragraph (a)(ii) does not apply;

(b)   in any other case, from the day the decision made in accordance with the Employment and Support Allowance (Transitional Provisions, Housing Benefit and Council Tax Benefit) (Existing Awards) Regulations 2010 takes effect.]

[¹² [¹³ (15)   A decision to which regulation 7A(2) applies shall take effect–

(a)   on the day of decision, where the determination in accordance with regulation 13C(3) of the Housing Benefit Regulations or regulation 13C(3) of the Housing Benefit (State Pension Credit) Regulations (when maximum rent (LHA) is to be determined) was made on the first day of the benefit week; and

(b)   in any other case, on the first day of the benefit week following the week in which the determination in accordance with regulation 13C(3) of the Housing Benefit Regulations or regulation 13C(3) of the Housing Benefit (State Pension Credit) Regulations (when maximum rent (LHA) is to be determined) was made.]]

Modifications

Para (6A) amended and para (15) substituted by reg 4(4) Housing Benefit (Local Housing Allowance, Miscellaneous and Consequential) Amendment Regulations 2007 SI No.2870, as amended by reg 6(2)(b) of SI 2008 No.586, as from 7 April 2008, save that for a person to whom reg 1(3) of those regulations applied (see p1235), the amendments came into force on the day on or after 7 April 2008 when the first of the events specified in reg 1(4) applied to her/him, or on 6 April 2009 if none had before that date.

Amendments

1.   Inserted by reg 9(c) of SI 2002 No 490 as from 1.4.02.
2.   Amended by reg 28(a) of SI 2003 No 325 as from 6.10.03.
3.   Inserted by reg 4(2) of SI 2003 No 1050 as from 5.5.03.
4.   Amended by reg 24(2) of SI 2003 No 1338 as from 6.10.03.
5.   Amended by reg 5(5) of SI 2003 No 2275 as from 6.10.03.
6.   Inserted by reg 16 of SI 2003 No 2399 as from a date specified in Sch 8 in relation to each particular authority.
7.   Inserted by reg 34(2) of SI 2004 No 14 as from 5.4.04.
8.   Revoked by reg 33 of SI 2004 No 14 as from 5.4.04.
9.   Inserted by Reg 10(4) of SI 2005 No 2677 as from 6.4.06.
10.   Amended by reg 5 and sch 2 para 17(3) of SI 2006 No 217 as from 6.3.06.
11.   Revoked by reg 8 of SI 2007 No 2470 as from 24.9.07.
12.   Amended by reg 4(4) of SI 2007 No 2870 as from 7.4.08 (or if reg 1(3) of that SI applies, on the day on or after 7.4.08 when the first of the events specified in reg 1(4) applies, or from 6.4.09 if none have before that date).
13.   Substituted by reg 6(2)(b) of SI 2008 No 286 as from 7.4.08.

14.   Inserted by reg 3(4) of SI 2008 No 1082, as substituted by reg 26 of SI 2008 No 2428, as from 27.10.08.
15.   Amended by Sch 1 para 154 of SI 2008 No 2683 as from 3.11.08.
16.   Amended by reg 9(4) of SI 2010 No 1160 as from 1.4.10.
17.   Amended by reg 27 And Sch 5 para 3(3) of SI 2010 No 1907 as amended by reg 15 of SI 2010 No 2430 as from 1.10.10.
18.   Amended by reg 6(2) of SI 2010 No 2449 as from 1.11.10.

Analysis
Paragraph (1): The general rule
Para (1) reflects the general rule as set out in Sch 7 para 4(5) CSPSSA, namely that a supersession takes effect on the date that the superseding decision was made or the date of the application, as the case may be. Exceptions to the general rule are found in paras (2) to (15).

Paragraphs (2), (3), (6) and (10): Changes of circumstances
Para (2) provides that superseding decisions made on the ground of change of circumstances generally take effect from the date on which the change falls to be taken into account under reg 79 HB Regs, regs 59 or 60 HB(SPC) Regs, reg 67 CTB Regs or regs 50 or 51 CTB(SPC) Regs. See the commentary to those provisions. Similarly, under para (6), where a rent officer has made a redetermination or other altering decision, that will be treated as a change of circumstances and will have similar effect.

Where a change of circumstances is one which someone is required to report (other than one under the regulations listed), para (3) effectively sets a one-month time limit for reporting the change, if the resulting superseding decision is to the advantage of the claimant. Note that regs 68A HB Regs and reg 59A CTB Regs were revoked in September 2002 subject to savings and transitional protection. Note also that by reg 2(4) HB&CTB(CP) Regs, the references to reg 68B HB Regs and reg 59B CTB Regs should be read as reg 60 HB(SPC) Regs and reg 51 CTB(SPC) Regs.

If such a change is reported within one month, the decision takes effect in accordance with para (2). The day of the change will be excluded, so a change occurring on 25 May and notified on 25 June is notified within the time period. Where notification of a change is made more than a month after it occurs and the new decision is advantageous to the claimant, the date of notification is treated as the date the change occurred: para (3). In such a case, this will normally be less beneficial to the claimant. An "advantageous" decision includes where it falls within reg 17(2): see para (5). The one-month period can be extended under reg 9. Note also that it was held in *CIS 1277/2002* (paras 13-15) that "notified to an appropriate office" in reg 7(2)(a)(ii) SSCS D&A Regs could include a case where a different office of the DWP passed the information to the office dealing with the relevant claim as well as a case where the claimant made the notification. Since that provision is in different form to reg 8(2), it is open to argument as to whether that analysis can be applied here, although there is nothing explicit to prevent its application.

Para (10) provides that where the change of circumstances is that there has been a change in the legislation in relation to HB/CTB, the superseding decision takes effect from the date the change in legislation has effect. Note that Art 3 Civil Partnership (Pensions, Social Security and Child Support) (Consequential, etc. Provisions) Order 2005 (see p1193) disapplies para (10) and provides transitional provisions for setting the effective date of a supersession for some claimants who are members of a couple who live together as if they are civil partners on or after 5 December 2005, and have an award of HB or CTB on 5 December 2005.

For the possibility of carrying out a "closed period" supersession where there has been more than one change of circumstance with the consequence that the claimant ceased to be entitled to benefit for a fixed period but has regained entitlement before the date on which the superseding decision is taken, see p142.

Paragraph (4): Decisions based on incorrect facts and supersession advantageous to the claimant
In such a case, the superseding decision has effect from the first day of the benefit week in which an application for a supersession was received *or* the authority had the relevant information justifying the supersession before it.

An "advantageous" decision includes where it falls within reg 17(2): see para (5).

Paragraphs (6A) and (6B): Supersession where rent officer determination required
Paras (6A) and (6B) deal with supersessions made under reg 7(2ZA). Except where entitlement to HB ceases, where a rent officer has made a determination following a local authority application under reg 14(1)(f) or (g) of either the HB or the HB(SPC) Regs, a supersession decision which adopts that determination takes effect as follows:
(1)   If the determination is the same or has increased and rent is payable weekly or in multiplies of weeks, it takes effect from the first day of the benefit week which includes the day after the end of the period covered by the previous determinations: sub-para (a)(i).
(2)   If the determination is the same or has increased and rent is payable at intervals of other than a week, it takes effect from the day after the end of the period covered by the previous determinations: sub-para (a)(ii).
(3)   If the determination has decreased, it takes effect from the first day of the week after the local authority receives it: sub-para (b).

Paragraph (7): Erroneous appeal decisions

If a First-tier Tribunal or Upper Tribunal decision was based on incorrect facts and was more advantageous to the claimant than it would otherwise have been, a decision superseding it takes effect from the date on which the appeal decision took (or was to take) effect. For the reasons given in the Analysis of reg 7(4), it is not presently possible to supersede a decision of a former appeal tribunal or of a social security commissioner.

Note that if an *authority's* decision was based on incorrect facts and was more advantageous to the claimant, it can be revised at any time under reg 4(2)(b), taking effect from the date of the original decision: reg 6.

Paragraph (8): Supersession following a "test case"

If a decision is being superseded because of a decision by the Upper Tribunal or a court in a "test case" (a relevant determination for the purposes of Sch 7 para 18 CSPSSA) the supersession is effective from the date of the Upper Tribunal's or court's decision.

Paragraph (9): Supersession where decision affected by "loss of benefit" provisions

Where a decision is affected by a DWP decision stopping or restricting benefit and is superseded under reg 7(2)(g) or (h), the supersession is effective from the first day of the disqualification period.

Paragraph (11): Supersession where decision made pending a "test case"

The ground for supersession in reg 7(2)(d)(ii) is not currently relevant for the reasons stated in the commentary on p1021.

Paragraph 14: Supersession on entitlement to a "relevant benefit" or an increase in its rate

Where a decision is superseded under reg 7(2)(i), the superseding decision has effect from the date of entitlement to the relevant benefit or the increase in its rate.

Paragraph 14A: Supersession on opting for or repaying a lump sum on deferring claiming pension

Where a decision is superseded under reg 7(2)(j), the superseding decision has effect from the day on which a lump sum (or a payment on account of a lump sum) is paid or repaid if that day is the first day of the benefit week. If not, it takes effect from the first day of the following benefit week.

Effective date for late notification of change of circumstances

9.–(1) For the purposes of making a decision under paragraph 4 of Schedule 7 to the Act a longer period of time may be allowed for the notification of a change of circumstances in so far as it affects the effective date of the change where the conditions specified in the following provisions of this regulation are satisfied.

(2) An application for the purposes of paragraph (1) shall–

(a) include particulars of the change of circumstances and the reasons for the failure to notify the change of circumstances on an earlier date; and

(b) be made within 13 months of the date on which the change occurred.

(3) An application for the purposes of paragraph (1) shall not be granted unless the appropriate relevant authority is satisfied that–

(a) it is reasonable to grant the application;

(b) the change of circumstances notified by the applicant is relevant to the decision which is to be superseded; and

(c) special circumstances are relevant and as a result of those special circumstances it was not practicable for the applicant to notify the change of circumstances within one month of the change occurring.

(4) In determining whether it is reasonable to grant the application, the appropriate relevant authority shall have regard to the principle that the greater the amount of time that has elapsed between the date one month after the change of circumstances occurred and the date the application for a superseding decision is made, the more compelling should be the special circumstances on which the application is based.

(5) In determining whether it is reasonable to grant an application, no account shall be taken of the following–

(a) that the applicant was unaware of, or misunderstood, the law applicable to his case (including ignorance or misunderstanding of the time limits imposed by these Regulations); or

(b) that [¹ the Upper Tribunal] or a court has taken a different view of the law from that previously understood and applied.

(6) An application under this regulation which has been refused may not be renewed.

Amendment

1.   Amended by Sch 1 para 155 of SI 2008 No 2683 as from 3.11.08.

Analysis

Reg 9 deals with the circumstances in which a notification of a change of circumstances made more than one month after it occurs may nonetheless be treated as if made in time. In this situation a superseding decision takes effect as set out in reg 8(2) rather than in reg 8(3), to the advantage of the claimant. The structure of reg 9 is similar to that of reg 5.

Para (2) deals with applications for an extension of time to report a change of circumstances and is similar to reg 5(3), save that the operative decision need not be identified and there is no provision for the place at which disclosure must be made (which is dealt with by reg 88 HB Regs, reg 69 HB(SPC) Regs, reg 74 CTB Regs and reg 59 CTB(SPC) Regs). An application must be made within 13 months of the date the change of circumstances occurred.

Para (3) is similar to reg 5(4), save that there is no need for the application to have merit – instead, the change of circumstances must be relevant. Practicability "involves a test of feasibility, not a test of desirability or convenience or anything of that sort": *CH 282/2006* applying *Singh v Post Office* [1973] ICR 437 at 440. Moreover, as the impracticability must result from the special circumstances, those circumstances must in some way relate to or affect the practicability of reporting the change of time within one month.

Paras (4), (5) and (6) are comparable to paras (6), (5) and (7) of reg 5 respectively.

Notice of a decision against which an appeal lies

10.–(1)   A person affected who has a right of appeal against a relevant decision shall be given written notice–

(a)   of the decision against which the appeal lies;

(b)   in a case where that notice does not include a statement of reasons for the decision, that he may [¹ , within one month of the date of notification of that decision (or, if the decision was notified before 1st November 2010, before 1st December 2010),] request the relevant authority to provide him with a written statement of the reasons for that decision; and

(c)   of his right of appeal against that decision.

(2)   Where a written statement of the reasons for the decision is not included in the written notice of the decision and is requested under paragraph (1)(b), the relevant authority shall, so far as practicable, provide that statement within 14 days.

Amendment

1.   Amended by reg 6(3) of SI 2010 No 2449 as from 1.11.10.

Definition

"person affected" – see reg 3.

Analysis

If there is a right of appeal against a decision, written notice of it must be given of it to a person affected by the decision. It must contain information as specified in paras (b) and (c). "Person affected" is defined in reg 3. The obligation in reg 10(1) is additional to those set out in Sch 9 HB Regs, Sch 8 HB(SPC) Regs, Sch 8 CTB Regs and Sch 7 CTB(SPC) Regs.

If a request for a written statement of reasons is made (where not already provided), the local authority must provide one within 14 days if this is practicable. The onus to provide a statement of reasons within 14 days if "practicable" is a heavy one. Days between the date a request is received by the authority and the date on which it is provided are ignored when calculating the one-month time limits for seeking a revision and appealing: see commentary to reg 4(4) on p1013. Since 1 November 2010, any request for a statement of reasons for a decision must be made within a month of the date on which the decision was notified or, if the decision was made before 1 November 2010, by 1 December 2010. The effect, taken together with the changes to Sch. 1 TP(FT) Rules, is to close the loophole by which it was possible to circumvent the 13-month time limit for appealing (see pp994 and 1039 of the 22nd edition).

[¹ Correction of accidental errors

10A.–(1)   Accidental errors in a relevant decision, or a revised decision, or the record of such a decision, may be corrected by the relevant authority at any time.

(2)   A correction made to a relevant decision, or a revised decision, or the record of such a decision, shall be deemed to be part of the decision, or of that record, and the relevant authority shall give a written notice of the correction as soon as practicable to the claimant.

(3)   In calculating the time within which an application can be made under regulation 4(1)(a) for a relevant decision to be revised [²] there shall be disregarded any day falling

before the day on which notice was given of a correction of the decision or to the revision or record thereof under paragraph (2).

Definition

"relevant decision" – see reg 1(2) above and Sch 7 para 19(2) CSPSSA.

Amendments

1. Inserted by reg 25 of SI 2002 No 1379 as from 20.5.02.
2. Amended by Sch 1 para 156 of SI 2008 No 2683 as from 3.11.08.

General Note

Accidental errors in decisions can be corrected under reg 10A. Written notice of the correction must be given to the claimant as soon as it is practicable. In calculating the time limit for seeking a revision under reg 4(1)(a), days before the day on which notice is given of the correction must be ignored.

<hr>

PART III
Suspension and Termination of Benefit and Other Matters

<hr>

Cases where a relevant authority may suspend

 11.–(1) A relevant authority may suspend, in whole or in part–
 (a) any payment of housing benefit or council tax benefit;
 (b) any reduction (by way of council tax benefit) in the amount that a person is or will become liable to pay in respect of council tax,
in the circumstances prescribed in paragraph (2).
 (2) The prescribed circumstances are where–
 (a) it appears to the relevant authority that an issue arises whether–
  (i) the conditions for entitlement to housing benefit or council tax benefit are or were fulfilled; or
  (ii) a decision as to an award of such a benefit should be revised under paragraph 3 of Schedule 7 to the Act or superseded under paragraph 4 of that Schedule;
 (b) an appeal is pending against–
  (i) a decision of [² the First-tier Tribunal, the Upper Tribunal] or a court; or
  (ii) a decision given by [² the Upper Tribunal] or a court in a different case,
  and it appears to the relevant authority that if the appeal were to be determined in a particular way an issue would arise whether the award of housing benefit or council tax benefit in the case itself ought to be revised or superseded; or
 (c) an issue arises whether–
  (i) an amount of housing benefit is recoverable under section 75 (overpayments) of the Administration Act or regulations made under that section; or
  (ii) an excess payment of council tax benefit under section 76 of the Administration Act or regulations made under that section has occurred.
 [¹ (3) For the purposes of paragraph 13(3)(c) of Schedule 7 to the Act the prescribed circumstances are that a decision of an appeal tribunal, a Commissioner or a court has been made and the relevant authority–
 (a) is waiting to receive that decision, or in the case of an appeal tribunal decision, is considering whether to apply for a statement of reasons for it, or has applied for such a statement and is waiting to receive it; or
 (b) has received that decision or, in the case of an appeal tribunal decision, the statement of reasons for it, and is considering whether to apply for leave to appeal, or where leave to appeal has been granted, is considering whether to appeal,
and the relevant authority shall as soon as reasonably practicable give written notice of its intention to apply for a statement of the reasons for a tribunal decision, to apply for leave to appeal, or to appeal.]

Amendments

1. Inserted by reg 4(2) of SI 2008 No 2667 as from 30.10.08.

2.   Amended by Sch 1 para 157 of SI 2008 No 2683 as from 3.11.08.

General Note

Reg 11 is made under Sch 7 para 13 CSPSSA (see p153). Reg 12 sets out the situations in which a suspension must be lifted.

Analysis

Para (1) specifies that the power to suspend may be exercised in the whole amount of the benefit payable or only part thereof. Payments of HB (whether or not made to the claimant) and CTB may be suspended. A reduction in council tax may also be suspended, but a claimant will only in this instance become liable to pay an increased amount of council tax where a fresh bill is sent to her/him: reg 18 Council Tax (Administration and Enforcement) Regulations 1992.

Suspension is discretionary, and the discretion must be exercised reasonably even if one of the specified circumstances exists. Thus if, for example, an issue arises as to whether a few hundred pounds of benefit was overpaid and the claimant has capital of that sum, it might not be reasonable for the authority to suspend ongoing entitlement to benefit under para (2)(c) if it could readily be recovered. However, as there is no right of appeal against a decision to suspend (see Schedule para 5) the claimant's only remedy against an unreasonable suspension is judicial review. It is often quicker, easier and less expensive to seek to provide the authority with the information and evidence it needs to resolve the question that has arisen.

Para (2) specifies the circumstances in which a suspension can be made. There is a degree of overlap between the provisions.

(1)   There may be a suspension where current or past entitlement is in issue, or when a revision or supersession is being considered: sub-para (a). It need not be clear that an existing decision was incorrect; all that is required is that "an issue arises" through a reasonable doubt existing as to the correctness of a decision. The power to suspend where an issue arises cannot be used merely to check the accuracy of an existing award where there are no particular grounds for doubting that it is correct. In *CH 2995/2006*, the commissioner stated:

> "26.   The second of the two situations I mentioned earlier as the ones that I presume were envisaged by Parliament is where a local authority has no particular doubt, or only a weak doubt, about the claimant's entitlement to . . . benefit but, as a matter of good administration, wishes the claimant to provide information and evidence in order, in effect, to update the information and evidence provided on the original claim and check its accuracy. Parliament seems to have expected that there would be no suspension of payment while that information was awaited but, if it was not forthcoming within the time allowed, there would be a suspension and, if the information was still not forthcoming, there would eventually be a termination of entitlement".

(2)   Pending appeals may give rise to a suspension under sub-para (b).

The appeals referred to in head (i) must, by implication, apply to appeals involving the claimant whose benefit is suspended. Note that the appeal must be pending: see Sch 7 para 13(3) CSPSSA on p153 for the extended definition of "pending". It includes cases where an application for permission to appeal has been lodged or where the time limit for applying for permission or lodging an appeal has not expired. It does not, however, appear to extend to a situation where a statement of reasons has been requested under reg 53 SSCS D&A Regs, though it may be arguable that sub-para (a)(i) can apply in such a situation. It would not be reasonable to continue a suspension where a decision had been taken by an authority not to pursue an appeal.

Under head (ii), appeals in other cases may also result in a suspension. However, this power only applies to an appeal *from* the Upper Tribunal or a court. It does not, therefore, apply where an appeal is pending *to* the Upper Tribunal. For discussion of "different case", see Sch 7 para 13(4) CSPSSA and the commentary on p153.

(3)   Suspected overpayments may also give rise to a right to suspend: sub-para (c). Again, "an issue arises" means it need not be clear that an overpayment has occurred. All that is necessary is reasonable grounds to suspect that too much benefit has been paid.

Making or restoring of payments or reductions suspended

12.–(1)   Subject to paragraph (2), the prescribed circumstances for the purposes of paragraph 13(1)(c) of Schedule 7 to the Act (the subsequent making, or restoring, of any or all of the payments or reductions so suspended) are–

(a)   in a case to which regulation 11(2)(a) applies, where the relevant authority is satisfied that the benefit so suspended is properly payable and no outstanding issues remain to be resolved;

(b)   in a case to which regulation 11(2)(b) applies, an appeal is no longer pending and the benefit suspended remains payable following the determination of that appeal.

(2)   Where any of the circumstances in paragraph (1) is satisfied, the relevant authority shall, so far as practicable, make the payment, or as the case may be, restore the reduction within 14 days of the decision to make or restore that payment or reduction.

Analysis

Reg 12 deals with the circumstances in which a suspension must be lifted under Sch 7 para 13(1)(c) CSPSSA. It is not well drafted.

Para (1) first, by sub-para (a), requires that accrued arrears be paid where any issues referred to in reg 11(2)(a) have been resolved. Note that there must be "no outstanding issues" and so if an authority has been satisfied that its initial concerns had no basis but further issues have arisen as a result of its inquiries, the suspension can remain in force.

Sub-para (b) deals with suspension pending appeals. For the question of when an appeal is "pending", see Sch 7 para 13(3) CSPSSA on p153 and reg 11(2)(b) above. The phrase "determination of that appeal" is inapt in the context of a suspension having been imposed during the period when the time limit for applying for permission or appealing has yet to expire but no application for permission has actually been made. In that situation, it is suggested that the "determination" of the appeal occurs once a final decision is taken not to pursue an appeal.

Para (2) requires an authority to make good a suspension which is brought to an end under para (1). Curiously, there is no specific provision governing suspensions under reg 11(2)(c) for suspected overpayments. However, if a suspension is revoked, it is suggested that the ordinary provisions as to payment in the HB and HB(SPC) Regs and the CTB and CTB(SPC) Regs would then become enforceable by a claimant by way of a debt action or a claim for judicial review.

Suspension for failure to furnish information etc.

13.–(1)   The relevant authority may suspend in whole or in part–

(a)   any payment of housing benefit or council tax benefit;

(b)   any reduction (by way of council tax benefit) in the amount that a person is or will become liable to pay in respect of council tax,

in relation to persons who fail to comply with the information requirements (as defined in paragraph 14 of Schedule 7 to the Act) as provided for in regulations made pursuant to section 5(1)(hh) and 6(1)(hh) of the Administration Act (person required to satisfy the information provisions).

(2)   For the purposes of section 5(1)(hh) in so far as it applies to housing benefit and section 6(1)(hh) of the Administration Act the prescribed persons are–

(a)   a person in respect of whom payment of benefit or a reduction has been suspended under regulation 11(2)(a);

(b)   a person who has made an application for a decision of the relevant authority to be revised or superseded;

(c)   a person in respect of whom a question has arisen in connection with his award of benefit and who fails to comply with the requirement in [¹ regulation 86 of the Housing Benefit Regulations, regulation 67 of the Housing Benefit (State Pension Credit) Regulations, regulation 72 of the Council Tax Benefit Regulations or regulation 57 of the Council Tax Benefit (State Pension Credit) Regulations] to furnish information or evidence needed for a determination whether a decision on an award should be revised under paragraph 3 or superseded under paragraph 4 of Schedule 7 to the Act.

(3)   The relevant authority shall notify any person to whom paragraph (2) refers of the requirements of this regulation.

(4)   A person to whom paragraph (2) refers must–

(a)   furnish the information or evidence needed within a period of–

(i)   one month beginning with the date on which the notification under paragraph (3) was sent to him; or

(ii)   such longer period as the relevant authority considers necessary in order to enable him to comply with the requirement; or

(b)   satisfy the relevant authority within the period provided for in paragraph (4)(a) that–

(i)   the information or evidence so required does not exist; or

(ii)   it is not possible for him to obtain the information or evidence so required.

(5)　Where a person satisfies the requirements in paragraph (4), the relevant authority shall, so far as practicable, make, or as the case may be restore, the payment within 14 days of the decision to make or restore that payment.

Amendment

1.　Amended by reg 5 and Sch 2 para 17(3) of SI 2006 No 217 as from 6.3.06.

Analysis

Reg 13 provides a power to suspend which is additional to those set out in reg 11. It deals with cases in which a person is required to provide information to an authority. The relationship between regs 11 and 13 was explained by Commissioner Rowland in *CH 2995/2006* as follows:

"21.　The 2001 Regulations make adequate, albeit complicated, provision for the . . . [situation]. . . where a local authority considers that there may be a question as to the claimant's continued entitlement to benefit and perhaps also as to his or her entitlement in the past. In those circumstances, payments may be suspended under reg 11(1) and (2)(a) while investigations are carried out. When the investigations have been concluded, the local authority must either restore the payments under regulation 12 or else revise or supersede the decision awarding benefit. If, as part of the investigation, the local authority asks the claimant for further information or evidence, the case falls within regulation 13(2)(a) and the claimant must be given the notice required by regulation 13(3) and in particular must be informed of the time within which the information must be provided under regulation 13(4)(a). If the claimant then fails to provide the information within the time allowed under regulation 13(4)(a), the local authority may, instead of restoring the payments or revising or superseding the award on any other ground, terminate the award under regulation 14 with effect from the date of the suspension under regulation 11(1) and (2)(a)."

The commissioner also notes (at para 24) that paras (2) to (4) "apply where there has been a suspension under reg 11(1) and (2)(a) just as much as where there has been a suspension under regulation 13(1)".

Paras (1) and (2) set out the situation in which the power to suspend may be exercised. The two provisions in the SSAA referred to give power to require information during the currency of a claim. The extended versions of reg 86(1) HB Regs, reg 67(1) HB(SPC) Regs, reg 72(1) CTB Regs and reg 57(1) CTB(SPC) Regs are made under ss5(1)(hh) and 6(1)(hh) SSAA respectively.

In order for a suspension to be lawful, the authority must show that the person of whom information is required falls into one of the categories in para (2).

In *AA v London Borough of Hounslow* [2008] UKUT 13 (AAC), the judge decided that the requirement to supply information (eg, under reg 86 HB Regs) must actually have been communicated to the person in question; proof of posting to the last known address is not sufficient.

There cannot be any suspension under para (1) until there has been at least one failure to comply with a request for information (although suspension may still be possible under reg 11). However, the suggestion in the 21st edition that para 2(c) might require a failure to comply with two requests is wrong for the reasons given by Deputy Judge Ovey in *AA v Leicester City Council* [2009] UKUT 86 (AAC). Note that a refusal to allow a home visit does not amount to a failure to comply with an information requirement (see *CH 2995/2006* (para 35)) although in some circumstances, it might give rise to a question about entitlement that would justify suspension under reg 11. The same would, presumably, be true of a failure to attend an interview under caution.

Paras (3) to (5) deal with the procedure for operating the regulation. The first step is for the authority to give the person notice under para (3) of "the requirements of this regulation". Failure to do so invalidates any subsequent termination: *AA v London Borough of Hounslow* [2008] UKUT 13 (AAC). Those requirements are set out in para (4) and are as follows:

(1)　**The information or evidence that is needed.** It is suggested that the information or evidence required by the authority must be specified in sufficient detail for the person to know what is required and for it to be possible to demonstrate whether or not the requirement has been complied with for the purposes of reg 14. For example, telling the person to telephone the benefits office is not, in itself, a request for information or evidence.

(2)　**The time limit for the provision of the evidence.** The clamant must be given a "firm deadline" for the provision of the information (*CH 2995/2006* para 43) and that deadline must be at least one month after the date on which the notification is sent (para (4)(a)). Despite the fact that the one-month time limit is explicitly set out in the regulations, many local authorities purport to impose shorter periods in practice. Time limits of seven and 14 days that have no basis in law and appear to have been plucked from the air by optimistic benefit officers – or, more probably, by the companies responsible for their computer software – are particularly common. A failure to specify a time limit of at least one month will invalidate any subsequent termination of benefit under reg 14.

The notice should also advise the person of the possibility of applying for an extension of time under para (4)(a)(ii) if s/he needs longer than a month in which to comply with the requirement.

(3)　**Evidence that does not exist or cannot be obtained.** As an alternative to providing the information within the one-month (or longer) time limit, the person may instead seek to persuade the authority that

that information does not exist or that it is not possible for her/him to obtain it. The standard-form notices issued by many authorities fail to mention this alternative and the deputy judge in *AA v Leicester City Council* [2009] UKUT 86 (AAC) held (at paras 54-56) that the failure invalidated the subsequent termination.

Alternatively, it could be argued that a person who does not provide information that does not exist, or that s/he cannot obtain, does not "fail" to comply with an information requirement for the purposes of reg 14(1) but merely omits to comply with that requirement. The word "failure" carries connotations of breach of duty (see, for example, *B v SSWP* [2005] EWCA Civ 929, [2005] 1 WLR 3796 (reported as *R(IS) 9/06*) and tribunals should be slow to find that a person is under a duty to perform the impossible.

Unfortunately, it is not all that uncommon to find authorities purporting to impose information requirements with which claimants obviously cannot comply: an example is demanding that a claimant who has just started work and is paid monthly should produce her/his "three most recent pay slips" within a month.

Para (3) does not require an authority to tell the person that her/his entitlement to benefit may be terminated under reg 14 if the information requirement is not satisfied. However, it is good practice to do so. By definition, the person's benefit has already been suspended (which a claimant is likely to see as "stopped"). S/he may therefore not understand the serious consequences of failing to comply unless these are explained. In those circumstances, it is in the authority's interests as well as the claimant's to give the explanation: a claimant who understands the nature of the penalty for non-compliance is more likely to comply.

In *CH 2995/2006*, the commissioner left open the possibility that some failures to comply with para (3) might not be fatal to a subsequent termination (para 43). However, it is suggested that that possibility ought not to be accepted. As the commissioner acknowledges, reg 14 imposes a procedural penalty for failing to provide information on a person who may well be otherwise entitled to benefit. In general terms, all para (3) requires is that, before such a penalty is imposed, the authority must tell the person in sufficient detail what s/he has to do and when s/he has to do it by. It is very difficult to imagine cases in which it would be just to impose a penalty where that information had not been given.

Under para (5), once the person has satisfied the requirements of para (4), the suspension imposed under reg 13 must be lifted.

Termination in cases of a failure to furnish information

14.–(1)   A person in respect of whom payment of benefit or a reduction has been suspended–

(a)   under regulation 11 and who subsequently fails to comply with an information requirement; or

(b)   under regulation 13 for failing to comply with such a requirement,

shall cease to be entitled to the benefit from the date on which the payments or reduction were so suspended, or such earlier date on which entitlement to benefit ceases.

(2)   Paragraph (1) does not apply–

[¹ (a)   subject to sub-paragraph (b), before the end of the period under regulation 13(4) for the provision of information;]

(b)   where payment of benefit or a reduction has been suspended in part under regulation 11 or regulation 13.

Amendment

1.   Substituted by reg 4 of SI 2005 No 2894 as from 10.11.05.

Analysis

Under reg 14, a claimant ceases to be entitled to benefit if, following suspension under regs 11 or 13, s/he fails to comply with a request for information.

There must be a failure to comply with "an information requirement". To be an information requirement for these purposes, the request must be for documents which are reasonably required by the local authority to determine the claimant's continuing entitlement to benefit: *R(H) 1/09*. Further, if a document which is the subject of an information requirement does not exist at the time that the information requirement is notified to the claimant an omission to produce it is not a "failure" for the purposes of reg 14.

Decisions made by virtue of reg 14 are "decisions superseding earlier decisions" within Sch 7 para 4 CSPSSA: *R(H) 4/08*. It follows that they can be revised under Sch 7 para 3 CSPSSA and that they carry a right of appeal to a tribunal: *R(H) 4/08* and *CH 2995/2006*. That right is expressly preserved by para 5 of the Schedule to these regulations. Given the decision of the ECtHR in *Tsfayo v United Kingdom* (application no: 60860/00) 2006, 14 November, unreported, ECtHR, any other arrangement would be an infringement of the claimant's Convention Rights.

It also follows that any person affected by the decision to terminate must be properly notified of that decision and of her/his right to appeal against it. In the absence of such a notification, the time for bringing an appeal will not normally begin to run.

The view expressed in previous editions that termination is "a third mechanism for altering decisions to add to revision and supersession" is wrong: *CH 2995/2006* (para 22). So is the DWP advice in Circular HB/CTB A2/2006 that "decisions given under Regulations 11-14 of the HB/CTB Decision and Appeals Regulations are made outside the normal revision/supersession rules" and instead are "administrative decisions" that do not carry a right of appeal: *R(H) 4/08* (in particular para 24). The word "termination" (which only appears in the heading to reg 14, and not in the operative words) describes the *outcome* of the process established by regs 11, 13 and 14 and not the process itself.

The scope of the appeal against a decision under reg 14 is less clear. It is certainly open to the claimant to argue that s/he did not "cease to be entitled to benefit" because the original decision to suspend was invalid, or because mandatory procedural requirements (particularly in reg 13) have not been observed, or because s/he did not in fact fail to comply with an information requirement. It is suggested, however, that where a claimant accepts (or the tribunal finds) that that the procedure in regs 11-14 was validly operated, and that the claimant did not produce the necessary information and evidence at the time, the tribunal has no power to reinstate benefit on the basis that, by the time of the appeal hearing, the necessary information and evidence has been supplied. This is because, whatever might have been the case if the claimant had produced the information or evidence on time, the fact that s/he did not do so caused her/his entitlement to cease from the date on which payments were suspended. The position is therefore different from an appeal against a decision where the authority does not rely on the Part III procedure, but instead draws an adverse inference against the claimant and supersedes on the basis that entitlement has ended on substantive, rather than procedural, grounds: *CH 3736/2006* (para 27).

It is suggested that the only remedy open to a claimant whose entitlement has been validly terminated under reg 14 but who is subsequently in a position to provide the information and evidence requested, is to ask the authority to extend time for the production of that information and evidence under reg 13(4)(a)(ii) and then to revise the termination decision. A refusal to revise the termination decision may, in some circumstances, give rise to a technical right of appeal against that decision but that right may be of little practical value because the tribunal has no jurisdiction to interfere with the authority's refusal to extend time under reg 13: see Sch para 5 on p1046.

Para (1). Termination can take place in two circumstances. First, there are cases where there has been a suspension under reg 11 and then a failure to comply with a requirement to supply information: see the definition of "information requirement" in Sch 7 para 14(3) CSPSSA on p154. The latter must have taken place "subsequently". If a reg 11 suspension is imposed as a result of a failure to provide information (when reg 13 could have been used instead), then a further chance would have to be given to the claimant before reg 14 can operate.

Secondly, there are cases where a requirement imposed by reg 13 is not complied with.

It is important for authorities to ensure (and, on appeal, for tribunals to satisfy themselves) that all the procedural safeguards (particularly in reg 13(3)) have been complied with. A failure to give a valid notice under reg 13(3) will almost always be fatal to a termination under reg 14. In particular, the claimant must be given a "firm deadline" by which to provide the evidence and information: *CH 2995/2006* (paras 43 and 44). See further the commentary to reg 13 on p1033.

CH 2995/2006 also confirms (para 41) that termination under reg 14 cannot be effective from any date before the date on which the decision to suspend was made. Para (1) appears to allow the possibility that termination might take effect from "such earlier date on which entitlement to benefit ceases" but those words are either meaningless or *ultra vires*. From a formal point of view, the provision is circular: stripped of irrelevant words it states that: "A person . . . shall cease to be entitled to the benefit . . . from such earlier date on which entitlement to benefit ceases". That proposition conveys no useful information whatsoever. Secondly, if entitlement to benefit ceases from some "earlier date" then that can only be because there are substantive grounds on which to revise or supersede the decision awarding benefit with effect from that earlier date. An authority that had such grounds would not need to rely upon reg 14 in the first place. Finally, reg 14 is made under para 15 Sch 7 CSPSSA, which only empowers the Secretary of State to make regulations that bring entitlement to HB to an end "not earlier than the date on which payments were suspended". It follows that, if reg 14 did permit a termination from an earlier date, it would be *ultra vires*: *CH 3736/2006* (para 27). At best, the words "or such earlier date on which entitlement to benefit ceases" should be interpreted as confirming that the possibility of a termination under reg 14 does not prevent an authority from making a substantive revision or supersession with effect from an earlier date where there are grounds upon which to do so.

An example demonstrates this. Benefit is awarded on 1 February, but on 1 June a question arises about the award, a reg 11 suspension is imposed and the claimant is required to supply information. By 1 September, the claimant has failed to comply with the information requirement. Entitlement can be terminated from 1 June, but in order to deprive the claimant of the award from any earlier date, grounds for revision or supersession must be shown.

Para (2) prevents termination of an award in two situations: where the suspension was only partial: sub-para (b), and before the end of the period specified in reg 13(4) for the provision of information: sub-para (a). Although an authority is not obliged to accept information late, it is suggested that it will rarely, if ever, be appropriate for an authority to proceed to terminate entitlement in circumstances in which the information requirement is complied with a few days late. This will be a trap for many authorities which were prone to reject or 'cancel' claims automatically if a claimant was even one day late with supplying information.

Decisions involving issues that arise on appeal in other cases

15.–(1)   For the purposes of paragraph 16(3)(b) of Schedule 7 to the Act (prescribed cases and circumstances in which a decision may be made) the prescribed cases and circumstances are those in which the claimant would be entitled to benefit to which the decision which falls to be made relates, even if the appeal in the other case referred to in paragraph 16(1)(b) of that Schedule were decided in the way which is most unfavourable to him.

(2)   For the purposes of paragraph 16(3)(b) of Schedule 7 to the Act (prescribed basis) the prescribed basis on which the relevant authority may make a decision is as if–

(a)   the appeal in the other case referred to in paragraph 16(1)(b) of that Schedule 7 had already been determined; and

(b)   the appeal had been decided in the way which is most unfavourable to the claimant.

Analysis

Sch 7 para 16 CSPSSA generally excuses an authority from making a decision where there is an appeal pending in a test case. Sch 7 para 16(3) gives a discretion to issue a decision where regulations so prescribe. Reg 15 exercises that power. If it chooses to issue a decision, the authority must make its decision on the assumption that the appeal is decided in the way most unfavourable to the claimant: para (2)(b).

The discretion conferred by Sch 7 para 16(3) and reg 15 must be exercised reasonably. Where it is clear that the claimant is entitled to a substantial award of HB or CTB whatever the outcome of the appeal, it would not be reasonable to refuse to make a decision. Persons affected will, however, have to ensure that they then appeal against the authority's decision in order to protect their interests.

PART IV

Rights of Appeal and Procedure for Bringing Appeals

Decisions against which no appeal lies

16.–(1)   No appeal shall lie against a decision specified in the Schedule to these Regulations.

[¹ (2)]

(3)   In this regulation references to a decision include references to a determination embodied in or necessary to a decision.

Amendment

1.   Amended by Sch 1 para 158 of SI 2008 No 2683 as from 3.11.08.

Analysis

See p1044 for those decisions which are excluded from the appeal regime. All other decisions may be appealed, but note that an appeal may only lie against an "outcome decision": see the commentary to Sch 7 para 6(1) CSPSSA on p145. Reg 16(3) reflects the distinction between decisions and determinations referred to in that commentary. The effect of para (3) is to confirm that it is not possible to appeal against a determination embodied in a decision which falls within the Schedule.

Appeal against a decision which has been revised

17.–(1)   An appeal against a decision of the relevant authority shall not lapse where the decision is revised under paragraph 3 of Schedule 7 to the Act before the appeal is determined and the decision as revised is not more advantageous to the appellant than the decision before it was so revised.

(2)   For the purposes of this regulation, a decision which is more advantageous includes any decision where–

(a)   any housing benefit or council tax benefit paid or any reduction in the amount that a person is liable to pay in respect of council tax is greater or is awarded for a longer period in consequence of a decision made under paragraph 3 of Schedule 7 to the Act;

(b)　the amount of housing benefit or council tax benefit in payment or reduction in the amount a person is liable to pay in respect of council tax would have been greater but for the operation of the Administration Act in suspending the payment of, or disqualifying a claimant from receiving, some or all of the benefit;

(c)　as a result of the decision, a denial of, or disqualification for the receiving of, housing benefit or council tax benefit is lifted, wholly or in part; or

(d)　in consequence of the revised decision, housing benefit or council tax benefit paid is not recoverable by virtue of or as a consequence of section 75 or 76 of the Administration Act, or an amount so recoverable is reduced.

(3)　Where a decision as revised under paragraph 3 of Schedule 7 to the Act is not more advantageous to the appellant than the decision before it was revised, the appeal shall be treated as though it had been brought against the decision as revised.

(4)　The appellant shall have a period of one month from the date of notification of the decision as revised to make further representations as to the appeal.

(5)　After the expiration of the period specified in paragraph (4), or within that period if the appellant consents in writing, the appeal to the [¹ First-tier Tribunal] shall proceed except where, in the light of further representations from the appellant, the relevant authority further revises its decision and that decision is more advantageous to the appellant than the decision before it was revised.

Amendment

1.　Amended by Sch 1 para 159 of SI 2008 No 2683 as from 3.11.08.

Analysis

Sch 7 para 3(6) CSPSSA provides that if a decision is revised while an appeal against it is pending, the appeal lapses except in the circumstances prescribed by regulations. Reg 17 is made under that power.

Para (1) sets out the general rule, which is that an appeal will only lapse if the decision is "more advantageous" to the claimant than the appealed decision was. The claimant has a fresh right of appeal against the revised decision: see Sch 7 para 6(1) CSPSSA on p145. However, it is inevitable that some claimants will find the procedures confusing and will assume that their appeal is still pending. Authorities ought to emphasise that the appeal is no longer proceeding in their correspondence with a claimant in these circumstances. The time limit for appealing runs from the date of notification of the new decision: Sch 7 para 3(5) CSPSSA.

If the fresh appeal is late then, as long as 13 months have not passed since the revision, an extension of time is possible under reg 19(5A) or rr23(2), (4) and (5) and 5(3)(a) TP(FT) Rules. The fact (if it be) that the local authority had failed to advise the appellant that the previous appeal had lapsed and/or of the need to make a fresh appeal would probably amount to a "special circumstance" within reg19(6)(b). If, however, the local authority had correctly advised the appellant but the appellant failed to make the appeal on time because s/he misunderstood, or disbelieved, that advice, that would not be a circumstance that could be taken into account (see reg 19(9)(a)). Note, however, that the First-tier Tribunal's power to extend time under r5(3)(a) is not constrained by regs 19(6)-(9).

In some circumstances, particularly where an appeal has already been part-heard and adjourned and where the revision will not give the appellant everything s/he seeks from the appeal, it will often be preferable for the authority to make a supplementary submission to the tribunal, asking the tribunal to substitute the proposed new decision rather than to issue the revised decision itself so as to cause the appeal to lapse and force the appellant to re-start the process from the beginning.

Para (2) offers a partial definition of "more advantageous". It only "includes" the four comparisons set out in sub-paras (a) to (d) and so if other changes make a decision better for a claimant, they may also fall within para (1). Some revisions may amount to a curate's egg and result in changes both for the good and bad from the claimant's perspective. In such circumstances, the best approach is to look at the result in pure money terms: is the claimant entitled to and/or receiving more money as a result of the revised decision?

Sub-para (a) deals with the most common situation, which is an increase in the amount of benefit payable or period for which it is awarded. Sub-para (b) deals with the same situation where the claimant's right to receive benefit is suspended. Revisions which lift disqualifications and reduce or eliminate recoverable overpayments are also "more advantageous".

Para (3) confirms that where the appeal does not lapse, it continues as if it was against the original decision as revised.

Paras (4) to (5) provide that an appeal will proceed after the claimant has a period of one month to make further representations. It is suggested that it will be open to a claimant to raise new issues for consideration if s/he wishes. At the end of the one-month period (or earlier if the appellant agrees in writing), the appeal must proceed unless the decision is further revised and is then more advantageous.

[² Time within which an appeal is to be brought
18.]

Amendments
1. Amended by reg 26 of SI 2002 No 1379 as from 20.5.02.
2. Omitted by Sch 1 para 160 of SI 2008 No 2683 as from 3.11.08.

Late appeals
19.–[⁵ (1)]
[⁵ (2)]
[⁵ (3)]
[⁵ (4)]
[² [⁵ (5)   Where a dispute arises as to whether an appeal was brought within the time specified under Tribunal Procedure Rules the dispute shall be referred to, and determined by, the First-tier Tribunal.

(5A)   The relevant authority may treat a late appeal as made in time in accordance with Tribunal Procedure Rules if the relevant authority is satisfied that it is in the interests of justice.];

(6)   For the purposes of paragraph [⁵ (5)], it is not in the interests of justice to [⁵ treat the appeal as made in time unless the relevant authority] is satisfied that–
(a)   any of the special circumstances specified in paragraph (7) are relevant [⁵]; or
(b)   some other special circumstances exist which are wholly exceptional and relevant [⁵],
and as a result of those special circumstances, it was not practicable for the [⁵ appeal notice to be submitted in accordance with Tribunal Procedure Rules.]

(7)   For the purposes of paragraph (6)(a), the special circumstances are–
(a)   the [⁵ appellant] or a partner or dependant of the [⁵ appellant] has died or suffered serious illness;
(b)   the [⁵ appellant] is not resident in the United Kingdom; or
(c)   normal postal services were disrupted.

(8)   In determining whether it is in the interests of justice to [⁵ treat the appeal as made in time], [⁴ regard shall be had] to the principle that the greater the amount of time that has elapsed between the expiration of the time [⁵ limit under Tribunal Procedure Rules and the submission of the notice of appeal, the more compelling should be the special circumstances.]

(9)   In determining whether it is in the interests of justice to [⁵ treat the appeal as made in time], no account shall be taken of the following–
(a)   that the applicant was unaware of or misunderstood the law applicable to his case (including ignorance or misunderstanding of the time limits imposed by [⁵ Tribunal Procedure Rules]); or
(b)   that [⁵ the Upper Tribunal] or a court has taken a different view of the law from that previously understood and applied.

[⁵ (10)]
[⁵ (11)]
[⁵ (12)]

Definition
"partner" – see reg 1(2).

Amendments
1. Amended by reg 27(a) of SI 2002 No 1379 as from 20.5.02.
2. Substituted by reg 27(b) of SI 2002 No 1379 as from 20.5.02.
3. Amended by reg 27(c) of SI 2002 No 1379 as from 20.5.02.
4. Amended by reg 27(d) of SI 2002 No 1379 as from 20.5.02.
5. Amended by Sch 1 para 161 of SI 2008 No 2683 as from 3.11.08.

Analysis

Paragraph (5)

As the appeal must be delivered to the authority (see r23(1) and (2) TP(FT) Rules), the authority must first decide whether to treat a late appeal as made in time under paras (5A) to (9). If the authority does not treat the appeal as made in time (and "objects" to the First-tier Tribunal doing so: see below), then the dispute must be referred to the First-tier Tribunal: see r23(7) on p1062

If the authority grants an extension, section 4 of its submission to the First-tier Tribunal should include a statement to that effect (Code of Appeals Procedure para 2060).

Paragraphs (5A) to (9): Criteria for late appeals

These set out the criteria by reference to which an authority may "treat a late appeal as made in time in accordance with the Tribunal Procedure Rules". The reference to the Tribunal Procedure Rules is puzzling because those rules do not require a decision maker to make a positive decision to treat a late appeal as made in time. Rather r23(4) provides that where an appeal is late "it will be treated [ie, treated by the First-tier Tribunal, not the decision maker] as having been made in time if the decision maker does not object". The position therefore appears to be that even if the authority cannot treat the decision as having been made in time (ie, because the criteria in paras (6)-(9) are not satisfied), it may nevertheless force the First-tier Tribunal to do so, simply by not objecting. That interpretation is confirmed by CAP Bulletin 03/08, para 16.

Under para (5A), the authority must be satisfied that it is "in the interests of justice" before it can treat the appeal as made in time. Paras (6) to (9) qualify that test. The reference in para (6) to "paragraph (5)" is an obvious drafting error for "paragraph (5A)".

"the interests of justice". The meaning of this phrase is extensively modified by paras (6) to (9). However, once any relevant modifications made by those rules have been taken into account, it will still be necessary for the local authority or panel member to stand back and consider the overall interests of justice. Given the highly deserving nature of the "special circumstances" that need to be shown under paras (6) and (7), however, it will be a rare case where such circumstances exist and yet an extension of time is refused.

Paras (6) and (7) set up an exclusionary rule. An appellant must bring her/himself within either sub-para (a) or (b) in para (6). Effectively, this means that one of the following must be shown:

(1)   The appellant, her/his partner or a dependant has died or suffered serious illness: paras (6)(a) and (7)(a). Whether an illness is "serious" is a question of fact and degree. "Partner" is defined in reg 1(2).

(2)   The appellant is not resident in the UK: paras (6)(a) and (7)(b). On first impression, this is an odd provision in regulations dealing with benefits where, to be entitled at all, the claimant must (for HB) occupy a dwelling in Great Britain as her/his home (s130(1)(a) SSCBA) or (for CTB) is "liable to pay council tax [a tax only levied on dwellings in the UK] for a dwelling of which he is a resident" (s131(3)(a) SSCBA). It is suggested that the provision might apply to landlords who are resident abroad but in receipt of direct payments of HB or where an appellant was resident in the UK at the time of the events that gave rise to the appeal but has since become resident elsewhere. The view expressed in previous editions of this book, that the provision applies whenever the appellant is not physically present in the UK at the relevant time, cannot be correct. If that was what was intended by the regulation, it is what it would have said. Absence from the country may nevertheless amount to a special circumstance within para (6)(b), as to which see below.

(3)   Normal postal services were disrupted: paras (6)(a) and (7)(c). Strike action need not be shown; it will be sufficient if there is some delay in a decision letter or a letter of appeal reaching its destination. The caselaw on reg 19(7)(c) SSCS D&A Regs, which is in similar terms, will also be relevant here. See, in particular, the decisions of Commissioner Angus in *CIS 4901/2002* and Deputy Commissioner Poynter in *CJSA 3960/2006*. For postal delays over the Christmas period, see *R(IS) 16/04*.

(4)   There are some other special circumstances which are "wholly exceptional" and "relevant to the application": para (6)(b). "Wholly" emphasises the need for the circumstances to be unusual in nature, though not necessarily unique to the appellant. "Relevant" must simply mean that the circumstances are relevant to the question of whether it is in the interests of justice to admit the appeal. "Special circumstances" are not defined, but are likely to be interpreted in a similar way to "special reasons" under the former reg 78(3) HB Regs 1987. See the commentary to reg 9 SSCP Regs.

Once it is shown that the appellant can bring her/himself within one of the four situations above, s/he must also show that it was not practicable for the appeal to be made within the reg 18 time limit as a result of the circumstances. "Practicable" is a stiffer test than "reasonably practicable", but the phrase "as a result" does not require that the circumstances should be the sole cause of the delay, though it will have to be a substantial cause. Questions of reasonableness may well enter into consideration – eg, was it reasonable to expect an appellant to deal with an appeal even though her/his partner was in hospital? In considering such matters, it may be legitimate for the local authority or panel member to consider other deserving factors even where these do not fall within any of the categories set out above.

It is suggested that there is no rigid rule that every single day of delay after the one-month period must be explained, in the way that good cause for a late claim must be shown. All that is necessary is that the additional period of delay was broadly caused by the special circumstances on which reliance is placed. Some support for this approach can be seen in para (8).

Para (8) requires the common-sense approach that the later the appeal is, the more compelling the special circumstances must be for it to be regarded as being in the interests of justice to admit the appeal.

Para (9) requires two factors, which would otherwise be relevant, to be left out of account. First, under sub-para (a), ignorance of, or mistakes as to, the law on the part of the appellant (or, it is suggested, her/his adviser) cannot be taken into account. This includes ignorance of the time limit. The rule applies, on the face of it, irrespective of the reasonableness of the mistake. However, it is suggested that the view expressed in previous editions that it might prevent an extension of time even where the appellant's mistake arose from incorrect advice given by a local authority officer is itself mistaken. In such a case, the incorrect advice would be the cause of the delay, would amount to a special circumstance under para (6)(b) and would not be excluded from consideration under para (9).

Second, under sub-para (b), the fact that the Upper Tribunal or a court has interpreted the law in a different way than previously "understood and applied" cannot be taken into account. This aims to prevent a torrent of late appeals relying on a favourable "test case" decision of a commissioner or a court. However, "understood and applied" will cause difficulties. Understood and applied by whom? It is likely that the phrase refers to the views of the local authorities and DWP practice, though this cannot be regarded as certain. And what about cases where a provision is not being applied consistently?

The 3 November 2008 amendments (substituting the words "the Upper Tribunal" for the words "a commissioner") have the effect that where a social security commissioner (as opposed to the Upper Tribunal) has taken a different view of the law from that previously understood and applied, that can now be taken into account even though it could not have been taken into account before that date.

An appellant who is refused an extension of time by the authority should always insist that the application be referred to the tribunal under para (3).

[² **Notice of appeal**]

20.–[² (1)   A notice of appeal made in accordance with Tribunal Procedure Rules must be made on a form approved by the relevant authority, or in such other format as the relevant authority may accept, and sent or delivered to the relevant authority.]

[² (2)   Except where paragraph (3) applies, where a form does not contain the information required under Tribunal Procedure Rules the form may be returned by the relevant authority to the sender for completion in accordance with the Tribunal Procedure Rules.]

(3)   Where the relevant authority is satisfied that the form, although not completed in accordance with the instructions on it, includes sufficient information to enable the appeal [²] to proceed, it may treat the form as satisfying the requirements of [² Tribunal Procedure Rules].

(4)   Where [² a notice of appeal] is made in writing otherwise than on the approved form ("the letter"), and the letter includes sufficient information to enable the appeal [²] to proceed, the relevant authority may treat the letter as satisfying the requirements of [² Tribunal Procedure Rules].

(5)   Where the letter does not include sufficient information to enable the appeal [²] to proceed, the relevant authority may request, in writing, further particulars.

(6)   Where a person to whom a form is returned or from whom further particulars are requested duly completes and returns the form or sends the further particulars and the form or particulars, as the case may be, are received by the relevant authority within–

(a)   14 days of the date on which the form was returned to him, the time for making the appeal shall be extended by 14 days from the date on which the form was returned;

(b)   14 days of the date on which the relevant authority's request was made, the time for making the appeal shall be extended by 14 days from the date of the request;

(c)   such longer period as the relevant authority may direct, the time for making the appeal shall be extended by a period equal to that longer period directed by the relevant authority.

(7)   Where a person to whom a form is returned or from whom further particulars are requested does not complete and return the form or send further particulars within the period of time specified in paragraph (6)–

(a)   the relevant authority shall forward a copy of the form, or as the case may be, the letter, together with any other relevant documents or evidence to [² the First-tier Tribunal]; and

(b)   the [² First-tier Tribunal] shall determine whether the form or the letter satisfies the requirements of [² Tribunal Procedure Rules]

(8)   Where–

(a)   a form is duly completed and returned or further particulars are sent after the expiry of the period of time allowed in accordance with paragraph (6); and

(b)   no decision has been made under paragraph (7) at the time the form or the further particulars are received by the relevant authority,

the form or further particulars shall also be forwarded to the [² First-tier Tribunal which] shall take into account any further information or evidence set out in the form or further particulars.

(9)   The relevant authority may discontinue action on an appeal where [² the notice of appeal] has not been forwarded to the [² First-tier Tribunal] and the appellant or an authorised representative of the appellant has given written notice that the appellant does not wish the appeal to continue.

Amendments

1.   Deleted by Sch 2 para 8(e) of SI 2002 No 1703 as from 30.9.02.
2.   Amended by Sch 1 para 162 of SI 2008 No 2683 as from 3.11.08.

General Note

Reg 20 contains the rules for making appeals. The requirements for a valid appeal are found in para (1). Where an appeal does not meet the requirements or does not contain sufficient information, paras (2) to (8) allow an authority to give an appellant an opportunity to put things right. It is important to note that although a local authority can treat an appeal as validly made under paras (3) and (4), only the First-tier Tribunal can reject an appeal as invalidly made: para (7)(b).

There is no provision in the regulations for dealing with the process by which local authorities refer appeals to the Tribunals Service where a tribunal member is required to rule on the validity of an appeal under paras (7) and (8). In particular, there is no time limit within which this is required to be done. However, the Local Government Ombudsman has made it clear in *Complaint No 01/C/13400 against Scarborough BC* that authorities should aim to refer all appeals to the Tribunals Service within 28 days. The power to revise a decision under reg 4(1)(c) is still available to authorities after an appeal has been referred to the Tribunals Service, until such time as the appeal has been determined.

In *CH 3497/2005*, there had been serious delay in the local authority's referral of a claimant's appeals to the Appeals Service (now the Tribunals Service). Deputy Commissioner Mark pointed out that under Article 6 of the European Convention on Human Rights, a claimant is entitled to have her/his appeal heard within a reasonable time by an appeal tribunal and that this could be particularly important in HB appeals, where delay could cost claimants their homes. Under s6(1) HRA 1998, it is unlawful for a public authority to act in a way which is incompatible with a Convention right. By s6(6), "an act" includes a failure to act – eg, a failure to refer an appeal to the Tribunals Service in a reasonable time. The deputy commissioner said at para 6 of his decision:

> "In any event, it is wholly unacceptable to the proper operation of the system of appeals in housing benefit and council tax benefit appeals that delays of this sort should occur. If a local authority receives an appeal, it must be processed promptly and passed to the Appeals Service without delay. This applies also in cases where there is an issue which requires to be dealt with by a legally qualified panel member under regulation 20(7) or (8) of the 2001 Regulations."

What if a local authority does not refer an appeal to the Tribunals Service? In *R(H) 1/07* Commissioner Jacobs considered whether, in such a case, a tribunal has power to deal with the appeal until it is referred. The local authority argued that where an appeal is not referred to the Tribunals Service, the claimant had to apply for judicial review of the local authority's failure or refusal to refer. The commissioner disagreed. He said that the usual principle is exclusivity of jurisdiction; if an issue is allocated to a judicial body, only that body has jurisdiction over it. A tribunal has power to determine whether it has jurisdiction and any challenge should be by appeal to the commissioners and from them to the Court of Appeal. Reg 20 does not deal with a challenge by the local authority to the tribunal's jurisdiction. However, its structure is relevant to whether a tribunal can deal with an appeal when it has not been referred to it by the local authority. The commissioner said:

> "31. . . .
>
> First, so long as regulation 20(1) is satisfied, the appeal tribunal has jurisdiction. Second, the only role of the local authority is to receive the appeal documents and to ensure, as far as it can, that they contain the necessary information. It has no power to decide whether the information provided is sufficient. That is for the legally qualified panel member and there is an express duty to refer the issue to that member. The local authority's function is essentially administrative.
>
> 33.   If the appeal were lodged with the tribunal, there would be no problem. However, as the appeal is lodged elsewhere, there has to be a procedure by which it comes to the notice of the clerk or the tribunal. It is possible for legislation expressly to provide for an appeal that is lodged with one body to

be referred to the tribunal. In the case of housing benefit, there is no express provision. The referral is but one of the many necessary administrative steps that have to be taken to bring a case before a tribunal. Others include the notification of sittings to the members of a tribunal and the photocopying and sending of the papers to the members. Most of these tasks are not spelt out in the legislation. They are assumed as necessary to allow the statutory powers and duties of the tribunal to operate. In legal terms, that assumption takes effect by implication, either as a general duty and power or as a series of specific duties and powers. It is not rational to interpret the legislation as making the tribunal's jurisdiction depend on a particular exercise of these administrative tasks. That would be incompatible with their function, which is to ensure that the tribunal established by the legislation can discharge its statutory function and do so efficiently and effectively. They are supportive not jurisdictional.

34.   In other words, an administrative task need not be performed by a particular person or in a particular way. So long as there is an appeal that satisfies the conditions of regulation 20(1), the tribunal has jurisdiction to deal with any issues that arise in respect of it, regardless of how they are brought to the tribunal's attention. This does not mean that the parties are free to disregard the usual procedures at will. Claimants cannot simply bypass the local authority and lodge appeals with the tribunal. Likewise, they cannot usually expect the tribunal to deal with a case before the local authority has had a chance to prepare the submission and assemble the papers for the parties and the tribunal. But what the tribunal is free to do is to allow matters to be handled differently if circumstances require it. The circumstances of this case did require it for two reasons. First, the local authority was refusing to refer the cases to the tribunal on the basis of an issue which the tribunal had (perhaps exclusive) jurisdiction to decide. Second, the local authority was trying to force the claimant to embark on an expensive legal procedure, which was risky in that the Administrative Court might not accept jurisdiction."

Analysis

Para (1). To be valid, the appeal must be made in writing, either on a form approved by the authority or "in such other format as the . . . authority may accept". It must be sent or delivered to the authority (see also r23(1) TP(FT) Rules on p1062).

Paras (2) and (3) apply where the appeal has been made on the approved form. If that form has not been completed in accordance with the instructions on it, then under para (3), the authority may nevertheless treat it as satisfying the requirements of the Tribunal Procedure Rules (ie, r23(6)) if it is satisfied that it "includes sufficient information to enable the appeal to proceed". Otherwise, para (2) applies and the authority "may" – which, in practice, means "must" – return the form to the sender "for completion in accordance with the Tribunal Procedure Rules". It is implicit in the difference in wording between the two paragraphs (ie, "does not contain the information required by the Tribunal Procedure Rules" and "not completed in accordance with the instructions on it") that the authority may not reject a form that contains the information required by the Rules even if (as is all too common) it has drafted its approved form so that the instructions on it require additional information. A form that complies with r23(6) will inevitably include sufficient information to enable the appeal to proceed.

Paras (4) and (5) apply where the appellant has appealed in writing but has not used the approved form. Where the letter of appeal includes sufficient information, the authority may – and, again, this means "must" – treat it as satisfying the Tribunal Procedure Rules under para (4). Where it does not include sufficient information, the authority should request "further particulars" under para (5). The further particulars an authority requires should be clearly set out in a letter to the appellant.

Paras (6)-(8). If the form is returned for completion or the further particulars are sought, an extension of time for appealing of 14 days is automatically conferred if the completed form or further particulars are received back by the authority within 14 days. An authority may grant a longer period, which then allows an equivalent extension of time: sub-para (c). This need not be done at the same time that the form is returned or particulars sought and it is suggested that it may be done after the 14-day period has expired.

If the authority's request is not complied with, it is required under para (7) to send all relevant documentation to the First-tier Tribunal, which will then decide whether the appeal has been validly made. If the completed form or further particulars are received by the authority after the time limit has expired, they must be sent to the First-tier Tribunal under para (8) for consideration. Any further details provided must be taken into account. If the First-tier Tribunal refuses to admit the appeal, it remains to be decided whether there is a further right of appeal to the Upper Tribunal: see the commentary on s11 TCEA 2007 on p176.

Para (9). If an appeal has not yet been passed to the First-tier Tribunal, an authority is absolved from taking action on it where it is withdrawn by a notice in writing. An "authorised representative" can withdraw an appeal on behalf of an appellant. A representative is only "authorised" where there is a validly given authorisation to act on behalf of the person affected. If an appeal is withdrawn but subsequently a second appeal on the same or similar grounds is made within the time limit, there seems to be no reason why the withdrawal of the first appeal affects the validity of the second appeal.

An appeal that has been passed to the First-tier Tribunal can be withdrawn under r17 TP(FT) Rules.

Death of a party to an appeal

21.–(1)   In any proceedings, on the death of a party to those proceedings, the relevant authority may appoint such person as it thinks fit to proceed with the appeal in the place of the deceased.

(2)   A grant of probate, confirmation or letters of administration in respect of the deceased, whenever taken out, shall have no effect on an appointment made under paragraph (1).

(3)   Where a person appointed under paragraph (1) has, prior to the date of such appointment, taken any action in relation to the appeal on behalf of the deceased, the effective date of appointment shall be treated as the day immediately prior to the first day on which such action was taken.

[¹ (4)   For the purposes of this regulation only, ''appeal'' means an appeal to an appeal tribunal, a Commissioner or a court.]

Amendment

1.   Inserted by reg 4(3) of SI 2008 No 2667 as from 30.10.08.

Analysis

Where an appellant dies in the course of an appeal to a tribunal, the local authority has power to appoint another person to act in her/his place. If, following reasonable enquiries, no one is available to be appointed then the appeal will abate (see below).

Unfortunately, reg 21 is unclear in parts and, where it is clear, it is less helpful than would be desirable. To understand the problems, it is necessary to go back a stage to the claim for benefit and the authority's decision on that claim. It is not possible for a new claim for HB or CTB to be made on behalf of someone who is dead (see, by analogy, *R(IS) 3/04*: reg 30 Social Security (Claims and Payments) Regulations 1987, and in particular, reg 30(5), probably does not extend to HB or CTB). But if a claimant dies after having made a claim, it is possible for the authority to pay any benefit due to her/his personal representative or next of kin under reg 97 HB Regs, reg 78 HB (SPC) Regs, reg 80 CTB Regs and reg 65 CTB (SPC) Regs. Unfortunately, those regulations contain no provision equivalent to reg 30(1) Social Security (Claims and Payments) Regulations 1987, which allows the Secretary of State to appoint a person "to proceed with the claim" of someone who has died.

This probably does not matter too much in a case where the authority needs further information before it is able to reach a decision. The personal representative or next of kin cannot be compelled to produce the necessary information (because, at this stage s/he is neither a "person who makes a claim" or "a person to whom . . . benefit has been awarded" for the purposes of reg 86 HB Regs etc or a "person by whom . . . . sums payable by way of . . . benefit are receivable" for the purposes of reg 88 HB Regs etc). But if s/he does not do so, the authority will take a decision on the basis of the information it does have. That decision will inevitably be to refuse the claim on the basis that the claimant has not established entitlement.

It does, however, matter where the personal representative or next of kin wishes to appeal against the authority's decision. Reg 97 HB Regs etc does not expressly give them standing to appeal and reg 21 does not assist because the opening words "In any proceedings" and the phrase "*proceed* with the appeal" (emphasis added) show that an appeal must already exist before the power of appointment can be exercised. It might be possible for the personal representative or next of kin to make an appeal even though s/he had no standing to do so, seek appointment under para (1) and then rely on para (3) to validate the appeal retrospectively but such a solution would be unsatisfactory because of the circularity involved: the appeal would not become valid until the appointment was made and the appointment could not be made in the absence of a valid appeal.

It is suggested that the answer is for the personal representative or next of kin to make the appeal as a person affected *in her/his own right* rather than as representing the deceased. Although not listed as a person affected in reg 3(1), *CH 3817/2004* holds that that list is not exhaustive and that other people may show that they are a person affected in the ordinary meaning of that term. The personal representative or next of kin would appear to satisfy reg 3(2) by virtue of the fact that any benefit awarded would be payable to her/him under reg 97 HB Regs etc.

Even once that hurdle is surmounted, there are still problems with reg 21. As noted by Commissioner Levenson in *CH 3631/2007* (at para 13):

(1)   It is unclear whether the authority's power to appoint "such person as it thinks fit" includes the power to appoint someone who does not consent to be appointed and may refuse to act under the appointment.

(2)   It is also unclear whether a power to appoint a person "to proceed with the appeal" includes a power to appoint someone to act as respondent to an appeal brought by the local authority.

However, the previous question is academic because such a situation could only arise on an appeal to the Upper Tribunal (local authorities having no right of appeal to the First-tier Tribunal against their own decisions) and *CH 3631/2007* held that reg 21 did not apply to appeals to the commissioner because the word "appeal" in the phrase "proceed with the appeal" was defined by reg 1(2) as meaning "an appeal to an appeal tribunal". Since 3

November 2008, that definition has changed and "appeal" now means "an appeal to the First-tier Tribunal". Therefore, by the same reasoning, reg 21 does not apply to appeals to the Upper Tribunal.

In *CH 3631/2007* (a case concerning the recovery of an overpayment), the commissioner held, following *R(IS) 6/01*, that the estate of a deceased claimant is not itself a legal person and cannot be a party to an appeal. In the absence of a grant of probate or letters of administration, there was no one with power to represent the estate before the commissioner and the appeal to the commissioner therefore abated. Although the commissioner's reasoning about the status of the deceased's estate is uncontroversial, the conclusion that the appeal must therefore abate may require further consideration. The authorities relied on by the commissioner at paras 14 and 15 are all cases in which the appeal abated on the death of the *appellant* and *R(SB) 25/84* states expressly that abatement is not appropriate where the deceased is the respondent to the appeal and the appellant is not willing to withdraw it. However, as abatement does not bring the appeal permanently to an end but merely suspends it, leaving open the possibility that it will be revived in the future (eg, by a grant of probate or letters of administration – see *R(I) 7/62* and *R(I) 2/83*), it may be that nothing turns on what procedure is followed.

Local authorities who wish to recover overpayments from unrepresented estates may consider applying for a grant of limited representation under s116 Supreme Court Act 1981 – see *R(IS) 6/01* (para 38).

Part V
Appeal Tribunals

[² Composition of appeal tribunals
22.]

Amendments

1. Omitted by reg 3(2) of SI 2004 No 3368 as from 21.12.04.
2. Omitted by Sch 1 para 163 of SI 2008 No 2683 as from 3.11.08.

[⁵ Procedure in connection with appeals
23.]

Amendments

1. Amended by reg 28 of SI 2002 No 1379 as from 20.5.02.
2. Amended by reg 3(3) of SI 2004 No 3368 as from 21.12.04.
3. Amended by reg 3(4) of SI 2005 No 337 as from 18.3.05.
4. Substituted by reg 9(3) of SI 2005 No 2878 as from 5.12.05.
5. Omitted by Sch 1 para 163 of SI 2008 No 2683 as from 3.11.08.

Schedule
Decisions Against Which No Appeal Lies

General Note

The Schedule, made under reg 16, sets out the categories of decisions which would otherwise fall within the right of appeal but which cannot be subject to an appeal to a tribunal. See the commentary to reg 16 (see p1036) and Sch 7 para 6(1) CSPSSA (see p145) for discussion of the types of decisions that can be appealed.

Note that certain exclusions of the right of appeal may infringe Art 6 of the European Convention on Human Rights: see *R(IS) 6/04*, discussed in the commentary to Art 6 on p125.

1. No appeal shall lie against a decision made by virtue of, or as a consequence of, any of the provisions in Part X (claims), Part XII (payments) and Part XIII (overpayments) of the Housing Benefit Regulations except a decision under–

[² (a) regulations 83 (time and manner in which claims are to be made), 84(1) and 85(1) and (4) (date of claim);

(b) regulation 93(3) (adjustments to payments to take account of underpayment or overpayment on account of rent allowance);

(c) regulation 95 (circumstances in which payment is to be made to a landlord);

(d) regulation 96 (circumstances in which payment may be made to a landlord);

(e) regulation 100 (recoverable overpayments);

(f) regulation 101 (person from whom recovery may be sought);

(g) regulation 103 (diminution of capital); or

(h) regulation 104 (sums to be deducted in calculating recoverable overpayments).]

Amendments

1. Substituted by reg 3(4)(a) of SI 2004 No 3368 as from 21.12.04.

2.   Substituted by reg 5 and para 17(3) of SI 2006 No 217 as from 6.3.06.

[¹**1A.** No appeal shall lie against a decision made by virtue of, or as a consequence of, any of the provisions in Part 9 (claims), Part 11 (payments) and Part 12 (overpayments) of the Housing Benefit (State Pension Credit) Regulations except a decision under–

(a)   regulations 64 (time and manner in which claims are to be made), 65(1) and 66(1) and (4) (date of claim);

(b)   regulation 74(3) (adjustments to payments to take account of underpayment or overpayment on account of rent allowance);

(c)   regulation 76 (circumstances in which payment is to be made to a landlord);

(d)   regulation 77 (circumstances in which payment may be made to a landlord);

(e)   regulation 81 (recoverable overpayments);

(f)   regulation 84 (diminution of capital); or

(g)   regulation 85 (sums to be deducted in calculating recoverable overpayments).]

Amendment

1.   Inserted by reg 5 and sch 2 para 17(3)(e)(ii) of SI 2006 No 217 as from 6.3.06.

2.   No appeal shall lie against a decision made by virtue of, or as a consequence of, any of the provisions in Part VIII (claims), Part X (awards or payments of benefit) and Part XI (excess benefit) of the Council Tax Benefit Regulations except a decision under–

[² (a)   regulations 69 (time and manner in which claims are to be made), 69(1) and 70(1) and (4) (date of claim);

(b)   regulation 83 (recoverable excess benefit);

(c)   regulation 85 (persons from whom recovery may be sought);

(d)   regulation 88 (diminution of capital); or

(e)   regulation 89 (sums to be deducted in calculating recoverable excess benefit).]

Amendments

1.   Substituted by reg 3(4)(b) of SI 2004 No 3368 as from 21.12.04.

2.   Substituted by reg 5 and Sch 2 para 17(3)(e) of SI 2006 No 217 as from 6.3.06

[¹**2A.** No appeal shall lie against a decision made by virtue of, or as a consequence of, any of the provisions in Part 7 (claims), Part 9 (awards or payments of benefit) and Part 10 (excess benefit) of the Council Tax Benefit (State Pension Credit) Regulations except a decision under–

(a)   regulations 53 (time and manner in which claims are to be made), 54(1) and 55(1) and (4) (date of claim);

(b)   regulation 68 (recoverable excess benefit);

(c)   regulation 70 (persons from whom recovery may be sought);

(d)   regulation 73 (diminution of capital); or

(e)   regulation 74 (sums to be deducted in calculating recoverable excess benefit).]

Amendment

1.   Inserted by reg 5 and Sch 2 para 17(3)(e)(iv) of SI 2006 No 217 as from 6.3.06.

Analysis

Paras 1, 1A, 2 and 2A effectively reverse the presumption that an appeal lies against any "decision" not within the scope of the Schedule and provide that in relation to decisions on claims, payments and overpayment, an appeal only lies against the decisions listed. They are:

(1)   A decision as to the time and manner in which a claim was made and the date on which a claim was made.

(2)   A decision as to whether a claim should be backdated for good cause.

(3)   A decision to make, or not to make, adjustments to ongoing payments of HB to reflect underpayments or overpayments made where payments on account under reg 93(3) HB Regs or 74(3) HB(SPC) Regs are made.

(4)   A decision as to whether direct payments of HB should be made to a landlord. This includes decisions on whether a landlord is a "fit and proper person" to receive direct payments.

(5)   A decision as to whether an overpayment is recoverable, and if so how much is recoverable.

(6)   A decision as to from whom an overpayment is recoverable. See also the commentary to para 3.

(7)   A decision as to the amount of a recoverable overpayment taking into account the diminishing capital rule and the rules in reg 104 HB Regs, reg 85 HB(SPC) Regs, reg 89 CTB Regs or reg 74 CTB(SPC) Regs.

3.   Subject to paragraphs 1(f) and 2(c), no appeal shall lie against a decision as to the exercise of discretion to recover an overpayment of housing benefit or, as the case may be, excess council tax benefit.

Analysis

Whatever the correctness of the Court of Appeal's decision in *Secretary of State for Work and Pensions v Chiltern District Council* [2003] EWCA Civ 508 (reported as *R(H) 2/03*) and the tribunal of commissioner's decision in *R(H) 3/04* in respect of the regime in place prior to October 2001 (and the correctness of the Court of Appeal's decision is strongly doubted in *R(H) 6/06*), the tribunal of commissioner's decision in *R(H) 6/06* holds that rights of appeal only attach to decisions going to the recoverability of an overpayment and do not attach to decisions concerning the recovery (or enforcement) of such recoverable overpayment decisions. As the tribunal of commissioners said:

"under the legislation in force from 1 October 2001 to 9 April 2006, an overpayment of housing benefit is always recoverable from any person within the scope of reg 101(2) as well as, if different, the person to whom the overpayment was made, except where reg 101(1) applies in which case it is recoverable only from any person within the scope of reg 101(2). No non-justiciable issues fall within the scope of the right of appeal and so there is no longer any need to apply *R(H) 3/04* and construe that right as being limited to points of law."

So the only appealable point (apart from whether there has in fact been an overpayment and whether it is recoverable) under s75(3) of the SSAA 1992 and reg 101 HB Regs is whether the person does in fact fall within reg 101. Once that point has been finally decided, *R(H) 6/06* makes it clear that no appeal right attaches to the enforcement decision of the local authority as to from whom the recoverable overpayment should actually be recovered.

4. No appeal shall lie against a decision of a relevant authority under paragraph 16(3)(a) or (b) and (4) of Schedule 7 to the Act (decisions involving issues that arise on appeal in other cases).

Analysis

Sch 7 para 16(3) CSPSSA and reg 15 of these regulations permit an authority to postpone a decision pending a decision in a "test case", while giving it a discretion to issue a decision in certain cases. Para 4 confirms that there is no appeal against a decision to issue, or not to issue, a decision. The only remedy is judicial review.

5. No appeal shall lie against a decision under Part III of these Regulations of a relevant authority relating to—

(a) suspension of a payment of benefit or of a reduction; or

(b) restoration following a suspension of payment of benefit or of a reduction,

except a decision that entitlement to benefit is terminated under regulation 14.

Analysis

There is no appeal against a decision to suspend or restore benefit under Pt III of these regulations. There is, however, an appeal against a termination of benefit under reg 14: see *R(H) 4/08*.

[¹**6.** No appeal shall lie against the calculation or estimate of the claimant's, or the claimant's partner's, income or capital used by a relevant authority in accordance with [² regulation 27(1) of the Housing Benefit (State Pension Credit) Regulations or regulation 17(1) of the Council Tax Benefit (State Pension Credit) Regulations] (calculation of claimant's income in savings credit only cases), as modified, in both cases, by the Housing Benefit and Council Tax Benefit (State Pension Credit) Regulations 2003.]

Amendments

1. Inserted by reg 3 of SI 2003 No 1581 as from 18.6.03.
2. Amended by reg 5 and sch 2 para 17(3)(e) of SI 2006 No 217 as from 6.3.06.

Analysis

Reg 27(1) HB(SPC) Regs and 17(1) CTB(SPC) Regs provide for local authorities to use the calculation or estimate of a claimant's (or her/his partner's) income and capital provided by the DWP (known as the "assessed income figure") where there is entitlement to the "savings credit" of pension credit only. There is no appeal against the local authority use of the DWP calculation or estimate of income and capital. An appeal would need to be made against the DWP income/capital decision instead.

Note that if the local authority modifies the "assessed income figure" under reg 27(4) HB(SPC) Regs or reg 17(4) CTB(SPC) Regs as the case may be, there *is* a right of appeal against the modification. There is therefore a potential for appeals against both the income/capital decision made by the DWP and the modification decision made by the local authority. It is suggested that it would be good practice to deal with both appeals together and that the former appeal should be dealt with first.

If a claimant wrongly lodges an appeal against the DWP income/capital decision with the local authority, the DWP's *Housing Benefit and Council Tax Benefit Pension Credit Handbook* (at Part 1 para 1103) reminds a local authority what it should do. The local authority should advise the claimant to lodge an appeal with the DWP. It should also advise the claimant that the appeal lodged with the local authority will be processed as "out of jurisdiction" (see regs 1(3) and 46 SSCS D&A Regs). The guidance rightly suggests that if the situation is ambiguous, claimants should be advised to consider lodging an appeal with the DWP as well as with the local authority.

The Tribunal Procedure (First-tier Tribunal) (Social Entitlement Chamber) Rules 2008
2008 No. 2685 (L. 13)

PART 1

Introduction

1.   Citation, commencement, application and interpretation
2.   Overriding objective and parties' obligation to co-operate with the Tribunal
3.   Alternative dispute resolution and arbitration

PART 2

4.   Delegation to staff
5.   Case management powers
6.   Procedure for applying for and giving directions
7.   Failure to comply with rules etc.
8.   Striking out a party's case
9.   Substitution and addition of parties
10.   No power to award costs
11.   Representatives
12.   Calculating time
13.   Sending and delivery of documents
14.   Use of documents and information
15.   Evidence and submissions
16.   Summoning or citation of witnesses and orders to answer questions or produce documents
17.   Withdrawal
18.   Lead cases
19.   Confidentiality in child support or child trust fund cases
21.   *Expenses in social security and child support cases*

PART 3
Proceedings before the Tribunal
CHAPTER 1
Before the hearing
23.   Cases in which the notice of appeal is to be sent to the decision maker
24.   Responses and replies

CHAPTER 2
Hearings
27.   Decision with or without a hearing
28.   Entitlement to attend a hearing
29.   Notice of hearings
30.   Public and private hearings
31.   Hearings in a party's absence

CHAPTER 3
Decisions
32.   Consent orders
33.   Notice of decisions
34.   Reasons for decisions

PART 4
Correcting, setting aside, reviewing and appealing Tribunal decisions
35.   Interpretation

36.   Clerical mistakes and accidental slips or omissions
37.   Setting aside a decision which disposes of proceedings
38.   Application for permission to appeal
39.   Tribunal's consideration of application for permission to appeal
40.   Review of a decision
41.   Power to treat an application as a different type of application

SCHEDULE 1
Time limits for providing notices of appeal to the decision maker

PART 1
Introduction

General Note on TP(FT) Rules

Each chamber of the First-tier Tribunal has its own procedural rules. These rules govern all appeals assigned to the Social Entitlement Chamber and, therefore, HB and CTB appeals.

In addition to social security appeals, the Social Entitlement Chamber deals with appeals relating to child support, vaccine damage payments, national insurance credits, industrial accident declarations, asylum support, criminal injuries compensation, diffuse mesothelioma payments and decisions in relation to NHS charges. Where a rule applies solely to one of those other jurisdictions, it has been omitted for reasons of space. However, there may be other rules which, while technically applicable to HB/CTB appeals, are designed for use in one or more of the other jurisdictions and are best understood in that context.

The rules are made by the Tribunal Procedure Committee, which is constituted by s22 and Sch 5 TCEA 2007. One of the major benefits of the November 2008 reforms is that procedural rules are now made by an independent body with a majority of judicial members, rather than by the Secretary of State for Work and Pensions who, through the subsidy system, is responsible for paying any HB/CTB that may be awarded as a result of a successful appeal. However, under Sch 5 para 28 (not reproduced in this book) the rules must be submitted to the Lord Chancellor who may allow or disallow them. The Lord Chancellor also has power to require the Committee to make rules to achieve a specified purpose (Sch 5 para 29). There is therefore scope for the DWP (and other government departments) to influence the content of the rules by making representations to the Lord Chancellor (who, since the Constitutional Reform Act 2005, is a government minister and no longer the head of the judiciary). One may speculate that certain aspects of the Rules, notably the requirement in r23 that social security appeals should be made to the decision maker rather than the First-tier Tribunal itself and the absence of any meaningful time limit for the decision maker to respond to the appeal once it has been received (r24(1)(b)), reflect such influence.

Citation, commencement, application and interpretation

1.–(1)   These Rules may be cited as the Tribunal Procedure (First-tier Tribunal) (Social Entitlement Chamber) Rules 2008 and come into force on 3rd November 2008.

[² (2)   These Rules apply to proceedings before the the Social Entitlement Chamber of the First-tier Tribunal.]

(3)   In these Rules–

"the 2007 Act" means the Tribunals, Courts and Enforcement Act 2007;

"appeal" includes an application under section 19(9) of the Tax Credits Act 2002;

"appellant" means a person who makes an appeal to the Tribunal, or a person substituted as an appellant under rule 9(1) (substitution of parties);

"decision maker" means the maker of a decision against which an appeal has been brought;

"dispose of proceedings" includes, unless indicated otherwise, disposing of a part of the proceedings;

"document" means anything in which information is recorded in any form, and an obligation under these Rules to provide or allow access to a document or a copy of a document for any purpose means, unless the Tribunal directs otherwise, an obligation to provide or allow access to such document or copy in a legible form or in a form which can be readily made into a legible form;

"hearing" means an oral hearing and includes a hearing conducted in whole or in part by video link, telephone or other means of instantaneous two-way electronic communication;

''legal representative'' means [¹ a person who, for the purposes of the Legal Services Act 2007, is an authorised person in relation to an activity which constitutes the exercise of a right of audience or the conduct of litigation within the meaning of that Act], an advocate or solicitor in Scotland or a barrister or solicitor in Northern Ireland;

''party'' means–
(a)   a person who is an appellant or respondent in proceedings before the Tribunal;
(b)-(c) *[Omitted]*
(d)   if the proceedings have been concluded, a person who was a party under paragraph (a), (b) or (c) when the Tribunal finally disposed of all issues in the proceedings;

''practice direction'' means a direction given under section 23 of the 2007 Act;

''respondent'' means–
(a)   in an appeal against a decision, the decision maker and any person other than the appellant who had a right of appeal against the decision;
(b)-(c) *[Omitted]*
(d)   a person substituted or added as a respondent under rule 9 (substitution and addition of parties);

''Social Entitlement Chamber'' means the Social Entitlement Chamber of the First-tier Tribunal established by the First-tier Tribunal and Upper Tribunal (Chambers) Order 2008;

''social security and child support case'' means any case allocated to the Social Entitlement Chamber except an asylum support case or a criminal injuries compensation case;

''Tribunal'' means the First-tier Tribunal.

Amendments

1.   Amended by r3 of SI 2010 No 43 as from 18.1.10.
2.   Substituted by r5(2) of SI 2010 No 2653 as from 29.11.10.

General Note

Rule 1 defines words and phrases that are used elsewhere in the Rules. Where appropriate, an analysis of those definitions will be given in the commentary to the individual rules.

Overriding objective and parties' obligation to co-operate with the Tribunal

2.–(1)   The overriding objective of these Rules is to enable the Tribunal to deal with cases fairly and justly.
(2)   Dealing with a case fairly and justly includes–
(a)   dealing with the case in ways which are proportionate to the importance of the case, the complexity of the issues, the anticipated costs and the resources of the parties;
(b)   avoiding unnecessary formality and seeking flexibility in the proceedings;
(c)   ensuring, so far as practicable, that the parties are able to participate fully in the proceedings;
(d)   using any special expertise of the Tribunal effectively; and
(e)   avoiding delay, so far as compatible with proper consideration of the issues.
(3)   The Tribunal must seek to give effect to the overriding objective when it–
(a)   exercises any power under these Rules; or
(b)   interprets any rule or practice direction.
(4)   Parties must–
(a)   help the Tribunal to further the overriding objective; and
(b)   co-operate with the Tribunal generally.

General Note

The overriding objective of the rules is that the First-tier Tribunal should deal with appeals "fairly and justly": para (1). Under para (3), the tribunal must seek to give effect to that objective when it exercises any power conferred by the Rules or interprets any rule or practice direction.

"Fairly and justly" is probably best regarded as a composite phrase that does not gain from being broken down into its individual words – "just and equitable" in relation to child support variations would be another example. However, if further analysis is required it is tentatively suggested that "fairly" requires the tribunal to adopt a fair procedure and "justly" to achieve the correct outcome in accordance with the law. A "just" outcome is, of course, far more likely if a "fair" procedure is followed.

The overriding objective was considered by the Upper Tribunal in *MA v SSWP* [2009] UKUT 211 (AAC), a case concerning the refusal of an adjournment. Judge Jacobs confirmed (para 10) that the principles listed in rule 2(2) are "illustrative, not comprehensive". He continued:

"11.   It is unlikely that these principles will dictate the decision for the tribunal. In the majority of cases, there will be factors pointing both for and against a proposed adjournment. The nature of the decision is likely to require the tribunal to undertake a balancing exercise between competing considerations. And it is the nature of such an exercise that different tribunals might properly make different assessments of the factors. On appeal, the Upper Tribunal will not find an error of law simply because it would have made a different assessment. . .

12.   The introduction of the overriding objective into the rules of procedure governing social security cases frees tribunals from the binding effect of previous authorities. They may continue to be relevant, but only to the extent that their principles are compatible with the overriding objective (*Albon (trading as NA Carriage Co) v Naza Motor Trading Sdn Bhd (No 5)* [2008] 1 WLR 2380 at [18])."

Para (2) contains a non-exhaustive list of the factors that are included in dealing with a case fairly and justly. They are largely self-explanatory and, as the tribunal is required to have regard to them by virtue of para (3), appellants, their representatives and presenting officers will be well advised to address them in any submission about how the tribunal should exercise its case management powers.

Some of the factors are similar to those in the list in r1.1 Civil Procedure Rules (CPR) 1998. However, the overriding objective in the civil courts is differently worded ("justly" rather than "fairly and justly") and the two lists are not identical. Caution must therefore be exercised when applying authorities relating to the overriding objective under the CPR to the First-tier Tribunal. In particular, para (2) (unlike r1.1(2)(e) CPR) does not oblige the tribunal to allot a share of the tribunal's resources to an appeal, while taking into account the need to allot resources to other cases.

There is, however, one way in which comparison with the CPR is instructive. Rule 1.1(2)(c)(i) and (ii) CPR mentions both "the amount of money involved" and "the importance of the case" as factors to be taken into account when deciding what is proportionate. It is to be inferred that "the importance of the case" and "the amount of money involved" are not the same thing.

Para (2)(a) while directing the tribunal to have regard to (among other things) "the importance of the case" makes no mention of "the amount of money involved". This is significant for social security appeals, including those relating to HB/CTB. Such appeals can involve large amounts of money – often so large that the County Court would not have jurisdiction over a civil dispute of the same size without the consent of the parties. In other cases, however, the amount of money involved is so small that the expense of holding a hearing to decide the appeal will inevitably exceed the potential benefit to the claimant. If the amount of money involved were a relevant factor, it might be argued that considering the appeal at all – or at any rate devoting any significant resources to it – was disproportionate. However, as it is not a relevant factor, there is no scope for such an argument. Claimants have a statutory right of appeal even in the smallest cases and it is the First-tier Tribunal's duty to decide such appeals in accordance with the law. To take any other approach would be to give decision makers carte blanche to make wrong decisions whenever the sum of money at stake was small and thus would ultimately undermine the rule of law.

The comparison between para (2)(a) and r1.1(2)(c)(i) and (ii) CPR also raises the question of what is meant by "the importance of the case" if it is not related to the amount of money involved. It is suggested that the case is important if it involves a point of law of general application (particularly if it has been selected as a lead case under r18). Any other interpretation inevitably raises the question, "Important to whom?" And answering that question will almost inevitably force the tribunal to consider the amount of money involved. An appeal involving, say, an alleged HB overpayment of £100 is likely to be more important to a single claimant under 25 with a JSA entitlement of £50.95 a week than it is to an authority with a budget of millions of pounds. However, it has already been established that the amount of money involved is a separate factor and one that is not relevant under para (2)(a).

The parties to an appeal have always been under an obligation to obey directions given by a tribunal: see, for example, *Davies v Child Support Commissioner and Child Support Agency* [2008] EWHC 334 (Admin), QBD, (Black J), in which (at paras 11-14) a refusal by the Secretary of State for Work and Pensions to obey a direction to give disclosure of a CSA file was formally declared to be irrational. However, that obligation is now spelled out in para (4). The parties must help the tribunal to further the overriding objective and co-operate with the tribunal generally. A failure to comply with directions can lead to the appeal (or part of it) being struck out or, in the case of a failure by a respondent, to her/his being barred from taking further part in the proceedings (r8). A failure to co-operate can lead to a strike out or a barring order even if no directions have been disobeyed, if that failure has the effect that the tribunal cannot deal with the proceedings fairly and justly (r8(3)(b) and (7)).

The parties' duty to co-operate with the tribunal generally involves "ensuring as far as possible that their case is ready by the time of the hearing" (see *MA v SSWP* above).

In *RF v CMEC (CSM)* [2010] UKUT 41 (AAC), the Upper Tribunal considered how the duty to co-operate affected the obligation on respondents to arrange for a presenting officer to attend a hearing when directed to do so. The judge stated:

"12.   The appeal tribunal directed that a presenting officer attend. . . . One was not sent. That was wrong. The tribunal had given a direction and the parties were under a duty to obey it. That duty is now incorporated into the duty on all parties 'to co-operate with the Tribunal generally' . . . . They do so by complying with the direction. If a party is unable to comply or finds it difficult to do so, the proper course is to apply under rule 6(5) for the tribunal to amend, suspend and set aside its direction. A party is not entitled to disregard a direction."

Alternative dispute resolution and arbitration

3.–(1)   The Tribunal should seek, where appropriate–

(a)   to bring to the attention of the parties the availability of any appropriate alternative procedure for the resolution of the dispute; and

(b)   if the parties wish and provided that it is compatible with the overriding objective, to facilitate the use of the procedure.

(2)   Part 1 of the Arbitration Act 1996 does not apply to proceedings before the Tribunal.

General Note

At present, r3 is easy to apply to HB/CTB. There is no alternative dispute resolution (ADR) procedure for HB/CTB appeals and therefore the tribunal cannot bring the parties' attention to such a procedure. Rule 3 does, however, raise issues about the possible role of ADR in the social security decision making and appeals system. It is suggested that the scope for any such role is limited. To begin with tribunals are themselves a form of ADR. The average HB/CTB appeal is dealt with in a single hearing lasting about 50 minutes and held within three or four months of the appeal being submitted to the Tribunals Service. It is unlikely that a civil court would be able to deal with the same issues in so short a time and with such a relatively short delay. Moreover, generalist judges in the civil courts would be unlikely to possess the specialist knowledge that allows tribunals to adopt an enabling role, thereby reducing the need for representation.

Diverting the appeal into ADR risks taking up a disproportionate amount of the time of a tribunal judge (which could be used simply to decide the appeal at a hearing) and if ADR is unsuccessful, it will have added to the delay. There is no reason to suppose that there will be an improved outcome to the appeal in return for those disadvantages.

In addition, while ADR (and, in particular, mediation) may be a useful aid to settling disputes between citizens, it is doubted whether it can be appropriate for disputes between the citizen and the state that relate to specified statutory entitlements. Given the facts of an individual case, a claimant is either entitled to a prescribed amount of HB/CTB or s/he is not entitled at all. Particularly given the vast disparity of bargaining power between the state and the citizen, it is not appropriate to involve the latter in any procedure in which s/he may either feel under pressure to accept less than full entitlement in order to avoid the perceived risks of a hearing or may, in effect, be bribed to give up an appeal by being offered more than s/he is strictly entitled to. The purpose of the social security decision making and appeals system is not to make disputes go away but to ensure that those who are entitled to benefit receive that entitlement and those who are not entitled do not. To be appropriate for social security appeals, any system of ADR adopted must not compromise that principle.

In January 2010, a report to the Ministry of Justice, *Early neutral evaluation pilot in the Social Security and Child Support Tribunal* (available from the Ministry of Justice website) concluded that a scheme piloting "early neutral evaluation" (a form of ADR) did not achieve swifter resolution of cases and was less cost-effective than the traditional tribunal process.

PART 2
General powers and provisions

Delegation to staff

4.–(1)   Staff appointed under section 40(1) of the 2007 Act (tribunal staff and services) may, with the approval of the Senior President of Tribunals, carry out functions of a judicial nature permitted or required to be done by the Tribunal.

(2)   The approval referred to at paragraph (1) may apply generally to the carrying out of specified functions by members of staff of a specified description in specified circumstances.

(3)   Within 14 days after the date on which the Tribunal sends notice of a decision made by a member of staff under paragraph (1) to a party, that party may apply in writing to the Tribunal for that decision to be considered afresh by a judge.

Case management powers

5.–(1) Subject to the provisions of the 2007 Act and any other enactment, the Tribunal may regulate its own procedure.

(2) The Tribunal may give a direction in relation to the conduct or disposal of proceedings at any time, including a direction amending, suspending or setting aside an earlier direction.

(3) In particular, and without restricting the general powers in paragraphs (1) and (2), the Tribunal may–

   (a) extend or shorten the time for complying with any rule, practice direction or direction;

   (b) consolidate or hear together two or more sets of proceedings or parts of proceedings raising common issues, or treat a case as a lead case (whether in accordance with rule 18 (lead cases) or otherwise);

   (c) permit or require a party to amend a document;

   (d) permit or require a party or another person to provide documents, information, evidence or submissions to the Tribunal or a party;

   (e) deal with an issue in the proceedings as a preliminary issue;

   (f) hold a hearing to consider any matter, including a case management issue;

   (g) decide the form of any hearing;

   (h) adjourn or postpone a hearing;

   (i) require a party to produce a bundle for a hearing;

   (j) stay (or, in Scotland, sist) proceedings;

   (k) transfer proceedings to another court or tribunal if that other court or tribunal has jurisdiction in relation to the proceedings and–

      (i) because of a change of circumstances since the proceedings were started, the Tribunal no longer has jurisdiction in relation to the proceedings; or

      (ii) the Tribunal considers that the other court or tribunal is a more appropriate forum for the determination of the case; or

   (l) suspend the effect of its own decision pending the determination by the Tribunal or the Upper Tribunal of an application for permission to appeal against, and any appeal or review of, that decision.

General Note

The case management provisions in r5 are the heart of the First-tier Tribunal's powers under the Rules.

By r5(1), the tribunal may regulate its own procedure except that it may not do anything that conflicts with TCEA 2007 or any other enactment. In doing so (and in exercising the case management powers in r5(2)) it must seek to give effect to the overriding objective.

The powers conferred by r5(2) are self-explanatory. It is, however, worth pointing out that, before 3 November 2008, appeal tribunals did not have the following powers:

(1)   to shorten a time limit;

(2)   to consolidate appeals or treat an appeal as a lead case;

(3)   to stay (or sist) proceedings;

(4)   to transfer proceedings to another court or tribunal;

(5)   to suspend the effect of a decision pending appeal.

Representatives and presenting officers should make themselves familiar with the full range of the First-tier Tribunal's case management powers and be prepared to ask the tribunal to use them in an appropriate case. When exercising the power to extend time for appealing (r5(3)(a)), the First-tier Tribunal need not have regard to the considerations listed in Rule 3.9(1) of the Civil Proceedings Rules, which apply when a court is considering whether to apply a sanction for a breach of procedural rules (see *CD v First-tier Tribunal (SEC) (CIC)* [2010] UKUT 181 (AAC).

In *MA v SSWP* [2009] UKUT 211 (AAC), the Upper Tribunal gives helpful guidance on the approach to be taken by the First-tier Tribunal when considering an application for adjournment in the context of the overriding objective in rule 2. Judge Jacobs stated that it was likely the tribunal's inquiries would focus on three issues: (1) what would be the benefit of an adjournment; (2) why was the party not ready to proceed; and (3) what impact will an adjournment have on the other party and the operation of the tribunal system? As regards (1), the application to adjourn had been to obtain further evidence. The judge advised that:

"A tribunal is always entitled to consider whether further evidence is likely to be helpful. In making its assessment, it is relevant to take into account: (i) the evidence that is already before the tribunal; (ii) the evidence that is likely to be obtained if the proceedings are adjourned; (iii) how long it will take to obtain it; and (iv) whether the tribunal could use its expertise to compensate for the lack of additional evidence."

As regards (2), the parties' duty is to co-operate with the tribunal generally under rule 2(4)(b). That involves ensuring as far as possible that their case is ready by the time of the hearing. It will be relevant to consider the advice given to claimants by the tribunal when an appeal is lodged. In relation to (3), the Secretary of State's interest in the appeal is not contentious and, except in an overpayment case when the Secretary of State may be concerned to avoid delaying tactics, is limited to "assisting the tribunal to ensure that it makes the correct decision in fact and law on the claimant's entitlement to benefit". The interests of the functioning of the tribunal system as a whole are unlikely to be of great significance in most cases and it will be "exceptional" for an adjournment that would otherwise be granted to be refused solely on account of the needs of the system as a whole.

The power in para (3)(b) to treat a case as a lead case may be delegated to a Regional Tribunal Judge but not a District Tribunal Judge (see para 10 of the Senior President's Practice Statement on the Composition of Tribunals on p1107)

Procedure for applying for and giving directions

6.–(1)   The Tribunal may give a direction on the application of one or more of the parties or on its own initiative.

(2)   An application for a direction may be made–

(a)   by sending or delivering a written application to the Tribunal; or

(b)   orally during the course of a hearing.

(3)   An application for a direction must include the reason for making that application.

(4)   Unless the Tribunal considers that there is good reason not to do so, the Tribunal must send written notice of any direction to every party and to any other person affected by the direction.

(5)   If a party or any other person sent notice of the direction under paragraph (4) wishes to challenge a direction which the Tribunal has given, they may do so by applying for another direction which amends, suspends or sets aside the first direction.

General Note

The tribunal may give directions on its own initiative and need not wait for an application from the parties: para (1). Under para (2), an application by a party must be in writing unless it is made at a hearing in which case it can be made by word of mouth. In either case, reasons must be given: para (3) and also simple common sense.

The requirement that an application be in writing is unnecessarily bureaucratic. Taken literally, it prevents an appellant (or a presenting officer) who is taken ill on the day of the hearing from telephoning the tribunal and requesting a postponement (because the "application" is neither in writing nor made at a hearing). It is hoped that the tribunal would exercise its powers under r7(2)(a) to waive the requirement for writing in such circumstances.

There is no requirement that the tribunal should seek the views of the parties before giving a direction (although it will often be sensible – and fairest – to do so). Once a direction has been made, however, any party may challenge it by applying for another direction which amends, suspends or sets aside the first direction. It cannot be over-emphasised that unless and until the first direction is amended, suspended or set aside, it must be obeyed.

If the tribunal gives a direction, a copy must normally be sent to every party: para (4).

Failure to comply with rules etc.

7.–(1)   An irregularity resulting from a failure to comply with any requirement in these Rules, a practice direction or a direction, does not of itself render void the proceedings or any step taken in the proceedings.

(2)   If a party has failed to comply with a requirement in these Rules, a practice direction or a direction, the Tribunal may take such action as it considers just, which may include–

(a)   waiving the requirement;

(b)   requiring the failure to be remedied;

(c)   exercising its power under rule 8 (striking out a party's case); or

(d)   exercising its power under paragraph (3).

(3)   The Tribunal may refer to the Upper Tribunal, and ask the Upper Tribunal to exercise its power under section 25 of the 2007 Act in relation to, any failure by a person to comply with a requirement imposed by the Tribunal–

(a)   to attend at any place for the purpose of giving evidence;

(b)   otherwise to make themselves available to give evidence;

(c)   to swear an oath in connection with the giving of evidence;

(d)   to give evidence as a witness;

(e)   to produce a document; or

(f)   to facilitate the inspection of a document or any other thing (including any premises).

General Note

A failure to comply with a rule, practice direction or direction has no practical consequences unless and until the tribunal decides to take action under para (2). Having regard to the overriding objective and, in particular, to the aim of "avoiding unnecessary formality and seeking flexibility in the proceedings" (r2(2)(b)) it will often be appropriate to waive the requirement, as long as this can be done without prejudicing the other party.

Under s25 TCEA 2007, the Upper Tribunal has the same powers as the High Court or the Court of Session in relation to the attendance and examination of witnesses, the production and inspection of documents and all other matters incidental to its functions. In principle, this includes power to punish for contempt of court. In practice, it is suspected that any prospect of a party going to prison for failure to comply with a requirement imposed by the First-tier Tribunal is an illusion.

The powers of the Upper Tribunal under s25 TCEA 2007 were considered by a three-judge panel in *PA v CMEC* [2009] UKUT 283 (AAC) and *MR v CMEC* [2009] UKUT 284 (AAC), [2009] UKUT 285 (AAC), [2010] UKUT 38 (AAC). In the former case, the tribunal stated:

"In our judgement these provisions [ie, rr7(3) and (4) of the TP(UT) Rules] mean that the Upper Tribunal can only exercise its powers under section 25 upon a referral by the First-tier Tribunal in respect of the requirement imposed by that tribunal. It is not open to the Upper Tribunal to impose a different requirement in substitution for that imposed by the First-tier Tribunal. It is the First-tier tribunal that knows what issues arise in the appeal and what material is required to assist in its resolution. It is therefore of the first importance that the First-tier tribunal consider carefully the terms of any direction to produce documents. Plainly any such documents require to be relevant to the resolution of the issues before it. The Direction Notice should articulate with precision what documents it requires and the period for which they are required. In the case of bank statements, for example, the dates specified must be related to the subject matter of the appeal before the First-tier tribunal."

Further consideration was given by a three-judge panel of the Upper Tribunal in *MD v SSWP (Enforcement Reference)* [2010] UKUT 202 (AAC). The panel stressed the importance of complying with procedural requirements in contempt cases (in that case the letter serving the summons misspelled the name of the person to whom it was addressed and contained no indication of the address to which it had been sent, and the summons made no provision for the payment of expenses as required by rule 16(2)(b)). It is also important that the First-tier Tribunal should investigate for itself whether there has actually been a breach of an order (rather than, for example, a failure of communication) before making the reference. The panel also pointed out that under para 10 of the Senior President's Practice Statement on the Composition of Tribunals, the power to refer to the Upper Tribunal is reserved to the Chamber President. That power may be delegated to a Regional Tribunal Judge (though not a District Tribunal Judge) but, at least at the time of the decision, no such delegation had actually been made.

Striking out a party's case

8.–(1)   The proceedings, or the appropriate part of them, will automatically be struck out if the appellant has failed to comply with a direction that stated that failure by a party to comply with the direction would lead to the striking out of the proceedings or that part of them.

(2)   The Tribunal must strike out the whole or a part of the proceedings if the Tribunal–

(a)   does not have jurisdiction in relation to the proceedings or that part of them; and

(b)   does not exercise its power under rule 5(3)(k)(i) (transfer to another court or tribunal) in relation to the proceedings or that part of them.

(3)   The Tribunal may strike out the whole or a part of the proceedings if–

(a)   the appellant has failed to comply with a direction which stated that failure by the appellant to comply with the direction could lead to the striking out of the proceedings or part of them;

(b)   the appellant has failed to co-operate with the Tribunal to such an extent that the Tribunal cannot deal with the proceedings fairly and justly; or

(c)   the Tribunal considers there is no reasonable prospect of the appellant's case, or part of it, succeeding.

(4)   The Tribunal may not strike out the whole or a part of the proceedings under paragraph (2) or (3)(b) or (c) without first giving the appellant an opportunity to make representations in relation to the proposed striking out.

(5)   If the proceedings, or part of them, have been struck out under paragraph (1) or (3)(a), the appellant may apply for the proceedings, or part of them, to be reinstated.

(6)   An application under paragraph (5) must be made in writing and received by the Tribunal within 1 month after the date on which the Tribunal sent notification of the striking out to the appellant.

(7)   This rule applies to a respondent as it applies to an appellant except that–

(a)   a reference to the striking out of the proceedings is to be read as a reference to the barring of the respondent from taking further part in the proceedings; and

(b)   a reference to an application for the reinstatement of proceedings which have been struck out is to be read as a reference to an application for the lifting of the bar on the respondent from taking further part in the proceedings.

(8)   If a respondent has been barred from taking further part in proceedings under this rule and that bar has not been lifted, the Tribunal need not consider any response or other submission made by that respondent [¹ and may summarily determine any or all issues against that respondent].

Amendment

1.   Amended by r5(3) of SI 2010 No 2653 as from 29.11.10.

General Note

Rule 8 sets out the tribunal's powers to strike out all or part of an appeal (and to bar a respondent from participating in the proceedings). In the past, striking out was most common under reg 46(1)(d) of the former SS D&A Regs – ie, where an appellant did not return the TAS1 questionnaire that was sent out at the beginning of an appeal and which asked for information (eg, does the appellant want a hearing, does s/he need an interpreter) that is then used for listing purposes. However, from 3 November 2008, such appeals are no longer automatically struck out. Instead they are referred to a tribunal judge who may decide to list them for hearing or (as, in the absence of an Enquiry Form (as the TAS1 is now called), it is probable that no party will have objected to a decision without a hearing) decide them without a hearing under r27. The tribunal judge may also strike out the appeal under reg 8(3)(a). However, there is power to strike out an appeal merely because the appellant has not completed and returned the enquiry form. That form (which may be downloaded from the Tribunals Service website) tells the appellant "Please complete in BLOCK CAPITALS and return this form to us within 14 days". That is not, by any stretch of the imagination, a direction within r8(3)(a). That rule is referring to a direction given by the tribunal in relation to an individual case. By contrast, the quoted part of the form is a general administrative instruction (and is issued by the Tribunals Service rather than by the First-tier Tribunal itself or of any individual Tribunal Judge); it uses the language of request rather than direction; and it does not "state that failure to comply could lead to the striking out of the proceedings or part of them" as is required by r8(3)(a). In any case, the exercise of that power is subject to the overriding objective and it is not immediately apparent how striking out the proceedings thereby depriving the claimant of access to the tribunal is a "fair and just" response to a failure to return an administrative form. Deciding such appeals rather than striking them out will sometimes be an unnecessary use of the resources of the tribunal. But the tribunal's resources, as opposed to the resources of the parties, are not listed as a relevant factor in r2(2). It might also be argued that deciding, rather than striking out, appeals in which the appellant may have lost interest will produce delay. However, under r2(2)(e) avoiding delay is only part of the overriding objective to the extent that it is "compatible with proper consideration of the issues": striking out the appeal prevents the issues from being considered at all, let alone properly.

Analysis

Failure to comply with Directions: paras (1), (3)(a), (5) and (6)

Paras (1) and (3)(a) both provide for an appeal, or part of it, to be struck out where the appellant has failed to comply with a direction. Which paragraph applies depends upon the warning that was given as part of the direction that has been disobeyed. If the direction states that a failure to comply "will" lead to the striking out of the proceedings, then those proceedings will automatically be struck out under para (1) as soon as the time limit for compliance has expired. If, however, the warning said that the proceedings "could" be struck out (or, presumably, used some similar word such as "can", "might" or "may"), the tribunal has a discretion to strike out under para (3)(a).

The power to strike out in para (3)(a) must be exercised in accordance with the overriding objective. As para (1) does not confer a power, no consideration is given to the overriding objective before the proceedings are automatically struck out. However, the tribunal judge who gave the original direction (ie, the direction containing the warning that failure to comply would lead to an automatic strike out) must have been satisfied that it was in the interests of the overriding objective to include such a warning in the first place.

Where the proceedings have been struck out under paras (1) or (3)(a), the appellant may apply under para (5) for them to be reinstated. Under para (6) that application must be in writing. The tribunal is unlikely to grant the application unless, belatedly, the appellant complies with the original direction or, possibly, explains why it is not practicable to do so. Any application to reinstate must be received by the tribunal within a month after notice of the striking out was sent to the parties. That time limit can be extended under reg 5(3)(a) if it is in accordance with the overriding objective to do so.

Out of jurisdiction appeals: paras (2) and (4)

Where the First-tier Tribunal does not have jurisdiction, it must either transfer the appeal to another court or tribunal under r5(3)(k)(i) (para (2)(b)) or strike it out. An appeal may be out of jurisdiction either because it is not a decision that carries a right of appeal under Sch 7 para 6 TCEA 2007, or because it is listed in the Schedule to the D&A Regs or because it is out of time and no decision has been made to treat it as in time under r23 or reg 19 D&A Regs or to extend time under r5(3)(a).

Before striking an appeal out under para (2), the tribunal must give the appellant an opportunity to make representations in relation to the proposed striking out: para (4). The tribunal may (r5(3)(f)), but does not have to (r27(3)), hold a hearing to give the appellant that opportunity.

There is no power to reinstate an appeal that has been struck out under para (2). It is unclear whether the decision to strike out is a "direction" that may therefore be amended, suspended or set aside by a subsequent direction under r5(2). It is also unclear whether there is a right of appeal to the Upper Tribunal against such a decision.

Failure to co-operate: paras (3)(b) and (4)

Under para (3)(b), the tribunal may strike out the appeal if the appellant has "failed to co-operate with the tribunal to such an extent that the tribunal cannot deal with the proceedings fairly and justly". It is difficult to envisage circumstances in which such a failure to co-operate did not involve a failure to comply with a specific direction (in which case, the proceedings would be more safely struck out under paras (1) or (3)(a)). One possible example may be where an appellant misconducts her/himself during a hearing to an extent that makes it impossible to continue with the hearing. However, the power in para (3)(b) is subject to the obligation in para (4) to give the appellant an opportunity to make representations in relation to the proposed striking out. It is unclear how the tribunal could give the appellant that opportunity without first adjourning. If the tribunal has to adjourn in any event, it may be preferable to give a direction under rule 30(5)(a) excluding the appellant from future hearings.

There is no power to reinstate an appeal that has been struck out under para (3)(b). It is unclear whether the decision to strike out is a "direction" that may therefore be amended, suspended or set aside by a subsequent direction under r5(2). It is also unclear whether there is a right of a appeal to the Upper Tribunal against such a decision.

No reasonable prospects of success: paras (3)(c) and (4)

It is suggested that the power in para (3)(c) should be exercised sparingly. Almost every tribunal judge will have experience of appeals which, on the papers, could not possibly succeed but, in the event, did so. There is also little to gain administratively from striking such appeals out. Once again, the power cannot be exercised without giving the appellant an opportunity to make representations in relation to the proposed striking out (para (4)) and making those representations may involve holding a hearing: rr5(3)(f) and 27(3). If, having received those representations, the tribunal is satisfied that the appeal has no reasonable prospects of success then the better course is to give a decision disallowing it on the merits rather than striking it out. That course also has the advantage that if the First-tier Tribunal has made an error, the appellant can appeal to the Upper Tribunal against a decision refusing the appeal but it is unclear whether there is a right of appeal against a decision to strike out.

There is no power to reinstate an appeal that has been struck out under para (3)(c). It is unclear whether the decision to strike out is a "direction" that may therefore be amended, suspended or set aside by a subsequent direction under r5(2).

Barring respondents from further participation in the proceedings: paras (7) and (8)

One innovation of the November 2008 changes is that a respondent may now be barred from taking further part in the proceedings in the same circumstances as an appellant's appeal may be struck out.

Under para (8) the effect of a barring order is that the tribunal need not consider the response to the appeal or any other submission. It is unclear whether para (8) permits the tribunal to disregard the evidence which, under r24, must accompany the response or whether a barred respondent and/or her/his representative may be excluded from future hearings of the appeal. It is suggested that the purpose behind paras (7) and (8) is to place a barred respondent in the same position as an appellant whose appeal has been struck out and that para (8) should therefore be interpreted in a way that excludes the respondent totally from the proceedings. Any other result would seem to raise issues of "equality of arms" under Art 6 of the European Convention on Human Rights.

Although the tribunal "need not" consider the response of a barred respondent, it may do so where, for example, that response includes concessions or other information that assists the appellant.

The tribunal may lift a bar in the same circumstances as it may reinstate an appeal that has been struck out. It is unclear whether the decision to impose a bar is a "direction" that may therefore be amended, suspended or set aside by a subsequent direction under rule 5(2). It is also unclear whether a barred respondent has a right of appeal to the Upper Tribunal against the barring order.

Barring a respondent is a draconian response and should be a matter of last resort. The tribunal should consider whether more proportionate means are available to the same end. If, for example, a local authority is in default of a direction to produce evidence, a witness summons – or the threat of one – addressed to the Chief

Executive or the Leader of the Council can work wonders. Often the tribunal needs the participation of the respondent which may be the only party with relevant evidence.

Substitution and addition of parties

9.–(1)   The Tribunal may give a direction substituting a party if–

(a)   the wrong person has been named as a party; or

(b)   the substitution has become necessary because of a change in circumstances since the start of proceedings.

(2)   The Tribunal may give a direction adding a person to the proceedings as a respondent.

(3)   If the Tribunal gives a direction under paragraph (1) or (2) it may give such consequential directions as it considers appropriate.

No power to award costs

10.   The Tribunal may not make any order in respect of costs (or, in Scotland, expenses).

Representatives

11.–(1)   A party may appoint a representative (whether a legal representative or not) to represent that party in the proceedings.

(2)   Subject to paragraph (3), if a party appoints a representative, that party (or the representative if the representative is a legal representative) must send or deliver to the Tribunal written notice of the representative's name and address.

(3)   In a case to which rule 23 (cases in which the notice of appeal is to be sent to the decision maker) applies, if the appellant (or the appellant's representative if the representative is a legal representative) provides written notification of the appellant's representative's name and address to the decision maker before the decision maker provides its response to the Tribunal, the appellant need not take any further steps in order to comply with paragraph (2).

(4)   If the Tribunal receives notice that a party has appointed a representative under paragraph (2), it must send a copy of that notice to each other party.

(5)   Anything permitted or required to be done by a party under these Rules, a practice direction or a direction may be done by the representative of that party, except signing a witness statement.

(6)   A person who receives due notice of the appointment of a representative–

(a)   must provide to the representative any document which is required to be provided to the represented party, and need not provide that document to the represented party; and

(b)   may assume that the representative is and remains authorised as such until they receive written notification that this is not so from the representative or the represented party.

(7)   At a hearing a party may be accompanied by another person whose name and address has not been notified under paragraph (2) or (3) but who, with the permission of the Tribunal, may act as a representative or otherwise assist in presenting the party's case at the hearing.

(8)   Paragraphs (2) to (6) do not apply to a person who accompanies a party under paragraph (7).

General Note

A party may appoint a representative who need not be legally qualified: para (1). Appointment is effected by sending written notice of the representative's name and address to the tribunal (para (2) or, if the party appointing the representative is the appellant, by giving such notice to the decision maker before the decision maker provides the tribunal with a response to the appeal under r24: para (3). If the tribunal receives notice under para (2), it must send a copy to all the other parties: para (4).

Once appointed, the representative may do anything permitted or required to be done by the party s/he represents except signing a witness statement: para (5). However, it is doubted that para (5) entitles a representative to give oral evidence at a hearing instead of an appellant. Once the tribunal and the other parties have been notified that a representative has been appointed, they may deal with her/him instead of the appellant and may continue to do so until notified that the representative has ceased to act. In particular, they must provide the representative with any relevant document and need not also provide a copy to the appellant. As many representative organisations are unable to attend hearings for funding reasons, the effect of the rule about documents is likely to be that more appellants attend tribunal hearings without the papers. Representatives who are unable to attend hearings themselves should ensure that they give the appeal papers to the appellant in good time and tell the appellant to take those papers to the hearing.

In *MP v SSWP* (DLA) [2010] UKUT 103 (AAC), the Upper Tribunal considered the position where under r11(3), the appellant notifies the decision maker of the details of her/his representative before the decision maker delivers the response to the First-tier Tribunal. Judge Turnbull stated:

"The Tribunals Service would therefore have been justified, under the express terms of Rule 11(6)(b), in sending the Enquiry Form to the solicitors only, but I do not think that there was any procedural irregularity in it being sent (and sent only, it appears) to the Claimant. The Enquiry Form does not appear to have been a document which was required to be provided, within the meaning of Rule 11(3)(a) *[sic, an obvious typographical error for 11(6)(a)]*, and so there was strictly no breach of the Rules in it being sent only to the Claimant. Nor do I think that the sending of it to the Claimant, rather than to the solicitors, involved a breach of natural justice. The Claimant of course had the opportunity to complete the Enquiry Form properly, and the fact that a paper hearing took place without her solicitors' knowledge was caused by the fact that she did not complete it properly. One might nevertheless question whether, in cases where the Tribunals Service is notified by the decision maker, in accordance with the procedure in Rule 11, that a representative has been appointed, it is sensible for the Tribunals Service to send the Enquiry Form to the claimant rather than to the representative. (I have examined the files in a number of other cases, and that does indeed appear to be the general practice of the Tribunals Service.) In many cases where a representative is appointed initially the reason may be that the claimant is hampered in dealing with his or her affairs, and there is therefore the potential for errors of the nature which occurred in this case to result. But it seems to me that the safeguard, if an error which causes unfairness does occur, lies in the power to set aside in Rule 37, and at the end of the day no harm should therefore result."

Calculating time

12.–(1) Except in asylum support cases, an act required by these Rules, a practice direction or a direction to be done on or by a particular day must be done by 5pm on that day.

(2) If the time specified by these Rules, a practice direction or a direction for doing any act ends on a day other than a working day, the act is done in time if it is done on the next working day.

(3) In this rule "working day" means any day except a Saturday or Sunday, Christmas Day, Good Friday or a bank holiday under section 1 of the Banking and Financial Dealings Act 1971.

General Note

Para (1) provides that time for doing anything required by the Rules, a practice direction or a direction expires at 5.00 pm on the day in question.

Paras (2) and (3) provide that a time limit can only expire on a working day.

Sending and delivery of documents

13.–(1) Any document to be provided to the Tribunal under these Rules, a practice direction or a direction must be–

(a) sent by pre-paid post or delivered by hand to the address specified for the proceedings;

(b) sent by fax to the number specified for the proceedings; or

(c) sent or delivered by such other method as the Tribunal may permit or direct.

(2) Subject to paragraph (3), if a party provides a fax number, email address or other details for the electronic transmission of documents to them, that party must accept delivery of documents by that method.

(3) If a party informs the Tribunal and all other parties that a particular form of communication (other than pre-paid post or delivery by hand) should not be used to provide documents to that party, that form of communication must not be so used.

(4) If the Tribunal or a party sends a document to a party or the Tribunal by email or any other electronic means of communication, the recipient may request that the sender provide a hard copy of the document to the recipient. The recipient must make such a request as soon as reasonably practicable after receiving the document electronically.

(5)   The Tribunal and each party may assume that the address provided by a party or its representative is and remains the address to which documents should be sent or delivered until receiving written notification to the contrary.

Use of documents and information

14.–(1)   The Tribunal may make an order prohibiting the disclosure or publication of–

(a)   specified documents or information relating to the proceedings; or

(b)   any matter likely to lead members of the public to identify any person whom the Tribunal considers should not be identified.

(2)   The Tribunal may give a direction prohibiting the disclosure of a document or information to a person if–

(a)   the Tribunal is satisfied that such disclosure would be likely to cause that person or some other person serious harm; and

(b)   the Tribunal is satisfied, having regard to the interests of justice, that it is proportionate to give such a direction.

(3)   If a party (''the first party'') considers that the Tribunal should give a direction under paragraph (2) prohibiting the disclosure of a document or information to another party (''the second party''), the first party must–

(a)   exclude the relevant document or information from any documents that will be provided to the second party; and

(b)   provide to the Tribunal the excluded document or information, and the reason for its exclusion, so that the Tribunal may decide whether the document or information should be disclosed to the second party or should be the subject of a direction under paragraph (2).

(4)   The Tribunal must conduct proceedings as appropriate in order to give effect to a direction given under paragraph (2).

(5)   If the Tribunal gives a direction under paragraph (2) which prevents disclosure to a party who has appointed a representative, the Tribunal may give a direction that the documents or information be disclosed to that representative if the Tribunal is satisfied that–

(a)   disclosure to the representative would be in the interests of the party; and

(b)   the representative will act in accordance with paragraph (6).

(6)   Documents or information disclosed to a representative in accordance with a direction under paragraph (5) must not be disclosed either directly or indirectly to any other person without the Tribunal's consent.

Evidence and submissions

15.–(1)   Without restriction on the general powers in rule 5(1) and (2) (case management powers), the Tribunal may give directions as to–

(a)   issues on which it requires evidence or submissions;

(b)   the nature of the evidence or submissions it requires;

(c)   whether the parties are permitted or required to provide expert evidence;

(d)   any limit on the number of witnesses whose evidence a party may put forward, whether in relation to a particular issue or generally;

(e)   the manner in which any evidence or submissions are to be provided, which may include a direction for them to be given–

    (i)   orally at a hearing; or

    (ii)   by written submissions or witness statement; and

(f)   the time at which any evidence or submissions are to be provided.

(2)   The Tribunal may–

(a)   admit evidence whether or not–

    (i)   the evidence would be admissible in a civil trial in the United Kingdom; or

    (ii)   the evidence was available to a previous decision maker; or

(b)   exclude evidence that would otherwise be admissible where–

(i)   the evidence was not provided within the time allowed by a direction or a practice direction;

(ii)   the evidence was otherwise provided in a manner that did not comply with a direction or a practice direction; or

(iii)   it would otherwise be unfair to admit the evidence.

(3)   The Tribunal may consent to a witness giving, or require any witness to give, evidence on oath, and may administer an oath for that purpose.

General Note

Para (1) confers supplementary case management powers on the tribunal in relation to evidence and submissions.

Para (2)(a) provides that the tribunal "may" admit evidence whether or not the evidence would be admissible in a civil trial or was available to the decision maker. Predecessors to the First-tier Tribunal (eg, social security appeal tribunals) were not bound by the rules on admissibility of evidence (see, for example, *CDLA 2014/2004* and the list of cases cited in para 10 of that decision): the only evidential issues were whether the evidence was relevant and, if so, how much weight to attach to it. Given that background, it is suggested that, unless para (2)(b) applies, the tribunal not only "may" but "must" admit all evidence that is relevant to the issues it has to decide.

It is also suggested that the First-tier Tribunal should be slow to exercise the power in para (2)(b) to exclude evidence. The overriding objective is unlikely to be served by excluding relevant evidence and, while the late production of evidence is an irritating obstacle to the smooth running of the tribunal's list, it is rare for late evidence to prejudice the other parties to the appeal or, indeed, to affect its outcome. If so, why create a collateral ground of appeal by refusing to consider it? And in those cases where the late evidence is determinative, it is unjust to exclude it and thereby reach the wrong result.

Para (3) permits the tribunal to take evidence on oath. Tribunal judges hold differing views on how helpful this is. However, it would be rare for the tribunal to refuse to allow a party or witness who wanted to give evidence on oath to do so.

Summoning or citation of witnesses and orders to answer questions or produce documents

16.–(1)   On the application of a party or on its own initiative, the Tribunal may–

(a)   by summons (or, in Scotland, citation) require any person to attend as a witness at a hearing at the time and place specified in the summons or citation; or

(b)   order any person to answer any questions or produce any documents in that person's possession or control which relate to any issue in the proceedings.

(2)   A summons or citation under paragraph (1)(a) must–

(a)   give the person required to attend 14 days' notice of the hearing or such shorter period as the Tribunal may direct; and

(b)   where the person is not a party, make provision for the person's necessary expenses of attendance to be paid, and state who is to pay them.

(3)   No person may be compelled to give any evidence or produce any document that the person could not be compelled to give or produce on a trial of an action in a court of law in the part of the United Kingdom where the proceedings are due to be determined.

(4)   A summons, citation or order under this rule must–

(a)   state that the person on whom the requirement is imposed may apply to the Tribunal to vary or set aside the summons, citation or order, if they have not had an opportunity to object to it; and

(b)   state the consequences of failure to comply with the summons, citation or order.

General Note

The power in r16(1)(b) to order any person to produce documents does not extend to the production of documents that are subject to legal professional privilege, see *LM v LB Lewisham* [2009] UKUT 204 (AAC): [2010] AACR 12.

Withdrawal

17.–(1)   Subject to paragraph (2), a party may give notice of the withdrawal of its case, or any part of it–

(a)   at any time before a hearing to consider the disposal of the proceedings (or, if the Tribunal disposes of the proceedings without a hearing, before that disposal), by sending or delivering to the Tribunal a written notice of withdrawal; or

(b)   orally at a hearing.

(2)   In the circumstances described in paragraph (3), a notice of withdrawal will not take effect unless the Tribunal consents to the withdrawal

(3)   The circumstances referred to in paragraph (2) are where a party gives notice of withdrawal–

(a)   under paragraph (1)(a) in a criminal injuries compensation case; or

(b)   under paragraph (1)(b).

(4)   A party who has withdrawn their case may apply to the Tribunal for the case to be reinstated.

(5)   An application under paragraph (4) must be made in writing and be received by the Tribunal within 1 month after–

(a)   the date on which the Tribunal received the notice under paragraph (1)(a); or

(b)   the date of the hearing at which the case was withdrawn orally under paragraph (1)(b).

(6)   The Tribunal must notify each party in writing of an withdrawal under this rule.

General Note

A party may withdraw its case by giving written notice of withdrawal or by word of mouth at a hearing. In HB/CTB appeals, withdrawal is only relevant to appellants. An authority that became persuaded that the grounds of appeal were correct would instead revise the decision against which the appeal was brought, thereby causing the appeal to lapse.

If notice of withdrawal is given during a hearing, then the tribunal's consent is needed (paras (1)(b) and (3)(b)). Withdrawal by written notice under para (1)(a) does not require the tribunal's consent and is effective as soon as it is received by the tribunal.

Paras (4) and (5) contain a welcome new power for the tribunal to reinstate a withdrawn appeal. The time limit in para (5) may be extended under rule 5(3)(a) if it is in accordance with the overriding objective to do so.

Lead cases

18.–(1)   This rule applies if–

(a)   two or more cases have been started before the Tribunal;

(b)   in each such case the Tribunal has not made a decision disposing of the proceedings; and

(c)   the cases give rise to common or related issues of fact or law.

(2)   The Tribunal may give a direction–

(a)   specifying one or more cases falling under paragraph (1) as a lead case or lead cases; and

(b)   staying (or, in Scotland, sisting) the other cases falling under paragraph (1) (''the related cases'').

(3)   When the Tribunal makes a decision in respect of the common or related issues–

(a)   the Tribunal must send a copy of that decision to each party in each of the related cases; and

(b)   subject to paragraph (4), that decision shall be binding on each of those parties.

(4)   Within 1 month after the date on which the Tribunal sent a copy of the decision to a party under paragraph (3)(a), that party may apply in writing for a direction that the decision does not apply to, and is not binding on the parties to, a particular related case.

(5)   The Tribunal must give directions in respect of cases which are stayed or sisted under paragraph (2)(b), providing for the disposal of or further directions in those cases.

(6)   If the lead case or cases lapse or are withdrawn before the Tribunal makes a decision in respect of the common or related issues, the Tribunal must give directions as to–

(a)   whether another case or other cases are to be specified as a lead case or lead cases; and

(b)   whether any direction affecting the related cases should be set aside or amended.

General Note

For the first time, r18 establishes a formal procedure for dealing with related or "lookalike" appeals. Note that, under paras 9 and 10 of the Senior President's Practice Statement *Composition of Tribunals in Social Security and Child Support Cases in the Social Entitlement Chamber on or after 3 November 2008*, the decision to treat a case as a lead case (whether under r18 or otherwise) can only be made by the Chamber President or a Regional Tribunal Judge.

Expenses in social security and child support cases

21.–(1)   This rule applies only to social security and child support cases.

(2)   The Secretary of State may pay such travelling and other allowances (including compensation for loss of remunerative time) as the Secretary of State may determine to any person required to attend a hearing in proceedings under section 20 of the Child Support Act 1991, section 12 of the Social Security Act 1998 or paragraph 6 of Schedule 7 to the Child Support, Pensions and Social Security Act 2000.

PART 3
Proceedings before the Tribunal
CHAPTER 1
Before the hearing

Cases in which the notice of appeal is to be sent to the decision maker

23.–(1)   This rule applies to social security and child support cases (except references under the Child Support Act 1991 and proceedings under paragraph 3 of Schedule 2 to the Tax Credits Act 2002).

(2)   An appellant must start proceedings by sending or delivering a notice of appeal to the decision maker so that it is received within the time specified in Schedule 1 to these Rules (time limits for providing notices of appeal to the decision maker).

(3)   If the appellant provides the notice of appeal to the decision maker later than the time required by paragraph (2) the notice of appeal must include the reason why the notice of appeal was not provided in time.

(4)   Subject to paragraph (5), where an appeal is not made within the time specified in Schedule 1, it will be treated as having been made in time if the decision maker does not object.

(5)   No appeal may be made more than 12 months after the time specified in Schedule 1.

(6)   The notice of appeal must be in English or Welsh, must be signed by the appellant and must state–

(a)   the name and address of the appellant;

(b)   the name and address of the appellant's representative (if any);

(c)   an address where documents for the appellant may be sent or delivered;

(d)   details of the decision being appealed; and

(e)   the grounds on which the appellant relies.

(7)   The decision maker must refer the case to the Tribunal immediately if–

(a)   the appeal has been made after the time specified in Schedule 1 and the decision maker objects to it being treated as having been made in time; or

(b)   the decision maker considers that the appeal has been made more than 12 months after the time specified in Schedule 1.

[¹ (8) Notwithstanding rule 5(3)(a) (case management powers) and rule 7(2) (failure to comply with rules etc.), the Tribunal must not extend the time limit in paragraph (5).]

Amendment

1.   Inserted by r3 of SI 2009 No 1975 as from 1.9.09.

General Note

Paras (1), (2) and (7). Under paras (1) and (2), in all social security cases (including HB/CTB appeals) the appeal must be made by sending or delivering a notice of appeal to the decision maker (ie, in HB/CTB appeals, the local authority) within the time limit specified in Sch 1. Broadly speaking, this is one month from the date on which notice of the decision was sent to the claimant, but see the commentary to Sch 1 on p1075.

If the appeal is late, the notice of appeal must explain why: para (3). Note, however, that in an appropriate case, the tribunal may waive that requirement under r7(2)(a).

No appeal may be made more than 12 months after the time limit specified in Sch 1 (para (5)). Subject to that absolute limit:

(1)   The decision maker may treat a late appeal as having been made in time if the criteria in reg 19(6)-(9) D&A Regs are satisfied.

(2)   If the decision maker cannot treat the appeal as having been made in time, the tribunal must nevertheless do so as long as the decision maker does not object: para (4).

(3)   If the decision maker does object, the tribunal may still extend the time for appealing under rule 5(3)(a) if it is in accordance with the overriding objective to do so.

Under para (7) the decision maker must refer the appeal to the tribunal immediately if it considers that it has been made outside the absolute time limit or if, although made within that limit, the authority objects to the appeal being treated as having been made in time.

Para (6) sets out the requirements for a valid appeal.

(1)   The notice must be in English or Welsh.

(2)   The notice must be signed by the appellant.

The decision in *R v Lambeth LBC ex p Crookes* [1998] 31 HLR 59, QBD suggests that this requirement cannot be met by a signature of a solicitor. However, the correctness of *Crookes* on this point has been undermined by the decision of the Privy Council in *General Legal Council ex parte Basil Whitter v Barrington Earl Frankson* [2006] UKPC 42, 27 July, and its holding that in *re Prince Blucher* [1931] 2 Ch D 70 (an authority on which *Crookes* strongly relied) was wrongly decided.

(3)   The notice must state the appellant's name and address, the name and address of any representative, an address for service of documents, details of the decision being appealed and the grounds of appeal.

The details of the decision being appealed must be sufficient for that decision to be identified. The grounds of appeal need only be in general terms (the requirement is to state the "grounds on which the appellant relies", not to give particulars of those grounds). It is unrealistic to expect an unrepresented appellant to identify all the relevant points with precision. Simply to say "I want to appeal" is insufficient, but, for example, "I disagree with your decision that I have no liability for rent" is probably sufficient, since that raises questions of fact and law. Authorities may well want to seek further details of the challenge on an informal basis in order to respond to the appeal.

Appellants and their representatives are advised to remember that under Sch 7 para 6(9(a) CSPSSA, the tribunal "need not consider any issue that is not raised by the appeal" (see p148). It is therefore important to raise all possible issues at the earliest opportunity.

Responses and replies

24.–(1)   When a decision maker receives the notice of appeal or a copy of it, the decision maker must send or deliver a response to the Tribunal–

(a)   *[Omitted]*; and

(b)   in other cases, as soon as reasonably practicable after the decision maker received the notice of appeal.

(2)   The response must state–

(a)   the name and address of the decision maker;

(b)   the name and address of the decision maker's representative (if any);

(c)   an address where documents for the decision maker may be sent or delivered;

(d)   the names and addresses of any other respondents and their representatives (if any);

(e)   whether the decision maker opposes the appellant's case and, if so, any grounds for such opposition which are not set out in any documents which are before the Tribunal; and

(f)   any further information or documents required by a practice direction or direction.

(3)   The response may include a submission as to whether it would be appropriate for the case to be disposed of without a hearing.

(4)   The decision maker must provide with the response–

(a)   a copy of any written record of the decision under challenge, and any statement of reasons for that decision, if they were not sent with the notice of appeal;

(b)   copies of all documents relevant to the case in the decision maker's possession, unless a practice direction or direction states otherwise; and

(c)   in cases to which rule 23 (cases in which the notice of appeal is to be sent to the decision maker) applies, a copy of the notice of appeal, any documents provided by the appellant with the notice of appeal and (if they have not otherwise been provided to the Tribunal) the name and address of the appellant's representative (if any).

(5)   The decision maker must provide a copy of the response and any accompanying documents to each other party at the same time as it provides the response to the Tribunal.

(6)   The appellant and any other respondent may make a written submission and supply further documents in reply to the decision maker's response.

(7)   Any submission or further documents under paragraph (6) must be provided to the Tribunal within 1 month after the date on which the decision maker sent the response to the party providing the reply, and the Tribunal must send a copy to each other party.

General Note

An authority that receives a notice of appeal under r23 must prepare a response and send it to the tribunal "as soon as reasonably practicable after the decision maker received the notice of appeal".

The "response" is, in effect, the document that was referred to colloquially as the "submission" in appeals to the former appeal tribunals. It must contain the information specified in para (2) and be accompanied by the documents specified in para (4), namely:

Head (a): a copy of the written record of the decision under challenge, and any statement of reasons for that decision. The reference in head (a) to "if they were not sent with the notice of appeal" applies to appeals (not social security appeals) which are commenced by sending the notice of appeal to the tribunal rather than to the decision maker. Setting out in black and white that the decision maker must let the tribunal know the precise terms of the decision it is considering might be thought superfluous. Unfortunately, experience with HB/CTB appeals since 2001 shows that it is not. Being required to tell the tribunal what decisions they have made will involve a significant change of culture at some authorities.

Head (b): copies of all documents relevant to the case in the decision maker's possession. The important words here are "relevant to the case". Relevant documents must be produced even if the decision maker does not wish to rely upon them and even if – one might say particularly if – they do not assist the authority's case. It will be particularly important for the authorities to comply with head (b) in overpayment cases. Submissions to the tribunal in such cases regularly fail to include the decision notices for the original (ie, allegedly incorrect) awards and a proper schedule explaining how the alleged overpayment has been calculated. The tribunal has an inquisitorial role. Without the former information it can be difficult for the tribunal to understand how the overpayment is said to have arisen and – more importantly – verify that the original decision has been properly revised or superseded so that there is an overpayment in the first place.

Head (c): again, one might have thought it would be unnecessary to make regulations requiring authorities to include a copy of the notice of appeal in the appeal papers. For a minority of authorities, however, head (c) will be a useful reminder.

"As soon as reasonably practicable". Decision makers in social security and child support cases are the only parties that are not required by the rules to comply with a proper time limit – ie, expressed by reference to a finite period of time. Even the time limit imposed on the tribunal – which in practice means a judge, not a party to the appeal – is subject to a primary time limit of one month in which to produce a statement of reasons under r34(5). This exemption of government departments and local authorities, from the rules that apply to ordinary citizens is an unfortunate anomaly in the rules and may raise issues of "equality of arms" under Art 6 of the ECHR. It may be argued that the exemption is necessary because it takes longer to produce a response (which has to be properly structured and argued and be accompanied by all relevant documents) than it does to produce an appeal (which need only say, for example, "I do not agree with your decision that my tenancy is uncommercial"). But even if one accepts that point, it only justifies there being a longer time limit for decision makers than exists for claimants and landlords. It does not justify an indefinite time limit.

The leading authority on what is "practicable" in the context of social security law is *R v Secretary of State for Social Services ex p CPAG* [1990] 2 QB 540, CA, (Balcombe, Woolf and Russell LJJ). The Court was considering s99(1) Social Security Act 1975 which provided that "[a]n adjudication officer to whom a claim or question is submitted . . . shall take . . . , so far as practicable, dispose of it . . . , within 14 days of its submission to him." The Court held that:

"[t]here is nothing in the language of section 99(1) which means that it is not permissible to look at factors other than those involved in an individual claim in deciding whether it was practicable to come to a decision within 14 days. Section 99(1) does not require matters independent of the claim to be ignored in deciding what is practical. The volume of claims awaiting determination and the number of investigating officers available to deal with the claims are examples of matters which can be relevant to the decision as to whether or not it was practicable to come to a determination within the 14 day period."

Except, perhaps, in the case of a flagrant delay, it will therefore be difficult for a claimant to show that an authority has taken longer than is "reasonably practicable" to produce a response because s/he will have no information as to the resources available to the decision maker or what other demands there are on those resources.

It is unclear whether the tribunal can shorten the authority's time for producing a response by giving a direction under its power (in r5(3)(a)) to "shorten the time for complying with any rule". To do so the tribunal would either have to direct the authority to deliver the response "sooner than reasonably practicable" or within a specified number of days. The former would probably be perverse. The latter does not involve "shortening" (or "extending") a time limit as much as substituting a definite time limit for an indefinite one or, arguably, imposing a time limit where none previously existed. However, such difficulties do not mean that the tribunal is powerless in the face of local authority delay. As is clear from *R(H) 1/07*, as long as a valid appeal has been made, the tribunal has jurisdiction over it even if it has not been registered. Under r5(1), the tribunal may regulate its own procedure. In an appropriate case, it may therefore decide the appeal in the absence of a response (possibly waiving the requirement to provide one under r7) as long as it is satisfied that the authority has had a reasonable opportunity to provide one. Alternatively, it could use its case management powers under rr5 and (in particular) 15 to direct the authority to make submissions and produce evidence equivalent (in substance, if not in name) to a response. A finite time limit may be imposed as part of such directions and, ultimately, an authority may be barred from further participation under r8(7) if those time limits are not met.

Further submissions: paras (6) and (7). Other parties may make a submission in reply and supply further documents within one month from the date the response is sent to them. It is suggested that the effect of these provisions is that (unless it expressly shortens the time limit) the tribunal cannot decide the appeal – or, at least, decide it in a manner that is adverse to the appellant or a respondent other than the decision maker – without giving a month for further comment. It does not mean that no further documents can be produced (or written submissions made) after the one-month limit has expired unless the tribunal gives leave. Even if that interpretation is wrong, the power to exclude evidence under r15(2) does not apply to evidence that is late merely because the limit in para (7) has expired. That power applies where "the evidence was not provided within the time allowed by a **direction or practice direction**" (emphasis added). It does not apply to evidence produced later than is allowed by a **rule**. And if the tribunal has no power to exclude such evidence, it inevitably follows that, provided the evidence is relevant, the tribunal must consider it.

CHAPTER 2
Hearings

Decision with or without a hearing

27.–(1)   Subject to the following paragraphs, the Tribunal must hold a hearing before making a decision which disposes of proceedings unless–
(a)   each party has consented to, or has not objected to, the matter being decided without a hearing; and
(b)   the Tribunal considers that it is able to decide the matter without a hearing.
(2)   This rule does not apply to decisions under Part 4.
(3)   The Tribunal may in any event dispose of proceedings without a hearing under rule 8 (striking out a party's case).
(4)-(6)   *[Omitted]*

General Note

"Hearing" is defined by r1(2) as meaning "an oral hearing". That phrase includes hearings conducted by telephone, video link or other means of instantaneous two-way electronic communication. Before the establishment of the First-tier Tribunal, it was common to refer colloquially to the process of deciding an appeal by considering only the written submissions and documentary evidence as a "paper hearing". That terminology will probably continue but, given the definition in r1(2) a "paper hearing" is now a contradiction in terms and the phrase "oral hearing" is tautologous.

Under r5(3)(f), the tribunal may hold a hearing in relation to any matter. Rule 27 is concerned with when the tribunal must hold a hearing. It says that, with four exceptions, the tribunal must hold a hearing "before making a decision which disposes of proceedings" – ie, a final decision of the appeal. Those four exceptions are: consent of all the parties (para (1)); absence of objection from any party (para (1)); post-hearing interlocutory decisions (para (2)) and striking out under rule 8 (para (3)). The first two of those exceptions only apply if, *in addition*, the tribunal considers it is able to decide the matter without a hearing.

Once an authority has prepared a response to the appeal, it must submit it to the Tribunals Service accompanied by a covering sheet (Form AT37). That form requires the authority to state whether it requires a hearing of the appeal. The Tribunals Service then sends the response to the appellant (and any other respondent) together with an Enquiry Form (the former TAS1). The Enquiry Form asks "Do you want to have a hearing where you and your representative, if you have one, can meet the Tribunal and put your case?"

It is very important that appellants should answer 'yes' to that question and should attend the hearing that will then be held. Many people do not like the prospect of having to attend a hearing but the advantages of doing so are clear as the Guidance Notes to the Enquiry Form state:

"The advantage of a hearing is that you have an opportunity to speak to the Tribunal and the Tribunal has an opportunity to learn more about your case than it could gather from the appeal papers alone. Most people who appeal opt for a hearing. Statistically, *more than twice as many* appeals are successful with a hearing." (emphasis added).

Why is it that an appeal is more than twice as likely to succeed if there is a hearing? There are a number of factors:
(1)   In most cases, it is ultimately for the appellant to prove that s/he is entitled to the benefit s/he has claimed and not for the authority to prove that s/he is not. This means that the authority, not the appellant gets the

benefit of any doubt. If the appeal papers leave the tribunal in doubt – eg, if they fail to mention a necessary fact, the appellant will lose unless there is a hearing and the tribunal can ask questions to elicit the missing evidence.

(2)   It is quite likely that an appellant will not include all the necessary facts in the papers. Social security law is complex and – at least where s/he is unrepresented – the appellant may simply not realise that a particular fact is relevant and needs to be mentioned.

(3)   Experience suggests that appellants tend to overestimate their powers of written explanation. (The same is also true of local authorities but that is not relevant to this discussion.) Their case is clear to them and they therefore assume it will be clear to everybody. Often, however, an appellant's explanation of her/his case assumes background knowledge that the tribunal does not share and will never learn unless the appellant comes to a hearing and answers the tribunal's questions. Most tribunal judges (and other members) will be able to give examples of appeals that seemed hopeless on paper, but which eventually succeeded because the appellant attended a hearing.

(4)   Many appeals turn on an assessment of credibility – ie, on whether the tribunal accepts that the appellant is telling the truth. Except for cases in which the appellant's case is wholly implausible, it is often difficult for the tribunal to assess who is telling the truth without being able to ask questions. Again, the appellant will not usually get the benefit of any doubt.

The procedure at a tribunal hearing is more formal than, say, at most meetings an appellant will attend, but it is much less formal than a court. The tribunal judge and other members will not wear robes and will normally sit on the other side of a table from the parties, rather than on a raised "bench". The tribunal has an enabling role and, although it must remain impartial, will try to help appellants put their cases in the best way possible. The tribunal (and any presenting officer from the authority) will want to ask the appellant questions (and appellants should not assume that their version of events will automatically be accepted) but hostile cross-examination of the type portrayed in television "court-room dramas" is strongly discouraged. Finally, hearings are normally held in public: if an appellant is concerned about attending a hearing or wants to know what happens at a hearing s/he can go to the local tribunal venue and sit in on a hearing as an observer before her/his own appeal is heard.

If, nevertheless, the appellant answers that s/he does not want a hearing, the Enquiry Form advises that "we will go ahead on the basis that you have no objection to your appeal being decided by the Tribunal in your absence. You can still write to us with anything you would like the Tribunal to take into consideration, but please do so within the next 14 days". There are difficulties reconciling that the 14-day time limit is consistent with r24(6) and (7) which allows a minimum of one month in which to reply to the response unless that time limit is shortened by a case management direction under r5(3)(a) – ie, a direction made by a judge in an individual case not an administrator as part of a general form. Even if the Enquiry Form is returned on the last day of the 14-day period that is allowed, a further 14 days will expire 28 days from the date on which the response was sent to the appellant. Except for February (and even then only three times every four years) 28 days is less than a month. Nevertheless, an appellant who requests a decision without a hearing but cannot obtain all the evidence s/he wants to submit within the 14 day period would be well advised to write in within that time limit and request an extension.

Where the appellant does not return the Enquiry Form at all, the appeal will be submitted to a tribunal judge for case management directions or a decision. In such cases the appellant will not have "objected to" a decision without a hearing and the tribunal judge may therefore decide the appeal there and then, request further evidence and submissions, or list the decision for a hearing. In *RM v SSWP* [2009] UKUT 256 (AAC), the Upper Tribunal allowed a DLA appeal where the First-tier Tribunal had refused the appeal without a hearing. The appellant suffered from fits and told the First-tier Tribunal that she could not attend a hearing because she was scared that lights would trigger her fits off. Judge Williams stated:

> "In my view this is precisely the sort of case where a tribunal's decision to hear the case on paper creates a danger of prejudging the outcome decision. The appellant clearly wanted to attend a hearing, and clearly knew it was to her advantage to do so, but felt unable to do so for precisely the reason she was claiming the allowance. There is no indication that the tribunal considered the reasons why the appellant stated that she could not attend the hearing and therefore did not. It did not consider whether it should adjourn for a domiciliary visit or for further evidence. But there was the clearest evidence from both the appellant and from her general practitioner of the reasons why she could not attend a tribunal where there was a risk that the lights would set off a fit. So do crowds of people. Nor, in common experience, could a tribunal hearing be held in the normal way in conditions that involved no such risks. So the appellant's approach to not attending the tribunal was entirely consistent with her claim for the allowance. In my view this is one of those rare cases where the inquisitorial function of the tribunal required that it consider whether it was being fair in taking no steps to deal with this justified fear of the appellant about attempting to attend the tribunal hearing."

Even when an appellant does not object to the appeal being decided without a hearing, s/he is still entitled to at least a month in which to make a written submission and supply further documents in response to the decision maker's response (see rr26(6) and (7)). Unless the appellant indicates that s/he does not have anything further to say or wishes to produce further evidence, a decision made within that period will be liable to be set aside under r37(2)(d) (see *MP v SSWP* (DLA) [2010] UKUT 103 (AAC)).

Under para (1)(b), even if the parties have consented (or have not objected) to a decision without a hearing, the tribunal may only make such a decision if it "considers that it is able to do so" It may therefore over rule the parties' wishes (or lack of objection) if it considers that it will further the overriding objective to hold a hearing.

'Post-hearing' decisions: para (2)

The tribunal may make a decision under Part 4 of the Rules to correct, set aside, or review a decision (or not to correct it, set it aside or review it) and to grant or refuse permission to appeal without holding a hearing.

Striking out: para (3)

In most cases, the whole point of striking out an appeal will be to bring it to an end without the trouble and expense of a hearing. Para (3) therefore excludes decisions under r8 from the requirement to hold a hearing before disposing of proceedings.

Rule 32(2)

Note, finally, that the tribunal need not hold a hearing if it disposes of the appeal by a consent order under r32.

Entitlement to attend a hearing

28. Subject to rule 30(5) (exclusion of a person from a hearing), each party to proceedings is entitled to attend a hearing.

Notice of hearings

29.–(1) The Tribunal must give each party entitled to attend a hearing reasonable notice of the time and place of the hearing (including any adjourned or postponed hearing) and any changes to the time and place of the hearing.

(2) The period of notice under paragraph (1) must be at least 14 days except that–

(a) *[Omitted]*; and

(b) the Tribunal may give shorter notice–

    (i) with the parties' consent; or

    (ii) in urgent or exceptional circumstances.

General Note

The tribunal must "give" the parties "reasonable notice" of the date, time and place of the hearing. Under para (2), that period of notice must normally be at least 14 days but the primary requirement of "reasonable notice" in para (1) leaves open the possibility that in some cases the parties may be entitled to more than 14 days' notice.

The Rules contain no equivalent to reg 2(2) D&A Regs under which notice sent to a claimant by post is deemed to have been "given" on the date it is posted. In those circumstances, the date on which notice of the hearing is given would appear to be governed by s7 Interpretation Act 1978 which is in the following terms:

"References to service by post.

7. Where an Act authorises or requires any document to be served by post (whether the expression "serve" or the expression "give" or "send" or any other expression is used) then, unless the contrary intention appears, the service is deemed to be effected by properly addressing, pre-paying and posting a letter containing the document and, unless the contrary is proved, to have been effected at the time at which the letter would be delivered in the ordinary course of post."

Para (2)(b) allows the tribunal to give less than 14 days' notice if the parties consent or in urgent or exceptional cases. It is suggested that it will be rare for a social security case to be so urgent that a hearing is required in less than 14 days even when the parties do not consent.

Public and private hearings

30.–(1) Subject to the following paragraphs, all hearings must be held in public.

(2) *[Omitted]*

(3) The Tribunal may give a direction that a hearing, or part of it, is to be held in private.

(4) Where a hearing, or part of it, is to be held in private, the Tribunal may determine who is permitted to attend the hearing or part of it.

(5) The Tribunal may give a direction excluding from any hearing, or part of it–

(a) any person whose conduct the Tribunal considers is disrupting or is likely to disrupt the hearing;

(b) any person whose presence the Tribunal considers is likely to prevent another person from giving evidence or making submissions freely;

(c) any person who the Tribunal considers should be excluded in order to give effect to a direction under rule 14(2) (withholding information likely to cause harm); or

(d) any person where the purpose of the hearing would be defeated by the attendance of that person.

(6)   The Tribunal may give a direction excluding a witness from a hearing until that witness gives evidence.

General Note

The general rule is that hearings must be in public: para (1). However, the tribunal may give a direction in an individual case that the hearing, or part of it, should be private (para (3)) and as to who may attend it (para (4)). In addition, the tribunal may exclude witnesses who have yet to give evidence (para (6)) and anyone (including a party – see r28) who is disrupting or likely to disrupt the hearing or who is likely inhibit others from giving evidence or making submissions or to give effect to a direction under r14(2).

Hearings in a party's absence

31.   If a party fails to attend a hearing the Tribunal may proceed with the hearing if the Tribunal–

(a)   is satisfied that the party has been notified of the hearing or that reasonable steps have been taken to notify the party of the hearing; and

(b)   considers that it is in the interests of justice to proceed with the hearing.

CHAPTER 3
Decisions

Consent orders

32.–(1)   The Tribunal may, at the request of the parties but only if it considers it appropriate, make a consent order disposing of the proceedings and making such other appropriate provision as the parties have agreed.

(2)   Notwithstanding any other provision of these Rules, the Tribunal need not hold a hearing before making an order under paragraph (1), or provide reasons for the order.

Notice of decisions

33.–(1)   The Tribunal may give a decision orally at a hearing.

(2)   Subject to rule 14(2) (withholding information likely to cause harm), the Tribunal must provide to each party as soon as reasonably practicable after making a decision which finally disposes of all issues in the proceedings (except a decision under Part 4)–

(a)   a decision notice stating the Tribunal's decision;

(b)   where appropriate, notification of the right to apply for a written statement of reasons under rule 34(3); and

(c)   notification of any right of appeal against the decision and the time within which, and the manner in which, such right of appeal may be exercised.

(3)   *[Omitted]*

Reasons for decisions

34.–(1)   *[Omitted]*

(2)   In all other cases the Tribunal may give reasons for a decision which disposes of proceedings (except a decision under Part 4)–

(a)   orally at a hearing; or

(b)   in a written statement of reasons to each party.

(3)   Unless the Tribunal has already provided a written statement of reasons under paragraph (2)(b), a party may make a written application to the Tribunal for such statement following a decision which finally disposes of all issues in the proceedings.

(4)   An application under paragraph (3) must be received within 1 month of the date on which the Tribunal sent or otherwise provided to the party a decision notice relating to the decision which finally disposes of all issues in the proceedings.

(5)   If a party makes an application in accordance with paragraphs (3) and (4) the Tribunal must, subject to rule 14(2) (withholding information likely to cause harm), send a written statement of reasons to each party within 1 month of the date on which it received the application or as soon as reasonably practicable after the end of that period.

General Note

The tribunal may give its reasons orally at a hearing (para (2)(a)) and by issuing a written statement of reasons on its own initiative: para (2)(b). If it does not issue a written statement under para (2)(b), any party may make a written application for one under para (3) within one month: para (4). Note that this right exists in relation to "a decision which finally disposes of all issues in the proceedings" and therefore applies to decisions to strike out under r8 as well as decisions on the merits of the appeal. However, reasons for decisions to strike out are likely to be brief. The tribunal must then send the statement to the parties within one month of receiving the application "or as soon as reasonably practicable after the end of that period". For "reasonably practicable", see the General Note to r24 on p1064.

If an application for permission to appeal is made when no written statement of reasons has been issued, then the tribunal must treat the application as being for a statement of reasons: r38(7)(a).

The one-month limit for applying for a statement can be extended under r5(3)(a). However, parties should not assume that such an extension will be granted. The overriding objective is to enable the tribunal to deal with cases fairly and justly. Before there has been a final decision, that objective tends to favour reasonable extensions of time that enable the parties to put their cases to the tribunal. Once a decision has been made, however, the case has been "dealt with" and, although there are rights of appeal, the public interest in the finality of judicial decisions must be weighed when an application is made to exercise those rights other than in accordance with the rules.

PART 4
Correcting, setting aside, reviewing and appealing Tribunal decisions

Interpretation

35. In this Part–

''appeal'' means the exercise of a right of appeal–

  (a)-(b) *[Omitted]*

  (c) on a point of law under section 11 of the 2007 Act; and

''review'' means the review of a decision by the Tribunal under section 9 of the 2007 Act.

Clerical mistakes and accidental slips or omissions

36. The Tribunal may at any time correct any clerical mistake or other accidental slip or omission in a decision, direction or any document produced by it, by–

  (a) sending notification of the amended decision or direction, or a copy of the amended document, to all parties; and

  (b) making any necessary amendment to any information published in relation to the decision, direction or document.

General Note

Rule 36 contains what is known colloquially as the "slip-rule". It allows the tribunal to correct a decision notice, directions notice or a statement of reasons where as a result of "any clerical mistake or other accidental slip or omission" the notice or statement fails to reflect the decision (or directions) the tribunal intended to make or the reasons it intended to give.

It is common for unsuccessful appellants – and sometimes also authorities to apply for a tribunal's decision to be "corrected" because it decided against them and was "incorrect" to do so. The slip rule cannot be used for that purpose. Parties who are dissatisfied with the tribunal's substantive decision must apply for permission to appeal against it.

Setting aside a decision which disposes of proceedings

37.–(1) The Tribunal may set aside a decision which disposes of proceedings, or part of such a decision, and re-make the decision, or the relevant part of it, if–

  (a) the Tribunal considers that it is in the interests of justice to do so; and

  (b) one or more of the conditions in paragraph (2) are satisfied.

  (2) The conditions are–

  (a) a document relating to the proceedings was not sent to, or was not received at an appropriate time by, a party or a party's representative;

  (b) a document relating to the proceedings was not sent to the Tribunal at an appropriate time;

(c) a party, or a party's representative, was not present at a hearing related to the proceedings; or

(d) there has been some other procedural irregularity in the proceedings.

(3) A party applying for a decision, or part of a decision, to be set aside under paragraph (1) must make a written application to the Tribunal so that it is received no later than 1 month after the date on which the Tribunal sent notice of the decision to the party.

General Note

The setting aside procedure provides an expeditious alternative to appealing where there has been some procedural difficulty, but it is important to bear in mind that setting aside is not a substitute for an appeal in all cases and to consider carefully which course is appropriate. If a set aside is refused, an application for leave to appeal to the commissioner can still be made and under r38(3)(c) the time limit for applying for permission to appeal is extended to one month from the date on which the tribunal notifies the party that the application to set aside has been unsuccessful, but only where that application was made in time: reg 38(4).

In *MP v SSWP* (DLA) [2010] UKUT 103 (AAC), Upper Tribunal Judge Turnbull accepted a concession from the Secretary of State for Work and Pensions that a refusal to set aside a decision of the Social Entitlement Chamber of the First-tier Tribunal under r37 TP(FTT) Rules was appealable. In that case, the Upper Tribunal set aside the First-tier Tribunal's substantive decision. However, it stated that, had it not done so, it would have set aside the refusal to set aside and re-made that decision by setting aside the substantive decision.

Setting aside for procedural reasons under this rule must be distinguished from setting aside on review under s9 TCEA 2007 and rule 40.

Analysis

Paras (1) and (2): Grounds for setting aside

Under para (1) there are two grounds for setting aside. Both must be satisfied. The first is that "the Tribunal considers that it is in the interests of justice" to set the decision aside and the second is that one of the conditions in para (2) is satisfied.

The conditions

The first two of those conditions relate to missing documents. This could be a notice of hearing that went astray or a piece of evidence that was missing. It could also be documents relevant to the production of a statement of reasons for a tribunal's decision (under r34(3) and (4)) going astray after the decision has been given: *CDLA 1685/2004*. The grounds will be made out if the document was not received by the applicant, her/his representative or was not sent to the tribunal. Comparison of paras 2(a) and (b) shows that, by a curious quirk of drafting, there is no power to set aside under those paras where a document is sent to the tribunal but not received by it. However, that circumstance would probably constitute "some other procedural irregularity in the proceedings" within para (2)(d). The document must be one that existed at the appropriate time, rather than one which has, for example, been brought into existence in response to the tribunal's decision. It is not possible to send or receive a non-existent document.

Para (2)(c) applies where the applicant or representative "was not present at a hearing related to the proceedings". If there has been a hearing, then this condition is self-explanatory. But what if there has been no hearing because the applicant did not ask for one or asked for the appeal to be decided without a hearing and then regrets that omission or choice? Is it possible to say that someone "was not present" at a hearing that did not take place? It is suggested that it is. The former reg 57(1)(b) SS D&A Regs used almost identical wording and was followed by reg 55(2) which made it clear that reg 57(1)(b) did apply to decisions made without a hearing under the former reg 39. It is suggested that the absence of any provision equivalent to reg 57(2) in these rules is merely to remove the former requirement that a decision without a hearing could only be set aside because of the absence of a party where "the interests of justice manifestly so require".

Para (2)(d) allows the tribunal to set aside a decision where there has been "some other procedural irregularity in the proceedings". This wording is deliberately wide so as to allow justice to be done in a wide range of individual cases. It has some similarity with the old ground for setting aside "where the interests of justice so require" under reg 86(1)(c) HB Regs 1987 (revoked on 2 July 2001). One difference, however, is that the tribunal now has an express power to waive procedural irregularities under r7(2)(a). Presumably, an irregularity that has been waived under that rule cannot subsequently form the basis of a decision to set aside under r37(2)(d).

A procedural irregularity that affected, or might have affected, the outcome of the appeal will also be an error of law and may therefore form the basis of an appeal to the Upper Tribunal.

The interests of justice

Even if one or more of the para (2) conditions are satisfied, the tribunal need not set the decision aside if it considers it to be "in the interests of justice to do so". This will not always be so. For example, the applicant may have made a deliberate decision not to attend the hearing, or a procedural mistake may have made no difference to the outcome.

Procedure

Under para (3), an application to set aside must be made in writing and received by the tribunal within one month of the decision notice. That limit may be extended under r5(3)(a) where to do so would further the overriding objective. Note that an application for a written statement of reasons under r34(3) does not automatically extend the time for applying to set the decision aside. This is a change from the former reg 57 SS D&A Regs. Moreover, the tribunal's express power under r41 to treat certain applications as other applications does not permit an application to set aside to be treated as an application under r34(3). However, if the tribunal chooses to do so, it may (r34(2)) issue a written statement on its own initiative at any time.

Application for permission to appeal

38.–(1) This rule does not apply to asylum support cases or criminal injuries compensation cases.

(2) A person seeking permission to appeal must make a written application to the Tribunal for permission to appeal.

(3) An application under paragraph (2) must be sent or delivered to the Tribunal so that it is received no later than 1 month after the latest of the dates that the Tribunal sends to the person making the application–

(a) written reasons for the decision;

(b) notification of amended reasons for, or correction of, the decision following a review; or

(c) notification that an application for the decision to be set aside has been unsuccessful.

(4) The date in paragraph (3)(c) applies only if the application for the decision to be set aside was made within the time stipulated in rule 37 (setting aside a decision which disposes of proceedings) or any extension of that time granted by the Tribunal.

(5) If the person seeking permission to appeal sends or delivers the application to the Tribunal later than the time required by paragraph (3) or by any extension of time under rule 5(3)(a) (power to extend time)–

(a) the application must include a request for an extension of time and the reason why the application was not provided in time; and

(b) unless the Tribunal extends time for the application under rule 5(3)(a) (power to extend time) the Tribunal must not admit the application.

(6) An application under paragraph (2) must–

(a) identify the decision of the Tribunal to which it relates;

(b) identify the alleged error or errors of law in the decision; and

(c) state the result the party making the application is seeking.

(7) If a person makes an application under paragraph (2) when the Tribunal has not given a written statement of reasons for its decision–

(a) if no application for a written statement of reasons has been made to the Tribunal, the application for permission must be treated as such an application;

(b) unless the Tribunal decides to give permission and directs that this sub-paragraph does not apply, the application is not to be treated as an application for permission to appeal; and

(c) if an application for a written statement of reasons has been, or is, refused because of a delay in making the application, the Tribunal must only admit the application for permission if the Tribunal considers that it is in the interests of justice to do so.

General Note

An application for permission to appeal must be in writing: para (3). By para (6) it must identify the tribunal decision which the applicant wishes to appeal, identify the alleged error or errors of law and state the result the applicant is seeking – ie, how s/he wishes the Upper Tribunal to exercise its powers under s12 TCEA 2007.

The application must be received by the tribunal within one month from the latest of the dates on which the tribunal sent the applicant the written statement of reasons under r34, notification that the decision (or the reasons for it) has been amended following review under s9 TCEA 2007 and r40, or notice that an in-time application to set aside has been refused: paras (3) and (4). That time limit may be extended under r5(3)(a) either on an application under para (5) or (by waiving para(5) under r7(2)(a)) on the tribunal's own initiative.

Para (7) sets out what should happen when, as is common, an application for permission to appeal is made when no written statement of reasons has been made under r34. The application must be treated as being for a statement of reasons. It will also be treated as not being an application for permission to appeal unless the tribunal is prepared to give permission to appeal and directs that para (7)(2) should not apply. Where there is no written statement of reasons because of delay in applying for one, the tribunal may only admit the application for permission to appeal where it is in the interests of justice to do so. In practice it will be difficult for the tribunal to be persuaded that a decision contains an arguable error of law where no statement of reasons has been given.

Tribunal's consideration of application for permission to appeal

39.–(1)   On receiving an application for permission to appeal the Tribunal must first consider, taking into account the overriding objective in rule 2, whether to review the decision in accordance with rule 40 (review of a decision).

(2)   If the Tribunal decides not to review the decision, or reviews the decision and decides to take no action in relation to the decision, or part of it, the Tribunal must consider whether to give permission to appeal in relation to the decision or that part of it.

(3)   The Tribunal must send a record of its decision to the parties as soon as practicable.

(4)   If the Tribunal refuses permission to appeal it must send with the record of its decision–

(a)   a statement of its reasons for such refusal; and

(b)   notification of the right to make an application to the Upper Tribunal for permission to appeal and the time within which, and the method by which, such application must be made.

(5)   The Tribunal may give permission to appeal on limited grounds, but must comply with paragraph (4) in relation to any grounds on which it has refused permission.

General Note

The tribunal must first consider whether to review the decision under s9 TCEA 2007 and r40: para (1). If it decides not to review the decision, or reviews the decision but does not take any action in respect of it, it must consider the application for permission to appeal: para (2). Reasons must be given for any refusal: para (4). A decision to review the tribunal's decision but take no action implies that the reviewing judge considers that the decision contained an error of law (see r40(2)(b)). Therefore, any subsequent refusal of permission to appeal should be based on the discretion not to grant permission to appeal where there is an error of law rather than on the absence of an error of law: see *VH v Suffolk County Council* [2010] UKUT 203 (AAC). Permission to appeal may be given on limited grounds, in which case reasons must be given for the refusal of any other grounds: para (5). It is not unlawful for a judge of the First-tier Tribunal to consider an application for permission to appeal from her/ his own decision: see *AA v Cheshire and Wirral Partnership NHS Foundation Trust* [2009] UKUT 195 (AAC) (paras 26-27) and *DL v LB Redbridge* [2010] UKUT 293 (AAC).

Reasons given for refusing permission to appeal may not add to the tribunal's reasons in order to bolster its decision in the light of the grounds of appeal.

Review of a decision

40.–(1)   This rule does not apply to asylum support cases or criminal injuries compensation cases.

(2)   The Tribunal may only undertake a review of a decision–

(a)   pursuant to rule 39(1) (review on an application for permission to appeal); and

(b)   if it is satisfied that there was an error of law in the decision.

(3)   The Tribunal must notify the parties in writing of the outcome of any review, and of any right of appeal in relation to the outcome.

(4)   If the Tribunal takes any action in relation to a decision following a review without first giving every party an opportunity to make representations, the notice under paragraph (3) must state that any party that did not have an opportunity to make representations may apply for such action to be set aside and for the decision to be reviewed again.

General Note

This rule establishes the procedure under which the tribunal may review its decision under s9 TCEA 2007.

Para (2) provides that the power to review may only be exercised on an application for permission to appeal (which presumably includes an application treated as an application for permission to appeal under r41) and where the original decision contains an error of law. A three-judge panel of the Upper Tribunal has held that the power to review should only be exercised where the decision is clearly wrong in law so as not to usurp the Upper Tribunal's function of deciding contentious points of law. The power of review was not intended to enable the judge to take a different view on the law from that previously reached when both views are tenable: see *R (RB) v First-tier Tribunal (Review)* [2010] UKUT 160 (AAC).

The view expressed in previous editions, that the requirement that there should be an application for permission to appeal is *ultra vires*, may be incorrect. It is now considered that para 6 of Sch 1 TCEA 2007 may confer the necessary power, even though – for the reasons given at p 1038 of the 22nd edition – s9 TCEA 2007 does not.

By para 11 of the Senior President's Practice Statement on the Composition of Tribunals in Child Support and Social Security Cases in the Social Entitlement Chamber (see pp1067-1068), the review must be carried out by a salaried tribunal judge. Where the judge who constituted or chaired the tribunal was a salaried judge, s/he must carry out the review unless it would be impracticable or cause undue delay. *AA v Cheshire and Wirral Partnership NHS Foundation Trust* [2009] UKUT 195 (AAC) (paras 26-27) confirms that it is not unlawful for a tribunal judge to carry out a review of her/his own decision.

The first step the reviewing judge must take is to consider whether there was an error of law in the original decision. Until such an error has been identified, no review can be carried out and the powers listed in s 9(4) TCEA 2007 do not arise see *SE v SSWP* [2009] UKUT 163 (AAC) and *AM v SSWP* [2009] UKUT 224 (AAC). The purported exercise of the powers before an error of law has been identified, renders the review a nullity (*AM v SSWP* at para 15).

In *LM v SSWP* [2009] UKUT 185 (AAC), the tribunal judge made a bizarre attempt to pre-empt the exercise of the review power by purporting to consider when the original decision was made whether it was wrong in law, concluding (unsurprisingly!) that it was not, and then declaring that the issue was *res judicata* (ie, that it was an issue that had been finally determined by the tribunal and could not be re-opened). The decision of the Upper Tribunal confirms that this is not permissible.

On the assumption that the original decision did contain an error of law, the salaried tribunal judge may review it and may (under s9(4) TCEA 2007) correct accidental errors in the decision, amend the decision, or set the decision aside. Those powers are cumulative and not exclusive so that the First-tier Tribunal may exercise more than one of them on a review, (*AM v SSWP* (above) at para 7).

Particular problems arise in relation to the amendment of statements of reasons. To begin with, the reviewing judge will probably not be the same judge who heard (or presided over) the appeal and wrote the statement. In *AM v SSWP* (above), Judge Agnew of Locknaw considered those circumstances and gave the following advice:

"11.   If, following representations, the salaried judge determines that the tribunal should be given such an opportunity, then the appeal should be remitted to the fee-paid chairman to determine whether or not to amend the Statement of Reasons together with a note of any representations made to the salaried judge. In light of the Practice Statement, the salaried chairman having received any proposed amendments to the Statement of Reasons from the fee-paid judge, if so advised, the salaried chairman should the take the action to amend the Statement of Reasons."

However, the problems are not just procedural. Issues also arise as to the extent of the power and as to whether the statement of reasons ought to be amended even when there is power to do so.

Upper Tribunal Judge White gave guidance on the former issue in *SE v SSWP* (above):

"28.   In cases where (as in this case) the tribunal which decided the case consisted of a panel of three, any subsequent variation of the statement of reasons must reflect issues which were discussed by all three members of the tribunal, but which were then inadvertently not included in the statement written by the chair of the tribunal. If this is not the case, then the decision will not be that of the tribunal which heard the case, but in part that of just one of its members. It would follow that in such cases the chair in revising the statement of reasons should state explicitly (1) that the issue which is the subject of revision was expressly considered and discussed by all members of the tribunal, and (2) what is now added to the statement of reasons represents actual conclusions of the whole tribunal (rather than something which the chair thinks they would have concluded if they had considered the point in issue).

29.   It would not be right in my view for the power in rule 40 to be used in some informal way as a means of adding to the reasons when prompted by an application for permission to appeal, and in order to address issues raised in the application which had not been fully considered by the tribunal in its deliberations."

Paragraph 28 above was quoted with approval in *AM v SSWP* (above).

As to the latter issue Judge Agnew stated:

"21.   Section 9(4)(b) of the 2007 Act does give the tribunal a power to amend a Statement of Reasons and therefore supersedes Mr Levenson's decision in CA/4297/2004 that it was not competent to amend a Statement of Reasons. The issue therefore is the circumstances in which such a power ought to be exercised. Considerable guidance is given in both *Barke v SEETEC Business Technology Centre Ltd* [2005] EWCA Civ 578 and *English v Emerty Reimgold & Strick Ltd* [2002] 1 WLR 2409. It is clear from those cases that a tribunal that has failed to give reasons or failed to deal with a particular point may deal with such a lacuna and provide those reasons. I consider the same approach applies to a tribunal, which will generally be expected to act professionally in amending a Statement of Reasons and therefore may, as the tribunal purported to do in this case, deal with the lacuna.

. . .

22.   However, a tribunal that has to decide whether or not to exercise the power to amend a Statement of Reasons should consider whether or not in the particular circumstances it ought to do so. Where a Statement of Reasons deals with a point, but in retrospect can be seen to have dealt with it inadequately or unclearly, then it may be reasonable to amend the reasons to amplify or clarify the point. If an argument is not dealt with in the Statement of Reasons at all, then more careful consideration might have to be given to whether or not the lacuna should be filled by new material in the Statement of Reasons on this point. The length of time since the hearing might be relevant, as might be the availability of contemporary material showing what was the decision and the reasons of the tribunal at the time. These are all matters upon which the parties might want to make representations, which could be of assistance to the tribunal in determining whether or not to consider amending the Statement of Reasons."

If the judge sets the decision aside, the tribunal must either re-make the decision or refer it to the Upper Tribunal: s9(5). As almost all HB/CTB appeals are decided by a single judge sitting alone, this will probably mean that the judge who carries out the review also re-decides the appeal. Appeals involving other benefits (eg, disability living allowance or employment and support allowance) are decided by a judge sitting with at least one other member. The reviewing judge will therefore refer the reviewed appeal to an appropriately constituted panel to be re-decided.

For the procedural safeguards which must be observed on a review, particularly where the proposed outcome is amended reasons for the same result: see *SE v SSWP* [2009] UKUT 163 (AAC). Where (as is the case with HB/CTB decisions) the decision is one that may be heard by a single tribunal judge, the tribunal may re-make the decision immediately and may make new findings of fact: s9(8). In some other social security cases, the appeal will be listed before a two- or three-member panel for decision.

Where the decision is referred to the Upper Tribunal, it must re-decide the matter (s9(6)) and may make any decision the First-tier Tribunal could have made: s9(7).

Para (4) of r40 provides that where the tribunal takes any action in relation to a decision following a review without first giving every party an opportunity to make representations, then the notice of the review decision must inform the parties that any party who did not have an opportunity to make representations may apply for the action taken following the review decision to be set aside and for the decision to be reviewed again.

This rule can probably be reconciled with s9(10) TCEA 2007 which provides that a decision of the Tribunal may not be reviewed more than once by drawing a distinction between the review itself (the formal process of re-considering the decision) and the action taken following that review (ie, the steps listed in s9(4) TCEA): although the review cannot be set aside, the consequential action can.

In *SE v SSWP* and *AM v SSWP* (above), the Upper Tribunal held that a failure to follow the procedure in rule 40(4) renders the review a nullity. This partially solves any problem that might be thought to exist despite the previous paragraph: where the First-tier Tribunal does not either seek representations from the parties before the review or inform them of the possibility that the action taken following the review may be set aside, then the first review will be a nullity and s9(10) therefore has no application. However, in a case where the Tribunal does not seek representations before the review but *does* give the notice required by rule 40(4), the review is not a nullity and the problem remains.

In those circumstances, it is suggested that the tribunal should usually seek representations from all parties before taking any action under s9(4).

Power to treat an application as a different type of application

41.   The Tribunal may treat an application for a decision to be corrected, set aside or reviewed, or for permission to appeal against a decision, as an application for any other one of those things.

SCHEDULE 1
TIME LIMITS FOR PROVIDING NOTICES OF APPEAL TO THE DECISION MAKER

Type of proceedings	Time for providing notice of appeal

[² Cases other than those listed below]	[² The latest of–
	(a) one month after the date on which notice of the decision being challenged was sent to the appellant;
	(b) if a written statement of reasons for the decision was requested within that month, 14 days after the later of–
	  (i) the end of that month; or
	  (ii) the date on which the written statement of reasons was provided; or
	(c) if the appellant made an application for revision of the decision under–
	  (i) regulation 17(1)(a) of the Child Support (Maintenance Assessment Procedure) Regulations 1992,
	  (ii) regulation 3(1) or (3) or 3A(1) of the Social Security and Child Support (Decision and Appeals) Regulations 1999, or
	  (iii) regulation 4 of the Housing Benefit and Council Tax Benefit (Decisions and Appeals) Regulations 2001,
	and that application was unsuccessful, one month after the date on which notice that the decision would not be revised was sent to the appellant.]

Amendments

1. Substituted by r4 of SI 2009 No 1975 as from 1.9.09.
2. Substituted by r5(4) of SI 2010 No 2653 as from 29.11.10.

General Note

Sch 1 contains the time limits for appealing. In social security cases, the limit is normally one month from the date on which the decision being appealed was sent to the appellant: para (a). However, where the appellant requests a written statement of reasons for the decision under appeal (ie, under reg 90(2) HB Regs, reg 71 HB(SPC) Regs, reg 76(2) CTB Regs and reg 61 CTB(SPC) Regs) within that one-month period, the time limit for appealing is extended until 14 days after the one-month period or 14 days after the date on which the statement of reasons was provided. Until 1 November 2010, the effect of para (b) was to circumvent the (supposedly) absolute 13-month time limit (see p1039 of the 22nd edition).

Until 1 September 2009, the drafting of para (c) was also defective. See p1101 of the 21st edition for details.

The Qualifications for Appointment of Members to the First-tier Tribunal and Upper Tribunal Order 2008
2008 No.2692

1.–(1)   This Order may be cited as the Qualifications for Appointment of Members to the First-tier Tribunal and Upper Tribunal Order 2008 and shall come into force on 3rd November 2008.

[¹ (2)   In this Order ''registered medical practitioner'' means a fully registered person within the meaning of the Medical Act 1983 whether or not they hold a licence to practise under that Act.]

Amendment
1.   Amended by Art 3 of SI 2009 No 1592 as from 16.11.09.

2.–(1)   A person is eligible for appointment as a member of the First-tier Tribunal or the Upper Tribunal who is not a judge of those tribunals if paragraph (2), (3) or (4) applies.
  (2)   This paragraph applies to a person who is–
  (a)   a registered medical practitioner;
  (b)   a registered nurse;
  (c)   a registered dentist;
  [¹ (ca) a registered optometrist;]
  (d)   a clinical psychologist;
  (e)   an educational psychologist;
  (f)   a pharmacologist;
  (g)   a veterinary surgeon or a veterinary practitioner registered under the Veterinary Surgeons Act 1966;
  (h)   a Member or Fellow of the Royal Institution of Chartered Surveyors; or
  (i)   an accountant who is a member of–
      (i)   the Institute of Chartered Accountants in England and Wales;
      (ii)   the Institute of Chartered Accountants in Scotland;
      (iii) the Institute of Chartered Accountants in Ireland;
      (iv)   the Institute of Certified Public Accountants in Ireland;
      (v)   the Association of Chartered Certified Accountants;
      (vi)   the Chartered Institute of Management Accountants; or
      (vii) the Chartered Institute of Public Finance and Accountancy.
  (3)   This paragraph applies to a person [¹] who is experienced in dealing with the physical or mental needs of disabled persons because they–
  (a)   work with disabled persons in a professional or voluntary capacity; or
  (b)   are themselves disabled.
  [¹ (3A)   A person is not eligible for appointment under paragraph (3) if they are a registered medical practitioner.]
  (4)   This paragraph applies to a person who has substantial experience–
  (a)   of service in Her Majesty's naval, military, or air forces;
  (b)   of educational, child care, health, or social care matters;
  (c)   of dealing with victims of violent crime;
  (d)   in transport operations and its law and practice;
  (e)   in the regulatory field;
  (f)   in consumer affairs;
  (g)   in an industry, trade or business sector and the matters that are likely to arise as issues in the course of disputes with regulators of such industries, trades or businesses;
  (h)   in tax matters and related tax procedures;
  (i)   in a business, trade [¹ , charity] or not-for-profit organisation.

[¹ (j) in immigration services or the law and procedure relating to immigration;
(k) of data protection;
(l) of freedom of information (including environmental information) rights;
(m) of service as a Member or Senior Officer of a local authority in England.]

Amendment

1. Amended by Art 4 of SI 2009 No 1592 as from 1.9.09.

The Tribunal Procedure (Upper Tribunal) Rules 2008
2008 No. 2698 (L. 15)

PART 1
Introduction

Citation, commencement, application and interpretation

1.–(1) These Rules may be cited as the Tribunal Procedure (Upper Tribunal) Rules 2008 and come into force on 3rd November 2008.

(2) These Rules apply to proceedings before the Upper Tribunal [² except proceedings in the Lands Chamber].

(3) In these Rules–

"the 2007 Act" means the Tribunals, Courts and Enforcement Act 2007;

[¹ "appellant" means–

- (a) a person who makes an appeal, or applies for permission to appeal, to the Upper Tribunal;
- (b) in proceedings transferred or referred to the Upper Tribunal from the First-tier Tribunal, a person who started the proceedings in the First-tier Tribunal; or
- (c) a person substituted as an appellant under rule 9(1) (substitution and addition of parties);]

[³ "applicant" means–

- (a) a person who applies for permission to bring, or does bring, judicial review proceedings before the Upper Tribunal and, in judicial review proceedings transferred to the Upper Tribunal from a court, includes a person who was a claimant or petitioner in the proceedings immediately before they were transferred; or
- (b) a person who refers a financial services case to the Upper Tribunal;]

[² "appropriate national authority" means, in relation to an appeal, the Secretary of State, the Scottish Ministers or the Welsh Ministers, as the case may be;

"authorised person" means an examiner appointed by the Secretary of State under section 66A of the Road Traffic Act 1988(10), or a person acting under the direction of such an examiner, who has detained the vehicle to which an appeal relates;]

"dispose of proceedings" includes, unless indicated otherwise, disposing of a part of the proceedings;

"document" means anything in which information is recorded in any form, and an obligation under these Rules or any practice direction or direction to provide or allow access to a document or a copy of a document for any purpose means, unless the Upper Tribunal directs otherwise, an obligation to provide or allow access to such document or copy in a legible form or in a form which can be readily made into a legible form;

"hearing" means an oral hearing and includes a hearing conducted in whole or in part by video link, telephone or other means of instantaneous two-way electronic communication;

"interested party" means–

- (a) a person who is directly affected by the outcome sought in judicial review proceedings, and has been named as an interested party under rule 28 or 29 (judicial review), or has been substituted or added as an interested party under rule 9 [⁴ (addition, substitution and removal of parties)]; [⁴]
- (b) in judicial review proceedings transferred to the Upper Tribunal under section 25A(2) or (3) of the Judicature (Northern Ireland) Act 1978 or section 31A(2) or (3) of the Supreme Court Act 1981, a person who was an interested party in the proceedings immediately before they were transferred to the Upper Tribunal; [⁴ and
- (c) [Omitted]

"judicial review proceedings" means proceedings within the jurisdiction of the Upper Tribunal pursuant to section 15 or 21 of the 2007 Act, whether such proceedings are started in the Upper Tribunal or transferred to the Upper Tribunal;

[¹]

"party" means a person who is an appellant, an applicant, a respondent or an interested party in proceedings before the Upper Tribunal, a person who has referred a question [⁴ or matter] to the Upper Tribunal or, if the proceedings have been concluded, a person who was an appellant, an applicant, a respondent or an interested party when the Tribunal finally disposed of all issues in the proceedings;

"permission" includes leave in cases arising under the law of Northern Ireland;

"practice direction" means a direction given under section 23 of the 2007 Act;

"respondent" means–
(a) in an appeal, or application for permission to appeal, against a decision of another tribunal, any person other than the appellant who–
  (i) was a party before that other tribunal;
  [¹ (ii)]
  (iii) otherwise has a right of appeal against the decision of the other tribunal and has given notice to the Upper Tribunal that they wish to be a party to the appeal;
(b) in an appeal against any other decision [² except a decision of a traffic commissioner], the person who made the decision;
(c) in judicial review proceedings–
  (i) in proceedings started in the Upper Tribunal, the person named by the applicant as the respondent;
  (ii) in proceedings transferred to the Upper Tribunal under section 25A(2) or (3) of the Judicature (Northern Ireland) Act 1978 or section 31A(2) or (3) of the Supreme Court Act 1981, a person who was a defendant in the proceedings immediately before they were transferred;
  (iii) in proceedings transferred to the Upper Tribunal under section 20(1) of the 2007 Act, a person to whom intimation of the petition was made before the proceedings were transferred, or to whom the Upper Tribunal has required intimation to be made.
[¹ (ca) in proceedings transferred or referred to the Upper Tribunal from the First-tier Tribunal, a person who was a respondent in the proceedings in the First-tier Tribunal;]
(d) *[Omitted]*; [⁴
(da) *[Omitted]*;]
(e) a person substituted or added as a respondent under rule 9 (substitution and addition of parties);

[² "tribunal" does not include a traffic commissioner;]

"working day" means any day except a Saturday or Sunday, Christmas Day, Good Friday or a bank holiday under section 1 of the Banking and Financial Dealings Act 1971.

Amendments

1. Amended by r5 of SI 2009 No 274 as from 1.4.09.
2. Amended by r8 of SI 2009 No 1975 as from 1.9.09.
3. Substituted by r4(a) of SI 2010 No 747 as from 6.4.10.
4. Amended by r4(c)-(f) of SI 2010 No 747 as from 6.4.10.

Overriding objective and parties' obligation to co-operate with the Upper Tribunal

2.–(1) The overriding objective of these Rules is to enable the Upper Tribunal to deal with cases fairly and justly.

(2) Dealing with a case fairly and justly includes–
(a) dealing with the case in ways which are proportionate to the importance of the case, the complexity of the issues, the anticipated costs and the resources of the parties;

(b)   avoiding unnecessary formality and seeking flexibility in the proceedings;

(c)   ensuring, so far as practicable, that the parties are able to participate fully in the proceedings;

(d)   using any special expertise of the Upper Tribunal effectively; and

(e)   avoiding delay, so far as compatible with proper consideration of the issues.

(3)   The Upper Tribunal must seek to give effect to the overriding objective when it–

(a)   exercises any power under these Rules; or

(b)   interprets any rule or practice direction.

(4)   Parties must–

(a)   help the Upper Tribunal to further the overriding objective; and

(b)   co-operate with the Upper Tribunal generally.

General Note
See the commentary to r2 TP(FT) Rules 2008 on p1049.

Alternative dispute resolution and arbitration

3.–(1)   The Upper Tribunal should seek, where appropriate–

(a)   to bring to the attention of the parties the availability of any appropriate alternative procedure for the resolution of the dispute; and

(b)   if the parties wish and provided that it is compatible with the overriding objective, to facilitate the use of the procedure.

(2)   Part 1 of the Arbitration Act 1996 does not apply to proceedings before the Upper Tribunal.

PART 2
General powers and provisions

Delegation to staff

4.–(1)   Staff appointed under section 40(1) of the 2007 Act (tribunal staff and services) may, with the approval of the Senior President of Tribunals, carry out functions of a judicial nature permitted or required to be done by the Upper Tribunal.

(2)   The approval referred to at paragraph (1) may apply generally to the carrying out of specified functions by members of staff of a specified description in specified circumstances.

(3)   Within 14 days after the date on which the Upper Tribunal sends notice of a decision made by a member of staff under paragraph (1) to a party, that party may apply in writing to the Upper Tribunal for that decision to be considered afresh by a judge.

General Note
Certain case management powers of the Upper Tribunal have been delegated to Registrars (the former "legal officers"). According to the Upper Tribunal website, Registrars "deal with matters of procedure before an Upper Tribunal judge decides whether to give permission for an appeal to be made . . . [and] with matters such as directing submissions from parties and directing hearings, until the case is ready to be decided by the Upper Tribunal judge. They also undertake research for Upper Tribunal judges." However, Registrars do not grant or refuse permission to appeal or decide appeals.

Case management powers

5.–(1)   Subject to the provisions of the 2007 Act and any other enactment, the Upper Tribunal may regulate its own procedure.

(2)   The Upper Tribunal may give a direction in relation to the conduct or disposal of proceedings at any time, including a direction amending, suspending or setting aside an earlier direction.

(3)   In particular, and without restricting the general powers in paragraphs (1) and (2), the Upper Tribunal may–

(a)   extend or shorten the time for complying with any rule, practice direction or direction;

(b) consolidate or hear together two or more sets of proceedings or parts of proceedings raising common issues, or treat a case as a lead case;
(c) permit or require a party to amend a document;
(d) permit or require a party or another person to provide documents, information, evidence or submissions to the Upper Tribunal or a party;
(e) deal with an issue in the proceedings as a preliminary issue;
(f) hold a hearing to consider any matter, including a case management issue;
(g) decide the form of any hearing;
(h) adjourn or postpone a hearing;
(i) require a party to produce a bundle for a hearing;
(j) stay (or, in Scotland, sist) proceedings;
(k) transfer proceedings to another court or tribunal if that other court or tribunal has jurisdiction in relation to the proceedings and–
    (i) because of a change of circumstances since the proceedings were started, the Upper Tribunal no longer has jurisdiction in relation to the proceedings; or
    (ii) the Upper Tribunal considers that the other court or tribunal is a more appropriate forum for the determination of the case;
(l) suspend the effect of its own decision pending an appeal or review of that decision;
(m) in an appeal, or an application for permission to appeal, against the decision of another tribunal, suspend the effect of that decision pending the determination of the application for permission to appeal, and any appeal;
[¹ (n) require any person, body or other tribunal whose decision is the subject of proceedings before the Upper Tribunal to provide reasons for the decision, or other information or documents in relation to the decision or any proceedings before that person, body or tribunal.]
[(4)-(6) *[Omitted]*]

Amendment
1.   Substituted by r9 of SI 2009 No 1975 as from 1.9.09.

General Note
See the commentary to r5 TP(FT) Rules 2008 on p1052.

Procedure for applying for and giving directions

6.–(1) The Upper Tribunal may give a direction on the application of one or more of the parties or on its own initiative.
(2) An application for a direction may be made–
(a) by sending or delivering a written application to the Upper Tribunal; or
(b) orally during the course of a hearing.
(3) An application for a direction must include the reason for making that application.
(4) Unless the Upper Tribunal considers that there is good reason not to do so, the Upper Tribunal must send written notice of any direction to every party and to any other person affected by the direction.
(5) If a party or any other person sent notice of the direction under paragraph (4) wishes to challenge a direction which the Upper Tribunal has given, they may do so by applying for another direction which amends, suspends or sets aside the first direction.

General Note
See the commentary to r6 TP(FT) Rules 2008 on p1053.

Failure to comply with rules etc.

7.–(1) An irregularity resulting from a failure to comply with any requirement in these Rules, a practice direction or a direction, does not of itself render void the proceedings or any step taken in the proceedings.

(2)   If a party has failed to comply with a requirement in these Rules, a practice direction or a direction, the Upper Tribunal may take such action as it considers just, which may include–
(a)   waiving the requirement;
(b)   requiring the failure to be remedied;
(c)   exercising its power under rule 8 (striking out a party's case); or
(d)   except in [¹ a mental health case, an asylum case or an immigration case], restricting a party's participation in the proceedings.
(3)   Paragraph (4) applies where the First-tier Tribunal has referred to the Upper Tribunal a failure by a person to comply with a requirement imposed by the First-tier Tribunal–
(a)   to attend at any place for the purpose of giving evidence;
(b)   otherwise to make themselves available to give evidence;
(c)   to swear an oath in connection with the giving of evidence;
(d)   to give evidence as a witness;
(e)   to produce a document; or
(f)   to facilitate the inspection of a document or any other thing (including any premises).
(4)   The Upper Tribunal may exercise its power under section 25 of the 2007 Act (supplementary powers of the Upper Tribunal) in relation to such non-compliance as if the requirement had been imposed by the Upper Tribunal.

Amendment
1.   Amended by r5 of SI 2010 No 44 as from 15.2.10.

General Note
See the commentary to r7 TP(FT) Rules 2008 on p1053.

Striking out a party's case
8.– [(1A)   *[Omitted]*]
(1)   The proceedings, or the appropriate part of them, will automatically be struck out if the appellant or applicant has failed to comply with a direction that stated that failure by the appellant or applicant to comply with the direction would lead to the striking out of the proceedings or that part of them.
(2)   The Upper Tribunal must strike out the whole or a part of the proceedings if the Upper Tribunal–
(a)   does not have jurisdiction in relation to the proceedings or that part of them; and
(b)   does not exercise its power under rule 5(3)(k)(i) (transfer to another court or tribunal) in relation to the proceedings or that part of them.
(3)   The Upper Tribunal may strike out the whole or a part of the proceedings if–
(a)   the appellant or applicant has failed to comply with a direction which stated that failure by the appellant or applicant to comply with the direction could lead to the striking out of the proceedings or part of them;
(b)   the appellant or applicant has failed to co-operate with the Upper Tribunal to such an extent that the Upper Tribunal cannot deal with the proceedings fairly and justly; or
(c)   in proceedings which are not an appeal from the decision of another tribunal or judicial review proceedings, the Upper Tribunal considers there is no reasonable prospect of the appellant's or the applicant's case, or part of it, succeeding.
(4)   The Upper Tribunal may not strike out the whole or a part of the proceedings under paragraph (2) or (3)(b) or (c) without first giving the appellant or applicant an opportunity to make representations in relation to the proposed striking out.
(5)   If the proceedings have been struck out under paragraph (1) or (3)(a), the appellant or applicant may apply for the proceedings, or part of them, to be reinstated.
(6)   An application under paragraph (5) must be made in writing and received by the Upper Tribunal within 1 month after the date on which the Upper Tribunal sent notification of the striking out to the appellant or applicant.

(7)   This rule applies to a respondent [¹ or an interested party] as it applies to an appellant or applicant except that–

(a)   a reference to the striking out of the proceedings is to be read as a reference to the barring of the respondent [¹ or an interested party] from taking further part in the proceedings; and

(b)   a reference to an application for the reinstatement of proceedings which have been struck out is to be read as a reference to an application for the lifting of the bar on the respondent [¹ or an interested party] [¹] taking further part in the proceedings.

(8)   If a respondent [¹ or an interested party] has been barred from taking further part in proceedings under this rule and that bar has not been lifted, the Upper Tribunal need not consider any response or other submission made by that respondent [¹ or interested party, and may summarily determine any or all issues against that respondent or interested party].

Amendment

1.   Amended by r6 of SI 2009 No 274 as from 1.4.09.

General Note

See the commentary to r8 TP(FT) Rules 2008 on p1054.

Substitution and addition of parties

[¹ **9.**–(1)   The Upper Tribunal may give a direction adding, substituting or removing a party as an appellant, a respondent or an interested party.

(2)   If the Upper Tribunal gives a direction under paragraph (1) it may give such consequential directions as it considers appropriate.

(3)   A person who is not a party may apply to the Upper Tribunal to be added or substituted as a party.

(4)   If a person who is entitled to be a party to proceedings by virtue of another enactment applies to be added as a party, and any conditions applicable to that entitlement have been satisfied, the Upper Tribunal must give a direction adding that person as a respondent or, if appropriate, as an appellant.]

[(5)   *[Omitted]*

(6)   *[Omitted]*]

Amendment

1.   Substituted by r10 of SI 2009 No 1975 as from 1.9.09.

[¹ Orders for costs

10.–(1) The Upper Tribunal may not make an order in respect of costs (or, in Scotland, expenses) in proceedings [² transferred or referred by, or on appeal from,] another tribunal except–

[(aa) *[Omitted]*]

(a)   in proceedings [² transferred by, or on appeal from,] the Tax Chamber of the First-tier Tribunal; or

(b)   to the extent and in the circumstances that the other tribunal had the power to make an order in respect of costs (or, in Scotland, expenses).

[(1A)   *[Omitted]*]

(2)   The Upper Tribunal may not make an order in respect of costs or expenses under section 4 of the Forfeiture Act 1982.

(3)   In other proceedings, the Upper Tribunal may not make an order in respect of costs or expenses except–

(a)   in judicial review proceedings;

[² (b)]

(c)   under section 29(4) of the 2007 Act (wasted costs); [³]

(d)   if the Upper Tribunal considers that a party or its representative has acted unreasonably in bringing, defending or conducting the proceedings.[³ or

(e)   *[Omitted]*]

(4)   The Upper Tribunal may make an order for costs (or, in Scotland, expenses) on an application or on its own initiative.

(5)   A person making an application for an order for costs or expenses must–

(a)   send or deliver a written application to the Upper Tribunal and to the person against whom it is proposed that the order be made; and

(b)   send or deliver with the application a schedule of the costs or expenses claimed sufficient to allow summary assessment of such costs or expenses by the Upper Tribunal.

(6)   An application for an order for costs or expenses may be made at any time during the proceedings but may not be made later than 1 month after the date on which the Upper Tribunal sends–

(a)   a decision notice recording the decision which finally disposes of all issues in the proceedings; or

(b)   notice of a withdrawal under rule 17 which ends the proceedings.

(7)   The Upper Tribunal may not make an order for costs or expenses against a person (the "paying person") without first–

(a)   giving that person an opportunity to make representations; and

(b)   if the paying person is an individual and the order is to be made under paragraph (3)(a), (b) or (d), considering that person's financial means.

(8)   The amount of costs or expenses to be paid under an order under this rule may be ascertained by–

(a)   summary assessment by the Upper Tribunal;

(b)   agreement of a specified sum by the paying person and the person entitled to receive the costs or expenses ("the receiving person"); or

(c)   assessment of the whole or a specified part of the costs or expenses incurred by the receiving person, if not agreed.

(9)   Following an order for assessment under paragraph (8)(c), the paying person or the receiving person may apply–

(a)   in England and Wales, to the High Court or the Costs Office of the Supreme Court (as specified in the order) for a detailed assessment of the costs on the standard basis or, if specified in the order, on the indemnity basis; and the Civil Procedure Rules 1998(6) shall apply, with necessary modifications, to that application and assessment as if the proceedings in the tribunal had been proceedings in a court to which the Civil Procedure Rules 1998 apply;

(b)   in Scotland, to the Auditor of the Court of Session for the taxation of the expenses according to the fees payable in that court; or

(c)   in Northern Ireland, to the Taxing Office of the High Court of Northern Ireland for taxation on the standard basis or, if specified in the order, on the indemnity basis.]

Amendments

1.   Substituted by r7 of SI 2009 No 274 as from 1.4.09.

2.   Amended by r11 of SI 2009 No 1975 as from 1.9.09.

3.   Amended by r6 of SI 2010 No 747 as from 6.4.10.

Representatives

11.–(1)   A party may appoint a representative (whether a legal representative or not) to represent that party in the proceedings [³ save that a party in an asylum or immigration case may not be represented by any person prohibited from representing by section 84 of the Immigration and Asylum Act 1999].

(2)   If a party appoints a representative, that party (or the representative if the representative is a legal representative) must send or deliver to the Upper Tribunal [¹] written notice of the representative's name and address.

[¹ (2A)   If the Upper Tribunal receives notice that a party has appointed a representative under paragraph (2), it must send a copy of that notice to each other party.]

(3)   Anything permitted or required to be done by a party under these Rules, a practice direction or a direction may be done by the representative of that party, except signing a witness statement.

(4)   A person who receives due notice of the appointment of a representative–

(a)   must provide to the representative any document which is required to be provided to the represented party, and need not provide that document to the represented party; and

(b)   may assume that the representative is and remains authorised as such until they receive written notification that this is not so from the representative or the represented party.

(5)   At a hearing a party may be accompanied by another person whose name and address has not been notified under paragraph (2) but who, subject to paragraph (8) and with the permission of the Upper Tribunal, may act as a representative or otherwise assist in presenting the party's case at the hearing.

(6)   Paragraphs (2) to (4) do not apply to a person who accompanies a party under paragraph (5).

(7)-(8)   *[Omitted]*

[¹ (9)   In this rule "legal representative" means [² a person who, for the purposes of the Legal Services Act 2007, is an authorised person in relation to an activity which constitutes the exercise of a right of audience or the conduct of litigation within the meaning of that Act,][³ a qualified person as defined in section 84(2) of the Immigration and Asylum Act 1999,] an advocate or solicitor in Scotland or a barrister or solicitor in Northern Ireland.]

[(10)   *[Omitted]*]]

Amendments

1.   Amended by r8 of SI 2009 No 274 as from 1.4.09.
2.   Amended by r8 of SI 2010 No 43 as from 18.1.10.
3.   Amended by r8 of SI 2010 No 44 as from 15.2.10.

General Note

See the commentary to r11 TP(FT) Rules 2008 on p1057.

Calculating time

12.–(1)   An act required by these Rules, a practice direction or a direction to be done on or by a particular day must be done by 5pm on that day.

(2)   If the time specified by these Rules, a practice direction or a direction for doing any act ends on a day other than a working day, the act is done in time if it is done on the next working day.

(3)-(5)   *Omitted*

General Note

See the commentary to rule 12 TP(FT) Rules 2008 on p1058.

Sending and delivery of documents

13.–(1)   Any document to be provided to the Upper Tribunal under these Rules, a practice direction or a direction must be–

(a)   sent by pre-paid post or [¹ by document exchange, or delivered by hand,] to the address specified for the proceedings;

(b)   sent by fax to the number specified for the proceedings; or

(c)   sent or delivered by such other method as the Upper Tribunal may permit or direct.

(2)   Subject to paragraph (3), if a party provides a fax number, email address or other details for the electronic transmission of documents to them, that party must accept delivery of documents by that method.

(3)   If a party informs the Upper Tribunal and all other parties that a particular form of communication, other than pre-paid post or delivery by hand, should not be used to provide documents to that party, that form of communication must not be so used.

(4)   If the Upper Tribunal or a party sends a document to a party or the Upper Tribunal by email or any other electronic means of communication, the recipient may request that the sender provide a hard copy of the document to the recipient. The recipient

must make such a request as soon as reasonably practicable after receiving the document electronically.

(5)   The Upper Tribunal and each party may assume that the address provided by a party or its representative is and remains the address to which documents should be sent or delivered until receiving written notification to the contrary.

[² (6)   Subject to paragraph (7), if a document submitted to the Upper Tribunal is not written in English, it must be accompanied by an English translation.

(7)   In proceedings that are in Wales or have a connection with Wales, a document or translation may be submitted to the Tribunal in Welsh.]

Amendments

1.   Amended by r10 of SI 2009 No 274 as from 1.4.09.
2.   Inserted by r10 of SI 2010 No 44 as from 15.2.10.

Use of documents and information

14.–(1)   The Upper Tribunal may make an order prohibiting the disclosure or publication of–

(a)   specified documents or information relating to the proceedings; or
(b)   any matter likely to lead members of the public to identify any person whom the Upper Tribunal considers should not be identified.

(2)   The Upper Tribunal may give a direction prohibiting the disclosure of a document or information to a person if–

(a)   the Upper Tribunal is satisfied that such disclosure would be likely to cause that person or some other person serious harm; and
(b)   the Upper Tribunal is satisfied, having regard to the interests of justice, that it is proportionate to give such a direction.

(3)   If a party (''the first party'') considers that the Upper Tribunal should give a direction under paragraph (2) prohibiting the disclosure of a document or information to another party (''the second party''), the first party must–

(a)   exclude the relevant document or information from any documents that will be provided to the second party; and
(b)   provide to the Upper Tribunal the excluded document or information, and the reason for its exclusion, so that the Upper Tribunal may decide whether the document or information should be disclosed to the second party or should be the subject of a direction under paragraph (2).

[¹ (4)]

(5)   If the Upper Tribunal gives a direction under paragraph (2) which prevents disclosure to a party who has appointed a representative, the Upper Tribunal may give a direction that the documents or information be disclosed to that representative if the Upper Tribunal is satisfied that–

(a)   disclosure to the representative would be in the interests of the party; and
(b)   the representative will act in accordance with paragraph (6).

(6)   Documents or information disclosed to a representative in accordance with a direction under paragraph (5) must not be disclosed either directly or indirectly to any other person without the Upper Tribunal's consent.

(7)   Unless the Upper Tribunal gives a direction to the contrary, information about mental health cases and the names of any persons concerned in such cases must not be made public.

[¹ (8)   The Upper Tribunal may, on its own initiative or on the application of a party, give a direction that certain documents or information must or may be disclosed to the Upper Tribunal on the basis that the Upper Tribunal will not disclose such documents or information to other persons, or specified other persons.

(9)   A party making an application for a direction under paragraph (8) may withhold the relevant documents or information from other parties until the Upper Tribunal has granted or refused the application.

(10)   In a case involving matters relating to national security, the Upper Tribunal must ensure that information is not disclosed contrary to the interests of national security.

(11)   The Upper Tribunal must conduct proceedings and record its decision and reasons appropriately so as not to undermine the effect of an order made under paragraph (1), a direction given under paragraph (2) or (8) or the duty imposed by paragraph (10).]

Amendment

1.   Amended by r13 of SI 2009 No 1975 as from 1.9.09.

Evidence and submissions

15.–(1)   Without restriction on the general powers in rule 5(1) and (2) (case management powers), the Upper Tribunal may give directions as to–

(a)   issues on which it requires evidence or submissions;

(b)   the nature of the evidence or submissions it requires;

(c)   whether the parties are permitted or required to provide expert evidence, and if so whether the parties must jointly appoint a single expert to provide such evidence;

(d)   any limit on the number of witnesses whose evidence a party may put forward, whether in relation to a particular issue or generally;

(e)   the manner in which any evidence or submissions are to be provided, which may include a direction for them to be given–

(i)   orally at a hearing; or

(ii)   by written submissions or witness statement; and

(f)   the time at which any evidence or submissions are to be provided.

(2)   The Upper Tribunal may–

(a)   admit evidence whether or not–

(i)   the evidence would be admissible in a civil trial in the United Kingdom; or

(ii)   the evidence was available to a previous decision maker; or

(b)   exclude evidence that would otherwise be admissible where–

(i)   the evidence was not provided within the time allowed by a direction or a practice direction;

(ii)   the evidence was otherwise provided in a manner that did not comply with a direction or a practice direction; or

(iii)   it would otherwise be unfair to admit the evidence.

[(2A)   *[Omitted]*]

(3)   The Upper Tribunal may consent to a witness giving, or require any witness to give, evidence on oath, and may administer an oath for that purpose.

General Note

See the commentary to r15 TP(FT) Rules 2008 on p1060.

Summoning or citation of witnesses and orders to answer questions or produce documents

16.–(1)   On the application of a party or on its own initiative, the Upper Tribunal may–

(a)   by summons (or, in Scotland, citation) require any person to attend as a witness at a hearing at the time and place specified in the summons or citation; or

(b)   order any person to answer any questions or produce any documents in that person's possession or control which relate to any issue in the proceedings.

(2)   A summons or citation under paragraph (1)(a) must–

(a)   give the person required to attend 14 days' notice of the hearing or such shorter period as the Upper Tribunal may direct; and

(b)   where the person is not a party, make provision for the person's necessary expenses of attendance to be paid, and state who is to pay them.

(3)   No person may be compelled to give any evidence or produce any document that the person could not be compelled to give or produce on a trial of an action in a court of law in the part of the United Kingdom where the proceedings are due to be determined.

[¹ (4)   A person who receives a summons, citation or order may apply to the Upper Tribunal for it to be varied or set aside if they did not have an opportunity to object to it before it was made or issued.

(5)   A person making an application under paragraph (4) must do so as soon as reasonably practicable after receiving notice of the summons, citation or order.

(6)   A summons, citation or order under this rule must–

(a)   state that the person on whom the requirement is imposed may apply to the Upper Tribunal to vary or set aside the summons, citation or order, if they did not have an opportunity to object to it before it was made or issued; and

(b)   state the consequences of failure to comply with the summons, citation or order.]

Amendment

1.   Substituted by r11 of SI 2009 No 274 as from 1.4.09.

Withdrawal

17.–(1)   Subject to paragraph (2), a party may give notice of the withdrawal of its case, or any part of it–

(a)   at any time before a hearing to consider the disposal of the proceedings (or, if the Upper Tribunal disposes of the proceedings without a hearing, before that disposal), by sending or delivering to the Upper Tribunal a written notice of withdrawal; or

(b)   orally at a hearing.

(2)   Notice of withdrawal will not take effect unless the Upper Tribunal consents to the withdrawal except in relation to an application for permission to appeal.

(3)   A party which has withdrawn its case may apply to the Upper Tribunal for the case to be reinstated.

(4)   An application under paragraph (3) must be made in writing and be received by the Upper Tribunal within 1 month after–

(a)   the date on which the Upper Tribunal received the notice under paragraph (1)(a); or

(b)   the date of the hearing at which the case was withdrawn orally under paragraph (1)(b).

(5)   The Upper Tribunal must notify each party in writing of a withdrawal under this rule.

[(6)   *[Omitted]*]

General Note

See the commentary to r17 TP(FT) Rules 2008 on p1060.

Notice of funding of legal services

18.   If a party is granted funding of legal services at any time, that party must as soon as practicable–

(a)   (i)   if funding is granted by the Legal Services Commission or the Northern Ireland Legal Services Commission, send a copy of the funding notice to the Upper Tribunal; or

(ii)   if funding is granted by the Scottish Legal Aid Board, send a copy of the legal aid certificate to the Upper Tribunal; and

(b)   notify every other party in writing that funding has been granted.

General Note

In *CSG 336/2003* the commissioner (at para 10) expressed concern that what he described as "responsible solicitors" had made a request for an oral hearing when they were unsure whether they would be able to appear at such a hearing due to funding considerations. He suggested that it would be good practice for solicitors appearing in appeals to the commissioners for claimants to indicate, when applying for oral hearings, whether they had applied for legal aid (or other funding) and the outcome of that funding application. Thereafter, it would also be good practice for such solicitors to keep the Commissioners' Office up to date with the progress of any such applications for funding, and inform that Office of any other reasons why they may not be able to appear at the oral hearing.

Now r18 sets out what an appellant must do if granted funding of legal services by the Legal Services Commission (the Legal Aid Board in Scotland). A copy of the funding notice (or legal aid certificate) must be sent to the Upper Tribunal and notice that funding has been granted must be given to all other parties.

Power to pay expenses and allowances

20.–(1) *[Omitted]*

(2) Paragraph (3) applies to proceedings on appeal from a decision of–

(a) the First-tier Tribunal in proceedings under the Child Support Act 1991, section 12 of the Social Security Act 1998 or paragraph 6 of Schedule 7 to the Child Support, Pensions and Social Security Act 2000;

(b)-(c) *[Omitted]*

(3) The Lord Chancellor (or, in Scotland, the Secretary of State) may pay to any person who attends any hearing such travelling and other allowances, including compensation for loss of remunerative time, as the Lord Chancellor (or, in Scotland, the Secretary of State) may determine.

[¹ Procedure for applying for a stay of a decision pending an appeal

20A.–(1) This rule applies where another enactment provides in any terms for the Upper Tribunal to stay or suspend, or to lift a stay or suspension of, a decision which is or may be the subject of an appeal to the Upper Tribunal ("the substantive decision") pending such appeal.

(2) A person who wishes the Upper Tribunal to decide whether the substantive decision should be stayed or suspended must make a written application to the Upper Tribunal which must include–

(a) the name and address of the person making the application;

(b) the name and address of any representative of that person;

(c) the address to which documents for that person should be sent or delivered;

(d) the name and address of any person who will be a respondent to the appeal;

(e) details of the substantive decision and any decision as to when that decision is to take effect, and copies of any written record of, or reasons for, those decisions; and

(f) the grounds on which the person making the application relies.

(3) In the case of an application under paragraph (2) for a stay of a decision of a traffic commissioner–

(a) the person making the application must notify the traffic commissioner when making the application;

(b) within 7 days of receiving notification of the application the traffic commissioner must send or deliver written reasons for refusing or withdrawing the stay–

(i) to the Upper Tribunal; and

(ii) to the person making the application, if the traffic commissioner has not already done so.

(4) If the Upper Tribunal grants a stay or suspension following an application under this rule–

(a) the Upper Tribunal may give directions as to the conduct of the appeal of the substantive decision; and

(b) the Upper Tribunal may, where appropriate, grant the stay or suspension subject to conditions.

(5) Unless the Upper Tribunal considers that there is good reason not to do so, the Upper Tribunal must send written notice of any decision made under this rule to each party.]

Amendment

1.   Inserted by r14 of SI 2009 No 1975 as from 1.9.09.

PART 3

[¹ Procedure for cases in] the Upper Tribunal

Amendment

1.   Amended by r13 of SI 2009 No 274 as from 1.4.09.

Application to the Upper Tribunal for permission to appeal

21.–[¹ (1)]

(2)   A person may apply to the Upper Tribunal for permission to appeal to the Upper Tribunal against a decision of another tribunal only if–

(a)   they have made an application for permission to appeal to the tribunal which made the decision challenged; and

(b)   that application has been refused or has not been admitted.

(3)   An application for permission to appeal must be made in writing and received by the Upper Tribunal no later than–

(a)-(ab) *[Omitted]*;

(b)   otherwise, a month after the date on which the tribunal that made the decision under challenge sent notice of its refusal of permission to appeal, or refusal to admit the application for permission to appeal, to the appellant.

[(3A)   *[Omitted]*]

(4)   The application must state–

(a)   the name and address of the appellant;

(b)   the name and address of the representative (if any) of the appellant;

(c)   an address where documents for the appellant may be sent or delivered;

(d)   details (including the full reference) of the decision challenged;

(e)   the grounds on which the appellant relies; and

(f)   whether the appellant wants the application to be dealt with at a hearing.

(5)   The appellant must provide with the application a copy of–

(a)   any written record of the decision being challenged;

(b)   any separate written statement of reasons for that decision; and

(c)   if the application is for permission to appeal against a decision of another tribunal, the notice of refusal of permission to appeal, or notice of refusal to admit the application for permission to appeal, from that other tribunal.

(6)   If the appellant provides the application to the Upper Tribunal later than the time required by paragraph (3) or by an extension of time allowed under rule 5(3)(a) (power to extend time)–

(a)   the application must include a request for an extension of time and the reason why the application was not provided in time; and

(b)   unless the Upper Tribunal extends time for the application under rule 5(3)(a) (power to extend time) the Upper Tribunal must not admit the application.

(7)   If the appellant makes an application to the Upper Tribunal for permission to appeal against the decision of another tribunal, and that other tribunal refused to admit the appellant's application for permission to appeal because the application for permission or for a written statement of reasons was not made in time–

(a)   the application to the Upper Tribunal for permission to appeal must include the reason why the application to the other tribunal for permission to appeal or for a written statement of reasons, as the case may be, was not made in time; and

(b)   the Upper Tribunal must only admit the application if the Upper Tribunal considers that it is in the interests of justice for it to do so.

Amendment

1.   Omitted by r15 of SI 2009 No 1975 as from 1.9.09.

General Note

A party who wishes to appeal to the Upper Tribunal must first apply to the First-tier Tribunal for permission to appeal under r38 TP(FT) Rules 2008. If the First-tier Tribunal refuses permission (or refuses to admit the application) a further application may be made to the Upper Tribunal: para (2). The application to the Upper

Tribunal must be in writing (para (3)), include the information specified in para (4) and be accompanied by the documents specified in para (5) (and, if applicable, paras (6)(a) and (7)(a)).

The Upper Tribunal must receive the application no later than a month from the date on which notice of the First-tier Tribunal's decision to refuse permission to appeal (or to admit the application) was sent to the appellant: para (2). That limit may be extended under r5(3)(a) either on an application under para (6) or of its own initiative by waiving para (6) under r7(2)(a). Where the application for permission to appeal to the First-tier Tribunal was late and the First-tier Tribunal refused to admit it on that ground, the Upper Tribunal may only admit the application if it is in the interests of justice to do so.

Decision in relation to permission to appeal

22.–(1) If the Upper Tribunal refuses permission to appeal, it must send written notice of the refusal and of the reasons for the refusal to the appellant.

(2) If the Upper Tribunal gives permission to appeal–

(a) the Upper Tribunal must send written notice of the permission, and of the reasons for any limitations or conditions on such permission, to each party;

(b) subject to any direction by the Upper Tribunal, the application for permission to appeal stands as the notice of appeal and the Upper Tribunal must send to each respondent a copy of the application for permission to appeal and any documents provided with it by the appellant; and

(c) the Upper Tribunal may, with the consent of the appellant and each respondent, determine the appeal without obtaining any further response.

(3)-(5) *[Omitted]*

Definitions

"appellant" – see r1(3).
"respondent" – see r1(3).

General Note

Rule 22(2)(b) provides for the continuation of the long-standing practice of treating the application for permission to appeal as the notice of appeal once permission is granted.

Rule 22(2)(c) gives the Upper Tribunal a power to finally determine an appeal once permission is granted without obtaining any further response, provided that the appellant and all respondents consent.

Notice of appeal

23.–[¹ (1)   This rule applies–

(a) to proceedings on appeal to the Upper Tribunal for which permission to appeal is not required, except proceedings to which rule 26A [² or 26B] applies;

(b) if another tribunal has given permission for a party to appeal to the Upper Tribunal; or

(c) subject to any other direction by the Upper Tribunal, if the Upper Tribunal has given permission to appeal and has given a direction that the application for permission to appeal does not stand as the notice of appeal.

[(1A)   *[Omitted]*

(2)   The appellant must provide a notice of appeal to the Upper Tribunal so that it is received within 1 month after–

(a) the date that the tribunal that gave permission to appeal sent notice of such permission to the appellant; or

(b) if permission to appeal is not required, the date on which notice of decision to which the appeal relates was sent to the appellant.]

(3)   The notice of appeal must include the information listed in rule 21(4)(a) to (e) (content of the application for permission to appeal) and, where the Upper Tribunal has given permission to appeal, the Upper Tribunal's case reference.

(4)   If another tribunal has granted permission to appeal, the appellant must provide with the notice of appeal a copy of–

(a) any written record of the decision being challenged;

(b) any separate written statement of reasons for that decision; and

(c) the notice of permission to appeal.

(5)   If the appellant provides the notice of appeal to the Upper Tribunal later than the time required by paragraph (2) or by an extension of time allowed under rule 5(3)(a) (power to extend time)–

(a)   the notice of appeal must include a request for an extension of time and the reason why the notice was not provided in time; and

(b)   unless the Upper Tribunal extends time for the notice of appeal under rule 5(3)(a) (power to extend time) the Upper Tribunal must not admit the notice of appeal.

[¹ (6)   When the Upper Tribunal receives the notice of appeal it must send a copy of the notice and any accompanying documents–

(a)   to each respondent; or

(b)   *[Omitted]*]

Amendments

1.   Substituted by r17 of SI 2009 No 1975 as from 1.9.09.
2.   Amended by r8 of SI 2010 No 747 as from 6.4.10.

General Note

Where the First-tier Tribunal gives permission to appeal (or where the Upper Tribunal gives permission but gives a direction under r22(2)(b) that the application for permission should not stand as the notice of appeal), the appellant must provide a notice of appeal meeting the requirements of para (3) and (4) within one month from notice of the grant of permission. The one-month limit may be extended: para (5) and rr5(3)(a) and 7(2)(a).

Response to the notice of appeal

24.–[² (1)   This rule and rule 25 do not apply to an appeal against a decision of a traffic commissioner, in respect of which Schedule 1 makes alternative provision.

(1A)   Subject to any direction given by the Upper Tribunal, a respondent may provide a response to a notice of appeal.]

(2)   Any response provided under paragraph [³ (1A)] must be in writing and must be sent or delivered to the Upper Tribunal so that it is received–

[⁴ (a)   if an application for permission to appeal stands as the notice of appeal, no later than one month after the date on which the respondent was sent notice that permission to appeal had been granted;] [⁴]

[(aa)   *[Omitted]*]

(b)   in any other case, no later than 1 month after the date on which the Upper Tribunal sent a copy of the notice of appeal to the respondent.

(3)   The response must state–

(a)   the name and address of the respondent;

(b)   the name and address of the representative (if any) of the respondent;

(c)   an address where documents for the respondent may be sent or delivered;

(d)   whether the respondent opposes the appeal;

(e)   the grounds on which the respondent relies, including [² (in the case of an appeal against the decision of another tribunal)] any grounds on which the respondent was unsuccessful in the proceedings which are the subject of the appeal, but intends to rely in the appeal; and

(f)   whether the respondent wants the case to be dealt with at a hearing.

(4)   If the respondent provides the response to the Upper Tribunal later than the time required by paragraph (2) or by an extension of time allowed under rule 5(3)(a) (power to extend time), the response must include a request for an extension of time and the reason why the [¹ response] was not provided in time.

(5)   When the Upper Tribunal receives the response it must send a copy of the response and any accompanying documents to the appellant and each other party.

Amendments

1.   Amended by Art 15 of SI 2009 No 274 as from 1.4.09.
2.   Amended by r18 of SI 2009 No 1975 as from 1.9.09.
3.   Amended by r9 of SI 2010 No 43 as from 18.1.10.

4.   Amended by r15 of SI 2010 No 44 as from 15.2.10.

General Note
    See the commentary to r24 TP(FT) Rules 2008 on p1064 (except that, in the Upper Tribunal, there is a proper
    time limit of one month in which to provide a response to the appeal).

Appellant's reply
25.–(1)   Subject to any direction given by the Upper Tribunal, the appellant may
provide a reply to any response provided under rule 24 (response to the notice of appeal).
    (2)   [¹ Subject to paragraph (2A), any] reply provided under paragraph (1) must be
in writing and must be sent or delivered to the Upper Tribunal so that it is received within
one month after the date on which the Upper Tribunal sent a copy of the response to the
appellant.
    [(2A)   *[Omitted]*]
    (3)   When the Upper Tribunal receives the reply it must send a copy of the reply and
any accompanying documents to each respondent.

Amendment
    1.   Amended by r16 of SI 2010 No 44 as from 15.2.10.

General Note
    The appellant has a month in which to reply to the response.

[¹ Cases transferred or referred to the Upper Tribunal, applications made directly to the Upper Tribunal and proceedings without notice to a respondent
26A.–[² (1)   Paragraphs (2) and (3) apply to–
    (a)   a case transferred or referred to the Upper Tribunal from the First-tier Tribunal;
           or
    (b)   a case, other than an appeal or a case to which rule 26 (references under the
           Forfeiture Act 1982) applies, which is started by an application made directly to
           the Upper Tribunal.]
    (2)   In a case to which this paragraph applies–
    (a)   the Upper Tribunal must give directions as to the procedure to be followed in
           the consideration and disposal of the proceedings; and
    (b)   the preceding rules in this Part will only apply to the proceedings to the extent
           provided for by such directions.
    (3)   If a case or matter to which this paragraph applies is to be determined without
notice to or the involvement of a respondent–
    (a)   any provision in these Rules requiring a document to be provided by or to a
           respondent; and
    (b)   any other provision in these Rules permitting a respondent to participate in the
           proceedings
does not apply to that case or matter.]
    (4)   *[Omitted]*

Amendments
    1.   Inserted by Art 16 of SI 2009 No 274 as from 1.4.09.
    2.   Substituted by r19 of SI 2009 No 1975 as from 1.9.09.

PART 4
Judicial review proceedings in the Upper Tribunal

General Note on Part 4
    See the General Note to ss15–21 TCEA 2007 on p186.

Application of this Part to judicial review proceedings transferred to the Upper Tribunal
27.–(1)   When a court transfers judicial review proceedings to the Upper Tribunal,
the Upper Tribunal–

(a)   must notify each party in writing that the proceedings have been transferred to the Upper Tribunal; and

(b)   must give directions as to the future conduct of the proceedings.

(2)   The directions given under paragraph (1)(b) may modify or disapply for the purposes of the proceedings any of the provisions of the following rules in this Part.

(3)   In proceedings transferred from the Court of Session under section 20(1) of the 2007 Act, the directions given under paragraph (1)(b) must–

(a)   if the Court of Session did not make a first order specifying the required intimation, service and advertisement of the petition, state the Upper Tribunal's requirements in relation to those matters;

(b)   state whether the Upper Tribunal will consider summary dismissal of the proceedings; and

(c)   where necessary, modify or disapply provisions relating to permission in the following rules in this Part.

Applications for permission to bring judicial review proceedings

28.–(1)   A person seeking permission to bring judicial review proceedings before the Upper Tribunal under section 16 of the 2007 Act must make a written application to the Upper Tribunal for such permission.

(2)   Subject to paragraph (3), an application under paragraph (1) must be made promptly and, unless any other enactment specifies a shorter time limit, must be sent or delivered to the Upper Tribunal so that it is received no later than 3 months after the date of the decision [¹ , action or omission] to which the application relates.

(3)   An application for permission to bring judicial review proceedings challenging a decision of the First-tier Tribunal may be made later than the time required by paragraph (2) if it is made within 1 month after the date on which the First-tier Tribunal sent–

(a)   written reasons for the decision; or

(b)   notification that an application for the decision to be set aside has been unsuccessful, provided that that application was made in time.

(4)   The application must state–

(a)   the name and address of the applicant, the respondent and any other person whom the applicant considers to be an interested party;

(b)   the name and address of the applicant's representative (if any);

(c)   an address where documents for the applicant may be sent or delivered;

(d)   details of the decision challenged (including the date, the full reference and the identity of the decision maker);

(e)   that the application is for permission to bring judicial review proceedings;

(f)   the outcome that the applicant is seeking; and

(g)   the facts and grounds on which the applicant relies.

(5)   If the application relates to proceedings in a court or tribunal, the application must name as an interested party each party to those proceedings who is not the applicant or a respondent.

(6)   The applicant must send with the application–

(a)   a copy of any written record of the decision in the applicant's possession or control; and

(b)   copies of any other documents in the applicant's possession or control on which the applicant intends to rely.

(7)   If the applicant provides the application to the Upper Tribunal later than the time required by paragraph (2) or (3) or by an extension of time allowed under rule 5(3)(a) (power to extend time)–

(a)   the application must include a request for an extension of time and the reason why the application was not provided in time; and

(b)   unless the Upper Tribunal extends time for the application under rule 5(3)(a) (power to extend time) the Upper Tribunal must not admit the application.

(8)   When the Upper Tribunal receives the application it must send a copy of the application and any accompanying documents to each person named in the application as a respondent or interested party.

Amendment

1.   Amended by r17 of SI 2009 No 274 as from 1.4.09.

Acknowledgment of service

29.–(1)   A person who is sent a copy of an application for permission under rule 28(8) (application for permission to bring judicial review proceedings) and wishes to take part in the proceedings must send or deliver to the Upper Tribunal an acknowledgment of service so that it is received no later than 21 days after the date on which the Upper Tribunal sent a copy of the application to that person.

(2)   An acknowledgment of service under paragraph (1) must be in writing and state–

(a)   whether the person intends to [¹ support or] oppose the application for permission;

(b)   their grounds for any [¹ support or] opposition under sub-paragraph (a), or any other submission or [² information which they consider may] assist the Upper Tribunal; and

(c)   the name and address of any other person not named in the application as a respondent or interested party whom the person providing the acknowledgment considers to be an interested party.

(3)   A person who is sent a copy of an application for permission under rule 28(8) but does not provide an acknowledgment of service may not take part in the application for permission, but may take part in the subsequent proceedings if the application is successful.

Amendments

1.   Amended by r18 of SI 2009 No 274 as from 1.4.09.
2.   Amended by correction slip 9.09.

Decision on permission or summary dismissal, and reconsideration of permission or summary dismissal at a hearing

30.–(1)   The Upper Tribunal must send to the applicant, each respondent and any other person who provided an acknowledgment of service to the Upper Tribunal, and may send to any other person who may have an interest in the proceedings, written notice of–

(a)   its decision in relation to the application for permission; and

(b)   the reasons for any refusal of the application, or any limitations or conditions on permission.

(2)   In proceedings transferred from the Court of Session under section 20(1) of the 2007 Act, where the Upper Tribunal has considered whether summarily to dismiss of the proceedings, the Upper Tribunal must send to the applicant and each respondent, and may send to any other person who may have an interest in the proceedings, written notice of–

(a)   its decision in relation to the summary dismissal of proceedings; and

(b)   the reasons for any decision summarily to dismiss part or all of the proceedings, or any limitations or conditions on the continuation of such proceedings.

(3)   Paragraph (4) applies where the Upper Tribunal, without a hearing–

(a)   determines an application for permission to bring judicial review proceedings and either refuses permission, or gives permission on limited grounds or subject to conditions; or

(b)   in proceedings transferred from the Court of Session, summarily dismisses part or all of the proceedings, or imposes any limitations or conditions on the continuation of such proceedings.

(4)   In the circumstances specified in paragraph (3) the applicant may apply for the decision to be reconsidered at a hearing.

(5)   An application under paragraph (4) must be made in writing and must be sent or delivered to the Upper Tribunal so that it is received within 14 days after the date on which the Upper Tribunal sent written notice of its decision regarding the application to the applicant.

Responses

31.–(1)   Any person to whom the Upper Tribunal has sent notice of the grant of permission under rule 30(1) (notification of decision on permission), and who wishes to contest the application or support it on additional grounds, must provide detailed grounds for contesting or supporting the application to the Upper Tribunal.

(2)   Any detailed grounds must be provided in writing and must be sent or delivered to the Upper Tribunal so that they are received not more than 35 days after the Upper Tribunal sent notice of the grant of permission under rule 30(1).

Applicant seeking to rely on additional grounds

32.   The applicant may not rely on any grounds, other than those grounds on which the applicant obtained permission for the judicial review proceedings, without the consent of the Upper Tribunal.

Right to make representations

33.   Each party and, with the permission of the Upper Tribunal, any other person, may–

(a)   submit evidence, except at the hearing of an application for permission;

(b)   make representations at any hearing which they are entitled to attend; and

(c)   make written representations in relation to a decision to be made without a hearing.

PART 5

Hearings

Decision with or without a hearing

34.–(1)   Subject to paragraph (2), the Upper Tribunal may make any decision without a hearing.

(2)   The Upper Tribunal must have regard to any view expressed by a party when deciding whether to hold a hearing to consider any matter, and the form of any such hearing.

General Note

The Upper Tribunal is not obliged to hold a hearing of the appeal. The decision whether to hold one is made by judge of the Upper Tribunal who must have regard to the parties' views. It is probable that the former practice (ie, in appeals to the commissioner) will continue to apply and that the Upper Tribunal will hold a hearing if any of the parties requests one, unless the judge considers that the appeal can be determined properly without one. The Upper Tribunal may also hold a hearing even if no party has requested it.

Entitlement to attend a hearing

35.[[1] –(1)]   Subject to rule 37(4) (exclusion of a person from a hearing), each party is entitled to attend a hearing.

[[1] (2)   *[Omitted]*]

Amendment

1.   Amended by r11 of SI 2010 No 43 as from 18.1.10.

Notice of hearings

36.–(1)   The Upper Tribunal must give each party entitled to attend a hearing reasonable notice of the time and place of the hearing (including any adjourned or postponed hearing) and any change to the time and place of the hearing.

(2)   The period of notice under paragraph (1) must be at least 14 days except that–

(a)   in applications for permission to bring judicial review proceedings, the period of notice must be at least 2 working days; [[1]]

[(aa)   *[Omitted]*]

(b)   [[1] in any case other than a fast-track case] the Upper Tribunal may give shorter notice–

(i)   with the parties' consent; or

(ii)   in urgent or exceptional cases.

Amendment
1.   Amended by r17 of SI 2010 No 44 as from 15.2.10.

General Note
See the commentary to r29 TP(FT) Rules 2008 on p1067. In a judicial review case, only two working days' notice is required.

Public and private hearings

37.–(1)   Subject to the following paragraphs, all hearings must be held in public.

(2)   The Upper Tribunal may give a direction that a hearing, or part of it, is to be held in private.

(2A)   *[Omitted]*

(3)   Where a hearing, or part of it, is to be held in private, the Upper Tribunal may determine who is entitled to attend the hearing or part of it.

(4)   The Upper Tribunal may give a direction excluding from any hearing, or part of it–

(a)   any person whose conduct the Upper Tribunal considers is disrupting or is likely to disrupt the hearing;

(b)   any person whose presence the Upper Tribunal considers is likely to prevent another person from giving evidence or making submissions freely;

(c)   any person who the Upper Tribunal considers should be excluded in order to give effect to [2 the requirement at rule 14(11) (prevention of disclosure or publication of documents and information)] ; [1]

(d)   any person where the purpose of the hearing would be defeated by the attendance of that person. [1 ; or

(e)   a person under the age of eighteen years.]

(5)   The Upper Tribunal may give a direction excluding a witness from a hearing until that witness gives evidence.

Amendments
1.   Amended by r19 of SI 2009 No 274 as from 1.4.09.
2.   Amended by r20 of SI 2009 No 1975 as from 1.9.09.

General Note
See the commentary to r30 TP(FT) Rules 2008 on p1067.

Hearings in a party's absence

38.   If a party fails to attend a hearing, the Upper Tribunal may proceed with the hearing if the Upper Tribunal–

(a)   is satisfied that the party has been notified of the hearing or that reasonable steps have been taken to notify the party of the hearing; and

(b)   considers that it is in the interests of justice to proceed with the hearing.

PART 6
Decisions

Consent orders

39.–(1)   The Upper Tribunal may, at the request of the parties but only if it considers it appropriate, make a consent order disposing of the proceedings and making such other appropriate provision as the parties have agreed.

(2)   Notwithstanding any other provision of these Rules, the Tribunal need not hold a hearing before making an order under paragraph (1) [1].

Amendment
1.   Amended by r20 of SI 2009 No 274 as from 1.4.09.

Decisions

40.–(1)   The Upper Tribunal may give a decision orally at a hearing.

(2)   [¹] [³ Except where rule 40A (special procedure for providing notice of a decision relating to an asylum case) applies,] the Upper Tribunal must provide to each party as soon as reasonably practicable after making a decision which finally disposes of all issues in the proceedings (except a decision under Part 7)–

(a)   a decision notice stating the Tribunal's decision; and

(b)   notification of any rights of review or appeal against the decision and the time and manner in which such rights of review or appeal may be exercised.

(3)   [¹ Subject to rule [² 14(11) (prevention of disclosure or publication of documents and information)] ,] The Upper Tribunal must provide written reasons for its decision with a decision notice provided under paragraph (2)(a) unless–

(a)   the decision was made with the consent of the parties; or

(b)   the parties have consented to the Upper Tribunal not giving written reasons.

(4)   The [² Upper] Tribunal may provide written reasons for any decision to which paragraph (2) does not apply.

(5)   *[Omitted]*

Amendments

1.   Amended by r21 of SI 2009 No 274 as from 1.4.09.
2.   Amended by r21 of SI 2009 No 1975 as from 1.9.09.
3.   Amended by r19 of SI 2010 No 44 as from 15.2.10.

General Note

The Upper Tribunal may give its decision by word of mouth (para (1)) but must then provide a written notice (para (2)(a)) and a written statement of reasons: para (3). There is no obligation to give reasons where the decision is made by consent or all parties have consented to a decision without reasons: para (3)(a) and (b).

PART 7

Correcting, setting aside, reviewing and appealing decisions of the Upper Tribunal

Interpretation

41.   In this Part–

"appeal" [¹ , except in rule 44(2) (application for permission to appeal),] means the exercise of a right of appeal under section 13 of the 2007 Act; and

"review" means the review of a decision by the Upper Tribunal under section 10 of the 2007 Act.

Amendment

1.   Amended by Art 22 of SI 2009 No 274 as from 1.4.09.

Clerical mistakes and accidental slips or omissions

42.   The Upper Tribunal may at any time correct any clerical mistake or other accidental slip or omission in a decision or record of a decision by–

(a)   sending notification of the amended decision, or a copy of the amended record, to all parties; and

(b)   making any necessary amendment to any information published in relation to the decision or record.

General Note

See the commentary to r36 TP(FT) Rules 2008 on p1069.

Setting aside a decision which disposes of proceedings

43.–(1)   The Upper Tribunal may set aside a decision which disposes of proceedings, or part of such a decision, and re-make the decision or the relevant part of it, if–

(a)   the Upper Tribunal considers that it is in the interests of justice to do so; and

(b)   one or more of the conditions in paragraph (2) are satisfied.

(2)   The conditions are–

(a)   a document relating to the proceedings was not sent to, or was not received at an appropriate time by, a party or a party's representative;

(b)   a document relating to the proceedings was not sent to the Upper Tribunal at an appropriate time;

(c)   a party, or a party's representative, was not present at a hearing related to the proceedings; or

(d)   there has been some other procedural irregularity in the proceedings.

(3)   [¹ Except where paragraph (4) applies,] A party applying for a decision, or part of a decision, to be set aside under paragraph (1) must make a written application to the Upper Tribunal so that it is received no later than 1 month after the date on which the Tribunal sent notice of the decision to the party.

[(4)-(5)   *[Omitted]*]]

Amendment

1.   Amended by r21 of SI 2010 No 44 as from 15.2.10.

General Note

See the commentary to r37 TP(FT) Rules 2008 on p1069.

Application for permission to appeal

44.–(1)   A person seeking permission to appeal must make a written application to the Upper Tribunal for permission to appeal.

(2)   Paragraph (3) applies to an application under paragraph (1) in respect of a decision–

(a)   on an appeal against a decision in a social security and child support case (as defined in the Tribunal Procedure (First-tier Tribunal) (Social Entitlement Chamber) Rules 2008;

(b)-(c) *[Omitted]*

(3)   Where this paragraph applies, the application must be sent or delivered to the Upper Tribunal so that it is received within 3 months after the date on which the Upper Tribunal sent to the person making the application–

(a)   written notice of the decision;

(b)   notification of amended reasons for, or correction of, the decision following a review; or

(c)   notification that an application for the decision to be set aside has been unsuccessful.

[(3A)-(3D)   *[Omitted]*]

(4)   Where paragraph (3) [¹ [² , (3A) or (3D)]] does not apply, an application under paragraph (1) must be sent or delivered to the Upper Tribunal so that it is received within 1 month after the latest of the dates on which the Upper Tribunal sent to the person making the application–

(a)   written reasons for the decision;

(b)   notification of amended reasons for, or correction of, the decision following a review; or

(c)   notification that an application for the decision to be set aside has been unsuccessful.

(5)   The date in paragraph (3)(c) or (4)(c) applies only if the application for the decision to be set aside was made within the time stipulated in rule 43 (setting aside a decision which disposes of proceedings) or any extension of that time granted by the Upper Tribunal.

(6)   If the person seeking permission to appeal provides the application to the Upper Tribunal later than the time required by paragraph (3) [¹ , (3A)][² ,(3D)] or (4), or by any extension of time under rule 5(3)(a) (power to extend time)–

(a)   the application must include a request for an extension of time and the reason why the application notice was not provided in time; and

(b)   unless the Upper Tribunal extends time for the application under rule 5(3)(a) (power to extend time) the Upper Tribunal must refuse the application.

(7)　An application under paragraph (1) must–
(a)　identify the decision of the Tribunal to which it relates;
(b)　identify the alleged error or errors of law in the decision; and
(c)　state the result the party making the application is seeking.

Amendment
1.　Amended by r22 of SI 2010 No 44 as from 15.2.10.
2.　Amended by r10 of SI 2010 No 747 as from 6.4.10.

General Note
Rule 44 deals with applications for permission to appeal from the Upper Tribunal to the Court of Appeal or Court of Session. The application for permission to appeal must be in writing (para (1)) and made within three months of the latest of the decisions listed in para (4). That time limit may be extended under para (6) and rr5(3)(a) and 7(2)(a).

Upper Tribunal's consideration of application for permission to appeal

45.–(1)　On receiving an application for permission to appeal the Upper Tribunal may review the decision in accordance with rule 46 (review of a decision), but may only do so if–
(a)　when making the decision the Upper Tribunal overlooked a legislative provision or binding authority which could have had a material effect on the decision; or
(b)　since the Upper Tribunal's decision, a court has made a decision which is binding on the Upper Tribunal and which, had it been made before the Upper Tribunal's decision, could have had a material effect on the decision.
(2)　If the Upper Tribunal decides not to review the decision, or reviews the decision and decides to take no action in relation to the decision or part of it, the Upper Tribunal must consider whether to give permission to appeal in relation to the decision or that part of it.
(3)　The Upper Tribunal must send a record of its decision to the parties as soon as practicable.
(4)　If the Upper Tribunal refuses permission to appeal it must send with the record of its decision–
(a)　a statement of its reasons for such refusal; and
(b)　notification of the right to make an application to the relevant appellate court for permission to appeal and the time within which, and the method by which, such application must be made.
(5)　The Upper Tribunal may give permission to appeal on limited grounds, but must comply with paragraph (4) in relation to any grounds on which it has refused permission.

General Note
See the commentary to r39 TP(FT) Rules 2008 on p1072. The grounds upon which the Upper Tribunal may review its decision in response to an application for permission to appeal are restricted to those in para (1)(a) and (b).

Review of a decision

46.–(1)　The Upper Tribunal may only undertake a review of a decision–
(a)　pursuant to rule 45(1) (review on an application for permission to appeal); or
(b)　*[Omitted]*
(2)　The Upper Tribunal must notify the parties in writing of the outcome of any review and of any rights of review or appeal in relation to the outcome.
(3)　If the Upper Tribunal decides to take any action in relation to a decision following a review without first giving every party an opportunity to make representations, the notice under paragraph (2) must state that any party that did not have an opportunity to make representations may apply for such action to be set aside and for the decision to be reviewed again.

General Note
See the commentary to r40 TP(FT) Rules 2008 on p1072. The relevant provision of the TCEA 2007 is s10.

[¹ Power to treat an application as a different type of application

48. The Tribunal may treat an application for a decision to be corrected, set aside or reviewed, or for permission to appeal against a decision, as an application for any other one of those things.]

Amendment

1.   Inserted by r8 of SI 2010 No 2653 as from 29.11.10.

The Transfer of Tribunal Functions Order 2008
(2008 No.2833)

Citation, commencement, interpretation and extent

1.–(1)   This Order may be cited as the Transfer of Tribunal Functions Order 2008 and comes into force on 3rd November 2008.

(2)   A reference in this Order to a Schedule by a number alone is a reference to the Schedule so numbered in this Order.

(3)   Subject as follows, this Order extends to England and Wales, Scotland and Northern Ireland.

(4)   Except as provided by paragraph (5) or (6), an amendment, repeal or revocation of any enactment by any provision of Schedule 3 extends to the part or parts of the United Kingdom to which the enactment extends.

(5)-(6)   *[Omitted]*.

Transfer of functions of certain tribunals

3.–(1)   Subject to paragraph (3), the functions of thetribunals listed in Table 1 of Schedule 1 are transferred to the First-tier Tribunal.

(2)   Subject to paragraph (3), the functions of the tribunals listed in Table 2 of Schedule 1 are transferred to the Upper Tribunal.

(3)   *[Omitted]*

Abolition of tribunals transferred under section 30(1)

4.   The tribunals listed in Table 1 and Table 2 of Schedule 1 areabolished except for–

(a)-(b) *[Omitted]*

Transfer of persons into the First-tier Tribunal and the Upper Tribunal

5.–(1)   A person holding an office listed in a table in Schedule 2 who was, was a member of, or was an authorised decision-maker for, a tribunal listed in the corresponding table in Schedule 1 immediately before the functions of that tribunal were transferred under article 3 shall hold the corresponding office or offices.

(2)   In paragraph (1) "corresponding" means appearing in the corresponding entry in the table below.

Table in Schedule 1	Table in Schedule 2	Office or offices
Table 1	Table 1	Transferred-in judge of the First-tier Tribunal
Table 1	Table 2	Transferred-in other member of the First-tier Tribunal
Table 1	Table 3	Transferred in judge of the First-tier Tribunal and deputy judge of the Upper Tribunal
Table 2	Table 4	Transferred-in judge of the Upper Tribunal
Table 1 or 2	Table 5	Transferred-in other member of the Upper Tribunal

SCHEDULE 1
Articles 3, 4 and 5
Functions transferred to the First-tier Tribunal and Upper Tribunal

Table 1: Functions transferred to the First-tier Tribunal

Tribunal	Enactment
Appeal tribunal	Chapter 1 of Part 1 of the Social Security Act 1998 (c.14)

Table 2: Functions transferred to the Upper Tribunal

Tribunal	Enactment
Social Security Commissioner	Schedule 4 to the Social Security Act 1998 (c.14)

SCHEDULE 2

Article 5

Persons transferred as judges and members of the First-tier Tribunal and Upper Tribunal

Table 1: Members becoming transferred-in judges of the First-tier Tribunal

Tribunal Member	Enactment
A legally qualified panel member	Section 6 of the Social Security Act 1998 (c.14)

Table 2: Members becoming transferred-in other members of the First-tier Tribunal

Tribunal Member	Enactment
A financially qualified panel member, a medically qualified panel member or a panel member with a disability qualification	Section 6 of the Social Security Act 1998 (c.14)

Table 3: Members becoming transferred-in judges of the First-tier Tribunal and deputy judges of the Upper Tribunal

Tribunal Member	Enactment
The President	Section 5 of the Social Security Act 1998 (c.14)
A deputy Commissioner	Paragraph 1(2) of Schedule 4 to the Social Security Act 1998 (c.14)

Table 4: Members becoming transferred-in judges of the Upper Tribunal

Tribunal Member	Enactment
The Chief Social Security Commissioner or a Social Security Commissioner	Paragraph 1 of Schedule 4 to the Social Security Act 1998 (c.14)

SCHEDULE 4

Article 6

Transitional provisions

1. Subject to article 3(3)(a) any proceedings before a tribunal listed in Table 1 of Schedule 1 which are pending immediately before 3rd November 2008 shall continue on and after 3rd November 2008 as proceedings before the First-tier Tribunal.

2. Subject to article 3(3)(b) any proceedings before a tribunal listed in Table 2 of Schedule 1 which are pending immediately before 3rd November 2008 shall continue on and after 3rd November 2008 as proceedings before the Upper Tribunal.

3.–(1) The following sub-paragraphs apply where proceedings are continued in the First-tier Tribunal or Upper Tribunal by virtue of paragraph 1 or 2.

(2) Where a hearing began before 3rd November 2008 but was not completed by that date, the First-tier Tribunal or the Upper Tribunal, as the case may be, must be comprised for the continuation of that hearing of the person or persons who began it.

(3) The First-tier Tribunal or Upper Tribunal, as the case may be, may give any direction to ensure that proceedings are dealt with fairly and, in particular, may–

    (a) apply any provision in procedural rules which applied to the proceedings before 3rd November 2008; or

    (b) disapply provisions of Tribunal Procedure Rules.

(4) In sub-paragraph (3) ''procedural rules'' means provision (whether called rules or not) regulating practice or procedure before a tribunal.

(5) Any direction or order given or made in proceedings which is in force immediately before 3rd November 2008 remains in force on and after that date as if it were a direction or order of the First-tier Tribunal or Upper Tribunal, as the case may be.

(6) A time period which has started to run before 3rd November 2008 and which has not expired shall continue to apply.

(7) An order for costs may only be made if, and to the extent that, an order could have been made before 3rd November 2008.

4. Subject to article 3(3)(a) and (b) where an appeal lies to a Child Support or Social Security Commissioner from any decision made before 3rd November 2008 by a tribunal listed in Table 1 of Schedule 1, section 11 of the 2007 Act (right to appeal to Upper Tribunal) shall apply as if the decision were a decision made on or after 3rd November 2008 by the First-tier Tribunal.

5. Subject to article 3(3)(b) where an appeal lies to a court from any decision made before 3rd November 2008 by a Child Support or Social Security Commissioner, section 13 of the 2007 Act (right to appeal to Court of Appeal etc.) shall apply as if the decision were a decision made on or after 3rd November 2008 by the Upper Tribunal.

6. Subject to article 3(3)(a) and (b) any case to be remitted by a court on or after 3rd November 2008 in relation to a tribunal listed in Schedule 1 shall be remitted to the First-tier Tribunal or Upper Tribunal as the case may be.

The Appeals from the Upper Tribunal to the Court of Appeal Order 2008

(SI 2008 No.2834)

1.   This Order may be cited as the Appeals from the Upper Tribunal to the Court of Appeal Order 2008 and shall come into force on 3rd November 2008.

2.   Permission to appeal to the Court of Appeal in England and Wales or leave to appeal to the Court of Appeal in Northern Ireland shall not be granted unless the Upper Tribunal or, where the Upper Tribunal refuses permission, the relevant appellate court, considers that–

(a)   the proposed appeal would raise some important point of principle or practice; or

(b)   there is some other compelling reason for the relevant appellate court to hear the appeal.

The First-tier Tribunal and Upper Tribunal (Composition of Tribunal) Order 2008

(2008 No.2835)

Citation and commencement

1. This Order may be cited as the First-tier Tribunal and Upper Tribunal (Composition of Tribunal) Order 2008 and comes into force on 3rd November 2008.

Number of members of the First-tier Tribunal

2.–(1) The number of members of the tribunal who are to decide any matter that falls to be decided by the First-tier Tribunal must be determined by the Senior President of Tribunals in accordance with paragraph (2).

(2) The Senior President of Tribunals must have regard to–

(a) where the matter which falls to be decided by the tribunal fell to a tribunal in a list in Schedule 6 to the Tribunals, Courts and Enforcement Act 2007 before its functions were transferred by order under section 30(1) of that Act, any provision made by or under any enactment for determining the number of members of that tribunal; and

(b) the need for members of tribunals to have particular expertise, skills or knowledge.

Number of members of the Upper Tribunal

3.–(1) The number of members of the tribunal who are to decide any matter that falls to be decided by the Upper Tribunal is one unless determined otherwise under paragraph (2).

(2) The tribunal may consist of two or three members if the Senior President of Tribunals so determines.

Tribunal consisting of single member

4.–(1) Where a matter is to be decided by a single member of a tribunal, it must be decided by a judge of the tribunal unless paragraph (2) applies.

(2) The matter may be decided by one of the other members of the tribunal if the Senior President of Tribunals so determines.

Tribunal consisting of two or more members

5. The following articles apply where a matter is to be decided by two or more members of a tribunal.

6. The number of members who are to be judges of the tribunal and the number of members who are to be other members of the tribunal must be determined by the Senior President of Tribunals.

7. The Senior President of Tribunals must select one of the members (the ''presiding member'') to chair the tribunal.

8. If the decision of the tribunal is not unanimous, the decision of the majority is the decision of the tribunal; and the presiding member has a casting vote if the votes are equally divided.

General Note

The Senior President has exercised the powers under Art 2(1) to make the Practice Statement Composition of Tribunals in Social Security and Child Support Cases in the Social Entitlement Chamber on or after 3 November 2008 as follows:

"1.   In this Practice Statement;

   a.   "the 2008 Order" means the First-tier Tribunal and Upper Tribunal (Composition of Tribunal) Order 2008;

   b.   "the Qualifications Order" means the Qualifications for Appointment of Members to the First-tier Tribunal and Upper Tribunal Order 2008;

   c.   "the 2008 Rules" means the Tribunal Procedure (First-tier Tribunal) (Social Entitlement Chamber) Rules 2008;

d.   "social security and child support case" has the meaning given in rule 1(3) of the 2008 Rules.

2.   In exercise of the powers conferred by the 2008 Order the Senior President of Tribunals makes the following determinations and supplementary provision:–

3.   The number of members of the Tribunal must not exceed three.

4.   *[Omitted]*

5.   *[Omitted]*

6.   In any other case the Tribunal must consist of a Tribunal Judge.

7.   The Chamber President may determine that the Tribunal constituted under paragraph 5 or 6 must also include–

   a.   a Tribunal Member who is an accountant within the meaning of Article 2(i) of the Qualifications Order, where the appeal may require the examination of financial accounts;

   b.   an additional Member who is a registered medical practitioner, where the complexity of the medical issues in the appeal so demands;

   c.   such an additional Tribunal Judge or Member as he considers appropriate for the purposes of providing further experience for that additional Judge or Member or for assisting the Chamber President in the monitoring of standards of decision-making.

8.   *[Omitted]*

9.   The powers of the Chamber President referred to in paragraphs 7, 8, 10 and 12 may be delegated to a Regional Tribunal Judge and those referred to in paragraphs 7, 8 and 12 may be delegated to a District Tribunal Judge.

10.   A decision, including a decision to give a direction or make an order, made under, or in accordance with, rules 5 to 9, 11, 14 to 19, 25(3), 30, 32, 36, 37 or 41 of the 2008 Rules may be made by a Tribunal Judge, except that a decision made under, or in accordance, with rule 7(3) or rule 5(3)(b) to treat a case as a lead case (whether in accordance with rule 18 (lead cases) or otherwise) of the 2008 Rules must be made by the Chamber President.

11.   The determination of an application for permission to appeal under rule 38 of the 2008 Rules and the exercise of the power of review under section 9 of the Tribunals, Courts and Enforcement Act 2007 must be carried out–

   a.   where the Judge who constituted or was a member of the Tribunal that made the decision was a fee-paid Judge, by a salaried Tribunal Judge; or

   b.   where the Judge who constituted or was a member of the Tribunal that made the decision was a salaried Judge, by that Judge or, if it would be impracticable or cause undue delay, by another salaried Tribunal Judge, save that, where the decision is set aside under section 9(4)(c) of the Act, the matter may only be re-decided under section 9(5)(a) by a Tribunal composed in accordance with paragraph 4, 5 or 6 above.

12.   Where the Tribunal consists of a Tribunal Judge and one or two Tribunal Members, the Tribunal Judge shall be the presiding member. Where the Tribunal comprises more than one Tribunal Judge, the Chamber President must select the presiding member. The presiding member may regulate the procedure of the Tribunal.

13.   Under rule 34(2) of the 2008 Rules it will be for the presiding member to give any written statement of reasons.

14.   *[Omitted]*

LORD JUSTICE CARNWATH SENIOR PRESIDENT OF TRIBUNALS 30 October 2008"

The effect is that HB/CTB appeals will almost always be heard by a single tribunal judge.

The Contracting Out (Administrative Work of Tribunals) Order 2009

(2009 No.121)

1.   This Order may be cited as the Contracting Out (Administrative Work of Tribunals) Order 2009 and comes into force on 2nd March 2009.

2.   The Lord Chancellor may enter into such contracts with other persons for the provision, by them or their sub-contractors, of staff to carry out the administrative work of–

(a)   the First-tier Tribunal;

(b)   the Upper Tribunal;

(c)-(e) *[Omitted]*

The First-tier Tribunal and Upper Tribunal (Chambers) Order 2010
(2010 No.2655)

Citation, commencement and revocations

1.–(1) This Order may be cited as the First-tier Tribunal and Upper Tribunal (Chambers) Order 2010 and comes into force on 29th November 2010.

(2)   The Orders listed in the first column of the Schedule to this Order are revoked to the extent specified in the second column.

First-tier Tribunal Chambers

2.   The First-tier Tribunal shall be organised into the following chambers–

(a)   the General Regulatory Chamber;

(b)   the Health, Education and Social Care Chamber;

(c)   the Immigration and Asylum Chamber;

(d)   the Social Entitlement Chamber;

(e)   the Tax Chamber;

(f)   the War Pensions and Armed Forces Compensation Chamber.

Functions of the Immigration and Asylum Chamber of the First-tier Tribunal

5.   To the Immigration and Asylum Chamber of the First-tier Tribunal are allocated all functions related to immigration and asylum matters, with the exception of matters allocated to–

(a)   the Social Entitlement Chamber by article 6(a);

(b)   *Omitted*

Functions of the Social Entitlement Chamber

6.   To the Social Entitlement Chamber are allocated all functions related to appeals–

(a)   in cases regarding support for asylum seekers, failed asylum seekers, persons designated under section 130 of the Criminal Justice and Immigration Act 2008, or the dependants of any such persons;

(b)   in criminal injuries compensation cases;

(c)   regarding entitlement to, payments of, or recovery or recoupment of payments of, social security benefits, child support, vaccine damage payments, health in pregnancy grant and tax credits, with the exception of–

　(i)   appeals under section 11 of the Social Security Contributions (Transfer of Functions, etc.) Act 1999 (appeals against decisions of Her Majesty's Revenue and Customs);

　(ii)   appeals in respect of employer penalties or employer information penalties (as defined in section 63(11) and (12) of the Tax Credits Act 2002);

　(iii)   appeals under regulation 28(3) of the Child Trust Funds Regulations 2004;

(d)   regarding saving gateway accounts with the exception of appeals against requirements to account for an amount under regulations made under section 14 of the Saving Gateway Accounts Act 2009;

(e)   regarding child trust funds with the exception of appeals against requirements to account for an amount under regulations made under section 22(4) of the Child Trust Funds Act 2004 in relation to section 13 of that Act;

(f)   regarding payments in consequence of diffuse mesothelioma;

(g)   regarding a certificate or waiver decision in relation to NHS charges;

(h)   regarding entitlement to be credited with earnings or contributions;

(i)   against a decision as to whether an accident was an industrial accident.

Upper Tribunal Chambers

9.   The Upper Tribunal shall be organised into the following chambers–

(a)   the Administrative Appeals Chamber;

(b)   the Immigration and Asylum Chamber of the Upper Tribunal;

(c)   the Lands Chamber;
(d)   the Tax and Chancery Chamber.

Functions of the Administrative Appeals Chamber

10.   To the Administrative Appeals Chamber are allocated all functions related to–
(a)   an appeal–
     (i)   against a decision made by the First-tier Tribunal, except an appeal allocated to the Tax and Chancery Chamber by article 13(a) or the Immigration and Asylum Chamber of the Upper Tribunal by article 11(a);
     (ii)-(vi) *Omitted*
     (vii)   transferred to the Upper Tribunal from the First-tier Tribunal under Tribunal Procedure Rules, except an appeal allocated to the Tax and Chancery Chamber by article 13(1)(e);
     (viii) *Omitted*
(b)   an application, except an application allocated to another chamber by article 11(c), 12(c) or 13(g), for the Upper Tribunal–
     (i)   to grant the relief mentioned in section 15(1) of the Tribunals, Courts and Enforcement Act 2007 (Upper Tribunal's "judicial review" jurisdiction);
     (ii)   to exercise the powers of review under section 21(2) of that Act (Upper Tribunal's "judicial review" jurisdiction: Scotland);
(c)   a matter referred to the Upper Tribunal by the First-tier Tribunal–
     (i)   under section 9(5)(b) of the Tribunals, Courts and Enforcement Act 2007 (review of decision of First-tier Tribunal), or
     (ii)   under Tribunal Procedure Rules relating to non-compliance with a requirement of the First-tier Tribunal,
     except where the reference is allocated to another chamber by article 11(b) or 13(f);
(d)   a determination or decision under section 4 of the Forfeiture Act 1982;
(e)   proceedings, or a preliminary issue, transferred under Tribunal Procedure Rules to the Upper Tribunal from the First-tier Tribunal, except those allocated to the Tax and Chancery Chamber by article 13(1)(e).

General Note

All HB/CTB appeals are assigned to the Social Entitlement Chamber of the First-tier Tribunal. Since 1 September 2009, the Upper Tribunal has consisted of three chambers: the Administrative Appeals Chamber, the Tax and Chancery Chamber and the Lands Chamber. Appeals relating to social security benefits (including HB/CTB) continue to be assigned to the Administrative Appeals Chamber.

Resolution of doubt or dispute as to chamber

14.   If there is any doubt or dispute as to the chamber in which a particular matter is to be dealt with, the Senior President of Tribunals may allocate that matter to the chamber which appears to the Senior President of Tribunals to be most appropriate.

Re-allocation of a case to another chamber

15.   At any point in the proceedings, the Chamber President of the chamber to which a case or any issue in that case has been allocated by or under this Order may, with the consent of the corresponding Chamber President, allocate that case or that issue to another chamber within the same tribunal, by giving a direction to that effect.

Part 6

Other primary legislation

Local Government Finance Act 1992
(1992 c14)

General Note to the Act

This Act introduced the council tax and CTB to replace the former community charge (or poll tax) and community charge benefit. The council tax itself is outside the scope of this work – see CPAG's *Council Tax Handbook*. The parts of the Act reproduced below are those which are most necessary for a full understanding of CTB, usually because they are referred to in the CTB and the CTB(SPC) Regulations.

Section 103 and Sch 9 to the Act substantially amended the Social Security Contributions and Benefits Act 1992 and the Social Security Administration Act 1992 so as to introduce CTB. Those provisions are not reproduced here as their effects have been incorporated in the text of the amended Acts as Part 1.

PART I
Council Tax: England and Wales
Chapter I: Main ProvisionsLiability to tax

Persons liable to pay council tax

6.–(1)   The person who is liable to pay council tax in respect of any chargeable dwelling and any day is the person who falls within the first paragraph of subsection (2) below to apply, taking paragraph (a) of that subsection first, paragraph (b) next, and so on.

(2)   A person falls within this subsection in relation to any chargeable dwelling and any day if, on that day–

(a)   he is a resident of the dwelling and has a freehold interest in the whole or any part of it;

(b)   he is such a resident and has a leasehold interest in the whole or any part of the dwelling which is not inferior to another such interest held by another such resident;

(c)   he is both such a resident and a statutory [¹ ...secure or introductory tenant] of the whole or any part of the dwelling;

(d)   he is such a resident and has a contractual licence to occupy the whole or any part of the dwelling;

(e)   he is such a resident.

(3)   Where, in relation to any chargeable dwelling and any day, two or more persons fall within the first paragraph of subsection (2) above to apply, they shall be jointly and severally liable to pay the council tax payable in respect of that dwelling and that day.

(4)   Subsection (3) above shall not apply as respects any day on which one or more of the persons there mentioned fall to be disregarded for the purposes of discount by virtue of [³ paragraph 2 (severely mentally impaired) or 4 (students etc.) of Schedule 1 to this Act] and one or more of them do not; and liability to pay the council tax in respect of the dwelling and that day shall be determined as follows–

(a)   if only one of those persons does not fall to be so disregarded, he shall be solely liable;

(b)   if two or more of those persons do not fall to be so disregarded, they shall be jointly and severally liable.

(5)   In this Part, unless the context otherwise requires–

"owner", in relation to any dwelling, means the person as regards whom the following conditions are fulfilled–

(a)   he has a material interest in the whole or any part of the dwelling; and

(b)   at least part of the dwelling or, as the case may be, of the part concerned is not subject to a material interest inferior to his interest;

"resident", in relation to any dwelling, means an individual who has attained the age of 18 years and has his sole or main residence in the dwelling

(6)   In this section–

[² "introductory tenant" means a tenant under an introductory tenancy within the meaning of Chapter I of Part V of the Housing Act 1996] "material interest" means a freehold interest or a leasehold interest which was granted for a term of six months or more;

"secure tenant" means a tenant under a secure tenancy within the meaning of Part IV of the Housing Act 1985;

"statutory tenant" means a statutory tenant within the meaning of the Rent Act 1977 or the Rent (Agriculture) Act 1976.

Amendments

1.   Substituted by Art 2 and Sch para 8(a) of SI 1997 No. 74 as from 12.2.97.
2.   Substituted by Art 2 and Sch para 8(b) of SI 1997 No. 74 as from 12.2.97.
3.   Amended by Local Government Act 2003 s74(1) (for financial years beginning on or after 1.4.04).

Amounts of tax payable

Discounts

11.–(1)   The amount of council tax payable in respect of any chargeable dwelling and any day shall be subject to a discount equal to the appropriate percentage of that amount if on that day–

(a)   there is only one resident of the dwelling and he does not fall to be disregarded for the purposes of discount; or

(b)   there are two or more residents of the dwelling and each of them except one falls to be disregarded for those purposes.

(2)   Subject to [¹ sections 11A and 12] below, the amount of council tax payable in respect of any chargeable dwelling and any day shall be subject to a discount equal to twice the appropriate percentage of that amount if on that day–

(a)   there is no resident of the dwelling; or

(b)   there are one or more residents of the dwelling and each of them falls to be disregarded for the purposes of discount.

(3)   In this section [²] "the appropriate percentage" means 25 per cent. or, if the Secretary of State by order so provides in relation to the financial year in which the day falls, such other percentage as may be specified in the order.

(4)   No order under subsection (3) above shall be made unless a draft of the order has been laid before and approved by resolution of the House of Commons.

(5)   Schedule 1 to this Act shall have effect for determining who shall be disregarded for the purposes of discount.

Amendments

1.   Amended by Local Government Act 2003 s127(1) and Sch 7 para 41.
2.   Repealed by Local Government Act 2003 s127(2) and Part 1 Sch 8 (18.11.03).

Reduced Amounts

13.–(1)   The Secretary of State may make regulations as regards any case where–

(a)   a person is liable to pay an amount to a billing authority in respect of council tax for any financial year which is prescribed; and

(b)   prescribed conditions are fulfilled.

(2)   The regulations may provide that the amount he is liable to pay shall be an amount which–

(a)   is less than the amount it would be apart from the regulations; and

(b)   is determined in accordance with prescribed rules.

(3)   This section applies whether the amount mentioned in subsection (1) above is determined under section 10 above or under that section read with section 11[¹ , 11A] or 12 above.

(4)   The conditions mentioned in subsection (1) above may be prescribed by reference to such factors as the Secretary of State thinks fit; and in particular such factors may include the making of an application by the person concerned and all or any of–

(a)   the factors mentioned in subsection (5) below; or

(b)   the factors mentioned in subsection (6) below.

(5)   The factors referred to in subsection (4)(a) above are–

(a)   community charges for a period before 1st April 1993;

(b)   the circumstances of, or other matters relating to, the person concerned;

(c)   an amount relating to the authority concerned and specified, or to be specified, for the purposes of the regulations in a report laid, or to be laid, before the House of Commons;

(d)   such other amounts as may be prescribed or arrived at in a prescribed manner.

(6)   The factors referred to in subsection (4)(b) above are–

(a)   a disabled person having his sole or main residence in the dwelling concerned;

(b)   the circumstances of, or other matters relating to, that persons;

(c)   the physical characteristics of, or other matters relating to, that dwelling.

(7)   The rules mentioned in subsection (2) above may be prescribed by reference to such factors as the Secretary of State thinks fit; and in particular such factors may include all or any of the factors mentioned in subsection (5) or subsection (6)(b) or (c) above.

(8)   Without prejudice to the generality of section 113(2) below, regulations under this section may include–

(a)   provision requiring the Secretary of State to specify in a report, for the purposes of the regulations, an amount in relation to each billing authority;

(b)   provision requiring him to lay the report before the House of Commons;

(c)   provision for the review of any prescribed decision of a billing authority relating to the application or operation of the regulations;

(d)   provision that no appeal may be made to a valuation tribunal in respect of such a decision, notwithstanding section 16(1) below.

(9)   To the extent that he would not have power to do so apart from this subsection, the Secretary of State may–

(a)   include in regulations under this section such amendments of any social security instrument as he thinks expedient in consequence of the regulations under this section;

(b)   include in any social security instrument such provision as he thinks expedient in consequence of regulations under this section.

(10)   In subsection (9) above "social security instrument" means an order or regulations made, or falling to be made, by the Secretary of State under the Social Security Acts, that is to say, the Social Security Contributions and Benefits Act 1992 and the Social Security Administration Act 1992.

Amendment

1.   Amended by Local Government Act 2003 s127(1) and Sch 7 para 42.

Chapter III: Setting of Council Tax

Substituted amount

31.–(1)   Where a billing authority has set amounts for a financial year under section 30 above and at any later time–

(a)   it makes substitute calculations under section 37 or 60 below; or

(b)   it is issued with a precept for the year (originally or by way of substitute) by a major precepting authority,

it shall as soon as reasonably practicable after that time set amounts in substitution so as to give effect to those calculations or that precept.

(2)   Any amount set in substitution under subsection (1) above must be set in accordance with section 30 above, but subsection (6) of that section shall be ignored for this purpose.

(3)   Where a billing authority sets any amount in substitution under subsection (1) above (a new amount), anything paid to it by reference to the amount from which it is substituted (the old amount) shall be treated as paid by reference to the new amount.

(4)   If the old amount exceeds the new amount, the following shall apply as regards anything paid if it would not have been paid had the old amount been the same as the new amount–

(a)   it shall be repaid if the person by whom it was paid so requires;

(b)   in any other case it shall (as the billing authority determines) either be repaid or be credited against any subsequent liability of the person to pay in respect of any council tax set by the authority in accordance with section 30 above.

(5)   Where an authority sets amounts in substitution under subsection (1)(b) above, it may recover from the major precepting authority administrative expenses incurred by it in, or in consequence of, so doing.

<hr>

PART II
Council Tax: Scotland
Liability to tax

<hr>

Persons liable to pay council tax

75.–(1)   The person who is liable to pay council tax in respect of any chargeable dwelling and any day is the person who falls within the first paragraph of subsection (2) below to apply, taking paragraph (a) of that subsection first, paragraph (b) next, and so on.

(2)   A person falls within this subsection in relation to any chargeable dwelling and any day if, on that day–

(a)   he is the resident owner of the whole or any part of the dwelling;

(b)   he is a resident tenant of the whole or any part of the dwelling;

(c)   he is a resident statutory tenant, resident statutory assured tenant or resident secure tenant of the whole or any part of the dwelling;

(d)   he is a resident sub-tenant of the whole or any part of the dwelling;

(e)   he is a resident of the dwelling.

(3)   Where, in relation to any chargeable dwelling and any day, two or more persons fall within the first paragraph of subsection (2) above to apply, they shall be jointly and severally liable to pay the council tax payable in respect of that dwelling and that day.

(4)   Subsection (3) above shall not apply as respects any day on which one or more of the persons there mentioned fall to be disregarded for the purposes of discount [¹ either] by virtue of paragraph 2 of Schedule 1 to this Act (the severely mentally impaired) [¹ or, being a student, by virtue of paragraph 4 of that Schedule] and one or more of them do not; and liability to pay the council tax in respect of the dwelling and that day shall be determined as follows–

(a)   if only one of those persons does not fall to be so disregarded, he shall be solely liable;

(b)   if two or more of those persons do not fall to be so disregarded, they shall be jointly and severally liable.

(5)   In this section–

[² "Scottish secure tenant" means a tenant under a Scottish secure tenancy within the meaning of the Housing (Scotland) Act 2001 (asp 10)];

"statutory tenant" means a statutory tenant within the meaning of the Rent (Scotland) Act 1984;

"statutory assured tenant" means a statutory assured tenant within the meaning of the Housing (Scotland) Act 1988.

Amendments

1.   Amended by Education (Graduate Endowment and Student Support) Act 2001 s4 (1.6.01).

2.   Amended by Housing (Scotland) Act 2001 Sch 10 para 19.

Amounts of tax payable

<hr>

Discounts

79.–(1)   The amount of council tax payable in respect of any chargeable dwelling and any day shall be subject to a discount equal to the appropriate percentage of that amount if on that day–

(a)   there is only one resident of the dwelling and he does not fall to be disregarded for the purposes of discount; or

(b)   there are two or more residents of the dwelling and each of them except one falls to be disregarded for those purposes.

(2)   The amount of council tax payable in respect of any chargeable dwelling and any day shall be subject to a discount equal to twice the appropriate percentage of that amount if on that day–

[¹ (a)]

(b)   there are one or more residents of the dwelling and each of them falls to be disregarded for the purposes of discount.

(3)   In this section "the appropriate percentage" means 25 per cent. or, if the Secretary of State by order so provides in relation to the financial year in which the day falls, such other percentage as may be specified in the order.

(4)   No order under subsection (3) above shall be made unless a draft of the order has been laid before and approved by resolution of the House of Commons.

(5)   Schedule 1 to this Act shall have effect for determining who shall be disregarded for the purposes of discount.

Amendment

1.   Repealed by reg 2 of SI 2005 No 51 as from 1.4.05.

Reduced amounts

80.–(1)   The Secretary of State may make regulations as regards any case where–

(a)   a person is liable to pay an amount to a [¹ ...local] authority in respect of council tax for any financial year which is prescribed; and

(b)   prescribed conditions are fulfilled.

(2)   The regulations may provide that the amount he is liable to pay shall be an amount which–

(a)   is less than the amount it would be apart from the regulations; and

(b)   is determined in accordance with prescribed rules.

(3)   This section applies whether the amount mentioned in subsection (1) above is determined under section 78 above or under that section read with section 79 above.

(4)   The conditions mentioned in subsection (1) above may be prescribed by reference to such factors as the Secretary of State thinks fit; and in particular such factors may include the making of an application by the person concerned and all or any or–

(a)   the factors mentioned in subsection (5) below; or

(b)   the factors mentioned in subsection (6) below.

(5)   The factors mentioned in subsection (4)(a) above are–

(a)   community charges for a period before 1st April 1993;

(b)   the circumstances of, or other matters relating to, the person concerned;

(c)   an amount–

[²(i)   relating to the local authority whose council tax constitutes the amount referred to in subsection (1) above;] and

(ii)   which is specified, or is to be specified, in a report laid, or to be laid, before the House of Commons;

(6)   The factors referred to in subsection (4)(b) above are

(a)   a disabled person having his sole or main residence in the dwelling concerned;

(b)   the circumstances of, or other matters relating to, that person;

(c)   the physical characteristics of, or other matters relating to, that dwelling.

(7)   The rules mentioned in subsection (2) above may be prescribed by reference to such factors as the Secretary of State thinks fit; and in particular such factors may include all or any of the factors mentioned in subsection (5) or subsection (6)(b) or (c) above.

(8)   Without prejudice to the generality of section 113(2) below, regulations under this section may include–

(a)   provision requiring the Secretary of State to specify in a report, for the purposes of the regulations, an amount in relation to each local authority;

(b)   provision requiring him to lay the report before the House of Commons;

(c)   provision for the review of any prescribed decision of a [¹ ...local] authority relating to the application or operation of the regulations;

(d)   provision that no appeal may be made to a valuation appeal committee in respect of such a decision, notwithstanding section 81(1) below.

(9)   To the extent that he would not have power to do so apart from this subsection, the Secretary of State may–

(a)   include in regulations under this section such amendments of any social security instrument as he thinks expedient in consequence of the regulations under this section;

(b)   include in any social security instrument such provision as he thinks expedient in consequence of regulations under this section.

(10)   In subsection (9) above "social security instrument" means an order or regulations made, or falling to be made, by the Secretary of State under the Social Security Acts.

Amendments

1.   Substituted by Local Government Etc. (Scotland) Act 1994 c.39 s180(1) and Sch 13 para 176(4)(a).
2.   Substituted by Local Government Etc. (Scotland) Act 1994 c.39 s180(1) and Sch 13 para 176(4)(b).

Setting of the tax

Substituted and reduced settings

94.–(1)   Subject to subsection (3) below, a local authority may set, in substitution for an amount of council tax already set or deemed to have been set, a lesser amount of council tax for the same financial year.

(2)   Schedule 7 to this Act has effect for the purpose of making provision as to the reduction of council tax where the Secretary of State is satisfied, in accordance with that Schedule, that the total estimated expenses mentioned in section 93(3) above of a local authority are excessive or that an increase in those expenses is excessive.

(3)   A local authority may not set a substitute amount of council tax during the period between the approval by the House of Commons of a report in respect of that authority made by the Secretary of State under paragraph 1 of that Schedule and the setting or deemed setting of a reduced amount of council tax under paragraph 3 of that Schedule.

(4)   Section 93(2) above shall not apply for the purposes of this section.

(5)   A local authority who, in respect of any financial year, set (or are deemed to have set) a substituted or reduced council tax shall neither wholly nor partially offset the difference between–

(a)   the amount produced by that substituted or reduced setting; and

(b)   the amount which would have been produced had they not substituted or reduced their setting,

with sums advanced from their loans fund established under Schedule 3 to the 1975 Act: Provided that such offsetting may nevertheless be permitted by the Secretary of State in any case on such terms and conditions as he considers appropriate.

(6)   If the Secretary of State is of the opinion that subsection (5) above, or any term or condition imposed under the proviso thereto, has been contravened, the local authority shall, on such opinion being intimated to them, reimburse their loans fund forthwith or within such time as the Secretary of State may allow.

(7)   Anything paid by reference to one setting of council tax shall be treated as paid by reference to a substitute setting by virtue of paragraph 3 of Schedule 7 to this Act.

(8)   Where a person has paid by reference to one setting of council tax more than is due under a substituted or reduced setting–

(a)   the balance shall be repaid to the person if s/he so requires;

(b)   in any other case the balance shall (as the [1 ...local] authority determine) either be repaid to the person or be credited against any subsequent liability of the person to pay in respect of any council tax due to the authority.

(9)   Where–

(a)   a substitute amount of council tax has been set under subsection (1) above; or

(b)   a reduced amount of council tax has been set or been deemed to have been set under paragraph 3 of that Schedule, the regional council shall levy and collect that substituted or reduced amount in place of the previous amount of council tax and may recover from the district council any administrative expenses incurred in so doing in relation to a substituted or reduced amount of district council tax.

Amendment

1.   Substituted by Local Government Etc. (Scotland) Act 1994 c.39 s180(1) and Sch 13 para 176(9).

SCHEDULE 1

PERSONS DISREGARDED FOR PURPOSES OF DISCOUNT

Persons in detention

1.–(1)   A person shall be disregarded for the purposes of discount on a particular day if on the day–
(a)   he is detained in a prison, a hospital or any other place by virtue of an order of a court to which sub-paragraph (2) below applies;
(b)   he is detained under paragraph 2 of Schedule 3 to the Immigration Act 1971 (deportation);
(c)   he is detained under Part II or section 46, 47, 48 or 136 of the Mental Health Act 1983; or
(d)   he is detained under Part V or section 69, 70, 71 or 118 of the Mental Health (Scotland) Act 1984.
(2)   This sub-paragraph applies to the following courts–
(a)   a court in the United Kingdom; and
(b)   a Standing Civilian Court established under the Armed Forces Act 1976.
(3)   If a person–
(a)   is temporarily discharged under section 28 of the Prison Act 1952, or temporarily released under rules under section 47(5) of that Act; or
(b)   is temporarily discharged under section 27 of the Prisons (Scotland) Act 1989, or temporarily released under rules under section 39(6) or that Act,
for the purposes of sub-paragraph (1) above he shall be treated as detained.
(4)   Sub-paragraph (1) above does not apply where the person–
(a)   is detained under regulations made under paragraph 8 of Schedule 4 to this Act;
(b)   is detained under section 76 of the Magistrates' Courts Act 1980, or section 9 of the Criminal Justice Act 1982, for default in payment of a fine; or
(c)   is detained only under section 407 of the Criminal Procedure (Scotland) Act 1975.
(5)   In sub-paragraph (1) above "order" includes a sentence, direction, warrant or other means of giving effect to the decision of the court concerned.
(6)   The Secretary of State may by order provide that a person shall be disregarded for the purposes of discount on a particular day if–
(a)   on the day he is imprisoned, detained or in custody under the Army Act 1955, the Air Force Act 1955 or the Naval Discipline Act 1957; and
(b)   such conditions as may be prescribed by the order are fulfilled.

The severely mentally impaired

2.–(1)   A person shall be disregarded for the purposes of discount on a particular day if
(a)   on the day he is severely mentally impaired;
(b)   as regards any period which includes the day he is stated in a certificate of a registered medical practitioner to have been or to be likely to be severely mentally impaired; and
(c)   as regards the day he fulfils such conditions as may be prescribed by order made by the Secretary of State.
(2)   For the purposes of this paragraph a person is severely mentally impaired if he has a severe impairment of intelligence and social functioning (however caused) which appears to be permanent.
(3)   The Secretary of State may by order substitute another definition for the definition in sub-paragraph (2) above as for the time being effective for the purposes of this paragraph.

Persons in respect of whom child benefit is payable

3.–(1)   A person shall be disregarded for the purposes of discount on a particular day if on the day he–
(a)   has attained the age of 18 years; but
(b)   is a person in respect of whom another person is entitled to child benefit, or would be so entitled but for paragraph 1(c) of Schedule 9 to the Social Security Contributions and Benefits Act 1992.
(2)   The Secretary of State may by order substitute another provision for sub-paragraph (1)(b) above as for the time being effective for the purposes of this paragraph.

Students etc

4.–(1)   A person shall be disregarded for the purposes of discount on a particular day if–
(a)   on the day he is a student, student nurse, apprentice or youth training trainee; and
(b)   such conditions as may be prescribed by order made by the Secretary of State are fulfilled.
(2)   In this paragraph "apprentice", "student", "student nurse" and "youth training trainee" have the meanings for the time being assigned to them by order made by the Secretary of State.

5.–(1)   An institution shall, on request, supply a certificate under this paragraph to any person who is following or, subject to sub-paragraph (3) below, has followed a course of education at that institution as a student or student nurse.

(2)   A certificate under this paragraph shall contain such information about the person to whom it refers as may be prescribed by order made by the Secretary of State.

(3)   An institution may refuse to comply with a request made more than one year after the person making it has ceased to follow a course of education at that institution.

(4)   In this paragraph–

"institution" means any such educational establishment or other body as may be prescribed by order made by the Secretary of State; and

"student" and "student nurse" have the same meanings as in paragraph 4 above.

Hospital patients

6.–(1)   A person shall be disregarded for the purposes of discount on a particular day if on the day he is a patient who has his sole or main residence in a hospital.

(2)   In this paragraph "hospital" means–

(a)   a health service hospital within the meaning of the National Health Service Act 1977 or section 108(1) (interpretation) of the National Health Service (Scotland) Act 1978; and

(b)   a military, air-force or naval unit or establishment at or in which medical or surgical treatment is provided for persons subject to military law, air-force law or the Naval Discipline Act 1957.

(3)   The Secretary of State may by order substitute another definition for the definition in sub-paragraph (2) above as for the time being effective for the purposes of this paragraph.

Patients in homes in England and Wales

7.–(1)   A person shall be disregarded for the purposes of discount on a particular day if on the day–

(a)   he has his sole or main residence in a [¹ care home, independent hospital] or hostel in England and Wales; and

(b)   he is receiving care or treatment (or both) in the home [¹ , hospital] or hostel.

[¹ (2)   In this paragraph–

"care home" means–

(a)   a care home within the meaning of the Care Standards Act 2000; or

(b)   a building or part of a building in which residential accommodation is provided under section 21 of the National Assistance Act 1948;

"hostel" means anything which falls within any definition of hostel for the time being prescribed by order made by the Secretary of State under this sub-paragraph;

[² "independent hospital"–

(a)   in relation to England, means a hospital as defined by section 275 of the National Health Service Act 2006 that is not a health service hospital as defined by that section; and

(b)   in relation to Wales, has the same meaning as in the Care Standards Act 2000.]

(3)   The Secretary of State may by order substitute another definition for any definition of [¹ "care home" or "independent hospital"] for the time being effective for the purposes of this paragraph.

Amendments

1.   Amended by the Care Standards Act 2000 Sch 10 para 20.
2.   Substituted by Art 9 of SI 2010 No 813 as from 1.10.10.

Patients in homes in Scotland

8.–(1)   A person shall be disregarded for the purposes of discount on a particular day if on the day–

[¹ (a)   either–

(i)   he has as his sole or main residence a private hospital in Scotland; or

(ii)   a care home service provides, in Scotland, accommodation which is his sole or main residence; and

(b)   he is receiving care or treatment (or both) in the hospital or in the accommodation so provided.]

(2)   In this paragraph–

[¹ "care home service" has the same meaning as in the Regulation of Care (Scotland) Act 2001 (asp 8); and]

[¹ . . .]

"private hospital" means a private hospital within the meaning of section 12 (registration of private hospitals) of the Mental Health (Scotland) Act 1984;

[¹ . . .]

(3)   [¹ . . .]

(4)   The Secretary of State may by order substitute another definition for any definition of [¹ . . .] "private hospital" or [¹ "care home service"] for the time being effective for the purposes of this paragraph.

Amendment

1.   Amended by the Regulation of Care (Scotland) Act 2001 Sch 3 para 18.

Care workers

9.–(1)   A person shall be disregarded for the purposes of discount on a particular day if–

(a)   on the day he is engaged in providing care or support (or both) to another person or other persons; and

(b)   such conditions as may be prescribed are fulfilled.

(2)   Without prejudice to the generality of sub-paragraph (1)(b) above the conditions may–

(a)   require the care or support (or both) to be provided on behalf of a charity or a person fulfilling some other description;

(b)   relate to the period for which the person is engaged in providing care of support (or both);

(c)   require his income for a prescribed period (which contains the day concerned) not to exceed a prescribed amount;

(d)   require his capital not to exceed a prescribed amount;

(e)   require him to be resident in prescribed premises;

(f)   require him not to exceed a prescribed age;

(g)   require the other person or persons to fulfil a prescribed description (whether relating to age, disablement or otherwise).

Residents of certain dwellings

10.–(1)   A person shall be disregarded for the purposes of discount on a particular day if on the day he has his sole or main residence in a dwelling to which sub-paragraph (2) below applies.

(2)   This sub-paragraph applies to any dwelling if–

(a)   it is for the time being providing residential accommodation, whether as a hostel or night shelter or otherwise; and

(b)   the accommodation is predominantly provided–

    (i)   otherwise than in separate and self-contained sets of premises;

    (ii)   for persons of no fixed abode and no settled way of life; and

    (iii)   under licences to occupy which do not constitute tenancies.

Persons of other descriptions

11.   A person shall be disregarded for the purposes of discount on a particular day if–

(a)   on the day he falls within such descriptions as may be prescribed; and

(b)   such conditions as may be prescribed are fulfilled.

Housing Act 1996

(1996 c52)

Functions of rent officers in connection with housing benefit and rent allowance subsidy

122.–(1)   The Secretary of State may by order require rent officers to carry out such functions as may be specified in the order in connection with housing benefit and council tax benefit.

(2)   Without prejudice to the generality of subsection (1), an order under this section may contain provision–

(a)   enabling a prospective landlord to apply for a determination for the purposes of any application for housing benefit which may be made by a tenant of a dwelling which he proposed to let;

(b)   as to the payment of a fee by the landlord for that determination;

(c)   requiring the landlord to give a copy of the determination to the appropriate local authority; and

(d)   enabling the appropriate local authority to seek a redetermination when a claim for housing benefit or rent allowance subsidy is made.

(3)   Regulations under section 130(4) of the Social Security Contributions and Benefits Act 1992 (housing benefit: manner of determining appropriate maximum benefit) may provide for benefit to be limited by reference to determinations made by rent officers in exercise of functions conferred under this section.

(4)   In relation to rent allowance subsidy, the Secretary of State may by order under section 140B of the Social Security Administration Act 1992–

(a)   provide for any calculation under subsection (2) of that section to be made,

(b)   specify any additions and deductions as are referred to in that subsection, and

(c)   exercise his discretion as to what is unreasonable for the purposes of subsection (4) of that section,

by reference to determinations made by rent officers in exercise of functions conferred on them under this section.

(5)   The Secretary of State may by any such regulations or order as are mentioned in subsection (3) or (4) require a local authority in any prescribed case–

(a)   to apply to a rent officer for a determination to be made in pursuance of the functions conferred on them under this section; and

(b)   to do so within such time as may be specified in the order or regulations.

(6)   An order under this section–

(a)   shall be made by statutory instrument which shall be subject to annulment in pursuance of a resolution of either House of Parliament;

(b)   may make different provision for different cases or classes of case and for different areas; and

(c)   may contain such transitional, incidental and supplementary provisions as appear to the Secretary of State to be desirable.

(7)   In this section ''housing benefit'' and ''rent allowance subsidy'' have the same meaning as in Part VIII of the Social Security Administration Act 1992.

Commencement

1.4.97.

General Note

This section allows the Secretary of State to further expand the role of rent officers in HB matters. See the Rent Officers (Housing Benefit Functions) Order 1997 (p592) and the Scottish equivalent (p614).

Subs (1) is a general power to give rent officers additional functions in relation to HB and rent allowance subsidy. The Secretary of State's powers are not restricted to those in Subs (2).

Subs (2) allows landlords to know, prior to the entry of a tenancy agreement, precisely what level of rent will be met by a rent allowance. It is the landlord's responsibility to obtain that assessment. Note, however, that provision may be made for a local authority to seek a fresh determination on a claim for HB. See also regs 13D(8)and 14(1)(e) of both the HB and the HB(SPC) Regs.

Subs (3) authorises the form of regs 13 and 13D of both the HB and the HB(SPC) Regs.

Welfare Reform and Pensions Act 1999
(1999 c30)

General Note to the Act

The principal innovation made by the Act, as far as this book is concerned, was a greatly expanded role for local authorities as providers of benefit services.

Miscellaneous

Supply of information for certain purposes

72.–(1)   The Secretary of State may by regulations make such provision for or in connection with any of the following matters, namely–

  (a)   the use by a person within subsection (2) of social security information [⁵ , or information relating to employment or training,] held by that person,

  (b)   the supply (whether to a person within subsection (2) or otherwise) of social security information [⁵ , or information relating to employment or training,] held by a person within that subsection,

  (c)   the relevant purposes for which a person to whom such information is supplied under the regulations may use it, and

  (d)   the circumstances and extent (if any) in and to which a person to whom such information is supplied under the regulations may supply it to any other person (whether within subsection (2) or not), as the Secretary of State considers appropriate in connection with any provision to which subsection (3) applies or in connection with any scheme or arrangements to which subsection (4) applies.

  (2)   The persons within this subsection are–

  (a)   a Minister of the Crown;

  (b)   a person providing services to, or designated for the purposes of this section by an order of, a Minister of the Crown;

  (c)   a local authority (within the meaning of the Administration Act); [⁴]

  [⁶ (ca)   a county council in England; and]

  (d)   a person providing services to, or authorised to exercise any function of, [⁶ any authority mentioned in paragraph (c) or (ca)].

  (3)   This subsection applies to any provision made by or under–

  (a)   any of the sections of the Administration Act inserted by section 57, 58 or 71 of this Act,

  [¹ (aa) section 2AA of the Administration Act,]

  (b)   section 60 of this Act, [³]

  (c)   the Jobseekers Act 1995. [² or

  (d)   Part 1 of the Welfare Reform Act 2007.]

  (4)   This subsection applies to–

  (a)   any scheme designated by regulations under subsection (1), being a scheme operated by the Secretary of State (whether under arrangements with any other person or not) for any purposes connected with employment or training in the case of persons of a particular category or description;

  (b)   any arrangements of a description specified in such regulations, being arrangements made by the Secretary of State for any such purposes.

  (5)   Regulations under subsection (1) may, in particular, authorise information supplied to a person under the regulations–

  (a)   to be used for the purpose of amending or supplementing other information held by that person; and

  (b)   if it is so used, to be supplied to any other person, and used for any purpose, to whom or for which that other information could be supplied or used.

  (6)   In this section–

"relevant purposes" means purposes connected with–

  (a)   social security, child support or war pensions, or

(b)   employment or training;

"social security information" means [⁶ (subject to subsection (6A))] information relating to social security, child support or war pensions; and in this subsection "war pensions" means war pensions within the meaning of section 25 of the Social Security Act 1989 (establishment and functions of war pensions committees).

[⁶ (6A)   References in subsection (1)(a) and (b) to social security information held by a county council do not include social security information about any person to whom the council is not required to make support services available under section 68(1) of the Education and Skills Act 2008 (support services: provision by local education authorities).]

(7)   Any reference in this section to [⁵ information relating to, or purposes connected with, employment or training includes information relating to, or purposes connected with,] the existing or future employment or training prospects or needs of persons, and (in particular) assisting or encouraging persons to enhance their employment prospects.

Commencement

11.11.99: see s89(4)(c).

Amendments

1.   Inserted by the Employment Act 2002 s53 and Sch 7 para 55 (5.7.03).
2.   Inserted by WRA s28 and Sch 3 para 18 (18.3.08 for making regulations and 27.10.08).
3.   Omitted by WRA s67 and Sch 8 (27.10.08).
4.   Amended by s169 and Sch 2 Education and Skills Act 2008 as from 26.1.09.
5.   Inserted by s34(4) Welfare Reform Act 2009 as from 12.1.09.
6.   Amended by s169 and Sch 1 para 74 Education and Skills Act 2008 as from 30.3.10.

General Note

This permits regulations governing the passing of information between the people listed in s72(2), including between a local authority and other public officials.

Supplementary

Regulations and orders

83.–(1)   Any power under this Act to make regulations or orders (other than orders under section 72(2)) shall be exercisable by statutory instrument.

(2)   A statutory instrument–

(a)   which contains (whether alone or with other provisions) regulations made under this Act, and

(b)   which is not subject to any requirement that a draft of the instrument be laid before and approved by a resolution of each House of Parliament, shall be subject to annulment in pursuance of a resolution of either House of Parliament.

(3)   A statutory instrument containing an order under section 27(3) shall be subject to annulment in pursuance of a resolution of either House of Parliament.

(4)   Any power under this Act to make regulations or orders may be exercised–

(a)   either in relation to all cases to which the power extends, or in relation to those cases subject to specified exceptions, or in relation to any specified cases or classes of case;

(b)   so as to make, as respects the cases in relation to which it is exercised–

(i)   the full provision to which the power extends or any less provision (whether by way of exception or otherwise);

(ii)   the same provision for all cases in relation to which the power is exercised, or different provision for different cases or different classes of case or different provision as respects the same case or class of case for different purposes of this Act;

(iii)   any such provision either unconditionally or subject to any specified condition.

(5)   Where any such power is expressed to be exercisable for alternative purposes it may be exercised in relation to the same case for any or all of those purposes.

(6)   Any such power includes power–

(a)   to make such incidental, supplementary, consequential, saving or transitional provision (including provision amending, repealing or revoking enactments) as appears to the authority making the regulations or order to be expedient; and

(b)   to provide for a person to exercise a discretion in dealing with any matter.

(7)   Any power to make regulations or an order for the purposes of any provision of this Act is without prejudice to any power to make regulations or an order for the purposes of any other provision of this or any other Act.

(8)   Any power conferred by this Act to make regulations or an order relating to–

(a)   housing benefit, or

(b)   council tax benefit, includes power to make different provision for different areas or different authorities; and regulations under section 60 or 79 may make different provision for different areas.

(9)   Without prejudice to the generality of any of the preceding provisions of this section, regulations under section 60 or 72 may provide for all or any of the provisions of the regulations to apply only in relation to any area or areas specified in the regulations.

(10)   Any power to make regulations under Part IV, except sections 28 and 48, shall, if the Treasury so direct, be exercisable only in conjunction with them.

(11)   Before exercising any power to make regulations under Part IV, the authority on whom the power is conferred, or, if the power is the subject of a direction under subsection (10), that authority and the Treasury acting jointly, shall consult such persons as the authority, or the authority and the Treasury, may consider appropriate.

Consequential amendments etc

84.–(1)   The consequential amendments specified in Schedule 12 shall have effect.

(2)   The Secretary of State may by regulations make such amendments or revocations of any instrument made under an Act as he thinks necessary or expedient in consequence of the coming into force of any of the provisions specified in subsection (4).

(3)   The Secretary of State may, for the purposes of or in connection with the coming into force of any of the provisions specified in subsection (4), make by regulations any provision which could be made by an order bringing the provision into force.

(4)   The provisions mentioned in subsections (2) and (3) are–

(a)   Part IV;

(b)   subsection (1) above so far as relating to paragraphs 14 to 63 of Schedule 12; and

(c)   section 88 so far as relating to Part III of Schedule 13.

Transitional provisions

85.–(1)   The Secretary of State may, for the purposes of or in connection with the coming into force of any provisions of Parts I and II, by regulations make such transitional adaptations or modifications–

(a)   of those provisions, or

(b)   in connection with those provisions, of any provisions of–

    (i)   this Act,

    (ii)   the Pension Schemes Act 1993, or

    (iii)   the Pensions Act 1995, then in force, as he considers necessary or expedient

(2)-(8)   *[Omitted]*

General financial provisions

86.–(1)   There shall be paid out of money provided by Parliament–

(a)   any expenditure incurred by a Minister of the Crown or government department under this Act; and

(b)   any increase attributable to this Act in the sums which under any other Act are payable out of money so provided.

(2)   There shall be paid into the Consolidated Fund any increase attributable to this Act in the sums which under any other Act are payable into that Fund.

Repeals

88. The enactments specified in Schedule 13 (which include certain enactments no longer of practical utility) are hereby repealed to the extent specified in the third column of that Schedule.

Commencement

89.–(1) Subject to the provisions of this section, the provisions of this Act shall not come into force until such day as the Secretary of State may by order appoint.

(2) The following provisions shall not come into force until such day as the Lord Chancellor may by order appoint–

(a) sections 19, 21 and 22;

(b) section 84(1) so far as relating to paragraphs 1 to 4 and 64 to 66 of Schedule 12;

(c) section 85(3) and (4); and

(d) section 88 so far as relating to the entries in Part II of Schedule 13 in respect of the Matrimonial Causes Act 1973, the Matrimonial and Family Proceedings Act 1984 and sections 9(8) and 16 of the Family Law Act 1996.

(3) The following provisions shall not come into force until such day as the Treasury may by order appoint–

(a) sections 73 to 78;

(b) section 84(1) so far as relating to paragraphs 74, 76 to 78 and 84 to 86 of Schedule 12; and

(c) section 88 so far as relating to Parts VI and VII of Schedule 13.

(4) The following provisions come into force on the day on which this Act is passed–

(a) sections 52, 57, 58, 60, 68 and 71;

(b) section 70 so far as relating to Part V of Schedule 8;

(c) section 72;

(d) sections 79 to 83;

(e) section 84(1) so far as relating to paragraphs 13, 79 to 83 and 87 of Schedule 12;

(f) section 84(2) to (4);

(g) section 85(1), (2), (6) and (7); and

(h) sections 86 and 87, this section and sections 90 and 91.

(5) The following provisions come into force on the day on which this Act is passed, but for the purpose only of the exercise of any power to make regulations–

(a) Parts I to IV;

(b) sections 59 and 61; and

(c) section 70 so far as relating to paragraph 23 of Schedule 8.

Without prejudice to section 83, an order under this section may appoint different days for different purposes or different areas.

Extent

90.–(1) The following provisions extend to England and Wales only–

(a) section 15;

(b) paragraph 2 of Schedule 2, and section 18 so far as relating thereto;

(c) sections 19, 21 and 22 and Schedules 3 and 4;

(d) paragraphs 1 to 4, 64 to 66 and 70 to 72 of Schedule 12, and section 84(1) so far as relating thereto; and

(e) section 85(3) and (4).

(2) The following provisions extend to Scotland only–

(a) sections 13 and 16;

(b) paragraph 1 of Schedule 2, and section 18 so far as relating thereto;

(c) section 20;

(d) paragraphs 5 to 12 and 67 to 69 of Schedule 12, and section 84(1) so far as relating thereto; and

(e) section 85(5).

(3) The following provisions extend to England and Wales and Scotland only–

(a) Part I;
(b) sections 9 to 12, 14 and 17;
(c) Schedule 2 (except for paragraphs 1, 2, 3(1), 7(2) and 16), and section 18 so far as relating thereto;
(d) sections 23, 24 and 26;
(e) Part IV except sections 42 to 44;
(f) Chapter I of Part V (except paragraph 1 of Schedule 8, and section 70 so far as relating thereto);
(g) sections 73, 75 and 77 and Schedule 9;
(h) section 79;
(i) paragraphs 1 to 8, 20 to 23, 32(b), 33, 35 and 37 of Schedule 11, and section 81 so far as relating thereto;
(j) paragraphs 14 to 63, 66(17), 76 to 80, 82, 83 and 87 of Schedule 12, and section 84(1) so far as relating thereto; and
(k) section 84(2) to (4).
(4) The following provisions extend to England and Wales, Scotland and Northern Ireland–
(a) paragraphs 3(1) and 16 of Schedule 2, and section 18 so far as relating thereto;
(b) sections 42 to 44;
(c) paragraph 1 of Schedule 8, and section 70 so far as relating thereto;
(d) section 80;
(e) paragraphs 29 to 31 and 32(a) of Schedule 11, and section 81 so far as relating thereto;
(f) sections 82 and 83;
(g) paragraphs 13, 73 to 75 and 81 of Schedule 12, and section 84(1) so far as relating thereto;
(h) sections 85(1), (2), (6) and (7) and 86; and
(i) section 89, this section and section 91.
(5) The following provisions extend to Northern Ireland only–
(a) paragraph 7(2) of Schedule 2, and section 18 so far as relating thereto;
(b) sections 74, 76 and 78 and Schedule 10;
(c) paragraphs 9 to 19, 24 to 28, 34, 36 and 38 of Schedule 11, and section 81 so far as relating thereto;
(d) paragraphs 84 to 86 of Schedule 12, and section 84(1) so far as relating thereto; and
(e) section 87.
(6) Nothing in the preceding provisions of this section applies to any repeal made by this Act; and the extent of any such repeal is the same as that of the enactment repealed.

Short title, general interpretation and Scottish devolution
91.–(1) This Act may be cited as the Welfare Reform and Pensions Act 1999.
(2) In this Act–
"the Administration Act" means the Social Security Administration Act 1992;
"the Contributions and Benefits Act" means the Social Security Contributions and Benefits Act 1992.
(3) In this Act, except sections 84(2) and (3), 85(1) and (6) and 89, and in any Act amended by this Act, references to the coming into force of any provision of this Act are to its coming into force otherwise than for the purpose of authorising the making of regulations.
(4) For the purposes of the Scotland Act 1998, the following provisions shall be taken to be pre-commencement enactments within the meaning of that Act–
(a) paragraphs 8(3) and (4) and 10 of Schedule 12; and
(b) so far as relating to those provisions, sections 83, 84(1) and 89(1) and (5).

SCHEDULE 8
Part VIII
Administration of benefits

34.–(1)   In each of the provisions of the Administration Act to which this paragraph applies–

(a)   any reference to a person authorised to exercise any function of a relevant authority relating to housing benefit or council tax benefit shall include a reference to a person providing services to a relevant authority which relate to such a benefit; and

(b)   any reference to the exercise of any function relating to such a benefit shall include a reference to the provision of any services so relating.

(2)   This paragraph applies to the following provisions of the Administration Act–

(a)   [¹ . . .];

(b)   sections 122C, 122D and 122E (supply of information in connection with administration of housing benefit or council tax benefit);

(c)   section 126A (power to require information from landlords etc. in connection with claims for housing benefit);

(d)   section 182B (information about redirection of post); and

(e)   Schedule 4 (persons covered by offence relating to unauthorised disclosures).

(3)   In this paragraph ''relevant authority'' means an authority administering housing benefit or council tax benefit.

Commencement

6.4.03. See SI 2003 No.936.

Amendment

1.   Repealed by CSPSSA s85(1) and Sch 9 Pt VI (1.4.01).

Immigration and Asylum Act 1999
(1999 c33)

Exclusion from benefits

115.–(1)   No person is entitled to income-based jobseeker's allowance under the Jobseekers Act 1995 or to–

  [. . . .]

  (j)   housing benefit, or

  (k)   council tax benefit,

under the Social Security Contributions and Benefits Act 1992 while he is a person to whom this section applies.

  (2)   No person in Northern Ireland is entitled to–

  (a)   [. . . .]

  (b)   any of the benefits mentioned in paragraphs (a) to (j) of subsection (1),

under the Social Security Contributions and Benefits (Northern Ireland) Act 1992 while he is a person to whom this section applies.

  (3)   This section applies to a person subject to immigration control unless he falls within such category or description, or satisfies such conditions, as may be prescribed.

  (4)   Regulations under subsection (3) may provide for a person to be treated for prescribed purposes only as not being a person to whom this section applies.

  (5)   In relation to [¹ child benefit], "prescribed" means prescribed by regulations made by the Treasury.

  (6)   In relation to the matters mentioned in subsection (2) (except so far as it relates to [¹ child benefit]), "prescribed" means prescribed by regulations made by the Department.

  (7)   Section 175(3) to (5) of the Social Security Contributions and Benefits Act 1992 (supplemental power in relation to regulations) applies to regulations made by the Secretary of State or the Treasury under subsection (3) as it applies to regulations made under that Act.

  (8)   Sections 133(2), 171(2) and 172(4) of the Social Security Contributions and Benefits (Northern Ireland) Act 1992 apply to regulations made by the Department under subsection (3) as they apply to regulations made by the Department under that Act.

  (9)   "A person subject to immigration control" means a person who is not a national of an EEA State and who–

  (a)   requires leave to enter or remain in the United Kingdom but does not have it;

  (b)   has leave to enter or remain in the United Kingdom which is subject to a condition that he does not have recourse to public funds;

  (c)   has leave to enter or remain in the United Kingdom given as a result of a maintenance undertaking; or

  (d)   has leave to enter or remain in the United Kingdom only as a result of paragraph 17 of Schedule 4.

  (10)   "Maintenance undertaking", in relation to any person, means a written undertaking given by another person in pursuance of the immigration rules to be responsible for that person's maintenance and accommodation.

Amendment

1.   Amended by TCA Sch 4 para 21 (1.4.03).

Commencement

1.1.2000 for the purpose only of making regulations: Immigration and Asylum Act 1999 (Commencement No.1) Order 1999 SI No.3190.

3.4.2000 for all other purposes: Immigration and Asylum Act 1999 (Commencement No.3) Order 2000 SI No.464.

General Note

Although s115 appears in Part VI of the Act headed "Support for Asylum-Seekers", it has an impact on the entitlements of a wider range of claimants than asylum seekers. The scheme of the section is to introduce a general exclusion from HB and CTB in respect of "persons subject to immigration control" with exceptions to be set out in regulations. In order to work out whether a particular claimant is excluded from entitlement, it is necessary to consider two separate questions:

(1)   Is the claimant a "person subject to immigration control" within the meaning of s115? If so, s/he is excluded from entitlement to HB and CTB unless s/he can show that s/he falls within para (1), (4)(a) or (6) of reg 2 Social Security (Immigration and Asylum) Consequential Amendments Regulations 2000 (see p1169).

(2)   Is the claimant a "person from abroad" within the meaning of reg 10 of both the HB and the HB(SPC) Regs or reg 7 of both the CTB and the CTB(SPC) Regs (see p266)? If so, s/he is excluded from benefit. It was confirmed in *Yesiloz v LB Camden and SSWP* [2009] EWCA Civ 145 (reported as *R(H)7/09*) that those subjected to immigration control who were not excluded from benefit because they were within the Consequential Amendments Regulations still needed to have a right to reside.

Analysis

Subsections (1) to (6): The general exclusion

Subs (1)(j) and (k) exclude a person to whom s115 applies from entitlement to HB and CTB in England, Wales and Scotland and subs (2) makes similar provision in relation to Northern Ireland in respect of the separate HB scheme there (council tax does not apply to Northern Ireland).

Subs (3) states that s115 applies to "a person subject to immigration control" subject to the wide powers to make regulations provided for in that subsection. This critical phrase is defined in subs (9) and is discussed below. It should be noted that the regulation-making powers do *not* include powers to create further categories of people within the definition; the powers are to exclude people from the effect of s115 only: subs (4).

Subsections (9) and (10): "Person subject to immigration control"

Two general points need to be made at the outset. Firstly, it is for the decision making body (the local authority for HB and CTB) to show that a claimant is a person subject to immigration control, the onus does not lie on the claimant to show that s/he is not a person subject to immigration control: *CIS 1697/2004*. In cases where the position is not clear (eg, what part a sponsorship undertaking in fact played in the decision to grant the claimant leave to remain in the UK), then the responsibility for obtaining the information necessary to decide the point will rest with the decision maker: *R(PC) 1/09*. Secondly, for the purposes of s115, a national of a member state of the European Economic Area (EEA) can never be a person subject to immigration control (whatever may be the effect of other immigration legislation in relation to them). The member states are: UK, Austria, Belgium, Bulgaria, Cyprus, the Czech Republic, Denmark, Estonia, Finland, France, Germany, Greece, Hungary, Iceland, Ireland, Italy, Latvia, Liechtenstein, Lithuania, Luxembourg, Malta, the Netherlands, Norway, Poland, Portugal, Romania, Slovakia, Slovenia, Spain and Sweden.

Subject to that consideration, there are four categories of "person" listed in subs (9):

(1)   "A person who requires leave to enter or remain in the United Kingdom but does not have it". The *Statement of Changes in Immigration Rules* (HC 395) para 7 defines such a person as someone who is not a British citizen, a person with a right of residence under the Immigration (European Economic Area) Regulations 2006 (SI 2006 No.1003), or a Commonwealth citizen with a right of abode.

For those who fall into the latter category, see s2(1)(b) of the Immigration Act 1971 which requires that the person should have fallen within s2(1)(d) or (2) of the 1971 Act at the time that the British Nationality Act 1981 came into force on 30 October 1981. Those that fall into this category of claimant will include illegal entrants, overstayers and those with temporary admission under Sch 2 para 21 Immigration Act 1971 – ie, asylum seekers who had been entitled to HB and CTB under reg 7A HB Regs 1987 and reg 4A CTB Regs 1992 prior to April 2000.

With regard to the 2006 regulations, note that although, as mentioned above, EEA nationals cannot be persons subject to immigration control for the purposes of s115 due to the wording of subs (9), it is also possible for non-EEA nationals to have rights of residence under the 2006 Regulations as the family member of an EEA national with such a right. Furthermore, s7 Immigration Act 1988 provides that a person with an "enforceable Community right" also does not require leave to enter or remain in the UK and therefore those who have a right of residence in EU law, provision for which is not mirrored in the 2006 regulations, are not persons subject to immigration control for the purposes of s115.

(2)   "A person who has leave to enter or remain in the United Kingdom which is subject to a condition that he does not have recourse to public funds". It should be clear from the stamp on a claimant's passport whether or not there is such a condition. Most of the categories of limited leave granted under the *Immigration Rules* are subject to such a condition: see, for example, para 41(vi) (visitors), para 56K(vii) (students), para 128(v) (holders of work permits) and para 281(v) (spouses). An eventual grant of indefinite leave to remain which carries no public funds condition operates from the date of grant and is not retrospective: *SSWP v IG* [2008] UKUT 5 (AAC).

(3)   "A person who has leave to enter or remain in the UK given as a result of a maintenance undertaking". See the definition in subs (10). Under para 35 of the *Immigration Rules* a person may be given leave to enter as a result of a sponsor giving an undertaking to be responsible for her/his maintenance and accommodation "for the period of any leave granted, including any further variation". Typically such an undertaking is given for five years (unless a shorter period of leave is granted). The undertaking need not be on the standard RON 112 form but may be, for example, in a letter: see *R(Begum) v Secretary of State for Work and Pensions* [2003] EWHC 3380 Admin, reported as *R(IS) 11/04*. There must be a necessary causal connection between the giving of the undertaking and the granting of leave to enter or remain, which must be investigated by the First-tier Tribunal if necessary. However, it need not be shown that the undertaking was the sole matter taken into account by the immigration officer as long as it was taken into account: *Shah v Secretary of State for Social Security* [2002] EWCA Civ 285, CA (reported as *R(IS) 2/02*); *CIS 3508/2001* paras 10, 24; *CIS 47/2002* para 27. Note, however, that in order for it to count as an undertaking it must amount to a promise, and not simply a general willingness, to maintain the person: *Secretary of State for Work and Pensions v Ahmed* [2005] EWCA Civ 535 (reported as *R(IS) 8/05*).

A person who falls within s115(9)(c) because of a maintenance undertaking would be excluded from HB and CTB indefinitely but for the fact that regulations have been made under s115(4) of the Act. These regulations operate to make such people eligible once they have been resident in the UK for five years from the later of their date of entry to the UK or the date on which the maintenance undertaking was given. That rule is relaxed further if the person (or all persons) who gave the undertaking ("the sponsor(s)") die before the end of that period – see the commentary to para 2 of Part 1 to the Schedule to the Social Security (Immigration and Asylum) Consequential Amendment Regulations 2000 on p1172.

(4)   "A person who has leave to enter or remain in the United Kingdom only as a result of paragraph 17 of Schedule 4". That provision deems leave to enter or remain to continue while an appeal is pending under s61 or 69(2) of the 1999 Act. These relate to appeals against variations or refusals to vary limited leave, and appeals to an adjudicator against a decision to require someone to leave following a refusal of asylum. However, given that the effect of s3C Immigration Act 1971 is that anyone who makes an in-time application to vary her/his leave and is then appealing (within the time limit) against a refusal to grant the variation will also be deemed to continue to have whatever form of leave s/he had before the variation (even if that has now expired), it is difficult to see how anyone could fall within s115(9)(d).

Back-dating of benefits where person recorded as refugee
[⁴**123.**]

Amendments
1.   Inserted by TCA Sch 4 para 22(2) (1.4.03).
2.   Amended by TCA Sch 4 para 22(3) (1.4.03).
3.   Amended by SPCA Sch 2 para 42 (2.7.02 for making regulations). Commencement from October 2003.
4.   Repealed by the Asylum and Immigration (Treatment of Claimants, etc.) Act 2004 s12(1) (for those recorded as refugees after 14.6.07).

Commencement
1.1.2000 for the purpose only of making regulations: Immigration and Asylum Act 1999 (Commencement No.1) Order 1999 SI No.3190.
3.4.2000 for all other purposes: Immigration and Asylum Act 1999 (Commencement No.3) Order 2000 SI No.464.

General Note
The section ceased to have effect from 14 June 2007 for those recorded as refugees after that date: s12(1) Asylum and Immigration (Treatment of Claimants, etc.) Act 2004, brought into effect by the Asylum and Immigration (Treatment of Claimants, etc.) Act 2004 (Commencement No.7 and Transitional Provisions) Order 2007 SI No.1602. For these purposes, a person is "recorded as a refugee" on the day the Secretary of State notifies her/him that s/he has been recognised as a refugee and granted asylum in the UK. For the full text of the section, see pp985-86 of the 19th edition.

The section authorised the making of regulations to permit backdated claims by asylum seekers who succeeded in establishing refugee status for benefits for the whole of that period. The relevant provisions in relation to HB and CTB were reg 10A and Sch A1 of both the HB and the HB(SPC) Regs and reg 7A and Sch A1 of both the CTB and the CTB(SPC) Regs as inserted by Sch 4 HB&CTB(CP) Regs (see p1225). There were specific powers to provide for one authority to determine all the entitlement over the period during which a person's status was being determined. The power to deduct the value of any asylum support provided was not exercised in relation to HB or CTB (compare reg 3(5) Social Security (Immigration and Asylum) Consequential Provisions Regulations 2000 which provided for the value of support to be deducted from backdated IS).

Children (Leaving Care) Act 2000
(2000 c35)

General Note to the Act

The Children (Leaving Care) Act 2000 makes provision for assistance by local authority social services departments to children formerly "looked after" by a local authority. The Act makes detailed provision for a package of assistance for children in such a position, of a financial and practical nature. Such children are generally excluded from entitlement to IS, income-based JSA and HB to prevent duplication of provision. However, children will always be entitled either to assistance or to benefits and advisers should be prepared to press authorities to act where there is a dispute between benefits and social services departments as to whether a child has a right to assistance. Note that, to date, such children have not been excluded from entitlement to ESA.

The bulk of this Act only applies to England and Wales, but by s8(6), s6 also applies to Scotland.

Exclusion from benefits

6.–(1) No person is entitled to income-based jobseeker's allowance under the Jobseekers Act 1995, or to income support or housing benefit under the Social Security Contributions and Benefits Act 1992, while he is a person to whom this section applies.

(2) Subject to subsection (3), this section applies to–

(a) an eligible child for the purposes of paragraph 19B of Schedule 2 to the Children Act 1989;

(b) a relevant child for the purposes of section 23A of that Act; and

(c) any person of a description prescribed in regulations under subsection (4).

(3) The Secretary of State may by regulations provide that this section does not apply to a person who falls within subsection (2)(a) or (b) but who also falls within such category or description, or satisfies such conditions, as may be prescribed in the regulations.

(4) The Secretary of State may make regulations prescribing descriptions of person who do not fall within subsection (2)(a) or (b) but who–

(a) have been looked after by a local authority in Scotland (within the meaning of section 17(6) of the Children (Scotland) Act 1995); and

(b) otherwise correspond (whether or not exactly) to eligible or relevant children.

(5) The Secretary of State may in regulations make such transitional, consequential and saving provision as he considers necessary or expedient in connection with the coming into force of this section.

(6) Section 175(3) to (5) of the Social Security Contributions and Benefits Act 1992 (supplemental power in relation to regulations) applies to regulations made under this section as it applies to regulations made under that Act.

(7) Powers to make regulations under this section include power to make different provision for different areas.

(8) Powers to make regulations under this section are exercisable by statutory instrument.

(9) No statutory instrument containing regulations under subsection (4) is to be made unless a draft of the instrument has been laid before Parliament and approved by a resolution of each House of Parliament.

(10) A statutory instrument containing regulations under subsection (3) or (5) shall be subject to annulment in pursuance of a resolution of either House of Parliament.

Commencement

10.9.01 for making regulations and 1.10.01 for other purposes: Art 2 of SI 2001 No.3070.

General Note

This section excludes children who receive assistance under the 2000 Act from entitlement to IS, income-based JSA and HB. Subs (2) to (4) refer to regulation-making powers. The relevant regulations are the Children (Leaving Care) Social Security Benefits Regulations 2001 SI No.3074, made under subs (3) and the Children (Leaving Care) Social Security Benefits (Scotland) Regulations 2004 No.747, made under subs (4).

The Children (Leaving Care) (Wales) Regulations 2001 SI No.2189 (amended by the Children (Leaving Care) (Wales) Amendment Regulations 2002 SI No.1855) and the Children (Leaving Care) (England) Regulations 2001

SI No.2874 deal with the definitions of "eligible child" and "relevant child". These are not identical and are referred to below as the "Wales Regulations" and "England Regulations".

Analysis

Subs (1) has the effect of excluding children to whom the arrangements apply from entitlement to HB, unless such a child is brought back into entitlement by regulations made under subss (3) or (4). The Children (Leaving Care) Social Security Benefits Regulations 2001 SI No.3074, made under subs (3), do not apply to HB. The Children (Leaving Care) Social Security Benefits (Scotland) Regulations 2004 No.747 bring certain children back into entitlement to IS and income-based JSA, but not to HB. So at present any child falling within subs (2) is excluded from HB.

Subs (2) and (4) set out the categories of children to whom the exclusion applies.

(1)   An "eligible child". Sch 2 para 19B Children Act 1989, inserted by s1 of the 2000 Act, defines such a child as being aged 16/17 who has been looked after by a local authority. S/he must have been looked after for at least 13 weeks and have been looked after some point since the age of 14: reg 3(1) of both the Wales and the England Regulations. Both sets of regulations then exclude specified categories of child. Reg 3(2)(a) of the Wales Regulations and reg 3(3) of the England Regulations excludes a child who has had a series of short-term placements of less than four weeks' duration before returning to her/his parent or guardian. The local authority social services department is required to prepare for the child to become independent by preparing a "pathway plan".

(2)   A "relevant child", which is defined by s23A(2) of the 1989 Act, as inserted by s2(4) of the 2000 Act, is a child aged 16/17 who is not presently being looked after by a local authority but who was an "eligible child" when last looked after. By s23A(3)(a), there is power to prescribe additional categories of "relevant child", and by s23A(3)(b), there is a power to exclude people from the definition. Reg 4(2) of the Wales Regulations includes a child who was in detention or in hospital at the age of 16 and who has been accommodated by the local authority for at least 13 weeks between the ages of 14 and 16. Reg 4(2) of the England Regulations has the same effect provided that there is no care order in force in respect of the child. Reg 4(4) of the Wales Regulations excludes a child who has had a family placement of at least six months' duration, except where the placement breaks down and it is more than six months since the placement began: reg 4(6). Reg 4(5) of the England Regulations also makes the same exclusion, save where the family placement "breaks down": see reg 4(7).

(3)   Those prescribed under subs (4). See the note to subs (1).

Social Security Fraud Act 2001
(2001 c11)

General Note to the Act

This was the second Act of Parliament in four years, following the Social Security Administration (Fraud) Act 1997, to be explicitly dedicated in its short title to the prevention of social security fraud. It amended the provisions for obtaining information in Pt VI of the SSAA. In addition controversial provisions were put into place for reducing the entitlement of recidivist benefit fraud offenders. There is an expansion of the powers to offer the payment of a penalty rather than prosecution.

The next group of sections, ss6A, 6B and 7 to 13, provide "loss of benefit" provisions. See p1185 for the Social Security (Loss of Benefit) Regulations 2001, made under those sections.

Obtaining and sharing information

Code of practice about use of information powers

3.–(1)   The Secretary of State shall issue a code of practice relating to the exercise of–

(a)   the powers that are exercisable by an authorised officer under section 109B of the Administration Act in relation to the persons mentioned in subsection (2A) of that section; and

(b)   the powers conferred on an authorised officer by sections 109BA and 110AA of that Act.

(2)   The Secretary of State may from time to time–

(a)   revise the whole or any part of the code for the time being in force under this section; and

(b)   issue a revised code.

(3)   Before issuing or revising the code of practice under this section, the Secretary of State shall–

(a)   prepare and publish a draft of the code, or of the revised code; and

(b)   consider any representations made to him about the draft;

and the Secretary of State may incorporate in the code he issues any modifications made by him to his proposals after their publication.

(4)   The Secretary of State shall lay before each House of Parliament the code of practice, and every revised code, issued by him under this section.

(5)   The code of practice issued under this section and any revisions of the code shall come into force at the time at which the code or, as the case may be, the revised code is issued by the Secretary of State.

(6)   An authorised officer exercising any power in relation to which provision must be made by the code of practice under this section shall have regard, in doing so, to the provisions (so far as they are applicable) of the code for the time being in force under this section.

(7)   A failure on the part of any person to comply with any provision of the code of practice for the time being in force under this section shall not of itself render him liable to any civil or criminal proceedings.

(8)   The code of practice for the time being in force under this section shall be admissible in evidence in any civil or criminal proceedings.

(9)   In this section ''authorised officer'' has the same meaning as in Part 6 of the Administration Act.

Commencement

28.1.02: SI 2002 No.117.

General Note

This welcome provision, added during passage of the Act through Parliament as a result of concerns about the absence of any comprehensive guidance for investigators, requires a Code of Practice to be issued. The critical provision is subs (6), which only requires an officer to "have regard" to the provisions. It is therefore clear that a breach of the Code will not require evidence to be excluded in a criminal prosecution, although such a breach would no doubt be a ground on which to base a submission to exclude such evidence under s78 Police and

Criminal Evidence Act 1984. Under subs (7), a failure to comply with the Code cannot give rise to civil or criminal proceedings and so could not give rise, for example, to a claim for misfeasance in a public office unless the elements of that tort were present in the absence of a breach of the Code.

The first version of the Code was included in Circular HB/CTB F2/2002.

Arrangements for payments in respect of information

4.–(1) It shall be the duty of the Secretary of State to ensure that such arrangements (if any) are in force as he thinks appropriate for requiring or authorising, in such cases as he thinks fit, the making of such payments as he considers appropriate in respect of compliance with relevant obligations by any of the following–

(a) a credit reference agency (within the meaning given by section 145(8) of the Consumer Credit Act 1974 (c. 39)) or any servant or agent of such an agency;

(b) a person providing a telecommunications service (within the meaning of the Regulation of Investigatory Powers Act 2000 (c. 23)) or any servant or agent of such a person;

(c) a water undertaker or [¹ Scottish Water] or any servant or agent of such an undertaker or [¹ that body],

(d) any person who (within the meaning the Gas Act 1986 (c. 44)) supplies gas conveyed through pipes, or any servant or agent of such a person;

(e) any person who (within the meaning of the Electricity Act 1989 (c. 29)) supplies electricity conveyed by distribution systems, or any servant or agent of such a person;

(f) any person added to the list of persons falling within subsection (2A) of section 109B of the Administration Act by an order under subsection (6) of that section, or any person's servant or agent who falls within that subsection by virtue of such an order.

(2) In subsection (1) ''relevant obligation''–

(a) in relation to a person falling within paragraph (a), (b) or (f) of that subsection, means–

(i) an obligation to provide information in pursuance of a requirement imposed on that person under section 109B of the Administration Act by virtue only of his falling within subsection (2A) of that section; or

(ii) any obligation to comply, for the purpose of enabling an authorised officer to obtain information which might otherwise be obtained by the imposition of such a requirement, with any requirements imposed on that person under section 109BA or 110AA of that Act; and

(b) in relation to a person falling within any of paragraphs (c) to (e) of that subsection, means any obligation to provide information in pursuance of a requirement imposed by such an exercise of the powers conferred by section 109B of that Act as is mentioned in subsection (2D) of that section.

(3) For the purpose of complying with his duty under this section, the Secretary of State may make arrangements for payments to be made out of money provided by Parliament.

(4) It shall be the duty of an authority administering housing benefit or council tax benefit to comply with such general or specific directions as to the making of payments as may be given by the Secretary of State in accordance with any arrangements for the time being in force for the purposes of subsection (1).

Commencement
  1.4.02: SI 2002 No.1222.

Amendment
  1. Amended by Art 2 and Sch para 19 of SI 2004 No. 1822 as from 14.7.04.

General Note
  Section 4 gives powers to pay for information. Not every body will be paid; only those bodies specified in subs (1) and then only to the extent that they have complied with "relevant obligations" as defined in subs (2).
  The Secretary of State may issue directions under subs (4) to local authorities to make payments.

Loss of benefit provisions

Meaning of "disqualifying benefit" and "sanctionable benefit" for purposes of sections 6B and 7

6A.–(1)   In this section and sections 6B and 7–

"disqualifying benefit" means (subject to any regulations under section 10(1))–

- (a)   any benefit under the Jobseekers Act 1995 or the Jobseekers (Northern Ireland) Order 1995;
- (b)   any benefit under the State Pension Credit Act 2002 or the State Pension Credit Act (Northern Ireland) 2002;
- (c)   any benefit under Part 1 of the Welfare Reform Act 2007 or Part 1 of the Welfare Reform Act (Northern Ireland) 2007 (employment and support allowance);
- (d)   any benefit under the Social Security Contributions and Benefit Act 1992 or the Social Security Contributions and Benefits (Northern Ireland) Act 1992 other than–
    - (i)   maternity allowance;
    - (ii)   statutory sick pay and statutory maternity pay;
- (e)   any war pension;

"sanctionable benefit" means (subject to subsection (2) and to any regulations under section 10(1)) any disqualifying benefit other than–

- (a)   joint-claim jobseeker's allowance;
- (b)   any retirement pension;
- (c)   graduated retirement benefit;
- (d)   disability living allowance;
- (e)   attendance allowance;
- (f)   child benefit;
- (g)   guardian's allowance;
- (h)   a payment out of the social fund in accordance with Part 8 of the Social Security Contributions and Benefits Act 1992;
- (i)   a payment under Part 10 of that Act (Christmas bonuses).

(2)   In their application to Northern Ireland sections 6B and 7 shall have effect as if references to a sanctionable benefit were references only to a war pension.

Commencement

Inserted by WRA 2009 s24 as from 12.1.10 for making regulations; 1.4.10 for all other purposes.

General Note

This section provides the definitions of "disqualifying benefit" and "sanctionable benefit" for the purposes of the schemes for loss of benefit following commission of offences under ss6B and 7 respectively, often referred to as the "one strike" and the "two strikes" schemes. "Disqualifying benefit" and "sanctionable benefit" both include HB and CTB within the definition, subject to subs (2).

Loss of benefit in case of conviction, penalty or caution for benefit offence

6B.–(1)   Subsection (4) applies where a person ("the offender")–

- (a)   is convicted of one or more benefit offences in any proceedings,
- (b)   after being given a notice under subsection (2) of the appropriate penalty provision by an appropriate authority, agrees in the manner specified by the appropriate authority to pay a penalty under the appropriate penalty provision to the appropriate authority by reference to an overpayment, in a case where the offence mentioned in subsection (1)(b) of the appropriate penalty provision is a benefit offence, or
- (c)   is cautioned in respect of one or more benefit offences.

(2)   In subsection (1)(b)–

- (a)   "the appropriate penalty provision" means section 115A of the Administration Act (penalty as alternative to prosecution) or section 109A of the Social Security Administration (Northern Ireland) 1992 (the corresponding provision for Northern Ireland);
- (b)   "appropriate authority" means–

(i)   in relation to section 115A of the Administration Act, the Secretary of State or an authority which administers housing benefit or council tax benefit, and

(ii)   in relation to section 109A of the Social Security Administration (Northern Ireland) Act 1992, the Department (within the meaning of that Act) or the Northern Ireland Housing Executive.

(3)   Subsection (4) does not apply by virtue of subsection (1)(a) if, because the proceedings in which the offender was convicted constitute the later set of proceedings for the purposes of section 7, the restriction in subsection (2) of that section applies in the offender's case.

(4)   If this subsection applies and the offender is a person with respect to whom the conditions for an entitlement to a sanctionable benefit are or become satisfied at any time within the disqualification period, then, even though those conditions are satisfied, the following restrictions shall apply in relation to the payment of that benefit in the offender's case.

(5)   Subject to subsections (6) to (10), the sanctionable benefit shall not be payable in the offender's case for any period comprised in the disqualification period.

(6)-(9)   *[Omitted]*

(10)   The Secretary of State may by regulations provide that, where the sanctionable benefit is housing benefit or council tax benefit, the benefit shall be payable, during the whole or a part of any period comprised in the disqualification period, as if one or more of the following applied–

(a)   the rate of the benefit were reduced in such manner as may be prescribed;

(b)   the benefit were payable only if the circumstances are such as may be prescribed.

(11)   For the purposes of this section the disqualification period, in relation to any disqualifying event, means the period of four weeks beginning with such date, falling after the date of the disqualifying event, as may be determined by or in accordance with regulations made by the Secretary of State.

(12)   This section has effect subject to section 6C.

(13)   In this section and section 6C–

"benefit offence" means–

(a)   any post-commencement offence in connection with a claim for a disqualifying benefit;

(b)   any post-commencement offence in connection with the receipt or payment of any amount by way of such a benefit;

(c)   any post-commencement offence committed for the purpose of facilitating the commission (whether or not by the same person) of a benefit offence;

(d)   any post-commencement offence consisting in an attempt or conspiracy to commit a benefit offence;

"disqualifying event" means the conviction falling within subsection (1)(a), the agreement falling within subsection (1)(b) or the caution falling within subsection (1)(c);

"post-commencement offence" means any criminal offence committed after the commencement of this section.

Commencement

Inserted by WRA 2009 s24 as from 12.1.10 for the power to make regulations; 1.4.10 for all other purposes.

General Note

This section sets up the "one strike" scheme for loss of benefit following commission of one or more benefit offences. A conviction for the offence is not always required. Note that where a person is convicted of two or more benefit offences within five years, a longer sanction can be imposed under s7, instead of a sanction under s6B.

The regulations made under this section are the Social Security (Loss of Benefit) Regulations 2001 (see p1185).

In essence, the scheme operates by providing for loss of benefit for an offender (under s6B) or a member of her/his family (under s9). HB and CTB are both "disqualifying benefits" (those which can trigger a sanction if an offence is committed) and "sanctionable benefits" (those which may be affected by an offence). HB and CTB can be partly reduced, though only in circumstances where a claimant is not in receipt of IS, income-based JSA, income-related ESA or PC in which case the sanction applies to those benefits alone: reg 18 Social Security (Loss of Benefit) Regulations 2001 (see p1185). Section 6C deals with matters supplementary to s6B, including what is to happen if a conviction is quashed or a person withdraws agreement to pay a penalty.

As the decision to impose the sanction is one made the Secretary of State (not the local authority), an appeal lies to the First-tier Tribunal against a decision made under s6B by virtue of Sch 3 para 3(f) SSA 1998.

Analysis
Subsections (1) to (4) and (12): The conditions for operation of the scheme
A sanction may be applied in three situations:

(1)   The claimant has been convicted of one or more "benefit offences": subs (1)(a). However, a sanction cannot be applied on this ground if the proceedings in which the claimant was convicted are a later set of proceedings for the purposes of s7 and hence the longer sanction under s7(2) applies: subs (3). s6C(5)(a) deals with the date of the conviction and s6C(b) with what references to a conviction includes.

(2)   The claimant has agreed to pay a penalty instead of being prosecuted for an offence ("the appropriate penalty provision"): subs(1)(b). The offence must be one mentioned in s115A(1)(b) SSAA 1992 or the equivalent NI provision which means that there must be grounds for instituting proceedings for an offence relating to an overpayment.

(3)   The claimant has been cautioned in respect of one or more "benefit offences": subs (1)(c). Note that "cautioned" is defined in s13 and means cautioned after the person concerned has admitted the offence. "Benefit offence" is widely defined in subs (13) to cover offences relating to claims and receipt of benefit, as well as aiding and abetting or attempting or conspiring to commit such an offence. Critically, it does not include any offence committed on or before the commencement date – ie, 1 April 2010: see the definition of "post-commencement offence", also in subs (13).

In all three cases, the offender must be a person who is, or is to become, entitled to a "sanctionable benefit" at any time within the "disqualification period", defined in subs (11): subs (4). "Sanctionable benefit" is defined in s6A and includes HB and CTB.

Section 6B has effect subject to s6C: subs (12). See s6C(1) where a a sanction is based on a conviction for an offence and the conviction is quashed and s6C(2) and (3) where the sanction is based on an agreement to pay a penalty and the agreement is withdrawn or it is decided on appeal that the overpayment to which the agreement related is not recoverable or due.

Subsections (5) and (10): Imposition of the sanction
The general rule under subs (5) is that the "sanctionable benefit" shall not be payable in respect of any period during the "disqualification period", defined in subs (11). However, in the case of HB and CTB, subs (10) and reg 17 Social Security (Loss of Benefit) Regulations 2001 provide for a reduction of benefit instead (see p1188). However, no reduction is to be made to HB and CTB where reg 18 of those regulations applies – ie, where a claimant is in receipt of IS, income-based JSA, income-related ESA or PC, the sanction applies to those benefits alone.

Subsection (11): The disqualification period
The period is four weeks from the date specified in reg 2 Social Security (Loss of Benefit) Regulations 2001: subs (11).

Section 6B: supplementary provisions
6C.–(1)   Where–

(a)   the conviction of any person of any offence is taken into account for the purposes of the application of section 6B in relation to that person, and

(b)   that conviction is subsequently quashed,

all such payments and other adjustments shall be made as would be necessary if no restriction had been imposed by or under section 6B that could not have been imposed if the conviction had not taken place.

(2)   Where, after the agreement of any person (''P'') to pay a penalty under the appropriate penalty provision is taken into account for the purposes of the application of section 6B in relation to that person–

(a)   P's agreement to pay the penalty is withdrawn under subsection (5) of the appropriate penalty provision, or

(b)   it is decided on an appeal or in accordance with regulations under the Social Security Act 1998 or the Social Security (Northern Ireland) Order 1998 that the overpayment to which the agreement relates is not recoverable or due,

all such payments and other adjustments shall be made as would be necessary if no restriction had been imposed by or under section 6B that could not have been imposed if P had not agreed to pay the penalty.

(3)   Where, after the agreement (''the old agreement'') of any person (''P'') to pay
a penalty under the appropriate penalty provision is taken into account for the purposes
of the application of section 6B in relation to P, the amount of the overpayment to which
the penalty relates is revised on an appeal or in accordance with regulations under the
Social Security Act 1998 or the Social Security (Northern Ireland) Order 1998–
(a)   section 6B shall cease to apply by virtue of the old agreement, and
(b)   subsection (4) shall apply.
(4)   Where this subsection applies–
(a)   if there is a new disqualifying event consisting of–
    (i)   P's agreement to pay a penalty under the appropriate penalty provision in
    relation to the revised overpayment, or
    (ii)   P being cautioned in relation to the offence to which the old agreement
    relates,
the disqualification period relating to the new disqualifying event shall be
reduced by the number of days in so much of the disqualification period relating
to the old agreement as had expired when section 6B ceased to apply by virtue
of the old agreement, and
(b)   in any other case, all such payments and other adjustments shall be made as
would be necessary if no restriction had been imposed by or under section 6B
that could not have been imposed if P had not agreed to pay the penalty.
(5)   For the purposes of section 6B–
(a)   the date of a person's conviction in any proceedings of a benefit offence shall be
taken to be the date on which the person was found guilty of that offence in
those proceedings (whenever the person was sentenced) or in the case mentioned
in paragraph (b)(ii) the date of the order for absolute discharge; and
(b)   references to a conviction include references to–
    (i)   a conviction in relation to which the court makes an order for absolute or
    conditional discharge or a court in Scotland makes a probation order,
    (ii)   an order for absolute discharge made by a court of summary jurisdiction
    in Scotland under section 246(3) of the Criminal Procedure (Scotland) Act
    1995 without proceeding to a conviction, and
    (iii)   a conviction in Northern Ireland.
(6)   In this section ''the appropriate penalty provision'' has the meaning given by
section 6B(2)(a).

Commencement
Inserted by WRA 2009 s24 as from 12.1.10 for the power to make regulations; 1.4.10 for all other purposes.

General Note
Section 6B is subject to this section which contains supplementary provisions.

Analysis
Subs (1) provides that where a conviction taken into account for the purposes of a sanction under s6B is
quashed, and the sanction could not have been applied unless that conviction stood, payment of the sanctionable
benefit should be made as normal. The words "could not have been imposed" are, however, of importance. If a
claimant is convicted of two offences and only one is quashed, then if the remaining conviction falls to be taken
into account under s6B(1)(a) the sanction will remain in place.
Subs (2) sets out when, after an agreement to pay a penalty has been taken into account for the purposes of
a sanction under s6B, payment of the sanctionable benefit should be made as normal. There are two possible
situations.
(1)   The agreement to pay a penalty is withdrawn: subs (2)(a).
(2)   It is decided on appeal or in accordance with regulations made under specified provisions (eg, on
    revision) that the overpayment to which the agreement relates is not recoverable or due: subs (2)(b).
In both cases, this only applies if the sanction could not have been applied had the claimant not agreed to pay
the penalty. As with subs (1) above, the words "could not have been imposed" are of importance.
Subs (3) and (4) deal with the situation when the amount of an overpayment to which a penalty relates is
revised on appeal or in accordance with regulations made under specified provisions and this happens after the
agreement to pay a penalty is taken into account for the purposes of a sanction under s6B. In this case, the
sanction under s6B ceases to apply in relation to the old agreement and payment of the sanctionable benefit

should be made as normal: subs (4)(b). However, if there is a new agreement to pay a penalty in relation to the revised overpayment, or the claimant is cautioned in relation to the offence to which the old agreement applied (a "new disqualifying event", defined in s6B(13)), a new sanction may be applied. In this case, the days in the disqualification period relating to the old agreement are offset against the days in the new disqualification period: subs (4)(a).

Subs (5)(a) confirms that the date of conviction is the date on which a claimant was "found guilty" rather than the date of sentence. "Found guilty" will include cases where the defendant pleads guilty as well as those where s/he is convicted on a plea of not guilty. If a guilty plea is subsequently changed to a plea of not guilty, it is suggested that the relevant date will be the date on which either a subsequent plea of guilty is entered or on which the claimant is convicted.

Subs (5)(b) confirms that "conviction" includes convictions in Northern Ireland or convictions in respect of which probation is imposed in Scotland or a *conditional* discharge in England. South of the border, s14(1) Powers of Criminal Courts (Sentencing) Act 2000 provides that absolute and conditional discharges are not to be treated as convictions, and s14(3) prevents either type of discharge biting in relation to legislation which imposes a "disqualification or disability" on convicted persons. Quite clearly, this Act falls within that description. There is no specific exception to s14(3) for other legislation which specifically imposes a disqualification on those subjected to a conditional discharge, so there is a conflict between s14(3) of the 2000 Act and s6C(5)(b) of this Act. It is likely that the courts will apply the rule of statutory construction that the general provision is overridden by the specific provision and that s6C(5)(b) of this Act prevails over s14(3) of the 2000 Act, particularly since this Act was passed on a later date.

Loss of benefit for [⁵ second or subsequent conviction of benefit offence]

7.–(1) If–

(a) a person (''the offender'') is convicted of one or more benefit offences in each of two separate sets of proceedings,

(b) the benefit offence, or one of the benefit offences, of which he is convicted in the later proceedings is one committed within the period of [³ five years] after the date, or any of the dates, on which he was convicted of a benefit offence in the earlier proceedings,

(c) the later set of proceedings has not been taken into account for the purposes of any previous application of this section or section 8 or 9 in relation to the offender or any person who was then a member of his family,

(d) the earlier set of proceedings has not been taken into account as the earlier set of proceedings for the purposes of any previous application of this section or either of those sections in relation to the offender or any person who was then a member of his family, and

(e) the offender is a person with respect to whom the conditions for an entitlement to a sanctionable benefit are or become satisfied at any time within the disqualification period,

then, even though those conditions are satisfied, the following restrictions shall apply in relation to the payment of that benefit in the offender's case.

(2) Subject to subsections (3) to (5), the sanctionable benefit shall not be payable in the offender's case for any period comprised in the disqualification period.

(3)-(4) *[Omitted]*

[² (4A)] *[Omitted]*

[⁴ (4B)] *[Omitted]*

(5) The Secretary of State may by regulations provide that, where the sanctionable benefit is housing benefit or council tax benefit, the benefit shall be payable, during the whole or a part of any period comprised in the disqualification period, as if one or both of the following applied–

(a) the rate of the benefit were reduced in such manner as may be prescribed;

(b) the benefit were payable only if the circumstances are such as may be prescribed.

(6) For the purposes of this section the disqualification period, in relation to the conviction of a person of one or more benefit offences in each of two separate sets of proceedings, means the period of thirteen weeks beginning with such date, falling after the date of the conviction in the later set of proceedings, as may be determined by or in accordance with regulations made by the Secretary of State.

(7)   Where–
(a)   the conviction of any person of any offence is taken into account for the purposes of the application of this section in relation to that person, and
(b)   that conviction is subsequently quashed,
all such payments and other adjustments shall be made as would be necessary if no restriction had been imposed by or under this section that could not have been imposed if the conviction had not taken place.
(8)   In this section–
''benefit offence'' means–
(a)   any post-commencement offence in connection with a claim for a disqualifying benefit;
(b)   any post-commencement offence in connection with the receipt or payment of any amount by way of such a benefit;
(c)   any post-commencement offence committed for the purpose of facilitating the commission (whether or not by the same person) of a benefit offence;
(d)   any post-commencement offence consisting in an attempt or conspiracy to commit a benefit offence;
[⁵ ''post-commencement offence'' means an offence committed on or after 1 April 2002 (the day on which this section came into force)."]
[⁵]
[⁵]
(9)   For the purposes of this section–
(a)   the date of a person's conviction in any proceedings of a benefit offence shall be taken to be the date on which he was found guilty of that offence in those proceedings (whenever he was sentenced [⁵ or in the case mentioned in paragraph (b)(ii) the date of the order for absolute discharge]); and
[⁵ (b) references to a conviction include references to–
(i)   a conviction in relation to which the court makes an order for absolute or conditional discharge or a court in Scotland makes a probation order,
(ii)   an order for absolute discharge made by a court of summary jurisdiction in Scotland under section 246(3) of the Criminal Procedure (Scotland) Act 1995 without proceeding to a conviction, and
(iii)   a conviction in Northern Ireland.]
(10)   In this section references to any previous application of this section or section 8 or 9–
(a)   include references to any previous application of a provision having an effect in Northern Ireland corresponding to provision made by this section, or either of those sections; but
(b)   do not include references to any previous application of this section, or of either of those sections, the effect of which was to impose a restriction for a period comprised in the same disqualification period.
[⁵ (11)]

Commencement
17.11.01 for making regulations and 1.4.02 generally: SI 2001 No.3689.

Amendments
1.   Repealed by TCA Sch 6 (8.4.03).
2.   Amended by SPCA Sch 2 para 45 (2.7.02 (for making regulations) and 6.10.03).
3.   Amended by WRA 2007 s49(1) (1.4.08).
4.   Amended by WRA 2007 s28 and Sch 3 para 23 (18.3.08 (for making regulations) and 27.10.08).
5.   Amended by WRA 2009 s24 and Sch 4 para 2 (12.1.10 for making regulations; 1.4.10 for all other purposes).

General Note
This section sets up the "two strikes" scheme for loss of benefit following commission of one or more benefit offences in two separate sets of proceedings. Note also the "one strike" scheme under ss6B and 6C.
    The regulations made under this section are the Social Security (Loss of Benefit) Regulations 2001 (see p1185).

In essence, the scheme operates by providing for loss of benefit for a repeat offender (under s7) or a member of her/his family (under s9). HB and CTB are both "disqualifying benefits" (those which can trigger a sanction if an offence is committed) and "sanctionable benefits" (those which may be affected by a repeat offence). HB and CTB can be partly reduced, though only in circumstances where a claimant is not in receipt of IS, income-based JSA, income-related ESA or PC in which case the sanction applies to those benefits alone: reg 18 Social Security (Loss of Benefit) Regulations 2001.

As the decision to impose the sanction is one made by the Secretary of State (not the local authority), an appeal lies to the First-tier Tribunal against a decision made under s7 by virtue of Sch 3 para 3(f) SSA 1998.

Analysis

Subsection (1): The conditions for operation of the scheme

There are three conditions under s7(1) for the scheme to bite upon a particular claimant who has been guilty of repeated benefit fraud offences:

(1)   The claimant has been convicted of offences in "each of two separate sets of proceedings": para (a). Note the definition of conviction in subs (9). There are provisions in paras (c) and (d) and in subs (10)(b) to prevent a particular set of proceedings being taken into account more than once. Para (c) provides that the later conviction can only affect benefit entitlement of the claimant or a member of his family under s9 on one occasion. Para (d) prevents the earlier conviction triggering a loss of benefit in relation to a third conviction. Subs (10)(b) prevents double counting if, for example, both s7 and s9 can apply because both a claimant and a member of her/his family are convicted twice. However, it is clear that a fourth conviction would then trigger a second loss of benefit. By subs (10)(a), the previous offence may have been committed in Northern Ireland. One uncertainty relates to the meaning of "separate". Does it apply to a case where an indictment is severed or separate trials take place of different charges on a summons? It is suggested that the two trials remain part of the same set of proceedings and a further conviction on a separate indictment or summons would be required in order to allow a loss of benefit.

(2)   The offence giving rise to the later conviction was committed within five years of the earlier conviction: para (b). The time period was three years before 1 April 2008. See s49 Welfare Reform Act 2007 for transitional provisions. See subs (9)(a) for the date of a conviction. There may be some difficulties in determining when an offence was committed where it involves an omission to notify a change of circumstances. It is suggested that the wording of the charge will be critical. Thus if the claimant is charged in the later proceedings with a failure to notify, the date on which it is said in the charge that notification should have occurred will be the relevant date for the purposes of para (b). If no date is specified in the charge, then it will have to be determined at what point the offence was committed.

(3)   The claimant must be, or must become, entitled to a "sanctionable benefit" during the "disqualification period" which is defined in subs (6): para (e). "Sanctionable benefit" is defined in s6A and includes HB and CTB.

Subsections (2), (5) and (7): Imposition of the sanction

The general rule under subs (2) is that the "sanctionable benefit" shall not be payable in respect of any period during the "disqualification period". However, in the case of HB and CTB, subs (5) and reg 17 Social Security (Loss of Benefit) Regulations 2001 provide for a reduction of benefit instead. However, no reduction is to be made to HB and CTB where reg 18 of those regulations applies – ie, where a claimant is in receipt of IS, income-based JSA, income-related ESA or PC, the sanction applies to those benefits alone.

Subs (7) provides that where a conviction is quashed and the sanction could not have been applied unless that conviction stood, payment of the sanctionable benefit should be made as normal. The words "could not have been imposed" are, however, of importance. If a claimant is convicted of two offences on the latter occasion and only one is quashed, then if the remaining conviction falls to be taken into account under subs (1) the sanction will remain in place.

Subsection (6): The disqualification period

The period is 13 weeks from the date specified in reg 2 Social Security (Loss of Benefit) Regulations 2001.

Subsections (8) and (9): Definitions

The definition of **"benefit offence"** is the same as in s6B (see the discussion on p1138) save that here, the commencement date is 1 April 2002: see the definition of "post-commencement offence" also in subs (8).

Subs (9) is identical to s6C(5), for which see the discussion on p1140.

Effect of offence on benefits for members of offender's family

9.–(1)   This section applies to–

(a)   income support;

(b)   jobseeker's allowance;

[¹ (bb) state pension credit;]

[² (bc)   employment and support allowance;]

(c)   housing benefit; and

(d)   council tax benefit.

(2)   The Secretary of State may by regulations make provision in accordance with the following provisions of this section in relation to any case in which–

    (a)   the conditions for entitlement to any benefit to which this section applies are or become satisfied in the case of any person (''the offender's family member'');

    (b)   that benefit falls to be paid in that person's case for the whole or any part of a period comprised in a period (''the relevant period'') which is the disqualification period in relation to restrictions imposed under [³ section 6B or 7] in the case of a member of that person's family; or

    (c)   that member of that family (''the offender'') is a person by reference to whom–

        (i)   the conditions for the entitlement of the offender's family member to the benefit in question are satisfied; or

        (ii)   the amount of benefit payable in the case of the offender's family member would fall (apart from any provision made under this section) to be determined.

(3)-(4B)   *[Omitted]*

(5)   In relation to cases in which the benefit is housing benefit or council tax benefit, the provision that may be made by virtue of subsection (2) is provision that, in the case of the offender's family member, the benefit shall be payable, during the whole or a part of any period comprised in the relevant period, as if one or both of the following applied–

    (a)   the rate of the benefit were reduced in such manner as may be prescribed;

    (b)   the benefit were payable only if the circumstances are such as may be prescribed.

(6)   Where–

    (a)   the conviction of any member of a person's family for any offence is taken into account for the purposes of any restriction imposed by virtue of any regulations under this section, and

    (b)   that conviction is subsequently quashed,

all such payments and other adjustments shall be made in that person's case as would be necessary if no restriction had been imposed that could not have been imposed had the conviction not taken place.

[³ (7)   Where, after the agreement of any member of a person's family (''M'') to pay a penalty under the appropriate penalty provision is taken into account for the purposes of any restriction imposed by virtue of any regulations under this section–

    (a)   M's agreement to pay the penalty is withdrawn under subsection (5) of the appropriate penalty provision, or

    (b)   it is decided on an appeal or in accordance with regulations under the Social Security Act 1998 or the Social Security (Northern Ireland) Order 1998 that the overpayment to which the agreement relates is not recoverable or due,

all such payments and other adjustments shall be made as would be necessary if no restriction had been imposed that could not have been imposed had M not agreed to pay the penalty.

(8)   Where, after the agreement (''the old agreement'') of any member of a person's family (''M'') to pay a penalty under the appropriate penalty provision is taken into account for the purposes of any restriction imposed by virtue of any regulations under this section, the amount of the overpayment to which the penalty relates is revised on an appeal or in accordance with regulations under the Social Security Act 1998 or the Social Security (Northern Ireland) Order 1998–

    (a)   if there is a new disqualifying event for the purposes of section 6B consisting of M's agreement to pay a penalty under the appropriate penalty provision in relation to the revised overpayment or M being cautioned in relation to the offence to which the old agreement relates, the new disqualification period for the purposes of section 6B falls to be determined in accordance with section 6C(4)(a), and

    (b)   in any other case, all such payments and other adjustments shall be made as would be necessary if no restriction had been imposed by or under this section that could not have been imposed had M not agreed to pay the penalty.

(9)   In this section ''the appropriate penalty provision'' has the meaning given by section 6B(2)(a).]

Commencement

17.11.01 for making regulations and 1.4.02 generally: SI 2001 No.3689.

Amendments

1.   Inserted by SPCA Sch 2 para 46 (2.7.02 (for making regulations) and 6.10.03).
2.   Amended by WRA s28 and Sch 3 para 23 (18.3.08 (for making regulations) and 27.10.08).
3.   Amended by WRA 2009 s24 and Sch 4 para 4 (12.1.10 (for making regulations) and 1.4.10 for all other purposes).

General Note

This section deals with cases where the offender is not the person claiming benefit on behalf of the family. The effect is that equivalent reductions in HB or CTB are still imposed.

The effect of s9 may in some cases be to impose a sanction on a blameless claimant. There is no requirement that the offender should have been part of the claimant's family at the time that the offence was committed. There may well be arguments that the imposition of a sanction in such a case infringes Art 8 of the European Convention on Human Rights (because it shows a lack of respect for the home which cannot be justified) or Art 14 (because there is discrimination in comparison with those who do not have a benefit offender in their households).

As the decision to impose a sanction is taken by the Secretary of State (not the local authority), an appeal lies to the First-tier Tribunal against a decision made under s7 by virtue of Sch 3 para 3(f) SSA 1998.

Analysis

Subsection (2): Cases where section 9 is applicable

The conditions for imposing a sanction under s9 are the following:

(1)   A person is claiming benefit to which s9 applies: subs (a).
(2)   The claimant will be paid that benefit for a period which forms part or the whole of the "disqualification period" under s6B or s7 in respect of a member of the claimant's family: subs (b). "Member of . . . . family" refers to a person falling to be treated as part of the claimant's family under s137(1) SSCBA and Pt 4 HB and HB(SPC) Regs or Pt 2 CTB and CTB(SPC) Regs: see the definition of "family" in s13 on p1145.
(3)   The offender is a person in relation to whom the conditions of entitlement are satisfied (such as where HB is claimed by in respect of a partner's liability for rent) or who falls to be taken into account in calculating benefit: subs (c). Although non-dependents would fall within the latter description, it is suggested that s9 cannot bite in such cases because they are not members of the claimant's family for the purposes of subs (b).

Subsections (5) to (7): Imposition of the sanction

Subs (5) imposes identical sanctions in s9 cases to those imposed by ss6B(10) and 7(5) above. Subs (6) is the equivalent of ss6C(1) and 7(7). Subs (7) to (9) are the equivalent of s6C(3) to (6).

Power to supplement and mitigate loss of benefit provisions

10.–(1)   The Secretary of State may by regulations provide for any social security benefit to be treated for the purposes of [⁴ sections 6A to 9]–

(a)   as a disqualifying benefit but not a sanctionable benefit; or
(b)   as neither a sanctionable benefit nor a disqualifying benefit.

(2)   The Secretary of State may by regulations provide for any restriction in section [⁴ 6B,] 7, 8 or 9 not to apply in relation to payments of benefit to the extent of any deduction that (if any payment were made) would fall, in pursuance of provision made by or under any enactment, to be made from the payments and paid to a person other than the offender or, as the case may be, a member of his family.

(3)   In this section "social security benefit" means–

(a)   any benefit under the Social Security Contributions and Benefits Act 1992 or the Social Security Contributions and Benefits (Northern Ireland) Act 1992; [² . . .]

(b)   any benefit under the Jobseekers Act 1995 or the Jobseekers (Northern Ireland) Order 1995;

[¹ (bb) any benefit under the State Pension Credit Act 2002 or under any provision having effect in Northern Ireland corresponding to that Act;

[² (bc) any benefit under Part 1 of the Welfare Reform Act 2007 (employment and support allowance) or under any provision having effect in Northern Ireland corresponding to that Part;] or]

(c)   any war pension.

Commencement

17.11.01 for making regulations and 1.4.02 generally: SI 2001 No.3689.

Amendments

1. Inserted by SPCA Sch 2 para 47 (2.7.02 (for making regulations) and October 2003).
2. Amended by SPCA Sch 3 (2.7.02 (for making regulations) and October 2003).
3. Amended by WRA s28 and Sch 3 para 23 (18.3.08 (for making regulations) and 27.10.08).
4. Amended by WRA 2009 s24 and Sch 4 para 5 (12.1.10 (for making regulations) and 1.4.10).

General Note

None of the powers conferred by subs (1) or (2) have been exercised in relation to HB or CTB.

Loss of benefit regulations

11.–(1)   In [³ sections 6B to 10] ''prescribed'' means prescribed by or determined in accordance with regulations made by the Secretary of State.

(2)   Regulations under any of the provisions of [³ sections 6B to 10] shall be made by statutory instrument which (except in the case of regulations to which subsection (3) applies) shall be subject to annulment in pursuance of a resolution of either House of Parliament.

(3)   A statutory instrument containing (whether alone or with other provisions)–

(a)   a provision by virtue of which anything is to be treated for the purposes of section [³ 6B or] 7 as a disqualifying benefit but not a sanctionable benefit,

(b)   a provision prescribing the manner in which the applicable amount is to be reduced for the purposes of section [³ 6B(6),] 7(3) or 9(3),

(c)   a provision the making of which is authorised by section [³ 6B(7), (8), (9) or (10),] 7(4) [¹ , (4A)] [² , (4B)] or (5), 8(4) or 9(4) [¹ , (4A)] [² , (4B)] or (5), or

(d)   a provision prescribing the manner in which the amount of joint-claim jobseeker's allowance is to be reduced for the purposes of section 8(3)(a),

shall not be made unless a draft of the instrument has been laid before, and approved by a resolution of, each House of Parliament.

(4)   Subsections (4) to (6) of section 189 of the Administration Act (supplemental and incidental powers etc.) shall apply in relation to a power to make regulations that is conferred by any of the provisions of [³ sections 6B to 10] as they apply in relation to the powers to make regulations that are conferred by that Act.

(5)   The provision that may be made in exercise of the powers to make regulations that are conferred by [³ sections 6B to 10] shall include different provision for different areas.

Commencement

17.11.01 for making regulations and 1.4.02 generally: SI 2001 No.3689.

Amendments

1. Amended by SPCA Sch 2 para 48 (2.7.02 (for making regulations) and 6.10.03).
2. Amended by WRA s28 and Sch 3 para 23 (18.3.08 (for making regulations) and 27.10.08).
3. Amended by WRA 2009 s24 and Sch 4 para 6 (12.1.10 (for making regulations) and 1.4.10).

Interpretation of [³ sections 6A to 12]

13.   In this section and [³ sections 6A to 12]–

''benefit'' includes any allowance, payment, credit or loan;

[³ ''cautioned'', in relation to any person and any offence, means cautioned after the person concerned has admitted the offence; and ''caution'' is to be interpreted accordingly;]

[³]

''family'' has the same meaning as in Part VII of the Social Security Contributions and Benefits Act 1992;

''income-based jobseeker's allowance'', ''joint-claim jobseeker's allowance'' and ''joint-claim couple'' have the same meanings as in the Jobseekers Act 1995;

[² ''income-related allowance'' has the same meaning as in Part 1 of the Welfare Reform Act 2007 (employment and support allowance);]

[³]

"sanctionable benefit" has the meaning given by [³ section 6A(1)];

[¹ "state pension credit" means state pension credit under the State Pension Credit Act 2002;]

"war pension" has the same meaning as in section 25 of the Social Security Act 1989 (establishment and functions of war pensions committees).

Commencement

17.11.01 for making regulations and 1.4.02 generally: SI 2001 No.3689.

Amendments

1.   Amended by SPCA Sch 2 para 49 (2.7.02 (for making regulations) and 6.10.03).
2.   Inserted by WRA s28 and Sch 3 para 24 (18.3.08 (for making regulations) and 27.10.08).
3.   Amended by WRA 2009 s24 and Sch 4 para 7 (12.1.10 (for making regulations) and 1.4.10).

Supplemental

Meaning of "the Administration Act"

18.   In this Act "the Administration Act" means the Social Security Administration Act 1992 (c. 5).

Commencement

20.–(1)   The preceding provisions of this Act shall come into force on such day as the Secretary of State may by order made by statutory instrument appoint.

(2)   Subject to subsection (3), different days may be appointed under this section for different purposes.

(3)   The power under this section to appoint a day for the coming into force of the provisions of sections 1 and 2 shall not authorise the appointment for those purposes of any day before the issue of the code of practice that must be issued under section 3.

Short title and extent

21.–(1)   This Act may be cited as the Social Security Fraud Act 2001.

(2)   Sections 5(2), [¹ 6A, 6B and 6C] 7, 10, 11, 12(3), 13 and 20, and this section, extend to Northern Ireland; and the other provisions of this Act do not so extend.

Amendment

1.   Amended by WRA 2009 s24 and Sch 4 para 8 (12.1.10 (for making regulations) and 1.4.10).

Tax Credits Act 2002

(2002 c21)

General Note to the Act

The Tax Credits Act 2002 replaced working families tax credit, disabled person's tax credit, amounts for children within the IS and JSA schemes, increases to non-means-tested benefits for children and other allowances with two tax credits: working tax credit (WTC) and child tax credit (CTC). Child benefit is paid in addition to CTC. HB and CTB continue to contain personal allowances for children who are members of the claimant's "family".

WTC and CTC are administered by HM Revenue and Customs (referred to as the Revenue in this book). For full details of the rules for WTC and CTC, see CPAG's *Welfare Benefits and Tax Credits Handbook*.

For HB and CTB, the only directly relevant parts of the Act are those concerning the sharing of information between local authorities and the Revenue.

SCHEDULE 5
USE AND DISCLOSURE OF INFORMATION
Exchange of information between Board and authorities administering certain benefits

7.–(1) This paragraph applies to information which is held for the purposes of functions relating to tax credits, child benefit or guardian's allowance–
(a)   by the Board, or
(b)   by a person providing services to the Board, in connection with the provision of those services.
(2)   Information to which this paragraph applies may be supplied by or under the authority of the Board–
(a)   to an authority administering housing benefit or council tax benefit, or
(b)   to a person authorised to exercise any function of such an authority relating to such a benefit,
for use in the administration of such a benefit.
(3)   Information supplied under this paragraph is not to be supplied by the recipient to any other person or body unless it is supplied–
(a)   to a person to whom the information could be supplied directly by or under the authority of the Board,
(b)   for the purposes of any civil or criminal proceedings relating to the Social Security Contributions and Benefits Act 1992 (c. 4), the Social Security Administration Act 1992 (c. 5) or the Jobseekers Act 1995 (c. 18) or to any provision of Northern Ireland legislation corresponding to any of them, or
(c)   under paragraph 8 below.

8.–(1) The Board may require–
(a)   an authority administering housing benefit or council tax benefit, or
(b)   a person authorised to exercise any function of such an authority relating to such a benefit,
to supply benefit administration information held by the authority or other person to, or to a person providing services to, the Board for use for any purpose relating to tax credits, child benefit or guardian's allowance.
(2)   In sub-paragraph (1) "benefit administration information", in relation to an authority or other person, means any information which is relevant to the exercise of any function relating to housing benefit or council tax benefit by the authority or other person.

Civil Partnership Act 2004
(2004 Chapter 33)

General Note

The Civil Partnership Act 2004 (Relationships Arising Through Civil Partnership) Order 2005 SI No.3137 sets out the provisions to which s246 of this Act applies for HB and CTB purposes (see p1195).

Interpretation of statutory references to stepchildren etc.

246.–(1)   In any provision to which this section applies, references to a stepchild or step-parent of a person (here, ''A''), and cognate expressions, are to be read as follows–

A's stepchild includes a person who is the child of A's civil partner (but is not A's child);

A's step-parent includes a person who is the civil partner of A's parent (but is not A's parent);

A's stepdaughter includes a person who is the daughter of A's civil partner (but is not A's daughter);

A's stepson includes a person who is the son of A's civil partner (but is not A's son);

A's stepfather includes a person who is the civil partner of A's father (but is not A's parent);

A's stepmother includes a person who is the civil partner of A's mother (but is not A's parent);

A's stepbrother includes a person who is the son of the civil partner of A's parent (but is not the son of either of A's parents);

A's stepsister includes a person who is the daughter of the civil partner of A's parent (but is not the daughter of either of A's parents).

(2)   For the purposes of any provision to which this section applies–

''brother-in-law'' includes civil partner's brother,

''daughter-in-law'' includes daughter's civil partner,

''father-in-law'' includes civil partner's father,

''mother-in-law'' includes civil partner's mother,

''parent-in-law'' includes civil partner's parent,

''sister-in-law'' includes civil partner's sister, and

''son-in-law'' includes son's civil partner.

Provisions to which section 246 applies: Acts of Parliament etc.

247.–(1)   Section 246 applies to–

(a)   any provision listed in Schedule 21 (references to stepchildren, in-laws etc. in existing Acts),

(b)   except in so far as otherwise provided, any provision made by a future Act, and

(c)   except in so far as otherwise provided, any provision made by future subordinate legislation.

(2)   A Minister of the Crown may by order–

(a)   amend Schedule 21 by adding to it any provision of an existing Act;

(b)   provide for section 246 to apply to prescribed provisions of existing subordinate legislation.

(3)   The power conferred by subsection (2) is also exercisable–

(a)   by the Scottish Ministers, in relation to a relevant Scottish provision;

(b)   by a Northern Ireland department, in relation to a provision which deals with a transferred matter;

(c)   by the National Assembly for Wales, if the order is made by virtue of subsection (2)(b) and deals with matters with respect to which functions are exercisable by the Assembly.

(4)   Subject to subsection (5), the power to make an order under subsection (2) is exercisable by statutory instrument.

(5)   Any power of a Northern Ireland department to make an order under subsection (2) is exercisable by statutory rule for the purposes of the Statutory Rules (Northern Ireland) Order 1979 (S.I. 1979/1573 (N.I. 12)).

(6)   A statutory instrument containing an order under subsection (2) made by a Minister of the Crown is subject to annulment in pursuance of a resolution of either House of Parliament.

(7)   A statutory instrument containing an order under subsection (2) made by the Scottish Ministers is subject to annulment in pursuance of a resolution of the Scottish Parliament.

(8)   A statutory rule containing an order under subsection (2) made by a Northern Ireland department is subject to negative resolution (within the meaning of section 41(6) of the Interpretation Act (Northern Ireland) 1954 (c. 33 (N.I.))).

(9)   In this section–

''Act'' includes an Act of the Scottish Parliament;

''existing Act'' means an Act passed on or before the last day of the Session in which this Act is passed;

''existing subordinate legislation'' means subordinate legislation made before the day on which this section comes into force;

''future Act'' means an Act passed after the last day of the Session in which this Act is passed;

''future subordinate legislation'' means subordinate legislation made on or after the day on which this section comes into force;

''Minister of the Crown'' has the same meaning as in the Ministers of the Crown Act 1975 (c. 26);

''prescribed'' means prescribed by the order;

''relevant Scottish provision'' means a provision that would be within the legislative competence of the Scottish Parliament if it were included in an Act of that Parliament;

''subordinate legislation'' has the same meaning as in the Interpretation Act 1978 (c. 30) except that it includes an instrument made under an Act of the Scottish Parliament;

''transferred matter'' has the meaning given by section 4(1) of the Northern Ireland Act 1998 (c. 47) and ''deals with'' in relation to a transferred matter is to be construed in accordance with section 98(2) and (3) of the 1998 Act.

Social security, child support and tax credits

254.–(1)   Schedule 24 contains amendments relating to social security, child support and tax credits.

(2)   Subsection (3) applies in relation to any provision of any Act, Northern Ireland legislation or subordinate legislation which–

(a)   relates to social security, child support or tax credits, and

(b)   contains references (however expressed) to persons who are living or have lived together as husband and wife.

(3)   The power under section 259 to make orders amending enactments, Northern Ireland legislation and subordinate legislation is to be treated as including power to amend the provision to refer to persons who are living or have lived together as if they were civil partners.

(4)   Subject to subsection (5), section 175(3), (5) and (6) of the Social Security Contributions and Benefits Act 1992 (c. 4) applies to the exercise of the power under section 259 in relation to social security, child support or tax credits as it applies to any power under that Act to make an order (there being disregarded for the purposes of this subsection the exceptions in section 175(3) and (5) of that Act).

(5)   Section 171(3), (5) and (6) of the Social Security Contributions and Benefits (Northern Ireland) Act 1992 (c. 7) applies to the exercise by a Northern Ireland department of the power under section 259 in relation to social security and child support as it applies to any power under that Act to make an order (there being disregarded for the purposes of this subsection the exceptions in section 171(3) and (5) of that Act).

(6)   The reference in subsection (2) to an Act or Northern Ireland legislation relating to social security is to be read as including a reference to–

(a)   the Pneumoconiosis etc. (Workers' Compensation) Act 1979 (c. 41), and (b)　the Pneumoconiosis, etc., (Workers' Compensation) (Northern Ireland) Order 1979 (S.I. 1979/925 (N.I. 9));

and the references in subsections (4) and (5) to social security are to be construed accordingly.

SCHEDULE 21
SECTION 247
REFERENCES TO STEPCHILDREN ETC. IN EXISTING ACTS

24　　Section 113(2) of the Housing Act 1985 (c. 68) (members of a person's family).

25　　Section 186(2) of that Act (members of a person's family).

44　　Section 62(2) of the Housing Act 1996 (c. 52) (members of a person's family: Part 1).

45　　Section 140(2) of that Act (members of a person's family Chapter 1).

46　　Section 143P(3) of that Act (members of a person's family: Chapter 1A).

47　　The definition of ''relative'' in section 178(3) of that Act (meaning of associated person).

Part 7

Other secondary legislation Common and transitional provisions

Social Security (Persons From Abroad) Miscellaneous Amendments Regulations 1996
(SI 1996 No.30)

Saving

12.–(1)   Where, before the coming into force of these Regulations, a person who becomes an asylum seeker under regulation 4A(5)(a)(i) of the Council Tax Benefit Regulations, regulation 7A(5)(a)(i) of the Housing Benefit Regulations or regulation 70(3A)(a) of the Income Support Regulations, as the case may be, is entitled to benefit under any of those Regulations, those provisions of those Regulations as then in force shall continue to have effect [¹ (both as regards him and as regards persons who are members of his family at the coming into force of these Regulations)] as if regulations 3(a) and (b), 7(a) and (b) or 8(2) and (3)(c), as the case may be, of these Regulations had not been made.

(2)   Where, before the coming into force of these Regulations, a person, in respect of whom an undertaking was given by another person or persons to be responsible for his maintenance and accommodation, claimed benefit to which he is entitled, or is receiving benefit, under the Council Tax Benefit Regulations, the Housing Benefit Regulations or the Income Support regulations, as the case may be, those Regulations as then in force shall have effect as if regulations 3, 7 or 8, as the case may be, of these Regulations had not been made.

Amendment

1.   Amended by the Asylum and Immigration Act 1996 Sch 1 para 5 from 24.7.96. The effect of this amendment is preserved by reg 12(11)(a) of SI 2000 No 636 from 3.4.00 following the repeal of Sch 1 of the 1996 Act on the same date.

Modifications

The amendments made by SI 2006 No.1026 to the HB Regs, HB(SPC) Regs, CTB Regs and CTB(SPC) Regs do not affect the continued operation of the transitional and savings provided for in reg 12 Social Security (Persons From Abroad) Miscellaneous Amendments Regulations 1996, reg 6 Social Security (Habitual Residence) Amendment Regulations 2004 or Sch 3 para 6 HB&CTB(CP) Regs. See reg 11 of SI 2006 No.1026 (on p1226).

General Note

This important saving provision prevents retrospective effect of the draconian restrictions on the receipt of benefit by asylum seekers which were introduced by these Regulations. The belief of the Government that the UK was seen as an easy target for economic migrants masquerading as asylum seekers resulted in these Regulations being made. An asylum seeker, B, and the Joint Council for the Welfare of Immigrants commenced judicial review proceedings claiming that the removal of benefit conflicted with the right to have an asylum claim determined in accordance with the Asylum and Immigration Appeals Act 1993 and the Regulations were therefore *ultra vires*. It was pointed out that asylum seekers were forbidden from obtaining employment while their claims were determined. Many would arrive in this country without means to support themselves. If they could not rely on public funds, then they would be destitute and unable to maintain themselves. Ultimately, they would be unable to survive while their claims were being determined.

At first instance, the Divisional Court refused the application but the Court of Appeal in *R v Secretary of State for Social Security ex p B and JCWI* [1997] 1 WLR 275 held, by a majority, that the regulations were indeed *ultra vires*. In a judgment that is a high watermark of judicial activism, Simon Brown LJ said (at 292E-F, 293C):

".... the 1993 Act confers on asylum seekers fuller rights than they had ever previously enjoyed, the right of appeal in particular. And yet these regulations for some genuine asylum seekers at least, must now be regarded as rendering these rights nugatory. Either that, or the 1996 regulations necessarily contemplate for some a life so destitute that, to my mind, no civilised nation can tolerate it. .... Parliament cannot have intended a significant number of genuine asylum seekers to be impaled on the horns of so intolerable a dilemma: the need either to abandon their claims to refugee status or alternatively to maintain themselves as best they can but in a state of utter destitution. Primary legislation alone could in my judgement achieve that sorry state of affairs."

However, the Asylum and Immigration Act 1996 was making its way through Parliament at the time of the Court of Appeal's decision and the Government took the opportunity to legislate to ensure that the "sorry state of affairs" continued by introducing an amendment to enact s11 and Sch 1, which effectively resurrected the 1996

Regulations, with amendments. Suggestions that a better way of solving the alleged difficulties (the existence of which was unsupported by any reliable evidence) would be to employ more special adjudicators to reduce the lengthy delays in the determination of asylum claims, fell on deaf ears.

The enduring result of the striking down of these Regulations by the decision of the Court of Appeal in *ex p B* and their subsequent resurrection by the 1996 Act is that there has been considerable difficulty in determining which claimants were entitled to transitional protection.

Where someone was entitled to HB or CTB by virtue of reg 12(1) or (2) of SI 1996 No.30 immediately before 6 March 2006, the modifications to the current CTB and CTB(SPC) Regs and the current HB Regs and HB(SPC) Regs are now to be found in Sch 3 para 6 HB&CTB(CP) Regs.

Under reg 12(11)(b) Social Security (Immigration and Asylum) Consequential Provisions Regulations 2000 SI No.636, the effect of the saving provisions of reg 12 of these Regulations remains the same, despite the repeal of much of the then reg 7A HB Regs 1987 and reg 4A CTB Regs 1992 by the 2000 Regulations.

Analysis

Paragraph (1)

".... before the coming into force of these Regulations ....". The unusual method chosen by the Government of re-activating the Regulations struck down in *ex p B and JCWI* rather than simply granting itself the powers to pass such Regulations and enacting a new set caused difficulties in determining the scope of the transitional protection.

Before the Court of Appeal's decision, the meaning of paras (1) and (2) in relation to the two categories of claimants was clear enough. Where the claim was made or treated as made before 5 February 1996, the Regulations had no effect on her/his entitlement. It appears that this would have applied to a claimant who had the date of her/his claim backdated under reg 72(15) HB Regs 1987 or reg 64(16) CTB Regs 1992 to before 5 February 1996 for good cause. Where the claim was made or treated as made after that date, the exclusions in the Regulations took effect.

The question that arose was as to the effect of the Court of Appeal's decision in *ex p B and JCWI* on reg 12. The order made by the court did not declare the Regulations as a whole to be *ultra vires*: merely those parts that purported to exclude asylum seekers from benefit. That being so, when was "the coming into force" of the Regulations? Was it on 5 February 1996, or was it on 24 July 1996, when the Regulations were revived by Sch 1 of the 1996 Act (with the amendment made by para 5 to reg 12(1))? The question arises in relation to "in country" asylum seekers whose claims were made or treated as made between 5 February and 23 July ("the window period").

In *ex p T*, it was held that the date referred to was the earlier date of 5 February. Because reg 12(1) had not been altered by the 1996 Act to refer to 24 July, it was reasonable to assume that the earlier commencement date represented Parliament's intention. Therefore asylum seekers who claimed benefits in the window period are not entitled to receive benefit. Potts J's ruling was upheld by the Court of Appeal [1997] 5 CL 619.

".... those provisions of those Regulations then in force ....". It is important to recall that prior to the enactment of these regulations, all asylum seekers were a group of "persons from abroad" who were exempted from the general exclusion from benefit. See reg 10(6)(a)(i) of both the HB and the HB(SPC) Regs and reg 7(6)(a)(i) of both the CTB and the CTB(SPC) Regs as provided by Sch 3 para 6(1)-(3) HB&CTB(CP) Regs.

After these Regulations were enacted, only "on arrival" applicants for asylum were exempt: see reg 10(1) of both the HB and the HB(SPC) Regs and 7(1) of both the CTB and the CTB(SPC) regs as modified by Sch 3 para 6(10)-(13) HB&CTB(CP) Regs. The question is therefore which "in country" applicants are protected by reg 12.

".... is entitled to benefit .... shall continue to have effect ....". The provisions can only have effect if the claimant is entitled to benefit on the date these Regulations came into force, which, following the decision in *ex p T* referred to above, is to be taken to be 5 February 1996. It is not sufficient that a claimant has been in receipt of benefit at some time prior to that date and then seeks to claim again after it: *R v Secretary of State for Social Security ex p Vijeikis* [1998] COD 49, QBD; *CIS 16992/1996* para 20. As Dyson J said in *Vijeikis* at 50, "for something to continue, it must exist; it cannot be something that once existed, but no longer exists."

This analysis applies even where the claimant has found work and later has to go back onto benefit, no matter how unfair that is. Parliament, by resurrecting the regulations, clearly intended to produce that unfair result: *Vijeikis* at 50. The decision in that case was upheld by the Court of Appeal [1998] unreported, 5 March.

However, what happens where there is a break in claim for a period after 5 February 1996? Is the transitional protection lost? It was suggested in previous editions of this book that the transitional protection should not cease. A number of commissioners, however, issued decisions on the effect of para (1). All the cases were where there were breaks in claims for IS. In *CIS 3955/1997* the claimant went to India for 11 weeks and in *CIS 1115/1999* and *CIS 6258/1999* the claimant obtained employment for a period. The commissioners all ruled that the transitional protection was lost once the previous claim for IS ended. The commissioner in *CIS 6258/1999* expressed some doubt about the reasoning in the other two cases that preceded his decision but decided that he could not be satisfied that those decisions were wrongly decided so as to entitle him to decline to follow them.

In *Yildiz v Secretary of State for Social Security* [2001] *The Independent* 9 March, [2001] EWCA Civ 309, CA, the Court of Appeal allowed an appeal from the decision in *CIS 6258/1999*. The court held (para 15 of the judgment of Buxton LJ) that the only pre-condition for the application of the transitional protection in para (1) is that the claimant must have been in receipt of benefit on 5 February 1996. Once that is shown, the protection remains until the claimant's claim for asylum is determined, regardless of any intervening period of employment or other non-entitlement to benefit.

"*.... both as regards him and as regards persons who are members of his family at the coming into force of these Regulations ....*". The effect of this amendment is to confirm that the claimant's immigration status determines the entitlement to benefit for the rest of the family. Suppose an asylum seeker arrived in Britain and did not claim on her arrival, but claimed benefit on 1 February 1996, and her partner arrived in the UK on 1 March with their son. They remain members of her family – eg, by virtue of reg 21(1) HB Regs. The claimant is entitled to claim benefit in respect of both of them. If the claimant and her partner separate, the partner can claim in his own right, even though he arrived after the cut-off date. If the son reaches the age of 16, he can claim in his own right.

However, it must be remembered that this only applies where the claimant and partner were a couple on 5 February 1996. If the relationship broke down before then, the partner will not be entitled to the transitional protection if s/he claims after that date: *R v Department of Social Security ex p Okito* [1998] COD 48 at 49, QBD (this case was heard with *Vijeikis*).

Paragraph (2)

This paragraph provides transitional protection for sponsored immigrants, who were not "persons from abroad" until 5 February 1996. These parts of the 1996 Regulations were not challenged in *Okito*. Note that where someone is entitled to HB/CTB by virtue of reg 12(2) when the consolidating regulations came into force on 6 March 2006, the HB and CTB Regs have effect subject to the modifications provided in Sch 3 para 6(2) and (3) HB&CTB(CP) Regs: Sch 3 para 6(4) HB&CTB(CP) Regs.

Claimants whose entitlement was terminated before 5 February 1996. In *CIS 16992/1996* (para 7) it was said that the scope of the transitional protection was the same as for para (1) above, so that the claimant could not rely on a period of entitlement that terminated prior to 5 February 1996. This was also assumed by Dyson J in *Vijeikis*, although none of the three cases before him were concerned with sponsored immigrants. However, there is a significant difference in language between paras (1) and (2). Para (1) refers to a claimant who "is entitled to benefit" on 5 February, for whom the old rules "continue to have effect". The language there clearly refers to a claimant who is entitled on the commencement date. Nothing else will do.

Para (2), however, refers to a person who "*before* the coming into force of the Regulations . . . *claimed* benefit to which he *is* entitled, *or is* receiving benefit". Para (2) clearly contemplates two separate categories of claimant. The second category covers those who are receiving benefit on 5 February. The first category could be read in two ways. Either it covers those who made a claim prior to 5 February which was not adjudicated until after that date, or it covers all those who made a claim for some period prior to 5 February. Which construction is to be preferred?

The difficulty with adopting the first construction is that the first category is then *otiose*, since a claimant who claimed on 1 February and whose claim was adjudicated on 1 March "is receiving benefit" for the four weeks in February, including the critical date of 5 February. It can therefore be said that s/he falls within the second category. The first category must therefore mean something different. If it was not intended to do so, why include it?

The second, wider construction is not altogether satisfactory either. The past tense of the word "claimed" supports it. The difficulty lies with the word "is". That would suggest that the entitlement must be a current one, as Dyson J thought. However, it can be explained by the need to exclude from the provision those claimants who claimed, and were awarded, benefit on a false basis. Although it could be said that such a claimant *was* entitled to benefit following the award on the claim, if the award was subsequently reviewed before or after the 5 February threshold, it could not be said that the claimant *is* entitled to the award of benefit on that claim. It is therefore suggested that if the first category of claimants is to have any meaning, the second, wider construction is to be preferred.

Breaks in claim after 5 February 1996. It is suggested that the same analysis applies for para (2) as for para (1) (see above). In *CIS 1077/1999* and *CIS 6088/1999* (para 120), Commissioner Jacobs suggested that once an award of IS ceases, the transitional protection is lost. Although this decision was issued prior to and without the benefit of the analysis in *Yildiz*, on a further appeal to the Court of Appeal (*Shah v Secretary of State for Social Security* [2002] EWCA Civ 285, CA (reported as *R(IS) 2/02*), the argument based on para (2) was abandoned in the light of the House of Lords' decision in *M (A Minor) v Secretary of State for Social Security* [2001] 1 WLR 1453.

The Housing Benefit (Permitted Totals) Order 1996
(SI 1996 No.677)

General Note

This Order sets out the basis for calculating the permitted totals of rebates or allowances for the year 1996/1997 and subsequent years for authorities granting rebates or allowances under Part VIII of the Social Security Administration Act 1992. The Order limits the amount by which HB payments may be increased on the exercise of the discretions formerly provided by reg 61(2) and (3) HB Regs 1987, and to war widows through modified schemes.

Citation, commencement and interpretation

1.–(1) This Order may be cited as the Housing Benefit (Permitted Totals) Order 1996 and shall come into force on 1st April 1996.

(2)   In this Order–

"the Act" means the Social Security Administration Act 1992;

"housing benefit" means either rent rebate or rent allowance as the circumstances may require;

"the Housing Benefit Regulations" means the Housing Benefit (General) Regulations 1987;

"increase in housing benefit" means the difference between–

(a)   the amount of housing benefit granted in a case in which an authority makes a determination under regulation 61(2) of the Housing Benefit Regulations (increase in the appropriate maximum housing benefit)(e), and

(b)   the amount of housing benefit which would have been granted in that case if the authority had not made a determination under regulation 61(2) of those Regulations; and

"increase above maximum rent" means the difference between–

(a)   the amount of housing benefit granted in a case in which an authority makes a determination under regulation 61(3) of the Housing Benefit Regulations, and

(b)   the amount of housing benefit which would have been granted in that case if the authority had not made a determination under regulation 61(3) of those Regulations.

Permitted total of benefit awarded in exercise of a discretion

2.   For the purpose of section 134(11) of the Act, the permitted total of housing benefit–

[1 (a) for the year commencing on 1st April 1996 in relation to an authority shall be the total of the amounts obtained by the calculations set out in articles 3 and 4 below.

(b)   for the year commencing on 1st April 1997 in relation to an authority shall be the total of the amounts obtained by the calculations set out in articles 3 and 4 below; and

(c)   for any year commencing on or after 1st April 1998 in relation to an authority shall be the total of the amount obtained by the calculation in article 3 below and the amount specified in the Schedule to this Order.]

Amendment

1.   Amended by reg 2 of SI 1998 No 566 from 31.3.98.

Increase in housing benefit

3.   The calculation referred to in article 2 above shall be the amount obtained by deducting 100% of any increases in housing benefit in cases in which that authority has during that year made a determination under regulation 61(2) of the Housing Benefit Regulations from the total housing benefit granted by that authority during that year, after deduction of any increase above maximum rent, and multiplying the resulting figure by [1 100.025%].

Amendment

1.   Amended by reg 2 SI 2001 No 1129 as from 1.04.01.

Increase above maximum rent

4.–(1)   The calculation referred to in article 2 above shall be the amount obtained by deducting 100% of any increases above maximum rent in cases in which that authority has during that year made a determination under regulation 61(3) of the Housing Benefit Regulations from the total housing benefit granted by that authority during that year, less the deductions specified in paragraph (2) below, and multiplying the resulting figure by [¹ 101.08%]

(2)   The deductions referred to in paragraph (1) above are–

(a)   all rent rebates granted during that year;

(b)   subject to paragraph (3) below, all rent allowances granted during that year in cases where the local authority did not refer a claim for housing benefit, in relation to the dwelling in respect of which that allowance was granted, to the rent officer pursuant to regulation 12A of the Housing Benefit Regulations; and

(c)   any increase in housing benefit.

(3)   No rent allowance shall be deducted pursuant to paragraph (2) above, if that case was not referred to the rent officer by reason of paragraph (2) of regulation 12A of those Regulations.

Amendment

1.   101.08% substituted for 100.9% by art 2 of SI 1996 No 2326 as from 7.10.96.

Permitted total of benefit in modified schemes

5.   For the purpose of section 134(9) of the Act (modifications other than war disablement pension or war widows pension within the Act), the permitted total of housing benefit for [¹ any year commencing on or after] 1st April 1996 in relation to an authority shall be the total of the amounts obtained by deducting 100% of any housing benefit awarded as a consequence of any determination to disregard made by that authority during that year pursuant to a modification adopted by them under section 134(8) of the Act (power to modify housing benefit schemes as prescribed) and regulation 7 of the Income Related Benefits Schemes Amendment (No. 2) Regulations 1995 (power to modify in respect of certain pensions to war widows) from the total housing benefit granted by that authority during that year and multiplying the resulting figure by 100.7%.

Amendment

1.   Amended by reg 3 of SI 1998 No 566 from 31.3.98.

Revocation

6.   The Housing Benefit (Permitted Totals) Order 1995 is hereby revoked.

SCHEDULE 1

[² TOTALS FOR INCREASES ABOVE MAXIMUM RENT

Authority	Permitted total £	Authority	Permitted total £
England		Basildon	21,576
Adur	11,073	Basingstoke and Deane	12,982
Allerdale	14,001	Bassetlaw	14,013
Alnwick	2,832	Bath and NE Somerset	31,322
Amber Valley	12,361	Bedford	25,697
Arun	41,402	Berwick upon Tweed	3,833
Ashfield	12,423	Bexley	49,763
Ashford	12,112	Birmingham	198,165
Aylesbury Vale	13,412	Blaby	4,376
Babergh	10,044	Blackburn with Darwen	33,307
Barking	38,065	Blackpool	117,965
Barnet	133,375	Blyth Valley	8,004
Barnsley	31,155	Bolsover	13,007
Barrow in Furness	23,278	Bolton	46,138

Housing Benefit (Permitted Totals) Order 1996

Authority	Permitted total £	Authority	Permitted total £
Boston	5,138	East Hampshire	11,956
Bournemouth	95,696	East Hertfordshire	10,036
Bracknell Forest	13,822	East Lindsey	32,105
Bradford	123,752	East Northamptonshire	8,204
Braintree	14,434	East Riding of Yorkshire	57,413
Breckland	12,774	East Staffordshire	12,968
Brent	193,395	Eastbourne	42,495
Brentwood	7,087	Eastleigh	12,311
Bridgnorth	4,120	Eden	5,083
Brighton and Hove	180,857	Ellesmere Port and Neston	5,910
Bristol	96,138	Elmbridge	22,072
Broadland	8,928	Enfield	109,407
Bromley	50,991	Epping Forest	20,508
Bromsgrove	4,359	Epsom and Ewell	9,885
Broxbourne	13,260	Erewash	13,294
Broxtowe	11,299	Exeter	35,462
Burnley	25,828	Fareham	9,844
Bury	29,838	Fenland	17,307
Calderdale	28,108	Forest Heath	6,146
Cambridge	16,167	Forest of Dean	10,316
Camden	132,750	Fylde	17,760
Cannock Chase	6,657	Gateshead	27,463
Canterbury	33,324	Gedling	12,914
Caradon	20,600	Gloucester	38,822
Carlisle	13,889	Gosport	11,207
Carrick	24,764	Gravesham	21,343
Castle Morpeth	3,056	Great Yarmouth	40,174
Castle Point	21,278	Greenwich	56,280
Charnwood	17,868	Guildford	17,990
Chelmsford	14,838	Hackney	159,737
Cheltenham	24,155	Halton	17,626
Cherwell	23,520	Hambleton	8,380
Chester	16,699	Hammersmith and Fulham	92,023
Chester le Street	5,524	Harborough	4,066
Chesterfield	14,802	Haringey	254,022
Chichester	15,367	Harlow	10,481
Chiltern	4,842	Harrogate	24,943
Chorley	9,480	Harrow	74,970
Christchurch	6,318	Hart	6,633
City of London	1,439	Hartlepool	20,158
Colchester	28,238	Hastings	70,070
Congleton	4,887	Havant	15,981
Copeland	12,193	Havering	36,693
Corby	12,013	Herefordshire	31,035
Cotswold	9,367	Hertsmere	10,520
Coventry	67,163	High Peak	11,583
Craven	6,118	Hillingdon	48,018
Crawley	7,786	Hinckley and Bosworth	6,864
Crewe and Nantwich	13,121	Horsham	11,381
Croydon	145,919	Hounslow	81,898
Dacorum	13,429	Huntingdonshire	12,412
Darlington	19,355	Hyndburn	23,110
Dartford	15,715	Ipswich	23,448
Daventry	4,365	Isle of Wight	48,692
Derby	48,483	Isles of Scilly	112
Derbyshire Dales	3,813	Islington	75,538
Derwentside	10,221	Kennet	6,553
Doncaster	39,071	Kensington and Chelsea	95,011
Dover	36,954	Kerrier	23,573
Dudley	21,784	Kettering	11,336
Durham	5,937	Kings Lynn & West Norfolk	19,448
Ealing	158,493	Kingston upon Hull	61,181
Easington	10,063	Kingston upon Thames	23,020
East Cambridgeshire	7,026	Kirklees	61,583
East Devon	18,050	Knowsley	24,691
East Dorset	6,974	Lambeth	166,917

Authority	Permitted total £	Authority	Permitted total £
Lancaster	52,083	Reigate and Banstead	13,661
Leeds	161,079	Restormel	32,194
Leicester	51,758	Ribble Valley	5,025
Lewes	24,395	Richmond upon Thames	34,918
Lewisham	118,483	Richmondshire	4,019
Lichfield	3,550	Rochdale	43,229
Lincoln	20,575	Rochford	10,624
Liverpool	201,524	Rossendale	11,986
Luton	63,742	Rother	22,310
Macclesfield	16,110	Rotherham	23,596
Maidstone	17,903	Rugby	7,523
Maldon	18,921	Runnymede	9,170
Malvern Hills	7,025	Rushcliffe	9,619
Manchester	195,674	Rushmoor	11,126
Mansfield	14,897	Rutland	1,986
Medway	108,499	Ryedale	5,138
Melton	3,109	Salford	77,097
Mendip	21,594	Salisbury	19,512
Merton	57,194	Sandwell	31,220
Mid Bedfordshire	8,266	Scarborough	37,313
Mid Devon	12,064	Sedgefield	7,215
Mid Suffolk	6,806	Sedgemoor	21,337
Mid Sussex	13,107	Sefton	84,267
Middlesbrough	30,388	Selby	6,559
Milton Keynes	30,589	Sevenoaks	10,096
Mole Valley	6,461	Sheffield	52,222
New Forest	19,869	Shepway	51,579
Newark and Sherwood	12,775	Shrewsbury and Atcham	12,479
Newcastle under Lyme	8,317	Slough	36,269
Newcastle upon Tyne	75,679	Solihull	11,316
Newham	236,456	South Bedfordshire	10,573
North Cornwall	22,078	South Bucks	3,586
North Devon	33,937	South Cambridgeshire	8,860
North Dorset	5,647	South Derbyshire	11,106
North East Derby	5,846	South Gloucestershire	20,227
North East Lincoln	42,198	South Hams	19,260
North Hertfordshire	15,823	South Holland	5,045
North Kesteven	6,418	South Kesteven	13,603
North Lincolnshire	20,707	South Lakeland	15,835
North Norfolk	19,096	South Norfolk	9,469
North Shropshire	6,383	South Northants	5,306
North Somerset	58,091	South Oxfordshire	19,106
North Tyneside	49,049	South Ribble	6,160
North Warwickshire	3,801	South Shropshire	6,168
North West Leicester	5,509	South Somerset	22,317
North Wiltshire	9,457	South Staffordshire	4,463
Northampton	32,163	South Tyneside	32,453
Norwich	26,986	Southampton	73,593
Nottingham	59,030	Southend on Sea	97,336
Nuneaton and Bedworth	14,606	Southwark	90,007
Oadby and Wigston	4,630	Spelthorne	10,818
Oldham	34,150	St Albans	9,953
Oswestry	4,760	St Edmundsbury	8,585
Oxford	48,078	St Helens	23,507
Pendle	19,716	Stafford	7,452
Penwith	23,242	Staffordshire Moorlands	7,006
Peterborough	41,089	Stevenage	9,376
Plymouth	95,680	Stockport	51,884
Poole	29,167	Stockton on Tees	28,021
Portsmouth	67,055	Stoke on Trent	34,205
Preston	23,230	Stratford on Avon	11,053
Purbeck	7,603	Stroud	14,432
Reading	51,780	Suffolk Coastal	17,852
Redbridge	142,324	Sunderland	53,243
Redcar and Cleveland	22,464	Surrey Heath	7,169
Redditch	5,822	Sutton	34,929

Authority	Permitted total £	Authority	Permitted total £
Swale	41,749	Wyre	22,173
Swindon	23,721	Wyre Forest	11,956
Tameside	36,307	York	29,336
Tamworth	9,172	**Scotland**	
Tandridge	7,092	Aberdeen	17,118
Taunton Deane	21,426	Aberdeenshire	15,810
Teesdale	2,865	Angus	10,333
Teignbridge	29,864	Argyll and Bute	17,435
Telford and Wrekin	18,049	Comhairle Nan Eilean Sair	2,249
Tendring	44,271	Clackmannanshire	3,067
Test Valley	6,818	Dumfries and Galloway	19,846
Tewkesbury	8,100	Dundee	23,135
Thanet	88,716	East Ayrshire	8,128
Three Rivers	8,128	East Dunbartonshire	5,812
Thurrock	24,684	East Lothian	12,140
Tonbridge and Malling	9,546	East Renfrewshire	5,656
Torbay	85,563	Edinburgh	116,558
Torridge	18,849	Falkirk	8,674
Tower Hamlets	45,003	Fife	43,080
Trafford	35,417	Glasgow	122,279
Tunbridge Wells	14,206	Highland	18,909
Tynedale	3,800	Inverclyde	9,892
Uttlesford	6,206	Midlothian	5,423
Vale of White Horse	9,747	Moray	9,487
Vale Royal	7,303	North Ayrshire	17,642
Wakefield	27,358	North Lanarkshire	12,042
Walsall	18,945	Orkney	2,857
Waltham Forest	158,176	Perth and Kinross	21,140
Wandsworth	121,014	Renfrewshire	14,138
Wansbeck	6,844	Scottish Borders	7,350
Warrington	13,911	Shetland	775
Warwick	15,350	South Ayrshire	22,019
Watford	16,358	South Lanarkshire	17,803
Waveney	51,698	Stirling	7,290
Waverley	13,121	West Dunbartonshire	5,438
Wealdon	21,509	West Lothian	12,617
Wear Valley	7,507	**Wales**	
Wellingborough	10,445	Blaenau Gwent	10,753
Welwyn Hatfield	9,713	Bridgend	25,789
West Berkshire	10,976	Caerphilly	24,394
West Devon	12,775	Cardiff	60,004
West Dorset	11,805	Carmarthenshire	32,572
West Lancashire	13,010	Ceredigion	18,702
West Lindsey	9,532	Conwy	37,048
West Oxfordshire	11,866	Denbighshire	30,347
West Somerset	10,899	Flintshire	16,400
West Wiltshire	20,797	Gwynedd	31,422
Westminster	189,131	Isle of Anglesey	18,958
Weymouth and Portland	23,141	Merthyr Tydfil	9,430
Wigan	26,933	Monmouthshire	9,465
Winchester	8,637	Neath and Port Talbot	20,810
Windsor and Maidenhead	17,452	Newport	22,985
Wirral	104,453	Pembrokeshire	26,943
Woking	10,638	Powys	16,586
Wokingham	11,843	Rhondda Cynon Taff	38,661
Wolverhampton	28,921	Swansea	52,344
Worcester	24,231	Torfaen	7,729
Worthing	33,956	Vale of Glamorgan	30,658
Wychavon	6,710	Wrexham	14,500
Wycombe	12,804		

Amendments

1. Schedule added by reg 2 of SI 1998 No 566 from 31.3.98.
2. Amended by reg 3 of SI 2001 No 1129 as from 1.04.01.

The Council Tax Benefit (Permitted Totals) Order 1996
(SI 1996 No.678)

General Note

This Order sets out the basis for calculating the permitted totals of CTB for any year for authorities granting such benefit under Part VIII of the Social Security Administration Act 1992. The Order limits the amount by which CTB allowed by an authority may be increased on the exercise of the discretion formerly provided by regs 51(5) and 54(4) of the CTB Regs 1992, and to war widows where the authority's scheme has been modified.

Citation, commencement and interpretation

1.–(1)   This Order may be cited as the Council Tax Benefit (Permitted Totals) Order 1996 and shall come into force on 1st April 1996.

(2)   In this Order–

"the Act" means the Social Security Administration Act 1992;

"council tax benefit" means council tax benefit under Part VII of the Contributions and Benefits Act;

"the Council Tax Benefit Regulations" means the Council Tax Benefit (General) Regulations 1992;

"increase in council tax benefit" means the difference between–

(a)   in a case in which an authority makes a determination under regulation 51(5) or 54(4) of the Council Tax Benefit Regulations (increase in the appropriate maximum council tax benefit or alternative maximum council tax benefit)(f), the amount of council tax benefit granted; and

(b)   the amount of council tax benefit which would have been granted in that case if the authority had not made a determination under the said regulation 51(5) or 54(4).

Permitted total of benefit allowed in exercise of a discretion

2.   For the purpose of section 139(9) of the Act, the permitted total of council tax benefit for any year commencing on or after 1st April 1996 in relation to an authority shall be the amount obtained by deducting 100% of any increases in council tax benefit allowed by that authority during that year from the total council tax benefit granted by that authority during that year and multiplying the resulting figure by [¹ 100.025%].

Amendment

1.   Amended by reg 2 of SI 2001 No 1130 as from 1.04.01.

Permitted total of benefit in modified schemes

3.   For the purpose of section 139(7) of the Act (modifications other than war disablement pension or war widows pension within the Act), the permitted total of council tax benefit for any year commencing on or after 1st April 1996 in relation to an authority shall be the total of the amounts obtained by deducting 100% of any council tax benefit awarded as a consequence of any determination to disregard made by that authority during that year pursuant to a modification adopted by them under section 139(6)(b) of the Act (power to modify council tax benefit schemes as prescribed) and regulation 8 of the Income-related Schemes Amendment (No. 2) Regulations 1995 (power to modify in respect of certain pensions to war widows) from the total council tax benefit granted by that authority during that year and multiplying the resulting figure by 100.7%.

Revocation

4.   The Council Tax Benefit (Permitted Total) Order 1994 and the Housing Benefit (Permitted Totals) and Council Tax Benefit (Permitted Total) (Pensions for War Widows) Amendment Order 1995 are hereby revoked.

The Housing Benefit (Information from Landlords and Agents) Regulations 1997
(SI 1997 No.2436)

General Note

These regulations implemented s126A SSAA 1992 by setting out the circumstances in which local authorities may require information from landlords and agents, the information which must be supplied, the time limit for supplying it and the manner in which the information must be provided. Failure to comply with a notice requiring information under s126A is a criminal offence and would be a factor which a local authority could take into account when considering whether a landlord is a "fit and proper person" to receive payments of HB under regs 95 and 96 HB Regs (or regs 76 and 77 HB(SPC) Regs).

These regulations were not amended or revoked when the consolidating regulations came into force on 6 March 2006. However, the provisions are now also in the HB and the HB(SPC) Regs as follows:

Reg 1 is now, in part, reg 113 HB Regs (see p503) and reg 94 HB(SPC) Regs (see p874).

Reg 2 is now reg 117 HB Regs (see p507) and reg 98 HB(SPC) Regs (see p878).

Reg 3 is now reg 118 HB Regs (see p508) and reg 99 HB(SPC) Regs (see p878).

Reg 4 is now reg 119 HB Regs (see p508) and reg 100 HB(SPC) Regs (see p879).

Reg 5 is now reg 120 HB Regs (see p511) and reg 101 HB(SPC) Regs (see p880).

Reg 6 is now reg 121 HB Regs (see p511) and reg 102 HB(SPC) Regs (see p880).

See the commentary to regs 117-121 HB Regs (pp508-511).

Citation, commencement and interpretation

1.–(1)   These Regulations, which may be cited as the Housing Benefit (Information from Landlords and Agents) Regulations 1997, shall come into force on 3rd November 1997.

(2)   In these Regulations, unless the context otherwise requires–

"the Act" means the Social Security Administration Act 1992;

"the Housing Benefit Regulations" means the Housing Benefit (General) Regulations 1987;

"the notice" means the notice prescribed in regulation 3(1)(b);

"relevant information" means such information as is prescribed in regulation 4;

"the requirer" means a person within regulation 2, who requires information pursuant to that regulation;

"the section" means section 126A of the Act and references to a subsection are to a subsection of the section;

"the supplier" means an appropriate person who is required, pursuant to regulations 2 and 3, to supply relevant information and any person who is not so required is not, for the purposes of supplying information pursuant to the section and these Regulations, an appropriate person,

and other expressions used both in these Regulations and in the Housing Benefit Regulations shall have the same meanings in these Regulations as they have in the Housing Benefit Regulations.

(3)   In these Regulations a reference to a numbered regulation is to the regulation in these Regulations bearing that number and, unless the context otherwise requires, a reference in a regulation to a numbered or lettered paragraph is to the paragraph bearing that letter or number in that regulation and a reference in a paragraph to a lettered or numbered sub-paragraph is to the sub-paragraph in that paragraph bearing that letter or number.

Requiring information

2.   Pursuant to the section, where a claim is made to an authority, on which a rent allowance may be awarded, then, in the circumstances prescribed in regulation 3, that authority, or any person authorised to exercise any function of the authority relating to housing benefit, may require an appropriate person to supply to that authority or person relevant information, in the manner prescribed in regulation 5.

Circumstances for requiring information

3.–(1)   A person is required to supply information in the following circumstances–

(a) he is an appropriate person in relation to any dwelling in respect of which–
  (i) housing benefit is being paid to an appropriate person pursuant to regulation 93 or 94 of the Housing Benefit Regulations (circumstances in which payment is to be or may be made to a landlord); or
  (ii) a request has been made by an appropriate person or by the claimant for housing benefit to be so paid; and
(b) the requirer serves upon that appropriate person, whether by post or otherwise, a written notice stating that the requirer–
  (i) suspects that there is or may be an impropriety in relation to a claim in respect of any dwelling wherever situate in relation to which he is an appropriate person; or
  (ii) is already investigating an allegation of impropriety in relation to that person.
(2) Information required to be supplied under paragraph (1) shall be supplied to the requirer at the address specified in the notice.

Relevant information
4.–(1) The information the supplier is to supply to the requirer is that prescribed in paragraphs (2) and (3) (referred to in these Regulations as ''the relevant information'').
(2) For a supplier who falls within paragraph (4) or sub-section (2)(b) (''the landlord''), the information is–
(a) where the landlord is a natural person–
  (i) his appropriate details;
  (ii) the relevant particulars of any residential property in which he has an interest; and
  (iii) the appropriate details of any body corporate, in which he is a major shareholder or of which he is a director and which has an interest in residential property;
(b) where the landlord is a trustee, except a trustee of a charity, in addition to any information that he is required to supply in accordance with sub-paragraph (a) or (c), as the case may be, the relevant particulars of any residential property held by the trust of which he is a trustee and the name and address of any beneficiary under the trust or the objects of that trust, as the case may be;
(c) where the landlord is a body corporate or otherwise not a natural person, other than a charity–
  (i) its appropriate details;
  (ii) the relevant particulars of any residential property in which it has an interest;
  (iii) the names and addresses of any directors of it;
  (iv) the appropriate details of any person–
    (aa) who owns 20 per cent. or more of it; or
    (bb) of whom it owns 20 per cent. or more; and
  (v) the names and addresses of its major shareholders.
(d) where the landlord is a charity or is a recognised body the appropriate details relating to the landlord and particulars of the landlord's registration as a charity.
(3) For a supplier who falls within subsection (2)(c) or paragraph (5) (''the agent''), the information is–
(a) the name and address of any person (''his principal'')–
  (i) to whom the agent has agreed to make payments in consequence of being entitled to receive relevant payments; or
  (ii) for whom the agent is acting on behalf of or in connection with any aspect of the management of a dwelling,
  as the case may be;
(b) the relevant particulars of any residential property in respect of which the agent–
  (i) has agreed to make payments in consequence of being entitled to receive relevant payments; or

(ii)   is acting on behalf of his principal in connection with any aspect of its management;

(c)   where the agent is a natural person–

    (i)   the relevant particulars of any residential property in which he has an interest;

    (ii)   the appropriate details of any body corporate or any person otherwise not a natural person, in which he is a major shareholder or of which he is a director and which has any interest in residential property; or

(d)   where the agent is a body corporate or other than a natural person–

    (i)   the relevant particulars of any residential property in which it has an interest;

    (ii)   the names and addresses of any directors of or major shareholders in the agent; and

    (iii)   the appropriate details of any person–

        (aa)   who owns 20 per cent. or more of the agent; or

        (bb)   of whom the agent owns 20 per cent. or more.

(4)   A supplier falls within this paragraph (landlord receiving the rent), if he falls within subsection (2)(a), but does not fall within paragraph (5).

(5)   A supplier falls within this paragraph (agent receiving the rent), if he falls within subsection (2)(a) and has agreed to make payments, in consequence of being entitled to receive relevant payments, to a person falling within subsection (2)(b).

(6)   For the purposes of this regulation, except where the context otherwise requires–

''appropriate details'' means the name of the person and (in the case of a company) its registered office and, in any case, the full postal address, including post code, of the principal place of business of that person and the telephone and facsimile numbers (if any) of that place;

''charity'' means a charity which is registered under section 3 of the Charities Act 1993 and is not an exempt charity within the meaning of that Act;

''major shareholder'' means, where a body corporate is a company limited by shares, any person holding one tenth or more of the issued shares in that company and, in any other case, all the owners of that body;

''recognised body'' has the same meaning as in section 1(7) of the Law Reform (Miscellaneous Provisions) (Scotland) Act 1990;

''relevant particulars'' means the full postal address, including post code, and number of current lettings of or within that residential property and, if that property includes two or more dwellings, that address and the number of such lettings for each such dwelling;

''residential property'' includes any premises, situated within the United Kingdom–

    (i)   used or which has, within the last six months, been used; or

    (ii)   which may be used or is adapted for use,

as residential accommodation,

and other expressions used in this regulation and also in the Companies Act 1985 shall have the same meaning in this regulation as they have in that Act.

Manner of supply of information

[¹5.–(1)   Subject to paragraph (2) the relevant information shall be supplied–

(a)   in typewritten or printed form; or

(b)   with the written agreement of the requirer, in electronic or handwritten form,

within a period of 4 weeks commencing on the date on which the notice was sent or given.

(2)   Where–

(a)   within a period of 4 weeks commencing on the date on which the notice was sent or given, the supplier requests that the time for supply of the relevant information be extended; and

(b)   the requirer provides written agreement to that request,

the time for supply of the relevant information shall be extended to a period of 8 weeks commencing on the date on which the notice was sent or given.]

Amendment
1.   Substituted by reg 2 of SI 2000 No 4 as from 1.4.00 or 3.4.00.

Criminal offence

6.   Any failure by the supplier to supply relevant information to the requirer as, when and how required under these Regulations shall be an offence under section 113 of the Act and there may be recovered from the supplier, on summary conviction for this offence, penalties not exceeding–

    (a)   for any one offence, level 3 on the standard scale; or

    (b)   for an offence of continuing any such failure after conviction, £40 for each day on which it is so continued.

The Social Security (Penalty Notice) Regulations 1997
(SI 1997 No.2813)

General Note

These regulations implement the provisions of s115A SSAA 1992 which allows payment of an administrative penalty as an alternative to prosecution for an offence in relation to an overpayment of benefit. The regulations specify in detail the contents of the written notice referred to in s115A(2) in which a local authority may invite a claimant or landlord to pay such a penalty. For details of the penalty scheme, see p63.

The purpose of prescribing the content of a notice is to provide the recipient with the information that s/he needs to consider whether or not to accept the penalty. It is therefore suggested that a failure to supply the notice in the required form will render the penalty a nullity if the claimant is prejudiced by the omission: *Warwick DC v Freeman* [1994] 27 HLR 616, CA; *Haringey LBC v Awaritefe* [1999] 32 HLR 517.

Citation and commencement

1. These Regulations may be cited as the Social Security (Penalty Notice) Regulations 1997 and shall come into force on 18th December 1997.

Notice

2.–(1) Where the Secretary of State or authority gives to a person a written notice under section 115A(2) of the Social Security Administration Act 1992, the notice shall contain the information that–

(a) the penalty only applies to an overpayment which is recoverable under section 71, 71A, 75 or 76 of the Social Security Administration Act 1992;

(b) the penalty only applies where it appears to the Secretary of State or authority that the making of the overpayment was attributable to an act or omission by the person and that there are grounds for instituting proceedings for an offence relating to the overpayment;

(c) the penalty is 30 per cent. of the amount of the overpayment, is payable in addition to repayment of the overpayment and is recoverable by the same methods as those by which the overpayment is recoverable;

(d) a person who agrees to pay a penalty may withdraw the agreement within 28 days (including the date of the agreement) by notifying the Secretary of State or authority in the manner specified by the Secretary of State or authority; if the person withdraws the agreement, so much of the penalty as has already been recovered shall be repaid and he will no longer be immune from proceedings for an offence;

(e) if it is decided on review or appeal (or in accordance with regulations) that the overpayment is not recoverable or due, so much of the penalty as has already been recovered shall be repaid;

(f) if the amount of the overpayment is revised on review or appeal, except as covered by a new agreement to pay the revised penalty, so much of the penalty as has already been recovered shall be repaid and the person will no longer be immune from proceedings for an offence;

(g) the payment of a penalty does not give the person immunity from prosecution in relation to any other overpayment or any offence not relating to an overpayment.

(2) The notice shall set out–

(a) the manner specified by the Secretary of State or authority by which the person may agree to pay a penalty;

(b) the manner specified by the Secretary of State or authority by which the person may notify the withdrawal of his agreement to pay a penalty.

The New Deal (Miscellaneous Provisions) Order 1998
(SI 1998 No.217)

General Note

This Order specifies when participation in options of the "New Deal" is to be treated as training (rather than employment) under s2 Employment and Training Act 1973. In consequence, any payment received by the trainee (other than a trading receipt) is to be treated as a training allowance for the purposes of HB and CTB. See also the New Deal (Miscellaneous Provisions) Order 2001 on p1174, the New Deal (Lone Parents) (Miscellaneous Provisions) Order 2001 on p1182, the Flexible New Deal (Miscellaneous Provisions) Order 2009 on p1245, the Community Task Force (Miscellaneous Provisions) Order 2010 on p1246 and the Jobseeker's Allowance (Work for Your Benefit Pilot Scheme) Regulations 2010 on p1247.

Citation, commencement and interpretation

1.–(1)   This Order may be cited as the New Deal (Miscellaneous Provisions) Order 1998 and shall come into force on 2nd March 1998.

(2)   In this Order, unless the context otherwise requires–

[¹ "facilities" means facilities provided for the participant in pursuance of one or more of the New Deal Components;]

"the New Deal" means the arrangements known by that name and made under section 2 of the 1973 Act for which only persons who are aged 18 years or over and less than 26 years immediately prior to entry are eligible and which are designed to help New Deal Participants to obtain work or to improve their prospects of obtaining work;

"the New Deal Components" means any of the following, that is to say, the programmes of employment or employment-related training under the New Deal known individually as "the Full-time Education and Training Option", "the Voluntary Sector Option" [¹ , "the Employment Option"] and "the Environment Task Force Option";

[¹ "trading receipt" means, in relation to a New Deal Participant under the Employment Option, any payment made to him in consideration of goods or services supplied by him in the course of his participation under that option;]

"training allowance" means a payment made directly by the Secretary of State to a New Deal Participant in connection with his participation in one or more of the New Deal components;

and a person is, or, as the case may be, was, at any material time, a "New Deal Participant" if he is, or, as the case may be, was, at that time, using facilities. [¹ ...]

Amendment

1.   Amended by reg 2 of 1998 SI No 1425 as from 3.7.98.

Treatment of persons and payments for the purposes of the Social Security Contributions and Benefits Act 1992, the Jobseekers Act 1995 and specified subordinate legislation

[¹**2.**–(1)   The provisions of this article apply for the purposes of–

(a)   Part I of the Social Security Contributions and Benefits Act 1992,

(b)   the Jobseekers Act 1995 and

(c)   the subordinate legislation specified in the Schedule to this Order.

(2)   If, for any period or periods commencing with or falling after the date on which this Order comes into force, during which a person is a New Deal Participant and is participating in either the Full-time Education and Training Option, the Voluntary Sector Option or the Environment Task Force Option, that person receives, or is eligible to receive, a training allowance, he is to be treated for that period or those periods and in respect of his participation as not being employed but as participating in arrangements for training under section 2 of the 1973 Act; and accordingly any payment made to such a person during that period or those periods in connection with his use of facilities shall be treated in the same manner as a payment of training allowance made in respect of such training.

(3)   If, for any period or periods commencing with or falling after the date on which this paragraph comes into force, during which a person is a New Deal Participant and is participating in the Employment Option in a capacity other than that of employee, that person receives, or is eligible to receive, a training allowance, he is to be treated for that period or those periods and in respect of his participation as not being employed but as participating in arrangements for training under section 2 of the 1973 Act; and accordingly any payment, other than a trading receipt, made to such a person during that period or those periods in connection with his use of facilities shall be treated in the same manner as a payment of training allowance made in respect of such training.

Amendment

1.   Substituted by reg 3 of 1998 SI No 1425 as from 3.7.98.

SCHEDULE
ARTICLE 2
LIST OF SUBORDINATE LEGISLATION

[. . .]

[¹ The Housing Benefit Regulations 2006;]

[¹ The Housing Benefit (Persons who have attained the qualifying age for state pension credit) Regulations 2006;]

[¹ The Council Tax Benefit Regulations 2006;]

[¹ The Council Tax Benefit (Persons who have attained the qualifying age for state pension credit) Regulations 2006;]

Amendment

1.   Substituted by reg 5 and Sch 2 para 14 of SI 2006 No 217 as from 6.3.06.

The Social Security (Immigration and Asylum) Consequential Amendments Regulations 2000
(SI 2000 No.636)

Citation, commencement and interpretation

1.–(1)   These Regulations may be cited as the Social Security (Immigration and Asylum) Consequential Amendments Regulations 2000.

(2)   These Regulations shall come into force on 3rd April 2000.

(3)   In these Regulations–

"the Act" means the Immigration and Asylum Act 1999;

"the Contributions and Benefits Act" means the Social Security Contributions and Benefits Act 1992;

[¹]

[¹]

"the Persons from Abroad Regulations" means the Social Security (Persons from Abroad) Miscellaneous Amendments Regulations 1996;

(4)   In these Regulations, unless the context otherwise requires, a reference–

(a)   to a numbered regulation or Schedule is to the regulation in, or the Schedule to, these Regulations bearing that number;

(b)   in a regulation or Schedule to a numbered paragraph is to the paragraph in that regulation or Schedule bearing that number.

Amendment

1.   Revoked by reg 3 and Sch 1 of SI 2006 No 217 as from 6.3.06.

Persons not excluded from specified benefits under section 115 of the Immigration and Asylum Act 1999

2.–(1)   For the purposes of entitlement to income-based jobseeker's allowance, income support, a social fund payment, housing benefit or council tax benefit under the Contributions and Benefits Act, [² income-related employment and support allowance] [¹or state pension credit under the State Pension Credit Act 2002] as the case may be, a person falling within a category or description of persons specified in Part I of the Schedule is a person to whom section 115 of the Act does not apply.

(2)-(3)   *[Omitted]*

(4)   For the purposes of entitlement to–

(a)   income support, a social fund payment, housing benefit or council tax benefit under the Contributions and Benefits Act, [² or income-related employment and support allowance,] as the case may be, a person who is entitled to or is receiving benefit by virtue of paragraph (1) or (2) of regulation 12 of the Persons from Abroad Regulations is a person to whom section 115 of the Act does not apply;

(b)   [. . .]

[¹(c)   state pension credit under the State Pension Credit Act 2002, a person to whom sub-paragraph (a) would have applied but for the fact that they have attained the qualifying age for the purposes of state pension credit, is a person to whom section 115 of the Act does not apply.]

(5)   *[Omitted]*

(6)   For the purposes of entitlement to housing benefit, council tax benefit or a social fund payment under the Contributions and Benefits Act, as the case may be, a person to whom regulation 12(6) applies is a person to whom section 115 of the Act does not apply.

(7)-(8)   *[Omitted]*

Amendments

1.   Inserted by reg 6 of SI 2003 No 2274 as from 6.10.03.

2.   Amended by reg 69 of SI 2008 No 1554 as from 27.10.08.

General Note

Reg 2 is the primary provision which creates the six categories of claimant that are exempted from the effect of s115.

Analysis

Para (1) exempts the four categories listed in Part I of the Schedule.

Para (4) exempts those who retain their transitional protection under reg 12 Social Security (Persons from Abroad) Miscellaneous Amendments Regulations 1996 SI No.30 (see p1153). Broadly, it relates to those who did not claim asylum "on arrival".

Such claimants only retain their transitional protection if they were in receipt of HB on 5 February 1996 and their entitlements have continued since then. It will only apply to those who are still receiving benefit (or to those who are not receiving benefit but have an underlying entitlement) pursuant to those rules, not to those who once did so.

The effect of the saving provision in reg 12 of the 1996 Regulations is that the rules as now found in Sch 3 para 6(1)-(4) of the HB&CTB(CP) Regs apply (see p1215). A person remains an asylum seeker while the Secretary of State has yet to record the claim as determined or, if the asylum claim was recorded as determined prior to 5 February 1996, while an appeal was pending. A person does not retain her/his status as an asylum seeker while a second appeal is pending from an adverse decision on the first appeal: *CIS 3418/1998* para 45. Note also the effect of reg 12(11)(b) below.

Para (6) exempted those falling within reg 12(6).

Transitional arrangements and savings

12.– [² (1)]

[² (2)]

(3)-(5) *[Omitted]*

[¹ (6)-(8)]

(9)   In paragraphs (4) and (7) "the Common Travel Area" means the United Kingdom, the Channel Islands, the Isle of Man and the Republic of Ireland collectively and "the Convention" means the Convention relating to the Status of Refugees done at Geneva on 28th July 1951 as extended by Article 2(1) of the Protocol relating to the Status of Refugees done at New York on 31st January 1967

(10)   *[Omitted]*

(11)   In the Persons from Abroad Regulations–

(a)   *[Omitted]*

(b)   notwithstanding the amendments and revocations in regulations 3, 6 and 7, regulations 12(1) and (2) of the Persons from Abroad Regulations shall continue to have effect as they had effect before those amendments and revocations came into force.

Amendments

1.   Revoked by reg 3 and Sch 1 of SI 2006 No 217 as from 6.3.06.

2.   Ceased to have effect by s12(1) of the Asylum and Immigration (Treatment of Claimants, etc.) Act 2004 (for those recorded as refugees after 14.6.07).

General Note

This regulation contained transitional arrangements and savings.

Analysis

Paragraphs (1) and (2): Amendments to backdated entitlements of refugees

Paras (1) and (2) ceased to have effect from 14 June 2007 for those recorded as refugees after that date: s12(3) Asylum and Immigration (Treatment of Claimants, etc.) Act 2004, brought into effect by the Asylum and Immigration (Treatment of Claimants, etc.) Act 2004 (Commencement No. 7 and Transitional Provisions) Order 2007 SI No.1602. For these purposes, a person is "recorded as a refugee" on the day the Secretary of State notifies her/him that s/he has been recognised as a refugee and granted asylum in the UK. For the full text, see p1030 of the 19th edition. Paras (1) and (2) prevented the amendments made to the entitlements of refugees to backdated HB and CTB from having effect where the claimant sought asylum prior to 2 April 2000. Reference should be made to the version of the provisions listed in para (2) that is reproduced in the 12th edition of this book for the provisions as they stood in relation to those claimants.

Paragraphs (6) to (9)
These paragraphs prevented certain asylum seekers either from falling foul of reg 7A HB Regs 1987 by being a person from abroad and also, by virtue of reg 2(6) above, from exclusion from HB under s115 of the 1999 Act. These savings rules are now to be found in Sch 3 para 6(10)-(11) HB&CTB(CP) Regs (see p1215). See the detailed commentary on p1220.

Paragraph (11)(b): Preservation of the effect of the 1996 Regulations
The effect of this provision is to prevent the repeal of large parts of reg 7A HB Regs 1987 and reg 4A CTB 1992 Regs from affecting the scope of the transitional protection afforded by reg 12 Social Security (Persons from Abroad) Miscellaneous Amendments Regulations 1996 SI No.30 (see p1153) and hence the scope of reg 2(4)(a).

<hr/>

SCHEDULE
Persons not excluded under section 115 of the Immigration and Asylum Act 1995 from entitlement to income-based jobseeker's allowance, income support, [¹ income-related employment and support allowance] a social fund payment, housing benefit or council tax benefit

Amendment
1.   Amended by reg 69(5)of SI 2008 No 1554 as from 27.10.08.

General Note
These categories of claimant are exempted from the operation of s115 of the Immigration and Asylum Act 1999 by virtue of reg 2(1) above.

<hr/>

1.   A person who–
(a)   has limited leave (as defined in section 33(1) of the 1971 Act) to enter or remain in the United Kingdom which was given in accordance with the immigration rules (as defined in that section) relating to–
   (i)   there being, or to there needing to be, no recourse to public funds, or
   (ii)   there being no charge on public funds,
   during that limited leave; and
(b)   having, during any one period of limited leave (including any such period as extended), supported himself without recourse to public funds, other than any such recourse by reason of the previous application of this sub-paragraph, is temporarily without funds during that period of leave because remittances to him from abroad have been disrupted, provided that there is a reasonable expectation that his supply of funds will be resumed.

Analysis
There are three requirements here: first that the claimant has a relevant "limited leave", secondly that the claimant should have supported her/himself without recourse to public funds and thirdly that there has been a disruption to her/his funds coming from abroad.

"Limited leave" means leave to enter the UK which is limited to duration: s33(1) Immigration Act 1971. It should be clear from the stamp on the claimant's passport whether s/he has limited leave or not.

Most of the categories of limited leave granted under the Immigration Rules make it a condition that there be no recourse to public funds. The words may not appear on the claimant's passport, but the claimant may have been sent a letter making it clear. Failing this, reference should be made to the Rules or to the UK Border Agency. The definition of "public funds" in para 6 of the Rules includes HB and CTB.

If the immigrant's money is disrupted, s/he may be treated as not being a person from abroad for a maximum of 42 days in any one period of leave to enter (see reg 10(4) of both the HB Regs and the HB(SPC) Regs and reg 7(5) of both the CTB Regs and the CTB(SPC) Regs).

" . . . having during any one period of limited leave . . . supported himself without recourse to public funds . . . ". A period which has been extended on application to the immigration authorities counts as a single period. The protection is lost if, contrary to the condition attached to the limited leave, the claimant has made use of public funds. However, the words "any one period" seem to suggest that where a claimant has had a previous period of limited leave during which the condition was not broken but has broken it during the present period, s/he may still fulfil para 1.

A previous use of public funds due to a previous disruption of money from abroad does not prevent this condition being fulfilled. It might be arguable that the reference to "this sub-paragraph" might include a reference to a person who received HB under the old reg 7A(4A) and (6) HB Regs 1987 during a temporary disruption: see p166 of the 12th edition. Para 1(b) might be viewed as a re-enactment of reg 7A(4A) with amendments, so as to require the reference to "this sub-paragraph" to include a reference to the predecessor legislation under the Interpretation Act 1978.

"*. . . . is temporarily without funds . . . . because remittances to him from abroad have been disrupted . . . .*". It must be noted that only immigrants whose funds from abroad have been disrupted may benefit. The phrase "is temporarily without funds" refers to the state of affairs at the date of the claim or the date of the award: *CH 4248/2006*. It is not sufficient that the claimant has been without funds at some point in the past, but that ceased before the date of claim. An immigrant whose sponsor is failing to meet her/his obligations in the UK cannot benefit from its provisions. It is suggested that the disruption need not be to funds directly sent to the claimant. So if a sponsor is receiving money in the UK and that flow of funds has been disrupted, then provided that part of that money is designated for the immigrant, the immigrant is entitled to the benefit of this provision.

Whether there is a reasonable expectation that the supply of funds will be resumed is a question of fact.

2.   A person who has been given leave to enter or remain in, the United Kingdom by the Secretary of State upon an undertaking given by another person or persons pursuant to the immigration rules within the meaning of the Immigration Act 1971, to be responsible for his maintenance and accommodation and who has not been resident in the United Kingdom for a period of at least five years beginning on the date of entry or the date on which the undertaking was given in respect of him, whichever date is the later and the person or persons who gave the undertaking to provide for his maintenance and accommodation has, or as the case may be, have died.

Analysis
Under the Immigration Rules, a sponsor of a person seeking leave to enter may be required to give an undertaking to be responsible for that person's maintenance and accommodation. If the sponsor is dead, para 2 excludes the sponsored person from the effect of s115 of the 1999 Act. If there is more than one sponsor, all must be deceased.

3.   A person who–
(a)   has been given leave to enter, or remain in, the United Kingdom by the Secretary of State upon an undertaking given by another person or persons in writing in pursuance of immigration rules within the meaning of the 1971 Act, to be responsible for his maintenance and accommodation; and
(b)   he has been resident in the United Kingdom for a period of at least five years beginning from the date of entry or the date on which the undertaking was given in respect of him, whichever date is the later.

Analysis
If a sponsored immigrant is resident for five years from the *later* of the date of entry or the date of the undertaking, para 3 excludes him/her from the effect of s115.

In *R(IS) 2/02*, Commissioner Jacobs held that where a claimant has been present with leave in the UK prior to the undertaking being given, the five year period runs from the date the undertaking is given. When the undertaking was given before leave, time runs from the time that leave was granted: paras 67 to 71. He also held that the five year period need not be continuous, but may be the sum of several different periods of residence: paras 72 to 75. Although this issue was discussed by one of the judges on a further appeal to the Court of Appeal – *Shah v Secretary of State for Social Security* [2002] EWCA Civ 285, CA (reported as *R(IS) 2/02*) – the court did not interfere with the commissioner's conclusion on this point. See also the commentary to reg 12 Social Security (Persons from Abroad) Miscellaneous Amendments Regulations 1996 on p1154.

4.   A person who is a national of a state which has ratified the European Convention on Social and Medical Assistance (done in Paris on 11th December 1953) or a state which has ratified the Council of Europe Social Charter (signed in Turin on 18th October 1961) and who is lawfully present in the United Kingdom.

Analysis
The relevant states. This paragraph applies to nationals of states that have ratified the ECSMA or the European Social Charter. All ECSMA states are at present signatories of the European Social Charter. At the time of writing, the following states had ratified the Social Charter, namely the UK, Austria, Germany, France, Belgium, Luxembourg, the Netherlands, Denmark, Norway, Sweden, Finland, Iceland, Ireland, Spain, Portugal, Italy, Cyprus, the Czech Republic, Hungary, Malta, Poland, Slovakia, Turkey, Croatia, Greece, Latvia and Macedonia. It is not sufficient if the state of nationality has signed the Social Charter and so nationals of Liechtenstein, Romania, Slovenia, Switzerland and the Ukraine cannot fall within para 4.

An up-to-date list of signatories and ratifications is available at http://conventions.coe.int.

"Lawfully present" is a phrase defined in Art 11 of ECSMA. Any person who has "a permit or such other permission as is required by the laws and regulations of the country concerned to reside therein" is lawfully present in the host state. It will encompass anyone who has leave to remain in the UK. It will include those with limited leave, including those who have their leave automatically extended under the immigration legislation pending the determination of an application for an extension of leave.

A person who is present in the UK by virtue of having been granted temporary admission is "lawfully present": *Szoma v Secretary of State for Work and Pensions* [2005] UKHL 64, [2006] 1 All ER 1 (reported as *R(IS) 2/06*).

Note, however, that most ECSMA country nationals entitlement to HB/CTB will now be governed by whether they can satisfy the "right to reside test" in regs 10 and 7 of the HB (and HB(SPC)) and CTB (and CTB(SPC)) Regs respectively.

New Deal (Miscellaneous Provisions) Order 2001
(SI 2001 No.970)

General Note

This Order specifies when participation in "Intensive Activity Period" options is to be treated as training (rather than employment) under s2 Employment and Training Act 1973. In consequence any payment received by the trainee (other than a specified trading payment) is to be treated as a training allowance for the purposes of HB and CTB. See also the New Deal (Miscellaneous Provisions) Order 1998 on p1167, the New Deal (Lone Parents) (Miscellaneous Provisions) Order 2001 on p1182, the Flexible New Deal (Miscellaneous Provisions) Order 2009 (on p1245), the Community Task Force (Miscellaneous Provisions) Order 2010 (on p1246) and the Jobseeker's Allowance (Work for Your Benefit Pilot Scheme) Regulations 2010 (on p1247).

Citation, commencement and interpretation

1.–(1)   This Order may be cited as the New Deal (Miscellaneous Provisions) Order 2001 and shall come into force on 9th April 2001.

(2)   In this Order–

"facilities" means facilities provided for the participant in pursuance of the Intensive Activity Period or the Intensive Activity Period for 50 plus;

"the Intensive Activity Period" means the arrangements known by that name and made under section 2 of the 1973 Act for which only persons who are aged 25 years or over and less than 50 years on the day of entry are eligible and which are designed to help participants to obtain work or to improve their prospects of obtaining work;

"the Intensive Activity Period for 50 plus" means the arrangements known by that name and made under section 2 of the 1973 Act for which only persons who are aged 50 years or over on the day of entry are eligible and which are designed to help participants to obtain work or to improve their prospects of obtaining work;

"training allowance" means a payment made directly by the Secretary of State to a participant in the Intensive Activity Period or the Intensive Activity Period for 50 plus in connection with his participation.

Treatment of persons and payments for the purposes of the Social Security Contributions and Benefits Act 1992, the Jobseekers Act 1995 and specified subordinate legislation

2.–(1)   The provisions of this article apply for the purposes of–

(a)   Part I of the Social Security Contributions and Benefits Act 1992,

(b)   The Jobseekers Act 1995, and

(c)   The subordinate legislation specified in the Schedule to this Order.

(2)   If, for any period or periods commencing with or falling after the date on which this Order comes into force, during which a person is participating in the Intensive Activity Period or the Intensive Activity Period for 50 plus, that person receives, or is eligible to receive, a training allowance, he is to be treated for that period or those periods and in respect of his participation as not being employed but as participating in arrangements for training under section 2 of the 1973 Act; and accordingly, subject to paragraph (3), any payment made to such a person during that period or these periods in connection with his use of facilities shall be treated in the same manner as a payment of training allowance made in respect of such training.

(3)   Paragraph (2) shall not apply in respect of any trading payment made to a person receiving assistance in pursuing self-employed earner's employment whilst participating in the Intensive Activity Period or the Intensive Activity Period for 50 plus.

SCHEDULE
LIST OF SUBORDINATE LEGISLATION

[¹ The Housing Benefit Regulations 2006;]

[¹ The Housing Benefit (Persons who have attained the qualifying age for state pension credit) Regulations 2006;]

[¹ The Council Tax Benefit Regulations 2006;]

[¹ The Council Tax Benefit (Persons who have attained the qualifying age for state pension credit) Regulations 2006;]

Amendment

1.   Amended by reg 5 and Sch 2 para 14 of SI 2006 No 217 as from 6.3.06.

The Discretionary Financial Assistance Regulations 2001
(SI 2001 No.1167)

General Note to the Regulations

The DFA Regs, made under s69 CSPSSA, provide the detail of the discretionary housing payments ("DHPs") scheme, which replaced the provisions formerly found in reg 61 HB Regs 1987 and regs 51(5) and 54(4) CTB Regs 1992, for increases in HB and CTB on the grounds of exceptional circumstances of hardship.

The regulations are considerably more flexible than the repealed provisions as to the circumstances in which DHPs may be made. However, a downside of the scheme from the point of view of claimants is its exclusion from the right of appeal to the First-tier Tribunal. The government's reason for doing this was to keep the discretion firmly in the hands of the relevant local authority, and it is said that as the making of DHPs is discretionary, there is no breach of Art 6 of the European Convention of Human Rights in failing to provide for an appeal. See the commentary to Art 6 in the Human Rights Act 1998 on p125 for discussion, and the commentary to Art 8 on p127 on the question of whether a refusal to make a DHP might interfere with the right to respect for the home.

The absence of a right of appeal means that there is some scope for judicial review proceedings in relation to DHPs.

DHPs are disregarded as income for HB and CTB purposes: Sch 5 para 62 HB Regs; Sch 4 para 62 CTB Regs; they do not come within the definition of income under the HB(SPC) Regs or the CTB(SPC) Regs. Arrears of (or concessionary payments of) DHPs are disregarded as capital for HB and CTB purposes: Sch 6 para 9(1)(d) HB Regs; Sch 5 para 9(1)(d) CTB Regs; Sch 6 para 21 HB(SPC) Regs; Sch 4 para 20 CTB(SPC) Regs.

Citation, commencement and interpretation

1.–(1)   These Regulations may be cited as the Discretionary Financial Assistance Regulations 2001 and shall come into force on 2nd July 2001.

[¹ (2)   In these Regulations–

"the Housing Benefit Regulations" means the Housing Benefit Regulations 2006; and

"the Housing Benefit (State Pension Credit) Regulations" means the Housing Benefit (Persons who have attained the qualifying age for state pension credit) Regulations 2006.]

Amendment

1.   Amended by reg 5 and Sch 2 para 18(2) of SI 2006 No 217 as from 6.3.06.

Discretionary housing payments

2.–(1)   Subject to paragraphs (2) and (3) and the following regulations, a relevant authority may make payments by way of financial assistance ("discretionary housing payments") to persons who–

(a)   are entitled to housing benefit or council tax benefit or to both; and

(b)   appear to such an authority to require some further financial assistance (in addition to the benefit or benefits to which they are entitled) in order to meet housing costs.

(2)   Subject to paragraph (3) and regulations 4 and 5, a relevant authority has a discretion–

(a)   as to whether or not to make discretionary housing payments in a particular case; and

(b)   as to the amount of the payments and the period for, or in respect of which, they are made.

(3)   Paragraphs (1) and (2) shall not apply in respect of housing costs incurred in any period before 2nd July 2001–

(a)   in the case of a person entitled to council tax benefit who requires further financial assistance in order to meet his liability to pay council tax;

(b)   in the case of a person entitled to housing benefit who requires further financial assistance in order to meet housing costs (other than costs in respect of council tax) arising from his liability to make periodical payments in respect of the dwelling which he occupies as his home.

Analysis

Para (1) reproduces the basic conditions of entitlement found in s69(1) CSPSSA. A claimant need not be in receipt of both HB and CTB to qualify; entitlement to either will suffice. "Housing costs" is not defined and so in principle could cover any expenditure that is related to the provision of accommodation for the claimant and her/his family. Reg 3 excludes certain categories of need but does not otherwise cut down the breadth of the phrase. It would appear that it could cover, for example, payments of capital to a mortgagee where a CTB claimant is in danger of losing her/his home. It could also cover payments in respect of a second home that are not met by HB.

The claimant must "require" financial assistance. While there is no need to show that the claimant's circumstances are exceptional, it is likely that authorities will impose a fairly high threshold. If, for example, a claimant has any savings or other realisable capital asset at all, it is unlikely that an application for a DHP would succeed unless it could be shown that there was a need to utilise those savings in some other way (eg, to discharge a different debt) or to retain the asset. However, it is suggested that a claimant need not show that her/his circumstances are desperate – eg, by showing that eviction is imminent. It would be sufficient to show that the household budget simply cannot be balanced and that debts will inevitably mount up unless a DHP is paid. An authority considering refusal of a DHP on the ground that the claimant could obtain a loan would have to be prepared to show how such a loan could be financed.

While a claimant is not "entitled" to benefits unless they are claimed, there seems to be no reason why an authority could not refuse a DHP on the basis that a claimant should be entitled to some other benefit if a claim is made. The same would apply where other forms of social assistance are available such as social fund payments, social services assistance and housing grants. However, as s73(14) SSCBA requires the mobility component of DLA to "be disregarded in applying any enactment or instrument under which regard is to be had to a person's means", it is suggested that any amount of that benefit must be ignored.

Para (2) gives a very broad discretion as to the amount of a DHP and the form that the payments take. Except as specified in reg 4, there is no restriction on the amount of a DHP and one-off payments may be made as well as weekly payments.

It is suggested that the amounts specified in the Discretionary Housing Payments (Grants) Order 2001 may provide some indication as to the annual expenditure that each authority should be making on DHPs. If an authority is spending considerably less, then it may be possible to challenge a decision by way of judicial review on the ground that it is adopting an approach to its discretion that is too restrictive, as its permitted expenditure is a relevant factor in the exercise of its discretion: *R v Gloucestershire CC ex p Barry* [1997] AC 584, HL. However, in *CH 1175/2002* (para 10), Commissioner Fellner expressed scepticism about a similar suggestion made in this book in relation to the old exceptional hardship payments: see p399 of the 14th edition. Note: the Discretionary Housing Payments (Grants) Order 2001 is in Part 8 of the online edition of this book. See pvii for information about obtaining a copy.

There is also a broad discretion as to the period for, or in respect of which, payments can be made, subject to reg 5.

Para (3) prevents a DHP being paid in respect of the liabilities set out arising prior to 2 July 2001. Note, however, that it appears that a CTB claimant who is not receiving HB could claim a DHP in respect of arrears of rent or mortgage payments arising prior to that date.

Circumstances in which discretionary housing payments may be made

3. For the purposes of section 69(2)(a) of the Child Support, Pensions and Social Security Act 2000, the prescribed circumstance in which discretionary housing payments may be made is where a person has made a claim for a discretionary housing payment and the requirement for financial assistance does not arise as a consequence of–

(a) a liability to meet any of the ineligible service charges specified in [³ Schedule 1 to the Housing Benefit Regulations or Schedule 1 to the Housing Benefit (State Pension Credit) Regulations] (ineligible service charges);

(b) a liability to meet charges for water, sewerage or allied environmental services;

(c) a liability to meet council tax payments in a case where the person is entitled to housing benefit but not council tax benefit;

(d) a liability to make periodical payments in respect of such housing costs as are referred to in [⁴ regulation 12 of the Housing Benefit Regulations or regulation 12 of the Housing Benefit (State Pension Credit) Regulations] in a case where the person is entitled to council tax benefit but not housing benefit;

(e) a liability to meet council tax where the conditions in section 131(4) and (5) of the Social Security Contributions and Benefits Act 1992 are not satisfied and alternative maximum council tax benefit is payable;

(f) a liability to meet the increase in such payment as is referred to in [⁴ regulation 11(3) of the Housing Benefit Regulations or regulation 11(2) of the Housing Benefit (State Pension Credit) Regulations];

(g) a reduction of an amount of benefit by virtue of [⁴ section 46(5)] of the Child Support Act 1991;

(h)   a reduction of a specified amount of benefit by virtue of section 2A of the Social Security Administration Act 1992;

(i)   a reduction in the amount of a jobseeker's allowance payable by virtue of section 17 of the Jobseekers Act 1995;

(j)   the non-payability of a jobseeker's allowance or a reduction in the amount of a jobseeker's allowance payable, pursuant to a decision made by virtue of [⁶ regulation 27A of the Jobseeker's Allowance Regulations 1996 or] section 19 or 20A *[or regulations made under section 17A]* of the Jobseekers Act 1995;

(k)   the suspension of payment of an amount of benefit by virtue of section 21, 22 or 24 of the Social Security Act 1998 or section 68 of, and paragraphs 13 and 14 of Schedule 7 to, the Child Support, Pensions and Social Security Act 2000.

[¹(l)   a restriction in relation to the payment of benefit imposed pursuant to [⁵] [² section [⁷ 6B,] 7, 8 or 9 of the Social Security Fraud Act 2001] (loss of benefit provisions).]

[(m)   See Modifications below]

[⁴ (n)   a reduction in the amount of benefit due to recovery of an overpayment under Part 13 of the Housing Benefit Regulations or Part 12 of the Housing Benefit (State Pension Credit) Regulations, or recovery of excess benefit under Part 11 of the Council Tax Benefit Regulations 2006 or Part 10 of the Council Tax Benefit (Persons who have attained the qualifying age for state pension credit) Regulations 2006.]

Modifications

Reg 3 was modified in respect of people to whom the Housing Benefit (Loss of Benefit) (Pilot Scheme) (Supplementary) Regulations 2007 SI No.2474 applied. See pp1188 to1192 of the 22nd edition of this book. Sub-paragrah (m) was inserted. The modification applied until 31 October 2009.

Reg 3(j) is modified by reg 19 Jobseeker's Allowance (Work for Your Benefit Pilot Scheme) Regulations 2010 SI No.1222 (see p1247) as from 22 November 2010 but only for those ordinarily resident in a pilot area or whose address for payment of JSA is located within such an area. The modifications are shown in italics above. They cease to have effect on 21 November 2013.

Amendments

1.   Inserted by reg 2(6) of SI 2001 No 1711 as from 15.10.01.
2.   Amended by reg 10 of SI 2002 No 490 as from 1.4.02.
3.   Amended by reg 5 and sch 2 para 18(3) of SI 2006 No 217 as from 6.3.06.
4.   Amended by reg 2 of SI 2008 No 637 as from 7.4.08.
5.   Amended by reg 5 of SI 2010 No 424 as from 2.4.10.
6.   Amended by reg 4(3) of SI 2010 No 509 as from 6.4.10.
7.   Amended by reg 8 of SI 2010 No 1160 as from 1.4.10.

Analysis

Reg 3 requires that a claim must be made for a DHP. In addition, a number of circumstances are set out in which DHPs cannot be paid, that is, where the need for financial assistance arises as a consequence of:

(1)   A liability for specified ineligible service charges: sub-para (a). See the commentary to Sch 1 HB Regs on p513.

(2)   A liability for water, sewerage or "allied environmental services": sub-para (b). The latter phrase would cover, for example, charges for the emptying of a septic tank.

(3)   Council tax liabilities where a person is entitled to HB but not to CTB, or liabilities for payments listed in reg 12 of both the HB Regs and the HB(SPC) Regs where a person is entitled to CTB but not to HB: sub-paras (c) and (d).

(4)   Council tax liabilities where a person is not entitled to main CTB and "alternative maximum CTB" is payable: sub-para (e). See the commentary to s131(6) SSCBA (see p12) and reg 62 CTB Regs (see p704).

(5)   Increases in rent to cover arrears of rent or other charges, whether on the present or a previous claim: sub-para (f).

(6)   Reductions in benefit for failure to co-operate in the pursuit of child support maintenance or for failing to participate in a work-focused interview: sub-paras (g) and (h).

(7)   JSA being reduced or stopped because the claimant failed to attend an interview as required or left her/his job voluntarily or lost a job because of misconduct: sub-paras (i) and (j).

(8)   Suspension of benefit under the provisions listed – eg, pending an appeal or for non-provision of information: sub-para (k).

(9)   Reductions in benefit under the provisions of ss6B, 7, 8 or 9 Social Security Fraud Act 2001 (loss of benefit for benefit offences): sub-para (l). Until 2 April 2010, in addition, DHPs could not be paid where the need arose as a consequence of reductions under the provisions of ss62 or 63 CSPSSA (failure to comply with a community order).

(10)   Reductions in the amount of HB or CTB due to recovery of an overpayment: sub-para (n).

Note: until 31 October 2009, DHPs could not be paid where the need arose as a consequence of reductions in benefit under the provisions of s130B SSCBA (loss of housing benefit following eviction on certain grounds): sub-para (m). This sub-para applied in pilot areas only and only until 31 October 2009. See the Housing Benefit (Loss of Benefit) (Pilot Scheme) (Supplementary) Regulations 2007 SI No.2474 and the Housing Benefit (Loss of Benefit) (Pilot Scheme) Regulations 2007 SI No.2202.

Limit on the amount of the discretionary housing payment that may be made

4.   The amount of a discretionary housing payment (if calculated as a weekly sum) shall not exceed, in a case where the need for further financial assistance arises as a consequence of the liability to make–

[¹ [² (a) periodical payments in respect of the dwelling which a person occupies as his home, other than payments in respect of council tax, an amount equal to the aggregate of the payments specified in–

(i)   regulation 12(1) of the Housing Benefit Regulations less the aggregate of the amounts referred to in regulation 12B(2) of those Regulations calculated on a weekly basis in accordance with regulations 80 and 81 of those Regulations; or

(ii)   regulation 12(1) of the Housing Benefit (State Pension Credit) Regulations less the aggregate of the amounts referred to in regulation 12B(2) of those Regulations, calculated on a weekly basis in accordance with regulations 61 and 62 of those Regulations; or]]

(b)   payments in respect of council tax, an amount equal to the weekly amount of council tax liability of that person calculated on a weekly basis.

Modifications

Para 4(a) substituted by reg 5 of the Housing Benefit (Local Housing Allowance, Miscellaneous and Consequential) Amendment Regulations 2007 SI No.2870 as from 7 April 2008, save that for a person to whom reg 1(3) of those regulations applied (see p1235), the amendments came into force on the day on or after 7 April 2008 when the first of the events specified in reg 1(4) applied to her/him, or on 6 April 2009 if none had before that date.

Amendments

1.   Amended by reg 5 and sch 2 para 18(4) of SI 2006 No 217 as from 6.3.06.

2.   Substituted by reg 5 of SI 2007 No 2870 as from 7.4.08 (or if reg 1(3) of that SI applies, on the day on or after 7.4.08 when the first of the events specified in reg 1(4) applies, or from 6.4.09 if none have before that date).

Analysis

Reg 4 imposes a limit on DHPs paid weekly. Larger sums could, therefore, be paid by way of a lump sum.

In relation to periodical payments of rent or similar payments, DHPs may not be more than the weekly amount of the payments which can be met by HB, less the amounts referred to in reg 12B(2) of both the HB and the HB(SPC) Regs. However, HB entitlement need not be deducted, and so, in theory, the total payment (of HB and DHPs) could be greater than the amount of the rent liability. Liabilities that do not fall within reg 12(1) HB Regs (reg 12(1) HB(SPC) Regs), such as those listed in reg 12(2), cannot be the subject of weekly payments, though that does not prevent a lump sum being awarded.

In *Gargett, R (on the application of) v London Borough of Lambeth* [2008] EWCA Civ 1450 (18 December 2008), the Court of Appeal considered whether a local authority can exercise its power to make DHPs by paying arrears of rent, if the claimant is currently in receipt of full HB and CTB. The claimant had asked for a lump sum DHP to pay rent arrears. The local authority argued that by reg 2(1)(b) Discretionary Financial Assistance Regulations 2001, there had to be a continuing shortfall between the benefits which the claimant is currently receiving and the housing costs which s/he is currently incurring (up to the eligible rent then applying). The Court of Appeal disagreed. It held that the regulations do not expressly place such a limit on the council's discretion. The limit imposed by reg 4 applies to a DHP, whether it takes the form of a lump sum payment for the past, or a weekly payment for the future. Once a local authority has used reg 5 to determine the past or future period in respect of which the DHP is to be restricted, that period must then be divided into weeks for the purpose of calculating the amount of the DHP as a weekly sum. Reg 4 sets the amount that the DHP must not exceed, by reference to the amount of the claimant's rent with various specified deductions. Note though that although the amount of HB already received for the relevant period is not expressly specified as a deduction, by virtue of the provisions in reg 2 that DHPs are "further financial assistance" with "housing costs", the Court decided that HB already paid for past housing costs must also be deducted.

As far as liabilities for council tax are concerned, weekly DHPs may not exceed the weekly council tax liability.

[¹ Period for, or in respect of which, discretionary housing payments may be made

5.–(1)   Subject to paragraph (2), a relevant authority may restrict the period for or in respect of which discretionary housing payments may be made to such period as it considers appropriate in the particular circumstances of a case.

(2)   A relevant authority may make discretionary housing payments to a person only in respect of a period during which that person is or was entitled to housing benefit or council tax benefit or to both.]

Amendment
1.   Substituted by reg 3 of SI 2008 No 637 as from 7.4.08.

Analysis
It is important to note that claims can be made in respect of a past period as well as the future, without any need to explain a delay in seeking a DHP. However, the claimant must have been entitled to HB or CTB during the period.

Form, manner and procedure for claims

6.–(1)   A relevant authority may accept a claim for discretionary housing payments–

(a)   in such form and manner as it approves;

(b)   from–

    (i)   a person entitled to either housing benefit or, as the case may be, council tax benefit; or

    (ii)   where it appears reasonable in the circumstances of a particular case, a person acting on behalf of a person so entitled.

(2)   A relevant authority may pay discretionary housing payments to either the person entitled to housing benefit or council tax benefit, or where it appears reasonable in the circumstances of a particular case, such other person as the authority thinks appropriate.

(3)   A relevant authority shall give a person who has claimed discretionary housing payments or who has requested a review of a decision made in respect of his claim, written notice of its decision in respect of that claim or review and the reasons for that decision as soon as is reasonably practicable.

Analysis
Para (1) gives an authority a broad discretion as to the form that claims for DHPs may take. An authority could accept an oral claim and interesting arguments could arise as to the circumstances in which an individual officer can bind the authority as to the validity of a claim. Claims may be accepted from agents where it appears reasonable to do so. Authorities ought to be ready, for example, to accept claims made by solicitors and social landlords on behalf of claimants.

Para (2) gives a power to make payments to a third party where it is reasonable to do so. Thus rent arrears can be directed to a landlord. However, it seems doubtful whether an authority can effectively pay itself (eg, where there are arrears of CTB) since it is not "such other person".

Para (3) is an important provision. First, it is suggested that it confers a right to a review of a decision on a DHP, even though reg 8(1) appears to make it discretionary as to whether a review is carried out. It is suggested that reg 8(1) is concerned with the situation where a local authority wishes to review a decision of its own motion rather than on a request. If that is right, there is no specific time limit for a request, although a substantial delay in applying for a review could possibly be relevant to the exercise of a discretion on the review. The review need not take any particular form, although good administrative practice would suggest that at minimum a different officer should reconsider the case.

Secondly, there must be a written decision for which adequate reasons must be given. It is likely that the courts would expect, as a minimum, a clear explanation for why an application had failed or only succeeded in part. A failure to comply with reg 6(3) would render a decision liable to be quashed on judicial review, although it is likely that a court would expect a claimant to seek a review first where one was available.

Provision of information

7.   A person claiming or receiving discretionary housing payments shall provide a relevant authority with the following information–

(a)   particulars of the grounds of claim or, as the case may be, particulars of the grounds for a review;

(b)   changes in circumstances which may be relevant to the continuance of discretionary housing payments,

and such other information as may be specified by the relevant authority within such time as that authority thinks appropriate.

Analysis

The requirement to specify particulars of the grounds for a review is a further indication that there is a right to a review rather than it purely being in the discretion of the authority. Changes of circumstances must be disclosed by the claimant, but other information must be specified by the authority. Note that there is no prohibition on requiring information about payments such as those specified in reg 86(4) HB Regs (see p453).

Reviews

8.–(1)   A relevant authority may review any decision it has made with respect to the making, cancellation or recovery of discretionary housing payments in such circumstances as it thinks fit.

(2)   Without prejudice to the generality of paragraph (1) above, a relevant authority may, on any such review, cancel the making of further such payments and recover a payment already made where that authority has determined that–

(a)   whether fraudulently or otherwise, any person has misrepresented, or failed to disclose, a material fact and, as a consequence of that misrepresentation or failure to disclose, a payment has been made; or

(b)   an error has been made when determining the application for a payment, and as a consequence of that error, a payment had been made which would not have been made but for that error.

Analysis

Para (1) states that an authority "may" review a decision on whatever grounds it sees fit. However, it is suggested that reg 6(3) has the effect of conferring a right to a review on application. If that is not right, then the discretion to review must still be exercised reasonably and the decisions in *R (Sibley) v West Dorset DC* [2001] EWHC Admin 365, Silber J and *R (Naghshbandi) v Camden LBC* [2001] EWHC Admin 813; [2003] HLR 280, CA, Rafferty J may assist as to the circumstances in which a refusal to review may be challenged.

Para (2) deals with the effect of a review. The making of further payments may be cancelled on any basis, but the circumstances in which there can be recovery of overpayments are limited.

A review of the decision awarding a DHP is a necessary precondition of recovery. Under sub-para (a), a DHP may be recovered on similar grounds to those in s71 SSAA and reg 101(2)(a) HB Regs (see the Analysis on p488). Sub-para (b) requires the error to take place during the course of the determination, but need not necessarily be that of the officer making the decision. It would be sufficient if an officer carrying out some inquiries made an error. "Error" must, however, mean a mistake as to law or fact. It cannot apply to a situation where a reviewing officer takes the view that s/he disagrees with the first officer's judgement or exercise of discretion.

The New Deal (Lone Parents) (Miscellaneous Provisions) Order 2001
(SI 2001 No.2915)

General Note

This Order specifies that payments received during participation in the self-employment route of the "New Deal for Lone Parents" are to be treated as a training premium for the purposes of HB and CTB. See also the New Deal (Miscellaneous Provisions) Order 1998 on p1167, the New Deal (Miscellaneous Provisions) Order 2001 on p1174, the Flexible New Deal (Miscellaneous Provisions) Order 2009 (on p1245), the Community Task Force (Miscellaneous Provisions) Order 2010 (on p1246) and the Jobseeker's Allowance (Work for Your Benefit Pilot Scheme) Regulations 2010 (on p1247).

Citation, commencement and interpretation

1.–(1) This Order may be cited as the New Deal (Lone Parents) (Miscellaneous Provisions) Order 2001 and shall come into force on 13th September 2001.

(2) In this Order–

"the New Deal for Lone Parents" means the arrangements known by that name and made under section 2 of the 1973 Act for which only persons who are lone parents are eligible and which are designed to help participants to obtain work or to improve their prospects of obtaining work;

"lone parent" means a person who has no partner and who is responsible for, and a member of the same household as, a child or young person;

"the self-employment route" means receiving assistance in pursuing self-employed earner's employment whilst participating in the New Deal for Lone Parents.

Treatment of payments for the purposes of the Social Security Contributions and Benefits Act 1992, the Jobseekers Act 1995 and specified subordinate legislation

2.–(1) The provisions of this article apply for the purposes of–

(a) Part I of the Social Security Contributions and Benefits Act 1992;

(b) the Jobseekers Act 1995; and

(c) the subordinate legislation specified in the Schedule to this Order.

(2) If during any period or periods commencing with or falling after the date on which this Order comes into force a person is participating in the New Deal for Lone Parents within the self-employment route and that person receives, or is eligible to receive, either a top-up payment or other payment made to him in order to assist with the expenses of participation, any such payments made to such a person during that period or those periods in connection with his use of those facilities shall be treated–

(a) for the purposes of regulation 6(1)(d) of the Income Support (General) Regulations 1987, as a training allowance;

(b) for all other purposes, as a training premium.

The Social Security (Notification of Change of Circumstances) Regulations 2001
(SI 2001 No.3252)

General Note to the Regulations

Possible offences under ss111A and 112 SSAA 1992 include where someone fails to give prompt notification of a change of circumstances. Reg 4 of these regulations prescribes to whom, and the manner in which, a change must be reported for these purposes. Note that although for the purposes of the general duty to report a change of circumstances in reg 88 HB Regs, reg 69 HB(SPC) Regs, reg 74 CTB Regs and reg 59 CTB(SPC) Regs, notice can be accepted in a form other than in writing, for the purposes of ss111A and 112, until 1 November 2010 notice had to generally be in writing. The only exception was where reg 4(1A) applied, and then only from 5 April 2010.

Para (1A) applies where the change is a birth or a death. In such cases, the change can be reported in person at a local authority office (or in England a county council office), if such an office has been specified for reporting these changes. If the change is a death, this can also be notified by telephone to a number specified for this purpose. This provision is sometimes referred to as "Tell Us Once".

Citation and commencement

1. These Regulations may be cited as the Social Security (Notification of Change of Circumstances) Regulations 2001 and shall come into force on 18th October 2001.

Notification for purposes of sections 111A and 112 of the Social Security Administration Act 1992

2. Regulations 3 to 5 below prescribe the person to whom, and manner in which, a change of circumstances must be notified for the purposes of sections 111A(1A) to (1G) and 112(1A) to (1F) of the Social Security Administration Act 1992 (offences relating to failure to notify a change of circumstances).

Change affecting housing benefit or council tax benefit

4.–[³ (1)   to paragraphs (1A) to (1C), where the benefit affected by the change of circumstances is housing benefit or council tax benefit, notice must be given to the relevant authority at the designated office–
(a)   in writing; or
(b)   by telephone–
  (i)   where the relevant authority has published a telephone number for that purpose or for the purposes of making a claim unless the authority determines that in any particular case or class of case notification may not be given by telephone; or
  (ii)   in any case or class of case where the relevant authority determines that notice may be given by telephone; or
(c)   by any other means which the relevant authority agrees to accept in any particular case.]

[? (1A)   In such cases and subject to such conditions as the Secretary of State may specify, notice may be given to the Secretary of State–
(a)   where the change of circumstances is a birth or death, through a relevant authority, or a county council in England, by personal attendance at an office specified by that authority or county council, provided the Secretary of State has agreed with that authority or county council for it to facilitate such notification; or
(b)   where the change of circumstances is a death, by telephone to a telephone number specified for that purpose by the Secretary of State.

(1B)   Paragraph (1A) only applies if the authority administering the claimant's housing benefit or council tax benefit agrees with the Secretary of State that notifications may be made in accordance with that paragraph.]

[³ (1C)   Notice may be given to the appropriate DWP office by telephone where all the following conditions are met–

    (a)   the claimant or the claimant's partner is in receipt of income support or a jobseeker's allowance;

    (b)   the change of circumstances is that the claimant or the claimant's partner starts employment;

    (c)   as a result of the change, either entitlement to housing benefit or council tax benefit will end, or the amount of benefit will be reduced; and

    (d)   a telephone number has been provided for that purpose.]

    (2)   In this regulation [3 "appropriate DWP office",] [2 "claimant",] "designated office" and "relevant authority" have the same meaning as in the Housing Benefit (General) Regulations 1987 and the Council Tax Benefit (General) Regulations 1992.

Amendments

    1.   Amended by reg 5 and Sch 2 para 19 of SI 2006 No 217 as from 6.3.06.

    2.   Amended by reg 4(3) of SI 2010 No 444 as from 5.4.10.

    3.   Amended by reg 7 of SI 2010 No 2449 as from 1.11.10.

The Social Security (Loss of Benefit) Regulations 2001
(SI 2001 No.4022)

General Note to the Regulations

ss6A to 13 of the Social Security Fraud Act 2001 (see p1134) provide "loss of benefit" provisions where a claimant or a member of her/his family is convicted of repeat benefit offences. These regulations deal with the commencement of the disqualification period and the amount by which HB and CTB can be reduced.

PART I
GENERAL

Citation, commencement and interpretation

1.–(1) These Regulations may be cited as the Social Security (Loss of Benefit) Regulations 2001 and shall come into force on 1st April 2002.

(2) In these Regulations, unless the context otherwise requires–

"the Act" means the Social Security Fraud Act 2001;

"the Benefits Act" means the Social Security Contributions and Benefits Act 1992;

[¹ "the Council Tax Benefit Regulations" means the Council Tax Benefit Regulations 2006;]

[¹ "the Council Tax Benefit (State Pension Credit) Regulations" means the Council Tax Benefit (Persons who have attained the qualifying age for state pension credit) Regulations 2006;]

[³ "the determination day" means (subject to paragraph (2A)) the day on which the Secretary of State determines that a restriction under–

(a) section 6B or 7 of the Act would be applicable to the offender were the offender in receipt of a sanctionable benefit;

(b) section 8 of the Act would be applicable to the offender were the offender a member of a joint-claim couple which is in receipt of a joint-claim jobseeker's allowance; or

(c) section 9 of the Act would be applicable to the offender's family member were that member in receipt of income support, jobseeker's allowance, state pension credit, employment and support allowance, housing benefit or council tax benefit;]

[¹ "the Housing Benefit Regulations" means the Housing Benefit (General) Regulations 1987;]

[¹ "the Housing Benefit (State Pension Credit) Regulations" means the Housing Benefit (Persons who have attained the qualifying age for state pension credit) Regulations 2006;]

"the Income Support Regulations" means the Income Support (General) Regulations 1987;

"the Jobseekers Act" means the Jobseekers Act 1995;

"the Jobseeker's Allowance Regulations" means the Jobseeker's Allowance Regulations 1996;

"claimant" in a regulation means the person claiming the sanctionable benefit referred to in that regulation;

"disqualification period" means the period in respect of which the restrictions on payment of a relevant benefit apply in respect of an offender in accordance with section [² 6B(11) or] 7(6) of the Act and shall be interpreted in accordance with [² regulations 1A and 2]; and

"offender" means the person who is subject to the restriction in the payment of his benefit in accordance with section [² 6B or] 7 of the Act.

[³ "pay day" in relation to a sanctionable benefit means the day on which that benefit is due to be paid;]

[³ "relevant authority" in relation to housing benefit or council tax benefit means the relevant authority administering the benefit of the offender or the offender's family member.]

[³ (2A)   Where, for the purposes of section 6B of the Act, the disqualifying event is an agreement to pay a penalty as referred to in section 6B(1)(b) of the Act, the determination day is the 28th day after the day referred to in the definition of that term in paragraph (2).]

(3)   Expressions used in these Regulations which are defined either for the purposes of the Jobseekers Act or for the purposes of the Jobseeker's Allowance Regulations shall, except where the context otherwise requires, have the same meaning as for the purposes of that Act or, as the case may be, those Regulations.

(4)   In these Regulations, unless the context otherwise requires, a reference–

(a)   to a numbered regulation is to the regulation in these Regulations bearing that number;

(b)   in a regulation to a numbered paragraph is to the paragraph in that regulation bearing that number.

Amendments

1.   Amended by reg 5 and Sch 2 para 20(2) of SI 2006 No 217 as from 6.3.06.
2.   Amended by reg 2(2) of SI 2010 No 1160 as from 1.4.10.
3.   Inserted by reg 2(2) and (3) of SI 2010 No 1160 as from 1.4.10.

[¹ Disqualification period: section 6B(11) of the Act

1A.–(1)   The first day of the disqualification period for the purposes of section 6B(11) of the Act ("DQ-day") shall be as follows.

(2)   This paragraph applies where on the determination day–

(a)   the offender is in receipt of a sanctionable benefit;

(b)   the offender is a member of a joint-claim couple which is in receipt of a joint-claim jobseeker's allowance; or

(c)   the offender's family member is in receipt of income support, jobseeker's allowance, state pension credit, employment and support allowance, housing benefit or council tax benefit.

(3)   Where paragraph (2) applies and paragraph (4) does not apply (but subject to paragraph (7))–

(a)   in relation to a sanctionable benefit which is paid in arrears, DQ-day is the day following the first pay day after the end of the period of 28 days beginning with the determination day; and

(b)   in relation to a sanctionable benefit which is paid in advance, DQ-day is the first pay day after the end of the period of 28 days beginning with the determination day.

(4)   This paragraph applies where on the determination day the offender or (as the case may be) the offender's family member is in receipt of–

(a)   either housing benefit or council tax benefit or both of those benefits; and

(b)   no other sanctionable benefit.

(5)   Where paragraph (4) applies–

(a)   in relation to housing benefit or council tax benefit which is paid in arrears, DQ-day is the day following the first pay day after the end of the period of 28 days beginning with the first day after the determination day on which the Secretary of State is notified by the relevant authority that the offender or the offender's family member is in receipt of either housing benefit or council tax benefit (or both of those benefits) or has been awarded either or both of those benefits; and

(b)   in relation to housing benefit or council tax benefit which is paid in advance, DQ-day is the first pay day after the end of the period of 28 days beginning with the first day after the determination day on which the Secretary of State is so notified by the relevant authority.

(6)   Where neither paragraph (2) nor paragraph (4) applies, DQ-day is the first day after the end of the period of 28 days beginning with the determination day.

(7)   Where on the determination day–

(a)   paragraph (2) applies in the case of an offender or (as the case may be) the offender's family member, but

(b)   that person ceases to be in receipt of a benefit referred to in that paragraph before the first day of the disqualification period that would apply by virtue of paragraph (3),

DQ-day is the first day after the end of the period of 28 days beginning with the determination day.]

Amendment

1.   Inserted by reg 2(3) of SI 2010 No 1160 as from 1.4.10.

Definitions

"determination day" – reg 1(2).
"disqualification period" – reg 1(2).
"sanctionable benefit" – s6A(1) SSFA 2001.

General Note

Made under s6B(11) SSFA 2001 (see p1136), reg 1A sets the commencement date of the "disqualification period" for those subject to loss of benefit under the "one strike" scheme ("DQ-day"). For HB and CTB purposes, DQ-day is set as follows. If on the "determination day" (defined in reg 1):

(1)   the offender or a family member of the offender is in receipt of HB or CTB or both and no other sanctionable benefit, DQ-day is set under para (5);

(2)   the offender is in receipt of a sanctionable benefit other than HB or CTB (or a sanctionable benefit in addition to HB or CTB) or the offender is in receipt of joint-claim JSA, or a family member of the offender is in receipt of HB, CTB, IS, JSA, ESA or PC, DQ-day is set by para (3). However, where the offender or the family member ceases to be in receipt of any of the benefits referred to in para (2) before the first day of the disqualification period, DQ-day is instead set by para (7). Note that if the offender or family member is an HB or CTB claimant and is in receipt of IS, *income-based* JSA, *income-related* ESA or PC, the reduction is applied to those benefits and not to HB or CTB: reg 18;

(3)   neither (1) or (2) applies (eg, neither the offender nor her/his partner is in receipt of any sanctionable benefit or joint-claim JSA), DQ-day is set by para (6).

The procedure is that the Secretary of State determines whether a restriction is applicable and notifies local authorities of the persons in relation to whom a restriction is imposed. The local authority then notifies the Secretary of State that an award of benefit has been made. The Secretary of State then requires a reduction in HB or CTB to be imposed.

[⁵ Disqualification period: section 7(6) of the Act

2.–(1)   The first day of the disqualification period for the purposes of section 7(6) of the Act (''DQ-day'') shall be as follows.

(2)   This paragraph applies where on the determination day–

(a)   the offender is in receipt of a sanctionable benefit;

(b)   the offender is a member of a joint-claim couple which is in receipt of a joint-claim jobseeker's allowance; or

(c)   the offender's family member is in receipt of income support, jobseeker's allowance, state pension credit, employment and support allowance, housing benefit or council tax benefit.

(3)   Where paragraph (2) applies and paragraph (4) does not apply–

(a)   in relation to a sanctionable benefit which is paid in arrears, DQ-day is the day following the first pay day after the end of the period of 28 days beginning with the determination day; and

(b)   in relation to a sanctionable benefit which is paid in advance, DQ-day is the first pay day after the end of the period of 28 days beginning with the determination day.

(4)   This paragraph applies where on the determination day the offender or (as the case may be) the offender's family member is in receipt of–

(a)   either housing benefit or council tax benefit or of both of those benefits; and

(b)   no other sanctionable benefit.

(5)   Where paragraph (4) applies–

(a)   in relation to housing benefit or council tax benefit which is paid in arrears, DQ-day is the day following the first pay day after the end of the period of 28 days beginning with the first day after the determination day on which the Secretary of State is notified by the relevant authority that the offender or the offender's

family member is in receipt of either housing benefit or council tax benefit (or both of those benefits) or has been awarded either or both of those benefits; and
(b)   in relation to housing benefit or council tax benefit which is paid in advance, DQ-day is the first pay day after the end of the period of 28 days beginning with the first day after the determination day on which the Secretary of State is so notified by the relevant authority.

(6)   Where neither paragraph (2) nor paragraph (4) applies, DQ-day is the first day after the end of the period of 28 days beginning with the determination day on which the Secretary of State decides to award–
(a)   a sanctionable benefit to the offender;
(b)   a joint-claim jobseeker's allowance to a joint-claim couple of which the offender is a member; or
(c)   income support, jobseeker's allowance, state pension credit or employment and support allowance to the offender's family member.

(7)   For the purposes of the preceding provisions of this regulation, DQ-day is to be no later than 5 years and 28 days after the date of the conviction of the offender for the benefit offence in the later proceedings referred to in section 7(1) of the Act; and section 7(9) of the Act (date of conviction and references to conviction) shall apply for the purposes of this paragraph as it applies for the purposes of section 7 of the Act.]

Amendments
1.   Amended by reg 2 of SI 2002 No 486 as from 1.4.02.
2.   Amended by reg 25(2) of SI 2002 No 1792 as from 6.10.03
3.   Amended by Art 3 of SI 2008 No 787 as from 1.4.08.
4.   Amended by reg 56 of SI 2008 No 1554 as from 27.10.08.
5.   Substituted by reg 2(3) of SI 2010 No 1160 as from 1.4.10.

Definitions
"determination day" – reg 1(2).
"sanctionable benefit" – s6A(1) SSFA 2001.

General Note
Made under s7(6) SSFA 2001 (see p1136), reg 2 sets the commencement date of the "disqualification period" for those subject to loss of benefit under the "two strikes" scheme ("DQ-day"). For HB and CTB purposes, DQ-day is set as follows. If on the "determination day" (defined in reg 1):
(1)   the offender or a family member of the offender is in receipt of HB or CTB or both and no other sanctionable benefit, DQ-day is set under para (5);
(2)   the offender is in receipt of a sanctionable benefit other than HB or CTB (or a sanctionable benefit in addition to HB or CTB) or the offender is in receipt of joint-claim JSA, or a family member of the offender is in receipt of HB, CTB, IS, JSA, ESA or PC, DQ-day is set by para (3). Note that if the offender or family member is an HB or CTB claimant and is in receipt of IS, *income-based* JSA, *income-related* ESA or PC, the reduction is applied to those benefits and not to HB or CTB: reg 18;
(3)   neither (1) or (2) applies (eg, neither the offender nor her/his partner is in receipt of any sanctionable benefit or joint-claim JSA), DQ-day is set by para (6).
In all cases, the date cannot be more than five years and 28 days after the conviction for the later offence: reg 2(7). The period was three years and 28 days prior to 1 April 2008. See also the transitional provisions in s49(2) WRA 2007 on p167.
The procedure is the same as under reg 1A (see p1186).

PART V
HOUSING BENEFIT AND COUNCIL TAX BENEFIT

Circumstances where a reduced amount of housing benefit and council tax benefit is payable
17.–(1)   Subject to [³[²]] regulation 18, any payment of housing benefit or, as the case may be, council tax benefit which falls to be made to an offender in respect of any week in the disqualification period or to an offender's family member in respect of any week in the relevant period shall be reduced–
(a)   where the claimant or a member of his family is pregnant or seriously ill, by a sum equivalent to 20 per cent.;

(b)   in any other case, by a sum equivalent to 40 per cent.,
of the amount which is or, where he is not the claimant or is not single, would be
applicable to the offender in respect of a single claimant for those benefits on the first day
of the disqualification period or, where the payment falls to be made to an offender's
family member, on the first day of the relevant period and specified in [¹ paragraph 1 of
Schedule 3 to the Housing Benefit Regulations or, as the case may be, in paragraph 1(1)
of Schedule 3 of the Housing Benefit (State Pension Credit) Regulations, in paragraph
1(1) of Schedule 1 to the Council Tax Benefit Regulations, or in paragraph 1(1) of
Schedule 1 of the Council Tax Benefit (State Pension Credit) Regulations.

(2)   A reduction under paragraph (1) shall, if it is not a multiple of 5p, be rounded to
the nearest such multiple or, if it is a multiple of 2.5p but not of 5p, to the next lower
multiple of 5p.

(3)   Where the rate of housing benefit or council tax benefit payable to a claimant
changes, the rules set out above for a reduction in the benefit payable shall be applied to
the new rates and any adjustment to the reduction shall take effect from the beginning of
the first benefit week to commence for the claimant following the change and in this
paragraph "benefit week" shall have the same meaning as in [¹ regulation 2(1) of the
Housing Benefit Regulations or, as the case may be, regulation 2(1) of the Housing
Benefit (State Pension Credit) Regulations, regulation 2(1) of the Council Tax Benefit
Regulations, or regulation 2(1) of the Council Tax Benefit (State Pension Credit)
Regulations.]

[³ [² (4)]]
[³ [² (5)]]

Amendments

1.   Amended by reg 5 and Sch 2 para 20(3) of SI 2006 No 217 as from 6.3.06.
2.   Inserted by reg 7 of SI 2007 No 2202 as from 1.11.07. The amendment ceases to have effect on 31.10.09
     unless revoked with effect from an earlier date.
3.   Omitted by reg 2(9) of SI 2010 No 1160 as from 1.4.10.

General Note

The amount of the reduction imposed is normally 40 per cent of the personal allowance for a single claimant of
the offender's age as at the first day of the disqualification period or the relevant period. If, however, the claimant
or any member of the family is pregnant or seriously ill, the reduction is 20 per cent. Where both HB and CTB are
being claimed, it appears that the reduction is applicable to both.

A reduction will be recalculated from the next benefit week where there is a change in the amount of
entitlement: para (3).

Note that where a reduction was being applied under both this regulation and s130B SSCBA 1992 (loss of
benefit following eviction on certain grounds), under paras (4) and (5), the reduction was the greater of the
amounts. See pp1206-1207 of the 21st edition for the text of those paragraphs. The Housing Benefit (Loss of
Benefit) (Pilot Scheme) Regulations 2007 only applied in Pilot Areas and only until 31 October 2009.

Circumstances where housing benefit and council tax benefit is payable

18.   Regulation 17 shall not apply and housing benefit or, as the case may be, council
tax benefit shall be payable to an offender or to an offender's family member–
   (a)   where the offender is the claimant, he is entitled to either of those benefits during
         the disqualification period;
   (b)   where the offender's family member is the claimant, he is entitled to either of
         those benefits during the relevant period,
and the claimant is, at the same time, also entitled to income support [¹ , an income-
related employment and support allowance, state pension credit,] or to an income-based
jobseeker's allowance.

Amendment

1.   Amended by reg 2(10) of SI 2010 No 1160 as from 1.4.10.

General Note

Reg 18 confirms that where the HB or CTB claimant is entitled to IS, income-based JSA, income-related ESA or
PC, the reductions will be applied to those benefits and not to HB or CTB.

The Contracting Out (Functions of Local Authorities: Income-Related Benefits) Order 2002

(2002 No.1888)

General Note to the Order

The Deregulation and Contracting Out Act 1994 confers power on ministers to make orders permitting public bodies to contract out work to private contractors. Prior to this, powers of delegation and contracting out were limited. This Order permits local authorities to contract out most of their benefit-related functions, with the limited exceptions set out in Art 3(2). Authorities are not obliged to contract the functions out.

Local authorities are obliged to carry out random checks on decisions made by contractors: Art 4. Art 5 prohibits any contractor or employee of a contractor making a decision on a claim if s/he is a person to whom rent is payable for a dwelling in respect of which the claim is made or in which s/he has a financial interest by reason of payment of HB under that claim.

The Order was made on 18 July 2002 and so came into force, by virtue of Art 1, on 25 July 2002.

Citation and commencement

1. This Order may be cited as the Contracting Out (Functions of Local Authorities: Income-Related Benefits) Order 2002 and shall come into force on the seventh day after the day on which it is made.

Interpretation

2. In this Order–

"the Administration Act" means the Social Security Administration Act 1992;

"the Benefits Act" means the Social Security Contributions and Benefits Act 1992;

"council tax benefit" means the benefit to which section 123(1)(e) of the Benefits Act refers;

"decisions on claims" means any decisions in relation to those benefits or payments referred to in article 3(1) that fall to be made under or by virtue of–

(a) the Administration Act;
(b) the Benefits Act;
(c) section 34 of the Social Security Act 1998; and
(d) the Child Support, Pensions and Social Security Act 2000

and any Regulations and Orders made under those provisions for the time being in force and, for the purposes of this Order, references to decisions include references to any determinations embodied in, or necessary to, a decision;

"discretionary housing payment" means any payment made by virtue of regulations under section 69 of the Child Support, Pensions and Social Security Act 2000;

"housing benefit" means the benefit to which section 123(1)(d) of the Benefits Act refers;

"local authority" means a billing authority, housing authority or local authority as they are defined in section 191 of the Administration Act;

"subsidy" means rent rebate subsidy, rent allowance subsidy or council tax benefit subsidy as referred to in section 140A(2) of the Administration Act or any grant made under section 70 of the Child Support, Pensions and Social Security Act 2000 (grants towards costs of discretionary housing payments).

Functions which may be contracted out

3.–(1) In so far as it is not already lawful for functions of a local authority in relation to council tax benefit, discretionary housing payments and housing benefit under the provisions of–

(a) the Benefits Act,
(b) the Administration Act,
(c) section 34 of the Social Security Act 1998, and
(d) the Child Support, Pensions and Social Security Act 2000,

and any Regulations and Orders made under those provisions for the time being in force, to be exercised by, or by employees of, such a person (if any) authorised to do so by that authority, any such function of an authority under those provisions (not being a function excluded from section 70 of the Deregulation and Contracting Out Act 1994 by section 71(1) of that Act), other than a function specified in paragraph (2), may, if and in so far as that authority may authorise, be so exercised.

(2)   The functions referred to in paragraph (1) are–

(a)   any function relating to the claiming and receipt of subsidy;

(b)   the issue of a certificate under section 116(3)(b) of the Administration Act (as to the date on which evidence sufficient to justify prosecution came to the local authority's knowledge);

(c)   the grant or withdrawal of authorisations under section 110A(3) to (7) of the Administration Act (to exercise the powers of inspection);

(d)   the function of requiring a person to enter into arrangements under section 110AA of the Administration Act (to allow access to electronic records); and

(e)   any function under sections 139D to 139H of the Administration Act (directions by the Secretary of State).

Checking requirement attaching to the exercise of functions

4.–(1)   Subject to paragraph (5) an authorisation given under this Order in relation to any function involving decisions on claims shall include the checking requirement specified in paragraph (2), and the authorisation shall be subject to the inclusion of that requirement.

(2)   The checking requirement shall require the authorised person to–

(a)   provide a random sample of decisions on claims made on a day, of not less than 10 per cent. of those decisions, to the local authority for checking within two working days of that day;

(b)   take all reasonable steps to prevent errors identified by the local authority from recurring.

(3)   When providing a random sample for the purposes of paragraph (2)(a) above, the authorised person shall use such method of random selection as may be specified by the local authority in the authorisation or, where no such method has been specified, the authorised person shall notify the local authority of the method of random selection that has been used.

(4)   When taking reasonable steps to prevent identified errors from recurring for the purposes of paragraph (2)(b) above, the authorised person shall take such steps to prevent that error from recurring as may be required by the local authority.

(5)   An authorised person shall be subject to the checking requirement only if he employs at least one other person to carry out the work in relation to the exercise of any function involving decisions on claims.

(6)   For the purposes of this article "working day" means any day other than a Saturday, a Sunday, Christmas Day, Good Friday or a day which is a bank holiday under the Banking and Financial Dealings Act 1971 in any part of the United Kingdom.

Extent of an authorisation

5.–(1)   An authorisation given under this Order in relation to any function involving decisions on claims shall not extend to any decisions on any claims where the authorised person–

(a)   is a person to whom rent is payable for a dwelling in respect of which the claim is made; or

(b)   may otherwise be affected financially by reason of a payment of housing benefit under that claim.

(2)   An authorisation given under this Order in relation to any function involving decisions on claims shall not extend to a decision made by an employee of an authorised person on any claim where that employee–

(a)   is a person to whom rent is payable for a dwelling in respect of which that claim is made; or

(b)   may otherwise be affected financially by reason of a payment of housing benefit under that claim.

The Social Security (Habitual Residence) Amendment Regulations 2004
(SI 2004 No.1232)

Citation, commencement and interpretation

1.–(1) These Regulations shall be cited as the Social Security (Habitual Residence) Amendment Regulations 2004 and shall come into force on 1st May 2004.

(2) In these Regulations–

[¹]

Amendment

1.   Revoked by reg 3 and Sch 1 of SI 2006 No 217 as from 6.3.06.

Transitional arrangements and savings

6.–(1) Paragraph (2) shall apply where a person–

(a) is entitled to a specified benefit in respect of a period which includes 30th April 2004;

(b) claims a specified benefit on or after 1st May 2004 and it is subsequently determined that he is entitled to that benefit in respect of a period which includes 30th April 2004;

(c) claims a specified benefit on or after 1st May 2004 and it is subsequently determined that he is entitled to such a benefit in respect of a period which is continuous with a period of entitlement to the same or another specified benefit which includes 30th April 2004;

[(d) Omitted]

(2) Where this paragraph applies–

[¹ (a)]

[(b)-(d) Omitted]

(3) The provisions saved by paragraph (2) shall continue to have effect until the date on which entitlement to a specified benefit for the purposes of paragraph (1) ceases, and if there is more than one such specified benefit, until the last date on which such entitlement ceases.

(4) In this regulation ''specified benefit'' means income support, housing benefit, council tax benefit, jobseeker's allowance and state pension credit.

Amendment

1.   Revoked by reg 3 and Sch 1 of SI 2006 No 217 as from 6.3.06.

General Note

The transitional protection provided by reg 6 is now replicated in Sch 3 para 6(5)-(7) HB&CTB(CP) Regs (see p1215). Reg 10 of both the HB and the HB(SPC) Regs and reg 7 of both the CTB and the CTB(SPC) Regs are modified for those with transitional protection by those paras.

Note that the amendments made by SI 2006 No.1026 to the HB Regs, HB(SPC) Regs, CTB Regs and CTB(SPC) Regs do not affect the continued operation of the transitional and savings provided for in reg 12 Social Security (Persons From Abroad) Miscellaneous Amendments Regulations 1996, reg 6 Social Security (Habitual Residence) Amendment Regulations 2004 or para 6 Sch 3 HB&CTB(CP) Regs. See reg 11 of SI 2006 No.1026 (on p1226).

The Civil Partnership (Pensions, Social Security and Child Support) (Consequential, etc. Provisions) Order 2005

(SI 2005 No.2877)

Citation and commencement

1. This Order may be cited as the Civil Partnership (Pensions, Social Security and Child Support) (Consequential, etc. Provisions) Order 2005 and shall come into force on 5th December 2005.

Transitional provision relating to housing benefit and council tax benefit

3.–(1) Paragraph (2) applies in the case of a claimant who is a member of a couple who live together as if they were civil partners on or after 5th December 2005, in respect of whom there is an award of housing benefit or council tax benefit on 5th December 2005.

(2) In such a case, subject to paragraphs (3) and (4)–

(a) the provisions of regulation 8(2) and (10) of the Decisions and Appeals Regulations shall not apply; and

(b) a superseding decision made in consequence of the amendments made by paragraph 15, 16, 21 or 22 of Schedule 3 to this Order shall take effect–

   (i) from the date that the claimant reports to the relevant authority that the couple live together as if they were civil partners; or

   (ii) from the date on which the relevant authority otherwise becomes aware that the couple are living together as if they were civil partners; or

   (iii) where there exists an award of a relevant benefit on 5th December 2005, from the date the superseding decision is made in relation to the relevant benefit that is consequential on the amendments made by paragraph 13, 26 or 35 of Schedule 3 to this Order,

whichever is the earliest date.

(3) The relevant authority may, where the provisions of paragraph (2)(b)(i) or (ii) apply, determine such earlier effective date for the superseding decision as it considers appropriate if it is satisfied that the claimant could reasonably have been expected to report that he is a member of a couple who live together as if they were civil partners earlier than the date which would otherwise apply under that paragraph.

(4) The provisions of regulation 8(2) and (10) of the Decisions and Appeals Regulations shall apply in a case falling within paragraph (1) where the application of those provisions is advantageous to the claimant.

(5) In this article–

"couple" has the same meaning as in regulation 2(1) of the Housing Benefit (General) Regulations 1987;

"the Decisions and Appeals Regulations" means the Housing Benefit and Council Tax Benefit (Decisions and Appeals) Regulations 2001;

"relevant authority" has the same meaning as in regulation 2(1) of the Housing Benefit (General) Regulations 1987;

"relevant benefit" means income support, income-based jobseeker's allowance or a guarantee credit awarded under section 2(1) of the State Pension Credit Act 2002.

General Note

Reg 3 provided a transitional provision on the coming into force of the Civil Partnership Act 2004 on 5 December 2005. It sets out when a supersession of a decision on an award of HB or CTB is to take effect where a claimant in respect of whom there was an award on 12 December 2005, is a member of a same sex couple on or after that date. As with most social security transitional provisions, it is densely worded.

The first point to note is that the transitional rules in reg 3 only apply if the claimant is a member of a same sex couple who are not civil partners but are living together as if they were civil partners. The rule has no application to same sex couples who have entered into a contract of civil partnership.

Same sex couples who are living together as if they were civil partners will have their claims altered under reg 8(2) or (10) DA Regs, if this is advantageous to them: para (4). Otherwise, they will not have their claim(s) for HB and CTB altered (ie, they will not be treated as a "couple"), until the earliest of the following.

(1)   The date the claimant reports to the authority that s/he and her/his partner are living together as if civil partners, unless the claimant could reasonably have been expected to report that s/he was living together with someone as a civil partner from an earlier date: paras (2)(b)(i) and (3).

(2)   The date when, other than being told by the claimant, the authority first became aware that the claimant and her/his partner were living together as if civil partners, unless the claimant could reasonably have been expected to report that s/he was living together with someone as a civil partner from an earlier date: paras (2)(b)(ii) and (3). However, it is understood that the DWP advised authorities to adopt a softly softly approach to the changes introduced by the Civil Partnership Act 2004 and to not enter into proactive and intrusive investigations, and so (initially at least) most awards were only to be superseded from the date one of the couple reported that they were living together as if civil partners.

(3)   If there has been a supersession of the claimant's (or her/his partner's) award of IS, income-based JSA or the guarantee credit of PC on "civil partnership" grounds, from the same date that the IS, income-based JSA or PC award was superseded: paras (2)(b)(iii) and (5).

The Civil Partnership Act 2004 (Relationships Arising Through Civil Partnership) Order 2005

(2005 No.3137)

Citation and commencement

1. This Order may be cited as the Civil Partnership Act 2004 (Relationships Arising Through Civil Partnership) Order 2005 and comes into force on 5th December 2005.

References to stepchildren etc. in existing subordinate legislation

3.–(1) Section 246 of the Civil Partnership Act 2004 (interpretation of statutory references to stepchildren etc.) applies to the provisions of existing subordinate legislation listed in the Schedule.

(2) The application of section 246 of the Civil Partnership Act 2004 to the provisions in the Regulations set out in paragraphs 24 and 44 of the Schedule applies to those Regulations as modified in their application to persons to whom regulations 2(1) and 12(1) of the Housing Benefit and Council Tax Benefit (State Pension Credit) Regulations 2003 apply and to those Regulations as not so modified.

(3) The application of section 246 of the Civil Partnership Act 2004 to the provisions in the Regulations set out in paragraphs 27 and 47 of the Schedule applies to those Regulations as modified in their application to persons to whom regulations 2(1) and 12(1) of the Housing Benefit and Council Tax Benefit (State Pension Credit) Regulations 2003 apply.

SCHEDULE

Article 3

REFERENCES TO STEPCHILDREN ETC. IN EXISTING SUBORDINATE LEGISLATION

24. The definition of "close relative" in regulation 2(1) of the Housing Benefit (General) Regulations 1987 (interpretation).

25. Paragraphs 34(4)(b)(i) and (ii) and 34(5)(b)(i) and (ii) of Schedule 4 to those Regulations (sums to be disregarded in the calculation of income other than earnings).

26. Paragraphs 23(4)(b)(i) and (ii) and 23(5)(b)(i) and (ii) of Schedule 5 to those Regulations (capital to be disregarded).

27. Paragraphs 16(4)(b)(i) and (ii) and 16(5)(b)(i) and (ii) of Schedule 5ZA to those Regulations (Part I: capital to be disregarded).

44. The definition of "close relative" in regulation 2(1) of the Council Tax Benefit (General) Regulations 1992 (interpretation).

45. Paragraphs 35(4)(b)(i) and (ii) and 35(5)(b)(i) and (ii) of Schedule 4 to those Regulations (sums to be disregarded in the calculation of income other than earnings).

46. Paragraphs 23(4)(b)(i) and (ii) and 23(5)(b)(i) and (ii) of Schedule 5 to those Regulations (capital to be disregarded).

47. Paragraphs 16(4)(b)(i) and (ii) and 16(5)(b)(i) and (ii) of Schedule 5ZA to those Regulations (Part I: capital to be disregarded).

The Housing Benefit and Council Tax Benefit (Consequential Provisions) Regulations 2006
(2006 No.217)

Citation, commencement and interpretation

1.–(1) These Regulations may be cited as the Housing Benefit and Council Tax Benefit (Consequential Provisions) Regulations 2006 and shall come into force on 6th March 2006.

(2) In these Regulations–

"the Act" means the Social Security Contributions and Benefits Act 1992;

"the 1987 Regulations" means the Housing Benefit (General) Regulations 1987;

"the 1992 Regulations" means the Council Tax Benefit (General) Regulations 1992;

"Council Tax Benefit Regulations" means the Council Tax Benefit Regulations 2006;

"the Council Tax Benefit (State Pension Credit) Regulations" means the Council Tax Benefit (Persons who have attained the qualifying age for state pension credit) Regulations 2006;

"the Housing Benefit Regulations" means the Housing Benefit Regulations 2006;

"the Housing Benefit (State Pension Credit) Regulations" means the Housing Benefit (Persons who have attained the qualifying age for state pension credit) Regulations 2006;

"the consolidating Regulations" means the Council Tax Benefit Regulations, the Council Tax Benefit (State Pension Credit) Regulations, the Housing Benefit Regulations and the Housing Benefit (State Pension Credit) Regulations.

Continuity of the law

2.–(1) The coming into force of the consolidating Regulations does not affect the continuity of the law.

(2) Anything done or having effect as if done under or for the purposes of a provision revoked by these Regulations has effect, if it could have been done under or for the purposes of the corresponding provision of the consolidating Regulations, as if done under or for the purposes of that provision.

(3) Any reference, whether express or implied, in the consolidating Regulations or any other instrument or document to a provision of the consolidating Regulations shall, in so far as the context permits, be construed as including, in relation to the times, circumstances and purposes in relation to which the corresponding provision of any regulation revoked by these Regulations has effect, a reference to that corresponding provision.

(4) Any reference, whether express or implied, in any instrument or document to a provision of a regulation revoked by these Regulations shall be construed, so far as is required for continuing effect, as including a reference to the corresponding provision of the consolidating Regulations.

Documents referring to revoked provisions

4. Any document made, served or issued after the consolidating Regulations comes into force which contains a reference to any of the regulations revoked by these Regulations shall be construed, except so far as a contrary intention appears, as referring or, as the context may require, including a reference to the corresponding provision of the consolidating Regulations.

Transitional provisions and savings

6.–(1) The provisions of Schedule 3 to these Regulations (which contains transitional provisions and savings) shall have effect.

(2) The revocation by these Regulations of any provision previously repealed subject to savings does not affect the continued operation of those savings.

Transitory modifications
7. The transitory modifications in Schedule 4 to these Regulations shall have effect.

Amending Orders
8. An order which is made under section 150 of the Social Security Administration Act 1992 after the consolidating Regulations have been made and which amends any of the Regulations scheduled to be revoked by these Regulations shall have the effect also of making a corresponding amendment of the consolidating Regulations.

SCHEDULE 3
REGULATION 6(1)
TRANSITIONAL AND SAVINGS PROVISIONS

1.–(1)   Where a change of circumstances occurs as a result of the payment of arrears of any income (and for the avoidance of doubt income includes any benefit within the meaning of the Act) which affects a determination or decision in respect of entitlement to, or the amount of, housing benefit or council tax benefit before 6th March 1995, the provisions specified in paragraph (2) shall apply subject to the omissions specified in relation to that provision.

(2)   The provisions specified in this paragraph (which all relate to the date on which changes of circumstances are to take effect) are–
- (a)   regulations 79 of the Housing Benefit Regulations which shall apply as if paragraph (7) was omitted;
- (b)   regulation 59 of the Housing Benefit (State Pension Credit) Regulations which shall apply as if paragraph (7) was omitted;
- (c)   regulation 67 of the Council Tax Benefit Regulations which shall apply as if paragraph (9) was omitted;
- (d)   regulation 50 of the Council Tax Benefit (State Pension Credit) Regulations which shall apply as if paragraph (9) was omitted.

General Note

This is a saving provision. The Housing Benefit and Council Tax Benefit (Amendment) Regulations 1995 SI No.511 amended reg 68 HB Regs 1987 following the decision in *R v Middlesborough BC ex p Holmes* [1995] unreported, 15 February, QBD. The transitional protection provided in that SI is now in para 1. The sub-paras in the regulations cited in para 1(2) are not to have affect where arrears of income are to be taken into account for a period prior to 6 March 1995. The amendment may be of continuing relevance in overpayment cases involving a failure to disclose receipt of income.

Persons incapable of work

2.–(1)   Where, on 12th April 1995, the disability premium was applicable to a claimant by virtue of paragraph 12(1)(b) of Schedule 2 to the 1987 Regulations or paragraph 13(1)(b) of Schedule 1 to the 1992 Regulations, as in force on that date, the disability premium shall continue to be applicable to that claimant from 13th April 1995 and for so long as he is incapable of work in accordance with the provisions of, and regulations made under, Part 12A of the Act (incapacity for work).

(2)   Where, on 12th April 1995, the disability premium was applicable to a claimant and in the period from 13th April 1995 to 1st October 1995 paragraph (1) either did not apply or ceased to apply in his case, if–
- (a)   for the period for which paragraph (1) did not apply or ceased to apply, the claimant was incapable of work or was treated as incapable of work in accordance with the provisions of, and regulations made under, Part 12A of the Act (the period of incapacity); and
- (b)   any break in the period of incapacity did not exceed a period of 56 continuous days,

with effect from 2nd October 1995 for so long as he is incapable of work or is treated as incapable of work, the disability premium shall be applicable in his case.

(3)   Paragraphs (1) and (2) shall not apply to a claimant who ceases to be incapable of work or ceases to be treated as incapable of work in accordance with the provisions of, and regulations made under, Part 12A of the Act (incapacity for work) for a period of more than 56 continuous days.

(4)   Where, in any period immediately preceding 13th April 1995, the circumstances mentioned in paragraph 12(6) of Schedule 2 to the 1987 Regulations, or paragraph 13(6) of Schedule 1 to the 1992 Regulations, as in force on 12th April 1995, applied to a claimant to whom the disability premium was not applicable, that claimant shall be treated for the purposes of–
- (a)   regulations 28(8)(c) and 56(2)(e) of, and paragraph 13(1)(b) of Schedule 3 to, the Housing Benefit Regulations;
- (b)   regulations 18(11)(e) and 45(3)(e) of, and paragraph 13(1)(b) of Schedule 1 to, the Council Tax Benefit Regulations; or as the case may be,

as if he had been incapable of work in accordance with the provisions of, and regulations made under, Part 12A of the Act (incapacity for work) throughout that period.

General Note to paras 2 and 3

The Housing Benefit and Council Tax Benefit (Miscellaneous Amendments) (No.2) Regulations 1995 SI No.626 introduced amendments to the conditions for qualifying for various premiums payable as part of HB and CTB. The transitional and savings provisions for those receiving the disability or higher pensioner premium on 12 April 1995 are now in paras 2 and 3.

Analysis of paras 2 and 3

Para 2. Prior to 12 April 1995, the requirement for the disability premium under, for example, Sch 2 para 12(1)(b) HB Regs 1987 was that the claimant was incapable of work for the purposes of the sickness and invalidity benefit legislation. Under para 2, disability premium continues to be applicable to a claimant to whom it was applicable on 12 April 1995 so long as s/he is incapable of work. Gaps of up to 56 days in incapacity between 13 April and 1 October 1995 were ignored if the claimant was incapable of work on 2 October 1995. A subsequent gap of 56 days in incapacity will destroy the transitional protection. For the text of the para, see the 1994-5 edition of this book.

Para 3. Prior to 12 April 1995, the requirement for the higher pensioner premium under, for example, Sch 2 para 12(1)(a)(ii) HB Regs 1987 was that the claimant or her/his partner must have been receiving invalidity pension. The transitional rules apply where the higher pensioner premium was "applicable" (as to which see *CIS 11293/1996*) to a claimant on 12 April 1995 or during the 56 days preceding that day. *R v Secretary of State for Social Security ex p Smithson* (case C-243/90) [1992] ECR I-467, ECJ dealt with the former version of Sch 3 para 11 HB Regs (the conditions for receipt of higher pensioner premium). It was an attempt to argue that the paragraph offended against EC Directive 79/7 in that it discriminated on the grounds of sex because women lost their right to opt for invalidity benefit at 65 and not 70. It was held that HB did not fall within the directive because it was a benefit calculated on the basis of the relationship between notional and actual income, even though the notional income was calculated by reference to a risk which was within the directive – ie, sickness or invalidity.

Note that higher pensioner and other pensioner premiums were omitted from the HB Regs by SI 2008 No.1042 as from 19 May 2008 and are not relevant for the HB(SPC) Regs.

3.–(1)   Where the higher pensioner premium was applicable to a claimant on, or at any time during the 56 days immediately preceding, 12th April 1995 by virtue of [¹ paragraph 12(1)(a)(ii) of Schedule 2 to the 1987 Regulations], or paragraph 13(1)(a)(ii) of Schedule 1 to the 1992 Regulations, as in force on that date, paragraph 13 of each of the Schedules specified in sub-paragraph (2) shall, in so far as it applies to those claimants, apply subject to the amendments specified in sub-paragraph (3).

(2)   Those Schedules (which all relate to the applicable amount) are–

(a)   Schedule 3 to the Housing Benefit Regulations; and

(b)   Schedule 1 to the Council Tax Benefit Regulations.

(3)   The amendments specified in this sub-paragraph are–

(a)   in sub-paragraph (1)(a)(i), for the words "long-term incapacity benefit", substitute "an invalidity pension" and for the words "in the case of long-term incapacity benefit", substitute "in the case of invalidity pension";

(b)   in sub-paragraph (1)(a)(ii) for the words "long-term incapacity benefit" substitute "invalidity pension";

(c)   for head (b) of sub-paragraph (1), substitute–

"(b)   the circumstances of the claimant fall, and have fallen, in respect of a continuous period of not less than 28 weeks, within sub-paragraph (6) or, if he was in Northern Ireland for the whole or part of that period, within one or more comparable Northern Irish provisions.";

(d)   in sub-paragraph (3), for the words "or to be incapable of work", substitute "for the purposes of the provisions specified in that provision";

(e)   for sub-paragraphs (6) and (7), substitute–

"(6)   For the purposes of sub-paragraph (1)(b) the circumstances of a claimant fall within this sub-paragraph if–

(a)   he provides evidence of incapacity in accordance with regulation 2 of the Social Security (Medical Evidence) Regulations 1976 (evidence of incapacity for work) in support of a claim for sickness benefit, invalidity pension or severe disablement allowance within the meaning of sections 31, 33 or 68 of the Act, provided that an adjudication officer has not determined he is not incapable of work, or

(b)   he is in receipt of statutory sick pay within the meaning of Part 11 of the Act.".

Amendment

1.   Amended by reg 7(2) of SI 2008 No 1042 as from 19.5.08.

[¹ **Eligible rent**

Amendment

1.   Substituted by reg 6(2) of SI 2007 No 2870 as from 7.4.08 (or if reg 1(3) of that SI applies, on the day on or after 7.4.08 when the first of the events specified in reg 1(4) applies, or from 6.4.09 if none have before that date).

Modifications
Paras 4 and 5 substituted by reg 6(2) Housing Benefit (Local Housing Allowance, Miscellaneous and Consequential) Amendment Regulations 2007 SI No.2870 as from 7 April 2008, save that for a person to whom reg 1(3) of those regulations applied (see p1235), the amendments came into force on the day on or after 7 April 2008 when the first of the events specified in reg 1(4) applied to her/him, or on 6 April 2009 if none had before that date.

4.–(1)   Subject to the following provisions of this paragraph, the eligible rent of a person–

(a)   who was entitled to housing benefit on both the first date and the second date; or

(b)   who is liable to make payments in respect of a dwelling occupied by him as his home, which is exempt accommodation,

shall be determined in accordance with–

(i)   regulations 12 (rent) and 13 (maximum rent) of the Housing Benefit Regulations, or, as the case may be,

(ii)   regulations 12 (rent) and 13 (maximum rent) of the Housing Benefit (State Pension Credit) Regulations,

as set out in paragraph 5.

(2)   Sub-paragraph (1)(a) shall not apply to–

(a)   any determination of a person's eligible rent in a case where a relevant authority is required to determine a maximum rent (LHA) by virtue of regulation 13C of the Housing Benefit Regulations or, as the case may be, regulation 13C of the Housing Benefit (State Pension Credit) Regulations; or

(b)   any subsequent determination of his eligible rent.

(3)   Sub-paragraph (1)(a) shall only apply in a case where–

(a)   either–

(i)   the dwelling occupied as his home by a person to whom sub-paragraph (1)(a) refers is the same on both the first date and the second date; or

(ii)   the dwelling so occupied was not the same by reason only that the change was caused by a fire, flood, explosion or natural catastrophe rendering the dwelling occupied as the home on the first date uninhabitable; and

(b)   the person–

(i)   was continuously entitled to and in receipt of housing benefit between the first date and the second date in respect of the dwelling to which head (a) above applies; or

(ii)   was not entitled to or receiving housing benefit for a period not exceeding 4 weeks, but was in continuous occupation of the dwelling to which head (a) above refers between the first date and the second date; or

(iii)   is a person to whom sub-paragraph (4) applies.

(4)   This sub-paragraph applies in the case of a person (''the claimant'') who becomes, or whose partner becomes, a welfare to work beneficiary, and–

(a)   the claimant ceases to be entitled to housing benefit in respect of his residence in the dwelling he occupies as his home;

(b)   the claimant subsequently becomes re-entitled to housing benefit–

(i)   in respect of the same dwelling, or

(ii)   in respect of a different dwelling in a case to which sub-paragraph (3)(a)(ii) applies; and

(c)   the first day of that entitlement is within 52 weeks of the claimant or his partner becoming a welfare to work beneficiary.

(5)   A person shall be deemed to fulfil the requirements of sub-paragraphs (1)(a) and (3), where–

(a)   he occupies the dwelling which he occupied on the relevant date;

(b)   this paragraph applied to the previous beneficiary on the relevant date; and

(c)   the requirements of sub-paragraphs (6) and (7) are satisfied in his case.

(6)   The requirements of this sub-paragraph are that the person was, on the relevant date–

(a)   the partner of the previous beneficiary; or

(b)   in a case where the previous beneficiary died on the relevant date, was a person to whom sub-paragraph (10)(b), (c) or (d) of regulation 13 (restrictions on unreasonable payments), as specified in paragraph 5, applied and for the purposes of this sub-paragraph ? claimant" in that paragraph of that regulation shall be taken to be a reference to the previous beneficiary.

(7)   The requirements of this sub-paragraph are that a claim for housing benefit is made within 4 weeks of the relevant date and where such a claim is made it shall be treated as having been made on the relevant date.

(8)   The eligible rent of a person to whom–

(a)   regulation 10A of and Schedule A1 to the Housing Benefit Regulations (entitlement to housing benefit by refugees), or, as the case may be,

(b)   regulation 10A of and Schedule A1 to the Housing Benefit (State Pension Credit) Regulations (entitlement to housing benefit by refugees)

apply, shall be determined in accordance with–

(i)   regulations 12 (rent) and 13 (maximum rent) of the Housing Benefit Regulations, or, as the case may be,

(ii)   regulations 12 (rent) and 13 (maximum rent) of the Housing Benefit (State Pension Credit) Regulations,

as set out in paragraph 5.

(9)   Sub-paragraphs (1) to (8) above shall continue to have effect in the case of a claimant who has ceased to be a welfare to work beneficiary or whose partner has ceased to be such a beneficiary where the claimant is entitled to housing benefit at the end of the 52 week period to which sub-paragraph (4)(c) refers.

(10)   In this paragraph–

"the first date" means 1st January 1996, except in a case to which sub-paragraph (5) applies, when it shall be the relevant date;

"the second date" means any day after the first date for which a claimant's entitlement to housing benefit is to be determined;

"eligible rent" means as the case may require, an eligible rent determined in accordance with–

(a)   regulations 12B (eligible rent), 12C (eligible rent and maximum rent), 12D (eligible rent and maximum rent (LHA)) or any of regulations 12E to 12K (transitional protection for pathfinder cases) ; or

(b)   regulations 12 (rent) and 13 (restrictions on unreasonable payments) as set out in paragraph 5 of Schedule 3 to the Consequential Provisions Regulations in a case to which paragraph 4 of that Schedule applies;

"exempt accommodation" means accommodation which is–

(a)   a resettlement place provided by persons to whom the Secretary of State has given assistance by way of grant pursuant to section 30 of the Jobseekers Act 1995 (grants for resettlement places); and for this purpose "resettlement place" shall have the same meaning as it has in that section; or

(b)   provided by a non-metropolitan county council in England within the meaning of section 1 of the Local Government Act 1972, a housing association, a registered charity or voluntary organisation where that body or a person acting on its behalf also provides the claimant with care, support or supervision;

"imprisoned" means detained in custody pending sentence upon conviction or under a sentence imposed by a court;

"previous beneficiary" means a person–

(a)   who died, left the dwelling or was imprisoned, as the case may be;

(b)   who was on that date in receipt of housing benefit or was on that date within 52 weeks of having become a welfare to work beneficiary; and

(c)   to whom this regulation applied on that date;

and, in this paragraph, a reference to a person occupying a dwelling as his home shall be taken to include a person who is treated as occupying a dwelling as his home by virtue of regulation 7 of the Housing Benefit Regulations or, as the case may be, regulation 7 of the Housing Benefit (State Pension Credit) Regulations;

"the qualifying age for state pension credit" means (in accordance with section 1(2)(b) and (6) of the State Pension Credit Act 2002)–

(a)   in the case of a woman, pensionable age; or

(b)   in the case of a man, the age which is pensionable age in the case of a woman born on the same day as the man;

"relevant authority" means an authority administering housing benefit;

"the relevant date" means the date–

(a)   of the death of a previous beneficiary;

(b)   on which a previous beneficiary who was the claimant's partner left the dwelling so that he and the claimant ceased to be living together as husband and wife; or

(c)   on which a previous beneficiary, other than a beneficiary to whom regulation 7(13) of the Housing Benefit Regulations or, as the case may be, regulation 7(13) of the Housing Benefit (State Pension Credit) Regulations applied, was imprisoned, but only where on that date he was the partner of the claimant,

as the case may be;

"state pension credit" means state pension credit under the State Pension Credit Act 2002;

"welfare to work beneficiary" means a person to whom regulation 13A(1) of the Social Security (Incapacity for Work) (General) Regulations 1995 applies.

General Note

Reg 10 Housing Benefit (General) Amendment Regulations 1995 SI No.1644 provided important protection for the residents of certain types of supported accommodation ("exempt accommodation") and for certain existing claimants and their families, from the "local reference rent" rules on rent restrictions which were originally introduced on 2 January 1996. For those residents and categories of claimant, reg 11 HB Regs 1987 applied in its old form. This scheme, referred to in this book as the "pre-January 1996" rules, is now in paras 4 and 5. See p297 for a summary of the three rent restriction schemes and when these can potentially apply.

If the pre-January 1996 rules apply, "rent" and "eligible rent" for the purposes of para 4(1) are assessed under reg 12 and "maximum rent" under reg 13 of both the HB Regs and the HB(SPC) Regs as set out in para 5. In simple terms, "eligible rent" is the contractual rent, minus ineligible services unless the authority decides that it should be restricted. If it does, it reduces eligible rent to the amount it considers appropriate. Reductions can also be made if eligible rent increases during an award of HB: reg 13ZA as inserted by para 5(3).

Analysis

The general rule, as set out in sub-para (1), is that there are two categories of claimants whose eligible rent is to be assessed under the "pre-January 1996" rules. The eligible rent of those in "exempt accommodation" is assessed under these rules indefinitely. The eligible rent of those who have been entitled to HB since 1 January 1996 is assessed under these rules while they retain transitional protection, as is the eligible rent of those who inherit the protection.

Sub-paragraphs (1)(b) and (10): Exempt accommodation

Under sub-para (1)(b), the eligible rent of claimants living in "exempt accommodation" must be determined under regs 12 and 13 as set out in para 5 (on p1203). The language of para 4(1) makes this mandatory, even though such claimants are not excluded from the requirement for an authority to apply to the rent officer for a determination under reg 14 of both the HB Regs and the HB(SPC) Regs (the "local reference rent" rules). Such claimants are also excluded from assessment under the "local housing allowance" rules by reg 13C(5)(b) of both the HB Regs and the HB(SPC) Regs.

"Exempt accommodation" is defined in sub-para (10). It is the dwelling occupied by the claimant as her/his home which must come within the definition of exempt accommodation. If a building contains two or more dwellings, the definition of "exempt accommodation" must be applied in relation to each dwelling, and not in relation to the building as a whole: *CH 1289/2007*. The accommodation must either be a "resettlement place" (as described in sub-para (a) of the definition) or accommodation provided by specified bodies where care, support or supervision is provided to the claimant by that body or a person acting on its behalf (as described in sub-para (b) of the definition). For "housing association" and "voluntary organisation", see reg 2 HB Regs on pp213 and 217.

"Provided by" means that the accommodation is provided by the owner or other person (eg, a tenant or intermediate landlord) who, but for the grant to the claimant of the tenancy or licence, would have the right to possession, and therefore the right to permit occupation of it, and to whom the obligation to pay rent or licence fee is owed: *CH 2726/2008*; *Chorley BC v IT* (HB) [2009] UKUT 107 (AAC); [2010] AACR 2. The definition does not encompass persons who have played a part, however important, in the accommodation becoming available, but who have no proprietary interest in the accommodation and no entitlement to the rent. In *CH 3900/2005*, Commissioner Pacey said that the accommodation must actually be provided by one of the bodies listed. This does *not* include instructing, arranging or facilitating privately rented accommodation through a third party: *R(H) 2/07* considered and applied.

In *CH 1289/2007*, Commissioner Turnbull said that the definition of "exempt accommodation" turns on whether the landlord provides "the claimant" with care, support or supervision. A claimant's accommodation will not be exempt if no (or only minimal) care, support or supervision is provided to her/him by the landlord, however much care, support or supervision may be provided to other tenants of the landlord. He pointed out that this "does not of course mean that it will always, or perhaps even usually, be necessary, in a case where a landlord has a number of tenants in a building (or even several buildings) to obtain and present evidence directed to the provision of care, support or supervision to each occupant individually. The landlord may be able to present evidence showing that the level of support provided is broadly similar in relation to all of them. Or there may be evidence of an assessment process whereby only applicants with at least a particular level of need are accepted as tenants."

In *R(H) 2/07*, Commissioner Turnbull concluded – when dealing with the same definition of exempt accommodation in reg 10(6) Housing Benefit (General) Amendment Regulations 1995 (SI 1995 No.1644), which sub-para 10(b) replaces – that the definition does not extend to a situation where the accommodation provider (ie, the landlord) neither provides nor has provided on its behalf the care, support or supervision. The landlord must either actually provide the care itself or have contracted for it to be provided on its behalf. Accordingly if the care provider is not the landlord and instead has a contract with the local authority Supporting People section to provide support, the accommodation will not normally be exempt. The same commissioner, in *R(H) 7/07*, emphasises that if the landlord is providing the care, support or supervision s/he need not be the main provider, nor must s/he be providing it pursuant to some contractual or statutory obligation; but the care support or supervision provided by the landlord must be more than a token or minimal amount. Note that an application for judicial review was dismissed in *R(S) v a Social Security Commissioner and Another* [2009] EWHC 2221 (Admin), in which the claimant sought to argue that *R(H) 2/07* was wrongly decided.

The care, support or supervision must be provided either by, or on behalf of, the landlord. The words "or acting on its behalf" in sub-para (b) of the definition means acting on its behalf in providing the care support, or supervision. It is not sufficient that a third party is acting on behalf of the landlord in some other respect. The third party must also be acting on the landlord's behalf in providing care, etc: *R(H) 6/08*, an interim decision of Commissioner Turnbull.

In his interim decision in *R(H) 4/09*, Commissioner Turnbull considered to what extent it is permissible to take into account support which is available to tenants generally, but not taken advantage of by a particular tenant. "Care" and "supervision" must actually be provided by the landlord. It is not enough that they are available should the tenant wish to call for them. However, it may be that the making available of certain types of service itself amounts to the provision of "support", but the support provided must be more than minimal. He said that there were at least two factors to which regard must be had. The first is the extent of the support services which are in reality available, having regard to the resources devoted by the landlord to providing the support and the number of tenants among whom those resources are spread. The second factor is the extent to which there is in practice any real likelihood that the claimant would need the available support.

In *Salford CC v PF* [2009] UKUT 150 (AAC), Judge Turnbull decided that provided the support would benefit the claimant to a significant extent, and therefore is needed, there is no additional test of whether it is in all the circumstances reasonable to provide support. He said that what matters is simply whether support is provided to more than a minimal extent, and that it was implicit that support is not "provided" unless there is in fact some need for it.

In *Bristol CC v AW* [2009] UKUT 109 (AAC), the claimant's rent of £503.75 included a sum of £10 for "supporting people charges". The authority argued that the amount indicated support at only a minimal level. However, Judge Turnbull said that £10 was not an amount so small that it indicated that the support to be provided by the landlord, over and above its ordinary property management functions, must be minimal. £10 a week is not an obviously nominal or token payment. The judge accepted an argument from the claimant that a satisfactory test for determining whether support of more than a minimal amount is provided is to ask whether the support provided was likely to make a real difference to the claimant's ability to live in the property.

The final decisions in *R(H) 4/09* and *R(H) 6/08* (and a third appeal, *CH 2805/2007*) were made by Commissioner Turnbull after a joint hearing. In all three cases he found that the claimants did not have "exempt accommodation". In his decision, he made a number of points about what amounted to "provides . . . support" for the purposes of the definition in sub-para (10).

(1)   The word "support" connotes the giving of advice and assistance to the claimant in coping with the practicalities of everyday life. It does not extend to scrutinising the arrangements for the provision of care, support and supervision by some other body, with a view to remedying perceived defects or to recommending improvements.

(2)   The word "support" involves the landlord doing something more than, or different from, the exercise of its ordinary property management functions. A landlord does not "provide . . . support" to a tenant by doing what any prudent landlord would do in the management of its property – eg, by complying with its repairing obligations.

(3)   The making available of certain types of support is capable of amounting to the provision of support within the ordinary meaning of the words "provides . . . support", even if no advantage is taken of it in the period under consideration, if what is being offered by way of advice and remedial action extends beyond ordinary housing management. The commissioner cited the example of a landlord making a properly staffed telephone service available whereby tenants could seek advice which, if given, amounts to "support". This would amount to the provision of support during any particular period, whether or not the tenant in fact makes use of the service during that period, subject to the proviso that there had to be a real prospect that the tenant would find the service of use from time to time. In determining whether such a service or facility amounts to the provision of support to any particular tenant to a more than minimal extent, regard must be had to the degree of likelihood that the particular tenant will ever need to take advantage of it and in determining that regard must be had to the extent to which support is available from elsewhere.

(4)   The words "provides . . . support" imply a degree of continuity in the available support. They therefore do not include any activities of the landlord which were involved in setting up the scheme nor, for example, advice and consultation in relation to the acquisition of the building and the tenant's move to it, nor the making of adaptations to the building which are carried out before or within a short time after the commencement of the tenancy.

(5)   The willingness and ability to intervene in situations where there appears to be a serious failing in the care and support regime in exceptional cases does not fall within the words "provides . . . support".

In *Chorley BC v IT* (HB) [2009] UKUT 107 (AAC); [2010] AACR 2, Judge Turnbull decided that "support" is not confined to counselling, advising, encouraging etc, the claimant. Although carrying out repairs is normally no more than the fulfilment of the landlord's repairing obligations, and therefore does not go beyond ordinary housing management, if the landlord is arranging for the carrying out of repairs which clearly go beyond ordinary housing management, this can amount to support. For example, if, owing to the nature of the tenant's disabilities, performance of the landlord's repairing obligations imposes a materially greater burden on the landlord than would otherwise be the case, performance of that greater burden may be capable of amounting to the provision of support.

In *Bristol CC v AW* [2009] UKUT 109 (AAC), Judge Turnbull said that a landlord's help in taking an appeal to the First-tier Tribunal could not be taken into account as an item of "support" going beyond ordinary property management. He said that if a landlord is not providing support within the meaning of the definition of "exempt accommodation", accommodation cannot be brought within the definition by virtue of the fact that the landlord intends to support the tenant by taking an adverse decision on an HB claim to appeal. In his judgment it could not be right that what would otherwise be a bad case can be made into a good one by virtue simply of the landlord's willingness to support the tenant by taking the case to appeal.

Sub-paragraphs (1) to (4): Entitlement to HB since 1 January 1996
Under sub-para (1)(a), transitional protection that was provided by reg 10 Housing Benefit (General) Amendment Regulations 1995 SI No.1644, continues for those who have been continuously entitled to HB since 1 January 1996, who (generally) continue to occupy the same dwelling, and who fulfil other conditions. If sub-para (1)(a) applies, eligible rent must be determined under regs 12 and 13 as set out in para 5. Note that para (1)(a) cannot apply where the authority is required to determine a "maximum rent (LHA)" by virtue of reg 13C HB Regs: sub-para (2). Unless any of the exceptions in reg 13C(5) apply (for which see p317), an authority will be required to determine a maximum rent (LHA) where a claim for HB is made on or after 7 April 2007 or where there is a change of dwelling during an award of HB after that date: reg 13C(2)(a) to (c) of both the HB Regs and the HB(SPC) Regs. In this event, transitional protection will be lost.

Linking rules are provided in sub-paras (3) and (4) where there is a break in entitlement to, and receipt of, HB of no more than four weeks (52 weeks if the claimant or her/his partner is a welfare to work beneficiary). In addition, there is provision for protection to be inherited under sub-paras (5) to (7). However, because of the effect of sub-para (2), the linking rules will only apply where the authority is *not* required to determine a "maximum rent (LHA)" by virtue of reg 13C HB Regs – ie, where any of reg 13C(5)(a) to (e) of either the HB Regs or the HB(SPC) Regs applies.

Sub-para (3): Further conditions. The claimant must be occupying the same dwelling throughout the whole period, save for any period in which the dwelling was uninhabitable as a result of one of the disasters mentioned in sub-para (3)(a)(ii). If the dwelling is permanently uninhabitable then the transitional protection is presumably retained at the claimant's new property, unless sub-para (2) above now applies: see, for example, reg 13C(2)(c) HB Regs. If the property is repaired, it appears that the transitional protection is lost unless the claimant moves back. Clearly, a certain period of time will have to be allowed to enable her/him to move back in. Note that by virtue of the definition of "previous beneficiary" in sub-para (10), the question of whether a person can be treated as occupying a dwelling must be resolved by reference to reg 7 of both the HB Regs and the HB(SPC) Regs.

Sub-paras (3)(b)(ii) and (4). Breaks in entitlement to (or receipt of) HB of up to four weeks are ignored, extended to 52 weeks if the claimant or her/his partner is a "welfare to work beneficiary", as defined in sub-para (10) (but see the discussion above on the application of sub-para (2)). Note: the 52-week linking period was not extended when the linking period for welfare to work beneficiaries was extended to 104 weeks.

Welfare to work beneficiaries are broadly those who have stopped receiving benefits claimed on the basis of their incapacity for work to try out paid work or training. The rules allow the welfare to work beneficiary to return to the same level of benefit that s/he was receiving before starting the work or training, so long as this was within a 104 week linking period. See CPAG's *Welfare Benefits and Tax Credits Handbook* for further details. Note that oddly, sub-para (4) has not been amended with the introduction of ESA from 27 October 2007.

Sub-paragraphs (5) to (7): Inherited protection
Under these provisions, a claimant is deemed to fall within sub-paras (1)(a) and (3) above if s/he fulfils four conditions. The common theme is that the claimant takes over the protection from a "previous beneficiary" who was claiming in respect of the same home. That person must have died, left the dwelling or been imprisoned. However, see the discussion above about the application of sub-para (2).

(1) The claimant occupies the same dwelling as was occupied on the relevant date: sub-para (5)(a). "Relevant date" is defined in sub-para (10).

(2) The previous beneficiary had the benefit of the transitional protection: sub-para (5)(b). It would appear that the previous beneficiary need not have fallen within the above two categories her/himself – it is sufficient if s/he also inherited the transitional protection under these provisions. An example will show how this might work. A and B were living in a property on 31 December 1995. A claimed HB. A then left B on 1 April 1996. B claimed HB herself. On 1 November 1997 C moved in with B. B dies on 1 January 1999. C is entitled to the transitional protection if he satisfies all the other conditions.

(3) Under sub-para (6), the claimant must either have been the partner of the previous beneficiary or a person to whom para (10)(b), (c) or (d) of reg 13 as set out in para 5(2) below applied in relation to the previous beneficiary. See the Analysis of reg 13ZA HB Regs on p315, which refers to the same categories of person.

(4) The claimant claims HB within four weeks of the relevant date: sub-para (7). The claim is then treated as made on the relevant date.

[¹**5.**–(1) For the purposes of paragraph 4(1), regulation 12 of both the Housing Benefit Regulations and the Housing Benefit (State Pension Credit) Regulations is as follows–
''**Rent**
12.–(1) Subject to the following provision of this regulation, the payments in respect of which housing benefit is payable in the form of a rent rebate or allowance are the following periodical payments which a person is liable to make in respect of the dwelling which he occupies as his home–
(a) payments of, or by way of, rent;
(b) payments in respect of a licence or permission to occupy the dwelling;
(c) payments by way of mesne profits or, in Scotland, violent profits;
(d) payments in respect of, or in consequence of, use and occupation of the dwelling;

(e) payments of, or by way of, service charges payment of which is a condition on which the right to occupy the dwelling depends;

(f) mooring charges payable for a houseboat;

(g) where the home is a caravan or a mobile home, payments in respect of the site on which it stands;

(h) any contribution payable by a person resident in an almshouse provided by a housing association which is either a charity of which particulars are entered in the register of charities established under section 3 of the Charities Act 1993 (register of charities) or an exempt charity within the meaning of that Act, which is a contribution towards the cost of maintaining that association's almshouses and essential services in them;

(i) payments under a rental purchase agreement, that is to say an agreement for the purchase of a dwelling which is a building or part of one under which the whole or part of the purchase price is to be paid in more than one instalment and the completion of the purchase is deferred until the whole or a specified part of the purchase price has been paid; and

(j) where, in Scotland, the dwelling is situated on or pertains to a croft within the meaning of section 3(1) of the Crofters (Scotland) Act 1993, the payment in respect of the croft land.

(2) A rent rebate or, as the case may be, a rent allowance shall not be payable in respect of the following periodical payments–

(a) payments under a long tenancy except a shared ownership tenancy granted by a housing association or a housing authority;

(b) payments under a co-ownership scheme;

(c) payments by an owner;

(d) payments under a hire purchase, credit sale or conditional sale agreement except to the extent the conditional sale agreement is in respect of land; and

(e) payments by a Crown tenant.

(3) Subject to any apportionment in accordance with paragraphs (4) and (5) and to regulations 13 and 13ZA (restrictions on unreasonable payments and rent increases), the amount of a person's eligible rent shall be the aggregate of such payments specified in paragraph (1) as he is liable to pay less–

(a) except where he is separately liable for charges for water, sewerage or allied environmental services, an amount determined in accordance with paragraph (6);

(b) where payments include service charges which are wholly or partly ineligible, an amount in respect of the ineligible charges determined in accordance with Schedule 1; and

(c) where he is liable to make payments in respect of any service charges to which paragraph (1)(e) does not apply, but to which paragraph 3(2) of Schedule 1 (unreasonably low service charges) applies in the particular circumstances, an amount in respect of such charges determined in accordance with paragraph 3(2) of Schedule 1.

(4) Where the payments specified in paragraph (1) are payable in respect of accommodation which consists partly of residential accommodation and partly of other accommodation, only such proportion thereof as is referable to the residential accommodation shall count as eligible rent for the purposes of these Regulations.

(5) Where more than one person is liable to make payments in respect of a dwelling, the payments specified in paragraph (1) shall be apportioned for the purpose of calculating the eligible rent for each such person having regard to all the circumstances, in particular, the number of such persons and the proportion of rent paid by each such person.

(6) The amount of the deduction referred to in paragraph (3) shall be–

(a) except in a case to which sub-paragraph (c) applies, if the dwelling occupied by the claimant is a self-contained unit, the amount of the charges;

(b) in any other case except one to which sub-paragraph (c) applies, the proportion of those charges in respect of the self-contained unit, which is obtained by dividing the area of the dwelling occupied by the claimant by the area of the self-contained unit of which it forms part; or

(c) where the charges vary in accordance with the amount of water actually used, the amount which the appropriate authority considers to be fairly attributable to water and sewerage services, having regard to the actual or estimated consumption of the claimant.

(7) In this regulation and Schedule 1–

"service charges" means periodical payments for services, whether or not under the same agreement as that under which the dwelling is occupied, or whether or not such a charge is specified as separate from or separately identified within other payments made by the occupier in respect of the dwelling; and

"services" means services performed or facilities (including the use of furniture) provided for, or rights made available to, the occupier of a dwelling."

General Note

As noted above, reg 10 of SI 1995 No.1644 provided important protection for the residents of certain types of accommodation (and certain existing claimants and their families) from the rules on rent restrictions which were introduced on 2 January 1996. For those categories of claimant, reg 10 HB Regs 1987 applied in its old form. The old form of reg 10 is now provided in the version of reg 12 of both the HB Regs and the HB(SPC) Regs as set out in para 5(1). The regulation is largely the same as the current version of provisions in the HB Regs and the HB(SPC) Regs, so reference to the commentary in the HB Regs can be made. For:

– paras (1), (2) and (8), see reg 12(1), (2) and (8) HB Regs;

– paras (4) to (6), see reg 12B(3) to (5) HB Regs;
– para (3)(a) to (c), see reg 12B(2)(a) to (c) HB Regs.
Note that under this version of reg 12, eligible rent is, subject to any apportionment under paras (4) and (5), and to reg 13 (as set out in para 5(2)) and reg 13ZA (as set out in para 5(3)), the aggregate of the payments specified in para (1), less the charges set out in para (3)(a) to (c).

---

(2)   For the purposes of paragraph 4(1), regulation 13 of both the Housing Benefit Regulations and the Housing Benefit (State Pension Credit) Regulations is as follows–

"Restrictions on unreasonable payments

13.–(1)   Where a rent is registered in respect of a dwelling under Part 4 or 5 of the Rent Act 1977 or Part 4 or 7 of the Rent (Scotland) Act 1984 and the rent recoverable from a claimant is limited to the rent so registered, his eligible rent determined in accordance with regulation 12 (rent) shall not exceed the rent so registered.

(2)   Where a rent has been determined by a rent assessment committee or a private rented housing committee in respect of a dwelling under Part 1 of the Housing Act 1988 or Part 2 of the Housing (Scotland) Act 1988, the claimant's eligible rent determined in accordance with regulation 12 shall not exceed the rent determined by the committee during the twelve months beginning with the first day on which that determination had effect.

(3)   The relevant authority shall consider–

(a)   whether by reference to a determination or re-determination made by a rent officer in exercise of a function conferred on him by an order under section 122 of the Housing Act 1996 or otherwise, whether a claimant occupies a dwelling larger than is reasonably required by him and others who also occupy that dwelling (including any non-dependants of his and any person paying rent to him) having regard in particular to suitable alternative accommodation occupied by a household of the same size; or

(b)   whether by reference to a determination or re-determination made by a rent officer in exercise of a function conferred on him by an order under section 122 of the Housing Act 1996 or otherwise, whether the rent payable for his dwelling is unreasonably high by comparison with the rent payable in respect of suitable alternative accommodation elsewhere,

and, where it appears to the authority that the dwelling is larger than is reasonably required or that the rent is unreasonably high, the authority shall, subject to paragraphs (4) to (7), treat the claimant's eligible rent, as reduced by such amount as it considers appropriate having regard in particular to the cost of suitable alternative accommodation elsewhere and the claimant's maximum housing benefit shall be calculated by reference to the eligible rent as so reduced.

(4)   If any person to whom paragraph (10) applies–

[⁴ (a)   has attained the qualifying age for state pension credit; or]

[¹ (b)   is incapable of work for the purposes of Part 12A of the Act; or]

(c)   is treated as capable of work in accordance with regulations made under section 171E of the Act; or

[² (ca) has limited capability for work [³ within the meaning of section 1(4)] of the Welfare Reform Act 2007; or

(cb)   is treated as not having limited capability for work in accordance with regulations made under paragraph 1(a) of Schedule 2 to that Act (employment and support allowance: supplementary provisions); or]

(d)   is a member of the same household as a child or young person for whom he or his partner is responsible,

no deduction shall be made under paragraph (3) unless suitable cheaper alternative accommodation is available and the authority considers that, taking into account the relevant factors, it is reasonable to expect the claimant to move from his present accommodation.

(5)   No deduction shall be made under paragraph (3) for a period of 12 months from the date of death of any person to whom paragraph (10) applied or, had a claim been made, would have applied, if the dwelling which the claimant occupies is the same as that occupied by him at that date except where the deduction began before the death occurred.

(6)   For the purposes of paragraph (5), a claimant shall be treated as occupying the dwelling if paragraph (13) of regulation 7 (circumstances in which a person is to be treated as occupying a dwelling) is satisfied and for that purpose sub-paragraph (b) of that paragraph shall be treated as if it were omitted.

(7)   Without prejudice to the operation of paragraph (4), but subject to paragraph (8), where the relevant authority is satisfied that a person to whom paragraph (10) applies was able to meet the financial commitments for his dwelling when they were entered into, no deduction shall be made under paragraph (3) during the first 13 benefit weeks of the claimant's award of housing benefit.

(8)   Paragraph (7) shall not apply where a claimant was previously entitled to benefit in respect of an award of housing benefit which fell wholly or partly less than 52 weeks before the commencement of his current award of housing benefit.

(9)   For the purposes of this regulation–

(a)   in deciding what is suitable alternative accommodation, the relevant authority shall take account of the nature of the alternative accommodation and the facilities provided having regard to the age and state of health of all the persons to whom paragraph (10) applies and, in particular, where a claimant's present dwelling is occupied with security of tenure, accommodation shall not be treated as suitable alternative accommodation unless that accommodation will be occupied on terms which will afford security of tenure reasonably equivalent to that presently enjoyed by the claimant; and

(b)   the relevant factors in paragraph (4) are the effects of a move to alternative accommodation on–

    (i)   the claimant's prospects of retaining his employment; and

    (ii)   the education of any child or young person referred to in paragraph (4)(d) if such a move were to result in a change of school.

(10)   This paragraph applies to the following persons–

(a)   the claimant;

(b)   any member of his family;

(c)   if the claimant is a member of a polygamous marriage, any partners of his and any child or young person for whom he or a partner is responsible and who is a member of the same household;

(d)   subject to paragraph (11), any relative of the claimant or his partner who occupies the same dwelling as the claimant, whether or not they reside with him.

(11)   Paragraph (10)(d) shall only apply to a relative who has no separate right of occupation of the dwelling which would enable him to continue to occupy it even if the claimant ceased his occupation of it.''

Amendments

1.   Amended by reg 7(3) of SI 2008 No 1042 as from 19.5.08.

2.   Inserted by reg 2 of SI 2008 No 1082 as from 27.10.08.

3.   Amended by reg 25 of SI 2008 No 2428 as from 27.10.08.

4.   Substituted by reg 41 of SI 2009 No 1488 as from 6.4.10.

General Note

As noted above, reg 10 of SI 1995 No.1644 provided important protection for the residents of certain types of accommodation (and for certain existing claimants and their families) from the rules on rent restrictions which were introduced on 2 January 1996. For those categories of claimant, reg 11 HB Regs 1987 applied in its old form. The old form of reg 11 is now provided in the version of reg 13 of both the HB Regs and the HB(SPC) Regs as set out in para 5(2).

Analysis of reg 13 as set out in para 5(2)

Much of the large body of caselaw concerned with the old reg 11 HB Regs 1987 consists of cases decided on the facts and evidence before the court. However, many of these offer useful illustrations of the approach of the court.

Paragraphs (1) and (2): Set rents

Para (1) only affects tenancies created before 15 January 1989 or, in Scotland, 2 January 1989. The Rent Acts do not apply to any tenancies created after those dates. Where they do apply – and a rent has been registered – the tenant is not legally liable to pay the landlord more than the registered rent so the eligible rent could never exceed the registered rent in any event. This paragraph merely makes that explicit.

A register of the accommodation in respect of which a fair rent has been registered in any particular area is maintained by the local Valuation Office and is open to public inspection. It is also available at www.voa.gov.uk.

If a "fair rent" has been registered but the authority uses its powers under para (3) to restrict the eligible rent to a lower figure, the tenant remains liable to the landlord for the balance. This is unlikely to happen in practice unless the claimant's accommodation is unreasonably large under sub-para (3)(a).

Para (2). Rent Assessment Committees (in Scotland, Private Rented Housing Committees) have the power to assess market rents for certain assured and assured shorthold tenancies under the 1988 Acts. These were created on or after 15 January 1989 or, in Scotland, 2 January 1989. The restriction of eligible rent imposed by this paragraph lasts only for 12 months from the time when the Committee's determination first takes effect. Again, this requirement is in addition to the general power under para (3).

Paragraph (3): Introduction

The scope of this provision requires careful application by authorities. The duty imposed on authorities by this paragraph is to consider whether the circumstances of the tenancy are such as are set out in sub-paras (a) or (b) and, if so, to reduce the eligible rent by an amount which it "considers appropriate having regard in particular to the cost of suitable alternative accommodation elsewhere".

It is plain from the word "or" that appears at the end of sub-para (a) that the authority is obliged to reduce the claimant's eligible rent if either of the sub-paras is satisfied. It is not necessary that both should be satisfied: *R v Kensington and Chelsea RBC ex p Pirie* [1997] unreported, 26 March, QBD.

Once it is shown that one of the sub-paras is applicable, before reducing the eligible rent the authority should be sure that it has given proper consideration to the limiting provisions in paras (4) to (8). For a discussion as to what "suitable alternative accommodation" is and the evidence that must be produced by the authority, see the Analysis to para (9)(a) on p1211.

Paragraph (3)(a): Size of the accommodation

The authority must consider whether the accommodation is "larger than is reasonably required" by the claimant's household. In reaching this decision, the authority must have regard to any suitable alternative accommodation occupied by a "household of the same size". The use of the phrases "or otherwise" and "in particular" make it clear that other factors may also be relevant. Some assistance may be obtained from the size criteria set out in Sch 2 Rent Officers (Housing Benefit Functions) Order 1997 and its Scottish equivalent, but the regulation requires a more general approach and the particular needs of any person in the household need close consideration. For the importance of the rent officer's determination generally, see the Analysis to para (3)(b) below.

In *Pirie* it was confirmed that the word "required" means "needed" and not, as the claimant suggested "demanded" (transcript at 2F-3B).

Although the regulation refers to the comparison being with alternative accommodation "occupied by a household of the same size", it is suggested that "household" in this context cannot be restricted to its normal meaning in social security law, which requires a degree of financial and social interdependence between the members of the household: see the Analysis to SSCBA s137 on p22. This is because the regulation provides that the requirements of others occupying the dwelling are to be taken into account, including non-dependants and lodgers, which need not be living in the same "household" as the claimant. The comparison must be with alternative accommodation which is suitable for that group, not with a narrower group comprised simply of the claimant and the members of her/his household within the dwelling.

Paragraph (3)(b): Cost of the accommodation

The authority is told to consider whether the claimant's rent "is unreasonably high by comparison with the rent payable in respect of suitable alternative accommodation elsewhere". "Rent" for these purposes includes all payments eligible under reg 12: *R v Beverley DC HBRB ex p Hare* [1995] 27 HLR 637, QBD.

In determining the application of para (3)(b), a number of principles can be derived from the authorities and are set out below.

The rent must be "unreasonably" higher. The question is not whether the restricted rent is reasonable but whether the full rent is unreasonably higher than rents for comparable properties. In any market for rented property there will be a range of rents which are being charged for similar properties. The fact that one such rent is higher than another does not per se make the former rent unreasonably high. That conclusion can only be justified if the rent is beyond the top end of the range of rents which a landlord might reasonably charge. Authority for this approach may be found in the decision of Lord Clyde in *Malcolm v Tweeddale District HBRB* [1994] SLT 1212, CS(OH). Discussing the examples of alternative accommodation provided by the authority, Lord Clyde said at 1215E-G:

"Even if the examples given were of comparable accommodation and even if the rents quoted were reasonable, it does not follow that the petitioner's rent, although higher, was unreasonably high. There may well be a band of rentals within which all may be reasonable. That one is higher than the others does not necessarily mean that it is unreasonably higher."

On this point *Malcolm* followed the earlier decision of Lord Weir in *McLeod v HBRB for Banff and Buchan District HBRB* [1988] SLT 753, CS(OH). Although these were Scottish cases and the former was concerned with the meaning of a pre-1987 predecessor of the old reg 11 rather than this version of reg 13, they should be treated as highly persuasive authority in England and Wales. *McLeod*, in particular, has been cited with approval by Hutchison J in *R v Sefton MBC ex p Cunningham* [1991] 23 HLR 534 at 538, QBD and by the Court of Appeal in *R v East Devon DC HBRB ex p Gibson* [1993] 25 HLR, CA – although in the latter case it was suggested that in some respects the test which *McLeod* imposes may be "higher than the statute strictly requires".

The comparison is with the range of rents charged for alternative accommodation. This is another point originating in the judgment of Lord Weir in *McLeod*. The Housing Benefit Review Board in that case had decided that because the claimant's rent was higher than the lowest rents charged for suitable alternative accommodation, it was entitled to apply the regulation then being considered (under the pre-1988 HB scheme). Lord Weir made it clear, at 756C, that this approach was incorrect and that there had to be an "overall examination of the spectrum of rents".

It follows from this that, where it is demonstrated that the claimant's rent falls into the "spectrum of rents" charged elsewhere, it will be impossible for the authority to conclude rationally that para (3)(b) is applicable. In one of the cases heard together in *R v Coventry CC ex p Waite* [1995] unreported, 7 July, QBD, the bracket of comparable rents was said to be £25 to £37. The claimant's rent was £37. A finding that the rent was unreasonably high was quashed. In *R v Kensington and Chelsea RBC ex p Abou-Jaoude* [1996] unreported, 10 May, QBD, the evidence before the Housing Benefit Review Board was that two-thirds of comparable properties had rents of below £240 and the rest had higher rents. The claimant's rent was £275, but Turner J held that in the absence of more detail of the rents payable under the more expensive comparators, it was impossible to conclude that his rent was unreasonably high.

The combination of the first two principles produces the result that even if the claimant's rent is in excess of the top end of the spectrum of rents, a conclusion that the rent was unreasonably high will still not be justified where the difference is small: *Waite* (transcript at 31F-G).

The local authority's financial position is irrelevant. The use of concepts of "reasonableness" and "appropriateness" in para (3) mean that the decision to be made by the authority does contain elements of discretion and judgment. However, this discretion is a narrow one and the only factors which are relevant to its exercise are those which relate to the personal circumstances of the claimant and her/his household and the existence and state of the market in suitable alternative accommodation. Successive Subsidy Orders have contained strong incentives to authorities to restrict eligible rents to a "threshold" level or to the level specified in the rent officer's determination and authorities have often succumbed to the temptation to do so, some even adopting formal policies to this effect.

However tempting this may be for authorities, it is clear from the case of *R v Brent LBC HBRB ex p Connery* [1989] 22 HLR 40 at 44, QBD, that to take the amount of subsidy payable into consideration under sub-paras (a) or (b) is impermissible.

The role of the rent officer's determination. On one reading of sub-paras (a) and (b), the authority would seem to be entitled to make decisions under those sub-paragraphs solely "by reference to" a determination under s122 Housing Act 1996. However, such a conclusion cannot always be reconciled with the terms of the Rent Officers (Housing Benefit Functions) Orders made under that section.

For example, Art 3 and Sch 1 para 1 obliges rent officers to make a "rent determination" as to whether the rent "is significantly higher than the rent which the landlord might reasonably have been expected to obtain from the tenancy at that time" having regard to "the level of rent under similar tenancies of similar dwellings in the vicinity" but on the assumption that no one who would have been entitled to HB has sought or is seeking the tenancy. The following points need to be made.

(1)   A "significantly high" rent is not necessarily the same as an "unreasonably high" one.

(2)   "Similar" accommodation is not necessarily the same as "suitable" alternative accommodation: the former concept does not pay as much regard to the individual circumstances of the claimant and her/his household as the latter, and those circumstances are directly relevant to the decision to be made by the authority under para (3).

(3)   As the rent officer's determination is predominantly for subsidy purposes, it includes an artificial assumption as to the type of tenant who is seeking the tenancy which is not reflected in the real world. The result is that the rent officer's determination is unlikely ever to be the same as an actual market rent. Under reg 13(3) no such assumption is made and, as stated above, it is impermissible to take subsidy considerations into account when reaching decisions under sub-paras (a) and (b).

Although the link between a rent officer determination and an unreasonably high rent may be stronger if the rent officer makes an exceptionally high rent determination (the assumptions underlying the determination are different and an "exceptionally" high rent is more likely to be unreasonably high than a "significantly" high one), the distinction between "suitable" and "similar" accommodation still remains. In these circumstances, it is inconceivable that an authority could, in practice, be satisfied of all matters which must be established before applying para (3) simply on the basis of a rent officer's significantly high rent determination.

It follows that, while an authority may have regard to such a determination in reaching its decision, the simple fact that the reasonable rent determined by the rent officer is lower than the contractual rent is not sufficient on its own to justify a reduction under sub-para (b).

This is supported by *R v Coventry CC ex p Waite* [1995] unreported, 7 October, QBD. However, it is clear that the rent officer's determination will often be a factor of great weight and may be conclusive in some cases: *Waite*; *R v East Devon DC HBRB ex p Gibson* [1993] 25 HLR, CA. In the absence of any evidence to the contrary, it is to be assumed that the rent officer is doing her/his job properly and the local authority may simply produce the determinations to a tribunal: *R v Manchester CC ex p Harcup* [1993] 26 HLR 402 at 408, QBD; *R v Kensington and Chelsea RBC ex p Pirie* [1997] unreported, 26 March, QBD.

In *R v Sandwell MBC ex p Wilkinson* [1998] 31 HLR 22, QBD, Laws J emphasised the separation of the functions of the Rent Officer and the Housing Benefit Review Board in determining whether a claimant's rent should be restricted under the old reg 11. He robustly rejected criticisms of the way in which the rent officer had made his recommendations, both on the basis that his decision was not the subject-matter of the application for judicial review and because, as he correctly pointed out, the valuation was only "a starting point for the Board to consider". He further confirmed, that in any case, authorities concerning the duties of Rent Officers and Rent Assessment Committees under the Rent Act 1977 and the Housing Act 1988 were of no assistance in examining whether the correct approach had been taken to a determination for HB purposes for the purposes of the old reg 11.

Suitable alternative accommodation. See the Analysis to para (9)(a) on p1211.

The approach of tribunals. Many of the cases brought against decisions of Housing Benefit Review Boards under the old reg 11 have complained (often successfully) of failures on the part of the Boards to comply with their statutory obligations to make findings of fact and give full reasons under the former reg 83(4) HB Regs 1987. As with other areas of the Regulations which are particularly replete with pitfalls, a systematic approach will assist the First-tier Tribunal considering a case under para (3)(b). One such approach was that put forward by Schiemann J in *R v Beverley DC HBRB ex p Hare* [1995] 27 HLR 637, QBD. It involves six stages.

(1)   Establish the rent, in the wide definition including all of the elements which are set out in reg 12(1), for the current dwelling: reg 12 as set out in para 5(1) on p1203.

(2)   Indicate what type of accommodation is regarded as a suitable alternative (this involves expressing a view on what services are necessary for this particular claimant).

(3)   Indicate the rent (in the wide sense) which is considered to be payable in respect of such accommodation.

(4)   Find whether the rent (in the wide sense) is unreasonably high in comparison with the rent payable in respect of suitable alternative accommodation elsewhere.

(5)   If so, indicate the reduction found appropriate.

(6)   Indicate how the First-tier Tribunal arrived at that amount.

Paragraph (3): Making the reduction

Once it has been established that either sub-para (a) or (b) is applicable, the claimant's eligible rent must be reduced and the question of the amount of the reduction needs to be considered. As originally enacted, the paragraph did not oblige authorities to reduce the claimant's eligible rent but merely gave them a discretion to do so where one of the sub-paras applied. That discretion was removed by SI 1991 No.235 with effect from 1 April 1991. Previous editions have suggested that the authority could elect to impose a nil reduction. However, it does not appear that this is an option open to the authority in view of the removal of the discretion not to apply a reduction, though Collins J thought, without resolving the point, that this was a possible construction: *R v Coventry CC ex p Waite* [1995] unreported, 7 July, QBD (transcript at 28B-29B). However, substantially the same effect could be achieved in an appropriate case by imposing a nominal reduction, such as one penny.

In determining the appropriate reduction, the authority may have regard to its financial position: *R v Brent LBC HBRB ex p Connery* [1989] 22 HLR 40 at 44, QBD. However, *Connery* also makes it clear that the rent may not be reduced below the level paid for suitable alternative accommodation. Neither, it is suggested, will an authority normally be justified in reducing the eligible rent to a figure at the bottom of the rental brackets. A rough average ought to be the starting point.

The language of the closing words to reg 13(3) makes it clear that any relevant factors may be taken into account in determining the level to which the claimant's rent should be reduced. The "relevant factors" listed in para (9)(b) may also be relevant here, as may other factors which exist in individual cases. The fact that the authority must consider all relevant factors when deciding whether to reduce the claimant's eligible rent and, if so, by how much, was confirmed in *R v Westminster CC HBRB ex p Mehanne* [1999] 2 All ER 319, CA. Although the cost of suitable accommodation elsewhere was "singled out for special mention and is thereby given the status of a mandatory consideration which carries the most weight", other factors could be taken into account. In particular, the pregnancy of the claimant's wife, his difficulty in obtaining other accommodation and the consequences of having to move from his present home were all matters relevant to the claimant's ability to pay his rent and so should have been considered by the Housing Benefit Review Board. *The House of Lords* [2001] 1 WLR 539 unanimously dismissed the authority's appeal. Lord Bingham and Lord Hope, who gave the two substantial speeches, both emphasised the generality of the language in the then para (2) (now para (3)) and the breadth of the discretion thereby conferred, along with the purpose of the HB Regs as being to prevent homelessness: see paras 13 and 24-26 at 546B-C, 548E-549E.

The First-tier Tribunal must consider the amount of the reduction to be made and give reasons for its decision or it will err in law: *CH 4970/2002* para 14.

Paragraph (4): Vulnerable families

Para (4) modifies the application of para (3) so as to forbid any reduction unless certain factors are shown to be present. A local authority should consider three questions.

Is there a relevant vulnerable person? Anyone falling within the categories of person set out in para (10) needs to be considered. The categories are exactly the same as those provided for in the definition of "linked person" in reg 2(1) of both the HB Regs and the HB(SPC) Regs – see the Analysis of reg 13ZA HB Regs (on p315) for a discussion.

A relevant person is "vulnerable" if s/he falls into any of the categories of person set out in the six sub-paras in para (4). "Vulnerable" is not a term used by the regulations but is simply used here as a convenient label. The categories are as follows:

(1)   Those aged at least the qualifying age for PC (defined in reg 2(1)): sub-para (a).

(2)   Those incapable of work: sub-para (b). The test for incapacity for work is that which arises under the current incapacity for work regime rather than the law which was in place to determine this question when reg 11(3)(b) HB Regs 1987 (now this version of reg 13(4)(b) HB Regs) was originally enacted: *R(H) 3/06* para 15. That decision also decided that, because of the terms of reg 11 Social Security and Child Support (Decisions and Appeals) Regulations 1999, it is for the Secretary of State (ie, the DWP) to determine whether the claimant is incapable of work (under Part XIIA of the SSCBA 1992); it is not a matter which the HB decision maker can determine.

(3)   Those who are only to be treated as capable of work because they have been disqualified from receipt of incapacity benefit: sub-para (c). Disqualification can be made for up to six weeks under reg 18 Social Security (Incapacity for Work) (General) Regulations 1995 on the grounds set out in that provision. The effect of this sub-para is that such disqualification does not prevent the claimant falling within the scope of para (4).

(4)   Those that have limited capability for work: sub-para (ca). The test is that which arises under the ESA regime within the meaning of s1(4) WRA 2007 – ie, the person's capability for work is limited by her/his physical or mental condition and the limitation is such that is is not reasonable to require her/him to work.

(5)   Those who are only to be treated as not having limited capability for work: sub-para (cb). This includes where there has been a failure to provide information or to attend a medical examination without good cause. See the Employment and Support Allowance Regulations 2008 SI No.794.

(6)   Those responsible for a child or young person who is a member of the same household: sub-para (d). For whether a relevant person is responsible for a child or young person, see reg 20 of both the HB and the HB(SPC) Regs.

Is suitable alternative accommodation available? This is discussed in the Analysis to para (9)(a) on p1211.

    Is it reasonable to expect the claimant to move? This question must be considered separately by the authority, and if the First-tier Tribunal fails to mention it in its decision, it will be presumed not to have applied its mind to it: *R v Sefton MBC ex p Cunningham* [1991] 23 HLR 534 at 538, QBD; *R v Allerdale DC HBRB ex p Doughty* [2000] COD 462, QBD. The question must be determined "taking into account the relevant factors". These are those set out in para (9)(b) and are the following:

(1)   The effect of a move on claimant's prospects of retaining her/his employment: sub-para (b)(i).

(2)   The effect on any child taken into account under the sixth category of relevant person in relation to her/his education. This factor appears only to be relevant if the move would force a change of school. In *R v Kensington and Chelsea RBC ex p Sheikh* [1997] unreported, 14 January, QBD a Housing Benefit Review Board came to the conclusion that even if the applicant was forced to move to the other side of London, travel arrangements could be made to enable the applicant's child to remain at her school. Latham J described this conclusion as "not very sensible" but decided that enough consideration had been given to the effect of a move on the child.

The factors to be taken into account

In *R v Kensington and Chelsea RBC ex p Carney* [1997] COD 124 at 125, QBD, Carnwath J decided that only the two factors in the then para (6)(b) (now para (9)(b)) were relevant. The medical evidence produced by the applicant in that case to the effect that a move would have a detrimental effect on her health could not therefore be relied upon. The same conclusion was reached by Buxton J in *R v Oadby and Wigston DC ex p Dickman* [1995] 28 HLR 807 at 817. He pointed to the fact that the then para (3) (now para (4)) referred to "the relevant factors" and suggested that the intention was to determine what was relevant and what was not relevant.

    In *R v Camden LBC HBRB ex p W* [1999] 21 May, unreported, QBD (Turner J), a case concerning an HIV-positive claimant, the judge, referring to the old reg 11 HB Regs 1987, decided that "reasonableness as to the expectation that the applicant should move finds no place in the authority's determination, unless reg 11(6)(b) is satisfied". In support of the decisions in these cases, a contrast can usefully be made with Sch 3 para 13(5) Income Support (General) Regulations 1987, which is cast in substantially wider terms than para (9)(b).

    The decision in *ex p W* was upheld by the Court of Appeal (1999) 32 HLR 879. The Court held that only the two factors set out in the then para (6)(b) of old reg 11 (now para (9)(b)) may be considered by the authority in deciding whether it is reasonable for the claimant to move.

    "As both of those counsel [for the authority and the Secretary of State] submit, credible reasons why a claimant cannot move can properly be considered under other aspects of regulation 11. That, as it seems to me, is a powerful argument. In my judgment, [counsel for the authority and the Secretary of State] are right in relation to this issue of construction. The authority can only properly conclude that it is reasonable to expect the claimant to move if it has regard to relevant factors and not to irrelevant ones. Paragraph 11(6)(b) sets out what, for the purposes of paragraph 11(3) are 'the relevant factors'. The use of the definite article in both paragraphs is important. It makes it clear that all other factors are irrelevant .... the closely confined wording of regulation 11(3) can be contrasted with the more open wording of regulation 11(2) where the authority makes its decision 'having regard in particular to ....'. Clearly the draftsman was well able to qualify an obligation when he chose to do so, but in the subsequent paragraph he deliberately chose precise words."

This decision must be treated as authoritatively resolving the question of whether other factors besides those set out in para (9)(b) can be taken into account. However, it is suggested that it is highly arguable that these cases were wrongly decided on this point. The use of the words "taking into account" would certainly suggest that other factors may be relevant. Schiemann J expressed doubts about the correctness of the position set out in the previous paragraph in *R v Canterbury CC ex p Woodhouse* [1994] unreported, 2 August, QBD. Moreover, the decisions are arguably inconsistent with the decision of the Court of Appeal in *R v Westminster CC HBRB ex p Mehanne* [1999] 2 All ER 319, CA (see the Analysis to para (3) above). The court's conclusion in *Mehanne* was that the words "having regard to" did not require only the factors set out in para (3) to be considered, merely that those factors were to be regarded as being particularly persuasive. There is, it is suggested, no difference between the wording used in the two sections. The fact that certain matters are to be considered to be relevant does not mean that other matters are necessarily irrelevant. In *R v Allerdale DC HBRB ex p Doughty* [2000] COD 462, QBD, Elias J gave powerful reasons why the analysis in *Carney* and *Dickman* should not be followed (paras 58 to 64). However, it appears that the decision of the Court of Appeal in *ex p W* was not cited and therefore his reasoning should not be adopted by authorities or tribunals, unless the House of Lords ever has occasion to pronounce on the matter.

    However, there is comfort for claimants in the acknowledgment by the Court of Appeal, dealing with the old reg 11 in *ex p W*, that "credible reasons why a claimant cannot move can properly be considered under other aspects of regulation 11". It is suggested that the Court is here referring to the question of whether the alternative accommodation identified by the council is in truth suitable. If the claimant cannot move, alternative accommodation cannot be suitable for him. The Court is thereby effectively approving the approach taken in *R v Westminster CC HBRB ex p Pallas* [1997] unreported, 23 September, QBD discussed in the Analysis to para (9)(a) below. If correct, this allows the interpretation of para (6)(b) (now para (9)(b)) propounded in *Carney, Dickman* and *ex p W* to be avoided.

Paragraphs (5) to (8): Delaying the restriction

These provisions allow for the effect of para (3) to be delayed in two circumstances:

(1) Where any of the people to whom para (10) applies dies and the claimant occupies the same dwelling as s/he did before the relevant death: paras (5) and (6). No deduction can be made for 12 months from the date of death unless a deduction began before the death occurred.

(2) Where the financial committments for the dwelling could be met by a person to whom para (10) applies when they were taken on: paras (7) and (8). No deduction can be made for the first 13 weeks of the award, provided the claimant was not entitled to HB in the 52 weeks before her/his current award.

Paragraph (9)(a): Suitable alternative accommodation

This phrase occurs at several places in the regulation. The wording used is not always consistent. The basic concepts that must be applied, however, remain the same throughout.

Para (9)(a) does not purport to provide an exclusive definition of "suitable alternative accommodation".

There is nothing that limits the factors relevant to whether the alternative accommodation is suitable. Para (9)(a) must be read against the background of a general, undefined requirement that the accommodation be suitable: *CH 3528/2006.*

Thus other factors may be taken into account, though if the factors mentioned give rise to a satisfactory result, the accommodation will *prima facie* be considered to be suitable: *R v Waltham Forest LBC ex p Holder* [1996] 29 HLR 71 at 78-9. In *R v Slough BC ex p Green* [1996] unreported, 15 November, QBD, Collins J referred to the phrase as "a composite phrase .... the Court in construing it must indeed give appropriate weight to each of the words that are used". The factors specifically mentioned in para (9)(a) relate mainly to the question of suitability. It is worth making the point, however, that the accommodation must be "alternative", that is accommodation other than the present accommodation: *R v East Devon DC HBRB ex p Gibson* [1993] 25 HLR, CA.

The question for consideration is whether alternative accommodation is suitable for the claimant. In *R v Canterbury CC ex p Woodhouse* [1994] unreported, 2 August, QBD, the applicants were a brother and sister who occupied a two-bedroom flat together. They had separate tenancy agreements under which both paid £299 a month rent. Both claimed HB to meet their rent. The only evidence of suitable alternative accommodation before the Housing Benefit Review Board was that of one two-bedroom flat for rent at £380 a month. The Board's approach was to treat the applicants as paying a combined rent of nearly £600, and reduced their HB entitlement accordingly. Schiemann J held that this approach was erroneous (transcript at 13A-14A) and that each claimant had to be viewed as an individual, despite their close relationship. However, he pointed out that in view of this conclusion, the authority would have been entitled to compare the rent paid with comparable one-bedroom flats.

R(H) 2/05 concludes that the wording of old reg 11(6)(a) (now reg 13(9)(a)), and particularly the use of the word "shall", means that the authority must actually take each of the relevant factors below into account in every case and is not entitled to assume that they are met unless the claimant specifically raises them. That is, the onus of proof rests with the local authority. However, he went on:

"In the case of a claimant who is elderly, for example, it may be sufficient for the authority to show that there is a supply of accommodation to rent designed or adapted for elderly residents, and in such a case it will not be necessary for the authority to identify any specific properties actually available for occupation by the claimant": para 18.

Relevant factors in deciding suitability. Bearing those general observations in mind, the factors in determining whether accommodation is suitable for the claimant include the following.

(1) ".... the nature of the .... accommodation". This would encompass matters that do not relate so much to the facilities available, but have more to do with whether it comprises a flat, maisonette or house, the arrangement of the rooms, and the standard of repair it is in. For example, if a claimant was unable to walk, accommodation containing one toilet accessible only up a flight of stairs could not be said to be suitable.

(2) ".... the facilities provided ....". Sufficient detail must be provided by the local authority to enable it to be demonstrated that the facilities are broadly comparable. In *R v Lambeth LBC HBRB ex p Harrington* [1996] unreported 22 November, QBD, the Board's decision was quashed because the comparable bed and breakfast accommodation was only specified to have heating, furnishings and a lounge available, which was insufficient (transcript at 17B-18D). See also *Malcolm v Tweeddale District HBRB* [1994] SLT 1212, CS(OH).

(3) ".... the age and state of health of all the persons to whom paragraph (10) applies ....". For the identity of these people, see the Analysis to the current reg 13ZA HB Regs on p315.

(4) ".... security of tenure reasonably equivalent ....". This is to be regarded as a particularly important factor. An assured shorthold tenancy is not to be regarded as "reasonably equivalent" to an assured tenancy: *R v Coventry CC ex p Waite* [1995] unreported, 7 October, QBD (transcript at 29B-G); *R v Kensington and Chelsea RBC ex p Pirie* [1997] unreported, 26 March, QBD (transcript at 4D-E). Nor should an assured

tenancy be viewed as being equivalent to a protected tenancy under the Rent Acts: the rent control is much less strict and the grounds for seeking possession less onerous. There is a conflict of authorities on whether public sector tenancies can be taken into account when the claimant is a private sector tenant. In *McLeod v HBRB for Banff and Buchan District HBRB* [1988] SLT 753, CS(OH), it was suggested that this was possible but Collins J dissented from this view in *Waite* at 30E-G. However, in *R(H) 2/05* the commissioner rejected an argument that it is necessary for a local authority to show a mix of public and private sector tenancies in order to show an "active market" in houses of the appropriate type (para 15) in a case involving a private sector tenancy. Different durations of assured shorthold tenancies may be permissible: *R v Sefton MBC HBRB ex p Brennan* [1996] 29 HLR 735 at 741, QBD ("very difficult" to see how six- to 12-month tenancy equivalent to five-year tenancy, though decision not perverse); *R v Kensington and Chelsea RBC ex p Sheikh* [1997] unreported, 14 January, QBD (six-month tenancy equivalent to three year tenancy). Latham J in the latter case said (transcript at 14F-15B) that the words "security of tenure" were concerned not with the length of the tenancy but with the claimant's rights to resist possession. Such a narrow construction seems at odds with the general wording of the paragraph.

(5) Size of the accommodation. In *Sheikh*, a claimant had been living with a friend in a three-bedroom flat, and then moved to a two-bedroom property to relieve financial difficulties. It was held that in the circumstances, the local authority should have considered some three- bedroom flats in their comparison (transcript at 20A-22C). Some flexibility therefore needs to be shown.

(6) Area covered by the comparators. In *Holder*, it was said that the alternative accommodation had to be reasonably local. That does not mean, however, that it has to be within the same borough, at any rate in London: *Sheikh* (transcript at 15C-16B). GM A4.1172 states that alternative accommodation need not necessarily be "in the same immediate area as the current accommodation. You may, if you consider it appropriate, compare the current accommodation with the cost of similar accommodation outside your authority's area if that would be suitable for the claimant's needs. This might be appropriate when it is not possible to make valid comparisons with accommodation within your area. However, do not make comparisons with other parts of the country where accommodation costs differ widely from those which apply locally."

(7) The effect of a move on the claimant. In *Pallas* there was evidence before the Housing Benefit Review Board from the claimant's GP that moving house would cause grave risk to his health. The claimant suffered from chronic heart disease. George Bartlett QC, sitting as a deputy judge, held that "if there is evidence that moving to other accommodation would be likely to give rise to the risk of the claimant's death, that is a material consideration for the purposes of deciding whether suitable alternative accommodation exists".

One factor which the local authority may leave out of account is the fact that claimants will usually have taken on a liability for rent which, if their eligible rent is reduced, they will not be in a position to meet and that no other accommodation is therefore "available" or "suitable" for the claimant. That would deprive this regulation of any real effect: *Woodhouse* (transcript at 15E-G)

Evidence of comparable accommodation. It is for the authority to provide sufficient evidence to justify restricting the rent: *CH 3528/2006*. One of the most controversial issues is the type of evidence that has to be produced by the local authority relating to the alternative accommodation. It was argued that it was necessary to identify specific comparable properties. That was accepted, at least implicitly, in *Malcolm*. However, the argument was categorically rejected by the Court of Appeal in *Gibson*. Referring to the old reg 11, Lord Bingham MR stated at 494:

"It is not part of the local authority's function and no part of the Review Board's function to identify specific property available for a recipient's occupation . . . Neither the local authority nor the Review Board is an accommodation agency; neither of them can be expected to assume what would be an inappropriate role. A situation should never arise, therefore, where the local authority or the Review Board is in the position of saying: 'Number 3, Laburnum Avenue is the same size as the house you are now occupying, it is available for letting at a rent substantially below what you are now paying; why do you not move there?' That would, as I say, be an entirely inappropriate approach to this matter. Moreover, it must be borne in mind that details of payment of HB are confidential matters and it can therefore never be incumbent on local authorities to disclose the names or addresses of beneficiaries to whom the benefit is paid. It is, in my judgment, quite sufficient if an active market is shown to exist in houses of the appropriate type in an appropriate place at the level of rent to which rent is restricted. There must, however, be evidence at least of that in a case falling within paragraph 11(3); otherwise the recipient, if he had to move, would have nowhere to go. It is, however, sufficient, as I wish to stress, to point to a range of properties, or a block of property, which is available without specific identification of particular dwelling-houses."

In that case, the Housing Benefit Review Board's decision on suitable alternative accommodation was based on the monitoring of HB claims over the previous month (and showed that there had been 400 new or renewed claims, some of which related to the type of accommodation required by the claimants and their families) and on the fact that local "surgeries" had not revealed any general difficulty in obtaining rented accommodation. The claimants, on the other hand, presented detailed evidence of the searches they had actually made for somewhere cheaper to live and the reasons why those attempts had been unsuccessful. The Court was not prepared to say that there was no evidence on which the Board could have based its decision that the actual rent was unreasonably high by comparison with that payable for suitable alternative accommodation but remitted the decision to the Board because it had failed to supply adequate reasons as to why it had reached its conclusion and rejected the claimants' evidence.

The possible inconsistency between *Gibson* and *Malcolm* would require a Scottish court to consider whether it considered itself bound by *Gibson*, but there is no doubt as to the position in England and Wales. In *R v Sandwell MBC ex p Wilkinson* [1998] 31 HLR 22, QBD, an extremely bold submission was made that *Gibson*, a decision of the Court of Appeal, was wrongly decided. Unsurprisingly, Laws J held that he was bound to apply the decision in *Gibson*.

The English courts have followed and applied *Gibson* reasonably consistently. The practice has developed of local authorities providing comparables showing properties on the market around the relevant time. These need not actually be available when the claimant, hypothetically, is looking on the market. In *Brennan*, evidence of 16 properties coming onto the market over a seven month period was held to be sufficient. Further, the First-tier Tribunal may be entitled to use its local knowledge to conclude that some of the properties on a list provided by the authority would be suitable for the claimant: *Abou-Jaoude*.

If local authorities choose to provide evidence based on claims made by other claimants, then any breach of the Data Protection Act 1998 in the provision of such information to the First-tier Tribunal does not render the evidence inadmissible: *CH 4970/2002* para 19.

Availability of the accommodation. The question of the extent to which the local authority must prove the availability of the alternative accommodation has also been a vexed one. A contrast needs to be drawn between paras (3) and (4). In para (3), there is no express requirement to show that the accommodation "is available". Evans LJ stated in *Gibson* at 501-2 that it was implicit in the wording "suitable alternative" that there had to be "some degree of availability". However, this part of his judgment was *obiter* and later decisions have consistently declined to read a requirement of availability into the legislation: *Malcolm*; *R v Ipswich BC ex p Flowers* [1994] unreported, 1 March, QBD (transcript at 14E-15E); *Waite* (transcript at 26B-28A). So under para (3), it is not necessary to exclude properties which are not, in practice, available to a claimant because s/he cannot afford to pay a deposit: *Holder, Green*.

In *Wilkinson* at 31, it was confirmed that the words "or otherwise" now in para (3)(b) cannot require the local authority to take the personal or other circumstances of the applicant into account. All that they meant was that the Rent Officer's decision was not determinative of whether the claimant's eligible rent should be restricted.

By contrast, under para (4) the authority must prove that the accommodation is available, and the availability or otherwise of properties for which a deposit is required may then be considered: *Holder* at 79; *R v Oadby and Wigston DC ex p Dickman* [1995] 28 HLR 807 at 816. In the latter case, Buxton J referred at 816 to "material about the difficulty of new tenants in obtaining properties and difficulties about deposits" being relevant. It was reiterated that the test was whether the applicant was in fact able to obtain such accommodation and not whether it was, as had been found by the Housing Benefit Review Board in that case, generally available. Buxton J explained the *Gibson* decision as being about the *evidence* required to prove availability, stating at 816:

"I quite accept that the starting point in realistic terms must be the availability of a pool or market of accommodation in general terms. It is then in accordance with the approach in *Gibson* for the applicant to put forward grounds which are unlikely to prove persuasive unless they are supported by evidence of some sort as to why that pool is either not available to her at all or only available in such a limited way or to such a limited extent that the Review Board feels that it cannot realistically say that suitable alternative accommodation is indeed available."

The First-tier Tribunal in considering whether suitable alternative accommodation "is available" must consider evidence that a claimant requires accommodation of the same type and with the same facilities. Where a vulnerable young single mother was staying in sheltered accommodation and there was evidence from her GP and from social services stating that she required the support that the accommodation provided, if the Housing Benefit Review Board rejected that evidence it had to state explicitly that it was doing so and give reasons for that rejection. As it had failed to do so, its decision was quashed: *R v East Devon DC HBRB ex p Preston* [1998] 31 HLR 936, QBD.

The old form of reg 11 was applied to the context of sheltered accommodation in two joined cases, *CH 1992/2002* and *CH 1993/2002*. The claimants were two men with learning disabilities who had been placed in accommodation adapted to their physical needs and which had room for a carer to sleep. The local authority restricted their rent on the ground that the "bricks and mortar" element of the rent was unreasonably high in relation to other suitable alternative accommodation. The commissioner emphasised that it was for the tribunal to decide the questions of fact on the evidence before it and that he was unable to overturn the decision: paras 25-26. In para 24, he concluded that the word "is" in the phrase "suitable alternative cheaper accommodation is available" now in para (4) did not require that the accommodation was available for occupation immediately, since the claimant's existing tenancy would first have to be terminated by notice. Thus alternative accommodation could be suitable if it was capable of being easily adapted. On the other hand, it would not be suitable if it could only be provided after a delay of 18 months while modifications were carried out.

(3)   For the purposes of regulation 12(3) of both the Housing Benefit Regulations and the Housing Benefit (State Pension Credit) Regulations, as inserted by paragraph (1) above, regulation 13ZA of both those Regulations is as follows–

"**Restrictions on rent increases**

13ZA.–(1)   Subject to paragraph (2), where a claimant's eligible rent is increased during an award of housing benefit, the relevant authority shall, if it considers, whether by reference to a determination or re-determination made by a rent officer in exercise of a function conferred on him by an order under section 122 of the Housing Act 1996, or otherwise, either–

(a)   that the increase is unreasonably high having regard in particular to the level of increases for suitable alternative accommodation, or

(b)   in the case of an increase which takes place less than 12 months after the date of the previous increase, that the increase is unreasonable having regard to the length of time since that previous increase,

treat the eligible rent as reduced either by the full amount of the increase or, if it considers that a lesser increase was reasonable in all the circumstances, by the difference between the full amount of the increase and the increase that is reasonable having regard in particular to the level of increases for suitable alternative accommodation, and the claimant's maximum housing benefit shall be calculated by reference to the eligible rent as so reduced.

(2)   No deduction shall be made under this regulation for a period of 12 months from the date of death of any person to whom paragraph (11) of regulation 13 (restrictions on unreasonable payments) applied or, had a claim been made, would have applied, if the dwelling which the claimant occupies is the same as that occupied by him at that date except where the deduction began before the death occurred.

(3)   For the purposes of paragraph (2), a claimant shall be treated as occupying the dwelling if paragraph (13) of regulation 7 (circumstances in which a person is to be treated as occupying a dwelling) is satisfied and for that purpose sub-paragraph (b) of that paragraph shall be treated as if it were omitted."]

General Note

Reg 12 of the HB Regs 1987 was repealed by reg 3(3) Housing Benefit and Council Tax Benefit (General) Amendment Regulations 1997 SI No.852 as from 6 October 1997.

Before the repeal, reg 12 dealt with an authority's powers to restrict rent and applied to claimants who were already receiving HB and whose rent was increased while they were claiming. The reason for the repeal was that, given the introduction of the January 1996 changes to the old form of reg 11 HB Regs 1987 and the abolition, also on 6 October 1997, of the 50 per cent taper a change in contractual rent during the period when a rent officer's determination is in force has no effect on the level of HB actually payable. It is therefore no longer possible for landlords to abuse the scheme by imposing unreasonable rent increases.

This, however, is not the case where the January 1996 changes do not apply because the accommodation (or the claimant) is exempt (see para 4 on p1199). Reg 4(3) of SI 1997 No.852 preserved reg 12 as it stood immediately before 6 October 1997. This is now in reg 13ZA as set out in para 5(3).

Analysis

Para (1). A restriction must be applied if para (1) is applicable, unless any of the following paragraphs apply. The terms on which eligible rent may be restricted are two-fold.

(1)   Where the authority thinks the increase is "unreasonable" having regard to the level of increases for suitable alternative accommodation: sub-para (a).

(2)   Where the increase is considered unreasonable because it is less than 12 months since the last increase: sub-para (b).

In so deciding, as mentioned above, the authority may take a rent officer's determination into account but does not have to do so, and if the authority always simply follows the rent officer's determinations it has wrongfully fettered its discretion.

In deciding whether an increase is reasonable, GM A4.1310 suggests that the authority take into account first the general level of rent increases locally for similar accommodation, and second any improvements made to the accommodation that might justify an increase even if the last increase had taken place less than 12 months before. This view can be criticised, however, in that the comparison under reg 13ZA(1)(a) is with the level of increase for *suitable alternative* accommodation, not similar accommodation in general. "Suitable alternative" is not defined here but arguably it has a similar meaning to the version of reg 13 in para 5(2) as it is part of the same "code" of restrictive measures.

BM v Cheshire West and Chester Council [2009] UKUT 162 (AAC) is the first decision to deal directly with how reg 12 HB Regs 1987 (now reg 13ZA as inserted by Sch 3 para 5(3)) should be interpreted. It concerns the rule as it was before benefit periods were abolished in April 2004, but nothing turns on this. The claimant lived in "exempt accommodation". When her rent was increased (by 81 per cent), the authority did not include the full increase in the weekly eligible rent but allowed an increase of 3.5 per cent only. The tribunal accepted on the evidence that the weekly increase was unreasonably high, accepted the comparator evidence produced as evidence of suitable alternative accommodation with rent increases significantly lower than that of the claimant's accommodation and confirmed the decision to only allow an increase of 3.5 per cent.

As regards whether a rent increase was unreasonably high, Judge Williams considered whether the reasonableness of the level of an increase should be measured in terms of a percentage increase from the base rent, or in terms of a cash increase as it merges into the resulting rent. He took the view that the regulation must be interpreted as involving consideration of both aspects. It is not enough to consider the increase simply as a percentage increase from the base rent (the rent before the increase is applied, taken in isolation from any other information). It must also be considered as a cash sum and compared for reasonableness to the equivalent weekly or other rents payable, after the increase, in comparator accommodation. This was because the power in reg 12 was a power to control individual rent increases given to local authorities and, on appeal, to local tribunals. It is a power to stop individual abusive claims. It is not a power to set a national guide figure for rent increases, such as that given to the former Housing Corporation. The judge felt this interpretation was supported by the consideration that this is an exception to the general rule that rent increases are eligible for HB. He said:

"The effect of a regulation 12 decision is to face a tenant or licensee with a shortfall in benefit as compared with rent. It is taking away resources from those who already have limited resources. Such a power is not to be interpreted too liberally."

In the his view, it therefore followed that the identification of what is reasonable by reference to what is "suitable alternative accommodation" must have in mind not only the increases applied in those comparators but also the base rents from which those increases are applied and the resulting rents after they are applied in those comparators.

Prior to the decision in *BM v Cheshire West and Chester Council*, CH 2214/2003 was the only decision that approached the topic. *CH 2214/2003* emphasised that it is the *increase* in rent, rather than the level of the total rent itself, with which this regulation is concerned, and holds that any decision on this issue will need to be based on adequate evidence as to the level of increases in rents for suitable alternative accommodation. On the facts, it was decided that an increase in rent from £10,920 pa to £15,600 pa was not unreasonably high in London where there had been no previous rent increase for three years. The decision further holds that the level of increases for suitable alternative accommodation is not the only factor which can be taken into account (because of the words "in particular"), and that other factors which may be relevant are:

(1)   Whether the claimant would have to move if the increase were not met.
(2)   The quality of the accommodation.
(3)   The effect on the claimant of having to move.
(4)   The length of time the claimant has lived in the accommodation.
(5)   The age, state of health and social mobility of the claimant.
(6)   The effects on job prospects of having to move.
(7)   The effect on other members of the household of having to move.

In *BM v Cheshire West and Chester Council*, Judge Williams' view was that *CH 2214/2003* was an "own facts" decision – ie, it would be an error to apply it generally. However, he did not agree that the factors listed, could be identified as irrelevant as a matter of law. He also concluded that the tribunal had erred in law when it said that the security of tenure of properties is not a relevant issue and did not consider the point.

If it is considered that either paragraph of reg 13ZA is satisfied, the authority must treat either the whole or part of the increase as "ineligible". However, Judge Williams stressed that if the authority or the First-tier Tribunal considers that a lesser increase is "reasonable in all the circumstances" it must identify the lesser increase and reduce the allowable increase to that amount. The levels of increase at identified suitable alternative accommodation have importance here. The authority or tribunal must consider, judged by the comparators it has already considered, what rent increase is reasonable, and any judicial decision must state why. This poses a difficult issue for the tribunal; what is required is for a local authority, and on appeal the First-tier Tribunal, to take its own view not only about whether a particular rent increase is unreasonable but also on the considerably more difficult and judgmental question of *what* rent increase is reasonable.

Paras (2) and (3) provide the same restrictions on an authority's powers under this regulation as found in reg 13(5) and (6) as set out in para 5(2) (see p1205).

Persons from abroad

6.–(1)   Where, immediately before the coming into force of the Consolidating Regulations, a person is entitled to council tax benefit or, as the case may be, housing benefit, by virtue of regulation 12(1) of the Social Security (Persons From Abroad) Miscellaneous Amendments Regulations 1996 ("the 1996 Regulations"), the modifications specified in relation to council tax benefit in paragraph (2) or, as the case may be, in relation to housing benefit in paragraph (3), shall continue to have effect both as regards that person and as regards persons who are members of his family on 5th February 1996.

(2)   The modifications specified in this paragraph are that for regulation 7 of both the Council Tax Benefit Regulations and the Council Tax Benefit (State Pension Credit) Regulations there shall be substituted–
    "Persons from abroad
    7. –(1)   A person from abroad is a person of a prescribed class for the purposes of section 131(3)(b) of the Act.
    (2)   In paragraph (1) a "person from abroad" means a person other than a person to whom paragraph (3) or (6) applies, who has limited leave (as defined in section 33(1) of the 1971 Act) to enter or remain in the

United Kingdom which was given in accordance with any provision in the immigration rules (as defined in that section) relating to–
- (a)   there being, or to there needing to be, no recourse to public funds, or
- (b)   there being no charge on public funds,

during that limited leave.

(3)   Subject to paragraph (7) this paragraph applies to a person who–
- (a)   is a national of a European Economic Area State, a state which is a signatory to the European Convention on Social and Medical Assistance (done in Paris on 11th December 1953), a state which is a signatory to the Council of Europe Social Charter (signed in Turin on 18th October 1961), the Channel Islands or the Isle of Man; or
- (b)   having, during any one period of limited leave (including any such period as extended), supported himself without recourse to public funds other than any such recourse by reason of the previous application of this sub-paragraph, is temporarily without funds during that period of leave because remittances to him from abroad have been disrupted, provided that there is a reasonable expectation that his supply of funds will be resumed.

(4)   In paragraph (1) "person from abroad" also means any person other than a person to whom paragraph (6) applies who–
- (a)   having a limited leave (as defined in section 33(1) of the 1971 Act) to enter or remain in the United Kingdom, has remained without further leave under that Act beyond the time limited by the leave; or
- (b)   is the subject of a deportation order being an order under section 5(1) of the 1971 Act (deportation) requiring him to leave and prohibiting him from entering the United Kingdom except where his removal from the United Kingdom has been deferred in writing by the Secretary of State; or
- (c)   is adjudged by the immigration authorities to be an illegal entrant (as defined in section 33(1) of the 1971 Act) who has not subsequently been given leave under that Act to enter or remain in the United Kingdom except a person who has been allowed to remain in the United Kingdom with the consent in writing of the Secretary of State; or
- (d)   is a national of a European Economic Area State and is required by the Secretary of State to leave the United Kingdom; or
- (e)   is not habitually resident in the United Kingdom, the Republic of Ireland, the Channel Islands or the Isle of Man, but for this purpose no person shall be treated as not habitually resident in the United Kingdom who is–
  - (i)   a worker for the purposes of Council Regulation (EEC) No. 1612/68 or (EEC) No. 1251/70 or a person with a right to reside in the United Kingdom pursuant to Council Directive No. 68/360/EEC or No. 73/148/EEC; or
  - (ii)   a refugee within the definition in Article 1 of the Convention relating to the Status of Refugees done at Geneva on 28th July 1951, as extended by Article 1(2) of the Protocol relating to the Status of Refugees done at New York on 31st January 1967; or
  - (iii)   a person who has been granted exceptional leave to remain in the United Kingdom by the Secretary of State; or
  - (iv)   person to whom paragraph (5) applies; or
  - (v)   the subject of a deportation order, being an order under section 5(1) of the 1971 Act (deportation) requiring him to leave and prohibiting him from entering the United Kingdom, and whose removal from the United Kingdom has been deferred in writing by the Secretary of State; or
  - (vi)   adjudged by the immigration authorities to be an illegal entrant (as defined in section 33(1) of the 1971 Act), has not subsequently been given leave under that Act to enter or remain in the United Kingdom but has been allowed to remain in the United Kingdom with the consent in writing of the Secretary of State.

(5)   Subject to paragraph (7) this paragraph applies to a person who, having, during any one period of limited leave (including any such period as extended), supported himself without recourse to public funds other than any such recourse by reason of the previous application of this sub-paragraph, is temporarily without funds during that period of leave because remittances to him from abroad have been disrupted, provided that there is a reasonable expectation that his supply of funds will be resumed.

(6)   This paragraph applies to a person who–
- (a)   is an asylum seeker, and for this purpose a person–
  - (i)   becomes an asylum seeker when he has submitted a claim for asylum to the Secretary of State that it would be contrary to the United Kingdom's obligations under the Convention relating to the Status of Refugees done at Geneva on 28th July 1951, and the protocol to that convention, for him to be removed from, or required to leave, the United Kingdom and that claim is recorded by the Secretary of State as having been made; and
  - (ii)   ceases to be an asylum seeker when his claim is recorded by the Secretary of State as having been finally determined or abandoned; or
- (b)   is awaiting the outcome of an appeal under Part 2 of the 1971 Act (including any period for which the appeal is treated as pending under section 33(4) of that Act); or

(c)   has no or no further right of appeal under the 1971 Act but has been allowed to remain in the United Kingdom while an application so to remain is, or representations on his behalf are, being considered by the Secretary of State; or

(d)   except where he is a person to whom paragraph (4)(b) applies, has been granted permission to remain in the United Kingdom pending the removal from the United Kingdom of a person who is the subject of a deportation order but whose deportation has been deferred in writing by the Secretary of State; or

(e)   is subject to a direction for his removal from the United Kingdom but whose removal has been deferred in writing by the Secretary of State; or

(f)   is in receipt of income support.

(7)   Paragraphs (3)(b) and (5) shall not apply to a person who has been temporarily without funds for any period, or the aggregate of any periods, exceeding 42 days during any one period of limited leave (including any such period as extended).

(8)   In this regulation–

"the 1971 Act" means the Immigration Act 1971; and

a "European Economic Area State" means a Member State, or Norway, Sweden, Iceland, Austria or Finland..".

(3)   The modifications specified in this paragraph are that for regulation 10 of both the Housing Benefit Regulations and the Housing Benefit (State Pension Credit) Regulations, there shall be substituted–

"Persons from abroad

10.–(1)   A person from abroad who is liable to make payments in respect of a dwelling shall be treated as if he were not so liable.

(2)   In paragraph (1) a "person from abroad" means a person, other than a person to whom paragraph (3) or (6) applies, who has limited leave (as defined in section 33(1) of the 1971 Act) to enter or remain in the United Kingdom which was given in accordance with any provision in the immigration rules (as defined in that section) relating to–

(a)   there being, or to there needing to be, no recourse to public funds, or

(b)   there being no charge on public funds,

during that limited leave.

(3)   Subject to paragraph (7) this paragraph applies to a person who–

(a)   is a national of a European Economic Area State, a state which is a signatory to the European Convention on Social and Medical Assistance (done in Paris on 11th December 1953), a state which is a signatory to the Council of Europe Social Charter (signed in Turin on 18th October 1961), the Channel Islands or the Isle of Man; or

(b)   having, during any one period of limited leave (including any such period as extended), supported himself without recourse to public funds other than any such recourse by reason of the previous application of this sub-paragraph, is temporarily without funds during that period of leave because remittances to him from abroad have been disrupted, provided that there is a reasonable expectation that his supply of funds will be resumed.

(4)   In paragraph (1) "person from abroad" also means any person other than a person to whom paragraph (6) applies who–

(a)   having a limited leave (as defined in section 33(1) of the 1971 Act) to enter or remain in the United Kingdom, has remained without further leave under that Act beyond the time limited by the leave; or

(b)   is the subject of a deportation order being an order under section 5(1) of the 1971 Act (deportation) requiring him to leave and prohibiting him from entering the United Kingdom except where his removal from the United Kingdom has been deferred in writing by the Secretary of State; or

(c)   is adjudged by the immigration authorities to be an illegal entrant (as defined in section 33(1) of the 1971 Act) who has not subsequently been given leave under that Act to enter or remain in the United Kingdom except a person who has been allowed to remain in the United Kingdom with the consent in writing of the Secretary of State.

(d)   is a national of a European Economic Area State and is required by the Secretary of State to leave the United Kingdom; or

(e)   is not habitually resident in the United Kingdom, the Republic of Ireland, the Channel Islands or the Isle of Man, but for this purpose no person shall be treated as not habitually resident in the United Kingdom who is–

(i)   a worker for the purposes of Council Regulation (EEC) No. 1612/68 or (EEC) No. 1251/70 or a person with a right to reside in the United Kingdom pursuant to Council Directive No. 68/360/EEC or No. 73/148/EEC; or

(ii)   a refugee within the definition in Article 1 of the Convention relating to the Status of Refugees done at Geneva on 28th July 1951, as extended by Article 1(2) of the Protocol relating to the Status of Refugees done at New York on 31st January 1967; or

(iii)   a person who has been granted exceptional leave to remain in the United Kingdom by the Secretary of State; or

(iv)   a person to whom paragraph (5) applies; or

(v)   the subject of a deportation order, being an order under section 5(1) of the 1971 Act (deportation) requiring him to leave and prohibiting him from entering the United Kingdom, and whose removal from the United Kingdom has been deferred in writing by the Secretary of State; or

(vi) adjudged by the immigration authorities to be an illegal entrant (as defined in section 33(1) of the 1971 Act), has not subsequently been given leave under that Act to enter or remain in the United Kingdom but has been allowed to remain in the United Kingdom with the consent in writing of the Secretary of State.

(5) Subject to paragraph (7) this paragraph applies to a person who, having, during any one period of limited leave (including any such period as extended), supported himself without recourse to public funds other than any such recourse by reason of the previous application of this sub-paragraph, is temporarily without funds during that period of leave because remittances to him from abroad have been disrupted, provided that there is a reasonable expectation that his supply of funds will be resumed.

(6) This paragraph applies to a person who–

(a) is an asylum seeker, and for this purpose a person–

(i) becomes an asylum seeker when he has submitted a claim for asylum to the Secretary of State that it would be contrary to the United Kingdom's obligations under the Convention relating to the Status of Refugees done at Geneva on 28th July 1951, and the protocol to that convention, for him to be removed from, or required to leave, the United Kingdom and that claim is recorded by the Secretary of State as having been made; and

(ii) ceases to be an asylum seeker when his claim is recorded by the Secretary of State as having been finally determined or abandoned; or

(b) is awaiting the outcome of an appeal under Part 2 of the 1971 Act (including any period for which the appeal is treated as pending under section 33(4) of that Act); or

(c) has no or no further right of appeal under the 1971 Act but has been allowed to remain in the United Kingdom while an application so to remain is, or representations on his behalf are, being considered by the Secretary of State; or

(d) except where he is a person to whom paragraph (4)(b) applies, has been granted permission to remain in the United Kingdom pending the removal from the United Kingdom of a person who is the subject of a deportation order but whose deportation has been deferred in writing by the Secretary of State; or

(e) is subject to a direction for his removal from the United Kingdom but whose removal has been deferred in writing by the Secretary of State; or

(f) is in receipt of income support.

(7) Paragraphs (3)(b) and (5) shall not apply to a person who has been temporarily without funds for any period, or the aggregate of any periods, exceeding 42 days during any one period of limited leave (including any such period as extended).

(8) In this regulation–

"the 1971 Act" means the Immigration Act 1971;

a "European Economic Area State" means a Member State or Norway, Sweden, Iceland, Austria or Finland..".

(4) Where, immediately before the coming into force of the Consolidating Regulations, a person is entitled to council tax benefit or, as the case may be, housing benefit, by virtue of regulation 12(2) of the Social Security (Persons From Abroad) Miscellaneous Amendments Regulations 1996–

(a) the Council Tax Benefit Regulations shall have effect in relation to him subject to the modifications set out in paragraph (2);

(b) the Housing Benefit Regulations shall have effect in relation to him subject to the modifications set out in paragraph (3).

(5) Sub-paragraph (6) applies where a person–

(a) is entitled to a specified benefit in respect of a period which includes 30th April 2004;

(b) claims a specified benefit on or after 1st May 2004 and it is subsequently determined that he is entitled to that benefit in respect of a period which includes 30th April 2004;

(c) claims a specified benefit on or after 1st May 2004 and it is subsequently determined that he is entitled to such a benefit in respect of a period which is continuous with a period of entitlement to the same or another specified benefit which includes 30th April 2004;

(d) claims jobseeker's allowance on or after 1st May 2004 and it is subsequently determined that he is entitled to jobseeker's allowance in respect of a period of entitlement to that benefit which is linked to a previous period of entitlement which includes 30th April 2004 by virtue of regulations made under paragraph 3 of Schedule 1 to the Jobseekers Act 1995.

(6) Where this sub-paragraph applies–

(a) the Council Tax Benefit Regulations and the Council Tax Benefit (State Pension Credit) Regulations shall both have effect as if in regulation 7 (persons from abroad)–

(i) in paragraph (2)(a) the words "or a person who is an accession State worker requiring registration who is treated as a worker for the purpose of the definition of "qualified person" in regulation 5(1) of the Immigration (European Economic Area) Regulations 2000 pursuant to regulation 5 of the Accession (Immigration and Worker Registration) Regulations 2004" were omitted; and

(ii) paragraph (3) were omitted.

(b)   the Housing Benefit Regulations and the Housing Benefit (State Pension Credit) Regulations shall both have effect as if in regulation 10 (persons from abroad)–

(i)   in paragraph (2)(a) the words "or a person who is an accession State worker requiring registration who is treated (i) as a worker for the purpose of the definition of "qualified person" in regulation 5(1) of the Immigration (European Economic Area) Regulations 2000 pursuant to regulation 5 of the Accession (Immigration and Worker Registration) Regulations 2004" were omitted; and

(ii)   paragraph (3) were omitted.

(7)   The provisions saved by sub-paragraph (6) shall continue to have effect until the date on which entitlement to a specified benefit for the purposes of sub-paragraph (5) ceases, and if there is more than one such specified benefit, until the last date on which such entitlement ceases.

(8)   In sub-paragraphs (5) and (7), "specified benefit" means income support, housing benefit, council tax benefit, jobseeker's allowance and state pension credit.

(9)   In regulation 12 of the 1996 Regulations–

(a)   in paragraph (1), for the words "those provisions" to the end of the paragraph, substitute "the provisions of the Income Support Regulations as then in force shall continue to have effect as if regulation 8(2) and (3)(c) of these Regulations had not been made"; and

(b)   in paragraph (2), for the words "those Regulations as then in force" to the end of the paragraph, substitute "the Income Support Regulations as then in force shall have effect as if regulation 8 of these Regulations had not been made".

(10)   For the purposes of–

(a)   regulation 10(1) of the Housing Benefit Regulations;

(b)   regulation 10(1) of the Housing Benefit (State Pension Credit) Regulations;

(c)   regulation 7(1) of the Council Tax Benefit Regulations; and

(d)   regulation 7(1) of the Council Tax Benefit (State Pension Credit) Regulations,

a person who is an asylum seeker within the meaning of sub-paragraph (11) who has not ceased to be an asylum seeker by virtue of sub-paragraph (12), is not a person from abroad within the meaning of paragraph (1) of those regulations.

(11)   An asylum seeker within the meaning of this paragraph is a person who–

(a)   submits on his arrival (other than on his re-entry) in the United Kingdom from a country outside the Common Travel Area a claim for asylum on or before 2nd April 2000 to the Secretary of State that it would be contrary to the United Kingdom's obligations under the Convention for him to be removed or required to leave, the United Kingdom and that claim is recorded by the Secretary of State has having been made before that date; or

(b)   on or before 2nd April 2000 becomes, while present in Great Britain, an asylum seeker when–

(i)   the Secretary of State makes a declaration to the effect that the country of which he is a national is subject to such a fundamental change of circumstances that he would not normally order the return of a person to that country; and

(ii)   he submits, within a period of three months from the date that declaration was made, a claim for asylum to the Secretary of State under the Convention relating to the Status of Refugees; and

(iii)   his claim for asylum under that Convention is recorded by the Secretary of State has having been made.

(12)   A person ceases to be an asylum seeker for the purposes of this paragraph when his claim for asylum is recorded by the Secretary of State as having been decided (other than on appeal) or abandoned.

(13)   In paragraph (11) "the Common Travel Area" means the United Kingdom, the Channel Islands, the Isle of Man and the Republic of Ireland collectively and "the Convention" means the Convention relating to the Status of Refugees done at Geneva on 28th July 1951 as extended by Article 2(1) of the Protocol relating to the Status of Refugees done at New York on 31st January 1967.

General Note

Paras (1)-(4). The Social Security (Persons from Abroad) Miscellaneous Amendments Regulations 1996 SI No.30 provided a savings provision for entitlement to HB and CTB by some asylum seekers. The modifications to the HB Regs, HB(SPC) Regs, CTB Regs and CTB(SPC) Regs to effect this are now in para 6(1)-(4). See the commentary to SI 1996 No.30 on p1153.

Paras (5)-(8). The Social Security (Habitual Residence) Amendment Regulations 2004 SI No.1232 provided a savings provision for those entitled to HB and CTB when the "right to reside" test was introduced from 1 May 2004. The modifications of the HB Regs, HB(SPC) Regs, CTB Regs and CTB(SPC) Regs to effect this are now in para 6(5)-(7). See the commentary on p1192.

Note that the amendments made by SI 2006 No.1026 to the HB Regs, HB(SPC) Regs, CTB Regs and CTB(SPC) Regs do not affect the continued operation of the transitional and savings provisions in reg 12 Social Security (Persons From Abroad) Miscellaneous Amendments Regulations 1996, reg 6 Social Security (Habitual Residence) Amendment Regulations 2004 or para 6 Sch 3 HB&CTB(CP) Regs. See reg 11 of SI 2006 No.102 on p1226.

Analysis

Paragraphs (10) to (13): Introduction

These prevent certain asylum seekers either from falling foul of reg 10 of either the HB or the HB(SPC) Regs or reg 7 of either the CTB or CTB(SPC) Regs by being a person from abroad and also, by virtue of reg 2(3) Social Security (Immigration and Asylum) Consequential Amendments Regulations 2000 SI No.636, from exclusion from HB under s115 of the 1999 Act. In summary, they are those who claimed asylum on or before 2 April 2000, and either claimed asylum "on...arrival" in the UK or who were present in the UK and claimed asylum within three months of an "upheaval declaration" having been made in relation to the country of her/his nationality.

The notes below discuss these two categories of asylum seeker in more detail and then go on to outline how a person loses her/his status as a relevant asylum seeker.

Paragraphs (11)(a) and (13): Those who claimed asylum "on . . . arrival"

"On his arrival". For the (now almost moribund) debate on whether these three words mean claiming asylum on the very moment of a person arriving in the UK (ie, before s/he passes immigration control), see pp1073-1075 of the 19th edition.

A definitive answer to this debate has been given in *Kola and Another v Secretary of State for Work and Pensions* [2007] 28 November, UKHL 54, reported as *R(IS) 1/08*. The House of Lords decided that an asylum seeker could have submitted her/his asylum claim "on arrival" even if s/he did not submit the claim to an immigration officer on duty at the port of entry. It held that the provision is ambiguous as to what is meant by "on arrival" and that the Secretary of State's very narrow interpretation of it would produce obvious unfairness in many cases. Lord Brown of Eaton-Under-Haywood said: "If the asylum seeker could not reasonably have been expected to claim asylum any earlier than he did, having regard both to his practical opportunity for doing so and to his state of mind at the time, including the effect on him of anything said by his facilitating agent, then I see no good reason why his claim should not properly be accepted as one made "on his arrival"."

" . . . other than on his re-entry". This is presumably intended to prevent a person present in the UK who wishes to claim asylum but who wishes to avoid being found to be a person from abroad from simply leaving the UK and re-entering to claim asylum "on his arrival". It is suggested that it does not mean that a person cannot come within the exception if s/he has visited the UK before. It only makes sense if it is read as meaning "re-entry during the same period of limited leave". That prevents the possible evasion of the "on his arrival" requirement while ensuring that a person who has visited the UK 20 years previously is not prevented from fulfilling the criterion.

"... in the United Kingdom from a country outside the Common Travel Area". The common travel area (CTA) is the UK, Channel Islands, Isle of Man and the Republic of Ireland: para (13). The phrase does not prevent the claimant from having been in another part of the CTA before arrival in the UK. If that were so, an asylum seeker from Columbia who landed in Ireland before claiming asylum in the UK could not fulfil the "on his arrival" criterion. It is suggested that a period of travel through another part of the CTA must be ignored.

"... a claim for asylum". There is no set procedure for making a claim for asylum under the Immigration Rules, save that para 328 provides that an application made at a port or airport will be referred to the Secretary of State by the immigration officer. In particular, it does not need to be done in writing and it is probable that most applications are made orally. In *CIS 1137/1997*, the claimant asserted that he had tried to speak to an official at the airport and a policeman but had been unable to communicate with them. The fact that the commissioner remitted the case for further consideration of these points (para 9) suggests that such attempts could amount to a claim for asylum. Note also *CIS 4341/1998*.

" . . . and that claim is recorded by the Secretary of State as having been made before that date". In order for the claimant to fall within the scope of para (11)(a), or indeed para (6)(b), the claim for asylum must not merely have been made but must have been recorded by the Secretary of State prior to 3 April 2000. The date on the claimant's Standard Acknowledgment Letter will be the best available evidence of this.

Paragraph (11)(b): Asylum seekers claiming after declarations

In conditions of extreme turmoil in a state, the Home Secretary may make a declaration that there will normally be no return of people to that country. These vary according to the conditions of the moment and last for three months at a time.

Any national of such a state making a claim for asylum from within the UK within three months of the declaration falls within this category of asylum seekers. It only applies to nationals of that state and not to those of other states: *R v Secretary of State for Social Security ex p Grant* [1997] unreported, 31 July, QBD.

The relevant claimants will be nationals of the former Zaire who claimed asylum between 16 May–16 August 1997 and those from Sierra Leone who claimed between 1 January–1 October 1997.

Paragraph (12): Loss of asylum seeker status

By para (12), a person ceases to be an asylum seeker on the date on which her/his claim is "recorded as determined" by the Secretary of State. The question then arises as to when a claim is "recorded as determined". In *R (Anufrijeva) v Secretary of State for the Home Department* [2003] 3 WLR 353, HL, the House of Lords ruled that it was contrary to fundamental constitutional principles for an uncommunicated administrative decision to affect the rights of a person to whom that decision related. Accordingly, the claimant did not lose her entitlement to IS until the refusal of her asylum claim was communicated to her. The same will apply to HB entitlement.

Frequency of payment of rent allowance

7.–(1) The regulations specified in sub-paragraphs (3) to (5) shall apply in accordance with the amendments so specified where the claimant–

(a) was entitled to and in receipt of housing benefit on account of his liability to make payments in respect of a dwelling, which he occupied or was treated as occupying as his home, on 06 October 1996;

(b) regulation 11 of the Housing Benefit (General) Amendment Regulations 1996 applied in the case of payments made to the claimant immediately before the consolidating Regulations came into force; and

(c) continues to be entitled to and in receipt of housing benefit on account of such occupation of that dwelling.

(2) In this regulation, "claimant" includes the deceased partner of a claimant in any case where a claim is made by the surviving partner within 4 weeks of the death, provided that this regulation or regulation 11 of the Housing Benefit (General) Amendment Regulations 1996 applied to that deceased on the day of his death.

(3) Regulation 91 of the Housing Benefit Regulations shall have effect as if, in paragraph (3), for the words "Subject to regulations 92 to 97 (frequency of payment of and payment on account of rent allowance, payment provisions)," there are substituted the words "Subject to regulations 93 to 97 (payment on account of rent allowance, payment provisions)".

(4) Regulation 72 of the Housing Benefit (State Pension Credit) Regulations shall have effect as if, in paragraph (3), for the words "Subject to regulations 73 to 78 (frequency of payment of and payment on account of rent allowance, payment provisions)," there are substituted the words "Subject to regulations 74 to 78 (payment on account of rent allowance, payment provisions)".

(5) Regulation 92 of the Housing Benefit Regulations and regulation 73 of the Housing Benefit (State Pension Credit) Regulations (frequency of payment of a rent allowance) shall both have effect as if–

(a) for paragraph (2), there is substituted–

"(2) A payment of a rent allowance in accordance with paragraph (1) shall be made insofar as it is practicable to do so, 2 weeks before the end of the period in respect of which it is made unless the liability to pay rent of the person entitled is in respect of a past period, in which case payment of the rent allowance may be made at the end of that period.";

(b) paragraphs (3) and (4) are omitted;

(c) in paragraphs (5) and (6), the words "Except in a case to which paragraph (3) applies," are omitted; and

(d) in paragraph (7) the words "Subject to paragraphs (2), (3) and (5)," are omitted.

General Note

The effect of this saving provision, formerly found in reg 11 Housing Benefit (General) Amendment Regulations 1996 SI No.965, is that the payment rules (either payment to the claimant or direct to the landlord – see reg 92(2) HB Regs) do not apply to claimants who were entitled to and in receipt of HB in respect of dwellings which they occupied on 6 October 1996, and who continue to be entitled to and in receipt of HB on the same dwelling. New claimants are also protected if they were the partner of a former claimant who would have been entitled to the protection of the savings rule but who has died. Such new claimants must claim HB in their own name within four weeks from the date of death: sub-para (2).

If para 7 applies, HB in the form of a rent allowance is paid, if practicable, two weeks before the end of period in respect of which it is made. So payments for two weeks are made in advance and payments for four weeks or a month, mid-way through the period: reg 92(2) as substituted by sub-para (5)(a).

A dispute has arisen in at least one authority as to the meaning of "in receipt of" in reg 11(1)(a) of SI 1996 No.965 (now in para 7(1)(a)). The circumstances were that a number of former council tenants had their homes transferred into the ownership of a registered social landlord, which was then paid the HB entitlements of those tenants direct. The social landlord argued that the transitional protection continued to apply to claimants who had been in continuous receipt of HB since 1996. It is suggested that the wording "in receipt of" is loose enough to include a claimant whose HB is paid direct to her/his landlord, since it cannot have been intended that the mode of payment should make a difference. The words "in receipt of" are used in a number of other contexts in the HB Regs where the mode of payment cannot have been intended to affect their applicability: see, for example, the definition of "prospective occupier" in reg 14(8) HB Regs as well as reg 50(2) HB Regs. The matter may, however, be open to argument.

[¹ Local reference rent taper

Amendment

1. Substituted by reg 6(3) of SI 2007 No 2870 as from 7.4.08 (or if reg 1(3) of that SI applies, on the day on or after 7.4.08 when the first of the events specified in reg 1(4) applies, or from 6.4.09 if none have before that date).

Modifications

Para 8 substituted by reg 6(3) Housing Benefit (Local Housing Allowance, Miscellaneous and Consequential) Amendment Regulations 2007 SI No.2870 as from 7 April 2008, save that for a person to whom reg 1(3) of those regulations applied (see p1235), the amendments came into force on the day on or after 7 April 2008 when the first of the events specified in reg 1(4) applied to her/him, or on 6 April 2009 if none had before that date.

8.–(1) Regulation 13 of both the Housing Benefit Regulations and the Housing Benefit (State Pension Credit) Regulations (maximum rent) shall have effect in the case of a claimant to whom any of sub-paragraphs (3) to (6) applies subject to the amendment specified in sub-paragraph (2).

(2) In paragraph (3) of regulation 13 at the end, add "plus 50 per cent. of the amount by which the claim related rent exceeds the local reference rent."

(3) This sub-paragraph applies to a claimant who has been continuously entitled to and in receipt of housing benefit–
  (a) in respect of the same dwelling for a period which includes 5th October 1997; and
  (b) which included an addition by virtue of paragraph (3) or (4) of regulation 11 of the 1987 Regulations as they had effect on 5th October 1997.

(4) Sub-paragraph (3) above shall continue to have effect in the case of a person who has ceased to be a welfare to work beneficiary or whose partner has ceased to be such a beneficiary where the person is entitled to housing benefit at the end of the 52 week period to which sub-paragraph (5) refers.

(5) This sub-paragraph applies in the case of a person–
  (a) who was entitled to housing benefit in respect of the dwelling he occupied as his home on or before 5th October 1997;
  (b) whose entitlement to housing benefit in respect of that dwelling was continuous from that date until it ceased because either the person or his partner became a welfare to work beneficiary;
  (c) who on the day before entitlement to housing benefit ceased, was in receipt of an addition to benefit by virtue of paragraph (4) or (5) of regulation 11 of the 1987 Regulations as they had effect on 5th October 1997; and
  (d) who subsequently becomes re-entitled to housing benefit in respect of that dwelling within 52 weeks of him or his partner becoming a welfare to work beneficiary.

(6) In this paragraph, "welfare to work beneficiary" means a person to whom regulation 13A(1) of the Social Security (Incapacity for Work) (General) Regulations 1995 applies.]

General Note

Para 8 preserves a "50 per cent taper" (see p314) for specified claimants whose maximum rent is calculated under the "local reference rent" scheme.

Analysis

Sub-paras (1) and (2) provide an amended version of reg 13 of both the HB Regs and the HB(SPC) Regs where any of sub-paras (3) to (6) apply.

Sub-para (3) provides transitional protection to a claimant if s/he was actually benefiting from the 50 per cent taper on 5 October 1997 and has been continuously entitled to, and in receipt of, HB in respect of the same dwelling since then. The transitional protection continues until the claimant ceases to be entitled to HB or moves home. It would seem that even a single day's non-entitlement to HB is sufficient to bring the protection of this sub-paragraph to an end. Note also that a new claim for HB or a move to a new dwelling during an HB award on or after 7 April 2008 may also result in the HB claim being assessed under the "local housing allowance" scheme for rent restriction instead of the "local reference rent" scheme to which para 8 applies. See Part 3 of the HB Regs, and in particular, regs 12D, 13C and 13D.

Sub-paras (4) and (5). The transitional protection under sub-para (3) is also retained even if the claimant or her/his partner ceases to be a welfare to work beneficiary as long as entitlement to HB is re-established by the end of the specified 52-week period. Note: this was not extended when the linking period for welfare to work beneficiaries was extended to 104 weeks.

Sub-para (5) applies to a welfare to work beneficiary (or her/his partner) who would, under sub-para (3), have been entitled to transitional protection but for the fact that s/he had returned to work. S/he can regain the protection if s/he has to re-claim HB within 52 weeks.

"Welfare to work beneficiary" is defined in sub-para (6) by reference to reg 13A Social Security (Incapacity for Work) Regulations 1995 SI No.311.

A "welfare to work beneficiary" is a claimant who has been incapable of work for at least 196 days and comes off benefit to try out paid work or training. Welfare to work beneficiaries enjoy a number of advantages in the social security system as an incentive to return to work where possible.

Oddly, para 8 was not amended when ESA was introduced in October 2008.

Care homes

9.–(1) In regulation 2(1) of both the Housing Benefit Regulations and the Housing Benefit (State Pension Credit) Regulations there shall be inserted in the appropriate place–
  " "the 1987 Regulations" means the Housing Benefit (General) Regulations 1987;"

(2) Sub-paragraph (3) shall apply to a person who, on 3rd October 2005 was a person to whom paragraph (2) of regulation 7 of the 1987 Regulations as in force on that date applied.

(3) Where this paragraph applies–

(a)   regulation 9 of both the Housing Benefit Regulations and the Housing Benefit (State Pension Credit) Regulations shall have effect as if–
    (i)   in paragraph (1)(k), at the beginning there were inserted the words ''except where paragraph (1A) applies'';
    (ii)   after paragraph (1) there were inserted–

''(1A)   This paragraph applies to a person who–
(a)   was or became entitled immediately before 30th October 1990 to housing benefit in respect of residential accommodation; or
(b)   became or becomes entitled to housing benefit in respect of such accommodation on or after that date but only if the claim was made or, as the case may be, the appropriate authority is satisfied that the claim was sent or delivered to the appropriate DWP office or designated office in accordance with regulation 83(4) [¹ regulation 64(5) *[substituted for regulation 83(4) in respect of reg 9 of the HB(SPC) Regs]*] (time and manner in which claims are made), before that date.'';

    (iii)   for paragraph (4) there were substituted paragraph (3) of regulation 7 of the 1987 Regulations as in force on 23rd October 2005;
(b)   regulation 52 of the Housing Benefit Regulations shall have effect as if–
    (i)   paragraph (4) there were substituted–

''(4)   For the purposes of paragraph (3), the prescribed circumstances are that the claimant–
(a)   occupies residential accommodation as his home; or
(b)   is a person to whom paragraph (1A), as inserted by paragraph 9(3)(a)(ii) of Schedule 3 to the Consequential Provisions Regulations (exceptions to circumstances in which a person is to be treated as not liable to make payments in respect of a dwelling) applies.'';

    (ii)   for paragraph (9), there were substituted–
''(9)   Paragraph (8) shall not apply to residential accommodation of the type referred to in sub-paragraph (b) or (c) of paragraph (8) where such accommodation is residential accommodation for the purposes of regulation 9 and paragraph (4)(b) does not apply to the claimant in respect of that accommodation.''.

(4)   Sub-paragraph (5) shall apply to a person who, on 3rd October 2005, was a person to whom paragraph (5) of regulation 7 of the 1987 Regulations as in force on that date applied.
(5)   Where this paragraph applies–
(a)   regulation 9 of both the Housing Benefit Regulations and the Housing Benefit (State Pension Credit) Regulations shall have effect as if–
    (i)   for paragraph (4) there were substituted paragraph (3) of regulation 7 of the 1987 Regulations as in force on 23rd October 2005;
    (ii)   after paragraph (4), there was inserted–

''(5)   Subject to the following provisions of this regulation, paragraph (6) applies to a person who–
(a)   occupies or is treated by regulation 6(8) of the 1987 Regulations as occupying residential accommodation on 31st March 1993;
(b)   is or was liable to pay rent in respect of that accommodation for that day;
(c)   is a person to whom sub-paragraph (a) or (b) of paragraph (2) of regulation 7 of the 1987 Regulations applies immediately before 1st April 1993; and
(d)   is or was entitled to housing benefit in respect of the liability mentioned in sub-paragraph (b).
(6)   In the case of a person to whom this paragraph applies, regulation 9 of these Regulations shall continue to apply to him as if the amendments to the 1987 Regulations specified in regulation 5(2) of the Social Security Benefits (Amendments Consequential Upon the Introduction of Community Care) Regulations 1992 had not been made.
(7)   Subject to paragraph (8), where on 1st April 1993 paragraph (6) applies to a person that paragraph shall cease to apply to him–
(a)   on the day on which he is first absent from the accommodation which he occupied or was treated under regulation 7(8) of the 1987 Regulations as occupying on 31st March 1993; and
(b)   on any day which falls after that day.
(8)   For the purposes of paragraph (7), any absence shall be disregarded during which the person is treated as occupying the accommodation as his home pursuant to regulation 7(12), (13) or (17) of these Regulations.
(9)   Where a person–
(a)   ceases to be entitled to housing benefit; and
(b)   was before he ceased to be entitled a person to whom paragraph (6) applied,
that paragraph shall not apply to him in the case of any subsequent claim for housing benefit.'';

(b)   regulation 52 of the Housing Benefit Regulations shall have effect as if–
    (i)   for paragraph (4) there were substituted–

''(4)   For the purposes of paragraph (3), the prescribed circumstances are that the claimant–
(a)   occupies residential accommodation as his home; or

(b)   is a person to whom paragraph (6), as inserted by paragraph 9(5)(a)(ii) of Schedule 3 to the Consequential Provisions Regulations (exceptions to circumstances in which a person is to be treated as not liable to make payments in respect of a dwelling) applies.'';

    (ii)   for paragraph (9), there were substituted–

''(9)   Paragraph (8) shall not apply to residential accommodation of the type referred to in sub-paragraph (b) or (c) of paragraph (8) where such accommodation is residential accommodation for the purposes of regulation 9 and paragraph (4)(b) does not apply to the claimant in respect of that accommodation.''.

(6)   Sub-paragraph (7) shall apply to a person who, on 3rd October 2005, was a person to whom paragraph (7) of regulation 7 of the 1987 Regulations as in force on that date applied.

(7)   Where this paragraph applies–

(a)   regulation 9 of both the Housing Benefit Regulations and the Housing Benefit (State Pension Credit) Regulations shall have effect as if–

    (i)   for paragraph (4) there were substituted paragraph (3) of regulation 7 of the 1987 Regulations as in force on 23rd October 2005;

    (ii)   after paragraph (4), there was inserted–

''(5)   Subject to the following provisions of this regulation, paragraph (6) applies to a person who–

(a)   occupies or is treated under regulation 5(7C), (8) or (8C) of the 1987 Regulations as occupying accommodation in an establishment which on 1st April 1993 is registered as a small home under Part I of the Registered Homes Act 1984 or is deemed to be so registered under section 2(3) of the Registered Homes (Amendment) Act 1991 (registration of small homes where application for registration not determined);

(b)   was occupying, or was treated under regulation 7(8) of the 1987 Regulations as occupying, that accommodation on 31st March 1993;

(c)   is or was liable to pay rent in respect of that accommodation for 31st March 1993; and

(d)   is or was entitled to housing benefit in respect of that liability.

(6)   In the case of a person to whom this paragraph applies, paragraph (4), as substituted by paragraph 9(7)(a)(i) of Schedule 3 to the Consequential Provisions Regulations, shall apply as if sub-paragraph (a) of the substituted paragraph was omitted.

(7)   Subject to paragraph (8), where on 1st April 1993 paragraph (6) applies to a person that paragraph shall cease to apply to him–

(a)   on the day on which he is first absent from the accommodation which he occupied or was treated under regulation 7(8) of the 1987 Regulations as occupying on 31st March 1993; and

(b)   on any day which falls after that day.

(8)   For the purposes of paragraph (7), any absence shall be disregarded during which the person is treated as occupying the accommodation as his home pursuant to regulation 7(12), (13) or (17) of these Regulations.

(9)   Where a person–

(a)   ceases to be entitled to housing benefit; and

(b)   was before he ceased to be entitled a person to whom paragraph (6) applied,

that paragraph shall not apply to him in the case of any subsequent claim for housing benefit.

(10)   Where on 31st March 1993 a person occupies or is treated as occupying an establishment mentioned in paragraph (5)(a) and on a day subsequent to that date the establishment–

(a)   if it was registered under Part I of the Registered Homes Act 1984, ceases to be so registered; or

(b)   if it was deemed to be so registered is neither registered nor deemed to be registered,

then on that day and on any day thereafter paragraph (9) shall not apply to that person.

(11)   In this regulation, ''small home'' has the same meaning as it had in Part 1 of the Registered Homes Act 1984 by virtue of section 1(4A) of that Act.''.

(b)   regulation 52 of the Housing Benefit Regulations shall have effect as if–

    (i)   for paragraph (4) there were substituted–

''(4)   For the purposes of paragraph (3), the prescribed circumstances are that the claimant–

(a)   occupies residential accommodation as his home; or

(b)   is a person to whom paragraph (6), as inserted by paragraph 9(7)(a)(ii) of Schedule 3 to the Consequential Provisions Regulations (exceptions to circumstances in which a person is to be treated as not liable to make payments in respect of a dwelling) applies.'';

    (ii)   for paragraph (9), there were substituted–

''(9)   Paragraph (8) shall not apply to residential accommodation of the type referred to in sub-paragraph (b) or (c) of paragraph (8) where such accommodation is residential accommodation for the purposes of regulation 9 and paragraph (4)(b) does not apply to the claimant in respect of that accommodation.''.

Amendment

1.   Amended by reg 7(4) of SI 2008 No 1042 as from 19.5.08.

SCHEDULE 4
REGULATION 7
TRANSITORY MODIFICATIONS
PROVISIONS NOT YET IN FORCE

1.–(1) If–
(a)   no date has been appointed as the date on which a provision mentioned in column 1 of the following
       Table is to come into force before 24th February 2006; or
(b)   a date has been appointed which is later than 24th February 2006,
    then the paragraph of this Schedule mentioned in column 2 of the Table opposite that provision shall have
effect until the appointed day.

TABLE

Provision	*Paragraph of this Schedule*
Section 12(2)(e) of the Asylum and Immigration (Treatment of Claimants, etc.) Act 2004.	Paragraph 2
Section 12(2)(g) of the Asylum and Immigration (Treatment of Claimants, etc.) Act 2004.	Paragraph 3
Section 12(3) of the Asylum and Immigration (Treatment of Claimants, etc.) Act 2004.	Paragraph 4

    (2)   If a date has been appointed as the date on which a provision mentioned in column 1 of the Table
above is to come into force for some purposes of that provision but not for others, then the paragraph of this
Schedule mentioned in column 2 of the Table opposite that provision shall have effect for those other purposes
of that provision (in so far as it is capable of doing so) until the provisions are brought into force for the
remaining purposes.

General Note
    Section 12 Asylum and Immigration (Treatment of Claimants, etc.) Act 2004 came into force on 14 June 2007 by
the Asylum and Immigration (Treatment of Claimants, etc.) Act 2004 (Commencement No.7 and Transitional
Provisions) Order 2007 SI No.1602. The commencement does not apply to those recorded as refugees on or
before 14 June 2007. For these purposes, a person is "recorded as a refugee" on the day the Secretary of State
notifies her/him that s/he has been recognised as a refugee and granted asylum in the UK. For those to whom
the commencement applies, the following provisions lapse:
(1)   Reg 10A and Sch A1 of both the HB Regs and the HB(SPC) Regs, as inserted by Sch 4 para 2(1) and
       (2). These dealt with a refugee's retrospective entitlement to HB.
(2)   Paras 55A and 55B of Sch 5 and paras 48A and 48B of Sch 6 of the HB Regs, as inserted by Sch 4 para
       2(5) and (6). These provided income and capital disregards for retrospective HB and IS paid to the
       refugee.
(3)   Reg 7A and Sch A1 of both the CTB Regs and the CTB(SPC) Regs, as inserted by Sch 4 para 3(1) and
       (2). These made similar provisions to those in (1) above for CTB.
(4)   Paras 56A and 56B of Sch 4 and paras 53A and 53B of Sch 5 of the CTB Regs, as inserted by Sch 4
       para 3(5) and (6). These made similar provisions to those in (2) above for CTB.
(5)   The modifications made to the above, as made by Sch 4 para 4.
See pp1125-1133 of the 20th edition for the full text of the provisions and commentary.
    Note that reg 10A and paras 3 and 7 of Sch A1 of both the HB regs and the HB(SPC) Regs, as inserted by
para 2, were substituted by reg 6 Housing Benefit (Local Housing Allowance, Miscellaneous and Consequential)
Amendment Regulations 2007 SI No.2870 as from 7 April 2008, save that for a person to whom reg 1(3) of those
regulations applied, the amendments came into force on the day on or after 7 April 2008 when the first of the
events specified in reg 1(4) applied to her/him, or on 6 April 2009 if none had before that date. Sch 4 para 3(4)
was amended by reg 7(5) Social Secuity (Miscellaneous Amendments)(No.2) Regulations 2008 SI No.1042 as
from 19 May 2008.
    Note also that paras 4(2)(b) and (c) and 4(4)(b) and (c) of Sch 4 were omitted by reg 9 of SI 2008 No.3157 as
from 5 January 2009.

The Social Security (Persons from Abroad) Amendment Regulations 2006

(SI 2006 No.1026)

Citation and commencement

1. These Regulations shall be cited as the Social Security (Persons from Abroad) Amendment Regulations 2006 and shall come into force on 30th April 2006.

Nationals of Norway, Iceland, Liechtenstein and Switzerland

10. The following provisions shall apply in relation to a national of Norway, Iceland, Liechtenstein or Switzerland or a member of his family (within the meaning of Article 2 of Council Directive No. 2004/38/EC) as if such a national were a national of a member State–

(a) regulation 7(4A)(a) to (e) of the Council Tax Benefit Regulations 2006;

(b) regulation 7(4A)(a) to (e) of the Council Tax Benefit (Persons who have attained the qualifying age for state pension credit) Regulations 2006;

(c) regulation 10(3B)(a) to (e) of the Housing Benefit Regulations 2006;

(d) regulation 10(4A)(a) to (e) of the Housing Benefit (Persons who have attained the qualifying age for state pension credit) Regulations 2006;

(e)-(h) *[Omitted]*

Revocations and savings

11.–(1) *[Omitted]*

(2) Nothing in these Regulations shall affect the continued operation of the transitional arrangements and savings provided for in–

(a) regulation 12 of the Social Security (Persons From Abroad) Miscellaneous Amendments Regulations 1996;

(b) regulation 6 of the Social Security (Habitual Residence) Amendment Regulations 2004; or

(c) paragraph 6 of Schedule 3 to the Housing Benefit and Council Tax Benefit (Consequential Provisions) Regulations 2006.

The Housing Benefit and Council Tax Benefit (War Pension Disregards) Regulations 2007
(SI 2007 No.1619)

General Note on the Regulations

In the assessment of income for HB and CTB £10 of certain war pensions must be disregarded. ss134(8) and 139(6) SSAA 1992 allow an authority to resolve to disregard more of (or all of) prescribed war pensions as income for the purposes of its HB and CTB schemes. The prescribed pensions are in the Schedule to these regulations. Note that "war widow's pension" includes any corresponding pension payable to a widower or a surviving civil partner: see, for example, s134(14) SSAA on p79.

Citation and commencement
1.   These Regulations may be cited as The Housing Benefit and Council Tax Benefit (War Pension Disregards) Regulations 2007 and shall come into force on 3rd July 2007.

War disablement pensions
2.   The war disablement pensions that are prescribed for the purpose of sections 134(8)(a) and 139(6)(a) of the Social Security Administration Act 1992, are specified in Part 1 of the Schedule.

War widow's pensions
3.   The war widow's pensions that are prescribed for the purpose of sections 134(8)(a) and 139(6)(a) of the Social Security Administration Act, are specified in Part 2 of the Schedule.

[¹ [³THE SCHEDULE

Regulations 2 and 3
War disablement and war widow's pensions

PART 1

War disablement pensions
1.   The war disablement pensions prescribed are–
(a)   any retired pay or pension or allowance payable in respect of disablement under an instrument specified in section 639(2) of the Income Tax (Earnings and Pensions) Act 2003;
(b)   any retired pay or pension payable, to a member of the armed forces of the Crown in respect of a disablement which is attributable to service, under–
    (i)   an Order in Council made under section 3 of the Naval and Marine Pay and Pensions Act 1865,
    (ii)   the Army Pensions Warrant 1977,
    [⁴ (iia)   the Army Pensions (Armed Forces Pension Scheme 1975 and Attributable Benefits Scheme) Warrant 2010;]
    (iii)   any order or regulations made under section 2 of the Air Force (Constitution) Act 1917,
    (iv)   any order or regulations made under section 4 of the Reserve Forces Act 1996,
    (v)   any instrument amending or replacing any of the instruments referred to in paragraphs (i) to (iv), or
    (vi)   any power of Her Majesty otherwise than under an enactment to make provision about pensions for or in respect of persons who have been disabled or have died in consequence of service as members of the armed forces of the Crown; and
(c)   a payment made under article 14(1)(b) of the Armed Forces and Reserve Forces (Compensation Scheme) Order 2005.

PART 2

War widow's pensions
2.   The war widow's pensions prescribed are–
(a)   any pension or allowance payable to a widow, widower or surviving civil partner under an instrument specified in section 639(2) of the Income Tax (Earnings and Pensions) Act 2003 in respect of the death or disablement of any person;
(b)   a pension payable, to a widow, widower or surviving civil partner of a member of the armed forces of the Crown in respect of death which is attributable to service, under–

      (i)   an Order in Council made under section 3 of the Naval and Marine Pay and Pensions Act 1865,

      (ii)   the Army Pensions Warrant 1977,

      [⁴ (iia) the Army Pensions (Armed Forces Pension Scheme 1975 and Attributable Benefits Scheme) Warrant 2010;]

      (iii)   any order or regulations made under section 2 of the Air Force (Constitution) Act 1917,

      (iv)   any order or regulations made under section 4 of the Reserve Forces Act 1996,

      (v)   any instrument amending or replacing any of the instruments referred to in paragraphs (i) to (iv), or

      (vi)   any power of Her Majesty otherwise than under an enactment to make provision about pensions for or in respect of persons who have been disabled or have died in consequence of service as members of the armed forces of the Crown; and

  (c)   a payment made under article 21(1)(a) of the Armed Forces and Reserve Forces (Compensation Scheme) Order 2005.]]

Amendments

  1.   Substituted by reg 10 of SI 2008 No 3157 as from 5.1.09.

  2.   Omitted by reg 10 of SI 2009 No 2655 as from 26.10.09.

  3.   Substituted by reg 2 of SI 2009 No 3389 as from 26.1.10.

  4.   Amended by reg 8 of SI 2010 No 2449 as from 1.11.10.

The Social Security (Claims and Information) Regulations 2007
(SI 2007 No.2911)

Citation, commencement and interpretation
1.–(1) These Regulations may be cited as the Social Security (Claims and Information) Regulations 2007 and shall come into force on 31st October 2007.

(2) In regulations 4 and 5 "the Administration Act" means the Social Security Administration Act 1992.

(3) In regulations 2 to 4–

"specified benefit" means one or more of the following benefits–

   (a)   attendance allowance;

   (b)   bereavement allowance;

   (c)   bereavement payment;

   (d)   carer's allowance;

   (e)   disability living allowance;

   [¹ (ee) employment and support allowance;]

   (f)   incapacity benefit;

   (g)   income support;

   (h)   jobseeker's allowance;

   (i)   retirement pension;

   (j)   state pension credit;

   (k)   widowed parent's allowance;

   (l)   winter fuel payment;

"the Secretary of State" includes persons providing services to the Secretary of State;

"local authority" includes persons providing services to a local authority and persons authorised to exercise any function of a local authority relating to housing benefit or council tax benefit.

Amendment

1.   Inserted by reg 8 of SI 2010 No 840 as from 28.6.10.

Use of social security information: local authorities
2.–(1) This regulation applies where social security information held by a local authority was supplied by the Secretary of State to the local authority and this information–

   (a)   was used by the Secretary of State in connection with a person's claim for, or award of, a specified benefit; and

   (b)   is relevant to that person's claim for, or award of, council tax benefit or housing benefit.

(2) The local authority must, for the purposes of the person's claim for, or award of, council tax benefit or housing benefit, use that information without verifying its accuracy.

(3) Paragraph (2) does not apply where–

   (a)   the information is supplied more than twelve months after it was used by the Secretary of State in connection with a claim for, or an award of, a specified benefit; or

   (b)   the information is supplied within twelve months of its use by the Secretary of State but the local authority has reasonable grounds for believing the information has changed in the period between its use by the Secretary of State and its supply to the local authority; or

   (c)   the date on which the information was used by the Secretary of State cannot be determined.

Use of social security information: Secretary of State
3.–(1) This regulation applies where social security information held by the Secretary of State was supplied by a local authority to the Secretary of State and this information–

   (a)   was used by the local authority in connection with a person's claim for, or award of, council tax benefit or housing benefit; and

(b)   is relevant to that person's claim for, or award of, a specified benefit.

(2)   The Secretary of State must, for the purposes of the person's claim for, or award of, a specified benefit, use that information without verifying its accuracy.

(3)   Paragraph (2) does not apply where–

(a)   the information is supplied more than twelve months after it was used by a local authority in connection with a claim for, or an award of, council tax benefit or housing benefit; or

(b)   the information is supplied within twelve months of its use by the local authority but the Secretary of State has reasonable grounds for believing the information has changed in the period between its use by the local authority and its supply to the Secretary of State; or

(c)   the date on which the information was used by the local authority cannot be determined.

Social security information verified by local authorities

4.–(1)   This regulation applies where social security information is verified by a local authority by virtue of regulations made under section 7A(2)(e) of the Administration Act and forwarded by that local authority to the Secretary of State.

(2)   The Secretary of State must, for the purposes of a person's claim for, or award of, a specified benefit, use this information without verifying its accuracy.

(3)   Paragraph (2) does not apply where–

(a)   the Secretary of State has reasonable grounds for believing the social security information received from the local authority is inaccurate; or

(b)   the Secretary of State receives the information more than four weeks after it was verified by the local authority.

Specified benefits for the purpose of section 7B(3) of the Administration Act

5.   The benefits specified for the purpose of section 7B(3) of the Administration Act are–

(a)   a ''specified benefit'' within the meaning given in regulation 1(3);

(b)   housing benefit; and

(c)   council tax benefit.

The Housing Benefit (Local Housing Allowance and Information Sharing) Amendment Regulations 2007

(SI 2007 No.2868)

Citation and commencement

1.–(1) These Regulations may be cited as the Housing Benefit (Local Housing Allowance and Information Sharing) Amendment Regulations 2007.

(2) This regulation and regulations 2 (amendment of the Housing Benefit Regulations 2006) and 3 (amendments relating to information sharing) shall come into force on 7th April 2008.

(3) Subject to paragraph (6) (which relates to non-local housing allowance cases), regulations 4 to 19 (amendment of the Housing Benefit Regulations 2006 relating to determination of appropriate maximum housing benefit) shall come into force on 7th April 2008 immediately following the coming into force of regulation 3.

(4) *[Omitted]*

(5) This paragraph applies to a case where no reference was made to a maximum rent (standard local rate) in determining the amount of the eligible rent which applied immediately before 7th April 2008 and in this paragraph–

"eligible rent" shall be construed in accordance with–

    (i)   regulations 12 or 12A of the Housing Benefit Regulations 2006 as in force immediately before 7th April 2008; or

    (ii)   in a case to which paragraph 4 of Schedule 3 to the Housing Benefit and Council Tax Benefit (Consequential Provisions) Regulations 2006 applies, regulations 12 and 13 of those Regulations as set out in paragraph 5 of that Schedule as in force immediately before 7th April 2008; and

"maximum rent (standard local rate)" means a maximum rent (standard local rate) determined in accordance with regulation 13A of the Housing Benefit Regulations 2006 as in force immediately before 7th April 2008.

(6) In a case to which paragraph (5) applies regulations 4 to 19 shall come into force on the day when, on or after 7th April 2008, the first of the following sub-paragraphs applies–

    (a)   a relevant authority is required to apply to a rent officer by virtue of regulation 14 of the Housing Benefit Regulations;

    (b)   sub-paragraph (a) would apply but for the case falling within regulation 14(4)(a) of, or 14(4)(b) of and paragraph 2 of Schedule 2 to, the Housing Benefit Regulations (no application to rent officer required as an existing rent officer determination may be used);

    (c)   a relevant authority is required to determine an eligible rent in accordance with regulation 12(3)(b) of the Housing Benefit Regulations; or

    (d)   a relevant authority is required to determine an eligible rent in accordance with regulation 12(3) of the Housing Benefit Regulations 2006 as set out in paragraph 5 of Schedule 3 to the Consequential Provisions Regulations,

and in this paragraph "relevant authority" means an authority administering housing benefit.

(7) Where paragraph (6) does not apply before 6th April 2009, regulations 4 to 19 shall come into force on that date.

(8) In this regulation–

    (a)   "the Housing Benefit Regulations" means the Housing Benefit Regulations 2006 as in force immediately before the coming into force of regulations 4 to 19 in that case; and

    (b)   "the Consequential Provisions Regulations" means the Housing Benefit and Council Tax Benefit (Consequential Provisions) Regulations 2006 as in force immediately before the coming into force of regulations 4 to 19 in that case.

Analysis

These regulations provided for the national introduction of the "local housing allowance" scheme for HB rent restriction, found in regs 12D, 13C and 13D HB Regs, which had been piloted in Pathfinder areas from 2003. They made many amendments to the HB Regs, all of which are incorporated into the relevant provisions in this edition.

Reg 1 is reproduced here because of the rather complex commencement provisions found in it. In most situations, the amendments came into force on 7 April 2008. So the amended HB regulations applied on any new claim for HB on or after 7 April 2008, or where a claimant with an award of HB moved to a new dwelling on or after that date. However, for those to whom para (5) applied, all claimants with a current award of HB on 7 April 2008, the amendments did not come into force until the first of various specific events occurred, or on 6 April 2009 if earlier: paras (6) and (7). In these cases, "eligible rent" continued to be determined under the old form of regs 12 and 12A HB Regs or Sch 3 para 4 HB&CTB(CP) Regs, as the case may be. This did not apply if the claimant's HB was determined by reference to a "maximum rent (standard local rate)", that is, in a former Pathfinder area under the pilot local housing allowance scheme rules (for which see the 20th edition of this book, pp510-518).

For any individual claimant, the specific events in para (6) are as follows:

(1)   The authority is required to apply to a rent officer for determinations under the old version of reg 14, or would have been required to do so were there not existing determinations it could use, that is, where "eligible rent was determined under the "local reference rent" rules: sub-paras (a) and (b). This would occur for example where the number of occupiers has changed. But see the commentary to reg 14 HB Regs (on p324) where it is more than 52 weeks since the last reference to the rent officer was made.

(2)   The authority is required to determine an "eligible rent" under the old version of reg 12(3)(b), that is, where no rent restriction rules applied: sub-para (c). This would occur, for example, where there has been a rent increase or where a non-dependant moves in or out of the household.

(3)   The authority is required to determine an "eligible rent" under the old version of reg 12(3) set out in Sch 4 para 5 HB&CTB(CP) regs, that is where the "pre-January 1996" rules applied: sub-para (d).

It is important to note that the effect of the amendments coming into force for an individual claimant does not mean that the claim is dealt with under a particular, or a different rent restriction scheme. It is important to consider all the provisions in Part 3 HB Regs carefully and, in particular, any modifications or transitional protection provided.

The Housing Benefit (State Pension Credit) (Local Housing Allowance and Information Sharing) Amendment Regulations 2007
(SI 2007 No.2869)

Citation and commencement

1.–(1)   These Regulations may be cited as the Housing Benefit (State Pension Credit) (Local Housing Allowance and Information Sharing) Amendment Regulations 2007.

(2)   This regulation and regulations 2 (amendment of the Housing Benefit (Persons who have attained the qualifying age for state pension credit) Regulations 2006) and 3 (amendments relating to information sharing) shall come into force on 7th April 2008.

(3)   Subject to paragraph (6) (which relates to non-local housing allowance cases), regulations 4 to 19 (amendment of the Housing Benefit (Persons who have attained the qualifying age for state pension credit) Regulations 2006 relating to determination of appropriate maximum housing benefit) shall come into force on 7th April 2008 immediately following the coming into force of regulation 3.

(4)   *[Omitted]*

(5)   This paragraph applies to a case where no reference was made to a maximum rent (standard local rate) in determining the amount of the eligible rent which applied immediately before 7th April 2008 and in this paragraph–

"eligible rent" shall be construed in accordance with–

   (i)   regulations 12 or 12A of the Housing Benefit (Persons who have attained the qualifying age for state pension credit) Regulations 2006 as in force immediately before 7th April 2008; or

   (ii)   in a case to which paragraph 4 of Schedule 3 to the Housing Benefit and Council Tax Benefit (Consequential Provisions) Regulations 2006 applies, regulations 12 and 13 of those Regulations as set out in paragraph 5 of that Schedule as in force immediately before 7th April 2008; and

"maximum rent (standard local rate)" means a maximum rent (standard local rate) determined in accordance with regulation 13A of the Housing Benefit (Persons who have attained the qualifying age for state pension credit) Regulations 2006 as in force immediately before 7th April 2008.

(6)   In a case to which paragraph (5) applies regulations 4 to 19 shall come into force on the day when, on or after 7th April 2008, the first of the following sub-paragraphs applies–

   (a)   a relevant authority is required to apply to a rent officer by virtue of regulation 14 of the Housing Benefit (State Pension Credit) Regulations;

   (b)   sub-paragraph (a) would apply but for the case falling within regulation 14(4)(a) of, or 14(4)(b) of and paragraph 2 of Schedule 2 to, the Housing Benefit (State Pension Credit) Regulations (no application to rent officer required as an existing rent officer determination may be used);

   (c)   a relevant authority is required to determine a new eligible rent in accordance with regulation 12(3)(b) of the Housing Benefit (State Pension Credit) Regulations; or

   (d)   a relevant authority is required to determine a new eligible rent in accordance with regulation 12(3) of the Housing Benefit (Persons who have attained the qualifying age for state pension credit) Regulations 2006 as set out in paragraph 5 of Schedule 3 to the Consequential Provisions Regulations,

and in this paragraph "relevant authority" means an authority administering housing benefit.

(7)   Where paragraph (6) does not apply before 6th April 2009, regulations 4 to 19 shall come into force on that date.

(8)   In this regulation–

"the Housing Benefit (State Pension Credit) Regulations" means the Housing Benefit (Persons who have attained the qualifying age for state pension credit) Regulations 2006 as in force immediately before the coming into force of regulations 4 to 19 in that case; and ''the Consequential Provisions Regulations'' means the Housing Benefit and Council Tax Benefit (Consequential Provisions) Regulations 2006 as in force immediately before the coming into force of regulations 4 to 19 in that case.

General Note

See the General Note to the Housing Benefit (Local Housing Allowance and Information Sharing) Amendment Regulations 2007 on p1231 on these rather complex commencement provisions.

The Housing Benefit (Local Housing Allowance, Miscellaneous and Consequential) Amendment Regulations 2007

(SI 2007 No.2870)

Citation, commencement and interpretation

1.–(1)   These Regulations may be cited as the Housing Benefit (Local Housing Allowance, Miscellaneous and Consequential) Amendment Regulations 2007.

(2)   This regulation and, subject to paragraph (4) (which relates to non-local housing allowance cases), regulations 2 to 6, shall come into force on 7th April 2008.

(3)   This paragraph applies to a case where no reference was made to a maximum rent (standard local rate) in determining the amount of the eligible rent which applied immediately before 7th April 2008 and in this paragraph–

"eligible rent" shall be construed in accordance with–

    (i)   regulations 12 or 12A of the Housing Benefit Regulations 2006 or the Housing Benefit (Persons who have attained the qualifying age for state pension credit) Regulations 2006 as in force immediately before 7th April 2008; or

    (ii)   in a case to which paragraph 4 of Schedule 3 to the Housing Benefit and Council Tax Benefit (Consequential Provisions) Regulations 2006 applies, regulations 12 and 13 of the Housing Benefit Regulations 2006 or the Housing Benefit (Persons who have attained the qualifying age for state pension credit) Regulations 2006 as set out in paragraph 5 of that Schedule as in force immediately before 7th April 2007.

"maximum rent (standard local rate)" means a maximum rent (standard local rate) determined in accordance with regulation 13A of the Housing Benefit Regulations 2006 or the Housing Benefit (persons who have attained the qualifying age for state pension credit) Regulations 2006 as in force immediately before 7th April 2008.

(4)   In a case to which paragraph (3) applies, these Regulations shall come into force on the day when, on or after 7th April 2008, the first of the following sub-paragraphs applies–

(a)   a relevant authority is required to apply to a rent officer by virtue of regulation 14 of the Housing Benefit Regulations or the Housing Benefit (State Pension Credit) Regulations;

(b)   sub-paragraph (a) would apply but for the case falling within regulation 14(4)(a) of, or regulations 14(4)(b) of and paragraph 2 of Schedule 2 to, the Housing Benefit Regulations or the Housing Benefit (State Pension Credit) Regulations (no application to rent officer required as an existing rent officer determination may be used);

(c)   a relevant authority is required to determine an eligible rent in accordance with regulation 12(3)(b) of the Housing Benefit Regulations or the Housing Benefit (State Pension Credit) Regulations; or

(d)   a relevant authority is required to determine an eligible rent in accordance with regulation 12(3) of the Housing Benefit Regulations 2006 or regulation 12(3) of the Housing Benefit (Persons who have attained the qualifying age for state pension credit) Regulations 2006 as set out in paragraph 5 of Schedule 3 to the Consequential Provisions Regulations,

and in this paragraph "relevant authority" means an authority administering housing benefit.

(5)   Where paragraph (4) does not apply before 6th April 2009, these Regulations shall come into force on that date.

(6)   In paragraph (4) of this regulation–

"the Housing Benefit Regulations" means the Housing Benefit Regulations 2006 as in force immediately before the coming into force of regulations 4 to 19 of the Housing Benefit (Local Housing Allowance and Information Sharing) Amendment Regulations 2007 in that case;

"the Housing Benefit (State Pension Credit) Regulations" means the Housing Benefit (persons who have attained the qualifying age for state pension credit) Regulations 2006 as in force immediately before the coming into force of regulations 4 to 19 of the Housing Benefit (State Pension Credit) (Local Housing Allowance and Information Sharing) Amendment Regulations 2007 in that case;

"the Consequential Provisions Regulations" means the Housing Benefit and Council Tax Benefit (Consequential Provisions) Regulations 2006 as in force immediately before the coming into force of regulations 2 to 6 of these regulations in that case.

General Note

See the General Note to the Housing Benefit (Local Housing Allowance and Information Sharing) Amendment Regulations 2007 on p1231 on these rather complex commencement provisions.

The Welfare Reform Act 2007 (Commencement No.4, and Savings and Transitional Provisions) Order 2007

(SI 2007 No.2872)

Citation and interpretation

1.–(1) This Order may be cited as the Welfare Reform Act 2007 (Commencement No.4, and Savings and Transitional Provisions) Order 2007.

(2) In this Order–

"the Act" means the Welfare Reform Act 2007;

"the Administration Act" means the Social Security Administration Act 1992;

"the Contributions and Benefits Act" means the Social Security Contributions and Benefits Act 1992;

"the Consequential Provisions Regulations" means the Housing Benefit and Council Tax Benefit (Consequential Provisions) Regulations 2006;

"the Housing Act" means the Housing Act 1996;

"the Housing Benefit (State Pension Credit) Regulations" means the Housing Benefit (Persons who have attained the qualifying age for state pension credit) Regulations 2006;

"the Regulations" means the Housing Benefit Regulations 2006.

Appointed days

2.–(1) 7th April 2008 is the appointed day for the coming into force of–

(a)-(b) *[Omitted]*

(c) Schedule 8 to the Act (repeals), in so far as it relates to the repeal of–

    (i) section 130(4) of the Contributions and Benefits Act (housing benefit);

    (ii) section 5(3) of the Administration Act (power to make regulations about information or evidence required by rent officer);

    (iii) section 122(3) of the Housing Act (functions of rent officers in connection with housing benefit and rent allowance subsidy);

    (iv) in section 122(5)(b) of the Housing Act, the words "or regulations"; and

    (v) paragraph 3(2) of Schedule 13 to the Housing Act (housing benefit and related matters: consequential amendments);

    and section 67 of the Act (repeals) in so far as it relates to those repeals; and

(d) paragraph 12 of Schedule 5 to the Act (minor and consequential amendments relating to Part 2) so far as it relates to the amendment of section 122(5) of the Housing Act and section 40 of the Act in so far as it relates to that consequential amendment.

(2)-(3) *[Omitted]*

(4) This article is subject to the savings and transitional provisions in articles 3 to 5.

Transitional provisions and savings in relation to section 130(4) of the Contributions and Benefits Act and section 122(3) and (5) of the Housing Act

3.–(1) Notwithstanding article 2 and subject to article 4–

(a) section 130(4) of the Contributions and Benefits Act and section 122(3) and (5) of the Housing Act shall continue to have effect as they were in force immediately before 7th April 2008 so far as is required for the purpose of conferring power to amend or revoke the regulations referred to in paragraph (2), until 7th April 2009; and

(b) any regulations made under any of the provisions referred to in sub-paragraph (a) shall continue to have effect in relation to the period ending on the date specified in paragraph (3), (4), (5) or (6) except for paragraphs 11 and 12 of Schedule 2 to the Consequential Provisions Regulations.

(2) The regulations are–

(a) the Regulations;

(b) the Housing Benefit (State Pension Credit) Regulations; and

(c) the Consequential Provisions Regulations.

(3)   In relation to a case in which reference was made to a maximum rent (standard local rate) in determining the eligible rent which applied immediately before 7th April 2008, the date is 7th April 2008.

(4)   In relation to a case where–

(a)   either–

    (i)   a claim for housing benefit is made, delivered or received on or after 7th April 2008 but the date the claim is made or is treated as being made is a date before 7th April 2008 by virtue of regulations 83, 83A, 84 or 85 of the Regulations or regulations 64, 64A, 65 or 66 of the Housing Benefit (State Pension Credit) Regulations; or

    (ii)   a claim was made or was treated as made before 7th April 2008 but the decision on the claim was not made by that date; and

(b)   reference to a maximum rent (standard local rate) would have been made in determining the eligible rent which applied immediately before 7th April 2008 had the decision on the claim been made before that date,

the date is 7th April 2008.

(5)   In relation to a non-local housing allowance case the date is the relevant date for that case.

(6)   In relation to a case where–

(a)   either–

    (i)   a claim for housing benefit is made, delivered or received on or after the 7th April 2008 but the date the claim is made or is treated as being made is a date before that date by virtue of regulations 83, 83A, 84 or 85 of the Regulations or regulations 64, 64A, 65 or 66 of the Housing Benefit (State Pension Credit) Regulations; or

    (ii)   a claim was made or was treated as made before 7th April 2008 but the decision on the claim was not made by that date; and

(b)   the case would have been a non-local housing allowance case had the decision on the claim been made before 7th April 2008,

the date is the relevant date for that case.

(7)   In this article–

"eligible rent" shall be construed, except in the definition of "the relevant date", in accordance with–

(a)   regulations 12 or 12A of the Regulations or the Housing Benefit (State Pension Credit) Regulations as in force immediately before the 7th April 2008; or

(b)   in a case to which paragraph 4 of Schedule 3 to the Consequential Provisions Regulations applies, regulations 12 and 13 of the Housing Benefit Regulations 2006 or the Housing Benefit (Persons who have attained the qualifying age for state pension credit) Regulations 2006 as set out in paragraph 5 of that Schedule as in force immediately before the 7th April 2008;

"maximum rent (standard local rate)" means a maximum rent (standard local rate) determined in accordance with regulation 13A of the Regulations or the Housing Benefit (State Pension Credit) Regulations as in force immediately before 7th April 2008;

"non-local housing allowance case" means a case where no reference was made to a maximum rent (standard local rate) in determining the amount of the eligible rent which applied immediately before 7th April 2008;

"the relevant date" means, in relation to a non-local housing allowance case–

(a)   the day on or after 7th April 2008 when any of the following sub-paragraphs first applies–

    (i)   a relevant authority is required to apply to a rent officer by virtue of regulation 14 of the Regulations or the Housing Benefit (State Pension Credit) Regulations as in force immediately before that day;

    (ii)   sub-paragraph (i) would apply but for the case falling within regulation 14(4)(a) of, or 14(4)(b) of and paragraph 2 of Schedule 2 to, the Regulations or the Housing Benefit (State Pension Credit) Regulations as in force immediately before that day;

(iii)   a relevant authority is required to determine an eligible rent in accordance with regulation 12(3)(b) of the Regulations or the Housing Benefit (State Pension Credit) Regulations as in force immediately before that day;

(iv)   a relevant authority is required to determine an eligible rent in accordance with regulation 12(3) of the Housing Benefit Regulations 2006 or the Housing Benefit (Persons who have attained the qualifying age for state pension credit) Regulations 2006 as set out in paragraph 5 of Schedule 3 to the Consequential Provisions Regulations as in force immediately before that day; or

(b)   6th April 2009 in any case where paragraph (a) does not apply before that date;
"relevant authority" means an authority administering housing benefit.

Transitional provisions and savings in relation to section 130(4) of the Contributions and Benefits Act and extended payments

4.–(1)   Notwithstanding article 2, regulations 72 and 73 of, and Schedules 7 and 8 to, the Regulations, and regulation 53 of, and Schedule 7 to, the Housing Benefit (State Pension Credit) Regulations shall continue to have effect in relation to the period ending on 6th October 2008 or such later date as is provided by paragraphs (2) or (3).

(2)   Where an extended payment award is determined before 6th October 2008 and the extended payment period will end after that date, the date shall be the end of that extended payment period.

(3)   Where a claim for an extended payment is made or treated as made on a date before 6th October 2008 but the extended payment award was not determined by that date, the date shall be the end of that extended payment period.

(4)   In this Article–
"extended payment" means a payment of housing benefit pursuant to–

(a)   regulation 72 of the Regulations (extended payments);

(b)   regulation 73 of the Regulations (extended payments (severe disablement allowance and incapacity benefit)); or

(c)   regulation 53 of the Housing Benefit (State Pension Credit) Regulations (extended payments severe disablement allowance and incapacity benefit),

where the date on which the claimant ceased to be entitled to housing benefit in accordance with regulation 77 or 78 of the Regulations or regulation 58 of the Housing Benefit (State Pension Credit) Regulations was before 6th October 2008; and
"extended payment period" means the period during which a person is entitled to housing benefit in accordance with regulation 72(6) or 73(6) of the Regulations or regulation 53(6) of the Housing Benefit (State Pension Credit) Regulations.

Transitional provisions and savings in relation to section 5(3) of the Administration Act

5.   Notwithstanding article 2, any regulations made under both section 5(1)(h) and 5(3) of the Administration Act shall continue to have effect for all purposes relating to the furnishing of information or evidence required by a rent officer under section 122 of the Housing Act 1996 in relation to a claim for or an award of housing benefit which relates to any period before 7th April 2008.

The Social Security (Local Authority Investigations and Prosecutions) Regulations 2008

(SI 2008 No.463)

Citation, commencement and interpretation

1.–(1) These Regulations may be cited as the Social Security (Local Authority Investigations and Prosecutions) Regulations 2008.

(2) These Regulations shall come into force on 7th April 2008.

(3) In these Regulations, "the Act" means the Social Security Administration Act 1992.

Authorisations by local authorities

2.–(1) An authority must not proceed for a purpose mentioned in section 109A(2)(a)(authorisations for investigators) of the Act unless the authorisation concerns one or more of the benefits listed in paragraph (5).

(2) An authority must not proceed for a purpose mentioned in section 109A(2)(c) of the Act unless the authorisation concerns relevant social security legislation relating to one or more of the benefits listed in paragraph (5).

(3) An authority must not proceed for a purpose mentioned in section 109A(2)(d) of the Act unless the authorisation concerns a benefit offence relating to one or more of the benefits listed in paragraph (5).

(4) An authorisation made for a purpose mentioned in section 109A(2)(a), (c) or (d) of the Act has effect in relation to a particular case only if in relation to that case an authorised officer has commenced an investigation for a purpose mentioned in section 110A(2) of that Act.

(5) The benefits are–

(a) income support;

(b) a jobseeker's allowance;

(c) incapacity benefit;

(d) state pension credit;

(e) an employment and support allowance.

Exercise of powers by local authorities to prosecute benefit fraud

3. For the purposes of paragraph (2)(a) of section 116A of the Act (local authority powers to prosecute benefit fraud), the benefits prescribed are all relevant social security benefits except for–

(a) income support;

(b) a jobseeker's allowance;

(c) incapacity benefit;

(d) state pension credit;

(e) an employment and support allowance.

The Welfare Reform Act 2007 (Commencement No. 7, Transitional and Savings Provisions) Order 2008

(SI 2008 No.2101)

Citation and interpretation

1.–(1)   This Order may be cited as the Welfare Reform Act 2007 (Commencement No. 7, Transitional and Savings Provisions) Order 2008.

(2)   In this Order ''the Act'' means the Welfare Reform Act 2007.

Transitional and savings provisions

3.–(1)   The following provisions of the Local Government Act 2000 continue to have effect after 31st August 2008 in relation to information supplied on or before that date by virtue of section 94 of that Act–

(a)   section 94(4), (5) and (6) (which permits the onward supply of information received by virtue of section 94(3) to a person providing qualifying welfare services); and

(b)   section 95 (under which a person is guilty of an offence if he makes an unauthorised disclosure of information).

(2)   Paragraph (1) applies notwithstanding article 2(2) (which brings into force on 1st September 2008 the repeal of sections 94 and 95).

(3)   *[Omitted]*

The Social Security (Use of Information for Housing Benefit and Welfare Services Purposes) Regulations 2008

(SI 2008 No.2112)

Citation and commencement
1. These Regulations may be cited as the Social Security (Use of Information for Housing Benefit and Welfare Services Purposes) Regulations 2008 and shall come into force on 1st September 2008.

Interpretation
2. In these Regulations–

"the 2007 Act" means the Welfare Reform Act 2007;

"benefit or welfare services information" means information falling within section 42(3) of the 2007 Act (information relating to certain benefits);

"claimant" means a person claiming housing benefit;

"excluded tenancy" means a type of tenancy falling within any of paragraphs 4 to 11 of Schedule 2 to the Housing Benefit Regulations (excluded tenancies) or paragraphs 4 to 11 of Schedule 2 to the Housing Benefit (State Pension Credit) Regulations (excluded tenancies), as the case may require;

"exempt accommodation" has the meaning given by sub-paragraph 4(10) of Schedule 3 to the Housing Benefit and Council Tax Benefit (Consequential Provisions) Regulations 2006(3) (transitional and savings provisions);

"hostel" has the same meaning as it has in the Housing Benefit Regulations or the Housing Benefit (State Pension Credit) Regulations, as the case may require;

"the Housing Benefit Regulations" means the Housing Benefit Regulations 2006(4);

"the Housing Benefit (State Pension Credit) Regulations" means the Housing Benefit (Persons who have attained the qualifying age for state pension credit) Regulations 2006(5);

"landlord" includes a person to whom rent is payable by the person entitled to a rent allowance for the purposes of regulation 95 of the Housing Benefit Regulations (circumstances in which payment is to be made to a landlord) or regulation 76 of the Housing Benefit (State Pension Credit) Regulations (circumstances in which payment is to be made to a landlord), as the case may require;

"registered social landlord" has the same meaning as in Part 1 of the Housing Act 1996(6);

"relevant person" means a person falling within any of paragraphs (c) to (h) of section 42(4) of the 2007 Act;

"rent" has the same meaning as it has in the Housing Benefit Regulations or the Housing Benefit (State Pension Credit) Regulations, as the case may require.

Prescribed purposes in section 42(2) of the 2007 Act
3. Regulations 4, 5 and 6 prescribe meanings of "prescribed purpose" in section 42(2) of the 2007 Act (information relating to certain benefits) for the purposes set out in those regulations.

Holding purposes relating to welfare services
4.–(1) This regulation prescribes the purposes for which a relevant person holds benefit or welfare services information ("holding purposes").

(2) The holding purposes are purposes relating to welfare services which may indicate–

    (a) whether a claimant is likely to have difficulty in managing his financial affairs;

    (b) the probability that a claimant will pay his rent;

    (c) whether a landlord–

        (i) was or is to provide qualifying welfare services within the meaning of section 42(6) of the 2007 Act, but

        (ii) has not provided those services or is unlikely to provide those services;

(d) whether–
 (i) a claimant's landlord is a registered social landlord [¹ or a private registered provider of social housing],
 (ii) a claimant occupies as his home a dwelling which is exempt accommodation,
 (iii) a claimant's tenancy is an excluded tenancy,
 (iv) a claimant occupies a houseboat, caravan or mobile home as his home, or
 (v) a claimant resides in a hostel.

Amendment

1.   Amended by Art 4 and Sch 1 para 71 of SI 2010 No 671 as from 1.4.10.

Using purposes relating to housing benefit

5.–(1) This regulation prescribes meanings of "prescribed purpose" for which benefit or welfare services information may be used ("using purposes") by–
 (a) the relevant person in relation to whom regulation 4 applies; or
 (b) another relevant person to whom the benefit or welfare services information has been provided.

(2) The using purposes are purposes relating to housing benefit connected with applying any of the following regulations–
 (a) regulation 13C(5) of the Housing Benefit Regulations(7) (when a maximum rent (LHA) is to be determined);
 (b) regulation 96(3) and (3A)(b)(i) or (ii) of the Housing Benefit Regulations(8) (circumstances in which payment may be made to a landlord), if a relevant authority is considering making direct payments in accordance with regulation 96(3A)(b)(i) or (ii);
 (c) regulation 13C(5) of the Housing Benefit (State Pension Credit) Regulations(9) (when a maximum rent (LHA) is to be determined);
 (d) regulation 77(3) and (3A)(b)(i) or (ii) of the Housing Benefit (State Pension Credit) Regulations(10) (circumstances in which payment may be made to a landlord), if a relevant authority is considering making direct payments in accordance with regulation 77(3A)(b)(i) or (ii).

Identifying purposes

6.–(1) This regulation prescribes meanings of "prescribed purpose" for the purposes of determining whether a relevant person holds benefit or welfare services information related to any holding purpose prescribed by regulation 4 ("identifying purposes").

(2) The identifying purposes are any purposes relating to housing benefit connected with identifying a claimant.

The Welfare Reform Act (Relevant Enactment) Order 2009
(SI 2009 No.2162)

Citation and commencement

1.–(1)   This Order may be cited as the Welfare Reform Act (Relevant Enactment) Order 2009.

(2)   It comes into force on 1st September 2009.

Relevant enactment

2.   A relevant enactment for the purposes of section 42(1) of the Welfare Reform Act 2007 (information relating to certain benefits) is section 31 of the Local Government Act 2003 (power to pay grant).

The Flexible New Deal (Miscellaneous Provisions) Order 2009
(SI 2009 No.1562)

This Order specifies when participation in the "Flexible New Deal" is to be treated as training (rather than employed). In consequence, any payments received by the trainee (other than the trading payments specified) are to be treated as a training allowance for the purposes of HB and CTB. See also the New Deal (Miscellaneous Provisions) Order 1998 (on p1167), the New Deal (Miscellaneous Provisions) Order 2001 (on p1174), the New Deal (Lone Parents) (Miscellaneous Provisions) Order 2001 (on p1182), the Community Task Force (Miscellaneous Provisions) Order 2010 (on p1246) and the Jobseeker's Allowance (Work for Your Benefit Pilot Scheme) Regulations 2010 (on p1247).

Citation, commencement and interpretation

1.–(1)   This Order may be cited as the Flexible New Deal (Miscellaneous Provisions) Order 2009.

(2)   It shall come into force on 5th October 2009.

(3)   In this Order–

"the Flexible New Deal" means the employment programme specified in regulation 75(1)(a)(v) of the Jobseeker's Allowance Regulations 1996;

"facilities" includes the provision of services;

"New Deal participant", in relation to any time, means a person who is at that time participating in the Flexible New Deal;

"trading payment" means a payment made to a Flexible New Deal participant in consideration of goods or services supplied by that person in the course of participating in the Flexible New Deal;

"training allowance" means a payment made by the Secretary of State to a person in connection with that person's participation in the Flexible New Deal.

Treatment of persons and payments for the purposes of the Social Security Contributions and Benefits Act 1992, the Jobseekers Act 1995 and specified subordinate legislation

2.–(1)   The provisions of this article shall apply to the following legislation–

(a)-(b) *[Omitted]*

(c)   the subordinate legislation specified in the Schedule to this Order. .

(2)   If, for any period commencing on or after the day on which this Order comes into force, a Flexible New Deal participant receives, or is eligible to receive, a training allowance, that person is to be treated for that period and in respect of participation in the Flexible New Deal as not being employed but as participating in arrangements for training under section 2 of the Employment and Training Act 1973.

(3)   Except as mentioned in paragraph (4), any payment made to a Flexible New Deal participant during that period in connection with that person's use of facilities provided in pursuance of those arrangements shall be treated in the same manner as a payment of training allowance made in respect of such training.

(4)   Paragraph (3) does not apply in respect of any trading payment made to a Flexible New Deal participant who is receiving assistance in pursuing self-employed earner's employment whilst participating in that programme.

Schedule
ARTICLE 2(1)(C)

LIST OF SUBORDINATE LEGISLATION

[Various omitted]

The Housing Benefit Regulations 2006

The Housing Benefit (Persons who have attained the qualifying age for state pension credit) Regulations 2006

The Council Tax Benefit Regulations 2006

The Council Tax Benefit (Persons who have attained the qualifying age for state pension credit) Regulations 2006

The Community Task Force (Miscellaneous Provisions) Order 2010
(SI 2010 No.349)

This Order specifies when participation in the "Community Task Force" is to be treated as training (rather than employment). In consequence, any payment received by the trainee is to be treated as a training allowance for the purposes of HB and CTB. See also the New Deal (Miscellaneous Provisions) Order 1998 (on p1167), the New Deal (Miscellaneous Provisions) Order 2001 on (p1174,) the New Deal (Lone Parents) (Miscellaneous Provisions) Order 2001 (on p1182), the Flexible New Deal (Miscellaneous Provisions) Order 2009 (on p1245), and the Jobseeker's Allowance (Work for Your Benefit Pilot Scheme) Regulations 2010 (on p1247).

Citation, commencement and interpretation

1.–(1)   This Order may be cited as the Community Task Force (Miscellaneous Provisions) Order 2010.

(2)   It shall come into force on 15 March 2010.

(3)   In this Order–

"the Community Task Force" means a programme known by that name and provided pursuant to arrangements made by the Secretary of State under section 2 of the Employment and Training Act 1973 for any individual aged 18 years or over and less than 25 on the first required entry date to the programme and which includes for that individual work experience and job search;

"facilities" includes the provision of services;

"Community Task Force participant", in relation to any time, means a person who is at that time participating in the Community Task Force;

"training allowance" means a payment made by the Secretary of State to a person in connection with that person's participation in the Community Task Force and includes a training premium.

Treatment of persons and payments for the purposes of the Social Security Contributions and Benefits Act 1992, the Jobseekers Act 1995 and specified subordinate legislation

2.–(1)   The provisions of this article apply to the following legislation–

(a)   Part 1 of the Social Security Contributions and Benefits Act 1992(3);

(b)   the Jobseekers Act 1995(4); and

(c)   the subordinate legislation specified in the Schedule to this Order.

(2)   If, for any period commencing on or after the day on which this Order comes into force, a Community Task Force participant receives, or is eligible to receive, a training allowance, that person is to be treated for that period and in respect of participation in the Community Task Force as not being employed but as participating in arrangements for training under section 2 of the Employment and Training Act 1973.

(3)   Any payment made to a Community Task Force participant during that period in connection with that person's use of facilities provided in pursuance of those arrangements shall be treated in the same manner as a payment of training allowance made in respect of such training.

Schedule
ARTICLE 2(1)(C)

LIST OF SUBORDINATE LEGISLATION

[Various omitted]

The Housing Benefit Regulations 2006

The Housing Benefit (Persons who have attained the qualifying age for state pension credit) Regulations 2006

The Council Tax Benefit Regulations 2006

The Council Tax Benefit (Persons who have attained the qualifying age for state pension credit) Regulations 2006

Jobseeker's Allowance (Work for Your Benefit Pilot Scheme) Regulations 2010

(2010 No.1222)

This Order deals with the treatment of income and capital payments received as a consequence of participation in the "Work for Your Benefit Pilot Scheme" for the purposes of HB and CTB. See also the New Deal (Miscellaneous Provisions) Order 1998 on p1167, the New Deal (Miscellaneous Provisions) Order 2001 on p1174, the New Deal (Lone Parents) (Miscellaneous Provisions) Order 2001 on p1182, the Flexible New Deal (Miscellaneous Provisions) Order 2009 on p1245 and the Community Task Force (Miscellaneous Provisions) Order 2010 on p1246.

Citation, commencement and duration

1.–(1)   These Regulations may be cited as the Jobseeker's Allowance (Work for Your Benefit Pilot Scheme) Regulations 2010.

(2)   They come into force on 22nd November 2010.

(3)   They cease to have effect on 21st November 2013.

Interpretation

2.   In these Regulations–

"the Council Tax Benefit Regulations" means the Council Tax Benefit Regulations 2006;

"the Housing Benefit Regulations" means the Housing Benefit Regulations 2006;

"pilot area" means any of the following Jobcentre Plus districts–

(a)   Cambridgeshire and Suffolk;

(b)   Greater Manchester Central;

(c)   Greater Manchester East and West;

(d)   Norfolk;

"Work for Your Benefit Pilot Scheme" means a scheme within section 17A(1) (schemes for assisting persons to obtain employment: "work for your benefit" schemes etc.) of the Act known by that name and provided pursuant to arrangements made by the Secretary of State that is designed to assist claimants to obtain employment, including self-employment, and which includes for any individual work experience and job search.

Part 6
Consequential Modifications

Definitions

13.–(1)   Paragraph (2) applies to the following provisions (which relate to interpretation)–

(a)   regulation 2(1) of the Council Tax Benefit Regulations;

(b)   regulation 2(1) of the Housing Benefit Regulations;

(c)-(d) [Omitted]

(2)   Each of the provisions to which this paragraph applies has effect as if the following definition were inserted in the appropriate place–

""the Work for Your Benefit Pilot Scheme" means a scheme within section 17A(1) of the Jobseekers Act 1995 known by that name and provided pursuant to arrangements made by the Secretary of State that is designed to assist claimants to obtain employment, including self-employment, and which includes for any individual work experience and job search;".

(3)   The definition of "the self-employment route" in each of the provisions mentioned in paragraph (1)(a), (b) and (d) above has effect as if–

(a)   at the end of sub-paragraph (a) "or" were omitted; and

(b)   at the end of sub-paragraph (b) "; or" and the following sub-paragraph were inserted–

"(c)   the Work for Your Benefit Pilot Scheme;".

(4)   *[Omitted]*

Notional income
14.–(1)   This regulation applies to the following provisions (which relate to notional income)–
(a)   regulation 32(7) of the Council Tax Benefit Regulations;
(b)   regulation 42(7) of the Housing Benefit Regulations;
(c)-(d) *[Omitted]*
(2)   Each of the provisions to which this regulation applies has effect as if the following sub-paragraph were inserted after sub-paragraph (c)–
(ca)   in respect of a person's participation in the Work for Your Benefit Pilot Scheme;''.

Notional capital
15.–(1)   This regulation applies to the following provisions (which relate to notional capital)–
(a)   regulation 39(4) of the Council Tax Benefit Regulations;
(b)   regulation 49(4) of the Housing Benefit Regulations;
(c)-(d) *[Omitted]*
(2)   Each of the provisions to which this regulation applies has effect as if the following sub-paragraph were inserted after sub-paragraph (b)–
''(ba) in respect of a person's participation in the Work for Your Benefit Pilot Scheme;''.

Income to be disregarded
16.–(1)   This regulation applies to the following Schedules (which relate to sums to be disregarded in the calculation of income other than earnings)–
(a)   Schedule 4 to the Council Tax Benefit Regulations;
(b)   Schedule 5 to the Housing Benefit Regulations;
(c)-(d) *[Omitted]*
(2)   Each Schedule to which this regulation applies has effect as if the following paragraph were inserted at the beginning–
"A1.   Any payment made to the claimant in respect of any child care, travel or other expenses incurred, or to be incurred, by him in respect of his participation in the Work for Your Benefit Pilot Scheme.".

Capital to be disregarded
17.–(1)   This regulation applies to the following Schedules (which relate to capital to be disregarded)–
(a)   Schedule 5 to the Council Tax Benefit Regulations;
(b)   Schedule 6 to the Housing Benefit Regulations;
(c)-(d) *[Omitted]*
(2)   Each Schedule to which this regulation applies has effect as if the following paragraph were inserted at the beginning–
"A1.   Any payment made to the claimant in respect of any child care, travel or other expenses incurred, or to be incurred, by him in respect of his participation in the Work for Your Benefit Scheme but only for 52 weeks beginning with the date of receipt of the payment.".

Consequential modifications relating to sanctions
19.–(1)   Paragraph (2) applies to the following provisions–
(a)   regulation 2(4)(a) and (b) (interpretation) of the Council Tax Benefit Regulations;
(b)   regulation 2(4)(a) and (b) (interpretation) of the Council Tax Benefit (Persons who have attained the qualifying age for state pension credit) Regulations 2006;
(c)   regulation 3(j) (circumstances in which discretionary housing payments may be made) of the Discretionary Financial Assistance Regulations 2001;
(d)   regulation 2(3)(a) and (b) (interpretation) of the Housing Benefit Regulations;
(e)   regulation 2(3)(a) and (b) (interpretation) of the Housing Benefit (Persons who have attained the qualifying age for state pension credit) Regulations 2006;
(2)   Each of the provisions to which this paragraph applies has effect as if the words ''or regulations made under section 17A'' were inserted after ''section 19 or 20A''.
(3)-(4)   *[Omitted]*

Index

Entries against the bold headings direct you to the general information on the subject, or where the subject is covered most fully. Sub-entries are listed alphabetically and direct you to specific aspects of the subject.

(CTB) Council tax benefit
(PC) Pension credit

(HB) Housing benefit

A
A2 nationals 278
A8 nationals 278
abroad
  calculation of capital abroad
    CTB 681
    CTB over PC age 950
    HB 383
    HB over PC age 833
  dwelling outside GB
    HB 233
    HB over PC age 785
  payment for employment abroad
    CTB 740
    HB 549
  payment in currencies other than sterling
    CTB 740, 746, 753
    CTB over PC age 987
    HB 549, 559
    HB over PC age 893
absence from home
  CTB 658, 661
  CTB over PC age 930
  detention in custody
    CTB 659
    CTB over PC age 928
    HB 236
    HB over PC age 787
  domestic violence
    HB 237
    HB over PC age 788
  HB 236, 335
  HB over PC age 787, 810
  repairs
    HB 234
    HB over PC age 785
  students
    CTB 659
    HB 236, 401
    HB over PC age 788
  temporary absence
    CTB 659
    CTB over PC age 928
    HB 236, 242
    HB over PC age 787
  trial stay in care home
    CTB 659
    CTB over PC age 928
    HB 235
    HB over PC age 787

absence from work
  CTB 656
  CTB over PC age 925
  HB 230, 430
  HB over PC age 784
academic year
  CTB 687
  HB 395
access funds
  definition 395
    CTB 687
  treatment as capital
    CTB 697
    HB 417
  treatment as income
    CTB 696
    HB 416
accommodation
  size criteria
    HB 609, 628
adaptations to home
  claiming before moving home 786
  HB 235
administration of benefits
  benefits administration information 71
    CTB 726
    CTB aged 60 or over 981
    HB 511
    HB aged 60 or over 881
  contracting out benefit functions by local
    authorities 1190
  reports on local authorities 83
Administrative Appeals Chamber 173
  functions 1110
adoption
  disregard of allowances
    CTB 744
    HB 557
  treatment as member of household
    CTB 661
    CTB over PC age 930
    HB 335
    HB over PC age 810
adoption leave
  definition of adoption leave
    CTB 645
    CTB over PC age 916
    HB 210
  in remunerative work
    CTB 668
    CTB over PC age 940

HB 350
 HB over PC age 821
advance claims
 CTB 711
 CTB over PC age 967
 HB 235, 447, 450
 HB over PC age 856
advance payment of rent
 HB 244
 HB over PC age 789
advantage
 taking advantage of benefit scheme
  CTB 655
  CTB over PC age 924
  HB 262
age rules 23
 HB 248
agents 77
aggregation
 applicable amount 15
  CTB 662
  CTB over PC age 931
  HB 337
  HB over PC age 810
 income and capital 16
  CTB 13
 treatment of child's income and capital
  CTB 681
 treatment of family's income and capital
  CTB 663
  CTB over PC age 932
  HB 344
  HB over PC age 811
almshouses
 HB 300
 HB over PC age 793
alternative dispute resolution 1051, 1080
alternative maximum council tax benefit 704,
715, 959
 aggregation 13
 amount 704, 736, 959
  CTB over PC age 996
 duty to notify change of circumstances 715
 entitlement 11, 705, 959
 notification 761, 999
 students 690
amending a claim
 CTB 714
 CTB over PC age 970
 HB 456
 HB over PC age 858
amount of benefit
 alternative maximum CTB 704, 736, 959
 couples
  CTB 13
 CTB 11
 CTB over PC age 996
 HB 5, 418
 maximum amount
  CTB 697
  CTB over PC age 953
  HB 418
  HB over PC age 837
 minimum
  HB 432
  HB over PC age 844
 non-dependant deductions

CTB 698
 CTB over PC age 954
 tapers
  CTB 700
  CTB over PC age 956
  HB 393
 weekly amount
  HB 437
  HB over PC age 850
annuities
 disregarded
  CTB 752
  CTB over PC age 989
  HB 570
  HB over PC age 895
 notional capital/income
  HB 377
 self-employed earners
  CTB 674
  CTB over PC age 945, 946
  HB 366
  HB over PC age 828
 treatment as income
  CTB 677
  HB 372
anti-social behaviour
 eviction
  HB 7, 162
 pilot scheme 10, 418
anti-test case rule 157
appeal tribunals
 abolition 170, 1102
 functions transferred to First-tier and Upper
  tribunals 193, 1102
 transitional provisions 1103
appeals 136, 139, 1005
 appeals structure 107
 decisions which can be appealed 144, 1029
 decisions with no right of appeal 1036, 1176
 effect of other appeal 155
 late appeals 1038
 legal aid 1088
 lookalike appeals 1061
 notice of appeal 1040, 1062, 1091
 recovery of overpayments 147
 revised decision
  HB/CTB 1036
 right to appeal to Court of Appeal 183
 right to appeal to First-tier Tribunal 145
 right to appeal to Upper Tribunal 176
 service of notices and documents
  HB/CTB 1007
 setting aside tribunal decisions 201
 test case pending
  HB/CTB 1036
 time limits 1075
  HB/CTB 1038
 who has right of appeal 1009
applicable amounts 15
 CTB 662, 726
 CTB over PC age 931, 981
 HB 337, 521
 HB over PC age 810
 hospital patients
  CTB 663
  HB 339
 personal allowance

CTB 726
CTB over PC age 981
HB 521
polygamous marriages
CTB 663
HB 338
applications
permission to appeal 1071, 1090, 1099
appointees
acting on behalf of the claimant
HB 443
person to receive benefit for claimant
CTB 707, 717
CTB over PC age 963, 974
HB 442, 469
HB over PC age 852, 863
recovery of overpayments
HB 490
apportionment
alternative maximum CTB 704, 959
council tax 697
non-dependants 842
CTB 698
CTB over PC age 955
HB 428
rent 304
student grant income
CTB 693
HB 410
student loans
CTB 695
HB 414
appropriate DWP office
CTB 645
CTB over PC age 916
HB 210
HB over PC age 771
approved training
HB 333
armed services
mobility supplement disregarded
CTB 742
HB 552
arrears
disregard of benefit arrears
CTB 752
CTB over PC age 994
HB 568
HB over PC age 902
offsetting against overpayments
CTB 718
CTB over PC age 974
HB 476
HB over PC age 866
rent arrears
HB 299
HB over PC age 792
treatment of arrears of income
CTB 707
CTB over PC age 961
HB 435
HB over PC age 846
treatment of benefit arrears
CTB 706
CTB over PC age 961
HB 437

assessment period
definition
CTB 645
CTB over PC age 916
HB 210
HB over PC age 771
employed earners
CTB 669
HB 353
income other than earnings
CTB 669
HB 355
self-employed earners
CTB 669
HB 355
assured tenancy
definition
HB 592, 594, 614
asylum seekers 1129, 1218
calculation of income
CTB 677
HB 371
exclusion from benefits 1129
loss of status 1220
on arrival claims 1220
retrospective claim for benefit
CTB 1170
HB 1170
transitional protection 1153, 1170
upheaval declarations 1220
attendance allowance
disregarded
CTB 742
CTB over PC age 934
HB 552
HB over PC age 815

B
backdating
HB 432, 451
refugees 1131, 1170
CTB 658
HB 542
bankruptcy
HB 491
recovery of overpayments 99
treatment of payments from pension
schemes
CTB 679, 682
HB 374, 384
beneficial interest
CTB 686, 743
CTB over PC age 953
HB 391, 555
benefit changes
treatment as income
HB 374, 378
HB over PC age 831
benefit offences
definition 1141
disqualification from benefit 1186
effect on family's benefit 1142
loss of benefit 167, 1136, 1140
one strike scheme 1137
reduction of benefit
HB/CTB 1188

benefit week
CTB 645
CTB over PC age 917
HB 210, 432
HB over PC age 772
bereavement benefits
disregarded income
CTB 743
HB 555
bereavement premium
CTB 729
HB 526
billing authority
administration
CTB 82
definition 18
blind
non-dependant deductions
CTB 698
CTB over PC age 955
HB 428
HB over PC age 842
blind homeworkers' scheme
CTB 756
HB 576
board
definition
HB over PC age 772
boarders
board and attendance determinations 503, 598, 618
board and attendance redeterminations 599
date entitlement begins
HB 432
HB over PC age 844
exceptions to determinations 600
insufficient information for rent officer 600, 620
non-dependants
HB 226, 431
HB over PC age 783
payments disregarded
CTB 744
CTB over PC age 989
HB 561
HB over PC age 894
substitute determinations 599
bonus of wages
treatment as earnings
CTB 671
CTB over PC age 942
HB 358
HB over PC age 824
broad rental market area 596, 612, 617, 631
definition 323, 603
business
assets disregarded as capital
CTB 751
CTB over PC age 991
HB 568
HB over PC age 899
costs of accommodation
HB 304
expenses/debts
CTB 674
CTB over PC age 945

HB 365
HB over PC age 828
business partners
calculation of net profit
HB 365
HB over PC age 828

C
calculations
CTB 697
CTB over PC age 953
campsite fees
HB 601, 612, 621, 631
HB over PC age 793
capital 16
abroad
CTB 681
CTB over PC age 950
HB 383
HB over PC age 833
arrears of benefit
CTB 752
HB 568
HB over PC age 833
calculation
CTB 680
CTB over PC age 932, 949
HB 380
HB over PC age 812, 833
calculation of capital in UK
CTB 681
CTB over PC age 950
HB 382
HB over PC age 833
calculation of capital outside UK
CTB 681
CTB over PC age 950
HB 383
HB over PC age 833
capital limit 15
CTB 680
CTB over PC age 949
HB 380
HB over PC age 832
capital limit increase backdating a claim
HB 432
charitable payments
CTB 681
HB 381
child/young person's
CTB 681
HB 344, 380
HB over PC age 811
CTB 680
deprivation of capital
CTB 681
CTB over PC age 950
HB 383
HB over PC age 833
difference between income and capital
HB 339
diminishing notional capital rule
CTB 683
CTB over PC age 950
HB 388
HB over PC age 834
diminution of capital

CTB 721
CTB over PC age 976
HB 494
HB over PC age 869
disregards
CTB 680, 751
CTB over PC age 949, 991
HB 380, 565, 566
HB over PC age 833, 898
family's capital 16
CTB 13, 663
CTB over PC age 932
HB 344
HB over PC age 811
HB 339, 379
income from capital 16
CTB 664, 681, 686, 743
CTB over PC age 935, 936
HB 381, 393, 555
HB over PC age 816, 898
income treated as capital 16
CTB 681, 746
HB 381, 559, 572
instalments of capital
CTB 677
HB 372
jointly held capital
CTB 686
CTB over PC age 953
HB 391
HB over PC age 837
non-dependant's
CTB 664
CTB over PC age 932
HB 345
HB over PC age 812
notional capital
CTB 681
CTB over PC age 950
HB 383
HB over PC age 833
partner's
CTB 663
CTB over PC age 932
HB 344
qualifying age for PC 17
tariff income 16
CTB 664, 686
CTB over PC age 936
HB 393
third party payments
CTB 682
HB 384
treatment as income 16
CTB 665, 677, 753
HB 346, 369, 372
treatment of guarantee credit
CTB over PC age 932
HB over PC age 812
treatment of savings credit
CTB over PC age 932
HB over PC age 813
valuation of capital
CTB 681
CTB over PC age 950
HB 382
HB over PC age 833

care
child/young person
HB 335
HB over PC age 810
care homes
absence from home
CTB 659, 660
CTB over PC age 929
HB 237
HB over PC age 788
counselling and care charges 108
definition
CTB 660
HB 237
HB over PC age 772, 788
HB 1222
not liable to make payments on a dwelling
HB 250, 262
HB over PC age 790
public bodies 117
rent officer determinations 600
residents disregarded for council tax
discount 1120
tariff income
HB 393
trial period
CTB 659
CTB over PC age 928
HB 235
HB over PC age 787
care leavers
exclusion from benefits 1132
career development loans
HB 372
carers
cost of care paid by employer
CTB 671
CTB over PC age 942
HB 358
HB over PC age 825
disregard of care payments
HB 558
disregarded for council tax discount 1121
earnings disregard
CTB 739
CTB over PC age 985
HB 545
HB over PC age 891
non-dependants
CTB 654
CTB over PC age 924
HB 227
HB over PC age 783
students entitled to benefit
CTB 691
HB 403
treatment of care payments
CTB 673
HB 364
HB over PC age 827
carer's premium
amount
CTB 733
CTB over PC age 985
HB 535
HB over PC age 890
CTB 732

CTB over PC age 984
earnings disregards
  CTB 739
  HB 545
HB 533
HB over PC age 889
Chamber President 172
change of circumstances
arrears of income 1197
CTB 713
CTB over PC age 969
date change takes effect
  CTB 706
  CTB over PC age 960
  HB 434
  HB over PC age 845
duty to notify
  CTB 714
  CTB over PC age 970
  HB 457
  HB over PC age 859
duty to report
  HB/CTB 1183
HB 434, 453
HB aged 60 or over 845, 857
pension credit
  CTB over PC age 961, 971
  HB over PC age 847, 860
supersessions 1024
supersessions – late application
  HB/CTB 1028
charitable payments
disregarded
  CTB 743, 755
  HB 553, 575
students
  CTB 694
  HB 413
treatment as income and capital
  CTB 681
  HB 381
child benefit
CTB 661, 1119
CTB aged 60 or over 930
disregarded
  CTB 750
  CTB over PC age 934
  HB 565
  HB over PC age 815
HB 333
HB aged 60 or over 809
child support
payments disregarded
  CTB 748
  HB 562
child tax credit 1147
arrears treated as capital
  HB 381
calculation of average weekly income 356
  HB 356
  HB over PC age 822
notional income/capital
  CTB 682
  HB 373
treatment as income
  CTB 676
  CTB over PC age 935

HB 369
HB over PC age 816
childcare
deduction of charges
  CTB 664
  HB 346, 347
  HB over PC age 818
eligible charges
  CTB 666
  CTB over PC age 937
estimating relevant charges
  CTB 667
  CTB over PC age 938
  HB 349
  HB over PC age 820
maternity leave
  HB 350
parental leave
  CTB 668
  CTB over PC age 940
relevant charges
  HB 348
  HB over PC age 819
student grant income – disregards
  CTB 693
treatment of charges
  CTB 665
  CTB over PC age 936
childminders
calculation of net profit
  CTB 674, 675
  CTB over PC age 946
  HB 366, 368
  HB over PC age 828, 829
costs paid by employer
  CTB 671
  CTB over PC age 942
  HB over PC age 825
children
applicable amount
  CTB 662
  CTB over PC age 931
claiming for a child
  HB 335
  HB over PC age 809
death of a child
  HB 334
definition 18
  CTB 645, 660
  CTB over PC age 929
  HB 210
  HB over PC age 772
disregarded capital
  CTB 681
  HB 380
disregarded for council tax discount 1119
duty to notify changes in family
  CTB 715
  CTB over PC age 971
  HB 457
  HB over PC age 859
landlord's child – responsibility for
  HB 249
  HB over PC age 789
leaving care 1132
member of household
  CTB 661

CTB over PC age 930
HB over PC age 809
non-dependants
CTB 654
CTB over PC age 924
HB 226
HB over PC age 782
payments from child disregarded
CTB 744
HB 556
responsibility for child
CTB 661, 691
CTB over PC age 930
HB 334, 402
HB over PC age 809
treatment of income and capital
CTB 681, 740
HB 344, 549
HB over PC age 811

children in care
disregard of care payments
CTB 673
HB 364, 558
HB over PC age 827
leaving care 1132
treatment as member of household
CTB 661
CTB over PC age 930
HB 335
HB over PC age 810

children in need
payments disregarded
CTB 753
HB 571

civil partners
close relatives 1148
definition of couple 18, 1006
stepchildren 1148, 1195
transitional arrangements 1193

claim forms
CTB 708
CTB over PC age 964
HB 443
HB over PC age 853

claim-related rent 635, 637
HB 312, 314, 606, 626
HB over PC age 798

claims 28
advance claims
CTB 711
CTB over PC age 967
HB 447, 450
HB over PC age 856
amending a claim
CTB 714
CTB over PC age 970
HB 456
HB over PC age 858
backdating
HB 432, 451
claim forms
CTB 708
HB 443
claiming procedure
CTB 708
CTB over PC age 964
HB 443

HB over PC age 853
date entitlement begins
CTB 706
CTB over PC age 960
HB 432
HB over PC age 844
date of claim
CTB 646
CTB over PC age 917, 965
HB 211, 445
HB over PC age 773
defective claims
CTB 710
CTB over PC age 966
HB 446
HB over PC age 855
discretionary housing payments 1180
electronic claims
CTB 712
CTB over PC age 968
HB 452, 590
HB over PC age 857
end of claim
CTB 706
CTB over PC age 960
HB 434
HB over PC age 845
evidence to support claim
CTB 712
CTB over PC age 969
HB 453
HB over PC age 857
information required by local authority
CTB 723
CTB over PC age 978
HB 501
HB over PC age 872
late claims
HB 451
national insurance number requirement 28
power to make regulations about
administration of claims 35
CTB 37
retrospective effect of requirement for claim
30
telephone claims
CTB 708
CTB over PC age 964
HB 444
HB over PC age 853
where to claim
CTB 708
HB 444, 448
HB over PC age 853
who can claim
CTB 707
CTB over PC age 963
HB 442
HB over PC age 852
withdrawing a claim
CTB 714
HB 456
HB over PC age 858
written claims
CTB 708
CTB over PC age 964

HB 443
HB over PC age 853
close relatives
civil partners 1148
definition
CTB 645
CTB over PC age 917
HB 210
HB over PC age 772
landlord
HB 249, 256
HB over PC age 789
co-ownership scheme
definition
HB over PC age 772
HB 211, 300
HB over PC age 793
coastguard
earnings disregard
CTB 739
CTB over PC age 985
HB 546
HB over PC age 891
HB 546
commencement
Council Tax Benefit (Persons who have
attained the qualifying age for state
pension credit) Regulations 2006 916
Council Tax Benefit Regulations 2006 644
Housing Benefit (Persons who have attained
the qualifying age for state pension credit)
Regulations 2006 771
Housing Benefit Regulations 2006 209
Rent Officers (Housing Benefit Functions)
(Scotland) Order 1997 614
Rent Officers (Housing Benefit Functions)
Order 1997 592
Social Security Act 1998 110
Social Security Administration Act 104
Social Security Contributions and Benefits
Act 25
Tribunal Procedure (First-tier Tribunal)
(Social Entitlement Chamber) Rules 2008
1048
Tribunal Procedure (Upper Tribunal) Rules
2008 1078
commercial basis
CTB 655
CTB over PC age 924
HB 226, 249, 250
HB over PC age 783, 789, 790
non-commercial agreements
HB 252
commission
treatment as earnings
CTB 671
CTB over PC age 942
HB 358
HB over PC age 824
common travel area 268
communal areas
definition
HB 517
HB over PC age 884
fuel charges
HB 515
HB over PC age 883

community care
direct payments
CTB 750
HB 564
Community Task Force 1246
treatment of payments 1246
compensation
for unfair dismissal
CTB 671
HB 358
income/capital disregards
CTB 753, 757
HB 568, 570, 577
HB over PC age 902
treatment as income or capital 342
components
entitlement to components
CTB 733
HB 536
concessionary payment
CTB 752
definition
CTB 645
CTB over PC age 917
HB 210
HB over PC age 772
disregards
CTB 742
HB 552
HB 534, 568
conditional sale agreement
HB 300
HB over PC age 793
continuity of the law 106
contrived tenancy
CTB 655
CTB over PC age 924
HB 249
taking advantage of benefit scheme
CTB 664
CTB over PC age 932
HB 250, 262, 345
HB over PC age 790, 812
convictions
conviction quashed 1138
loss of benefit 1136
council tax 1113
discounts 719, 1114, 1116
disregards for discount 1119
joint liability 697, 704, 959
liability 1113, 1116
reduction 1114
reduction of liability 718, 975
reductions 1117
setting amounts 1115, 1118
council tax benefit 641
adminstration 82
claiming other benefits 39
disregarded as income
HB 563
entitlement 11
over PC age 913
permitted totals 1161
power to modify scheme 82
councillors' allowances
HB 361

counselling services
    grants to organisations to provide services
        166
    rent officer referrals 602, 622
    service charges 108
    supported accomodation 1200
couples
    alternative maximum CTB 704, 959
    applicable amount
        CTB 662
        CTB over PC age 931
        HB 337
    capital of partner
        HB 344
        HB over PC age 811
    change of circumstances
        CTB 706
        CTB over PC age 960
    claiming
        CTB 707
        CTB over PC age 963
        HB 244, 442
        HB over PC age 789, 852
    definition
        CTB 646
        CTB over PC age 917
        HB 211
        HB over PC age 772, 776
    entitlement to CTB 13
    estrangement
        CTB 652
        CTB over PC age 923
    eviction
        HB 9
    former partner is landlord
        HB 249
        HB over PC age 789
    income of partner 16
        CTB 13, 663
        CTB over PC age 932
        HB 344
    maximum CTB 697
    member of household
        CTB 661
        CTB over PC age 930
        HB 335
        HB over PC age 809
    non-dependant deductions
        CTB 698
        CTB over PC age 955
        HB 428
        HB over PC age 842
    partner
        CTB 648
        CTB over PC age 920
        HB 215
    partner absent from home
        HB 335
    recovery of overpayments
        HB 492
    same sex couples 18
    student partners
        CTB 691, 696
        HB 244, 402, 409, 417
        HB over PC age 789

course of study
    definition
        CTB 687
        HB 396
court action
    delays in payment
        HB 465
    recovery of overpayments
        CTB 45, 721
        CTB over PC age 976
        HB 42, 494
Court of Appeal
    proceedings on appeal 185
    right to appeal to 183, 1105
Court of Protection
    CTB 707
    CTB over PC age 963
    HB 442
    HB over PC age 852
covenants
    CTB 687, 693, 694
    HB 396, 412, 417
credit sale
    HB 300
    HB over PC age 793
Creutzfeldt-Jakob disease
    payments from trusts
        CTB 758
        CTB over PC age 992
        HB over PC age 900
criminal offences
    disclosure of information 75, 166
    dishonesty 55
    failure to provide information
        HB 511
        HB over PC age 880
    false representations 59
    obstructing inspector 55
    penalty alternatives 62, 1166
    time limits 68
croft land
    disregarded as capital
        CTB 751
        HB 566
    HB 300
    HB over PC age 781, 793
Crown tenants
    HB 300
    definition
        HB 211
        HB over PC age 773
    HB over PC age 793

D
date of claim
    CTB 706
    CTB over PC age 960, 965
    HB 432, 445
    HB over PC age 844
deafness
    students
        HB 402
death
    appeals
        HB/CTB 1043
    change of circumstances
        CTB 706

CTB over PC age 960
disregard of compensation
   CTB 757
   HB 577
duty to report 1183
effect on carer premium
   HB 534
inherited protection from rent restrictions
   HB 307, 315
   HB over PC age 797
payments on death
   CTB 718
   CTB over PC age 974
   HB 476
   HB over PC age 865
recovery of overpayments
   HB 493
decisions
appeal tribunals 1068, 1098
delayed – appeal pending 154
no right of appeal 1036
notice of decisions which can be appealed
   1029
person affected 1009
quashing orders 188
relevant 140
revision of decisions 1010
setting aside tribunal decisions 201
time limits for appeals 1038
decisions by local authority 107
duty to determine claim
   CTB 716
   CTB over PC age 972
notification to claimant 107
   CTB 716, 759
   CTB over PC age 972, 997
   HB 461, 580
   HB over PC age 861, 904
statement of reasons
   CTB 716
   CTB over PC age 973
   HB 461
   HB over PC age 861
validation of decisions 108
deductions from benefits
non-dependant
   CTB 698
   CTB over PC age 954
prescribed benefits
   HB 498
   HB over PC age 870
recovery of overpayments
   CTB 676, 720, 722
   CTB over PC age 977
   HB 490, 492, 493, 498
   HB over PC age 868, 870
recovery of overpayments from other
   benefits
   CTB 45
   HB 42, 369
deductions from eligible rent
HB 304, 513
HB over PC age 881
defective claims
CTB 710
CTB over PC age 966

HB 446
HB over PC age 855
delays
in making payments
   CTB 717
   CTB over PC age 973
   HB 464
   HB over PC age 862
moving home
   HB 235
   HB over PC age 786
deprivation of resources
CTB 681
CTB over PC age 950
diminishing notional capital rule
   CTB 683
   CTB over PC age 950
   HB 388
   HB over PC age 834
HB 376, 383
HB over PC age 833
income
   CTB 678
   CTB over PC age 947
designated authority
definition
   CTB 646
   CTB over PC age 917
   HB 211
   HB over PC age 773
designated office
definition
   CTB 646
   CTB over PC age 917
   HB 211
detention
absence from home
   CTB 659
   CTB over PC age 929
disregarded for council tax discount 1119
determinations by local authority
amended determinations
   HB 332
   HB over PC age 808
board and attendance
   HB 598, 618
broad rental market area
   HB 596, 617
categories of dwelling 610
   HB 629
definition
   HB 592, 614
definition of relevant period
   HB 593, 594, 614
definition of relevant time
   HB 593
errors
   HB 601, 621
exceptions 600, 621
HB 603, 615
indicative rent calculation
   HB 608, 627
local housing allowance 617
   HB 596
notifications
   HB 608, 627
redeterminations

HB 329
HB over PC age 806
significantly high rent
HB 603
substitute determinations
HB 331, 617
HB over PC age 808
diminishing notional capital rule
calculating the reduction
HB 391
CTB 683
CTB over PC age 950
HB 388
HB over PC age 834
tariff income
HB 393
direct payments to landlord
death of claimant
HB 476
HB over PC age 866
frequency of payment
HB 466, 470
HB over PC age 862
HB 473
HB over PC age 864
information requirements
HB 1162
notification
HB 462, 583
HB over PC age 906
obligation to make direct payments
HB 471
payments on account
HB 468
person affected
HB 462
disability
childcare costs 665, 937
CTB 667
HB 347
HB over PC age 818, 938
council tax reductions 1115, 1117
disability living allowance
disregarded
CTB 742
CTB over PC age 934
HB 552
HB over PC age 815
disability premium
amount
CTB 732
HB 535
CTB 729
earnings disregard
HB 544
HB 527
incapable of work 1197
disability reduction 719, 975, 1115, 1117
disabled child premium
amount
CTB 733
CTB over PC age 985
HB 535
HB over PC age 890
CTB 732
CTB over PC age 984

HB 533
HB over PC age 889
disabled students
CTB 690
disabled students' allowance
CTB 691
HB 402
discount
council tax 719, 975, 1114, 1116
disregarded for discount 1119
discretionary housing payments 136, 1176
circumstances in which payments may be
made 1177
claims 1178, 1180
disregard of payments
CTB 750
HB 565
excluded from right to appeal 1176
grants to local authority 137
HB 419
information 1181
maximum weekly payments 1179
reviews 1181
discretionary powers
CTB 82
HB 80
recovery of overpayments
HB 42
dishonesty 55
disqualification from benefit
benefit offences 1140
effect on offender's family 1142
period of disqualification 1186
disqualifying benefits
definition 1136
disregards
benefits
CTB 741
CTB over PC age 934
HB 550
HB over PC age 815
capital
CTB 680, 751
CTB over PC age 949, 991
HB 380, 566
HB over PC age 833, 898
changes in tax and contributions
CTB 670
CTB over PC age 942
HB 357
HB over PC age 824
child's capital
CTB 681
HB 380
child's earnings
CTB 740
employee's earnings
CTB 672, 737, 740
CTB over PC age 985
HB 362, 542
HB over PC age 890
income other than earnings
CTB 669, 676, 741
CTB over PC age 988
HB 369, 550
HB over PC age 893
non-dependant's income

CTB 699
CTB over PC age 955
HB 429
HB over PC age 843
second adult's income
CTB 737
self-employed earnings
CTB 673, 675, 740
CTB over PC age 944, 945, 946
HB 364, 365, 368
HB over PC age 827, 829
student loans
CTB 695
HB 414
student's income
CTB 692, 694, 696, 697
HB 409, 413, 417
war pensions
CTB 83
CTB over PC age 988
HB 80
HB over PC age 893
divorce
former partner pays the mortgage
HB 249
HB over PC age 789
dwelling
change of dwelling 210
definition 18, 102
CTB 646
CTB over PC age 918
HB 219, 592, 614
HB over PC age 773, 780
disregarded as capital
CTB 751, 754
HB 566, 573
liability to make payments
HB 244
over PC age 788
not liable to make payments
HB 249
over PC age 789
occupation of home
CTB 651, 658
CTB over PC age 923
HB 233, 401
HB over PC age 785
rent officer categories 610, 629
size criteria
HB 603, 623, 1206

E

earnings
child/young person's earnings
CTB 740
HB 549
deduction of childcare costs
CTB 664
CTB over PC age 936
definition
CTB over PC age 942
HB over PC age 824
disregards from employed earnings
CTB 672, 737, 740
CTB over PC age 985
HB 362, 368, 542
HB over PC age 890

disregards from self-employed earnings
CTB 673, 675, 740
CTB over PC age 944, 945, 946
HB 364
HB over PC age 827, 829
employed earner
CTB 671
CTB over PC age 942
employed earner average weekly earnings
CTB 669
HB 353, 357
HB over PC age 822
employed earner calculation of net earnings
CTB 671
CTB over PC age 943
HB 362
HB over PC age 825
fluctuating earnings of employed earner
CTB 669
HB 353
low earnings-notional income
CTB 679
HB 374
self-employed assessment period
HB 355
self-employed average weekly earnings
CTB 669
HB 355
self-employed calculation of net profit
CTB 673
CTB over PC age 945
HB 364
HB over PC age 827
self-employed earner
CTB 673
CTB over PC age 944
HB 363
HB over PC age 826, 827
education authority
CTB 687
education maintenance allowance
CTB 742
HB 552
EEA nationals 270
family members 277
former worker 278
right of residence 282
self-employed
CTB 657
HB 267
sickness 273
unemployment 274
workers
CTB 657
CTB over PC age 926
HB 267
HB over PC age 791
Eileen Trust
definition
CTB 646
HB 211
disregarded as capital
CTB 681, 754
CTB over PC age 993
HB 381, 572
HB over PC age 900
disregarded as income

CTB 746
HB 559
disregarded from second adult's income
CTB 737
third party payments
CTB 678, 682
HB 373, 384
electronic communications
claims
CTB 712, 763
CTB over PC age 968
HB 452, 590, 591
HB over PC age 857, 911, 912
CTB 646
CTB over PC age 918
HB 212
HB over PC age 773
notification of changes 459
use by local authorities
CTB 762
CTB over PC age 1000
HB 590
HB over PC age 911
eligible housing costs
calculation
HB 437
HB over PC age 792, 850
HB 298
HB over PC age 792
rent-free periods
HB 440
HB over PC age 851
students
HB 408
eligible rent 299, 304, 794
calculation
HB 304, 437
HB over PC age 794
exempt accommodation 1199
maximum rent
HB 306, 307
HB over PC age 795
transitional protection 1198
employed earners
average weekly earnings
CTB 669
HB 353, 357
HB over PC age 822
calculation of net earnings
CTB 671
CTB over PC age 943
HB 362
HB over PC age 825
definition
CTB 646
CTB over PC age 918
HB 212
HB over PC age 773
disregards
CTB 672, 737
CTB over PC age 985
HB 362
HB over PC age 890
earnings
CTB 669, 671
CTB over PC age 942
HB 358

HB over PC age 824
fluctuating earnings
CTB 669
HB 353
loans and advances from employer
CTB 681
HB 381
employers
colluding in fraud 65
employment and support allowance
assessment phase
CTB 733
HB 536
change of circumstances
CTB 714
HB 457
components
CTB 733
HB 536
converted ESA
CTB 645, 734
HB 211, 221, 538
CTB 652
CTB over PC age 923
disregarded income
CTB 740, 742
HB 551
HB 219
HB over PC age 780
non-dependant deductions
CTB 699
CTB over PC age 955
HB 429
HB over PC age 843
person from abroad 282
students on ESA
CTB 690
HB 401
employment zone programme
definition
CTB 646
HB 212
disregard of payments
CTB 750, 757
HB 565, 577
end of claim
date entitlement ends
CTB 706
CTB over PC age 960
HB 434
HB over PC age 845
enduring power of attorney
CTB over PC age 963
HB 442
enforcement notices 88
enhanced disability premium
amount
HB 535
HB over PC age 890
CTB 731
CTB aged 60 or over
HB over PC age 985
CTB over PC age 984
HB 532
HB over PC age 889

entitlement
conditions of entitlement
CTB 11, 13
HB 4
date entitlement begins
CTB 706
CTB over PC age 960
HB 432
HB over PC age 844
end of entitlement
CTB 706
CTB over PC age 960
HB 434
HB over PC age 845
exclusions 15
occupation of dwelling
CTB 651, 658
CTB over PC age 923
persons from abroad
CTB 657
CTB over PC age 926
HB 266
restriction in cases of error 156
work-focused interview 31
entry
inspectors' powers of entry 51
equity release schemes
treatment as income
CTB over PC age 935
HB over PC age 816
equity sharing schemes
HB 221
errors
correction 158, 201, 1029, 1069, 1098
First-tier Tribunal errors 1069
official error – definition
HB/CTB 1006, 1007
overpayment caused by official error
CTB 719, 721
CTB over PC age 975, 976
HB 478, 494
HB over PC age 866, 869
rent officer
HB 601, 621
rent officer application
HB 331
HB over PC age 808
restriction on benefit entitlement 156
Upper Tribunal errors 1098
estrangement
CTB 652
CTB over PC age 923
European Commission on Human Rights 113
European Convention on Human Rights 112
Articles 124
declaration of incompatibility 115
impact on UK law 114
judicial remedies 119
legal proceedings 117
European Court of Human Rights 113
eviction
loss of HB 6, 162
pilot scheme 10
evidence
in support of claims
CTB 712
CTB over PC age 969

HB 453
HB over PC age 857
of liability for rent
HB 246
required by rent officer
HB over PC age 877
tribunals 200, 1059, 1087
exceptional leave to remain
CTB 657
HB 282
exceptionally high rent
HB 604, 623
excluded tenancies
HB 517
HB over PC age 884
referrals to rent officers
HB 325
HB over PC age 805
exempt accommodation
definition 1200
expectation of payment for work
HB 232
expenses
disregarded income
CTB 741
HB 551
paid work
CTB 741
HB 551
self-employed
CTB 674
CTB over PC age 945
service user group
CTB 741
treatment as earnings
CTB 671
CTB over PC age 942
HB 358
HB over PC age 825
tribunals 193, 200, 1062, 1083, 1089
voluntary/charity work
CTB 741
HB 551
extended payments 162
amount of payments
CTB 701, 703
CTB over PC age 957
HB 421, 426
HB over PC age 839
CTB 162, 647, 700
CTB over PC age 918, 954, 958
decision notice
CTB 760
CTB over PC age 998
HB 582
HB over PC age 905
HB 162, 212, 419
HB over PC age 773, 837, 841
information to be supplied
CTB 725
CTB over PC age 980
HB 507
HB over PC age 877
moving home
CTB 701, 703
CTB over PC age 957
HB 423, 426, 506

HB over PC age 840
payment period
  CTB 701, 702, 703
  CTB over PC age 957
  HB 212, 421, 425
  HB over PC age 774, 839
qualifying contributory benefits
  CTB 702
  CTB over PC age 956
  HB 425
  HB over PC age 838
rules prior to 6 Oct 08 580

F
failure to
disclose a material fact
  CTB 720, 721
  CTB over PC age 976
disclose overpayments
  HB 486, 489, 494
  HB over PC age 867, 869
supply information
  HB 511
  HB over PC age 880
fair rent
  HB 1206
families
aggregation
  CTB 13
aggregation of applicable amounts
  CTB 662
  CTB over PC age 931
  HB 337
  HB over PC age 810
death of a child
  HB 334
definition 18
  CTB 647, 660
  CTB over PC age 929
  HB 332
duty to notify changes in family
  CTB 715
  CTB over PC age 971
  HB 457
  HB over PC age 859
EEA nationals 277
membership of family
  HB 332
  HB over PC age 809
non-dependants
  CTB 654
  CTB over PC age 924
  HB 226
  HB over PC age 782
responsibility for a child
  HB 334
  HB over PC age 809
treatment of income and capital 16
  CTB 13, 663, 681, 739
  CTB over PC age 932
  HB 344, 380, 545
  HB over PC age 811
family premium
amount
  HB 523
  HB over PC age 887
CTB 727

CTB over PC age 982
HB 523
HB over PC age 887
firefighters
earnings disregard
  CTB 739
  CTB over PC age 985
  HB 546
  HB over PC age 891
  HB 546
First-tier Tribunal 169
administration 196
appealing First-tier Tribunal decisions in
  Upper Tribunal 150, 176
application for permission to appeal 1071
case management powers 1052
composition of tribunals 170, 1106
consent orders 1068
costs and expenses 193, 200, 1062
decision-making approach 145
decisions which can be appealed 144
decisions which cannot be appealed 144
delegation to staff 1051
enforcement of decisions 192
evidence and submissions 1059
expert assistance 192
failure to comply with rules 1053
fees 197
hearings 1065
judges 170, 172
lookalike appeals 1061
mediation 191, 1051
membership of tribunal 1076
notice of appeal 1062
notice of decisions 1068
notice of hearings 1067
obligation to cooperate 1049
organisation 1109
overriding objective 1049
practice directions 190
procedures for giving directions 1053
public and private hearings 1067
reasons for decisions 1068
representatives 1057
response to the tribunal 1063
review of decisions 174, 1072
right to appeal to First-tier tribunal 144
sending documents 1058
setting aside a decision 1069
sitting places 191
striking out a case 1054
time limits 1075
transfer of functions 193
transitional provisions 1103
Tribunal Procedure Rules 189, 199, 1048
withdrawal of a case 1060
witnesses 1060
Flexible New Deal 1245
fluctuating earnings
  CTB 669
  CTB over PC age 941
  HB 353
  HB over PC age 822, 824
fluctuating hours of work
  CTB 656
  CTB over PC age 925, 941

HB 230
HB over PC age 784
former pathfinder authority
definition
HB 512
HB over PC age 881
list of authorities 586, 633, 637, 907
maximum rent 512
transitional protection
HB 310, 587
HB over PC age 797, 908
fostering
allowances
HB 364
HB over PC age 827
treatment as member of household
CTB 661
CTB over PC age 930
HB 335
HB over PC age 810
fraud
authorisation of inspectors 46
employers colluding 65
landlords
HB 472
local authorities power to prosecute 1240
local authorities requirement to prevent fraud
84
loss of benefit 1134
penalties 55, 59
penalty as alternative to prosecution 62
powers of entry 51
powers to require information 47
prevention affecting subsidy 91
prosecution of offences 67
recovery of overpayments
CTB 721
CTB over PC age 976
HB 486, 494
HB over PC age 867, 869
redirected mail 97
reports on local authorities administration 85
fuel
definition
HB 517
HB over PC age 884
fuel costs
communal areas
HB 515
HB over PC age 883
deductions from eligible rent
HB 515
HB over PC age 883
service charges
HB 515
HB over PC age 883
full-time course of study
definition
CTB 687
HB 396
sandwich course
CTB 689
HB 398
full-time education
definition
HB 396

non-advanced education
HB 333
Fund, The
definition
CTB 647
HB 212
disregarded as capital
CTB 681, 754
HB 381, 572
disregarded as income
CTB 746
HB 559
disregarded from second adult's income
CTB 737
notional income
CTB 678
third party payments
CTB 682
HB 373, 384

G
gay couples 18
George Cross payments
CTB 742, 757
HB 552, 577
good cause
absence from work 656
CTB 656
CTB over PC age 925
HB 230
HB over PC age 784
granny annexe 228
grants
student
CTB 688, 692
HB 397, 409
guarantee payments
treatment as earnings
CTB 671
HB 359
guaranteed income payment
disregarded
CTB 743
HB 554
guardian's allowance
CTB 749
CTB over PC age 934
HB 563
HB over PC age 815

H
habitual residence 293, 1217
CTB 657
CTB over PC age 926
HB 266
HB over PC age 790, 792
transitional arrangements 1192
haemophilia
CTB 746
CTB over PC age 993
HB 559, 572
HB over PC age 900
health benefits
CTB 748, 756
HB 561

health in pregnancy grant
disregarded
CTB 756
CTB over PC age 995
HB over PC age 904
heritable securities 4
HB 297
higher education
CTB 688
higher pensioner premium
amount
CTB 732
CTB 729
HB 526, 527
hire purchase agreement
HB 300
HB over PC age 793
holiday pay
CTB 671, 681
CTB over PC age 942
HB 358, 381
HB over PC age 825
treatment as earnings
CTB 671
CTB over PC age 942
holidays
treatment of hours of work
CTB 656
CTB over PC age 925
HB over PC age 784
home
disregarded as capital
CTB 751, 754
CTB over PC age 991
HB 566, 573
HB over PC age 898
occupation of home
CTB 658
CTB over PC age 923
HB 401
HB over PC age 785
two homes
HB 234
HB over PC age 785
homeless
disregarded for council tax discount 1121
homeowner
definition
HB 215
HB over PC age 776
hospital
absence from home
CTB 659
CTB over PC age 928
HB 236
HB over PC age 788
applicable amount
CTB 663
HB over PC age 811
child care charges
HB 347
definition of patient
HB 237, 352
HB over PC age 788
disregarded for council tax discount 1120
HB 339
non-dependant deductions

CTB 699
CTB over PC age 955
HB 428
HB over PC age 843
students
HB 401
hostels
date entitlement begins
HB 432
HB over PC age 844
definition
HB 212
NINO requirement
HB 229
HB over PC age 783
rent officer determinations
HB 325, 600, 621
HB over PC age 805
residents disregarded for council tax
discount 1120, 1121
treatment as home 234
hours of work
CTB 656
CTB over PC age 925
HB 230
HB over PC age 784
house sale
CTB 751, 755
HB 566, 573
two homes
HB 234, 235
HB over PC age 785
houseboats
CTB 653
HB 220, 300, 601, 612, 621, 631
HB over PC age 781, 793
household
definition 22
duty to notify changes in family
CTB 715
CTB over PC age 971
HB 457
HB over PC age 859
treated as member of
CTB 661
CTB over PC age 930
HB 335
HB over PC age 809
housing association
co-ownership scheme
HB 211
HB over PC age 772
CTB 752
definition
HB 213
HB over PC age 774
disregard of deposits 569
excluded tenancies 519
HB 608, 627
registered housing association 216, 224
housing authority
definition 80
housing benefit
absence from home 236, 787
administration 79
entitlement 4

over PC age 767
power to modify scheme 80
housing costs
calculation
HB 437
HB over PC age 850
eligible rent
HB 304
HB over PC age 794
HB 298
HB over PC age 792
ineligible housing costs 4
rent-free periods
HB 440
HB over PC age 851
students
HB 408
housing revenue account 79
human rights
benefits treated as possessions 132
freedom of thought, conscience and religion
128
limitation on use of restrictions on rights 132
prohibition of abuse of rights 132
prohibition of discrimination 129
prohibition of torture 125
protection of property 132
public bodies – definition 116
remedies through the courts 119
right to a fair trial 125
right to education 134
right to respect for private and family life 127
taking legal action 117
Human Rights Act
commencement 124

I
Iceland 1226
Immigration and Asylum Chamber 1109
immigration authority
CTB 647
incapacity for work 1197
students able to claim benefit
CTB 690
HB 402
income 16
arrears of income
CTB 707
CTB over PC age 961
HB 435
HB over PC age 846
assessment period
CTB 669
CTB over PC age 916
HB 210, 355
average weekly income other than earnings
CTB 669
HB 355
calculation of income
CTB 664, 670
CTB over PC age 932, 936, 940
HB 344, 346, 357, 369
HB over PC age 811, 812, 817, 822
calculation of income other than earnings
CTB 675
HB 355
capital treated as income 16

CTB 665, 677, 753
HB 346, 369, 372, 572
change in income
CTB 706
CTB over PC age 961
HB 435
HB over PC age 846
chargeable income
HB 368
child/young person's income
HB 344
HB over PC age 811
CTB 664, 675
CTB over PC age 936
definition
CTB over PC age 934
HB over PC age 815, 817
deprivation of income
CTB 678
CTB over PC age 947
HB 373
HB over PC age 830
difference between capital and income
HB 339
disregards
CTB 670, 676, 741
CTB over PC age 942, 988
HB 355, 369, 550
HB over PC age 893
effect of PC on calculation
CTB over PC age 932
HB over PC age 812
family's income 16
CTB 13, 663
CTB over PC age 932
HB 344
HB over PC age 811
HB 339
income from capital 16
CTB 664, 681, 686, 743
CTB over PC age 935, 936
HB 346, 381, 393, 555
HB over PC age 816, 898
income other than earnings
CTB 741
CTB over PC age 988
HB 550
HB over PC age 893
income treated as capital 16
CTB 681, 746
HB 381, 559
non-dependant's income
CTB 664, 698
CTB over PC age 932, 954
HB 345, 427
HB over PC age 812, 842
notional income
CTB 665, 678
CTB over PC age 947
HB 346, 373
HB over PC age 830
partner's income
HB 344
HB over PC age 811
qualifying age for PC 17
second adult's income
CTB 736

CTB over PC age 996
student grants
CTB 692
HB 409
student loans
CTB 695
HB 413
tariff income 16
CTB 664, 686
CTB over PC age 935
HB 346, 381, 393
HB over PC age 817
third party payments
CTB 678
HB 373
treatment of guarantee credit
CTB over PC age 932
HB over PC age 812
treatment of savings credit
CTB over PC age 932
HB over PC age 813
weekly income
CTB 664, 670
CTB over PC age 936, 940
HB 346
HB over PC age 817
income related benefits 3
CTB 3
definition 102
HB 3
income support
change of circumstances
CTB 714
HB 457
disregarded income
CTB 740, 742
CTB over PC age 991
HB 551
information passed between authorities 79
non-dependant deductions
CTB 699
CTB over PC age 955
HB 429
HB over PC age 843
persons from abroad
HB 282
students on IS
CTB 690
HB 401
income tax
calculating net profit
CTB 675
deducted from earnings
CTB 672
CTB over PC age 943
HB 362
HB over PC age 825
deducted from notional earnings
CTB 680
HB 375
deducted from self-employed net profit
CTB 674, 675
CTB over PC age 946
HB 365, 366, 368
HB over PC age 828, 829
disregard of changes
CTB 670

CTB over PC age 942
HB 357
HB over PC age 824
disregarded from income other than earnings
CTB 741
HB 551
refund of tax
CTB 697, 753
HB 381, 417, 572
Independent Living Funds
definition
CTB 647
HB 213
HB over PC age 774
disregarded as capital
CTB 681, 754
CTB over PC age 900, 993
HB 381, 572
disregarded as income
CTB 746
HB 559
disregarded from second adult's income
CTB 737
third party payments
CTB 678, 682
HB 373, 384
indicative rent levels
HB 608, 627
information 71
benefits administration information 71
CTB 726
CTB over PC age 981
collection of information
CTB 723
CTB over PC age 978
HB 501
HB over PC age 872
disclosure by First-tier Tribunal 1059
disclosure by Upper Tribunal 1086
discretionary housing payments 1181
electronic information 54
failure to supply 880
forwarding information
CTB 724
CTB over PC age 979
HB 502
HB over PC age 873
fraud investigations 47
holding information
CTB 723
CTB over PC age 978
HB 502
HB over PC age 873
in support of claim
CTB 712
CTB over PC age 969
HB 453
HB over PC age 857
included in notification of decision
CTB 759
CTB over PC age 997
HB 581
HB over PC age 904
local authority powers
HB/CTB 1123
local housing allowances 634, 636
HB 324

HB over PC age 804
passed between benefit authorities
  CTB 724, 725
  CTB over PC age 979
passed between local authorities
  CTB over PC age 979
  HB 506
  HB over PC age 877
payments on account
  HB 468
  HB over PC age 863
penalty notices 1166
possessions 9
relevant information
  HB 508
  HB over PC age 879
requesting information
  CTB 724
  CTB over PC age 979
  HB 502
  HB over PC age 873
required by rent officers
  HB 503
  HB over PC age 874, 877
required by Upper Tribunal 191
required from appropriate person
  HB 508
  HB over PC age 878
required from landlords and agents 77
  HB 507, 1162
  HB over PC age 878
social security information 41, 1229
suspension of benefit 154
  HB/CTB 1032
to/from Secretary of State 1229
verifying information
  CTB 723
  CTB over PC age 978
  HB 501
  HB over PC age 873
wrongful disclosure 71, 75
inspection
  administration of benefits 83
  authorisation of inspectors 46
  directions for improvement 85
  enforcement determinations 89
  enforcement notices 88
  obstruction of inspectors 55
  power to require information 47
  powers 52, 69
  powers of entry 51
instalments
  capital
    CTB 677, 753
    HB 372, 571
Intensive Activity Period
  50 plus 1174
  definition 1174
interim payments
  HB 43, 467
  HB over PC age 863
invalid vehicles
  definition
    CTB 647
    CTB over PC age 919
    HB 213
    HB over PC age 775

investigators
  administration of benefits 83
  authorisation 46
  code of practice 1134
  powers of investigators 52, 69
investments
  valuation of capital
    CTB 681
    HB over PC age 833

J
jobseeker's allowance
  change of circumstances
    CTB 714
  CTB 651
  CTB over PC age 923
  disregarded income
    CTB 740, 742
    CTB over PC age 991
    HB 551
  HB 219, 457
  HB over PC age 780
  information passed between authorities 79
  non-dependant deductions
    CTB 699
    CTB over PC age 955
    HB 429
    HB over PC age 843
  persons from abroad
    HB 282
  students on JSA
    CTB 690
    HB 401
  Work for Your Benefit 1247
joint beneficial interest
  CTB 686
  CTB over PC age 953
  HB 223, 391
joint capital
  CTB 686
  CTB over PC age 953
  HB 391
  HB over PC age 837
joint liability for council tax
  alternative maximum CTB 704, 959
  amount of CTB 697
  non-dependants 654, 698, 924, 955
joint occupiers
  liability for rent
    HB 249
    HB over PC age 789
  non-dependants
    CTB 698
    CTB over PC age 955
    HB 226, 428
    HB over PC age 782, 842
joint owner
  CTB 686
  CTB over PC age 953
  HB over PC age 837
joint tenants
  HB 228, 392
judicial review 186
  Upper Tribunal 187, 1093

jury service
  allowances
    CTB 747
    HB 560

K
kinship carers
  payments disregarded
    CTB 745
    HB 557

L
landlords
  assessment of rent level 1122
  close relative
    HB 249
    HB over PC age 789
  connected trust or company
    HB 249, 258
    HB over PC age 789
  direct payments
    HB 470, 473
    HB over PC age 864
  duty to notify change of circumstances
    HB 457
    HB over PC age 859
  fit and proper person
    HB 472
  former partner
    HB 257
    HB over PC age 789
  information required by local authority
    HB 507, 508, 1162
    HB over PC age 878, 879
  notification of decision
    HB 583
    HB over PC age 906
  overpayments which are not recoverable
    HB 486
    HB over PC age 867
  payments on account
    HB 468
  recovery of overpayments
    HB 500
    HB over PC age 872
  resident landlord
    HB 249
    HB over PC age 789
  responsibility for landlord's child
    HB 249, 257
    HB over PC age 789
late claims
  HB 451
learner support funds
  CTB 687
  HB 396
legal aid
  funding for appeals 1088
lesbian couples 18
liability to make payments for a home
  evidence of liability
    HB 246
  HB 244
  liability defined
    HB 245
  persons from abroad
    HB 266

  persons treated as not liable
    HB 249
  who can be treated as liable
    HB 245
licence
  HB 300, 793
Liechtenstein 1226
life insurance policy
  definition
    CTB 649
    CTB over PC age 920
    HB 215
    HB over PC age 776
  payments disregarded
    CTB 746
    HB 559
  surrender value disregarded
    CTB 753
    CTB over PC age 992
    HB 571
    HB over PC age 899
lifeboat crew
  earnings disregard
    CTB 739
    CTB over PC age 985
    HB 546
    HB over PC age 891
  HB 546
limited capability for work
  CTB 734
  HB 537
  students 402
limited capability for work-related activity
  CTB 734
  HB 537
limited leave to enter or remain 1171
linked person
  definition
    HB 213
loans
  business loans disregarded
    CTB 674
    CTB over PC age 946
    HB 365
    HB over PC age 828
  from employer
    CTB 681
    HB 381
  student
    CTB 695
    HB 413
local authorities
  acting on behalf of another authority 79
  benefit administration information 71
    CTB 726
    CTB over PC age 981
  children leaving care 1132
  collection of information
    CTB 723
    CTB over PC age 978
    HB 501
    HB over PC age 872
  contracting out benefit functions 1190
  directions for improvement 85
  disclosure of information
    CTB 724, 725
  duty to publicise benefit schemes 4

enforcement notices 88
forwarding information
  CTB 724
  CTB over PC age 979
  HB 502
  HB over PC age 873
holding information
  CTB 723
  CTB over PC age 978
  HB 502
  HB over PC age 873
information between authorities
  CTB 724
  CTB over PC age 979
  HB 506
  HB over PC age 877
information from landlords
  HB 507, 1162
information to/from Secretary of State 1229
inspection of benefits administration 83
joint arrangements 93
permitted spending totals
  CTB 1161
  HB 1156
power to appoint inspectors 52, 69
powers to prosecute fraud 1240
relevant decisions 140
requesting information
  CTB 724
  CTB over PC age 979
  HB 502
  HB over PC age 873
second authority
  CTB 649
  CTB over PC age 921
  HB 216
  HB over PC age 777
standards of service 87
local housing allowance
calculation of maximum rent
  HB 319
  HB over PC age 801
cap from April 2011 322, 598, 610
categories of dwellings 610, 611, 629
definition 322
eligible rent
  HB 307
  HB over PC age 795
excluded tenancies
  HB 517
information for rent officers
  HB over PC age 874
introduction 297, 1231
local authority pilot areas 632
publication of LHAs
  HB 324
  HB over PC age 804
rent officer determinations 592, 596, 634, 635
when LHA rules are used
  HB 317
  HB over PC age 800
local reference rent
definition
  HB 313
  HB over PC age 799
HB 314, 604, 624
information for rent officers

HB over PC age 874
maximum rent
  HB 312
  HB over PC age 798
taper 1221
transitional protection 1200
locality
definition 603
London Bombings Relief Charitable Fund
definition
  CTB 647
  CTB over PC age 919
  HB 213
disregarded as capital
  CTB 754
  CTB over PC age 993
  HB 572
  HB over PC age 900
third party payments
  CTB 682
  HB 384
lone parents
childcare costs
  CTB 665
  CTB over PC age 936
  HB 347
  HB over PC age 818
definition
  CTB 648
  CTB over PC age 919
  HB 214
  HB over PC age 775
earnings disregards
  CTB 739
  CTB over PC age 985
  HB 545
  HB over PC age 890
family premium
  CTB 727
  CTB over PC age 982
  HB 523
New Deal 1182
students – occupation of home
  HB 234
  HB over PC age 785
students able to claim benefit
  CTB 690
  HB 401
long tenancy
HB 300
definition
  HB 214
  HB over PC age 775
HB over PC age 793
looked after children
leaving care 1132
treatment as member of family
  CTB 661
treatment of payments
  HB 557
low paid work
earnings and notional income
  CTB 679
  HB 374

M
Macfarlane Trusts
definition
CTB 651
CTB over PC age 919
HB 214
HB over PC age 775
disregarded as capital
CTB over PC age 993
HB 381, 572
HB over PC age 900
disregarded as income
CTB 746
HB 559
third party payments
CTB 678
HB 373, 384
mail
Post Office requirement to report redirected
mail 98
return of redirected mail 97
maintenance
disregard of payments
CTB 748
CTB over PC age 990
HB 562
maintenance undertaking
definition for asylum seekers 1129
maternity leave
definition
CTB 648
CTB over PC age 919
earnings disregards
HB 359, 543
in remunerative work
CTB 668
CTB over PC age 940
HB 350
HB over PC age 821
not in remunerative work
CTB 656
CTB over PC age 926
HB 231
HB over PC age 784
maximum benefit
CTB 11, 697
CTB over PC age 953
HB 4, 418
HB over PC age 837
maximum rent 306, 795
calculation
IID 313, 319
HB over PC age 801
definition
HB 214
HB over PC age 775
former pathfinder authorities 586
increases above
HB 1157
local housing allowance
HB 214, 307
HB over PC age 775, 795
local reference rent
HB 306, 312
HB over PC age 795, 798
protection from restrictions
HB 315

HB over PC age 798
rent officer determinations 592
transitional arrangements
HB 586
when LHA rules are used
HB 317
HB over PC age 800
meals
excluded from HB 514, 882
service charges
HB 513, 514, 625
HB over PC age 881, 882
mediation 191, 1051, 1080
medical treatment 108
absence from home
CTB 659
CTB over PC age 928
HB 236
HB over PC age 788
mental illness
charges for counselling/support 108
liability to pay rent
HB 248
mesne profits
HB 300
HB over PC age 793
minimum benefit 15
HB 432
HB over PC age 844
misrepresentation
criminal offences 59
overpayment
CTB 720, 721
CTB over PC age 976
HB 486, 489, 494
HB over PC age 867, 869
mistakes
leading to overpayment
HB 478, 479
HB over PC age 866
revisions 1011
mobile homes
campsite fees
HB 300
HB over PC age 793
CTB 653
excluded tenancies 519
HB 220, 601, 612, 621, 631
HB over PC age 781
mobility supplement
disregarded
CTB 742
CTB over PC age 988
HB 552
HB over PC age 894
Montserrat volcanic eruption
CTB 657
CTB over PC age 927
HB 267, 282
HB over PC age 791
mooring charges
HB 300, 601, 612, 621, 631
HB over PC age 793
mortgage payments 4
disregard of mortgage protection payments
CTB 746
HB 559

HB 297, 300
HB over PC age 793
moving home
date entitlement begins
HB 432
HB over PC age 844
definition of mover
CTB 648
CTB over PC age 919
HB 214
HB over PC age 776
extended payments
CTB 701, 703
CTB over PC age 957
HB 423, 426
HB over PC age 840
liaison between local authorities
CTB 725
HB 506
two homes
HB 234, 235
HB over PC age 785

N
national insurance contributions
deducted from earnings
CTB 672
CTB over PC age 943
HB 362
HB over PC age 825
deducted from notional income
CTB 680
HB 375
deducted from self-employed net profit
CTB 674, 675
CTB over PC age 947
HB 365, 368
HB over PC age 828, 829
disregard of changes
CTB 670
HB 357
HB over PC age 824
national insurance number requirement 28
CTB 655
CTB over PC age 925
HB 229
HB over PC age 783
neighbourhood
rent officer determinations
HB 603
net earnings
CTB 648
definition
CTB over PC age 919
HB 214
HB over PC age 776
net profit
CTB 648, 673
deductions of tax and national insurance
CTB 675
definition
CTB over PC age 919
HB 214
HB over PC age 776
HB 364
HB over PC age 827
self-employed earners

CTB 673
CTB over PC age 945
New Deal 1167
definition
CTB 648
disregard of payments
CTB 678, 682
Flexible New Deal 1245
lone parents 1182
notional income
CTB 679
HB 374
payments to trainees 1167
payments treated as capital
CTB 681
self-employed earnings
HB 381
third party payments
HB 384
treatment of payments 1174, 1182
next of kin
definition 476
CTB 718
CTB over PC age 974
HB over PC age 865
nil award 141
no fixed abode
disregarded for council tax discount 1121
non-advanced education
HB 333
non-dependants 760
calculation of non-dependant's income
CTB 698
CTB over PC age 954
HB 427
HB over PC age 842
deductions
CTB 698
CTB over PC age 954
HB 427
HB over PC age 842
definition
CTB 654
CTB over PC age 924
HB 226
HB over PC age 782
disregard of payments
CTB 744
HB 556
exceptions 654
CTB over PC age 924
HB 226
HB over PC age 782
exclusions from non-dependant deductions
HB 428
HB over PC age 842
income/capital
CTB 664
CTB over PC age 932
HB 345
HB over PC age 812
notification of decisions
HB 584
HB over PC age 906
taking advantage of benefit scheme
CTB 655, 664
CTB over PC age 924, 932

HB 345
HB over PC age 812
Norway 1226
notice
payments in lieu
CTB 671
CTB over PC age 942
HB 358, 543
HB over PC age 825
notification
board and attendance
HB 598, 618
decisions 107
CTB 716, 759
CTB over PC age 972, 997
HB 461, 580
HB over PC age 861, 904
rent officer determinations
HB 608, 627
notional capital
CTB 681
CTB over PC age 950
diminishing notional capital rule
CTB 683
CTB over PC age 950
HB 388
HB over PC age 834
HB 383
HB over PC age 833
notional income
CTB 665
CTB over PC age 947
HB 346, 373, 378
HB over PC age 830
nursing care 108

O

obstruction of inspector 55
occupation
normally occupied
HB 238
of home
CTB 651, 658
CTB over PC age 923
HB 233, 401
occupational pensions
contributions deducted from earnings
CTB 672
CTB over PC age 943
HB 362
HB over PC age 825
contributions deducted from notional
earnings
CTB 680
HB 375
definition
CTB 648
CTB over PC age 920
HB 214
HB over PC age 776
disregarded
CTB 755
HB 574
notional capital/ income
CTB over PC age 948
HB 373, 383
HB over PC age 830

third party payments
CTB 678, 682
HB 373, 384
treatment as earnings
CTB over PC age 943
HB 359
HB over PC age 825
treatment as income
CTB 671
occupier
definition
HB 593, 594, 614
official error
causing overpayment
CTB 719
CTB over PC age 975
HB 478
HB over PC age 866
revisions 1011
ombudsman
HB 461
ONE 33
one bedroom shared accommodation 319
one strike scheme 1137
disqualification period 1187
overlapping benefits
CTB 728
CTB over PC age 983
HB 526
overpayments
appeals 147
arising from arrears
HB 437
calculation
CTB 721
CTB over PC age 976
HB 495
HB over PC age 869
challenging a decision 147
challenging a decision on recovery 147
challenging method of recovery 147
court action
CTB 45, 721
CTB over PC age 976
HB 42, 494
CTB 44
deductions from recoverable overpayments
CTB 721
CTB over PC age 977
HB 496
HB over PC age 869
definition
HB 477
HB over PC age 866
diminution of capital
CTB 721
CTB over PC age 976
HB 494
HB over PC age 869
discretion to recover
CTB 44
HB 42
HB 42
involvement of relevant person
HB 483
knowledge of overpayment 484
landlord, payments direct 42

local housing allowance
  HB over PC age 867
method of recovery
  CTB 720
  CTB over PC age 976
  HB 490
  HB over PC age 868
mistakes
  HB 479
notification of recoverable overpayments
  CTB 762
  CTB over PC age 999
  HB 585
  HB over PC age 906
official error
  CTB 719
  CTB over PC age 975
  HB 478
  HB over PC age 866
offsetting against arrears
  CTB 718
  CTB over PC age 974
  HB 476
  HB over PC age 866
payments on account
  HB 468, 478
person from whom recovery may be sought
  CTB 44
  HB 42
prescribed benefits
  HB 498
  HB over PC age 870
recoverable overpayments
  CTB 718, 720
  CTB over PC age 975, 976
  HB 478, 486
  HB over PC age 866
recovery by court action
  CTB 721
  CTB over PC age 976
recovery from benefits
  CTB 45, 720, 722
  CTB over PC age 977
  HB 42, 490, 498
  HB over PC age 867, 868, 870
recovery from landlord
  HB 500
  HB over PC age 872
reduced council tax liability
  CTB 718
  CTB over PC age 975
time limit for recovery
  HB 494
treatment as rent arrears
  HB 471
two homes
  HB 240
overseas assets
  CTB 681
  CTB over PC age 950
  HB 383
  HB over PC age 833
owner
  beneficial interest
    CTB 686
    CTB over PC age 953
    HB 391

definition
  HB 215
  HB over PC age 776

P
parental contribution
  covenant income
    CTB 693
    HB 412
  definition
    CTB 687
    HB 396
  disregarded
    CTB 744
    CTB over PC age 990
    HB 555
    HB over PC age 896
part-time work
  earnings disregards
    HB 544
  HB 549
partner
  definition
    CTB 648
    CTB over PC age 920
    HB 215
    HB over PC age 776
paternity leave
  definition
    CTB 648
    CTB over PC age 920
    HB 215
    HB over PC age 776
  in remunerative work
    CTB 668
    CTB over PC age 940
    HB over PC age 821
pay in lieu of notice
  treatment as earnings
    CTB 671
    HB 358
    HB over PC age 825
payment in kind
  CTB 671
  CTB over PC age 943
  treatment as earnings
    HB 359
    HB over PC age 825
payment of benefit
  death of person entitled
    CTB 718
    CTB over PC age 974
    HB 476
    HB over PC age 865
  frequency of payment
    HB 464, 1221
    HB over PC age 862
  landlord direct
    HB 470
    HB over PC age 864
  late payment
    CTB 717
    CTB over PC age 973
    HB 464
    HB over PC age 862
  method
    CTB 82, 716

CTB over PC age 973
HB 79
power to make regulations about
administration of payments 35
CTB 37
rent allowance
HB 466
HB over PC age 862
underpayment 717
CTB 45
CTB over PC age 974
who is paid
CTB 717
CTB over PC age 974
HB 469
HB over PC age 863
payments on account 43
HB 467, 478
HB over PC age 863
penalties 62, 1166
withdrawn 1138
pension credit
change of circumstances
CTB over PC age 961
HB over PC age 847
extended payments
CTB 958
HB 841
guarantee credit
CTB over PC age 932
HB over PC age 812
non-dependant deductions
CTB over PC age 955
notifying change of circumstances
CTB over PC age 971
HB over PC age 860
persons from abroad
HB over PC age 791
qualifying age 17, 18, 22
CTB 655
CTB over PC age 925
HB 215, 230, 777
HB over PC age 783
savings credit
CTB over PC age 932
HB over PC age 813
pension fund holder
CTB 648
definition
CTB over PC age 920
HB 215
HB over PC age 776
pensionable age
definition 18, 782
equalisation 782
HB 224
pensioner premium
amount
CTB 732
CTB 729
HB 526
period of experience
definition
CTB 689
HB 397

period of study
definition
CTB 688
HB 397
permitted totals
CTB 83, 1161
HB 80, 1156
person affected
CTB 716
CTB over PC age 973
definition
CTB over PC age 920
HB 215
HB over PC age 776
HB 462
HB/CTB 1009
person subject to immigration control
definition 1129
entitlement to claim benefits 1169, 1171
personal allowances
CTB 726
CTB over PC age 981
HB 521
HB over PC age 886
rates
CTB 726
CTB over PC age 981
HB 521
HB over PC age 886
personal injuries
disregard of compensation
CTB 678, 753
CTB over PC age 990, 993
HB 373, 383, 570
HB over PC age 896, 901
periodical payments
CTB 677
HB over PC age 896
personal pensions
contributions deducted from earnings
CTB 672, 675
CTB over PC age 943, 946
HB 362, 366
HB over PC age 826, 829
contributions deducted from notional
earnings
CTB 680
HB 375
definition
CTB 649
CTB over PC age 920
HB 215
HB over PC age 776
disregarded
CTB 755
HB 574
information to be provided
CTB 713
CTB over PC age 969
HB 453
HB over PC age 858
notional income/capital
CTB 682
CTB over PC age 948
HB 373, 377, 383
HB over PC age 830
qualifying contribution

CTB 672
CTB over PC age 943
HB 362
third party payments
CTB 678, 682
HB 373, 384
persons from abroad 1215
asylum seekers 1130
definition
CTB 657
CTB over PC age 926
HB 266
HB over PC age 790
entitlement to claim benefits 1169, 1171
CTB 657
CTB over PC age 926
HB 266
HB over PC age 790
exceptions
HB 267
students
CTB 690
transitional protection 1153
polygamous marriages
alternative maximum CTB 705, 959
applicable amounts
CTB 663
HB 338
claims
CTB 707
CTB over PC age 963
HB 442
HB over PC age 852
CTB 14
definition
CTB 649
CTB over PC age 920
HB 215
HB over PC age 777
earnings disregards
CTB 738
HB 544
non-dependants
CTB 654, 698
CTB over PC age 924, 955
HB 226, 428
HB over PC age 842
occupation of home
HB 233
HB over PC age 785
treatment of income and capital
CTB 663
CTB over PC age 932
HB 344
HB over PC age 811
possession orders
loss of HB 7
post
return of redirected post 97
Post Office
reporting redirected mail 98
power of attorney
CTB over PC age 963
HB 442, 443
HB over PC age 852

premiums
amounts
CTB 732
CTB over PC age 985
HB 535
CTB 728
CTB over PC age 983
HB 524
HB over PC age 888
prescribed benefits
CTB 722
CTB over PC age 977
HB 499
HB over PC age 871
prisoners
absence from home
CTB 659
CTB over PC age 928
HB 236
HB over PC age 787
child care charges
HB 347
disregard of payments for visits
CTB 748, 756
HB 562
disregarded for council tax discount 1119
non-dependant deductions
HB 428
HB over PC age 843
temporary release
CTB 660
HB 236
HB over PC age 787
property
benefits treated as possessions 132
valuation of capital
HB 382
HB over PC age 833
public authority
definition
CTB 649
CTB over PC age 920
HB 215
HB over PC age 777
public bodies
definition 117
human rights 116
Public Lending Right payments
CTB 673
HB 364

Q
qualifying benefits
contributory benefits
CTB 649
CTB over PC age 920
HB 215
HB over PC age 777
extended payments
CTB 700, 702
CTB over PC age 956
HB 212, 425
HB over PC age 838
income-related benefits
CTB 649
CTB over PC age 920

HB 215
HB over PC age 777
qualifying contribution
definition
HB over PC age 826
qualifying course
definition
CTB 689
HB 397
qualifying person
definition
CTB 649
CTB over PC age 920
qualifying premium
CTB 673
CTB over PC age 945
HB 365
HB over PC age 828
quashing order 188

R
rapid reclaim
HB 448
reckonable rent
change in reckonable rent
HB 316
HB over PC age 800
definition
HB 316
recourse to public funds 1171
recovery of benefits
appeals relating to overpayments 147
court action
CTB 45, 721
CTB over PC age 976
HB 42, 494
deduction from benefits
CTB 45, 676, 720, 722
CTB over PC age 977
HB 42, 369, 498
HB over PC age 868, 870
discretion to recover
CTB 44
HB 42
from landlord
HB 500
HB over PC age 872
methods of recovery
CTB 720
CTB over PC age 976
HB 490
HB over PC age 868
notification to claimant
CTB 762
CTB over PC age 999
HB 585
HB over PC age 906
payments on account
HB 468
HB over PC age 863
person from whom recovery made
CTB 44, 720
CTB over PC age 976
HB 42, 486
HB over PC age 867
recoverable overpayments
CTB 719

CTB over PC age 975
HB 478
HB over PC age 866
redeterminations
appeals by tribunal 149
board and attendance
HB 599, 619
challenging decision of rent officer
HB 329
HB over PC age 807
definition
HB 593, 614
errors
HB 601, 621
exceptions 600, 621
HB 329
HB over PC age 806
rent officer
HB 595, 616, 629
substitute redeterminations
HB 331, 617
HB over PC age 808
reduction of benefit 153
benefit offences
HB/CTB 1188
failure to provide information
HB/CTB 1032
HB/CTB 1030
reduction lifted
HB/CTB 1031
reductions for council tax 1114, 1117
redundancy
CTB 671
CTB over PC age 942
HB over PC age 825
treatment as earnings
CTB 671
CTB over PC age 942
HB 358
refugees
CTB 658, 726
CTB over PC age 927, 981
definition
CTB over PC age 927
HB 268
HB over PC age 791
evidence to support a claim
HB 453
HB over PC age 857
HB 296
HB over PC age 792
not persons from abroad
CTB 657
CTB over PC age 927
HB 267
HB over PC age 791
retrospective claim for benefit 1131
CTB 1170
HB 1170
transitional protection 1170
regulations
parliamentary control 101, 110
power to make 24, 100, 109
rehabilitation allowance
CTB 678
HB 373

relative
definition
CTB 649
CTB over PC age 920
HB 216
HB over PC age 777
relevant authority
decisions 140
CTB 716
CTB over PC age 972
HB 460
HB over PC age 861
definition
CTB over PC age 921
HB 216
HB over PC age 777
religious orders
HB 250, 261
HB over PC age 790
remunerative work
definition
CTB 656
CTB over PC age 925
HB 230, 231
HB over PC age 784
rent
advance payments
HB 244
claim-related rent
HB 312, 314, 606, 626
HB over PC age 798
definition
CTB 649
CTB over PC age 921
HB 216, 300, 301
HB over PC age 777, 793
disregards
CTB 744
HB 556
eligible rent
HB 304
HB over PC age 794
exceptionally high rent
HB 604, 623
increases in rent 1214
increases to cover arrears
HB over PC age 792
indicative rent levels
HB 608, 627
liability to pay
HB 244
local reference rent
HB 314, 604, 624
maximum rent
HB 214
rent increase
HB 518
HB over PC age 884
rent officer determinations
HB 603, 623
rent-free periods
HB 244, 418, 440, 516
HB over PC age 789, 851, 884
significantly high rent
HB 314, 603, 623
single room rent
HB 312, 314, 605, 625

size criteria
HB 314, 603, 609, 623, 628
unreasonably high
HB 1207
weekly rent
HB 437
HB over PC age 850
rent allowance
definition 79
frequency of payment
HB 466
HB over PC age 862
information for rent officers
HB over PC age 874
payments on account
HB 467
HB over PC age 863
when rent allowances are paid
HB 465
HB over PC age 862
rent arrears
overpayments of benefit to landlord
HB 471
payment direct to landlord
HB 470, 473
HB over PC age 864, 865
payment on account to landlord
HB 468
rent increases to cover arrears
HB 299
HB over PC age 792
rent assessment committee determinations
HB 1206
rent officer
challenging decision of rent officer
HB 329, 592
HB over PC age 807
claim-related rent
HB 606, 626
determinations 592, 594, 615
HB 603, 623
errors
HB 601, 621
evidence/information required
HB over PC age 877
excluded tenancies
HB 517
HB over PC age 884
functions 1122
indicative rent calculation
HB 608, 627
information from local authority
HB 503
HB over PC age 874
local reference rent
HB 312
HB over PC age 798
notifications
HB 608, 627
pre-tenancy determination
HB 325
HB over PC age 805
redeterminations
HB 329, 595, 616, 629
HB over PC age 806
rent increases
HB over PC age 884

requirement to refer to rent officers 324, 804
substitute determinations
  HB over PC age 808
time limit for referrals
  HB 325
  HB over PC age 805
rent rebate
  definition 79
  recovery of overpayment
    HB 493
  subsidy 93
rent restrictions 297
  increases of rent 1214
  local housing allowance 297
  local reference rent 297
  pre-Jan 96 scheme 297
  protection from restrictions
    HB 308, 1206
    HB over PC age 797, 798
  transitional protection
    HB 1198
rent-free period
  HB 244, 418, 440, 516
  HB over PC age 789, 837, 851, 884
rental purchase agreements
  HB 300, 601, 613, 621, 631
  HB over PC age 793
repairs
  disregard of dwelling awaiting repairs
    CTB 755
    HB 574
  set-off against rent
    HB 244, 440
    HB over PC age 789
  temporary accommodation
    HB 234
    HB over PC age 785
resident
  definition
    CTB 12
retainer fee
  treatment as earnings
    CTB 671
    CTB over PC age 942
    HB 358
    HB over PC age 825
retirement
  annuity contracts
    HB 377
  earnings disregards
    CTB 738
    HB 543
retirement pensions
  notional income
    CTB over PC age 947
    HB over PC age 830
  treatment as income
    HB over PC age 815, 817
reviews
  discretionary housing payments 1181
  First-tier Tribunal decisions 174, 1072
  replacement of reviews 139
  Upper Tribunal decisions 175
revision 136, 139
  any grounds revision 1010
  any time revisions 1015
  appeal pending 1011

appealing a revised decision
  HB/CTB 1036
date revision takes effect 1018
difference between revision and
  supersession 143
late application
  HB/CTB 1016
official error 1011
refusal to revise 141
revision of decisions 142, 1010
revision or supersession 1020
right to reside
  HB 267
rounding up of benefit
  CTB 651, 717
  CTB over PC age 923, 973
  HB 438
royalties
  CTB 673
  HB 364

S
same sex couples
  definition 18, 1006
  transitional arrangements 1193
sanctionable benefits
  definition 1136
sanctions
  anti-social behaviour
    HB 7
  benefit offences 1140
  conviction then quashed 1138
  disqualification from benefit 1186
  effect on offender's family 1142
  one strike scheme 1137
sandwich courses
  CTB 689, 693
  HB 397, 398, 410
school holidays
  treatment of hours of work
    CTB 656
    CTB over PC age 925
    HB 230
    HB over PC age 784
second adult
  alternative maximum CTB 704, 959
  duty to notify change of circumstances
    CTB 715
    CTB over PC age 971
  income
    CTB 736
    CTB over PC age 996
second adult rebate 12
Second World War
  ex-gratia payments
    CTB 758
    CTB over PC age 992
    HB 578
    HB over PC age 899
self-employed earner
  average weekly earnings
    CTB 669
    HB 355
  calculation of net profit
    CTB 673
    CTB over PC age 945
    HB 364

HB over PC age 827
chargeable income
  HB 368
definition
  CTB 649
  CTB over PC age 921
  HB 216
  HB over PC age 777
disregards from earnings
  CTB 673, 675
  CTB over PC age 944, 946
  HB 364, 365, 368, 544
  HB over PC age 827, 829
earnings
  CTB 673
  CTB over PC age 944
  HB over PC age 826
earnings defined
  CTB over PC age 945
  HB 363
  HB over PC age 827
EEA nationals
  CTB 657
  HB 267
expectation of payment
  HB 232
notional capital
  CTB 683
  HB 384
self-employment route
definition
  CTB 649
  HB 216
Senior President of Tribunals 169, 173
reports 198
separation
date change of circumstances takes effect
  CTB 706
  CTB over PC age 960
disregard of home
  CTB 754
  HB 573
estrangement
  CTB 652
  CTB over PC age 923
former partner
  HB 244
  HB over PC age 789
former partner is landlord
  HB 249, 257
  HB over PC age 789
service charges
counselling and support 108
definition
  HB 301
  HB over PC age 794
excessive
  HB 515
  HB over PC age 883
fuel
  HB 515
  HBover PC age 883
HB 300
HB over PC age 793
ineligible service charges 635, 636
  HB 304, 513, 605, 607, 624, 626
  HB over PC age 881

meals
  HB 513
  HB over PC age 881
rent officer determinations
  HB 605, 622, 624
validated charges 108
service of notices for appeals
HB/CTB 1007
service user group
definition
  CTB 650
  CTB over PC age 921
  HB 216
  HB over PC age 777
disregard of expenses
  CTB 738
  HB 551
notional income
  CTB 680
  CTB over PC age 948
  HB 375
  HB over PC age 831
treatment of expenses
  CTB 671
  HB 359
services
definition
  HB 301
  HB over PC age 794
setting aside decision 158, 201, 1069, 1098
severe disability premium
amount
  CTB 733
  CTB over PC age 985
  HB 535
  HB over PC age 890
CTB 731
CTB over PC age 983
earnings disregards
  CTB 738
  HB 544
HB 531
HB over PC age 888
severe mental impairment
disregarded for council tax discount 1119
share fishermen
CTB 673
HB 365
shared accommodation
HB 227
shared ownership tenancy
definition
  HB 217
  HB over PC age 778
HB 300
shares
valuation of capital
  CTB 681
  CTB over PC age 950
  HB 382
  HB over PC age 833
sickness
earnings disregards
  HB 543
EEA nationals 273
not in remunerative work
  CTB 656

CTB over PC age 926
HB 231
HB over PC age 784
students entitled to benefit
CTB 691
HB 403
significant rent
HB 625
significantly high rent
HB 314, 603, 623
single room rent
HB 312, 314, 605, 625
transitional arrangements
HB 595, 616
site fees
HB 300, 612, 631
size criteria
definition
HB 593, 615
future restrictions 322
HB 603, 609, 623, 628
transitional protection
HB 311
HB over PC age 798
size-related rent
HB 314, 623, 628
Skipton Fund
definition
CTB 650
CTB over PC age 921
HB 217
HB over PC age 778
disregarded as capital
CTB 754
CTB over PC age 993
HB 572
HB over PC age 900
third party payments
HB 384
Social Entitlement Chamber 173
functions 1048, 1109
Social Security Advisory Committee 94
Social Security Commissioners
abolition 170, 1102
functions transferred to First-tier and Upper
Tribunals 193, 1102
transitional provisions 1103
special account 217
sponsorship of people from abroad
transitional protection 1153
sports award
definition
CTB over PC age 921
HB 217
HB over PC age 778
disregard of payments
CTB 750, 757
HB 364, 564
HB over PC age 827
not in remunerative work
CTB 656
CTB over PC age 926
HB 231
HB over PC age 784
standard maintenance allowance
CTB 689
HB 398

statement of reasons
CTB 716
CTB over PC age 973
decisions which can be appealed
HB/CTB 1029
HB 461
HB over PC age 861
statutory adoption pay
HB 359
treatment as earnings
CTB 671
CTB over PC age 943
HB over PC age 825
statutory instruments
parliamentary control 101, 110
power to make 24, 100, 109
statutory maternity pay
treatment as earnings
CTB 671
CTB over PC age 942
HB 359
HB over PC age 825
statutory paternity pay
HB 359
treatment as earnings
CTB 671
CTB over PC age 942
HB over PC age 825
statutory sick pay
treatment as earnings
CTB 671
CTB over PC age 942
HB 359
HB over PC age 825
student loans
definition
CTB 689
fee loans
CTB 696
HB 416
giving up course
CTB 676
HB 369
treatment as income
HB 369
students
absence from home
CTB 659
CTB over PC age 928
HB 236
HB over PC age 788
academic year
CTB 687
HB 395
accommodation during vacations
HB 401
accommodation owned by institution
HB 408
alternative maximum CTB 690
breaks from study
HB 406
course of study
CTB 687
HB 396
covenants
CTB 693, 694
HB 412

CTB 686
deaf students
  CTB 691
  HB 402
definition
  CTB 689
  HB 398, 404
disabled students
  CTB 690
disregarded for council tax discount 1119
disregards
  CTB 692
  HB 409, 413
eligible housing costs
  HB 408
entitlement to benefit
  CTB 690
  HB 401
excluded from benefit
  CTB 690
  HB 401
exemptions from exclusion from benefits
  CTB 690
  HB 401, 405
failing exams
  HB 406
frequency of payment
  HB 467
  HB over PC age 863
full-time course
  CTB 687
  HB 396
giving up course
  CTB 676
  HB 369
grant income
  CTB 688, 692
  HB 397, 409
HB 394
income treated as capital
  CTB 697
  HB 417
last day of course
  CTB 688
  HB 397
loans
  CTB 695
  HB 413
lone parents
  CTB 690
  HB 401
modular courses
  HB 405
non-dependant deductions
  CTB 699
  CTB over PC age 955
  HB 428
  HB over PC age 843
occupation of home
  HB 234, 401
  HB over PC age 785
overseas students
  CTB 690
period of study
  CTB 688
  HB 397
receiving IS/JSA/ESA

CTB 690
HB 401
student partners
  CTB 691
  HB 244, 402, 417
  HB over PC age 789
summer vacations
  CTB 697
  HB 417
two homes
  HB 234
  HB over PC age 785
subordinate legislation
  power to make regulations 24, 100
subsidiary limit
  CTB 83
  HB 80
subsidy 90
  calculation 91
  discretionary housing payments 137
  fraud prevention 91
  payment 92
  rent rebate 93
  rent-free periods
    HB 418
    HB over PC age 837
suitable alternative accommodation
  HB 1206, 1211
supersession 139, 143, 1018
  change of circumstances after decision 141
  closed period supersessions 142
  date of taking effect 1024
  difference between supersession and
    revision 143
  grounds for 1018, 1021
  refusal to supersede 141
  revision or supersession 1020
support charges
  ineligible charges
    HB 607, 626
  rent officer referrals 602
support component
  amount
    CTB 734
    HB 538
  CTB 734
supported accommodation
  definition 1200
surrender value
  valuation of investments
    CTB 681
    CTB over PC age 950
suspension of benefit 153
  failure to provide information
    HB/CTB 1032
  HB/CTB 1030
  lifting of suspension
    HB/CTB 1031
  suspension leading to termination
    HB/CTB 1034
Switzerland 1226

T
tapers
  CTB 700
  CTB over PC age 956
  HB 314, 393, 419, 1214

HB over PC age 837
transitional protection
HB 1222
tariff income 16
CTB 686
CTB over PC age 935, 936
HB 346, 393
HB over PC age 817
tax year
definition
CTB over PC age 922
HB 217
HB over PC age 778
teachers
student loans disregarded
CTB 743
temporary accommodation
HB on two homes 234, 785
tenancy
definition
HB 593, 615
tenancy in common
HB 392
termination of benefit
HB/CTB 1034
Territorial Army
earnings disregard
CTB 739
CTB over PC age 985
HB 546
HB over PC age 891
test case pending
HB/CTB 1022, 1036
third party payments
capital
CTB 682
HB 384
income
CTB 678
notional capital
CTB 682
HB 384
notional income
CTB 678
CTB over PC age 949
HB 373, 377
HB over PC age 832
tied accommodation
HB 250, 261
HB over PC age 790
time limits 861
appeals
HB/CTB 1038
applying for revision of decision
HB/CTB 1010
challenging decision of rent officer
HB 330
HB over PC age 807
criminal proceedings 68
first payment of benefit
CTB 717
CTB over PC age 973
HB 464
HB over PC age 862
First-tier Tribunals 200, 1075
landlord to supply information
HB 511

HB over PC age 880
notice of appeal 1040, 1062, 1091
notice of decisions which can be appealed
HB/CTB 1029
notification of decision
CTB 716
CTB over PC age 972
HB 461
notification of rent officer determinations
HB 608
recovery of overpayment
HB 494
referrals to rent officers
HB 325
HB over PC age 805
statement of reasons
CTB 716
CTB over PC age 973
HB 461
HB over PC age 861
supplying information to support a claim
HB 453
HB over PC age 857
Upper Tribunals 200
training
Community Task Force 1246
definition of training course
CTB 660
disregard of payments
CTB 743
HB 553, 575
New Deal payments 1167
non-dependant deductions
CTB 699
CTB over PC age 955
training allowance
definition
CTB 650
CTB over PC age 922
HB 217
HB over PC age 778
disregarded
CTB 743
HB 553
New Deal payments
HB/CTB 1167
non-dependant deductions
HB 428
HB over PC age 843
training course
definition
HB 237
HB over PC age 788
transitional arrangements
asylum seekers 1153, 1170
civil partnerships 1193
employment and support allowance
CTB 734
HB 538
former pathfinder cases
HB 310, 587
HB over PC age 797
habitual residence 1192
persons from abroad 1153
rent restrictions 311, 798, 1198
single room rent 595

travel expenses
  treated as earnings
    CTB 671, 741
    CTB over PC age 942
    HB 358
    HB over PC age 825
  voluntary/charity work
    CTB 741
    HB 551
treatment as member of household
  HB 335
trusts
  CTB 678, 682
  HB 373, 383
  landlord is a connected trust
    HB 249, 258
    HB over PC age 789
two homes
  HB 234
  HB over PC age 785
  students
    HB 234
    HB over PC age 785

U
udal tenure
  definition
    HB 224
underpayments 717
  CTB 45
  CTB over PC age 974
  offsetting against overpayments
    CTB 718
    CTB over PC age 974
    HB 476
    HB over PC age 866
  payments on account
    HB 468
    HB over PC age 863
unemployment
  EEA nationals 274
unfair dismissal
  CTB 671
  HB 358, 543
unmarried couple 20
unreasonable rent restriction
  HB over PC age 885
  transitional protection 1205
unreasonably large accommodation
  HB 603, 609, 623, 1206
  HB over PC age 885
  size criteria
    HB 628
Upper Tribunal 112, 169
  administration 196
  appealing against an Upper Tribunal decision
    151, 183, 1105
  appeals against First-tier Tribunal decisions
    150, 176
  application for permission to appeal 1090,
    1099
  case management powers 1080
  composition 171, 1106
  consent orders 1097
  costs and expenses 193, 200, 1083, 1089
  delegation to staff 1080
  enforcement of decisions 192

  evidence and submissions 1087
  expert assistance 192
  failure to comply with rules 1081
  fees 197
  hearings 1096
  judges 171, 172
  judicial review powers 187
  judicial review proceedings 1093
  mediation 191, 1080
  membership of tribunal 1076
  notice of appeal 1091
  notice of decisions 1098
  notice of hearings 1096
  obligation to cooperate 1079
  organisation 1109
  overriding objective 1079
  practice directions 190
  procedures for giving directions 1081
  proceedings on appeal 182
  public and private hearings 1097
  quashing order 188
  representatives 1084
  review of decisions 175, 1100
  right to appeal to 176
  sending documents 1085
  setting aside a decision 1098
  sitting places 191
  striking out a case 1082
  transfer of functions 193
  transitional provisions 1103
  Tribunal Procedure Rules 189, 199
  withdrawal of a case 1088
  witnesses 1087

V
vacations
  summer vacations for students
    CTB 697
    HB 417
  treatment of hours of work
    CTB 656
    CTB over PC age 925
    HB 230
    HB over PC age 784
vaccine damage payment
  HB 376
validated charges 108
valuation of capital
  CTB 681
  CTB over PC age 950
  HB 382, 383
  HB over PC age 833
vicinity
  rent officer determinations
    HB 602
Victoria Cross payments
  CTB 742, 757
  HB 552, 577
violence
  absence from home
    HB 237
    HB over PC age 788
  housing costs for two homes
    HB 234, 235
    HB over PC age 785, 787
  treated as occupying former home

HB 235
HB over PC age 787
violent profits
HB 300
HB over PC age 793
voluntary payments
disregards
CTB 743
HB 553
students
CTB 694
HB 413
treatment as income/capital
CTB 681
HB 381
voluntary work
expectation of payment
HB 232
expenses
CTB 741
HB 551
notional income
CTB 679
unpaid work and notional income
CTB 679
HB 374
voluntary organisation defined
CTB 651
CTB over PC age 922
HB 217
HB over PC age 779
vouchers
non-cash vouchers
HB 359
HB over PC age 825

W
waiting days
HB 219
HB over PC age 780
war disablement pension
definition 1227
disregarded
CTB 83, 743, 1227
CTB over PC age 988, 1227
HB 80, 554, 1227
HB over PC age 893, 1227
war pension scheme
definition 18
war pensions
definition
CTB 651
CTB over PC age 922
HB 218
HB over PC age 779
disregarded
CTB 83, 743, 756, 1227
CTB over PC age 988, 1227
HB 80, 554, 575, 1227
HB over PC age 893, 1227
water and sewerage charges
deductions from rent 304
definition
CTB 651
CTB over PC age 922
HB 218
HB over PC age 779

week
definition for
CTB 18
HB 210
HB over PC age 772
Welfare Reform and Pensions Act 1999
commencement 1126
welfare to work beneficiary 530
withdrawal of claim 139
CTB 714
CTB over PC age 970
HB 456
HB over PC age 858
witnesses
allowances
CTB 747
HB 560
summoned to tribunals 200, 1060, 1087
Upper Tribunal's power to call 191
work
starting or increasing work
extended CTB 162, 700
extended HB 162, 419
working away from home
HB 335
HB over PC age 810
work experience 374, 679
Work for Your Benefit Pilot Scheme 218, 1247
Work for Your Benefit pilot scheme
CTB 651
work-focused interview
condition of benefit entitlement 31
optional 34
work-related activity component
amount
CTB 734
HB 538
CTB 734
HB 537
workers
definition 271
not persons from abroad
CTB 657
HB 267
working tax credit 1147
arrears treated as capital
HB 381
calculation of average weekly income 356
CTB 670
CTB over PC age 940
HB 356
HB over PC age 822
income/notional capital
CTB 682
HB 373
treatment as income
CTB 676
CTB over PC age 935
HB 369
HB over PC age 816

Y
young individual
definition
HB 218
HB over PC age 779
one bedroom shared accommodation 319

rent officer determinations
    HB 600, 621
single room rent
    HB 314
young people
    applicable amount
        CTB 662
        CTB over PC age 931
        HB 337
        HB over PC age 811
    definition
        CTB 660
        CTB over PC age 929
        HB 333
    disregarded for council tax discount 1119
    duty to notify changes in family
        CTB 715
        CTB over PC age 971
        HB 457
        HB over PC age 859
    leaving care 1132
    liability to pay rent
        HB 248
    member of household
        CTB 661
        CTB over PC age 930
        HB over PC age 809
    non-dependants
        CTB 654
        CTB over PC age 924
        HB 226
        HB over PC age 782
    payments from young person disregarded
        CTB 744
        HB 556
    qualifying young person
        HB over PC age 809
    responsibility for
        CTB 661, 691
        CTB over PC age 930
        HB 334, 402
        HB over PC age 809
    treatment of income and capital
        CTB 740
        HB 344, 380, 549

Z
Zimbabwe
    CTB 657
    HB 267